DICTIONARY OF GARDENING

THE ROYAL HORTICULTURAL SOCIETY

DICTIONARY OF GARDENING

A PRACTICAL AND SCIENTIFIC
ENCYCLOPAEDIA OF HORTICULTURE

Edited by

FRED J. CHITTENDEN, O.B.E., F.L.S., V.M.H.

Assisted by Specialists

SECOND EDITION
by
PATRICK M. SYNGE, M.A. (Cantab.), F.L.S.

VOLUME IV: PT—ZY

OXFORD
AT THE CLARENDON PRESS

Oxford University Press, Walton Street, Oxford OX2 6DP
Oxford New York Toronto
Delhi Bombay Calcutta Madras Karachi
Kuala Lumpur Singapore Hong Kong Tokyo
Nairobi Dar es Salaam Cape Town
Melbourne Auckland
and associated companies in
Beirut Berlin Ibadan Nicosia

Oxford is a trade mark of Oxford University Press

First published 1951
Second edition 1956
Reprinted from corrected sheets of the
second edition 1965
Reprinted (with corrections) 1974, 1977, 1981,
1984, 1986

ISBN 0 19 869106 8

Printed in Great Britain
at the University Printing House, Oxford
by David Stanford
Printer to the University

ABBREVIATIONS USED FOR TITLES OF WORKS CONTAINING ILLUSTRATIONS CITED IN THIS DICTIONARY

(Works are octavo unless otherwise mentioned)

A.B.G.C. CALCUTTA, ROYAL BOTANIC GARDENS. Annals. Calcutta. 1887–1936. Vols. 1–14, pt. i. Folio.

A.B.R. ANDREWS, HENRY C. The Botanist's Repository. London. 1797–1812. 10 vols. 4to. (For dates of publication, see *J. Bot. (London)*, **54**. 236; 1916.)

ADD. Addisonia: coloured Illustrations and popular Descriptions of Plants. New York. 1916– . Vol. 1– . Ref. to plate nos.

A.G. ANDREWS, HENRY C. Geraniums. London. 1805–24. 2 vols. 4to. Ref. to plate nos.

A.G.S.B. ALPINE GARDEN SOCIETY. Bulletin. Capel, Surrey, &c., 1930– . Vol. I– .

A.H. ANDREWS, HENRY C. The Heathery; or a Monograph of the Genus Erica. London. 1804–12. 6 vols. Ref. to plate nos.

A.P.J. TAKEDA, HISAYOSHI. Alpine Plants of Japan. Tokyo. 1938. Ref. to plate nos.

ANN. MUS. LUGDUNO-BAT. MIQUEL, FREDERIK ANTON WILHELM. Annales Musei botanici Lugduno-Batavorum. Amsterdam, &c. 1863–9. 4 vols. Folio. (For dates of publication see *J. Arnold Arb.* **6**. 212; 1925.)

B.B. BRITTON, NATHANIEL LORD, and BROWN, ADDISON. An Illustrated Flora of the Northern United States, Canada, and the British Possessions from Newfoundland to Virginia. New York. Ed. 2. 1913. 3 vols. Ref. to vol. and page.

B.C.F. SCHNEIDER, GEORGE. The Book of choice Ferns. London. 1892–4. 3 vols.

B.H. La Belgique Horticole. Liége. 1851–85. 35 vols. Ref. to date and plate nos.

B.J.O. BOLUS, HARRY. Icones Orchidearum Austro-Africanarum extra-tropicarum. London. 1893–1913. 3 vols. Ref. to plate nos.

B.M. Curtis's Botanical Magazine. London. 1787–1947. 164 vols. Ref. to plate nos.

B.M. n.s. Idem 1948– . Vol. 165– . Ref. to plate nos.

B.O. BATEMAN, JAMES. A Monograph of Odontoglossum. 1864–74. Folio. Ref. to plate nos.

B.O.M.G. BATEMAN, JAMES. The Orchidaceae of Mexico and Guatemala. London. 1843. Folio.

B.R. The Botanical Register by SYDENHAM EDWARDS. London. 1815–28. 14 vols. 8vo. *Cont. as* Botanical Register or Ornamental Flower Garden. Ed. by JOHN LINDLEY. 1829–47. 19 vols. Ref. to plate nos. for vols. 1–23 (1815–37), to vol. and plate nos. for vols. 24–47 (1838–49).

B.R.C. BRITTON, NATHANIEL LORD, and ROSE, JOSEPH NELSON. The Cactaceae: Descriptions and Illustrations of Plants of the Cactus Family. Washington, D.C. 1919–23. 4 vols. 4to. Ref. to vol. and plate or fig. nos.

B.T.S. BEAN, WILLIAM JACKSON. Trees and Shrubs hardy in the British Isles. 1914. 2 vols. Vol. 3. 1933. Ref. to vol. and page.

BAIRD, VIOL. BAIRD, VIOLA BRAINERD. Wild Violets of North America. Berkeley and Los Angeles. 1942.

BULL. ALP. GARD. SOC. *See* A.G.S.B. *above*.

C.B. CLINTON-BAKER, HENRY WILLIAM. Illustrations of Conifers. Hertford. 1909–13. 3 vols. 4to. Ref. to vol. and plate nos.

C.B.J. CLINTON-BAKER, HENRY WILLIAM, and JACKSON, ALBERT BRUCE. Illustrations of new Conifers. Hertford. 1935. 4to. Ref. to plate nos.

C.F.K. COVENTRY, B.O. Wild Flowers of Kashmir. Calcutta, Simla, London. 1925–30. 3 vols.

C.H.P. *See* H.I.H. *below*.

C.I.N.Z. CHEESEMAN, THOMAS FREDERICK. Illustrations of the New Zealand Flora. Wellington, N.Z. 1914. 2 vols. 4to. Ref. to plate nos.

D.C.PL.G. CANDOLLE, AUGUSTIN PYRAMUS DE. Plantarum succulentarum Historia; ou Histoire naturelle des Plantes grasses. Paris. 1798–1829. 2 vols. Folio. Ref. to plate nos. (For dates of publication, see *Cactus J.* **7**. 37; 1938.)

D.J.C. DALLIMORE, WILLIAM, and JACKSON, ALBERT BRUCE. A Handbook of Coniferae including Ginkgoaceae. London. 1923. Ref. to pages.

E.B. SYME, JOHN THOMAS BOSWELL. English Botany. London. 1863–86. 12 vols. 8vo. Supplementary vol. (13) by NICHOLAS EDWARD BROWN. 1891–2. Ref. to plate nos.

E.H. ELWES, HENRY JOHN, and HENRY, AUGUSTINE. The Trees of Great Britain and Ireland. Edinburgh. 1906–13. 7 vols. 4to. Ref. to plate nos.

E.L. ELWES, HENRY JOHN. A Monograph of the Genus Lilium. London. 1877–80. Folio. Ref. to plate nos. (For dates of publication, see WOODCOCK, H. B. D., and STEARN, W. T., Lilies, 396; 1950.)

E.L.S. GROVE, ARTHUR STANLEY, and COTTON, ARTHUR DISBROWE. A Supplement to Elwes' Monograph of the Genus Lilium. London. 1934–40. Folio. Ref. to plate nos.

E.R.G. FARRER, REGINALD. The English Rock-garden. London. 1919. 2 vols. Ref. to pages.

F.A.O. FITZGERALD, ROBERT DAVID. Australian Orchids. Sydney. 1875–94. 2 vols. Folio. Ref. to vol. and part.

F. & S. Flora and Sylva; a monthly Review for Lovers of Garden, Woodland, Tree or Flower. Ed. by WILLIAM ROBINSON. London. 1903–5. 3 vols. 4to. Ref. to vol. and plate nos.

F.B.A. HOOKER, Sir WILLIAM JACKSON. Flora Boreali-Americana: or the Botany of the northern Parts of British America. London. 1829–40. 2 vols. 4to. Ref. to plate nos. (For dates of publication, see *J. Bot. (London)*, **47**. 106; 1909.)

F.B.I. BEDDOME, RICHARD HENRY. The Ferns of British India. Madras. 1865–70. 3 vols. 4to.

F.C. KNOWLES, GEORGE BEAUCHAMP, and WESTCOTT, FREDERIC. The Floral Cabinet and Magazine of exotic Beauty. London. 1837–40. 3 vols. 4to.

F.d.S. Flore des Serres et des Jardins de l'Europe. Ghent. 1845–83. 23 vols. Ref. to plate nos.

F.G. SIBTHORP, JOHN, and SMITH, Sir JAMES EDWARD. Flora Graeca: sive Plantarum rariorum Historia. London. 1806–40. 10 vols. Folio. Ref. to plate nos.

FL.ATL. DESFONTAINES, RENÉ LOUICHE. Flora Atlantica. Paris. 1798–9. 2 vols. 4to. Ref. to plate nos. (For dates of publication, see *J. Soc. Bibl. Nat. Hist.* **1**. 147; 1938.)

F.M. The Floral Magazine. London, 1st series 1861–71. 10 vols. 8vo. 2nd series 1872–81. 10 vols. 4to.

F.P.R. BICKNELL, CLARENCE. Flowering Plants and Ferns of the Riviera and neighbouring Mountains. London. 1885. 4to. Ref. to plate nos.

F.P.S.A. The Flowering Plants of South Africa. London &c. 1921–44. Vols. 1–24. *Cont. as* The Flowering Plants of Africa. Vol. 25– . 1945– . Ref. to plate nos.

F.S.A. MARLOTH, RUDOLF. The Flora of South Africa: with synoptical Tables of the Genera of the Higher Plants. Cape Town and London. 1913–32. Vols. 1–4. 4to. Ref. to plate nos.

F.S.I. BEDDOME, RICHARD HENRY. The Ferns of Southern India; being Descriptions and Plates of the Ferns of the Madras Presidency. Madras. 1863–4. Ref. to plate nos.

G. & F. Garden and Forest: A Journal of Horticulture, Landscape, Art, and Forestry. New York. 1888–97. 10 vols. 4to. Ref. to vol. and plate nos.

G.C. The Gardeners' Chronicle. London. 1841–3. 3 vols. 4to. The Gardeners' Chronicle and Agricultural Gazette. 1844–73. 30 vols. The Gardeners' Chronicle, new series 1874–86. 26 vols.; 3rd series 1887– . Vol. 1– . Ref. to vol., date, and page.

GEN. WILKIE, DAVID. Gentians. London. 1936.

GENTES HERB. BAILEY, LIBERTY HYDE. Gentes Herbarum. Ithaca, N.Y. 1920– . Vol. 1– .

G.F. Gartenflora. Erlangen. 1852–85. 34 vols. *Cont. as* Gartenflora, Zeitschrift, &c. 1886–1938. Berlin. Vols. 35–87. Ref. to plate nos., or to vol. and page.

G.I. Gardening Illustrated. London.

GN. The Garden: an illustrated weekly Journal of Gardening in all its Branches. London. 1871–1927. 91 vols. 4to. Ref. to vol., date, and page.

GTF. Gartenflora. *See* G.F. *above.*

H.B.F. HOOKER, Sir WILLIAM JACKSON. The British Ferns. London. 1861. 8vo. Ref. to fig. nos.

H.C.I.S. HU, HSEN-HSU, and CHUN, WOON YOUNG. Icones Plantarum Sinicarum. Shanghai. 1927–9. Folio. 2 parts. Ref. to plate nos.

H.E.F. HOOKER, Sir WILLIAM JACKSON. Exotic Flora. Edinburgh. 1822–7. 3 vols. Ref. to plate nos.

HENSHAW MT.W.FL. HENSHAW, JULIA WILLMOTTE. Wild Flowers of the North American Mountains. London and New York. 1916.

H.F.A. HOOKER, Sir JOSEPH DALTON. Flora Antarctica. London. 1844–60. 2 vols. 4to. (For dates of publication, see *J. Bot. (London)*, **51**. 356; 1913.)

H.F.T. HOOKER, Sir JOSEPH DALTON. Flora Tasmaniae. London. 1855–60. 2 vols. 4to. (For dates of publication, see *J. Bot. (London)*, **51**. 358; 1913.)

H.G.F. HOOKER, Sir WILLIAM JACKSON. Genera Filicum; or Illustrations of Ferns. London. 1842. Ref. to fig. nos.

H.I.H. HOOKER, Sir JOSEPH DALTON. Illustrations of Himalayan Plants. London. 1855. Folio. Ref. to plate nos. (For date of publication, see *Calcutta, R. Bot. Gard., Anniv. Vol.*, 115; 1942.)

H.I.P. HOOKER, Sir WILLIAM JACKSON. Icones Plantarum. London. 1837–53. 10 vols. 8vo. *Cont. as* Hooker's Icones Plantarum *under various editors.* Ref. to plate nos.

H.S. / H.S.F. HOOKER, Sir WILLIAM JACKSON. Species Filicum. London. 1846–64. 5 vols. Folio.

H.S.C.F. HOOKER, Sir WILLIAM JACKSON. A Second Century of Ferns. London. 1860.

H.T. HALL, Sir ALFRED DANIEL. The Genus Tulipa. London. 1940. Ref. to plate nos.

HOOK.I. *See* H.I.P. *above.*

HOUSE, W. F. HOUSE, HOMER DOLIVER. Wild Flowers of New York. New York. 1918. 4to.

J.H.S — HORTICULTURAL SOCIETY OF LONDON. Journal. London. 1846–55. 9 vols. Ref. to vol. and page.

J.L. — JORDAN, ALEXIS, and FOURREAU, JULES. Icones ad Floram Europae novo fundamento instaurandam spectantes. Paris. 1866–1903. 3 vols. Folio. Ref. to plate nos.

J.L.S. — LINNEAN SOCIETY OF LONDON. Journal: Botany. London. 1865– . Vol. 8– . 8vo. Ref. to vol. and plate nos.

J.R.H.S. — ROYAL HORTICULTURAL SOCIETY. Journal. London. 1866. Vol. 1– . Ref. to vol. and page.

K.B. — KEW, ROYAL BOTANIC GARDENS. Bulletin of Miscellaneous Information. London. 1887. Ref. to date and page.

L. — LINDEN, JULES, and LINDEN, LUCIEN. Lindenia: Iconographie des Orchidées. Ghent. 1885–1901. 17 vols. Folio. Ref. to plate nos.

L.B.C. — LODDIGES, CONRAD. The Botanical Cabinet: coloured Delineations of Plants from all Countries. London. 1818–33. 20 vols. 4to. Ref. to plate nos.

L.F. — LOWE, EDWARD JOSEPH. Ferns British and exotic. London. 1856–60. 8 vols. 8vo. Ref. to vol. and plate nos.

L.Y.B. — ROYAL HORTICULTURAL SOCIETY. Lily Year Book. London. 1932– . Ref. to year and fig. nos.

LAING AND BLACKWELL — LAING, ROBERT MALCOLM, and BLACKWELL, E. W. Plants of New Zealand. Christchurch, N.Z. 1906. Ref. to pages.

M.A.S. — SALM - REIFFERSCHEID - DYCK, JOSEPH, Prince. Monographia Generum Aloes et Mesembryanthemi. Bonn. 1836–63. 2 vols. 4to. Ref. to vol. and plate nos. (For the modern names of the plants figured, see *Cactus J.* **1**. 34–44, 66–85; 1938–9.)

M.C. — MAW, GEORGE. A Monograph of the Genus Crocus. London. 1886. 4to. Ref. to plate nos.

M.F.M. — MOGGRIDGE, JOHN TRAHERNE. Contributions to the Flora of Mentone. London. 1865–71. (3rd ed. 1874.) Ref. to plate nos.

MOGGRIDGE, FL. MENTONE — *See* M.F.M. *above.*

N. — BURBIDGE, FREDERICK WILLIAM, and BAKER, JOHN GILBERT. The Narcissus, its History and Culture. London. 1875. Ref. to plate nos.

N.E.BR. — BROWN, NATHANIEL EDWARD, FISCHER, A., and KARSTEN, M. C. Mesembryanthema. Ashford. 1931. 8vo. Ref. to pages.

N.F.S. — The New Flora and Silva. London. 1928–40. 12 vols. 8vo. Ref. to vol. and fig. nos.

N.R.B.G.E. — EDINBURGH, ROYAL BOTANIC GARDEN. Notes. Glasgow and Edinburgh. 1900– . Vol. 1– . Ref. to vol. and page.

O.R. — The Orchid Review: and illustrated monthly Journal devoted to Orchidology. London. 1893– . Vol. 1– . 8vo. Ref. to date and page.

P.F.G. — LINDLEY, JOHN, and PAXTON, Sir JOSEPH. Paxton's Flower Garden. London. 1850–3. 3 vols. 4to. Ref. to vol. and plate nos.

P.F.S. — POST, GEORGE EDWARD. Flora of Syria, Palestine and Sinai. Beirut. 1896. Ref. to pages.

P.L. — SALISBURY, RICHARD ANTHONY. Paradisus Londinensis. London. 1805–8. 2 vols. 4to. Ref. to plate nos.

P.M.B. — Paxton's Magazine of Botany. London. 1834–49. 16 vols. 4to. Ref. to vol. and plate nos.

PARSONS, WILD FLOWERS OF CALIFORNIA. — PARSONS, MARY ELIZABETH . The Wild Flowers of California, their Names, Haunts, and Habits. San Francisco. 1897.

PESCATOREA — LINDEN, JEAN JULES. Pescatorea: Iconographie des Orchidées. Brussels. 1860. Folio. Ref. to plate nos.

R. — SANDER, FREDERICK. Reichenbachia. St. Albans. 1888–94. 4 vols. Folio. Ref. to plate nos.

REF.B. — SAUNDERS, WILLIAM WILSON. Refugium Botanicum. London. 1869–73. 5 vols. Ref. to vol. and plate nos.

R.H. — La Revue Horticole. Paris. 1842– . 12mo. and 8vo. Ref. to date and plate nos.

R.H.B. — Revue de l'Horticulture belge et étrangère. 1875–1914. 40 vols. Ghent. Ref. to date and plate nos.

R.I.F.G. — REICHENBACH, HEINRICH GOTTLIEB, and others. Icones Florae Germanicae et Helveticae. Leipzig. 1834–1912. 25 vols. 4to. Ref. to vol. and plate nos.

R.L. — REDOUTÉ, PIERRE JOSEPH. Les Liliacées. Paris. 1807–16. 8 vols. Folio. Ref. to plate nos. (For dates of publication, see *J. Bot.* (*London*), **43**. 26; 1905.)

R.M.F. — CLEMENTS, FREDERIC EDWARD, and CLEMENTS, EDITH SCHWARTZ. Rocky Mountain Flowers. New York. 1914. Ref. to fig. nos.

R.S.H. — HOOKER, Sir JOSEPH DALTON. The Rhododendrons of Sikkim-Himalaya. London. 1849–51. Folio. Ref. to plate nos.

R.X.O. — REICHENBACH, HENRICH GUSTAV. Xenia orchidacea. Leipzig. 1854–1900. 3 vols. 8vo. Ref. to plate nos.

RHODORA — NEW ENGLAND BOTANICAL CLUB. Rhodora. Boston. 1899– . Vol. 1– .

ROYLE ILL. B.H. — ROYLE, JOHN FORBES. Illustrations of the Botany of the Himalayan Mountains, and of the Flora of Cashmere. London. 1833–40. 2 vols. 4to. Ref. to plate nos. (For dates of publication, see *J. Arnold. Arb.* **24**. 484; 1943.)

S.AFR.GARD. — South African Gardening. Cape Town. 1915– . Vols. 1– . 4to. Ref. to vol., date, and page.

S.B.F.G. — SWEET, ROBERT. The British Flower Garden. London. 1st series 1823–9. 3 vols. Ref. to plate nos.

S.B.F.G.2	SWEET, ROBERT. The British Flower Garden. London. 2nd series 1831–8. 4 vols. Ref. to plate nos.
S.C.	SWEET, ROBERT. Cistineae. London. 1825–30. Ref. to plate nos.
S.D.	*See* M.A.S. *above.*
S.E.B.	SMITH, Sir JAMES EDWARD. Exotic Botany. 1804–5. 2 vols. 4to. Ref. to plate nos.
S.G.	SWEET, ROBERT. Geraniaceae. London. 1820–30. 5 vols. Ref. to plate nos.
S.MAN.	SARGENT, CHARLES SPRAGUE. Manual of the Trees of North America (exclusive of Mexico). Boston. 1905.
S.P.	STERN, FREDERICK CLAUDE. A Study of the Genus Paeonia. London. 1946. 4to. Ref. to plate nos.
S.S.	SARGENT, CHARLES SPRAGUE. The Silva of North America. Boston. 1891–1902. 14 vols. 4to. Ref. to plate nos.
S.T.S.	SARGENT, CHARLES SPRAGUE. Trees and Shrubs; Illustrations of new or little known ligneous Plants. 1902–13. Boston and New York. 2 vols. 4to.
S.Z.F.J.	SIEBOLD, PHILIPP FRANZ VON, and ZUCCARINI, JOSEPH GERHARD. Flora Japonica. 1835–70. Leyden. 2 vols. Folio. Ref. to plate nos. (For dates of publication, see *Bot. Mag. Tokyo*, **40**. 362; 1926.)
SIBTH, SM., FL. GRAECA	*See* F.G. *above.*
STOKER, GARDENER'S PROGRESS.	STOKER, FRED. A Gardener's Progress. London. 1938. 8vo. Ref. to fig. nos.
T.A.P.E.	THOMPSON, HAROLD STUART. Alpine Plants of Europe: together with cultural Hints. London. 1911. Ref. to pages.
T.H.S.	HORTICULTURAL SOCIETY OF LONDON. Transactions. 1805–48. 10 vols. 4to. Ref. to vol. and plate nos.
T.L.S.	LINNEAN SOCIETY OF LONDON. Transactions. London. 1791–1876. 30 vols. 4to. 2nd series, Botany. 1875– . Vol. 1– . Ref. to vol. and plate nos.
T.S.A.P.	THOMPSON, HAROLD STUART. Subalpine Plants or Flowers of the Swiss Woods and Meadows. London. 1912. 8vo. Ref. to pages.
USEFUL PL. JAP.	AGRICULTURAL SOCIETY OF JAPAN. Useful Plants of Japan described and illustrated. Tokyo. 1895. 3 vols. of plates. 1 vol. of text.
W.A.P.	WOOSTER, DAVID. Alpine Plants. London. 1st series 1872. 2nd series 1874. 2 vols. 4to. Ref. to plate nos.
W.I.C.P.	WEBB, PHILIP BARKER, and BERTHELOT, SABIN. Histoire naturelle des Iles Canaries: Tome 3, Partie 2, Phytographia Canariensis. Paris. 1836–50. 3 vols. 4to. Ref. to plate nos. (For dates of publication, see *J. Soc. Bibl. Nat. Hist.* **1**. 49; 1937.)
W.I.I.B.	WRIGHT, ROBERT. Illustrations of Indian Botany. Madras. 1840–50. 2 vols. 4to. Ref. to plate nos.
W.O.A.	WARNER, ROBERT, &c. The Orchid Album. Coloured Figures and Descriptions of new, rare, and beautiful orchidaceous Plants. London. 1882–97. 11 vols. 4to. Ref. to plate nos.
W.P.A.R.	WALLICH, NATHANIEL. Plantae Asiaticae rariores. London. 1829–32. 3 vols. Folio. Ref. to plate nos.
W.R.	WILLMOTT, ELLEN ANN. The Genus Rosa. London. 1910–14. 2 vols. 4to. Ref. to plate nos. (For dates of publication, see *J. Arnold Arb.* **3**. 230; 1922.)
W.S.	WOODCOCK, HUBERT DRYSDALE, and STEARN, WILLIAM THOMAS. Lilies of the World, their Cultivation and Classification. London. 1950. Ref. to pages.
W.S.O.	WARNER, ROBERT. Select Orchidaceous Plants. London. 1862–5. 2nd series 1865–75. 3rd series 1878–91. Folio. Ref. to plate nos.
WIGHT ICON.	WIGHT, ROBERT. Icones Plantarum Indiae orientalis. Madras. 1838–40. 6 vols. 4to. Ref. to plate nos. (For dates of publication, see *J. Arnold Arb.* **22**. 222; 1941.)

See also Vol. I, p. xiv, for additions.

ABBREVIATIONS USED IN TEXT

A indicates entries to be found in the Additions, Part II of Supplement
A→ indicates new headings to be found in the Additions, Part II of Supplement

cal.	calyx
cau.	caudex (rootstock of ferns)
Cent.	Central
cor.	corolla
Dist.	Distribution
E.	East(ern)
FAM.	Botanical Family (formerly called Natural Order)
fl.	flower(s)
-fld.	-flowered
fr.	fruit
ft.	foot (approximately 30 cm.)
h.	high
in.	inch (2·5 cm.)
infl.	inflorescence
infruct.	infructescence
Is.	Isle(s), Island(s)
l.	leaf (leaves)
lflets.	leaflets
lvs.	leaves
Mts.	Mountains
N.	North(ern)
NE.	North east(ern)
NW.	North west(ern)
per.	perianth
pet.	petal(s)
rhiz.	rhizome
S.	South(ern)
SE.	South east(ern)
SW.	South west(ern)
seg.	segment(s)
sep.	sepal(s)
sti.	stipe (leaf-stalk of ferns)
SYN.	Synonym
W.	West(ern)
*	of special merit
×	hybrid
+	graft chimaera graft hybrid

The scale of illustrations is indicated by the line e.g. ——— which is included in each drawing and represents one inch.

The year given in many descriptions represents the date of first introduction of the plant to Great Britain as far as is known.

PTYCHOSPER'MA (*ptyche*, a fold, *sperma*, seed; the albumen of the seed being folded). FAM. *Palmaceae*. A genus of a few species of Palms with smooth ringed stems and a dense crown of foliage. Leaves pinnately cut; leaflets slender-pointed, jagged or entire at tip. Spadix simple or rarely branched, from below the leaves. Flowers monoecious in the same spadix. Fruit an ovoid drupe. Cultivation as for Archontophoenix.

P. Alexand'rae. A synonym of *Archontophoenix Alexandrae.*

P. Cunninghamia'num. A synonym of *Archontophoenix Cunninghamiana.*

P. e'legans. A low or very tall Palm. *l.* several ft. long; segs. numerous, about 2 ft. long, linear, more or less toothed or jagged at tip. *Spadices* lateral, 1 to 1½ ft. long and as wide, branches many, slender, ends flexuous. Australia. (B.M. 7345.) SYN. *Seaforthia elegans* a name which has also been applied in gardens to *Archontophoenix Cunninghamiana.*

P. Macarth'urii. A synonym of *Actinophloeus Macarthurii.*

P. Sanderian'um. A synonym of *Actinophloeus Sanderianus.*

P. Seeman'nii. A synonym of *Balaka Seemannii.*

PUAWANANGA. *See* **Clematis indivisa.**

pu'bens, downy.

puberulous, minutely pubescent.

pubes'cens, pubescent, covered with soft hair or down.

pubi'genus -a -um, pubi'gerus -a -um, hairy.

A→

PUCCIN'IA. A large genus of Rust fungi (Uredinales) containing some serious plant parasites (*see* **Rusts**). In this genus the characteristic features of the fungus are that in the autumn stage the teleutospores are stalked and have 2 cells, each having 1 germ pore and the spring aecidiospore stage (perhaps on another host) is formed in cup-like aecidia. Perhaps the best known of all Rust fungi is *P. graminis*, the Black Rust of Cereals, with its aecidial stage produced as Clustercups on the leaves of *Berberis vulgaris*, the common Barberry. Other well-known rust diseases due to Puccinia species are seen on Hollyhocks, Mint, Violas, Asparagus, Gooseberry, Plum, and Iris.

D. E. G.

PUCCOON, RED. *See* **Sanguinaria canadense.**

PUCHA-PAT. Indian name of *Pogostemon Heyneanus.*

PUCHERO. *See* **Talinum patens.**

PUDDING BERRIES. *See* **Cornus canadensis**: the berries are edible.

PUDDING-PIPE TREE. *See* **Cassia fistula.**

PUDDLING. (1) Dipping roots of young vegetable plants, small trees, and shrubs into a thin mixture of clay and water to keep them moist until planted. (2) Rendering impervious by means of clay, as the bottom of a pond; wet clay being rammed or trampled heavily so as to form a continuous coating without crevices through which water can find its way.

pudi'cus -a -um, bashful, modest.

PUERA'RIA (in honour of M. N. Puerari, 1765–1845, Professor at Copenhagen). FAM. *Leguminosae*. A genus of about 10 species of climbing herbs or sub-shrubs, closely related to Dolichos and Phaseolus, natives of Trop. Asia and Japan, distinct by the beardless style, swollen nodes of the raceme and monadelphous stamens. Leaves pinnately 3-foliolate, leaflets large, ovate or rhomboid, entire or sinuately lobed, stipellate. Flowers blue or purplish on long axillary peduncles or on clustered racemes at ends of branches, papilionaceous; standard obovate or roundish, auricles inflexed; bracts small or narrow, falling very soon. Pods long, 2-valved. For treatment *see* **Clitoria.**

P. loba'ta. Kudzu Vine. Climber with twining, scarcely woody stems growing many ft. long in a season; roots thick, fleshy, starchy. *l.* 3-foliolate, middle lflet. 6 or 7 in. long, rhombic-ovate, side ones smaller, ovate; stalks 4 to 8 in. long. *fl.* in racemes up to 10 in. long, fragrant, violet-purple, ½ to ¾ in. long, papilionaceous. July, August. China, Japan. 1885. SYN. *P. hirsuta, P. Thunbergiana.* It does not fl. with us and rarely survives our winters except in the warmer counties, but it is unequalled for clothing a temporary structure rapidly. Raised from imported seeds, which should be sown singly in pots in a warm house and planted out as soon as there is no danger of frost. In good soil growths 20 ft. long may be expected by autumn.

P. tubero'sa. Roots tuberous. Shrubby, about 3 ft. h. *lflets.* 6 to 12 in. long, rhomboid or obliquely ovate, nearly smooth above, densely whitish-hairy beneath; stipules ovate, subcordate. *fl.* bluish in slender, dense, often panicled racemes 6 to 9 in. long, standards about ½ in. long, cal. densely silky; pedicels very short. June. *Pods* 2 to 3 in. long, constricted, long silky-haired. India. 1806. SYN. *Hedysarum tuberosum.*

P. Wallich'ii. Shrubby, about 3 ft. h. *lflets.* obliquely slender-pointed, entire, stipules lanceolate, falling very soon. *fl.* reddish, pedicels slender; standard ¾ in. long, base with a short, narrow claw, June. India. 1826.

PUFF-BALLS. The popular name given to certain large spherical fleshy fungi of the class Basidiomycetes and usually those in the genera Lycoperdon and Bovista. They grow from May to December on the ground in pastures, orchards, &c. They resemble large balls of a white or yellowish colour nearly a foot across, and some in America have been known to measure 4 or 5 ft. across. Most of the British species are edible when young and tender. When mature the outer rind ruptures and the spores filling the inside are released in dustlike clouds, thus suggesting the name puff-ball.

D. E. G.

pugioniform'is -is -e, dagger-shaped.

PUHERETAIKO. *See* **Senecio rotundifolius.**

PUKA. *See* **Griselinia lucida, Mertya Sinclairi.**

PUKATEA. *See* **Laurelia novae-zelandiae.**

PULAS TREE. *See* **Butea frondosa.**

pulchel'lus -a -um, pretty.

pul'cher -chra -chrum, beautiful.

pulcher'rimus -a -um, very beautiful.

PULE'GIUM. A synonym of Mentha.

pul'lus -a -um, black or nearly black.

PULMONA'RIA (*pulmo*, lung; the spotted leaves of *P. officinalis* were supposed to resemble diseased lungs). FAM. *Boraginaceae*. Low hairy perennial herbs, about 6 to 12 in. high, spring-flowering. Basal leaves stalked, those produced in summer providing the best specific characters; stem-leaves alternate. Flowers pink, purple, or blue, occasionally white, pedicellate, in terminal 2-fid cymes; calyx 5-fid; corolla funnel-shaped, tube cylindric, hairy inside, without scales, lobes 5, broad, rounded, spreading. Stamens borne on corolla tube, not protruding. Nutlets 4, smooth. Pulmonarias grow well in any moderately good garden soil which does not dry out. Propagate by division of clumps in early spring. The species are difficult to distinguish and interbreed promiscuously.

P. affi'nis. *Summer basal l.* oblong or lanceolate, bristly, white-spotted, rather abruptly narrowed into stalk. *fl.* at first pink, then purplish-blue. France.

P. angustifo'lia. Blue Cowslip. *Summer basal l.* mostly very narrowly elliptic, bristly, unspotted, narrowed gradually into stalk. *fl.* at first pink, then bright blue. Cent. Europe (Sweden to N. Italy). Before 1823. SYN. *P. azurea.* var. **al'ba,** *fl.* white. **Mawson's var.** a selected good garden form.

P. arvernen'sis. Garden name for a plant with deep purple-blue *fl.* var. **al'ba,** *fl.* white.

P. longifo'lia. *Summer basal l.* mostly very narrowly elliptic, bristly, white-spotted, gradually narrowed into stalk. *fl.* at first pink, then purplish-blue. W. Europe, including England. (E.B. 1097.) Often confused with *P. angustifolia*.

P. mol'lis. *Summer basal l.* elliptic or narrowly ovate, softly hairy, unspotted, gradually narrowed into stalk. *fl.* at first pink, then violet, Spring. Cent. and E. Europe, N. Asia. 1816. (B.M. 2422; L.B.C. 1492.)

P. officina'lis. Jerusalem Cowslip, Lungwort, Spotted Dog. *Summer basal l.* ovate, bristly, white-spotted, cordate. *fl.* at first pink, then purplish-blue. Europe. Before 1597. SYN. *P. maculosa.* var. **immacula'ta,** *l.* unspotted. SYN. *P. obscura.*

Pulmonaria angustifolia (p. 1713)

P. rub'ra. *Summer basal l.* oblong, softly hairy, bright green, usually unspotted, abruptly narrowed into stalk. *fl.* bright brick red, never blue or purple. SE. Europe (Carpathians), Balkan Peninsula. Before 1914. var. **albocorolla'ta,** *fl.* white.

P. sacchara'ta. *Summer basal l.* elliptic or narrowly ovate, bristly, profusely white-blotched, gradually or rather abruptly narrowed into stalk. *fl.* first rose, then blue. Origin uncertain, probably Italy. Before 1683. SYN. *P. picta.*

PULQUE. *See* Agave americana.

PULSATIL'LA (of unknown origin, used first by Mattioli). FAM. *Ranunculaceae.* A genus of about a dozen species closely related to Anemone (with which it is often grouped), differing especially in the feathery styles lengthening, often to 2 in., after flowering. The plants have a tufted habit, feathery foliage, often very hairy, dying down in autumn, except in *P. vernalis*; in many instances they flower before the foliage is fully developed in spring. The Pulsatillas are plants of open places and need well-drained soil. They do not resent lime.

KEY

1. *Involucral lvs. similar to foliage lvs., shortly stalked, not dividing into narrow linear segs. at tip; nectary absent*	2
1. *Involucral lvs. sessile, usually distinctly narrower than foliage lvs., with narrow-linear tips; nectary present, capitate*	3
2. *Fl. 2 to 2½ in. across*	P. alpina
2. *Fl. 1½ to 2 in. across*	P. occidentalis
3. *Lvs. remaining over winter*	P. vernalis
3. *Lvs. dying down in autumn*	4
4. *Fl. erect or ascending*	5
4. *Fl. nodding*	8
5. *Basal lvs. digitate*	6
5. *Basal lvs. pinnate*	7
6. *Fl. 2 to 3 in. across; l. segs. linear-lanceolate, hairy*	P. patens
6. *Fl. larger; l.-segs. narrower, very hairy*	P. hirsutissima
7. *Lvs. 2 or 3 times pinnate*	P. vulgaris
7. *Lvs. 3 or 4 times pinnate*	P. Halleri
8. *Fl. bell-shaped*	9
8. *Fl. wide-bell-shaped, bright violet*	P. Regeliana
9. *Stamens half length of sep.*	P. montana
9. *Stamens one-third length of sep. or less*	P. pratensis
9. *Stamens three-quarters as long as sep.*	P. albana
9. *Stamens two-thirds as long as sep.*	P. armena

P. alba'na. Related to *P. pratensis* but segs. of *l.* wider and much longer; invol. l. separate to base. *fl.* yellowish or blue, bell-shaped, nodding, silky-hairy without; sep. oblong, apex reflexed; stamens three-quarters as long as sep. Early spring; flowering nearly at the time l. develop. Caucasus, Persia. SYN. *Anemone albana.*

P. alpi'na.* *l.* long-stalked, 2-ternate, more or less hairy; segs. pinnate, deeply serrated; involucre of same form; 4 to 12 in. h., up to 16 in. in fruit. Rootstock black. *fl.* white, or white within, flushed violet to red outside, or yellowish, long-stalked, almost erect, up to 2½ in. across; sep. generally 6, spreading, elliptic or sometimes ovate; stamens yellow. May. N. Spain, France, Italy, Balkans, Caucasus. 1658. SYN. *Anemone alpina.* var. **Burseria'na,*** *fl.* white, at times flushed blue or reddish outside, *l.* with revolute margins at flowering-time, therefore appearing narrower, 16 in. h. Western Alps, Croatia, Dalmatia. SYN. *Anemone myrrhidifolia, A. alpina apiifolia*; **sulphu'rea,*** *fl.* sulphur-yellow, 2 to 2½ in. across, but sometimes cup-shaped, sep. 6 with silky-down outside, stamens golden. May and June. A very beautiful variety. Sometimes sterile. Pyrenees, France, Alps, Italy, Balkans, Caucasus. Large plants of this species do not transplant satisfactorily and plant collectors should only take seed or young seedlings.

P. arme'na. Dwarf. Near *P. montana* but fl. starry, l. longer and wider; than *P. albana* the l. are much shorter and fl. smaller. *l.* ovate, 2-pinnatifid, white-hairy; segs. short, crowded, linear-oblong. *fl.* purple-violet, nodding, bell-shaped, covered with appressed hairs without; sep. oblong, acute. Early spring; in nature flowering with the melting of the snow. Armenia.

P. Hal'leri.* *Basal l.* (usually doubly) pinnate, very hairy, with narrow-linear segs. 12 in. h., reaching 2 ft. in fruit. Rootstock black. *fl.* purplish inside, rarely white, hairy outside, campanulate at first, later spreading, erect; sep. generally 6, 1¼ to 1¾ in. long, oblong-ovate, acute. April. Switzerland, Austria, 1816. SYN. *Anemone Halleri.* This species varies in the fineness of the l.-divisions and in the colour of the fl.

Pulsatilla hirsutissima

P. hirsutis'sima. *Basal l.* stalked, much divided into narrow-linear acute segs., villose with long, silky hairs. 4 to 9 in. h., becoming taller in fruit. *fl.* bluish-purple or whitish, nearly always erect; styles becoming 2 in. long. April. United States and Siberia. 1826. SYN. *P. patens Nuttalliana, Anemone patens Nuttalliana.*

P. monta'na. *Basal l.* broad-ovate, pinnate, 3-partite, lobes narrow-linear, acute; involucral l. sessile, similar, all strongly hairy. 4 to 10 in. h. Rootstock black. *fl.* violet, rose, or white, white hairy without, nodding, at first campanulate, later starry; stamens yellow, bent near tips, half length of sep. March, April. Italy eastwards to Transcaucasia, Siberia, and Manchuria. SYN. *Anemone montana, A. pratensis montana.* The var. **ochroleu'ca** has creamy-white fl.

P. occidenta'lis. *l.* 2-parted, deeply pinnatifid with linear-toothed lobes; involucral l. similar, almost sessile. 4 to 15 in. h. *fl.* white or purplish at base; sep. 5 or 6, oval or broadly elliptic, $\frac{3}{4}$ in. long. June. Western N. America.

P. pa'tens.* *Basal l.* palmately lobed, lobes 2- or 3-partite with linear lanceolate segs., toothed, rough with spreading hairs. 3to 6 in. h., reaching 18 in. in fruit. Rootstock brown. *fl.* blue-violet or lilac outside with spreading hairs erect; sep. 6, narrow-ovate, acute, $1\frac{1}{4}$ to $1\frac{3}{4}$ in. long; stamens yellow, many times shorter than sep. March to May. N. Europe, Siberia. 1752. SYN. *Anemone patens.*

P. praten'sis. *l.* pinnate with narrow-linear divisions $\frac{1}{25}$ to $\frac{1}{8}$ in. wide at tip, whitish-hairy. 3 to 12 in. h., up to 18 in. in fruit. Rootstock erect, dark. *fl.* bright or black purple, rarely reddish, greenish-yellow or yellowish-white, thickly hairy without, usually nodding, campanulate; sep. reflexed at tips, $\frac{1}{2}$ to $1\frac{1}{4}$ in.; stamens yellow, the longest less than one-third as long as sep. May. Italy to S. Russia. 1731. SYN. *Anemone pratensis.*

P. Regelia'na. *l.* pinnately divided. 4 to 6 in. h. *fl.* bright violet, nodding, widely campanulate, with sep. curving outwards from middle, $1\frac{1}{4}$ to $1\frac{3}{4}$ in. wide. April. Siberia. (B.M. 9056.)

P. verna'lis. *fl.* white, or tinged violet outside, and covered with silky, bright-brown down outside, erect, campanulate or somewhat spreading; sep. 6, $\frac{3}{4}$ to $1\frac{1}{2}$ in. long, acute; stamens greenish-yellow. April. Europe. 1816. SYN. *Anemone vernalis, Pulsatilla sulphurea.*

P. vulga'ris.* Pasque Flower. *l.* pinnate, segs. many-partite, linear-lanceolate. 2 to 8 in. h. Rootstock almost black, fibrous. *fl.* violet or rarely white, erect, campanulate, somewhat spreading at mouth; sep. 6 with curved points, outside shaggy, like the stem and involucre; stamens egg-yolk yellow, the longer half length of sep. April. England, Europe. SYN. *Anemone Pulsatilla.* Of this there are many varieties, both in size and colour. var. **gran'dis,** *fl.* larger. Cent. Europe. SYN. *Anemone grandis.*

PULTENAE'A (in honour of Dr. Richard Pulteney, botanical historian, born in 1730 at Mt. Sorrel in Leicestershire, died at Blandford, Dorset, in 1801). FAM. *Leguminosae.* A genus of about 126 species of evergreen shrubs confined to Australia and Tasmania. Leaves mostly alternate, rarely opposite, simple. Flowers papilionaceous, mostly axillary and solitary but often collected into terminal leafy heads; they are usually yellow, often with a brown or reddish keel, rarely pink. A distinctive feature of this and allied genera is in the 5-lobed calyx, having the 2 upper lobes united and forming a 'lip', usually larger than the 3 lower ones combined. Cool greenhouse plants, mostly of considerable beauty but neglected in recent times. Fibrous peat with some silver sand, and like other Australian hard-wooded plants, firm potting and careful watering, are necessary. Seeds and cuttings of nearly ripe points of shoots give means of propagation. The latter should be put into very sandy peat in a close frame, shaded, and given an intermediate temperature.

KEY

1.	*L.-margins recurved*	2
1.	*L.-margins not recurved, often incurved*	9
2.	*Shrub erect or spreading*	3
2.	*Shrub prostrate; lvs. small*	P. pedunculata
3.	*Fl. in dense terminal sessile heads; inner bracts longer than pedicels*	4
3.	*Fl. few in small heads; bracts shorter than pedicels*	8
4.	*Stipules minute*	5
4.	*Stipules conspicuous*	7
5.	*Lvs. wedge-shaped, rounded or truncate at apex*	6
5.	*Lvs. linear*	P. retusa
6.	*Lvs.* $\frac{1}{2}$ *to* $1\frac{1}{2}$ *in. long*	P. daphnoides
6.	*Lvs. under* $\frac{1}{2}$ *in. long*	P. stricta
7.	*Bracts deciduous; fl.-heads softly hairy*	P. polifolia
7.	*Bracts persistent, glabrous or nearly so*	P. paleacea
8.	*Lvs. ovate, lanceolate, or oblong*	P. Gunnii
8.	*Lvs. obovate or broadly wedge-shaped*	P. scabra
9.	*Fl. in dense terminal heads, not intermixed with lvs.*	10
9.	*Fl. axillary, solitary, or in leafy heads*	13
10.	*Lvs. stipulate*	11
10.	*Lvs. without stipules*	P. subumbellata
11.	*Lvs. under* $\frac{1}{2}$ *in. long*	12
11.	*Lvs. 1 to* $1\frac{1}{2}$ *in. long, stipules long, overlapping*	P. stipularis
12.	*Lvs. very concave; fl. yellow and brown*	P. dentata
12.	*Lvs. terete; fl. pink*	P. rosea
13.	*Lvs. not spine-tipped*	14
13.	*Lvs. spine-tipped*	P. juniperina
14.	*Lvs. concave or nearly flat*	15
14.	*Lvs. terete, channelled above; fl. solitary*	P. tenuifolia
15.	*Plant glabrous*	16
15.	*Plant hairy; lvs. up to* $\frac{1}{3}$ *in. long*	P. villosa
16.	*Bracteoles on the cal. near its base*	P. flexilis
16.	*Bracteoles beneath the cal.*	P. euchila

P. argen'tea. A synonym of *P. dentata.*

P. corda'ta. A synonym of *P. juniperina latifolia.*

P. daphnoi'des. Shrub 3 to 6 ft., shoots downy, angular. *l.* $\frac{3}{4}$ to $1\frac{1}{2}$ in. long, $\frac{1}{4}$ to $\frac{1}{2}$ in. wide, oblanceolate, rounded and mucronate at apex, cuneate, glabrous or nearly so, pale or silvery beneath. *fl.* in a terminal stalkless head about 1 in. across; standard and wings yellow, $\frac{1}{3}$ in. long; keel short, scarlet. Summer. Australia, Tasmania. 1792. (B.M. 1394.) var. **obcorda'ta,** *l.* shorter and broader. (A.B.R. 574 as *P. obcordata.*)

P. densifo'lia. Rigid shrub, 2 to 3 ft., shoots downy, but at first concealed by the closely appressed and overlapping l. and stipules. *l.* $\frac{1}{10}$ to $\frac{1}{6}$ in. long, crowded, obovate or oblong, cuneate, concave above, glabrous, mostly recurved at the tip. *fl.* axillary, stalkless, crowded into terminal leafy heads; standard and wings yellow; keel crimson. April, May. Victoria, S. Australia.

P. denta'ta. Heath-like shrub 1 to 3 ft., shoots silky-downy. *l.* linear to narrowly lanceolate, $\frac{1}{4}$ to $\frac{1}{2}$ in. long, usually glabrous. *fl.* in dense terminal stalkless clusters $\frac{5}{8}$ in. across; cal. silky-hairy, $\frac{1}{8}$ in. long; standard orange-yellow, $\frac{1}{5}$ in. long; keel dark brown. June. Australia, Tasmania. 1820. SYN. *P. argentea.*

P. euchi'la. Glabrous, very leafy shrub, $3\frac{1}{2}$ to 7 ft., shoots slender. *l.* narrowly cuneate, blunt, $\frac{1}{3}$ to 1 in. long, $\frac{1}{12}$ to $\frac{1}{8}$ in. wide, rather glaucous. *fl.* $\frac{3}{8}$ in. long, axillary on stalks $\frac{1}{8}$ to $\frac{1}{4}$ in. long; cal. $\frac{1}{4}$ in. long, with long lobes; standard orange-yellow; keel incurved. Queensland, New S. Wales. 1824.

Pultenaea flexilis

P. fle'xilis.* Shrub 2 to 3 ft. and upwards, shoots slender, glabrous or thinly hairy. *l.* $\frac{1}{2}$ to 1 in. long, $\frac{1}{8}$ to $\frac{1}{6}$ in. wide, linear-cuneate, blunt-ended, mucronate. *fl.* axillary, solitary, yellow, shortly stalked; cal. $\frac{1}{6}$ in. long, lobes triangular-pointed; standard $\frac{1}{4}$ in. wide, with a darker patch at base, slightly notched. May. New S. Wales. 1801. (B.R. 1694.)

P. Gunn'ii.* Densely bushy shrub, 1 to 5 ft., shoots very slender, downy or hairy. *l.* densely set, linear-oblong, $\frac{1}{8}$ to $\frac{1}{3}$ in. long, blunt-ended, margins recurved, shining green above, pale beneath. *fl.* up to 8 in compact terminal heads; cal. downy or hairy, $\frac{1}{8}$ in. long; standard orange-yellow, $\frac{3}{8}$ in. long; keel deep reddish-brown or purple. Victoria, Tasmania. 1855.

P. juniperi'na.* Shrub up to 8 ft. or more, shoots hairy. *l.* stiff, prickly pointed, linear, $\frac{1}{4}$ to $\frac{5}{8}$ in. long, spreading, concave above, usually glabrous. *fl.* yellow or orange, few at end of smallish twigs; cal. $\frac{1}{6}$ in. long; standard $\frac{1}{5}$ in. long, keel dark brown. June. Victoria, Tasmania. 1824. Distinct by its prickly character. var. **latifo'lia,** *l.* broader, lanceolate, rounded or slightly cordate at base, pungent. Tasmania. 1832. (B.M. 3443 as *P. cordata.*)

P. linophyl'la. A variety of *P. retusa.*

P. obcorda'ta of Andrews, a variety of *P. daphnoides*.

P. palea'cea. Shrub 1 to 2 ft., shoots very slender, silky-downy when young. *l.* ½ to ¾ in. long, linear, pointed, glabrous above, silky-hairy beneath. *fl.* yellow with a brown keel, densely packed in a terminal stalkless head 1 in. across; cal. silky-hairy, ¼ in. long; standard ⅓ in. long; bracts very prominent, lanceolate. New S. Wales, Victoria. 1789. (L.B.C. 291.)

P. peduncula'ta. Heath-like prostrate shrub, often forming patches, shoots slender, downy or hairy. *l.* ⅙ to ½ in. long, narrow-linear, pointed, sessile. *fl.* solitary or in pairs near end of short, densely leafy twigs, each on a slender stalk ½ to ¾ in. long; standard cream to yellow, ⅜ in. long; keel short, yellow or red. May. Australia, Tasmania. 1820. (B.M. 2859.) Distinct by its long fl.-stalks.

P. polifo'lia. Shrub 2 ft., shoots virgate, softly hairy when young. *l.* linear, ½ to 1½ in. long, up to ⅛ in. wide, pointed, downy beneath and hairy on the midrib. *fl.* crowded in terminal globose heads about 1 in. across; standard yellow, ¼ in. long; wings and keel short. May. New S. Wales, Victoria. 1824. (B.R. 1584, as *P. rosmarinifolia.*)

P. retu'sa. Shrub up to 4 ft., shoots slender, virgate, angular, downy. *l.* ⅙ to ⅓ in. long, linear-cuneate, widest at notched apex, usually glabrous. *fl.* yellow, few in terminal heads; cal. silky-hairy, ⅛ in. long; standard ⅓ in. long; keel dark reddish-brown. April, May. Australia. 1789. (B.M. 2081.) var. **linophyl'la,** shoots more downy, *l.* ½ to ¾ in. long, *fl.* larger. Syn. *P. linophylla.*

P. ro'sea. Erect, heath-like shrub, 3 ft., shoots nearly or quite glabrous. *l.* narrow-linear, ¼ to ½ in. long, densely set, channelled above, pointed, silky-hairy when quite young, scabrous, stalkless. *fl.* rose-lilac, in terminal heads about 1 in. wide; cal. silky, ⅕ in. long, lobes ovate-lanceolate; standard ⅓ to ½ in. h.; keel the same in length. April. Victoria. 1874. (B.M. 6941.)

P. rosmarinifo'lia. A synonym of *P. polifolia.*

P. scab'ra. Shrub 3 or 4 ft., shoots softly downy or hairy, often rust-coloured. *l.* obovate to narrowly cuneate, widest at end, up to 1½ in. long, notched or slightly 2-lobed, mucronate, scabrous above, downy to shaggy beneath; stipules thread-like. *fl.* yellow, few in stalkless terminal clusters; cal. ⅙ in. long; standard ⅓ in. long; wings and keel shorter, the latter dark. New S. Wales, Victoria. 1803. var. **monta'na,** *l.* often as wide as long, not mucronate.

P. stipula'ris. Erect shrub 2 to 3 ft., shoots very densely crowded with l. and small appressed stipules. *l.* ¾ to 1½ in. long, $\frac{1}{16}$ to $\frac{1}{12}$ in. wide, narrowly linear, slender-pointed, ciliate. *fl.* crowded 20 or more in a terminal head 1¼ in. across, stalkless, yellow; cal. ¼ in. long, the 5 lobes pointed ciliate. April, May. New S. Wales. 1792. (B.M. 475.) Shoots completely hidden by the foliage.

P. stric'ta. Shrub 1 to 3 ft., shoots silky when young. *l.* ¼ to ⅓ in. long, obovate to oblong, blunt except for a short mucro, silky-white beneath. *fl.* in small terminal heads of 4 to 6, scarcely stalked; standard bright yellow streaked with red at base, ⅜ in. wide; keel dark purple at end. June. Australia, Tasmania. (B.M. 1588.)

P. subumbella'ta. Erect or straggling shrub, 2 ft., shoots hairy. *l.* densely set, linear to narrowly oblong or oval, ¼ to ½ in. long, blunt, glabrous. *fl.* ⅝ in. long, in dense, terminal heads ¾ in. wide, stalkless; standard obovate, almost keeled at back, yellow; keel dark. April, May. Australia, Tasmania. 1831. (B.M. 3254.)

P. tenuifo'lia. Prostrate, heath-like shrub, the very slender shoots and l. softly downy. *l.* heath-like, densely set, ⅓ to 1½ in. long, concave above. *fl.* yellow, stalkless or nearly so, solitary or in pairs terminating short side twigs; standard $\frac{3}{16}$ in. wide, streaked with red. April, May. Australia, Tasmania. 1817. (B.M. 2086.)

P. villo'sa. Low, spreading shrub up to 3 ft., shoots downy. *l.* ⅙ to ⅓ in. long, densely set, oblong-cuneate to linear or obovate, concave above with incurved margins, hairy or tubercular beneath. *fl.* solitary, axillary, often in short leafy racemes, usually entirely yellow; standard ¼ in. wide. April, May. 1790. (B.M. 967.)

W. J. B.

pulvera'ceus, powdery.

pulverulen'tus -a -um, as though dusted with powder.

PULVINAR'IA vitis. *See* **Scale Insects.** A

pulvina'tus -a -um, pulvinate, cushion-shaped.

PULVINUS. A cushion, an enlargement or swelling at the base of the leaf or leaflet or at the top of a leaf-stalk.

pumil'io, dwarf.

pu'milus -a -um, low, or small.

PUMPKIN. *See* **Cucurbita Pepo.**

puncta'tus -a -um, dotted.

puncticula'tus -a -um, minutely dotted.

punctis'simus -a -um, much spotted.

punctula'tus -a -um, dotted.

pun'gens, ending in a sharp point, as does the holly leaf.

PU'NICA (old Latin name of the plant, the *Malum Punicum* of Pliny). Fam. *Punicaceae.* A genus of 2 species in the E. Mediterranean eastwards to NW. India and in Socotra. Deciduous shrubs or small trees with usually opposite, clustered, entire leaves without stipules. Flowers perfect, 1 to 5 at ends of both terminal and axillary branches; calyx tube more or less tubular, sepals 5 to 8, fleshy, valvate; petals 5 to 7, imbricate, perigynous; stamens very numerous; style 1, carpels in 2 series, one above the other, the lower of 3 or 4 carpels with axile placentae, the upper of 3 to 7 with parietal placentae. Fruit a berry with a leathery pericarp and pulpy flesh formed by the fleshy outer seed-coats of the numerous seeds. The Pomegranate rarely ripens fruit in England but is worth growing where wall-space can be given it for its flowers. In the open it is liable to be cut to the ground-level in all but the mildest winters. It grows well in good, loamy, well-drained soil against a south or west wall and flowers over a long period from June to September. It can be propagated by cuttings, layers, or grafting and if the last is undertaken the stock should be a seedling of the type. The named varieties do not come true from seed.

P. Grana'tum. Pomegranate. Deciduous shrub or small tree, 15 to 30 ft. h. with spiny branches, angled, glabrous. *l.* obovate to oblong, ¾ to 3½ in. long, glabrous, shining above. *fl.* about 1¼ in. across, scarlet, pet. crumpled, cal. purple, on short stalks. June to September. *fr.* deep yellow, 2½ to 3½ in. wide. SE. Europe to Himalaya. 16th century. (B.M. 1832.) var. **albes'cens,** *fl.* whitish; **albo-ple'na,** *fl.* double white; **flore-ple'no,** *fl.* double red; **Legrel'lii,** *fl.* double, striped red and yellowish-white; **na'na,** a shrub with narrow *l.*, possibly hardier than the type. 1723. (B.M. 634.); **rubro-ple'na,** a synonym of *flore-pleno.*

PUNICA'CEAE. Dicotyledons. A family with a single genus. *See* **Punica** for characters.

punic'eus -a -um, crimson.

PUPA. The inactive, resting stage of insects which undergo a complete metamorphosis. During this phase —the Chrysalis stage—the larva (caterpillar, grub, or maggot) undergoes a remodelling both externally and internally to adapt it to the requirements of the future adult insect. Most pupae remain motionless, but some possess a considerable (Mosquitoes) or a limited (certain Moths with burrowing caterpillars) capacity for movement which becomes evident towards the end of the pupal period and facilitates the emergence of the adult.

There are 3 main types of pupae, viz.: (1) free Pupae of such Orders as *Neuroptera* (e.g. Lacewing Flies), *Trichoptera* (Caddis Flies), and *Hymenoptera* (Sawflies, Gall-Wasps, Ichneumon Flies, Wasps, Bees, and Ants); (2) the Pupae of most *Lepidoptera* (Butterflies and Moths) and the *Diptera Orthorrhapha* (Crane Flies, Mosquitoes, Gall-Midges, &c.); and (3) those of the *Diptera Cyclorrhapha* (Hover Flies, Carrot Flies, Cabbage and Onion Flies, &c.), in which the last larval skin is retained as a covering to the pupa, becoming hardened and capsule-like and known as a Puparium.

The inactive state of most pupae renders them vulnerable to the attacks of enemies, and they are usually concealed in earthen cells in the ground, within silken cocoons, between the folds of a leaf and in other sheltered positions.

It is seldom possible to take active measures against the pupae of insects for they are as a general rule in a sheltered position. Insects which pupate in the soil, however, are affected to some degree by cultural operations, especially winter digging, which both exposes them to severe weather conditions and to insectivorous birds, or injures them mechanically, and may result in their deep burial which prevents the adult insects from making their way to the air.

G. F. W.

PUPA'LIA (native name in E. Indies). FAM. *Amaranthaceae.* A genus of about 10 species of trichotomously branched herbs or sub-shrubs, natives of Trop. Asia and Africa. Leaves opposite, ovate or roundish, obtuse or slender-pointed, entire, stalked. Flowers green, in interrupted simple or panicled spikes; perfect flowers solitary, 5-parted, segments lanceolate, almost equal, stamens 5, with filaments shortly connate at base; imperfect flowers clustered. *P. atropurpurea* grows in sandy loam. It needs stove conditions and may be increased by cuttings in sand, under a glass in heat.

P. atropurpu'rea. Evergreen sub-shrub, 1½ to 2 ft. h.; stem striated; branches purplish, ascending. *l.* ovate, 2½ to 3 in. long, 1 in. or more wide, obsoletely mucronate, slightly dotted, long-stalked. *fl.* dark purple; spikes 3 to 7 in. long. September. Tropics. 1759.

pural'bus -a -um, very white.

Pur'domii, in honour of William Purdom, 1880–1921, collector for Messrs. Veitch in China, and companion of R. Farrer.

Pur'dyi, in honour of Carl Purdy, 1861–1945, collector and student of Californian plants, especially bulbs.

pur'gans, purgative.

PURIRI. *See* **Vitex lucens.** A

PURPLE LOOSESTRIFE. *See* **Lythrum Salicaria.**

PURPLE MEDICK. *See* **Medicago sativa.**

PURPLE OSIER. *See* **Salix purpurea.**

PURPLE WREATH. *See* **Petrea volubilis.**

purpuras'cens, becoming purple.

purpura'tus -a -um, purplish.

purpu'reus -a -um, purple.

Purpus'ii, in honour of Joseph Anton Purpus, 1860–1932, for 40 years Curator, Botanic Garden, Darmstadt, who collected in Mexico, or sometimes his brother, C. A. Purpus, born 1853.

Purpuso'rum, of C. A. and J. A. Purpus.

PURSH'IA (in honour of Frederick T. Pursh, 1774–1820, German who travelled in N. America and wrote (1817) *Flora Americae Septentrionalis*). FAM. *Rosaceae.* A genus of a single N. American deciduous shrub, with alternate 3-lobed leaves with solitary small yellowish flowers and fruit a hairy achene. Needs a light soil, is hardy in all but the most severe of winters and is propagated by layers.

P. tridenta'ta. Spreading bush, 3 to 6 ft. h. with downy young shoots. *l.* wedge-shaped at base, 3-lobed at apex, up to 1¼ in. long, ⅛ to ¼ in. wide, grey-green above, white tomentose below. *fl.* about ⅛ in. wide, yellow, usually solitary at ends of branches. May. Western N. America. 1826. (B.R. 1446.) var. **glandulo'sa,** *l.* smaller, glandular, smooth above, more tender than type. 1898.

PURSLANE (*Portulaca oleracea*). The young shoots of Purslane are sometimes used in salads especially on the Continent, and the older ones used as a potherb or for pickling. It is an annual and grows best in a sunny open position in well-drained soil and is sown outdoors in March in drills a foot apart, the plants being thinned to 9 in. apart in the rows. The only cultivation necessary in summer is to keep the plants free of weeds. The name Purslane is also sometimes applied to *Claytonia perfoliata*, &c., which, though not often grown for the purpose, is sometimes used as a salad. *C. perfoliata* is naturalized on well-drained banks and makes its growth in early spring.

PURSLANE TREE. *See* **Portulacaria afra.**

PUSCHKIN'IA (in honour of Count Apollos Apollosovich Mussin-Pushkin, died 1805, Russian chemist who collected plants in Caucasus and Ararat). FAM. *Liliaceae.* A genus of 2 species of bulbous plants, natives of Asia Minor, Caucasus, and Afghanistan, related to Chionodoxa but with connate filaments. Leaves radical, few, the first usually oblong, the others linear. Flowers few, sometimes solitary, usually in a raceme on a leafless scape; perianth tube short, bell-shaped, segments longer, almost equal, somewhat spreading. *P. scilloides* is hardy and grows well in a compost of sandy loam and leaf-mould. Increase by division of bulbs every 2 or 3 years.

P. libano'tica. A synonym of *P. scilloides.*

P. scilloi'des.* Striped Squill. *l.* few, lanceolate, 4 to 6 in. long, concave, dark green. *fl.* ½ to 1 in. across, blue or whitish with distinct blue median stripe on segs.; scape 4 to 8 in. h., pedicels slender, distant, 1- to 6-fld., arching, fls. secund. Orient. 1819. (B.M. 2244; F.d.S. 2220 as *P. sicula*; G.F. 310 as *Adamsia scilloides.*) var. **compac'ta,** more compact and with more numerous fl.

P. si'cula. A synonym of *P. scilloides.*

pusil'lus -a -um, weak and slender.

PUSS MOTH, *Cerura vinula*, is a pest of Poplars and Willows, the leaves of which may be stripped by the caterpillars. The moth has a wing expanse of 2½ to 3 in., the body being thick-set, furry, and silver grey, with the hind-wings striped black. The eggs are laid on the leaves in May and early June, and the caterpillar is conspicuous both on account of its colour and shape. There is a purplish-brown saddle-shaped marking with a white border on a green body, a marked hump on the last thoracic segment, and a pair of flexible tubes which conceal long purplish whips on the hind segment. The fully fed caterpillar constructs a cocoon formed of bark fragments spun together with silk and glued firmly to a branch, making detection difficult. The pupal stage lasts some 6 or 8 months. The emergence of the moth from its prison is aided by an injection of a fluid which softens the cocoon wall and by a head-shield which breaks through the pupal shell.

The caterpillars are readily destroyed by lightly spraying the attacked leaves in June or July with D.D.T. or arsenate of lead.

G. F. W.

pustula'tus -a -um, covered with excrescences, often glandular, like blisters.

PUSTULE. Small raised spot or intumescence on the surface of leaf or shoot, sometimes characteristic of the species, sometimes due to disturbance in the cells of that area. The cause of disturbance may be the presence of an organism, e.g. bacterium, fungus, mite, or insect within the tissues, or lack of balance between the intake and transpiration of water (see, for example, Oedema).

D. E. G.

PUTAMEN. The stone (endocarp) of a drupe.

PUTAPUTAWETA. *See* **Carpodetus serratus.**

PUTO'RIA (*putor*, a strong smell; in allusion to the smell of the leaves). FAM. *Rubiaceae.* A genus of 2 or 3 species of low, spreading, unpleasantly smelling shrubs occurring in the Mediterranean region from Spain to Syria. Leaves opposite, entire; flowers in terminal fascicles; fruit a linear-oblong drupe. Rather tender shrub suitable for a sunny spot in a rock-garden in the milder counties.

P. calab'rica. Evergreen, low, scrubby, spreading shrub; bark peeling; shoot slender, downy. *l.* linear-lanceolate, tapered to both ends, ⅓ to 1 in. long, $\frac{1}{16}$ to $\frac{3}{16}$ in. wide, margins recurved. *fl.* in terminal clusters of up to 12; cor. very slenderly tubular with a limb ½ in. across of 4 slender lobes, bright red or purple-rose. June, July. *fr.* a small red juicy berry. Mediterranean region. 1820.

W. J. B.

PUTTERLICK'IA (in honour of A. Putterlick, 1810–45, assistant in the Botanical Museum of Vienna). FAM. *Celastraceae.* Two species of glabrous S. African shrubs sometimes united to Celastrus, which differs from Putterlickia in having only 2 ovules in each ovary-cell, whereas Putterlickia has about 6. Leaves alternate, mostly on spurs, toothed or entire; parts of the flower 5 or (rarely) 4. Fruit a 3-angled capsule. They require greenhouse treatment.

P. pyracan'tha. Shrub 2 to 6 ft. glabrous, spiny. Spines strong, horizontal, ½ to 2 in. long. *l.* mostly clustered on short, stunted twigs, but alternate on fully grown shoots, 1 to 1½ in. long, obovate or elliptic, usually broadest towards the rounded apex. *fl.* 3 to 12 or more on axillary panicles 1 to 1½ in. long; cor. creamy-white, ¼ in. wide. Summer. *Capsule* red, obovoid, ½ to ¾ in. long. S. Africa. 1742. (B.M. 1167 as *Celastrus pyracanthus.*)

P. verruco'sa. Shrub with warted shoots (which distinguish it from the other sp.); spines ½ to 1½ in. long, stout. *l.* 1 to 2 in. long, obovate, tapered to a short stalk, blunt, notched, minutely prickle-toothed. *fl.* 8 to over 20 on slender axillary panicles 1 to 2 in. long; cor. greenish, $\frac{1}{12}$ in. long. *fr.* 3-angled, ½ to ¾ in. long. S. Africa.

W. J. B.

PU'YA (native name of the plant in Chile). FAM. *Bromeliaceae.* A genus of about 80 Andean herbaceous or woody plants mostly dying after seeding, but in some species branching from the lower leaves or rarely stoloniferous. The long often very spiny foliage ending in a hard sharp point is produced in dense rosettes either without an evident stem or with a woody stem or trunk, some species, e.g. *P. chilensis,* reaching a height of many feet. Closely related to Dyckia but distinguished by having petals free. The flowers are generally showy in a simple or paniculate inflorescence on a tall scape. They mostly require greenhouse or stove treatment (but *P. alpestris* is fairly hardy) and need a mixture of loam and peat. Propagation is effected either by seed or, where they are produced, by suckers.

P. alpes'tris. *fl.* pet. metallic greenish blue, about 2 in. long, with orange anthers, in a large many-fld. pyramidal panicle, the tips of the branches with reddish bracts but devoid of fl., on a scape 2 to 3 ft. or so h. *l.* tufted, crowded, remotely spiny, scurfy beneath. Chile. Before 1868. (B.M. 5732, J.R.H.S. 74, 144, as *P. Whytei.*) Almost hardy, a good plant for the cool greenhouse, often confused with *P. caerulea.*

P. Altenstein'ii. A synonym of *Pitcairnia Altensteinii.*

P. caeru'lea. *fl.* pet. deep blue, about 2 in. long, with orange anthers, in a many-fld. pyramidal panicle, the tips of the branches crowded with fl., on a scape 3 to 4 ft. h. *l.* tufted, crowded, remotely spiny, scurfy beneath. Chile. Before 1838. (B.R. 1840, 11.) SYN. *Pitcairnia caerulea.*

P. chilen'sis. *fl.* pet. greenish-yellow; 2¼ in. long; sep. 1¼ in. long, green; panicle many-fld., dense, rhomboid, 2 to 3 ft. long, with crowded branches; lower bracts 1 in. long; peduncle erect, much longer than the l., bearing many sterile bracts. July. *l.* 100 or more in a rosette, ensiform, acuminate, 3 to 4 ft. long, 2 in. broad, vertically lined on the back, with large, distant, horny spines. Stem 6 to 10 ft. long, sometimes branched. Chile, &c. 1820. (B.M. 4715; F.d.S. 869–70; G.F. 1858, 225.) var. **gigante'a,** *fl.* smaller. *l.* erect, with shorter and more robust prickles, stem 10 to 15 ft. long.

P. coarcta'ta. A synonym of *P. chilensis.*

P. flocco'sa. *fl.* pet. blue, half as long again as the hairy sep.; panicle many-fld., lax, with numerous ascending, spicate branches, densely white-floccose, about 2½ ft. long; peduncle as long as the l. *l.* about 100 in a dense rosette, ensiform, acuminate, 2½ to 3 ft. long, 1 in. broad, spiny, 3 ft. h. Brit. Guiana, Colombia, Venezuela. 1847. SYN. *Pitcairnia floccosa.*

P. gi'gas. *fl.* white or rose, in erect spikes, from 18 to 30 ft. in height. *l.* tufted, agave-like, linear-lanceolate, spiny-toothed, mealy white beneath. Colombia. 1881. (R.H. 1881, 315.)

P. grandiflo'ra. A synonym of *Pitcairnia ferruginea.*

P. heterophyl'la. A synonym of *Pitcairnia heterophylla.*

P. longifo'lia. A synonym of *Pitcairnia longifolia.*

P. maidifo'lia. A synonym of *Pitcairnia maidifolia.*

P. spatha'cea. *fl.* pet. pale blue, 1¼ in. long; infl. many-fld., paniculate, up to 2 ft. long, axis, bracteoles and sep. rose. *l.* in a basal rosette, about 15 in. long, ¾ in. wide, somewhat scaly below. 3 ft. h. Argentine. 1896? (B.M. 7966.)

P. sulphu'rea. A synonym of *Pitcairnia Wendlandi.*

P. viola'cea.* *fl.* pet. deep violet, 2¼ in. long, with yellow anthers; infl. many-fld., lax, usually with horizontally spreading branches 6 to 14 in. long, borne on a stem 6 ft. h. *l.* long, narrow, 18 in. long, ⅝ in. wide; recurving, glaucous, spiny. Chile. 1890. (B.M. 8194.)

Puya alpestris

P. vires'cens. A synonym of *Guzmania virescens.*

P. Warszewic'zii. A synonym of *Pitcairnia atrorubens.*

P. Whyte'i. A synonym of *P. alpestris.*

PYCNAN'THEMUM (*pyknos,* dense, *anthos,* flower; the flowers are densely arranged). FAM. *Labiatae.* Mountain Mint. A genus of about 21 species of N. American perennial herbs with a pungent Mint-like flavour, allied to Origanum. Stems often branched corymbosely above. Leaves entire, nearly sessile. Flowers in dense many-flowered whorls, crowded with bracts and forming a terminal head as in Monarda but smaller and hairy, whitish or purplish; calyx about 13-nerved, throat naked; corolla somewhat 2-lipped, short; stamens 4, lower pair rather shorter than upper. The following, treated like other hardy perennials, succeed in any good ordinary soil, growing from 1 to 3 ft. h. Sometimes listed under Koellia, a name now discarded. For a revision of the genus by E. Grant and C. Epling, see *Univ. California Publ. Bot.* 20, 195–240 (1943).

P. flexuo'sum. Stem slender, about 2 ft. h. *l.* narrow-linear, 1 to 2 in. long, about ⅛ in. wide. *fl.* purplish, cal. teeth awl-shaped, bristle-tipped. Eastern N. America. SYN. *P. linifolium.*

P. lanceola'tum. A synonym of *P. virginianum.*

P. mu'ticum. Minutely hoary, pleasantly aromatic, up to 2½ ft. h. *l.* ovate, broadly ovate-lanceolate or lanceolate, rather rigid, acute, mostly sessile. *fl.* white. Summer, autumn. N. America. 1897.

P. virginia'num. Stem rather hairy. *l.* lanceolate to nearly linear, very numerous, obtuse at the stalkless base. *fl.* purplish; bracts ovate. Summer. N. America.

PYCNI'DIUM (pl. **Pycnidia**). The type of fungus fruit-body mostly found in the class *Fungi Imperfecti* but also formed by some of the Ascomycetes and many other fungi. Formed by the hyphae, it is typically more or less globular and may be embedded among fungus threads or, where parasitic fungi are concerned, may be formed in the plant tissues and open out to the surface by means of a definite pore or ostiole. A pycnidium has a definite wall composed of several layers of fungus cells with the inside surface of the wall lined with conidiophores which produce spores. The spores accumulate inside the pycnidium and are later forced out through the ostiole either separately or something, by sticking together, appear as long sticky coils or tendrils (e.g. Phoma). Pycnidia are barely visible to the naked eye and are pale, black, or even coloured red. They are generally stimulated to release their spores by sudden wetting, as by rain, during which the spores are ejected.

D. E. G.

***pycno-*,** in compound words, signifying dense.

***pycnocar'pus -a -um*,** thick- or dense-fruited.

PYCNODOR'IA. Included in **Pteris.**

***pycnolo'bus -a -um*,** dense-lobed, or conspicuously lobed.

PYCNOP'TERIS. Included in **Dryopteris.**

PYCNOSTA'CHYS (*pyknos*, dense, *stachys*, spike; in allusion to the dense flower-spikes). FAM. *Labiatae.* A genus of over 40 species of erect annual or perennial herbs, natives of Trop. and S. Africa and Madagascar. Leaves stalked, linear-lanceolate to broadly ovate, coarsely toothed. Flowers in whorls in dense, terminal spikes; corolla blue, its tube exserted and bent down, limb 2-lipped, upper lip 4-toothed, lower entire and concave; calyx ovoid-bell-shaped with 5 equal awl-shaped spiny teeth; stamens 4. Nutlets almost round, smooth. For cultivation of these stove plants *see* **Ocimum.**

P. caeru'lea. Annual. About 18 in. h., stem 4-angled. *l.* oblong or linear-lanceolate, 2 to 3 in. long, acute, deeply toothed, narrowed to base, glandular beneath. *fl.* blue in a spike 1 to 2 in. long. Madagascar. 1825. (H.E.F. 202.)

P. Daw'ei. Stout perennial 4 to 6 ft. h., loosely branched, pyramidal. *l.* narrow-lanceolate, slender-pointed, toothed. *fl.* cobalt-blue in short spikes; cal. teeth needle-like. Uganda. (B.M. 8450.)

P. urticifo'lia. Perennial, about 3 ft. h. *l.* ovate, slender-pointed, obtuse at base, deeply toothed, downy beneath; stalk long. *fl.* blue in a large thyrse-like ovate spike. August. Trop. Africa. 1862. (B.M. 5365.)

***pygmae'us -a -um*,** dwarf, very small.

PYGMY PINE. *See* **Dacrydium laxifolium.**

***py'lius -a -um*,** of Pylia Navarin, Messina; ancient name, Pylos.

***Pylzow'ii*,** in honour of Mikhai Alexandrovich Pylzov, Russian companion of Przewalski in his botanical exploration of W. China 1870–3, officer in the Russian Asiatic Land Department.

PYRACAN'THA (*pyr*, fire, *acanthos*, thorn). FAM. *Rosaceae.* A genus of 6 or 7 species of evergreen shrubs, more or less thorny, allied to Crataegus. Flower always white, ¼ to ⅓ in. wide, borne in clusters on short leafy twigs. Fruit a small red, orange, or yellow pome with the calyx adhering at the top. All are hardy or nearly so and love a good loamy soil. Propagation is by seeds or cuttings.

KEY

1.	*Cal. and lvs. beneath glabrous*	2
1.	*Cal. and lvs. beneath downy*	P. angustifolia
2.	*Corymbs downy*	P. coccinea
2.	*Corymbs glabrous*	3
3.	*Lvs. over 1½ in. long*	4
3.	*Lvs. ½ to 1½ in. long*	5
4.	*Lvs. oblong to obovate*	P. atalantioides
4.	*Lvs. oblanceolate, rounded at apex*	P. crenatoserrata
5.	*Lvs. finely toothed, narrowly oval, obtuse*	P. crenulata taliensis
5.	*Lvs. narrowly obovate to oblanceolate, tapered to base*	P. Rogersiana

Pyracantha angustifolia

Pyracantha angustifolia

P. angustifo'lia. Evergreen shrub up to 10 or 12 ft., often much lower and spreading, young shoots thickly downy. *l.* narrow-oblong, round-ended, 1 to 2¼ in. long, ⅛ to ½ in. wide, faintly toothed, grey tomentose beneath. *fr.* at first grey with down, finally brilliant orange-yellow, flattish-globose, ¼ to ⅜ in. wide. China. June, July. 1889. The early introduced plants were less hardy and more tomentose than the later of Forrest's finding. (B.M. 8345.)

P. atalantioi'des. Evergreen tree up to 20 ft. *l.* oblong, elliptic or obovate, 1½ to 3 in. long, about half as wide, sometimes slightly or not at all toothed. *fr.* orange-shaped, ¼ in. wide, scarlet, persisting till March. China. June. 1907. (B.M. 9099.) SYN. *P. Gibbsii.* The tallest and largest-leaved species.

P. coccin'ea.* Fire thorn. Evergreen round-headed tree up to 20 ft., more often a bushy, very leafy shrub, young shoots downy. *l.* narrowly obovate or oval, pointed, finely toothed, 1 to 2½ in. long, ¼ to ¾ in. wide. *fl.* white, ⅓ in. across. June. *fr.* orange-shaped, about ¼ in. wide, bright red. S. Europe, Asia Minor. 1629. (B.T.S. 2, 268.) var. **Lalan'dei** vigorous form with wider, less deeply toothed *l.*, and bright orange-red *fr.* (R.H.B. 1882, 145 as *Crataegus Pyracantha Lalandei.*) These 2 shrubs are perfectly hardy and bear fine crops of brilliantly coloured fr. which, if unmolested by, or protected from birds, persist for 5 months. They are also valuable as evergreen covering for walls.

P. crenatoserra'ta. Evergreen shrub up to 12 or 18 ft. distinguished from the other sp. by its oblanceolate, glabrous *l.* having a broad rounded apex; they are 1½ to 3 in. long, ⅓ to 1 in. wide. *fl.* June. It has been considered a form of *P. atalantioides*, but apart from differences in the foliage, it has smaller, later maturing red fr. which persist till March. China. 1906. (B.M. 9099.) SYN. *P. yunnanensis.*

P. crenula'ta. It may be that, in its true Himalayan form, this species is not now in cultivation. In any case it is an inferior shrub for gardens and probably more tender than *P. coccinea*, from which it differs by its round-ended *l.* A var. of it, called **talien'sis** in gardens, has l. of the proper shape but smaller, *fr.* shining yellow falling earlier than that of *P. coccinea.* Presumably from the Tali Range, NW. Yunnan.

P. Gibb'sii. A synonym of *P. atalantioides.*

P. Laland'ei. A variety of *P. coccinea.*

P. Rogersia'na.* Evergreen shrub of dense, ultimately spreading habit up to 10 or 12 ft. *l.* ½ to 1½ in. long, ⅛ to ½ in. wide, oblanceolate or narrowly obovate, slenderly tapered to base. *fl.* ¼ in. wide, white, in small corymbose racemes. June. *fr.* ¼ in. wide, globose, golden yellow to reddish-orange. China. 1911. (B.M. n.s. 74.) The smallest-leaved and least vigorous species and of quite dainty beauty when young, producing enormous crops of fruit which in var. **auranti'aca,** are orange-yellow, in **flav'a** are bright yellow. var. **semiple'na** has 10 or more pet. to each fl. The best species for small gardens.

P. yunnanen'sis. A synonym of *P. crenatoserrata.*

pyramida'lis -is -e, conical.

A→

PYRENA. 'Stone' caused by hardening of the endocarp of drupaceous fruits, e.g. Cotoneaster.

pyrenae'us -a -um, pyrena'icus -a -um, of the Pyrenees.

PYRENOMYCE'TES. Ascomycetous fungi which, in their perfect (ascospore-forming) stage produce flask-shaped perithecia opening by a pore or ostiole, and have their asci arranged in parallel rows on the floor of the perithecia.

D. E. G.

PYRETH'RUM. Included in **Chrysanthemum.**

PYRETHRUM. A very effective insecticide made from the powdered flower-heads of *Chrysanthemum cinerariifolium* and *C. roseum.* The flower-heads are collected just as they open and dried gently. When quite dry they are ground to a fine powder and may be used either in that form for dusting affected plants, &c., or an extract may be made and used as a spray. In either form it is valuable against many types of insects and being non-poisonous it may be used on plants intended for food even when approaching maturity. **A**

pyriform'is -is -e, pear-shaped.

+**PYROCYDONIA.** FAM. *Rosaceae.* Graft chimaeras (graft hybrids) of Pyrus and Cydonia.

+**P. Daniel'ii.** Graft-hybrid between *Cydonia oblonga* and *Pyrus communis* (Williams's Bon Chrêtien). Tree resembling the quince. *l.* ovate, 1½ to 3 in. long, 1 to 1½ in. wide, base rounded, apex pointed, toothed, more or less downy; stalk scarcely ¼ in. long. Appeared in 1902 at the junction of a scion of the pear grafted on common quince in the garden of St. Vincent College, Rennes, France. var. **Wink'leri,** *l.* elliptic-ovate, up to 2 in. long, slender-pointed, more downy. Appeared in 1913 in the same garden.

PY'ROLA (from *Pyrus*, so called from a fancied resemblance in the foliage). FAM. *Pyrolaceae.* Wintergreen. A genus of about 14 species of perennial, stoloniferous, glabrous dwarf herbs, natives of Europe, N. and Cent. Asia, and N. America as far south as Mexico. Leaves radical or cauline, alternate, usually long stalked, persistent. Flowers white, pink, yellowish, or pale purple, nodding, in racemes on erect, bracteate scapes; calyx 5-partite, persistent; petals 5, concave, sessile, more or less incurved; stamens 10, anther cells short, obtuse. Fruit a 5-celled globose capsule with numerous minute seeds. The plants are difficult to establish after moving or division and although they may live long yet often fail to grow when the long-ranging stolons are damaged. Light woodland soil, in cool positions on the rock-garden with partial shade or on the edge of woodland suits them. Careful division or seed serves for propagation. They are hardy.

KEY

1.	*Style straight; pet. erect; stamens not beaked*	2
1.	*Style curving; pet. spreading; stamens usually beaked*	4
2.	*Style included or almost so*	3
2.	*Style exserted*	P. secunda
3.	*Stamens as long as style; fl. ¼ in. across*	P. minor
3.	*Stamens shorter than style; fl. ½ in. across; plant larger*	P. media
4.	*Lvs. thick*	5
4.	*Lvs. thin; fl. whitish or pinkish*	P. elliptica
5.	*Fl. reddish or flesh-coloured*	P. asarifolia
5.	*Fl. white or greenish-white*	6
6.	*Lvs. green*	7
6.	*Lvs. mottled*	P. picta
7.	*Fl. white*	8
7.	*Fl. greenish-white*	9
8.	*Lvs. 1 to 1½ in. long*	P. rotundifolia
8.	*Lvs. 2 in. long*	P. americana
9.	*Lvs. spatulate, sharply toothed*	P. picta dentata
9.	*Lvs. orbicular*	P. virens

P. america'na. Habit of *P. minor*, but 5 to 12 in. h. *l.* orbicular, 2 in. long, thick, shorter than stalk. *fl.* numerous, white; pet. thick; cal. lobes lanceolate or oblong-lanceolate, up to ½ as long as pet.; bracts conspicuous. Summer. Eastern N. America. SYN. *P. rotundifolia* of some authors, *P. rotundifolia* var. *americana.*

P. asarifo'lia.* *l.* broadly elliptic to kidney-shaped, rather thin but leathery, shining, teeth rounded. *fl.* purple, ⅜ to ⅝ in. across, on scapes 1 to 15 in. long, with ovate-lanceolate bracts; cal. lobes triangular-ovate, acute. June to August. Canada, E. United States, Asia. var. **incarna'ta,*** *fl.* pink or rose, *l.* more or less cordate to obovate, dull.

P. bractea'ta. A synonym of *P. rotundifolia.*

P. chloran'tha. A synonym of *P. virens.*

Pyrola uliginosa (p. 1721)

P. ellip'tica. About 6 in. h. or more. *l.* elliptic or obovate, 1 to 2½ in. long, scarcely toothed; stalk rather shorter than blade, margined. *fl.* white, bell-shaped, on 5- to 10-fld. scapes; bracts short; pedicels slender; cal. lobes ovate, short. June, July. N. America, Japan. 1818.

P. me'dia.* About 4 in. h. Much like *P. minor* but larger and stouter. *l.* roundish-ovate up to 1¾ in. wide. *fl.* white, tinged red, ½ in. across, in many-fld. racemes. July, August. Europe, including Britain. (E.B. 897.)

P. mi'nor.* Stem 1 to 3 in. long. *l.* sometimes alternate, roundish-ovate, 1 to 1½ in. across, stalk longer than blade. *fl.* white tinged rose, globose, ¼ in. across, on a slender scape 8 to 12 in. long. June to August. Europe including Britain, N. America. (E.B. 898.)

P. pic'ta. *l.* ovate or elliptic, 1 to 2 in. long, nearly entire, blotched white above, purplish beneath, slightly revolute. *fl.* greenish-white (sometimes tinged pink); pet. ⅕ in. long; sep. short, broadly ovate; scapes 6 to 12 in. long, few- to many-fld. Summer. Western N. America. var. **denta'ta,** *l.* not mottled, spatulate-oblong, sharply toothed, stalk short.

P. rotundifo'lia.* About 6 in. h. *l.* roundish-obovate, shorter than the slender stalks. *fl.* white, ½ in. across on 10- to 20-fld. scapes 6 to 12 in. long; bracts few. Summer. Europe, including Britain, N. America. (E.B. 895; B.M. 8710B as *P. bracteata.*) var. **arena'ria,*** *l.* smaller, bracts more numerous. (E.B. 896.)

P. secun'da. Branches straggling, ascending, 1 to 4 in. long. *l.* ovate, acute, 1 to 1¼ in. long, toothed, rather thin, veined; stalk shorter than blade. *fl.* greenish-white, ¼ in. across, horizontal; scapes slender, 2 to 5 in. long; racemes 1 to 2 in. long, secund. July. Europe, including Britain, W. Asia, N. America. (E.B. 899.)

P. uligino'sa. Rootstock long, creeping. Stem very short. *l.* nearly round or ovate-elliptic, up to 3 in. long and nearly as wide, crenulate, dull dark green above, sometimes reddish beneath; stalk up to 4 in. long. *fl.* bright red-purple or rose, especially without, about ¾ in. across, fragrant, nodding; pet. concave, obovate or elliptic; scapes 6 to 12 in. h., racemes 5- to 20-fld., 2½ to 4 in. long. N. America. 1916. (B.M. 8710A.) Syn. *P. asarifolia* var. *purpurea.*

P. umbella'ta. A synonym of *Chimaphila.*

P. uniflo'ra. A synonym of *Moneses uniflora.*

P. vi'rens. 6 to 10 in. h. *l.* orbicular or kidney-shaped, ⅓ to 1 in. wide, dull, veined above, scarcely or not toothed. *fl.* 1 to 10, greenish-yellow, about ⅜ in. across; cal. lobes short, obtuse. June, July. N. America. Syn. *P. chlorantha.*

PYROLA'CEAE. Dicotyledons. A family of about 40 species of herbaceous or sub-shrubby plants in 11 genera. Some species are non-chlorophyllose parasites. Inhabitants of arctic and north temperate parts of the world. Leaves alternate, without stipules; flowers regular with 5-parted calyx (sometimes absent), 5 (rarely 4) free petals, 10 stamens dehiscing by apical pores or by slits, and a superior 5-celled, many-ovuled ovary with a single style and stigma; fruit a capsule, splitting into 5 valves. The genera dealt with here are Chimaphila, Moneses, Monotropa, Pyrola.

PYROLI'RION (*pyr*, fire, *lirion*, lily, from the colour of the flowers). Fam. *Amaryllidaceae.* A genus of about 5 species of bulbous plants closely related to Zephyranthes with which it is often combined, natives of the Andes of Bolivia and Peru. Habit as in Zephyranthes but spathe with 2 segments completely free and opposite in the upper part, perianth erect with a narrow cylindrical tube dilated at the throat into a bell-shaped-cylindrical limb with the upper parts of the segments only recurved; stamens inserted at the mouth of the true tube; stigma deeply trifid, its lobes spatulate, not linear. Cultivation as for Zephyranthes.

P. au'reum.* About 1 ft. h. *l.* 1 or 2, linear, channelled, narrowed and recurved near tip, dark green. *Scape* terete, shorter than l. in cultivation, longer in nature; spathe rather longer than perianth tube. *fl.* solitary, sessile, pale golden-yellow, 3 to 4 in. long; segs. lanceolate, acute. May. (B.R. 1724.) Syn. *Zephyranthes flava.*

×PYRO'NIA. Fam. *Rosaceae.* Sexual hybrids between Pyrus and Cydonia. *See also* **+Pyrocydonia.**

×P. Veitch'ii. Hybrid (sexual) between *Cydonia oblonga* and *Pyrus communis.* Shrub or tree. *l.* oval, 1½ to 3 in. long, tapered to both ends, toothless. *fl.* white tinged rose, 2 in. across, often borne in threes; stamens 20, anthers violet. *fr.* oval, 3½ in. long, almost as wide, shortly stalked, greenish-yellow, spotted with red; flesh white, firm, juicy, lightly acid; pips absent. Fruited first in 1907. The fruit is edible. Raised in the nursery of Messrs. Veitch about 1895. var. **luxembergia'na,** *l.* 3 to 4 in. long, *fl.* pale rose, *fr.* pear-shaped. Of the same origin.

W. J. B.

PYROSTE'GIA (*pyr*, fire, *stega* roof; from the colour and form of the upper lip of the flower). Fam. *Bignoniaceae.* A genus of about 20 species of Brazilian shrubs climbing by tendrils, nearly related to Bignonia but the corolla lobes are valvate in bud and the flowers are tubular or almost club-shaped. Leaves of 2 or 3 leaflets, tendrils 3-fid. Flowers in terminal panicles, corolla tubular-funnel-shaped, curved; stamens longer than corolla tube. For treatment *see* **Clytostoma.**

P. venus'ta. *lflets.* oblong-ovate, slender-pointed, oblique at base. *fl.* crimson-orange, in many-fld. drooping panicles; cor. tubular, 2 to 3 in. long, lobes oblong, obtuse, reflexed; hairy inside. Brazil. 1816. (B.M. 2050; B.R. 249.) Syn. *P. ignea, Bignonia venusta.*

F. G. P.

PYRRHEI'MA Loddiges'ii. A synonym of *Tradescantia fuscata.*

PYRULA'RIA (a diminutive from Pyrus, the pear; in allusion to the shape of the fruit). Fam. *Santalaceae.* A genus of 3 species of deciduous trees or shrubs, 2 Asiatic, 1 N. American. Leaves alternate; flowers small, in parts of 4 or 5, 1-sexual or 2-sexual, the sexes sometimes on separate racemes. For cultivation *see* **Buckleya.**

P. oleif'era. A synonym of *P. pubera.*

P. pu'bera. Elk-nut; Oil nut. A straggling, deciduous shrub up to 13 ft., shoots and l. downy when young. *l.* oval to obovate-oblong, 2 to 5 in. long, ¾ to 1½ in. wide, pointed, cuneate, entire; stalk ⅛ to ⅓ in. long. *fl.* greenish, very small, in terminal racemes; males many-fld., 1 to 2 in. long, females few-fld. and shorter. *fr.* pear-shaped, 1 in. long, permeated with an acrid oil, crowned with the cal. lobes. Pennsylvania to Georgia on the mountains. 1800. Said to be parasitic on the roots of *Tsuga carolina.* For cultivation *see* **Buckleya.**

W. J. B.

PY'RUS (from Pyrus, the Latin for pear-tree). Pear. Fam. *Rosaceae.* A genus of about 20 species of deciduous, often thorny trees of small or medium size. Leaves alternate, simple, toothed or (rarely) entire. Flower in umbel-like clusters, white or pinkish; stamens 20 to 30; styles 2 to 5, free. Fruit top-shaped to sub-globose, the flesh with many grit-cells. The chief aggregation of species is in the E. Mediterranean region; others come from NE. Asia.

The pears have not on the whole the same ornamental value as the crabs although some, including *P. communis,* are very beautiful in flower. The snowy white down that covers the young growths of *P. nivalis* and *P. salicifolia* is very attractive, but the pears generally are not conspicuously notable for beauty of fruit or autumn colour, though the foliage of some varieties of the orchard pear takes on good colour in autumn (*see* **Pear**). They are perfectly hardy and grow freely in good, well-drained loam, in full sunshine. Propagated by seed or by grafting on wild pear stock.

Their chief botanical difference from Malus is in the latter having the styles united at or near the base.

Many species formerly listed under Pyrus are to be found here under Aronia, Malus, or Sorbus. Species of Cydonia, Chaenomeles, Mespilus, and even Amelanchier may be found under the name Pyrus in lists and gardens. Cydonia and Mespilus, and frequently Chaenomeles, are distinct from Pyrus by their solitary flowers; Amelanchier has flowers in racemes; Sorbus and Aronia have flowers in corymbs or panicles.

KEY

1.	*Cal. persistent on fruit*	2
1.	*Cal. deciduous or nearly so*	9
2.	*Lvs. not lobed*	3
2.	*Lvs. or some of them pinnatifid*	P. Regelii
3.	*Lvs. entire or with rounded teeth*	4
3.	*Lvs. with bristle-tipped teeth, usually ovate*	P. ussuriensis
4.	*Lvs. with small roundish projections beneath*	P. amygdaliformis
4.	*Lvs. without such papillae*	5
5.	*Lvs. entire, usually downy beneath*	6
5.	*Lvs. with rounded teeth*	8
6.	*Lvs. linear-lanceolate to lanceolate, shining above*	P. salicifolia

6. *Lvs. broader* 7
7. *Lvs. lanceolate to narrow-elliptic* P. elaeagrifolia
7. *Lvs. elliptic to obovate* P. nivalis
8. *Lvs.* $1\frac{1}{2}$ *to* $3\frac{1}{2}$ *in. long, ovoid* P. communis
8. *Lvs. under* $1\frac{1}{2}$ *in. long, cordate* P. cordata
9. *Lvs. sharply toothed* 10
9. *Lvs. with rounded teeth; styles* 3 *to* 5 P. Pashia
10. *Teeth of lvs. appressed* P. pyrifolia
10. *Teeth of lvs. spreading* P. betulaefolia

P. amygdaliform'is. Tree up to 20 ft. or more, sometimes a shrub. *l.* ovate, oval, or obovate, $1\frac{1}{2}$ to $2\frac{1}{2}$ in. long, shallow-toothed or entire, slightly downy at first, finally smooth and lustrous. *fl.* white, 1 in. wide, in clusters of 8 to 12. April. *fr.* sub-globose, 1 in. wide, yellowish-brown, thick-stalked. Europe. 1810. (B.T.S. 2, 273.) Several vars. exist varying mainly in shape of l. such as **cuneifolia, lobata, oblongifolia.**

P. betulaefo'lia. Graceful tree, 20 to 30 ft., shoots grey-felted for a whole season. *l.* ovate to roundish-ovate, 2 to 3 in. long, coarsely toothed, shining green. *fl.* white, $\frac{3}{4}$ in. wide, downy-stalked, 8 to 10 in a cluster; anthers red. April. *fr.* about the size of a large pea, on a stalk about 1 in. long, brown, dotted, cal. deciduous. China. 1882. (J.F.M. 20.)

P. × **canes'cens.** Intermediate between *P. nivalis* and *P. salicifolia* and probably a hybrid from them. (J.F.M. 19.)

P. commu'nis. Wild pear. Tree often of pyramidal shape, 40 to 50 ft., sometimes spiny. *l.* ovate to almost round or cordate, $1\frac{1}{2}$ to $3\frac{1}{2}$ in. long. *fl.* white, 1 to $1\frac{1}{2}$ in. wide, in corymbs 2 to 3 in. across. April. *fr.* obovoid or sub-globose, 1 to 2 in. long. Europe (naturalized in Britain.) (E.B. 488; E. and H. 356, 357; J.F.M. 1.) The species from which garden pears have been derived. Beautiful in fl. var. **Achras** has elongated fr. and l. is woolly when young; **Pyraster** is glabrous when the growths are mature and the fr. is rounded.

P. corda'ta. Often regarded as a var. of *P. communis*, but distinct by its small, often heart-shaped *l.* being usually less than $1\frac{1}{2}$ in. long, in its smaller *fl.*, and in its globose or pear-shaped *fr.* being only $\frac{3}{8}$ to $\frac{1}{2}$ in. long, brown specked with white, its cal. deciduous. France, Portugal, and found apparently wild in Devon and Cornwall in 1865. (E.B. 488 a (suppl.); J.F.M. 3.) SYN. *P. communis Briggsii.*

P. elaeagrifo'lia. Tree 20 to 30 ft., often thorny. *l.* lanceolate to narrowly obovate, entire, $1\frac{1}{2}$ to 3 in. long, up to 1 in. wide, grey-downy. *fl.* white, 1 in. wide. April. *fr.* roundish, or pear-shaped, 1 in. wide, green, short-stalked. Asia Minor. 1800. (J.F.M. 17.) Near *P. nivalis* but with narrower l. and greyer pubescence.

P. heterophyl'la. A synonym of *P. Regelii.*

P. loba'ta. A synonym of × *Crataego-mespilus grandiflora.*

P. niva'lis.* Small tree, shoots thickly woolly. *l.* oval to obovate, 2 to 3 in. long, entire, covered when young with white wool. *fl.* pure white, 1 to $1\frac{1}{2}$ in. wide, abundant. April. *fr.* sub-globose, 1 to $1\frac{1}{2}$ in. wide, yellowish-green, long-stalked. Asia Minor. (J.F.M. 21.) Very pleasing in the simultaneous whiteness of fl. and young l.

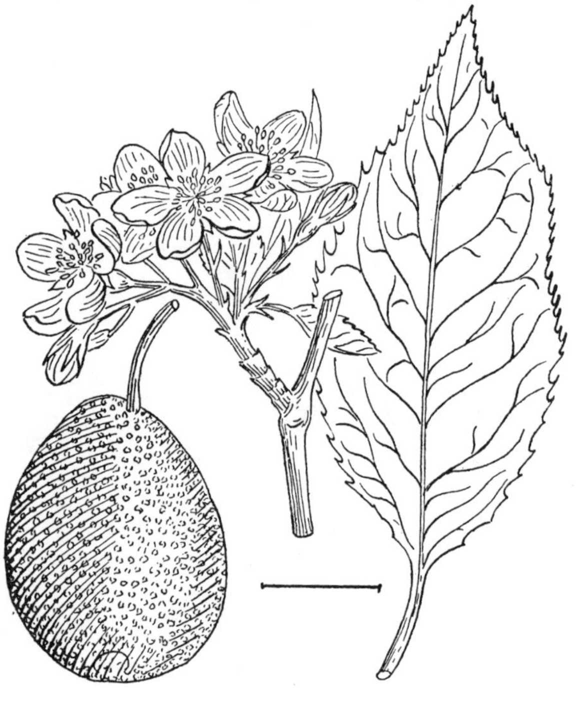

Pyrus pyrifolia Stapfiana

P. Pash'ia. Tree 25 to 35 ft. *l.* ovate 2 to 4 in. long, finely toothed. *fl.* densely packed in clusters $1\frac{1}{2}$ to 2 in. across, rose-tinted, afterwards white, $\frac{3}{4}$ in. wide; stamens 25 to 30; anthers red. April. *fr.* globose or ovoid-globose, speckled brown. (J.F.M. 7.) In the type the young shoots, l., and infl. are woolly; in var. **kuma'oni** (B.M. 8256), they are glabrous. N. India. 1825.

P. pyrifo'lia. Sand Pear. Tree 30 to 40 ft. *l.* ovate-oblong, slender-pointed, 3 to 5 in. long, toothed. *fl.* white, $1\frac{1}{4}$ in. wide, in clusters of 6 to 8. April. *fr.* sub-globose, $1\frac{1}{3}$ in. wide, brown with pale dots. China. 1909. (B.R. 1248.) var. **Stapfia'na,** *fr.* 2 to $2\frac{1}{2}$ in. long, pear-shaped. (B.M. 8226.) SYN. *P. serotina, P. sinensis.* Edible vars. are grown in China and Japan.

P. Rege'lii. Tree up to 30 ft., shoots at first downy. *l.* remarkably variable; one type divided pinnately into narrow strips like the cut-leaved form of common alder (*imperialis*); the second type ovate, 2 to $3\frac{1}{2}$ in. long, merely toothed. *fl.* white, 1 in. wide. April. *fr.* globose, $1\frac{1}{4}$ in. across. Turkistan. 1891. (B.T.S. 2, 284.) In foliage the most remarkable of pears. SYN. *P. heterophylla.*

P. salicifo'lia.* Tree 15 to 25 ft., shoots densely covered with white down. *l.* narrowly lanceolate, entire, $1\frac{1}{2}$ to $3\frac{1}{2}$ in. long, $\frac{1}{3}$ to $\frac{1}{2}$ in. wide, covered at first with silvery-white down, afterwards glabrous and glossy. *fl.* pure white, $\frac{3}{4}$ in. wide, closely packed in rounded clusters. April. *fr.* brown, pear-shaped, 1 to $1\frac{1}{4}$ in. long. SE. Europe, Asia Minor. 1870. var. **pend'ula,** elegant, weeping tree. (B.R. 514.) Both distinct and beautiful in their silky-white l. and fl. opening together.

P. × **salvifo'lia.** Hybrid between *P. nivalis* and *P. communis.* (B.R. 1482.)

P. sambu'cifolia. A synonym of *Sorbus decora.*

P. serot'ina. A synonym of *P. pyrifolia.*

P. theif'era. A synonym of *Malus hupehensis.*

P. ussurien'sis. Snow Pear. Tree up to 40 ft., shoots and l. glabrous or nearly so. *l.* orbicular to ovate, slender-pointed, 2 to 4 in. long, bristly toothed. *fl.* 1 to $1\frac{1}{2}$ in. wide, dense in hemispherical clusters. April. *fr.* globose, 1 to $1\frac{1}{2}$ in. wide, short-stalked, yellowish-green. NE. Asia. 1855. Grown sometimes as *P. sinensis.* Handsome in fl. and for bronzy-red l. in autumn.

P. vesti'ta. A synonym of *Sorbus cuspidata.*

W. J. B.

PYTH'IUM. A genus of fungi belonging to the Phycomycetes (q.v.). Many species of Pythium are serious plant parasites. *P. de Baryanum*, the cause of damping off in many kinds of seedlings, is the best known. On the attacked plants the fungus forms spherical bodies (sporangia) which burst to release 2-ciliate spores having the power of movement, i.e. zoospores. Later, in the rotting plant tissues, the fungus forms thick-walled resting bodies (oospores) which are very resistant to adverse circumstances and contaminate the soil. On germination the oospores may either produce zoospores or may infect directly by hyphae. (*See* **Damping off.**)

D. E. G.

PYXIDAN'THERA (*pyxis*, a small box, *anthera*; the anthers opening like the lid of a box). FAM. *Diapensiaceae.* A monotypic genus. Leaves alternate or opposite, sessile, imbricate towards end of shoot; sessile, solitary, terminal flowers, tubular corolla with 5 spreading, slightly decurved, broad lobes, calyx subtended by bracts with 5 oblong, obtuse, hairy, thin lobes, anthers opening transversely, a 3-celled ovary and a sessile, rounded, loculicidal capsule. *P. barbulata* is very attractive in nature but reluctant to flower and difficult to keep in British gardens. A very sandy or gravelly, well-drained, lime-free soil with moisture well beneath, a slightly shady position, and association with a dwarf, deciduous plant like *Salix reticulata* perhaps gives it the best chance.

P. barbula'ta. Pyxie, Pine-barren Beauty, Flowering Moss. Evergreen, moss-like, creeping little shrub 1 in. or so h. *l.* sessile, narrow-lanceolate, or linear-oblong, pointed or sub-acute, $\frac{1}{6}$ to $\frac{1}{3}$ in. long, $\frac{1}{16}$ to $\frac{1}{12}$ in. wide, downy at base when young. Cor. white or pinkish, $\frac{1}{6}$ to $\frac{1}{4}$ in. across, tube $\frac{1}{8}$ in. or a trifle more long. March to May. E. United States. 1806. SYN. *Diapensia barbulata.* (B.M. 4592.)

F. S.

pyxida'tus -a -um, box-like.

pyxidif'erus -a -um, bearing boxes (usually referring to the fruits).

A→

PYXIS. A capsule dehiscing by a lid as in Anagallis.

Q

quadrangula'ris -is -e, 4-angled.

quadri- in compound words, signifying four, as *quadrifid,* 4 times cut.

QUAKING GRASS. *See* **Briza.**

QUA'LEA (native name in Guiana). FAM. *Vochysiaceae.* A genus of about 25 species of curious, resinous trees, natives of Brazil and Guiana. Leaves opposite, or whorled, leathery, stalked; stalks with 2 glands at base. Flowers yellow, pink or blue, rather large, in lateral or terminal racemes or panicles; sepals 5, free; petal 1, clawed, obovate or obcordate. *Q. rosea* needs stove conditions and a peat-leaf-mould compost. Seeds should be sown on a hotbed; or cuttings of half-ripe shoots may be struck in sand under a bell-glass, with bottom heat.

Q. ro'sea. Tree of about 30 ft. *l.* elliptic, slender-pointed, smooth on both sides. *fl.* both pet. and the large seg. of cal., white without, rose within; pet. entire; spur shorter than cal. Guiana. SYN. *Q. violacea.*

Quam'ash, North American Indian name of Camassia.

QUA'MOCLIT (Derivation uncertain; ? from Greek *kuamos,* bean). FAM. *Convolvulaceae.* A genus of about 12 species of American annual twining herbs, some of which are perennial in the tropics. Sometimes included in Ipomoea from which it differs by the shape of the corolla tube and the cup-shaped limb of the corolla and by the exserted stamens and style. Best treated as half-hardy annuals though some can be raised by sowing outdoors in May, or they may be grown as greenhouse twiners. **A**

Q. cocci'nea. Star Ipomoea. Twiner to 8 ft. *l.* cordate or at base sagittate or hastate, slender-pointed, entire, angled or toothed, stalks slender. *fl.* scarlet with yellow throat, fragrant; cor. ¾ to 1½ in. long, limb obscurely lobed, ½ to ¾ in. wide. N. Mexico, Arizona. (B.M. 221.) var. **hederifo'lia,** *l.* 3- to 5-lobed, middle lobe ovate-lanceolate, lateral much narrower, sinuate-angled. Mexico. (B.M. 1769 as *Ipomoea sanguinea.*) SYN. *Ipomoea hederifolia, Mina sanguinea*; **luteo'la,** *fl.* yellow to orange.

Q. grandiflo'ra. *l.* 3-lobed, cordate-hastate, finely downy. *fl.* scarlet, cor. about 2 in. long, slender, bent, limb 5-angled, under 1 in. across; panicles long. S. Mexico. SYN. *Ipomoea grandiflora.*

Q. Kerb'eri. *l.* cordate. *fl.* vivid scarlet, very freely produced. Summer. S. America. 1894. SYN. *Ipomoea Kerberi.*

Q. loba'ta.* Vigorous climber. *l.* 3-lobed, cordate at base. *fl.* bright crimson, becoming orange then yellow; cor. salver-shaped, tube swollen, baggy; racemes scorpioid. June to September. S. Mexico. 1841. (B.M. 7689; B.R. 1842.) SYN. *Ipomoea versicolor, Mina lobata.*

Q. Nation'is. Slender, branched, glabrous twiner. *l.* cordate, slender pointed, entire, 3 to 6 in. long; stalk 2 to 4 in. long. *fl.* rich orange-scarlet, salver-shaped, 2 in. across, 5-lobed, tube cylindrical, whitish, 2 to 2½ in. long, minutely downy; cal. ½ in. long, mucronate; peduncles 3-fld. in l.-axils. Peru. 1863. (B.M. 5432.) SYN. *Ipomoea Nationis.*

Quamoclit vitifolia

Q. penna'ta.* Cypress Vine, Indian Pink. Smooth, slender twiner to 6 or 8 ft. *l.* pinnate, segs. filiform; sessile or almost so. *fl.* scarlet; cor. tube narrow funnel-shaped, inflated above, limb nearly flat, 5-lobed; peduncles few-fld., occasionally twin. Trop. America. 1629. (B.M. 244.) SYN. *Ipomoea Quamoclit.* var. **al'ba** has white *fl.*

Q. sangui'nea. A synonym of *Q. coccinea hederifolia.*

Q. vitifo'lia. Glabrous twiner. *l.* entire or 3-lobed, middle lobe constricted below. *fl.* scarlet, cor. limb 5-lobed; tube yellowish, 1 in. long; peduncle several-fld., long. July, August. 1820. S. Mexico. SYN. *Calboa vitifolia.*

F. G. P.

QUARARIB'EA (derivation?). FAM. *Bombacaceae.* A genus of about 7 species of evergreen trees, natives of Trop. S. America, having an aromatic odour. Leaves entire or almost so, oblong or elliptic. Flowers white; calyx more or less funnel-shaped, 2- to 5-lobed; petals oblong; staminal tube indistinctly 5-toothed; ovary 2-celled. Peduncles 1-flowered, short, opposite leaves. *Q. turbinata* needs stove conditions, and a rich sandy loam soil. It can be propagated by cuttings of half-ripe shoots in sand under glass in heat.

Q. turbina'ta. Shrub of 8 to 20 ft. Branches few. *l.* elliptic, quite entire. *fl.* white, very fragrant; peduncles nearly as long as l.-stalks. May. Antibes to Brazil. 1793. SYN. *Myrodia turbinata.* The fl. and l. when dry smell strongly of Fenugreek (*Trigonella Foenum-Graecum*).

F. G. P.

QUAS'SIA (name given by Linnaeus to a tree of Surinam, in honour of a Negro, Quasi or Coissi, who employed the bark as a remedy for fever). FAM. *Simarubaceae.* A genus of a single species of tall tree much like the common ash, of interest from its use. A compost of rich sandy loam and leaf-mould suits it and it needs stove conditions. Propagated by cuttings of ripe shoots.

Q. ama'ra. Bitter Quassia; Surinam Quassia. Tree of 20 ft. *l.* alternate, unequally pinnate, stalks winged; lflets. opposite, entire. *fl.* scarlet, large, tubular, in terminal clusters. Trop. America. 1790. (B.M. 497.) The wood is without scent but intensely bitter and has therefore been used as a tonic; the root and bark have been used in treating dysentery.

QUASSIA CHIPS. Chips of the wood of *Picrasma excelsa,* a tree related to *Quassia amara,* were at one time largely used as the source of an insecticide, especially in spraying against green-fly, but their use is now almost entirely superseded. 4 oz. of the chips were boiled for 10 min. in a gallon of water; the liquor was then strained off and 4 oz. soft soap added and thoroughly stirred in as the liquor cooled. Quassia extract was also used with sugar in the making of fly-papers. It is said that insects cannot live in boxes made of quassia wood.

QUEEN LILY. *See* **Phaedranassa.**

QUEEN OF THE MEADOWS. See **Filipendula Ulmaria.**

QUEENSLAND ITCH TREE. *See* **Davidsonia pruriens.**

QUEENSLAND KAURI. *See* **Agathis Brownii.**

queenslan'dicus -a -um, of Queensland, Australia.

Queh'lii, in honour of L. Quehl, who had a fine collection of Cacti at Halle, Germany.

QUEKET'TIA (in honour of E. J. Quekett, an eminent microscopist, &c.). FAM. *Orchidaceae.* About 5 species are known in this Brazilian epiphytic genus, all are of botanical rather than horticultural interest. The very small flowers have erect sepals, the lower in some species shortly connate; the petals are similar in shape. The lip is free, as long as or longer than the sepals, sessile on the base of the short column. Pollinia 2. The tiny pseudobulbs are terminated by a single leaf, usually linear and terete. The scapes are produced from the base of the pseudobulbs, few- or many-flowered. The plants should be suspended in small pans in the intermediate house, shaded from sunlight. Free drainage should be ensured. Compost should consist of 2 parts of Osmunda fibre and 2 parts of Sphagnum moss cut fine and well mixed.

Q. Jenman'i. *fl.* small, white. *l.* about 2 in. long, rigid. Brazil? 1906.

Q. microscop'ica. *fl.* yellow and white, nearly sessile, 1/8 in. long, segs. nearly erect, the lateral shortly connate giving a tubular shape to the fl., tips spreading, panicle about 3 in. long. *Pseudobulbs* oblong, very small. *l.* terete, subulate, about 3 in. long, mottled with light green, deep green, and purple. Brazil. 1839. SYN. *Q. chrysantha.*

E. C.

QUEL'TIA. Included in **Narcissus.**

QUENOUILLE. A form of tree, usually trained against a wall, having a central stem with branches in horizontal tiers, progressively shorter from below upwards, forming a triangle in outline. The upper part of the wall is largely wasted unless filled with a fan-trained tree on a long stem; and trees so trained tend to make much wasteful growth towards the top, requiring frequent root-pruning.

QUERCIFI'LIX (*Quercus*, oak, *filix*, fern; from the form of the fronds). FAM. *Polypodiaceae.* A single species native of Ceylon with fronds of 2 forms, the main veins distinct nearly to the margin. Sori without indusia. For general treatment *see* **Bolbitis.**

Q. zeyla'nica.* *rhiz.* stout, wide-creeping. *sti.* of barren fronds 1 to 2 in. long, clothed with brownish hairs. *Barren fronds* 3 to 4 in. long, 1½ to 2 in. broad, the terminal pinnae with blunt, rounded lobes. *Fertile fronds* with terminal pinna, 1 to 2 in. long, 1/12 in. broad, the 2 lateral smaller, with slender stipes 6 to 9 in. long, hairy at base. Ceylon. Stove. (L.F. 7, 49.) SYN. *Acrostichum Neitneri* (of gardens), *A. quercifolium, Gymnopteris quercifolia.*

quercifo'lius -a -um, having leaves like those of oak.

QUERCITRON. *See* **Quercus velutina.**

QUER'CUS (ancient Latin name). Oak. FAM. *Fagaceae.* A genus of about 230 species of deciduous or evergreen trees, rarely shrubs. They are natives of the cool and warm temperate regions of the N. hemisphere or of tropical and sub-tropical regions in Asia and America at altitudes sufficiently high to afford conditions approximately similar. Leaves alternate, often lobed, sometimes deeply, sometimes shallowly or merely toothed, rarely entire. The pubescence is mostly stellate. Flower 1-sexual and monoecious, the males numerous in slender, pendulous catkins and usually with 6 stamens, the females solitary to many on a spike. Fruit a nut (popularly acorn), ovoid to globose, more or less (sometimes almost wholly) enclosed by a cup; they take 1 or 2 seasons to attain maturity.

There is no large genus of trees in temperate regions that includes a greater proportion of noble species, or one whose timber is of greater economic value. The bark is often rich in tannin and at one time, more than now, was extensively employed for tanning leather.

Oaks, apart from forestry, are essentially trees for parks or large gardens, valued for their size and robust beauty, their often fine foliage and rich leafiness, and for their autumn tints. They love best of all a good deep loam which may even be on the stiff side. If possible they should always be raised from acorns, which should be sown as soon as ripe or kept moist. Acorns stored away in paper bags or dry places soon lose their vitality. It is advisable to get young trees into their permanent places as soon as possible. Grafting is often unavoidable where acorns are unobtainable and where stocks of weeping, fastigiate, or coloured-leafed varieties are required. Many evergreen species can be rooted from cuttings.

The chief sections into which the species are grouped are as follows:

1. CYCLOBALANOPSIS. Cup with rings instead of scales. Evergreens with pointed entire or serrate leaves. E. Asia. *acuta, glauca, lamellosa, myrsinifolia, oxyodon, stenophylla.*

2. CERRIS. Cup usually with long scales. Styles linear. Bud scales usually long and persistent. The deciduous species have often triangular lobes tipped with bristles, the evergreen species small variously toothed leaves. Old World.

(*a*) Deciduous species. *acutissima, Aegilops, castaneifolia, Cerris, libani, trojana, variabilis.*

(*b*) Evergreen species. *alnifolia, calliprinos, coccifera, phillyraeoides, semecarpifolia, Suber.*

3. MESOBALANUS. Intermediate between the last and the next sections. Often ornamental trees with large leaves. All are deciduous. Old World. *dentata, Farnetto, macranthera, pontica, Toza.*

4. LEPIDOBALANUS. Styles short. Acorn not woolly inside. The deciduous species have leaves more or less resembling those of the common oak.

(*a*) Old World Deciduous and half-evergreen species. *aliena, canariensis, crispula, fruticosa, glandulifera, infectoria, lusitanica, petraea, pubescens, Robur.*

(*b*) American deciduous species. These rarely thrive in this country. *alba, bicolor, Garryana, lobata, lyrata, macrocarpa, prinoides, Prinus, stellata, utahensis.*

(*c*) Evergreen species. *Engleriana, Ilex, leucotrichophora, virginiana.*

5. PROTOBALANUS. Differs from the last in the acorn woolly inside. All evergreen. Western N. America. *chrysolepis.*

6. ERYTHROBALANUS. Styles long, spatulate. Abortive ovules apical. America. Usually thriving well in this country.

(*a*) Willow Oaks. Deciduous species with narrow entire leaves. *imbricaria, laurifolia, nigra, Phellos.*

(*b*) Red Oaks. Deciduous species with often large leaves with triangular bristle-pointed lobes. Often colouring red in autumn. *arkansana, borealis, Catesbaei, coccinea, falcata, georgiana, ilicifolia, Kelloggii, marilandica, palustris, Shumardii, velutina.* This section includes the best oaks for autumn colour; the acorns take 2 seasons to attain maturity. Leaves sharply cut.

(*c*) Evergreen species; Leaves more or less holly-like. *agrifolia, Wislizenii.*

For information on the oaks in cultivation in the British Isles see an article by Sir Oscar Warburg and E. F. Warburg in J.R.H.S. 58, 176–88.

For other evergreen species often included under Quercus *see* **Lithocarpus.**

DISEASES. The most conspicuous disease of young oak trees is Powdery Mildew, which whitens the young leaves in spots or patches and sometimes severely injures them. This is caused by the fungus *Microsphaera quercina* and though it rarely does serious damage in Great Britain, in other countries it often has to be controlled by spraying with Bordeaux mixture. The roots of oaks in wet soil may be attacked by *Rosellinia quercina,* which in habit is somewhat similar to the Honey Fungus, *Armillaria mellea,* spreading by means of rhizomorphs. The fungus *Stereum hirsutum,* closely related to the Silver

Leaf fungus (q.v.), may damage oaks by entering the branches through wounds; it forms a flat or bracket-like yellowish fruiting body with a hairy upper surface. Old oaks are very liable to the entrance through wounds of certain bracket fungi (*see* **Bracket fungi**) mostly species of Polyporus, Fomes, &c., as well as the Beef Steak fungus, *Fistulina hepatica* (*see* **Beef Steak fungus**).

(D. E. G.)

PESTS. The Oak Leaf-roller Moth, *Tortrix viridana*, is chiefly responsible for the serious defoliation of Oak trees that occurs from time to time in the southern counties of England. Of the 2 native species of Quercus, *Q. pedunculata* suffers to a greater degree from this pest than *Q. sessiflora*. The moth, which has a wing expanse of about ¾ in., has bright-green fore-wings and greyish hind-wings, and is on the wing during late June and July, when vast swarms fly about the trees and undergrowth. The flat, circular eggs are laid on the young twigs in midsummer, and hatch in the following May into greenish-white caterpillars with black spots and a dark-brown head. They feed on the developing buds and leaves, which are folded over—the upper surface outwards and downwards—in a manner characteristic of many Tortricid leaf-rollers. Pupation takes place in the folded leaves, or the caterpillars may descend and pupate under cover of the folded leaves of other plants (Rhododendrons) growing beneath the attacked Oaks. A threatened outbreak may often fail to occur owing to weather conditions—countless numbers of the newly hatched caterpillars being washed off or blown from the leaves and shoots by heavy rainstorms and gales. The cumulative effect of this pest and of the Oak Mildew (q.v.) is to reduce the vigour of the tree and to produce conditions which often result in 'stag-headed' trees.

There is no method of controlling an outbreak on Oaks in this country, though success is obtained on the Continent by the aid of aeroplanes with dust-distributing apparatus. There are a number of natural agencies (climatic conditions, insectivorous birds, and parasitic and predaceous insects) which aid in reducing it.

(G. F. W.)

Q. acu'ta (1).* Evergreen tree, 20 to 40 ft., often a shrub of bushy habit in gardens; shoots and l. soon glabrous. *l.* oval to oblong-lanceolate, pointed or bluntish, 2½ to 5 in. long, ¾ to 2¼ in. wide, dark glossy green, stout and leathery; margins toothless, wavy; stalk up to 1 in. long. *Acorns* hemispherical, crowded on a spike, the cup concentrically ringed with scales and enclosing the lower third. Japan. 1878. (Gn. 79 (1915), 386.) SYN. *Q. Buergeri*. Unsuitable for chalky soils.

Quercus agrifolia

Q. acutis'sima (2*a*). Deciduous tree, 40 to 50 ft., shoots downy at first. *l.* oblong to narrowly oval, 3 to 7 in. long, 1½ to 2 in. wide, glabrous and shining green above also bright green beneath but with axil tufts of down; veins parallel in 12 to 16 pairs, each ending in a bristle-like tooth ⅛ in. long. *Acorns* ½ to ¾ in. long; cup sessile enclosing half to two-thirds of the nut and covered with spreading, slender, recurved scales. China, Japan, Korea. 1862. Akin and similar to *Q. variabilis* whose l. are distinct by being dull and tomentose beneath. SYN. *Q. serrata*.

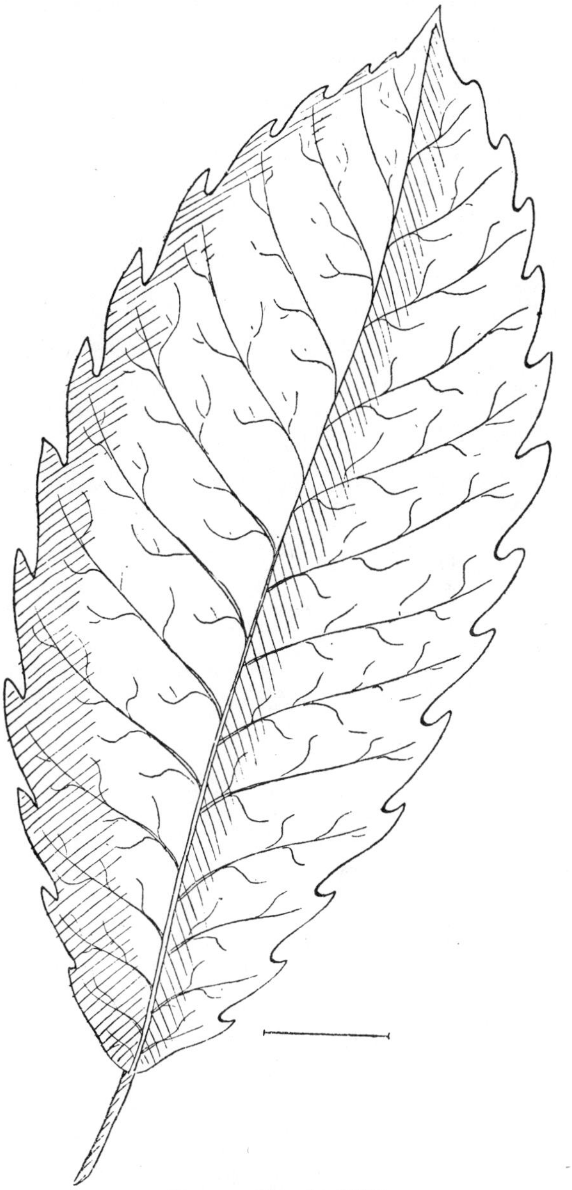

Quercus aliena (p. 1726)

Q. Aeg'ilops (2*a*). Valonia Oak. Deciduous tree, 30 to 80 ft., shoots grey-downy. *l.* 2 to 4 in. long, 1½ to 2½ in. wide, oval to oblong, downy beneath, with 4 to 6 pairs of angular, bristle-tipped teeth or small lobes on each margin; stalk ½ to 1¼ in. long. *Acorns* sub-globose, ordinarily ¾ to 1½ in. long (occasionally 2 to 2½ in. long), the cup very large and up to 2 in. wide. SE. Europe, Asia Minor. 1731. (E.H. 322.) Remarkable for the great size of its acorn cups, once very highly prized for the tannin they contain. Over 8,000 tons of these cups, known as 'valonia', were imported in 1896.

Q. Afa'res. A synonym of *Q. castaneifolia algeriensis*.

Q. agrifo'lia (6*c*). Evergreen tree, 80 to 100 ft. and wide-spreading, but often shrubby, shoots downy. *l.* hard in texture, broadly ovate to roundish, mostly convex, 1 to 2 in. long, spiny-toothed, usually glabrous except for vein-axil tufts of down beneath. *Acorns* conical, pointed, stalkless, ¾ to 1¼ in. long, one-third enclosed in the cup which is silky within. California. 1849. (S.S. 403.) (J.R.H.S. 58 (1933), 182.) Neat and rounded in habit as a young tree. Hardy if not too exposed.

Q. al'ba (4*b*). White Oak. Deciduous tree, 100 to 150 ft. with a trunk girth of up to 20 ft., and perhaps the finest deciduous oak of the

E. United States. In general outline, especially when leafless, it resembles the British Oak. It was introduced to England in 1724 but has never succeeded for any great length of time. *l.* obovate, 5 to 9 in. long, nearly half as wide, and 5- to 9-lobed. *Acorns* ¾ in. long, one-fourth enclosed in the cup. (S.S. 356–8.)

Q. alie'na (4*a*). Deciduous tree, 60 ft. or more h., shoots yellowish, glabrous. *l.* obovate to oblong-lanceolate, always cuneate, coarsely wavily and bluntly toothed; 4 to 8 in. long, half as wide, strongly parallel-veined, dark lustrous green and glabrous above, pale and greyish-felted beneath. *Acorns* mostly, but not always, solitary, ½ to 1 in. long, one-third to half enclosed in the stalkless cup. Japan, Korea, China. 1908. (J.R.H.S. 58 (1933), 182.) var. **acuteserra'ta,** marginal teeth of *l.* pointed, incurved, often mucronate. Both are promising trees. Japan, China.

Q. alnifo'lia (2*b*). Golden Oak. Evergreen small tree or shrub, shoots densely grey-downy. *l.* hard in texture, roundish or broadly obovate, rather convex, shallowly toothed, 1 to 2¼ in. long, dark lustrous green above, covered beneath with a close yellow (ultimately grey) felt. *Acorns* 1 to 1½ in. long, ⅓ to ½ in. wide, tapering downwards truncheon-like; cup ½ in. deep. Mts. of Cyprus. 1885. Fairly hardy but very slow growing. (Gn. 40 (1891), 95.)

Q. ambig'ua. A synonym of *Q. borealis.*

Q. america'na. *See* **Q. coccinea, Q. palustris, Q. borealis maxima.**

Q. america'na splen'dens. A synonym of *Q. coccinea splendens.*

Q. aquat'ica. A synonym of *Q. nigra.*

Q. arkansa'na (6*b*). Deciduous tree, 20 to 30 ft. *l.* obovate or broadly cuneate, often 3-lobed at the apex, 3 to 5½ in. long, half as wide, at first covered with starry hairs but finally glabrous except for vein-axil tufts of down beneath; stalks about ½ in. long. *Acorns* single or in twos on a short stalk, roundish-ovoid, ½ in. wide, with a shallow cup. United States. 1909. (S.T.S. 2, 152.) Related and often similar in l. to *Q. marilandica.*

Q. × Auzan'dri. A hybrid between *Q. coccifera* and *Q. Ilex. l.* felted beneath. *Acorns* 2 or 3 together. S. France, Algeria.

Q. Ballot'a. A synonym of *Q. Ilex Ballota.*

Q. bambusifo'lia. A synonym of *Q. myrsinifolia.*

Q. Banister'i. A synonym of *Q. ilicifolia.*

Q. bicolor (4*b*). Swamp White Oak. Deciduous tree, 60 to 70 (rarely 100) ft. *l.* obovate, 3 to 7 in. long, shallowly 6- to 8-lobed on either side, dark lustrous green and soon smooth above, closely whitish-felted beneath. *Acorns* 1 in. long, solitary or in pairs on a stalk up to 3 in. long, one-third enclosed by the cup. N. America. 1800. (E.H. 329.) Akin to *Q. macrocarpa* which is well distinguished by the much deeper lobing of the l. One of the best of the American white oaks for Britain.

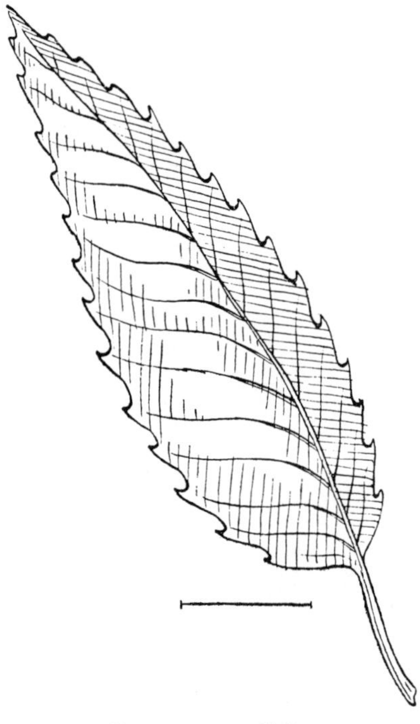

Quercus castaneifolia

Q. borea'lis (6*b*). Deciduous tree 60 to 80 ft., shoots glabrous. *l.* 5 to 9 in. long, oblong, with 3 to 5 pairs of triangular-ovate lobes, dull green above, greyish beneath and with hair-tufts in the vein axils. *Acorns* ovoid, ¾ to 1 in. long, the cup enclosing the lower third. N. America. 1800. (B.B. ed. 2, 1, 618.) Closely akin to *Q. borealis maxima*, but a smaller tree with smaller acorns. Colours beautiful red in autumn. SYN. *Q. ambigua.*

Q. borea'lis max'ima.* Red Oak. Deciduous tree, 80 to 150 ft., with a wide-spreading rounded habit, shoots glabrous. *l.* oval to obovate, 4 to 9 in. long, 3 to 6 in. wide, with 3 to 5 pairs of obliquely triangular or ovate, pointed lobes; dark green above, dull green or greyish and with vein-axil tufts beneath. *Acorns* 1¼ in. long, ovoid; cup shallow. N. America. 1691. (S.S. 409, 410; E.H. 314.) SYN. *Q. rubra* (in part). Finest of American oaks in Britain. Autumn tints dull or brownish-red. var. **au'rea,** *l.* beautiful soft yellow in spring, changing to green later. Much less vigorous than the type.

Q. Buer'geri. A synonym of *Q. acuta.*

Q. Bungea'na. A synonym of *Q. variabilis.*

Q. califor'nica. A synonym of *Q. Kelloggii.*

Q. callipri'nos (2*b*). Palestine Oak. Evergreen tree, sometimes of large size with a trunk 10 ft. or more in girth; closely akin and very similar to *Q. coccifera* (q.v.) in general character but with larger more oblong l. and larger acorns with a cup sometimes 1 in. deep. The famous Oak of Mamre or Abraham's Oak growing at Hebron (K.B. 1920, 257) belongs to this sp. SYN. *Q. coccifera pseudococcifera.*

Q. canarien'sis. Deciduous tree 100 to 120 ft., almost wholly glabrous. *l.* 3 to 7 in. long, half as wide, firm in texture, oval to obovate, rich green above, rather, glaucous beneath; ribs parallel, in 8 to 14 pairs, each ending in a triangular tooth. *Acorns* in pairs or threes, ovoid, one-third enclosed by the cup. N. Africa, Portugal. 1845. (E.H. 323, 332.) Handsome shapely tree notable for retaining its foliage well into the New Year. SYN. *Q. Mirbeckii.*

Q. castaneifo'lia (2*a*).* Chestnut-leaved Oak. Wide-spreading, rounded tree up to 100 ft., shoots downy. *l.* sweet chestnut-like, 4 to 7 in. long, narrowly oval to oblong, with 8 to 12 pairs of parallel veins each ending in a triangular tooth; dark lustrous green above, greyish and minutely downy beneath. *Acorns* ¾ to 1¼ in. long, cup shaggy. Caucasus, Persia. 1840. (B.T.S. 2, 304; E.H. 323.) A magnificent oak. var. **algerien'sis,** more pyramidal in shape, *l.* 3 to 5 in. long, 1 to 2 in. wide, shoots more downy. Algeria. SYN. *Q. Afares.*

Q. Cates'baei (6*b*). Deciduous tree usually 20 to 30 ft., but occasionally twice as h., buds rusty-downy. *l.* obovate to triangular in main outline, but deeply cut into 3, 5, or 7 lobes, each lobe terminated by a few sharp bristle-tipped teeth; 4 to 8 in. long, shining green on both surfaces and glabrous except for vein axil-tufts of reddish down beneath; stalks only ¼ to ¾ in. long. *Acorns* usually solitary, roundish-ovoid, ¾ in. long, one-third enclosed by the shortly stalked cup. SE. United States. 1823. (S.S. 417.) Distinct in the 'red' oak group by its very short l.-stalks.

Q. Cer'ris (2*a*).* Turkey Oak. Deciduous tree of noble proportions, up to 120 ft., the trunk girthing 12 to 18 ft., shoots grey-downy; winter buds with linear, persistent, downy stipules. *l.* 3 to 5 in. long, oval to oblong, very coarsely toothed or lobed, dark green and harsh above, downy on both surfaces; stalk ½ to ¾ in. long. *Acorns* solitary or up to 4 together, 1 to 1¼ in. long, half enclosed by the cup. S. Europe, Asia Minor. 1735. The quickest growing of cultivated oaks, but of little timber value. (E.H. 316–18.) var. **austri'aca,** *l.* shallowly lobed, more downy. SE. Europe, 1824; **lacinia'ta** (*dissecta*), *l.* lobed almost to the midrib; **pend'ula,** branches pendulous; **variega'ta,** *l.* edged with white; a good variegated tree.

Q. chrysole'pis (5). Maul Oak. Evergreen tree, 40 to 60 ft. h. much more in width, shoots yellowish-downy. *l.* leathery, 1½ to 4 in. long, half as wide, ovate to oval, rounded to cordate at the base, spiny-toothed on young trees, entire on old ones, bright green and at maturity glabrous above, dull with yellowish down beneath. *Acorns* in ones or twos, ovoid, ¾ to 1 in. long, ¼ enclosed by the cup. Western N. America. 1877. (S.S. 398, 399.) A tree of majestic proportions and sometimes 150 ft. in spread. var. **vaccinifo'lia,** a shrubby form with small entire *l.* found at high altitudes. (S.S. 400.)

Q. cleistocar'pa. A synonym of *Lithocarpus cleistocarpa.*

Q. coccif'era (2*b*).* Kermes Oak. Evergreen shrub or small tree, 12 to 20 ft., of dense sturdy habit. *l.* broadly oval to ovate-oblong, stiff and hard, ½ to 1½ in. long, glabrous and glossy green, with a terminal spine and 3 to 5 more on each margin. *Acorns* in ones or twos, about 1 in. long, more than half enclosed by the spiny cup. S. Europe, Asia Minor, N. Africa. 1683. (B.T.S. 2, 306.) The host plant of the Kermes insect, which, when collected and treated, formed a famous medieval scarlet dye known as 'grain'. var. **pseudococcif'era,** a synonym of *Q. calliprinos.*

Q. coccin'ea (6*b*).* Scarlet Oak. Deciduous tree up to 80 ft., and 10 ft. in girth of trunk; shoots soon glabrous; winter buds downy above the middle. *l.* 3 to 6 in. long, 2½ to 4½ in. wide, obovate to oval, deeply 7- or 9-lobed, the lobes with 2 to 5 bristle-tipped teeth towards the apex; both surfaces shining and smooth except for tufts of down in the vein-axils beneath; stalk 1½ to 2½ in. long. *Acorns* ½ to 1 in. long, one-half to two-thirds enclosed by the hemispherical cup. N. America. 1691. (S.S. 412, 413.) The most notable oak for its scarlet, long lasting autumn colour. var. **splen'dens,** the best form of Scarlet Oak. SYN. *Q. americana splendens.*

Q. Concord'ia. *See* **Q. Robur.**

Q. confer'ta. A synonym of *Q. Farnetto.*

Q. cris'pula. Deciduous tree up to 100 ft., shoots glabrous. *l.* obovate 4 to 9 in. long, about half as wide, with 10 to 15 conspicuous teeth on each margin, the largest $\frac{1}{2}$ to $\frac{3}{4}$ in. deep; glabrous except on the midrib and veins; stalk $\frac{1}{8}$ to $\frac{1}{3}$ in. long. *Acorns* 1 to 3 on a short stalk, ovoid, $\frac{3}{4}$ in. long. Japan. 1893. Distinct by its large, very shortly stalked, large-toothed l. SYN. *Q. grosseserrata.*

Quercus dentata

Q. cunea'ta. A synonym of *Q. falcata.*

Q. cuspida'ta. Evergreen shrub in cult. but naturally a tree 40 ft. or more, shoots glabrous. *l.* narrowly oval or oblong, tapering at the apex to a long, slender, blunt tip; 2 to $3\frac{1}{2}$ in. long, scarcely half as wide, dark glossy green, greyish beneath. *Acorns* about $\frac{3}{4}$ in. long, $\frac{3}{8}$ in. wide, tapering to a point, 6 to 10 of them borne on an erect stalk, enclosed completely by the stalkless cup. Japan. 1830. (G.C. 12 (1879), 233.) This is now more often referred to the genus Castanopsis as *C. cuspidata.*

Q. Dai'mio. A synonym of *Q. dentata.*

Q. Dauves'sei. A synonym of *Q. pedunculata pendula.*

Q. densiflor'a. A synonym of *Lithocarpus densiflora.*

Q. denta'ta (3). Daimyo Oak. Deciduous tree up to 60 or 80 ft., shoots stout, very hairy. *l.* obovate, 4 to 12 in. long, two-thirds as wide, with 5 to 9 rounded lobes or undulations on each side, at first with down above and whitish felt beneath which mostly falls away later. *Acorns* roundish-ovoid, $\frac{1}{2}$ to $\frac{3}{4}$ in. long, clustered, half or more enclosed by the nearly stalkless cup. Japan, Korea, China. 1830. (J.R.H.S. 58 (1933), 189.) Remarkable in a young state for its large l. but rarely a permanent success through injury by spring frost. SYN. *Q. Daimio.*

Q. digita'ta. A synonym of *Q. falcata.*

Q. ed'ulis. A synonym of *Lithocarpus edulis.*

Q. Engleria'na (4*c*). Evergreen tree, 20 to 30 ft., shoots densely grey-downy. *l.* narrowly ovate to oblong, slender-pointed, sharply and prominently toothed, 3 to 7 in. long, one-third as wide, conspicuously ribbed in 9 to 13 pairs, glabrous and dark lustrous green above, brown-woolly beneath at first; stalk $\frac{1}{4}$ to $\frac{5}{8}$ in. long. *Acorns* stalkless, solitary or in twos or threes, ovoid, $\frac{1}{2}$ in. long, half enclosed in a cup $\frac{5}{8}$ in. wide. China. 1900.

Q. fagin'ea. A synonym of *Q. lusitanica.*

Q. falca'ta (6*b*). Spanish Oak. Deciduous tree, 70 to 80 ft. *l.* obovate, terminally 3-lobed with a cuneate base, or ovate and 3- to 7-lobed; 4 to 7 in. long, $3\frac{1}{2}$ to 5 in. wide, dark glossy green above, dull grey and downy beneath; stalk $\frac{3}{4}$ to 2 in. long. *Acorns* sub-globose, $\frac{1}{2}$ in. long and wide, base enclosed by a short-stalked, saucer-shaped or turbinate cup. N. America. 1763. (S.S. 8. 420, 421 as *Q. digitata.*) SYN. *Q. cuneata, Q. rubra* (in part).

Q. Farnet'to (3). Hungarian Oak. Deciduous oak of stately proportions, up to 130 ft. and 12 ft. in trunk girth. *l.* 6 to 8 in. long, half as wide, obovate, deeply 6- to 10-lobed on each side, the lobes themselves coarsely toothed, dark green above, dull and greyish-green beneath; stalk $\frac{1}{3}$ in. or less long. *Acorns* in clusters of up to 4, $\frac{1}{2}$ to $\frac{3}{4}$ in. long, half enclosed by the cup. SE. Europe. 1837. (E.H. 331.) SYN. *Q. conferta, Q. pannonica.*

Q. frutico'sa (4*a*). Semi-evergreen shrub or small tree varying from 1 to 12 ft. *l.* oval, spiny-toothed, closely covered with appressed whitish down beneath, 1 to 2 in. long, marginal teeth in 4 to 7 pairs; $\frac{1}{3}$ in. long. *Acorns* clustered on short spikes; cup hemispherical, $\frac{1}{2}$ in. deep, enclosing one-third of the acorn. Portugal and Spain (including Gibraltar). 1827. (G.C. 1 (1874), 113 as *Q. humilis.*)

Q. Garrya'na (4*b*). Oregon Oak. Deciduous tree 60 to 80 ft., with a wide compact head of branches, shoots and buds downy. *l.* obovate with 3 to 5 pairs of blunt rounded lobes reaching half-way to the midrib, 3 to 6 in. long, dark green and glabrous above, bright green beneath. *Acorns* ovoid, 1 in. long, one-third enclosed by the stalkless cup. Western N. America. (S.S. 364, 365.) In general appearance resembles Durmast Oak, but does not grow well in Britain.

Q. georgia'na (6*b*). Deciduous shrub up to 10 ft., sometimes a small tree. *l.* 2 to 3 in. long, half as wide, oval or obovate, cuneate, divided half-way to the midrib in 3 to 7 lobes, the lobes often toothed. *Acorns* ovoid or subglobose, $\frac{1}{3}$ to $\frac{1}{2}$ in. long. Georgia, U.S.A. 1876. Interesting as a shrubby 'red' oak, the l. turning dull orange and scarlet in autumn. (S.S. 425.)

Q. glab'ra. A synonym of *Lithocarpus glabra.*

Q. glandulif'era (4*a*). Deciduous tree 30 to 40 ft., shoots at first silky-downy. *l.* obovate to narrowly oval, 2 to 7 in. long, 1 to $2\frac{1}{2}$ in. wide, with 6 to 12 pairs of incurved gland-tipped teeth on each margin; veins parallel, in 8 to 14 pairs; both surfaces white with appressed silvery hairs at first, the upper one finally glabrous and lustrous green. *Acorns* ovoid, about $\frac{1}{2}$ in. long, one to several on a short stalk; cup shallow, Japan, Korea, China. 1893. Attractive small oak retaining its foliage late.

Q. glau'ca (1). Evergreen tree, 40 to 50 ft., mostly shrubby in gardens. *l.* narrowly oval to ovate-oblong, the terminal half toothed; 3 to 5 in. long, glaucous and with appressed silky hairs beneath; stalk $\frac{1}{2}$ to 1 in. long. *Acorns* ovoid, $\frac{5}{8}$ in. long; cup shallow composed of a concentric ring of silky scales. Japan, China, Himalaya. 1835. (A.B.G.C. 2, 23.)

Q. Gramun'tia. A synonym of *Q. Ilex Gramuntia.*

Q. grosseserra'ta (4*a*).* A synonym of *Q. crispula.*

Q. Hen'ryi. A synonym of *Lithocarpus Henryi.*

Q. × **heterophyl'la** (6*b*). Bartram's Oak. A hybrid between *Q. borealis maxima* and *Q. Phellos.* Deciduous tree up to 80 ft. *l.* very variable in shape from oblong to oval and from having 3 to 5 pairs of bristle-tipped lobes to being almost entire; 3 to 6 in. long, 1 to $2\frac{1}{2}$ in. wide. Originally found wild in a field belonging to John Bartram near Philadelphia about 1812. (S.S. 436.)

Q. Hinds'ii. A synonym of *Q. lobata.*

Q. × **hispa'nica** var. **Lucombea'na.** Lucombe Oak. Deciduous or semi-evergreen tree and a hybrid between *Q. Cerris* and *Q. Suber* raised accidentally in the nursery of Lucombe and Pince at Exeter about 1765. It attains 100 ft. with a trunk-girth of 10 to 16 ft. *l.* oval or ovate, 2 to 5 in. long, grey-felted beneath. *Acorns* single or in pairs, $\frac{3}{4}$ to 1 in. long, more than half enclosed by the cup. It produces fertile acorns and the seedling trees vary considerably in l., stature, corkiness of bark, &c. (B.T.S. 2, 316; E.H. 320, 321.) var. **crisp'a** shows strongly the influence of *Q. Suber* in its small size, corky bark, compact habit, and nearly evergreen character; **diversifo'lia** is quite evergreen and has *l.* of extraordinarily diverse shapes from spoon-shaped to fiddle-shaped, bark corky; **fulhamen'sis** is nearer to *Q. Cerris* and quite deciduous.

Q. hu'milis. A synonym of *Q. fruticosa.*

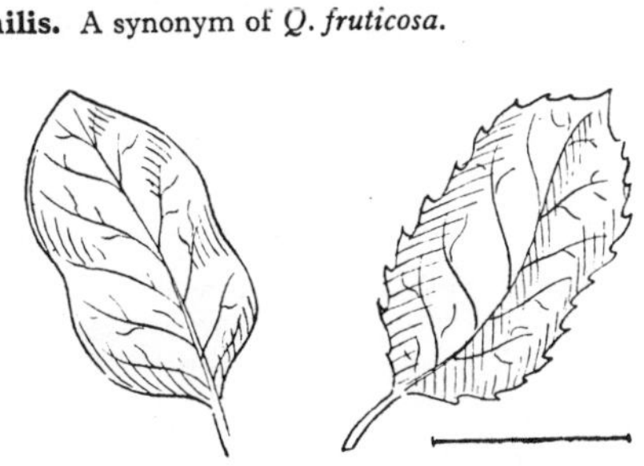

Quercus Ilex (p. 1728)

Q. I'lex (4*c*).* Holm Oak. Evergreen, rounded, densely leafy tree, 70 to 90 ft. with a trunk-girth of up to 18 ft., shoots grey-felted. *l.* narrowly ovate to ovate-lanceolate, $1\frac{1}{2}$ to 3 in. long, soon glabrous and dark shining green above, grey-felted beneath; mostly entire or with wavy margins on old trees, more or less toothed on young ones. *Acorns* $\frac{1}{2}$ to $\frac{3}{4}$ in. long, ovoid to sub-globose, 1 to 3 together, often very abundantly produced. Mediterranean region. 1580. (E.H. 324–6.) The finest of our evergreen trees apart from conifers; may be clipped into formal shapes or as a high hedge. var. **Ballot'a,** acorns large, edible. Spain, N. Africa. SYN. *Q. Ballota*; **cris'pa,** *l.* orbicular, $\frac{1}{2}$ in. long, margins decurved; a curiosity merely; **Ford'ii,** small tree, *l.* narrow, 1 to 2 in. long, margins wavy; **Gena'bii,** *l.* up to 5 in. by $2\frac{1}{2}$ in., coarsely toothed; **Gramun'tia,** *l.* oval to roundish, 2 in. long, often cordate, spiny-toothed. SYN. *Q. Gramuntia*; **latifo'lia,** *l.* up to 4 or 5 in., half as wide, not so rigid as those of *Genabii.*

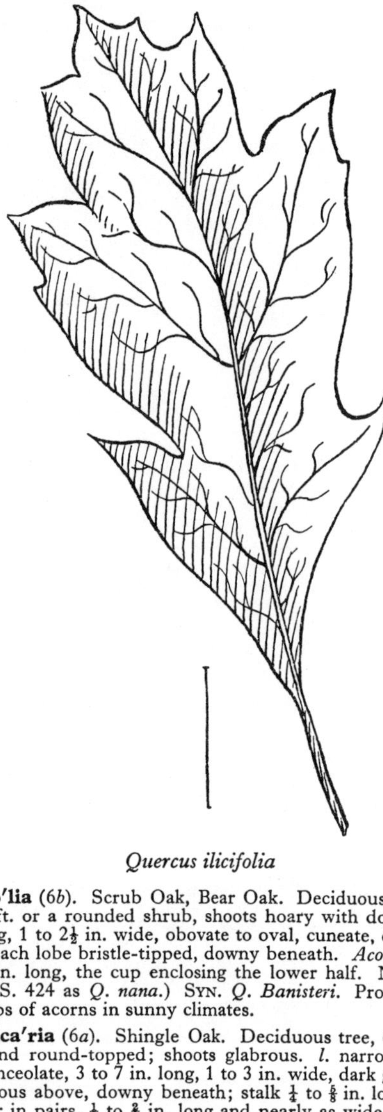

Quercus ilicifolia

Q. ilicifo'lia (6*b*). Scrub Oak, Bear Oak. Deciduous small tree, 15 to 25 ft. or a rounded shrub, shoots hoary with down. *l.* 2 to $4\frac{1}{2}$ in. long, 1 to $2\frac{1}{2}$ in. wide, obovate to oval, cuneate, deeply 5- or 7-lobed, each lobe bristle-tipped, downy beneath. *Acorns* globose-ovoid, $\frac{1}{2}$ in. long, the cup enclosing the lower half. N. America. 1800. (S.S. 424 as *Q. nana.*) SYN. *Q. Banisteri.* Produces enormous crops of acorns in sunny climates.

Q. imbrica'ria (6*a*). Shingle Oak. Deciduous tree, 60 to 90 ft., shapely and round-topped; shoots glabrous. *l.* narrowly oval to oblong-lanceolate, 3 to 7 in. long, 1 to 3 in. wide, dark glossy green and glabrous above, downy beneath; stalk $\frac{1}{4}$ to $\frac{5}{8}$ in. long. *Acorns* solitary or in pairs, $\frac{1}{2}$ to $\frac{5}{8}$ in. long and nearly as wide, cup short-stalked, enclosing the lower third. N. America. 1786. (S.S. 432.) Near *Q. Phellos* but with larger wider l. fading reddish.

Q. inca'na. A synonym of *Q. leucotricophora.*

Q. infector'ia (4*a*). May be regarded as an eastern form of *Q. lusitanica* with the same habit and slowness of growth and the same variability in shape of l. which usually have blunter teeth, but differing in pubescence. At first downy the shoots and l. are ultimately glabrous. *Acorns* as in *Q. lusitanica*, but with the cup-scales somewhat thickened. SE. Europe, Asia Minor, Cyprus; abundant on Mt. Lebanon. Retains its foliage until December.

Q. Kellog'gii (1).* Californian Black Oak. Deciduous, round-topped tree, 80 to 100 ft., shoots hoary with down. *l.* oval, oblong, or obovate, 3 to 6 in. long, 2 to 4 in. wide, usually 7-lobed, the lobes oblong with 2 to 4 bristle-tipped teeth; dark shining and glabrous above, glabrous to tomentose beneath; stalk yellowish, 1 to $1\frac{1}{2}$ in. long. *Acorns* ovoid to oblong, 1 to $1\frac{1}{4}$ in. long, two-thirds enclosed by the shortly and thickly stalked cup. Western N. America. The only species of the 'red' oak type from west of the Rocky Mts. (S.S. 416 as *Q. californica.*)

Quercus imbricaria

Q. × kewen'sis (6*c*). Evergreen tree of erect growth, probably 40 to 50 ft. *l.* oblong-ovate, with 5 or 6 triangular, mucronate lobes on each side; $1\frac{1}{2}$ to $3\frac{1}{2}$ in. long, half as wide, dull green above, glossy beneath, with a fine network of veins. *Acorns* $\frac{3}{4}$ to 1 in. long, taking 2 years to mature. Hybrid from *Q. Wislizenii* fertilized with pollen of *Q. Cerris*; raised at Kew in 1914.

Q. lamello'sa (1).* Large evergreen tree up to 120 ft., trunk-girth up to 15 ft., shoots tawny with down. *l.* oval to oblong, pointed, sharply toothed, 6 to 15 in. long, $2\frac{1}{2}$ to 9 in. wide, dark lustrous green above, glaucous beneath, with 20 to over 30 pairs of sunken veins; stalk 1 to 2 in. long. *Acorns* stalkless, 1 to 4 on a short, stout spike, flattish, 1 in. or more wide, almost enclosed by a cup consisting of about 10 thin, superposed, concentric rings. N. India. (I.H. 1857, 125.) Tender, but growing well in Cornwall and the Isle of Wight. Foliage magnificent; has been termed 'noblest of all oaks'.

Q. lanugino'sa. A synonym of *Q. pubescens.*

Q. laurifo'lia (6*a*). Laurel Oak. Deciduous or semi-evergreen tree, 60 to 100 ft., shoots slender, glabrous. *l.* oblong to oblong-obovate, $2\frac{1}{2}$ to 4 in. long, $\frac{1}{2}$ to 1 in. wide, lustrous dark green; entire in adult trees, but on young ones variable in shape and size, often lobed and up to 6 in. long by 2 in. wide. *Acorns* almost stalkless, solitary or rarely in pairs, globose-ovoid, the cup saucer-shaped. SE. United States. 1786. (S.S. 429, 430.) Akin to *Q. Phellos*, but not so hardy and best suited for the warmer counties.

Q. × Lea'na (6*a*) (*Q. imbricaria × Q. velutina*). Deciduous tree up to 80 ft. *l.* oblong, 3 to 7 in. long, 1 to 3 in. wide, mostly irregularly and deeply or shallowly lobed, glossy green above, duller and scurfy beneath. *Acorns* usually solitary, sub-globose, half to two-thirds enclosed by the short-stalked cup. Originally found near Cincinnati about 1830. (S.S. 434.)

Q. leucotricophora (4*c*). Evergreen tree up to 80 ft., bark peeling off in flakes, shoots grey-felted. *l.* oblong-lanceolate to narrowly oval, toothed or waved, $2\frac{1}{2}$ to 6 in. long, 1 to 2 in. wide, dark green above, clothed beneath with close, pure-white, persistent felt; veins prominent, in 8 to 12 pairs. *Acorns* 1 to 3 on a short stalk, ovoid to conical, half enclosed by the cup. N. India. 1810. Only suitable for the S. and SW. counties and similar climates. Almost invariably associated with *Rhododendron arboreum* in its wild state. SYN. *Q. incana.*

Q. liba'ni (2*a*).* Lebanon Oak. Deciduous tree up to 30 ft. of elegant habit, shoots downy at first only. *l.* oblong-lanceolate, rounded at the base, pointed, 2 to 4 in. long, $\frac{1}{2}$ to 1 in. wide; veins in 9 to 12 pairs, each terminated by a bristle-tipped tooth; dark glossy green above, paler beneath and downy on midrib and veins, or thinly so all over. *Acorns* solitary or in pairs, 1 in. long, two-thirds enclosed by the cup. Syria, Asia Minor. 1855. (B.T.S. 2, 315.) Attractive and interesting for small gardens.

Q. loba'ta (4*b*). Valley Oak. Deciduous, wide-spreading tree, 100 to 130 ft.; trunk-girth 20 to 30 ft. *l.* oval or obovate, 2 to 3½ in. long, half as wide, deeply 4- or 5-lobed, dark green above, dull and downy beneath. *Acorns* slenderly conical, pointed, 1 to 2 in. long, about one-third enclosed in the nearly stalkless cup. California. 1874. (S.S. 362.) SYN. *Q. Hindsii.* A magnificent tree in its home but not a great success in Britain. Acorn very distinct.

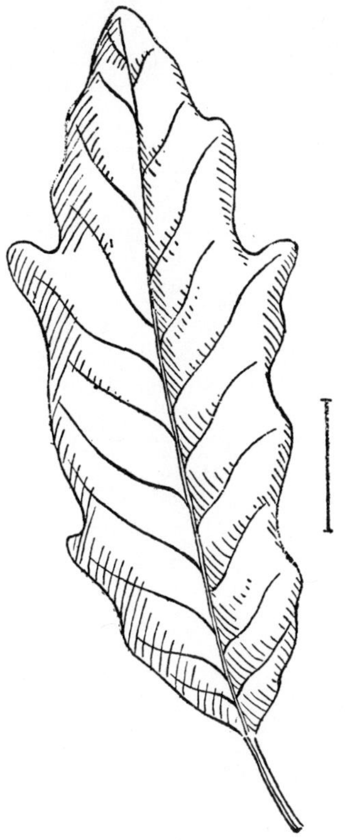

Quercus × *Leana* (p. 1728)

Q. Louet'tii. A synonym of *Q. sessiliflora mespilifolia.*

Q. × **Lucombea'na.** *See under* **Q. hispanica** var. **Lucombeana.**

Q. lusitan'ica (4*a*). Portuguese Oak. Deciduous tree up to 60 ft. and 10 ft. in girth of trunk, shoots densely downy. *l.* leathery, 2 to 3 in. long, very variable in shape but most commonly oval or obovate, blunt at the apex, and cuneate or rounded at the base, with 5 to 9 incurved teeth on each side; greyish-green and ultimately nearly glabrous above, grey-downy beneath. *Acorns* 2 or 3 together, ¾ in. long, quarter to one-third enclosed by the cup. SW. Europe. 1824. SYN. *Q. faginea.*

Q. lyra'ta (4*b*). Overcup Oak. Deciduous round-topped tree up to 100 ft., shoots downy at first. *l.* obovate-oblong, deeply 5- to 9-lobed, the basal lobes much smaller than the terminal ones; 6 to 9 in. long, nearly half as wide, dark green above, white with down beneath. *Acorns* sub-globose to ovoid, ½ to 1 in. long, almost entirely enclosed by the cup. S. United States. 1786. (S.S. 374.)

Q. macedon'ica. A synonym of *Q. trojana.*

Q. macran'thera (3). Deciduous tree up to 60 ft., very downy in nearly all its parts but especially on the shoots and beneath the l. *l.* 4 to 7 in. long, 2 to 4 in. wide, obovate, cuneate, conspicuously 7- to 11-lobed on each side, the lobes rounded, ½ to 1 in. deep; stalk ½ to ⅝ in. long. *Acorns* stalkless, solitary or up to 4 in a cluster, 1 in. long, half enclosed in the cup. Caucasus, Persia. 1895. Akin to *Q. conferta* but slower in growth and much more downy.

Q. macrocar'pa (4*b*). Burr Oak. Deciduous tree 80 to (occasionally) 170 ft., shoots and buds downy. *l.* 4 to 12 in. long, obovate, 5- to 7-lobed, the terminal lobe much the largest, the lower ones nearly reaching the midrib. *Acorns* ¾ to 1½ in. long, usually solitary, the lower half enclosed in a curious cup, the rim of which is thickly fringed with thread-like, curling scales on account of which it is sometimes called 'Mossy-cup Oak'. N. America. 1811. (S.S. 371–3.) There are trees 40 ft. h. in England but the species has no great value.

Q. marilan'dica (6*b*). Black Jack Oak. Deciduous tree, 20 to 50 ft. with a spreading head of branches, shoots scurfy. *l.* 3 to 7 in. long, nearly as wide, broadly obovate, tapering towards the base, widest and 3-lobed at the apex, glabrous and dark polished green above, scurfy beneath; stalk ¼ to ½ in. long. *Acorns* solitary or in pairs, oblong, ¾ in. long, up to two-thirds enclosed by the cup. SE. United States. 1723. (S.S. 426, 427.) SYN. *Q. nigra* (of Wangenheim). The strikingly shaped l. turn brown or yellow in autumn.

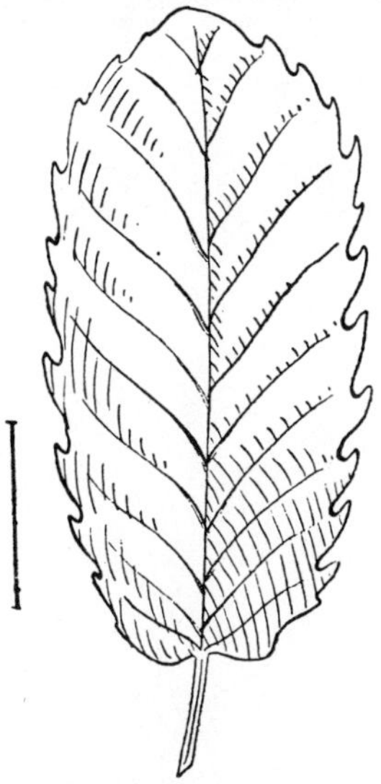

Quercus lusitanica

Q. mi'nor. A synonym of *Q. stellata.*

Q. Mirbeck'ii. A synonym of *Q. canariensis.*

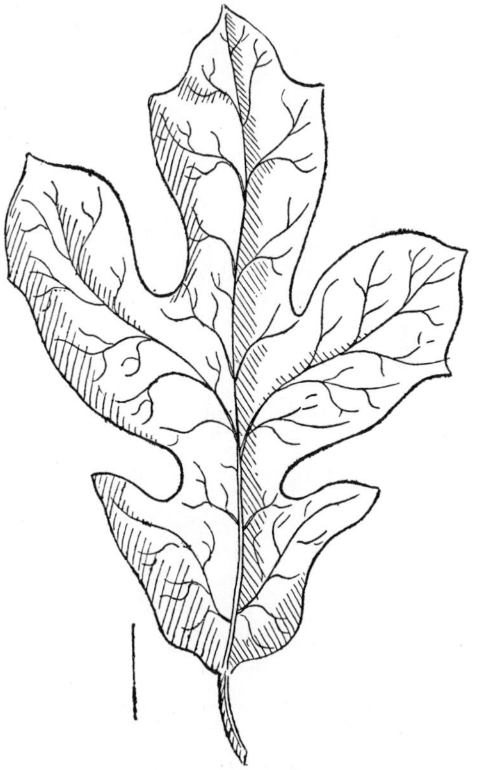

Quercus marilandica

Q. myrsinifo'lia (1). Evergreen tree, 30 to 60 ft., much smaller and mostly shrubby in cultivation, shoots and l. glabrous. *l.* lanceolate, 2½ to 4 in. long, ⅝ to 1¼ in. wide, toothed, slender-pointed, at first purplish-red, then lustrous green above, rather glaucous beneath; stalk ½ in. long. *Acorns* 2 to 4 on a spike, each ½ to ¾ in. long, the lower third enclosed in a ringed glabrous cup. Japan. 1854. SYN. *Q. bambusifolia, Q. Vibrayeana.* Distinct in its group by the narrow l.

Q. na'na. A synonym of *Q. ilicifolia.*

Q. nig'ra (6*a*). Water Oak. Deciduous tree up to 80 ft., symmetrical, rounded, soon glabrous except for tufts of down in the vein-axils beneath the l. *l.* 1½ to 4 in. long, very variable in shape but mostly obovate and shallowly lobed at the end; some are oval to oblong and entire. *Acorns* ½ in. long and wide, one-third enclosed by the short-stalked cup. N. America. 1723. (E.H. 312; S.S. 428.) Syn. *Q. aquatica*. Often found wild near water but succeeds with us in ordinary good loam. Popular street tree in the S. United States. Retains its foliage until January. *Q. nigra* (of Wangenheim) is *Q. marilandica.*

Quercus Mirbeckii (p. 1729)

Q. obtusilo'ba. A synonym of *Q. stellata*.

Q. oxyo'don (1). Evergreen tree up to 30 ft., with a wide, flattened head of branches, shoots soon glabrous. *l.* 3 to 8 in. long, 1 to 3 in. wide, narrow-oblong, slender-pointed, prominently toothed, dark shining green above, glaucous and closely felted beneath; midrib and the 12 to 20 pairs of veins yellow and conspicuously raised beneath. *Acorns* ⅓ in. long, clustered on a spike 1 to 1½ in. long, third to half enclosed by the ringed cup. China, Assam. 1900. (J.R.H.S. 58 (1933), 176.) Not very hardy and best suited for the south-western counties.

Q. palus'tris (6*b*).* Pin Oak. Deciduous tree of densely leafy, graceful growth, 70 to 100 ft., and up to 15 ft. in trunk-girth, soon glabrous except for conspicuous tufts in the vein-axils beneath. *l.* 4 to 6 in. long, 2 to 4 in. wide, obovate to oval, deeply 5- to 7-lobed, the lobes toothed near the apex; shining green on both surfaces. *Acorns* ½ in. long, one-third enclosed by the thin, shallow cup. N. America. 1800. (S.S. 422, 423; E.H. 315.) Often confused with *Q. coccinea*, from which it is readily distinguished by its quite glabrous buds; the vein-axil tufts are also much more evident; autumn colour inferior.

Q. pannon'ica. A synonym of *Q. Farnetto*.

Q. peduncula'ta. A synonym of *Q. Robur*.

Q. petrae'a (4*a*).* Durmast Oak. In size, habit, and foliage very like *Q. Robur* with which it was united by Linnaeus. Its most marked distinctions are in producing stalkless acorns and in having the l. distinctly stalked. The l. are also somewhat larger and with stellate hairs along the midrib beneath. A curious and valuable characteristic is that it is nearly or quite immune from the attacks of the Tortrix Moth, which in some seasons defoliates *Q. Robur* almost entirely. (E.B. 1289; E.H. 92.) Syn. *Q. sessiliflora*. var. **cochlea'ta,** *l.* decurved at the margins making them hooded or shell-shaped; **Geis'leri,** *l.* of unusual length, deeply and unequally lobed; **mespilifo'lia,** *l.* 4 to 8 in. long, ½ to 2 in. wide, entire or only shallowly lobed; very distinct. Syn. *Q. Louettii*; **rubicun'da,** young *l.* reddish-purple.

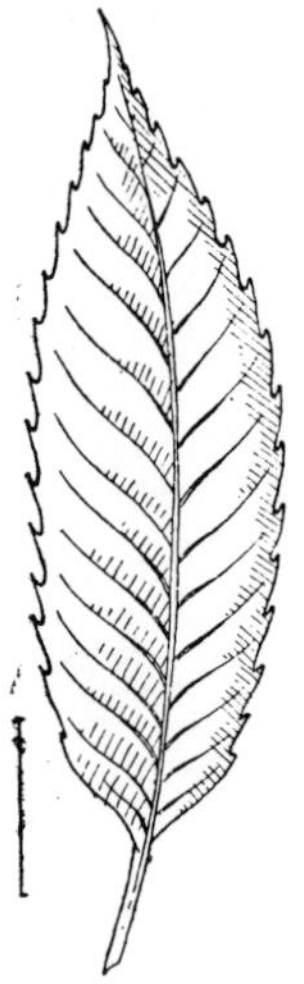

Quercus oxyodon

Q. Phel'los (6*a*).* Willow Oak. Deciduous tree 60 to 70 (rarely 100) ft., of columnar or rounded shape, densely leafy, shoots and l. soon glabrous. *l.* linear-oblong, 2 to 5 in. long, ⅓ to 1 in. wide, pointed, entire, light green, thin in texture. *Acorns* nearly stalkless, globose, ½ in. wide, the cup saucer-shaped, shallow. N. America. (S.S. 435.) Handsome tree distinct by its narrow, pale-green l. which fade to yellow.

Q. phillyraeoi'des (2*b*).* Evergreen shrub or tree up to 30 ft., shoots downy. *l.* obovate or oval, cordate or rounded at the base, the terminal part shallowly and bluntly toothed, 1¼ to 2½ in. long, about half as wide, glossy green on both surfaces, almost glabrous. *Acorns* ½ to ¾ in. long, cup thin, cup-shaped. Japan, China. 1861. (J.R.H.S. 58 (1933), 184.) Pleasant evergreen shrub, at present rare.

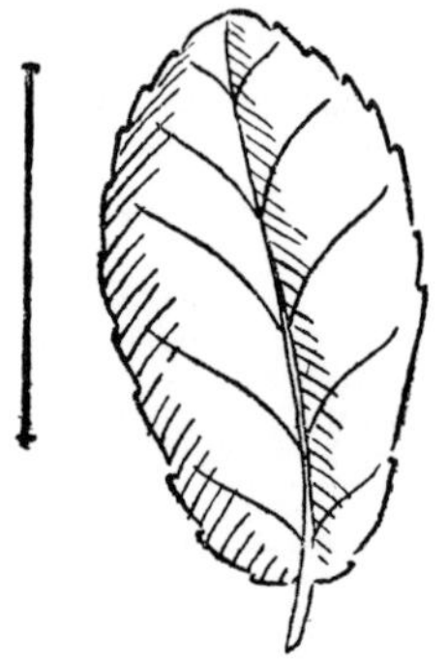

Quercus phillyraeoides

Q. platanoi'des. A synonym of *Q. bicolor*.

Q. pon'tica (3).* Armenian Oak. Shrub-like deciduous tree, 10 to 20 ft., often broader than h., shoots glabrous, ribbed. *l.* 4 to 6½ in. long, about half as wide, oval to obovate, sharply, coarsely, and unequally toothed, bright green, glabrous, the midrib yellow above, glaucous and slightly hairy beneath; there are 13 to 20 pairs of prominent parallel ribs each running out to an incurved tooth. *Acorns* ovoid, half enclosed in the cup. Armenia, Caucasus. 1885. Notable for its very large silky winter buds, noble foliage, and low, wide habit.

Q. prinoi'des (4*b*). Chinquapin Oak. Deciduous, suckering shrub forming dense masses up to 6 or 7 ft., rarely a small slender tree. *l.* obovate, with 4 to 7 pairs of triangular teeth, 3 to 6 in. long, bright green above, dull and thinly downy beneath. *Acorns* ovoid, ¾ in. long, nearly half enclosed by the stalkless cup. N. America. 1828. (S.S. 378.) Easily distinguished from all other cultivated oaks by its suckering habit, but of no great merit.

Q. Pri'nus (4*b*). Chestnut Oak. Deciduous, broad-headed tree, 60 to 70, sometimes 100, ft. h., shoots soon glabrous. *l.* obovate, 4 to 7 in. long, half as wide, dark glossy green above, dull and minutely downy beneath, veins parallel in 10 to 15 pairs, each running out to a large, oblique, rounded tooth. *Acorns* ½ to 1¼ in. long, third to half enclosed by the short-stalked cup. N. America. 1800. (S.S. 375, 376.) Rare but grows well; foliage turns rich crimson.

Q. pubescens. Deciduous tree, 40 to 60 ft., shoots very downy. *l.* obovate, 2 to 4 in. long, with 4 to 8 lobes on each side; lower surface thickly downy; stalk ¼ to ¾ in. long. *Acorns* nearly or quite stalkless, solitary or up to 4 in a cluster, half enclosed in the cup. S. Europe to Asia Minor. (E.H. 2, 92; J.R.H.S. 45 (1919), 171.) Very closely akin to *Q. petraea* but a smaller, much more downy tree. SYN. *Q. lanuginosa*, *Q. sessiliflora lanuginosa*. var. **dissec'ta,** *l.* deeper lobed; **pend'ula,** branches pendulous with deeper-lobed *l.*

Q. Ro'bur. Common Oak. Deciduous, glabrous tree, 60 to 100 ft., of wide-spreading habit in open situations. *l.* very shortly stalked, obovate to oblong, 2 to 4 in. long, 3- to 6-lobed on each side, and with 2 small lobes or auricles at the base. *Acorns* ¾ to 1¼ in. long, 1 to several on a slender stalk 2 to 4 in. long; cup saucer-shaped. Europe (Britain), Asia Minor. SYN. *Q. pedunculata*. (E.H. 81 to 91; E.B. 1288.) Under cultivation the common oak has produced many vars. of which the following are the most notable: **aspleni-fo'lia,** Fern-leaved Oak, *l.* long-stalked, cut almost to the midrib into narrow, slender lobes. SYN. *Q. filicifolia*, *Q. pectinata*; **atropur-pu'rea,** *l.* purple. SYN. var. *purpurascens*; **Concor'dia,** *l.* yellow during the summer, a weak grower; **cris'pa,** *l.* small, very wrinkled; **fastigia'ta** (Cypress Oak), slender tree with erect branches. (E.H. 80; J.R.H.S. 45 (1919), 203.); **heterophyl'la,** *l.* variously shaped, some long and narrow, some almost entire; **nig'ra,** *l.* darker purple than *atropurpurea;* **pend'ula,** Weeping Oak, branches pendulous. (J.R.H.S. 45 (1919), 202.); **variega'ta,** occurs in various forms, *l.* variegated with white or yellow, sometimes on the margins only; one form has its first growth ordinary green, its second variegated. *Q. Robur* differs from its companion British species (*Q. petraea*) by its long, slender acorn-stalk, also by the *l.* being very shortly stalked and with 2 auricles at the base (absent in *petraea*). Hybrids exist. The name was formerly used to include *petraea* also.

Q. ru'bra. An ambiguous name. A synonym in part of *Q. borealis maxima* and in part of *Q. falcata*.

Q. Schneck'ii. A synonym of *Q. Shumardii Schneckii*.

Q. semecarpifo'lia (2*b*). Evergreen or sub-evergreen tree up to 100 ft., with a trunk-girth of 18 ft., shoots rusty-downy. *l.* oval to oblong, cordate, spiny-toothed on young trees, 2 to 4 in. long, dark green above, reddish-downy beneath; veins in 8 to 12 pairs; stalk $\frac{1}{16}$ to ⅛ in. long. *Acorns* single or in pairs on a short stalk, globose to ovoid, ½ to 1 in. wide; cup thin, shallow. Himalaya, China. 1900. (J.R.H.S. 40 (1914), 80.) Has been successfully grown in Hants, and is 40 ft. h. in Cornwall.

Q. serra'ta. A synonym of *Q. acutissima*.

Q. sessiliflo'ra. A synonym of *Q. petraea*.

Q. Shumar'dii (6*b*). Deciduous tree up to 150 ft., shoots glabrous. *l.* obovate, oval, or oblong, 3 to 7 in. long, 5- to 9-lobed, dark shining green above, paler and with conspicuous axil tufts beneath. *Acorns* ovoid, up to 1¼ in. long, cup shallow, saucer-shaped. N. America. 1907. One of the Red Oak group and akin to *Q. coccinea* which has less conspicuous vein-axil tufts. var. **Schneck'ii,*** magnificent tree occasionally nearly 200 ft. h. with a trunk-girth of 25 ft. It has a deeper acorn cup than the type, enclosing one-third of the nut. S. United States. 1901. (S.S. 411 as *Q. texana*.) SYN. *Q. Schneckii*. Autumn tints golden-brown to rich red.

Q. stella'ta (4*b*). Post Oak. Deciduous tree, 40 to 60 ft. or more, of dense, rounded habit, shoots downy. *l.* 4 to 8 in. long, 3 to 5 in. wide, from obovate and deeply 5-lobed (the basal lobes small with a very wide sinus above them) to almost triangular; dark green and harsh to the touch above, dull and stellately hairy beneath. *Acorns* ¾ to 1 in. long, third to half enclosed by the stalkless cup. N. America. 1800. (S.S. 368, 369 as *Q. minor*.) SYN. *Q. obtusiloba*.

Q. stenophylla (1). Evergreen tree. *l.* lanceolate, 2½ to 4 cm. long, ⅝ to 1 in. wide, serrate in the upper part, acuminate, green above, glaucous and waxy beneath; stalk about ½ in. long. *Acorns* 1 or 2 on a very short stalk, each about ⅝ in. long, half enclosed in a ringed silky cup. Japan, Korea. Allied to *Q. myrsinifolia* but differing in the l. white with wax below. Has been confused with *Q. glauca* but has longer, narrower l., whiter below.

Q. Su'ber (2*b*). Cork Oak. Evergreen tree up to 60 ft., bark thick and corky, shoots grey-downy. *l.* 1 to 2½ in. long, oval, ovate, or oblong, shortly toothed, occasionally entire, dark lustrous green above, closely grey-felted beneath; stalk ¼ to ½ in. long. *Acorns* single or in pairs, ¾ in. long, half enclosed by the cup, ripening the first year. S. Europe, N. Africa. 1699. (E.H. 328.) This tree furnishes the cork of commerce, imported most extensively from Portugal and Spain. var. **occidenta'lis** differs from the type by its acorns taking 2 seasons to mature, *l.* less persistent. Hardier than the type, no doubt most of the cultivated cork oaks belong to it.

Q. texa'na (in part). A synonym of *Q. Shumardii Schneckii*.

Q. tincto'ria. A synonym of *Q. velutina*.

Q. To'za (3). Deciduous tree 50 to 70 ft., shoots and buds densely downy. *l.* 3 to 7 in. long, half as wide, with 4 to 7 deep, often toothed, lobes each side; deep green above, thickly and closely velvety beneath. *Acorns* ¾ in. long, 2 to 4 clustered on a stalk ½ to 1½ in. long, half enclosed in the cup. SW. Europe. 1822. (E.H. 330.) Notable for its deeply lobed l. and very downy parts. var. **splen'dens,*** *l.* up to 9 in. long.

Q. troja'na. Macedonian Oak. Small deciduous tree up to 30 ft., or a shrub, of neat close habit; shoots grey-scurfy. *l.* ovate-oblong, rounded at the base, 1½ to 3 in. long, ½ to 1½ in. wide, lustrous green above, almost or quite glabrous on both surfaces when fully grown; stalk ⅛ in. long; veins in 8 to 12 pairs, parallel, each ending in a triangular incurved tooth. *Acorns* usually solitary, ovoid, ¾ to 1¼ in. long, more than half enclosed by the cup. SE. Europe. 1890. Akin to and often confused with *Q. libani*, which has a l.-stalk ½ in. long and the teeth more bristle-like. SYN. *Q. macedonica*.

Q. × Tur'neri. Turner's Oak. Deciduous or semi-evergreen tree with a short, thick trunk and rounded shape; up to 50 ft. h. and usually wider. *l.* oblong-obovate, 2½ to 4½ in. long, one-third as wide, with 4 to 6 lobes on each margin. *Acorns* ¾ in. long, single or in pairs on a stalk 1 to 2 in. long, half enclosed in the cup. (J.R.H.S. 45 (1919), 219.) Raised in the nursery of Mr. S. Turner, Holloway Down, Essex, about 1750 and conjectured to be a hybrid between *Q. Ilex* and *Q. Robur*. Several forms raised from its seed are in cultivation, such as *austriaca*, *austriaca splendens*, *pseudoturneri*, &c. The foliage persists until February or March, dropping gradually.

Q. utahen'sis (4*b*). Deciduous shrub or a tree 20 to 40 ft., shoots grey-downy. *l.* 3 to 5 in. long, narrowly obovate with 3 to 5 lobes; dark shining green above, softly downy beneath; stalk ¼ to ⅝ in. long. *Acorns* in ones or twos, ½ to ¾ in. long, ovoid, the cup enclosing the lower one-third. SW. United States, including the Grand Canyon. 1912. (S.M. 297.)

Q. varia'bilis (2*a*).* Deciduous tree up to 80 ft., bark thick and corky, shoots soon glabrous. *l.* oblong or narrowly oval, 3 to 7 in. long, the margins set with bristle-like teeth $\frac{1}{10}$ in. long, each terminating one of the 9 to 16 pairs of parallel veins; glabrous above, closely grey-felted beneath. *Acorns* almost stalkless, globose-ovoid, ½ to ¾ in. long, nearly enclosed by a cup with long curly scales. China, Japan, Korea. Akin to *Q. acutissima* whose l. are glossy and glabrous beneath except in the vein-axils.

Q. veluti'na (6*b*).* Black Oak. Deciduous tree 70 to 100, occasionally 150, ft., buds and shoots downy. *l.* oval, ovate, to obovate, 5 to 12 in. long, more than half as wide, 5- or 7-lobed; lobes bristle-toothed, shining dark green above, thinly downy beneath. *Acorns* ½ to ¾ in. long, ovoid, half enclosed in the short-stalked cup. Bark and acorns permeated by a yellow principle from which 'quercitron', a yellow dye, is obtained. (S.S. 414, 415; E.H. 313.) SYN. *Q. tinctoria*. var. **rubrifo'lia** is the finest-leaved of American oaks and is known as 'Champion's Oak'. Its l. on young trees are not unusually 12 to 15 in. long.

Q. Vibrayea'na. A synonym of *Q. myrsinifolia*.

Q. vi'rens. A synonym of *Q. virginiana*.

Q. virginia'na (4*c*). Live Oak. Evergreen tree up to 60 or 70 ft., with a heavy, wide-spreading head of branches. *l.* oval to oblong, 2 to 5 in. long, entire or with a few teeth towards the apex, dark shining green above, white with down beneath. *Acorns* ovoid, 1 in. long, one-third enclosed by the cup. S. United States. 1739. (S.S. 394, 395.) SYN. *Q. virens*. The most beautiful of American evergreen oaks, but never successfully cultivated in Britain.

Q.×Warbur'gii (6*c*). Half-evergreen tree up to 40 ft. or more, glabrous almost throughout. *l.* obovate, up to 4 in. long and 2 in. wide, rather leathery, green above with the veins impressed, somewhat glaucous below and with raised veins, margins sinuately toothed and wavy, rounded at the apex; stalk ⅓ to ½ in. long. *Acorns* usually 2 on a stalk about 2 in. long; cup hemispherical about ⅝ in. across with numerous small appressed scales. A hybrid probably between *Q. Robur* and a Mexican species, perhaps *Q. rugosa*, probably originating at Genoa about 1869. SYN. *Q. obtusata* of gardens (not of H.B.K.), *Q. genuensis*. Succeeds well at Kew and Cambridge.

Q. Wislize'nii (6*c*). Evergreen round-topped tree, 70 to 80 ft., with a trunk-girth of 12 to 20 ft. *l.* roundish, ovate, or oval, spiny-toothed and from 1 to 2 in. long, or, ovate-lanceolate, entire, and up to 2¾ in. long on adult trees; glabrous and shining on both surfaces. *Acorns* oblong-oval, slender, ¾ to 1½ in. long, two-thirds enclosed by a short-stalked cup. California. 1874. (S.S. 406.) Akin to *Q. agrifolia* and hardy, but slow-growing

W. J. B.

QUESNEL'IA (named in honour of M. Quesnel, a French Consul at Cayenne, through whom the genus was introduced to Europe). FAM. *Bromeliaceae*. A genus of about 12 herbaceous perennials, natives of Brazil, Guiana, and Argentine, sometimes caulescent and sometimes epiphytic. The linear spiny leaves form a rosette from which the pedunculate inflorescence of blue or red flowers projects. Closely related to Aechmea but sepals usually without awns and inflorescence unbranched. Treatment as for Aechmea.

Q. arven'sis. *fl.* deep purple, about 1½ in. long, in a cylindrical spike; bracts undulate, flesh-coloured, upper variegated with white, 6 ft. h. Brazil. 1874. An erect-growing species, with the same habit as *Q. roseo-marginata*, but having the l. more acuminate, and deep green, 8 ft. long. (B.H. 1882, 115, t. 16 as *Q. rufa*; F.d.S. 1028 and G.F. 1875, 834–6 as *Billbergia Quesneliana*.) SYN. *Lievena princeps*.

Q. blan'da. *fl.* 1½ in. long; pet. greenish-blue, twice as long as farinose sep.; infl. ellipsoid, about 3½ in. long, bracts sharp-pointed. *l.* few, in a rosette, linear, ending in a brown spine, spiny, about 2 ft. long, 1½ in. wide. Brazil. 1885. SYN. *Q. strobilispica*.

Q. End'eri. A synonym of *Q. lateralis*.

Q. latera'lis. *fl.* pet. violet, twice as long as the sep.; spike oblong, few-fld., about 6 in. long; bracts tinged red, the lower 1 ft. long; peduncle slender, above 1 ft. long. *l.* 8 to 10 in a rosette, lorate, 2½ ft. long, 2 in. broad, rounded to a cusp at apex, spiny. Brazil. 1880. (G.F. 1886, 1217 as *Billbergia Enderi;* G.F. 1888, 195, f. 41–3 as *Q. Enderi*.)

Q. Libonia'na.* *fl.* sep. coral red; pet. twice as long, deep blue; infl. few-fld. in a simple spike, bracts acute, Winter. *l.* few, linear, narrowed to apex, spiny, about 2 ft. long, 1½ in. wide. 1 ft. h. Brazil. 1858. (B.M. 5090; F.d.S. 1048; G.F. 1866, 224, t. 514 as *Billbergia Liboniana*.)

Q. Morrenia'na.* *fl.* in a lax, sub-erect, few-fld. spike 3 to 4 in. long, with a red, flexuous rachis; pet. green, tipped violet-blue, 1 in. longer than sep.; peduncle shorter than l., bract-l. red. December. *l.* 8 to 10 in a rosette, connivent in the lower 3 to 4 in., over 8 in. long, 2 in. broad, whitish on the back, scarcely spiny. Brazil? 1887. SYN. *Billbergia Morreniana*.

Q. roseo-margina'ta.* *infl.* a dense oblong spike of light blue, subtended by large, broad, plane, deep rose bracts, with scarious margins; pet. about twice as long as sep. January. *l.* sheathing at the base, about 2 ft. long, 1½ in. wide, channelled, spiny, marked with transverse mealy bands. 1½ ft. h. Guiana? 1880. (B.H. 1881, 82, t. 4.) SYN. *Q. rufa, Billbergia roseo-marginata*.

Q. ru'fa. *See* **Q. arvensis** *and* **Q. roseo-marginata.**

Q. Skin'neri. A synonym of *Q. roseo-marginata*.

Q. strobilispi'ca. A synonym of *Q. blanda*.

Q. Van Houtt'ei. A synonym of *Aechmea Van Houtteana*.

Q. Wittmackia'na. A synonym of *Aechmea Wittmackiana*.

QUICK, QUICKTHORN. Hawthorn, *Crataegus Oxyacantha*, so called especially when used as a hedge: hence Quick-set hedge.

QUILLAI TREE. *See* **Quillaja Saponaria.**

QUILLAJ'A (from the Chilean name, *Quillai* or *Cullay*). FAM. *Rosaceae*. A genus of about 4 species of glabrous evergreen trees, some of them remarkable for the properties of their bark, natives of Chile, Peru, and S. Brazil. Leaves scattered, simple, thickly leathery, almost entire, stalked. Flowers rather large, hairy, lateral male, central ones purplish; calyx leathery, persistent, 5-lobed, valvate; petals 5, spatulate; peduncles axillary and terminal, 3- to 5-flowered. *Q. Saponaria* needs greenhouse protection and general treatment as for Kageneckia.

Q. Sapona'ria. Quillai; Soap Bark Tree; Soap Bush. Tree of 50 to 60 ft. *l.* oval, usually toothed, smooth, shining, short-stalked. *fl.* white, solitary or 3 to 5 on peduncle, usually terminal. April. Chile. 1832. (R.H. 1873, 254.) The bark contains a considerable amount of carbonate of lime and other minerals and saponin, and because of its content of the last it is used for washing and cleansing clothes, &c.

QUILLWORT. *See* **Isoetes.**

***quin-*,** in compound words, signifying five.

QUINA, QUINO, or **QUINQUINA.** The bark of several species of Cinchona (q.v.). *See* **Cinchona.**

quinary, arranged in fives.

***quina'tus -a -um*,** with 5 divisions.

QUINCE (*Cydonia oblonga*). The Quince has been in cultivation in S. Europe and in S. England from time immemorial and its native country, though probably in Cent. Asia, is not certainly known. It is, if not native, widely naturalized in S. Europe. It grows best in moist soil and is perhaps best of all by the side of a pond or stream, but it will grow in good deep loam and even in sandy soil provided the trees are well mulched in spring. It needs an open sunny position and in northern districts unless given protection from cold winds by a wall or fence it rarely ripens its fruit. In the south it is grown as a bush or in warm districts as a standard, but in the north as a fan-shaped tree or espalier against a wall or fence. It lives to a great age and forms a spreading tree with usually contorted branches, making a picturesque object if given the little attention it calls for in the way of pruning, merely removing overcrowding branches. Attempts at training into a special form are rarely easily consummated or desirable, and such pruning as is necessary should be done in early autumn. Early autumn is the best time for planting and bushes should be about 10 ft. apart, half standards 15 ft., and standards 20 ft.

The chief value of the Quince in horticulture is in providing a dwarfing stock for pears, especially the Angers Quince and the Common Quince. The fruit is mainly used for adding in small quantities to Apples when cooking to enhance their flavour. It also makes a good preserve and an excellent jelly. It is too acid and astringent to be eaten raw and its aroma when ripe is so strong that it should not be stored with apples or pears lest their flavour be affected. The fruit should be allowed to hang until ripe, about the end of October, unless unusually early frosts occur, and stored in a cool frost-free place laid on clean straw; it becomes yellow when ripe and will keep 2 or 3 months.

The Quince can be easily propagated by layers, stools, hard-wood cuttings, or suckers: for the production of rootstocks for pears the stooling method is usually used.

The varieties of Quince best worth growing will be found noted and described in the Supplement.

DISEASES. The most common disease of the Quince is Leaf Spot or Leaf Blight due to the fungus *Fabraea maculata* which results in spotting of foliage and fruit and may be serious on young stools or layers which are grown in quantity as stocks for pears. Fallen leaves should be raked up at the end of the season and burnt or buried deeply and the foliage sprayed during summer with Bordeaux mixture. Another leaf blotch is due to the fungus *Sclerotinia cydoniae* which may cause much damage in wet seasons. It produces blackish blotches with a sweetish odour on the leaves near the midrib about the time the trees begin to flower and these discoloured areas soon develop a whitish mould. It should be sufficient control to pick off the infected leaves as soon as they are seen. Other quince diseases are similar to those of apple such as Mildew due to *Podosphaera leucotricha* (*see* **Apple diseases**), Brown Rot (*Sclerotinia fructigena*), *see* **Brown Rot diseases,** Bitter Rot (*Glomerella cingulata*), *see* **Apple Rots.** Cluster cups on the leaves constitute a stage in the life of the Rust fungus *Gymnosporangium confusum* which also attacks medlars and produces its teleutospore stage on *Juniperus Sabina* (*see* **Medlar**).

(D. E. G.)

QUINCE, BENGAL. *See* **Aegle.**

quincuncial, a term applied to the arrangement of sepals and petals in the bud, when there are 2 sepals or petals with both margins overlapping, 2 with both margins covered, 1 with 1 margin overlapping, the other covered, as seen in the calyx of Ranunculaceae.

quincunx, an old term for 'planting alternately', plants or trees in one row standing midway between those in the next.

QUININE. The chief source of Quinine, so valuable in feverish complaints, is the bark of *Cinchona Calisaya*, *C. Ledgeriana*, *C. officinalis*, *C. succirubra*, and *Remijia pedunculata*. *See* **Cinchona.**

QUINOA. Native name of *Chenopodium Quinoa*.

A→

quinque-, in compound words, signifying 5; as quinquefoliolate, having 5 leaflets.

QUINSY BERRY. The fruit of the Black Currant, *Ribes nigrum*.

QUINTIL'IA. A synonym of Stauranthera.

QUINTIN'IA (in honour of La Quintinie, French botanist). FAM. *Saxifragaceae*. A genus of 2 species of New Zealand shrubs or trees. Leaves alternate. Flowers in axillary or terminal racemes, white or lilac; calyx tube 5-toothed; petals 5; stamens 5. Seeds winged. For treatment of these greenhouse plants *see* **Carpodetus.**

Q. acutifo'lia. Slender shrub or tree of quick growth. *l.* more or less oblong, 3 to 7 in. long, yellowish with green veins, margins crinkled. *fl.* showy, white; racemes 6 in. long. New Zealand.

Q. serra'ta. Tawhewheo. Small tree to 20 ft.; shoots clammy. Whole plant covered with whitish scales. *l.* oblong, 3 to 6 in. long, leathery, coarsely toothed. *fl.* pale lilac, 1/4 in. across; racemes axillary, 3 to 4 in. long. N. Island, New Zealand.

QUISQUAL'IS (*quis*, who, *qualis*, what kind; from original uncertainty as to its family). FAM. *Combretaceae*. A genus of 2 species of climbing shrubs with slender shoots, natives of Trop. Asia and Africa extending to S. Africa. Leaves opposite or nearly so, rather thin, oblong or obovate, slender-pointed, entire. Flowers white or red, showy, in short axillary and terminal spikes or racemes: calyx tube rather long: petals 5, sometimes large, obtuse. Fruit rather large, dry, oblong, leathery, 5-winged, 1-seeded. *Q. indica* grows in a compost of peat and loam and may be propagated by cuttings of young shoots with a heel in sand under a glass with bottom heat. It needs stove conditions. **A**

Q. in'dica. Rangoon Creeper. Sometimes hairy. *l.* ovate, slender-pointed. *fl.* varying from orange to red, fragrant, beautiful; pet. oval-oblong, with appressed hairs. May to August. Trop. Asia and Africa. 1815. (B.M. 2033; B.R. 492; B.R. 30, 15 as *Q. sinensis*.) SYN. *Q. glabra*, *Q. pubescens*.

QUITCH. *See* **Couch-grass.**

QUIVER-TREE. *See* **Aloe dichotoma.**

QUIVIS'IA (*Bois de Quivi*, local name in the Isle de France). FAM. *Meliaceae*. A genus of about 6 species of trees and shrubs, natives of Mauritius and Madagascar. Leaves alternate or nearly opposite, simple, entire or pinnately lobed often on the same branch, shining above, venation netted. Flowers axillary, solitary or in short

Quisqualis indica

cymes: calyx 4- or 5-toothed, persistent; petals 4 or 5, oblong or linear. Requires stove conditions with a compost of sandy loam and fibrous peat. Cuttings of ripe shoots will strike in brisk heat.

Q. chilosan'tha. Glabrous tree or shrub. *l.* entire, obtuse or acute, 4 to 6 in. long, firm, short-stalked. *fl.* white, in sessile clusters from old wood; cor. 3/4 to 1 in. long, tubular, at first silky without. April. Mauritius. 1816. SYN. *Turraea rigida*.

Q. heterophyl'la. 10 to 15 ft. h. *l.* oval or obovate, entire, sinuate-toothed, or pinnatifid. *fl.* white; pedicels in axillary pairs, 1-fld. Mauritius. 1822.

Quoya'nus -a -um, in honour of J. R. C. Quoy, 1790–1861, surgeon in the French navy on the de Freycinet expedition.

R

RABBIT (*Oryctolagus cuniculus*). This is a most destructive pest on farms and in gardens throughout the British Is. Its food is similar to that of the hare and considerable damage is done to cereals, vegetables, the leaves of shrubs and hedge plants, and to trees and shrubs, the bark of which is often completely ringed, especially during severe weather.

Damage to trees by Rabbits and Hares may be prevented by placing wire-netting round the trunks with the top portion bent outwards to prevent them from climbing the trees and gnawing the branches, and by smearing the bark with a preparation which repels them. Other measures for avoiding damage to crops and ornamental plants in gardens, especially those adjoining woodland areas, commons, and open country, are the erection of wire-netting fences, the lower portion of which should be buried some inches in the ground and bent outwards; shooting; gassing the warrens; ferreting; and the dusting of low-growing plants such as Carnations with commercial Pepper which repels attacks.

G. F. W.

RABBIT BERRY. *See* **Shepherdia argentea.**

RACE. (1) A variety so fixed that it is reproduced by seed. (2) Related individuals without regard to rank.

RACEME. An inflorescence in which the distinctly stalked flowers are arranged singly at intervals along a stem. Cf. **Spike.**

racemi-, in compound words implying arrangement in a raceme.

racemo'sus -a -um, racemose, arranged in a raceme.

RACHIS, RHACHIS. The axis of an inflorescence or of a compound leaf.

Raddea'nus -a -um, in honour of Gustav Ferdinand Richard Radde, 1831–1903, of Danzig, director of Caucasian Museum, Tiflis, &c.

ra'dens, rasping.

RADERMACH'ERIA (in honour of J. C. M. Radermacher, resident and amateur of plants in Java). FAM. *Bignoniaceae*. A genus of about 8 species of vigorous evergreen trees and shrubs, native of SE. Asia. Leaves large, opposite, pinnate or 2-pinnate. Flowers large, bell-shaped, in terminal panicles; stamens 4 or 5, included. The species require a large, warm greenhouse and are propagated by seed, by cuttings, and by layers.

R. Paget'ii. Tree, 30 to 60 ft. h. *l.* pinnate, up to 6½ in. long; lflets. oblong-lanceolate or ovate-lanceolate, oblique at base. *fl.* white or pale lilac; cor. 2½ in. long, tube hairy within below insertion of stamens; cal. densely tuberculate, especially near base, ½ in. long; peduncle short, terminal. *fr.* brown, 6 in. long, densely tuberculate; seed including wing about 1½ in. across. Siam?

R. pentan'dra. Evergreen glabrous shrub or tree up to 20 ft. *l.* 2-pinnate, bold, stalks stout; lflets. oblong to oblong-lanceolate, 3 to 6 in. long. *fl.* yellow, unpleasantly scented, tube about 2 in. long; limb spreading, about 3 in. across; panicles about 12 in. long. Early summer. SW. China. 1903. SYN. *Oroxylum flavum.*

R. sin'ica. Fast-growing symmetrical, evergreen tree or shrub. *l.* 2-pinnate, fern-like; lflets. bluntly pointed, glabrous, about 2 in. long. *fl.* pale sulphur-yellow, 3 in. long; lobes spreading, roundish, with crisped margins. Spring, early summer. SE. China. SYN. *Stereospermum sinicum.*

F. G. P.

radia'tus -a -um, radiate, spreading from or arranged round a common centre, as the arms of an umbel or the ligulate florets of a Daisy.

radical, belonging to or proceeding from a root or from a root-like part of the stem at or below soil level.

radi'cans, radicant, having rooting stems.

radica'tus -a -um, having a distinct or conspicuous root.

radiciflo'rus -a -um, apparently flowering from the root.

RADICLE. The first root of a plant, rudimentary in the embryo.

radico'sus -a -um, having a large root.

RADIC'ULA. A synonym of Roripa.

radiiflo'rus -a -um, having flowers with radiating perianth segments.

radi'nus -a -um, slender.

RADISH (*Raphanus sativus*). The radish is a hardy, quick-growing annual, cultivated from very early times, mainly for the use of its fleshy roots as salad, but also for the young green pods for pickling. The radish is in greatest demand in spring and early summer when it grows quickly. It is tender and fit for eating for but a short time, while the roots are large enough to use and the plant has a few rough leaves before there are signs of a flowering stem. When the flower-stem develops the roots become stringy and have a hot flavour. Though most easily grown in spring, with care radishes may be had the year round, and so long as they are crisp and tender they will be in demand. Quick growth and frequent small sowings are necessary and rich, moist soil, not recently heavily manured, with a fine tilth is the only soil which gives really good results. The young plants must never be allowed to be short of water and the roots must be gathered as soon as they are large enough.

The soil should be deeply dug and a good tilth secured before the seed is sown. The seed is usually broadcast but may be sown in drills 6 to 8 in. apart, especially if grown for winter use. The seed should be sown thinly and covered with not more than ½ in. of soil. Birds are fond of the seed and some method of protecting it from them may be necessary. The seedlings under glass should not stand closer than 3 in. apart.

The earliest supplies of radishes are grown in frames on a hot-bed. They may be sown with other crops in the frame coming to use before they will interfere with their neighbours. Varieties with small tops should be used for this purpose and the plants must never be allowed to stand thickly. All small plants should be removed as soon as the usable bulk is collected so that they do not interfere with the other crop. A temperature of 50° F. is sufficient and ventilation must be given whenever possible. Sowing may also be made on a hot-bed in the open in February, the fermenting material being covered with about 3 in. of fine soil. The bed should be covered with litter or with mats at night, the covering being removed during the day except in frosty weather.

For early crops from the open ground, raised beds are best, so that the ground, while moist, never remains really wet. It is useless to sow in heavy, close, wet soil. If thorough drainage and a good tilth are secured on a warm site, sowings may be made in December and January and protected by long litter, daily removed during daylight after germination occurs and replaced whenever frost or snow threatens. The plants should not be closer together than 1½ in. and small-topped varieties are best for all early sowings. This crop will be succeeded by those sown in open ground in March and April. For later successional sowings in May to August, cool moist ground must be chosen and frequent waterings will be necessary. Crops may often be secured from between other crops which grow more slowly, but thin sowing is essential. For sowing from August to the end of October, provided the ground is moist from showers, open sites may be used, but the plants may need protection with litter or mats supported on bent sticks when frost threatens.

Radish seed retains its vitality, under good conditions of storage, for about 5 years. About 4 oz. will sow 1 sq. rod.

Radishes are subject to the same pests as other Cruciferous crops and are also sometimes affected by ailments common to Cruciferae, especially Brassicas. Among thickly sown crops, Damping off (due to *Pythium de Baryanum*) and White Blister (due to *Cystopus candidus*) may occur, as well as the common Downy Mildew (*Peronospora parasitica*). It is possible also for Finger and Toe (*Plasmodiophora brassicae*) to damage radishes but some authorities believe that there are different strains of the fungus and that the one on radish is not the same as that which attacks cabbages. There is also Scab disease caused by the fungus *Actinomyces scabies* which makes circular sunken scabby areas on the edible part of the root. This organism causes the very similar Potato Common Scab and is discussed under that heading.

A considerable variety is found in the form and colouring of the roots, which may be globose or long and tapering, red, white, or red above and white below. As already indicated the leaf growth also differs in size in different varieties. A typical long-rooted variety for frames is Wood's Early Frame, and a small-topped variety for general growth is French Breakfast, but there are many others, a selection of which is given in the Supplement. Varieties with very large roots are sometimes grown but have little to recommend them. Those most frequently offered are Black Spanish, with a black skin, and China Rose, red. The seed is sown in July or August and the plants thinned to 8 or 9 in. apart, grown on as quickly as possible, lifted in autumn, and stored in sand in a cool place. The flesh, however, is usually hard. *See* Supplement for varieties.

RADIUS. Distance from centre to outside of a circle, applied to umbels or heads.

RADIX. Root; the descending axis; the part developed from the radicle. *See* **Root.**

RAFFENAL'DIA (in honour of Alire Raffeneau Delile, Professor of Botany, Montpellier, in early 19th century). FAM. *Cruciferae.* A genus of about 3 species of dwarf perennial herbs, natives of N. Africa, related to Raphanus, but the fruit has no distinct basal joint and a very evanescent septum. It resembles Morisia in habit and while hardy is best grown in the alpine house, since it flowers normally in winter, the flowering continuing for several weeks. It does not need a rich soil either in the house or on the rock-garden.

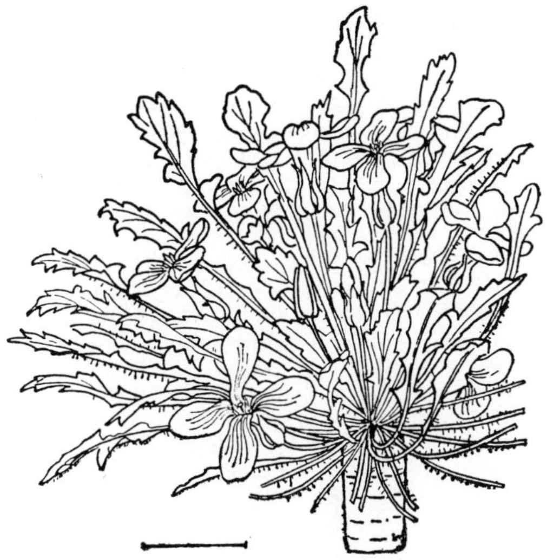

Raffenaldia primuloides

R. primuloi'des. Root stout, fleshy, long. Stem short, thick. *l.* in a spreading rosette, pinnatipartite, 1 to 4 in. long, terminal lobe large, obovate, lateral lobes distant, small; stalk short. *fl.* many, axillary, on pedicels up to 2 in. long, thickened upwards; sep. often flushed lilac, appressed to cor.; pet. primrose-yellow or lilac with darker veins, spreading; cor. about $1\frac{1}{4}$ in. across. Morocco, Algeria. (B.M. 9267.) SYN. *Cossonia africana.*

RAFFIA. (1) Malagasy name for *Raphia Roffia.* (2) Fibrous material obtained from *Raphia pedunculata* and *R. vinifera.*

Raffill'ii, in honour of Charles Percival Raffill, 1876–1951, of the Royal Botanic Gardens, Kew.

Rafines'quii, in honour of the American botanist Constantine Samuel Rafinesque, 1783–1840; see Merrill *Index Rafinesquianus* (1949).

RAF'NIA (in honour of Karl G. Rafn, 1769–1808, Danish botanist, author of a Flora of Denmark). FAM. *Leguminosae.* A genus of 22 species of evergreen, glabrous, often glaucous shrubs and sub-shrubs, confined to S. Africa. Leaves alternate, entire, simple; calyx 5-lobed or toothed; corolla papilionaceous; stamens 10. The following species require cool greenhouse conditions and thrive in a compost of fibry loam, peat, and sand. Propagated by cuttings of firm side shoots.

R. angula'ta. Shrub up to $1\frac{1}{2}$ ft., shoots ribbed. *l.* densely set, erect, $\frac{3}{4}$ to $1\frac{1}{2}$ in. long, varying from oblong-cuneate to lanceolate and linear-filiform, $\frac{1}{20}$ to $\frac{1}{2}$ in. wide, sometimes glaucous. *fl.* yellow, $\frac{1}{2}$ to $\frac{5}{8}$ in. long, in the l.-axils of forked branchlets; cal. $\frac{3}{8}$ in. long, lobes awl-shaped; keel beaked, longer than cal. by $\frac{1}{4}$ in. S. Africa. 1819.

R. ellip'tica. Shrub to 3 ft., shoots angled. *l.* 2 to 3 in. long, $\frac{1}{2}$ to $1\frac{1}{2}$ in. wide, varying in shape from narrowly oval and ovate to narrowly and broadly obovate, pointed to blunt. *fl.* solitary in upper l.-axils, yellow, $\frac{3}{4}$ in. long; cal. $\frac{3}{4}$ in. long, lobes awl-shaped, up to $\frac{3}{8}$ in. long. S. Africa. 1819.

R. triflo'ra.* Glaucous shrub, 3 to 4 ft., shoots angled. *l.* crowded and overlapping, ovate to orbicular, 1 to 3 in. long, $\frac{1}{2}$ to $2\frac{1}{2}$ in. wide, very variable in size and shape. *fl.* yellow, 1 to 3 in uppermost l.-axils, making terminal leafy racemes 3 to 6 in. long; standard roundish-cordate, $\frac{3}{4}$ in. wide, reflexed; wings about $\frac{1}{2}$ in. long. August, September. S. Africa. 1784. (B.M. 482 as *Crotalaria triflora.*)

W. J. B.

RAGGED-ROBIN. *See* **Lychnis Flos-Cuculi.**

RAGWORT. *See* **Senecio Jacobaea.** A

RAGWORT, SEA. *See* **Cineraria maritima.**

RAILINGS. Railings may be of wood or of iron. For dividing open spaces iron railings are to be preferred as they are practically invisible at a distance and do not obstruct the view as do wooden railings. Wooden railings, however, have much to recommend them especially when made of oak and well put up. The posts should be charred or tarred at the base, a strong, durable, and sightly barrier is then made capable of keeping cattle out of plantations and of protecting young fences of Quick, Beech, Holly, or Hornbeam, &c., until large enough to act as an effective barrier themselves.

RAILLARD'IA (in honour of A. M. L. Raillard, an officer in the French Marine Service). FAM. *Compositae.* A genus of over 20 species of shrubs or small trees confined to the Sandwich Is. Leaves opposite, in threes or alternate, stalkless, entire. Flower-heads without ray-florets. *R. ciliolata* requires a warm greenhouse.

R. ciliola'ta. Evergreen shrub, 3 to 4 ft., shoots downy but almost hidden by the foliage. *l.* linear to linear-lanceolate, varying very much in size from $\frac{1}{2}$ to $1\frac{1}{2}$ in. long, in pairs or threes, downy especially on margins. *fl.-heads* $\frac{3}{4}$ in. long, $\frac{1}{2}$ in. wide, in terminal racemes of 6 to 8; florets bright-yellow, crowded. July. Hawaii on the slopes of volcanoes up to 10,000 ft. 1858. (B.M. 5517.)

W. J. B.

RAIMAN'NIA. Included in **Oenothera.**

RAIN. A familiar example of the origin and nature of Rain is seen in the formation of a miniature shower, when steam escapes from a steam-engine into the air. When water is heated, it becomes an invisible vapour; and this rises, and mixes with the air, if the air is warm. When the warm air, full of water in this state, mixes with cold air, or touches any cold object, the vapour returns to the state of water; but, for a time, it remains in the form of very small particles, like fine dust—so light that they can still float in the air. In this state, they form clouds when high above the earth, or mist when lying close to the earth. Among mountains, clouds and mists are often seen to be directly continuous. But mists often cling to the mountain-tops while the sky is nearly cloudless. This is owing to the rocks and soil being colder than the air, and causing the vapour to become visible as mist, by cooling the air near them below the temperature at which the water can remain vapour. As the wind carries the mist from the mountain into the warmer air around, it resumes the form of vapour, and becomes invisible; but new mist is formed, and supplies the place of that carried away, so that the mist seems to remain unchanged on the peaks for hours. Clouds form and disappear in the sky according as the air filled with vapour meets colder or warmer winds. When the minute drops of water that form clouds are very crowded they join together and form drops, too large to be supported in the air. These then fall as Rain. Sometimes a cloud will be seen raining high up in the sky, though Rain does not reach the ground. This happens when the Rain has to fall through a layer of warm, dry air, in which it is all turned into vapour again. Light Rain sometimes falls out of a sky cloudless or nearly so; but this is a rare occurrence. The greater amount of rainfall during the night is due to the cooling of the air when the sun's heat is withdrawn. The vapour forms drops of water, and falls as Rain. The sources of the vapour in the air are various. Much of it is given off by growing plants, and a little by animals. More is taken up by warm, dry winds blowing over the surface of the land, with its marshes, rivers, and lakes; but most of all is absorbed by the winds in passing over the oceans, such as the Atlantic Ocean. Such winds are saturated, or nearly so; that is, they carry away as much vapour as they can dissolve at the temperature they had while passing over the water. If this is higher than that of the land at which they first arrive, they will give up, as Rain, the vapour that no longer can be dissolved when the temperature falls. Hence, countries near oceans receive more Rain than those at a distance from them in the middle of continents. Mountainous countries near the sea are especially rainy, since air becomes colder the higher it rises along the slopes, and a very great part of the vapour is thus lost. For the reasons just stated, as well as from local peculiarities of situation, the frequency and amount of the rainfall vary widely in different localities, and at different seasons. The total amount of Rain that falls in any given time is measured by means of instruments (*see* **Rain gauge**). Careful observations have been carried on in many countries, and in many localities, for a considerable number of years, as to the total amount of Rain that falls during the year, as well as during the various periods of the year, in each locality. The amount is expressed in the number of inches or millimetres in depth that the Rain would reach in any given time if it could all be confined to the exact area on which it has fallen.

It has been found that in some countries in the tropics, e.g. in Upper Egypt and the Sahara Desert, and on part of the coast of Peru, little Rain, if any, falls. On the other hand, the heaviest recorded rainfall occurs among mountain ranges in the neighbourhood of tropical oceans. Thus, in the Himalaya, about 100 miles from Calcutta, a rainfall of about 524 in., or about 44 ft., has been observed within a year. In the British Is. the rainfall is considerably greater on the west side than on the east, the winds from the Atlantic Ocean losing much of their vapour among the mountains. The heaviest rainfall in Britain is recorded from the Cumberland mountains, near Keswick, where over 150 in., or 12½ ft. of Rain has been collected in a year. Along our western coasts, the average annual rainfall varies from about 36 to 66 in., and on the eastern side of our islands from about 20 to 30 in.

The actual rainfall bears no definite relation to the number of rainy days in a year, for often the heaviest fall is met with in districts where it is almost limited to certain seasons. When much Rain falls in a limited time, the greater part of it necessarily flows off the surface of the ground, and it is apt to carry away the fertile soil, and to cause disastrous floods. Where, on the other hand, the period during which it falls is more prolonged, the Rain sinks into the soil and supplies the underground reservoirs of springs.

In passing through the atmosphere, the Rain becomes of the same temperature, and, as this in summer is almost always higher than that of the soil, the latter becomes warmed, and the plants in it are stimulated to more active growth. Moreover, the rain-water has oxygen, and, it may be, also minute traces of ammonia and of nitric acid, obtained from the atmosphere, dissolved freely in it, and these also are beneficial to the plants. It is unnecessary to dilate on the importance of a good supply of water in the soil ensured to plants by regular Rains.

Rain-water is very generally preferred for watering plants in pots, and it has the great advantage over that drawn from springs, or from underground pipes, of usually being at the temperature of the air, and of containing in it the oxygen, and other substances, mentioned above, and, if pure, leaves no deposit on plants sprayed with it. Its use is, of course, similar, in its effects, to the watering of plants by Rain in the open air and, when rain-water can be had, the employment of it is therefore to be recommended, but if it is collected from roofs it is apt to contain spores of mosses and algae and even of disease-producing fungi and bacteria and may therefore, unless it can be collected in an uncontaminated state, be less recommendable than deep well water.

RAIN BERRY. *See* **Rhamnus catharticus.**

RAIN GAUGE. An instrument for measuring the amount of rain falling in any place in a given time. There are several forms, but they are alike in essentials. In all there is a collecting surface of known size. This is usually a brass funnel with an upright rim about 1½ in. high around it to prevent the drops splashing over the rim. The rain falling on the funnel runs down a tube into a receiver which is protected from water getting into it except by the tube and which prevents the water entering it from evaporating. At known intervals the water collected is poured into a graduated vessel and carefully measured either in 100ths of an inch or in millimetres. The receiver is usually made to hold 3 in. depth of rainfall, and may need attention when exceptional rainfall occurs as occasionally happens during very heavy storms when 4 in. or more may fall within an hour. The collecting funnel may be of any size so long as it is accurately known, but 5 in. is the usual diameter. The instrument must be placed in an open position, the more open the better, to avoid eddies of air, &c. The funnel must be accurately horizontal and its rim should be about 6 in. above the surface on which it stands. If raised too much it will catch less rain than it should. Snow and hail must be melted and calculated as water. The depth of snow alone cannot be taken as a guide since the packing varies very much with the size of the flakes and the general atmospheric conditions. Very slight rain-showers cannot be accurately measured as the moisture is apt to evaporate from the funnel without running into the receiver, and if such showers are frequent the total amount measured in a given time will be somewhat lower than the actual fall.

RAIN-TREES. Trees, which being frequently attacked by insects such as Cicadas, are injured so that sap exudes from them, have become associated with the legend that rain is continually falling beneath them, as, for example, some species of Acer and Andira, and *Pithecolobium Saman* of Trop. S. America.

RAINBOW FLOWER. Name sometimes applied to the genus Iris.

RAISIN. Dried grape, the fruit of *Vitis vinifera.*

RAISIN-TREE, JAPANESE. *See* **Hovenia dulcis.**

RAKES. Rakes are among the indispensable garden tools for levelling ground previous to seed-sowing in order to secure a fine tilth, for collecting weeds, grass, leaves, &c., and for various other purposes. They are of different forms: some have heads entirely of iron, some have wooden heads with iron teeth, some are entirely of wood. The ordinary iron rakes have heads of different sizes, 6 in., 8 in., 10 in., and so on, the teeth being set at 1 in. apart, or rather less in the small sizes. The 10-tooth iron rake with an ash handle of 5 to 6 ft. is probably the most useful. It is the best tool for preparing fine seed-beds and for collecting weeds on cropped ground. The rake with a wooden handle and bar and iron teeth is suitable for breaking lumps of soil and collecting stones from the soil-surface where wooden teeth would soon be mutilated. The wooden rake of ordinary make is best for raking over uncropped ground on which it may very usefully be employed in spring after the action of frost, for collecting grass and leaves on lawns, and for levelling gravel on paths as well as for its more ordinary use in the hay-field. Worn teeth may be replaced by pegs of hard wood. Daisy-rakes, used for removing daisy flowers and the like from lawns, have broad teeth sharpened on both edges. Spring-toothed rakes with 4 to 8 curved-wire teeth are very useful for raking out moss and breaking the stolons of grasses on lawns during the autumn and early spring cultivations and before the last and first cutting with the lawn-mower.

ramala'na, of Mt. Ra-ma-la in W. China.

RAMBU'TAN. *See* **Nephelium lappaceum.**

RAMENTA. Thin, chaffy scales with which the stems of some plants, especially ferns, are covered.

A→

ramenta'ceus -a -um, covered with ramenta.

rami-, in compound words, signifying branches.

ramiflo'rus -a -um, bearing flowers on the branches.

RAMMERS. Rammers are frequently needed in the garden, the large size in various garden works, the hand size for use during potting. The large rammers are needed when transplanting trees for consolidating the soil about the roots when treading is insufficient, and in firming the earth round posts, &c. They are also needed when new walks are being made to ensure that the ground beneath is firm and solid. The ordinary form is made of wood, tapering upwards from a circular base, having handles at the side for lifting. A usual form is that with a rounded cast-iron head with a central socket in which a wooden handle is fixed. The hand-rammer for use in potting is made from any hard piece of wood, such as an old spade handle, shaped to a convenient size for firming the soil in a pot around the ball of roots, &c.

RAMON'DA (in honour of L. F. Ramond, French botanist and traveller, d. 1827). FAM. *Gesneriaceae.* A genus of about 3 species of stemless herbs, natives of S. Europe. Leaves in a basal rosette, softly rugose. Flowers showy, 1 or a few on leafless scapes; calyx segments 4 to 6, ovate or oblong; corolla violet to pale purple with 4 to 6 broad, overlapping lobes; stamens affixed to base of corolla. Fruit a many-seeded capsule. Alpine plants for the rock-garden or alpine-house, best grown in north-facing cracks of the rock-garden in well-drained peaty soils. Propagated by seed or division.

R. Heldreich'ii. A synonym of *Jankaea Heldreichii.*

R. Myco'ni.* *l.* in a rosette, about 6 in. across, ovate, deeply toothed, having long, reddish hairs. *Scape* about 3 in. h., usually several-fld. *fl.* purple; sep. and pet. 5; cor. lobes somewhat obovate. Pyrenees, &c. 1731. (B.M. 236 as *Verbascum Myconi.*) SYN. *R. pyrenaica.* Variable in form of l. and in fl. colour. var. **al'ba,** *fl.* white; **ro'sea,*** *fl.* rose, in its best form a very beautiful plant.

R. Nathal'iae.* Habit of *R. Myconi* but *l.* ovate, corrugated, bright glossy green, cilia dark, *fl.* lavender-blue with orange eye, sep. and pet. 4; fls. more numerous. Colour varies to pale lavender and pure white. Bulgaria, Serbia. (B.M. n.s. 152.)

R. × permix'ta (*R. Myconi × R. serbica*). Intermediate between parents.

R. pyrena'ica. A synonym of *R. Myconi.*

R. ser'bica. Habit of *R. Myconi* but *fl.* smaller and more cup-shaped; lilac-blue; sep. and pet. 5; style shorter. Balkans. (B.M. 8765.)

ramo'sus -a -um, branching.

RAMPION (*Campanula Rapunculus*). Hardy biennial, native of Europe, naturalized in Britain, grown for its fleshy roots to be used, either raw (the usual fashion) or boiled, in salads. The leaves also are used in winter salads. The minute seeds are sown in very shallow drills about the end of May (not earlier otherwise there is danger of the plants running to seed before winter). The drills should be 6 in. apart and the seedlings should be thinned to 4 in. apart as soon as large enough to handle. Rich, light soil is best for it and a somewhat shady situation. Frequent waterings are usually needed. The fleshy, white roots are ready for use from November through the winter. They need scraping before being eaten.

RAMPION, HORNED. *See* **Phyteuma.**

RAM'S HEAD. *See* **Cypripedium arietinum.**

RAM'S HORNS. *See* **Orchis mascula.**

RAMULA'RIA. A genus of fungi placed among the Imperfect Fungi (Deuteromycetes) as its members form no known perfect stage. Some species are well-known plant parasites, e.g. *Ramularia vallisumbrosae* causing White Mould on Narcissus leaves. *See* **Narcissus diseases.**

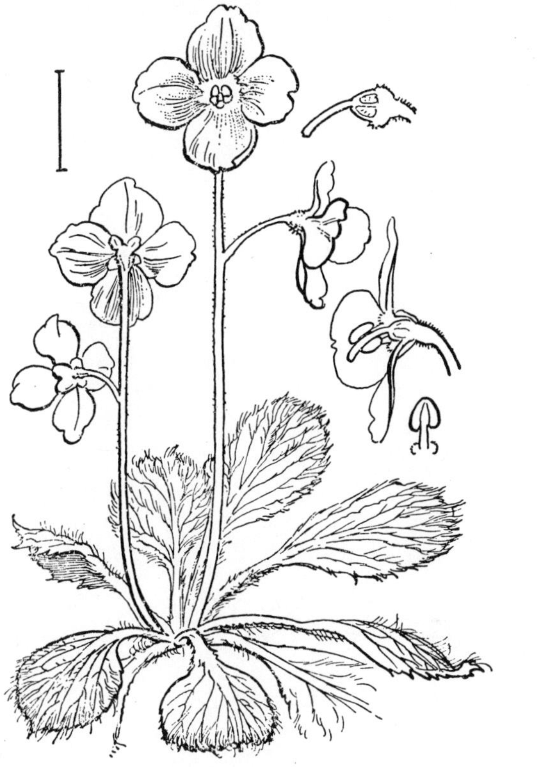

Ramonda Nathaliae

ramulo'sus -a -um, twiggy.

RAND'IA (in honour of Isaac Rand, a former Praefectus of the Chelsea Physic Garden). FAM. *Rubiaceae.* A genus of about 150 species of erect or climbing, unarmed or spiny, evergreen shrubs, natives mostly of the tropics of Asia and Africa, related to Gardenia. Leaves obovate, oblong, or lanceolate, usually leathery. Flowers white or yellow, rarely pink, small or large, solitary, in corymbs or clusters, axillary, rarely terminal; calyx tube ovoid, obovoid, or turbinate, limb usually tubular, rarely toothed or lobed; corolla funnel-, bell-, or salver-shaped, with a long or short tube, and 5 (rarely more) acute or obtuse, twisted lobes; stamens 5. For cultivation *see* **Gardenia.**

R. dumeto'rum. Much-branched shrub or small tree, with rigid, axillary spines. *l.* opposite or clustered, obovate-cuneate, smooth. *fl.* white, finally yellow; cal. tube longer than the lanceolate cor. lobes; cor. silky without. July. *fr.* large, ovate-cordate, shining. E. Indies. 1825. SYN. *R. floribunda.*

R. longiflo'ra. Tree with opposite, recurved spines. *l.* lanceolate-oblong, smooth. *fl.* in terminal or axillary few-fld. cymes, white, cor. tube long and slender; cal. tubular, 5-lobed. *Berry* smooth, as large as a cherry. E. India.

R. macran'tha. Unarmed climbing shrub or small tree, 9 to 30 ft. h. *l.* obovate-oblong, slender-pointed, short-stalked, membranous, slightly hairy beneath and on veins. *fl.* pale yellow, fragrant, axillary or terminal on ultimate branchlets, solitary; cal. lobes somewhat leaf-like; cor. tube very long. June. Trop. Africa. 1815. (B.M. 3409 as *R. Bowieana.*)

R. macula'ta. Small, unarmed, glabrous tree. *l.* oblong, somewhat leathery, shining, smooth; stalk very short. *fl.* purple with white lobes, solitary; cor. sometimes downy, tube very long. Sierra Leone. 1843. (B.M. 4185 as *Gardenia Stanleyana.*)

R. mallei'fera. 4 to 6 ft. h. *l.* in whorls of 3, obovate, cuspidate, wedge-shaped at base, glabrous; stalks short. *fl.* white, solitary, terminal, hairy; cor. tube cylindrical, club-shaped, expanded into a broad, funnel-shaped limb. July. Sierra Leone. 1843. (B.M. 4307 as *Gardenia malleifera.*)

R. Moor'ei. Shrub of 8 ft., glabrous, often thorny. *l.* ovate, $1\frac{1}{2}$ to 3 in. long; stalks short, stipules broad, acute. *fl.* white, solitary, axillary, on a slender, short pedicel; cor. tube about $\frac{1}{3}$ in. long, cylindrical, slightly widened at mouth; lobes 5, obtuse. New S. Wales.

R. penduliflo'ra. Tree up to 60 ft. h., young branches rusty hairy. *l.* up to 8 in. long, 3½ in. wide; stalk short. *fl.* white without, purplish within, in pendulous, lax clusters of 3 or 4; cor. 1½ to 2 in. long, bell-shaped, silky without; cal. ½ to ¾ in. long, deeply lobed. Tropics. SYN. *R. sericantha.*

Randia maculata (p. 1737)

R. serican'tha. A synonym of *R. penduliflora.*

F. G. P.

Rand'ii, in honour of E. S. Rand, Esq., of Para, who sent Orchids to Kew, *c.* 1894.

RANEV'EA (in honour of Louis Ranevé, horticulturist of Berlin). FAM. *Palmaceae.* A genus of about 9 species of slender Palm nearly related to Hyphorbe. Needing stove conditions and treatment as for Areca.

R. Hildebrandt'ii. About 10 ft. h. with graceful habit like some Chamaedoreas. *l.* pinnate; lflets. lanceolate, very acute, smooth, light green, rachis cylindrical; stalk long. *fl.* greenish-white, dioecious; spadix simply branched, fleshy, stalked; cal. cup-shaped, 3-lobed; pet. 3, oblong-lanceolate. Comoro Is. 1878. (B.M. 6776 as *Ravenea Hildebrandtii.*)

RANTIL OIL. Oil expressed from the seed of *Guizotia abyssinica.*

RANTY. *See* **Sorbus Aucuparia.**

RANUNCULA'CEAE. Dicotyledons. A family of 48 genera with about 1,300 species mostly in the north temperate regions but a few south of the Equator. Herbs or shrubs with alternate or opposite leaves often much cut. Flowers perfect (rarely 1-sexual); sepals 2 to 15, usually 5; petals 2 to 15, rarely absent; stamens many, rarely few, carpels 1 to many, separate, ovary superior. Fruit an achene or a follicle, rarely berry-like. Most of the Ranunculaceae have acid sap, in some instances, as *Ranunculus sceleratus*, apt to raise blisters, and several are poisonous, as the Hellebores and Aconites. The genera dealt with here are Aconitum, Actaea, Adonis, Anemone, Anemonella, Anemonopsis, Aquilegia, Callianthemum, Caltha, Cimicifuga, Clematis, Clematoposis, Coptis, Delphinium, Eranthis, Helleborus, Hepatica, Hydrastis, Isopyrum, Knowltonia, Naravelia, Nigella, Paeonia, Paraquilegia, Pulsatilla, Ranunculus, Semiaquilegia, Thalictrum, Trautvetteria, Trollius, Xanthorrhiza. **A**

RANUN'CULUS (name used by Pliny, from *rana*, frog, as some species grow in moist places). FAM. *Ranunculaceae.* A genus of about 250 species of annual or perennial herbs widely distributed over the globe but most numerous in temperate and cold regions of the N. Hemisphere. The tropical species are confined to high mountains. Leaves entire or variously divided, those of the stem often small. Flowers white, yellow, or red, solitary or in panicles, usually terminal; sepals 3 to 5, caducous, free; petals 3 or 5, or more up to 15, with a nectar-bearing scale at base, often conspicuous, sometimes minute: stamens shorter than sepals and petals, often numerous. Fruit compressed or sub-globose achenes, smooth or variously striated, wrinkled, ribbed, or bristly. The species are generally hardy and are nearly all easily grown in borders or on the rock-garden, usually preferring moist situations in loamy soil. *R. asiaticus*, a variable plant, was at one time a great favourite and ranked among the most prized florists' flowers. It needs different treatment from most other species but the striking colouring and form of the flowers, where the plants succeed, compensate for the extra trouble they give in cultivation. The system found to suit them was to prepare special beds by removing the ordinary soil to the depth of 1½ to 2 ft., putting in drainage material at the bottom if there was the least suspicion of stagnant moisture, and filling up with a prepared compost. The compost consisted of 2 parts loam to 1 part leaf-soil and thoroughly decayed cow-dung with plenty of sharp river or road sand. Road sand in the present day would, of course, be worse than useless. The beds were made up some time before the planting time which was towards the end of February if weather and soil conditions were favourable. Roots planted in autumn are liable to die during the winter. The soil needed to be brought to a fine tilth and the beds were raised a little above the paths. The roots of this Ranunculus are small and somewhat like small claws. They should be planted 6 in. apart and 1½ to 2 in. deep. The claws must be set downwards and pressed firmly into place, a little sand being afterwards scattered about them and then a covering given of fine soil. When the flowers begin to open it is well to give shelter and shade by stretching a light awning over the bed, though this is not essential. If the weather is dry enough water must be given to prevent the soil cracking, the evening being the best time. The plant likes plenty of moisture, but if it receives too much the leaves are apt to turn yellow and die prematurely. A top-dressing of fine soil is a great aid towards retaining moisture in the soil. When the leaves ripen and turn yellow after flowering is over, the roots should be lifted and stored in a dry, airy place, or suspended in paper bags until the next planting time arrives. This part of the treatment is most important. Two main sections of the florists' Ranunculus are recognized, one, the Persian, of compact, symmetrical growth, with well-shaped flowers of beautiful colours, and the Turban, which is somewhat coarser in habit of growth with perhaps larger flowers and is of a somewhat hardier constitution. At the height of its popularity very many varieties received names, just as, for example, Narcissi do to-day, but now the main aim should be to secure plants of a good strain, and with suitable care they will give a rich reward. The various species are propagated by seed and the perennials also by division. Several species have been added of recent years for their value on the rock-garden and some species have been introduced from time to time that try the skill of the most experienced, such as *R. Lyallii*, the white-flowered giant species of New Zealand. Most, however, are amenable to ordinary methods of treatment and those mentioned below are hardy unless the contrary is indicated. Even in its native land *R. Lyallii* is difficult to grow in gardens, though much attempted for garden decoration and desired for cutting. It grows in its home in loamy or peaty soil over-lying stony ground both in full sun and under shrubs in great colonies at an elevation of 3,000 to 4,500 ft. Its massive rhizomes collected in late autumn or early spring flower freely in their first season, but rarely does it take kindly to garden conditions. Perhaps collected rhizomes may be transmitted to England now transport is so rapid, or even in cold store. Some other related large-flowered New Zealand species appear equally difficult, e.g. the white-flowered *R. Buchanani* and the yellow-flowered *R. Godleyanus* and the various hybrids between the 2 known as *R.* × *Matthewsii*. Some other New Zealand species, e.g. *R. insignis*, *R. lobulatus* and *R. Monroi*, as well as species with smaller flowers appear less difficult to accommodate.

R. aconitifo'lius. White Batchelors' Buttons. 6 in. to 2 ft. h., branching. *l.* spining, palmately 3- to 5-lobed, lobes deeply toothed; upper l. sessile, lobes linear-lanceolate. *fl.* white, few or many; cal. smooth; pet. oblong, wedge-shaped, or orbicular. May, June. Europe. 1596. Borders. var. **flore-ple'no,*** *fl.* double. Fair Maids of France, Fair Maids of Kent; **grandiflo'rus,*** *fl.* very large.

R. ac'ris. Common Buttercup, Gold Knots. Hairy, 8 in. to 3 ft. h. *l.* lower stalked, orbicular or 5-angled, 3- to 7-partite; segs. of lower l. wedge-shaped, deeply cut and lobed; uppermost sessile; segs. linear, entire. *fl.* yellow, 1 in. across; sep. and pet. spreading; sep. hairy; peduncles not furrowed. Europe, including Britain, N. Asia. (E.B. 33.) var. **flore-ple'no,** *fl.* double. Yellow Batchelor's Buttons.

R. alpes'tris.* 3 to 6 in. h. *l.* roundish-heart-shaped, 3-lobed or 3-fid, blunt, apex deeply crenate. *fl.* white, usually solitary; pet 5, obcordate or 3-lobed. March to August. European Alps. var. **Traunfellneri,*** smaller than type, *l.* duller green, more finely cut, *fl.* always solitary. Eastern Alps. Rock-garden in deep, rich, moist soil, or moraine.

R. amplexicau'lis.* 3 to 9 in. h. *l.* ovate-lanceolate, slender-pointed, stem-clasping, glabrous or with a few hairs on edges, glaucous. *fl.* white, large, occasionally double; scapes 3- to 6-fld., smooth. April, May. Pyrenees. 1633. (B.M. 266; G.C. 19 (1883), 788.) Rock-garden.

R. anemonoi'des. A synonym of *Callianthemum rutifolium.*

R. aquati'lis. Water Buttercup. *l.* floating or submerged, variously cut, the submerged l. 2- or 3-multifid, segs. very narrow. *fl.* white, solitary on usually l.-opposed peduncles. May. Temperate regions, including Britain. Extremely variable and often divided into many species. Ponds and streams but apt to become invasive.

R. asia'ticus.* Garden Ranunculus. Erect, 9 to 15 in. h. or more. Stem simple or branched from base. *l.* 3- or 2-biternate, segs. toothed or deeply 3-fid. *fl.* of various colours, large; cal. spreading but at length reflexed; pet. large, obovate, blunt. May, June. Orient. 1596. Very variable in cultivation and fl. then almost always double. See note in introduction. The great red-flowered single form, wild in the Levant, is most striking and may be the 'Lily of the Field' of Matt. vi. 28. var. **albiflo'rus,*** tall, much-branched, downy, segs. of lower *l.* wedge-shaped, 2 in. long, 1 in. wide, lobed in upper part, *fl.* white with a green flush at base of pet., 4 in. across, with up to 7 in a cyme. Crete. 1928. (B.M. 9380.) Several varieties have received names.

R. bi'lobus.* Related to *R. alpestris* but with dark-green, evergreen, orbicular or kidney-shaped *l.* merely crenate, not lobed, the white *fl.* with more numerous and more deeply notched pet. May to August. Tyrol. Rock-garden. Sometimes confused in gardens with *R. crenatus.*

R. brevifo'lius. Related to *R. Thora.* About 3 in. h. *l.* grey-green, much wider than long, 3- to 5-lobed, stalks long, thin; upper l. more deeply lobed, smaller and more acute. *fl.* yellow, smaller, solitary. Asia Minor Rock-garden.

R. Breynia'nus. A synonym of *R. Villarsii.*

R. Brot'eri. Hairy perennial with a short rhizome, somewhat bulbous at base. Stem erect or ascending, hollow, up to 2 ft. h., usually branched, many-fld., covered with yellowish hairs. *Radical l.* heart-shaped at base, roundish or ovate in outline, deeply 3-sect; segs. incised; lobes rounded, crenate. *fl.* 1 in. across, yellow; cal. reflexed, yellowish; pet. widely ovate. March to May. Spain, Portugal.

R. bru'tius. Perennial, related to *R. acris.* Stem erect, *l.* hairy. 3- to 5-partite; segs. 3-partite; lobes lanceolate, 2-fid, hairy above. *fl.* yellow; cal. appressed; pet. twice as long; peduncles terete, many-fld. April, May. Italy, Greece.

R. Buchan'ani. Related to *R. Lyalli.* About 12 in. h. *l.* kidney-shaped, 3-lobed, mid-lobe often stalked. *fl.* large, white; pet. many. New Zealand. 1890. See introduction.

R. bulbo'sus. Buttercup. About 1 ft. h. *l.* 3-foliolate or 3-sect, hairy; segs. lobed. *fl.* yellow, sep. reflexed; receptacle hairy; peduncles furrowed. Spring, summer. Europe, Asia, N. Africa. (E.B. 35.) One of the common Buttercups. Poultry are fond of the bulbous base of the plant and may be used to diminish it on lawns. var. **pleniflo'rus,** *fl.* double, is the only form of value.

R. bulla'tus. 6 to 12 in. h. from a tuberous root. *l.* all basal, ovate, blistered, toothed, stalked. *fl.* solitary on a naked scape, golden-yellow, large, fragrant. May. S. Europe. 1640. Rather tender. Border or rock-garden.

Ranunculus calandrinioides

R. calandrinioi'des. Perennial, about 4 in. h., from a thick, cylindrical, unbranched rootstock, with fleshy roots. *l.* about 8, at flowering time, lanceolate or ovate-lanceolate, $1\frac{1}{2}$ to $2\frac{1}{2}$ in. long, entire, wavy at margins, glaucous green. *fl.* 1 to 3, about 2 in. across; sep. reddish, thin, about $\frac{3}{8}$ in. long; pet. white, flushed pink, about 1 in. long; anthers yellow. March, April. Morocco. 1928. (B.M. n.s. 38.)

R. carpati'cus. About 1 ft. h. from a creeping rootstock. *l.* roundish in outline, palmate, crenate. *fl.* golden-yellow, about 2 in. across. May. E. Hungary. 1892. (B.M. 7266.) Sometimes called *R. Gouani* (q.v.). Border.

P. cassu'bicus. About 6 in. h. *l.* smooth, lower kidney-shaped. crenate, stalked; upper divided into linear, toothed lobes; upper 3- or 5-partite, lobes linear, toothed. *fl.* yellow; cal. downy, shorter than pet. June, July. N. and E. Europe. 1794. (B.M. 2267.)

R. cauca'sicus. Related to *R. carpaticus.*

R. chaerophyl'lus. Erect perennial; stems 1- to 2-fld. *Radical l.* somewhat hairy, 3-sect; segs. mostly 2- or 3- partite, acute. *fl.* 1 to 2 to a stem; cal. spreading. Mediterranean region.

R. Chi'us. Annual. Stem erect, hairy. *l.* roundish-heart-shaped, with wide teeth. *fl.* yellow; peduncles opposite l; cal. reflexed; carpels with hooked bristles. S. Europe, Asia Minor.

R. cortusaefo'lius.* About 2 ft. h., slightly hairy. Stem branched, corymbose. *l.* at base, somewhat heart-kidney-shaped, slightly lobed, broadly crenate; upper l. sessile or nearly so, 3- to 5-parted, narrow. *fl.* yellow; cal. spreading. June, July. Teneriffe. 1826.

(B.R. 1432.) Not quite hardy. Best in full sun in well-drained light soil.

R. crena'tus. 3 to 4 in. h. *l.* roundish-heart-shaped, apex toothed, dull dark green. *fl.* white, as large as in *R. bilobus*, which it much resembles, but the 5 pet. almost entire, obovate; cal. glabrous. June, July. Hungary, Macedonia. 1818. Rock-garden.

R. cre'ticus. 1 ft. or more h., slightly hairy. Stem branched, many-fld. *l.* deeply lobed, toothed, teeth somewhat rounded. *fl.* golden-yellow, large. April, May. Grecian Is. 1658.

R. Cymbala'ria. Dwarf. *Radical l.* roundish ovate with large rounded teeth, rather fleshy; stalk glabrous. *fl.* yellow; pet. linear; scape naked, 1- to 3-fld., ascending. N. temperate region.

R. falca'tus. Annual, differing from most species of Ranunculus by its fewer stamens, 5 to 15 only. S. Europe. SYN. *Ceratocephalus falcatus.*

R. Fica'ria. Figwort, Lesser Celandine, Pilewort. Root tuberous. Glabrous. Stem short, decumbent, branched at base. *l.* variable, heart-shaped, obtusely angled or with rounded teeth, shining; stalks stout, dilated at base. *fl.* bright yellow, about 1 in. across; pet. several, sometimes none; peduncles ascillary, stout. 1-fld. March to May. Europe, including Britain. (E.B. 39.) Sometimes forms axillary tubers, especially in shady places. Apt to become a weed. Variable. var. **al'bus,** *fl.* white; **grandiflo'rus,*** larger in all parts. Mediterranean region. (B.M. 9199.) There are two double forms, one with more green in the fl. than the other.

R. flabella'tus. Very close to *R. chaerophyllus* but l.-segs. ovate, toothed, much 3-sect. N. Africa. Often regarded as a variety of *R. chaerophyllus.*

R. Flam'mula. Lesser Spearwort. Prostrate or erect. *Lowest l.* ovate, stalked; *upper* more lanceolate, sessile. *fl.* yellow, usually less than ½ in. across. June to August. (E.B. 29.) Damp or swampy places. *R. Lingua* is a much finer plant. var. **re'pens,** plant prostrate.

R. fumariifo'lius. A synonym of *R. millefoliatus.*

R. geraniifo'lius.* About 6 in. h., stem 1-fld., appressed, hairy at top. *l.* smooth; radical orbicular. 3-partite, segs. blunt, 3-fid, stalked; stem-l. 3- to 5-partite, sessile, segs. linear, entire. *fl.* yellow, rather larger than in *R. acris*, but variable; cal. smoothish; stigma revolute. May to July. Europe. 1775. (B.M. 3022.) SYN. *R. montanus.* A variable species. Rock-garden.

R. glacia'lis.* 3 to 6 in. h. Roots stout, long. Stem 1- to 3-fld. *l.* usually glabrous, upper sometimes hairy, radical l. palmately 3-partite, or 3-lobed, lobes 3-fid, rather blunt, grey-green. *fl.* white or pink or suffused with purple, pet. rounded, bluntly emarginate, as long as the very hairy cal. June to August. European Mts., Greenland, Iceland. 1775. Stony loam with water running below suits it best.

R. Goua'ni. About 1 ft. h. Related to *R. geraniifolius* but *l.* deeply-cut, scarcely flattened, velvety. *fl.* yellow. Pyrenees. Rock-garden, but rather leafy. *See also* **R. carpaticus.**

R. grami'neus.* Erect, glabrous, 6 to 12 in. h. Stem fibrous below, 1- to 3-fid. *l.* linear-lanceolate, glaucous. *fl.* citron-yellow, large, pedicels long; scales of pet. tubular. April to June. SW. Europe. (B.M. 164.) Variable. var. **flore-ple'no** has double *fl.*; **phoenicifo'lius,** *l.* lanceolate.

R.×hyb'ridus. A synonym of *R. Phthora.*

R. illy'ricus. Roots tuberous. Stem erect, many-fld., about 18 in. h. *l.* covered with silky wool; lower entire, linear-lanceolate, upper 3-partite, lobes 3-partite or entire, linear. *fl.* pale yellow, large; cal. somewhat reflexed. May. S. Europe. 1596. Borders.

R. insig'nis. Related to *R. Lyallii* but brown, hairy and with large, round or kidney-shaped *l.* with rounded teeth, and large golden-yellow *fl.*, 2 in. or more across in panicles of 10 to 40, up to 3 ft. h. New Zealand. It has the reputation of being much more easily grown in New Zealand than *R. Lyallii.*

R. lanugino'sus. Erect perennial. Stem covered with reflexed hairs, many-fld., terete. *l.* 3-fid, lobes somewhat incised, wide. *fl.* yellow. Europe, Caucasus. Woodland plant.

R. Lin'gua.* Greater Spearwort. Roots densely fibrous. Stem 2 to 3 ft. h., hollow. *l.* lanceolate, 6 to 10 in. long, ½ to 1 in. wide, entire or toothed, sessile, half-stem-clasping. *fl.* yellow, 2 in. across, somewhat panicled; sep. and pet. 5. July to September. Europe, including Britain. (E.B. 31.) For damp, marshy places. var. **grandiflo'rus** is a large-fld. form.

R. Lyall'ii. Stem up to 4 ft. h., paniculately branched with 10 to 60 ft. *rhiz.* thick, far-spreading. *l.* peltate, up to 12 in. or more wide, stalks long, stout; blade orbicular, concave, thick and leathery, crenate. *fl.* white, up to 4 in. across, sometimes semi-double; sep. 5, broad, hairy; pet. broadly wedge-shaped, basal gland-obscure, oblong. Spring, summer. New Zealand. 1879. (G.C. 15 (1881), 724; B.M. 6888.) See introduction.

R.×Matthews'ii. See introduction.

R. millefolia'tus. About 12 in. h. Stem almost leafless, erect, hairy, 1-fld. *l.* decompound, multifid; lobes linear, smooth. *fl.* yellow. May to July. S. Europe. 1820. (B.M. 3009.) var. **grandiflo'rus** has larger *fl.* Rock-garden.

R. monspeli'acus. Stem erect, few-fld., about 18 in. h. *l.* woolly; radical 3-lobed; lobes wedge-shaped, 3-fid toothed; upper l. 3-partite, lobes linear, entire. *fl.* golden-yellow; cal. reflexed. April, May. Mediterranean region. Borders. var. **cunea'tus,** *l.* wedge-shaped, with 3-fid teeth at tip. (S.B.F.G. 94); **rotundifo'lius,** *l.* roundish, 3-fid, lobes toothed, obtuse.

R. monta'nus. A synonym of *R. geraniifolius.*

R. nissa'nus. A synonym of *R. psilostachys.*

R. parnassifo'lius. 3 to 6 in. h. Stem hairy, 1- to 6-fld. *Radical l.* stalked, somewhat heart-shaped, roundish-ovate, stalks dilated at base; *stem-l.* sessile, ovate-lanceolate; all dark green, veins woolly, edges reddish, ciliate. *fl.* white, somewhat pinkish without; pet. round, not notched, overlapping; peduncles hairy. June, July. Alps, Pyrenees. 1769. (B.M. 386.) Rock-garden.

Ranunculus geraniifolius

R.×Phtho'ra (*R. brevifolius×R. Thora*). Root tuberous. Stem about 9 in. h., erect, many-fld. *l.* glabrous; radical l. long-stalked, kidney-shaped, crenately lobed; stem-l. 1 or 2, lobed at apex, stalks short. Austrian Alps. 1820. SYN. *R. hybridus.*

R. platanifo'lius. Related to *R. aconitifolius* but taller and larger, *l.* less divided, *fl.* white, less stiffly carried. May. Europe.

R. psilosta'chys.* Perennial, up to 16 in. h. Stem branched above, from a tufted mass of thickened roots. *l.* radical, roundish, up to 4 in. across, deeply 3-partite; segs. wedge-shaped, lobed, hairy, hairs silky. *fl.* glossy yellow up to 2½ in. across, in a branched infl.

of 1 to 14 fl.; sep. reflexed, silky without, glabrous within. May. E. Mediterranean, especially Balkans. 1895. (B.M. 9188.) SYN. *R. nissanus*.

R. pyrenae'us.* About 1 ft. h. *l.* linear or lanceolate, entire. *fl.* white; scape 1- to several-fld., hairy in upper part. June to August. Alps, Pyrenees. 1807. Rock-garden in rich soil.

Ranunculus psilostachys (p. 1740)

R. re'pens. Creeping Buttercup. The double-fld. form (**flore-ple'no**) is sometimes offered, but the single-fld. form is apt to be a troublesome weed.

R. rupes'tris. 9 to 12 in. h. *l.* hairy, roundish-kidney-shaped, 3-fid. *fl.* golden-yellow, 2 in. across; scapes 1- to 4-fld. Spain. Rock-garden.

R. rutifo'lius. A synonym of *Callianthemum rutifolium*.

R. Seguie'ri. About 3 in. h. Stem 1- to 3-fld. *l.* 3-parted, each seg. 3-fid, acute or bluntish, entire; upper small, sessile, sometimes 3-fid. *fl.* white, $\frac{3}{4}$ in. across, pet. 5, entire, orbicular, longer than cal. June, July. Alps. 1819. (G.F. 1192.) Rock-garden.

R. Tho'ra. Root tuberosus. Stem 9 in. h. *l.* glabrous; radical l. stalked; stem-l. sessile, reniform, crenate. *fl.* yellow, 2 or 3 on a glabrous scape. May. S. Europe. 1710. Rock-garden.

R. Traunfell'neri. A variety of *R. alpestris*.

R. Villar'sii.* Related to *R. montanus*, but dwarfer and with larger yellow *fl.* W. Alps. Rock-garden. SYN. *R. Breynianus*.

RAOU'LIA (in honour of Edouard Raoul, 1815–52, French naval surgeon who collected in New Zealand in 1842 and described his plants in *Choix de Plantes de la Nouvelle Zélande*). FAM. *Compositae*. A genus of about 22 species related to Helichrysum, natives of New Zealand and Australia. There are two growth forms, the shrubby species which seem never to have been successfully cultivated and the mat-forming species of which a few have been introduced and proved useful on the well-drained rock-garden. They are creeping plants with very small leaves often covered with stiff, close wool, overlapping the stems, which end in flower-heads with silvery bracts much resembling those of the mat-forming Helichrysums. Flowers all tubular with a toothed corolla. Achenes with a pappus. The most striking species is the New Zealand *R. eximia* which forms large mounds the younger parts of the much and closely branched plant rooting into the old decaying portions so that a great grey mass is produced, much resembling in appearance at a distance a procumbent sheep and aptly known as a Vegetable Sheep. Cultivation as for Helichrysum, needing a warm site. Propagated by seed or by rooted pieces from an established plant.

R. austra'lis. Carpet silvery. *l.* $\frac{1}{15}$ to $\frac{1}{8}$ in. long, grey tomentose above and below. *fl.-heads* pale yellow, $\frac{1}{8}$ to $\frac{1}{4}$ in. across. New Zealand.

R. glab'ra. Carpet green. *l.* $\frac{1}{8}$ to $\frac{1}{5}$ in. long, glabrous or slightly hairy. *fl.-heads* white, $\frac{1}{4}$ to $\frac{1}{3}$ in. across. New Zealand.

R. lutes'cens. Carpet greyish. *l.* minute, $\frac{1}{20}$ to $\frac{1}{12}$ in. long, tomentose above and below. *fl.-heads* lemon-yellow $\frac{1}{8}$ to $\frac{1}{6}$ in. across. New Zealand.

R. subseri'cea. Carpet green. *l.* $\frac{1}{6}$ to $\frac{1}{4}$ in. long, almost glabrous above, tomentose below. *fl.-heads* white, $\frac{1}{3}$ in. across. New Zealand, (B.M. 9145 B.)

RAPA'NEA. Included in **Suttonia.**

RAPE, *Brassica Napus*, a biennial native of Britain, the young seedlings of which are frequently used as a salad in substitution for Mustard and grown in a similar way. Varieties with a large leaf winter-hardy are also grown as Kale (q.v.) and a form with edible-roots is occasionally grown. The roots are carrot-shaped, long and white, about as thick as the thumb. The seed is sown in January on rather poor soil not recently manured (on freshly manured ground the roots are apt to fork) and these will be ready for use in May. The roots are scraped and boiled like Turnips. For later supplies seed should be sown in a cool place shaded during the hottest part of the day. The seedlings need to be thinned to 10 in. apart.

RAPE, BROOM. *See* **Orobanche.**

RAPHA'NUS (ancient Greek name used by Theophrastus). FAM. *Cruciferae*. A genus of about 6 species of hardy annual or biennial branching herbs natives of Europe and temperate Asia. Roots often succulent. Lower leaves lyrate. Flowers white or yellow with purple veins; pedicels slender; lateral sepals somewhat saccate at base; racemes long, terminal, opposite leaves. Pods long, more or less erect, jointed. *R. sativus* is the common Radish, and *R. caudatus* produces long, edible pods. For cultivation *see* **Radish.**

R. cauda'tus. Annual. Stems purplish, glaucous, at first erect. then prostrate. *fl.* purplish-veined, as large as those of a Wallflower. *Pods* flattish, slender-pointed, as long as the whole plant. Java? 1815. (G.F. 594.) Widely grown in W. India for its edible pods

R. isatoi'des. A variety of *R. sativus* with the general aspect of *Isatis tinctoria*. *l.* lyrate-pinnatisect; stem-l. ovate-lanceolate, stem-clasping, thick, glaucous. 1886. (R.H. 1886, 372.)

R. sati'vus. Annual. Root reddish, white, yellowish or deep black-brown, fusiform, half-globular, or turnip-shaped. *l.* rough, lyrate or sometimes lobed, terminal lobe longest and broadest. *fl.* white to pale violet with dark veins; in an erect panicle about 3 ft. long. May. *Pods* usually smooth, with a terminal beak. Temperate regions of Old World, long cultivated, perhaps a derivative of the wild *R. Raphanistrum*.

RAPHE. Part of the stalk (funicle) of an anatropous ovule, lying along the side of the ovule and fused with it.

RAPH'IA (*raphis*, needle; in allusion to the beaked fruit). FAM. *Palmaceae*. A genus of about 15 species of unarmed palms or with the sheaths only armed, natives of Trop. Africa and the Mascarene Is. one in Trop. S. America. Monocarpic. Stem tall, erect, simple or dichotomously branched, densely ringed. Leaves in a terminal crown, long, pinnatisect, thickly leathery, leaflets linear-lanceolate, slender-pointed, recurved, bristly at base. Spadices monoecious, large, pendulous, cylindrical, much-branched, branches thick, compressed, densely set with cup-shaped bracts. Flowers solitary in the axils of bracts, male at base of branchlets of spadix, female at tip. Fruit large, oblong, ovoid or elliptic, beaked, 1-seeded, the spikes sometimes weighing 200 to 300 lb. Cultivation as for Cocos.

R. Gentilia'na. *l.* pinnate, prickles small. *Infl.* dense, pendent, nearly 3 ft. long. *fr.* pear-shaped, beaked, 2 to 2½ in. long, with 9 or 10 rows of fringed scales. Congo.

R. Laurent'ii. Stem up to 6 ft. *l.* 15 to 40 ft. long; lflets. linear, up to 2½ ft. long, 2 in. wide, acute, with short blackish spines. *infl.* compact, over 3 ft. long. *fr.* ovoid, 2 in. long, with 12 rows of scales. Congo.

R. Ruf'fia. Raffia or Roffia Palm. Stem 6 to 25 ft. long. *l.* 50 to 60 ft. long; the stalk 12 or 13 ft. long, about 1 in. thick. *fr.* obovate or pear-shaped with usually 12 (13 to 15) ribs, scales shining, very convex. Mascarene Is.

R. taedi'gera. Raffia or Roffia Palm. Stem 6 to 8 ft. long. *l.* forming a plume 70 ft. h., 40 ft. across; lflets. with weak prickles on margins. *fr.* about 2½ in. long, oblong, scales large. Amazon. 1847.

R. vini'fera. Bamboo or Wine Palm. Stem of moderate height. *l.* 6 to 7 ft. long; lflets. spiny. *fr.* elliptic, 3 in. long, with 8 or 9 rows of deeply groved chestnut scales. Trop. Africa. The sap is used by the natives for wine called 'bourdon'. *See also* **Raffia.**

RAPHIDES. Crystals, often needle-shaped and of calcium oxalate, contained in the cells of plants. These crystals frequently cause skin irritation which can be prevented to a large extent when, e.g., gathering or handling quantities of Daffodils, by greasing the hands and wrists with tallow, and by washing them well after handling the flowers.

RAPHIDO'PHORA (*raphis*, needle, *phora*, to bear; from the raphides in the cells). FAM. *Araceae.* A genus of about 60 species of creeping or climbing plants, rooting from the stems, and with leaves in 2 ranks, natives of the E. Indies and S. Asia. Leaf-stalk long, sharply bent at base of blade, more or less sheathing, blade lanceolate or oblong, usually large. Flowers usually hermaphrodite, naked; stamens 4. Fruits joined, many-seeded. Spathe boat-shaped. Spadix densely flowered; shorter than spathe. For cultivation *see* **Caladium.**

R. decur'siva. Branches about 1 in. thick, round, bearing long roots. *l.-stalk* 16 to 20 in. long, channelled, blade leathery, green above, paler beneath, oblong, 20 to 30 in. long, acute, in the adult cut to midrib in linear segs. *Peduncle* 4 to 6 in. long. *Spathe* fleshy, ovate-oblong, slender-pointed, yellow, paler at margins, 7 in. or more long. *Spadix* ashy green, shorter than spathe. SE. Asia. (B.M. 7282.)

RAPHIOLE'PIS (*rhapis*, a needle, *lepis*, a scale; in allusion to the awl-shaped bracts). FAM. *Rosaceae.* Evergreen shrubs, with short-stalked, toothed, firm-textured leaves and white or pink flowers in terminal racemes or panicles; petals 5; stamens 15 to 20; styles 2 or 3 united at the base. Fruit purplish or bluish-black, 1- or 2-seeded, the calyx fallen away. These shrubs grow well in fertile loam or peaty soil and should have a sunny position. Increased by cuttings.

R. × Delacour'ii.* (*R. indica × R. umbellata.*) Raised at Cannes about 1896. A shapely shrub up to 6 ft. h. *l.* obovate, toothed towards the end, 1½ to 3½ in. long, ¾ to 1½ in. wide. *fl.* in erect terminal panicles 3 or 4 in. h., each fl. ½ to ¾ in. wide, the 5 obovate pet. rosy-pink. (R.H. 1900, 698.) Like *R. indica* its flowering season is variable and may extend intermittently from January to August. This charming shrub was injured in exposed sites by the winter of 1939–40. (B.M. n.s. 362.)

R. in'dica. A cold greenhouse shrub a few feet h., with narrow, toothed, lanceolate or oblanceolate *l.* 2 to 3 in. long. *fl.* narrow-petalled, ¾ in. wide, white tinged with pink borne in racemes 2 to 3 in. tall. Blooms intermittently February to August. Hardy in S. Cornwall. S. China. 1806. (B.R. 468; B.M. 1726 as *Crataegus indica.*)

R. japo'nica. A synonym of *R. umbellata.*

R. ova'ta. A synonym of *R. umbellata ovata.*

Raphiolepis umbellata ovata

R. umbella'ta. A sturdy shrub of rounded shape, 6 to 10 ft. *l.* very stout and leathery, oval to obovate, tapered towards both ends, inconspicuously toothed, 1½ to 3 in. long. *fl.* pure white, fragrant, ¾ in. wide, on a stiff, erect, terminal infl. 3 or 4 in. h. June. *fr.* pear-shaped, ⅓ in. long, blue-black, 1-seeded. Japan. 1862. SYN. *R. japonica.* Normally hardy; a fine healthy plant 8 ft. though in an open position at Kew, withstood 30 or more winters uninjured until that of 1939–40 which was fatal. var. **ova'ta,** *l.* entire or nearly so. (B.M. 5510 as *R. japonica integerrima.*)

W. J. B.

RAPHISTEM'MA (*raphis*, needle, *stemma*, crown; the lobes of the corolla needle-shaped). FAM. *Asclepiadaceae.* A genus of 2 species of twining, glabrous shrubs or sub-shrubs, natives of E. Indies and Malaya. Leaves opposite, membranous. Flowers white, rather large, in long-stalked umbels; calyx deeply 5- cut or -parted; corolla somewhat bell-shaped with 5 lobes twisted in bud, overlapping to the right; corona scales 5, adnate at base in a staminal tube. Treatment as for Stephanotis.

R. pulchel'lum. Shrub. *l.* cordate, slender-pointed, membranous, smooth, glandular. *fl.* pure white; sep. broad; cor. segs. ovate, obtuse, erect; stigma rather prominent. July. Himalayan region, Burma. 1852. (F.d.S. 228.)

F. G. P.

ra'rus -a -um, uncommon.

RASPA'LIA (in honour of F. V. Raspail, a celebrated French chemist and botanist, 1794–1878). FAM. *Bruniaceae.* A genus of 10 species of evergreen shrubs, bushy and twiggy in habit with a close leaf arrangement resembling that of some cypresses and New Zealand Veronicas, natives of S. Africa. Greenhouse, should be grown in sandy peat. Propagated by cuttings.

R. microphyl'la. Densely branched shrub, 1 to 2 ft., twigs together with the minute, closely appressed, scale-like l. $\frac{1}{16}$ in. wide. *l.* opposite, scoop-shaped, ciliolate, rhomboid-ovate, obtuse, $\frac{1}{24}$ to $\frac{1}{12}$ in. long. *fl.* minute, white, crowded in woolly globose heads $\frac{1}{6}$ to $\frac{1}{4}$ in. wide; cal. 5-lobed, pet. 5. July. S. Africa. 1804.

W. J. B.

RASPBERRY (*Rubus idaeus*). The Raspberry is a native of most European countries including Great Britain and is the parent of the great majority of the Raspberries cultivated in the British Isles. In America the related species, *R. occidentalis* with black or yellow fruits and *R. strigosus* with light red or occasionally white or yellow fruits, have been the main elements in the development of the American varieties of Raspberry, the varieties derived from *R. idaeus* being less amenable to local conditions there. Some of the American varieties have been introduced to cultivation in Britain but only a few of them compete successfully with varieties of British type.

The Raspberry is a deciduous perennial with biennial stems making their growth in their first year and producing lateral shoots from the buds thereon at the ends of which fruit is borne in the second. The chief feature of the American varieties, which is an advantage over the British, is that they are of more open habit and hold their fruits out in a way that makes them somewhat easier to gather. After the fruit is ripe the whole stem (cane) on which they were borne dies and is replaced in the same year by new canes from the rootstock or from suckers from the old plant. The old canes should be cut away at the base, soon after the fruit is picked, and burnt, about 6 of the new canes from each root being retained and tied in, the weak and superfluous canes being cut away; this treatment means that at the end of the autumn only the new canes for fruiting in the following year are left. A few varieties produce fruit in autumn on canes of the current year and these require different treatment: all the canes are cut down to the ground in February. The fruit is extensively grown for cooking and dessert and is largely used for preserving as jam and by bottling, and is used in the manufacture of Raspberry brandy, wine, and vinegar. It has a fine flavour and aroma when it first ripens but this is not generally retained for more than 2 or 3 days. If allowed to hang after ripening the fruit soon shrivels and becomes useless. The Raspberry has been long cultivated, but in comparatively recent years virus diseases (see below) have spread in it so seriously that many varieties once highly valued are now either not procurable or are so much infected that they are not worth planting. Where attention is paid to the maintenance of clean stock they form an important crop and large areas are devoted to them, especially in Scotland.

The soil best suited for Raspberries is a light or medium loam, deep and well-drained. They do not grow very well on very heavy soils but light sandy soils suit them if a sufficient supply of decaying organic matter can be maintained to ensure that they do not dry out in periods of drought. An open situation is best but they are more tolerant of some shade than most other fruit crops. Water-logging is bound to cause much loss and dry conditions in summer check growth and diminish the crop in that and the following year.

Planting is best done in early autumn on ground that has been deeply worked and thoroughly cleaned. The ground should be enriched by digging in at least 20 tons of farmyard manure or its equivalent to the acre and on very light soils at least 30 tons, working it into the body of the soil, not making a manure sandwich. The planting must be shallow, the roots being covered by not more than 3 in. of soil well firmed over them. At no subsequent time should the cultivation be deep, however carried out, otherwise the roots and suckers will be damaged. The canes are best planted in rows, allowing 2 ft. from plant to plant and 6 ft. from row to row. Thus about 3,600 canes are required for the acre, about 25 for the square rod.

The canes planted should be taken from a nursery bed where they have been thoroughly inspected for possible infection with virus diseases, rather than from the fruiting stock, and the young canes coming up away from the rows should be avoided, using only strong, healthy canes from near the base of the old stock. The canes selected should be well-provided with fibrous roots and of medium size, avoiding both weak canes and those which have made very vigorous growth. As soon as they are planted the canes should be cut down to about 24 in. in length. In spring they are further shortened to a live, growing bud, 10 to 12 in. above ground.

The canes will probably need support which, since the life of the row, if healthy, should be 7 or 8 years, may be permanent. For this nothing is better than 2 strands of 12- or 13-gauge galvanized wire stretched between stout posts and supported at wide intervals by lighter posts. The canes are tied to this as they grow or at least after they have been topped in early spring. Support may be given at fruiting time only by stakes along the row and a double line of twine.

The ground should be frequently cultivated through the spring and summer but the cultivation must be shallow. Regular mulching with farmyard manure or its equivalent will be necessary every spring, not only as a means of supplying mineral deficiencies but especially as a means of conserving moisture, without which the Raspberries cannot thrive. As Raspberries need potash, an application of sulphate of potash (not kainit) should be given in early spring or in autumn at the rate of 3 oz. to the yard run of row. If the canes are weak, and only then, nitrogenous manures should be given. The mulching already referred to will usually supply all the nitrogen needed. In February the weak tops of the canes and any dead parts should be cut away and burnt, leaving sturdy growths for the production of fruit.

The ripe fruit should be gathered daily, for it does not all ripen at once. If the fruit is required for dessert it is picked with the stalk attached, but if for other purposes the fruit is pulled from the stalk, i.e. plugged, leaving the core of the cluster on the plant. All the ripe fruits should be picked and that which is attacked by grubs separated and burnt as a means of checking the increase of the Raspberry beetle (q.v.). The fruit is soft and needs careful handling. For market, dessert fruit is picked into 1 lb. punnets lined with greaseproof paper and covered with cellophane; the main crop is picked into 2-lb. punnets or sometimes into 3-lb. chip-baskets. Anything larger than this is too large if the fruit has to be carried far. For jam-making the fruit is sent in tubs.

As soon as the fruit is gathered the old canes are cut completely down and burnt. (But see the note on Autumn-fruiting varieties above.)

Seed is used for propagation only when new varieties are desired. For this purpose the selected fruits are lightly crushed and all the pulp washed away, the remaining seeds dried of superfluous moisture and sowed in pans of light soil, or in the open in a mixture of sand and leaf-mould.

Considerable variation is seen in the height and vigour of plants so raised, in the colour and armature of the canes, and in the size, colour, and season of the fruits. The yellow varieties are grown only for dessert. Selection is necessary for colour, not only at the moment of ripening but subsequently, for ease of plugging and for cohesion of the druplets, for size and for solidity of the ripe fruit, and ease of picking, as well as for flavour. There is considerable difference, too, among the varieties as regards their fitness for bottling or jam-making. For a selection of varieties for planting *see* Supplementary volume.

DISEASES. Raspberries are subject to several fungus attacks, but with ordinary care and good cultivation they should not be serious. Where the soil conditions are unsuitable or waterlogging occurs Crown Rot due to *Nectria rubi* or *Fusarium* spp., in which there is a rotting of the canes at the crown and whitish pustules of spores or red perithecia, may develop on the rotting bark. Attention to drainage and general cultivation should eliminate such troubles. On the leaves rust due to *Phragmidium rubi-idaei* produces all its stages, first yellow pustules on the upper surface in June (aecidiospores), then orange pustules on the under surface (uredospores), and later black pustules of the overwintering stage (teleutospores) are seen. This rust is rarely serious. Mildew (*Sphaerotheca humuli*) may produce its white powdery or mealy covering on leaves and even on the fruit, but can be checked by dusting with sulphur. The most serious foliage disease is the virus disease called Mosaic showing as mottling with light- and dark-green areas over the leaf surface. The symptoms produced may be a mild even mottling over the leaf surface without any curling or distortion, or deformed yellow patches near the midrib or sharply defined yellow spots with much crumpling and twisting of the leaf-blade, but all are in general a yellowish speckling with gradual reduction in size of leaf and stunting of canes with scanty fruiting. Some varieties, however, may last for years and seem to resist the ill-effects, but others are very susceptible, notably the variety Lloyd George. As with most virus diseases all affected plants must be destroyed when seen, and if a stock is seriously affected it should be grubbed out and burnt and a new stock planted. No young canes should be saved from the Mosaic-infected stock. The canes of raspberries may be affected by several diseases. Occasionally they show Crown Gall (due to *Bacterium tumefaciens*) at ground-level or even on the canes some feet above the ground, and all such canes should be cut out and burnt. Blue Stripe Wilt is due to the fungus *Verticillium dahliae* living in the rootstock and so interfering with the flow of sap that the leaves of the young canes in June or July show yellowish areas in stripes between the veins, and these areas turn brown and die, giving a striped effect. Such leaves fall prematurely and some of the ends of the canes may also die. It is necessary to dig up and burn any affected stools and not to take young canes or 'spawn' from them for replanting. Cane Blight is seen on the fruiting canes in summer when the leaves wilt and wither and the canes are liable to snap off at ground-level. This is due to the fungus *Leptosphaeria Coniothyrium* which may be producing its small, blackish, spherical fruit bodies on the cracked and discoloured bark at the base of the canes. All such affected canes should be cut out well below soil-level and burnt. Cane Spot or Anthracnose is due to the fungus *Elsinoe veneta* and although not so serious as Cane Blight will reduce the vigour of the plants considerably. It also causes a spotting of the fruit in some cases. The symptoms are seen on the young canes about May or June, which develop small circular purplish spots. As the canes grow these spots become elliptical and the centres turn whitish-grey. They gradually become sunken and on the older fruiting canes are very like small cankers, giving the cane a rough and cracked appearance. The leaves when infected show small circular spots with a white centre and dark border and the fruit if affected may be misshapen or one-sided. The treatment is to cut out badly affected canes and spray the others with Lime Sulphur or Bordeaux mixture, giving 2 applications: (*a*) Delayed Dormant when the cane buds have pushed out about ½ in. with Lime Sulphur 1 part to 15 parts water or Bordeaux mixture 6–6–50 (*b*) Preblossom when the first flower-buds show white tips with Lime Sulphur 1 part to 40 parts water, or Bordeaux mixture 6–6–100. Spur Blight shows as dark-purplish blotches on the canes mostly at the nodes but sometimes between them as well. The purple patches increase in size and then gradually become pale grey with very small black dots, the fruiting bodies of the fungus *Didymella applanata* on them. Young canes are infected in wet weather by these fungus fruit-bodies as they release their spores, especially if the canes are crowded. Where the disease is severe overcrowding should be avoided by removing superfluous young canes and the rest should be sprayed with Bordeaux mixture as for Cane Spot. Black Blotch (*Cryptosporium minimum*) may almost cover the canes with a black superficial blotchiness, but the canes remain quite smooth and are not likely to be much affected. The Grey Mould fungus, *Botrytis cinerea*, may in wet weather do damage to young canes if overcrowded and all infected should be at once removed (*see* **Grey Mould fungus**). Cases have been known where raspberry plants have been attacked by the Silver Leaf fungus, but the foliage although whitish does not become very silvery (*see* **Silver Leaf**).

(D. E. G.)

PESTS. Aphides. Several species of Aphides feed on Raspberry, but a few only are of special concern. Massee in *The Pests of Fruits and Hops*, 1937, pp. 206–7, names 4, the Raspberry Aphis, *Amphorophora rubi*: the Leaf-curling Raspberry Aphis, *Aphis idaei*; and 2 species of *Macrosiphum*, *M. fragariae*, and *M. funestum*. *Amphorophora rubi* is the most common and widely distributed, and has been proved in the United States of America to be the carrier of the virus disease called Raspberry Mosaic. The Aphides occur on the leaves during May and June, and may cause partial or complete leaf-curl and severe stunting of the shoots. Control measures against these Aphides may be unnecessary unless the invasions are heavy and the injury severe. The thorough application of a 5 per cent. Tar-distillate wash during the dormant season will destroy the eggs of those that overwinter on the canes. As winged forms migrate from wild Blackberries in spring it is sometimes necessary to spray the under-side of the leaves and the shoots with Nicotine-Soap wash, and several applications may be essential in some seasons in order to keep the canes clear of these migratory forms.

Raspberry Beetle, *Byturus tomentosus*, is the most serious pest of Raspberry, Loganberry, and cultivated Blackberries, the fruits of which are damaged by the grubs. It has become of great importance since the advent of the canning industry in this country as the presence of the grubs floating in the syrup of canned fruits will condemn the sample. The small, yellowish-brown, later greyish-brown, beetles emerge from the soil in May and visit the blossoms of fruit and ornamental trees and bushes where they feed on the floral organs. They eat also the flower-buds of the host plants. The eggs are laid in the fertilized blossoms during June and July, and the grubs feed on the drupelets and, later, tunnel into the fruit 'plugs'. When fully fed they descend to the soil and pupate within an earthern cell; the adults emerge the following May.

The most severe attack may be controlled by the thorough application of Derris washes and dusts, a double application being necessary in the heaviest attacks. The first application should be made to Raspberries 10 days, to Loganberries 15 days, after flowering begins; the second application 10 to 15 days after the first. It is essential to direct the wash in the form of a fine mist into the base of the blooms, the object being to destroy the grubs while they are feeding on the outside of the fruits and before they tunnel inside. Derris dust may be substituted for the liquid spray, and should be applied in mid-June for Raspberries and Loganberries, and in early July for Blackberries. Late dusting is not recommended otherwise the fruits will be rendered unsightly by the dust deposit.

RASPBERRY MOTH, *Lampronia rubiella.* A pest of primary importance which causes considerable damage to the canes. Its presence on the plants is readily detected towards the end of April and in early May by the withered shoots, the interior of which are tunnelled by the red caterpillars of this small Moth. The Moth has a wing expanse of about ½ in., the wings being shiny and purplish-brown with yellow spots on the fore-wing. It is on the wing in May and June, and flies during the daytime. The eggs are laid in the open flowers, and the young caterpillars bore their way into the plug or receptacle of the fruit. The caterpillars soon crawl from the developing fruits and seek hibernating quarters at the base of the canes, in crevices of support-stakes, among rubbish, and in the soil. They leave their cocoons in April and ascend the canes where they burrow into the base of the shoots. They feed on the pith inside the shoots, which shrivel, and eventually pupate within the burrows. Light infestations in gardens may be checked by hand-picking and burning all wilted shoots as soon as they appear. Clean cultivation in and around the canes is advisable, and all accumulations of rubbish and fallen leaves should be removed. Success is claimed from the spraying of the canes in December or January with 8 per cent. Tar Oil wash.

(G. F. W.)

RASPBERRY JAM TREE. *See* **Acacia acuminata.**

RATA. *See* **Metrosideros.**

RATHBUN'IA (in honour of Dr. Richard Rathbun, 1852–1918, Assistant Secretary of the Smithsonian Institute). FAM. *Cactaceae.* Bushy plants with slender stems; ribs few, prominent; spines awl-shaped; flowers diurnal, red; stamens longer than the perianth; flower persisting on the ovary; fruit round, spiny or smooth. A

R. alamosen'sis. Stems erect at first, rooting near the tip; ribs blunt, radial spines spreading, centrals much stouter. *fl.* scarlet, up to 4 in. long. *fr.* round, red. Mexico. (B.R.C. 2, t. 25.) SYN. *Cereus alamosensis.*

V. H.

RATIBID'A. Included in **Rudbeckia.**

RATS are less destructive in gardens and nurseries than Mice and Voles. Of the 2 British species the Brown Rat (*Rattus norvegicus*) is a hardier, more indiscriminate feeder, and is more widely distributed than the Black Rat (*Rattus rattus*), which is again becoming common following a period of scarcity in this country. Confusion often arises by the term 'Water Rat' being applied to the Water Vole (*Arvicola amphibius*), which is distinguishable from Rats by being more heavily built and having a broad head, blunt muzzle, inconspicuous ears, and a hairy tail. The Brown Rat will invade gardens and glasshouses where it has been known to climb vine rods for the ripening grapes, carry away ripe fruits from orchard houses, devour tomato fruits, and eat the larger seeds of plants both in storage and after sowing. It is fond of burrowing in banks, leaf-mould, and rubbish heaps and even in glasshouse borders, and is a good swimmer, following water-courses in its search for fresh homes. Both Rats are omnivorous, but they are vegetarian under wild conditions. Their large incisor teeth enable them to gnaw through wood, brickwork, and lead in their effort to reach a store of food. Their rate of breeding is high, the average litter being 8 with 5 or 6 litters in a year.

Measures against these destructive pests include both preventive and remedial methods. The former are aimed at preventing their access to places where damage can be done by rendering buildings rat-proof. Remedial measures included hunting by ferrets and dogs, shooting, gassing, trapping, and the employment of poison baits and Rat viruses. Particulars of the methods of destroying Rats are published in the Ministry of Agriculture's Bulletin No. 30, entitled *Rats and Their Extermination.*

G. F. W.

RAT'S-TAIL CACTUS. *See* **Cereus flagelliformis.** A

RATTAN CANE. *See* **Calamus.**

Rattan'ii, in honour of Volney Rattan, Californian botanist, 19th century.

RATTLE, RED. *See* **Pedicularis palustris.**

RATTLE, YELLOW, is *Rhinanthus minor.* A

RATTLESNAKE FERN. *See* **Botrychium virginianum.**

Rattray'i, in honour of Major Rattray who sent *Crinum Rattrayi* to England from his garden at Eutelobe, Uganda.

RAT'TUS. *See* **Rats.**

RAUPO, is **Typha angustifolia.** A

RAUTINI. *See* **Senecio Huntii.**

RAUWOLF'IA (in honour of Leonhard Rauwolf, physician at Augsburg, traveller in Palestine and other eastern countries, 1753–5). FAM. *Apocynaceae.* A genus of about 45 species of usually glabrous trees or shrubs, mostly natives of the tropics and S. Africa. Leaves opposite or in whorls of 3 or 4. Flowers and fruit rather small; calyx short, 5- fid or -parted, without glands; corolla salver-shaped, tube cylindrical, constricted at throat, lobes 5, twisted and overlapping to left; peduncles alternate with terminal leaves, few-flowered, the cymes usually umbel-like. Drupes 2, distinct or united into a 2-stoned fruit. They grow in a compost of loam, peat, and sand, and cuttings root readily in sand under glass. The following are all shrubs.

R. chinen'sis. Small evergreen shrub. *l.* dark green. *fl.* white in dense terminal trusses. *Berries* bright red. China. 1889. Greenhouse, needing plenty of water.

R. densiflo'ra. About 6 ft. h. *l.* lanceolate, slender-pointed, close, sometimes ternate. *fl.* white, limb about as long as tube; in a short, many-fld. cyme. June. *fr.* 1-seeded. E. Indies. 1824. (B.R. 1273 as *Tabernaemontana densiflora.*)

R. ternifo'lia. Branches rarely warted. About 3 ft. h. *l.* ternate, oblong, 1½ to 2 in. long, slender-pointed, acute at base, net-veined; stalks very short. W. Indies. 1823. (B.M. 2440.)

R. vomito'ria. Shrub to 18 ft. *l.* in whorls of 4, narrowly obovate, acutely slender-pointed, up to 6 in. long, 3 in. wide. *fl.* whitish, small, in many-fld. forked cymes. *Berry* large, round, smooth, scarlet, containing large seeds ½ in. long. Trop. Africa. The liquid in which roots have been boiled is said to cure jaundice, the bark of the roots mixed with Guinea Grain (*Aframomum Melegueta*) and the sap of the Banana stem applied to swellings is said to give relief.

RAVENA'LA (native name of plant in Madagascar). FAM. *Musaceae.* A genus of 2 erect tree-like plants, having the trunk formed of parts of the concave, woody leaf-stalks from which the blades, &c., have fallen, one a native of Guiana, the other of Madagascar. The very large leaves are arranged in 2 ranks and spread out fan-wise at the top of the trunk. Flowers large in axillary racemes, bracts large; stamens 5 or 6; ovary 3-celled. *R. madagascarensis* is known as the Travellers' Tree, owing to the water contained in the cup-shaped sheaths of the leaf-stalks. Its seeds are edible. Stove conditions are necessary. For cultivation *see* **Musa.**

R. guianen'sis. Tree dwarf or up to 25 to 30 ft. h. *l.* large, elliptic, about 3 ft. long with a l.-stalk equally long. *Spathes* 7, boat-shaped, deflexed, 1 to 1½ ft. *fl.* white; stamens 5. Brazil, Guiana. 1848.

R. madagascaren'sis. Tree with a tall trunk to 90 ft. h. *l.* Banana-like, about 10 ft. long, long-stalked. *Spathes* up to 12, about 7 in. long. *fl.* white; stamens 6. Madagascar. (F.d.S. 1355.)

RAVEN'EA. *See* **Ranevea.**

RAVEN'IA (named in honour of J. F. R. Ravin, *c.* 1656–1708, pupil of Tournefort, collected in interior of Brazil). FAM. *Rutaceae.* A genus of probably only 2 species of beautiful, almost glabrous, shrubs with terete branchlets, one native of Cuba, the other of Brazil. Leaves opposite with 1 to 3 leaflets, somewhat leathery, slightly dotted, entire. Flowers white or scarlet, few on long axillary peduncles; sepals unequal, overlapping, outer 2 larger, somewhat foliaceous; corolla tube straight, limb somewhat oblique, of 5 oblong lobes; stamens 5, adnate to throat of corolla. They need peat and sand and stove or warm greenhouse conditions, and can be propagated by cuttings of half-ripe shoots.

R. ro'sea. About 2 ft. h. *lflets.* 3, elliptic-obovate, shining. *fl.* rose-red, axillary, 2½ to 3 in. across. Summer. Brazil. 1880.

R. specta'bilis. About 2 ft. h. Branchlets downy. *lflets.* 3, longer than the downy stalk, obovate, obtuse. *fl.* deep reddish-scarlet; cor. fleshy, salver-shaped, segs. obtuse. July, August. Cuba. 1839. (B.R. 26, 59 as *Lemonia spectabilis.*)

F. G. P.

RAVENSA'RA (*raven*, leaf, *sara*, good; Malaguay words referring to the clove scent of the foliage.) FAM. *Lauraceae.* A genus of 3 or 4 species of strongly aromatic glabrous trees, all natives of Madagascar. Leaves sparse, leathery, pinnately veined. Flowers small; perianth tube turbinate or obovoid, segments 6, nearly equal; perfect stamens 9; panicles few-flowered, in upper axils. Fruit enclosed by the persistent calyx. Stove in a compost of light rich loam, easily increased by cuttings. Of economic interest only.

R. aromat'ica. Madagascar Nutmeg. Tree up to 30 ft. h. *l.* alternate, obovate, obtuse, leathery, entire, smooth. *fl.* white. Madagascar. 1823. SYN. *Agathophyllum aromaticum.*

F. G. P.

ra'vus -a -um, grey or tawny.

RAY FLOWERS. Flowers around the margin of a circular flower cluster, as in a daisy; they differ from those of the disk, being usually larger.

RAZOR-STROP FUNGUS. *See* **Bracket Fungi.**

REAUMU'RIA (in honour of René A. Ferchault de Reaumur, 1683–1757, a French entomologist). FAM. *Tamaricineae.* A genus of about 13 species of shrubs, natives of W. to Cent. Asia, often in dry desert regions. Leaves alternate, entire. Half-hardy. Should be grown in a compost of loam, peat, and sand; easily raised from cuttings of youngish wood.

R. hypericoi'des. Deciduous shrub, 1 to 2 ft., shoots slender, erect, glabrous, often springing from a thick woody base. *l.* linear to ovate and narrow-oblong, ⅛ to ⅜ in. long, $\frac{1}{16}$ to ⅛ in. wide, entire, glandular-dotted. *fl.* purple, 1 to 1½ in. across, solitary and terminal on short, lateral, leafy twigs; cal. deeply 5-lobed; pet. 5; stamens numerous, purple; anthers blue. May to August. Syria, Persia, Armenia, &c. 1800. (B.M. 2057; B.R. 845.)

W. J. B.

REBUT'IA (in honour of P. Rebut, a French cactus dealer). FAM. *Cactaceae.* Plants solitary or in clumps, round, without ribs but with low tubercles arranged in spirals. Flowers diurnal from old areoles at the side or base of the plant, funnel-shaped, red or orange. Fruit small, red, not spiny. These plants grow well and flower freely even when young. A number of new species have recently been discovered. They are easily raised from seed, which they produce freely, and which often germinates round the parent plant within a few days of the ripening and splitting of the fruit. **A**

R. aureiflo'ra. Spines variable, so that there are many varietal names. *fl.* golden or orange-yellow. Argentina. SYN. *Mediolobivia aureiflora.*

R. deminu'ta. Plants round or short-cylindrical; tubercles low; spines numerous, stiff. *fl.* red or orange. Argentina. SYN. *Echinocactus deminutus, Echinopsis deminuta.*

R. Fiebrig'ii. Stem globose, depressed, tuberculate; spines 30 to 40, bristle-like, white. *fl.* red, from the side of the plant. Bolivia. (B.R.C. 3, f. 59.)

R. minus'cula. Stems small, globular, depressed; spines numerous, very small. *fl.* scarlet, very freely produced round the base of the plant. Argentina. (B.M. 8583; B.R.C. 3, t. 4.) SYN. *Echinocactus minusculus, Echinopsis minuscula.* A cristate form is in cultivation.

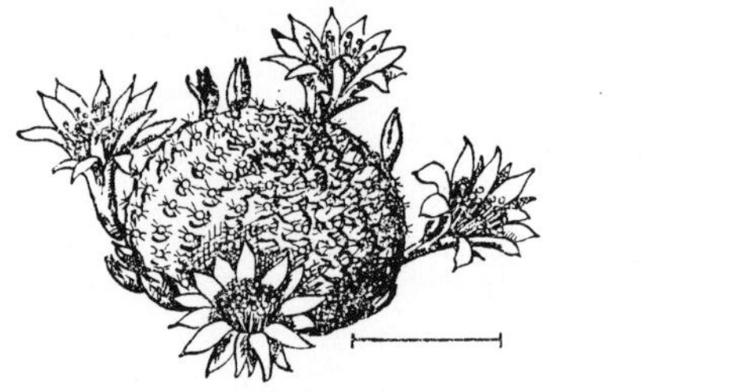

Rebutia minuscula

P. pseudodeminu'ta. Like *R. deminuta* but *fl.* golden-orange and spines longer. Argentina.

R. pseudominus'cula. Solitary or in clumps, round or short-cylindric, strongly tuberculate; spines bristle-like, short, yellow. *fl.* red, from the lower half of the plant. Argentina. Very similar to *R. minuscula* but pistil different. (B.R.C. 3, f. 58.)

R. pyg'mea. Stems ovoid, very small, with a much thickened root; tubercles very small, spines numerous, tiny. *fl.* rose-purple, from the base of the plant. Bolivia, Argentina. (B.R.C. 3, f. 60.)

R. sen'ilis. Stems round or short-cylindric; spines long, white, bristle-like. *fl.* red, from the sides of the plant. Argentina.

R. Spegezzinia'na. Forming clumps; spines short, yellowish-brown. *fl.* dark red, freely produced. Argentina.

R. Steinman'nii. Plants small, oblong, tubercles low, spines about 8, short and slender. *fl.* in varying shades of red. Bolivia. (B.R.C. 3, f. 60a.)

R. Stuemeria'na. Like *R. minuscula* but considerably larger. Argentina.

V. H.

rece'dens, departing from, in the sense that the species is different from its congeners.

RECEPTACLE. (1) The torus: that axile portion of the flower which bears sepals, petals, stamens and pistils. (2) The part of the axis bearing the flowers in the heads of the Compositae and similar inflorescences.

reclina'tus -a -um, reclining, falling or turning backwards so that the upper part rests on the ground or some other object.

rec'tus -a -um, straight.

recur'vus -a -um, curved backwards (cf. *reflexus, revolutus.*)

RED ADMIRAL BUTTERFLY. *See* **Butterflies.**

RED APPLE. *See* **Eugenia brachyandra.**

RED BERRY, AUSTRALIAN. *See* **Rhagodia.**

RED-BERRY DISEASE. *See* **Blackberry Mite.**

RED BUCKEYE. *See* **Aesculus Pavia.**

RED BUD. *See* **Cercis canadensis.**

RED BUD-BORER, *Thomasiniana oculiperda*, causes considerable damage to freshly budded fruit-trees, especially Apple, Pear, Peach, and Plum, and to Roses. The minute brick-red maggots work their way under the bark of the stock at the point of incision for the bud, and are found during late August. There appear to be 3 broods a year, but only the third generation injures grafts and buds. The eggs are laid in the graft-slits and near the cut bark of budded stocks, and the maggots feed on the sap between the 2 cambium layers. The fully fed maggots descend to the soil in late September and October and overwinter in the ground prior to pupation. This pest may be prevented by thoroughly coating the buds and tying material with Vaseline or Petroleum jelly, which repels the females and prevents egg-laying.

G. F. W.

RED CAMPION. *See* **Lychnis diurna.**

RED CEDAR. *See* **Juniperus virginiana.**

RED CEDAR, AUSTRALIAN. *See* **Cedrela Toona.**

RED CORE. *See* **Strawberry diseases.**

RED CURRANT. *See* **Currant.**

RED GUM. *See* **Eucalyptus ficifolia.**

RED HORSE-CHESTNUT. *See* **Aesculus × carnea.**

RED-HOT POKER. *See* **Kniphofia uvaria.**

RED-LEAF APHIS. *See* **Apple Aphides.**

RED-LEGGED WEEVIL, *Otiorrhynchus clavipes.* This widely distributed weevil feeds on a great variety of plants, including Apricot, Gooseberry, Nectarine, Peach, Plum, Raspberry, and Strawberry, and is often found attacking some of these plants in company with the Clay-Coloured Weevil (q.v.). The weevil, which is black with reddish legs and about ½ in. long, appears towards the end of April and in May, and feeds at night on blossoms and developing fruitlets, gnaws the rind of shoots, eats out holes in the leaves, and bores into the base of Raspberry canes thereby checking growth. The eggs are laid in the ground, and the creamy-white, legless grubs feed on the roots of various trees, shrubs and other plants, but far less damage is done by the grubs than by the adults. The grubs feed throughout the winter, and pupate in spring in earthen cocoons. This pest is a difficult one to eradicate completely from a heavily infested plantation, but persistence with the measures advocated will reduce the amount of injury to fruits. The trunks of standard and half-standard fruit-trees should be greasebanded to deter the wingless weevils from ascending the stems. Clean cultivation, including the clearing of ditches and headlands round Raspberry and Strawberry plantations will result in the abolition of natural sites for the weevils. Many weevils may be shaken from the branches of fruit-trees and bushes and from Raspberry canes after dark on to sticky boards placed beneath the infested plants—this operation should be done without the aid of a light otherwise the weevils drop to the ground before the boards are placed in position. A poison bait consisting of Apple pomace or Raisins (10 lb.), Sodium fluosilicate (1 lb.), and Bran (10 lb.) has proved successful against these weevils in the United States. D.D.T. emulsion applied to the shoots is also effective.

G. F. W.

RED LYCHNIS. *See* **Melandrium rubrum.**

RED MAHOGANY. *See* **Eucalyptus resinifera.**

RED MAPLE. *See* **Acer rubrum.**

RED MOROCCO. *See* **Adonis autumnalis.**

RED OSIER DOGWOOD. *See* **Cornus stolonifera.**

RED PEPPER. *See* **Capsicum annuum.**

RED PERU BARK. *See* **Cinchona succirubra.**

RED PUCCOON. *See* **Sanguinaria canadensis.**

RED ROOT. *See* **Lachnanthes tinctoria.**

RED SPIDER MITE, Greenhouse (*Tetranychus telarius*). This mite is a familiar and serious pest of glasshouse plants. It attacks Peach and Vine, Cucumber and Tomato, Arums, Carnations, Hydrangeas, Salvias and, in frames, Violets; and occurs on Hops, Strawberries, and many weeds. All stages are to be found on the underside of leaves, where the mites pierce the tissues and abstract the sap, causing mottling, yellowing, and bleached areas. The immature mites are found in a thick web over the leaves, fruits (e.g. Grapes) and flowers (e.g. Carnations and Hydrangeas) interfering with the normal functions of the foliage and rendering fruits and flowers unsaleable. The majority of the mites overwinter as bright-red adults in crevices in walls and woodwork, in Bamboo-canes and wooden supports, in straw and dried plant-stems, and even between overlapping glass-panes. They become active in spring and wander on to various plants when the minute, spherical, golden or pinkish eggs are laid among the fine webbing produced by the females. The newly hatched mites are pale, globular, and 6-legged, becoming 8-legged after the first moult. The adult females are straw-coloured, broadly-oval, and about $\frac{1}{15}$ in. long, while the males are about one-half the size of the females and elongate in shape. Breeding is continuous throughout the spring and summer, and overlapping of the broods occurs.

The complete eradication of Red Spider in heavily infested houses, especially in mixed collections, is possible with Azobenzene in the form of a vapour. Cultural methods will aid in reducing their numbers considerably. All weeds in and around glasshouses should be relentlessly destroyed, especially in autumn when they provide winter shelter for the mites. Brickwork in houses should be pointed or regularly whitewashed, split Bamboo-canes should be burned, while serviceable canes and support-stakes should be steeped in a strong concentration of Lime Sulphur, and all plant debris removed from the house to reduce available shelter. Cucumber houses should be fumigated with Azobenzene as soon as the crop is harvested, and empty plant-houses should be thoroughly cleaned by spraying wood- and metal-work, glass and walls with Cresylic acid emulsion. Cucumbers and plants (e.g. Carnations) may be fumigated with Grade 16 Naphthalene during the growing season (*see* Fumigants). Spraying the underside of the leaves of infested plants with White or Refined Petroleum emulsions is desirable provided that such washes are not applied to glaucous-foliaged (Carnation) and tender-leaved plants, nor too frequently to such plants as Tomato, otherwise Dropsy or Oedema may develop. Success has followed the application of Lime Sulphur at 1 per cent. concentration to the leaves of many ornamental tender shrubs, while the routine spraying of plants with Derris and Pyrethrum washes will reduce infestation. The daily forceful syringing of Peach and Nectarine trees with clear water will render conditions distasteful to the mites. Plants grown in dry, over-crowded glasshouses with high temperatures are especially liable to infestation. **A**

G. F. W.

RED SANDALWOOD TREE. *See* **Adenanthera pavonina.**

RED VALERIAN. *See* **Kentranthus ruber.**

RED-WATER TREE. *See* **Erythrophloeum.**

RED WEED. *See* **Papaver Rhoeas.**

RED WOOD. *See* **Sequoia sempervirens.**

REDHEAD. *See* **Asclepias curassavica.**

redivi'vus -a -um, renewed.

reduplicate, folding and projecting outwards.

REED, REED GRASS. *See* **Arundo.**

REED INDIAN. *See* **Canna indica.**

REED MACE. *See* **Typha latifolia.**

REED, PAPER. *See* **Cyperus Papyrus.**

REEL AND LINE. Garden lines are indispensable when drawing drills, planting, cutting grass edges, and so on. They should be of stout cord which will bear stretching tightly without breaking, and should be wound on an iron reel as this permits them to dry after use. If rolled on a stick they are less convenient to use and are apt to rot quickly if rolled up, as they frequently are, when wet. Suitable cords are usually sold in lengths of 60 ft. or 120 ft. The iron reel is made to revolve on an iron pin by means of a small handle on the upper bar of the reel, and a similar projection on the lower bar serves to prevent the reel turning when the line is tightly stretched. The end peg and the pin of the reel are useful in measuring distances between rows when sowing seeds, being made as a rule 12 in. and 18 in. long respectively. The pin has an eye at the end by which it may be suspended as a further help towards drying.

REEVES'IA (in honour of John Reeves, F.L.S., of Canton, botanist). FAM. *Sterculiaceae.* A genus of 5 species of deciduous trees or shrubs, 1 from China, 1 from Formosa, 2 from the Himalaya and 1 from Siam. Leaves alternate, entire. Flowers 2-sexual, white, numerously massed in terminal panicles or corymbs: calyx 3- to 5-lobed: petals 5: anthers sessile, closely packed in a globose head at summit of staminal column. They require warm greenhouse conditions.

Reevesia thyrsoidea

R. thyrsoi'dea. Tree 15 to 25 ft., shoots glabrous. *l.* lanceolate to ovate-lanceolate, 2 to 5 in. long, ½ to 2 in. wide, pointed, base rounded to tapered. *fl.* in terminal clusters 2 to 3 in. across; cor. white or cream-coloured; pet. 5; anthers at top of staminal column standing ¼ to ½ in. clear above pet. July. China. 1826. (B.M. 4199.)

R. Wallich'ii. Tree 40 to 50 ft. *l.* broadly ovate, 2½ to 4 in. long, 1 to 2 in. wide, base rounded or subcordate, apex pointed. *fl.* scented, in terminal panicles or corymbs 3 to 3½ in. wide; cor. white, 1½ in. wide; staminal column protruded ¾ in. above pet., capsule 1 to 2 in. long. E. Himalaya, 4,000 to 6,000 alt.

W. J. B.

reflex'us -a -um, reflexed, abruptly bent back or down.

refrac'tus -a -um, sharply bent backwards from the base.

rega'lis -is -e, royal, of outstanding merit.

REGEL'IA (in honour of Dr. E. Regel, Superintendent of the Imperial Botanic Gardens at St. Petersburg, now Leningrad). FAM. *Myrtaceae.* Three species of evergreen shrubs natives of W. Australia. Leaves opposite, entire. Flowers in dense heads: calyx 5-lobed; petals 5; stamens numerous, arranged in 5 bundles. Cultivation as for Beaufortia.

R. cilia'ta. Spreading shrub, 3 to 5 ft., shoots hairy. *l.* roundish ovate to obovate, closely superposed in 4 rows, overlapping, ⅛ to ⅓ in. long, stiff, grey-hairy. *fl.* closely packed in globose terminal heads ¾ in. wide, pale reddish-purple; stamens in clusters of about 12. September. *fr.* woody, in a globose head. SW. Australia, 1874. (B.M. 6100.) Cool greenhouse shrub.

W. J. B.

REGEL'IA of Lemaire. *See* **Aregelia.**

region, area of distribution.

Regi'nae, in honour (in Tradescantia) of the Queen of the Belgians.

reg'ius -a -um, royal.

A→

regular, uniform and symmetrical: a regular flower can be divided into similar halves along any line passing through its centre. Cf. irregular, actinomorphic, zygomorphic.

Rehderi, in honour of Jacob Heinrich Rehder, 1790–1852, Park Inspector, Moscow, as *Robinia Rehderi*; or of Prof. Alfred Rehder, 1863–1949, Curator of the Herbarium, Arnold Arboretum, U.S.A., from 1918 to 1940.

REHDERODEND'RON (in honour of Prof. Alfred Rehder, 1863–1949, Curator of the Herbarium, Arnold Arboretum, U.S.A., 1918–40). FAM. *Styracaceae.* A genus of 8 species of deciduous trees from S. and W. China, closely allied to Styrax. The first species was discovered only in 1931. Only one species, *R. macrocarpum*, is in cultivation. Branchlets glabrous, leaves petioled, serrulate, exstipulate. Flowers small, white in axillary leafless panicles or racemes, calyx 5-lobed, petals 5, connate only at base. Fruit large, woody, oblong or ellipsoid, seeds 1 to 3.

R. macrocar'pum. Tree up to 30 ft. h., petioles reddish, *l.* elliptic to oblong-ovate, finely serrate, apex acute, 3 to 4 in. long. Racemes 6- to 10-fld., flowering before the l., cal. lobes triangular, pet. elliptic-oblong ½ in. long, pubescent on both sides, white. Anthers yellow and conspicuous. *fr.* oblong, 3 in. long, 8- to 10-ribbed. Mt. Omei, W. China. (J.R.H.S. 63, p. 386 and fig. 101.) Introduced by Prof. Hu about 1934. Has flowered in Cornish gardens and in Northamptonshire.

P. M. S.

REHMAN'NIA (in honour of Joseph Rehmann, 1799–1831, physician in Leningrad). FAM. *Scrophulariaceae.* A genus of about 5 species of perennial herbs with showy flowers. Stems leafy, clammy-hairy. Leaves alternate, obovate or oblong, deeply toothed. Flowers rather large, in terminal, leafy racemes; calyx ovoid-bell-shaped, 5-cleft at top; corolla hairy, tube rather broadly-ventricose, limb obliquely 2-lipped, its lobes spreading, throat deeply coloured; stamens 4. Fruit a many-seeded capsule. All the species are natives of China or Japan and do best in the cool greenhouse potted in ordinary well-drained loam. Propagation is by seeds or cuttings. Several hybrids have been raised. *See* e.g. **R. × Briscoei, R. × Kewensis.**

R. angula'ta. 1 to 3 ft. h. *l.* about 6 in. long, pinnately lobed, lobes toothed, or l. without distinct lobes, many toothed; bracts l.-like, broadest at wedge-shaped base. *fl.* smaller than in *R. elata*, red with band of scarlet on margin of upper lip and orange dots on lower lip. China. var. **Pink Perfection,** *fl.* bright pink; **tric'olor,** *fl.* at first bright purple, later more rose, upper lip shaded vermilion, throat whitish, spotted purple. China. *R. angulata* is frequently confused with *R. elata.*

R. × Briscoe'ei (*R. elata* × *R. Henryi*). Intermediate in habit between parents. *fl.* soft pink, *l.* with dark veining as in *R. Henryi* but less velvety than in that species. Of garden origin.

R. chinen'sis. A synonym of *R. glutinosa.*

R. ela'ta. A much larger plant than *R. angulata. l.* 2- to 6-lobed on each side, lobes entire; bracts long wedge-shaped at base. *fl.* rather larger than in *R. angulata*, 3 to 4 in. long, lips bright rose-purple, throat yellow, dotted red. China. (B.M. 8177 as *R. angulata.*) Best treated as a biennial.

R. glutino'sa. 1 to 2 ft. h., stem often purplish, downy. *l.* obovate, 1 to 3 in. long, narrowed to a short stalk, coarsely toothed. *fl.* large, about 1 in. long, yellowish-buff or purplish, throat purple with deeper veins; cal. tube oval, often purplish. April. China. (B.M. 3653; B.R. 1960; F.d.S. 1134 as *R. chinensis.*)

Rehmannia elata (p. 1748)

R. Hen'ryi. 6 to 18 in. h., hairy. *l.* elliptic-oblong, narrowed to stalk, lowest 3 to 7 in. long, more or less pinnately lobed, toothed. *fl.* ascending, 1¾ to 2 in. long, downy, tube dirty-yellow, spotted red, limb white, throat yellow, dotted red. China. (B.M. 8302.)

R. × kewen'sis (*R. glutinosa* × *R. Henryi*). Stems about 2 ft. h. *l.* glossy, ovate. *fl.* 2 in. long, cor. segs. broad, creamy-yellow, upper segs. with dark crimson blotch. Of garden origin.

R. Oldham'ii. A synonym of *Titanotrichum Oldhamii.*

R. rupes'tris. 1 to 1½ ft. h. *l.* Central one erect, lateral drooping. *l.* ovate, fleshy, silky-haired, toothed. *fl.* white tinged rose, tubular. July. W. China. 1890. (B.M. 7191.)

Reich'ei, in honour of Dr. Karl Reiche, 1860–1929, who collected in Chile and Mexico.

Reichenbach'ii, in honour of Heinrich Gottlieb Ludwig Reichenbach, Germany.

REID'IA. Included in **Phyllanthus.** *R. glaucescens* is a synonym of *P. pulcher.*

REINECK'IA (in honour of J. Reinecke, German gardener, successful cultivator of tropical plants). FAM. *Liliaceae.* A genus of a single species of perennial herb, with a creeping rhizome, native of China and Japan, with the characters given below. It is hardy, not particular as to soil, and easily propagated by division.

R. carn'ea. *rhiz.* thick. *l.* 6 to 12, almost erect, 12 to 18 in. long, channelled. *fl.* flesh-pink, fragrant, in a loose spike; perianth tube cylindrical, lobes spreading, recurved; scape leafless. April. *fr.* a globular red berry, ¼ in. across with 1 or a few seeds in each cell. China, Japan. (B.M. 739 as *Sanseviera sessiliflora*; A.B.R. 361 as *S. carnea.*) var. **variega'ta,** *l.* striped. (I.H. 323.)

REINHARDTIA (in honour of Herr Reinhardt). FAM. *Palmaceae.* A genus of about 5 species of dwarf Palms, natives of Cent. America. Leaves on long stalks, irregularly pinnate in a crown on slender stems. Flowers 1-sexual on simply branched spikes from the axils of the lower leaves. For these stove palms abundance of water and perfect drainage are essential; they grow best in a compost of peat and sand with a little sandy loam and are excellent and elegant plants for a Wardian Case.

R. gra'cilis. Stems slender, 2 to 4 ft. h. *l.* dark green on very slender stalks, segs. toothed, and split in middle. Guatemala. 1862. (B.M. 5291.) SYN. *Geonoma fenestrata, Malortiea gracilis.*

R. sim'plex. Much like *R. gracilis* but without the window-like holes in l. *l.* dark green, oblong, simple or 2-fid. Costa Rica. (B.M. 5247 as *Malortiea simplex.*)

REINWARDTIA (in honour of K. G. K. Reinwardt, 1773–1822, director of the Botanic Garden, Leiden). FAM. *Linaceae.* A genus of 1 species of shrub or subshrub, native of the mountains of N. India. Leaves alternate, membranous, often serrated, penninerved. Flowers yellow, rather large, in very short, clustered racemes, solitary in the leaf-axils or in dense corymbs at tips of branches; sepals 5, petals 5, twisted, fugacious; stamens connate at base, hypogynous. *R. trigynum* is a winter-flowering warm greenhouse plant well worth growing. Cuttings should be taken from the strongest points of old plants in April or May and inserted in sandy soil in a close frame. When rooted they should be grown on singly in 5- or 6-in. pots in an intermediate temperature until established. They need to be pinched frequently to induce a compact habit. The best position for them in autumn is a frame where plenty of air and sunlight can be admitted as it is necessary for the recently formed shoots to be thoroughly ripened for winter-flowering. A temperature of 55° F. will be necessary to open the flowers properly and keep them from damping off. Old plants may be cut back and grown on a second year with similar treatment, but they are generally weaker and less satisfactory than those raised annually from good cuttings. Red Spider Mite (q.v.) is a troublesome pest, and the frequent syringing through the summer which is desirable in order to keep this pest in check is also beneficial to the plants.

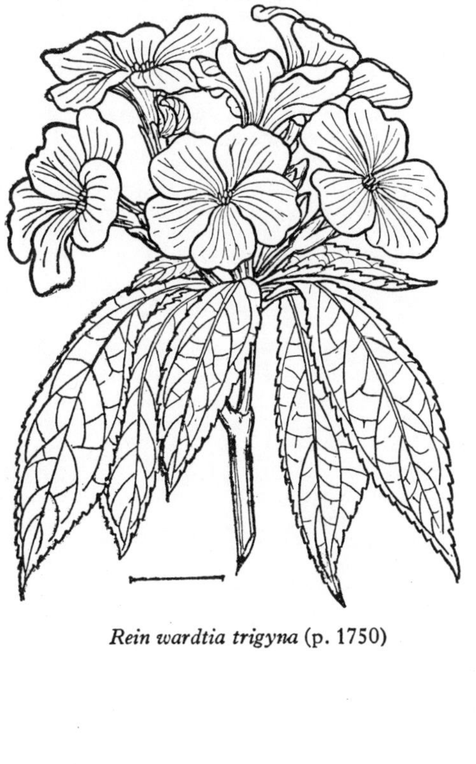

Rein wardtia trigyna (p. 1750)

R. trigy'na. Shrub of 2 to 3 ft. *l.* ovate-oblong, entire, with a distinct, awn-like mucro; stipules minute. *fl.* yellow, solitary or a few clustered in an umbel-like infl.; pet. obovate, emarginate, claws connate into a tube. October onwards. N. India. 1799. (B.M. 1100 as *Linum trigynum.*)

religio'sus -a -um, holy or sacred; connected with religious rites.

REMIJ'IA (in honour of Dr. Remijo, who made known in Brazil the febrifugal property of the bark of the plants). FAM. *Rubiaceae.* A genus of about 13 species of trees or small shrubs allied to Cinchona, natives of Trop. America. Leaves opposite or in threes, sometimes large and very leathery; stipulars often large. Flowers white or pink, scented, downy, hairy, in long-stalked interrupted axillary racemes; stamens 5, inserted below the middle of the tube. *R. pedunculata* needs a warm, moist atmosphere and fresh, spongy heath soil broken coarsely, kept moist by frequent watering. Not easy to grow and perhaps better in a cooler house. Propagated as for Cinchona.

R. peduncula'ta. Shrub. *l.* opposite, ovate, about 6 in. long, acute, nerves evident, shortly stalked. *fl.* pink, peduncles as long as l. Colombian Andes. 1887. (Gn. 1889, 343; R.H. 1887, 84.)

remo'tus -a -um, scattered, not close together.

REMUSA'TIA (in honour of Abel Remusat, 1785–1832, celebrated orientalist and physician). FAM. *Araceae.* A genus of 2 species of tropical herbs with tuberous roots, differing from Gonatanthus by its parietal ovules and from Steudnera by the absence of staminodes. Leaves on long slender stalks, peltate, ovate-cordate or lanceolate. For treatment *see* **Caladium.**

R. vivip'ara. Tuber large, flattish-round. Shoots erect or ascending, reddish purple; scales of bulbs each ending in a hooked bristle. *l.* wide cordate-ovate, 12 to 16 in. long, 8 to 10 in. long, thinly leathery, dark green above, the main veins pale; stalk 16 to 20 in. long. *Peduncle* 4 to 6 in. long. *Spathe* yellow, trapezoid, 3 to 3½ in. long. Himalaya, E. Indies. (L.B.C. 281 as *Caladium viviparum.*)

RENANTAND'A. FAM. *Orchidaceae.* Hybrids combining species of the genera Renanthera and Vanda.

RENANTH'ERA (*renes*, a kidney, *anthera*, an anther; in reference to the shape of the anthers or pollinia). FAM. *Orchidaceae.* A genus of 10 or more species of epiphytic orchids, natives of Trop. Asia and Malaya. Flowers showy, numerous; sepals spreading, free, petaloid, the lateral ones broader and often longer than the narrow, more or less erect dorsal, which the petals resemble but are usually narrower, spreading; lip short, sessile at the base of the column, articulated, saccate or shortly spurred; column short and thick; anthers terminal, convex; pollinia 2, ovoid or oblong; peduncles lateral, elongated, branched; panicles loose, ample. Leaves distichous, spreading, strap-shaped, somewhat leathery, fleshy or rigid, often obliquely 2-lobed at apex, their bases clasping the stems. Stem leafy, branched in some species. The genus is allied to Aerides, Arachnis, Vanda, &c., but is distinguished by the prevailing reduction in width of the upper sepal and petals and the enlargement of the lateral sepals, which have narrowed bases, their inner margins more or less parallel and straighter than the outer but, like them, somewhat waved. Several species sometimes included under Renanthera should be sought under Arachnis. General treatment, compost, &c., should be as advised for Vandas and Aerides but the harder texture of the leaf denotes the need for, and greater resistance, to light. Shading is required but it should be thin and removed early in the autumn. *R. coccinea*, a free-growing but shy-flowering species, has been successfully flowered by attaching the plant to a long birch log, with a little compost and suspending it lengthwise in a greenhouse, the winter temperature of which fell to 50° F. The plant was fully exposed to sunlight, so much so that the leaves were dwarfed and browned. *R. Imschootiana* is better suited in the intermediate than in the warm house throughout the year. In summer the syringe may be freely used and the plants watered liberally. In winter water must not be withheld entirely but only given often enough to prevent the foliage approaching the shrivelling point and the compost becoming really dry. Propagation can be effected as in Vandas and Aerides. When the stems become too long or bare and leafless at the base the leafy portion, provided it has stem roots, may be severed and potted in late spring. Young growths may develop from the stump. *R. coccinea* lends itself to treatment more readily and long stems may be cut into lengths of 2 or 3 ft., with roots, and laid in a propagating case or on a damp stage in a warm house. The plants occasionally branch, particularly if the main growing point has been damaged.

R. annamen'sis. Allied to *R. Imschootiana*, but rather smaller. *fl.* in panicles, orange-yellow, spotted crimson; lobes of lip and tips of pet. deep crimson; lower sep. 1¼ in. long. *l.* about 3 in. long, ¾ in. wide, set rather closely. Annam. About 1904. (B.M. 8116.)

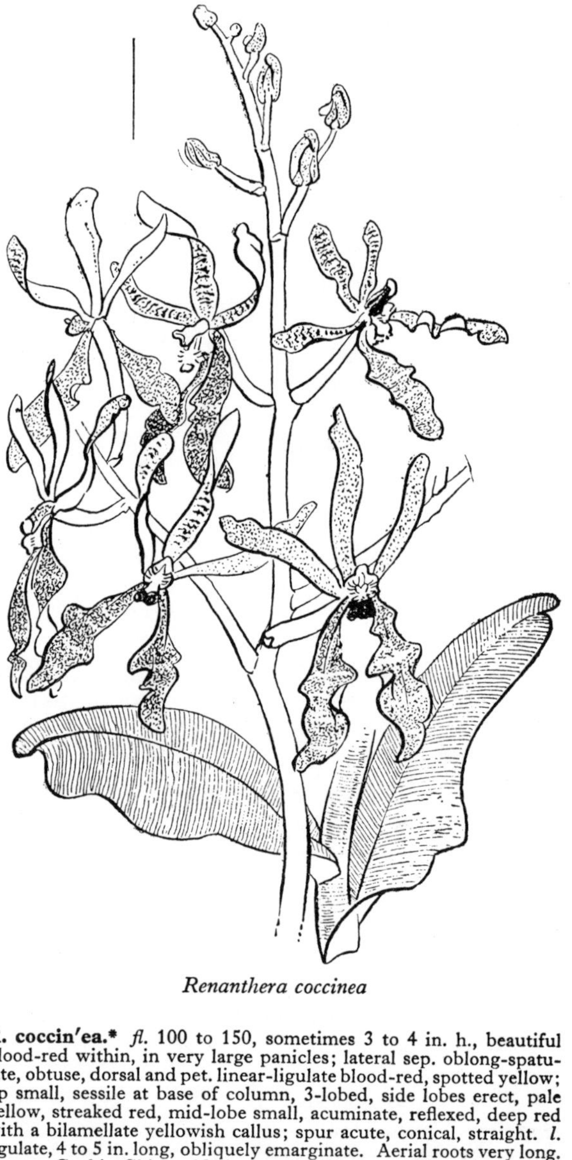

Renanthera coccinea

R. coccin'ea.* *fl.* 100 to 150, sometimes 3 to 4 in. h., beautiful blood-red within, in very large panicles; lateral sep. oblong-spatulate, obtuse, dorsal and pet. linear-ligulate blood-red, spotted yellow; lip small, sessile at base of column, 3-lobed, side lobes erect, pale yellow, streaked red, mid-lobe small, acuminate, reflexed, deep red with a bilamellate yellowish callus; spur acute, conical, straight. *l.* ligulate, 4 to 5 in. long, obliquely emarginate. Aerial roots very long. Burma, Cochin China. 1816. A splendid plant, will attain a length of 30 ft. or more under cultivation. (B.M. 2997; B.R. 1131; W.S.O. 2, 37.) var. **al'ba,** *fl.* white.

R. elonga'ta. *fl.* many, rather small, purplish or yellow and red-marked; lateral sep. unguiculate; lateral lobes of lip sometimes sinuate, mid-lobe triangular and very short, with 2 calli at base;

spur obtuse, conical; panicle elongated, nodding. *l.* broadly linear, oblique, emarginate, 4 in. long. Java, Sumatra, Kuripan. (B.R. 29, 41 as *R. matutina.*)

R. histrion'ica. *fl.* sep. and pet. yellow, bordered with purplish blotches; lip white, with purplish blotches on the side lobes; spur orange; racemes short, few-fld. *l.* acuminate. Malaya (?). 1878.

R. Imschootia'na.* *fl.* 20 to 50 or more, about 2 in. h.; upper sep. and pet. yellow marked with vermilion, lower sep. vermilion-red; lip with a short spur and small side lobes. Slight variation occurs in the colour which may be wholly vermilion. Assam. 1892. (B.M. 7711.) A fine species, flowering in late spring.

R. matuti'na.* *fl.* about 2 in. h., bright orange-yellow, becoming yellowish with age, almost covered with scarlet-crimson, slightly raised, softly tomentose spots; dorsal sep. with slightly wavy margins, lateral sep. clawed then widening abruptly, inner edges often parallel and appearing to interlock, diverging with age; lip very small, crimson-scarlet, side lobes almost clasping the column, mid-lobe like a hooked tongue. *l.* much as in *R. Imschootiana*, but more leathery and longer. Java. 1846. (Pesc. t. 12.) SYN. *Aerides matutinum.*

R. pulchel'la. Allied to *R. Imschootiana*. *fl.* half as large, buff-yellow, side lobes and upper half of lip and pet. tips crimson. *l.* about 3 in. long. Stem (under cultivation) 7 in. or more long. Assam. 1913.

R. Storiei.* *fl.* even finer than in *R. coccinea*, lower sep. dark crimson with lighter shading and spots. Summer, autumn. Philippines. 1880. (B.M. 7537; W.O.A. 513.) Will flower when 3 ft. h.

E. C.

RENANTHOP'SIS. FAM. *Orchidaceae*. Hybrids combining species of the genera Phalaenopsis and Renanthera.

RENEA'LMIA (in honour of the French Botanist Paul Reneaulme, 1560–1624, who in 1611 published *Specimen Historia Plantarum*). FAM. *Zingiberaceae*. A genus of nearly 60 Trop. American species of perennial herbs related to Alpinia, but like Burbidgea and Pommereschea, having an erect lip with a long claw and differing from these two by the short flat filament, flat anther, and absence of appendages to the connective. Leaves 2-ranked on a leafy stem. Inflorescence paniculate or racemose sometimes terminating the leafy stem, sometimes on a distinct stem from the somewhat fleshy rhizome. The plants are aromatic. Cultivation as for Alpinia.

R. exalta'ta. Robust perennial up to 12 ft. h. but usually much less. *l.* sessile or nearly so, long, lanceolate or oblanceolate, 1 to 3 ft. long, glabrous. *fl.* many in a panicle 8 to 12 in. long, peduncle, pedicels, &c. somewhat hairy, red; cor. rose, tube about ¾ in. long, lobes ⅓ in. W. Indies, Guiana. 1820. (B.M. 2494 and B.R. 777 as *Alpinia tubulata.*)

renifor'mis -is -e, reniform, kidney-shaped.

repan'dus -a -um, slightly uneven at margin.

re'pens, prostrate, creeping, flat upon ground.

replica'tus -a -um, doubled down.

REPLUM. Partition between the two carpels in Cruciferae left when the valves fall away on dehiscence of the fruit.

rep'tans, creeping on ground, crawling.

Requien'ii, in honour of Esprit Requien, 1788–1851, student of the Flora of S. France and Corsica.

RESE'DA (ancient Latin name used by Pliny, from *resedo*, to calm, because the application of the plant to external bruises was considered useful by the Latins). FAM. *Resedaceae*. A genus of over 50 species of annual or biennial, erect or decumbent, glabrous or hairy herbs, natives of S. Europe and N. Africa and extending to Persia. Leaves entire, lobed or pinnatisect; stipules glandular. Flowers in bracteate racemes; calyx 4- to 7-parted; petals 4 to 7, hypogynous, 2- to many-fid; receptacle sub-sessile. Capsule indehiscent, 3-lobed at apex. *R. lutea* and *R. Luteola* are natives; the latter at one time used in dyeing, *R. Luteola* has been known as Dyer's Rocket, Woad or Weld or Dyer's Yellow weed. *R. odorata*, Mignonette, is greatly valued for its sweet scent and *R. alba* is sometimes grown for ornament and as a pot plant, otherwise the genus is of no horticultural interest.

R. al'ba. Hardy biennial. About 2 ft. h. *l.* pinnatifid or interruptedly pinnate, segs. lanceolate, smooth, rarely wavy. *fl.* with white pet. and brownish anthers, in dense spikes; cal. 5- or 6-parted. May to September. S. Europe. 1596. (S.F.G. 459.)

R. frutes'cens. A shrubby form of *R. odorata.*

R. odora'ta. Mignonette. Diffuse annual or perennial. Sometimes shrubby (var. **frutes'cens**). *l.* lanceolate, bluntish, entire or 3-fid. *fl.* with yellowish-white pet. and saffron anthers, in loose racemes; cal. 6-parted, as long as pet.; pet. cleft into many club-shaped divisions. June to October. N. Africa, Egypt. 1752. (B.M. 29; B.R. 227.)

RESEDA'CEAE. Dicotyledons. A family of 6 genera with about 45 species of herbs, mostly Mediterranean, but also represented in other parts of Europe, Africa, Asia, and California. Leaves alternate, sometimes lobed, stipulate. Flowers in racemes, zygomorphic, perfect, the axis develops a large disk at the back of the flower and the petals, &c., are there better developed; sepals 4 to 8; petals absent or up to 8; stamens 3 to 40; ovary superior of 2 to 6 carpels, open at top, with one to many ovules in each, carpels sometimes free. Fruit a capsule. The only genera of importance in the gardens are Astrocarpus and Reseda.

RESERVE GARDEN. It is desirable in most gardens to set aside part in which to grow on trees and hardy plants for future use, such as filling up gaps, growing to such a size that they may take their place with others, planting for succession in herbaceous borders, preparing for forcing to be lifted and potted in due season, and so on. Such a space properly looked after is a very valuable section of a garden.

RESIN. A compound having the formula $C_{44}H_{62}O_4$ held in solution in terebene, the mixture being the well-known turpentine found in many conifers. It is a waste-product which helps to protect wounds in the trees in which it occurs. **A**

RESIN PLANT. A name applied to a variety of plants, including *Agathis australis*, *Bursera acuminata*, *B. Simaruba*, *Guaiacum officinale*, *Pistacia Lentiscus*, &c.

RESIN, ANIME. *See* **Hymenaea Courbarii.**

RESIN, SANDERACH. *See* **Callitris.**

RESINOSIS. The abnormal production of resin or pitch from pines, firs, spruces, &c. A limited exudation is often seen, but when this becomes abnormal it may indicate the presence of conditions such as might be caused by parasitic bracket fungi or some of the rust fungi.

D. E. G.

resino'sus -a -um, resin-producing.

RESISTANCE. Among plants even of the same variety there are often individuals which are outstanding in their ability to resist certain diseases, and from these varieties or strains showing resistance to specific diseases may be bred and are much valued among plant growers. There are wide degrees of resistance and the factors determining the methods by which plants achieve the condition are somewhat complex. Resistance may be inherited as a simple genetic factor and then wherever grown the plants resist the disease, but the resistance may also depend on some morphological advantage such as a thick cuticle, &c., in which case environmental conditions retarding the development of the cuticle can weaken the resistance. When resistance is inherited it often happens that disease organisms succeed in entering epidermal cells but are then killed by some substance possessed by the cell sap which is toxic to the parasite. At the same time it must be remembered that a plant resistant to one disease may be susceptible to

another. In commercial practice, although a variety may be resistant to a disease, it must also possess other desirable characters such as good habit, flowers, or fruits, and much research is devoted to breeding plants which show these advantages combined with resistance to diseases.
D. E. G.

A→

resplen'dens, very splendid.

RESTING. Plants are said to be resting during any period when growth in them appears to be inactive. The term applies only to such plants as live over 1 year; nearly all these plants require a resting stage after a period of active growth, corresponding as a rule with the colder season of the year or with annual periods of drought.

RESTING SPORES are spores formed by fungi to survive the winter. In the Phycomycetes they are formed by certain genera as the result of fusion of 2 sexual cells which may be similar and produce a zygospore or may be differentiated into male anteridium and female oogonium when the result is an oospore. In the rust fungi (*see* **Rusts**) the resting spore stage is the teleutospore. In many other fungal genera very thick-walled resting cells may be formed out of the cells in the vegetative mycelium without any sexual fusion, and these are called chlamydospores. Some resting spores (e.g. teleutospores of rusts) are formed regularly in the autumn, but many form when growing conditions become adverse to the fungus, no matter what time of the year this may happen.
D. E. G.

RESTIONAC'EAE. Monocotyledons. A family of 19 genera with about 250 species, natives of temperate and sub-tropical regions of the S. Hemisphere, only a few in the tropics. Mostly perennial herbs, leaves somewhat like rushes, with a creeping rootstock and 2-ranked sheathing leaves. Flowers dioecious (occasionally monoecious or perfect), regular, in spikelets; perianth in 2 whorls, one often absent; stamens 3 or 2; ovary superior, 1- to 3-celled with 1 ovule in each cell. Fruit a capsule or nut.

RESTREP'IA (in honour of Joseph E. Restrep, a naturalist who travelled in S. America). FAM. *Orchidaceae.* A genus of epiphytic orchids, with tufted stems, or simple, creeping branches. About 40 species have been described, natives of Trop. America, from Brazil as far as Mexico. The genus is very closely related to Pleurothallis, but is distinguished by having 4 pollen masses; the habit is very similar. Two divisions may be made. The species generally seen in cultivation are tufted, the peduncles 1-flowered, the upper sepal narrowly lanceolate, then filiform, the petals similar but smaller, the 3 segments often slightly clubbed or knobbed at apex, the lower sepals enlarged, connate the greater part of their length, sometimes with only the tips separate, the ovate or oblong lip resting on the lateral sepals. The plants often flower several times from the same axis. The second division has a creeping rhizome, the sepals and petals are more equal, and 1 or more species have several flowers on a common peduncle. In all the stems are 1-leaved and sheathed with 1 to 3 membranous bracts. The atmosphere and general treatment of the Odontoglossum house suit them and similar compost to that given Odontoglossums may be used. *R. antennifera* and *R. maculata* have the largest and showiest flowers but all are free-flowering. Propagation is by division.

R. antennif'era.* Differs from *R. maculata*, with which it has been confused, by being slightly smaller in all parts and by the connate lower sep. each marked with 7 reddish-purple stripes on a yellowish-white ground. Colombia, Venezuela. 1815. (B.M. 7930.)

R. Daya'na. *fl.* of medium size, dorsal sep. and pet. violet-brown, filiform, clavate; connate, lateral sep., broad, 2-fid, yellowish and brown; lip yellow, mottled purple, strap-shaped. *l.* roundish acute, nearly cordate at base. Costa Rica. 1875. Habit tufted.

R. ecuadoren'sis. Near *R. antennifera. fl.* of similar size with shorter lateral sep. which are densely spotted maroon on a whitish-ground; lip similarly spotted on a yellowish-ground; upper sep. white lined maroon at base, tipped yellow; pet. similar, smaller, tipped purple. Ecuador. 1892?

R. el'egans. *fl.* smaller than in *R. maculata*, lateral sep. connate, oblong, concave, yellow, dotted purple, dorsal sep. and pet. white with purple streaks at base, pet. smaller; lip linear, clawed, retuse, hollowed and dilated at base, with a tooth each side. *l.* oval, about 3 in. long, sheaths straight. Stem, ½ to 2 in. h. Caracas. 1872. (B.M. 5966; F.d.S. 743.)

R. guttula'ta. Similar to *R. maculata* but larger in all parts, *fl.* darker and without tendrils at base of lip. Ecuador. 1836.

R. Lansberg'ii. Dorsal sep. and pet. crimson; lateral sep. white with crimson dots; lip yellow with purple blotches, linear, truncate, hollowed and broader at base. *l.* oval, as long as stem, sheaths, straight, closely overlapping. Venezuela, Guatemala. 1861. (R.X.O. 1, 60.) *R. Lansbergii* of Hooker is *R. xanthophthalma.*

Restrepia maculata

R. macula'ta.* *fl.* lower sep. 1½ to 2 in. long, forming an oblong body 2-fid at apex, with edges near base slightly raised, yellow with brown-purple spots more or less in rows, upper sep. pale yellow, dotted with red, shorter than the lower, lanceolate at base then filiform with knobbed ends; pet. similar but smaller, lip oblong, ½ to ¾ in. long, coloured like the lateral sep. Stems 2 to 4 in. h. *l.* ovate, 2½ to 3½ in. long. Variable. Colombia. (B.M. 6288 as *R. antennifera.*) So far the largest fld. in the genus.

R. pandura'ta. *fl.* several in succession; lateral sep. connate, whitish with lines of crimson spots; dorsal sep. short-tailed, whitish with purple veins and tip; pet. smaller with 3 purple lines at base; lip fiddle-shaped, front very broad, oblong, warted, hairy, whitish with many purplish spots; column with 2 orange spots at base. September. *l.* 2½ to 4 in. long. Stems 1 to 2 in. long. Colombia. 1884.

R. prore'pens. *fl.* yellow, solitary, nodding on a long, very slender peduncle; the 2 straight, linear pet. pointing forward;

lateral sep. connate, boat-shaped, much narrower than dorsal; lip very small, fiddle-shaped, sub-acute with small angle before base. *l.* very small, narrow. *rhiz.* creeping, in large masses. Costa Rica. 1877. (R.X.O. 4, 11–17.)

R. Reichenbachia'na. *fl.* canary-yellow, on filiform peduncles 4 in. long, tips of connate lateral sep. dark purple; pet. and lateral sep. with 1, dorsal sep. with 2, dark purple lines at base. *l.* spatulate-oblong, obovate, about 2 in. long. Costa Rica. 1875. Densely tufted. (R.X.O. 2, 5–10.)

R. sanguin'ea. *fl.* crimson, yellowish at base of column and lateral sep.; peduncle 2 in. long. *l.* elliptic, 2 in. long. Otherwise like *R. pandurata.* Colombia. 1896. var. **gem'ma,** *fl.* about 2 in. h., lower sep. whitish, thickly spotted with crimson-purple, yellowish at base, upper sep. whitish at base with 2 narrow crimson lines and a broad central line, pet. similar, smaller. 3 to 5 in. h. Colombia. Before 1927.

R. stria'ta. Similar to *R. elegans* but with striped, not spotted sep.; lateral sep. connate for more than half their length. Colombia. 1891. (B.M. 7233.)

R. trichoglos'sa. Dorsal sep. and smaller pet. white, marked with purple at base, thickened tips yellowish; lower sep. yellowish-white, densely spotted crimson-purple; lip similarly coloured. Colombia. 1899. Resembles a small *R. antennifera* in habit.

R. xanthophthal'ma. *fl.* yellow, purple-blotched; lateral sep. connate, 2-fid. Stems 1 to 2 in. h. *l.* narrow, 1 to 2 in. long. Guatemala, Venezuela. 1860. (B.M. 5257 as *R. Lansbergii.*)

resupina'tus -a -um, reversed so that the true lower part becomes uppermost as in the flowers of most Orchids.

RESURRECTION PLANTS. *Selaginella lepidophylla* is the best known of the plants which deserve this name. It is a native of Mexico and S. Texas which in the dry season curls up into a tight ball apparently dead, but which on the return of rain expands again and continues its growth. It may break loose from its hold on the soil and be rolled about by the wind and still revive when wetted, and is sometimes sold in the dry state as a curiosity. It does not retain its life for an unlimited length of dry period but even when dead will expand and show its green leaves when placed in water. The British moss, *Leucobryum glaucum,* often grows in a ball form and becoming loosened from its hold on the woodland soil as it dries in hot weather may be rolled about and revive on wetting. The Rose of Jericho, *Anastatica Hierochuntica,* is sometimes called a resurrection plant, but it is an annual which as the dry season in the Mediterranean region from Algeria to Syria comes on curls up (after dropping its leaves) into a wicker-work ball with the ripe fruits still intact. This, too, may break loose and be rolled about by the wind. When it is wetted by dropping into water or by the coming of the rainy season, the branches again expand and the fruits then burst and shed their seeds. The original plant, of course, is dead. The opening of seed capsules and the shedding of seed usually occurs in dry weather, but *Anastatica Hierochuntica* shares with *Odontospermum pygmaeum,* an inhabitant of the same region, and with several species of Mesembryanthemum, the peculiarity of opening its capsules and shedding its seeds when moistened after drought.

RETA'MA. Included in **Genista.**

RETARDING. By keeping resting plants in artificially cooled chambers the season of growth or flowering may, in many instances, be postponed so that certain plants may be had, by bringing the retarded crowns, bulbs, or plants out of the cool chamber at intervals, all the year round. Some Lilies, like *Lilium longiflorum,* Lily of the Valley, Spiraeas, *Azalea mollis,* for example, may be so treated with success. The provision of a suitable cool chamber cannot be made in every garden, but much may be done to retard the development of plants so as to prolong their season of usefulness even without this special means. Thus by planting flowering plants in different parts of the garden in varying aspects the season of beauty may be extended; Gooseberries and Currants planted against a north wall and kept dry overhead will provide these fruits until November if protected from birds, and so on.

reticula'tus -a -um, netted.

RETINACULA. Hook-like outgrowths from the stalks of seeds of Acanthaceae aiding in their ejection from the ripe fruit; the threads attaching the pollinia to the sticky body of the translator in Asclepias, &c.

RETINIS'PORA, RETINOS'PORA. Unnecessary names often applied to juvenile forms of species of Chamaecyparis.

retro-, in compound words, implying backwards.

retroflex'us -a -um, reflexed, turned backwards.

retrors'us -a -um, directed backwards or downwards.

retu'sus -a -um, the leaf having a shallow notch at its rounded tip, retuse. **A**

RETZ'IA (in honour of Anders Johan Retzius, 1742–1821, Professor of Natural History in the University of Lund). FAM. *Solanaceae,* or, by some authors, made into a Family by itself—Retziaceae. Monotypic. Greenhouse, in sandy soil.

R. capen'sis. Compact evergreen shrub, 2 to 3 ft., shoots erect, rigid, densely leafy. *l.* in whorls of 6 or 8, erect, stalkless, $1\frac{3}{4}$ in. long, $\frac{1}{8}$ to $\frac{1}{6}$ in. wide, linear-lanceolate, entire, glabrous. *fl.* stalkless, solitary in the axils of the upper l., $1\frac{1}{2}$ in. long, the lower part concealed by the foliage; cor. tubular, erect, reddish-orange, $\frac{1}{4}$ in. wide; limb erect, 5- (rarely 6- or 7-) lobed, purple, almost black; stamens 5; *fr.* an oblong, pointed, 2-valved capsule. S. Africa, where it is in danger of becoming extinct. In the wild state the foliage of this shrub is described as having an orange hue.

W. J. B.

Reut'eri, in honour of Georges Francois Reuter, 1805–72, Swiss botanist.

Revelieri, in honour of Eugéne Revelière, *c.* 1823–92, student of the Corsican flora.

REVERSION. The term reversion is applied to certain changes seen in plants from the idea that they at times 'revert' to an ancestral form. Reversion in this sense is extremely rare, though the term might properly be applied in some instances where a mixed lot of varieties of a species are grown together and allowed to seed without selection: some of the seedlings might then show the characters of the species from which they had originally sprung. Occasionally, too, a sport may produce shoots resembling the form from which it originally sported. The term is, however, used for such occurrences as the swamping of a variety grafted or budded on a stock, where the stock has been allowed to grow and, indeed, outgrow the variety budded or grafted upon it. This is not infrequent where Manetti stock has been used for Roses, and in neglected orchards with Apples or Plums. Another form popularly attributed to 'reversion' is the multiplication of one strong variety and the disappearance of weaker varieties from some cause, as is sometimes seen when the double Van Sion Daffodil or *Narcissus poeticus* multiplies and other less vigorous varieties die out. Still another misapplication of the term is found when the appearance of, for example, the grass *Bromus secalinus* is very evident in a field of oats; the Bromus is not an ancestral form of oat, but has been unwittingly sown. A very common misapplication also occurs in calling the 'Nettle-head disease' of Black Currants reversion, whereas it is a disease brought about by a virus.

revolu'tus -a -um, rolled back, often applied to the leaf margin, revolute.

REWAREWA. *See* **Knightia excelsa.**

A→

RHABDOTHAM'NUS (*rhabdos,* rod, *thamnos,* bush; the shrub having many branches). FAM *Gesneriaceae.*

A genus of a single New Zealand shrub with spreading, slender branches. Leaves small, opposite, roundish, coarsely toothed. Flowers solitary in leaf-axils; red-striped: calyx deeply 5-cut, segments thin, slender-pointed; corolla tubular-bell-shaped, limb rather oblique, lobes 5, roundish, nearly equal; stamens 4, perfect. Fruit a leathery, 4-valved capsule. Only half-hardy and requiring similar soil to Gesneria. Slow-growing.

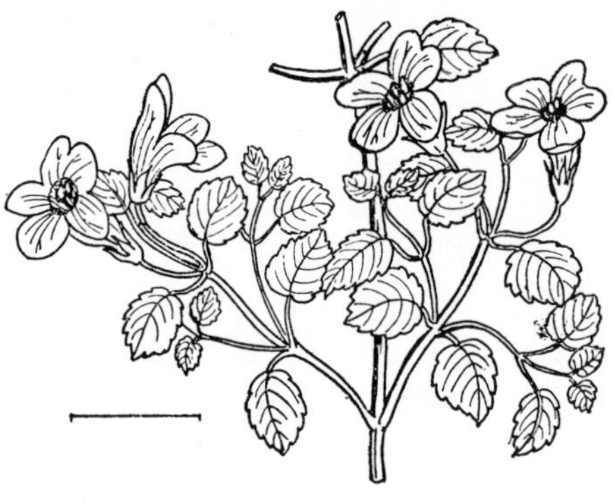

Rhabdothamnus Solandri

R. Soland'ri. Waiuatua. Shrub to 5 ft. h., branches roughly hairy, slender, somewhat entangled, greyish. *l.* more or less roundish, coarsely toothed and rough-haired. *fl.* up to 1 in. long, open at mouth, orange, striped purple in throat, red on margin of lobes. N. Island, New Zealand. (B.M. 8019.)

rhabdo'tus -a -um, striped.

RHACHIS. *See* **Rachis.**

RHADINOCERAE'A mi'cans. *See* **Iris Sawfly.**

rhae'ticus -a -um, from the old name of inhabitants of the Central (Rhaetian) Alps.

RHAGO'DIA (*rhax*, *rhagos*, a berry; in reference to the characteristic fruit). FAM. *Chenopodiaceae.* Australian Red Berry. A genus of about 15 species confined to Australia. They have no attractiveness in foliage or flower, but are useful fodder plants in dry climates. Of no value in Britain.

R. nu'tans. Saltbush. Evergreen herbaceous perennial, prostrate or climbing 3 ft. or more; stems almost woody at the base. *l.* mostly opposite, stalked, linear, lanceolate or halberd-shaped, ¼ to 1 in. long, cordate with angular basal lobes. *fl.* very small, green, 1-sexual and 2-sexual, few in short axillary racemes. *fr.* a red berry (sometimes yellow) $\frac{1}{12}$ to ⅛ in. wide, falling with the persisting perianth attached. Australia. 'One of the most fattening and relished of all the pastoral saltbushes; wonderfully resistant to drought.'

W. J. B.

RHAGOLE'TIS cerasi. *See* **Cherry Fruit-Fly.**

RHAMNAC'EAE. Dicotyledons. A family of about 40 genera with about 500 species, mostly in the tropics. Shrubs or trees, rarely herbs, often climbing. Leaves simple, commonly 3- to 5-nerved, with small stipules. Flowers small, greenish or yellowish, frequently in axillary corymbs, sepals 5 or 4, perigynous or epigynous, petals small or 0, stamens 5 or 4, carpels 5 to 2 joined. Fruit a drupe or dry, splitting or not. Closely related to Vitaceae, but distinct by the simple leaves, small petals, the receptacle, and the endocarp. Some are of economic importance. Genera dealt with are Berchemia, Ceanothus, Colletia, Discaria, Helinus, Hovenia, Noltia, Palinurus. Phylica, Pomaderris, Rhamnella, Rhamnus, Spyridium, Trevoa, Trymalium, Ventilago, Zizyphus.

RHAMNEL'LA (diminutive of *Rhamnus*). FAM. *Rhamnaceae.* About 6 species of E. Asiatic trees or shrubs with alternate leaves. Flowers 2-sexual, small, 5-parted. Fruit a black, oblong drupe with a 1-seeded nutlet. (Rhamnus differs in having a roundish drupe with 2 to 3 1-seeded nutlets.)

R. franguloi'des. Deciduous shrub or tree up to 20 or 30 ft. *l.* 2 to 4½ in. long, ¾ to 2 in. wide, oval-oblong, tapered abruptly to a slender point, finely toothed, downy only on veins beneath; stalk ¼ in. long. *fl.* yellowish-green, crowded in very shortly stalked, axillary clusters of 5 to 15. May, June. *fr.* a black, cylindric drupe ⅓ in. long. China, Japan, Korea. Hardy but of little garden merit.

W. J. B.

RHAM'NUS (Ancient Greek name). Buckthorn. FAM. *Rhamnaceae.* A genus of about 100 species of mostly small trees or shrubs, the majority deciduous, a few evergreen, often spiny. Leaves usually alternate, sometimes opposite, mostly toothed, rarely entire, more or less conspicuously parallel-veined. Flowers perfect or 1-sexual, sometimes dioecious, the parts in fours or fives; petals occasionally absent. Fruit a black or purplish-black drupe, usually globose to top-shaped, generally ⅛ to ⅓ in. wide and with 2 to 4 seeds. Some species are of economic value in yielding dyes and many possess violent purgative properties. They are mostly natives of the temperate parts of the N. Hemisphere, but some are to be found in S. America and S. Africa.

On the whole, the buckthorns have no great value in gardens, the flowers being tiny and their colour green. But some species like *R. imeritina* and *R. costata* have good foliage and others give fine crops of fruits. They can be propagated by seed, layering, or cuttings. Any reasonably good soil will suit them.

R. catharticus and *R. frangula* often bear the aecidospore stage of the rust fungus *Puccinia coronata*, which forms its uredospore and teleutospore stages on oats, causing the disease known as Crown Rust of oats.

R. Alater'nus.* Evergreen, bushy, rounded shrub, usually 8 to 10 ft., occasionally 20 ft.; shoots closely, minutely downy. *l.* ¾ to 2 in. long, oval to oblong, sometimes slightly obovate, abruptly pointed but little toothed, shining green; veins in 3 to 5 pairs. *fl.* yellow-green, ⅛ in. wide, in short axillary clusters. April. *fr.* black, ¼ in. wide. SW. Europe. 17th cent. var. **angustifo'lia,** *l.* linear to narrowly lanceolate, ⅛ to ⅝ in. wide, conspicuously toothed. SYN. *R. angustifolia*, *R. Perrieri*; **integrifo'lia,** *l.* entire; **variega'ta,** *l.* narrower than in type, bordered with creamy-white.

R. alnifo'lia. Deciduous, low, spreading shrub, rarely more than 3 ft., shoots minutely downy. *l.* oval, 2 to 4 in. long, half as wide, unevenly toothed; veins in 6 to 8 pairs, downy beneath. *fl.* yellow-green, usually in twos or threes; pet. absent. *fr.* black, ¼ in. long, 3-seeded. N. America. 1778.

R. alpi'na. Alpine Buckthorn. Deciduous shrub up to 10 ft. *l.* oval, 2 to 4 in. long, rounded or shortly pointed at apex, rounded or slightly cordate at base, finely toothed, glabrous; veins in 9 to 12 pairs. SW. Europe. 1752. (L.B.C. 1077.) Closely akin to *R. fallax* and similar in fl. and fr.

R. angustifo'lia. A variety of *R. Alaternus.*

R. califor'nica. Evergreen bush, 10 to 15 ft., shoots downy. *l.* 1½ to 4 in. long, oval to oblong, rounded at base, blunt or short-pointed at apex, scarcely toothed, downy on the 8 to 12 pairs of veins beneath. *fl.* in downy, short-stalked umbels. *fr.* orange-shaped, ¼ in. wide, red, finally black-purple. Western N. America. var. **oleifo'lia,** *l.* smaller, narrower, toothed; **tomentel'la,** very distinct by the shoots and *l.* being covered with a close yellowish or greyish velvety down. Has medicinal properties similar to *R. Purshiana.* 1858. SYN. *R. tomentella.*

R. carolinia'na. Indian Cherry. Tree to 30 or 40 ft. or a shrub, shoots downy. *l.* oval to narrowly oblong, 2 to 6 in. long, obscurely toothed; veins in 8 to 10 pairs. *fl.* in downy-stalked umbels of 2 to 8; stalk ⅛ to ⅖ in. long. May. *fr.* globose, black, ⅓ in. wide. E. United States. 1819.

R. cathar'tica. Common Buckthorn. Rhine Berry. Deciduous shrub 10 to 20 ft., shoots often spine-tipped in age, shoots glabrous. *l.* both opposite and alternate on the same shoot, 1 to 2½ in. long, oval or ovate, finely toothed; veins in 3 to 5 pairs. *fl.* small, green, borne in lower l.-axils in crowded clusters of 2 to 5. *fr.* black, ¼ in. wide, globose. Europe (Britain on limy soils). (E.B. 318.) Violently purgative.

R. costa'ta.* Deciduous shrub up to 15 ft., shoots stout, glabrous. *l.* opposite, 3 to 6 in. long, ovate-oblong, shortly pointed, narrowly cordate or rounded at base, wrinkled above; veins in about 20 pairs, conspicuous, downy; stalk ⅛ in. long. *fl.* on slender stalks up to 1 in. long, green. *fr.* top-shaped, black, ⅓ in. wide. Japan. 1900. Handsome shrub of the many-veined group.

R. cro'cea. Evergreen shrub, usually low and spreading (but in **insula'ris** a tree 20 to 30 ft.). Sometimes spiny. *l.* oval to orbicular, ½ to 1 in. long, spiny toothed, of leathery texture, yellowish beneath, very shortly stalked. *fl.* with minute pet. or none. *fr.* ⅛ to ¼ in. long, red, obovoid. California, 1848. Notable for its red fr., rather tender.

R. davu'rica. Spreading, deciduous shrub or small tree up to 30 ft., shoots glabrous. *l.* 2 to 4 in. long, oblong or oval, cuneate, slender-pointed, finely toothed; veins in 4 to 6 pairs. *fl.* in dense clusters at the base of the shoots, green. June. *fr.* black, $\frac{1}{4}$ in. wide, roundish. Siberia to N. China. 1817.

R. erythrox'ylon. Spreading deciduous shrub, spiny, 3 to 6 ft., shoots finely downy. *l.* linear to linear-lanceolate, $\frac{3}{4}$ to 3 in. long, $\frac{1}{12}$ to $\frac{3}{8}$ in. wide, pointed, indistinctly toothed, downy beneath. *fl.* with stalk $\frac{1}{8}$ to $\frac{1}{3}$ in. long, borne on short spurs. *fr.* black, $\frac{1}{6}$ in. wide, globose. Siberia. 1823. Distinct by the narrow l.

R. fal'lax.* Deciduous shrub, 5 to 10 ft., shoots glabrous. *l.* 2 to 5 in. long, oval to oblong-obovate, rounded or cordate at base, shortly pointed, finely toothed; veins in 12 to 20 pairs, with axil-tufts beneath; stalk $\frac{1}{2}$ in. or less long. *fl.* yellowish-green, in axillary clusters of 2 to 7. May. *fr.* roundish, $\frac{1}{4}$ in. wide, black. Alps of SE. Europe. 1800. Handsome for its large, many-veined l.

R. Frang'ula. Alder Buckthorn. Deciduous shrub or small tree up to 18 ft., shoots downy. *l.* oval or obovate, $1\frac{1}{2}$ to 3 in. long, cuneate to rounded at base, abruptly pointed, toothless, glossy green, glabrous except sometimes beneath; veins in 8 or 9 pairs; stalk $\frac{1}{4}$ to $\frac{1}{2}$ in. long. *fl.* 2 to 8 in axillary, glabrous clusters, green. June. *fr.* $\frac{1}{4}$ in. wide, red, finally dark purple, 2-seeded. Europe (Britain), Asia Minor, N. Africa. (E.B. 319.) Its charcoal once much valued for gunpowder-making. var. **angustifo'lia,** *l.* narrowly oblong or oblanceolate, $\frac{1}{2}$ to 1 in. wide, with jagged margins; **asplenifo'lia,** *l.* $\frac{1}{8}$ to $\frac{1}{4}$ in. wide, up to 2 in. long; **latifo'lia,** *l.* up to $3\frac{1}{2}$ in. long, 2 in. wide. Caucasus.

R. × **hyb'rida.** Evergreen or semi-deciduous shrub up to 12 ft., shoots glabrous. *l.* ovate to oblong, $1\frac{1}{2}$ to 4 in. long, finely toothed, glabrous; veins in about 7 pairs; stalk $\frac{1}{8}$ to $\frac{1}{3}$ in. long. *R. alpina* × *R. Alaternus.* 1788. var. **Billard'ii,** *l.* smaller, narrower, more lanceolate, and more coarsely toothed.

Rhamnus imeritina

R. imeriti'na.* Deciduous shrub up to 10 ft., shoots thick, sparsely downy. *l.* 4 to 10 in. long, half as wide, oblong or oval, pointed, finely toothed; veins in 15 to 28 pairs, downy on both surfaces, especially beneath; stalk $\frac{1}{2}$ to $\frac{3}{4}$ in. long. *fl.* green, in small axillary clusters. June. *fr.* $\frac{1}{3}$ in. wide. Caucasus. (B.M. 6721 as *R. libanotica.*) Handsomest and largest-leaved of the buckthorns; bronzy purple in autumn.

R. infecto'ria. Avignon Berry. Spreading, deciduous shrub up to 7 ft., shoots downy, eventually spine-tipped. *l.* oval, ovate, or obovate, $\frac{1}{2}$ to $1\frac{1}{2}$ in. long, finely toothed, nearly or quite glabrous; veins in 3 or 4 pairs. *fr.* black, 2-seeded, once used by dyers as 'Graine d'Avignon'. SW. Europe.

R. japon'ica. Deciduous shrub, 8 or 9 ft., shoots glabrous, often ultimately spine-tipped. *l.* 1 to 3 in. long, obovate, cuneate, rounded or shortly pointed at apex, finely toothed, bright green; veins in 3 to 5 pairs. *fl.* greenish-brown, fragrant, very abundant, borne in dense, hemispherical clusters on short spurs. *fr.* black, globose, $\frac{1}{4}$ in. wide. Japan. 1888.

R. lanceola'ta. Erect deciduous shrub 6 to 7 ft., shoots downy. *l.* 1 to 3 in. long, ovate-lanceolate to oblong-lanceolate, bright green, cuneate to rounded at the base, finely toothed, downy or glabrous beneath, veins in 6 to 9 pairs; stalk $\frac{1}{8}$ in. long. *fl.* on some plants short-stalked, in clusters, and with a short style; in others few or solitary and longer-styled. May. *fr.* $\frac{1}{4}$ in. wide, black, top-shaped. United States. 1870.

R. latifo'lia. Akin to *R. Frangula,* this has larger *l.*, 4 to 7 in. long, with 10 to 16 pairs of veins, downy beneath; stalk $\frac{1}{2}$ to $1\frac{1}{4}$ in. long. *fl.* in axillary clusters; stalks $\frac{5}{8}$ in. long and (like the cal.) downy. *fr.* red then black, $\frac{1}{3}$ to $\frac{1}{2}$ in. wide. Azores. 1778. (B.M. 2663.) Not so hardy as most sp. but grows well in the west and south.

R. libanot'ica. Nearly related to *R. imeritina,* which is figured under its name B.M. 6721. It has smaller, oblong-obovate *l.* with only 10 to 15 pairs of veins; stalk $\frac{1}{8}$ in. long. *fr.* $\frac{1}{3}$ in. wide. Syria.

R. pu'mila. Dwarf Buckthorn. Deciduous, low, often procumbent shrub usually only a few inches h., shoots downy. *l.* roundish to narrowly oval, $\frac{3}{4}$ to $2\frac{1}{4}$ in. long, cuneate, finely toothed; veins in 5 to 8 pairs; stalk downy, $\frac{1}{8}$ to $\frac{1}{3}$ in. long. *fl.* pale green. *fr.* globose, blue-black. Alps of Europe. 1752. Often found wild in crevices of rock. Rock-garden.

R. Purshia'na. Cascara Sagrada. Deciduous tree 35 to 45 ft., shoots downy. *l.* oval, oblong, or obovate, rounded at the base, slightly or not toothed, 2 to 6 in. long; veins parallel in 10 to 15 pairs, downy beneath; stalk $\frac{1}{2}$ to $\frac{3}{4}$ in. long. *fl.* green, in stalked umbels. July. *fr.* top-shaped, $\frac{1}{3}$ in. long, purplish black, usually 3-seeded. N. America, 1826. Bark yields the drug 'Cascara Sagrada'.

R. saxat'ilis. Rock Buckthorn. Low, spreading, deciduous shrub, 2 to 3 ft., spiny; shoots minutely downy. *l.* $\frac{1}{2}$ to 1 in. long, $\frac{1}{4}$ to $\frac{1}{2}$ in. wide, narrowly oval, ovate, or obovate, cuneate, finely toothed, glabrous; veins in 2 to 4 pairs. *fl.* very small, greenish-yellow. *fr.* black, top-shaped, 3-seeded. Mts. of Cent. and S. Europe. 1752.

R. tomentel'la. A variety of *R. californica.*

W. J. B.

RHAPIDES. *See* Raphides.

RHAPHIDOPH'ORA (*rhaphidos*, needle, *phero*, to bear; needle-like hairs abound in the intercellular spaces in all parts of the plants). FAM. *Araceae.* A genus of about 30 species of climbing shrubs with very long rooting branches, natives of Trop. Asia, the Malay Archipelago, N. Australia, the Pacific Is., and a few in Africa. Leaves distichous, often large, lanceolate or ovate-oblong, entire, perforated or pinnatifid, rarely pinnatipartite; segments broad at base; sides unequal; stalk short or long with a long sheath. Flowers densely arranged on a sessile, thick, cylindrical, usually inappendiculate spadix; usually hermaphrodite; spathe thick, boat-shaped, including the spadix, at first oblong and convolute, afterwards opening, often rostrate, marcescent, finally deciduous: peduncles terminal, solitary or many. They need stove conditions and a compost of rich loam and fibrous peat in equal parts. They should be planted in the border near a wall or the dead stump of a tree up which they can climb. They need a moist atmosphere. Propagation by seeds or by cuttings in sandy loam and peat under a hand glass with bottom heat.

R. decur'siva. *l.* oblong, unequally pinnatisect; segs. on adult l. 15 or more on each side, nearly equal, linear; stalk one-third shorter than l. *Spathe* yellowish with paler margins, very thick, longer than l.-stalk; spadix greyish-green, long, thick. India, &c. 1859.

R. lancifo'lia. Stem cylindrical. *l.* lanceolate, cuspidate, 9 to 10 in. long, sides unequal, dark, shining green, glabrous. *Spathe* apricot with green spots without, salmon within, 3 to 4 in. long, $2\frac{1}{2}$ to 3 in. wide, ovate, acuminate, open; spadix white, cylindrical, erect, obtuse. Khasia, Sylhet. 1874. (G.C. 2 (1874), 612.)

R. Peep'la. *l.* oblong or elliptic-oblong, base rounded or wedge-shaped, apex acute, long-cuspidate. *Spathe* yellowish without, reddish-yellow within, shorter than l.-stalk; spadix yellowish. E. Indies.

R. pertu'sa. *l.* unequal-sided, heart-shaped at base, shortly cuspidate, entire, pinnatifid or perforated; stalk one quarter shorter than l. E. Indies.

RHAPHIOLE'PIS. *See* Raphiolepis.

RHAPHITHAM'US (*rhapis*, a needle, *thamnos* a shrub: in reference to the spiny character of some of the species). FAM. *Verbenaceae*. About 10 species of shrubs or trees natives of Chile. Leaves opposite, small, simple, entire; calyx bell-shaped, 5-toothed: corolla tubular with 4 or 5 unequal lobes; stamens 4; fruit a fleshy drupe. The following species is most satisfactory in the south-west counties and similar places. Its tenure is insecure in inland places, even against a wall. Thrives in loamy soil and is easily propagated by cuttings.

R. cyanocarp'us.* Evergreen, much-branched shrub 20 to 25 ft., shoots hairy, armed with slender, axillary spines $\frac{1}{2}$ to 1 in. long. *l.* often in threes, $\frac{1}{4}$ to $\frac{3}{4}$ in. long, $\frac{1}{8}$ to $\frac{1}{2}$ in. wide, broadly ovate, pointed, bristly on the midrib beneath. *fl.* axillary, crowded near the summit of the twigs; cor. tube $\frac{1}{2}$ in. long, pale blue. April. *fr.* bright blue; drupe $\frac{1}{3}$ to $\frac{1}{2}$ in. wide. Chile. 1843. (B.M. 6849.) Beautiful in fr.

W. J. B.

RHAPIDOPHYL'LUM (*Raphis*, *phyllon*; resembling Raphis in producing suckers freely). FAM. *Palmaceae*. A genus of a single species of dwarf Palm with a short, erect or creeping stem. For treatment *see* **Chamaerops.**

R. Hys'trix. Blue Palmetto. Trunk of 3 to 4 ft. *l.* almost orbicular, deeply and unequally plicate, 3 to 4 ft. long, segs. numerous, 2- to 4-toothed, silvery beneath; stalks 3-edged, rough; sheaths persistent of numerous oblique fibres interwoven with many strong, erect spines. *fl.* yellow, very small; spadix small, short-stalked; spathes about 4, oblong, woolly, sharply 2-lipped. June, July. S. United States. 1801. (I.H. 1883, 304 as *Chamaerops Hystrix.*)

RHAP'IS (*rhapis*, needle; in allusion to the needle-like leaf-segments). FAM. *Palmaceae*. A genus of 4 or 5 species of dwarf Chinese and Japanese Palms with long densely-tufted, reed-like, leafy stems. Leaves alternate and terminal, rather membranous, connate or half-round, deeply cut into 3 to many linear, wedge-shaped or elliptic, truncate, entire or toothed segments; stalks short, 2-convex, margins smooth or toothed; sheaths split into a fibrous network. Flowers yellowish; spathes 2 or 3, incomplete, membranous; spadices shorter than leaves with spreading branches, peduncles slender. For treatment of these greenhouse plants *see* **Chamaerops.**

R. asp'era. A synonym of *R. excelsa*.

R. cochinchinen'sis. Stem 8 ft. h. *l.* fan-shaped, palmately divided; segs. oblong, obtuse, much plaited; stalks short, straight, prickly. *Spadix* short, branched. *fr* ovate, inedible. Cochin China.

R. excel'sa. Ground Rattan Cane. Stem about $1\frac{1}{2}$ ft. h., as thick as the thumb, sheathed by the persistent fibrous base of l. *l.* 5- to 7-parted; segs. somewhat plaited, ciliate and spiny on margin and keels of plaits, erose at tip; stalks roundish, 2-edged, naked, obscurely toothed. *Male fl.* yellowish, sessile, thickly covering spikelets; spadix sparse, paniculately branched, 4 to 5 in. long. China, Japan. 1774. (B.M. 1374 as *R. flabelliformis.*) SYN. *R. aspera*, var. **foliis-variega'tis,** *l.* striped white. Japan. 1861.

R. flabellifor'mis. A synonym of *R. excelsa*.

R. hu'milis. Similar in general aspect to *R. excelsa*; *l.* cut into 7 to 10 spreading segs., stalks unarmed. Japan.

RHAPONT'ICUM. Included in **Centaurea.**

RHATANY ROOT. The root of *Krameria triandra*.

RHAZ'YA (in honour of the Arabian physician Abu Bekr-er-Rasi, author of medical works in 9th and 10th centuries). FAM. *Apocynaceae*. A genus of 2 species of glabrous, erect shrubs or under shrubs, natives of the Levant and Arabia, closely related to Vinca. Leaves alternate, rather thick. Flowers densely corymbose or somewhat thyrsoid at tips of branches. *R. orientalis* should be planted in a sunny place on a warm, well-drained slope.

R. orienta'lis. About 10 in. h. with simple, short, erect, thickly leafy branches. *fl.* bright blue to dark violet, about $\frac{1}{2}$ in. long, in terminal cymes among the uppermost l. Late summer. Orient. 1889. (G.F. 1891, t. 1346; B.M. 9119.)

RHE'A. *See* **Boehmeria nivea.**

RHEED'IA (in honour of Hen. van Rheede, 1635–91, a Dutch resident in Malabar, author of *Hortus Malabaricus*). FAM. *Guttiferae*. A genus of about 30 species of trees, natives of Madagascar and Trop. Africa and Asia. Leaves rigidly leathery, pinnately-veined. Flowers usually rather small; sepals 2; petals 4; peduncles axillary or lateral, 1-flowered. *R. brasiliensis* is the source of the Bakupari (Bakury) fruit of commerce, but the species are of little horticultural interest. They need stove conditions.

Rhazya orientalis

R. lateriflo'ra. Tree. *l.* opposite, ovate, entire; stalked. *fl.* on lateral unbranched 1-fld. peduncles, numerous. *fr.* yellow. Trop. America.

RHEKTOPHYL'LUM (*rechtos*, torn, *phyllon*, leaf; the leaf is cut and perforated). FAM. *Araceae*. A genus of perhaps 2 species of tall climbers rooting at the nodes, natives of W. Trop. Africa. Stem thick. Leaves long-stalked, in young plants widely cordate-hastate, more or less undulate, in adult plants ovate or oblong-ovate, perforated or laciniate between the veins. Peduncles shorter than the spathe, which is rather thick and almost cylindrical, scarcely constricted. Flowers with 3 or 4 stamens. Related to Nephthytis, and needing similar treatment.

R. mira'bile. Climber to over 30 ft. In young plants *l.-stalk* 10 to 16 in. long; blade membranous, dark green with paler variegation between veins, hastate or cordate-hastate, 8 to 12 in. long. In adult l.-stalk 12 to 30 in. long, blade not variegated, ovate with large linear perforations or long slits. *Peduncle* about 2 in. long. *Spathe* 4 in. long, green without, red-purple within. Congo. 1887. SYN. *Nephthytis picturata.*

RHEUM (*rha*, ancient Greek name for Rhubarb: *Rheon barbarum* being corrupted into our Rhubarb). FAM. *Polygonaceae.* A genus of possibly 20 species of stout, perennial herbs, with thick, somewhat woody rhizomes, natives of Siberia, the Himalaya, and E. Asia. Leaves large, sinuately toothed or palmately lobed, 3- to 8-nerved at base. Flowers like those of Rumex, but coloured and insect-pollinated, clustered, the clusters disposed in narrow panicles: perianth of 6 spreading segments: stigmas large as in wind-pollinated plants. The introduction of Rhubarbs into our garden was due to the medicinal value of the roots and for a long time this was the sole object of their cultivation. The first species to be introduced was *R. Rhaponticum*, one, possibly the chief, parent of our culinary Rhubarbs. It seems to have reached this country prior to 1573 and other species followed at intervals, but it was not until the 18th century that it came into use for making tarts and considerably later before it became a market commodity (*see* **Rhubarb**). *R. officinale* seems now to be the main source of medicinal Rhubarb, though possibly *R. palmatum* may also provide some. Several species are very handsome in foliage and inflorescence and well adapted for the wild garden, margins of shrubberies, and even the large herbaceous border. They do best in rich soil of good depth but will grow in almost any soil. Propagation by seed or by division in early spring.

R. acumina'tum. About 3 ft. h. from a slender root many feet long. *l.* broadly heart-shaped with a deep basal sinus, and a long tapered apex, opaque green above, downy beneath; stalk slender, channelled above. *fl.* lurid-purple, blood-red, or brownish-purple, ¼ in. across; in a slightly branched panicle. Sikkim. 1837. (B.M. 4877.)

R. Alexan'drae. Stem erect, simple. *l.* long-stalked, ovate-oblong with a heart-shaped base, obtuse, entire, glabrous, passing into greenish-yellow membranous sessile bracts. Branches of panicle only shortly exserted beyond bracts. Szechwan, Tibet.

R. austra'le. A synonym of *R. emodi.* A

R. Collinia'num. About 3 ft. h., robust. *l.* ovate, scarcely heart-shaped, deeply cut into broad lobes, red beneath at first, margin unequally cut. *fl.* dull red, very numerous. China.

R. compac'tum. *l.* large, somewhat obtusely lobed, leathery, glabrous or nearly so, strongly veined, lobes sharply toothed, margins wavy. Branches of panicle nodding. China.

R. emo'di. Stem 6 to 10 ft. h., leafy. *l.* broadly ovate, heart-shaped at base, obtuse, 5- to 7-nerved, margins slightly wavy. *fl.* whitish, in a dense fastigiate panicle. Summer. Himalaya.

R. Forrest'ii. 2 to 2½ ft. h. *l.* slightly lobed, somewhat heart-shaped at base and slightly pointed. *fl.* white in a long panicle; pedicels very slender. Lowest panicle branches lowest; scape glabrous at base, downy above. W. China.

R. × hyb'ridum. A name given to various hybrids between different species, e.g. *R. Collinianum* × *R. officinale, R. Rhaponticum* × *R. undulatum.*

R. Moorcroftia'num. About 2 ft. h. *l.* large, oblique, nearly glabrous. *fl.* bright red, in a dense pyramidal panicle, shorter than in most species, its branches hairy. Himalaya. 1895. (G.C. 17 (1895), 765.)

R. nob'ile.* Over 3 ft. h. from a thick, fleshy root, sometimes many feet long. *Radical l.* large, bright glossy green; stalks and veins red; stipules pink, easily torn. *fl.* small green, in short branched panicles; bracts straw-coloured, shining, almost transparent, concave, overlapping, hiding the fl., upper ones with pink edges. Summer. Himalaya. (G.C. 13 (1880) 793.)

R. officina'le.* 8 to 10 ft. h., leafy and much branched. *l.* large with a roundish-kidney-shaped outline, 5-nerved, cut into 5 short lobes at margin, lobes unequally cut. *fl.* greenish, small, in a dense panicle. Summer. Tibet. 1871. (B.M. 6135; R.H. 1874, 13.) var. **dissec'tum.** *l.* deeply lobed.

R. palma'tum.* About 5 ft. h. *l.* roundish-heart-shaped in outline, palmately lobed, glabrous or somewhat rough above, 3- or 5-veined; lobes oblong-ovate or lanceolate, acute, variously cut into, sometimes entire; stalk almost cylindrical. *fl.* deep red, in a large panicle. China. 1763. (B.M. 9200.) var. **tangu'ticum,** *l.* longer and more deeply lobed than in type.

R. Rhapon'ticum. Common Rhubarb. About 4 ft. h. *l.* roundish in outline, deeply cordate at base, undulate, 5-veined, glabrous above, downy beneath and on veins; upper l. ovate or acuminate; stalks long, thick, fleshy, channelled above, rounded at edges. *fl.* in a dense, leafy, fastigiate panicle. June. Siberia. 1573.

R. Ri'bes. Stem tall, thick, leafy in lower part, leafless above, forming a large, much-branched, fastigiate panicle. *l.* roundish-heart-shaped or kidney-shaped in outline, 4 to 12 in. long, 6 in. to 2 ft. wide, minutely toothed, often roughly papillose beneath. *fl.* green and white, in clusters. May. Persia. 1724. (B.M. 7591.) Somewhat tender.

R. undula'tum. Stem 4 to 5 ft. h., smooth, green. *l.* ovate-heart-shaped, undulate, 5- to 7-veined, glabrous above, downy beneath; upper l. almost sessile, 2 or 3 times as long as wide; stalks half-round, somewhat channelled above, margins rounded. Siberia, &c. 1734.

RHEX'IA (*rhexio*, rupture). FAM. *Melastomaceae.* A genus of about 7 species of erect herbs or sub-shrubs, natives of extra-tropical Eastern N. America. Leaves oblong, shortly stalked, 3-veined, entire or bristly toothed. Flowers of various colours, solitary or in cymes: calyx tube oblong, bell- or urn-shaped, limb of 4 triangular or subulate lobes; petals 4, obovate; stamens 8. The Rhexias do best in a bed of peat but may be grown in pots in peaty soil. They are readily propagated by division. The species referred to below are hardy herbs.

Rhexia ciliosa

R. cilio'sa. Stem simple, 1 to 1½ ft. h., smooth, 4-angled above. *l.* ovate, rarely up to 1 in. long, bristly above. *fl.* purple, 1 to ½ in. across, in a few-fld. leafy cyme. July, August. 1812. (S.B.F.G. 298.)

R. maria'na. Bristly, 1 to 2 ft. h. Stem branched, terete or 6-angled. *l.* lanceolate, acute, bristly toothed; stalk short. *fl.* purple or white, 1½ to 2 in. across, hairy without; cal. usually smooth. July to September. 1759. (L.B.C. 366; S.B.F.G. 41.) Variable in l.-form and fl.-colour.

R. virgin'ica. Deer Grass; Meadow Beauty. Bristly. Stem scarcely branched 4-angled, 6 to 12 in. h. *l.* ovate or ovate-lanceolate, sometimes 5-veined, lowest roundish. *fl.* bright purple. July, August. 1759. (B.M. 968; Gn. 11 (1877), 294.)

RHINACAN'THUS (*rhinos*, rose, *Acanthus*; from the curious shape of the corolla). FAM. *Acanthaceae.* A genus of about 4 species of rather straggling, sometimes almost climbing shrubs, natives of S. Africa, Madagascar, E. Indies, and Malaya. Leaves entire. Flowers few, almost sessile and sometimes clustered in the axils of bracts: calyx deeply 5-cleft, segments narrow: corolla a long tube, 2-lipped; stamens 2, attached in throat of corolla. For treatment *see* **Justicia.**

R. commu'nis. Ringworm Root. About 2 ft. h. *l.* oblong or ovate-oblong, about 4 in. long. *fl.* white with straight linear upper lip, often clustered on long terminal spreading, dichotomous or trichotomous panicles, covered with dusky down. June. India. 1790. (B.M. 325 as *Justicia Nasuta.*)

RHINE BERRY. *See* **Rhamnus catharticus.**

RHINOPET'ALUM. Included in **Fritillaria.**

RHIPIDOP'TERIS (*rhipis*, fan, *pteris*, fern; from the peculiar fronds). FAM. *Polypodiaceae.* Four species related to Elaphoglossum with fronds of 2 forms, the fertile ones small, orbicular and undivided, the sori without indusia. Veins arranged in a fan-like manner. Barren fronds forked with very narrow divisions. Soil may be as for Elaphoglossum but *R. peltata* requires a place naturally moist with a liberal water-supply all the year round; with a moist atmosphere it grows freely in a mixture of partly decayed leaf-mould, fibrous peat, and silver sand in equal parts; it does not like root-disturbance.

R. foenicula'cea.* *rhiz.* slender, creeping. *sti.* distant, slender, 2 to 8 in. long, scaly. *Barren fronds* 1 to 2 in. broad, usually dichotomously forked, with filiform divisions. *Fertile fronds* 3/8 in. broad, 2-lobed. Andes of Ecuador. SYN. *Acrostichum foeniculaceum.* Stove species.

R. pelta'ta.* *rhiz.* slender, wide creeping. *sti.* distant, slender, 1 to 4 in. long, scaly throughout. *Barren fronds* 1 to 2 in. each way, repeatedly dichotomously forked, with very narrow linear ultimate divisions. *Fertile fronds* 1/2 in. broad, often 2-lobed. Trop. America. (R.H. 1899, 266; B.C.F. 1, 216.) SYN. *Acrostichum peltatum.* Stove or greenhouse. var. **gracil'lima** has larger fronds more finely divided than in the type. It is more easily grown.

RHIPOG'ONUM (*rhips*, rod, *gonu*, knee or joint; the stalk is jointed). FAM. *Liliaceae.* A genus of tall climbing shrubs, one native of New Zealand, the others of E. Australia. Leaves generally mostly opposite, sometimes all alternate, 3- to 5-veined, net-veined; stalks not bearing tendrils. Flowers hermaphrodite, rather small, in short axillary spikes or racemes or in a terminal panicle; segments 6, free, equal or the outer shorter. They do not take kindly to cultivation but rich soil and shade should suit them. General treatment as for Asparagus species.

R. al'bum. Main branches often prickly. *l.* elliptic or oblong, ovate to lanceolate, shortly slender-pointed, narrowed at base, 3 to 4 in. long. *fl.* white, rather distant, in axillary, simple racemes, usually shorter than l. June, July. *fr.* at first red, drying black, 1/3 in. thick. Australia. 1820.

R. scan'dens. Supple Jack. Lofty twiner; stems eventually naked below, black. *fr.* handsome, bright red. New Zealand.

RHIPSALIDOP'SIS (*Rhipsalis*, *opsis*, like; the plant being like a Rhipsalis in some ways). FAM. *Cactaceae.* Shrubby plants, erect or pendent; joints 3- to 5-angled; areoles small, sometimes with bristles. Flowers terminal, pink, large for the group and with a short tube (a distinction from Rhipsalis); fruit unknown.

R. ro'sea. The only species. Brazil. SYN. *Rhipsalis rosea.* (B.R.C. 4, f. 210.) For cultivation *see* **Cactus.**

V. H.

RHIPSA'LIS (*rhips*, wickerwork; on account of the pliability of the interlacing branches). FAM. *Cactaceae.* Epiphytic cacti, stems much branched, sometimes making aerial roots; the stems may be slender and cylindrical, angled or flattened: areoles are borne on the margins of the flattened forms or scattered irregularly on the cylindrical ones, bearing hairs, wool, or bristles: spines never strongly developed. Flowers usually solitary at an areole, diurnal or nocturnal, very small: tube short or absent, perianth leaves few, widespread. Fruit round, juicy, white or coloured. This genus gives its name to the sub-tribe Rhipsalidanae (*see under* **Cactus**), species formerly classed as Rhipsalis being now separated into 8 genera, not all of which are in cultivation (see synonyms below). These plants, which all come from Trop. America, require different treatment from the desert types and should be given a moister atmosphere. For cultivation *see under* **Cactus.**

R. ala'ta. A synonym of *Pseudorhipsalis alata.*

R. capilliform'is. Stems much-branched, slender, very weak, pendent. *fl.* cream. *fr.* white. Brazil. (B.R.C. 4, t. 25, 26.)

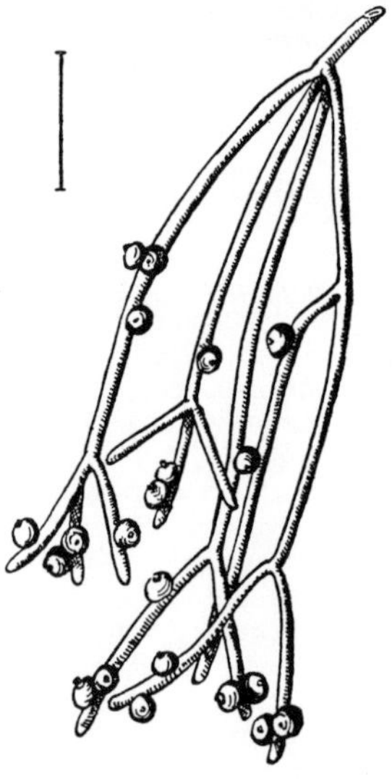

Rhipsalis Cassutha

R. Cassu'tha. Stems cylindrical, weak, and pendent, hanging in large clusters; sometimes producing aerial roots; areoles scattered with bristles when young. *fl.* cream. Florida, Mexico, Cent. America to Peru; also found in Ceylon and Trop. Africa, which is unusual as Cacti are otherwise natives of America only; it may have been introduced by birds. *R. Cassytha* is an incorrect spelling. (B.R.C. 4, t. 27; B.M. 3080; L.B.C. 865.) **A**

R. caverno'sa. A synonym of *Lepismium cruciforme.*

R. cereus'cula. Stems cylindrical, slender, long and often erect, crowned with a cluster of short branches; areoles with short bristles. *fl.* terminal, pink or white. *Berries* white. Uruguay, Brazil. (B.M. 4039; B.R.C. 4, t. 27.)

R. commu'nis. A synonym of *Lepismium cruciforme.*

R. cribra'ta. Plants woody, stems cylindrical, branches short and in whorls; areoles small with 1 or 2 bristles. *fl.* terminal, pendulous, white. *fr.* pinkish. Brazil. (B.R.C. 4, t. 23, 26.) SYN. *R. penduliflora.*

R. crispa'ta. Stems wide and flat, the margins crenate, divided into joints which are narrowed at the ends. *fl.* cream to pale yellow. *fr.* white. Brazil. (B.R.C. 4, t. 35.)

R. dissim'ilis. Plants forming large clumps, stems various, some with numerous bristly hairs from the areoles, others naked; hairy branches faintly ribbed, naked ones 5-angled. *fl.* pinkish. Brazil. (B.M. 8013; B.R.C. 4, t. 29, 32.)

R. Houlletia'na. Stems long, cylindrical below, flattened above, up to 2 in. across, margin serrate. *fl.* numerous, cream with a red eye. *fr.* red. Brazil. (B.R.C. 4, t. 33, 34; B.M. 6089.)

R. Knight'ii. A synonym of *Lepismium cruciforme.*

R. lumbricoi'des. Stems thicker than in some species, cylindrical when growing, angled when dormant; white bristles in young areoles; old branches naked. *fl.* white or greenish. *fr.* white. Uruguay, Paraguay. (B.M. 5136.)

R. micran'tha. Stems flattened, 3- or 4-angled; areoles small, distant, with 1 to 4 bristles. *fl.* white, lateral; *fr.* round, white or reddish. Ecuador, Peru.

R. pachyp'tera. Stems flat, pendulous, jointed; joints about 3 in. long, 2 in. wide, margins crenate. *fl.* solitary, small, pale brownish-yellow, buds pinkish. *fr.* red, about as large as a red currant. 1839. Brazil. Nearly related to *R. crispata.*

R. paradox'a. Stems pendent, producing aerial roots freely; branches forking or sometimes in whorls, 3-angled, joints short; areoles very woolly and with bristles when young. *fl.* large, white, towards the ends of the branches. Brazil. (B.R.C. 4, t. 28.)

R. pentap'tera. Stems 5- or 6-ribbed, indented at the areoles; areoles distant, subtended by broad bracts, usually with 1 or 2 bristles. *fl.* cream, scattered the whole length of the branches. Brazil, Uruguay. (B.R.C. 4, t. 30.)

R. pilocar'pa. A synonym of *Erythrorhipsalis pilocarpa.*

R. prismat'ica. Stems prostrate, much-branched, cylindrical; upper branches short and sometimes angled; areoles usually with bristles. *fl.* white. *fr.* white. Brazil, Madagascar. (B.R.C. 4, t. 32.)

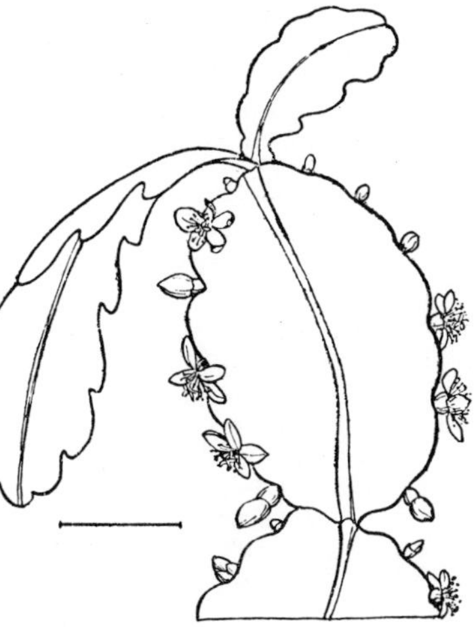

Rhipsalis pachyptera (p. 1758)

R. ro'sea. *Rhipsalidopsis rosea.*

R. salicornoi'des. A synonym of *Hatiora salicornoides.*

R. Schwartzia'na. A synonym of *Pseudorhipsalis alata.*

R. squamulo'sa. A synonym of *Lepismium cruciforme.*

R. te'res. Stems erect or spreading, much-branched into short ultimate branches, cylindrical. *fl.* pale yellow, more or less terminal. Brazil. (B.R.C. 4, t. 26.)

R. Tonduz'ii. Stems erect at first, then pendent, thick, normally 4- or 5-angled but the terminal branches 3-angled and even flattened; areoles close, in notches. *fl.* small, white. Costa Rica. (B.R.C. 4, t. 30.)

R. Warmingia'na. Stems hanging, branches long, jointed, narrow and flattened with crenate margins; green blotched with red or purple. *fl.* white. *fr.* nearly black. Brazil. (B.R.C. 4, t. 30, 34.) A

V. H.

rhizanthous, flowering from the root, or apparently so.

rhizocarpous, producing subterranean flowers and fruit, also used for a plant having a perennial root but a stem which perishes annually: herbaceous perennial.

RHIZOCTO'NIA. A genus of Fungi Imperfecti peculiar in that they form a very characteristic type of fungal thread for vegetative growth but produce no kind of spore body, although some of them produce sclerotia. Some fungi previously known as Rhizoctonia have now been placed in other genera, one being *Rhizoctonia solani*, which since the discovery that it produced basidiospores has been called *Corticium solani*. Some Rhizoctonia species are known to be serious parasites, living in the soil and attacking a great variety of plants, including lettuce, potato, carrot, seakale, tomato, cabbage, &c., usually attacking them when young. Examples are Potato Black Speck and Collar Rot disease and various damping-off diseases in seedling plants. In general the Rhizoctonias are difficult fungi to eradicate and where a species forms sclerotia there may be need to sterilize the soil.

D. E. G.

RHIZOGLYPH'US echino'pus. *See* **Bulb Mite.**

RHIZOID. A root-like filament, such as attaches a moss to the soil.

RHIZOME. Creeping underground stem, thick and swollen, rooting, and sending up successively from the apex leafy shoots or flowering stems.

RHIZOMORPH. In certain fungi the vegetative threads become aggregated into long firm cord-like strands varying from slender threads to good-sized strings which may branch to form a network. These strands are called rhizomorphs and may be whitish, dark brown, or even black, but their purpose is to enable the fungus to grow considerable distances through the soil in search of nourishment. In this way a parasitic fungus on tree roots may spread out to infect adjacent trees. A good example is the Honey Fungus which forms conspicuous black cord-like strands which has led to many other names such as Bootlace fungus, Shoestring fungus, &c., being applied to it. Before the fruiting sporophores of the Honey Fungus (*Armillaria mellea*) had been identified as connected with its rhizomorphs the latter were referred to by the separate title of *Rhizomorpha subterranea.*

D. E. G.

RHIZOMORPH'A. *See* **Rhizomorph.**

rhizomorphous, having the appearance of a root.

RHIZOPHORE. The downward-growing structure of Selaginella which roots at its tip.

rhizophyl'lus -a -um, root-leaved.

RHIZO'PUS. A genus of fungi in the class Phycomycetes. The resting spores of the genus are the result of fusion of 2 very similar cells, so are called zygospores. There are several species which grow on fruits in store or preserved foods, &c., causing a mould. The most common is *Rhizopus nigricans* with its very small black spherical sporangia produced on aerial stalks. Another species, *R. necans*, causes rotting of stored lily bulbs if the storage conditions are unsuitable.

D. E. G.

RHODAM'NIA (*rhodamnus*, a small branch: from the size of the plants). FAM. *Myrtaceae.* A genus of about 12 species of shrubs or small trees, natives of Trop. Asia and Australia. Leaves opposite, ovate to lanceolate, 3-nerved, not pinnately veined as in Rhodomyrtus, often hoary or downy beneath. Flowers often small: calyx tube ovoid, or nearly globose: limb of 4 persistent lobes: petals 4, spreading: pedicels short, clustered in axils or loosely racemose, bracteoles small, caducous. Fruit a globular berry. For treatment *see* **Myrtus.**

R. argen'tea. Shrub with close silvery-white hairs on young shoots, infl. and under surface of l. *l.* ovate-oblong, rather blunt, 3-veined. *fl.* white; pet. about $\frac{1}{8}$ in. long. Australia.

R. trinerv'ia. Tall shrub or small tree, young shoots velvety-hairy. *l.* ovate-oblong or ovate-lanceolate, slender-pointed, glabrous, net-veined above, prominently 3-veined from base, beneath and velvety-hairy there. *fl.* white in axillary clusters of 3 or on a short, common peduncle. India, Australia. 1823. (B.M. 3223 as *Eugenia trinervia.*) Greenhouse.

RHODAN'THE. Included in **Helipterum.** *See* **H. Manglesii.**

RHODES WOOD. *See* **Amyris balsamifera.**

RHODIOLA. Included in **Sedum.**

RHODI'TES ro'sae. *See* **Bedeguar Galls.** A

rhodo-, in compound words, signifying red.

RHODOCHI'TON (*rhodo*, red, *chiton*, cloak: in allusion to the large, coloured calyx). FAM. *Scrophulariaceae.* A genus of 1 species of herb with the leaf-stalks and peduncles twisting to assist climbing, related to Maurandia. For treatment of this greenhouse plant *see* **Maurandia.**

R. atrosangui'neum. Climber to about 10 ft. *l.* alternate, cordate, slender-pointed, with a few acute teeth, sparsely glandular-downy. *fl.* dark blood-red, rather large with 5 erecto-patent lobes; cal. pale reddish, large, broadly bell-shaped, 5-toothed. June. Mexico. (B.M. 3367; B.R. 1755.) SYN. *R. volubile.*

R. volu'bile. A synonym of *R. atrosanguineum.*

rhodochlo'rus -a -um, reddish coloured.

RHODOCIS'TUS Berthelotia'nus. A synonym of *Cistus candidissimus.*

Rhodochiton atrosanguineum (p. 1759)

RHODODEN'DRON (Of Greek origin from *rhodon*, rose, and *dendron*, tree). FAM. *Ericaceae.* This genus, which now includes Azalea and Rhodora—kept distinct in earlier times—is a very large one. The number of wild species attributed to it varies very much in accordance with the views of the chief authorities as to the degree of distinction that constitutes a species, but even a conservative estimate will allow over 500 of them. The greatest aggregation occurs in a vast area including adjoining parts of W. and Central China, SW. Tibet, NW. India, and NE. Burma. Japan and N. America have comparatively few 'true' rhododendrons but contribute many charming Azaleas. Europe has very few species, Africa and S. America none. A few warm greenhouse species have been introduced from Java and the Malay Islands, one from Australia, and a number, not yet seen in gardens, exist on the mountains of New Guinea and the Philippine Is.

The leading characters of the genus are: shrubs or trees; leaves alternate, simple, entire; flowers in clusters mostly terminal but sometimes axillary, sometimes solitary; corolla generally bell- or funnel-shaped, sometimes saucer-shaped or tubular, mostly 5-lobed but varying also from 6- to 10-lobed; calyx usually with the same number of lobes as the corolla, but frequently almost obsolete; stamens mostly 5 or 10 but generally twice the number of the corolla lobes; seed-vessel hard, woody, splitting lengthwise to release the numerous minute seeds. The genus may be divided into 2 great sections by the existence or non-existence of scales on the various parts. They are termed respectively 'lepidote' or 'elepidote' and members of one section have only once hybridized with the other.

The chief authority for the dates of the introduction of the earlier cultivated exotic plants is Aiton's *Hortus Kewensis*, the last edition of which (in the form of an epitome) was published in 1814. According to this work the first rhododendron introduced to Britain was *R. hirsutum*, in 1656. Why it should have come nearly 100 years earlier than *R. ferrugineum* (1752), its much more abundant neighbour on the Alps, is difficult to understand. In the first decade of the 19th century the total number of species (including Azaleas) in cultivation was 15. An important acquisition from N. India in 1815 was *R. arboreum*, but the first great impulse to the cultivation of this genus came in 1849–51, when Joseph D. Hooker explored the Himalaya. Previous to that, the varieties and hybrids of the American Azaleas, and of *R. catawbiense*, *R. maximum*, *R. caucasicum*, and *R. ponticum* constituted the chief representation of the genus in gardens. Hooker's introductions provided an entirely new conception of Rhododendron, especially by reason of such species as *R. Griffithianum*, *R. Falconeri*, *R. grande*, &c.: but owing to their tenderness this was manifested chiefly in Cornwall and similar climates. **A**

The use of *R. arboreum* by hybridizers and the production thereby of *R.* × *Nobleanum*, *R.* × *Russellianum*, &c., introduced the first red-flowered varieties to gardens, and it still remains the chief source of that colour in the very hardy garden hybrids of the 'Doncaster' and 'Michael Waterer' types. Amongst Hooker's introductions were 4 excellent red-flowered species, viz. *barbatum*, *fulgens*, *Hookeri*, and *Thomsonii*.

Subsequent to Hooker's labours, the chief new Rhododendrons of the 19th century came intermittently and in small numbers. An interesting one was *R. Fortunei* from E. China, for long the only species from that great country, soon found on its western side to be by far the richest Rhododendron area on the globe.

The first revelation of the wealth of Rhododendrons hidden away in the mountains of this region came through the French missionaries stationed there. Notable amongst them were David, Delavay, and Farges. They sent home much botanical material in the way of dried specimens but very little seed, although some arrived in Paris as early as 1889. The first genuine attempt to tap the riches of the flora of Western and Central China was made in 1899–1900 by Messrs. Veitch of Chelsea, when they sent out E. H. Wilson. From that time onwards until 1939 and from 1946 onwards, a band of collectors, prominent amongst whom, besides Wilson himself, were Forrest, Kingdon-Ward, Farrer, Rock, Ludlow, Sherriff, and Taylor, introduced to Britain a continuous stream of new species they had discovered, thereby widening our conception of the genus to an astonishing degree.

At the present time Rhododendron is one of the most important and popular genera in horticulture, although its garden value is greatly limited by the inability of practically all its species to thrive on a chalky or limy soil. *R. hirsutum*, well known on the European Alps, succeeds in limy areas and collectors in SW. China have found large quantities there on limestone, but always overlaid with a layer of peat. The flowering season of the genus in the open air extends over eight months, beginning with *R. mucronulatum* in January and ending with *R. auriculatum*, *Kyawi*, and *viscosum* in August, but its maximum period is from mid-April to mid-June. Much of the value of Rhododendrons, apart from their blossom, is due to their evergreen character, many of the species, but more especially the garden hybrids, making shapely bushes densely clad with dark green foliage, and excellent for shelter or screening. The young growth of many species is also most decorative, being in species such as *R. concatenans* a brilliant glaucous colour, and in others such as *R. Bureavii* or *R. coriaceum* covered in rufous or silvery-white indumentum.

Rhododendrons can be grown on most lime-free or 'acid' soils except those of a dry, arid nature, or heavy and clayey. Peaty soil is generally considered most suitable, but a sweet, well-drained, sandy loam, 1½ to 2 ft. deep, is almost if not quite as good. Even heavy soils, by generous additions of decayed leaves and other lightening material, may be made available for the more vigorous hybrids and species. The two chief adverse conditions are dryness at the root and too much sunshine. They are ill-adapted for growing in places where there is competition with the roots of hungry trees like elm, lime, beech, sycamore, &c. In such places it may be necessary to keep the tree roots at bay by cutting a trench occasionally between them and the Rhododendrons. Top-dressings of straw-manure, leaves, or bracken are helpful, especially in dry seasons. In places where these aids are not available, nor artificial watering possible, it is a good plan to select those kinds which 'feather' themselves with their own foliage down to the ground, thereby keeping it shaded and decreasing evaporation.

The best tree to associate with and give shade to rhododendrons is common oak, which roots deeply enough to avoid competition with them. The best of all situations is oak woodland, not thickly or densely planted, but sufficiently so to give light shadows. This applies more especially to species and hybrids with large leaves like those belonging to the *Falconeri*, *grande*, *auriculatum*, and *Fortunei* series. There is, nevertheless, a very large selection of kinds that will succeed in full sunlight. All the common hybrids of the 'Waterer' type are usually grown in nurseries and are happy enough in open fields like other shrubs, and most of the smaller-leaved, smaller-flowered types such as belong to the *lapponicum* series tolerate sunshine quite well. But with all these and even with Azaleas and other deciduous species (which of course are best fitted for sunny places) a light shade cast over the plants during the hot hours of the day will help to prevent wilting of the blossom and lengthen its duration.

Where time and labour are available it is very desirable, as soon as the flowers have faded, that the trusses should be picked off, thereby preventing the production of seed and concentrating the energies of the plant on the new growths and, concurrently, on the following season's crop of blossom.

Few shrubs, especially evergreen ones, are more easily or safely transplanted than Rhododendrons. Their root system is usually so close to the stem and so dense that it can be removed nearly or quite entire. Thus, none of the problems as regards the time of year that are encountered in transplanting evergreens with more or less naked roots like hollies, barberries, &c., arise with Rhododendrons. They can be removed during open weather at any time from October to mid-April. Two matters have to be borne in mind; the new soil round the 'balls' should be made very firm, and the danger of too deep planting must be avoided. Plants with a single clean stem not uncommonly decay at the collar if it is condemned to perpetual darkness and dampness by being buried several inches deep. As these deaths may occur several years after the transplanting, without the cause being apparent, they are often regarded as mysterious. A generous watering after planting is useful in settling the soil firmly about the 'ball'.

The four chief methods of propagation, viz. seed-sowing, grafting, layering, and by cuttings, are all available for Rhododendrons. All the large-leaved types should be raised either by seeds or by layering. For garden hybrids of the common hardy evergreen type, grafting is most commonly adopted, using *R. ponticum* as a stock, just as stocks of *R. luteum* are used for the hardy deciduous azaleas. This method is often absolutely necessary so that batches of a new hybrid or variety may become available within a reasonable (and remunerative) period. But for established kinds the use of layering is becoming more general and plants so raised are worth the larger price usually required for them, because the nuisance of suckers springing from the stock is eliminated.

Seeds should be sown in well-drained pots or pans of very sandy, peaty soil. They are very small and should be sown thinly and only partially covered with a sprinkling of silver sand. They are best in a slightly heated house or frame and need careful watering with a very fine rose to avoid 'washing'. It is useful to cover the pot with a sheet of glass to reduce evaporation until germination occurs. As soon as the seedlings are large enough to handle they should be 'pricked off'—say, 1½ to 2 in. apart—in shallow boxes of soil similar to, but not quite so sandy as, that used for the seeds. When large enough they can go to the nursery border where a suitable soil, properly fined down, has been prepared for them.

Layering is only convenient when there are branches low enough for them to be bent down sufficiently to bury part of the stem with 2 or 3 in. of soil. They must be held quite securely in place with a hooked peg firmly set in the ground: and the terminal part, if long enough, can be secured to a short stake. Roots will usually come more quickly if the buried piece of stem has a slit or tongue cut in it, but it is not always possible to do this without breaking when the branches are thick and stiff.

The larger-leafed rhododendrons and most of the elepidote species are so difficult to raise from cuttings that the operation is not of much practical use, but the smaller-leafed ones such as belong to the lapponicum, triflorum, and other lepidote series are usually quite easily raised in this way. They are usually taken in a half-ripe state and set in very sandy, peaty soil in a close, moderately warm house. If room in a propagator's frame can be found for them, so much the better. A

For lists of recommended hybrids see Supplement.

GREENHOUSE RHODODENDRONS may be divided into 3 sections. The first is represented by the large-growing evergreen species, such as *R. stamineum*, *R. Nuttallii*, *R. Kyawi*, *R. eriogynum*, *R. Griffithianum*, &c. They are mostly natives of the Himalaya, and although hardy in the more favoured parts of the country, in less favoured parts they require the shelter of a cold greenhouse. With them must be included some of the newer introductions from China, the flower-buds and young growths of which are apt to be injured by spring frosts, even if they are otherwise winter-hardy. Many of them are too large for the ordinary greenhouse, and are only seen at their best when they can be planted out in large houses.

The second section is also with few exceptions evergreen, but being of much more moderate growth, they are better suited for small or moderate-sized houses. The older and better-known species are mostly native of the Himalaya. Newer introductions from China and Burma include *R. bullatum*, *R. burmanicum*, and *R. Taggianum*. The older species include *R. ciliatum*, *R. ciliicalyx*, *R. Dalhousiae*, *R. Edgworthii*, *R. formosum*, *R. Johnstoneanum*, *R. Lindleyi*, *R. Oldhamii*, recently reintroduced from Formosa, *R. obtusum*, the 'Kurume Azalea', which include many beautiful varieties ideal for growing in small pots, and *R. Simsii*, 'Indian Azalea', which includes numerous single- and double-flowered varieties. In this section there are many beautiful hybrids, mostly between *R. Dalhousiae*, *R. Edgworthii*, *R. formosum*, *R. Nuttallii*, and *R. Veitchianum*, many of them, especially the Edgeworthii hybrids, being very fragrant. They include 'Forsterianum', 'Fragrantissimum', 'Sesterianum', 'Victorianum', Countess of Haddington, Countess of Sefton, Lady Alice Fitzwilliam, Princess Alice, &c. All are suitable for growing in pots or tubs, or planted out in well-drained beds or borders in a cold house from which frost can be excluded.

Some of the species are at times more or less epiphytic in nature, and they require a very freely drained compost.

The third section known as the Javanese or Malayan Rhododendrons are natives of Java, Sumatra, Borneo, Penang, and Malacca. They are all evergreen and include a few species and many garden hybrids and varieties, all derived from the epiphytic *R. Brookeanum*, *R. jasminiflorum*, *R. javanicum*, *R. Lobbii*, *R. Malayanum*, *R. multicolor*, and *R. Teysmannii*. The original species were first introduced by Messrs. James Veitch & Sons, late of Chelsea, who grew them so successfully, and raised many beautiful hybrids and varieties, ranging in colour through many varying shades from white, pink, rose, yellow, orange, crimson, and scarlet. With a good collection they may be had in flower practically every week throughout the year, for during 1897 Messrs. J. Veitch cut flowers of them at every fortnightly meeting held by the Royal Horticultural Society. They have never been generally cultivated from a mistaken idea that they were difficult. Cultivators generally failed to realize that the original species are more or less epiphytic on trees and rocks, thus even the garden forms require a very free and open compost, with a restricted root-run. They require a warm greenhouse for their successful cultivation, although the hybrids succeed during the summer in a cool greenhouse. They are ideal for growing in small pots. Planted out, some of them make large specimens, and are somewhat straggling in habit, but by judicious pruning and tying in the shoots they can be kept well furnished.

Plants of the first section, whether planted out or grown in tubs, succeed in a compost consisting of 3 parts medium lime-free loam to 1 of brown fibrous peat, with enough clean coarse sand to keep the whole open and porous, ample drainage and firm potting being essential. The species may be raised from seed, but generally both they and the many hybrids are increased by grafting or layering.

Plants of the second section generally benefit by a larger proportion of peat, most of them succeed in equal proportions of brown fibrous peat and a medium lime-free loam, with enough clean coarse sand to ensure free drainage, but much depends on the class of loam used; with heavy loam it may be advisable to use a larger proportion of peat. Many in this section are readily propagated by ripened shoots of the current year's growth, all the obtusum varieties rooting very readily in a compost of sandy peat, in a close case with slight bottom heat, as also do many of the Indian Azaleas, although it is the practice in the trade to graft them on to stocks of a strong-growing variety.

Plants of the third section require a very free root run, and succeed best in a mixture of brown fibrous peat, broken charcoal, and sand, with just a dusting of light loam; potting should not be so firm as in the other sections. They should be repotted every year, rubbing down the 'balls' to get them into the same-sized, or slightly larger, pots as the plants increase in size. They can also be successfully grown planted out in a shallow well-drained bed, using a compost similar to that recommended for pots, a little decayed leaf-soil collected under oak or beech trees, where it has decayed naturally, may with advantage be added to the compost, while pieces of sandstone partially buried or laid on the surface help to conserve moisture, thus doing away with the need of too frequent watering: usually such a bed requires fresh compost every second or third year. Grown in this way some of the varieties soon make large specimens. They are readily propagated by short ripened shoots of the current year's wood, inserting the cuttings in sandy peat in a warm propagating case.

Greenhouse Rhododendrons are worthy of more general cultivation, for generally they require only enough heat to exclude frost, and there are few other greenhouse plants so free from insect pests and diseases. (J. C.)

DISEASES. Rhododendrons may be attacked by Crown Gall (q.v.), and the roots are frequently affected by *Armillaria mellea*, the Honey fungus (q.v.). The leaves may show one or two leaf spots, notably that caused by the fungus *Pestalozia rhododendri* which causes brown spots that later have greyish-white areas in the centre, and *Lophodermium rhododendri* in which the spots are large and silvery-white with raised reddish margins, but neither should be very serious and can be controlled by removing the affected leaves. A rare rust of Rhododendrons is caused by *Chrysomyxa rhododendri*, which forms yellow and brown spots on the under surface of the leaves (uredospores and teleutospores) and its aecidial stage on the needles of the spruce, *Picea Abies*. Rhododendron seedlings may suffer from damping off (q.v.), but the most common disease is that known as Gall, which affects many kinds of small-leaved Rhododendrons (especially those grown under glass). The parasite responsible for the galls which occur on the leaves, shoots, and flowers is *Exobasidium vaccinii*, and all such galls should be removed before they turn white, which is when the fungus is releasing its spores. Spraying with Bordeaux mixture would increase the protection. 'Bud Blast' has become a serious disease of Rhododendrons, especially in the south of England since 1948. The scales of infected buds begin to turn brown in September and later the whole bud may turn a silvery-grey colour and be covered with small black hair-like stalks about 1 mm. long and bearing at their tips a knob. These are the fruiting bodies (Coremia) of the fungus *Sporocybe Azaleae*. Infected buds at this stage often look black in colour. Work is proceeding on the control of this disease; in the meantime, it is recommended that all infected buds be picked off and burnt and diseased shoots pruned back for 2 in. Buds damaged by bud blast are superficially similar to those damaged by frost, but they remain firm while those damaged by frost can be easily broken off. Reference should be made to the Supplement, where the latest results will be published, if available before the Supplement is printed. (D. E. G.)

PESTS. AZALEA LEAF MINER (*Gracilaria azaleella*) was first recorded in England in 1926, and has now become an important pest of Azaleas in forcing-houses, having been introduced from Belgium and Holland and originally from the Far East. The small active moths measure about ½ in. across the wings, and fly about in glass-houses where infested plants are grown. The female lays her eggs singly on the underside of the leaves, and the young caterpillars pierce the epidermis and tunnel into the tissues, causing the foliage to become yellow and, later, to turn brown, shrivel and fall. The larvae move from leaf to leaf until they are full fed, when they travel to uninjured leaves and there construct cocoons within the folded leaf edges. The damage is more evident from November to March on plants brought into glass-houses for forcing. Owing to overlapping generations control is possible only when spraying or fumigating is continued throughout the season. Handcrushing the caterpillars within the mined and folded leaf-tips is possible in small outbreaks; severe attacks are controlled by spraying the foliage with D.D.T. wash or by fumigating with Tetrachlorethane at the rate of ¼ pint to 1,000 cubic ft. of space with an exposure of 12 hours.

RHODODENDRON BUG (*Stephanitis rhododendri*) is a native of the north-eastern States of America, it was introduced into Europe prior to 1900 and into England about 1910. It is now widely distributed in England, especially in the south. This sucking pest causes the leaves to become 'rusty', the upper surface being marbled or mottled, the lower having rusty or chocolate spots scattered over the surface. This bug is more partial to some species and hybrids than others and, whereas *R. ponticum* is not a favoured host, *R. catawbiense*, *R. fastuosum fl. pl.*, and others are frequently attacked. The adult bug is a sun-lover and prefers the southern and western sides of a bush, and plants grown in dense shade are seldom infested. It is about $\frac{1}{8}$ in. long, oval, with a shiny black body, which is covered by the lace-like wings. The eggs are laid in summer and autumn, being inserted within the tissues alongside the midribs on the lower leaf surface. The young bugs are minute, spiny, black and grey, wingless insects, which feed in colonies on the underside of the leaves from mid-May. As they grow, the wing-buds appear and, when mature, they are fully winged. The insect in all stages is rather sluggish, and the adults are seldom seen in flight. It is distributed from one district to another on infested plants.

Light attacks on small bushes can be controlled by handpicking and burning the leaves upon which the colonies of young bugs are to be seen in May and June, or by hand-crushing the colonies. Spraying with Nicotine and Soap, Derris, or Pyrethrum extract will be found effective provided the wash is directed to the underside of the leaves so that the insects are thoroughly wetted by the insecticide, and provided the spraying is carried out in late May and in June when the immature bugs are present. Dusting infested bushes with Nicotine dust is an efficient method of controlling infestations in closely grown plants. Heavily infested banks of Rhododendrons should be drastically pruned back in March and the prunings burned to destroy the eggs which are laid chiefly in the younger leaves.

RHODODENDRON WHITE FLY (*Dialeurodes chittendeni*) is a pest of certain species and of hybrid Rhododendrons in the south of England, and may occur elsewhere if introduced on plants from infested districts. The signs of attack resemble somewhat those produced by the Rhododendron Bug (q.v.), but there is no chocolate-spotting or rusty appearance on the lower leaf surface. The small, white, mealy-winged adults swarm on the underside of the topmost leaves of the shoots from mid-June to mid-July, and are easily disturbed when the bush is shaken though they quickly resettle on the foliage. The female lays a number of eggs which are scattered over the lower surface. The freshly emerged nymphs or 'scales' wander about for a time seeking for a spot on which to settle down to a sedentary existence. Quantities of honeydew are excreted by the nymphs, and this falls on to the upper surface of the lower leaves and provides a medium for the growth of Sooty Moulds. The larvae feed on the underside of the leaves from August to the following April, when pupation takes place, and the adults emerge from the flattened, whitish pupa-cases in June. Some species of Rhododendron are more susceptible to attack than others, and *R. catawbiense*, *R. caucasicum*, and *R. ponticum*, as well as their hybrids, are favoured hosts.

The foliage of all smooth-leaved species and hybrids, particularly those received from an infested district, should be examined before planting for the presence of eggs and 'scales'. Remove and burn all infested leaves, allowing the older leaves upon which only empty pupa-cases will be found to remain. The underside of infested leaves should be thoroughly and forcibly sprayed in early September and in late March with a Nicotine and White Oil emulsion (*see* **Insecticides**). The adult White Flies are readily killed by dusting the topmost leaves in mid-summer, when they are seen on the foliage, with a Nicotine dust. **A**

(G. F. W.)

In order to facilitate the study of the vast group of plants constituting the genus Rhododendron, and to make them more intelligible to the horticulturist, Prof. Bailey Balfour and Dr. Hutchinson and those working with them, especially upon the numerous Chinese and Himalayan species, proposed to arrange the species in 'Series', each of the series to contain those species which from their form and geographical range appeared to be most nearly related. The series containing species described in this Dictionary are set out below. A fuller account of them is contained in *The Species of Rhododendron* and modifications which, from time to time as fuller knowledge is acquired, appear desirable are published in the Royal Horticultural Society's Rhododendron Year-books and the *Rhododendron Handbook* which is revised quinquennially. The number given in brackets following each specific name below refers to the Series in which it has been placed in this classification. **A**

1. ALBIFLORUM Series. A single deciduous elepidote shrub, its flowers scattered along the shoots singly or in pairs.

albiflorum.

2. ANTHOPOGON Series. Small lepidote shrubs; corolla slender-tubed; style very short, thick, and glabrous; calyx usually large; stamens 5 to 10. *See* Series 13. CEPHALANTHUM.

anthopogon, cephalanthum, hypenanthum, kongboense, primulaeflorum, Sargentianum, trichostomum.

3. ARBOREUM Series. Mostly trees, elepidote; flowers numerous, densely packed in rounded trusses; stamens not less than 10, but sometimes 12 or 14.

(*a*) Arboreum subseries:
arboreum, Campbelliae, cinnamomeum, Delavayi, Kingianum, niveum, zeylanicum.

(*b*) Argyrophyllum subseries:
argyrophyllum, floribundum, Hunnewellianum, hypoglaucum, insigne, Ririei, Thayerianum.

4. AURICULATUM Series. Two species of elepidote shrubs marked by their long, slender-pointed leaf-buds and flower-buds beset with long narrow scales.

auriculatum, Griersonianum.

5. AZALEA Series. Elepidote shrubs, a large portion of which are deciduous; stamens usually 5, but occasionally 10; calyx usually small.

(*a*) Canadense subseries:
Albrechtii, canadense, Vaseyi.

(*b*) Luteum subseries:
arborescens, calendulaceum, japonicum, luteum, molle, nudiflorum, occidentale, prunifolium, speciosum, viscosum.

(*c*) Nipponicum subseries:
nipponicum.

(*d*) Obtusum subseries:
indicum, linearifolium, mucronatum, obtusum, Oldhamii, scabrum, serpyllifolium, Simsii, yedoense.

(*e*) Schlippenbachii subseries:
quinquefolium, reticulatum, Schlippenbachii, Weyrichii.

6. BARBATUM Series. Elepidote trees and shrubs, mostly bristly or glandular-hairy to a greater or lesser degree on shoot and leaf.

(*a*) Barbatum subseries:
barbatum, Smithii.

(*b*) Crinigerum subseries:
Bainbridgeanum, crinigerum.

(*c*) Glischrum subseries:
diphrocalyx, glischroides, glischrum, habrotrichum.

(*d*) Maculiferum subseries:
longesquamatum, maculiferum, monosematum, pachytrichum, strigillosum.

7. BOOTHII Series. Small lepidote shrubs, occasionally epiphytic; calyx lobes usually large; corolla mostly yellow; stamens 10, hairy; style short, often curved.

Boothii, leucaspis, megeratum, mishmiense, sulfureum, tephropeplum, xanthostephanum.

8. CAMELLIAEFLORUM Series. Lepidote shrub; calyx well developed; stamens 12 to 16.

camelliaeflorum.

9. CAMPANULATUM Series. Elepidote shrubs or small trees; leaves usually rounded at one or both ends, woolly beneath; ovary glabrous.

campanulatum, fulgens lanatum, Sherriffii, Wallichii.

10. CAMPYLOGYNUM Series. Small lepidote shrubs; leaves small, thick; flowers mostly solitary, purple, long-stalked, less than 1 in. wide; style short, thick, glabrous.
campylogynum, myrtilloides.

11. CAMTSCHATICUM Series. Differs from all other series in producing its flowers on the leafy young shoots; deciduous.
camtschaticum.

12. CAROLINIANUM Series. Small lepidote shrubs; calyx small, ciliate; stamens 10, downy; ovary scaly; style glabrous.
carolinianum, minus.

13. CEPHALANTHUM Series. Small lepidote shrubs; calyx well developed; stamens 5, very short and included in the corolla-tube; style very short and thick.
Now combined with Series 2. ANTHOPOGON.
primulaeflorum.

14. CINNABARINUM Series. Lepidote shrubs; leaves more or less glaucous; calyx small; corolla tubular-cylindric with erect or sub-erect lobes; stamens 10; style downy.
cinnabarinum, concatenans, Keysii.

15. DAURICUM Series. Deciduous or semi-evergreen lepidote shrubs; flowers solitary or in pairs from each of several terminal buds; winter flowering.
dauricum, mucronulatum.

16. EDGEWORTHII Series. Lepidote, mostly epiphytic shrubs; calyx large; corolla funnel-shaped, fleshy; stamens 10; style long and stout; leaves woolly as well as scaly beneath—an unusual combination.
bullatum, Edgeworthii.

17. FALCONERI Series. Elepidote trees or shrubs; leaves large, tomentose; calyx small, corolla 7- to 10-lobed; stamens 12 to 18; flowers mostly 20 to 30 in the truss.
arizelum, basilicum, coriaceum, eximium, Falconeri, fictolacteum, galactinum, Hodgsonii.

18. FERRUGINEUM Series. Lepidote alpine shrubs 2 to 4 ft. high; flowers ½ to ¾ in. wide, crowded in small trusses; stamens 10.
ferrugineum, hirsutum, Kotschyi.

19. FORTUNEI Series. Elepidote shrubs mostly of large size; foliage glabrous or soon becoming so; corolla large, funnel- or bell-shaped, occasionally 5-lobed, but mostly 6- or 7-lobed, white, pink, or rose, never red or yellow; stamens 12 to 25, rarely 10.
(*a*) Calophytum subseries:
calophytum.
(*b*) Davidi subseries:
praevernum, sutchuenense.
(*c*) Fortunei subseries:
decorum, diaprepes, discolor, Fortunei, serotinum, vernicosum.
(*d*) Griffithianum subseries:
Griffithianum.
(*e*) Orbiculare subseries:
orbiculare.
(*f*) Oreodoxa subseries:
Fargesii, oreodoxa.

20. FULVUM Series. Elepidote shrubs or small trees with long narrow leaves broadest on the terminal half and felted beneath; flowers with long thin stalks in loose trusses; ovary glabrous.
fulvum, uvarifolium.

21. GLAUCUM Series. Lepidote shrubs, usually small or dwarf; leaves stout in texture, often glaucous beneath; calyx large, deeply 5-lobed; stamens 10; style short, thick, often recurved.
brachyanthum, charitopes, Genestierianum (calyx small), *glaucophyllum, pemakoense, tsangpoense.*

22. GRANDE Series. Elepidote trees with large leaves, akin to the Falconeri Series; calyx minute; corolla 7- to 10-lobed, usually bellied at the base; stamens 14 to 20; the indumentum is usually closer and more 'plastered' than in the Falconeri Series.
coryphaeum, giganteum, grande, Macabeanum, magnificum, praestans, protistum, sinogrande.

23. HELIOLEPIS Series. Lepidote shrubs or trees; calyx very small; corolla always scaly outside; stamens 10. Very close to the Triflorum Series, but more densely lepidote; inflorescence 3- to 6-flowered.
brevistylum, desquamatum, heliolepis, rubiginosum.

24. IRRORATUM Series. Elepidote shrubs; leaves finally glabrous, the margin cartilaginous; corolla nearly always tubular and 5-lobed; calyx very small or almost obsolete; stamens 10 to 14.
(*a*) Irroratum subseries:
Aberconwayi, anthosphaerum, araiophyllum, irroratum, laxiflorum, tanastylum.
(*b*) Parishii subseries:
agapetum, Elliottii, eriogynum, facetum, Kyawi, venator.

25. LACTEUM Series. Elepidote shrubs or small trees always with some type of indumentum on the leaf beneath; stamens 10, always downy at the base; with the exception of *lacteum* and *Wightii* which have yellow flowers, the colour is white or rose.
Beesianum, lacteum, Wightii.

26. LAPPONICUM Series. Dwarf, lepidote shrubs; leaves very small, densely scaly beneath; flower-stalks very short; calyx usually small; stamens 5 or 10.
chryseum, cuneatum, Edgarianum, fastigiatum, flavidum, hippophaeoides, impeditum, intricatum, orthocladum, rupicola, russatum, scintillans, setosum, telmateium, verruculosum.

27. LEPIDOTUM Series. Small lepidote shrubs; leaves usually wholly covered with scales beneath; calyx well developed; stamens 8 or 10, style short, thick, often bent, glabrous.
Baileyi, elaeagnoides, imperator, lepidotum, Ludlowii patulum.

28. MADDENII Series. Lepidote, often epiphytic shrubs of large or medium size; flowers usually 2 to 6 in a truss, large to very large; corolla mostly funnel-shaped and white but sometimes yellow; stamens 10 to 25; style nearly always scaly.
(*a*) Ciliicalyx subseries:
ciliatum, ciliicalyx, formosum, Johnstoneanum, taronense, Valentinianum, Veitchianum.
(*b*) Maddenii subseries:
crassum, Maddenii, manipurense.
(*c*) Megacalyx subseries:
Dalhousiae, Lindleyi, megacalyx, Nuttallii, rhabdotum, sinonuttallii, Taggianum.

29. MICRANTHUM Series. A single lepidote shrub, with white flowers ⅓ to ½ in. across, numerous in the truss; stamens 10, glabrous.
micranthum.

30. MOUPINENSE Series. Small lepidote shrubs; leaves leathery, ciliate; flowers solitary or in pairs, white or rosy; stamens 10.
moupinense.

31. NERIIFLORUM Series. Elepidote shrubs; flowers never congested in the truss; corolla almost invariably unspotted; ovary usually densely hairy and often glandular as well; stamens 10 or 12.
(*a*) Forrestii subseries:
Forrestii, repens.
(*b*) Haematodes subseries:
Beanianum, catacosmum, chaetomallum, haematodes, mallotum, pocophorum.

(*c*) Neriiflorum subseries:
euchaites, neriiflorum, sperabile, sperabiloides.
(*d*) Sanguineum subseries:
aperantum, apodectum, citriniflorum, dichroanthum, didymum, haemaleum, sanguineum.

32. OVATUM Series. Elepidote slender-twigged shrubs; flowers solitary, from axillary buds near the end of the shoot; stamens 5; ovary bristly.
Bachii, leptothrium, ovatum.

33. PONTICUM Series. Elepidote shrubs or small trees; main flower-stalk elongated, often making a racemose inflorescence; corolla deeply 5-lobed, the lobes almost equalling the tube in length; stamens 10 (14 in *Metternichii*).
(*a*) Caucasicum subseries:
adenopodum, brachycarpum, caucasicum, chrysanthum, Degronianum, Makinoi, Metternichii, Smirnowi, Ungernii, yakusimanum.
(*b*) Ponticum subseries:
californicum, catawbiense, maximum, ponticum.

34. SALUENENSE Series. Lepidote, low, often prostrate shrubs; leaves often ciliate; flowers solitary, in pairs or threes; calyx large, ciliate; corolla open and flat; stamens 10.
calostrotum, chameunum, keleticum, prostratum, radicans, saluenense.

35. SCABRIFOLIUM Series. Lepidote, slender-twigged shrubs; flowers springing from axillary buds; calyx well developed; corolla tubular; stamens 10.
hemitrichotum, mollicomum, pubescens, scabrifolium, spinuliferum.

36. STAMINEUM Series. Elepidote shrubs or trees; inflorescence axillary, 1- to 3-flowered; calyx obsolete; stamens 10; style glabrous.
oxyphyllum, stamineum, stenaulum, Wilsonae.

37. TALIENSE Series. Elepidote shrubs mostly between 3 ft. and 10 ft. high; all but a few characterized by a woolly or felted covering beneath the leaf; stamens 10, downy at the lower part; floral rachis short.
(*a*) Adenogynum subseries:
Bureavii.
(*b*) Roxieanum subseries:
proteoides, Roxieanum.
(*c*) Taliense subseries:
Clementinae.
(*d*) Wasonii subseries:
Wasonii, Wiltonii.

38. THOMSONII Series. Elepidote shrubs; leaf broad as compared with its length, usually glabrous, often glaucous; inflorescence loose, often few-flowered; often glandular on the flower-stalk, ovary, and style; stamens 10.
(*a*) Campylocarpum subseries:
callimorphum, caloxanthum, campylocarpum, cyclium, myiagrum, telopeum.
(*b*) Martinianum subseries:
Martinianum.
(*c*) Selense subseries:
selense.
(*d*) Souliei subseries:
astrocalyx, croceum, litiense, puralbum, Souliei, Wardii, Williamsianum.
(*e*) Thomsonii subseries:
cerasinum, cyanocarpum, eclecteum, Hookeri, Meddianum, Stewartianum, Thomsonii.

39. TRICHOCLADUM Series. Lepidote shrubs, mostly deciduous or nearly so; inflorescence 2- to 4-flowered, yellow; style usually glabrous, often sharply bent; stamens 10.
chloranthum, melinanthum, rubrolineatum, trichocladum, viridescens.

40. TRIFLORUM Series. Evergreen, rarely deciduous, lepidote, slender-twigged shrubs; flowers usually 3 or 4, sometimes 6 to 8 in a loose truss; calyx quite small, corolla usually spotted; stamens 10; style glabrous.
(*a*) Augustinii subseries:
Augustinii, chasmanthoides, chasmanthum, villosum.
(*b*) Oreotrephes subseries:
artosquameum, bracteatum, exquisitum, Hanceanum, oreotrephes, timeteum.
(*c*) Polylepis subseries:
concinnum, pseudoyanthinum.
(*d*) Triflorum subseries:
ambiguum, Keiskei, lutescens, triflorum, xanthocodon.
(*e*) Yunnanense subseries:
caeruleum, Davidsonianum, Searsiae, yunnanense zaleucum.

41. VIRGATUM Series. Lepidote shrubs producing their flowers from several or many axillary buds; stamens 10, hairy at the base; ovary densely scaly.
oleifolium, racemosum, virgatum.

The few Malayan species included in the following notes have not yet been serialized. They come from Java, Borneo, and other Malay islands, and require warm greenhouse conditions. They will not hybridize with any other group. See Introduction.

In the following descriptive list each name is followed by a capital letter from A to F—which denotes approximately the degree of hardiness of the species concerned. This is the same plan as is adopted in the *Rhododendron Handbook* of the R.H.S. The asterisk, as elsewhere, marks species of exceptional beauty or interest.

A. Hardy anywhere (at ordinary altitudes) in the British Isles.
B. Hardy anywhere in the British Isles but requires some shelter to obtain the best results.
C. Hardy along the seaboard and in warm gardens inland.
D. Hardy in the south and west but needs shelter even in warm gardens inland.
E. Requires shelter in the most favoured gardens.
F. A greenhouse plant.

R. Aberconwa'yi (24*a*). B. Evergreen shrub up to 4 ft. h. Young shoots glandular and minutely hairy. *l.* 2 to 3 in. long, 1 to 1½ in. wide, brittle, oblong-elliptic, apex acute, distinctly mucronate. *fl.* 6 to 12 in a racemose umbel, cor. flatly campanulate or even saucer-shaped, 1 to 1½ in. wide, white or white tinged pink, stamens 10, unequal. May. W. China, Yunnan. 1937. (Rh.Y.B. 1948, p. 42, fig. 17.) An unusual and beautiful species, distinct in its saucer-shaped flowers.

R. adenopo'dum (33*a*). B. Evergreen shrub 4 to 10 ft., young shoots felted. *l.* 4 to 8 in. long, 1 to 2 in. wide, pointed, dark green above, white-felted beneath. *fl.* 6 to 10 in a racemose cluster; cor. widely bell-shaped, 5-lobed, 2½ to 3 in. wide, pale rose; stamens 10, hairy at base; cal. ciliate. April. China. 1901. (G.C. 45 (1909), 291.) Distinguished by its glandular pedicels and ovary.

R. aerugino'sum (9). A. Nearly related to *R. campanulatum*, differing mainly in the young foliage, which is brilliant verdigris coloured and constitutes its chief beauty in spring. The shrub itself is more compact in habit with stiffer foliage. *fl.* lilac-rose to reddish-purple. April, May. Himalaya. 1849. (R.S.H. 22.) SYN. *R. campanulatum aeruginosum.*

R. agape'tum (24*b*). E. Very closely akin to *R. Kyawi*, differing by the pedicels only about ½ in. long, and style glandular at base only. June. Burma.

R. aiolosal'pinx. A synonym of *R. Stewartianum.*

R. albiflo'rum (1). C. Deciduous shrub, 5 to 6 ft., young shoots hairy. *l.* narrow-oval, 1 to 2½ in. long, with a few long hairs on both surfaces, or glabrous. *fl.* solitary or in pairs from axillary buds of the previous year's naked shoots; cor. white, ¾ in. wide, bell-shaped, 5-lobed, lobes erect; stamens 10, downy. June, July. Rocky Mts. (B.M. 3670.) A remarkably distinct species in its method of flowering; difficult to cultivate. SYN. *Azalea albiflora.*

R. Albrech'tii* (5*a*). B. Deciduous shrub, 3 to 5 ft. *l.* in fives a end of twigs, obovate, 2 to 4 in. long, thinly hairy above, grey-downy beneath. *fl.* in clusters of 3 to 5; cor. 1½ to 2 in. wide, with 5 rounded lobes, bright purplish-rose with green spots; stamens 10; ovary, pedicels, and the small cal. covered with pale glandular hairs; style glabrous. April, May. Japan. 1892. (B.M. 9207.) Distinguished from *R. Vaseyi* by its 10 stamens and deeper colour.

R. ambig'uum (40*d*). A. Evergreen shrub, 5 to 6 ft., young shoots scaly. *l.* ovate-lanceolate to oval, slender-pointed, 2 to 3 in. long, dark green, scaly (especially beneath). *fl.* in clusters of 3 to 6; cor. funnel-shaped, 5-lobed, 2 in. wide, yellow spotted with green; stamens 10, downy. April, May. China. 1904. (B.M. 8400.) One of the few sp. in its series with yellow fl. The best of the forms (which vary in merit) are quite attractive.

R. anthopo'gon (2). B. Evergreen strongly aromatic shrub, 2 ft. h., compact; young shoots brown, scurfy. *l.* oval or obovate, pointed, 1 to 1½ in. long, glossy green above, densely scaly beneath. *fl.* 4 to 6 in a compact cluster; cor. pink or whitish, ¾ in. wide, narrowly tubular at base, spreading into 5 rounded lobes; stamens 5 to 8, glabrous; ovary scaly; style glabrous, very short and thick. April. N. India, Tibet. (B.M. 3947.) *See also* **R. hypenanthum.**

R. anthosphae'rum (24*a*). C. Evergreen shrub or small tree, 20 to 30 ft. h. *l.* oblong-lanceolate, tapering to both ends, 3 to 6 in. long, 1 to 2 in. wide, finally glabrous. *fl.* in clusters of 6 to 12, 4 to 5 in. across; cor. bell-shaped, 5- to 7-lobed, 2 in. wide, rich rose-magenta deeping to crimson in throat with a dark crimson blotch at base; stamens 10 to 14; ovary and style glabrous. March. China. 1906. (B.M. 9083). Richly and distinctly coloured.

R. aperan'tum* (31*d*). B. Dwarf, spreading, evergreen shrub, 6 to 20 in. h., sometimes in nature 20 ft. across; young shoots with long-persisting l.-bud scales. *l.* oval-obovate, ¾ to 1¾ in. long, glaucous beneath. *fl.* in clusters of 3 to 6; cor. broadly funnel-shaped, 1½ to 1¾ in. long, very diverse in colouring, ranging from white to different shades of rose, orange-red, and yellow; stamens 10, glabrous, ovary hairy; style glabrous. May. Burma. 1925. (B.M. 9507.) Its low spreading habit and glabrous under surface distinguish it. A very slow-growing species which does not flower freely as a young plant.

R. apodec'tum* (31*d*). A. Evergreen shrub up to 4 ft. *l.* oval, 1½ to 3 in. long, dark green and smooth above, covered beneath with close, greyish, matted hairs. *fl.* in pairs, threes, or fours; cor. tubular bell-shaped, 1 to 1¾ in. long, 5-lobed, lobes erect, varying from orange to crimson and yellowish-scarlet; stamens 10; ovary clad with fasciate hairs; style glabrous; cal. cup-shaped, ⅓ to ½ in. long, 5-lobed, coloured like cor. June. China. 1912. (B.M. 9014.) Akin to *R. dichroanthum.*

R. araiophyl'lum* (24*a*). D. Evergreen shrub up to 16 ft. *l.* lanceolate, sharply and slenderly pointed, 3 to 5 in. long, ⅝ to 1¼ in. wide, firm, entirely glabrous. *fl.* in trusses of about 8; cor. open bell-shaped, 5-lobed, 1½ in. long, white often flushed rose or lavender, with a basal crimson blotch and crimson dots; stamens 10; ovary slightly downy; style smooth. May. China. 1913.

R. arbores'cens* (5*b*). A. Deciduous shrub, 8 to 18 ft. *l.* obovate, 1½ to 3½ in. long, ½ to 1 in. wide, bright green above, glaucous beneath, ciliate. *fl.* 3 to 6 in a cluster, fragrant; cor. 2 to 2½ in. wide, white or pinkish, funnel-shaped, 5-lobed; stamens 5, much protruded, downy at base, reddish-purple above; cal. with 5 linear, downy or bristly lobes. June, July. E. United States. 1818. (L.B.C. 1632 as *Azalea verticillata.*) Distinguished by the hay-like, persistent fragrance of its dried l. and its late fl.

R. arbor'eum* (3*a*). D. Evergreen tree, 20 to 40 ft. h. and wide. *l.* hard, oblong-lanceolate, 4 to 8 in. long, dark green and wrinkled above, silvery beneath. *fl.* up to 20 in compact rounded trusses 4 to 5 in. wide; cor. bell-shaped, 1½ to 2 in. across, 5-lobed, blood-red with 5 dark blotches at base; stamens 10, white, glabrous. March, April. Himalaya, Ceylon. 1815. (B.R. 890; S.B.F.G. 250.) This is the typical form, but there are several vars. or sub-sp.: var. **al'bum,** *l.* rusty brown beneath, *fl.* white. (B.M. 3290; B.R. 1684.); **Campbell'iae,** *l.* reddish beneath, *fl.* purplish-rose. (R.S.H. 6.); **cinnamo'meum.** C. *fl.* white or nearly so, spotted; *l.* cinnamon-coloured beneath. (B.R. 1982.); **limba'tum,** *l.* silvery beneath, *fl.* rosy-purple. (B.M. 5311.) The typical *R. arboreum,* discovered in 1796, first flowered at the Grange, Northington, near Alresford in 1825 and was the chief source of the red colouring of the early hybrids. The tree is at its best in Cornwall and similar mild climates. The silvery-leafed type is the tenderest form, **cinnamomeum** the hardiest. **A**

R. argen'teum. A synonym of *R. grande.*

R. argyrophyl'lum (3*b*). A. Evergreen shrub, 6 to 20 ft. *l.* oblong-lanceolate, tapered to both ends, 2½ to 5 in. long, dark bright green above, silvery beneath. *fl.* up to 15 in a loose truss; cor. bell-shaped, 1½ in. wide, white or flushed with rose, the 5 lobes shallow, spreading; stamens 10 to 14, shorter than cor., downy at base; ovary white with down; style glabrous. May. China, Tibet. 1904. var. **leian'drum** has glabrous stamens. (B.M. 8767.) Akin to *R. hypoglossum* which has glandular parts and fewer fl. in the truss. **A**

R. arize'lum* (17). C. Evergreen shrub or small tree, 10 to 20 ft., young shoots and under surface of l. velvety with cinnamon-brown felt. *l.* 5 to 9 in. long, 2 to 3½ in. wide, obovate, upper surface wrinkled as in *R. Falconeri. fl.* crowded 15 to 20 together in trusses 6 in. across; cor. bell-shaped, 1½ to 2 in. wide, 8-lobed, white, creamy-yellow or yellow tinged with rose and with a crimson blotch at base; stamens 16; ovary not glandular but very downy. April. China, Burma, Tibet. 1917. Closely akin to *R. Falconeri* which is a bigger tree with larger l. and a glandular ovary. **A**

R. artosqua'meum (40*b*). B. Evergreen shrub, 3 to 6 ft., closely related to *R. oreotrephes* but with more rounded cordate l. and rose fl. without spots, cor. not scaly outside. *fl.* in clusters of 3 to 5, each 2 in. wide. May. Tibet. 1917.

R. astroca'lyx (38*d*). C. Evergreen shrub, 4 to 5 ft., closely akin to *R. Wardii* and with similar bowl-shaped fl., yellow but smaller. *l.* also smaller, up to 2½ in. long, and scarcely cordate at base. Cal. distinct by its 5 narrow lobes, spreading star-like as implied by the specific name; ovary, style, and cal. all glandular. May. China. 1917.

R. atlanti'cum (5*b*). B. Deciduous stoloniferous shrub up to 2 ft. h. *fl.* 4 to 10 in a cluster, very fragrant, cor. funnel-form, about 1½ in. across, white, flushed pink or purple on outside. Eastern N. America. Distinguished by its fragrant fl. and conspicuous row of stipitate glands on the back of the cor. lobes. An early-flowering species. Varieties with white and yellow fl. have been found. (Rh. Y.B. 1946, p. 37.)

R. Aucklan'dii. A synonym of *R. Griffithianum.*

Rhododendron Augustinii

R. Augusti'nii* (40*a*). B, C. Evergreen shrub, 6 to 10 ft., erect, young shoots downy. *l.* lanceolate, taper-pointed, dark green, 1½ to 4 in. long, ½ to 1 in. wide, scaly and with a conspicuous line of hairs along midrib beneath. *fl.* in clusters of 3 to 5; cor. 2½ in. wide, deeply 5-lobed, mauve and grey-blue to deep blue; greenish in throat; stamens 10, hairy at base; ovary scaly and downy; cal. ciliate. May. China. 1901. (B.M. 8497; F. & S. 3, 162.) Generally considered the most beautiful of the blue species, the deepest-coloured ones being the most tender. The hairy under side of the mid-rib is a good distinction.

R. aureum. A synonym of *R. xanthostephanum.*

R. auricula'tum (4). B. Evergreen shrub or small tree, 10 to 20 ft. *l.* 6 to 12 in. long, 2 to 4 in. wide, oblong, rounded but with a mucro at apex and with 2 distinct lobes (auricles) at base, rich green above paler and glandular-hairy beneath. *fl.* 7 to 15 in a rounded cluster; cor. 7-lobed, white or pinkish, 3 to 4 in. deep, scarcely so wide; pedicels 1 to 1½ in. long, densely glandular; stamens 14, up to 1¾ in. long, glabrous. China. 1900. (B.M. 8786.) Remarkable in not starting into growth, nor beginning to flower until well into July. Does not flower as a young plant.

R. × **azaleoi'des.*** A. A hybrid between a fragrant N. American Azalea and a Rhododendron of the ponticum series. *l.* 2 to 3½ in. long, 1 to 1½ in. wide, glaucous beneath; *fl.* in several clusters of 8 to 20 often making a compound truss of up to 50; cor. 1 to 1½ in. wide, white in the tube, the 5 lobes tinged with pale purple, unspotted. June, July. 1820. 6 to 8 ft. h. Charming, very fragrant, perfectly hardy.

R. Ba'chii (32). E. Evergreen, diffusely branched shrub, 8 ft. or more, young shoots softly downy. *l.* oval to ovate, tapered at both ends, ¾ to 2 in. long, half as wide, glabrous except for midrib. *fl.* solitary from several terminal axillary buds; cor. 1¼ in. wide, with 5 deep, spreading lobes, pale rosy-lilac, spotted; stamens 5, hairy; ovary densely glandular; style glabrous; cal. large, deeply 5-lobed, margined with glands. April, May. China. 1900. (B.M. 9375.) Akin to *ovatum* but differs by the glandular cal.

R. bae'ticum is the form of *R. ponticum* found wild on the Iberian Peninsula, not now considered distinct enough to justify a separate name.

R. Bai'leyi (27). C. Evergreen shrub, 3 to 5 ft., young shoots scaly. *l.* oblong or obovate, 1 to 2½ in. long, scaly on both sides. *fl.* in racemose clusters of 5 to 14; cor. flattish, dark red-purple, spotted on the upper lobes, 1½ in. wide, deeply 5-lobed; stamens 10, rosy purple, hairy; ovary scaly; style rosy purple, thick, much bent over; pedicels very slender, scaly. 1 to 1½ in. long. May. Tibet. 1913. (B.M. 8942.)

R. Bainbridgea'num (6*b*). C. Evergreen shrub up to 6 ft., young shoots, l.-stalks, fl.-stalks, and cal. glandular-bristly. *l.* 3 to 5 in. long, 1 to 2 in. wide, loosely felted beneath. *fl.* in trusses of 6 to 8; cor. bell-shaped, 1½ in. long, 5-lobed, white or creamy yellow, sometimes flushed with rose or blotched with crimson; stamens 10; ovary densely glandular. April. Tibet. 1922. Closely allied to *R. crinigerum* but with comparatively wider, less slenderly pointed l.

Rhododendron barbatum

R. barba'tum* (6*a*). B. Evergreen tree, 15 to 40 ft.; bark smooth, grey, peeling; young shoots mostly bristly. *l.* oblong; 4 to 9 in. long, 1½ to 3 in. wide, glabrous at maturity. *fl.* closely packed in a hemispherical truss 4 to 5 in. wide; cor. bell-shaped, 1½ in. wide, 5-lobed, blood-red, with 5 black-crimson blotches at base; stamens 10, white, glabrous; anthers purple-black; ovary glandular; style glabrous. April. Himalaya. 1849. (R.S.H. 3.) Outstanding characters are the smooth grey back, the bristly shoots, and rich crimson fl. Type sp. of its series.

R. basi'licum (17). B. Evergreen shrub or tree, 10 to 30 ft., young shoots clad with red-brown felt. *l.* oval to obovate, 6 to 12 in. long, about half as wide, with red-brown felt beneath; stalk 1¼ in. long, very stout, flattened on upper side. *fl.* densely packed in trusses of 20 or more 5 to 6 in. across; cor. widely bell-shaped, 8-lobed, 1½ in. across, pale yellow tinged with crimson and blotched at base; stamens 16, glabrous, ovary densely tomentose. May. China. 1913. Marked by its distinct decurrent l.-stalk.

R. Beania'num* (31*b*). B. Evergreen shrub up to 5 ft. h. Young shoots clad with red-brown floccose hairs. *l.* thinly leathery, oblong to oblong-obovate, 2½ to 4 in. long, apex rounded, upper surface dark green, shining, rugulose, under surface covered with persistent chestnut-brown woolly indumentum. *fl.* 6 to 10 in a terminal umbel; cal. cup-shaped, fleshy; *cor.* tubular-campanulate, waxy, about 1½ in. long, deep blood red with 5 black nectar pouches at base. May. SE. Tibet, Upper Burma. (N.F. and S. 10 (1938), p. 80.) Related to *R. haematodes*, but distinguished by the bristles on the stems and by the oblong shining rugulose l. Pink flowered forms also occur. **A**

R. Beesia'num (25). C. Evergreen shrub or small tree, 15 to 20 ft. *l.* elliptic-oblanceolate, 6 to 12 in. long, 1½ to 3 in. wide; dark green and glabrous above clad beneath with rich red-brown felt. *fl.* 20 or more closely clustered in a truss 6 in. across; cor. open bell-shaped, 2 in. wide, 5-lobed, white to deep rose, with a crimson basal blotch; stamens 1 in. long, 10; ovary brown-woolly; style smooth, longer than stamens. April. China. 1906. (B.M. n.s. t. 125.) Not easy to cultivate.

R. blandfordiaeflo'rum. A variety of *R. cinnabarinum*.

R. Booth'ii* (7). F. Evergreen, often epiphytic shrub, 6 to 10 ft., young shoots hairy. *l.* ovate, ovate-lanceolate, or oval, slender-pointed, 3½ to 5 in. long, 1¼ to 2½ in. wide, hairy on midrib, ciliate, scaly beneath; stalk shaggy. *fl.* in compact trusses of 7 to 10; cor. funnel-shaped at base, with 5 spreading lobes and 1 to 1½ in. wide, bright unspotted yellow; pedicel scaly; stamens 10, hairy at base; ovary scaly; style thick, short, much decurved; cal. large, with 5 membranous lobes ½ in. long. April, May. Bhutan. 1852. (B.M. 7149.) Type sp. of its series.

R. brachyan'thum (21). A. Evergreen shrub, 4 or 5 ft., young shoots reddish, scaly. *l.* oblong to narrowly oval, 1½ to 2½ in. long, scaly and very glaucous beneath. *fl.* usually 3 or 4 (up to 8) in a cluster; cor. bell-shaped, ¾ to 1 in. wide, shortly 5-lobed, clear pale yellow or tinged with green; cal. proportionately very large, ⅜ to ¾ in. wide, deeply 5-lobed, lobes green and spreading; stamens 10; ovary scaly; style glabrous. June, July. China. 1906. (B.M. 8750.) Notable for its very large cal. *See* **R. hypolepidotum.**

R. brachycar'pum (33*a*). A. Evergreen shrub, 6 to 10 ft. *l.* oblong, 4 to 6 in. long, 1½ to 2 in. wide, thinly felted beneath. *fl.* 10 to 20 in rounded clusters 4 to 6 in. across; cor. 2 in. wide, broadly funnel-shaped, deeply 5-lobed, creamy-white flushed with pink; stamens 10, hairy at the base; ovary brown-felted; style shorter than the stamens, glabrous. June. Japan. 1861. (B.M. 7881.) The short style is distinctive.

R. bractea'tum (40*b*). B. Evergreen shrub, 3 to 6 ft., compact, slow-growing, sparingly scurfy in all its parts. *l.* ovate or elliptic, rounded at base, ¾ to 2 in. long, with an odour when crushed of black currants. *fl.* in trusses of 3 to 6; cor. bell-shaped at base, spreading openly to a width of 1 to 1¼ in., the 5 lobes are white, but the basal part is richly blotched and spotted with red. June. China. 1908. (B.M. 9031.) The name refers to long persisting scales (or 'bracts') that come beneath the leaf proper. *fl.* small but daintily coloured.

R. Bret'tii. A synonym of *R. longesquamatum*.

B. brevisty'lum (23). B. Evergreen shrub up to 10 ft., young shoots, l., and ovary scaly. *l.* oblong-lanceolate, 2 to 4 in. long, 1 to 1¾ in. wide. *fl.* in clusters of 4 to 8; cor. widely funnel-shaped, 5-lobed, loosely scaly outside, pale to deep rose, with crimson markings on upper side; stamens 10, very downy; style very short, lower part downy. June, July. China. 1906. Distinct by its short style and late flowering. (B.M. 8898.)

R. Brookea'num.* F. Evergreen, often epiphytic shrub; young wood and l.-stalks purplish. *l.* elliptic-lanceolate, pointed, 5 to 9 in. long, leathery. *fl.* in trusses of 6 to 10 and 6 in. across; cor. orange or golden tawny, funnel-shaped below with a 5-lobed limb 2 in. wide; stamens 10, downy at base; anthers yellow, curiously incurved; ovary downy; style glabrous. April onwards. Borneo, up to 7,800 ft. on Mt. Kinabalu. (B.M. 4935.) Warm greenhouse.

Rhododendron bullatum

R. bulla'tum* (16). D. Closely akin to *R. Edgeworthii*, especially in shoot, leaf, and flower, but of much stiffer growth and hardier, and the cal. differs in being hairy only on margin. The style also is scaly (not so in *R. Edgeworthii*). April to June. China. 1904. (J.R.H.S. 41, 197.)

R. Burea'vii (37*a*). B. Evergreen shrub up to 6 ft., young shoots thickly felted. *l.* leathery, ovate or oval, $2\frac{1}{2}$ to $4\frac{1}{2}$ in. long, 1 to 2 in. wide, clad beneath with thick red wool. *fl.* in clusters of 10 to 15; cor. funnel-shaped, $1\frac{1}{2}$ in. long, rose with crimson spots; stamens 10, very downy at base; ovary, base of style, pedicels and cal. all glandular and hairy. April. China. 1908.

R. caerul'eum (40*e*). D. Evergreen shrub up to 6 ft. h. Annual shoots short, purplish, not scaly. *l.* elliptic, leathery, about $1\frac{1}{4}$ in. long and $\frac{1}{2}$ to $\frac{3}{4}$ in. broad, slightly scaly below. *fl.* in terminal clusters of 3 to 4; cor. $\frac{3}{4}$ in. long, 5-lobed, deep rose-lavender, sometimes white. Yunnan, W. China. SYN. *R. rarosquameum*, *R. eriandrum.*

R. calendula'ceum* (5*b*). A. Deciduous shrub, 4 to 10 ft., shoots bristly-hairy. *l.* elliptic to obovate-oblong, 2 to $3\frac{1}{2}$ in. long, downy beneath especially on midrib. *fl.* in clusters of 5 to 7, not much scented; cor. funnel-shaped, 2 in. wide, of various shades of orange-scarlet or yellow, glandular-hairy, lobes 5, longer than the tube; stamens 5, thrice as long as the cor. tube; cal., pedicels, and ovary glandular-hairy. May. N. America. 1806. (B.R. 145; L.B.C. 1324 as *Azalea calendulacea.*) One of the most brilliantly coloured of the Azaleas and the source of the fine orange and scarlet garden vars. **cro'ceum** is the yellow-flowered form. (B.M. 1721.)

R. californ'icum (38*b*). A. Evergreen shrub, up to 12 ft. *l.* elliptic, 4 to 6 in. long, dark green, glabrous. *fl.* 20 or more in clusters 6 to 8 in. wide; cor. 2 in. across, broadly bell-shaped, rosy-purple, the 5 lobes wavy; stamens 10, shorter than cor., downy at base; ovary white-downy; fl.-stalk $1\frac{1}{2}$ in. long. May. California. 1849. (B.M. 4863.) The W. American representative of *R. catawbiense* which is distinguished by its rusty pubescent ovary and fl.-stalks. SYN. *R. macrophyllum.*

R. callimor'phum* (38*a*). B. Evergreen shrub up to 10 ft. in a wild state, but usually much smaller and of rounded habit in gardens; quite young shoots glandular. *l.* round to roundish-ovate, base cordate, $1\frac{1}{2}$ to 3 in. long, shining green above, glaucous beneath, with glands on midrib and stalk. *fl.* in trusses of 5 to 8; cor. open bell-shaped, 5-lobed, $1\frac{1}{2}$ in. wide, pale rose with a crimson blotch; stamens 10, glabrous; cal., fl.-stalk, ovary, and base of style covered with red glands. April, May. China. 1912. (B.M. 8789.) Akin to *R. campylocarpum.*

R. calophy'tum* (19*a*). B. Evergreen tree of 30 to 40 ft., mostly a shrub in gardens up to 10 ft. young shoots very stout. *l.* obovate to oblanceolate, 8 to 12 in. long, 2 to $3\frac{1}{2}$ in. wide, almost glabrous. *fl.* up to 30 in trusses 6 to 8 in. across; cor. bell-shaped, 5- to 7-lobed, $2\frac{1}{2}$ to 3 in. wide, white or rosy-pink with a conspicuous dark crimson blotch at base; stamens 15 to 20, shorter than the cor.; ovary glabrous; stigma yellow, knob-like, $\frac{1}{4}$ in. wide. March, April. China, Tibet. 1904. (B.M. 9173.) One of the noblest of Chinese sp., often confused with *R. sutchuenense*, which has a 5-lobed cor. up to 3 in. wide and a much smaller reddish stigma.

R. calostro'tum* (34). A. Evergreen shrub, about 12 in., young shoots and fl.-stalks scaly. *l.* oval to obovate, $\frac{3}{8}$ to $1\frac{1}{8}$ in. long, $\frac{1}{3}$ to $\frac{1}{2}$ in. wide, ciliate, scaly beneath. *fl.* mostly in pairs; cor. open and flattish, $1\frac{1}{2}$ in. wide, pale pink to purplish-crimson, lobes 5 overlapping, downy outside; stamens 10, purple-tufted at base; ovary scaly; style glabrous or nearly so; cal. large, scaly, and fringed with hairs. May. Burma. 1919. (B.M. 9001.) Differing from *R. saluenense* in the absence of bristles from the shoots and fl.-stalks. Charming for rock-garden.

R. caloxan'thum * (38*a*). B. Evergreen shrub, 3 to 5 ft., young shoots glandular. *l.* oval to roundish, $1\frac{1}{2}$ to $2\frac{1}{2}$ in. long, pale glaucous green beneath, glabrous. *fl.* in trusses of 4 to 9; cor. bell-shaped, $1\frac{3}{4}$ in. wide, 5-lobed, scarlet in bud, opening from sulphur- to orange-yellow; stamens 10, glabrous; ovary, base of pistil, cal., and fl.-stalk all densely glandular. April, May. Burma. 1919. One of a charming group of yellow-fld. species including *R. campylocarpum*, *R. telopeum*, and *R. Wardii.*

R. camel'liaeflorum (8). D. Evergreen, often epiphytic shrub up to 6 ft., of straggling growth, all its parts more or less scaly. *l.* oblong-lanceolate, $2\frac{1}{2}$ to 4 in. long, glistening with scales beneath. *fl.* usually in pairs; cor. white tinged with rose, $1\frac{1}{2}$ in. wide, flattish, 5-lobed; stamens 12 to 16; style glabrous, bent over; cal. $\frac{1}{4}$ in. long, deeply 5-lobed. July. Himalaya. 1851. (B.M. 4932; R.S.H. 28.) Its series contains one other species only—*R. lucidum*—not in cultivation.

R. campanula'tum (9). B. Evergreen widely-spreading shrub, 6 to 12 ft. *l.* oval, often rather cordate at the base, 3 to $5\frac{1}{2}$ in. long. nearly half as wide, covered with red-brown felt beneath. *fl.* about 8 in a loose cluster; cor. broadly bell-shaped, 2 in. wide, 5-lobed, rosy-purple in various shades, upper lobes darker spotted; stamens 10; ovary and style glabrous. April. Himalaya. 1825. (B.M. 3759; S.B.F.G. s. 2, 241; L.B.C. 1944.) var. **aerugino'sum.** *See* **R. aeruginosum.**

R. Campbel'liae (3*a*). A subspecies of *R. arboreum.*

R. campylocar'pum* (38*a*). B. Evergreen shrub, 4 to 8 ft., bushy. *l.* 2 to 4 in. long, ovate to elliptic, cordate to rounded at base, blue-white beneath; petiole glandular, 1 in. long. *fl.* 6 to 8 in a loose cluster; cor. widely bell-shaped, $2\frac{1}{2}$ to 3 in. wide, 5-lobed, pale, soft yellow; stamens 10; anthers reddish; ovary and cal. very glandular. May. Himalaya. 1851. (B.M. 4968; R.S.H. 30.) One of the very best of yellow species (apart from Azaleas), and valued for hybridizing. var. **ela'tum** is of more erect habit and when used for hybridizing 'throws' pinks or ivory-whites. With the more bushy type, the yellow colouring remains dominant in the progeny.

Rhododendron campylogynum

R. campylogy'num* (10). A. Evergreen, low, dense, compact shrub. *l.* obovate, rounded and mucronate at apex, margins recurved, $\frac{1}{3}$ to 1 in. long, $\frac{1}{8}$ to $\frac{1}{2}$ in. wide, dark glossy green. *fl.* 1 to 4 at end of shoot, each on a slender erect stalk 1 to 2 in. long; cor. nodding, bell-shaped, $\frac{5}{8}$ in. long with 5 rounded scarcely recurved lobes, rosy-purple, plum-coloured, or almost black-purple; stamens 8, 10, or 12; ovary scaly; style bent downwards, glabrous; cal. with 5 lobes $\frac{1}{5}$ in. long. May. China, Tibet, Burma. 1912. (B.M. 9407.) Its cushion-like habit renders it admirable for the rock-garden.

R. camtschat'icum (11). A. Deciduous shrub 4 to 8 in. h., spreading by underground stems, all the parts more or less hairy. *l.* stalkless, obovate, $\frac{3}{4}$ to 2 in. long, conspicuously veined. *fl.* borne singly or in pairs on the young, growing, leafy shoots (not from buds formed the previous year); cor. $1\frac{1}{2}$ to $1\frac{3}{4}$ in. wide, rosy-crimson, with 5 deep, oblong, spreading lobes, the 3 upper spotted; stamens 10, reddish-purple; cal. large, leaf-like, $\frac{3}{4}$ in. wide with 5 deep oblong lobes. May. NE. Asia, NW. America. 1799. (B.M. 8210.) SYN. *Therorhodion camtschaticum.*

R. canaden'se (5*a*). A. Deciduous shrub, 1 to 3 ft., shoots erect, soon glabrous. *l.* oval, 1 to 2 in. long, sparingly bristly above, downy beneath, finally glabrous. *fl.* 4 to 6 in a cluster; cor. rose-purple, 1 to $1\frac{1}{2}$ in. wide, 2-lipped, the upper lip of 3 very short lobes, the lower one of 2 long, narrow lobes divided to the base; stamens 10; anthers purple; ovary bristly. April. N. America. 1767. (B.M. 474 as *Rhodora canadensis.*) Very distinct by its 2-lipped cor.

R. canta'bile (26), now regarded as synonymous with *R. russatum*, was originally kept distinct because of the more numerous fl. in a truss. They are united by intermediates. (B.M. 8963.)

R. carolinia'num (12). A. Evergreen shrub up to 3 or 4 ft., shoots scaly. *l.* oval to oval-obovate, 1 to 3 in. long, densely covered beneath with dark scales. *fl.* 4 to 10 in a truss; cor. $1\frac{1}{2}$ in. wide, funnel-shaped, pale rosy-purple, the 5 lobes longer than the tube, slightly or not scaly outside. In other respects resembling *R. minus* to which it is very closely akin but which has its corolla densely scaly outside. N. America. (B.R. 37; Add. 1.) Both have been called *R. punctatum.*

R. catacos'mum (31*b*). B. Very closely related to *R. haematodes*, but with a huge, cupped cal., which is $\frac{3}{4}$ in. long. *l.* larger and more rounded, and cor. more bell-shaped and crimson-rose. April. Tibet. 1921.

R. catawbien'se (33*b*). A. Evergreen shrub, 6 to 10 ft. *l.* elliptic to oblong, 3 to 6 in. long, $1\frac{1}{4}$ to 2 in. wide, glabrous. *fl.* in trusses of 15 to 20, 5 to 6 in. across; cor. 2 in. across the 5 lobes, lilac-purple with yellow-green spots on the upper side; stamens 10, white, downy at the base; ovary brown-felted, style glabrous. May, June. N. America. 1809. (B.M. 1671; L.B.C. 1176.) A valuable hardy species from which the best of the very hardy 'Waterer' hybrids have been raised. Distinct from *R. ponticum* by its broader leaves, sturdier habit, and felted ovary.

R. caucas'icum (33*a*). A. Evergreen shrub, $1\frac{1}{2}$ to 3 ft. *l.* narrow, ovate to obovate, 2 to 4 in. long, with brownish down beneath. *fl.* 7 to 10 in a truss; cor. yellowish-white tinged with pink; stamens 10; ovary white tomentose; style glabrous, pink. Seed-pods erect; fl.-

stalks 2 in. or more long. May. Caucasus. 1803. (B.M. 1145.) Interesting as a parent of some of the early hybrids, of which 'Cunningham's White' is one. var. **stramin'eum,** *fl.* straw-coloured. (B.M. 3422.)

R. cephalanthoi'des. A variety of *R. primulaeflorum.*

Rhododendron canadense (p. 1768)

Rhododendron carolinianum (p. 1768)

R. cephalan'thum* (2). C. Evergreen shrub, 2 to 4 ft., young shoots thickly scaly. *l.* oval or oblong, blunt, ½ to 1¼ in. long, flaky beneath, margins recurved. *fl.* about 8 clustered densely in a head 1½ in. wide; cor. tubular at base, ½ in. long and wide, 5-lobed, white; stamens 5, enclosed in cor. tube; ovary scaly; style very short; cal. ciliate, scaly outside. April, May. China. 1908. (B.T.S. 3, 361.) var. **crebreflo'rum,** dwarf. *fl.* pink, stamens 6, filaments glabrous.

R. cerasi'num (38*e*). C. Evergreen shrub, up to 12 ft. *l.* oblong-elliptic, 2 to 3 in. long, at first loosely flossy and rather glaucous beneath. *fl.* pendulous, in trusses of 5 or 6; cor. bell-shaped, 1½ to 2 in. long, creamy-white with cherry-red lobes, sometimes entirely crimson, but always having 5 almost black blotches at the base; stamens 10, glabrous; ovary, style, cal., and fl.-stalk all glandular. May. Tibet. 1924. (B.M. 9538.) Close akin to *R. Stewartianum* which is also variable in colour but has a glabrous style.

R. chaetomal'lum* (31*b*). C. One of a group of which *R. haematodes* is regarded as the central species. It differs from that species by young shoots being very bristly, not woolly, and by the cal. being usually much larger (up to ⅜ in. long). Cor. variable in colour but deep crimson in the type; cal. also red. April. Tibet, China. 1917. (B.M n.s. t. 25.) var. **citriniflo'rum,** *fl.* lemon-yellow; var. **xanthan'thum,** *fl.* cream-yellow, flushed rose.

R. chameu'num (34). A. Evergreen shrub, 1 to 2 ft. closely akin to *R. prostratum* and *R. saluenense. fl.* in the usual twos or threes of this series, deep purple-rose with crimson markings and about 1½ in. wide. Differs from *R. prostratum* by its more erect growth and from *R. saluenense* in having no (or very few) scales on the cal. June. China. 1914.

R. charito'pes* (21). C. Evergreen shrub up to 18 in. *l.* obovate, 1 to 2½ in. long, ⅝ to ⅞ in. wide, glossy green above with yellowish shining scales beneath. *fl.* in clusters of 2 to 5, usually 3; cor. bell-shaped, 5-lobed, 1 in. wide, clear pink spotted with crimson on upper lobes; cal. with 5 deep lobes ⅛ in. long, scaly outside; ovary densely scaly; style very stout, glabrous. April, May. Burma. 1920. (B.M. 9358.) Charming rock-garden shrub.

R. chasmanthoi'des (40*a*). C. Differs chiefly from *R. chasmanthum* by its very small, unlobed cal. and its more abruptly pointed l. May. China, Tibet. 1918.

R. chasman'thum* (40*a*). C. Evergreen shrub, 6 to 8 ft., young shoots glabrous. *l.* lanceolate, taper-pointed, 2½ to 4 in. long, softly hairy on midrib beneath. *fl.* 4 or 5 in a cluster; cor. deeply 5-lobed, 1½ to 2 in. wide, pale lavender to deep lavender-mauve, spotted with green on upper part; cal. deeply 5-lobed, scaly; stamens 10. May. China, Tibet. (B.M. n.s. t. 79.) 1907. Akin to *R. Augustinii* with hairy midrib, but that species has downy shoots and flowers a fortnight earlier.

R. chloran'thum (39). B. Deciduous shrub up to 4 ft., shoots nearly glabrous. *l.* obovate, rounded at apex, 1 in. long, ⅝ in. wide, glaucous green at first, glabrous above, scaly and bristly on midrib beneath. *fl.* in clusters of 2 to 5; cor. yellow tinged with green, 1 in. wide, bell-shaped, 5-lobed; stamens 10; ovary scaly; style stout, curved, glabrous, 1 in. long. June. China. 1917. (B.M. n.s. 79.) Distinguished by its long, slender, glabrous fl.-stalks.

R. chrysan'thum (33*a*). B. Dwarf evergreen usually under 1 ft. *fl.* yellow, 1½ in. wide, erect in clusters of 5 to 8. Akin to and resembling *R. caucasicum* in l. May. N. Asia. Very rare and difficult to cultivate.

R. chry'seum (26). A. Evergreen shrub, 1½ to 2½ ft., shoots scurfy *l.* oval to obovate, ½ to ⅞ in. long, scaly, glaucous beneath. *fl.* 4 to 6 in a cluster; cor. deep sulphur to bright yellow, ¾ to 1 in. wide, tube short and downy, lobes 5 spreading scaly on the back; stamens normally 5; anthers brown; ovary very scaly; cal. with 5 oblong, scaly, ciliate lobes, ⅛ in. long. May. China. 1912. (B.M. 9246.) Distinct by its yellow fl. and 5 stamens.

R. cilia'tum* (28*a*). C. Evergreen shrub, 4 to 8 ft., usually wider than h., young shoots, l., l.-stalks, fl.-stalks, and cal. all more or less bristly. *l.* elliptic, 2 to 3½ in. long, scaly beneath. *fl.* in clusters of 3 to 5; cor. rosy-red in bud, pale pink on opening, becoming white, 2½ in. across, widely bell-shaped, 5-lobed; stamens 10; ovary scaly; style smooth. April. Himalaya. 1850. (B.M. 4648.) Has been much used for hybridizing.

R. ciliica'lyx* (28*a*). F. Evergreen shrub, up to 10 ft. *l.* narrowly oval, 2½ to 4½ in. long, pointed, glaucous and scaly beneath, stalk bristly. *fl.* usually in threes, fragrant; cor. funnel-shaped at base, spreading into 5 deep lobes, 4 in. wide, pure white or tinged with rose with a yellow stain on upper side; stamens 10, 2 in. long, very hairy at the base; ovary scaly; cal. 5-lobed, the lobes ⅛ to ¼ in. long, conspicuously fringed with bristles. March, April. China. 1892. (B.M. 7782.)

R. cinnabari'num* (14). B. Evergreen erect shrub, 6 to 8 ft. *l.* 2 to 4 in. long, oval, greyish-green above, scaly and rather glaucous beneath. *fl.* 5 to 8 in a cluster, short-stalked and drooping; cor. tubular, 1½ to 2 in. long, with 5 erect lobes, cinnabar red; stamens 10, scarcely as long as the corolla. May, June. Himalaya. 1849. Very distinct, beautiful species whose flowers resemble those of Lapageria. They vary much in colour and size. Three forms are recognized in gardens but intermediates exist. Type as above. (R.S.H. 8.); **blandfordiaeflor'um,** *fl.* red outside, yellow within. (B.M. 4930.); **Roylei,** *fl.* 1½ in. long, intense rosy-red. (B.M. 4788.) A

R. cinnamo'meum (3*a*). C. Subspecies of *R. arboreum.*

R. citriniflo'rum (31*d*). C. Evergreen shrub 2 to 5 ft. *l.* obovate, 1½ to 3½ in. long, very woolly beneath. *fl.* in trusses of 6 to 8, stalks ½ to 1 in. long, bristly-hairy, glandular; cor. clear unspotted lemon-yellow, bell-shaped, 1¾ in. long, 5-lobed; stamens 10; ovary matted with tawny hairs and glandular bristles; style glabrous. April, May. China. 1917. Its yellow fl. (sometimes flushed with pink) make it distinct.

R. Clementi'nae (37*c*). B. Evergreen shrub up to 10 ft. *l.* oval, mostly cordate at the base, 2½ to 5 in. long, with thick, soft, red-brown felt beneath. *fl.* closely set in trusses of about 15, 6 in. wide; cor. bell-shaped, 2 to 2½ in. wide, 6- or 7-lobed, creamy-white flushed with rose or bright rose, crimson-dotted; stamens 12 or 14; ovary and style glabrous. April, May. China. 1913. (B.M. 9392.) Distinct by its 6- or 7-lobed cor.

Rhododendron ciliicalyx (p. 1769)

Rhododendron cinnabarinum (p. 1769)

R. concate'nans* (14). C. Evergreen shrub up to 6 ft. h., allied to *R. cinnabarinum.* Young growth markedly glaucous. *l.* obovate-elliptic, rounded to a mucronate apex, up to 3 in. long and 1¾ in. broad, densely scaly and glaucous below. *fl.* in loose trusses of 7 to 8, cor. campanulate with 5 half-spreading ovate-rounded lobes, apricot, faintly tinged outside with pale purple, conspicuously veined. April to May. SE. Tibet. 1925. A beautiful species distinguished by the glaucousness of its young foliage, often persisting throughout the year, and its apricot bell-like fl.

R. concin'num (40*c*). B. Evergreen shrub, 5 to 7 ft. *l.* oblong-lanceolate, 1 to 2 in. long, scaly on both surfaces. *fl.* 2 to 4 in a cluster; cor. purple, 1½ to 2 in. wide, funnel-shaped, 5-lobed, densely scaly outside; stamens 10, densely hairy near the base; ovary scaly; style glabrous. May. China. 1904. (B.M. 8620; 8280 as *R. coombense.*) **A**

R. coomben'se. A synonym of *R. concinnum.*

R. corea'num. A synonym of *R. yedoense poukhanense.*

R. coria'ceum (17). C. Evergreen shrub or small tree up to 25 ft. *l.* oblanceolate, 5 to 10 in. long, pale green and glabrous above, greyish-white with down beneath. *fl.* in a rather loose truss of 15 to 20; cor. narrowly bell-shaped, 1½ in. long, 5- to 7-lobed, white- or rose-tinted with a crimson blotch and spots; stamens 10 to 14; ovary hairy; style glabrous. April. China, Tibet. Distinct by its narrow l. and slender branchlets.

R. coryphae'um (22). C. A form of *R. praestans* with creamy-white fl. China. 1918.

R. cras'sum* (28*b*). D. Evergreen shrub or small tree up to 20 ft. very nearly akin to the Himalayan *R. Maddenii* and having the same scaly branchlets, l., cor., ovary, and style. *fl.* in clusters of 3 to 6, fragrant; cor. white, funnel-shaped, 3½ in. long. Differs from *R. Maddenii* in having 15 to 20 stamens and by cal. lobes being up to ½ in. long. It is also hardier. Several forms are in cultivation, varying in size and shape of l. June, July. China. 1906. (B.M. 9673.)

R. crebreflo'rum* (2). A dwarf form of *R. cephalanthum.*

Rhododendron crinigerum

R. crinig'erum (6*b*). B. Evergreen shrub, 8 to 14 ft., young shoots viscid, glandular-bristly. *l.* lanceolate to oblanceolate, slender pointed, 3 to 7 in. long, ½ to 2 in. wide, felted beneath; midrib very glandular. *fl.* about 12 in. the truss; cor. bell-shaped, 1½ in. long, 5-lobed, white or cream, often flushed with rose with a large blotch at base, sometimes heavily spotted; stamens 10, ovary glandular; cal. and fl.-stalk bristly. April. China, Tibet. 1914. Near *R. glischrum,* but distinguished by the velvety pale to buff felted l. (B.M. 9464.) Syn. *R. ixeuticum.*

R. cro'ceum* (38*d*). C. Evergreen shrub said to be 15 to 25 ft. h. in a wild state, much dwarfer in cultivation. *l.* oval-oblong, slightly cordate at base, distinctly mucronate, 2½ to 4½ in. long, glabrous. *fl.* in loose trusses of 7 or 8; cor. open saucer-shaped, 5-lobed, 2 to 3 in. wide, clear soft yellow, sometimes with a crimson blotch; stamens 10, glabrous; ovary and style glandular; cal. ⅝ to ¾ in. wide, fringed with glands. May. China. 1915. (B.T.S. 3, 367.) Distinct by l. being green (not glaucous) beneath.

R. cunea'tum (26). A. Evergreen shrub, 4 to 6 ft. *l.* oval, 1 to 2 in. long, rusty with brown-red scales beneath. *fl.* in clusters of 3 to 6; cor. widely funnel-shaped, 1 to 1½ in. long and wide, downy in tube, deep rose; stamens 10, white; anthers brown; ovary scaly; style glabrous; cal. large, reddish with 5 scaly lobes ¼ to ⅓ in. long. April. China. 1906. One of the few with rosy fl.

R. cyanocar'pum (38*e*). C. Evergreen shrub, up to 20 ft. closely akin to *R. Thomsonii* and once considered a var. of it. It is well distinguished by its white or rose-coloured fl. Cal. large and cup-shaped as in *Thomsonii*; both have purple or purplish seed vessels. March, April. China. 1906. (B.M. n.s. 155.)

R. cy'clium (38*a*). B. Evergreen shrub, 4 to 6 ft., very closely related to *R. callimorphum* and with similar glandular young shoots, cal., fl.-stalks, l.-stalks, and ovary. *fl.* in trusses of 5 to 8, the bell-shaped cor. 1½ in. wide, but deeper rose and with a darker blotch. *l.* rounder and more leathery. May. China. 1917.

R. Dalhou'siae* (28*e*). F. Evergreen shrub, up to 6 or 8 ft., usually an epiphyte in nature, bark papery, young shoots bristly and scaly. *l.* obovate to oblanceolate, 3 to 6 in. long, glaucous and scaly beneath. *fl.* in clusters of 3 to 5, fragrant, stalks hairy and scaly; cor. funnel-shaped, 5-lobed, $3\frac{1}{2}$ in. long and wide, yellow at first turning white (pure or rose-tinted); stamens 10, downy; anthers $\frac{1}{2}$ in. long, brown; ovary and base of style scaly. May, June. Himalaya. 1850. (B.M. 4718; R.S.H. 1, 2.) Has been used for hybridizing, now rare.

R. dau'ricum (15). A. Deciduous or semi-evergreen shrub, 4 to 6 ft. *l.* oval, $\frac{1}{2}$ to $1\frac{1}{2}$ in. long, densely scaly beneath. *fl.* borne singly from several buds at the apex of the shoot; cor. bright rosy-purple, 1 to $1\frac{1}{2}$ in. wide, 5-lobed, widely open; stamens 10; ovary scaly; style glabrous. January to March. N. Asia. 1780. (B.M. 636; L.B.C. 605, 1446.) var. **sempervi'rens** is a superior, evergreen form. (B.M. 1888; L.B.C. 1584.) A parent of the valuable *R.* × *praecox.* **A**

R. Davidsonia'num* (40*e*). B. Evergreen shrub up to 10 ft. *l.* narrowly oblanceolate, 1 to $2\frac{1}{2}$ in. long, dull brown and scaly beneath. *fl.* in clusters of 2 to 4 from each of several terminal buds; cor. 5-lobed, $1\frac{3}{4}$ to 2 in. wide, pale rose with red spots on the upper lobe; stamens 10, well exserted; anthers yellow; ovary scaly; style glabrous. April, May. China. 1908. (B.M. 8759 as *R. siderophyllum.*) Very profuse bloomer. A distinctive character is the bending upwards of the 2 halves of the l. from the midrib, giving it a **V**-shape in cross-section. **A**

Rhododendron decorum

R. deco'rum* (19*c*). C. Evergreen sturdy shrub, 6 to 10 ft. *l.* oblong-lanceolate, 4 to 6 in. long, mucronate, stout in texture, glabrous. *fl.* in lax trusses of 8 to 10, fragrant; cor. funnel-shaped, with 7, spreading, overlapping lobes, 3 to $3\frac{1}{2}$ in. wide, white to shell pink; cal. cup-shaped, glandular; stamens 14 to 16, downy; ovary and style glandular. March to May. China. (B.M. 8659.) 1889. Attractive fragrant species, variable in habit and time of flowering. Akin to *R. Fortunei* and *R. discolor,* which have glabrous stamens.

R. Degronia'num (33*a*). B. Evergreen shrub, 4 to 6 ft. *l.* oblong to oval, 4 to 6 in. long, glabrous above, reddish-downy beneath. *fl.* in trusses of about 12, 5 in. across; cor. $2\frac{1}{2}$ in. wide, 5-lobed, soft purplish-pink, unspotted; stamens 10; anthers yellow; ovary covered with white down; style glabrous. April, May. Japan. (B.M. 8403 as *R. japonicum pentamerum.*) Syn. *R. Metternichii pentamerum.*

R. Delava'yi* (3*a*). E. Really only the Chinese form of the Himalayan *R. arboreum. fl.* as in that species vary in colour from crimson to rose and there is a white var. (**al'bum**); habit and l. the same. The only botanical difference is in the character of the indumentum beneath the l. March to May. 1889. (B.M. 8137.)

R. deleiense. A synonym of *R. tephropeplum,* which is a very variable species. Forms found in gardens under the name *deleiense* tend to be those with larger and deeper coloured fl.

R. desquama'tum (23). D. Evergreen shrub or small tree up to 25 ft. *l.* oblong-lanceolate, slender-pointed, $2\frac{1}{2}$ to 4 in. long, glabrous above, densely scaly beneath. *fl.* in loose cluster of 6 to 8; cor. widely funnel-shaped, 5-lobed, $2\frac{1}{4}$ to $2\frac{3}{4}$ in. wide, mauve with crimson dots, scaly outside; stamens 10, downy; ovary scaly; style red, glabrous. May. Tibet, China, Burma. 1917. (B.M. 9497.) The largest fl. of its series. Of varying merit; its best forms are charming.

R. diapre'pes (19*c*). D. Closely related to *R. decorum,* but with larger l. (up to 12 in. long) and white fl. 5 in. across. Not so hardy. Evergreen tree, 10 to 25 ft. July. China, Burma. 1913. (B.M. 9524.)

R. dichroan'thum* (31*d*). B. Evergreen shrub, 3 to 5 ft., young shoots white with down. *l.* obovate to oblanceolate, 2 to 4 in. long, glabrous above, white with scurf beneath. *fl.* in clusters of 4 to 8; cor. tubular bell-shaped, $1\frac{3}{4}$ in. long, 5-lobed, very variable in shade, normally orange suffused with pink, or salmon-pink; stamens 10, pinkish; ovary white with down; style glabrous; cal. coloured like cor., very variable in size of lobes which are $\frac{1}{8}$ to 1 in. long. May, June. China. 1906. (B.M. 8815.)

R. did'ymum (31*d*). B. Evergreen shrub, 1 to 3 ft., shoots bristly. *l.* obovate, 1 to $2\frac{1}{2}$ in. long, soon glabrous above, grey-white with down beneath. *fl.* in clusters of 4 to 8; stalk glandular, 1 in. long; cor. narrowly bell-shaped, 1 in. long, black-crimson; stamens 10, red, glabrous; ovary glandular; style red, glabrous. June, July. Tibet. 1917. (B.M. 9217.) Remarkable for the very dark fl. (*See also* **R. haemaleum.**)

R. dilata'tum. A synonym of *R. reticulatum pentandrum.*

R. diphroca'lyx* (6*c*). C. Evergreen shrub up to 15 ft., shoots glandular-bristly, downy. *l.* $2\frac{1}{2}$ to 6 in. long, oblong to oval, rather glaucous beneath, nearly glabrous except on midrib. *fl.* up to 20 in a truss; cor. bell-shaped, $1\frac{1}{4}$ in. long, bright red to rosy-crimson, with a crimson blotch and spots; cal. very large, $\frac{1}{2}$ to $\frac{3}{4}$ in. long, unequally 5-lobed, red, ciliate. April. China. 1912. Very distinct by the large, coloured cal., fl.-stalks having no glands, and l. glaucous beneath.

R. dis'color* (19*c*). B. Evergreen tree up to 20 ft., or a shrub. *l.* oval to oblong, 4 to 8 in. long, glabrous, pale beneath. *fl.* in loose trusses of about 10; cor. funnel-shaped at base, 6- or 7-lobed, $2\frac{1}{2}$ to 4 in. across, white to pale pink; stamens 12 to 16, glabrous; cal., ovary, and style glandular. June, July. China. (B.M. 8696.) 1900. A fine species valuable for its hardiness and its beautiful late fl. Much used for hybridizing. Closely akin to *R. Fortunei* which blooms earlier and is more shrubby.

R. eclec'teum (38*e*). C. Evergreen shrub, 5 to 10 ft., branchlets stout. *l.* mostly obovate or oblong, $2\frac{1}{2}$ to 5 in. long, glabrous except on the midrib, very short-stalked, sometimes almost sessile. *fl.* in clusters of 6 or more; cor. widely funnel-shaped, $1\frac{1}{2}$ to 2 in. long, 5-lobed, very variable in colour, white, rose, purple, rarely yellow; stamens 10, short; ovary very glandular; cal. $\frac{1}{3}$ in. long, glabrous. Jan. to March. Tibet. Its very short l.-stalks distinguish it.

R. Edgaria'num (26). A. Evergreen shrub, 2 to 3 ft., shoots scurfy. *l.* oval, $\frac{1}{4}$ to $\frac{1}{2}$ in. long, scaly on both surfaces, scales beneath contiguous or overlapping. *fl.* solitary or in pairs; cor. $\frac{3}{4}$ to 1 in. wide, deeply 5-lobed, rose-purple, not scaly outside; stamens 10; anthers pale yellow-brown; ovary scaly; style purple, glabrous; cal. 5-lobed, scaly, ciliate. May. China. 1908. Suitable for the rock-garden.

R. Edgewort'hii* (16). F. Straggling, often epiphytic, evergreen shrub, 6 to 10 ft., shoots clad with thick tawny felt. *l.* oval to ovate, 2 to $4\frac{1}{2}$ in. long, wrinkled with sunken veins above, thickly tawny-felted beneath. *fl.* 2 to 4 together, richly fragrant; cor. funnel-shaped, $2\frac{1}{2}$ to 4 in. long, 5-lobed, waxy-white tinged pink; cal. deeply 5-lobed, densely hairy outside and on margins; stamens 10; ovary hairy; style not scaly, but woolly on lower part. April, May. Himalaya. 1851. (B.M. 4936; R.S.H. 21.) A fine group of hybrids has been raised from it.

R. elaeagnoi'des (27). A. Evergreen shrub usually under 1 ft. with thin, warty twigs. *l.* roundish-oval or obovate, $\frac{1}{4}$ to $\frac{5}{8}$ in. long, covered with overlapping scales. *fl.* usually solitary, cor. flat and open, $\frac{3}{4}$ to $1\frac{1}{8}$ in. wide, 5-lobed, usually of some shade of yellow, but sometimes rose, or red-purple in the Chinese and Burmese forms; stamens 8 or 10. Resembling *R. lepidotum* in its colour variation from yellow to purple, but differing by its smaller, rounder, proportionately wider leaves. June. Himalaya. 1850. China, Burma. 1906. (R.S.H. 23.) Syn. *R. sinolepidotum.* In the broad sense this is a form of *R. lepidotum* with which species it is now generally included.

R. Elliott'ii* (24*b*). D. Evergreen shrub, 8 to 12 ft. *l.* oblong-elliptic, 4 to 6 in. long, dull green above, paler beneath, nearly or quite glabrous and shining at maturity. *fl.* in trusses of about 12, 5 in. across; cor. funnel-shaped, 2 in. long, 5-lobed, scarlet, much spotted with crimson; stamens 10, red, glabrous; ovary and style glandular. May, June. India. 1927. (B.M. 9546.)

R. × **emas'culum** (15). Evergreen hybrid between *R.* × *praecox* and *R. dauricum* up to 6 ft. *l.* 1 to 2 in. long, oval. *fl.* solitary or in pairs, pale, unspotted rosy-lilac. March, April. Stamens aborted or absent.

R. eriogy'num* (24*b*). D. Evergreen shrub up to 10 ft. *l.* oblong-elliptic, 4 to 8 in. long, loosely downy beneath at first, ultimately glittering green. *fl.* in trusses of 12 to 16, 5 in. across; cor. bell-shaped, 2 in. wide, 5-lobed, bright red, with 5 dark pouches at bare and spotted; stamens 10, downy below, ovary and lower half of style densely downy. June. China. 1914. Brilliantly coloured and useful in the production of tender hybrids. (B.M. 9337.)

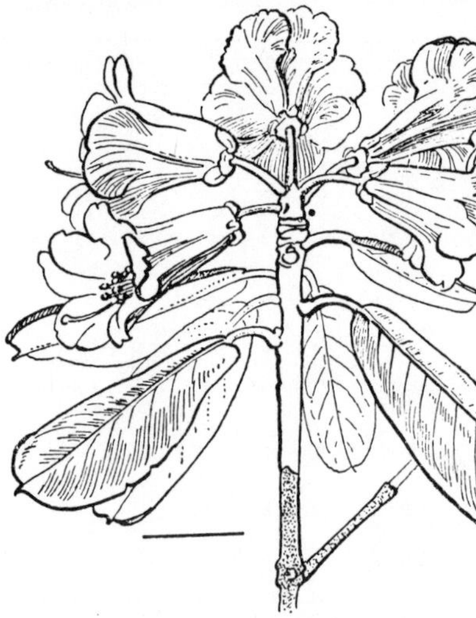

Rhododendron euchaites

R. euchai'tes* (31*c*). C. Often regarded as one of several subspecies of *R. neriiflorum*. It is a taller shrub and said to become 15 to 20 ft. h. in a wild state; as yet much smaller in gardens. *fl.* larger and of a brighter crimson; young shoots sometimes bristly and glandular. Considered the finest of the neriiflorum group. April. China, Burma. 1913.

R. exim'ium* (17). C. Closely related to *R. Falconeri* and similar in general appearance. Differs by upper surface of l. covered with a dense tomentum, which, being orange on the unfolding new growth, is then very attractive; cor. tinged with rose, not yellow. April, May. Bhutan. (B.M. 7317 as *R. Falconeri eximium.*)

Rhododendron Fargesii

R. exquisi'tum (40*b*). D. Evergreen shrub up to 4 ft. h. *l.* broadly elliptic, widely rounded at base, 2 to 3 in. long, 1 to 1½ in. broad, glabrous above, glaucous and scaly below. *fl.* in a loose terminal cluster of 8 to 10; cor. widely funnel-shaped, 5-lobed, tube about 1 in. long, pink, unspotted. May. SW. Szechuan, W. China. 1922. (B.M. 9597.)

R. face'tum* (24*b*) D. Probably only a subspecies of *R. eriogynum* from which it differs in l. of thinner texture and in fl.-stalks more or less glandular. Coming from Burma, it is of larger size and grows in a moister region. June. 1914.

R. Falcone'ri* (17). C. Evergreen tree up to 40 ft., young shoots stout, woolly. *l.* oval to oblong, 6 to 12 in. long, about half as wide, wrinkled with deep-set veins above, rusty-woolly beneath. *fl.* 20 or more in a close rounded truss 6 to 9 in. across; cor. bell-shaped, 2 in. wide, 8- to 10-lobed, creamy-white to pale yellow, purple blotched at the base; stamens 12 to 16, shorter than cor.; stigma knob-like. April. Himalaya. 1850. (B.M. 4924; R.S.H. 10.) One of the most magnificent in stature, foliage, and blossom. Trunk occasionally 2 ft. through. var. **exim'ium,** a synonym of *R. eximium.*

R. Farge'sii (19*f*). B. Evergreen shrub or small tree. *l.* oblong-ovate, apex rounded, 2 to 3½ in. long, rather glaucous beneath. *fl.* 6 to 10 in a truss; cor. open bell-shaped, 2 in. wide, 6- or 7-lobed, pale rose to purplish-pink; stamens 14, glabrous; cal. and ovary glandular. April. China. 1901. (B.M. 8736.) Often confused with *R. oreodoxa*, which is distinct by its glabrous ovary and proportionately narrower l.

R. fastigia'tum (26). A. Small evergreen shrub up to 3 ft. *l.* elliptic-oblanceolate ⅓ in. long, densely scaly on both surfaces. *fl.* in terminal clusters of 4 to 5; cor. ½ in. long; light-purple but variable in colour. Yunnan, W. China. An attractive dwarf species when grown in a mass.

R. ferrugin'eum (18). A. Alpine rose. Evergreen shrub, 3 to 4 ft., of dense habit. *l.* narrow-oblong, pointed, 1 to 1¾ in. long, glossy green, thickly covered beneath with golden brown, finally rust-coloured scales. *fl.* in clusters of 6 to 12; cor. rose-scarlet or deep rose, ½ to ¾ in. wide with 5 rounded lobes, tubular at base; stamens 10, hairy; cal. and ovary very scaly. June. Cent. Europe. 1752. (L.B.C. 65.) Well known to travellers in the Alps where it blooms in July and August, according to altitude. var. **al'bum,** *fl.* white; **atrococcin'eum,** *fl.* nearly scarlet; **myrtifo'lium,** a synonym of *R. Kotschyi.*

Rhododendron fictolacteum

R. fictolac'teum (17). B. Evergreen tree, in nature 15 to 45 ft., shoots tomentose. *l.* elliptical to obovate, 5 to 12 in. long, brown-felted beneath. *fl.* 12 to 15 in trusses 5 to 7 in. across; cor. bell-shaped, 2½ in. wide, 7- or 8-lobed, white, creamy, or rose-tinted, always crimson-blotched. Stamens 14 to 16, shorter than cor.; anthers red-brown; ovary felted. April, May. China. 1889. (B.M. 8372 as *R. lacteum.*) Very variable, some forms being poor compared with the best, which are very handsome.

R. Fittia'num (15). A. Low evergreen shrub akin to, but quite distinct from *R. dauricum*. The violet-purple fl., each ⅝ in. wide, come singly, not only from a cluster of buds at the apex of the shoot, but also in the axils of l. lower down; 20 or more may be open simultaneously on one shoot. April, May. China. 1912. Sometimes included in *R. dauricum.*

R. flav'idum (26). A. Evergreen bushy shrub, 1 to 2 ft., shoots densely scaly. *l.* ovate-oblong, ½ to 1 in. long, scaly on both surfaces, especially beneath. *fl.* 3 to 6 in a cluster; cor. 1¼ in. wide, with a short, downy tube and 5 spreading or slightly decurved crinkled lobes, soft primrose yellow; stamens 10; ovary scaly; style downy towards base; cal. with 5 oblong, scaly lobes ¼ in. long. April. China. 1905. (B.M. 8326.) SYN. *R. primulinum.*

R. fla'vum. A synonym of *R. luteum.*

R. floribun'dum (3*b*). B. Evergreen shrub up to 15 ft., of stiff habit. *l.* elliptic-lanceolate, 3 to 6 in. long, margins recurved, stiff and leathery, glabrous above, white-felted beneath. *fl.* in compact trusses of 8 to 12; cor. widely bell-shaped, 2 to 2½ in. across the 5 lobes, purplish-lavender with a maroon blush; stamens 10; ovary bristly; cal. and fl.-stalk white-felted. April. China. 1903. The fl. vary in colour and some of the better lavender ones are quite attractive. (B.M. 9609.)

R. formo'sum (28*a*). D. Evergreen shrub 8 to 10 ft., scaly in most parts. *l.* oblanceolate to obovate, 1½ to 3 in. long, glaucous beneath, margins and stalks ciliate. *fl.* 2 to 4 in a cluster, fragrant; cor. funnel-shaped, 2 to 2½ in. long, 5-lobed, white tinged with pink, yellow in the throat; stamens 10, shorter than the cor., hairy; ovary 6-celled, scaly; cal. very small. May, June. Assam. 1845. (B.M. 4457.) SYN. *R. Gibsonii.*

R. Forres'tii* (31*a*). B. Creeping evergreen shrub a few in. h. *l.* broadly obovate to roundish, ½ to 1½ in. long, veins conspicuously grooved, undersurface more or less purple-stained. *fl.* often solitary, sometimes in twos or even threes, cor. deep crimson, narrowly bell-shaped, 1⅜ in. long and wide, lobes 5, deeply notched; stamens 10, glabrous; ovary densely glandular; style glabrous; cal. very short, glandular. April, May. China, Tibet. 1914. Creeping habit very distinctive; has been found climbing 3 to 5 ft. h. up the face of moist rocks. (B.M. 9186.)

R. Fortu'nei* (19*c*). B. Evergreen, wide-spreading shrub up to 10 or 12 ft. *l.* oblong, 4 to 8 in. long, rather glaucous beneath. *fl.* in a loose truss of 6 to 12, fragrant; cor. 2½ to 3 in. wide, pale rose, 7- or 8-lobed; stamens 14, glabrous; ovary and style glandular. May. E. China. 1855. (B.M. 5596.) Charmingly fragrant species and a parent of many fine hybrids such as *Loderi, kewense, Luscombei.*

R. ful'gens (9). B. Evergreen shrub or small tree up to 12 ft., bark peeling; leaf-bud-scales crimson. *l.* oval, 3 to 4 in. long, rounded or cordate at the base, thickly tawny-felted beneath. *fl.* 10 or 12 in a compact rounded truss 3 to 4 in. wide. cor. bell-shaped, 5-lobed, 1 to 1½ in. wide, blood-red, unspotted; stamens 10, glabrous; anthers chocolate-brown. March. Himalaya. 1849. (B.M. 5317; R.S.H. 25.)

R. fulvoi'des (20). B. Very near *R. fulvum* but the down on leaf beneath differs in being buff to tawny and the ovary is 5- or 6-chambered whilst that of *R. fulvum* is 8- to 10-chambered. Cor. similar in range of colour. April. China, Tibet. 1918. Now regarded as inseparable from *R. fulvum.*

Rhododendron fulvum

R. fulvum (20). B. Evergreen shrub or small tree; shoots brown-felted. *l.* oblong to oval, 4 to 8 in. long, glabrous above, clad beneath with cinnamon-coloured down. *fl.* up to 20 in a close rounded truss 4 in. across; cor. bell-shaped, 1½ in. long, 5- or 6-lobed, white flushed with rose to bright rose, crimson blotched; stamens 10; ovary and style glabrous. March, April. China. 1912. (B.M. 9587.) A distinctive and beautiful feature of this species is the richly coloured pubescence beneath the l.

R. galacti'num (17). A. Evergreen shrub or small tree up to 25 ft. *l.* oblong-ovate to oblanceolate, 4 to 10 in. long, 2 to 4 in. wide, glabrous above, velvety beneath with pale grey or brown pubescence. *fl.* about 15 in a rounded truss; cor. bell-shaped, 1¼ in. long, 7-lobed, white tinged with pink outside, blotched and spotted with crimson inside; stamens 14; ovary and style glabrous. April, May. China. 1908. Only species of its series with a glabrous ovary.

R. Genestieria'num (21). D. Evergreen shrub, 4 to 12 ft. *l.* lanceolate, tapered at both ends, 2 to 4 in. long, ¼ to 1½ in. wide, thin, glaucous beneath. *fl.* in racemes of 12 or more, their stalks slender, 1 in. long; cor. narrowly bell-shaped, ½ in. long, plum-purple, with 5 erect lobes; stamens 10, glabrous; ovary scaly; style glabrous, bent over. April. China. 1919. (B.M. 9310.) Very distinct by its racemose inflorescence, small purple fl., small cal., and few scales.

R. Gib'sonii. A synonym of *R. formosum.*

R. gigan'teum (22). E. Evergreen tree, 80 ft. h. at its largest; trunk 2 ft. thick. *l.* elliptic, 9 to 16 in. long, glabrous above, covered with red-brown down beneath in mature plants, glabrous in younger plants. *fl.* in trusses of 20 to 25; cor. bell-shaped, 2½ in. long, deep rose-crimson with a slight blotch at base, 8-lobed; stamens 16, glabrous; ovary downy; style glabrous. April. China. 1919. The most gigantic of rhododendrons; very tender. (B.M. n.s. 253.)

R. glaucophyl'lum (21). B. Evergreen, resinous-scented shrub, 3 to 6 ft., young shoots, l., fl.-stalks, and cal. covered with red-brown scales. *l.* oval to oblong, 1 to 3 in. long, ½ to 1 in. wide, dull green above, glaucous beneath. *fl.* 5 or 6 in a truss; cor. 1 in. wide, bell-shaped, rosy-red, the 5 lobes rounded, overlapping; cal. lobes ⅓ in. long; stamens 10; ovary scaly; style glabrous, thickening towards the stigma. May. Himalaya. 1850. (B.M. 4721; R.S.H. 17.) SYN. *R. glaucum.*

R. glau'cum. A synonym of *R. glaucophyllum.*

R. glischroi'des (6*c*). D. Differs from *R. glischrum* in the white or creamy-white fl. crimson blotched at base and flushed with rose, the glabrous style, and l. covered beneath with pale grey hairs. March. Burma. 1925.

R. glis'chrum (6*c*). C. Evergreen shrub or small tree up to 25 ft.; shoots, l.-stalks, fl.-stalks, and cal. very bristly. *l.* narrow-oblong to lanceolate, 6 to 10 in. long, soon glabrous above, more or less bristly beneath. *fl.* 15 or more in trusses 5 to 6 in. across; cor. bell-shaped, 2 in. wide, 5-lobed, pink, magenta pink, rosy-lilac, or

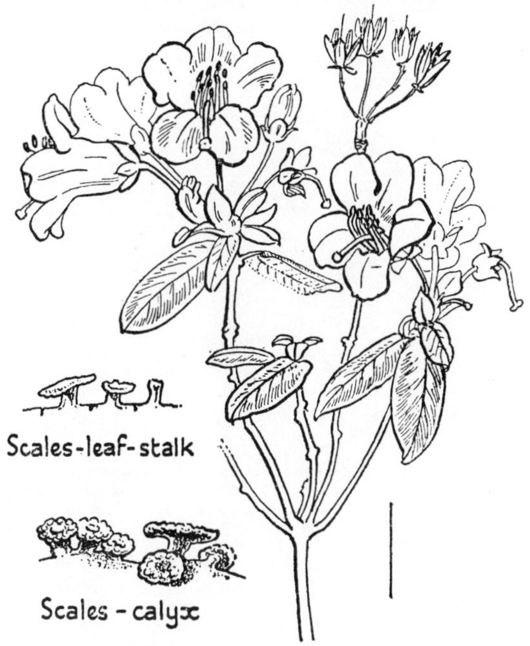

Rhododendron glaucophyllum

Rhododendron glischrum

purplish-rose, with a dark blotch; stamens 10, ovary and style glandular-bristly. May. China. 1914. (B.M. 9035.) Of variable quality, sometimes pretty, sometimes poor. **A**

R. gran'de* (22). E. Evergreen tree up to 30 ft. *l.* oblong to oblanceolate, 6 to 15 in. long, silvery-white or with tawny down beneath. *fl.* 25 to 30 in a rounded truss 7 in. wide; cor. bell-shaped, 2 to 3 in. long and wide, 8-lobed, ivory-white, purple-blotched at base; stamens 16; ovary downy and glandular; stigma large, disk-like. February to April. Himalaya. 1849. One of the finest Himalayan species in l. and blossom. *R. argenteum* (B.M. 5054) is usually made synonymous with *R. grande*, but some keep it separate because of its silvery l. as distinct from the tawny undersurface in *grande* proper. var. **ro'seum** (B.M. 6948) is probably a hybrid with *R. arboreum*; cor. 6-lobed, bright rose.

Rhododendron Griersonianum

R. Griersonia'num* (4). C. Evergreen shrub, 7 ft. or more; shoots and l.-stalks bristly, glandular; winter buds enclosed by much-prolonged scales. *l.* lanceolate, 4 to 8 in. long, woolly beneath. *fl.* 5 to 12 in loose clusters; cor. $2\frac{1}{2}$ in. wide, trumpet-shaped with a fluted cylindrical tube; lobes 5, very downy outside; stamens 10, geranium-scarlet, 1 to $2\frac{1}{2}$ in. long; ovary and style hairy. June. China. 1917. (B.M. 9195.) Fine, distinct species much used by hybridists. Unique in the genus for its brilliant colour. Its young growth starts to grow late and in exposed places is often damaged by autumn frosts.

R. Griffithia'num* (19*d*). E. Evergreen shrub or small tree up to 20 ft. *l.* oblong, 6 to 12 in. long, glabrous, rather glaucous beneath. *fl.* 4 to 6 in a lax truss, slightly fragrant; cor. open bell-shaped, 5 to 6 in. across, 5-lobed, white or flushed pink; cal. saucer-shaped, $\frac{3}{4}$ to 1 in. wide; stamens 12 to 16, glabrous, shortish; ovary and style glandular; stigma knob-like. May. Himalaya. 1849. (B.M. 5065 as *R. Griffithianum Aucklandii.*) Finest of all white-fld. species and the largest-fld. of all. Hardy in Cornwall. A parent of many hybrids.

R. habrot'richum (6*c*). C. Bushy evergreen up to 10 ft., shoots densely glandular-bristly. *l.* ovate-oblong, rounded or cordate at base, 3 to $6\frac{1}{2}$ in. long, l.-stalks, margins, and midrib underneath bristly. *fl.* 9 to 12 in a truss; cor. bell-shaped, $1\frac{1}{2}$ to 2 in. wide, 5-lobed, white or pale rose, purple-blotched; stamens 10; ovary, style, cal. and fl.-stalk glandular-bristly. April. China. 1913. (B.T.S. 3, 382.)

Rhododendron haematodes

R. haema'leum (31*d*). A. Evergreen shrub, 2 to 4 ft. very similar in habit, l., infl., and fl. to *R. didymum*, but differs by having no glands on young shoots, cal., and fl.-stalk. *l.* larger, up to $3\frac{1}{2}$ in. long. Cor. of the same black-crimson, but larger. May, June. Tibet 1904. (B.M. 9263 as *R. sanguineum.*)

R. haematochi'lum. A synonym of *R. oreodoxa.*

R. haemato'des* (31*b*). B. Evergreen of close growth, 3 to 4 ft., shoots woolly. *l.* obovate, $1\frac{1}{2}$ to $3\frac{1}{2}$ in. long, densely felted beneath. *fl.* in clusters of 6 to 10; cor. funnel-shaped, $1\frac{1}{2}$ in. long, 5-lobed, brilliant scarlet-crimson; stamens 10; ovary woolly; style glabrous; cal. red, $\frac{1}{3}$ in. long, 5-lobed. May. China. 1911. (B.M. 9165.) One of the richest coloured of dwarf species.

R. halen'se. A hybrid between *R. ferrugineum* and *R. hirsutum.*

Rhododendron Hanceanum

R. Hancea'num (40 *b*). Evergreen shrub, 3 to 4 ft.; shoots glabrous. *l.* lanceolate to narrow obovate, $\frac{1}{2}$ to 4 in. long, hard, dark green and rather scaly above, pale and scaly beneath. *fl.* in terminal many-fld. clusters; cor. 1 in. long, funnel-shaped, white to yellow, lobes deep; cal. lobes $\frac{3}{16}$ in. long, scaly; stamens 10, protruded, downy in lower part; ovary scaly; style glabrous. March, April. China. 1909. (B.M. 8669.) var. **na'num,** a dwarf variety up to $1\frac{1}{2}$ ft., *fl.* pale yellow. A good plant for the rock-garden as it usually flowers freely.

R. heliole'pis (23). C. Evergreen shrub up to 10 ft.; shoots under-surface of l., cal., cor., fl.-stalks, and ovary all scaly. *l.* ovate-lanceolate, 3 to 4 in. long. *fl.* 4 to 7 in a loose cluster; cor. widely funnel-shaped, 1 to $1\frac{1}{3}$ in. long and wide, rose-purple to pale old rose, with crimson markings; stamens 10, very downy below; style downy. June. China. 1912.

R. hemitricho'tum (35). C. Evergreen shrub, 3 to 5 ft., shoots softly downy. *l.* scattered along shoots, oblong, 1 to $1\frac{3}{4}$ in. long, downy above, glaucous and scaly beneath. *fl.* mostly in pairs from several buds at end of shoots; cor. funnel-shaped, $\frac{1}{2}$ to $\frac{3}{4}$ in. wide, 5-lobed; stamens 10; ovary scaly; style glabrous. April. China. 1919. The glaucous undersurface of l. is distinctive.

R. hippophaeoi'des* (26). A. Evergreen shrub, 4 to 5 ft.; shoots slender, scurfy. *l.* oblong to narrowly elliptical, $\frac{3}{4}$ to $1\frac{1}{2}$ in. long, greyish beneath, scaly on both sides. *fl.* 4 to 8 in a cluster; cor. $1\frac{1}{2}$ to 2 in. wide, with short hairy tube and 5 rounded overlapping lobes, purplish-blue, rosy-purple, rarely rose-pink; stamens 10, purple, $\frac{1}{6}$ in. long; ovary scaly; style red, smooth. April. China. 1913. (B.M. 9156.) Useful and easily grown.

R. × **hirsutiform'e.** A hybrid between *R. ferrugineum* and *R. hirsutum.*

R. hirsu'tum (18). A. Alpine rose. Similar to *R. ferrugineum* in habit and fl., but the young shoots, l.-margins, cal., and fl.-stalks are all bristly. *l.* less scaly, greener beneath; cal. lobes larger. Grows in similar alpine regions but always on limestone. June. 1656. (B.M. 1853; L.B.C. 479.) var. **albiflo'rum** has white fl.

R. Hodgson'ii (17). B. Evergreen shrub or small tree, up to 20 ft. *l.* 6 to 12 in. long, oval to obovate, very leathery, brown-woolly beneath, stalk cylindric, very stout. *fl.* 15 to 20 in a compact truss 6 to 8 in. across; cor. $1\frac{1}{2}$ to 2 in. wide, bell-shaped, usually 7- to 8-lobed (sometimes 6- or 10-lobed), magenta-lilac; stamens usually 16, shortish; ovary and fl.-stalk downy. April. Himalaya. 1849. (B.M. 5552; R.S.H. 15.) Fine foliaged species, l. have been found 18 in. long.

R. Hook'eri* (38*e*). E. Evergreen shrub, 12 to 14 ft., entirely glabrous except for tufts of down spaced on the veins beneath the l.—a distinctive character. *l.* oval-oblong, 3 to 5 in. long, rather glaucous beneath. *fl.* in compact trusses of 12 to 15; cor. bell-shaped, 5-lobed, $1\frac{1}{2}$ to 2 in. wide, blood-red, lobes rounded and notched in middle; stamens 10, shortish; cal. $\frac{1}{4}$ in. long. March, April. Bhutan. 1852. (B.M. 4926.)

R. Hunnewellia'num (3*b*). B. Evergreen shrub up to 15 ft., shoots felted. *l.* oblanceolate, 2 to $4\frac{1}{2}$ in. long, $\frac{1}{2}$ to 1 in. wide, grey-white-felted beneath. *fl.* 5 to 8 in a cluster; cor. bell-shaped, 5-lobed, 2 in. wide, pink to pale rosy-lilac spotted with maroon; stamens 10, white; anthers dark brown; ovary and base of style white-downy. March–April. China. 1908. Chiefly distinct by its very narrow, slender-pointed l., white-woolly beneath.

R. hypenan'thum (2). C. Long confused with *R. anthopogon* and similar to it in habit and foliage, but *fl.* sulphur-yellow (not pink), and scales that surround base of winter l.-buds persist for several years, whereas in *R. anthopogon* they fall away almost immediately. April. Himalaya. 1820.

R. hypoglau'cum (3*b*). B. Evergreen shrub or small tree, 10 to 20 ft. *l.* narrow-elliptic, 2½ to 4½ in. long, glossy green above, with appressed white scurf beneath. *fl.* 6 to 8 in a truss; cor. bell-shaped, 1½ in. wide, 5-lobed, white flushed with rose, spotted dark rose; stamens 10; ovary woolly and glandular. May. China. 1900. (B.M. 8649.) Near *R. argyrophyllum*, *fl.* fewer.

R. hypolepido'tum (21). B. Evergreen aromatic shrub, 4 to 6 ft. *l.* oval to obovate, 1 to 2 in. long, ½ to ⅞ in. wide, densely scaly and rather glaucous beneath. *fl.* in clusters of 4 to 8, sometimes 10; cor. yellow, bell-shaped, 5-lobed, ¾ in. wide; cal. 5-lobed almost to base, scaly outside; stamens 10, downy; anthers brown; ovary densely scaly; style very thick and stout, glabrous. May, June. China. Tibet. (B.M. 9259.) Closely related to *R. brachyanthum* and sometimes regarded as a variety of that species.

R. impedi'tum* (26). A. Dwarf, densely twiggy, evergreen shrub, 6 to 18 in., shoots scaly. *l.* oval to ovate, ⅜ to ⅝ in. long, ¼ in wide, very scaly on both sides. *fl.* 2 or 3 together, slightly fragrant; cor. 1 in. wide, mauve or pale purplish-blue, with a short tube and 5 or 6 spreading lobes; stamens 10, purple; cal. with 5 lobes, ⅛ in. long. May. China. 1911. Dainty, free-flowering rock-garden shrub.

R. impera'tor* (27). A. Dwarf evergreen shrub, forming a mat-like growth a few in. high. *l.* aromatic, oblanceolate to narrowly elliptic, 1 to 1½ in. long, glaucous and very thinly scaly beneath. *fl.* solitary or in pairs; cor. funnel-shaped, 1 to 1½ in. wide, with 5 recurved lobes, downy all over outside, pinkish-purple in various shades without spots; stamens 10, downy; ovary scaly; style glabrous, crimson, fl.-stalk red, ½ to 1 in. long. May. Burma. 1926.

R. in'dicum (5*d*). C. Evergreen shrub, 3 to 6 ft., shoots covered with flattened bristles. *l.* lanceolate to oblanceolate, 1 to 1½ in. long, bristly on both sides. *fl.* solitary or in pairs; cor. broadly funnel-shaped, 1½ in. long, bright red, scarlet, or sometimes rosy-red; stamens 5; ovary bristly; style glabrous. June. Japan. 1833. (B.R. 1700; L.B.C. 275 as *A. indica.*) (This is not the 'Indian Azalea' of greenhouses, which is *R. Simsii*, with 10 stamens, larger l., and is not so hardy.) var. **balsaminaeflo'rum,** *fl.* very double, salmon-red. Japan. 1877. SYN. *Azalea rosaeflora*; **crispiflo'rum,** cor. bright rose with wavy margins. 1850. (B.M. 4726.) SYN. *Azalea crispiflora*; **variega'tum,** cor. striped red and white.

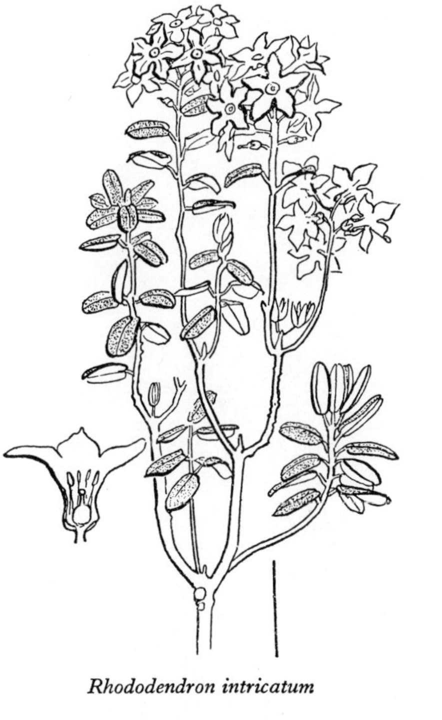

Rhododendron intricatum

R. insi'gne (3*b*). A. Evergreen shrub of stocky growth, said to attain 5 to 12 ft. *l.* narrowly elliptic, 3 to 5 in. long, glossy green, silvery beneath. *fl.* long-stalked, in trusses of 15 or more and 4 to 5 in. across; cor. bell-shaped, 5-lobed, 2 in. wide, pink with crimson spots; stamens 10 to 14; ovary silky-hairy. May. China. 1908. At present a low, stocky bush in gardens but fl. freely. (B.M. 8885.)

R. × **interme'dium** (18). One of several hybrids between *R. ferrugineum* and *R. hirsutum*. Tyrol.

R. intrica'tum* (26). A. Evergreen shrub, 6 to 12 in., shoots scurfy with reddish scales. *l.* roundish-ovate, ¼ to ½ in. long, scaly on both sides. *fl.* in clusters of 4 to 6; cor. ⅝ in. wide, with a short downy tube and 5 rounded spreading lobes, violet-purple in bud, pale mauve or lilac when fully open; stamens 10, almost completely enclosed in cor. tube; ovary scaly; style glabrous, very short; cal. lobes 5, short triangular. April, May. China. 1904. (B.M. 8163.)

R. irrora'tum (24*a*). C. Evergreen shrub or small tree, 12 to 25 ft. *l.* narrowly elliptical, 2 to 5 in. long, firm, glabrous at maturity. *fl.* about 15 in a rounded truss 4 in. across; cor. narrowly bell-shaped, with 5 rounded notched lobes, 1½ to 2 in. wide, of varied colouring, being sometimes pure white, sometimes creamy, yellow, or suffused with rose, nearly always spotted, occasionally conspicuously so; stamens 10, white or yellow; ovary, style, and fl.-stalk glandular. March, April. China. 1890. (B.M. 7361.) Of variable merit; the best forms are attractive.

R. ixeu'ticum. A synonym of *R. crinigerum.*

R. japon'icum* (5*b*). A. Deciduous shrub, 4 to 8 ft. *l.* narrowly oblanceolate to oboval, 2 to 4 in. long, glaucous beneath. *fl.* 6 to 10 in a cluster, not fragrant; cor. 2½ to 3½ in. wide, funnel-shaped at the base, soft rose, orange-red, salmon-red; stamens 5; anthers dark brown; ovary and the small cal. hairy. May. Japan. 1861. (B.M. 5905 as *R. sinense.*) Mostly grown as 'Azalea mollis' and the parent of a beautiful race of garden vars. and hybrids. (*See* **R. molle** with which this has been much confused.)

R. jasminiflo'rum. F. Evergreen, often epiphytic shrub, 8 to 10 ft. *l.* oval, ovate, or obovate, often cordate at the base, 1 to 2½ in. long, very shortly stalked, leathery, glabrous. *fl.* crowded in a truss of up to 20; cor. white, slenderly tubular, tube 1½ in. long, the limb deeply 5-lobed and 1 in. wide; stamens 10, downy; anthers deep pink and just visible at mouth of tube. May to September. Malacca. 1845. (B.M. 4524.) Needs warm greenhouse conditions.

Rhododendron javanicum

R. java'nicum.* F. Evergreen shrub, 4 to 6 ft. *l.* elliptic-lanceolate, slender-pointed, 4 to 7 in. long, dark glossy green, scaly beneath. *fl.* up to 12 in shapely trusses 6 in. wide; cor. rich orange-yellow, with funnel-shaped base and 5-lobed limb 1½ to 2½ in. wide; stamens 10; anthers dark purple; fl.-stalk 1 to 2 in. long. Various seasons. Java. 1844. (B.M. 4336.) Perhaps the finest of the Javan species. Warm greenhouse. var. **tubiflo'rum** has smaller orange-red fl. with a comparatively longer cor. tube. (B.M. 6850.)

R. Johnstonea'num* (28*a*). D. An evergreen shrub up to 6 ft. h. *l.* elliptic, 2 to 4 in. long, up to 1½ in. broad. *fl.* in trusses of 4; cor. 2 to 2½ in. long, white to pale yellow spotted with red inside the back lobe which also has a yellow blotch at the base, fragrant. May. Manipur. An attractive loose-growing shrub for the sheltered garden.

R. Keis'kei (40*d*). A. Evergreen shrub of low compact growth but said to be 6 ft. h. in nature. *l.* ovate-lanceolate, 1½ to 2½ in. long, pointed, scaly (especially beneath). *fl.* in clusters of 3 to 5; cor. widely bell-shaped, 1½ to 2 in. wide, 5-lobed, yellow, not spotted. April, May. Japan. 1908. (B.M. 8300.) Interesting as one of the few yellow-fld. in the series. The colour varies in different shrubs, sometimes dull but in better forms clear lemon-yellow.

R. kelet'icum (34). A. Evergreen shrub up to 12 in. *l.* obovate or oval, ½ in. long, bright green, very scaly beneath. *fl.* solitary or in pairs; cor. open, ¾ in. wide, deeply 5-lobed, purplish-crimson; stamens 10, woolly near base; ovary scaly; style glabrous; cal. with

5 deep lobes $\frac{3}{16}$ in. long; pedicel $\frac{3}{4}$ to $1\frac{1}{4}$ in. long. June. Tibet. 1919. Charming rock-garden plant.

R. Key'sii (14). C. Evergreen shrub, 6 to 12 ft., shoots, l.-stalk, undersurface of l., and fl.-stalk densely scaly. *l.* oblong-lanceolate, 2 to 4 in. long. *fl.* in clusters of about 6, several of which spring from axillary buds; cor. a cylindrical tube $\frac{3}{4}$ in. long, $\frac{1}{4}$ in. wide, red except at apex where are 5 small, erect, yellowish lobes. May, June. Bhutan. 1851. (B.M. 4875.) Very distinct by its Correa-like cor. **var. unic'olor** has cor. lobes similar in colour to tube.

R. Kingia'num* (*3a*). D. A subspecies of *R. arboreum*, differing from it chiefly by the l. which is broader, very convex, very wrinkled and peculiarly puckered (bullate), *fl.* borne later in trusses 4 or 5 in. wide, rich blood red. June. Himalaya. 1882. (B.M. 7696 as *R. arboreum Kingianum.*)

R. kongboen'se (2). A. Dwarf evergreen shrub, shoots scaly. *l.* aromatic, oblong to oblong-lanceolate, $\frac{1}{2}$ to 1 in. long, scaly on both sides. *fl.* up to 10 in a cluster 1 in. wide; cor. deep rose, tube hairy, $\frac{1}{8}$ to $\frac{1}{2}$ in. wide with 5 spreading glabrous lobes; stamens 5, hidden in cor. tube; ovary very scaly; style glabrous, very short and thick; cal. with 5 lobes, $\frac{1}{8}$ in. long, erect, scaly down middle. April, May. Tibet. 1925. (B.M. 9492.) Adapted for the rock-garden.

R. Kotsch'yi (18). A. Evergreen shrub, about $1\frac{1}{2}$ ft. *l.* $\frac{1}{2}$ to $\frac{3}{4}$ in. long, elliptic-oblong, blunt, with rusty brown scales beneath. *fl.* up to 8 in a cluster; cor. 1 in. wide, clear rose, with 5 spreading lobes; stamens 10, hairy, enclosed in the cor. tube; ovary very scaly; style very short. June. Cent. Europe. (B.M. 9132.) SYN. *R. ferrugineum myrtifolium.* Distinct by its dwarf habit, small l., downy cor., and enclosed stamens. Often grows on limestone.

R. Kyaw'i* (*24b*). E. Evergreen shrub or small tree, 15 to 20 ft. *l.* oblong-oval, 6 to 12 in. long, one-third as wide, loosely downy at first, finally shining green beneath. *fl.* 12 to 16 in fine trusses 6 to 7 in. across; cor. funnel-shaped, 2 to 3 in. wide, 5-lobed, rich crimson, with blackish blotches at the base; stamens 10, crimson; ovary and fl.-stalk downy; style crimson, glandular. July, August. Burma. 1919. (B.M. 9271.) One of the richest coloured of all, late to grow and late to flower.

R. lac'teum* (25). C. Evergreen shrub, or a tree up to 30 ft., shoots $\frac{1}{2}$ in. thick. *l.* stout, oblong, ovate, often cordate, 4 to 8 in. long, tawny-felted beneath. *fl.* 15 to 30 packed in a truss 6 in. across; cor. bell-shaped, 5-lobed, $1\frac{1}{2}$ to 2 in. wide, lovely soft sulphur-yellow; stamens 10; ovary whitish-downy; style glabrous. April. China. 1910. (B.M. 8988.) One of the finest yellow. Not very easily grown, particularly resentful of hot sunshine.

R. lana'tum (9). C. Evergreen shrub 5 to 7 ft.; shoots, l. beneath, and fl.-stalks all thickly felted. *l.* $2\frac{1}{2}$ to 5 in. long, obovate to narrowly oval. *fl.* 6 to 7 in a truss; cor. bell-shaped, 2 in. wide, pale yellow with purple-red spots; stamens 10; ovary woolly; style glabrous. April. Himalaya. 1849. (F.d.S. 684; R.S.H. 16.) Distinguished by its yellow fl. Not easy to grow and very rare.

R. laxiflo'rum (*24a*). E. Evergreen shrub, 12 to 20 ft., shoots very slender, soon glabrous. *l.* oblong-lanceolate, tapered at both ends, 3 to $5\frac{1}{2}$ in. long, glabrous. *fl.* in loose trusses of 6 to 12; cor. widely bell-shaped, 5-lobed, 2 in. wide, white unspotted but suffused with rose; stamens 10, glabrous; ovary and style glandular; fl.-stalk 1 to $1\frac{1}{2}$ in. long, glandular. April. China. 1919. (B.M. n.s. 385.)

R. ledoi'des (2). C. Evergreen shrub, 2 to 4 ft., shoots slender, scaly, hairy. *l.* linear to narrowly lanceolate, $\frac{3}{4}$ to $1\frac{1}{4}$ in. long, dull green, yellowish with dense scales beneath. *fl.* fragrant, 12 to 20 closely packed in rounded trusses 1 to $1\frac{1}{2}$ in. wide; cor. slenderly tubular with 5 spreading lobes, white to clear rose, $\frac{1}{2}$ in. wide; stamens 5, hidden in the cor. tube, glabrous; ovary very scaly; style red, thick, very short; cal. ciliate. May. China. 1914. (B.M. 6631; 8831.) *See* **R. trichostomum.**

R. lepidan'thum. A variety of *R. primulaeflorum.*

R. lepido'tum (27). A–C. Evergreen, resinously scented, scaly shrub, 2 to 4 ft., shoots slender. *l.* $\frac{1}{2}$ to $1\frac{1}{2}$ in. long, narrowly obovate to elliptic. *fl.* 2 to 4 (rarely 6) in a truss; stalks slender, up to 1 in. long; cor. $\frac{3}{4}$ to 1 in. wide, 5-lobed, pale yellow, pink or dull purple; stamens 8, hairy below; style thick, short, glabrous. June. Himalaya, Tibet. 1850. (B.M. 4657; R.H.S. 23 as *R. salignum.*) Variable in colour of fl. and in hardiness and in the broad sense may be taken to include *R. elaeagnoides.*

R. leptoth'rium (32). E. Evergreen, diffusely branched shrub, up to 20 ft., shoots very slender, minutely downy, becoming grey. *l.* oval-lanceolate, pointed, $1\frac{1}{2}$ to 3 in. long, purplish at first then dark glossy green, glabrous except on midrib. *fl.* solitary from several terminal axillary buds; cor. $1\frac{1}{2}$ in. wide, 5-lobed, deep magenta-rose; stamens 5; ovary viscous, glandular; style glabrous. April, May. China. 1914. Differs from *R. ovatum* by its ciliate, glandular cal.

R. leucas'pis* (7). C. Evergreen shrub, 1 to 2 ft.; shoots and l.-stalks hairy. *l.* elliptic to obovate, rounded at apex, tapered at base, $1\frac{1}{2}$ to $2\frac{3}{4}$ in. long, glaucous and scaly beneath. *fl.* single, in pairs, or in threes; cor. flat and open, 2 in. wide, pure white, with 5 overlapping lobes; stamens 10, short, white, hairy; anthers brown; ovary densely scaly; style thick, bent over, glabrous; cal. deeply 5-lobed. February to April. Tibet. 1925. (G.C. 85 (1929), 135; B.M. 9665.) Distinguished by its pure white fl. Seedlings will flower at 3 years old.

R. Lin'dleyi (*28c*). E. Evergreen shrub, often epiphytic and straggling in its wild state. *l.* elliptic, $2\frac{1}{2}$ to 6 in. long, glaucous and scaly below. *fl.* in clusters of 4 to 6, fragrant; cor. funnel-shaped, $3\frac{1}{2}$ in. long and wide, white. Now quite rare, this species is closely akin to, and has been confused with, *R. Dalhousiae*, but young shoots and pedicels not bristly, cal. ciliate, and anthers about half as long. April. Himalaya. 1849. (B.M. n.s. 363.)

R. linearifo'lium (*5d*). B. Evergreen shrub, 2 to 4 ft., shoots, l., and fl.-stalks very hairy. *l.* 2 to 3 in. long, less than $\frac{1}{4}$ in. wide. *fl.* fragrant, in clusters of about 3; cor. with 5 lobes up to $1\frac{1}{2}$ in. long, but only $\frac{3}{16}$ in. wide, rosy-lilac; stamens 5; cal. narrowly linear, hairy, $\frac{1}{2}$ in. long. May. Japan. 1865. (B.M. 5769.) A narrow-leafed garden form of the Japanese *R. macrosepalum* which has lanceolate to ovate l. and fl. 2 in. wide, with the lobes $\frac{1}{2}$ to $\frac{5}{8}$ in. wide.

Rhododendron leucaspis

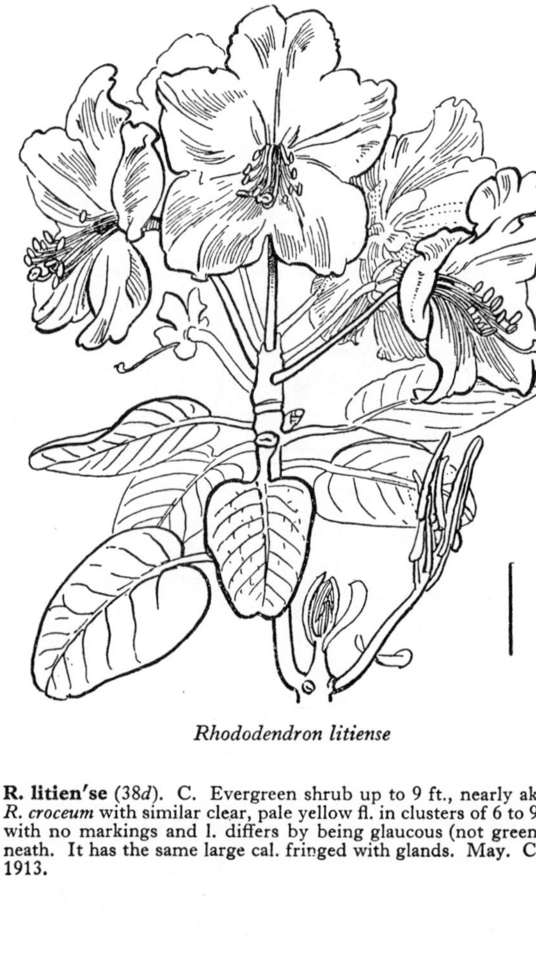

Rhododendron litiense

R. litien'se (*38d*). C. Evergreen shrub up to 9 ft., nearly akin to *R. croceum* with similar clear, pale yellow fl. in clusters of 6 to 9, but with no markings and l. differs by being glaucous (not green) beneath. It has the same large cal. fringed with glands. May. China. 1913.

R. Loch'ae. Evergreen shrub up to 20 ft., often epiphytic. *l.* elliptic to obovate, 2 to 3 in. long, glabrous, leathery, dark glossy green above, minutely scaly beneath. *fl.* pendulous, few in the cluster; cor. 1½ to 2 in. long, 1¼ in. wide, cylindric at base, 5-lobed, bright red; stamens 10, hairy at base; style and ovary scaly and downy. Queensland, on a few mountain tops at about 5,000 ft. alt. 1936. The only known Australian Rhododendron and of the same group as *R. javanicum* and needs the same warm greenhouse treatment. It flowered at Kew in September 1939, in 3 years from seed. **A**

R. × Lod'eri. C. (*R. Griffithianum* × *R. Fortunei*). A very fine hybrid raised at Leonardslee, Sussex, by Sir Edmund Loder. An evergreen shrub up to 20 ft. *l.* oblong, 6 to 10 in. long. *fl.* in trusses of 6 to 10, large, white or flushed pink. A number of varieties of this hybrid have been selected. The best are **King George,** *fl.* white flushed pink in bud; **Sir Joseph Hooker,** *fl.* pale pink; **Pink Diamond,** *fl.* pink in bud and on first opening; **Princess Marina,** *fl.* very large, white flushed pink; **Sir Edmund**; and **Venus.**

R. longesquama'tum (6*d*). B. Evergreen shrub up to 10 ft. or more; shoots, l.-stalks, and fl.-stalks clad with long, rusty, branched hairs. *l.* 3 to 5 in. long, oblanceolate, glabrous above except on the midrib, ciliate. *fl.* in trusses of 7 to 12; cor. bell-shaped, 5-lobed, 2 in. wide, soft pink; cal. with oblong lobes up to ½ in. long; stamens 10; ovary bristly; style glabrous. May. China. 1904. (B.M. 9430.) SYN. *R. Brettii.* Very distinct by its large, long-persisting l.-bud scales and large cal.

Rhododendron lutescens

R. Ludlo'wii (27). A. Dwarf evergreen shrub up to 1 ft. h. *l.* leathery, obovate, ¾ in. long, ½ in. broad. *fl.* single or in pairs, terminal; cor. broadly tubular with broad open lobes ½ to ¾ in. wide, 1 to 1½ in. long, primrose yellow, spotted yellowish from wide tube, softly silky, pubescent on outside, style longer than stamens. S. Tibet. A species of recent introduction closely allied to *R. pumilum*, still a very rare plant in cultivation. (B.M. n.s. 412.)

R. lutes'cens* (40*d*). C. Evergreen shrub of loose habit, up to 10 ft., shoots slender. *l.* lanceolate, slenderly pointed, 1½ to 3½ in. long, scaly beneath. *fl.* solitary or in pairs from each of several buds at the end of the shoot; cor. funnel-shaped, 1½ in. wide, soft primrose-yellow; stamens 10, very prominent, 1 to 1½ in. long. February to April. China, Tibet. 1904. (B.M. 8851.) Valuable for its early yellow fl. which open successively for 6 weeks or more.

R. lu'teum* (5*b*). A. Deciduous shrub, 6 to 12 ft. *l.* linear-oblong to oblanceolate, 2½ to 4½ in. long, hairy along the midrib and margins. *fl.* in clusters of 6 to 12, very fragrant; cor. 1½ to 2 in. across, yellow, glandular and viscous outside; stamens 5 and, like the style, downy at the base, ovary glandular; cal. 5-lobed, the lobes ⅛ in. long, glandular like the fl.-stalk. May. E. Europe and Asia Minor. 1793. (B.M. 433 as *Azalea pontica.*) SYN. *R. flavum.* Vigorous free-flowering shrub, giving fine autumnal tints. Parent of many hybrids.

R. Macabea'num* (22). C. A large evergreen tree up to 45 ft. in its native habitat. Young branches densely tomentose with chestnut-brown indumentium. *l.* large, leathery, oblong-elliptic up to 12 in. long, 8 in. broad, upper surface glabrous, deep green, under surface greyish-white with a compact woolly indumentum. *fl.* in a compact umbel of many fl.; cor. ventricose campanulate, 2 to 2½ in. long, yellow or pale yellow with large purplish spots at base, pouched at base, lobes 8. One of the finest large-leaved species both for its foliage and its fl., the colour of which in the best forms is a rich yellow. April, May. Manipur, Assam. (1928.) (B.M. n.s. 187.)

R. Mackenziea'num. A synonym of *R. stenaulum.*

R. maculif'erum (6*d*). C. Evergreen shrub, 8 to 10 ft. *l.* oblong to obovate, 3 to 5½ in. long, woolly on midrib beneath. *fl.* in loose trusses of 6 to 10; cor. widely bell-shaped, 1½ in. wide, 5-lobed, white to pale rose with a black-crimson blotch; stamens 10; anthers black-purple; ovary cylindrical, covered with pale hairs; style glabrous. April. Distinct by its woolly midrib, the very conspicuous blotch on cor. and its erect lobes.

R. Mad'denii* (28*b*). E. Evergreen shrub up to 9 ft., bark papery, nearly all its parts scaly. *l.* lanceolate to oblong-lanceolate, 3 to 6 in. long, glaucous beneath. *fl.* very fragrant, in pairs, threes, or fours; cor. funnel-shaped, 4 in. long and wide, 5-lobed, white often flushed with rose; stamens, 20, glabrous; lobes of cal. ⅛ in. long. June to August. Himalaya. 1849. (B.M. 4805; R.S.H. 18.) var. **obtusifo'lium,** a synonym of *R. manipurense.*

R. magnifi'cum (22). D. Evergreen shrub or small tree up to 60 ft. h. in native habitat. *l.* oblong to oblong-obovate 10 to 15 in. long, 4 to 6 in. broad, apex broadly rounded, upper surface mat green, rugulose, under surface with a thin loose web-like white tomentum disappearing on older l. *fl.* in a large umbel of 20 to 30; cor. campanulate or tubular, up to 2½ in. long, Fuchsine-pink. Burma-Tibet frontier. 1931. A fine-leaved species allied to *R. protistum* and *R. sinogrande*, but differing in the colour of the fl. Like other members of this series does not flower as a young tree.

R. Makino'i (33*a*). B. Evergreen shrub up to 7 ft., shoots loosely woolly. *l.* narrowly lanceolate, 4 to 7 in. long, 1¼ in. wide, margins recurved, stiff, glabrous, thickly woolly beneath. *fl.* in trusses of 6 or more, stalks 1⅓ in. long, bristly; cor. 1½ in. wide, 5-lobed, soft pink; stamens 10; ovary densely woolly; style glabrous, white. June. Japan. SYN. *R. Metternichii angustifolium.* Spoilt by its rough-looking foliage.

R. malaya'num. F. Evergreen shrub or small tree; shoots, l., fl.-stalks, cal., and ovary all covered with minute red-brown scales. *l.* oblanceolate to elliptic-lanceolate, 2 to 4 in. long, dark green above, red-brown beneath. *fl.* 6 to 10 in a loose, almost stalkless cluster; cor. with a dull scarlet cylindrical tube ⅝ in. long, the more rosy limb ⅛ in. across, 5-lobed, the lobes rounded. Malay Is. 1854. (B.M. 6045.) Warm greenhouse.

R. mallo'tum* (31*b*). C. Evergreen shrub, 6 to 15 ft., shoots downy. *l.* obovate to elliptic, 3 to 6 in. long, dark dull green and wrinkled above, clad beneath with a dense, soft, red-brown wool. *fl.* 12 to 18 in a close truss 4½ in. wide; cor. widely funnel-shaped, 5-lobed, 1¾ in. wide, rosy-scarlet to rich crimson, with 5 black pouches at the base; stamens 10, glabrous; ovary woolly. March, April. China, Burma. 1914. (B.M. 9419.) The l. bears a strong likeness to that of *R. Falconeri*, but is much smaller. SYN. *R. aemulorum.*

R. manipuren'se (28*b*). D. So near is this to *R. Maddenii* that it has been regarded and figured as a var. of it. It is still closer to *R. crassum*, having the same scaly character, the same lovely, white, fragrant, funnel-shaped fl. 3½ in. wide in clusters of 4 or 5. It is distinct from *R. Maddenii* by its downy stamens and its ½-in. long cal. lobes; and from *R. crassum* by the wider, broad-ended l. and 12-celled ovary. June. Himalaya. 1882. (B.M. 8212 as *R. Maddenii obtusifolium.*)

R. Martinia'num* (38*b*). C. Evergreen shrub, 3 to 6 ft., shoots glandular. *l.* in a terminal cluster, oval, 1 to 2 in. long, glabrous or nearly so. *fl.* in loose clusters of 3 to 6; cor. broadly funnel-shaped, 5-lobed, 1 in. long, 1½ to 2 in. wide, pale rose with a dark blotch. Stalk slender up to 1½ in. long, glandular; stamens 10, downy at base; ovary and base of style glandular. April. China. 1914.

R. max'imum (33*b*). A. Evergreen bushy tree up to 30 to 40 ft. in a wild state; in cultivation a shrub rarely more than 8 to 10 ft. *l.* 4 to 10 in. long, narrowly oval to oblanceolate; soon glabrous or nearly so. *fl.* in trusses of 16 to 24; cor. bell-shaped, deeply 5-lobed, 1½ in. wide, pale rose to purplish-pink; stamens 8 to 12, mostly 10; ovary, cal.-lobes, and fl.-stalk glandular. June, July. N. America. 1736. (B.M. 951.) Not particularly ornamental but late-flowering. Used by the early hybridizers. var. **al'bum,** *fl.* white.

R. Meddia'num (38*e*). D. Sturdy evergreen shrub, up to 6 ft. or more, entirely glabrous. Popularly known as the 'Chinese Thomsonii', it differs from its Himalayan ally in its stouter branchlets, its larger, less-rounded l., larger fl., and red cal. Cor. normally deep, rich crimson, ovary glabrous; but some cultivated plants have bright scarlet blossom and in the var. **atrokermesi'num** (very deeply coloured) the ovary is glandular. March, April. China, Burma. 1914. (B.M. 9636.)

R. megaca'lyx* (28*c*). E. Evergreen shrub, 10 to 15 ft. *l.* elliptic-oblong, often inclined to obovate, 4 to 6 in. long, strongly veined, glabrous above, scaly beneath. *fl.* in stalked clusters of 3 to 5, nutmeg-scented, drooping; cor. funnel-shaped, with 5 spreading lobes, 3 or 4 in. wide, white stained with yellow at base, often flushed with pinkish-purple, cal. very large, $\frac{3}{4}$ to $1\frac{1}{8}$ in. long; stamens 10, short; ovary and base of style scaly. April, May. Burma. 1914. (B.M. 9326.)

R. megera'tum (7). D. Evergreen shrub, 1 to 2 ft., shoots, l.-stalks, and fl.-stalks bristly. *l.* elliptic, $\frac{1}{2}$ to $1\frac{1}{2}$ in. long, glossy green above, very glaucous beneath. *fl.* mostly solitary, sometimes in pairs or threes; cor. $1\frac{1}{4}$ in. wide, with 5 much overlapping lobes, bright yellow; stamens 10; anthers red-brown; ovary scaly; style bent over; cal. with 5 membranous lobes nearly $\frac{1}{2}$ in. long. March, April. Himalaya. 1914. (B.M. 9120.) Akin to *R. leucaspis* which has white fl. with stalks not bristly.

R. melinan'thum* (39). B. Deciduous or sub-evergreen shrub, 6 to 8 ft., closely related to *R. trichocladum* and with the same bristly shoots and 10 stamens; it differs by the l. soon becoming glabrous above. *fl.* yellow. May. Burma. Regarded as the best of its series. (B.M. 8903.)

R. Metternich'ii (33*a*). B. Evergreen shrub up to 8 ft. *l.* 4 to 6 in. long, 1 to $1\frac{3}{4}$ in. wide, reddish-downy beneath. *fl.* 10 to 15 in a truss; cor. rose-coloured, 7-lobed, $1\frac{3}{4}$ in. wide; stamens 14, white; ovary reddish-downy; style glabrous. Japan. Distinct by its 7-lobed cor. Very rare in gardens. var. **angustifo'lium,** a synonym of *R. Makinoi*; **pentam'erum,** a synonym of *R. Degronianum.*

R. micran'thum (29). A. Evergreen bush. 6 ft. or more; twigs very slender. *l.* narrowly oblanceolate, $\frac{3}{4}$ to $1\frac{1}{2}$ in. long, scaly beneath. *fl.* densely clustered in a raceme $1\frac{1}{2}$ in. across; cor. dull white, $\frac{1}{3}$ to $\frac{1}{2}$ in. wide, with 5 spreading ovate lobes; stamens 10, glabrous. May. China. 1901. Quite distinct from any other species by its small fl. and one of the least effective. (B.M. 8198.)

R. mi'nus (12). C. Evergreen shrub up to 6 ft., shoots scaly. *l.* ovate-lanceolate to narrowly obovate, $1\frac{1}{2}$ to $3\frac{1}{2}$ in. long, densely scaly beneath. *fl.* 6 or more in a loose cluster; cor. 1 to $1\frac{1}{2}$ in. wide, funnel-shaped, the 5 lobes shorter than the tube, pale pinkish-purple, spotted, scaly outside; stamens 10; ovary scaly; style glabrous; cal. 5-lobed, $\frac{1}{8}$ in. long, hairy on the margin. June. N. America. 1786. (A.B.R. i. 36 as *R. punctatum.*)

Rhododendron moupinense

R. mishmien'se (7). E. Epiphytic evergreen, 2 to 4 ft., shoots bristly. *l.* elliptic to oblong-elliptic, pointed, $2\frac{1}{2}$ to 5 in. long, densely scaly beneath, stalk and lower part of midrib bristly. *fl.* in erect trusses of 4 to 8; stalk up to 1 in. long, tawny-bristly, cor. flattish, $2\frac{1}{2}$ in. across, 5-lobed (lobes reflexed) pale yellow, 3 upper lobes spotted brownish-red; stamens 10, short, thick, hairy; anthers $\frac{1}{8}$ in. long reddish-brown; ovary densely scaly, style very short, bent over. Cal. deeply 5-lobed, lobes rounded, $\frac{1}{2}$ in. long, ciliate. April. Assam. 1928. (G.C. 107 (1940), 196.)

R. mol'le* (5). C. There has been great confusion between this Azalea and the one popularly known as 'Azalea mollis' (*see* **R. japonicum**). It was for long known as *R. sinense.* In growth, l., and general appearance the two are much alike, but in *R. molle* the l. are densely and softly downy beneath, the 5 stamens are relatively shorter in comparison with the cor., and, more than all, the fl. are golden-yellow. May. China. 1824. (S.B.F.G. 290.) Syn. *Azalea sinensis flavescens.*

R. mollico'mum (35). D. Evergreen shrub, up to 6 ft., shoots, l., fl.-stalks, and cal. softly downy. *l.* narrowly oval or oblong, $\frac{3}{4}$ to 2 in. long. *fl.* usually in pairs from each of several terminal l.-axils, making altogether a cluster 2 to 3 in. across; cor. rose $\frac{3}{4}$ to 1 in. wide, 5-lobed; stamens 10; ovary and style pubescent. April. China. 1913. Near *R. hemitrichotum* which has l. glaucous beneath.

R. monosema'tum (6*d*). B. Evergreen shrub, 5 to 8 ft. with trusses of about 12 fl.; cor. white suffused with pink and with a smallish purple blotch at base. April. China. 1904. (B.M. 8675.) Closely related to *R. pachytrichum,* but the hairs on young shoots, l.-stalks, and fl.-stalks are straight. *R. strigillo'sum,* also allied, has brilliant red fl.

R. moupinen'se* (30). B. Evergreen shrub, 2 to 3 ft., shoots hairy at first. *l.* obovate or oval, rounded at both ends, covered with tiny scales beneath. *fl.* single, in pairs or threes, fragrant; cor. tubular at base, 5-lobed, 2 to $2\frac{1}{2}$ in. wide, white or pink, dotted with red on upper side; stamens 10; ovary scaly; style glabrous; cal. $\frac{1}{8}$ in. long, glandular, slightly ciliate. February, March. Tibet, China. 1909. (B.M. 8598.) Valuable for its early blossoms and for flowering when a few in. h.

R. mucrona'tum* (5*d*). C. Evergreen shrub, 4 to 6 ft., shoots bristly. *l.* 1 to $2\frac{1}{2}$ in. long, $\frac{1}{3}$ to 1 in. wide, hairy all over. *fl.* mostly in pairs or threes, fragrant; cor. open bell-shaped, pure white, $2\frac{1}{2}$ in. wide; stamens 10, glabrous; ovary bristly; style glabrous; cal. with 5 glandular-hairy, lanceolate lobes, $\frac{1}{2}$ in. long. May. 1819. (B.M. 2901 as *Azalea ledifolia.*) var. **narcissflo'rum** is double white-fld.; **ple'num** is double, rose-purple. (B.M. 2509 as *Azalea indica plena.*) *R. mucronatum,* much cultivated in Japan and China, has never been found wild. It originated as a white-fld. sport from an azalea with rose-purple fl. spontaneous in S. Japan and now called var. *ripense.*

R. mucronula'tum* (15). B. Deciduous shrub, 6 to 8 ft., erect and thinnish in growth. *l.* $1\frac{1}{2}$ to 4 in. long, lanceolate. *fl.* borne singly from each of a cluster of buds at top of the naked shoot; cor. bright rose purple, 5-lobed, $1\frac{3}{4}$ in. wide, downy outside; stamens 10; anthers dark purple; ovary scaly; style glabrous. December to February. NE. Asia. 1907. (B.M. 8304.) Sometimes made a var. of *R. dauricum* but more vigorous with larger l. and fl. In open winters it will be in bloom by Christmas.

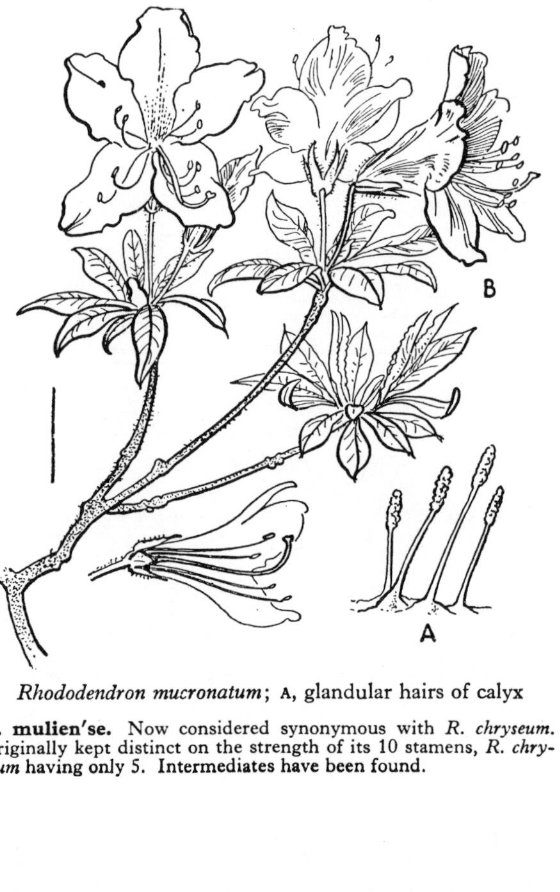

Rhododendron mucronatum; A, glandular hairs of calyx

R. mulien'se. Now considered synonymous with *R. chryseum.* Originally kept distinct on the strength of its 10 stamens, *R. chryseum* having only 5. Intermediates have been found.

R. myia'grum (38*a*). C. Evergreen shrub, 3 to 5 ft., nearly related to *R. callimorphum* and with the same glandular young shoots, cal., and fl.-stalks, the last so viscid that they act as fly-catchers and become plastered with dead flies; hence the specific name. It is distinct in its white *fl.* which are bell-shaped, $1\frac{1}{4}$ to $1\frac{1}{2}$ in. wide and in trusses of 4 or 5. May to June. China. 1919.

R. myrtilloides* (10). A. Evergreen dwarf shrub found in low tufts 6 in. h. in nature; shoots warted. *l.* narrowly obovate, $\frac{1}{2}$ to $\frac{3}{4}$ in. long, glossy green above, thinly scaly and glaucous beneath. *fl.* solitary, nodding at the end of a slender, warted stalk 1 to $1\frac{1}{2}$ in. long; cor. bell-shaped, $\frac{1}{2}$ in. long, with 5 erect rounded lobes; plum-coloured outside, maroon within; stamens 10; anthers white; cal. with 5 rounded lobes $1\frac{1}{2}$ in. long. May. Burma. 1914. (B.T.S. 3, 399.) Charming for the rock-garden.

R. neriiflo'rum* (31*c*). C. Evergreen shrub, 4 to 8 ft., shoots reddish, woolly at first. *l.* oblong to narrowly obovate, 2 to 4 in. long, glaucous-white beneath. *fl.* in trusses of 6 to 12; cor. rich crimson, $1\frac{1}{2}$ to $1\frac{3}{4}$ in. long, scarcely as wide, lobes 5; stamens 10, white, glabrous; ovary felted; style white or pinkish; cal. variable in size, sometimes very large, reddish. March, April. China. 1906. (B.M. 8727.) In its rich colour it compares with *R. fulgens* and *R. Thomsonii*.

R. nilagi'ricum. D. Subspecies of *R. arboreum*; *fl.* from deep crimson to rose. (B.M. 4381.) See also *R. zeylanicum*.

R. niphar'gum. A synonym of *R. uvarifolium*.

R. nippon'icum (5*c*). B. Deciduous shrub, 3 to 6 ft., shoots glandular-bristly. *l.* obovate, 2 to 6 in. long, half as wide, ciliate, bristly on both surfaces. *fl.* in clusters of 6 to 15; cor. white, narrowly bell-shaped, scarcely 1 in. long, the 5 lobes almost erect and $\frac{1}{2}$ in. long; stamens 10; cal., l.-stalks, fl.-stalks, and ovary glandular-hairy. June. Japan. 1914. The fl. are inconspicuous and hidden in the foliage, but the latter turns brilliant orange and crimson.

R. ni'veum (3*a*). B. Evergreen shrub, 10 to 15 ft., shoots white-felted. *l.* narrow oblong, 4 to 7 in. long, $1\frac{1}{2}$ to $2\frac{1}{2}$ in. wide, covered at first with white wool which persists on the lower surface and turns pale brown. *fl.* about 20 in compact, rounded trusses 4 to 5 in. across; cor. bell-shaped, $1\frac{1}{2}$ in. wide, 5-lobed, purplish-lilac; stamens 10, short, glabrous; ovary densely pubescent. March, May. Himalaya. 1849. (B.M. 4730.) 'Niveum' refers to the snow-white young shoots and l. The blossom varies in beauty, but forms with fl. most nearly approaching blue are attractive.

R. nudiflo'rum (5*b*). A. Deciduous, much-branched shrub, 4 to 8 ft., shoots bristly. *l.* oval or obovate, $1\frac{1}{2}$ to 4 in. long, often bristly on midrib and margins. *fl.* in clusters of 6 to 12, faintly scented; cor. $1\frac{1}{2}$ in. wide, pink or whitish with a tube $\frac{3}{4}$ in. long; stamens 5, thrice as long as cor. tube, pink; ovary bristly; cal. very small, ciliate. May. N. America. 1734. (B.R. 120.) A parent of many early hybrids.

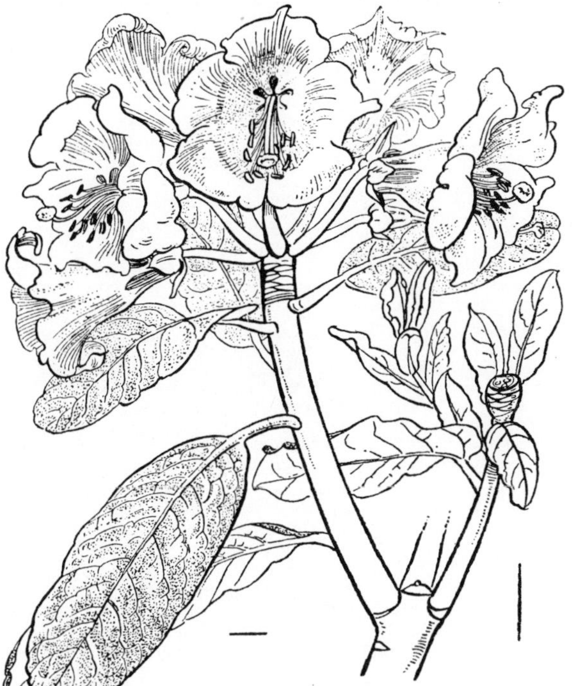

Rhododendron Nuttallii

R. Nu'ttallii* (28*c*). F. Evergreen shrub or tree up to 30 ft., sometimes epiphytic, of thin, erect habit, branchlets very stout. *l.* elliptic, 5 to 12 in. long, $2\frac{1}{2}$ to $4\frac{1}{2}$ in. wide, bullate and strongly net-veined. *fl.* 3 to 6 in a cluster, fragrant; cor. funnel-shaped, 4 to 5 in. or more long and wide, ivory-white, suffused with yellow, thick in texture; stamens 10, $2\frac{1}{2}$ in. long; ovary scaly, style 3 in. long, scaly at base; cal. with 5 deep lobes 1 in. long, $\frac{1}{2}$ in. wide. April, May. Bhutan. 1852. (B.M. 5146.) Largest-flowered of rhododendrons.

R. obtu'sum* (5*d*). A. Evergreen or nearly deciduous shrub, 3 ft. and upwards; shoots covered with flattened brown hairs. *l.* oval to ovate, $\frac{1}{2}$ to $1\frac{1}{4}$ in. long, glossy green. *fl.* solitary or in twos or threes; cor. funnel-shaped, 1 in. wide, variable in colour, salmon, pink, magenta, rosy-mauve, scarlet, crimson and (in var. **al'bum**) white; stamens 5, glabrous; ovary densely hairy; style glabrous; cal. ciliate. May. Japan. 1844. (B.R. 32, 37.) A very variable species cultivated for centuries in Japan, where hundreds of vars. have been raised. The best-known of them is **amoe'num** (*Azalea amoena*, B.M. 4728), a hardy, dark-leafed, densely bushy evergreen up to 5 ft., with copious rosy-purple fl. var. **Kaemp'feri** is up to 8 ft., nearly deciduous, and very hardy; fls. purplish-rose to rosy-scarlet. In 1919 some 50 vars. were introduced from Japan under native names but collectively as 'Kurume' azaleas; some of these are tender. The following are recommended: Hinodegiri, Hinomayo, Kirin, Kurai No Himo, Kureno-Yuki, Kumo No Uye, Takasago. (See J.R.H.S. 74, pp. 144–53.)

R. occidenta'le* (5*b*). A. Deciduous bushy shrub, up to 10 ft. *l.* oblanceolate to oblong-lanceolate, 2 to 4 in. long. *fl.* in clusters of 6 to 12, fragrant; cor. funnel-shaped, 2 to 3 in. wide, white (sometimes pink-tinted) with a yellow blotch; stamens 5, and like the style 2 to $2\frac{1}{2}$ in. long and downy at base; ovary glandular; cal. ciliate. June, July. N. America. 1851. (B.M. 5005 as *Azalea occidentale*.)

R. Old'hamii. E. Evergreen shrub 5 to 10 ft., shoots, l., and l.-stalks very hairy. *l.* oblong-lanceolate, tapered at both ends, $1\frac{1}{2}$ to $3\frac{1}{2}$ in. long, dull green. *fl.* 2 to 4 in a loose cluster; cor. funnel-shaped, 2 in. wide, 5-lobed, orange-red spotted with purple; stamens 10, red; anthers purple; ovary bristly; cal. and fl.-stalks glandular-hairy. May. Formosa. 1878. (B.M. 9059.) SYN. *Azalea Oldhamii*. Distinguished by its extreme hairiness and orange-red fl.

R. oleifo'lium (41). E. Evergreen shrub, 2 to 4 ft., shoots slender, scaly. *l.* oblong-lanceolate, 1 to $2\frac{1}{2}$ in. long, glaucous and very scaly beneath. *fl.* borne singly or in pairs from numerous l.-axils at end of shoot; cor. 1 to $1\frac{1}{4}$ in. wide, tubular with 5 spreading lobes, scaly and downy outside, pale rose or white; stamens 10, rosy purple; ovary scaly; style standing clear of stamens. April, May. China. 1906. Closely akin to *R. virgatum* which has no pubescence outside cor. (B.M. 8802.)

R. orbicula're (19*e*). B. Evergreen shrub of very compact rounded shape, said to be 13 ft. h. in its wild state, about half as much in cultivation. *l.* orbicular, 2 to 4 in. long, deeply notched at the base, glaucous beneath. *fl.* in lax trusses of 7 to 10, rose (often with a bluish tinge), 2 to $2\frac{1}{2}$ in. across, widely bell-shaped, 7-lobed; stamens 14, white, glabrous; ovary glandular; style glabrous. April, May. China. 1904. (B.M. 8775.) Distinct in its symmetrically rounded shape; usually wider than h.

R. oreodo'xa (19*f*). B. Evergreen shrub or small tree. *l.* 2 to 4 in. long, oblong, rather glaucous beneath. *fl.* 8 to 12 in a truss; stalk glandular; cor. open bell-shaped, 7-lobed, 2 in. wide, pale rose; stamens 14, white; ovary and style glabrous. March, April. China. 1904. (B.M. 8518 as *R. haematochilum*.)

R. oreotre'phes* (40*b*). B. Evergreen shrub, 6 to 8 ft. *l.* oval, rounded at both ends, $1\frac{1}{2}$ to 3 in. long, half as wide, grey-green and smooth above, glaucous and scaly beneath. *fl.* 4 to 10 in a cluster; cor. funnel-shaped, 2 to $2\frac{1}{2}$ in. across the 5 lobes, lavender-rose with darker spots, but varying in depth of shade; stamens 10, white; ovary scaly. April, May. China, Tibet. 1906. (B.M. 8784.) Well marked by the attractive strikingly glaucous colouring of some of its better forms.

R. orthocla'dum* (26). A. Evergreen shrub, densely twiggy and bushy, up to 4 ft.; shoots slender, scaly. *l.* narrowly oblong to lanceolate, $\frac{1}{3}$ to $\frac{3}{4}$ in. long, scaly on both surfaces. *fl.* 2 to 4 in a cluster 1 in. wide; col. pale mauve or lavender blue, $\frac{3}{4}$ in. wide with a very short downy tube and 5 rounded lobes $\frac{1}{4}$ in. long; stamens 10, purple; anthers red; ovary scaly; style glabrous, reddish, short. April. China. 1913.

R. ova'tum (32). E. Evergreen shrub, 4 to 12 ft., shoots, l.-stalk, midrib, and fl.-stalk downy. *l.* ovate, pointed, 1 to 2 in. long. *fl.* borne singly from each of several buds at end of shoot; cor. white to pale pink or purplish, spotted, 1 in. wide, lobes 5, spreading; stamens 5; ovary bristly; style glabrous; lobes of cal. $\frac{3}{16}$ in. long. May, June. China. 1844. (B.M. 5064 as *Azalea ovata*.)

R. oxyphyl'lum (36). F. Evergreen glabrous shrub or small tree up to 18 ft., *l.* narrow-oblong to oblanceolate, 3 to 6 in. long. *fl.* fragrant, in several clusters of 3 to 5 near end of branchlet; cor. tubular with 5 spreading lobes, $2\frac{1}{2}$ to 3 in. wide, white with a yellow stain; stamens 10. April. Siam and China. (B.T.S. 3, 405.) Differs from *R. stamineum* in its larger l. and much shorter stamens. Very beautiful but tender. Blooms when quite small.

R. pachytrich'um (6*d*). C. Evergreen shrub, 10 to 15 ft., shoots, fl.- and l.-stalks, densely coated with moss-like branched hairs. *l.* 3 to 6 in. long, narrowly oblong to obovate, bristly on midrib beneath, ciliate. *fl.* in trusses of 7 to 10; cor. bell-shaped, $1\frac{1}{2}$ in. wide, white to pale rose with a basal purplish blotch; stamens 10, shorter than cor., downy; ovary bristly. April. China. 1903. There is an unpleasantly magenta-tinted form, but at its best the species is very attractive. Akin to *R. strigillosum*, the hairs on which are long and unbranched.

R. patu'lum (27). B. A dwarf evergreen prostrate shrub with spreading branches. *l.* lanceolate to oblanceolate, apex acute ½ to ¾ in. long, scaly above, glaucous and scaly below. *fl.* solitary or in pairs; cor. funnel-shaped, 5-lobed, purple, the upper lobe spotted crimson-purple, ¾ to 1¼ in. long. Assam frontier. Closely related to *R. imperator*. Quite hardy but a rather difficult species to grow satisfactorily.

R. pemako'ense (21). A. Dwarf evergreen shrub up to 2 ft. h. and a valuable plant for the rock-garden. *l.* obovate, apex rounded, ½ to ¾ in. long, under surface slightly glaucous and scaly. *fl.* solitary or in pairs, purple in varying shades; cor. pubescent all over, broadly funnel-shaped, up to 1¼ in. long and 1½ in. across. Tibet, Tsangpo Gorge. 1930. Unique in the genus for its habit of suckering almost like a Pernettya.

R. pocoph'orum (31*b*). C. A near relative of *R. haematodes* and *R. catacosmum* but distinguished by its glandular young shoots, cal., l.-stalks, fl.-stalks, and ovary. The fl. are in trusses of 15 to 20 and of various shades of crimson. March. Tibet. 1922.

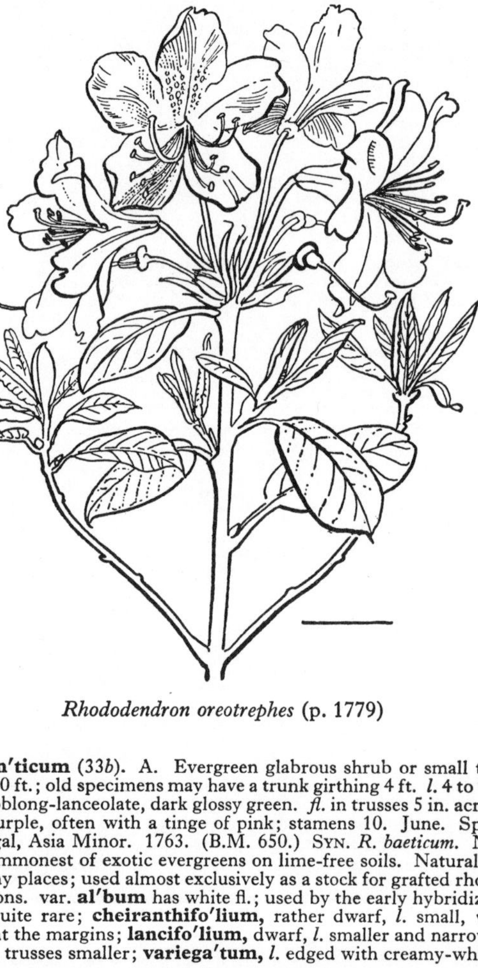

Rhododendron oreotrephes (p. 1779)

R. pon'ticum (33*b*). A. Evergreen glabrous shrub or small tree, 12 to 20 ft.; old specimens may have a trunk girthing 4 ft. *l.* 4 to 9 in. long, oblong-lanceolate, dark glossy green. *fl.* in trusses 5 in. across; cor. purple, often with a tinge of pink; stamens 10. June. Spain, Portugal, Asia Minor. 1763. (B.M. 650.) SYN. *R. baeticum.* Now the commonest of exotic evergreens on lime-free soils. Naturalized in many places; used almost exclusively as a stock for grafted rhododendrons. var. **al'bum** has white fl.; used by the early hybridizers, now quite rare; **cheiranthifo'lium,** rather dwarf, *l.* small, very wavy at the margins; **lancifo'lium,** dwarf, *l.* smaller and narrower, *fl.* and trusses smaller; **variega'tum,** *l.* edged with creamy-white.

R. × **prae'cox.*** A. A hybrid between *R. ciliatum* and *R. dauricum*, raised about 1855 by Mr. J. Davies of Ormskirk. *l.* dark glossy green, 2 to 3 in. long, scaly. *fl.* in clusters of about 3, bright rosy-purple, 1½ to 2 in. wide. Semi-evergreen, 3 to 5 ft. h. February, March. (R.H. 1868, 211.)

R. prae'stans (22). C. Evergreen shrub or tree up to 30 ft. *l.* oblong to oblanceolate, 10 to 15 in. long, 5 in. wide, glossy black-green above, scurfy and grey or fawn beneath; stalk flattened. *fl.* in trusses of 15 to 20; cor. obliquely bell-shaped, 2 in. long, 8-lobed, magenta or flushed with that colour, crimson-blotched at base; ovary downy; style glabrous; stamens 16. China. 1914. SYN. *R. semnum.* Fine foliaged species.

R. praevern'um (19*b*). C. Very closely related to *R. sutchuenense*, this differs by being of dwarfer more spreading growth, by the l. having a quite glabrous midrib, and by the cor. having a fine wine-red blotch at base. February, March. China. 1907. Although hardy, its early fl. are very apt to be spoiled by spring frost, but in favourable seasons it may be very beautiful.

R. primulaeflo'rum* (2). B. Evergreen, strongly aromatic shrub, 4½ ft. *l.* oval-oblong, ½ to 1 in. long, ¼ to ⅜ in. wide, covered with reddish scurf beneath. *fl.* 6 to 15 in a compact truss 1½ in. wide; cor. ⅜ in. long, with a yellow tube and 5 rounded, white lobes, tube hairy; stamens 5, enclosed in the tube; ovary scaly; style very short and thick; stigma broad and flat; cal. ⅛ in. long, ciliate. April, May. Tibet. 1917. SYN. *R. tsarongense.* Differs from *R. hypenanthum* by the soon-falling l.-bud scales and from *R. anthopogon* by its yellow fl. var. **cephalanthoi'des,** cor. tube densely downy without; **lepidan'thum,** cor. tube densely scaly without.

R. primuli'num. A synonym of *R. flavidum.*

R. prostra'tum (34). A. Evergreen prostrate shrub about 4 in. in its wild state, shoots and fl.-stalks hairy. *l.* oblong to oval, ½ to ¾ in. long, glabrous above, scaly beneath. *fl.* borne singly, in pairs, or threes; cor. flat and open, 1 to 1¼ in. wide, rosy-purple, with 5 rounded lobes; stamens 10, purple, hairy at base; ovary scaly; style glabrous; cal. deeply 5-lobed, ciliate. April. China (where it grows at almost the limit of vegetation). 1910. (B.M. 8747.) Suitable for the rock-garden.

R. proteoi'des (37*b*). B. Evergreen shrub of dense habit, 1 to 3 ft. *l.* oblong, oval, or obovate, margins much recurved, ¾ to 2 in. long, ¼ to ½ in. wide, reddish-woolly beneath; stalk short, very thick. *fl.* about 8 in compact trusses 2 to 3 in. wide; cor. creamy-yellow, sometimes flushed with rose, crimson-spotted, bell-shaped, 1 to 1½ in. long; ovary clad with branched hairs. April. China. 1917. Distinct by its dwarf dense habit, small l., and yellow fl.

R. protis'tum (22). E. Evergreen tree, 25 to 45 ft. *l.* oblanceolate to obovate, 8 to 18 in. long, 4 to 7½ in. wide, glabrous in young plants. *fl.* in trusses of 20 to 30; cor. bell-shaped, 2 in. long, creamy-white flushed with rose, 8-lobed; stamens 16; ovary clad with pinkish down; style glabrous. May (in its wild state). China. 1919. Closely related to *R. giganteum.*

R. pruniflo'rum* (21). C. Evergreen strong-smelling shrub, 2 to 3 ft. *l.* obovate-elliptic, rounded at apex, more tapered at base, 1 to 2½ in. long, glabrous above, greyish and very densely scaly beneath. *fl.* up to 6 in a cluster, stalks slender, 1 to 1½ in. long, very scaly; cor. bell-shaped, 1 in. wide, 5-lobed, plum-purple, or nearly crimson, or violet; stamens 10, downy; ovary scaly; style short, recurved, glabrous. May, June. Burma. 1926. Distinct by its purple fl. but very close to *R. tsangpoense*, of which it is now generally considered as a variety.

R. prunifo'lium (5*b*). C. Deciduous shrub up to 9 ft., shoots purplish-red, glabrous. *l.* oval, obovate, or oblong, 1½ to 4 in. long, mostly quite glabrous except on midrib. *fl.* in clusters of 4 or 5; cor. crimson, funnel-shaped, 1 to 1½ in. wide, tube ¾ to 1 in. long; stamens 2 to 2½ in. long; ovary hairy. July. N. America. 1918. Notable for its rich colour, its late-flowering, and in being the most glabrous of American species.

R. pseudoyanthi'num* (40*c*). B. A species close to *R. concinnum*, but distinguished by the larger fl. of deeper purple. A striking plant in the garden

R. pubes'cens (35). B. Evergreen shrub, 4 to 8 ft.; shoots, l., fl.-stalk, and cal. all very pubescent. *l.* scattered along the twigs, ½ to 1½ in. long, ⅛ to ⅜ in. wide, narrowly oblong. *fl.* produced in twos or threes from each of a cluster of buds near end of shoots; cor. ½ to ⅝ in. wide, tubular at base, pinkish-white or rose, lobes 5 spreading, rounded; stamens 10; ovary very downy; style glabrous. April, May. China. 1919. (B.M. 9319.) Akin to *R. mollicomum* which has a pubescent style and un-lobed cal.

R. puncta'tum. A synonym of *R. carolinianum* and *R. minus.*

R. pural'bum (38*d*). C. Evergreen shrub 12 to 15 ft., very closely related to *R. croceum* and with similar loose trusses of 7 to 9 flat, saucer-shaped fl. each 1½ to 2 in. wide; they are, however, pure white (yellow in *R. croceum*). May, June. China. 1913.

R. quinquefo'lium (5*e*). B. Deciduous shrub, 3 ft. or more h. (said to be a small tree in its wild state); shoots very slender, glabrous. *l.* obovate to rhomboid, 1½ to 2 in. long, in whorls of 5, pale green with a purple margin. *fl.* solitary or in pairs, coming with the young l.; cor. widely funnel-shaped, 1½ in. wide, 5-lobed, white; stamens 10, greenish; ovary and style glabrous. April, May. Japan. 1896. Young l., tender green edged with purple, are very pretty.

R. racemo'sum* (41). A. Evergreen shrub, 4 to 6 ft. *l.* elliptic, ¾ to 2 in. long, densely scaly on the glaucous undersurface. *fl.* from terminal l.-axils in clusters of 3 to 6; cor. funnel-shaped, 5-lobed, 1 in. wide, soft pink to bright pink, sometimes white; stamens 10; cal. and fl.-stalk very scaly. March to May. China. 1889. (B.M. 7301.) Rather variable in size, colour of blossom, and time of flowering.

R. radi'cans (34). B. Evergreen prostrate shrub, forming a close tuft up to 4 in. *l.* oblanceolate, tapered to both ends, ¼ to ½ in. long, dark bright green, densely scaly beneath. *fl.* solitary on a stalk ½ to 1 in. long; cor. purple, ¾ in. wide, deeply 5-lobed, downy and scaly outside; stamens 10, woolly near base; ovary scaly; style glabrous; cal. lobes ciliate, scaly, ⅛ in. long. May. Tibet. 1921. A pygmy of the genus, charmingly suited for the rock-garden.

R. radi'num (2). C. Evergreen, twiggy shrub up to 4 ft. *l.* narrowly oblanceolate, ⅓ to ¾ in. long, ⅛ to ½ in. wide, scurfy on both surfaces. *fl.* 8 to 10, crowded in compact clusters about 1 in. wide; cor. white, flushed with rose, ⅓ in. wide, tubular at base; stamens 5, glabrous; ovary scaly; style very short, top-shaped, glabrous; cal.

scaly and ciliate. May. China. 1917. Only species in its series with cor. scaly outside. *See* **R. trichostomum.**

R. re'pens (31*a*). A. By some authorities this is not considered specifically distinct from *R. Forrestii*. The description of that species may be repeated for this, except that the fl.-stalk and ovary are less glandular and the l. beneath is pale green (not purple). Cultivators generally keep them distinct, the fl. being usually more scarlet than that of *R. Forrestii*. China. Tibet. var. **chamaethau'ma** is of taller growth and has carmine fl. 4 or 5 in a truss. **A**

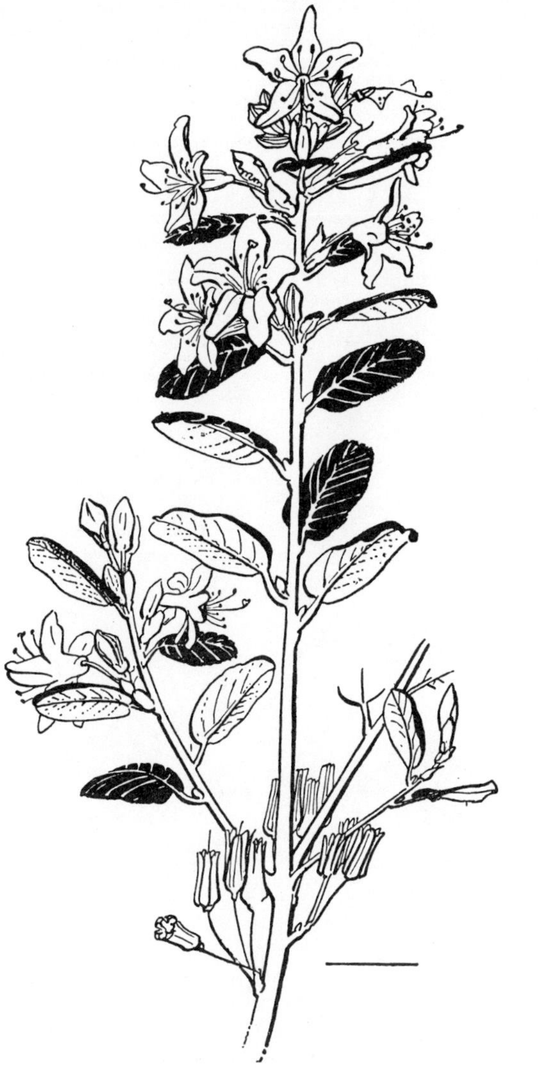

Rhododrendon racemosum (p. 1780)

R. reticula'tum (5*e*). B. Deciduous shrub, 4 to 20 ft. *l.* often in pairs or threes, rhomboid, $1\frac{1}{2}$ to 2 in. long, not so wide, hairy above when young. *fl.* solitary or in pairs (rarely more); cor. rose-purple, $1\frac{1}{2}$ to 2 in. wide, 5-lobed; stamens 10, glabrous, 5 quite short; ovary and style hairy. April. Japan. (B.M. 6972 as *R. rhombicum.*) var. **pentan'drum** differs in having only 5 stamens, ovary glandular (not hairy), style glabrous. It is more attractive in its autumnal hues which are brilliant red instead of purple. (B.M. 7681 as *R. dilatatum.*)

R. retu'sum.* F. Evergreen shrub, 2 to 4 ft. *l.* scarcely stalked, obovate, 1 to 2 in. long, glabrous, margins decurved, apex notched or blunt, thinly scaly beneath. *fl.* in loose trusses of 6 to 9; cor. about 1 in. long, tubular with a shallowly lobed limb $\frac{5}{8}$ in. wide, bright scarlet outside, yellowish in the tube; stamens 10, glabrous; ovary scaly; cal. ciliate; fl.-stalk hairy. May. Java, Sumatra. 1850. (B.M. 4859.) Warm greenhouse.

R. rhabdo'tum* (28*c*). E. Evergreen shrub up to 13 ft. *l.* narrowly oblong-elliptic, 3 to 6 in. long, $1\frac{1}{4}$ to 2 in. wide, glaucous green and scaly beneath. *fl.* in trusses of 3 or 4; stalks scaly and downy; cor. widely funnel-shaped, 4 in. wide, 5-lobed, white tinged with yellow and with a conspicuous crimson stripe running down the back of each lobe; stamens 10; anthers $\frac{1}{2}$ in. long; cal. $\frac{5}{8}$ in. long, deeply 5-lobed, downy outside. June. Bhutan. 1915. (B.M. 9447.) Related to *R. Dalhousiae* but hardier and made very distinct by the striped cor.

R. Rhodo'ra. A synonym of *R. canadense.*

R. rhom'bicum. A synonym of *R. reticulatum.*

R. Rir'ei (3*b*). C. Evergreen shrub up to 18 ft. *l.* narrowly oval to oblanceolate, 3 to 6 in. long, 1 to 2 in. wide, glabrous above, clad beneath with close white scurf. *fl.* in clusters of 8 to 10; cor. widely bell-shaped, 5-lobed, 2 in. wide, dull purple with blackish-purple spots at base; stamens 10, glabrous; ovary grey-felted. March. China. 1904. Its colour is distinct in its series.

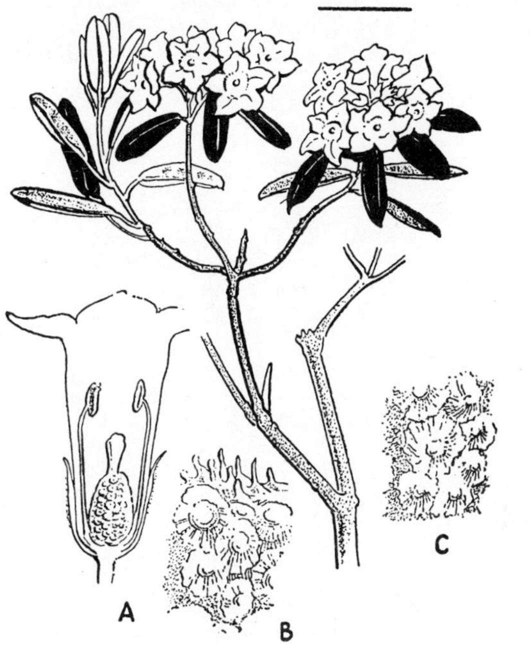

Rhododendron radinum. A. Section of flower. B. Scales of calyx. C. Scales of flower (p. 1780)

Rhododendron repens

R. Roxiea'num (37*b*). B. Evergreen shrub, 4 ft. and upwards, close and compact. *l.* linear-oblong or oblanceolate, 2 to 4 in. long, $\frac{1}{3}$ to $\frac{3}{4}$ in. wide, woolly beneath, margins much decurved. *fl.* 10 to 20 in a compact truss 3 to 4 in. across; cor. bell-shaped, $1\frac{1}{2}$ in. long, shallowly 5-lobed, white or creamy-white, flushed with rose, crimson-spotted on the upper lobe; ovary downy; cal. very small. April, May. China. 1913. (B.M. 9383.) Very slow growing.

R. Royl'ei. A synonym of *R. cinnabarinum Roylei.*

R. rubigino'sum* (23). A. Evergreen shrub, 6 to 10 ft. *l.* elliptic-lanceolate, pointed, $1\frac{1}{2}$ to $3\frac{1}{2}$ in. long, $\frac{3}{4}$ to $1\frac{1}{4}$ in. wide, densely scaly beneath. *fl.* in clusters of 4 to 8; cor. funnel-shaped, $1\frac{1}{2}$ to 2 in. wide, scaly outside, rosy-lilac; stamens 10, downy at base; ovary scaly; style glabrous. April, May. China. 1889. (B.M. 7621.) Hardy, floriferous, easily grown.

R. rubrolinea'tum (39). C. Semi-evergreen shrub, up to 5 ft. *l.* obovate-elliptic, $1\frac{1}{4}$ in. long, scaly beneath, stalk slender, $\frac{1}{4}$ in. long.

fl. 2 to 4 from 1 or more buds near apex; cor. funnel-shaped, ¾ in. wide, 5-lobed, yellow lined and flushed with rose on outside; stamens 10, longer than cor.; ovary densely scaly; style glabrous, erect. May. China. 1918. The long stamens, straight style, and rose-flushed fl. distinguish it.

R. rupic'ola (26). A. Evergreen shrub, 2 to 4 ft., very scaly on nearly all its parts except the style. *l.* oval to oblong, ½ to ¾ in. long, ⅙ to ⅓ in. wide, yellowish-grey beneath. *fl.* short-stalked, in clusters of 3 to 5; cor. ⅞ in. wide, rich plum-purple, the short hairy tube spreading into 5 rounded lobes; stamens normally 10, sometimes 7, purple with tufts of white down at base; anthers pale brown; cal. ⅛ in. long, with 5 purple, ciliate lobes. April, May. China. 1910. Remarkable for the fl. being entirely purple except the anther.

Rhododendron rubiginosum (p. 1781)

Rhododendron saluenense
A. Scales on shoots. B. Scales and hairs on calyx

R. russa'tum* (26). A. Evergreen shrub 2 to 4 ft., shoots very scaly. *l.* oval or ovate, ¾ to 1½ in. long, rusty-yellow beneath. *fl.* 5 to 10 in close clusters; cor. 1 in. wide with a short hairy tube and 5 overlapping, widespreading lobes, rich violet-purple; stamens 10, conspicuously exposed; anthers brown; ovary scaly; style longer than stamens, red; cal. deeply 5-lobed, lobes ⅛ in. long, ciliate. One of the finest of the Lapponicum series. (B.M. 8963 as *R. cantabile.*)

R. salig'num. A synonym of *R. lepidotum.*

R. saluenen'se* (34). A. Evergreen shrub, 1½ to 2 ft., shoots, fl.-stalks, and cal. margins very bristly. *l.* oblong to oval, ¾ to 1 in. long, scaly especially beneath. *fl.* in pairs or threes; cor. 1⅜ in. wide, rose-purple to purplish-crimson with darker stains, the 5 lobes spreading and overlapping, scaly and downy outside; stamens 10, with a tuft of down at base; cal. and ovary scaly, style glabrous. April, May. China. 1914. (B.M. 9095.) One of the most charming of a beautiful group of dwarf species.

R. sanguin'eum (31*d*). B. Evergreen compact shrub up to 3 ft. *l.* oblong-obovate to oval, 2 to 3½ in. long, covered beneath with grey-white, close layer of appressed hairs. *fl.* in clusters up to 6; cor. bell-shaped, 1 to 1½ in. long, 5-lobed, crimson; stamens 10, white, glabrous; ovary densely tomentose; style glabrous. May. China, Tibet. Of uncertain identity but closely akin to, if not identical with, *R. haemaleum.*

R. Sargentia'num (2). A. Evergreen, aromatic shrub up to 2 ft., shoots scaly. *l.* oval, ½ to ⅝ in. long, glossy above, scurfy beneath, stalk ⅛ in. long. *fl.* 6 to 12 in a cluster; cor. ½ in. wide, pale yellow, cylindrical at base and hairy inside, lobes 5, spreading; stamens 5; hidden in the cor. tube; ovary scaly; style very short and thick; cal. with 5 erect, oblong, scaly, ciliate lobes. May. China. 1903. (B.M. 8871.)

R. scabrifo'lium (35). D. Evergreen shrub, 6 to 8 ft., of thin, erect habit; shoots slender, hairy. *l.* scattered along the shoot, oblong-lanceolate, 1½ to 3½ in. long, ¾ to 1 in. wide, shortly hairy and rough to the touch above, downy beneath, ciliate. *fl.* in twos or threes from each of several terminal buds; cor. white or pale pink, deeply 5-lobed, 1¼ in. wide; stamens 10, pink; ovary densely scaly and hairy. April. China. 1888. (B.M. 7159.) The composite fl. clusters may be 3 or 4 in. across.

R. scab'rum (5*d*). E. Evergreen shrub, 3 to 6 ft., shoots clad with flattened hairs. *l.* oval-lanceolate to oblanceolate, 1½ to 3½ in. long. *fl.* 3 or 4 in a cluster; cor. broadly funnel-shaped, 2½ to 3 in. wide, rosy-red to blood-red; stamens 10; ovary glandular-bristly; cal. with usually rounded ciliate lobes ¼ in. long. May. Liukiu Isles. 1909. (B.M. 8478 as *R. sublanceolatum.*) Richly coloured but tender species.

Rhododendron Schlippenbachii

R. Schlippenbach'ii* (5*e*). C. Deciduous shrub, 6 to 15 ft., shoots glandular-downy. *l.* in terminal whorls of 5, obovate to rhomboid, 2½ to 4½ in. long, almost glabrous except on midrib and veins beneath. *fl.* in clusters of 3 to 6; cor. pale pink to soft rose spotted with red-brown, 3 to 3½ in. across; stamens 10, hairy in lower half; cal., ovary, and fl.-stalk glandular and viscid. April, May. Japan, Korea. 1893. (B.M. 7373.) Of exquisite beauty, but subject to injury by late frost. Foliage turns to lovely shades of orange, yellow, and crimson.

R. scin'tillans* (26). A. Evergreen, twiggy, scaly shrub, 2 to 3 ft., shoots very slender, erect. *l.* oblong-lanceolate, ¼ to ⅝ in. long, ⅛ to ⅜ in. wide, greyish beneath. *fl.* 3 to 6 in clusters 1½ in. wide; cor. lavender-blue to purplish-blue, ¾ to 1 in. wide, deeply 5-lobed;

stamens 10, $\frac{1}{2}$ in. long; ovary scaly; style purple, glabrous; cal. lobes fringed at end. April. China. 1913. One of the bluest of the genus in its best forms.

R. Sear'siae (40*e*). B. Evergreen scaly shrub, 6 to 12 ft. h. *l.* oblanceolate, slender-pointed, 2 to $3\frac{1}{2}$ in. long, $\frac{1}{2}$ to $\frac{7}{8}$ in. wide, glaucous beneath. *fl.* in loose clusters of 4 to 8; cor. 1 to $1\frac{1}{2}$ in. long, rather wider across the 5 lobes, pale lavender to almost white, with pale-green spots; stamens 10; anthers brown. April, May. China. 1908. (B.M. 8993.) Very floriferous; distinctive characters are its narrow l. and the cal. fringed with long hairs.

R. selen'se (38*c*). C. Evergreen shrub, 4 to 7 ft. *l.* oval to obovate, $1\frac{1}{2}$ to 3 in. long, glabrous at maturity. *fl.* in trusses of 4 to 8; cor. bell-shaped, $1\frac{1}{2}$ in. long and wide, 5-lobed, white to shades of rose, sometimes with a crimson blotch; stamens 10, downy at base; ovary glandular, style glabrous; cal., fl.-stalks, and l.-stalks glandular. April, May. China. 1917. Type species of its subseries which is one of the least ornamental and least distinguished in the genus.

R. sem'num. A synonym of *R. praestans.*

R. serot'inum (19*c*). C. Related to *R. decorum* but very lax and sprawling in habit. It differs in having a red blotch and spots on the cor. and in flowering as late as September. China. 1889. (B.M. 8841.)

R. serpyllifo'lium (5*d*). D. Evergreen shrub, 2 to 4 ft., shoots thickly covered with flattened hairs. *l.* narrowly oval or obovate, $\frac{1}{4}$ to $\frac{3}{4}$ in. long, half as wide, slightly hairy. *fl.* mostly solitary; cor. $\frac{3}{4}$ in. wide, pale rose or almost white, 5-lobed; stamens 5; cal. and ovary bristly. May. Japan. Distinguished in the *obtusum* (*indicum*) group by its tiny l. and very slender twigs. (B.M. 7503.) SYN. *Azalea serpyllifolia.*

R. seto'sum (26). A. Dwarf evergreen shrub, suitable for the rock-garden. Branchlets densely setose. *l.* oblong-elliptic $\frac{1}{3}$ to $\frac{1}{2}$ in. long, about $\frac{1}{4}$ in. broad. *fl.* in terminal clusters of 3, purplish-pink; cor. openly funnel-shaped, deeply divided, up to 1 in. long. Sikkim, S. Tibet. 1850. (B.M. 8523.)

R. Sherrif'fii (9). Evergreen shrub up to 10 ft. h., branchlets hairy. *l.* oval or obovate, 2 to $2\frac{1}{2}$ in. long, $1\frac{1}{2}$ to $1\frac{3}{4}$ in. broad, upper surface glabrous at maturity, under surface covered with a thick brown indumentum. *fl.* in short raceme of 4 to 6; cor. funnel-campanulate, fleshy, $1\frac{1}{2}$ in. long, rich deep carmine with small deep magenta patches at the base of each pet. Tibet. 1936. A distinctive species, as yet little known in cultivation. (B.M. n.s. 337).

R. Sims'ii (5*d*). F. Evergreen shrub up to 5 ft. or more; shoots clad with flattened hairs. *l.* lanceolate to narrowly oblanceolate, $1\frac{1}{2}$ to $3\frac{1}{2}$ in. long, bristly. *fl.* in clusters of 2 to 5; cor. funnel-shaped, 2 to 3 in. wide, rosy-red to dark red; stamens 10 (sometimes 8); cal. lobes $\frac{1}{12}$ to $\frac{1}{4}$ in. long, bristly, ciliate. May. China. 1808. SYN. *A. indica* of gardens. (B.M. 1480.) This is the so-called 'Indian' azalea of our greenhouses, of which so many vars. with popular names have been raised, the fl. varying from pure white to rose, salmon, violet-purple, magenta, orange, scarlet, and crimson; also double and single. The true *R. indicum* (q.v.) is from Japan and has only 5 stamens.

R. sinogran'de* (22). D. Evergreen tree, 30 to 50 ft. *l.* oval, oblong, or obovate, 10 to 20 in. long, 6 to 12 in. wide, sometimes over 2 ft. long, very dark green, silvery-grey beneath, stalk up to $\frac{1}{2}$ in. thick. *fl.* 20 to 30 in compact trusses 9 in. wide; cor. bell-shaped, 2 in. wide, 8- to 10-lobed, creamy-white to soft yellow, usually blotched at base; stamens 18 or 20, shorter than the cor.; ovary densely downy; style glabrous, its stigma disk-like and $\frac{3}{8}$ in. wide. April. China, Burma, Tibet. 1913. (B.T.S. 3, 419.) The most wonderful in the genus for the size of its l., which have, in Cornwall, been $2\frac{1}{2}$ ft. long. It is variable in shape as well as in size of l., also in the shades of fl. colour. var. **borea'le** has soft-yellow fl. either unspotted or with a crimson blotch. **A**

R. sinolepido'tum. A synonym of *R. elaeagnoides.*

R. sinonut'tallii* (28). F. Similar in most respects to the Himalayan *R. Nuttallii* and its equal in beauty and distinction, but the fl.-stalks and cal. lobes are softly downy (as well as scaly) and the seed vessels are twice as long—$2\frac{1}{2}$ in. April, May. Tibet. 1919.

R. Smir'nowi (33*a*). A. Evergreen sturdy shrub, 5 to 7 ft., shoots white-felted. *l.* oblong-lanceolate, 3 to 6 in. long, felted beneath. *fl.* 10 to 12 in a truss 5 or 6 in. across; cor. 2 to 3 in. wide with 5 frilled lobes, pale to deep rose-purple; stamens 10, hairy; ovary downy; style glabrous. May. Caucasus. 1886. (B.M. 7495) Very hardy species of varying merit.

R. Smith'ii (6*a*). B. This is so near to *R. barbatum* that it can scarcely be regarded as more than a var. of it. It is a smaller tree from 10 to 15 ft. h. and the young shoots and fl.-stalks are more bristly. *fl.* a fine scarlet-crimson. March. Bhutan. 1852. (B.M. 5120.)

R. Sou'liei* (38*d*). B. Evergreen shrub, 6 to 10 ft., shoots purplish, glandular. *l.* broadly ovate to almost orbicular, often with a cordate base, 2 to $3\frac{1}{2}$ in. long, glabrous, glaucous green, stalk glandular. *fl.* in a loose truss of 5 to 8; cor. saucer-shaped, 2 to $2\frac{1}{2}$ in. wide, 5- or 6-lobed, white or pale rose; stamens usually 10, $\frac{1}{2}$ in. long; cal. with 5 oblong, rounded lobes and like the ovary, style, and fl.-stalk glandular. May. China. 1905. (B.M. 8622.) Distinct and very charming.

R. specio'sum* (5*b*). A. Deciduous shrub up to 6 ft., shoots downy and bristly. *l.* obovate to oblong, $1\frac{1}{2}$ to $2\frac{1}{2}$ in. long, bristly above, downy beneath. *fl.* in clusters of 6 to 15; cor. $1\frac{3}{4}$ in. long, $1\frac{1}{2}$ to 2 in. wide, scarlet or bright red with a large orange blotch; stamens 5; ovary bristly; cal. very small, ciliate. May. N. America. 1789. (B.M. 180 as *A. nudiflora coccinea.*) The most brilliantly coloured of American azaleas, and the one to which many of the finest hybrids owe their vivid hues of red and scarlet.

R. spera'bile (31*c*). C. Evergreen shrub, 3 to 5 ft., shoots at first woolly and glandular. *l.* oblong to lanceolate, 2 to 4 in. long, thickly woolly beneath. *fl.* in loose trusses of 4 to 6; cor. bell-shaped, $1\frac{1}{2}$ in. long, 5-lobed, clear scarlet with 5 black-crimson blotches at base; stamens 10, glabrous; ovary densely glandular and downy; cal. small, glandular-hairy. May. Burma. 1919. (B.M. 9301.)

R. sperabiloi'des* (31*c*). C. Evergreen shrub up to 4 ft., shoots whitish-scurfy. *l.* oblong to oblanceolate, $1\frac{1}{2}$ to 3 in. long, scurfy beneath. *fl.* in clusters of 6 to 10, cor. narrowly bell-shaped, 1 to $1\frac{1}{2}$ in. long, of various shades of crimson; stamens 10; ovary densely woolly; cal. with 5 unequal lobes from $\frac{1}{12}$ to $\frac{1}{8}$ in. long. April. Tibet. 1922. *R. sperabile* differs by the glandular ovary, cal., fl.-stalk, and shoots.

R. sphaeran'thum (2). C. So closely related is this to *R. ledoides* and so closely resembling it in general appearance as to be scarcely distinguishable. *fl.* white or rose, stamens downy towards the base (glabrous in *ledoides*). May. China. *See R. trichostomum.*

R. spinuli'ferum (35). C. Evergreen shrub, 6 to 8 ft., shoots hairy and bristly. *l.* lanceolate to oblanceolate, 2 to 3 in. long, scaly and downy. *fl.* in erect clusters of 3 to 5; cor. tubular, about 1 in. long, the 5 lobes incurved at the top, brick-red to crimson; stamens 10, exposed, glabrous; ovary very downy; cal. small and, like the short fl.-stalk, very downy. April. China. 1910. (B.M. 8408.) Most distinct on account of the incurved top of the cor.

Rhododendron spinuliferum

R. × spinulo'sum. Hybrid between *R. spinuliferum* and *R. racemosum.* *fl.* axillary, pink.

R. stamin'eum (36). E. Evergreen glabrous shrub of loose habit, 6 to 15 ft., shoots slender. *l.* whorled and persisting 2 or 3 years, narrowly elliptical to oblanceolate, slender-pointed, 2 to 4 in. long, glossy. *fl.* fragrant, in threes or fours from each of several buds at end of shoots; cor. white with yellow stains, $1\frac{1}{2}$ to 2 in. wide, funnel-shaped at base, deeply 5-lobed; stamens 10, $1\frac{1}{2}$ to 2 in. long; style still longer. April, May. China. 1900. (B.M. 8601.)

R. stenau'lum (36). F. Evergreen glabrous shrub of thin lanky growth, 16 to 40 ft. but with very beautiful, very fragrant fl. of a soft purplish-rose, darker in the tube and stained with greenish-yellow; they come singly, in pairs or in threes from several buds near the apex of the shoots, each $2\frac{1}{2}$ in. long. *l.* oblong-lanceolate, slender-pointed, 3 to 5 in. long. (G.C. 81 (1927), 193 as *R. Mackenzieanum.*) **A**

R. Stewartia'num (38*e*). C. Evergreen shrub or small tree. *l.* obovate to oval, 2 to $4\frac{1}{2}$ in. long, rounded at apex, mucronate, yellowish with powdery down beneath. *fl.* in trusses of 3 to 7; cor. broadly funnel-shaped, $1\frac{3}{4}$ in. long and wide, 5-lobed, colour very varied and described as pure white, cream, all shades of pink to deep rose, scarlet-red, and deep crimson; ovary glandular; cal. bowl-shaped, $\frac{1}{3}$ in. wide. February, March. Burma, Tibet, China. 1904. SYN. *R. aiolosalpinx.*

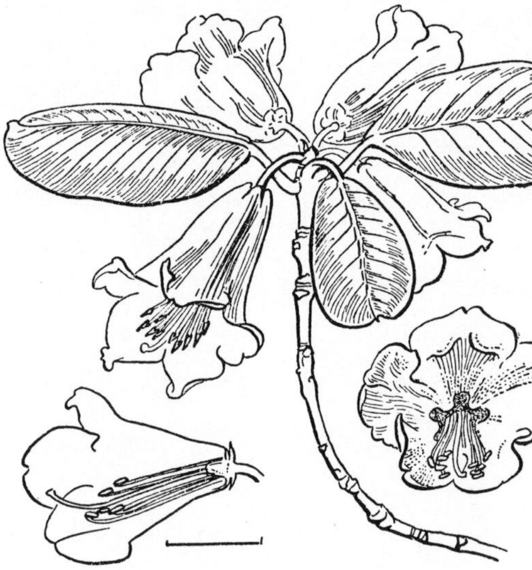

Rhododendron Stewartianum (p. 1783)

R. strigillo'sum (*6d*). D. Evergreen shrub, 6 to 15 ft., shoots, l.-stalks, and ovary bristly. *l.* narrowly oblong-lanceolate, 3 to 6 in. long, hairy beneath, especially on midrib. *fl.* 8 to 12 in trusses 4 to 5 in. across; cor. bell-shaped, with 5 spreading, rounded lobes, $1\frac{1}{2}$ to 2 in. wide, brilliant crimson-scarlet with 5 small, black-purple spots at base; stamens 10. March. China. 1904. Related to *R. pachytrichum*, which has non-glandular, branched hairs giving a rather mossy appearance. (B.M. 8864.)

R. sublanceola'tum. A synonym of *R. scabrum.*

R. sulfu'reum (7). E. Evergreen shrub, 2 to 4 ft. *l.* oval, $1\frac{1}{2}$ to 3 in. long, glaucous and densely covered with minute scales beneath. *fl.* in clusters of 4 to 8; cor. 1 in. wide, flattish, with 5 spreading lobes and a tubular base, bright yellow, slightly dotted; stamens 10, $\frac{3}{8}$ in. long, densely hairy at the base; ovary scaly; style sharply bent over; cal. deeply 5-lobed. April. China. 1905. (B.M. 8946.) The fl. are perhaps the richest hued of all yellow species.

Rhododendron sutchuenense

R. sutchuenen'se* (19*b*). B. Evergreen small tree 20 ft. in a wild state, usually a wide shrub up to 10 or 12 ft. in gardens; shoots $\frac{1}{2}$ in. thick. *l.* oblong-oval, 6 to 10 in. long. *fl.* about 10 in a truss 8 in. across; cor. widely bell-shaped, 3 in. wide, 5-lobed, rosy-pink unblotched but with purple spots; stamens 12 to 15, white; anthers black-purple; stigma large, reddish. March. China. 1901. (B.M. 8362.) One of the finest Chinese species closely akin to *R. praevernum* (q.v.). var. **Geral'dii** has deeper, rose-coloured fl. with a large chocolate blotch.

R. Taggia'num* (28*c*). E. Evergreen shrub, 6 to 7 ft., shoots scaly. *l.* oblong-elliptic, 3 to 6 in. long, one-third as wide, glaucous and scaly beneath. *fl.* usually 3 or 4 in a cluster, very fragrant; cor. pure white except for a yellow blotch, funnel-shaped, 3 to 4 in. long and wide, 5-lobed; stamens 10, 2 in. long, downy at base; ovary and base of style scaly. April, May. Burma. 1925. Fine species distinguished by its large, glandular seed-vessel (2 in. long). **A**

R. tanasty'lum* (24*a*). E. Evergreen shrub 8 to 20 ft. *l.* elliptic-lanceolate, slender-pointed, 3 to $5\frac{1}{2}$ in. long, 1 to $1\frac{3}{4}$ in. wide, glabrous. *fl.* in racemose clusters of about 8; cor. funnel-shaped, 2 in. long, 5-lobed, deep crimson, sometimes purplish or pink; stamens 10; ovary and style glabrous, latter standing clear of stamens and cor. April. Burma. Distinct by its richly coloured fl. and long style.

R. taronen'se* (28*a*). F. Evergreen shrub 10 to 15 ft., often growing as an epiphyte on large trees. *l.* obovate to elliptic, 4 to 6 in. long, glaucous and laxly scaly below. *fl.* fragrant, 4 to 6 in a shapely cluster 6 to 7 in. across; cor. widely bell-shaped, 5-lobed, $3\frac{1}{2}$ in. wide, white tinged with pink and stained with yellow in throat; stamens 10, $1\frac{1}{2}$ in. long; ovary, the long style, fl.-stalk, and small cal. all scaly. April. China. 1922. (B.M.N.S. t. 1.)

R. × Tay'lori. F. Hybrid between *R. jasminiflorum* and *R. javanicum* and an evergreen shrub of vigorous growth, producing large trusses of soft salmon-rose *fl.* paling to ivory-white in the tube; cor. 1 in. across, the tube $\frac{3}{4}$ in. long. Warm greenhouse.

R. telmatei'um (26). A. Evergreen shrub up to 3 ft. of erect habit; shoots very scurfy. *l.* elliptic-lanceolate, $\frac{1}{4}$ to $\frac{1}{2}$ in. long, $\frac{1}{10}$ to $\frac{1}{8}$ in. wide, very scaly on both surfaces. *fl.* solitary or in pairs; cor. $\frac{1}{2}$ in. wide, broadly funnel-shaped, deep rosy-purple, white in throat, 5-lobed, scaly outside; stamens 10; ovary scaly; style glabrous; cal. small, very scaly, ciliate. April, May. China. 1914. Dainty shrub for the rock-garden.

R. telo'peum (38*a*). B. Evergreen shrub, 3 to 4 ft., closely akin to *R. caloxanthum. fl.* pale yellow, in trusses of as many as 10, each $1\frac{1}{2}$ in. wide. It differs from *R. caloxanthum* by having a glabrous style and downy stamens. May. Tibet. 1919.

R. tephropep'lum* (7). C. Evergreen shrub up to 4 ft., shoots scaly. *l.* oblong-obovate, tapered at base, distinctly mucronate, $1\frac{1}{2}$ to $2\frac{1}{2}$ in. long, $\frac{1}{2}$ to 1 in. wide, glaucous and scaly beneath. *fl.* in clusters of 3 to 5; cor. narrowly bell-shaped, 5-lobed, 1 to $1\frac{1}{2}$ in. wide, bright purplish-rose, pink, or rosy-crimson; stamens 10; ovary densely scaly; style slender, erect; stigma large, crimson; cal. deeply 5-lobed. May. Tibet, Burma. 1921. (B.M. 9343.) Distinct by fl. colour and the straight stigma. *See* **R. deleiense.**

R. Tey'smannii. F. Evergreen shrub up to 4 ft. or more, epiphytic in a wild state. *l.* elliptic-lanceolate, pointed, 3 to 7 in. long, 1 to $2\frac{1}{2}$ in. wide. *fl.* in loose clusters of 6 to 12; cor. apricot-yellow with 5 slightly clawed lobes, fl.-stalks 1 in. long. Malay Peninsula. Blooms at various seasons. Warm greenhouse.

R. Thayeria'num (3*b*). B. Evergreen shrub up to 12 ft., shoots viscid. *l.* oblanceolate, pointed, $2\frac{1}{2}$ to 8 in. long, with very close, yellowish-brown felt beneath. *fl.* 10 to 16 in a loose, erect, graceful cluster 4 or 5 in. across; cor. broadly funnel-shaped, 5-lobed, $1\frac{1}{4}$ in. long, white with a pink tinge especially outside, spotted inside; stamens 10, ovary, style, cal., and fl.-stalk all glandular. June, July. China. 1910. Distinguished by the whorls of narrow l. persisting for 4 or 5 years and by most of the younger parts being viscidly glandular. (B.M. 8983.)

Rhododendron Thomsonii

R. Thom'sonii* (38). B. Evergreen shrub, 8 to 12 ft., of spreading habit. *l.* roundish-oval, 2 to 4 in. long, often slightly cordate at base, glabrous, dark green above, glaucous beneath. *fl.* 5 to 8 in a loose truss; cor. blood-red, open bell-shaped, 2 to $2\frac{1}{2}$ in. wide; stamens 10, glabrous. March. Himalaya. 1849. (B.M. 4997; R.S.H. 12.)

One of the finest red-flowered species; has been much used for hybridizing; distinguished by its large cal. (cup-shaped and ⅝ in. wide) and entirely glabrous character. **A**

R. timet'eum* (40*b*). C. Evergreen shrub up to 4 ft. Similar in general character to *R. oreotrephes* but dwarfer, flowering later and with scales on l. only half as dense. *fl.* pink, slightly spotted. May. China. 1918.

R. trichocla'dum (39). B. Deciduous or partly evergreen, stiff-habited shrub, up to 4 ft.; shoots bristly. *l.* oblong or obovate, 1 to 1½ in. long, dull green and hairy above, paler and scaly beneath, bristly on margins. *fl.* 3 to 5, closely clustered; cor. flat and open, 1 to 1¼ in. wide, yellow tinged and spotted with green, woolly in the throat, 5-lobed; stamens 10, ½ in. long, downy; ovary scaly but not bristly; style bent over at a right angle. May. China. 1910. (B.M. 9073.)

R. trichosto'mum (2). The three species regarded as distinct here, viz. *R. ledoides*, *R. radinum*, and *R. sphaeranthum*, appear to be very close to one another and to *R. trichostomum* of Franchet of which species they are sometimes considered varieties. The characters given under the 3 species will define *R. trichostomum* if that name is adopted. (B.M. 9202 as *R. hedyosmum*.)

R. triflo'rum (40*d*). D. Evergreen shrub up to 8 ft., the older bark peeling off in cinnamon-coloured flakes. *l.* lanceolate, 1½ to 3 in. long, glabrous above, very scaly and glandular beneath. *fl.* in threes, fragrant; cor. pale yellow, green-spotted, 1½ to 2 in. wide, 5-lobed; stamens 10; ovary very scaly; style glabrous. May, June. Himalaya. 1850. (R.S.H. 19.) Rare and of no great merit.

R. tsangpoen'se (21). B. Evergreen shrub, 1 to 2 ft., shoots thinly scaly. *l.* obovate, rounded at apex, more tapered at base, ¾ to 1½ in. long, glabrous above, thinly scaly and glaucous beneath. *fl.* in clusters of 3 to 5; stalk slender, 1 in. long; cor. 1 in. long, open-bell-shaped, 5-lobed, pink to deep cerise; cal. lobes ¼ in. long; stamens 10, hairy; style sharply bent down. May. Tibet. 1924. Least scaly of its series. *See* **R. pruniflorum.**

R. tsarongen'se. A synonym of *R. primulaeflorum*.

R. Unger'nii (33*a*). A. Evergreen shrub up to 20 ft. h. in nature, but slow-growing and much dwarfer in cultivation. *l.* oblong-lanceolate, 4 to 7 in. long, 1 to 2¼ in. wide, distinctly mucronate, felted beneath. *fl.* 20 or more in trusses 6 in. wide; cor. funnel-shaped with 5 spreading lobes, 1½ to 2 in. wide, white to pale rose; stamens 10; fl.-stalks, ovary, and margin of cal. glandular-hairy. July. Caucasus. 1886. (B.M. 8332.) Distinct by its late fl. and conspicuous mucro terminating the l.

R. uvarifo'lium (20). B. Evergreen tree or shrub, 15 to 25 ft. *l.* oblanceolate, 5 to 9 in. long, 1½ to 2¾ in. wide, closely white-woolly beneath. *fl.* in rounded, compact trusses of 15 to 20 and 5 to 6 in. across; cor. 2 in. wide, bell-shaped, 5-lobed, rosy white to pale rose with a crimson blotch; stamens 10; anthers dark brown; ovary minutely downy; style glabrous. March, April. China. 1913. (B.M. 9480.) Distinct by the white undersurface of the l. SYN. *R. niphargum*.

R. Valentinia'num (28*a*). D. Evergreen shrub, 3 to 4 ft., shoots very bristly. *l.* 1 to 2 in. long, half as wide, oval, bristly above, ciliate, very scaly beneath. *fl.* 2 to 6 in a cluster; cor. widely funnel-shaped, 1½ in. long, bright yellow; stamens 10; anthers pink; ovary very scaly; cal. ⅓ in. long, 5-lobed, scaly, ciliate. April. China. 1917. Distinct in the *ciliicalyx* group for its yellow fl.

R. Va'seyi* (5*a*). B. Deciduous shrub, 8 to 15 ft., shoots soon glabrous. *l.* ovate-lanceolate, much tapered at both ends, 2 to 4 in. long, slightly bristly. *fl.* in clusters of 4 to 8; cor. 1½ in. across, clear pale pink, deeply 5-lobed, upper lobes red-spotted; stamens 5 to 7, glabrous; ovary, cal., and fl.-stalk glandular. April, May. N. America. 1878. (B.M. 8081.) SYN. *Azalea Vaseyi*. Akin to *R. canadense* and *R. Albrechtii* and with the same very deeply lobed cor.

R. Veitchia'num* (28*a*). F. Epiphytic evergreen, 3 to 5 ft., scaly in all parts. *l.* 2 to 4 in. long, obovate, glaucous beneath. *fl.* in trusses of 3 to 5; cor. widely funnel-shaped, 4 in. or more across the 5 crinkled lobes, pure white, softly downy outside; stamens 10, downy; ovary very scaly, cal. usually more or less ciliate. April, May. Burma, Siam. 1850. (B.M. 4992.)

R. vena'tor* (24*a*). C. Evergreen shrub, 8 to 10 ft., shoots at first scurfy. *l.* oblong-lanceolate, 2½ to 5 in. long, sharply pointed, soon glabrous. *fl.* in close trusses of 5 to 10, stalks scurfy; cor. 1½ in. long, funnel-shaped, 5-lobed, scarlet with 5 black-crimson pouches at base; stamens 10; anthers purplish-black; ovary downy; style glabrous. May. Tibet. 1924.

R. vernico'sum (19*c*). B. Evergreen shrub, 6 to 25 ft. *l.* oval, 2½ to 5 in. long, glabrous, rather glaucous beneath. *fl.* in trusses of about 10; cor. widely funnel-shaped, 2½ in. across, 7-lobed, pale clear rose; stamens 14, glabrous; ovary very glandular; style clad over its whole length with dark-red glands which make the species distinct in the Fortunei series. The 'varnish' on the l. can only be developed by heating them. May. China. 1904. (B.M. 8834.) **A**

R. verruculo'sum (26). A. Evergreen shrub, 1½ to 3 ft. *l.* oval, ⅓ to ¾ in. long, thickly scaly above, less so beneath. *fl.* solitary, shortly stalked; cor. ¾ to 1 in. wide, purple, 5-lobed, scaly outside; stamens 7 or 8, purple; anthers yellowish; cal. deeply 5-lobed, $\frac{1}{10}$ in. long, ciliate. May. China. 1908. Suitable for the rock-garden.

R. villo'sum (40*a*). B. Evergreen shrub, up to 10 ft. or more; shoots densely bristly. *l.* oblong-lanceolate, 2 to 4 in. long, ¾ to 1⅓ in. wide, at first bristly above, bristly on midrib and scaly beneath. *fl.* in clusters of 3 or 4; cor. bright magenta-purple 1¾ in. wide, hairy outside, funnel-shaped, deeply 5-lobed; ovary bristly and scaly; cal. saucer-shaped and, like the l.-stalk, very bristly. May. China. 1904. Notable for its bristliness. (B.M. 8880.)

Rhododendron Vaseyi

R. virga'tum (41). E. Evergreen shrub, up to 3 ft., branchlets slender, scaly. *l.* oblong, 1½ to 3 in. long, ⅓ to 1 in. wide, scaly beneath; stalk ⅛ to ¼ in. long. *fl.* solitary or in pairs from several l.-axils at top of shoots; cor. tubular below, 1 to 1½ in. across the 5 spreading lobes, pale purplish-pink; stamens 10 or 12; ovary very scaly; style downy and scaly. April to June. N. India. 1849. (B.M. 5060; R.S.H. 26.)

R. virides'cens (39). B. Evergreen shrub, 1½ to 2 ft., shoots very bristly for 2 seasons. *l.* oblong-elliptic, rounded at apex, ¾ to 1½ in. long, scaly and glaucous beneath when young; stalks slender, 1 in. long, hairy. *fl.* pale yellowish-green, sometimes tinged crimson at margin, 1½ in. wide, 5-lobed; stamens 10; style curved, glabrous; cal. scaly and ciliate. June. Tibet. 1924. Distinguished by its glabrous l. and fringed cal.

R. visco'sum (5*b*). A. Deciduous shrub, 6 to 8 ft., shoots hairy. *l.* obovate, 1 to 2 in. long, glabrous above, hairy beneath. *fl.* in clusters of 6 to 10, exquisitely fragrant; cor. 1 to 1¼ in. long, 1 in. wide, narrowly tubular at base, white or pink, glandular and hairy; cal. very small, glandular-ciliate; stamens 5; ovary bristly. July. N. America. 1734. SYN. *Azalea viscosa*. Valuable for its late fl.; the parent of many of the early hybrids with small but numerous fragrant fl.

R. Wallich'ii (9). C. Very nearly akin to *R. campanulatum* and often regarded as a var. of it. The felt beneath the *l.* is sparse and sprinkled—not continuous as in *campanulatum*. The cor. is not spotted. April. N. India. 1849. (R.S.H. 5; B.M. 4928 as *R. campanulatum Wallichii*.)

R. War'dii* (38*d*). C. Evergreen shrub up to 12 or 15 ft. *l.* roundish oval to oval, base cordate, 2 to 4 in. long, glaucous beneath, glabrous. *fl.* in trusses of 7 to 14; cor. bowl-shaped, 5-lobed, 2 to 2½ in. wide, clear bright unspotted yellow; stamens 10, ½ to ¾ in. long, glabrous; ovary and style glandular; cal. distinctly 5-lobed, very glandular like the fl.-stalk. May. China. 1913. Allied to *R. Souliei* but with beautiful yellow fl.

R. Wa'sonii (37*d*). A. Evergreen shrub 2 to 5 ft. *l.* oval to ovate, 2 to 3 in. long, leathery, rusty-brown-felted beneath. *fl.* in trusses of 6 to 9; cor. bell-shaped, 1½ in. wide, 5-lobed, lobes erect, creamy-white or lemon-yellow shaded with rose (wholly rose in one form); stamens 10 with black-brown anthers; ovary white-downy; style glabrous, pale yellow; cal. and fl.-stalk downy. April. China. 1904. (B.M. 9190.)

R. Weyrich'ii* (5*e*). C. Deciduous shrub, 5 to 15 ft. *l.* often in threes, obovate, ovate, or rhomboid, 1½ to 3½ in. long. *fl.* 2 to 4 in a cluster; cor. bright brick-red, 2 in. wide, funnel-shaped with

5 spreading lobes, upper one spotted; stamens 6 to 10, much exserted, red; cal., ovary, and fl.-stalk clad with reddish hairs. April, May. Japan. 1915. (B.M. 9475.) SYN. *Azalea Weyrichii.* Distinguished by the unusual shade of red of the fl.

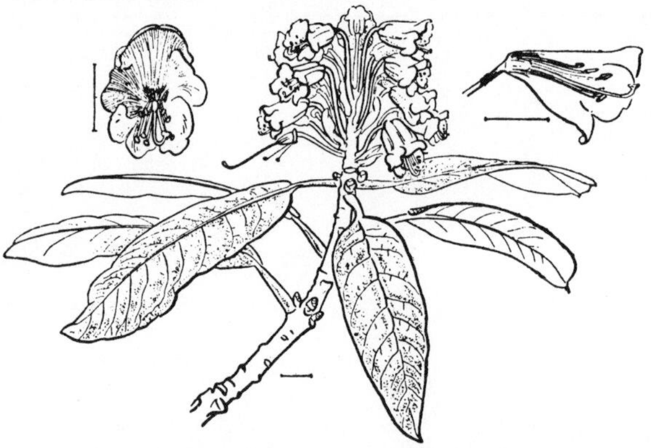

Rhododendron Wightii

R. Wight'ii (25). B. Evergreen shrub, sometimes tree-like, 10 to 15 ft. *l.* oblong, elliptic, or obovate, 6 to 8 in. long, reddish-brown-felted beneath. *fl.* in rather loose trusses of 12 to 20; cor. bell-shaped, 1½ in. wide, pale yellow with a crimson blotch and crimson spots; stamens 10, much shorter than cor.; ovary densely woolly; style glabrous, much longer than stamens. April. Himalaya. 1851. (B.M. 8492; R.S.H. 27.) Handsome, rare, and not easily cultivated.

R. Williamsia'num* (38). C. Evergreen shrub of compact, rounded shape, 4 to 5 ft., dense and leafy. *l.* orbicular to ovate, usually cordate at the base, 1 to 2 in. long, at first bronzy, then dark green, glaucous beneath; stalk glandular-bristly. *fl.* often solitary or in pairs, sometimes 4 in a loose truss; cor. bell-shaped, 2¼ in. wide, 5- or 6-lobed, soft unspotted rosy-red; cal. minute and, like the ovary, style, l.-stalk, and fl.-stalk, glandular. April. China. 1908. (B.M. 8935.) Distinct and attractive, notable for its compact, hemispherical shape and bronzy young foliage.

R. Wil'sonae (36). D. Evergreen, glabrous shrub, 6 or 7 ft., shoots slender. *l.* in whorls, persisting 2 years, oval, short-pointed, 2½ to 4½ in. long, 1 to 1¾ in. wide, of hard texture. *fl.* produced singly or in pairs from several buds at apex of shoot; cor. funnel-shaped, 2 in. wide across the 5 lobes, pale flesh-pink; stamens 10; ovary and style glabrous. April. China. 1904.

R. Wil'tonii (37*d*). B. Evergreen shrub, 4 to 10 ft., shoots brown-woolly. *l.* oblanceolate, 2 to 3½ in. long, glossy green and deeply wrinkled above, woolly like the shoots beneath. *fl.* in loose clusters of 8 to 10, stalks slender, 1 in. long, downy; cor. bell-shaped, 1½ in. long with 5 erect lobes, pale pink to nearly white with a crimson stain; stamens 10, shorter than the cor., ovary white-woolly. April, May. China. 1904. (B.M. 9388.)

R. xanthoco'don (40*d*). C. Evergreen slender tree, in nature 15 to 25 ft., shoots scaly. *l.* oval, 1½ to 3 in. long, scaly, glaucous green beneath. *fl.* in clusters of 5 or more; cor. bell-shaped, 1 in. long, 5-lobed, creamy-yellow, unspotted; stamens 10, creamy-white; anthers pale brown; ovary densely scaly; cal. small, scaly. May. Tibet. 1924. Interesting for its unspotted yellow fl.

R. xanthostepha'num (7). D. Evergreen shrub, 4 to 6 ft. *l.* lanceolate, 1½ to 3½ in. long, ⅜ to 1⅛ in. wide, grey-glaucous and scaly beneath. *fl.* in clusters of 3 to 5; cor. broadly tubular at base, 5-lobed, 1 to 1½ in. wide, of varying shades of yellow, usually bright, sometimes tinged green; stamens 10, more or less hairy; ovary densely scaly; style 1 in. long, slender, not bent; cal. deeply 5-lobed, membranous, scaly. April, May. China. 1906. (B.M. 8882.) Distinct by its straight style. SYN. *R. aureum.*

R. yakusima'num (33 *a*). B. Evergreen rounded shrub, about 2 ft. 6 in. h., nearly related to *R. Metternichii. l.* very similar to *R. Degronianum. fl.* at first pink, becoming white, in compact, erect trusses; cor. 5-lobed, 2½ in. across, lobes broad, emarginate. May. Japan. 1939? (J.R.H.S. 72, 395.)

R. yedoen'se poukhanen'se (5*d*). B. Deciduous shrub, 3 to 6 ft. *l.* lanceolate to oblanceolate, 1½ to 3 in. long, bristly on both surfaces, ciliate. *fl.* 2 to 4 together, rosy-purple, spotted on the upper lobe, funnel-shaped, 1½ in. long, 5-lobed; stamens 10; anthers purple; ovary bristly; style 1¾ in. long. April. Korea. 1913. SYN. *R. coreanum.* Although known as 'var. *poukhanense*' to botanists this is really the wild form of this Azalea. A form of garden origin with double fl., but of earlier introduction, is given the specific name. (B.M. n.s. 455.)

R. yunnanen'se* (40*e*). B. Evergreen bush of rounded shape, 10 ft. by 12 ft. *l.* elliptic-lanceolate or oblanceolate, 1½ to 3 in. long, slightly hairy above, ciliate. *fl.* in clusters of 3 to 6; cor. 1½ to 2 in. wide, white or pinkish freely spotted with crimson; stamens 10; ovary densely scaly; style smooth. May. China. 1889. (B.M. 7614; F.S. 2, 360.) Valuable for its profuse and never-failing blossom.

R. zaleu'cum (40*e*). D. Seen only as an evergreen shrub in gardens, this is said to have been found wild in damp rain forest as a thin tree of 20 to 30 ft. *l.* oval-lanceolate, 1 to 3 in. long, dark green above, very glaucous or blue-white beneath. *fl.* in clusters of 3 to 6, slightly fragrant; cor. rosy-white, lavender-blue, or mauve, funnel-shaped, with 5 spreading lobes, 1 to 1¾ in. wide, scaly outside. April. China, Burma. 1912. The whiteness beneath the l. is, in this species, purer perhaps than in any other rhododendron. Collectors have recorded that the fl. vary greatly in colour. (B.M. 8878.)

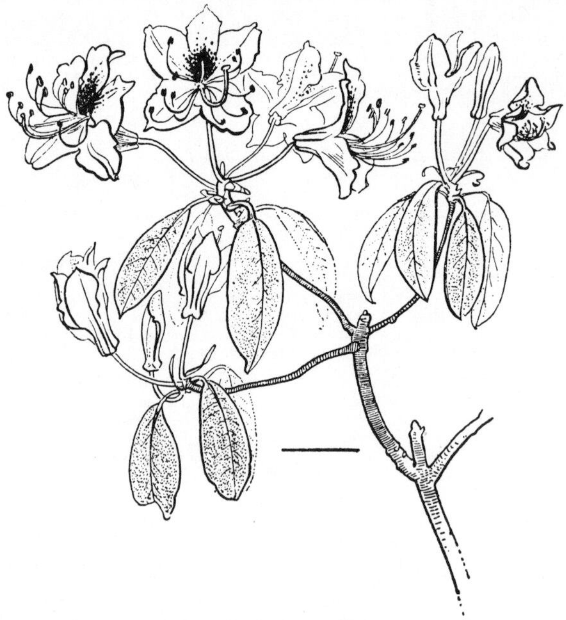

Rhododendron yunnanense

R. zeylan'icum (3*a*). E. A subspecies of *R. arboreum* resembling *R. Kingianum* in its bullate *l.* but with rich pink *fl.* Ceylon. (P.F.G.I. 7 as *R. Rollissonii.*) Dr. O. Stapf considered *R. nilagiricum* to be the same. (B.M. 9323.)

F. J. C. and P. M. S.

RHODOHYPOX'IS (*rhodon*, rose, *Hypoxis*; from the colour of the flower and its relationship). FAM. *Hypoxidaceae.* A genus of a single species of perennial herb closely related to Hypoxis and at one time included in it, but differing by the perianth pieces being joined at the base instead of quite free and the stamens being in 2 series adnate to the perianth tube while the anthers have 2 short horn-like projections above the anther-lobes. A second species *R. rubella* is probably not a Rhodohypoxis and is apparently not in cultivation. A light soil in a sunny position, provided the plant has sufficient moisture in summer, suits this plant which, however, is impatient of winter damp, though capable of withstanding the cold of most winters. It makes an excellent alpine-house plant.

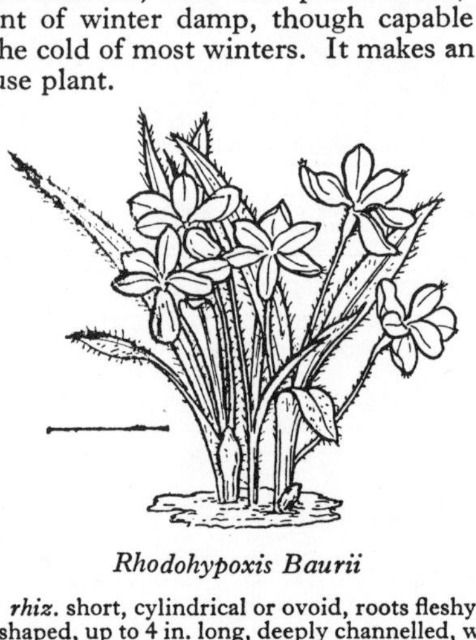

Rhodohypoxis Baurii

R. Baur'ii. *rhiz.* short, cylindrical or ovoid, roots fleshy. *l.* radical, erect, strap-shaped, up to 4 in. long, deeply channelled, with spreading silky hairs near base on upper and all over lower surface, base sheathing. *fl.* solitary in l.-axils on a stiff pedicel about 4 in. long;

perianth rose-red, pale outside; segs. in 2 series, outer obovate-elliptic, hairy without near base and on midrib, inner glabrous, all spreading above the tube, about ⅜ in. long. S. Africa. 1877. (B.M. 9412.) SYN. *Hypoxis Baurii, R. rubella* of gardens. var. **platypet'ala,** *fl.* white, otherwise like type. (B.M. 9412.) SYN. *Hypoxis platypetala.*

R. rubel'la of gardens. A synonym of *R. Baurii.*

RHODOLEI'A (*rhodon*, rose, *leios*, smooth). FAM. *Hamamelidaceae.* A genus of 7 small, glabrous trees with the habit of Rhododendron, 1 native in China and the E. Indies. Leaves crowded at tip of branchlets, alternate, spreading, evergreen, oblong, entire, thickly leathery, glaucous beneath; stalk long. Flowers in an axillary, stalked, nodding, 5-flowered head surrounded by a coloured, many-leaved involucre; petals rose, 2 to 4, very unequal, clawed; stamens 7 to 10, inserted with petals. For treatment *see* **Gardenia.** *R. Forrestii* has been grown outdoors in Cornwall but is a tender plant even there.

R. Champion'ii. *l.* elliptic-obovate, obtuse, bright green. *fl.* 2½ in. across; outer leaves of involucre, about 12; inner about 18. February. *fr.* of 5 radiating capsules, each as large as a hazel-nut. Hong Kong. 1852. (B.M. 4509.)

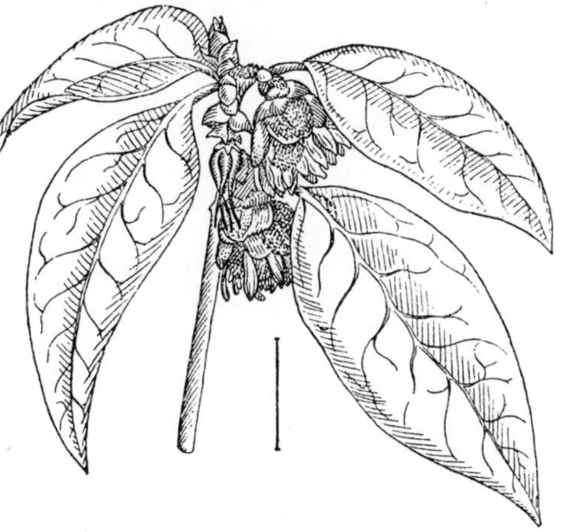

Rhodoleia Forrestii

R. Forrestii. Tree or shrub, stellately hairy at first, then glabrous. *l.* elliptic, 3 to 6 in. long, 1 to 3 in. wide, densely red-hairy at first, finally shining above; stalk about 2 in. long. *fl.* in a pedunculate head; pet. narrow-spatulate, about 1 in. long; stamens 8. Yunnan, Burma. 1920. (B.M.N.S. t. 27.)

RHODOMYR'TUS (*rhodon*, rose, *myrtos*, myrtle; in allusion to the rosy, myrtle-like flowers). FAM. *Myrtaceae.* Five species in Trop. Asia; closely akin to Myrtus, but well distinguished by the prominently 3-veined leaves.

R. tomento'sa. Evergreen shrub, sometimes a small tree, nearly all parts densely downy. *l.* opposite, 1 to 3 in. long, ½ to 1½ in. wide, oval to obovate, apex blunt, base cuneate, with 3 strong veins united by fine cross-veins. *fl.* ¾ to 1¼ in. wide, axillary, solitary or 3 in a stalked cluster; pet. broadly obovate, rosy, downy outside; stamens very numerous. June. *fr.* ovoid, ⅓ in. long, purple, capped by the cal. lobes, pleasantly flavoured. Very widely spread in Trop. Asia. 1766. (B.M. 250 as *Myrtus tomentosa.*) Warm greenhouse.

W. J. B.

rhodopen'sis -is -e, of the Rhodope Mt., Bulgaria.

RHODOR'A. Included in **Rhododendron.**

RHODOSPATH'A (*rhodon*, rose, *spatha*, spathe; the spathe is rose in some species). FAM. *Araceae.* A genus of about a dozen species of climbing shrubs, natives of Trop. America, closely related to Stenospermation, differing mainly in the arrangement of the ovules. Branches rooting. Leaves closely arranged in 2 ranks, petiole sharply bent at base of blade, oblong-elliptic, more or less oblique; stalks about as long as leaves, sheaths long. Flowers hermaphrodite; naked; stamens 4; ovary 2-celled. Fruit a small, many-seeded berry. Spathe widely ovate or oblong-ovate, cuspidate. Spadix dense-flowered. Stove conditions with a moist atmosphere and sandy loam and peat suit these plants which are propagated by seed or by cuttings.

R. blan'da. Climber, lower internodes about 1½ in. long. *l.-stalk* 5 to 6 in. long, sharply bent, blade oblong-elliptic, somewhat curved near apex, 5 to 8 in. long. *Peduncle* about 3 in. long. *Spathe* greenish-ochre; spadix about 3 in. long, narrowed to tip. Brazil. 1860.

R. Forget'ii. Glabrous climber, upper internodes about ½ in. long. *l.-stalk* about 18 in. long, sheathing, margin of sheath entire, blade oblong, up to 24 in. long, dark green, veins prominent beneath. *Peduncle* about 12 in. long, clasped by uppermost l.-sheath. *Spathe* creamy-white with pink outer edge at first, salmon within, soon deciduous, oblong, about 6 in. long, 1½ in. wide, slender-pointed; spadix about 5 in. long. Costarica. 1912? (B.M. 9105.)

R. pic'ta. Stem round. *l.-stalk* about 10 in. long, sharply bent, blade thinly leathery, ovate-elliptic, 12 to 18 in. long, dark green irregularly spotted with orange. *Peduncle* round, about 6 in. long. *Spathe* flesh-coloured, ovate-oblong, 8 to 9 in. long, about 3 in. wide; spadix 6 to 8 in. long. S. America. SYN. *Spathiphyllum pictum.*

RHODOSPHAER'A (*rhodon*, rose, *sphaeron*, globe; in allusion to the reddish globose fruit). FAM. *Anacardiaceae.* A genus of a single species of Australian tree, closely related to Rhus and sometimes included in that genus from which it differs by the 10 stamens instead of 5. Leaves odd-pinnate, rather leathery, evergreen. Flowers red, in axillary and terminal panicles, polygamo-dioecious; stamens 10; styles 3, free. Fruit a globose drupe. *R. rhodanthema* needs greenhouse conditions and treatment as for the tender Eucalypti.

R. rhodan'thema. Yellow-wood. Glabrous, evergreen tree to 60 or 70 ft. *lflets.* 7 to 9, oblong-ovate with a blunt point, 2 to 2½ in. long, shining dark green above, paler beneath with tufts of hair in vein-axils. *fl.* crimson or pink, about ⅛ in. across, in panicles 4 in. long. *fr.* globose, ½ in. across, reddish-brown. Queensland, New S. Wales. SYN. *Rhus rhodanthema.* The wood of this handsome-foliaged tree is used in cabinet-making and yields a yellow dye.

RHODOSTACH'YS. *See* **Fascicularia.**

RHODOTHAM'NUS (*rhodon*, rose, *thamnos*, a shrub; in allusion to the rosy flowers). FAM. *Ericaceae.* A monotypic genus characterized by 5-merous flowers, rotate corolla, glandular-hairy calyx lobes, 10 projecting stamens, a capsular, rounded, hairy, septicidal fruit and almost sessile, bristly ciliate leaves. Differs from Rhododendron by its regular rotate (i.e. circular and flat-spreading) corolla, that of Rhododendron, when rotate, being irregular in outline. Thrives in light, humous, lime-free soil although in nature it is found on limestone mountains. Seed affords the best means of propagation, but cuttings and layers may also be used.

R. Chamaecis'tus. Evergreen, slender-stemmed shrub, erect at first, later procumbent, seldom more than 9 in. h. with glandular-hairy young wood. The difficulty sometimes found in cultivating this shrub may be considerably overcome by protecting the rooting area from strong sunshine; in nature this is effected by other herbage and rocks. *l.* oval to obovate, ¼ to ½ in. long, about half as wide. *fl.* on long, glandular-hairy stalks in terminal clusters of 2 to 4; cor. shell-pink, spreading, 1 in. across, deeply divided into 5 lobes; cal. lobes 5, about half length of cor., glandular-hairy, narrowly ovate, acute. April, May. E. European Alps, E. Siberia. 1786. (B.M. 488 as *Rhododendron Chamaecistus.*)

F. S.

RHODOTY'POS (*rhodon*, rose, *typos*, a type or model; from the resemblance of the flowers to a rose). FAM. *Rosaceae.* A genus of a single species, a shrub, native of China and Japan, related to Kerria, from which it is readily distinguished by its opposite (not alternate) leaves and 4- (not 5-) petalled white (not yellow) flowers. Hardy and easily grown in ordinary soil, and propagated by seed or by moderately soft cuttings in sand with bottom heat.

R. kerrioi'des. A twiggy deciduous bush about 5 or 6 ft. h. with erect branches. *l.* ovate, slender-pointed, acutely toothed, silky-hairy beneath, stalked, stipules free. *fl.* white, 1½ to 2 in. across, solitary at end of twig, pet. 4, rounded, sep. 4, toothed, persistent. May to July. *fr.* shining black, about as large as small peas. China, Japan. 1866. (B.M. 5805.) SYN. *R. scandens.*

RHOE'O (? derivation). FAM. *Commelinaceae.* A monotypic genus, native of Cent. America, related to Tradescantia, and distinct by the boat-like involucre which subtends the flower-clusters. A perennial herb with nearly erect stiff leaves crowded on a short stem arising from the underground rhizome, and congested flowers borne in an involucre of overlapping boat-like bracts. Petals equal, not clawed. Fruit a sessile capsule. Moist rich soil and a warm-house are its requirements.

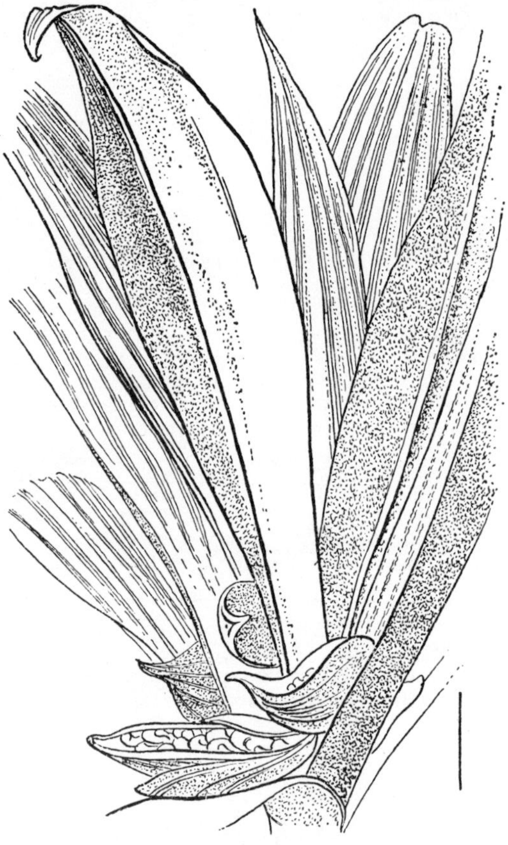

Rhoeo discolor

R. dis'color. Boat Lily. *l.* 8 to 15 in. long, blades thick, broad-linear, acute, often purple especially beneath. *fl.* white or blue, about ¼ in. long, crowded; spathes 1 to 1¾ in. long. All year. Florida to Mexico. (B.M. 1192, 5079.)

RHOICIS'SUS (*rhoia*, pomegranate, *Cissus*). FAM. *Vitaceae.* A genus of about 8 species of shrubby climbers or sub-climbers, mostly natives of extra-tropical Africa, related to Cissus. Inflorescence a tendril bearing cyme. Flowers 5-merous, petals triangular-oblong, more or less marcescent. Fruit a 1- to 4-seeded berry. Cultivation as for Cissus.

R. rhomboi'dea. Moderate climber. *l.* rhomboid with a wedge-shaped base, acute, with few acute teeth above middle, brownish hairy at first, becoming almost glabrous; stalked. Peduncle shortly hairy. Tendril simple. *fr.* edible. Natal. Greenhouse.

rhom'bicus -a -um, rhomboid, diamond-shaped with obtuse lateral angles.

rhomboi'deus -a -um, rhomboid.

RHOMBOPHYL'LUM. Included in **Mesembryanthemum.**

RHOPA'LA. *See* **Roupala.**

rhopalo-, in compound words, signifying club-shaped.

RHOPALOBLAS'TE (*rhopalon*, club, *blaste*, sprout; the embryo has a club-shaped appendage). FAM. *Palmaceae.* A genus of 3 species of Malayan Palms with simple spineless stems and a large crown of equally pinnatisect leaves. Leaf-segments slender-pointed, 1-nerved. The short-stalked, much-branched spadix appears among the leaves; spathes 2, caducous, the lower shorter, 2-keeled; stamens 6. Fruit red. Cultivation as for Archontophoenix.

R. hexand'ra. Stem stoutish, about 4 ft. h. *l.* numerous; lflets. lanceolate, thick leathery, acute. *fl.* rather large; spadix thick; spathes large, the lower velvety-hairy. Moluccas. 1890.

RHOPALOC'ERA. *See* **Lepidoptera.** A

RHOPALOSIPH'UM. *See* **Brown Currant Aphis, Oat-apple Aphis, Water-lily Aphis.** A

RHOPALOSTIG'MA. Included in **Staurostigma.**

RHOPALOSTYL'IS (*rhopalon*, club, *stylos*, pillar; from the club-shaped spadix). FAM. *Palmaceae.* A genus of 2 species of palms, natives of New Zealand and Norfolk Island. Stems of moderate size, spineless, ringed. Leaves in a terminal cluster, equally pinnatisect; segments equidistant, numerous, narrowly sword-shaped, slender-pointed, recurved at base but not thickened; stalk short; sheath long. Spadix short, spreading, branches thick, densely flowered; spathes 2, oblong, flattened, lower 2-winged. Flowers of medium size. Fruit elliptic, smooth. Graceful greenhouse palms requiring conditions similar to Areca.

R. Bau'eri. About 20 ft. h. or more. Stem about 4 in. thick. *l.* 6 to 9 ft. long, pinnate; lflets. closely set, 2 ft. long, 1½ in. wide, stiff, slender-pointed, ribbed and plaited; stalk scaly as are rachis and veins. *Spathes* white, 8 to 20 in. long, narrow-oblong; spadix 1 to 2 ft. long. *fl.* white. *fr.* scarlet. Norfolk and Kermadec Is. (B.M. 5735 as *Areca Baueri.*)

R. sap'ida. Nikau Palm. 6 to 30 ft. h. Stem 6 to 9 in. thick, often glaucous. *l.* 4 to 6 ft. long, pinnate; lflets. very narrow, linear; margin recurved; veins, midrib, and l.-stalk scurfy. *Spadix* 18 to 24 in. long, half-enclosed, much-branched. *fl.* pale-pinkish. *fr.* ovoid, brown. New Zealand. (B.M. 5139 as *Areca sapida.*) SYN. *Kentia sapida.*

RHUBARB (*Rheum Rhaponticum*, &c.). In spite of the fact that *Rheum Rhaponticum* had reached British gardens in the latter half of the sixteenth century, the cultivation of Rhubarb as an article of food did not become general until much later and it was not until the beginning of the nineteenth century that it began to come into the London market. It is indeed doubtful whether Rhubarb would have become so popular as it is or of such importance in the market if varieties of *Rheum Rhaponticum* alone were concerned. It is probable that *R. undulatum* and possibly also *R. hybridum*, which some botanists have considered to be derived from a cross between *R. Rhaponticum* and *R. palmatum*, have a part in the parentage of the culinary Rhubarbs of to-day. Many varieties were raised in English gardens in the first half of the nineteenth century, several of which persist at the present time, and others have been added since, seedlings selected for their earliness, colour, flavour, and especially for their amenability to forcing. Stocks of some seedling forms have been adopted by individual growers and grown exclusively by them since they have found that they suit the particular conditions under which they are cultivated and the markets they are intended to supply. An account of the history of the introduction of the species of Rheum and of the development of the culinary varieties with many references to the literature of the subject is given by Miss D. M. Turner, B.Sc., in 'Economic Rhubarbs', in the *Journal R.H.S.* 63, p. 355. At the present time Rhubarb is an important article of cultivation in private and market gardens all over the country, its leaf-stalks being used either in a blanched or a natural state in pies, or stewed, either by itself or mixed with apples or gooseberries, and for bottling and in making preserves, while Rhubarb wine is also sometimes made. It should be noted that the green leaves themselves are unwholesome and cases of poisoning through their use are on record.

Rhubarb can be grown in almost any soil but does best in a rich, rather light soil, and in an open situation unshaded by trees, &c. It has sometimes been grown between fruit-trees, but this is inadvisable, not only because of the shade, but because of the spraying operations necessary in successful fruit-growing.

Rhubarb is readily raised from seed sown in spring on a gentle hot-bed, the seedlings being transplanted to the open ground when large enough, but the plants so obtained will vary greatly between themselves and the most satisfactory results are to be obtained by the use of established varieties propagated by division. Strong, healthy roots should be divided in March so that each piece has a crown and these single crown divisions should be planted out at once, 3 ft. apart each way, keeping the crown slightly above the surface. The ground should previously have been deeply cultivated and well manured. No leaves should be removed in the year of planting, but in the next year a moderate crop may be taken and in the third year a good crop should be available. The plantation should have an annual dressing of manure or compost each winter, and be kept free from weeds. With this treatment it should be good for several years, though it may be desirable to renew it after 4 or 5 years if pulling has been hard.

Early supplies are produced by forcing during winter and early spring. The forcing of very early supplies must be done in houses where the temperature can be kept at 55 to 60° F. For this purpose 3-year-old roots are best, though older ones may be used. The roots are lifted and brought into the forcing house at intervals from November onwards. They appear to respond to forcing most readily after exposure to some frost. The roots are stood nearly close together on the floor of the house, either a greenhouse where light can be excluded, or a mushroom house, and some soil scattered amongst and over them, water being occasionally given. When growth begins the temperature may be raised to the point mentioned, but premature heating often results in decay.

Rhubarb may also be forwarded in the open ground by covering the roots where they have been growing with large flower-pots, seakale pots, or boxes and burying them with a good depth of fermenting material, such as stable litter and leaves, or by any of the methods used in forcing seakale. This should be done early in January or February. Less active growth may be promoted by covering the roots with a good layer of straw but this will, of course, not produce the blanched leaf-stalks that the other methods secure; the produce will be similar to that where the plants are allowed to grow naturally, though a little earlier.

Varieties to be recommended will be found in the Supplement and full descriptions of most varieties in the records of trials carried out at Wisley published in the *Journal R.H.S.*

DISEASES. Of the few diseases attacking Rhubarb the most likely to be troublesome is Crown Rot caused by *Bacterium rhaponticum* in which the terminal bud rots following rotting in the pithy tissues beneath it. Infection seems to be through wounds and the organism causes brownish rot of the inside, often so extensive that a blackened discoloured cavity is formed and the top of the plant may be knocked or pulled off quite easily. With the failure of the terminal bud there may be only spindly side shoots developed and these may later die away. If this disease is seen in an old plant being divided up for sets the plant should not be used for the purpose and is better destroyed. Rhubarb foliage is often attacked by leaf-spotting fungi and sometimes the spots are very numerous. The commonest is *Ramularia rhei* which causes brown spots on the leaves, but it does not seem to weaken rhubarb to any great extent. The Grey Mould fungus, *Botrytis cinerea*, may cause injury to forced Rhubarb but should be checked with proper ventilation and destruction of infected material. Outdoors this grey mould is only likely to harm Rhubarb in very wet seasons.

A mosaic virus disease attacks Rhubarb, causing yellowish mottling and spotting of the leaves which are smaller and with thinner leaf-stalks than normal, and this is followed by marked weakening of the crown. Plants attacked should be removed and burnt.

(D. E. G.)

RHUBARB, PRICKLY. *See* **Gunnera manicata.**

RHUS (ancient Greek name for the genus, used by Theophrastus). FAM. *Anacardiaceae*. Sumach. A genus of about 150 species of trees or shrubs, mostly with poisonous properties in a greater or less degree. They are distributed over the temperate regions of both hemispheres, and especially in S. Africa, but rarely occur within the tropics. Leaves alternate, simple, 3-foliolate or unequally pinnate; leaflets entire or serrate. Flowers small, polygamous, in axillary and terminal panicles; calyx 4- to 6-parted, persistent, segments overlapping; petals 4 to 6, spreading, overlapping; stamens 4, 5, 6, or 10. Fruit a small, dry, compressed drupe. Some American species, including *R. Toxicodendron* and *R. vernix*, seriously affect those touching them, the hands and arms, and sometimes the whole body, becoming greatly swollen, the swelling being accompanied with great pain and inflammation, and ending in ulceration. These effects are not, however, felt by everyone, for some can handle the plants with impunity. *R. Coriaria*, the leaves being finely ground, provides the well-known tanning and dyeing material, Sumac, and from the wood of *R. Cotinus* the dyeing material known as 'young fustic' is obtained. The notched bark of *R. verniciflua* yields the Japanese lacquer and the crushed berries of *R. succedanea* yield wax. The chief value in gardens of several of the following species lies in the fine autumn tints and the striking masses of coloured fruits they produce. Most of them are hardy and can be propagated by cuttings or layers and some of them propagate freely by cuttings of the roots.

KEY

1.	*Lvs. simple*	2
1.	*Lvs. compound*	3
2.	*Lvs. wedge-shaped at base, usually obovate*	R. cotinoides
2.	*Lvs. abruptly narrowed at base, usually oval*	R. Cotinus
3.	*Lflets.* 3	4
3.	*Lflets.* 5 *or more*	11
4.	*Lvs. more or less evergreen*	5
4.	*Lvs. deciduous*	7
5.	*Lflets. obovate, up to* $2\frac{1}{2}$ *in. long*	6
5.	*Lflets. ovate, slender-pointed,* 3 to 5 *in. long*	R. laevigata
6.	*Lflets. obtuse*	R. lucida
6.	*Lflets. mucronate*	R. mucronata
7.	*Lflets. usually over* 1 *in. long*	8
7.	*Lflets. not over* 1 *in. long, lobed or with few rounded teeth*	R. trilobata
8.	*Lflets. and red fr. downy; fl. in dense spikes*	R. aromatica
8.	*Fl. in loose panicles; fr. whitish*	9
9.	*Lflets. entire or coarsely toothed*	10
9.	*Lflets. with rounded teeth, sometimes lobed*	R. diversiloba
10.	*Fr. glabrous or shortly pubescent*	24
10.	*Fr. bristly*	R. orientalis
11.	*Infl. terminal; fr. red, hairy*	12
11.	*Infl. axillary; fr. whitish*	19
12.	*Fruiting panicles pendulous*	13
12.	*Fruiting panicles upright*	14
13.	*Lflets. oblong-lanceolate, finely pointed*	R. Potaninii
13.	*Lflets. oblong-ovate, entire*	R. punjabensis sinica
14.	*Common stalk of lvs. winged throughout*	15
14.	*Common stalk of lvs. not, or only in upper part, winged*	17
15.	*Lflets. oval or ovate, bluntish*	R. Coriaria
15.	*Lflets. acute, usually over* 2 *in. long*	16
16.	*Lflets. mostly entire*	R. copallina
16.	*Lflets. toothed*	R. javanica
17.	*Shoots hairy*	18
17.	*Shoots glabrous*	R. glabra
18.	*Lvs.* 8 *to* 12 *in. long, yellowish-downy beneath*	R. Michauxii

18. *Lvs.* 12 *to* 24 *in. long*	R. typhina
19. *Lvs. more or less downy*	20
19. *Lvs. glabrous*	C. succedanea
20. *Lflets.* 3 *to* 9 *in. long*	21
20. *Lflets.* 2 *to* 4 *or* 5 *in. long*	22
21. *Lvs. shining above, velvety beneath*	R. insignis
21. *Lvs. downy at least on midrib beneath*	R. verniciflua
22. *Lflets.* 7 to 13	23
22. *Lflets.* 13 *to* 17	R. trichocarpa
23. *Lflets. more or less downy, veins numerous, conspicuous*	R. sylvestris
23. *Lflets. at length glabrous, veins* 8 *to* 12 *pairs*	R. vernix
24. *Plant climbing with aerial roots*	R. radicans
24. *Plant not climbing; no aerial roots*	R. Toxicodendron

R. aromat'ica. Low, spreading, pleasantly aromatic, deciduous shrub, 3 to 4 ft., shoots downy. *l.* 3-foliolate; lflets. 1½ to 3 in. long, side ones ovate, terminal one larger, obovate, all coarsely toothed, very downy beneath. *fl.* small, yellowish, in clusters ½ to ¾ in. long, forming short terminal panicles. April. *fr.* red, hairy, ¼ in. wide, globose. E. United States. 1759. SYN. *R. aromatica.* var. **triloba'ta,** a synonym of *R. trilobata.*

R. canaden'sis. A synonym of *R. aromatica.*

R. chinen'sis. Tree 20 ft. or more with a rounded head; shoots yellowish-downy; winter buds brown-velvety. *l.* pinnate, 8 to 15 in. long; lflts. 7 to 13, ovate-oblong, 2½ to 5 in. long, half as wide, pointed, toothed, velvety-downy beneath. *fl.* yellowish-white, in panicles 6 to 10 in. long. August. *fr.* orange-red, ⅙ in. wide, densely downy. China, Japan. (R.H. 1867, 111 as *R. Osbeckii.*) SYN. *R. semialata Osbeckii.*

R. copallin'a.* Deciduous shrub in Britain but a tree up to 30 ft. in the S. United States; shoots reddish, downy. *l.* pinnate; common stalk winged; lflets. 9 to 21, lanceolate, mostly entire, 2 to 3½ in. long, dark shining green, changing to reddish-purple, downy beneath. *fl.* greenish-yellow, in 1-sexual panicles 4 to 6 in. long. July to September. *fr.* hairy, crimson. N. America. 1688. (S.S. 3, 104–5.) Beautiful in autumn.

R. Coriar'ia. Shrub 4 to 10 ft., shoots downy. *l.* pinnate; lflts. 7 to 15, oval to ovate, 1 to 3 in. long, coarsely, bluntly toothed, downy; common stalk more or less winged. *Panicles* terminal, 3 to

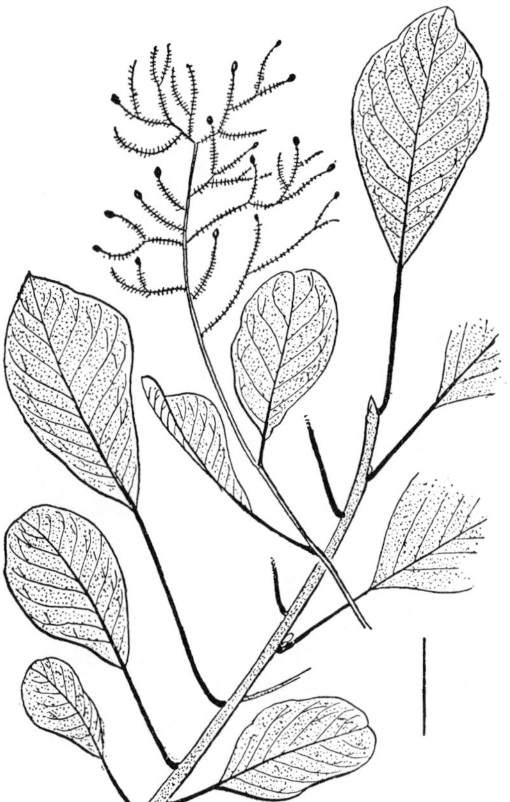

Rhus Cotinus

6 in. long. *fl.* small, whitish. July, August. *fr.* sub-globose, ⅛ in. wide, brown-purple, roughly hairy. Europe. 1629. The milk-white sap is venomous. Tan made from the l. and shoots is used in the preparation of morocco leather. Greenhouse.

R. cotinoi'des.* Shrub of roundish habit, or a small tree up to 30 ft. *l.* simple, obovate or oval, 2 to 5 in. long, apex rounded, rather transparent. *fl.* dioecious, few and inconspicuous on large panicles. Very beautiful in autumn for its scarlet, orange, and purple hues. SE. United States. 1882. (S.S. 3, 98–9.) SYNS. *Cotinus americanus, Cotinus obovatus.*

R. Coti'nus. Venetian Sumach, Wig Tree, Smoke Tree. Bushy shrub, 6 to 10 ft., often wider than high. *l.* simple, orbicular or oval to obovate, 1½ to 3 in. long, glabrous. *fl.* few, small, on loose, terminal, much-branched panicles, most of the ultimate subdivisions flowerless, hairy. June, July. In autumn the plant is densely furnished with these panicles turned smoky-grey, giving a striking and unique effect. S. Europe, Caucasus. 1656. (G.C. 29 (1901), 92.) SYN. *Cotinus Coggygria.* var. **atropurpu'rea,*** *l.* and *infl.* purple; one of the best purple shrubs, superior to the var. **purpu'rea; pendula,** pendulous.

R. diversilo'ba. Erect shrub up to 8 or more ft., or a climber much taller, with aerial roots. *l.* 3-foliolate; lflts. variable, mainly ovate to oval or obovate, 1½ to 3 in. long, coarsely lobed, obtuse. *fl.* in axillary panicles 2 or 3 in. long, greenish-white, ¼ in. wide. *fr.* whitish, ¼ in. wide. California. 1845. (B.R. 31, 38.) Closely akin to *R. Toxicodendron*; poisonous.

R. glab'ra.* Smooth Sumach. Shrub, usually 4 to 6, but up to 10 ft. *l.* pinnate, 12 to 18 in. long; lflets. oblong-lanceolate, 2 to 4½ in. long, toothed, glabrous, glaucous beneath. *fl.* 1-sexual, small, densely packed in pyramidal panicles 4 to 10 in. long, downy. July, August. *fr.* scarlet, ⅛ in. wide, hairy. N. America. 1726. var. **lacinia'ta,** *l.* very handsomely, deeply lobed. Both type and var. turn brilliant red in autumn. (R.H. 1863, 7.)

R. Hen'ryi. A synonym of *R. Potaninii.*

R. hir'ta. A synonym of *R. typhina.*

R. insig'nis. Tree 12 to 40 ft. *l.* pinnate, 12 to 18 in. long; lflets. 7 to 11, ovate-oblong, pointed, 6 to 9 in. long, half as wide, entire, velvety beneath, glabrous and shining above; veins very numerous, parallel. *Panicles* axillary, up to 10 in. by 5 in. *fr.* globose, ⅓ in. wide, waxy-white beneath the skin. Assam. Fine-foliaged tree. Warm greenhouse.

R. laeviga'ta. Glabrous, semi-evergreen tree up to 50 ft., or a shrub. *l.* 3-foliolate; lflets. ovate-acuminate, 3 to 5 in. long, entire (toothed in var. **denta'ta**). *Panicles* terminal and axillary, lax, 6 to 12 in. long; fl. minute, yellowish-white. *fr.* shining red, ⅕ in. wide. S. Africa. Greenhouse.

R. lu'cida. Evergreen shrub, 5 to 10 ft., shoots downy, sometimes resinous. *l.* 3-foliolate; lflets. obovate, entire, apex rounded, shining dark green and leathery; terminal one up to 2½ in. long, lateral ones smaller. *Panicles* axillary and terminal, ¾ to 2 in. long. *fl.* whitish, minute. *fr.* globose, brown, shining, ⅛ in. wide. S. Africa. 1697.

R. Michaux'ii. Stoloniferous shrub up to 3½ ft., shoots hairy. *l.* pinnate, 8 to 12 in. long; lflets. 9 to 15, ovate or oblong, 2 to 4 in. long, base rounded, downy above, densely yellowish-downy beneath, coarsely toothed. *fl.* greenish-yellow in erect, terminal, hairy panicles 6 to 8 in. long. *fr.* globose, ⅙ in. wide, scarlet, very downy. SE. United States. 1901. (G. and F. 8, 405.)

R. mucrona'ta. Evergreen erect shrub, 3 to 8 ft. *l.* 3-foliolate; lflets. obovate to oblanceolate, ½ to 2½ in. long, base cuneate, apex rounded to acute, mucronate, glabrous, pale beneath. *Panicles* terminal and axillary, 2 to 4 in. long. *fl.* minute, whitish. *fr.* globose, ⅛ in. wide, yellow or red. S. Africa. Greenhouse.

R. orienta'lis. Climbing shrub, poisonous. *lflets.* entire, with axil tufts of down beneath. Very near *R. radicans*, but well distinguished by its bristly fr. and by being a native of China, Japan. 1865. SYN. *R. Toxicodendron orientalis.*

R. Osbeck'ii. A synonym of *R. chinensis.*

R. Potanin'ii.* Round-headed tree up to 25 ft., shoots finely downy. *l.* pinnate, 10 to 16 in. long; lflets. 7 to 11, oblong-lanceolate, 3 to 5 in. long, finely pointed, base obliquely rounded. *fl.* whitish, small, in pyramidal panicles 4 to 8 in. long. June. *fr.* rich red, downy, ⅙ in. wide. Cent. and W. China. 1902. Autumn colour rich red. SYN. *R. Henryi.*

R. punjaben'sis. The typical Himalayan tree is probably not in cultivation. var. **sin'ica** is Chinese and a tree up to 40 ft., shoots downy. *l.* pinnate; lflets. 7 to 11, oblong-ovate, 3 to 5 in. long, entire, downy beneath. *fl.* small, whitish, in downy panicles 5 to 8 in. long. *fr.* roundish, ⅙ in. wide, red, hairy, in large pendulous masses. 1890. Cent. and W. China. SYN. *R. sinica.*

R. radi'cans. Poison Ivy or Vine. Climbing shrub supporting itself by aerial roots. *lflets.* 3, ovate or rhomboid up to 4½ in., turning scarlet and orange in autumn. *fl.* dull white, ⅛ in. across in panicles up to 2½ in. long. *fr.* whitish, ¼ in. wide, usually glabrous. N. America. 1640. (B.M. 1806 as *R. Toxicodendron vulgare.*) SYN. *Toxicodendron vulgare.* Sap extremely poisonous, causing painful blisters. Should not be planted where it can come in contact with passers-by or as a climber on houses.

R. semiala'ta Osbeck'ii. A synonym of *R. chinensis.*

R. sin'ica. A variety of *R. punjabensis.*

R. succeda'nea. Wax Tree. Deciduous tree up to 30 ft. *l.* pinnate, 9 to 12 in. long; lflets. 9 to 15, ovate-oblong, long-pointed, entire, 2 to 4 in. long, glabrous, glossy, often purplish; veins in 10 to 20 pairs. *fl.* very small, yellowish in axillary panicles 3 to 5 in. long. *fr.* ⅜ in. wide, subglobose, in pendulous clusters, white; they yield a wax or tallow used as an illuminant. Autumn colour lovely soft red. China, Japan. Not quite hardy except in the warmest counties.

R. sylves'tris. Tree up to 30 ft., shoots downy. *l.* pinnate; lflets. 7 to 13, ovate to oblong, 2 to 5 in. long, downy beneath, veins numerous and conspicuous. *fl.* small, in a crowd of lateral panicles, 3 to 7 in. long, brownish-downy. *fr.* brownish-yellow, obliquely flattened, ⅜ in. across. China, Japan, Korea. 1881. Autumn colour deep red to scarlet.

R. Toxicodendron. Poison Oak. Loosely growing shrub up to 2 ft., spreading by underground stolons, not climbing nor with aerial roots. *lflets.* 3, variously lobed, rarely entire, turning scarlet and orange in autumn. *fl.* dull white in panicles. *fr.* usually pubescent, greenish to buff. N. America. Highly poisonous, *see* **R. radicans.** SYN. *R. quercifolia.*

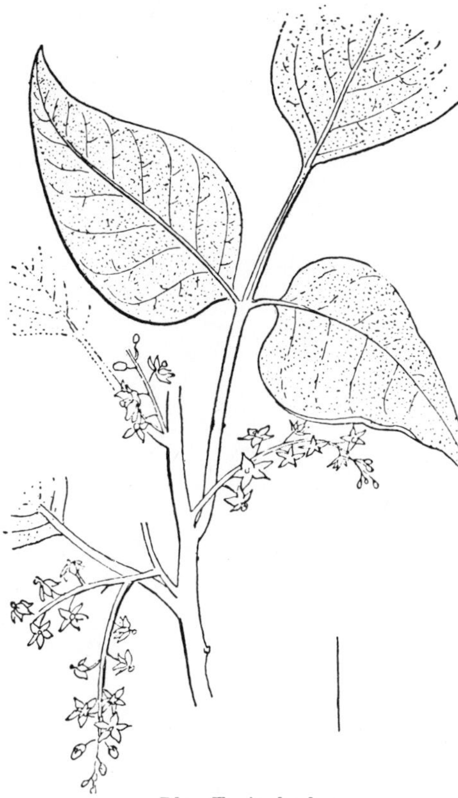

Rhus Toxicodendron

R. trichocar'pa.* Small tree 20 to 25 ft., shoots downy. *l.* pinnate, 12 to 20 in. long; lflets. 13 to 17, broadly ovate to oblong, 2 to 4 in. long; downy on both sides. *Panicles* slender, downy, axillary with a stalk 3 to 6 in. long. *fl.* inconspicuous. June. *fr.* yellowish, ¼ in. wide, bristly, in pendulous clusters. Japan. 1894. (G. and F. 10, 384.) Autumn colour deep orange-scarlet.

R. triloba'ta. Closely akin to *R. aromatica* but unpleasantly scented, more erect in growth and up to 6 ft., the 3 lflets. smaller, ½ to 1 in. long; terminal one fan-shaped, usually 3-lobed. *fl.* greenish-yellow. April. *fr.* rather smaller than in *R. aromatica,* red. Western N. America. 1877. SYN. *R. aromatica trilobata.*

R. typhi'na.* Stag's horn Sumach. Shrub or tree 20 ft. or more; branches thick, very pithy, densely hairy; sep. whitish, thick, ultimately black on exposure. *l.* 1 to 2 ft. long, pinnate; lflets. 13 upwards, oblong-lanceolate, 2 to 4½ in. long, toothed, hairy. *Female panicles* pyramidal, 4 to 8 in. long, very hairy. *fl.* greenish, male panicle larger. *fr.* hairy, crimson. Eastern N. America. 1629. Autumn colour scarlet. SYN. *R. hirta, R. viridiflora* (the male).

R. venena'ta. A synonym of *R. vernix.*

R. vernicif'era. A synonym of *R. verniciflua.*

R. verniciflu'a. Lacquer tree. Tree 30 ft. and upwards. *l.* pinnate, 1 to 2 ft. long; lflets. 7 to 13, broadly ovate, 3 to 8 in. long, entire, downy beneath. *fl.* small, yellowish-white, in lax drooping panicles up to 10 in. long and 6 in. wide. *fr.* ¼ in. wide, yellow, ornamental; contains an oil used for candle-making. Japan, China. 1823. Yields the varnish or lacquer of Japan. SYN. *R. vernicifera.*

R. vern'ix. Poison Sumach. Shrub or tree up to 20 ft., shoots grey, glabrous. *l.* pinnate, 1 to 2 ft. long; lflets. 7 to 13, ovate to obovate, 2 to 4 in. long, entire, soon glabrous. *fl.* greenish-yellow, ⅛ in. wide, in slender, drooping, axillary panicles, 4 to 8 in. long. *fr.* ⅕ in. wide, yellowish-white. Eastern N. America. 1713. SYN. *R. venenata.* Attractive for its rich autumnal colours and graceful panicles of fr. Sap very poisonous.

R. viridiflo'ra. A synonym for ♂ form of *R. typhina.*

W. J. B.

RHYNCHAN'THERA (*rhynchos*, beak, *anthera*, anther; from the beaked anthers). FAM. *Melastomataceae.* A genus of about 25 species of glandular, often bristly, annual or perennial herbs or shrubs, natives of Trop. S. America. Leaves ovate, cordate, or oblong. Flowers purple, often large, showy, in panicles; calyx tube ovoid or bell-shaped, lobes 5, awl-shaped, lanceolate or bristle-like, often persistent; petals obovate; stamens 10, very unequal. *R. grandiflora* is a handsome, stove, evergreen shrub, needing rich sandy peat and fibrous loam with ample drainage. Propagation by cuttings in sandy loam in heat under a bell-glass, care being needed to give free circulation of air and prevent damping off.

R. grandiflo'ra. Shrub of 6 ft., branches nearly round, hairy or slightly hispid. *l.* rather large, long-stalked, ovate-heart-shaped, with a short point, toothed, 7- to 9-nerved, slightly bristly. *fl.* purple, numerous, terminal in a forked corymb-like panicle; cal. tube shorter than the narrow teeth. Autumn. N. Brazil. 1873. (B.M. 6011.)

RHYNCHAN'THUS (*rhynchos*, beak, *anthos*, flower; from the peculiar form of the flower). FAM. *Zingiberaceae.* A genus of 2 slender, glabrous, perennial herbs with tuberous base, natives of Burma. Stems leafy, erect; leaves sessile. Flowers sessile in a terminal spike with coloured bracts. Corolla lobes very short, tube slender, somewhat widened in middle; lip very small; filament much exserted beyond the corolla, petaloid with its margins curved to resemble a long canoe. Cultivation as for Heliconia.

R. Bluthia'nus. About 12 in. h., roots not thickened. *l.* 4, oblong-lanceolate, about 4 in. long, sheath green. *fl.* 2, about 2 in. long; cal. and cor. red, filament white, anther yellow. September. 1897. Burma? (G.F. 38, 1464.)

R. longiflo'rus. About 18 in. h. *l.* 8 to 12, in 2 regular ranks oblong-lanceolate, 5 to 7 in. long, margin reddish, sheath red-spotted. *fl.* 4 or 5, nearly 4 in. long, bracts red, cor. tube 2 in. long, pale yellowish-green, lobes green, filament yellow, anther orange. July. Burma. 1885. (B.M. 6861.)

RHYNCHI'TES. A genus of weevils many of which are harmful to fruit and broad-leaved deciduous trees, to Strawberry, Helianthemum, and some other cultivated plants. *See* **Apple Fruit Weevil** under **Apple, Pests;** *see also* **Strawberry, Pests.**

G. F. W.

RHYNCHO'SIA (*rhynchos*, beak; from the shape of the keel). FAM. *Leguminosae.* A genus of about 100 species of twining, prostrate or rarely erect shrubs, sub-shrubs, or herbs, natives of the warmer regions of the world. Leaves 3-foliolate, lflets. resin-dotted beneath, sometimes stipellate. Flowers yellow, the standard often darkly lined, rarely purple, in axillary racemes, rarely solitary in the axils; the 2 upper sepals more or less connate; standard obovate or round, spreading or reflexed; keel incurved at tip. The plants need stove or greenhouse conditions, and a light sandy soil. They are increased by seed. Few of the species have any special beauty.

R. Chrysos'cias. Climbing sub-shrub, young parts covered with tawny or golden hairs. *l.* short-stalked; lflets. oblong-lanceolate, 1½ in. long, margins revolute, dark above, reddish-hairy beneath. *fl.* golden-yellow or orange; standard large; peduncles 3- or 4-fld. May. S. Africa. 1871. (B.M. 5913.) Greenhouse.

R. phaseoloi'des. Twining sub-shrub, stem cylindrical. *lflets.* ovate or ovate-rhomboid, pointed. *fl.* standard striped purple; racemes many-fld. June, July. *Seed* black with a scarlet-yellow ring around the hilum. Trop. America. 1818. (B.M. 2284 as *Glycine phaseoloides.*) Stove.

RHYNCHOSPERM'UM of Lindley. A synonym of Trachelospermum.

RHYNCOS'TYLIS (*rhynchos*, beak, *stylos*, a pillar; from the shape of the column). FAM. *Orchidaceae.* A genus of 2 or 3 beautiful epiphytic orchids in the E. Indies and Malaya. Flowers rather large, short-stalked; lateral sepals broader than dorsal; lip attached to the column, produced into a short, compressed, blunt spur pointing backwards; column short, thick; racemes lateral, long, densely flowered. Leaves distichous, leathery or fleshy, flat, sheaths persistent, hiding the stem. Treatment as for Saccolabium to which they are closely allied, and under which genus they have been placed.

R. coeles'tis.* *fl.* crowded, ¾ in. across; pedicels erect, white or pale blue; sep. white with indigo tip; basal half of lip white, upper half indigo; column very short. Stem stoutish. *l.* fleshy, 4 to 6 in. long. Siam. 1891. (L. 300; W.O.A. 361 as *Saccolabium coeleste.*)

R. garwal'ica. A synonym of *R. retusa.*

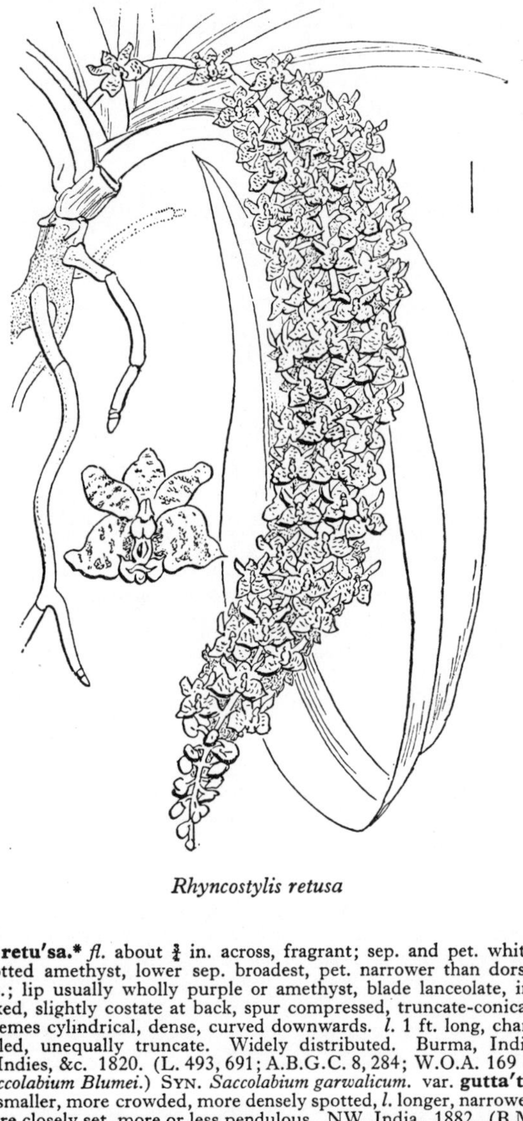

Rhyncostylis retusa

R. retu'sa.* *fl.* about ¾ in. across, fragrant; sep. and pet. white, spotted amethyst, lower sep. broadest, pet. narrower than dorsal sep.; lip usually wholly purple or amethyst, blade lanceolate, inflexed, slightly costate at back, spur compressed, truncate-conical; racemes cylindrical, dense, curved downwards. *l.* 1 ft. long, channelled, unequally truncate. Widely distributed. Burma, India, E. Indies, &c. 1820. (L. 493, 691; A.B.G.C. 8, 284; W.O.A. 169 as *Saccolabium Blumei.*) SYN. *Saccolabium garwalicum.* var. **gutta'ta,** *fl.* smaller, more crowded, more densely spotted, *l.* longer, narrower, more closely set, more or less pendulous. NW. India. 1882. (B.M. 4108 as *Saccolabium guttatum*; B.M. 1443 as *Sarcanthus guttatus.*) SYN. *Saccolabium Rheedii*; **Heath'ii,** *fl.* white, spike often longer than in type. Java. 1885; **Holfordia'na,** *fl.* richer in colour, spikes longer, *l.* broader, truncate (W.S.O. 2, 18 as *Saccolabium guttatum* var.); **ma'jus,** stronger and *fl.* larger on a longer spike than in type. Moulmein (I.H. 545); **praemor'sa,** *fl.* pale with fewer spots, racemes longer, *l.* shorter and broader, distinctly truncate at apex, plant more robust. SYN. *R. praemorsa, Saccolabium praemorsum, S. guttatum giganteum*; **Russellia'num,** *fl.* larger than type, beautifully spotted, spikes 2 ft. long (W.O.A. 238 as *Saccolabium Blumei* var.).

RHYTICO'COS (*rhytis*, a wrinkle, *Cocos*; the albumen of the seed is ruminated). FAM. *Palmaceae.* A genus of a single species of Palm, a native of Martinique and other W. Indian Is., closely related to Cocos, but with ruminate, not regularly distributed, albumen in the seed. Characters given below. Treatment as for Cocos.

R. ama'ra. Tree of 50 to 100 ft. or more. Habit of *Cocos nucifera. l.* with linear, slender-pointed segs. Inner perianth segs. of male fl. linear-oblong; of females ovate-globose. *fr.* ovoid-oblong, blunt at both ends, 3 in. long. Jamaica, &c. SYN. *Cocos amara.*

RHYTIDOPHYL'LUM (*rhytidos*, a wrinkle, *phyllon*, leaf; the leaves are rugose). FAM. *Gesneriaceae.* A genus of about 10 species of usually hairy or white-woolly shrubs or small trees, natives of the W. Indies and Colombia. Leaves alternate, often long, entire or crenate, softly rugose or harshly hairy, sometimes woolly beneath. Flowers often softly hairy or woolly; calyx tube adnate, turbinate or nearly hemispherical; corolla usually greenish outside, coloured within, tube incurved, widened above, lobes short, broad, erecto-patent; peduncles axillary, long, many-flowered. For cultivation of these stove plants *see* **Gesneria.**

R. auricula'tum. About 1 ft. h. *l.* sessile, base narrow, half stem-clasping, and dilated; toothed, harshly hairy above, somewhat hoary beneath. *fl.* red-spotted within; cor. bell-shaped, hairy; peduncles glandular. August. Brazil. 1824. (B.M. 3562.)

R. Humbold'tii. A synonym of *Campanaea Humboldtii.*

R. Oersted'ii. A synonym of *Campanaea Oerstedii.*

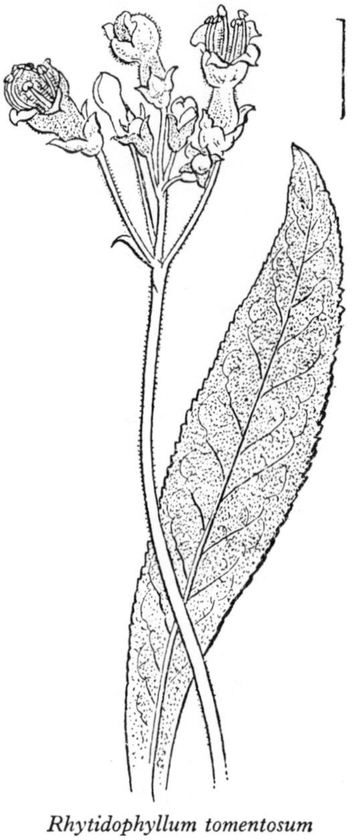

Rhytidophyllum tomentosum

R. tomento'sum. 2 to 3 ft. h. *l.* lanceolate or oblong-lanceolate, 4 to 8 in. long, toothed, harsh above, hairy beneath. *fl.* greenish-yellow, spotted purple, or purple, ¾ in. long, hairy; peduncles at least as long as l. Summer. W. Indies. (B.M. 1023 as *Gesneria tomentosa.*)

RHYTIS'MA. A genus of fungi in the Ascomycetes containing a few parasitic species the best known of which is *Rhytisma acerinum* causing Black Blotch or Tar Spot on leaves of sycamore and maple. (*See* **Acer.**)

RIB. One of the main veins of the leaf.

RIBBON FERN. *See* **Vittaria.**

RIBBON GRASS. *See* **Phalaris arundinacea picta.**

RIBBON TREE. *See* **Hoheria, Plagianthus.**

RIBBON WOOD. *See* **Hoheria, Plagianthus.**

RI'BES (an Arabian name belonging properly to Rheum). Currant, Gooseberry. FAM. *Saxifragaceae.* A genus of some 150 species of deciduous and evergreen shrubs widely spread in the cool and temperate parts of the N. Hemisphere, also in the Andes as far south as Patagonia. Important for its economic value in including the gooseberries and the red, white, and black currants; the ornamental value of the genus is nothing like commensurate with its size. The species are divisible into 2 large groups: (1) the gooseberries, distinguished by their spiny character and the jointed (articulate) flower-stalks, sometimes kept generically apart as Grossularia, and (2) the currants which are unarmed and whose flower-stalks are not jointed, sometimes kept separate as Ribes. There are a few species in which these distinctions break down. Leaves alternate, simple but mostly 3- or 5-lobed, toothed, very frequently glandular. Flowers rarely more than $\frac{1}{3}$ in. wide, usually green or greenish-white, mostly racemose in the currant section, solitary or few in the gooseberries, often functionally unisexual, the parts in fives, rarely in fours: sepals usually larger and more spreading than the petals. Fruit a juicy, many-seeded berry. A few cultivated species, mostly from California or S. America are rather tender, but on the whole they are very hardy and easily accommodated if given a loamy soil of at least moderate quality. They are readily propagated by cuttings of leafless hardwood under a handlight. The better class currants are more readily increased by July or August cuttings placed in gentle bottom heat.

KEY

1.	*Branches unarmed*	2
1.	*Branches more or less spiny or bristly*	24
2.	*Evergreen*	3
2.	*Deciduous*	7
3.	*Lvs. usually over 2 in. long*	4
3.	*Lvs. usually less than 2 in. long*	5
4.	*Lvs. oblong, bristly glandular*	R. Henryi
4.	*Lvs. ovate-oblong, glabrous*	R. laurifolium
5.	*Fl. yellow*	6
5.	*Fl. dull pink; lvs. broadly ovate to oval*	R. viburnifolium
6.	*Lvs. almost round, 3- to 5-lobed, downy*	R. Gayanum
6.	*Lvs. ovate to 3-lobed, with numerous shiny yellow glands beneath*	R. punctatum
7.	*Fl. unisexual; usually in erect racemes*	8
7.	*Fl. perfect; usually in drooping racemes*	12
8.	*Fl. solitary or in clusters of 2 to 9*	R. fasciculatum
8.	*Fl. in racemes, many*	9
9.	*Shoots glandular or hairy*	11
9.	*Shoots glabrous or nearly so*	10
10.	*L.-lobes acute, glandular bristly*	R. glaciale
10.	*L.-lobes bluntish, minutely downy on veins beneath*	R. luridum
11.	*Lvs. to $1\frac{1}{2}$ in. long, 3- to 5-lobed; fl. greenish-yellow*	R. alpinum
11.	*Lvs. $1\frac{3}{4}$ to 4 in. long, scarcely lobed; fl. red; fr. bristly*	R. Maximowiczii
12.	*Shoots glabrous or nearly so at maturity*	13
12.	*Shoots downy or glandular*	17
13.	*Lvs. up to 2 in. wide; fl. yellow*	R. aureum
13.	*Lvs. 3 in. or more wide*	14
14.	*Lvs. glabrous or nearly so.*	15
14.	*Lvs. downy at least on veins beneath*	16
15.	*Racemes spreading, 2 to 4 in. long*	R. rubrum
15.	*Racemes drooping, up to 12 in. long, slender*	R. longiracemosum
16.	*Lvs. 3-lobed; racemes spreading, up to 4 in. long*	R. petraeum
16.	*Lvs. deeply 5- to 7-lobed; fl. racemes erect, 8 in. long*	R. bracteosum
17.	*Fr. prickly*	R. californicum
17.	*Fr. smooth or slightly glandular*	18
18.	*Fr. red*	19
18.	*Fr. black or blue-black*	21
19.	*Lvs. less than 2 in. wide*	R. cereum
19.	*Lvs. usually 2 in. or more wide*	20
20.	*Downy at least on veins beneath; lvs. up to 3 in. wide*	R. sativum
20.	*Densely grey-hairy beneath; lvs. up to 4 in. wide*	R. multiflorum
21.	*Lvs. rarely up to 2 in. wide with black stalked glands on stalk*	R. ciliatum
21.	*Lvs. usually 2 in. or more wide*	22
22.	*Lvs. with clammy glands beneath, softly downy; fl. red*	R. sanguineum
22.	*Lvs. resin-dotted beneath*	23
23.	*Cal. tube tubular-bell-shaped; racemes many-fld.*	R. americanum
23.	*Cal. tube widely bell-shaped; racemes few-fld.*	R. nigrum
24.	*Lvs. glabrous or slightly bristly*	25
24.	*Lvs. more or less downy*	27
25.	*Shoots glabrous*	26
25.	*Shoots often bristly glandular; lvs. slightly bristly, sometimes persistent; fl. bright red, stamens exserted*	R. speciosum
26.	*Fl. 2 to 4, white*	R. niveum
26.	*Fl. 1 or rarely 2, orange-red*	R. pinetorum
27.	*Lvs. rarely 1 in. wide, 3- to 5-lobed*	28
27.	*Lvs. 1 in. or more wide*	29
28.	*Lvs. up to $\frac{3}{4}$ in. long, deeply 3- to 5-lobed, sometimes bristly; fl. white or pinkish*	R. leptanthum
28.	*Lvs. up to 1 in. long, downy; fl. purple and white*	R. Roezlii
29.	*Fl. white, sometimes tinged purple*	30
29.	*Fl. purple or red*	34
30.	*Sep. white or greenish-white*	31
30.	*Sep. green or greenish tinged purple*	32
31.	*Shoots glabrous; lvs. more or less downy; fr. purple, smooth*	R. curvatum
31.	*Shoots bristly; lvs. deeply 5-lobed; fr. red, smooth*	R. oxyacanthoides
32.	*Fr. prickly, not glandular*	R. Cynosbati
32.	*Fr. smooth or hairy*	33
33.	*Ovary glabrous*	R. divaricatum
33.	*Ovary downy or glandular*	R. Grossularia
34.	*Fr. densely glandular*	R. Lobbii
34.	*Fr. glandular-bristly*	R. Menziesii

R. alpin'um. Mountain Currant. Deciduous, unarmed, unisexual shrub, 6 to 8 ft., of dense bushy growth; shoots more or less glandular. *l.* $\frac{1}{2}$ to $1\frac{1}{2}$ in. long, broadly ovate to roundish, 3- (rarely 5-) lobed, coarsely toothed, with scattered bristles. *fl.* greenish-yellow, produced in erect racemes of 20 to 30 on the males, half as many on the females. *fr.* red, not palatable. N. Europe (Britain). (E.B. 519.) With little floral beauty, this makes a neat shapely bush excellent for shady places. var. **au'reum,** *l.* bright yellow when young; **lacinia'tum,** *l.* more deeply lobed and toothed; **pu'milum,** dwarf, 2 to 3 ft., more in width, *l.* smaller.

R. america'num. American Wild Black Currant. Deciduous, unarmed shrub, 5 to 6 ft., shoots glandular-downy. *l.* 3- or 5-lobed, roundish-cordate, $1\frac{1}{2}$ to $3\frac{1}{2}$ in. wide, yellowish-glandular beneath. *fl.* yellowish-white in pendulous racemes. *fr.* black. Eastern N. America. 1729. Closely related to common Black Currant and with the same heavy odour. Grown chiefly for its rich autumn colours of crimson and yellow. SYN. *R. floridum, R. missouriense.*

R. au'reum.* Golden Currant. Buffalo Currant. Deciduous, unarmed shrub 6 to 8 ft., of lax habit. *l.* usually 3-lobed, coarsely toothed, $\frac{3}{4}$ to 2 in. wide, mostly glabrous. *fl.* spicily fragrant, bright golden yellow, in drooping racemes 1 to 2 in. long. April. *fr.* globose, black, $\frac{1}{4}$ in. wide. Western N. America. 1812. (B.R. 1274 as *R. tenuiflorum.*) Some plants in their native wilds are described as having crimson or yellow fr. the latter known as var. *chrysococcum.*

R. Beat'onii. A synonym of *R.* × *Gordonianum.*

R. Billiard'ii. A synonym of *R. fasciculatum chinense.*

R. bracteo'sum. Deciduous unarmed shrub, 6 to 8 ft., shoots soon glabrous. *l.* 5- or 7-lobed (very deeply), 3 to 7 in. wide, sharply and irregularly toothed, dotted beneath with resin-glands; stalk often longer than the blade. *fl.* in erect, cylindrical racemes up to 8 in. long, greenish-white or yellow. May. *fr.* globose, $\frac{1}{3}$ in. wide, resin-dotted, black with blue-white bloom. California. 1826. (B.M. 7419.) Interesting Black Currant with maple-like l. sometimes 10 in. wide, and long slender racemes.

R. californ'icum. Related to *R. Menziesii* but branches not bristly. *l.* glabrous or nearly so. *fl.* greenish or purplish. California.

R. ce'reum.* Deciduous, unarmed shrub, up to 6 ft., shoots downy and glandular. *l.* 3- or 5-lobed, roundish to kidney-shaped, $\frac{1}{2}$ to $1\frac{1}{2}$ in. wide, greyish-green, glandular-downy, especially beneath; stalk as long as the blade. *fl.* tubular, $\frac{1}{3}$ to $\frac{1}{2}$ in. long, 2 to 6 together on a downy glandular stalk, white tinged rose. April. *fr.* bright red, $\frac{1}{4}$ in. wide. Western N. America. 1827. (B.M. 3008.) Free-flowering.

R. cilia'tum. Deciduous unarmed shrub up to 10 ft., of bushy rounded shape, shoots slender, downy, glandular. *l.* 3- or 5-lobed, doubly toothed, cordate, $1\frac{1}{2}$ to 2 in. wide, appressed bristly above, downy and glandular beneath. *fl.* nearly $\frac{1}{2}$ in. long, in nodding racemes of 6 to 10, greenish, downy outside. April. *fr.* globose, black, shining, $\frac{1}{3}$ in. wide. Mexico. SYN. *R. jorullense.* The stalked glands on l.-stalk and fl.-stalk are black.

R. cruen'tum. A variety of *R. Roezlii.*

R. curva'tum.* Deciduous spiny shrub 3 to 4 ft. shoots purplish, glabrous; spines simple or 3-pronged. *l.* roundish, $1\frac{1}{4}$ in. or less wide, 3- or 5-lobed, toothed, slightly downy. *fl.* white, single or in pairs (sometimes up to fives) on a slender stalk; cal. bell-shaped, sep. $\frac{1}{4}$ in. long, much reflexed; pet. very short. *fr.* globose, glabrous, $\frac{1}{3}$ in. wide, purplish. SE. United States. 1910. Closely akin to

R. niveum which has a glabrous ovary; in *R. curvatum* it is covered with resinous glands.

R. Cynosba'ti. Deciduous, armed but spines often absent and bristles few or none. *l.* deeply 3- to 5-lobed, usually downy, up to 2 in. wide. *fl.* 1 to 3, green, glabrous; ovary prickly. *fr.* usually prickly, globose, to elliptic, wine-red, edible. Eastern N. America. A parent of the American gooseberries. var. **inerm'e** has smooth fr.

R. diacan'thum. Deciduous, armed, unisexual shrub, 4 to 6 ft., shoots glabrous; spines in pairs, ⅛ to ¼ in. long. *l.* obovate to ovate, ¾ to 2 in. wide, often slightly 3-lobed, coarsely toothed, glabrous, glossy green. *Male fl.* yellowish, in erect glandular racemes, 1 to 1½ in. long; *female fl.* in shorter racemes. April. *fr.* roundish oval, ¼ in. long, glabrous, scarlet. Siberia, Manchuria, &c. 1781. Although spiny, its affinities are with the currants, especially *R. alpinum*, which it resembles.

R. divarica'tum. Deciduous shrub to 9 ft., usually stoutly armed, shoots sometimes bristly; spines about ½ in. long. *l.* usually 5-lobed, 1 to 2½ in. long, cordate, coarsely toothed, sometimes downy beneath. *fl.* 2 to 4, greenish purple; peduncles slender; sep. much longer than cal.-tube; pet. white or purplish shorter than sep. *fr.* black or purple, about ⅜ in. wide. Western N. America. (B.R. 1359.)

R. fascicula'tum. Deciduous, unarmed, unisexual shrub, 4 or 5 ft., shoots and l.-stalks finely downy. *l.* 3- or 5-lobed, roundish, 2 or 3 in. wide, coarsely toothed, usually downy, *Male fl.* cup-shaped, 4 to 9 in stalkless umbels (fascicles) each on a stalk ½ to 1 in. long, yellow, fragrant; *female fl.* 2 to 4 together. April. *fr.* erect, glabrous, bright scarlet, ⅓ to ½ in. wide, long persisting, unpalatable. Japan, Korea. 1881. var. **chinen'se,** taller, semi-evergreen, *l.* larger more downy. China. SYN. *R. Billiardii.*

R. flor'idum. A synonym of *R. americanum.*

R. Gaya'num.* Evergreen, unarmed shrub, 4 to 5 ft., shoots, l.-stalks, fl.-stalks, ovary, and cal. all shaggy with soft hairs. *l.* 1½ in. wide, roundish-ovate, stout, 3-lobed, round-toothed, downy on both sides. *fl.* bell-shaped, ¼ in. wide, yellow, honey-scented, closely packed in erect, cylindrical racemes 1 to 2 in. long. June. *fr.* purple-black, hairy, ¼ in. wide. Chile. 1855. (B.M. 7611 as *R. villosum.*)

R. glacia'le. Habit of *R. alpinum* but mid-lobe of *l.* longer, acute; *fl.* brownish, cup-shaped. Himalaya, China. 1823. *See also* **R.** × **Wallichii.**

R. × **Gordonia'num** (*R. aureum* × *R. sanguineum.*) Intermediate in most of its characters, but not as beautiful as either. *fl.* in racemes of about 20, reddish outside, yellow within. April. Sterile. (F.d.S. 165.) Raised at Shrubland Park, Ipswich, about 1837. SYN. *R. Beatonii.*

R. grac'ile. A synonym of *R. niveum.*

R. Grossula'ria. Gooseberry. Catberry. Deciduous, spiny shrub about 4 ft., shoots bristly. *l.* 3- or 5-lobed, 1 to 2 in. wide. *fl.* single, in pairs or threes, greenish, ¼ in. wide. *fr.* bristly in one group, smooth in another (var. **uva-crisp'a**). (E.B. 518.) The wild gooseberry from which the varieties cultivated for their fruits have been derived is a native of the mountainous parts of Europe and N. Africa. The gooseberries found wild in Britain are regarded as descendants of garden plants.

R. Hen'ryi. Evergreen, unarmed, unisexual shrub up to 4 ft., shoots glandular-bristly. *l.* obovate to rhomboid, tapered to both ends, 2 to 4 in. long, half as wide, glandular-toothed, glandular and bristly beneath. *fl.* greenish-yellow, ⅓ in. wide, in racemes 1 to 2 in. long; stalk glandular-hairy. February, March. *fr.* narrowly oval, ½ in. long, glandular-hairy. China. 1908. Closely akin to *R. laurifolium* but distinct by its glandular bristliness.

R. Jesson'iae. A synonym of *R. Maximowiczii floribundum.*

R. jorullen'se. A synonym of *R. ciliatum.*

R. lacus'tre. Deciduous armed shrub, 3 to 5 ft., stems covered with bristles, the spines at each node 3 to 9, semicircularly arranged. *l.* 1 to 2½ in. wide, cordate, 3- or 5-lobed, lobes deeply cut; veins bristly. *fl.* 12 to 20, in drooping glandular racemes 2 to 3½ in. long; cal. funnel-shaped with short, spreading, brownish-crimson sep., pet. white. April, May. *fr.* round, ¼ in. wide, glandular-bristly. N. America. 1812. (B.M. 6492.)

R. laurifo'lium. Evergreen, unarmed, unisexual shrub, shoots glabrous at first, glandular. *l.* leathery, ovate or oval, pointed, 2 to 4 or 5 in. long, 1 to 2 in. wide, glabrous, coarsely toothed; stalks bristly. *fl.* greenish-yellow, ⅓ in. wide, in pendent racemes of 6 to 12; cal. and fl.-stalk downy. February, March. *fr.* oval, ½ in. long, purplish-black. China. 1908. (B.M. 8543.) Interesting for its early fl.

R. leptan'thum. Deciduous shrub, 3 to 6 ft., shoots slender, very leafy, spines solitary, up to ⅓ in. long. *l.* roundish to somewhat kidney-shaped, ½ to ¾ in. long, deeply and narrowly 3- or 5-lobed. *fl.* white or pinkish, ⅜ in. wide, 1 to 3 on a short stalk; cal. cylindrical, with downy sep. *fr.* black, shining, oval. Western N. America. 1893. Pleasing for its tiny l. and graceful habit.

R. Lobb'ii. Deciduous spiny shrub, 4 to 6 ft., shoots downy, spines in threes, ½ in. long. *l.* roundish-cordate, ¾ to 2 in. wide, 3- to 5-lobed, slightly downy and glandular. *fl.* usually 2 on a pendulous-glandular stalk; cal. purplish-red, sep. reflexed; pet. white, erect; stamens much protruded. April, May. *fr.* oblong, red-brown, glandular. Western N. America. 1830. (G.C. 19 (1883), 11.) Nearly akin to *R. Menziesii* whose bristly shoots distinguish it.

R. longiracemo'sum. Deciduous unarmed shrub up to 10 ft., shoots glabrous. *l.* 3- to 5-lobed, 3 to 5 in. long and wide, long-stalked, cordate, glabrous. *Racemes* quite pendulous, 12 to 18 in. long; *fl.* ½ in. long, greenish, very thinly disposed. April, May. *fr.* jet black, about the size of the common black currant; flavour good. China. 1908. Remarkable for its long, slender racemes.

Ribes laurifolium

R. lu'ridum. Deciduous unarmed shrub 4 to 8 ft., shoots glabrous, bark peeling. *l.* roundish-ovate to kidney-shaped, ¾ to 2 in. wide, 3- or 5-lobed, lobes coarsely toothed, minutely downy on veins beneath. *fl.* dark purple or brownish-red, in erect racemes ¾ to 2 in. long. *fr.* black, glabrous, ⅓ in. long. Himalaya, W. China. 1900. *See* **R.** × **Wallichii.**

R. Maximowicz'ii. Deciduous, unarmed shrub, 6 to 9 ft., shoots hairy. *l.* of the Black Currant type, 3- or 5-lobed, 2 to 5 in. wide, downy beneath. *Racemes* slender, erect, 2 to 4 in. long, ½ in. wide; stalks glandular-downy. *fl.* ¼ in. wide, dull lurid red; cal. funnel-shaped. May. *fr.* globose, ⅜ in. wide, orange-coloured or red, covered with stalked glands. China. 1904. var. **floribun'dum** has more numerous *fl.* in racemes 4 to 6 in. long, *fr.* reddish-yellow. (B.M. 8840 as *R. Jessoniae.*)

R. Menzies'ii. Deciduous spiny shrub up to 6 ft., shoots downy and bristly, spines about ½ in. long. *l.* roundish-ovate, 1 to 2 in. wide, 3- or 5-lobed, more or less cordate, toothed, velvety and glandular beneath. *fl.* 1 or 2 on a slender glandular stalk; cal. red-purple, ⅓ in. long; pet. white. May. *fr.* globose, spiny, ½ in. wide. Western N. America. 1830. (G.C. 45 (1909), 242.) SYN. *R. subvestitum.*

R. missourien'se. A synonym of *R. americanum.*

R. multiflo'rum. Deciduous, unarmed shrub up to 6 ft., shoots downy. *l.* roundish, up to 4 in. wide, 3- or 5-lobed, grey-downy beneath. *fl.* greenish-yellow, crowded on slender, cylindrical racemes up to 4 or 5 in. long; stamens well protruded. April, May. *fr.* globose, red, ⅓ in. wide, glabrous. E. Europe. 1818. (B.M. 2368.) Remarkable for its long slender racemes.

R. ni'grum. Common Black Currant. Unarmed shrub, 5 or 6 ft., the wild parent of the cultivated vars. of Black Currant. *l.* 2 to 4 in. wide, with a heavy very distinctive odour due to the yellow glands beneath. *fl.* dull white, in racemes of 4 to 10. April, May. *fr.* black. Europe to Himalaya, naturalized in, but probably not a native of Britain.

R. niv'eum.* Deciduous armed shrub up to 9 ft., shoots glabrous; spines $\frac{1}{2}$ in. long, solitary or in threes. *l.* roundish, 1 to 1$\frac{1}{2}$ in. wide, 3- or 5-lobed, lobes shallow, bluntly toothed, nearly or quite glabrous. *fl.* 2 to 4 together in drooping clusters, white; sep. much recurved; stamens protruded $\frac{1}{3}$ in. April. *fr.* globose, blue-black, $\frac{1}{3}$ in. wide, glabrous. Western N. America. 1826. (B.M. 8849.) Syn. *R. gracile.*

R. oxyacanthoi'des. Deciduous armed low shrub, branches slender, often reclining, usually bristly; spines stout about $\frac{1}{4}$ in. long. *l.* cordate or broadly wedge-shaped, 1 to 1$\frac{1}{2}$ in. long, lobes 5, deep, toothed, usually wrinkled in age. *fl.* 1 or 2, greenish-white; pet. and stamens shorter than sep. *fr.* red, smooth, about $\frac{3}{8}$ in. across. N. America. Of little value.

R. petrae'um. Deciduous usually glabrous upright unarmed shrub up to 6 ft. *l.* roundish, more or less cordate, wrinkled and downy above at first, 3 to 4 in. wide, 3-lobed, downy on veins beneath. *fl.* red or pink; sep. short, rounded, ciliate; pet. about half as long as sep. with stamens slightly longer. *fr.* dark red, acid. W. and Cent. Europe. 1794. A variable plant, parent with *R. rubrum* and *R. sativum* of the Red Currants.

R. pinetor'um. Deciduous shrub up to 6 ft., shoots glabrous; spines solitary, in pairs, or in threes. *l.* about 1 in. wide, usually 5-lobed, almost glabrous. *fl.* solitary, rarely in pairs, orange-red; sep. hairy, reflexed; pet. erect. *fr.* black-purple, $\frac{1}{2}$ in. long, globose, bristly. Arizona, New Mexico. 1902. Interesting for the unusual colour of its fl. Often wild in pine woods.

R. puncta'tum. Evergreen unarmed shrub, 4 to 6 ft. *l.* ovate to 3-lobed, jaggedly and bluntly toothed, $\frac{3}{4}$ to 2$\frac{1}{2}$ in. long, with numerous yellowish, shining resin-glands beneath. *fl.* yellow, in slender racemes 1$\frac{1}{2}$ to 3 in. long. April, May. *fr.* globose, $\frac{1}{6}$ in. wide, red. Chile. 1826. (B.R. 1658.)

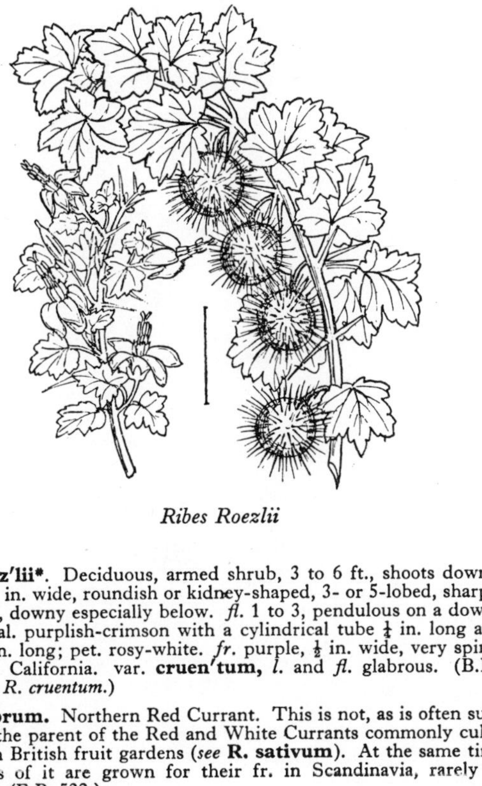

Ribes Roezlii

R. Roez'lii*. Deciduous, armed shrub, 3 to 6 ft., shoots downy. *l.* $\frac{1}{2}$ to 1 in. wide, roundish or kidney-shaped, 3- or 5-lobed, sharply toothed, downy especially below. *fl.* 1 to 3, pendulous on a downy stalk; cal. purplish-crimson with a cylindrical tube $\frac{1}{4}$ in. long and sep. $\frac{1}{3}$ in. long; pet. rosy-white. *fr.* purple, $\frac{1}{2}$ in. wide, very spiny, bristly. California. var. **cruen'tum,** *l.* and *fl.* glabrous. (B.M. 8105 as *R. cruentum.*)

R. ru'brum. Northern Red Currant. This is not, as is often supposed, the parent of the Red and White Currants commonly cultivated in British fruit gardens (*see* **R. sativum**). At the same time varieties of it are grown for their fr. in Scandinavia, rarely in Britain. (E.B. 522.)

R. sanguin'eum.* Deciduous, unarmed shrub, 6 to 9 ft., shoots downy. *l.* 3- or 5-lobed, 2 to 4 in. wide, roundish cordate, unequally toothed, soft with pale down beneath. *fl.* deep rosy-red, $\frac{1}{2}$ in. long and wide, in racemes 2 to 4 in. long. April, May. *fr.* globose, $\frac{1}{4}$ in. wide, blue-black. Western N. America. 1826. (B.M. 3335.) Most ornamental of the Currant section. var. **al'bidum,** *fl.* white, slightly pink-tinted, not so robust as type; **atroru'bens,** *fl.* deep red, in smaller racemes; **Brocklebank'ii,** *l.* a good yellow; **carn'eum,** *fl.* pink; **fl. plens,** *fl.* double; **King Edward VII,** *fl.* deep crimson, dwarfer; **splen'dens,** no form of this currant has fl. of genuine blood colour, but this and the previous one come the nearest.

R. sati'vum. Red and White Currant. The wild type of this species is a native of Europe and the parent of the garden vars. of Red and White Currants. It is often called *R. rubrum* but the true shrub of that name is different. Neither has any recommendations outside the fruit garden. (E.B. 520 as *R. rubrum sativum.*)

R. specio'sum.* Deciduous or partly evergreen shrub 6 to 10 ft., spiny; shoots usually glandular-bristly. *l.* 3- sometimes 5-lobed, $\frac{3}{4}$ to 1$\frac{1}{2}$ in. wide, roundish to obovate, glabrous or slightly glandular-bristly. *fl.* bright red, hanging in rows like tiny Fuchsias in clusters of 2 to 5. Sep. 4, erect; pet. 4, as long as the sep.; stamens 4, red, protruding $\frac{3}{4}$ in. May, June. *fr.* red, glandular-bristly, $\frac{1}{2}$ in. long. California. 1828. (B.M. 3530.) The most beautiful of the Gooseberry group.

R. subvesti'tum. A synonym of *R. Menziesii.*

R. tenuiflo'rum. A synonym of *R. aureum.*

R. viburnifo'lium. Evergreen, unarmed shrub, 7 or 8 ft. *l.* broadly ovate to oval, $\frac{3}{4}$ to 1$\frac{3}{4}$ in. long, with a rounded base and blunt apex, thickly set with resin-glands which, when rubbed, give off a pleasant, turpentine-like odour. *fl.* $\frac{1}{3}$ in. wide, on erect racemes 1 in. long, dull pink. April. *fr.* red, oval, $\frac{1}{3}$ in. long. Lower California, Santa Catalina Is. Requires a wall. (B.M. 8094.)

R. villo'sum. A synonym of *R. Gayanum.*

R. × Wallich'ii (*R. glaciale* × *R. luridum.*) *l.* as in *R. luridum. fl.* as in *R. glaciale*, brownish-purple, saucer-shaped or somewhat turbinate; sep. ovate; staminate racemes up to 1$\frac{1}{2}$ in. long, 7- to 30-fld.; pistillate 3- to 6-fld., fl. smaller. 1907.

W. J. B.

RIB-GRASS OR RIB-WORT. *See* **Plantago lanceolata marginata.**

RICE. *See* **Oryza.** **A**

RICE, CANADA. *See* **Zizania aquatica.**

RICE FLOWER. *See* **Pimelea.**

RICE-PAPER PLANT OF MALAY. *See* **Scaevola Koenigii.**

RICE-PAPER TREE, CHINESE. *See* **Fatsia papyrifera.**

RICHARD'IA. *See* **Zantedeschia.**

Richard'ii, in honour of L. C. Richard, 1754–1821, French Botanist.

Richardson'ii, in honour of Dr. Richardson, friend and companion of Sir John Franklin.

RICH'EA (in honour of Col. A. Riche, a French naturalist who died in 1791 when taking part in the Australian voyage of D'Entrecasteaux in search of La Peyrouse.) Fam. *Epacridaceae.* A genus of about 18 species of shrubs and trees commonest in Tasmania, but one species is found in Australia and several in Madagascar. Leaves sheathing, narrow and more resembling in mode of growth a monocotyledonous genus like Cordyline or Pandanus than an Epacris to whose family it belongs. Flowers in dense terminal simple heads or in compound spikes like or branched panicles; corolla is cut off after opening near the base leaving the filaments persisting long after flowering is over. In most parts of the country the Tasmanian species will require a cool greenhouse temperature but will no doubt succeed in such counties as Cornwall. For cultivation *see* **Epacris.**

R. pandanifo'lia. Evergreen tree with a slender trunk from 6 to 30 ft., carrying one or more terminal heads of crowded, arching l. like a Cordyline. *l.* 3 to 5 ft. long, tapering from a base 3 or 4 in. wide to a long, slender, frayed apex, minutely toothed or entire. *fl.* quite inconspicuous, very small, in erect axillary compound panicles 4 to 6 in. long, growing out of a sheath of lanceolate bracts. Tasmania. 1884. (G.C. 91 (1932), 163.)

R. scopa'ria. Evergreen, bushy shrub up to 5 ft., branching freely from the base. Stem clothed with sheathing, imbricated, lanceolate. *l.* up to 3 in. long, stiff and pointed. *fl.* $\frac{1}{3}$ in. long, white to pink (also, according to Hooker, orange) borne densely in terminal, erect, cylindrical spikes up to 12 in. long; filaments short. Tasmania. 1930. (G.C. 95 (1934), 93; B.M. 9632.) Hardy in Sussex, see J.R.H.S. 74, 1949, fig. 105.

R. sprengelioi'des. Usually glabrous, low shrub from 1 to 3 ft., of bushy, spreading growth. *l.* broadly ovate, $\frac{1}{4}$ to $\frac{1}{2}$ in. long, tapered to a stiff point. *fl.* reddish in small, terminal, globular, leafy heads, each nearly sessile within a floral l.; sep. $\frac{1}{5}$ in. long, pointed, concave; cor. much longer. Tasmania. 1836. Syn. *Cystanthe sprengelioides.*

W. J. B.

RIC'INUS (*ricinus*, a tick, which the seeds resemble). FAM. *Euphorbiaceae.* A genus of a single species, native of Trop. Africa probably, but now cultivated and often wild in most tropical and many temperate countries. A tall annual herb in our gardens, but in warmer regions a tree-like shrub, with large, peltate, palmately 5- to 12-lobed leaves, the lobes toothed, the stalk conspicuously glandular. Flowers monoecious in terminal panicles, often appearing lateral as the plant branches repeatedly below the inflorescence; petals and disk absent; calyx 3- to 5-parted, valvate; stamens much branched; pistillate flowers in lower part of inflorescence, with longer pedicels than staminate; styles 3; ovary generally covered with soft spines, 3-celled, with 1 ovule in each cell. Fruit a capsule. Seed large with a well-developed caruncle and variously marked shell-like testa. *R. communis* is half-hardy and is readily raised from seed sown in early March in heat. It is best sown singly in small pots so as to avoid breaking the roots in potting on or planting out. The young plants must be kept growing under glass until early June, when, after hardening off, they should be planted in their permanent positions outside. They are handsome foliage plants very useful in sub-tropical bedding. *R. communis* is widely grown in the tropics, especially in India, for its seed which yields Castor-oil, used in medicine, in the arts, and as a lubricant. The seeds contain a poisonous principle known as ricinin. The plant is very variable and several forms, mostly with purplish- or bronzy-green leaves have been named and are sometimes offered under different specific names, but they intercross very freely and are connected by intermediates and there seems no doubt they are variants of one species.

R. commu'nis.* Castor Bean; Castor-oil Plant; Palma Christi. Half-hardy herb of 3 to 5 ft. *l.* variable in size and colour, usually glabrous, or nearly so; stalks long. *fl.* green, upper male, clustered; lower female, shortly pedicellate. July. *Capsule* smooth or prickly. 1590. (B.M. 2209; S.F.G. 952.) var. **borbonien'sis arbor'eus,** tall form, *l.* bronzy-green, useful as an isolated plant; **cambodgen'sis,** *l.* purple, large, stems and branches blackish; **Gib'soni,** *l.* reddish-crimson, height 4 to 5 ft.; **sanguin'eus,** *l.* reddish; **zanzibaren'sis,** *l.* about 2 ft. across, bright green, veins whitish, height 6 to 8 ft., seeds much larger than type. 1894.

RICO'TIA (derivation?). FAM. *Cruciferae.* A genus of about 4 species of glabrous, branching herbs, natives of the eastern Mediterranean. Leaves 2-pinnatisect. Flowers pale lilac in long racemes; petals obcordate, clawed. Pods oblong, much compressed, sessile. A light sandy soil suits the hardy annual *R. Lunaria*, seed of which should be sown where the plant is to flower.

R. Luna'ria. Annual about 9 in. h. *l.*-lobes oblong, sinuate margined, angular. *fl.* lilac, claws of pet. white. June, July. *Pods* ovate-lanceolate. Syria, Egypt. 1757. (B.R. 49 as *R. aegyptiaca.*)

RIDDLING. Sifting. An operation needed when fine seeds are to be sown on the soil surface, a fine riddle or sieve being used. It is also of value for the removal of such unwanted things as broken pieces of pot from soils it is intended to use. The use of the fine riddle is, however, apt to be abused for potting soils may often be too fine.

RIDERS. Tall-stemmed fruit-trees used for covering the upper part of high walls, temporarily or permanently, while the lower part is furnished with dwarf trees.

RIDGES. It is often desirable to arrange heaps of soil, manure, &c., in ridges for various cultural purposes. Ridge Cucumbers, for instance, may often be grown better on ridges of soil and manure than on level ground. Land dug or trenched in autumn is usually thrown up into uneven ridges to expose a greater surface to the action of the frost; these ridges may readily be broken and levelled down in spring after exposure through the winter and heavy soils are thereby greatly improved.

ri'gens, stiff, rigid.

RIGIDEL'LA (diminutive of *rigidus*, rigid; the fruit-stalks are erect). FAM. *Iridaceae.* A genus of perhaps 2 species of bulbous perennials, natives of Mexico and Cent. America. Radical leaves few, long, sometimes broad, plicate, sometimes contracted into a long stalk; bracts long-slender-pointed. Flowers several in a spathe, sometimes numerous, long-stalked, bright red, short-lived, cup-shaped at base, without a tube, outer lobes 3, spreading or reflexed, inner very small, ovate, erect, thus differing from Tigridia where they are larger, fiddle-shaped, and spreading; stamens 3, filaments connate into a cylindrical tube; spathes long, membranous. For cultivation *see* **Tigridia.**

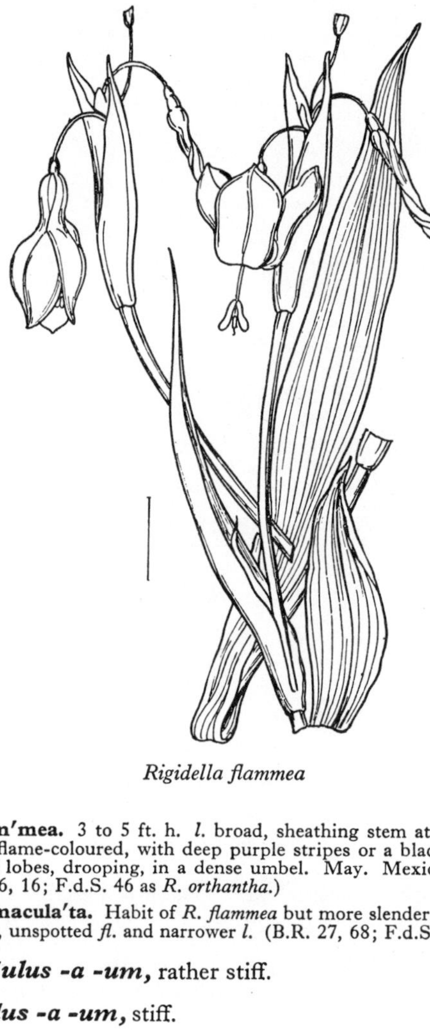

Rigidella flammea

R. flam'mea. 3 to 5 ft. h. *l.* broad, sheathing stem at base. *fl.* bright flame-coloured, with deep purple stripes or a black spot at base of lobes, drooping, in a dense umbel. May. Mexico. 1839. (B.R. 26, 16; F.d.S. 46 as *R. orthantha.*)

R. immacula'ta. Habit of *R. flammea* but more slender and with smaller, unspotted *fl.* and narrower *l.* (B.R. 27, 68; F.d.S. 502.)

rigid'ulus -a -um, rather stiff.

rig'idus -a -um, stiff.

rimo'sus -a -um, having chinks or cracks on the surface like those of old bark.

RIMU. *See* **Dacrydium cupressinum.**

RIND'ERA (in honour of A. Rinder, M.D., of Orenburg). FAM. *Boraginaceae.* A genus of 15 species of narrow-leaved perennial herbs with terminal racemes, natives of E. Europe and extra-tropical Asia, one in N. Africa. Flowers with cylindrical corolla, $1\frac{1}{2}$ times to twice as long as calyx, the oblong-linear lobes about equalling or shorter than the tube, sometimes with scales at throat; stamens inserted at the middle or top of the corolla tube, exserted, filaments flattened, Nutlets coherent with the style, widely winged. Cultivation as for Cynoglossum.

R. caespito'sa. Tufted perennial with yellow or ashy hairy. Stem erect, simple, densely leafy, 2 to 8 in. h. *Basal l.* linear-lanceolate, long-stalked, 1 to 3 in. long, 1-nerved, acute, upper narrower, sessile. *fl.* in a corymbose racemes, rose or bluish, narrowly cylindrical, ½ in. long, lobes shorter than tube. May to August. Asia Minor.

R. graec'a. Tufted silvery-scaly perennial. Stem 3 to 8 in. h. *l.* linear-lanceolate, 2 to 5 in. long, 1-nerved, lower stalked, upper sessile. *fl.* in umbellate-racemes, purple, ½ in. long, cylindrical, lobes shorter than tube. April to July. Greece.

R. umbella'ta. Perennial with erect, simple stem, loosely hairy, 8 to 24 in. h. *l.* linear or lanceolate or oblong, 3 to 10 in. long, hairy, acute, 1-nerved, stalked; upper l. numerous, sessile. *fl.* in umbellate racemes, reddish-yellow or dark brown, ⅜ in. long, cylindrical, tube and lobes of equal length. May, June. SE. Europe. (G.C. 42 (1907), f. 97, 98.)

RIND-GRAFTING. *See* **Grafting.**

RING-BARKING. The removal of a complete or partial ring of bark from the stem or branch of a tree prevents or impedes the downward flow of the sap containing sugar and nitrogenous materials made in the parts above the ring to those below. If the ring is complete and too wide to be healed over in a reasonable time, and it is made below the parts of the tree bearing leaves, the roots will eventually be starved and die; if it is partial or able to heal over before the stores of food below the cut are exhausted it will tend to check the vigorous growth of the root and diminish the flow of water up to wood to the leaves as a consequence. It has therefore the same effect as root-pruning and may be used as a substitute for that operation. Constriction of a stem or branch by a ring of wire placed tightly round it has a somewhat similar effect and will eventually cause death unless the wire be loosened. The tight ring of wire, however, is rather more drastic in its action since it constricts the vessels of the wood and thus impedes the upward flow of water which may result in the death of the upper part from lack of water long before the root is seriously affected by lack of food. This bad effect is not infrequently seen when the wire or even string of a label or tie around a tree stem is allowed to remain too long and constrict the part to which it is attached. Ring-barking cannot well be applied to plums and other stone-fruits which appear to be too vigorous to be fruitful, for a wound of this nature in them is liable to lay them open to gumming, but it can be used for apples and pears in place of root-pruning. There are 2 ways of doing it. A complete ring of bark ⅛ to ¼ in. wide may be removed by the aid of a sharp knife or chisel down to the wood, about a foot below the lowest branch, the ring being forthwith covered by adhesive tape or by grafting wax to protect it from infection by fungi or bacteria; or 2 half rings ½ to ¾ in. wide and about 4 in. apart are made one on one side of the stem the other on the other and the half rings painted over with lead paint.

A less severe method of ringing is to make a ring round the stem down to the wood with a sharp knife without removing any bark and this is a useful method for young trees or trees of restricted growth. Where it is desired to increase the vigour of a shoot or bud a nick of bark may be taken out just above the shoot or bud, and conversely the making of a similar nick close below the bud or shoot will tend to restrict the vigour of its growth and this gives a useful method of obtaining balance of growth on trained trees. All these operations are best done in May.

Where the wire-ring method is used, the ring must be loosened or removed a year after it is first applied.

RING-BUDDING. *See* **Budding.**

rin'gens, gaping, as the mouth of an open 2-lipped corolla.

RINGING. A method of preparing layers for propagation. *See under* **Layering.**

Rin'go. Japanese name for *Malus Ringo.* **A**

RINGWORM ROOT. *See* **Rhinacanthus communis.**

A→

ripa'rius -a -um, growing by streams.

RIPE ROT. *See* **Apple Rot** and **Vine diseases.**

RIPENING WOOD. Fine fruit and flowers depend to a large extent upon the thorough ripening of the wood of the previous year, i.e. upon its complete lignification and full storage of food resulting from ample exposure to light and air during the summer and autumn and the gradual check to the water-supply as winter approaches. Unripened wood is more liable to frost injury than well ripened and if growth is prolonged beyond the normal time the cork which normally covers the shoot and helps to protect it during winter is not developed towards the tip of the shoot and that part at least is liable to be killed. Summer pruning, so long as it is not unduly delayed is an aid towards exposing what is left to sun and air.

RIPERS'IA. *See* **Mealy Bug.**

Ri'riei, in honour of the Rev. B. Ririe of the China Inland Mission.

RITCH'IEA (in honour of Joseph Ritchie, a Yorkshire explorer, killed in Cent. Africa, 1819). FAM. *Capparidaceae.* A genus of about 4 species of erect or scrambling shrubs, natives of Trop. Africa. Leaves simple or 3- to 5-foliolate. Flowers yellowish, large, fragrant, on long pedicels in corymbs; sepals 4, large, valvate; petals 4 or many, oblong, undulate, long-clawed; torus hemispherical, fleshy. For treatment of these stove plants *see* **Euadenia.**

R. polypet'ala. Erect, glabrous shrub of 3 to 4 ft. *l.* alternate, 3- to 5-foliolate; lflets. 3 to 5 in. long, oblong or obovate-lanceolate; stalks 3 to 5 in. long. *fl.* large, pale straw-coloured, 4 in. across, 3 to 5 in a terminal, erect corymb; pet. about 14, very narrow. 1859. (B.M. 5344.)

riva'lis -is -e, growing by streams.

RIV'EA (in honour of Auguste de la Rive, physiologist of Geneva). FAM. *Convolvulaceae.* A genus of 2 species of E. Indian twining perennials. Leaves broad, woolly or silky beneath. Flowers large; peduncles axillary, 1- to 3-flowered; sepals ovate or oblong, obtuse; corolla salver-shaped, tube long, cylindrical, lobes angled and somewhat cut; stamens included, filaments short, bracts narrow. For treatment of these stove plants *see* **Ipomoea.** Related to Argyreia.

R. hypocrateriform'is. Midnapore Creeper. *l.* roundish-heart-shaped or roundish, sometimes hairy beneath. *fl.* white, large, opening at sunset, very fragrant of cloves; very wide; peduncles shorter than l.-stalks. July. W. India, &c. 1799.

R. orna'ta. Stem white, silky. *l.* roundish-heart-shaped or kidney-shaped, with ashy hairs beneath. *fl.* white, silky without; peduncles mostly 3-fld. June. 1824.

Rivier'i, in honour of M. Riviere, head gardener of the Luxemburg Palace Gardens, Paris.

RIVI'NA (in honour of A. Q. Rivinus, 1652–1722, Professor of Botany at Leipzig). FAM. *Phytolaccaceae.* A genus of 3 species of erect herbs with forked stems, shrubby at base, natives of the warmer parts of America. Leaves alternate, ovate, ovate-lanceolate, or cordate-ovate, somewhat crenate, membranous. Flowers hermaphrodite, in racemes; perianth corolla-like, 4-parted; segments obovate-oblong, obtuse, concave, coloured, remaining unchanged in fruit; stamens 4. Fruit red, pea-shaped. Rivinas need warm-house conditions and a rich, loamy soil. Propagated by seeds or cuttings taken in spring and rooted in heat, or by leaf cuttings of the entire leaf taken near the axil. Very attractive in winter when covered with berries.

R. hu'milis. Rouge Plant; Bloodberry. Stem shrubby at base, 18 to 24 in. h. with spreading branches, slightly hairy. *l.* ovate, slender-pointed, 1 to 2 in. long, nearly entire, rather thick, more or less hairy. *fl.* whitish-rose, scarcely $\frac{1}{12}$ in. long, rather reflexed, in racemes longer than l. January to October. Berries bright scarlet. Caribbean Is., &c. 1699. (B.M. 1781.) SYN. *R. laevis.*

Rivina humilis (p. 1797)

rivula'ris -is -e, by the water-side.

ROADS. *See* **Drive.**

ROAN or **ROWAN TREE.** *See* **Sorbus Aucuparia.**

ROBBER FLIES. Two-winged flies, often large, of the family Asilidae, which feed on a variety of insects, including Aphides, Dragonflies, Moths, Beetles, and Sawflies. Their maggots live in the soil, in leaf-mould, and in decayed wood and either prey on other insects or act as scavengers.

G. F. W.

ROBERTSON'IA. Included in **Saxifraga.**

ROBIN'IA (after Jean Robin, herbalist to Henry IV of France; d. 1629). FAM. *Leguminosae.* A genus of about 20 species of deciduous trees and shrubs, mostly very attractive, confined in a wild state to the United States and Mexico. Leaves alternate, unequally pinnate, stipules often developing into thorns; shoots and pods frequently glandular-bristly; leaflets entire. Flowers in pendulous racemes, papillionaceous, often fragrant, varying from white to various shades of pink and purple; standard petal large, reflexed. Pod flat, 3- to 10-seeded. They blossom mostly in June. They are naturally brittle and easily broken by rough winds, for which reason they are better in a well-drained soil of moderate quality than in a very rich one which promotes lush growth, especially in young specimens, and renders them more vulnerable in storms. They are best propagated by seed; when this is not obtainable they can be grafted on stocks of *R. Pseudacacia.* The named varieties of *R. Pseudacacia,* of which there are many, are often offered as species but should be sought here under their proper name as varieties of *R. Pseudacacia.* They can be had true only as grafted plants.

KEY

1. *Shoots glabrous or downy only* 2
1. *Shoots and peduncles more or less hispid, glandular or clammy* 5
2. *Pods smooth; shoots nearly glabrous* R. Pseudacacia
2. *Pods hispid or glandular* 3
3. *Shoots glabrous or minutely downy at first* 4
3. *Shoots hairy when young; peduncles and lflets. beneath greyish downy* R. Elliottii
4. *Shoots without stipulary spines; peduncles smooth* R. Boyntonii
4. *Shoots with stipulary spines; peduncles somewhat glandular-hairy* R. Kelseyi
5. *Shoots and peduncles usually hispid; lflets. 7 to 15* R. hispida
5. *Shoots and peduncles glandular or clammy; lflets. 13 to 25* 6
6. *Main axis of lvs. downy, not glandular* R. luxurians
6. *Main axis of lvs. glandular and clammy* 7
7. *Shoots and l.-stalks with stalked glands* R. Hartwigii
7. *Shoots and l.-stalks clammy* R. viscosa

R. × ambig'ua (*R. Pseudacacia × R. viscosa*). Shoots slightly viscid. *lflets.* 13 to 21. *fl.* light pink. SYN. *R. dubia.* var. **bella-ro'sea,** shoots more viscid, *fl.* deeper rose, *lflets.* small. Elegant small tree.

R. Boynton'ii. Shrub up to 10 ft., shoots unarmed. *l.* 6 to 10 in. long; lflets. 7 to 13, oblong, 1 to 2 in. long, glabrous. *fl.* 6 to 12 in loose racemes $2\frac{1}{2}$ to 4 in. long; cor. pink or rose-purple, 1 in. long, standard pet. $\frac{3}{4}$ to 1 in. wide; cal. and pod bristly. May, June. SE. United States. 1919.

R. du'bia. A synonym of *R. × ambigua.*

R. Elliott'ii. Shrub to 5 or 6 ft., its erect stems branched only near top; shoots grey-downy beneath. *fl.* rose-purple or purple and white, about 1 in. long, borne in racemes of 5 to 10; cal. and fl.-stalk grey-downy. June. *Pod* bristly, narrow. SE. United States. 1901. The dwarfest species.

R. glutino'sa. A synonym of *R. viscosa.*

R. Hartwig'ii. Shrub to 12 ft., shoots, l.-stalks, fl.-stalks, cal., and pod all glandular-bristly and downy. *l.* 6 or 7 in. long; lflets. 11 to 23, oval to narrowly ovate, up to $1\frac{1}{2}$ in. long, downy on both sides. *fl.* whitish to rosy-purple, 1 in. long, crowded 20 to 30 together on racemes up to $4\frac{1}{2}$ in. long. June. *Pod* 2 to $3\frac{1}{2}$ in. long. SE. United States. 1904. (G.C. Nov. 1931 (supplement).)

R. his'pida.* Rose Acacia. Shrub, 5 or 6 ft., suckering, shoots glandular-bristly. *l.* 6 to 9 in. long; lflets. 7 to 15, roundish, oval, or broadly ovate, $1\frac{1}{2}$ to 2 in. long, bristle-tipped, glabrous. *fl.* in pendent racemes of 5 to 10, deep rose, 1 to $1\frac{1}{4}$ in. long, standard pet. as wide. May, June. *Pod* (rarely seen even in wild plants) 2 to 3 in. long, glandular-bristly. SE. United States. 1743. (B.M. 311.) Usually grafted on *R. Pseudacacia.* var. **macrophyl'la,*** branches and l.-stalks not bristly, lflets. rounder, *fl.* larger and more richly coloured. Perhaps the most beautiful fl. in the genus; **ro'sea,** a synonym of *R. Elliottii* and *R. Boyntonii.*

R. × Holdt'ii (*R. luxurians × R. Pseudacacia*). *Racemes* looser than in *R. luxurians. fl.* paler pink or rose; standard pet. pale rose; keel and wing pet. still paler.

R. Kel'seyi.* Shrub or small tree up to 10 ft., shoots slender, glabrous, prickly. *l.* 4 to 6 in. long; lflets. 9 to 11, oblong to ovate, 1 to 2 in. long, pointed, glabrous. *fl.* bright rose, $\frac{3}{4}$ in. long, in short clusters of 3 to 7; standard pet. $\frac{3}{4}$ in. across; cal. $\frac{1}{4}$ in. long, downy. June. *Pod* 2 in. long, glandular-bristly. SE. United States. 1901. (B.M. 8213.)

R. luxu'rians. Shrub or small tree, 20 to 40 ft., shoots downy. *l.* 6 to 12 in. long; lflets. 15 to 25, oval or ovate, 1 to $1\frac{1}{2}$ in. long, bristle-tipped. *fl.* $\frac{3}{4}$ in. long, pale rose, in many-fld. racemes; cal. glandular, shaggy. June. *Pod* 3 to 4 in. long, covered with glandular bristles. SW. United States. 1887. (B.M. 7726 as *R. neomexicana.*)

R. × Margaret'ta (*R. hispida × R. Pseudacacia*). Shrub. *lflets.* downy beneath. *fl.* pale pink, $\frac{3}{4}$ in. long; cal. downy and slightly glandular.

R. Pseudoaca'cia. Locust; False Acacia. Tree 70 to 80 ft., bark deeply furrowed. *l.* 6 to 10 in. long; lflets. 11 to 23, oval or ovate, 1 to 2 in. long. *fl.* $\frac{3}{4}$ in. long, white, fragrant, in pendulous racemes 4 to 7 in. long; standard pet. blotched with yellow at base. June. *Pod* 2 to 4 in. long, glabrous, 4- to 10-seeded. N. America. 1601. Naturalized in many parts of Europe. (S.S. 3, 112–13.) The tree produces suckers sometimes very freely and they spring up profusely from the roots of fallen trees; they are very thorny. An extraordinary number of very variable forms have been raised from seed. This is a selection: var. **angustifo'lia,** *lflets.* narrow, $\frac{1}{4}$ in. wide; elegant, fern-like; **au'rea,** *lflets.* at first yellow; **Bessonia'na,** a compact, round-headed tree; **coluteoi'des,** *fl.* and *lflets.* small, free-flowering; **Decaisnea'na,*** *fl.* deep rose. France. 1862; **fastigia'ta,** stems and branches quite erect, tree more slender than Lombardy Poplar; **inerm'is,** mop-headed small tree, rarely or never blossoms. SYN. var. *umbraculifera*; **microphyl'la,** *lflets.* $\frac{1}{2}$ by $\frac{1}{3}$ in.; **monophyl'la,** *lflets.* reduced to 1, 2, or 3, much larger (4 by $1\frac{1}{2}$ in.); there is an erect form of it (*fastigiata*); **Rehd'eri,** dwarf bush or slow-growing small tree; **Rosynskia'na,** *l.* long and pendulous, *lflets.* large, distinct; **semperflor'ens,** continues to blossom intermittently throughout the summer; **stria'ta,** upright in growth but not so slender as *fastigiata*; **tortuo'sa,** branches contorted; **Ubricia'na,** best pendulous form.

R. × **Slavin'ii** (*R. Kelseyi* × *R. Pseudacacia*). More tree-like than *R. Kelseyi*, the seed parent, with more numerous rosy-pink *fl.* 1914.

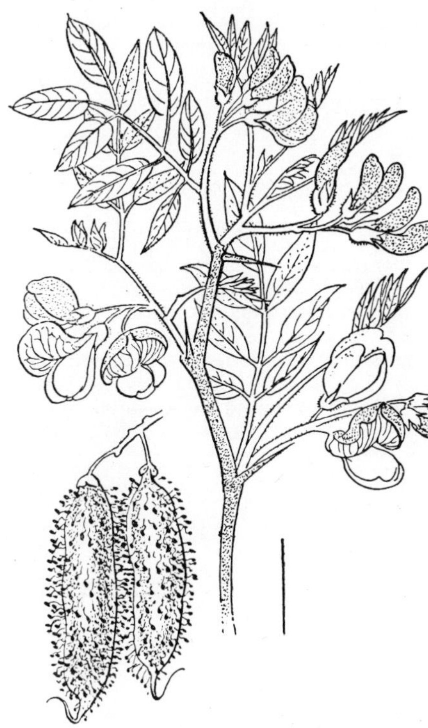

Robinia Kelseyi (p. 1798)

R. vis'cosa. Clammy Locust. Tree 30 to 40 ft., shoots viscid. *l.* up to 8 or 10 in. long; lflets. 11 to 25, oval or ovate, 1 to 2 in. long, usually downy beneath, main stalk viscid. *fl.* $\frac{3}{4}$ in. long, 10 to 15 in short racemes, pale rose with a yellow spot on standard; cal. dark red, downy. June. *Pod* 2 to 3 in. long, glandular, viscid. SE. United States. 1797. (B.M. 560 as *R. glutinosa*.)

W. J. B.

ROBIN'S PINCUSHION. A common name for the Bedeguar gall of the rose.

Robinsonia'nus -a -um, in honour of Sir Hercules Robinson, K.C.M.G., Governor of New S. Wales, 1869.

robus'tus -a -um, strong and stout in growth.

ROCAMBOLE (*Allium Scordoprasum*). A hardy perennial grown for its bulbs which are used in a somewhat similar way to those of Garlic. Increase is effected by dividing the bulbs which form annually both at the base of the stems and also on the tops. When separated they are planted singly in rows at the end of February or in March leaving 8 in. between the bulbs and putting them in about 2 in. deep. As soon as the leaves die the plants are lifted and the bulbs dried in the sun and then stored like shallots for future use.

ROCH'EA (in honour of François de la Roche (d. 1813), a French botanical writer). FAM. *Crassulaceae.* A genus containing 4 species from S. Africa, closely allied to Crassula from which it differs chiefly in the tubular corolla; the leaves are opposite, leathery, but not very succulent. The flowers are showy and the plants are used for house decoration. For cultivation *see* **Cotyledon. A**

R. coccin'ea. Stem 12 in. h. *l.* crowded in 4 ranks, green, leathery. *fl.* long-tubed, in false umbels, scarlet or carmine. (B.M. 495.) SYN. *Cotyledon coccinea, Crassula coccinea, Kalosanthes coccinea.*

R. falca'ta. A synonym of *Crassula falcata.*

R. jasmin'ea. Stem prostrate. *l.* crowded along it. *fl.* white, turning pink later. (B.M. 2178.) SYN. *Cotyledon jasminea, Crassula jasminea, Kalosanthes jasminea.*

R. versico'lor. Stem 12 in. h. *l.* closely crowded along it. *fl.* in false umbels, white, pink, yellow, sometimes bright red outside. (B.M. 2356.) SYN. *Crassula versicolor, Kalosanthes versicolor.*

V. H.

ROCK BEAUTY. *See* **Petrocallis pyrenaica.**

ROCK BRAKE. *See* **Cryptogramma crispa.**

ROCK BROOM. *See* **Genista.**

ROCK CARROT. *See* **Thapsia edulis.**

ROCK CRESS. *See* **Arabis, Aubrieta deltoidea.**

ROCK JASMINE. *See* **Androsace.**

ROCK LYCHNIS. *See* **Viscaria alpina.**

ROCK PINK. *See* **Dianthus Kitaibelii**

ROCK ROSE. *See* **Cistus** and **Helianthemum.**

ROCK TOBACCO. *See* **Primulina Tabacum.**

A→

ROCK-GARDEN PLANTS. The plants grown on rock-gardens, on dry walls, and in the Alpine-house are often termed Alpine Plants but this is misleading for true alpine plants (q.v.) form a comparatively small proportion of the plants which are given a home in these quarters. In addition to some true alpines, many sub-alpine plants are best accommodated in these places and other dwarf plants, especially those needing moisture and thorough drainage, find conditions better fitted for them than in the flower border or the wild garden. A considerable number of small shrubs are also well adapted for growing in the rock-garden, indeed any plant that looks and feels at home among rocks comes in this category and the ultimate choice must depend largely upon the size of the garden, the various aspects it presents, and the tastes of the gardener. The extreme conditions which may be presented in the rock-garden will call for special consideration and careful choice and lists of some such as Moraine, Scree, and Water plants will be found under their respective headings. Many of the plants mentioned may be grown on borders, and consultation of the notes in the body of the Dictionary will be helpful in selecting these. Plants that specially demand shade are indicated by *, those that are particularly good on a dry wall by †. It often happens, however, that there are in a genus species that are especially fitted for each of the varied sites a well-built rock-garden can provide. Examples of this are seen in the genus Saxifraga and in Campanula and here, as a rule, only the generic name is given. For the special requirements of some of the species the descriptions and notes under the generic headings must be consulted. The plants mentioned below are generally hardy but some may need winter protection against wet and foggy weather or spring protection in bleak places and frost-ridden areas, because they are apt to start too early into growth. Notes in the body of the Dictionary will be helpful in dealing with these. See also Rock-Garden Construction (Suppl.)

Abies balsamea hudsonia; Abronia; Acaena; Acantholimon; Acanthophyllum; Acer palmatum; Achillea; Aciphylla; Adenophora; Adenostyles; Adiantum pedatum; Adonis; †Aethionema; Agave (on large rock-gardens); Ajuga; Alchemilla; Allectorurus yedoensis; Allium; Allosurus crispus; Alopecurus lanatus; Alsine; Alyssoides; †Alyssum; Amaracus; Amphicome; Amsonia; Anacyclus; Anagallis; Anaphalis; Anarrhinum bellidifolium; Andromeda polifolia; Androsace; Anemone; Anemonella; †Antennaria; Anthemis; Anthericum; Anthyllis; †Antirrhinum; Aphyllanthes; Aplopappus; Aquilegia; Arabis; Arctostaphylos alpina; *Arenaria; Arisaema (moist soils); Arisarum; Armeria; Arnica; Artemisia; Asarum; Asperula; Asphodeline; †Asplenium; Aster; Astilbe; Astragalus; Astrantia; Asyneuma; †Aubrieta; Azorella; Bellis; Bellium; Biscutella; Blechnum; Blepharoglottis; Bletia; Boenninghausenia; Bolax; Bongardia; Borago; Boykinia; Brachycome; Braya; Brodiaea Bruckenthalia spiculifolia; Brunnera; Bulbinella; Bulbocodium; Buxus; Calamintha; Calandrinia; Calceolaria; Callianthemum; Calluna; Caltha; *†Campanula; Cardamine; Cardaminopsis; Carduncellus; Carex; Carlina; Cassandra calyculata; Cassiope; Castilleia;

Caulophyllum; Cautlea; Cedronella; Celmisia; Celsia; Centaurea; Centaurium; *Cephalanthera; †Cerastium; Ceratostigma plumbaginoides; Chamaecyparis; *Chamaelirium luteum; †Cheiranthus; Chevreulia stolonifera; Chimaphila; *Chiogenes; Chionodoxa; Chrysanthemum; Chrysogonum; Chrysopsis; Chrysosplenium; Cistus; Cladothamus pyrolaefolius; *Claytonia; Clintonia; Codonopsis; Colchicum; Colobanthus; Comarella; Conandron; *Convallaria; Convolvulus; Coprosma; Coptis; Coreopsis; Coris; Cornus; Coronilla; Cortusa; Corydalis; Corynephorus; Cotoneaster; Cotula; Cotyledon; Craspedia; Crassula sarcocaulis; Cremanthodium; Crepis; Crocus; Cyananthus; Cyathodes; Cyclamen; Cypripedium; Cystopteris; Cytisus; Daboecia; Daphne; *Deinanthe; Delphinium; *Dentaria; Dianella; †Dianthus; Diapensia; Dicentra; Dictamnus; Didissandra; Dierama; Digitalis; Dionysia; Diosphaera; Diphylleia; Diplarrhena; Disporum; Dodecatheon; Dondia; Doronicum; Douglasia; Draba; Dracocephalum; Drosera; Dryas; Drypis; Ebenus; Edraianthus; Empetrum; Eomecon; Ephedra; *Epigaea; Epilobium; Epimedium; Epipactis; Eranthis; Erica; †Erigeron; Erinacea; Erinus; Eriogonum; Eriophyllum; Eritrichium; Erodium; Eryngium; Erysimum; Erythraea (Centaurium); Erythronium; Euonymus; Euphorbia; Farsetia; Festuca; Filipendula; Fragaria; Francoa; Frankenia; Frasera; Fritillaria; Fuchsia; Gagea; Galanthus; *Galax; Gaultheria; Genista; Gentiana; Geranium; Geum; Gilia; Gillenia; Gladiolus; Globularia; Gnaphalium; Goodyera; Grevillea; Gymnadenia; Gypsophila; Habenaria; Haberlea; Halenia; Halimium; †Helianthemum; Helichrysum; Helionopsis; Heliosperma; Helonias; Helxine; Hepatica; Herminium; Herniaria; Heuchera; Hieracium; Himantoglossum; Hippocrepis; *Homogyne; Horminum; Hosta; Houstonia; †Hutchinsia; Hyacinthus; Hydrocotyle; Hypericum; Hypochaeris; Hypolepis; Hypsela; Hyssopus; †Iberis; Incarvillea; Inula; Ionopsidium; Iris; Isopyrum; Jankaea; Jasione; Jasminum; Jeffersonia; Jovellana; Juniperus; Kalmia; Kentranthus; Kirengeshoma; Kniphofia; Lagenophora; Lancea; Laurentia; †Lavandula; Ledum; Leiophyllum; Leontice; Leontopodium; Leptospermum; Leucocrinum; Leucojum; Lewisia; Liabum; Libertia; Lilium; Limonium; †Linaria; Lindelofia; Linnaea; Linum; *Liparis; Lippia; Liriope; *Listera; Lithospermum; Lloydia; Lobelia; Loiseleuria procumbens; Lonicera; Lotus; Luetkea; Lupinus; Luzula; Lychnis; *Lysimachia; Macrotomia; Maianthemum; Malvastrum; Margyricarpus; Matthiola; Mazus; Meconopsis; Melandrium; Melittis; Mentha; Merendera; Mertensia; Meum; Micromeria; Millegania; Mimulus; Minuartia; *Mitella; Moehringia; Moltkia; Moneses; Morisia; Muehlenbeckia; Muscari; Myosotis; Myrica; Myrtus; Nama; Narcissus; Nardostachys; Narthecium; Neotinea; Nepeta; Nertera; Nierembergia; Nigritella; Noccaea; Nomocharis; Nothoscordon; Notothlaspi; Odontospermum; Oenothera; Omphalodes; Omphalogramma; Ononis; Onosma; Ophrys; Opuntia; Orchis; Oreocharis; Oresitrophe; Origanum; Ornithogalum; Ornithopus; Orobus; Orphanidesia; Ourisia; Oxalis; Oxycoccus; Oxytropis; Pachysandra; Pachystigma; Paederota; Paeonia; Papaver; Paraquilegia; Pardanthus; Paris; Parnassia; Parochetus; Paronychia; Parosella; Parrya; Patrinia; *Pelargonium Endlicherianum*; Penstemon; Pentachondra; Perezia; Pernettya; Petasites; Petrocallis; Petrocoptis; Phacelia; Philesia; Phlomis; Phlox; Phyllodoce; Phyllothamnus; Phyteuma; Picea; Picrorrhiza; Pimelea; Pinguicula; Pinus; Plantago; Platycodon; Podocarpus; Podolepis; Podophyllum; Polemonium; Polygala; Polygonatum; Polygonum; Polypodium; Polystichum; Potentilla; Pratia; Prenanthes; Primula; Prunella; Pteridophyllum; Pterocephalus; Ptilotrichum; Pulmonaria; Pulsatilla; Puschkinia; Putoria; Pyrola; Pyxidanthera; Raffenaldia; Ramonda; Ranunculus; Raoulia; Reineckia; *Rhamnus alpina*; Rhazya; Rhexia; Rhododendron; Rhodothamnus; Rohdea; Romanzoffia; Romulea; Rosa; Roscoea; Rosmarinus; Rubus; Ruscus; Ruta; Sabbatia; Sagina; Salix; Samolus; Sanguinaria; Santolina; Saponaria; Sarracenia; Satureia; Saxifraga; Scabiosa; Schivereckia; Schizocodon; Schizostylis; Scilla; Scleranthus; Scorzonera; Scutellaria; Sedum; Selaginella; Selliera; Sempervivella; Sempervivum; Senecio; Serapias; Sesile; Shortia; Sibbaldia; Sibthorpia; Sieversia; Silene; Sisyrinchium; Sobolewskya; Soldanella; Solidago; Solms-Laubachia; Spenceria; Sphaeralcea; Spigelia; Spiraea; Spiranthes; Spraguea; Stachys; Stellera; Sternbergia; Stokesia; Stylomecon; Suksdorfia; Sullivantia; Swertia; Symphyandra; Synthyris; Tanacetum; Tanakaea; Taxus; Tecophilaea; Tellima; Teucrium; Thalictrum; Thlaspi; Thuja; Thymus; Tiarella; Tolmiea; Townsendia; Traunsteinera; Tricyrtis; Trientalis; Trifolium; Trillium; Triptilion; Trollius; Tropaeolum; Tsuga; Tulipa; Tunica; Turritis; Tussilago; Umbilicus; Urospermum; Uvularia; Vaccaria; Vaccinium; Valeriana; Vancouveria; Velezia; Vella; Verbascum; Verbena; Veronica; Vicia; Viola; Wahlenbergia; Waldsteinia; Weldenia; Wulfenia; Zauschneria; *Zephyranthes candida*; Zygadenus.

ROCKET, SWEET. *See* **Hesperis matronalis.**

ROCKET CANDYTUFT. *See* **Iberis amara coronaria.**

ROCKET, DAME'S. *See* **Hesperis matronalis.**

ROCKET, DYERS'. *See* **Reseda Luteola.**

ROCKET LARKSPUR. *See* **Delphinium Ajacis.**

ROCKET, SEA. *See* **Cakile.**

ROCKET, YELLOW. *See* **Barbarea praecox.**

ROCKFOIL. Sometimes used for Saxifraga.

Rock'ii, in honour of Joseph Francis Rock, b. 1884. American collector of plants in China and Tibet, *c.* 1920–48.

ROCKSPRAY. *See* **Cotoneaster horizontalis.**

RODGERS'IA (in honour of Admiral John Rodgers, 1812–82, of the United States Navy, commander of the expedition during which *R. podophylla* was discovered). FAM. *Saxifragaceae.* A genus of 5 species of erect, herbaceous perennials with thick scaly rhizomes. Leaves alternate, large, peltate or digitately or pinnately divided. Flowers numerous, small, in large panicles on tall stems; calyx lobes 5, coloured; petals usually absent; stamens 10; carpels 2 or 3, joined. The Rodgersias are natives of China and Japan and, while they will grow in ordinary good moist garden ground and are hardy, they are best in moist peaty soil. They should have a sunny position not exposed to high winds. Propagated by seeds or by division of the rhizome.

R. aesculifo'lia.* 2½ to 6 ft. h. *Basal l.* up to 18 in. across, digitately compound; lflets. 7, 4 to 10 in. long, narrowed to base, coarsely toothed; stalk and veins covered with long brown hairs. *infl.* 1 to 2½ ft. long. *fl.* white, in large clusters; sep. rounded. China.

R. japon'ica. A synonym of *R. podophylla.*

Rodgersia pinnata

R. pinna'ta.* 3 to 4 ft. h., somewhat branched; stem hollow. *l.* digitately pinnate, long-stalked; lflets. 5 to 9, 6 to 8 in. long, obovate or oblanceolate. *fl.* reddish, in a large, much-branched panicle; rachis rosy-red; cal. downy, lobes ovate, red without, white within. July. China. 1902. (B.M. 7892.) Variable in colour. var. **al'ba,** *fl.* white, *infl.* looser and larger. 1905; **el'egans,** *fl.* rose-pink; **ro'sea,** *fl.* rose; **ru'bra,** *fl.* deeper red; **super'ba,** taller with infl. 21 in. long, *fl.* pale rose.

R. podoph'ylla. 3 to 4 ft. h. *l.* large, basal long-stalked, palmately or peltately 5-sect., 6 to 8 in. across; stem-l. 3-lobed; lflets. sessile, sharply toothed, 5 to 10 in. long, 3 to 6 in. wide. *fl.* yellowish-white in a large naked panicle, somewhat nodding; cal. lobes spreading. June, July. Japan. 1880. (B.M. 6691; G.F. 708 as *R. japonica.*)

R. sambucifo'lia. 2 to 3 ft. h. *Basal l.* long-stalked, 9 to 15 in. long, bright green; lflets. in 3 to 5 widely separated pairs and an odd terminal, oblong-lanceolate. *fl.* white, small, in a small terminal, dense panicle; sep. fleshy, ovate, more or less acute. China.

R. tabula'ris. About 3 ft. h. *l.* peltate, 1 to 3 ft. across, with many short lobes; lobes broadly acuminate, with a few bristly hairs; stalks long. *fl.* small, white, in a many-fld. infl. resembling Astilbe; sep. broad, obovate-oblong, rounded; pet. obovate-oblong. China.

Rodigasia'nus -a -um, in honour of Señor Rodigas who collected in S. America.

RODRIGUE'ZIA (in honour of Emanuel Rodriguez, a Spanish physician and botanist). FAM. *Orchidaceae.* Including Burlingtonia. A genus of 30 or more species of epiphytic orchids, natives of Trop. America. Flowers usually showy; inflorescence a simple, many-flowered raceme; dorsal sepal free, petaloid, lateral narrow, connate usually their whole length, boat-shaped; petals like dorsal sepal; lip continuous, or very shortly connate with base of column, the base often produced into a short spur, blade spreading, obovate or obcordate, often longer than the sepals, disk usually crested; column erect, slender, club-shaped or with 2 auricles at the apex; pollinia 2; scapes axillary under the pseudobulbs. The small pseudobulbs may be set close together or at intervals along the rhizome; they are usually 1-leaved, but sometimes 2-leaved. Leaves oblong or elongated, leathery. The species with a more or less tufted habit should be placed in small pans or baskets. Those with somewhat scandent habit on rafts. Several of the species form quantities of roots which extend into the atmosphere. Within reason this should be encouraged; when repotting is necessary they may be considerably reduced. Compost should consist of half Osmunda fibre and half Sphagnum moss. Ample drainage must be provided, as during the growing season liberal waterings are necessary and the compost should not be allowed to dry in winter. Distinction must be made between those with hard bulbs and hard leaves and those of softer nature. When growing they may be suspended in the warm house, but their winter night temperature should be about 60° F. Scale insects often lodge in the axils of the basal leaves and the mealy bug is partial to the same position. They must be carefully removed, which is often difficult as the leaves fit closely to the pseudobulbs. Tobacco powder may be dusted in the axils or flowers of sulphur, and syringed out after a couple of days. Thrips will attack the flowers and sometimes the foliage. Propagation is by dividing the plants in late spring.

R. amoe'na. A synonym of *R. decora.*

R. anom'ala. A synonym of *R. uliginosa.*

R. Batemann'i.* *fl.* fragrant; sep. about 1 in. long, the lower connate, whitish; pet. whitish, often streaked with rose-purple; lip exceeding 1 in., oblong, white, streaked or flushed with rose-purple, emarginate, disk with 2 keels extending to base; spur short; scape arched or pendulous. *Pseudobulbs* clustered, 1 to 2 in. h. *l.* 3 to 5 in. long, about 1 in. wide. Brazil, Peru. 1866. (Ref. B. 128.) SYN. *R. candida Batemanni, Burlingtonia rubescens.*

R. Bungeroth'ii. *fl.* purplish; sep. and pet. like those of *R. secunda*; lip cuneate-obovate, 2-lobed, with a well-developed, triangular, descending spur; column naked, white; infl. dense. Venezuela. 1887. (L. 127.) A near ally of *R. secunda.*

R. caloplec'tron. *fl.* light yellowish-white, twisted; lateral sep. forming a long, compressed, horn-like, acute body, wrapping round the spur of the emarginate lip; column square-winged; infl. usually pendulous, few-fld. *Pseudobulbs* small, oblong-ligulate. *l.* solitary, thick, lanceolate, acuminate. Colombia. 1871. (G.F. 1372.)

R. can'dida.* *fl.* fragrant; 4 to 7, 2 to 3 in. h., satin-white; dorsal sep. obovate-oblong, clawed, emarginate, lateral sep. narrow, connate two-thirds, their bases embracing the short spur; pet. about 1 in. long, ½ in. wide; lip 1 to 1¾ in. long, about 1 in. wide, tip with a central stripe of yellow and 8 to 10 fleshy lamellae; peduncle arching. April, May. *Pseudobulbs* 1½ to 2 in. h., clustered. *l.* rigid, 4 to 6 in. long, 1 to 1½ in. wide. Demerara, Brazil. 1834. (B.R. 1927 and W.O.A. 18 as *Burlingtonia candida.*)

R. dec'ora.* *fl.* 10 to 15, 1½ in. long; sep. and pet. white, spotted red, sometimes flushed rose; dorsal sep. elliptic-oblong, lateral sep. connate for two-thirds, narrow; pet. larger; lip clawed, the claw with 5 raised lines, red-spotted, blade about 1 in. broad, white, 2-lobed, peduncle erect, 12 to 15 in. long. Summer. *Pseudobulbs* at long intervals about 1 in. h. *l.* 3 to 6 in. long, ½ in. or more wide. Should be grown on a raft. Brazil. 1851. (B.M. 4834 as *Burlingtonia decora.*) var. **pic'ta,** *fl.* brighter. (B.M. 5419.)

R. Farm'eri. A synonym of *R. candida.*

R. frag'rans. A synonym of *R. venusta.*

R. Fuerstenberg'ii. *fl.* 2 in. long, more than 1 in. broad; sep. rose; pet. and lip white, blotched yellow; raceme 1 ft. long, 3-fld. *l.* and *pseudobulbs* small. Habitat? 1890. Allied to *R. Leeana.*

R. granaden'sis. *fl.* 5 to 7, white, 1 in. or more across; dorsal sep. and pet. about equal, ovate, acute; lateral sep. connate into a boat-shape; lip clawed, 1½ in. long, obovate, emarginate, white with yellow blotch on disk; scape pendulous. *Pseudobulbs* small, 1-leaved. *l.* 3 to 4 in. long, lanceolate. Allied to *R. pubescens.* Colombia. *c.* 1887. SYN. *Burlingtonia granadensis.*

Rodriguezia candida

R. Knowles'ii. A variety of *R. venusta.*

R. lanceola'ta. A synonym of *R. secunda.*

R. Leea'na.* *fl.* fragrant, segs. white with yellowish middle line; dorsal sep. about 1 in. long, lateral connate; pet. strap-shaped; lip clawed, with 2 long linear keels, each with 4 small keels spreading outwards; column white with mauve spots; ovary mauve. *Pseudobulbs* 2-edged. *l.* linear, acute, 12 in. long. Brazil. 1883. var. **pic'ta,** *fl.* covered with mauve-purple lines and spots. 1885.

R. Lehmann'ii. *fl.* whitish-ochre, tinged brown; dorsal sep. gibbous-arched in middle, lateral connate into a narrow, falcate spur-like structure, blade-like near apex; pet. wedge-shaped-obovate, emarginate; lip with a solid acute spur between lateral sep., free part clawed, blade blotched and spotted cinnamon. Colombia, Ecuador. 1882.

R. Lin'denii. A synonym of *R. pubescens.*

R. luteo'la. *fl.* yellowish, small; sep. narrow, tip of dorsal sep. recurved, lateral connate; lip narrow, clawed, margin crisped, emarginate with a small apiculus in sinus. *l.* 3 to 5 in. long, about 1 in. wide. British Guiana. 1883.

R. macula'ta. *fl.* 6 to 10, rather small, fragrant, yellowish, with cinnamon spots; lip whitish at base, emarginate. Brazil. 1836. (B.R. 1839, 44.) Very variable.

R. pubes'cens.* *fl.* fragrant, 10 to 15, nearly 1½ in. across, pure white; dorsal sep. oblong-lanceolate, acute, lateral sep. narrow, connate; lip somewhat heart-shaped, yellowish at base, emarginate, 2-lobed, the base with 2 small erect, downy auricles, disk with 3 or more unequal raised lines; column densely pubescent; racemes pendulous. Summer. *Pseudobulbs* clustered, about 1 in. h. *l.* 2 to 5 in. long, narrow. Brazil. 1846. (L. 306.) SYN. *R. Lindenii.*

R. refract'a. *fl.* yellow-salmon, few; dorsal sep. cuneate-obovate, lateral connate, narrow boat-shaped; pet. like dorsal sep.; lip clawed, blade emarginate, with 4 or 5 angular keels each side. *l.* cuneate-oblong, acute. Brazil. 1854. (L. 212; Ref. B. 129.)

R. rig'ida. *fl.* fragrant, white, flushed rose; sep. about 1 in. long, dorsal concave, lateral connate; pet. larger; lip clawed, blade broadly obovate-obcordate, 2 in. long, 1½ in. wide, purplish marked, deeply emarginate with an apiculus in the sinus, disk with 4 short lamellae; scape 10 to 20 in. long, sometimes branched, fl. set rather densely. *Pseudobulbs* ovoid-oblong. *l.* rigid, 2½ to 4½ in. long, ¾ to 1¼ in. wide. Habit much as in *R. decora.* Brazil. 1838. (F.d.S 1845, 8 as *Burlingtonia rigida.*)

R. rubes'cens. A synonym of *R. Batemannii.*

R. secun'da.* *fl.* distichous, secund, rather small, rose-pink; dorsal sep. oval-oblong, concave, lateral connate into a boat-shape, gibbous at base, narrow at apex; pet. broader than dorsal sep.; lip deep rose, obovate-oblong, emarginate, with a furrowed callus; scape arched, many-fld. *Pseudobulbs* oval-oblong, compressed, 1 to 2 in. h. *l.* linear-lanceolate, tapered, 5 to 9 in. long, leathery. Trinidad, Colombia. 1818. (B.R. 930; B.M. 3524; W.O.A. 351.) SYN. *R. lanceolata.*

R. uligino'sa. *fl.* 12 or more, very small, fragrant; segs. crystalline white with a central pale reddish suffusion; dorsal sep. erect or hooded; pet. larger; lip spreading, rounded, base slightly saccate, crest yellow, bicallose; lower sep. spread laterally; peduncles 1 in. long, wiry, rachis 1 to 1½ in. *Pseudobulbs* clustered, teretely oblong, about ¾ in. h. *l.* cylindrical, tapered, 2 in. long. Brazil before 1891. (G.C. 9 (1891), 729 as *R. anomala.*) SYN. *Capanemia uliginosa.* A very small but pretty species.

R. venus'ta.* *fl.* few or many, fragrant, 1½ in. long, pure white or flushed with rose; lip with an oblong yellow blotch, upper sep. broadly ovate, concave; lateral connate, boat-shaped; lip clawed, broadly obovate with a deep sinus in which is a small triangular lobule; disk with 2 orange-margined keels; column with 2 horn-like auricles and 2 purple teeth; scapes usually pendulous. *Pseudobulbs* clustered, about 1 in. h. *l.* rigid, 3 to 6 in. long, ½ to 1 in. wide. Brazil. 1840. (I.H. 1858, 188 as *Burlingtonia venusta*; W.O.A. 363 as *Burlingtonia fragrans.*) var. **Knowles'ii,** *fl.* white faintly tinged lilac-pink, more robust and with longer spikes than type.

RODRIGUEZIELLA. *See under* **Theodorea.**

RODS, MEASURING. *See* **Measures.**

Roebelin'ii, in honour of the Swiss M. Roebelin who collected in the Philippines, &c., for Messrs. Sanders.

ROEL'LA (in honour of W. Roell, Professor of Anatomy at Amsterdam). FAM. *Campanulaceae.* A genus of about 10 species of sub-shrubs or rarely herbs, natives of S. Africa, with alternate, usually narrow, stiff leaves, and terminal flowers, solitary or in clusters, sessile. Calyx cylindrical, 5-toothed; corolla funnel- to bell-shaped, large, 5-lobed; stamens 5, anthers free; ovary 2-celled, stigmas 2, thick. Fruit a cylindrical capsule, opening by a large terminal pore; seeds numerous. Roellas need greenhouse treatment and a compost of sandy loam and peat. Propagation is by seeds or by cuttings of young shoots put into the compost above-named under a bell-glass.

Roella ciliata

R. cilia'ta. African Harebell. Perennial with a branched, hairy stem 6 to 12 in. h. *l.* clustered, linear, ciliate with white hairs nearly ½ in. long. *fl.* blue or rose with a deep-purple or blue circle at the base of the lobes, up to 1 in. or even more long, funnel-shaped, solitary. September. S. Africa. (B.M. 378; L.B.C. 1156; F.d.S. 517.) A variable plant.

R. decur'rens. A synonym of *Wahlenbergia capensis.*

R. el'egans. Herbaceous perennial, stem branched, 9 or 10 in. h., hairy. *l.* spatulate, about 1½ in. long, hairy, opposite, sessile. *fl.* bright blue with a purple stain in the throat; solitary in the axils of l., about 1 in. long. February to May. Habitat? 1836. (P.M.B. 6, 27.) Perhaps not a Roella.

Roella elegans

ROEME'RIA (in honour of Johann Jakob Roemer, 1763–1819, Professor of Botany at Zurich). FAM. *Papaveraceae.* A genus of about 6 species of slender annuals with yellow sap, natives of the Mediterranean region for the most part. Leaves pinnatipartite with narrow, much-cut lobes often ending in an acute mucro. Flowers solitary on leaf-opposed peduncles, violet or reddish. Distinct from Glaucium by the 1- (not 2-) celled ovary and from Cathcartia by the 2 to 4 (not 3 to 6) carpels; sepals 2; petals 4, corrugated in bud; stamens numerous. Fruit siliqua-like. Seeds should be sown in spring where the plants are to flower. Ordinary garden soil.

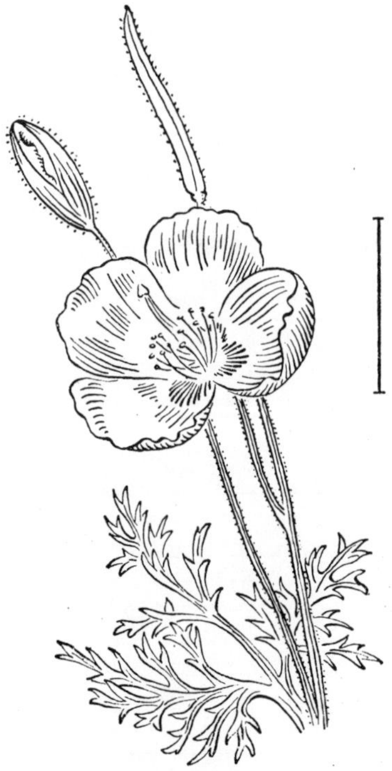

Roemeria hybrida

R. hyb'rida. Violet-flowered Horned Poppy; Wind Rose. Annual herb, about 18 in. h., more or less hairy. *l.* much-cut into narrow segs. *fl.* violet-purple; pet. about 1 in. long; peduncles erect. *Capsule* bristly hairy. May, June. Mediterranean region, Britain. (E.B. 64.)

R. refrac'ta. Annual herb about 12 in. h. with ascending stem less hairy than in *R. hybrida*. *fl.* on erect, rarely refracted peduncles; pet. ¾ to 1¼ in. long, reddish with a black blotch at base. *Capsule* almost smooth. Armenia, Persia. There is a variety (**albomargina'ta**) with a white ring round the black pet.-blotch, from Turkistan; and var. **seto'sa** with *fl.* dark scarlet with a black basal blotch, sometimes surrounded by a white ring and a bristly capsule. Armenia to Afghanistan. (B.M. 9242.)

ROESTE'LIA. An elongated cylindrical tubular structure, either straight or slightly curved and horn-shaped. Term now almost obsolete but at one time used as a generic name for the stage of the fungi belonging to the genus Gymnosporangium, where the peridermium was of the form indicated.

ROEZ'LIA. Included in **Monochaetum.**

Roez'lii, in honour of Benedikt Roezl, Austrian collector in Mexico and Cent. America, &c., 1824–85.

ROFFIA. *See* **Raphia.**

ROGATION FLOWER. *See* **Polygala vulgaris.**

Rogers'ii, in honour of Charles Gilbert Rogers of the Indian Forest Service.

Rohania'nus -a -um, in honour of Camille de Rohan, of Czechoslovakia, enthusiastic gardener.

ROH'DEA (in honour of Michael Rohde, physician and botanist of Bremen). FAM. *Liliaceae.* A genus of a single perennial herb, native of Japan, with a short thick rhizome and oblanceolate leaves. Scape short, axillary. Flowers densely arranged, bracts short-ovate; perianth tube bowl-shaped, lobes short; stamens adnate to tube almost whole length; style very short, stigma 3-lobed. Fruit a berry, often 1-seeded. For treatment *see* **Reineckia.**

R. japon'ica. *l.* 9 to 12 in basal rosette, sub-erect, oblanceolate, 1 ft. long, 2 to 3 in. wide, glabrous, acute. *Scape* 2 to 3 in. long. *fl.* white, fleshy, ⅛ in. long, in a dense spike 1 to 2 in. long. January to April. Japan. 1783. (B.M. 898 as *Orontium japonicum.*)

×**ROLFEA'RA** (in honour of R. A. Rolfe, 1855–1921, botanist at Kew). FAM. *Orchidaceae.* Hybrids combining species of Brassavola, Cattleya, and Sophronitis.

ROLLERS and ROLLING. Rollers are necessary for keeping walks both of gravel and grass in good condition, for lawns, and at times in preparing a seed-bed. Where walks are narrow or turnings intricate a narrow roller must be used, for broader areas a wider roller is to be preferred. Cast-iron rollers for wide areas are usually made with the cylinder in 2 parts revolving separately on the axle so that less damage is likely when turning to a new direction. For newly laid gravel a light roller should be used at first, later a heavy one for if properly made a heavy one can be supported at any time after the gravel is set. Rolling of gravel paths should be done only when the gravel is too dry to cling, yet while the walk is sufficiently damp for the roller to make an impression. Concrete rollers are also sometimes used. Iron rollers with cylinders made to hold water give a means of altering the weight of the roller according to circumstances. The use of a heavy roller on grass while it is wet is unwise and generally a light roller is sufficient and less liable to 'pack' the surface soil and lead to the exclusion of air from the roots. A wooden roller is often sufficient as it is in preparation for sowing of seeds such as grass and onion. A spiked roller of the type known as Sarel's Patent is useful on lawns subject to much traffic for the spikes help the ventilation of the soil so that the roots of grasses obtain fresh air and water reaches them more easily. Like the larger iron rollers this is built up in sections, here about 12 in. long and 9 in. in diameter.

Rollison'ii, in honour of George Rollison, nurseryman of Tooting, 1800–80, and his brother W. Rollison (d. 1875).

Romanet'tii, in honour of Romanet de Caillaud, of Périgueux, who introduced Vitis sp., &c., from China, *c.* 1881.

roma'nus -a -um, of Rome.

roma'nicus, of Roumania.

ROMANZOFF'IA (in honour of Nicholas Romanzoff, Russian who originated and financed an expedition round the world, 1816–17). FAM. *Hydrophyllaceae.* A genus of 4 species of dwarf perennial herbs with the aspect of Saxifrages, natives of Western N. America and NE. Asia. Leaves basal, long-stalked, kidney-shaped, palmately or crenately lobed. Flowers solitary or in spikes from basal peduncles; calyx divided to the base; corolla bell- to funnel-shaped, glabrous, lobes widely ovate, obtuse. Stamens included. Fruit a many-seeded capsule. Plants for a damp spot in the rock-garden, rather shaded, with a rather peaty soil.

R. californ'ica. *Rhiz.* bulbiferous. Smooth or whitish hairy herb, 2 to 6 in. h. *l.* 1 to 2 in. wide, base of l.-stalk dilated. *fl.* white, bell- to funnel-shaped; cor. nearly thrice as long as sep.; peduncles straight; pedicels longer than cal. in fr. April. Western N. America. 1873. (B.M. 6109.)

R. sitchen'sis of Bot. Mag. A synonym of *R. californica.*

R. unalaschken'sis. Spreading, more or less dark hairy, 2 to 6 in. h. *l.* 5- to 11-lobed; those of stem very few, alternate. *fl.* pale purple or whitish, about ½ in. long; in a dense short 1-sided raceme; pedicels not exceeding cal. in fr. May. E. Siberia, W. Canada, Alaska. (B.M. 9683*b*.)

ROM'NEYA (in honour of the Rev. T. Romney Robinson, 1792–1882, astronomer of Armagh). FAM. *Papaveraceae.* A genus of 2 species of tall herbaceous perennials, natives of SW. California. Glabrous or almost so, glaucous, with branched stems and pinnatifid leaves with 2 or 3 pairs of lobes with hardened tips, somewhat distant, spreading; stalks about a quarter as long as blades. Flowers solitary at ends of corymbose branches, large, white, and showy; sepals 3, ovate, leathery, quickly falling; petals 6 in 2 series, obovate; stamens very numerous. Fruit an ovate capsule, very many seeded, covered with rigid golden bristles. A good deep soil and a sunny position suits the Romneyas which are hardy in all but cold localities and very handsome. They spread by underground stems and may, with care, be divided or raised from seed.

R. Coul'teri.* Stems 6 to 8 ft. h., somewhat flexuous, much-branched above. *l.* somewhat glaucous, with in lower l. 6 lanceolate lobes below and a terminal ovate lobe; upper toothed or entire; all somewhat leathery. *fl.* white, about 4 or 5 in. across. Summer, autumn. Fruit with spreading bristles. SW. California. 1875. (G.C. 65 (1919), 40; Gn. 26 (1884), 400.)

R. trichocal'yx.* Somewhat more erect and less branched than *R. Coulteri* with sub-globose (not ovate-conical) buds, somewhat bristly (not all but smooth) at apex, and with the bristles on the capsule appressed, not spreading. Flowers equally freely produced and fine. *R. trichocalyx* appears to spread more widely than *R. Coulteri* by underground shoots but these root more slowly. SW. California. Hybrids, first raised by Mr. W. B. Fletcher of Aldwick, Sussex, are now well distributed under the name *R.* × *hybrida* (SYN. *R. Vandedeni*). They are intermediate between the parents. (B.M. 8002.)

ROMU'LEA (after *Romulus*, founder and first king of Rome). FAM. *Iridaceae.* A genus of about 50 species of small herbs related to Crocus, natives of W. Europe, the Mediterranean region, and W. and S. Africa, distinguished from Crocus by the stem appearing out of the ground at flowering time and the short perianth tube. Corm with brown crust-like to leathery tunic. Leaves few, linear or awl-shaped, sheaths rarely dilated. Stem sometimes branched and leafy. Flowers 1 to a spathe; perianth lilac, yellow, or white; tube shortly funnel-shaped, segments equal, erecto-patent; stamens affixed to throat. Fruit 3-celled, oblong, papery; seeds dark chestnut. The species mostly need frame or greenhouse protection but some are hardy and all like a compost of peat and sandy loam. Propagation by seed or offsets.

Romneya Coulteri (p. 1803)

R. bulbocodioi'des. About 6 in. h. *Basal l.* hollow, sheathing; *stem-l.* 2 or 3, rarely solitary. *fl.* greenish-yellow; outer spathe valve boat-shaped, inner very slender and dark-striped; scape terete. June. S. Africa. 1810. (B.M. 1392 as *Trichonema caulescens.*) Greenhouse.

R. Bulboco'dium. About 6 in. h., 1- (rarely 2- or 3-) fld. *l.* erect or recurved, linear, green, channelled. *fl.* bright violet, rarely white, yellow at base, large; segs. elliptic-lanceolate; spathe valves unequal, upper half as long as perianth, inner purple-spotted. March. W. France, Mediterranean region. 1739. (B.M. 265 as *Ixia Bulbocodium.*) Hardy. (B.R. 30, 40 shows a form (fig. 1) with white fl. margined blue as *Trichonema palustre*, and (fig. 2) white fl. marked purple on a many-fld. scape as *T. Pylium.*)

R. Clusia'na. Stem 2 to 3 in. h., usually forked at base. *l.* 3 or 4, setaceous, arching, 6 to 12 in. long. *fl.* large, bright yellow at base, white near middle, bright violet above; segs. overlapping, lanceolate, acute, outer segs, broader; stamens about half as long as segs., anthers bright yellow; stigmatic branches white. Spring. Spain. 1860. SYN. *Trichonema Clusianum.*

R. Colum'nae. *l.* erect or recurved, 2 to 4 in. long, grooved above. fl.-stem short, 1- to 3-fld. *fl.* blue, violet, or whitish, yellow at base, small; segs. oblong-lanceolate, acute, distinctly 3-nerved; spathe longer than perianth tube. March, April. *fr.* ovate, 6-angled. W. Europe including Britain, Mediterranean region. (E.B. 1492.) Hardy.

R. cors'ica. *l.* erect or recurved, longer than scape. *Scape* 2- or 3-fld. *fl.* small, violet, with violet stripes near base; segs. acute. Corsica.

R. crucia'ta. A synonym of *R. longifolia.*

R. longifo'lia. About 6 in. h. *l.* undulately recurved, with a long basal sheath, 4-ribbed both sides. *Scape* simple or branched. *fl.* rose; outer spathe valve striped and purple-spotted; inner dark-striped and dotted. S. Africa. 1758. (B.M. 575 as *Trichonema cruciatum.*) Half-hardy.

R. Linare'sii. Nearly related to *R. Requienii.* Italy to Greece.

R. Macow'anii. Stem short, 1- to 4-fld. *l.* sub-terete, long, spreading. *fl.* bright golden yellow in lower, paler in upper part, often tinged red at tips, 1 to 1½ in. across; stamens half as long as segs. S. Africa. (G.C. 1 (1887), 180, 184, f. 42.) Greenhouse.

R. pudi'ca. A variety of *R. rosea.*

R. ramiflo'ra. Stem long, 2- or 3-fld. *l.* stout, straight or recurved, 6 to 12 in. long. *fl.* small, yellow in throat, outer segs. yellowish without, deep or pale lilac in upper part, inner purple in upper part within and without; filaments hairy to middle. May. S. Europe. 1830. (M.F.M. 92.)

R. Requie'nii. Corm very small, globose, tunic leathery. *l.* cylindrical, nearly prostrate. *fl.* 1 to 3, medium-sized, deep violet; tube very short; segs. oblanceolate, obtuse; stamens half as long as segs., anthers yellow, stigmas violet, overtopping anthers. February, March. Corsica, Sardinia. (B.M. 9555.) SYN. *R. Linaresii Requienii.*

R. Revelier'i. Corm very small. *l.* filiform, rigid, much longer than fl. *fl.* 1 or 2, small, violet, pedicels reddish; segs. lanceolate, acute, outer deeper in colour, streaked green outside; anthers yellow; stigmas pale, rather below stamens. March. Corsica.

R. ro'sea. About 6 in. h. *l.* recurved, long-sheathing at base, often ciliate on ribs. *Scape* terete, simple, leafy. *fl.* rose, yellow at base, bell-shaped; spathe valves broadly ovate, acute, striped, purple-spotted. July. S. Africa. 1818. (B.M. as *Trichonema roseum.*) Greenhouse. var. **pudi'ca,** *fl.* pink, spotted violet at base. (B.M. 1244 as *T. pudicum.*); **specio'sa,** *fl.* deep carmine, yellow, and violet-striped at base of segs. (B.M. 1476 as *T. speciosum*; S.B.F.G. 300 as *Spatalanthus speciosus.*)

R. specio'sa. A variety of *R. rosea.*

RONDELET'IA (in honour of William Rondelet, 1507–66, physician and student of fishes and algae). FAM. *Rubiaceae.* A genus of about 80 species of evergreen shrubs or, rarely, trees, natives of the W. Indies and Trop. America. Branchlets terete. Leaves opposite, rarely in whorls of three, sometimes sessile, leathery or membranous; stipules broad, interpetiolar, deciduous or persistent. Flowers white, yellow, or red, small, stalked, in axillary or terminal corymbs or panicles; calyx 4- or 5-lobed, persistent; corolla funnel- or salver-shaped, lobes 4 or 5, spreading; stamens 4 or 5. Fruit a capsule, seeds small, not winged. Many of the species are pretty and well worthy of a place in the stove. A compost of loam, peat, and sand, in which they should be firmly potted, suits them. Propagation by half-ripe cuttings in heat under a close frame.

R. amoe'na.* Shrub of about 4 ft. *l.* broadly oblong, 2 to 5 in. long, with a slender point. *fl.* pink, with a golden beard at throat, lobes emarginate; clustered. June. Guatemala. 1838. (F.d.S. 442 as *Rogiera amoena.*)

R. Backhous'ei. *See* **R. erythroneura.**

R. corda'ta. About 4 ft. h. *l.* ovate or ovate-lanceolate, slender-pointed, cordate at base, leathery, downy beneath and on veins at first, stipules ovate-lanceolate, leafy, reflexed. *fl.* pink or flesh-coloured with a yellow throat, 4-parted; in many-fld. terminal corymbs. Summer. Guatemala. 1844. (B.M. 8540; F.d.S. 754 as *Rogiera cordata.*)

R. erythroneu'ra. Shrub of 3 or 4 ft., smooth except minutely downy infl. Stem slender, terete. *l.* ovate, 4 to 9 in. long, green, the short stalk and veins beneath red; stipules appressed, persistent. *fl.* pink, darker without, ⅓ in. across; cal. tube nearly globose, segs. linear-obovate; cor. tube slender, twice as long as segs., hairy, throat glabrous; panicle terminal, loosely many-fld. Trop. America. (B.M. 6290 as *R. Backhousei.*)

R. gratis'sima.* *l.* lanceolate-elliptic, 1 to 2 in. long, rounded at base; stalk short. *fl.* pinkish, fragrant, tube bright rose, long, lobes 5, paler; corymbs dense, terminal, not unlike those of the Laurustinus. Trop. America. 1866. (F.d.S. 1570–1 and G.F. 490 as *Rogiera gratissima*). For cool stove.

R. latifo'lia. *l.* large, heart-shaped, slender-pointed; stalk short. *fl.* in corymbose cymes; cor. tube pink, lobes white; cal. lobes obtuse, oval. Guatemala. SYN. *Rogiera latifolia.*

R. odora'ta.* Shrub of about 3 ft., branches straggling, downy. *l.* in opposite, distant pairs, ovate, acute, entire, waved; stalk very short. *fl.* bright vermilion with conspicuous yellow throat, fragrant, in terminal trichotomous corymbs; cor. tube narrow, lobes spreading; pedicels hairy. November. Cuba. 1836. (B.M. 3953; B.R. 1905; L.B.C. 1893 as *R. speciosa.*) var. **breviflo'ra,** *fl.* scentless, cor. shorter than in type, about ½ in. across. W. Indies. (B.M. 6350): **ma'jor,** *fl.* larger than in type.

R. Purd'iei. Shrub of about 4 ft., almost silky-hairy. *l.* ovate-oblong to oblong-lanceolate, 3 to 8 in. long, blunt, narrowed to a very short stalk or somewhat cordate, midrib red above. *fl.* pale yellow, fragrant, ½ in. across, in crowded terminal and axillary corymbs; cor. with a thickened ring at throat. Summer. Colombia. 1867. (B.M. 5669.)

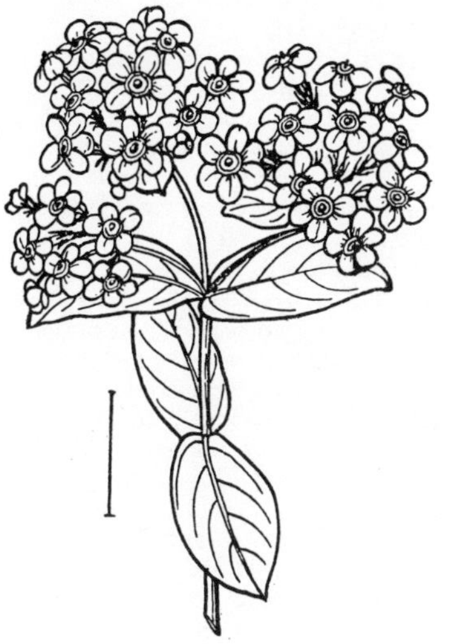

Rondeletia odorata (p. 1804)

R. Roez'lii. *l.* 1 to 4 in. long, slender-pointed, rather thin. Cor. tube gradually widened upwards; filaments above middle of cor. tube; anthers slightly exserted. Guatemala.

R. specio'sa. A synonym of *R. odorata.*

R. thyrsoi'dea. Shrub of about 6 ft. *l.* ovate or elliptic, 3 to 6 in. long, acute, glabrous above, with minute, scattered down beneath; stipules deltoid-awl-shaped, strigose. *fl.* rusty-yellowish, downy without, in hairy, axillary, pyramidal panicles. July. Jamaica. 1819.

R. vers'icolor. Shrub of 5 or 6 ft., branches 4-angled, silky-hairy when young. *l.* ovate, 4 in. or more long, slender-pointed, obtuse or subcordate at base, hairy and paler beneath; stalk ½ in. long, stipules deciduous. *fl.* pale pink within, deeper without, tube orange, cal. tube small, globose; cor. salver-shaped, 5-lobed; panicle rather dense, many-fld., downy. Cent. America. 1838. (B.M. 4579.)

F. G. P.

RONNBERG'IA (in honour of M. Ronnberg, Director of Agriculture and Horticulture). Fam. *Bromeliaceae.* A genus of 3 herbaceous perennials in Colombia, 1 in Brazil. Closely related to Chevalieria but with rather loosely spicate inflorescence raised above the leaf rosette. For treatment *see* **Billbergia.**

R. columbia'na. *l.* about 12 in a rosette, lorate, arching, 1 ft. long, 1½ in. wide, brown beneath, spines close and minute. *fl.* violet; pet. twice as long as cal.; spike few-fld., loose, simple, erect, 2 to 3 in. long; peduncle thick, hidden by the l.-bases. March. Colombia. 1882. SYN. *Quesnelia columbiana.*

R. Morrenia'na. *l.* few, ovate, large, entire, long-stalked, slender-pointed, subcordate at base, bright green, zoned with bars and spots of very deep green. *fl.* blue, in a dense, spike-like thyrse; scape slender, suberect, with many narrow, unarmed l. Colombia. 1874. (I.H. 1874, 177.)

Rood'ae, in honour of Mrs. Rood of Van Rhynsdorp, Namaqualand.

ROOM PLANTS. A large number of different kinds of plants can be grown in the dwelling-house provided elementary precautions are taken. Frequent causes of failure are the introduction of plants not specially prepared for the conditions in a room; bad treatment, especially in regard to watering; attempts to right wrong by the application of nostrums including artificial manures; bad-potting and too frequent interference with the root system; ill-advised attempts to increase the stock; frost; draughts; dust; bad drainage. Pests and disease-causing organisms are rarely the cause of trouble with these plants or when they occur are readily dealt with.

Plants to be grown in rooms, especially those with large leaves which in nature inhabit countries with a hot, moist climate, need special care in preparing them for growing under these conditions. If they have been brought on in circumstances approximately to those natural to them they will quickly succumb to the dry conditions of the dwelling-house. Such plants should be purchased from a reliable nurseryman who has prepared them for the treatment they are likely to undergo, and they should be bought in spring or summer, not in autumn or winter. Plants grown for quick sale are almost certain to be ephemeral.

Frost and draughts are the greatest enemies against which to contend. Plants must have plenty of sunlight and the best place for them generally in the day-time is the window. At night in winter they may well be too much exposed to low temperatures there unless the room is uniformly heated and it is therefore desirable to remove them to a place in the room for the night where they will be free from draughts and where danger of frost will be greatly reduced, returning them to their light quarters in the morning. Plants used for the decoration of the hall are particularly liable to suffer from draughts and this must be guarded against.

The leaves of plants not only take in and give out gases through tiny pores in their surface during their life-processes but also need unobstructed exposure to sunlight. Dust on the foliage interferes with these essential needs and where plants such as Palms, Euryas, Aspidistras, Indiarubber plants, Fatsias and the like are grown they must be carefully freed from dust and dirt on their leaves by sponging with soft, lukewarm water twice a week, or oftener in very dusty places.

Good drainage is an all-important need for plants in pots or boxes. If the water has not free movement through the soil a sour condition soon develops to the detriment of the roots and if water stands in the soil roots cannot get the air they need to breathe and the plant quickly dies. The drainage material must be of a suitable nature and must be properly arranged in the pot. Further, the nature of the plant must be considered. Some need to be potted on as soon as the pot becomes full of roots, others succeed better the less they are interfered with so long as they are periodically top-dressed. Palms are much better if not allowed too much room for their roots. So long as the roots are not too crowded and drainage is ample while the plant appears healthy it should not be repotted. The soil in potting needs to be made very firm for some plants, e.g. Palms and Chrysanthemums, and especially hard-wooded plants like Heaths and Azaleas, whereas it should not be nearly as firm for soft-wooded plants like Pelargoniums and for Ferns. Some growers recommend that in potting Palms the surface of the soil in the pot should be sloped gradually from the side down to the centre but usually it is better that the surface should be finished off level and equally firm all through.

Never repot a plant when the soil is thoroughly dry. It should be moist but not wet and the pots should be clean and dry. Pots that have been washed and new pots that have been soaked, as they should be before use, should be thoroughly dried before potting begins. Most plants are best repotted in spring as growth becomes more active.

For watering rain-water is best or that from a stream or well. No hard-and-fast rules can be laid down as to how often a plant should be watered. The only rule is that it should have water when it needs it. A good method of ascertaining when water is needed by a growing plant is to rap the pot with the knuckles or with the handle of a knife. If a clear ringing sound is given out it may be assumed that water is needed, but if the sound is dull and heavy there is usually sufficient water present. This method is apt to be misleading if a pot is cracked, and it does not hold good with Palms for with them the pot should be crowded with roots and the sound given out will be deceptive. The condition of the leaves, especially the ends of the leaves, will be the best guide for Palms—they should be stiff, not easily rolled up.

The best time of day for watering depends upon the season. In winter the morning is best if there is no danger of frost and in summer early morning before the sun is too hot is best. If it cannot be done then evening is best, but watering should be thorough, merely wetting the surface of the soil is useless or worse; the soil should have a good soaking. With most plants it is important that the roots should never be thoroughly dry and with hard-wooded plants if the ball of soil is allowed to dry it is almost impossible to get water into it again and the plant is doomed. There is no better test of the efficiency of a gardener than his skill in keeping plants properly supplied with water at all their stages—and his recognition of the fact that requirements vary greatly at different stages.

Most of the plants suitable for growing in rooms can be potted in the 'standard' type of potting soil (q.v.), a mixture of good loam, peat, and sand, but special plants such as Cacti, Heaths, and some Ferns need modifications of this and the articles dealing with them in this Dictionary should be consulted. If leaf-soil is used it is best prepared from Oak and Beech leaves and care must be taken that it is not collected from a place where it has become sodden with stagnant water at any time.

Where it is really necessary in addition to top-dressings of good soil, liquid manure may be used from time to time. Soot-water made by sinking a bag of soot in a large tub of soft water, or liquid cow or sheep manure, will supply a certain amount of nitrogen and help to give colour to the foliage of such plants as Palms and Aspidistras, or a suitable mixture of artificials prepared by a reliable firm for the purpose may be used.

The following list of plants suitable for rooms, large and small, and for various purposes therein may be useful. It is not exhaustive but contains the names of plants which experience shows can be grown in this position if care is exercised. Size and other characters of importance can be ascertained by consulting the articles dealing with them in the body of the Dictionary.

FOLIAGE PLANTS include the following Palms: *Archonophoenix Cunninghamiana*, *Arecastrum Romanzoffiana*, *Howea Belmoreana*, *H. Forsteriana*, *Jubaea spectabilis*, *Livistona chinensis*, *Nannorhops Ritchieana*, *Phoenix reclinata*, *P. rupicola*, *Rhapis excelsa*, *Sabal minor*, *S. umbraculifera*, *Syagrus Weddeliana*, and *Trachycarpus Fortunei*. Other good plants for the purpose, several of them suitable only for very large rooms, are *Agave americana* and its variety *variegata*, *Aglaonema modestum*, *Araucaria Bidwillii*, *A. excelsa*, *Asparagus plumosus*, *Aspidistra lurida* (*elatior*) and var. *variegata*, *Begonia Rex* and its many varieties, *Carex Morrowii*, *Coleus*, *Cordyline australis*, *C. indivisa*, *Cyperus alternifolius* and its variegated form, *Dasylirion acrotrichum*, *D. glaucophyllum*, *Dieffenbachia nobilis*, *Dracaena fragrans*, *Eurya japonica*, *Fatsia japonica* (which should be freely watered from late spring to late summer and given a shaded place), *Ficus elastica* (Indiarubber plant), *Maranta major* (which must be kept from the direct rays of the sun), *Miscanthus japonicus* and its variegated form, *Monstera deliciosa*, *Mondo Jaburan* and its variegated form, *Pandanus utilis*, *P. Veitchii*, *Phormium tenax* and especially its variegated forms, *Sanseviera trifasciata Laurentii*, *Yucca aloifolia*, and *Y. filamentosa variegata*.

FLOWERING PLANTS. Cacti and other Succulents including species of Crassula, Echeoeria, Kalanchoe, Mesembryanthemum and its relations, Sedum, all of which are dealt with under their special headings. Bulbous and tuberous plants including Crocus, Hyacinth, Narcissus, Scilla, Snowdrop, Tulip, tuberous Begonia, Cyclamen, especially *C. persicum*, Lilies such as *L. auratum*, *L. formosanum* Price's var., *L. longiflorum*, *L. speciosum*, Solomon's Seal (*Polygonatum multiflorum*), *Vallota purpurea*, Ixia, Sparaxis, *Lapeyrousia cruenta*, Lachenalia, Nerine, Montbretias, Schizostylis, Watsonia, early flowering Gladioli, Zephyranthes, Hippeastrum, bulbous Irises. Annuals such as Stocks, Asters, Mignonette, Forget-me-not, Schizanthus. Various flowering plants including Fuchsia, Pelargoniums, Musk, *Primula obconica*, *P. sinensis*, *P. malacoides*, Cineraria, Astilbe, Francoa; shrubs such as Hydrangea, *Genista fragrans* and *G. racemosus*, and *Deutzia gracilis*. Many of these cannot be regarded as permanent occupants of the rooms but may be brought in during their flowering period after proper preparation.

FERNS. Among the most suitable ferns are *Asplenium bulbiferum*, *A. Nidus*, and *A. Trichomanes*, *Cyrtomium falcatum*, *C. caryotideum*, *Lomaria Spicant*, *Nephrolepis exaltata* and its varieties, *Pellaea rotundifolia*, *Pteris cretica*, *P. multifida*?, *P. quadriaurita*, *Polypodium vulgare cambricum*, *Phyllitis Scolopendrium*. *See also* **Ferns.**

BASKET-PLANTS. *Campanula isophylla*, *C. fragilis*, Ivy-leaved Pelargoniums, *Lysimachia nummularia*, and its variegated forms, Ivies, especially variegated forms, Sedum sp., *Othonna crassifolia*, *Nierembergia gracilis*, Fuchsias, *Saxifraga sarmentosa*, *Scirpus cernuus*, *Linaria Cymbalaria*, *Tropaeolum majus*, *T. polyphyllum*, *Tradescantia fluminensis*, *Zebrina pendula*. Many ferns also make good basket-plants (*see* **Ferns**).

Roo'peri, in honour of Capt. Rooper, who sent *Kniphofia Rooperi* from Kaffraria, *c.* 1873.

ROOT. From the earliest period in the life of a flowering plant or fern there is usually a clear distinction between the root and the shoot. It is readily seen in the embryo in the seed where the difference between radicle and plumule is marked. The radicle develops into the root, usually the first part to emerge from the seed on germination, and it differs from the shoot by growing downwards, bearing no lateral members differing from itself (whereas the shoot bears not only branches like itself but leaves and reproductive organs), produces root-branches from its inner tissues (not from the tissues at the growing-point as does the shoot), and usually bears a root-cap.

Not only is there marked dissimilarity in structure but the normal functions of the root are quite distinct. They are the absorption of water and earth-salts from the soil and anchoring the plant. Only in very rare instances does the root contain chlorophyll and if exposed to light, take part in photosynthesis. Roots may develop not only from the growth of the radicle but from the inner tissues of the shoot (even at times from leaves) and this power is commonly made use of by horticulturists in propagating plants. Roots formed directly from stems and leaves and also those produced from other roots but not in the usual order (i.e. from successively younger parts) are sometimes called adventitious roots, those from the radicle being known as true roots, but there is no essential difference of structure or function between them, only of their place of origin.

The growth in length of a root takes place by the formation of new cells at its tip just behind the dead-cells which form the protecting root-cap which is continually being worn away as the root is forced forward between the soil particles and continually renewed within by the cells at the growing-point. The elongation of the new cells lengthens the root and forces forward its tip into the soil. The tip of the root is sensitive to various influences which serve to direct it into a position where it can most effectively perform its functions. Its response to gravity is such that it grows, so far as it is not mechanically prevented, vertically downwards, but it is also sensitive to the presence of water causing it to grow towards the damper parts of the soil, and to light, causing it to grow away from light. In ordinary land-plants although moisture attracts the root, if the soil is water-logged the root cannot grow downwards for long. As with all other living parts it needs supplies of oxygen for respiration and without an adequate supply it dies. As soon as the cells produced at the growing-point have attained their full length some of the outer ones grow out more or less at right angles to the parent-root into root-hairs thus greatly extending the area of the root-surface in contact with the soil and increasing the opportunity for absorbing water and earth-salts from the film covering the soil particles around it. The life of the root-hairs is not long but they are continually renewed near the growing-point as the root increases in length. This region is sometimes called the piliferous region. Just behind it branches of the root begin to form, arising from within in definite order, and the youngest nearest the tip of the root burrowing their way through the cortex of the root. These root-branches will be in vertical ranks, the number of ranks depending upon the number of xylem bundles in the primary root. The lateral roots are not affected to the same extent as the primary root by the pull of gravity but grow out more or less horizontally, and the roots arising from these are still less affected, so that eventually the whole body of soil about the primary or tap-root for some distance laterally becomes filled with the root-branches and the whole of this mass is tapped for water and earth-salts. Light and dryness of the atmosphere tends to keep the roots from appearing above the surface, but in dim light and a very humid atmosphere some of them, not infrequently make their way out. As the root ages in most Dicotyledons and Conifers, a thickening process takes place by means of a cambium and as the root increases in thickness the primary cortex is shed with its root-hairs, and its place is taken by a secondary cortex and often a layer of cork so that the function of absorption can no longer be performed by the older parts of the root. This function devolves therefore upon the young roots with their root-hairs and in this lies the great importance of encouraging the production of a fibrous-root system, often induced in cultivation by transplanting and by judicious watering. The great part of this fibrous-root system may lie beyond the circumference of the circle of the branches or foliage, the older roots growing in thickness, and therefore in the extent of their transport tissue, to keep pace with the growth of the stem and the continually increasing demand upon water and earth-salts as the assimilatory system of stem and foliage increases; but where cultivation is carefully done the ground beneath the branches may still be maintained in part as a collecting area as well as an anchorage. Where large trees are concerned the older roots often increase so greatly in thickness that they form buttress roots very effective in withstanding the strains and stresses imposed by winds upon the aerial parts.

While the production of root-hairs is the main means of securing an adequate absorbing area, in some plants, especially in forest trees, their place is taken by mycorrhiza (q.v.), while in saprophytes (q.v.) the root absorbs organic food supplies from decaying vegetable remains, and in parasitic plants (q.v.) these supplies or part of them are absorbed directly from the living host.

In many plants most of the root system is composed of adventitious roots produced from the base of the stem. In these as a rule the primary root is often of limited growth and the adventitious roots are of equal length and importance. In spite of this limitation roots of such plants often attain a length of many feet in suitable soils. This type of root system is common in Monocotyledons where, as a rule, no thickening of the root takes place since cambium is absent, but it is seen in many other herbaceous plants and induced in many plants in gardens by transplanting, propagation by cuttings and layering, and so on.

While the variations in roots are not so obvious as in aerial portions of plants the observant gardener may nevertheless find many characteristic differences. The coarseness of roots of many bulbous plants and differences in their capacity for branching, the thickness of roots of many xerophytic plants, the fine roots of ferns and many peat plants, often combined in the latter with a pinkish coloration at their tips, the distinct colouring of certain roots such as the yellow roots of Berberis, the characteristic odour of others such as the Acacias will often give a guide to the plant being handled and in some instances suggestions for the best types of soil, methods of potting, and so on.

While the two principal functions of roots are absorption from and anchorage in the soil, many roots are fitted to perform these functions in special circumstances and also to take on other duties. Roots which serve as special means of support are well seen in Pandanus, some Palms, and species of Ficus which spring from the stem at some distance above the soil surface and grow down more or less obliquely to the earth acting as pillars to take the weight of the tree. Aerial roots for the absorption of moisture from the air are seen in many Orchids and in many Araceae. In the latter these roots often elongate sufficiently to enter the soil and perform their functions more normally. A curious instance is afforded by Selaginellas where special organs (rhizophores) are produced by the stems; these grow vertically downwards and form roots when they reach the earth. Roots also may act as clasping and climbing organs as they do in many Araceae, Ivy, Ficus, Metrosideros, and in many climbing Ferns. A special instance of root growth is afforded by some Tree ferns which produce many roots from their stems, provided they are in a sufficiently humid atmosphere, which ramify among the scales and fibres of old leaf bases on the stems and obtain food materials and water for the plant from this environment. As already noted parasitic plants such as Cuscuta, Viscum, Rhinanthus, Lathraea, and Orobanche send special sucker roots into living stems or roots of their host plants. Myrmecophilous plants (q.v.) often provide hollowed roots in which their partner ants live and the roots of Leguminoseae provide nodules for their partner bacteria.

The most marked modification of roots for special purposes is perhaps seen in storage roots. The roots of trees and many perennial herbaceous plants contain reserve food and frequently the form is greatly altered for this purpose as seen in Beet, Carrot, Parsnip, Dahlia, terrestrial Orchids, Dandelion, Horseradish, *Ranunculus Ficaria*, some Anemones, &c.

In perennial and biennial plants with basal leaf-rosettes the main root not infrequently contracts in length as it ages and so draws the crown of the plant, which would naturally with growth of the axis be gradually raised above soil level, down to about the surface of the soil. Contractile roots of a special type are seen also in some plants with corms or bulbs which are annually drawn down to about a uniform depth by their action. The new Crocus corm, e.g. formed above the old one, is so drawn down each year.

A few roots, including the aerial roots of Orchids, contain chlorophyll and thus play the part of assimilatory organs.

Buds are formed adventitiously on many roots, sometimes normally as in Anemone, Rheum, Populus, *Convolvulus arvensis*, Dandelion, Horseradish, and so on, sometimes, or more readily, after injury as in Prunus and Malus. The faculty of producing buds from roots is possessed by a considerable number of plants and made wide use of in propagating plants. *See* **Root-cuttings.**

Reference has been made to the essential character of a fibrous root system for the production of healthy trees, &c. To attain such a system a suitable rooting medium is necessary. Except for aquatic and Bog plants thorough drainage is requisite, for stagnant water prevents respiration and the finer roots are the first to suffer. Many trees may withstand a wet condition of soil for perhaps 6 weeks in winter and possibly 3 weeks in summer, but not for more and some for less than that. The practice of standing pots in a basin or saucer of water to avoid frequent watering, while less common than formerly, is, unhappily, still practiced and many pot-plants succumb or suffer only a lingering existence because of it, for it inevitably interferes with proper root respiration. Another cause of damage to roots is the presence of so much lime or soda that the soil is alkaline. The whole family of Ericaceae suffers from this and so do many plants when planted near the sea. Most fruit-trees, however, are the better for a somewhat alkaline soil or at least for a neutral soil condition and this applies especially to Stone-fruit. A loose soil into which roots can easily penetrate suits most plants with thick roots, but others, especially the Vine and Fig and indeed most fruits, give the best results when the soil is firm. They then produce a mass of fibrous roots followed by short-jointed, sturdy wood, capable of producing satisfactory crops. Care must be exercised in cultivating land under trees lest the roots should be mutilated. In fact, in some plants, such as Raspberries and Rhododendrons anything more than surface cultivation is very injurious as the best roots are sure to be destroyed. Care in transplanting that the fine fibrous root system is disturbed as little as possible is always desirable and from the time of lifting until replanting roots should be kept moist. If they are allowed to become dry or damaged by exposure to frost between lifting and planting a serious check is bound to follow.

ROOT, BITTER. *See* **Lewisia rediviva.**

ROOT CUTTINGS. Many plants are capable of forming adventitious buds upon their roots. This may occur normally, but is probably more commonly seen after a root has been injured. This capacity for forming buds on roots is made use of in propagation. A length of root is cut and inserted in sandy soil kept moist and at a suitable temperature according to the type of plant. The production of the bud takes place at the end of the piece of root which was nearest to the stem, roots being formed at the other end; this in spite of the direction towards which the piece of root has been inserted. With thick roots it is well to plant vertically and when making the cutting to cut square at the end nearest to the parent stem, slanting at the other end, so that there is no doubt as to the way the cutting should be inserted in the soil. Thick roots are used in propagating, for example, *Papaver orientale*, *Anchusa azurea*, Horseradish, and Seakale. The pieces of the first 2 are usually 1 to 1½ in. long, of the others 3½ in. upwards. The root-cuttings of, for example, *Phlox decussata*, Gaillardia, and Drosera sp. are quite thin and are usually about 1 in. long and strewn on the moist sand in the propagating pan and lightly covered with sand. Romneya, *Acanthus mollis*, *Anemone hupehensis* and its varieties, *A. sylvestris*, *Euphorbia Cyparissias*, Bouvardias, some Pelargoniums, Apple stocks, some Plums, Poplars are among the plants that are readily propagated by root-cuttings. As a rule root-cuttings reproduce the parent true to type but in some instances where the parent is a periclinal chimera the exact type of plant produced depends upon whether the bud develops from the outer or the inner tissues of the root-cutting. The faculty of producing buds on roots may prove a nuisance in the garden as it does with *Convolvulus arvensis*, every broken piece of root being capable of reproducing the plant, the common Docks, the Dandelion, most Plums, and some Apples where shoots arise from roots injured in cultivation. *See also* **Propagation.**

ROOT GRAFTING. Propagation by grafting in which a piece of root only is used as the stock, the scion being a piece of the current year's wood of the plant it is desired to increase. Hybrid Clematises are often propagated on roots of *C. Vitalba* or *C. Viticella*, varieties of *Paeonia suffruticosa* on roots of *P. officinalis*, Rhododendrons on roots of *R. ponticum* and so on. Apples may also be grafted on roots of the selected stock and as this work can be done under cover during winter, the method is not infrequently employed in countries with a long, snowy winter. The type of graft is either the cleft or the whip and as the cut surfaces will be buried as soon as the graft is completed, only tying is needed.

ROOT HAIRS. Unicellular outgrowths from the outer layer of cells of the root a short distance behind the growing point. Their function is to absorb water and substances dissolved therein from the soil and incidentally to assist in anchoring the plant firmly. Their life is of short duration and they are continually renewed as on the newly formed part of the root it pushes forward through the soil. They are extremely fine, much finer than the root on which they are produced. The roots of almost all land plants produce root-hairs, but they are usually absent or few from the roots of water plants and from those of small-leaved flowering plants (when their presence is often compensated for by mycorrhiza (q.v.)), and from saprophytes as well as from aerial roots (unless they come in contact with a moist surface) such as those of Orchids.

ROOT-KNOT EELWORM (*Heterodera marioni*). This microscopic eelworm is a pest primarily of glasshouse crops, especially Cucumber, Tomato, and Lettuce, upon the roots of which it produces swellings varying in size from a pin's head to a walnut. These root galls often coalesce to produce distorted, misshapen root systems. The male eelworm retains its shape throughout its life, but the female swells into a glistening, white, pear-shaped body or cyst, which is just visible to the naked eye and is found within the galled tissue. A single female may lay from 300 to 1,200 eggs, which are present in a gelatinous mass adhering to the body. On hatching, some of the larval eelworms penetrate deeper into the galled tissue, others move to new roots, while others may descend to 3 ft. or more in the soil and are capable of surviving for many weeks or months according to the conditions. This pest is most serious in light and open glasshouse borders, and may even survive in the open in more favourable districts and attack the roots of herbs, Carrot, Parsnip, and Celery. These outdoor infections usually arise from soil from Tomato borders which has been removed from a glasshouse and spread over the vegetable garden. An indoor Tomato crop, though heavily infected, may produce a satisfactory crop of fruit provided that conditions for plant growth are good and a top-dressing is given into which surface roots may penetrate, but diseased plants invariably wilt more readily during warm weather owing to the failure of the deeper roots to act. This eelworm is practically cosmopolitan, and has a very wide range of host plants, both cultivated and wild. Unlike the closely related Beet and Potato Eelworm, *H. rostochiensis* (q.v.), the Root-knot Eelworm has no specialized races or strains, and attacks indiscriminately any one of its very numerous host plants.

The most effective method of treating infected soil is by steam sterilization and, though the initial cost of sterilizing outfits is heavy, the operation is effective and essential in commercial concerns. Diseased roots should be lifted carefully and burned since any galled portion left in the soil will act as a source of infection to succeeding crops. All weeds occurring in infected glasshouse borders should be cleared out and destroyed for they serve as 'bridging hosts' from one season to another. Chemical control by the use of Formaldehyde and Cresylic acid is only partially successful owing to the difficulty of reaching the eelworms or their eggs within galled tissues or in lumps of dry soil. Infected Tomato plants may be induced to complete their growth by mulching with peat to induce surface rooting. It should be remembered that the eelworm is readily dispersed on the roots of young plants, on tools, boxes, pots, and on the feet of workmen walking over infected borders, and all such possible sources of infection should be guarded against.

G. F. W.

ROOT OF SCARCITY. Name once applied to the Mangel-wurzel (*Beta vulgaris macrorhiza*, q.v.).

ROOT, PAINT. *See* **Lachnanthes tinctoria.**

ROOT-PRUNING. The pruning of roots is sometimes resorted to when a fruit-tree is making rampant growth and bearing little or no fruit. Judicious root-pruning will check excessive growth and tends to throw the trees into a fruit-bearing condition. The process is now superseded to a large extent by bark-ringing or constriction by means of a ring of wire. In carrying out root-pruning the size of the tree and other conditions must be considered. In dealing with a large tree which has not been disturbed for many years it is advisable to root-prune only one side at a time. To do it all round at once would be to risk severe injury the effects of which would be seen over many years and might result in death. In dealing with a large tree a deep trench should be dug about as far from the stem as the branches extend or with trained trees 8 to 12 ft. away from the trunk. The trench should be deep enough to enable all the roots extending laterally to be cut through. Afterwards, with a fork the soil should be worked from amongst the roots towards the trunk and roots striking directly downwards should be cut; other roots should be carefully preserved and kept moist. When all the roots nearly to the trunk are bared, those badly injured should be cut back and then all laid evenly in the soil again, using fresh soil if possible. The soil should be trodden firmly to encourage the development of fibrous roots near the surface. In 2 years the other side of the tree may be similarly treated.

Smaller trees may be lifted bodily and all the long straggling roots cut back, and replanted, thus checking superabundant growth. In nurseries specimen trees are lifted every 2 years to ensure good balls of earth being attached to the roots when they are finally transplanted.

As with all pruning the cuts made should be clean and bruising should be avoided.

ROOT-ROTS. The roots of plants, whether woody or fleshy, may be attacked by bacteria or fungi which cause rapid or slow rotting of the tissues. Fleshy roots such as beet, carrot, turnip, &c., may develop soft rots such as are caused by *Bacterium carotovorum* and similar organisms or may show a hard dry rot such as results from the attack of *Phoma lingam* on swedes and *Alternaria radicina* on carrots. On the other hand, large trees and shrubs suffer root-rots chiefly due to *Armillaria mellea*, the Honey fungus (q.v.), but in some cases resulting from smaller fungi such as *Verticillium dahliae*, *Rosellinia necatrix*, &c. Rotting of the roots in small herbaceous plants may be due to various fungi; in seedlings the condition is often called damping off (q.v.) and various fungi such as Pythium spp., Phytophthora spp., *Rhizoctonia solani*, and Fusarium spp. are held responsible. In some plants, especially Tomatoes, seedling root-rots are followed by several other root diseases due to such fungi as species of Verticillium, Colletotrichum, and Fusarium, which may weaken or destroy large and mature plants. Probably the most notable of these is the Sleepy disease of Tomatoes due to *Verticillium alboatrum* (*see* **Tomato diseases**). Many root-rots are primarily due to unsuitable soil conditions such as waterlogging, &c., which weaken the roots and render them liable to attack from soil fungi such as Fusarium spp. which would not enter healthy roots. Similarly where a root system suffers mechanical injury many fungi and bacteria may enter the wounded parts and be able to destroy them.

ROOTLET. A very slender root or branch of a root.

ROOTSTOCK. (1) A rhizome or other underground stem from which the aerial branches spring, the separate parts of which are capable of separate existence. (2) The stock upon which a scion is grafted.

ROOT-SUCKERS. Shoots which proceed from the root of a plant as distinct from underground stems as seen, for example, in plums, many poplars, and some apple-root stocks. At times they provide a method of increase.

ror'idus -a -um, dewy.

RORIP'A (Latinized form of old Saxon name Rorippen.) FAM. *Cruciferae*. A genus of about 50 branching, glabrous, or hairy herbs of various habits, terrestrial or aquatic, natives of the temperate and warmer regions of the N. Hemisphere. Leaves entire or variously lobed or pinnatisect. Flowers white or yellow, small. Pods short or long. SYN. Radicula.

R. Nasturtium-aquaticum. Watercress. Hardy perennial. Stem much-branched, sometimes short and creeping or floating in shallow water, sometimes scrambling on banks or bushes and 2 ft. or more long. *l.* pinnate; lflets. 3 to 11, roundish or oblong, nearly entire. *fl.* white, small, in short racemes. June. Europe, including Britain, W. Asia, introduced in N. America, &c., and apt to choke New Zealand rivers. (E.B. 125 as *Nasturtium officinale.*) SYN. *R. officinalis. See* **Watercress.**

R. officina'lis. A synonym of *R. Nasturtium-aquaticum.*

rorulen'tus -a -um, dewy.

RO'SA (ancient Latin name). FAM. *Rosaceae*. A genus of about 125 species recognized by recent authors of which 95 are Asiatic, 18 American, the remainder chiefly natives of Europe or NW. Africa. Great variation and frequent occurrence of hybrids has led to many thousands of forms receiving specific or varietal Latin names. They occur throughout the N. Hemisphere from Alaska and Siberia, south to Mexico, S. India, the Philippine Is., and Abyssinia.

Shrubs, generally with prickly stems, ranging from a few inches to many feet in height, in many instances climbers. Leaves alternate, generally deciduous, odd-pinnate and stipulate (except *R. persica*). Flowers solitary or up to 100 or more in corymbs at ends of short growths of the current year; sepals and petals 5 (except 4 in *R. sericea* and *R. omeiensis*); sepals usually persistent on fruit, often pinnate; stamens and styles numerous, latter surrounded by receptacle which becomes fleshy at maturity to form the hip, enclosing few to many bony achenes ('seeds').

They are plants of considerable garden ornament for their plentiful flowers, white or some tone of pink or red, from May to July, often followed by decorative red fruits in autumn and winter. Some are useful for informal hedges (e.g. *R. virginiana*, *R. nutkana*), others for rock-gardens (*R. Serafinii*, *R. sicula*), pergolas, covering old tree stumps, walls, &c. Not usually particular in requirements, some enjoy heavy soils and those containing lime, others thrive in poor sandy ground, a few in damp situations. Propagation is by seeds (leading frequently to variation or hybrid forms), suckers, if the form is on its own roots, cuttings inserted in late summer, preferably in frames, budding in July, or grafting under glass in early spring.

The dried petals of *R. gallica officinalis* have been used in France since the 14th century for conserves, potpourri, &c., *R. damascena* is cultivated in SE. Europe for attar of roses, *R. moschata* in India for essential oil. The hips of *R. canina* are a source of vitamin C and may be made into jam or jelly, like those of *R. rugosa*, *R. villosa*, and other species. **A**

For treatment of Roses of the florists' types *see* **Rose.**

KEY

1. *Lvs. pinnate with stipules* 2
1. *Lvs. simple, without stipules* R. persica
2. *Styles much protruded beyond mouth of receptacle* 3
2. *Styles not or scarcely protruded* 28
3. *Styles united into a column about as long as stamens* 4
3. *Styles free, about half as long as stamens* 25
4. *Stipules entire or toothed only. Prickles scattered* 5
4. *Stipules comb-like. Prickles mostly beneath stipules* R. multiflora
5. *Growth trailing or prostrate* 6
5. *Growth erect at first, then arching or climbing* 9
6. *Lvs. evergreen or nearly so, shining* 7
6. *Lvs. deciduous, greyish beneath; lflets. usually* 7 R. arvensis
7. *Lflets.* 7 *or* 9, *blunt, under* 1 *in. long* 8
7. *Lflets., usually* 5, *acuminate,* 1 *to* 2 *in. long* R. sempervirens
8. *Lflets.* 7 *or* 9. *Fl.* $1\frac{1}{2}$ *to* 2 *in. across* R. Wichuraiana
8. *Lflets.* 5 *or* 7. *Fl.* $\frac{3}{4}$ *to* $1\frac{1}{4}$ *in. across* R. Luciae
9. *Lflets.* 3 *or* 5, *hairy on veins beneath* 10
9. *Lflets.* 5 *to* 9 12
10. *Lflets. ovate to ovate-lanceolate* 11
10. *Lflets. linear-lanceolate* R. Watsoniana
11. *Fl. pink,* 2 *in. across* R. setigera
11. *Fl. white, smaller, double* R. triphylla
12. *Lflets. acute or acuminate, over* 1 *in. long. Climbers* 13
12. *Lflets. blunt or almost so, up to* 1 *in. long, greyish* R. Soulieana
13. *Lflets. hairy at least beneath, sometimes only on veins* 14
13. *Lflets. glabrous or nearly so* 18
14. *Lflets. hairy chiefly on veins beneath* 15
14. *Lflets. hairy all over beneath. Fr. subglobose, about* $\frac{3}{8}$ *in. long* 17
15. *Lflets.* 5 *or* 7 16
15. *Lflets.* 7 *or* 9. *Fr. ovoid, about* $\frac{1}{2}$ *in. long* R. Helenae
16. *Lflets.* 5, *purple when young. Fr. globose, about* $\frac{1}{3}$ *in. long* R. Ernestii
16. *Lflets.* 5 *or* 7, *blunt. Fr. ovoid,* $\frac{1}{2}$ *in. long* R. phoenicea
17. *Lflets. usually* 5, *glabrous above* R. Rubus
17. *Lflets. usually* 7, *hairy above* R. Brunonii
18. *Lflets. usually* 5, *up to* 3 *in. long, greyish beneath* R. cerasocarpa
18. *Lflets. usually* 5 *or* 7, *sometimes* 9, *green beneath* 19
19. *Fl.* $\frac{3}{4}$ *to* 2 *in. across* 20
19. *Fl. white,* 3 *in. across* R. Leschenaultii
20. *Fl.* 1 *in. across or less* 21
20. *Fl.* 1 *to* 2 *in. across* 22
21. *Styles glabrous* R. crocacantha
21. *Styles hairy* R. filipes
22. *Lflets.* 2 *to* 3 *in. or more long* 23
22. *Lflets.* 1 *to* 2 *in. long. Fl. buds abruptly narrowed to a point; styles glabrous* R. Maximowiczii
23. *Young shoots reddish* 24
23. *Young shoots olive-green* or *-brown* R. moschata
24. *Fl. buds rounded, short-pointed; sep. as long as pet.* R. sinowilsonii
24. *Fl. buds long-pointed; sep. longer than pet.* R. longicuspis
25. *Evergreen or almost so* 26
25. *Deciduous. Fl. many in a corymb* R. Noisettiana
26. *Fl.* 2 *to* 3 *in. across* 27
26. *Fl.* 4 *to* 5 *in. across, white or pale yellow, solitary* R. gigantea
27. *Lflets.* 3 *or* 5 R. chinensis
27. *Lflets.* 5 *or* 7 R. odorata
28. *Stipules small, free or adnate only at base* 29
28. *Stipules adnate more than half their length* 33
29. *Shoots glabrous* 30
29. *Shoots hairy. Fl. with large bracts at base* R. bracteata
30. *Receptacles and pedicels not prickly or bristly* 31
30. *Receptacles and pedicels bristly* R. laevigata
31. *Fl. white, double, about* 3 *in. across* R. Fortuniana
31. *Fl. small, white or yellow* 32
32. *Branches unarmed or almost so* R. Banksiae
32. *Branches slender with hooked prickles* R. cymosa
33. *Receptacle smooth or hispid only* 34
33. *Receptacle prickly* 118
34. *Lflets. on flowering branches* 3 *or* 5 35
34. *Lflets. on flowering branches* 5 *to* 11 40
35. *Lflets. glandular-toothed. Prickles very unequal* 36
35. *Lflets. simply toothed, not glandular. Prickles equal* R. damascena
36. *Lflets. firm, leathery. Pedicels erect* 37
36. *Lflets. thin, teeth sometimes simple. Pedicel nodding* 38
37. *Stem densely bristly and prickly. Fr. brick-red, subglobose* R. gallica
37. *Stem with hooked prickles. Fr. ovate, orange-red* R. collina
38. *Fl. large* 39
38. *Fl. small. Prickles paired* R. sancta
39. *Prickles straight. Fl. double* R. centifolia
39. *Prickles hooked. Receptacle smooth* R. Richardii
40. *Fl. usually in corymbs or bracteate* 41
40. *Fl. usually solitary, without bracts* 107
41. *Prickles of one kind, usually hooked. Sometimes with glandular bristles* 42
41. *Prickles usually straight, bristles if present at base of stem* 59
42. *Lvs. more or less glandular or with glandular teeth* 43
42. *Lvs. not glandular* 52
43. *Prickles slender, straight or almost so. Lflets. hairy* 44
43. *Prickles hooked. Lvs. glabrous or hairy beneath* 47
44. *Sep. upright, persistent. Fl. large, over* $\frac{3}{4}$ *in. across* 45
44. *Sep. deciduous. Fr. smaller* R. tomentosa
45. *Shrub of* 6 *ft. Fr.* 1 *in. across, hispid. Lflets. over* 1 *in. long* R. villosa
45. *Shrub dwarf. Fr. smaller* 46
46. *Shoots purplish. Fr. not hispid* R. mollis
46. *Shoots densely hairy. Lflets. up to* $\frac{4}{5}$ *in. long* R. orientalis
47. *Lvs. roundish. Sep. long-lasting; styles hairy* 48
47. *Lvs. ovate to oval, acute. Sep. soon deciduous; styles glabrous* 50
48. *Shrub of* 6 *ft. Prickles strong, hooked* R. Eglanteria
48. *Shrub dwarf. Prickles straight* 49
49. *Prickles about equal. Fl. over* 1 *in. across* R. sicula
49. *Prickles unequal, partly bristly, numerous. Fl. small* R. glutinosa
50. *Shrub of* 6 *ft. Prickles uniform, curved. No bristles* R. micrantha
50. *Shrub dwarf. Prickles not uniform* 51
51. *Lflets.* $\frac{2}{5}$ *to* $\frac{3}{5}$ *in. long. Fl. white* R. horrida
51. *Lflets.* $\frac{1}{5}$ *to* $\frac{2}{5}$ *in. long. Fl. pink* R. Serafini
52. *Styles exserted* R. stylosa
52. *Styles not or only slightly exserted* 53
53. *Lvs. hairy at least beneath* 54
53. *Lvs. glabrous* 55
54. *Shrub to* 10 *ft. Pedicels long. Sep. deciduous* R. corymbifera
54. *Shrub to* 6 *ft. Pedicels short. Sep. long-lasting* R. coriifolia
55. *Lvs. blue-green tinged red, dull above* R. rubrifolia
55. *Lvs. green, shining above* 56
56. *Fl.* 2 *in. or more across* 57
56. *Fl.* $1\frac{1}{2}$ *in. across. Branches smooth, without prickles* R. Montezumae
57. *Prickles stout, hooked. Fl. about* 2 *in. across* R. canina
57. *Prickles slender* 58
58. *Lflets.* 7 *to* 11. *Fl. about* $1\frac{1}{2}$ *in. across* R. britzensis
58. *Lflets.* 3 *to* 7. *Fl.* 2 *to* 3 *in. across* R. marginata
59. *Sep. spreading after flowering, deciduous* 60
59. *Sep. erect after flowering, usually persisting* 64
60. *Stipules flat. Teeth of lvs. rather coarse* 61
60. *Stipules convolute. Teeth of lvs. fine* R. palustris
61. *Lflets.* 7 *to* 11 62
61. *Lflets.* 5 *or* 7, *glabrous or almost so* R. carolina
62. *Prickles beneath stipules usually curved. Lflets.* 7 *or* 9 R. virginica
62. *Prickles beneath stipules usually straight. Lflets.* 7 *to* 11 63
63. *Branches densely bristly. Pedicels* $\frac{1}{2}$ *to* $1\frac{1}{4}$ *in. long* R. nitida
63. *Branches not bristly. Pedicels* $\frac{1}{5}$ *to* $\frac{2}{5}$ *in. long* R. foliolosa
64. *Without prickles below stipules* 65
64. *With prickles below stipules* 72
65. *Shoots and prickles hairy* 66
65. *Shoots and prickles glabrous* 67
66. *Stem stout. Fl.* $2\frac{1}{2}$ *to* $3\frac{1}{2}$ *in. across* R. rugosa
66. *Stem slender. Fl. smaller* R. kamtschatica
67. *Stem bristly* 68
67. *Stem unarmed or weakly bristly when young only* 70
68. *Fl. solitary or few. Lflets.* 3 *to* 7, *or rarely* 9 69
68. *Fl. in corymbs. Lflets.* 7 *to* 11 R. arkansana
69. *Branches often unarmed. Lvs. simply toothed, downy beneath* R. acicularis
69. *Branches bristly. Lvs. doubly toothed, glabrous beneath* R. Engelmannii
70. *Lflets.* 5 *or* 7, *teeth simple. Fr. nearly globose* R. blanda
70. *Lflets.* 7 *or* 9, *teeth double. Fr. usually oblong* 71
71. 10 *to* 12 *ft. h. Stem somewhat prickly* R. oxyodon
71. 3 *to* 5 *ft. h. Stem smooth* R. pendulina
72. *Stipules more or less convolute* 73
72. *Stipules flat* 76
73. *Prickles usually curved* 74
73. *Prickles straight* 75
74. *Lflets.* 5 *or* 7. *Fl. purple, solitary or few. Pedicels smooth* R. cinnamomea
74. *Lflets.* 7 *or* 9. *Fl. white, several. Pedicels glandular* R. laxa
75. *Pedicels* $1\frac{1}{2}$ *in. or more long, glandular* R. davurica
75. *Branches dark purple. Pedicels smooth* R. Marettii
76. *Sep. deciduous with disk. Fl. solitary* 77
76. *Sep. persistent* 80
77. *Stem without bristles. Teeth of lvs. simple* R. Willmottiana
77. *Stem bristly and prickly* 78
78. *Prickles straight* 79
78. *Prickles hooked* R. Beggeriana
79. *Shrub to* 8 *ft. h. Lflets. glabrous. Fl. white* R. gymnocarpa
79. *Shrub to* 3 *ft. Lflets. hairy beneath. Fl. white* R. Alberti
80. *Lflets.* 3 *to* 7. *Branches prickly, not bristly* 81
80. *Lflets.* 7 *to* 13 87

81. *Styles not exserted* 82
81. *Styles exserted* R. corymbulosa
82. *Fl. usually several, less than* 2 *in. across* 83
82. *Fl. solitary,* 2 *in. or more across* R. nutkana
83. *Prickles curved* 84
83. *Prickles straight* 85
84. *Teeth of lvs. simple. Branches upright* R. californica
84. *Teeth of lvs. double. Branches spreading* R. yainacensis
85. *Lflets. downy beneath* 86
85. *Lflets. glabrous, bluish-green* R. Woodsii
86. *Lflets. bright green* R. pisocarpa
86. *Lflets. pale or glaucous beneath* R. Macounii
87. *Fl. in corymbs* 88
87. *Fl. usually solitary or few on short branches* 95
88. *Branches prickly and bristly* 89
88. *Branches prickly or unarmed, not bristly* 90
89. *Teeth of lvs. simple* R. setipoda
89. *Teeth of lvs. double* R. Hemsleyana
90. *Styles exserted* 91
90. *Styles not exserted* 93
91. *Lflets. blunt, up to* $\frac{3}{8}$ *in. long* 92
91. *Lflets. acute,* $1\frac{1}{2}$ *to* $2\frac{1}{2}$ *in. long* R. Davidi
92. *Shrub up to* 10 *ft. h. Corymbs many-fld.* R. multibracteata
92. *Shrub up to* 3 *ft. h. Corymbs up to* 5-*fld.* R. Forrestiana
93. *Lflets.* 7 *or* 9 94
93. *Lflets.* 9 *or* 11, *elliptic-ovate* R. macrophylla
94. *Stem prickly. Fl.* $1\frac{1}{2}$ *to* 2 *in. across. Lvs. glabrous and glaucous beneath* R. caudata
94. *Stem not prickly or scarcely so. Fl. about* 1 *in. across. Lvs. hairy beneath* R. banksiopsis
95. *Styles exserted. Lflets. blunt,* $\frac{1}{3}$ *to* $\frac{1}{2}$ *in. long* R. multibracteata
95. *Styles not exserted* 96
96. *Lflets. hairy beneath, at least on midrib* 97
96. *Lflets. glabrous* 102
97. *Branches with prickles and bristles* 100
97. *Branches with prickles only. Teeth of lvs. simple* 98
98. *Lflets.* 7 *to* 13, $\frac{1}{2}$ *to* $1\frac{1}{2}$ *in. long* R. Moyesii
98. *Lflets. up to* 2 *in. long* 99
99. *Shoots prickly. Fr. up to* $2\frac{1}{4}$ *in. long* R. holodonta
99. *Shoots almost unarmed. Fr. up to* $\frac{3}{4}$ *in. long* R. saturata
100. *Up to* 15 *ft. h. Prickles large. Fl. rose. Fr.* 1 *in. long* R. Sweginzowii
100. *Up to* 8 *ft. h. Prickles slender or straight. Fr. about* $\frac{3}{4}$ *in. long* 101
101. *Lflets.* 5 *or* 7 R. Fedschenkoana
101. *Lflets.* 9 *to* 15 R. Murielae
102. *Lflets. blunt, rounded or oblong,* $\frac{3}{4}$ *to* $\frac{3}{4}$ *in. long* 103
102. *Lflets. acute, elliptic or ovate,* $\frac{1}{2}$ *to* 1 *in. long* R. bella
103. *Lflets. toothed above middle. Pedicels short* R. Webbiana
103. *Lflets. sharply toothed from below middle. Pedicels up to over* 1 *in. long* 104
104. *Lvs. glandular* R. sertata
104. *Lvs. hairy at least on veins beneath* 105
105. *Lflets.* 7 *or* 9 106
105. *Lflets.* 11 *to* 15, *finely hairy on midrib* R. Prattii
106. *Lflets. hairy on both sides, teeth simple* R. Giraldi
106. *Lflets. glaucous, hairy on midrib beneath, teeth often double* R. elegantula
107. *Pet.* 5*; styles not exserted. Prickles scattered* 108
107. *Pet.* 4, *rarely* 5; *fl. white* 117
108. *Lflets. usually* 9. *Prickles straight. Sep. entire* 109
108. *Lflets.* 5 *or* 7. *Prickles hooked. Outer sep. pinnate* 115
109. *Flowering branches prickly and bristly* 110
109. *Flowering branches not prickly or bristly* 112
110. *Internodes short* 111
110. *Internodes long. Branches acutely angled* R. pimpinellifolia
111. *Shoots brown. Lflets. glabrous beneath. Fr. black* R. spinosissima
111. *Shoots red. Lflets. woolly beneath. Fr. red* R. koreana
112. *Lvs. without glands* 113
112. *Lvs. glandular, fragrant* 114
113. *Shoots bristly. Lvs. glabrous* R. Hugonis
113. *Shoots not bristly. Lvs. hairy at first* R. xanthina
114. *Fl. about* 1 *in. across, golden yellow. Fr. red* R. Ecae
114. *Fl. about* $1\frac{1}{2}$ *in. across, pale yellow. Fr. maroon* R. Primula
115. *Prickles hooked* 116
115. *Prickles straight. Fl. deep yellow, odour unpleasant* R. foetida
116. *Climber to* 10 *ft. h. Fl. double* R. hemisphaerica
116. 2 *to* 5 *ft. h. Fl. single* R. Rapinii
117. *Lflets.* 9 *or* 11, *almost glabrous. Fr. red, pedicel thickened* R. omeiensis
117. *Lflets.* 7 *to* 11, *silky beneath. Pedicel not thickened* R. sericea
118. *Lflets.* 3 *to* 7, *wedge-shaped-obovate* 119
118. *Lflets.* 7 *to* 15, *elliptic to elliptic-oblong* 120
119. *About* 2 *ft. h., young shoots with starry hairs* R. stellata
119. *About* 5 *ft. h., shoots without starry hairs* R. mirifica
120. *Lflets. up to* 1 *in. long. Sep. pinnate* R. Roxburghii
120. *Lflets. up to* $2\frac{1}{4}$ *in. long. Sep. not pinnate* R. praelucens

R. acicula'ris. About 3 ft. h., erect, densely bristly; prickles straight, slender. *lflets.* 3 to 7, elliptic to oblong, downy beneath, simply toothed; stalks glabrous or slightly hairy; stipules broad. *fl.* pink, $1\frac{1}{2}$ to 2 in. across, solitary, fragrant; pet. obovate, notched; receptacle and usually pedicels glabrous or sometimes glandular. May, June. *fr.* red, often pear shaped, $\frac{1}{2}$ to $\frac{3}{4}$ in. long. Canada, N. United States, NE. Asia. 1805. (W.R. 147, 149.) SYN. *R. Bourgeauiana, R. Sayi.* var. **Engelman'nii,** *see* **R. Engelmannii; nipponen'sis,** pedicels glandular-bristly, *fr.* ovoid, *lflets.* 7 or 9, simply toothed, glabrous, stalks bristly. E. Asia. 1894. (B.M. 7646.) SYN. *R. nipponensis*; **Schrenkia'na,** pedicels shorter, $\frac{3}{4}$ to $1\frac{1}{4}$ in. long, receptacle densely glandular, *lflets.* 3 or 5, branches without bristles. Cent. Asia. SYN. *R. Schrenkiana.*

R. × al'ba.* (*R. canina × R. damascena*). 6 to 8 ft. h.; stems stout, few, upright or arching; prickles hooked, scattered. *lflets.* 5 or 7, ovate to oblong, simply toothed, grey-green, upturned at edges, hairy beneath; stalk glandular, hairy. *fl.* white, single or double, $2\frac{1}{2}$ to 3 in. across, fragrant, in small corymbs; sep. pinnate, deciduous, glandular on back; pedicels glandular. June. *fr.* oblong, red, 1 in. long. Origin unknown. Cultivated in England in 16th century, and much earlier in Italy. (W.R. 409, 411.) A long-lived shrub. var. **incarna'ta,** *fl.* double, pink. (W.R. 413.) Many garden roses of merit and marked fragrance belong here. var. **suaveo'lens**, largely grown in SE. Europe, is one of the chief sources of Attar of Roses.

R. Albert'i. 3 ft. h.; branches numerous, long, arching; prickles small, straight, often paired, mixed with bristles. *lflets.* 7 or 9, orbicular to elliptic, usually hairy only on veins beneath, margin glandular, teeth compound; stalk hairy. *fl.* white, 1 to 3, 1 to $1\frac{1}{2}$ in. across; buds long, pointed; sep. usually entire, glabrous or glandular on back, deciduous with disk; pet. slightly notched; pedicels glandular. June. *fr.* ovoid, smooth, $\frac{3}{4}$ in. long, neck narrow. E. Turkestan. 1877. Allied to *R. Willmottiae* and *R. Beggeriana*; perhaps not now in cultivation.

R. alpi'na. A synonym of *R. pendulina.*

R. alta'ica. A variety of *R. pimpinellifolia.*

R. amblyo'tis. A synonym of *R. davurica.*

R. andegaven'sis. A variety of *R. canina.*

R. Anderson'ii. A variety of *R. collina.*

R. anemoneflo'ra. A synonym of *R. triphylla.* **A**

R. × anemonoi'des* (*R. laevigata × R. odorata*?). Vigorous climber, needing a warm wall in most districts. *lflets.* 3, or sometimes 5, glabrous, shining; stipules half free. *fl.* pale pink, single, 3 in. across, on bristly pedicels; receptacle slightly prickly. Originated at Erfurt, Germany, before 1896. (W.R. 121 as *R. laevigata × R. chinensis.*) SYN. *R. sinica Anemone.* **Ramona** is a form with carmine pet. Origin in California. 1913.

R. arkansa'na. 2 ft. h.; stems prickly and bristly. *lflets.* 9 or 11, elliptic, 1 to 2 in. long, acute, sharply toothed, shining above, glabrous on both sides or hairy on veins beneath. *fl.* bright pink, $1\frac{1}{2}$ in. across, in corymbs; sep. glabrous or glandular on back, reflexed, outer often pinnate; pedicels glabrous. June, July. *fr.* subglobose, $\frac{1}{2}$ in. wide, red. Cent. and W. United States. 1917. SYN. *R. blanda arkansana, R. suffulta.* Related to *R. acicularis*, but dwarfer, and flowering for a longer period on suckers as well as on laterals.

R. arven'sis. Stems 5 to 10 ft. long, trailing, purplish, glaucous; prickles stout, uniform, strongly hooked. *lflets.* 5 or 7, ovate to elliptic, glabrous, or hairy on midrib beneath, or sparsely on both sides, deeply toothed. *fl.* white or pink, 1 to $1\frac{1}{2}$ in. across, scentless, solitary or in few-fld. corymbs; sep. oval, much shorter than pet., pointed, smooth on back, deciduous; styles united in a column, glabrous. June, July. *fr.* ovoid or oblong, up to $\frac{3}{4}$ in. long, bright red. Europe, Asiatic Turkey. 1750. (B.M. 2054 as *R. capreolata*; W.R. 11.) SYN. *R. repens.* Parent of the Ayrshire Roses.

R. Banks'iae.* Banksian Rose. Vigorous climber to 20 ft. or more, almost devoid of prickles or bristles. *lflets.* 3 to 5, oblong-lanceolate, 1 to over 2 in. long, obtuse or acute, often waved, hairy on midrib beneath, teeth simple; stalk usually glabrous. *fl.* white or yellow, single or double, numerous, small; sep. entire, pointed, reflexing, deciduous; receptacle hemispherical; pedicels glabrous or hairy, very slender. May, June. *fr.* globose, $\frac{1}{4}$ in. wide, red. China. 1796. var. **albo-ple'na,** *fl.* white, double, fragrant. 1807. (B.M. 1954; B.R. 397); **lu'tea,*** *fl.* yellow, double, less fragrant than *albo-plena.* 1824. (B.R. 1105.) Needs a sunny wall. **A**

R. banksiop'sis. 6 to 10 ft. h.; stems upright, reddish-purple; prickles few, sometimes paired. *lflets.* 7 to 9, oblong, 1 in. or more long, glabrous, or downy beneath, teeth simple. *fl.* rose-red, 1 in. across, in umbellate corymbs; sep. leafy at tip, longer than pet., glabrous on back, persistent; pedicels glabrous. June, July. *fr.* flask-shaped, orange-red. W. China. 1907. (W.R. 505.) Scarcely distinct from *R. caudata.*

R. Beggeria'na. 5 to 8 ft. h., sometimes climbing; branches bristly at base; prickles unequal, hooked, flattened, often paired. *lflets.* 5 to 9, oval to elliptic, glabrous or hairy beneath, $\frac{1}{2}$ to $1\frac{1}{2}$ in. long, fragrant, teeth glandular, simple or compound. *fl.* white, rarely pink or yellowish, usually in few-fld. corymbs; buds long-pointed; sep. usually entire, glabrous, hairy, or glandular, deciduous; pedicels $\frac{1}{2}$ in. long. June, July. *fr.* nearly globose, $\frac{1}{2}$ in. long, smooth, red. Temperate Asia. 1868. (W.R. 171.) SYN. *R. cabulica.* Allied to *R. Willmottiae* but prickles hooked, *fl.* usually white, stems bristly.

R. bel'la. 6 to 10 ft. h.; stems bristly at base; prickles few, slender, straight. *lflets.* 7 to 9, elliptic or ovate, glaucescent, glabrous, glandular on midrib beneath, teeth simple. *fl.* bright rose, fragrant, 1 to 3 together, $1\frac{1}{2}$ to 2 in. across; sep. leafy at tip, shorter than pet., glandular on back; pet. obcordate; short pedicels, bracts and fr. glandular. June. *fr.* elliptic-ovate, as long as pedicel, tapering, orange-scarlet. N. China. 1910. Closely allied to *R. Moyesii* but distinct by pink fl., smaller lflets., bristly stems, &c. var. **mongol'ica,** *lflets.* more numerous, smaller, downy beneath; **pal'lens,** *fl.* pale rose.

Rosa Banksiae (p. 1811)

R. berberifo'lia. A synonym of *R. persica.*

R. blan'da. 4 to 6 ft. h.; almost unarmed or with scattered, straight, deciduous prickles. *lflets.* 5 or 7, elliptic or oblong, blunt, pale, finely downy beneath, coarsely, simply toothed; stipules large. *fl.* rose-pink, 1 to 3, 2 in. across; pedicels and receptacle smooth. May, June. *fr.* subglobose, $\frac{1}{2}$ in. wide, red. Eastern and Cent. N. America. 1773. (W.R. 307.) Related to *R. pendulina.*

R. Blondaea'na. A variety of *R. canina.*

R. × borbonia'na.* (*R. chinensis* × *R. damascena*). Stems stout, upright; prickles strong, hooked. *lflets.* 5 to 7, acute, glossy, slightly hairy beneath, teeth simple. *fl.* rose-pink, usually semi-double, solitary or in few-fld. corymbs; pedicels and back of sep. glandular. Originated in Réunion (Isle de Bourbon). 1817. (W.R. 339 as *R. borbonica.*) Parent of Hybrid Perpetuals. Includes many good garden roses.

R. Bourgeauia'na. A synonym of *R. acicularis.*

R. bractea'ta.* Macartney Rose. 6 to 12 ft. h., rambling; branches hairy; prickles strong, recurved, often paired. *lflets.* 5 to 9, obovate, $\frac{3}{4}$ to $1\frac{1}{2}$ in. long, slightly toothed, shining, glabrous; stipules nearly free, laciniate. *fl.* white, large, solitary, terminal, delicately fragrant; sep. and short pedicels densely hairy; bracts large, surrounding cal. July, August. *fr.* globose, orange-red, $1\frac{1}{4}$ in. long, hairy. China. 1793. (B.M. 1377.) Naturalized in SE. United States. Rather tender in Britain. Has yielded some fine garden roses by hybridizing, including Mermaid.

R. britzen'sis. 4 to 6 ft. h., with a few, upright stems; prickles few, slender, varying in size. *lflets.* 7 to 11, ovate to elliptic, 1 to $1\frac{1}{2}$ in. long, glabrous except for a few glands on stalk and midrib beneath, teeth usually simple. *fl.* pale pink, becoming white, solitary, about 3 in. across, sep. 1 in. long, shorter than pet., glandular-bristly without, outer pinnate, persistent; pet. deeply notched; receptacle and pedicels glandular-bristly. May, June. *fr.* ovoid, 1 in. long, deep blood red. Kurdistan. 1901. Closely related to *R. marginata.*

R. Brunon'ii.* Himalayan Musk Rose. Strong climber of 10 to 25 ft. or more, branches usually hairy and glandular when young; prickles stout, hooked. *lflets.* 5 or 7, elliptic- or lanceolate-oblong, 1 to 2 in. long, acuminate, softly hairy, especially beneath, teeth fine; stalk downy and prickly. *fl.* white, 1 to 2 in. across, fragrant, in many-fld. corymbs; sep. narrow-lanceolate, sparsely hairy and glandular on back, reflexed, deciduous; pedicels slightly hairy and glandular. June, July. *fr.* ovate, $\frac{1}{3}$ in. wide, brown. Himalaya. 1822. (B.R. 829 as *R. moschata nepalensis.*) Nearly allied to *R. moschata.*

R. cabu'lica. A synonym of *R. Beggeriana.*

R. californ'ica. 4 to 8 ft. h.; branches upright, sometimes bristly; prickles stout, recurved, usually paired below l. *lflets.* 5 or 7, broadly elliptic to oblong, usually blunt, dull with appressed hairs above, hairy beneath, occasionally glandular, teeth simple. *fl.* pink, $1\frac{1}{2}$ in. across, in corymbs; sep. leafy, toothed at tips; pet. obcordate, $\frac{3}{4}$ to 1 in. long; pedicels usually hairy and glandular. June, July. *fr.* globose or ovoid, with a neck, up to $\frac{3}{4}$ in. wide. California. 1878. Very variable in pubescence, number of fl., and shape of fr. var. **bidenticula'ta,** *lflets.* usually $\frac{1}{2}$ in. long, glandular, coarsely toothed, stems slender, upright, about 2 ft. long; **na'na,** a dwarf form, otherwise like type; **ple'na,** *fl.* semi-double. (W.R. 223.)

R. × calocarp'a* (*R. chinensis* × *R. rugosa*). 7 to 10 ft. h., robust, upright; prickles dense, straight, mixed with bristles. *fl.* rose-red, single, smaller than in *R. rugosa*, in large corymbs; sep. glandular, bristly, finally deciduous; pedicels bristly. June, July. *fr.* numerous, globose, bright red. September to November. Originated in France. Before 1891. (W.R. 189, 191.)

R. cani'na. Dog Rose. 6 to 10 ft. h.; branches long, arching. *lflets.* 5 or 7, oval to elliptic, glabrous or thinly hairy, acute, sharply toothed. *fl.* white to deep pink, solitary or clustered; sep. usually glabrous, reflexed, pinnate; styles hairy. June. *fr.* ovoid to nearly globose, scarlet, disk conspicuous. Europe (including Britain). (W.R. 379, 380.) A very variable species. var. **andegaven'sis,** *lflets.* glabrous, teeth usually simple, without glands, sep. and pedicels glandular. Europe, Turkey, Syria. Syn. *R. andegavensis*; **Anderson'ii,** *see* **R. collina**; **Blondaea'na,** *lflets.* glabrous, teeth compound, glandular, back of sep. and pedicels usually glandular. Sweden to S. Europe. Syn. *R. Blondaeana*; **leucochro'a,** *lflets.* glabrous or hairy only on midrib beneath, teeth simple, without glands, sep. smooth or slightly glandular on back; pedicels mostly smooth. S. England to Alps and Pyrenees. Syn. *R. surculo'sa*; **tomentel'la,** *lflets.* hairy at least on veins beneath, teeth glandular, compound, *fl.* white or flesh-pink up to 2 in. across, sometimes in corymbs, back of sep. and short pedicels glabrous. Distribution as type. Syn. *R. tomentella.*

R. × cantabrigien'sis.* (*R. Hugonis* × *R. sericea Hookeri*). 7 to 9 ft. h., stiff, erect. *lflets.* 7 to 11, hairy on veins and densely glandular beneath and on compound teeth. *fl.* pale yellow, $2\frac{1}{4}$ in. across, solitary; pedicels $\frac{3}{4}$ in. long, glandular; sep. glandular on back. June. Originated at Cambridge.

R. caroli'na. 2 to 3 ft. h., stems bristly when young; prickles straight, slender. *lflets.* 5, elliptic, acute, dull above, pale beneath; stipules narrow. *fl.* rose, usually solitary, 2 in. across; sep. lanceolate, acuminate or dilated at tip, pinnate, deciduous, glandular and hairy; pedicels glandular, hairy. June. *fr.* flattish-globose, rather bristly. E. United States. 1826. (W.R. 201 as *R. humilis.*) Syn. *R. Deamii.* var. **grandiflo'ra,** *lflets.* usually 7, oval to obovate, *fl.* 2 to $2\frac{1}{2}$ in. across. NE. United States. (W.R. 207 as *R. humilis grandiflora.*)

R. cathayen'sis. A synonym of *R. multiflora Gentiliana.*

R. cauda'ta.* 6 to 10 ft. h.; stems upright, reddish; prickles few, straight. *lflets.* 7 or 9, distant, elliptic to ovate, 1 to 2 in. long, paler beneath, hairy on midrib, teeth simple; stalk downy; stipules large, without glands. *fl.* pink, $1\frac{1}{4}$ to $1\frac{1}{2}$ in. wide, in large corymbs; sep. entire, dilated at tip, as long as pet., glabrous on back, persistent; pedicels $\frac{1}{2}$ to $\frac{3}{4}$ in. long, glandular-bristly; receptacle glandular, bristly. June. *fr.* flask-shaped, 1 in. long, poppy red to vermilion. W. China. About 1896. (W.R. 497.) Similar to *R. Davidi* but styles not exserted.

R. centifo'lia.* Cabbage or Provence Rose. 3 to 5 ft. h.; prickles scattered, nearly straight, scarcely dilated at base. *lflets.* usually 5 or 7, ovate, flat, glandular on margin, hairy beneath, rather limp, teeth simple. *fl.* large, double, rose-pink, fragrant; sep. spreading, persistent; pet. incurved; pedicels very glandular, slender. June, July. *fr.* ovate to subglobose. E. Caucasus. 1596. (W.R. 341.) Many forms and hybrids have been raised. var. **musco'sa,** Moss Rose, *fl.* rose, pedicels and sep. glandular-mossy. (B.M. 69.); **parvifo'lia,** Burgundian Rose, dwarf, *lflets.* small, $\frac{1}{2}$ to $\frac{3}{4}$ in. long, finely and simply toothed. *fl.* red-purple, 1 in. across, solitary, very double, overtopped by young shoots. (B.R. 452 as *R. parvifolia.*); **pompo'nia,** Rose de Meause, dwarf, *lflets.* smooth above, 1 in. long, *fl.* pink or white, double, $1\frac{1}{4}$ in. across. (W.R. 353 as *R. pomponia.*)

R. cerasocar'pa.* Strong climber up to 12 ft. h.; prickles few, stout, hooked. *lflets.* 5, rather leathery, up to 3 in. long, $1\frac{1}{2}$ in. wide, acuminate, glabrous, teeth simple; stalk glabrous; stipules entire, narrow. *fl.* white, 1 to $1\frac{1}{2}$ in. across, in panicles; sep. entire or pinnate, $\frac{1}{4}$ in. long, hairy and glandular on back, deciduous; pedicels $\frac{3}{4}$ to 1 in. long, glabrous, densely glandular. June. *fr.* globose, $\frac{5}{16}$ in. wide, red. W. China. 1914. (B.M. 8688.) Related to *R. Helenae*; differing by 5 larger lflets., glabrous l.-stalks, shorter sep., &c.

R. chinen'sis.* China Rose, Monthly Rose. 4 to 20 ft. h., often climbing in wild state; branches stout; prickles brown, hooked, sometimes very few. *lflets.* 3 or 5, ovate to oblong, acuminate, 1 to $2\frac{1}{2}$ in. long, shining, toothed; stalk glabrous, often prickly; stipules very narrow, gland-edged. *fl.* crimson to pink or almost white, 2 in. across; sep. simple or nearly so, acuminate, glabrous without, shorter than pet., deciduous; pedicels usually glandular. June to September. *fr.* scarlet, obovate, $\frac{1}{2}$ to $\frac{3}{4}$ in. long. Cent. China. 1768. (W.R. 79 as *R. indica.*) var. **min'ima,** Fairy Rose, up to 12 in. h., prickly or bristly or nearly smooth, *lflets.* ovate, obtuse, purplish, *fl.* rose-red or pink, 1 in. across, single or double. (B.M.

1762 as *R. semperflorens minima.*) SYN. *R. Lawranceana, R. Rouletii*; **semperflo'rens,** Crimson China Rose, stems slender, dwarf, prickly or almost unarmed, *lflets.* thin, purplish, lanceolate or ovate, *fl.* crimson, on long slender pedicels, solitary. (B.M. 284 as *R. semperflorens.*) Many good garden roses belong here. A parent of the Boursault, Bourbon, and Noisette Roses and of *R.* × *ruga.* (B.R. 1389.)

R. cinnamo'mea. Cinnamon Rose. 6 ft. h.; prickles paired, curved, sometimes absent. *lflets.* 5 or 7, ovate-oblong, hairy, teeth simple; stipules dilated. *fl.* purple to rose, solitary or 2 or 3 together, about $2\frac{1}{2}$ in. across; sep. very narrow, longer than pet.; bracts conspicuous, upfolded over pedicels. May, June. *fr.* bright red, globose, $\frac{1}{2}$ in. wide. Europe, N. and W. Asia. 1596. (W.R. 141; L.R. 5.) var. **ple'na,** Rose de Mai, *fl.* double. (W.R. 143.)

R. colli'na. Possibly *R. canina* var. × *R. gallica.* About 6 ft. h., erect; stem smooth; prickles strong, hooked, greyish, reddish when young. *lflets.* 5, rarely 7, finely toothed, glabrous above, paler and hairy at least on veins beneath; stalk hairy, sometimes glandular, prickly; stipules acute. *fl.* flesh-pink, fragrant, about 2 in. across, 1 to 3 on short spurs; sep. leafy at tip, glandular on back, persistent, outer pinnate; pedicels bristly, glandular; receptacle sometimes glandular; styles hairy. June, July. *fr.* ovate, shining, orange-red as in *R. canina.* Chiefly Cent. Europe. var. **Anderson'ii,*** *lflets.* sparsely hairy above, *fl.* up to 3 in. across, Phlox-pink at first, fading to fuchsine-pink. Of unknown origin. Before 1912. (W.R. 379, 383 as *R. canina Andersonii.*)

R. coriifo'lia. 5 to 6 ft. h.; stems erect or arching, green or bluish-green; prickles small, few, hooked. *lflets.* 5 or 7, ovate to oblong, grey-green, downy, teeth simple or double; stalk hairy. *fl.* white or pale pink, 1 to 4 together; sep. distinctly pinnate, glabrous on back, persistent; receptacle glabrous. June. *fr.* nearly globose, bright red, 1 in. long. Europe, Caucasus, Armenia. 1878. (W.R. 391.) Allied to *R. canina.* Very variable. **A**

R. × **Corya'na** (*R. macrophylla* × *R. Roxburghii*). About 8 ft. h. *l.* resembling *R. Roxburghii. fl.* single, dark pink, about $2\frac{1}{2}$ in. across.

R. corymbif'era. 6 to 10 ft. h., spreading; prickles stout, hooked. *lflets.* 5 to 9, oval to elliptic, up to $2\frac{1}{2}$ in. long, hairy, especially on veins beneath, usually simply toothed. *fl.* usually white or pale pink, $1\frac{1}{2}$ to 2 in. across, in corymbs; sep. glabrous, rarely slightly glandular at back, deciduous; pedicels usually glabrous. June. *fr.* ovoid, $\frac{1}{2}$ to $\frac{3}{4}$ in. long, orange-red. Europe, N. Africa, W. Asia. 1838. (W.R. 397 as *R. dumetorum.*) Closely related to *R. canina*, differing mainly by the hairy lflets.

R. corymbulo'sa.* 4 to 6 ft. h., erect or somewhat climbing, smooth; prickles few, small, mostly paired. *lflets.* 3 or 5, elliptic or ovate, $\frac{3}{4}$ to 2 in. long, sparsely hairy above, more densely beneath, finely and doubly toothed; stalk and stipules glandular. *fl.* rose-pink with white eye, $\frac{3}{4}$ to 1 in. across, few or in up to 12-fld. corymbs; sep. shortly acuminate, about $\frac{1}{4}$ in. long, hairy on back, persistent; receptacle glandular; pedicels slender, $\frac{3}{4}$ in. long, glandular. July. W. China. 1907. (B.M. 8566.) Allied to *R. Davidi* but fl. and fr. smaller. Lvs. become purplish-red in autumn.

R. crocacan'tha.* 8 to 12 ft. h., arching; pedicels hooked, orange-yellow. *lflets.* 5 or 7, elliptic, acuminate, up to 2 in. long, glabrous above, sometimes hairy on veins beneath, deeply toothed; stalk glandular, prickly; stipules narrow, gland-edged. *fl.* white, small, slightly scented, in branched panicles; bud short, pointed; sep. $\frac{1}{2}$ in. long, leafy at tip, slightly pinnate, as long as or longer than pet., hairy on back; pet. narrow; pedicels slender, up to $\frac{3}{4}$ in. long, glabrous or slightly hairy, glandular. June, July. *fr.* globose or ovoid, $\frac{5}{16}$ in. long, orange-red. W. China. About 1919. Nearly related to *R. filipes* but *fl.* smaller, styles glabrous.

R. cymo'sa. Climber up to 15 ft. h. with slender branches; prickles few, hooked. *lflets.* 3 to 5, distant, elliptic to ovate-lanceolate, dark shining green above, paler beneath, usually glabrous, teeth simple; stipules filiform or wanting. *fl.* small, white, very numerous, in compound corymbs; styles woolly, free, exserted; pedicels about $\frac{1}{2}$ in. long; bracts deciduous. June. *fr.* scarlet, like Hawthorn. China. 1904? (L.R. as *R. microcarpa*; G.C. 37 (1905), 227 as *R. sorbifolia.*) Characters variable. Common all over China; rarely grown in Britain.

R. dalmat'ica. A variety of *R. glutinosa.*

R. damasce'na.* Damask Rose. 3 to 5 ft. h.; prickles numerous, unequal, dilated towards base. *lflets.* 5 to 7, ovate, often grey-green, convex, downy beneath. *fl.* white to red, large, fragrant, in corymbs; sep. reflexed, glandular-hispid; pedicels glandular-hispid. June, July. *fr.* obovate, 1 in. long, red, bristly. Asia Minor. 1573. (W.R. 369.) var. **versico'lor,** York and Lancaster Rose, *fl.* semi-double, white, pale pink, or half-white, half-pink. Many garden roses are grouped here and it is one parent of the Hybrid Perpetual Roses. **A**

R. Da'vidii.* 5 to 9 ft. h.; stems upright; prickles straight, stout, dilated at base. *lflets.* usually 7 or 9, elliptic to ovate-oblong, $\frac{3}{4}$ to 2 in. long, downy at least on veins beneath, teeth simple or somewhat glandular; stalk hairy, glandular, prickly. *fl.* rose, 1 to $1\frac{1}{2}$ in. across, in corymbs; sep. prominent, often longer than pet., dilated at tip, smooth or glandular at back, persistent; styles woolly exserted, $\frac{1}{4}$ in.; pedicels slender, $\frac{1}{2}$ to $1\frac{1}{2}$ in. long. June, July. *fr.* flask-shaped, $\frac{3}{4}$ in. long, Mandarin-red. E. Tibet, W. China. 1908. (B.M. 8679.) var. **elonga'ta,** *fl.* 3 to 7, *lflets.* and *fr* larger. W. China. 1908; **Fang'ii,** *lflets.* densely hairy below, almost entire, *fl.* pale rose, back of sep., receptacle and pedicels hairy. Szechwan; **perseto'sa,** stems densely bristly. SW. China. 1898. (J.R.H.S. 1902, 487, 488 as *R. macrophylla acicularis.*) SYN. *R. persetosa.* Best in the wild garden.

Rosa Davidii

R. davu'rica. 3 to 5 ft. h.; branches nearly smooth; prickles large, paired below l., slightly hooked. *lflets.* 7, 1 to $1\frac{1}{2}$ in. long, oblong-lanceolate, acute, glandular and hairy beneath, teeth double; stalks downy; stipules narrow. *fl.* rose-red, 1 to 3; sep. longer than pet., leafy at tip, persistent, margin downy. June, July. *fr.* ovate, red, nearly $\frac{1}{2}$ in. long, smooth. NE. Asia. 1910. SYN. *R. amblyotis.* Closely related to *R. cinnamomea.* A parent of *R.* × *kamtchatica.*

R. Deam'ii. A synonym of *R. carolina.*

R. dumeto'rum. A synonym of *R. corymbifera.*

R. × **Dupont'ii*** (? *R. gallica* × *R. moschata*). 8 to 10 ft. h.; branches at first upright, then spreading; prickles few, weak. *lflets.* usually 5, elliptic to ovate, up to 2 in. long, hairy chiefly on veins beneath, teeth often compound, glandular; stalks hairy, glandular. *fl.* opening white from a pink bud, 3 in. across, fragrant, usually in 4- to 7-fld. corymbs, single; sep. often glandular on back, deciduous; anthers sometimes petaloid; receptacle oblong; styles free, silky-hairy; pedicels glandular. June. *fr.* elliptic, about $\frac{1}{2}$ in. long, red. October to January. Originated in France. Before 1817. (B.R. 861 as *R. moschata nivea*; W.R. 43, 46.)

R. Ec'ae. Small shrub, densely branched, very prickly. *lflets.* 5 or 11, ovate to nearly round, $\frac{1}{4}$ in. long, glandular beneath, toothed. *fl.* golden yellow, 1 in. or less across, solitary; pedicels $\frac{1}{2}$ in. long. May, June. *fr.* globose, shining, glabrous, red, $\frac{1}{4}$ in. wide, crowned by reflexed sep. Afghanistan, Turkistan. 1880. (W.R. 277 as *R. xanthina.*) Needs a sunny position and good drainage.

R. Eglante'ria. Sweetbrier. 5 to 7 ft. h.; branches densely interlaced; prickles hooked, mixed with bristles. *lflets.* 5 to 9, oval, glabrous above, hairy beneath, glandular on both surfaces, fragrant. *fl.* bright pink, 1 to 3, $1\frac{1}{4}$ to 2 in. across; sep. pinnate, densely glandular, semi-persistent; pedicels densely glandular. June. *fr.* ovoid, orange-scarlet, up to 1 in. long, $\frac{5}{8}$ in. wide. Europe, including Britain. SYN. *R. rubiginosa.* var. **du'plex,*** *fl.* double. (W.R. 449 as Janet's Pride.) The single form is one parent of the Penzance Briers. The type makes a good low hedge if clipped annually before growth starts in spring.

R. elegan'tula. 4 to 6 ft. h., suckering; young shoots densely branched; prickles rather few. *lflets.* 7 or 9, elliptic to ovate, $\frac{1}{2}$ to $\frac{3}{4}$ in. long, glaucous on both sides, downy on midrib beneath, teeth usually simple; stalk sparingly glandular and prickly; stipules narrow, $\frac{1}{4}$ in. long, minutely gland-edged. *fl.* deep rose, 1 to $1\frac{1}{4}$ in.

across, solitary or few; sep. leafy at tip, finely downy, $\frac{3}{8}$ in. long, spreading, persistent; pet. broadly obcordate; pedicels $\frac{3}{4}$ in. long, slender, glabrous. June. *fr.* bright red, receptacle oblong, glabrous; obcordate, $\frac{1}{3}$ to $\frac{1}{2}$ in. long. W. China. 1900. Related to *R. Giraldii* and *R. sertata.*

R. Engelman'nii. Related to *R. nutkana* but dwarfer. About 3 ft. h.; stems arching, sparingly bristly; prickles straight, slender, paired below l. *lflets.* 5 or 7, doubly glandular-toothed, slightly hairy and glandular beneath. *fl.* much as in *R. acicularis.* June. *fl.* up to $\frac{3}{4}$ in. wide, usually pendent on slender pedicels up to $1\frac{1}{4}$ in. long. Rocky Mts. 1891. Syn. *R. acicularis Engelmannii.* Probably a hybrid between *R. acicularis* and *R. nutkana.*

R. Ernest'ii. Climber of 10 to 15 ft.; stems purplish, glabrous or downy; prickles hooked. *lflets.* 5, ovate to oblong-ovate, $1\frac{1}{2}$ to 4 in. long on shoots, acuminate, finely toothed, glabrous or softly downy beneath, purplish. *fl.* white, $1\frac{1}{4}$ in. across, fragrant, in 30- to 40-fld. panicles; sep. glandular and downy; styles united in a hairy column; pedicels glandular, downy. June, July. *fr.* globose, dark red, $\frac{1}{4}$ to $\frac{1}{3}$ in. wide. W. China. 1907. Syn. *R. Rubus* of Rehder and Wilson. Distinct from *R. Helenae* by 5 larger, thinner, downy lflets., purple beneath when young. **A**

R. Farges'ii. A synonym of *R. Moyesii.* **A**

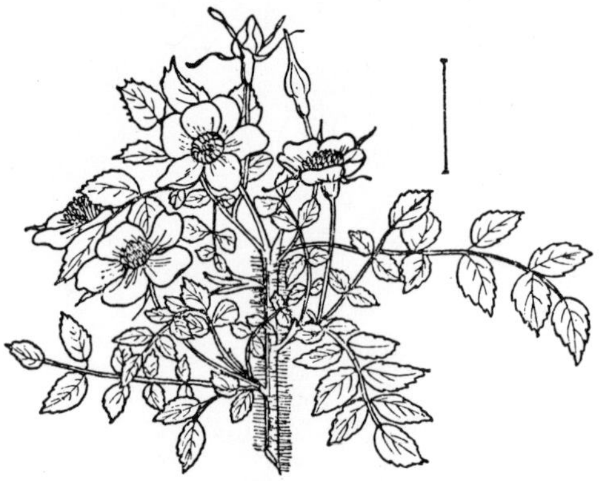

Rosa Farreri persetosa

R. Far'reri.* 5 to 8 ft. h.; stems densely bristly at base, branches with a few short prickles or none. *lflets.* 7 or 9, ovate to elliptic, usually blunt, about $\frac{3}{4}$ in. long, gland-toothed, glabrous; stalk slightly hairy, prickly, glandular; stipules narrow. *fl.* pale pink to white, $1\frac{1}{4}$ to $1\frac{1}{2}$ in. across, solitary; sep. filiform, persistent, tip leafy, back smooth; receptacle glabrous; pedicels very slender, 1 in. long, glabrous. May, June. *fr.* ovoid to ellipsoid, $\frac{1}{2}$ in. long, red. NW. China. 1914. var. **perseto'sa,** Threepenny-bit Rose, branches entirely covered with bristly spines, *fl.* smaller, salmon-pink. (B.M. 8877.)

R. Fedtschenkoa'na. 5 to 7 ft. h.; branches bristly, upright; prickles in pairs below l., almost straight. *lflets.* 5 or 7, elliptic, acute, 1 in. long, glaucous on both sides, finely toothed; stalk sparsely bristly; stipules acuminate. *fl.* white, or sometimes pink, 2 in. across, solitary or 2 to 4 at ends of shoots, scent unpleasant; sep. glandular on back, shorter than pet., persistent, tips filiform; receptacle glandular; pedicels glandular. June, July. *fr.* ellipsoid to pear-shaped, red, over $\frac{1}{2}$ in. long. August, Turkistan. 1876? (B.M. 7770.) Related to *R. Webbiana*; distinct by its bristly stems and usually white fl.

R. Fend'leri. A variety of *R. Woodsii.*

R. fe'rox. A synonym of *R. horrida.*

R. ferrugin'ea. A synonym of *R. rubrifolia.*

R. fil'ipes. Climber of 10 to 20 ft.; prickles few, hooked. *lflets.* 5 or 7, ovate to lanceolate, 2 to 3 in. long, glabrous, glandular beneath, simply toothed; stipules narrow, gland-edged. *fl.* white, $\frac{3}{4}$ to 1 in. across, in very many-fld. panicles; sep. narrowed, dilated at tip, glabrous or slightly hairy on back, pinnate, nearly as long as the narrow pet., deciduous; pedicels very slender, 1 to $1\frac{1}{4}$ in. long, glabrous or glandular; styles hairy, united in a column. June, July. *fr.* globose or ovoid, red, $\frac{3}{8}$ in. long. W. China. 1908. (B.M. 8894.) Related to *R. moschata*, but fl. smaller, on short pedicels in a panicle, lflets. glandular beneath.

R. foe'tida.* Austrian Brier. 3 to 5 ft. h.; stems erect, chestnut-brown; prickles few, straight. *lflets.* 5 to 9, elliptic-ovate to orbicular, $\frac{1}{2}$ to over 1 in. long, glandular beneath and on margin, teeth compound; stipules glandular. *fl.* rich yellow, 1 or few, 2 to $2\frac{1}{2}$ in. wide, odour heavy; sep. leafy, acuminate, $\frac{1}{2}$ to $\frac{3}{4}$ in. long, sometimes pinnate, bristly; pet. obcordate; receptacle globose, often bristly; pedicels usually glabrous. June. Armenia, Kurdistan, N. Persia. Before 1600. (B.M. 363 as *R. lutea unicolor*; W.R. 267.) Possibly an ancient hybrid between *R. Rapinii* and *R. spinosissima.* var. **bi'color,** Austrian Copper, pet. scarlet within, yellow without. Before 1590. (B.M. 1077 as *R. lutea bicolor*; W.R. 269.); **persia'na,** Persian Yellow, *fl.* fully double, golden-yellow, globose. Introduced 1838. (F.d.S. 374.) Has been used as a pollen parent of several hybrids, imparting noticeable colour and fragrance.

R. foliolo'sa.* 1 to 3 ft. h.; stems reddish, rather weak; prickles short, straight, often few. *lflets.* 7 to 9, narrow-oblong, $\frac{1}{2}$ to 1 in. long, shining above, glabrous, or hairy on veins beneath. *fl.* bright rose, 1 to few, $1\frac{1}{2}$ in. across; sep. lanceolate, finely acuminate, up to 1 in. long, glandular-bristly, receptacle and the short pedicel glandular-bristly. July, August. *fr.* subglobose, red, $\frac{5}{16}$ in. wide. SE. United States. 1880. (B.M. 8513.) var. **al'ba,** *fl.* white. Useful for its late flowering.

Rosa filipes

R. Forrestia'na. 3 ft. h.; stems upright, stiff; prickles in pairs, straight or pointing upwards, pale brown. *lflets.* 5 to 7, oval or orbicular, up to $\frac{1}{2}$ in. long, blunt, glabrous or hairy or glandular on midrib beneath, teeth simple or double; stalk glabrous, glandular; stipules large, gland-edged. *fl.* bright or pale pink, $\frac{3}{4}$ to $1\frac{1}{4}$ in. across, solitary or up to 5 in a corymb; sep. small, tip filiform, glabrous or glandular on back, much shorter than pet., persistent; pedicels about $\frac{1}{2}$ in. long, glandular; bracts large, oval or orbicular, glandular; styles projecting from disk. June, July. *fr.* ovoid, red, glabrous or bristly, up to $\frac{1}{2}$ in. long. SW. China. 1918. Closely related to *R. multibracteata*, flowering at same time but fls. fewer and bush much smaller.

R. × Fortunea'na.* (*R. Banksiae × R. laevigata*). Scrambling, branches slender; prickles small, falcate, sparse. *lflets.* 3 to 5, ovate-lanceolate, finely toothed, thin, bright green, shining; stipules small, subulate, deciduous. *fl.* white, double, about 3 in. across, solitary, on short, bristly pedicels; sep. ovate, entire; pet. loosely and irregularly arranged. June. China. 1850. (W.R. 109.) Rarely grown; needs a sheltered position. The yellow *R. odorata pseudindica* has also been called *R. Fortuneara* but is quite distinct from this.

R. gal'lica.* 2 to 3 ft. h., prickly and bristly. *lflets.* 3 or 5, ovate, leathery, rugose, deflexing; stipules narrow. *fl.* pink to crimson, $1\frac{1}{2}$ to 3 in. across, erect; sep., receptacle, and pedicels glandular; pedicels stout. June. *fr.* brick red. S. Europe to W. Asia. (W.R. 325.) Dr. Hurst considered the name should be *R. rubra.* A parent of many old garden roses. var. **Agatha,** *fl.* purple, small, very double, sep. more or less pinnate, outer pet. spreading, inner concave; **incarna'ta,** stems smooth or nearly so, *lflets.* elliptic-ovate, hairy beneath, doubly glandular-toothed, *fl.* larger, light crimson, receptacle ovoid, glandular. France. (B.M. 7035 as *R. incarnata*); **officina'lis,** *fl.* double, otherwise like type. (W.R. 359 as *R. provincialis.*); **pu'mila** dwarf and creeping, lflets. roundish-ovate, rarely lanceolate, *fl.* red, single, sep. and pedicels glandular-hispid; **versico'lor,** *fl.* semi-double, striped red and white. (B.M. 1794.) Syn. *Rosamundi.*

R. Gentilia'na. A variety of *R. multiflora.*

R. gigante'a. Rampant climber to 40 ft. or more; prickles thick, hooked; branches often without prickles. *lflets.* 5 or 7, lanceolate, acuminate, about 3 in. long, glossy, glabrous, deeply and often glandular-toothed; stalks glabrous; stipules long, narrow with linear tips. *fl.* white or pale yellow, fragrant, usually solitary, 4 to 5 in. across; sep. $1\frac{1}{4}$ in. long, sometimes dilated at tip, smooth on back, reflexed, generally deciduous, usually much shorter than entire pet.; receptacle glabrous; pedicels glabrous, as long as sep. May, June. *fr.* globular or shortly pear-shaped, 1 in. or more long, yellow or orange, thick-walled. Upper Burma, SW. China. 1889. (B.M. 7972.) Syn. *R. odorata gigantea.* var. **erubes'cens,** *fl.* blush-pink. W. China. Tender. Has flowered in some districts on a south wall.

R. Girald'ii. 5 to 8 ft. h.; stems upright; prickles straight, often paired, frequently absent from branches. *lflets.* 7 or 9, small, $\frac{1}{2}$ to 1 in. long, oval or elliptic, hairy on both sides, sometimes glandular beneath, teeth often compound; stalk hairy. *fl.* pink, solitary or in clusters of 3 to 5, $\frac{1}{2}$ to 1 in. across; sep. up to $\frac{1}{2}$ in. long, glandular on back, persistent; receptacle glandular; pedicels very short, hairy or glandular, often hidden by large bracts. June, July. *fr.* globular or ovoid, red, $\frac{1}{2}$ to $\frac{3}{4}$ in. long. N. and Cent. China. 1897? Related to *R. Webbiana* but fl. much smaller, almost sessile. var. **venulo'sa,** *lflets.* markedly net-veined beneath, sometimes nearly glabrous. W. China. 1907.

R. glutino'sa. 6 in. to 3 ft. h. forming a low dense bush; prickles on stem unequal, some stout and straight or nearly so, others bristle-like, glandular. *lflets.* 3 to 7, rounded to elliptic, small, doubly toothed, densely glandular on both sides, on the margin, prickly stalk and stipules. *fl.* blush-pink, small, solitary on short pedicels; pinnate sep., receptacle and pedicels bristly glandular; styles hairy. June. *fr.* scarlet, shining, hispid, crowned by hoary sep. SE. Europe, W. Asia. 1821. (W.R. 467.) SYN. *R. pulverulenta.* var. **dalmat'ica,** *lflets.* $\frac{1}{2}$ to 1 in. long, less hairy, prickles straight, *fr.* ovoid, larger, up to 1 in. long. Dalmatia. 1882. (B.M. 8826.)

R. graciliflo'ra. Bush with slender purplish branches; prickles few, straight or slightly hooked, about $\frac{1}{4}$ in. long. *lflets.* 7 or 9, oval or elliptic, $\frac{1}{2}$ to $\frac{3}{4}$ in. long, narrow, blunt, glabrous or slightly hairy on midrib beneath, glandular and doubly toothed; stalk glabrous or glandular. *fl.* solitary on short branches, pale pink, $1\frac{1}{2}$ in. across; sep. dilated and often toothed at tip, at least as long as notched pet.; pedicels glabrous or hairy, $\frac{1}{2}$ to 1 in. long, without bracts. July. *fr.* not known. W. China. 1908. Related to *R. Farreri*, but with much broader stipules and longer sep. Perhaps not now in cultivation.

R. gymnocar'pa. 1 to 5 ft. h.; branches glabrous with slender prickles and bristles. *lflets.* 5 to 9, glabrous, rather distant, oval, elliptic or round, sharply doubly gland-toothed. *fl.* very small, rose-pink, solitary or sometimes in pairs; sep. ovate, acuminate, deciduous with disk. June. *fr.* red, as large as a small pea, glabrous. Western N. America. 1893. (W.R. 221.) Suitable for rock-gardens, but not showy.

R. haemato'des. A synonym of *R. oxyodon.*

R. × Hard'ii (*R. clinophylla* × *R. persica*). *l.* pinnate, glabrous, stipulate. *fl.* pale yellow with red eye, 2 in. across; receptacle scarcely prickly. Originated in Paris. Before 1836. Scarcely hardy outside, except in S. England, and even these best planted at the foot of a sunny wall.

R. × Haris'onii.* (*R. foetida* × *R. spinosissima*). 2 to 3 ft. h. *lflets.* 5 to 9, elliptic, doubly toothed, slightly glandular beneath and on the thinly hairy stalk. *fl.* semi-double, solitary, light yellow, $2\frac{1}{2}$ in. across; sep. lobed at tip, glandular on back; receptacle and pedicel bristly. Originated in New York. About 1830. (S.B.F.G. 410 as *R. lutea Hoggii.*)

R. Hel'enae.* Vigorous climber of 10 to 20 ft. h.; prickles stout, hooked; young shoots reddish. *lflets.* usually 7 or 9, ovate to ovate-lanceolate, shortly acuminate, 1 to 2 in. long, nearly glabrous or hairy on veins and grey-green beneath, sharply, usually simply, toothed. *fl.* white, $\frac{3}{4}$ to $1\frac{1}{4}$ in. across, in many-fld. umbels or panicles, fragrant; buds short, rounded; sep. lanceolate, going to a fine point, slightly pinnate, shorter than pet., deciduous; pet. reflexing; receptacle glabrous; pedicels $\frac{1}{2}$ to 1 in. long, glabrous, glandular. June, July. *fr.* ovoid, red, about $\frac{1}{2}$ in. long. China. 1907. (N.F.S. 12, 120.)

R. hemisphae'rica. Up to 10 ft. h. on a wall. *lflets.* 5 to 9, obovate, pale beneath, hairy on veins, glaucescent. *fl.* yellow, solitary, 2 in. across, very double; cal. tube hemispherical; sep. leafy, toothed at tip; pet. obovate; pedicel short. July. W. Asia. Before 1625. (W.R. 273; B.R. 46 as *R. sulphurea.*) Rare and difficult in cultivation. Fls. fail to open well in cold wet summers. *See* **R. Rapinii.** A

R. Hemsleya'na. 5 to 7 ft. h.; branches few, strong, reddish; prickles sparse, short, usually straight, dilated at base. *lflets.* usually 7 or 9, oval to elliptic, 1 to 2 in. long, glabrous or hairy on veins beneath, glandular beneath and on margin, doubly toothed; stalk glandular, spiny; stipules large. *fl.* rose-pink, $1\frac{1}{2}$ to 2 in. across; corymbs 3- to 11-fld.; sep. at least as long as pet., pinnate, dilated and toothed at apex, about 1 in. long, often glandular on back, persistent; receptacle long, glandular; pedicels $\frac{1}{2}$ to 1 in. long, glandular. June, July. *fr.* flask-shaped, red, glandular-bristly, 1 in. long. N. China. 1907. (B.M. 8569 as *R. setipoda.*)

R. × hibern'ica (*R. canina* × *R. spinosissima*). 3 to 8 ft. h.; stems dark red, upright or arching; prickles scattered, curved, mixed with a few bristles. *lflets.* 7 or 9, ovate, $\frac{3}{4}$ in. long, usually glabrous, sharply toothed. *fl.* pink, $1\frac{1}{2}$ to $2\frac{1}{4}$ in. across, solitary or in pairs or threes, slightly scented; sep. persistent, glabrous; receptacle and pedicel glabrous. *fr.* globular to ovate, $\frac{1}{2}$ in. wide, dull red. N. Ireland, N. England, Scotland. (W.R. 289, 291.)

R. × highdown'ensis.* (*R. Moyesii* × ?). Erect. 6 to 10 ft. A very fine hybrid resembling *R. Moyesii* in habit and foliage. *fl.* deep pink, $1\frac{1}{2}$ to $2\frac{1}{2}$ in. across. *fr.* flask shaped, scarlet, borne in clusters. June. One of the best roses for colour and number of its hips.

R. his'pida. A synonym of *R. spinosissima hispida.*

R. holodon'ta.* Similar to *R. Moyesii* but *lflets.* up to 2 in. long, 1 in. wide, loosely hairy beneath, especially on veins. *fl.* rose or pink, about 2 in. across, solitary or in umbels of 2 to 6, *fr.* bottle shaped, red to scarlet, bristly or smooth, up to $2\frac{1}{4}$ in. long. W. China. 1908. (B.M. 9248.) SYN. *R. Moyesii rosea.*

R. hor'rida. Dwarf, much-branched, branches stout; prickles short, unequal, strongly hooked, dilated at base. *lflets.* 5 or 7, ovate or elliptic, glandular beneath, on doubly toothed margins, stalk and stipules. *fl.* white, solitary, 1 to $1\frac{1}{2}$ in. across; sep. pinnate, glandular on back, often leafy at tip, as long as pet., deciduous; receptacle long, glandular-hispid; pedicel short, glandular-hispid. June. *fr.* blood-red, ovate to almost globose, smooth or bristly. SE. Europe, Turkey, Caucasus. 1796. (W.R. 477 as *R. ferox.*)

R. Hugo'nis.* 6 to 9 ft. h.; stems dark brown, straight or arching, branching at top, bristly below; prickles straight, varying in number. *lflets.* 7 to 13, obovate to elliptic, $\frac{1}{4}$ to $\frac{3}{4}$ in. long, usually blunt, glabrous or slightly hairy beneath at first, teeth simple. *fl.* pale yellow, 2 in. across, solitary on short, stiff branches; sep. lanceolate, finely acuminate, glabrous on back, entire, persistent; receptacle and pedicel glabrous. May, June. *fr.* round, small, dark red, ripening July, August. Cent. China. 1899. (B.M. 8004; W.R. 279.) Distinct from *R. xanthina* by its bristly shoots, glabrous lflets., and paler fl. Vigorous and ornamental when not in flower by its fern-like foliage.

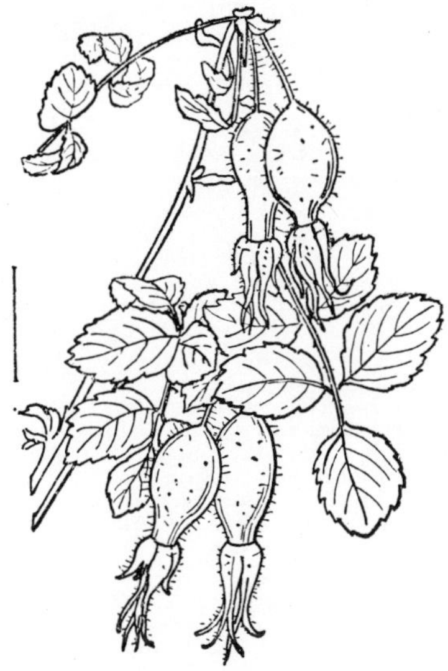

Rosa holodonta

R. hu'milis. A synonym of *R. carolina.*

R. incarna'ta. A variety of *R. gallica.*

R. in'dica. A synonym of *R. chinensis.* var. **odoratis'sima,** a synonym of *R. odorata.*

Rosa Hugonis

R. × involu'ta (*R. spinosissima* × *R. villosa* or *R. tomentosa*). 2 to 5 ft. h., old wood chocolate-brown, bristly and spiny; bush suckering freely. *lflets.* 7 or 9, overlapping, ovate, up to $\frac{5}{8}$ in. long, blunt, grey, green, hairy at least on veins beneath, teeth coarse, usually simple. *fl.* white, striped red in bud, solitary, on short spurs, 2¼ in. across; back of sep., receptacle and pedicels smooth; pedicels ¾ in. long. June. *fr.* globular to pyriform, about ½ in. wide, dark maroon. N. Scotland, Hebrides. (W.R. 281, 283.) Similar hybrids in W. Ireland and SE. France.

R. × **Jack'sonii** (*R. rugosa* × *R. Wichuraiana*). Stems long, arching. *lflets.* 7 or 9, shining, glabrous or nearly so, teeth shallow. *fl.* crimson, 2 in. across, in corymbs; sep. leafy at tips. *fr.* bright red. Originated at Arnold Arboretum, United States. Before 1897. (W.R. 63, 65.)

R. Jundzill'ii. A synonym of *R. marginata.*

R. × **kamtchat'ica** (*R. davurica* × *R. rugosa*). 8 to 10 ft. h.; branches upright, chocolate-brown, thickly bristly with scattered prickles, downy and glandular at least when young. *lflets.* 7 or 9, oblong-elliptic, 1 to 1¾ in. long, half as wide, veins conspicuous on both sides, densely hairy, glaucous and glandular beneath; stipules with large divergent tips; stalks softly hairy, prickly. Kamtchatka. About 1770. (B.M. 3149.) SYN. *R. rugosa kamtchatica.*

R. korea'na. Dwarf bush with densely bristly and spiny dark red branches. *lflets.* 7 to 15, ½ to ¾ in. long, sparsely woolly beneath, sharply toothed, margin and stalk glandular. *fl.* white, 1 to 1¼ in. across, solitary; back of sep. and pedicels glandular; sep. lanceolate. *fr.* ovoid to oblong, ⅓ in. long. N. Korea. 1917. Closely related to *R. spinosissima* but with more numerous lflets. and longer fr.

R. laeviga'ta.* Cherokee Rose. Strong climber; stem usually glabrous, branches with stout, curved prickles. *lflets.* evergreen, 3 or 5, ovate to lanceolate, shining, glabrous, midrib and stalk sometimes prickly; stipules free or deciduous. *fl.* white, solitary, 2 to 3 in. across, fragrant; sep. very bristly, entire, upright, persistent. May, June. *fr.* orange-red, pyriform, bristly, ¾ to 1 in. wide. China; naturalized in SE. United States. 1759. (B.M. 2847 and B.R. 1922 *R. sinica.*) Tender. The rose known as *R.* × *anemonoides* is a hybrid from this and is hardier.

R. lax'a. 5 to 8 ft. h., branches slender, bark green, often glaucescent; prickles stout, hooked, paired, dilated at base. *lflets.* 5 to 9, oval to elliptic, simply or doubly toothed, glabrous above, usually hairy beneath; stipules rather large, without glands. *fl.* white, 1 to several; sep. entire, smooth or glandular, persistent; pet. yellowish at base, somewhat cordate; pedicels very short, glandular, glabrous. July. *fr.* ovoid or globose, red, ½ to ¾ in. long, sep. upright. Cent. Asia, Siberia NW. China. 1800.

R. Lawrancea'na. A synonym of *R. chinensis minima.*

R. Leschenaultia'na. Rampant climber, reaching 60 ft. h.; branches purplish, mealy; prickles few, small, hooked, dilated at base. *l.* evergreen, glabrous. *lflets.* 5 to 9, usually 7, firm, ovate to elliptic, 1½ to 2½ in. long, acuminate, teeth simple, stalk and margin of narrow stipules glandular. *fl.* white, 3 in. across, fragrant, in few-fld. corymbs; sep. 1 in. long, acuminate, entire or pinnate, deciduous, glandular; receptacle and pedicel glandular; pedicel prickly; pet. notched, strongly reflexing; styles united in a column. *fr.* globose, red, ½ in. long, rough. S. India. Probably not now in cultivation. Needs protection in Britain.

R. longicus'pis. Strong climber; shoots reddish at first; prickles few, small, hooked, often absent from flowering branches. *l.* evergreen; lflets. 5 or 7, reddish when young, ovate-lanceolate, shining, firm, long-acuminate, sharply toothed, 2 in. or more long, usually glabrous, netted beneath; stalk glabrous; stipules very narrow. *fl.* white, 1¾ in. across, in corymbs; sep. finely acuminate, often dilated at tip, up to 1 in. long, hairy, often glandular on back, deciduous; pet. silky-hairy on back; receptacle hairy and glandular; pedicel about 1 in. long, hairy and glandular. May to July. *fr.* globose, ½ to ¾ in. long, deep red or orange. Assam. 1904? SYN. *R. lucens.* Rather tender inland. var. **Willmottia'na,** *lflets.* hairy on veins beneath, scarcely netted, pedicels and sep. shorter. Yunnan, W. China. (W.R. 521 as *R. Willmottiana.*) Perhaps not now in cultivation. *R. lucens* is said to have glabrous pet.

R. lu'cens. A synonym of *R. longicuspis.*

R. Lu'ciae. Climbing to 12 ft. or prostrate; branches green; prickles small, slightly hooked, pale brown, scattered. *lflets.* semi-evergreen, glossy, usually 5 or 7, ovate, glabrous or near so, teeth simple, sharp; stipules laciniate, on margin tip lanceolate. *fl.* white, ¾ to 1¼ in. across; corymbs 3- to 20-fld.; fragrant; sep. very short, oval, with a sharp point, reflexing, deciduous; pedicels and receptacle glabrous or glandular; styles united into a hairy column; bud short, rounded. July, August. *fr.* purple or red, ¼ in. long, globose or ovoid. Japan, Korea, E. China. 1880? Closely related to *R. Wichuraiana* but *lflets.* usually fewer, *fl.* and *fr.* smaller.

R. lu'cida. A synonym of *R. virginiana.*

R. lu'tea. A synonym of *R. foetida.*

R. lutes'cens. A synonym of *R. spinosissima hispida.*

R. Macdoug'alii. A synonym of *R. nutkana hispida.*

R. Macoun'ii. Stems reddish when young, bristly at base; prickles straight, slender, brittle, paired below l., small. *lflets.* 9 or 11, ¾ to 1½ in. long, oval to obovate, pale and finely downy beneath, coarsely toothed. *fl.* bright pink, solitary, 2 to 2½ in. across; sep. acuminate, entire, persistent, erect in fr.; pedicels slender. June, July. *fr.* globose, scarlet. W. Canada, United States S. to Texas. Before 1826. (B.R. 976 as *R. Woodsii.*) Closely related to *R. Woodsii.*

R. × **macran'tha.*** (*R. canina* × *R. gallica*). 4 to 5 ft. h.; stems green, arching; prickles hooked, scattered, with a few bristles in young state. *lflets.* 5 or 7, ovate, about 1½ in. long, hairy at least on veins beneath, teeth simple or double; stalk hairy and glandular. *fl.* pale pink becoming almost white, single or semi-double, 3 in. across, in 2- to 4-fld. corymbs; fragrant, back of sep., receptacle, and pedicels glandular; sep. pinnate, deciduous. June, July. *fr.* subglobose, dull red, ¾ in. wide, ripening in October. Originated in France in early 18th century. (W.R. 403, 405.) SYN. *R. canina grandiflora.* **A**

R. macrophyl'la.* Upright, 10 to 15 ft. h.; branches dark red or purple; prickles few, light brown, hard, straight. *l.* 3 to 8 in. long; lflets. 9 or 11, elliptic-ovate, acute or acuminate, up to 1¼ in. long, finely toothed, hairy and glandular beneath; stalk glandular and prickly. *fl.* bright rose, solitary or in few-fld. corymbs, 2 to 3 in. across; sep. nearly as long as pet., persistent, usually glandular-bristly; pet. broadly obcordate; receptacle and pedicels usually glandular-bristly. June. *fr.* flask shaped, 1½ to 2 in. long. Poppy-red, bristly. Himalaya. 1818. (L.R. 35; W.R. 157.) Handsome both in fl. and fr. var. **acicula'ris,** a synonym of *R. Davidii persetosa*; **crasse-aculea'ta,** a synonym of *R. setipoda*; **Korolkow'ii,** 10 to 15 ft. h., *lflets.* 9, stalked, 1¼ to 2¼ in. long, half as wide, stipules large, glandular on back and edges, *fl.* pale pink, 2½ in. across, sep. glandular on back, pedicels hairy and glandular, bracts conspicuous, glandular on margin. Late June. *fr.* vermilion-red, 1½ to 2 in. long, glandular-bristly. Turkistan. Before 1902. (G.C. 60 (1916) 28.)

R. margina'ta. Upright, 3 to 10 ft. h.; prickles few, slender, straight or slightly hooked, often mixed with bristles. *lflets.* 5 to 9, or 11, on shoots, obovate or elliptic, 1 to 2 in. long, glabrous, or hairy on veins beneath, teeth usually compound, glandular like margin of stipules. *fl.* pink, becoming white, solitary or few, up to 3 in. across; sep. pinnate, glandular on back, shorter than pet., ¾ to 1 in. long; pedicels glandular. June. *fr.* ovoid, dark scarlet, about 1 in. wide. Cent. Europe, W. Asia. 1870. (W.R. 463 as *R. Jundzillii.*)

R. Marret'ii. Upright, 5 to 7 ft. h.; branches purplish; prickles few, paired, slender, straight, pointed upwards. *lflets.* 7 to 9, oblong, ¾ to 1½ in. long, green, glabrous or nearly so, teeth simple. *fl.* pink, few, 1½ to 2 in. across; sep. dilated at tip, hairy on back, longer than pet., persistent; pedicels glabrous. June. *fr.* globose or top-shaped, about ½ in. wide, red. Saghalin. 1908. (W.R. 495.) Closely related to *R. cinnamomea* and *R. davurica* but lflets. glabrous beneath, prickles pointing upwards not curved.

R. Maximowicz'ii. Climbing and densely branched; prickles few, hooked, small, mixed with bristles on young shoots. *lflets.* 7 or 9, oval to elliptic, 1 to 2 in. long, glabrous, shining, teeth simple; stalk hairy, sparsely prickly, glandular; stipules very narrow, glandular-ciliate. *fl.* white 1 to 1¼ in. across, in small corymbs; sep. long, narrow, pinnate, reflexing, deciduous; pedicels ½ to ¾ in. long, smooth or glandular; bracts persistent; styles united in a glabrous column. June, July. *fr.* ovoid, ¼ to ½ in. wide, smooth, red. Manchuria, Korea. var. **Jack'ii,** shoots without bristles, *lflets.* up to 2½ in. long, corymbs up to 20-fld. Korea. 1905. *R. Kelleri* belongs here.

R. micran'tha. 4 to 5 ft. h.; branches arching; prickles uniform, curved. *lflets.* 5 or 7, small, ovate, acute, usually glabrous above, densely glandular and downy beneath. *fl.* white or pale pink, 1 in. across; sep. pinnate, deciduous, enlarged at tip, densely glandular; styles glabrous or nearly so. June. *fr.* scarlet, ½ to ¾ in. long, ovoid. Europe and Mediterranean region. (W.R. 461.) Distinct from *R. Eglanteria* by the glabrous styles, deciduous sep., and lflets. only glandular beneath.

R. microcar'pa. A synonym of *R. cymosa.*

R. microphyl'la. A synonym of *R. Roxburghii.*

R. mirif'ica.* 2½ to 3 ft. h., densely branched, suckering, forming clumps, glabrous, densely glandular; prickles straight, slender, pale yellow, paired, mixed with bristles. *lflets.* 3 or 5, or 5 to 9 on shoots, obovate, wedge shaped, small, glabrous or almost so, deeply toothed; stalk unarmed. *fl.* deep rose becoming pale pink, solitary, 2 to 3 in. across; sep. shorter than pet., narrowed, entire or pinnate, persistent; receptacle glabrous or bristly; stamens up to 150; pedicels about ¼ in. long, without bracts, glabrous or bristly. June, July. *fr.* globose, bristly, dull red, ½ to ¾ in. wide. New Mexico. 1917. (B.M. 9070.) SYN. *R. stellata mirifica.* Closely related to *R. stellata*, chiefly distinguished by glabrous, glandular stems and few stamens. Needs a sunny position. **A**

R. mol'lis. 3 to 5 ft. h.; branches erect, bloomy; prickles uniform, scattered, slender, nearly straight. *lflets.* 5 or 7, very hairy, somewhat glandular beneath, doubly toothed. *fl.* rose, 1 to 4, 1½ to 2 in. across; sep. slightly pinnate, glandular-bristly, persistent; pedicels short, glandular-bristly. June, July. *fr.* subglobose, scarlet, usually prickly, ripening early. Europe, including Britain. W. Asia. 1818. (W.R. 417.) SYN. *R. mollissima.* Very closely related to *R. villosa* but *lflets.* smaller and rounder.

R. mollis'sima. A synonym of *R. mollis.*

R. Montezu'mae. 3 to 6 ft. h., glabrous, without prickles. *lflets.* 3 to 7, ovate, acute, rounded at base, ½ to ¾ in. long, glabrous, much paler beneath; stalks prickly; stipules gland-edged. *fl.* pink, solitary, 1½ in. across, fragrant; sep. oval, pinnate with filiform tips, hairy on back; receptacle elliptic, glabrous; pedicels glabrous. *fr.* red. New Mexico. Related to *R. canina.*

R. moscha'ta.* Musk Rose. Rampant climber to 40 ft.; branches olive-green to -brown; prickles hooked, broader than long, scattered. *lflets.* 5 or 7, elliptic-lanceolate, 2 to 3 in. long, nearly half as wide, acuminate, glabrous, simply toothed; stalk slightly hairy, prickly; stipules narrow, glandular-ciliate. *fl.* cream-white, 1½ to 2 in. across, fragrant, in loose corymbs; sep. 1 in. long, often pinnate, narrow-lanceolate, hairy on back, at least as long as pet., reflexing, persistent; receptacle glandular and sparsely hairy; pet. obovate; pedicels 1 to 2 in. long, glandular, sparsely hairy; styles forming a silky column. June, July. *fr.* ovoid, ⅜ in. long, hairy, orange-red. Persia to Himalaya. 1590. (W.R. 33.) Best when allowed to grow over other shrubs. Distinct from *R. Brunonii* by its smooth branches and lflets. var. **nastara'na,** *lflets.* smaller, densely and sharply toothed, glaucous, glabrous, stalks glandular, *fl.* crowded. N. Persia. 1879. SYN. *R. Pissardii*; **nepalen'sis,** a synonym of *R. Brunonii*; **ple'na,** *fl.* semi-double, *lflets.* hairy beneath, prickles fewer and weaker. Before 1629. *R. moschata* has been crossed with other roses and given rise to several good hybrids.

Rosa Moyesii

R. Moyes'ii.* Erect 6 to 12 ft. h.; branches smooth; prickles few, straight. *lflets.* 7 to 13, elliptic to oblong-ovate, ½ to 1½ in. long, midrib silky-downy beneath; stalk downy, prickly, glandular; stipules purplish, gland-edged. *fl.* blood-red, 1½ to 2½ in. across, 1 or 2; sep. ovate, nearly 1 in. long, dilated at tip, sparsely hairy and glandular on back, persistent, connivent; pet. orbicular, 1 in. wide; receptacle purple, glandular; pedicels about 1 in. long, glabrous or glandular; bracts with glandular margins. June. *fr.* vermilion-red, flask shaped, 1¼ in. long. NW. China. 1894. (W.R. 229.) var. **Farges'ii,** not separable from type. SYN. *R. Fargesii*; **pubes'cens,** *lflets.* densely hairy beneath, stalk densely hairy, prickles dilated at base. E. Tibet. A good form, **Geranium,** of compact growth with fine red fl. and fr. has been raised at Wisley and other good roses have *Moyesii* blood in them, e.g. *R. highdownensis* and possibly **Nevada.** **A**

R. multibractea'ta.* 6 to 10 ft. h. with a few long, arching stems, branches glabrous; prickles paired, straight, ½ in. long. *lflets.* 5 to 9, obovate to orbicular, ¼ to ⅝ in. long, blunt, silky-hairy on veins beneath; stalks and stipules prickly and glandular. *fl.* pink, 1 in. across, usually in narrow terminal panicles, sometimes few; sep. ovate, ½ in. long, acuminate, hairy and glandular on back, persistent; pet. deeply notched; receptacle hairy and glandular; pedicels short; bracts very crowded; styles hairy, protruding ¼ in. Late June, July. *fr.* globose or ovoid, ¼ to ½ in. wide, orange-red, glandular. W. China. 1910. (G.C. 100 (1936), 23.)

R. multiflo'ra.* 10 to 20 ft. h.; branches, peduncles and sep. hairy; prickles slender, scattered. *lflets.* usually 9, ovate-lanceolate, ¾ to nearly 2 in. long, glabrous or hairy on veins beneath; stipules pectinate. *fl.* white or pink, in many-fld. corymbs; sep. short, ovate, entire, deciduous; styles glabrous. June, July. *fr.* bright red, globular, about ¼ in. wide. Korea, Japan. Before 1886. (B.M. 7119.) SYN. *R. polyantha.* One parent of the Polyantha roses. var. **car'nea,** *fl.* double, pink. 1804. (B.R. 425 as *R. multiflora.*) SYN. var. *plena*; **Gentilia'na,** *lflets.* downy or glabrous, *fl.* pinkish, 1 in. across, in few- or many-fld. corymbs. China. 1907. (W.R. 515 as *R. Gentiliana.*) SYN. *R. cathayensis, R. multiflora cathayensis.* Very variable in fl. and foliage; **platyphyl'la,** Seven Sisters Rose, *lflets.* broader than in type, *fl.* purple, large, double. 1817. (B.R. 1372); **Watsonia'na,** a synonym of *R. Watsoniana. R. Thunbergii* belongs here. It has stronger stems, longer l., and larger but fewer fl. The rose-stock **de la Grifferaie** also belongs here and is worth growing for its roundish double fl. opening carmine and becoming pinkish-lilac. **A**

R. Muriel'ae. Erect or spreading, 5 to 10 ft. h.; branches slender, reddish; prickles few, slender, straight or none. *lflets.* 9 to 15, thin, elliptic to oblong, about ¾ in. long, glabrous except on midrib beneath, gland-toothed; stalk woolly, prickly; stipules glabrous, sparingly glandular on margin. *fl.* white, ¾ to 1 in. across, in small corymbs; sep. ½ in. long acuminate, leafy at tip, densely hairy or nearly glabrous on back, persistent; pet. nearly orbicular; pedicels very slender, about 1 in. long, often glandular. June, July. *fr.* ellipsoid, tapering to neck, ½ in. or more long, orange-red. W. China. 1904. Rare in cultivation.

R. muta'bilis. A form of *R. chinensis.*

R. × Nevada (*R. Moyesii* ? × R. La Giralda). Erect. 6 to 7 ft. *fl.* creamy-white. One of the finest large shrub roses with a very long season of flower. *See* Supplement.

R. nipponen'sis. A synonym of *R. acicularis nipponensis.*

R. ni'tida.* 2 to 3 ft. h., suckering freely; branch erect, covered with slender prickles and brown bristles. *lflets.* 7 or 9, narrow-lanceolate shining dark green, becoming red or purple in autumn, glabrous or slightly hairy; stipules gland-edged, dilated. *fl.* bright red, solitary or few, up to 2 in. across; sep. very narrow, usually entire; pet. obcordate, nearly erect; pedicels bristly. July. *fr.* scarlet, about ⅜ in. wide, subglobose, slightly bristly. Eastern N. America. 1807. (W.R. 215.)

R. × Noisettia'na.* (*R. chinensis* × *R. moschata*). Climbing to 7 to 10 ft. or spreading. *lflets.* 5 or 7, glabrous or nearly so, simply toothed. *fl.* white or pink, semi-double, in many-fld. corymbs; back of sep., receptacle, and pedicels glabrous; styles loosely joined, exserted, hairy. Originated in S. Carolina. Early 19th century. (W.R. 93.) *R. Manettii* frequently used as a stock is a form of this hybrid.

R. nutka'na.* 7 to 9 ft. h.; branches purplish-brown; prickles slender, easily rubbed off, paired below l. *lflets.* usually 5, ovate-elliptic, up to 1¼ in. long, ¾ in. wide, glandular and slightly hairy beneath, coarsely and doubly glandular-toothed. *fl.* pink, rarely white, about 2 in. across, usually solitary; sep. entire, narrow, long-acuminate, glandular on back, persistent; pedicels 1 in. long, glandular. June, July. *fr.* globose, ½ to ¾ in. wide, Turkey red, tapering to neck, lasting to December or later. Western N. America. About 1876. (W.R. 231.) Useful especially for its persistent fr. var. **his'pida,** *lflets.* coarsely toothed, receptacle glandular-bristly. SYN. *R. Macdougalii.*

R. ochroleu'ca. A synonym of *R. pimpinellifolia ochroleuca.*

R. odora'ta.* Tea Rose. Often climbing, 6 to 12, up to 40 ft. h.; prickles scattered, hooked. *l.* half-evergreen; *lflets.* 5 or 7, elliptic to oblong-ovate, ¾ to 2¾ in. long, acute or acuminate, glabrous, shining above, sharply toothed; stipules sometimes sparsely glandular. *fl.* white, pale pink or yellowish, double or semi-double, 2 to 3 in. across, solitary or few, fragrant; sep. entire or slightly pinnate; pedicels short, often glandular; styles free exserted. June to September. Cultivated in China. 1810. (B.R. 804 as *R. indica odoratissima.*) var. **gigante'a,** a synonym of *R. gigantea*; **pseudin'dica,** Fortune's Double Yellow, Beauty of Glazenwood, climbing or scrambling to 20 ft. or more, *fl.* rose-pink tinged coppery-yellow double, fragrant, 3 to 4 in. across. SW. China. 1845. (B.M. 4679 as *R. chinensis pseudo-indica.*) A somewhat tender plant of unusual colouring.

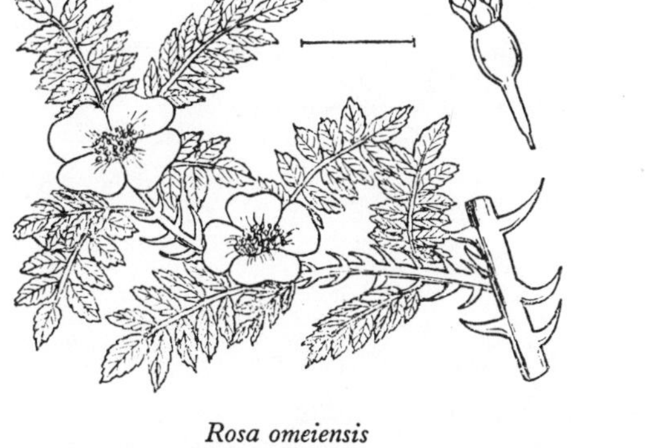

Rosa omeiensis

R. omeien'sis.* 7 to 12 ft. h.; stems upright, grey-brown, densely bristly; prickles hard, flattened, straight, paired below l. *l.* short; lflets. 7 to 13, oblong to elliptic, blunt, ½ to 1 in. long, toothed nearly to base, hairy on veins beneath; stipules narrow, revolute, glandular-ciliate. *fl.* white, rarely pale yellow or pink, usually 4-petalled, 1 to 2 in. across, solitary; sep. ovate, acuminate, silky within and on back, persistent; receptacle glabrous; pedicels short, glabrous May, June. *fr.* pear-shaped, edible, ½ to 1 in. long, smooth, yellow scarlet, deep red or 2-coloured, tapering at base, falling early. W. China. 1901. (B.M. 8471.) Close relative of *R. sericea*, but *lflets.* more numerous, more toothed, less hairy, *fr.* on a thickened pedicel. var. **prae'cox,** bush of open habit, 7 to 8 ft. h. branches olive- or yellow-green without bristles, prickles few, slender, paired below l., *fl.* mid-May, *fr.* Capsicum-red in July. SW. China; **pteracan'tha,** shoots and prickles deep red when young, prickles up to 1 in. long, contiguous. W. China. 1890. (B.M. 8218 as *R. sericea pteracantha.*) A form, **lu'tea,** has Empire-yellow pet. Of garden origin.

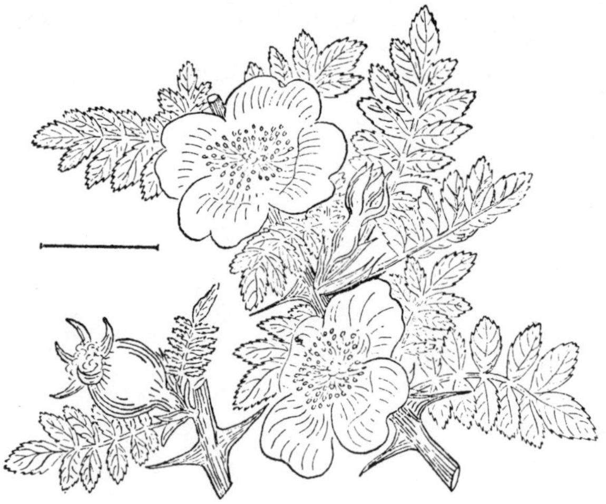

Rosa omeiensis pteracantha

R. oxyo'don. Upright shrub of 10 to 12 ft.; branches reddish; prickles sparse. *lflets.* 7 or 9 as a rule, distant, elliptic, 1 to 2 in. long half as wide, hairy on veins beneath, margin doubly toothed, often glandular; stalk downy, prickly, glandular; stipules large, mid-vein tinged red, edged with crimson glands. *fl.* Fuchsine-pink, 1½ to 2 in. across, faintly fragrant, in 3- to 7-fld. corymbs; sep. entire, dilated at tip, often glandular on back, nearly as long, or longer than pet.; pedicels slender, about 1 in. long, glandular, with a pair of bracts. June. *fr.* ovoid to flask shaped, ¾ to 1¼ in. long, shining, Capsicum-red. E. Caucasus. 1904. Syn. *R. haematodes, R. pendulina oxyodon.*

R. palus'tris. Stems slender, upright, purplish-brown, 4 to 6 ft. h.; prickles hooked, paired below l. *lflets.* 5 to 7, rarely 9, oblong or elliptic, 1 to 2 in. long, acute, finely toothed, pale beneath, downy; stalk prickly, downy; stipules incurved. *fl.* bright pink, nearly 2 in. across, in corymbs; sep., receptacle, and pedicels glandular; sep. leafy at tip; receptacles globose; pedicels short. July. *fr.* ⅓ in. wide, bright red, glandular. Eastern N. America. 1726. (W.R. 211 as *R. carolina.*) Syn. *R. pensylvanica.* One of the latest species to flower, retaining fr. long into winter.

R. penduli'na. Upright, 3 to 5 ft. h.; young stems reddish, normally smooth. *lflets.* 5 to 9, or 11, ovate to elliptic, ¾ to 1½ in. long, usually doubly gland-toothed to base, paler beneath, hairy at least on veins, often glandular; stipules conspicuous, up to 1 in. long, gland-edged. *fl.* rose-purple, solitary or few, 1½ to 2 in. across; sep. ovate-lanceolate, often leafy at tip, persistent, sometimes glandular. June. *fr.* ovate to flask shaped, ¾ to 1 in. long, scarlet. Cent. and S. Europe. 1789. (B.R. 424 as *R. alpina*; W.R. 293.) Distinct by its smooth, cane-like, reddish stems. var. **oxyo'don,** a synonym of *R. oxyodon*; **pyrena'ica,** pedicels and *fr.* glandular, *lflets.* mostly oval, glandular on veins beneath and on doubly toothed margin. Pyrenees. 1815. (B.M. 6724 as *R. alpina.*)

R. pensylvan'ica. A synonym of *R. palustris.*

R. perseto'sa. A synonym of *R. Davidii.*

R. pers'ica. Upright, 12 to 24 in. h.; branches slender, yellow-brown, prickly; thorns yellow or reddish, frequent below l. *l.* simple, obovate to oblong, bluish-green, ½ to 1 in. long, toothed chiefly near tip, hairy; stalk short; stipules absent. *fl.* solitary, 1 in. across, rich yellow with dark-red eye; sep. lanceolate, persistent, simple; sep., pedicels and receptacle bristly. May to July. *fr.* globose, green, prickly. Persia, Afghanistan. 1790. (B.R. 1261 as *Lowea berberifolia*; W.R. 1, 5 (fr.).) Very rare in British gardens and difficult to grow except under glass. Sometimes placed in a separate genus, Hulthemia.

R. phoeni'cea. Strong climber; prickles hooked, few, small. *lflets.* 5 to 7, usually ovate-elliptic, obtuse, sharply and simply toothed, hairy especially beneath; stalks hairy, prickly. *fl.* white, 1¼ to 2 in. across, in corymbs; bud rounded; sep. shorter than pet., pinnate, narrowed at tip, deciduous; receptacle glabrous as are the columnar styles. June. *fr.* ovoid, red, ½ in. long. Turkey, Syria. About 1885. Of little garden value. Thought to be one parent of the Damask rose.

R. pimpinellifo'lia.* Upright, suckering; stems 2½ to 6 ft. h. or more, purple-brown, becoming grey; prickles very numerous, straight, slender, densely mixed with bristles towards base, sometimes only slightly prickly. *lflets.* 5 to 11, usually 7 to 9, orbicular to elliptic, blunt to rounded at tip, ¼ to ¾ in. long, deeply simply toothed, rarely glandular on margin. *fl.* solitary, 1 to 2 in. across, white, creamy or pale yellow; sep. entire, persistent, much shorter than notched pet.; pedicels 1 to 1¼ in. long, smooth, without bracts. Mid-May to early June. *fr.* globose or somewhat flattened, ¾ in. wide, black or nearly so like the thickened pedicels. Mts. of Europe, Caucasus, Armenia eastwards to Siberia. Differs from *R. spinosissima* by its alpine habitat, straight, acute-angled shoots with long internodes and in chromosome constitution. var. **alta'ica,*** 5 to 7 ft. h., stems dark brown, prickles, slender, mixed with bristles near base, branches with few or none, *lflets.* usually 9, ½ to ¾ in. long, stipules narrow, gland-edged, *fl.* 2 to 2½ in. wide, scented, creamy-white, sep. narrow-lanceolate, tips often expanded, pet. broadly obovate, speckled yellow at base, pedicels ½ to ¾ in. long, *fr.* dark maroon-purple, shining, seeds few, red. Altai Mts., Siberia. 1818. (B.R. 888 as *R. grandiflora*; W.R. 257 as *R. spinosissima altaica.*) Syn. *R. altaica*; **lu'tea,** 3 ft. h., suckering freely, *lflets.* broadly oval, up to 1 in. long, ¾ in. wide, downy beneath, *fl.* bright yellow, 2 in. across (G.C. 60 (1916), 27 as *R. spinossisima lutea*). Origin unknown; **ochroleu'ca,** creeping, stems densely bristly and prickly, 5 to 10 ft. h., *lflets.* 9 to 13, elliptic to oval, up to ¾ in. long, coarsely toothed, stalk prickly, stipules lanceolate, prickly, *fl.* cream, fragrant, 1½ to 2 in. across, sep. lanceolate, acuminate, slightly woolly, shorter than obcordate pet., pedicels glabrous, 1 in. long, *fr.* globose, dark purple, fleshy. Russia. Before 1802. (W.R. 255 as *R. spinosissima ochroleuca.*)

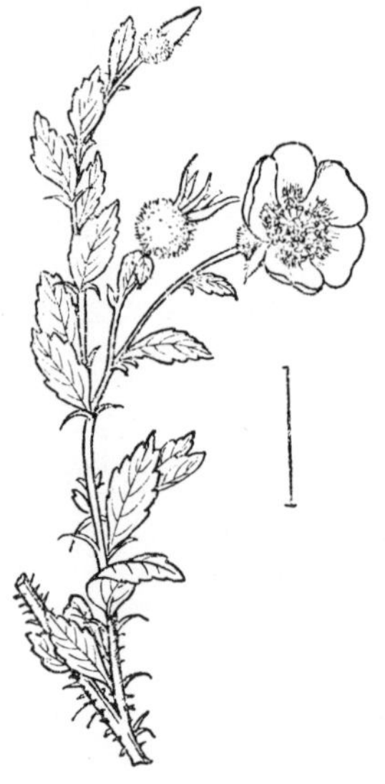

Rosa persica

R. pisocar'pa. Upright, dense bush, 5 to 7 ft. h.; stems slender, sparsely prickly, bristly at base. *l.* 2 to 3 in. long; lflets. 5 to 7, ¾ in. long, oblong-elliptic, blunt, coarsely toothed, finely downy beneath; stalk finely downy. *fl.* pink, 1 in. across, solitary or few; sep. ovate, acuminate, dilated at tip, glandular at back, persistent. June, July. *fr.* red, ¼ to ⅜ in. long, subglobose. Brit. Columbia to California. 1882. (B.M. 6857; W.R. 227 (fr.).)

R. Pissard'ii. A synonym of *R. moschata nastarana.*

R. polyan'tha. A synonym of *R. multiflora.*

R. pomif'era. A synonym of *R. villosa.*

R. Pratt'ii. 4 to 8 ft. h.; stems reddish, glabrous, unarmed or with a few straight, needle-like, straw-coloured prickles. *l.* 2 to 3 in. long; lflets. 11 to 15, oval to lanceolate, scarcely 1 in. long, obscurely toothed, finely hairy on midrib; stalk very short; stipules entire, acute. *fl.* pink, about 1 in. across, 3 to 7 in a corymb; sep. abruptly acuminate, sometimes dilated at tip, hairy on both sides, finally deciduous; receptacle and pedicels densely glandular-bristly; pedicels slender. June, July. *fr.* scarlet, ovoid, ⅓ in. long, glandular. W. China. 1908. Related to *R. Davidii* but *fl.* in a smaller corymb, styles only slightly protruding from throat.

R. praelu'cens. Shrub; stems stout, glabrous, purple-brown; prickles few, dilated at base, ½ in. long, none on branches. *lflets.* 7 to 13, obovate to elliptic, ¾ to 2¼ in. long, ½ to ¾ in. wide, rounded at tip, coarsely glandular-serrate, finely hairy, grey beneath; stalk hairy; stipules narrow, gland-edged. *fl.* red or rose, 3 in. across, fragrant; sep. leafy near tip, toothed, woolly on both sides, slightly shorter than obovate pet., persistent; receptacle glandular prickly; pedicels thick, 2½ in. long; bracts broad, leafy. July. *fr.* flattish-globose, slightly prickly, green or brown, ¾ in. wide. SW. China. A very desirable Rose apparently not in cultivation in Britain. Allied to *R. Roxburghii*, but sep. not pinnate, fr. less prickly, lflets. generally fewer, larger, more hairy.

R. Prim'ula. More or less upright, dense bush, 7 to 10 ft. h.; stems red-brown at first, prickles stiff, flattened at base, broad, in pairs below l. *l.* 1½ to 2½ in. long, fragrant, glandular beneath and on margin; lflets. 7 to 13, elliptic to oblong, ¼ to ½ in. long, glabrous, doubly toothed; stipules narrow, glandular, tips filiform. *fl.* pale yellow, saucer shaped, about 1½ in. across, fragrant, solitary; sep. reflexed, persistent or finally deciduous; pet. obcordate with a shallow notch; pedicels slender, glabrous, coloured like fr. Late May, early June. *fr.* globose, smooth, ½ to ⅝ in. wide, maroon-red. Turkistan. 1911. (N.F.S. 2, 193 and 8, 242 as *R. Ecae.*) Distinct from *R. Ecae*, with which it has been confused, by its taller habit, larger, paler fl., and much larger maroon fr.

Rosa Primula

R. provincia'lis. A synonym of *R. gallica provincialis.*

R. pseudin'dica. A synonym of *R. odorata pseudindica.*

R. Puget'ii. A synonym of *R. marginata.*

R. pulverulen'ta. A synonym of *R. glutinosa.*

R. punic'ea. A synonym of *R. foetida bicolor.*

R. pyrena'ica. A synonym of *R. pedulina pyrenaica.*

R. pyrif'era. A synonym of *R. Woodsii.*

R. ra'pa. A synonym of *R. virginiana plena.*

R. Rapin'ii. 2 to 5 ft. h.; stems with hooked prickles sometimes mixed with fine bristles. *l.* up to 2½ in. long; lflets. usually 7, obovate to elliptic, glabrous above, velvety-hairy at least on veins beneath, blunt, glaucous, toothed mainly in upper part; stalk glandular-downy; stipules linear, gland-edged. *fl.* solitary or 2 or 3, sulphur-yellow, 1¾ to 2⅜ in. across; sep. acuminate, leafy at tip, entire or slightly pinnate, much shorter than the obovate pet., persistent; receptacle hemispherical, bristly-downy; pedicels glabrous or slightly hairy or prickly, up to ¾ in. long, usually without bracts. May. *fr.* globose, smooth, ½ to ¾ in. long, yellow or red. Asiatic Turkey to NW. Persia. 1933. The wild single form of *R. hemispherica.* Rarely cultivated and difficult under our conditions. A

R. re'pens. A synonym of *R. arvensis.*

R. Richard'ii. Low spreading bush about 3 ft. h. with green glabrous stems; prickles many, small, hooked, very unequal. *lflets.* 3 or 5, elliptic to oblong, acute, glandular on margin, slightly hairy beneath, wrinkled above; stalk and shortly acuminate stipules hairy. *fl.* pale pink, 2 to 3 in. across, in small corymbs; sep. large, pinnate, leafy at tip, glandular on back and margins; styles downy; pedicels glandular-bristly, 1 to 1½ in. long; receptacle smooth. June. Abyssinia. 1902. (W.R. 337 as *R. sancta.*) Fr. apparently does not mature. Possibly a hybrid *R. gallica* × *R. phoenicea.*

R. Roulet'tii. A synonym of *R. chinensis minima.*

R. Roxburgh'ii.* Bush 5 to 7 ft. h. and as wide; branches stiff, smooth, light brown, peeling; prickles paired below l., ½ in. long, slightly hooked. *l.* 3 to 4 in. long; lflets. 9 to 15, elliptic to lanceolate, ½ to 1 in. long, slightly hairy, finely toothed almost to base; stalk sparsely prickly; stipules, narrow, acuminate, gland-tipped. *fl.* usually solitary, on short branches, double, pale pink to carmine, 2½ to 3 in. across, slightly scented; sep. broad ovate, acuminate, leafy, pinnate, back prickly, persistent, much shorter than pet.; receptacle and pedicels prickly. June. *fr.* of the single form flattish-round, 1 to 1½ in. wide, green, falling in August. China. 1823. (W.R. 135; B.M. 3490 as *R. microphylla.*) var. **hirt'ula,** *lflets.* sparsely hairy above, mainly on veins beneath, *fl.* single, Phlox-pink becoming nearly white. Japan. Before 1880. (B.M. 6548 as *R. microphylla.*); **norma'lis,** *lflets.* obovate or elliptic, rounded or acute, glabrous, *fl.* single. China. 1908; **ple'na,** *fl.* double. Original form of the species, first introduced from Canton to Calcutta.

R. × **rubel'la** (*R. pendulina* × *R. spinosissima*). Intermediate between parents. SYN. *R.* × *reversa.*

R. rubifo'lia. A synonym of *R. setigera tomentosa.*

R. rubigino'sa. A synonym of *R. Eglanteria.*

R. rubrifo'lia.* 5 to 8 ft. h.; stems more or less upright, few, arching, sparsely branched; prickles few, small, straight or curved, usually paired below l. *lflets.* 5 to 9, elliptic-lanceolate, ¾ to 1¼ in. long, toothed, glabrous. *fl.* rose to purplish-red, 1 to 2 in. across, in few-fld. corymbs; sep. lanceolate, entire or slightly pinnate, dilated at tip, glandular on back, as long as or longer than pet., usually soon deciduous, purplish-red, glaucous; receptacle, young l., and shoots purplish-red, glaucous. June. *fr.* ovoid, red, about ½ in. long. Pyrenees to Jugoslavia. 1814. (B.R. 430; W.R. 399, 401.) SYN. *R. ferruginea.* Ornamental by its purple shoots and l.

R. Ru'bus. Climbing to 20 ft.; prickles few, short, hooked. *lflets.* 5, or 3 on fl.-shoots, obovate to elliptic, up to 2½ in. long, toothed, glabrous above, downy at least on veins beneath; stalk downy; stipules narrow with lanceolate tips. *fl.* white, about 1 in. across, up to 12 in a corymb; sep. 1 in. long, entire, or slightly pinnate, downy and slightly glandular on back, ½ in. long, deciduous; styles hairy, long; pedicels short, downy, slightly glandular. June. *fr.* globose, ⅓ in. wide, red. Cent. and W. China. 1907. (W.R. 507.) Related to *R. moschata* and *R. Brunonii* but fl. and sep. smaller. A

R. rugo'sa.* Ramanas Rose. 5 to 8 ft. h.; branches stout, hairy; prickles dense, mixed with bristles. *lflets.* 5 to 9, 1 to 2 in. long, acute, toothed, much wrinkled, glabrous and shining above, hairy and net-veined beneath. *fl.* usually solitary, red or white, 2½ to 3 in. across, fragrant; sep. reflexed, hairy, dilated at tip, becoming erect, persistent; pedicels short, bristly-glandular. June, July. *fr.* orange-red, 1 in. wide, showy, flattish-round, ripening in early autumn. N. China, Korea, Japan. 1845. (W.R. 181.) Conspicuous both in fl. and fr., l. turn rich yellow in autumn. Useful for hedges. *fr.* sometimes used in conserves. var. **al'ba,** *fl.* white. (Gn. (1876), 452.); **albo-ple'na,** *fl.* double, white; **fimbria'ta,** pet. fringed, white; **kamtchat'ica,** a synonym of *R. kamtchatica*; **ple'na** *fl.* double, purple. A parent of many good hybrid roses.

R. sanc'ta. St. John's Rose. Dwarf shrub with decumbent branches; prickles paired. *lflets.* lanceolate, small, toothed. *fl.* small, pink, flat, double; receptacle globose. Italy. 1826. Possibly a hybrid of *R. chinensis.* Probably not now in cultivation. The plant usually grown under this name is *R. Richardii.*

R. satura'ta. 3 to 8 ft. h.; flowering shoots without prickles; stems brown. *lflets.* 7 or 9, oblong, 1½ to 2 in. long, quite glabrous or hairy on veins beneath, thin, simply and sharply toothed; stalk glabrous; stipules with ovate tips. *fl.* 1 to 3, rose-red or pink, about 2 in. across; sep. entire, leafy at tip, longer than pet., persistent; receptacle glabrous; pedicels smooth or slightly prickly. July. *fr.* coral-red, ¾ in. long, ovoid with a narrow neck. Cent. and W. China. 1907. Closely allied to *R. bella* and *R. Moyesii* but lflets. longer, sep. and receptacle glabrous.

R. Say'i. A synonym of *R. acicularis.*

R. Schrenkia'na. A variety of *R. acicularis.*

R. semperflo'rens. A variety of *R. chinensis.*

R. sempervi'rens. Strong climber or trailer to 20 or 30 ft.; stems green, prickles small, usually hooked. *l.* evergreen; lflets. 5 to 7, ovate to lanceolate, shortly acuminate, 1 to 2½ in. long, firm, glossy on both sides, glabrous, teeth simple; stipules gland-edged or laciniate. *fl.* white, 1 to 2 in. wide, slightly fragrant, in small corymbs; sep. ovate, dilated at tip, shortly pointed, deciduous, glandular on back; styles hairy; receptacle globose, glandular; pedicels long, glandular. June, July. *fr.* ovoid to globose, about ½ in. long, orange-red. S. Europe, NW. Africa. 1629. (B.R. 465; W.R. 19.) Related to *R. Wichuraiana.* var. **prostra'ta,** *fl.* few or solitary, styles normally glabrous, receptacle oval-oblong. S. France.

R. Serafin'ii. 1 to 4 ft. h.; stems stout, interlacing, thickly set with strong, hooked prickles. *lflets.* 5 or 7, roundish-ovate, blunt, ¼ to ½ in. long, slightly hairy beneath, densely glandular on doubly toothed margin and prickly stalk; stipules narrow, tips dilated. *fl.* usually solitary, bright pink, rather small; sep. ovate, acuminate, outer usually pinnate, glandular on back, finally deciduous; styles glabrous or nearly so; pedicels short, glabrous. June. *fr.* globose to ovate, bright red, ⅓ to ½ in. wide. Italy and adjacent islands. 1914 or earlier. (W.R. 475.) Of low habit, suitable for sunny rock-garden. Distinct from *R. sicula* by hooked prickles and glabrous styles.

R. seric'ea. 6 to 8 ft. h., stiffly upright; branches brown to grey; prickles large, often flattened, straight or upturned, paired or below l. *l.* 1 to 3 in. long, crowded; *lflets.* 7 to 11, small, roundish to elliptic, obtuse, sharply toothed towards tip, silky chiefly on veins beneath. *fl.* white, rarely pink or pale yellow, solitary, 1 to 2 in. wide, without bracts; sep. glabrous or downy, shorter than the 4 obcordate pet., persistent; pedicels short, glabrous, not thickened in fr. May. *fr.* globose to pear-shaped, about ½ in. long, red to yellow. Himalaya. 1822. (B.M. 5200; W.R. 163.) Closely related to *R. omeiensis* but *lflets.* usually fewer, seeds set at base of receptacle only, pedicels not thickened in fr. var. **Hook'eri,** glandular in most parts. Kumaon.

R. serta'ta. 3 to 8 ft. h.; stems red-brown, glaucous, arching; prickles few, straight, slender, paired. *l.* $2\frac{1}{2}$ to 4 in. long; lflets. 7 to 11; elliptic, $\frac{1}{2}$ to $\frac{3}{4}$ in. long, glabrous, glaucous beneath, sharply toothed; stalk sparsely glandular, prickly; stipules narrow, gland-edged. *fl.* rose, 1 to 2 in. across, up to 4 at ends of short branches; sep. acuminate, entire, downy or glabrous, shorter than pet., persistent; pedicels $\frac{1}{2}$ to 1 in. long, glabrous or glandular; receptacle narrowly ovoid, glabrous or glandular. June. *fr.* ovoid, tapering, $\frac{3}{4}$ in. long, deep red. China, Kansu to Yunnan. 1904. (B.M. 8473.) Related to *R. Webbiana* but fl. larger and more richly coloured, pedicels shorter, lflets. more toothed, habit taller and laxer.

Rosa sertata

R. setig'era. Prairie Rose. Spreading or climbing, shoots reaching 10 to 15 ft. in a season, glabrous; prickles stout, nearly straight. *lflets.* 3 or 5, ovate, acute, 1 to 3 in. long, sharply toothed, downy on veins beneath. *fl.* rose, becoming pale pink, about 2 in. across, in few-fld. corymbs.; sep., pedicels, and receptacle glandular-bristly; styles glabrous. July. *fr.* globose, small, ripening in late autumn, reddish. Eastern and Cent. N. America south to Florida and Texas. 1810. (W.R. 71.) Useful for its hardiness and late flowering. var. **tomento'sa,** *fl.* smaller, more numerous, *lflets.* downy beneath. 1800. SYN. *R. rubifolia.*

R. setipo'da. 6 to 10 ft. h., upright; stems stout, reddish; prickles few, straight, broad, dilated at base, pale brown, sometimes many. *lflets.* 7 or 9, ovate to elliptic, up to $2\frac{1}{2}$ in. long, glabrous or glandular or downy on midrib beneath, usually simply, deeply toothed; stalks and stipules glabrous, often prickly and glandular; stipules large. *fl.* pink, $1\frac{1}{2}$ to 2 in. across, 12 or more in a panicle; sep. lanceolate, dilated at tip, about as long as notched pet., persistent; pet. silky without; bracts leafy, conspicuous, glandular; pedicels 1 to $1\frac{3}{4}$ in. long; receptacle glandular. July. *fr.* flask shaped, red, 1 in. long. W. China. 1895. (J.R.H.S. 1902, 485–6 as *R. macrophylla crasseaculeata* ; B.M. 8569.) A handsome species but rarely seen.

R. sic'ula. 6 in. to 3 ft. h., suckering; branches stiff; prickles many, straight or slightly curved; young shoots red. *lflets.* 5 to 9, orbicular or obovate, $\frac{1}{4}$ to $\frac{3}{4}$ in. long, shining, glabrous or nearly so, glandular beneath and on compound teeth; stalk and narrow stipules glandular beneath; fragrant. *fl.* pink, $\frac{3}{4}$ to 1 in. across, usually solitary; sep. glandular on back, pinnate, dilated at tip, becoming upright, persistent; styles hairy; pedicels $\frac{3}{4}$ in. long or less. June. *fr.* globose or ovoid, about $\frac{1}{2}$ in. long, red. Mediterranean region. Before 1894. (B.M. 7761 as *R. Serafinii.*) Dwarf, compact, prickly shrub for a sunny position.

R. simplicifo'lia. A synonym of *R. persica.*

R. sin'ica. A synonym of *R. laevigata.*

R. sinica Anemone. A synonym of *R.* × *anemonoides.*

R. sinowilson'ii.* Strong climber to 20 ft.; stem reddish when young, glabrous; prickles few, short, hooked. *l.* more or less evergreen; lflets. 5 or 7, oblong or elliptic, 3 in. or more long, 1 to 2 in. wide, long acuminate, shining dark green, firm, slightly hairy on main veins beneath, sharply toothed; stalk glabrous, prickly; stipules 1 in. long, gland-toothed. *fl.* white, $1\frac{1}{2}$ to 2 in. across, in loose corymbs; sep. ovate, tailed, up to 1 in. long, often pinnate, glabrous or nearly so, deciduous; pet. entire, broad, hairy without; pedicels stout, reddish, sparsely glandular. June, July. *fr.* ellipsoid, red, $\frac{1}{2}$ in. long. SW. China. 1905. Handsome species allied to *R. longicuspis,* but buds rounded, shortly pointed, sep. about as long as pet. **A**

R. sorbifo'lia. *See* **R. cymosa.**

R. Souliea'na. About 10 ft. h.; young shoots green, glaucous; prickles reddish, on older shoots brown, hard, numerous, straight, dilated at base. *lflets.* 5 to 9, $\frac{3}{8}$ to $\frac{7}{8}$ in. long, oblong-elliptic, glabrous, glaucous, simply toothed; stalk prickly; stipules narrow, gland-edged. $\frac{1}{2}$ in. long. *fl.* ivory-white, $1\frac{1}{2}$ in. across, in corymbs of 1 to 5, slightly scented; sep. ovate, shortly pointed, reflexed, glabrous or slightly hairy or glandular beneath, entire or slightly pinnate, deciduous; receptacle glandular; styles sparsely hairy, persisting in fr.; pedicels short, often glandular. June, July. *fl.* ovate to subglobose. $\frac{3}{8}$ in. long, apricot. W. China. 1896. (B.M. 8158; W.R. 57.) Dense, prickly, rounded bush, ornamental in foliage, fl., and fr. var. **sungpanen'sis,** corymbs broad, many-fld., *lflets.* up to $1\frac{1}{4}$ in. long, obovate or elliptic-obovate, rounded at tip, toothed. Szechwan.

R. spinosis'sima.* Burnet or Scots Rose. 1 to 3 ft. h., suckering freely; prickles crowded, very unequal, nearly straight, passing into stiff bristles or hairs. *l.* small, slightly or not glandular; lflets. usually 7 to 9, or 11, orbicular to oblong, simply or doubly toothed, about $\frac{1}{2}$ in. long. *fl.* white, pale yellow or pink, 1 to $2\frac{1}{2}$ in. wide, solitary without bracts; sep. simple, shorter than pet., persistent, erect in fr.; pedicels glabrous, sometimes glandular, thickening. May, June. *fr.* rounded, black or dark brown, $\frac{1}{2}$ to $\frac{3}{4}$ in. wide. Europe to N. Spain, N. and W. Asia, Iceland. (W.R. 247.) Grows on sand-dunes and in dry places. Distinct from *R. pimpinellifolia* by its short-jointed, tortuous, horizontal branches and difference in chromosome constitution. var. **his'pida,** 4 to 6 ft. h., stems upright, thickly covered with slender prickles and bristles, *lflets.* 7 to 11, oval to obovate, $\frac{3}{4}$ to $1\frac{1}{4}$ in. long, glabrous, teeth simple, *fl.* pale yellow, $2\frac{1}{4}$ to $2\frac{1}{2}$ in. across, sep. entire, generally glabrous, receptacle and pedicels glabrous, *fr.* ovate, black, $\frac{3}{4}$ in. wide. Siberia. Before 1781. (B.M. 1570 as *R. hispida.*); **myriacan'tha,** 2 to 3 ft. h., prickles very slender, dense, mixed with bristles, *lflets.* densely glandular, *fl.* usually smaller than in type, sep. densely glandular on back. Spain to Armenia. Before 1820. (W.R. 261.); **Ripart'ii,** *lflets.* glandular on veins beneath, sep. glandular on margin only, *fr.* red becoming black, up to $\frac{1}{2}$ in. wide, otherwise as in var. *myriacantha.* Cent. and W. Europe.

R. stella'ta. $1\frac{1}{2}$ to 2 ft. h.; stems downy when young, densely branched; prickles slender, straight, often paired, sometimes mixed with bristles. *l.* up to $1\frac{1}{4}$ in. long; lflets. 3 to 5, up to $\frac{1}{2}$ in. long, obovate to wedge shaped, glabrous or slightly hairy, deeply toothed near tip; stipules gland-edged. *fl.* solitary, $1\frac{3}{4}$ to $2\frac{1}{2}$ in. across, bright rose; sep. bristly on back, pinnate, usually dilated at tip, upright, persistent, shorter than pet.; styles woolly; stamens 160 or more; receptacle bristly; pedicels about $\frac{1}{4}$ in. long without bracts. June, July. *fr.* globose, bristly, brownish-red, $\frac{1}{2}$ to $\frac{3}{4}$ in. wide, rarely producing seed. SW. New Mexico. 1912. (W.R. 305.) Needs a sunny, dry place. var. **mirif'ica,** a synonym of *R. mirifica.* **A**

R. stylo'sa. 6 to 10 ft. h.; stems arching; prickles stout, hooked, broadest at base. *lflets.* elliptic, acute, usually shining, simply toothed, hairy beneath, rarely above. *fl.* pale pink to nearly white, clustered, up to 2 in. across; sep. pinnate, glabrous or slightly glandular on back, finally deciduous; pedicels long, glandular; styles usually much exserted from the conical disk, free, glabrous. June. *fr.* ovoid, red. Europe, W. Asia. 1838. (W.R. 47.) SYN. *R. systyla.* Closely related to *R. canina* and *R. corymbifera,* distinct by the normally exserted styles without hair.

R. sufful'ta. A synonym of *R. arkansana.*

R. sulphu'rea. A synonym of *R. hemisphaerica.*

R. surculo'sa. A synonym of *R. canina leucochroa.*

R. Sweginzow'ii. Upright, 6 to 10 ft. h.; shoots reddish, glabrous; prickles large up to $\frac{1}{2}$ in. wide, flattened, straight, mixed with smaller prickles or bristles, few on flowering branches. *lflets.* 7 to 11, oval, $\frac{3}{4}$ to $1\frac{1}{4}$ in. long, acute, doubly toothed, paler beneath, hairy on veins; stalk and margin of stipules prickly and hairy. *fl.* 1 to 3, rose-pink, $1\frac{1}{2}$ in. across; sep. up to $\frac{3}{4}$ in. long, tailed, outer pinnate, glandular-bristly, slightly shorter than notched pet., persistent; receptacle narrow-oblong, glandular-bristly; styles densely woolly pedicels glandular-bristly; bracts prominent, as long as pedicels, glandular-ciliate. June. *fr.* orange-scarlet, 1 in. long, flask shaped, bristly. Kansu, NW. China. 1909. (G.C. 72 (1922), 135.)

R. systy'la. A synonym of *R. stylosa.*

R. tomentel'la. A synonym of *R. canina tomentella.*

R. tomento'sa. 5 to 9 ft. h.; branches often zigzag, or long and arching; prickles stout, straight or slightly curved, often paired. *lflets.* 5 or 7, often greyish, orbicular to elliptic, 1 to $1\frac{1}{2}$ in. long, hairy, especially beneath, teeth compound, glandular; stalk and stipules glandular and hairy. *fl.* white to bright pink, $1\frac{1}{2}$ to $2\frac{1}{4}$ in. across, corymbs up to 5-fld.; sep. dilated at tip, pinnate, glandular on back, up to 1 in. long, usually deciduous; styles hairy; pedicels short, glandular. June, July. *fr.* globose to ovoid, $\frac{1}{2}$ to 1 in. long, generally glandular, orange-red. Europe, including Britain, Caucasus, W. Asia. 1820. (W.R. 421.) var. **cineras'cens,** *lflets.* simply toothed, almost or quite without glands. Chiefly in Cent. Europe.

R. triphyl'la. Climber; prickles few, small, hooked. *lflets.* 3, rarely 5, ovate-lanceolate, acuminate, simply toothed, glabrous, stipules narrow, toothed; stalk glabrous. *fl.* white, 1 to 2 in. across, in small corymbs or panicles, single in wild form, or double in cultivated form; sep. acuminate, generally slightly pinnate, up to $\frac{1}{2}$ in. long, styles united in a column; inner pet. of double form narrow, distinct from outer; receptacle ovoid, glabrous; pedicels $\frac{1}{2}$ to 1 in. long, glabrous or slightly glandular. June, July. *fr.* E. China. 1844 (double form). (W.R. as *R. anemoneflora.*) Distinct and rather tender; perhaps best grown on a wall. **A**

R. ultramonta'na. A synonym of *R. pisocarpa.*

R. villo'sa. Apple Rose. Stiffly upright, 3 to 6 ft. h., often suckering; shoots reddish and pruinose when young; prickles usually straight, not uniform, scattered. *lflets.* 5 to 9, elliptic, very variable in size up to 2 in. long, resin-scented, grey-green, softly hairy, glandular at least beneath and on margins, teeth compound; stipules and downy stalk glandular; stipules large. *fl.* Phlox- or Fuchsine-pink, 1 to 2½ in. across, solitary or in few-fld. corymbs, slightly or not scented; sep. pinnate, dilated and toothed at tip, reflexing, glandular on back, persistent; receptacle globose, hidden by large bracts, glandular; pedicels short, glandular. June. *fr.* globose or ovoid, ¾ to 1 in. wide, very bristly, dark red, many-seeded. N. Europe to Asiatic Turkey. 1771. (W.R. 435 as *R. pomifera.*) Remarkable for the dark-red Gooseberry-like fruits. var. **du'plex,** Double Apple Rose, *fl.* semi-double, Cyclamen-purple, 2½ in. across. 1797, or earlier. (W.R. 436 as *R. pomifera* var.) Also known as Wolley-Dod's Rose.

R. virginia'na. 3 to 6 ft. h., suckering; young shoots bristly; prickles often hooked. *lflets.* 7 or 9, elliptic or oblong, sharply toothed, glabrous or hairy on veins beneath. *fl.* bright rose, 2 in. across, solitary or few; sep. and pedicels glandular-hairy. May to July. *fr.* more or less globose, ½ in. wide, smooth. Eastern N. America. Before 1807. (W.R. 197, 198.) SYN. *R. lucida.* Valuable for red autumnal foliage and useful for hedges. var. **ple'na,** Rose d'Amour, *fl.* double. 1820. SYN. *R. rapa.*

R. Watsonia'na. Stems climbing or arching, slender; prickles small, scattered, slightly hooked. *lflets.* usually 3, linear-lanceolate, 1 to 2 in. long, entire, waved, often mottled, hairy at least on midrib beneath; stipules very narrow, with linear points, entire. *fl.* pink, ½ in. across, in long panicles; sep. hairy, entire, as long as narrow pet.; styles joined in a column, glabrous; pedicels about ¼ in. long, hairy. June. *fr.* globose, as large as a pea, red, rarely containing seeds. Japan, unknown wild. 1870. (W.R. 53.) SYN. *R. multiflora Watsoniana.* Distinct by its very narrow lflets. and very small fr. Not very ornamental. A

R. Webbia'na. 4 to 7 ft. h.; branches slender; prickles, few, straight, pale, ⅜ in. long, paired. *lflets.* 5 to 9, orbicular to broad-elliptic or obovate, usually ½ to ⅝ in. long, glabrous or slightly hairy on paler underside, simply toothed, entire towards base, blunt; stalk often prickly, glandular and hairy; stipules glandular-ciliate. *fl.* pale pink, 1½ to 2 in. across, solitary or up to 3; sep. glandular and sometimes hairy on back, often dilated at tip, shorter than pet., persistent; receptacle oblong; pedicels glandular or glabrous. June. *fr.* ovoid or flask shaped, ½ to 1 in. long, Capsicum- or signal-red. W. Himalaya. 1879. (W.R. 233.) Related to *R. sertata* and *R. Giraldii.* var. **Winterbot'tomii,** *lflets.* ½ in. long, oval, hairy and densely glandular beneath, simply or doubly toothed, *fl.* 1½ in. across, back of sep., receptacle, and pedicels glandular. Garhwal, Himalaya.

R. Wichuraia'na. Trailer of 10 to 20 ft. *lflets.* 7 or 9, sub-orbicular, obovate or elliptic, ½ to 1¼ in. long, glabrous; stalk often glandular and prickly. *fl.* white, 1½ to 2 in. across, fragrant; sep. much shorter than pet., glabrous or slightly glandular on back; receptacle ovoid, sometimes slightly glandular; pedicels short, glabrous or glandular. July, August. *fr.* dark red, ovoid, nearly ½ in. long. E. China, Korea, Formosa, Japan. 1891. (B.M. 7421 as *R. Luciae*; W.R. 59.) Distinct by its trailing habit, semi-evergreen l. with laciniate stipules, and its late flowering season. Closely related to *R. Luciae.*

R. Willmot'tiae.* 5 to 8 ft. h.; branches purplish, erect or somewhat arching; prickles paired, straight, slender, pale brown, ¼ to ½ in. long; bristles absent. *lflets.* usually 7 or 9, oval to obovate, ¼ to ½ in. long, simply or doubly toothed, glaucous, especially beneath, glabrous; stalk glabrous; stipules glandular-ciliate. *fl.* rose-purple, 1¼ to 1½ in. across, slightly fragrant, solitary, rarely more; sep. lanceolate, acuminate, finally deciduous with the disk, much shorter than pet; receptacle smooth; pedicels ¼ to ½ in. long, smooth. Late May, June. *fr.* ovoid to pyriform, tapering to apex, ⅜ in. long, orange-scarlet. W. China. 1904. Early flowering species related to *R. Webbiana* but distinct by its deciduous sep. (B.M. 8186.)

R. Willmottia'na. A synonym of *R. longicuspis.*

R. Woods'ii. Upright, 4 to 6 ft. h.; stems reddish, becoming grey; prickles straight or somewhat curved, slender, paired, few on flowering branches. *lflets.* 5 or 7, obovate to oblong, up to 1¼ in. long, rather sharply simply toothed, paler and glabrous or almost so beneath; stalk downy, prickly; stipules convolute, usually slightly glandular. *fl.* pink, solitary or up to 5, about 1½ in. across; sep. entire or nearly so, slightly hairy on back, persistent; receptacle glabrous; pedicel glabrous. June, July. *fr.* globose to ovoid, ½ in. wide. Cent. and Western N. America to Kansas. 1880. (W.R. 235; 236, the white form.) SYN. *R. pyrifera.* var. **Fend'leri,** *lflets.* usually doubly gland-toothed, stalks and stipules glandular. Western N. America to N. Mexico. 1888. (W.R. 175, 177 as *R. Fendleri.*)

R. xanthi'na. Dense upright bush up to 8 ft. h.; young branches dark chocolate becoming grey-brown, minutely warted; prickles thin, flexible, broad at base. *lflets.* 7 to 13, ovate to elliptic, up to ⅝ in. long, blunt, simple toothed to base, hairy chiefly on veins, stalk and stipules thinly hairy; stipules narrow, revolute, glandular-ciliate. *fl.* semi-double, Empire yellow, 1¾ in. across, solitary or in pairs; sep. acuminate, somewhat leafy and toothed near tip, back sparsely hairy; pet. about 20, nearly orbicular; pedicels ¾ to 1 in. long, glabrous; receptacle glabrous; styles poorly developed. May, June. *fr.* ? Cultivated in N. China. 1907. var. **sponta'nea,** *lflets.* often hairy along midrib above, *fl.* 2 to 2½ in. across, saucer shaped, single, *fr.* more or less globose, ½ to ⅝ in. wide, bright red, sep. persistent, upright. N. China, Mongolia, Turkistan. 1907. SYN. *R. xanthina normalis.*

Rosa Willmo ttiae

R. yainacen'sis. Low bush, branches stiff, spreading; prickles only in pairs below l., stout, long, curved. *lflets.* 5, oval, blunt, doubly glandular-toothed, glabrous above, finely downy and paler beneath, veins, stalk, and large stipules glandular. *fl.* rose, about 1½ in. across, 1 to 3; sep. glandular on back and margin; pedicels glabrous. Oregon. 1928. Related to *R. nutkana* but fl. more numerous and fr. smaller. SYN. *R. myriadena.*

B. O. M.

Rosa sinensis, Chinese rose. *See* **Hibiscus Rosa-sinensis.**

ROSA'CEAE. Dicotyledons. A family of about 90 genera including about 2,000 species of herbs, shrubs, and trees found in all parts of the world. Leaves alternate, usually stipulate, the stipules often adnate to the petiole. Flowers usually regular, usually perfect, terminal, in racemes or cymes. Calyx of 5 sepals, often with an epicalyx of smaller leaves, petals 5, like the sepals usually overlapping in the bud, stamens 2, 3, or 4 times as many as the petals, or indefinite, bent inwards in the bud; carpels 2 or 3 times as many as petals or indefinite, rarely 1 to 4, free as a rule, and usually superior but sometimes completely united to the receptacle and inferior. Fruits various. Many members of the family are ornamental and some are of economic importance, especially as producers of fruits, including Almond, Apple, Apricot, Blackberry, Cherry, Medlar, Nectarine, Peach, Pear, Plum, Quince, Raspberry, Service Berry, and Strawberry. *Chrysobalanus Icaco* is the Cocoa Plum of the W. Indies. *Parinarium excelsum,* the Grey or Roughskin Plum, and *P. macrophyllum,* the Gingerbread Plum. Genera treated of are: Acaena, Adenostoma, Agrimonia, Alchemilla, Amelanchier, ×Amelosorbus, Aronia, Aruncus, Bencomia, Cercocarpus, Chaenomeles, Chamaebatia, Chamaebatiaria, Chrysobalanus, Cliffortia, Coluria, Comarum, Cotoneaster, Cowania, ×Crataego-Mespilus, Crataegus, Cydonia, Dalibarda, Dichotomanthes, Docynia, Dryas, Eriobotrya, Exochorda, Fallugia, Filipendula, Fragaria, Geum, Gillenia, Heteromeles, Holodiscus, Kageneckia, Kelseya, Kerria, Lindleyella, Luetkea, Lyonothamnus, Maddenia, Malus, Margyricarpus, Mespilus, Moquilea, Neillia, Neviusia, Osmaronia, Osteomeles, Parinarium, Peraphyllum, Petrophytum,

Photinia, Physocarpus, Potentilla, Prinsepia, Prunus, Purshia, Pyracantha, ×Pyronia, Pyrus, Quillaja, Raphiolepis, Rhodotypos, Rosa, Rubus, Sanguisorba, Sibbaldia, Sibiraea, Sorbaria, ×Sorbaronia, ×Sorbopyrus, Sorbus, Spiraea, Stephanandra, Stranvaesia, Waldsteinia.

rosa'ceus -a -um, rose-like in some way; arranged like the 5 petals of a rose; coloured like a rose.

rosa'tus -a -um, rose-coloured.

ROSCHE'RIA (derivation?). FAM. *Palmaceae*. A genus of a single species of slender, erect Palm with many aerial roots. Cultivation as for Phoenix.

R. melanochae'tes. 15 to 25 ft. h. Stem 2 to 3 in. thick, with a ring of spines beneath each l.-scar when young. *l.* 3 to 5 ft. long, 2 to 3 ft. wide, entire at first, becoming pinnate, pale green; pinnae 1 to 1½ ft. long, 3-fid at tip, scaly beneath; stalks 1½ to 2½ ft. long, smooth, somewhat 3-angled, with a few black spines arising from a flattish cushion. *fl.* in 2-fld. clusters arranged spirally on the slender branches of the much-branched spadix. *Spadix* axillary, peduncle long, flattish, glabrous. *fr.* black, elliptical, about ⅛ in. long. Seychelles. 1871. (I.H. 1871, 54 as *Verschaffeltia melanochaetes.*) SYN. *Dypsis gracilis.*

ROSCO'EA (in honour of William Roscoe, 1753–1831, founder of Liverpool Botanic Garden, 1802, author of *Monandrian Plants*, 1828). FAM. *Zingiberaceae*. A genus of about 14 Himalayan and Chinese perennial rhizomatous herbs with clusters of fleshy roots. Leaves lanceolate or oblong. Flowers usually blue or purple, rarely yellowish or white, in a terminal spike or head; calyx long, tubular, 2- or 3-toothed; corolla tube often long, somewhat enlarged above, lobes 3, the dorsal one erect, incurved, the lateral ones spreading or recurved. Roscoea differs from Cautlea by the posterior petal being much wider than the others and by the longer ovary, producing a capsule slow to dehisc. Roscoeas grow best in light turfy loam or rich woodland soil, for *R. cautleoides*, *R. Humeana*, and *R. purpurea* are generally hardy if planted at least 6 inches deep, in spite of belonging to a family so many of which need warm conditions. They may be propagated by division.

KEY

1. *Fl. purple*	2
1. *Fl. yellow*	R. cautleoides
2. *Fl. solitary*	R. alpina
2. *Fl. 2 to 4*	3
3. *Lvs. linear-lanceolate; lip longer than wide*	R. purpurea
3. *Lvs. wide-lanceolate; lip wider than long*	R. Humeana

R. alpi'na. 4 to 8 in. h. with commonly 2 wide sheaths at base. *l.* usually 3, lanceolate or linear-lanceolate, slender-pointed, up to 4½ in. long. *fl.* solitary, purple, scarcely exceeding l.; cal. green, about 1½ in. long, 2-lobed; cor. tube slender, longer than cal., dorsal pet. round, erect; lip obovate, 2-lobed. Summer. Himalaya.

R. cautleoi'des.* Slender, 10 to 12 in. h., lower part of stem with usually 2 sheaths. *l.* usually sessile, lanceolate or oblong-lanceolate, slender-pointed, glabrous, grey or glossy green, up to about 5 in. long. *fl.* up to 6 or 7 in a close spike, clear yellow, large, cor. tube often much longer than cal., dorsal pet. hooded, lip obovate, 1¼ in. long, 2-lobed, lobes acute. Summer. China. 1912. (B.M. 9084.) var. **Bees'ii,** *fl.* pale yellow.

R. Humea'na.* About 8 in. h., root fusiform. *l.* 4 to 6, more or less expanded at fl.-time, sessile, wide-lanceolate or ovate-lanceolate, glabrous, 4 to 8 in. long. *fl.* 2 to 4, violet-purple, large, cor. tube longer than cal., dorsal pet. about 1½ in. long, erect, concave, rounded; lip 1 in. long, 1¼ in. wide, squarish. Summer. W. China. 1916. (B.M. 9075.)

R. purpu'rea. Stem about 12 in. h., lower parts usually with 2 sheaths. *l.* sessile, linear-lanceolate or widely linear, long-slender-pointed. *fl.* in a short head, little raised above bracts, 2 to 4, purple or purplish-blue; dorsal pet. arching, longer than lateral; lip large, obovate, deeply 2-lobed. Summer. Kumaon and Sikkim. 1820. (B.M. 4630; L.B.C. 1404.) var. **proce'ra,** taller, with wider l.-sheaths, and much larger fl., the lip 2 in. long. SYN. var. *superba.*

ROSE. The wild species of the genus Rosa form but a small part of the roses seen in British gardens and it is probably true that no group of plants in cultivation is of such mixed parentage as the roses commonly seen there, and few decorative plants can have had so long a horticultural history. Roses attracted peoples of nearly all the early civilizations of the northern hemisphere and many allusions to them occur in the writings and poems of most northern countries from the most ancient times. It

Roscoea Humeana

is, of course, certain that not all the allusions to the rose in ancient writings refer to the plants we now call roses, but it is equally certain that very many of them do, although the most generally admired garden roses of to-day are comparatively modern productions and were certainly unknown to the ancients. Their fragrance, freedom, and colour commended them in olden times as they do to-day, and in olden times also great medicinal virtue was claimed for them. Dr. Lindley, who wrote a monograph on roses, tells us that one of the most earnest defenders of their medicinal worth has not hesitated to assure the world that 'the Pharmacopoeia should be formed of Roses alone'. In modern times the value of the hips of some kinds of Roses has been widely recognized and exploited as a source of vitamins.

Our native wild roses have, in spite of their great variety, contributed little directly to the development of our garden roses. The commonest species, *Rosa canina*, seems to be directly concerned with none, for the rose called *Andersonii*, sometimes given as a variety of *R. canina*, seems rather to be a hybrid between *R. canina* and *R. gallica*. Dundee Rambler with white flowers tinged pink certainly comes near *R. arvensis* and may be a variety of that beautiful species. The Scotch roses, as they are called, have possibly derived from *R. spinosissima*, but many varieties that have been grown under that name seem rather to belong to the nearly related *R. pimpinellifolia*, *R. eglanteria*, the Sweet Brier, has come in on account of its fragrant foliage and is often used as a dwarf hedge, cut over each spring, but by crossing with exotic species their contribution is not small.

The rose of which the ancient poets sang and which was early grown in the gardens of S. Europe was probably the fragrant *R. centifolia* in its double forms. It was one of the roses from which Attar of Roses was obtained, and it was used in many extravagant ways in classical times. In due course it reached England. It was certainly known here in the sixteenth century and in its many forms was widely cultivated until in the nineteenth and twentieth centuries the hybrid perpetual and hybrid tea races outdistanced it in popular favour. It is the Cabbage or Provence Rose of old times often pictured by artists and it has given rise to the Moss Roses (the history of which is recounted by Dr. Hurst in J.R.H.S. 47, p. 26), the miniature Burgundy Rose with double flowers about 1 in. across, the Crested Moss Rose (not a true Moss Rose), and the dwarf Pompon Roses. *R.* × *alba*, a cross between *R. canina* and *R. damascena*, which had long been cultivated in Italy, was also in cultivation in England at that time. To it belong the White Rose of York and few other varieties still seen in old gardens. *R. damascena*, brought it is said from Damascus by a crusader, gave rise to the York and Lancaster Rose, the place of which is usually taken in gardens by the better variety *versicolor* of *R. gallica* with similarly striped flowers. The double form of *R. gallica* from S. Europe, sometimes called *R. provincialis*, *R. foetida* from the orient which introduced deep yellow into garden roses, and *R. moschata*, another Eastern rose with fragrant flowers also reached these shores before the end of the sixteenth century and all have been successfully used in crossing to produce eventually a great variety of roses widely cultivated ever since. All these roses were more or less variable themselves, but the combination of their characters with those of other species has widened the range of variation to an unimaginable extent.

With the exception of *R. moschata* all these early introductions were bush roses and, except *R. foetida*, all were largely grown abroad for the making of Attar of Roses.

In 1629 a climbing rose, *R. sempervirens*, was introduced from the Mediterranean region, but perhaps more important still was the coming in 1768 of *R. chinensis*. *R. chinensis* had a very long-flowering period and from it the China or Monthly Roses were derived, as well as the little Fairy Roses of which the forms called *R. Lawranceana* and *R. Roulettii* are examples, and by crossing the Boursault, Bourbon, Noisette, and other hybrid forms and races, all of which had their day.

Still more important for present-day roses was the coming of *R. odorata*, closely related to *R. chinensis*, for from it, either as variants or hybrids, the Teas and Hybrid Teas have come. The very valuable character of continuous flowering is seen not only in the groups mentioned but in the Hybrid Musks, Hybrid Rugosas, and Hybrid Perpetuals, as well as in some of derivatives of crosses with *R. multiflora* and *R. Wichuraiana*. We can look to no other hardy shrub to give a succession of flowers over so long a period as some varieties of these groups, for in favourable seasons one plant may be in bloom from May to Christmas and after. From time to time other species have been introduced from N. America, China, and Japan especially, and some of these have played their part in originating new hybrid races, and there is no reason to suppose that the end is in sight.

Each of the races or groups of hybrids has become popular in its turn, only to be more or less neglected when a new race with some feature that has caught popular fancy has been introduced, just as there is a call for new varieties in the popular groups of the day. Today the popular groups are the Hybrid Teas and the Polyantha and Wichuraiana hybrids. But each group has left behind in our gardens some representatives which have proved to possess characters greatly recommending them, and many perhaps an increasing number of garden lovers appreciate and desire to grow some of these old-fashioned varieties as well as new forms bearing some resemblance to them. Many of these 'old-fashioned' roses are of less formal type, more fragrant or with a different fragrance, and not infrequently longer-lasting than varieties that owe much of their charm to the perfect form and delicate colouring of their half-open flowers.

The wild species of the genus Rosa can be arranged in more or less natural groups, though these are not always clearly distinct, as will be seen in the key preceding the description of the species (q.v., p. 1810). Crossing has, however, occurred so freely that the roses most popular in gardens will in many instances fail to find a place in these natural groups. This has led to many attempts to arrange these 'garden roses' into groups of hybrids of similar type having in the main the same horticultural requirements. The usual basis of these groupings is descent, and some of them are fairly distinct, but their boundaries are being continually threatened or broken down as new crossings are made and new varieties, of which there is a continuous stream, appear. This is not to be wondered at, for raisers of new roses are busy not only in the British Isles, but in N. America, France, Germany, Holland, Belgium, and Australia, and on the whole each country has its own ideals towards which to work, for the roses of one country are not necessarily aesthetically acceptable to rose-lovers in another, but different climates and situations call for differences in constitution in the roses to be grown in them. To meet these changes of varieties and attempt to map out the directions in which the spread of the stream appears to tend, new classes are from time to time proposed. In one such recent classification no fewer than 48 classes are named and even then some groups which have distinct horticultural characteristics are combined with others. So great a subdivision to a large extent defeats its own ends and rather tends to confuse than to clarify.

The following notes aim at giving some idea of the principal groups to which particular names have been given but are not by any means exhaustive. The characters of varieties of roses derived directly from the wild species are set out broadly in the specific descriptions under Rosa.

1. Hybrid Tea Roses are the result of crossing Hybrid Perpetual varieties with Tea-scented Roses. The group was first distinguished about 1890, though the first Hybrid Tea (Cheshunt Hybrid) was introduced in 1873. It is now the most popular and the largest group and is annually being added to. As a group these Roses are hardy, often of strong growth with smooth stems armed with strong prickles, green or bronzy foliage, often glossy, flower from June to November, with long pointed buds, and are more or less tea-scented. Most are mildew-resistant. The colour range is wide, especially since the introduction of the Pernetiana strain, now included in this group. The habit varies from dwarf bush varieties through the more vigorous pillar roses to climbers. The pruning must vary according to the purpose the plants are designed to serve, but many varieties lightly pruned will make large floriferous bushes, while some, apt to form shoots 6 or more feet long, are excellent for pillars, and for this need some support. This type may be used

for bedding if pegged down. Hard pruning of these vigorous varieties is apt to lead to rank growth and few flowers. The group includes single, semi-double, and fully double varieties. The group also provides many varieties suitable for pots or for planting out under glass.

2. HYBRID PERPETUAL ROSES. This group for long held pride of place in our gardens in early and mid-Victorian times, first appearing about 1825. It originated in the crossing of the Damask Rose with the Hybrid China varieties. Many of the varieties so-raised flowered well into autumn, but they were generally surpassed in this as well as in brilliancy of colour by the Hybrid Teas, but not in the 'old-rose perfume' which the Damask Rose brought in. The roses in this group are hardy and need no protection. The flowers are usually fully double and often rather flat when fully open, the buds being more or less rounded. The habit varies from dwarf bushes to vigorous climbers as in the Hybrid Teas. They are, on the whole, more subject to mildew and rust than the Hybrid Teas.

3. CHINA AND HYBRID CHINA ROSES. These were derived from the crossing of *R. chinensis* and *R. semperflorens*. The varieties with much blood of *R. chinensis* usually make big bushes with white to deep pink flowers, while the derivatives of *R. semperflorens*, such as Fabvier, are dwarf, mostly deep crimson, and if pruned hard make good bedding varieties. Their long flowering period was a distinct advance on earlier roses, and the 'monthly roses' found a wide acceptance, and some varieties are still highly valued. They are quite hardy, not particular as to soil, and the *chinensis* forms, which need only thinning, make good hedges.

4. TEA-SCENTED ROSES, derived from *R. odorata*. The earliest roses of this group, and indeed most of those raised subsequently, were produced in France. They were too tender to be trusted in the open in England. A hardier race appeared in 1853 in Gloire de Dijon which proved excellent on a wall, as it still is, and a few others were raised capable of growing into good-sized bushes in the open, but it was under glass that most gave good results in England. Their usually high centre and perfect form, their delicate colouring, and above all their delightful scent recommend them. For exhibition they became great favourites, but they need special attention for this purpose, including as a rule severe disbudding. Outdoors they mostly hang their heads and suffer damage from rain so that the buds fail to expand properly.

5. NOISETTE ROSES. These roses were named after their original raiser who crossed *R. moschata* and the Common Blush China, *R. chinensis*, obtaining a hardy, vigorous race characterized by their distinctive perfume and their habit of producing their flowers in corymbs, not singly as in the Teas. Later they were crossed with the Tea-scented Roses and gained in size, while the number of flowers in a corymb decreased, so that it was at last difficult to distinguish between the Noisette and the Tea-scented Roses, except by scent. Maréchal Niel illustrates this and may be compared with the white, almost evergreen, Aimée Vibert, introduced in 1828. These two are among the few survivors of the many Noisette Roses once grown. William Allan Richardson is another.

6. DWARF POLYANTHA ROSES probably originated by a cross between *R. multiflora* and a Tea-scented variety. They appeared about 1875 and are now widely grown for bedding and edging. They are hardy, of compact growth, with small, more or less double flowers very freely produced in clusters from summer to autumn. They are usually about 2 ft. high with foliage much as in *R. multiflora*, flowers white to scarlet, the orange varieties being liable to sport.

7. HYBRID POLYANTHA ROSES. These are taller than the Roses in Group 6, 2½ to 4 ft. high, and were raised by crossing the dwarf Polyantha varieties with Hybrid Tea Roses. The flowers are usually larger than in Group 6 varieties, and either single or double, in large clusters produced from June onwards. Both groups are excellent for bedding (when they may be pruned fairly hard in spring) or for growing as bushes (when little pruning beyond the removal of old shoots is needed).

8. HYBRID MUSK ROSES. *R. moschata* crossed with various modern roses has given a group of perpetual flowering roses producing a good crop of flowers in summer with usually a better one in autumn. The flowers are of medium size, single, semi-double, or double, in large clusters, and musk-scented. The plants are of bushy habit, 5 to 6 ft. high, or occasionally more, with good foliage and make good hedges.

9. PENZANCE BRIERS, raised by crossing *R. Eglanteria* with Hybrid Perpetual Roses. They are shrubs 6 to 8 ft. high, or, if left unpruned, up to 12 ft. high, needing support and merely thinning and removal of spent wood. They flower from June with semi-double, brightly coloured flowers and have the Sweet Brier fragrance. Some varieties produce showy fruits.

10. HYBRID WICHURAIANAS AND OTHER CLIMBING ROSES. The introduction of *R. Wichuraiana* and its crossing with various garden roses led to the production in the present century of a great number of roses suitable for training over arches, pergolas, walls and fences, and for planting to cover banks, and at the same time increased the use of climbing forms nearer to *R. multiflora*, which may be called Climbing Polyanthus. An endeavour is sometimes made to distinguish between Climbing Wichuraianas and Rambling Wichuraianas but the forms run so close to one another that such distinction serves little purpose. These roses have in common, in addition to the climbing habit, the production of flowers in clusters and the cultural need for pruning out old flowered wood in autumn after flowering, the encouragement of growth from the base of the plant, and the training out of new growth in autumn. The flowers and foliage vary greatly as between the different varieties and the duration of the flowering period, which is mainly in summer, also varies, but more and more it is being prolonged into autumn. Many of the varieties make good weeping standards if budded on tall rugosa or brier stocks.

The foregoing are the chief groups, and selected examples of each will be found described in the Supplement, but there are several smaller groups which are indicated in the list under **Rosa.** Among them forms of *R. alba*; the Ayrshire Rose (*R. arvensis* hybrids); Banksian Roses (*see* **R. Banksiae**); the Bourbon Roses (*R. chinensis* ×) the Damask Perpetual—a chance seedling in the Isle of Bourbon (Redouté, Les Roses) crossed again with *R. chinensis* forms. Plants with thick, smooth stems with few scattered prickles and white, blush, or rose double flowers. Souvenir de la Malmaison and Hermosa illustrate the two extreme forms, and Zephyrine Drouhin, still widely grown; the Boursault Roses (hybrids of *R. alpina*, pillar roses with reddish smooth stems, sometimes without prickles); Bracteata hybrids (hybrids of *R. bracteata*, the Macartney Rose); Miniature Provence (varieties of the Provence or Cabbage Rose with dwarf habit, and small rosette-like double flowers about 1 in. across); Moss Roses (see above); Ramanas Roses (forms as hybrids of *R. rugosa*, e.g. Blanche double de Coubert, Fambriata, Conrad F. Meyer); Persian Roses or Austrian Briers (forms of *R. lutea*, e.g. Persian Yellow with deep orange-yellow flowers and Harisonii with double canary yellow flowers, globular in bud, opening out flat); Scotch Roses (forms or hybrids of *R. pimpinellifolia* or *P. spinosissima*, with usually small, double-white or yellow, sometimes pink flowers, early to bloom, but with a short season, suckering with prickly stems and small foliage). An interesting article on the older shrub roses by G. S. Thomas will be found in J.R.H.S. 73 (1948), 170.

Roses Outdoors. Roses provide material for the decoration of many parts of the garden both formal and informal. Only strong-growing species and hybrids should be planted near a shrub border or even in an herbaceous border where their roots have to compete with those of their neighbours with strong roots. A background of ever-green shrubs may be desirable but it should be well separated from the area the roses are to occupy. Roses for garden beds should therefore have the beds to themselves and if they are on land tilted towards the south or south-west, with trees to act as a windbreak but neither to shade them nor compete with the rose-roots, they will have an ideal site; failing this a level spot in the open with a rose-hedge around it will be best. The roses themselves for the beds should be hardy, dwarf, or at least not tall enough to need support, free-flowering and capable of giving a succession of flowers from June to October or later. The majority of bedding roses will be found among the Hybrid Teas, Hybrid Perpetuals, Polyantha, and Hybrid Polyantha varieties and the type of flower which best pleases the planter can be judged at a Show, but the Show is not the best place to select roses for bedding, for habit, vigour, and continuity of flowering are not seen there; they are best seen in other gardens and nurseries.

The bedding roses, treated as they are more or less like herbaceous perennials, are not the only, and, except in the formal garden, the most satisfying type of rose for garden decoration. Many of the Hybrid Tea and Hybrid Perpetual Roses of somewhat robust growth make most decorative rose-bushes, calling for little pruning, except the removal of spent or dead shoots in spring and such pruning as results from the cutting of flowers for house decoration. The individual flowers will probably not be quite as fine as those resulting from hard pruning but they will be more abundant and produced over a longer period. Such roses may have a border to themselves or be used with other shrubs or as isolated plants on lawns, and they include several of the species. For a further account of shrub roses by G. S. Thomas see J.R.H.S. 75 (1950), 6.

The more vigorous of the Hybrid Tea, Hybrid Perpetual, and Hybrid Musk Roses may be grown as pillar roses tied up to a supporting stake, and these have their place both in the informal rose bed and in the formal garden.

Also for the formal garden roses budded high on brier or rugosa stocks and grown as standards or weeping standards make excellent features so long as they are given room to grow and firmly staked at the time of planting. The weeping standards need 9 or 10 ft. from plant to plant and the standards of Hybrid Teas and Hybrid Perpetuals at least 2 ft. 6 in., whereas bedding roses are planted, according to their vigour, 21 to 24 in. apart, but if to be grown as bushes the spaces should be 3 or 4 ft. or even more.

Some of the Polyantha varieties are dwarf enough to be used as edging plants to rose beds (*see* Supplement) and the Roses like Lawranceana and Roulettii and their 'Fairy Rose' relatives are dwarf and compact enough for the rock garden or alpine house.

Climbing Roses for Pergolas, Fences, and Walls are provided by several of the groups of garden roses as well as several species and need pruning according to the type of growth on which they produce their flowers. The extremes are seen in the Banksian Rose which flowers on the twigs and should not be pruned unless strong young growth has to be cut out, and, say, American Pillar which may have all but its strong young growths cut out annually.

Several Roses also make good hedges, from the dwarf Sweet Brier (*Rosa eglanteria*), about 2 ft. 6 in. high, to the taller Penzance Briers and the less formal *R. rugosa* in several varieties. Still other uses for roses are seen in such very vigorous species as *R. multiflora* and *R. moschata* in some of its varieties which may be allowed to ramble over trees and strong hedges without harming them but providing beautiful features in summer, while at the other extreme are the roses suited for covering banks by their sprawling or almost prostrate habit of growth, such as *R. Wichuraiana* and the Ayrshire Roses.

No matter in what form or for what purpose roses are grown the soil should be well prepared for them before planting by attention to securing thorough drainage, deep digging combined with the thorough mixing of manure, cow or pig manure being best for light soils, and bone-meal being beneficial on most soils, and the addition of enough powdered chalk to counteract any tendency to acidity, but not more. Garden roses on the whole are best suited by a rich loamy soil and for most, where light soils only are available, it is desirable to add clay or strong loam, but the Wichuraiana climbers thrive on a lighter soil. Where hard pruning is practised, as with most bedding roses, annual dressings of garden compost or well-decayed manure are necessary, and this may be augmented by bone-meal and sulphate of potash. This annual dressing may be put on in autumn and forked in after pruning is done in spring.

The best time for planting is the latter end of October or in November, though it may be done when necessary at any time when the weather is open and the soil workable up to the end of March. The holes made for planting should be wide enough to permit the roots to be spread out evenly, but it is important that they should be only deep enough to allow the junction of stock and scion to be buried 1 in. below the surface when the soil has settled down after planting. Too deep planting is detrimental and a frequent cause of failure. If the junction is just buried, rooting of the scion often occurs, and this is an advantage. The planting should always be firm and for the rest the ordinary rules for planting trees and shrubs apply.

If the planting is delayed until March the roses should be watered freely in the evening during dry periods in early summer and a mulch of decayed garden compost will be a help to them.

Newly planted bush and standard (not weeping) roses should be pruned back to 3 or 4 in. in the March or April following planting, the more vigorous being left with more buds than the weaker ones. Pruning should be to a bud pointing outwards. Newly planted climbing roses should also be pruned back, but one or two of the strongest shoots may be left after cutting back one-third to half and these should at once be tied in. Newly planted weeping standards should have all weak shoots cut back and the stronger ones left half or one-third their length.

Notes have already been given on pruning, and the general treatment should be as follows. For all roses cut away all dead, and (except Banksian Roses which flower on their twiggy growth) all unripe and old spent wood. Bedding roses and ordinary standards are cut back like newly planted bush roses, but less hard unless for exhibition flowers. This should be done in March or April. Climbing, Rambling, and Pillar Roses, Rugosas, Scotch, Austrian Briers, Provence Roses, and Moss Roses need little pruning—only the removal of dead or worn-out wood. The Wichuraiana and Climbing Polyantha varieties should be pruned soon after flowering finishes in Autumn. In addition to the Banksian Roses many other species described under Rosa need little pruning, e.g. *Rosa bracteata*, *R. hemisphaerica*, *R. Hugonis*, *R. laevigata*, *R. omeiensis*, *R. Primula*, *R. sericea*, *R. Willmottiae*, and *R. xanthina*, and their varieties and species allied to them. Where the special value of the plant is its fruit, the old exhausted wood should be pruned away in March, the best flowers and fruit being produced from wood of the previous year. Where fruit is not so important the shoots may be left to grow and flower for three years and then, unless still strong and vigorous, they should be pruned away. All cuts should be clean, made with a sharp knife or secateurs a little way above a bud, not quite close to it. Blunt tools crush or bruise and leave wounds difficult or impossible to heal, inviting decay and death.

Roses that have been budded or grafted need constant attention for the removal of suckers from the stock. Where brier or rugosa stocks have been used the suckers are usually readily recognized from their stems or leaves, but the growths of Manetti and perhaps some other types of stocks are not so easily distinguished and call for more careful observation. Where roses have been propagated by cuttings the sucker problem is not a serious one and growth from below ground, being of the same type and variety as the plant desired, may indeed be an advantage.

ROSES IN POTS AND UNDER GLASS. In most conservatories and cool greenhouses it is possible to find space for roses which can be planted out and trained up under the roof glass, on pillars, or on the back wall of lean-to houses. Some of the older varieties are especially suitable for these positions, e.g. Devoniensis, Lamarque, Maréchal Niel, and Niphetos; most of the climbing forms of the Tea and Hybrid Tea Roses also lend themselves to this method of treatment. It is not always easy to find suitable planting positions in these structures owing to the arrangement of the hot-water pipes, benches, and so on, but so far as possible the planting sites should be at least 2½ to 3 ft. deep. This will allow for ample drainage, an essential for success with Roses. The compost should consist of a good medium loam, some well-rotted manure, a 5-in. pot of bone-meal to each bushel of soil, and enough clean, coarse sand to keep the whole open. The same compost will serve for Roses in pots.

All the stronger-growing varieties of Tea Roses are specially suitable for growing in pots and they were at one time commonly so grown. They have, however, now been largely superseded by the many fine varieties of Hybrid Teas now available. Some of these are grown on a very large scale commercially to supply the great demand for Roses cut with long stiff stems, such as Columbia, Ophelia, Madame Butterfly, Richmond, and Roselandia. Many of the dwarf Polyantha varieties can also be grown with advantage in pots for decoration, and many of the Ramblers are also useful grown in this way.

For growing in pots plants may be lifted from the open ground and potted up in October. Under cool treatment they will give a good display in the following year, but if intended for forcing they should be established for a season in their flowering pots.

After potting the Hybrid Teas may be plunged outdoors in a sheltered place for the winter, protecting them with some dry litter or bracken; the more tender Tea varieties are better wintered in a cold pit or house.

If healthy and well furnished with roots the Roses will not need to be repotted every year, but some of the top soil should be removed and replaced with fresh compost. When growing and flowering occasional applications of liquid manure or some well-tried fertilizer will be helpful.

For forcing Roses established in pots, for flowering in early spring, artificial heat is necessary. They should be pruned, top-dressed, examined to see that the drainage is satisfactory, and if not have it corrected, and brought into a little heat in December or early January. A temperature of 45 to 50° F. is enough to start with and when growth begins and the days lengthen this should be gradually raised to about 65° F., giving plenty of air on all favourable occasions, but taking care at all times to avoid draughts, for exposure to draughts often lays them open to attacks of mildew. The plants should be sprayed several times a day with tepid water until the flowers begin to open; they may then be moved to a cool house, but if they are required only to supply flowers for cutting they should remain in the warmer house.

After flowering the pots should be plunged outdoors in an open sunny place where they must on no account be neglected, but must be regularly watered and fed so as to ensure strong matured wood for the next season.

Indoors a sharp lookout must be kept for attacks of greenfly which must be dealt with by light fumigations, and for mildew which often proves troublesome where ventilation has been faulty (*see below*).

The pruning of dwarf Roses in pots consists in cutting them more or less hard back according to the strength of the variety. Climbing Roses planted out will require to have all the weak growth thinned out during the growing season, and early in the year, when they are being started, some at least of the strong shoots should be cut hard back. Varieties such as Maréchal Niel, which give only one crop of flowers in the season, should be pruned hard back as soon as flowering is finished, and the young shoots that form should be trained up about 1 ft. apart to fill the allotted space; wherever possible 2 permanent shoots should be trained horizontally at the height of the eaves and the lateral shoots trained up from these; this method of training is also suitable for other strong-growing varieties.

(J. C.)

PROPAGATION. *Budding*. The chief method of propagating roses is by budding (*see* **Budding**). For all roses except standards budding is best done so low down on the shoot that the union can be buried, and in order that this shall be possible the stocks should be earthed up after planting to a height of 3 or 4 in. The earth is removed from the base of the stock on the side where the bud is to be inserted just before budding is done, so that the bud may be put in a little way above the roots, and where the bark is soft and easily manipulated. It is often found well to bud on the north side of the stock for drying out is less liable to occur there.

Several different stocks are, or have been, used for roses and each has its advocates, but the general opinion is that for British conditions for plants to be grown in the open, the common brier (*Rosa canina*) is to be preferred, whether raised from cuttings or from seed. Among other stocks are *R. rugosa*, used perhaps most frequently for standards; Manetti, originated in Italy as a seedling selected by Signor Manetti at Monza about 1835, and propagated by cuttings; *R. multiflora*, raised from cuttings which root freely; *R. laxa*, introduced about 1803, recommended for its thin bark and the earliness at which it is ready for budding compared with other stocks, but useful for the purpose over only a short season; other selected stocks are known as Brogs, Deegen's, Kokulensky's, and Senff's, while Blush China has been frequently used. A comparison of these stocks will be found in the J.R.H.S., vol. 58, 1933, pp. 344–71.

The cuttings of stocks are made and treated as described below and though these rooted cuttings are often planted in autumn, if well-rooted it is better that they should be laid in until the following February and then planted in single rows 2½ ft. apart and 1 ft. between, or if space is important, in double rows, 1 ft. between each and 3 ft. before the next double row. The single row is, however, best. The shoots taken for cuttings should be well-ripened and the cuttings 9 to 12 in. long. They are put in only sufficiently deep to keep them in place and well earthed up.

Budding takes place in the following June, July, or August, when after the base is exposed as already mentioned, the area in which the bud is to be inserted is rubbed clean of soil by the aid of a piece of coarse cloth such as hessian, and any root in the way removed. Before beginning the operation the readiness with which the bark lifts should be ascertained, for everything should be done to ensure the carrying out of the operation with a minimum of delay.

The scions are taken from the varieties desired, preferably the day before the buds are put in, shoots that have flowered being selected and cut about 1 ft. long, tied in bundles of one variety and labelled and stood in water until the following day, the leaves having been cut off to the leaf-stalk and the stem cleared of prickles. The best buds are usually about the middle of the shoot. In making the bud ready the cut should be made through the bark about ½ in. above the bud and carried down behind it, dipping a little to avoid injuring it, and brought out about 1 in. below, but not severing it entirely. The cut strip is then held and the separation finished by peeling the bark off still further down. The piece removed is held by the leaf-stalk and the wood removed by a quick movement, leaving the core of the bud in place and uninjured. The lower end of the bark is then trimmed to a rounded end about ½ in. below the bud. Where numbers of buds have to be put in the buds are usually prepared very shortly before insertion and kept moist (as they must be) in a tin box with a moist felt lining.

The ordinary T-budding is practised and the wound tied in with moist, flat raffia, leaving the bud itself uncovered. The proximity of moist earth should obviate the need for waxing, or other protection. Usually only one bud is inserted on a stock, but two buds may be put in one above the other in the same longitudinal slit and so provide some ensurance against failure. It is desirable that the newly inserted buds should remain dormant, but if they start into growth not later than August they will probably be able to withstand the winter. If they start later than this it is well to shorten them back somewhat in September to encourage the growth to ripen. The first sign that the bud has taken will be the readiness with which the stalk of the parent leaf falls away when touched.

The top of the stock should be cut back in February following the budding and a stake should be in position ready to tie the growth from the bud and long enough to keep it tied during its first year.

Stocks to be budded as standards are strong shoots from the roots of the Dog-rose, one year old and about ¾ in. thick, showing dark-green mottling with streaks of brown on the bark; the summer shoots with waxy green bark are too pithy and soft to make good stocks. The shoots are cut away from the parent, leaving a piece of hard root, but not part bearing buds, with a few fibrous roots at the base. If these have been got some time before they can be planted they should be stood with their bases in water until well soaked, but it is best if they can be put in the moist earth at once. The length left for the stem depends upon the maturity of the growth and the purpose for which the standard is needed. For half-standards they may be shortened to about 3 ft. from the ground, for ordinary standards 4 ft. to 4 ft. 6 in., for weeping standards 6 to 8 ft., cutting back in all to a good eye. The budding is done in the following summer on the new shoots formed at the top of the stem (not in the old wood as for dwarfs) and all the lower shoots must be rubbed out as they are seen in spring, leaving the shoots near the top from which to select three equally spaced on which to bud. The buds are prepared as already described and are inserted on the lower side of each of the three selected shoots, the remainder are removed. The longitudinal slit to receive the bud is begun as near as possible to the base of the shoot and no transverse cut is made, the bud being slipped in sideways, raising the bark with the handle of the knife so as to enable this to be done. The budded shoot is not cut back until the following spring when it is shortened. Tying should be done with soft budding cotton which will remain through the winter and act as a protection to the young bud until the time for shortening the budded shoot arrives.

Grafting is much less practised than budding and is usually done to obtain early roses from maidens under glass, the stocks being rooted in pots and the scions put on by whip or cleft grafting, tied with raffia. Grafting may be done in January and February under glass, and is sometimes done in March in the open. When done under glass the stocks are started in a little heat and so obtained in advance of the scions which are cut from the open, pieces of ripe wood, about 6 in. long, being used. Shorter pieces may be used as scions for cleft-grafting. The junction of stock and scion may be waxed or clayed to keep the moisture in. Manetti stocks are often used on which to graft, and the resulting plants grown on under glass, but they may, after the union is made, be hardened off and planted in the open.

Cuttings. Roses on their own roots have the advantage that any suckers produced are of the same nature as the variety desired, and if, through bad weather or other cause, the upper part of the plant is killed, shoots from below ground will replace it. Many of the species can be propagated readily by cuttings made in the same way and treated like those of black currants, and so can many of the garden roses. In taking them no buds should be removed and care must be taken that the earth about them is firmed after frost. The tops of some may die, but the part underground may still remain and grow. The plants so raised will usually be ready to move in the following autumn. Some of the garden roses with wide pith and somewhat soft shoots are not easy to raise and some of the more tender roses must be raised under glass, the cuttings being put in sandy soil in pots, being dibbled in rather close and stood in cold frames for the winter and then given a little bottom heat in spring. Only well-ripened shoots taken in autumn are fit for use as cuttings treated in these ways.

Leafy shoots taken in summer when the wood is half ripe, made with 2 or 3 eyes, may usually be readily rooted. Such shoots taken from roses forced under glass and put in a close frame with a little heat, or on a gentle hot bed, kept moist and shaded will, as a rule, soon root and may then be potted off singly and later hardened gradually before going into the open air.

Cuttings may be with or without a heel and the usual precautions taken in propagation by cuttings must of course be observed.

Layers. Dwarf and weeping roses where the shoots can be brought to the ground can be propagated with certainty by layering firm wood in June and early July. The layer is made with a tongue and pegged down in the usual way. It should have rooted by the autumn and can then be detached from the parent and planted. If suitable shoots are not available by this time the layering must be deferred and the rooting will not be sufficiently forward to warrant the detachment and transplanting until the following year.

Suckers produced by roses growing on their own roots may be taken off in autumn and used for increasing stock. Even if without roots the suckers will usually form them if planted in sandy soil and slightly protected from strong winds through the winter.

Seeds. Roses are raised from seed to produce new varieties and for providing stocks, *R. canina* being the principal form used for the latter purpose. The hips should remain on the plant until fully ripe, and when gathered dried in the sun, the seed being then rubbed out. It may be sown in a warm, sheltered position outdoors or in shallow boxes or pots of sandy soil stood in a cold frame at once, or it may be stored in sand or soil until spring, guarding them very carefully against rats and mice. Birds are also destructive when the seed is sown in the open. Autumn-sown seeds usually germinate in the following spring but may lie dormant for a year; indeed, germination is usually irregular. Seedlings raised in pots, &c., usually need pricking off as soon as large enough; they are allowed to grow on in the open until the autumn when all that are large enough are transplanted from 6 to 12 in. apart.

If the seedlings are from seed obtained after cross-pollination or from naturally pollinated flowers of garden forms they are often used as material for budding, every bud being utilized, since except for colour they do not show the full characters of the flower in the first flowering from seed; or they may be allowed to flower and the character judged after cutting-back for the following year. A large proportion of such seedlings will probably be no advance upon existing varieties and should be discarded, but something can be done to minimize this by careful selection of the parents, both seed and pollen. The most certain results can be obtained by carrying out the process of pollination under glass where the flowers can be protected from chance pollination by insects or wind. Timely emasculation of the seed parents is necessary to obviate self-pollination.

DISEASES. Rose roots may suffer from Crown Gall (q.v.). The stems may show various brown lesions or even deep corrugated cankers due to the fungi *Coniothyrium Fuckelii* or *C. rosarum*, the latter generally causing graft canker and entering at the junction of graft and scion. All cankered stems should be cut out and burnt. The Grey Mould fungus, *Botrytis cinerea*, can damage weak or soft sappy rose stems, often entering through dead buds, but should not seriously affect vigorous and hardy shoots. On the foliage of roses under glass the downy mildew fungus, *Peronospora sparsa*, may cause brown spots on the leaves and defoliate the trees, and spraying with Bordeaux mixture may be required. Powdery Mildew (*Sphaerotheca pannosa*) is very common, causing an obvious white powdery growth on leaves and stems and should be checked by spraying with lime-sulphur 1 part in 60 parts of water, or with Bordeaux mixture, or by dusting with green sulphur. This mildew may be serious in rambler roses, especially if the roots suffer from dryness, so that ramblers growing against walls, &c., in dry summers need watering or mulching above the roots to keep the soil moist. Black Spot (*Diplocarpon rosae*) causes circular black blotches on the leaves and requires to be combated by spraying with Bordeaux mixture from June onwards and burning or burying deeply all fallen leaves in autumn. Some varieties are also affected on the shoots as black scabby patches, this occurs severely in some rose species. Such affected shoots should be destroyed. Some varieties, on the other hand, are very resistant to Black Spot. Rose Rust (*Phragmidium mucronatum*) forms all its stages (*see* **Rusts**) on the rose. The spring (aecidiospores) stage is seen as a yellowish-orange powder on shoots which may become twisted and malformed; these shoots should be destroyed. Some rose species are severely affected by this spring stage. The summer (uredospore) and autumn (teleutospore) stages appear on rose leaves generally on the under-surface as yellow and black spots respectively and the leaves lose vigour. Spraying with Bordeaux mixture is advised for rust starting in mid-June and repeating if necessary, in addition to which the fallen leaves should be burnt or dug in deeply. Where roses suffer severely from either Rust or Black Spot it is possible that the plants are weak from some other cause and thus fall easy prey to these fungus parasites. Although spraying may help such plants it is essential to make sure that the soil conditions are suitable and provided with food and moisture so that the plants can develop healthy roots and be encouraged to grow vigorously.

(D. E. G.)

PESTS. APHIDES. A number of Aphid species infest cultivated Roses, and these pests are the bane of all who grow these plants owing to their high rate of increase, their persistence, the amount of serious injury done to the young shoots and foliage, and the quantity of honeydew excreted by them. The winged forms that appear on Roses during some part of the year are important in that they migrate either to neighbouring Rose bushes or to secondary hosts, which include many weeds. Among the more important Rose-infesting species are: *Macrosiphum rosae*, which is the commonest and largest Green Fly found on Roses. It overwinters in the egg stage on Rose and on Teazle and, in mild winters and in sheltered positions may continue to live and breed on the Rose throughout the year. The green or pinkish Aphides cluster thickly on the shoots, which shrivel and die. *M. dirhodum* is an abundant species though less important as a pest than the former. It migrates to various Grasses and Cereals, and later returns to the Rose for winter egg-laying. *Chaetosiphon tetrahodus* and *Myzaphis rosarum* appear to be confined entirely to Roses, and are smaller insects than *Macrosiphum* and somewhat less common. *Longicaudus trirhodus* overwinters in the egg stage on Roses and lives on the leaves in spring and early summer, when winged forms appear and migrate to Columbines (*Aquilegia*), upon which plants serious damage is done. *Maculolachnus rosae* is a root-feeder, and occurs on the lower part of the stem and on the roots of Bush Roses, especially on those imported from the Continent. These root lice are attended by Ants that swarm round the infested roots.

Rose Aphides have many natural enemies, including birds, ladybirds and their grubs, hover fly maggots, lacewing fly grubs, and numerous parasitic Hymenopterous 'wasps', all of which aid in reducing their numbers but upon which no reliance can be placed to eradicate an infestation.

Control measures include thorough spraying of the infested shoots and underside of the leaves, as soon as the insects are seen to be present, with a Nicotine-Soap wash or with a Derris or Pyrethrum preparation. Spraying should be carried out on dull days or in the evening as the leaves of certain varieties are tender and very susceptible to spray injury, especially by soap-containing washes. Dusting with Nicotine or Derris dusts is also effective. At least 2 applications of any wash or dust is essential within a week owing to the high rate of reproduction in this group of insects. Any wingless, viviparous female Aphid that escapes the first application is capable of producing a large colony of young within a few days. The roots of newly acquired Roses should be thoroughly washed clear of all soil prior to planting to avoid introducing the root pests. Certain species of garden Ants invade Aphis-infested plants for the honeydew excreted by the lice, and may even transport them from one bush to another, so that the destruction of Ants' nests in and near Rose beds is advisable. A narrow band of grease round the stems of standard Roses will prevent the passage of Ants to the branches and shoots. It is safe to spray older and well-established bushes, standards, and climbers in December with 3 per cent. tar-distillate egg-killing wash.

CATERPILLARS. The caterpillars of a large number of Moths attack the buds, leaves, and blossoms of cultivated Roses, some being of common occurrence and consistently destructive (Tortrix larvae), while others appear in isolated attacks (the larvae of the Brindled Beauty, Mottled Umber, and Winter Moths). There is considerable variation in the larval habits, the caterpillars of some Moths feeding openly on the leaves (Buff Tip, Dagger, Gold Tail, Lackey, Vapourer, and the Geometers previously mentioned); some burrowing into the blossom buds and rolling the leaves (Tortrix Moths or Rose Maggots); and others mining the foliage (Tineid Moths, e.g. *Nepticula anomalella*). The more important species of Macro-lepidoptera, including the Buff Tip, Lackey, and Vapourer Moths, are dealt with under their respective headings.

Among the Micro-lepidoptera are found some of the most serious pests—the so-called Rose Maggots—which not only eat the foliage but roll the leaves and burrow into the flower-buds. The fleshy stout caterpillars of a number of Tortricid Moths occur on Roses, and the following list includes those that are widely distributed. After each species, in parentheses, is given the months of appearance and the general body colour of the caterpillar; *Cacoecia podana* (5, 6: green); *C. rosana* (5, 6: dark olive-green); *Eucosma tripunctana* (4, 5: reddish-brown); *Notocelia roborana* (5, 6: reddish-brown); *Peronia holmiana* (5, 6: yellowish); and *P. variegana* (6, 7: greenish-yellow). Several of these species have a wide range of host plants, including fruit and forest trees, especially Oak, and various ornamental shrubs. They pupate as a rule within the tightly rolled leaves, from which the empty chrysalides may be seen protruding after the moths have emerged.

The measures of control will depend upon the larval habits, and upon the number of bushes attacked and the severity of the infestation. Caterpillars which feed openly on the foliage are readily destroyed when young with Nicotine-Soap wash or Nicotine dust. If this early spraying has been neglected, it is necessary to spray the foliage lightly with D.D.T. emulsion. The destruction of the leaf-rolling Tortricid caterpillars is more difficult as they are protected from the action of contact washes within the tightly curled leaves. Hand picking is an effective method of dealing with small outbreaks, the maggots within the rolled leaves and flower buds being collected and destroyed or crushed *in situ*. Thorough application of a Nicotine-Soap wash to both leaf surfaces early in the year, in mid-April and repeating once or twice during May, will control leaf-eating caterpillars other than Tortricids. Nicotine dust correctly applied will kill a number of caterpillars living within tightly rolled leaves. Rose bushes attacked by leaf-mining larvae should be looked over in June and July, and the mined leaves removed and burned.

ROSE GALLS. Of the several types of galls produced on Roses as a result of Gall-wasp attacks, the Bedeguar, Moss, or Robin's Pincushion is the best known. This gall consists of moss-like filaments, greenish and later reddish, surrounding a cluster of cells containing the grubs of *Rhodites rosae*. It occurs chiefly on wild Roses, but also occasionally on cultivated Roses. No control measures are necessary other than the cutting off and burning of the galls as soon as they are seen.

ROSE-HIP FLY, *Spilographa alternata*. This marbled-winged fruit fly attacks the hips of many species of *Rosa*. The fruits may be speckled due to the oviposition punctures of the female fly. The legless maggots feed within the fruits, which shrivel, and the yellowish-white, barrel-shaped puparia are found in the fruits and in the soil beneath attacked plants. No measures are necessary against this pest, but it is advisable to examine all Rose seeds for the presence of the puparia, which may be floated out in water.

ROSE LEAF-HOPPER, *Typhlocyba rosae* is a sucking insect responsible for the pale, mottled areas on Rose leaves during the spring and summer. In severe attacks the foliage becomes chlorotic and falls prematurely. The active, jumping and flying, yellowish-green adult hoppers are on the foliage throughout the year, but become most abundant during dry weather in May and June. They take flying leaps into the air when the bush is disturbed. The eggs are laid in the leaves, and the pale yellowish, wingless larvae occur on the underside of the leaves where they suck the sap and give rise to mottled and marbled areas. All stages are found on the leaves during mid-summer, together with the dry greyish cast-skins which are anchored by their feeding stylets and persist for months, so that they are sometimes mistaken for the living insects. A second brood appears in August and September, and the winter is passed in the immature and adult stages. Some varieties of Roses are more susceptible to attack than others, and those with thin, papery leaves are severely affected.

The foliage should be thoroughly sprayed with a Nicotine-Soap wash as soon as the nymphs are seen on the leaves in spring, or the plants may be dusted with Nicotine dust. It is essential to direct the wash to the underside of the leaves so that the hoppers are wetted by the liquid. The ground beneath attacked plants should be sprayed immediately after the foliage to destroy the hoppers which fall to the ground during the spraying.

ROSE SAWFLIES. Among the most destructive pests of cultivated Roses are the larvae of Sawflies, of which nearly 20 species are recorded in this country, some being widely distributed while others are less common and confined to the south. The larval habits of the species vary, some feeding openly on the leaves (*Emphytus cinctus*); some rolling the leaves (*Blennocampa pusilla*); and others boring into the shoots (*Ardis brunniventris*).

The Rose Emphytus, *E. cinctus*, is double-brooded, the dark-green larvae devouring the foliage in May and June, and in July and August. Pupation takes place either in the soil, among rubbish, or within the shoots.

Symptoms of attack by Leaf-rolling Sawfly

The Rose Leaf-rolling Sawfly, *B. pusilla*, causes the leaves to fold downwards and inwards, which is not only disfiguring but prevents their proper functioning. The small, black, shiny Sawflies appear in May and June, and the female inserts an egg in the leaf-margin. The result is that the leaf reacts to the stimulus, so that there is a marginal folding of the foliage soon after the egg is inserted. The greyish-green larva may be seen later within the leaf-fold. Pupation takes place in the soil.

The Rose Slugworm, *Endelomyia aethiops*, is named from the slug-like appearance of the larva, which is pale greenish-yellow but is devoid of any slimy exudation. It feeds during May and June, and in August, on the upper leaf surface, the lower skin remaining intact, so that the leaves become partially or completely skeletonized. Pupation takes place in the soil.

The Rose-leaf Sawfly, *Arge ochropus* (*rosae*), is a pest of cultivated Roses in the southern counties, where the brightly coloured larvae occur on the leaves during July and August. Pupation takes place in the soil.

The Rose Shoot-borer Sawfly, *Ardis brunniventris*, bores downwards during its larval stage in the shoots of wild and cultivated Roses.

The chief remedies against Rose Sawflies are hand-picking and burning the attacked and rolled leaves and tunnelled shoots; washing the roots of newly acquired bushes free of soil in which may be lodged the larval cocoons; lightly spraying the foliage with D.D.T. emulsion; and forcibly spraying or dusting the attacked leaves at the first sign of larval attack with Nicotine-Soap wash or Nicotine dust.

ROSE SCALE INSECTS. The 2 species that occur on Roses are the European Brown or Peach Scale, *Lecanium corni*, and the Scurfy Scale, *Diaspis rosae*. These pests multiply to a considerable extent only on old and neglected plants, being comparatively uncommon on plants that are given regular sprayings of Nicotine washes.

ROSE THRIPS, *Thrips fuscipennis*, occurs on Roses and on several herbaceous plants in the open, but is specially harmful to the flowers of forced Roses and, occasionally, to Cucumbers. The eggs are laid in the outer petals of Roses as the sepals begin to open—the effect of which is to cause malformation of the blooms—and in the weak shoots known as 'water shoots'. The adult Thrips over-winter in glasshouses in cracks and crevices of the woodwork, and begin to feed and to lay their eggs from early March.

High temperatures, dry soil conditions, and a humid and static atmosphere are factors predisposing plants to attacks by Thrips in glasshouses. Regular syringing of the plants with clear water will wash off large numbers of their nymphs, which are unable to regain their host plants. Remove and burn all severely infested blooms as it is difficult to reach the minute insects deep within the flowers, and spray the developing buds at intervals with a Nicotine-Soap wash.

(G. F. W.)

ROSE ACACIA. *See* **Robinia hispida.**

ROSE, ALPINE. *See* **Rhododendron ferrugineum, R. hirsutum.**

ROSE APPLE. *See* **Eugenia Jambos.**

ROSE BAY. *See* **Epilobium angustifolium, Nerium Oleander.**

ROSE BEDEGUAR. *See* **Rose,** PESTS, ROSE GALLS.

ROSE BOX. *See* **Cotoneaster.**

ROSE CAMPION. *See* **Lychnis.**

ROSE CHAFER. *See* **Chafers.**

ROSE, CHRISTMAS. *See* **Helleborus niger.**

ROSE, ELDER. *See* **Viburnum Opulus.**

ROSE, GUELDER. *See* **Viburnum Opulus.**

ROSE, JAMAICA. *See* **Blakea trinervis, Meriania.**

ROSE, JAPANESE. *See* **Rosa rugosa;** occasionally used for **Camellia japonica.**

ROSE, JUNO'S. *See* **Lilium candidum.**

ROSE, LENTEN. *See* **Helleborus orientalis.**

ROSE MALLOW. *See* **Hibiscus Moscheutos.**

ROSE OF HEAVEN. *See* **Silene Coeli-rosa.**

ROSE OF JERICHO. *See* **Anastatica hierochuntica; Resurrection Plants.**

ROSE OF SHARON. *See* **Hypericum calycinum. A**

ROSE PINK. *See* **Sabbatia angularis.**

ROSE, ROCK. *See* **Cistus, Helianthemum.**

ROSE ROOT. *See* **Sedum roseum.**

ROSE SCURFY SCALE. *See* **Rose Scale Insects.**

ROSE SLUGWORM. *See* **Rose Sawflies.**

ROSE WILLOW. *See* **Salix rubra.**

ROSE, WIND. *See* **Roemeria hybrida.**

ROSE WOOD. *See* **Dalbergia.**

ROSELLIN'IA. A genus of fungi among the Ascomycetes. This genus contains several parasitic species which are interesting in being root parasites, living in the soil and spreading by means of rhizomorphs. They therefore resemble the Honey fungus which is a Basidiomycete (*see* **Honey fungus**) in their mode of life but Rosellinia spp. of course produce their final fructifications as perithecium (q.v.). Two of the best-known species are *R. quercina*, the cause of root rot in young oak trees (*see* **Quercus diseases**), and *R. necatrix* causing White Root Rot in grape vines where the drainage is not satisfactory.

D. E. G.

ROSEMARY (*Rosmarinus officinalis*). A hardy, evergreen shrub the foliage of which has been used for making Rosemary Tea, a decoction sometimes used for relieving headache. It was also used in making Rosemary Wine. The young fresh leaves and stems, and the flowers, have also been used in flavouring stews and fish and meat sauces, and in small quantities in cider cup and claret cup and in salads. Mrs. Marian Cran gives a recipe for moth destroyer consisting of ½ lb. dried Rosemary, ½ lb. dried Mint, ¼ lb. dried Tansy, ¼ lb. dried Thyme, thoroughly mixed with 2 tablespoonfuls of fresh ground cloves, to be scattered freely among the clothes it is desired to protect. Seeds may be sown on a warm, sunny border. Cuttings about 6 in. long, taken in summer and dibbled in a shady border, under a hand-glass will form plants ready for transplanting into permanent quarters the following autumn, or shoots may be layered in summer. Rosemary does best in light, rather dry soil and with some shelter from wind. The common green-leaved form is hardier than the gold- or silver-striped varieties.

ROSEMARY, WILD. *See* **Ledum palustre.**

Rosenbachia'nus -a -um, in honour of General Nikolai O. von Rosenbach, Governor of Turkistan.

Rosenbergia'nus -a -um, in honour of C. B. H. Baron von Rosenberg, 1817–88, of Darmstadt, who collected in Sumatra and New Guinea.

Rosenstock'ii, in honour of E. Rosenstock, b. 1856, of Frankenberg.

ROSES, ATTAR OF. *See* **Rosa.**

ROSETTE DISEASE. *See* **Lilium Diseases.**

ROSETTE MULLEIN. *See* **Ramonda Myconi.**

ro'seus -a -um, rosae- or ***rosi-*** in compound words, rose-coloured.

ROSIN. When resin obtained by tapping the trunks of the Scots Pine, *Pinus sylvestris*, is distilled, the distillate being oil of turpentine, the residue is rosin.

rosmarinifo'lius -a -um, with leaves like Rosmarinus.

ROSMARI'NUS (sea-dew, the ancient Latin name for rosemary). FAM. *Labiatae.* Although usually regarded as monotypic, various authors have made as many as 12 species of rosemary. Dr. Turrill, in the Kew Bulletin for 1920, p. 105, reduces these to 4, viz. *R. officinalis*, *R. laxiflorus*, *R. Tournefortii*, and *R. lavandulaceus.* The last is the plant that has been grown as var. *prostratus* and proved not hardy.

R. lavandula'ceus. Prostrate. *l.* about ½ in. long, $\frac{1}{25}$ in. wide. *fl.* crowded in a many-fld. infl. about 1¼ in. long; cal. much more hairy than in *R. officinalis* and not glandular as in that plant. SYN. *R officinalis prostratus* of gardens. Not hardy.

R. officina'lis. Evergreen shrub up to 6 or 7 ft., usually much less; shoots downy. *l.* opposite, linear, ¾ to 2 in. long, $\frac{1}{16}$ to ⅛ in. wide, sessile, margins revolute, dark shining green above, white-downy beneath. *fl.* few in axils of previous year's shoots; cor. 2-lipped, ½ to ¾ in. wide, pale violet. May. S. Europe, Asia Minor. (S.B.F.G. 14.) var. **albiflo'rus** (or *al'bus*), *fl.* white; **angustifo'lius,** *l.* about $\frac{1}{16}$ in. wide, dark green, cor. large, bright blue; **au'reus,** *l.* marked with yellow; **erect'us** (or *fastigiatus* or *pyramidalis*), branches erect; **hu'milis,** (or *prostratus*), prostrate with spreading branches; **prostra'tus** of gardens, *see* **R. lavandulaceus.** The rosemary has been valued in Britain during 4 or 5 centuries for its attractive appearance and pleasant aromatic fragrance. It is only injured by very severe winters and is easily propagated by August-made cuttings placed in a cold frame in very sandy soil.

ros'sicus -a -um, Russian.

Ross'ii, in honour of (1) Rear-Admiral Sir John Ross, 1777–1856, arctic navigator, (2) Herman Ross, d. 1942, German botanist.

Rossianus -a -um in honour of Henry James Ross, 1820–1902, who grew a large collection of orchids near Florence.

rostella'tus -a -um, beaked.

ROSTELLUM. A small beak; the narrow extension of the upper edge of the stigma of some orchids.

rostra'tus -a -um, gradually ending in a long, straight, hard point, like the pod of a Radish.

rostrif'erus -a -um, nose-like, or nose-bearing.

ROSULA'RIA (*rosula*, a little rose; referring to the characteristic leaf-rosettes). FAM. *Crassulaceae.* There are some 20 species from Asia Minor to Cent. Asia, which have sometimes been included in Cotyledon (q.v.); they form stemless rosettes of narrow, stalkless leaves and usually produce numerous offsets. The inflorescence is terminal or lateral, the flowers bell-shaped. Most of the Rosularias will grow out of doors in sheltered places, otherwise they need the protection of a cold house or frame, but no heat.

R. Aizo'on. *l.* very small, tongue-shaped, ciliate, in crowded rosettes. *fl.* yellowish, in a loose, few-fld. spray. Asia Minor. SYN. *Cotyledon Aizoon, Umbilicus Aizoon.*

R. glab'ra. *l.* spatulate, bright green, bare. *fl.* pale yellow or greenish, tips pink. E. Turkistan. SYN. *Cotyledon glabra, Umbilicus glaber.*

R. globulariaefo'lia. *l.* 1½ in. long, spatulate. *fl.* pinkish. Asia Minor. SYN. *Cotyledon globulariaefolia, Umbilicus globulariaefolius, Sedum globulariaefolium.*

R. pal'lida. *l.* small, surface and edge with numerous grey hairs. *fl.* white or cream, erect, large. Asia Minor. SYN. *Cotyledon chrysantha, Umbilicus chrysanthus, U. pallidus.*

R. platyphyl'la. Whole plant hairy and glandular. *fl.* white. Altai. SYN. *Cotyledon platyphylla, Umbilicus platyphyllus.*

Rosularia pallida

R. Sempervi'vum. *l.* spatulate, hairy and glandular. *fl.* pale to deep pink. Caucasus, Asia Minor. SYN. *Cotyledon Sempervivum, C. libanotica, C. Pestalozzae, Umbilicus Sempervivum.* A variable species.

R. serra'ta. *l.* 1 to 1½ in. long, with a finely toothed edge. *fl.* white, marked with red. Grecian Archipelago and Asia Minor. SYN. *Cotyledon serrata, Umbilicus serratus.*

R. turkesta'nica. *l.* with rough hairs on surface and edge. *fl.* white, striped with red outside. Turkistan. SYN. *Cotyledon turkestanica, Umbilicus turkestanicus.*

V. H.

rosulate, collected in a rosette.

ROSY APPLE APHIS. *See* **Apple Aphides.**

ROSY RUSTIC MOTH, *Hydroecia micacea*, is widely distributed throughout N. and Cent. Europe and is a pest in the British Is., especially in Scotland and the Northern Counties. The caterpillars are stem-borers, and feed primarily on weeds, including Docks, Couch-grass, Horsetails (*Equisetum*), and Plantains. It is important economically owing to the larvae tunnelling in Potato haulm, Tomato stems, Hop bines, and Rhubarb crowns, especially when they are grown in freshly broken pasture and waste-land and weedy ground. The moth has a wing expanse of 1 to 1½ in., the fore-wings have a rosy hue interrupted by a grey band at the outer margin, and the hind-wings are grey with a narrow dark median line. The caterpillars are pinkish with a reddish stripe along the back, and with a number of dark-brown wart-like spots, each armed with a bristle, on the sides; the head is reddish-brown, and the second segment bears a polished, brown, semicircular plate with a somewhat similar plate on the last segment. The eggs are laid on the lower leaves of the host plants in August and September, and the young caterpillars overwinter in the soil, becoming active again in spring when they tunnel into the stems of their food plants. They are fully grown in late July, when they pupate in earthen cells in the ground. Injury to Potatoes and other crops becomes evident in June and early July.

Collect and burn all attacked shoots and stems in June and July. Destroy weed hosts, especially Docks and Plantains, by regular hoeing throughout the growing season. Careful watch should be kept upon Potatoes and Tomatoes in summer, especially on plants grown in ground that has been overgrown with weeds in the previous year.

G. F. W.

Ro'tang, Malayan name for a palm.

rotate, wheel-shape; circular and spreading horizontally, e.g. a gamopetalous corolla with a very short tube and spreading lobes.

Rothia'nus -a -um, in honour of A. W. Roth, 1757–1834, physician and botanist of Dotlingen.

Rothschildia'nus -a -um, in honour of Baron Lionel Walter Rothschild, 1868–1945, of Tring, or of Ferdinand James de Rothschild of Lodgehill, Aylesbury, *c.* 1888.

rotomagen'sis, of Rouen.

Rottboel'lii, in honour of Chr. Fr. Rottboel, 1727–97, of Copenhagen, botanist, correspondent of Linnaeus.

Rott'leri, in honour of J. P. Rottler, 1749–1836, orientalist of Strassburg and India.

ROTATION CROPPING. Cropping by Rotation is a term used in reference to kitchen-garden management. It implies that the ground on which a certain crop is grown shall be planted in Rotation, by another crop of, as far as possible, quite a different character. This system is pretty generally believed in and practised in large gardens; in small ones, there is often neither sufficient space nor variety in the crops annually grown to give an opportunity for changing the situation for each. Where plenty of manure can be added for each crop, rotation is of not so much consequence, as additional nutriment will thereby be supplied to take the place of that which the preceding one will have absorbed. It is, however, a good plan to adopt a system of Rotation Cropping, so far as possible, as one sort of vegetable will not, as a rule, require exactly the same constituent parts of the soil to nourish it as another which is of an entirely different nature and habit. In changing crops, it is best to avoid planting any to succeed others which belong to the same Family, as, for instance, the different representatives of the extensive Brassica or Cabbage tribe. These should be made to follow such crops as Beans, Onions, Peas, Potatoes, &c. It is invariably a good arrangement to grow Peas on land which has, during the previous year, been planted with Celery. Many other instances might be named, but they would not be generally applicable as, for various reasons, ground has to be cropped at certain times and seasons, when it is impossible to pay very much attention to planting under such a system as that indicated. Crops grown for the use of their roots should not follow one another if it can be avoided; such, for instance, as Carrots, Parsnips, and other plants of the family Umbelliferae. Onions may follow and be followed by plants of the Brassica tribe.

Not only is rotation a means of economizing manure but it is also an important aid in avoiding infection by disease organisms and pests, for only a few of these attack many kinds of plants. It is furthermore an aid to carrying out thorough cultivation, for by it successive thirds of the kitchen garden can be kept clear for deep autumn digging each year.

ROTHMAN'NIA. Included under **Gardenia.**

ROTTING. This word covers many kinds of putrefaction and decay caused by the growth of fungi and bacteria in plant tissues whether living or dead. The term is usually qualified to describe the type of rot in certain diseases, so we have Brown Rot in Apples (Sclerotinia sp.); Dry Rot in Potatoes (*Fusarium caeruleum*), in Gladioli (*Sclerotinia gladioli*), in Swedes (*Phoma lingam*); Soft Rot in Carrot, Turnip, Swede, Parsnip, Arum lily, Iris, Cabbage, Hyacinth (*Bacterium carotovorum*); Hard Rot in Gladioli (*Septoria gladioli*); Heart Rot in deciduous and coniferous trees (Bracket fungi of various kinds); Heart Rot in Celery (*Bacterium carotovorum*); Crown Rot in Rhubarb (*Bacterium rhaponticum*); Grey Bulb Rot in Tulips (*Sclerotium tuliparum*); Foot Rot in Tomatoes and Cineraria (*Phytophthora cryptogea*), in Dwarf Beans (Fusarium spp.), in Cucumber (*Bacterium carotovorum*); Black Rot in Cabbage, Turnip, Seakale, &c. (*Pseudomonas campestris*); Buck Eye Rot in Tomatoes (*Phytophthora parasitica*), Stem Rot in Tomatoes (*Didymella lycopersici*). The foregoing rots are all caused by fungal or bacterial parasites, but some rots are of the non-parasitic class, e.g. Blossom End Rot in Tomato fruits due to excessive shortage of water when the young fruits are forming, or Heart Rot in Turnip and Beetroot due to boron deficiency. In general, fleshy structures may be expected to show a soft type of rot and woody tissues a dry rot, but this is by no means always the case. Most of the above rots are mentioned under their various plant headings and root rots are discussed under that title. It must not be forgotten that many wood-rotting fungi and bacteria which destroy poles, posts, and structural timber are purely saprophytic and enter the tissues in the presence of moisture and air usually at ground-level, thus creating the necessity of treating wooden posts at their bases with some kind of preservative.

D. E. G.

ROTT'LERA. *See* **Chirita hamosa.**

rotunda'tus -a -um, rounded, especially at ends.

rotun'dus -a -um (***rotundi-*** in compound words), round in outline.

ROUGE PLANT. *See* **Carthamus tinctorius.**

ROUGH LEAVES. The first leaves produced after the Cotyledons.

ROUND WORMS. *See* **Eelworms.**

ROUPA'LA (native name in Guiana). FAM. *Proteaceae.* A genus of over 60 species of handsome trees or shrubs, natives of Trop. America. Leaves alternate, leathery, rigid, entire or toothed, simple or pinnate (sometimes on the same tree). Flowers regular, in pairs on axillary or terminal racemes; perianth cylindrical, the 4 segments eventually recurved at apex, 1 stamen inserted on the middle of each. Fruit a hard, obliquely 2-valved, short-stalked capsule. The Roupalas need stove conditions and a compost of peat and loam. They can be propagated by cuttings in sand under a glass with bottom heat.

R. au'rea. Shrub or small tree. Young shoots and l.-stalks densely clothed with golden hairs. Brazil. 1866.

R. Boissieria'na. *l.* simple, 4 to 5 in. long including stalk, 1½ to 2 in. wide, ovate, narrowly pointed, rounded at the base, remotely bluntly toothed, glabrous. *fl.* yellow, ½ in. long, in solitary or paired racemes 5 to 6 in. long. Colombia. 1852.

R. complica'ta. Shrub 6 to 8 ft. *l.* ovate, 1½ to 5 in. long, 1 to 3 in. wide, thick, leathery, glaucous, entire or occasionally slightly bluntly toothed, slender-pointed, base rounded; stalk about 1 in. long. *Racemes* 3 to 5 in. long; fl. fragrant; perianth pale, rufous. Colombia. 1853.

R. heterophyl'la.* Shrub or small tree, 10 ft. *l.* pinnate, 2 ft. long; lflets. 9 to 13, ovate, pointed, shallowly bluntly toothed, 3 to 5 in. long, shining green above, veins prominent. *Racemes* about 3 in. long, axillary and terminal, solitary or in pairs. Brazil. (G.F. 402.) var. **variab'ilis,** *l.* simple, pinnately lobed.

R. macrophyl'la. Shrub 4 to 6 ft. *l.* pinnate, 2 to 3 ft. long; lflets. 9 to 15, ovate-oblong, pointed, irregularly coarsely toothed, 8 or 9 in. long, 2½ to 4 in. wide, shining on the upper side. Brazil. (G.F. 1863.)

R. monta'na. Shrub or small tree, 8 to 10 ft. *l.* simple, ovate to oval, slender-pointed, 2 to 4 in. long, about half as wide, rather plicate, 3 to 6 in. long. Perianth with 4 obovate, spreading segs. ½ in. long, white above, yellow beneath; 1 stamen (as in other species) stands erect on the upper surface. French Guiana. 1823.

R. obova'ta. Tree 18 to 24 ft. *l.* simple, 3 to 6 in. long, 1½ to 2½ in. wide, obovate, shortly pointed, sparsely toothed or entire, glabrous. *Racemes* solitary, axillary and terminal, 6 in. long. Colombia. 1855.

R. Pohl'ii.* Tree up to 20 ft., shoots densely covered with bright, rust-coloured wool. *l.* pinnate, 1 ft. or more long; lflets. 11 to 17, 3 to 5 in. long, up to 3 in. wide, obliquely ovate, coarsely sharply toothed, bright green above, paler and at first downy beneath. *fl.* densely set in erect, axillary, slender racemes, 3 to 5 in. long; perianth orange-red, ½ in. long, club-shaped at first. Brazil. (B.M. 6095.) SYN. *R. corcovadensis.*

W. J. B.

ROUPEL'LIA. *See* **Strophanthus.**

ROVE BEETLE. *See* **Devil's Coach Horse.**

ROWAN or **ROAN TREE.** *See* **Sorbus Aucuparia.**

Roxburgh'ii, in honour of Dr. W. Roxburgh, 1751–1815, director, Botanic Garden, Calcutta.

Roxiea'nus -a -um, in honour of Mrs. Roxie Hanna of Tali-fu, China.

ROYAL BAY. *See* **Laurus nobilis.**

ROYAL FERN. *See* **Osmunda regalis.**

ROYAL PALM. *See* **Roystonea regia.**

ROYAL PEACOCK FLOWER. *See* **Poinciana regia.**

ROYD'SIA (in honour of Sir John Royds, sometime an Indian judge and patron of science). FAM. *Capparidaceae.* A genus of 4 species of shrubs natives of E. Indies and Philippine Is. Leaves large, simple, oblong, short-stalked, without stipules. Flowers yellow, small, fragrant, axillary, and in terminal panicles; sepals 6, coloured, petals none, torus short, stamens very many. Fruit orange-yellow or red, olive-shaped. *R. suaveolens* will flower freely as a pot plant and is worth growing thus for its fragrance; it is a rather coarse, rambling bush suitable only for large houses when planted out. It needs warm-house treatment and a rich loamy soil. It can be readily increased by cuttings.

Roydsia suaveolens

R. suaveo'lens. *l.* alternate, oblong or oblong-lanceolate, 4 to 12 in. long, acute, entire, shining, pale beneath; stalks about ½ in. long. *fl.* numerous, ¾ in. across, fragrant; stamens about 100, spreading; racemes axillary or rather above axils, 3 to 7 in. long. January to May. *fr.* 1 to 1½ in. long, orange-yellow with white specks. E. Indies. (B.M. 6881.)

ROYEN'A (in honour of Adrian van Royen, d. 1779; he and his son David were successively professors of botany at Leyden). FAM. *Ebenaceae.* A genus of about 20 species of shrubs or small trees inhabiting S. and Trop. Africa. Leaves normally alternate, entire. Flowers usually solitary (sometimes 3) in the leaf-axils; calyx 4- or 5-parted, accrescent in fruit; corolla urn-shaped at the base with a 5-parted, reflexed limb; stamens usually 10. Fruit globose to ovoid, ½ to 1 in. long, seated in the persistent calyx. Greenhouse plants requiring a loamy soil. Cuttings are easily struck in a close frame. *R. lucida* and *R. glabra* are grown out of doors in Scilly.

R. glab'ra. Evergreen shrub 2 to 8 ft., shoots densely leafy. *l.* narrowly oval, tapered to both ends, stiff, flat, finally glabrous and shining above, ½ to 1½ in. long, ⅛ to ⅕ in. wide. *fl.* whitish, nodding, ¼ in. long, 1 to 5 on slender, axillary, hairy stalks. *fr.* oval, ½ in. long, purple. S. Africa.

R. lu'cida. Small evergreen tree, shoots downy. *l.* 1 to 1½ in. long, half as wide, ovate, pointed, more or less cordate, white with down when young, shining above at maturity. *fl.* solitary on an axillary stalk, ½ to 1 in. long; cor. pale yellow to white, ½ in. wide, lobes reflexed. *fr.* ovoid to sub-globose, ½ to 1 in. long, red or purple and fleshy when ripe. S. Africa. 1690. (B.R. 32, 40.)

R. pal'lens. Evergreen or sometimes deciduous shrub or tree, usually under 15 ft., sometimes much larger, shoots silky-downy. *l.* oblanceolate, blunt, cuneate, ¾ to 2 in. long, ¼ to ¾ in. wide, silky beneath at first. *fl.* whitish to yellow, solitary, axillary, ⅜ in. long, nodding; cor. spreading or reflexed. June. S. Africa. 1752. (B.R. 500 as *R. pubescens.*)

R. villo'sa. Scandent or trailing shrub up to 50 ft. long, young shoots downy or hairy. *l.* obovate-oblong, 1 to 5 in. long, half as wide, rounded to more or less cordate at the base, rounded at the apex, hairy beneath. *fl.* yellow, fragrant, solitary or rarely 3 on a densely downy stalk ⅓ to ½ in. long; cor. ½ in. wide, downy outside, deeply 5-lobed. S. Africa.

W. J. B.

ROYL'EA (in honour of Dr. John Forbes Royle, 1799–1858, Professor of Materia Medica, King's College, London, Superintendent, Botanic Gardens, Saharanpur, India). FAM. *Labiatae.* *R. elegans*, the only species, is a greyish, erect, much-branched shrub with almost terete, spreading branches. It is best in a light, rich soil and needs greenhouse protection. Cuttings root readily in a close frame.

R. el'egans. Shrub of 3 to 5 ft., grey, leafy. *l.* ovate, acute, sub-cordate, deeply toothed, 1 to 1½ in. long, green above, hoary beneath, lemon-scented. *fl.* in loose 6- to 10-fld. whorls; cal. over ½ in. long, hairy; cor. ½ in. long, pale rose. July. Himalaya. 1824.

ROYSTONEA (in honour of General Roy Stone, 1836–1905). FAM. *Palmaceae.* A genus of 6 or 7 species of slender unarmed Palms, natives of Trop. America, with ringed stems and a terminal crown of large pinnate leaves with long sheathing stalks forming a cylinder round the summit. Leaves equally pinnatisect, segments narrow, linear-lanceolate, narrowed at apex, unequally 2-fid. Flowers white, monoecious, small, the spadices enclosed in double, somewhat woody spathes. Several species are excellent for indoor decoration. They are also good for sub-tropical gardens provided protection can be given from winds. For general treatment *see* **Phoenix.**

R. Borinque'na. Royal Palm of Porto Rico. Trunk 30 to 35 ft. h., usually with a bulge about the middle. *l.* much like *R. regia. fl.* on a more densely branched spadix covered with dark-brown hairs. *Seeds* narrower. Porto Rico. SYN. *Oreodoxa Borinquena.*

R. olera'cea. Cabbage Palm. 100 to 120 ft. h., swollen at base. *l.* 10 to 14 ft. long, gracefully arched, segs. linear-lanceolate, 1 to 3 ft. long, dark green. *fr.* obovoid-oblong, ¾ in. long. W. Indies. 1844. The plants are cut down when about 8 years old for the central l. which are tender and edible. SYN. *Oreodoxa oleracea.*

R. re'gia.* Royal Palm. 30 to 40 ft. h., usually with a bulge about the middle. *l.* 8 to 10 ft. long, segs. up to 2½ ft. long, about 1 in. wide, bright green. *fr.* ovoid, ½ in. long. Cuba. 1836. SYN. *Oreodoxa regia.* A slender and elegant species when young.

Rozyns'kii, in honour of Oberfürster Rozynski of podzancze, *c.* 1900.

RUBBER-PLANT. *See* **Ficus elastica.**

RUBBER-TREE, AFRICA. *See* **Landolphia.**

RUBBER-TREE, PARA. *See* **Hevea.**

rubel'lus -a -um, reddish.

ru'bens, blush red.

ru'ber -ra -rum (***rubri-*** or ***rubro-,*** in compound words), red.

rubes'cens, reddish; turning red.

RUBIAC'EAE. Dicotyledons. A family of about 350 genera with about 4,500 species of herbs, shrubs, or trees, mostly tropical, but some in temperate and a few in arctic regions. Leaves opposite and usually entire, stipules variable, sometimes united so as to form a sheath round the stem or leaf-like as in Galium and some related genera. Flowers usually in cymes or panicles, usually regular, perfect, their parts in fours or fives, one sepal being sometimes much larger than the others and coloured; stamens attached to the corolla, ovary inferior, usually 2-, rarely many-celled, with 1 ovule in each cell. Fruit a capsule, berry, or schizocarp. Several are of economic importance, e.g. Coffea, Cinchona, Rubia, and many are ornamental. Genera dealt with are: Adina, Alberta, Alibertia, Anthospermum, Antirrhoea, Asperula, Bouvardia, Burchella, Calycophyllum, Catesbaea, Cephaelis, Cephalanthus, Chiococca, Cinchona, Coccocypselum, Coffea, Coprosma, Cosmibuena, Coutarea, Craterispermum, Crucianella, Damnacanthus, Deppea, Emmenopterys, Erithalis, Exostemma, Faramea, Fernelia, Galium, Gardenia, Genipa, Geophila, Glycosmis, Guettarda, Hamelia, Hamiltonia, Heinsia, Hillia, Hindsia, Hoffmannia, Houstonia, Hydnophytum, Hymenodictyon, Isertia, Ixora, Keltoggia, Knoxia, Leptactina, Leptodermis, Lindenia, Luculia, Macrocnemum, Macrosphyra, Manettia, Mitchella, Mitriostigma, Morinda, Mussaenda, Myrmecodia, Nauclea, Nertera, Opercularia, Oxyanthus, Paederia, Palicourea, Pavetta, Pentagonia, Pentas, Petunga, Phuopsis, Phyllis, Pinckneya, Platycarpum, Pogonopus, Pomax, Portlandia, Posoqueria, Psychotria, Putoria, Randia, Remijia, Rondeletia, Rudgea, Sabicea, Sarcocephalus, Serissa, Sherbournia, Timonia, Tocoyena, Uncaria, Vanguieria, Wendlandia.

rubia'ceus -a -um, Rubia-like.

ru'bidus -a -um, reddish.

rubiflo'rus -a -um, with Rubus-like flowers.

rubigino'sus -a -um, brownish, rusty-red.

RU'BUS (ancient Latin name). Bramble, Raspberry. FAM. *Rosaceae*. A genus probably of some 400 species, but difficult to estimate because of the different interpretations of what constitutes a species by different authorities. Bentham, for instance, included all the shrubby British brambles under 1 name, *R. fruticosus*, whilst others make over 100 species of them.

The genus includes shrubby, sub-shrubby, and herbaceous plants, very often creeping or scandent, usually more or less spiny or prickly; evergreen or deciduous. Stems perennial or biennial. Leaves alternate, simple, digitate, or pinnate. Flowers white or pink, usually in terminal and axillary racemes or panicles, sometimes solitary; calyx 5-lobed, persistent, petals 5; stamens numerous. Fruit 1-seeded drupes borne, few or many, on a cone-shaped receptacle. In the raspberry section the fruits come away from the receptacle in a rounded or helmet-shaped group, but in the bramble or blackberry section they adhere to it.

The ornamental qualities of the genus are far from being commensurate with its size, but a few are really handsome in blossom, such as *R. deliciosus*, *R. odoratus*, and *R. spectabilis*. Floral beauty is about entirely absent from the Chinese species, but they are very variable, interesting, and often attractive in foliage or in their white stems. Fruit often edible and handsome.

The genus is most abundant in the N. Hemisphere, but is represented also in S. and Trop. Africa, Australia, New Zealand, and the Pacific Is. Most of the cultivated species are very hardy; a few succeed best in our warmer counties and others need greenhouse conditions. Cultivation is easy. All succeed in a good loamy soil and can be propagated, preferably by seeds, but also by layering or by division. The species with biennial stems should have those that have flowered or borne fruit cut out just as is done with garden raspberries. Even those with perennial stems are improved by an occasional clearing out of old, worn-out growths. The slender-stemmed, scandent species are best trained loosely up rough poles. *See also* **Blackberry, Loganberry, Raspberry.** A

R. adenoph'orus. Deciduous shrub, 8 ft. or more; stems biennial arching, densely clothed with bristles and stalked glands, spiny. *l.* on virgin shoots mostly pinnate with 5 lflets. which are 2 to 5 in. long, ovate to obovate, tapered to cordate at base, dull and hairy on both surfaces; on fertile shoots in threes and smaller. *fl.* pink, small, in cylindrical panicles 4 to 5 in. long. July. *fr.* black, ½ in. wide, edible. China. 1907. Remarkable for the black-headed glands mixed with bristles on the stems, &c.

R. alleghenien'sis. Deciduous shrub; stems, midrib, and l.-stalks glandular-downy, prickly. *l.* with 5 lflets. on barren shoots, 3 on fertile ones, ovate, 2 to 8 in. long, doubly toothed, downy beneath; veins in 10 to 14 pairs. *fl.* white, in racemes 4 to 8 in. long, stalks glandular. *fr.* black, conical, ½ in. long, sweet. N. America. SYN. *R. nigrobaccus*. Original type of a group of Blackberries, cultivated in N. America; fr. ¾ to 1 in. long.

R. amab'ilis.* Graceful deciduous shrub, 6 or 7 ft.; stems downy and slightly prickly. *l.* pinnate, 4 to 8 in. long; lflets. 7 to 11, ovate, pointed, sharply and doubly toothed, ¾ to 2 in. long, ½ to 1 in. wide, terminal one larger; all downy and prickly on veins beneath. *fl.* white, solitary at end of short twigs, 1 to 2 in. wide; pet. overlapping. June, July. *fr.* conical, red, ⅝ in. long, edible. China. 1908. Notable for its large solitary fl.

R. arc'ticus. Stems herbaceous, 4 to 8 in. h., erect, springing from a creeping rootstock. *l.* 3-foliolate, the lflets. roundish-ovate to obovate, coarsely and bluntly toothed, ¾ to 1½ in. long, glabrous or nearly so. *fl.* usually solitary near top of stem, ¾ in. wide; pet. 5 to 7, roundish, notched, rose. June. *fr.* with a few amber drupes, sweet and palatable. N. Hemisphere.

R. austra'lis. Bush Lawyer. Tall evergreen climber; stems slender, zigzag, glabrous, very prickly. *l.* of 3 or 5 lflets. which are very variable in shape, ovate-oblong, linear-oblong, ovate-lanceolate, or linear, truncate or cordate, prickly on stalk and midrib, 2 to 5 in. long, 1 to 2 in. wide. *fl.* white, ¼ to ½ in. wide, in panicles up to 2 ft. long, dioecious, males the larger. *fr.* ½ in. wide, reddish-orange. New Zealand. This climber, so strongly armed as to be almost impenetrable, may be regarded as the type of a very variable species. *R. cissoides* and *R. parvus* are sometimes treated as distinct species, sometimes as varieties of *R. australis*; they are not generally hardy.

R. bambusa'rum. A synonym of *R. Henryi bambusarum*.

R. biflo'rus.* Deciduous shrub; stems erect, 8 to 10 ft., covered like the twigs with a white waxy coating, spiny, biennial. *l.* 4 to 10 in. long with 3 or 5 ovate, pointed lflets., 2 to 4 in. long, unevenly toothed, dark green above, white beneath. *fl.* white, ¾ in. wide, in twos or threes, terminal and axillary. July. *fr.* yellow, roundish, ¾ in. wide, pleasantly flavoured. Himalaya. 1818. One of the 'whitewashed' brambles. var. **quinqueflo'rus,** *fl.* usually in fives but occasionally up to 8 in a cluster. China. 1908.

R. cae'sius. Dewberry. Prostrate shrub; stems slender, prickly, glabrous, glaucous at first. *lflets.* mostly in threes, 1½ to 3 in. long, coarsely toothed, green on both surfaces; lateral scarcely stalked. *fl.* white, 1¼ in. wide, few in a cluster. July. *fr.* with only a few large, blue-white drupes, edible. Europe (Britain). (E.B. 456.)

R. canaden'sis. American Dewberry. Deciduous shrub; stems 6 to 8 ft., erect or arching, nearly or quite unarmed and soon glabrous. *l.* of usually 5 oval, ovate, or obovate lflets. 2 to 6 in. long, glabrous or nearly so. *fl.* white, 1 in. wide, borne in terminal racemes 3 to 6 in. long. July. *fr.* black, juicy, sour. N. America. 1902. (B.M. 8264.) SYN. *R. Millspaughii*. Pretty in blossom.

R. Chamaemo'rus. Cloudberry. Stem herbaceous, erect, 3 to 10 in. h., very slender, unarmed, with 1 to 4 l., springing from a woody rootstock. *l.* simple, rounded to oblate, 5- to 7-lobed, cordate, 1½ to 3½ in. across. *fl.* solitary, pure white, about 1½ in. wide, dioecious. June. *fr.* ¾ to 1 in. long; the drupes few, large, pale orange, and edible. N. Europe (Britain), usually in boggy mountainous districts. (E.B. 440.)

R. chroosep'alus. Semi-evergreen, straggling bush; stems prickly. *l.* broadly ovate, cordate, with a long tapering apex, 3 to 7 in. long, finely and sharply toothed, silvery-felted beneath; stalk 1 to 2½ in. long. *fl.* ½ in. wide, with no pet., borne in terminal panicles 6 to 9 in.

long; cal. purple inside. July. *fr.* small, black. China. 1900. In shape, size, and in the silvery undersurface, the l. resembles that of *Tilia tomentosa.*

R. cissoi'des. *l.* 2 to 5 in. long, narrowly ovate to linear-lanceolate; panicles 2 to 6 in. long. *fl.* yellowish; pet. narrower. var. **paupera'-tus,** *l.* almost wholly reduced to a prickly midrib. Related to *R. australis* and not reliably hardy.

R. Cockburnia'nus.* Deciduous shrub; stems up to 8 or 10 ft., biennial, much-branched at the top, covered with a pure-white wax. *l.* pinnate, 5 to 8 in. long, with 7 or 9 lflets., which are $1\frac{1}{2}$ to $2\frac{1}{2}$ in. long, ovate, rhombic, or oval-lanceolate, rather coarsely toothed, slender-pointed, white beneath. *fl.* small, purple, in a terminal panicle 4 or 5 in. long. June. *fr.* black. China. 1907. The best of the 'whitewashed' brambles. SYN. *R. Giraldianus.*

R. corchorifo'lius. Deciduous, suckering shrub; stems erect, 6 to 8 ft. h., minutely downy. *l.* simple, 3 to 7 in. long, ovate to ovate-lanceolate, cordate (often deeply 3-lobed on the sucker shoots), downy on veins beneath; stalk 1 to $1\frac{1}{2}$ in. long. *fl.* white, solitary or a few together on short side twigs. June. *fr.* large, bright red, of good flavour. China, Japan. 1907.

R. corea'nus. Deciduous shrub, 8 to 20 ft.; stems biennial, erect, ultimately arching, blue-white; spines broad, $\frac{1}{2}$ in. long. *l.* pinnate; lflets. 5 or 7, ovate or broadly oval, $1\frac{1}{2}$ to 3 in. long, terminal largest and rounded or cordate at base; all coarsely toothed or lobed and with parallel veins. *fl.* in clusters of 3 to 8 on short shoots; pet. pink, shorter than sep. June. *fr.* small, red or black, of poor flavour. Korea, China. 1907.

R. crataegifo'lius. Deciduous shrub; stems erect, 6 to 8 ft., prickly, biennial. *l.* on virgin shoots 3- or 5-lobed, 5 to 8 in. (sometimes more) across, cordate, toothed, maple-like, downy beneath; on the fruiting shoots 3-lobed, smaller. *fl.* white, $\frac{3}{4}$ to 1 in. wide, several in a cluster on short twigs. June. *fr.* red. China, Korea, Japan. 1875. Handsome foliage turning red and yellow in autumn.

R. delicio'sus.* Deciduous, unarmed shrub, 6 to 10 ft., shoots downy at first. *l.* $1\frac{1}{2}$ to 3 in. long, rather wider, 3- sometimes 5-lobed, broadly ovate, coarsely toothed, glandular and downy beneath. *fl.* white, 2 in. across, usually solitary on short twigs. May, June. *fr.* $\frac{1}{2}$ in. wide, purplish, with no flavour. Rocky Mts. 1870. (B.M. 6062.) One of the most beautiful of Rubi; fl. like single roses.

R. flagelliflo'rus. Evergreen climbing shrub; stems slender, graceful, whitish-felted, prickly. *l.* up to 6 or 7 in. long, broadly ovate to ovate-lanceolate, cordate, long-pointed, toothed and shallowly lobed, downy beneath. *fl.* white, small, in axillary clusters. June. *fr.* black, $\frac{1}{2}$ in. wide, edible. China. 1901. Without beauty of fl., it is very graceful trained up a support, making shoots 5 or 6 ft. long in a season.

R. flosculo'sus. Deciduous shrub, 10 to 12 ft.; stems biennial, erect, arching and much-branched the second year, purplish-brown, spines few. *l.* pinnate with 5 or 7 lflets. which are ovate, $\frac{3}{4}$ to 2 in. long (terminal larger and often 3-lobed), closely white-felted beneath. *fl.* pink, $\frac{1}{4}$ in. wide, in slender panicles 2 to 4 in. long. July. *fr.* small, dark red or nearly black. China. 1907.

R. frutico'sus. A comprehensive Linnaean term for the common blackberries or brambles not much used now. Botanists have split them up into scores of species and varieties, based on variations in l., fl., and size and edible quality of the fruit. The shrub may be deciduous or nearly evergreen; the stem prickly, bristly or glabrous; the l. 3- or 5-foliolate, glabrous or downy, green or glaucous beneath; the fl. pure white to pink, with differences in the size and character of the infl. The British flora is particularly rich in this type of Rubi.

R. Giraldia'nus. A synonym of *R. Cockburnianus.*

R. grac'ilis. Deciduous shrub; stems biennial, up to 20 ft., 1 to $1\frac{1}{2}$ in. thick, densely velvety, thinly prickly. *l.* with 3 or 5 broadly ovate to cordate lflets. 3 to 5 in, long, white-felted beneath. *fl.* white or pale pink, $\frac{1}{2}$ in. wide in few-fld. clusters; pet. shorter than sep. June, July. *fr.* blue-black, small. Himalaya, China. 1901. Most robust of all the Rubi.

R. Hen'ryi. Evergreen, slightly prickly scandent shrub, up to 20 ft.; stems slender, downy when young. *l.* 3-lobed, 4 to 6 in. long, closely white-felted beneath; lobes deep, $\frac{3}{4}$ to 1 in. wide, slender, pointed, finely toothed. *fl.* in racemes of 6 to 10, $\frac{3}{4}$ in. wide, pink; sep. glandular-hairy with a tail-like point. June. *fr.* black, shining. China. 1900. var. **bambusa'rum,*** *l.* of 3 distinct lflets. 3 to 5 in. long. Both are very elegant, quick-growing climbers. (H.I.P. 1705; G.C. 42 (1907), 251; B.M. n.s. 33.) as *R. bambusarum.*

R. his'pidus. Swamp Dewberry. Low, semi-evergreen shrub; stems prostrate, wiry, spiny, bristly. *l.* of 3 or 5 glabrous, obovate lflets., sharply and coarsely toothed, 1 to $1\frac{3}{4}$ in. long, $\frac{1}{2}$ to 1 in. wide, glabrous or nearly so. *fl.* white, $\frac{1}{2}$ to $\frac{3}{4}$ in. across, few in a cluster; stalks downy. June, July. *fr.* red then purple-black, drupes few, sour. N. America. 1768.

R. hupehen'sis. Semi-evergreen, climbing shrub; shoots dark, slender, cobwebby, slightly spiny. *l.* oblong-lanceolate, 3 to $4\frac{1}{2}$ in. long, $1\frac{1}{2}$ in. wide, finely toothed, long-pointed, grey-downy beneath; stalk $\frac{1}{4}$ to $\frac{1}{2}$ in. long. *fl.* 3 to 7 in short glandular racemes of no beauty; cal. grey-felted. *fr.* black-purple, austere. China. 1907. (G.C. 51 (1912), 166 as *R. Swinhoei.*)

R. ichangen'sis. Deciduous scandent or prostrate shrub; stems slender, spiny, bristly. *l.* ovate-cordate, often with 2 basal lobes, $3\frac{1}{2}$ to 7 in. long, 1 to 2 in. wide, glabrous, sparsely toothed. *fl.* white, $\frac{1}{4}$ in. wide, in slender terminal panicles 8 to 12 in. or more long; sep. erect. July. *fr.* red, small, well flavoured. China. 1900. (G.C. 48 (1910), 275.)

R. idae'us. Wild Raspberry. Deciduous shrub; stems 4 to 6 ft., erect, biennial, slightly or not prickly. *lflets.* 3 or 5, $1\frac{1}{2}$ to 4 in. long, ovate, coarsely and doubly toothed, white-felted beneath. *fl.* white, small, in racemes terminating short twigs of the year-old stems. June. *fr.* red. Europe (Britain), N. Asia. (E.B. 442.) Of interest as the parent of cultivated raspberries but of no ornamental value. var. **strigo'sus,** a synonym of *R. strigosus.*

R. illecebro'sus. Strawberry-Raspberry. Sub-shrubby or herbaceous plant with a creeping, woody rootstock; stems 6 to 15 in., erect, angular, prickly, glabrous. *l.* pinnate, 5 to 9 in. long; lflets. 3 to 15, ovate to ovate-lanceolate, slender-pointed, sharply toothed, $1\frac{1}{2}$ to 3 in. long, nearly glabrous. *fl.* solitary or in threes, terminal, white, 1 to $1\frac{1}{2}$ in. across; stamens very numerous, anthers yellow. July. *fr.* red, roundish-oval, $1\frac{1}{4}$ in. long, sweet but rather insipid. Japan. (B.M. 8704.) SYN. *R. sorbifolius.*

R. iner'mis. A variety of *R. ulmifolius.*

R. innomina'tus. Deciduous shrub; stems biennial, 6 to 10 ft., erect, velvety, densely glandular, prickles few. *l.* pinnate; lflets. 3 to 5, the side ones 2 to 4 in. long, 1 to $2\frac{1}{2}$ in. across, terminal larger, broader, often 3-lobed; all closely white-felted beneath. *fl.* pink, $\frac{1}{3}$ to $\frac{1}{2}$ in. wide, borne in large, glandular, terminal panicles 1 to $1\frac{1}{2}$ ft. long. August. *fr.* orange-red, rounded, $\frac{1}{2}$ to $\frac{3}{4}$ in. wide, well flavoured. China. 1901. var. **Kuntzea'nus,** differs by the stems and infl. being without glands. China. 1907.

R. irenae'us. Evergreen prostrate shrub; stems slender, prickly, and densely downy. *l.* 6 in. or more wide, roundish-cordate, abruptly pointed, dark green and glabrous above, brownish-felted beneath. *fl.* white, $\frac{5}{8}$ in. wide, in the l.-axils and in terminal clusters. July. *fr.* red, large. China. 1900. Not very hardy, but useful for making an evergreen ground cover in the milder counties; likes shade.

R. Koehnea'nus. Deciduous shrub of bushy habit; stems 3 or 4 ft., biennial, purplish blooms, almost unarmed. *l.* broadly ovate, cordate to triangular, 3- or 5-lobed, $1\frac{1}{2}$ to 5 in. long and nearly as wide, sharply toothed, glabrous above, white beneath. *fl.* white, $\frac{3}{4}$ in. wide, slender-stalked, usually in threes terminating short, leafy twigs; anthers purplish-red. June, July. *fr.* small, drupes few, orange. Japan. 1890. (B.M. 8246.)

R. lacinia'tus.* Deciduous scandent shrub, 6 to 8 ft., stems angled; spines stout, recurved. *l.* of 5 (sometimes 3) lflets. which are 2 to $3\frac{1}{2}$ in. long, deeply pinnately lobed or even pinnate, coarsely toothed, spiny on stalk and midrib, downy beneath. *fl.* in large terminal panicles; pet. pinkish, obovate, $\frac{2}{5}$ in. long, sometimes lobed. *fr.* black, $\frac{1}{2}$ to $\frac{3}{4}$ in. long, sweet. Europe (Britain); naturalized in N. America. One of the best of wild blackberries and now much grown for its fr. Origin uncertain.

R. Lambertia'nus. Semi-evergreen, very eafy, scandent or straggling shrub; stems slender, angled, spiny. *l.* 3 to 5 in. long, ovate to oblong-ovate, cordate, obscurely 3-or 5-lobed, toothed, hairy beneath. *fl.* white, $\frac{1}{3}$ in. wide, in terminal panicles 3 to 5 in. long. June, July. *fr.* red, small. China. 1907. (G.C. 48 (1910), 276.)

R. lasiosty'lus. Deciduous shrub; stems to 6 ft., biennial, blue-white, prickles bristle-like. *l.* of 3 to 5 lflets., lateral 2 to 4 in. long, ovate, coarsely toothed; terminal much larger; all white-felted beneath. *fl.* small, solitary to 5 in a cluster; pet. reddish-purple, shorter than cal., soon falling. June. *fr.* $\frac{3}{4}$ in. wide, roundish, red, agreeably acid. China. 1899. (B.M. 7426.)

R. leucoder'mis. Deciduous shrub; stems erect, 4 to 8 ft., blue-white, prickly. *l.* with 3 or (on barren shoots) 5 lflets. which are broadly ovate, coarsely toothed, 1 to 3 in. long, white beneath. *fl.* white, few in terminal clusters; pet. shorter than cal. June. *fr.* purple-black, well flavoured. Western N. America. 1829. Garden vars. are cultivated in the United States.

R. linea'tus.* Deciduous or semi-evergreen, rambling shrub, up to 10 ft.; stems slender, downy, almost unarmed. *l.* with usually 5 radiating lflets. which are oblong-lanceolate to oblong, evenly toothed, the central one 4 to 9 in. long, the others smaller, all dark green with a downy midrib above, completely silky-downy beneath; veins parallel in 30 to 50 pairs. *fl.* white, small, in short axillary clusters. *fr.* small, red or yellow. Himalaya, China. Remarkable for the numerous parallel veins and the beautiful silvery sheen beneath the l. Only suitable for the milder counties.

R. × loganobac'cus. *See* **Loganberry.**

R. malifo'lius.* Deciduous prostrate or climbing shrub, up to 10 ft.; stems sparingly armed with hooked prickles. *l.* oval to ovate, 2 to 5 in. long, rounded at base, glabrous above, downy on the 7 to 10 pairs of veins beneath, stalk $\frac{1}{4}$ to $\frac{5}{8}$ in. long. *fl.* 1 in. wide, white, on terminal racemes up to 5 in. long. June. *fr.* black, not palatable. China. 1904. Handsome in fl.

R. mesogae'us. Very vigorous, deciduous shrub; stems up to 10 ft., arching, velvety; prickles very small. *l.* of 3 ovate to roundish lflets. on a velvety stalk, coarsely toothed; terminal up to 7 in. long, and from half to nearly as much wide; lateral much smaller. *fl.* pinkish-white, small, in axillary clusters. June. *fr.* black, round, $\frac{1}{3}$ in. wide. China. 1907.

R. nigrobac'cus. A synonym of *R. allegheniensis.*

R. × **nob'ilis.** Hybrid between *R. odoratus* and *R. idaeus.* Stems erect with peeling bark. *l.* of 3 lflets., downy on both surfaces. *fl.* purplish-red in terminal clusters. June, July. In general appearance and in the fl. it resembles *R. odoratus,* but the l. is 3-foliolate. 1855.

R. nu'tans.* Evergreen, unarmed, prostrate shrub; stems creeping, very bristly. *l.* of 3 bristly stalked lflets., the middle one 1 to $2\frac{1}{2}$ in. long, rhombic; the lateral smaller, glossy green, bristly on the veins beneath. *fl.* white, $1\frac{1}{2}$ in. wide, borne 1 to 3 in the l.-axils and terminating erect bristly shoots. June. *fr.* globose, purple, edible. Himalaya. 1850. Makes a charming ground cover.

R. nutka'nus. A synonym of *R. parviflorus.*

R. occidenta'lis. Deciduous shrub; stems biennial, 6 to 10 ft., arching, very glaucous or purplish; spines scattered. *l.* pinnate with 3 or 5 ovate lflets. $1\frac{1}{2}$ to 4 in. long, shortly pointed, coarsely toothed, white-felted beneath. *fl.* white, $\frac{1}{2}$ in. across, few in terminal clusters. June. *fr.* purple-black, hemispherical. N. America, and the parent of garden varieties there. var. **pal'lidus,** *fr.* amber-yellow.

R. odora'tus.* Unarmed deciduous shrub, 6 to 8 ft., increasing by new shoots from the base, glandular-hairy on stems, l.-stalks, and fl.-stalks. *l.* 5-lobed, 4 to 10 or even 12 in. wide, vine-like, jaggedly toothed, at first soft and velvety beneath. *fl.* fragrant, purple, $1\frac{1}{2}$ to 2 in. across, up to 20 or 30 together on broad, irregularly branched panicles. July to September. *fr.* red, flattish, $\frac{5}{8}$ in. wide. N. America. 1770. (B.M. 323.) One of the handsomest species, closely akin to *R. parviflorus*; distinct by the more numerous purple fl.

R. omeien'sis. A synonym of *R. setchuenensis.*

Rubus palmatus

R. palma'tus. Deciduous shrub; stems up to 20 ft., glabrous, prickly. *l.* maple-like, palmately 5-lobed, $1\frac{1}{2}$ to 4 in. long, nearly or quite as wide, sharply and deeply toothed, green on both surfaces. *fl.* white, solitary, axillary, $1\frac{1}{2}$ in. wide; pet. narrowly oval, blunt; lobes of cal. $\frac{1}{2}$ in. long, linear-lanceolate. May. *fr.* roundish, yellow, juicy, $\frac{3}{4}$ in. wide. China, Japan. 1895. (B.M. 7801.) Very distinct by its long spreading pet. Rather tender.

R. Par'keri. Deciduous climbing shrub; stems thickly covered with greyish hairs, slightly spiny. *l.* 4 to 7 in. long, ovate and oblong to lanceolate, cordate, margins wavy and finely toothed, bristly above, densely covered with reddish-brown down beneath. *fl.* white, $\frac{1}{3}$ in. wide, in panicles 6 in. or more long, of no beauty; cal. covered with reddish glandular hairs. June. *fr.* small, black. China. 1907. Very distinct in l.

R. parviflo'rus.* Salmon Berry. Unarmed, glandular-hairy, deciduous shrub, 6 to 8 ft., increasing by young shoots from the base and forming dense thickets. *l.* 4 to 8 in. or more across, 5-lobed, vine-like, irregularly toothed. *fl.* pure white, $1\frac{1}{2}$ to $2\frac{1}{2}$ in. wide, in terminal clusters of 3 to 9. June. *fr.* hemispherical, $\frac{5}{8}$ in. wide, red, insipid. Western N. America. 1827. (B.M. 3453.) SYN. *R. nutkanus.*

R. parvifo'lius. Low, deciduous, bushy shrub; stems slender, downy, prickly. *l.* of 3 or sometimes 5 lflets. which are usually roundish, broadly obovate, $\frac{3}{4}$ to 2 in. long, coarsely toothed, dark green and glabrous above, white-felted beneath; terminal one the largest. *fl.* small, in clusters 1 to 2 in. wide; pet. bright rose, erect. June. *fr.* roundish, red, edible. China, Japan. 1818. (B.R. 496.) SYN. *R. triphyllus.*

R. par'vus. Dwarf prostrate shrub; stem creeping, rooting at the joints. *l.* 1-foliolate, 1 to 3 in. long, linear to linear-lanceolate. *fl.* white. *fr.* $\frac{1}{2}$ to 1 in. long, juicy. Related to *R. australis* and not reliably hardy.

R. phoenicola'sius.* Deciduous shrub, 8 to 10 ft.; stems biennial, densely covered with reddish gland-tipped bristles and scattered prickles. *l.* 3-foliolate; lflets. 2 to 4 in. long, broadly ovate, coarsely toothed and lobed, white-felted beneath. *fl.* in terminal racemes; cal. $1\frac{1}{2}$ in. wide, lobes narrow, glandular, bristly; pet. $\frac{1}{4}$ in. long, pink. June, July. *fr.* conical, $\frac{3}{4}$ in. long, red, sweet. Japan, N. China. 1876. (B.M. 6479.) Notable for its large handsome fr. and stems covered with red bristles.

R. Playfairia'nus. Evergreen or semi-deciduous, climbing shrub; stems slender, string-like, armed with tiny hooked prickles, cobwebby when young. *l.* of 3 or 5 lflets. radiating from the end of a stalk up to $2\frac{1}{2}$ in. long, lanceolate, sharply toothed, the terminal one up to 6 in. long, the others 1 to 3 in. *fl.* $\frac{1}{2}$ in. wide in small racemes of no beauty. May, June. *fr.* black. China. 1907. (G.C. 51 (1912), 165.)

R. polyt'richus. A synonym of *R. tricolor.*

R. rosaefo'lius. Evergreen shrub, stems erect, prickly, downy. *l.* pinnate, with 3 to 7 ovate-lanceolate lflets., slender-pointed, sharply and doubly toothed, $1\frac{1}{2}$ to $3\frac{1}{2}$ in. long, downy beneath. *fl.* solitary or few in a cluster, white, 1 to $1\frac{1}{2}$ in. wide. August. *fr.* conical, $\frac{7}{8}$ in. long, drupes very small, red, insipid. Himalaya, E. Indies; naturalized in many warm countries. (B.M. 6970.) Greenhouse. var. **corona'rius,** *fl.* very double, $1\frac{3}{4}$ in. wide. (B.M. 1783.) Can be grown as small plants in pots.

R. rustica'nus. A synonym of *R. ulmifolius.*

R. saxa'tilis. Rootstock woody; stems semi-woody, creeping, very slender, self-layering. Flowering shoots erect, 4 to 6 in. h., minutely prickly. *l.* 3-foliolate; lflets. ovate, ovate-lanceolate, or rhomboid, coarsely and sharply toothed, 1 to 3 in. long, nearly glabrous; stalk slender, 2 to 3 in. long. *fl.* $\frac{3}{8}$ in. wide, dull white or greenish, 1 to 3 in the upper l.-axils. *fr.* red with 1 to 4 large drupes. N. Temperate and Arctic regions (Britain).

R. Schlechtenda'lii.* A bramble widely spread over Great Britain and Ireland, belonging to the Silvatici group and notable as bearing one of the largest and best blackberries. *lflets.* 5, often very large, sharply toothed, grey-downy beneath. *fl.* white with a pink claw or wholly pink; stamens pink. *Panicles* terminal and axillary, 4 to 10 in. long. Britain. (G.C. 68 (1920), 83.) Inhabits open thickets and hedges rather than woods.

R. setchuenen'sis. Deciduous, very vigorous, straggling shrub; stems unarmed, self-layering, downy, 10 to 12 ft. long in a season on young healthy plants. *l.* maple-like, 5- or 7-lobed, cordate, 3 to 7 in. long and wide, downy beneath; stipules $\frac{1}{2}$ to $\frac{3}{4}$ in. long, deeply divided. *fl.* purple, $\frac{1}{2}$ in. wide, numerous in terminal panicles. July. *fr.* black, well flavoured. China. 1903. The stipules, cut up into linear segs., are distinctive. SYN. *R. omeiensis.*

R. sorbifo'lius. A synonym of *R. illecebrosus.*

R. specta'bilis.* Deciduous shrub; stems erect, 4 to 6 ft., glabrous, prickly. *l.* 3-foliolate; lflets. ovate, $1\frac{1}{2}$ to 4 in. long, doubly toothed, nearly glabrous. *fl.* fragrant, borne singly or few on lateral leafy shoots, purplish-red, 1 in. wide. April. *fr.* orange, large, ovoid, edible. Western N. America. 1827. (B.R. 1424.)

R. strigo'sus. Deciduous shrub; stems 3 to 6 ft., densely bristly. *l.* pinnate with 3 or 5 lflets. which are ovate to oblong, $1\frac{1}{2}$ to 3 in. long, grey-felted beneath. *fl.* white, $\frac{3}{4}$ in. wide, axillary and terminal. *fr.* red, conical. The American counterpart of *R. idaeus* but distinct in its bristly, often glandular stems. The 'Cuthbert' and 'Hansall' raspberries are derived from it. SYN. *R. idaeus strigosus.*

R. thibeta'nus.* Deciduous shrub; stems biennial, erect, 6 ft., purplish, prickles slender. *l.* pinnate, 4 to 9 in. long; lflets. 7 to 13, oval or ovate, coarsely toothed or lobed, whitish-felted beneath; the basal pair 1 to 2 in. long, the others gradually smaller towards the terminal one which is itself, however, 2 to 3 in. long, ovate-lanceolate, deeply cut. On fertile shoots the l. are considerably smaller. *fl.* small, purple, in terminal panicles a few in. long, *fr.* $\frac{5}{8}$ in. wide, blue-black. China. 1908. SYN. *R. Veitchii.* One of the most handsome in foliage of the Chinese species.

R. thyrsoi'deus. Deciduous, arching or spreading shrub of vigorous growth; stems glabrous or nearly so, prickly. *lflets.* 5, the large terminal one ovate, long-stalked, 3 or 4 in. long; glabrous or nearly so above, dull white-felted beneath. *fl.* in erect panicles 6 or 8 in. long, white or pinkish. *fr.* black. Europe (Britain). var. **fl. pleno,** *fl.* white, very double. July, August. An admirable late-flowering shrub for rough, even semi-shady places.

R. trian'thus. Deciduous, glabrous shrub; stems biennial, erect, 4 to 6 ft. ultimately spreading, glaucous. *l.* 5 to 6 in. long, 2 to 4 in. wide, ovate to triangular and 3-lobed on the virgin stems, smaller on flowering ones. *fl.* pinkish-white, insignificant. *fr.* dark red. China. 1900.

R. tric'olor. Evergreen (or in cold districts deciduous) unarmed, creeping shrub, 1 ft. or more h. bristly on nearly all its parts. *l.* cordate, 3 or 4 in. long, dark green, whitish-felted beneath; stalk 1 to 1½ in. long. *fl.* white, 1 in. wide, solitary in l.-axils and in a terminal raceme. July. *fr.* bright red, palatable. China. 1908. (B.M. 9534.) SYN. *R. polytrichus.* Makes an admirable evergreen ground cover for shady places in mild districts.

R. trif'idus. Evergreen or semi-evergreen, unarmed shrub; stems erect, 4 to 7 ft., glandular-hairy at first. *l.* deeply 5- or 7-lobed, 4 to 10 in. wide; lobes ovate, doubly toothed, pointed; stalks 1 to 2½ in. long. *fl.* 1 to 1¼ in. wide, rosy-white, borne singly in the terminal l.-axils and in a few-fld. terminal cluster; cal. very downy. May. *fr.* red, edible. Japan. 1908. Notable for its large, maple-like, handsomely cut l.

R. triphyl'lus. A synonym of *R. parvifolius.*

R. ulmifo'lius. Spreading, semi-evergreen shrub with purplish, downy stems armed with broad prickles. *lflets.* 3 or 5, white-felted beneath, 1½ to 3½ in. long. *fl.* rosy-red, in cylindrical panicles 1 ft. or more long. July. *fr.* small, of no edible value. Europe (S. Britain). SYN. *R. rusticanus.* var. **bellidiflo'rus,*** *fl.* very double, ¾ in. wide, bachelor-button-like. Useful July, August flowering shrub, especially for roughish places; **inerm'is,** quite devoid of spines; **variega'tus,** midrib and veins bright yellow.

R. Veitch'ii. A synonym of *R. thibetanus.*

R. xanthocar'pus. Sub-shrub with a woody rootstock, stems annual, erect, angular, prickly. *l.* pinnate with 3 sometimes 5 lflets. which are 1½ to 3½ in. long, ovate to lanceolate, slender-pointed, coarsely toothed terminal one much the largest, very prickly on stalk and midrib. *fl.* white, terminal. June. *fr.* shining golden-yellow, ¾ in. long, rather raspberry flavoured. China. 1885.

W. J. B.

Ruc'keri, in honour of Mr. Rucker of Wandsworth, who, *c.* 1873, successfully cultivated orchids.

RUDBECK'IA (in honour of Olaf Rudbeck, 1660–1740, and his son, Professors of Botany at Uppsala). FAM. *Compositae.* A genus of about 30 species of usually perennial herbs, natives of N. America. Leaves usually alternate, sometimes deeply cut but often entire. Flower-heads often large with yellow rays and a conical disk of brownish to deep purple tubular florets; disk flowers fertile, 5-lobed; involucral bracts overlapping in 2 to 4 series; scales of receptacle chaffy, usually persistent. Achenes 4-angled, blunt at apex, pappus if present of 2 to 4 teeth. The genera Echinacea and Lepachys are very closely related to Rudbeckia and though kept separate here can scarcely be distinguished on botanical grounds. The ray florets of Echinacea, however, are rose or purple, not yellow, and the scales of the disk in Lepachys are deciduous, not persistent. The Rudbeckias dealt with below are hardy and good border plants, growing well in ordinary good garden soil, but to succeed with *R. laciniata* and *R. maxima* and their forms a moist soil during the hotter part of the year is necessary. *R. hirta* on the other hand thrives in dry soil. Propagation by seed sown outdoors or by division. The following plants are all perennial unless otherwise stated.

R. amplexicau'lis. Annual of 1 to 2 ft., glabrous and somewhat glaucous. *Lower l.* oblong-spatulate, entire or almost so; *upper l.* stem-clasping. *fl.-heads* with oblong yellow rays about ½ in. long; disk brownish, finally cylindrical. July. Texas, &c. 1793. (B.M. 3716 as *Dracopis amplexicaulis.*)

R. bi'color. Annual of 1 to 2 ft., bristly hairy. *Lower l.* entire or nearly so, 1 to 2 in. long. *fl.-heads* with yellow rays sometimes purplish at base, ½ to ¾ in. long, disk dark purple, conical. July. Arkansas, Texas, &c. var. **semiple'na,** rays in more than one series; **superb'a,** *fl.-heads* 2 in. across, rays yellow above, brownish-purple beneath.

R. califor'nica.* Unbranched, 3 to 6 ft. h., roughly hairy. *l.* ovate to oblong-lanceolate, usually 2-cleft, at least in lower part of plant; upper l. sessile. *fl.-heads* solitary, up to 5 in. across; rays 7 to 9, lemon-chrome often 2 in. across, up to 2½ in. long; disk green to citron-yellow. W. United States. 1891.

R. columna'ris. A synonym of *Lepachys columnaris.*

R. Drummond'ii. A synonym of *Lepachys columnaris pulcherrima*

R. ful'gida. Slightly hairy, 1 to 3 ft. h. *l.* spatulate-oblong or lanceolate, partly stem-clasping, 3-nerved; upper l. entire, obtuse. *fl.-heads* with 12 to 14 orange-yellow rays about 1 in. long, disk dark purple. July. SE. United States. 1760. (B.M. 1996.) var. **compac'ta,** dwarf of close habit; **variab'ilis,** about 3 ft. h., stems many, rigid, ray-fl. yellow and brown.

R. grandiflo'ra. Branched, about 3½ ft. h., stem angled. *Lower l.* ovate, with rounded teeth; *upper* lanceolate, rough, scarcely toothed, all stalked, acute. *fl.-heads* with drooping rays about 2 in. long, disk dark purple, convex. September. 1830. N. America. (S.B.F.G. s. 2, 87 as *Centrocarpha grandiflora.*)

Lepachys columnaris (sometimes included in *Rudbeckia*)

R. hir'ta. Black-eyed Susan. Annual or biennial. Roughly and bristly hairy, 1 to 2 ft. h., sometimes branched near base. *Lower l.* spatulate, 2 to 5 in. long, 3-nerved; *upper* oblong or lanceolate, all entire, sessile. *fl.-heads* solitary, rays about 14, longer than involucre, golden-yellow, sometimes orange at base, disk dull brown. Summer. N. America. 1714. (S.B.F.G. s. 2.) var. **hyb'rida,** *fl.-heads* of various shades; **vomeren'sis,** *fl.-heads* larger, of various shades of yellow.

R. lacinia'ta. Cone Flower. 2 to 7 ft. h., branched, smooth. *Lower l.* pinnatisect, segs. often deeply cut; *lower stem-l.* 3- to 5-partite, *upper* 3-cleft or entire. *fl.-heads* large, rays few or several, yellow, oblanceolate, soon drooping, disk greenish. Summer. Canada, United States. 1640. Needs moist soil. var. **angustifo'lia,** *l.* narrow; **fl. ple'no,** disk *fl.* ligulate; **Golden Glow,*** a full double form, *fl.-heads* up to 3½ in. wide; **nitida,** *see R. nitida.*

R. laeviga'ta. A synonym of *R. nitida.*

R. max'ima.* 4 to 10 ft. h. *l.* glaucous, lowest 8 to 12 in. long, upper stem-clasping. *fl.-heads* with pure yellow, drooping, disk columnar, long. August. Texas. Moist soil.

R. New'manii. A synonym of *R. speciosa.*

R. nit'ida. Up to 4 ft. h. *l.* entire or nearly so, bright green but in cultivation sometimes running up to 6 ft. or more, thus coming near to *R. laciniata* in stature. var. **Herbstsonne,*** with large single fl.-heads with bright primrose-yellow rays and a greenish disk possibly belongs here. Late summer.

R. palus'tris. 1½ to 2½ ft. h., glabrous or nearly so, at least in lower part. *Lower l.* ovate-lanceolate, remotely toothed or nearly entire. *fl.-heads* with yellow rays. ½ to ¾ in. long; involucral scales linear, blunt. September. Tennessee to Kentucky. Moist soil. Allied to *R. fulgida.*

R. pinna'ta. A synonym of *Lepachys pinnata.*

R. purpu'rea. A synonym of *Echinacea purpurea.*

R. specio'sa.* 2 to 3 ft. h., branched below. *Lower l.* ovate, strongly nerved, coarsely irregularly toothed, stalks 6 to 9 in. long, slender; *upper* narrower, uppermost sessile. *fl.-heads* 2½ to 4 in. across, rays orange, disk black-purple. Summer. (G.C. 16 (1881), 373.) SYN. *R. Newmanii.* (B.M. n.s. 238.)

R. subtomento'sa. Softly ashy-hairy, 2 to 5 ft. h. *l.* ovate, sharply toothed, terminal lobe ovate, lateral oblong or lanceolate. *fl.-heads* with numerous golden rays, 1 to 1½ in. long, disk black, scarcely raised. Summer. N. America.

R. trilo'ba. Biennial, 2 to 5 ft. h., hairy, much-branched. *Upper l.* ovate-lanceolate, little toothed; *lower* 3-lobed, narrowed to base, coarsely toothed; radical l. pinnately partite or undivided. *fl.-heads* small, many, showy, rays 8, yellow, ¾ in. long, disk blackish-purple. United States. 1699. (B.R. 525.)

RUDDLES. An old name for Marigolds.

ruden'tus -a -um, rope-like.

rudera'lis -is -e, of waste places or rubbish heaps.

RUDG'EA (in honour of Edward Rudge, 1763–1846, English botanist, author of *Plantarum Guianae Icones*). FAM. *Rubiaceae*. A genus of about 110 species of shrubs or small trees, natives of Trop. America. Leaves opposite, sometimes sessile, leathery; stipules cartilaginous but sometimes thickly leathery and inflated. Flowers of moderate size, usually in panicles, rarely in heads; calyx tube ovoid or obconic; limb short, segments 4 or usually 5, persistent; corolla cylindrical or funnel-shaped, tube usually straight and long, throat naked or bearded, lobes 5 (or rarely 4) erect or spreading; stamens 5 (or 4). Treatment as for Coffea.

R. leucoceph'ala. Shrub to 6 ft. *l.* large, obovate-oblong, narrowed to base, nearly sessile. *fl.* cream, densely clustered in globose heads; pet. obtuse; peduncles short. Summer. Brazil. (B.M. 5653 and F.d.S. 1720 as *R. macrophylla.*)

R. macrophyl'la. A synonym of *R. leucocephala.*

R. nivo'sa. Erect, stem cylindrical. *l.* resembling those of *Prunus Laurocerasus. fl.* snow-white, few together; cor. tube 1 in. or more long, segs. 5, each with a horn-like projection below its apex. Brazil. 1866. SYN. *Psychotria nivosa.*

F. G. P.

rudimentary, imperfectly developed; incomplete.

ru'dis -is -e, wild.

RUE (*Ruta graveolens*). Hardy evergreen, somewhat shrubby, native of S. Europe, grown in garden for its medicinal value for treating croup in poultry and for certain cattle diseases. The leaves have a very strong odour and an exceedingly acrid taste and are sometimes used in claret cup. Rue is not particular as to soil so long as it is well drained, but is less liable to injury by frosts if planted in a sheltered, dry situation. It can be raised from seed sown outdoors in spring, or by cuttings or rooted slips also in spring, placed for a time in a shady border.

RUE ANEMONE. *See* **Anemonella thalictroides.**

RUE, GOAT'S. *See* **Galega.**

RUE, MEADOW. *See* **Thalictrum.**

RUE, WALL. *See* **Asplenium Ruta-muraria.**

RUEL'LIA (in honour of Jean de la Ruelle of Soissons, 1474–1537, botanist and physician to Francis I; he wrote *De Natura Plantarum* in 1536). FAM. *Acanthaceae*. A genus of about 200 species of annual or perennial herbs, sub-shrubs or shrubs, mostly American but with representatives in Africa, Asia, and Australia. Leaves opposite, usually entire. Flowers sessile or nearly so in the axils of leaves or bracts, sometimes solitary or clustered, sometimes in panicles; calyx deeply 5-cut; corolla tube straight, curved, or abruptly bent with 5 ovate or rounded, twisted lobes; stamens 4. Bracts narrow or small as a rule. The Ruellias are pretty, free-flowering plants, mostly needing stove temperatures and a light rich soil. They may be increased readily by cuttings in a close frame. Several make handsome pot plants, including *R. formosa, R. Herbstii, R. macrantha, R. macrophylla. R. ciliosa* and *R. strepens* are hardy or nearly so.

R. acutang'ula.. Large herb. *l.* elliptic-ovate, 6 to 8 in. long, slender-pointed, nerves depressed. *fl.* scarlet, 2 in. across, sessile on axillary, branched peduncles; cal. cylindrical, ½ in. long; cor. tube 1 to 1½ in. long, slightly curved, sometimes yellow in throat. May. Brazil. (B.M. 6382.) var. **hirsu'ta,** stems densely hairy.

R. affin'is. A synonym of *R. speciosa.*

R. amoe'na. *l.* broadly elliptic, usually entire, glabrous, lower up to 7 in. long; stalks about 1 in. long. *fl.* crimson, streaking yellow within, 1¼ in. long, on axillary peduncles about 4 in. long; cal. with 1 seg. longer than others; cor. tube cylindric for ¼ in. then much swollen, lobes short, erect. S. America.

R. Baik'eli. Herb of 2 to 3 ft. *l.* ovate-lanceolate, up to 9 in. long, slender-pointed, narrowed to stalk. *fl.* crimson in a large terminal much-branched panicle; cal. small, segs. linear; cor. tube about 2 in. long, curved, trumpet-shaped, swollen above middle. Winter. Nigeria. (B.M. 5111 as *Stephanophysum Baikiei.*)

R. Blum'ei. Herb. *l.* narrow-oblong, 4 in. long, blunt, rough, margins crenulate. *fl.* whitish, small, lobes tipped pink; cor. ¾ in. long, tube narrow in lower half, then suddenly funnel-shaped; spikes few-fld., axillary, shorter than l. Java.

R. ciliatiflo'ra. Herb with roughly hairy stem, about 2 ft. h. *l.* ovate, hairy, toothed, stalked. *fl.* lavender; cal. with 1 awl-shaped seg. longer than others; cor. tube 1 in., curved, enlarging upwards, lobes 1 in. across. September. Buenos Aires. (B.M. 3718.)

R. cilio'sa. Hairy herbaceous perennial. *l.* oblong or oval, 1 to 2 in. long, almost sessile. *fl.* blue, about 2 in. long; cor. tube twice as long as tube, throat obconic. July. N. America. 1824. Variable in all parts, up to 2 ft. h., but often flowering when about 3 in. h. Hardy or nearly so.

R. Devosia'na. Sub-shrub with purple stems. *l.* lanceolate, distantly toothed, deep green and veins whitish above, purple beneath. *fl.* white, tinted rose, cor. tube suddenly dilated and bent in middle. Brazil. 1877. (B.H. 1877, 19; B.M. 8406.) Pretty foliage plant.

R. Dipteracan'thus. Low, spreading herb. *l.* oblong-lanceolate, obtuse, hairy. *fl.* purple, 1½ in. long, narrow part of tube about 1 in. long, lobes large, 1¼ in. across; fl. axillary, solitary, almost sessile. Mexico. Needs feeding as flowers expand.

R. formo'sa. Shrub to 2 ft. *l.* ovate, somewhat acute, shortly hairy on both sides, stalks short. *fl.* scarlet; cor. tube 1½ in. long; peduncles 2- or 3-fld., twice or thrice as long as l., axillary. Summer. Brazil. 1808. (B.M. 1400.) Free-flowering stove plant.

R. ful'gida. *l.* ovate, acute, hairy, margins with rounded teeth. *fl.* red, small, in axillary, stalked heads; cor. tube narrow trumpet-shaped, ¾ in. long, lobes unequal. Colombia.

R. Harveya'na. Perennial with trailing or ascending 4-angled stems. *l.* oblong or elliptic-oblong, stalked. *fl.* pale lilac with white throat, sessile in upper l.-axils; cor. lobes rounded; cal. segs. very unequal. Mexico. (B.M. 8485.)

R. Herbst'ii. Erect small shrub to 3 ft. h. *l.* lanceolate, slender-pointed, downy, 5 to 7 in. long, toothed, deep dull green. *fl.* pale rose, in sessile axillary clusters of 3 to 5, about 3 in. long; cor. tube narrow for about 2 in. then bent and wider, upwards, lobes short, equal. September. Brazil. 1859. (B.M. 5156 as *Dipteracanthus Herbstii.*)

R. insig'nis. Shrub of 6 to 10 ft., branched, branches 4-angled at first. *l.* elliptical or rhomboid, 1½ to 2½ in. long, leathery, hairy; stalked. *fl.* lilac, solitary in axils of upper l.; cor. funnel-shaped, tube 1¼ in. long, expanded into rounded lobes ½ in. long, glabrous within, sparsely hairy without. Socotra.

R. latebro'sa. A synonym of *Hemigraphis latebrosa.*

R. lilaci'na. A synonym of *R. Schaueriana.*

R. longifo'lia. Glabrous perennial herb of 2 to 3 ft. *l.* oblong-lanceolate to oblong, narrowed to both ends, more or less toothed. *fl.* vermilion, cor. lobes notched; on many-fld. axillary peduncles shorter than l. July. Brazil. 1820.

R. Lorentzia'na. Nearly related to *R. ciliatiflora* but l. entire. Erect with 4-sided stem. *l.* oval, 3 to 4 in. long, rough beneath. *fl.* violet-blue about 1½ in. across in loose terminal panicles about 6 in. long; heads 3-fld., cor. tube funnel-shaped above the narrow base. Uruguay. (R.H. 1902, 136.)

R. macran'tha.* Shrub. *l.* long lanceolate. *fl.* rose with veined throat, about 3½ in. long, 2¼ in. across, axillary; cor. tube expanding from a narrow base. Winter and spring. Brazil. (B.M. 7872; R.H. 1881, 410.) Cultivation as for Justicias with spring propagation and a summer rest.

R. macrophyl'la. Sub-shrub of 3 to 4 ft. *l.* ovate, slender-pointed, wavy at margin or slightly toothed, downy. *fl.* bright scarlet, in spreading somewhat 1-sided axillary panicles; cor. tube about 3 in. long, curved, and as in *R. amoena* compressed, lobes large, reflexed. Summer. Colombia. 1844. (B.M. 4448 and B.R. 32, 7 as *Stemonacanthus macrophyllus.*) Similar to *R. amoena* but with much longer cor. tube.

R. Makoya'na. Low, spreading herb. *l.* olive-green shaded violet above, purple beneath. *fl.* solitary, rosy-carmine; cor. tube long, swollen upwards. Brazil. 1895. Foliage plant for pans.

R. macula'ta. Shrubby. *l.* oblong-lanceolate, cordate at base, blunt, spotted white above, appressed hairy; stalked. *fl.* blue, 1¼ to 1½ in. long. July. India. (W.P.A.R. 3, 250.) SYN. *Strobilanthes maculatus.*

R. panicula'ta. Christmas Pride of Jamaica. Perennial herb to 3 ft. h. *l.* oblong-ovate, narrowed to both ends, downy. *fl.* bluish-purple in axillary dichotomously branched cymes; cor. funnel-shaped, ½ in. long, sharply bent in middle of tube. August. W. Indies. 1768. (B.R. 585.)

R. Pearc'ei. Erect, glabrous sub-shrub. *l.* lanceolate, 5 to 6 in. long, long slender-pointed, obtusely toothed, brownish-purple beneath. *fl.* scarlet, 2 to 2½ in. long, erect, on few-fld. axillary peduncles; cor. tube slender, curved, very gradually widened upwards, lobes small, recurved. Bolivia, 1867. (B.M. 5648 as *Stemonacanthus Pearcei.*)

R. persicifo'lia. A synonym of *Strobilanthes anisophyllus.*

R. Portel'lae. Low annual or perennial, spreading herb, about 1 ft. h. *l.* elliptic-ovate, 2 to 3 in. long, more or less pointed, narrowed to the slender stalk, red-purple beneath. *fl.* rose, 1½ in. or more long, 1 in. wide, hairy without, solitary in l.-axils; cor. tube slender, lobes flat. Winter. Brazil. 1879. (B.M. 6498.) Best in pans.

Ruellia macrantha (p. 1838)

R. Purdiea'na. Glabrous sub-shrub up to 18 in. h. *l.* ovate, slender-pointed, stalked. *fl.* crimson, large, in terminal pairs in axils of a pair of large bracts; cor. tube long, lobes wavy. Jamaica. (B.M. 4298.)

R. ro'sea. Very hairy sub-shrub with angled stems. *l.* ovate, obtuse, about 1 in. long. *fl.* rose, 2 in. long, solitary on a peduncle with 2 bracts near apex. Mexico.

R. rubicau'lis. Glabrous, erect sub-shrub; branches 4-angled, warted, purple. *l.* oblong-lanceolate, acute, narrowed to nearly entire base, repand, fleshy. *fl.* yellow, funnel-shaped, solitary in axils or in a head of 3-fld. cymes. Pacific Is. SYN. *Dipteracanthus rubicaulis.*

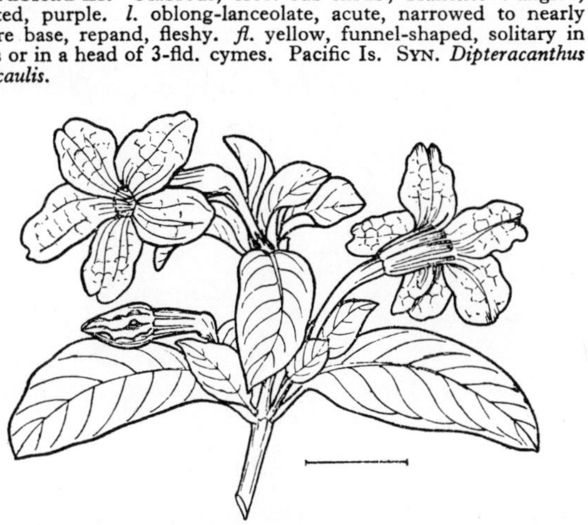

Ruellia Schaueriana

R. Schaueria'na. Low sub-shrub to about 2 ft. *l.* ovate, shining. *fl.* lilac, veined, solitary in l.-axils; with 2 large bracts about 1 in. long; cor. tube funnel-shaped, very long, bent below middle, lobes rounded. Brazil. 1844. (B.M. 4147; B.R. 32, 45 as *R. lilacina.*)

R. solitar'ia. Sub-shrub to 2 ft. *l.* oblong to ovate-lanceolate, 1 to 2 in. long, shortly stalked, sometimes with middle white blotch, pale and sometimes purplish beneath. *fl.* lavender-blue, lined or streaked purplish, solitary or twin, nearly sessile, the bracts smaller than in *R. Schaueriana*; cor. tube long, funnel-shaped. Winter. Brazil. (B.M. 5106 as *Dipteracanthus calvescens*; B.M. 4366 and F.d.S. 346 as *Strobilanthes lactatus.*)

R. specio'sa.* Shrub with pendent flexuous branches in nature up to 20 ft. long. *l.* oval, lower obtuse, upper acute. *fl.* scarlet, 3¼ in. long, solitary in l.-axils; cor. tube funnel-shaped. July. Brazil. 1859. (B.M. 5414 as *Dipteracanthus affinis.*) Somewhat like *R. macrantha.*

R. spectab'ilis.* Annual or perennial herb to 2 ft. or more h. *l.* ovate, slender-pointed, ciliate, slightly downy above. *fl.* purplish-blue with dark veins, 3½ in. long, lobes large, rounded; tube funnel-shaped, curved, fls. in pairs, sessile or nearly so. Peru. 1849. (B.M. 4494 as *Dipteracanthus spectabilis.*)

R. strep'ens. Spreading. *l.* ovate to obovate-oblong. *fl.* purplish, 1 to 3 in every l.-axil, large; cor. tube long, funnel-shaped; cal-segs. ciliate. N. America. Best in a large pan or basket.

R. tubero'sa Hairy herb with root of several fleshy tubers. *l.* oval or ovate, 2 to 3 in. long. *fl.* blue, 1½ to 2 in. long, solitary or in pairs on long axillary or terminal peduncles making a terminal panicle. W. Indies and SW. United States.

rufes'cens, reddish, or becoming red.

rufi'nus -a -um, red.

ru'fus -a -um (***rufi-,*** in compound words), pale red with a brown tone.

rugilo'bus -a -um, having wrinkled lobes.

rugo'sus -a -um, wrinkled.

rugulo'sus -a -um, somewhat wrinkled.

Ruhm'eri, in honour of G. F. Ruhmer, 1853–83, writer on flora of Brandenburg.

RUIZ'IA (in honour of Don Hippolite Ruiz Lopez, 1754–1815, joint author with Pavon of *Florae Peruvianae et Chilensis*). FAM. *Sterculiaceae.* A genus of 3 species of shrubs, natives of Bourbon. Leaves palmately veined, entire, lobed, sometimes densely hairy beneath. Calyx 5-parted; petals 5, lop-sided, flat, persistent; staminal cup with 20 to 30 fertile stamens; peduncles axillary, many-flowered. Stove plants needing a compost of loam, peat, and sand. Propagated by cuttings which root freely under a glass in heat in a similar compost.

R. loba'ta. Shrub of 6 ft. *l.* cordate, 3- to 5-lobed, mid-lobe longest and slender-pointed, crenate, whitish-hairy beneath, smooth above. *fl.* pale reddish. May. 1818.

R. variab'ilis. Shrub of 10 ft. *l.* of fl.-branches palmatifid, on sterile branches palmatipartite, whitish-hairy beneath. *fl.* pale reddish. May. 1792.

F. G. P.

RULING'IA (in honour of John Phillip Rüling of Gottingen, author about 1766 of an essay on the Natural Orders of Plants). FAM. *Sterculiaceae.* A genus of about 15 species of evergreen shrubs, undershrubs or rarely small trees, all except one, a native of Madagascar, confined to Australia. Leaves alternate, stellately downy or hairy, mostly terminal or from the same node as a leaf but on the opposite side; calyx 5-lobed, larger than the corolla; petals 5, broad-based, but narrowed to a slender, linear apex; stamens 10, 5 without anthers. Cool greenhouse plants easily cultivated and propagated by cuttings but not very ornamental.

KEY

1. *Lvs. up to 1 in. long*		2
1. *Lvs. 1 to 3 in. long*		3
2. *Lvs. about ½ in. long, soon glabrous above*	R. hermanniaefolia	
2. *Lvs. ½ to 1 in. long, densely hairy, often lobed*	R. parviflora	
3. *Lvs. downy especially beneath, ovate; fls. many in cluster*	R. corylifolia	
3. *Lvs. softly woolly, lanceolate; fls. few in cluster*	R. pannosa	

R. corylifo'lia. Shrub 3 to 7 ft., erect; shoots hairy. *l.* up to 3 in. long, 2 in. wide, broadly ovate, cordate, cuneate to slightly cordate at base, downy especially beneath. *fl.* white, crowded in stalked clusters 1½ in. across, near the top of the shoots, forming leafy panicles, cal. prominently 5-angled, lobes about ⅓ in. long. May. W. Australia. 1824. (B.M. 3182.)

R. hermanniaefo'lia. Shrub 2 or 3 ft., shoots slender, downy when young. *l.* narrow-oblong to linear, ¼ to ⅓ in. long, 1/12 to ¼ in. wide, much wrinkled, soon glabrous above, pale and downy beneath. *fl.* white, ½ in wide, in small terminal or lateral clusters. New S. Wales. 1818. (L.B.C. 1564 as *Lasiopetalum dumosum.*)

R. panno'sa. Shrub 3 to 6 ft. rarely a tree 20 ft., softly woolly in all its parts. *l.* lanceolate to ovate-lanceolate, 1 to 3 in. long, ¼ to 1 in. wide, rounded or slightly cordate at the base, pointed, bluntly toothed. *fl.* white, ¼ to ⅓ in. across, few in short-stalked lateral of terminal clusters. May. Australia. 1819. (B.M. 2191.)

R. parviflo'ra. Low shrub or undershrub up to 1½ ft., shoots slender and, like l. and infl., densely hairy. *l.* ¼ to 1 in. long, ⅛ to ⅝ in. wide, broadly ovate to oblong, often lobed, coarsely bluntly toothed. *fl.* white, ½ in. across, few in short lateral and terminal clusters; cal. spreading, downy outside. April. W. Australia. 1867. (Ref. B. 3.)

W. J. B.

rumel'icus -a -um, of Roumelia, SE. Europe.

RU'MEX (old Latin name used by Pliny). FAM. *Polygonaceae.* A genus of about 100 species, widely distributed over the world but especially in the North Temperate zone. Most are perennial herbs, some annuals, some sub-shrubs, rarely tall shrubs. Leaves sometimes all radical, sometimes alternate on stems and branches. Flowers clusters at the nodes, often in terminal racemes or panicles. Few species have any horticultural value and several, the Docks, are troublesome deep-rooting weeds forming buds on any piece of root left in the ground. *R. Acetosella*, the Sheep Sorrel, and *R. Acetosa*, the Sorrel, are typical plants of acid soils, and are best eradicated by liming. *R. Acetosella* runs widely underground with underground stems at different subterranean levels, and forms buds on extremely slender stems which may be left in trying to root it out. The leaves of *R. Acetosa* and *R. Patientia* are sometimes used as Spinach.

R. Aceto'sa. Sorrel. Rather succulent glabrous perennial tufted herb, 1 to 2 ft. h. *l.* radical, sagittate, 3 to 6 in. long, long-stalked, upper sessile. *fl.* dioecious in an erect leafless panicle; male fl. in dense 4- to 8-fld. clusters. N. Temperate and Arctic regions (Britain). Salad and pot herb.

R. alpi'nus. Monk's Rhubarb. Downy perennial with a stout rootstock, 2 to 4 ft. h. *l.* broadly ovate-cordate, 6 to 24 in. long with waved margins, long-stalked. *fl.* monoecious in erect much-branched panicles. N. and alpine Europe (Britain). Formerly used as a pot herb.

R. Hydrolap'athum. Great Water Dock. Glabrous perennial, 3 to 6 ft. h. *l.* broad oblong-lanceolate, 1 to 2 ft. long, acute, with rounded teeth; stalk 6 to 10 in. *fl.* in very large panicles. Europe (Britain). A good foliage plant for the side of ponds or slow streams, not spreading unduly.

R. flexuo'sus. Spreading, much-branched perennial with reddish-brown foliage. *Lower l.* narrow-lanceolate: *upper* gradually smaller but all longer than fl. *fl.* bisexual, few, in distant clusters; inner sep. toothed, acute, netted in fr. Australia, New Zealand.

R. Patien'tia. Herb Patience. Glabrous perennial herb, up to 5 ft., scarcely branched. *Radical l.* elliptic-ovate, tapered above and below, 8 to 12 in. long, margins undulate; *upper*, ovate-lanceolate with a long slender point. *fl.* in a long panicle, dense in fr. Europe. Leaves used as Spinach, earlier than Sorrel.

R. veno'sus. Glabrous branched perennial up to 18 in. h. *l.* oblong-ovate or ovate-lanceolate, entire. *fr.* 1 in. or more across, red-veined and showy, drooping. Montana, United States. Sometimes grown for its showy fr.

ru'micis, Rumex-like.

rumina'tus -a -um, thoroughly mingled.

rum'pens, bursting.

Rumphia'nus -a -um, in honour of G. E. Rumpf, 1628–1702, Dutch botanist writer on flora of Amboyna.

run, *see* **Bolt.**

runcina'tus -a -um, having saw-toothed or sharply incised leaves. **A**

RUNNER. A prostrate slender branch rooting at its extremity or elsewhere, affording a means of propagating.

rupes'tris -is -e, growing on rocks.

RUPI'COLA (*rupis*, rock, *colere*, dwelling, from the habitat). FAM. *Epacridaceae.* A genus of a single species of evergreen shrub related to Epacris, a native of Australia. Characters as below. Treatment as for Epacris.

R. sprengelioi'des. Shrub with densely leafy slender branches, about 30 in. h. *l.* linear lanceolate, ⅜ to ¾ in. long, narrowed to a short stalk, rigid. *fl.* solitary in l.-axils, forming a spike with a leafy apex; milk-white, about ⅓ in. across, notate, tube very short; anthers 1-celled. April. New S. Wales. 1906. (B.M. 8438.)

rupi'cola, growing in rocky places.

rupif'ragus -a -um, growing in rock crevices.

Ruppellia'nus -a -um, in honour of E. Ruppell, 1794–1884, of Frankfort, who collected in Egypt, Arabia, &c.

Ruprechtia'nus -a -um, in honour of Franz J. Ruprecht, 1814–70, of Prague, keeper of the herbarium of St. Petersburg.

RUPTUREWORT. *See* **Herniaria.**

rupturing, bursting in an irregular manner.

rura'lis -is -e, of country places.

Rus'byi, in honour of Dr. Rusby, traveller in New Mexico, *c.* 1885, who discovered *Primula Rusbyi.*

rusciform'is -is -e, Ruscus-like.

RUS'CUS (old Latin name used by Virgil, &c.). FAM. *Liliaceae.* A genus of 4 evergreen, sub-shrubs with a creeping rootstock and more or less woody stems, rigid, bearing a small, scale-like or bract-like leaf about the middle in the axil of which 1 or a few small, usually dioecious flowers are produced. Perianth segments 6, spreading, distinct; stamens 3, connate into a tube; ovary 1-celled with 2 ovules: fruit a red berry. All are natives of the Mediterranean region. They grow in almost any soil and thrive in shady places. Propagation is by division of the creeping rootstock in spring. The young growths which are frequently produced from the base are used in some parts of Europe like Asparagus.

R. aculea'tus. Butcher's Broom. *Cladodes* stiff and spiny, about ¾ to 1½ in. long, rather glossy on grooved stems, 1½ to 3½ ft. h., with rigid branches near top. *fl.* 1 or 2, from middle of cladode, about ¼ in. across, greenish, inner segs. shorter. March, April. *fr.* globose, red, about ½ in. thick. England, Mediterranean region to Persia. (E.B. 1516.) Beautiful when covered with berries, but being usually male, berries are not very frequent. Hermaphrodite forms are known. var. **angustifo'lius** has narrower cladodes than the type; **latifo'lius,** cladodes up to 2 in. long, ¾ to 1 in. wide, glossy.

R. androgy'nus. A synonym of *Semele androgyna.*

R. Hypoglos'sum. Growth compact, tufted; stems 8 to 18 in. h., unbranched, more or less arching, scarcely woody. *Cladodes* 3 to 4½ in. long, 1 to 1½ in. wide, tapering to both ends, lower narrow-oval, upper oblanceolate. *fl.* 3 to 5 small, yellow in axil of a leaf-like bract 1 to 1½ in. long on upper side of cladode. April, May. *Berry* (rarely produced) red, globose, ¼ to ½ in. wide. S. Europe, before 1600. Excellent for planting in shade among tree-roots. SYN. *R. Hypophyllum Hypoglossum.*

R. Hypophyl'lum. Habit of *R. Hypoglossum* but about 6 to 12 in. h., *cladodes* oval or ovate, 1½ to 3 in. long, 1 to 1½ in. wide, *fl.* 5 or 6, white, on slender stalks in axil of small bract on lower side of cladode. March, April. *fr.* about ⅜ in. thick. Madeira to Caucasus. 1625. (B.M. 2049.) Less hardy than *R. Hypoglossum.*

R. hyrcan'us. Closely related to *R. aculeatus* but with branches in whorls and fls. in groups of 2 to 5. Transcaucasus to N. Persia.

R. racemo'sus. A synonym of *Danae racemosa.*

RUSH. *See* **Juncus.**

RUSH FERN. *See* **Schizaea.**

RUSH, FLOWERING. *See* **Butomus.**

A→

russa'tus -a -um, reddened.

RUSSEL'IA (in honour of Dr. Alexander Russel, F.R.S., author of *Natural History of Aleppo*, 1756). FAM. *Scrophulariaceae.* A genus of about 20 species of evergreen shrubs with showy flowers, natives of Mexico and Cent. America. Leaves opposite or whorled, those of the often nodding or pendulous branchlets frequently reduced to scales. Calyx deeply cut, segments 5, closely overlapping; corolla scarlet, tube cylindrical, limbs 5-fid, 2-lipped; stamens 4; cymes forked, sometimes many-flowered, sometimes with but one flower. Rich light soil suits these excellent basket plants almost continuously in bloom. Cuttings readily strike in light soil under a glass in heat.

R. × elegantiss'ima. *See* **R. × Lemoinei.**

R. floribun'da. A synonym of *R. rotundifolia.*

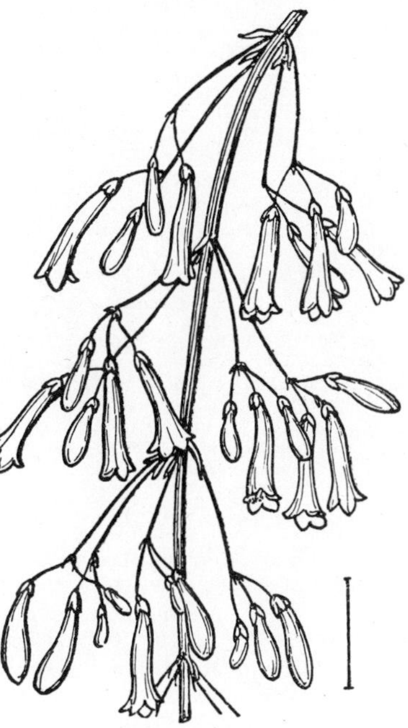

Russelia juncea

R. junc'ea. Coral Plant. Shrub of 3 to 4 ft. with twiggy, rush-like branches with drooping ends. *l.* linear, lanceolate or ovate, small; of branchlets minute and scale-like. *fl.* scarlet, 1 in. long, in loose racemes; peduncles long. Summer. Mexico. 1833. (B.R. 1773.)

R. × Lemoin'ei (*R. juncea* × *R. sarmentosa*). Intermediate between parents but more floriferous, particularly in winter. Of garden origin. 1897. Syn. *R. juncea Lemoinei. R. × elegantissima* is of the same origin with similar characters. (B.M. n.s. 315.)

R. multiflo'ra. A synonym of *R. sarmentosa.*

R. rotundifo'lia. Shrub to 4 ft. *l.* round, deeply cordate at base, 2 to 4 in. long and broad, netted beneath, softly hairy. *fl.* as in *R. sarmentosa*, peduncles many-fld. June. Mexico. 1824. Syn. *R. floribunda.*

R. sarmento'sa. Shrub to 4 ft. *l.* opposite or in whorls of 3 or 4, wedge- or somewhat heart-shaped at base, variable in most characters. *fl.* appearing whorled or in loose cymes; peduncles 3- or 4- to 30- or 40-fld., sometimes axillary, sometimes crowded; cor. more or less bearded in throat below lip. July. Cent. America. 1812. (B.M. 1528 as *R. multiflora.*)

F. G. P.

Russellia'nus -a -um, in honour of Dukes of Bedford, whose family name is Russell or of Mr. Russell of Falkirk.

RUSSETING. Although russeting may be a normal character there are instances where this roughening is an abnormal symptom on a surface which should be normally smooth. On apples, for instance, there may be some russeting owing to the powdery mildew fungus *Podosphaera leucotricha* and on the other hand some varieties (especially Cox's Orange Pippin) display russeting after injury by frost or after spraying with Bordeaux mixture. If the attack of a parasite causes more pronounced injury than russeting it is described as Scurf or Scab as in Apple Scab, Pear Scab, Potato Common Scab, &c.

D. E. G.

rustica'nus -a -um, of wild places.

RUSTS. This term is apt to be used for any reddish-brown or rusty discoloration of foliage, but this usage should not be encouraged. The true rust diseases on plants are a definite and special group caused by fungus parasites known as the Rusts or Uredinales. These constitute a large group containing several genera and all members depend entirely on their parasitic habit and, except in resting spore (teleutospore) form, cannot exist apart from their living host-plant or plants. Many are specific parasites attacking only one species of plant or even one part of a plant, being confined to leaf or stem or fruit. The hyphae are septate and ramify through the tissues of the host in the intercellular spaces of the cells, putting out specialized suckers or haustoria into the cells to obtain nourishment. Sometimes this does not immediately kill the cells but causes them to grow abnormally and present the enlarged appearance known as hypertrophy. Sometimes the rust fungus remains perennial in the host, e.g. Weymouth Pine Rust, and produces the spore stage year after year. The rust fungi have definite stages in their life-cycle and each stage produces characteristic spores for reproduction of the next and the common name Rusts is suggested by the conspicuous reddish or orange appearance of the spore stages shown in most rust diseases. The summer stage produces the uredospores which are usually pale brown or yellow, thin-walled and borne in sori on leaves and stems. These uredospores spread the infection during summer and several generations may be produced for this purpose. Later in the autumn in the same spots (sori) or in fresh places on the same foliage or stems appear the winter or resting teleutospores. These are thick-walled and dark brown and mostly have a resting period before germinating to produce a short broad, tubular hypha known as a promycelium which in turn forms and releases basidiospores. These basidiospores will germinate to infect their host and the resulting mycelium will, in spring, give rise to aecidiospores formed in some cases in cup-shaped structures commonly known as cluster cups. The aecidiospores carry on the infection and the resulting mycelium produces the uredospore stage again. This is roughly the life-cycle of a complete rust fungus. Where all the stages are formed on the same plant the rust is termed autoecious, but many species form their aecidiospores on a different and perhaps unrelated plant from the one on which they produce the teleutospores and these are described as heteroecious rusts. Furthermore some species are devoid of uredospores and some devoid of both uredospores and aecidospores but the teleutospore stage is always formed. Among autoecious rusts, the Broad Bean rust, *Uromyces fabae*, forms 3 kinds of spores on the bean plant, as does the Mint rust *Puccinia menthae* on the mint. On Antirrhinums the rust fungus *Puccinia antirrhini* produces only uredospores and teleutospores, while the Hollyhock rust *Puccinia malvacearum* produces only teleutospores. Among the heteroecious rusts there is great variety of genera and of different host plants. Of interest in horticulture are Cineraria rust, *Coleosporium senecionis*, which produces its uredospores and teleutospores as orange-red pustules on the leaves of cultivated Cinerarias and wild Senecio species while its aecidiospores are formed as yellowish-white blisters on the needles of the Scots Pine; Gooseberry rust, *Puccinia Pringsheimiana*, forms reddish-orange aecidia or cluster cups on the fruits, leaves, and shoots of gooseberries while the teleutospores and uredospores are produced on various sedges. The classical example of a heteroecious rust is Wheat rust caused by *Puccinia graminis* which causes great loss when in its uredospore and teleutospore stages it destroys Wheat and other cereals but forms the aecidiospores on the common Barberry, *B. vulgaris*, in the well-known cluster-cup stage.

The classification of rusts is based upon the teleutospores which fall into 2 groups: (1) those in which the teleutospores are without stalks, and (2) those in which they possess stalks although these may be short. The first group contains the 3 families Melampsoraceae, Coleosporiaceae, and Cronartiaceae and the second the one family, Pucciniaceae. In these families genera are classified according as to whether the teleutospore is 1-celled

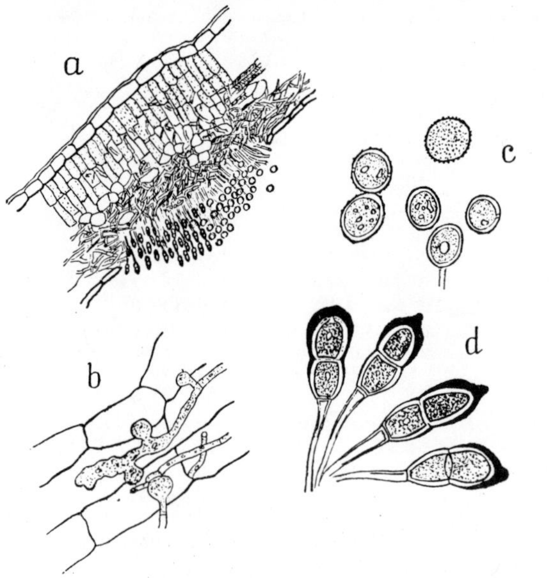

Puccinia antirrhini—Antirrhinum Rust

a. Fungus in leaf producing uredo- and teleutospores.
b. Fungus showing haustoria.
c. Uredospores.
d. Teleutospores.

or more. Genera with teleutospores 1-celled are Melampsora and Uromyces; 2-celled, Puccinia; and 2- to several-celled, Phragmidium and Gymnosporangium. These genera containing many species which are of importance as parasites of cultivated plants. Nevertheless our present knowledge of rust fungi is not sufficient to enable a thorough system of classification to be made.

D. E. G.

RU'TA (*Rute* was the old Greek name, probably from ***ruomai***, to preserve: in allusion to the effect of the plant on health). FAM. *Rutaceae*. A genus of about 40 species of hardy shrubs, sub-shrubs, or perennial herbs, strong smelling and gland-dotted, natives of S. Europe, the Mediterranean region, and W. Asia. Leaves alternate, varying from simple to 3-foliolate, pinnate, and decompound. Flowers in terminal corymbs or panicles; calyx 4- or 5-lobed; petals 4 or 5, sometimes toothed or ciliate; stamens 8 or 10. Any good open soil will suit them and they are propagated by seeds or cuttings.

KEY

1. *Lvs. pinnate or 2-pinnate*	2
1. *Lvs. simple, entire*	R. suaveolens
2. *Shrub or sub-shrub*	3
2. *Perennial with woody rootstock; l.-segs. linear to lanceolate, ¼ to 1½ in. wide*	R. divaricata
3. *Stems downy*	R. patavina
3. *Stems glabrous*	4
4. *Fl. ½ in. wide*	5
4. *Fl. ¾ in. wide; plant glabrous*	R. graveolens
5. *Lvs. 3 to 4 in. long; lflets. obovate*	R. bracteosa
5. *Lvs. up to 6 in. long; lflets. narrow-linear*	R. chalepensis

R. angustifo'lia. A synonym of *R. chalepensis*.

R. bracteo'sa. Evergreen shrub about 3 ft., glabrous. *l.* 3 to 4 in. long, mostly 2-pinnate; lflets. oblanceolate to obovate, ¼ to ¾ in. long, apex rounded. *fl.* yellow, ½ in. wide, in loose terminal corymbs 3 to 5 in. across; pet. recurved at the point, margins hairy. June to September. S. Europe. 1772.

R. chalepen'sis. Sub-shrub up to 2½ ft., glabrous; stems semi-woody. *l.* up to 6 in. long, pinnate or 2-pinnate; lflets. ¼ to ¾ in. long, 1/12 to 3/16 in. wide, narrowly oblong-cuneate to linear, apex rounded. *fl.* yellow, ½ in. wide, in axillary and terminal corymbs; pet. incurved at the tip, margins hairy. June to September. Mediterranean region. 1772. SYN. *R. angustifolia*.

R. divarica'ta. Perennial plant with a woody rootstock, 10 to 20 in. h. *l.* 2 to 4 in. long, pinnate or 2-pinnately compound; final subdivisions ¼ to 1 in. long, 1/12 to ¼ in. wide, linear-oblong to lanceolate, apex rounded. *fl.* dullish yellow, ½ in. wide, in terminal compound corymbs 3 to 5 in. across; pet. 4, concave with the apex incurved. June, July. Cent. and E. Europe.

R. grave'olens. Rue. Herb of Grace. Evergreen acrid shrub about 3 ft., shoots erect, glabrous, semi-woody. *l.* 3 to 5 in. long, glaucous, pinnately compound, ultimate segs. obovate, ⅛ to ½ in. long. *fl.* in terminal corymbs, ¾ in. across, rather dull yellow; sep. and pet. 4 or 5, pet. concave; stamens 8 or 10. *fr.* a 4- or 5-celled capsule. June to September. S. Europe. 1562. var. **variega'ta,** *lflets.* bordered white. *See also* **Rue.**

R. macrophyl'la. A synonym of *R. bracteosa*.

R. patavi'na. Sub-shrub, 6 to 15 in., stems semi-woody, downy. *Lower l.* erect, oblong-cuneate to linear-spatulate, ½ to 1¼ in. long, 1/16 to 3/16 in. wide, apex blunt; *upper* 3-fid or 3-lobed. *fl.* ½ in. wide, in a compact, terminal head, 1 to 2 in. across, pet. 5 with a green central rib. June, July. Orient. 1819. A useful rock plant for a sunny place.

R. suave'olens. Sub-shrub up to 2 ft., stems erect, hairy. *l.* entire, simple, erect, narrowly oval or lanceolate, ½ to 1¼ in. long, ⅛ to ¼ in. wide, downy, ciliate, densely set. *fl.* ½ to ⅝ in. wide, closely set in terminal corymbs, 1½ to 2½ in. across, cowslip scented; pet. 5; cal. ciliate. June to September. E. Europe. 1800. SYN. *Haplophyllum Biebersteinii, H. suaveolens*. var. **grandiflo'ra,** *fl.* and corymbs larger. (B.M. 2254, as *Ruta linifolia grandiflora*.)

W. J. B.

Ruta-mura'ria, Wall-rue.

RUTA'CEAE. Dicotyledons. A family of about 100 genera with about 900 species in tropical and temperate regions, especially in S. Africa and Australia. Usually shrubs or trees with alternate or opposite leaves, gland-dotted, simple or often compound, with stipules. Flowers usually in cymes, regular or zygomorphic, sometimes unisexual. Sepals 5 or 4, overlapping in bud; petals 5 or 4; stamens 10 or 8, but sometimes fewer; ovary superior of 5 or 4 carpels, rarely fewer or indefinite, often free at the base and united above, many-celled, ovules 2 to many in each cell. Fruit various. Several species are important for the oil they yield and Citrus and allied genera for their fruits. Genera dealt with are: Acmadenia, Acradenia, Acronychia, Adenandra, Aegle, Agathosma, Almeidea, Atalantia, Balsamocitrus, Barosma, Boenninghausenia, Boronia, Calodendron, Casimiroa, Chloroxylon, Choisya, Chomelia, Citropsis, Citrus, Clausenia, Coleonema, Correa, Crowea, Cusparia, Dictamnus, Diosma, Diplolaena, Empleurum, Eriostemon, Erythrochiton, Euchaetis, Evodia, Feronia, Geijera, Macrostylis, Medicosma, Melicope, Murraya, Orixa, Peganum, Peltostigma, Phebalium, Philotheca, Pilocarpus, Poncirus, Ptelea, Ravenia, Ruta, Severinia, Skimmia, Spatelia, Spiranthera, Ticorea, Toddalia, Triphasia, Xanthoxylum, Zieria.

ruta'ceus -a -um, resembling Ruta.

rutaefo'lius -a -um, with Rue-like leaves.

ruthen'icus -a -um, of Ruthenia, Cent. Carpathians.

ru'tilans, ru'tilus -a -um, glowing deep red.

rutrif'er -fera -ferum, shovel-shaped.

Rutt'neri, in honour of Fr. Ruttner, b. 1882, of Vienna, travelled in Sumatra, &c.

RUT'TYA (in honour of Dr. John Rutty, 1697–1775 Irish naturalist). FAM. *Acanthaceae*. A genus of 5 species of shrubs, natives of S. Africa, with spikes of flowers with small, linear bracts. Calyx 5-parted nearly to base, with narrow equal segments; corolla with wide tube, 2-lipped, segments 5, ovate; stamens 2, fertile, 1-celled; style with 2 small equal branches. Fruit an ellipsoid capsule, 4-seeded. For treatment *see* **Eranthemum.**

R. ova'ta. Shrub. *l.* ovate, tapering at both ends, up to 5 in. long, stalked. *fl.* bright red in a densely fld., terminal, cone-like spike with awl-shaped bracts; cor. 2-lipped, upper lip erect, flat, lower deflexed, 3-lobed. S. Africa.

RUYSCH'IA (in honour of Frederick Ruysch, 1638–1731, Professor of Botany, Amsterdam; died 1731). FAM. *Marcgraviaceae.* A genus of about 8 species of epiphytic or climbing shrubs, rarely trees, natives of Trop. America. Leaves entire, leathery. Flowers in terminal, often long racemes, with sessile 3-lobed bracts at tip of pedicels; sepals 5, closely overlapping; petals 5, overlapping, joined at base; stamens 5; bracteoles sepal-like. *R. clusiifolia* needs stove conditions and grows in a compost of vegetable mould and loam, and can be increased by cuttings of ripe wood in sand in heat.

R. clusiifo'lia. Undershrub about 4 ft. h. *l.* alternate, obovate, about 4 in. long, thick, shining. *fl.* purple in many-fld. racemes about 1 ft. long; peduncles short; bracts scarlet, dotted red, obovate, acute, thick, deflexed. June. Guiana and Caribbean Is. 1823.

RYAN'IA (in honour of Dr. John Ryan, F.R.S., correspondent of Vahl). FAM. *Flacourtiaceae.* A genus of about 6 species of stellately hairy trees, natives of Trop. America. Leaves entire, not dotted, pinnate-veined. Flowers axillary, often showy, solitary or somewhat clustered; sepals 5, lanceolate or oblong, overlapping, persistent; petals absent; stamens indefinite. *R. speciosa* needs stove conditions and a compost of peat and loam. Ripe cuttings will root in sand in heat.

R. specio'sa. About 10 ft. h. *l.* green, stellately hairy on veins beneath. *fl.* large, creamy; peduncles 1-fld. W. Indies. 1823.

F. G. P.

RYDBERG'IA. Included in **Actinella.**

RYSSOP'TERYS (*ryssos*, wrinkled, *pteris*, wing; in allusion to the wing of the fruit). FAM. *Malpighiaceae.* A genus of about 12 species of slender, twining shrubs, natives of the E. Indies and Australia. Leaves opposite or nearly so, entire, margins glandular beneath, stalks slender, with 2 glands at apex; stipules rather large. Flowers whitish; calyx 5-parted; petals scarcely clawed; stamens 10, all fertile, inflorescence terminal or apparently axillary, corymbose; pedicels thickened upwards. Samaras 1 to 3 with broad wings at apex bearing lateral tubercles. They need stove heat and should have a compost of fibrous peat and sandy loam. Cuttings will root in sand with bottom heat.

R. microste'ma. *l.* broadly ovate, 3 to 5 in. long, up to 3 in. wide, somewhat cordate, mucronate, somewhat wavy at margin, grey-downy beneath. *infl.* at least as long as l.; pet. 3 or 4 times as long as cal.; anthers minute. August. Java. 1820.

F. G. P.

rytido- (***rhytido-***, in compound words), signifying wrinkled.

S

SABADIL'LA. A synonym of Schoenocaulon. A

SA'BAL (said to be a native name in S. America; not explained by the author of the genus). FAM. *Palmaceae.* A genus of about 20 species of Palms of varying stature, spineless, natives of the hotter parts of America. Stem slender or stout, creeping or erect, smooth or ringed, clothed above with persistent leaf-sheaths. Leaves in a terminal crown, round or wedge-shaped at base, deeply cut fan-wise; segments linear, 2-fid, margins fimbriate; stalks concave above, margins smooth, acute; sheaths large. Spadix long, much branched, erect at first, the branches and branchlets slender, recurving, pendent; spathes tubular. Flowers small, glabrous, white or green. Fruits small, black, globose, the short style basal. Most species will succeed under greenhouse conditions except those from Trop. S. America which need a higher temperature. A light loam suit them. They are handsome Palms, some of which are good decorative pot plants. A few suckers are sometimes formed and these can be taken off when about a foot long. They need careful nursing at first, especially when they have no roots. Seeds afford the best means of propagating. There is much confusion, as with several other palms, in the nomenclature of these Fan Palms.

S. Adanson'ii. A synonym of *S. minor.*

S. Blackburn'ia. Fan or Thatch Palm. Stem 30 to 40 ft. h., thickened at middle. *l.* 20 to 30, large, orbicular, glaucous, rather rigid; segs. about 40, ensiform, 2-fid., filamentous stalks 6 to 8 ft. long. *Spadix* much branched. *fr.* inverted pear-shaped, about 1½ in. long. W. Indies. 1825. A good window plant when small, and for the sub-tropical garden in summer. This name has been used in gardens for several palms including *S. umbraculifera.*

S. glauces'cens. A synonym of *S. mauritiiformis.*

S. mauritiiform'is. Trinidad Palm. Stem sometimes to 80 ft., somewhat ringed, 12 to 15 in. thick. *l.* up to 12 ft. across, suborbicular, glaucous beneath, multifid to middle, with loose fibres between the 2-fid lobes; stalks 7 to 8 ft. long. *Spadix* longer than l., branches paniculate. *fr.* black, as large as a pea. W. Indies. SYN. *S. glaucescens.*

S. mexica'na. This name is sometimes used in gardens for *S. Palmetto.*

S. mi'nor. Dwarf Palmetto. Stem very short or not above ground. *l.* orbicular, fan-shaped, glaucous, 2 to 3 ft. long, slightly pinnatifid; segs. 20 to 30, slightly 2-fid, slightly fibrous in sinuses; stalks stout, concave, smooth at edges, shorter than l. *Spadix* erect, 3 to 6 ft. h., smooth, slender. S. United States. 1810. (B.M. 1434 as *S. Adansonii.*) Greenhouse or half-hardy.

S. Palmet'to. Cabbage Palmetto; Palmetto Palm. Stem erect, 20 to 80 ft. h. *l.* 5 to 8 ft. long, cordate, recurved at summit, shorter than stalk; segs. numerous, deeply cleft, fibrous in sinuses; stalks smooth. *Spadix* smooth and spreading, usually shorter than l. *fr.* black. S. United States. 1825. Greenhouse.

S. serrula'ta. A synonym of *Serenoa repens.*

S. umbraculif'era. Stem 60 to 80 ft. *l.* 4 to 6 ft. across, suborbicular, somewhat glaucous, multifid to ⅓ or ⅔, fibrous between segs., segs. 2-fid. *Spadix* 4 to 5 ft. long, paniculate. *fr.* greenish-black, ½ in. wide. W. Indies. 1825. Greenhouse.

sabau'dus -a -um, of Savoy.

SABBAT'IA (in honour of L. Sabbati, Italian botanist, author of *Synopsis Plantarum*, 1745). FAM. *Gentianaceae.* A genus of about 12 species of annual or biennial herbs, erect and sometimes branched above, natives of N. America and Cuba. Leaves opposite, sessile or stem-clasping. Flowers white or rose-purple, handsome; calyx 5- to 12-parted or cleft; corolla tube very short, limb rotate with 5 to 12 ovate or narrow twisted lobes; stamens 5 to 12; anthers recurved or revolute. These hardy plants are rarely seen but are handsome in flower and worth growing. Seeds should be sown in peaty soil as soon as ripe, either thinly in pots or in a shady border. As the plants grow naturally in boggy and marshy places the pots may be stood in shallow pans of water. Some of the species, however, succeed in the ordinary border and *S. chloroides* has been found to make a good bedding plant. The following species are all N. American and flower in summer. The name is sometimes spelt Sabatia.

S. angula'ris. Rose Pink. 1 to 2 ft. h. *l.* ovate, more or less acute, cordate and clasping at base. *fl.* rose-pink, rarely white, 1½ in. across, eye yellowish or green; cal. lobes ½ to ¾ in. long, infl. pyramidal, many-fld., peduncles short. 1826.

S. calyco'sa. 5 to 20 in. h., stem forking frequently. *l.* oblong or lanceolate-oblong, narrowed at base. *fl.* almost white; cal. lobes $\frac{2}{3}$ to 1 in. long, exceeding cor.; peduncles long, 1-fld. 1812. (B.M. 1600.)

S. campes'tris. About 12 in. h. Stem 4-angled, forked; branchlets 1-fld. *l.* ovate, lower obtuse. *fl.* rose, 5-parted; cal. lobes as long as cor. 1855. (B.M. 5015; G.F. 73.)

S. chloroi'des.* 12 to 24 in. h., branched above. *l.* oblong-lanceolate. *fl.* deep rose, rarely white, 9- to 12-parted; cor. twice as long as cal., cal. lobes linear; infl. a panicle. 1817. (J.R.H.S. 63, 92.)

Sabbatia gracilis

S. grac'ilis. 12 to 18 in. h. Stem erect, slender, angled, glabrous. *l.* crowded at base, obovate; upper narrower, pale green, glabrous. *fl.* pale pink with yellow base, in a dichotomous cyme; pedicels long. July. 1805. Eastern N. America.

S. panicula'ta. 1 to 2 ft. h., much branched. *l.* linear, lower oblong, obtuse. *fl.* white; cal. lobes linear, much shorter than cor.; infl. a many-fld. corymb. 1817.

S. stella'ris. 6 to 20 in. h., forked, spreading. *l.* oblong to ovate-lanceolate, upper linear. *fl.* bright rose-purple; cal. lobes awl-shaped, up to nearly as long as cor.; peduncles 1-fld. 1827.

Sabdariff'a, from a W. Indian name.

SAB'IA (derived from *Sabja-lat*, its Indian name). FAM. *Sabiaceae.* A genus of about 20 species of Asiatic, deciduous, or evergreen climbers. Leaves alternate, entire. Flowers in small axillary clusters or solitary; calyx and corolla 5- or (rarely) 4-parted. Fruit in 2 closely attached globose or kidney-shaped parts (mericarps). The 2 following species are hardy, but the flowers are inconspicuous and their beauty is in their blue fruits. Increased by cuttings.

S. latifo'lia. Deciduous scandent shrub up to 10 ft., shoots yellowish-green or purplish. *l.* oval, oval-oblong or obovate, 2 to 5 in. long, $1\frac{1}{2}$ to 3 in. wide, hairy on midrib and veins beneath; stalk $\frac{1}{4}$ to $\frac{1}{2}$ in. long. *fl.* usually 3 in axillary cymes $\frac{1}{4}$ to $\frac{1}{2}$ in. long; cor. $\frac{1}{4}$ in. wide, pet. greenish-yellow, incurved to make the fl. somewhat globose. *fr.* bright blue in 2 (often 1 suppressed) kidney-shaped parts $\frac{1}{3}$ in. long. China. 1908. (B.M. 8859.)

S. Schumannia'na. Deciduous climber up to 10 ft., shoots glabrous. *l.* 1 to 4 in. long, $\frac{1}{3}$ to $1\frac{1}{2}$ in. wide, narrowly oblong to oval-lanceolate, slender pointed, glabrous. *fl.* $\frac{1}{4}$ in. long, cup-shaped, 3 to 6 in axillary cymes with a stalk up to $1\frac{1}{2}$ in. long; pet. greenish to dull purple. oval. May. *fr.* blue, in 2 globose parts each $\frac{1}{4}$ in. wide. China. 1908.

W. J. B.

SABIA'CEAE. Dicotyledons. A family of about 70 species of trees and shrubs, sometimes climbing, in 4 genera, mostly natives of Trop. Asia and America, but some in temperate E. Asia. Leaves alternate, odd-pinnate or simple, without stipules. Flowers perfect or polygamous, in terminal or axillary cymes or panicles; sepals 4 or 5, imbricate, unequal; petals 5, rarely 4, imbricate, often unequal; stamens opposite petals, 3 outer sometimes changed to staminodes; ovary superior, usually 2-, rarely 3-celled. Fruit 1-, rarely 2-celled, indehiscent, 1-seeded. The genera treated here are Meliosma, Sabia.

SABIC'EA (from *Sabisabi*, native name in Guiana). FAM. *Rubiaceae.* A genus of about 40 species of twining shrubs, often markedly hairy, natives of the tropics of America, and Africa including Madagascar. Leaves opposite, oblong; stipules intrapetiolar, usually persistent, erect or recurved. Flowers clustered in axillary, sessile or stalked corymbose cymes or heads; calyx tube nearly globose, limb long, 3- to 6-lobed; corolla funnel- or salver-shaped, lobes 4 or 5, short, valvate; stamens 5. A compost of peat, loam, and sand suits these stove plants, which may be propagated by cuttings in heat.

S. asp'era. Twiner to 6 ft. *l.* elliptic, slender-pointed, roughly hairy above, softly beneath; stipules oval-oblong, acute. *fl.* white, somewhat whorled, sessile. June. Guiana. 1824. SYN. *S. edulis, S. velutinus.*

S. hir'ta. Closely allied to *S. aspera*, perhaps only a variety. *l.* ovate-lanceolate, slender-pointed, hairy on both sides; stipules large, cordate-ovate, membranous. *fl.* white; involucre of 4 lflets; umbels 3-fld. short stalked. Jamaica. 1825.

F. G. P.

SAB'INEA (in honour of Joseph Sabine, F.L.S., F.R.S., 1770–1837, a founder and later Secretary of the Horticultural Society of London). FAM. *Leguminosae.* A genus of 2 or 3 species of small trees or shrubs, natives of the W. Indies. Leaves equally pinnate, deciduous, leaflets entire, without stipels; flowers pink, clustered, papilionaceous; calyx with very short teeth; standard roundish, spreading or reflexed; wings falcate-oblong, free; keel incurved; bracts small; bracteoles absent. Pods linear, flattish, 2-valved. Stove plants needing a compost of well-drained sandy loam. Young shoots will strike in sand in heat, under a glass.

S. carinal'is. *Lflets.* in 6 to 8 pairs, distant oblong, 5 about $\frac{1}{2}$ in. long, mucronulate. *fl.* bright scarlet, 3 to 5 in a cluster, standard and wings about 1 in. long, keel $1\frac{1}{2}$ in. long.

S. flo'rida. *Lflets.* in 8 to 15 pairs, oblong or elliptic oblong, $\frac{1}{3}$ in. long. *fl.* rosy; wings and standard $\frac{1}{2}$ in. long; keel $\frac{2}{3}$ in. long, half-round.

F. G. P.

Sabinia'nus -a -um, *see above.*

Sabi'nus -a -um, from old Latin name of Sabini.

sabuli'cola, a dweller on sand.

sabulo'sus -a -um, of sandy ground.

Saccardia'nus -a -um, in honour of P. A. Saccardo, 1845–1920, director, Academy of Botany, Padua, a noted mycologist.

saccatus -a -um, sacco- in compound words, bag-shaped.

saccharif'erus -a -um, sugar-producing.

sacchariform'is -is -e, Saccharum-like.

SACCHA'RUM (*saccharon*, old Greek name for sugar). FAM. *Gramineae.* A genus of about a dozen species of tall grasses, inhabiting tropical and sub-tropical regions. Spikelets at the sides of the branchlets, dense, or ample and twin, one sessile, the other stalked; glumes 4, 3 of which are empty, acute, or somewhat bristly acuminate; panicle terminal, densely pilose, sometimes ample and densely bundle-flowered, sometimes contracted into a dense spike. Leaves flat or narrow, convolute when dry. The most important species is *S. officinarum*, the Sugar-cane of commerce. It has been cultivated from time immemorial, being propagated by cuttings. Some of the species are ornamental plants. They are all easily grown in a light, rich soil, with a good heat. Propagation may be effected by suckers; or by cuttings of the stems, which produce shoots at their joints. The undermentioned species require stove treatment, except where otherwise stated.

S. aegypt'icum. A synonym of *S. spontaneum.*

S. arundina'ceum. *fl.* panicle diffuse, branches whorled, compound and decompound. July. *l.* ensiform, midrib white, margins slightly hispid. Stems erect, 10 to 20 ft. h. Bengal. 1822. Allied to *S. officinarum.*

S. Mun'ja. *fl.* all hermaphrodite; panicle large, oblong, spreading, branches whorled, decompound. Summer. *l.* hispid, long-linear, white-nerved, channelled. Stems 8 to 10 ft. h. Benares. 1805. Plant wholly glabrous, except on inside of l. at base.

S. officina'rum. Sugar-cane. *fl.* palea half as long as third glume; outer glumes pointed, half to one-third as long as wool; panicle large, pyramidal, common axis sulcate, joints and pedicels glabrous below wool. July. *l.* long and broad, dark green, hanging in graceful curves. Stems yellowish-green, stout, erect. 10 ft. h. E. Indies. 1597. var. **sinen'se,** *fl.* 2-valved, unilateral, panicle ovate, branches whorled, simple and compound, stems 6 to 10 ft. h. China. 1822. Greenhouse; **viola'ceum,** *fl.* midrib of the second glume suppressed, stems rich violet or plum-colour. W. Indies. 1824.

S. sponta'neum.* *fl.* panicle silvery-silky, crowded; 10 to 12 in. long; lower branches compound. July. *l.* numerous, long, ribbon-like, with white midrib, covered with soft, silky hairs, which impart a greyish appearance to the plants. Stems about 7 ft. h. Algeria. 1866. A vigorous grass, forming a gigantic tuft, rivalling Bambusa, Cortadeiria, and Erianthus.

saccif'erus -a -um, bag-bearing.

SACCOLA'BIUM (*saccos*, bag, *labium*, lip; alluding to the baggy lip). FAM. *Orchidaceae.* Revisions of this genus have been made from time to time and a number of sections have been given generic names, but though as treated here the genus does contain species which are slightly at variance, practically all have long been known in gardens as Saccolabiums and it is convenient horticulturally to keep the larger grouping. All are epiphytic. As originally defined over 100 species have been included in the genus distributed through the East from Ceylon to Java. The inflorescence is lateral, racemose, or scattered, spicate, panicled, or sub-corymbose. The flowers have sub-equal, free, spreading sepals, flat or concave, petals similar, sometimes narrower or broader, adnate to the column base which is not produced into a foot, lip 3-lobed, sessile at base of column, spurred (spur more or less conical) or saccate at base, lateral lobes erect, often very small, mid-lobe polymorphous, spreading or erect, usually small. Column short, pollinia 2. Stems comparatively short; leaves distichous, leathery, fleshy, broad or slender, flat or arched, sometimes terete. The genus is allied to Rhynchostylis (which was formerly included), Aerides, and Vanda, but none of the species appears to attain the stem heights of the larger Vandas and Aerides.

Temperatures and compost should be as for Aerides. The species with rather hard foliage should be given more light than softer-leaved kinds. The roots are usually large and fleshy, and baskets which can be suspended are preferable to pots; for the smaller species pans are handier. They should be hung near the glass in winter, the plants 12 to 18 in. away. As with Aerides, Phalaenopsis, &c., repotting should be done only when absolutely necessary; it is better to remove old compost carefully and replace with new. Water is required throughout the year, with, in winter, slight differentiation denoted by leaf texture. 60° F. should be regarded as a winter minimum.

The plants do not lend themselves readily to propagation. Occasionally basal growths are produced and when rooted can be separated or allowed to remain and form a larger, more effective plant. Thrips and scale insects will attack them, but the moist atmosphere suitable to the plants usually prevents infestation; occasional spongings are a preventive, but weak insecticides or fumigation should be used if the insects are present.

The chief genera into which Saccolabium has been divided are:

1. ANOTA, in which the lip is produced backwards with a short funnel-shaped spur parallel with the ovary. Some consider it should be united with Rhynchostylis and not kept separate. (Type, *S. violaceum.*)
2. ASCOCENTRUM. Species similar to *S. ampullaceum*, with short thickly leaved stems, narrow leaves, short peduncles and a more or less erect rachis crowded with flowers; lip protracted into a straight swollen bag-like spur, mid-lobe of lip ligulate, side lobes erect pressed against the column. (Type, *S. ampullaceum.*)
3. The section CALCEOLARIA of Hooker (LATILABELLATAE of the Genera Plantarum), marked by the hemispheric sac to the labellum, and the short somewhat corymb-like inflorescence, has been titled Gastrochilus but that name has already been applied to a genus of the Scitaminae. (Type, *S. acutifolium.*)
4. MALLEOLA. Small flowers with a long funnel-shaped spur. Sepals and petals very similar. The lip is open with small erect side lobes, the front lobe is also very small and smooth. Stalks to the pollinia broadened above. (Type, *S. penangianum.*)
5. ROBIQUETIA, differentiated chiefly through the mid-lobe of the lip which is set with small tooth-like tubercles, is comparatively long, and is expanded in front. The spur is often sharply curved. Pollinia separate. (Type, *S. Mooreanum.*)
6. SCHOENORCHIS. The fleshy foliage is more or less awl-shaped. The pollinia have one stalk with a large viscid disk. The flowers are small with comparatively long spurs or sacs. (Type, *S. gemmatum.*)

The species are as far as possible numbered below according to the divisions or genera in which they have been placed.

S. acutifo'lium* (3). *fl.* about ¾ in. across, in small corymbs on stiff peduncles 2 to 3 in. long; sep. and slightly narrower pet. yellow, spotted red-brown, obovate, acute; lip with comparatively large sub-globose sac, bright yellow spotted red, mid-lobe small, somewhat triangular, whitish, fringed with hairs. *l.* sessile, flat, oblong-lanceolate, 6 in. long, ¾ to 1½ in. wide, acute. Khasya, Burma. 1837. (A.B.G.C. 8, 302; B.M. 4772 as *S. denticulatum.*)

S. ampulla'ceum* (2). *fl.* about ¾ in. across, crowded in erect racemes, bright rose-carmine; sep. and pet. sub-equal, broad-obovate; lip shorter, linear, reflexed; spur cylindric, compressed, longer than blade of lip, with 2 rounded protuberances at mouth. Stem about 6 in. h. *l.* linear-ligulate, 5 to 6 in. long, irregularly toothed at tip. Burma. 1847. (B.M. 5595; W.O.A. 191; L. 485; A.B.G.C. 8, 293.) SYN. *Aerides ampullaceum.* var. **moulmeinen'se,** more robust, *fl.* deep rich rose, *l.* spotted dull brown on both sides. SYN. *S. roseum.*

S. × belli'no-bigib'bum (3). Natural hybrid (*S. bellinum* × *S. bigibbum*). *fl.* variable; sep. and pet. red-brown, margins yellowish; lip white, spotted purple; base of sac yellow spotted brown; column carmine. Burma. 1893.

S. belli'num* (3). *fl.* usually 4 to 6, 1 to 1¾ in. wide, in a sub-corymb on a stout decurved peduncle, somewhat fleshy; sep. and pet. nearly equal, yellow blotched red-brown or blackish-purple; lip with a large sac, blade white with orange-yellow purple-spotted disk, spreading, 2-lobed, pubescent, fimbriate-toothed on margin. February, March. *l.* lorate, 7 to 12 in. long, obliquely 2-fid. Stems erect, short. Burma. 1884. (B.M. 7142; W.O.A. 156; L. 330.)

S. Berke'leyi. A synonym of *Rhynchostylis retusa.*

S. bigib'bum* (3). *fl.* 8 or more; infl. sub-corymbose, short-stalked, drooping; sep. and pet. pale yellow, spatulate; lip white or yellowish with a few red markings at edge of sub-hemispherical laterally compressed sac, blade white, triangular with jagged ciliate margins. November. *l.* persistent, linear-oblong, 2-fid, bright green, about 4 in. long. Stems very short. Rangoon. 1868. (B.M. 5767.) Compact.

S. bivittat'um. *fl.* small; infl. lax, drooping; sep. and pet. yellowish with 2 purplish-brown stripes; lip white, about as long as sep. *l.* strap-shaped, leathery. E. Indies. 1890.

S. Blu'mei. A synonym of *Rhynchostylis retusa.*

Saccolabium bellinum (p. 1845)

S. borneen'se.* *fl.* a peculiar ochre-cinnamon something like a Sarcanthus; infl. a nodding, dense raceme; sep. and pet. oblong, acute, connivent; spur clavate and depressed, with abrupt, broad top; side lobes rounded and toothed, mid-lobe almost terete, apiculate. *l.* broad, short, unequally 2-lobed. Borneo. 1881.

S. bucco'sum. *fl.* small, yellowish, with a few dark purplish-brown dots on side lobes of lip and on spur, erect; sep. oblong, acute; pet. ovate, shorter than sep.; blade of lip 3-fid, side lobes ovate, acute, mid-lobe lanceolate, acute, keeled; neck of spur contracted, base globose; raceme sometimes branched. *l.* ligulate obliquely obtusely 2-lobed at apex. Moulmein. 1871. Syn. *S. parvulum.*

S. calceola're* (3). *fl.* $\frac{1}{2}$ to $\frac{2}{3}$ in. across, yellow or greenish, speckled, barred or blotched reddish-brown; lip with a sub-globose sac, white at top, orange-yellow at base, with a few red spots on margin; blade of lip fringed white; infl. almost umbellate, short-stalked. *l.* 4 to 5 in. long, 2-lobed. India. (A.B.G.C. 8, 300.) Very near *S. acutifolium. S. calceolare* of Paxton is *S. intermedium.*

S. calop'terum. A synonym of *Ascoglossum calopterum.*

S. ceri'num (2). *fl.* orange, waxy; spur apricot; infl. many fl. April. *l.* dark, ligulate, 2-lobed. Malaya. 1888.

S. coeles'te. A synonym of *Rhynchostylis coelestis.*

S. curvifo'lium* (2). *fl.* about 1 in. h., cinnabar-red, crowded in erect, axillary racemes, freely produced; sep. and pet. ovate-oblong; lip linear-oblong with an orange keel and 2 tubercles at base; spur, slender, cylindrical, with a rounded erect lobe each side. May, June. *l.* linear, 7 to 10 in. long, deflexed, channelled, light green. Stem erect, 6 to 12 in. h. E. Indies. (W.O.A. 107; B.M. 5326 as *S. miniatum.*) Syn. *S. rubrum.* Compact. var. **lat'eum,** *fl.* clear yellow. Moulmein.

S. dasypo'gon (3). Probably a form of *S. calceolare.* (A.B.G.C. 8, 299.)

S. denticulat'um. A synonym of *S. acutifolium.*

S. di'ves. *fl.* small, whitish-yellow, very numerous. *l.* straight, linear-ligulate, unequally 2-lobed at tip, 7 in. long, $\frac{3}{8}$ in. wide. India. 1875.

S. flex'um. *fl.* red; sep. and pet. ligulate, obtuse or acute; lip 3-lobed, side lobes obtuse, minute, mid-lobe triangular; racemes small. New Guinea. 1882.

S. frag'rans. *fl.* small, violet-scented, numerous, in decurved, short, dense racemes; sep. and narrower pet. rose-red or purplish, whitish at base; lip pandurate, lanceolate, contracted into a spur inflated at top, broadly clavate, at right angles to blade of lip, blade spatulate, fleshy, acute. Stem short. *l.* 5 to 8 in. long, 1 in. wide, channelled. Burma. 1882.

S. furca'tum. A garden name for, probably, a form of *Rhynchostylis retusa. fl.* white, spotted with rose. July, August. India, Java.

S. gemma'tum (6). *fl.* $\frac{1}{8}$ in. long, numerous, in flexuous racemes; sep. and pet. whitish or green tinted, spotted purple; lip white. Stem 6 to 12 in. long. *l.* terete, 2 to 4 in. long. N. India. 1838. (A.B.G.C. 5, 70.) A pretty species with straggling habit. Should be placed on a raft. Winter temperature 55° F.

S. gigant'eum* (1). *fl.* 1 in. or more wide, very fragrant, freely produced in long, dense, drooping racemes; sep. and narrower pet. white spotted amethyst; lip mauve, undulate, produced backwards into a short funnel-shaped compressed spur; side lobes rounded, mid-lobe oblong. Winter. *l.* broadly lorate, 12 in. long, 3 in. wide, obliquely 2-lobed at tip, stout, streaked. Stem very stout, short, erect. Burma, Cochin China, Siam, &c. 1862. (B.M. 5635; W.O.A. 56; R. 1, 22.) Syn. *Vanda densiflora.* var. **illust're,** colouring richer, *fl.* larger, infl. looser, longer, *l.* broader and longer, more prominently veined. Cochin China. (I.H. 31, 517; L. 83.); **Petotia'num,** *fl.* dull white with a slight yellow tinge, large, Cochin China. 1885. (L. 605.); **Regnie'ri,** *fl.* $1\frac{1}{2}$ in. across. 1889.

S. glomera'tum (4). Allied to *S. penangianum. fl.* small, yellow; sep. and pet. spotted and side lobes of lip striped brownish-red; racemes short, dense-fld. Borneo. 1913.

S. Graeff'ei. *fl.* deep purple, pendent, conspicuous; lip blade short, 3-toothed, with a transverse lamella in front of base of mid-lobe; spur cylindrical, blunt, constricted; peduncle strong. *l.* broad, ligulate, notched. Fiji. 1881.

S. gurwal'icum. A synonym of *Rhynchostylis retusa.*

S. gutta'tum. A synonym of *Rhynchostylis retusa.*

S. hainanen'se (6). *fl.* white and purple; dorsal sep. and pet. oblong-lanceolate, purplish; lateral sep. and lip whitish; spur blunt; panicle many-fld., 6 in. long. *l.* lanceolate-linear, $2\frac{1}{2}$ in. long. Hainan. 1895.

S. Harrisonia'num. A variety of *S. violaceum.*

S. Heath'ii. A variety of *Rhynchostylis retusa.*

S. Hendersonia'num* (2). *fl.* numerous, in erect, axillary racemes; sep. and pet. rose, lip paler, the 3 lobes tooth-like, spur comparatively large, cylindric, compressed. *l.* about 6 in. long, ligulate, keeled, bright green. Borneo. 1862. Small, compact. (B.M. 6222; W.O.A. 275; L. 313.)

S. Hutton'ii. A synonym of *Aerides Huttonii.*

S. interme'dium* (3). Allied to *S. calceolare* of which it may be a form. *fl.* smaller; sep. and pet. yellow spotted red-purple; lip whitish with fimbriate blade, sac yellow, stem slender, taller than in *S. calceolare, l.* narrower. N. India, Burma. (A.B.G.C. 301.)

S. longicalcara'tum (2). *fl.* pink to rose, small, many; raceme 6 in. long or more; lobes of lip very small, spur large, $\frac{1}{2}$ in. long, swollen. *l.* 4 to 8 in. long, about $1\frac{1}{2}$ in. wide, leathery. Burma. 1894.

S. mim'us. *fl.* rose-purplish, tipped green; sep. and pet. ligulate; side lobes of lip semi-ovate, erect, mid-lobe triangular; spur slender, cylindrical, with a bent dilated tip, equalling the stalked ovary; racemes 1-sided. *l.* oblong-ligulate, unequally lobed at tip, 5 in. long, about 2 in. wide. South Sea Is. 1878.

S. minia'tum* (2). *fl.* about $\frac{3}{4}$ in. wide, brilliant orange-red; raceme 10- to 20-fld., short, erect, cylindrical; lip linear-oblong, obtuse, recurved; spur slender, cylindric, with a small lobe on each side of aperture. March, April. *l.* lorate, channelled, obliquely truncate. Stem short, erect. Java, Siam, Philippines. (B.R. 33, 58.) var. **citri'num,** *fl.* lemon-yellow with dark centre; infl. dense. Philippines. 1884. *S. miniatum* of Hooker is *S. curvifolium.*

S. Moorea'num (5). *fl.* small, rose-pink or purplish, rarely white with green tips; lip with spur nearly $\frac{1}{2}$ in. long, panicle short, crowded, 8 in. long. Stem 12 in. long. *l.* 6 in. long, $1\frac{1}{2}$ in. wide. New Guinea, Sumatra. 1893. (B.M. 7428.) Syn. *S. Sanderianum.* var. **candid'ulum,** *fl.* white.

S. papillo'sum. A synonym of *Acampe papillosum.*

S. Pech'ei* (3). *fl.* ochre with red spots; sep. and pet. oblong, wedge-shaped; lip with few yellow spots at base of spur, side lobes retuse, mid-lobe nearly white; raceme few-fld. *l.* broad ligulate, blunt, 2-lobed at tip, 7 in. long, nearly 2 in. wide. Allied to *S. bellinum* but larger. Moulmein. 1887.

S. penangia'num (4). *fl.* very small, crowded in a cylindrical infl. about 1 in. h.; sep. light yellow, downy without; pet., lip, and spur whitish; side lobes of lip and wings of column with narrow purple margin; spur twice as long as sep., narrowed at tip. Stem a few inches long. *l.* narrow, acute, 2 to 3 in. long, $\frac{1}{4}$ in. wide. Penang. 1891. (A.B.G.C. 5, 71.)

S. platycalcara'tum (3). Allied to *S. calceolare.* Sep. and pet. yellow, spotted brown; lip whitish with a greenish centre to front lobe; spur flattened. Burma. 1909.

S. pumil'io. *fl.* very small; raceme bent, cylindrical, dense, shorter than l.; sep. and pet. yellowish, ligulate, obtuse; lip white with purplish marks on blade. *l.* about 3 in. long, nearly 1 in. wide, oblong, unequally lobed at tip, dark green above, purple beneath. Manila. 1875. (A.B.G.C. 8, 294.)

S. retu'sum. A synonym of *Rhynchostylis retusa.*

S. rubes'cens* (2). *fl.* small, numerous, on erect scapes, light rose-purple; spur often slightly curved; column tipped yellow. Stems 6 to 12 in. h. *l.* leathery, 5 to 6 in. long, 1 in. or more wide, unequally 2-lobed. Allied to *S. ampullaceum.* Annam. 1906. (B.M. 8121.)

S. ru'brum. A synonym of *S. curvifolium* or *Aerides radicosum.*

S. Sanderia'num. A synonym of *S. Mooreanum.*

S. Smeea'num. *fl.* small; sep. and pet. greenish-white with mauve mid-veins, becoming whitish-ochre with brown-purple stripes; sep. oblong-ligulate, pet. nearly so; lip white becoming yellow with age, mid-lobe oblong, acute, disk mauve turning brown, side lobes very small; peduncles 2-fid, each branch densely racemose. Habitat? 1887.

S. Turn'eri. *fl.* lilac-spotted, racemes 2 ft. long, dense-fld. June. India. Probably a variety of *Rhynchostylis retusa.*

S. undulatum. *See* **S. Woodfordii.**

S. viola'ceum* (1). *fl.* about 1 in. across, very fragrant; racemes about 1 ft. long, densely fld., axillary; sep. and pet. pure white, spotted mauve; lip dark mauve-amethyst, marked with lines of deeper colour, oblong, undulate, with 3 ridges and a small apical lobule, spur sub-conic, rather short, compressed, greenish. January, February. *l.* 1 ft. or more long, up to 2 in. wide, recurved, deep green, lined with deeper green. Stems stout, erect. Manila. 1839. (W.S.O. 1, 14; B.R. 33, 30 as *Vanda violacea.*) var. **Harrisonia'num** *fl.* pure white, racemes up to 2 ft. long, *l.* lighter green, broadly oblong, keeled beneath, unequally lobed at tip. Pulo Copang. 1864. (W.O.A. 236; B.M. 54, 33 as *S. Harrisonianum.*)

S. Wightia'num. A synonym of *Aerides radicosum.*

S. Wittea'num. *fl.* in a loose, long raceme; sep. and pet. orange with reddish spots, lip white with some purple markings, spur green at tip, its mouth covered by 3 teeth. *l.* cuneate-oblong, tip toothed, 2 ft. or more long. Java. Habit of *S. giganteum.*

S. Woodford'ii. *fl.* pale vermilion; lip tipped brown; raceme dense. Solomon Is. 1925. This species and *S. undulatum* appear to be confused.

E. C.

SACCUS, a bag or cup; a term occasionally applied to the crown of Stapelia, &c.

sachalinen'sis -is -e, of the island of Sachalin, E. Asia.

SACRED BEAN of the Egyptians. *See* **Nymphaea Lotus,** and **Nelumbo.**

SACRED LOTUS. *See* **Nelumbo nucifera.**

sacro'rum, of the holy places.

SADDLE GRAFTING. *See* **Grafting.**

saddle-shaped, oblong with sides hanging down like the laps of a saddle.

SADDLE-TREE. *See* **Liriodendron Tulipifera.**

SADLER'IA (in honour of Joseph Sadler, 1791–1841, Professor of Botany at Budapest). FAM. *Polypodiaceae.* A genus of 7 species of tree-like ferns, natives of the Sandwich Is. and Sumatra. Sori continuous in a line close to the midrib on both sides on a raised receptacle; indusium narrow, rather leathery, at first covering the sorus later spreading. *S. cyatheoides* is a fine plant combining the fructification of a Blechnum with the habit of a Cyathea. It is vigorous and needs no special care, thriving under warm treatment in a compost of 2 parts peat, 1 loam, 1 silver-sand with abundant moisture at all times. Usually propagated by spores obtained from wild plants.

S. cyatheoi'des. *Caudex* 3 to 4 ft. h. *sti.* strong, erect, 6 to 18 in. long, naked except at base, there clothed with long-linear scales. *Fronds* 4 to 6 ft. long, 9 to 18 in. wide; pinnae 8 to 12 in. long, ½ to ¾ in. wide, cut to rachis into very numerous connected linear pinnules, ⅜ to ½ in. long, acute or bluntish. Sandwich Is. 1877.

SAD-TREE. *See* **Nyctanthes Arbor-tristis.**

saep'ium, of a hedge.

SAFFLOWER. *See* **Carthamus tinctorius.**

SAFFRON. *See* **Crocus sativus.**

SAFFRON, MEADOW. *See* **Colchicum autumnale.**

SAFFRON THISTLE. *See* **Carthamus tinctorius.**

SAGE (*Salvia officinalis*). The culinary Sage is an evergreen undershrub about 1 ft. high with a strong aromatic odour in all parts. Though a native of S. Europe it is sufficiently hardy to withstand any ordinary winter outdoors without protection. It does best in a warm, rather dry position, but will also grow well in almost any garden soil so long as it is not very acid. It is occasionally raised from seed but much more commonly from cuttings or from rooted pieces taken from the base of old plants. Cuttings are best made in early summer from the growing tips. Pieces about 3 in. long, put into sandy soil under a cloche in a shady place root readily. The plants should be put a foot apart and kept clear of weeds. The chief use of sage at the present time is in making stuffing and for this purpose the narrow-leaved form with white flowers is said to be the best. It was at one time much used in medicine and is still used in home-cures. The purple-leaved and variegated forms are useful in the pleasure garden, the purple-leaved form is one of the best evergreen plants of its colour and height.

SAGE BRUSH. *See* **Artemisia tridentata.**

SAGE, JERUSALEM. *See* **Phlomis fruticosa.**

SAGE OF BETHLEHEM. *See* **Pulmonaria officinalis.**

SAGE ROSE. An old name for Cistus.

SAGI'NA (*sagina,* fatness; from the nourishing qualities of Spurrey, once called *Sagina Spergula,* for sheep). FAM. *Caryophyllaceae.* Pearlwort. A genus of about 20 species of small, tufted annual or perennial mat-forming herbs, many of them weeds, natives of the temperate and Arctic regions of the N. Hemisphere southwards to Mexico and Chile and the mountains of Trop. Africa. Closely related to Minuartia but with carpels as many (5 or 4) as petals and sepals and capsule opening by as many valves to the base. Leaves awl-shaped or filiform, flowers small, white, usually long-stalked, umbels few-flowered: petals entire, usually very small; stamens 4, 5, 8, or 10. Treatment as for Arenaria. The value of the following which are all perennial unless otherwise stated, lies in their habit of making a close green carpet and their place is on the rock-garden or occasionally as an edging. *S. pilifera* and *S. procumbens* have been suggested as lawn plants dibbled in 2 in. apart but in many places they are apt to become patchy.

S. Boyd'ii. Forms a dense cushion, ½ in. h., stem underground, much branched. *l.* subulate, ¾ in. long, much and regularly recurved, rigid, somewhat fleshy, mucronate, dark, shining green. *fl.* solitary; sep. 5 (or 4), erect; pet. none. Scotland. 1892. (J.B. 30, 226.) Very slow growing.

S. glab'ra. Stem creeping or prostrate, often rooting at lower nodes, ¾ to 4 in. h. *l.* narrow-linear to almost filiform, shortly mucronate, glabrous. *fl.* nodding, becoming erect in fr.; pet. 1½ times as long as cal. Summer. W. Alps to Corsica, Scotland.

S. Linna'ei. Stems usually numerous, prostrate, ascending, branched, making a mat up to a foot across, ¾ to 4 in. h., glabrous or nearly so. *l.* linear to almost filiform, grass-green, with a short awn-like point. *fl.* solitary, rarely twin on slender pedicels; pet. ovate, about as long as cal. Summer. Europe, including Scotland, N. Africa, N. Asia, Greenland, N. America to Mexico.

S. pilif'era. Stem creeping, branched, tufted, about 2 in. h. *l.* linear, rather stiff, in clusters, glabrous, long-awned. *fl.* on very long pedicels; pet. twice as long as cal. Summer. Corsica, Sardinia. var. **au'rea,** *l.* yellow. SYN. *Spergula pilifera.*

S. procum'bens. Perennial but sometimes annual or biennial. Often forming a flat mat, the stem springing from the axils of the l. of the basal rosette, ¾ to 2 in. h., often rooting at base, generally much branched. *l.* linear, mucronate, ⅛ to ⅜ in. long, usually glabrous. *fl.* solitary; sep. broadly ovate. May onwards. Widely distributed, including Britain and variable.

S. subula'ta. Stem very much branched forming a dense mat, ascending, up to 4 in. long, filiform. *l.* linear-awl-shaped, long-awned. *fl.* usually 2 or 3, on hair-like pedicels up to 1¼ in. long; sep. roundish-ovate with a narrow border; pet. roundish-ovate, about as long as sep. Summer. W. Europe to Italy, including Britain, N. Greece.

saginoi'des, Sagina-like.

sagitta'lis -is -e, arrow-shaped.

SAGITTA'RIA (*sagitta*, arrow; in allusion to the prevailing form of leaf). FAM. *Alismataceae.* A genus of about 30 species of marsh or water-side, usually erect, perennial herbs, natives of temperate and tropical regions of the world. Leaves on long and often thick stalks, elliptic-lanceolate or sagittate, often with pellucid dots or lineolate. Flowers white, usually in whorls of 3, in spikes or panicles, pedicellate, 3- (or rarely 1-) bracted at nodes; perianth segments 6, the inner larger, petaloid, deciduous; stamens 9 or more, usually numerous; scape erect, slender or stout. They need a moist or wet loamy soil and are readily increased by division. The under-mentioned species are all hardy and flower in summer.

S. angustifo'lia. A variety of *S. lancifolia.*

S. Engelmannia'na. Related to *S. latifolia* but *l.* narrow, pale green. *fl.* white; scape 2½ ft. long. N. America. Nearly hardy.

S. gramin'ea. *l.* ovate-lanceolate to linear, or reduced to broad acute phyllodes, very rarely sagittate. *fl.* small, white, in 2 or 3 whorls, lower fertile; bracts usually connate; scapes very slender, erect, 1 to 2 ft. h.; pedicels slender. N. America. 1812. Water 3 to 5 in. deep. Greenhouse. SYN. *S. acutifolia.*

S. heterophyl'la. *l.* lanceolate or ovate-lanceolate, entire or with 1 or 2 basal acute lobes. *fl.* of lowest whorl fertile, almost sessile, sterile fl. long-pedicelled; bracts obtuse; scape weak, at length procumbent. N. America. 1822. var. **rig'ida,** *see* **S. rigida.**

S. isoetiform'is. Very slender. *Floating l.* small round. *fl.* very small; scape 12 in. h. Shallow water.

S. japon'ica. A synonym of *S. sagittifolia.*

S. lancifo'lia. *l.* lanceolate or lanceolate-oblong, rarely linear, all tapering at base, 6 to 18 in. long, never sagittate; stalks long, stout. *fl.* of several of lower whorls fertile; bracts acute; scape 2 to 5 ft. long, pedicels slender. W. Indies. 1787. Greenhouse. (B.M. 1792.) var. **angustifo'lia,** blades of *l.* very narrow or wanting, plant much smaller in all parts. (B.R. 1141 as *S. angustifolia.*)

S. latifo'lia. Duck Potato; Wapato. *l.* mostly broadly sagittate with long basal lobes, but variable and sometimes very narrow. *fl.* white, about 1 in. across, usually monoecious, filaments slender; scape variable in length, 3 in. to 4 ft., angled. *fr.* winged, the beak more than a quarter as long; N. America. 1818. SYN. *S. variabilis.* In water 3 to 5 in. deep. var. **flore ple'no,** *fl.* double. SYN. *S.variabilis fl.-pl.* Several forms have been named from variations in leaf-shape but such variations and variations in stature are almost infinite. The tuberous roots of this species formed a favourite food of the Indians; carp are very fond of it.

S. macrophyl'la. *l.* large, dark green, becoming yellow and bronzy-red. *fl.* white, of medium size; scape 3 ft. long. Mexico. Water about 8 in. deep.

S. monteviden'sis.* Giant Arrowhead. *l.* sagittate, 1 to 2 ft. long, basal lobes diverging, sharp-pointed. *fl.* white with a purple blotch at base of pet., 2 to 3 in. across, monoecious in loose whorls; scape up to 6 ft., that bearing female fl. stouter and pedicels shorter than those of males. Argentine to Peru. 1884. (B.M. 6755; Gn. 27 (1885), 8.) Greenhouse. Shallow water.

S. na'tans. *l.* floating, oblong or oval, obtuse, somewhat cordate at base; submerged l. narrow. *fl.* small, white, floating. Carolina. Shallow water or aquarium.

S. platyphyl'la. *l.* large, arrow-shaped. *fl.* white; scape about 2½ ft. long. N. America.

S. pugioniform'is. *l.* dagger-shaped. *fl.* white, anthers yellow; scape slender, 2½ ft. long. Guiana. Tender.

S. pusil'la. A synonym of *S. subulata.*

S. rig'ida. Allied to *S. heterophylla* but with rigid, narrow lanceolate *l.*, acute at both ends; stalks stout. Scape 3 ft. long. (B.M. 1632.) Greenhouse. Water 12 to 18 in. deep.

S. sagittifo'lia. Common Arrow-head. Water Archer. Stoloniferous, root-stock swollen. *l.* hastate, 2 to 8 in. long, acute or obtuse, erect, basal lobes long, spreading, acuminate, the earliest submerged; stalks stout, 8 to 18 in. long. *fl.* ½ in. across, male larger; pet. with purple claws; whorls 3 to 5, distant, 3- to 5-fld.; scape 6 to 18 in. h. Europe, including Britain. (E.B. 1436; B.M. 1631 with different leaf-form as *S. sinensis.*) var. **flore-ple'no,*** *fl.* double. SYN. *S. japonica fl.-pl.* Water 12 to 18 in. deep.

S. subula'ta. *l.* linear or narrowly oblanceolate, rigid. *fl.* usually in a single whorl, white, ½ to ¾ in. across, filaments broad; scape only a few in. long. N. America.

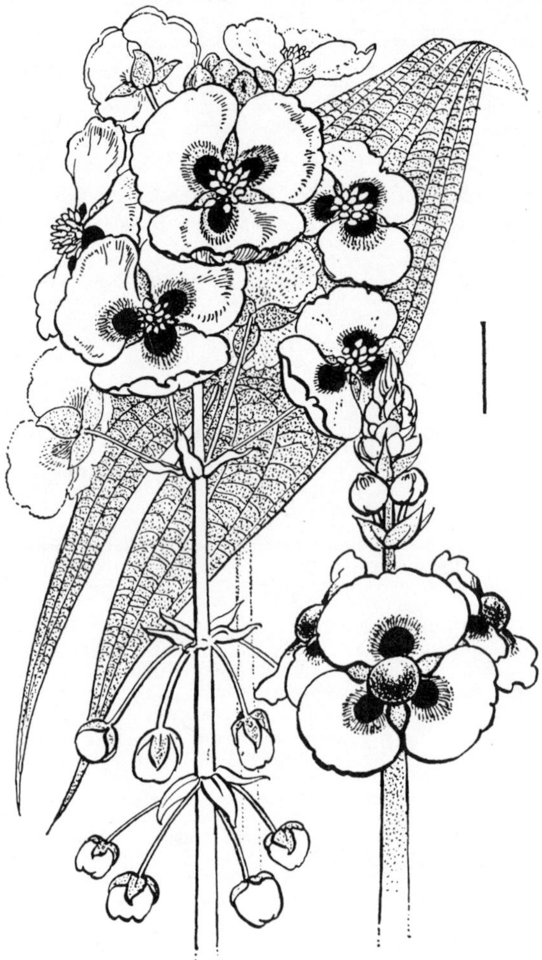

Sagittaria montevidensis

S. variab'ilis. *See* **S. latifolia.**

sagitta'tus -a -um, sagitti-, in compound words, arrow-shaped.

Saglio'nis -is -e, in honour of the Frenchman who first grew *Gymnocalycium Saglionis* in Europe.

SAGO. Starchy reserve obtained from the pith of *Arenga pinnata, Caryota urens, Cycas circinalis, Metroxylon Rumphii, M. Sagu, and Roystonea oleracea.*

SAGRAE'A (in honour of Ramon de la Sagra, who wrote in 1827 an account of the Botanic Garden, Havana, of which he was Director). FAM. *Melastomataceae.* A genus of about 50 species of bristly, or hairy, rarely glabrous shrubs, closely related to Clidemia, natives of Trop. America. Leaves sessile or stalked, ovate, oblong, or heart-shaped, 3- to 7-nerved, entire or toothed. Flowers small, in small or large axillary, solitary or clustered panicles; calyx 4-lobed; petals 4, obtuse or notched; stamens 8. Berries 4-celled, often hairy. For treatment *see* **Melastoma.**

S. hirsu'ta. *See* **Ossaea hirsuta.**

S. pilo'sa. Shrub, rusty hairy on branches and l.-stalks. *l.* oblong, 5-nerved, acute, smooth above, hairy, especially on nerves beneath. *fl.* whitish, spotted at base, small; in an axillary panicle. W. Indies.

S. sessiliflo'ra. Shrub to 4 ft., branches round, densely reddish-hairy. *l.* oval, slender-pointed, 7-nerved, ciliate, densely bristly hairy above, softly hairy beneath. *fl.* red, crowded in axils; pet. oval, obtuse. April. Trop. America. 1793.

S. umbro'sa. Shrub of 6 ft. *l.* broadly ovate, slender pointed, toothed, ciliate, densely hairy on veins; stalks 1½ in. long. *fl.* red; pet. obovate; panicles axillary, loosely branched, slightly hispid, as long as l.-stalks. March. W. Indies. 1824.

F. G. P.

SAINFOIN. *See* **Onobrychis viciifolia.**

ST. ANDREW'S CROSS. *See* **Ascyrum hypericoides.**

ST. BARBARA'S HERB. *See* **Barbarea vulgaris.**

ST. BERNARD'S LILY. *See* **Anthericum Liliago.**

ST. BRUNO'S LILY. *See* **Paradisea Liliastrum.**

ST. DABEOC'S HEATH. *See* **Daboecia.**

ST. GEORGE'S HERB. *See* **Valeriana officinalis.**

ST. JOHN'S BREAD. *See* **Ceratonia.**

ST. JOHN'S WORT. *See* **Hypericum perforatum.**

ST. JOSEPH'S LILY. *See* **Lilium candidum.**

ST. MARK'S FLY, *Bibio marci*, is so called because it appears on the wing about St. Mark's Day, 25 April. The legless, dark-brownish, caterpillar-like maggots are provided with short fleshy processes arranged in a band round each body segment, which enables them to progress through the soil. They frequently occur in vast colonies in leaf-mould heaps and among decaying vegetation, and may abound on neglected lawns and in turf. They feed on the roots of Grasses and, occasionally, of Cereals and Hops. The hairy black flies are frequent visitors to the blossoms of hardy fruits. For control measures *see* **Fever Fly.**

G. F. W.

ST. MARTIN'S FLOWER. *See* **Alstroemeria Ligtu pulchra.**

ST. MARTIN'S HERB. *See* **Sauvagesia erecta.**

ST. MARY'S WOOD. *See* **Calophyllum Inophyllum.**

ST. PATRICK'S CABBAGE. *See* **Saxifraga umbrosa.**

SAINTPAUL'IA (in honour of Baron Walter von Saint Paul-Illaire, 1860–1910, of Berlin, who discovered *S. ionantha*). FAM. *Gesneriaceae*. African Violet. A genus of 6 species of hairy, mostly stemless perennial herbs, natives of Trop. Africa. Leaves ovate, long-stalked. Flowers 1 to many in a loose cyme, on a peduncle 1 to 5 in. long; calyx small, deeply 5-lobed; corolla widely bell-shaped, with a short tube and elliptic blue lobes; perfect stamens 2; ovary hairy. Fruit a many-seeded, 2-valved capsule; seeds small. The 3 species mentioned need a warm house and soil as for Achimenes. They can be raised from seed treated like Gloxinia and sown in March, they may be had in flower from August onwards, or may be grown from leaf-cuttings, the fully developed leaf being taken with about 1 in. of stalk and inserted in sand, burying only a small part of the blade. The sand should not be too wet. They are very decorative pot plants. An article on this genus by B. L. Burtt will be found in Gard. Chron. 122 (1947), 22. Numerous garden forms have been raised in America and are described by H. V. P. Wilson, *The African Violet*, 1948.

S. diplo'tricha. Very similar to *S. ionantha*, but *l.* entire with many long white hairs of varying length; cal. lobes much broader and shaggy-white hairy. Trop. Africa. (B.M. 7408 as *S. ionantha.*)

S. ionan'tha. African Violet, Usambara Violet. Hairy, stemless perennial. *l.* ovate or oblong-cordate, 1½ to 2 in. long, obtuse, crenate, with a few white hairs of uniform length on both surfaces; stalks short, stout. *fl.* violet-blue, 2-lipped, 1 in. across, upper lip 2-lobed, much the smaller; cal. lobes linear; cymes several-fld., peduncles radical. Almost continuously flowering. E. Trop. Africa near sea level. 1893. (Gn. 47 (1895), 133.) var. **albes'cens,** *fl.* white tinged blush-pink; **grandiflo'ra,** *fl.* much larger than type, deep violet; **purpu'rea,** *fl.* very dark violet; **variega'ta,** *l.* variegated with yellow, becoming white.

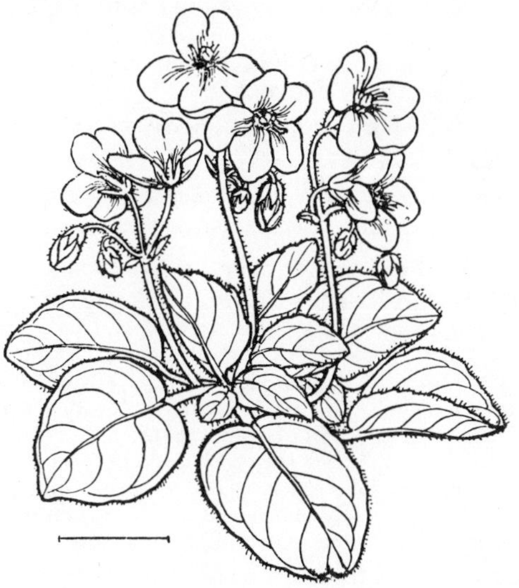

Saintpaulia ionantha

S. tongwen'sis. Very similar to *S. ionantha*, but with leaf-blades elliptic or ovate-elliptic, subacute at the apex, somewhat fleshy, dark green above, lighter green or in young leaves purplish-red below. *Inflor.* up to 6 in. h. cor. purple, capsule longer than in *S. ionantha*, densely covered with crisped hairs. (B.M. n.s. 11.) NE. Tanganyika. Warm greenhouse. Grown as an edging in orchid houses at Kew.

ST. PETER'S WORT. A name variously applied to *Ascyrum stans, Hypericum Ascyron, Primula vulgaris*, and species of Symphoricarpos.

SALAC'IA (mythological, Salacia, wife of Neptune). FAM. *Hippocrateaceae*. A genus of about 100 species of climbing or creeping shrubs or small trees, natives of the warmer parts of Asia, Africa, and America. Leaves generally opposite, leathery, shining above, entire or with rounded teeth, stalked, without stipules. Flowers usually on short axillary branchlets, clustered or cymose, rarely solitary or in pairs, sometimes in panicles; calyx small, 5-parted; pet. 5, spreading, overlapping; stamens 2 to 4, usually 3. Fruit 1- to 3-celled, sometimes large and edible. Most of these plants are of little beauty, require stove conditions and sandy loam and can be propagated by ripe cuttings in heat.

S. prionoi'des. Climber. *l.* toothed. *fl.* greenish-yellow, small, solitary, axillary. June. *fr.* about size and shape of a small cherry, 1-seeded. E. Indies. 1820.

S. pyriform'is. Shrub of 5 ft. *l.* oblong, slightly toothed. *fl.* greenish-yellow, small, clustered in axils. June. *fr.* about as large as a Bergamot Pear. Upper Guinea. 1825.

S. Roxburgh'ii. Small tree. *l.* broad lanceolate, entire. *fl.* orange, small, solitary axillary. June. *fr.* dull red, 2- or 3-seeded, pulp white. India. 1822.

F. G. P.

SALAD. Herbs prepared for food without cooking. The term is now used, however, to include several vegetables which need cooking before use, and which are mixed with the uncooked herbs or even used alone with suitable seasoning. The original salad (or sallet) was usually seasoned with salt. The character common to all salad plants is absence of tough fibre, and to secure this most require to be grown quickly and are thus best suited by a warm, open, moist soil. Several need blanching to secure tender growth or absence of strong flavour. Particulars of cultivation will be found under the several headings including: American or Land Cress, Beet, Celeriac, Celery, Chervil, Chicory and Witloof Chicory,

Chives, Corn Salad or Lamb's Lettuce, Cress, Cucumber, Dandelion, Endive, Lettuce, Mustard, Nasturtium, Onion, Purslane, Radish, Rampion, Salsify, Shallot, Sorrel, Tarragon, Tomato, Watercress. In addition to these among other plants the following may also form a constituent of a Salad, or even be the only plant in it: Cabbage, Carrot, Cauliflower, Brussels Sprouts, Jerusalem Artichoke, Potato.

SALAD BURNET. *See* **Burnet,** *Sanguisorba minor.*

SALAL or **SHALLON.** *See* **Gaultheria Shallon.**

salaman'icus -a -um, of Salamanca, Spain.

salebro'sus -a -um, rough, rugged.

salhutuen'sis -is -e, of Salhoetoe, Amboina.

SALICA'CEAE. Dicotyledons. A family of 2 genera containing about 330 species of mostly hardy trees or shrubs, scattered over the north temperate zone, generally deciduous, with alternate, simple, stipulate leaves. Flowers dioecious, in catkins, usually before the leaves, each flower in the axil of a bract; stamens 2; stigmas 2 to 4. Fruit a dehiscent many-seeded capsule, the seeds surrounded by tufts of long silky hairs. The poplars (Populus) with usually pendulous catkins and the willows (Salix) with usually upright catkins constitute the family.

salica'ria, from the resemblance of some part to a willow.

salicifo'lius -a -um, with willow-like leaves.

salici'nus -a -um, resembling a willow.

SALICORN'IA (*sal*, salt, *cornu*, horn; from the horn-like branches). FAM. *Chenopodiaceae.* A genus of about 8 species of annual or perennial leafless herbs with very succulent cylindrical jointed stems and opposite branches, minute flowers, 2 together sunk in pits at the nodes, fruit enclosed in the swollen perianth. *S. fruticosa* is sometimes offered but is of no horticultural value. At one time the plants which are abundant in salt marshes of S. Europe (including Britain) and N. Africa were among the plants the ashes of which, called Barilla, were imported as a source of the soda used in making soap and glass (hence the name Glasswort). The name Marsh Samphire, sometimes applied to them, has sometimes caused confusion with Samphire (*see* **Crithmum**).

S. frutico'sa. 6 to 24 in. h. Perennial with creeping woody stem and erect cylindrical or club-shaped cylindrical branches. Stamens 2. Shores of Europe, including Britain, S. Africa, America.

salicornioi'des, Salicornia-like.

A→

salig'nus -a -um, willow-like.

SALIGOT. *See* **Trapa natans.**

sali'nus -a -um, growing in a salt-marsh.

SALISBUR'IA adiantifolia. A synonym of *Ginkgo biloba.*

Salis'ii, in honour of Adalbert Ulysses von Salis-Marschlins, 1795–1886, of Landquart, who wrote on the flora of Corsica and S. France.

SA'LIX (Old Latin name). FAM. *Salicaceae.* A genus of deciduous trees and shrubs comprising some 250 or more species, supplemented by many natural hybrids, and almost entirely confined to the cooler latitudes and altitudes of the N. Hemisphere. Buds with a single bud-scale. The typical willow leaf is long, narrow, slenderly pointed and toothed, but in many species they vary from roundish to ovate, obovate, or broadly oblong and some are toothless. Stipules vary from large and persistent to small and deciduous and may often be entirely absent.

The plants are usually unisexual, with the flowers in cylindrical catkins. Each flower is in the axil of a scale and there are no sepals or petals. The male has most often 2 stamens, occasionally 1, and in 1 group there are 3 to 9 (usually 5). The female flower has an ovary of 2 carpels and the seed-vessel (capsule) is conical, splitting from the top into 2 recurving halves. Seeds minute, with a tuft of hairs at one end which promotes their dispersal by wind.

The chief economic value of willows is in the toughness and suppleness of the shoots which makes them invaluable for wicker work and basket making. The best cricket bats are made from the timber of *S. coerulea.* Willows are easily raised from leafless cuttings varying from the thickness and length of a broom handle to mere twigs. More than any other genus willows are valued for planting in wet, ill-drained, or intermittently inundated situations, also for holding up the erosion of riversides, &c. Several species are of picturesque habit and of value from the colour of the bark of young shoots in winter. For this effect, hard pruning in early spring is necessary.

DISEASES. Willows may be affected by Crown Gall disease (*see* **Crown Gall**) and by the fungus *Nectria galligena* which is so well known as causing canker on apple-trees (*see* **Apple Canker**). They may also occasionally show Silver Leaf disease (*see* **Silver Leaf**). On the trunks of old willows certain Bracket fungi such as *Fomes igniarius* and *Polyporus sulphureus* may appear and begin to destroy the tree (*see* **Bracket fungi**). The roots are sometimes affected by the Honey Fungus (q.v.). The disease called Anthracnose due to the fungus *Marssonina salicicola* causes brown spots on the leaves and lesions on the shoots and often requires much cutting out followed by spraying to check it. A more serious disease is Black Canker of Osier Willows (*Physalospora Miyabeana*) which causes serious leaf spotting and cankers on the stems so that the latter are useless for basket-making. The remedy is to remove cankered parts and to spray the young shoots during spring with Bordeaux mixture. There are several rusts of willows due to species of the Rust fungus Melampsora (q.v.) which particularly affect Osier Willows and spoil the rods. These rusts are heteroecious forming their dark-brown pustules of teleutospores on the willow rods and their aecidial stages on species of Allium, e.g. *A. ursinum.* There is a Scab disease of certain willow shoots due to the fungus *Fusicladium saliciperdum*, control of which is similar to Anthracnose above. There is also a special disease of cricket-bat willow (*Salix coerulea*) due to *Bacterium salicis* which is called Watermark because the crown is invaded and dieback occurs and the wood when cut across is found to be deeply stained. Such wood is then useless for making good-quality cricket bats. This disease is most prevalent on wet subsoils and where the trees are overcrowded and it is necessary to provide good drainage, adequate spacing, and to destroy any affected trees in the early spring.

(D. E. G.)

PESTS. There are few trees that are more liable to the attacks of insect pests than species of *Salix.* The chief pests are: Aphides, of which three species are widely distributed; Willow Leaf Beetles, *Phyllodecta vitellinae, P. vulgatissima,* and *Galerucella lineola*; Willow Weevil, *Cryptorrhynchus lapathi*; Willow Sawfly, *Nematus salicis*, and the Gall Sawflies, *Pontania gallicola,* &c.; Clearwing Moths, *Trochilium crabroniforme*, and *Aegeria formiciformis*; Tortrix *Eucosma cruciana*, and Tineid Moths, *Depressaria conterminella*; and several Gall Midges, including *Rhabdophaga heterobia* and *R. terminalis* (q.v.). An account of the several insect pests and fungus diseases of Basket Willows is given in the Ministry of Agriculture's Bulletin No. 29.

WILLOW APHIDES, of which there are several species, cause considerable injury to Osiers and Willows by sucking the sap and causing thereby the staining of the wood, and malformation and subsequent death of the rods, shoots, and leaves. They excrete quantities of honeydew which coats the leaves and allows the growth of Sooty Moulds, the presence of which hinders the normal functions of the leaves. Among the more common Salix-feeding species are: *Siphocoryne capreae*, *S. pastinaceae*, *Pterocomma populea*, *Melanoxantherum salicis*, and *Pterochlorus saligna*; the last two occur in vast colonies on the stems and branches. **A**

These pests are readily destroyed by timely applications of Nicotine-Soap wash, care being taken to direct the spray to the underside of the leaves, to the shoot tips and the stems where the pests congregate and feed. The destruction of weeds in and around Willow beds is desirable as a means of discouraging those species, e.g. *Siphocoryne*, which migrate from Willows to wild Umbelliferous plants.

WILLOW GALL SAWFLY. *See* **Sawflies.**

WILLOW LEAF BEETLES include two species of *Phyllodecta*, namely, *P. vitellinae* and *P. vulgatissima*, and *Galerucella lineola*, all of which cause considerable damage to Willow leaves. Phyllodectids are metallic bluish or dark-green beetles, which appear on the leaves in spring and early summer. There are two broods a year, but the generations overlap and both larval and adult stages are found together for a period. The white eggs are laid in groups on the underside of the leaves, and develop into dirty grey or yellowish grubs, whose bodies are covered with regular rows of black, spiny, conspicuous patches from some of which a protective fluid is emitted from special glands. They feed on the under-surface of the leaves which become skeletonized. Pupation takes place in the soil. The second brood beetles cluster in large numbers during August on the upper sides of the leaves and feed on the terminal shoots which become malformed. The beetles overwinter among rubbish, beneath bark, in tree stumps and similar situations, and reappear again the following spring.

Galerucella lineola is a yellowish-brown beetle with dark markings on its upper surface. This pest is also double-brooded. The white eggs are deposited on the terminal leaves in May or early June, and the grubs skeletonize the leaves and, when fully fed, pupate in the soil. The second brood adults appear in early August and devour the entire leaf with the exception of the mid-rib. Hibernation takes place in damper situations, and exposure to flooded conditions does not appear to affect them. Control measures to be successful must be directed against the very young larvae, especially with Phyllodectids, which protect themselves from the effect of insecticides by the secretion mentioned. Thorough application of a Nicotine-Soap wash to both leaf surfaces and to the terminal shoots in mid-June will effect a control.

WILLOW MOTHS. The caterpillars of a great many Moths attack Willows, some feeding openly on the leaves, some spinning the terminal shoots together, others burrowing in the rods and stumps. The most common species of leaf- and shoot-tiers are the Tortricid, *Eucosma cruciana*, and the Tineid, *Depressaria conterminella*; while the tunnelling species include the Willow Hornet Clearwing, *Trochilium crabroniforme*, and the Red-Tipped Clearwing, *Aegeria formiciformis*.

The presence of spun leaves at the shoot tips indicates an attack by one or other of the two first mentioned pests, which feed on the leaves and buds and eventually pupate within the 'nest' formed on the terminal shoots. The result is that growth is checked, and the condition known as 'Bushy Top' results. The grub-like caterpillars of the Clearwing Moths are white with brown heads and tunnel in the stumps and rods. Pupation takes place within the burrows, and the moths emerge in June or July. The Hornet Clearwing more closely resembles a Hornet or large Wasp than a Moth, while the Red-Tipped Clearwing resembles an Ichneumon Fly owing to their colour and the almost complete absence of scales on the wings.

Both groups of pests are difficult to control because of the protection afforded the caterpillars by the closely spun leaves or by their tunnelling habits. Their control in large beds of Willows must depend upon the value of the timber, but specimen trees in gardens and parks and those in nursery beds may be dusted with Nicotine dust in the case of the leaf-spinning caterpillars, and with the placing of crystals of Sodium cyanide (highly poisonous) or of Paradichlorbenzene in the tunnels of the burrowing larvae—the entrances to the burrows being plugged later with clay, putty, or wax to prevent the escape of the fumes.

WILLOW SCALE. *See* **Scale insects.**

WILLOW WEEVIL or BORER, *Cryptorrhynchus lapathi*, attacks also Poplar and Alder, into the stems and branches of which the grubs burrow. Attacked trees exhibit irregular lesions in the outer bark where the legless grubs are tunnelling in the wood, and such ruptured tissues are frequently invaded by bacteria and fungi which extend the initial injury. Young trees are more seriously affected than older trees, and considerable injury may be done to the cricket-bat Willow, *Salix coerulea*. The weevil is dark brown with lighter areas, and possesses a blunt, broad snout or proboscis, which is pushed into the soft growing portions of the tree causing the fracture of the young rods in early summer. The eggs are laid in the stumps, stem, or rods, and the white, legless grubs burrow into the wood, later pupating within their tunnels, and emerging as adult weevils the following year. The methods of control used on the Continent and in the United States include the jarring of the weevils from the trees into a beating-tray in early summer, and the spraying of the stems and stumps in autumn or winter with a Tar-distillate wash. (G. F. W.)

S. acutifo'lia. Very closely akin to, and often made a var. of, *S. daphnoides*, having a similar plum-coloured bloom on the shoots and *l.* similarly glaucous blue beneath. The l. are narrower, the shoots more slender and the tree not so tall. Russia, Turkistan. (E.B. 1366.) SYN. *S. pruinosa.*

S. adenophyl'la. Furry Willow. Shrub of loose habit, up to 8 ft. h., shoots coated thickly with silvery hairs. *l.* 1 to 2 in. long, half as wide, ovate, rounded or cordate at base, shortly pointed, finely toothed, silky-downy especially beneath. *Male catkins* cylindrical, 1 to 1½ in. long; *female* 2 to 3 in. N. America. 1900. Handsome and distinct in its closely set, very silky, comparatively broad l.

S. aegyptia'ca. *See* **S. Medemii.**

S. al'ba.* White Willow. Tree 70 to 80 ft. h., of elegant shape; trunk 15 to 20 ft. in girth; branches pendulous at ends; young shoots silky, springing at angles of 30 to 45° from the older branches. *l.* lanceolate, 1½ to 4 in. long, finely toothed, permanently silky-grey beneath. *Catkins* 1½ to 2 in. long; stamens 2, silky at base; ovary sessile. Europe (Britain), N. Asia. (E.B. 1309.) One of the most attractive of native trees. var. **argen'tea,** Silver Willow, *l.* silvery grey-white, very striking but not so robust as the type. SYN. var. *splendens*, *S. regalis*; **coeru'lea,** synonym of *S. coerulea*; **vitelli'na,** *see* **S. vitellina.**

S. × ambig'ua. Hybrid between *S. aurita* and *S. repens*. Shrub 1 to 3 ft. h., branches erect or procumbent. *l.* oblong, obovate, oval or oblanceolate, about 1 in. long, usually glaucous and silky beneath, resembling those of *S. aurita* but smaller and less wrinkled, stipules less conspicuous. Europe (Britain). As with many hybrid willows, the l. vary much, especially in shape.

S. america'na pen'dula. A variety of *S. purpurea.*

S. amygdali'na. Almond-leaved Willow. Shrub or small tree up to 30 ft. h., shoots downy at first, becoming glabrous and red-brown later. *l.* 2 to 4 in. long, lanceolate, finely toothed, pale green beneath. *Catkins* 1½ to 3 in. long, males with 3 stamens. April, May. Europe (Britain), N. Asia. SYN. *S. triandra.* (E.B. 1313–5.) Of great value for basket making. Osiers known in the trade as Black Hollander, Black Italian, Black Maul, French, Glibskins, Jelstiver, Mottled Spaniards and Pomeranian all belong to it or its vars.

S. angustifo'lia. A synonym of *S. Wilhelmsiana.*

S. Arbus'cula. Shrub 1 to 3 ft. h., varying from decumbent (var. **hu'milis**) to bushy and miniature-tree-like (var. **erec'ta**). *l.* oval, sometimes inclined to obovate or lanceolate, ½ to 1½ in. long, about half as wide, entire or shallowly toothed, usually more or less glaucous beneath. *Catkins* ½ to 1 in. long, slender. May. Europe (Mts. of Scotland). (E.B. 1371–4.)

S. argen'tea. A variety of *S. repens.*

S. auri'ta. Bushy shrub, 3 to 7 ft., shoots slender, at first very downy. *l.* 1 to 2 in. long, obovate to roundish, abruptly pointed, dull dark green, much wrinkled above, grey-downy beneath; stipules conspicuous, kidney-shaped. *Male catkins* $\frac{1}{2}$ to $\frac{3}{4}$ in. long, stalkless; stamens 2; *female* longer. April. Europe (Britain), N. Asia. (E.B. 1330.) Of no particular garden value.

S. babylon'ica.* Weeping Willow. Tree 30 to 50 ft. h., of wide-spreading growth, branches very pendulous, trunk short and rugged; shoots glabrous, very slender. *l.* 3 to 5 in. long, linear-lanceolate, slender-pointed, about $\frac{1}{2}$ in. wide, finely toothed, blue-grey beneath, soon quite glabrous. *Catkins* slender; female 1 to $1\frac{1}{2}$ in. long, male shorter. April. China. (B.T.S. 1, 64.) Introduced 1730 from the River Euphrates region but not native there. Most notable of weeping trees but not so hardy as most willows. var. **annula'ris,** l. curiously curled and twisted. A curiosity merely: **ramu'leis au'reis,** *see* **S. vitellina.**

S. Bebbia'na. Beak Willow. Shrub or small tree up to 25 ft. h., shoots downy, becoming glabrous and dark brown. *l.* oval, oblong-lanceolate, often inclined to obovate, entire or sparsely toothed, dull green above, glaucous beneath. *Male catkins* 1 to $1\frac{1}{3}$ in. long; stamens 2. N. America. 1889. (S.S. 477.) The popular name refers to the stalked long-beaked seed vessels.

S. × blan'da (*S. babylonica × S. fragilis*). Elegant tree up to 50 ft. h. with a spreading head of pendulous branches; twigs rather brittle. *l.* lanceolate up to 6 in. long, glabrous, broader and more lustrous green than in *S. babylonica* and not so glaucous beneath. Hardier than *S. babylonica* and sometimes grown as such on the Continent. Syn. *S. Petzoldii pendula*, *S. pendulina*, and *S. elegantissima* are very similar.

S. Bock'ii.* Shrub of neat spreading habit, up to 10 ft. in a wild state; shoots slender, densely grey-downy. *l.* oblong to obovate, $\frac{1}{4}$ to $\frac{3}{4}$ in. long, entire or nearly so, dark bright green above, glaucous and silky-hairy beneath. *Female catkins* $1\frac{1}{2}$ in. long; *male* shorter; stamens 2, united up to the anthers. September, October. China. 1910. Attractive shrub notable for its small l., late flowering, and pretty male catkins. Somewhat tender. (B.M. 9079.)

S. britzen'sis. A variety of *S. vitellina.*

S. cae'sia. Shrub 2 to 4 ft., of spreading habit; shoots very leafy, dark brown, glabrous; buds yellow. *l.* $\frac{3}{4}$ to $1\frac{1}{2}$ in. long, $\frac{1}{3}$ to $\frac{3}{4}$ in. wide, quite glabrous, blue-white beneath; stalk $\frac{1}{16}$ to $\frac{1}{8}$ in. long. *Catkins* $\frac{1}{2}$ to $\frac{3}{4}$ in. long; stamens 2, united in lower half. April. Alps of Cent. Europe to Cent. Asia. 1824. Sometimes grafted on standards and made into a small weeping tree and in that guise sold as *S. Zabelii pendula.*

S. can'dida. Sage Willow. Shrub 4 to 6 ft., shoots white-woolly, afterwards red. *l.* linear to oblong-lanceolate, $1\frac{1}{2}$ to $4\frac{1}{2}$ in. long, $\frac{1}{8}$ to $\frac{7}{8}$ in. wide, wrinkled and at first white with down above, permanently and thickly white-woolly beneath. *Male catkins* about 1 in. long; stamens 2; anthers red. April. N. America. 1811. Very distinct by its white-woolly l. and shoots.

S. Cap'rea. Goat Willow. Sallow. Shrub or low tree 10 to 25 ft., bushy. *l.* $2\frac{1}{2}$ to 4 in. long, roundish-oval to oblong or obovate, wrinkled above, soft grey-woolly beneath. *Male catkins*, 1 to $1\frac{1}{2}$ in. long, half as wide; stamens 2; *females* larger. March, April. Europe (Britain) NE. Asia. (E.B. 1331–2.) Often found in hedgerows and out of the way places where the seed has been brought by wind and germinated. Flowers gathered at Easter and known as 'Palm'. var. **pen'dula,** Kilmarnock Willow, branches stiffly pendulous; **varie-ga'ta,** *l.* stained and blotched with white.

S. cine'rea. Grey Willow. Sallow. Shrub 6 to 12 ft., occasionally a small tree; almost wholly covered with grey down which remains on the shoots through the second season. *l.* obovate or oval, 2 to $3\frac{1}{2}$ in. long, entire or obscurely toothed. *Catkins* very silky; males 1 in. long; stamens 2. March, April. Europe (Britain). (E.B. 1327–9.) Akin to *S. Caprea* but with smaller, narrower l. This is also called Palm. var. **tric'olor,** *l.* mottled with yellow and white. Syn. var. *argentea variegata.*

S. coeru'lea.* Cricket Bat Willow. Tree 70 to 100 ft. h., of pyramidal habit, especially when young. *l.* lanceolate, $1\frac{1}{2}$ to 4 in. long, finely toothed, blue-grey and ultimately glabrous beneath. Closely akin to *S. alba*, it differs in habit, in the l. becoming glabrous, in the ovary being slightly stalked. Only known wild in the eastern counties of England and as a female tree. Probably *S. alba × S. fragilis.* (B.T.S. 2, 480.) Syn. *S. alba coerulea.*

S. corda'ta. Shrub 10 to 12 ft., sometimes tree-like; shoots very leafy, glabrous by late summer. *l.* 2 to 6 in. long, $\frac{1}{2}$ to $1\frac{1}{2}$ in. wide, closely set on shoot, rounded or cordate at base, slender-pointed, sharply toothed, green on both surfaces, but paler beneath and glabrous or nearly so; stalk $\frac{1}{2}$ to 1 in. long; stipules large, persistent. *Catkins* 1 to 2 in. long. April. N. America. 1812.

S. cuspida'ta. A synonym of *S. × Meyeriana.*

S. daphnoi'des.* Tree up to 40 ft. h., or a large shrub; shoots at first downy, then purple with waxy bloom. *l.* oval-lanceolate, 2 to $4\frac{1}{2}$ in. long, $\frac{1}{2}$ to 1 in. wide, slender-pointed, finely glandular-toothed, soon glabrous, dark green and glossy above, glaucous blue beneath. *Male catkins* 2 in. long, $\frac{1}{2}$ to $\frac{3}{4}$ in. wide; *female* more slender. March. Europe to Siberia and Himalaya. Naturalized in Britain. Known in the osier trade as 'violets'. Winter effect of the young branches attractive.

S. dis'color. Shrub or low tree up to 20 ft. h., shoots soon glabrous and purplish-brown. *l.* 2 to $4\frac{1}{2}$ in. long, oblong, oval, or obovate, tapered at both ends, often nearly entire, at first downy above, then glabrous and bright green, blue-white beneath. *Male catkins* $1\frac{1}{2}$ in. long; *female* up to 3 in. in fr. March, April. N. America. 1811. (S.S. 478.)

S. elegantis'sima. *See* **S. × blanda.**

S. Farge'sii.* Shrub 6 to 10 ft., shoots stout, glabrous, ultimately dark shining brown; winter buds red. *l.* 3 to 7 in. long, $1\frac{1}{4}$ to 3 in. wide, oval to oval-lanceolate, pointed, tapered at base, finely toothed, silky-hairy beneath; veins in 15 to 20 pairs. *Catkins* erect on short leafy shoots, cylindrical, 2 to $2\frac{1}{2}$ in. long. May. China, 1911. Handsome and well marked by its glossy young shoots, red buds, and many-veined l.

S. frag'ilis. Crack Willow. Tree 90 to 100 ft.; trunk up to 20 ft. in girth, deeply furrowed; shoots glabrous. *l.* lanceolate, up to 6 or 7 in. long, slender-pointed, cuneate, regularly toothed (teeth gland-tipped), glabrous except at first; stalk $\frac{1}{4}$ to $\frac{3}{4}$ in. long. *Catkins* 2 to $2\frac{1}{2}$ in. long on short leafy shoots; stamens 2; ovary conic, stalked. April, May. Europe (Britain), N. Asia. (E.B. 1306.) The largest of European Willows. The popular name refers to the ease with which the twigs snap off when bent. var. **basfordia'na,** twigs shining, orange, changing to red. Ardennes. 1882.

S. × Friesia'na* (*S. repens × S. viminalis*). Rosemary Willow. Bushy shrub 2 to 4 ft. with brown twigs. *l.* $1\frac{1}{2}$ to 3 in. long, $\frac{1}{8}$ to $\frac{1}{4}$ in. wide, linear to linear-lanceolate, tapered towards both ends, entire, densely silky-white beneath. Europe (Britain). (E.B. 1364.) Syn. *S. rosmarinifolia.*

Salix gracilistyla

S. gracilisty'la.* Shrub up to 6 ft., buds prominent; shoots grey-downy. *l.* 2 to 4 in. long, $\frac{1}{2}$ to $1\frac{1}{4}$ in. wide, oblong, oval or narrowly ovate, tapered at both ends, indistinctly toothed, grey-green and at first silky above, glaucous and silky beneath; veins numerous, parallel. *Male catkins* 1 to $1\frac{1}{2}$ in. long; stamens 2; anthers orange and scarlet. March, April. Japan, Korea. 1895. Pretty for its early coloured fl. and distinct for its many-veined l. (B.M. 9122.)

S. × Graham'ii. Shrub 1 to 3 ft. *l.* 1 to $1\frac{1}{2}$ in. long, oval to roundish-oval or obovate, obtuse, bluntly toothed, glossy green and glabrous above, hairy on veins beneath. *Catkins* terminal on leafy shoots, $\frac{1}{2}$ in. long. Probably a hybrid between *S. herbacea* and *S. phylicifolia.* Originally found in Sutherlandshire about 1865. (E.B. 1378.)

S. hasta'ta. Shrub of bushy habit up to 5 ft., shoots at first downy, purplish in second year. *l.* ovate, oval, or obovate, 1 to $3\frac{1}{2}$ in. long, tapered, rounded or cordate at base, acutely pointed, toothed, glabrous, dull green above, glaucous beneath. *Catkins* $1\frac{1}{2}$ to 2 in. long; stamens 2, glabrous. May. Europe, NE. Asia. 1780.

S. helvet'ica. Shrub up to 2 ft. *l.* ½ to 1½ in. long, ¼ to ½ in. wide, oblong to oval-lanceolate, entire, glabrous or nearly so above, silvery-downy beneath. *Catkins* 1½ to 2 in. long. European Alps. Closely akin to *S. Lapponum*, but smaller in stature and l.

S. herba'cea. Dwarf Willow. Small shrub (not herbaceous) 2 to 4 in. h.; stems creeping, rooting and often buried. *l.* few (2 to 4, rarely 6) on each shoot, round, broadly oval or ovate, ¼ to ¾ in. long, toothed, shining green on both sides, soon glabrous. *Catkins* ¼ to ½ in. long; stamens 2. April. N. Hemisphere (Britain). (E.B. 1378.)

S. hu'milis. Prairie Willow. Shrub up to 6 ft. or more, sometimes a small tree; shoots downy. *l.* 2 to 4 in. long, ½ to 1 in. wide, oblanceolate, tapered to both ends, slightly toothed, dark dull green above, glaucous beneath; stalk ⅛ to ¼ in. long. *Catkins* stalkless, oval, ¾ to 1 in. long. April. N. America. 1876.

S. hypoleu'ca. Shrub 5 to 10 ft., shoots glabrous, brown. *l.* 1 to 2 in. long, half as wide, oval-obovate or oblong, pointed, entire or obscurely toothed, glabrous, thin, dark-green above, glaucous beneath. *Catkins* stalked, slender, cylindric, 1 to 2 in. long. China. 1911. var. **platyphyl'la** has comparatively broader, rounder l.

S. inca'na. Shrub of bushy, leafy growth, up to 8 or 10 ft., usually wider than h., shoots grey-downy when young. *l.* 2 to 5 in. long, ⅛ to 3/16 in. wide, linear, tapering at both ends, dark green above, white-felted beneath. *Catkins* erect, slender; female 1 to 1½ in. long, male shorter; stamens 2. April, May. Europe, Asia Minor. 1820.

S. irrora'ta. Upright shrub to 10 ft., shoots smooth, purple or yellow, waxy. *l.* 2 to 4 in. long, oblong-lanceolate, slender-pointed, shining bright green above, glaucous beneath, smooth, sometimes slightly toothed. *Catkins* short and dense, ¾ to 1 in. long; stamens 2. April. SW. United States.

S. lana'ta.* Shrub 2 to 3 ft., shoots covered thickly with soft grey wool. *l.* 1 to 2½ in. long, ¾ to 1½ in. wide, oval to roundish or obovate, shortly pointed, mostly entire, silvery-hairy on both sides. *Male catkins* 1 to 2 in. long, golden yellow; *female* up to 3 in. long when ripe. May. N. Europe (Scotland), N. Asia. (E.B. 1367.) Handsome dwarf shrub, especially when in fl.

S. Lappo'num. Spreading, much-branched shrub, 2 to 4 ft., shoots more or less downy, later dark brown. *l.* 1 to 3 in. long, ¼ to 1¼ in. wide, oval to lanceolate, inclined to obovate, usually entire, pointed, softly silvery-downy above and beneath. *Male catkins* stalkless, 1 in. long; *female* shortly stalked, 1¼ in. long; both very silky. April, May. Europe (Scotland), Siberia. (E.B. 1368–70.) var. **Stuartia'na,** *l.* woolly above, densely silky and cottony beneath, more lanceolate, scarcely distinct. (E.B. 1369.)

S. lasian'dra. Tree up to 60 ft. h., shoots downy at first. *l.* narrowly oval-lanceolate, 3 to 6 in. long, ½ to 1½ in. wide, minutely glandular-toothed, shining dark green above with a yellow midrib, more or less glaucous beneath; stalk ¼ to ½ in. long with a few wart-like glands. *Male catkins* cylindrical, 1 to 1½ in. long; stamens 5 up to 9; anthers hairy. Spring. Western N. America. (SS. 469–70.) Akin to *S. pentandra.*

S. laurifo'lia. A synonym of *S. pentandra.*

S. lu'cida. Shining Willow. Shrub or tree up to 25 ft. h., shoots glossy, glabrous. *l.* 3 to 5 in. long, ¾ to 1½ in. wide, lanceolate with a long tail-like point, glandular-toothed, shining green on both surfaces; stalk ¼ to ½ in. long, glandular; stipules large, cordate, glandular, usually persistent. *Male catkins* erect, 1½ to 2½ in. long; stamens usually 5. April, May. N. America. 1830. (S.S. 473.)

S. magnif'ica.* Glabrous shrub or small tree up to 20 ft. h., stems stout, purple changing to reddish; buds purple. *l.* 4 to 8 in. long, 3 to 5 in. wide, oval or inclined to obovate, entire, rounded to cordate at base, abruptly pointed, dull grey-green above, glaucous beneath; stalk ½ to 1½ in. long. *Male catkins* 4 to 7 in. long; *female* 7 to 12 in. long. China. 1910. Most remarkable of willows in size and shape of l. On young vigorous plants they may be 10 in. by 5 in.

S. Matsuda'na.* Tree 40 to 60 ft. h., shoots slender, downy at first and yellowish, becoming brownish-grey. *l.* 2 to 4 in. long, linear-lanceolate, slender-pointed, finely toothed, glaucous and soon glabrous beneath. *Catkins* ½ to 1 in. long. China, Korea. 1913. (B.T.S. 3, 448.) Beautiful willow closely akin to *S. babylonica.* Said to grow wild on dry lands with a scanty summer rainfall. var. **pen'dula,** of weeping habit.

S. Medem'ii. Shrub up to 12 or 14 ft., shoots downy. *l.* 3 to 5 in. long, sometimes inclined to obovate, pointed, broadly cuneate at the base, margin rounded- to sharp-toothed, downy on both sides at first, becoming glabrous above, glaucous beneath. *Male catkins* 1½ to 2 in. long; stamens united half-way up; anthers yellow. January, February. Armenia, Persia. (Gn. 87 (1923), 121; B.M. n.s. 91 as *S. aegyptiaca.*) Akin to *S. cinerea* which has quite detached stamens. SYN. *S. aegyptiaca.* One of the earliest to flower.

S. × Meyeria'na (*S. fragilis × S. pentandra*). Tree 50 or 60 ft. h., shoots glabrous. *l.* oval, ovate, or obovate, 1½ to 4½ in. long, ½ to 1½ in. wide, finely glandular-toothed, shining, glabrous. *Male catkins* cylindric, 1½ to 2 in. long; stamens 3 to 5, usually 4. Europe (wild in Shropshire). (E.B. 1304.) Inherits much of the beauty and distinction of *S. pentandra.* SYN: *S. cuspidata.*

S. microstach'ya. A variety of *S. Wilhelmsiana.*

S. moupinen'sis.* Shrub or small tree, 10 to 20 ft. h., shoots glabrous, reddish-brown, winter buds slender, up to ½ in. long. *l.* 2 to 5 in. long, oval to obovate, tapered to rounded at base, finely and regularly glandular-toothed, glabrous or silky on midrib beneath. *Catkins* very slender; female 3 to 5 in. long. May. China. 1912. Handsome and distinct.

S. myrsinifo'lia. A synonym of *S. nigricans.*

S. myrsini'tes. Shrub 1 to 1½ ft., bushy, often partly procumbent; shoots slender, silky-hairy at first, afterwards dark brown, shining. *l.* ½ to 1½ in. long, ⅙ to ½ in. wide, bright green on both sides, narrowly oval to roundish, glandular-toothed; stalk ⅛ in. or less long. *Catkins* erect, up to 1 in. long. N. Hemisphere (Britain). (E.B. 1375–6.) Resembles the whortleberry in habit and l.

S. myrtilloi'des. Shrub 6 in. to 2 ft., of bushy, spreading habit, glabrous; stems often procumbent and rooting. *l.* ⅓ to 1½ in. long, ⅙ to ⅞ in. wide, oblong, obovate or ovate, entire, dark dull green above, glaucous or purplish beneath. *Male catkins* ½ to ¾ in. long, cylindrical. N. Hemisphere. High mountain plant, not British.

S. nig'ra. Black Willow. Tree 30 to 40 ft. h., shoots yellowish, soon glabrous. *l.* linear-lanceolate, 3 to 5 in. long, ¼ to ½ in. wide, slender-pointed, finely toothed, pale green, almost or quite glabrous. *Male catkins* 1 to 2 in. long, cylindric, slender; stamens 3 to 5, or even 7. N. America. 1811. (SS. 9, 462.) var. **falca'ta,** *l.* narrower and more curved. (S.S. 9, 463.)

S. nig'ricans. Very variable species of which more than a dozen varieties have been named, not one of any real garden value. Bushy shrub, 10 to 12 ft. *l.* very variable in size and shape, from 1 to 4 in. long and ½ to 2 in. wide, orbicular, oval, ovate, obovate, or oblanceolate, dull green above, grey-green beneath, usually slightly downy. *Male catkins* ¾ to 1¼ in. long, oblong, stamens 2; *female* more slender. April. Europe (Britain). (E.B. 1347–54.) Often found in gardens, having grown from wind-blown seed. *l.* turns black in drying. SYN. *S. myrsinifolia.*

S. penduli'na. *See* **S. × blanda.**

S. pentan'dra.* Bay-leaved Willow. Tree 30 to 50 ft., shoots shining, brownish-green, glabrous; buds yellow. *l.* 1½ to 4½ in. long, half as wide, ovate to oval, rounded or slightly cordate at the base, shortly pointed, finely glandular-toothed, glabrous, lustrous green; midrib yellow. *Male catkins* 1½ to 2 in. long, golden-yellow; stamens 5 to 7. May. Europe (Britain). NW. Asia. (E.B. 1393.) SYN. *S. laurifolia.* Handsome bright-foliaged tree.

S. petiola'ris. Shrub 4 to 6 ft., shoots slender, soon glabrous, afterwards purple. *l.* 1½ to 3½ in. long, ¼ to ⅝ in. wide, narrowly lanceolate, tapered at both ends, soon quite glabrous, rather glaucous beneath; stalk ⅛ to ⅜ in. long. *Male catkins* ½ to ¾ in. long; *female* 1 to 1½ in. long; seed vessel slenderly stalked. April. N. America, where it is valued for basket-making.

S. Petzold'ii pend'ula. A synonym of *S. × blanda.*

S. phylicifo'lia. Shrub 6 to 10 ft., shoots glabrous or slightly downy, shining brown. *l.* 1 to 3½ in. long, varying from orbicular, oval and ovate to obovate, glossy-green above, glaucous beneath. *Male catkins* 1 in., *female* 1½ to 2 in. long. Europe (Britain). (E.B. 1334–46.) Very variable; over a dozen varieties having been named. Nearly akin to *S. nigricans* but with brighter shining foliage and young shoots. Of little garden value.

S. Pierot'ii. Shrub up to 6 or 8 ft., shoots shining brown, glabrous. *l.* 2 to 5 in. long, ½ to 1½ in. wide, lanceolate, slender-pointed, finely toothed, shining dark green above, vividly glaucous beneath, soon glabrous. *Catkins* ¾ to 2 in. long; stamens 2. Japan. 1903. SYN. *S. japonica* (not of Thunberg). Handsome bushy, very leafy shrub.

S. × Pontedera'na (*S. cinerea × S. purpurea*). Shrub 8 to 12 ft. *l.* 1 to 2½ in. long, ⅓ to ¾ in. wide, narrowly obovate to lanceolate, tapering to both ends, toothed, dark shining green above, glaucous and at first silky beneath. *Male catkins* 1 in. long; stamens 2, the lower halves of each pair united. April. Europe (not British). SYN. *S. sordida.*

S. pruino'sa. A synonym of *S. acutifolia.*

S. purpu'rea.* Purple Osier. Spreading bush 10 ft. or more, sometimes a small tree; shoots very slender, glabrous, purplish. *l.* 1½ to 3 in. long, ⅛ to ⅓ in. wide, linear to narrow-oblong, widest above middle, pointed, toothed towards end, often opposite, soon glabrous. *Catkins* ½ to 1 in. long; stamens solitary. Bark very bitter and rich in salicine. Europe (Britain), N. and Cent. Asia. (E.B. 1316.) Basket-making osiers known as Dicks, Kecks, Red-bud, and Welch belong to this species. var. **grac'ilis,** a slender-branched form with narrow l. SYN. var. *uralensis*; **Lambertia'na,** *l.* larger, broader, and up to 4 in. by ¾ in.; **pen'dula,** naturally prostrate, this makes a weeping tree when grafted on standards 8 or 10 ft. h. SYN. var. *scharfenbergensis, S. americana pendula.*

S. rega'lis. A synonym of *S. alba argentea.*

S. Rehderia'na. Shrub or small tree up to 30 ft., shoots with little or no down, reddish-brown. *l.* 2 to 5 in. long, ½ to 1 in. wide, lanceolate or oblanceolate, slender-pointed, rounded at the base, glandular and bluntly toothed, grey-silky or sometimes glaucous and glabrous beneath. *Catkins* stalkless, about 1 in. long; stamens 2; anthers purple. April, China. 1908.

S. re'pens. Creeping Willow. Low shrub, 1 to 4 ft. with creeping rootstock, prostrate stems, and upright branches; shoots silky. *l.* oval to oblong and lanceolate, ½ to ¾ in. long (larger in gardens), densely covered beneath with glistening, silky hairs. *Male catkins* ½ to ¾ in. long, roundish; stamens 2. April, May. Europe (Britain), N. Asia. (E.B. 1356–62.) Of numerous varieties, mostly with larger l., the most attractive is **argen'tea** with both surfaces silky-hairy.

S. reticula'ta. Low prostrate shrub only 5 or 6 in. h., stems rooting; shoots shining brown, angled, soon glabrous. *l.* 2 to 4 on a twig, ½ to 1½ in. long, round, roundish-oval or broadly obovate, entire, conspicuously net-veined, glaucous white and soon glabrous beneath; stalk up to ¾ in. long. *Catkins* ½ to 1 in. long, cylindrical on a stalk up to 1 in. long. May. Europe (Scotland), N. Asia. (E.B. 1379.) Distinct species for the rock-garden.

S. retu'sa. Low prostrate shrub a few inches h., stems creeping and self-rooting; shoots glabrous. *l.* obovate to rhombic and oblong, ¼ to ¾ in. long, $\frac{1}{10}$ to ⅓ in. wide, entire or nearly so, green on both sides, glabrous or slightly downy beneath. *Catkins* erect on leafy twigs, ½ to ¾ in. long. May, June. Cent. and E. Europe. 1763. Makes a neat ground cover.

S. rosmarinifo'lia. A synonym of *S.* × *Friesiana.*

S. × ru'bra (*S. purpurea* × *S. viminalis*). Highly valued by basket-makers as yielding the osiers known as Mawdesley's Long Skein and Tulip Willow. Shrub or small tree. *l.* linear-lanceolate, sparsely toothed, 2 to 5½ in. long, ¼ to ⅜ wide. var. **Forbya'na,** *l.* broader. The Fine Basket Osier of the trade.

S. Russellia'na. *See* **S. × viridis.**

S. × Salamon'ii (*S. alba* × *S. babylonica*). Female tree up to 50 or 60 ft. h., graceful and pendulous but not so much so as *S. babylonica. l.* 2½ to 5 in. long, ½ to ⅞ in. wide, more or less silky, especially beneath on first opening, but soon becoming as glabrous as *S. babylonica.* (B.T.S. 1, 98.) It is an admirable substitute for *S. babylonica* in places too cold for that species. First noticed about 1860 on the estate of Baron de Salamon, Manosque, Basse-Alpes.

S. serpyllifo'lia. Very near *S. retusa* of which it has been considered a variety with smaller l. In a wild state it is a close tufted shrub a few inches h. with l. ⅛ to ⅓ in. long. In gardens it grows more freely and has l. up to ⅝ in. long, obovate. *Catkins* ½ in. long. European Alps.

S. × Smithia'na (*S. Caprea* × *S. viminalis*). Shrub up to 15 ft. or a small tree, shoots reddish, softly downy. *l.* oblong-lanceolate or ovate-lanceolate, 3 to 6 in. long, nearly entire, glaucous and downy beneath. *Male catkins* 1 to 1½ in. long. March, April. Europe (Britain). Often handsome in fl.

S. sor'dida. A synonym of *S.* × *Pontederana.*

S. × subalpi'na (*S. incana* × *S. repens*). Shrub 3 to 5 ft., shoots downy. *l.* 1 to 2½ in. long, ½ to 1 in. wide, oval-lanceolate, tapered towards both ends, entire or slightly toothed, bright green above, grey-woolly beneath. *Male catkins* 1 to 1¼ in. long, slender, yellow. April, May. Switzerland.

S. trian'dra. A synonym of *S. amygdalina.*

S. vimina'lis. Common Osier. Erect shrub or small tree, 15 to 20 or more ft. *l.* linear-lanceolate, 3 to 10 in. long, long and slender-pointed, dark dull green above, shining silky grey beneath. *Catkins* about 1¼ in. long. March, April. Europe (Britain). (E.B. 1332.) Very common on the banks of rivers and lakes and useful for preventing erosion. Very much used for basket-making. Selected kinds for this purpose are: Yellow Osier, Long Skein, Brown Merrin.

S. × vi'ridis. Tree up to 70 or 80 ft. h., generally regarded as a hybrid between *S. alba* and *S. fragilis.* Twigs not readily broken off. *l.* lanceolate, silky at first, glabrous at maturity, glaucous beneath; ovary conical, glabrous, slightly stalked. It has presumably the same origin as *S. coerulea* and resembles it in many characters, but has not the same pyramidal shape. Britain. (E.B. 1308.) It varies considerably in the intermediates between the parents. One of its forms known as *S. Russelliana* (Bedford Willow) leans towards *S. fragilis.*

S. vitelli'na.* Golden Willow. Tree up to 65 ft. h., shoots downy near the buds, ultimately glabrous and yellow. *l.* lanceolate, 2 to 4 in. long, ½ in. wide, tapering to a long slender point, bright green above, glaucous and slightly silky beneath. Akin to, and sometimes regarded as, a variety of *S. alba,* but the l. is not so silky, the catkins are longer, and the stamens are occasionally three to a fl. Chiefly planted for winter effect, pruned back annually to produce thickets of young shoots. var. **britzen'sis,*** winter shoots bright red; **pen'dula,*** a very beautiful weeping tree with the same habit as *S. babylonica.* Shoots slender, perfectly pendulous, bright yellow in winter. SYN. *S. vitellina ramuleis aureis.*

S. Wilhelmsia'na. Shrub 10 to 15 ft., shoots slender, silky. *l.* linear, 1 to 2 in. long, $\frac{1}{12}$ to ⅛ in. wide, indistinctly toothed, silky on both sides when young, becoming glabrous, scarcely stalked. *Catkins* slender, ¾ in. long; stamens 2, united up to the yellow anthers. May. Caucasus and N. Asia. SYN. *S. angustifolia.* var. **microstach'ya,** *l.* up to 1½ in. long, ⅛ in. wide. SYN. *S. microstachya.*

S. Zabel'ii pend'ula. *See* **S. caesia.**

SALLOW. A name for Willows such as *Salix Caprea, S. cinerea.*

SALLOW THORN. *See* **Hippophae rhamnoides.**

SALMA'LIA malab'ricum. *See* **Bombax.**

Salm'ii, in honour of Joseph Maria Franz Anton Hubert Ignaz Salm-Reifferscheid-Dyck, 1773–1861, of Dusseldorf, writer on succulent plants.

SALMON BERRY. *See* **Rubus spectabilis.**

SALPICHLAE'NA. Included in **Blechnum.**

SALPICHRO'A (*salpinx,* tube, *chroos,* skin; from the form and texture of the flowers). FAM. *Solanaceae.* A genus of about 10 species of herbs, sub-shrubs, and shrubs, natives of extra-tropical S. America and the Andes. Leaves entire, often rather small, stalks rather long. Flowers white or yellow, up to 2 or 3 in. long, calyx 5-fid or -parted; corolla long-tubular, or urn-shaped, lobes 5, acute, often short, erect or spreading; stamens affixed above middle of tube; pedicels solitary. Treatment as for Juanulloa.

S. glandulo'sa. Sub-erect, much branched, 2 ft. h. *l.* twin, cordate-ovate, ½ to 1 in. long, glandular-hairy, often hoary. *fl.* yellow, cor. 1½ in. long, throat ½ in. across; pedicels filiform, nodding at apex. July. Chile. 1844. Stove.

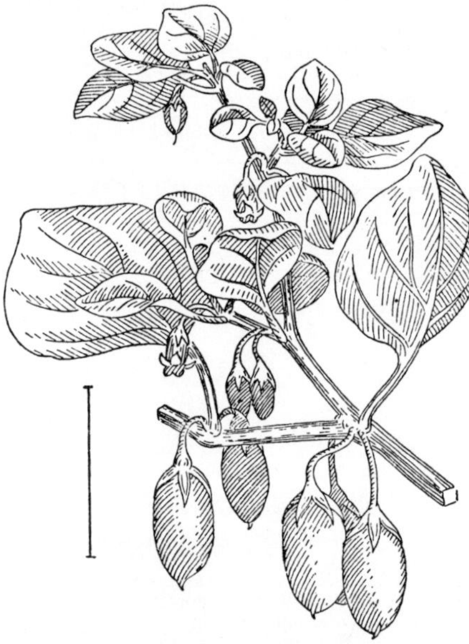

Salpichroa rhomboidea

S. rhomboi'dea. Stem slender. *fl.* small, rhomboid-ovate, rounded at base, narrowed to stalk, glabrous or almost so, ciliate. *fl.* white, solitary or twin; cor. short, tubular. *fr.* white. Buenos Aires. (R.H. 1897, f. 159.) Greenhouse or half-hardy; suitable for trellises.

SALPIGLOS'SIS (*salpinx,* tube, *glossa,* tongue; from the tongue-like style at the mouth of the corolla). FAM. *Solanaceae.* A genus of about 8 species of annual, biennial, or perennial, clammy-hairy herbs, natives of Chile. Leaves entire, sinuately toothed or pinnatifid. Flowers few, often rather large, Alstroemeria-like; calyx tubular, 5-fid; corolla obliquely funnel-shaped, throat open bell-shaped; lobes 5, plicate, emarginate, erecto-patent; perfect stamens 4, included. *S. sinuata* is a very ornamental and useful border plant needing the same cultural treatment as Schizanthus. Plants are apt to suffer from a foot-rot disease caused by a species of

Phytophthora. This may be controlled by the use of Cheshunt Compound (*see* **Fungicides**), and the destruction of affected plants. Seedlings are best raised in sterilized soil.

S. integrifo'lia. A synonym of *Petunia violacea.*

S. linea'ris. About 1 ft. h., erect, branched, leafy. *l.* linear-oblong, somewhat spatulate, obtuse, narrowed to the sessile base, entire, 1 to 1½ in. long. *fl.* axillary or opposite l.; cor. ¾ in. across, glandular-hairy without, tube yellow, striped, longer than cal., limb purple with a paler margin; peduncles ½ to 1 in. long, filiform. August. (B.M. 3256; B.R. 1931 as *Petunia intermedia*; S.B.F.G. s. 2, 237 as *Nierembergia intermedia.*)

S. sinua'ta.* About 2 ft. h., sub-erect, branched, clammy-hairy. *Lower l.* stalked, elliptic-oblong, sinuately toothed or pinnatifid; *upper* more entire. *fl.* dark-purple, straw-coloured, or various marked, often striped, showy; cor. about 1½ in. long or more. Summer. August. Greenhouse or hardy annual. Variable. Many names have been given to it on account of its variability in colouring in wild forms and others to garden-raised forms. (B.M. 2811, B.R. 1518, and S.B.F.G. 271 as *S. atropurpurea*; S.B.F.G. s. 2, 112 as *S. Barclayana*; B.M. 3365, L.B.C. 1652, and S.B.F.G. 258 as *S. picta*; S.B.F.G. 231 as *S. straminea.*) Other names are *S. coccinea, S. flava,* and *S. variabilis.* The last name well expresses the variety of colouring exhibited by this plant.

SALPING'A (*salpinx*, trumpet; from the shape of the calyx). FAM. *Melastomaceae.* A genus of erect, branching herbs, natives of S. America, related to Bertolonia, cultivated for their attractive foliage. Stems 4-angled. Leaves often unequal, oblong or lanceolate, often purple beneath, long-stalked. Flowers in spikes on terminal simple or forked peduncles; calyx tube cylindrical or bell-shaped; petals 5; stamens 10; ovary oblong, 3-celled. Requires stove conditions and treatment like the Bertolonias.

S. longifo'lia. *l.* oblong, rounded or slightly cordate at base, glabrous and bright green above, paler and downy beneath. *fl.* white. Brazil. SYN. *Bertolonia longifolia.*

S. margarita'cea. *l.* ovate, base rounded or more or less cordate, dull green with white spots between veins above, pale green, reddish, or bright rose beneath. *fl.* white or pale rose. Brazil. SYN. *Bertolonia margaritacea, Gravenia guttata margaritacea.*

S. secund'a. *l.* narrow-ovate, base rather obtuse, light green above, paler beneath. Brazil.

sal'pinx, trumpet.

SALSIFY (*Tragopogon porrifolius*). A hardy biennial grown for its long, white, fleshy roots which are ready for use from mid-October through the winter following the sowing at the end of March or in April, and for its tender young shoots in the following spring (*see* **Chards**). It is best in a deep, moist, and rather light soil but can be grown in heavier soils if they are double-dug and thoroughly worked throughout. As with other long-rooted vegetables fresh manure should not be added for this crop, unless it is put below the top spit, otherwise the roots branch and are fanged and have an earthy flavour. Manuring is better done for the previous crop. The seed should be sown when the surface is dry in drills 1 in. deep and 10 to 12 in. apart, the seedlings being thinned when large enough to handle to a few inches apart and finally to 8 or 9 in. The crop must be kept free from weeds and the surface soil kept crumbly throughout the summer to conserve soil moisture and check the tendency to run to seed in dry soil. The roots may be lifted, like Parsnips, as required, or stored in a clamp or in moist sand or earth in a shed, and care should be taken not to damage them in lifting. The plant is sometimes known as Oyster Plant or Vegetable Oyster.

DISEASES. Salsify has few diseases. The leaves may be attacked by White Blister (*Cystopus cubicus*), a very similar trouble to White Blister on cabbage, but except in very young and overcrowded plants this is not likely to be serious and can be checked by thinning. Powdery Mildew (*Erysiphe cichoracearum*) may appear but should have little effect on plants which are not too crowded. There is also a rust disease due to *Puccinia hysterium* which is not very common. It shows first as orange and then dark-brown pustules on both surfaces of the leaves and, as the fungus is considered to hibernate in the crowns, affected plants should be destroyed in stocks intended for seed production.

(D. E. G.)

Salsil'la, native name of a Bomarea in Chile.

SALSO'LA (*sal*, salt). FAM. *Chenopodiaceae.* A genus of about 40 species of herbs and sub-shrubs, mainly found in salt soil in temperate regions, of no horticultural value but a source of the impure carbonate of soda called Barilla, mainly obtained from the native *S. Kali* and the S. European *S. Soda* (*see* **Salicornia**).

salsugino'sus -a -um, growing in places liable to inundation with salt-water.

salsu'lus -a -um, salt-loving.

SALT. In the chemist's sense a salt is the compound formed when chemical action takes place between an acid and a base. All acids contain hydrogen (H) and the formation of a salt by the action of an acid upon a base is due to the redistribution of the atoms composing the molecules of the 2 compounds in such a way that some or all of the hydrogen atoms in the acid molecules change places with the metallic atoms (or the molecules of the compound acting as a base) of the base. Thus if carbonic acid (H_2CO_3) interacts with sodium (Na) either sodium carbonate (Na_2CO_3), where both atoms of hydrogen have been displaced, or sodium bi-carbonate ($HNaCO_3$), where only 1 atom of hydrogen has been displaced is produced. Similarly if sulphuric acid (H_2SO_4) interacts with ammonia (NH_4), sulphate of ammonia ($(NH_4)_2SO_4$) is produced.

In the special sense when Salt is referred to, common salt which is the compound resulting from the interaction of hydrochloric acid (HCl) with sodium giving the compound sodium chloride (NaCl) is indicated. Salt has been used as a manure from very early times although actual need for adding either of its constituents, sodium or chlorine, to the soil is problematical. Used in excess it is certainly injurious. In dry soil 1 part in 1,000 of soil is likely to be injurious while in wet soils probably 2 parts in 1,000 could be endured. It is thought that with light soils a moderate dressing of common salt helps in maintaining a moist condition and possibly in some instances action of a beneficial nature takes place upon humus material in the soil. Seakale and Asparagus appear to benefit by an annual dressing of salt in spring.

In strong solutions, at the rate of 1 lb. to the gallon of water, salt is sometimes used as a weed-killer on paths. It kills young seedlings and moss but its effects are not very lasting.

saltato'rius -a -um, dancing.

Saltia'nus -a -um, in honour of H. Salt, 1780–1827, of Lichfield, who travelled in Abyssinia.

SALTPETRE. Potassium nitrate is often known by this name. It has considerable value as a manure, supplying both potash and nitrogen, but is usually too expensive to use on a large scale. *See* **Potash.**

SALT-TREE. *See* **Halimodendron.**

SALTWORT. *See* **Salicornia** and **Salsola.**

saluenen'sis -is -e, of the Salween River, Tibet.

saluta'ris -is -e, healing.

SALVADO'RA (in honour of Juan Salvador y Bosca, 1598–1681, apothecary of Barcelona). FAM. *Salvadoraceae.* A genus of 2 or 3 species of evergreen trees or shrubs, natives of E. Africa, Arabia, and India. Leaves opposite, entire, rather thick, often pale. Flowers small, in racemes or spikes, forming axillary or terminal panicles; calyx lobes 4, overlapping; corolla bell-shaped, tube with 4 small teeth between the bases of the filaments, lobes 4, overlapping; stamens 4. *S. persica* is by many considered to be the mustard tree of Matt. xiii. 32. It will grow in well-drained soil under stove conditions, and may be increased by cuttings in sand under a glass, in heat.

S. in'dica. A synonym of *S. persica.*

S. pers'ica. Kiknel Oil-plant, Mustard Tree. Small, glabrous tree. *l.* ovate or oblong, obtuse, 1¾ in. long. *fl.* white, stalked, scattered; panicles 2 to 5 in. long, often numerous in upper axils. *fr.* aromatic. Arabia, India, &c. 1850. SYN. *S. indica.*

SALVADORA'CEAE. Dicotyledons. A family of 9 species of trees and shrubs falling into 3 genera, natives of Africa and Trop. or Sub-tropical Asia. Leaves opposite, entire, usually with awl-shaped stipules. Flowers usually numerous in short, axillary panicles or in dense, sessile clusters; sometimes dioecious; regular; calyx free, bell-shaped or ovoid, 4- or 5-toothed; corolla gamopetalous and bell-shaped or polypetalous, lobes or petals 4 or 5; stamens 4 or 5; carpels 2. Fruit a berry or drupe, usually 1-seeded. The bark of the root of *Salvadora persica* is acrid, that of the stem tonic. The genera dealt with are Azima and Salvadora.

SAL'VIA (ancient Latin name used by Pliny, from *salveo* to save or heal, from the alleged medicinal qualities of some species). FAM. *Labiatae.* A genus of over 500 species of annual, biennial, or perennial herbs, sub-shrubs, or shrubs of various habit, widely dispersed over the temperate and warmer regions of the globe. Leaves entire or variously toothed or pinnatisect; stem-leaves usually of different form from the lower leaves. Flowers mostly showy, sessile or shortly pedicellate in 2- to many-flowered whorls, usually forming a spike, raceme, or panicle, rarely axillary; calyx 2-lipped, upper lip entire or with 3 minute teeth, lower 2-fid; corolla tube cylindrical or swollen or enlarged above, limb 2-lipped, upper lip erect, concave or arched, entire or scarcely notched, lower spreading, 3-lobed, mid-lobe often notched or divided; perfect stamens 2, the connective often variously modified. Fruit of 4 nutlets, ovoid, triquetrous or slightly compressed, smooth. *S. officinalis* is the common sage (q.v.). Many other species are very ornamental. Some are hardy, some need greenhouse or even stove conditions. Seeds should be sown thinly and are usually better for a little warmth. The tender species can be raised from cuttings very readily in heat and many varieties must be so raised to obtain them true. The cuttings should be quite soft and in a growing condition. Some species are excellent for autumn- or winter-flowering in the greenhouse, among them *S. azurea* and its variety *grandiflora*, *S. cacaliifolia*, *S. involucrata* and its variety *Bethellii*, *S. rutilans*, and *S. splendens*, especially the variety *Bruantii*. For spring-flowering under glass *S. fulgens* and *S. gesneriiflora* are good. *S. patens* is one of the most distinct and beautiful of deep blue-flowered plants in cultivation and is equally well suited for greenhouse decoration in summer or for planting in beds outside for the same season. Salvias like a rich soil, especially if grown in pots; loam and manure in about equal parts is not too strong for them. The tender species may be grown outdoors in summer but they must be housed before frost occurs as they cannot stand severe weather. Salvias are not well adapted for room decoration for in the atmosphere of rooms their flowers soon fall. Propagation should be done in spring. Except where otherwise stated the species described below are hardy herbaceous perennials.

S. acau'lis. Related to *S. lyrata.* Stem erect, herbaceous, little branched. *l.* obovate, entire, sinuate, roughly hairy above. *fl.* blue-purple in remote, 6-fld. whorls on an almost simple raceme. E. Indies.

S. Aethio'pis. Perennial white-woolly herb, 6 to 12 in. h., erect. *l.* broad-ovate, lower narrowed to a stalk, upper stem-clasping, all deeply toothed; bracts very broad, long-pointed, concave, persistent. *fl.* in a panicle, whorls 6- to 10-fld., distinct; cal. bell-shaped, teeth spiny, awl-shaped; cor. white, upper lip often reddish; tube narrowed at middle, without a ring of hairs inside; connectives not toothed. Mediterranean region.

S. algerien'sis. Annual, nearly related to *S. bicolor* but l. narrower, crenate, not coarsely toothed, pedicels shorter. Stem erect, hairy. *l.* ovate or oblong, glabrous or hairy only on veins beneath. *fl.* violet-blue; cor. 3 times as long as cal.; whorls numerous, 6-fld. remote. Algiers.

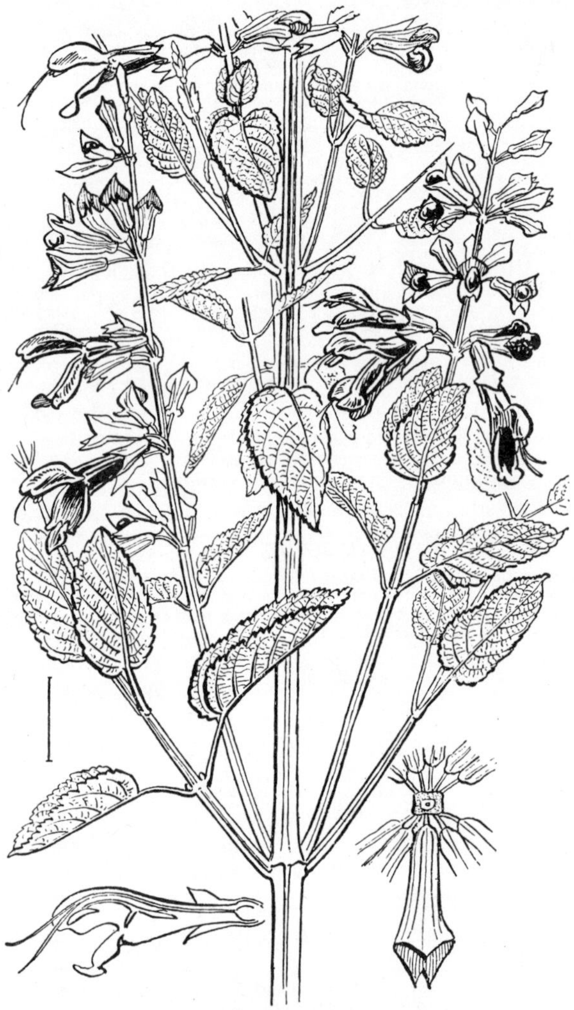

Salvia ambigens

S. am'bigens.* Sub-shrubby perennial up to 5 ft. h. Stems 4-angled, hairy. *l.* ovate, 2 to 5 in. long, acute, toothed, shortly hairy. *fl.* dark- to violet-blue or bluish-rose with a whitish base; cal. tubular, ciliate; cor. about 1½ to 2 in. long, tube flattened sideways, glabrous; raceme of 5 or 6 whorls, somewhat 1-sided. September, October. S. America. 1925. (B.M. 9178 as *S. caerulea.*) Half-hardy. May be grown as half-hardy annual.

S. angustifo'lia. Perennial of about 2 ft. *l.* linear, 1½ to 3 in. long, entire or nearly so, acute, stalk short. *fl.* blue, lower lip as wide as long, its mid-lobe emarginate; cal. lips half as long as tube; pedicels very short; infl. twiggy, slender, whorls few, distant. Mexico. 1816. (B.R. 1554; S.B.F.G. s. 2, 219.) Greenhouse.

S. argen'tea. Biennial, erect, shaggy, up to 3 ft. h. *Radical l.* stalked; *stem-l.* sessile, 6 to 8 in. h., wedge-shaped at base, sinuately lobed, white-woolly, wrinkled, margin irregularly toothed; *floral l.* very broad, concave, long-pointed, hairy, persistent. *fl.* in a slightly branched large panicle, the whorls 6- to 10-fld., remote; cor. pinkish-white, 2 in. long or more, about 3 times as long as cal. Mediterranean region. 1759. (S.B.F.G. 27.)

S. azu'rea. Glabrous or downy perennial up to 6 ft. h. *Lower l.* lanceolate or oblong, obtuse, toothed, narrowed to a short stalk; *upper l.* narrower, often linear, entire; *floral l.* awl-shaped, somewhat persistent. *fl.* in a spike, pedicels very short; cor. deep blue (sometimes white), lower lip 3-lobed, emarginate; cal. oblong bell-shaped, scarcely 2-lipped. August. N. America. 1806. (B.M. 1728.) var. **grandiflo'ra,** ashy-downy, *infl.* denser than in type; cal. silky-hairy. Mexico. (G.C. 14 (1880), 685 as *S. Pitcheri.*)

S. Beck'eri. Herbaceous perennial. Stem erect, 18 in. h., hairy. *l.* ovate, up to 2½ in. long and as wide, more or less cordate at base, repand, glabrous above, appressed hairy beneath. *fl.* violet, cal. blue, one-third as long as corolla; upper lip falcate. *Raceme* 6 in. long, whorls distant, 2- to 4-fld. Caucasus.

S. Bertolo'nii. Hairy herbaceous perennial with habit of *S. pratensis* and *fl.* much like *S. Verbenaca,* but *l.* wider ovate, somewhat cordate at base, hairy beneath, stalked. *fl.* in a branched raceme. Dalmatia.

S. Bethell'ii. A variety of *S. involucrata.*

S. bi'color. Clammy-hairy biennial. Stem stout, 2 to 3 ft. h., scarcely branched. *Lower l.* large, ovate, pinnatifid or palmately lobed, stalked; *middle-l.* narrower; *upper l.* sessile; all heart-shaped at base. *fl.* in many, distinct, 6-fld. whorls, in a raceme 1½ to 2 ft. long; cal. clammy, about ⅓ in. long, teeth awl-shaped; cor. 1 in. long or more, upper lip bluish-violet with golden dots, lower lip whitish. June. N. Africa. 1793. (B.M. 1774.) Hardy.

S. blepharophyl'la. Sub-shrubby, stoloniferous, stolons fleshy. About 1 ft. h. *l.* ovate, dark green, irregularly toothed, ciliate, but otherwise almost glabrous; stalk long, slender. *fl.* scarlet; cal. slightly clammy-hairy; cor. tube ¾ in. long, swollen in middle, lower lip large, upper hooded, downy without. Mexico. About 1930. Half-hardy. Needs a sunny position.

S. brachyca'lyx. Perennial of 2½ to 5 ft., somewhat hairy, leafy below. *Lower l.* ovate, 2½ to 12 in. long, somewhat lobed, irregularly toothed; *stem-l.* triangular-ovate, sessile; *floral l.* shorter. *fl.* in a panicle about 18 in. long; cal. bell-shaped, clammy, about ⅓ in. long, teeth short, broad; cor. bluish, about 1½ in. long; stamens and style long-exserted. May to July. Asia Minor, Syria.

S. brevilab'ra. Closely related to *S. hians* but with smaller fl. with shorter lips, and with irregularly, coarsely toothed l. Perennial, about 2 ft. h. *l.* ovate, up to 4½ in. long, green, sparsely hairy. *fl.* violet streaked with long, white blotches, tube about ¾ in. long with a ring of hairs near base within, upper lip ⅙ in., lower ⅓ in. long; infl. branched, whorls 2- to 6-fld. W. China. 1904. (B.M. 8848.) SYN. *S. Souliei* of Duthie and gardens.

S. cacaliifo'lia. Erect herbaceous perennial, about 3 ft. h., stem hairy. *l.* broadly deltoid, more or less hastate-cordate at base, rather thick, hairy above, reddish or whitish softly hairy beneath. *fl.* in branched racemes; whorls 2-fld.; cal. bell-shaped, teeth spiny; cor. deep blue, much longer than cal., tube broad, not hairy within. June. Mexico. 1858. (B.M. 5274; B.H. 1862, 10.) Greenhouse.

S. caeru'lea. Shrubby. *l.* roundish, with a truncate base, toothed all round. *fl.* violet. S. Africa. Probably not in cultivation. *S. caerulea* of B.M. 9178 is *S. ambigens.*

S. canarien'sis. Shrub up to 6 ft. h., stem white-woolly. *l.* lanceolate, hastate-triangular, almost smooth; bracts ovate-lanceolate, coloured. *fl.* in branched racemes, whorls about 6-fld., distinct but close; cal. bell-shaped, lips membranous, coloured; cor. purplish, hood curved. Canary Is. Greenhouse.

S. candelab'rum.* Sub-shrub, strongly aromatic, 3 to 4 ft. h., erect. *l.* oblong-lanceolate, rather blunt, 3 to 4 in. long, crenulate, loosely wrinkled, gland-dotted, hairy, stalked. *fl.* in an erect panicle with spreading branches each bearing a cyme of several fl.; cal. sharply ribbed, tinged purple; cor. white with pale-purple lines, 3 times as long as cal., hairy without; lower lip rich purple with white markings in throat. July. S. Spain. 1845. (B.M. 5017; F.d.S. 1344.) Half-hardy.

S. candidis'sima. Sub-shrub up to 3 ft. with ascending to erect branches. *l.* ovate-lanceolate, slender-pointed, about 3 in. long, heart-shaped at base, with rounded teeth, wrinkled, white-hairy; lower stalked, upper sessile; bracts shorter than pedicels, persistent. *fl.* in a much-branched panicle about 12 in. long; whorls 2-fld., about 1 in. apart, pedicels short; cal. bell-shaped, hairy; cor. white, about 3 times as long as cal., upper lip curved, flattened. Baghdad. 1804. Greenhouse. SYN. *S. odorata.*

S. cardua'cea.* Perennial, about 1 ft. h., stem stout, simple, naked above, leafy below. *l.* thistle-like, oblong, pinnatifid, loosely woolly beneath, lobes ovate, teeth spiny, slender; bracts overlapping, very spiny. *fl.* in a dense, many-fld. infl., whorls distant; cal. inflated, long-woolly; cor. lavender, 1 in. long, tube slightly exserted; upper lip toothed or fringed, 2-cleft; lower with small toothed lobes and a larger, deeply, many-cut mid-lobe. July. California. (B.M. 4874.) Alpine house or greenhouse.

S. carno'sa. Sub-shrub, much-branched evergreen, 1 to 2 ft. h. bark shredding, shoots hairy. *l.* obovate, ½ to 1½ in. long, blunt, entire, tapering to a short stalk; bracts orbiculate to obovate, downy, ciliate, tinged rose or purple. *fl.* in terminal panicles 6 in. or more long, in whorls; cal. ¼ in. long, 2-lipped, downy, tinged red; cor. blue, ½ in. or more long, lower lip ⅜ in. wide. Summer. NW. America. 1826. (B.R. 1469 as *Audibertia incana.*) Hardy.

S. clandesti'na. A variety of *S. Verbenaca.*

S. coccin'ea. Annual or perennial, about 2 ft. h., of variable hairiness. *l.* cordate or ovate, veiny, usually acute, with rounded teeth, usually softly hairy beneath; stalk slender. *fl.* in a twiggy raceme, clusters rather distant, few- or many-fld.; cal. lips half as long as tube; cor. deep scarlet, about 1 in. long, more or less hairy without, lower lip twice as long as upper. July. Cent. and S. America. 1772. Half-hardy or greenhouse. A variable species. var. **bi'color,** upper lip of cor. white, lower bright carmine-red; **lac'tea,** *fl.* white; **ma'jor,** sub-shrub up to 4½ ft. with larger bright scarlet-red fl.; **na'na,** bushy, much-branched; **na'na compac'ta,** more compact than var. *nana*; **pseu'do-cocci'nea,** up to 4 ft. h., stem, l.-stalks, and margins of bracts long-haired. Mexico. (B.M. 2864 as *S. pseudo-coccinea.*); **punic'ea,** *fl.* brighter red, more velvety, and closer, plant larger, more slender and flowering later than type; **splen'dens,** a synonym of var. *punicea.* Apt to be confused with *S. splendens* which has thinner l., is usually taller, with glabrous branches, &c.

Salvia carduacea

S. coeru'lea of Bentham. A synonym of *S. ambigens.*

S. col'orans. A synonym of *S. splendens.*

S. Columba'riae. Annual. Stem slender, 6 to 20 in. h. *l.* once or twice deeply pinnatifid or pinnatipartite, lobes oblong, more or less toothed, blunt, wrinkled; bracts broadly ovate, entire. *fl.* small in many-fld. heads; cal. naked within; cor. blue, scarcely longer than cal., upper lip 2-lobed at apex, lower lip with small later and larger 2-lobed mid-lobe. Summer. California. (B.M. 6595.) Half-hardy.

S. cya'nea. Shrubby. Branches 4-angled, sometimes hairy. *l.* ovate, long-pointed, toothed, hairy beneath, sometimes whitish-hairy; stalked; bracts ovate, deciduous. *fl.* in a simple somewhat 1-sided raceme; whorls loosely 6- to 10-fld.; cal. tubular, bluish, glandular-hairy; cor. blue, exserted, tube somewhat swollen. Mexico, Cent. America. Greenhouse.

S. cypria. Shrub of 3 to 5 ft. Stem with erect opposite branches, appressed grey-hairy. *l.* small, obtusely lobed, crenate; stalked. *fl.* violet with yellow spots in throat, in a glandular raceme. May. Cyprus. SYN. *S. triloba cypria.*

S. dichro'a.* Glandular-hairy perennial, 2 to 3 ft. h., little-branched. *Lower l.* oblong-ovate or ovate-lanceolate, 6 to 8 in. long, sinuately toothed with rounded lobules, hairy, narrowed to a stalk;

upper stem-l. sessile. *fl.* in a many-fld. raceme 1 ft. or more long; cal. ⅜ in. long; cor. 1¼ in. long, upper lip bright blue, hairy, arched, side lobes of lower lip pale blue, mid-lobe white, drooping. August. Atlas Mt. 1871. (B.M. 6004.) Half-hardy. Nearly related to *S. bicolor* and sometimes regarded as a variety of it. A var. **mag-nif'ica** with larger fl. is listed.

S. ele'gans. Perennial herb 3 to 4 ft. h., glabrous or nearly so. *l.* ovate, 1 to 1½ in. long, slender-pointed, toothed, more or less rounded at base, slightly hairy above, smooth beneath, stalked; bracts sessile. *fl.* in racemes 2 to 6 in. long, whorls remote, about 6-fld.; pedicels short; cal. short, bell-shaped, glandular-hairy; cor. blood-red, over 1 in. long. Summer. Mexico, Guatemala. (B.M. 6448.) Greenhouse.

S. farina'cea.* Perennial. Stems many, clustered, about 3 ft. h. *Lower l.* ovate-lanceolate or ovate, usually obtuse at base, toothed, on slender stalks; *upper* lanceolate or linear-lanceolate, sometimes entire; bracts awl-shaped or ovate-lanceolate. *fl.* in a spike-like raceme on a long, naked, interrupted peduncle, whorls densely many-fld.; cal. densely white-hairy, often tinged violet; cor. violet-blue, tube short, lower lip obcordate. Summer. Texas. 1847. (R.H. 1873, 90.) var. **al'ba,** *fl.* white. Nearly hardy. Best grown as half-hardy annual. var. **Blue Bedder** compact in habit, *fl.* deeper blue than in type.

S. fla'va megalan'tha. A synonym of *S. Bulleyana.*

S. ful'gens. Perennial shrub 2 to 3 ft. h., much-branched. *l.* ovate, 1 to 3 in. long, acute, with rounded teeth, heart-shaped at base, hairy above, white-hairy or woolly beneath. *fl.* showy, in racemes 6 to 12 in. long, whorls 6-fld., nearly 1 in. apart; cal. ½ to ⅝ in. long, tubular bell-shaped; cor. scarlet, nearly 2 in. long, hairy, tube exserted and swollen. July. Mexico. 1829. (B.R. 1355; L.B.C. 1910; S.B.F.G. s. 2, 59.) Greenhouse.

S. gesneriiflo'ra. Related to *S. fulgens,* 2–6 ft. but *fl.* more abundant and showy, upper lip of cor. flatter and less shaggy, tube longer, style less feathery. Colombia. 1840. (F.d.S. 2131; I.H. 1, 32.) Greenhouse.

S. glutino'sa. Jupiter's Distaff. Perennial, about 3 ft. h., erect. Stem hairy, glutinous. *l.* ovate-oblong, long-pointed, cordate-sagittate at base; lower often 7 to 8 in. long, upper smaller; bracts ovate, slender-pointed, shorter than cal. *fl.* in a simple raceme, whorls distant, loosely few-fld.; cal. tubular, ½ in. long; cor. pale yellow, about 1½ in. long, tube exserted, swollen. July. Europe and Cent. Asia. 1759. (S.B.F.G. 140 as *S. nubicola.*) Hardy.

S. Goudo'tii. Shrub of about 2 ft., branchlets sometimes reddish-hairy. *l.* ovate or ovate-lanceolate, about 3 in. long, slender-pointed, narrowed at base, teeth roundish, hairy. *fl.* in a simple, somewhat 1-sided raceme about 6 in. long; cal. tubular bell-shaped, about ½ in. long; cor. bright crimson, about 1 in. long, tube long-exserted, swollen above, lips nearly equal. Colombia. 1870. (Ref. B. 229.) Greenhouse.

S. Graham'ii. Shrub up to about 4 ft., shoots glabrous or nearly so. *l.* oval, obtuse, rounded or wedge-shaped at base, irregularly roundish-toothed, nearly glabrous; bracts ovate, slender-pointed, ciliate. *fl.* in racemes 1 ft. long or more; whorls 2-fld.; cal. often coloured, tubular, hairy; cor. deep crimson, becoming purplish, twice as long as cal., lower lip twice as long as hood. Mexico. 1829. (B.R. 1370; L.B.C. 1798.) Mexico. 1829.

S. grandiflo'ra. Shrub up to over 2 ft. h., stems white-woolly. *l.* ovate, acute, rounded or cordate at base, hairy, stalked; *lower l.* woolly beneath; bracts rather thin. *fl.* blue in little-branched racemes; whorls distinct, 6- to 10-fld.; cal. bell-shaped, coloured, roughly hairy. June, July. Asia Minor.

S. Greg'gii. Shrub about 3 ft. h. *l.* linear-oblong, blunt, 1 to 1½ in. long, narrowed to base, closely gland-dotted, dull pale green; stalk very short. *fl.* carmine in 6- to 8-fld. racemes about 2 in. long; cal. narrow bell-shaped, lips one-third to half as long as tube, nearly straight; cor. tube twice as long as cal., swollen in throat, contracted at mouth; lower lip large. Texas, Mexico. 1885. (B.M. 6812.) Greenhouse. var. **al'ba,** *fl.* white.

S. haemato'des.* More or less biennial. About 3 ft. h. *Lower l.* in a rosette, ovate with a cordate base, about 9 in. long, 6 in. wide, sinuate-crenate, rugose, almost glabrous above, hairy on veins beneath; stalk flattish, channelled, 4 in. long, hairy. *fl.* bluish-violet in 4- to 6-fld. whorls about 1 in. apart, forming large panicles, peduncles scarcely leafy, hairy; pedicels and bracts very short; cal. bell-shaped, ½ in. long, purplish on veins and teeth, hairy; cor. tube included, upper lip about ⅝ in. long, arching, hairy without. June to September. Greece. 1938.

S. hi'ans. Allied to *S. glutinosa.* Erect herbaceous perennial, softly hairy, about 2 ft. h. *l.* broadly ovate, heart-shaped, or broadly truncate at base, long-stalked; bracts ovate, shorter than cal. *fl.* showy, blue, in slightly branched racemes; whorls 6-fld.; cal. bell-shaped, bluish, clammy; cor. 3 times as long as cal., tube large, exserted, limb short, gaping. June. Kashmir. 1830. (B.M. 6517; B.R. 1841, 39.) Hardy. var. **plectranthifo'lia** has rather smaller, less hairy, fl. of a deeper violet than type.

S. hispan'ica. Annual, hairy, 1 to 2 ft. h. *l.* ovate, 2 to 4 in. long, slender-pointed, toothed; long-stalked; bracts ovate, longer than pedicels. *fl.* blue in spike-like racemes; whorls close, many-fld., pedicels short; cal. bell-shaped, hairy; cor. shortly exserted, glabrous, ⅓ to ½ in. long. July. W. Indies. 1739. (B.R. 359.) Hardy.

S. Hor'minum. Erect, hairy annual, about 18 in. h. *l.* oval-oblong, blunt, somewhat rounded at base, teeth rounded, hairy, stalked; bracts very broad, acute, persistent, uppermost coloured, rather longer than cal. *fl.* purple in unbranched racemes; whorls distant, about 6-fld.; cal. hairy; cor. 1½ times as long as cal. June to August. S. Europe. 1596. (F.G. 20.) Hardy. var. **al'ba,** bracts white; **Bluebeard,** a synonym of var. *violacea*; **Oxford Blue,** bracts very broad, Oxford blue; **purpu'rea,** bracts carmine-rose to bright purple with darker veins; **viola'cea,** bracts light violet-blue, large, veins darker; **vulga'ris,** bracts violet-blue, veins darker.

S. Ho'veyi of gardens. A synonym of *S. ianthina.*

S. ianthi'na. Perennial about 2 ft. h., downy. Stem erect. *l.* more or less ovate heart-shaped, long-pointed with rounded teeth, wrinkled, paler beneath. *fl.* large, deep violet-purple, clustered in 6-fld. whorls; bracts coloured, ovate; cor. nearly 3 times as long as cal., tube funnel-shaped, upper lip erect. June. Peru or Mexico? 1850. (F.d.S. 884 and G.C. 15 (1881), 145 as *S. Hoveyi.*) Greenhouse.

S. incarna'ta. A synonym of *S. elegans.*

S. interrup'ta. Clammy-downy more or less erect perennial, 3 to 4 ft. h. *l.* pinnatisect, 6 to 10 in. long, spreading, coarsely wrinkled above, white-hairy beneath; terminal lobe 2 to 3 in. long; oblong-ovate; side lobes distant. *fl.* dark violet-purple with a white throat, tube red-purple, in a raceme of numerous whorls 2 to 3 in. apart, 5- to 10-fld., nearly sessile; cal. ½ in. long, deeply grooved; cor. 1¼ in. long, 1 in. across, tube nearly straight. Morocco. 1867. (B.M. 5860; G.F. 1210.) Hardy or nearly so. *S. interrupta* of Sweet is *S. confusa.*

Salvia involucrata

S. involucra'ta. Sub-shrub attaining several ft. h., sparsely branched. *l.* ovate, 2 to 3 in. long, long-pointed, teeth rounded; stalked; bracts sessile, broadly ovate, coloured. *fl.* rose, in rather close 6-fld. whorls forming a spike-like raceme; pedicels as long as cal.; cal. often coloured, tubular bell-shaped, clammy; cor. long-exserted, 3 to 5 times as long as cal., tube swollen, lips nearly equal. August. Mexico. 1824. (B.M. 2872; B.R. 1205.) Greenhouse or hardy in favoured districts. var. **Bethel'lii,*** *l.* large, ovate heart-shaped, *fl.* bright rosy-crimson, in large spikes at ends of branches, in bud each whorl is surrounded by a pair of large coloured bracts. 1881. Of garden origin (G.C. 15 (1881), 49 as *S. Bethellii*); **Deschampsia'na,** 3 ft. h. or more, *fl.* bright rose, tube much swollen, raceme ovate, spike-like, cal. and the caducous bracts bright red. 1869. Raised in France.

S. japo'nica. Perennial, glabrous herb, about 18 in. h., stem hard, erect, branched. *l.* pinnatisect, 3 to 4 in. long or more, stalked, lobes ovate, long-pointed, toothed or pinnatifid; bracts lanceolate. *fl.* dark lilac in racemes 4 to 5 in. long, scarcely branched, whorls distinct, about 6-fld.; cal. tubular bell-shaped, striate; cor. tube scarcely exserted. Japan. var. **al'ba,** *fl.* white. Hardy.

S. Jurisic'ii. Herbaceous perennial, hairy, 8 to 16 in. h. *Lower l.* crenate, long-stalked; *upper* cut into linear segs., short-stalked.

fl. violet-blue, inverted, lower lip of 2 pet. with long violet-blue hairs. *infl.* branched, up to 8 in. long, whorls 2- to 7-fld., ⅛ to ⅜ in. apart at flowering, pedicels ⅛ in. long. June. Serbia. 1922 **A**

S. leucan'tha. Shrub of about 2 ft., branches woolly. *l.* narrow oblong-lanceolate, acute, wrinkled, almost glabrous above, downy beneath. *fl.* white and woolly, cal. covered with dense violet or lavender wool, paler beneath, in a long raceme, the rachis covered with violet wool, whorls 6- to 8-fld.; cal. ovate-cylindrical; cor. twice as long as cal., tube thick, curved upwards. Mexico. 1847. (B.M. 4318.) Greenhouse.

S. longisty'la. Erect perennial up to 14 or 15 ft. h., hairy. *l.* broad-ovate, 3 to 5½ in. long, slender-pointed, base broadly cordate, teeth rounded, softly hairy on both sides; bracts ovate, ciliate, deciduous. *fl.* red-pink, in a raceme 15 to 25 in. long; whorls 6- to 16-fld.; cal. long-tubular, striate at base, softly hairy, teeth long-bristly; cor. exserted, about 1 in. long. Mexico. (B.M. 8590.) Greenhouse.

S. lyra'ta. Root thick, perennial. Stem 8 to 24 in. h., little-branched, hairy. *Basal l.* lyrate, 2 to 3 in. long, coarsely toothed, rough-haired; *stem-l.* few, oblong-lanceolate, narrowed gradually to base. *fl.* blue-purple; in an interrupted, little-branched panicle; whorls loose, 6-fld., distant; cal. tubular bell-shaped, nodding, hairy; cor. about 1 in. long. May, June. United States. Hardy.

S. mexica'na mi'nor. Shrubby perennial up to 12 ft. h. Stem 4-angled, densely and finely hairy. *l.* ovate, often oblique, 3 to 5 in. long, upper much smaller, teeth minutely gland-tipped; stalk up to 2 in. long. *infl.* in terminal spikes up to 4 in. long. *fl.* rich violet-blue, about 1¼ in. long; tube long exserted, about as long as lip. February. Mexico. 1720. Related to *S. cyanea*. Tender.

S. Moorcroftia'na. Related to *S. argentea* but *l.* less cut and scarcely woolly above, lower *l.* about 12 in. long, cor. long, violet, hairy without, stamens long exserted, whorls 6-fld., remote, in a panicle. Himalaya.

S. nemoro'sa of gardens. A synonym of *S.* × *superba.*

S. neure'pia.* Sub-shrub up to 6 or 7 ft. h. related to *S. Grahami. l.* ovate, light green or yellowish-green, aromatic, 2 in. long, toothed except at rounded base, softly hairy beneath; stalk about 1 in. long. *fl.* clear carmine, large, lip flat; whorls 2-fld. August onwards. Mexico.

S. nubic'ola. A synonym of *S. glutinosa.*

S. nu'tans. Herbaceous perennial, 2 to 3 ft. h. Stem hairy, nearly simple. *l.* ovate-oblong, 4 to 5 in. long, doubly toothed, wrinkled, long-stalked; bracts minute, roundish. *fl.* violet, drooping, in spike-like racemes 1 to 1½ in. long, peduncles long; whorls close, about 6-fld.; cal. scarcely ⅙ in. long; cor. about ⅓ in. long, hood straight, spreading. July. E. Europe. 1780. (B.M. 2436.) Hardy.

S. odora'ta. A synonym of *S. candidissima.*

S. officina'lis.* Common Sage. Shrub about 1 ft. h. Stem white-woolly. *l.* oblong, 1 to 1½ in. long, rounded or narrowed to a stalk, entire, wrinkled; lower more or less woolly on both sides or only beneath; bracts ovate, slender-pointed, sessile. *fl.* purple, blue, or white, in a nearly simple raceme with few dense 10- to 20-fld. whorls; cal. about ½ in. long, bell-shaped, hairy; cor. nearly 1 in. long. June. S. Europe, &c. 1597. Hardy. Long grown as a sweet-herb, *see* **Sage.** Variable. var. **albiflo'ra,** *l.* 3 to 4 times as long as wide, *fl.* white; **au'rea,** habit compact, *l.* golden-yellow; **cris'pa,** *l.* broad, crisped, variegated; **icteri'na,** *l.* variegated green and gold; **latifo'lia,** *l.* twice as long as wide; **Mil'leri,** *l.* reddish, spotted; **purpuras'cens** (Purple Sage), *l.* reddish-purple, a useful bedding plant; **purpu'rea,** *see* var. **purpurascens; rubriflo'ra,** *l.* 3 to 4 times as long as wide, *fl.* red; **salicifo'lia,** *l.* 4 to 7 times as long as wide; **sturni'na,** *l.* variegated green and white; **tenu'ior,** *l.* about 3 to 4 times as long as wide, *fl.* blue; **tric'olor,** *l.* grey-green, veined yellowish-white, and pink, becoming pink or red.

S. pa'tens.* Perennial about 30 in. h. Stem erect, hairy. *l.* ovate-deltoid, with rounded teeth, rough-haired, base variable, stalked; bracts linear-lanceolate. *fl.* blue in a few remote whorls; cal. bell-shaped, ½ in. or more long; cor. 2 in. long or more, tube broad, lips slightly gaping. September. Mexico. 1838. (B.M. 3808; B.R. 25, 23.) Half-hardy. var. **al'ba,** *fl.* white; **Cambridge Blue,** *fl.* pale Cambridge blue.

S. Pit'cheri. A synonym of *S. azurea grandiflora.*

S. Pithier'i of gardens. A synonym of *S. blepharophylla.*

S. praten'sis. Perennial of 2 ft. h. or more. *l.* oblong or ovate, blunt, 3 to 6 in. long, sometimes 2-lobed at base, with large irregular crenatures, wrinkled; stem-l. few, smaller with shorter stalks. *fl.* bright blue, in spikes up to 18 in. long, whorls 4-fld.; cal. (and bracts) coloured; cor. about 1 in. long, glabrous within, upper lip long, much-arched, lower broad. June to August. Europe, including Britain. (E.B. 1058; S.B.F.G. 26 as *S. Tenorii.*) Hardy. Variable. var. **al'ba,** *fl.* white; **atroviola'cea,** *fl.* dark violet; **Baumgar'tenii,** *fl.* violet; **lupinoi'des,** *fl.* bluish-purple and white; **ro'sea,** *fl.* rosy-purple; **rubicun'da,** *fl.* rose-red; **Tenor'ii,** *fl.* deep blue, very free; **variega'ta,** *fl.* light blue, mid-lobe of lower lip white.

S. Przewal'skii. Herbaceous perennial, with ascending stems, 3 to 5 ft. h., hairy, glandular above. *Basal l.* oblong-heart-shaped, acute, hoary-haired beneath, with rounded teeth, long-stalked; *stem-l.* hastate heart-shaped, acute. *fl.* violet in branching spike-like racemes, the whorls distant, about 2-fld.; cal. bell-shaped, striate, glandular-hairy, teeth acute, short; cor. tube long-exserted. June. China. Hardy.

S. pseudo-coccin'ea. A variety of *S. coccinea.*

S. rin'gens. Shrub about 18 in. h. *l.* pinnatisect, segs. unequal, ovate-oblong, rounded at base, hairy; bracts deciduous. *fl.* reddish-purple in remote, loose, 6-fld. whorls; cal. striate; cor. 4 times as long as cal., tube swollen, recurved, upper lip erect, more or less curved, lower large with reflexed lobes. Summer. Greece. (G.F. 59; S.F.G. 18.) Hardy.

S. Roemeria'na. Perennial of 1 to 2 ft., often slightly hairy below. *l.* or terminal lflet. roundish or heart-kidney-shaped, coarsely repand- or crenate-toothed; lower l. often with 2 or 3 similar or smaller lateral lflets.; bracts usually shorter than pedicels. *fl.* deep scarlet, in long, loose racemes; cal. somewhat hairy, naked within; cor. downy, 1 in. or more long, narrow tubular funnel-shaped, somewhat arched. July. Texas. 1852. (F.d.S. 1080 as *S. porphyrantha*; B.M. 4939 as *S. porphyratra.*) Greenhouse. (The name *S. Roemeriana* is sometimes applied to *S. coccinea major.*)

S. Roez'lii. A synonym of *S. Sessei.*

S. rubes'cens. Shrub of about 18 in. h. Stems 4-angled. *l.* ovate-cordate, 4 to 10 in. long, crenate, acute or long-pointed, downy above, hoary beneath, long-stalked. *fl.* scarlet in a panicle 1 ft. or more long, without bracts; whorls 4- to 8-fld., distant; cal. purple-brown, ½ in. long, densely glandular-hairy; cor. twice as long as cal., tube somewhat ascending. Colombia. 1872. (B.M. 5947.) Stove.

S. ru'tilans. Pine-apple-scented Sage. Sub-shrubby, 2 to 3 ft. h. *l.* cordate-ovate, acute, softly downy. *fl.* bright scarlet in a leafy panicle of spike-like racemes; cor. tube slender, lower lip deflexed. Summer. Habitat? (G.C. 15 (1881), 117.) Greenhouse.

S. scabiosifo'lia. Diffuse perennial with woolly stems 1 to 1½ ft. long, leafy. *l.* pinnatisect, segs. in 3 to 5 pairs, often ternate or twin, entire or pinnatisect, oblong or linear, acute. *fl.* whitish in racemes 4 to 6 in. long; whorls 6- to 10-fld., distinct; cal. large, bell-shaped, hairy; cor. twice as long as cal., upper lip 2-fid. August, Tauria. 1818. (B.M. 5209; 1429 as *S. Hablitziana.*)

S. Scla'rea.* Clary. Biennial, 2 to 3 ft. h. with a clammy-hairy, erect stem. *l.* ovate, often 8 to 9 in. long, irregularly crenate at base, wrinkled, sometimes hoary-stalked; stem-l. stem-clasping; bracts coloured, very broad concave, slender-pointed. *fl.* bluish-white in a panicle of distant 6-fld. whorls; cal. whitish at base, bell-shaped, rough-haired; cor. twice as long as cal., tube contracted, upper lip curved and compressed. August. Europe. (B.M. 2320 as *S. bracteata*; B.R. 1003 as *S. Simsiana.*) Hardy. var. **turkesta'nica,*** stems 4-angled, tinged pink, *fl.* white, tinged pink. The true *S. bracteata* is a smaller plant with purplish fl., native of W. Asia.

S. Ses'sei. Sub-shrub about 18 in. h., branches nearly smooth. *l.* broadly ovate or ovate-oblong, slender-pointed, base variable; stalked; bracts smaller, deciduous. *fl.* scarlet in a short, loose panicle, its whorls few-fld.; cal. inflated, bell-shaped, scarlet, glabrous; cor. nearly 2 in. long, downy. Summer. Mexico. (F.d.S. 1407 as *S. Roezlii.*) Greenhouse.

S. Simsia'na. A synonym of *S. Sclarea.*

S. Sou'lei. A synonym of *S. brevilabra.*

S. spatha'cea. Stem glandular, roughly hairy. *Lower l.* hastate, 3 to 8 in. long, blunt, coarse, woolly beneath. *fl.* in dense clusters; cor. red or purplish, 1 to 1½ in. long. California. Reputed a good bee plant. SYN. *Audibertia grandiflora.*

S. splen'dens.* Scarlet Sage. Sub-shrub up to 3 ft. h., with glabrous branches. *l.* ovate, long-pointed, with rounded teeth, base variable, glabrous, stalked, bracts coloured, deciduous. *fl.* scarlet in a spike-like raceme about 6 in. long, its whorls 2-fld.; cal. coloured, bell-shaped, with 3 broad-ovate teeth; cor. 2 to 2½ in. long, glabrous, tube exserted and somewhat enlarged, lower lip short. Summer onwards. Brazil. 1822. (B.R. 687; L.B.C. 1889; I.H. 432 as *S. brasiliensis.*) Best grown as a half-hardy annual. Excellent for bedding out. A variable species. var. **al'ba,** *fl.* white; **atropurpu'rea,** *fl.* dark violet-purple; **atrosanguin'ea,** *fl.* dark crimson; **bi'color,** *fl.* scarlet and white; **Bruan'tii,** dwarfer than type, *fl.* very bright scarlet. (Gn. 21, 328.); **compac'ta,** dwarfer with denser racemes and bright scarlet *fl.*; there is a white form of this and one with dark-scarlet *fl.*; **grandiflo'ra,** tall with larger *fl.*; **Issan'chon,** *fl.* with white cal., cor. striped red and rose-white, and habit of var. *compacta*; **na'na,** dwarf, *fl.* bright red; **semperflo'rens,** *fl.* continuously; **Souchet'ii,** much like var. *compacta*, with a white variant; **viola'cea,** *fl.* purplish.

S. × **super'ba*** (? *S. sylvestris* × *S. villicaulis*). Perennial herb with numerous branching stems about 3 ft. h., branches twiggy, 4-angled, softly hairy. *l.* ovate-oblong, up to 3 in. long but mostly smaller, rounded at base, toothed, finely rugose, minutely hairy beneath; sessile or nearly so. *fl.* blue-purple in stiffly erect spikes up to 8 in. or more long, with close whorls; bracts red and still conspicuous after fl. fall. Origin unknown. 1900? (B.M. 9169; R.H. 1913, 471 as *S. nemorosa.*) SYN. *S. sylvestris superba, S. virgata nemorosa.* Hardy.

S. sylves'tris. Perennial of 6 in. to 3 ft. h. *l.* oblong-lanceolate, rounded or cordate at base, 2 to 4 in. long, pale green and downy or hoary beneath, lower stalked, upper sessile. *fl.* purplish-violet in long, somewhat branched long racemes, lower whorls about ½ in. apart, 6- to 12-fld. August, S. Europe, Asia Minor. 1759. Hardy. **al'ba,** *fl.* white; **super'ba,** a synonym of *S.* × *superba.*

S. taraxacifo'lia. Perennial with many ascending or erect stems 6 to 18 in. h. *l.* pinnatisect, 2 to 4 in. h., sometimes sessile; lower lobes few or many; terminal 1 to 1½ in. long, ovate, blunt or cuspidate, irregularly wavy-toothed; snowy-hairy beneath, bracts sessile, ovate, with a terminal bristle. *fl.* pale pink with a yellowish disk on lower lip and a purple-speckled hairy palate in a raceme of 6- to 10-fld. whorls; pedicels very short; cal. ½ in. long, teeth bristle-tipped. July, Morocco. 1872. (B.M. 5991.)

S. Teno'rii. A variety of *S. pratensis.*

S. tiliifo'lia. Herbaceous perennial with slender, erect, slightly hairy stems. *l.* widely ovate, 1 to 3 in. long. *fl.* blue, cor. scarcely longer than cal.; raceme simple, 2 to 3 in. long. Mexico.

S. turkista'nica. A variety of *S. Sclarea.*

Salvia uliginosa

S. uligino'sa.* Perennial herb up to 8 ft., usually much less. Stem branched, bluntly 4-angled, grooved, appressed-hairy. *l.* oblong-lanceolate, up to 3½ in. long, smaller in upper part of stem, deeply toothed, glabrous above, somewhat hairy and black-dotted beneath; lower stalked, upper sessile. *fl.* blue, about ⅝ in. long, tube very narrow at base; infl. branched, racemes spike-like up to over 4 in. long, lateral shorter; whorls 7 to 20-fld., the ciliate bracts soon falling. Summer. Eastern S. America, Brazil to Uruguay. 1912. (B.M. 8544.) Hardy, except in cold localities.

S. verbascifo'lia. Perennial with an erect, clammy-hairy stem. *l.* broadly ovate, wavy-lobed, irregularly toothed, cordate at base, much-wrinkled, thick, scarcely woolly above, white woolly beneath; bracts very wide, concave, persistent, long-haired. *fl.* white, covered with blue hairs in a twiggy panicle with 2- to 6-fld. whorls, distinct but close, the uppermost abortive; cal. bell-shaped, striate, clammy-hairy; cor. with a very large curved hood. Caucasus. Hardy.

S. Verbena'ca. Vervain; Wild Clary. Perennial, with a leafy, erect stem, 1 to 2 ft. h. *Basal l.* oblong, 2 to 4 in. long, wrinkled, blunt, irregularly toothed, stalked; *upper l.* oblong or deltoid-ovate, sessile. *fl.* blue-purple in long bracteate spikes, whorls 6-fld.; cal. bell-shaped, upper lip with minute spiny teeth; cor. about ½ in. long, upper lip short, compressed. June to September. Europe, including Britain, W. Asia. (E.B. 1056.) Hardy. var. **clandesti'na,** smaller and more slender than type with narrower *l.*, less spiny cal. teeth, and longer *fl.* Channel Is. (E.B. 1057.) SYN. *S. clandestina.*

S. verticilla'ta. Herbaceous perennial of 2 to 3 ft. Stems erect, rough-haired. *l.* lyrate with a cordate base, uppermost lobe the largest, ovate-rotund, margin sinuate-crenate, rough-hairy or woolly on both surfaces. *fl.* lilac-blue in distant whorls of 20 to 40 fl.; cal. hairy; cor. tube included. July, August. Europe, Asia Minor, Caucasus. Hardy.

S. virga'ta. Herbaceous perennial of 2 ft. h. or more. Stems branched, long-haired. *Basal l.* broad-ovate, cordate at base, stalked; *higher l.* oblong to cordate with shorter stalks, *uppermost* stem-clasping; all irregularly toothed, slightly hairy above, hairy or hispid on veins beneath. *fl.* light blue in long, branched racemes with a few distant 6-fld. whorls, pedicels short; cal. bell-shaped, striate, clammy-hairy; cor. tube included. E. Mediterranean region. Hardy. var. **al'ba,** *fl.* white; **nemoro'sa,** a synonym of *S.* × *superba.*

S. visco'sa. Herbaceous perennial, erect, clammy-hairy. *l.* ovate, almost entire, lower 8 in. long, stem-l. 3 to 4 in. long, uppermost much smaller, all rugose. *fl.* blue, ¾ in. long, glabrous without. Italy.

S. yunnanen'sis. Herbaceous perennial about 1 ft. h. with fusiform tubers on creeping rhizomes. *l.* oblong, 1½ to 3 in. long, with rounded teeth, green above, purple beneath. *fl.* cobalt-blue in simple spikes, the whorls 4- to 6-fld.; cal. glandular; cor. about 1 in. long, hairy outside. China. Hardy.

salviifo'lius -a -um, having Salvia-like leaves.

SALVIN'IA (named in honour of Antonio Maria Salvini, 1633–1729, Professor of Greek at Florence). FAM. *Salviniaceae.* A genus of about 10 species found floating on still water (like *Lemna*), widely dispersed over the N. Hemisphere, and in Trop. and S. America. *S. natans* is a pretty little floating aquatic, which, like Azolla, is suitable for a stove, greenhouse, or indoor aquarium, is easily managed in summer, simply requiring to be let alone or have its water changed, if necessary, but is often lost in winter. The mature plant floats on the water, has no true roots, a row of divided leaves on the under side looking like roots assuming their functions. Among these the sporangia are developed, and from them the plant must be grown annually, as the old plants die in the winter. The best way to preserve the spores is to half-fill a broad pan with sandy loam, and then fill up with water; when the water has cleared, put a number of the plants upon it and stand the pan in a cool greenhouse. In winter the plants will die, but the spores will remain in the loam, which must not become dry, and the next spring they will reproduce the plant.

S. na'tans. *fr.* globular bags, composed of a double membrane, at length bursting irregularly. *l.* sub-elliptic, entire, floating, not circinate when young. *rhiz.* floating, thread-like, leafy above, with long root-like l. and fruit on short, leafless branches below. The young plant closely resembles a young Selaginella, apart from the 2 cotyledon-like processes.

SALVINIA'CEAE. A family of 2 genera with about 16 species allied to Marsileaceae and the ferns, all floating plants. The sporangia are in a sorus which is enclosed in a sporocarp, developed in Azolla from the lobe of an ordinary leaf and in Salvinia from a submerged leaf. The sporocarps contain either microsporangia (male) or macrosporangia (female). When mature the spores are shed and sink where they germinate, producing minute male (1-celled) prothallia with an antheridum or small female prothallia which remain enclosed in the burst spore, the subsequent development being like that of ferns. Both genera are in cultivation: Azolla, Salvinia.

salviodo'rus -a -um, Sage-scented.

Salzman'nii, in honour of Philipp Salzmann, 1781–1851, of Montpellier, who botanized in Brazil, 1827–30, Spain, N. Africa, and south France.

Sam'an, native name in S. America.

SAMA'NEA. Included in **Pithecellobium.**

SAMARA. An indehiscent fruit with a wing on back or end, as in Maple.

samarangen'sis -is -e, of Samarang, north coast of Java.

Sam'bac, Persian name for plant.

sambuci'nus -a -um, having the scent of Elder.

SAMBU'CUS (old Latin name of the Elder). FAM. *Caprifoliaceae.* Elder. A genus of about 20 herbs or deciduous shrubs or small trees with opposite, odd-pinnate leaves with toothed leaflets, regular, usually white or creamy-white flowers with parts in fives and a rotate corolla, fruits a 3- to 5-seeded berry. They are found in temperate and sub-tropical regions of both hemispheres. A moist loamy soil suits these plants best and though they will put up with some shade their value is only seen when in a sunny place. The herbaceous species can be propagated by division, the shrubby ones by cuttings of bare shoots in autumn in the open ground, or of half-ripe shoots with a heel in sandy soil in frames. Several varieties of *S. nigra* and other species have been selected for their ornamental foliage and these should be pruned in late autumn or early spring before growth begins. The following species are hardy.

KEY

1.	*Herbaceous perennial*	S. Ebulus
1.	*Deciduous shrub*	2
2.	*Infl. flattish umbel-like*	3
2.	*Infl. paniculate*	6
3.	*Fr. grey with mealy bloom*	4
3.	*Fr. not grey*	5
4.	*Foliage glabrous*	S. caerulea
4.	*Foliage densely downy*	S. velutina
5.	*Lflets. usually 5, fr. normally black*	S. nigra
5.	*Lflets. usually 7, fr. normally dark purple*	S. canadensis
6.	*Fr. black*	S. melanocarpa
6.	*Fr. red or yellow*	7
7.	*Plant glabrous*	8
7.	*Plant more or less hairy*	9
8.	*Infl. compact; lflets. 5 to 7, coarsely toothed*	S. racemosa
8.	*Infl. rather loose; lflets. 7 or more, finely toothed*	S. Sieboldii
9.	*Infl. nearly hemispherical; l. hairy on midrib*	S. callicarpa
9.	*Infl. taller than broad; l. finely downy when young*	S. pubens

S. au'rea. A synonym of *S. nigra aurea.*

S. caeru'lea. Shrub of 5 to 10 ft., much larger wild, with smooth, somewhat glaucous, young shoots. *lflets.* usually 5 or 7, 2½ to 6 in. long, oblong, coarsely toothed, bright green. *fl.* yellowish-white, cymes convex, 4 to 6 in. across. June, July. *fr.* blue-black, densely covered with bloom. Western N. America. 1850. (S.S. 222.) var. **veluti'na,** a synonym of *S. velutina.*

S. califor'nica. A synonym of *S. velutina.*

S. callicar'pa. Shrub of 6 ft. *lflets.* 5 or 7, 2 to 4 in. long, sharply toothed, slender-pointed, hairy on midrib. *fl.* whitish, cymes hemispherical, about 3 in. across. June, July. *fr.* scarlet. California, Oregon. 1900.

S. canaden'sis. Shrub up to 12 ft., young branches smooth. *lflets.* usually 7 (5 to 11), oval, 2 to 6 in. long, sharply toothed, bright green, slightly downy beneath, slender-pointed, lowest often lobed. *fl.* white in convex umbels 4 to 8 in. across. July. *fr.* purple-black. Canada, E. United States. 1761. var. **au'rea,** *l.* golden-yellow, *fr.* cherry-red; **chlorocar'pa,** *fr.* greenish, *l.* pale green; **lacinia'ta,*** *l.* much-divided, lower lflets. pinnatifid, a graceful form; **max'ima,*** very vigorous, *l.* up to 18 in. long, lflets. often 11, cymes up to 18 in. across. SYN. *S. pubens maxima.*

S. Eb'ulus. Herbaceous perennial, 2 to 4 ft. h., stem stout, grooved. *lflets.* 9 to 13, oblong-lanceolate, 4 to 6 in. long, toothed. *fl.* white, tipped pink, in corymbs 3 to 4 in. across. July, August. *fr.* black. Europe, including Britain, N. Africa. (E.B. 638.) A plant for rough banks, &c.

S. lacinia'ta. A variety of *S. racemosa.*

S. melanocar'pa. Shrub up to 12 ft. *lflets.* 5 or 7, oblong-lanceolate, 3 to 6 in. long, with long slender point, coarsely toothed, dark green, hairy below when young. *fl.* yellowish-white, cyme rounded, 2 to 3 in. across. July, August. *fr.* black. Western N. America. 1894.

S. ni'gra. Shrub or tree to 30 ft., young branches smooth, lenticels conspicuous. *lflets.* usually 5 (3 to 7), ovate, 1½ to 5 in. long, sharply toothed, almost smooth. *fl.* yellowish or dull white, in flat cymes, 5 to 8 in. across, odour heavy. June. *fr.* shining black. Europe, including Britain. (B.M. 137; E.B. 637.) Many varieties have arisen, including **al'ba,** with white fruit; **albo-variega'ta,** *l.* bordered creamy-white; **argentea variega'ta,** a synonym of var. *albo-variegata*; **aurea-variega'ta,** *l.* variegated yellow; **au'rea,*** *l.* golden-yellow; **chlorocar'pa,** *see* **alba; flo're ple'no,** pet. 10, there is a rose-tinted form of this, **ros'eo flo're ple'no; fruc'tu-al'bo,** *see* **alba** *and* **viridis; heterophyl'la,** parts of l. reduced to midrib only; **lacinia'ta,*** *lflets.* deeply and regularly divided, of this there is a variegated form; **leucocar'pa,** *see* var. **viridis; macula'ta au'rea,** *l.* spotted yellow; **pen'dula,** branches weeping; **pulveru-lent'a alba,** *l.* spotted white; **pyramid'alis,** branches stiffly upright; **rotundifo'lia,** *lflets.* broader and rounder, usually 3; **vi'ridis,** with greenish *fr.*

S. pu'bens. Shrub up to 12 ft. or more, very similar to *S. racemosa* but shoots, l., and fl.-stalks downy, the W. American form, however, being nearly glabrous leaving the somewhat looser infl. with spreading instead of reflexed branches the main distinction. N. America. 1812. var. **leucocar'pa** has white *fr.*; **xanthocar'pa,** golden-yellow *fr.*; var. **max'ima,** *see* **S. canadensis,** it does not belong here.

S. racemo'sa. Shrub, 8 to 10 ft. h., young shoots smooth. *lflets.* 5, oval or ovate, 2 to 4 in. long, slender-pointed, sharply toothed. *fl.* yellowish-white in panicles 1½ to 3 in. h. April. *fr.* scarlet, ripening June and July. Europe, Asia Minor to N. China. Long cultivated. Unfortunately rarely fruits freely. Many varieties have arisen, including **lacinia'ta,** *l.* regular and deeply cut, divisions about $\frac{1}{12}$ in. wide; **lacinia'ta au'rea,** *see* var. **plumo'sa aurea; plumo'sa,** *lflets.* cut to about half-way to midrib, up to 5 in. long, the form **serratifo'lia,** a synonym of var. *laciniata*; **plumo'sa au'rea*** being golden-yellow; **purpu'rea,** *fl.* rosy without; **specta'bilis,** *fl.* whiter than type; **tenuifo'lia,** *lflets.* divided to midrib into long narrow segs., purplish when unfolding.

S. Siebold'ii. Shrub up to 18 ft. h., shoots smooth. *lflets.* usually 7 (to 11), oblong, or oblong-lanceolate, 2 to 8 in. long, slender-pointed, finely toothed. *fl.* yellowish-white in ovoid panicles about 3 in. long. April, May. *fr.* scarlet. Japan, China. 1907.

S. xanthocar'pa. A variety of *S. pubens.*

SAMBUL PLANT. *See* **Ferula Sumbul.**

sa'mius -a -um, of the Isle of Samos.

samoen'sis, of Samoa.

SAM'OLUS (name used by Pliny). FAM. *Primulaceae.* A genus of 9 species, *S. Valerandi* being cosmopolitan, 2 N. American, the others natives of temperate parts of the S. Hemisphere. Herbs sometimes woody at the base. Leaves alternate, rarely forming a loose basal rosette, linear to spatulate, entire. Flowers in terminal racemes or corymbs, small, white; corolla 5-lobed; stamens 5 with 5 staminodes alternating; ovary half-inferior; seeds many. Of little horticultural merit. The 2 species mentioned grow well in ordinary soil in a moist place and may be increased by seed or by division.

S. re'pens. Erect or sometimes ascending, more or less woody at base; stem 6 to 12 in. covered with glands. *l.* linear to spatulate-ovate, *fl.* about ⅓ in. across in a terminal corymb, pinkish-white. Australia, S. America. 1806. (L.B.C. 435 as *S. littoralis.*) Hardy.

S. Valeran'di. Erect herb, 4 to 12 in. h., with several stems from base. *l.* ovate or oblong-ovate, basal stalked, cauline, almost sessile. *fl.* small, white, in a raceme; staminodes as long as stamens. Cosmopolitan, including Britain. (E.B. 1151.)

SAMPHIRE (*Crithmum maritimum*). A perennial native of cliffs near the sea-coast, the succulent leaves of which are occasionally used in salads and pickled as a condiment. It is the plant of Shakespeare's 'Samphire-gatherer's fearful trade'. It is not readily cultivated away from the sea-coast. It needs a warm spot, as under a south wall, and protection in winter, and a well-drained soil. Seed should be sown as soon as ripe in autumn.

SAMPHIRE, GOLDEN. *See* **Inula.**

SAMPHIRE, MARSH. *See* **Salicornia** sp.

Samp'sonii, in honour of Thomas Sampson, 1831–97, consul in S. China.

SAN JOSÉ SCALE, *Aspidiotus perniciosus,* is the most notorious Scale insect, being practically cosmopolitan in its distribution and attacking a wide range of forest, fruit, and ornamental trees. Though imported into this country on fruit and plants from time to time, it has never become established in the British Is. It is considered the most injurious orchard pest in many American States, having been introduced into California about 1870 on some flowering Peach trees from China.

SANCHEZ'IA (in honour of Josef Sanchez, Professor of Botany, Cadiz). FAM. *Acanthaceae.* A genus of about 10 species of handsome perennial herbs or sub-shrubs, natives of Trop. America. Stems erect. Leaves opposite, large, entire or almost so. Flowers sessile in axils of bracts or shortly stalked and clustered, or rarely solitary; calyx deeply 5-cut; corolla tube long; cylindrical or slightly swollen above the middle, lobes 5, spreading, rounded, bracts sometimes large, forming a cup, sometimes narrow or small; bracteoles resembling calyx segments. Handsome flowering and foliage plants requiring similar cultivation to Barleria.

S. longiflo'ra. Sub-shrub, stems 4-angled. *l.* oblong to lanceolate, large. *fl.*, pedicels, and panicle branches rich wine-purple in long, drooping panicles; cor. tube about 2 in. long. April. Guayaquil. 1866. (B.M. 5588 as *Ancylogyne longiflora.*)

Sanchezia nobilis

S. nob'ilis. Sub-shrub, 1 to 3 ft. h. *l.* oblong to lanceolate, up to 9 in. long, slender-pointed, teeth blunt, narrowed to broadly winged stalk, connate at base. *fl.* yellow, 2 in. long, in an erect, terminal densely fld. panicle with purple branches; bracts bright red, 1 to 1½ in. long, each with 8 to 10 fls. in its axil. June. Ecuador. 1866. (B.M. 5594; F.d.S. 2437.) var. **glaucophyl'la,** *l.* glaucous green, striped white or yellow. (I.H. 580.) SYN. *S. nobilis variegata.* A handsome foliage plant.

S. parvibractea'ta. Allied to *S. nobilis* but petioles not winged, bracts smaller. *fl.* fewer, staminodes larger. Trop. S. America.

Sancti-Johan'nis, in honour of St. Ivan Rilski, the patron saint of the Rila monastery, the largest in Bulgaria.

sanc'tus -a -um, sacred.

SAND. Sand consists of small pieces of quartz, the crystalline form of silica, found in the primitive rocks and set free by weathering of these or their derivative sandstones. At first-weathering the grains are angular, but by rubbing over one another through the action of wind or running water they become more or less rounded and etched. They vary in size, the fraction of the soil reckoned as sand in soil analysis consisting of particles from $\frac{1}{80}$ to $\frac{1}{25}$ in. in diameter. Pure sand is almost insoluble in water, but sand as found in nature usually includes tiny particles of other minerals, and the finer the sand usually the greater the proportion of other minerals. The main characteristic of sand is that its particles fail to cohere when dry. Sand, if pure, provides no nutrient for plants. It is, nevertheless, an essential ingredient of potting composts (*see* **Composts**) for it helps to keep the soil open and to ensure drainage away of surplus water and circulation of air in the soil. Clean, sharp sand is also an excellent medium in which to root cuttings of many plants, though as the sand contains no nutrient the rooted cuttings need to be moved on into soil soon after the roots are formed. Silver sand contains little iron, the presence of which often colours river- or sea-sand. Sand suitable for potting composts contains some particles larger than those constituting sand in the analytical sense, particles which would fall into the category of fine gravel, up to about ⅛ in. diameter.

SAND LEEK. *See* **Allium Scordoprasum.**

SAND MYRTLE. *See* **Leiophyllum.**

SAND PEAR. *See* **Pyrus pyrifolia.**

SAND VERBENA. *See* **Abronia latifolia.**

SANDAL-TREE. *See* **Sandoricum indicum.**

SANDAL-WOOD. *See* **Santalum album.**

SANDAL-WOOD, FALSE. *See* **Ximenia americana.**

SANDARACH GUM-TREE. *See* **Tetraclinis articulata.**

SANDBOX TREE. *See* **Hura crepitans.**

Sandemania'nus -a -um, in honour of Mr. Sandeman, who collected in S. America.

San'derae, San'deri, -ianus -a -um, in honour of members of the Sander family, nurserymen of St. Albans and Bruges. (Henry F. C. Sander, 1847–1920.)

SANDERA'RA (*see above*). FAM. *Orchidaceae.* Hybrids combining species of Brassia, Cochlioda, and Odontoglossum.

SANDERSON'IA (in honour of John Sanderson, 1820?–81, Hon. Secretary of the Hort. Soc. of Natal). FAM. *Liliaceae.* Related to Gloriosa but with more or less erect stems with axillary urn-shaped-globose orange flowers. For cultivation *see* **Gloriosa.**

S. auranti'aca. About 18 in. h. *l.* lanceolate, sometimes with a cirrhose point, upper stem-l. and floral l. similar or the uppermost smaller. *fl.* orange, showy, nodding on axillary, solitary pedicels, without bracts; perianth persistent, urn-shaped-globose, slightly inflated, shortly 6-lobed, and with 6 short nectariferous spurs at base; stamens much shorter than the perianth. Natal. 1852. (B.M. 4716.)

SANDFLY BUSH. *See* **Zieria Smithii.**

SANDOR'ICUM (from *Santoor*, Malayan name of genus). FAM. *Meliaceae.* A genus of about 10 species of evergreen, glabrous (sometimes downy) trees natives of the Moluccas. Leaves 3-foliolate; leaflets large, nerved.

Flowers yellow, few or clustered, bracteate; calyx cup-like, lobes 5, short, overlapping; petals 5, free, overlapping; panicles axillary. Fruit yellow, somewhat like a small orange, fleshy, sweetish, acid, edible. *S. indicum* is cultivated in the tropics. It needs stove conditions and a compost of loam and peat. Propagated by cuttings in sand, under a glass, in heat.

Sandersonia aurantiaca (p. 1862)

S. ind'icum. Sandal-tree. Tall tree. *lflets.* ovate-oblong, entire, downy. *fl.* in axillary panicles. *fr.* agreeably acid, containing 5 ovate-compressed nuts. 1820.

F. G. P.

sandwicen'sis -is -e, of the Sandwich Is.

SANDWORT. *See* **Arenaria.**

sangia'nus -a -um, of the Island of Sangian, Sonda Straits.

SANGUINAIRE PLANT. *See* **Paronychia argentea.**

sanguina'lis -is -e, blood-red.

SANGUINAR'IA (*sanguis*, blood, all parts of the plant have copious orange-red sap). FAM. *Papaveraceae.* A genus of a single, low-growing N. American herb with a long, thick, horizontal rootstock. Leaves usually one from each bud on the rootstock, more or less heart-shaped, stalk about 6 in. long. Flowers solitary; sepals 2, quickly shed; petals 8 to 12, oblong or obovate. *S. canadensis* is a beautiful spring-flowering plant, growing best in rather sandy soil, but not very particular so long as the soil is not water-logged. It thrives either in sun or shade and is excellent for planting under deciduous trees and even in grass if the grass is cut before the leaves fade. Its white flowers open before the blue-grey leaves are fully expanded. It is propagated by division and is best transplanted in August just after the leaves ripen.

Sanguinaria canadensis

S. canaden'sis.* Bloodroot; Red Puccoon. *l.* heart- or kidney-shaped, lobed or scalloped, blue-grey above, smooth beneath. *fl.* white, about 3 in. across; stamens many; peduncles up to 6 in. long. April. Eastern N. America. 1680. (B.M. 162.) A variable species. var. **grandiflo'ra** has larger *fl.*; **ple'na*** has more numerous pets. which are often narrower.

sanguin'eus -a -um, sanguinolen'tus -a -um, blood-red; dull red passing into brownish-black.

SANGUISORB'A (*sanguis*, blood, *sorbere*, soaking up; reputed to have styptic qualities). FAM. *Rosaceae.* A genus of about 30 species distributed over the whole north temperate zone. Large and often striking, usually perennial herbs with pinnate leaves. Flowers all, or at least the lower or middle ones, hermaphrodite, the upper, if unisexual, female; stamens numerous, or 4, or 2; stigmas many or few, brush-like; sepals in fruit dry-rot coloured, pitted, wrinkled, or winged. Ordinary good garden soil suits them. Propagation by division or by seed.

S. canaden'sis. 5 to 6 ft. h. *lflets.* oblong to triangular-oblong, truncate or cordate at base, blunt, sharply toothed, long-stalked. *fl.-heads* cylindrical, 2 to 6 in. long; fl. all perfect, whitish. Summer. Eastern N. America. SYN. *Poterium canadense.* Borders or moist places in grass.

S. dodecan'dra. Robust. Stem erect, 18 in. to 3 ft. h., nodding at tip. *l.* rather long, linear in outline; lflets. 13 to 19, oblong-ovate to linear-oblong, blunt, bluish-green beneath, stalked. *fl.-spikes* long-stalked, over 2 in. long, nodding, greenish-yellow to whitish; stamens many, longer than cal. July, August. Alps. SYN. *S. Vallistellinae.*

S. hakusanen'sis. A synonym of *S. obtusa.*

S. mi'nor. Burnet. 1 to 2½ ft., sometimes slightly hairy. *l.* long, odd-pinnate; lflets. in 6 to 10 pairs, small, roundish to oblong, deeply toothed. *fl.* in terminal, small, globular or oblong heads, lower fl. bisexual or staminate, upper female; stigmas purple, exserted. Summer. Europe, including Britain. Asia. SYN. *Poterium Sanguisorba.* *See* **Burnet.**

S. obtu'sa.* About 4 ft. h. *Radical l.* long-stalked, 5 to 20 in. long; lflets. 5 to 16, bluntly ovate or elliptic, 1½ to 2½ in. long, pale green above, somewhat glaucous beneath, toothed, stalked. *fl.* in cylindrical spikes, 2 to 3½ in. long, rose-purple, all perfect; stamens usually 6, 4 times as long as cal. Summer. Japan. 1910 (B.M. 8690.) SYN. *S. hakusanensis.* var. **al'ba,** *fl.* white.

S. officina'lis. Glabrous with erect, branching stem, 1 to 3 ft. h. or more, leafy. *Basal l.* large, with usually 7 to 13 stalked lflets.; lflets. oblong, sharply toothed, blue-green beneath. *fl.-spikes* usually long-stalked, roundish or oblong, brownish-red; stamens 4, as long as, or scarcely longer than, cal. June to September. N. Hemisphere, including Britain. SYN. *Poterium officinale.*

S. tenuifo'lia. Perennial. *l.* oblong-lanceolate, sharply toothed, glabrous, nearly sessile. *fl.* red, in a cylindrical spike, bracts ciliate. China. SYN. *Poterium tenuifolium.*

S. Vallistelli'nae. A synonym of *S. dodecandra.*

SANSEVIER'IA (in honour of Raimond de Sansgrio, Prince of Sanseviero, 1710–71). FAM. *Liliaceae.* A genus of over 50 species of herbaceous perennials with short, thick, sometimes stoloniferous rhizomes, natives of Trop. and S. Africa and the E. Indies. Leaves in a rosette, thick, cartilaginous, fibrous within, often long, nearly flat or terete. Flowers of medium size or long, in racemes; perianth tube sometimes very long, scarcely enlarged at apex, lobes narrow, equal and slightly spreading; stamens 6; pedicels jointed at top; scape simple, tall. Sansevierias are grown for their stiff, erect, decorative leaves which are usually variegated or mottled. They are tender plants growing well in a sandy loam compost and propagated by suckers or by leaf cuttings about 3 in. long placed in sand. The plants should be watered sparingly when dormant. The genus is important in yielding fibre which is used for fine mats, hats, rope, and by the natives for bowstrings, &c.

S. aethiop'ica. *l.* 5 to 16 in. long, somewhat tufted, nearly erect, linear-lanceolate, acute, tipped white. *fl.* white, tube 1 in. long, slightly swollen at base, lobes ½ to ¾ in. long, 1 in. wide, subspatulate, linear, revolute; stamens far exserted; style exceeding stamens; racemes 1½ to 2½ ft. long. July. S. Africa. 1895. (B.M. 8487.)

S. cylind'rica. *l.* 3 to 4 ft. long, 1 in. thick, cylindrical, arching, rigid, leathery. *fl.* whitish, tinged pink, 1 to 1¼ in. long, segs. as long as the slender tube; anthers exserted; raceme 2 to 2½ ft. long, 2½ to 3 in. thick; scape nearly 1 ft. long, firm. August. S. Trop. Africa. 1856. (B.M. 5093.)

S. gran'dis. *l.* few, obovate-oblong, up to 3 to 4 ft. long, 6 in. broad, dull green with broad bands of deeper green, margins red-brown. *fl.* white, sessile, in dense spike-like panicles, 2 to 3 ft. long. Trop. Africa. 1896. (B.M. 7877.) Yields a good fibre.

S. guineen'sis. A synonym of *S. thyrsiflora.*

S. Kirk'ii. *rhiz.* stout. *l.* 3 or 4, oblanceolate, 2 to 3 ft. long, 3 in. wide, obscurely mottled, bordered reddish-brown. *fl.* white in a dense globose raceme, 6 to 8 in. across; tube cylindrical, 4 to 6 in. long; lobes recurved, 1 in. long. February. SE. Trop. Africa. About 1881. (B.M. 7357.)

S. Laurent'ii. A variety of *S. trifasciata.*

S. longiflo'ra. *l.* sub-erect, oblanceolate, 1 to 2 ft. long, 3 to 4 in. wide, spotted white, red-margined, cartilaginous, not thick. *fl.* greenish-white, 3½ to 4 in. long, at length drooping; segs. one-third as long as tube; raceme dense, 1 to 1½ ft. long, 8 to 9 in. thick; scape 1 ft. or more long. July. Trop. W. Africa. 1824. (B.M. 2634.) Much like *S. thyrsiflora* but with much longer perianth tube.

S. Roxburghia'na. Stem very short. *l.* 8 or 9, 2 to 2½ ft. long, 1 in. wide, dagger-shaped, concave above, pale green marked with darker green, with a narrow red border. *fl.* pale greenish-white, 1 in. long, cylindric, in clusters of 3 to 6 in a cylindrical raceme, 1 to 1½ ft. long. July. E. Indies. 1895. (B.M. 7487.)

S. subspica'ta. *l.* oblanceolate, nearly flat, 8 to 9 in. long, gradually narrowed to base. *fl.* whitish, solitary in a dense spike-like infl.; perianth 2 in. long. October. S. Africa. 1889. Greenhouse.

S. thyrsiflo'ra. *l.* sub-erect, oblanceolate, 6 to 18 in. long, cartilaginous, 1½ to 3 in. wide, cuspidate, with close paler green transverse bands which nearly disappear with age, margin whitish or dull red. *fl.* whitish, tinged greenish-brown, 2 in. long segs. as long as tube, in a simple raceme 1½ to 2 ft. long, 3 in. wide; scape 1 to 1½ ft. long, glaucous, purplish-green. September. S. Africa. 1701. (B.M. 1179 as *S. guineensis.*)

S. trifascia'ta. *Rhizome* creeping, ½ to 1 in. thick. *l.* erect, stiff, straight, 1 to 4 ft. long, linear-lanceolate, acute with a stout green awl-shaped point, gradually narrowing from near the middle to a concave channelled stalk, transversely banded on both sides with distinct, light, dull or clear whitish-green and deep grass- to almost blackish-green, slightly glaucous over all. *fl.* pale greenish or greenish-white, solitary, clustered or in scattered groups of 2 or 3 on a loose raceme; scape 1 to 2½ ft., dotted pale green. *fr.* bright orange, ⅓ in. across. W. Trop. Africa. SYN. *S. zebrina.* Long grown in England but confused with *S. thyrsiflora.* var. **Laurent'ii,** *l.* margin longitudinally striped golden-yellow, otherwise like type. W. Trop. Africa. Leaf-cuttings of this variety give rise to the type; to obtain it true division must be resorted to.

S. zeylan'ica. Bow-string Hemp. *l.* falcate, ensiform, sub-terete, 1 to 2 ft. long, ¾ to 1 in. thick at base, deeply channelled, dull green with white markings, margins scarious and distinctly red-lined. *fl.* greenish-white, 1¼ to 1½ in. long, segs. equalling tube; raceme 1 ft. or more long, 2 to 2½ in. thick; scape 1 ft. or more h. September. E. Indies. 1731. (B.R. 160.)

SANTALA'CEAE. Dicotyledons. A family of about 250 species of herbs or shrubs in 35 genera of parasitic or semiparasitic plants. Leaves undivided, sometimes scale-like, without stipules. Flowers perfect or 1-sexual, perianth simple, 4- to 6-lobed, stamens as many, ovary usually inferior. Fruit a 1-seeded nut or drupe. The genera treated here are Buckleya, Leptomeria, Osyris, Pyrularia, Santalum.

SANTAL'UM (from Persian *Shandal,* the name of the tree). FAM. *Santalaceae.* A genus of about 18 species of evergreen, glabrous trees or shrubs, natives of SE. Asia, Australia, and Pacific Is. Leaves opposite or rarely alternate, stalked, entire, leathery or slightly fleshy, pinnately veined, midrib conspicuous. Flowers in small panicles usually shorter than leaves; perianth tube bell-shaped or obovate, lobes 4 or rarely 5, with a tuft of hairs inside behind each stamen. *S. album,* the source of Sandalwood, like other species, is difficult to grow, on account of its parasitic habit on roots of other plants. It must have stove conditions and is raised from seed, sown in heat on receipt.

S. al'bum. Sandalwood. Tree to 15 ft. *l.* ovate-elliptic, usually narrowed to both ends, 1½ to 2½ in. long, pale beneath, membranous. *fl.* reddish within, 4-fid, in many-fld. panicles; pedicels as long as perianth tube. *fr.* a drupe, black, as large as a cherry. E. Indies. 1804. (B.M. 3235.) The white or citron-coloured wood develops a sweet scent when dry, and is used for making boxes, necklaces, fans, and other fancy articles, and yields an aromatic oil used in perfumery and ceremonially. var. **myrtifo'lium,** *l.* narrower and paler beneath.

S. obtusifo'lium. Slender shrub of 6 ft. *l.* opposite, or upper alternate, linear-oblong, lanceolate or broadly oblong, obtuse, 1 to 2 in. long, rather thick, rather livid. *fl.* red, few, in short-stalked axillary racemes. June. Australia. 1823.

SANTOLI'NA (from *Sanctum linum,* holy flax, old name for *S. virens*). FAM. *Compositae.* A genus of about 8 species of aromatic, evergreen shrubs, sub-shrubs or herbs, native of the Mediterranean region. Leaves alternate, pinnate or pinnatisect. Flowers crowded in terminal long-stalked heads, all perfect and without ray-florets; yellow or white.

These plants do not require a rich soil and dislike wet conditions at the root. The whiteness of the foliage of *S. Chamaecyparissus* and *S. neapolitana*—not excelled in any other hardy shrubs—is most highly developed in light sandy soil and full sunshine. Easily increased by cuttings.

KEY

1. *Mature foliage green*	2
1. *Mature foliage white*	3
2. *Fl. yellow*	S. virens
2. *Fl. white*	S. pinnata
3. *Earliest l. green, later white-felted; l. pinnatisect, segs. in 2 or 4 rows, short, thick*	S. Chamaecyparissus
3. *Lvs. white-felted, pinnate or with segs. in 4 rows, up to ⅜ in. long, very slender*	S. neapolitana

S. alpi'na. A synonym of *Anthemis montana.*

S. Chamaecyparis'sus.* Lavender Cotton. Bushy shrub 1½ to 2½ ft., shoots and l. white-felted. *l.* very crowded, 1 to 1½ in. long, about ⅛ in. wide, pinnatisect, the segs. short, thick, and set in 2 to 4 rows. *fl.-heads* yellow, ½ to ¾ in. across, terminating a stalk up to 6 in. long, and very freely borne. July, August. S. Europe. 1596. The earliest l. are green. (B.T.S. 2, 498.) SYN. *S. incana.* var. **na'na,*** charming dwarf form.

S. neapolita'na. Evergreen shrub, 2 to 2½ ft., shoots and l. white-felted. *l.* 1½ to 3 in. long, either pinnate or with 4 rows of lflets. which are $\frac{1}{12}$ to ⅜ in. long and the thickness of stout thread. *fl.-heads* bright yellow, ¾ in. across on slender erect stalks up to 6 in. long. July. S. Italy. Often grown as *S. rosmarinifolia.*

S. pinna'ta. Evergreen shrub, 1½ to 2½ ft., bushy, very leafy, glabrous or nearly so. *l.* green, 1 to 1½ in. long; segs. ⅛ to 3/16 in. long in 2 to 4 rows. *fl.-heads* dull white in hemispherical heads ⅝ in. wide, solitary on stalks up to 6 in. long. July. Italy. 1791. SYN. *S. leucantha.*

S. rosmarinifo'lia. *See* **S. neapolitana.**

S. vir'ens. Evergreen bush about 2 ft. *l.* 1 to 2 in. long, about ⅛ in. wide, dark green, glabrous. *fl.-heads* yellow, ¾ in. across, solitary at top of slender erect stalks 6 to 10 in. long. July. S. Europe. 1727. SYN. *S. viridis.* The other green-leaved species, *S. pinnata*, has white fl.

W. J. B.

SANVITA'LIA (in honour of the Sanvitali family of Parma). FAM. *Compositae.* A genus of about 4 species of annual or perennial herbs, natives of Mexico. Leaves all opposite, entire. Flower-heads yellow or whitish, rather small, disk often purplish; ray-florets in 1 or 2 series; involucral bracts in 2 or 3 series; receptacle flat or convex; achenes glabrous, those of rays with 3 arms. *S. procumbens* may be grown as an annual, the seeds being sown in March or April under glass, the seedlings planted out in late May. A light sandy loam with peat suits it best.

S. procum'bens. Stem procumbent or wide spreading. *l.* ovate, entire. *fl.-heads* small, like those of a Rudbeckia, ray-fl. bright yellow, disk dark; outer achenes of disk muricate. July. 1798. (B.R. 707.) var. **fl. ple'no,** *fl.-heads* double.

SAP, the fluid which exists in living plants, enclosed in the cells or passing up the vessels of the wood (xylem) or down the sieve-tubes of soft bast (phloem). The ascending current passing from the roots to the leaves through the xylem consists mainly of water in which the minerals absorbed by the roots are dissolved. It is in fact nearly pure water during the actively growing period of the plant's life. Much of the water is lost by transpiration from the leaves and other green parts and in the green parts the sap acquires many other substances manufactured there, such as sugars, soluble proteins, and other materials which are conveyed to the parts where they are immediately required, as at the growing-points and where leaves, flowers, fruits, and roots are growing, or to storage places. This 'elaborated sap' as the older books called it is conveyed mainly through the phloem, but passes also in its final disposal through the cell-walls from cell to cell where it is required. The effects of notching, ringing, and constriction upon stems are due in large measure to the relative position of the vessels along which the 2 main currents of sap flow and can be seen only in those plants, i.e. in most Dicotyledons, where the 2 tissues phloem and xylem are in concentric cylinders in the stem and not in those in which the fibro-vascular bundles are scattered, as in Monocotyledons and a few Dicotyledons.

SAPER'DA. *See* **Populus, Poplar borers.**

sap'idus -a -um, having a pleasant taste.

sapient'um, of the wise.

SAPINDA'CEAE. Dicotyledons. A family of about 1,050 species in about 120 genera, mostly trees and shrubs in tropical regions, a few are herbs and a few temperate plants. Leaves usually alternate, usually pinnate, sometimes 2-pinnate or 3-foliolate, without stipules. Flowers 1-sexual but with both stamens and pistils, regular or irregular, small as a rule, usually in panicles; sepals 4 or 5, usually overlapping in bud; petals 4 or 5 (or wanting); disk outside the 8 or 10 stamens (rarely 7 or 6); ovary superior, usually 3-celled, deeply 3-lobed. Fruit a capsule, berry, drupe, nut, or winged fruit. The genera treated here are Aitonia, Alectryon, Blighia, Cardiospermum, Cossignia, Cupania, Diploglottis, Dodonaea, Euphoria, Filicium, Greyia, Hippobromus, Koelreuteria, Litchi, Melicocca, Paullinia, Sapindus, Serjania, Talisia, Ungnadia, Xanthoceras.

SAPIND'US (contraction of *Sapo-indicus*, Indian soap). FAM. *Sapindaceae.* A genus of 15 species in tropical regions, a few extending into temperate regions. Trees or shrubs with pubescent winter scales. Leaves alternate, in 1 species simple, in others abruptly pinnate, entire. Flowers small, regular, in large terminal or axillary panicles. Propagated by seeds. *S. Drummondii* is probably the hardiest but is not likely to survive long in the British climate. The outer covering of the seeds of some species is edible, and the aril of *S. Saponaria* (Soapberry) is used as soap by the N. American Indians. The seeds are poisonous and in some species the hard, round, black seeds are made into rosaries, necklaces, bracelets, &c.

S. Drummond'ii. Wild Chena Tree. Deciduous tree to 50 ft. with scaly red bark; shoots hairy. *lflets.* 8 to 18, shoot stalked, obliquely lanceolate, 2 to 3 in. long, hairy beneath. *fl.* yellowish-white, ⅕ in. across in loose hairy panicles, up to 10 in. long. May, June. *fr.* black. SW. United States.

S. Mukoros'si. Evergreen tree. *lflets.* 8 to 13, oblong-lanceolate, 3 to 6 in. long, smooth beneath. *fr.* brown or yellow. Japan.

SA'PIUM (Pliny's name for a resinous pine; the wounded stem exudes a greasy sap). FAM. *Euphorbiaceae.* A genus of about 100 species, natives of tropical regions and there grown for their economic value, especially as a source of rubber. Evergreen glabrous trees or shrubs with poisonous milky juice. Leaves usually alternate, stalked, usually entire, simple, with small stipules and 2 conspicuous glands at the apex of the stalk. Flowers generally in terminal spikes, the female singly above, male in threes below, all without petals; calyx of staminate flowers 2- or 3-lobed, lobes over-lapping; stamens 2 or 3, free; ovary 1- to 3-celled. Fruit a capsule. The species require stove cultivation and are easily grown but, except *S. sebiferum*, are not ornamental. *S. sebiferum* is grown, especially in China, for the wax which covers the seed and which is used for candles, in soap-making, and for dressing cloth. Propagation is by seed or by cuttings. Some 'jumping beans' (q.v.) belong to species of Sapium.

S. Hippoma'ne. Milk Tree, Poison Tree. *l.* thick, elliptic, tip hooded. W. Indies to Brazil. Juice extremely poisonous.

S. in'dicum. Tree with white bark. *l.* oblong, willow-like. India. Juice very poisonous.

S. Jenman'ii. Large tree. *l.* oblong-lanceolate, suddenly acuminate. *fl.* with 1-celled ovary and deciduous style. British Guiana. Important source of rubber there.

S. Pavonia'num. Tree. *l.* oblong, lanceolate, or oblanceolate. *fl.-spikes* solitary, long; style deciduous; seeds with red covering. Colombia. Yields a medium grade rubber. *S. verum*, now rare in Colombia, yields a better grade and differs by the *l.* oblong-lanceolate or elliptic, base narrowed, apex rounded; style persistent.

S. sebif'erum. Chinese Tallow Tree, Vegetable Tallow. Tree of 25 to 30 ft. *l.* broad-ovate, 1 to 3 in. wide. *fl.* in terminal racemes; seeds with white covering. China. The leaves becoming bright red in age.

S. ve'rum. *See* **S. Pavonianum.**

SAPLING. A young tree.

SAPODILLA. *See* **Achras Sapota.**

sapona'ceus -a -um, soapy; lather-forming.

SAPONA'RIA (*sapo*, soap; the juice of the leaves of *S. officinalis* forms a lather with water and is similar to soap in its power to remove grease, &c.). FAM. *Caryophyllaceae.* A genus of about 20 species of hardy or half-hardy annuals somewhat resembling Gypsophila, or biennials or perennials resembling Silene, natives of middle and S. Europe and temperate Asia, differing from Dianthus by the absence of bracts at the base of the calyx and from Vaccaria, which is sometimes combined with it, by the presence of distinct outgrowths on the petals at the throat, and the cylindrical, not winged, herbaceous calyx. Saponarias mostly grow readily in well-drained soils, and except for the annual or biennial species and *S. officinalis* are well accommodated on the rock-garden, perhaps best in the lime-free areas. They are readily increased by seed and the perennials also by cuttings, need open sunny places, and flower in summer. *S. pumila* seems to be a difficult plant, needing perfect drainage, complete absence of lime, rich soil, very deep, and full sun.

KEY

1.	*Lvs. spatulate; fl. in umbels or panicles; cal. narrow-cylindrical*	2
1.	*Lvs. narrow-linear-lanceolate to narrow-spatulate; cal. not sticky; pet. entire, rarely cordate, claw not longer than cal.*	7
2.	*Pet. entire, claw longer than cal.; fl. in loose umbel-like groups*	3
2.	*Cal. long, usually sticky, main nerves white; pet. 2-lobed; stem erect or ascending*	5
3.	*Stem 12 to 24 in. h., erect; lvs. 3-nerved, acute*	S. officinalis
3.	*Stem creeping, or ascending at tip, glandular-hairy. Plant cushion-like*	4
4.	*Annual, erect, 6 to 12 in. h.*	S. calabrica
4.	*Perennial, prostrate*	S. ocymoides
5.	*Fl. small, claw not longer than cal.*	S. glutinosa
5.	*Fl. large; pet. cordate, claw scarcely longer than cal.*	6
6.	*Rhizome thin; lvs. short-stalked*	S. cypria
6.	*Rhizome thick, woody; lvs. long-stalked*	S. depressa
7.	*Fl. large, solitary or in a head, rose; cal. swollen; pet. ovate*	8
7.	*Fl. small, in a head; pet. yellow*	10
8.	*Rather loosely tufted; pet. narrow*	S. caespitosa
8.	*Forming a tight cushion*	9
9.	*Fl. solitary*	S. pumila
9.	*Fls. up to 7*	S. pulvinaris
10.	*Tufted perennial*	S. bellidifolia
10.	*Mat-forming perennial*	S. lutea

S. bellidifo'lia. Tufted perennial with woody root. Stem simple, smooth, erect, 8 to 15 in. h. *Basal l.* oblong-spatulate, long-stalked; *stem-l.* smaller, narrower; *bract-l.* ciliate. *fl.* yellow, almost sessile in a small head at the apex of the stem; stamens yellow. S. Europe. Somewhat tender.

S. × Boissier'i* (*S. caespitosa × S. ocymoides*). Mat-forming with spreading stems. *fl.* clear pink, much larger than *S. ocymoides.* (G.C. 119 (1946), 170.) Raised by Sündermann. 1898.

S. caespito'sa. Tufted perennial, 2 to 3 in. h. *l.* linear, glabrous, mostly radical, scarcely toothed, acute. *fl.* rose, almost umbellate; cal. hairy, deeply lobed, lobes acute; pet. notched, narrow. Pyrenees. 1824. Rather tender.

S. calab'rica. Annual. Stem erect, forked, sticky-hairy above, 6 to 12 in. h. *l.* obovate-spatulate, smooth, opposite, oblong-lanceolate, ciliate at base. *fl.* in a forked corymbose cyme, pale rose; cal. cylindrical, segs. obtuse; pet. roundish. August (or if sown in autumn, spring). Italy, Greece. 1830. Hardy. Variable. var. **al'ba,** *fl.* white; **compact'a,** of closer growth; **Scarlet Queen,** *fl.* redder.

S. cyp'ria. Allied to *S. depressa* but with a more slender rhizome. Stems 1 to 2 in. h., sticky. *l.* oblong-spatulate, obtuse, about $\frac{7}{8}$ in. long; stem-l. small, oblong-linear. *fl.* few, rose; cal. about $\frac{3}{8}$ in. long, almost as long as the claw of the pet. Mt. Troodos, Cyprus.

S. depres'sa. Tufted or mat-forming, rhizome thick, somewhat woody. Stems 3- to 12-in. h., sticky. *l.* obovate-elliptic, smooth, bluish-green. *fl.* more or less umbellate, large, pink; pet. notched; cal. very long, 5-angled, sticky. Sicily, Greece.

S. glutino'sa. Biennial, whole plant covered with glandular hairs. Stem erect, 10 to 20 in. h., branched above. *l.* 3- to 5-nerved, basal spatulate; stem-l. ovate-oblong, acute. *fl.* purple, in panicles; pet. narrow, 2-lobed at top. E. Mediterranean region. 1817. Hardy. (B.M. 2855.)

S. lu'tea. Perennial, mat-forming, root woody. Stem 3 to 6 in. h. *l.* mostly radical, linear, pale green. *fl.* yellow, in a head at apex of stem; cal. hairy; pet. linear; stamens violet. W. Alps. 1804. Rather tender.

S. ocymoi'des.* Perennial. Rootstock branching, woody. Stem prostrate, branching from base. *Lower l.* obovate to obovate-lanceolate with a short broad petiole; *upper* oblong-lanceolate, sessile, grass-green ciliate. *fl.* rose, about $\frac{1}{2}$ in. across, in umbel-like groups; cal. cylindrical, hairy, purplish. Alps and Jura. 1768. Hardy. Good for trailing over rocks. Variable. var. **al'biflor'a,** *fl.* white; **carn'ea,** *fl.* flesh-pink; **splen'dens,** *fl.* deeper rose; **splendidis'sima,** *fl.* larger; **vers'icolor,** *fl.* at first white, then rose.

S. officina'lis.* Bouncing Bet. Soapwort. Perennial herb. Rootstock creeping, branched. Stem erect, 1 to 3 ft. h., stout, rather rough, cylindrical, sometimes branched. *l.* elliptical to oblong-lanceolate, acute, 3-nerved, 2 or 5 in. long, 2 in. wide, connate at base. *infl.* many-fld. in terminal and axillary umbels. *fl.* 1 to $1\frac{1}{2}$ in. across, white to reddish, short-stalked; pet. clawed, limb obovate; cal. cylindrical. August, September. Europe, temperate Asia (naturalized in Britain). Hardy. (E.B. 197.) var. **albo-plena, roseo-plena, rubro-plena,** double forms respectively white, rose, and red. The black anthers sometimes seen owe their colour to the presence of a smut-fungus that infests them and is perennial in the affected plant.

S. × peregri'na (*S. bellidifolia × S. ocymoides*). Of stronger growth than *S. ocymoides,* with larger *l.,* much denser *infl.,* and smaller pale yellow *fl.* with a rosy flush.

S. pulvinar'is. Densely tufted perennial forming a tight cushion. Stem short, 1- to 7-fld. *l.* small, linear, somewhat keeled. *infl.* hairy. *fl.* bright rose. Lebanon, Anatolia.

S. pu'mila. Deep-rooting perennial with thick, woody, branching rootstock, forming a dense cushion. *l.* in rosettes, linear, $\frac{1}{2}$ to 1 in. long, very narrow, somewhat fleshy, grass-green, almost glabrous. Stem usually very short from centre of rosette, with usually only 1 pair of l. *fl.* about 1 in. across, rose with whitish claws to pet., rarely entirely white; cal. inflated, veins netted; styles usually 3. June. Alps. Difficult to grow and flower; soon dying on limy soils. SYN. *Silene pumila, S. Pumilio.*

S. × Suenderman'nii (*S. bellidifolia × S. caespitosa*). Mat-forming. *fl.* rose.

S. Vacca'ria. A synonym of *Vaccaria segetalis.*

S. × Wiemann'ii (*S. caespitosa × S. lutea*). Mat-forming with decumbent stems, 2 to 3 in. h. *fl.* in heads, bright rose. Raised by Herr Wiemann.

sapona'rius -a -um, soapy.

SAPONIN. A constituent of the sap of many plants, including Saponaria, many Sapindaceae, such as Horse-chestnut seeds, having many of the properties of soap, including the formation of a copious lather with water, and the faculty of wetting surfaces usually difficult to wet. The latter property has led to its use as a wetting or spreading agent for mixing with insecticides and fungicides where soap is unsuitable; it enables waxy surfaces to be wetted without destroying the wax as soap is apt to do.

SAPO'TA Ach'ras. *See* **Achras Sapota.**

SAPOTA'CEAE. Dicotyledons. A family of sub-tropical and tropical trees and shrubs with milky juice, including about 600 species in over 30 genera. Leaves alternate, more or less leathery, without stipules. Flowers usually perfect, regular, small, in axillary clusters, sometimes solitary; calyx sepals 5 or in 2 whorls of 2, 3, or 4; corolla gamopetalous, lobes as many as sepals or twice as many, overlapping; stamens opposite corolla lobes, staminodes often present; ovary superior, 4- to many-celled. Fruit a drupe. Several produce edible fruit, e.g. *Lucuma mammosa* (Marmalade of W. Indies), *Achras Sapota* (Sapodilla), Bassia, Chrysophyllum, Imbricaria, &c. Species of Sideroxylon and Argania (Ironwood) have very hard timber used in building. The Malayan *Dichopsis gutta* is a source of gutta-percha. The genera treated here are Achras, Argania, Bumelia, Chrysophyllum, Lucuma, Madhuca, Palaquium.

SAPOTE, WHITE. *See* **Casimiroa edulis.**

Sappan, native Malayan name.

SAPROPHYTE. A plant living entirely upon dead vegetable or animal matter. In this manner live many bacteria and fungi and in many instances bring about changes (decay) in dead matter which fit it for use by higher plants. Here also belong several flowering plants devoid of chlorophyll, such as *Monotropa Hypopitys,* belonging to the heath family, and *Neottia Nidus-avis,* an Orchid, both found in beech woods in Britain. Saprophytes are to be distinguished from parasites (q.v.) which obtain their food in whole or part from living things, and some, which may be partial saprophytes, have become partners with higher plants. (*See* **Symbiosis, Mycorrhiza.**)

saprophyt'icus -a -um, living on decaying material.

SAP-ROT. Some bracket fungi (q.v.) attacking trees live first in the sap-wood, soft and rich in manufactured plant-foods, like sugar and proteins, causing sap-rot, which may eventually spread to girdle the tree and destroy it.

SAP-WOOD. The wood most recently produced just within the cambium in a dicotyledonous or coniferous tree, softer, and containing more water than the heart-wood.

SAPUCAIA NUT. *See* **Lecythis.**

Sar'a, native Hindustan name.

SARAC'A (*Sarac*, native name in India). FAM. *Leguminosae.* A genus of about 6 species of tropical trees. Leaves equally pinnate, leaflets usually in few pairs, leathery; stipules small, caducous. Flowers yellow, rose or scarlet, in short, much-branched panicles; calyx segments 4, petal-like, closely overlapping; petals absent; stamens 3 to 9, free; bracts small, deciduous. Pods oblong or linear, 2-valved. For treatment *see* **Brownea.**

S. cauliflo'ra. *lflets.* 10 to 12, upper oblanceolate-oblong, acute, 1 ft. or more long, lower shorter, more oblong. *fl.* scarlet, in dense, nearly sessile corymbs. India.

S. declina'ta. Closely related to *S. indica. lflets.* in 6 to 8 pairs, oblong, reddish when young. *fl.* yellowish-orange, in clustered panicles. *Pods* bright red. Java, Sumatra.

S. in'dica. *lflets.* 6 to 10, oblong, shining, 4 to 9 in. long; young l. in long, drooping, greyish-white bunches. *fl.* rich orange, fragrant, in roundish panicles on stems and branches, shorter than l.; bracts red; stamens crimson, exserted; style long curved. Summer. India, Malaya. 1796. (B.M. 3018 as *Jonesia Asoca.*)

F. G. P.

saracen'icus -a -um, Arabian.

SARACH'A (in honour of Isidore Saracha, 1733–1803?, a Bendictine monk who sent many rare plants to the Royal Gardens, Madrid). FAM. *Solanaceae.* A genus of about 12 species of erect or spreading herbs natives of Bolivia to Mexico. Leaves entire or with broad wavy teeth. Calyx broadly bell-shaped, 5-toothed; corolla sub-rotate or very broadly bell-shaped, deeply 5-lobed; stamens 5; peduncles short. The 2 species mentioned may be grown as hardy annuals in ordinary garden soil.

S. stapelioi'des. Erect, sometimes woody at base, 18 in. h. *l.* heart-shaped or rounded at base, ovate, entire or with wavy teeth, lower solitary, upper twin. *fl.* pale yellow with 5 reddish-brown, yellow-veined blotches; cor. rotate, lobes rounded apiculate; peduncles usually solitary, 1-fld. Summer. 1865. (G.F. 465.)

S. umbella'ta. 2 to 4 ft. h. *l.* ovate, wrinkled, entire, shining, acute, rough; upper ones twin. *fl.* cream or greenish-white; cor. plicate; umbels 5- to 10-fld., axillary, pedunculate. June, July. Peru. 1822. (S.B.F.G. 85.)

SARAN'THE (*saron*, broom, *anthos*, flower). FAM. *Marantaceae.* A genus of 8 species of S. American perennial herbs with thickened rhizomes and tuberous roots. Like Maranta the leaves are not inverted but the bracts are arranged dorsiventrally not distichally as in that genus; from Myrosma it is distinguished by the pairs of flowers being solitary and not 2 or many together and in the bracts falling away quickly. For cultivation *see* **Calathea** and **Maranta.**

S. compos'ita. Robust stemless perennial about 18 in. h. *l.-stalk* about 2 in. long, its apical swelling flattened, slightly downy, blade oblong to ovate-lanceolate, about 15 in. long, often less. *fl.* in a panicle; peduncle about 8 in. long, crowded. Brazil.

S. leptostach'ya. Stemless perennial about 2½ ft. h. *l.-stalk* about 8 in. long, its apical swelling flattened, glabrous, blade linear up to 18 in. long, bright green, sometimes banded with greenish-white. *fl.* in a solitary raceme from the centre of the foliage, peduncle about 6 in. long, cor. white. Brazil. 1884. SYN. *Maranta leptostachya, M. speciosa.*

Sarasin'ii, Sarasino'rum, in honour of Paul (1856–1921) and Friedrich (1859–?) Sarasin of Basel who botanized in Ceylon, New Caledonia, Siam, &c.

Saras'sa, native name in Molucca.

sarawacen'sis -is -e, of Sarawak, N. Borneo. Several spellings have been used.

SARCAN'THUS (*sarkos*, flesh, *anthos*, flower; flowers fleshy). FAM. *Orchidaceae.* A polymorphic genus to which over 70 species have been referred. Under further revision that number may be altered. All are epiphytic, distributed from Ceylon, through the East: India, Burma, S. China, New Guinea, &c. The flowers are in leaf-opposed racemes sometimes branched. The sepals and petals are free, equal or sub-equal, spreading, slightly fleshy. The 3-lobed fleshy lip is affixed to the column base and is shortly spurred, the spur being partially, often obscurely, divided internally. The lateral lobes of the lip are short, often ear-like or oblique, the mid-lobe ovate, oblong, or lanceolate. Column usually semi-terete. Pollinia 2. The stems vary in height, in some species short and moderately stout, in others long and slender. The leaves are distichously arranged and vary from flat to terete or quill shape. The genus is allied to Saccolabium and similar compost and temperatures should be given. Pans may be used for the smaller species. Those with taller stems should be supported; a narrow raft or board, with the base fixed in a pot or pan and inclined obliquely answers. A thin layer of compost should be placed between the plant and support. Water must not be withheld in the winter, but the varied texture of the leaves must be studied as to the frequency. The genus contains a number of interesting species, with small, rather attractive inflorescences, but as a whole of little horticultural value.

S. appendicula'tus. *fl.* 10 to 20, ⅜ in. across; sep. and pet. linear-oblong, yellowish, striped red-brown; lip 3-lobed, side lobes small, mid-lobe pointed, purplish; spur conical, short, yellowish, purplish-striped. Stem 1 to 2 ft. h. *l.* 2 to 4 in. long, slenderly terete. *Scape* simple or branched, 12 to 18 in. long. Burma, N. India. 1819. (A.B.G.C. 8, 318; B.R. 676 as *Vanda teretifolia.*) SYN. *S. teretifolius* (Rchb. f.).

S. arieti'nus. A synonym of *S. Williamsonii.*

S. auricula'tus. *fl.* greenish-white, lined purple. Allied to *S. Parishii*, but differing by a pair of ear-like lobes at base of lip. Habitat? 1895.

S. beloph'orus. *fl.* ochre, with 2 longitudinal, purple-brown stripes on sep., pet. and lip, small. *l.* ligulate, equally 2-lobed, undulate. 1883. A small species.

S. chrysom'elas. *fl.* yellowish, disk of sep. and pet. blackish-purple, in a large panicle, small. *l.* broad, lorate, unequally 2-lobed. Moulmein. 1869. Probably a form of *S. paniculatus.*

S. erina'ceus.* *fl.* white, or suffused pink with a rose-tinted lip, numerous; spikes pendent, 3 to 6 in. long, axillary; rachis and ovaries red and hairy. Stems 4 to 6 in. h. *l.* fleshy, flat, lanceolate. Moulmein. 1867. (B.M. 5630.) SYN. *Aerides dasypogon.*

S. filiform'is. *fl.* violet-scented, very small; sep. and pet. chocolate, reflexed; lip pale yellow or white, tipped pink; callus broad, hispid; raceme 6 to 8 in. long, 7- or 8-fld. *l.* filiform, 8 to 10 in. long. Stem pendulous, up to 4 ft. long. N. India, Siam, E. Indies. 1842. Allied to *S. teretifolius.* (B.M. 4639; A.B.G.C. 8, 319.)

S. flex'us. Sep. yellowish-brown, tipped outside reddish-brown; pet. yellowish-brown; spur of lip whitish-yellow, blade at first of the same colour, afterwards yellow; panicle zigzag. *l.* short, ligulate, 2-lobed. Borneo. 1881. Robust.

S. gutta'tus. A synonym of *Rhynchostylis retusa.*

S. Hincksia'nus. *fl.* small; sep. and pet. green, with 3 equal red stripes; side lobes of lip blunt, callus with medium angles; spur longer and more attenuated. Otherwise like *S. teretifolius*, but more slender. Habitat?, 1878.

S. hongkongen'sis.* *fl.* pale lilac, small, numerous, in axillary racemes 5 in. long; column and front of lip bright purple. *l.* terete, recurved, 4 in. long. Stem 1 ft. h. Hong Kong. 1893. Allied to *S. filiformis.*

S. infla'tus. *fl.* small, in small panicles; sep. and pet. greenish, striped brown; lip comparatively large, inflated. *l.* 2-lobed. Annam. 1906.

S. insect'ifer. *fl.* small, few, clustered on short spikes; sep. and pet. yellow, shaded green, striped red-brown; lip white marked with purple, mid-lobe pointed. Stem 6 to 12 in. h. *l.* short, broad, leathery, obliquely 2-lobed. Burma. 1857. (A.B.G.C. 5, 78.)

S. lax'us. *fl.* dirty-white, somewhat fleshy; sep. oblong, blunt-acute; pet. linear-ligulate, blunt-acute; side lobes of lip erect, oblong, lobed; mid-lobe ruby, triangular, apiculate, hollowed out; spur conical; raceme long, many-fld., lax, hairless. *l.* close together, few short, very thick, oblong, bluntly 2-lobed, keeled beneath, and with numerous purple spots. Stems very short. Moulmein. 1865. (Ref. B. 109.)

S. Lendya'nus. *fl.* in a small, loose panicle; sep. and pet. greenish, with purple disk; side-lobes of lip orange, with 2 purple lines, roundish, with introrse angles; mid-lobe white, with purple spots, oblong; spur as long as purple ovary. *l.* linear, blunt, 2-lobed. Saigon. 1884.

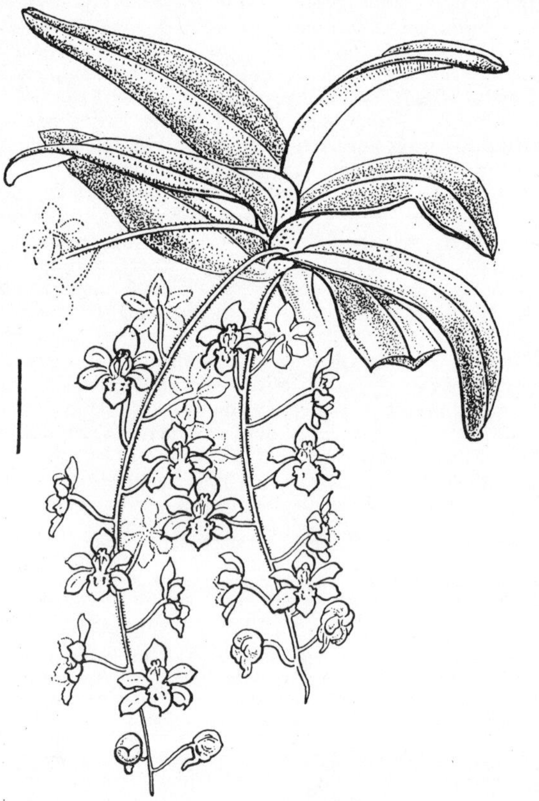

Sarcanthus erinaceus (p. 1867)

S. macro'don. *fl.* yellowish, streaked purple; sep. and pet. oblong, nearly straight; lip 3-fid; bracts very minute; raceme elongated, loosely many-fld. *l.* short, oblong-ligulate, toothed at apex. India. 1872. Small, not particularly ornamental.

S. mirab'ilis. *fl.* yellowish, with a cylindric, somewhat curved, purplish spur, small, in an erect panicle 18 in. long; sep. oblong; pet. ligulate. *l.* 6 in. long. India. 1878. Not worthy of its name.

S. ornithorrhyn'chus. *fl.* small; sep. and pet. yellowish, flushed rose-purple in centre; lip amethyst-purple; spur whitish or rose flushed. Habit dwarf. *l.* 3 to 4 in. long, spike longer. Habitat? 1856.

S. pal'lidus. *fl.* small, many; sep. and pet. purplish, edged yellow; lip white; spur shorter than ovary, a cylindric obtuse sac. Stem stout, 1 to 2 ft. h. *l.* 10 to 14 in. long, 2 in. wide, leathery. *Panicle*, with peduncle, 2 to 3 ft. long, branches long. N. India, Burma, Siam. 1840. (A.B.G.C. 8, 320.) SYN. *S. racemifer*, *S. tricolor*, *Saccolabium racemiferum*, *Aerides racemiferum.*

S. panicula'tus. *fl.* small, yellowish; sep. and pet. with 2 red-brown stripes, linear-oblong, undulate; blade of lip 2-horned; spur straight; spike paniculate, many-fld. *l.* long, lorate, leathery, obliquely 2-lobed at obtuse tip. China. SYN. *Aerides paniculatum. See* **S. chrysomelas.**

S. Parish'ii. *fl.* small in slender spikes; sep. and pet. yellow, lined red; lip yellow and rose-red; spur narrowly conical. Stem short. *l.* lorate, obliquely tipped, 4 to 6 in. long. Moulmein. 1861. (B.M. 5217.)

S. pugioniform'is. *fl.* yellowish-white, striped red, small, sessile; spike pendulous, many-fld., 7 in. long. *l.* lanceolate, 8 in. long, fleshy. Stem flattish, 9 in. long. Habitat? 1894.

S. rostra'tus. *fl.* in a simple, horizontal spike equalling l.; sep. and pet. yellowish-green, with reddish stripes; lip violet, produced into a beak. *l.* lanceolate, acute, flat, sub-recurved. China. 1824. (B.R. 891.)

S. striola'tus. *fl.* sep. and pet. orange, with 2 parallel, longitudinal cinnamon bars; lower part of spur white, upper part of lip orange. Philippine Is. 1882.

S. succis'us. *fl.* sep. and pet. yellowish-green, purple in middle, obtuse; lip yellow, red at apex; spike simple, horizontal or deflexed, longer than l. *l.* oblong, slightly undulate, blunt, toothed at apex. China. 1824. (B.R. 1014.)

S. teretifo'lius. *fl.* small, sep. and pet. yellowish-green, marked with reddish veinings, obtuse, reflexed; lip white, margins of throat violet; spur straight, obtuse, pubescent within; spike simple, horizontal, equalling l. *l.* terete. China. 1819. (B.M. 3571.) SYN. *Vanda teretifolia* of Reichenbach is *S. appendiculatus.*

S. Williamson'ii. *fl.* small, numerous; sep. and pet. pink-lilac; lip deeper lilac with amethyst side-lobes. Stems 3 to 6 in. h. *l.* rigid, curved, terete. Racemes sometimes branched. Assam. 1865.

E. C.

sarco- in compound words signifying fleshy.

SARCOBA'TUS (*sarkos*, fleshy, *batia*, bush; its pale bark gives the plant a fleshy appearance). FAM. *Chenopodiaceae.* A genus of 2 species in Western N. America. Deciduous loose-habited shrubs with rigid spine-tipped branches, fleshy linear leaves, and small green 1-sexual flowers, the staminate (without perianth, of 1 to 3 stamens beneath a peltate scale) in a crowded spike, the pistillate with a calyx which later enlarges and becomes a thin papery disk about $\frac{1}{3}$ in. across, axillary and sessile, solitary or twin. *S. vermiculatus* is hardy, grows well in ordinary soil, is increased by seed, but has little beauty to recommend it.

S. Maximilian'ii. A synonym of *S. vermiculatus.*

S. vermicula'tus. Greasewood. Dense shrub 6 to 9 ft. h. and wider; branches arching; shoots whitish, smooth or sometimes hairy. *l.* alternate, linear, $\frac{1}{2}$ to $1\frac{1}{2}$ in. long, up to $\frac{1}{8}$ in. wide, grey, stalkless. *fl.* as above; staminate spikes about 1 in. long, terminal on short lateral twigs. Western N. America.

SARCOCAP'NOS (*sarkos*, fleshy, *kapnos*, Greek name for fumitory; the leaves are fleshy). FAM. *Papaveraceae.* A genus of 3 species of dwarf, tufted, perennial herbs, natives of Spain and N. Africa. Leaves compound, segments broad and rather thick. Flowers white, yellow, or purplish; sepals 2, scale-like; petals 4, erecto-connivent, one of outer ones spurred at base, the other flat, the inner ones narrow, coherent at tip; stamens 6; in few-flowered terminal racemes. Hardy plants for the rock-garden, readily increased by seed or cuttings, but not showy.

S. enneaphyl'la. Shrubby at base, stems slender, 2 to 5 in. h., much-branched. *l.* 3-ternately cut; stalks long, slender; segs. roundish-ovate, sometimes cordate, mucronulate, terminal one usually larger. *fl.* yellow marked with purple above, about $\frac{3}{4}$ in. long, including spur; racemes short, about 10-fld. June. SW. Europe, 1714. (B.M. 9525.)

S. specio'sa. Perennial. *l.* simple or 3-sect; segs. ovate. *fl.* pale yellow; bracts ovate, small. Morocco, &c. SYN. *S. crassifolia.*

SARCOCARP. (1) A fleshy fruit such as a berry. (2) The fleshy part of a drupe between the epicarp (or skin) and the endocarp (or stone).

SARCOCAUL'ON (*sarkos*, fleshy, *caulon*, stem; in reference to the fleshy stems). FAM. *Geraniaceae.* A genus of 3 species of herbs or sub-shrubs with rigid spreading branches and fleshy stems armed with spines which are the persistent, hardened leaf-stalks, natives of S. Africa. Leaves small, sometimes tufted, petioles becoming spines on leaf-fall. Flowers purple on axillary, 1-flowered peduncles; sepals 5, overlapping; petals 5, overlapping; stamens 15. Greenhouse conditions and a compost of loam, peat or leaf-mould, and sand suits them. Root-cuttings or cuttings of young shoots in sand under a glass afford means of propagation.

S. Burmann'i. About 1 ft. h. *l.* obovate-cuneate, $\frac{1}{2}$ to $\frac{3}{4}$ in. long, crenately toothed, glabrous or downy, fleshy, on short stalks. *fl.* $1\frac{1}{2}$ to 2 in. across; pet. twice as long as the mucronate sep.; stamens 5 long, 10 shorter. May. 1800. (B.M. 5729.)

S. L'Heritier'i. About 1 ft. h. *l.* obovate or obcordate, acute or obtuse, entire, glabrous. *pet.* about as long as the cuspidate, narrowly pointed sep. May. 1790.

S. Paterson'ii. About 2 ft. h. *l.* wedge-shaped or obcordate, obtuse or mucronulate, entire, glabrous. *fl.* smaller than in other species; pet. not twice as long as the obtuse, mucronate sep. May. 1827.

SARCOCEPHA'LUS (*sarkos*, fleshy, *kephale*, head; referring to the fleshy heads of fruit). FAM. *Rubiaceae*. A genus of about 30 species of shrubs or trees, sometimes climbing, with terete or obtusely 4-angled branchlets, natives of Trop. Asia, Africa, and Australia. Leaves opposite, rather leathery, stalked; stipules interpetiolar, of variable size. Flowers white, yellow, red, or pale pink; calyx truncate, 5- or 6-toothed, hairy; corolla tubular funnel-shaped, lobes 5 or 6, rounded; heads terminal and axillary, pedunculate sometimes in panicles, without bracts. Fruit globose, 1-celled. Stove conditions with a compost of loam, peat, and sand suit these plants. Cuttings will root in sand under a glass in heat.

S. corda'tus. Tree of 10 ft. or more. *l.* broadly ovate, 4 to 10 in. long, obtuse, sometimes softly hairy beneath; stipules large, quickly deciduous. *fl.* yellow, in dense, globular heads over 1 in. across without the styles; cor. about ¼ in. long. May. Australia, India. 1820. SYN. *Nauclea coadunata.*

S. esculen'tus. Guinea, Negro, or Sierra Leone Peach. Tall tree or climbing shrub to 20 ft. *l.* roundish-oval, shining above, hairy in vein-axils beneath; stipules triangular, solitary. *fl.* pinkish, white, or yellow in short, terminal, globular heads resembling pin-cushions. *fr.* brownish, warted, in heads as large as a peach, pulp soft, reddish, watery, edible. Sierra Leone. 1822.

S. ova'tus. *l.* ovate or elliptic, 7 in. long, 3½ in. wide, acute at base, obtuse at apex, glabrous, leathery. *fl.* reddish in stalked heads, cal. with club-shaped, hairy, deciduous appendages. Philippines. 1906.

F. G. P.

SARCOCHIL'US (*sarkos*, flesh, *cheilos*, lip; the lip is distinctly fleshy). FAM. *Orchidaceae*. A large polymorphic genus into which about 200 species have been put, all epiphytic, caulescent orchids natives of the E. Indies, Malaya, the Pacific Is., and Australia. Camarotis are sometimes included, but as it is horticulturally distinct is kept separate here. Thrixspermum is sometimes separated but is included here. The group still contains many anomalies and no doubt further investigation will result in some rearrangement.

Flowers of medium size or small; sepals and usually narrower petals spreading, the lateral sepals often more or less adnate to the foot of the column; lip sessile or clawed, often saccate, 3-lobed, side-lobes small or large, fleshy or petaloid, sometimes toothed, mid-lobe variable, fleshy, sometimes much reduced, almost solid, often hairy; column erect, short or long, pollinia 2, globose, or 4 more or less connate in a pair; peduncles lateral, simple or rarely branched. Leaves variable, leathery or fleshy, oblong or linear, distichous, or sometimes very few, deficient or fugacious, thin. Stems long or short, stout or slender.

The genus is so widely distributed and the species vary so much that cultivation must largely be governed by the temperatures of the localities in which the particular plants are native and by the character of the foliage. *S. unguiculatus* resembles a Phalaenopsis in habit and coming from the Philippines should have similar compost and treatment to that given Phalaenopsis. *S. luniferus*, practically a mass of roots, from N. India and Burma, is suited with the temperatures of the intermediate house and should be attached to a block of wood, with very little compost, few if any waterings being given in the resting period. *S. Fitzgeraldii* and *S. Hartmannii*, with several other species from Australia, may be placed in small pans and grown with Odontoglossums. Species from warm parts of Australia would require more heat. A general compost can consist of Osmunda fibre, cleaned and cut rather short, to an equal quantity of Sphagnum moss, also cut. Thorough drainage is essential as very few of the species can withstand a really dry or a sour compost. For the greater number, watering must be continued through the winter. In summer the syringe may be freely used. Species with tufted habit may be increased by division of plants with several stems. With the exception of *S. Fitzgeraldii* and *S. Hartmannii*, little desire will probably be found to increase stock, as on the whole the genus, though including some pretty species, is of little garden value.

S. Berk'eleyi.* *fl.* creamy-white, with a purple stain on lip, crowded, 1½ in. h.; lip clawed, side lobes falcately linear; racemes pendulous, longer than l. *l.* ligulate, spreading, 5 to 9 in. long, obtuse or emarginate. Stem 3 to 6 in. h. Nicobar Is. 1891. (A.B.G.C. 5, 66; W.O.A. 436 as *Thrixspermum Berkeleyi.*)

S. borneen'sis. *fl.* yellowish, in a short spike, on a long peduncle; sep. narrow, spreading; pet. about 1½ in. long; lip spotted. Erect. Borneo. 1892. (I.H. 39, 161.)

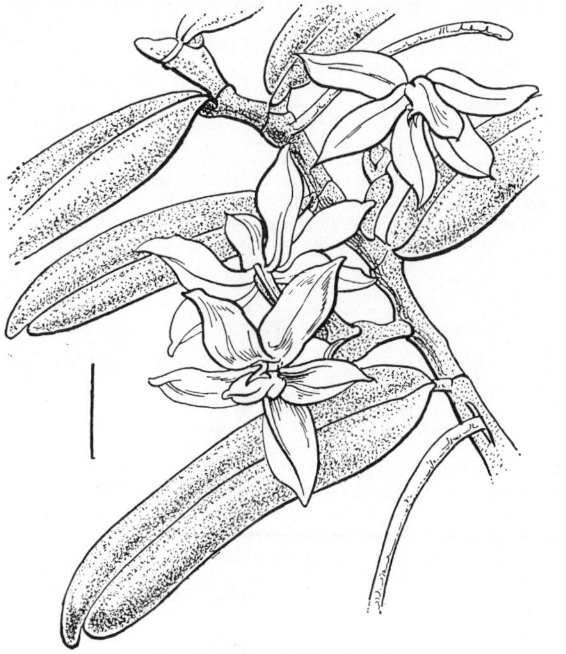

Sarcochilus Calceolus

S. Calceo'lus. *fl.* 2½ in. across, white; sep. and pet. fleshy, oblong, acute; mid-lobe of lip slipper-like, but closed up, side lobes ascending, triangular; peduncles short, 2-fld. *l.* oblong, fleshy, obliquely emarginate, obtuse. Stem elongated. Manila. 1844. (B.R. 32, 19.)

S. Cecil'iae. *fl.* somewhat campanulate, small, pinkish, fragrant; mid-lobe of lip short, broad, with dense white ciliation, side lobes longer; racemes erect, may reach 9 in. h., few-fld. *l.* linear or linear-lanceolate, 2 to 4 in. long, obscurely spotted. Australia. 1910 or before.

S. cochinchinen'sis. *fl.* yellowish, glutinous; sep. striped brown over middle nerves outside and with some dark-yellow patches under column; racemes small. *l.* rather narrow, linear-ligulate, 2-lobed at apex. Cochin China. 1877. SYN. *Camarotis cochinchinensis.*

S. crassifo'lius. *fl.* yellowish or yellowish-white, few, small; mid-lobe of lip yellow with orange blotch behind crest; scape short. *l.* short, ovate-oblong, fleshy. Stem flattened, climbing. Habitat? 1894.

S. falca'tus.* *fl.* 3 to 10, 1½ in. across, white, with red streaks on an orange ground on side lobes of lip, distant; lateral sep. adnate to basal projections of column; peduncles scarcely exceeding, sometimes shorter than, l. *l.* oblong, often falcate, 2 to 4 in. long. Stems 2 to 3 in. h. Australia. 1821. (B.R. 1832.) A variable species.

S. Fitzger'aldii.* *fl.* 1 in. across, up to 12, snowy-white, spotted rich lake or maroon, the saccate lip not half length of sep., side lobes falcate; peduncle, with raceme, 6 to 12 in. long. *l.* 3 to 6 in. long. Australia. 1877. Habit of *S. falcatus* but stronger. var. **al'bus,** *fl.* pure white. (B.M. n.s. 201.)

S. Freeman'ii. *fl.* yellow, with brownish spots and streaks, numerous in a raceme; sep. very long, narrow-linear; pet. a little shorter than sep.; lip small, saccate, 3-dentate. *l.* ligulate, here and there undulate, 2-dentate, 6 to 7 in. long, 1¼ in. wide. Assam. 1876. Dwarf. SYN. *Thrixspermum Freemanii.*

S. hainanen'sis. *fl.* light yellow, pendent; sep. and pet. 2 in. long; lip shorter, white, finely papillose; raceme 3 in. long, with imbricate bracts. *l.* linear-oblong, 4 in. long. Stem slender, 12 in. long. Hainan. 1896. (B.M. 7489.)

S. Hartmann'ii.* *fl.* creamy-white, ¾ in. across; sep. and pet. with brick-red spots at base; side-lobes of lip spotted and streaked brick-red, semifalcate or oblong, mid-lobe yellow; callus yellow with red spots; raceme dense erect. *l.* generally 4, rather thick, ligulate, 2-dentate. Queensland. 1877. (B.M. 7010.) SYN. *Thrixspermum Hartmannii* *See* **S. rubricentrum.**

S. indusia'tum. *fl.* small, in several-fld. drooping racemes; sep. and pet. yellowish, spotted red; lip white; spur cylindric, inflated at apex. *l.* soft, shining, oblong, 3 in. broad. Sunda Is. 1886. SYN. *Thrixspermum indusiatum.*

S. lunif'erus.* *fl.* ½ in. across; sep. and pet. yellow, spotted orange-red, obtuse; lip white, saccate, side lobes erect; racemes drooping, many-fld.; peduncles 1 to 2 in. long. *l.* usually wanting, but sometimes small ones present. Moulmein. 1868. (B.M. 7044; A.B.G.C. 8, 276.) SYN. *Thrixspermum luniferum.*

S. minu'tiflos. *fl.* small, numerous, blush white; lip with purple stripes on the side lobes, an orange crest, front lobe a globular mass of white hairs; spikes slender. *l.* very narrow. Habit tufted, 3 to 4 in. h. Queensland. 1917.

S. Moor'ei. *fl.* many in a raceme; sep. and pet. light yellow, with numerous brown blotches; lip sac-like, with short lobes; peduncle 6 in. long. *l.* nearly 1 ft. long, over 2 in. wide. Solomon Is. 1880. SYN. *Thrixspermum Moorei.*

S. muricula'tus. *fl.* light yellow, in very short racemes, sweet-scented, about ½ in. across; sep. and pet. with 2 purple bars; lip short-clawed; peduncles and rachis viscid. *l.* 6 to 9 in. long, lorate, obliquely notched. Stem 6 to 8 in. long, stout, rooting below. Andaman Is. 1881. SYN. *Thrixspermum muriculatum.*

S. musco'sus. *fl.* yellow and purple, small, on a short, hairy scape; lip whitish with brown marks. *l.* distichous, oblong. Stem dwarf. Andaman Is. 1893.

S. obtu'sus. A synonym of *Camarotis obtusa.*

S. oliva'ceus. *fl.* 3 to 12, slightly scented; sep. and pet. narrow, dull pale purple or yellowish-brown, much contracted below middle; lip white, streaked red, about half as long as sep.; racemes loose. *l.* oblong, often falcate, 2 to 3 in. long. Stems less than 1 in. long. Australia.

S. pal'lidus. *fl.* pale yellow, rather small, 8 to 15 in a short raceme. *l.* broadly linear, arcuate, oblique at apex, somewhat 3-toothed. Sylhet? SYN. *Micropera pallida.*

S. purpu'reus. A synonym of *Camarotis purpurea.*

S. rubricent'rum.* *fl.* white, centre red, spotted darker red, 12 to 20 in a raceme; lip banded red across front. *l.* oblong, about 5 in. long. Australia. 1880. Perhaps a form of *S. Hartmannii.*

S. Sillemia'nus. *fl.* milk-white, slightly tinted pale yellow; lip striped purple, mid-lobe yellow inside, marked with 2 purple spots outside; peduncle 2-fld. *l.* elongated, terete. Burma? 1882. Habit of *Vanda teres*, but not quite so robust. SYN. *Thrixspermum Sillemianum.*

S. te'res. Sep. and pet. white, spotted, fleshy, obtuse; lip white with a few violet stains and a deep purple round knob at end. *l.* ovate-oblong or oblong, unequal at tip, flat, fleshy, pale green, 5 in. long, ½ in. wide. Java? SYN. *Ornitharium striatulum.*

S. unguicula'tus. *fl.* 2 in. across, scented; sep. and pet. light straw; lip clawed, 3-lobed, side lobes large, white, streaked crimson, mid-lobe rounded, fleshy, dotted crimson; raceme on a stout peduncle, 4 to 6 in. long, rachis thickened. Continues to flower for some time, usually producing 2 fl. at a time, each lasting but a few hours. *l.* resemble those of *Phalaenopsis amabilis.* Manilla. 1848. (L. 756; W.O.A. 266 as *Thrixspermum unguiculatum.*) SYN. *Phalaenopsis fugax, P. Ruckeriana.*

E. C.

SARCOCOC'CA (*sarkos*, fleshy, *kokkos*, a berry; alluding to the fleshy fruits). FAM. *Buxaceae.* A genus of 5 or 6 species of low, evergreen shrubs, natives of India, China, and the Malayan Archipelago. Leaves alternate, entire, glabrous. Flowers white, 1-sexual, both sexes on the same short, axillary clusters; petals none; sepals and stamens 4 to 6; styles 2 or 3. Fruit a fleshy, ovoid or globose berry. Differing from Pachysandra by the entire (not toothed) leaves, short flower-clusters, and short styles.

S. confusa, S. Hookeriana digyna, S. humilis are more hardy than *S. ruscifolia, S. Hookeriana,* and *S. saligna.* All grow easily in any well-drained soil of moderate richness and all thrive in shady situations. Spreading by means of sucker growths, they are readily propagated by division; also by cuttings or seed. The flowers of all species except *S. saligna* are very fragrant and are useful for bringing into the house during the winter.

KEY

1.	*Lvs. ovate to ovate-elliptic*	2
1.	*Lvs. lanceolate*	3
2.	*Fruits scarlet*	S. ruscifolia
2.	*Fruits black*	S. confusa
3.	*Young shoots glabrous; fl. greenish*	S. saligna
3.	*Young shoots downy; fl. white*	4
4.	*Densely tufted shrub* 12 *to* 18 *in. h., anthers pink*	S. humilis
4.	*Looser growing shrub, sometimes up to 6 ft. stems often purplish, anthers cream*	S. Hookeriana var. digyna

S. confu'sa. Evergreen shrub up to 6 ft. h., dense, much branched from base; branches downy, green. *l.* elliptic to elliptic-ovate, 1¼ to 2½ in. long (usually 1¼ to 2 in.), glabrous, dark green above; paler beneath; stalk short. *fl.* as in *S. humilis* but anthers cream, female *fl.* with 2 or 3 styles. Winter. Very fragrant. *fr.* black, shining. Habitat? (B.M. 9449 as *S. humilis.*) SYN. *S. ruscifolia chinensis* of gardens.

Sarcococca Hookeriana var. *digyna*

S. Hookeria'na. Evergreen shrub up to 6 ft. h., shoots minutely downy. *l.* 2 to 3½ in. long, ½ to ¾ in. wide, narrowly lanceolate to oblong-lanceolate, slender-pointed, cuneate; stalk ¼ in. long. *fl.* fragrant, white, crowded in the l.-axils; styles 3. September to November. *fr.* nearly globose, ¼ in. wide, black. Himalaya. SYN. *S. pruniformis Hookeriana.* var. **digy'na,** young stems sometimes purplish, female *fl.* with 2 styles. China. 1908.

S. hum'ilis. Evergreen shrub of dense, tufted growth, 1 to 1½ ft. h., stems minutely downy when young, branched above. *l.* elliptic to lanceolate, pointed, cuneate, 1 to 2½ in. long, glabrous, shining. *fl.* in short axillary clusters, white, very fragrant; stamens flattened, petal-like, female fl. with 2 styles, anthers pink. January to March. *fr.* globose, ¼ in. across, black. China. 1907.

S. pruniform'is. A synonym of *S. saligna.* var. **Hookeria'na,** a synonym of *S. Hookeriana.*

S. ruscifo'lia. Evergreen shrub, 2 to 3 ft. h., shoots downy at first. *l.* 1 to 2½ in. long, half as wide, ovate, slender-pointed, glossy-green; stalk ⅛ to ¼ in. long. *fl.* milk-white, fragrant, in few-fld. axillary clusters; styles 3, stamens ¼ in. long. December to March. *fr.* globose, ¼ in. wide, scarlet or crimson. China. 1901. (B.M. 9045.)

S. salig'na. Evergreen shrub 2 to 4 ft. h., stems glabrous. *l.* 3 to 5 in. long, ½ to 1⅛ in. wide, narrow-lanceolate, slenderly tapered to both ends, glabrous, shining green, with a marginal vein. *fl.* greenish in short axillary clusters, stamens ¼ in. long, anthers yellow; styles 2. December to March. *fr.* ovoid, ⅓ in. long, purple. Himalaya. 1820. (B.R. 1012 as *S. pruniformis.*) Not fragrant.

W. J. B.

SARCOCOL'LA (name used by Pliny for a kind of gum, from *sarx*, flesh, and *kolla*, glue; in reference to the resinous secretion from some of the species). FAM. *Penaeaceae.* A small genus of low S. African shrubs, evergreen and thickly set with imbricated leaves which change beneath the flowers to leaf-like coloured bracts; flowers terminal; perianth tubular, cylindrical; stamens 4, inserted in the throat of the perianth.

S. squamo'sa. Shrub, 1½ to 2 ft. h., shoots glabrous. *l.* closely set on the stems, imbricate, obovate to ovate, ⅓ to ⅜ in. long, nearly as wide, glandular, pointed. *fl.* red, ⅝ in. wide, in terminal heads of about 6; perianth tube ⅓ in. long, with a limb of 4 ovate, pointed lobes; lower bracts larger than the l., ciliate. Spring. S. Africa. (B.R. 106 as *Penaea squamosa.*) Greenhouse.

W. J. B.

sarco'des, flesh-like.

SARCOGLOS'SUM. A synonym of Cirrhaea.

SARCOPO'DIUM. *See* **Bulbophyllum.** The name has also been used for a section of Dendrobium.

SARCOSTEM'MA (*sarkos*, fleshy, *stemma*, crown; from the fleshy corona). FAM. *Asclepiadaceae.* Climbing or straggling plants with slender, succulent stems, jointed and leafless, exuding a milky juice when damaged. The small flowers, which are produced in an umbel, are usually white, greenish, or yellowish; in structure they resemble Stapelia, but the corona is fleshy and conspicuous. Sarcostemmas can be treated in the same way as Ceropegias and Stapelias, grown in a well-drained soil and dried in the winter, but on the whole they prefer more heat as they come from Trop. and Sub-trop. Africa, Asia, and Australia. *S. viminale* was for long known and grown as *Euphorbia pendula* until it flowered in the Darrah collection, Manchester, in 1915 and was recognized as an Asclepiad.

S. Brunonia'num. *fl.* yellow. In habit very similar to *S. viminale* but with slightly thicker stems. E. Indies. (B.M. 6002.)

S. vimina'le. *fl.* greenish-white or yellowish, in clusters from the upper joints. Stems about ¼ in. or less in diameter, long-jointed, weak. Abyssinia to Cape Province. SYN. *Euphorbia pendula.*

V. H.

sarden'sis -is -e, of Sardis, near to Smyrna.

sardo'us -a -um, of Sardinia.

Sargentia'nus -a -um, in honour of Prof. Charles Sprague Sargent, 1841–1927, Founder and Director, Arnold Arboretum, Mass., U.S.A.

SARGENTODOX'A (*doxe*, glory; in honour of Prof. C. S. Sargent). FAM. *Sargentodoxaceae.* A genus of a single species, a deciduous twining shrub, related to Sinofranchetia, but with lateral leaflets 2- or 3-nerved at base, with forked nerves, flowers dioecious, pistillate, with many 1-ovuled carpels, fruits berry-like. Greatly resembling Sinofranchetia in appearance but needing the protection of a wall in most parts of England.

S. cunea'ta. Deciduous glabrous twining shrub, 25 ft. or more h. *l.* alternate, 3-foliolate, dark shining green, lateral lflets. obliquely ovate, about 4 in. long, terminal lflet. obovate to oblong, smaller than lateral. *fl.* in drooping racemes 4 to 6 in. long, greenish-yellow, sep. 6, petaloid, ½ in. long, narrow-oblong; staminate fragrant, bell-shaped, with 6 stamens; pistillate with carpels crowded on a central cone. May. *fr.* a cluster of purplish-blue 1-seeded berries on stalks about ⅓ in. long; seed black. E. and Cent. China. 1907. (B.M. 9111, 9112.) SYN. *Holboellia cuneata.*

SARGENTODOXA'CEAE. Dicotyledons. A family of but 1 species related to Lardizabalaceae and Schizandraceae. Characters given under genus and species above. The stalked 1-seeded berries on a conical torus are peculiar.

sari, of the River Sar, Asia Minor.

sarmat'icus -a -um, of Sarmatia, ancient name for part of E. Europe.

sarmento'sus -a -um, having long runners, as in the Strawberry.

SARMIENT'A (in honour of Mart. Sarmiento, a Spanish botanist). FAM. *Gesneriaceae.* A genus of 1 creeping, wiry-stemmed, glabrous, Chilean shrub. Leaves opposite, rather fleshy. Flowers stalked, solitary in the axils of the leaves, corolla tube swollen, somewhat oblique at mouth, lobes 5, rounded, spreading. Stamens 2, front pair represented by staminodes; ovary superior. A difficult plant to grow well. It is best in a compost of soft peat mixed with Sphagnum, small crocks, and charcoal, planted in a pan or orchid-basket, in a shady place near the glass of a moist greenhouse such as suits Lapagerias. It needs abundant water. In nature it climbs over trees and rocks.

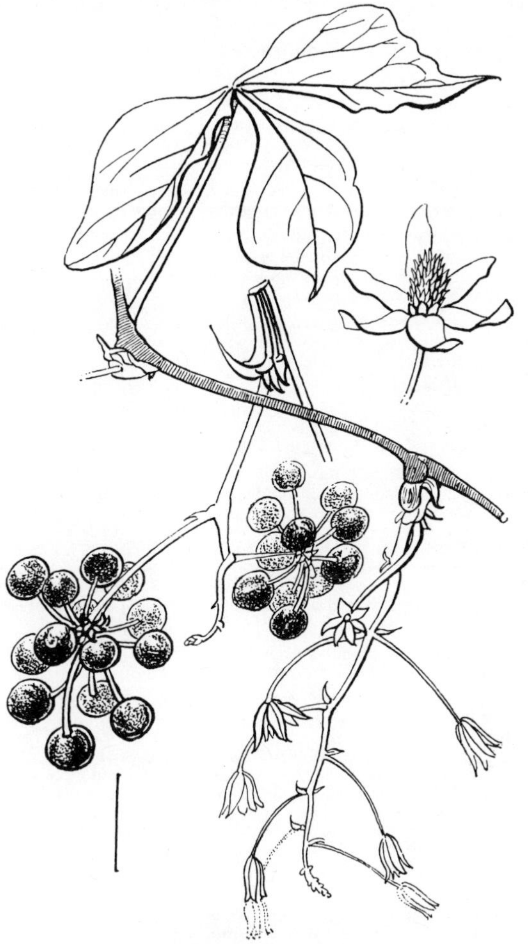

Sargentodoxa cuneata

S. re'pens.* *l.* rather small, entire or slightly toothed. *fl.* crimson, numerous, solitary in l.-axils; tube long, lobes spreading; sep. 5, free. Chile. 1862. (B.M. 6720; F.d.S. 1646.)

sarnien'sis -is -e, of Guernsey.

saro- in compound words signifying broom-like.

SAROTHAM'NUS scopar'ius. A synonym of *Cytisus scoparus.*

SARRACE'NIA (in honour of Dr. Sarrazin of Quebec who first sent species from N. America to Europe in the 17th century). FAM. *Sarraceniaceae.* A genus of about 7 species of curious herbaceous perennials, natives of N. America, with pitcher-like leaves serving as fly-traps, the plants making use of the insects caught as food (*see* **Carnivorous Plants**). Leaves radical, pitcher-shaped. Flowers on 1-flowered scapes with 3 bracteoles close beneath the calyx; sepals 5, spreading; petals 5, connivent; style expanded into an umbrella-like disk. Fruit a many-seeded capsule. Many names have been given these curious plants: e.g. Indian Cup, Pitcher Plant, Side-saddle Flower, Trumpet Leaf, and their curious form has encouraged many to attempt their cultivation. *S. flava*, *S. psittacina*, and *S. purpurea* are sometimes grown in boggy spots in the open, but generally the plants are half-hardy and succeed best in a moderately cool greenhouse. They must never be allowed to get dry, and some, e.g. *S. psittacina*, are best treated as semi-aquatics. Good fibrous peat and Sphagnum make the best compost for them as it does not readily become sour as other composts are apt to do with the large quantities of water needed for successful cultivation. A moderately cool house with a moist, close atmosphere is best. Many hybrids have been raised in gardens and several occur in nature where the species grow in proximity to one another. A few are mentioned below.

S. × Atkinsonia'na (*S. flava maxima* × *S. purpurea*). Much resembling *S. flava*. *l.* long, narrow, erect, green, with slight red ribs and veins; blade broad, heart-shaped, green, with red veins. Of garden origin. Cf. *S.* × *Stevensii* which is of the same parentage.

S. × cantabrigien'sis (*S. Drummondii* × *S. minor*). Intermediate between parents. Raised at Cambridge Botanic Garden.

S. × Cates'baei* (*S. flava* × *S. purpurea*). Pitchers very large, with a flat, roundish heart-shaped wing, veined red. SYN. *S. flava Catesbaei*, *S. flava picta*. A natural hybrid. Florida. Long known and described by John Ray.

S. × chelson'ii* (*S. purpurea* × *S. rubra*). *l.* with brighter colouring than either parent. Pitchers long as in *S. rubra* but broader as in *S. purpurea*, ascending. Of garden origin. (G.C. 13 (1880), 725.)

S. × Courtii* (*S. psittacina* × *S. purpurea*). *l.* bright crimson-purple above the middle when young with darker veins, becoming deep blood-red with blackish-purple veins with age. Pitchers semi-decumbent. Of garden origin. 1885. (G.F. 1886, 29.)

S. Drum'mondii.* Pitchers 2 ft. long, erect, trumpet-shaped with narrow wings; blade erect, rounded, shortly pointed, hairy within, white, like the upper part of the pitcher, veined with purple. *fl.* purple, 3 in. long on scapes longer than l. April. SE. United States. 1829. (F.d.S. 560, 1071.) Produces a second crop of pitchers late in summer, remaining during winter. var. **al'ba,** pitchers tall, green, with white areas above. (G.C. 10 (1878), 281.); **ru'bra,** pitchers shorter, narrowed, deep purple above; **undula'ta,** margins of lamina wavy.

S. × Farnha'mii (*S. Drummondii* × *S. rubra*). Intermediate between parents. Of garden origin.

S. fla'va. Pitchers erect, 2 ft. h., yellowish, narrowly winged; lamina yellow, erect, orbicular, 3 to 4 in. wide, slender-pointed, hairy within, reddish at base or with purple veins. *fl.* yellow, 4 to 5 in. across; pet. obovate-spatulate, undulate; stigma 2 in. wide; scapes as long as l. April, May. SE. United States. 1752. (B.M. 780; L.B.C. 1957.) var. **atrosanguin'ea,** pitcher and lid becoming rich deep blood-red. (G.C. 16 (1881), 13.); **Cates'baei,** a synonym of *S. Catesbaei*; **gigan'tea,** larger than type. Of garden origin; **orna'ta,** up to 32 in. h., throat of pitcher and base of lid with purple lines. 1881. (G.C. 15 (1881), 114 as *S. ornata*.) SYN. *S. Fildesii*.

S. × illustra'ta (*S. flava* × *S.* × *Stevensii*). Habit of *S. flava*. Pitchers strongly marked with longitudinal crimson ribs united by crimson veins. Of garden origin.

S. × Maddisonia'na (*S. minor* × *S. psittacina*). Pitchers somewhat erect, short, broad, green with dull veins outside; mouth with translucent spots; lid broad-ovate, curved over the tube, wavy, strongly ribbed with deep purple veins. Of garden origin. The reciprocal cross raised by Messrs. Veitch was called *S.* × *formosa* and is intermediate between parents.

S. × melanorho'da (*S. purpurea* × *S.* × *Stevensii*). Pitchers 6 to 12 in. long, more or less decumbent, long funnel-shaped, widest at mouth, blood-red veined, blackish-crimson when mature; wing broad; lid erect, crisped reddish-yellow with blackish-crimson veins, hairy above.

S. mi'nor. Pitchers 6 to 12 in. long, erect, trumpet-shaped, green to purple, spotted white near yellowish summit; wings broad; lid ovate, concave, arching over mouth of tube, hairy and netted with purple within. *fl.* yellow, 2 in. across; pet. bent over stigma; scapes shorter than l. May. E. United States. 1803. (B.M. 1710 and L.B.C. 803 as *S. variolaris*.)

S. × Mitchellia'na.* (*S. Drummondii rubra* × *S. purpurea*). Pitchers curved, funnel-shaped, broadest at mouth, olive-green profusely netted with fine red veins, becoming reddish-crimson with age; lid heart kidney-shaped, wavy, boldly netted deep crimson-red.

S. × Moorei (*S. Drummondii* × *S. flava*). Pitchers 2 ft. long, green, 4 in. wide at mouth. (G.C. 16 (1881) 44.) The first hybrid Sarracenia raised by Moore at Glasnevin. The hybrid occurs in nature and is called *S. Mandaiana*.

S. psittaci'na.* Pitchers 2 to 4 in. long, spreading, tube slender; wings broad, marked with white spots and purple veins; lid round, inflated, with incurved beak, almost closing the mouth of the tube. *fl.* purple; scapes 12 in. long. April, May. SE. United States. 1866. (F.d.S. 2063; G.C. 15 (1881) 816.)

S. purpu'rea.* Pitchers 4 to 6 in. long, spreading, inflated, contracted at throat, broadly winged; lid kidney-shaped, erect, hairy within, often veined with purple. *fl.* purple; pet. inflected over stigma; scapes 12 in. long. April, May. E. United States. 1640. (B.M. 849; F.d.S. 1076.)

Sarracenia purpurea

S. ru'bra. Pitchers 10 to 18 in. long, erect, slender, narrowly winged, paler above, netted with purple veins; lid ovate, erect, tip beaked, hairy within. *fl.* reddish-purple, smaller than in *S. purpurea*; pet. obovate; scapes longer than l. May. 1786. (L.B.C. 1163.) var. **acumina'ta,** pitchers pale green with crimson netting near top; lid acuminate, much larger than mouth. (B.M. 3515 and H.E.F. 13.)

S. × Sanderia'na* (*S. Drummondii rubra* × *S.* × *Farnhamii*). Intermediate between parents. Of garden origin. 1897.

S. × Stevens'ii (*S. flava* × *S. purpurea*). Similar to *S.* × *Catesbaei* (q.v.). Raised by Mr. Stevens at Trentham. (G.C. 16 (1881), 40.)

S. × Swania'na* (*S. minor* × *S. purpurea*). Pitchers funnel-shaped, slightly incurved, greenish-purple, closely netted with crimson within; wings broad; lid ovate heart-shaped, 2-lobed at tip. Of garden origin.

S. × Tollia'na (*S. Drummondii alba* × *S. flava*). Pitchers long, slender, funnel-shaped, margin of mouth recurved, greenish or deep purple-red with darker ribs and veins; lid broadly kidney-shaped, wavy, netted reddish-purple. Of garden origin.

S. × vitta'ta (*S.* × *Chelsonii* × *S. purpurea*). Striped and spotted red-purple.

S. × Wil'lisii (*S.* × *Courtii* × *S.* × *melanorhoda*). Combining the characters of 3 species. Pitchers pale green, white, and crimson. Of garden origin.

S. × Wilsonia'na (*S. flava* × *S. purpurea*). Of same parentage as *S.* × *Catesbaei* and *S.* × *Stevensii* (q.v.).

SARRACENIA'CEAE. Dicotyledons. A family of about 9 species in 3 genera, all carnivorous perennial herbs inhabiting turfy or marshy bogs in America. Leaves all radical with a tubular pitcher and a small, rounded lid lying on or over the orifice of the pitcher. The pitcher-shaped leaves are effective insect-traps, a sugary secretion near the mouth attracting the insects which enter the pitcher, exit being obstructed by downward-pointing hairs. The captives fall into the liquid at the bottom of the pitcher where they are digested and absorbed. Flowers solitary or few in a raceme, large, nodding; sepals 4 or 5, free, closely overlapping from the base, more or less petaloid, persistent, petals 5, free, overlapping, deciduous (wanting in Heliamphora); stamens numerous, hypogynous, free, filaments filiform; anthers 2-celled; ovary superior. Scapes naked or with a few bracts. The genera are Darlingtonia, Heliamphora, Sarracenia.

sarrace'nicus -a -um, Arabian.

SARSAPARILLA. Name applied to the roots of several distinct plants, especially those of species of Smilax.

SA'SA (Japanese name for dwarf bamboos). FAM. *Gramineae.* A genus containing numerous species wild in E. Asia, of which 3 or 4 are in cultivation. These have, until recently, been included in Arundinaria, from which, however, they are abundantly distinct in their combination of a dwarf habit, large leaves, slender stems with 1 to few branches at a joint, and in their numerous secondary veins. All are rampant growers of dense growth and are only useful as isolated patches, preferably in thin woodland. Associated with other shrubs they are apt to become a nuisance. (*See also* **Arundinaria.**)

KEY

1.	*Lvs.* 4 *to* 8 *in. long; margins becoming drab in autumn*	S. Veitchii
1.	*Lvs.* 9 *to* 24 *in. long*	2
2.	*Veins in* 7 *to* 13 *pairs*	S. senanensis
2.	*Veins in* 15 *to* 18 *pairs*	S. tessellata

S. senanen'sis. Stems 4 to 8 ft., slender, waxy below joints. *l.* 9 to 13 in. long, 2 to 3 in. wide, ribbed, with a tail-like point, dark glossy-green, glaucous beneath; secondary veins in 7 to 13 pairs. Japan. 1889. (B.T.S. i. 218.) var. **nebulo'sa,** stems purple-tinged; sheaths spotted. Except for *S. tessellata*, this has the largest l. among hardy bamboos. A very strong, rapid spreader which should have an isolated position. SYN. *Arundinaria palmata, Bambusa metallica.*

S. tessella'ta. Stems 4 to 6 ft., slender; stem-sheaths 8 to 10 in. long, fringed with hairs, persistent. *l.* 12 to 24 in. long, 3 to 4 in. wide, very slenderly pointed, glaucous beneath, slightly ribbed; secondary veins in 15 to 18 pairs. Japan. 1845. (B.T.S. i. 78.) Notable as having the largest l. of all hardy bamboos. Spreads rapidly by creeping rootstocks and forms dense thickets. SYN. *Arundinaria Ragamowskii.*

S. Veitch'ii. Stems 1½ to 4 ft., ⅛ in. wide, with a single branch at a joint; stem-sheaths persistent, very downy at first, with tufts of bristles at top. *l.* 4 to 8 in. long, 1 to 2 in. wide, abruptly pointed, withering at margins in autumn; secondary veins in 5 to 9 pairs. Japan. 1880. SYN. *Arundinaria Veitchii.* Of little garden value. Spreads rapidly.

W. J. B.

Sasan'qua, from the Japanese name.

SASHES. The framework of a glass structure in which the glass is held, especially the glazed frames which open for ventilating a house or are used in pits, &c., where they can be moved or entirely removed at will. In houses the ventilating sashes are usually made to open by means of iron gearing and levers, making effective working much easier than when each had to be opened independently.

SAS'SAFRAS (from the Spanish *salsafras*). FAM. *Lauraceae.* A genus of 3 species of deciduous trees, one each in America, China, and Formosa. The flowers are 1-sexual, have a 6-lobed calyx and 9 stamens. Fruit a drupe. *S. albidum*, the only one now in cultivation, was long supposed to have many medicinal virtues; an oil used in perfumery is still obtained from it. It is a very handsome, pleasantly aromatic, distinct tree, but with little beauty of flower. Good specimens are rare in cultivation, but it is quite hardy. Propagated by seed or by root suckers. Likes a rich loamy soil.

S. albi'dum.* Sassafras. Deciduous tree 70 to 100 ft. h. *l.* 3 to 6 in. long, alternate, variable in shape and size, oval, ovate or obovate, entire or 3-lobed, cuneate, 3-veined, glaucous beneath; stalk ½ to 1½ in. long. *fl.* ¼ in. wide, greenish-yellow, in racemes 1 to 2 in. long. May. *fr.* roundish-ovoid, dark blue, ⅜ in. long. N. America. Before 1633. (B.T.S. ii. 501.) The foliage puts on orange and scarlet tints in autumn. SYN. *S. officinale.*

S. officina'le. A synonym of *S. albidum.*

S. Tzu'mu. A single tree raised from Chinese seed in 1900 grew vigorously in the Coombe Wood Nursery until it was closed down in 1913. The tree was then removed to Kew but, owing no doubt to its never having been transplanted before, it did not survive. Botanically it is very near *S. officinale*, but the *l.* were much larger and there are certain differences in floral structure.

W. J. B.

SASSAFRAS, CALIFORNIAN. *See* **Umbellularia californica.**

SASSAFRAS, SWAMP. *See* **Magnolia virginiana.**

SASSAFRAS, TASMANIAN. *See* **Atherosperma moschatum.**

SASSAFRAS-TREE. *See* **Sassafras albidum.**

sasuroi'des, like Sasuru, the native name of *Osmoxylon umbelliferum.*

SATIN FLOWER. *See* **Sisyrinchium.**

SATINWOOD-TREE. *See* **Chloroxylon Swietenia.**

sati'vus -a -um, sown or planted, not spontaneous.

satsuma'nus -a -um, of Satsuma, SW. Japan.

satura'tus -a -um, full or extreme.

SATUREI'A (old Latin name used by Pliny). FAM. *Labiatae.* A genus of about 14 species of highly aromatic, hardy herbs or under-shrubs; one is a native of Florida, and the rest of the Mediterranean region. Flowers whorled; calyx 5-toothed or very obscurely bilabiate: corolla tube equalling the calyx or bracteoles, the limb bilabiate; stamens 4, distant. Leaves small, entire or toothed, often fascicled; floral and cauline ones similar, or the uppermost ones reduced to small bracts. The leaves of both species usually cultivated are employed, like other sweet herbs, for seasoning in cookery. They were noticed by Virgil as among the most fragrant of herbs, and on this account were recommended to be grown near bee-hives. Vinegar, flavoured with Savory and other aromatic herbs, was much used by the ancient Romans as Mint-sauce is at the present day with us. *See* **Savory.**

S. horten'sis. Summer Savory. Annual aromatic herb with erect downy stems 6 to 8 in. h. *l.* ½ to ⅝ in. long, linear-oblong, pointed, scarcely stalked. *fl.* pale lilac or nearly white in axillary whorls of about 6, forming dense spikes. S. Europe. 1562.

S. monta'na. Winter Savory. Pleasantly aromatic, semi-evergreen sub-shrub 12 to 15 in. h.; stems erect, minutely downy. *l.* ½ to 1 in. long, narrow-oblong to oblanceolate, entire, glandular, margins bristly. *fl.* pale purple, ⅜ in. long, in axillary whorls forming slender terminal panicles. June. S. Europe, N. Africa. 1562.

W. J. B.

SATY'RIUM (*Satyrion*, name given by Dioscorides to an Orchid). FAM. *Orchidaceae.* A rather large genus of about 70 species of stove, terrestrial, deciduous, tuberous-rooted orchids, inhabiting the E. Indies, the Mascarene Is., and, for the most part, S. and Trop. Africa. Flowers mediocre or rather large, rarely small, in dense spikes; sepals and petals free, much-spreading or reflexed; lip superior, sessile at the base of the column, broad, concave, galeate, or cucullate, undivided with 2 spurs or sacs; bracts membranous or somewhat leafy. Leaves few on the lower part of the stem, rarely many at the sides of a tall stem; in some only 2 more or less orbicular leaves lie close to the compost. Species from cool regions can be grown in a cold frame, in a compost of turfy peat, fibry loam, and sand, with plenty of drainage, but should be wintered in a temperature near 50° F. *S. ciliatum* and *S. nepalense* thrive under similar treatment as regards compost, but require a greenhouse temperature, and species from warm localities must have correspondingly higher temperatures. Growth is rapid. Water should be given infrequently as growth begins but more and more liberally as roots become numerous. For S. African species very occasional watering should be given while the tubers are dormant. As with many tuberous-rooted orchids, propagation by division can rarely be effected. The genus is allied to Disa and Orchis. Where no locality is mentioned below the species is S. African.

S. auranti'acum. A synonym of *S. coriifolium.*

S. au'reum. A variety of *S. coriifolium.*

S. bicallo'sum. *fl.* small, whitish, densely set; spur small; bracts bristle-like, long. *l.* ovate, stem-clasping.

S. bicorn'e. *fl.* green, with an unpleasant odour; dorsal sep. longer than pet., linear, obtuse, lateral larger, all connate at base; lip acute, fleshy; spurs pendulous; bracts concave, reflexed. June. *l.* twin, orbicular, scabrous-ciliate; sheaths inflated, distant, furfuraceous-ciliate. 9 in. h. 1786. (B.R. 416 as *S. cucullatum.*) SYN. *Orchis bicornis.*

S. × **Bolus'ii.** Natural hybrid, *S. carneum* × *S. coriifolium.*

S. can'didum.* *fl.* white or rose-tinted, very sweetly scented; sep. linear, spreading; pet. smaller, ascending, recurved at apex; lip inflated, obtuse. September. *l.* twin, somewhat roundish-ovate, glabrous. Sheath inflated, holding water. Sometimes 1½ ft. h. 1836.

S. carn'eum.* *fl.* white, suffused flesh-colour, large; sep. obtuse; pet. unequal-sided; lip galeate, apiculate, reflexed; bracts rose-margined. June. *l.* radical, twin, orbicular, fleshy; sheaths leafy, cucullate. 1½ ft. h. or more. 1797. (B.M. 1512.) var. **ro'seum,** *fl.* rose, 1889.

S. cilia'tum. A synonym of *S. nepalense.*

S. coriifo'lium.* *fl.* yellow; sep. and pet. linear, obtuse, glabrous, shorter than the orbicular lip; spur cylindrical, obtuse, bearded within; bracts ovate, reflexed; spike few-fld. October. *l.* oblong-lanceolate, acute, spreading, slightly scabrous on margins. 1 ft. h. or more. 1787. (B.M. 2172; B.R. 703; S.B.F.G. s. 2, 3; L.B.C. 104 as *S. cucullatum.*) var. **au'reum,** *fl.* deep golden-yellow shaded rich crimson. July, August. 1842. SYN. *S. aureum;* **macula'tum,** *fl.* deep yellow, spotted red. May be a natural hybrid. (B.M. 7289.)

S. cuculla'tum of Thunberg. A synonym of *S. bicorne* of Lindley or *S. coriifolium.*

S. erec'tum. *fl.* yellowish-orange or pale purple; sep. and pet. scarcely longer than the galeate lip; spurs filiform; bracts concave, reflexed, longer than fl.; spike many-fld. February. *l.* oblong, obtuse, leathery, with cartilaginous margins, scabrous, much-spreading, changing to convolute imbricated sheaths. Stem 1½ to 2 ft. h. wholly sheathed. 1838. (B.R. 26, 18 as *S. pustulatum.*) *S. erectum* of Lindley is *S. coriifolium.*

S. folio'sum. *fl.* pale purplish, small, erect; lateral sep. spreading, middle one decurved; pet. obtuse, sub-erect; galea hemispherical, longer than the filiform spurs; bracts longer than fl.; spike dense, obtuse, imbricate. July. *l.* oblong-lanceolate, erect, cucullate, imbricate, nearly as long as stem. Stem 1 to 1½ ft. h., leafy. 1828.

S. × **Guthrie'i.** Natural hybrid? (*S. bicallosum* × *S. candidum*). Possibly a form of *S.* × *Bolusii.* SYN. *S. bicalloso-candidum.*

S. macrophyl'lum. *fl.* rose-pink; spike many-fld. *l.* erect, oblong-lanceolate, pointed, about 9 in. long. 1½ to 2 ft. h.

S. membrana'ceum.* *fl.* bright or pale carmine or white and pink, nodding, 1 in. broad; pet., serrate beyond middle; lip with a recurved, serrulate tip; spike dense, 3 to 5 in. long. May. *l.* 2, 4 to 6 in. long, spreading, rounded-ovate. Stem 1 to 2 ft. h., very stout. S. Africa. 1889. (B.M. 7104.)

S. milita're. A synonym of *S. sphaerocarpum.*

S. nepalense.* *fl.* rose-pink, dark pink, or white, fragrant; lateral sep. oblong, dorsal and pet. linear; lip galeate, apiculate; spurs filiform; bracts reflexed, at least as long as fl.; spike oblong, loose, many-fld. *l.*, radical ones ovate or lanceolate or orbicular; cauline ones shorter, spreading, sheathing at base. 1 ft. h. or more. Himalaya, Nepal. 1882. (B.M. 6625; A.B.G.C. 8, 444.) var. **Wightian'um,** has a short, dense spike and few broad, radical *l.* (SYN. *S. Wightianum.*)

S. odo'rum. *fl.* inconspicuous, green, very fragrant. 1906.

S. pustula'tum. A synonym of *S. erectum.*

S. sphaerocarp'um. *fl.* white with red spots and lines, Orchis-like, 1 in. long; lip hooded, spur slender; spike about 20-fld., erect. *l.* ovate-oblong, erect, acute. 1893. (B.M. 7295.) SYN. *S. militare.*

S. Wightia'num. A variety of *S. nepalense.*

E. C.

SAUCERS. Saucers are made to suit all the smaller sizes of flower-pots. They are occasionally useful for standing pots in while they are in rooms, and for this purpose glazed non-porous saucers are best. They also serve as reservoirs of water where aquatic or semi-aquatic plants are grown in pots, but generally plants are quickly injured when the pots are stood for any length of time in pots of water. The roots are likely to be killed, possibly from lack of air, and the leaves soon show browning of the tips and finally, if the condition is allowed to continue, die. A means of preserving a plant from the attacks of slugs and crawling insects like ants is afforded by placing an inverted pot in the middle of a saucer of water and standing the plant on top of it.

SAUNDERS'IA (in honour of William Wilson Saunders, F.R.S., 1809–79, ardent collector and cultivator of rare plants at Reigate). FAM. *Orchidaceae.* A genus of a single epiphytic species, needing stove conditions. For general treatment *see* **Epidendrum.**

S. mirab'ilis. Sep. and pet. free, inclined forward; sep. ¼ in. long, two-thirds as broad, concave-ovate, yellowish, transversely barred purple; pet. similar but narrower; lip shortly connate with the column towards base, white, over ½ in. long, the 2-lobed apex ⅓ in. wide, twice as wide as the long claw; column short; pollen masses 2; scape short, recurved, many-fld.; bracts ovate. *l.* oblong, fleshy-leathery, 3 to 6 in. long, about ½ in. wide. Stem very short, 1-leaved, scarcely pseudobulbous. Brazil.

E. C.

Saunders'iae, in honour of Mrs. Kathleen Saunders of Zululand, amateur botanist.

SAURAU'JA (in honour of Fr. J. von Saurau, 1760–1832, Italian botanist). FAM. *Actinidiaceae.* A genus of about 200 species of usually hairy trees or shrubs, natives of the warmer parts of Asia and America. Leaves usually toothed. Flowers usually hermaphrodite; sepals 5, closely overlapping; petals 5, overlapping, joined or nearly free at base; stamens numerous, adherent to base of corolla, peduncles axillary or lateral, many-flowered, rarely short and few-flowered. The species mentioned below are stove shrubs (except *S. subspinosa*) with fine flowers and foliage, needing a compost of loam and peat. Propagated by cuttings of ripe wood in sand, under a glass, in heat.

S. excel'sa. About 10 ft. h. *l.* oblong-obovate, entire, rough above, hairy on veins beneath. *fl.* white, in trichotomous panicles on long, brown-hairy peduncles. June. Venezuela. 1820.

S. lanceola'ta. Stout shrub. *l.* oblong-lanceolate, slender-pointed, teeth very small, bright green, at first red-scaly on veins beneath, finally glabrous. *fl.* in axillary umbels. Java. 1882.

S. nepaulen'sis. About 6 ft. h., branches, &c., brown-downy. *l.* lanceolate, 9 in. long, 2 to 3 in. wide, slender-pointed, smooth above, brown-downy beneath. *fl.* white in many-fld. panicles on long peduncles. August. Nepal. 1824.

S. specta'bilis. About 10 ft. h., branches, &c., reddish-brown bristles. *l.* obovate-lanceolate, with short slender-points, connate at base, double-toothed, naked in vein-axils beneath; stalked. *fl.* white in large panicles; pet. obcordate, twice as long as cal. Brazil. 1838. (B.M. 3982.)

S. subspino'sa. Shrub of 8 ft. *l.* oblanceolate, 5 to 6 in. long, 2 in. wide, glabrous above, sparsely hairy on veins beneath, base rounded, apex acute; stalks densely hairy. *fl.* pale pink, tube deep red within, in axillary, many-fld. panicles; peduncles bristly; sep. overlapping; cor. widely bell-shaped. *fr.* a berry. Upper Burma. 1926. (B.M. 9472.) Cool greenhouse.

sauroceph'alus -a -um, resembling a lizard's head.

SAUROMA'TUM (*sauros,* lizard: the interior of the spathe is speckled). FAM. *Araceae.* A genus of 4 species of perennial Trop. Asiatic and African herbs with tuberous roots, the tubers producing 1 long-stalked pedate leaf. Spathe with an inflated tube with its margins more or less connate, the blade lanceolate, long. Related to Eminium but the rudimentary flowers between the male and female flowers on the spadix club-shaped. *S. guttatum* needs warm greenhouse treatment and a compost of light loam and peat in equal parts. It is propagated by offsets. The tubers are sometimes grown in rooms without soil as curiosities, the large inflorescences being produced before the leaves.

S. gutta'tum. Tuber large, about 6 in. across. *l.* produced after fl., rarely at the same time; stalk about 18 in. long, thick at base, sometimes spotted; blade roundish-cordate, palmately pedate, or pedatifid, segs. oblong or oblong-lanceolate, about 10 in. long, the lateral smaller. *Peduncle* very short. *Spathe* tube 2 to 4 in. long, about 1 in. wide, blade oblong-lanceolate, 12 to 25 in. long, purplish below, green above with large irregular dark purple spots; spadix terete-conical. May. Himalaya, E. Indies. 1815. (B.R. 1017 as *Arum venosum.*) A variable plant. var. **peda'tum** has a green unspotted l.-stalk and a pedatisect blade, the blade of the spathe being about 12 in. long, yellowish and spotted purple within; **puncta'tum,** only known in gardens, has the spathe unspotted except for brown spots near the base; **veno'sum,** has a spotted l.-stalk and a pedate blade with 7 to 11 segs. (B.M. 4465 as *S. guttatum.*)

Sauromatum guttatum (p. 1874)

SAURO'PUS (*sauros*, lizard, *pous*, foot). FAM. *Euphorbiaceae.* A genus of about 14 species of shrubs with the habit of Phyllanthus, natives of the E. Indies and Malaya. Leaves alternate, distichous, membranous, entire. Flowers clustered in leaf-axils, pedicellate, male minute, female solitary or twin, sometimes in same axil with male. For treatment *see* **Phyllanthus.** Stove conditions are required.

S. al'bicans Gardneria'nus. Branches and branchlets slender, green, angular. *l.* oblong-ovate, somewhat rounded at base, acute at apex, small, deep green with a greyish central blotch. Ceylon. 1861.

SAURURA'CEAE. Dicotyledons. A family of about 4 species in 4 genera of water or marsh herbs of E. Asia and N. America. Flowers without calyx or corolla, stamens 6 to 8 or fewer, carpels 3 or 4, somewhat united when the placentation is parietal. Related to and sometimes united with Piperaceae. The genera treated here are Anemopsis, Houttuynia, Saururus.

SAURUR'US (*sauros*, lizard, *oura*, tail; from the form of the inflorescence). Lizard's Tail. FAM. *Saururaceae.* A genus of 2 aquatic, perennial herbs, one native of E. Asia, the other N. American. Leaves alternate, broad, cordate; stipules membranous, adnate to petioles. Flowers small, numerous, in a terminal raceme, each with a small bract: perianth wanting; stamens 6 or 8 or fewer. Fruit sub-globose. The plants are hardy and should be grown in loam in a pond or cistern. They may be propagated by division or by seeds.

S. cern'uus. American Swamp Lily. *l.* cordate, 3 to 6 in. long, 2 to 3½ in. wide, slender-pointed, thin, veins 5 to 9 palmately converging, dark green, downy at first, without distinct stipules. *fl.* white, fragrant, in a dense spike, 4 to 6 in. long, nodding at end; bracts lanceolate; filaments long, capillary. N. America. 1759.

Saururus chinensis

S. chinen'sis. *rhiz.* stout. Stem stout, 12 to 18 in. long. *l.* alternate, ovate, cordate at base, 4 to 5 in. long, acute, bright green. *Spikes* cylindrical, 4 to 5 in. long in axils of upper l. *fl.* yellowish-white, filaments very short. Late summer. China, Japan. 1819. (R.H. 1908, 395 as *S. Loureiri.*)

S. Loureir'i. A synonym of *S. chinensis.*

SAUSSU'REA (in honour of the Swiss philosopher Horace Benedict de Saussure, 1740–99). FAM. *Compositae.* A genus of about 125 species of glabrous or white-hairy, perennial herbs, mostly natives of the mountains of Europe, Asia, and N. America. Leaves alternate, usually toothed or lobed but not spiny. Flower-heads purplish or bluish, sometimes narrow and corymbose, sometimes broader and pedunculate, solitary or in loose panicles: involucre ovoid or globose, with many closely overlapping bracts, the outer long; receptacle flat or convex, densely bristly scaly, rarely naked; rays deeply 5-fid, achenes glabrous, bristles of pappus in 1 or 2 series. Few of the species are very ornamental but some of the most curious, looking like cones or mounds of wool, natives of the mountains of Yunnan, &c., are not yet in cultivation, among them *S. gossypiphora,* and *S. leucoma.* No special soil is needed, but good drainage and full sun are desirable.

S. albes'cens. About 2 ft. h. *l.* white-hairy beneath, oval, blunt, almost entire, sessile. *fl.-heads* purple; involucre oblong, slightly hoary, scales with long slender points; corymbs many-headed, compound. July. Nepal. 1837.

S. alpi'na. 6 to 8 in. h., stem unbranched, stout, erect, leafy. *l.* oblong-lanceolate, toothed, cottony beneath; lower 4 to 7 in. long, stalked, long-pointed; upper smaller, sessile. *fl.-heads* purple, 2 to 3 in. across; involucre ovoid, bracts woolly, blunt; corymbs dense. August. Northern and Arctic regions, including Britain. (E.B. 703.)

S. dis'color. *Lower l.* cordate, stalked, coarsely toothed; *upper* oblong-lanceolate, entire, nearly sessile'; all glabrous above, densely white-hairy beneath acuminate. *fl.-heads* purple in corymbs involucral bracts appressed, shaggy. Switzerland, Siberia. SYN. *Serratula discolor.*

S. el'egans. About 2 ft. h. *Lower l.* lyrate-pinnatifid or toothed; *upper l.* oblong, nearly entire, narrowed to ends; all somewhat rough above, cobwebby beneath. *fl.-heads* pink, in corymbs; involucre nearly cylindrical, hoary-hairy, outer scales ovate, inner oblong. July. Caucasus. 1820.

S. japon'ica. About 2 ft. h. *l.* pinnatifid, somewhat rough, segs. linear acute, slightly toothed; stem-l. somewhat decurrent, upper entire. *fl.-heads* purple, globose, in corymbs; outer involucral scales hairy, inner coloured. July. Siberia, &c. 1835. (B.R. 28, 18 as *S. pulchella*; B.M. 2589 as *Serratula pulchella.*)

S. macrophyl'la. A synonym of *S. alpina.*

S. pulchel'la. A synonym of *S. japonica.*

S. pyg'maea. About 1 ft. h.; stems sparsely leafy, 1-headed. *l.* linear, usually clustered, almost entire, with revolute margins, slightly hairy beneath; sessile. *fl.-heads* purple; involucral scales slightly hairy, slender-pointed. July. E. Europe. 1816.

S. stel'la. *l.* in a stellate rosette, long linear, 2½ to 8 in. long, entire, leathery, glabrous, deep green, inner mauve or reddish at base. *fl.-heads* sessile, 1 in. h., ⅓ in. across, cor. purplish; receptacle flat with straw-coloured bristles. Tibet. 1938. (B.M. n.s. 85.)

S. Veitchia'na. About 18 in. h., hairy. Stems many, woolly in upper part. *Basal l.* many, narrow oblong-lanceolate, about 10 in. long; *upper l.* narrower, uppermost ovate-lanceolate with inflated bases, finely toothed and undulate on margins, passing to blush or purplish bracts. *fl.-heads* ovoid, over 1 in. long; florets deep purple, 4-lobed; anthers alternately black with woolly tails. Cent. China. 1901. (B.M. 8381.)

S. yak'la. Stemless with a woody rootstock. *l.* linear-oblong, sessile, 10 to 15 in. long, pinnate or pinnatifid, white-hairy beneath, lobes broadly ovate or more or less triangular. *fl.-heads* 1 to 3, 1 to 3 in. across, sessile-rays purple, nearly 1 in. long; involucral bracts erect, narrow-lanceolate. Achenes ⅛ in. long, angled. Himalaya.

SAUVAGE'SIA (in honour of Francis Boissier de Sauvages, 1706–67, Professor of Botany, Montpellier, correspondent of Linnaeus). FAM. *Ochnaceae*. A genus of about 10 species of glabrous, Trop. American herbs or sub-shrubs. Leaves alternate, rather rigid: stipules ciliate. Flowers white, pink or violet, axillary or in terminal racemes: sepals nearly equal: petals equal, convolute. *S. erecta* is a pleasing annual the seed of which should be sown in March in pots of loam and peat, the seedlings being treated like those of other stove annuals.

S. erec'ta. Iron Shrub; St. Martin's Herb. About 6 in. h., stem branched, erect or decumbent. *l.* lanceolate, toothed. *fl.* pink or purple-red; sep. bristly pointed; pet. obovate, apiculate. May to October. Mexico. 1824. SYN. *S. geminiflora.*

S. geminiflo'ra. A synonym of *S. erecta.*

SAVANNAH FLOWER. *See* **Echites.**

savanni'cola, of the grassy plains.

SAVIN. *See* **Juniperus Sabina.**

SAVORY, SUMMER (*Satureia hortensis*), is used as an ingredient of stuffings, pork-pies, and sausages, in sauces used with veal, pork, duck, and goose, and in stews. Fresh sprigs are sometimes boiled with broad beans and peas like Mint, and for garnishing like Parsley and Chervil. The stems cut, when flower-buds appear, and dried, are used in making syrups and conserves and are regarded as better for this purpose than the winter savory. Summer Savory is also credited with medicinal virtues and is said to alleviate the pain of bee-stings if rubbed on the affected part. An annual fragrant in all parts, the seed of which should be sown in early April in shallow drills about 1 ft. apart in a sunny spot. The seedlings should be thinned when large enough to 6 in. apart. The plants when cut down for drying will sprout again.

SAVORY, WINTER (*Satureia montana*). Used for the same purposes as Summer Savory but regarded as inferior and of little or no value medicinally. It is a hardy perennial which can be grown from seed like the Summer Savory or from cuttings of young side shoots with a heel rooted under a glass or on a shady border outside. The plants may also be divided in March or April; the plants obtained from rooted cuttings should be planted out 1 ft. apart in showery weather in the latter part of summer.

SAVOURY AKEE. *See* **Blighia sapida.**

SAVOY CABBAGE (*Brassica oleracea bullata sabauda*). The Savoy Cabbage differs from the bulk of the hearting Cabbages by its wrinkled foliage and its greater hardiness. There are several varieties, the variations being in size, rate of reaching maturity, and hardiness. Seed is sown in the open in the same way as that of other Cabbages, according to the variety in March or April, but care should be taken that it is not put in too early since the object is to have good hearts to cut during the winter, and early May will not be too late for sowing in some localities. Transplanting to permanent quarters should not be delayed so long that the plants become hard in the seed-bed and should be done in June or July during showery weather, the plants being put out 15 to 30 in. apart according to the variety. Treatment is the same as for other Cabbages but no nitrogenous manure should be applied towards autumn otherwise soft growth and danger of damage from low temperatures will be incurred. The Cabbage January King, of somewhat recent introduction, partakes of the hardiness of the Savoys but has less-wrinkled foliage.

SAW PALMETTO. *See* **Serenoa repens.**

SAWDUST. The main value of sawdust probably lies in its power of absorbing moisture, and it has greater power of absorbing ammonia than peat or garden soil. It has, however, a value as bedding for animals, though straw litter is to be preferred. It may be added to the compost heap. Used directly on soil it decays too slowly to show much immediate effect but it eventually adds to the humus content of the soil and is therefore of value. The idea that the use of sawdust encourages the growth of injurious fungi is erroneous, for none of the fungi likely to grow upon it are likely to attack living plants. Sawdust is sometimes used as a medium in which to grow plants, but it contains very little plant nutriment and success can only be looked for with it alone for a short time. As a mulch it stifles annual weeds.

SAWFLIES. The true Sawflies (Family *Tenthredinidae*, Order *Hymenoptera*), of which there are over 400 British species, are recognized by having 2 pairs of membranous wings, biting mouthparts, and a broadly sessile abdomen which, in the female, is provided with a pair of saw-like organs which aid in puncturing the tissues of plants to enable the eggs to be deposited in the shoots and leaves of the food plants. The larvae are termed 'false caterpillars' as most of them resemble closely those of Noctuid Moths, but possess 6, 7, or 8 pairs of sucker feet or abdominal legs (prolegs), instead of 5 pairs, and have only a single pair of simple eyes (ocelli) instead of 4 or 5 pairs. The larvae of *Caliroa* are exceptional, as they are slug-like and are covered with slimy exudation (Pear and Cherry Slugworm). The sawfly larvae feed only on plants, and show a diversity of habits. Some are solitary (Iris Sawfly) and others gregarious or 'social' (the Nut, Social Pear, and Pine Sawflies). Some feed in fruits (Apple and Plum Sawflies), some are leaf-miners (Geum Sawfly), some are leaf-rollers (Rose Leaf-rolling Sawfly), some burrow into shoots (Rose Shoot Sawfly), while others live in leaf-galls (Willow Leaf Sawflies). The signs of attack on the foliage are diverse for, while some larvae partially (as Pear and Cherry Slugworm) or completely (as Spiraea Sawfly), skeletonize the leaves, others make clean-cut holes (Solomon's Seal Sawfly) and may even completely defoliate the plant (Gooseberry Sawfly). The larva when fully grown, with certain exceptions (first brood Pine Sawfly), descend to the ground and spin a cocoon in which pupation takes place. Some species have a single, others 2 or even 3 broods in a season. Control measures against the many species that attack crops and cultivated plants vary according to the larval habits, and are considered under their respective headings, e.g. Apple Sawfly, Pear and Cherry Slugworm, &c.

G. F. W.

SAWS. Saws of various kinds are in constant demand in the garden. Ordinary saws with the teeth set rather wide answer well for sawing wood, for cutting down trees, &c., but are too coarse for most pruning operations. Cross-cut saws are useful where large branches or trees too large to cut down with an ordinary saw have to be dealt with. Pruning-saws (*see* **Pruning**) should be used for removing branches or spurs in ordinary pruning; carried to a point they can be used without damage where the ordinary saw would be likely to wound branches that should not be injured. All saws should be kept clean and in a dry place when not in use: a little sweet oil rubbed over the blade will prevent them from rusting.

SAW-WORT. *See* **Serratula tinctoria.**

saxa'tilis -is -e, growing among rocks.

SAXE-GOTH'AEA (in honour of His Royal Highness, Prince Albert). Prince Albert's Yew. FAM. *Taxaceae.* A monotypic genus.

Saxe-Gothaea conspicua (male flowers)

Saxe- G othaea conspicua (female cone)

S. conspi'cua. Small, evergreen tree of Yew-like character, 30 to 40 ft. h. with dense branches and drooping branchlets. Young shoots smooth, green at first, purple later. Winter buds small, rounded, purplish, hidden by leaves. *l.* alternate and scattered or, on lateral branches, in 2 more or less opposite rows, lasting several years, $\frac{1}{2}$ to $\frac{3}{4}$ in. long, slightly curved or twisted, dark green above with 2 silvery bands of stomata beneath, sharply pointed. *Male and female fl.* on same tree, male in short-stalked catkins from l.-axils; female terminal, of several glaucous, 3-sided, overlapping scales, the upper with 2 inverted ovules; ripe cones $\frac{1}{3}$ to $\frac{1}{2}$ in. wide with fleshy grooved scales carrying 6 to 12 seeds. Chile, W. Patagonia. 1847. (B.M. 8664.) Of great botanical interest, the connecting link between the Taxaceae and the Pinaceae with affinities with Podocarpus and Araucaria. It grows slowly in ordinary garden soil in the warmer parts of the country, under similar conditions to the Cypresses. Young trees, 6 to 8 ft. h., were killed at Bedgebury during the winter of 1939–40. Propagation is usually effected by cuttings.

W. D.

saxi'cola, a rock-dweller.

SAXIFRA'GA (*saxum,* rock, *frango,* to break; either from the roots of some species penetrating crevices in rocks and assisting in breaking them, or from the supposed value in breaking stones in the bladder). FAM. *Saxifragaceae.* A genus of about 300 species of mostly perennial herbs, usually alpine, in the north and south temperate regions, rare in Asia and S. America and absent from Australia and S. Africa. Leaves variable, the radical ones frequently in rosettes, stem-leaves usually alternate, petioles sheathing at base. Flowers white or yellow, rarely purple or rose, in panicles or corymbs: calyx tube short or long, free or adnate at base to the ovary, calyx lobes 5, erect or spreading, overlapping: petals 5, rarely unequal, sometimes fringed; stamens 10, rarely 5, inserted with the petals; carpels 2, styles 2, spreading. With few exceptions Saxifrages are easy to grow in an open soil, and they usually prefer to be surrounded by stones. They are mostly hardy perennials, the exceptions among those described being noted below. Propagation is readily effected by offsets or by division of the tufts, but many, especially the hybrids of the Kabschia section (*see below*), are best propagated by very small cuttings, rooted in sand in a cold frame soon after flowering in spring.

A rust occurs on Saxifrages due to *Puccinia Pazschkei* which produces only teleutospores on the leaves in dark reddish-brown pustules. Species likely to be affected are *S. Aizoon*, *S. elatior*, and *S. longifolia*, as well as various hybrids.

The majority of the species are best grown as rock-plants or in the alpine house, the genus, with the genera Campanula, Dianthus, Draba, Sedum, and Sempervivum constituting by far the most important groups of plants suitable for this purpose. They show great diversity of habit and this enables the different sections into which the genus has been divided to be readily recognized, a valuable help being thereby afforded in very many instances as to their cultural requirements. Engler and Irmscher in their great monograph on Saxifraga in *Das Pflanzenreich* have divided the genus into 15 sections, Section 12 being here sub-divided into 2 (12 and 13). It will be convenient to take these in order and give the main characters by which they are distinguished and to facilitate reference to number these sections and the sub-section consecutively, 1 to 16. The number of the group to which each species described is given in parentheses immediately after its name in the following list. A few plants at times included in Saxifraga are now regarded as belonging to other genera and should be sought there. They are the plants with broad, leathery leaves often called Megaseas, in the genus Bergenia, the old group Isomeria, now the genus Boykinia, and the water-side plant once called *Saxifraga peltata,* now *Peltiphyllum peltatum.*

Section 1. BORAPHILA. Leaves all radical in a few-leaved rosette, softly leathery. Flowers in spikes or loose panicles, white or spotted. These are plants of cool or damp places in peaty soils, flowering in summer. The British *S. nivalis* and *S. stellaris* are typical.

KEY TO SPECIES

1.	*L.-margin more or less toothed*	2
1.	*L.-margin entire or nearly so*	5
2.	*Basal lvs. ovate-oblong or kidney-shaped*	3
2.	*Basal lvs. spatulate*	6
3.	*Basal lvs. ovate or oblong*	4
3.	*Basal lvs. kidney-shaped*	7
4.	*Carpels partly inferior, joined above*	S. pallida
4.	*Carpels wholly superior, free or nearly so*	9
5.	*Fl. white. Plant of 4 ft. h.*	S. Forbesii
5.	*Fl. yellowish-white. Plant of 3 ft. h. or more*	S. pensylvanica
6.	*Bracts much smaller than lvs.*	S. stellaris
6.	*Bracts large, leaf-like but somewhat smaller upwards*	S. Clusii

7. *L.-teeth simple. Pet.* $\frac{1}{10}$ *to* $\frac{1}{6}$ *in. long*	8*
7. *L.-teeth double. Pet.* $\frac{1}{5}$ *in. long*	S. Mertensiana
8. *Stem 3 to 4 in. h. Fl. in a loose infl.*	S. punctata*
8. *Stem 14 in. h. Fl. in a dense sub-globose infl.*	S. manshuriensis
9. *Fl. close in a head*	S. nivalis
9. *Fl. loose, in a corymb or panicle*	10
10. *Infl. corymbose*	S. rufidula
10. *Infl. paniculate. Pet. 3 times as long as sep.*	S. virginiensis

* See also *S. arguta.*

Section 2. HIRCULUS. Mat-forming plants with undivided, deciduous, oval leaves and orange or yellow flowers on leafy stems. These species need bog or damp scree conditions, and flower in summer or autumn. Our native *S. Hirculus* is typical.

KEY TO SPECIES

1. *Base of petiole only reddish-hairy. Fl. secund, nodding*	S. nutans
1. *Base of stem with crisped reddish hairs*	2
1. *Stem without reddish hairs*	6
2. *Stem leafy throughout. Lower lvs. not larger than median*	S. turfosa
2. *Lvs. gradually smaller upwards; basal lvs. present*	3
3. *Basal lvs. not cordate; stem lvs. about 4 times as long as wide or more*	4
3. *Stem lvs.* $1\frac{1}{2}$ *to 2 times as long as wide*	5
4. *Stem lvs. oblong-lanceolate, about* $\frac{1}{2}$ *in. long, narrowed to base*	S. Hirculus
4. *Stem lvs. linear, not over* $\frac{1}{3}$ *in. long. Fls. solitary*	S. aristulata
5. *Plant small, not over 2 in. h.*	S. palpebrata
5. *Plant 4 to 16 in. h.*	S. diversifolia
6. *L.-margin with transparent fringe. Cushion-forming small*	S. Eschscholtzii
6. *L.-margin not transparent*	7
7. *Stem leafy throughout*	8
7. *Lvs. unequally distributed, crowded at base*	10
8. *Stem unbranched. Lvs. entire, lanceolate*	9
8. *Stem branched. Lvs. spatulate with roundish blades*	S. signata
8. *Stem branched. Lvs. linear*	S. filicaulis
9. *Fl. solitary. Lvs. somewhat stem-clasping, spiny*	S. brachypoda
9. *Fl. 1 to 3. Lvs. not stem-clasping, teeth cartilaginous*	S. filicaulis
10. *Plant without runners*	11
10. *Plant with runners from basal rosette*	14
11. *Plant of 5 to 10 in. Basal lvs. over* $\frac{1}{2}$ *in. long*	S. candelabrum
11. *Plant smaller. Basal lvs. not* $\frac{1}{2}$ *in. long*	12
12. *Stem many-fld. Fl. golden, not spotted*	S. umbellulata
12. *Stem 1-fld.*	13
13. *Stems leafy*	S. chrysantha
13. *Stems with few lvs.*	S. serpyllifolia
14. *Pet. obovate*	S. flagellaris
14. *Pet. oblong. Stem with few lvs.*	S. Brunoniana

Section 3. ROBERTSONIA. All or nearly all leaves in basal rosettes. Leaves more or less spoon-shaped, leathery, undivided, variously toothed. Flowers small, white, pink, or spotted, in loose, open panicles. All are easily grown in moist shady positions and flower in early summer. *S. umbrosa* is typical of this section.

KEY TO SPECIES

1. *Basal lvs. cordate at base*	S. Geum
1. *Basal lvs. wedge-shaped at base, not cordate*	2
2. *Basal lvs. oblong or obovate-oblong*	S. umbrosa
2. *Basal lvs. obovate or roundish*	S. cuneifolia

Section 4. MISCOPETALUM. Tufted plants. Leaves leathery, round to oval, variously toothed, all stalked. Stems upright, more or less leafy, with a terminal open panicle of rather small flowers, with often unequal petals. Flowers usually white, sometimes spotted. Shade-loving easily grown plants of which *S. rotundifolia* is typical.

KEY TO SPECIES

1. *Blade at junction of l.-stalk wedge-shaped*	S. chrysosplenifolia
1. *Blade at junction of l.-stalk not distinctly wedge-shaped*	2
2. *L.-teeth 12 to 20*	S. rotundifolia
2. *L.-teeth 5 to 9*	S. taygetea

Section 5. CYMBALARIA. Small much-branched annuals. Leaves more or less ivy-shaped, flowers golden, starry. Plants of this section, of which *S. Sibthorpii* is typical, will seed themselves in any cool, shady spot and crevice.

KEY TO SPECIES

1. *Pet. white or sulphur, scarcely twice as long as sep.*	S. hederacea
1. *Pet. yellow, double sep. or more*	2
2. *Sep. reflexed*	S. Sibthorpii
2. *Sep. not reflexed*	3
3. *L.-teeth 5 to 13 acute*	S. Cymbalaria
3. *L.-teeth 5 to 7, wide, obtuse*	S. Huetiana

Section 6. TRIDACTYLITES. Annual or biennial plants with basal rosettes of undivided or 3-pointed flimsy leaves and more or less leafy branching stems. Flowers very small, white. Plants of this section are for the most part unimportant horticulturally. They succeed in sandy soils in sun or shade. *S. tridactylites*, a native species, is typical.

KEY TO SPECIES

1. *Pet. not over 3 times as long as sep.*	2
1. *Pet. over 3 times as long as sep.*	S. Blavii
2. *Annual*	S. tridactylites
2. *Biennial. Pet. 2 or 3 times as long as sep.*	S. adscendens

Section 7. NEPHROPHYLLUM. Small herbs, leafless in winter, often bearing bulbils at the base or even in the leaf-axils of the flower-stems. Leaves usually kidney-shaped, rather soft, variously lobed. Flowers usually white. Some of the very small northern species are difficult to grow and have few and small flowers. Of the more easily grown species the handsome native *S. granulata* is the type.

KEY TO SPECIES

1. *Fl. lemon-yellow*	S. arachnoidea
1. *Fl. white, rarely yellowish-white or pale rose*	2
2. *Axils of lvs. without bulbils*	3
2. *Axils of basal or stem lvs. with bulbils*	4
3. *Fl.-stems branched from middle*	S. irrigua
3. *Fl.-stems branched from base*	S. latepetiolata
4. *Lower stem-lvs. more or less wedge-shaped or ovate, rarely biternate*	5
4. *Stem lvs. usually kidney-shaped, cordate, or widely 3-lobed*	11
5. *Lvs. kidney-shaped or ovate, sometimes 3-lobed*	6
5. *Lvs. biternate. Pet.* $\frac{3}{4}$ *in. long. Plant tall*	S. biternata
6. *Fl.-stem many-lvd.*	7
6. *Fl.-stem with few lvs. or none*	10
7. *Bulbils in axils of basal lvs.*	8
7. *Bulbils in axils of stem lvs.*	S. bulbifera
8. *Stem lvs. deeply cut*	S. atlantica
8. *Stem lvs. with rounded teeth*	9
9. *Fls. at tip of stem in corymbose cymes*	S. Hervieri
9. *Fls. in corymbose panicles in upper half of stem*	S. Haensleri
10. *Lvs. kidney-shaped, with rounded teeth*	S. granulata
10. *Lvs. 3-lobed, lobes 3- to 5-lobed*	S. Cossoniana
11. *Base of l.-stalks dilated*	12
11. *Base of l.-stalks sheathing*	S. rivularis
12. *Stem lvs. without bulbils in axils*	13
12. *Stem lvs. with bulbils in axils*	S. cernua
13. *Pet. 3 times as long as sep. or more*	S. sibirica
13. *Pet. scarcely twice as long as sep.*	S. carpathica

Section 8. DACTYLOIDES. All the well-known 'mossy' Saxifrages belong to this section, and of these there are more hybrids and garden forms than species, for they vary within wide limits and cross readily. The more easily grown forms form more or less dense carpets composed of rosettes of variously cleft hairy or glabrous leaves with multitudes of white, pink, rose, or deep red flowers on stems of varying length in spring. They are happiest in partial shade and fairly moist spots in an open, gritty soil. Of these *S. decipiens* and *S. hypnoides* are typical. Old mats are apt to become brown in the middle when they need to be divided and replanted. Some of the small cushion forming species of this section from high alpine situations are difficult to grow.

KEY TO SPECIES

1. *Lvs. all entire, or rarely 3- to 5-toothed at apex*	2
1. *Basal lvs. more or less palmately lobed or cut*	9
2. *Lvs. tipped with a colourless bristle*	3
2. *Lvs. not bristle-tipped*	4
3. *Lvs. with transparent margin*	S. tenella
3. *Lvs. not margined*	S. sedoides
4. *Basal lvs. linear*	5
4. *Basal lvs. wedge-shaped or spatulate*	6
5. *Pet. twice as long as sep.*	S. muscoides
5. *Pet. scarcely longer than sep.*	S. Facchinii
6. *Basal lvs. wedge-shaped, 3-fid at apex. Pet. little longer than sep.*	S. aphylla
6. *Basal lvs. spatulate, rarely 3-fid, but usually 2- to 5-toothed at apex*	7
7. *Pet. about as long as sep.*	S. Seguieri
7. *Pet. twice as long as sep. or more*	8

8. *Lvs. long-haired. Sometimes with* 1 *or* 2 *lvs. beneath fls.*	S. androsacea
8. *Lvs. short-haired. Stem hairs long. Plant* 1 *to* 1½ *in. h.*	S. tridens
9. *Fl.-stems from axils of lower lvs.*	S. ajugifolia
9. *Fl.-stems terminal*	10
10. *Fl.-stems robust, branching from base*	S. aquatica
10. *Fl.-stems usually branching from middle, rarely* 1-*fld.*	11
11. *More or less woody at base and mat-forming. Lvs. usually rigid. Fl.-stems leafy*	12
11. *Herbaceous, or if woody, forming dormant buds*	22
12. *Sep. linear*	13
12. *Sep. wider*	15
13. *L.-stalks short, wide. Basal-lvs. palmately lobed*	S. pedemontana
13. *L.-stalks long, narrow*	14
14. *L.-blade narrowed gradually to stalk*	S. Prostii
14. *L.-blade abruptly narrowed to stalk*	S. geranioides
15. *Sep. triangular or oblong*	16
15. *Sep. wide-ovate, obtuse*	S. Vayredana
16. *Blade narrowed to a wide stalk. Glabrous*	S. Camposii
16. *Blade narrowed to a slender stalk*	17
17. *Basal lvs. widely obovate in general outline*	S. cuneata
17. *Basal lvs. more or less kidney-shaped, contracted to a slender stalk*	18
18. *Blade roundish-kidney-shaped, deeply lobed*	S. maderensis
18. *Blade kidney-shaped, pedately cut*	19
19. *Whole plant glandular-hairy*	S. pedatifida
19. *Whole plant glabrous*	20
20. *L.-segs. not curved*	21
20. *L.-segs. curved outwards*	S. trifurcata
21. *Tips of l.-segs. mucronate*	S. canaliculata
21. *Tips of l.-segs. blunt, or somewhat acute*	S. valentina
22. *Dormant buds with more or less chaffy scales*	23
22. *Dormant buds without chaffy scales*	27
23. *Sep. mucronate*	24
23. *Sep. blunt*	25
24. *Lvs. undivided*	S. conifera
24. *Basal lvs.* 3- *to* 5-*cut*	S. hypnoides
25. *Pet. about* ⅓ *in. long*	S. globulifera
25. *Pet. about* ½ *in. long*	26
26. *L.-blade heart- to kidney-shaped,* 3-*partite, segs.* 3- *to* 5-lobed	S. Maweana
26. *L.-blade spatulate,* 3-*cut*	S. Rigoi
27. *Pet.* 3 *or* 4 *times as long as sep.*	28
27. *Pet.* 1½ *to* 2 *times as long as sep.*	31
28. *Pet.* 3 *times as long as sep.*	29
28. *Pet.* 4 *times as long as sep.*	S. lactea
29. *Lvs. with more or less long glandular hairs*	30
29. *Whole plant densely glandular-downy*	S. adenodes
30. *Basal lvs.* 3- *to* 11-*fid, hairs long*	S. decipiens
30. *Basal lvs.* 3- *to* 5-*lobed, hairs short*	S. caespitosa
31. *Lvs. deep green, often clammy*	32
31. *Lvs. bright green, not clammy*	S. moschata
32. *Lvs. resinous, deeply* 3-*cut, segs. linear, side lobes* 2-*fid*	S. pentadactylis
32. *Lvs. glandular-hairy*	33
33. *Pet. white, occasionally rose*	34
33. *Pet. whitish or purplish, rarely white*	S. exarata
34. *Whole plant covered with long glandular hairs*	35
34. *Lvs. with short glandular hairs*	S. intricata
35. *Stem lvs. linear*	S. cebennensis
35. *Stem lvs.* 3- *to* 5-*cut*	S. pubescens

Section 9. Trachyphyllum. Small mat-forming plants with narrow, undivided leaves, bristly on margin and at apex. Flowers fairly large, dingy white, pale or almost orange-yellow, in sparsely branched stems about 4 in. high. The plants of this section seem to inhabit lime-free places in nature, and are easy to grow but undistinguished horticulturally. *S. aspera* and *S. bronchialis* are good examples of this section.

KEY TO SPECIES

1. *Lvs. more or less lanceolate, bristle-edged*	2
1. *Lvs.* 3-*toothed at apex*	4
2. *Pet. shortly clawed at base*	S. aspera
2. *Pet. rounded at base, scarcely clawed*	3
3. *Lvs. flat*	S. bronchialis
3. *Lvs. concave or apex incurved*	S. cherlerioides
4. *Lvs. usually reddish*	S. tricuspidata
4. *Lvs. dark green*	S. azorelloides

Section 10. Xanthizoon. This section contains only the many forms of *S. aizoides*, found all over the N. Hemisphere except Asia. *S. aizoides* makes loose mats of tangled stems, with scattered, narrow, undivided leaves (rarely in rosettes) sometimes with bristly or toothed margins. Flowers solitary or in loose cymes, pale to rich yellow or orange, rarely purple or deep red. In nature they grow on shingly water-margins but put up with less water in gardens.

Species one only. S. aizoides.

Section 11. Euaizoonia. Broad-leaved, silver-encrusted Saxifrages. Rosette-forming, usually with many offset rosettes producing clumps or cushions. Flower-stems more or less tall, branching, with loose or dense panicles of flowers in summer. The rosettes that have flowered die, and the younger rosettes grow on to flowering size in succeeding years. The species that produce offsets are readily propagated by division or cuttings. Seed-raising generally results in a host of hybrids and intermediate forms and as seeds are so unreliable should be resorted to only with monocarpic species like *S. longifolia*. Many species are extremely variable and have given rise in nature as well as in the garden to a great number of varieties. All the species of this section are easily grown and most appreciate some lime-rubble and full exposure to sun, but some of the larger species will tolerate, and may do better in, partial shade.

KEY TO SPECIES

1. *Fl. white, usually spotted purple, rarely rose or purplish*	2
1. *Fl. rose or yellow*	11
2. *Lvs. entire or nearly so*	3
2. *Lvs. distinctly toothed*	7
3. *Fl.-stem branched from base*	S. longifolia
3. *Fl.-stem branched from middle or at top*	4
4. *Lvs. linear or linear-spatulate, over* ½ *in. long*	5
4. *Lvs. linear-spatulate, small, about* ¼ *in. long, or shell-like*	6
5. *Lvs.* ⅛ *to* ⅙ *in. wide at tip*	S. lingulata
5. *Lvs.* 1/12 *in. wide or less at tip*	S. crustata
6. *Lvs. shell-like-spatulate*	S. cochlearis
6. *Lvs. linear-spatulate*	S. valdensis
7. *Fl.-stem branched in upper part*	8
7. *Fl.-stem branched from base*	S. Cotyledon
8. *Rosette-lvs. straight or bent in. Branches of infl.* 1- *or* 2-*fld.*	9
8. *Rosette-lvs. deflexed at tip. Branches of infl.* 3- *or* 5-*fld.*	S. Hostii
9. *Lvs. obtuse or acute, not acuminate*	S. Aizoon
9. *Lvs. distinctly acuminate*	10
10. *Fl. white*	S. cartilaginea
10. *Fl. rose or deep purple*	S. Kolenatiana
11. *Fl. rose*	S. florulenta
11. *Fl. yellow*	S. mutata

Section 12. Kabschia. Here belong perhaps the most beautiful of the Saxifrages. Small cushion or hummock forming densely tufted plants; leaves more or less spiny or broader and more spreading, blunt or round-pointed. Flowers solitary or several on a short more or less branched stem, usually of fair size, pure white, soft or rich yellow, lilac, pink, or soft red, never spotted. Of the 36 species of this section only half are in cultivation, but there are perhaps a hundred hybrids to be grouped here. Cultivation needs care, watering must be dealt with especially carefully, and as they flower early in spring they are best grown in the alpine house. Propagation is best done by means of small cuttings in spring, put into sand under a bell-glass or in a cold frame. *S. Burseriana* and *S. marginata* are typical of this section.

KEY TO SPECIES

1. *Stamens as long as or longer than the yellow pet.*	2
1. *Pet. much longer than stamens*	7
2. *Lvs. acute or mucronate*	3
2. *Lvs. blunt, lower flat, upper channelled*	S. Kotschyi
3. *Leafy branches rarely in whorls*	4
3. *Leafy branches often whorled*	6
4. *Infl. a raceme*	S. juniperifolia
4. *Infl. more or less corymbose*	5
5. *Lvs. markedly ciliate, marginal lime glands present*	S. sancta
5. *Lvs. shortly ciliate with terminal lime glands only*	S. caucasica
6. *Lvs. almost erect*	S. subverticillata
6. *Lvs. reflexed*	S. scleropoda
7. *Fl. white or rose*	8
7. *Fl. golden-yellow*	21
8. *Lvs. spatulate, widest above middle*	9
8. *Lvs. linear, oblong, or subulate*	16
9. *Fl. solitary, rarely* 2 *or* 3	10
9. *Fl. several*	13

10. *L.-margin cartilaginous*	S. ramulosa
10. *L. cartilaginous near tip at most*	11
11. *Fl. stalked, lilac*	S. lilacina
11. *Fl. nearly sessile*	12
12. *Lvs. with 3 to 5 lime-glands*	S. likiangensis
12. *Lvs. with 1 lime gland only*	S. imbricata
13. *L.-margin cartilaginous*	14
13. *L. cartilaginous near tip at most*	15
14. *Lvs. acute*	S. scardica
14. *Lvs. blunt*	S. marginata
15. *Lvs. reflexed, spatulate*	S. Andersonii
15. *Lvs. erect, flat, widely obovate*	S. Spruneri
16. *Lvs. reflexed at base or apex*	17
16. *Lvs. never reflexed, erect*	18
17. *Lvs. recurved from base*	S. caesia
17. *Lvs. arched at tip*	S. squarrosa
18. *Lvs. acute or mucronate*	19
18. *Lvs. blunt*	S. diapensioides
19. *Fl. several*	20
19. *Fl. usually solitary*	S. Burseriana
20. *Lvs. about ⅛ in. long*	S. tombeanensis
20. *Lvs. about ¼ in. long*	S. Vandellii
21. *Lvs. glaucous*	22
21. *Lvs. dark green*	S. pravislavia
22. *Lvs. with cartilaginous margin*	S. aretioides
22. *L.-margins scarcely cartilaginous*	S. Ferdinandi-Coburgii

Section 13. ENGLERIA. This is usually regarded as a subsection under Kabschia. Most species are of similar habit to those of Section 11 (Euaizoonia) and have leafy flower-stems ending in a spike or branched raceme of small flowers with usually highly coloured calyces, the stem-leaves also being more or less highly coloured. They begin to flower very early in spring and are best grown in the alpine house. They need a very porous soil mixture containing lime. Provided the species are isolated at flowering time they produce seed from which plants true to type may be raised. The species have been much crossed with those of Section 12 (Kabschia) and it is often difficult to assign the resulting hybrids with definiteness to a place in either section 12 or 13. *S. Grisebachii* is typical of this section.

KEY TO SPECIES

1. *Pedicels longer than bracts. Infl. paniculate*	2
1. *Pedicels shorter than bracts. Infl. a simple raceme*	4
2. *Pet. rosy-purple*	3
2. *Pet. yellowish-green*	S. corymbosa
3. *Lvs. small, about ½ in. long. Pet. about ⅛ in. long*	S. media
3. *Lvs. larger, up to ¾ in. long. Pet. about ⅙ in. long*	S. Stribrnyi
4. *Lvs. small, ½ in. long or less*	S. porophylla
4. *Lvs. large, 1 to 1½ in. long*	S. Grisebachii

Section 14. PORPHYRION. Creeping mat-forming plants, usually with purple flowers, but a few white or bicolour forms are known. Leaves on creeping stems opposite and only where crowded at the ends of the shoots do they approach a rosette formation. A very gritty, porous soil suits them, and they are best in a cool, slightly moist but not sunless or airless position. Frequent top-dressings of grit and leaf-mould aid them. They can be propagated by division after flowering or by cuttings of shoots that have not flowered. *S. oppositifolia* and *S. retusa* illustrate the extremes of this section.

KEY TO SPECIES

1. *Sep. not ciliate. Median lvs. spreading or recurved, usually with 5 lime-glands*	S. retusa
1. *Sep. ciliate. Lvs. flat or at most recurved at tip, ciliate rarely with 5 lime-glands*	2
2. *Many-fld.*	S. biflora
2. *One-fld.*	3
3. *Tips of lvs. shortly ciliate*	S. oppositifolia
3. *Tips of lvs. long ciliate. Lvs. widely spatulate*	S. blepharophylla

Section 15. TETRAMERIDIUM. A very distinct group of Saxifrages, natives of Asia, only 1 species of which has so far been introduced. The flowers are distinct from those of all other sections by having only 4 sepals and no petals. They are solitary on short stems. The plants form short, dense tufts of many, short, branching stems thickly set with overlapping, opposite, small, narrow leaves. Treatment like that advised for plants of Section 14 will probably suit them and we may expect other species to be introduced in the future.

Only species introduced. S. nana.

Section 16. DIPTERA (sometimes called LIGULARIA). Tufted plants with broad-bladed, stalked leaves, more or less leathery. In autumn branching stems arise from the tufts bearing pure white or sometimes spotted flowers with 1 or 2 elongated petals often notched along the margins. Cool positions in rich humus soils appear to suit most species of this section but many are tender in most British gardens. Species which do not form stolons appear to be hardy. Those that produce stolons can be propagated at almost any time, others by careful division in spring. *S. cortusifolia* and *S. stolonifera*, both tender, may be regarded as typical of this section.

KEY TO SPECIES

1. *Forming runners*	2
1. *Not forming runners*	4
2. *Lvs. white-veined above*	3
2. *Lvs. not white-veined above*	S. Veitchiana
3. *Lvs. distinctly cordate at base, hairy above*	S. stolonifera
3. *Lvs. rounded at base, longer than wide, glabrous above*	S. cuscutiformis
4. *Lvs. prickly at margin*	S. aculeata
4. *Lvs. not prickly at margin*	5
5. *Lvs. bronzed beneath*	S. Fortunei
5. *Lvs. grey-green beneath*	6
6. *Lvs. thick, fleshy*	S. cortusifolia
6. *Lvs. thin, deeply cut*	S. madida

HYBRIDS. In addition to the wild species and their numerous varieties cultivated in our gardens, a large number of hybrids are also grown, and in some instances they have taken the place of their parents, or nearly so. Some of these hybrids have been found wild where their parents meet in nature, many have arisen in gardens, sometimes as the result of hand-pollination, sometimes by chance. The species readily cross especially with other species of the same section of the genus, and with many it is impossible, unless special precautions are taken, to be sure that seed will reproduce the characters of the plant from which it was gathered. To this may be attributed a good many of the errors of naming found in gardens and nurseries where seedlings have been raised from seeds saved in gardens. It must also be said that to this, too, we owe some of the most striking and useful additions to the Saxifrages available; we need mention only the fine Saxifrage Guildford Seedling which was a chance seedling found on an ash-heap in the Guildford Hardy Plant Nursery—an outstanding plant in its day. Most of these hybrids will not breed true to type, nor sufficiently true to warrant the retention of the original name for their seedlings unless the name is intended to cover a variable group, which is most unusual. They can only be had true by propagating them vegetatively, or by repeating the cross of the original parents. It is unfortunate that they have so frequently received names of Latin form, especially when raised on the Continent, instead of fancy names by which plants of garden origin are always best designated. Latin names usually imply to most people that the plant is capable of being reproduced reasonably true to its maternal characters, whereas a fancy name carries with it, at any rate so far as perennial plants are concerned, the warning that in all probability it can be increased, retaining its characters, only by vegetative means. To convert these names into names of desirable form would entail much confusion in nomenclature and we have therefore retained them here in alphabetical sequence with the species, indicating always the hybrid character of the plant to which they are attached. The hybrid plants which have received fancy names follow in a list by themselves, alphabetically arranged. These two lists do not pretend to be exhaustive, but like the rest of the Dictionary contain the names of plants known to be in cultivation at present.

As some indication of the characteristics of these hybrids which are of so much horticultural importance the following paragraphs show the sections of the genus to which they belong with the parents where they are known or the putative parents where they are reasonably certain.

Hybrid between species of Sections 3 and 4:
S. × tazetta (*S. cuneifolia × S. taygetea*).

Hybrid between species of Sections 3 and 10:
S. × Primulaize (*S. aizoides × S. umbrosa*).

Hybrids between species of Sections 3 and 11:
S. × Andrewsii and **S. × Wildiana** (*S. Aizoon × S. umbrosa*); **S. × Pseudo-Forsteri** (*S. crustata × S. cuneifolia*); **S. × Zimmeteri** (*S. Aizoon × S. cuneifolia*).

Hybrids between species of Sections 7 and 8:
S. × Arkwrightii (*S. decipiens × S. granulata*); and **S. × Clibranii.**

Hybrid between species of Sections 6 and 8;
S. × Farreri (*S. hypnoides × S. tridactylites*).

Hybrids between species of Section 8:
S. × Fergusonii (*S. decipiens × S. muscoides*); **S. × obscura** (*S. geranioides × S. pubescens*); **S. × Reyuri** (*S. sedoides × S. tenella*); **S. × Schraderi** (*S. hypnoides × S. trifurcata*), and the following of which the parents are not certainly known (often of complicated parentage); **Apple Blossom, Bakeri, bathoniensis, Beauty of Letchworth, Crimson King, Flower of Sulphur, Guildford Seedling, James Bremner, Lloyd Edwards, Mother of Pearl, Pompadour, Red Admiral, sanguinea superba, Sir Douglas Haig, Wenlock Peach.**

Hybrids between species of Sections 8 and 9.
S. × arguta and **S. × rigescens** (*S. tenella × S. tricuspidata*).

Hybrids between species of Sections 10 and 11:
S. × Hausmannii and **S. × Regelii** (*S. aizoides × S. mutata*).

Hybrid between species of Sections 10 and 12:
S. × patens (*S. aizoides × S. caesia*).

Hybrids between species of Section 11:
S. × bellunensis and **S. × Churchillii** (*S. Aizoon × S. Hostii*); **S. × Burnatii** and **S. × Esther** (*S. Aizoon × S. cochlearis*); **S. × calabrica, Cecil Davis,** and **Tumbling Waters** (*S. lingulata × S. longifolia*); **S. × canis dalmatica, S. × Gaudinii,** and **S. × speciosa** (*S. Aizoon × S. Cotyledon*); **S. × Dr. Ramsey** (*S. cochlearis × S. longifolia*); **S. × Engleri** (*S. crustata × S. Hostii*); **S. × florairensis** (*S. Hostii × S. lingulata*); **S. × Francis Cade** (*S. cochlearis × S. lingulata*); **S. × Macnabiana** (*S. Cotyledon × S. lingulata*); **S. × paradoxa** (*S. crustata × S. lingulata*); **S. × pectinata** and **S. × Portae** (*S. Aizoon × S. crustata*); **S. × imperialis, S. × splendida,** and **S. × superba** (*S. Cotyledon × S. longifolia*); and of undetermined parentage **S. × splendens** and **Kathleen Pinsent.**

Hybrids between species of Sections 11 and 12:
S. × stricta (parentage unknown); **S. × Forsteri** (*S. caesia × S. mutata*).

Hybrids between species of Section 12:
S. × Ada (*S. Burseriana × S. tombeanensis*); **S. × Amitie** (*S. lilacina × S. scardica*); **S. × apiculata** (*S. marginata × S. sancta*); **S. × arco-valleyi, S. × Irvingii, S. × rubella, Gem,** and **Harry Marshall** (*S. Burseriana × S. lilacina*); **S. × aretiastra** (*S. aretioides × S. Burseriana*); **S. × Bilekii** (*S. Ferdinandi-Coburgii × S. tombeanensis*); **S. × Borisii, S. Pseudo-Borisii,** and **S. × Kyrillii** (*S. Ferdinandi-Coburgii × S. marginata*); **S. × Boydii** (*S. aretioides × S. Burseriana*); **S. × Boydii alba, S. × kestoniensis, S. × Obristii, S. × Salamonii,** and **S. Suendermannii** (1) (*S. Burseriana × S. marginata*); **S. × bursiculata** (*S. × apiculata × S. Burseriana*); **S. × Cherry Trees** and **S. × Faldonside** (*S. aretioides × S. marginata*); **S. × Elizabethae, S. × Godseffiana,** and **S. × ochroleuca** (*S. Burseriana × S. sancta*); **S. × Etheline** (*S. Burseriana × S. tombeanensis*); **S. × Eudoxiana** and **S. × Haagii** (*S. Ferdinandi-Coburgii × S. sancta*); **S. × Fontanae** (*S. diapensioides × S. Ferdinandi-Coburgii*); **S. × grata** (*S. aretioides × S. Ferdinandi-Coburgii*); **S. × kewensis** (*S. Burseriana × S. porophylla*); **S. × Leyboldii** (*S. marginata × S. Vandellii*); **S. × Myra** (*S. lilacina × S. scardica*); **S. × Paulinae** (*S. Burseriana × S. Ferdinandi-Coburgii*); **S. × Petraschii** (*S. marginata × S. tombeanensis*); **S. × Pseudo-Kotschyi** (*S. Kotschyi × S. marginata*); **S. × pungens** (*S. juniperifolia × S. marginata*); **S. × Simplicity** (*S. lilacina × S. tombeanensis*); **S. × Steinii** (*S. aretioides × S. tombeanensis*); **S. × tirolensis** (*S. caesia × S. squarrosa*); and the following of undetermined parentage, **Affinis, Allenii, assimilis, Biegleri, Brilliant, Cerise Queen, Coombe White, Cranbourne, Delia, Franzii, Friesii, Funkii, Geuderi, Gloriosa, Grace Farwell, Hansii, Jenkinsii, Kolbiana, Loeflingii, Mrs. Lang, Pichleri, Rosinae, Schilleri, Schreineri, Semmleri, Stormonthii,** and **Vahlii.**

Hybrids between species of Sections 12 and 13:
S. × ambigua, S. × Benthamii, S. × Godroniana, S. × Lapeyrousii, and **S. × luteopurpurea** (*S. aretioides × S. media*); **S. × Bertolonii** (*S. porophylla × S. Stribrnyi*); **S. × Biasoletii** (*S. Grisebachii × S. porophylla*); **S. × Boeckleri** (*S. Ferdinandi-Coburgii × S. Stribrnyi*); **S. × Clarkei** (*S. media × S. Vandellii*); **S. × Edithae** (*S. marginata × S. Stribrnyi*); **S. × Friderici-Augusti** (*S. media × S. porophylla*); **S. × Heinrichii** (*S. aretioides × S. Stribrnyi*); **S. × Hoerhammeri** (*S. Grisebachii × S. marginata*); **S. × Hoffmannii** (*S. Burseriana × S. porophylla*); **S. × Kellereri** and **S. × Schleicheri** (*S. Burseriana × S. Stribrnyi*); **S. × Marie-Theresae** (*S. Burseriana × S. Grisebachii*); the following all *S. × Godroniana × S. lilacina*, **Beryl, Elysium, Priory Jewel, Sparkling,** and **Valerie Keevil**; from *S. lilacina × S. porophylla*, **Laurent Wood, Riverslea,** and **Sonia Prichard**; and of undetermined parentage **S. × Gaertneri, Iris Prichard,** and **megasiflora.**

Hybrids between species of Section 13:
S. × Doerfleri (*S. Grisebachii × S. Stribrnyi*); **S. × Fleischeri** (*S. corymbosa × S. Grisebachii*); **S. × Gusmusii** (*S. corymbosa × S. porophylla*); **S. × Schottii** (*S. corymbosa × S. Stribrnyi*); and of undetermined parentage, **S. × anomalis, Landaueri, Prosenii, Urumoffii,** and **Volgeri.**

Hybrid between species of Sections 12, 13, and 14:
S. × Lady Beatrix Stanley (*S. × Godroniana × S. oppositifolia*).

S. aconitifo'lia. A synonym of *Boykinia aconitifolia.*

S. aculea'ta (16). Tufted perennial about 12 in. h. without runners. Stems covered with reddish hairs. *l.* deeply cut, lobes bristle-pointed. *fl.* pink; pet. unequal. China. Deciduous and probably tender.

S. adeno'des (8). Nearly related to *S. caespitosa* but all green parts thickly covered with clammy hairs. *l.* of lateral shoots oblong-lanceolate, obtuse. Sep. narrow. Chilean Andes.

S. adscend'ens (6). Annual, 3 to 6 in. h., closely related to *S. tridactylites* and like that of no garden value. Mts. of N. Hemisphere. 1732. (B.M. 3026 as *S. petraea.*)

S. × aem'ula. A synonym of *Bergenia × media.*

S. × affin'is (2) (parentage?). Forming tiny, very compact, grey-green cushions. *fl.* white. Raised by Sündermann.

S. afghan'ica of gardens. A form of *Bergenia Stracheyi.*

S. aizoi'des (10). Mat-forming, loosely tufted perennial, branches decumbent or ascending. *fl.-stems* leafy, up to 12 in. long. *l.* crowded below, fleshy, linear-oblong, ⅛ to 1¼ in. long, usually entire, sometimes ciliate. *fl.* orange or yellow, dotted with red, about ½ in. across, branches of infl. usually 1-fld. June, July. Alpine and Arctic Europe (including Britain) and Asia. (E.B. 551.) Moisture-loving. Variable. var. **atroru'bens,** *fl.* blood-red; **aurant'ia,** *fl.* orange; **autumna'lis,** of compact habit, *fl.* larger, orange. August. Prefers limestone crevices to moist shingle. Hybrids with *S. mutata* and with *S. umbrosa primuloides* are known, for which *see* **S. × Hausmannii** and **S. × Primulaize.**

S. Aizo'on* (11). Densely tufted perennial with stolons 1 to 2 in. long. *fl.-stems* erect, 1½ to 12 in. long, loosely leafy. *Rosette-l.* incurved, fleshy, ciliate near base, obovate or tongue-shaped, about 2 in. long, margins white, cartilagenous, toothed; chalk glands evident; stem-l. smaller, spatulate, glandular-ciliate. Branches of infl. 1- to 3-fld., rarely more. *fl.* white or spotted purple, about ⅓ in. across. June. Europe, N. America. 1731. A very variable plant. Rock-garden in sun or partial shade and almost any well-drained soil suits this species. Increased by separation of individual rosettes. var. **alpi'cola,** *see* var. **rosularis; balca'na,** of medium size, stems 6 in. h., stout, *fl.* large, white, rounded, heavily spotted crimson. June. Of garden origin; **brevifo'lia,** *basal l.* obovate to spatulate, ⅛ to ⅜ in. long, toothed, *fl.-stem* 1½ to 6 in. long, branches of corymb 1- to 3-fld. Mts. of Europe; **bulga'rica,** *fl.* spotted rose; **carinthi'aca,** small, neat, *l.* narrow-spatulate, stems 4 to 6 in. h., glabrous, *fl.* in open panicle, cream; **cartilagin'ea,** *see* **S. cartilaginea; Churchil'lii,** *see* **S. × Churchillii; Correvonia'na,** very small, rosettes about ½ in. across, forming dense cushions stems, 3 in. h. *fl.* small, dull white; **crustat'a,** a synonym of *S. crustata*; **cultra'ta,** *l.* narrowly tongue-shaped, ¾ to 1¼ in. long, about ⅛ in. wide, teeth triangular, *fl.-stem* 6 to 14 in. h. Carpathians. Not very distinct; **elonga'ta,** rosettes large, *l.* long, narrow, scarcely silvery, stems up to 12 in. h., *fl.* few, large, creamy-white: good in semi-shade, the form **erubes'cens** has reddish stems and *fl.* densely spotted purple. E. and S. Alps; **flaves'cens,** rosettes greenish, 1 to 1½ in. across, stems about 6 in. h., *fl.* rounded, yellow; **Gaudin'ii,** *see* **S. × Gaudinii; grac'ilis,** rather small, intermediate between vars. *carinthiaca* and *Sturmiana.* Salzburg; **hirsu'ta,** rosettes of medium size, *l.* and stems densely downy, stems up to 6 in. h., *fl.* creamy-white with few red spots. Corsica; **hirtel'la,** a small form of var. *hirsuta*; **hirtifo'lia,** rosettes small, velvety-grey downy, stems 3 to 4 in. h., *fl.* creamy-white, sometimes regarded as a form of var. *Sturmiana.* Limestone mts.; **intact'a** (probably a hybrid, *S. Aizoon × S. Hostii*), rosettes large, *l.* long, more or less silvery, stems up to 12 in. or more, *fl.* creamy, often spotted red, in loose heads; **Kolenatia'na,** *see* **S. Kolenatiana; labrador'ica,** rosettes very small, ½ to ¾ in. across, very silvery, stems 3 in. h., *fl.* round, white; **lagravea'na,** small, rosettes ½ to ¾ in. across, forming dense cushions, stems 2 to 3 in. h., *fl.* round, white, *l.* with many rounded teeth. La Grave; **lu'tea,** rosettes 2 in. across, *l.* long, narrow, green with little silver-grey, forming large patches, stems 6 to 8 in. h., *fl.* large, round, soft yellow, in loose heads; **ma'jor,** rosettes large, incurving, *l.* usually margined with grey and stained red, the red colouring often involving the whole rosette in winter, stems 12 to 18 in. h., very clammy-hairy, *fl.* large, round, heavily speckled red. Mts. of Dalmatia. Here belong as synonyms vars. *flabellata, linguifolia, Malyi, recta, robusta,* and *valida*; **min'or,** small with densely silvered rosettes up to about 1 in. across, stems 3 in. h., *fl.* creamy-white; a form of this, **minor brevifo'lia,** is still more condensed; **minutifo'lia,** rosettes scarcely ½ in. across, very silvery, *l.* usually deep red, *fl.* small, starry, creamy-white. Mt. Baldo. 1911. SYN. *S. baldensis*;

Saxifraga Aizoon (p. 1881)

nota'ta, rosettes of medium size, *l.* incurved, usually stained red beneath, stems 6 in. h., covered with clammy red hair, *fl.* starry, poor, creamy-white. SYN. var. *Sturmiana notata*; **orienta'lis,** rosettes of medium size, *l.* variable, with fairly heavy silvering, stems 6 to 8 in. h., *fl.* creamy-white, sometimes lightly spotted. The varying forms of this connect *S. Aizoon* with the eastern species *S. cartilaginea* and *S. Kolenatiana.* Balkans; **parado'xa,** a synonym of *S. paradoxa*; **pectina'ta,** a synonym of *S.* × *pectinata*; **puncta'ta,** rosettes of medium size, *l.* strap-shaped, only lightly silvered, stems sturdy, about 8 in. h., *fl.* heavily spotted red; **punctatis'sima,** rosettes of medium size, *l.* incurved, heavily silvered, stems about 4 in. long, *fl.* round, very heavily spotted red; **rec'ta,** a synonym of var. *major*; **Rex,** *l.* spreading, rounded, very silvery, stems 8 in. h., mahogany red, *fl.* large, clear creamy-white without spots; **robus'ta,** a synonym of var. *major*; **ro'sea,** rosettes 1½ to 2 in. across, *l.* silvered only at margin, strap-shaped, triangular at apex, stems 8 to 10 in. h., branched freely, *fl.* many, clear rose-pink becoming, in strong sunlight, pale pink. Bulgaria; **rosular'is,** rosettes large, *l.* incurved, dark green margined only with lime glands, stems 12 in. h. or more, *fl.* large, creamy-white, spotted red. SYN. var. *alpicola*; **Sempervi'vum,** rosettes of medium size, *l.* incurved, thick, stems stout, *fl.* creamy-white; **Stabia'na,** rosettes scarcely 2 in. across, *l.* spatulate, thick, wedge-shaped at apex, stems 6 to 8 in. h., stiff, stout, *fl.* whitish. Italy; **stenoglos'sa,** near var. *cultrata,* but *l.* narrower, acute; **Sturmia'na,** rosettes 1 to 2 in. across, *l.* spatulate to wedge-shaped, sharply toothed, often mucronate, stems 6 in. h., *fl.* creamy-white. Cent. Alps, *see also* var. **notata**; **vene'tia,** almost as small as var. *minutifolia* but less humped in growth as a rule, *l.* toothed, silvery, deep mahogany-red beneath, stem 2 in. h., *fl.* pure white. Venetian Alps. SYN. var. *venusta.*

S. ajugifo'lia (8). Small, creeping perennial, 2 to 3 in. h. *l.* about ½ in. long, 5- to 7-lobed, densely arranged near tips of shoots. *fl.-stems* axillary. *fl.* white, usually in pairs on slender pedicels. May, June. Pyrenees on stony margins of lakes, &c. A difficult plant. Several forms of the hybrid *S. ajugifolia* × *S. aquatica* are known and some have been offered.

S. Albert'i of gardens, a form of *S. lingulata.* There is also a garden hybrid of this name similar to *S.* × *apiculata.*

S. × **Allenii** (12) (*S. Burseriana* × ?). Forming grey, humped cushions. *fl.* round, very pale yellow, pet. slightly crimped at margin. Raised at Birch Farm, Sussex. 1938.

S. Allion'ii. A variety of *S. moschata.* The name occurs also as a synonym of *S. cymosa* and *S. pedemontana.*

S. altis'sima. A variety of *S. Hostii.*

S. × **ama'bilis** (13) (*S. porophylla Sibthorpiana* × *S. Stribrnyi?*). Tufted perennial up to 4 in. h. *l.-rosettes* many, ½ to ¾ in. across. *l.* oblanceolate, about ⅕ in. long, firm, glaucous; stem-l. spatulate-oblanceolate, blunt, ¼ in. long, softly woolly, mauvish-purple. *fl.* 4 to 6 in a short nodding raceme, carmine; bracts mauve-purple. Origin? 1916?

S. × **ambi'gua** (12 × 13) (*S. aretioides* × *S. media*). A natural hybrid close to *S. media. fl.* with red sep. and pet. a little longer than cal. Pyrenees.

S. amoe'na of gardens (8). Closely approaches *S. moschata* and *S. muscoides.* Forms a small, mossy cushion. Stems about 1 in. h. *fl.* rose. Needs a cool position. Origin?

S. Anderson'ii (12). Loosely tufted perennial. Stems erect, 2 in. h. *l.* dense, spatulate, less than ¼ in. long, overlapping, recurved; stem-l. few. *fl.* 4 or 5, rather small, pink. Sikkim.

S. × **Andrews'ii** (3, xii) (*S. Aizoon* × *S. Geum hirsuta*). Perennial, 6 to 12 in. h. *Basal l.* narrow, leathery, with horny, toothed margin; stem-l. 1 or 2. *infl.* much as in *S. umbrosa. fl.* white, dotted purple above middle. Summer. 1848. SYN. *S.* × *Guthrieana.*

S. androsa'cea (8). Densely tufted. Rosettes few-leaved, flat. *l.* obovate-spatulate, entire or 3-toothed. Stems 2 to 3 in. h., solitary- to many-fld., sometimes almost stemless. *fl.* milk-white, about ⅝ in. across. June, July. Alps. 1792. Dislikes lime. Moisture-loving.

S. × **anorma'lis** (13) (Parentage?). About 2 in. h. *fl.* yellow. Spring. Raised by Sündermann.

S. apenni'na. A synonym of *S. cuneifolia capillipes.*

S. aphyl'la (8). Cushions very small. *l.* 3-cleft. Stems leafless up to 1¼ in. long. *fl.* solitary, yellow, small, starry. High European Alps. Moisture- and lime-loving. Of small garden value.

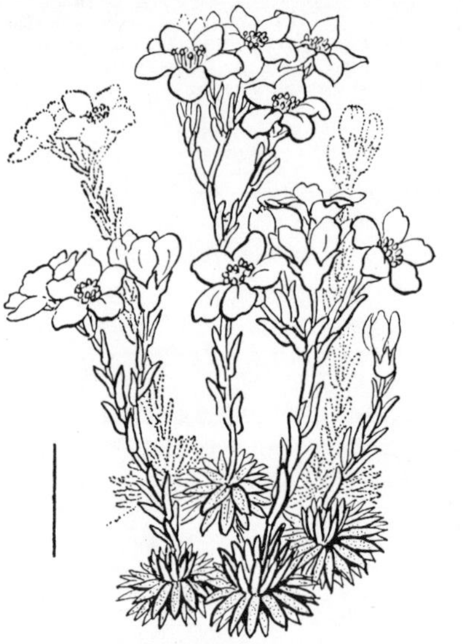

Saxifraga × *apiculata*

S. × **apicula'ta** (12) (*S. marginata Rocheliana* × *S. sancta*). Quick-growing, widespreading mat-plant. *l.* in rosettes, narrow, green, with 3 lime-glands near apex. Stems 3 to 4 in. long, leafy. *fl.* primrose-yellow in loose clusters, very free. March, April. Probably the earliest hybrid of the Kabschia section. 1894. var. **al'ba,** *fl.* white, equally free; **Primrose Bee,** free-flowering; probably a cross between *S. apiculata* and *S. marginata.* (B.M. 8048.)

S. aqua'tica (8). Cushion-forming, cushions large. *l.* leathery, deeply divided. *fl.-stems* branching, up to 1 ft. h. *fl.* snow-white, round, large. Summer. Pyrenees, on margins of streams. SYN. *S. adscendens.* var. **ap'rica,** smaller with smaller fl. SYN. *S. petraea. See note under* **S. ajugifolia.**

S. arachnoi'dea (7). Annual or biennial. *l.* oval, toothed, shaggy-grey-hairy. Stems procumbent, 4 to 12 in. long, slender. *fl.* small, pale yellow. Italian Alps, in grit and dust in dry limestone caves. Difficult to grow.

S. × **arco-val'leyi** (12) (*S. Burseriana minor* × *S. lilacina*). Very small with silver-grey rosettes and soft rose *fl.* on stems 1 in. h. Spring.

S. × **aretias'trum** (12) (*S. aretioides* × *S. Burseriana*). Differs from *S. aretioides* by its acute, not blunt, *l.* and by its larger, pale-yellow *fl.*

S. aretioi'des (12). Forms dense, hard, grey-green cushions. *l.* linear-ligulate, glaucous. Stems about 2 in. h., glandular. *fl.* yellow in a dense, few-fld. corymb; cal. baggy, glandular. May to July. Pyrenees. 1826. (B.M. 5849.) SYN. *Chondrosa aretioides.* Parent of many hybrids with better fl. and easier to grow. var. **primuli'na,** a synonym of *S. diapensioides lutea*; **micropet'ala,** a synonym of *S.* × *apiculata.*

S. argu'ta (1). Nearly related to *S. punctata* but with stamens about as long as pet. Arctic and sub-arctic regions. Of little garden value.

S. × **argu'ta** (8 × 9) (*S. tenella* × *S. tricuspidata*). Cushion-forming. *l.* 3-parted, bright green. Stems branching, 5 to 6 in. h. *fl.* snow-white. Easy to grow in partial shade.

S. aristula'ta (2). More or less deciduous, forming dense tufts. *l.* in small rosettes, undivided. Stems from centre of rosette, 2 in. long. *fl.* solitary, large, yellow. Himalaya.

S. × Arkwright'ii (8) (*S. decipiens* × *S. granulata?*). Vigorous, mossy, but of lax growth. Stems 6 to 9 in. long. *fl.* large, red. This needs frequent division and a moist, partially shaded position.

S. asp'era (9). Forms dense mats of mossy shoots. *l.* bristly edged. Non-flowering shoots condensed into buds. Stems long, rooting, branching, ascending, 3 to 4 in. h. *fl.* straw-yellow, flecked with orange spots, about ¾ in. across. European Alps. Easy to grow in open, gritty soil. var. **bryoi'des,** smaller, forming dense humped cushions, *fl.-stems* unbranched, 1-fld., often spotted red instead of orange; **Huguenin'ii,** *fl.* sessile or almost so, larger than in type, pet. touching, sep. ciliate. Pyrenees.

S. × assim'ilis (12) (Parentage ?). Cushions firm, grey, compact. Stems 1 to 1½ in. *fl.* white. Raised by Sündermann. Perhaps *S. Burseriana* × *S. tombeanensis.*

S. atlan'tica (7). Similar to *S. granulata* but with axillary, not basal bulbils. *fl.* white, large, fragrant, on slender stems about 8 in. h. W. Mediterranean region. 1895. Of easy cultivation in shady fibrous loam.

S. atropurpu'rea. A variety of *S. moschata.*

S. atroru'bens. A variety of *S. aizoides.*

S. austra'lis. *See* **S. lingulata.**

S. austromon'tana. A variety of *S. bronchialis.*

S. autumna'lis. A variety of *S. aizoides.*

S. azorelloi'des (9). Forms loosely humped cushions or mats of tangled shoots. *l.* 3-cleft, dark green. *fl.-stems* up to 6 in. h. *fl.* white, often spotted yellow or purple. Early summer. Grows well in moist cool spots with good drainage. SYN. *S. subtrifurcata.*

S. × Ba'keri (8). Rather coarse-growing, mossy plant. Possibly a derivative of *S. decipiens* × *S. granulata.*

S. Baldac'cii. *See* **S. pedemontana.**

S. balden'sis. A synonym of *S. Aizoon minutifolia.*

S. × bathonien'sis* (8) (Parentage ?). A strong-growing mossy Saxifrage. Stems branching, often reddish, about 9 in. h. *fl.* large, blood-red. Requires dividing frequently to keep it tidy. Possibly *S. decipiens* × *S. granulata.*

S. × bellunen'sis (11) (*S. Aizoon* × *S. Hostii*). *l.-rosettes* like those of *S. Aizoon. fl.* white, larger, in panicles on stems 12 to 16 in. h. Mt. Serva, near Belluno. 1900.

S. × Bentham'ii (12 × 13) (*S. aretioides* × *S. media*). Closely resembling *S. aretioides* but *fl.* varying from pale to rich yellow or orange. Natural hybrid. Mt. Beat, Cent. Pyrenees. 1901.

S. × Bertolon'ii (12 × 13) (*S. Stribrnyi* × *S. porophylla thessalica*). Close to *S. porophylla thessalica. l.* silver-grey, spiny. *fl.* in racemes, purple on stems 4 to 6 in. h. Spring. Garden hybrid.

S. × Biasolet'tii (12 × 13) (*S. Grisebachii* × *S. porophylla thessalica*). *l.-rosettes* intermediate. *fl.-stems* 4 in. h. *fl.* red in spikes. Early spring. Garden hybrid.

S. × Bieg'leri (12). Very compact and dwarf. Rosettes very small, silver-grey. Stems 1 in. h. *fl.* pure white. Raised by Sündermann. Perhaps *S. Burseriana* form × *S. tombeanensis.*

S. biflo'ra (14). Forms loose masses of trailing stems. *l.* opposite, very small, dark green. *fl.-stems* 2 in. h. *fl.* purple, in twos or threes, thin. May. Cent. Alps on granite. A high alpine difficult to grow, found on damp shale beds. var. **al'ba,** *fl.* white, good. SYN. *S. macropetala*; **Koch'ii,** *fl.* intense red. SYN. *S. Kochii.*

S. × Bilek'ii (12) (*S. Ferdinandi-Coburgii* × *S. tombeanensis*). Cushions very firm, silvery-grey. *l.* very small, incurved. *fl.* in threes or fours on 1- to 2-in. glandular stems, pale yellow. April, May. Best in alpine house.

S. biterna'ta (7). Evergreen hairy perennial. Stems leafy, 6 to 8 in. high. *l.* reniform to ternate, with bulbils in axils. *fl.* large, white, in loose clusters. June. Mediterranean region, in moist limestone crevices. Rather tender.

S. Blav'ii (6). Short-lived. *fl.* small. Near *S. tridactylites,* of no garden value. Balkans.

S. blepharophyl'la (14). Related to *S. oppositifolia* but with blunt l. ciliate to their tips. *fl.* starry, purple on stems 1 to 2 in. long. Cent. Alps on granite. A high alpine difficult to grow.

S. × Boeck'leri (12 × 13) (*S. Ferdinandi-Coburgii* × *S. Stribrnyi*). *l.-rosettes* up to 3 in. across. *fl.-stem* about 3 in. long. *fl.* numerous, small, orange or yellow tinted red. Spring.

S. × Boris'ii (12) (*S. Ferdinandi-Coburgii* × *S. marginata*). *l.-rosettes* grey-blue. Stems about 3 in. long, reddish glandular-hairy. *fl.* few, large, citron-yellow. Early spring. Of garden origin.

S. Bor'yi (12). Nearly related to *S. marginata* but more compact. *fl.* up to 5, large, round, pure white. Spring. Greece.

S. × Boyd'ii (12) (*S. aretioides* × *S. Burseriana*). *l.-rosettes* blue-grey, in dense firm tufts. *fl.-stems* tinged red. *fl.* 1 or 2, large, round, citron-yellow. Spring. The first hybrid of merit of its section to be raised in Britain. 1890. Needs careful cultivation.

S. × Boyd'ii alba (12) (*S. Burseriana* × *S. marginata Rocheliana*). *l.-rosettes* about 1 in. wide, in rounded cushions. *l.* silver-grey, blunt. *fl.* 2 or 3, large, white, on 2- to 3-in. stems. Spring. Of garden origin. 1890.

S. brachypo'da (2). Tufted. *l.* small, glossy above, grey-green beneath. Stem 3 to 4 in. h. *fl.* solitary, pale to rich yellow. Himalaya to China. Difficult.

S. brevifo'lia. A variety of *S. Aizoon.*

S. bronchia'lis (9). Densely tufted. Stems creeping, branched, densely leafy. *fl.-stems* 6 to 8 in. h. *l.* overlapping, narrow, sharply pointed, ciliate. *fl.* 3 to 5, yellow, spotted orange. May. N. Asia, N. America. 1819. SYN. *S. spinulosa, Ciliaria bronchialis.* var. **austromon'tana,** *fl.* spotted purple. N. America. SYN. *S. cognata S. congesta, Leptasea austromontana.*

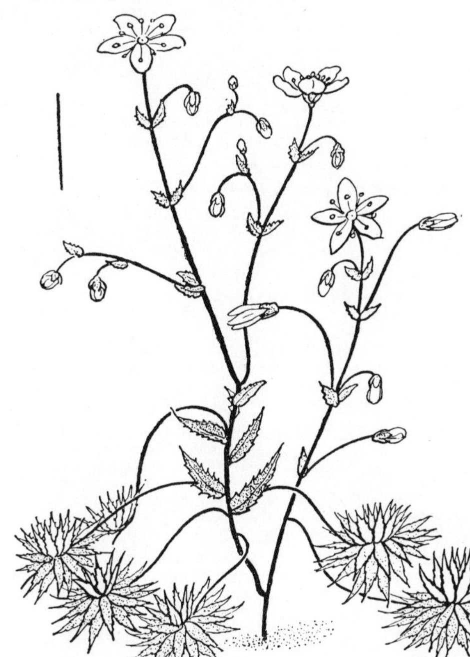

Saxifraga Brunoniana

S. Brunonia'na (2). In wide-spreading masses of l.-rosettes. *l.* spiny, pale green, bristle-margined. Stolons long, bright red, with a large terminal bud. *fl.* 3 or 4, large, rich yellow. Stems erect, 2 to 3 in. long, slender. Summer. Sikkim Himalaya. (B.M. 8189.)

S. bryoi'des. A variety of *S. aspera.*

S. Buckland'ii. *See* **S. cuneifolia subintegra.**

S. bulbif'era (7). Nearly related to *S. granulata.* Bulbils axillary. Stem tall. *fl.* 3 or 4, dingy white. Europe.

S. × Burna'tii (11) (*S. Aizoon* × *S. cochlearis*). Intermediate between parents. *l.* in rosettes, lime-beaded, recurved. *fl.* white in loose sprays on branching, reddish stems, 4 to 5 in. h. Maritime Alps. Natural hybrid.

S. Burseria'na* (12). Cushions large. *l.-rosettes* many-leaved. *l.* spiny, silver-grey. Stem about 2 in. h., tinted red. *fl.-buds* reddish, pet. glistening white, large. Early spring. E. Alps on limestone. 1826. A fine plant, parent of many good hybrids. var. **Brookside,** *fl.* large, of fine form; **crena'ta,** compact and close in growth, about 1 in. h.; pet. crimped and toothed on margins; **Gloria,** a fine form of var. *tridentina,* stems red, 4 in. h., *fl.* very large, white; **His Majesty,** *fl.* large, white flushed pink; possibly a hybrid; **ma'jor,** stems green, 1-fld., *fl.* large, white. SYN. var. *magna*; **mi'nor,** dwarf and compact, stems short, *fl.* round, white. Karawanken Mt.; **multiflo'ra,** stems about 3 in. h., *fl.* several, clustered, smaller; **sulphu'rea,** like type but *fl.* soft yellow; possibly a hybrid; **tridenti'na,*** robust, *fl.* large. Laentino, Italy. From this have been selected the taller large-fld. forms mentioned above; **Trimmersfield,*** 2 to 3 in. h., soft yellow. Spring. Of garden origin. Hindhead; possibly a hybrid.

S. × bursicula'ta (12) (*S.* × *apiculata* × *S. Burseriana*). Intermediate between parents. *fl.* in loose heads, white, 2 to 3 in. h. Early spring.

S. cae'sia (12). Forms dense spreading masses. *l.-rosettes* small, flattish, grey-green, with lime glands. Stems slender, about 2 in. long, branching. *fl.* white, round in a small panicle. May, June. Pyrenees to E. Alps. 1752. (L.B.C. 421.) Mostly in crevices or on cliffs, occasionally in earthy screes. var. **balden'sis,** many-fld., slightly glandular, 3 in. h. August. Trentino, Italy; **glandulosis'sima,**

more robust than type, 3 to 4 in. h., stems glandular. Styria; **ma'jor,** a garden name for the 2 foregoing forms; **subacau'lis,** unbranched, 1 in. h., *fl.* solitary. Another small plant belonging to Section 11 is in gardens under the name *S. caesia*, possibly a hybrid of *S. crustata*. *See* **S. × stricta.**

S. caespito'sa (8). Loosely leafy, shoots not columnar. *l.* deeply lobed, lobes narrow, more or less glandular-hairy. *fl.* on slender pedicels, pet. 2 or 3 times as long as sep., pet. not clawed. Early summer. N. Hemisphere including Britain. (E.B. 556.) An extremely variable plant of which botanists have named numerous forms and sub-forms. In gardens it has hybridized with other mossy Saxifrages and given rise to many coloured varieties that cannot be referred with any certainty to definite species. For most of the natural forms and for the almost endless synonyms Engler and Irmscher's monograph should be consulted. The most marked forms are var. **compac'ta,** dwarf and compact, forming rich green mossy cushions, *fl.* usually 1 or 2, white, round, on stems about 3 in. h. Spring. Syn. *S. groenlandica*; **palma'ta,** variable, of loose or compact habit, *l.* 3- to 7-lobed, lobes spatulate, often fleshy, very hairy to almost glabrous, stems 3 to 6 in. h., *fl.* white. Spring. Syn. *S. hibernica, S. hirta.* Most of the plants in gardens under this name are superior plants of hybrid origin; **ro'sea,** compact, *l.* hairy, *fl.-stems* 3 in. h., loosely branched, *fl.* soft pink. Spring. A similar form has been found on Clare Is., Ireland.

S. calab'rica. *See* **S. lingulata australis.**

S. × calab'rica (11) (*S. lingulata* × *S. longifolia*). Rosettes and infl. both finer than in parents. Here belong the forms **Alopecurea, Cecil Davies,** and the remarkable **Tumbling Waters.** The last makes many offsets and has *fl.* far finer than in *S. longifolia.*

S. callo'sa. A synonym of *S. lingulata.* **A**

S. calyciflo'ra. A synonym of *S. media.*

S. Campo'sii (8). Robust mossy plant forming neat cushions 4 to 6 in. h. *l.* sharply 3-cleft, clammy. *fl.-stems* stout, freely branched. *fl.* large, shapely, white in a close cluster. Summer. S. Spain. 1882. (B.M. 6440.) Syn. *S. Wallacei* of gardens.

S. canalicula'ta (8). Forming large, loose cushions, almost subshrubby at base. *l.* rigid, deeply cleft, stalks channelled. *fl.* large, white. Early summer. Spain. Syn. *S. Willcommiana.*

S. candelab'rum (2). *Basal l.* wedge-shaped. Stem 6 to 9 in. h. *fl.* starry, the narrow yellow pet. alternating with the green sep. Yunnan, China.

S. × canis-dalmat'ica (11) (*S. Aizoon balcana* × *S. Cotyledon*). *l.-rosettes* of medium size. *l.* slightly incurved. Stem 12 in. h., branching. *fl.* round, white heavily spotted purple. Early summer. Of garden origin.

S. capilla'ris. A synonym of *S. cuneifolia.*

S. capita'ta. A synonym of *S. ajugifolia, S. aquatica,* and *S. Aizoon brevifolia multicaulis.*

S. carinthi'aca. A variety of *S. Aizoon.*

S. carpath'ica (7). Allied to *S. granulata.* Deciduous. About 9 in. h. Bulbils in axils of lower stem-l. *fl.* 3 to 5, large, white. Carpathian Mts.

S. cartilagin'ea (11). Closely related to *S. Aizoon. l.-rosettes* about 1 to 1½ in. across. *l.* long-triangular, stiff, leathery, margin cartilaginous, with rounded teeth. Stems upright, branched, 5 to 6 in. h. *fl.* starry white. June to August. Caucasus. var. **atropurpu'rea,** *fl.* deep blood-red. Dargestan. 1935. A shy plant; **Kolenatia'na,** *see* **S. Kolenatiana**; **ma'jor,** rather taller, stems 9 to 12 in., *fl.* red. Syn. *S. Sendtneri*; **mi'nor,** smaller in all parts, 3 to 4 in. h.

S. catalaun'ica. A form of *S. lingulata.*

S. caterhamen'sis. A variety of *S. Cotyledon.*

S. cauca'sica (12). Tufted, dark green. *l.* spiny. Stems about 3 in. h. *fl.* yellow, pet. very short, concealed by anthers. Summer. Caucasus. var. **Desoulav'yi,** a slight variant. Of little garden value.

S. cebennen'sis (8). Forms dwarf, firm, hemispherical, mossy cushions. Stems 1 to 2 in. long, thread-like. *fl.* numerous, round, white. Cevennes, France. Best in alpine house. Syn. *S. Prostiana.*

S. ceratophyl'la. A synonym of *S. exarata Villarsii, S. Schraderi,* and *S. trifurcata.*

S. cer'nua (7). Like *S. granulata* but smaller, 6 to 9 in. h. *fl.* usually solitary, drooping, white. July. Bulbils in l.-axils of stem-l., bright red. Europe, including Britain, America. (E.B. 554.) Needs constant but not stagnant moisture.

S. cervicorn'is. A synonym of *S. pedemontana.*

S. cherlerioi'des (9). Very near *S. bronchialis* and of no garden value. Arctic regions. Syn. *S. compacta. S. pseudoburseriana* has also been so called.

S. chrysan'tha (2). Tufted, small. *l.* in rosettes, thyme-like. Stems 2 in. h. *fl.* golden-yellow. Rocky Mts. Grows in damp places at about 12,000 ft. Difficult to cultivate.

S. chrysosplenifo'lia (4). Similar to *S. rotundifolia* but smaller. Stems 4 to 6 in. h., branching. *fl.* small, white, spotted yellow or purple. Summer. Greece. var. **fra'gilis,** *l.* margins crenulate; **rhodo'pea,** rather larger, *l.* sharply toothed.

S. × Churchil'lii (11) (*S. Aizoon* × *S. Hostii*). Intermediate between parents. *l.-rosettes* large. *l.* stiff, margined with silvery glands. Stems 12 in. h. *fl.* large, white, numerous. Spring. Natural hybrid.

S. cilia'ta. *See* **Bergenia ligulata.**

S. circina'ta. A variety of *S. cristata.*

S. circuen'ta. A garden name for *S.* × *paradoxa* or *S. pectinata.*

S. citri'na. A variety of *S. moschata.*

S. × Clark'ei (12 × 13) (*S. media* × *S. Vandellii*). More nearly resembling *S. media* than its other parent in its rosettes but pet. twice as long as sep. and *fl.* as in the Kabschia section, soft rose. About 3 in. h. Garden hybrid raised by Sündermann. 1908.

S. × Clib'ranii (8) (Parentage?). Resembles *S. muscoides* but 3 to 4 in. h., fl. larger, deep red. Spring. Easily grown in partial shade and open soil. For an interesting account of this and related hybrids, see *Garden*, 77 (1913), p. 485.

S. Clu'sii (1). *Basal l.* in rosette, coarsely toothed, obovate. Stem branching, leafy. *fl.* white speckled red. Mts. of Cent. Europe on moist rocks or in shady places. 1882. Syn. *S. stellaris Clusii, S. stellaris leucanthemifolia.* var. **propagi'nea,** bulbils replace the *fl.* Doubtful whether now in cultivation.

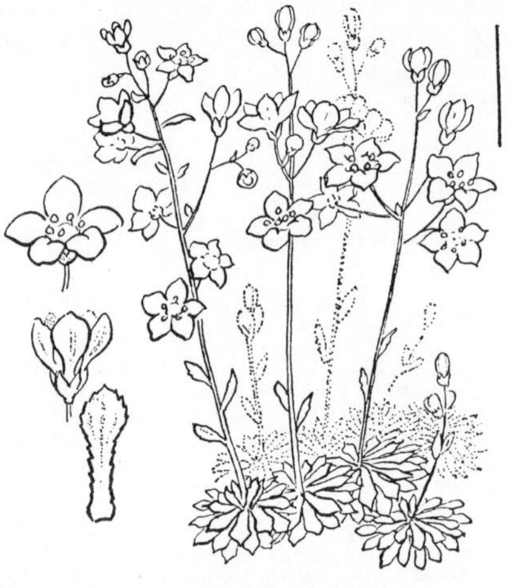

Saxifraga cochlearis

S. cochlear'is (11). *l.-rosettes* in humped masses, heavily encrusted. *l.* ½ to 1 in. long, tips thickened, reflexed. Stems 6 in., branching, reddish. *fl.* white in slender panicles. June. Maritime Alps. 1883. (B.M. 6688.) Syn. *S. lingulata cochlearis.* var. **ma'jor,** larger than type; **mi'nor,** small, *l.-rosettes* about ½ in. across, thickly encrusted, silvery, stems 3 to 4 in. h., *fl.* white. Good for crevices. Syn. *S. Probynii.* Sometimes confused with *S. valdensis.*

S. cochlea'ta. A synonym of *S. cochlearis major.*

S. cogna'ta. A synonym of *S. bronchialis austromontana.*

S. compact'a. A synonym of *S. Aizoon brevifolia, S. cherlerioides,* and *S. valdensis.* The name has also been used for a yellow-fld. plant from Siberia, like *S. Burseriana* in its rosettes but with offsets like a Sempervivum, otherwise unnamed unless it be *S. pseudoburseriana* which it much resembles.

S. conif'era (8). Small mossy Saxifrage related to *S. hypnoides* but with narrowly pointed, undivided *l.*, winter buds covered with grey hairs, and *fl.* small, white. Pyrenees, Spain.

S. corbarien'sis. A variety of *S. geranioides.*

S. cordifo'lia. A synonym of *Bergenia cordifolia.*

S. coriophyl'la. A variety of *S. marginata.*

S. Correvonia'na. A variety of *S. Aizoon.*

S. cor'sica. A variety of *S. granulata.*

S. cortusifo'lia (16). Tufted, deciduous, without runners. *l.* roundish, leathery, deeply cut, stalks stiff, 3 in. long. *fl.* white, with 1 or 2 pet. lengthened, peduncles branched. September. Japan. 1883. Considerable variety occurs in the foliage. var. **ro'sea,** *fl.* pink, dwarf. (B.M. 6680.)

S. corymbo'sa (13). Forms small tufts of a few rosettes, each about ½ in. across. *l.* narrow, broadly pointed, grey-green with marginal lime-glands. Stems 2 to 4 in. h., glandular, leafy with a terminal corymb of yellow *fl.*, partly enclosed by the large, green, glandular calyces. W. Asia Minor, Bulgaria. Prefers partial shade. A parent of many hybrids. Syn. *S. chlorantha, S. luteoviridis.* var. **luteovi'ridis,** *l.* narrower and more pointed, stems up to 6 in. h. Spring. Carpathians and Transylvania. Syn. *S. luteopurpurea, S. luteoviridis* of gardens, *S. mutata, S. Lapeyrousii, S. tecta.*

S. Cossonia'na (7). Deciduous, tufted. *l.* small, round, crenulate. Bulbils basal. Stems branching, with few l., 6 to 8 in. h. *fl.* large, white. June. Spain. SYN. *S. granulata ramosissima, S. paniculata.*

S. Cotyle'don* (11). Forms masses of broad-leaved rosettes. *l.* rounded at apex, finely toothed, each tooth with a lime-gland at its base. Stems 18 to 24 in. h., branched almost from base. *Panicles* large. *fl.* white. May to July. Pyrenees, SW. Alps north to Lapland and Iceland. 1596. SYN. *S. montavonensis, S. paniculata, S. pyramidalis.* Usually found on lime-free sites. A very fine plant of which many hybrids occur. var. **caterhamen'sis,*** *fl.* heavily spotted red; **iceland'ica,** *l.* iron-grey, stem up to 4 ft. h.; **launcestonen'sis,** *l.* broader than in type, stems 1 ft. h., *fl.* white, unspotted; **montavonen'sis,** *l.* broad, *fl.-stem* 1 ft. h., red, *fl.* white; **norveg'ica,** name given to plants from northern localities and otherwise inseparable from southern plants; **pauciflo'ra,** *l.-rosettes* about 1½ in. across, stems about 6 in. in height, a plant from high altitudes in Sweden, Switzerland, &c., not retaining its characters in cultivation; **prolif'era,** *fl.* replaced by small l.-rosettes by which the plant may be propagated; **pyramid'alis,** *l.* broad, rosettes tending to become mahogany-red in winter, stems branching from base, panicles large, pyramidal, *fl.* pure white. Pyrenees, Alps of Vallais.

S. crassifo'lia. A synonym of *Bergenia crassifolia.*

S. cro'cea. A variety of *S. moschata.*

S. crusta'ta (11). Forming dense cushions or mats. *l.* in rosettes, narrow, glossy green, silver-beaded at margin, recurved. Stems about 6 in. h., branched only in upper parts, each branch with 1 to 3 dingy-white *fl.* June, July. E. Alps. 1800. SYN. *S. cristata, S. crustacea, S. incrustata.* Occurs only on limestone. var. **vochinen'sis,** *l.-rosettes* 2 to 3 in. across, *l.* of very unequal length, stems 12 in. h., arching, free-flowering, *fl.* almost white. Julian Alps. Much like *S. lingulata Bellardii* when out of fl.

S. cultra'ta (11). A variety of *S. Aizoon.*

S. cunea'ta (8). Loosely tufted, mossy, stems woody at base. *l.* thick, leathery, 3- to 5-cleft, lobes entire or coarsely toothed. Stem up to 8 in. *fl.* in loose heads, white. Spain, Pyrenees. Prefers a light soil and sunny position.

S. cuneifo'lia (3). In spreading masses of dark-green rosettes. *l.* small, roundish, slightly scalloped, stalks thin. Stems 3 in. h., reddish. *fl.* numerous, small, white with 1 yellow spot at base of each pet. May, June. Alps. 1768. In woodlands. var. **apenni'na,** a synonym of var. *capillipes*; **capil'lipes,** smaller than type, paler green, stems green, *fl.* in addition to the yellow spot with very small pink spots. Apennines and SW. Alps. SYN. *S. apennina, S. capillaris* of gardens; **multicaul'is,** *l.* spatulate, wedge-shaped; a garden form **subinte'gra,** slightly larger, *l.* less scalloped, *fl.* with 2 instead of 1 basal yellow dot on each pet. Pyrenees, &c. SYN. var. *infundibulum.*

S. cuscutifor'mis (16). *Basal l.* roundish, bronze, often with white marbling, rather thick, more or less deeply toothed. Stem slender, 3 to 4 in. long. *fl.* white or pinkish, lanceolate-elliptic; 2 upper pet. short, 3 lower long, narrow; branches of panicle 2- or 3-fld. June, July. China? 1815. (B.M. 2631; L.B.C. 186.) Produces young plants at ends of slender runners. Best grown under glass.

S. Cymbala'ria (5). Small annual. Stem branching. *l.* in basal rosettes and on stem round or kidney-shaped, variously lobed. *fl.* small, golden-yellow, starry. May to August. Caucasus to Persia. var. **Huetia'na,** a form sometimes found in the Carpathians. SYN. *S. hederacea, S. orientalis, S. paradoxa, S. Sibthorpii* of gardens.

S. cymo'sa. A variety of *S. pedemontana.*

S. dalmat'ica of gardens. A synonym of *S. scardica obtusa.*

S. decip'iens (8). Cushions large or small, loose or compact. *l.* broad with blunt segs. or narrow with acute segs., glabrous or hairy. *fl.* white, pink to red, opening flat, buds erect. Widely distributed, very variable. var. **Clib'ranii,** *see* **S. × Clibranii**; **grandiflo'ra,** spreading freely, stems 6 in. h., *fl.* large, creamy-white; good in a shady position; **grandiflora hybrids,** covers a number of the larger loose-growing coloured mossy Saxifrages of garden origin. Most seem to have some trace of *S. granulata* in their constitution. Here might be placed *Bakeri, bathoniensis, Clibranii, Willmottiae,* for example. They are for the most part good handsome garden plants, often rather untidy in habit and needing frequent division or renewal by cuttings. Some shade is desirable, particularly for the more highly coloured forms; **groenland'ica,** *see* **S. caespitosa compacta**; **hybrids** (i.e. **decipiens hybrids**) may cover the smaller and neater-growing mossy Saxifrages which cannot with certainty be attributed to *S. moschata, S. muscoides,* or *S. rhoei.* Examples would be *S. Craven Gem, S. Fergusonii, S. Guildford Seedling, S. Stormonths' Seedling,* and there are hosts of others; **palma'ta,** *rossette-l.* 3- or 5-cleft, stem-l. entire or 3-cleft, lobes variable in width, more or less hairy, *fl.* white, rather small; **quinquef'ida,** very near next and of the same value; **sponhem'ica,** *l.-rosettes* round, closely tufted, *l.* large, 3-, 5-, or 7-cleft, *fl.* white. SYN. *S. sponhemica.* Now superseded by hybrid forms. For closely allied forms *see also* **S. Stansfieldii** and **S. Webbiana**; **Sternber'gii,** large, *l.* glabrous or nearly so, the stalk with a few hairs, segs. rather blunt. Ireland. **A**

S. Delavay'i. *See* **Bergenia Delavayi.**

S. delphinen'sis. A synonym of *S. moschata acaulis.*

S. demis'sa. A variety of **S. mutata.**

S. dens'a. A synonym of *S. bronchialis cherlerioides, S. hypnoides calabrica.*

S. denta'ta. A variety of *S. Geum.*

S. depres'sa (8). Forms little columns of l.-shoots. *l.* wedge-shaped, 3-toothed at apex. *fl.-stems* 3 to 4 in. h., almost leafless. *fl.* small, white, few. Spring. SYN. *S. androsacea, S. fassana.*

S. Desoulav'yi. A variety of *S. caucasica.*

S. diapensioi'des (12). Forms rigid, blue-grey masses. *l.* very small, crowded, blunt. Stems 1 to 2 in. h. *fl.* 1 or 2, round, milk-white. Spring. European Alps. 1825. SYN. *S. caesia, S. glauca.* Grows very slowly and needs care. Best in sunny, limestone crevices or in pans in alpine house. var. **lu'tea,** *fl.* yellow. SYN. *S. aretioides primulina*; **tombeanen'sis,** a misnomer.

S. diversifo'lia (2). Tufted. *Basal l.* long-stalked, heart-shaped, 1 to 2 in. long; *stem-l.* smaller, sessile. Stem 9 to 10 in. h., leafy. *fl.* few, yellow, small. July. Himalaya, Yunnan. 1882. (B.M. 6603.) SYN. *S. Moorcroftiana, S. parnassifolia. S. signata* is frequently grown under this name.

S. × Doerf'leri (13) (*S. Grisebachii × S. Stribrnyi*). Intermediate between parents, 4 to 5 in. h. *fl.* purple. Spring. Raised by Suendermann. 1915.

S. × E'dithae (12 × 13) (*S. marginata × S. Stribrnyi*). Habit of *S. marginata,* 2 to 3 in. h. *fl.* pink. Spring. Raised by Sündermann.

S. ela'tior. A synonym of *S. Aizoon major* and *S. Hostii.*

S. × Eliza'bethae (12) (*S. Burseriana × S. sancta*). Quick-growing, forming widespreading blue-green mats. *Rosette-l.* spiny. Stems 2 to 3 in. h. *fl.* soft yellow in heads, freely produced. Early spring.

S. elonga'ta. A variety of *S. virginiensis.*

S. × Eng'leri (11) (*S. crustata × S. Hostii*). *Rosette-l.* narrow, silvery. Stem branching. *fl.* white. Natural hybrid. Carinthian and Venetian Alps. Other plants are known in gardens as *S. Engleri,* including a form of *S. stellaris* and various hybrids of *S. Aizoon* and probably *S. longifolia.*

S. ero'sa (1). A synonym of *S. micranthidifolia.* Of no garden value.

S. erubes'cens. A form of *S. Aizoon elongata.*

S. erythran'tha. A variety of *S. scardica.*

S. Escholtz'ii. A synonym of *S. serpyllifolia.*

S. Eschscholt'zii (2). Forms dense cushions of erect stems, about 1 in. high, covered with overlapping obovate l. with hairy margins. *fl.* terminal sessile, very small, yellow. Arctic America. Not yet introduced. Of interesting habit.

S. × Eudoxia'na (12) (*S. Ferdinandi-Coburgii × S. sancta*). Cushions neat, of crowded rosettes. *l.* blue-grey, spiny. Stems 2 in. h. *fl.* pale yellow of medium size. Spring. Of garden origin, raised by Sündermann.

S. exara'ta (8). Distinguished from *S. moschata* by its dark-green, prominently nerved *l.,* 3-partite, with side lobes usually 2-fid or 2-lobed, tips obtuse. Pet. 2 to 2½ times as long as sep., white, yellowish, or rarely purplish. June, July. Alps east to Persia. 1800. A very variable plant. var. **adenoph'ora,** pet. obovate-oblong, at least twice as long as sep., *l.* of about equal length, nerves not prominent, shoots more or less columnar. Asia Minor; **Villars'ii,** *fl.* smaller, pet. obovate, not over twice as long as sep. or ⅛ in. long, white, yellowish, purple, or purple-spotted, densely tufted. Alps to Caucasus.

S. Facchin'ii (8). Small, densely tufted. *l.* short, blunt, scarcely divided, 3- to 5-nerved. Stem 1 to 2 in. h., erect, with few narrow l., glandular hairs short. *fl.* 2 or 3, pale or golden-yellow or purple. June. Crevices and screes in Dolomitic Alps. SYN. *S. muscoides Fachinii, S. planifolia.*

S. × Far'reri (8 × 6) (*S. hypnoides × S. tridactylites*). Ingleborough, Yorks. Of no garden value.

S. Federici-Augu'sti. A synonym of *S. porophylla. See* **S. × Frederici-Augusti.**

S. Ferdinandi-Cobur'gii (12). Much like *S. aretioides* but of eastern distribution. Forms neat clumps of silver-grey rosettes of spiny l. Stems 3 to 4 in. h. *fl.* roundish, bright yellow, buds often red. Spring. Rhodope Mts., Bulgaria.

S. × Ferguso'nii (8) (*S. decipiens? × S. muscoides purpurea?*). Forms neat mats. Stems 4 in. h., branching. *fl.* numerous, round, red.

S. filicau'lis (2). Loosely tufted. *Rosette-l.* narrow, minutely toothed. Stems 4 to 6 in. h., erect or ascending, with a few bulbils in lower part. *fl.* 1 or 2, white or yellow. Summer. Himalaya, Yunnan.

S. fimbria'ta (2). Stems 4 to 6 in. h., ascending, with a few bulbils in lower part. *fl.* 2 or 3, golden-yellow. Mts. of Cent. Asia.

S. firma'ta. A synonym of *S. moschata lineata.*

S. flagella'ris (2). Related to *S. Brunoniana.* Rosettes in masses, few-leaved. Stems short, leafy, with numerous slender stolons ending in bulbils. *fl.* 1 to 3, yellow. Arctic and sub-arctic. 1819.

S. flaves'cens. A synonym of *S. hypnoides condensata.*

S. × **Fleisch'eri** (13) (*S. Grisebachii* × *S. corymbosa luteoviridis*). Rosettes intermediate between parents. Stem 3 to 4 in. h. *fl.* varying from cinnabar-red to rich orange, upper fl. of spike sessile, lower long-stalked. Spring. Raised by Sündermann. 1915.

S. × **florarien'sis** (11) (*S. Hostii* × *S. lingulata lantoscana*). Forms handsome, wide-spreading masses of rosettes up to 3 in. across with rather narrow l., not recurved. *fl.* in branching sprays up to 18 in. long. Early summer.

S. florulent'a (11). Monocarpic. *l-rosettes* large, handsome, 4 to 6 in. across. *l.* numerous, narrow, dark green, points upturned, spiny. *fl.* dingy pink, pet. short, in a compact, many-branched panicle up to 18 in. h., cal. large, fluffy, styles 3. Summer. SW. and Maritime Alps. Slow to reach flowering and dying after seed production. Its beauty lies in the fine rosette. SYN. *Tristylea floribunda.*

S. × **Fontan'ae** (12) (*S. diapensioides* × *S. Ferdinandi-Coburgii*). Forms very compact humped masses of small grey rosettes. Stems 2 to 3 in. h. *fl.* 3, yellow. Difficult to grow.

S. Forbes'ii (1). A form of *S. pennsylvanica* up to 4 ft. h. *fl.* white. Illinois, United States, on moist rocks.

S. × **Forst'eri** (12) (*S. caesia* × *S. mutata*). Forms rather loose mats. Rosettes small, resembling those of *S. caesia*, but green. Stems very slender, 2 in. h. *fl.* 1 to 3, rounded, butter-yellow. Summer. N. Tyrol. 1877. A natural hybrid. Needs careful cultivation either in pans in the alpine house or in limestone scree in a rather moist, sunny, sheltered nook.

Saxifraga Fortunei

S. Fortu'nei (16). Forms deciduous clumps. *l.* large, glossy, leathery, roundish, variously toothed, brownish-red beneath. Stems 12 to 18 in. h., branching, leafy, stem-l. clasping at base, smaller. *fl.* white in loose panicles, 1 or 2 lower pet. long and toothed. Autumn. China, Japan. 1863. (B.M. 5377.) Hardy. Prefers a cool, partly shaded spot.

S. × **Franz'ii** (12) (parentage?). Clumps firm, rounded. *Rosette-l.* narrow, silver-grey. Stems 2 in. h. *fl.* several, pale yellow. Spring. Garden hybrid.

S. × **Frederici-Augu'sti*** of gardens (12) (probably *S. media* × *S. porophylla*). *l.-rosettes* like those of *S. media*, fl.-spike arching as in *S. porophylla*. *fl.* small, pink, partly enclosed in large claret calyces. Stem 6 in. h. Spring. Good for alpine house. Cf. *S. Federici-Augusti.*

S. × **Fries'ii** (12) (parentage?). Very small, forming very firm, almost hemispherical masses of silvery-grey rosettes. Stems 1 to 2 in. *fl.* white. Early spring.

S. × **Funk'ii** (12) (parentage?). Very compact, forming humped cushions of silvery-grey rosettes. Stems 2 to 3 in. h. *fl.* white. Early spring.

S. × **Gaert'neri** (12 × 13) (parentage?). Stem 2 in. h. *fl.* pink. Early spring.

S. × **Gaudin'ii** (11) (*S. Aizoon* × *S. Cotyledon pyramidalis*). Larger than most of the Aizoon section, intermediate in habit and appearance between parents. *l.* distinctly toothed. Stems tall, branching from near base. *fl.* white, Cent. Alps, Pyrenees. Natural hybrid.

S. geranioi'des (8). Of strong growth. *l.* fragrant, variously cut, stalks long, hairy, blade leathery, hairy, sometimes clammy. Stems 6 to 8 in. h. *fl.* white, not widely expanded, in a loose panicle. Early summer. Pyrenees, Spain. 1770. SYN. *S. ladanifera.* var. **corbarien'sis,** *l.* less deeply cut, glabrous or almost so, *fl.* more widely expanded. E. Pyrenees on limestone rocks. SYN. *S. Lapeyrousii, S. palmata, S. Prostii.*

S. × **Geud'eri** (12) (possibly *S. aretioides* × *S. Ferdinandi-Coburgii*). Small, cushions dense. *l.* spiny. Stem 2 to 3 in. h. *fl.* deep yellow. Early spring.

S. Ge'um (3). Forms wide mats. *l.* of basal rosettes long-stalked, round to kidney-shaped, leathery, often red beneath, more or less hairy, base cordate, margin crenate or serrate. Stem erect, 12 in. or more h., branching in upper third. *fl.* many, small, white, often yellow at base or spotted red. Early summer. SW. Europe, including Ireland and Scotland. SYN. *S. hirsuta.* var. **crena'ta,** larger than type, *l.* kidney-shaped, less hairy, bluntly crenate; **denta'ta,** *l.* round to kidney-shaped, sharply toothed, *fl.* white with pale-yellow base, rarely spotted; **grac'ilis,** *l.* widely oval or roundish, small, sharply toothed, smooth above. Of garden origin. SYN. *S. gracilis;* **hirsu'ta,** *l.* oval, densely hairy, l.-stalks hairy. Ireland, Yorkshire, Pyrenees; **ma'jor,** *l.* larger than type, round, crenate, deep red beneath. Probably a garden form; **mi'nor,** about half size of type, otherwise similar. Several other variations in fl. colour, l.-form, and size have received botanical names but they are of little horticultural interest. Grows well in a moist, shady place.

S. gibraltar'ica. A variety of *S. globulifera.*

S. glau'ca. A synonym of *S. diapensioides.*

S. globulif'era (8). Forms a bright-green mossy carpet, purplish-red in winter. Related to *S. hypnoides*, but with sep. rounded, not mucronate, pet. only about ⅙ in. long; distinct from other related species by numerous small fl. *l.* at base often spatulate, upper palmately 3- to 5-cleft, with globose bulbils in their axils. W. Mediterranean region. 1895. Very variable. var. **erioblast'a,** *basal l.* entire or shortly 3-lobed, bulbils obovoid, densely white-hairy at tip and within. Spain; **gibraltar'ica,** *basal l.* about two-thirds as long as stalks, 3-fid, bulbils stalked, sparsely hairy within. Gibraltar, Algiers; **granaten'sis,** strong-growing, 6 in. h., *l.* 5-cleft, bulbils sessile or nearly so, obovoid, long-hairy; **oranen'sis,** bulbils glabrous outside, oblong. Algiers; **spathula'ta,** densely tufted, lower l. long-stalked, spatulate, obtuse, or 3-lobed, fl.-stem about 8 in. h. Algiers.

S. × **Godronian'a** (12 × 13) (*S. aretioides* × *S. media*). Rosettes as in *S. media.* Stem 3 in. h. *fl.* pale yellow stained red. Spring. Pyrenees. Natural hybrid.

S. × **Godseffia'na** (12) (*S. Burseriana* × *S. sancta*). Closely resembling *S.* × *Elizabethae.* Quickly growing mats. *l.* spiny, blue-green. Stem reddish. *fl.* lemon-yellow, in loose clusters. Early spring. SYN. L. C. Godseff, *S. Burseriana speciosa, S. ochroleuca.*

S. grac'ilis of gardens. A synonym of *S. Geum gracilis.*

S. granaten'sis. A variety of *S. globulifera.*

S. grandiflo'ra villo'sa of gardens. A synonym of *S. sibirica.*

S. granula'ta (7). Meadow Saxifrage; Fair Maids of France. Deciduous. Tufted. *l.* kidney-shaped, thickish. Stem 12 in. or more h., sparsely leafy. *fl.* white, large, in loose panicles. Early summer. Bulbils clustered at base of stem. Europe, including Britain. (E.B. 555.) A parent with *S. decipiens* of many hybrids, usually of rather loose habit. var. **ple'na,** Pretty Maids. *fl.* fully double, about 1 in. across, more frequent in gardens than the single form; **cor'sica,** dwarfer, up to 8 in. h., *fl.* rarely exceeding 3, *l.* of fl.-stems 3-cleft only. Corsica. SYN. *S. Russii, S. corsica.*

S. × **gra'ta** (12) (*S. aretioides* × *S. Ferdinandi-Coburgii*). Intermediate between parents. Stems about 4 in. h. *fl.* 5 or 6 in corymbs, bright yellow. Raised by Sündermann.

S. Grisebach'ii* (13). Basal rosettes up to 3 in. across, eventually forming large humped cushions. fl.-stems from centre of rosette at first arching, then erect, to 9 in. h., leafy. *l.* silvery-grey; *stem-l.* and cal. densely covered with deep-red glandular hairs. *fl.* small, pink, partly concealed in the large cal. Early spring. Mts. of Macedonia, Greece, Albania. **Wisley var.,*** a very fine form, first seen at R.H.S. Gardens, Wisley, subsequently found wild in a gorge on Mt. Tsukala, Albania. Variants of this, less desirable, have occurred occasionally with pink or terra-cotta colouring instead of deep red. **A**

S. groenland'ica. *See* **S. caespitosa compacta.**

S. × **Gusmus'ii** (13) (*S. luteoviridis* × *S. porophylla thessalica*). About 4 to 6 in. h. Spikes short. *fl.* reddish-yellow. Early spring. Raised by Sündermann.

S. × **Guthriea'na.** A synonym of *S.* × *Andrewsii.*

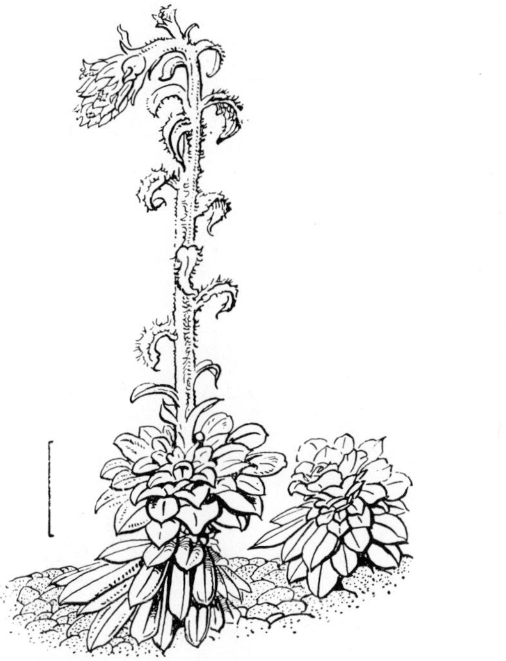

Saxifraga Grisebachii (p. 1886)

S. × **Haag'ii** (12) (*S. Ferdinandi-Coburgii* × *S. sancta*). Forms dark-green mats. Rosettes rather loose, *l.* spiny. Stems 2 to 3 in. h. *fl.* rather small, rich yellow, starry in open clusters. Free-flowering. Early spring.

S. Haens'leri (7). Clammy all over. *Basal l.* wedge-shaped, 3-cleft. Stems forked, 3 to 4 in. h. *fl.* large, white, few. Bulbils at base of stem. Spain.

S. × **Hans'ii** (12) (parentage doubtful, perhaps *S. tombeanensis* × ?). Very dwarf, cushions firm. Stems 1 to 2 in. h. *fl.* white. Spring. Raised by Sündermann.

S. × **Hausmann'ii** (10 × 11) (*S. aizoides* × *S. mutata*). Near *S. mutata* in general aspect. *fl.* starry, copper-orange. Stems short, stiff. Natural hybrid occurring where parents meet. 1851. Short-lived.

S. Haworth'ii (8). An indeterminate name attached to various white-fld. mossy Saxifrages in gardens.

S. hedera'cea (5). Small annual. *l.* small, ivy-shaped. *fl.* white, starry. Summer. Growth that of a small, creeping Linaria. 2 in. h. Asia Minor, Sicily, on damp rocks.

S. × **Hedwig'ii.** A synonym of *S.* × *Suendermannii purpurea.*

S. × **Heinrich'ii** (12 × 13) (*S. aretioides* × *S. Stribrnyi*). Habit intermediate between parents. Stem 3 to 4 in. h. *fl.* 6 to 8, almost bell-shaped, yellowish to purplish. Spring. Raised by Sündermann.

S. Hervier'i (7). Near *S. dichotoma.* A small *S. granulata* without bulbils. Stems 3 to 4 in. h., red. *fl.* white, nodding. Spain.

S. heucherifo'lia. A variety of *S. rotundifolia.*

S. hibern'ica. Used for varieties of *S. caespitosa, S. Geum,* and *S. palmata.*

S. Hirc'ulus (2). Tufted, forming mats. *Basall .* narrow, bright green, entire. Stems 6 to 9 in. h., more or less leafy. *fl.* 1 or more, large, golden-yellow speckled with orange. Summer. Widely distributed in the N. Hemisphere, including Britain. Cool and moist places suit it. A variable plant. var. **grandiflo'ra,** a synonym of var. *major*; **ma'jor,** taller, up to 12 in. h., *fl.* larger, usually densely red-hairy. Cent. Europe.

S. hirsu'ta. A synonym of *S. Geum.*

S. hir'ta. A synonym of *S. caespitosa palmata.*

S. × **Hoerham'meri** (12 × 13) (*S. Grisebachii* × *S. marginata coriophylla*). *Rosette-l.* blunt. Stems 3 in. h., stem-l. blunt. *fl.* reddish. Early spring.

S. × **Hofmann'ii** (12 × 13) (*S. Burseriana major* × *S. porophylla thessalica*). Habit of *S. porophylla thessalica.* Rosettes large. *l.* sharply pointed. Stems 4 to 6 in. h. *fl.* several, reddish. Early spring.

S. Hohenwar'tii. A variety of *S. sedoides.*

S. Host'ii* (11). Forms wide masses of clustered rosettes. *l.* narrow, flattish, margins beaded with lime glands. Stems 12 in. h. or more. *fl.* creamy-white in a short corymb of 5 to 9. May. E. and S. Alps. Always on limestone. SYN. *S. longifolia, S. elatior, S. Besleri. S. Hostii* is a parent with *S. Cotyledon* and *S. Aizoon* of many natural and garden hybrids. var. **altis'sima,** taller, up to 18 in. h., *l.* very long, recurving, beaded with lime glands, stem stained red, freely branched, *fl.* cream-white spotted red at base. Early summer. N. Alps; **ma'jor,** probably identical with *altissima*; **rhaet'ica,** similar to type but less desirable. Rhaetian Alps.

Saxifraga Huetiana

S. Huetia'na (5). Annual. *Basal l.* kidney-shaped, crenulate, in a round rosette. Stem 2 to 3 in. h. *fl.* yellow, starry on long pedicels. Continuously all summer. Carpathians to Iran.

S. Huguenin'ii. A variety of *S. aspera.*

S. hypnoi'des (8). Dovedale Moss. Eve's Cushion. Cushion forming. *l.* very finely 3- to 5-cleft with bulbils in axils. Stems 3 to 4 in. long. *fl.* white, rounded, usually 4 to 6 in cluster, of medium size. Early summer. Widely distributed in W. Europe, including Britain, N. America. A variable species often with very compact cushions. var. **cantab'rica,** *fl.* smaller, sep. acute. Cent. Spain; **carmin'ea,** a synonym of *S. moschata versicolor*; **condensa'ta,** compact in growth, *fl.* soft yellow; **den'sa,** very dense in growth, emerald-green, *fl.* creamy-white, 4 to 5 in. h.; **hir'ta,** *see* **S. caespitosa palmata**; **King'ii,** neat, of compact growth, forms large cushions turning red in winter, *l.* very narrow, 3-cleft, *fl.* white, often tipped pink in bud. Best in partial shade. Of garden origin; **lutes'cens,** a garden name for cream-fld. forms including *densa*; **purpu'rea,** *fl.* purplish-red, a parent of *S. Rhei superba* according to Mr. Arends of Ronsdorf; **Schra'deri,** *see* **S.** × **Schraderi**; **Sternberg'ii,** a synonym of *S. decipiens Sternbergii*; **Whitlav'ei,** compact in habit much as in var. *Kingii,* but stems 4 to 6 in. h., *fl.* white, round, more freely produced. Of garden origin. A variegated form (**variega'ta**) is sometimes offered.

S. imbrica'ta (12). Forms firm cushions of crowded small rosettes. *l.* densely overlapping. *fl.* white, round, almost sessile on the rosette. Sikkim at high elevations. 1843. SYN. *S. ciliata.* var. **rubes'cens,** *l.* more or less permanently stained red. Not yet introduced.

S. × **imperia'lis** (11) (*S. Cotyledon* × *S. longifolia*). Rosettes very large. *l.* long, narrow, intermediate in form between parents. *infl.* similar to that of *S. longifolia* but smaller. Raised at Petrograd Bot. Gard. 1887. Compare *S.* × *superba.*

S. incrusta'ta. A synonym of *S. crustata.*

S. intrica'ta (8). More or less tufted, *l.* often clammy and scented, with short glandular hairs. Distinguished from *S. exarata* by the usually creamy or white *fl.* Spring. Cent. Pyrenees in lime-free districts. SYN. *S. exarata compacta, S. exarata intricata.* var. **nervo'sa,** like type but *fl.* 2 or 3, white with yellowish or greenish veins, *l.* 3- to 5-cleft.

S. irrig'ua (7). Monocarpic. Related to *S. latepetiolata,* rather coarse in growth. Basal rosettes of much-cut, buttercup-like, hairy, and long-stalked *l.* Stems 12 in. h., hairy branching. *fl.* large, white, in loose panicles. Summer. Crimea. 1887. (B.M. 2207.) SYN. *S. aquatica, S. ranunculoides.*

S. × **Irving'ii*** (12) (*S. Burseriana* × *S. lilacina* ?). Cushion-forming. *l.-rosettes* blue-grey, spiny. Stems 1 to $1\frac{1}{2}$ in. *fl.* pale lilac-pink. Early spring. Free-flowering. Raised at Kew. SYN. *S. Burseriana elegans.*

S. × **Jenk'insae** (12). Slightly larger in growth and *fl.* than *S.* × *Irvingii*, and flowering at a slightly different time. 2 to 3 in. h. Probably of same parentage as *S.* × *Irvingii*.

S. juniperifo'lia (12). Juniper-scented. Forms dense, humped cushions. *l.* of rosettes sharply spiny, dark green. Stem 2 to 3 in. h. *fl.* not showy, yellow, in a small cluster; pet. small, usually 1- to 3-nerved; stamens prominent. Summer. Caucasus. SYN. *S. juniperina*. A variable species. var. **brachyphyl'la,** growth columnar, densely leafy, *l.* overlapping, *stem-l.* about $\frac{1}{8}$ in. long, erect; **Brot'heri,** *l.* erect, *stem-l.* $\frac{3}{4}$ in. long, otherwise like type; **ciner'ea,** old *stem-l.* reflexed, rosettes grey-green; **Kasnezowia'na,** tufted, grey-green, *l.* oblong-lanceolate, ciliate near base, pet. 5-nerved; **macedon'ica,** up to 3 in. h., *l.* lanceolate, $\frac{2}{5}$ in. long, ciliate, sep. glabrous (B.M. n.s. 137 as *S. macedonica*); **pseudosanc'ta,** about 2 in. h., *l.* linear-awl-shaped, about $\frac{1}{2}$ in. long, ciliate near base, *fl.* yellow, larger, sep. glabrous; **Steven'sii,** like var. *Brotheri* but *stem-l.* about $\frac{2}{5}$ in. long. B.M. n.s. 137 as *S. macedonica*.

S. juniperi'na. A synonym of *S. juniperifolia*.

S. karadzicen'sis. A variety of *S. marginata*.

S. × **Kel'lereri*** (12 × 13) (*S. Burseriana* × *S. Stribrnyi*). *l.* of rosettes long, silvery. Stems 3 to 4 in. h. *fl.* soft pink. Mid-winter or early spring. Raised by Sündermann. 1906.

S. × **kestonen'sis** (12) (*S. Burseriana* × *S. marginata*) ? Cushion-forming. *l.-rosettes* small, grey. *l.* blunt. Stems 2 to 3 in. h. *fl.* of medium size, white, round. January.

S. × **kewen'sis** (12 × 13) (*S. Burseriana macrantha* × *S. porophylla*) ? *l.* of *S. porophylla*, rosettes as in *S. Burseriana*. *fl.* lilac or pink, medium-sized. 3 in. h. Early spring. Raised at Kew. 1912.

S. King'ii. A variety of *S. hypnoides*.

S. Koch'ii. *See* **S. biflora.**

S. × **Kolbia'na** (12) (parentage ?). Rosettes resembling those of *S. marginata*. *fl.* yellow. Stem 2 to 3 in. h. January. Sündermann. 1918.

S. Kol'byi. A synonym of *S.* × *Kolbiana*.

S. Kolenatia'na (11). Closely related to *S. Aizoon*, and *S. cartilaginea*. Like the latter with distinctly acuminate *l.* but *fl.* rose or deep purple, not spotted; pet. 2 or 3 times as long as sep. Caucasus. var. **ma'jor,** rather taller, stems 9 to 12 in. h., *fl.* red. SYN. *S. Sendtneri*.

S. Kotsch'yi (12). Forms hummocks of densely crowded rosettes. *l.* blunt. *fl.* very small, in small heads; stamens prominent. Stems 2 to 3 in. h. Cilician Taurus. (B.M. 6065.) *S.* × *pseudo-Kotschyi* is often grown under this name.

S. × **Kyril'lii*** (12) (*S. Ferdinandi-Coburgii* × *S. marginata*). *l.-rosettes* clustered. *l.* grey-green, spiny. Stems 4 in. h. *fl.* clear lemon-yellow. Spring. Raised by Sündermann. Easily grown and free-flowering.

S. labrador'ica. A variety of *S. Aizoon*.

S. lac'tea (8). Loosely tufted, densely leafy. *l.* soft, slightly hairy, basal l. widely obovate, 5-fid, fan-like, segs. obtuse, not in one plane, upper l. 3-fid. *fl.-stem* 3 to 6 in. long, branched, branches slender, 2- to 4-fld. *fl.* white, about $\frac{1}{2}$ in. across. N. Asia.

S. laev'is (12). Loosely tufted. Stems 1 to 2 in. h., densely leafy. *l.* short, overlapping, deep green, ciliate. *fl.* few, small, yellow; pet. very small, stamens long. Early summer. Caucasus.

S. lagravea'na. A variety of *S. Aizoon*.

S. lanceola'ta. A synonym of *S. androsacea integrifolia*.

S. × **Landau'eri** (13) (parentage ?). Stems 3 in. h. *fl.* white flushed pink. Spring. Raised by Sündermann.

S. lantosca'na. A variety of *S. lingulata*.

S. lantosca'na hyb'rida. *See* **S.** × **florariensis.**

S. × **Lapeyrous'ii** (12 × 13) (*S. aretioides* × *S. media*). Closely resembles *S. aretioides*. Stems short. *fl.* 3 or 4, pale yellow. Spring. Pyrenees. The name is also a synonym of *S. corbariensis* and of *S. corymbosa luteoviridis*.

S. lasiophyl'la. A synonym of *S. rotundifolia*.

S. latepetiola'ta (7). Short-lived. *Basal l.* in densely hairy rosettes. Stem 9 to 12 in. h., leafy, hairy, clammy. *fl.* numerous, large, milk-white. Summer. Spain. 1889. Seeds itself freely.

S. lati'na. A variety of *S. oppositifolia*.

S. Leichtlin'ii. A synonym of *Bergenia ligulata*.

S leptophyl'la. A variety of *S. hypnoides*.

S. × **Leybold'ii** (12) (*S. marginata Rocheliana* × *S. Vandellii*). Similar to *S. Vandellii*, of slow growth, forming very hard, humped cushions. *l.* in rosettes, blue-grey, overlapping. Stems 2 in. h. *fl.* white. Spring. Raised by Sündermann.

S. ligula'ta. A synonym of *Bergenia ligulata*.

S. likiangen'sis (12). Small with habit of *S. lilacina*. *l.-tips* recurved. *fl.* white, sessile. 1 in. h. Spring. NW. Yunnan. Not yet introduced.

S. lilaci'na* (12). Habit of *S. caesia*. *l.-rosettes* green. Stems 1 to 2 in. h., slender. *fl.* solitary, amethyst. Spring. W. Himalaya. A parent of almost all the pink, reddish, and purple hybrids of this section, preferring slight shade and moisture, and best without lime.

S. × **Lindsaya'na.** *See* **S.** × **Macnabiana.**

S. linguaeform'is. A garden form of *S. Cotyledon*.

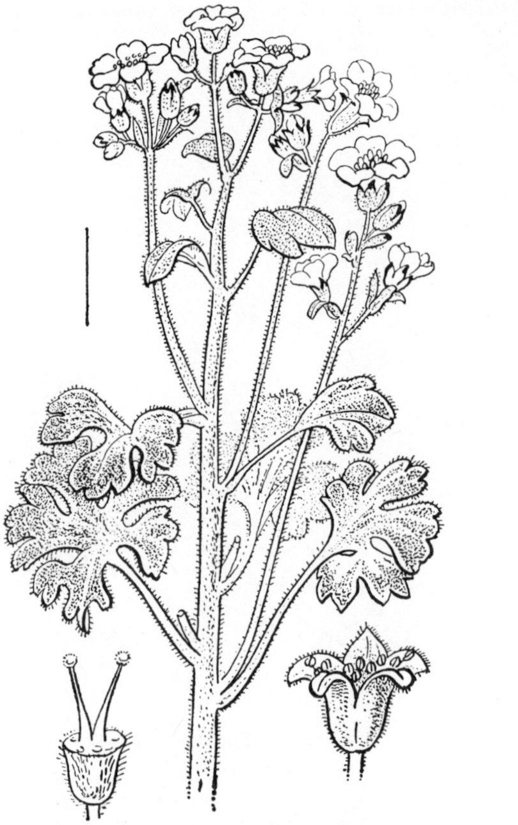

Saxifraga latepetiolata

S. lingula'ta* (11). *l.-rosettes* large, forming spreading mats. *l.* long, narrow, iron-grey, thickened and recurved at tips, margin beaded with lime-glands. Stem 12 to 18 in. h., often stained red. *fl.* white, in gracefully arching panicles. Early summer. W. and Maritime Alps. 1819. Lime-loving, growing well in sun and shade. SYN. *S. callosa*. var. **Albert'ii,** *see* var. **albida; al'bida,** 12 to 18 in. h., *l.* broader than in type, greyer, *fl.* numerous, white. A fine form which possibly originated in Mr. Beamish's garden at Queenstown, and possibly a hybrid with *S. cochlearis* or *S. longifolia*; **austra'lis,** rosettes large, *l.* stiff, greener than type, broadest in upper third, hairy towards base, margined with lime glands, stem 12 in. h., *fl.*

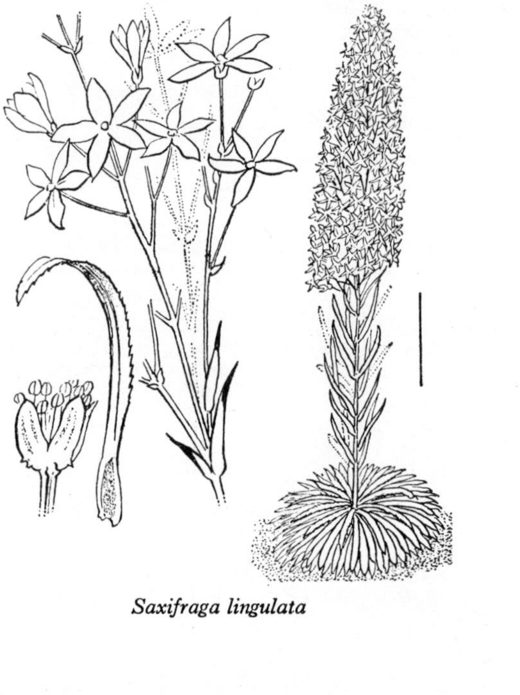

Saxifraga lingulata

white or spotted with pink. Apennines, Abruzzi Mts. variable. SYN. *S. Australis* best in partial shade; **Bellard'ii,*** rosettes less regular, *l.* longer and thinner, of varying lengths, panicles large, arching, *fl.* white. Alps and Apennines. Best in partial shade; **catalaun'ica,** *l.* much broader, shorter, and more pointed than in type, and fewer in rosette, panicle more upright and stiffer, 12 in. h. NE. Spain, Montserrat. SYN. *S. catalaunica*; **cochlea'ris,** a synonym of *S. cochlearis*; **lantosca'na,** rosettes more formal than in *S. lingulata* type. *l.* shorter, more recurved with markedly swollen tips, dark green to iron grey, with marginal lime-glands, stems shorter, 9 to 12 in., panicle denser, almost secund. Best in shade and likes lime; a fine garden form is called *lantoscana superba*. SYN. *S. lantoscana*. A fine hybrid with *S. cochlearis*, found by Farrer near Tenda, intermediate between its parents is probably not now in cultivation. For the hybrids with *S. longifolia see* **S. calabrica.** A

S. × Loefling'ii (12) (parentage?). Dwarf. Stem about 2 in. h. *fl.* deep yellow. Raised by Sündermann.

S. longifo'lia* (11). Differs from others of its section by the panicle being floriferous to the base. *l.-rosettes* 3 to 6 in. across, densely leafy. Stem erect, 8 to 24 in. long, densely leafy, very many-fld., glandular-hairy. *Basal l.* greyish, glabrous, linear-ligulate, 1¼ to 4 in. long, entire or slightly crenate. *fl.* white, rarely purple-spotted, about ½ in. across. June. Pyrenees. 1871. **Walpole's** var. (*Mt. Usher* var.) is a fine seedling form, possibly crossed with *S. lingulata*, 12 to 18 in. or more h., rosettes shapely, surrounded by many offsets; panicle somewhat smaller than in type. Easily grown. Many hybrids occur with *S. Aizoon*, all good garden plants, especially for crevices among large boulders, but scarcely worth special names. For the hybrid with *S. Cotyledon see* **S. × imperialis.** A cross with *S. marginata* has been reported but this may be an error as the flowering times are different and hybrids between species of Sections 11 and 12 are very rare. Hybrids derived from the cross *S. lingulata* × *S. longifolia* are very fine; *see* **S. × calabrica.**

S. × luteopurpu'rea (12 × 13) (*S. aretioides* × *S. media*). Rosettes similar to those of *S. media*. Stem 3 to 4 in. h. *fl.* 5 to 7, rather small, pale washy yellow. Early spring. A natural hybrid. The name is also applied to *S. × apiculata*, and to *S. corymbosa luteoviridis*.

S. luteovi'ridis. A variety of *S. corymbosa*.

S. macedon'ica. A variety of *S. juniperifolia*.

S. × Macnabia'na (11) (*S. Cotyledon* × *S. lingulata*). Two dissimilar plants were raised of this cross, one with foliage much as in *S. Cotyledon* and white *fl.* which should be called var. *Lindsayana*, the other with rosettes more nearly resembling those of *S. lingulata*, and *fl.* heavily spotted red, the spots sometimes confluent into a deep-red ring at the base of the fl. Edinburgh Bot. Gard. 1885.

S. macropet'ala. *See* **S. biflora.**

S. maderen'sis (8). More like Section 4 in general appearance. *l.* kidney-shaped, toothed. Stem 4 to 6 in. h. *fl.* white in a widely branched panicle. Early summer. Madeira. Rather tender.

S. mad'ida (16). Larger than *S. cortusifolia* with *l.* lobed, persistently hairy above, green or purple beneath. *fl.* very numerous, pet. 3 ovate, 2 lower larger, lanceolate, equal. Autumn. Japan. In the var. **stolonif'era** a few slender stolons are produced.

S. Mal'yi. A synonym of *S. Aizoon alpicola*, also applied in gardens to *S. × apiculata*.

S. manshurien'sis (1). Fleshy with a short, stout rootstock. *l.* radical, several, stalk 4½ in. long, reddish-hairy; blade roundish kidney-shaped, 2 to 2½ in. long, up to 3½ in. wide, coarsely roundish apiculate teeth, dark green and glabrous above, paler and sparsely hairy beneath. *fl.* 6- to 8-parted, in a dense, roundish panicle about 1½ in. across, on a solitary hairy scape 14 in. h.; pet. spatulate-oblong, ⅓ in. long; stamens conspicuous; pistils red. Manchuria, Korea. 1913. (B.M. 8707.) Rock-garden, moist shady places.

S. margina'ta (12). Forming mats, cushions, or loose hummocks of crowded rosettes. *l.* fleshy, green, blunt, with marginal band of lime-glands. Stems leafy, 2 to 3 in. h. *fl.* several, white, large. Early spring. Italy. 1883. (B.M. 6702.) A variable species the more eastern varieties of which have usually smaller rosettes than the type. var. **coriophyl'la,** stems rarely over 2-fld., 1 to 2 in. h., *l.* more silvery, rosettes less open. Spring. Carpathians to E. Greece. There is a form of this **rubes'cens,** not yet introduced, with pale-pink *fl.* SYN. *S. coriophylla*; **karazicen'sis,** very small, about as large as *S. caesia*, 1 to 1½ in. h., *fl.* 2 or 3, white. Early summer. N. Albania, **Rochelia'na,** more compact than type, with shorter stems, blunter *l.*, and slightly smaller *fl.*, cal. stained purple and buds often red in the form **purpu'rea,** pet. pale yellow in form **lu'tea.** Carpathians to Greece. SYN. *S. pseudocaesia*; **subuniflo'ra,** very small. *l.* blunt, stems 1-fld. Veliki Maglie, Bosnia. Not yet introduced.

S. × Marie-Mere'siae (12 × 13) (*S. Burseriana major* × *S. Grisebachii*). Intermediate between parents, differing from *S. Burseriana* by its 6- to 8-fld., branching stems and from *S. Grisebachii* by the pet. at least twice as long as sep. Stem 3 to 4 in. h. *fl.* pale purple. Early spring. Raised by Sündermann.

S. Mawea'na (8). *l.* fleshy, 3-lobed. Stems 4 to 6 in. h. *fl.* large, white. Summer. Tetuan, N. Africa. Perennial by tightly closed winter buds which in the var. **succulo'sa** become leafy shoots. Rather tender. Alpine house. Treat as *S. oranensis*.

S. me'dia (13). *Rosette-l.* about 1 in. long, silver-grey, with marginal line of lime-glands. Stems 4 to 5 in. h., leafy. *fl.* pink, cor. almost enclosed by the large red-haired cal. Early spring. Pyrenees on limestone. SYN. *S. calyciflora, S. Gouani*. Parent of many hybrids.

S. × megasiflo'ra (12) (*S. Burseriana* ? × ?). Habit of *S. Burseriana*. Stem 2 in. h. *fl.* large, clear rose, rather loosely arranged, pet. not overlapping. Spring. Raised by Prichard.

S. Melvil'lei (3). A variety of *S. umbrosa*.

S. Mertensia'na (1). Tufted. *Basal l.* round, leathery, glossy, with roundish teeth, stalk rather long. Stem 9 to 12 in. h., branched. *fl.* white, anthers red. Early summer. Western N. America. Needs a cool, shady spot. var. **bulbilif'era,** 18 in. h., with reddish bulbils in lower part of stem.

S. Miles'ii. *See* **Bergenia ligulata.**

S. mix'ta. A synonym of *S. pubescens*.

S. montavonen'sis. A variety of *S. Cotyledon*.

S. montenegri'na. A variety of *S. porophylla*.

S. moscha'ta (8). Forming bright green loose or dense tufts, sometimes glandular but not resinous. *l.* lobed, lobes obtuse. *fl.* usually yellowish-white, sometimes purplish, deep purple, or whitish; pet. 1¼ to 1½ times as long as sep., oblong or oblong-oval. Spring. Pyrenees to Caucasus. 1819. SYN. *S. varians*. The type plant is not often seen in gardens, where the name covers a number of pink-fld. forms of uncertain parentage. A variable plant. var. **acaul'is,** densely tufted, small and compact, *l.* closely overlapping, small, wedge-shaped, 3-cleft, stem 1 to 2 in. h., *fl.* 1 to 3, white with 3 red, branching veins. Alps; **atropurpu'rea,** densely tufted, 1 to 2 in. h., few-fld., *fl.* deep red or orange. SE. Alps; **citri'na,** see var. **laxa; Cloth of Gold,** densely tufted, quickly spreading, stems 2 to 3 in. h., *fl.* whitish, *l.* bronzy-gold at all seasons, and in this its chief value lies. Of garden origin; **cro'cea,** habit of type, but *fl.* yellow, stem 2 in. h. Alps; **Fairy,** *fl.* round, pink, stem 2 in. h. Perhaps a hybrid; **fl.-pleno,** *fl.* pale yellow, double; **interme'dia,** dense-growing. SYN. *S. pyrenaica*; **lax'a,** small, loosely tufted, *fl.* pale yellow; **linea'ta,** loosely tufted, stems 1 to 2 in., *fl.* white or pale yellow, small to medium size. Alps; **versicol'or.** Here belong the mossy saxifrages with pink or red fl., too small in growth to be classed under *S. decipiens*, e.g. '*S. muscoides Rhei superba*'. See also **S. amoena.**

S. muscoi'des (8). Often confused with *S. moschata* but densely tufted, with linear or lanceolate entire l., blunt and without a hyaline margin. Stem 2 to 3 in. h. *fl.* white or yellow, about ¼ in. across. Spring. High Alps in moist crevices and shingle beds. var. **citri'na,** *fl.* pale yellow. var. **Rhe'i,** a synonym of *S. moschata laxa*; **Rhei super'ba,** a form of *S. moschata versicolor* raised by Ahrends *See also* **S. hypnoides purpurea.**

S. musco'sa. A synonym of *S. moschata laxa*.

S. muta'ta (11). *l.-rosettes* resembling those of *S. Cotyledon*, dark green. Stems 9 to 12 in. h., branching. *fl.* golden-yellow, pet. narrow. Summer. E. Alps usually on limestone. 1779. Frequently dying after flowering in cultivation without forming side offsets but in nature offsets are common. var. **demis'sa,** smaller than type, 4 to 5 in. h. Carpathians on limestone in shade. SYN. *S. transylvanica*.

S. na'na (15). Forming a dense mat. Branches very short, up to 1½ in. covered with obovate-oblong l. about ⅛ in. long. *l.* opposite, overlapping. *fl.* solitary, sep. 4, pet. 0, stamens 4 or 8; pedicel about ⅛ in. long, terminal. Kansu, China.

S. Nelsonia'na. A synonym of *S. punctata coarctata*.

S. nepalen'sis of gardens is *S. Cotyledon* or sometimes a hybrid of that species.

S. nervo'sa. A variety of *S. intricata*.

S. niva'lis (1). *Basal l.* in rosettes, variable in form and toothing, leathery. Stems 2 to 4 in. h. *fl.* small, white, crowded. Early summer. N. and Arctic Europe and Asia, including Britain. Of no garden value.

S. nota'ta. A variety of *S. Aizoon*.

S. nu'tans (2). Tufted. Stem glabrous below, glandular-hairy above, 4 to 7 in. long. *l.* oblong, margined with long, pale hairs, ½ to 1 in. long, upper l. shorter. *fl.* 6 to 9, nodding, secund, yellow, about ¾ in. across. June, July. N. India, W. China.

S. × Obrist'ii* (12) (*S. Burseriana* × *S. marginata*). Intermediate between parents. *l.* larger and bolder than in *S. Burseriana*. Stems 2 to 3 in. h. *fl.* white, large, several on a stem, buds often stained red. Raised by Sündermann about 1900.

S. × obscu'ra (8) (*S. geranioides* × *S. pubescens*). Densely or loosely tufted, glandular-hairy. Stem woody at base. *lower l.* 3- to 5-fid, segs. linear, entire or somewhat lobed, side-lobes much cut. *fl.* 5 to 20, white, in a panicle. *fl.-stems* 2 to 8 in. h. Pyrenees.

S. × ochroleu'ca (12) (*S. Burseriana minor* × *S. sancta*). Habit of *S. Burseriana* but *rosette-l.* shorter. Stem 2 in. h. *fl.* pale yellow, small, somewhat starry, several. Spring. Raised by Sündermann.

S. odontophyl'la. A synonym of *S. arguta*.

S. olymp'ica. A synonym of *S. rotundifolia geoides*.

S. oppositifo'lia* (14). Stems many, creeping, densely leafy. *l.* mostly opposite, variable in size and shape, tips rounded, margin more or less ciliate; lime-glands usually 1 on a l. but sometimes 3, 5, or 9. *fl.* terminal, sessile or nearl so, rarely on short lateral leafy or naked branches, purple, pink, or red, very rarely white, starry or roundish. Early spring. Widely distributed over Europe, including Britain, N. Asia, and N. America, on both granite and limestone, the best garden forms being as a rule on limestone. Extremely variable. Some of the many forms are var. **al'ba,** probably the albino form of var. *Murithiana, fl.* poor, white, starry. White forms of vars. *latina* and *Vaccariana* are much to be desired; **amphib'ia,** straggling, *fl.* starry, remarkable for its ability to withstand long immersion during the snow-melting period. Shores of Lake Constance; **biflo'ra,** *see* **S. biflora; blepharophyl'la,** *see* **S. blepharophylla; coccin'ea,** *fl.* small, intensely red-purple; **compac'ta,** an indeterminate name for any close-growing form; **grandiflo'ra,** *l.* rather large, of variable shape, growth more upright than in type, *fl.* large, round-petalled, clear rose-red. Spring. SYN. var. *macrantha,* and var. *major*; **lati'na,*** more upright than type, 1 to 2 in. h., *l.* more silvery, *fl.* large, bright. March, April. SYN. *S. adenosepala*; **ma'jor,** *see* var. **grandiflora; Murithia'na,** stems trailing, *l.* rather distant, small, narrow, *fl.* starry, usually purple. A rather poor form native on granitic hills; **Nathorst'ii,** *l.* beneath fl. alternate, others opposite, *fl.* small, starry, sparse. Northern part of district; **pyrena'ica splen'dens,*** easily grown, free-flowering, *fl.* large, probably a form of var. *Vaccariana*; **pyrena'ica superb'a,** another good form of similar characters; **R. M. Prichard,*** *fl.* large, lilac purple; **Rudolphia'na,** forms wide mats of close upright shoots, densely leafy, *l.* overlapping, stems 1 in. h., *fl.* sessile bright rose-purple. Early summer. Alps. Difficult to cultivate; **specio'sa,** of loose habit, *fl.* large, rich rose-red, pet. frequently 6. S. Alps on limestone; **Vaccaria'na,** forms wide mats, very free-flowering, *fl.* large, intense reddish-purple, cupped. *See* var. **pyrena'ica; W. A. Clark,*** habit neat, *fl.* of medium size, intense bright crimson-rose, free-flowering; **Wetterhorn** var., *fl.* rather small, but of rich colour.

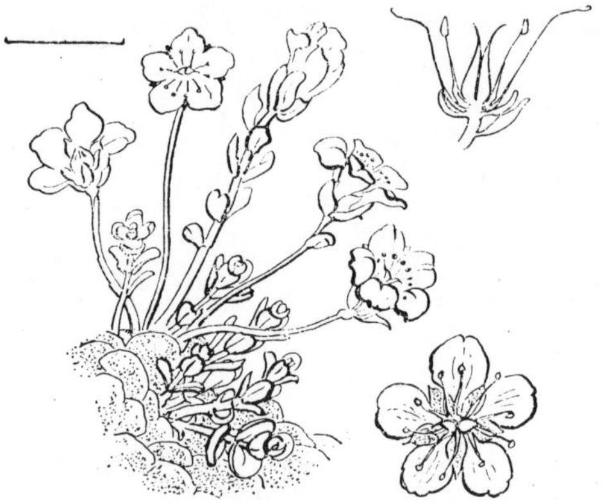

Saxifraga oppositifolia

S. oranen'sis (8). Closely related to *S. globulifera,* and sometimes regarded as a variety. Forming domes of flesh, wedge-shaped. *l.* 3-cleft at apex, green during growing season, often stained red in winter. Stem 2 to 3 in. h. with few undivided narrow l. *fl.* 2 or 3, large, milk-white, round. Oran, N. Africa. Rather tender and best in alpine house; if kept dry survives considerable cold.

S. orbicula'ris. A synonym of *Bergenia crassifolia.*

S. pal'lida (1). Basal *rosette-l.* few, hairy above, ovate, up to 3 in. long, more or less toothed. fl.-stem branched, hairy. *fl.* white, pet. about ⅛ in. long, 3-nerved, anthers violet. Himalaya. 1885. Of little garden value.

S. palma'ta. A variety of *S. decipiens.*

S. palpebra'ta (2). Rosettes small, hairy. Stem 2 to 3 in. h. with hairy *l. fl.* of medium size, golden-yellow, solitary. Early summer. Sikkim.

S. panicula'ta. A synonym of *S. Cossoniana* and *S. Cotyledon.*

S. paradox'a. A synonym of *S. moschata crocea, S. moschata pygmaea,* and *Zahlbruckneri paradoxa.*

S. ×paradox'a (11) (*S. crustata × S. lingulata* ?). Rosettes handsome. *l.* narrow, edged with lime-glands. *fl.* poor, creamy-white in short spike, 6 to 9 in. h. Early summer.

S. ×pa'tens (10 × 12) (*S. aizoides × S. caesia*). Habit of a loose-growing *S. caesia* but less silver-grey. Stem branching, 2 to 3 in. h. *fl.* butter-yellow. Early summer. A natural hybrid. Bavaria, Austria, &c. **Elliott's** var. (raised artificially) has apricot buds opening butter-yellow. SYN. *S. sulphurea.*

S. ×Paulin'ae (12) (*S. Burseriana minor × S. Ferdinandi-Coburgi*). Dwarf. Cushions tight; rosettes compact. Stems 2 in. h. *fl.* primrose, round. Early spring. Raised by Sündermann. 1900.

S. ×pectina'ta (11) (*S. Aizoon × S. crustata*). *Rosette-l.* long, narrow, dark green, toothed. Stems about 6 in. h. *fl.* creamy. Early summer. Carniola. 1870. SYN. *S. ×Fritschiana.*

S. pedatif'ida (8). Vigorous, quickly forming large emerald cushions. *l.-stalks* long, hairy, blade wide, 3-cleft, the two outside lobes again 2-cleft. Stem 6 in. h. *fl.* white in 8- to 10-fid. sprays, cup-shaped. Spring. Origin unknown. A good plant for shady places. SYN. *S. quinquefida.*

S. pedemonta'na (8). Tufted. Densely leafy. *Basal l.* palmately lobed or cut, obovate in general outline, narrowed to a short stalk, glandular-hairy. *fl.* 3 to 7, white, pet. 2 or 3 times as long as linear sep., pedicels of varying length, 1 to 2½ in. long. European Alps. 1824. SYN. *S. Allionii.* A variable plant. var. **Baldac'cii,** base woody, tufted, stem branching, 3 in. h., *fl.* pure white. Spring. Maritime Alps; **cervicorn'is,** *l.* clammy, aromatic, hairy. Corsica. Needs sunny, well-drained position without lime; **cymo'sa,** small, *l.* 3- to 5-cleft, wedge-shaped, hairs long, *fl.* few, large, white. Carpathians and Balkan Mts. Forms loose tufts.

S. pelta'ta. A synonym of *Peltiphyllum peltatum.*

S. pensylvan'ica (1). Swamp Saxifrage. *Basal l.* large, coarse, leathery, forming a rosette 12 in. or more across. Stem 3 ft. or more h., stout, sometimes branched. *fl.* numerous, small, yellowish-white; pet. narrow. Summer. N. America. 1732. Wild garden in shade. *See* **S. Forbesii.**

S. pentadact'ylis (8). Small, mat-forming. *l.* glabrous, clammy, aromatic, 5-cleft, segs. blunt, flesh, stalks grooved. Stems 3 in. h., much-branched. *fl.* 3 to 30, white tinged soft yellow at base, starry. Early summer. Pyrenees. 1815. SYN. *S. obtusifolia.* A scree plant avoiding limestone.

S. perdu'rans (8). Small, mossy plant. *l.* broadly wedge-shaped, 3- to 5-, rarely 7-, cleft. Stems 2 in. h. from l.-axils. *fl.* 3, white. Spring, early summer. Carpathian Mts. SYN. *S. axillaris.*

S. petrae'a. A synonym of *S. adscendens* and *S. aquatica aprica.*

S. ×Petrasch'ii (12)* (*S. marginata Rocheliana × S. tombeanensis*). Habit intermediate between parents, forming grey mounds. Stems 2 in. h. *fl.* 3 or 4, white, large, round. Raised by Sündermann, 1900.

S. ×Pich'leri (12) (parentage ?). Dwarf, compact, 1 to 2 in. h. *fl.* white. Early spring. Raised by Sündermann.

S. planifo'lia. A synonym of *S. muscoides.*

S.porophyl'la (13). *Rosette-l.* spatulate, or lignulate, ⅓ to ½ in. long, glaucous. Stems 4 to 6 in. h. flowering in upper third. *Stem-l.* narrow-spatulate, glandular-hairy. *fl.* sessile, pink, pet. short, cal. baggy, large, purple. Early spring. Apennines, Abruzzi Mts., Italy. SYN. *S. Gouani, S. Federici-Augusti* (not of gardens). var. **montenegri'na,** resembling a small *S. Grisebachii, rosette-l.* broad, spreading, blunt, margined with lime-glands, stem 6 in. h. or more, *infl.* as in type. Montenegro, Albania; **Sibthorpia'na,** *rosette-l.* spatulate, spreading, acute, *fl.* pale purple, cal. darker purple, 6 to 9 in. h. S. Balkans. SYN. *S. media Sibthorpiana*; **thessal'ica,** rosettes in dome-like clusters, *l.* spiny, silver-grey, 4 to 6 in. h., *fl.-spikes* as in type. Montenegro to Greece. A smaller form (*thessalica alpina*) comes from Montenegro.

S. Port'ae. A synonym of *S. lingulata australis.*

S. ×Port'ae (11) (*S. Aizoon × S. crustata*). Much like *S. ×pectinata.*

S. pravislav'ia (12). Forms rounded masses of rather dark green rosettes. *l.* spiny. Stem 2 in. h. *fl.* rich yellow, round. Spring. Macedonia.

S. primuloi'des. A variety of *S. umbrosa.*

S. propagin'ea. A variety of *S. Clusii.*

S. ×Prosen'ii (13) (parentage?). Rosettes small, flat. Stem 2 to 3 in. h., branching. *fl.* small-orange, successively produced early spring to midsummer.

S. Prostia'na. A synonym of *S. cebennensis.*

S. Prost'ii (8). Forms almost shrubby tufts with hard, woody stems. *l.* 5- to 11-cleft, segs. broad or narrow. *fl.-stems* 4 to 6 in. h. *fl.* white, pet. 3-nerved. Spring. Cevennes, &c.

S. ×pseudo-Boris'ii (12) (*S. Ferdinandi-Coburgi × S. marginata coriophylla*). Rosettes densely tufted, about ½ in. across, silver-grey. Stems 2 to 3 in. long. *fl.* 5 to 8, pale yellow, in a corymb. Spring. Raised by Sündermann.

S. ×pseudo-Forst'eri (3 × 11) (*S. crustata ? × S. cuneifolia ?*). *l.-rosettes* neat, green. *l.* round, margins somewhat cartilaginous. Stem 3 in. h. *fl.* white, starry, in panicles. Early summer. Augsburg.

S. ×pseudo-Kots'chyi (12) (*S. Kotschyi × S. marginata Rocheliana*). Much like *S. marginata lutea* and often confused with it. Habit of *S. marginata.* Stems 2 in. h. *fl.* pale yellow. Spring. Raised by Sündermann.

S. ×pseudo-Salomon'ii. *See* **S. × Salomonii.**

S. pseudo-sanct'a. *See* **S. juniperifolia pseudo-sancta.**

S. pubes'cens (8). Tufted, loosely or densely, shoots in alpine forms columnar. *l.* usually green, with long glandular hairs, clammy, aromatic, general outline obovate or oval, 3-, 5-, or 7-cleft or lobed, segs. linear, obtuse. *fl.-stem* 1 to 5 in. h., 3- to 20-fld., few-leaved. *fl.* white or with purple veins, rarely yellowish. Spain. var. **nevaden'sis,** dwarfer, *l.* densely overlapping, grey, *fl.-stems* 1 to 2 in. h., *fl.* 2 or 3, round, white, sometimes purple-veined. Sierra Nevada, Spain. SYN. *S. mixta.*

S. puncta'ta (1). Tufted. *Basal l.* kidney-shaped, leathery, broadly toothed; stalks long. Stem 3 to 4 in. long, stout, branching. *fl.* 2 or 3, white, at tip of each branch, ovaries purple. Early summer. Arctic and sub-arctic regions. var. **coarcta'ta,** *fl.* in a head.

S. × pung'ens (12) (*S. juniperifolia pseudosancta* × *S. marginata Rocheliana*). Resembling a very small *S. marginata*, but *l.* spine-pointed. Stem 2 in. h. *fl.* several, yellow. Spring.

S. purpuras'cens. A synonym of *Bergenia purpurascens.*

S. purpu'rea. A synonym of *S. retusa Baumgartenii.*

S. pyg'maea. A synonym of *S. moschata crocea.*

S. pyramid'alis. A variety of *S. Cotyledon.*

S. pyrena'ica. A synonym of *S. moschata intermedia.*

S. quinquef'ida. A variety of *S. decipiens.*

S. ramulo'sa (12). Closely related to *S. imbricata. l.-rosettes* very small. Stem glandular, about 1 in. long. *fl.* 1 or 2, large, white. Kashmir, Nepal. Not yet introduced.

S. ranunculifo'lia. A synonym of *Boykina ranunculifolia.*

S. ranunculoi'des. A synonym of *S. irrigua.*

S. rect'a. A synonym of *S. Aizoon major* and *S. marginata.*

S. recurvifo'lia. A synonym of *S. caesia.*

S. × Regel'ii (10 × 11) (*S. aizoides* × *S. mutata*). Similar to *S. aizoides. l.* narrow, with a few lime-glands. Cf. *S.* × *Hausmannii*, the reverse cross.

S. repand'a. A variety of *S. rotundifolia.*

Saxifraga retusa

S. retu'sa (14). Densely tufted, stem prostrate, much-branched, woody. *l.* overlapping, ovate or oblong-lanceolate, usually with 5 lime-glands, *fl.-stems* erect, up to 2 in. h., branched. *fl.* 1 to 5, in corymbs; pet. about $\frac{1}{5}$ in. long, rosy-purple, shorter than stamens, 3-nerved, sep. not ciliate, filaments purple, erect, anthers yellow. Summer. Pyrenees to Bulgaria. 1826. var. **Baumgarten'ii,** smaller than type, nearly glabrous, stem under 1 in. h. *fl.* 1 to 3, small. More difficult to grow than type.

S. × Rey'eri (8) (*S. sedoides* × *S. tenella*). *fl.* small, greenish. Natural hybrid, of no garden value.

S. rhaet'ica. A variety of *S. Hostii.*

S. Rhei globo'sa. *See* **S. muscoides Rhei.**

S. Rhei superb'a. *See* **S. muscoides Rhei superba.**

S. × riges'cens (8 × 9) (*S. tenella* × *S. tricuspidata*). Rosettes clustered. *l.* 3-pointed, acute, rigid. Stems 3 in. h., branching. *fl.* white. Raised by Sündermann. 1906.

S. Rigo'i (8). *fl.* large, white. Shoots closing into bud-like structure in summer. Spain.

S. rivula'ris (7). Tufted or solitary, creeping underground with usually many fl.-stems with bulbils on stolons from axils of rosette-l. *l.* fleshy, reddish, kidney-shaped or round, $\frac{1}{5}$ to $\frac{4}{5}$ in. long, palmately 3- to 7-lobed, lobes obtuse. *fl.* white or reddish, small, sometimes in heads. Difficult to keep healthy in gardens and of little beauty. Arctic and sub-arctic regions.

S. robus'ta. A variety of *S. stellaris.*

S. Rochelia'na. *See under* **S. marginata.**

S. × Rosi'nae (12) (parentage?). Cushion-forming. Stems 2 in. h. *fl.* white. Early spring. Origin unknown.

S. Ross'ii. A synonym of *Aceriphyllum Rossii.*

S. rotundifo'lia (4). Tufted. *Basal l.* rather fleshy, kidney-shaped. Stems 12 to 24 in. h., leafy. *fl.* white more or less speckled pink, starry, in loose panicles. Early summer. Widely distributed in N. Hemisphere in shady gorges and alpine wods. (B.M. 424.) 1596. var. **heucherifo'lia,** smaller than type, stems much less hairy, *fl.* heavily spotted, side branches of infl. longer than central one. Carpathians to Greece; **heucherifolia geoi'des,** *fl.-stems* about 8 in. h., leafless, densely glandular-hairy, *fl.* heavily spotted purple. Summer. Montenegro to N. Greece; **repand'a,** rather taller than type, stems glandular-hairy. Widely distributed; **tayget'ea,** *see* **S. taygetea.**

S. × rubel'la (12) (*S.* × *Irvingii* × *S. lilacina?*). Smaller than *S.* × *Irvingii. fl.* pink, flushed, buds deep pink. Stem 1 in. h. Raised by Sündermann.

S. Rudolphia'na. A variety of *S. oppositifolia.*

S. rufid'ula (1). Nearly evergreen. *Rosette-l.* oval, leathery, crenate, red-hairy beneath. Stems short, stiff, 2 to 3 in. h. *fl.* white, starry, anthers red. Sub-arctic N. America. Early summer. Needs shade.

S. rupest'ris. A synonym of *S. hypnoides* and *S. valdensis.*

S. × Salomon'ii (12) (*S. Burseriana* × *S. marginata Rocheliana*). Rosettes silver-grey. *l.* spine-tipped. Stem 3 to 4 in. h., tinged red. *fl.* 3 or 4, large, white, buds red, not very free-flowering. Early spring. Raised by Sündermann. SYN. *S. Salmonica.* **Boyd's** var.,* identical in fl. and habit but free-flowering. Raised by Dr. Boyd. SYN. *S. Burseriana multiflora.*

S. sanc'ta (12). Forms wide carpets. *l.* dark green, spine-tipped. Stems 2 in. h. *fl.* rich yellow. Spring. Greece, Asia Minor. 1882. Needs poor soil and full sun to ensure free-flowering. Indifferent to lime. (B.M. n.s. 137.)

S. × sanguin'ea superb'a* (8) (parentage?). Probably related to *S. decipiens.* Of neat habit. Stem 3 in. h. *fl.* dark red, freely produced. Holding colour well in partial shade.

S. sarmento'sa. A synonym of *S. stolonifera.*

S. Sartor'ii. A synonym of *S. scardica.*

S. scard'ica* (12). Densely clustered, hard mounds; rosettes more or less columnar. *l.* blue-grey, spine-tipped, with marginal lime-glands. Stems 4 in. h. *fl.* white, sometimes flushed pink, large, in a flattish head. June, July. Macedonia, on limestone cliffs and crevices. SYN. *S. Sartorii.* var. **erythran'tha,** like type but *fl.* permanently deep purple. Kyllene, Greece. Not yet introduced; **obtu'sa,** much smaller and less rigid than type, stem rarely over 2 in. h. (B.M. 8058.) SYN. *S. dalmatica* of gardens. Possibly a hybrid; **pseudo-coriophyl'la,** smaller than type, *l.* more spreading, less acute; **ro'sea** of gardens is typical *S. scardica.* **A**

S. × Schel'leri (12) (parentage?). Forms compact grey-green rosettes. Stem 2 in. h. *fl.* white, round. Raised by Sündermann.

S. Schleich'eri. A synonym of *S. stellaris.*

S. × Schleich'eri (12 × 13) (*S. Burseriana* × *S. Stribrnyi*). Stems 2 to 3 in. h. *fl.* pink. January.

S. Schmid'tii. A synonym of *Bergenia ligulata Schmidtii.*

S. × Schot'tii* (13) (*S. corymbosa luteoviridis* × *S. Stribrnyi*). Foliage resembling that of *S. corymbosa*, the branching infl. *S. Stribrnyi. fl.* yellowish. Stems 3 to 4 in. covered with reddish glandular hairs. Raised by Sündermann.

S. × Schrad'eri* (8) (*S. hypnoides* × *S. trifurcata*). Forms loose cushions. *l.* much-divided, firmer than in *S. hypnoides* without the rigidity and clamminess of *S. trifurcata*, evergreen. Stem 6 to 8 in. *fl.* white, freely produced. Spring. Useful for partially shaded walls and nooks.

S. × Schrein'eri (12) (parentage?). Rosettes silvery-grey. *l.* spine-tipped. *fl.* white, several. Stem 2 in. h. Spring. Raised by Sündermann.

S. sclerop'oda (12). Tufted. *l.* long, densely overlapping, acute, green, young l. nearly erect, older l. recurved. Stem 2 in. long. *fl.* clustered, yellow, sep. and pet. of equal length, overtopped by anthers. W. Caucasus.

S. sedoi'des (8). Forming close mats, tufts small. *l.* densely packed, small, undivided, ciliate. Stems 1 in. h., leafy. *fl.* greenish-yellow, starry. Alps and Pyrenees at high altitudes. SYN. *S. saginoides.* var. **Hohenwart'ii,** tips of pet. stained purple, anthers pink. Tyrol, &c.; **Hohenwartii pren'ja,** a condensed form. Bosnia.

S. Seguier'i (8). Small. *l.* in rosettes undivided. Stems 1 to 2 in. h. *fl.* 1 to 3, small, starry. Alps, usually on granite.

S. × Semm'leri (12) (parentage?). Cushions of medium size. Stem 2 to 3 in. *fl.* round, yellow, freely produced. Early spring. Raised by Sündermann.

S. Sempervi'vum. A synonym of *S. porophylla Sibthorpiana.*

S. Sendt'neri. A synonym of *S. Kolenatiana major.*

S. serpyllifo'lia (2). Stems creeping. *l.-rosettes* small. *fl.-stems* 1 to 2 in. h. *fl.* solitary, yellow, round. Arctic Asia and America. SYN. *S. Escholtzii, S. Fischeri.*

S. sibir'ica (7). Related to *S. granulata*, but with small growths rather than bulbils at base. Tufted. *l.* bright green, ivy-shaped; stalks fleshy. *fl.* few, large, white on 6 in. stems. Early summer. SYN. *S. grandiflora villosa.*

Saxifraga scardica (p. 1891)

S. Sibthorp'ii (5). Annual. *l.* kidney-shaped, fleshy, *fl.-stems* branching. *fl.* yellow; cal. reflexed. All summer. Greece. SYN. *S. Cymbalaria.* Usually sows itself freely.

S. signa'ta (2). Monocarpic. Basal rosette dense, 1 to 1¾ in. across. *l.* spatulate, ⅜ to ¾ in. long, fleshy, fringed, often flushed red or purple. *fl.-stems*, reddish, leafy, beset with purple glands. *fl.* in a panicle, branches 2- to 3-fld.; sep. linear-lanceolate, obtuse, about ⅕ in. long; pet. pale yellow in upper, greenish-yellow with bands and blotches of red in lower half, dull purple without. August, September. Yunnan, Szechwan. 1930. (B.M. 9441.)

S. spathula'ta. A variety of *S. globulifera.*

S. specio'sa. A variety of *S. oppositifolia.*

S. × specio'sa (11) (*S. Aizoon × S. Cotyledon*). Forms clumps of dark-green rosettes with distinct marginal lime-glands. Stems 6 in. h., rather stout. *fl.* white. Early summer.

S. × splendens (11) (*S. lingulata lantoscana* × ?). *l.-rosettes* well formed. *fl.* white; panicle arching, many-fld., 8 to 9 in. long. Early summer.

S. × splen'dida (11) (*S. Cotyledon × S. longifolia*). Rosettes wide, shapely, with marginal lime-glands. *fl.-stems* 6 in. long, stout. *fl.* many, whitish. The beauty of the plant lies in the l.-rosettes.

S. sponhem'ica. A variety of *S. decipiens.*

S. Sprun'eri (12). Much like *S. marginata* in habit, but *l.* closely glandular-hairy, in domed rosettes 2 to 3 in. across. *fl.-stems* short. *fl.* in a close corymb, white. Early summer. Olympus and Bulgaria.

S. squarro'sa (12). Rosettes flat, crowded, very small. Stems 2 to 3 in. h., usually glandular, branching. *fl.* white. Summer. Tyrol. Perhaps the smallest species of its group. Needs careful cultivation.

S. Stabia'na. A variety of *S. Aizoon.*

S. Stansfield'ii (8). A garden form of *S. decipiens* with white *fl.*, less worthy than many.

S. × Stein'ii (12) (*S. aretioides × S. tombeanensis*). Rosettes small, silvery, forming dense, firm clusters. Stems 2 in. h. *fl.* creamy-white, several in a loose corymb. Raised by Sündermann.

S. stellar'is (1). *Basal l.* in rosettes, dark green, toothed, of various shapes, leathery. Stems 2 to 6 in., branching. *fl.* white, starry. Northern regions. Needs gritty soil and constant moisture but good drainage. Of little garden value. Variable.

S. Stelleria'na. A synonym of *S. bronchialis cherlerioides.*

S. stenoglos'sa. A variety of *S. Aizoon.*

S. Sternberg'ii. A variety of *S. decipiens.*

S. stoloni'fera.* (16). Mother of Thousands, Aaron's Beard, Roving Sailor, Strawberry Geranium. Loosely tufted. *l.* round, marbled; stalks long. *fl.-stems* 9 to 12 in. h. *fl.* white, 2 inner pet. with yellow, central pet. with 2 red spots at base, 2 outer pet. large, drooping. July, August. Forms numerous creeping red stolons bearing young plants. China, Japan. 1815. (B.M. 92.) SYN. *S. chinensis, S. sarmentosa.* A good window plant. Nearly hardy. Will usually survive in poor soil with a northerly exposure. var. **mi'nor,** probably *S. cuscutiformis*; **tric'olor,** smaller than type and more tender, *l.* deeply cut, irregularly marked with green, white, and red blotches. For warm greenhouse; useful as an edging, in vases and hanging baskets.

S. × Stormonth'ii (12) (Parentage ?). *l.-rosettes* neat, dark green. *l.* spine-tipped. *fl.-stems* leafy, 2 to 3 in. h. *fl.* 5 or 6, light yellow.

S. Strach'eyi. A synonym of *Bergenia Stracheyi.*

S. Strib'rnyi (13). Rosettes of broad, silver-grey l. with marginal lime-glands. Stems 3 to 4 in. h., branching. *fl.* pink, cal. inflated, shaggy, purple. Spring to early summer. Rhodope Mts., Bulgaria. 1902. Parent of many garden hybrids. var. **apicula'ta,** has longer acute sep., concealing pet.; **Zollikof'feri,** pet. more prominent, soft-pink, cal. and stem covered with purple glandular hairs. Bulgaria.

S. stric'ta. A synonym of *S. nivalis tenuis.*

S. × stric'ta (11 × 12 ?) (*S. crustata* × ?). *See under* **S. caesia.**

S. × Stuart'ii (12 × 13 × 13) (*S. aretioides × S. media × S. Stribrnyi*). Rosettes resembling those of *S. media* but infl. branching, *fl.* usually pale yellow but variable, sometimes pink. Raised by Sündermann.

S. Sturmia'na. A variety of *S. Aizoon.*

S. subverticilla'ta (12). Loose-growing with *l.-rosettes* at intervals on weakly trailing stems. *fl.-stems* about 2 in. h. *fl.* yellow, pet. short, stamens long exserted. Summer. E. Caucasus.

S. × Suenderman'nii* (12) (*S. Burseriana × S. marginata*). Smaller than *S. × Obristii. Rosette-l.* about ⅕ in. long, grey, spine-tipped. *fl.* 1, large, white on a reddish stem, 2 in. h. Raised by Irving at Kew. 1911. SYN. *S. × Irvingii.* Another plant raised by Sündermann in 1915 also has been so named. It is *S. Burseriana × S. Stribrnyi* with dense, blue-grey cushions, *l.* spine-tipped. Stems 2 in. h. *fl.* soft rose, few. Spring. var. **ma'jor*** of this is larger and bolder, 3 in. h., and **purpu'rea,** dwarf, compact, free-flowering, 2 in. h., *fl.* 2 or 3, round, rich rose. 1920. Received award as *S. × Hedewigii.*

S. × superb'a (11) (*S. Cotyledon × S. longifolia*). *Rosette-l.* toothed as in *S. Cotyledon*, about 3 in. long. Pet. large, ciliate at base, obovate. Natural hybrid. Pyrenees. Compare *S. × imperialis.*

S. taygete'a (4). Basal *rosette-l.* kidney-shaped, leathery, crenulate. Stem 4 to 6 in., leafless. Panicle loose. *fl.* 1 to 6, white, spotted pink, pet. about ⅓ in. long, 3-nerved. Early summer. Greece. SYN. *S. rotundifolia taygetea.*

S. × tazet'ta (4) (*S. cuneifolia × S. taygetea*). Basal rosettes small. *l.* spatulate, leathery, stalks long, thin. *fl.-stem* leafless. *fl.* round, cupped, white dotted pink, in a loose panicle. A natural hybrid.

S. tellimoi'des. A synonym of *Boykinia tellimoides.*

S. tenel'la (8). Cushion-forming. *l.* undivided, narrow, keeled, acute, emerald green, in dense columns, sometimes with a few bristly hairs on margins. *fl.-stems* slender, branching, 3 to 4 in. h. *fl.* rather small, white. E. Alps. 1819. Best in shade in moist places. SYN. *S. arenarioides, S. nitida.*

S. thessal'ica. A variety of *S. porophylla.*

S. Thomasia'na (12 × 13) (*S. Stribrnyi × S. tombeanensis*). Habit of *S. tombeanensis.* Forms dense cushions, firm, domed. Stems 3 to 4 in. h. *fl.* several, small, pale rose, bell-shaped. Early spring. Raised by Sündermann. 1915.

S. × tirolen'sis (12) (*S. caesia × S. squarrosa*). Very small, intermediate between parents. SE. Alps. A natural hybrid. 1869. SYN. *S. × Pacheriana.*

S. tombeanen'sis (12). Forms dense, hard, domed cushions of crowded rosettes. Rosettes small. *l.* thick, silver-grey sometimes flushed red. Stems 2 in. h., glandular. *fl.* fairly large, snow-white, several. Early summer. Alps.

S. tric'olor. A variety of *S. sarmentosa.*

S. tricuspida'ta (9). Forms wide humped mats. Stems woody. *l.* evergreen, wedge-shaped, 3-cleft at apex, lobes toothed, often bristle-tipped, and sometimes bristly on l.-margin. *fl.-stems* 4 to 6 in. h., branched. *fl.* white, spotted yellow. Early summer. Arctic and sub-arctic regions.

S. tridactyli'tes (6). Annual. Very variable but of no garden value. *fl.* very small. Widely distributed including Britain.

S. tri'dens (8). Very small. Rosettes flat on ground. *l.* small, 3-toothed. Stems 1 to 2 in. h. *fl.* few, milk-white. Early summer. Italian Mts. in moist, peaty soils. SYN. *S. androsacea tridens.*

S. tridenta'ta. An erroneous rendering of *tridentina*, a variety of *S. Burseriana.*

S. × **trif'ida.** A synonym of *S.* × *rigescens.*

S. trifurca'ta* (8). Stems woody. *l.* 3-cleft, lobes cut into up to 13 triangular, stiffly recurved segs., glabrous, clammy, aromatic in summer. *fl.-stems* 6 in. h. or more, branching, reddish. *fl.* many, large, white. Summer. Spain. 1804. SYN. *S. ceratophylla.*

S. turfo'sa (2). Stems erect, 4 to 6 in. h., leafy, branched at top. *fl.* several yellow. Yunnan, China. 1912. Forms stolons from base of stem.

S. × **tyrolen'sis.** *See* **S. tirolensis.**

S. umbellula'ta (2). Rosette very small. *l.* oval, flat on ground. *fl.-stem* 2 to 3 in., sparsely leafy. *fl.* 6 or 7 in a loose umbel, yellow, starry. Summer. Himalaya.

S. umbro'sa (3). London Pride, St. Patrick's Cabbage. *Rosette-l.* spatulate, leathery, tapering to stalks, crenulate or toothed. *fl.-stems* 12 to 18 in. h. *fl.* in loose panicles, pink, starry. Early summer. Widely distributed in mountain woods and gorges, including Britain. Best in partial shade. A variable plant. var. **aeg'ilops,** *l.* narrow, twisted, much-toothed if grown in full sun, becoming like var. *serratifolia* in shade; **Colvil'lei,** smaller than type, *l.* toothed; **dentat'a,** *l.* distinctly toothed; **Melvil'lei,** *l.* rounded, abruptly stalked as in *S. Geum* with which it is possibly a hybrid, *fl.* as in *S. umbrosa*; **Ogilviean'a,** larger than type, *l.* deeply toothed, rosettes many-leaved, becoming rich bronze in sunny places, *fl.-stems* red, *fl.* pink spotted red; **primuloi'des,** small, *l.* small, *fl.-stems* 6 to 8 in. long, *fl.* rich pink. Pyrenees; **primuloi'des, Elliott's** var., smaller, *fl.-stems* 6 in. h., red, *fl.* rose in late spring. A good shade plant; **primuloides, Ingwersen's** var., still smaller, *l.* often bronze, stems 4 in. h., red. *fl.* rich rose; **serratifo'lia,** robust, *l.* deeply toothed, stalks long, *fl.-stems* 18 in. h. Well suited for planting among ferns in shade; **Smithii,** form wild in Ireland; **variega'ta,** *l.* mottled white and often pink at margins; **variegata au'rea,** *l.* spotted yellow, midribs often yellow. These 2 variegated forms should be grown in sun.

S. × **Urumof'fii** (13) (parentage ?). Stems 2 to 3 in. h. *fl.* rich yellow. Spring.

S. × **Vahl'ii** (12) (parentage ?). Very small. Rosettes small, firm, silver-grey, domed. Stems 1 to 2 in. h. *fl.* pure white. Spring.

S. valden'sis (11). Slow-growing. Much smaller than *S. cochlearis,* less domed, less grey. Stem 2 to 3 in. h., stiff, glandular. *fl.* round, white, in a clustered head. Early summer. French Alps. 1871. SYN. *S. caesia Morettii, S. compacta, S. rupestris.*

S. valenti'na (8). Related to *S. trifurcata.* Rosettes large. *l.* glabrous, clammy, 3-cleft with side lobes divided, all points blunt, long-stalked. Stem 6 to 9 in. h. *fl.* large, white, freely produced. Early summer. Mts. of Spain.

S. Vandel'lii (12). Slow-growing. Domed, grey, firm and rigid. *l.* spine-tipped. Stems 2 to 3 in. h., glandular. *fl.* large, in a flattish head. Early summer. Alps of Lombardy in limestone crevices. SYN. *S. Burseriana Vandellii, S. pungens.*

S. Vanhout'tii. A synonym of *Bergenia crassifolia.*

S. var'ians. A synonym of *S. moschata.*

S. Vayreda'na (8). Related to *S. trifurcata,* smaller. *Rosette-l.* wedge-shaped, 3-cleft at apex, clammy, aromatic. Stems 3 to 4 in. h. *fl.* 9 to 10, white, round. Early summer. Spain.

S. Veitchia'na (16). *l.* roundish-cordate; fleshy, dark green, sometimes marbled. Stem 6 to 9 in. h. *fl.* white with usually a few yellow spots at base, long pet. 1 or 2; in a panicle. W. Hupeh. 1900. Sometimes producing stolons or runners.

S. veronicifo'lia. A synonym of *S. atlantica.*

S. virginien'sis (1). Basal *rosette-l.* few, coarse, leathery. Stem 12 in. h., stout. *fl.* in a panicle, small, white. Early summer. N. America. 1790. Of little garden value. var. **elongat'a,** smaller, more graceful, few-fld. Needing a cool, shady place.

S. vochinen'sis. A variety of *S. crustata.*

S. × **Vol'geri** (13) (parentage ?). *fl.* light red.

S. Wallac'ei. A synonym of *S. Camposii.*

S. Webbian'a (8). A coarse-growing mossy Saxifrage of the *S. decipiens* group.

S. × **Wildia'na** (11 × 3) (*S. Aizoon* × *S. Geum hirsuta*). Basal rosettes glossy. *l.* oval, leathery, toothed, often hairy at first. *fl.* like those of *S.* × *Andrewsii.* Botanic Garden, Dresden. 1836.

S. Wilkomia'na. A synonym of *S. canaliculata.*

S. Wulfenia'na. A synonym of *S. retusa Baumgartenii.*

S. yunnanen'sis. A synonym of *Bergenia yunnanensis.*

S. Zelebor'i. A synonym of *S. Aizoon montana subaffinis.*

S. × **Zimmeteri*** (11 × 3) (*S. Aizoon* × *S. cuneifolia*). Rosettes glossy. *l.* leathery, margined grey. Stem 4 in. h., loosely branched. *fl.* white, starry; anthers orange. Early summer. Austria. 1870. A natural hybrid.

HYBRIDS WITH FANCY NAMES (see p. 1880).

Ada (12) (*S. Burseriana crenata* × *S. tombeanensis*). Rosettes dense, forming tight, firm cushions. *l.* short, narrow, slightly pointed. *fl.-stems* 2 in. h. *fl.* 2 or 3, white. Early spring. Of garden origin; **Amitie** (12) (*S. lilacina* × *S. scardica obtusa*). Forms dense, firm cushions of greyish-green rosettes. *fl.-stems* 1 in. h. *fl.* lilac fading to white, solitary; **Apple Blossom** (8) (*S. decipiens* hybrid × *S. muscoides*). Small, *fl.* pale pink. Possibly a selected colour-form; **Beauty of Letchworth** (8) (parentage ?). Habit neat and compact. *fl.* 3, round, old rose. Spring; **Bellisant** (12) (parentage ?). Forms neat spiny cushions. *fl.-stems* 2 in. h. *fl.* soft rose-pink. Early spring; **Beryl** (12 × 12 × 13) (*S.* × *Godroniana* × *S. lilacina*). Habit of *S. aretioides. fl.-stems* 2 in. h. *fl.* pink, resembling *S. lilacina.* Early spring; **Buttercup** (12) (parentage ?). Rosettes neatly rounded, dark green, spiny. *fl.-stems,* 2 in. h. *fl.* rich yellow, round. Spring; **Cecil Davis** (11) (? *S. lingulata* × *S. longifolia*). Of medium size. Rosettes handsome, silvery. *fl.* resembling *S. Aizoon.* Worth growing for its rosettes; **Cerise Queen** (12) (parentage ?). Forms firm, grey-green rosettes. *fl.-stems* short. *fl.* few, rich cerise-red, of medium size. SYN. *S.* × *Christine*; **Cherry Trees** (12) (*S. aretioides* × *S. marginata Rocheliana*). Forms very hard and compact humped rosettes of grey-green l. *fl.-stems* 3 in. h. *fl.* few, butter-yellow. Early spring. Rather difficult to cultivate. The earliest first-class hybrid Saxifrage of the Section, raised by Dr. J. B. Boyd about 1890; **Coombe White** (12) (*S. Burseriana* × ?). Habit of *S. Burseriana,* compact. *fl.-stems* 2 in. h. *fl.* large, white, round. Very free-flowering. Early spring. Raised by Mrs. Lloyd Edwards; **Cranbourne*** (12) (parentage ?). Forms neat cushions of grey-green rosettes about ½ in. across. *l.* blunt. *fl.-stems* 2 in. h. *fl.* large, rose, of good form. Spring; **Crimson King** (8) (parentage ?). Habit neat. *fl.* red, of good form; **Delia** (12) (parentage ?). Forms firm domes of very small, blunt-leaved rosettes. *fl.-stem* 2 in. h. *fl.* white, faintly tinged lilac. Early spring; **Dr. Ramsay** (11) (*S. cochlearis* × *S. longifolia*). Rosettes handsome. *fl.-stems* 12 in. h. *fl.* in fine panicles, pure white. Early summer. Seedlings of this produce inferior plants; **Elysium** (13 × 12) (*S.* × *Godroniana* × *S. lilacina*). Very small, forming silvery-grey cushions of small, flattish rosettes. *fl.-stems* 1 in. h. *fl.* soft pink. Early spring. Raised by Mr. Prichard; **Esther*** (11) (*S. Aizoon lutea* × *S. cochlearis*). Quickly forming masses of rosettes 1 to 2 in. across. *fl.-stems* branching up to 12 in. h. *fl.* numerous, soft yellow; **Etheline** (12) (*S. Burseriana minor* × *S. tombeanensis*). Forms dense, grey-silvery domes of very small, closely packed rosettes. *fl.-stems* 1 in. h. *fl.* white, flushed pink in bud. Raised by Mr. Prichard; **Faldonside*** (12) (*S. aretioides* × *S. marginata Rocheliana*). Forms dense, silver-grey tufts. *l.* spiny. *fl.-stems* 2 to 3 in. h., reddish. *fl.* citron-yellow, large, pet. overlapping. Early spring. Raised by Dr. Boyd. 1890; **Flower of Sulphur** (8) (parentage ?). Of neat habit. *fl.-stem* 3 to 4 in. h. *fl.* pale-yellow. Spring; **Francis Cade*** (11) (*S. cochlearis* × *S. lingulata*). Rosettes silvery. *fl.-stems* 8 to 10 in. h., arching. *fl.* many, large, white. Early summer; **Gem*** (12) (*S. Burseriana Gloria* × *S.* × *Irvingii*). Habit neat and compact. *l.* blue-grey, spiny. *fl.-stem* 1 to 2 in. h. *fl.* pale pink. Early spring. Raised by Mr. Prichard; **Gloriosa** (12) (*S. tombeanensis* ? × ?). Compact in habit. *fl.* small, round rich-red on stems 1 to 2 in. h. Early spring. Raised by Mr. Prichard; **Grace Farwell** (12 × 13) (parentage ?). Rosettes small, somewhat like those of *S. media,* forming mats. *fl.-stems* 2 to 3 in. h. *fl.* rich wine-red. Spring; **Guildford Seedling*** (8) (parentage ?). Tufted, compact, evergreen, of *decipiens-muscoides* type. *fl.-stems* 3 to 4 in. h. *fl.* deep red. Spring. Raised at Guildford; **Harry Marshall*** (12) (?*S.* × *Irvingii* × *S. lilacina*). Taller and with better habit and larger, more richly coloured fl. than *S.* × *Irvingii. fl.-stems* 2 in. h. Early spring. Raised by Mr. Prichard; **Iris Prichard*** (12 × 13) (*S.* × *Godroniana* × ?). Habit of *S. Bursiana. fl.-stem* 3 in. h. *fl.* of good shape, buff. Spring. Raised by Mr. Prichard; **James Bremner*** (8) (parentage ? probably *S. granulata* cross). *fl.-stems* 6 to 9 in. h. *fl.* white, larger than any other mossy Saxifrage. Early summer. Needs annual propagation by cuttings; **Kathleen Pinsent*** (11) (Probably *S. lingulata* × ?). *fl.-stem* 9 to 12 in. h. *fl.* soft rose-pink, numerous. May, June. Introduced by Mr. C. Elliott; **Lady Beatrix Stanley*** (12 × 13 × 14) (*S.* × *Godroniana* × *S. oppositifolia latina*). Rosettes intermediate between those of parents, dark green. *fl.-stems* 1 to 1½ in. h. *fl.* large, widely expanded, pink. Early spring. Best in alpine house; **L. C. Godseff.** A synonym of *S.* × *Godseffiana*; **Laurent Ward** (12 × 13) (*S. porophylla* × *S. lilacina*). Forms neat cushions. *fl.-stems* 2 in. h. *fl.* dark red. Early spring. Raised by Mr. Prichard; **Lloyd Edwards** (8) (parentage ?). Habit of Guildford Seedling. *fl.* red; **Mrs. Laing** (12), very near *S.* × *Elizabethae* and not superior to it; **Mother of Pearl** (12) (parentage ?). *fl.-stem* 2 in. h. *fl.* shell-pink, large. Early spring; **Myra** (12) (? *S. lilacina* × *S. scardica*). Rather slow in growth. Rosettes of type of *S. marginata. fl.-stem* 1 to 2 in. h. *fl.* large, deep red. Early spring. Introduced by Reginald Farrer; **Pompadour** (8) (parentage ?) Of untidy habit unless frequently propagated. Very large in growth and fl. *fl.-stems* 9 to 10 in. h. *fl.* dusky crimson, round. Spring; **Primrose Bee.** *See* **S.** × **apiculata**; **Primulaize*** (3 × 10) (*S. aizoides aurantia* × *S. umbrosa primuloides*). Dwarf, mat-forming, evergreen. *l.* narrow, slightly toothed. *fl.-stem* 2 to 3 in. h. *fl.* in panicles, carmine, salmon, or red. Summer. Best in partial shade. Raised by Mr. Prichard; **Priory Jewel** (13 × 12) (*S.* × *Godroniana* × *S. lilacina*). Forms very compact silvery-grey cushions. Small. *fl.-stems* 1 in. h. *fl.* pink. Early spring. Good in alpine house and for limestone crevices. Raised by Mr. Prichard; **Red Admiral** (8) (parentage?). Habit neat. About 4 in. h. *fl.* round, red, freely produced. Spring; **Riverslea*** (13 × 12) (*S. lilacina* × *S. porophylla*). Forms dense silvery mounds. *fl.-stems* 2 to 3 in. h. *fl.* of good size, deep purplish-rose. Early spring. Raised by Mr. Prichard; **Simplicity** (12) (*S. lilacina* × *S.*

tombeanensis). Very small, *fl.-stems* 1 to 2 in. h. *fl.* white. Early spring. Raised by Mr. Prichard; **Sir Douglas Haig** (8) (parentage?). Robust, *fl.-stems* 6 to 9 in. h. *fl.* deep crimson, large, round. Spring. Best in partial shade; **Sonia Prichard** (13 × 12) (*S. lilacina* × *S. porophylla*). Habit intermediate between parents. *fl.-stems* 2 in. h. *fl.* purplish-red. Early spring. Raised by Mr. Prichard; **Sparkling** (13 × 12 × 12) (*S.* × *Godroniana* × *S. lilacina*). Very dwarf. Rosettes small, clustered. *fl.-stem* 1 in. h. *fl.* clear bright pink, at first tubular then opening wide, almost sessile. Early spring. Raised by Mr. Prichard; **Tumbling Waters*** (11) (*S. lingulata* × *S. longifolia*). The finest of the hybrids of its group with fine rosettes and magnificent panicles of white fl. freely produced; **Valerie Keevil*** (13 × 12 × 12) (*S.* × *Godroniana* × *S. lilacina*). Forms firm, small, silvery-grey mounds. *fl.-stems* about 2 in. h. *fl.* deep rose-pink, about ⅜ in. across. Spring. Raised by Mr. Prichard; **Wenlock Peach** (8) (parentage?). Large in growth and fl. forming large tufts. *fl.-stem* 9 in. h. *fl.* peach-coloured. Spring. Needs frequent top-dressing or division to keep neat.

W. E. Th. I.

SAXIFRAGA'CEAE. Dicotyledons. A family of about 650 species of herbs, shrubs, or trees in about 80 genera distributed mainly over temperate and cold regions, rare in the tropics. Flowers usually hermaphrodite, rarely 1-sexual. Calyx usually 5-parted, rarely 4- to 12-parted, lobes valvate or overlapping; petals generally 5, or 4, rarely absent, usually perigynous, sometimes epigynous, rarely hypogynous; stamens as many or twice as many as petals, rarely indefinite, erect or spreading, filaments free. Fruit a capsule or berry, rarely a follicle or nut. The family contains no very important economic plants but is rich in plants of an ornamental character. Genera dealt with here are: Abrophyllum, Anopterus, Astilbe, Bauera, Bergenia, Boykinia, Brexia, Calacluvia, Callicoma, Cardiandra, Carpenteria, Cephalotus, Davidsonia, Decumaria, Deinanthe, Deutzia, Dichroa, Escallonia, Fendlera, Francoa, Geissois, Heuchera, × Heucherella, Hydrangea, Itea, Jimesia, Kirengeshoma, Lithophragma, Mitella, Parnassia, Penthorum, Philadelphus, Pileostegia, Platycrates, Quintinia, Ribes, Rodgersia, Saxifraga, Schizophragma, Tanakea, Tellima, Tiarella, Tolmiea, Valdivia.

SAXIFRAGE. *See* **Saxifraga.**

SAXIFRAGE, MEADOW. *See* **Saxifraga granulata.**

SCAB. A term loosely applied to disfigurements of the skin of plants resulting from the injury caused by fungus parasites. The usual appearance is that of small, more or less circular, raised areas on the skin of fruits, shoots, and tubers. At first the spots may be pimple-like but they gradually increase in size and the epidermis ruptures to show a scabby area with a ragged frayed edge. Although this does not usually cause the death of the attacked part, some of the most serious diseases are of the scab type owing to the great loss resulting from disfigurement, especially when grown for commercial use. Instances are Potato Common Scab where, although only skin deep, the scabby areas may almost cover the whole surface of the tuber; Apple and Pear Scab where a similar condition spoils the market value of the fruits; Peach Scab.

D. E. G.

sca'ber -ra -rum, rough.

scaber'ulus -a -um, roughish.

SCABIO'SA (*scabies*, the itch, a disease the common species are said to cure). FAM. *Dipsacaceae*. A genus of about 60 species of annual or perennial herbs, sometimes more or less shrubby at the base, natives of Europe, Asia, and Africa, mainly in the Mediterranean region. Leaves entire, toothed, lobed, or much divided. Flowers blue, rose, purple, yellowish-white, or white in terminal heads; involucral bracts in 1 or 2 series; involucels 2-, 4-, or 8-ribbed; calyx bristly; corolla limb 4- or 5-fid, lobes subequal, or often oblique or 2-lipped; stamens 4, very rarely 2, all perfect. The species of Scabious grow well in ordinary soil and may be increased by seeds or in some instances by division. The 2 most useful species for cut flowers are *S. atropurpurea* and *S. caucasica*. *S. atropurpurea* is an annual which may be grown in pots for winter flowering, for which purpose seed should be sown in June or July and the plants when large enough should be potted singly and grown in a cool frame. For summer flowering outdoors the seeds should be sown in March or early April. *S. caucasica* is a perennial which makes a good border plant, several fine varieties of which have been raised in recent years and are propagated by division. Seedlings are easily raised but do not come true to shade.

Scabious seedlings are apt to suffer from damping off (q.v.) and are sometimes attacked by other fungi, including *Thielaviopsis basicola*, but this is usually severe only where the soil is damp and cold. Leaf blotch due to a species of Ramularia occurs, but is not a serious disease. Powdery mildew due to *Erysiphe Polygoni* may be a nuisance. It may be controlled by spraying in good time with Bordeaux mixture or by dusting with green sulphur dust.

The species described below are perennial unless otherwise stated.

S. alpi'na. A synonym of *Cephalaria alpina*.

S. amoe'na. Perennial of 2 to 3 ft. *Radical l.* obovate, toothed or lyrate, rather hairy; *stem-l.* pinnatifid, lobes lanceolate, acute, nearly entire. *fl.-heads* lilac or rose; cor. rayed; peduncles long, hairy below heads. June, July. Russia. 1820.

S. anthemifo'lia. Annual or biennial. Habit, &c., of *S. Columbaria* and one of the S. African forms of that variable species. *fl.* rose, mauvish, or violet. S. Africa. 1920. (B.M. 9115.) SYN. *S. Columbaria dissecta*, *S. Columbaria rosea*.

S. arven'sis. A synonym of *Knautia arvensis*. *See* Supplement.

S. atropurpu'rea.* Mournful Widow, Sweet Scabious. Pincushion Flower. Egyptian Rose. Annual. Stem branched, 2 to 3 ft. h. *Radical l.* lanceolate-ovate, lyrate, coarsely toothed; *stem-l.* pinnatipartite, lobes oblong, toothed or cut. *fl.-heads* normally deep crimson, fragrant; cor. radiate, a little longer than involucre. July to September. SW. Europe. 1629. (B.M. 247.) Under the name of Saudade the fl. of this species have been largely used in Portugal, Brazil, &c., for funeral wreaths and similar purposes. There are many colour forms, the blue **Azure Fairy** being particularly pleasing, var. **flore ple'no** has double purple or white fl. (F.d.S. 1203.); **foliis au'reis,** *l.* yellow; **na'na,** about 1 ft. h., of compact habit; **stria'ta,** *fl.* spotted and streaked. Colour varieties may be had separately.

S. brachia'ta. More or less hairy annual of variable height, erect. *l.* variable, lower toothed or lyrate, rarely pinnatipartite, upper lyrate or pinnatipartite. *fl.-heads* of various colours, forms, and sizes; cor. radiate; segs. 3- to 6-cleft. Summer. Levant, &c. SYN. *S. palaestina*.

S. caucas'ica.* About 12 to 18 in. h. *Radical l.* lanceolate, acuminate, entire, glaucous; *stem-l.* more or less pinnatifid; *fl.-heads* pale blue, 3 in. across, radiate; cor. 5-cleft; involucre hairy. June to October. Caucasus. 1803. (B.M. 886.) Variable in shade of colour and size of fl.-head. *See* Supplement. var. **al'ba,** *fl.-heads* white; **el'egans,** *l.* whitish, *stem-l.* entire or nearly so. (R.H. 1212.); **fimbriata,** cor. pale lilac, finely fringed; **heterophyl'la,** *l.* hairy, pinnatisect, segs. linear-lanceolate, acute, *fl.-heads* pale purple, large. 1883. (G.F. 1084.)

S. Columba'ria. 1 to 2 ft. h. *l.* very variable, glabrous or hairy; radical narrow, stalked, entire or divided; stem-l. pinnatifid, segs. often cut. *fl.-heads* lilac or blue-purple, 1 to 1½ in. across; cor. hairy, of inner fl. in head regular, of outer rayed; peduncles slender. July to September. Europe, including Britain. (E.B. 678.) var. **ro'sea,** a synonym of *S. anthemifolia*.

S. cre'tica. Perennial. *l.* lanceolate, almost entire. *fl.-heads* blue-purple, cor. 5-fid. Crete, Sicily.

S. ela'ta. A synonym of *Cephalaria gigantea* (*C. tatarica*, p. 434).

S. Fisch'eri.* About 20 in. h. *l.* much cut. *fl.-heads* deep violet-blue, about 2½ in. across; peduncles long, stiff. July to October. Manchuria. 1934.

S. gigante'a. A synonym of *Cephalaria gigantea* (*C. tartarica*, p. 434.)

S. graminifo'lia.* About 9 in. h. from a woody rootstock. Loosely mat-forming. *l.* linear-lanceolate, entire, silvery-white. *fl.-heads* pale mauve to rose. S. Europe. 1683. (B.R. 835.) Rock-garden or border.

S. Hook'eri. Perennial from a woody rootstock. *l.* nearly all radical, 6 in. long, ¾ in. wide, linear-spatulate, runcinate or sometimes entire. *fl.-heads* globose, bluish, 1 to 1¾ in. wide; cor. ¾ in. long, tubular funnel-shaped, hairy without, not rayed. Himalaya. SYN. *Pterocephalus Hookeri*. (B.M. 8774.)

S. japo'nica. Biennial, about 1 ft. h. *fl.-heads* large, lavender. June to September. Japan. 1904.

S. lu'cida. 6 to 9 in. h. *l.* finely cut, silvery. *fl.-heads* rosy-lilac. May to September. E. Alps. Rock-garden.

Scabiosa graminifolia (p. 1894)

S. ochroleu'ca. About 2 ft. h. Softly hairy. *Lower l.* stalked, obovate, crenate; *upper* pinnatifid, lobes ovate or oblong, entire. *fl.-heads* primrose-yellow, on long peduncles; cor. nearly regular. July to November. SE. Europe. Border. var. **Webbia'na,** about 6 in. h., *l.* wrinkled, *fl.-heads* creamy-white. Mt. Ida. Rock-garden.

S. palaesti'na. A synonym of *S. brachiata.*

S. prolif'era. Annual, 1 to 2 ft. h., covered with appressed hairs. Stem stout, forked. *l.* oblong to oblong-lanceolate or linear. *fl.-heads* cream, on short peduncles or sessile, 1 to 1½ in. across. June. Syria.

S. Pterocephʹalus. A synonym of *Pterocephalus parnassi.*

S. silenifo'lia.* Habit of *S. graminifolia.* Tufted, about 6 in. h. *l.* dark, glossy green. *fl.-heads* violet. Hungary. Rock-garden.

S. stella'ta. Annual, about 18 in. h., branched. *l.* almost lyrate, end lobe largest, obovate, toothed. *fl.-heads* pink or bluish-white, on long peduncles; cor. radiate. July. Mediterranean region. 1823.

S. Succi'sa. Rootstock short, abruptly truncate. *l.* sometimes hairy; lower oblong or obovate, entire, stalked; upper few, toothed. *fl.-heads* blue-purple or white, ⅔ to 1½ in. across; involucral bracts shorter than hairy cor.; peduncles appressed-hairy. July to October. Europe, including Britain. (E.B. 677.) SYN. *Succisa pratensis.* **A**

S. vesti'ta. Habit of *S. graminifolia.*

S. Webbia'na. A variety of *S. ochroleuca.*

SCABIOUS. *See* Scabiosa.

SCABIOUS, SHEEP'S-BIT. *See* Jasione.

SCABIOUS, SWEET. *See* Scabiosa atropurpurea.

scabra -um, *see* ***scaber.***

scabrius'culus -a -um, somewhat rough.

scabro'sus -a -um, rather rough.

SCAE'VOLA (*scaevus*, left, in honour of Gaius Mucius, 507 B.C., left-handed king of Clusium; referring to the form of the corolla). FAM. *Goodeniaceae.* A genus of about 60 species of shrubs, sub-shrubs, or perennial herbs, mostly Australian with a few on tropical coasts of both hemispheres. Leaves alternate or rarely opposite, entire or toothed. Flowers solitary, axillary, or in forks of branches, white, blue, yellowish, or reddish; sepals very short, sometimes absent; corolla split to base at back; anthers free; ovary usually inferior, 2-celled, with 1 ovule in each cell, or 1-celled with 1 or 2 ovules. Fruit more or less soft, not dehiscing. Stove or greenhouse conditions are needed. The compost should be turfy loam, peat, and sand. Propagation by cuttings in a sandy compost, those of *S. Plumieri* in heat. The following species need greenhouse treatment, except the W. Indian *S. Plumieri*, and are Australian.

S. anchusifo'lia. Herb or sub-shrub, erect or prostrate. *l.* linear or oblanceolate, entire, or, if broad, coarsely toothed, 1 to 2 in. long; bracts less than ½ in. long. *fl.* blue, sessile or nearly so, in a terminal leafy spike; sep. very small; cor. ½ in. long, hairy without, bristly within. May.

S. attenua'ta. Erect shrub, 18 to 24 in. h. *l.* broadly lanceolate with few teeth, 2 to 3 in. long; upper linear, usually entire. *fl.* blue, sessile, in terminal, leafy spikes, at length interrupted; cal. prominent, annular; cor. ¾ in. long, hairy within, softly bristly in throat. June. 1844. (B.M. 4196.)

S. cuneiform'is. Erect or ascending herb. *l.* stalked, lower obovate, often 2 in. long, upper oblong wedge-shaped; bracts sessile, usually less than ½ in. long, entire. *fl.* blue, sessile, in a long, interrupted spike; cor. ⅔ in. long. 1824.

S. grandiflo'ra. A synonym of *Leschenaultia linarioides.*

S. Koenig'ii. Malay Rice Paper Plant. Erect shrub, 2 ft. h. *l.* oblong-obovate, 3 to 5 in. long, rounded and blunt, entire or rarely broadly crenate, stalks short. *fl.* pale red, in axillary cymes, shorter than l.; cal. lobes as long as, or longer than, tube; cor. ¾ in. long, hairy without. August. 1820. (B.M. 2732.)

S. microcarp'a. Erect or spreading perennial. *l.* obovate, ovate, or wedge-shaped, coarsely toothed, lower often 1 to 1½ in. long, upper shorter. *fl.* violet; spike usually long, interrupted; sep. small; cor. about ¾ in. long, hairy without. July. 1790. (L.B.C. 1327; B.M. 287 as *Goodenia laevigata.*) **A**

S. pilo'sa. Hispid perennial or sub-shrub, 1 to 3 ft. h. *Lower l.* stalked, obovate or oblong, coarsely toothed, 2 to 3 in. long; *upper* much smaller, sessile or stem-clasping, oblong wedge-shaped to lanceolate. *fl.* blue; cal. tube hairy; cor. ¾ to 1 in. long; peduncles axillary, longer than l., 1-fld. May. 1841.

S. platyphyl'la. Erect, hispid, 2 ft. h., woody at base, branches rigid, herbaceous. *l.* sessile or stem-clasping, ovate to oblong, entire or with few teeth, 1 to 1½ in., rarely 2 in., long, upper smaller. *fl.* white, sessile or nearly so, in a terminal, leafy spike; cal. lobes very small; cor. over 1 in. long, silky-hairy, lobes winged. May. 1841.

S. Plumie'ri. Shrub, 2 ft. h., *l.* obovate, fleshy, entire. *fl.* white, usually in axillary, stalked cymes; cal. truncate, slightly toothed; cor. ⅔ to ⅚ in. long, hairy within. August. W. Indies. 1724. Stove.

S. suaveo'lens. Prostrate or decumbent, sub-shrubby at times. *l.* stalked, obovate to oblong-spatulate, entire, thick, up to 2 to 3 in. long; upper smaller, often narrower. *fl.* blue, sessile, in interrupted, terminal, hairy spikes; cal. 5-lobed; cor. about ⅔ in. long, sometimes hairy without and toothed or bristly in throat. August. 1793. (A.B.R. 22 as *Goodenia calendulacea.*)

scalariform, ladder-like.

scala'ris -is -e, ladder-like.

SCALD. A term used for a type of skin injury which occurs on certain fruits not from the attack of a parasite but from some cause acting externally. On Tomatoes it is due to the action of the sun on fruits growing near or placed near the glass, which results in a creamy-white patch with wrinkled skin (*see* **Tomato diseases**). On Apples a brownish scald-like area may be seen on the skin of some fruits in very hot seasons (sun scald), but the trouble is far more common on Apples which have been kept in ordinary storage or gas storage, and is then seen more as irregular dark blotches often near the eye but possibly scattered all over the surface of the skin, the flesh underneath being still sound. Much apple storage scald can be prevented by the use of oiled wrappers, and these are essential for gas storage. On Grapes, insufficient ventilation during hot sunshine may result in sun scald if there is moisture on the berries. The usual appearance is a brown sunken area on the shoulder of affected berries, but the symptoms may vary a good deal (*see* **Vine diseases**).

D. E. G.

SCALE APHIS, *Cerataphis lataniae*, is so called because of its similarity to a Scale insect. It occurs under glass on Palms and Orchids, especially Cypripediums, on the leaves and flower-stalks of which it clusters and feeds, also between the sheaths and at the base of Orchid stems. The wingless female has a dark-reddish or purplish-brown scale-like body, around which is a fringe of short, white, waxen threads. They are sluggish, and their antennae and legs are hidden beneath the scale. The immature forms are also scale-like, pale yellow, and covered with white waxy powder. This pest may become very abundant in stoves and Orchid houses if measures are not taken to check it. For control measures *see* **Aphis.**

G. F. W.

SCALE FERN. *See* **Ceterach officinarum.**

SCALE INSECTS. These insects, with Mealy Bugs (q.v.), constitute the Homopterous family *Coccidae* and are among the most important plant pests. While closely related to Mealy Bugs, they differ from them in being inactive during the greater part of their life and by possessing a scaly covering. The shape, appearance, and colour of Scale insects vary considerably; the females are invariably wingless with no sharply defined body segments. The males of some species are rare or absent, and in others they may be wingless or provided with a single pair of simple wings with a pair of hooked halteres (balancing organs) to replace the second pair of wings. The mouth parts consist of a short, tubular lower lip enclosing the 4 long slender stylets, which are pushed into the tissues of plants and through which sap is abstracted. The eggs are usually deposited beneath the female Scale, after which the insect shrivels. The young nymphs or immature Scales are at first active and run about over the leaves and shoots of infested plants, but soon settle down to a sedentary existence and lose their limbs. As the larvae develop, the scaly covering is extended and may be hard and rounded (European Brown Scale, *Lecanium corni*) or soft and flat (Soft Scale, *L. hesperidum*).

Scales are serious pests of a great variety of plants, including fruit-trees (Mussel Scale, *Lepidosaphes ulmi*), forest trees (Felted Beech Coccus, *Cryptococcus fagi*), shrubs (*Lecanium corni* on Cotoneasters), hedge plants (Yew Scale, *L. cornicrudum*), Roses (Scurvy Scale, *Diaspis rosae*), Vines (Woolly Currant Scale, *Pulvinaria vitis*), greenhouse plants (Soft Scale, *L. hesperidum*), while Orchids and stove plants are attacked by a number of exotic species. The leaves of infested plants, especially those attacked by the Soft Scale, become covered with Sooty Moulds, which grow on the honeydew excreted by the young Scales. Ants are frequent attendants on Scales for the honeydew which they collect, and frequently build shelters of soil particles over them.

The measures for controlling Scale insects are dealt with under the headings Mussel Scale and others, and it is necessary here only to outline the general principles governing their successful eradication. Constant watch should be kept on plants for the presence of Scales, and action taken against them immediately they are detected to avoid widespread infestations. The young Scales are more readily destroyed than the adult Scales, so that applications of a Contact Wash (e.g. Nicotine and Soap) should be made soon after the eggs hatch. The wash should be applied in a thorough manner to ensure the wetting of all portions of plants, especially the underside of the leaves, shoots, and stems. Little trouble with these pests is experienced in orchards where routine winter washing with Tar Oils is carried out, or in glasshouses where routine fumigation is practised. Control measures to be successful must be of a routine nature, including spraying of outdoor plants, fumigation of glasshouse subjects, and sponging of tender stove plants. Newly acquired plants introduced into a garden or nursery should be carefully examined for Scale pests and, if found to be infested, treated prior to planting.

G. F. W.

SCALE LEAVES. Leaves which remain rudimentary and often perform some special function as, for example, the scales on the outside of the winter buds of many plants which protect the young foliage leaves or flowers from injury; but some scale leaves have no special function as the rudimentary leaves on stems which have taken over the usual functions of leaves, such as in the Gorse, or in parasitic and saprophytic plants which have abnormal methods of nutrition. They are sometimes used as storage organs as the thick leaves of a bulb, and sometimes act as a check to loss of water as in the tunic leaves of some bulbs and corms.

SCALLION. *See* **Allium ascalonicum.** Also applied to all Onions which do not bulb, but which instead form a long neck.

scalpelliform, resembling the blade of a penknife or scalpel.

scalptura'tus -a -um, engraved.

SCALY BULB. A bulb in which the leaves borne on the disk merely overlap as in the Lily, not completely enwrap it as in the Tulip.

SCAMMONY PLANT. *See* **Convolvulus Scammonia.**

scan'dens, scandent, climbing.

SCAPE. A long, naked, or nearly naked, peduncle, rising direct from the base of a plant, whether 1- or many-fld.

scaphi- or ***scapho-,*** in compound words, signifies boat-shaped.

SCAPHOSEP'ALUM (*skaphe*, boat, *sepalum*, sepal; in allusion to the form of the sepals). FAM. *Orchidaceae*. About 14 species formerly included in Masdevallia form this genus. They have a similar tufted habit but are readily distinguished by the diverging lateral sepals being uppermost, their bases boat-shaped, connate, more or less thickened and protracted into tails. The small, variously shaped lip, also superior, is practically concealed by the connate portion of the lateral sepals. The dorsal sepal, smaller than the lateral, is free or nearly so, inclined upwards, its base often inflated, covering the column and petals. A succession of flowers is maintained by the elongation of the usually slender scapes. With *S. octhodes* in particular the duration of flowering is almost indefinite. All are epiphytic, and natives chiefly in Brazil, Guiana, and Costa Rica. Cultivation is as for Masdevallias, and propagation is by dividing the plants when large enough. Though not showy the flowers are attractive by their quaint shapes and the freedom with which the scapes are produced. The bases of the lateral sepals usually exhibit brighter colouring than the remainder of the flower.

S. anchorif'erum. *fl.* small; lateral sep. greenish, spotted and ribbed maroon, tails rather short, drooping, greenish-yellow; dorsal sep. dark crimson-maroon. *Scape* about 6 in. long. *l.* 3 to 6 in. h. Costa Rica. 1884. SYN. *Masdevallia anchorifera.*

S. antennif'erum. *fl.* nearly 1 in. h., greenish-yellow lined with brown. *Scape* stout 12 to 18 in. h. *l.* about 6 in. h. Habitat? 1890. Allied to *S. pulvinare.*

S. bre've. *fl.* small; lateral sep. brownish, the thickened portions yellow, shaded purple, tails ⅓ in. long; dorsal sep. yellowish, spotted purple, tail shorter; the small lip whitish, purple-lined, margin fimbriate. *l.* rather rigid, 3 to 4 in. long including petiole. British Guiana. 1884. SYN. *Masdevallia brevis.*

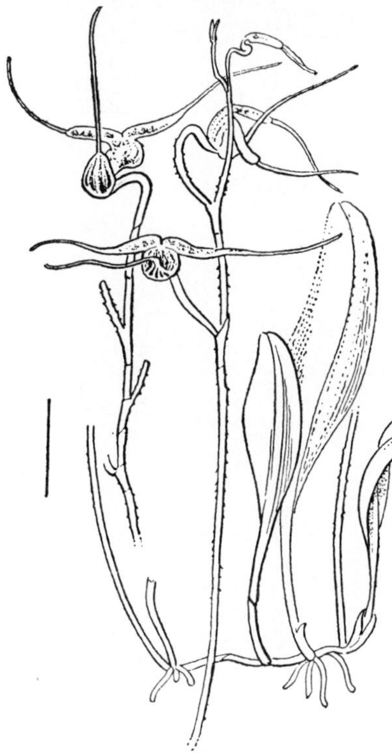

Scaphosepalum gibberosum

S. gibbero'sum.* *fl.* 3 to 5, comparatively large, slender; lateral sep. creamy-white or green, shaded and dotted with purple at base, spreading, with the tails, about 2½ in. across; tail of dorsal sep. much the largest; peduncle warted. *l.* 6 to 8 in. long including petiole. Colombia. 1876. (B.M. 6990 as *Masdevallia gibberosa.*)

S. octho'des. *fl.* small, tails very short, yellowish or greenish-yellow with brownish or purplish-brown lines; dorsal sep. ribbed. *Scape* slender, sometimes reaching 3 ft., minutely verrucose. *l.* 3 to 8 in. long. Colombia. 1888. SYN. *Masdevallia octhodes.*

S. pulvina're. *fl.* medium size; lateral sep. with bases much thickened, olive-green, ribbed brown, tails short, purplish; dorsal sep. olive-green blotched purplish, tail longer than those on the lateral. *Scape* longer than l., rather stout, warted. *l.* 5 to 9 in. long, leathery. Colombia. 1890. (B.M. 7151.) SYN. *Masdevallia pulvinaris.*

S. puncta'tum. *fl.* greenish or greenish-yellow, heavily spotted purple-brown; lateral sep. with a yellowish ground colour; tail of dorsal sep. the longest, all tails short. *Scape* drooping. *l.* 3 to 5 in. long. Allied to *S. anchoriferum.* Colombia. (B.M. 7165 as *Masdevallia punctata.*)

S. swertiifo'lium. *fl.* yellowish, spotted brown and shaded purple, tails of lateral sep. bent downward, tail of dorsal sep. shorter, bent upward. *Scape* lateral, short, freely produced. *l.* 3 to 6 in. long, thin. New Granada. 1880. SYN. *Masdevallia swertiaefolia.*

E. C.

SCAPHYGLOT'TIS (*skaphe*, boat, *glotta*, tongue; the lip is hollowed). FAM. *Orchidaceae.* Boat-lip Orchid. A genus of about 20 species of epiphytic, branching Orchids, natives of Trop. America from Brazil to Mexico. Flowers small, twin, or few in a cluster, on short stalks; lateral sep. lengthened at base and often connate with the foot of the rather long, erect column; petals similar but smaller; lip narrow, continuous with the column but turned up parallel with it. Pollinia 4, cohering in pairs. Leaves narrow, sometimes linear, leathery. Stems slender, straggling. Pseudobulbs small, linear, or sharply fusiform. Treatment should be similar to Cattleya. Their straggling habit entails a raft so suspended that they can grow downwards if so inclined. They have little decorative value. SYN. Cladobium.

S. Kienast'ii. A synonym of *Hartwegia Kienastii.*

S. stella'ta. *fl.* nearly pellucid, usually solitary, larger than in *S. violacea*, segs. more spreading, side lobes of lip equalling mid-lobe. Demerara.

S. viola'cea. *fl.* violet, small; lateral sep. oblique, twice as wide as dorsal; lip white, often shaded rose, fleshy, channelled. *l.* 3 to 6 in. long, linear or linear-lanceolate, acute. Stems terete, striate, jointed. Demerara. (B.M. 4071; B.R. 1901.)

E. C.

scapi-, in compound words, signifying a scape (q.v.), as *scapigerus*, having a scape.

SCAR. The mark left on a stem after the fall of the leaf, or on a seed, &c., by its detachment. Such places are covered with a healing, usually corky, tissue.

SCARAB BEETLES. *See* **Dung Beetles.**

scar'dicus -a -um, of Mt. Scardus, Albania.

SCARES. Devices to frighten birds from fruit-trees, seeds, &c. Few are really effective if stationary as birds soon become accustomed to them. Apparatuses for causing explosions at intervals need to be moved from place to place after standing a short time. Seed-beds and small trees and low-growing plants can be protected by stretching threads of black cotton over and about them. This, being almost invisible, scares birds when their wings are entangled in it and they avoid the place in future.

SCARIOLE. An old name for Endive. *See* **Cichorium Endivia.**

scario'sus -a -um, thin, dry, shrivelled, membranous.

scarlati'nus -a -um, bright red.

SCARLET RUNNER. *See* **Beans** and **Phaseolus coccineus.**

scattered, irregularly disposed; not whorled, opposite or ternate.

scelera'tus -a -um, wicked, noxious.

SCELE'TIUM. Included in **Mesembryanthemum.**

SCELOCHI'LUS (*skelos*, leg; *cheilos*, lip; in allusion to the shape of the divided lip). FAM. *Orchidaceae.* A genus of about 10 species of epiphytic Orchids, natives of the Andes of S. America. Flowers rather small, stalked, in few-flowered racemes; sepals erect, connivent, dorsal concave, lateral connate forming a sac or spur; petals rather wider than dorsal sepal; lip continuous with base of column, long-clawed, erect, 3-lobed, mid-lobe short, broad, disk often a callous; spur short, more or less dilated, enclosed in the base of the lateral sepals; columns erect, semi-terete. Pollinia 2, sub-globose. Scapes from base of pseudobulbs, erect, simple or slightly branched; bracts narrow. Leaves leathery, not plicate. Stem finally thickened into a narrow pseudobulb. General cultivation, temperatures, &c., should be as for Comparettia.

S. carina'tus.* *fl.* about 7, raceme short, pendulous; sep. bright yellow, ¾ in. long; pet. purple and white, ½ in. long; lip white, ½ in. long, with purple blotch at base of reflexed mid-lobe. *l.* lanceolate, 4 in. long. Andes. 1895.

S. Otton'is. *fl.* yellow, purple-striped within, short-stalked, on a short round, thread-like, smooth spike a little longer than l. covered by sessile, dry, lanceolate, slender-pointed bracts. May. *l.* oblong, leathery, waved, very acute, recurved. Caracas. 1841.

S. sacca'tus. *fl.* small; lateral sep. connate, narrow, straw-coloured, pet. rose; lip rose, clawed; scape sometimes branched, 9 in. long or more. *Pseudobulbs* 1 in. h. *l.* 6 in. long, 1 in. wide. Peru, Brazil. 1863.

S. variega'tus. *fl.* whitish, lined purple. *l.* erect or spreading, narrow-lanceolate, 4 to 5 in. long. *Pseudobulbs* flat, very thin. Colombia. 1895.

E. C.

SCENTED ORCHIS. *See* **Gymnadenia conopsea.**

SCENTED POLYPODY. *See* **Polypodium pustulatum.**

SCENTED VERBENA. *See* **Lippia citriodora.**

sceptrum, the staff which is the symbol of government.

SCHAEFFER'IA (in honour of James Christian Schaeffer, 1718–90, German naturalist). FAM. *Celastraceae.* A genus of 2 rigid, glabrous shrubs, natives of SW. United States and W. Indies. Leaves alternate or clustered, small, leathery, entire, without stipules. Flowers small, axillary; sepals and petals 4. Fruit a drupe as large as a pea. Of no particular beauty it needs stove temperature and a compost of loam, peat, and sand.

S. frutes'cens. Crabwood, False Box. Shrub up to 10 ft. *l.* elliptic, veiny, about 1½ in. long. *fl.* white, clustered in l.-axils. August. *fr.* scarlet. W. Indies. 1793.

F. G. P.

Schaf'ta, native name of *Silene Schafta* in Talysh, on the Caspian Sea.

schangulen'sis -is -e, of Beni Schangel, Trop. E. Africa.

Scharff'ii, in honour of Carl Scharff, who collected, *c.* 1888, in the island of Santa Catherina, Brazil.

Scharlok'ii, in honour of Karl Julius Adolf Scharlok, 1809–99, apothecary and botanist in W. Prussia.

Scharoja'ni, in honour of Herr Scharojan who collected *Crocus Scharojani* in the Caucasus, *c.* 1865.

SCHAUER'IA (in honour of John Conrad Schauer, professor at Greifswald, 1813–48). FAM. *Acanthaceae.* A genus of about 8 species of Brazilian sub-shrubs closely related to Jacobinia but with equal, parallel, anther lobes. Leaves entire. Flowers in terminal thyrses or spikes; calyx lobes bristly or linear; corolla tube slender, scarcely widened upwards, 2-lipped; stamens 2, staminodes wanting. The species mentioned need greenhouse treatment and general cultivation as for Justicia.

S. calycot'richa. About 2 ft. h. *l.* broadly ovate, glabrous, long-stalked. *fl.* yellow, in a subspicate terminal thyrse; cor. tube slender, about 1½ in. long, downy, upper lip entire; cal. and slender bracts yellowish-green, downy. February. 1824. (H.E.F. 212 as *Justicia calycotricha.*)

S. flavico'ma. Closely related to *S. calycotricha* but with lanceolate, slender-pointed *l.* with short stalks, minutely downy, midrib and main veins pale green or whitish and *fl.* with whitish cal., glandular-hairy, and cor. smooth, upper lip notched. (B.R. 1027 as *Justicia flavicoma*; B.M. 2816 as *J. calycotricha*; L.B.C. 1921 as *J. callitricha.*)

SCHEEL'EA (in honour of Karl Wilhelm Scheele, 1742–86, Swedish chemist). FAM. *Palmaceae.* A genus of tall palms, natives of Cent. and S. America.

S. gomphococ'ca. Stem 20 to 30 ft. h. *l.* 6 to 9 ft. long; segs. very many, linear or linear-lanceolate, bright green above, paler beneath; stalk short, very fibrous at base. *Spadix* reflexed; spathe slender, woody. Costa Rica. SYN. *Attalea gomphococca.*

S. Martia'na. Stem 90 to 100 ft. h. *l.* erect-spreading, large. *Female fl.* solitary at ends of branches of spadix. *fr.* acute at both ends. Brazil. 1826. SYN. *Attalea excelsa.*

Scheer'i, in honour of Frederick Scheer, 1792?–1868, amateur botanist who resided at Kew, author of *Kew and its Garden*, 1840.

SCHEER'IA. Included in **Achimenes.**

Schef'feri, in honour of R. H. C. C. Scheffer, 1844–80, Dutch horticulturist and botanist in Java.

SCHEFF'LERA (in honour of J. C. Scheffler of Danzig). FAM. *Araliaceae.* A genus of about 150 species of tall shrubs or trees widely distributed in the tropics. Leaves alternate, digitate, compound. Flowers 5- or 6-merous, in large panicles, racemose or umbellate. For cultivation *see* **Aralia.**

S. digita'ta. Low tree, or shrub, smooth. *l.* digitate, 7- to 10-foliolate; lflets. oblong to broad-lanceolate, 3 to 6 in. long, thin, sharply toothed; stalks long. New Zealand. Greenhouse.

Schefflera polybotrya

S. polybot'rya. Slender, little-branched tall shrub, branches covered with hemispherical warts. *l.* digitate; lflets. 5 to 7, 6 to 8 in. long, oblong-ovate to obovate-oblong, with long, slender point, entire, rounded or wedge-shaped at base; stalk 5 to 8 in. long, slender, swollen at base and apex, warted in lower half. *fl.* small, green, racemes 12 in. or more long, covered with minute starry down at first. Winter. *fr.* globose, 5-celled, as large as a peppercorn. (B.M. 6238.) Java. 1860. SYN. *Heptapleurum polybotryum.* Stove.

S. venulo'sa. Small glabrous tree with strong branches, or climbing shrub. *lflets.* entire, slender-pointed. *fl.* greenish in compound panicles. India. Stove. SYN. *Heptapleurum venulosum.* var. **erythrostach'ys,** branches spreading, *l.* very large, long-stalked, lflets. broad, *fl.* deep red, very tiny, in a branched, terminal panicle. Trop. Asia. 1895. (B.M. 7402.) Stove.

S. vitien'sis. *l.* digitate; lflets. obovate-oblong, obtuse, narrowed to stalk, entire, veins spreading horizontally. *fl.* 3 to 7 in an umbel. Fiji. 1887. SYN. *Heptapleurum vitiense.* Stove.

F. G. P.

Scheideck'eri, in honour of Peter Scheidecker, nurseryman of Munich, d. 1890, who raised *Malus* × *Scheideckeri.*

SCHELHAM'MERA (in honour of G. C. Schelhammer, 1649–1716, professor at Jena). FAM. *Liliaceae.* A genus of 2 species of perennial herbs with fibrous roots, creeping rhizome, and simple or branched stems, natives of E. Australia. Leaves ovate or lanceolate. Flowers small, lilac or white, solitary at the ends of branches or in umbels sessile between the uppermost leaves; perianth segments free, equal; stamens 6, shorter than perianth segments. A warm border with a mixture of peat and loam suits these plants in summer but they need ample protection in winter, such as a frame at the base of a warm greenhouse wall would provide. Propagation by division.

S. multiflo'ra. 6 to 12 in. h. *l.* 1 to 2 in. long, firmer than in *S. undulata*, but narrower at base, entire. *fl.* white in a terminal umbel; pedicels $\frac{3}{4}$ to 1 in. long, sometimes bracteate. June. 1824. (L.B.C. 1511.)

S. undula'ta. Stems slender, ascending or erect, 6 in. h., branching at base. *l.* ovate-lanceolate, 1 to 2 in. long, minutely undulate at margins. *fl.* pale lilac, solitary or rarely twin at ends of branches; pedicels $\frac{1}{2}$ to 1 in. long, without bracts. 1824. (B.M. 2712.)

SCHELLOLE'PIS. Included in **Polypodium.**

Scherzeria'nus -a -um, in honour of M. Scherzer, 1821–1903, of Vienna, who discovered *Anthurium Scherzerianum* in Guatemala.

Scheuch'zeri, in honour of Jakob J. Scheuchzer, 1672–1733, and J. Scheuchzer, 1684–1738, both professors in Zurich, students of the flora of Switzerland.

SCHEUCHZERIA'CEAE. Monocotyledons. A family of 4 genera with about 14 species of marsh or water plants with narrow leaves and terminal spikes of flowers. Flowers perfect or 1-sexual, 1 or many, perianth segments all alike or absent; carpels 1, 6, or 8, each with 2 ovules (some sometimes sterile). They are plants of temperate regions and the family is sometimes called Juncaginaceae. The only genus of any horticultural interest is Triglochin.

Schiedea'nus -a -um, in honour of Christian J. W. Schiede, d. 1836 in Mexico, German traveller with Deppe in Mexico.

Schiffneria'nus -a -um, in honour of Viktor Schiffner, b. 1862, of Prague and Vienna, and writer on Hepaticae.

Schildia'nus -a -um, in honour of J. Schild, b. 1865, botanist of Vienna.

Schilleria'nus -a -um, in honour of Herr Schiller, consul in Hamburg, who grew over 1,400 Orchids.

SCHI'MA (said to be the Arabic name). FAM. *Theaceae.* A genus of about 6 species of trees or shrubs native of Trop. and E. Asia and the E. Indies. Leaves evergreen. Flowers showy; sepals 5, almost equal; petals 5, much larger than sepals, connate at base, much overlapping; stamens numerous. Peduncles 2-bracteolate, 1-flowered, usually erect, solitary in the leaf-axils or upper ones clustered on a short raceme. Most species need a warm house but *S. argentea* is hardy in sheltered places in S. England except in very severe winters. Peaty soil suits them best and they may be propagated by cuttings in sandy peat with bottom heat.

Schima argentea

S. argen'tea. Shrub of 4 to 6 ft. in cultivation, much taller in the wild; young shoots silky. *l.* narrowly elliptic-oblong to oblanceolate, 3 to 5 in. long, acute, entire, green and glabrous above, glaucous beneath. *fl.* creamy-white, 2 in. across; sep. almost round, $\frac{1}{10}$ in. long; pet. roundish-obovate, up to 1 in. long, partly silky without; solitary in upper l.-axils on a short peduncle. August, September. Szechwan, Yunnan, &c. 1928?. (B.M. 9558.)

S. khasia'na. Tree. *l.* ovate, 5 to 6 in. long, 2 to $3\frac{1}{2}$ in. wide, acute, strongly toothed, glabrous. *fl.* white, $2\frac{1}{2}$ in. across, silky-hairy without; peduncles stout, $\frac{3}{4}$ in. long, minutely warted; from axils of fallen l. Khasia Hills. (B.M. n.s. 143.)

S. Noron'hae. Compact shrub with terete branches. *l.* elliptic-lanceolate, slender-pointed, entire, narrowed to a short stalk. *fl.* white; sep. markedly concave; pet. obovate, spreading; peduncles solitary, shorter than l. Trop. Asia. 1849. (B.M. 4539 as *Gordonia javanica.*)

S. Wallich'ii. Tree of 80 to 100 ft. *l.* elliptic-oblong, 6 to 7 in. long, 2 to 3 in. wide, entire or slightly toothed, glabrous and reddish-veined above, netted and hairy beneath; stalk $\frac{1}{2}$ in. long, hairy. *fl.* white, $1\frac{1}{2}$ to 2 in. across, fragrant, hairy without; peduncle $\frac{3}{4}$ to 2 in. long, minutely warted, racemes short, terminal. Sikkim, Nepal, E. Indies.

Schimp'eri, in honour of (1) W. Schimper, 1804–78, German botanist who collected in Abyssinia, Egypt, &c.; (2) A. F. W. Schimper, 1856–1901, of Strasbourg, writer of Plant Geography and botanist-explorer.

SCHI'NUS (from *Schinos*, Greek name for *Pistacia Lentiscus*, the mastic tree, some species yielding similar resinous mastic-like juices). FAM. *Anacardiaceae.* A genus of about 16 species of dioecious trees with alternate leaves mostly pinnate, but simple in the section known as Duvaua. Flowers small, white or yellow, borne in terminal or axillary panicles; calyx 5-lobed, petals 5, stamens 10. Fruit a globose drupe. Nearly all the species are from sub-tropical S. America. *S. dependens* is fairly hardy, the remainder need greenhouse conditions. Propagation is by cuttings.

KEY

1. *Lvs. simple*	S. dependens
1. *Lvs. pinnate*	2
2. *Lvs. downy when young*	S. Molle
2. *Lvs. glabrous*	S. terebinthifolius

S. depend'ens. Evergreen shrub up to 15 ft., shoots stiff, often spine-tipped. *l.* obovate, $\frac{1}{2}$ to 1 in. long, rounded at apex, base tapered, very shortly stalked, usually entire. *fl.* $\frac{1}{8}$ in. wide, yellow, very numerous in short, axillary racemes. May. *fr.* densely clustered, deep purple, the size of a peppercorn. Chile. (B.R. 1573.) SYN. *Duvaua dependens.* var. **ova'tus,** *l.* smaller, ovate, toothed or even slightly lobed near the base. (B.M. 7406.) Both are fairly hardy but suffer in very severe winters.

S. Mol'le. Pepper Tree. Peruvian Mastic Tree. Evergreen tree 20 to 50 ft. of rounded shape with graceful pendulous branches. *l.* 5 to 9 in. long, pinnate; lflets. 1 to $2\frac{1}{2}$ in. long, linear-lanceolate, toothed, pointed, glabrous. *fl.* yellowish-white, $\frac{1}{8}$ in. wide, in panicles 1 to $2\frac{1}{2}$ in. long. April. *fr.* the size of small peas, rosy-red. S. America. (B.M. 3339.) Not hardy. Used as a street tree in S. Europe and much planted in California.

S. terebinthifo'lius. Evergreen tree up to 20 ft. or more, shoots and l. downy when young. *l.* pinnate, 4 to 7 in. long, rachis winged; lflets. variable in shape, oval-lanceolate, obovate, pointed or rounded at apex, toothed, 1 to 2 in. long. fl. in axillary and terminal panicles, 2 to 6 in. long. *fl.* small, white. *fr.* red, the size of peppercorns. S. America. Greenhouse.

W. J. B.

Schinzianus -a -um, Schinzii, in honour of Dr. Hans Schinz, 1858–1941, Director, Botanical Garden, Zurich.

schipkaensis -is -e, of the Schipka Pass, Bulgaria, Balkans.

SCHISAN'DRA. *See* **Schizandra.**

SCHISMATOGLOT'TIS (*schismatos*, deciduous, *glotta*, tongue; the limb of the spathe quickly falls). FAM. *Araceae.* A genus of about 15 species of stoloniferous herbs, natives of Malaya. Caudex short. Leaves oblong- or ovate-cordate, rarely hastate or lanceolate, often marbled or spotted; stalks sheathing at base. Spathe cylindrical, tube convolute, scarcely constricted at throat, blade apiculate or acuminate; spadix sessile, not appendiculate, included in spathe, constricted at or below middle, male inflorescence cylindrical or club-shaped; female shorter or narrower, cylindrical or conical; peduncles solitary or clustered, shorter than leaf-stalks. They need a humid atmosphere and stove conditions with abundance of water and shade. Rich, well-drained, fibrous peat, leaf-mould, and sandy loam suits them. Propagation by division.

S. aspera'ta albomacula'ta. *l.* cordate-oblong, shortly cuspidate, dark green above, with a broad, irregular, greyish band on each side of midrib, midway between it and the margin, or with greyish stripes between veins; stalks with crisped, transparent edges. *Spathe* green in persistent basal part, creamy-white and open above; infl. subsessile. Borneo. 1881. (B.M. 6576 as *S. crispata.*)

S. deco'ra. A synonym of *S. pulchra.*

S. latifo'lia. A synonym of *S. rupestris.*

S. Lavall'eei. *l.* bright green above, variegated with irregular, grey blotches, light green beneath. Borneo, Sumatra. (I.H. 28, 418.) var. **immacula'ta,** *l.* uniform, unspotted bright green above, vinous purple beneath and on stalks. Java. 1882. (I.H. as var. *Lansbergiana.*); **purpu'rea,** *l.* as in type above, deep vinous purple beneath and on stalks. Sumatra. 1882.

S. longispath'a. Erect, tufted, shortly rhizomatous. *l.* obliquely ovate, about 4 in. long, pale green with a feathered middle silver-grey band, through which the green midrib runs; stalk as long as or longer than blades. Borneo. 1881. (I.H. 466.)

S. neoguineen'sis. *l.* ovate, acute, deeply cordate, bright green above with very irregular pale yellow-green blotches; stalks 9 to 12 in. long, terete. *Spathe* pale greenish, tube narrowly ellipsoid, obscurely trigonal, 1 in. long, limb acuminate, 1½ in. long; infl. solitary in l.-axils; scapes 1½ to 3 in. long, inclosed in l.-sheaths. New Guinea. 1879. (I.H. 380 as *Colocasia neoguineensis.*) SYN. *S. variegata* of gardens.

S. pic'ta. *l.* cordate-ovate, cuspidate, with a feathered greyish band down middle; stalk as long as blade. *Spathe* tube obliquely ovoid-oblong, limb greenish-yellow, gaping, shortly cuspidate; male infl. pale sulphur. Java. 1864.

S. pul'chra.* *l.* obliquely oblong-acute, cordate, 4 to 5 in. long, up to 2½ in. wide, glaucous green above with irregular silver-green spots. Borneo. 1884. (I.H. 520.) SYN. *S. decora.*

S. rupes'tris. Caudex thick. *l.* ovate, acute, deeply cordate, lobes half-ovate; stalks longer than blade, sheathing about one-third of length, slightly terete. *Spathe* yellow, tube oblong-ovoid, limb scarcely opening; peduncles many. Java. 1882. SYN. *S. latifolia.*

S. siamen'sis. Small, of neat habit. *l.* ovate, acuminate, glossy green spotted white. Siam. 1884.

S. variega'ta.* Stemless. *l.* oblong-lanceolate, blunt at base, narrowed to long cusp at apex, dark green with a broad, silvery, middle band beneath; stalk half length of blades. Borneo. 1862.

SCHIST. Rock splitting into thin layers, crystalline.

schista'ceus -a -um, splitting.

schisto-, in compound words, signifying split.

SCHIVERECK'IA (in honour of S. B. Schivereck of Innsbruck, Professor at Lemberg, *c.* 1782–1805). FAM. *Cruciferae.* A genus of 2 species of dwarf perennial plants with rosettes of silvery leaves allied to Alyssum and sometimes included in that genus. Flowers white, petals glabrous, longer stamens winged, inner toothed. Fruit an oblong to ovate capsule with swollen valves and 8 to 10 seeds. Rock-garden plants for sunny spots in well-drained soil.

S. Doerfl'eri. About 2 in. h. *l.* silvery, with large stellate hairs in a rosette. *fl.* white, freely produced. Balkan Peninsula, Asia Minor.

S. podoli'ca. 5 or 7 in. h. *l.* silvery, in a rosette, lanceolate, margin 2-toothed. *fl.* white, in corymbs on leafy stems; pet. entire; pedicels short. Spring. E. Europe. SYN. *Alyssum podolicum.*

SCHIZAE'A (*schizo*, to split; fronds fan-shaped or dichotomously multifid). Comb or Rush Fern. FAM. *Schizaceae.* A genus of about 30 species of small ferns with somewhat rush-like fronds widely distributed over the world. Sporangia sessile in 2 or 4 rows on one side of close 2-ranked spikes which form fertile segments at the ends of the fronds. These ferns are somewhat difficult to grow but are well worth a little extra attention. Where they thrive under cultivation they are invariably grown in a compost of roughly broken peat and loam, in about equal parts, with ample drainage; for, although growing naturally in swampy places, under cultivation they greatly dislike stagnant water. Frequent and copious waterings at the roots are, however, necessary, as is a well-ventilated position.

S. bif'ida.* *sti.* dense, chestnut-brown, passing gradually into fronds, which are 6 to 18 in. long, forked generally below middle, sometimes forked again, rarely simple, very wiry and rush-like, with a prominent, scabrous midrib and 2 narrow, thick wings; fertile segs. sub-erect or recurved, unilateral, ½ to ⅜ in. long, with 12 to 20 erecto-patent spikes each side. Australia, New Zealand. 1822. Greenhouse.

S. dichot'oma. *sti.* 6 to 18 in. long, firm, erect, channelled on face above. *Fronds* fan-like, 6 to 9 in. each way, many times dichotomously forked, ultimate divisions with 1 fertile seg. each; rachis with 4 to 10 close-spreading spikes on each side. Asia, Australia, Polynesia, Madagascar. Stove.

S. digita'ta. *sti.* dense, 1 to 2 in. long, brownish, sub-terete, passing gradually into fronds 1 ft. or more long, 1/12 to ⅛ in. broad, flattened, midrib beneath prominent, crowned at apex with 6 to 15 sub-triquetrous, fertile spikes 1½ in. long. Asia, Polynesia. Stove. (H.G.F. 49.)

S. el'egans. *sti.* 6 to 12 in. long, firm, erect, naked. *Fronds* **V**-shaped, 4 to 8 in. each way, dichotomously forked or cleft, divisions varying greatly in number and breadth (½ to 2 in.); fertile segs. many, stalked, ¼ to ⅜ in. long, rachis often recurved, with 6 to 15 close-spreading, linear-cylindrical spikes each side. Trop. America. 1819. Stove. (H.G.F. 34.) var. **latifo'lia** is a form with broad fronds.

S. pen'nula. *sti.* dense, 1 to 2 in. long, brownish, passing gradually into fronds 1 ft. or more long, nearly 1/12 in. thick, triquetrous, with 3 sharp angles, crowned at apex with 6 to 12 sub-triquetrous, fertile spikes ½ to 1½ in. long, pilose beneath, with capsules usually in 4 rows. Trop. America. 1816. Stove.

S. pusil'la. *sti.* dense. *Barren fronds* much shorter than fertile, much twisted and slightly flattened. *Fertile fronds* 3 to 4 in. long, terete, wiry, very slender; fertile segs. sub-erect, ¼ in. long, unilateral, with about 6 rather stout, erecto-patent spikes each side, lowest ⅛ in. long. New Jersey, Nova Scotia, Newfoundland. (B.B. ed. 2, 1, 9.) Hardy in S. England.

S. rupes'tris.* *sti.* lax, about 1 in. long, sub-terete, passing gradually into grass-like, flattened fronds 3 to 4 in. long, 1/12 in. broad, with a slender midrib; fertile segs. pinnate, solitary, sub-erect, ¼ to ½ in. long, with 6 to 10 slender, spreading, serrate spikes each side. Australia. 1822. (H.G.F. 42.) Greenhouse.

SCHIZAEA'CEAE. A family of usually small ferns with little stem, of about 160 species in 4 genera, chiefly in Trop. America, but a few in cooler districts. Lygodium is a leaf-climber. The sporangia are borne (except in Mohria) on special pinnae, are sessile and usually without indusia; at their apex is a cap-like annulus, and they split lengthwise. All 4 genera are in cultivation; Aneimia, Lygodium, Mohria, Schizaea.

SCHIZAN'DRA (*schisio*, splitting, division, *andros*, male, in allusion to the cleft anthers). FAM. *Magnoliaceae.* A genus of about 24 species of more or less aromatic, deciduous, or evergreen climbing shrubs; stems twining. One is native of N. America, the others are Asiatic. Leaves alternate, mostly cuneate, stalks slender. Flowers dioecious, solitary or few in axillary clusters. Sepals and petals indistinguishable, 7 to 12; stamens 5 to 15. In the female flowers the carpels are densely packed in a head, but as they ripen that part to which they are attached elongates very remarkably and the carpels develop into a large number of berries ultimately forming a spike several inches long. For a monograph *see* A. C. Smith in *Sargentia*, 7, 1947.

All the species here noticed except *S. coccinea*, the one American representative, are hardy, at any rate on walls. The fruits are sometimes more ornamental than the flowers. Propagated by seed or cuttings.

S. chinen'sis. Deciduous 1-sexual climber, 20 to 30ft., glabrous. *l.* 2 to 4 in. long, obovate to oval, cuneate, short-pointed, remotely toothed, glabrous except on young veins. *fl.* ½ in. across, pale rose, fragrant, each pendulous on a stalk 1 in. long; sep. and pet. 9 (together), stamens 5. April, May. *fr.* scarlet, berries ¼ in. wide on a close spike up to 4 in. long. China. 1860. (G.C. 50 (1919), 2.)

S. coccin'ea. Slender twining shrub, 10 to 15 ft. *l.* oval or ovate, 2 to 5 in. long, short-pointed, mostly cuneate, indistinctly toothed, glabrous or nearly so; stalk 1 to $2\frac{1}{2}$ in. long. *fl.* crimson, $\frac{1}{2}$ to $\frac{3}{4}$ in. long; stalk very slender, up to 2 in. long. June. *fr.* spike 2 to 3 in. long; berries oval, $\frac{2}{5}$ in. long, red. SE. United States. 1806. (B.M. 1413.) Cool greenhouse. Perhaps not now in cultivation.

S. glauces'cens. Deciduous climber, 20 ft., shoots much warted, glabrous. *l.* obovate, 2 to 4 in. long, $\frac{3}{4}$ to 2 in. wide, glabrous, glaucous beneath, faintly toothed, shortly pointed, much tapered at the base; stalk $\frac{1}{2}$ to $1\frac{1}{2}$ in. long. *fl.* orange-red, on slender stalks 2 in. long. May, June. *fr.* spikes scarlet, 2 to 4 in. long. China. 1907.

S. Hen'ryi.* Deciduous, glabrous climber, shoots triangular, winged. *l.* 3 to 5 in. long, oval, ovate, cordate or cuneate, sparsely toothed, shining green above, glaucous beneath; stalk red. *fl.* $\frac{1}{2}$ in. wide, 1-sexual, white, on slender stalks 2 to 3 in. long. April, May. *fr.* spikes 2 to 3 in. long, berries red. China. 1900.

S. nig'ra. A synonym of *S. repanda.*

S. propin'qua. Deciduous climber up to 30 ft., shoots angled. *l.* narrowly oval, ovate-lanceolate, 3 to 5 in. long, $\frac{3}{4}$ to $1\frac{1}{2}$ in. wide, cuneate to almost rounded at base, apex slenderly pointed, sparsely toothed or entire. *fl.* orange, $\frac{3}{5}$ in. wide, on axillary stalks $\frac{1}{4}$ to $\frac{1}{2}$ in. long. June. *fr.* clusters scarlet. Himalaya, Malaya. 1828. (B.M. 4614 as *Sphaerostema propinquum.*) var. **sinen'sis,** *l.* more slender, *fl.* smaller, yellowish. Both are distinct by the very short fl.-stalk. China. 1907. Hardier than type.

S. pubes'cens. Deciduous climber; shoots angular, downy at first. *l.* ovate to orbicular and obovate, 2 to 5 in. long, $1\frac{1}{2}$ to $2\frac{1}{2}$ in. wide, sparsely toothed, cuneate, shortly pointed, downy beneath. *fl.* creamy-yellow, $\frac{1}{2}$ in. wide, on slender stalks $1\frac{1}{2}$ in. long. *fr.* clusters orange, pendulous, 2 to 4 in. long. China. 1907. Distinct by its downiness.

S. repan'da. Vigorous climber, shoots brown. *l.* broadly ovate, obovate, or oval, 2 to 3 in. long, cuneate, short-pointed; stalk up to $1\frac{1}{2}$ in. long. *fl.* white, $\frac{3}{5}$ in. wide, stalk up to 1 in. long. May, June. *fr.* black, with a glaucous bloom; berries $\frac{3}{5}$ in. wide on stalks 2 to 4 in. long. Japan, Korea. 1892. Distinct by its black fr. SYN. *S. nigra.*

S. rubriflo'ra.* Deciduous climber, 16 to 20 ft., shoots slender, reddish, glabrous. *l.* obovate to oblanceolate, $2\frac{1}{2}$ to 5 in. long, toothed, cuneate, slender-pointed, glabrous. *fl.* solitary, axillary, 1 in. wide, pendulous on a red stalk 1 to 2 in. long, sep. and pet. 7, deep crimson. April, May. *fr.* spikes composed of closely packed, globose, red berries on a stalk 2 to 5 in. long. China. 1908. (B.M. 9146.) SYN. *S. grandiflora rubrifolia.*

S. sinen'sis. *See* **S. propinqua.**

Schizandra sphenandra

S. sphenan'dra. Deciduous climber up to 16 ft., glabrous; shoots reddish-brown. *l.* 2 to 4 in. long, obovate to oval or roundish, cuneate, distantly toothed; stalk slender, $\frac{3}{4}$ to $1\frac{1}{2}$ in. long. *fl.* 1-sexual, solitary, $\frac{3}{4}$ in. wide, axillary, pendulous on stalks 1 to 2 in. long, sep. and pet. 6 to 9, orange, concave; stamens numerous. April, May. *fr.* spikes 2 to 3 in. long, berries scarlet, globose, $\frac{1}{4}$ in. wide, terminating a stalk 4 to 8 in. long. China. 1907. (B.M. 8921.)

W. J. B.

SCHIZAN'THUS (*schizo*, to cut, *anthos*, flower; referring to the deeply cut corolla). FAM. *Solanaceae.* A genus of about 11 species of showy, erect, more or less sticky annual herbs, natives of Chile. Leaves often pinnatisect, segments entire or toothed. Flowers variously coloured; calyx deeply 5-cleft; corolla tube short or long, cylindrical; limb spreading, oblique, plicate, somewhat 2-lipped, overlapping, deeply cut, perfect stamens 2; cymes terminal. Fruit a many-seeded capsule. These free-flowering annuals are excellent border plants for summer-flowering in the open and for pot cultivation for flowering indoors in early spring. The half-hardy species should be sown in a little heat in spring and afterwards planted out; or in autumn and kept in a cool house or pit through the winter. *S. pinnatus* and its varieties are hardy and may be sown in the open ground in March or April. For flowering in pots in spring seed should be sown in August or September and the plants grown on singly in a frame or house where frost is excluded. They may be grown in 7- or 8-in. pots during early spring. They are the better for a rich soil as soon as the plants are large enough to profit by it and a rich soil is best from outdoors as well. For the plants in pots thin stakes should be provided. Seed is formed in considerable quantity.

Foot rot (q.v.) may attack the plants or root rot due to the fungus *Corticium solani.* Stem rot caused by *Sclerotinia sclerotiorum* also occasionally occurs. Powdery mildew due to an unnamed species of Oidium which sometimes attacks the leaves can be controlled by sulphur vaporization or dusting together with adequate ventilation. Leafy gall (q.v.) also attacks them as does the virus disease, spotted wilt. In Schizanthus this virus causes marked wilting of the topmost leaves with bronzing and browning followed by death.

S. Gra'hami. About 2 ft. h. *l.* once or twice pinnatisect; segs. entire or pinnatifidly toothed. *fl.* large, lilac or rose, upper lip yellow tipped lilac; tube as long as cal.; middle seg. of lower lip without a notch; stamens shortly exserted. June to October. 1831. (B.M. 3044; F.d.S. 712.) Several colour forms have been offered from time to time but they are scarcely distinguished now.

S. pinna'tus.* About 2 ft. h. *l.* once or twice pinnatifid, segs. entire, toothed or somewhat pinnatifid. *fl.* large, of various colours; upper lip often violet or lilac, the middle seg. hooded, 2-lobed; lower lip pale, middle seg. more or less yellowish spotted with purple or violet, notched, side lobes 4-lobed; cor. tube shorter than cal.; stamens long exserted. June to October. 1822. (B.M. 2404.) A very variable species of which many forms have received garden names. The race named *hybridus grandiflorus* or *grandiflorus* belongs here and fine strains varying in height and size of flower as well as colour-range have been selected. *See* Supplement.

S. retu'sus.* About 2 ft. h. *l.* pinnatisect, segs. variously cut or entire. *fl.* deep rose, middle seg. of upper lip orange except at tip, middle seg. of lower lip notched, lateral segs. falcate, acute, linear, longer than middle seg.; tube about as long as cal.; stamens shortly exserted. 1831. (B.M. 3045.) Of this also several colour forms have been offered but except var. **al'bus** with white *fl.* are not now usually distinguished.

S. × wisetonen'sis* (*S. Grahami* × *S. pinnatus*). Intermediate between parents. *fl.* resembling *S. Grahami* in form and of varying colours from white to reddish-brown with yellow on the middle lobe of the upper lip. Of garden origin. 1900.

schizo-, in compound words, signifying cut, or divided, as *schizochilus*, having a divided lip.

SCHIZOBA'SIS (*schizo*, to cut, *basis*, base; the withered perianth is pushed off by the swelling fruit by splitting at its base). FAM. *Liliaceae.* A genus of 5 species of bulbous plants, natives of Trop. and S. Africa. Stem leafless, slender, branched. Leaves radical, few, early, linear, rather thick, withering before flowering. Flowers small, in racemes or scattered at ends of branches; perianth marcescent, persistent, segments equal, spreading; stamens 6. Greenhouse or stove conditions and full sunshine are required. Light loam is the best soil. Increase by seeds or offsets.

S. intrica'ta. *l.* 4 to 10, awl-shaped, erect, fleshy, glabrous, 2 to 3 in. long. *fl.* white with a green dorsal rib; racemes finally very loose, $1\frac{1}{2}$ to 2 in. long; panicle 2 to 6 in. long and wide, its branches ascending; scape firm, slender, 2 to 6 in. long. S. Africa. 1875. Greenhouse.

SCHIZOCARP. A fruit which splits into 1-seeded pieces, as in many Malvaceae.

SCHIZOCA'SIA (*schizo*, to cut or split, *Casia*; in allusion to the divided leaves and its relation to Colocasia). FAM. *Araceae*. A genus of 4 species of erect herbs natives of the E. Indies. Leaves pinnatipartite, veins netted. Peduncle short with linear-lanceolate rolled scale-leaves. Spathe tube rolled, blade about 3 times as long as tube. Nearly allied to Alocasia, differing mainly in the form of the leaves, and in the form of the ovule. Treatment as for Alocasia.

S. Port'ei. Stem thick, finally rather tall. *l.* oblong-triangular, base sagittate, 12 to 20 in. long, deeply pinnatipartite, lobes usually oblong, obtuse; stalks about half as long again as blade. *Peduncle* slender, 4 to 7 in. long. *Spathe* tube ovoid-globose, about 1 in. long, blade oblong-lanceolate, slender-pointed, about 2 in. long. New Guinea. 1862.

S. Regnier'i. Showy and robust. *l.* narrowly ovate-lanceolate, base sagittate, 10 to 20 in. long, deeply pinnatifid, lobes ovate-lanceolate, obtuse, margins repand, thinly leathery, dark green above, midrib and main veins paler, greyish beneath; stalk 16 to 24 in. long, pale green or yellowish, marked with irregular rose or dull-purple spots. *fl.* unknown. Siam. (I.H. 1887, 6.)

SCHIZOCEN'TRON (*schizo*, to cut, *kentron*, spur; from the form of the flower). FAM. *Melastomataceae*. A genus of a single herbaceous plant, native of Mexico, needing a warm house. Compost of fibrous loam, peat, and sand. Propagated by rooted pieces or by seeds. Characters as below.

Schizocentron elegans

S. el'egans.* Creeping, forming a dense mat, stem rooting at nodes. Branches terete or nearly so, reddish, somewhat hairy, hairs appressed. *l.* ovate, obtuse, stalked, small. *fl.* deep purple, about 1 in. across, terminal on slender peduncles about ¾ in. long. *fr.* hairy. Mexico. 1902. SYN. *Heeria elegans, Heterocentron elegans.*

SCHIZOCO'DON (*schizo*, cut, *kodon*, bell; the bell-shaped corolla is fringed). FAM. *Diapensiaceae*. A genus of 1 species of perennial herb, closely related to Shortia, but with the flowers in a raceme, fringed corolla lobes and 4 filaments of varying length. Natives of Japan. These beautiful plants are somewhat exacting in their requirements and like Shortias resent root disturbance. On the whole the conditions suiting *Shortia galacifolia* are those required by the Schizocodons. Well-drained sandy loam and peat, in a cool, moist, but not wet position. In the drier parts of the country a somewhat shady position is best and even one quite shaded, but for the full development of the crimson autumn colouring of the leaves more exposure is necessary. Propagation by seed.

S. ilicifo'lius. A variety of *S. soldanelloides.*

S. macrophyl'lus. A synonym of *S. soldanelloides magnus.*

S. soldanelloi'des.* Mat-forming, 2 to 4 in. h. *l.* small, evergreen, ovate or orbicular, wedge-shaped or somewhat cordate at base, toothed. *fl.* deep rose in centre shading to blush-white or white, open bell-shaped, 1 in. across, pet. fringed; racemes 4- to 6-fld. March, April. 1892. (B.M. 7316.) var. **alpi'nus,** *l.* smaller, plant more compact; **ilicifo'lius,** l. smaller, teeth more holly-like and fewer; **mag'nus,** *l.* larger, margin crenate-diatate, teeth small, numerous, *fl.* rose-pink. (B.M. n.s. 110.)

SCHIZOLO'BIUM (*schizo*, cut, *lobos*, lobe). FAM. *Leguminosae*. A genus of possibly 2 species of tall evergreen trees, one a native of Brazil, the other of Panama. Leaves 2-pinnate, large, leaflets numerous, small. Flowers in racemes; calyx segments overlapping, reflexed; petals 5, clawed, ovate or rounded; stamens 10, free; racemes axillary or forming a terminal panicle; bracts small. Pods 1-seeded. Treatment as for Caesalpinia.

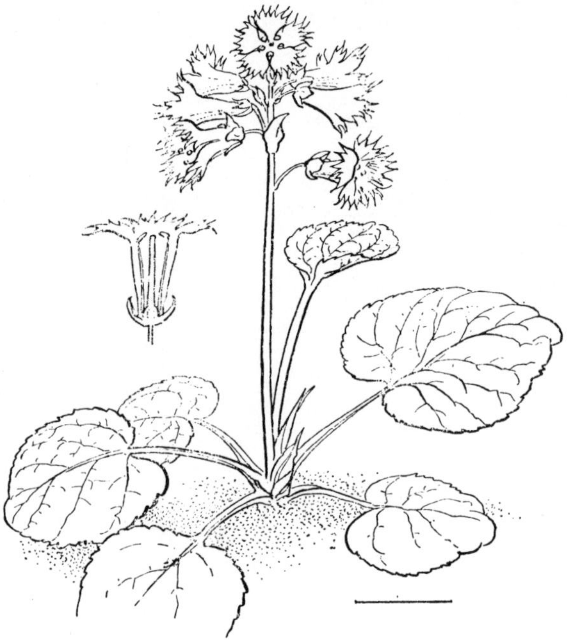

Schizocodon soldanelloides magnus

S. excel'sum. Tree of 120 ft. h. in nature. Pinnae in 18 pairs, 2 in. long, each with 20 pairs of lflets., oblong, white beneath, golden-hairy on middle nerve; common stalk 2 ft. long, glabrous. *fl.* yellow; pedicels appressed-hairy. Brazil. 1874.

SCHIZOLO'MA (*schizo*, cut, *loma*, margin; sori as in a slit in the margin of the frond). FAM. *Polypodiaceae*. A genus of 24 species of ferns related to Lindsaya but with opaque equilateral pinnae. Fronds entire or simply pinnate. For treatment *see* **Lindsaya.**

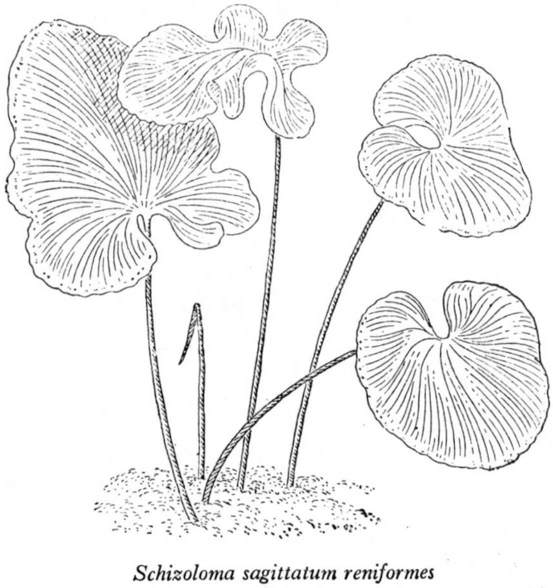

Schizoloma sagittatum reniformes

S. diver'gens. *rhiz.* creeping, wiry, fibrillose. *sti.* wiry, erect, 4 to 6 in. long, 1½ to 2 in. broad, simply pinnate; pinnae ⅜ to 1 in. long, 2 to 3 lines broad, obliquely truncate at the base below, auricled at the base above, margin entire, point bluntish. *Sori* in a continuous line along both edges. Malaya. (F.B.I. 250.) SYN. *Isoloma divergens, Lindsaya divergens.*

S. ensifo'lium. *rhiz.* creeping, stout, scaly. *sti.* 6 to 9 in. long, wiry, flexuose. *Fronds* 6 to 12 in. long, 3 to 4 in. broad, with a linear-lanceolate, simple or pinnatifid point, simply pinnate below; pinnae usually in numerous pairs, all stalked, 1½ to 6 in. long, ¼ to 1 in. broad, linear-acuminate to lanceolate, sterile a little toothed. *Sori* in a continuous marginal line. Hong Kong, Himalaya, &c. SYN. *Lindsaya ensifolia.* (H.G.F. 62; F.S.A. (2) 39.)

S. heterophyl'lum. *rhiz.* short-creeping. *sti.* 4 to 8 in. long, firm, naked, erect. *Fronds* 6 to 12 in. long, 3 to 6 in. broad, lanceolate or oblong-deltoid, varying from simply pinnate with large, linear-lanceolate, entire pinnae, to bipinnate with erecto-patent branches, 3 to 4 in. long, with oblong-lanceolate blunt pinnules, ½ to 1 in. long, ¼ in. broad. *Sori* in continuous marginal lines. S. India to Malaya. (F.S.I. 26.) SYN. *Lindsaya heterophyllum.*

S. sagitta'tum. *sti.* wiry, flexuose, 4 to 6 in. long, black, polished. *Fronds* sagittate-acuminate, with a deep basal sinus, 2 to 4 in. across, sometimes lobed. *Sori* continuous. Guadeloupe, French Guiana. (B.C.F. 2, 366.) SYN. *Lindsaya reniformis, Isoloma reniforme.*

SCHIZOME'RIA (*schizo*, cut, *meris*, a part; alluding to the cut petals). FAM. *Cunoniaceae.* A genus of 4 or 5 species, natives of Australia, New Guinea, &c. Leaves opposite, simple; petals small, toothed; stamens 10. *S. ovata* is a plant for the cool greenhouse, needing a compost of loam, sand, and peat. It can be propagated by cuttings.

S. ova'ta. Evergreen tree up to 50 or occasionally 80 ft. *l.* elliptical, tapered to both ends or ovate, 3 to 4 (sometimes over 6) in. long, margin shallowly toothed or merely wavy, leathery, glabrous; stalk ½ to 1 in. long. *fl.* white, ⅛ in. wide, in stalked cymes 2 to 3 in. long; cal. 5-lobed, pet. 5. *fr.* an ovoid or globose, translucent, white drupe, ½ in. long. New S. Wales, Queensland. 1825.

W. J. B.

SCHIZOMYCE'TES. *See* **Bacteria.**

SCHIZOPET'ALON (*schizo*, cut, *petalon*, a petal; the petals are lobed). FAM. *Cruciferae.* A genus of about 10 species of annual herbs, natives of Chile. Erect, slightly branched with alternate sinuate-toothed or pinnatifid leaves. Flowers purple or white in terminal, leafy racemes; sepals erect, petals clawed, pinnately lobed, aestivation involute. *S. Walkeri* is a half-hardy annual rather difficult to transplant, but otherwise needs treatment like plants of similar habit. It may be grown in pots and flowered in an airy greenhouse or planted out.

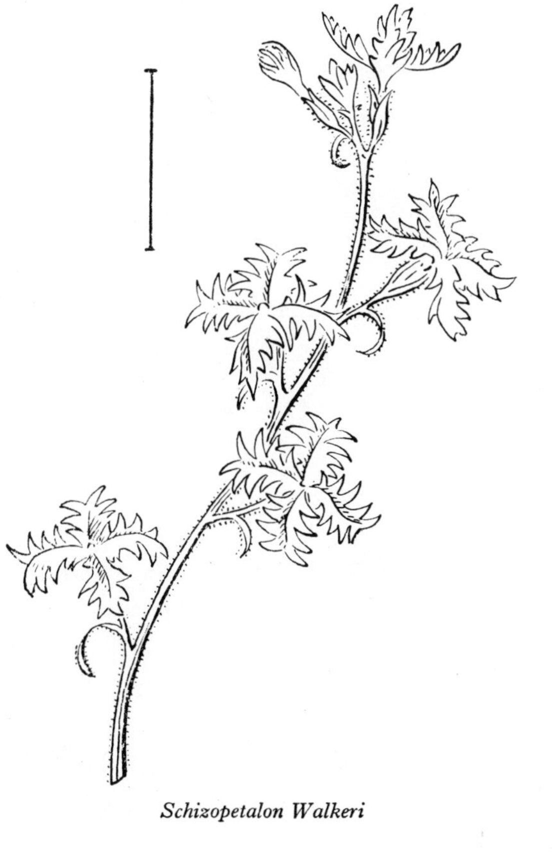

Schizopetalon Walkeri

S. Walk'eri. About 18 in. h., covered with branched down. *l.* sinuately pinnatifid. *fl.* white, in long racemes; bracts linear. May to August. Chile. 1821. (B.M. 2379; B.R. 752; S.B.F.G. 2, 387.)

SCHIZOPHRAG'MA (*schizo*, cut, *phragma*, to break; referring to parts of the vase-shaped fruits falling away and leaving them skeletonized). FAM. *Saxifragaceae.* Three species of deciduous climbers supporting their stems by aerial roots like the ivy, 2 from China, 1 from Japan. Leaves opposite, long-stalked. Flowers small, white, in flat cymes each section of the inflorescence developing 1 large stalked bract (really an enlarged sepal), white and 1½ to 3 in. long, giving the cyme its chief beauty and distinction. Akin to Hydrangea, whose sterile, bract-like flowers are distinct by having 4 or 5 sepals.

The 2 following species are easily grown. They require support similar to that given to ivy, i.e. walls, tree-trunks, &c. Easily propagated by cuttings of half-ripened shoots with a heel in July in a warm frame, or layers.

S. hydrangeoi'des. Deciduous climber up to 40 ft. *l.* 3 to 5 in. long, broadly ovate, coarsely toothed, nearly glabrous; stalk 1 to 2 in. long. *fl.* small, yellowish-white, in flattish cymes 6 to 8 in. across. Bracts ovate to cordate, yellowish-white, 1 to 1½ in. long. July. Japan. 1879. (B.M. 8520.) Easily distinguished from *integrifolia* by its coarsely toothed l.

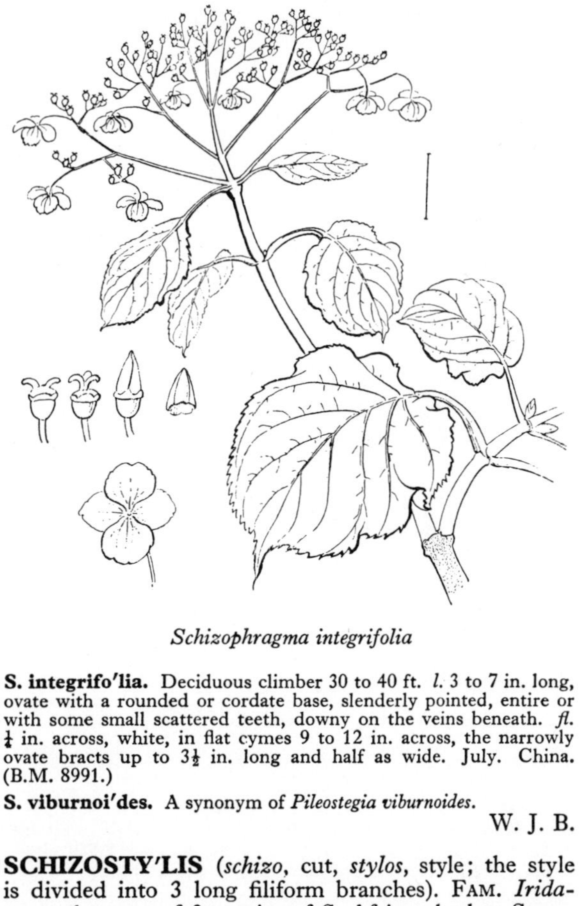

Schizophragma integrifolia

S. integrifo'lia. Deciduous climber 30 to 40 ft. *l.* 3 to 7 in. long, ovate with a rounded or cordate base, slenderly pointed, entire or with some small scattered teeth, downy on the veins beneath. *fl.* ¼ in. across, white, in flat cymes 9 to 12 in. across, the narrowly ovate bracts up to 3½ in. long and half as wide. July. China. (B.M. 8991.)

S. viburnoi'des. A synonym of *Pileostegia viburnoides.*

W. J. B.

SCHIZOSTY'LIS (*schizo*, cut, *stylos*, style; the style is divided into 3 long filiform branches). FAM. *Iridaceae.* A genus of 2 species of S. African herbs. Stems clustered, erect, from a rhizome, without a bulb or slightly bulbous at base. Leaves linear or narrow-ensiform. Flowers scattered on a simple peduncle, sessile in a spathe, red, showy; perianth tube slender, much enlarged at throat, lobes equal, oblong or ovate, spreading; stamens affixed to throat. *S. coccinea* flowers freely in a warm, sunny border, especially one at the front of a glass-house. The flowers last well. It is also useful for pot cultivation, the flowers coming to perfection in a glass-house and very useful for cutting. Propagation by dividing the clumps, leaving 4 to 6 shoots to each division, in spring. The divisions should be planted in good soil about 9 in. apart. Sandy loam and peat or leaf-soil make a good compost.

Schizostylis coccinea

S. coccin'ea. Crimson Flag; Kaffir Lily. About 3 ft. h. *l.* long, sheathing, sword-shaped, keeled, the longest at the base. *fl.* 10 to 14 in a distichous spike; perianth tube shorter than spathe, limb 2 in. across, of 6 uniform, spreading, acute, scarlet segs.; anthers yellow. October, November. 1864. (B.M. 5422; F.d.S. 1637.) Hardy in warm positions. **Viscountess Byng,** fl. pink, a good variety.

Schkuh'rii, in honour of Christian Schkuhr, 1741–1811, German botanist.

Schlechtenda'lii, in honour of (1) D. F. K. von Schlechtendal, 1767–1842, of Xanten, (2) D. F. L. von Schlechtendal, 1794–1866, Professor of Botany at Halle.

Schlecht'eri, in honour of F. R. Rudolf Schlechter, 1872–1925, of Berlin, authority on orchids.

Schleha'nii, in honour of Gustav Schlehan.

Schleich'eri, in honour of J. Christian Schleicher, 1768–1834, student of Swiss flora.

Schlei'denii, in honour of M. J. Schleiden, 1804–81, German botanist.

Schleinit'zii, in honour of G. E. G. von Schleinitz, 1834–1910, of the German navy, travelled in New Guinea.

SCHLIM'MIA (in honour of M. Schlimm, one of Linden's collectors, *c.* 1848). FAM. *Orchidaceae.* A genus of 3 closely related species of Orchids, natives of the Andes of Colombia. Epiphytes. Flowers rather large, fleshy, few in a raceme, shortly stalked; dorsal sepal free, concave, carinate; lateral very broad, saccate at base, connate with foot of the erect column; petals narrower, spreading at apex; lip variously lobed, apex reclining on foot of column; pollen masses 2. Bracts oblong. Scapes erect, recurved, simple, few-sheathed. Leaf leathery, narrowed to the stalk. Pseudobulbs oblong, somewhat fusiform, 1-leaved. The species should be grown in well-drained pots in the Cattleya house; compost and treatment as for Stanhopea, but water will be needed more frequently in winter.

S. jasminodo'ra.* *fl.* white and very fragrant; dorsal sep. linear, erect; pet. reflexed; lip fleshy, shorter than column and articulated with it, with 3 knobs near foot of column, another in middle, and a fifth, concave at the tip, which is prolonged into a thin, trowel-shaped limb; scape 1 ft. h. with 3 secund fl. *Pseudobulbs* long and slender. *l.* oval, long-stalked. Colombia. 1852.

S. trif'ida.* *fl.* with a scent between those of Jessamine and Bergamot; dorsal sep. declined; lateral waxy-white with a few purple spots inside, forming a helmet; pet. linear, acute, bent outwards; lip with a pandurate hypochil, 3-fid at tip, marked rich orange; scape lateral, drooping, deep purple, bearing a 1-sided raceme with about 4 fl. *Pseudobulbs* elongate-ovate, clustered, about 1 in. long. *l.* oblong, acute, 4 to 6 in. long. Colombia. 1877.

E. C.

Schlippenbach'ii, in honour of Baron Schlippenbach who collected in Russian Manchuria, *c.* 1854.

Schlos'seri, in honour of Josef Calasanz Schlosser, Ritter von Klekovski, 1808–82, student of the flora of Croatia, &c.

SCHLUMBERG'ERA (in honour of Frederick Schlumberger, an amateur student of plants). FAM. *Cactaceae.* Similar in habit to Zygocactus, with short joints but without the terminal bristles. Flowers purple to scarlet, regular, with a short, straight tube. Fruit hard. The plants are epiphytic and may be grown on their own roots or grafted (*see* **Cactus**). **A**

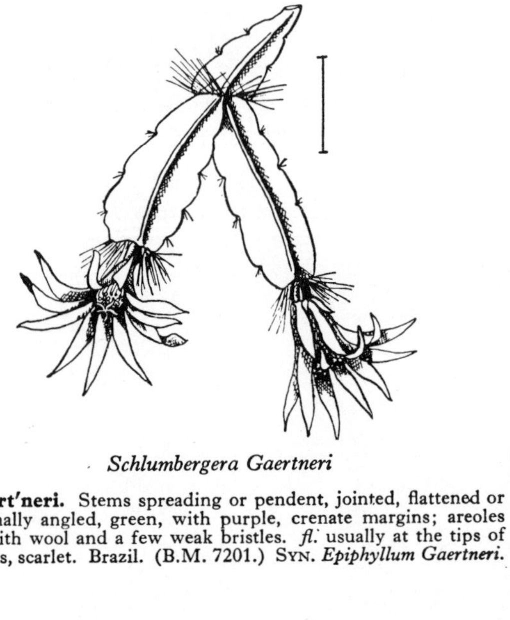

Schlumbergera Gaertneri

S. Gaert'neri. Stems spreading or pendent, jointed, flattened or occasionally angled, green, with purple, crenate margins; areoles small with wool and a few weak bristles. *fl.* usually at the tips of branches, scarlet. Brazil. (B.M. 7201.) SYN. *Epiphyllum Gaertneri.*

S. Russellia'na. Stems pendent or erect, jointed; old joints cylindrical, young ones flat, thin, serrate; areoles may bear weak spines. *fl.* terminal, reddish-purple. Brazil. (B.M. 3717.) SYN. *Epiphyllum Russellianum.*

V. H.

Schnei'deri, in honour of (1) Gustav Schneider, b. 1867, zoologist and Conservator of Zoology at Basle; (2) C. K. Schneider, 1876–1951, botanist and garden architect in Berlin.

schoen-, in compound words, signifying rush-like.

SCHOENORCH'IS. Included in **Saccolabium.**

schola'ris -is -e, of a school.

SCHOMBOCATT'LEYA. FAM. *Orchidaceae.* Hybrids between species of Cattleya and Schomburgkia including Myrmecophila.

SCHOMBOLAE'LIA. FAM. *Orchidaceae.* Hybrids between species of Laelia and Schomburgkia including Myrmecophila.

SCHOMBOLAELIOCATT'LEYA. FAM. *Orchidaceae.* The correct name for these trigeneric hybrids is now Lyonarci and includes species of Cattleya, Laelia and Schomburgkia.

SCHOMBURG'KIA (in honour of Sir Robert Hermann Schomburgk, 1804–65, traveller in Guiana and other parts of S. America, discoverer of *Victoria regia*). FAM. *Orchidaceae.* A genus of about 10 species in Trop. America. Originally about double the number were included, but those with hollow pseudobulbs are now separated (*see* **Myrmecophila**). Readily distinguished by their solid, more or less fusiform pseudobulbs, bearing 2 large, more or less elliptic-oblong leaves, and terminating in unbranched scapes often several feet long. Flowers numerous, somewhat aggregated at end of the scape into usually elongated heads, the segments rather narrow with numerous keels on the disk of the rather small lip. Pollen masses 8. Bracts rather long and narrow. The genus is closely allied to Laelia (*S. superbiens* is better known as a Laelia). In Schomburgkia the lip usually approaches that of the Labiata group of Cattleyas in shape, but is much smaller. *S. superbiens* and most of the other species attain considerable size apart from the long scapes, so that a large or moderately large house is required. Compost, temperatures, &c., as for Cattleyas. A rather decided rest should be given in winter when the plants are dormant. Difficulty is sometimes experienced in flowering the species. Exposure to light in autumn is required, and though old stale compost should be removed and new inserted when necessary, repotting should not be attempted until the plants have completely outgrown their pots. At least 1, sometimes 2, pseudobulbs, particularly in *S. superbiens*, should be allowed to project over the pot rim. Propagation can be effected as suggested for Cattleyas.

S. carina'ta. A synonym of *S. Lyonsii.*

S. chionodox'a. A synonym of *Myrmecophila chionodoxa.*

S. crisp'a. *fl.* 2 in. or more across; sep. and pet. narrow-oblong, brown, margins yellow, wavy; lip whitish or shaded rose, ovate-oblong, obtuse, slightly 3-lobed; raceme broad, crowded, pedicels long, whitish or rose-flushed, peduncle 3 to 4 ft. long. Winter. *Pseudobulbs* fusiform, 1 ft. h. *l.* 2, 8 to 10 in. long, oblong-lanceolate. Demerara. 1844. Best in a pot or basket. Fl. sometimes wholly dull brick-red. (B.R. 30, 23.)

S. Galeottia'na. A synonym of *Myrmecophila Galeottiana.*

S. grandiflo'ra. Probably a variety of *Myrmecophila tibicinis.*

S. Humboldt'ii. A synonym of *Myrmecophila Humboldtii.*

S. lepidis'sima. A synonym of *Myrmecophila lepidissima.*

S. Lueddemann'ii. Allied to *S. crispa.* *fl.* 12 to 20, about 3 in. across; sep. and pet. brown or brown-red with darker margins, lanceolate; lip rose-red with 3 bright yellow keels on disk. *Pseudobulbs* clavate, 8 to 10 in. h. *l.* rounded at tip. Venezuela. (B.M. 8427.)

4561.4

S. Lyon'sii.* *fl.* 10 to 15 on long pedicels, 1½ to 2 in. across; sep. and pet. white, spotted and transversely barred purple, ovate, obtuse, crisped; lip white, edged yellow, scarcely spotted, acute; raceme broad, many-fld.; scape 3 to 4 ft. long. August. *Pseudobulbs* about 1 ft. h. *l.* 9 to 12 in. long, narrow-oblong. Jamaica. 1853. (B.M. 5172.) SYN. *S. carinata.* Variable.

S. margina'ta.* Sep. and pet. dull brick-red, oblong, spreading, undulate at margin which is sometimes yellow; lip white, tinged pink, yellow at base, oblong-ovate, less waved than sep.; raceme or corymb broad; peduncle 1 to 1½ ft. long. *Pseudobulbs* oblong, furrowed, stalked, sheathed with brown scales, 2- or 3-leaved. *l.* large, oblong-lanceolate, leathery. Surinam. 1838. var. **immargina'ta,** *fl.* without yellow margin. 1887. (B.M. 3729.)

S. ro'sea.* *fl.* smaller than in *S. undulata*; sep. and pet. reddish-purple, margins wavy; lip rose-purple with 3 white keels; column white, spotted purple; spike rather short. Winter, spring. Colombia. 1892. (L. 475.)

S. Sanderia'na. A synonym of *Myrmecophila Sanderiana.*

S. splen'dida.* *fl.* 10 to 15, 4 in. across; sep. and pet. brownish-purple, undulate; lip rose-purple; scapes 4 ft. long. *Pseudobulbs* 12 to 15 in. h. Autumn. Colombia. 1905.

Schomburgkia superbiens

S. superb'iens.* *fl.* up to 20, 5 in. or more across; sep. and pet. similar, lanceolate, rosy-mauve, paler at base; lip shorter than sep. and pet., 3-lobed; side lobes convolute over column, yellow, streaked purple inside, mid-lobe bright rose-purple with purple veins, disk yellow with 5 serrated lamellae; column dull purple, cap white; scapes 4 to 12 ft. long. *Pseudobulbs* fusiform, 9 to 15 in. h. *l.* elliptic-oblong, 9 to 15 in. long. Guatemala. 1842. (B.M. 4090, W.S.O. 20, and W.O.A. 244 as *Laelia superbiens.*) SYN. *Bletia superbiens.*

S. Thomsonia'na. A synonym of *Myrmecophila Thomsoniana.*

S. tibici'nis. A synonym of *Myrmecophila tibicinis.*

S. undula'ta.* *fl.* in a dense raceme; sep. and pet. rich brown-purple, narrow, waved; longer than lip; lip clear violet-purple, cucullate, mid-lobe oval, side-lobes rounded, disk whitish with 5 raised lines; scape 3 to 4 ft. long; bracts very long. January. *Pseudobulbs* fusiform, 9 to 12 in. h. *l.* up to 9 in. long. Colombia. 1843. (W.S.O. 2, 21; B.R. 31, 53.)

S. Wallis'ii. *fl.* about 3 in. across; sep. and pet. narrow, undulate, yellowish; lip with broad obtuse side lobes, mid-lobe acute, apex of lobes brownish; crest of lip yellow in front of a convex disk with a depression above base. *Pseudobulbs* clavate, 8 to 10 in. h. *l.* 12 to 15 in. long. Colombia. 1913. Somewhat resembling *S. Lueddemannii.*

E. C.

Schomburgk'ii, in honour of Sir Moritz Richard Schomburgk, 1811–80, Director, Botanic Garden, Adelaide, or Sir R. H. Schomburgk (see above).

SCHOT'IA (in honour of Richard van der Schot, one-time head-gardener at Schoenbrunn, travelled with Jacquin in America; d. 1819). FAM. *Leguminosae.* A genus of 5 species of handsome, unarmed shrubs or small trees, natives of S. Africa. Leaves alternate, equally pinnate. Flowers crowded in axillary or terminal panicles (sometimes direct from the older branches); calyx 4-lobed; petals 5, nearly equal; stamens 10, much exserted, united at the base. Pod oblong, compressed. They require greenhouse conditions and succeed splendidly on the French and Italian Rivieras. Much of the floral beauty is due to the stamens.

KEY

1. *Lflets. 4 to 12*	2
1. *Lflets. up to 20 pairs, up to ¾ in. long*	S. speciosa
2. *Lflets. up to 2½ in. long; fl. crimson or carmine*	3
2. *Lflets. about 1 in. long; fl. pale rose*	S. latifolia
3. *Pet. minute, bristle-like*	S. brachypetala
3. *Pet. ¾ in. long, spatulate*	S. transvaalensis

S. brachypet'ala.* Glabrous tree, 20 to 30 ft. h. *lflets.* 6 to 10, ovate-oblong, obovate, apex rounded, ¾ to 2½ in. long, ½ to 1½ in. wide. *Panicles* terminal and axillary, often borne on old wood. *fl.* deep crimson, numerous, crowded; cal. ¾ in. long, tubular below, 4-lobed; pet. very minute, bristle-like, $\frac{1}{16}$ in. long; stamens ½ to 1 in. long. August. S. Africa.

S. latifo'lia. Elephant Hedge Bean Tree. Tree 15 to 45 ft. h. *lflets.* 4 to 8, obovate to oval, 1 to 2½ in. long, leathery, glabrous, apex notched and minutely mucronate. *Panicle* terminal, much-branched, 3 to 5 in. long, pyramidal. *fl.* crowded, scarcely stalked; pet. ½ in. long, recurved, pale rose; cal. green; stamens ⅝ in. long, pink. June. *Pod* 2 to 4 in. long, 1- to 3-seeded. S. Africa. 1815. (H.E.F. 159.)

S. specio'sa.* Shrub or small tree, 6 to 15 ft. h. *l.* 1 to 2½ in. long; lflets. in up to 20 pairs, very variable, from ⅓ to ¾ in. long, by $\frac{1}{16}$ to ½ in. wide, mostly oblong. *fl.* crowded in axillary panicles forming a terminal cluster up to 3 or 4 in. across; pet. ½ in. long, oval, rich crimson; cal. similar in colour but smaller; anthers yellow. Autumn. S. Africa. 1759. (A.B.R. 348.) var. **tamarindifo'lia,** the form with the broadest lflets. (B.M. 1153 as *S. tamarindifolia.*)

S. transvaalen'sis. Large shrub or a tree up to 30 ft. h. *lflets.* in 4 to 6 pairs, about 1 in. long, oval, oval-oblong, obovate, apex mucronate, glabrous; common stalk winged. *fl.* bright carmine, in a dense cluster 2½ in. long and wide; cal. ⅝ in. long, tubular at base; pet. ¾ in. long, spatulate; stamens 1 in. long. S. Africa.

W. J. B.

Scho'ttii, in honour of Dr. Arthur Schott, who collected *Agave Schottii,* &c., in Arizona, 1855.

Schou'teni, in honour of A. R. Schouten, 1877–1932, biologist in Malaya.

SCHOU'WIA (in honour of J. F. Schouw, 1787–1854, Danish botanist). FAM. *Cruciferae.* A genus of 3 species of tall, branched, glabrous herbs, natives of Arabia. Leaves entire. Flowers purple, at first in corymbs, afterwards racemose; pedicels slender; sepals sub-erect, lateral broader; stamens free. *S. arabica* is a hardy annual growing best in sandy soil.

S. arab'ica. About 1 ft. h. *Upper l.* auriculate and amplexicaul. *fl.* rosy-purple. June. 1837.

A→

SCHRA'DERA (in honour of Henry Adolf Schrader, 1767–1836, of Hildesheim, author of a monograph on Verbascum). FAM. *Rubiaceae.* A genus of about 5 more or less epiphytic species of glabrous shrubs, natives of S. America and the W. Indies. Branches thick, rooting. Leaves opposite, oblong, thick and leathery, stalked; stipules large, connate into a sheath. Flowers in compact, globose, terminal heads; calyx tube turbinate or hemispherical, superior; corolla thick and leathery, salver-shaped, limb of 5 to 10 narrow, spreading or reflexed lobes; stamens 5 to 10. *S. Cephalotes* does well in a compost of sandy loam and peat. Propagated by cuttings in sand, under a glass in heat.

S. Cephalo'tes. About 4 ft. h. *l.* elliptic or lanceolate-oblong; stipules spatulate-oblong, blunt, equally stalked. *fl.* white, 8- to 10-lobed, tube twice as long as cal. July. Jamaica. 1820.

Schra'deri, in honour of (1) H. A. Schrader, see above; (2) Carl Schrader, 1852–1930, astronomer and traveller.

SCHRANK'IA (in honour of F. von Paula von Schrank, 1747–1835, German botanist). FAM. *Leguminosae.* A genus of about 10 species of herbs or sub-shrubs, natives of America. Stems often prostrate, armed with recurved prickles. Leaves 2-pinnate, often sensitive; leaflets small; stipules bristly. Flowers rose or purplish, in globose heads or cylindrical spikes; calyx small; petals connate to middle, forming a funnel-shaped corolla. Pods linear, acute or acuminate, prickly. The leaves of the 2 species described droop at the slightest touch. A mixture of loam, peat, and sand suits them. Propagation by young cuttings in sand under a bell-glass in heat or by separation of the root tubers.

S. aculea'ta. Herbaceous perennial about 18 to 24 in. h. with creeping roots. Stem 4-angled. *l.* with 2 or 3 pairs of pinnae, each with numerous lflets. *fl.* red, in solitary heads. Vera Cruz. 1733. Stove

S. uncina'ta. Sensitive Brier. Herbaceous perennial, about 2 ft. h. Stem with hooked prickles. *lflets.* elliptic, veins netted. *fl.* rose, in globose heads. June to August. *Pods* 2 in. long, densely prickly. S. United States. 1789. Half-hardy.

SCHRE'BERA (in honour of J. C. D. von Schreber, 1739–1810, correspondent of Linnaeus). FAM. *Oleaceae.* A genus of trees or climbing shrubs, natives of India and Africa. Leaves opposite, unequally pinnate. Flowers in trichotomous terminal panicles. *S. Saundersiae* needs a store house.

S. Saunders'iae. Large, partly scandent shrub, up to 25 or 30 ft. h. *lflets.* 3 to 5, sessile, oblong-lanceolate to ovate, bluntly pointed. *fl.* white with dark purple velvety patches; stamens exserted. Trop. and S. Africa.

Schrenk'ii, in honour of Alexander Schrenk, 1816–76?, of the Botanic Garden, St. Petersburg, who collected in Russia and Turkiestan.

Schroeder'ae, Schroeder'i, in honour of (1) Baroness and Baron Henry von Schröder, 1825–1910, banker and noted grower of orchids at Englefield Green; (2) R. Schröder, head-gardener, Agricultural Institute, nr. Moscow.

Schroeteria'nus -a -um, in honour of Carl Schroeter, b. 1855, botanist of Zürich.

SCHUBERT'IA. *See* **Araujia.**

Schubert'ii, in honour of G. H. von Schubert, 1780–1860, physician of Munich, who travelled in Egypt and Palestine.

Schul'leri, in honour of J. G. H. F. Schuller tot Peursum, who sent orchids from Batavia, *c.* 1914.

Schultesia'nus -a -um, in honour of J. A. Schultes, 1773–1831, of Vienna, botanical writer.

Schult'zei, in honour of Leonhard Schultze of Jena, b. 1872, who travelled and collected widely.

Schultzia'nus -a -um, in honour of K. H. Schultz, 1805–67, physician, student of Compositae.

Schumacher'ae, in honour of Anna Koorders, *née* Schumacher, 1870–1934, of Bonn.

Schuman'ni, in honour of K. M. Schumann, 1851–1904, of the Botanical Museum, Berlin, writer on Cactaceae, Marantaceae, &c.

SCHWALBEA (in honour of C. G. Schwalbe, author of flora of Further India, *c.* 1719). FAM. *Scrophulariaceae.* A genus of a single species of perennial herb with entire 3-veined leaves and rather large, yellowish-purple flowers in a terminal bracteate spike. Hardy in ordinary soil.

S. america'na. Erect, 1 to 2 ft. h. *l.* oblong or ovate-oblong, acute, 1 to 1½ in. long, upper smaller; sessile. *fl.* nearly sessile, longer than bracts; cor. tube slightly longer than lower cal. lobes. *Capsule* enclosed by cal. May to July. SE. United States.

SCHWANNIA (in honour of Theodor Schwann, physician of Bonn). FAM. *Malpighiaceae.* A genus of about 5 species of climbing shrubs, natives of Brazil. Leaves opposite, entire, stalked, stipules inconspicuous. Flowers red; calyx deeply 5-cleft with 8 glands; petals with short claws, fringed; stamens 6, unequal, all fertile; filaments unequally monadelphous, glabrous; umbels or racemes 4-flowered, often in panicles, terminal; peduncles bracteate. A compost of loam, peat, and sand suits *S. elegans* which needs stove conditions. Propagation by ripe cuttings in sand under a glass in heat.

S. el'egans. Young branches silky. *l.* ovate or roundish, acuminate, softly and densely hairy beneath; stalks with 4 to 6 glands. *fl.* hairy; stamens scarcely exserted; peduncles and cal. silky. June. 1842.

Schwantes'ii, in honour of Dr. G. Schwantes of Kiel, Germany, botanist.

Schwarz'ii, in honour of Johannes Albert Traugott Schwarz, b. 1836, Dutch official in E. Indies.

SCHWEIGGER'IA (in honour of Aug. Frid. Schweigger, 1783–1821, Professor of Botany Königsberg). FAM. *Violaceae.* A genus of 2 species of erect shrubs, one Brazilian, the other Mexican. Leaves alternate; stipules minute. Flowers with 3 outer sepals larger than the 2 narrow inner ones; petals spurred at base; peduncles axillary, 1-flowered, jointed above the bracts. *S. fruticosa* grows well in a compost of loam, peat, and sand. Young cuttings strike readily in sand under a hand-glass in heat.

S. frutico'sa.* Tongue Violet. Shrub of 4 to 6 ft. *l.* obovate-spatulate, tapered to base, obtuse, crenately toothed. *fl.* white. December. Brazil. 1838. (B.R. 1841, 40.) SYN. *S. pauciflora.* Stove.

Schweinfurth'ii, in honour of Dr. Georg August Schweinfurth, 1836–1895, traveller and collector in Central Africa, &c.

SCHWENK'IA (in honour of J. T. Schwenck, 1619–71, Professor of Medicine, Jena). FAM. *Solanaceae.* A genus of about 20 species of herbs or sub-shrubs, natives of S. America, with one also in Trop. Africa. Leaves entire, ovate or narrow. Flowers yellowish-green or whitish; calyx 5-toothed or cleft; corolla with a long tube, limb 5-toothed, with 2 to 5 club-shaped glands between the teeth; stamens exserted or included; peduncles 1-flowered or in a panicle. *S. americana* is an annual for light soil and stove conditions.

S. america'na. Annual, 2 ft. h. *lower l.* ovate, 1 to 1½ in. long, narrowed to base; *upper* oblong; stalked. *fl.* lilac; cor. ⅓ in. long in a slender, many-fld. panicle; pedicels scarcely as long as cal. August. Brazil. 1781.

sciadi-, sciado-, in compound words, signifying shade or canopy.

SCIADOCA'LYX. Included in **Isoloma.**

SCIADOPHYL'LUM (*skias*, shade or canopy, *phyllon*, leaf; the large leaves afford much shade). FAM. *Araliaceae.* A genus of about 25 species of trees or shrubs, natives of Trop. America. Leaves digitately compound; leaflets entire; stipules often long. Flowers hermaphrodite or polygamous; petals 5, rarely 4; heads or small umbels in simple racemes, panicles, or umbels. Grown for their fine foliage in stove or greenhouse. A compost of loam, peat, and sand suits them. Propagated readily by cuttings in sand under a glass with moderate heat.

S. acumina'tum. Climber to 10 ft. *lflets.* 7 to 11, stalked, oblong, obliquely acuminate, leathery, glabrous, net-veined. *fl.* yellow, in heads little larger than a pea. May. Peru. Greenhouse.

S. Brown'ii. Galapee Tree. Tree 10 to 15 ft. h. *lflets.* 7 to 11, stalked, oblong-lanceolate, glabrous, unequal, central smallest. *fl.* white, almost capitate; heads in very long panicles. June. Jamaica. 1793. Stove.

S. con'icum. Shrub of 10 ft. *lflets.* 7 to 13, stalked, oblong, abruptly acuminate, leathery, glabrous, net-veined. *fl.* whitish-red in heads about as large as a pea; racemes 2 or 3, rather velvety. May. Peru. Stove.

S. leptophyl'lum. A synonym of *Dizygotheca leptophylla.*

SCIADOP'ITYS (*skias*, a parasol, *pitys*, a fir-tree; in reference to the spreading whorls of false leaves resembling the ribs of a parasol). FAM. *Pinaceae.* A monotypic genus.

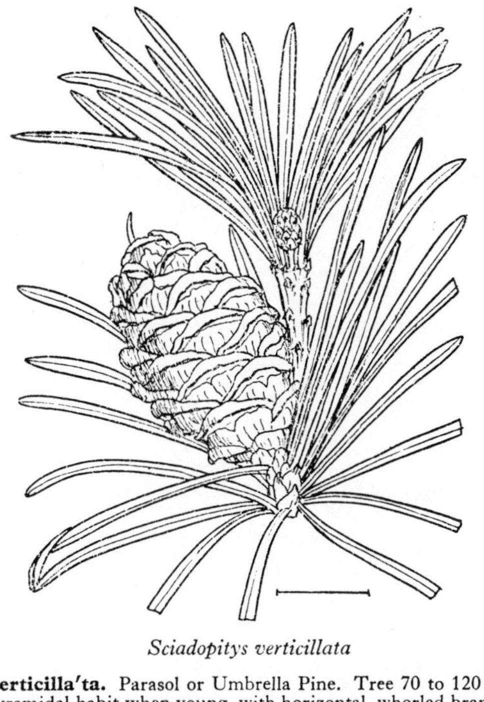

Sciadopitys verticillata

S. verticilla'ta. Parasol or Umbrella Pine. Tree 70 to 120 ft. h. of pyramidal habit when young, with horizontal, whorled branches. Young shoots smooth, green at first, light brown later, with small, scale-like l. pressed close to the bark. Winter buds rounded or broadly oblong, bright brown, surrounded by thick incurved greenish or dark-brown scales. *l.* of 2 kinds, (1) scale-like, triangular, ⅛ to ¼ in. long, light brown, irregularly disposed on lower part of shoot and forming 2 or more alternating rings near the apex; (2) cladodes or modified shoots functioning as l. in whorls of 10 to 30 at the apex of the shoots inside the rings of scale l.: they are glossy dark green or yellowish-green above, with a central yellowish furrow beneath, 2 to 5 in. long, grooved on each surface, with thickened entire margins, and a shallowly notched apex, faint stomatic lines are on the undersurface. *Male and female fl.* are on the same tree, male in terminal clusters of about 10 fl. each, female terminal made up of thin lance-shaped bracts attached to tiny scales. *Cones* oblong egg-shaped, short-stalked, 2½ to 4 in. long, 1½ to 2 in. wide, ripening second year, occasionally proliferous; scales woody, fan-shaped with a rounded or reflexed margin, much longer than bracts with 5 to 9 seeds on each fertile one. *Seeds* elliptical, ⅓ to ½ in. long, ⅜ in. wide, brown, surrounded by a thin narrow wing. Japan. 1861. (D.J.C. 487.) The tallest tree recorded in Britain in 1931 was 32 ft. at Bodnant, 51 ft. in 1948. var. **pend'ula,** branches pendulous; **variega'ta,** some cladodes are yellow. Two distinct forms are in cultivation, one growing much more freely than the other. The best one has a single leader, the other with several erect shoots from near the ground. A very decorative garden tree well suited for a lawn specimen. It is quite hardy but should not be exposed to cold and violent winds. Good loamy soil reasonably free from lime, to which a little peat or leaf-mould has been added suits it. It should be planted in a permanent place whilst quite small and should not be disturbed after it has once become established. Waterlogged soil must be avoided although moist conditions at the roots are an advantage. An annual surface dressing of decayed leaves will protect the surface roots from hot sun and provide food material. It needs no regular pruning. Propagation is usually by imported seeds sown in light soil indoors, although home-grown seeds are sometimes available. **A**

sciaph'ilus -a -um, shade-loving.

SCIA'RA. A genus of small, 2-winged flies. *See* **Fungus Gnats, Mushroom Sciarid Flies.**

SCIL'LA (name used by Greeks and Romans for *Urginea maritima*). FAM. *Liliaceae.* Squill, Wild Hyacinth. A genus of about 100 species of bulbous plants, natives of Europe and extra-tropical regions of Asia and Africa. Bulb tunicated. Leaves radical, linear, loriform, oblong or nearly ovate. Flowers small or of medium size in racemes on jointed pedicels, usually appearing with the leaves; segments nearly equal, distinct, or very shortly connate towards base, spreading or rarely somewhat bell-shaped towards base, 1-nerved; stamens 6, affixed at base or below middle of segments; bracts usually small; racemes sometimes long and many-flowered, sometimes flowers only 2 or 3, occasionally corymbiform; scape simple, leafless. The hardy Scillas are among the most beautiful of spring flowers. They succeed in any ordinary garden soil and need to be planted in early autumn while the bulbs are resting. *S. siberica* makes a good pot plant grown in a cold house or frame without heat. The greenhouse species grow well in sandy loam in 5-in. pots in the cool greenhouse along with other Cape bulbs. Propagation by seeds, taking 4 or 5 years to flower, or by offsets. Scillas are sometimes attacked by the Grey Bulb Rot due to *Sclerotium tuliparum,* which is described under Tulip. *S. bulborum* also attacks the bulbs as it does those of Hyacinth, and a soft rot also occurs. Bulbs so attacked should be destroyed. The bulbs may also be attacked by *Penicillium gladioli,* but this no doubt originates in bad storage conditions. Rust, due to *Uromyces scillarum,* is fairly common on *Scilla campanulata* and sometimes occurs on *S. non-scripta* and *S. bifolia.* Smut, caused by *Ustilago Vaillantii,* attacks *S. bifolia, S. verna,* and some other species, while a leaf-tip disease is caused by *Septoria scillae.*

S. Ad'lamii. *l.* single, linear, rather fleshy, 8 to 9 in long, $\frac{1}{2}$ in. wide. *fl.* mauve-purple, $\frac{1}{3}$ in. long, in a short raceme; pedicels $\frac{1}{2}$ to $\frac{3}{4}$ in. long; peduncle slender, 3 to 4 in. long. April. E. Natal. 1891. Greenhouse.

S. amoe'na. *l.* 4 or 5, flaccid, lorate, ascending, glabrous, 6 to 9 in. long, $\frac{1}{3}$ to $\frac{5}{8}$ in. wide. *fl.* blue, rarely whitish, $\frac{1}{2}$ in. long, segs. lanceolate; in a loose 3- to 6-fld. raceme 1 to 3 in. long; pedicels ascending, $\frac{1}{2}$ to $\frac{3}{4}$ in. long; scape weak, 4 to 6 in. long. March. Cyprus 1596. (B.M. 341; L.B.C. 1015.) var. **siber'ica,** a synonym of *S. siberica.*

S. autumna'lis. *l.* autumnal, after the fl., narrow, 3 to 6 in. long, half terete, grooved above. *fl.* reddish-purple, $\frac{1}{2}$ in. across in a short raceme; pedicels ascending or spreading; scapes several, as long as l. July to September. Europe, including Britain, N. Africa. (B.M. 919; E.B. 1526.) Hardy. The form **japon'ica** has rose *fl.*

S. Bel'lii. *l.* 2 or 3, oblong-lanceolate, 3 to 4 in. long, acute, fleshy. *fl.* brownish-blue, bell-shaped, $\frac{1}{3}$ in. long, segs. oblong-spatulate, in short, 10- to 12-fld. racemes; bracts white; scape slender, terete, 3 to 4 in. long. Spring. Laristan, Cent. Persia. 1884. Hardy.

S. Berthelot'ii. *l.* 5 or 6, slender, spreading, lorate, 6 to 12 in. long, $\frac{1}{2}$ to $\frac{3}{4}$ in. wide, with a long, narrow point. *fl.* pale lilac, $\frac{1}{4}$ in. long, in a 12- to 20-fld. raceme, bell-shaped; pedicels ascending as long as perianth; scape slender, 6 to 8 in. long. April. Trop. Africa. 1862. (B.M. 5308.) Greenhouse.

S. bifo'lia. *l.* usually 2, narrowed and hooded at tip, opposite, 4 to 8 in. long, $\frac{1}{3}$ to $\frac{1}{2}$ in. wide, concave on face. *fl.* blue, reddish, or whitish, $\frac{1}{3}$ in. long, in a deltoid 3- to 8-fld. raceme 1 to $1\frac{1}{2}$ in. wide; segs. spreading; pedicels ascending, $\frac{1}{2}$ to 1 in. long; scape solitary, 3 to 6 in. long. March. Mediterranean region. (B.M. 746; L.B.C. 283.) Hardy. var. **al'ba,** *fl.* creamy-white; **prae'cox,** more robust, *fl.* earlier, 10 to 15. (S.B.F.G. s. 2, 141 as *S. praecox.*); **ro'sea,** *fl.* rose; **taur'ica,** *l.* 3 to 5, pedicels longer. (G.F. 1860, 307; Gn. 44 (1893), 304.); **Whittal'lii,** *fl.* bright blue, in a close raceme. Asia Minor. 1891. A hybrid occurs between *S. bifolia* and *Chionodoxa Lucilliae. See* **Chionoscilla.** The chocolate anthers sometimes seen in this species and in the hybrids are due to the spores of the fungus *Ustilago Vaillantii* produced there.

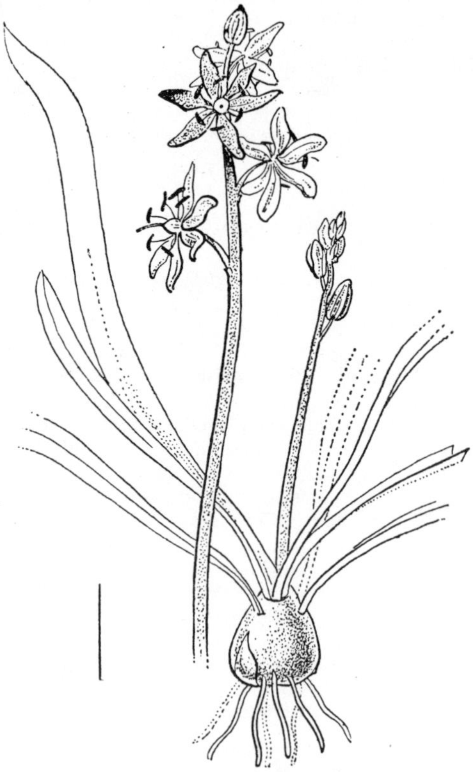

Scilla amoena

S. bipart'ita. A form of *S. lingulata.*

S. bithyn'ica. *l.* usually 3, linear, 3 to 12 in. long, shortly narrowed at tip. *fl.* pale purple-blue or white, $\frac{1}{3}$ in. long, elliptic, in an ovoid, compact, 7- to 15-fld. raceme; bracts pinkish, 2-auriculate, $\frac{1}{3}$ in. long; scapes 2 to a bulb, slender, 4 to 12 in. long. April. Bulgaria, Asia Minor. 1920. (B.M. 9230.) Hardy. Bracts much shorter than in *S. verna.*

S. Buchan'anii. *l.* 3, lanceolate. *fl.* green with purple filaments, $\frac{1}{8}$ in. long, in a dense, oblong raceme 2 in. long; scape flexuous, 6 to 8 in. long. May. Mozambique. 1893. Greenhouse.

S. campanula'ta. A synonym of *S. hispanica.*

S. chinen'sis. *l.* 2 or 3, rather hard, acute, channelled, as long as, or exceeding, the scape. *fl.* rose-purple, $\frac{1}{12}$ in. long, in a dense, 20- to 60-fld. raceme 1 to 2 in. long; pedicels ascending, lower often twin, about $\frac{1}{8}$ in. long; scape slender, straight, 1 ft. or more long. June. China. 1826. (B.M. 3788 and B.R. 1029 as *Barnardia scilloides.*) Half-hardy.

S. concin'na. *l.* 3 or 4, nearly erect, linear, 8 to 9 in. long, $\frac{1}{2}$ to $\frac{3}{4}$ in. wide, profusely spotted purple on back. *fl.* rose-purple within, oblong bell-shaped, $\frac{1}{6}$ in. long, in a dense, 30- to 50-fld. oblong raceme $1\frac{1}{2}$ to 2 in. long; scape firm, erect, terete, 2 to 6 in. long. Spring. S. Africa. 1862. (Ref. B. 235.) Greenhouse.

S. con'color. *l.* 5 or 6, falcate, ligulate-lanceolate, 5 to 8 in. long, $1\frac{1}{4}$ to $1\frac{1}{2}$ in. wide, obtuse or nearly so, slightly narrowed at base, not spotted. *fl.* greenish, rounded bell-shaped, about $\frac{1}{6}$ in. long, in dense, 30- to 50-fld., oblong-cylindrical racemes 3 to 4 in. long; pedicels $\frac{1}{8}$ to $\frac{1}{6}$ in. long, lower drooping; scapes 1 to 3, flexuous, 3 to 4 in. long. Spring. S. Africa. 1862. (Ref. B. 18 as *Drimia Cooperi.*) Greenhouse.

S. Coop'eri. *l.* 4 or 5, ascending, 10 to 12 in. long, $\frac{1}{2}$ to $\frac{3}{4}$ in. wide, green, streaked and spotted purple on back. *fl.* bright purple, segs. spreading, oblong, about $\frac{1}{4}$ in. long; raceme rather dense, 30- to 50-fld., 2 to 3 in. long, 1 in. wide; pedicels $\frac{3}{8}$ to $\frac{1}{2}$ in. long, spreading or lowest slightly nodding; scape firm, erect, 2 to 5 in. long. Spring. S. Africa. 1866. (B.M. 5580; F.P.S.A. 943.) Greenhouse.

S. Cupa'ni. *l.* 6 to 8, lorate-lanceolate, spreading, 3 to 4 in. long, $\frac{1}{2}$ to $\frac{5}{8}$ in. wide, margins pellucid, minutely ciliate. *fl.* purple, in a loose 6- to 12-fld. raceme, somewhat corymbose or deltoid, $1\frac{1}{2}$ to 2 in. long and wide; segs. oblong, obtuse, $\frac{5}{16}$ in. long; bracts whitish, slightly ciliate, $\frac{1}{2}$ to $\frac{3}{4}$ in. long; pedicels ascending, 1 to 2 in. long; scape slender, flexuous, 3 to 6 in. long. June. Sicily. 1834. (B.R. 1878.) Hardy.

S. festa'lis. A synonym of *S. non-scripta.*

S. floribun'da. *l.* nearly erect, lorate, about 1 ft. long, 1½ to 2 in. wide, acute, pale green blotched deeper green. *fl.* greenish without, rose-purple within, in rather dense, 60- to 100-fld. racemes 6 to 8 in. long, 2 in. wide; pedicels ½ to 2 in. long, central spreading, lower drooping; scape erect, 6 to 9 in. long. Spring. S. Africa. 1862. (Ref. B. 188.) Greenhouse.

S. Galpin'ii. *l.* 3 or 4, oblong-spatulate, sessile, 2 to 3 in. long. *fl.* bright mauve-purple, ⅛ in. long, in a dense, sub-globose raceme ¾ in. wide; filaments bright purple. Transvaal. (F.P.S.A. 864.) Greenhouse.

S. hispan'ica.* *l.* 5 or 6, linear-lorate, glabrous, ascending, ½ to 1 in. wide, somewhat blunt, convex at back. *fl.* typically blue, often rose-purple or whitish, sub-globose bell-shaped, ½ to ¾ in. long, in a rather loose, 6- to 8-fld. raceme; lower pedicels ½ to 1 in. long; scape 6 to 9 in. long. May. Spain, Portugal. 1683. (B.M. 127, 1102 as *S. campanulata.*) SYN. *S. patula.* A variable species. White, flesh-coloured, pink, and blue of various shades are offered, and forms with larger fl. and infl. than in the type, all of them worth growing. A

S. humifu'sa. *l.* 2 or 3, cordate-oblong, 3 to 4 in. long, 1½ to 2 in. wide, pale green with a few deep-green blotches. *fl.* reddish-green, small; raceme 3 to 4 in. long; pedicels very short; scape 3 to 4 in. long, purple at base, green above. Spring. Natal. 1881. Greenhouse.

S. hyacinthoi'des. *l.* 10 to 12, spreading, 1 to 1½ ft. long, ½ to 1½ in. wide, narrowed to both ends, minutely ciliate-toothed. *fl.* bluish-lilac, about ⅓ in. long, segs. ligulate, downy at tip; bracts whitish, minute, persistent; pedicels erecto-patent, lower 1 to 1½ in. long; racemes 50- to 150-fld., 6 to 18 in. long, 2 to 2½ in. wide; scape straight, 1 to 2 ft. long. August. Mediterranean region. 1585. (B.M. 1140.) Hardy. var. **stric'ta,** bulbs solitary, pedicels erect.

S. in'dica. *l.* oblong or lanceolate, 3 to 6 in. long, ½ to 1¼ in. wide, acute, narrowed to base, often with tiny bulbils on margins. *fl.* greenish-purple, ⅛ to ⅙ in. long, rounded bell-shaped, in a dense, 30- to 60-fld. raceme 2 to 4 in. long; segs. falcate; pedicels somewhat spreading, up to ⅓ in. long; scapes flexuous, 2 to 6 in. long. June. India. 1816. (B.M. 3226 as *Ledebouria hyacinthina.*) Greenhouse.

S. ital'ica. *l.* 4 to 6, lorate, 4 to 8 in. long, ¼ to ½ in. wide, spreading, flaccid, acute, keeled. *fl.* blue, about ¼ in. long, in 6- to 30-fld. conical raceme, later extending to 2 in. long, ¾ to 1 in. wide; segs. downy at tip; bracts twin; scape solitary, slender, 6 to 10 in. long. May. Italy, S. France. 1605. (B.M. 663; L.B.C. 1483.) Hardy. **S. purpu'rea** is a robust garden form with *fl.* of deeper colour.

S. Kraus'sii. Bulb 1½ to 2 in. wide. *l.* about 4, spreading, lanceolate, 2 to 3 in. long, distinctly ribbed, densely hairy. *fl.* bright blue, bell-shaped, ⅛ in. long, in a raceme 3 to 4 in. long; pedicels erecto-patent, ⅓ to ½ in. long; scape slender, 6 to 9 in. long. S. Africa. Greenhouse.

S. lanceola'ta. *l.* 5 or 6, lanceolate, 3 to 4 in. long, about ¾ in. wide, acute, green, not spotted. *fl.* greenish-purple, tubular bell-shaped, ⅓ in. long in very loose, 8- to 12-fld. racemes 1½ to 2 in. long, 1½ in. wide; pedicels dotted red, somewhat spreading, lower long; scape flexuous, 4 to 5 in. long. September. S. Africa. 1774. (A.B.R. 299 as *Lachenalia reflexa.*) SYN. *Drimia lanceolata.* Greenhouse.

S. lancifo'lia. *l.* 6 to 8, oblong, 4 to 6 in. long, 1½ to 2 in. wide, somewhat spreading, acute, scarcely narrowed to base, pale green, spotted above. *fl.* purple within, greenish at back, sub-globose bell-shaped, nearly ⅛ in. long in a dense, 30- to 50-fld., oblong raceme 2 to 3 in. long, 1¼ to 1½ in. wide; segs. ligulate-lanceolate; pedicels about ½ in. long, lower deflexed; scapes 1 to 3, firm, terete, 2 to 4 in. long, often decurved. May. S. Africa. 1818. (Ref. B. 182; B.M. 643 as *Lachenalia lanceaefolia*; L.B.C. 1041 as *Drimia acuminata.*) var. **ovatifo'lia,** *l.* broadly ovate, 2 to 3 in. long, 1½ to 2 in. wide. 1862. (Ref. B. 183 as *S. ovatifolia.*)

S. latifo'lia. *l.* 6 to 9, lanceolate, slender, 1 to 1½ ft. long, 1½ to 2 in. wide, narrowed to base and tip, glabrous. *fl.* lilac, bell-shaped, ⅓ in. long, in a dense 30- to 60-fld. raceme, 3 to 4 in. long, 1 to 1½ in. wide; segs. ligulate; pedicels spreading, lower about ½ in. long; scape straight, about 1 ft. long. May. Canary Is. 1777. Greenhouse. (B.M. 1999 as *S. lusitanica,* a robust form.)

S. laxiflo'ra. *l.* 3 or 4, oblong-lanceolate, up to 3 in. long, mottled. *fl.* green, ⅛ in. long, in a very loose oblong raceme 3 in. long; pedicels pale mauve, erect, ½ to ¾ in. long; scape slender, 3 in. long. S. Africa. 1891. Greenhouse.

S. Ledie'ni. Bulb 1 in. across. *l.* 5 or 6, lanceolate, 6 to 12 in. long, rooting at tip, glaucous, spotted. *fl.* greenish, bell-shaped, ¼ in. long, in a raceme 3 in. long; pedicels very short. Lower Guinea. 1889. (G.F. 1294.) Greenhouse.

S. leucophyl'la. Habit of Hyacinth but perianth segs. free to base. *fl.* bright purple tipped green. Persia. 1893. Hardy.

S. lilio-hyacinthus. Habit of *S. hyacinthoides* but *fl.* usually 6 to 20 in raceme, *l.* narrow-linear and longer, bracts about ½ in. long, *fl.* somewhat larger. W. France, N. Spain.

S. linearifo'lia. *l.* 4 to 6, linear, 9 to 12 in. long, ⅛ to ⅜ in. wide, nearly erect, acute, pale green, spotted purple at back. *fl.* greenish without, purple within, about ⅛ in. long, oblong bell-shaped in 30- to 40-fld., rather dense oblong racemes 2 to 3 in. long, 1¼ to 1½ in. wide; segs. falcate; scape flexuous, 3 to 4 in. long. Spring. S. Africa. 1862. (Ref. B. 184.) Greenhouse.

S. lingula'ta. *l.* 6 to 8, somewhat fleshy, lingulate-lorate, 2 to 3 in. long, ⅓ to ½ in. wide, ascending, glabrous. *fl.* blue, bell-shaped, starry, about ¼ in. long in a rather dense, oblong, 6- to 15-fld, raceme; scape 2 to 4 in. long. Spring. Algeria, Morocco. 1887. (G.F. 1261.) Hardy. var. **al'ba,** *fl.* white; **lilaci'na,** *fl.* lilac.

S. liv'ida. *l.* 6 to 8, lanceolate, 6 to 8 in. long, 1 to 1¼ in. wide, gradually narrowed to acute tip, green, not spotted. *fl.* green, tinged without very dull purple, ⅛ in. long, oblong, in a dense, oblong raceme, 3 to 4 in. long, about 1½ in. wide; pedicels erecto-patent, ¼ to ⅓ in. long; scape terete, 4 to 5 in. long. S. Africa. 1883. Greenhouse.

S. lora'ta. *l.* 5 or 6, lorate-lanceolate, 8 to 9 in. long, about 1 in. wide, nearly erect, acute, green, spotted purple at back. *fl.* livid-purple, green on back and margins of segs., ¼ in. long, oblong bell-shaped, in a rather dense, oblong-cylindrical, 30- to 60-fld. raceme, 3 to 4 in. long, up to nearly 2 in. wide; pedicels ⅓ in. long, lower drooping; scape terete, erect, 8 to 9 in. long, spotted below. S. Africa. 1862. (Ref. B. 19 as *Drimia apertiflora.*) Greenhouse.

S. MacOwani. Habit of *S. Cooperi. l.* 3 or 4, linear, green, about 6 in. long. *fl.* greenish, bell-shaped, in a dense, conical raceme with 20 to 30 fl.; scape as long as l. S. Africa. 1873. Greenhouse.

S. marit'ima. A synonym of *Urginea maritima.*

S. messeni'aca. Related to *S. pratensis* but *l.* 5 to 7, ½ to ⅝ in. wide, *fl.* pale blue, ¼ in. long, in ovate-oblong racemes of 10 to 20 fl. April. Greece. 1897. (B.M. 8035.) Hardy.

S. microscyph'a. *l.* 2 or 3, cordate-oblong, 12 in. long, 4 to 4½ in. wide, glaucous-green with purplish-brown bars near base, dark-green stripes in upper part. *fl.* green, in dense racemes 5 to 6 in. long; scape green, as long as l. Spring. Natal. 1881. Greenhouse.

S. monophyl'la. *l.* usually solitary, ascending, lorate, 6 to 9 in. long, ½ in. wide, acute. *fl.* blue, bell-shaped, up to ⅓ in. long in a loose, 6- to 20-fld. raceme, 1 to 2½ in. long, 1¼ to 1½ in. wide; pedicels ascending, lowest ½ to 1 in. long; scape slender, flexuous, 3 to 6 in. long. May. Spain, Portugal. 1821. (B.M. 3023 as *S. pumila.*) Hardy.

S. natalen'sis. *l.* 4 to 6, lorate-lanceolate, green, glabrous, 9 to 12 in. long, 3 to 4 in. wide, ascending, narrowed to acute tip. *fl.* blue, ¼ to ⅓ in. long, in a dense, 50- to 100-fld. raceme 6 to 12 in. long, 2½ to 3 in. wide; bracts solitary; pedicels ascending, lower ¾ to 1 in. long; scape terete, erect, up to 18 in. long, stout. April. Natal. 1862. (B.M. 5379; F.d.S. 1043; F.P.S.A. 365.) Greenhouse. var. **sord'ida,** *l.* tinged brown, up to 8 in. long, 1¼ to 1½ in. wide, scape slender, *fl.* smaller and fewer.

S. non-scrip'ta.* Bluebell; Harebell; Wild Hyacinth. *l.* linear, 10 to 18 in. long, ½ in. wide, sub-acute, concave. *fl.* blue, purple, white, or pink, drooping in 6- to 12-fld. racemes; bracts twin; pedicels short curved, erect in bud and fruit; scape solitary, tall, stout. April to June. W. Europe, including Britain. (E.B. 1528.) SYN. *S. festalis, S. nutans, Endymion non-scriptus, Hyacinthus non-scripta.* Hardy. Variable. var. **grandiflo'ra alba,** *fl.* large, white; **ro'sea,** *fl.* pink; **ru'bra,** *fl.* red. A form with bracts much longer than fl. is not infrequent (var. **bractea'ta**). A

S. nu'tans. A synonym of *S. non-scripta.*

S. odora'ta. *l.* 3 or 4, 6 to 9 in. long, bluntish, channelled down face, glabrous, narrowed to base. *fl.* blue, fragrant, bell-shaped. ⅓ in. long, in a loose, 6- to 20-fld. raceme 1 to 2½ in. long, 1¼ to 1½ in. wide; pedicels ascending, lower 4 to 6 in. long; scape slender, flexuous, 3 to 6 in. long. May. Spain, Portugal. 1818. Hardy.

S. ovatifo'lia. A variety of *S. lancifolia.*

S. pallidiflo'ra. A synonym of *S. rigidiflora.*

S. pa'tula. A synonym of *S. hispanica* but sometimes regarded as distinct.

S. paucifo'lia. *l.* 2 or 3, oblong-lanceolate, 2½ to 3 in. long, spreading, undulate, pale green and spotted on face, narrowed at base. *fl.* greenish, roundish bell-shaped, ¼ in. long, in a loose, oblong, 20- to 30-fld. raceme, 3 to 4 in. long, 1¼ to 1½ in. wide; segs. falcate; pedicels about ½ in. long, lower drooping; scape firm, terete, 3 to 4 in. long, without spots. S. Africa. 1862. (Ref. B. 181.) Greenhouse.

S. Paui. Bulb about 1 in. thick. *l.* 3 or 4 with fl., glabrous, about 6 in. long, ½ in. wide, margin narrowly white-cartilaginous. *fl.* blue, ⅝ in. across, segs. spreading, striped violet, in a dense 20- to 25-fld. raceme; pedicels erect-spreading; scape about 6 in. long. May, June. Spain. 1928. Related to *S. verna,* near var. *Ramburei.*

S. pen'dula. *l.* lorate, 12 to 15 in. long, about 1½ in. wide, acute, narrowed to base, nearly flat, pale green with very faint spots. *fl.* greenish without, purple within, ⅓ in. long, oblong bell-shaped, in rather dense, 30- to 60-fld. racemes 3 to 6 in. long, up to 3 in. wide; pedicels very slender, ¾ to 1¼ in. long, drooping; scape slender, flexuous, 8 to 9 in. long. Spring. S. Africa. 1862. Greenhouse.

S. peruvia'na.* Cuban Lily (a misnomer). *l.* 6 to 9, lorate, 6 to 12 in. long, ⅝ to 1 in. wide, narrowed to base and tip, densely white, bristly ciliate. *fl.* lilac, reddish or white, about ½ in. long, in a very dense, 50- to 100-fld. deltoid raceme, elongating to 4 to 6 in. long and as wide; segs. striped green; bracts solitary, whitish, persistent, 1 to 2 in. long; scape robust, striate, 6 to 12 in. long. May. Mediterranean region. 1607. (B.M. 749; B.R. 29, 48 as var. *discolor,* a dingy form.) var. **al'ba,** *fl.* white; **el'egans,** *fl.* red; **glab'ra,** *l.* not ciliate, *fl.* lilac, lower pedicels up to 2 in. long. 1873. *S. Hughii* is a more robust form with scape, &c., tinged red and *l.* up to 2½ in. wide.

S. plumb'ea. Very similar to *S. natalensis*. *fl.* dirty-blue. S. Africa. 1812. (B.R. 1355; F.P.S.A. 1006.) Greenhouse.

S. polyan'tha. Bulb 1½ to 2 in. thick. *l.* 4, lorate-oblong, 12 to 15 in. long, sub-erect, blotched with dark spots and purple at base. *fl.* green without, dull purple within, ⅛ in. long, in a dense, oblong raceme 4 to 5 in. long; pedicles ½ in. long; scape 6 to 9 in. long, spotted purple. S. Africa. 1878. Greenhouse.

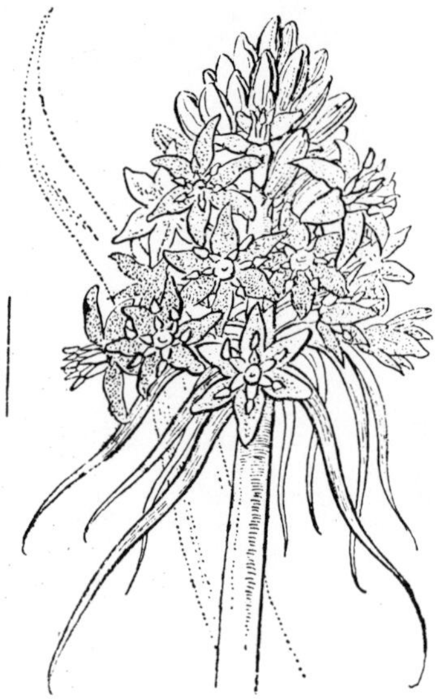

Scilla peruviana (p. 1909)

S. prae'cox. A variety of *S. bifolia*.

S. prasi'na. *l.* 5 or 6, oblong-lanceolate, 4 to 5 in. long, 1 to 1¼ in. wide, acute, spreading, narrowed below, often spotted purple. *fl.* green, sometimes faintly tinged purple, roundish bell-shaped, in a rather dense, sub-cylindrical, 30- to 50-fld. raceme, 1½ to 2 in. long, ½ to ¾ in. wide; segs. very narrow; central pedicels spreading, ⅛ in. long, lower deflexed; scape flexuous, deflexed, 3 to 4 in. long. Spring. S. Africa. 1870. Greenhouse.

S. praten'sis.* *l.* 3 to 6, narrow-ligulate, 6 to 12 in. long, up to ⅓ in. wide, narrowed to both ends, glabrous. *fl.* blue, ⅛ in. long, bell-shaped, in a dense, 12- to 30-fld. raceme, 1½ to 2½ in. long, 1¼ to 1½ in. wide; pedicels about ½ in. long, ascending or spreading. May. Dalmatia. 1827. (B.R. 25, 63.) Hardy.

S. prin'ceps. *l.* 5 or 6, lorate, 18 to 24 in. long, 2 to 2½ in. wide narrowed at base, acute, pale green, spotted. *fl.* greenish without, reddish-purple within, oblong bell-shaped, about ⅓ in. long, in a dense 100- to 200-fld. raceme 12 in. long, up to 3½ in. wide; pedicels 1 to 1¼ in. long, central spreading, lower drooping; scapes 2 or 3, 7 to 9 in. Spring. S. Africa. 1862. (Ref. B. 189.) Greenhouse.

S. pu'mila. A synonym of *S. monophylla*.

S. puschkinioides.* Habit much like *S. bifolia*. *l.* 2 to 4, broadly linear, obtuse. *fl.* pale blue, erect, starry. Spring. Turkistan. 1881. (G.F. 1051.)

S. rigidifolia. *l.* 5 or 6, lorate-lanceolate, 12 to 15 in. long, 1 to 1¼ in. wide, ascending, glabrous, green. *fl.* whitish tinged green, bell-shaped, in a dense, conical, 100- to 150-fld. raceme at first conical, 6 to 10 in. long, 3 in. wide; pedicels straight, lower spreading horizontally, 1 to 1¼ in. long; scape erect, 18 in. or more long, Spring. S. Africa. 1870. (Ref. B. 179.) Greenhouse.

S. serot'ina. A synonym of *Dipcadi serotinum*.

S. sibir'ica.* *l.* 2 to 4, narrow-lorate, 4 to 6 in. long, about ½ in. wide, ascending, slightly culcullate. *fl.* 1 to 3, deep blue, about ½ in. long, horizontal or slightly drooping, on short pedicels; scapes 1 to 6, fleshy, 3 to 6 in. long. March. E. Russia, Siberia. 1796. (L.B.C. 151; B.M. 1025 as *S. amoena siberica*; 2408 as *S. amoenula*.) SYN. *S. uniflora*. Several varieties are offered: **al'ba,** *fl.* white; **atrocoeru'lea,*** *fl.* deep blue, robust. SYN. Spring Beauty; **azu'rea,** *fl.* bright light blue; **tau'rica,*** *fl.* lighter blue than type, 3 weeks earlier. (Gn. 48 (1895), 162 as *S. siberica multiflora*.)

S. socia'lis. *l.* 3 or 4, oblong-lanceolate, 2 to 2½ in. long, ¾ to 1 in. wide, slightly narrowed to base, pale glaucous green, spotted above. *fl.* greenish, roundish bell-shaped, ⅛ in. long, in dense, 20- to 30-fld. oblong racemes, 1½ to 2 in. long, 1 in. wide; pedicels ⅛ in. long, lower drooping; scape firm, terete, not spotted, 2 to 3 in. long. Spring. S. Africa. 1862. (Ref. B. 180.) Greenhouse.

S. spathula'ta. *l.* 5 or 6, lorate-spatulate, 6 to 8 in. long, 1½ to 1¾ in. wide, pale glaucous-green with deeper green and purplish blotches. *fl.* greenish without, purple within, oblong bell-shaped, about ⅛ in. long, in dense, 30- to 40-fld. racemes 3 to 4 in. long, 1½ to 1¾ in. wide; pedicels about ½ in. long, lower drooping; scape flexuous, 3 to 4 in. long. Spring. S. Africa. 1862. (Ref. B. 187.) Greenhouse.

S. subglau'ca. *l.* 5 or 6, lorate-lanceolate, 9 to 10 in. long, 1 in. wide, acute, distinctly narrowed to base, pale glaucous-green above, purple spotted beneath. *fl.* greenish without, purple within, oblong bell-shaped, ¼ in. long, in a rather loose, 30- to 40-fld. raceme, 3 to 4 in. long, about 1½ in. wide; pedicels about ½ in. long, lower drooping; scape spotted, 3 to 4 in. long. Spring. S. Africa. 1862. (Ref. B. 186.)

S. subsecun'da. *l.* 6 to 8, lanceolate, 6 to 12 in. long, 1 to 1½ in. wide, tinged purple at back and somewhat blotched towards base. *fl.* green with brownish tinge outside towards base, ⅛ in. long, in a dense, secund raceme 6 in. long; filaments bright purple; scape drooping, nearly 12 in. long. June. S. Africa. 1881. Greenhouse.

S. tric'olor. *l.* 6 to 7, lanceolate, 12 in. long, 2 in. wide, narrowing to 1 in. at the channelled base, erecto-patent, dark green with lighter green blotches above, claret brown blotches beneath. *fl.* green in a dense oblong-conical raceme 2 to 3 in. long, 1¼ to 1½ in. wide; filaments bright mauve-purple; lower pedicels spreading, ½ in. or more long; scape flexuous, terete, 6 to 8 in. long. Spring. Port Elizabeth. 1880. Greenhouse.

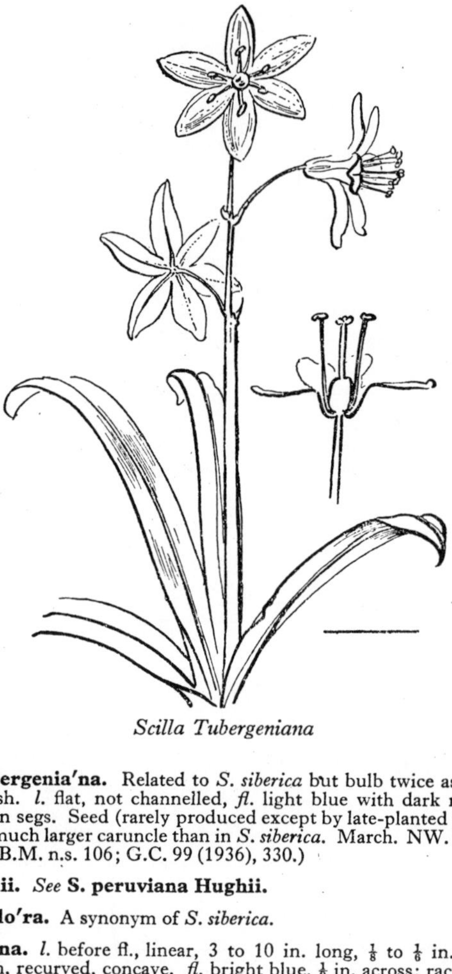

Scilla Tubergeniana

S. Tubergenia'na. Related to *S. siberica* but bulb twice as large, yellowish. *l.* flat, not channelled, *fl.* light blue with dark median stripe on segs. Seed (rarely produced except by late-planted plants) with a much larger caruncle than in *S. siberica*. March. NW. Persia. 1931. (B.M. n.s. 106; G.C. 99 (1936), 330.)

S. Ughii. *See* **S. peruviana Hughii.**

S. uniflo'ra. A synonym of *S. siberica*.

S. ver'na. *l.* before fl., linear, 3 to 10 in. long, ⅛ to ⅙ in. wide, bluntish, recurved, concave. *fl.* bright blue, ½ in. across; raceme 6- to 12-fld., sub-corymbose or deltoid, ¾ to 1½ in. wide; bracts equalling pedicels or longer; lower pedicels ½ in. long; scapes 1 or 2, shorter than l. April, May. Europe, including Britain. (E.B. 1527; L.B.C. 1736.) A beautiful species but difficult to grow. var. **Rambu'rei,** larger in all parts. Spain.

S. versicol'or. *l.* 6 to 8, linear-lorate, 6 to 9 in. long, about ½ in. wide, ascending, narrowed to acute apex, glabrous, green on both surfaces. *fl.* whitish, tinged green, ⅛ in. long, in a rather dense 50- to 80-fld. raceme, 6 to 8 in. long, 3½ in. wide; segs. ligulate, blunt; anthers blue; lower pedicels at length spreading, 1½ to 2 in. long. Spring. S. Africa. 1872. (Ref. B. 305.) Greenhouse.

S. villo'sa. *l.* 3 or 4, lorate, 3 to 5 in. long, ¼ to ½ in. wide, spreading, ciliate, somewhat hairy on face, channelled below. *fl.* blue, ⅓ in. or more long, in 6- to 8-fld. sub-corymbose racemes; segs. elliptic, blunt; pedicels erecto-patent, lower ¾ to 1¼ in. long. Spring. N. Africa. 1831. (B.M. 3211.) Hardy.

S. zebri'na. *l.* 5 or 6, ligulate-lanceolate, 8 to 12 in. long, 1 to 1¾ in. wide, nearly erect, slightly narrowed at base, glaucous-green above, marked with parallel vertical bars below and also with horizontal bars near base passing into blotches of purple. *fl.* greenish and purple, roundish bell-shaped, ½ in. long in a dense, 30- to 40-fld. raceme; pedicels ½ to ⅓ in. long, lower drooping; scape 4 to 6 in. long, spotted below. S. Africa. 1862. (Ref. B. 185.) Greenhouse.

SCIMITAR PODS. Pods of *Entada scandens.*

SCINDAP'SUS (ancient Greek name for a plant resembling Ivy). FAM. *Araceae.* A genus of about 20 species of climbing herbaceous plants usually rooting from the stem, natives of Trop. Asia, E. Indies, Fiji. Leaves ovate, oblong, or oblong-lanceolate, slender-pointed, abruptly bent at base of blade. Peduncle short. Spathe boat-shaped, deciduous. Spadix dense-flowered. Flowers hermaphrodite, naked; stamens 4. Fruit a rather large 1-seeded berry. Cultivation as for Caladium.

S. argyrae'us. Juvenile form of *S. pictus.*

S. au'reus.* Tall climber, much-branched; stem grooved. *l.-stalk* 12 to 14 in. long, abruptly bent, sheath long, blade thinly leathery, obliquely ovate or ovate-oblong, 12 to 18 in. long, deeply cordate, young l. entire, adult deeply lobed, bright green with numerous irregular golden spots and lines. Solomon Is.

S. officina'lis. About 4 ft. h., branches round. *l.-stalk* 5 to 6 in. long, abruptly bent, sheath expanded, blade thinly leathery, obliquely ovate-oblong, cuspidate, 6 to 10 in. long, rounded or slightly cordate at base. *Peduncle* about 2 in. long. *Spathe* oblong, 5 to 6 in. long, green without, dull yellow within. India, Burma, Malaya. 1820.

S. pic'tus. Silver Vine. Up to 40 ft. long, warted; branches slender, flexuous. *l.-stalk* about 1 in. long, abruptly bent, sheath narrowed from a wide base, blade leathery, obliquely ovate-oblong or ovate, 4 to 6 in. long, rounded at base, irregularly spotted and clouded with pale green on dark green above, unspotted beneath. *Peduncles* about 1 in. long. *Spathe* white, thick or fleshy, ovate-oblong, 2½ to 3 in. long. Malaya, Java. var. **argyrae'us,** a juvenile state with cordate *l.* with silver spots above. E. Indies. SYN. *S. argyraeus, Pothos argyraea.*

scin'tillans, sparkling.

SCION. A shoot used for grafting upon a rootstock; any young shoot.

scipio'num, wand-like.

scirpoi'deus -a -um, Scirpus-like, rush-like.

SCIRP'US (old Latin name used by Pliny for a Rush). FAM. *Cyperaceae.* A genus of about 200 species of annual or perennial herbs widely distributed over the world in marshy places and shallow water. Leaves few at the base of the stem, sometimes very long, sometimes small and grass-like, or all reduced to sheaths. The plants grow freely in loamy soil so long as it is sufficiently wet, the hardy species being best planted in bogs or in the shallow margins of ponds. All the species mentioned below are perennial and can be increased by suckers or by division.

S. cernu'us. Closely resembling *S. setaceus* but of close-tufted habit, sheaths brown or yellowish-brown tinged purple in lower part, fl.-stems weak, scarcely over 6 in. long. *Spikelets* 1 to 3, ovate. Wet places. W. Europe, including Britain, Mediterranean, &c. A useful greenhouse plant for damp pots. SYN. *S. gracilis, Isolepis gracilis* of gardens.

S. grac'ilis. A synonym of *S. cernuus.*

S. Holoschoen'us variega'tus. Stems erect, terete, 12 to 18 in. h., marked with alternate zones of whitish and green. *Spikelets* minute in crowded heads, ¼ to ½ in. across; stigmas 3. Summer. Hardy. The green form (up to 3 ft. h.) occurs on sandy shores in Europe, including SW. England, Mediterranean regions, Siberia, S. Africa.

S. hudsonia'nus. A synonym of *Eriophorum alpinum.*

S. lacus'tris. Bulrush. Stems terete or nearly so, 1 to 8 ft., grass- or yellow-green. *l.* wanting or short, flat and keeled in still water, long and strap-shaped in streams. *Spikelets* red-brown, 1 to 6, ¼ to ½ in. long, sessile, in a terminal branched cyme, the branches ½ to 3 in. long. July, August. Europe, including Britain, Asia, Africa, Australia, Polynesia, N. and Cent. America. Hardy. Used for matting, chair-bottoms, &c.

S. marit'imus variega'tus. Stems sharply 3-cornered, 2 to 3 ft. h. *l.* long, flat, about ¼ in. wide, variegated. *Spikelets* rich brown, about ¾ in. long, 2, frequently up to 8 or 10 in a cluster. Summer. Sea coasts of the world. Hardy.

S. seta'ceus. Densely tufted or somewhat creeping. Stem very slender, terete, erect or somewhat spreading, 1 to 12 in. h. *l.* with a purple sheath and a green blade. *Spikelets* usually 2, but up to 10, ovate-lanceolate, purple, often with a broad green stripe, rarely wholly green. June to autumn. Europe including Britain, S. Africa, Asia, Australia. (E.B. 1594.) SYN. *Isolepis setacea.*

S. Tabernaemonta'ni zebri'nus. Much like *S. lacustris* and often regarded as a variety of it, but with a more slender and dwarfer stem usually 18 in. to 6 ft. h., *l.* blades absent. *Spikelets* usually thicker and shorter. The stems are transversely banded with white and green. Japan. 1881. (I.H. n.s. 393 as *Juncus zebrinus.*) Hardy. A striking plant for shallow water.

S. zebri'na. *See* **S. Tabernaemontani zebrinus.**

SCISSORS. Scissors of various types find their uses in horticulture. Ordinary scissors about 7 in. long are occasionally of use, as, for instance, in cutting shreds, string, and so on, but special types are more often required. Among them are Flower Scissors, strong scissors about 6 in. long, shorter, more pointed, and with narrower blades than in ordinary type; Grape Scissors, used for thinning the berries in bunches of grapes, with long blades tapering to a blunt point, made in sizes from 6 to 8 in. long, those of 6½ or 7 in. being the most useful; Propagating Scissors, about 4 in. long with very thin, pointed blades, their work being done now more often by safety-razor blades; Pruning Scissors, about 5½ in. long (shorter and longer forms are made) with short, wide blades with rounded ends, useful for cutting stout stems for florists' work; Wire Scissors also for florists' work, about 4 in. long, for cutting mounting wires of various sizes up to 18 gauge. All these tools should be kept sharp and wiped with an oily rag before being put away. They are best hung up when not in use.

scit'ulus -a -um, neat, pretty.

sci'tus -a -um, fine.

sciuroi'des, like a squirrel's tail.

SCIU'RUS carolinen'sis. *See* **Grey Squirrel.**

SCLA'REA. Included in **Salvia.** Italian plant name.

SCLERENCHYMA. Tissue consisting of usually long cells which have generally lost their protoplasm and contain only air or water, the walls of the cells being much thickened so that the cavity is almost filled, and often lignified. Single cells of this nature are found in some fruits, e.g. Pears, where they constitute the 'grit', and in leathery leaves such as those of Camellia, Hakea, and Olea. These fibres, however, are usually arranged in masses disposed so as to give support to the organ containing them and in many stems they and collenchyma ensure the rigidity and erect pose necessary to bring the leaves into position to do their work. In fruits the sclerenchyma doubtless serves to protect the seeds.

sclero- in compound words, signifying hard.

SCLEROCAC'TUS (*scleros*, hard or cruel; from the formidable spines). FAM. *Cactaceae.* Plants solitary, but sometimes in clusters, with prominent wavy or tuberculate ribs; spines well developed, some hooked. Flowers from the young areoles, purple, bell-shaped. Fruit pear-shaped, smooth, dehiscing by a basal pore. **A**

S. polyancis'trus. Stems solitary, round but elongating with age to over 1 ft. h.; ribs about 13; spines 20, radials white; centrals up to 5 in. long, white and brown, the upper ones erect and flattened. *fl.* magenta, up to 3½ in. long. California, Nevada. (B.R.C. 3, f. 224.)

S. Whip'plei. Plants solitary or in small cluster, ribs 13 to 15, prominent; radial spines 7 to 11, flattened, white but some black; centrals 4, uppermost flattened and straight, 1 or 3 of the lower hooked, brown or black. *fl.* purplish-pink. Arizona, Utah, Colorado. (B.R.C. 3, t. 16.)

V. H.

SCLEROCARP'US (*skleros*, hard, *karpos*, fruit; the fruit is enclosed in hardened bracts). FAM. *Compositae.* A genus of about a dozen species of annual or perennial herbs, closely related to Gymnolomia, natives of warm or hot regions. Leaves usually alternate. Flower-heads yellow, rather small, terminal; ray-florets several, fertile. Pappus absent; achenes flattish at top. The treatment of *S. uniserialis* is that of a half-hardy annual.

S. uniseria'lis. Half-hardy annual, with much-branched stems, 3½ to 4½ ft. h. *l.* large, ovate, acute, irregularly toothed, crenulate, hairy beneath. *fl.-heads* orange-yellow, slightly scented, solitary at ends of branches. Texas. SYN. *Gymnolomia uniserialis, Gymnopsis uniserialis.*

SCLERODERMA. A genus of fungi in the class Basidiomycetes, growing on the ground in open places near trees. In *Scleroderma vulgare* the fruit-body, which is the part seen above ground, is globose, without a stem, whitish or yellowish, and the skin is often scaly. The interior is greyish-white at first, later becoming purplish-black marbled with white veins and often having a disagreeable smell. This fungus is fairly common and is edible, often being used in place of the French Truffle (*Tuber macrosporum*).

D. E. G.

SCLEROTHAM'NUS. Included in **Eutaxia.**

SCLEROTIN'IA. A large genus of fungi in the class Ascomycetes. The summer conidia are of various types such as Botrytis or Monilia but the ascospore stage is formed by an apothecium arising from a black sclerotium. Many species are most destructive parasites. One is *Sclerotinia sclerotiorum* which attacks a great diversity of plants and causes rotting of many kinds of root vegetables, tubers, &c., in storage. It may also attack plants such as Lettuces, Tomatoes, Artichokes, Antirrhinums, while growing and, as with other species, the chief danger lies in the sclerotia, which contaminate the soil for a succeeding crop. *S. fructigena* and *S. laxa* cause Brown Rot and allied troubles such as Blossom Wilt, Spur Blight, &c., in Apples, Pears, Peaches, Cherries, &c.

D. E. G.

SCLERO'TIUM (pl. Sclerotia). Resting body formed by many fungi for the purpose of surviving adverse conditions such as drying-up of food-supply or severe winter weather. It is usually a hard, compact body formed by a tightly compressed mass of fungus threads. In this condition the sclerotium can lie dormant until better conditions prevail, when it has the power of growing again. Sclerotia when mature are generally dark (black or brown) and become very hard. Their size varies greatly, some being pin-head size, some as large as a pea or bean, while some are 5 to 6 in. or more long. Possibly the outer cells die and form a crust to protect the inner ones, which retain their vitality. In many plant diseases these sclerotia are produced by the fungus-parasite either on the surface or inside the tissues as a means of survival and as the dead plant disintegrates they fall into the soil and contaminate it. Sclerotia vary in their methods of growing again and in some fungi this fact has a bearing on the classification of the fungus, as is mentioned later. Some on germination produce many fungus threads and infect the host plant directly while others give rise to a stalked apothecium from the inner surface of which the ascospores are released for infecting plants.

D. E. G.

SCLERO'TIUM spp. A parasitic fungus which produces only sclerotia as means of reproduction and these sclerotia on germination produce only germ tubes for infection is placed in the genus Sclerotium among the Fungi Imperfecti. If, however, the sclerotium produces an apothecium the fungus is placed in the genus Sclerotinia among the Ascomycetes. Examples of disease-producing fungi forming sclerotia are *Sclerotium cepivorum* (causing White Rot of onions) with its pin-head size sclerotia, and *Sclerotinia sclerotiorum* (rotting of carrot and many other plants both ornamental and vegetable) with its sclerotia from pea to dwarf-bean size. A parasitic fungus sometimes reduces the plant organ it has attacked to a blackened structure which is so permeated with the fungus that it is in effect a sclerotium and acts as such. For example, *Sclerotinia fructigena*, the fungus of Brown Rot in apples, reduces the infected fruits to a hard shrivelled 'mummy' and this, the following spring, will produce stalked apothecia.

D. E. G.

scobiform'is -is -e, resembling sawdust or shavings.

SCOLIO'PUS (*scolios*, tortuous, *pous*, foot; perhaps from the rhizome). FAM. *Liliaceae.* A genus of 2 species of rhizomatous perennials closely related to Medeola, natives of N. America. Leaves 2 at tip of stem, sessile or short-stalked. Perianth deciduous; segments distinct, outer 3 broadly lanceolate, spreading, inner 3 linear, erect. Treatment as for Trillium. Hardy or nearly so.

S. Bigelo'vii. *l.* radical, ovate-elliptic to narrow-lanceolate, 4 to 15 in. long, spotted, sessile or narrowed to base. *fl.* solitary, inner segs. purple, outer green lined purple, about ¾ in. long. February. California. (G.C. 15 (1894), 267.)

scolopendrioi'des, resembling a harts-tongue fern.

SCOLOPEN'DRIUM. A synonym of Phyllitis.

SCOLO'PIA (*skolops*, paling with a sharply pointed top; from the sharp thorns). FAM. *Bixaceae.* A genus of about 30 species of spiny trees, natives of Africa, Asia, and Australia. Spines often compound. Leaves alternate, entire, stipules minute or absent. Flowers small in axillary racemes, dioecious; sepals 4 to 6, almost alike; stamens many; ovary 1-celled. Fruit a 2- to 4-seeded berry. Stove conditions are needed.

S. Brown'ii. Glabrous. *l.* ovate to oblong-lanceolate, 1½ to 3 in. long, narrowed to a stalk, entire or almost so, thick; stalk ¼ in. long. *fl.* in short racemes or in a terminal panicle. Queensland, New S. Wales.

SCOLY'MUS (ancient Greek name, used by Theophrastus and earlier writers). FAM. *Compositae.* A genus of 3 species of erect herbs, natives of the Mediterranean region. Leaves alternate, rigid, sinuately toothed or pinnatifid, with spiny teeth or lobes, often spotted white above. Flower-heads yellow, terminal or lateral, sessile; involucre ovoid or sub-globose, involucral bracts in a few series mucronate or spine-tipped; receptacle conical or long; florets ligulate, truncate, 5-toothed. The roots of *S. hispanicus* are as good as those of Scorzonera and the leaves and stalks are sometimes eaten as Cardoons, while the flowers are used to adulterate Saffron. The annual *S. maculatus* is sometimes grown for the sake of its variegated leaves. It only needs to be sown in the open border. The other 2 species grow well in ordinary soil from seed or divisions.

S. grandiflo'rus. Stem very hairy, about 3 ft. h. *l.* slightly hairy, decurrent, winged. *fl.-heads* solitary, usually terminal; bracts subverticillate. May. Mediterranean region. 1828. Perennial.

S. hispan'icus. Golden Thistle; Spanish Oyster Plant. About 3 ft. h. *l.* decurrent, winged. *fl.-heads* 2-bracteate, somewhat clustered, in leafy spikes. August. SW. Europe. 1653. (F.G. 825.) Biennial.

S. macula'tus. Stem erect, glabrous, about 3 ft. h. *l.* leathery on margin, decurrent, winged, often spotted white. *fl.-heads* somewhat corymbose; bracts many, pectinate. July. S. Europe. (F.G. 824.) Annual.

SCOL'YTUS. *See* **Elm-bark Beetle** and **Fruit-bark Beetle.**

SCOOPS. Tools for levelling or smoothing the bottoms of drains when preparing for drain-pipes. They usually have long handles. They are made in several widths both hollowed and flattened in the sole. Some have the point of the scoop turned on an angle towards the workman when in use; others turn in the opposite direction.

sco'pa, a twining twig.

scopa'rius -a -um, broom-like.

scopella'tus -a -um, like a broom.

SCOPO'LIA (in honour of Giovanni Antonio Scopoli, 1723–88, Professor of Natural History at Pavia, and botanical writer). FAM. *Solanaceae.* A genus of 4 species of erect, scarcely branched, perennial herbs, 1 European, 1 Siberian, 1 Japanese, 1 Himalayan. Leaves membranous, entire. Flowers lurid purple or greenish, veined, nodding; calyx truncate or broadly and shortly 5-lobed; corolla large, limb 5-angled or very shortly 5-lobed; stamens 5; pedicels solitary, filiform. They grow well in light, dry soil in a shady position. Propagation by division, *S. carniolica* has pretty flowers in spring.

S. carnioli'ca.* 1 ft. or more h. *l.* entire, 3 to 3¼ in. long, ovate or obovate-oblong, sub-cuspidate; stalks ½ in. long. *fl.* ¾ in. long, solitary in l.-axils, nodding; cor. lurid-red, yellow, or green within; peduncles ¾ to 1¼ in. long. April. Russia. 1780. (B.M. 1126 as *Hyoscyamus Scopolia.*) var. **Hladnikia'na,** *fl.* pale yellow, scentless. E. Europe. 1893. (G.C. 13 (1893), 418 as *S. Hladnikiana.*)

S. lu'rida. 4 to 6 ft. h. *l.* ovate, up to 6 or 7 in. long, acute, undulate, wrinkled, mostly unequal, glabrous above, hairy and ash-coloured beneath; stalked. *fl.* axillary; cor. at first green, then yellowish, at length purplish; peduncles ½ to 2 in. long. Nepal. 1824. (S.B.F.G. 125 as *Whittleya stramonifolia.*)

S. physaloi'des.* 1 to 1½ ft. h. *l.* ovate, acute, somewhat repand or quite entire; stalked. *fl.* purplish-violet, terminal, in a capitate corymb; cal. much larger than capsule. March, April. Siberia. 1777. (B.M. 852 and S.B.F.G. 13 as *Hyoscyamus physaloides.*) SYN. *Physochlaina physaloides.*

scopuli'nus -a -um, twiggy.

scopulo'rum, of the rocks or cliffs.

SCORCHING. As used in horticulture scorching usually means injury that may occur to foliage as a result of spraying. It often follows if the leaves have been previously damaged by Aphides or smoke fumes but it may occur without this previous injury. Certain varieties of Apple, e.g. Stirling Castle and Lane's Prince Albert, are very susceptible to injury by lime-sulphur and must not be sprayed with it. Some Gooseberries and Black Currants also suffer from scorching after sulphur spraying. Many plants may be injured by Burgundy mixture but can be safely sprayed with Bordeaux mixture. Plants in glasshouses may suffer from scorching owing to the escape of furnace fumes into the house or to fumigation. Scorching may also follow, both indoors and out, the prevalence of dry heat and lack of moisture. Under glass in the early part of the year Vines quickly have the tender young foliage scorched unless ventilation is carefully attended to, especially in the morning, when the sun suddenly shines upon the house, running the temperature to a considerable height very quickly. Sometimes the berries are scorched for the same reason. To avoid this cause of scorching the ventilators should be opened early if the weather is mild, giving only a little air at first, gradually increasing it as the temperature rises, and reducing it as it falls. A very grave mistake is to throw the ventilators open suddenly with the object of lowering too high a temperature quickly. Sudden cooling is almost always followed by an attack of mildew.

SCORD'IUM. Included in **Teucrium.**

SCORODO'NIA. Included in **Teucrium.**

scorpioid, a term applied to an inflorescence coiled in the bud stage, the flowers produced on the upper side; the flowers are 2-ranked, being alternately thrown to right and left.

SCORPION GRASS. *See* **Myosotis.**

SCORPION SENNA. *See* **Coronilla Emerus.**

SCORPIU'RUS (*scorpios,* scorpion, *ura,* tail; from the twisted form of the legumes). FAM. *Leguminosae.* Caterpillar Plant. A genus of about 6 species of nearly stemless or decumbent herbs, natives of S. Europe, N. Africa, and W. Asia. Leaves simple, entire, tapering into the stalks. Flowers yellow, papilionaceous, often small, solitary or in umbels on axillary peduncles, nodding. Pods subterete, tubercled or muricate, circinate-involute. The plants have little beauty. *S. vermiculata* may be treated as a hardy annual.

S. vermicula'ta. *fl.* solitary; standard streaked red. June, July. *Pods* thick, glabrous, inner ribs almost obsolete, 10 outer ones covered with crowded tubercles, which are obtusely dilated at apex. 1621.

Scortechin'ii, in honour of Benedetto Scortechini, of Ancona, 1845–86, Roman Catholic missionary in Queensland and Straits Settlements.

scor'teus -a -um, leathery.

SCORZONE'RA (perhaps from old French *scorzon,* Catalonian *scurzon,* serpent, in allusion to the cooling, antifebrile effects of *S. hispanica,* which was formerly employed in Spain, on account of these properties, for the cure of snake-bites. Another supposition is that it derives from Italian *scorza,* bark, *nera,* black, in allusion to the roots). FAM. *Compositae.* A genus of about 100 species of perennial or rarely biennial or annual herbs, natives of the temperate regions of the Old World. Leaves alternate, sometimes entire and grass-like or broader, sometimes more or less pinnately lobed or cut. Flower-heads yellow or purple, often rather large, on long peduncles; involucre cylindrical or bell-shaped, with overlapping, acute or acuminate bracts in many series; receptacle naked or foveolate; florets ligulate, truncately 5-toothed at tip; achenes linear, sub-terete, or outer angled, glabrous or hairy. *S. hispanica* is grown for its long tapering roots which are cooked in the same way as Salsify. Their skin is black but the flesh is white. Seed should be sown at the end of March or in April, in drills 1 ft. apart and the plants thinned to 6 or 8 in. asunder. They need an open site and deep soil. The roots will be ready for use in November and through the winter. Some should be lifted and stored in sand in a cool shed before frost sets in, to be ready for use when required. All the species may be grown from seed sown in the open border in spring, the seedlings being afterwards thinned out. The perennial species may also be propagated by division in autumn or just as growth begins in spring. They are sometimes attacked by White Blister (*see* **Salsify, Diseases**).

S. coronopifo'lia. Stem erect, nearly simple, leafy at base, about 1 ft. h. *l.* lanceolate, mostly pinnatifid; lobes linear, unequal. *fl.-heads* yellow, terminal, solitary; involucral scales mucronate, outer ovate. June, July. N. Africa. 1818.

S. hispan'ica. Common Viper's Grass. Root carrot-shaped, but smaller and very dark, flesh white, of sweet and agreeable flavour. Stem branched, about 3 ft. h., branches naked. *l.* lanceolate, undulate or slightly toothed, sometimes hairy, stem-clasping. *fl.-heads* yellow, solitary, involucre oblong, scales somewhat glabrous, acuminate. June to September. S. Europe. 1576. Biennial.

S. lacinia'ta. Stem sub-erect, 2 ft. h., naked above. *l.* pinnatisect; lobes linear, entire. *fl.-heads* yellow, solitary; involucral bracts slightly hooked at tip. June, July. S. Europe. 1640. Biennial.

S. mol'lis. About 18 in. h. *l.* linear-subulate, keeled, at first woolly, becoming nearly glabrous; young leaves undulately crisped on margins. *fl.-heads* yellow, rays purplish beneath; involucre and the long sub-corymbose peduncles woolly-hairy. June, July. Caucasus. 1818. (B.M. 3027.) var. **undula'ta,** up to 2 ft. h., slender, branched, basal. *l.* with yellow midrib, about 1 ft. long, upper smaller, finely pointed, *fl.*-heads purplish-rose, 2 to 2½ in. across. July. Algeria, Morocco. 1874. (B.M. 6127 as *S. undulata.*)

S. purpu'rea. Root cylindrical-fusiform. Stem 2 ft. h., branched, 2- to 5-headed. *l.* linear-subulate, channelled, 3-angled. *fl.-heads* purplish; involucre cylindrical, scales broadly lanceolate, not ciliate. May, June. *Achenes* smooth. E. Europe. 1759. var. **grandiflo'ra,** more robust and showy with larger fl.-heads. (B.M. 2294.)

S. ro'sea. Stem 18 in. h., simple. *Radical l.* long, linear-lanceolate, flat, glabrous; *upper* few, keeled, linear. *fl.-heads* rose-pink, solitary; involucral bracts lanceolate, acuminate. July. *Achenes* sulcate, muricate above. E. Europe. 1807. SYN. *S. purpurea rosea.*

SCOTCH ASPHODEL. *See* **Tofieldia pusilla.**

SCOTCH BONNETS. *See* **Marasmius oreades.**

SCOTCH FIR. *See* **Pinus sylvestris.**

SCOTCH KALE. *See* **Kale.**

scoti'cus -a -um, Scottish.

scoti'nus -a -um, dusky, dark.

Scottia'nus -a -um, Scottii, in honour of Robert Scott, 1757–1808, Professor of Botany, Dublin.

Scoul'eri, in honour of Dr. John Scouler, 1804–71, of Glasgow, Professor of Zoology, Dublin, who collected with David Douglas, 1825, in NW. America.

SCRAPERS. Scrapers of some description should be placed in various positions in gardens, especially at points where there are paths cut in ordinary soil joining others with gravel or stone surface. The form matters little provided they are firmly fixed.

Scratchleya'nus -a -um, of Mt. Scratchley, New Guinea.

A→

A→

SCREENS. A shrubbery or belt of fast-growing trees is termed a Screen when planted to afford shelter to a garden or orchard. Gardens near the sea-coast always need a shelter or screen from the wind or salt spray even though only a low one when dwarf plants are grown. A belt of trees or shrubs should be planted, choosing those known to succeed in such situations. A good many shrubs do well near the sea and among trees the Austrian Pine and the Sycamore are both good for shelter belts. Inland the choice is greater but it is important to avoid trees which provide food for pests of the plants it is desired to protect. The term 'Screen' also denotes anything erected or grown to hide an unsightly object from any particular point, such as from one of the principal walks in a garden. Trellis with Ivy or other creeper trained upon it may often be used effectively and more extensively free-growing trees and evergreen shrubs may be planted. The choice of these is great but the precise fashion in which they and other types of screen are best used must depend upon the particular requirements of the locality.

SCREW PINE. *See* **Pandanus.**

scrip'tus -a -um, written upon, or marked with lines resembling writing.

scrobicula'tus -a -um, marked by tiny depressions or grooves.

SCROPHU'LARIA (*scrophula*, referring to supposed benefit against scrofula, as indicated by the roots of some species which bear a resemblance to scrofulous tumours). FAM. *Scrophulariaceae*. Figwort. A genus of about 120 species of herbs or sub-shrubs often with a fetid odour, widely distributed over the extra tropical regions of the N. Hemisphere. Leaves opposite, or upper alternate, sometimes entire, sometimes much cut, often with pellucid dots. Flowers greenish-purple, lurid-purple, or yellow, generally rather small, in paniculate, thyrsoid cymes; calyx deeply 5-cleft or -parted; corolla tube ventricose, globose or oblong; lobes 5, short and flat, 4 upper erect, lowest spreading; perfect stamens 4, fifth usually rudimentary. Some species, particularly *S. aquatica* and *S. nodosa* are occasional weeds of perennial duration, but few are of any horticultural merit. *S. chrysantha* is ornamental and will grow in ordinary garden soil as a pot plant in a cool frame or house, and is multiplied by seed.

S. chrysan'tha.* Stout, erect biennial, 6 to 18 in. h. *l.* ovate- or roundish-cordate, 2 to 3 in. long, lobed and toothed, convex, wrinkled. *fl.* golden-yellow, drooping, ½ in. long; cor. ovoid, turgid, contracted at mouth; cymes closely packed in upper l.-axils forming a rounded head, 2 in. in diameter. Caucasus. 1882. (B.M. 6629.)

S. no'dosa variega'ta. Perennial, about 2 ft. h. *l.* dark green, variegated with yellowish spots and blotches. Hardy.

SCROPHULARIA'CEAE. Dicotyledons. A family of about 2,600 species of herbs, shrubs, and trees falling into about 190 genera. Leaves, in a few genera, all alternate, in most the lowest, or all, are opposite or whorled, the upper and the bracts often alternate, entire, toothed, lobed or variously dissected; stipules none. Flowers hermaphrodite, often irregular; calyx inferior, persistent, with 5 (rarely 4) teeth or lobes; corolla gamopetalous; limb of 4 or 5, rarely 6 or 8, equally spreading lobes or more or less 2-lipped with the upper lip entire, emarginate or 2-lobed, lower 3-lobed and often spreading; stamens often 4, didynamous or 2, alternating with corolla lobes; anthers 2-celled, sometimes 1-celled; inflorescence variable. Fruit variable, often a dehiscent capsule, sometimes an indehiscent berry. Many of the species have medicinal value, the most important being the Foxglove (*Digitalis purpurea*). The family is an important one horticulturally for it contributes many beautiful plants to our gardens. The genera dealt with here are: Adenosma, Alonsoa, Anarrhinum, Angelonia, Antirrhinum, Aptosimum, Artanema, Bacopa, Bartsia, Bowkeria, Calceolaria, Campylanthus, Castelleja, Celsia, Chaenostoma, Chelone, Collinsia, Craterostigma, Dermatobotrys, Diascia, Digitalis, Erinus, Euphrasia, Freylinia, Gerardia, Gratiola, Hebenstreitia, Hemichaena, Hemiphragma, Isoplexis, Ixianthes, Jovellana, Lencocarpus, Leucophyllum, Linaria, Manulea, Maurandia, Mazus, Melampyrum, Mimulus, Nemesia, Oresitrophe, Orthocarpus, Ourisia, Pedicularis, Penstemon, Phygelius, Picrorhiza, Rehmannia, Rhodochiton, Russelia, Scrophularia, Selago, Seymeria, Sibthorpia, Synthyris, Teedia, Tetranema, Torenia, Uroskinnera, Verbascum, Veronica, Walafrida, Wulfenia, Zaluzianskya.

scrotiform'is -is -e, pouch-like.

SCRUB OAK. *See* **Quercus ilicifolia.**

SCRUBBY OAK. *See* **Lophira alata.**

sculptura'tus -a -um, appearing as though carved out.

SCURF. Loose, scaly matter on the skin of a plant.

SCURVY GRASS (*Cochlearia officinalis*). Sometimes used as a salad, and at one time valued as a cure for Scurvy, a disease induced by lack of fresh vegetables. Scurvy Grass will grow in any light porous soil. The seeds germinate quickly if sown as soon as ripe at the end of June or early in July in drills about 9 in. apart, lightly covering them. When large enough to handle the seedlings should be thinned out to about 9 in. apart in the rows; the thinnings may be planted out and if watered will make good plants by the following spring, when the leaves will be ready to pick for use.

scuta'tus -a -um, like a small, round buckler.

SCUTELLA'RIA (*scutella*, a small shield; from the form of the fruiting calyx). FAM. *Labiatae*. A genus of about 180 species of annual or perennial herbs or sub-shrubs, decumbent or diffuse, rarely erect and tall, still more rarely shrubby. Natives of temperate regions and tropical mountains. Leaves opposite, often toothed, sometimes pinnatifid or entire. Flowers blue, violet, yellow or white, solitary or in pairs, axillary or in terminal spikes or racemes; calyx bell-shaped, 2-lipped, tube dilated opposite the posterior lip into a broad, flattened, hollow pouch, both lip and pouch deciduous in fruit, the anterior lip closed after flowering, persistent; corolla tube long, naked within; limb 2-lipped, upper lip entire or notched, lower dilated, its lateral lobes spreading, usually connate with the upper lip, rarely with the lower; stamens 4. Nutlets sub-globose or depressed. The hardy species described below are, for the most part, handsome in flower and suitable for the front of flower borders or for the rock-garden. Any ordinary garden soil is usually suitable for them. The herbaceous species may be increased by division or by seed; the shrubby ones by cuttings. *S. Mociniana* is a beautiful stove plant easily grown in the cool stove or warm greenhouse. Its bunches of bright flowers are freely produced, one at the point of nearly every shoot. Cuttings of half-ripe shoots root readily in spring or at almost any season in a warm propagating frame. Young plants should have their points pinched out once or twice when growing to encourage a bushy habit and more abundant flowering shoots. They grow best in a compost of loam and leaf-soil or decayed manure with a little sand added, and flower well in 5-in. pots. The species described are hardy herbaceous perennials unless otherwise noted.

S. al'bida. Erect, branched, hairy. *l.* broadly ovate, coarsely crenately toothed, rounded or cordate at base, 1½ in. long, stalked. *fl.* dull white, ½ in. long, hairy without, in a secund raceme 9 in. to over 1 ft. long; pedicels very short. SE. Europe, Cent. Asia.

S. alboro'sea. Stem 1½ ft. h., 4-angled. *l.* ovate-oblong, cordate, undulate. *fl.* lilac, paler towards base of the long tube, in long terminal racemes. Summer. Upper Amazon. 1859. (I.H. 584.) Stove shrub.

S. alpi'na.* Stems procumbent, often rooting, about 1 ft. h. *l.* ovate, rounded or cordate at base, ½ to ⅝ in. long, crenately toothed, downy, very shortly stalked. Bracts coloured, overlapping. *fl.* purple or with lower lip yellow, 1 to 1½ in. long, in oblong, 4-angled spikes. August. Europe, Cent. Asia. 1752. (B.R. 1460; S.B.F.G. 90.) var. **al'ba,** *fl.* white; **bi'color,** *fl.* purple and white; **lupuli'na,** *fl.* wholly yellow. (B.R. 1493 as *S. lupulina.*); **ro'sea,** *fl.* rose.

S. altis'sima. Erect, branched. *l.* ovate to ovate-lanceolate, broadly cordate, crenately toothed. *fl.* creamy-yellow in pairs on a secund hairy raceme; cal. hairy, a quarter as long as cor. SE. Europe, Caucasus. (B.M. 2548.)

S. amoe'na. *See* **S. baicalen'sis.**

S. angustifo'lia. About 6 in. h. *l.* oblong-lanceolate to linear, narrowed to base, ½ to 1 in. long, entire. *fl.* deep violet-blue, ¾ to 1 in. long, tube slender, solitary in axils. NW. America. Moist soil.

S. aura'ta. Stem 18 in. h., 4-angled. *l.* ovate, obtuse, acuminate, auricled and cordate at base, the lobes approximate, entire or almost so; stalk long. *fl.* yellow, long tubular funnel-shaped, on short pedicels, in a many-fld., erect raceme; bracts linear, reflexed. Summer. Brazil. 1863. (I.H. 1862, 368.) Stove perennial. var. **sulphu'rea,** *fl.* pale sulphur, smaller than in type. (B.M. 5525.)

S. baicalen'sis.* About 1 ft. h., procumbent at base, ascending, often tinged purple, nearly glabrous. *l.* lanceolate, obtuse, entire, ciliate, otherwise glabrous or nearly so; sessile. *fl.* blue or purple, 1 in. long, tube dilated upwards, hood incurved, in simple secund racemes; cal. hairy, shorter than bracts. August. E. Asia. 1827. (B.M. 4420 as *S. macrantha.*) var. **coelesti'na,** *fl.* bright blue. **S. amoe'na** is closely related with oblong *l.* and large blue *fl.* China.

S. Britton'ii. Tuberous. Stem 4 to 8 in. h., branching from base, usually clammy-hairy. *l.* oblong or oval, entire and sessile or nearly so. *fl.* pale blue and white, solitary in l.-axils. W. United States.

S. cordifo'lia. A synonym of *S. splendens.*

S. costarica'na.* Stem 1½ to 3 ft. h., erect, dark purple. *l.* ovate, slender-pointed, toothed; long-stalked. *fl.* golden-scarlet, inside lips deep yellow, 2½ in. long, erect, tubular funnel-shaped, in many-fld. subsecund racemes; cal. and pedicel deep purple; cal. small. June. Costa Rica. 1863. (B.M. 5439.) Stove perennial.

S. formosa'na. Stem 2 to 3 ft. h., erect, shrubby. *l.* ovate or ovate-lanceolate, acuminate, faintly toothed, 2½ to 3 in. long. *fl.* dark violet-blue, green below, about 1 in. long, twin, in loose, terminal, sub-secund racemes. June. China. 1894. (B.M. 7458.) Greenhouse.

S. galericula'ta. Stem slender, 6 to 18 in. h. *l.* oblong to ovate, cordate, somewhat crenately toothed, ½ to 2 in. long. *fl.* blue with white markings within, ⅝ in. long, tube curved, solitary in axils in a downy, secund raceme; bracts leafy; pedicels very short. July to September. Europe, including Britain. (E.B. 1060.)

S. grandiflo'ra. A synonym of *S. orientalis.*

S. Hartweg'ii.* Sub-shrub, 1 to 2 ft. h. *l.* ovate, irregularly toothed, rounded or slightly cordate at base, green above, purple and downy on veins beneath; stalks downy. *fl.* bright red with lower lip violet, 1 in. long, scattered in a loose raceme. Summer. Quito. 1882. (B.M. 6615. Stove.

S. incarna'ta. Erect, hairy, 2 ft. h. *l.* ovate, 1 to 3 in. long, deeply toothed, green and downy above, hairy beneath. *fl.* flesh-coloured or pale reddish-violet, hairy; cor. 6 times as long as cal., limb spreading; cal. tubular, compressed; raceme terminal, secund. Summer. Cent. America. 1856. (B.M. 4268.) Stove perennial.

S. in'dica. 6 to 12 in. h., shoots procumbent at base, ascending. *l.* roundish, small, cordate at base, crenately toothed, downy, stalked. *fl.* bluish, lower lip broad, slightly hairy; cal. hairy; raceme dense, secund, 3 to 4 in. long; bracts short. June to August. China, Japan. var. **japon'ica,*** 6 in. h., l. ovate, grey-green, *fl.* blue or lilac, hairy. Japan. (P.M.B. 10, 123.)

S. lupuli'na. A variety of *S. alpina.*

S. macran'tha. A synonym of *S. baicalensis.*

S. Mociniana.* Shrub 18 in. h. *l.* ovate to long elliptical, somewhat crenate, slightly hispid above, glabrous or nearly so beneath, stalked, uppermost small, oblong. *fl.* showy, bright scarlet, 1¼ to 1½ in. long, yellow inside lip, tube finely hairy, limb erect; cor. 6 times as long as cal.; raceme secund. Summer. Mexico. 1868. (Gn. (1877), I.H. 562.)

S. orienta'lis.* Stem creeping and rooting, about 9 in. h., ascending, grey-hairy. *l.* ovate, sharply toothed, ⅓ to ¾ in. long, hoary beneath; upper entire, thin, slightly overlapping. *fl.* yellow or lower lip brownish or purplish, 1 to 1¼ in. long, in oblong, 4-sided spikes. July, August. S. Europe, Cent. Asia. 1729. (B.M. 2120; S.B.F.G. 45.) SYN. *S. grandiflora, S. pulchella.*

S. peregri'na. Procumbent with often purplish or reddish branches hairy near tip. *l.* ovate, obtuse, roundish at base, blunt, glabrous or nearly so. *fl.* violet, hairy without; cal. large, hairy; raceme secund. S. Europe, Asia Minor.

S. pulchel'la of gardens is nearly allied to *S. indica japonica* but is of more slender habit with darker fl.

S. purpuras'cens. 1 to 2 ft. h. *l.* broad-ovate, obtuse, margin wavy, somewhat hispid above or glabrous on both sides; stalk long. *fl.* ¾ in. long, tube and upper lip bright blue, lower lip dark violet with a median white stripe; infl. a terminal loose raceme. S. America. 1880. (B.M. 6464.) Stove perennial.

S. resino'sa. Much-branched, erect, about 1 ft. h., minutely hairy and glandular. *l.* ovate or spatulate-oblong, blunt, green on both surfaces, entire, resinous-glandular, not cordate at base. *fl.* blue, densely hairy; cal. hairy; raceme secund, leafy. Middle United States. (B.B. ed. 2, 3. 108.) SYN. *S. Wrightii.*

S. splen'dens. Hairy, about 1 ft. h., stems ascending, branched. *l.* broad-ovate, obtuse or almost so, 4 to 5 in. long, deeply cordate, hairy on both surfaces; stalked. *fl.* scarlet, nearly 1 in. long, tube long, slender, lobes short; scattered on a long raceme. October. Mexico. 1841. (B.M. 4290 as *S. cordifolia.*) Tender perennial.

S. Ventena'tii. Erect, branched, softly hairy perennial, about 18 in. h. *l.* cordate-ovate, rather blunt, deeply toothed, rather thick; long-stalked. *fl.* scarlet, long, upper lip 4-cleft; cal. small; bracts deciduous, narrow; racemes terminal, long, more or less secund. August. Colombia. 1844. (B.M. 4271.) Greenhouse.

S. viola'cea. Erect, branched from base, 18 to 24 in. h., downy, perennial. *l.* ovate, 1½ to 3 in. long, cordate or rounded at base, toothed, downy beneath especially on veins; stalk slender, 1¼ to 2¼ in. long. *fl.* violet with white blotches, about ¾ in. long, in opposite pairs in a terminal, many-fld. secund raceme up to 6 in. long. July. India, Ceylon. 1900. (B.M. 8320.) Warm house.

scutella'tus -a -um, shield-shaped.

SCUTICA'RIA (*scutica*, a whip; alluding to the shape of the leaves). FAM. *Orchidaceae.* A genus of 2 or 3 species of epiphytic orchids, found in Brazil and Guiana. Flowers very handsome; sepals sub-equal, erecto-patent, the lateral ones adnate with the foot of the column forming a prominent chin; petals rather smaller; lip sessile, articulated, broad and concave, the lateral lobes large, erect, the middle one small and spreading; pollen masses 4; peduncles short, stout, usually 2-flowered growing from the base of the stem. Leaves solitary, very long, fleshy, slender, subterete, furrowed, continuous with the small stem-like pseudobulbs, hardly distinguishable as such, carried on a rather stout branching rhizome. They thrive either on rafts or in baskets. Compost should consist of Sphagnum moss and Osmunda fibre in equal parts, or with slightly more fibre. A thin layer should be placed over the raft. If baskets are used they should be suspended vertically. For *S. Hadwenii* baskets are preferable and should be suspended in normal position. During the growing season abundance of water must be supplied to the roots. Propagation may be effected by divisions as growth begins, when plants are large enough. Exposure to light should be given in autumn. A minimum winter temperature of 55° F. is usually sufficient, but plants from warm localities are better suited with 60° F. The syringe may be freely used during the summer.

S. Dodgson'ii. *fl.* 2; sep. and pet. brownish, darker at base, blotched with yellow or red with a few whitish markings; lip white streaked with light rose and yellow, or veined with purple-red, veins hairy, strongly 3-lobed. Demerara? about 1877. Allied to *S. Hadwenii* and probably a variety of that species.

Scuticaria Hadwenii

S. Hadwen'ii.* *fl.* 3 to 4 in. across; pet. and sep. ½ in. broad, yellow-green, beautifully blotched rich brown; lip large, over 1 in. wide, white with broken lines of rose, downy within. June. *l.* erect ¼ in. h. 1½ ft., often less. Guiana, Brazil, 1851. (B.M. 4629 as *Bifrenaria Hadwenii.*) var. **bell'a** has sep. and pet. whitish-yellow without, brilliant shining cinnamon within, with a few spots, bars, and blotches of whitish-sulphur, lip wide, with one light-brown spot behind and a larger one in front of the callus, radiating light-brown lines on lateral lobes and mauve lines on anterior lobe; **Dodgson'ii,** *see* **S. Dodgsonii**; **pardali'na,** sep. and pet. light yellow with brown circles or polygonal figures, lip light ochre near base, white in front, with radiating mauve-purple streaks.

S. Steel'ii. *fl.* about 3 in. across, primrose yellow, with reddish-brown blotches, fragrant; lip marked with brownish-crimson especially on side lobes, mid-lobe 2-lobed in front, spreading crest with 3 orange teeth in front; scape 1- to 3-fld. *l.* terete, 2 to 4 ft. long, pendent, channelled, tapering to a fine point. British Guiana, Brazil. 1834. (W.O.A. 55; B.M. 3573 and B.R. 1986 as *Maxillaria Steelii.*) **S. Keyseria'na** is closely allied and probably a variety.

E. C.

SCYPHULA'RIA (*skyphos*, a cup). FAM. *Polypodiaceae.* A genus of 7 species of ferns related to Davallia with once-pinnate fronds with few linear, nearly entire segments. Sori as in Davallia. For treatment *see* **Davallia.**

S. pentaphyl'la.* *rhiz.* creeping, stout, densely fibrillose. *sti.* erect, strong, 2 to 4 in. long. *Fronds* with a terminal and 2 or 3 pairs of lateral segs.; terminal seg. of fertile frond linear, 4 to 6 in. long, ½ in. broad, of barren frond broader and shorter. *Sori* in 2 rows along the slightly toothed margins. Java, Polynesia. (L.F. 8, 18.) SYN. *Davallia pentaphylla.*

SCYTAL'IA chinen'sis. A synonym of *Litchi chinensis.*

SCYTHES. Little used in gardens nowadays except for cutting grass where a machine cannot conveniently be worked. A scythe for lawn-mowing should be hung differently from those used amongst long field-grass. The stick and handles should be attached so that the edge of the blade may be slightly raised above ground when the back is resting on the ground. The mower must be careful to avoid, as far as possible, any ribbing—that is, mowing so as to show the marks of the scythe after the grass has been swept up and taken away. This is scarcely possible unless the blade has been attached to the handle for the special purpose of cutting short grass.

scytophyl'lus -a -um, leather-leaved.

SEA BUCKTHORN. *See* **Hippophae.**

SEA HEATH. *See* **Frankenia.**

SEA HOLLY. *See* **Eryngium maritimum.**

SEA LAVENDER. *See* **Limonium.**

SEA ONION. *See* **Urginea maritima.**

SEA PINK. *See* **Armeria maritima.**

SEA RAGWORT. *See* **Senecio Cineraria.**

SEAFORTH'IA. *See* **Ptychosperma elegans.**

SEAKALE (*Crambe maritima*). A hardy herbaceous perennial; the blanched young leaf-stalks and shoots are used as a vegetable while still crisp and tender. The stronger the shoots are the better and the chief object in cultivation of Seakale is to secure good, large roots and crowns previous to forcing. The best type of soil, since the roots have often to be lifted in winter, is a sandy loam, but a well-cultivated, deep, rather heavy soil will grow the finest roots. In any case the soil must be rich, well-drained, deep, and in a sunny place free from trees. Before a plantation is made the soil must be deeply and thoroughly cultivated, and well manured with farmyard manure or its equivalent. If there is any tendency to sourness it should be limed. Cultivation should be carried out in autumn ready for the spring planting and the soil left in ridges to ensure good working later. In early March, as soon as weather permits, it should be levelled down and marked out ready for planting, the distance of planting being dependent on the type of forcing or growing to be adopted. Seakale may be raised from seeds or from cuttings. Though the amount of variation from seed is apparently not great, it has been found that the progeny of some seedlings is markedly inferior to that of others in the readiness with which it responds to forcing and there is also variation in colour, and though Seakale is easily raised from seed, growers, because of these variations usually resort to root-cuttings as the chief means of propagation, furthermore it takes 2 years from seed to obtain crowns fit for forcing, whereas 1 year is sufficient from cuttings.

The seed should be sown on beds of rich soil with a fine tilth in March in drills 1 in. deep and 12 in. apart. The seedlings should be thinned out (wherever possible choosing the strongest) to about 6 in. apart in the rows and the bed should be hoed frequently during the summer, a dressing of nitrate of soda or nitro-chalk being given to encourage growth, or watering with liquid manure may be substituted. The seedlings should be transferred to their permanent quarters in the following March, having the top cut off just below the crown before planting as this has a tendency to reduce the number of shoots formed and to retard flower with the result that stronger crowns are produced for forcing.

Cuttings, or thongs as they are frequently called, are clean straight pieces of the side roots about the thickness of an ordinary lead drawing pencil and they are obtained from the trimmings of the roots lifted and prepared for forcing. The best of the side roots are selected, cut in pieces 5 or 6 in. long, the upper end (nearest the main root) being cut off straight, the lower slanting. These thongs are then tied in bundles and stood in layers in damp sand or fine earth with 3 in. of sand between the layers until planting time in the following spring; or they may be put in a thick layer on a raised bed, to secure thorough drainage, with 3 in. of soil over them. The thongs by the spring will have developed several eyes or buds at the upper flat end and before planting all of these except the strongest must be rubbed off. In planting the thongs are dibbled in so that the crown is about 1 in. below the soil surface.

Both seedlings and plants raised from cuttings should have all flowers that tend to develop removed so as to avoid the drain that seed production involves.

Blanching is done both by lifting the plants in autumn (beginning about November) and forcing the roots in heat, and also on the ground where the plants are growing.

Planting where the plants are to be lifted for forcing, or for blanching on the ground by other means than Seakale pots, should be 15 to 18 in. apart each way. Where Seakale pots are to be used the plants should be set in clumps of 3 or 4, 4 in. apart, leaving 2 ft. between the clumps in the row and 3 ft. between the rows of clumps. Plants that are lifted for forcing are of no further use and should be thrown away, not, however, on to the compost heap since pieces of the root so readily grow, and for the same reason care should be taken to lift the plants completely, leaving none of the roots in the ground. Plants forced or blanched on the ground without forcing ('natural' Seakale) will, however, give a crop for several years in succession if well manured and prevented from flowering.

Seakale is very easily forced. For this purpose as soon as the leaves die down in autumn the roots are lifted and trimmed, leaving about 5 in. of the main axis with the crown on top. Those not wanted are put into moist sandy soil in a shed, or in a trench in the open with some dry litter over them to protect from frost, and drawn from as required. The roots to be immediately forced are planted about 3 in. apart in a bed of fine compost, half old hotbed manure, quarter garden soil, quarter sand with a little 'fallen' lime, all sifted and about 8 to 10 in. deep; when planted the soil is watered gently with tepid water and then covered to a depth of about 3 in. with fine dry soil or fine dry litter, chaff, for example. For this earliest forcing, about mid-November, the best roots should be selected and forcing can be done in any place where absolute darkness and a temperature of 50 to 55° and not more than 60° F. can be had, beginning with a low temperature, and raising it by the aid of hot-water pipes or fermenting material, preferably below the roots. Provided absolute darkness is secured pots or boxes covered with inverted pots or boxes can be used satisfactorily, or where hotbeds are available box frames with the lights covered with mats or with wooden coverings in place of lights answer admirably. If the conditions are right some of the Seakale will be ready for cutting about 4 weeks after the forcing begins. Temporary pits may also be easily constructed with a hotbed of fermenting material at the bottom and the compost recommended above, the sides banked up outside with the soil removed in making the pit, the pit covered with boards and these in turn by a good layer of litter. Beds may also be made without a hotbed where fermenting material cannot be obtained in sufficient quantity, raising them above the level to secure thorough drainage and planting the whole bed at once, covering part successively with frames and filling the space between the frames with hot manure well trodden down. Blanching on the ground where the plants are growing may be done where the soil is sandy by throwing the soil from between the beds on to the bed to a depth of 8 in. By this method Seakale may be had by the middle of March and through April, the cracking of the surface showing when cutting may begin. Care must be taken to see that any leaves breaking through are protected from light by a covering of dry litter. This 'natural' kale is of excellent quality.

DISEASES. Seakale may be attacked by Finger and Toe or Club Root disease (*Plasmodiophora brassicae*), but this is only likely to occur if the soil is very acid, and the remedy is the same as for other cruciferous crops affected by this disease. Violet Root Rot (*Helicobasidium purpureum*) may also be seen on Seakale with its reddish-purple net of fungus threads covering the surface of the root and causing injury. Such roots must be destroyed because this fungus can attack so many other vegetables. The most common Seakale trouble is Black Rot (*Pseudomonas campestris*) where the vascular system is blackened so that affected roots when cut across show a darkened or black-dotted ring-like appearance in the region of the vascular strands. Such crowns are likely to be weak and of little use in forcing and any root-cuttings (thongs) and mother crowns seen to be affected should be destroyed.

(D. E. G.)

SEAL FLOWER. *See* **Dicentra spectabilis.**

Searsiae, in honour of Sarah C. Sears, American artist and amateur botanist, *c.* 1908.

SEASIDE ALDER. *See* **Alnus maritima.**

SEASIDE BALSAM. *See* **Croton Eluteria.**

SEASIDE GRAPE. *See* **Coccoloba uvifera.**

SEASIDE PLANTING. The seaside, as generally understood, is the coast-land immediately adjoining the sea and consequently exposed to strong winds often more or less laden with salt spray. Both the strong wind and the salt spray have an evil effect on trees and shrubs and, with some exceptions, on plant life generally. In the formation of new gardens in such places the first important requisite is to establish a screen of some sort between the garden and the sea. This is best accomplished by the use of trees and shrubs that are most capable of withstanding violent winds. Where there is absolutely no protection from these, it is often useful at the beginning to erect some sort of artificial wind-break even if it is only made of wattled hurdles. Even with this protection both trees and shrubs must be planted in a small state to avoid rocking in the wind and the consequent loosening of the roots before they are established. It is well also to plant fairly thickly for mutual protection. Larger plants can, of course, be used but they must be very securely staked.

For building up this frontal rampart of vegetation there is not a very great variety of species available, and they should be either sturdy and stiff enough to hold their own, or sufficiently supple to give to the wind without breaking, as, for instance, willows and tamarisks. The following can be recommended:

Trees. *Pinus Pinaster* and *P. radiata* in the south, Austrian and Corsican pines in the colder north, especially the former. *P. halepensis*, the outstanding sea pine of the Adriatic, would no doubt be admirable for the south but at present it is not obtainable in quantity. The common Sycamore (*Acer Pseudoplatanus*) is extremely useful in the front line and so are the wild pear (*Pyrus communis*), the Swedish whitebeam (*Sorbus intermedia*), Hawthorn, and other species of Crataegus.

The choice of shrubs is greater. Amongst evergreens, *Quercus Ilex*, the Holm Oak, naturally of course a big tree, is very valuable in its smaller state, keeping as it does close-growing and compact. There may be recommended also the larger, stronger-growing Barberries and Cotoneasters, *Pinus montana* in its shrubby forms, *Olearia Haastii*, New Zealand Veronicas, the thick-leaved varieties of Holly. In the milder localities *Escallonia macrantha* and *Euonymus japonicus* are excellent.

Turning to deciduous subjects there is a larger variety. The common Tamarisks with their supple branches and minute foliage are indispensable. The shrubby Willows are also valuable for their suppleness. *Hippophaë rhamnoides*, wild as it is on our sea-shores, is, of course, perfectly at home. Then there are *Lycium chinense*, Sweet-brier, Dog-rose, *Salix Caprea*, oval-leaved Privet, and Blackthorn.

When once this rampart has been established, the choice of ornamental trees and shrubs that can be grown protected by it becomes practically unlimited, for the climatic influence of the sea is very favourable to the cultivation of the most beautiful species of S. Europe, New Zealand, Chile, Japan, China, and N. India.

W. J. B.

SEASIDE PLUM. *See* **Ximenia americana.**

SEASIDE POPPY. *See* **Glaucium flavum.**

SEATS. Seats are desirable in most gardens as resting places, and often as necessary adjuncts to outdoor features such as terraces or vistas, as well as for areas on which games are played. They may be of the simplest form in woodland or in a park away from buildings, such as a trunk sawn down the middle and fixed to two lengths of trunk sunk upright in the ground as supports, or even a fallen log. Such seats are lasting and not uncomfortable. If it is desirable that they should be sheltered from the wind to a greater extent than the wood itself affords, no attempt should be made to disguise them with 'rustic work', but thatched walls and roof (using reed, straw, or leather) or split wood hurdles will not be out of keeping with their surroundings. Such log or plank seats are also suitable for cricket and football grounds if permanent seats are to be provided in the open. For lawn tennis and croquet lawns and bowling greens, usually much nearer the house, more formal seats are needed as they are in the garden proper, and still more formal seats of a design in keeping with the house itself are more in keeping on a terrace. Seats may be of material and construction that will need to be taken into shelter when not in use, but if of a permanent character may be of various sizes with backs or even something in the nature of forms. They may be made of wood or have an iron frame with laths of pitch pine or other durable wood or light steel spring laths for the seat. Of whatever construction, they should be sturdy and stand steady in their position. Unless made of teak, cedar, or oak they will need to be well painted and kept painted regularly. If of teak, cedar, or oak, an annual dressing of oil will be an advantage. Wherever possible these seats should be stored under shelter in winter and before being placed in position in spring should have any necessary repairs made. Except as an architectural feature stone seats are not very desirable in our climate and they, of course, remain in position the year through.

Seats in the garden should be carefully placed in relation to their surroundings and where it will not be uncomfortable to sit upon them. Either they should be sited so that a pleasant picture is before the eyes of the occupant, or shade, seclusion, or shelter from wind may be the primary consideration. While a seat constructed around the bole of a large tree or well under a weeping tree may be pleasant, it is usually a mistake to place it near the periphery of the branches of a tree where drip will be frequent.

At one time, happily in the past, seats and shelters made of contorted limbs of trees were a vogue. Simple, sturdy lines are much better and more in keeping with a garden. Intricate patterns of scroll work, however beautiful for screens and gates, are not pleasing in seats.

SEAWEEDS belong to the Algae (q.v.). On some parts of the coast they are abundant and many, often of large size, are washed up after storms. They form valuable manure and are much used for this purpose where the distance of carting does not render them out of reach. They are not only rich in nutritive salts but decay rapidly when dug into the soil and so yield their components quickly for the use of plants. They vary in composition and often contain decaying animal matter mixed in the mass from dead sea animals which adds to their value. They are usually rich in potash and lime but rather deficient in phosphates which can be made good by the addition of bone-meal. They seem to be very useful in preparing the ground for potatoes and for turnips and members of the turnip family generally.

seba'ceus -a -um, wax-like, producing wax.

SEBAE'A (in honour of Albert Seba, 1665–1736, apothecary and botanical author of Amsterdam). FAM. *Gentianaceae.* A genus of over 20 species of erect annual herbs, natives of Trop. and southern Africa, Madagascar, Australia, and New Zealand. Leaves sessile or stem-clasping, often small. Flowers whitish or yellow, rather small, numerous, in corymbose cymes, rarely few or solitary and long-stalked or almost sessile on the branches; calyx 4- or 5-parted; corolla tube cylindrical then swollen, lobes 4 or 5, spreading, twisted; stamens 4 or 5, filaments short. The seeds of the 3 species mentioned below should be raised in a warm house, the seedlings being planted out in a warm sheltered border at the end of May, or grown in pans in the cool greenhouse.

S. al'bens. About 6 in. h. *l.* cordate-oblong. *fl.* whitish; cal. lobes obtuse; cor. lobes elliptic, obtuse, nearly as long as the wide tube. August. S. Africa. 1820.

S. au'rea. About 6 in. h. *l.* cordate-triangular in lower part, ovate or lanceolate above, all obtuse. *fl.* golden-yellow; sep. 5; cor. lobes elliptic-oblong, equalling the tube; cymes many-fld. July. S. Africa. 1824.

S. ova'ta. About 6 in. h. *l.* ovate, somewhat rounded at base, slightly obtuse. *fl.* yellow; sep. 5, ovate-lanceolate; cor. lobes ovate, rather acute, half as long as tube. August. Australia, Tasmania, New Zealand. 1820.

F. G. P.

SEBESTI'NA. *See* **Cordia Sebestena.** From the Arabian name of *C. Sebestena.*

seb'ifer, -a -um, wax-bearing.

secali'nus -a -um, rye-like.

SECATEUR. Small hand pruning-shears, in effect scissors with 1 or 2 short cutting blades strong enough to shear through shoots, and to make a clean cut. The best makes will cut woody shoots up to ¾ in. thick. In the French type the blades are curved and bevelled on one side, in the more modern Rolcut type the cutting-edge is straight, bevelled on both sides, and cuts against a soft-metal anvil with rounded edges which goes far to avoid the crushing action which often occurred when the older type was used and which made them much inferior to the knife as a pruning-tool. Secateurs are more expeditious in use than the knife and more comfortable to use with prickly stems but they must above all be kept keen if they are not to do delicate shoots considerable injury.

sechella'rum, of the Seychelle Is., Indian Ocean.

SECH'IUM (from the W. Indian name, *chacha*). FAM. *Cucurbitaceae.* The only species is a slightly hispid, tendril-climbing, perennial herb needing greenhouse protection and considerable room for its development. It is grown for its fruit in the W. Indies and in other warm regions and these fruits have occasionally found their way to our markets as Chayotes. They are interesting as containing only 1 seed which often germinates in the fruit, the cotyledons extending towards the base of the fruit and the hypocotyl emerging at its apex, forming roots which enter the soil, after which the stem grows from between the cotyledons. Ordinary soil suits it.

S. ed'ule. Chaco, Chayota, Chocho Plant. Climber to 12 ft. Root, developed in second year, large and fleshy, up to 20 lb. in weight, yam-like and, after cooking, with a similar flavour. *l.* heart-shaped, angled or lobed. *fl.* monoecious, yellow, in long racemes, somewhat clustered, shortly stalked; cor. rotate, deeply 5-parted. June. *fr.* obovoid or pear-shaped, deeply grooved, about 4 in. long, fleshy, 1-seeded. Trop. America. 1816. (B.M. 8738.)

SECOND GROWTHS. Growths from the buds of a shoot which is itself still actively lengthening; or shoots produced after the normal season, often formed after injury to the terminal bud.

SECRETION. A substance sorted out from the sap by a gland, as the chalk by the glands on a Saxifrage leaf.

secun'dus -a -um (*secundi-* in compound words), directed to one side, used especially of the flowers in an inflorescence.

SECURIDA'CA (*securis*, hatchet; from the shape of the wing at the end of the pod). FAM. *Polygalaceae.* A genus of about 30 species of shrubs, often climbing, mostly natives of Trop. America, but some of Trop. Asia or Africa. Leaves alternate, usually entire, 2-glandular. Flowers in terminal and axillary panicles or racemes. Sepals unequal, the 2 largest petaloid, wing-like; the 2 lateral adnate to the staminal tube towards its base, erecto-connivent; keel concave-hooded, erect, or broadly 3-lobed; stamens 8. The 2 species mentioned need a compost of loam, peat, and sand and stove conditions. They are readily propagated by cuttings in sand under a bell-glass in heat.

S. erec'ta. Erect shrub of 10 to 15 ft. *l.* ovate-lanceolate to oblong, 1½ to 2 in. long, puberulous beneath. *fl.* red, in dense panicles; dorsal sep. spatulate, blunt, wings orbicular as long as the shortly 2-lobed keel. July. Trop. America. 1824.

S. virga'ta. High climber. *l.* rounded at both ends or somewhat notched, about ¾ in. wide, but much smaller on flowering branches. *fl.* variegated, scented, distant; cor. yellow; wings rosy without, white within; racemes terminal, filiform, drooping. W. Indies. 1739.

SECURIG'ERA (*securis*, hatchet, *gero*, to bear; from the shape of the pods). FAM. *Leguminosae.* A single annual herb. To be treated as a hardy annual in any garden soil.

S. Coronil'la. Axe-weed. Hatchet Vetch. About 1 ft. h. *l.* unequally pinnate, lflets. entire; stipules small, membranous. *fl.* yellow, at tips of axillary peduncles, nodding; pet. free of staminal tube; standard nearly round. July. S. Europe, &c. 1562. (S.B.F.G. as *Coronilla Securidacea.*)

SECURINE'GA (*securis*, hatchet, *nego*, to refuse; in reference to the extreme hardness of the wood). FAM. *Euphorbiaceae.* A genus of about 10 species of branched shrubs inhabiting temperate and tropical regions. Leaves alternate, entire, often small. Flowers monoecious or dioecious, greenish-white, apetalous, clustered in the leaf-axils; males small, numerous, stamens usually 5 with a 5-lobed disk at the base, females fewer or solitary. The Securinegas grow well in any rich, loamy soil and can be propagated readily by cuttings of the half-ripe wood in sand under a glass in heat.

S. duris'sima. Otaheite Myrtle. Bois dur. Tree of about 35 ft. *l.* usually oblong-ovate, acute, shortly narrowed to the petioles. *fl.* white; cal. silky-downy; males almost sessile; females at length somewhat spreading. June. Mauritius, &c. 1793. Stove.

S. flueggeoi'des. Somewhat resembles *S. ramiflora* but branchlets soon become brownish or purple and *l.* more obtuse. China, Korea, Japan. SYN. *S. japonica.*

S. ramiflo'ra. Branchlets numerous, yellowish, 4-angled, leafy. *l.* ovate-lanceolate, 1 to 1¾ in. long, narrowed to both ends, glabrous, pale beneath. *fl.* male in small clusters, female solitary. E. Asia. SYN. *Flueggea suffruticosa, Phyllanthus ramiflorus, Xylophylla ramiflora.*

SEDGE. *See* **Carex.**

SEDGE, COTTON. *See* **Eriophorum.**

sedifo'lius -a -um, having Sedum-like leaves.

sedoi'des, Sedum-like.

SE'DUM (*sedo*, to sit; in reference to the manner in which some species attach themselves to rocks and walls). FAM. *Crassulaceae.* A genus of about 300 species of glabrous or glandular-downy, fleshy, erect or decumbent, sometimes tufted or moss-like herbs or more rarely subshrubs mostly natives of temperate or frigid regions of the N. Hemisphere, several on mountains in warmer regions as far south as the Philippines, Cent. Africa, and Bolivia. The plants are mainly perennial but there are several annual or biennial species. Leaves flat to cylindrical, entire or nearly so, usually alternate, sometimes opposite or whorled. Flowers usually 2-sexual and 5- (rarely 3-, 4-, 6-, or 7-) parted, white or yellow, more rarely red or purple, very rarely blue. Sepals, petals, and carpels equal in number, stamens usually twice as many; sepals often fleshy and leaf-like; petals free to base or slightly joined; stamens free or those opposite petals adnate to them in lower part; carpels free or nearly so. Fruit a number of usually many-seeded follicles. Sedum is very closely related to Crassula, Cotyledon, and Sempervivum and there is at times some doubt as to where a given plant should be placed. This has led to some small groups being cut off from the rest and constituted separate genera, but it seems best to retain those most nearly approaching the general character of Sedum within that genus, the new genus to which some botanists have assigned them being indicated in the synonyms. Sedums are usually very easily grown, some being best accommodated on the rock-garden, some do well on walls, or roofs, some are fine border plants, and *S. bithynicum minus* has been used in carpet bedding. The habit of the plant will be a guide as to the best position to give it. The soil should generally be of an open, loamy type but a few species (indicated below) are the better for a damp situation and the Telephium type do best in a rich moist loam. The majority of species in cultivation are hardy: those that are not (indicated below) are safe in the alpine-house as a rule, several of them, as well as the hardy species, making excellent plants for pans. Most Sedums are readily propagated by cuttings or by division as well as by seed and many will form plants from leaves and indeed do so in nature when by any chance leaves are knocked off. Some even of the monocarpic species like *S. indicum* will do so. Much information on the genus will be found in 'An account of the genus Sedum as found in cultivation', by R. Lloyd Praeger in *Journal, R.H.S.*, vol. 46, pp. 1–314, and on the classification in *The Genus Sedum: a Systematic Essay*, by Dr. Harald Fröderström (Meddelanden från Göteborgs Botaniska Trädgård, vols. v–x, 1930–5). **A**

KEY

1.	*Annual or monocarpic (some occasionally perennial through persistent winter buds)*	2
1.	*Perennial*	21
2.	*Lvs. flat; basal lvs. in a rosette*	3
2.	*Lvs. semi-terete or cylindrical; if flat not forming rosettes*	8
3.	*Rosettes scarcely Sempervivum-like. Fl. white with red markings*	4
3.	*Rosettes Sempervivum-like. Fl. white to purple. Plant more or less downy*	6
4.	*Stamens 10*	5
4.	*Stamens 5*	S. indicum
5.	*Lvs. fimbriate at tips*	S. fimbriatum
5.	*Lvs. spine-tipped, not fimbriate*	S. spinosum
6.	*Infl. broad-corymbose*	7
6.	*Infl. long; peduncle short. Rosette not downy*	S. Lampusae

7\. *Pet. free almost to base* S. sempervivoides
7\. *Pet. entire; cor. almost bell-shaped* S. pilosum
8\. *Lvs. flattish* 9
8\. *Lvs. semi-terete to cylindrical* 13
9\. *Fl. white to purplish* 10
9\. *Fl. yellow* 12
10\. *Fl. purplish. Lvs. spatulate, glabrous* S. stellatum
10\. *Fl. white* 11
11\. *Scales somewhat lobed. Plant tall, much-branched* S. Cepaea
11\. *Scales spatulate, concave. Plant weak* S. monregalense
12\. *Plant glabrous, more or less erect* S. formosanum
12\. *Plant clammy-downy* S. drymarioides (viscosum)
13\. *Fl. white to purple* 14
13\. *Fl. yellow* 19
14\. *Fl.* 4-*parted; stamens* 4 S. nevadense
14\. *Fl.* 5- *to* 9-*parted* 15
15\. *Fl. blue,* 7- *to* 9-*parted* S. coeruleum
15\. *Fl. not blue* 16
16\. *Downy* 17
16\. *Glabrous or almost so* 18
17\. *Infl. corymbose, few-fld.* S. villosum
17\. *Infl. with* 3 *or* 4 *erect branches. Fl.* 5-*parted* S. rubens
18\. *Branches few. Infl. a dense corymb. Stamens* 10. *Lvs. obovate* S. atratum
18\. *Branched from base. Infl. loose, flattish. Lvs. linear* S. hispanicum
19\. *Plant small* 20
19\. *Plant bushy, rather dense, to* 6 *in. h. Lvs. often in whorls of* 4. *Stamens* 5 S. Leblancae
20\. *Lvs. linear-oblong to obovate* (*some perennial forms are known*) S. annuum
20\. *Lvs. broad-oblong* S. Nuttallianum
21\. *Rootstock thickened. Stems annual or biennial* 22
21\. *Stems perennial with both barren and annual-flowering shoots* 64
22\. *Rootstock fleshy crowned with scales or lvs. with a broad clasping base in the axils of which the annual stems arise* 23
22\. *Rootstock without such scales* 35
23\. *Crown lvs. scale-like, sometimes green and fleshy when young* 24
23\. *Rootstock slender, not much thickened. Crown-lvs. with a distinct blade, usually stalked. Fl.* 5-*parted* 34
24\. *Rootstock subterranean usually without persistent dry stems* 25
24\. *Rootstock projecting above ground, branched, old stems persistent* 31
25\. *Fl. usually* 1-*sexual,* 4- *to* 6-*parted. Pet. yellow to purple* 26
25\. *Fl. hermaphrodite,* 5-*parted. Pet. reddish-white* 29
26\. *Stem stout, up to* 3 *ft. h.* 27
26\. *Stem slender, up to* 18 *in. h. Lvs. oblong to orbicular* S. bupleuroides
27\. *Lvs. broad or very large, toothed or somewhat lobed* 28
27\. *Lvs. linear, long* S. Kirilowii
28\. *Lvs. broad, toothed. Pet. oblong* S. roseum
28\. *Lvs. very large, sometimes lobed. Infl. somewhat thyrsoid* S. yunnanense
29\. *Lvs. alternate, entire. Pet. entire* 30
29\. *Lvs. crowded above. Pet. erose* S. linearifolium
30\. *Lvs. linear, up to* 2 *in. long. Stamens as long as pet.* S. Semenovii
30\. *Lvs. oblong, up to* 1 *in. long. Stamens shorter than pet.* S. rhodanthum
31\. *Fl. usually hermaphrodite,* 4- *to* 6-*parted* 32
31\. *Fl. usually* 1-*sexual,* 4-*parted* 33
32\. *Pet. fringed, large* S. dumulosum
32\. *Pet. entire, rather small. Plant stoloniferous* S. crassipes
33\. *Lvs. small, entire. Fl. white to purple* S. quadrifidum
33\. *Fl. and fr. larger. Fl. deep purple* S. fastigiatum
34\. *Stem lvs. toothed, acute* S. Hobsonii
34\. *Stem lvs. entire, blunt* S. primuloides
35\. *Rootstock usually thick and often with carrot-like tubers. Stems annual from beside or above bases of stems of previous year* 36
35\. *Roots slender* 50
36\. *Fl. dioecious,* 4-*parted* S. yunnanense
36\. *Fl. hermaphrodite,* 5-*parted* 37
37\. *Stems tall* (*up to* 36 *in.*), *stout, erect. Lvs.* 2 *to* 4 *in. long* 38
37\. *Stems short* (*about* 6 *in.*), *weak, not erect. Lvs. up to* 1 *in. long* 45
38\. *Rootstock broad, fleshy. Stem shrubby up to* 18 *in. Lvs. ovate, cordate, coarsely toothed, stalked* S. populifolium
38\. *Rootstock with carrot-like roots. Lvs. sessile or almost so* 39
39\. *Lvs. opposite or ternate as a rule* 40
39\. *Lvs. alternate or in whorls of* 4 *or* 5 43
40\. *Fl. white or greenish-white* 41
40\. *Fl. pink* 42
41\. *Lvs. deep green to purple. Fl. greenish-white* S. maximum
41\. *Lvs. pale glaucous green. Fl. white; carpels rosy* S. alboroseum
42\. *Lvs. pale glaucous green. Stamens* $1\frac{1}{2}$ *times as long as pet. Infl.* 4 *to* 6 *in. across* S. spectabile
42\. *Lvs. scarcely glaucous. Stamens* $1\frac{1}{2}$ *times as long as pet. Infl. about* 2 *in. across* S. pseudospectabile
43\. *Lvs. alternate* 44
43\. *Lvs. in whorls of* 4 *or* 5, *toothed. Fl. greenish-yellow* S. verticillatum
44\. *Scales of fl. broad* S. telephioides
44\. *Scales of fl. narrow* S. Telephium
45\. *Stems annual, arching or at least erect at base* 46
45\. *Stems perennial, creeping* 49
46\. *Lvs. deeply toothed* S. Tatarinowii
46\. *Lvs. cordate-ovate* 47
47\. *Lvs. ternate* S. Sieboldii
47\. *Lvs. opposite* 48
48\. *Lvs. stalked* S. caulicolum
48\. *Lvs. sessile* S. Ewersii
49\. *Lvs. obovate to orbicular* S. Anacampseros
49\. *Lvs. of fl.-shoots oblong to oblong-linear* S. cyaneum
50\. *Rootstock thick. Stems annual* (*except hybridum*). *Lvs. flat. Fl. yellow* 51
50\. *Rootstock thickening horizontally or contracted. Stems tufted, erect, at least at first, biennial, or if annual winter green* 56
51\. *Downy. Stems few, erect* S. Selskianum
51\. *Glabrous* 52
52\. *Stems few, erect, up to* 30 *in. h.* S. Aizoon
52\. *Stems slender, decumbent or spreading* 53
53\. *Stems decumbent, tufted* S. hybridum
53\. *Stems many, spreading, up to* 16 *in. h.* 54
54\. *Lvs. oblong. Sep. small* 55
54\. *Lvs. narrow. Sep. long* S. Middendorffianum
55\. *Stems unbranched. Lvs. light green. Fl.* $\frac{5}{8}$ *in. across* S. Ellacombianum
55\. *Stems finally branched. Lvs. dark green. Fl.* $\frac{3}{4}$ *in. across, orange-yellow* S. kamtschaticum
56\. *Stems* 6 *to* 12 *in. h. from a Sempervivum-like l.-rosette* 57
56\. *Stems* 3 *to* 6 *in. h., annual or biennial with basal rosette* 58
57\. *Glabrous throughout* S. glabrum
57\. *Downy throughout* S. ebracteatum
58\. *Fl. yellow* 59
58\. *Fl. white or flushed red* 60
59\. *Lvs. ovate, very blunt. Sep. not spurred* S. diversifolium
59\. *Lvs. oblong. Sep. spurred* S. Greggii
60\. *Lvs. linear to linear-oblong* 61
60\. *Lvs. spatulate* 63
61\. *Lvs. linear-oblong, papillose, crowded* S. alamosanum
61\. *Lvs. glabrous, linear to linear-lanceolate* 62
62\. *Lvs. at right angles to stem, papillose, green then red* S. mellitulum
62\. *Lvs. ascending, linear-terete, crowded on barren shoots* S. potosinum
63\. *Glabrous. Fl. white; about* $\frac{1}{2}$ *in. across; pet wavy* S. bellum
63\. *Downy. Fl. rosy; about* $\frac{3}{4}$ *in. across; pet. deflexed* S. versadense
64\. *Fl. white, red, or purple* 65
64\. *Fl. yellow* 99
65\. *Fl. white* 66
65\. *Fl. red or purple* 93
66\. *Sub-shrubs* 67
66\. *Herbs* 72
67\. *Stout or rather stout* 68
67\. *Slender with small sterile branches* 70
68\. *Lvs. spatulate-oblong, retuse. Stamens attached well above base of pet.* S. retusum
68\. *Lvs. lanceolate to obovate, pale glaucous, smooth* 69
69\. *Sep. oblong, about* $\frac{1}{6}$ *in. long. Lvs. terete, very blunt* S. allantoides
69\. *Sep. broader than long, about* $\frac{1}{25}$ *in. long. Lvs. flat on face* S. Adolphi
70\. *Roots fibrous* 71
70\. *Roots tuberous* S. guadalajarum
71\. *Scales of fl. linear. Branches red. Lvs. green, flat above* S. Bourgaei
71\. *Scales of fl. quadrate. Branches grey. Lvs. glaucous, sub-terete* S. griseum
72\. *Lvs. flat on face* 73
72\. *Lvs. terete or sub-terete* 81
73\. *Fl.* 4-*parted. Stamens* 8. *Lvs. in whorls of* 3, *obovate* S. ternatum
73\. *Fl. usually* 5-*parted. Stamens* 10 74
74\. *Basal lvs. spatulate to oblanceolate* 75
74\. *Lvs. small, more or less ovate* 77
75\. *Basal lvs. forming an Echeveria-like rosette* S. Weinbergii
75\. *Apical lvs. forming a more or less loose rosette* 76
76\. *Fl. almost sessile. Infl. of* 3 *or more spreading branches* S. Nevii
76\. *Fl. long-stalked. Infl. very loose, glandular panicle* S. adenotrichum
77\. *Infl. few-fld.* 78
77\. *Infl. a raceme or panicle* 80
78\. *Stem covered by persistent white l.-bases* S. Liebmannianum
78\. *Stems very short or spreading* 79
79\. *Stems very short, densely leafy, forming a grey mat* S. compactum
79\. *Stems spreading, bare and red in lower part* S. moranense
80\. *Infl. a raceme. Stems* 3 *to* 4 *in. h.* S. magellense
80\. *Infl. a loose panicle. Stems up to* 6 *in. h.* S. alsinefolium
81\. *Fl.-stems up to* 12 *in. h., erect* 82

81. *Fl.-stems* 1½ *to* 4 *in. h., usually tufted* 84
82. *Lvs. linear, acute, smooth* S. subulatum
82. *Lvs. obovate to rhomboid* 83
83. *Lvs. linear-oblong to obovate,* ¼ *to* ½ *in. long, glabrous* S. album
83. *Lvs. ovate to rhomboid,* ½ *in. long, minutely downy* S. gypsicola
84. *Glabrous or nearly so* 85
84. *Downy* 92
85. *Lvs. linear-terete* S. lydium
85. *Lvs. oblong to ovoid* 86
86. *Stems spreading and few-fld. Lvs. blunt, somewhat ovate* S. Candollei
86. *Fl.-stems more or less erect* 87
87. *Pedicels downy* S. dasyphyllum
87. *Pedicels glabrous* 88
88. *Lvs. oblong to nearly orbicular* 89
88. *Lvs. globose or elliptic* 91
89. *Sep. spurred* 90
89. *Sep. not spurred, short* S. gracile
90. *Scales large, stalked, emarginate* S. tenellum
90. *Scales cup-shaped* S. farinosum
91. *Lvs. opposite, mealy. Fl.* $\frac{3}{16}$ *in. across* S. brevifolium
91. *Lvs. alternate, broadest about middle. Fl.* ½ *in. across* S. anglicum
92. *Cor. almost bell-shaped. Sep. broad* S. Winkleri
92. *Lvs. almost ovoid. Sep. broad. Pet. oblong, scarcely joined* S. hirsutum
93. *Herbs* 94
93. *Sub-shrub, glabrous, erect,* 2 *to* 3 *ft. h. Pet. linear-lanceolate* S. oxypetalum
94. *Lvs. flat* 95
94. *Lvs. terete. Stem erect. Fl.* 4*-parted* S. pulchellum
95. *Lvs.* ¾ *to* 1 *in. long* 96
95. *Lvs.* ¼ *in. long. Shoots densely crowded, glaucous. Fl.* 6*-parted* S. bithynicum
95. *Lvs.* ⅛ *to* ⅜ *in. long. Sterile stems straggling. Fl. sometimes partly white* S. longipes
96. *Stem straggling, angles winged. Pet. erose* S. rhodocarpum
96. *Stem not winged* 97
97. *Fl. brownish-yellow, red-spotted at back. Branches prostrate with lvs. in rosettes at ends* S. atlanticum
97. *Fl. reddish to purplish* 98
98. *Lvs. narrowed to stalk-like base. Sep. unequal* S. stoloniferum
98. *Lvs. spatulate-oblong. Sep. equal* S. obtusifolium
98. *Lvs. broad, crenate, fringed with hyaline hairs* S. spurium
99. *Sub-shrubs* 100
99. *Herbs* 106
100. *Infl. large, panicled, many-fld.* 101
100. *Infl. small, corymbose, few-fld.* 104
101. *Sep. long, unequal. Carpels nearly erect. Lvs. very thick* S. nutans
101. *Sep. short, broad. Carpels spreading* 102
102. *Stamens short* S. dendroideum
102. *Stamens nearly as long as pet.* 103
103. *Pet. oblong, about* ⅓ *in. long* S. confusum
103. *Pet. lanceolate, about* ¼ *in. long* S. praealtum
104. *Sep. linear to oblanceolate* 105
104. *Sep. spatulate-club-shaped* S. pachyphyllum
105. *Sep. spurred, blunt* S. amecamecanum
105. *Sep. without spurs, rather acute* S. Treleasei
106. *Lvs. opposite or whorled* 107
106. *Lvs. alternate* 113
107. *More or less procumbent* 108
107. *Tufted or sub-erect. Lvs. linear, blunt* S. mexicanum
108. *Puberulent. Lvs. ovoid, easily falling* S. Stahlii
108. *Glabrous. Lvs. ovate or narrow, not readily falling* 109
109. *Lvs. in loose rosettes, obovate with short stalk* S. rubroglaucum
109. *Lvs. not in rosettes* 110
110. *Lvs. obovate-spatulate, spreading. Fl.* ¾ *in. across* S. divergens
110. *Lvs. lanceolate or oblanceolate* 111
111. *Lvs. ternate, blunt. Fl.-stems densely mamillate* S. Chauveaudii
111. *Lvs. ternate, more or less acute. Fl.-stems smooth* 112
112. *Sep. rather broad. Anthers narrow* S. sarmentosum
112. *Sep. linear-lanceolate. Anthers oblong* S. lineare
113. *Lvs. spatulate, flat* 114
113. *Lvs. ovate to linear, not broadest above middle* 120
114. *Sprawling. Stems bare and rooting in lower part* 115
114. *Barren stems very short with terminal rosette* 116
115. *Lvs. blunt, glaucous, narrowed to base* S. Palmeri
115. *Lvs. acute, pale green, rather thin* S. compressum
116. *Rootstock stoloniferous with terminal l.-rosettes* 117
116. *Rootstock without stolons, l.-rosettes small* S. pruinosum
117. *Pet. long, acute, erect; buds* ⅝ *in. long, tapering. Lvs. green* S. oreganum
117. *Pet. oblong-lanceolate, spreading; buds oblong-ovate* 118
118. *Lvs. usually glaucous; lower lvs. smooth* S. spathulifolium
118. *Lvs. green; lower lvs. mamillate* 119
119. *Infl. corymbose* S. yosemitense
119. *Infl. thyrsoid* S. Hallii
120. *Stems more or less procumbent or arching or with stolons* 121
120. *More or less erect or tufted* 130
121. *Stoloniferous with sterile branches flowering in 2nd year. Fl.* 7*- to* 10*-parted* S. Jaccardianum
121. *Stems more or less procumbent or arching* 122
122. *Stems arching* 123
122. *Stems more or less procumbent* 124
123. *Lvs. blunt. Pet. nearly free* S. nudum
123. *Lvs. more or less pointed. Pet. united* S. fusiforme
124. *Lvs. blunt linear-oblong, almost terete,* ½ *in. long* S. japonicum
124. *Lvs. linear, more or less pointed,* ½ *in. or more long* 125
125. *Stamens hairy at base* 126
125. *Stamens glabrous* 129
126. *Infl. drooping in bud* 127
126. *Infl. erect in bud* 128
127. *Lvs. quite flat above* S. rupestre
127. *Lvs. terete* S. reflexum
128. *Infl. flat in bud, fl., and fr.* S. anopetalum
128. *Infl. convex in fl., concave in fr.* S. sediforme
129. *Lvs. of sterile stems with* 3*-lobed spurs* S. amplexicaule
129. *Lvs. of sterile stems with narrow spurs* S. pruinatum
129. *Lvs. of sterile stems with broad spurs* S. stenopetalum
130. *Stems erect, up to* 12 *in. h. Lvs. slender-pointed. Pet. long-mucronate* S. Douglasii
130. *Stems more or less tufted* 131
131. *Lvs. ciliate in tiny Sempervivum-like rosettes. Fl. solitary* S. humifusum
131. *Lvs. not in rosettes* 132
132. *Stem woody at base, procumbent or ascending* 133
132. *Stem herbaceous, erect or spreading* S. alpestre
133. *Lvs. small, closely appressed. Fl.* 1 *to* 3*; sep. short, broad* S. cupressoides
133. *Lvs. not closely appressed* 134
134. *Stem continuously elongating, rooting. Lvs. obovate.* ¼ *in. long* S. oaxacanum
134. *Stem freely branched* 135
135. *Stem woody at base, procumbent or ascending* 136
135. *Stem herbaceous, erect or spreading* S. alpestre
136. *Lvs. narrow* 137
136. *Lvs. very broad* S. acre
137. *Stem covered with dry lvs. Lvs. linear-oblong,* ¼ *in. long, papillose* S. multiceps
137. *Stem leafy. Lvs. linear, more or less terete, spurred* 138
138. *Lvs. glaucous, slightly flattened,* ½ *in. long* S. Stribrnyi
138. *Lvs. green, linear, terete,* ⅛ *to* ¼ *in. long, smooth* S. sexangulare

S. a′cre. Stonecrop, Wallpepper. Creeping, mat-forming, glabrous evergreen, with barren shoots erect, ½ to 2 in. h., rooting at base. *l.* ⅛ to ¼ in. long, crowded, thick, conical, obtuse, widest and gibbous at base, having an acrid taste; l. on fl.-stems scattered. *fl.* yellow, numerous, ½ in. across; sep. like l. half as long as spreading pet.; cymes 2- or 3-forked, terminal on erect stems 2 to 3 in. h. Summer. Britain to Persia, Norway to Morocco. (J.R.H.S. 46, 246; E.B. 532.) A somewhat variable plant, the most marked forms being var. **au′reum,** *l.* and tips of stems bright golden-yellow in spring, useful for edging, &c.; **el′egans,** with *l.* and stem-tips silver; **ma′jus,** *fl.* ⅝ in. across, *l.* in 7 rows, ⅜ in. long, deltoid, pale green, plant larger and more robust than type. Morocco. SYN. *S. Maweanum.* Hardy.

S. acutifo′lium. A synonym of *S. subulatum.*

S. adenot′richum. *l.* glabrous, fleshy, obtuse, ⅝ to 1 in. long, in rosettes and scattered on barren shoots below rosettes. *fl.* white, ⅜ in. across in a lax, glandular-hairy panicle of 6 to 12 fls.; fl.-stem erect, slender, 3 to 4 in. long, sparingly leafy. April, May. Himalaya. (J.R.H.S. 46, 164.) Hardy.

S. Adol′phi. A loosely bushy, glabrous, very fleshy evergreen, the many branches ascending or sprawling, up to 1 ft. long. *l.* alternate, firm, very fleshy, flat on face, sub-acute, about 1½ in. long, yellowish-green with reddish margins, on fl.-stem smaller. *fl.* white, starry, about ¾ in. across, in a compact branched infl.; pedicels about ½ in. long. March, April. Mexico. (J.R.H.S. 46, 156.) Not hardy.

S. Ai′zoon. Herbaceous perennial with carrot-like roots and several erect, glabrous, sub-angular, mostly unbranched stems. *l.* distant, alternate, sessile, oblong-lanceolate, 2½ in. long, ¾ in. wide, coarsely and irregularly toothed, midrib prominent beneath. *fl.* yellow, numerous, ½ in. across, in a loose paniculate cyme 1 to 3 in. across, the lower peduncles axillary. July. Siberia to Japan. 1757. (G.F. 528 as *S. Maximowiczii*; J.R.H.S. 46, 109.) A variable species generally bright green but var. **auranti′acum** has stem dark red, *l.* dark green, *fl.* deep orange, and *fr.* red: a well-marked variety.

S. alamosa′num. Small, glaucous perennial with tufted, erect stems, densely leafy when young, later diffuse, 3 to 5 in. long. *l.* crowded, linear-oblong, ¼ in. long, obtuse, glaucous then reddish, papillose except on face. *fl.* reddish-white, at first spreading, ⅜ in. across, in small, few-fld. cymes; buds red. March. NW. Mexico. (J.R.H.S. 46, 134.) Not hardy. Stems dying after flowering, replaced by branches from base.

S. albes′cens. A form of *S. rupestre.*

S. alboro′seum. 1 to 2 ft. h., glaucous herbaceous perennial with thickened rootstock and carrot-like roots, and erect stems. *l.* usually opposite, ovate, 2 to 3 in. long, 1 to 1½ in. wide, pale glaucous green, bluntly toothed. *fl.* ½ in. across; pet. greenish-white; carpels pink. *infl.* a dense terminal (or sometimes also lateral) corymb. September. Japan, Manchuria, China. 1860. (G.F. 709; J.R.H.S. 46, 89.)

S. al'bum. Creeping, glabrous, mat-forming evergreen perennial with ascending branches. *l.* alternate, spreading, ½ in. long, linear-oblong, obtuse, contracted at base; those of fl.-stem larger, scattered. fl.-stem pinkish, erect, 4 to 6 in. h. *fl.* white, about ⅜ in. across; pet. lanceolate, spreading, twice as long as cal.; cymes corymbose, much-branched, many-fld. July. Europe (Britain), Siberia, W. Asia, N. Africa. (J.R.H.S. 46, 183; E.B. 529.) A very variable species especially in the l. var. **micran'thum** has *fl.* half the size of the type (Pyrenees) and a form of it; **mura'le** has all parts tinged red or purple. SYN. *S. murale*; **pal'lens** (*chloroticum*) has yellowish-green growth and greenish-white *fl.*

S. allantoi'des. Evergreen, glaucous sub-shrub, branching from base; branches leafy, erect, 1 ft. h. *l.* alternate, terete, obtuse, thickest near tip. *fl.* greenish-white, ⅝ in. across, in a loose panicle, 4 to 5 in. long, 3 in. across. June, July. Mexico. (J.R.H.S. 46, 154.) Not hardy.

S. alpes'tre. *l.* oblong-obovate, very fleshy, obtuse. *fl.* greenish-yellow; $\frac{3}{16}$ in. across in small clusters at ends of fl.-stems; pet. erect. June. Stems leafy with larger leaves in rosettes at tips, very short; fl.-stems 2 to 3 in. h. Mts. of Cent. and S. Europe, Asia Minor. (J.R.H.S. 46, 256.)

S. alsinefo'lium. Small, tufted, dark-green, shining, sticky, hairy with l. in close, flat rosettes about 1 in. across. *l.* of barren shoots, stalked, fleshy, ¼ to ⅜ in. long, obtuse; of fl.-stems larger, upper sessile. *fl.* few, ¼ in. across, white. June, July. fl.-stem, about 4 to 6 in. long, slender, weak, branched. S. France, N. Italy. (J.R.H.S. 46, 170.)

S. altis'simum. A synonym of *S. sediforme.*

S. amecameca'num. Erect, glabrous, evergreen sub-shrub, about 6 in. h., branches spreading, leafy towards tips, reddish. *l.* flat, oblanceolate, ⅜ in. long, ¼ in. wide, fleshy, green. *fl.* ⅝ in. across, pale buff-yellow in rather dense infl. about ¾ to 1 in. long and wide. May. Mexico. 1918. (J.R.H.S. 46, 214.) Not hardy.

S. amplexicau'le. Close to *S. pruinatum*, but *l*, with broad clasping base, *fl.* golden yellow. Mediterranean region.

S. Anacamp'seros. Procumbent, glaucous semi-evergreen rooting at nodes. *l.* round or obovate, obtuse, apiculate, auricled at base, ¾ in. long, half as wide, margins reddish. *fl.* violet, numerous when produced but the plant flowers rarely, ¼ in. across; cymes dense, terminal, globose on erect, terete, reddish stems. July. Cent. Europe. 1596. (B.M. 118; J.R.H.S. 46, 52.) var. **ma'jus** is a stronger, more erect plant with green *l.* up to 1½ in. long, ½ in. wide, and a larger *infl.* (J.R.H.S. 46, 51.)

S. an'glicum. Mat-forming, glabrous evergreen; stems slender, rooting. *l.* crowded, alternate, ⅛ to ¼ in. long, very thick, often tinged red; less crowded on the fl.-stems. *fl.* white or tinted rose, ½ in. across; pet. lanceolate, much longer than sep.; cymes dichotomous, few-fld.; fl.-stems 1 to 2 in. h. Summer. W. Europe, including Britain. (J.R.H.S. 46, 101; E.B. 531.)

S. an'nuum. Much-branched annual with yellow *fl.* about ⅜ in. across in the forks of the stem, about 1½ to 6 in. h. June, July. Caucasus, Asia Minor through Europe to Greenland. (J.R.H.S. 46, 306.)

S. anopet'alum. Glabrous, creeping evergreen with ascending branches 4 to 6 in. long, making a green or glaucous mat often tinged red. *l.* in 6 or more ranks, crowded, linear, about ⅜ in. long, slightly flattened above, spreading (on fl.-shoots ascending and longer), spiny and greyish-red at tip. *fl.* pale yellow, ½ in. across; sep. 5 to 7, lanceolate, erect, acute, grooved; pet. nearly erect, somewhat folded and keeled; cymes dense, flat or concave, umbellate, about 1 in. across. fl.-stems 6 to 9 in. h. June, July. Cent. and S. Spain, Asia Minor. 1818. (J.R.H.S. 46, 274.)

S. arbo'reum. A synonym of *S. moranense arboreum*, but sometimes attached to other species.

S. asiat'icum. A synonym of *S. crassipes.*

S. atho'um. A form of *S. album.*

S. atlan'ticum. *l.* ovate, fleshy, about ½ in. long, mostly at ends of 1 to 3 in. long, prostrate branches in rosettes of 20 to 30. *fl.* brownish-yellow with red spots on back, 6- or 7-parted, about ⅓ in. across, on slender pedicels; *infl.* 3- to 5-fld. April. Morocco. 1871. (B.M. 5988 as *Monanthes muralis.*)

S. atra'tum. Annual. fl.-stems ascending, little-branched, 1 to 3 in. h. *l.* obovate to round, ⅛ to ¼ in. long. *fl.* reddish- or greenish-white, about ⅛ in. across, in a short, dense corymb; pet. 5 or 6; stamens 10 or 12, very broad at base. S. Europe.

S. atropurpu'reum. A variety of *S. roseum.*

S. au'reum of gardens. A synonym of *S. acre aureum.*

S. azu'reum. A synonym of *S. coeruleum* and *S. Ewersii.*

S. bel'lum. Mealy glaucous perennial, with few unbranched leafy stems, 3 to 6 in. long, flowering in second year. *l.* glaucous, entire, spatulate, up to 1 in. long. *fl.* white, spreading, ½ in. across in a flat, leafy cyme. April, May. Mexico. (J.R.H.S. 46, 142.) Not hardy.

S. Beyrichia'num. A variety of *S. Nevii.*

S. bhutanen'se. *See* **S. bupleuroides.**

S. bithyn'icum. Allied to *S. hispanicum* but perennial with suffruticose basal creeping, rooting, stems, barren branches densely leafy, ¾ to 1½ in. h., fl.-stems erect, unbranched, 1 to 2½ in. long. *l.* linear, up to ¼ in. long, glaucous. *fl.* rose, 5- or 6-parted. Asia Minor and Balkans. SYN. *S. hispanicum bithynicum* and *minus.* Plants under the latter name are often grown as *S. glaucum* or *S. Lydium glaucum* and are rather more robust than the type. It was much used for carpet-bedding.

S. bolonien'se. A synonym of *S. sexangulare.*

S. Bor'deri. A variety of *S. Telephium.*

S. Bour'gaei. Slender, erect, sub-shrubby evergreen with smooth, red stems 6 to 12 in. h., woody and bare below, branched. *l.* alternate, green, linear, obtuse, flattened, ⅓ to ¾ in. long, $\frac{1}{16}$ in. broad in a loose infl. with spreading, curved branches, 1 to 2 in. long. *fl.* white, usually tipped red, spreading, ½ in. across. July, August. Cent. Mexico. Nearly hardy. (J.R.H.S. 46, 155.)

S. brevifo'lium. Creeping, mealy, evergreen perennial; stems 1 to 2 in. long. *l.* opposite, crowded in 4 rows, $\frac{1}{10}$ in. long, ovoid, pinkish, densely mealy downy. *fl.* ¼ in. across; *sep.* whitish, pet. white, both with reddish midrib; pet. ovate, acute; *infl.* few-fld. July. SW. Europe, Morocco. (J.R.H.S. 46, 99.) SYN. *S. Pittonii*, *S. farinosum*, *S. Pottsii.* By some considered a var. of *S. dasyphyllum* and like it demanding perfect drainage. var. **quinquefo'lium** has stems twice as thick and long, with larger *l.* in 5 ranks. (J.R.H.S. 46, 99.)

S. Brown'ii. A synonym of *S. kamtschaticum* and related species.

S. bupleuroi'des. Herbaceous perennial with thick rootstock, branched and usually scaly, with annual erect or spreading, slender often papillose stems. *l.* alternate or opposite, lanceolate to orbicular, entire or minutely toothed, usually papillose. *fl.* 1-sexual, 4- to 5-parted, small; male purple; female carpels broad, sub-erect; *infl.* a loose corymb, often with involucre. May, June. Himalaya, Tibet, W. China. (J.R.H.S. 46, 41–9.) SYN. *S. elongatum*, *S. Cooperi.* A fairly moist loam suits this very variable species best. Here Fröderström groups var. **rotunda'tum** with stout stems, *l.* broad-ovate to orbicular (Tibet, W. China). var. **dis'color** with erect, slender stem, *l.* small, broad-lanceolate to ovate (W. China). var. **purpureo'viride,** with several erect stems, *l.* oblong-lanceolate, denticulate, densely papillose, 1 to 1¼ in. (Yunnan). SYN. *S. purpureoviride.* The form called *S. bhutanense* (Bhutan) has sometimes pseudoternate l. dentate in upper part, about 1½ in. long.

S. caeru'leum. *See* **S. coeruleum.**

S. Candol'lei. Glabrous annual or sometimes perennial by small sterile shoots, ⅓ to 1 in. long. *l.* obovate to oblong, about ⅛ in. long, fl.-stems 1 to 4 in. long, arching, simple below, with few branches above, 1- to 5-fld., pedicels short; pet. white, $\frac{1}{10}$ in. long, stamens shorter. Mts. of N. Spain. SYN. *Cotyledon sedoides, C. sediformis.*

S. carn'eum. A synonym of *S. lineare variegatum.*

S. carpat'icum of gardens. A variety of *S. Telephium.*

Sedum cauticola

S. cautic'ola. Nearly related to *S. Sieboldii*, distinguished by its opposite stalked *l.* and lax *infl.* September. Japan. (J.R.H.S. 46, 100; B.M. n.s. 401.)

S. Cepae'a. Annual, appearing in autumn, flowering in early summer. Tall, slender, much-branched, usually hairy, up to 12 in. h. Stem dotted red, branches spreading, ascending. *l.* linear-obovate, flat, fleshy, smooth, sessile, red-spotted; basal l. obovate, stalked.

fl. white, ⅜ in. across; pet. spreading, lanceolate, nerve red; filaments white, anthers purple; panicle formed by whole plant. June, July. Cent. and S. Europe. 1610. (J.R.H.S. 46, 290.)

S. Chan'eti. *See* **S. fimbriatum Chaneti.**

S. Chauveau'dii. Creeping, rooting at nodes, glabrous, evergreen perennial with barren shoots 6 to 9 in. long, leafy; stem red, slightly rough. *l.* on barren shoots ternate, oblong-oblanceolate, obtuse, flat, ½ to ¾ in. long, widest near apex, green, pale below, with silvery margin when young. *fl.* yellow, streaked red on back, ⅝ in. across, in dense, flat cymes, 1 to 2 in. across. August to October. Yunnan. 1915. (J.R.H.S. 46, 225.) Hardy.

S. Clusia'num. A synonym of *S. album.*

S. coccin'eum. A synonym of *S. quadrifidum* and *S. spurium.*

S. coerules'cens. A form of *S. sediforme.*

S. coeru'leum. Annual, 2 to 3 in. h., branched, green or suffused red. *l.* alternate, ovoid, ½ to ¾ in. long, slightly flattened above. *fl.* pale blue, 5- to 7-parted, ¼ in. across; cyme loose, many-fld., 1 in. across with recurved branches. S. Europe, Algeria. (J.R.H.S. 46, 303.)

S. compac'tum. Close to *S. humifusum* but with glabrous leaves. *fl.* globular, white, scented of elder. July. Mexico. (J.R.H.S. 46, 96.) Not hardy.

S. compres'sum. Related to *S. Palmeri* but with acute l. and sep., larger fl., older l. often flushed red. *fl.* bright orange. March, April. Mexico. (J.R.H.S. 46, 235.) Nearly hardy.

S. confu'sum. Related to *S. praealtum* with smaller, broader *l.* 1 to 1½ in. long, ½ to ¾ in. broad, obtuse, *infl.* smaller and denser, 2 in. across. April, May. Origin doubtful, long in cultivation. (J.R.H.S. 46, 212.) Hardy in most districts.

S. coria'ceum. A synonym of *S. quadrifidum.*

S. cor'sicum. A synonym of *S. dasyphyllum glanduliferum.*

S. cras'sipes. Herbaceous, glabrous, erect perennial with thick rootstock, often spreading underground, branching. Stem unbranched, 6 to 12 in. h. *l.* many, alternate, bright green, flat, linear, ½ to ¾ in. long, coarsely toothed in upper half. *fl.* yellowish-white or greenish, ½ in. across, spreading or reflexed. *infl.* dense, flattish, 1 in. across. June. Himalaya, Tibet, W. China. (J.R.H.S. 46, 56–7.) Syn. *S. asiaticum, S. Wallichianum.* A more robust grey-green plant with *l.* 1 to 1½ in. long and green *fl.* is var. **cholaèn'ae** (J.R.H.S. 46, 59), and var. **Stepha'ni** (Syn. *S. Stephani*) with no underground runners, has usually 1-sexual *fl.* and deeply toothed green *l.* E. Siberia. (J.R.H.S. 46, 60.)

S. Cris'ta-gal'li. A form of *S. rupestre.*

S. cupressoi'des. Glabrous, evergreen, much-branched plant, 4 or 5 in. h., woody and rooting below. *l.* closely imbricate and appressed, very fleshy, ovate, ⅙ in. long, obtuse, flat on face, convex on back. *fl.* bright yellow, about ½ in. across, sessile, 1 to 3 at end of leafy shoots. August. Mexico. (J.R.H.S. 46, 245.)

S. cyan'eum. Creeping, glaucous, deciduous perennial with prostrate branched stems 2 to 3 in. h. *l.* alternate, oblanceolate, about ½ to ¾ in. long, entire, obtuse, glaucous. *fl.* very rare, rose-purple, in a loose corymb. NE. Siberia. *See also* **S. Ewersii homophyllum.** Hardy.

S. dasyphyl'lum. Tufted evergreen, 1 to 2 in. h., with wiry, much-branched stems, barren shoots very leafy; fl.-shoots taller, more distant, larger. *l.* crowded, sessile, oblong, ⅛ to ⅙ in. long, thick, spreading. *fl.* 5- or 6-parted, ¼ in. across; pet. lanceolate, white with pinkish midrib; cymes few-fld.; pedicels hairy. June. Mediterranean, Britain. (E.B. 530; J.R.H.S. 46, 177.) var. **glandulif'erum,** densely glandular-pubescent. (B.M. 6027.) Syn. *S. corsicum;* **macrophyl'lum,** larger in all its parts; **Suendermann'ii,** has densely overlapping *l.* and larger *fl.* Spain. Syn. *S. rivulare.* This species varies greatly in hairiness. Hardy.

S. dendroi'deum. Related to *S. praealtum* but much less common, the name being usually applied erroneously to *S. confusum* or *S. praealtum. l.* stalked, almost orbicular, about 1¾ in. long, rounded above, flat beneath. *infl.* very large and many-fld.; pet. larger than stamens. Mexico. (J.R.H.S. 46, 208.) Not hardy.

S. diver'gens. Glabrous, evergreen perennial with slender, prostrate, rooting stems and reddish, ascending, barren (2 to 3 in. h.) and flowering shoots (3 to 6 in. h.). *l.* opposite (or alternate if on fl.-stems), smooth, green, often flushed red, obovate, ¼ in. long, obtuse, very fleshy. *fl.* bright yellow, spreading, about ¾ in. across, in a rather loose, flattish infl. 1 to 2 in. across. June. Oregon to Brit. Columbia. (J.R.H.S. 46, 220.) Hardy.

S. diversifo'lium. Tufted, glabrousperennial with erect, densely leafy young branches from base which later elongate to 4 to 8 in., become decumbent and branched, flower and die. *l.* alternate, flat, fleshy, papillose, obovate, $\frac{3}{16}$ in. long; on fl.-stems quickly falling, bright green, convex on both sides, ¼ to ½ in. long. *fl.* yellow, ⅜ in. across, from 1 to 3 at apex of shoot. April, May. Mexico. (J.R.H.S. 46, 145.) Not hardy.

S. Douglas'ii. Stout, erect, glabrous, evergreen perennial, often tinged red, with barren shoots leafy near top up to 3 in. h., slightly branched, fl.-shoots 3 to 6 in. h. unbranched. *l.* alternate, crowded, linear, ½ to ¾ in. long, flattened above, acute (on fl.-stem often blunt). *fl.* bright yellow, about ½ in. across, in a few-fld. compact *infl.* June, July. Western N. America. The short shoots in l.-axils of upper part of fl.-stem drop off after l.-fall and take root. (J.R.H.S. 46, 257.) Syn. *S. himalense.*

S. drymarioi'des visco'sum. Annual or biennial, soft, downy, clammy. Stem erect, 4 to 18 in. h. with many red ascending branches. *l.* in a rosette in young plants, obovate. blade ½ in. long, bluntly pointed, stalk ¼ in. long. *fl.* yellow on slender pedicels about ½ in. long. June to August. W. China. (J.R.H.S. 46, 291–2 as *S. viscosum.*) Not hardy.

S. dumulo'sum. Glabrous, herbaceous perennial with a thick, branched rootstock, and many erect or arching, unbranched, reddish, slender, leafy stems 4 to 7 in. h. *l.* alternate, green, entire, linear, ½ to 1 in. long, acute, flat above, convex below. *fl.* white, bell-shaped, about ½ in. across, in *infl.* of 6 to 12 fl., very compact. N. China. (J.R.H.S. 46, 62.) Syn. *S. rariflorum, S. Farreri.*

S. ebractea'tum. Bright-green, fleshy, downy perennial, with densely leafy basal rosettes about 1 in. across in winter, becoming erect, stout, leafy. *fl.* shoots about 1 ft. h., marked with short, purple lines. Rootstock very fleshy. *l.* alternate, fleshy, ovate, 1 in. long, bluntly pointed, flat above, rounded below. *fl.* whitish, ½ in. across, in a few-fld., very lax, almost bractless *infl.* October. Mexico. 1865. (J.R.H.S. 46, 68.) Not quite hardy. var. **rubricau'le,** stems suffused with purple, *l.* ovate-oblong. Mexico.

S. el'egans. A name misused for several species.

S. Ellacombia'num. Related to *S. kamtschaticum* but stems not branched, green. *l.* broadly crenate. *infl.* dense. *fl.* ⅝ in. across, bright yellow. Japan. (J.R.H.S. 46, 118–19.) Regarded by some as a variety of *S. kamtschaticum.* Hardy.

S. elonga'tum. A synonym of *S. bupleuroides.*

S. Engleria'num. A synonym of *S. dasyphyllum.*

S. eriocarp'um. A form of *S. hispanicum.*

S. erythrostict'um. A synonym of *S. alboroseum.*

S. euphorbioi'des of gardens. A synonym of *S. Aizoon.*

S. Ewers'ii. Glaucous, herbaceous perennial with a twiggy, much-branched rootstock and many trailing or ascending, round, unbranched stems, 6 to 12 in. long. *l.* often opposite, sessile, roundish, somewhat stem-clasping, about ¾ in. wide, entire or faintly toothed. *fl.* pink or pale violet, numerous, about ½ in. across in dense, convex cymes. August, September. W. Himalaya to Mongolia. 1829. (J.R.H.S. 46, 97.) A much smaller var. (**homophyl'lum**) with barren and fl.-stems equal in length and entire l. is often wrongly known as *S. cyaneum.* (J.R.H.S. 46, 98.) var. **turkestan'icum** is not distinct.

S. Faba'ria. *See* **S. Telephium.**

S. farino'sum. Allied to *S. anglicum* but basal stems woody, slender, branched, sterile branches sub-erect, in loose tufts, about 1 in. h.; fl.-stems erect, 1 to 3 in. h. *l.* oblong to obovoid, blunt, ⅒ to ¼ in. long, spurred. *fl.* white, 5- to 7-parted, crowded in cymes. July. Madeira. (G.C. 10 (1878), 2.) The name is often wrongly applied to *S. brevifolium* in gardens. Not quite hardy.

S. Far'reri. A synonym of *S. dumulosum.*

S. fastigia'tum. Perhaps a form of *S. quadrifidum* but with larger *fl.* and *fr.* Herbaceous, glabrous perennial with many stems 3 to 6 in. h. *l.* ¼ to ½ in. long, narrow, fleshy, dark green, shining. Himalaya, W. Yunnan. (J.R.H.S. 46, 54.)

S. fimbria'tum. Glaucous, brittle, fleshy perennial, with very short barren stems, bearing short horizontal branches rosulate and rooting at tips. *l.* of rosettes linear, rounded at back, about 1 in. long, with a broad fimbriate cartilaginous tip and a long spine; of fl.-stems linear, acuminate. *infl.* many-fld., paniculate, dense, very leafy, pyramidal or oblong, about 2 in. wide; *fl.* pedicellate, ½ in. wide, starry; pet. white mottled red and green on back. Autumn. Szechwan, Kansu, &c. Syn. *Orostachys fimbriatus.* Not hardy. var. **Chanet'i** has rosette-l. with small cartilaginous tips scarcely dentate and a long spine and rather longer pet. (about ¼ in.) than the type. (J.R.H.S. 46, 166, 167 as *S. Chaneti.*)

S. florif'erum. *See* **S. kamtschaticum.**

S. formosa'num. Glabrous annual, 6 to 9 in. h., erect or procumbent, much-branched. Stem smooth, succulent, reddish, branches grooved. *l.* alternate or opposite, spatulate, about 1 in. long, flat, softly succulent, obtuse, recurved. *fl.* yellow, ½ in. across, bracteate; pet. lanceolate, spreading. Summer. Formosa, Korea. 1885. (J.R.H.S. 46, 296.) Not hardy.

S. Forsteria'num. A variety of *S. rupestre.*

S. fusifor'me. From a stout woody base 1 to 2 in. long, sterile branches erect, about 1½ in. long, l. crowded at tip; fl. branches nearly erect, about 3 in. long, not branched. *l.* lanceolate to oblong, about ¼ in. long. *fl.* greenish-yellow, spotted red at base of pet. within, about ⅔ in. across. Madeira. Not hardy.

S. gemmif'erum of gardens. A synonym of *S. obtusifolium Listoniae.*

S. glabrum. Pale green, glabrous, very fleshy with erect, round, leafy fl.-stems about 8 in. long; barren shoots very short, with l. in rosettes. *l.* alternate, oblong-obovate, 1¼ in. long, ½ in. wide, obtusely pointed. *fl.* flattish, ⅜ in. across; petals ovate, white with purple midribs. Mexico. (J.R.H.S. 46, 128.) Not hardy.

S. glandulif'erum. A synonym of *S. dasyphyllum glanduliferum.*

S. glandulo'sum. A synonym of *S. villosum.*

S. glau'cum. A synonym of *S. hispanicum.*

S. grac'ile. Glabrous, bright-green, much-branched, procumbent evergreen perennial with red, densely leafy shoots; fl.-shoots 1½ to 2 in. long, barren shorter. *l.* linear-oblong, about ¼ in. long, flattish above, rounded below, red-dotted. *fl.* about ¼ in. across, white, dotted red on black. June. Caucasus, N. Persia. (J.R.H.S. 46, 190.)

S. grandiflo'rum of gardens. A synonym of *S. reflexum.*

S. Gregg'ii. Tufted. fl.-stems slender, 3 to 6 in. long, ascending. *l.* oblong or obovate, $\frac{1}{10}$ to ⅛ in. long, smooth, obtuse, overlapping. *fl.* few, yellow, about ⅓ in. across, slender-pointed. Mexico. Not hardy.

S. gris'eum. Similar to *S. Bourgaei*, but stouter and more compact with greyish branches, glaucous, linear, tapering, sub-terete *l.* about ½ in. long. January, February. (J.R.H.S. 46, 158.) Not hardy. Probably Mexican.

S. guadalajara'num. Similar to *S. griseum* but with thickened rootstocks and tuberous roots, and thin, wiry stems, linear *l.* and a lax *infl.* with white pet. reddish at base. July, August. Mexico. (J.R.H.S. 46, 157.) Not hardy.

S. gypsic'ola. Creeping, downy, evergreen perennial, forming a greyish mat often tinged red, with short, densely leafy, barren shoots, and sparingly leafy fl.-stems 4 to 6 in. long. *l.* ovate-rhomboid, ¼ in. long, ⅛ in. thick, fleshy, obtuse, dull grey-green, tinged red. *fl.* similar to *S. album*, ¼ in. across. June, July. Spain, Portugal. (J.R.H.S. 46, 186.) By some regarded as a variety of *S. album.*

S. Hall'ii. A close ally of *S. yosemitense* but with a thyrsoid instead of flat *infl.* *l.* green, not glaucous as in *S. spathulifolium* to which it is also allied. *fl.* bright yellow. Yosemite, California. SYN. *Gormania Hallii.*

S. Hayes'ii. A synonym of *S. Ewersii homophyllum.*

S. heterodon'tum. A synonym of *S. roseum heterodontum.*

S. Hildebrand'ii. A variety of *S. sexangulare.*

S. himalen'se of gardens. A synonym of *S. Douglasii.* The true plant is allied to *S. quadrifidum.*

S. hirsu'tum. Tufted, hairy, evergreen perennial, green, often tinged red, with ascending barren shoots about 1 in. long, l. crowded at their tips, and erect. fl.-stems 2 to 3 in. h. with alternate l. *l.* oblanceolate, ¾ in. long, ⅛ in. wide, fleshy, obtuse. *fl.* white with distinct red vein at back of pet. ½ in. across in few-fld. *infl.*, buds drooping. June, July. SW. Europe. (J.R.H.S. 46, 188.) Requires thorough drainage. var. **baet'icum.** A synonym of *S. Winkleri.*

S. hispan'icum. Pinkish, glaucous annual or biennial with more or less hairy stems branched below and leafy. *l.* linear, ½ to 1 in. long, ⅛ in. broad, rather acute, glaucous, often reddish, generally more or less flattened. *fl.* white with red median vein to pet., ½ in. across, 4- to 6-parted, in a loose, leafy, flattish cyme. June. Caucasus and Asia Minor westwards to Italy. (J.R.H.S. 46, 300.) SYN. *S. glaucum.* Hardy. Tends in dry places to form barren shoots and become perennial. In the var. **polypet'alum,** *fl.* are pale yellow, 7- to 9-parted. For var. **bithyn'icum** and **mi'nus,** *see* **S. bithynicum.**

S. Hob'sonii. Glabrous, herbaceous perennial with a very short, thick, erect rootstock and thick woody roots a few in. long. *Root-l.* in a flat rosette 4 in. across, entire, green, fleshy, flat; stalk with broad, clasping base. Fl.-stems from axils of withered root-l. of previous year, decumbent, 4 to 6 in. long; their *l.* green, tipped red, linear oblong, rather blunt, ⅜ in. long, reflexed. *fl.* ovoid, rose, in lax terminal few-fld. cymes. July. Tibet. 1913. Hardy. (J.R.H.S. 46, 71–2 as *S. Praegerianum.*)

S. homophyl'lum. A variety of *S. Ewersii.*

S. humifu'sum. A spreading, mat-forming perennial with creeping shoots about 1 in. long and erect shoots with rosettes of l. about $\frac{3}{10}$ in. across. *l.* obovate, fleshy, ciliate, hairy at tip, closely imbricate, reddish when old. *fl.* solitary, terminal, bright yellow, about ⅜ in. across, on reddish fl.-stems up to ¾ in. long. April to June. Mexico. 1915. (J.R.H.S. 46, 244.) Not hardy.

S. hyb'ridum. Creeping and branching, with both barren and fl.-shoots, forming a loose evergreen mat from a woody rootstock. *l.* alternate, scarcely stalked, spatulate, about 1 in. long, coarsely toothed in upper half, entire and tapering in lower, teeth red-tipped. *fl.* yellow, ½ in. across, numerous in flattish, much-branched cymes 2 to 3 in. across; bracts large, spreading. Summer. Siberia. 1776. (J.R.H.S. 46, 126.)

S. iber'icum. Garden name for *S. reflexum.* *See also* **S. stoloniferum.**

S. in'dicum. Biennial; in first year with a loose rosette of l. on a very short stem, in second year with erect stem, 6 to 12 in. h., usually unbranched below, with alternate l. and a corymbose panicle of almost globular flowers. *l.* alternate, very fleshy, oblong-acuminate, 1½ to 2½ in. long, ⅜ to ⅝ in. broad, spine-tipped, rather glaucous, densely red-dotted when old. *fl.* about $\frac{3}{16}$ in. long, with pet. whitish in lower, crimson in upper part. September, October. Himalaya, W. China. 1915. (J.R.H.S. 46, 285–6.) SYN. *Crassula indica.* A very variable species. var. **Forrest'ii** has opposite, almost orbicular *l.*; **yunnanen'se** has small rosettes with glandular-pubescent, acute *l.* and fl.-stems 2 to 4 in. long, the *infl.* broad and dense.

S. integrifo'lium. A synonym of *S. roseum.*

S. involucra'tum. A synonym of *S. spurium.*

S. Jaccardia'num. Downy perennial; sterile shoots densely leafy at tip; fl.-shoots erect or spreading, about 3 in. long. *l.* obovate, about ½ in. long, stem-l. smaller. *fl.* yellow, 7- to 10-parted, nearly ½ in. across; pet. acute; in a loose cyme. Morocco. Not hardy.

S. japon'icum. Perennial with barren stems about 1½ in. long; fl.-stems slender, much-branched, ascending, 4 to 12 in. long. *l.* linear-spatulate or ovate, crowded, obtuse. *fl.* yellowish, small; sep. obtuse, with a broad spur, unequal. W. China to Japan. l. very variable.

S. kamtschat'icum. Allied to *S. hybridum* but without barren shoots, with short shoots in winter. *l.* dark green. *fl.* orange-yellow, ¾ in. across in a rather loose *infl.* June to September. N. China, Kamchatka, E. Siberia. 1829. (J.R.H.S. 46, 121.) var. **variega'tum** has *l.* with white margin. **S. florif'erum** is intermediate between *S. hybridum* and *S. kamtschaticum*, with similar habit. (J.R.H.S. 46, 123–4.)

S. Kirilow'ii. Herbaceous perennial with several slender, erect, unbranched stems 1 to 3 ft. long from the thick branched rootstock, pale green and glabrous. *l.* linear or oblong, up to 2 in. long, broadest at base, usually coarsely toothed. *fl.* 5- (rarely 4-parted), dioecious, about ¼ in. across, in a dense terminal cyme. April, May. W. China, Upper Burma, Tibet. (J.R.H.S. 46, 36, 38.) var. **linifo'lium** has brown-red *fl.*, is stouter, and has a denser *infl.*, the male form being the more showy; **ru'brum,** a synonym of var. *linifolium.* The tall-stemmed form has been called *S. longicaule.*

S. lacon'icum. A synonym of *S. acre* or *S. album.*

S. Lag'geri of gardens. A synonym of *S. Aizoon.*

S. Lampu'sae. Somewhat similar in growth to *S. fimbriatum*, biennial, pubescent. *l.* obovate, up to 2 in. long, fl.-stems erect, 4 to 8 in. long; *infl.* pyramidal, many-fld., occupying nearly the length of the stem. *fl.* small. June. Mt. Troodos, Cyprus. 1930.

S. lancerot'tense. A variety of *S. nudum.*

S. latifo'lium. A form of *S. maximum.*

S. Leblanc'ae. Annual or biennial, forming a shoot of 2 or 3 in. in the first year, usually unbranched and leafy (*l.* deciduous, in whorls of 3, or 4, narrow linear, obtuse, up to ½ in. long), and in the second year a bushy rounded plant with reddish branches, densely mammillate in upper part, up to 6 in. h. *fl.* small, yellow, about $\frac{5}{16}$ in. across; sep. as long as pet.; stamens 5. September, October. W. China. 1915. (J.R.H.S. 46, 307–8.) A somewhat variable species.

S. Liebmannian'um. Glabrous perennial, 2 to 6 in. h., with green ascending stems, the old parts clothed with the persistent white bases of the withered l., nearly deciduous. *l.* clustered, broad, short-spurred, more or less ovate, ⅛ to ¼ in. long. *fl.* white; pet. obtuse, with short mucro, ⅕ to ¼ in. long. June to August. Mexico. 1880. (J.R.H.S. 46, 175.) Not hardy. Allied to *S. moranense* and *S. cupressoides.*

S. linea're variega'tum. Straggling, glabrous, evergreen perennial, with generally decumbent, reddish stems, often rooting; fl.-stems about 6 in. long, ascending. *l.* in whorls of 3, linear-lanceolate, obtuse, ¾ to 1 in. long, with marginal stripe of white or cream. *fl.* yellow, starry, about ⅝ in. across, in a loose, terminal umbellate *infl.* about 1½ in. across. May to July. China, Japan. Not hardy.

S. linearifo'lium. Stems erect, slender, 3 to 7 in. h., unbranched, from a thick, branched rootstock. *l.* alternate, crowded towards top of stem, green, linear to obovate, 1½ to 3 in. long, deeply cut and toothed. *fl.* purple-red, ⅝ in. across, in a leafy, lax, flat cyme about 2 in. across. August, September. Himalaya, W. China. (J.R.H.S. 46, 64–5 as *S. trifidum.*)

S. Liston'iae. A variety of *S. obtusifolium.*

S. liv'idum. A name used for several species.

S. longicau'le. *See* **S. Kirilowii.**

S. long'ipes. Stems from a short, fibrous-rooted stock; sterile stems short, densely leafy; flowering stems up to 8 in. long, arching or decumbent, rooting, aerial roots often purple. *l.* rather distant, fleshy, obovate or spatulate, up to ⅜ in. long, slightly spurred. *fl.* purple or in part whitish, on filiform pedicels; pet. ovate, blunt; nectariferous scales very large with reflexed tips. January. Mexico. (J.R.H.S. 46, 203.) Greenhouse: will not withstand frost.

S. lyd'ium. Evergreen perennial forming a mat, mostly red tinged; stems rooting below, barren shoots about 1 in. h. *l.* linear, terete, ¼ in. long, green, minutely pimpled at tip. *fl.* white, ¼ in. across; sep. tipped pink; many in a corymbose cyme, on shoots 2 to 4 in. long. June. W. Asia Minor. 1867. (J.R.H.S. 46, 189.)

S. magellen'se. Evergreen perennial, with slender, twiggy, rooting stems, short, very leafy, barren shoots and erect or ascending, sparingly leafy fl.-stems, 3 or 4 in. h. *l.* glabrous, obovate, ¼ in. long, flat, fleshy, obtuse, on fl.-stem rather longer. *fl.* white or whitish, ¼ to ⅜ in. across in an erect raceme 1 to 2 in. long, about ¼ in. broad. May, June. Italy. (J.R.H.S. 46, 167.) var. **olympicum,** dwarfer with smaller, often rounder *l.*

S. Mawea'num. A synonym of *S. acre majus.*

S. Maximowicz'ii. A synonym of *S. Aizoon.*

S. max'imum. Herbaceous perennial with thick rootstock and carrot-like roots, glabrous. Stems 1 to 3 ft. h., green or red, unbranched, or branched only at top, erect. *l.* usually opposite or in threes, broad-ovate, 2 to 3 in. long, clasping stem, obtuse, slightly toothed, dark green. *fl.* crowded, greenish-white, $\frac{3}{4}$ in. across, in crowded terminal and lateral corymbs on slender pedicels. Europe. (J.R.H.S. 46, 80.) A very variable species of which marked forms are: **atropurpu'reum,** very robust with stem and *l.* purple, *fl.* pink, l. up to 5 in. long, often in threes (B.M. n.s. 429); **haemato'des,** *l.* purplish, stem deep purple, *fl.* whitish, tipped red, robust; **versicol'or,** *l.* variegated with silver, stems pink. (F. de S. as *S. Rodigasi.*)

S. mellit'ulum. Slender, glabrous, tufted perennial, stems terete, reddish, 3 to 4 in. h., occasionally branched. *l.* alternate, green then reddish, linear-subulate, $\frac{1}{4}$ to $\frac{3}{4}$ in. long, obtuse, glaucous when young. *fl.* white, greenish on back, $\frac{1}{2}$ in. wide. September, October. Mexico. (J.R.H.S. 46, 136.) Not hardy. Does best in half-shade.

S. mexica'num. Evergreen perennial with glabrous, light green, decumbent stems, rooting below, with many erect branches about 6 in. h. *l.* alternate or in 3's or 5's, linear, $\frac{1}{4}$ to $\frac{1}{2}$ in. long, nearly terete, obtuse. *fl.* golden-yellow, about $\frac{1}{2}$ in. across in flattish, leafy cymes. April to June. Mexico. 1875? (J.R.H.S. 46, 231.) SYN. *S. sarmentosum* of some. Not quite hardy.

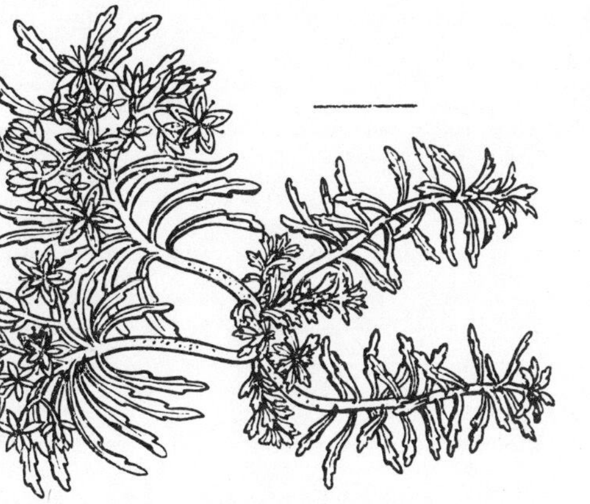

Sedum Middendorfianum

S. Middendorfia'num. Allied to *S. Aizoon* but more slender with narrower *l.* toothed only at apex and smaller *fl.* Stems unbranched. July, August. E. Siberia, Manchuria. var. **diffu'sum** is larger, more or less decumbent, rooting at base. (J.R.H.S. 46, 116.)

S. monregalen'se. Stems decumbent below, erect above, 1 to 2 in. h. *l.* on barren shoots in whorls of 4, crowded, spreading, thick, $\frac{1}{4}$ in. long, obtuse, green, glabrous or nearly so; on fertile shoots narrower, often spotted pink. *fl.* white, $\frac{3}{8}$ in. across in a loose, terminal, many-fld. panicle, glandular-pubescent. July, August. Italy, S. France, Corsica. (J.R.H.S. 46, 172.) Needs a damp, shady place.

S. monstros'um. *See* **S. reflexum cristatum.**

S. moranen'se. Bushy, about 3 to 4 in. h., with many wiry red branches, evergreen perennial. *l.* crowded, triangular, $\frac{1}{8}$ in. long, $\frac{1}{16}$ in. wide, glabrous, green. *fl.* $\frac{3}{8}$ in. across, white, tinged red at back, in small terminal groups. July. Mexico. (J.R.H.S. 43, 173.) var. **arbo'reum** is an erect, much-branched, fastigiate bush 6 to 11 in. h. SYN. *S. arboreum.* Not hardy.

S. mul'ticeps. Much-branched, bushy, 3 to 4 in. h.; stems covered below with withered l., leafy near tips. *l.* alternate, linear-oblong, $\frac{1}{4}$ in. long, fleshy, flat on face. *fl.* yellow, $\frac{1}{2}$ in. across, spreading, in few-fld. cymes on leafy 2 or 3 in. long shoots. July. Algeria. (J.R.H.S. 43, 263.)

S. mura'le. A synonym of *S. album murale.*

S. neglec'tum. A minor form of *S. acre.*

S. nevaden'se. Allied to *S. villosum* but annual. fl.-shoots sometimes branched from base, 1 to 4 in. h. *l.* linear or oblong, nearly round, about $\frac{1}{5}$ in. long. *fl.* reddish-white; pet. nearly erect, about $\frac{1}{4}$ in. across; stamens 5. Spain, N. Africa. SYN. *S. villosum nevadense.*

S. Nev'ii. Small, tufted evergreen, rather glaucous, pale green with l. in dense rosettes on barren shoots. fl.-shoots 3 to 4 in. h. *l.* alternate, spatulate, $\frac{1}{2}$ in. long, $\frac{1}{6}$ in. wide, entire, tapered below. *fl.* white, $\frac{1}{2}$ in. across on 3 terminal branches. June. E. United States. (J.R.H.S. 46, 162.) var. **Beyrichia'num** is more diffuse and slender.

S. nicaeen'se. A synonym of *S. sediforme.*

S. nu'dum. Weak, straggling, rooting, glabrous perennial. *l.* alternate, green or glaucous, obovate-oblong, about $\frac{3}{8}$ in. long, obtuse. *fl.* greenish-yellow, up to $\frac{3}{8}$ in. across, in a few-fld. cyme. May, June. Madeira. (J.R.H.S. 46, 252.) Not hardy. The var. **lancerotten'se** has ovate *l.*, sep. spurred. (J.R.H.S. 46, 253.)

S. nu'tans. Glabrous, evergreen perennial with erect, branched stem. *l.* at top of branches, oblong-ovate, 3 in. long, 2 in. wide, $\frac{5}{8}$ in. thick, dark green, flat above, rounded below. *fl.* greenish-yellow, in a nodding panicle about 3 in. long, $1\frac{1}{2}$ in. wide. March. Mexico. (J.R.H.S. 46, 207.) Not hardy.

S. Nuttallia'num. Small glabrous annual, branched from base, more or less decumbent, 2 to 4 in. h. *l.* short, about $\frac{1}{8}$ in. long, oblong, broad-spurred. *fl.* yellow along slender peduncles; pet. about $\frac{1}{8}$ in. long; stamens 10. Missouri to Texas.

S. oaxaca'num. Prostrate, much-branched, rough stems up to 6 in. long, rooting; sterile branches short, l. densely overlapping, more or less spreading. All *l.* spurred, oblong to obovate, blunt, $\frac{1}{8}$ to $\frac{1}{4}$ in. long. *fl.* yellow, pet. about $\frac{1}{3}$ in. long, nearly oblong, very broad below tip, with a small mucro; borne 1 to 3 together at tips of branches. Mexico. (J.R.H.S. 46, 250.) Not hardy.

S. obtusa'tum. Related to *S. rubroglaucum* but with smaller fl. Stems prostrate. Evergreen, glaucous, pruinose. *l.* in dense rosettes, spatulate, 1 in. long, $\frac{3}{8}$ in. across, entire, becoming reddish-green. *fl.* yellow, $\frac{1}{4}$ in. across, on short stalks in spreading, umbellate cymes, $1\frac{1}{2}$ to 2 in. across; pet. lanceolate; fl.-stems erect, reddish, finally leafless. June, July. California. SYN. *Gormania obtusata.* This name is frequently used in gardens for *S. oreganum.*

S. obtusifo'lium. Glabrous perennial with sterile shoots at first underground, pea-like, later lengthening to slender runners, with a flat winter rosette of obovate green l. fl.-stems erect, smooth, $2\frac{1}{2}$ to 5 in. h. *l.* opposite, spatulate-oblong, not spurred, up to $1\frac{1}{2}$ in. long, with rounded teeth, obtuse. *fl.* variable, reddish or white; pet. lanceolate, slender-pointed, about $\frac{1}{4}$ in. long or more. N. Persia, Armenia. var. **Liston'iae** is larger, *fl.* rose or light reddish-purple. Asia Minor. SYN. *S. proponticum.* Not hardy.

S. ochroleu'cum. A synonym of *S. sediforme* and *S. anopetalum.*

S. olym'picum. A variety of *S. magellense.*

S. oppositifo'lium. A synonym of *S. spurium.*

S. orega'num. Creeping, glabrous, evergreen perennial making a red-tinged mat, with ascending branches, barren shoots 1 to 3 in. h., leafy, fl.-stems unbranched, about 6 in. h., l. more distant. *l.* flat, fleshy, spatulate, $\frac{3}{4}$ in. long, $\frac{3}{8}$ in. wide, obtuse, tapered below, green, shining, red-tinged. *fl.* yellow, pet. tapering to a point, almost erect, in a flat *infl.* about $1\frac{1}{2}$ in. across. July, August. Western N. America. (J.R.H.S. 46, 242.) SYN. *Gormania oregana.*

S. oxypet'alum. Sub-shrubby, erect, 2 to 3 ft. h., much-branched, glabrous. *l.* alternate, obovate-spatulate, 1 to $1\frac{1}{2}$ in. long, rounded at apex, fleshy, green. *fl.* dull red, star-like, honey-scented, $\frac{1}{2}$ in. across, in a lax, flat cyme, 1 to 2 in. across. June, July. Mexico. 1880. Not hardy. (J.R.H.S. 46, 193.)

S. pachyphyl'lum. Allied to *S. allantoides* but infl. dense, flattish, *fl.* yellow, *l.* tipped red, young l. many. April. Mexico. Not hardy. (J.R.H.S. 46, 215.)

S. pal'lidum. A synonym of *S. hispanicum* and of *S. spurum.*

S. Palm'eri. Rather sprawling, glaucous evergreen with decumbent rooting branches, 6 to 9 in. h. *l.* spatulate, 1 in. long, $\frac{5}{8}$ in. wide, entire, obtuse, glaucous, more or less in a loose rosette at end of branch. *fl.* orange, $\frac{3}{8}$ in. across, in many-fld., spreading, somewhat drooping cymes, branches 1 to 4 in. long. May, June. Mexico. (J.R.H.S. 46, 233.) Nearly hardy.

S. pilos'um. Biennial. In first year with a dense, hairy rosette. *l.* incurved, linear-spatulate, $\frac{1}{2}$ in. long, obtuse, dark green; on the 2 to 4 in. long fl.-stem, $\frac{3}{4}$ in. long, $\frac{1}{2}$ in. broad, oblong-obovate. *fl.* rose, in dense, much-branched, panicled cyme, $1\frac{1}{2}$ to 3 in. across. May, June. Persia, Caucasus, Asia Minor. 1910. (B.M. 8503; J.R.H.S. 46, 284.)

S. Pitton'ii. A synonym of *S. brevifolium.*

S. populifo'lium. Rootstock broad and knotted, roots woody. Stems erect, 12 to 18 in. h., greenish or purplish, slender, glabrous, branched. *l.* alternate, ovate, $\frac{3}{4}$ in. long, acute, more or less cordate at base, coarse, irregularly toothed. *fl.* whitish or pinkish, about $\frac{3}{8}$ in. across, numerous, hawthorn scented in much-branched corymbose cymes. August. Siberia. 1780. (B.M. 211; J.R.H.S. 46, 78.) Hybrids with *S. Ewersii* and *S. maximum* with a general likeness to *S. populifolium* have occurred in gardens.

S. potosi'num. Glaucous or pinkish perennial with weak ascending, branched, pink stems, 3 to 6 in. h., rooting below. *l.* crowded, linear or linear-lanceolate on barren shoots $\frac{3}{5}$ in. on fl.-shoots $\frac{1}{2}$ in. long, pale, often pinkish, rather flattened. *fl.* white flushed red on back, spreading, $\frac{5}{8}$ in. across in 2- or 3-branched cymes. July, August. Mexico. (J.R.H.S. 46, 139.) Not hardy.

S. Pott'sii. A synonym of *S. brevifolium.*

S. praeal'tum. Evergreen, glabrous shrub, bushy, much-branched, 1 to 2 ft. h. and as wide, the green woody stems leafy near tips. *l.* alternate, green, shining, flat, very fleshy, lanceolate-spatulate, 2 to $2\frac{1}{2}$ in. long, entire, obtuse, flat on face, rounded at back. *fl.* $\frac{3}{4}$ in. across, bright yellow in a much-branched lax panicle, 3 to 4 in. long and broad. May, June. Mexico. 1850? (J.R.H.S. 46, 211.) Often wrongly named *S. dendroideum.* Hardy in milder parts of Britain.

S. Praegeria'num. A synonym of *S. Hobsonii.*

S. primuloi'des. Glabrous, almost deciduous sub-shrub, 2 or 3 in. h., with spreading much-branched stout stems shaggy with withered leaves. *l.* in dense flattish rosettes at branch ends, obovate, ⅜ in. long, ¼ in. broad, petiole flat, widened at reddish base. *fl.* white tinged green on back, pet. erect, ⅜ in. long, 1 to 3 at tips of short leafy branches. August. Yunnan. 1912. (J.R.H.S. 46, 70.)

S. propon'ticum. A synonym of *S. obtusifolium Listoniae.*

S. pruina'tum. Slender, very glaucous, evergreen perennial with 6 to 9 in. long prostrate barren shoots which die in autumn except for rooting tips, and erect fl.-stems about 6 in. h. *l.* alternate, linear, ¾ in. long, flattish above, acute, those at end of shoot crowded. *fl.* very pale yellow, 6- or 7-parted, ⅝ to ¾ in. across, spreading, in lax 2-branched *infl.* July. Portugal. 1890. (J.R.H.S. 46, 278.) This name has been applied to *S. rupestre* in error.

S. pruino'sum. Closely related to *S. spathulifolium.* A white-pruinose perennial with small sterile stems. *l.* as in *S. spathulifolium*, but rounder at apex. *fl.* stems stout but weak, branched just above base, up to 8 in. long. *fl.* rather long-stalked, smaller than in *S. spathulifolium*; pet. linear-lanceolate. N. California.

S. pseudospectab'ile. Allied to *S. spectabile* but with taller stems, green *l.* rounded at base, 1½ to 2 in. long, smaller *infl.* and *fl.* in all parts one-third shorter. China. 1910. (J.R.H.S. 46, 91.) August, September.

S. pulchel'lum. Evergreen tufted perennial with slender branches, trailing or ascending, 3 to 6 in. long, red. *l.* crowded, ascending, with a broadly cleft, half-clasping spur, narrow-linear-lanceolate, up to 1 in. long. *fl.* rosy-purple, ½ in. across, 4-parted, crowded on the leafy 3- to 5-branched cyme. July, August. (B.M. 6223; J.R.H.S. 46, 205.) Prefers a damp situation.

S. purpuras'cens. A form of *S. Telephium.*

S. purpureovi'ride. *See* **S. bupleuroides.**

S. purpu'reum. One of the many forms of *S. Telephium* in the wide sense. Stout, erect, glabrous, herbaceous perennial with thick rootstock and carrot-like roots, clustered leafy stems, 12 to 18 in. h. *l.* alternate, obovate-oblong, sessile, wedge-shaped or rounded at base, fleshy. *fl.* purplish-red, about ⅜ in. across, in dense terminal and lateral sub-globose corymbs. August, September. Japan to England. (E.B. 526.) Hardy.

S. quadrif'idum. Perennial with a fleshy, tufted rootstock bearing usually green, fleshy scale-leaves, often elongated; old fl.-stems persistent. Stems short, often papillose. *l.* entire, often rough, oblong to lanceolate. *fl.* 1-sexual, 4- to 5-parted, yellow or purple; *infl.* 1- to few-fld. May, June. Here come **S. fastigia'tum** with *l.* narrower than in *S. himalense*, glabrous, fleshy, shining dark green; *fl.* deep red-purple. Himalaya, W. China. **S. himalen'se** differs from *S. tibeticum* by its leafy *infl.*; *l.* dark green, ¾ to 1 in. long, stems red, both roughish; *fl.* dark purple. Himalaya. **S. quadrif'idum** proper, smaller in all parts, with rootstock clothed with old wiry, black stems; *l.* linear, acute, ½ in. long; *fl.* white or purple. Himalaya, Siberia. **S. tibet'icum,** glaucous, smooth; *infl.* leafless; *l.* about ¾ in. long; *fl.* dark purple, ⅜ in. across. Himalaya. (J.R.H.S. 46, 50, 52, 54.)

S. rariflo'rum. A synonym of *S. dumulosum.*

S. reflex'um. Stone Orpine. Evergreen perennial forming a loose mat with creeping, rooting stems. Barren shoots many, 1 to 4 in. long, leafy; fl.-shoots unbranched, 6 to 12 in. long with more distant reflexed l. *l.* linear, ½ in. long, acute, nearly terete. *fl.* bright yellow, 5- to 7-parted, ⅝ in. across in 3- to 5-branched cymes, 1½ in. across, sub-globose and drooping in bud. July. Cent. and W. Europe. (E.B. 534.) A variable species often confused with others. var. **crista'tum** is a fasciated form with stem up to 2 in. across, curious but not beautiful.

S. retu'sum. Evergreen sub-shrub about 1 ft. h., much-branched, glabrous, leafy mainly near tips. *l.* green, shining, obovate-oblong, notched at tips, ½ to 1 in. long. *fl.* white with red base, ⅜ in. across, in small, dense, terminal clusters. June, July. Mexico. 1880. (J.R.H.S. 46, 149.) Not hardy.

S. rhodan'thum. Herbaceous perennial, erect, glabrous, with unbranched, very leafy stems about 1 ft. h. from a thick rootstock. *l.* alternate, linear-oblanceolate, 1 in. long, ¼ in. wide, entire or somewhat toothed near apex. *fl.* rose, in a dense raceme up to 3 in. long, June. Arizona to Montana. (J.R.H.S. 46, 68.)

S. Rhodio'la. A synonym of *S. roseum.*

S. rhodocarp'um. Straggling light green perennial with weak unbranched stems 6 to 9 in. h., triangular (rarely square) in section with winged angles, only the base of the shoots persisting after fl. *l.* in whorls of 3 (rarely 4), lower spatulate, upper nearly round, ¾ in. long, entire, often notched at apex. *fl.* few, ½ in. across, stalked, greenish flushed red, spreading then reflexed. December. *fr.* deep red. Monterey, Mexico. (J.R.H.S. 46, 201.) Not hardy.

S. rivula're. A synonym of *S. dasyphyllum Suendermannii.*

S. ro'seum. Rose Root. Herbaceous perennial, glaucous, dioecious, with erect, unbranched, leafy stems, 6 to 12 in. h. from a thick, branched rootstock. *l.* scattered, strap-shaped to obovate, about 1½ in. long, by ¾ in. broad, flat, acute. *fl.* 4-parted, yellow or greenish in terminal compact cymes. May. N. Hemisphere in cold and temperate zones. (E.B. 525; J.R.H.S. 46, 29, 31, 33.) A variable species. var. **atropurpu'reum,** 3 to 7 in. h., glaucous, with light or dark purple *fl.*; **heterodon'tum,** 12 to 18 in. h., *l.* ½ to ¾ in. long, ½ in. broad, coarsely toothed, *fl.* yellowish or reddish. Himalaya, &c. SYN. *S. heterodontum.* (J.R.H.S. 46, 35.); **linifolium** has narrow *l.* and bright rose *fl.* with variants to orange (**auranti'acum**) or deep rose fl. (**ru'brum**); **Tachiro'i,** 3 to 7 in. h., with a long cylindrical rhizome and yellow *fl.* Japan; **vulga're,** 7 to 12 in. h., very glaucous, with yellow *fl.*, is a native. The dried roots are rose-scented.

S. rotunda'tum. Included in *S. bupleuroides.*

S. ru'bens. Annual, glandular-hairy, clammy. Stems erect, 2 to 4 in. h. *l.* crowded, oblong-linear, semicylindrical, ¾ in. long, glaucous green more or less tinged red. *fl.* pinkish-white, ½ in. across, in cymes with lax branches 2 to 3 in. long. July. Mediterranean, Canaries. (Ref. B. 242; J.R.H.S. 46, 304.)

S. rubricau'le. A variety of *S. ebracteatum.*

S. rubroglau'cum. Small dark green glaucous evergreen perennial related to *S. spathulifolium* but with pet. connate in lower part. Barren shoots procumbent; stems crimson at first then black, with runner-like axillary shoots with a rosette of l. at tip and rooting there. *l.* glaucous, very fleshy, about ¾ in. long, obovate-rounded with a short apiculus; stalk short, stem clasping. *fl.* few, yellow, ⅝ in. across on stems from centre of rosette, 2 in. h., erect; pet. blunt or apiculate. August. California. (J.R.H.S. 46, 219.) SYN. *Gormania rubroglauca.*

S. rupes'tre. Mat-forming glaucous evergreen, reddening with age and drought. *l.* linear-subulate, ½ in. long, incurved, convex beneath, flattish above, in numerous rows forming dense obconical rosettes ¾ to 1 in. across at ends of sterile shoots. *fl.* clear yellow, numerous, nearly ½ in. across, 5- to 8-parted, in umbellate 3- to 5-forked cymes on stalks 8 to 12 in. long; cymes drooping and sub-globose in bud, finally hollow-topped. July. W. Europe, including Britain. (E.B. 536; J.R.H.S. 46, 266.) var. **Forsteria'num** is slender, green, with round-topped *infl.*; **min'us** is about half the size of the type. The specific name is often misapplied to *S. reflexum.*

S. sarmento'sum. Prostrate evergreen glabrous perennial with decumbent reddish-brown shoots up to 1 ft. long, rooting at tip; fl.-shoots about 3 in. h., ascending. *l.* in threes, broadly lanceolate, 1 in. long, ¼ in. wide, fleshy, entire, slightly spurred at base. *fl.* bright yellow, ½ to ⅝ in. across in a flat-topped umbellate 3- to 5-forked cyme with a solitary fl. in the forks. July. China, Japan. (J.R.H.S. 46, 226.) Hardy. var. **variega'tum,** a synonym of *S. lineare variegatum.*

S. Sartoria'num. A synonym of *S. acre* applied in error to *S. Stribrnyi.*

S. sediform'e. Evergreen, glabrous, usually glaucous. Stems woody and branching at base, 6 in. to 2 ft. h. *l.* lanceolate, distinctly flattened, ½ to ¾ in. long, ⅛ to 3/16 in. wide, acute, upper scattered, nearly flat above. *fl.* greenish-white, many in a corymbose cyme; pet. 5 to 8, lanceolate, acute, spreading. July, August. Mediterranean. 1769. (J.R.H.S. 46, 272 as *S. altissimum.*) Variable in size (*l.* may be up to 1½ in. long and stem 2 ft. h. in var. **latifolium.** SYN. *S. nicaeense*) and in colour from pale or dark green to purple glaucous. A small purple form is **S. coerulescens.**

S. Selskia'num. Allied to *S. Aizoon* but with hairy stem, hairy narrow *l.*, and smaller *fl.* August. Manchuria, Amur. (J.R.H.S. 46, 114.) Hardy.

S. Semeno'vii. Similar to *S. rhodanthum* with a racemose *infl.* up to 3 in. long, but with whitish *fl.* and narrower entire *l.* 1 to 2 in. long. June, July. Turkistan. (J.R.H.S. 46, 66.) Hardy.

S. sempervivoi'des. Related to *S. pilosum* but with much looser rosettes of broader *l.* marked dark red, and with scarlet *fl.* Biennial and downy, 4 to 8 in. h. June, July. Asia Minor, Caucasus. (J.R.H.S. 46, 282.) SYN. *S. Sempervivum.* Hardy.

S. sexangula're. Evergreen, glabrous, mat-forming perennial with barren shoots ascending, 2 to 3 in. long, branched; fl.-shoots erect, very slender, 2 to 3 in. h. *l.* densely crowded in 6 or 7 rows, spreading or ascending, about ⅛ in. long, linear-cylindric. *fl.* yellow, ¾ in. across; *infl.* flat-topped, 1 to 2 in. across, 3-branched. Europe, including Britain. (E.B. 533; J.R.H.S. 46, 265.) The var. **bolonien'se** is more slender with greenish-yellow *fl.* Hardy.

S. Siebold'ii. Herbaceous perennial with low-arching, slender, terete, purplish stems about 9 in. long. *l.* in whorls of 3, sessile or nearly so, spreading, nearly round, blue-green, margins wavy, pinkish, base wedge-shaped. *fl.* pinkish, ½ in. across, numerous; pet. with green spot at back near top; *infl.* much-branched, umbellate, about 2 in. across; pedicels about as long as fl. October. Japan. 1836. (B.M. 5358; J.R.H.S. 46, 100.) var. **medio-variega'tum** has a large blotch of yellow in the middle of *l.* (I.H. 373.) Pot-plant for greenhouse. Not hardy.

S. spathulifo'lium.* Forming a close evergreen clump, often tinged red, with runner-like branches from base; fl.-stems erect, 3 to 5 in. h. *l.* on barren shoots about 15 in a terminal rosette 1 in. across, spatulate with an abrupt, pointed, recurved tip; on fl.-stem scattered, spreading, ½ in. long, ⅜ in. wide, club-shaped. *fl.* yellow, numerous, ½ to ¾ in. across in a flattish leafy cyme, 2 to 3 in. across. Western N. America. 1873. (J.R.H.S. 46, 239.) var. **ma'jus** has rosettes of up to 20 larger *l.* permanently green, and a larger *infl.*; **purpu'reum,** has rosettes up to 2 in. across, *l.* deep purple except when young, then mealy and white; *infl.* larger. A fine plant.

S. specta'bile.* Glaucous, herbaceous perennial, with stout, erect, leafy, unbranched stems, 12 to 18 in. h. *l.* opposite or in threes, spreading, nearly sessile, obovate, 3 in. long, 2 in. wide (or larger), fleshy, slightly toothed. *fl.* pink, ½ in. across, very numerous in flat-topped corymbs 4 to 6 in. across; the stamens longer than pet. September, October. China. (G.F. 709; I.H. 271 as *S. Fabaria*; J.R.H.S. 46, 93.) Forms with darker flowers are **atropurpu'reum,** 'Brilliant', **purpu'reum, ro'seum**; **al'bum** has whitish *fl.* A fine border plant especially in the darker fl. varieties.

S. spinos'um. *l.* in a dense basal rosette, close during winter, opening when in growth, oblong-spatulate, with a cartilaginous tip and narrow spine; stem-l. short. *fl.* yellowish-white; pet. about ⅛ in. long, joined at base; *infl.* very dense, narrow spike, sometimes branched. NE. and Cent. Asia. SYN. *Cotyledon spinosa, Umbilicus spinosus.* Produces offsets freely.

S. spu'rium. More or less evergreen, forming a large mat, with finely hairy, much-branched creeping stems, and fl.-stems reddish, about 6 in. h. *l.* opposite, obovate, 1 in. long, ¾ in. wide, cuneate in lower half, crenate-serrate in upper part, with a fringe of hairs on margin. *fl.* white to crimson, usually pink, ½ in. long; pet. almost erect; *infl.* a dense, flat, terminal, leafy umbellate cyme about 2 in. across. July, August. N. Persia, Caucasus. (B.M. 1807, 2370; J.R.H.S. 46, 195.) The white form is var. **al'bum**; **splen'dens** has rich crimson *fl.*; and there are other colour variations as **coccin'eum, ro'seum,** and **ru'brum.** Hardy.

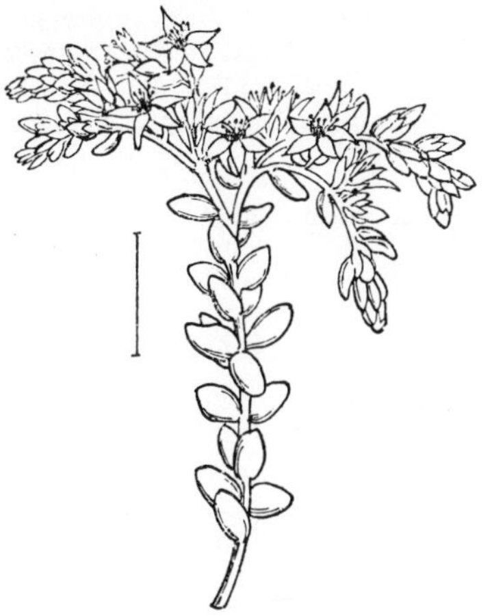

Sedum Stahlii

S. Stahl'ii.* Finely downy, evergreen perennial, reddish-brown, stems many, erect or spreading, slender, woody below, 4 to 8 in. long, rarely branched except at base. *l.* opposite, egg-shaped, ½ in. long, ¼ in. wide and thick, very blunt. *fl.* yellow, ½ in. across in a terminal cyme, 2 in. across. August, September. Mexico. 1900. (B.M. 7908; J.R.H.S. 46, 222.) Nearly hardy. The easily detached leaves are sometimes eaten by birds.

S. stella'tum. Annual. *l.* alternate, spatulate, rounded at apex. 2 to 6 in. h. *fl.* purplish, ½ in. long, pet. small. June. Crete to Portugal. (J.R.H.S. 46, 294.)

S. stenopet'alum. Glabrous tufted evergreen perennial. Stems 3 to 6 in. h., erect from a decumbent base, simple or somewhat branched. *l.* crowded on barren shoots, sessile, lanceolate, ½ to ¾ in. long, entire, obtuse, fleshy. *fl.* bright yellow, ½ in. across, in flattish compact cymes 1 to 2 in. across. June. Rocky Mts. (J.R.H.S. 46, 276.) Hardy.

S. Stepha'ni. A synonym of *S. crassipes Stephani.*

S. stolonife'rum. Allied to *S. spurium* but with smaller, more rhomboidal *l.* which are light green without marginal hairs, more slender bright red stem, and pink starry *fl.* in a small lax *infl.* June, July. N. Persia, Caucasus, Asia Minor. (J.R.H.S. 46, 197.)

S. Strib'rnyi. Glabrous, evergreen perennial, tufted with ascending stems rooting below, much-branched, up to 6 in. h. *l.* rather glaucous green, linear, ½ in. long, obtuse, slightly flattened. *fl.* bright yellow, ½ in. across on 2 or 3 almost erect cyme-branches (1 to 2 in. long). July. Bulgaria, Greece. 1912. (J.R.H.S. 46, 145.)

S. subula'tum. Allied to *S. album* with ascending barren shoots 1 to 2 in. h. and slender, unbranched fl.-shoots up to 8 in. h. *l.* close, linear, terete, very acute, about ⅜ in. long. *fl.* white larger than in *S. album*, in a dense corymb. N. Persia, Armenia. SYN. *S. acutifolium.*

S. sulphu'reum. A synonym of *S. sediforme latifolium.*

S. Tatarinow'ii. Glabrous herbaceous perennial with thick rootstock and small carrot-shaped roots. Stems annual, many, erect or arching, 4 to 6 in. long, smooth, unbranched, leafy. *l.* alternate, linear-lanceolate, ½ to 1 in. long, flat on face, convex at back, with few large scattered teeth, upper l. narrower, very fleshy. *fl.* pinkish-white, ½ in. across; pet. spreading. July, August. N. China. 1913. Hardy.

S. telephioi'des. Very near *S. Telephium* with slender erect stem up to 12 in. h., differing mainly by the very short stamens only two-thirds as long as pet., and the very broad nectar scales. Alleghany Mts.

S. Tele'phium. Orpine, Live for ever. Rootstock thick with a bunch of carrot-like roots. Stem stout, 12 to 18 in. h. *l.* scattered, rarely opposite, oblong-ovate, 2 to 3 in. long, 1 to 1¼ in. wide, obtuse, toothed, lower wedge-shaped, upper rather rounded at base. *fl.* red-purple, spreading, somewhat recurved, ⅜ in. across, in dense sub-globose terminal or lateral cymes. August, September. Europe, including Britain. **S. purpu'reum** is nearly related to *S. Telephium*, and **S. Faba'ria** may be regarded as a subspecies. It is more slender than *S. purpureum*, has *l.* deeper green, narrower, and thinner and *fl.* smaller. Many varieties have been named, among them **affi'ne** with rosy-pink *fl.*; **Bor'deri** with red stems and greyish *l.*; **purpuras'cens,** *fl.* purplish; **roseo-variega'tum** with young *l.* bright pink, later green. A good form is **Munstead Dark Red.**

S. tenel'lum. Habit of *S. lydium.* Stem woody and bare at base, ascending, 2 to 3 in. long; barren shoots short, densely leafy. *l.* crowded at tips, oblong to nearly round, smooth, up to $\frac{1}{10}$ in. long; fl.-shoots ascending or arched with l. up to ¼ in. long. *fl.* few, white, tinged red, about ⅓ in. across. N. Persia, Armenia, Caucasus.

S. terna'tum. Glabrous evergreen forming a pale green tuft with barren stems 3 to 6 in. long, prostrate, rooting below. *l.* in whorls of 3, roundish, spatulate, ½ in. long, crowded in rosettes at ends of branches; l. of fl.-shoots scattered, ascending or spreading, oblong, acute. *fl.* white ½ in. across, 4-parted, on a 3- or 4-branched cyme with spreading branches. May, June. E. United States. (B.M. 1977; B.R. 142.) A variety (**mi'nus**) with all parts smaller, only 2 or 3 in. h., is known.

S. tibet'icum. *See* **S. quadrifidum.**

S. Treleas'ei. Allied to *S. Adolphi* but with glaucous pruinose *l.* about 1½ in. long, ⅝ in. wide, and ⅜ in. thick, and bright-yellow *fl.* about ½ in. wide. April. Mexico. (J.R.H.S. 46, 217.) Not hardy.

S. trif'idum. *See* **S. linearifolium.**

S. turgid'um. A synonym of *S. album.*

S. turkestan'icum. *See* **S. Ewersii.**

S. valerianoi'des. A variety of *S. yunnanense.*

S. Verlot'i. A form of *S. anopetalum* or of *S. sediforme.*

S. versaden'se. Tufted, downy, evergreen perennial, 4 to 6 in. h. Stems decumbent at base, densely hairy at base, ascending, glabrous in upper part, unbranched, leafy. *l.* spatulate, up to 1 in. long, ½ in. wide, slightly spurred, bluntly pointed, downy, green, red at tip and edges, flat above, rounded beneath; upper l. smaller, narrower, glabrous. *fl.* on 2 or 3 secund drooping branches, white, flushed rose, rose at back of pet., ¾ in. across. Summer. Mexico. Not hardy. (J.R.H.S. 46, 142.)

S. verticilla'tum. Glabrous herbaceous perennial with thick rootstock and erect green stems 1 to 2 ft. h. at most with a few branches near the top. *l.* in whorls of 4 or 5, oblong-lanceolate, narrowed at ends. *fl.* green, ¼ in. across. September. Japan, Kamchatka. (J.R.H.S. 46, 95.)

S. villo'sum. Annual or biennial. Downy with erect, red stems, 2 to 6 in. h., usually branched from near base. *l.* linear-oblong, fleshy. *fl.* small, pink, ¼ in. across, in a loose corymb. June, July. Europe, including Britain, Algeria, Greenland. (J.R.H.S. 46, 302.) Needs a damp spot.

S. virens. A synonym of *S. rupestre.*

S. visco'sum. A variety of *S. drymarioides.*

S. Wallichia'num. A synonym of *S. crassipes.*

S. Weinberg'ii. Glaucous, herbaceous perennial, with Echeveria-like l.-rosette at first stemless, finally with a stem. *l.* fleshy, oblanceolate, pointed, infl. cymose, few-branched, axillary. *fl.* with 5 glaucous green sep., cor. white, pet. jointed at base; stamens 10, spreading; carpels reddish. Habitat? (Add. 37 as *Byrnesia Weinbergii.*) SYN. *Cotyledon paraguayensis, Echeveria Weinbergii, E. arizonica* of gardens, *Graptopetalum Weinbergii.* Shy to flower.

S. Wink'leri. Downy perennial, sometimes with underground runners. Barren shoots 1 to 2 in. long. *l.* crowded at tips; fl.-shoots erect or spreading up to 4 in. long, l. spatulate-oblong, ⅛ to ⅜ in. long, upper narrower. *fl.* white, green-veined, ½ in. across in a broad corymb. S. Spain. 1918. SYN. *S. hirsutum baeticum.*

S. Woodward'ii. A synonym of *S. Aizoon.*

S. yosemiten'se. Closely related to *S. spathulifolium* but *l.* fresh green, not glaucous, smaller than in *S. spathulifolium majus*; *fl.* as in *S. spathulifolium.* May. Yosemite, California. (J.R.H.S. 46, 241.)

S. yunnanen'se valerianoi'des. *S. yunnanense* is a very variable species and only this variety is in British cultivation. Tall, glaucous herbaceous perennial up to 3 ft. h. *l.* in whorls of 3, ovate 1½ in. long, ¾ in. wide. *fl.* small, green, 4-parted, dioecious, in a panicle. July. Yunnan. (J.R.H.S. 40, 74–6.) Of little garden value but of interest as coming between the Rhodiola and Telephium groups.

SEED. The seed is a structure peculiar to flowering plants. It consists essentially of a resting embryo plant enclosed in a protecting coat. The embryo plant has a rudimentary root (the radicle), a rudimentary shoot (the plumule), and one or more rudimentary leaves (the cotyledons). The coat (testa) is usually double, the outer one thick and hard and usually impervious to water or nearly so, its continuity broken only by a minute pore (the micropyle) lying near the tip of the radicle; it usually shows a scar (the hilum) where the seed separated from its attachment to the parent plant. The seed contains a store of food which has already been absorbed by the embryo (when the seed is said to be exalbuminous, e.g. Pea, Bean, Apple) or lying adjacent to the embryo (when the seed is said to be albuminous, e.g. Ash, Onion, Crinum). The food-store may have been formed within the embryo sac when it is called endosperm, or just outside it when it is known as perisperm. The difference between endosperm and perisperm, however, has little significance in horticulture though of botanical importance.

The testa frequently bears outgrowths of some kind, such as wings, hairs, or corrugations which usually aid in the distribution of the seed. Not infrequently an outgrowth from some part takes the form of an aril, arillode, or caruncle (q.v.). These outgrowths are frequently fleshy, sweet, or oily, and attractive to ants and other insects and animals which are induced to pick up the seeds and carry them where it is convenient to feed upon the outgrowths, leaving the hard seeds unharmed. The seeds are thus distributed. The arillode may, however, serve in an entirely different manner.

The seed is derived directly from the ovule, which in the Gymnosperms (the Conifers and their allies) is produced at or near the end of a shoot and is not enclosed in an ovary but is protected by scales of one sort or another, while in the Angiosperms (all other flowering plants) it is enclosed in an ovary which forms part of the pistil or gynoecium of the flower.

It should be noted that the 'seed' which the horticulturist handles is very often not the true seed but the true seed plus other parts of the flower or even other structures which help to protect or distribute it. The seeds of Antirrhinum, Pansy, Pea, Bean, and Cabbage, for example, are true seeds, but the horticulturist's 'seeds' of Coreopsis, Lettuce, Marigold, and Beet are not. The latter group contain seeds within their coverings, the former are seeds without extra coverings. It is only the seeds proper which are developed from the ovule, and the following is concerned only with a brief account of the changes that result in the rudimentary ovule developing into a seed. As between Gymnosperms and Angiosperms the development does not differ greatly from a horticultural point of view.

The number of ovules produced in a single female flower varies greatly; it may be only one, it may be hundreds. Each ovule arises as a minute outgrowth from near the growing-point of the shoot which bears it or from the wall of the ovary or on the edges of the carpels. From near the base of each young ovule 1 or 2 walls of cells grow up and completely surround it except for a minute pore (the micropyle) which may be at the top or near the base of the ovule which, during growth, is often bent or inverted so that the micropyle is brought down near the stalk (funicle) of the ovule. Strands of vascular tissue pass from the ovary into the funicle bringing food and water to the developing ovule. The mass of cells which these walls surround is often called the nucellus and is a stage of development corresponding with, say, the macrosporangium of Selaginella. As with that it develops a large cell within it, the embryo-sac, but unlike it, this occurs while the nucellus is still attached to the parent plant, and subsequent developments occur while this attachment is complete.

The embryo-sac at first contains one nucleus with its full complement of chromosomes (q.v.). The first division of this nucleus gives rise to 2 nuclei but no dividing wall is formed between them. One moves to the micropylar end of the sac, the other to its base, and then each divides into 2 and these again into 2. At one of these divisions, as in the formation of pollen grains (q.v.), the chromosomes fail to split lengthwise but half pass intact into each daughter nucleus. There are thus now 8 nuclei in the embryo-sac, 4 at each end, each containing only half the full complement of chromosomes (*see* **Mendel's Law**). Two of these nuclei pass, 1 from each end to the middle of the sac, leaving 3 at each end. The 3 at the end of the sac opposite to the micropyle, as a rule, take no further part in the development of the seed: of those at the micropylar end, 1 is the egg-cell, the other 2 are potential egg-cells (synergidae) which do not usually develop further.

At this stage the egg-cell is ready for fertilization, and until it is fertilized no further development takes place. Fertilization (q.v.), as we have seen, is effected by the fusion of a nucleus from a related pollen grain with the egg-cell, bringing the number of chromosomes up to normal and producing a cell containing characters derived partly from one, partly from the other parent.

Pollination is usually followed by fertilization with little delay if the stigma is receptive, but in some plants the delay is considerable. In Pines the pollen germinates at the mouth of the micropyle in the year it is shed, but growth is checked after a while and resumed only in the following year when fertilization is effected and the growth of the embryo begins. In orchids, at the time of pollination, no embryo-sacs are differentiated in the ovules and the growth of the pollen-tubes is very slow. Only after the stimulus given by pollination is the embryo-sac developed and fertilization becomes possible; even after fertilization in orchids the growth of the embryo is so slow that it is represented in the ripe seed only by a group of cells.

Pollen has a certain length of life and can, in some plants, be sent to distant places if precautions are taken to pack it dry, yet with ample access of air. It may, for instance, be collected, when ripe and dry, in a gelatine capsule and this enclosed in a glass tube containing at the bottom a small amount of dry calcium chloride covered with a layer of cotton-wool to keep the capsule from direct contact with it. The tube is tightly corked and enclosed in a wooden case and may then be consigned by air-mail almost anywhere with safety. Even surface mail may be fast enough to places as near as N. America.

As a rule, as soon as fertilization is effected, the fertilized egg-cell surrounds itself with a cell wall, divides transversely into 2, the upper cell dividing to form a temporary organ called the suspensor, the lower dividing transversely and longitudinally into 8, the uppermost of which contribute to the formation of the radicle, the others to the plumule and the cotyledons, thus laying the foundation of the embryo. Meanwhile, other cells are produced from the other nuclei in the embryo-sac, forming eventually a mass of storage cells, the endosperm. This endosperm may be partly or even entirely absorbed by the growing embryo before the seed is ripe.

Many variations from this sequence of events occur for which advanced botanical text-books should be consulted, but they do not materially affect the formation of the seed from the horticultural point of view. Generally, with the development of the embryo and the thickening and hardening of the coats of the ovule (testa), growth ceases for a time and the water-supply to the seed is gradually cut off by the formation of an absciss layer between it and its stalk; the amount of water retained in the seed being very greatly lessened, so that while the developing ovule may contain over 90 per cent. of its weight of water, the ripe seed has only 10 per cent. Then begins a period of rest which may be long or short according to the kind of plant and the circumstances surrounding the seed.

The seed contains, as a rule, only one embryo, but in some Gymnosperms several may be formed and seeds of some Angiosperms sometimes show the same phenomenon, e.g. Citrus, but one is the general rule. The food store, whether within or outside the embryo, consists mainly of starch or oil and protein, but other materials are sometimes found such as cellulose in the endosperm of the date-stone. When the growth of the embryo is resumed on germination these materials are made soluble by means of enzymes or ferments and used for growth until the young plant can fend for itself. Where endosperm is present the cotyledons usually absorb the food and pass it on before they emerge completely from the testa, and they may continue to do so even after normal leaves have been formed, as may be seen, for instance, in the coco-nut palm and in Crinums and other large seeds.

The size of the seed is determined on the one hand by the need for provision of food when germination begins, and on the other by the necessity of distributing the seed over as wide an area as possible. It is thus a compromise and some plants succeed by adopting a balance leaning towards one side, some to the other. The extremes may be illustrated by the large seeds of the double coco-nut palm which weigh about 40 lb. and the minute seeds of orchids scarcely distinguishable from dust. Though other factors come in, and no hard and fast line can be drawn, in general the plants that have succeeded in distributing themselves most widely over the surface of the earth have numerous small seeds with a moderate food store, or have developed some special means of insuring carriage over a wide area. The number of seeds produced by a plant is, however, determined not only by the number of seeds in a fruit but also by the number of flowers it may bear, and such a plant as Foxglove, Antirrhinum, or Mullein, with their many flowers may produce over a million seeds; a Poppy, in spite of the hundreds of seeds formed in a single capsule, since it has comparatively few flowers, is left far behind.

SEED BEETLES. *See* **Bruchid Beetles.**

SEED DISINFECTION. The term for the treatment of seed by chemical substances designed to kill disease-producing fungi and bacteria which may be on the surfaces of the seed or may to some extent be living in the seed tissues. The substance used may be a liquid or a dust. The seeds are steeped in liquid disinfectants such as Formalin solution or are well shaken up with a dust such as Zinc oxide. In many cases besides direct destruction of a parasite such treatments give protection against disease especially where dusts form a coating on the seeds (*see* **Seed dressing**). Sometimes hot water alone is sufficient to kill the parasite living within the seed tissues as in the Black Rot disease of Cabbage. A well-known seed treatment is the use of weak Formalin solution for steeping Celery seed to destroy the Celery Leaf Spot fungus living in the outer tissues (*see* **Celery diseases**). Seed disinfection, especially when using dusts, must be done carefully so as to avoid injury which may reduce germination.

SEED DRESSING. A method of seed disinfection. Dressing usually means that the seeds are covered with some chemical substance as a protective coating against disease. They are shaken up with some such substance as Cuprous oxide (red or yellow oxide of copper), Zinc oxide, or an organic Mercury dust. The result is to protect them from many soil fungi which may rot them in the ground, especially if the weather is wet and cold. The treatment is therefore most valuable for early spring- or late autumn-sown seeds especially Peas, Beans, and Brassicas. Care must be observed in such treatment so that injury which may reduce germination will not occur. For instance, Cuprous oxide is injurious to Brassica seeds but gives good results with Peas, Beans, Tomato, Cucumber, and Lettuce.

SEED ROOM. The room in which seeds are kept should be dry at all times. If the air is moist, the seeds will absorb some of the moisture and will be likely to respire more freely, reducing their capacity for germination. Changes or extremes of temperature are of little account if the seeds are dry.

A→

SEEDLING. A plant produced from a seed, especially, but not exclusively, a very young plant. An apple tree, for instance, raised from seed, is often, no matter what its age, referred to as a seedling to distinguish it from one raised by vegetative means and belonging to a clone.

A→

Seegeria'nus -a -um, in honour of the firm of Seeger and Tropp, florists of Dulwich, *c.* 1890.

Seelos'ii, in honour of Gustav Seelos, b. 1832, botanist of Briscen, Austria.

Seeman'nii, in honour of B. C. Seemann, 1825–71, of Hanover, who collected in Trop. America and the Pacific Is.

segeta'lis -is -e, segetum, of cornfields.

SEGMENT. One of the divisions into which an organ such as a leaf or a petal may be cut.

segregate. (1) to separate; (2) a separated part. The reverse of aggregate.

segrega'tus -a -um, selected from a group.

Seguier'i, in honour of Jean Francis Seguier, 1703–84, of Nimes, France, who botanized in many parts of Europe.

SELAGINEAE. An old Family now partly included in Scrophulariaceae (Hebenstreitia, Selago), partly forming the Family Globulariaceae.

SELAGINEL'LA (diminutive of *Selago*, the old name for another Lycopod). FAM. *Selaginellaceae.* A vast genus (upwards of 700 species) of stove, greenhouse, or hardy evergreen plants, much resembling Mosses. Chiefly Trop. American; a few in S. Africa, temperate Australia, and S. America, and 2 in Europe. Habit of Lycopodium, from which it differs by its dimorphic spores and sporangia. Stems much-branched, the ultimate branching usually flabellate-dichotomous, trailing, sub-erect, sarmentose, or scandent, with the root-fibres confined to the base, or in the trailing species extending to the upper nodes; in shape more or less distinctly quadrangular, or the faces flat. Leaves small, with a single central vein, usually in 4 rows and dimorphous, and more or less oblique, the 2 rows of the lower plane larger and more spreading, the 2 rows of the upper ascending, appressed to the stem and imbricate. Spikes usually 4-ranked and often sharply square, but in 2 sub-genera dimorphic on the same plan as the leaves, but mostly resupinate (i.e. the small bracts on the same plane as the large leaves, and vice versa). Selaginellas grow freely in any light soil, which should be kept open by mixing charcoal, or small potsherds, through it. They require to be kept quite moist at all times, and prefer shade. Propagated readily from cuttings, made from the creeping stems, which emit roots at nearly every joint. *S. Kraussiana* is useful for edgings to greenhouse beds, and for decorative purposes in pots. It may be propagated in quantity at any season. Cuttings should be made about February or March in the pots or pans in which they are to remain for the season. Stove and greenhouse Selaginellas succeed under somewhat similar conditions to stove and greenhouse Ferns respectively.

The layering of the fronds by pegging firmly on a constantly damp, mossy surface is a rapid method of producing very handsome plants, and this operation may be performed with equal success at almost any time of the year. In private establishments, especially where the demand for decorative plants is great, and where greater difficulties are encountered in the propagation of ferns, these useful plants may be increased at a rapid rate, and with comparatively little trouble.

With very few exceptions, Selaginellas require a warm, close, moist atmosphere, where draughts are carefully excluded, although some of them are quite at home in a temperate house, and a few are even hardy in a sheltered place out-of-doors. The temperature most suitable for the bulk of them is from 65 to 70° F., and they will, by growing more luxuriantly, give even more satisfaction if the atmosphere can be kept at from 70 to 75° F. all the year round.

There are various ways of growing Selaginellas. Growing them in shallow pans is the best method of cultivation, as, with the exception of the plants belonging to the *Rosulatae* section, they all require room to spread, and most of them root upon the surface of the soil only. They should be kept on the shady side, or at one end of the house; in any case it will be found beneficial to have them in such a position that there may be a certain amount of constant moisture about them. To that effect, they should be placed on a solid bed which constantly gives off moisture, or, if this is impracticable on account of the house being provided with permanent stages, these should be covered with Sphagnum, to be kept wet; and the pans should not be allowed to rest directly on the moss, but be set up above it upon 3 small pots or on an inverted pan, so as to avoid all direct contact with the saturated material. Plants so arranged will derive all the benefit of the surrounding moisture without their soil becoming sour. Although they have a particular dislike to standing permanently in the wet, Selaginellas require copious waterings at the roots, and for that reason it is necessary that their pots or pans shall be thoroughly well drained. They should not be syringed overhead, or only very sparingly during hot summer days, as their massive though feathery fronds cannot long endure being wetted. **A**

S. affin'is. Stems 1 ft. or more long, trailing, flat on back, 2-sulcate on face, jointed at nodes, forked low down and very pinnate, with erecto-patent, very compound branches. *l.* of lower plane obtuse on branchlets, ascending, oblong-lanceolate, acute, $\frac{1}{8}$ to $\frac{1}{6}$ in. long, bright green; l. of upper plane one-third as long, oblique-oblong, cuspidate, imbricate. *Spikes* $\frac{1}{4}$ to $\frac{1}{2}$ in. long; bracts ovate, cuspidate, strongly keeled. Guiana. Stove. SYN. *S. rigida* (of gardens).

S. africa'na. A synonym of *S. Vogelii.*

S. albo-ni'tens.* Stems slender, trailing, copiously pinnate, upper branches simple, lower slightly compound. *l.* of lower plane spaced on main stem, spreading, oblong-lanceolate, $\frac{1}{12}$ in. long, bright green, rather unequal-sided, rounded on upper side at base, shortly ciliate; l. of upper plane one-third as long, oblique-ovate, distinctly cuspidate. *Spikes* $\frac{1}{4}$ to $\frac{1}{2}$ in. long; bracts acute, very crowded, strongly keeled. W. Indies. Greenhouse.

S. albospi'ca. A form of *S. stenophylla.*

S. amoe'na. A variety of *S. caulescens.*

S. apo'da. A garden name for *S. apus.*

S. a'pus.* Stems slender, trailing, densely matted, 1 to 4 in. long, the short, distant, erecto-patent branches simple or forked. *l.* of lower plane spaced below tips of branches, upper spreading, lower reflexed, ovate, acute, $\frac{1}{24}$ in. long, unequal-sided; l. of upper plane half as long, shortly cuspidate. *Spikes* $\frac{1}{4}$ to $\frac{1}{2}$ in. long; bracts ovate, acute, about $\frac{1}{12}$ in. long, strongly serrulate. N. America. (B.B. ed. 2. 1. 49.) Greenhouse. SYN. *S. apoda* and *S. densa* (of gardens).

S. argen'tea. A variety of *S. caulescens.* The name *argentea* is also used in catalogues for *S. erythropus.*

S. ascen'dens. A form of *S. Martensii.*

S. atrovi'ridis.* Stems sub-erect, 6 to 12 in. long, flat on back, root-fibres confined to lower part, decompound, branching between pinnatifid and pinnate. *l.* of lower plane close, both on stem and branches, spreading or rather ascending, oblong-rhomboid, sub-obtuse, $\frac{1}{8}$ to $\frac{1}{4}$ in. long, bright green, unequal-sided, more or less ciliate; l. of upper plane half as long, oblong, long-cuspidate, much imbricate. *Spikes* square, $\frac{1}{2}$ to 1 in. long; bracts ovate, acute, strongly keeled. Stove. (Gn. 40 (1891), 359.) Trop. Asia.

S. azo'rica. Stems trailing, rooting nearly to tip, 2 to 3 in. long, with several short, compound branches. *l.* of lower plane contiguous on branches, oblique-oblong, nearly equilateral, acute, $\frac{1}{8}$ in. long, rounded at base, serrulate from base to apex along both branches, bright green; l. of upper plane much imbricate, more than half as long as others, oblique, oblong-lanceolate. Azores.

S. Bakeria'na.* Stems trailing, 6 to 9 in. long; lower branches copiously compound. *l.* bright green; those of lower plane spaced, spreading, oblong, obtuse, $\frac{1}{12}$ in. long; l. of upper plane half as long, ascending, acute. *Spikes* numerous, slender, square, 1 to 2 in. long. Queensland. SYN. *S. leptostachya.* Greenhouse.

S. bel'lula of Moore. A synonym of *S. inaequalifolia perelegans.*

S. brasilien'sis. Stems trailing, 2 to 4 in. long, copiously pinnate, branches erecto-patent, upper simple, lower slightly decompound. *l.* of lower plane spaced and spreading, except towards tips of branches, about $\frac{1}{12}$ in. long, bright green, cordate at base on upper side, distinctly ciliate and imbricate over stem; l. of upper plane half as long, distinctly cuspidate. *Spikes* $\frac{1}{4}$ to $\frac{1}{2}$ in. long; bracts ovate-lanceolate, strongly keeled. Brazil. Greenhouse. A near ally of *S. apus.*

S. Braun'ii. Stems 1 to $1\frac{1}{2}$ ft. long, erect, pale straw-colour, simple in lower half, decompound, deltoid, and flexuous in upper half; pinnae erecto-patent, deltoid; pinnules regular, short, deltoid, spaced; ultimate branchlets $\frac{1}{8}$ to $\frac{1}{4}$ in. long. *l.* of lower plane contiguous only on final branchlets, nearly spreading, ovate-rhomboid, $\frac{1}{24}$ in. long; l. of upper plane one-third to half as long, shortly cuspidate. *Spikes* short, square; bracts little longer than sporangia. W. China. Greenhouse.

S. Brown'ii. A form of *S. Kraussiana.*

S. bulbif'era. Stems decumbent, with many root-fibres in lower half; many of lower branchlets excurrent and whip-like at tip, bearing bulbils, which reproduce the plant. *l.* not distinctly ciliate. 1867. Stove or greenhouse.

S. cae'sia. A synonym of *S. uncinata.*

S. cae'sia arbor'ea. A synonym of *S. Willdenovii.*

S. canalicula'ta.* Stems sub-erect, sarmentose, 3 to 4 ft. long; pinnae deltoid, usually 4 to 6 in. long, sometimes flexuous and longer; lower branchlets very compound, tertiary divisions more erecto-patent, and not so close as in *S. inaequalifolia.* *l.* of lower plane crowded, oblong-rhomboid, $\frac{1}{12}$ to $\frac{1}{8}$ in. long on branchlets, bright green, cuneate-truncate on upper, nearly square on lower side at base; l. of upper plane half as long, ovate-lanceolate. *Spikes* square, $\frac{1}{4}$ to 1 in. long; bracts cuspidate, strongly keeled. E. Himalaya, &c. Stove. SYN. *S. caudata, S. chinensis, S. sinensis.* var. **robus'ta** is a very tall, strong-growing form. SYN. *S. robusta.*

S. caules'cens.* Stems generally 6 to 12 in. long, stiffly erect, unbranched in lower half, with spaced, appressed l., deltoid and decompound in upper half; pinnae close, deltoid, with copiously sub-flabellately compound lower pinnules, final branchlets ascending. *l.* of lower plane crowded, ovate, falcate, acute, $\frac{1}{24}$ to $\frac{1}{12}$ in. long, bright green, slightly ciliate on upper side at base; l. of upper plane a quarter to one-third as long, much imbricate. *Spikes* square, $\frac{1}{4}$ to $\frac{1}{2}$ in. long; bracts ovate, cuspidate. Japan, China, &c. Stove. var. **amoe'na,** stems erect, about 1 ft. h., upper part triangular, pinnately branched, with spreading, distant, acuminate l., branches horizontal, 2-pinnate. Mexico. Whole plant bright and cheerful green; **argen'tea** differs from type by the silvery sheen of under-surface. SYN. *S. argentea*; **grac'ilis,** stems dwarf, distantly branched, bright green. 1880; **japon'ica,** stems, pinnae less crowded, and not so decompound as in type, *l.* of lower plane broadly ovate, those of main stem and pinnae nearly as broad as long, those of unbranched part of stem rather spreading. Japan.

S. chinen'sis. A synonym of *S. canaliculata.*

S. cogna'ta. A synonym of *S. Lobbii.*

S. concin'na. Stems trailing, 1 ft. or more long, pinnately branched; lower branches flabellately compound. *l.* of lower plane crowded, ascending, oblong-lanceolate, $\frac{1}{12}$ to $\frac{1}{8}$ in. long, glossy, rigid, much dilated at base; l. of upper plane one-third as long, much imbricate with a long cusp. *Spikes* $\frac{1}{2}$ to 1 in. long, square; bracts cuspidate, strongly keeled. Mascarene Is. (Gn. 17 (1880), 214.) Stove.

S. confer'ta. Stems very slender, trailing, intermatted, 1 to 2 in. long, pinnate, lower branches slightly compound. *l.* of lower plane close, erecto-patent, linear-oblong, obtuse, $\frac{1}{24}$ in. long, equal-sided, strongly ciliate, a little imbricate; l. of upper plane one-third or one-quarter as long, acute. *Spikes* very short; bracts ovate, crowded, strongly keeled. Cuba. Stove.

S. convolu'ta. Stems densely tufted, 3 to 6 in. long, compound nearly to base, primary branching pinnate, short, broad, erecto-patent pinnae between pinnate and flabellate. *l.* of lower plane much imbricate, ascending, ovate, acute, $\frac{1}{24}$ in. long, serrulate, bright green; l. of upper plane half as long, acute. *Spikes* square, $\frac{1}{4}$ to $\frac{1}{2}$ in. long; bracts cuspidate, strongly keeled. Trop. America. Stove.

S. cuspida'ta.* Stems densely tufted, about 6 in. long, branched nearly or quite from base, primary branching pinnate; pinnae short, rhomboid, copiously compound, with contiguous branchlets. *l.* of lower plane crowded, ascending, oblique-ovate, cuspidate, dilated and ciliate on upper side at base, pale green, white-edged, $\frac{1}{24}$ to $\frac{1}{12}$ in. long; l. of upper plane nearly as long, cuspidate. *Spikes* square, $\frac{1}{4}$ to $\frac{1}{2}$ in. long; bracts cuspidate, strongly keeled. Mexico, &c. Stove. var. **cris'pa,** differs from type in its crisped stems. 1888; **elonga'ta,** stems 1 ft. or more long, simple in lower part, primary branches longer and more pinnate. SYN. *Lycopodium cordifolium*; **Emilia'na,*** stems, branches 6 to 9 in. long, abundant and much-branched, light green, erect when young, becoming darker and horizontal.

S. delicatis'sima. Stems densely matted, very slender, straw-colour, trailing to 6 to 12 in., forked and copiously pinnately branched, branches very compound. *l.* of lower plane spaced, except at tips of branches, spreading, oblong, obtuse, broadly rounded and densely ciliate on upper side at base; l. of upper plane half as long, acute, strongly auricled on outside at base. *Spikes* unknown. Colombia. Greenhouse. Leaves and branches curl up readily in drought.

S. densa. A synonym of *S. apus*.

S. denticula'ta.* Stems densely matted, pale, trailing, 6 in. long, copiously pinnately branched, lower branches flabellately compound. *l.* of lower plane close or slightly spaced, broadly ovate, oblique, subacute, about $\frac{1}{12}$ in. long, spreading or erecto-patent, flat, denticulate, cordate on upper side at base, much imbricate over stem; l. of upper plane half as long, cuspidate, rather diverging. *Spikes* sessile, square, about $\frac{1}{2}$ in. long; bracts acute, much imbricate, strongly keeled. Mediterranean region. (Bick. Fl.P.R. 82.) Greenhouse. In exposed places, whole plant sometimes turns bright red when old. The name *S. denticulata* is sometimes wrongly applied in gardens to *S. Kraussiana*.

S. dichro'a. A garden form of *S. Vogelii*.

S. distor'ta. Stems slender, trailing or sub-erect, intermatted, 3 to 6 in. long, obscurely jointed at nodes, pinnate, short, ascending branches sub-flabellately compound. *l.* of lower plane crowded on branchlets, deflexed, oblong-lanceolate, acute, about $\frac{1}{24}$ in. long; l. of upper plane more than half as long, imbricate, oblong, acute. *Spikes* short, square; bracts acute, strongly keeled. Brazil. Greenhouse. var. **ma'jor,** more luxuriant, with stouter stems, 1 ft. or more long, often excurrent at end; l. of lower plane often $\frac{1}{12}$ in. long, spreading, or rather ascending.

S. divarica'ta. A form of *S. Martensii*.

S. Douglas'ii. Stems trailing, 3 to 6 in. long, pinnately branched; lower branches very compound. *l.* of lower plane pale, firm, broadly oblong, obtuse, $\frac{1}{12}$ in. long, auricled and ciliate at base, upper side much imbricate over stem; l. of upper plane half as long, cuspidate. *Spikes* $\frac{1}{2}$ to 1 in. long; bracts cuspidate, much imbricate. British Columbia, &c. Greenhouse.

S. Emilia'na. A form of *S. cuspidata*.

S. erythro'pus.* Stems about 9 in. long, bright crimson, simple in lower half or third, deltoid and decompound upwards; lower pinnae deltoid, 3-pinnate; final branchlets ascending, contiguous. *l.* of lower plane contiguous, ascending, oblong or ovate-lanceolate, acute, $\frac{1}{12}$ to $\frac{1}{8}$ in. long, bright green, unequal-sided, strongly ciliate and imbricate over stem on upper side at base; l. of upper plane half as long, oblique-ovate, cuspidate. *Spikes* square; bracts cuspidate, strongly keeled. Trop. America. Greenhouse. var. **ma'jor** is more compound, unbranched part of stem longer, and all leaves appressed. *S. setosa* (of gardens) is a starved, small form of this species.

S. filici'na. A synonym of *S. haematodes*.

S. flabella'ta. Stems 1 to 2 ft. long, erect, simple in lower half, deltoid and decompound in upper half; pinnae deltoid, lower 3- or 4-pinnate; final branchlets contiguous, $\frac{1}{4}$ to 1 in. long. *l.* of lower plane contiguous, oblique-ovate, acute, ascending, bright green, obliquely inserted, much dilated, ciliate, much imbricate over stem on upper side at base; l. of upper plane a quarter to one-third as long, cuspidate. *Spikes* square, $\frac{1}{2}$ to 1 in. long; bracts cuspidate, strongly keeled. Tropics of Asia, America, and Polynesia. Greenhouse.

S. flagella'ta. Stems trailing, 6 in. long; branches erecto-patent, lower very compound; branches excurrent and whip-like at end. *l.* of lower plane ovate-lanceolate, very acute, above $\frac{1}{12}$ in. long, pellucid, bright green, more produced on upper side of midrib, rounded at base, shortly ciliate, imbricate over stem; l. of upper plane one-third as long, ovate, acuminate, falcate, converging. *Spikes* $\frac{1}{3}$ to $\frac{1}{2}$ in. long; bracts very acuminate, strongly keeled. French Guiana. Stove.

S. flagellif'era. A garden form of *S. plumosa*.

S. flagellifor'mis. A synonym of *S. plumosa flagellifera*.

S. flexuo'sa. Stems about 1 ft. long, flat on back, copiously branched, lower branches elongate and very compound, upper part assurgent; root-fibres often only in lower half. *l.* of lower plane close, spreading, bright green, oblong-rhomboidal, subacute, $\frac{1}{8}$ to $\frac{1}{6}$ in. long, more produced on upper side of distinct midrib, serrulate on upper side near base; l. of upper plane one-third as long, long-cuspidate. *Spikes* $\frac{1}{2}$ to 1 in. long, square; bracts $\frac{1}{24}$ in. long, crowded, sharply keeled. South Brazil. Stove.

S. formo'sa. A form of *S. Martensii*.

S. fulcra'ta. Stems $1\frac{1}{2}$ to 2 ft. long, stiffly erect, simple in lower half, with a few distant, small, appressed l., deltoid and decompound in upper half; pinnae deltoid, lower ones 3- or 4-pinnate, rachises pubescent; final branchlets contiguous, $\frac{1}{4}$ to $\frac{1}{2}$ in. long. *l.* of lower plane rather spaced even on branchlets, ascending, lanceolate, acute, $\frac{1}{12}$ to $\frac{1}{8}$ in. long, truncate; l. of upper plane half as long, incurved, not cuspidate. *Spikes* square, $\frac{1}{4}$ to $\frac{1}{2}$ in. long; bracts little longer than sporangia. E. Himalaya. Stove.

S. Galeot'tei. Stems 1 to 2 ft. long, sub-erect, with root-fibres from lower half, sometimes excurrent and whip-like at tip, copiously pinnate, branches pyramidal and decompound. *l.* of lower plane close on branchlets, spaced on branches and stem, ascending, lanceolate or oblong-lanceolate, acute, $\frac{1}{8}$ to $\frac{1}{6}$ in. long, more produced on upper side of midrib, broadly rounded and shortly ciliate on upper side at base, truncate and auricled on lower; l. of upper plane one-third to one-half as long, much imbricate. *Spikes* $\frac{1}{4}$ to $\frac{1}{2}$ in. long; bracts cuspidate, strongly keeled. Mexico. Stove. (Gn. 17 (1880), 214.)

S. grac'ilis.* Stems 2 to 3 ft. long, sub-erect, pinnately branched, rather rough; pinnae narrow-lanceolate, 4 to 5 in. long; pinnules simple, lower 1 in. long, $\frac{1}{8}$ in. broad. *l.* bright green, ovate-falcate; stipular ones narrow-lanceolate, cuspidate, parallel, close-set. *Spikes* terminal, tetragonal, $\frac{1}{2}$ to 1 in. long. South Sea Is. 1886. Stove.

S. gran'dis.* Stems erect, $1\frac{1}{2}$ to 2 ft. long, simple in lower half, deltoid and decompound in upper half, branching midway between flabellate and pinnate, contiguous final branchlets $\frac{3}{8}$ in. broad. *l.* of lower plane crowded, lanceolate, very acute, $\frac{1}{4}$ to $\frac{1}{3}$ in. long, bright green, equilateral except at base, slightly ciliate; l. of upper plane one-third as long, ovate-lanceolate, very acute, much imbricate. *Spikes* copious, square, tetragonal, 1 to $1\frac{1}{2}$ in. long; bracts strongly ciliate. Borneo. 1882. Stove. (B.C.F. 3, 407; G.C. 18 (1882), 40, 41.) SYN. *S. platyphylla* (of gardens).

S. Griffith'ii. Stems erect, 6 to 12 in. long, simple below, deltoid and decompound upwards; lower pinnae 3-pinnate; final branchlets $\frac{1}{4}$ to $\frac{1}{2}$ in. long. *l.* of lower plane ascending, oblong-rhomboid, $\frac{1}{8}$ to $\frac{1}{6}$ in. long, dilated, serrulate and imbricate; l. of upper plane minute, with a large cusp. *Spikes* square, $\frac{1}{4}$ to $\frac{1}{2}$ in. long; bracts cuspidate, strongly keeled. Trop. Asia. 1860. Greenhouse.

S. haemato'des.* Stems 1 to 2 ft. long, bright crimson, unbranched in lower half, with l. spaced and appressed, deltoid and decompound in upper half; pinnae deltoid, 3- or 4-pinnate, the contiguous, erecto-patent ultimate divisions $\frac{1}{4}$ to 1 in. long. *l.* of lower plane contiguous, ascending, ovate or oblong-rhomboidal, acute, $\frac{1}{6}$ to $\frac{1}{3}$ in. long, bright green, dilated on upper side at base, broadly rounded; l. of upper plane minute, with a large cusp. *Spikes* square, 1 to $1\frac{1}{2}$ in. long; bracts ovate-lanceolate. Andes. Stove. (R.H. 1907, 516.) SYN. *S. filicina*.

S. helvet'ica. Stems densely matted, slender, pale, trailing, 2 to 3 in. long, forked at base, distantly pinnately branched, with short, erecto-patent, slightly compound branches. *l.* of lower plane spreading, close or slightly spaced, about $\frac{1}{24}$ in. long, oblique, produced on upper side; l. of upper plane acute, half as long, rather divergent. *Spikes* distinctly pedunculate, $\frac{1}{2}$ to 1 in. long, terete; bracts imbricate. Cent. Europe to Japan. Hardy.

S. inaequalifo'lia. Stems sub-erect, sarmentose, 3 to 4 ft. long; pinnae oblong-lanceolate, 6 in. long, the erecto-patent branchlets considerably compound, with ascending tertiary divisions. *l.* of lower plane contiguous, oblong-rhomboid, $\frac{1}{12}$ to $\frac{1}{8}$ in. long, bright green; l. of upper plane half as long, shortly cuspidate. *Spikes* square, $\frac{1}{4}$ to $\frac{1}{2}$ in. long; bracts ovate, cuspidate, strongly keeled. E. Himalaya. Stove. var. **perel'egans,** stems not more than 1 ft. long, pinnae shorter, more deltoid, with more compound lower branches, *spikes* copious, often 1 in. long. (B.C.F. 3, 421.) SYN. *S. bellula* (of Moore).

S. invol'vens. Stems very densely tufted, 2 to 6 in. long, deltoid, 2- or 3-pinnate, branched nearly or quite from base, branching of all grades between flabellate and pinnate. *l.* of lower plane very crowded, ascending, ovate, with a distinct cusp, about $\frac{1}{12}$ in. long, bright green, very thick, serrulate, nearly equal-sided; l. of upper plane nearly as long, oblique, distinctly cuspidate. *Spikes* square; bracts acutely keeled. Japan, China, &c. Greenhouse. (G.C. 19 (1883), 404.) var. **tex'ta,** a peculiar garden form, with branches almost simple. SYN. *S. texta* (of Belgian gardens); **variega'ta** differs from type in having tips of some branches creamy-white.

S. japon'ica. A variety of *S. caulescens*.

S. Karstenia'na. Stems about 1 ft. long, erect from a decumbent base, 2-sulcate down face, copiously pinnate; branches short, erecto-patent, sparingly compound. *l.* of lower plane ovate, acute, dark green, sub-diaphanous, very unequal-sided, denticulate on upper margin, much produced on upper side at base and imbricate over stem; l. of upper plane one-third as long, ovate-oblong, cuspidate. *Spikes* short, often twin, but little flattened; bracts not very obviously dimorphous. New Grenada. Greenhouse.

S. Kraussia'na.* Stems trailing, 6 to 12 in. long, jointed at nodes, copiously pinnate, with very compound, erecto-patent branches. *l.* of lower plane contiguous on branchlets, spaced on branches and main stems, oblong-lanceolate, acute, $\frac{1}{8}$ to $\frac{1}{6}$ in. long, bright green, ciliate and broadly rounded at base; l. of upper plane one-third as long, not cuspidate. *Spikes* short, square; bracts cuspidate, strongly keeled. S. Africa. 1878. Greenhouse. (F.S.A. (2) 182.) *S. Brownii* is a dwarf form from the Azores. The form **au'rea** has yellow leaves; **variega'ta** is a variegated form.

S. laeviga'ta.* Stems erect, 1 to $1\frac{1}{2}$ ft. long, simple in lower half, l. small, distant and soon deciduous, deltoid in upper half, with petiolate, deltoid, once or twice pinnate pinnae; final divisions erecto-patent, 2 to 3 in. long. *l.* of lower plane crowded, oblong-lanceolate, sub-patent, very falcate, acute, $\frac{1}{8}$ to $\frac{1}{6}$ in. long, bright green, adnate by a broad base, decurrent on lower side; l. of upper plane minute, recurved. *Spikes* square, $\frac{1}{2}$ to 1 in. long; bracts acute, strongly keeled. Madagascar. Stove. (R.H. 1869, 286.) var. **Lyal'li,** lower pinnae 2-pinnate, with final divisions $\frac{1}{2}$ to 1 in. long.

S. lepidophyl'la.* Resurrection Club-moss, which is frequently exposed for sale as a vegetable curiosity, owing to the manner in which its curled-up stems unroll and resume a fresh appearance when placed in water. Stems densely tufted, 2 to 4 in. long, branched to base, the primary branching closely pinnate, the broad, cuneate, ascending pinnae sub-flabellately compound. *l.* of lower plane much imbricate, ascending, oblique, ovate, obtuse, $\frac{1}{24}$ in. long, minutely ciliate, when old tinted red-brown; l. of upper plane nearly as long, obtuse. *Spikes* square, $\frac{1}{4}$ to $\frac{1}{2}$ in. long; bracts deltoid, acutely keeled. Texas to Peru. Greenhouse. (Gn. 17 (1880), 400.)

S. leptostach'ya. A synonym of *S. Bakeriana.*

S. Lobb'ii. Stems sub-erect, sarmentose, 3 to 4 ft. long; pinnae regular, lanceolate-deltoid, about 6 in. long, cuneate at base; pinnules contiguous, erecto-patent, upper ones simple, lower forked. *l.* of lower plane contiguous, oblong-lanceolate, falcate, acute, $\frac{1}{8}$ in. long on pinnules, $\frac{1}{6}$ to $\frac{1}{5}$ in. on pinnae, bright green, truncate and rather dilated on both sides at base; l. of upper plane one-third as long, cuspidate. *Spikes* square, oblique-ovate, terminal on branchlets, $\frac{1}{4}$ to $\frac{3}{4}$ in. long; bracts cuspidate, strongly keeled. Borneo. Stove. SYN. *S. cognata.*

S. longis'sima. Stems 2 ft. or more long; branches deltoid, 6 to 9 in. long, with ascending simple upper and slightly compound lower branchlets; ultimate divisions 2 to $2\frac{1}{2}$ in. long. *l.* of lower plane close, oblique, ovate-oblong, acute, $\frac{1}{8}$ in. long, upper side strongly ciliate at base; l. of upper plane one-third as long, nearly erect, obscurely cuspidate. *Spikes* terminal on branchlets, square, 1 to 2 in. long; bracts erecto-patent, strongly keeled. Colombia, &c. 1881. Stove.

S. ludovicia'na. Stems slender, copiously pinnate, flat, 6 in. long, upper branches simple, lower slightly compound. *l.* of lower plane much spaced below tips of the branches, spreading, ovate-oblong, subacute, $\frac{1}{24}$ in. or more long, serrulate, imbricate over stem; l. of upper plane half as long, cuspidate. *Spikes* $\frac{1}{4}$ to $\frac{1}{2}$ in. long; bracts $\frac{1}{12}$ in. long, strongly keeled. United States. Greenhouse.

S. Lyal'li. A variety of *S. laevigata.*

S. Marten'sii.* Stems 6 to 12 in. long, trailing in lower half, with many long root-fibres, ascending in upper half, decompound, branching between pinnate and flabellate. *l.* of lower plane usually crowded, erecto-patent, oblong-lanceolate, sub-obtuse, bright green, unequal-sided, serrulate, a little imbricate; l. of upper plane half as long, with a long cusp, much imbricate. *Spikes* $\frac{1}{4}$ to $\frac{1}{2}$ in. long, square; bracts acute, strongly keeled. Mexico. (B.H. 1866, 129.) Greenhouse. There are numerous varieties, of which the most distinct are: **ascendens, divaricata, formosa,** the variegated **robusta,** and **stolonifera.**

S. Metten'ii. Stems slender, wide-trailing, distantly pinnate; branches short, flabellately compound. *l.* of lower plane nearly contiguous on branches, upper ascending, lower spreading, obtuse, $\frac{1}{8}$ in. long, bright green, not imbricate over stem; l. of upper plane one-third as long, not cuspidate. *Spikes* square. 1865. Greenhouse. Supposed to be a garden hybrid between *S. uncinata* and *S. inaequalifolia.*

S. mol'liceps. Stems erect, densely tufted, 6 to 9 in. long, very pinnate, base 2-sulcate; lower branches compound. *l.* of lower plane contiguous on branchlets, spaced on main stem, erecto-patent, obliquely oblong-lanceolate, acute, dark green, $\frac{1}{12}$ in. long, very unequal-sided, serrulate on upper edge, broadly rounded, shortly ciliate, and a little imbricate over stem on upper side at base; l. of upper plane one-half to one-third as long, ovate or ovate-lanceolate, cuspidate. *Spikes* copious, resupinate, $\frac{1}{4}$ to $\frac{1}{2}$ in. long; bracts of upper plane lanceolate-rhomboid, those of lower plane ovate, cuspidate. Upper Guinea. (F.S.A. (2) 183.) Stove. SYN. *S. rubricaulis.*

S. mutab'ilis. A synonym of *S. serpens.*

S. orega'na.* Stems pendent, flaccid, 1 to 6 ft. long, pinnate, much-branched. *l.* uniform, linear-lanceolate, convex and grooved at back, sparsely denticulate, scarcely $\frac{1}{12}$ in. long, acute, not bristle-tipped. *Spikes* square, very slender, resembling sterile branchlets. Oregon. Greenhouse.

S. pat'ula. Stems slender, pale, trailing, 6 to 9 in. long, with a long, whip-like tip, and numerous short, alternate, pinnately arranged branches with 3 to 7 branchlets. *l.* of lower plane crowded, erecto-patent, oblong-lanceolate, bright green, midrib distinct, ciliate and imbricate over rachis on upper side at base; l. of upper plane one-third as long, oblique-ovate, acute. *Spikes* square, $\frac{1}{4}$ to $\frac{1}{2}$ in. long; bracts cuspidate, much imbricate, strongly keeled. Jamaica. Stove.

S. perel'egans. A variety of *S. inaequalifolia.*

S. Pervil'lei. A synonym of *S. Vogelii.*

S. pilif'era. Stems densely tufted, 3 to 4 in. long, very compound, cuneate, branching midway between pinnate and flabellate, branches erecto-patent. *l.* of lower plane crowded on branches, rather spaced on main stem, ascending, oblique-ovate, $\frac{1}{24}$ in. long, distinctly cuspidate. *Spikes* square, $\frac{1}{4}$ to $\frac{1}{2}$ in. long; bracts strongly keeled. Texas. Greenhouse. (Gn. 67 (1905), 210.)

S. Pitcheria'na. A form of *S. erythropus.*

S. platyphyl'la. A synonym of *S. grandis.*

S. plumo'sa. Stems pale, trailing, 6 to 12 in. long, often forked low down, pinnately branched, branches copiously compound, root-fibres extending to upper nodes. *l.* of lower plane contiguous on branches, spreading or rather ascending, bright green, oblong- or ovate-lanceolate, acute, $\frac{1}{12}$ to $\frac{1}{8}$ in. long, ciliate at base, cordate on upper side and much imbricate over stem; l. of upper plane one-third as long, ovate, cuspidate, much imbricate. *Spikes* copious, square, $\frac{1}{4}$ to $\frac{1}{2}$ in. long; bracts acute, strongly keeled. E. Himalaya. Stove. *S. flagellifera* is a garden form of this species. SYN. *S. flagelliformis.*

S. Poeppigia'na. Stems trailing, 1 to 2 ft. long, forked at base, jointed at nodes, copiously pinnate, with very compound, erecto-patent branchlets. *l.* of lower plane spaced, except towards tips of branchlets, much spaced on main stem, ascending, oblong-lanceolate, $\frac{1}{8}$ to $\frac{1}{6}$ in. long, broadly rounded on upper side at base; l. of upper plane one-third as long, oblique, with a distinct cusp. *Spikes* square, $\frac{1}{4}$ to $\frac{1}{2}$ in. long; bracts acute, sharply keeled. Andes. Greenhouse.

S. Poul'teri.* Stems densely tufted, very slender, sub-erect, 2 to 3 in. long, 3 or 4 times trichotomously forked, with slender radicles from lower half. *l.* of lower plane distinctly spaced, spreading, sub-orbicular, obtuse, $\frac{1}{24}$ in. long, bright green; l. of upper plane nearly as long, acute, ascending. *Spikes* slender, $\frac{1}{2}$ to 1 in. long; bracts scarcely longer than sporangia. Azores. 1868. Greenhouse.

S. radia'ta.* Stems slender, sub-erect, 6 to 12 in. long, acutely angled down face, closely pinnate, sometimes stoloniferous at base; branches copiously compound. *l.* of lower plane contiguous on branchlets, spaced on main stem, erecto-patent, ovate, acute, $\frac{1}{24}$ to $\frac{1}{12}$ in. long, much imbricate on upper side at base, strongly ciliate; l. of upper plane half as long, cuspidate. *Spikes* square, $\frac{1}{4}$ to 1 in. long. Trop. America (up to 9,000 ft.). Stove or greenhouse. SYN. *S. Warscewiczii.*

S. radica'ta. A synonym of *S. plumosa.*

S. rig'ida. A synonym of *S. affinis.*

S. robus'ta. A synonym of *S. canaliculata robusta.*

S. rubel'la. Stems 1 ft. long, sub-erect, with root-fibres from lower half, reddish-brown, pinnately branched, lower branches cuneate, with 5 to 7 branchlets. *l.* lower plane ascending, crowded on branchlets, oblique-oblong, obtuse or obscurely cuspidate, $\frac{1}{12}$ to $\frac{1}{8}$ in. long, dark green, turning reddish with age, more produced and ciliate on the upper side at base; l. of upper plane half as long, ovate, cuspidate, much imbricate. *Spikes* square, $\frac{1}{2}$ to 1 in. long, bracts long-cuspidate, strongly keeled. Mexico. 1870. Greenhouse. (R.H. 1907, 516.)

S. rubricau'lis. A synonym of *S. molliceps.*

S. Schot'tii. A synonym of *S. Galeottei.*

S. selaginoi'des. A synonym of *S. spinosa.*

S. ser'pens. Stems densely matted, trailing, 6 to 9 in. long, pinnate, branched, with numerous, erecto-patent, slightly compound branches. *l.* of lower plane crowded, spreading, $\frac{1}{16}$ in. long, ovate-oblong, bright green with a distinct midrib, both sides rounded and ciliate at base; l. of upper plane one-third as long, acute. *Spikes* square, $\frac{1}{4}$ to $\frac{1}{2}$ in. long; bracts cuspidate, crowded, strongly keeled. W. Indies. Greenhouse. (Gn. 17 (1880), 216.) SYN. *S. mutabilis, S. variabilis, S. varians.*

S. seto'sa. A synonym of *S. erythropus.*

S. sinen'sis. A synonym of *S. canaliculata.*

S. spino'sa. Barren stems short, trailing, slender, little-branched, with short, ascending branches. *l.* lax and spreading on lower part of barren branches, dense and ascending upwards, lanceolate, $\frac{1}{24}$ to $\frac{1}{12}$ in. long, acute, bright green, ciliate. Fertile stems erect, simple, 2 to 3 in. long, with a leafy peduncle about as long as spike. *Spike* multifarious; bracts lax, ascending, lanceolate or ovate-lanceolate, $\frac{1}{8}$ to $\frac{1}{6}$ in. long, strongly ciliate, not acutely keeled. Europe (Britain), N. America. Hardy. (H.B.F. 52.) SYN. *S. selaginoides.*

S. spinulo'sa. Stems very slender, trailing, 1 to 2 in. long, little-branched. *l.* of lower plane spaced even on branchlets, oblong, obtuse, $\frac{1}{24}$ in. long, pale green, strongly ciliate; l. of upper plane one-quarter to one-third as long, oblong, acute. *Spikes* short, square; bracts cuspidate, strongly keeled. Java. Stove.

S. stenophyl'la. Stems pale straw-colour, sub-erect, 6 to 12 in. long, rooting from lower half, pinnate; lower branches very compound. *l.* of lower plane ascending, oblong-lanceolate, $\frac{1}{12}$ to $\frac{1}{8}$ in. long, serrulate and imbricate on upper side; l. of upper plane one-third to half as long, cuspidate. *Spikes* resupinate, short. Mexico. Stove. (Gn. 17 (1880), 216.) *S. albospica* is a form of this.

S. stolonif'era. A variety of *S. Martensii.*

S. subero'sa. Stems densely tufted, sub-erect, often above 1 ft. long, pale, shining brown, pinnate, branching erecto-patent and decompound, root-fibres sometimes extending half-way up to it. *l.* of lower plane spaced and erecto-patent on branches, very distant and spreading on main stem, oblique-lanceolate or ovate-lanceolate, acute, bright green, unequal-sided, much produced, broadly rounded, shortly ciliate; l. of upper plane half as long, long-cuspidate. *Spikes* copious, $\frac{1}{4}$ to $\frac{3}{4}$ in. long, resupinate; bracts of upper plane lanceolate, erecto-patent, of lower plane ascending, ovate, cuspidate. Khasia Mts. Greenhouse. (R.H. 1907, 517.)

S. sulca'ta. Stems trailing in lower half, usually assurgent in upper half, deeply 2-sulcate down face, jointed at nodes, flabellate-pinnate, final branchlets contiguous. *l.* of lower plane close on branchlets, spaced on stem, oblong-lanceolate, acute, $\frac{1}{8}$ to $\frac{1}{6}$ in. long, auricled on both sides at base; l. of upper plane one-third as long, long-cuspidate. *Spikes* $\frac{1}{4}$ to $\frac{1}{2}$ in. long, square; bracts acute, strongly keeled. S. Brazil. Greenhouse.

S. tassella'ta.* Stems erect; branches and branchlets flat, closely pinnate, tips furnished with fertile, quadrangular spikes about $1\frac{1}{2}$ in. long, giving the plant a tasselled appearance. Brazil. 1887. Stove.

S. tex'ta. *See* **S. involvens texta.**

S. uncina'ta.* Stems weak, slender, pale straw-colour, 2-sulcate on face, trailing, 1 to 2 ft. long, with a long, excurrent tip, and alternate, short, pinnately arranged, very compound branches. *l.* of lower plane sub-ovate, $\frac{1}{12}$ to $\frac{1}{8}$ in. long, close or rather spaced on branches, thin, bright blue-green, minutely petiolate, both sides cordate at base; l. of upper plane one-third as long, cuspidate, much imbricate. *Spikes* $\frac{1}{4}$ to $\frac{1}{2}$ in. long, square; bracts $\frac{1}{12}$ in. long, crowded, sharply keeled. China. Stove. SYN. *S. caesia.*

S. us'ta. Stems 9 to 12 in. long, erect, simple at base, compound above; branches erecto-patent, upper ones copiously compound. *l.* of lower plane crowded, erecto-patent, bright green, rigid, dilated, serrulate, imbricate on upper side at base; l. of upper plane one-third as long, acute, much imbricate. *Spikes* square, $\frac{1}{4}$ to $\frac{1}{2}$ in. long. New Caledonia. Stove.

S. variab'ilis. A synonym of *S. serpens.*

S. var'ians. A synonym of *S. serpens.*

S. Victor'iae. Stems sub-erect, sarmentose, 3 to 4 ft. long; pinnae lanceolate-deltoid, 6 to 9 in. long, caudate; upper pinnules erecto-patent and simple, contiguous, lower forked or slightly pinnate. *l.* of lower plane crowded, oblong-lanceolate, falcate, acute, $\frac{1}{12}$ in. long, dark bright green, obscurely petiolate; l. of upper plane a quarter as long, much imbricate. *Spikes* square, 1 to 2 in. long; bracts acutely keeled. Borneo, &c. 1879. Stove. (G.C. 11 (1879), 75; B.C.F. 3, 430.)

S. viridan'gula.* Stems sub-erect, sarmentose, 3 to 4 ft. long; pinnae deltoid, 1 ft. long, erecto-patent; pinnules with simple upper and compound lower erecto-patent tertiary divisions; ultimate segs. usually $\frac{1}{2}$ to 1 in. long, bright green at base. *l.* of lower plane contiguous or nearly so on branchlets, lanceolate-falcate, acute, $\frac{1}{8}$ to $\frac{1}{6}$ in. long ($\frac{1}{4}$ in. long and much spaced on pinnae), bright green, dilated; l. of upper plane very small, distinctly cuspidate. *Spikes* square, 1 to 2 in. long; bracts strongly keeled. Mts. of Fiji. 1884. Stove. (Gn. 25 (1884), 459.)

S. viticulo'sa. Stems about 9 in. long, straw-colour, simple in lower part, deltoid and decompound upwards; pinnae deltoid, 2- or 3-pinnate, root-fibres sometimes extending to axils of lowest pinnae, the contiguous, ascending final segs. $\frac{1}{2}$ to 1 in. long. *l.* of lower plane contiguous, ascending, lanceolate or oblique-ovate, acute, $\frac{1}{12}$ to $\frac{1}{8}$ in. long, bright green; l. of upper plane one-third as long, oblique-ovate, cuspidate. *Spikes* square; bracts cuspidate, strongly keeled. Cent. America, Venezuela. Greenhouse. (R.H. 1907, 517.)

S. Vogel'ii. Stems 1 to 2 ft. long, erect, simple in lower half, often pink-tinted, with a few distant, small, appressed leaves, deltoid and decompound in upper half; lower pinnae deltoid, petiolate, 3- or 4-pinnate, the contiguous, erecto-patent final divisions $\frac{1}{4}$ to $\frac{3}{4}$ in. long. *l.* of lower plane spaced even on branchlets, lanceolate or oblong-lanceolate, ascending, acute, $\frac{1}{12}$ to $\frac{1}{6}$ in. long, bright green, both edges liable to be revolute, truncate at base; l. of upper plane minute, with a large cusp. *Spikes* square, $\frac{1}{4}$ to $\frac{1}{2}$ in. long; bracts cuspidate, strongly keeled. W. Africa. Stove. (R.H. 1907, 517.) SYN. *S. africana.* There is a variegated form. *S. dichroa* is a garden form.

S. Wallich'ii.* Stems sarmentose, sub-erect, 2 to 3 ft. long; pinnae lanceolate, 6 to 9 in. long; pinnules invariably simple, crowded, erecto-patent, 1 to $1\frac{1}{2}$ in. long, end one sometimes 3 to 4 in. long. *l.* of lower plane crowded, oblong-lanceolate, slightly falcate, pointed at upper corner, equal-sided, lower pinnules $\frac{1}{12}$ to $\frac{1}{8}$ in. long, upper gradually smaller, dark bright green, obscurely petiolulate, truncate, or slightly cordate on both sides at base; l. of upper plane a quarter as long, much imbricate. *Spikes* square, terminal on pinnules, $\frac{1}{2}$ to 1 in. long; bracts cuspidate, strongly keeled. India. Stove.

S. Warscewicz'ii. A synonym of *S. radiata.*

S. Willdenov'ii.* Stems climbing 12 to 20 ft. or more; pinnae spreading, deltoid, 1 to 2 ft. long, pinnules deltoid and decompound; ultimate branches short and contiguous. *l.* of lower plane crowded, ascending, ovate or oblong, $\frac{1}{12}$ to $\frac{1}{8}$ in. long, green with a tint of blue, obscurely petiolate, cordate on both sides at base; l. of upper plane one-third as long, not cuspidate. *Spikes* square, $\frac{1}{2}$ to 1 in. long; bracts scarcely larger than sporangia. Cochin China, &c. Greenhouse. (R.H. 1907, 518; Gn. 6 (1874), 407.) SYN. *S. caesia arborea.*

SELAGINELLA'CEAE. A family of but 1 genus, Selaginella, with the characters given under the genus.

selaginoi'des, Selago-like.

SELA'GO (an old Latin name used by Pliny for a plant which the Druids gathered with mysterious ceremonies). FAM. *Scrophulariaceae.* A genus of about 140 species of evergreen, usually dwarf shrubs or undershrubs; rarely annual herbs. Most of them are S. African but a few occur in Trop. Africa. Leaves clustered or scattered. Flowers stalkless or nearly so, in spikes, heads, or panicles; calyx 5-lobed; corolla tubular with an unequally 5-lobed limb; stamens 4, in 2 pairs of different length. They require greenhouse conditions but some, no doubt, would be hardy in our warmest counties. They are easily grown in a compost of loam, peat, and sand. Propagation is by cuttings of half-ripened wood, in mild bottom heat, and under a bell-glass. (*See also* **Walafrida.**)

KEY

1. *Shoots downy at least at first*	2
1. *Glabrous*	5
2. *Lvs. clustered or densely packed*	3
2. *Lvs. not clustered*	S. fruticosa
3. *Fl. white*	4
3. *Fl. pink to purple*	S. Galpinii
4. *Fl. in spikes*	S. Bolusii
4. *Fl. in corymbose clusters*	S. corymbosa
5. *Lvs. linear to linear-lanceolate*	S. spuria
5. *Lvs. obovate*	S. serrata

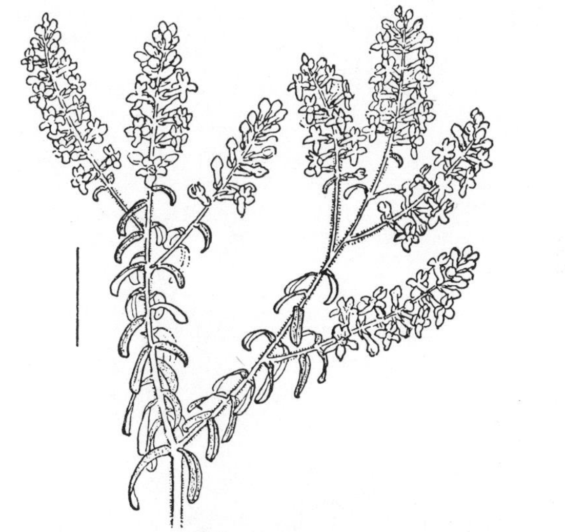

Selago Bolusii

S. Bolus'ii. Sub-shrub, 1 to $1\frac{1}{2}$ ft., much-branched, shoots minutely downy. *l.* clustered, linear, $\frac{1}{8}$ to $\frac{1}{4}$ in. long, nearly glabrous. *fl.* in spikes 1 to $1\frac{1}{4}$ in. long, terminating lateral twigs; cor. white, tube short, limb $\frac{1}{4}$ in. across, lobes of unequal length, obtuse. April. S. Africa. 1842. (B.R. 31, 46, as *S. distans.*)

S. corymbo'sa. Sub-shrub, 1 to 2 ft., shoots erect, downy. *l.* clustered, linear to filiform, $\frac{1}{16}$ to $\frac{1}{3}$ in. long. *fl.* white, small and very numerous, in corymbose clusters up to 4 in. across of terminal smaller clusters; tube of cor. oblong, lobes $\frac{1}{16}$ in. long. July, August. S. Africa. 1699.

S. dis'tans of Bot. Reg. A synonym of *S. Bolusii.*

S. fascicula'ta. A synonym of *S. serrata.*

S. frutico'sa. Sub-shrub, 1 to $1\frac{1}{2}$ ft., stems minutely downy, much-branched. *l.* $\frac{1}{12}$ to $\frac{1}{3}$ in. long, linear to oblong, not clustered, downy. *fl.* white or purple, in broad, oblong spikes $\frac{1}{2}$ to $1\frac{1}{4}$ in. long; tube of cor. slender, $\frac{1}{4}$ in. long, lobes $\frac{1}{12}$ in. long. S. Africa. 1774.

S. Galpin'ii.* Bushy shrub, 6 to 9 in., much-branched, shoots downy when young. *l.* densely set, linear, greyish, $\frac{1}{4}$ to $\frac{1}{2}$ in. long, becoming glabrous. *fl.* pink to purple, closely packed in terminal clusters 1 in. or more across; tube of cor. cylindrical, lobes roundish-blunt. Autumn. S. Africa. (G.C. 94 (1933), 413.) Half-hardy. A

S. Gil'lii. A synonym of *Walafrida myrtifolia.*

S. rapunculoi'des. A synonym of *S. spuria.*

S. rotundifo'lia. A synonym of *Walafrida rotundifolia.*

S. serra'ta. Glabrous sub-shrub, 1 to 2 ft. *l.* densely set, $\frac{1}{2}$ to 1 in. long, half as wide, obovate, stalkless, strongly toothed, stiff, dark green. *fl.* fragrant, in a compact rounded head $1\frac{1}{2}$ to 2 in. wide; cor. $\frac{1}{4}$ in. across, pale blue to purple; lobes oblong, rounded; tube funnel-shaped, whitish. July. S. Africa. 1774. (B.M. 9265; B.R. 184 as *S. fascicularis.*)

S. spu'ria. Sub-shrub up to 2 ft., branching at base. *l.* $\frac{1}{4}$ to $1\frac{1}{4}$ in. long, crowded at base, linear to linear-lanceolate, sharply toothed, usually glabrous. *fl.* in a dense cluster of corymbs up to 5 in. across, slightly fragrant; cor. purple, lilac, or white, tube very slender, lobes $\frac{1}{8}$ in. long. S. Africa. 1824. SYN. *S. rapunculoides.*

W. J. B.

selan'icus -a -um, from the Moluccan plant name, *Damar selan.*

seleben'sis -is -e, of Celebes.

SELE'NIA (from *Selene*, moon, in allusion to an affinity with Lunaria). FAM. *Cruciferae.* A genus of 3 species of small annual herbs, natives of Texas and Arkansas. Leaves pinnatisect. Flowers yellowish, in terminal, leafy racemes; sepals spreading, coloured, sub-equal; petals erect. *S. aurea* is worth growing for its sweet scent and long-lasting flowering. It needs treatment as a hardy annual and will grow in any ordinary soil.

S. au'rea. Hardy annual about 9 in. h. *l.* linear-oblong, 1 to 2 in. long, pinnatifid; segs. in 5 to 7 pairs. *fl.* erect, $\frac{1}{2}$ in. across, in a sub-corymbose raceme, lengthening after flowering; sep. greenish-yellow; pet. golden-yellow, twice as long as sep., obovate-spatulate. June. *Pods* flat. 1881. (B.M. 6607.)

SELENICE'REUS (*Selene*, the moon; the flowers being mostly nocturnal). FAM. *Cactaceae.* Slender, climbing plants, ribbed or angled, producing aerial roots; areoles small with small spines. Flowers nocturnal, very large, white; outer perianth leaves narrow, coloured; inner ones wider and widespread. Fruit large, covered with deciduous spines, juicy. These plants need fairly warm treatment; they grow a yard or more in one year and should be trained up a wall or over the roof.

S. Boeckman'nii. Stems slender, ribbed, spines yellowish. *fl.* up to 16 in. long, not scented. Mexico. (B.R.C. 2, t. 36.)

Selenicereus grandiflorus

S. coniflo'rus. Stems ribbed, margins wavy, spines short, yellow. *fl.* about 10 in. long. Mexico. (B.R.C. 2, t. 35.) SYN. *Cereus nycticalus armatus.*

S. grandiflo'rus. Queen of the Night. Stems ribbed, spines yellow, with white hairs. *fr.* yellow, streaked with red. *fl.* about 12 in. long, strongly scented. Jamaica. (B.M. 3381; B.R.C. 2, 32, 33.) SYN. *Cereus grandiflorus.*

S. hama'tus. Stems usually 4-angled with knobby, reflexed projections on the edges; spines few and weak. *fl.* 10 in. long, strongly scented. Mexico. (B.R.C. 2, 282–3.)

S. Kunthia'nus. Possibly a natural hybrid of *S. Macdonaldiae.*

S. Macdon'aldiae. Stems round when old, 5-angled when young, with prominent tubercles, spines small. *fl.* very large, not scented. Uruguay, Argentina. (B.M. 4707; B.R.C. 2, f. 279–81.) SYN. *Cereus Macdonaldiae, C. Donati.*

S. nyctica'lus. A synonym of *S. pteranthus.*

S. pteran'thus. Stems stout, bluish-green to purple, 4- to 6-angled, spines small, dark. *fl.* similar to *S. Macdonaldiae.* Mexico. (B.R.C. 2, t. 38.)

S. spinulo'sus. Stem producing many aerial roots, 5-ribbed; areoles on slight protuberances, spines very short, stiff, brown. *fl.* about 6 in. long. Mexico. (B.R.C. 2, t. 38.)

V. H.

SELENIPE'DIUM (Selenipe'dilum). Included in **Cypripedium.**

SELENOCYPRIPE'DIUM. FAM. *Orchidaceae.* A proposed name for hybrids between species of the groups Paphiopedilum and Phragmipedilum of Cypripedium.

selenop'teris, with a half-moon-shaped wing.

self or **self-coloured,** term used for a flower (or a plant) which is wholly of 1 colour.

self-fertile, producing seed with pollen from the same flower, from other flowers of the same plant, or from flowers of other plants of the same clone.

SELF-FERTILIZATION. In nature fertilization of the ovule by pollen of the same flower; or artificially, also by pollen of the same individual.

SELF-HEAL or All-heal. *See* **Prunella vulgaris.**

SELF-POLLINATION. Deposition of the pollen without extraneous aid (as of insects) upon the stigma of the flower which produced it, possibly by dropping upon the stigma from the anthers, or by some movement bringing the pollen in contact with the stigma.

self-sterile, in self-sterile plants the pollen is incapable of fertilizing the ovule of the same flower or of any flower on the same plant. This inability extends to all subdivisions of the plant, and is thus of great importance when plants belonging to a single clone are grown together, as, for example, in orchard practice. *See* **Pollination.** Self-sterility is quite common among plants; it may be absolute or only partial.

SELLIE'RA (in honour of Natale Sellier, French engraver who worked for Cavanilles). FAM. *Goodeniaceae.* A genus of 2 species of glabrous creeping perennial herbs rooting at the nodes, natives of Australia and New Zealand, one, *S. radicans*, also found in Chile. Leaves alternate, or clustered, entire. Flowers small, axillary; calyx 5-lobed; corolla 5-lobed, oblique, split down back; stamens 5; ovary 2-celled, sometimes incompletely. Fruit fleshy and indehiscent. *S. radicans* is hardy and needs a moist position on the rock-garden.

S. radi'cans. Form a spreading mat, stems sometimes several ft. long, creeping and rooting. *l.* obovate-spatulate, variable in size from very small to 4 in. long, obtuse, narrowed to a long stalk. *fl.* white, small, 1 or 2 on axillary peduncles $\frac{1}{8}$ in. long. *fr.* ovoid or obovoid, about $\frac{1}{2}$ in. long. (B.M. n.s. 395/A.)

Sellowia'nus -a -um, Sellow'ii, in honour of Friderich Sellow, 1789–1831, of Potsdam, who accompanied Prince Neuwied to Brazil as botanical collector.

Selskia'nus -a -um, in honour of Ilarion Sergiewitsch Selskey, 1808-61, officer of the Siberian branch of the Russian Geographical Society, Irkutsk.

SEMECARP'US (*semeion*, a mark, *karpos*, fruit; from the use to which the fruit-juice is put). FAM. *Anacardiaceae.* A genus of about 40 species of evergreen trees, natives of N. Australia and Trop. Asia, especially Ceylon. Leaves alternate, simple, leathery, stalked. Flowers small, calyx 5-cleft, segments overlapping, deciduous; petals 5, spreading, overlapping; stamens 5; panicles terminal or lateral, bracteate. Nuts or drupe kidney-shaped. For cultivation *see* **Anacardium.**

S. Anacard'ium. Kidney-bean of Malacca, Marking-nut Tree. Tree of about 50 ft. *l.* oblong, rather blunt, glaucous or with rough down on veins beneath. *fl.* greenish-yellow; panicle terminal, about as long as l., hairy. July, August. *Drupe* 1 in. long, smooth, black. Mts. of E. Indies. 1824. The black, acrid juice of the fruit is used by the natives for printing or marking cotton cloth.

F. G. P.

SEMEIAND'RA (*semeion*, a mark or signal, *andros*, a male; in allusion to the conspicuous shape of 1 of the stamens). FAM. *Oenotheraceae.* Two species of evergreen shrubs from the mountains of Mexico. The species here described—the only one introduced—requires greenhouse treatment and a loamy soil. The flowers are brightly coloured and of singular structure but the plant itself is of rather weedy growth. Akin to Fuchsia.

S. grandiflo'ra. Shrub up to 6 ft., shoots herbaceous. *l.* alternate or sub-opposite, lanceolate to ovate-lanceolate, pointed, shallowly toothed, 1 to 3½ in. long, ¼ to 1 in. wide, downy beneath. *fl.* wholly bright red, about 2 in. long, solitary in the l.-axils and often crowded at the end of short shoots; cal. petaloid, downy, ¾ in. long, the base swollen-tubular dividing into 4 linear segs., 3 of them reflexed, 1 erect; pet. 4, linear-awl-shaped; stamens 2, with very long filaments, 1 with a petal-like expansion, the other perfect; style and stigma protruded. March. Mexico. 1850. (B.M. 4727.)

W. J. B.

SEM'ELE (after the daughter of Kadmos, mother of Bacchus). FAM. *Liliaceae.* A single species in the Canary Is. related to Danae and Ruscus but climbing, with several (6 to 20) flowers in an umbel from the sides of the cladodes as a rule, and having the perianth segments joined. A greenhouse climbing shrub with a branched stem and evergreen cladodes, needing a rich soil and easily increased by division.

Semele androgyna

S. androgy'na. *Cladodes* alternate, ovate or ovate-lanceolate, slender-pointed, leathery, many-nerved. *fl.* small, greenish-white, lobes ovate, tube short, in umbels from edges, rarely face of cladode. April. Canary Is. 1713. (B.M. 1898, 3029 as *Ruscus androgynus.*)

Semeno'vii, in honour of Peter Petrowitsch von Semenow-Tian-Shansky, 1827–1914, Russian traveller in Cent. Asia.

semi-, in compound words, signifying half, as semi-hastate, hastate on one side only.

SEMIAQUILE'GIA (*semi*, half, *Aquilegia*; from its relationship to Aquilegia). FAM. *Ranunculaceae.* A genus of about 5 species of herbaceous perennials allied to Aquilegia, but with the petals gibbous at the base, not or only very slightly spurred, and to Isopyrum but with the inner stamens transformed into staminodes as in Aquilegia and carpels 3 to 10. *S. ecalcarata* is hardy and succeeds in an open sunny situation in ordinary soil in the border or the rock-garden.

S. ecalcara'ta.* About 15 in. h., stems hairy above, tinged purple. *Radical l.* 2-ternate, up to 12 in. long; lflets. 3-partite to base, glabrous or nearly so; segs. up to 1¼ in. long, deeply lobed, lobes blunt; stalks sheathing at base. *fl.* crimson, nodding, in a loose corymbose panicle; pedicels slender, about 3 in. long; pet. oblong-elliptic, about ½ in. long, glabrous, not spurred. June. W. China. 1915. (B.M. 9382.) SYN. *S. simulatrix, Aquilegia ecalcarata.*)

SEMIARUNDINA'RIA. Included in **Arundinaria.**

semiclau'sus -a -um, half-closed.

seminal, concerned with seed.

seminiferous, seed-bearing.

semita'lis -is -e, of a footpath.

semper-, a prefix signifying continuance, as *semperflorens*, ever-flowering.

sempervi'rens, evergreen.

SEMPERVIVEL'LA (from likeness to Sempervivum). FAM. *Crassulaceae.* A small genus (about 4 species) of Himalayan succulent plants distinguished from Sempervivum by the 6- to 8-parted gamopetalous corolla with a short acutely 6- to 8-angled tube. Cultivation as Sempervivum, the species nearly or quite hardy perennials.

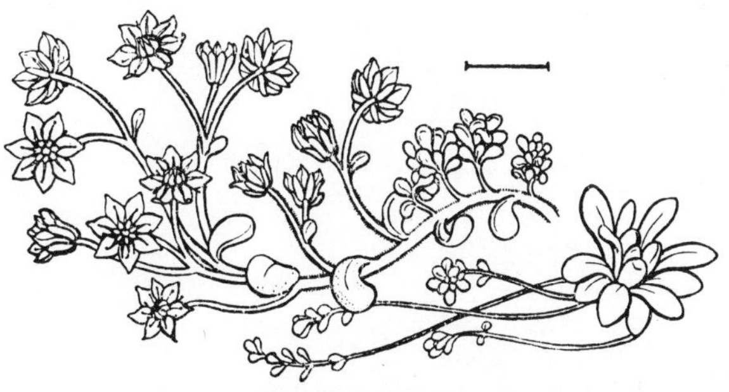

Sempervivella alba

S. al'ba. Rosettes 1 to 1¼ in. across, glandular. *l.* flat, obtuse, broadly oblong, ⅗ in. long, ⅛ to ¼ in. wide, green, partly tinged rose or red. fl.-stems axillary, procumbent, about 2 in. h., cymes few to 8-fld.; pedicels ⅕ to ⅓ in. long. *fl.* saucer-shaped, ½ in. across, white, bud red-tipped. Himalaya. 1910? (B.M. 8985.) SYN. *Sempervivum album.*

sempervivoi'des, Sempervivum-like.

SEMPERVIVUM (the Latin name used by Pliny, and derived from *semper vivo*, to live for ever). House Leek. FAM. *Crassulaceae.* A genus of about 25 species of hardy, thick, fleshy herbs, usually stemless, and producing young plants from the leaf-axils; they inhabit the mountains of Cent. and S. Europe (1 in Morocco). Flowers white, yellow, red, or purplish, in paniculate, often dense cymes; calyx green, fleshy, cup-shaped, 6- to 20-parted; petals free, as many as sepals; stamens twice as many, free; filaments filiform; scales small, more or less quadrate; ovaries as many as petals, immersed in base of receptacle. Leaves alternate in rosettes, crowded, entire, sessile, acute, ciliate, thickly fleshy, often revolute. *S. tectorum* is found growing on walls and houses in Britain, but it is not indigenous. Sempervivums succeed in any sandy soil, in a 'soil' consisting largely of brick-rubble broken fine or containing humus provided the drainage is adequate. The smaller species are best in rock crevices and in dry positions, needing very little soil provided it contains plenty of humus. The larger species need a richer soil. The rosettes die after flowering but the plants may be readily propagated from the young plants, which appear round old ones at the base, except in *S. Heuffelii* where the rootstock must be cut up. Most of the species hybridize readily and this seed cannot be depended upon to reproduce the species true to type, except in the Jovisbarbae section with 6- or 7-parted flowers, to which *S. Heuffelii* belongs.

Sempervivums are occasionally attacked by rust due to *Endophyllum sempervivi* which occurs on wild and cultivated Sempervivums. This rust fungus is perennial in the rootstock and forms only the teleutospores produced in small orange cup-like depressions on the leaves. Affected plants, besides showing the orange pustules, are more erect and not so rosette-like as healthy ones owing to the affected leaves being thinner and longer. Such plants must be destroyed and the remainder sprayed with Bordeaux mixture.

A full account of this group is given in *Sempervivums* by Dr. Lloyd Praeger (R.H.S. 1932) from which much of the information given below is taken. Many names which often appear under Sempervivum may be sought under Aeonium, Aichryson, Greenovia, or Monanthes. A very great number of names have been used for forms of Sempervivum and many still appear in various lists. They are often mere synonyms or names used without any description or attached to small variations of the numerous hybrids that occur both in nature and in the garden. Most of them—they are far too numerous for repetition here—are to be found with their proper allocation where it is possible to ascertain it in Dr. Praeger's book to which reference should be made.

KEY

1.	*Pet. 6 or 7, erect or sub-erect*	2
1.	*Pet. 9 to 20, spreading*	5
2.	*Slender-stemmed offsets absent*	S. Heuffelii
2.	*Slender-stemmed offsets many*	3
3.	*Lvs. finely hairy*	S. Allionii
3.	*Lvs. smooth*	4
4.	*Offsets high among leaves*	S. soboliferum
4.	*Rosettes open, 1 to 2 in. across*	S. hirtum
4.	*Rosettes of 60 to 80 leaves, 1/5 to 4/5 in. across*	S. arenarium
5.	*Fl. yellow or yellowish*	6
5.	*Fl. red or purple*	10
6.	*Lvs. smooth*	S. Wulfenii
6.	*Lvs. downy or hairy*	7
7.	*Offsets long, leafy, lvs. strongly scented*	S. grandiflorum
7.	*Not strongly scented*	8
8.	*Pet. without purple base*	9
8.	*Pet. with purple base*	S. Kindingeri, S. ruthenicum
9.	*Rosettes close, greyish, with long hairs in upper part*	S. ciliosum
9.	*Offsets on stems about 1 in. long*	S. Pittonii
9.	*Offsets on stems about 3 in. long*	S. leucanthum
10.	*L.-tips connected by cobwebby hairs*	S. arachnoideum
10.	*Lvs. not connected by cobwebby hairs*	11
11.	*All lvs. smooth*	12
11.	*Some or all lvs. downy*	13
12.	*Rosettes about 6 in. across, glaucous or glaucous purple*	S. × calcaratum
12.	*Rosettes 2 to 3 in. (or more), green often purple-tipped*	S. tectorum
13.	*Rosettes under 1 in. across*	S. pumilum
13.	*Rosettes usually over 2 in. across*	14
13.	*Rosettes usually between 1 and 2 in. across*	15
14.	*Young lvs. hairy; pet. with distinct white margin*	S. Schlehanii
14.	*Lvs. hairy, purple-tipped, offsets on long leafy stems*	S. Kosaninii
15.	*Greyish-green or usually greyish-purple, rosettes open*	S. erythraeum
15.	*Green, conspicuously ciliate, base white*	S. × Funckii
15.	*Dark dull green*	S. montanum
15.	*Pale green, offsets on very weak slender stems, older lvs. sometimes smooth*	S. atlanticum
15.	*Rather dull green, base white, tips not purple*	S. macedonicum
15.	*Fresh green, base red, tips red-purple*	S. dolomiticum

S. aizoi'des. *See* **Aichryson.**

S. Allion'ii. Similar in flower to *S. hirtum.* Rosettes about 1 in. across, almost globular, pale green, sometimes red- or brown-tipped, finely hairy. July. S. Alps, France to Tirol. (P.S. f. 32.) **A**

S. anom'alum. A synonym of *S. montanum.*

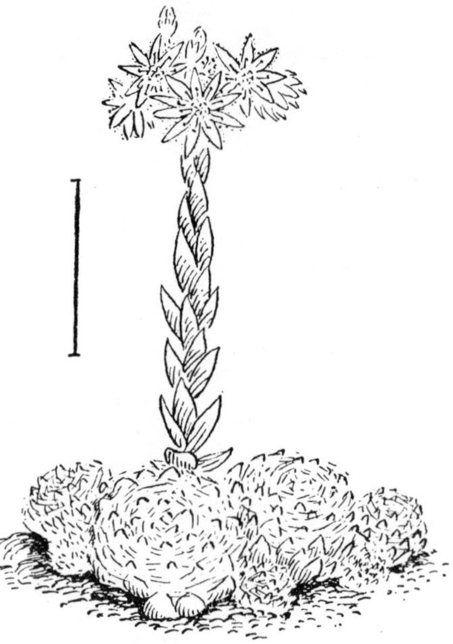

Sempervivum arachnoideum

S. arachnoi'deum.* Rosette about 2 in. across of densely arranged *l.*, half-open, reddish or green, tips of l. connected by cobweb-like hairs, from very small to an inch across. *fl.* 8- to 10-parted, 2/5 to 3/5 in. across, bright rose-red. July. Pyrenees to Carpathians. 1699. (B.M. 68; Gn. 6 (1874), 21; P.S. f. 3.) var. **glabres'cens,** rosettes ovoid, web rather lax. (B.M. 6610 as *S. Moggridgei.*); **tomento'sum,** rosettes flattish, web dense. A very variable species in the development of the 'cobweb' and one moreover that has given a great number of hybrids both in nature (with *S. grandiflorum, S. montanum, S. tectorum,* and *S. Wulfenii*) and in gardens with these and other species. These hybrids have more or less 'cobweb' or tufts of hair on the tips of the l. Most of them are fertile and may intercross between themselves or with their parents and give rise to an infinity of forms many of which have received names, a list of which will be found in the publication referred to above.

S. arbo'reum. *See* **Aeonium.**

S. arena'rium. Rosettes of 50 to 60 l., about 1/5 to 4/5 in. across, dense, light green. *l.* glabrous, often tipped brown. *fl.* 6-parted, 3/5 to 4/5 in. across; pet. erect, pale green, thrice as long as cal. August. Rosettes about half size of those of *S. soboliferum* and offsets very small and not perched among l. E. Alps. 1879. (Gn. 49 (1896), 220; P.S. f. 36.)

S. atlan'ticum. Rosettes 1 3/5 to 2 1/2 in. across, l. usually sub-erect. *l.* 4/5 to 1 1/2 in. long, 2/5 in. broad, green, rarely red-tipped, convex and finely hairy on both spaces. fl.-stem up to 1 ft. long, densely pilose; stem-l. red-purple. *fl.* 12-parted, 1 1/4 to 1 3/4 in. across, white with broad bright red-purple median band. June. Offsets large on short, slender stems. Morocco. 1871. (B.M. 6055 as *S. tectorum.*)

S. au'reum. *See* **Greenovia.**

S. × barbula'tum (*S. arachnoideum* × *S. montanum*).

S. Boris'ii. A synonym of *S. ciliosum.*

S. caespito'sum. *See* **Aeonium.**

S. × calcara'tum.* Rosettes up to 6 in. across. *l.* many, glaucous or rich glaucous purple, crimson at base, glabrous, nearly 3 in. long, 4/5 in. broad, flat on face, concave on back, ciliate. *fl.* 12- to 16-parted, 1 in. across, dull red-purple (pink with many fine lines); *infl.* 8 in. long, 6 in. broad. Stem 12 to 16 in. long with red l. July. Offsets large on stems over 2 in. long. Probably a hybrid with *S. tectorum* as one parent. (P.S. f. 19.) SYN. *S. Comolii.*

S. canarien'se. *See* **Aeonium.**

S. caucas'icum. Near *S. tectorum. Rosette-l.* ciliate with strong hairs, otherwise glabrous. *fl.* star-like, in a few-fld. corymb; pet. 14, linear-lanceolate, acuminate, shortly hairy, about twice as long as cal., rose-red with a median stripe. Caucasus. Little known.

S. × Christ'ii (*S. grandiflorum* × *S. montanum*).

S. cilio'sum. Rosettes 1 to 2 in. across, wholly or half-closed, grey-green, very hairy. *l.* many, imbricate, incurved, about 1 in. long, ⅛ in. broad, convex on both faces, light green, hairs translucent. *fl.* 10- to 12-parted, greenish-yellow, glandular-hairy. Stem about 4 in. long, with erect, overlapping leaves. *infl.* compact, about 1 in. across. July. Offsets on slender, at first leafy, stems. Bulgaria. (P.S. f. 28; E.R.G. 2, 40 as *S. ciliatum.*)

S. Comol'ii. A synonym of *S.* × *calcaratum.*

S. cruen'tum. *See* **Aeonium spathulatum.**

S. dolomit'icum. Rosettes about 1½ in. across, dense, flattish or half-open, whitish with hairs in centre. *l.* about ⅜ in. long, fresh green, generally red-tipped, red at base, glandular-hairy, tipped with white hairs. *fl.* 10- to 14-parted; pet. deep rose-red with darker median stripe and white flecks near margin. Stem about 4 in. h., shaggy white, l. purple-tipped. *infl.* about 1½ in. across, with 12 to 20 sessile fls. July. Offsets nearly globular, on slender stems under 1 in. long. E. limestone Alps. 1927. (P.S. f. 9.)

S. erythrae'um. Rosettes usually about 1½ to 2 in. across, flattish, wide open, generally soft greenish-purple, sometimes grey-green. *l.* 80 or more, about ½ in. long, ⅛ to ⅜ wide, purplish or rarely green, densely covered with minute white hairs. *fl.* 11- or 12-parted, ¾ in. across; cal. reddish, pet. red-purple. Stem 6 to 8 in. long, purple, shaggy especially in upper part. *infl.* very hairy. July. Offsets short-stemmed. Bulgaria. (P.S. f. 12.)

S. × **fimbria'tum.** Two hybrids have been so named. *S. arachnoideum* × *S. montanum*, a small plant with finely hairy leaves and a tuft of woolly white hairs at their apex, *fl.* intermediate. And *S. arachnoideum* × *S. Wulfenii*, resembling a small *S. Wulfenii* with light green glabrous l. and a tuft of woolly hair at their apex; *fl.* yellow with red lines.

S. flagellifor'me. A small form of *S. montanum* with long-stemmed offsets.

S. × **Funck'ii.** Rosettes crowded, compact, flattish, open, 1 to 1⅜ in. across, bright green, old l. tipped purple. *l.* ⅝ to ⅞ in. long, white at base, finely hairy, convex on both sides, hairs not tufted at apex. *fl.* 11- to 12-parted, nearly 1 in. across, purple-rose. Stem about 8 in. long, glandular-hairy, with erect, oblong-ovate leaves. *infl.* compact, flattish, branches 6- or 7-fld. July. Offsets numerous on stems about 1½ in. long. Probably a triple hybrid ((*S. arachnoideum* × *S. montanum*) × *S. tectorum*). (P.S. f. 8; E.R.G. 2, 42; B.H. 1873, 13.)

S. glau'cum. *See* **S. tectorum.**

S. glutino'sum. *See* **Aeonium.**

S. grandiflo'rum. Rosettes 2 to 4 in. (sometimes up to 9 in.) across, similar to *S. tectorum*, but with dull-green, clammy-hairy *l.*, long leafy offsets (3 to 9 in.) and a strong smell. *fl.* whitish to greenish-yellow with a purple stain at base. Stem 6 to 12 in. long, leafy. *infl.* about 4 in. across. June. Switzerland. (P.S. f. 21; B.M. 507, 2115 as *S. globiferum.*) This species hybridizes readily with *S. montanum* (with purplish fl.), *S. tectorum*, and *S. arachnoideum.*

S. Heuffel'ii. Rosettes 1 to 6 in. across, sometimes more, flattish, open. *l.* about 30 to 40, size variable, flat on face, convex at back, green or glaucous, sometimes brown-tipped, finely hairy. *fl.* 6- to 7-parted, narrow, ½ to ⅝ in. across; pet. erect, pale yellow or yellowish-white. Stem 4 to 8 in. long, with broad-based, clasping, lanceolate, purple-tipped l. *infl.* dense, flattish, about 2 in. across. August, &c. Rosettes divide into 2 or more rosettes of about equal size, rootstock very thick. S.E. Europe. (G.F. 858; P.S. f. 31.) SYN. *S. patens.* This species varies considerably in size and colour of l.

S. hirt'um. Rosettes 1 to 2 in. across, open and stellate except in drought. *l.* ⅜ to ⅝ in. long, about ⅛ in. wide, glabrous, ciliate, flattish on face, convex on back, green, or brown-tipped, or red-brown on back. *fl.* 6-parted, pale yellow to yellowish-brown; pet. erect, about ⅝ in. long. Stem 4 to 6 in. long, stout, hairy, with many l. *infl.* 2 to 3 in. across, 3-branched, each 5-fld. August. Offsets small, about ¼ in. across, globular, on short, very thin stems, arising from axils of upper as well as outer l. E. Alps, Hungary, Dalmatia. 1804. (P.S. f. 33, 34.)

S. holochry'sum. *See* **Aeonium.**

S. × **Hook'eri.** A very small neat form of the hybrid *S. arachnoideum* × *S. montanum.* *See* **S.** × **fimbriatum.**

S. Kinding'eri. Rosettes and fls. as in *S. ruthenicum.* *l.* with long hairs on face and back in upper part. Offsets on short stems. Macedonia. Of weak constitution. (P.S. f. 25.)

S. Kosanin'ii. Rosettes 2 to 3 in. across, open, flat, dense. *l.* very fleshy, about 1¼ in. long, ½ in. wide, dark green, purple at tip, white at base, glandular-hairy on both surfaces. *fl.* dull reddish-purple, 13- to 14-parted. Stem 6 to 8 in. long, with crowded, fleshy l., red in upper part. *infl.* 3 to 4 in. across, dense. July. Offsets on strong leafy stems up to 5 in. long. Macedonia. 1925.

S. Lag'geri. A synonym of *S. arachnoideum tomentosum.*

S. Lamot'tei. A synonym of *S. tectorum.*

S. leucan'thum. Rosettes 1⅜ to 3 in. across, flattish. *l.* about 70, curved, widest near cuspidate, purple tip, about 1⅜ in. long, ⅜ in. broad, glandular-hairy on both convex faces. *fl.* 11- to 13-parted, 1 in. across; pet. pale or greenish-yellow, spreading; filaments white, yellow, or purple. Stem 4 to 8 in. long, clothed with purple-tipped cuspidate l. *infl.* compact, 2 to 3 in. across, branches viscid. July. Offsets on stout 3-in. stems. Bulgaria. (P.S. f. 27.)

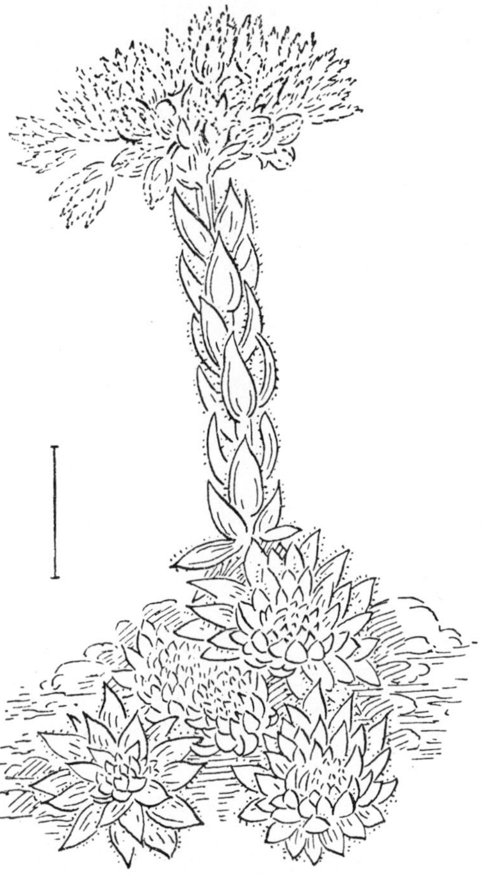

Sempervivum hirtum

S. macedon'icum. Characters of *S. erythraeum* but forming a loose mat owing to long, leafy stems of offsets (up to 2⅜ in. long), and rosettes (light green, only older l.-tips flushed red), fl.-stem, and *fl.* all smaller and pet. narrower. June. Macedonia. (P.S. f. 10.)

S. Moggridg'ei. A synonym of *S. arachnoideum glabrescens.*

S. Monan'thes. A synonym of *Monanthes polyphylla.*

S. monta'num. A small clustered plant with rather dense, open rosettes from ⅝ to 1⅝ in. across. *l.* dark green, dull, about ⅝ in. long, ⅛ in. wide, very fleshy, finely hairy. *fl.* short-stalked, 10- to 15-parted, 1⅛ to 1⅝ in. across, violet-purple; pet. narrow, white pubescent beneath. Stem 2 in. or more long, with ovate, acute l. *infl.* 3- to 10-fld. June to August. Offsets many on slender, leafy pubescent stems ⅝ to 1½ in. long. Pyrenees, Corsica, Alps, Carpathians. 1752. (P.S. f. 6.) A rather variable species of which the plant grown as *S. flagelliforme* is a small form with long-stemmed offsets; *S. montanum stiriacum* has rosettes up to 2 in. across, *l.* with marked brown-red tip, and *fl.* up to 2 in. across. E. Alps. (P.S. f. 6, A.) var. **Braun'ii** has white or yellowish-white *fl.* Carinthia; **Burna'tii** is much larger, up to 4 in. across, with strong long-stemmed offsets and tall fl.-stems. The finely hairy green *l.* and absence of strong odour distinguish this variety from *S. grandiflorum.* SW. Alps, Pyrenees. *S. montanum* also hybridizes with *S arachnoideum, S. grandiflorum, S. tectorum,* and *S. Wulfenii.*

S. Paiv'ae. *See* **Aeonium Castello-Paivae.**

S. Pitton'ii. Rosettes dense, flattish, 1 to 2 in. across. *l.* crowded, incurved, up to 1 in. long, ¼ in. wide, glandular-hairy on face, greyish-green, tip dark purple. *fl.* 9- to 12-parted, about 1 in. across, pale greenish-yellow. Stem 2 in. or more long, covered by erect, purple-tipped l. *infl.* flattish, 2 to 3 in. across, branches 3- to 9-fld. July. Offsets on slender naked stems about 1 in. long. Styria. (P.S. f. 27.)

S. × **Pomel'lii.** A hybrid of the same parentage as *S.* × *Thompsonii.*

S. pulchel'lum. *See* **Aeonium spathulatum cruentum.**

S. pu'milum. Rosettes small, about ½ to ¾ in. across, open. *l.* green, about ⅜ in. across, ⅛ in. wide, flattish on face, convex on back. glandular-hairy. *fl.* 10- to 12-parted, ½ in. across; pet. about ⅜ in. long, rosy-purple with pale margin. Stem 1½ to 4 in. long, leafy. *infl.* 4- to 8-fld. about 1 in. across. July. Offsets on slender stems about ⅜ in. long. Caucasus. 1926. (P.S. f. 13.)

S. ruthen'icum. Rosettes 1¾ to 3 in. across, open in summer, contracted in winter. *l.* about 1⅛ in. long, ⅜ in. wide, finely hairy, green, rarely tipped purple, older tinged rose in upper part. *fl.* 11- or 12-parted, up to 1 in. across, pale green or light yellow, purple at base. Stem 4 to 6 in. long, with oblong, hairy, purple-tipped l. *infl.* up to 3 in. across, densely hairy. July. Offsets flattish-globular, on hairy stems 1½ to 2 in. long. SE. Europe, Asia Minor. (P.S. f. 23.)

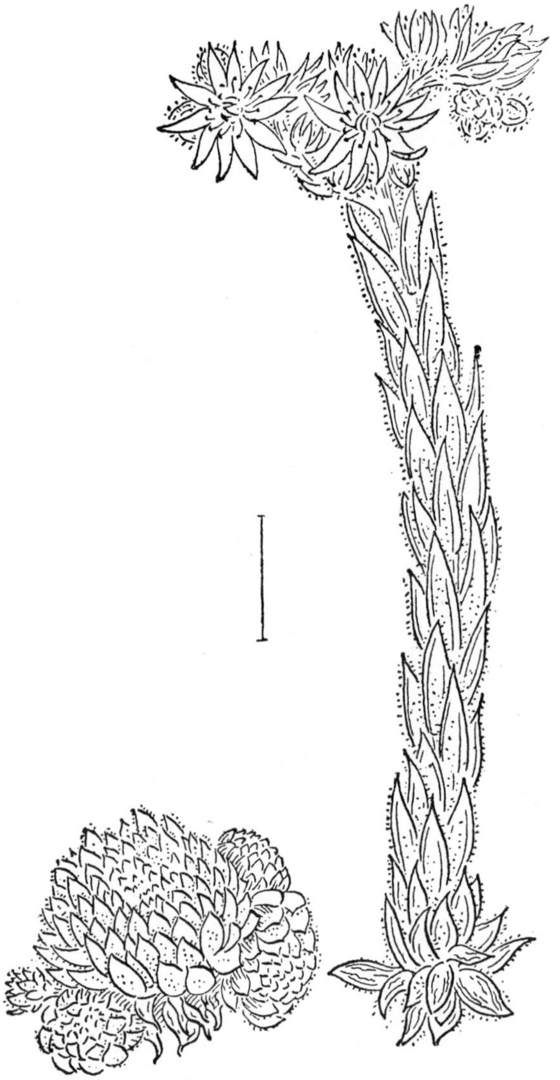

Sempervivum Pittonii (p. 1937)

S. Schlehan'ii.* Rosettes similar to *S. tectorum* but smaller and neater, l.-tips seldom purple, flushed red over centre and lower part of face, young l. hairy. *fl.* 12- to 13-parted, about 1 in. across; pet. with white margin, about ⅜ in. long. Stem 4 to 6 in. long, l. usually finely hairy. *infl.* compact, flattish, about 2 in. across. August. Offsets at first globular, on hairy stems about ¾ in. long. Hungary to Greece. (P.S. f. 14.) In the form **brunneifo'lium** *l.* are uniform brown, red in winter, glabrous when mature. SYN. *S. ornatum*, *S. rubicundum.* **A**

S. × Schot'tii. A hybrid between *S. montanum* and *S. tectorum*, resembling a small *S. tectorum* with denser rosettes and *l.* more or less glandular-hairy with a purple tip. *fl.* purple; pet. more tapering than in *S. tectorum*, and *infl.* smaller. (P.S. f. 7.)

S. Smith'ii. *See* **Aeonium.**

S. sobolif'erum. Hen and Chickens Houseleek. Rosettes crowded, flattened-globose, half-closed, about ⅘ in. across. *l.* incurved, about ⅗ in. long, ⅕ in. wide, fleshy, flattish above, very convex on back, light green, usually with red tipped at back, glabrous. *fl.* 6-parted, greenish-yellow; pet. erect, about ⅜ in. long. Stem 4 to 8 in. long, with many sub-erect, red-tipped leaves. *infl.* flattish, 2 to 3 in. across. July. Offsets many, globose, often among middle leaves, on short, very short-lived stems. N. Europe and Asia. (B.M. 1457; P.S. f. 35.) Distinguished from *S. Allionii* by its glabrous, not finely-hairy, very pale l.; from *S. arenarium* by its larger rosettes and l. and easily detachable offsets; and from *S. hirtum* by its half-closed rosettes and l. broadest two-thirds up, not one-third up.

S. tabulaeform'e. *See* **Aeonium.**

S. tecto'rum. Houseleek, St. Patrick's Cabbage. Rosettes 2 or 3 in. across (sometimes up to 8 in.), open, flattish. *l.* green, usually with large purple tip, up to 2 in. long, ⅕ to ⅜ in. wide, very fleshy, flat on face, rounded at back, red or white at base. *fl.* 12- to 16-parted, dark or light purplish-red, about 1 in. across. Stem 8 to 12 in. long, shaggy with white hairs, clothed with hairy lanceolate l. July. Offsets strong, on stout stems 1½ in. long, hairy at first. Pyrenees, Alps, Apennines, naturalized in Britain. (E.B. 1320; P.S. f. 16.) An extremely variable species that has hybridized with many others both in nature and in the garden, giving rise to forms which have received more names than all other Sempervivums put together. The following are marked varieties: var. **alpi'num,** rather small with rosettes 1 to 2½ in. across, *l.* reddish at base, fl.-stem 4 to 12 in. long, *infl.* compact, flattish. N. and Cent. Alps; **calcar'eum,** rosettes up to 2½ in. across, *l.* very glaucous with brown-purple tips, *fl.* rather smaller than type. French Alps; **glau'cum,** rosettes 2 to 3 in. across, *l.* glaucous or nearly so, whitish at base, fl.-stem 18 to 30 in. long, often branched. S. and E. Alps. (P.S. f. 17.) SYN. *S. calcareum*, *S. californicum.* *See also* **S. calcaratum.**

S. × Thomp'sonii. A hybrid between *S. arachnoideum* and *S. tectorum* with smaller rosettes than the latter, *l.* more or less hairy, with a tuft of straggling white hairs at tip; *infl.* about as large as in *S. arachnoideum* but *fl.* less bright. (P.S. f. 5.)

S. tris'te. A synonym of *S. tectorum.*

S. villo'sum. A synonym of *Aeonium spathulatum.*

S. Wulfen'ii. Rosettes about 3½ in. across, much like *S. tectorum* but *l.* fewer, younger, usually in a conical bud, glaucous or greyish-green without purple tips, base rosy-purple. *fl.* 12- to 15-parted, stellate, yellow or greenish-yellow, purple at base. Stem about 8 in. long, clothed with rather spreading hairy l. about ⅜ in. long. *infl.* compact, flattish. July. Offsets few, on very stout, at first leafy, stems about 4 in. long. Austrian and Swiss Alps. (P.S. f. 30.)

S. × villo'sum. A hybrid of the same parentage as *S. × Thompsonii.*

S. Youngia'num. A synonym of *Aeonium undulatum.*

SENECA, SENEGA, or **SENEKA SNAKE-ROOT.** *See* **Polygala Senega.**

Senecil'lis. A synonym of Ligularia.

SENEC'IO (old Latin name used by Pliny, from *senex*, an old man; referring to the usually white or grey hair-like pappus). FAM. *Compositae.* Probably the largest genus in the vegetable kingdom, containing about 1,300 species of plants of various habit and duration, but rarely attaining the size of trees. Some of them are gigantic herbs like those of the African mountains. The genus is cosmopolitan but most species are found in temperate or mountainous regions. S. Africa is richest in species in the Old World, the Andean region in the New. Leaves alternate or radical, entire, toothed, lobed, or variously, often pinnately, cut. Flower-heads radiate-heterogamous or discoid-homogamous, solitary or in corymbs, very rarely in pyramidal panicles, subracemose, or sessile on the sides of branches; involucral bracts in 1 series with sometimes a few smaller ones at base, at length often reflexed; receptacle flat or slightly convex; ray-florets, when present, various-coloured, in a single series, ligulate; disk yellow, whitish, or rarely purplish or violet. Achenes glabrous or slightly hairy, of variable form and size. Most Senecios are easy to grow; they succeed in almost any loamy soil. The annuals are readily increased by seed which is often produced in abundance, the perennials may be increased by division or by cuttings of shoots or roots. Some species are natives or have become naturalized, among them the annual Groundsel (*S. vulgaris*) and the ragworts which are apt to spread very rapidly if allowed to seed.

Rust caused by the heteroecious fungus *Coleosporium senecionis* occurs on many wild and cultivated species, including *S. vulgaris*, *S. Jacobaea*, *S. silvaticus*, *S. pulcher*, and cultivated Cinerarias. *S. pulcher* is apt to be very severely damaged by it and it is important on the Cineraria, appearing as orange pustules of uredospores and red, crust-like groups of teleutospores on the undersurface of the leaves. The alternate host is the Scots Fir, on the needles of which the aecidia appear as small yellowish blisters. This stage is not harmful to large pines, but where young trees are attacked in the nursery spraying with Bordeaux mixture may be necessary. Where

Cinerarias are attacked young plants can be protected by spraying with Bordeaux mixture, taking care to wet both surfaces of the leaves.

Many attempts have been made to divide this huge genus into smaller ones, but the characters which have been relied upon to effect this are usually very small and not readily observed and, what is more important, are such as defy the drawing of any rigid line between groups, and, for the most part, these divisions have been ignored here, but *see* **Cacalia, Cineraria, Kleinia,** and **Ligularia.** A

S. abrotanifo'lius.* Sub-shrub, 1 to 2 ft., woody at the base; shoots glabrous or slightly downy. *l.* at the base laciniately 2-pinnate, 1 to 3 in. long, ultimate segs. 1/16 to ⅛ in. wide, dark glossy green; upper l. simply pinnate. *fl.-heads* ¾ in. wide, 2 or more in a terminal head; ray-florets orange-yellow, linear-oblong. July to September. Cent. Europe. 1800. Rock-garden; peaty, well-drained soil, with stones.

S. adonidifo'lius. Glabrous perennial, 8 to 18 in. h. Stems erect, simple, terete. *l.* much cut, pinnatisect, stalked; lobes linear, acute, deep green. *fl.-heads* orange, in a compound corymb. S. France, Spain. SYN. *S. artemisiifolius.* Habit of *S. abrotanifolius* but less bright. Rock-garden.

S. alpi'nus. Perennial herb up to 3 ft. h. *l.* heart-shaped-ovate, pinnatifid, unequally toothed, thinly cobwebby beneath, stalked; upper lanceolate, auriculate at base. *fl.* yellow, rays spreading. July, August. European Alps.

S. ampulla'ceus. Half-hardy annual. Stems 1 to 2 ft. erect, glabrous. *l.* 3 to 5 in. long, thick and fleshy, oblong, sparsely toothed or entire, basal ones spatulate, stalkless, partially clasping the stem. *fl.-heads* 1 to 1½ in. across, yellow, borne on loose, long-stalked clusters 2 to 3 in. across; ray-florets 6 to 9, notched at end. July. Texas. 1834. (B.M. 3487.)

S. Anteuphorb'ium. A synonym of *Kleinia Anteuphorbium.*

S. artemisiifolius. A synonym of *S. adonidifolius.*

S. auranti'acus. A synonym of *S. campestris* and *S. palustris aurantiacus.*

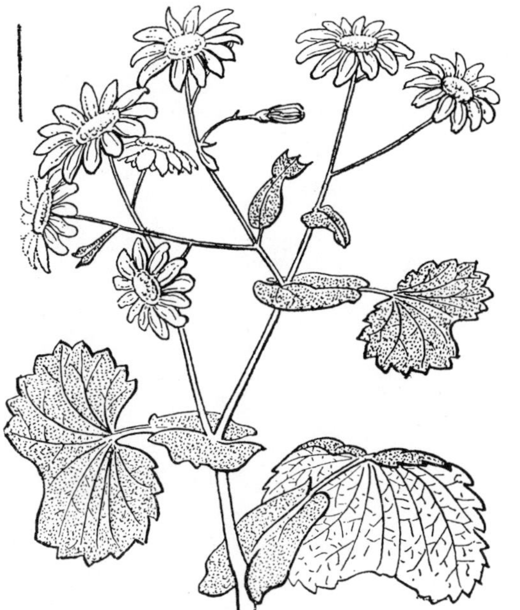

Senecio auriculatissimus

S. auriculatis'simus.* Climbing, evergreen, quite glabrous shrub. *l.* 2 to 2½ in. wide, less in length, transversely oblong or roundish kidney-shaped, coarsely and bluntly toothed; stalk 1 to 2 in. long, dilated at the base into an auricle ¾ in. wide. *fl.-heads* 1 in. wide, golden-yellow in loose clusters 5 or 6 in. across; ray-florets 12 to 15. Spring. Cent. Africa. 1896. (B.M. 7731.) Greenhouse.

S. Buchanan'ii. *See* **S. elaeagnifolius.**

S. campes'tris. Shaggy perennial. Stems 6 to 8 in. h., simple. *Radical l.* nearly entire, narrowed to base, woolly beneath; *stem-l.* small, lanceolate. *fl.-heads* yellow, erect, 1 to 6 in a simple corymb; involucre woolly in lower, nearly glabrous in upper half. June, July. Achenes hispid. Europe. (E.B. 760.) var. **marit'ima,** *fl.-heads* larger, lower *l.* toothed. SYN. *S. aurantiacus.* Hardy.

S. carniol'icus. A variety of *S. incanus.*

S. chordifo'lius. Glabrous, fleshy sub-shrub about 1 ft. h. Stem slightly branched. *l.* cylindric, 7 to 10 in. long, flattened above towards base, acute. *fl.-heads* yellow, few, narrow, about ⅜ in. long in very slender cymes, 6 to 10 in. long, branches erect; involucral bracts about 16 with a few bristle-shaped bracteoles at base. July. Pappus white. S. Africa. 1862. (B.M. 6216.) Greenhouse.

S. Cinera'ria.* Sea Ragwort. Sub-shrub with a woody base, the whole plant densely white-woolly, 1 to 2 ft. h. *l.* deeply pinnately lobed, thick, 2 to 6 in. long, 1½ to 4 in. wide, segs. ⅛ to ¼ in. wide broadening and with 3 or more blunt lobes at the apex. *fl.-heads* terminal in compound corymbs several in. across; ray-florets about 6, yellow. Summer, autumn. S. Europe. Naturalized in SW. England, Wales, and Ireland. (F.P.R. 29.)

S. clivo'rum. *See* **Ligularia clivorum.**

S. compac'tus. Evergreen compact shrub, 2 to 4 ft., more in width, shoots, under-surface of l. and fl.-stalks white-felted. *l.* ¾ to 2 in. long, ¼ to 1 in. wide, narrow-oblong, cuneate, apex rounded, margins wavy, dull green above; stalk ¼ to ½ in. long. *fl.-heads* ¾ to 1 in. wide, 3 to 10 of them in a terminal raceme; ray-florets about 12, bright yellow. July, August. New Zealand. Near *S. Monroi.* Hardy only with protection in hard weather.

S. con'color. Perennial, fleshy sub-shrub, 1 to 2 ft., stems angled, downy. *Basal l.* 4 to 10 in. long, oblanceolate, obtuse, entire or wavy-toothed, glabrous; *upper l.* smaller, linear, irregularly toothed. *fl.-heads* 1 to 1¼ in. across, on a tall, loose corymb 6 in. across; ray-florets 10 to 12, purple; disk white with purple anthers. July. S. Africa. 1880. (B.M. 6713.) Tender.

S. cremeiflo'rus.* Stout herbaceous perennial. *l.* 12 to 18 in. long, one-third as wide, oblong-ovate, more or less cordate, margin wavy and bluntly toothed, glaucous or purplish beneath; stalk as long as the blade, hollow. *fl.-heads* 1 in. across in axillary and terminal clusters, each 1½ to 2 in. wide, forming a large panicle 1 to 2 ft. h.; ray-florets 12 to 16, pale yellow, broadly oval, apex toothed. June. Chile, Argentine. 1890. Hardy. (B.M. 7422 as *S. Hualtata.*)

S. cruen'tus. Semi-herbaceous perennial, 2 to 3 ft., stems woolly. *l.* 4 to 8 in. wide, ovate to triangular-cordate, pointed, round-toothed. *fl.-heads* ¾ to 1¼ in. across, borne in loose terminal and axillary corymbs, making altogether a large flattish infl.; ray-florets 12 to 15, linear, purplish-red, disk darker. Spring to summer. Canaries. 1777. (B.M. 406 as *Cineraria cruenta.*) Greenhouse. Parent of garden Cinerarias.

S. Do'ria. Herbaceous perennial, 4 ft. *l.* glabrous, sub-glaucous, 3 to 5 in. long, oval-oblong to lanceolate, toothed. *fl.-heads* ¾ to 1 in. across, compactly clustered at the top of an erect stem; ray-florets 6 to 8 yellow; disk ½ in. wide. July to September. S. and Cent. Europe. 1570.

S. Doron'icum.* Herbaceous perennial. 6 in. to 2 ft., all the parts usually more or less cottony, sometimes nearly glabrous. *l.* stout, variable in shape from ovate and oblong to lanceolate and oblanceolate; 2 to 5 in. long. *fl.-heads* 2 in. wide, orange-yellow, mostly solitary but also from 2 to 4; ray-florets 10 to 20. Summer. S. and Cent. Europe. 1705. var. **hosmarien'sis,*** dwarf form 3 to 6 in. h., *l.* ovate-cordate, 1½ to 3 in. long, *fl.-heads* 1½ in. across. Morocco. 1871. (B.M. 6101.) Rock-garden.

S. Douglas'ii. Tufted perennial, white-floccose to glabrous. Stems 1 to 3 ft., woody below, leafy. *l.* linear, or more or less cut deeply into narrow divisions. *fl.-heads* in terminal corymbose cymes, rather small; ray-florets usually 13, yellow; involucre bell-shaped. July. Achenes downy. W. United States. 1833.

S. elaeagnifo'lius. Evergreen shrub, 5 to 15 ft., shoots, under-surface and stalk of l. and infl. pale buff-felted. *l.* 2 to 5 in. long, 1 to 3½ in. wide, oval to obovate, stout, leathery, smooth and glossy green above; stalk ½ to 1¾ in. long. *fl.-heads* ⅓ to ½ in. wide, 9 to 12 in terminal panicles 3 to 6 in. h.; ray-florets absent; of little beauty. New Zealand. Hardy only in mild districts. var. **Buchan'anii,** smaller shrub, *l.* only 1 to 2½ in. long, *infl.* a raceme.

S. el'egans. Annual or biennial, viscous-downy plant. Stems 1 to 2 ft., erect or diffuse. *l.* 1 to 3 in. long, very varied in shape and toothing, from entire to deeply pinnately lobed, stem-clasping at the base. *fl.-heads* 1 in. across in lax corymbs; ray-florets purple, disk yellow. S. Africa. 1700. (B.M. 238.) SYN. *Jacobaea erecta.* Half-hardy. var. **al'bus,** ray-florets white; **erect'us,** stems erect, slender; *l.* pinnately lobed, *fl.-heads* sometimes entirely of ray-florets. A double form is commonly grown.

S. Fa'beri. Stout herbaceous perennial, almost smooth, with several hollow, angled stems 4 to 5 ft. h. *l.* pinnatifid, coarsely toothed, l.-base partially clasping the stem; lowermost up to 2 ft. long. *fl.-heads* with 3 to 5 deep-yellow rays and 8 to 12 yellow disk-florets, in a corymbose head about 8 in. across. W. China. Hardy.

S. Fors'teri. A synonym of *Brachyglottis repanda.*

S. ful'gens. A synonym of *Kleinia fulgens.*

S. Galpin'ii. A synonym of *Kleinia Galpinii.*

S. glastifo'lius. Glabrous, erect, branching shrub, 4 ft. and upwards. *l.* oblong to oblong-lanceolate, 1 to 3 in. long, ½ to 1 in. wide, coarsely and unevenly toothed. *fl.-heads* 2 in. across, borne in loosely corymbose panicles built up of numerous 3- to 5-headed clusters; ray-florets 12 to 14, linear, purple; disk ½ in. wide, yellow. June. S. Africa. 1866. (B.M. 8624; B.R. 1342 as *S. lilacinus.*) Greenhouse.

S. grandiflo'rus. Herbaceous perennial. Stems 3 to 5 ft., erect, closely leafy at the base, sparsely so upwards. *l.* stalkless, partially clasping the stem, up to 6 in. long, pinnately lobed, the lobes linear, 1 to 3 in. long, $\frac{1}{16}$ to $\frac{1}{8}$ in. wide. *fl.-heads* 1 to $1\frac{1}{2}$ in. across in a tall, terminal, loose corymb 6 to 10 in. wide; ray-florets 12 to 15, purple; disk yellow. August. S. Africa. 1774. (B.R. 901 as *S. venustus.*) Greenhouse.

S. grandifo'lius.* Semi-woody shrub, 5 to 15 ft., often with a single or a few erect, stout, purplish stems. *l.* ovate to ovate-oblong, 6 to 18 in. long, half or more than half as wide, distantly shallowly to coarsely toothed, dark green above, sparsely downy beneath. *fl.-heads* in a terminal cluster of corymbs 12 to 18 in. across. Mexico. Magnificent winter-flowering shrub for planting in a cool greenhouse or growing in a large pot. SYN. *S. Ghiesbreghtii.*

S. Grey'ii.* Evergreen shrub up to 8 ft., usually much less, shoots, under-surface and stalks of l. white-felted. *l.* $1\frac{1}{2}$ to 4 in. long, 1 to $2\frac{1}{4}$ in. wide, dark green, oblong or oblong-obovate, blunt-ended, entire; stalk $\frac{1}{2}$ to $1\frac{1}{2}$ in. long. *fl.-heads* 1 in. across in terminal panicles 4 to 6 in. long, scarcely as wide; ray-florets 12 to 15, rich clear yellow; fl.-stalks glandular-downy. Summer. New Zealand. Rather tender. Rare in gardens, *S. laxifolius* being often grown under the name but differing in its more pointed l. and non-glandular infl.; it is also hardier.

S. Haas'tii. Low spreading plant with a stout, woody rootstock, keeping near the ground, white-felted all over. *l.* radical, 2 to 5 in. long, sometimes nearly as wide, broadly ovate to orbicular, obscurely toothed; stalk up to 6 in. long. *fl.-heads* 1 in. wide, 1 to 3 on an erect, slender stalk 12 to 15 in. h.; ray-florets yellow. Grown chiefly for its white foliage. New Zealand. Hardy on the south coast, &c.

S. Haworth'ii. A synonym of *Kleinia tomentosa.*

S. Hec'tori. Evergreen or semi-deciduous shrub, 6 to 14 ft., shoots stout, loosely woolly. *l.* 6 to 10 in. long, half as wide, oblanceolate to narrowly oval, conspicuously toothed and pinnately lobed at the narrowed base, thinly downy; stalk short. *fl.-heads* $1\frac{1}{2}$ to 2 in. across in flattish or rounded clusters up to 10 in. wide; stalks very glandular; ray-florets 12 to 14, pure white, disk yellow. July. New Zealand. 1910. (B.M. 8705.) Hardy only in mild districts.

S. Hen'ryi. A synonym of *S. tanguticus.*

S. Heritier'i.* Shrub 3 to 4 ft. of loose habit, shoots zigzag, slender, closely white-felted. *l.* broadly ovate-cordate, sparsely toothed or shallowly lobed, 4 to 6 in. across, white-felted beneath, long stalked. *fl.-heads* violet-scented, $1\frac{1}{2}$ in. across, in axillary and terminal corymbs 6 to 10 in. wide, forming a large compound panicle; ray-florets white and rosy-crimson, disk purple. May to July. Canaries. 1774. (B.M. 53 as *Cineraria lanata* and 3827 (var. **cyanophthal'mus,** with blue disk fl.).) Greenhouse.

S. Hunt'ii. Evergreen shrub or small tree, 6 to 20 ft., shoots stout, glandular-downy, clammy. *l.* 2 to $4\frac{1}{2}$ in. long, $\frac{3}{4}$ to 1 in. wide, narrowly oblong to oblanceolate, closely set at the end of the shoot, thinly rusty-downy beneath, stalkless. *fl.-heads* $\frac{1}{2}$ to $\frac{3}{4}$ in. wide, very numerous in terminal clusters 3 to 5 in. across; ray-florets 15 to 20, yellow. June, July. Chatham Islds. 1909. Hardy only in mild districts.

S. inca'nus.* Compact perennial covered with appressed white hairs. Tufted, 3 to 4 in. h. *l.* bright silvery, lower obovate with incised lobes, upper overlapping, oblong, with linear lflets. *fl.-heads* yellow, in a simple rather crowded corymb; involucre about half as long as florets, bracts few. August. European Alps. var. **carniol'icus,** cobwebby, stems ascending, *l.* oblong, deeply cut into entire lobes, *fl.-heads* twice as large as in *S. incanus* on longer pedicels. Hardy. Rock-garden.

S. japon'icus. A synonym of *Ligularia japonica.*

S. Kaemp'feri. A synonym of *Ligularia Kaempferi.*

S. Kirk'ii.* Erect, glabrous, evergreen shrub, 6 to 12 ft. *l.* very variable in shape and size, 2 to 5 in. long, $\frac{1}{3}$ to $1\frac{1}{2}$ in. wide, always cuneate, but either pointed or blunt-ended, shallowly toothed or entire. *fl.-heads* $1\frac{1}{4}$ to 2 in. wide, in flattish, terminal, much-branched clusters 4 to 12 in. across; ray-florets up to 10, pure white; disk yellow. April. New Zealand. (B.M. 8524.) Mild districts only.

S. Lago'pus. Crown of root covered with matted hairs. Perennial. *l.* broadly cordate-oblong, rounded at tip, 1 to 4 in. long, white-woolly beneath, wrinkled and bristly above; stalk short, stout, hairy. *fl.-heads* bright yellow, $\frac{1}{2}$ to 1 in. across; pedicels slender, scape 2 to 6 in. h., branched above, bearing 2 to 8 fl.-heads. Summer. Pappus white. New Zealand. 1882. Very much resembling *S. saxifragoides.* Rock-garden or alpine house.

S. laxifo'lius.* Evergreen shrub up to 4 ft., shoots grey-downy. *l.* $1\frac{1}{4}$ to $2\frac{1}{2}$ in. long, $\frac{3}{4}$ to $1\frac{1}{4}$ in. wide, oval to lanceolate, or ovate to obovate, cuneate, entire, grey-white with down especially beneath; stalk $\frac{1}{2}$ to 1 in. long. *fl.-heads* 1 in. across, in terminal broadly pyramidal panicles 5 to 8 in. long; ray-florets 12 to 15, golden-yellow, disk reddish-brown. Summer. New Zealand. (B.M. 7378.) Hardy in mild districts. Often confused with *S. Greyii.*

S. Ledebour'ii. A synonym of *Ligularia macrophylla.*

S. leucostach'ys. Tufted with white-hairy *l.* much like those of *S. Cineraria* but finely pinnatisect. Patagonia. 1893. (B.H. 1893, 37.) Tender.

S. lilaci'nus. A synonym of *S. glastifolius.*

S. long'ipes. A synonym of *Kleinia Grantii.*

Senecio laxifolius

S. macroglos'sus.* Cape Ivy. Tall, evergreen, quite glabrous climber, stems slender. *l.* of very much the same shape as common ivy, dark lustrous green, $1\frac{1}{2}$ to $2\frac{1}{2}$ in. long and wide, triangular but with 3- to 7-pointed lobes. *fl.-heads* 2 to $2\frac{1}{2}$ in. across, rich yellow, solitary on axillary or terminal stalks 3 to 5 in. long; ray-florets 8 or more, oval, 1 in. by $\frac{1}{2}$ in. Winter. S. Africa. (B.M. 6149.) Greenhouse. Admirable for training on rafters.

S. macrophyl'lus. Stout herbaceous perennial, 3 to 4 ft. h., smooth or nearly so. *Lower l.* obovate-oblong, 6 to 18 in. long, 1 to 4 in. broad, narrowed to winged stalk, pale green; *upper* sessile. *fl.-heads* in a terminal compound corymbose cyme. Caucasus. 1896. Hardy.

S. magnif'icus.* Shrub or under-shrub, shoots and l. glaucous and quite glabrous. *Lower l.* 6 in. long, $\frac{1}{2}$ to 1 in. wide, obovate-oblong to oblong-lanceolate, pointed, coarsely toothed, the base clasping half the stem. *fl.-heads* $1\frac{3}{4}$ in. wide in loose, axillary and terminal, few-flowered corymbs; ray-florets 8 to 12, oblong, golden-yellow. October. Australia. 1899. (B.M. 7803.) Greenhouse.

S. marit'ima. A synonym of *S. Cineraria.*

S. mikanioi'des. Quite glabrous evergreen climber many feet high. *l.* ivy-shaped, 2 to 4 in. wide; 3- to 5- or 7-lobed, rather fleshy, lobes shallow, triangular-pointed; stalk as long as the blade, sometimes twice as long. *fl.-heads* $\frac{1}{4}$ in. long, yellow, fragrant, numerously packed in axillary and terminal corymbs 1 to 3 in. wide; no ray-florets. December. S. Africa. 1855. Greenhouse.

S. Monro'i. Evergreen shrub 2 to 6 ft., shoots, undersurface, and stalk of l. and fl.-stalks whitish-felted. *l.* oblong, oval, or obovate, $\frac{1}{2}$ to $1\frac{1}{2}$ in. long, half as wide, margins conspicuously wavy, dull green above. *fl.-heads* $\frac{1}{2}$ to $\frac{3}{4}$ in. wide, in terminal, compound clusters, 4 to 6 in. across; ray-florets 10 to 15, bright yellow; fl.-stalks long, slender, glandular. July. New Zealand. (B.M. 8698.) Hardy in mild districts.

S. nemoren'sis. Herbaceous perennial, 3 to 4 ft. *l.* ovate, obovate, or oval-lanceolate, $1\frac{1}{2}$ to 5 in. long, $\frac{1}{2}$ to $1\frac{1}{2}$ in. wide, pointed, cuneate, toothed, finely downy beneath. *fl.-heads* 1 in. across, in erect, terminal, loose, corymbs 4 to 6 in. wide; ray-florets 6 to 8, oblong, bright yellow; disk $\frac{1}{3}$ in. wide. July, August. S. Europe. 1775.

S. palma'tus. Glabrous perennial, branched above, erect. *Stem-l.* wedge-shaped at base, pinnatipartite, rather hairy, lobes 3 to 7, oblong-lanceolate with a long point, unequally toothed. *fl.-heads* many; rays yellow. *Achenes* glabrous, reddish-brown. Siberia.

S. Palm'eri. 1 to 2 ft. h., densely white-felted. *l.* oblong-lanceolate, slightly toothed, narrowed to a long stalk. *fl.-heads* yellow, few, about 1 in. across, in a stalked corymb. Guadeloupe Is., California. 1890. Greenhouse. May be grown as a hardy annual.

S. palustris auranti'acus. Herbaceous perennial. Stems erect, up to 12 in., stout, white-woolly. *l.* oval or ovate, 2 to 3 in. long, blunt, obscurely toothed, stem-clasping, woolly; stem-l. smaller, narrower, entire. *fl.-heads* 1 to 1½ in. wide, fragrant, borne in close terminal clusters; ray-florets 14 to 16, linear, orange-brown changing to golden-yellow; disk ½ to ¾ in. wide. Summer. European Alps. (B.M. 2262 as *Cineraria aurantiaca.*) Hardy.

S. pend'ulus. A synonym of *Kleinia pendula.*

S. pentacti'nus. Herbaceous perennial of elegant climbing habit, quite glabrous; stems very slender, often pendulous. *l.* ½ to 1 in. wide, roundish, rather distant, shallowly 5-lobed, coarsely toothed, pale green; stalk nearly as long as the blade. *fl.-heads* ¾ to 1 in. wide, in loose, terminal, few-fld., long- and slender-stalked panicles; ray-florets 5, golden-yellow; disk orange-yellow; stalks pale red. Summer. S. Africa? (B.M. 7799 as *Cineraria pentactina.*) Greenhouse.

S. perdicioi'des. Evergreen shrub, 6 ft. or more, shoots slender, ribbed. *l.* 1 to 2 in. long, scarcely half as wide, oblong to slightly obovate, cuneate, toothed, apex rounded, dull green. *fl.-heads* ⅜ in. wide and long, funnel-shaped, in erect, much-branched, terminal clusters 3 to 6 in. wide; ray-florets 2 or 3; disk-florets 4 to 8. June, July. New Zealand. Only suitable for very mild districts.

S. Petasi'tes. Evergreen bushy shrub, 3 to 4 ft., shoots downy. *l.* 6 to 12 in. long and across, roundish-cordate, wavy-lobed, downy, especially beneath; stalk as long as the blade. *fl.-heads* 1¼ in. wide in large, erect, terminal panicles; ray-florets 5 or 6, bright yellow; disk brownish. December to February. Mexico. 1812. (B.M. 1536 as *Cineraria Petasites.*) Hardy in Cornwall.

S. populifo'lius. Sub-shrub, woody only at the base, 3 to 4 ft. *l.* ovate, cordate, irregularly lobed and toothed, 1½ to 2 in. wide, white-woolly beneath; stalk about 1 in. long. *fl.-heads* 1¼ in. wide in rounded terminal corymbs, fragrant; ray-florets 10 to 14, purple or pink; disk ½ in. wide. August, September. Canary Is. Greenhouse.

S. pteroneu'rus. A synonym of *Kleinia pteroneura.*

S. pulcher.* Cobwebby-hairy perennial, 1 to 2 ft. h. *l.* oblong-lanceolate, crenately toothed, leathery, dark green; basal l. stalked, upper somewhat stem-clasping and decurrent. *fl.-heads* large, in corymbs, ray-florets nearly 20, purple, longer than the yellow disk; involucre broadly bell-shaped, bracts woolly-hairy, blunt. Autumn. Uruguay, &c. 1872. (B.M. 5959.) Hardy in a warm spot, needing deep, rich, cool root-run.

S. pyramida'tus.* Succulent shrub about 2 ft. with a short, thick, erect stem. *l.* closely set, cylindrical, pointed, 3 to 4 in. long, ¼ in. thick, glaucous or cobwebby. *fl.-heads* 2 in. across, beautiful yellow, borne in an erect columnar raceme 8 in. long by 3 or 4 in. wide; ray-florets about 12. June. S. Africa. 1860. (B.M. 5396.) Greenhouse. Very beautiful and distinct.

S. × Reisach'ii (*S. alpinus × S. Jacobaea*). Intermediate between parents. Alps. Rock-garden.

S. re'pens. A synonym of *Kleinia repens.*

S. rotundifo'lius. Evergreen shrub or small tree varying from 6 to 30 ft., shoots, undersurface, and stalk of l., and fl.-stalks densely white-felted. *l.* 3 to 5 in. long and wide, shining dark green above, very stout and leathery; stalk up to 3½ in. long. *fl.-heads* yellowish, ½ in. long, ⅓ in. wide, in terminal clusters 5 to 10 in. across, of little beauty; ray florets absent. Summer. New Zealand. Nearly hardy; excellent sea-side shrub.

S. sagittifo'lius. Herbaceous biennial or perennial. *l.* 2 to 3 ft. long, 1 to 1½ ft. wide, arrow-head-shaped, pointed, sometimes lobed. upperside of the midrib curiously crested or frilled. *fl.-heads* 1½ to 2 in. across, borne near and at the top of an erect stem 6 or 7 (said sometimes to be 12) ft. h. in a rounded panicle 9 to 12 in. wide; ray-florets 20 to 40, creamy-white. Uruguay. 1892. (B.M. 7322.) Greenhouse.

S. saracen'icus. Herbaceous, nearly glabrous perennial; rootstock creeping. *Lower l.* 3 to 8 in. long, ¾ to 2 in. wide, oval to oblong and oblanceolate, finely and irregularly toothed; *upper l.* smaller and narrower. *fl.-heads* 1 to 1¼ in. across in terminal corymbs or compound corymbs; ray-florets 6 to 8, bright yellow; disk ⅜ in. wide. Autumn. Europe (Britain). (E.B. 757.)

S. saxifragoi'des. Perennial, densely purplish-hairy herb with a stout rhizome and a woolly crown; about 12 in. h. *Radical l.* widely oblong-elliptic or nearly round, somewhat heart-shaped at base, 3 to 5 in. long, leathery, toothed and wavy at margin. *fl.-heads* in a panicle on an erect scape, yellow; rays 18 to 20, about ½ in. long, disk about ⅝ in. across, yellow. Summer. New Zealand. 1908. (B.M. 8394.) Rock-garden or alpine house.

S. scan'dens. Evergreen climber up to 15 ft., shoots slender-ribbed. *l.* 2 to 4 in. long, one-third as wide, ovate to narrowly triangular, slender-pointed, rather coarsely triangular-toothed, sometimes lobed at the base. *fl.-heads* ½ in. long, in axillary and terminal clusters forming a large compound panicle; ray-florets 8 to 12, bright yellow. China, Japan. 1895.

S. scapo'sus. Fleshy-shrubby, 12 in. h., branched. *l.* broadly linear, 2 to 3 in. long, crowded at tips of shoots, blunt, terete, cobwebby at first, later glabrous. *fl.-heads* yellow, rays about 12; involucre cobwebby, peduncles scape-like, 12 to 18 in. long, usually with 3 to 5 fl.-heads on long pedicels. S. Africa. 1843. (B.M. 4011 as *S. calamifolius.*) Greenhouse.

S. Smith'ii.* Herbaceous perennial, 3 to 4 ft., loosely woolly. *l.* 8 to 10 in. long, ovate to oblong, cordate, coarsely blunt-toothed, leathery; stalk half as long to longer than the blade. *fl.-heads* 1½ in. across in a close terminal panicle 4 to 6 in. wide; ray-florets 20 to 30, white; disk ½ in. wide, yellow. June. S. Chile, Falkland Is. 1895. (B.M. 7531.) Hardy.

S. specio'sus.* Herbaceous perennial. *l.* 4 to 8 in. long, ¾ to 1½ in. wide, obovate-lanceolate to narrow, coarsely and bluntly toothed. clothed with glandular hairs. *fl.-heads* 2 in. wide, borne near and at the summit of a glandular-hairy stalk 9 to 14 in. long on which are small amplexicaul l., ray-florets up to 20, linear, bright purple. July. S. Africa. 1789. (B.M. 6488.) Greenhouse.

S. stenoceph'alus. *See* **Ligularia intermedia.**

S. subscan'dens. Tall herbaceous climber. *l.* 5 to 9 in. long, nearly half as wide, triangular in the main but very deeply 5- to 13-lobed; lobes widely triangular-toothed. *fl.-heads* yellow, ½ in. long, cylindric, in rounded clusters 1 to 1½ in. wide forming axillary and terminal panicles 6 to 10 in. long; florets about 10. January. Trop. Africa. (B.M. 6363.) Warm greenhouse.

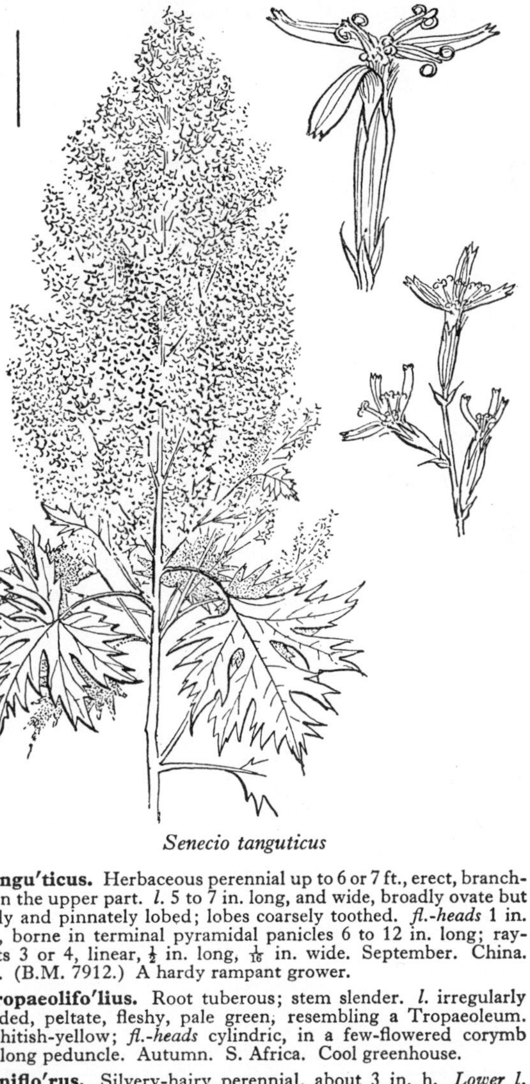

Senecio tanguticus

S. tangu'ticus. Herbaceous perennial up to 6 or 7 ft., erect, branching on the upper part. *l.* 5 to 7 in. long, and wide, broadly ovate but deeply and pinnately lobed; lobes coarsely toothed. *fl.-heads* 1 in. wide, borne in terminal pyramidal panicles 6 to 12 in. long; ray-florets 3 or 4, linear, ½ in. long, $\frac{1}{16}$ in. wide. September. China. 1902. (B.M. 7912.) A hardy rampant grower.

S. tropaeolifo'lius. Root tuberous; stem slender. *l.* irregularly rounded, peltate, fleshy, pale green, resembling a Tropaeoleum. *fl.* whitish-yellow; *fl.-heads* cylindric, in a few-flowered corymb on a long peduncle. Autumn. S. Africa. Cool greenhouse.

S. uniflo'rus. Silvery-hairy perennial, about 3 in. h. *Lower l.* oblong, cut, stalked; *upper* linear, entire, sessile. *fl.-heads* yellow, solitary or few on long pedicels; involucre urn-shaped, half as long as disk; rays flat. July. European Alps. 1785. Related to *S. incanus.*

S. Veitchian'us. *See* **Ligularia Veitchiana.**

S. Wilsonian'us. *See* **Ligularia Wilsoniana.**

SENE'GA. Included in **Polygala.**

SENEGA SNAKE-ROOT. *See* **Polygala Senega.**

senegalen'sis -is -e, of Senegal, W. Africa.

senen'sis -is -e, of Sena, Mozambique.

senes'cens, appearing old.

se'nez. grey-haired.

SENGREEN. *See* **Saxifraga nivalis, Sempervivum tectorum.**

seni'lis -is -e, grey-haired, appearing old.

Sen'na, from the Arabic name.

SENNA. Leaves or pulp of pods of *Cassia acutifolia, C. angustifolia,* &c. Used as a cathartic and emetic.

SENNA, BLADDER. *See* **Colutea.**

SENNA, SCORPION. *See* **Coronilla Emerus.**

sensib'ilis -is -e, sensitive.

SENSITIVE PLANT. *See* **Mimosa.**

sensiti'vus -a -um, sensitive, responding quickly to changes in surroundings.

sentico'sus -a -um, thorny.

SEPAL. One of the parts that together form the calyx or outermost whorl of the flower. The sepals are usually green and unlike the petals but they may resemble them as in the Tulip. They may be free but are often more or less united to form a tube or cup. They protect the more delicate inner parts of the flower while growing and sometimes help in the distribution of the fruits.

sepaline, relating to the sepals.

SEPALODY. A change of petals, &c., into sepals or sepal-like organs.

sepaloid, resembling a sepal.

sepia'rius -a -um, hedge-loving.

se'pium, hedge-growing.

septate, separated by a partition or septum.

septem- in compound words, signifying 7, as *septemfidus,* of 7 parts.

septentriona'lis -is -e, northern.

septicidal, applied to a capsule which dehisces through the lines of junction of the carpels.

SEPTO'RIA. A genus of Fungi Imperfecti containing many parasitic species, *S. apii,* the cause of leaf-spot of Celery, and *S. chrysanthemella* on Chrysanthemums being especially important.

D. E. G.

SEPTUM (pl. *septa*), a wall of tissue dividing the ovary, anther, fruit, &c., into cells or compartments.

sepulchra'lis -is -e, of a tomb.

SEQUOI'A (derivation obscure, but possibly modified from *See-qua-yah,* a word connected with the Cherokee Indians). FAM. *Pinaceae.* A genus of 2 species of gigantic, hardy, evergreen, Californian trees very dissimilar in appearance, which live to a very great age, the oldest reputed to be the oldest living trees in the world. Male and female flowers on the same tree, males in small, compact, axillary or terminal catkins, female small, terminal, egg-shaped or oblong bodies. Cones small. Both species require rich moist soil, and protection from violent winds. The best results are obtained by planting them in the alluvial soil of deep valleys where the tops are well sheltered; when planted in poor soil in exposed places they grow slowly and are of ragged appearance. Propagation is usually by imported seeds sown either in frames or out of doors, but the germination percentage may be low. Good trees, particularly of *S. sempervirens,* can also be raised from cuttings. When possible erect shoots should be used, but by rooting side shoots and cutting them down afterwards, strong, erect leading shoots can be procured from dormant buds. Cuttings may be made during late summer and inserted in a cold or slightly warm shaded frame, or under a handlight, in sandy soil; they usually root during winter or early spring. The timber is light in weight, sapwood yellow, heart-wood red. It has very good lasting properties and that of *S. sempervirens* is largely used for building purposes.

Seedlings and young trees may be attacked in the leading shoots by the Grey Mould fungus, *Botrytis cinerea.* It appears as a greyish-brown mould on the shoot which often curls and dies. Many other conifers are apt to be attacked in the same way and in nursery work removal of affected plants and thorough spraying with Bordeaux mixture may be required.

S. gigan'tea. A synonym of *S. Wellingtonia.*

S. sempervir'ens. Redwood. Large tree of about 130 ft. (tallest recorded 340 ft.) with diameter of 8 to 25 ft. Bark thick, reddish, fibrous. Branch-system dense, branches drooping and on isolated trees remaining healthy to ground line for 100 or more years, secondary branchlets deciduous. Young shoots smooth, green at first, brown later. *Winter buds* small, surrounded by loose scales. *l.* on leading points of main shoots surrounding the shoots on branchlets appearing in 2 lateral sets by reason of a basal twist, $\frac{1}{4}$ to $\frac{4}{5}$ in. long, $\frac{1}{10}$ in. wide, flat, dark green above with 2 broad, silvery, stomatic bands beneath, and broken stomatic lines on the surface, apex a short point. There are also smaller, scale-like l. on face of shoot. *Cones* oval or elliptical, $\frac{3}{4}$ to $1\frac{1}{8}$ in. long, $\frac{1}{2}$ to $\frac{7}{8}$ in. wide, brown when mature; scales woody, $\frac{1}{3}$ in. across at apex. *Seeds* light brown with very narrow wings. California. About 1843 or 1846. (D.J.C. 494.) When growing under forest conditions the trunk is clear of branches for one-third to half the height. Age of the very large trees up to 1,300 or more years. It gives excellent results in the British Is. and several trees exceeding 100 ft. in height have been recorded. Sometimes reproduces itself from self-sown seeds in this country and also renews itself from sprouts produced from dormant buds at the base of cut-down trees. An inconceivably large amount of timber is obtained from these very large trees and it is of considerable importance in N. America. It has very long-lasting properties and trunks fallen in the forest have been known to remain sound for many years. Young trees are sometimes injured by winter or spring cold, and very cold winds may turn the l. brown, but it is not a really tender tree. The following varieties are grown: **adpres'sa,** tips of shoots creamy-white, less vigorous than type. SYN. var. *albo-spica*; **glau'ca,** *l.* glaucous green, shoots more slender than in type.

S. Washington'ia. A synonym of *S. Wellingtonia.*

S. Wellington'ia. Big Tree, Mammoth Tree. Large tree 130 to 320 ft. h. with a girth up to 90 ft., of pyramidal outline with a long massive trunk swelling near ground into large buttresses. Bark reddish-brown, very thick, branches drooping acutely from near trunk. Young shoots smooth, green, closely covered by l.-bases. *Winter buds* small, hidden by l. *l.* widely awl-shaped, spirally densely arranged, closely overlapping, base clasping shoot, pointed tips free, deep green, lasting about 4 years. *Male fl.* in short catkins at points of shoots. *Cones* solitary, terminal on leafy stalks, 2 to 3 in. long, 1 to 2 in. wide, green at first then brown, taking 2 summers to mature; scales woody, apex much enlarged, 4-sided. *Seeds* thin, oblong with narrow marginal wing. California. 1853. (B.M. 4777–8; D.J.C. 491 as *S. gigantea.*) SYN. *S. Washingtonia, Wellingtonia gigantea.* The tallest tree in the British Is., at Leaton Knolls, Shropshire, recorded for the Conifer Conference in 1931, was $143\frac{1}{2}$ ft. h. Less common in California than *S. sempervirens,* limited to a few groves under government control, no cutting being allowed. The best known is the Calaveras Grove where some of the largest trees are found. The age of these trees has for long been a matter of speculation. One authority on Californian trees suggests an age of about 1,500 years for the largest trees, while another authority asserts that the largest trees are up to 4,000 years old. Succeeds under similar conditions to *S. sempervirens,* but is hardier when small. var. **au'rea,** *l.* golden, not of good constitution; **pen'dula,** grotesque tree with long pendent branches hanging close to trunk. These varieties are increased by grafting on to stocks of the type. A

W. D.

A→

serampuren'sis -is -e, of Serampur, near Calcutta.

Seraphi'ni, in honour of the Italian botanist Serafino.

SERAPHY'TA. Included in **Epidendrum.**

SERAP'IAS (old Greek name used by Dioscorides for an Orchid, derived from the Egyptian deity Serapis). FAM. *Orchidaceae.* A genus of 6 or more species of terrestrial orchids, natives of the Mediterranean region, 1 extending as far as the Azores. Flowers often rather large, few in a spike; sepals erect, connivent or coherent in a tube; petals sometimes smaller, sometimes scarcely shorter, but much narrower; lip 3-lobed, the side lobes erect, mid-lobe tongue-shaped and pendulous. Leaves narrow. Tubers undivided. In habit the species much resemble those of Orchis. So close is the affinity with Orchis that several natural hybrids have been found between species of the 2 genera and supposed natural hybrids between species of Serapias have also been recorded. Several species of Cephalanthera and Epipactis were, at one time, placed under Serapias. Though possibly hardy in suitable positions less risk is incurred if they are cultivated in pots which can be removed to a frost-proof position in winter. If pots are used they should be well drained; compost should consist of sandy loam, with a little leaf-mould. Generally the tubers require to be kept dry in the winter, or moderately so.

S. × **ambig'ua.** A natural hybrid between *S. cordigera* and *S. Lingua.*

S. cordig'era.* Heart-flowered Orchis. *fl.* brown and lavender to purple; side lobes of lip obtuse, erect, connivent; mid-lobe longer, ovate, often cordate at base, acuminate, disk pilose, basal callus deeply 2-lobed; bracts often longer than fl.; spike at first crowded, 1 ft. h. S. Europe. 1806. (B.M. 5868A; F.G. 932.)

S. gregar'ia. Very near to *S. Lingua*, the chief floral difference being in the lip. Vegetatively it is curious in that a third tuber is produced each year, hence the species rapidly increases. Hyères. 1921. (J. B. 1921, 241.)

S. Ling'ua. Tongue-flowered Orchis. *fl.* variable, reddish-brown; side-lobes of lip ovate, obtuse; mid-lobe longer and narrower, oblong-lanceolate, acuminate; basal callus obscure, sulcate or flat; bracts shorter than fl., violet-rose with darker nerves, spike at first loose, 1 ft. h. or more. S. Europe. 1786. SYN. *S. glabra.* (B.M. 5868B; L.B.C. 655; F.G. 931.) var. **luteol'a** has yellowish and purplish *fl.*

S. longipet'ala. *fl.* reddish-violet; side lobes of lip red-violet, mid-lobe brownish-red, yellowish in centre, hairy. 12 to 18 in. h. Allied to *S. Lingua.* S. Europe. SYN. *S. hirsuta, S. lancifera.*

S. neglec'ta. *fl.* with violet-purple sep.; side lobes of lip rounded, dark purple, mid-lobe oval, hairy, bright red, ochre-red in centre. 12 in. h. S. Europe. SYN. *S. pseudocordigera.*

S. occulta'ta. *fl.* small, reddish or green, variable; sep. violet-red with green nerves; pet. greenish or reddish; side lobes of lip dark purple; mid-lobe yellowish-red with brownish hairs, about 12 in. h. S. Europe. SYN. *S. laxiflora.*

S. papilionacea-ling'ua (a natural hybrid between *Orchis papilionacea* and *S. Lingua*). *fl.* 5 or 6 to a spike; sep. and pet. pale green and pale purple, veined; pet. erect, free, broad, spreading, and recurved; lip bright purple, large, broadly cordate, margins crenulate, base with 2 tubercles on the very short claw. *l.* narrow-lanceolate, acuminate, pale green, unspotted. Stem 1 ft. or more h. S. France. 1876. (B.M. 6255.)

E. C.

serb'icus -a -um, of Serbia, Servian.

SERENO'A (in honour of Sereno Watson, 1826–92, a distinguished American botanist). FAM. *Palmaceae.* A genus of 2 often low-growing, somewhat spiny palms, natives of SE. United States, with creeping, branched stems, covered with the fibrous bases of old leaves. Leaves terminal, roundish, leathery, deeply plaited, glaucous below, with narrow 2-fid segments; stalk toothed on margin. Spadix long, branched, hairy. Flowers white. Fruit ovid, black, 1 in. long. Good pot plants but slow in growth. For cultivation *see* **Sabal.**

S. arbores'cens. A synonym of *Paurotis Wrightii.*

S. re'pens. Saw Palmetto. Shrubby with creeping stem 4 to 8 ft. long. *l.* circular, fan-shaped, bright green, 2 to 4 ft. h., segs. 15 to 30, erect, slightly cleft, without fibres in sinuses; stalks slender, longer than l., more or less spiny-edged. *Spadix* densely downy, shorter than l. June. *Drupes* black, about $\frac{3}{4}$ in. long. S. United States. 1840. SYN. *Sabal serrulata, Serenoa serrulata.*

S. serrula'ta. A synonym of *S. repens.*

seric'eus -a -um, serici- in compound words, silky; covered with soft, straight, closely appressed hairs.

SERICOCARP'US (*serikos*, silky, *karpos*, fruit; the achenes are covered with silky hairs). FAM. *Compositae.* A genus of 5 species of perennial herbs almost indistinguishable from Aster, natives of N. America, mostly in the east. Leaves alternate, sessile. Flower-heads rather small, in corymbs or panicles; involucral bracts rather broad in many series; ray-florets white; disk pale yellow, becoming purplish. Achenes silky-hairy; scarcely compressed (compressed in Aster), pappus bristles many. Much like a small, whitish golden-rod. Cultivation, &c., as for Aster.

S. conyzoi'des. Silk Fruit. 1 to 2 ft. h. *l.* 1 to 3 in. long, rather firm, glabrous beneath, ciliate. *fl.-heads* sometimes solitary and stalked, usually in small clusters and sessile; involucre somewhat turbinate; pappus reddish-brown. 1778.

S. rigi'dus. Ascending, 6 to 8 in. h. *l.* spatulate, entire, scabrid on margin. *fl.-heads* few, in a small corymb; rays very short; disk-florets whitish with purple stamens, shorter than pappus.

S. solidagin'eus. About 2 ft. h. *l.* linear-oblanceolate or linear, obtuse, scabrid on margins, obscurely dotted. *fl.-heads* small, clustered at ends of erect peduncles; involucre cylindrical; pappus white. July to September. 1699.

sericof'era, from *Seres*, an ancient name for an eastern people, as Chinese, *fero*, bearing; meaning bearing Eastern stuff, e.g. silky.

SERING'IA (in honour of Nicholas Charles Seringe, 1776–1858, Director of the Botanic Gardens, Lyons). FAM. *Sterculiaceae.* A genus of 3 species of shrubs, 2 Australian, 1 from the Mascarene Is. Greenhouse shrub. The ordinary compost of loam, peat, and sand is suitable for it. Propagated by cuttings.

S. platyphyl'la. Evergreen shrub, 4 to 8 ft., shoots softly brownish-downy at first. *l.* alternate, ovate-lanceolate, $2\frac{1}{2}$ to $4\frac{1}{2}$ in. long, slender-pointed, sparsely coarsely toothed, velvety-downy beneath; stalk $\frac{1}{4}$ to $\frac{1}{2}$ in. long. *fl.* crowded in axillary and terminal, globose, short-stalked, downy clusters, 1 to $1\frac{1}{2}$ in. wide; cal. $\frac{1}{8}$ in. long, white; pet. none; stamens 5, alternating with 5 staminodes. June. 1822. Australia.

W. J. B.

SERIS'SA (from the Indian name). FAM. *Rubiaceae.* The only species is a branched shrub with glabrous or downy shoots. Bark fetid when bruised. Leaves opposite; stipules persistent. Flowers rather small, solitary or clustered; corolla 4- to 6-lobed, the lobes 3-lobed; stamens attached below middle of corolla tube. Fruit very fleshy. Distinguished from Coprosma by the very short 2-lobed style. *S. foetida* requires a greenhouse and succeeds in a compost of loam, peat, and sand. It can be increased by cuttings in sand under a close frame in heat.

S. foe'tida. Shrub of 2 ft. *l.* small, ovate, slender-pointed, rather leathery. *fl.* white, axillary or terminal. SE. Asia. 1787. (B.M. 361 as *Lycium japonicum.*) There is a double-fld. form and one with gold-margined l.

SERJAN'IA (in honour of Paul Serjeant, French friar and botanist). FAM. *Sapindaceae.* A genus of nearly 200 species of climbing or twining shrubs, natives of the warm parts of S. America. Leaves alternate, compound, stipules if present very minute, often with pellucid dots. Flowers yellowish, irregular, in racemes or panicles often with 2 tendrils; sepals 5 (or 4, 2 connate), overlapping; petals 4; disk with 4 glands, 2 larger than others; stamens 8. Fruit an indehiscent samara. *S. cuspidata* needs a warm house.

S. cuspida'ta. Climbing with triangular branches densely brown-hairy at the angles. *l.* ternate; lflets. somewhat heart-shaped, more or less 3-lobed, irregularly coarsely toothed. *fl.* yellowish, rather large; pet. usually glabrous. *fr.* ovate, 3-winged. Brazil. (B.R. 1077 as *Urvillea ferruginea.*)

seroti'nus-a-um, produced late in the season.

serp'ens, creeping.

SERPENT CUCUMBER. *See* **Trichosanthes Anguina.**

serpentar'ius -a -um, snake-like.

serpyllifo'lius -a -um, with thyme-like leaves.

serra-, in compound words, signifying saw-like.

SERRASTYL'IS modest'a. A synonym of *Macradenia modesta.*

SERRAT'ULA (*serrula*, a little saw; in reference to the serrate leaves). FAM. *Compositae.* A genus of about 40 species of perennial herbs, distributed over Europe, N. Africa, and Asia, related to Centaurea, from which it is distinguished by the long pappus hairs and from Carduus and other thistles by its unarmed bracts. Leaves alternate, radical simple, cauline usually pinnatifid. Flower-heads solitary, in corymbs, purple or white, sometimes dioecious; involucral bracts many, overlapping, inner more or less scarious at the tip. Corolla regular, tubular, lobes 5, narrow, oblique. Fruit oblong, compressed, smooth; pappus-hairs in many series. Few species are of horticultural value but the undermentioned are sometimes grown; they will succeed in any ordinary soil but *S. atricifolia* needs a fairly warm situation and a well-drained one. *S. tinctoria*, Saw-wort, of no garden value, is wild in Britain; its foliage has been used for the production of a yellow dye.

S. atriplicifo'lia. Vigorous, silvery, up to 5 ft. h. *Lower l.* heart-shaped, large; *upper* deeply cut. *fl.-heads* deep purple, horizontal or nodding, globular. Autumn. Cent. China.

S. corona'ta. *l.* deeply pinnately cut, lobes oblong-elliptic with large teeth, cartilaginous in upper part. *fl.-heads* in corymbs, purple, involucral bracts woolly or hairy, outer ovate, shortly mucronate, inner long-lanceolate; ray-florets few. Russia, Siberia.

S. nudicau'lis. 8 to 15 in. h., glabrous and grey-green. Stem simple or branched above. *Lower l.* ovate-lanceolate, entire at base, narrowed to stalk; *upper* toothed. *fl.-heads* purple, disk about ¾ in. across, involucral bracts glabrous, margins scarious, pale green, outer ovate, spotted brown at tip. June, July. France, Switzerland, Italy.

S. quinquef'olia. About 3 ft. h. *l.* deeply pinnately cut, lobes ovate-lanceolate, toothed, terminal largest. *fl.-heads* deep purple. July. Caucasus. (B.M. 1871.)

serrat'ulus -a -um, serratulate, edged with small teeth.

SERRATURE, one of the teeth of a serrate margin.

serra'tus -a -um, serrati- (in compound words), serrate, edged with forward-pointing teeth. **A**

SERRU'RIA (in honour of Dr. James Serrurier, Professor of Botany at Utrecht). FAM. *Proteaceae.* A genus of about 60 species of evergreen shrubs confined to S. Africa. Nearly related to Protea, they differ most noticeably in the leaves, which are pinnately to 3-pinnately divided into narrow segments, rarely undivided. Flowers in dense heads which are solitary or in clusters, terminal or axillary, subtended by floral and often involucral bracts. They require the same conditions and treatment as Protea, but are very rare and not easy to cultivate.

S. anethifo'lia. Shrub 2 to 3 ft., shoots glabrous. *l.* 2½ to 5½ in. long, pinnately and 2-pinnately divided into terete, pointed segs. 1 to 2 in. long, $\frac{1}{16}$ in. thick. *fl.* purple, numerous in globose heads ¾ in. wide, fragrant, forming terminal corymbose panicles 3 to 4 in. across. July. S. Africa. 1802. (A.B.R. 447 as *Protea argentiflora.*) SYN. *S. triternata.*

S. artemisiifo'lia. Shrub 5 to 6 ft., shoots downy or hairy. *l.* 1 to 2 in. long, 2-pinnately divided into linear segs. ¼ to ½ in. long, $\frac{1}{16}$ in. wide. *fl.-heads* terminal, 1 to 1¼ in. wide, on a downy stalk up to 3 in. long; floral bracts ⅓ in. long, pink; *fl.* ⅓ in. long, pale purple. July. S. Africa. 1789. (A.B.R. 264 as *Protea glomerata.*) SYN. *S. pedunculata.*

S. flor'ida.* Shrub 3 to 9 ft. Stems erect, glabrous, purplish. *l.* 1½ to 2¾ in. long, glabrous, pinnately and 2-pinnately divided into sharply pointed segs. $\frac{1}{16}$ in. wide. *fl.-heads* axillary and terminal, 2 to 2½ in. across, borne 3 to 6 towards the end of the branches; involucral bracts pure white, ovate-lanceolate, 1¼ in. long; floral bracts ¾ in. long, blush, linear or linear-lanceolate, ciliate; true fl. small and inconspicuous. July. S. Africa. 1824. The loveliest of the genus, known popularly as 'the blushing bride'. Has only a very restricted area in its wild state, now protected.

S. peduncula'ta. A synonym of *S. artemisiifolia.*

S. triterna'ta. A synonym of *S. anethifolia.*

W. J. B.

serta'tus -a -um, making a garland.

sertu'lifer -a -um, bearing a garland, floriferous.

SERVICE BERRY. *See* **Amelanchier ovalis.**

SERVICE TREE. *See* **Sorbus domestica.**

SES'AMUM (name used by the Greek Hippocrates). FAM. *Pedaliaceae.* A genus of about 16 species of erect or prostrate herbs all natives of India or Africa. Leaves opposite in lower part, alternate above, entire or variously cut, stalked. Flowers whitish or violet, solitary in leaf-axils, stalked; calyx rather small, 5-parted; corolla tube decurved; limb more or less 2-lipped, lobes 5, spreading; stamens 4. Fruit an oblong or ovoid capsule, 2-celled, with numerous oily seeds. *S. indicum* has been widely grown in tropical countries since ancient times for the oil contained in its seeds. This Gingelly- or Teel-oil is used in India for cooking and both oil and seeds are imported in large quantities into Europe for the manufacture of soap. The mucilaginous leaves are used in India, particularly in the north, in cases of dysentery and diarrhoea. For cultivation *see* **Martynia.**

S. in'dicum. Gingelly or Gingilie oil-plant; Sesame; Teel-oil plant, &c. Herb of 1 to 2 ft. *l.* oblong or ovate, 3 to 5 in. long, variable; upper often narrowly oblong, nearly entire, middle ovate, toothed, lower lobed or pedatisect. *fl.* whitish with red, purplish, or yellow marks; pedicels usually 1, rarely 2 or 3. July. India, &c. 1731. (B.M. 1688.) SYN. *S. orientale.*

SESBA'NIA (*Sesban*, the Arabic name for *S. aegyptica*). FAM. *Leguminosae.* A genus of about 30 species of herbs or shrubs, sometimes almost trees but short-lived, natives of the warmer parts of the world. Leaves abruptly pinnate; leaflets in many pairs, entire; stipules very quickly falling; stipels minute or absent. Flowers papilionaceous in loose, axillary racemes, yellow, dull scarlet, purple, variegated, or white, on slender pedicels; calyx broad; standard rounded or ovate, spreading or reflexed, wings falcate-oblong, keel incurved; bracts and bracteoles bristly. Pods linear or rarely oblong, compressed, 4-angled or 4-winged. All the species grow well in a compost of loam and sandy peat. The annual species are increased by seed, the shrubby ones by cuttings of half-ripe, stubby shoots in sand, under a bell glass, in heat. Most of the species need stove conditions, a few thrive in the greenhouse.

S. aculea'ta. A synonym of *S. bispinosa.*

S. aegyp'tica. Sesban. Short-lived shrub about 5 ft. h. *lflets.* in 10 pairs, oblong-linear, obtuse, shortly mucronate. *fl.* pale yellow, often spotted or tinged with purple; standards roundish, amarginate. July, August. Egypt, &c. 1680. SYN. *Aeschynomene Sesban.* Stove.

S. bispino'sa. Prickly shrub up to 10 ft. h. *lflets.* up to ½ in. long. *fl.* pale yellow spotted reddish-brown, in racemes 6 in. long. *Pods* 8 in. long. Tropics.

S. Cavanilles'ii. Shrub 3 to 7 ft. h. *l.* odd-pinnate; *lflets.* many, narrow-oblong, ½ to 1 in. long, pale, blunt. *fl.* yellow, ¼ to ¾ in. long, in racemes. *fr.* 4-winged. S. United States. SYN. *Danbentonia Cavanillesii.* The seeds are used as a substitute for coffee in its habitat.

S. exaspera'ta. Shrub, 8 to 10 ft. h. with slender branches. *l.* 6 to 10 in. long; lflets. in 30 to 50 pairs; stalk and rachis slender. *fl.* golden-yellow, large, spotted red on back of standard, in short racemes. *Pods* 8 to 12 in. long, drooping, many-seeded. Trop. America. Before 1894. (B.M. 7384.) SYN. *S. macrocarpa, Lotus palustris.*

S. grandiflo'ra. Tree, 14 to 26 ft. h. *lflets.*.many, glabrous. *fl.* pink or white, large; standard oval-oblong, shorter than wings; in few-fld. racemes. July, August. *Pods* 18 in. long, falcate, firm, not torulose. Mauritius, India to N. Australia. 1768. var. **coccin'ea,** *fl.* red, smaller than type, *l.* powdery; **flore al'bo,** *fl.* double, white. N. Australia. 1869. Stove. SYN. *Aeschynomene grandiflora, Agati grandiflora.*

S. longifo'lia. Shrub about 6 ft. h. *lflets.* in 11 or 12 pairs, lanceolate, acute. *fl.* yellow; racemes a little shorter than l. June to August. New Spain. 1820. Stove.

S. pic'ta. Biennial, 4 to 6 ft. h. *lflets.* in 12 to 16 pairs, oblong-linear, obtuse. *fl.* yellow; standard variegated with black dotted lines; racemes many-fld., nodding. July, August. New Spain. 1823. (B.R. 873.) SYN. *S. gracillima, Aeschynomene picta.* Stove.

S. platycarp'a. Annual, 5 to 7 ft. h. *lflets.* in many pairs on mature l. *fl.* yellow, few, loose; standard reniform, very short and broad; racemes stalked. July, August. Florida, Carolina. 1816. SYN. *S. vesicaria, Glottidium floridanum.* Greenhouse.

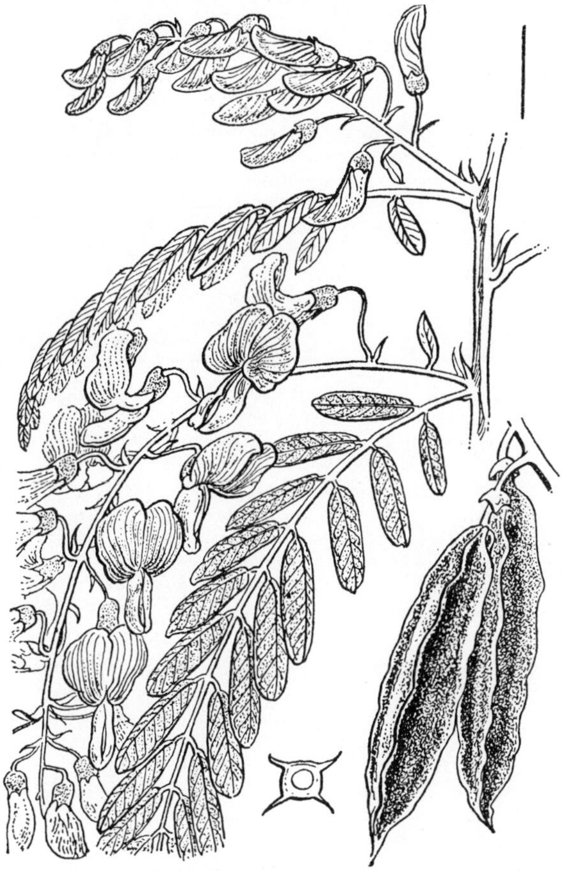

Sesbania punicea

S. punic'ea. Shrub, 3 ft. h. *lflets.* Robinia-like. *fl.* vermilion, in loose racemes; cal. truncate, teeth small, standards broad, roundish. July. *Pod* 2 to 4 in. long, thick, 4-angled with leathery wings. Brazil. 1820. (B.M. 7353.) SYN. *Aeschynomene miniata.* Stove.

S. Tripe'tii. About 6 ft. h. *lflets.* dull green above, somewhat glaucous beneath. *fl.* orange-red, in drooping racemes; standard scarlet, paler within with a yellow spot on claw; wings and keel pale. June to October. Brazil, Argentine. Greenhouse.

F. G. P.

SES'ELI (old Greek name used by Hippocrates for an umbelliferous plant). FAM. *Umbelliferae.* A genus of about 60 species of perennial (rarely biennial) erect herbs, nearly all natives of the north temperate regions. Leaves ternate-pinnate, dissected or decompound; segments sometimes filiform, sometimes broader and deeply cut. Flowers white, in compound umbels; petals rather broad; involucral bracts numerous, few, or sometimes absent. Fruit ovoid or elliptic, prominently ridged. Ordinary soil suits these hardy plants which are suitable for the border, or the dwarfer ones for the rock-garden.

S. caespito'sum. Perennial from a thick root. Stem simple, erect, 1-lvd. *Radical l.* densely tufted, glabrous, rigid, pinnately cut; *upper* with 3-fid. lflets. decurrent. *Umbel* usually 3-partite. Greece.

S. dichoto'mum. Perennial of 1 to 2 ft. Stem terete, finely downy; lower branches short. *l.* pinnate; lflets. multifid; segs. linear. *fl.* white, umbels without involucre. June, July. Tauria. 1818. (B.M. 2073.)

S. glau'cum. Branched. *Radical l.* 3-nate, 3-pinnatisect, triangular in outline: segs. linear; stalk canaliculate above. Involucre none or 1-lvd. Umbel 15- to 25-rayed. Mid-Russia ,Caucasus.

S. gummif'erum. Biennial of 3 to 4 ft. Stem thick, stiff, branched at top. *l.* 3-pinnate, glaucous; lflets. wedge-shaped, 3-fid. *fl.* white, tinged pink; involucre of few bracts, rarely wanting; umbel 20-rayed. July to September. Tauria. 1804. (B.M. 2259.) The stem yields a gum when cut.

sesqui-, in compound words, signifying 1½, as *sesquipedalis,* 1½ ft. long.

ses'silis -is -e, sessili-, in compound words, attached without a stalk.

SESUV'IUM (derivation ?). FAM. *Aizoaceae.* A genus of 5 species of tropical and sub-tropical, erect or prostrate, branched, succulent herbs or sub-shrubs, natives of sea-shores. Leaves opposite, fleshy, linear or oblong, stipules usually none. Flowers flesh-coloured or purple, axillary; calyx tube turbinate, the 5 lobes coloured within; petals absent; stamens 5. *S. Portulacastrum* is edible as a pot herb. The species need greenhouse protection and a well-drained, sandy soil. They may be propagated by cuttings in soil under glass. They should be allowed to become partially dry. Watering must be done very carefully.

S. Portulacast'rum. Sea Purslane or Samphire of the W. Indies. *l.* linear or oblong-lanceolate, flat. *fl.* greenish without, reddish within; stamens 25 to 30; pedicellate. June, July. Tropics. 1692. (A.B.R. 201 as *Aizoon canariense.*) var. **ses'sile,** *fl.* without pedicels.

S. revolutifo'lium. *l.* ovate-oblong, rather glaucous, margins revolute. *fl.* red and white, sessile; stamens very numerous; stigmas 5 or 6. July, August. Cuba. (B.M. 1701 as *S. Portulacastrum* var.)

SET WALL. *See* **Valeriana officinalis.**

seta'ceus -a -um, seti-, in compound words, bristle-like or furnished with bristles or stiff hairs or slender straight prickles.

A→

setiform, bristle-like.

setig'erus -a -um, bearing bristles.

seto'sus -a -um, bristly; covered with stiff hairs.

SETS. A term used for Potatoes, Dahlia tubers, and similar things used for propagation. The sets may be whole or parts of Potatoes.

SETTERWORT. *See* **Helleborus foetidus.**

SETTING. The fertilization of the flower. Some plants which, though forming many female flowers, produce few fruits, are said to be shy setters. *See* **Fertilization, Pollination.**

setulo'sus -a -um, slightly bristly.

SEVERIN'IA (in honour of M. A. Severino, 1580–1656, lecturer on anatomy at Naples). FAM. *Rutaceae.* A genus of a single species of spiny evergreen shrub, native of China, often included in Atalantia but differing by the black berry, the walls of the ovary becoming succulent as the fruit ripens. Leaves simple, on short wingless stalks. Flowers 5-merous, 2 or 3 together in leaf-axils; petals small, white; stamens 10, free; ovary 2- (or 3-) celled with 1 ovule in each cell. Treatment as for Citrus.

S. buxifo'lia. Spiny shrub of about 3 ft. *l.* simple, Box-like, up to 1½ in. long, leathery, evergreen, entire. *fl.* white, small, almost sessile, solitary or in small clusters. S. China, Hong Kong, Formosa. Greenhouse.

SEVILLE ORANGE. *See* **Citrus Aurantium.**

SEWERZOW'IA turkestan'ica. A synonym of *Astragalus Schmalhausenii.*

sex-, in compound words, signifying 6, as *sexangularis,* 6-cornered.

SEYMER'IA (in honour of Henry Seymer, English naturalist). FAM. *Scrophulariaceae.* A genus of 10 species of perennial or annual herbs, 9 in N. America, 1 in Madagascar. Leaves mostly opposite, toothed or much cut. Flowers yellow in interrupted spikes or racemes; calyx bell-shaped, lobes 5; corolla tube short, broad, lobes 5, broad or oblong, spreading; stamens 4, nearly equal; pedicels solitary, without bracts. The 2 species mentioned are hardy annuals and are best sown where they are to flower in rather light rich, well-drained soil.

S. pectina'ta. About 1 ft. h. *l.* pinnately cut into a few short or oblong-linear divisions, the upper with a few teeth or entire. Cal. lobes linear; cor. hairy without. July. SE. United States. 1820.

S. tenuifo'lia. 2 to 4 ft. h. *l.* pinnate or 2-pinnate, ½ in. long. *fl.* on filiform pedicels; cal. lobes bristly; cor. ½ in. long, lobes deeply cleft. July. SE. United States. 1730.

SHAD-BUSH. *See* **Amelanchier canadensis.**

SHADDOCK. *See* **Citrus maxima.**

SHADING. Nearly all indoor plants benefit by shading during sunny weather in summer, for almost all stove and greenhouse plants then need protection from the direct rays of the sun. Few of them can be successfully grown without shade unless they are in the open air. The shading given should be such as will allow light to pass but in a diffused manner, not as direct rays. A great variety of materials in various thicknesses is available for shading plants. The use of thin blinds on rollers which may be drawn up in dull weather is one of the best, and, because more durable, roller blinds of thin laths are even better. A drawback to the last is that foliage beneath them is apt to be barred with alternate horizontal bands of light and dark green owing to bands of brighter light filtering through the spaces between the laths on to parts of the leaves. This can be avoided by slightly shifting the plants at intervals. Permanent shading has the great disadvantage of preventing sufficient light to pass in dull weather to maintain the essential process of photosynthesis. If blinds cannot be provided the best alternative is to stipple the glass thinly with whiting mixed with milk or some oily substance which will not readily wash off. If white is objected to the shading may be tinted with Brunswick Green. It is very important that this permanent shading should be put on very lightly and the glass should be cleaned as soon as possible as light becomes less intense. Cutting-boxes, hand-glasses, and small propagating-frames may readily be shaded with sheets of paper which can be as easily removed in dull weather. Beds of seedlings in the nursery can also be screened from direct sun quite readily by wicker hurdles or frames of twigs made to rest on uprights placed at convenient distances apart, a few inches above the seedlings. Shading of this kind is most desirable for young seedling trees and shrubs.

SHAG-BARK HICKORY. *See* **Carya ovata.**

shaggy, covered with long, soft hairs.

SHAGGY CAPS. A common name for the edible fungus *Coprinus comatus.*

SHAKING OR QUAKING GRASS. *See* **Briza.**

SHALLON BUSH. *See* **Gaultheria Shallon.**

SHALLOT (*Allium ascalonicum*). A hardy perennial native of Palestine which has been cultivated since ancient times for its bulbs used in flavouring culinary preparations and for pickling, and sometimes for its leaves to be eaten while young and tender. It is essentially a cottage-garden crop though sometimes grown on a larger scale for pickling. The soil should be prepared as for the onion crop, and should be open, deeply worked, and well drained. Heavy, close soil is not suitable. The necessary enrichment of the soil should be effected by manuring for a previous crop. Early planting is essential. The old direction to plant on the shortest and harvest on the longest day should be obeyed in spirit at least, and all planting should be completed by early February and the crop lifted as soon as the leaves turn yellow in late June or July. Shallots may be raised from seed, but there is no advantage in this and the disadvantage that a certain amount of variation occurs, sometimes in the direction of early flowering which is undesirable and leads to some loss of crop. Single bulbs should be planted 4 to 6 in. apart in rows 9 to 12 in. apart, the ground having been lightly rolled, and the bulbs merely pressed in to about half their depth. Care should be taken to free the bulbs from loose scales and dead leaves which attract worms to draw them into their burrows with the result that some of the bulbs may be pulled out of the ground, and the soil should be firmed about the bulbs lest the formation of roots lift them out. Any so displaced should be replanted. Only firm bulbs should be planted. The only treatment needed during growth will be to keep weeds down by hoeing, taking care not to bury the bulbs in the process. The leaves turn yellow when growth is completed and the plants should then be lifted, spread to dry in the sun for 2 or 3 days and then taken in, cleaned of old scales and leaves, and stored in a cool, dry place free from frost. There are 2 or 3 varieties of Shallot, the old true Shallot being the best for most purposes. It is about the size of a small walnut but elongated and narrowed to a point, coppery-red near the base and lighter above, the foliage being green. It does not often run to seed and if thoroughly dried and properly stored keeps well, even until May or June. The Jersey Shallot is as large as a small onion, roundish, with a thin red skin all over, and the foliage is grey-green. It not infrequently runs to seed and though it produces a heavier crop of larger bulbs they keep less well, shrivelling in early spring.

SHAMROCK. Both the White Clover, *Trifolium repens*, and the Yellow Clover, *T. minus*, and possibly some other species of Trifolium as well as the Black Medick, *Medicago lupulina*, are at times said to be the 'true shamrock', the White Clover being the most commonly so named in Ireland. In England the Wood Sorrel, *Oxalis Acetosella*, is not infrequently so called. They all have small 3-foliolate leaves.

SHAMROCK, INDIAN. *See* **Trillium.**

SHAMROCK PEA. *See* **Parochetus communis.**

SHANKING. A term used for disease symptoms in certain plants. In Grapes shanking appears as browning and blackening of the pedicels of the berries, and the latter shrivel up. The trouble may show on all or part of the berries in a bunch, and serious loss may result. In Tulips shanking reveals itself in blackening of the roots and root plate, and when cut open the inside of the bulb is also seen to be discoloured towards the central shoot so that growth of the flower is prevented or dwarfed. Shanking in Grapes is due to poor root growth, while in Tulips the disease is due to attack by a species of Phytophthora.

D. E. G.

A→

SHARP CEDAR. *See* **Acacia Oxycedrus, Juniperus Oxycedrus.**

Shawia'nus -a -um, in honour of W. R. Shaw, 1871–3, botanist of Illinois and Manila.

SHE OAK. *See* **Casuarina stricta.**

SHEARS. Double-bladed cutting instruments, various kinds of which are required in gardens, some for trimming hedges, others for clipping grass edgings, others for pruning. Garden shears for clipping hedges and for topiary work are still in general use. They are made with blades 8 in., 9in., or 10 in. long, with or without a notch at the lower end of the blade to enable thick shoots to be cut. Grass-edging shears are of similar construction except that the blades are set at an angle with the handles and the handles are long so that the work can be done without stooping. The blades are usually 9 in. long, and sometimes a wheel is fitted at the cranked end of the lower blade, but this is rarely an advantage. Like all other cutting instruments the shears must be kept sharp and free from rust and the bolt joining the blades should have any wear taken up so that the edges of the blades meet effectively, and the joint should of course be lubricated. Where large-leaved plants are used for hedges such as Laurels, and even Holly, a knife is a more satisfactory implement for pruning since the work can be done without leaving unsightly cuts on leaves. Spring Grass-shears with flattish blades and metal shanks connected with a metal spring are sometimes used for trimming grass-edges and topiary work. They are about 7 in. long. Pruning-shears are made in several small sizes but are now almost superseded by secateurs (q.v.). A form with strong handles about 3 ft. long, called Parrot-bill shears, is one of the most useful pruning instruments for cutting branches too large for severing with a knife or any other kind of shears. The danger of crushing and bruising by such an instrument used carelessly or in a blunt condition must be borne in mind and guarded against. Hedge-cutting tools made on the principle of the grass-mower used in the hay-field have been made but their use is somewhat limited on account of weight.

SHEATH. A part of a plant rolled round a stem or other body, often formed by a leaf-base or by a spathe.

SHEEP BERRY. *See* **Viburnum Lentago.**

SHEEP LAUREL. *See* **Kalmia angustifolia.**

SHEEP, VEGETABLE. *See* **Raoulia.**

SHEEP'S BEARD. *See* **Urospermum.**

SHEEP'S-BIT SCABIOUS. *See* **Jasione montana.**

SHEEP'S SORREL, *Rumex Acetosella*, a troublesome weed on acid soil, running long distances underground, especially on light land. Where lime can be used without detriment to the plants it is desired to grow it will check and eventually destroy this weed.

SHEET GLASS. This is the best type of glass for glazing horticultural structures, since it is flat and of equal thickness. It may be had in large sheets for cutting up into panes of the sizes required. It is made in various thickness, the sizes being denoted by the weight of a square foot in ounces. 21-oz. glass is thus more expensive than 16-oz. glass as it contains the additional weight in each square foot of surface and is consequently thicker throughout. (*See* **Glass.**)

SHELF FUNGI. *See* **Bracket Fungi.**

SHELL-FLOWER. *See* **Chelone, Moluccella laevis.**

SHELLAC. *See* **Lac.**

SHELLS. Pounded shells have some manurial value, partly on account of their composition, mainly calcium carbonate, partly because of their value in assisting drainage. Broken Cockle-shells are sometimes used for covering benches in greenhouses in place of fine shingle.

SHELTER. The value of shelter in a garden cannot be overestimated. It is of great importance where the cultivation of rather tender trees and shrubs is attempted, and it is of value for fruit-trees, in the kitchen-garden, and in the garden generally. Where natural shelter is not available artificial methods of protection have to be resorted to. It is especially necessary against cold and unfavourable winds and, on the sea-coast, from the prevailing winds and salt spray. Young trees and shrubs in nursery plantations may be effectively sheltered by hedges planted at right angles to each other to form squares. These may be of Beech, Hornbeam, Thorn, Holly, or Yew, or where the climate permits of *Euonymus japonicus*. Any of these can be grown to the desired height and kept thin by trimming. For sheltering alpines and perennials which are not quite hardy, hand-glasses or bell-glasses or cloches are well adapted, and to make assurance doubly sure dry litter or bracken may be scattered over them as well in severe weather. Small hurdles, placed on the coldest or most exposed sides are good for protecting some of the larger specimens, and also for placing over half-hardy shrubs and trees on walls. A covering of bass or straw mats placed over frames in frosty weather, and even ordinary netting placed over wall-trees when in flower, will often enable a crop to be secured that would otherwise be lost. Branches of Spruce may be used for sheltering somewhat tender trees on walls or even in beds. Specimen plants such as shrubs may be preserved by tying stakes together so as to form a sort of hood, something like an extinguisher in shape, covered close down to the bottom with garden mats, so arranged that it may be taken off in mild weather during winter and easily replaced at need. A pane of glass placed over a woolly plant during the wet and cold months will often, though open at the sides, shelter it from excessive wet on the foliage, which is often a greater danger than low temperature.

SHELVES. Boards of various widths, generally about 1 in. thick, are used for standing plants upon in glass-houses. They should be painted the same colour as the rafters and other parts of the woodwork. These shelves may be fixed or movable. A single shelf on the back wall of a lean-to house or suspended by irons from the roof is often a valuable place for growing small plants that need plenty of light. Shelves are sometimes made of flat tiles resting on angle-irons, or slate, or even corrugated iron covered with ashes or small shingle.

SHEPHERD'IA (in honour of John Shepherd, 1764–1836, curator, Bot. Gard., Liverpool). FAM. *Elaeagnaceae*. A genus of 3 N. American deciduous or evergreen shrubs differing from Elaeagnus and Hippophae by their opposite leaves, and flowers with 8 (not 4) stamens, and from Elaeagnus by their dioecious flowers. Flowers in short axillary spikes, or the pistillate solitary. Fruit ovoid, drupe-like. The 2 species in cultivation are hardy silvery-leaved shrubs somewhat resembling Hippophaë, *S. argentea* being sometimes confused with *Elaeagnus argentea*. They grow well in ordinary moist well-drained soil.

S. argent'ea. Buffalo Berry. Deciduous shrub with opposite often spiny branches covered with silvery scales at first. 6 to 12 ft. h. *l.* oblong, ¾ to 2 in. long, obtuse, wedge-shaped at base, silvery-scaly on both sides, scales dentate. *fl.* yellowish. March. *fr.* ovoid, about ⅙ in. long, scarlet, acid but edible. Cent. United States. 1818.

S. canaden'sis. Deciduous shrub, 6 to 8 ft. h., not spiny, shoots covered with brown scales. *l.* wider than in *S. argentea*, oval, ½ to 2 in. long, dull dark green above, densely hairy with numerous brownish scales beneath, scales deeply cleft. *fl.* yellowish. April. *fr.* ovoid, about ⅙ in. long, yellowish-red, insipid, rarely produced in quantity here. Canada, United States. 1759. A yellow-fruited var. (**xanthocarp'a**) is known.

S. × gottingen'sis. (*S. argentea* × *S. canadensis*) has silvery scales cleft about half-way to middle.

Shepherd'ii, in honour of Mr. Henry Shepherd of Liverpool Botanic Garden.

shepherdioi'des, Shepherdia-like.

SHEPHERD'S CLOCK. *See* **Tragopogon pratensis.**

SHEPHERD'S CLUB. *See* **Verbascum Thapsus.**

SHEPHERD'S PURSE. Capsella Bursapastoris, a common English wild flower and weed of gardens.

SHERBOURN'IA (in honour of Mrs. Sherbourn who first flowered *S. foliosa* in England). FAM. *Rubiaceae.* A genus of a single species native in W. Trop. Africa, related to Genipa, and like that having axillary flowers with a single style, but with large sepals. *S. foliosa* needs stove temperature and treatment as for Gardenia.

Sherbournia foliosa

S. folio'sa. Climbing evergreen shrub. *l.* opposite, elliptic to ovate-oblong, acuminate, wedge-shaped, rounded or cordate at base, 2 to 9 in. long, up to 4½ in. wide; stipules caducous, ⅓ to ⅔ in. long. *fl.* white within, blood-red without or orange variegated with red-purple, 1 to 2¾ in. long, fleshy-leathery, rigid, solitary or twin; sep. ¾ to 1 in. long. 1842. (B.M. 4044 as *Gardenia Sherbourniae.*) SYN. *Amaralia bignoniaeflora.*

Sherriffii, in honour of Major G. Sherriff who, with Mr. F. Ludlow and Mrs. Sherriff, has collected extensively in Thibet and Bhutan between 1935 and 1950.

SHIBATAE'A (in honour of K. Shibata, a Japanese botanist). FAM. *Gramineae.* Two species in E. Asia, very distinct from Phyllostachys by the comparatively broad leaves, short branches, and dwarf habit. Quite hardy and easily increased by division.

S. kumasa'sa. Stems tufted usually under 3 ft., very zigzag, slender, flattened between the joints which are 2 to 3½ in. apart; branches 3 or 4 at each joint, each bearing 2 to 4 l. *l.* narrowly ovate, slender-pointed, 3 to 4 in. long, ¾ to 1 in. wide, bright-green, rather glaucous and downy beneath; nerves 5 to 7 each side the mid-rib. Japan. 1861. SYN. *Bambusa ruscifolia, B. viminalis, Phyllostachys ruscifolia.*

W. J. B.

SHIELD-BUDDING. *See* **Budding.**

SHIELD FERN. *See* **Dryopteris Filix-mas.**

SHIELD FLOWER. *See* **Aspidistra.**

shield-shaped, round, oval, or flat with the stalk attached to lower surface; *see* **clypeatus, peltatus, scutatus.**

SHIFT. To move from one receptacle to a larger one, as in 'potting-on'; to move a shrub or tree from one part of the garden to another.

SHINGLE OAK. *See* **Quercus imbricaria.**

SHINGLE PLANT. *See* **Monstera acuminata.**

SHIRLEY POPPY. A race of *Papaver Rhoeas* selected by the Rev. W. Wilks of Shirley, secretary, The Royal Horticultural Society: single poppies without a trace of black, and of shades from white through pink to scarlet (not bluish-purple), self-coloured or picotee-edged.

SHOE FLOWER, SHOEBLACK PLANT. *See* **Hibiscus Rosa-sinensis.**

SHOESTRING FUNGUS. *See* **Honey Fungus.**

SHOLA. *See* **Aeschynomene aspera.**

SHOOT. The developed bud while still green or only half-woody (when it becomes woody it is a branch); a twig; a vigorous stem. A shoot may be of unlimited growth when it terminates in a bud, as in the leading shoots of Conifers, or of limited growth when it ends in a flower or inflorescence, or when the terminal bud aborts, as in Ulmus and in the short shoots of Conifers.

SHOOTING STAR. *See* **Dodecatheon Meadia.**

SHORT-LEAF PINE. *See* **Pinus echinata.**

SHORT'IA (in honour of Dr. Charles W. Short, 1794–1863, botanist, of Kentucky, United States). FAM.

Shortia galacifolia (p. 1949)

Diapensiaceae. A genus of about 8 species of beautiful dwarf perennial herbs, natives of the mountains of Carolina, Formosa, and Japan, related to Galax. Leaves all radical, orbicular or cordate, toothed, persistent, scaly at base, long-stalked. Flowers white or pink, large, on a terminal scape, solitary, nodding or horizontal; calyx 5-parted, with scaly bracts; corolla bell-shaped, 5-lobed; staminodes 5, scale-like, the 5 stamens alternating. Fruit an erect, globose, 3-celled capsule. Woodland soil of leaf-mould or peat and sand in a cool, moist but well-drained spot with semi-shade suits these plants which are good also on the rock-garden and in pots or pans in the alpine house, where indeed *S. uniflora* and especially its fine variety *grandiflora* are seen at their best. The foliage of *S. galacifolia* becomes red in the open in winter and is an added virtue to an already beautiful plant. Seed is rarely available and propagation is by careful division. Transplanted plants need great care to establish them.

S. galacifo'lia.* Tufted, up to about 6 in. h. *l.* all radical, nearly orbicular, about 2 in. across, repand-toothed, shining green, leathery, on long stalks, becoming bronzy-crimson in autumn. *fl.* white, becoming tinged with pink, about 1 in. across; cor. lobes ovate-oblong, deeply crenate, tube short, funnel-shaped; scapes red, slender, 4 to 5 in. long. Spring, early summer. N. Carolina. 1881. (B.M. 7082.) Rock-garden or woodland. A pink-fld. form is known.

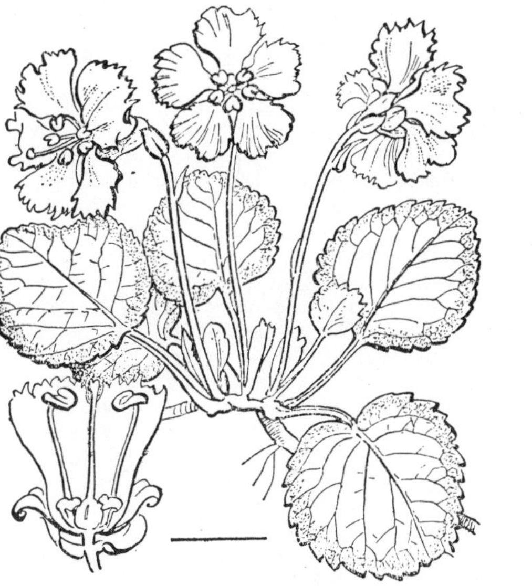

Shortia uniflora

S. uniflo'ra.* More apt to run than *S. galacifolia* with thinner *l.*, sinuately toothed, retuse at tip. *fl.* pale pink veined white, about 1 in. across; stamens white. Spring. Japan. (B.M. 8166.) var. **grandiflo'ra,*** *fl.* 1½ in. across, more freely produced than in the species. Rock-garden in semi-shade, or alpine house. A very beautiful plant. Colour of flower variable from white to rose.

SHOT, INDIAN. *See* **Canna indica.**

SHOT-BORER BEETLES, including the Shot Hole Borer, *Anisandrus dispar,* and the Flat-celled Shot Borer, *Xyleborus saxeseni,* are often referred to as 'Ambrosia Beetles'; they live in association with a fungus that occurs in their tunnels. They bore into the stem and branches of many deciduous fruit and forest trees, being partial to Plum, Apple, and Oak. *A. dispar* is a pitchy-black or dark-brownish beetle, the female being ⅛ in. long while the male is much smaller. The female bores into the heartwood of the stems and larger branches, and makes passages in which are deposited white eggs in cavities at the entrance to these tunnels. The white, legless grubs feed in the galleries during the summer months, though the adults are found in the tunnels throughout the year. Their exit holes resemble the effect of a charge of shot fired at the affected tree. *X. saxeseni* differs from *A. dispar* in the form of its gallery, the brood-tunnels being narrow and flat as compared with the cylindrical tunnels made by the Shot Hole Borer, and sapwood rather than heartwood is preferred. These beetles often abound in trees that are not in full vigour either as a result of unhealthy root action arising from waterlogging or prolonged periods of drought, or from bacterial and fungal infection, though healthy trees are occasionally attacked.

Their control is difficult because of their mode of feeding deep within the stems or branches. Dead and dying limbs are often the first to be attacked, so that all such branches should be removed from fruit and ornamental trees. The stems of standard and half-standard fruit-trees attacked by these pests should be sprayed in March or April with a 10 per cent. Tar-distillate wash. Special care should be taken in applying the wash to avoid spraying any growing portion of the tree, otherwise severe injury will be done to the young shoots, buds, and foliage. The effect is to drive the beetles from their galleries and they are killed as they come into contact with the deposit of spray liquid on the bark.

G. F. W.

SHOTHOLE or **SHOTHOLING.** A term for the lesions on leaves in which small areas of dead or diseased tissues fall out, leaving a circular or slightly irregular hole. The death of the areas may be caused by a bacterial or fungus parasite or may result from non-parasitic factors such as drought or frost injury, but the appearance is known as 'shothole'. In general the stone fruit trees seem to be more susceptible to this kind of trouble, which is common in Peaches. It must be remembered that perforations very much resembling shothole may be caused by the effect of spraying with a too strong spray solution.

D. E. G.

SHOVELS. Shovels are needed for various purposes in the garden. They are lighter than spades and better adapted for shifting light soil, short loose manure, sand, gravel, &c. Square-topped shovels have the 2 side edges slightly turned up and are the most generally useful. Stoke-hole shovels should be made chiefly or entirely of iron to withstand the heat to which they are subject in stoking. The pan of the stoking shovel is best made long and not very wide as it may then be readily emptied into the furnace without coming into contact with the front which is often narrow.

SHOWERS OF SULPHUR. The pollen of pines is often carried to the ground by showers and there forms sulphur-coloured patches.

SHREDS. Usually small pieces of cloth are used to secure wall-trees and their growths in their proper positions. Waste cloth may sometimes be purchased from tailors or drapers for the purpose. This is cut into narrow strips of a length to suit requirements, and after being passed round the shoot is nailed to the wall. Balls of suitable material and also specially treated—'medicated'—red or green cloth cut in pieces from 2 to 5 in. long are also procurable from horticultural sundriesmen. It is an excellent plan to take all wall-trees away from the wall and burn the shreds annually as they form harbours for insects and their eggs. To avoid the need for this and the damage liable to be caused to the walls by nailing, walls for trees and climbers are now furnished with wires stretched vertically or horizontally to which the shoots are tied.

SHRUB. A perennial plant with many persistent woody stems from or near the base. If the woody part is confined to the lower portion of the plant while the upper shoots are soft, the term sub-shrub is applied.

SHRUBBERY. Part of the garden devoted to shrubs. In the past it has too often been a neglected area overcrowded with quick-growing shrubs which, with age, have lost any charm they once possessed and having become a tangled mass of starved and leggy individuals of no interest or beauty, serving merely to fill the ground and perhaps hide something even more ugly than themselves. Initially well chosen and properly planted, and afterwards given the small amount of attention they annually need, a garden of shrubs can be a thing of beauty and of interest at all seasons of the year and for year after year for a long time. It may, instead of being a place of less than no account, give a feeling of peace and permanence to a garden which no other place except an old wood with healthy trees lifting up their straight trunks to hold up the green canopy above can give; and like such a wood it may give a home to the wild creatures which most lovers of gardens like to see and hear about them.

SHRUBS AND TREES FOR FORCING. There is a great variety of hardy trees and shrubs well suited for forcing, both for providing cut flowers and for the embellishment of the conservatory and greenhouse during the early months of the year.

Enormous quantities were imported before the war from the Continent, notably Indian Azaleas from Belgium, and hardy Azaleas of the Ghent type, and many other trees and shrubs from Holland.

Being specially grown for this purpose they arrived with a more or less restricted root system which rendered them suitable for immediate transference to small or moderate-sized pots, the Azaleas especially, with the fine and compact root system, being easily handled and forcing readily without being established for a season. This is not true of many of the trees and shrubs used for this purpose, the best results only being obtained when they are established in pots or tubs. This applies especially to the ornamental flowering-trees, such as the many beautiful varieties of Malus and Prunus. These give a better and more lasting display when established for a season in their flowering-pots, and they may be grown successfully for several years, provided they are given proper care in watering and feeding.

Some shrubs, if specially grown for the purpose, lifted from the open and potted up during October, will give quite good results. Whether for the embellishment of the conservatory or for exhibition it is very important to keep up a successful stock of young plants, either by home propagation, or by the purchase of young stock, for growing on.

Purchased plants should be potted as soon as received, and the pots plunged to the rim in a bed of ashes, in a sheltered but sunny position, protecting the pots from frost by loose litter or bracken. As already stated under Azalea, those of the Indian group need the protection of the cold frame or greenhouse. The longer they can be exposed in the open the more readily they will respond to forcing. It is important to start with the plants that naturally flower early. Some shrubs, such as Lilacs, Staphyleas, Spiraeas, and some Rhododendrons, may be had in flower at Christmas, but unless specially required there is not much to be gained by too early forcing. The quality and the lasting properties of the flowers are much inferior in those forced early than in those brought on later in much less heat. February, March, and April are the months when they are at their best, for at this period they come on more naturally and do not require so much heat. It is a mistake to give these shrubs too much heat to start with. For the first fortnight the temperature should not exceed 45 to 50° F., afterwards increasing it to 60° F. or more with sun heat. While in the forcing house the plants should be syringed several times during the day with tepid water.

Before removing them to the conservatory or show house they should be given more air and a slightly lower temperature.

The proper care and maintenance of a collection of forcing plants require a good deal of experience of the different plants used. After flowering they must on no account be neglected—as is too often the case—but should be returned to a cool house to complete their growth before they are put outdoor for the summer. Such as require it should be pruned and weak wood cut out. This applies especially to shrubs that flower on the previous year's wood. With such plants all the old flowering wood should be cut out and strong young growths encouraged. *Deutzia gracilis* and *Prunus triloba plena* may be taken as good examples of this class of plant. Beyond removing weak wood, most of the flowering trees should require little or no pruning. While some may be forced several years in succession, others require to be planted out for a season to recover, or be replaced by young stock. This applies to most of the Spiraeas, Ghent Azaleas, and Lilacs, the latter being pruned hard back and encouraged to make a restricted number of strong young shoots. When they have completed their growth the roots should be cut round with a sharp spade; this check helps to mature the wood and flower-buds to set, and they can then be lifted with a compact ball of roots.

The nursery ground should be in an open sunny position where the plants will get the full benefit of sun and air.

The following is a list of some of the most useful and popular shrubs and trees used for forcing: *Acer japonicum*, *A. palmatum* in variety, and *A. Negundo variegata*, all used for their foliage; *Amelanchier canadensis*, *A. laevis*, and *A. oblongifolia*, *Ceanothus divaricatus*, *C. dentatus*, *C. papillosus*, *C. rigidus*, and *C. Veitchianus*, *Clematis* in variety, *Crataegus* (the coloured thorns both single and double force readily), *Cytisus* (pot-grown brooms in variety are popular, but require frequent renewal as they are short-lived), *Deutzia corymbiflora*, *D. gracilis* and its varieties or hybrids, such as *campanulata*, *carminea*, *eximia*, and *rosea*, *D. Lemoinei* and *D. scabra*, *Diervilla* in variety, *Forsythia intermedia spectabilis* and *F. suspensa*, *Hydrangea opuloides* (*Hortensis*) in great variety and *H. paniculata grandiflora*, *Kerria japonica plena*, *Laburnum alpinum*, *L. Watereri*, and *L. Vossii*, *Magnolia denudata*, *M. Soulangiana*, and several hybrids, such as *Alexandrina*, *Norberti*, *speciosa*, *superba*, and *spectabilis*, all hybrids between *M. denudata* and *M. obovata*, also *M. stellata*, *Paeonia suffruticosa* (Tree Paeony) in many beautiful varieties, *Philadelphus* (many of the smaller growing hybrids, both single and double-flowered, are excellent for forcing), *Pieris floribunda* and *P. japonica*, *Prunus communis* (Almond), *P. cerasifera atropurpurea*, *Blireiana*, and *Moseri*, *P. japonica plena*, *P. persica* (double-flowering Peaches, of which there are many varieties ranging in colour from white to rose and deep crimson), the 'Japanese Cherries' in many varieties, *P. subhirtella* and *P. triloba plena*, *Malus floribunda* and var. *atrosanguinea*, *M. Scheideckeri*, and *M. spectabilis*; Rhododendron which includes the Ghent and Mollis Azaleas, and the many varieties of *R. obtusum* (Kurume) and *R. Kaempferi*. Many of the evergreen hybrid Rhododendrons are suitable for this purpose, especially those with *caucasicum* blood in them as they naturally flower early, such as Cunningham's White, *Nobleanum*, *Rosa Mundi*, *sulphureum*, and *venustum*; they, along with *R.* × *praecox* and *R. Rosy Bell*, may be had in flower from Christmas onwards. For later there is ample choice from the many earlier flowering garden hybrids; a few of them are Alice, Cynthia, *Everestianum*, *fastuosum flore pleno*, Gomer Waterer, Grand Arab, Loder's White, Mrs. E. C. Stirling, Pink Pearl, Prince Camille de Rohan, Prof. Hugo de Vries, and White Pearl.

(The individual flowers of the large-flowered Ghent and Mollis Azaleas are very short-lived, falling off in a few days. However, if a drop of floral gum is dropped into the base of each flower they will remain fresh on the plant for over a week.)

Spiraea arguta, S. prunifola plena, S. Thunbergii, and *S. Van Houttei, Staphylea colchica, Syringa* (Lilac); a few varieties are largely used by market growers for early forcing; they include Charles X, Marie Legraye, J. C. van Tol, Souv. de Louis Spath, Alphonse Lavallée, Mme. Lemoine, and President Grevy), *Viburnum Carlesii, V. Opulus plenum, V. Tinus,* and *V. tomentosum* and var. *plicatum, Wisteria chinensis, Zenobia speciosa, Z. pulverulenta.*

J. C.

Shuttlewor'thii, in honour of Mr. Shuttleworth who collected plants for Mr. Bull, nurseryman, of Chiswick, about 1875.

sia'mensis -is -e, of Siam.

SIBBALD'IA (in honour of Robert Sibbald, 1643–1720, Professor of Medicine in Edinburgh). FAM. *Rosaceae.* A genus of about 10 species of dwarf perennial herbs, mostly natives of the mountains of Asia, closely related to Potentilla and sometimes combined with it. The chief distinguishing characters lie in the fewer (5 to 12) carpels and (5, rarely 4 to 10) stamens. Leaves digitate. Flowers greenish, inconspicuous. *S. procumbens,* which occurs wild in Britain, is sometimes offered for the rock-garden and calls for a cool, shady place suitable for better plants.

S. procum'bens. More or less spreading perennial with many sterile leafy shoots with long stalks and flowering shoots 4 to 12 in. h. with scattered smaller, short-stalked l. *l.* 3-foliolate; lflets. obovate, ½ to 1 in. long, 3- to 6-toothed at tip. *fl.* in close terminal cymes, about ¼ in. across; pet. orange-yellow, small and narrow, or absent. Alpine and Arctic Europe, N. Asia, N. America.

SIBERIAN CEDAR. *See* **Pinus Cembra.**

SIBERIAN CRAB. *See* **Malus prunifolia.**

SIBERIAN PEA-TREE. *See* **Caragana arborescens.**

SIBIRAE'A (from *Siberia,* the home of *S. laevigata*). FAM. *Rosaceae.* A genus of 2 Asiatic species of deciduous shrubs allied to Spiraea and sometimes included in that genus, distinguished by the entire leaves; flowers small, frequently dioecious, in terminal panicles; carpels joined at base. Treatment as for Spiraea.

S. altaiens'is. A synonym of *S. laevigata.*

S. laeviga'ta. A glabrous shrub about 3 ft. h. and often twice as wide with purple or reddish-brown shoots. *l.* entire, oblong, narrower at base, 2 to 4½ in. long, mucronate, sessile, glaucous. *fl.* white, tinged with rose, dioecious; male panicles larger and looser, in longer, interrupted racemes; female panicles smaller and more dense, in closely packed, continuous racemes of smaller flowers. June. Siberia. 1774. SYN. *S. altaiensis, Spiraea laevigata.* The shrub when not in flower bears a great resemblance to *Daphne Mezereum,* or a Euphorbia. var. **angusta'ta** has narrow *l.* and a somewhat downy *infl.* China. 1908. A var. **croat'ica** occurs in SE. Europe.

S. tomento'sa. Shrub of about 18 in. *l.* oblong-lanceolate or oblong-obovate, acute, mucronate, densely silky-hairy beneath. *fl.* yellowish-green, in dense panicles about 2 in. long. SW. China. 1915.

sibi'ricus -a -um, Siberian.

SIBTHORP'IA (in honour of Dr. John Sibthorp, 1758–96, Professor of Botany, Oxford, originator of the magnificent *Flora Graeca*). FAM. *Scrophulariaceae.* A genus of about 6 species of prostrate, perennial, hairy herbs, rooting at the nodes and forming a carpet, natives of W. Europe, Trop. and NW. Africa, Nepal, and S. America. Leaves alternate or clustered, stalked, roundish kidney-shaped, deeply toothed. Flowers yellow or reddish in leaf-axils, small calyx bell-shaped, 4- or 5- to 8-cleft; corolla tube short, lobes and stamens as many as, or more than, calyx lobes, or stamens 1 less; petals spreading. The variegated form of the British *S. europaea* is sometimes grown in light well-drained soil on the rock-garden, but is best in a cool house. *S. peregrina* needs the greenhouse and should be raised so as to display the pendent branches with their small yellow flowers. Propagation by division or cuttings put in a shady place. **A**

S. europae'a. Cornish Moneywort. Hairy perennial with filiform creeping stems 6 to 14 in. long. *l.* 7- to 9-lobed, thin, up to ⅜ in. wide; lobes broad, rounded. *fl.* minute, pink and yellowish; stamens 4. W. England and Ireland, France, Spain, Portugal. (E.B. 969). var. **variega'ta,** *l.* slightly larger than in type, bright golden-green with silvery markings.

S. peregri'na. Hairy, trailing perennial. *l.* much crenated, small. *fl.* yellow, about ⅛ in. across, 5- to 8-parted; peduncles often clustered, 2 in. long. Madeira. 1771. (B.M. 218 as *Disandra prostrata.*) Greenhouse.

Sibthorp'ii, Sibthorpia'nus -a -um, in honour of Professor Dr. John Sibthorp. See above. **A**

SICA'NA (Peruvian name). FAM. *Cucurbitaceae.* A genus of 3 species of tall climbing herbs differing from Cucurbita by the somewhat reflexed calyx lobes, connate filaments, and usually free anthers. Leaves palmately 3- to 9-lobed. Flowers monoecious, rather large, solitary; corolla inflated bell-shaped, 5-lobed above the middle. Fruit large, fleshy, many-seeded, fragrant, edible. For treatment of these greenhouse plants *see* **Gourds.**

S. atropurpu'rea. Strong climbing herb. *l.* lobed, large, reddish-violet beneath. *fr.* purplish-violet, shorter than in *S. odorifera,* strongly perfumed. Uruguay. 1892. (R.H. 1894, 108.)

S. odorif'era. Curuba. Climber to 40 or 50 ft. *l.* nearly round, 5 to 10 in. across, deeply cordate, 5- to 7-lobed. *fl.* axillary; cor. small, urn-shaped, lobes reflexed; ovary 2 in. to 2½ in. long. *fr.* yellow then orange, cylindrical, glabrous, something like a large Cucumber, with a strong aromatic odour; flesh pale yellow, edible. Brazil. 1889. (R.H. 1890, 516.) Fruit said to act as a preventive of the attacks of noxious insects upon the person and upon garments.

S. sphaer'ica. Nearly glabrous climber. *l.* kidney-shaped, 3 to 4 in. across, deeply 3- to 5-lobed, deeply cordate. *Male fl.* golden-yellow, spreading bell-shaped, 4 in. across, downy without; anthers joined. September. *fr.* globose, about as large as a small orange.

F. G. P.

sic'ulus -a -um, Sicilian.

SIC'YOS (ancient Greek name used by Theophrastus for the related Cucumber). FAM. *Cucurbitaceae.* A genus of about 50 species of climbing or prostrate annual herbs, natives of the warmer parts of America, the Pacific Is., and Australia. They are very rapid climbers but have little beauty. Leaves angular or lobed, rarely deeply 3- to 5-lobed. Flowers small, monoecious. Fruit compressed or angular, rarely over an inch long. They are half-hardy but may be grown in the open where they are sown. *S. angulatus* is the most easily grown.

S. angulat'us. Bur Cucumber. Vigorous climbing annual. *l.* broadly ovate with 5 shallow lobes, stalk slender, glandular-hairy. *fl.* small, whitish. *fr.* ovoid, 1-seeded. United States.

F. G. P.

SI'DA (ancient Greek name used by Theophrastus for the Water-lily). FAM. *Malvaceae.* A genus of about 120 species of herbs, sub-shrubs, or shrubs, natives of the tropics, most species being American. Leaves alternate. Flowers sometimes showy, sessile or stalked, solitary or clustered, axillary or in terminal heads, spikes or racemes; calyx 5-toothed or cleft; petals 5; stamens numerous, their filaments joined into a columnar tube; bracteoles absent or distant from the calyx. The Sidas mostly need stove conditions and will grow in any rich soil. *S. Hermaphrodita* is hardy and can be increased by seeds; the others by cuttings in heat. Many plants once included here are now classed under Abutilon.

S. Hermaphrodi'ta. Herbaceous perennial, 4 to 10 ft. h., smooth. *l.* 5-cleft; lobes oblong, pointed, toothed. *fl.* white, in corymbs; carpels 10, pointed. Summer. N. America. (B.M. 2913 as *Sida Napaea.*) Hardy, succeeding with same treatment as the Hollyhock.

S. Napae'a of Bot. Mag. A synonym of *S. Hermaphrodita.*

S. rhombifo'lia. Evergreen sub-shrub. *l.* variable, lanceolate to rhomboid-lanceolate, often hoary beneath. *fl.* axillary, solitary, pale yellow (or rarely white), blotched red at base. Tropics. Grown in India for the excellent fibre it yields.

S. sessiliflo'ra. A synonym of *Abutilon crispum*.

F. G. P.

SIDAL'CEA (*Sida* and *Alcea*). FAM. *Malvaceae.* A genus of about 8 species of mostly perennial herbs with the habit of Malva, natives of Western N. America. Leaves palmately lobed or parted. Flowers sessile or shortly pedicellate, in terminal spikes or racemes; calyx 5-cleft, usually without bracteoles; corolla spreading, white to rose-purple; stamens many united in 2 series (in 1 only in Malva); styles with thread-like branches (stigma not capitate as in Sida and Sphaeralcea). Hardy border perennials so far as named below, and in recent years improved in habit and length of flowering as well as in colour by selection of seedlings mainly from *S. malvaeflora* and its variety *Listeri*. The named forms must be propagated by division; the species also by seed. Hollyhock rust (*see* **Hollyhock**) sometimes attacks Sidalceas.

S. campest'ris. 2 to 5 ft. h., somewhat hairy. *Lower l.* rounded, variously lobed; *upper* 5- to 7-parted, lobes narrow. *fl.* purplish, 1½ in. across, in strict spike-like racemes; pet. often toothed. Western N. America.

S. can'dida. 2 to 3 ft. h. *l.* roundish, 7-lobed, glabrous and glossy; stalks long. *fl.* white, 1 in. across, in spike-like racemes, freely produced. Colorado. 1882. var. **incarna'ta,** *fl.* flesh-coloured.

S. List'eri. A variety of *S. malvaeflora*.

Sidalcea malvaeflora

S. malvaeflo'ra. Slender, twiggy, 1½ to 3 ft. h. *Radical l.* roundish, 5- to 9-lobed or crenately cut; *stem-l.* deeply 7- to 9-cleft, segs. 3-lobed, toothed at tip, the uppermost entire. *fl.* lilac, about 2 in. across; racemes many-fld.; pedicels twice as long as cal. Summer. California. 1838. (B.R. 1036 as *Sida malvaeflora*; G.F. 737 as *Callirhoe spicata*.) var. **List'eri,** *fl.* pink, 1½ in. across, fringed, spreading. 1897. Of garden origin. Many forms of this species have been raised; **atropurpur'ea,** *fl.* dark purple; **maria'na,** *fl.* deep rosy crimson; **mexica'na,** *fl.* satiny rose. SYN. *S. mexicana*, a garden name.

S. orega'na. Related to *S. campestris* but stem only downy, the racemes branched and panicled, *fl.* smaller, cal. greyish-hairy. Oregon.

S. spica'ta. 1 to 3 ft. h., scarcely branched, usually more or less hairy, lobes of upper l. linear, often deeply cut. *fl.* about 1 in. across, purplish, in an oblong, interrupted spike; pedicels hardly developed. Western N. America.

SIDE-GRAFTING. A method of grafting enabling a branch or stem to be supplied when one is deficient; it may be practised without removal of the head of the stock. *See* **Grafting.**

SIDE-SADDLE FLOWER. *See* **Sarracenia.**

side'reus -a -um, iron-hard.

SIDERI'TIS (ancient Greek name used by Dioscorides, reputed to heal wounds inflicted by iron, *sideros*). FAM. *Labiatae.* A genus of about 50 species of woolly or softly hairy herbs, sub-shrubs, or shrubs, natives of the Canaries and the Mediterranean region, especially in the east. Leaves entire or toothed. Flowers small, often yellowish, produced in summer; calyx tubular with 5 usually spiny teeth; corolla tube within the calyx, limb bilabiate, upper lip, emarginate or 2-fid, lower 3-fid, middle lobe much the largest; stamens 4; whorls 6- to many flowered, axillary, or in interrupted or dense spikes. Nutlets ovoid, smooth. Some species are hardy, some half-hardy; they do best in dry, sandy or chalky soils. Propagation by seed, by cuttings, or by division.

S. canarien'sis. Shrub, several ft. h. *l.* ovate, crenate, cordate at base, 2 to 4 in. long, wrinkled, velvety. *fl.* with cor. scarcely longer than the cal., upper lip 2-fid, lower spreading; whorls 20- to 30-fld. in simple racemes. Teneriffe. 1869. (Ref. B. 160.) Greenhouse.

S. can'dicans. Habit of *S. canariensis*, but wholly white-woolly, about 3 ft. h. *l.* ovate, slightly crenate, truncately cordate at base, thick. *fl.* scarcely exceeding calyx, in usually 10-fld. whorls, lower distant. Teneriffe. 1714. Greenhouse.

S. inca'na. Sub-shrub about 1 ft. h. Branches white-woolly. *l.* oblong-linear, obtuse, entire, ½ to 1½ in. long, white-woolly, sessile. *fl.* in distant about 6-fld. whorls; cal. white-woolly. Spain. 1752. Half-hardy.

S. perfolia'ta. Sub-shrub, 1 to 1½ ft. h., branches erect. *l.* ovate-oblong to lanceolate, softly hairy, 1½ to 2 in. long, half amplexicaul; bracts spreading. *fl.* sessile, in distinct, rather distant whorls; cor. scarcely longer than cal. S. Europe. Half-hardy.

S. scordioi'des. Sub-shrub, about 1 ft. h. *l.* ovate, oblong or oblong-linear, narrowed at base, sharply toothed; bracts broad, spiny. *fl.* yellowish, upper lip paler or whitish, scarcely longer than cal.; spikes 1 to 3 in. long; whorls sometimes interrupted. S. Europe. 1597. Hardy, variable. var. **alpi'na,** branches short, decumbent. *l.* oblong-ovate, at first grey-hairy then glabrous, teeth few, *fl.* in dense whorls in a spike. Pyrenees. 1827; **angustifo'lia,** *l.* oblong-linear, almost glabrous. Pyrenees. 1597; **elonga'ta,** branches long, ascending or erect, *l.* oblong or oblong-lanceolate, sharply toothed, nearly glabrous, *fl.* in usually interrupted spikes. Spain. 1822.

S. tau'rica. Sub-shrub, 18 in. h. *l.* oblong-lanceolate or spatulate, narrowed at base, lower crenulate, densely white-woolly, thick. *fl.* with cor. slightly exceeding cal. Tauria. 1822. Hardy.

sideromal'lus -a -um, having rust-coloured hair.

SIDEROXY'LON dulcif'icum. Miraculous Berry of W. Africa, has a very sweet tasting fruit but is of no garden value in Britain.

Sie'beri, in honour of F. W. Sieber, 1785–1844, of Prague, botanist who travelled in the East, tropical E. Africa, Mauritius, and the W. Indies.

Sieboldia'nus -a -um, Siebold'ii, in honour of Philipp Franz von Siebold, 1796–1866, who travelled officially for Holland in, and introduced many plants from, Japan.

SIEGESBECK'IA (in honour of John George Siegesbeck, 1686–1755, physician and botanist of Leipzig, director of Botanic Garden, St. Petersburg). FAM. *Compositae.* A genus of 2 species of usually annual herbs, one widely distributed over warm regions of the world, the other a native of Peru. Leaves opposite, lobed. Flower-heads yellow or white, small, sub-radiate, panicled; involucral bracts few, green; receptacle small. Achenes glabrous. *S. orientalis* is half-hardy. Seeds should be raised in heat in spring and the seedlings planted outdoors at the end of May.

S. orienta'lis. About 2 ft. h. *l.* ovate-triangular, wedge-shaped at base, slender-pointed, deeply toothed. *fl.-heads* yellow; outer involucral bracts 3 or 4 times as long as inner. August. Tropics. 1824. (B.R. 1061; S.B.F.G. 203 as *S. droserioides.*) Several forms of this widely distributed species have received specific names.

Siehea'nus -a -um, in honour of Walther Siehe, 1859–1928, of Berlin, and Mersina, Asia Minor, who introduced many plants of Asia Minor into cultivation.

SIEVEKINGIA (in honour of Dr. Sieveking, Burgomaster of Hamburg in 1871). FAM. *Orchidaceae.* A genus of 5 or 6 species of epiphytic orchids, allied to Lacaena, natives of Ecuador, Guiana, Costa Rica, &c. Flowers in arching or pendulous few-flowered scapes; sepals fleshy, free or very nearly so; petals similar to the dorsal sepal, sometimes fringed on margins; lip sessile on the column base, somewhat ventricose, more or less 3-lobed; column erect. Pollinia 2. Pseudobulbs rather small, carrying a single, plicately veined shortly stalked leaf. Compost, temperature, &c., should be as for Stanhopeas.

S. Jenman'ii. *fl.* 2 or 3, reddish-yellow; disk of lip with serrated keels. Brazil, British Guiana. 1886.

S. peruvia'na. *fl.* 2 to 6, about 1 in. long, yellow; sep. and pet. elliptic, pointed; lip broad. Peru. Before 1911.

Sievekingia Reichenbachiana

S. Reichenbachia'na. *fl.* about 6, 2 in. across, in a pendulous corymb; sep. pale straw-colour, concave; pet. narrower, like lip fringed with deep-yellow hairs; lip blotched red; peduncle 2 in. long. *Pseudobulbs* 1 in. long, clustered. *l.* 6 in. long, 1½ in. wide, solitary, elliptic-lanceolate, plicate, prominently ribbed; petioles red-speckled. Ecuador. 1890. (B.M. 7576.) Sometimes placed in a separate genus as *Gorgoglossum Reichenbachiana.*

S. suav'is. *fl.* 2 to 3, short-lived; sep. ovate, acute, concave, ¾ in. long, greenish-yellow; pet. smaller, deep yellow; lip ventricose, deep yellow, dotted black. From the crest proceeds a narrow keel with a 2-lobed scale in middle. *Pseudobulbs* small, ovoid. *l.* elliptical-oblong, acute, 5 to 6 in. long. Costa Rica. 1868.

E. C.

SIEVERS'IA. Included in **Geum.**

Sievers'ii, in honour of Johann Sievers, 1731–1801, General and Governor of Novgorod 1783.

SIEVES. Sieves are in frequent demand in the garden for sifting soil, &c., for potting and for screening gravel and sand. The best for the potting-shed work are round sieves with elm rings 3½ in. deep and strong wire of $\frac{3}{16}$ in. *¼ in., ⅜ in., *½ in., *¾ in., and 1 in. mesh, those marked * being the most useful. There is a regrettable tendency to use too fine a sieve in the preparation of composts and this should be guarded against at all times. Only on rare occasions when very fine seed is sown should anything less than ¼ in. sieve be used for preparing the covering, and usually nothing finer than ½ in. for other purposes. Screens for cinders, gravel, &c., are oblong with deal frames 5½ to 6 ft. long and 2 ft. 9 in. to 3 ft. wide, strengthened with galvanized iron at the corners, the meshes ¼ in., ½ in., or ¾ in. Sieves for cleaning dry, ripe seeds are specially made in different sizes.

SIGMATOSTA'LIX (*sigma, sigmatos,* S-shaped, *stalix,* a stake). FAM. *Orchidaceae.* A genus comprising about a dozen species of dwarf, epiphytic orchids, natives of Trop. America. Flowers mediocre or rather small, short-stalked, scattered, racemose; sepals and petals free; claw of the lip long, often 2-keeled; the blade often acute or recurved at tip, peduncles axillary under the 1- or 2-leaved pseudobulbs. Leaves narrow, often grass-like. Few of the species are yet in cultivation. Though small the flowers are attractive from their numbers and graceful spikes. The intermediate house suits them as regards temperatures. The compost used should be that advised for Odontoglossums. Small pans which can be

Sigmatostalix costaricensis (p. 1954)

suspended can generally be used, but *S. radicans* and similar species which have the pseudobulbs slightly distant on the rhizome show to better advantage when placed on rafts. The flowering season is usually autumn, but irregular.

S. bicornu'ta. *fl.* small, yellow with a deep purple-red stripe on dorsal sep. and pet. The pet. bear a pair of fleshy conical horns. Allied to *S. graminea.* Peru. 1912.

S. costaricen'sis.* *fl.* 9 to 12, small; sep. and slightly narrower pet. about $\frac{1}{2}$ in. long, reflexed, greenish-yellow with a central zone of red-brown; lip broadly cordate, reflexed at sides, bright yellow with a half-circle of velvety red-brown at base, side lobes fleshy, yellow, hook-like; column nearly erect, yellowish-green, barred brown, cap bright yellow. Scapes thin, stiff. *Pseudobulbs* clustered, 1 to $1\frac{1}{2}$ in. h., 1-leaved. *l.* narrowly lanceolate, channelled, about 3 in. h. Costa Rica. 1915. (B.M. 8825.)

S. E'liae. *fl.* many, yellow, spotted with red-brown on lip; racemes comparatively long. Velez. 1908.

S. gramin'ea. *fl.* very small, light yellow, purple spotted; scapes short, few-fld. *Pseudobulbs* small, 1-leaved. *l.* linear, 1 to 2 in. long. Peru. 1852? (R.X.O. 1, 8.)

S. guatemalen'sis. Possibly the proper name of *S. costaricensis.*

S. malleif'era.* *fl.* yellow, brown-spotted; sep. and pet. ligulate-triangular, acute; lip 3-parted, divisions linear, emarginate; callus hammer-like; raceme slender. *Pseudobulbs* dark brown, oblong, $1\frac{1}{2}$ in. long, $\frac{1}{2}$ in. broad. *l.* light green, cuneate-ligulate, 5 in. long, $\frac{1}{2}$ in. broad. New Granada. 1883.

S. peruvia'na. Sep. and pet. straw- or stone-colour with a dark band at base of upper sep. and pet.; lip light yellow, disk orange-yellow. Smaller than *S. radicans.* Peru. 1910.

S. radi'cans.* *fl.* small, 6 to 12; sep. and pet. greenish-yellow, reflexed; lip broader, white, recurved with 2 small horn-like side lobes, crest tumid, yellow; column erect, dark brown or purplish; scapes about 6 in. h., slender. *Pseudobulbs* compressed, tapered, 1 to $1\frac{1}{2}$ in. h., at intervals on rhizomes, 2-leaved. *l.* linear, 6 in. long. Brazil. 1860? (B.M. 9307.)

E. C.

sigmoid, somewhat resembling the form of the letter S.

signa'tus -a -um, well marked.

sikkimen'sis -is -e, of Sikkim, N. India.

sikokia'nus -a -um, of the Is. of Shikoku, Japan.

SILE'NE (name quoted by Theophrastus for Viscaria). FAM. *Caryophyllaceae.* Catchfly. A genus of over 300 annual or perennial herbs, very rarely sub-shrubs, natives of the N. Hemisphere and S. Africa. Leaves opposite, entire. Flowers solitary or in 1-sided spikes, or in panicles; calyx tubular, 5-toothed or -cleft, usually 10-nerved; petals 5, entire, 2-fid or sometimes laciniate, with a narrow claw, and frequently with 2 scales at the base of the lamina; stamens 10; ovary superior, styles 3 or 5. Fruit a capsule with 3 or 5 divisions at base, opening with twice as many teeth as styles. Seeds many. Several species are useful rock-plants, others good for the open border, and most succeed in a light loamy soil. Many species, however, are weedy plants and are ignored below. They are propagated by seed, cuttings, or division. *S. pendula* is often grown for spring bedding the seed being sown early in the previous autumn. **A**

S. acau'lis. Moss Campion. Cushion Pink. Densely tufted, bright green, perennial cushion about 2 in. h. *l.* very close-set, linear, acute or obtuse, $\frac{1}{4}$ to $\frac{1}{2}$ in. long, ciliate at base, keeled beneath. *fl.* solitary, on a very short stem, $\frac{1}{8}$ to $\frac{1}{2}$ in. across; cal. reddish or purple, bell-shaped; cor. rose, pink, or white, pet. notched. June to August. N. Hemisphere from Arctic south to Spain, including Britain. (L.B.C. 568; E.B. 205.) Easily grown in light soil in sun, but rarely flowers freely; best on moraine. A very variable plant. var. **al'ba,** *fl.* white; **au'rea,** *l.* yellowish; **dianthifo'lia,** a synonym of var. *pannonica*; **elonga'ta,** *see* **S. elongata**; **exsca'pa,** *l.* very short, erect, *fl.* small, sessile or nearly so, pale pink. Pyrenees, Aragon, Nova Zembla; **flo're plen'o,** *see* **S. elongata Correvoniana**; **grandiflo'ra,** *fl.* brighter and larger than type, stems longer; **pannon'ica,** loosely tufted, often yellowish-green, *fl.* larger than type. Carpathians.

S. alpes'tris. A synonym of *Heliosperma alpestre. See also* **S. rupestris.**

S. alpi'na. A name variously applied, originally to *Heliosperma alpestre.*

S. alta'ica. Stem erect, branched from a woody base. *Lower l.* linear, rigid, somewhat spine-tipped, somewhat scabrid. *fl.* white, solitary or in small racemes; cal. long, clavate, 10-striate, rather hairy. Urals and Altai.

S. Arme'ria. Allied to *S. compacta.* Smooth, glaucous annual or biennial. Stem erect, 8 to 18 in. h., leafy, clammy below the upper nodes, little-branched. *Lower l.* spatulate; *upper* ovate-lanceolate, cordate at base. *fl.* $\frac{1}{8}$ to $\frac{1}{2}$ in. across, in corymbose panicles, short-stalked, purplish, rose, or white; pet. obcordate; cal. narrow, conical. May to September. Europe, naturalized in Britain. (E.B. 204.) For border, or moraine, or old walls.

S. Aster'ias. Smooth perennial, with non-flowering rosettes at base of erect, unbranched stem, 4 to 6 in. h., clammy below nodes. *Lower l.* lanceolate-spatulate, about 4 in. long; *upper* lanceolate or oblong, acute. *infl.* many-fld. in a head about 1 in. across. *fl.* almost sessile, purple; cal. cylindrical. June. Serbia, Macedonia, Bulgaria.

S. Bord'eri. Perennial. Stem very short, glabrous below, clammy above. *Lower l.* lanceolate-spatulate, with raised spots, ciliate. *fl.* rose, 1 to 4 in small cymes, erect; peduncles short; cal. large, hairy, 10-nerved, teeth obtuse; pet. 2-fid, ligules obtuse. August. E. Pyrenees.

S. Bo'ryi. Dull or grey-green tufted perennial from a creeping rhizome; clammy hairy. *l.* forming a terminal rosette, linear lanceolate, acute, hairy; stem-l. smaller. *fl.* pale rose, solitary or rarely twin, in a forked 3-fid cyme; pet. 2-fid, corona lobes acute. June to August. Spain.

S. bryoi'des. Probably a hybrid (*S. acaulis exscapa* × *S. elongata*). Differing from *S. elongata* by the rounded base of the cal., pet. not obcordate, capsule slightly exserted; and from *S. acaulis exscapa* by the size of the fl. and seed which are midway between the species mentioned. Pyrenees, Scandinavia, &c.

S. caespito'sa. Tufted perennial, glabrous, stems many, simple, erect. *l.* of radical rosette many, linear-awl-shaped, about 1 in. long, fleshy, entire, of stem much smaller. *fl.* greenish-white in a 5- to 10-fld. terminal panicle, pedicels short. June. Caucasus.

S. californ'ica. Indian Pink. Erect, 6 to 12 in. h., or sometimes ascending among bushes to 3 ft., very leafy, glandular-downy. *l.* elliptic-ovate to oblanceolate, $3\frac{1}{2}$ in. long, abruptly pointed. *fl.* crimson, 1 to $1\frac{1}{4}$ in. wide; pet. deeply 4-cleft, middle segs. longest, all toothed or rarely some or all entire, scales conspicuous; cal. oblong, $\frac{3}{4}$ in. long, teeth lanceolate. May, June. California. SYN. *Melandrium californicum.*

S. Campan'ula. Tufted perennial allied to *S. Saxifraga*, but with smooth, not clammy, stem, 4 to 8 in. h. *l.* almost all clustered at base, linear-lanceolate to grass-like, acute, those near fl. small, white-margined, ciliate. *fl.* 1 or 2 on long pedicels, cal. purple, pet. white within, tinged reddish outside, deeply notched. July, August. Maritime Alps.

S. caucas'ica. Allied to *S. vallesia* but velvety, not clammy. *stem-l.* shorter, almost sessile, peduncles shorter and cal. not inflated. In var. **ma'jor** *fl.* are more numerous and sometimes in whorls. Caucasus.

S. chloraefo'lia. Woody at base, about 18 in. h., glaucous, branches more or less erect, clammy above. *Lower l.* elliptic-spatulate, petiole slender, about 1 in. long; *upper* sessile, nearly round, about $\frac{3}{4}$ in. long. *fl.* white or pinkish, in loose panicles, pedicels slender; cal. 10-nerved, glabrous, pet. cleft to middle. July, August. W. Asia. 1796. (B.M. 807; B.R. 1989.)

S. cilia'ta. A dense mat from a woody rootstock. Stem from middle of l.-rosette, 4 to 6 in. h., sometimes roughly hairy. *Lower l.* linear-lanceolate, acute, ciliate near base; *upper* shorter, rather numerous, bracts ciliate. *fl.* 1 to 3 in a 1-side raceme, white inside, green or reddish without; pet. 2-lobed; cal. club-shaped, hairy. July to September. S. Europe.

S. Coeli-ro'sa. Rose of Heaven. Annual. Stem erect, 8 to 15 in. h., somewhat angled, smooth. *l.* oblong-linear, acute, ciliate. *fl.* purple to lilac or white; pet. 2-lobed; cal. club-shaped. June to August. Mediterranean region, Canary Is. 1713. Seed should be sown in April. var. **fimbria'ta,** pet. fringed. SYN. *Agrostemma Coeli-rosa, Eudianthe Coeli-rosa, Lychnis Coeli-rosa, Viscaria Burridgei, V. elegans, V. cardinalis, V. Dunnettii.*

S. compac'ta. Allied to *S. Armeria.* Annual or biennial. Grey-green, smooth, erect, 8 to 15 in. h., little-branched. *Lower l.* spatulate; *upper* ovate. *fl.* sessile, in a close corymb, rose; pet. almost entire. June, July. S. Russia, Asia Minor. Sow in early autumn. (L.B.C. 1638; S.B.F.G. 2, 64.) Not to be confused with *S. pendula compacta.*

S. cordifo'lia. Tufted perennial. Stems erect, 4 to 8 in. h., branched above, clammy. *Lower l.* small, ovate; *upper* larger, oval, somewhat cordate, acute, all shortly and softly hairy. *fl.* 1 to 4, very short-stalked, whitish to light rose; pet. notched; cal. wide-club-shaped, whitish, hairy, with linear-lanceolate teeth. June to August. Maritime Alps.

S. Correvonia'na. *See* **S. elongata.**

S. cre'tica. Glabrous or nearly glabrous annual, clammy above. Stem erect, about 18 in. h. *Lower l.* often in a rosette, spatulate-obovate, petiole ciliate; *upper* lanceolate, acute. *infl.* a loose panicle, middle fl. long-stalked. *fl.* reddish; cal. short, cylindric-bell-shaped, 10-ribbed; pet. 2-lobed. June, July. Mediterranean region.

S. Delavay'i. Habit of *Melandrium Elisabethae. Rosette l.* 1¼ to 3 in. long, pale green, rather thick, glabrous, ciliate. *fl.* 1 to 6 on a stem 3 to 8 in. long; pet. deep purple, twice as long as cal., 4-lobed side lobes linear, mid-lobes twice as wide, laciniate; throat with long oblong scales. Yunnan. 1884.

S. dianthifo'lia. A synonym of *S. acaulis pannonica.*

S. dianthoi'des. Tufted perennial. *fl.* white, terminal, on lateral peduncles, sessile between 2 small lflets. as in Dianthus; cal. striate; pet. 2-fid. Asia Minor.

S. dichot'oma. Hairy annual. Stem erect, 1 to 3 ft. h., sometimes branched from base. *Lower l.* spatulate to lanceolate, 3-nerved; *upper* lanceolate, acute, petioles short or absent. *fl.* numerous in 1-sided spikes, many stems bear female fl. only, about ½ to ¾ in. across, white, very rarely purplish-red; pet. 2-lobed; cal. oblong-cylindric, with bristly green nerves; pedicels short or absent. June to September. Europe, Asia Minor (introduced in Britain).

S. dinar'ica. Tufted perennial related to *S. acaulis* but cushion looser, fl.-stems longer, cal. oblong. *fl.* rose. July, August. Hungary.

S. Douglas'ii. Slender, downy perennial, scarcely clammy. Stems ascending, about 15 in. h. *l.* distant, linear or narrow-lanceolate. *fl.* white or pale pink in few-fld. racemes, pedicels long; cal. oblong, teeth blunt; pet. 2-lobed. Western N. America. A variable plant. **S. Macoun'ii** differs by its branched stems clammy above and somewhat taller, *l.* oblanceolate tapering to stalk, and blunt purple-tipped cal. teeth. Brit. Columbia and Washington. SYN. *S. multicaulis.*

S. Drummond'ii of gardens. A synonym of *S. glauca.*

S. Elisabeth'ae. A synonym of *Melandrium Elisabethae.*

S. elonga'ta. Differs from *S. acaulis* of which it is often regarded as a variety by its larger, looser mats and larger, brighter *fl.* on 2-in. long stems. W. Graian Alps east to Simplon Pass. var. **Correvonia'na** is a double-fld. form of this.

S. erioph'ora of gardens. A synonym of *Heliosperma glutinosum.*

S. exsca'pa. A variety of *S. acaulis.*

S. Faba'ria. Glabrous, glaucous perennial, 2 to 3 ft. h., densely leafy near base. *Lower l.* obovate; *upper* elliptic-lanceolate to linear. *fl.* in short racemose cymes, cymes in distant clusters, branches ½ to 1 in. long; pet. 2-fid, narrow, white; cal. inflated, glabrous. June. Greece. (F.G. 415.)

S. fimbria'ta. Hairy perennial, 2 to 4 ft. h. *l.* ovate-lanceolate, undulate, large, petiole long. *fl.* white, in large spreading panicles; pet. fringed; cal. much swollen, teeth broad. May to August. Caucasus. 1803. (B.M. 908.)

S. Fortun'ei. Rough-haired perennial, woody at base. Stems numerous, erect, 1½ to 3 ft. h., clammy near top. *l.* linear-lanceolate, acute, narrowed to a ciliate stalk. *fl.* rose or white, in a raceme, pedicels short; cal. tubular, smooth, teeth acute, white-margined; pet. 2-lobed more or less deeply. China, Formosa. (B.M. 7649.)

S. Frivaldskya'na. Glaucous perennial about 30 in. h. *Lower l.* linear-lanceolate, 4 in. long with stalk; *upper* narrower and shorter. *fl.* white in a raceme 6 to 8 in. long; pet. 2-fid, lobes linear-spatulate; cal. about ½ in. long, cylindrical. Rhodope Mt.

S. frutico'sa. Perennial with woody base. *l.* oblong-spatulate to oblanceolate, 1 to 2½ in. long, ciliate, grey-green. *fl.* pink in panicles, bracts long-linear, slender-pointed, ciliate; cal. glandular-hairy; pet. 2-cleft. S. Europe. 1877.

S. gigan'tea. Hairy perennial, up to 4 ft. h., clammy. Stem thick, 4-sided. *Lower l.* in a dense rosette, obovate-spatulate; *upper* oblong-lanceolate. *fl.* white in a long panicle of dense, whorled cymes, upper sessile; cal. obconical, slightly hairy, teeth ovate, blunt; pet. 2-cleft, lobes oblong. June to September. E. Mediterranean.

S. glau'ca. Shortly hairy, stout. *Lower l.* lanceolate, stalked; *upper* linear, sessile. *fl.* rose, small, closed at midday, in a very long raceme; cal. inflated, green-veined. April, May. Algeria, Spain.

S. Griffith'ii. Densely hairy robust perennial, 12 to 18 in. h. *l.* oblong to ovate-lanceolate, 2½ to 4 in. long, lower stalked. *fl.* white; pet. laciniate, without scales; cal. cylindric; cymes opposite, few-fld. N. India, Afghanistan.

S. gris'ea. Tufted, shrubby at base, grey-velvety. Stem slender, 8 to 12 in. h., clammy. *Lower l.* oblong-spatulate; *upper* linear. *fl.* yellowish-green, in a 1- to 7-fld. raceme; cal. cylindrical-obconical, glandular, teeth acute; pet. 2-lobed, lobes linear. Summer. Mt. Lebanon.

S. Heuf'fleri. A synonym of *Heliosperma glutinosum.*

S. Hook'eri. Perennial with many radiating decumbent stems. *l.* 2 to 3 in. long, pubescent; lower elliptic-spatulate, narrowed into long petioles; upper elliptic-lanceolate, acute or acuminate. *fl.* 2 to 2½ in. across, axillary on slender pedicels 2 in. long; cal. 1 in. long; pet. soft pink with white rays from throat where are 2 white scales to each pet., very deeply 2-fid, lobes often unequal. May to July. California. 1873. (B.M. 6051; F.d.S. 2093.) Needs a sunny, very well-drained position protected from winter wet. **A**

S. inapert'a. A synonym of *S. multicaulis.*

S. lacinia'ta. A synonym of *Melandrium laciniatum.*

S. legionen'sis. Tufted perennial from a thick rather woody rhizome. *l.* evergreen, rosette l. lanceolate, stem-l. shorter. *fl.* 2 to 6, white above, livid beneath; sep. margined white; stalks short. June, July. W. Spain.

S. Lerchenfeldia'na. Perennial tufted and glaucous. Stem smooth, decumbent, 4 to 6 in. h., lateral from the basal rosette. *l.* lanceolate, acute, sparingly ciliate near base, up to 2 in. long, ⅛ in. wide, upper shorter and broader. *fl.* 5 to 11 in more or less corymbose infl., rather small, rose; cal. shortly club-shaped, smooth, teeth ovate; pet. narrow, linear. June, July. E. Europe.

Silene Hookeri

S. linic'ola. Annual. Stem erect, slender, sparingly branched, up to 20 in. h., covered with short hairs. *l.* grass-green, hairy and ciliate; lower obovate to oblong, obtuse, narrowed to the petiole; upper linear-lanceolate, about 1½ in. long. *infl.* branched, pedicels about 1¼ in. long. *fl.* about ⅓ in. across, rose or bright pink, rarely white. June, July. N. Italy.

S. Macoun'ii. *See* **S. Douglasii.**

S. marit'ima. Sea Campion. Tufted blue-grey perennial with a woody rootstock and numerous prostrate leafy stems about 6 in. long. *l.* lanceolate to ovate. *fl.-stems* ascending. *fl.* sometimes dioecious, solitary or a few in a loose truss, white, large; cal. ovate, inflated; pet. with 2 acute scales at base of blade. July to September. W. Europe (including Britain) and N. Africa sea-shores. (E.B. 200.) var. **flor'e plen'o,** *fl.* double. The plant grown as **S. marit'ima ro'sea** is probably a variety of the closely allied *S. venosa* (SYN. *S. inflata*), *fl.* tinged dull red.

S. monacho'rum. A variety of *Heliosperma multifidum.*

S. multicau'lis. Densely tufted perennial. Stem ascending or erect, usually more or less branched, 8 to 15 in. h., smooth, clammy above. *l.* linear-lanceolate, ½ to 1 in. long, acute, hairy, ciliate. *fl.* usually many, whitish within, olive-green without, or rose within, reddish-brown without; pedicels long; cal. cylindrical-conical, main veins reddish. June to September. Corsica, Italy, Balkans. (F.G. 514, 14 as *S. inaperta.*)

S. nicaeen'sis. Annual or biennial, clammy. Stem erect or ascending, 4 to 12 in. h., often woody at base. *l.* fleshy, linear, lower often oblong-spatulate, upper grooved. *fl.* short-stalked, spike 1-sided; pet. white, dull purple to greenish-purple outside, 2-lobed. May to July. Mediterranean region.

S. ocula'ta. 12 to 18 in. h. *l.* linear-lanceolate, rough. *fl.* bright purple with a dark spot at base; pet. obovate, about 1½ in. across. May to August. N. Africa. (B.M. 4075 as *Viscaria aspera*; B.R. 53 as *V. oculata.*)

S. odontopet'ala. Densely pubescent perennial. Stems 4 to 6 in. h., leafy, little-branched, glandular. *l.* lanceolate or linear-lanceolate, 1-nerved. *infl.* 1- to 7-fld., cymose. *fl.* white; cal. clammy, whitish, bell-shaped; pet. 2-lobed. Summer. Asia Minor, Caucasus.

S. orienta'lis. A synonym of *S. compacta.*

S. orna'ta. A synonym of *Melandrium ornatum.*

S. paradox'a. Perennial with more or less woody base. Stem erect, 12 to 18 in. h., little-branched, white-hairy, clammy above. *Lower l.* lanceolate-spatulate to obovate; *upper* narrower, densely ciliate. *fl.* in a loose pyramidal panicle, branches 1- to 3-fld. *fl.* white, outside yellowish; cal. long, tubular, teeth margined white, nerves green, hairy, pet. 2-lobed. Summer. S. Europe.

S. parnas'sica. A variety of *S. Saxifraga.*

S. pend'ula. Annual, more or less white-hairy, glandular above, branched, trailing; branches about 12 in. long. *l.* oblong-spatulate, obtuse, densely ciliate; lower stalked. *fl.* axillary, drooping, about 1 in. across, bright rose, sometimes white; pet. obcordate, with 2 obtuse scales at base of blade; cal. oblong-club-shaped, veins green, clammy. May to September. S. Europe. 1731. (B.M. 114.) Variable in colour: **al'ba,** *fl.* white; **carn'ea,** *fl.* pale pink; **lilacin'a,** *fl.* lilac-purple; **ruber'rima Bonnet'tii,** *fl.* bright carmine-rose; whole plant purple-tinged, glabrous. Double forms of some of these occur. var. **compact'a,** dwarf, compact, cushions 9 to 12 in. across, 2 to 3 in. h., good for spring bedding. Also known with double fl.

S. pensylvan'ica. A synonym of *Melandrium pennsylvanicum.*

S. petrae'a. A synonym of *S. Saxifraga.*

S. pharnaceifo'lia. Tufted perennial about 3 in. h. Stem slender. *Lower l.* densely clustered, awl-shaped, grooved, hairy. *fl.* rose, in 1- to 5-fld. clusters; cal. obconical-bell-shaped, reddish, slightly hairy; pet. 2-lobed. June. Lebanon.

Silene oculata (p. 1955)

S. Pumil'is. A synonym of *Saponaria Pumilis.*

S. pusil'la. A variety of *Heliosperma quadrifidum.*

S. quadridenta'ta. A synonym of *Heliosperma quadrifidum.*

S. quadrifi'da. A synonym of *Heliosperma quadrifidum.*

S. Reichenbach'ii. Perennial. Stems 12 to 15 in. h., hairy below, smooth above. *Lower l.* spatulate, acute, narrowed to a petiole, hairy on margin and midrib beneath; *upper* linear, margined white. *fl.* greenish-white, nodding on short pedicels; cal. narrowly club-shaped; many-ribbed; pet. obcordate. July, August. Dalmatia. var. **umbro'sa,** larger in all parts, about 2 ft. h.

S. re'pens. Perennial with long creeping root. Stems 8 to 10 in. h., more or less roughly hairy. *l.* narrow-oblong, or lanceolate, acute. *fl.* white, on opposite, axillary, 1- to 5-fld. peduncles; cal. cylindrical-club-shaped, inflated, 10-ribbed, hairy; pet. 2-fid, lobes oblong. Summer. Russia east to Alaska.

S. rupes'tris. Blue-grey tufted perennial about 4 to 8 in. h. Stem branched from base, erect. *l.* lanceolate to oblong-lanceolate, lower acute, upper blunt. *infl.* a large, very loose panicle with long-stalked fl. *fl.* $\frac{1}{4}$ to $\frac{1}{3}$ in. across, white to pink; cal. 10-ribbed, teeth ovate, obtuse; pet. obovate. June to August. W. Europe, Siberia. Apt to be biennial under cultivation. Dislikes lime.

S. Saxifra'ga. Tufted perennial. Stem 4 to 8 in. h., ascending, slender, clammy above. *l.* rather short, linear to linear-lanceolate, finely ciliate. *fl.* usually solitary, on long pedicels, white within, greenish or reddish without; cal. whitish, shortly club-shaped, ribs green or reddish; pet. 2-fid, lobes oblong. May to August or later. S. Europe, Asia Minor. 1640. (L.B.C. 454.) A widely distributed variable plant. var. **parnas'sica,** *fl.* larger, cal. teeth acutish, claw of pet. smooth. Greece; **petrae'a,** *l.* usually acute, smooth or rough, usually not in a rosette.

S. Schaf'ta. Tufted perennial, up to 6 in. h. Stems many, usually unbranched, ascending from a woody rootstock. *l.* obovate, acute. *fl.* rosy-magenta, solitary or in twos; cal. over 1 in. long, 10-nerved, club-shaped; pet. broadly obovate, toothed. June to October. Caucasus. 1844. (B.R. 32, 20.) Valuable for its late flowering.

S. Scoul'eri. Hairy perennial, clammy above, 18 to 24 in. h. Stem simple, erect. *l.* narrowly oblanceolate or linear-lanceolate, slender-pointed. *fl.* white or purplish, in whorled spikes; cal. club-shaped, teeth ciliate; pet. 2-fid. Summer. Western N. America.

S. stella'ta. Hairy perennial, 2 to 3 ft. h. Stems erect, branched. *l.* usually in whorls of 4, ovate-lanceolate, 2 to 3 in. long, slender-pointed. *fl.* nodding, in an open panicle, white; cal. bell-shaped, inflated, downy; pet. laciniate, without scales at base of blade. Summer. N. America. (B.M. 1107 as *Cucubalus stellatus.*) *S. stellata* of Lapeyrouse is *S. ciliata.*

S. Tanak'ae. Shrubby, upright, about 2 ft. h. *l.* elliptic to lanceolate-spatulate, 1 to $2\frac{1}{2}$ in. long, downy. *fl.* purple; cal. $\frac{2}{3}$ in. long, downy; pet. notched, claw ciliate. Summer. S. Japan. 1884.

S. tatar'ica. Perennial. Stem erect, 1 to 2 ft., smooth or nearly so, often tinged red, with short leafy branches below, flowering above. *l.* lanceolate or linear-lanceolate, toothed. *fl.* in long panicles, white; cal. oblong-club-shaped, with green ribs; teeth ovate, acute, white-margined, ciliate; pet. 2-cleft, segs. oblong-linear, blunt. July, August. N. Europe, Siberia.

S. tejeden'sis. Allied to *S. Boryi.* Densely glandular-hairy perennial with slender prostrate branches, 1- or 2-fld. at tips. *l.* oblong-lanceolate. *fl.* flesh-pink; pet. 2-fid to middle, lobes oblong, scales oblong; cal. $\frac{3}{4}$ to 1 in. long, green-striped, sub-clavate. Summer. Spain, Lebanon to Persia.

S. valles'ia. Loosely tufted perennial, 4 to 6 in. h. with woody rootstock. *l.* grey-green, dull, lanceolate to oblong-lanceolate, acute, hairy, ciliate, lower stalked, upper sessile. *fl.-stems* from sides of rosette, 4-angled, clammy, 1- or 2-, rarely more, fld. *fl.* about $\frac{2}{3}$ in. across, pinkish within, blood-red outside, opening only in the evening; cal. oblong-club-shaped, teeth white-margined, acute, ciliate; pet. 2-lobed. July, August. W. Alps.

S. Veselskyi. A synonym of *Heliosperma glutinosum.*

S. virgini'ca. A synonym of *Melandrium virginicum.*

S. Wher'ryi. A synonym of *Melandrium Wherryi.*

S. Zawads'kii. A synonym of *Melandrium Zawadskii.*

sileniflo'rus -a -um, having flowers resembling a Silene.

silhetia'nus -a -um, of Sylhet, Bengal, India.

SILICA. A very abundant mineral in the soil, existing in the pure state and in combination with various elements forming silicates. Silica is an oxide (SiO_2) of the element Silicon. It occurs as flint, sand, quartz, rock crystal, and chalcedony, and in combination with calcium, magnesium, and aluminium it occurs in clay, mica, felspar, and other materials and forms a large number of the rocks constituting the crust of the earth. Silica is not soluble in water but in water containing carbonic acid it is very slightly soluble and is thus found in almost all soil water and is to some extent absorbed by plants. It is very doubtful whether it plays any part in the nutrition of plants although it is found in the ash of all plants. It is deposited in the cell-walls and is often particularly abundant there in the outer cells of many grass stems and horse-tails, while the walls of diatoms are very rich in it. Silicon is frequently combined with potassium and sodium and these silicates are an important storehouse of these elements in the soil and being to some extent soluble, probably of essential potash supplies to the plant.

SILICULA. A siliqua at least as broad as long.

siliculo'sus -a -um, having a siliqua at least as broad as long.

SILIQUA. The long pod-like fruits of Cruciferae. It has 2 valves applied to the frame on which the seeds grow. *See* **Replum.**

Siliquas'trum, ancient Latin name for a pod-bearing tree.

siliquo'sus -a -um, bearing siliquas or pods.

SILK COTTON TREE. *See* **Ceiba.**

SILK VINE. *See* **Periploca gracea.**

SILK-TREE. *See* **Albizzia Julibrissin.**

SILK-WEED. *See* **Asclepias syriaca.**

SILKWOOD-TREE. *See* **Muntingia Calabura.**

SILKWORM. The caterpillar of the mulberry silk moth, *Bombyx mori*, natural silk being the fibre spun in making its cocoon. It is usually fed with the leaves of *Morus alba*, local conditions (e.g. a well-drained soil, &c.) determining their suitability. Sericulture has been successful at only a few places in England, e.g. Eynsford, Kent.

SILKY OAK. *See* **Grevillea robusta.**

SILPH'A op'aca. *See* **Beet Carrion Beetle.**

SIL'PHIUM (ancient Greek name used by Hippocrates for a plant which produced some gum-resin, perhaps asafoetida). FAM. *Compositae.* A genus of about 25 species of tall, coarse, perennial herbs with resinous sap, natives of N. America. Leaves alternate, opposite or whorled, entire, toothed or lobed. Flower-heads yellow, large, in a corymbose panicle; involucre broad, rather flat, the scales in many overlapping rows; ray-florets only fertile. Achenes glabrous, surrounded by a wing notched at top. *S. laciniatum* is perhaps the most interesting species; in at least the young state the leaves often present their faces north and south whence its name of Compass Plant. Any ordinary soil suits these hardy plants which are best placed at the back of the border. They may be increased by division or seed.

S. albiflo'rum. Stem unbranched, 2 to 4 ft. h. Plant covered with short prickles. *l.* ovate, pinnatifid or 2-pinnatifid, leathery, upper linear; lobes linear, 2 to 5 in. long. *fl.-heads* pale straw or creamy-white, 3 in. across; rays narrowly oblong, 2-fid. Texas. (B.M. 6918.)

S. integrifo'lium. Stem sometimes smooth, 2 to 6 ft. h. *l.* entire, ovate-lanceolate, large, upper somewhat stem-clasping, acute, 3 to 5 in. long, glabrous or ashy-hairy. *fl.-heads* many, 1 to 2 in. across, shortly stalked, in corymbs. July, August. W. United States.

S. lacinia'tum.* Compass Plant, Pilot Weed, Polar Plant. Roughly bristly, 3 to 6 ft. h. *l.* pinnatipartite, lower ovate, 1 to 2½ ft. long; divisions lanceolate or linear, acute, much cut as a rule. *fl.-heads* few, somewhat racemose, 1 to 2 in. across; involucral bracts with rigid points. July, August. (B.M. 6534.)

S. perfolia'tum. Stem 4 to 6 ft. h., square. *l.* ovate, not lobed, 6 to 15 in. long, bases of upper l. united forming a cup around stem, lower l. with winged stalks connate at their bases. *fl.-heads* 2 to 3 in. across, in corymbs; rays 20 to 30. July. Eastern N. America. (B.M. 8354.)

S. terebinthina'ceum.* Prairie Dock. Stem smooth, 4 to 10 ft. h. *l.* ovate or ovate-oblong, somewhat heart-shaped at base, toothed, rough, especially beneath, 1 to 2 ft. long, on slender stalks. *fl.-heads* 1½ to 3 in. across, numerous in a terminal panicle; rays 12 to 20. July to September. Canada, middle U.S.A. (B.M. 3525.)

silvan'us -a -um, of bushy places or woods.

Silva-Tarouca'nus, in honour of Graaf Ernst Silva Tarouca, president of the Austrian Dendrological Society.

silvat'icus -a -um, of woods.

SILVER BERRY. *See* **Elaeagnus argentea** (fruit).

SILVER BUSH. *See* **Anthyllis Barba-Jovis.**

SILVER CEDAR. *See* **Juniperus virginiana glauca.**

SILVER FIR. *See* ***Abies.***

SILVER FISH, *Lepisma saccharina*, owes its common name to its scaly body, which is long (about ½ in.) and narrow, and its quickly gliding motion. These primitive insects are found in kitchens, pantries, cupboards, and beneath skirting-boards, and hot-water pipes. The minute eggs are laid in the haunts of the adults, and the newly hatched nymphs are devoid of scales though they otherwise resemble the adults. They often abound in old houses where they feed on starchy substances, such as paste on wall-paper, the starch on lace curtains and the like, the glue of book-bindings, bread crumbs, &c. Silver Fish are more serious pests in hot countries than in temperate regions. They may be destroyed by sprinkling a mixture of 6 parts sodium fluoride, 2 parts Pyrethrum powder, and 2 parts corn starch round skirtings, on shelves, beneath water-pipes, and elsewhere, care being taken to keep children and domestic animals away from the mixture and treated area. **A**

G. F. W.

SILVER GRAIN. The glittering plates in wood seen where medullary rays are cut.

SILVER LEAF. A disease caused by the fungus *Stereum purpureum* which may attack many kinds of plants. The usual result is that the affected plant develops a silvery discoloration of the leaves, thus giving rise to the name. Other factors not connected with any parasitic fungus may cause a silvery sheen in plant foliage and this is dealt with later. The true Silver Leaf disease is due to infection by the above fungus and is especially well known on Plums but attacks many other fruit and ornamental trees, Poplar, Portugal Laurel, Laburnum. It may attack Rhododendrons but here for some reason or other the foliage is not silvered. Although silvering is the first visible symptom of this disease it is not alone sufficient for positive identification and other signs must be looked for. One is that the wood on affected branches when cut across shows a dark-brown or black stain which may vary both in size and in shape but when present together with the leaf silvering is good evidence of the disease. Another symptom is the appearance of the fungus fructifications on the branch but this unfortunately only happens when the branch is dead. The fructifications appear on the bark as flat or bracket-like plates of fungus tissue which are dull brown when dry but have a very characteristic purplish or lilac colour when moist. On these bodies the spores (basidiospores) are formed for infection which occurs chiefly through wounds. In view of this, once young trees have been shaped they should be cut as little as possible and where necessary branches should be removed in early summer when infection is least likely. Branches should be cut off flush with the main stem or larger branch and wounds protected by painting with white-lead paint or tar. The Silver Leaf Order of 1923 requires growers to cut out and burn all dead wood from plum and apple trees before 15 July in each year. Treatment of affected plum trees depends on cutting affected branches back so far that no brown stain is seen in the wood and then encouraging the tree by good cultivation, liming, and applications of fertilizers so as to keep it vigorous, for vigorous trees, especially if young, have been known to recover.

Silvering of the foliage not due to the fungus *Stereum purpureum* or any other parasite occurs causing False Silver Leaf. This condition may be seen on Roses and Antirrhinum seedlings after frosts and in many other trees, shrubs, and herbaceous plants owing to extreme drought, or some obscure form of malnutrition possibly connected with poor root action. Peaches often show such symptoms and with such valuable trees it is always desirable to obtain expert advice before deciding on the destruction of the tree.

D. E. G.

SILVER ROD. *See* **Asphodelus.**

SILVER TREE. *See* **Elaeagnus** and **Leucadendron argenteum.**

SILVER VINE. *See* **Scindapsus pictus.**

SILVER WEED. *See* **Argyreia cuneata** and **Potentilla Anserina.**

SILVER Y MOTH, *Plusia gamma*, is so named from the characteristic silvery mark on the fore-wings resembling the Greek letter Gamma (γ) or the letter *Y*. The moths, whose wings are of various shades of grey and brown to velvety-black, fly freely in sunshine from May to September, and often migrate in enormous numbers to this country from the Continent. The caterpillars are semi-loopers possessing 3 instead of the normal 5 pairs of prolegs or sucker feet. They are delicate green to olive-green with transverse white wavy lines, and are slightly humped on the hind body segment. They feed from June to the following April on a great variety of plants, both wild and cultivated—Dead Nettle and Stinging Nettle, Bindweed, Sowthistles and Thistles, Cabbage, Peas, Marigold, Polyanthus, and are very partial to the leaves of Geraniums grown under glass during the winter. When fully fed in April they form blackish chrysalides enclosed in a whitish cocoon among the lower leaves of the food plant. This pest is encouraged by the presence of weeds, which should be destroyed by regular hoeing both in the garden and in and around glasshouses. The caterpillars may be hand-picked from glasshouse plants, or the foliage sprayed lightly with arsenate of lead. **A**

G. F. W.

SILVER-BELL TREE. *See* **Halesia carolina.**

silves'ter -is -e, of woods, thence growing wild in contrast to a cultivated plant.

Silves'trii, in honour of Dr. Philippo Silvestri, Argentine zoologist and plant-collector, who discovered *Chamaecereus Silvestrii* in Argentina.

silvic'ola, wood-dwelling.

SIL'YBUM (name applied by Dioscorides to some thistle-like plant). FAM. *Compositae.* A genus of 2 species of erect, glabrous, biennial herbs, natives of Europe, Asia, and Africa, allied to Carduus from which it is distinguished by the glabrous filaments connate into a sheath. Leaves alternate, spotted white above, sinuately lobed or pinnatifid, the teeth and lobes spiny. Flower-heads spiny; flowers purplish, all perfect; corolla tube slender, limb 5-cleft to middle or base; achenes smooth, obovate, oblong. *S. Marianum* will grow in any ordinary soil, and it has become naturalized in waste places. It was formerly grown for its root which was boiled as a pot-herb, the heads treated like those of the Artichoke and the leaves used as a spring salad.

S. Maria'num. Blessed Thistle, Holy Thistle, Our Lady's Milk Thistle. Biennial of 1 to 4 ft. *l.* large. *fl.-heads* rose-purple, globose, 1 to 2 in. across; involucral bracts leathery, closely appressed, with 1 very stout, terminal spine; receptacle hairy, not pitted, fleshy. July to September. S. Europe, Asia, N. Africa. (E.B. 681.)

SIMA'BA (native name in Guiana of 1 species). FAM. *Simarubaceae.* A genus of 19 species of evergreen or deciduous trees or shrubs, natives of S. America. Leaves alternate, pinnate or rarely 1- to 3-foliolate; leaflets entire, leathery. Flowers 4- to 5-merous; petals longer than calyx, spreading, valvate; disk narrow, erect; stamens 8 to 10, included; panicles loose. Fruit drupaceous, endocarp usually hard. *S. Cedron* is remarkable for the febrifugal properties of its seeds, which are used as a tonic and sedative and which have been used from time immemorial in its native place as a remedy for snake-bites. It needs stove conditions and a compost of well-drained turfy loam. Propagated by cuttings of ripe wood in sand under glass in heat or by imported seed.

S. Ced'ron. Tree with slender, simple, erect stem to 20 ft. h. *l.* large, pinnate; lflets. 20 or more, narrow-elliptic, livid-green above, paler beneath. *fl.* in racemes 3 to 4 ft. long. May. Colombia. 1846.

F. G. P.

SIMARU'BA (Carib name for *S. amara*). FAM. *Simarubaceae.* A genus of species of evergreen trees, natives of E. Trop. America, with equally pinnate leaves with alternate, entire, leathery leaflets. Flower dioecious, in axillary and terminal long, branched panicles; calyx small, 5-lobed; petals 5, spreading at tips, overlapping; stamens 10. Drupes 1 to 5, sessile. For treatment (warm-house), *see* **Quassia.**

S. ama'ra. Bitter or Mountain Damson; Stavewood; Bitter Wood. Tree, in cultivation about 10 ft. h., tall in nature. *l.* oblong or oblong-lanceolate, mucronate, green on both sides; lflets. glabrous or downy. *fl.* yellowish-white; pet. spreading; panicle shorter than l. May. W. Indies, Trop. America. 1789. SYN. *S. officinalis.* Yields Simaruba-bark.

S. Tu'lae. Tree of 15 to 25 ft. *lflets.* elliptic-oblong, short-pointed. *fl.* bright carmine, about ⅛ in. across, pet. much longer than in *S. amara*; branches of corymb tinted purple. Porto Rico. 1889. (G.F. 1889, 1298.)

F. G. P.

SIMARUBA'CEAE. Dicotyledons. A family of about 125 species in 28 genera of trees and shrubs, natives of the Tropics and sub-tropical regions of the world. They have alternate, pinnate or simple leaves without gland-dots; small, regular flowers in compound axillary panicles or cymose spikes; calyx and corolla 3- to 7-merous, sepals sometimes free, disk between stamens and ovary ring- or cup-like, sometimes becoming a gynophore; stamens twice as many as petals; carpels 4 or 5, or fewer, often free below, styles united. Fruit a drupe or capsule. A few have medicinal properties and some yield useful timber. The genera treated are: Ailanthus, Brucea, Picrasma, Quassia, Simaba, Simaruba.

simen'sis -is -e, of Arabia.

SIMETH'IS (after the nymph Simethis, mistress of Acis). FAM. *Liliaceae.* A genus of a single species of herbaceous perennial with clusters of stout fibrous roots, grass-like radical leaves, and a panicled, bracteate scape of flowers with 6 almost free perianth segments. Heathy mould and sand form the best compost for this hardy plant, which grows in fir-woods.

S. bi'color. Root fibres stout. *l.* radical, linear, 6 to 18 in. long, recurved, surrounded at base with torn brown sheaths. *Scape* 6 to 18 in. long; branched, forming a panicle. *fl.* ¾ in. across, white within, purple on back; segs. oblong, obtuse. SW. Europe, N. Africa. (E.B. 1541.)

sim'ilis -is -e, having a likeness to another species.

Simon'ii, in honour of Gabriel Eugène Simon, b. 1829, French consul and plant-collector in Asia Minor, Japan, and China.

Simonkaia'nus -a -um, in honour of Ludwig Simkovics, later Simonkai, 1851–1910, Professor in Budapest.

Simonsia'nus -a -um, in honour of Dr. J. C. Simons, who collected *Cymbidium Simonsianum,* &c., in Assam, *c.* 1895.

Simons'ii, in honour of the Rev. Jelinger Symons, 1778–1851, Vicar of Leyton, Essex.

simorrhi'num, monkey's nose; flat-nosed.

simple, consisting of 1 piece only, as a simple leaf, a leaf with but 1 blade.

SIMPLER'S JOY. *See* **Verbena officinalis.**

sim'plex (in compound words, ***simplici-***), undivided.

Sims'ii, in honour of John Sims, 1749–1831, of Dorking, sometime editor of the *Botanical Magazine.*

sim'ulans, imitating.

simula'tus -a -um, imitating.

sina'icus -a -um, of Sinai.

sinapifo'lius -a -um, with charlock-like leaves.

SIN'APIS (*Sinapi,* name used by Theophrastus for Mustard). FAM. *Cruciferae.* A genus of 8 species of mostly annual hairy herbs of the Mediterranean region growing on calcareous and sandy soils, closely related to Brassica, distinguished by the characters mentioned under that genus. *S. arvensis* is the common charlock, seeds of which are sometimes crushed for the oil they contain. *S. alba* is the White Mustard, used when young as a salad. *See* **Mustard.**

S. al'ba. White Mustard. Erect, hairy annual, 10 to 24 in. h., branched above. *Lower l.* lyrate-pinnatipartite, with 2 or 3 pairs of blunt lobes with roundish teeth, terminal lobe broadly ovate; *upper* with acute lobes; all usually hairy and bright green, sometimes spotted violet. *fl.* yellow, in 35- to 50- or more-fld. racemes; pet. usually nearly ½ in. long. *fr.* with a persistent, compressed, 2-edged, sword-shaped beak. *Seeds* 4 to 8, pale yellow as a rule, about 1/16 to 1/12 in. wide. Mediterranean region, &c. (E.B. 1677.) Sometimes considered the Mustard of the Bible, but *see* **Salvadora persica.**

S. arven'sis. Charlock. Much like *S. alba* but less leafy as a rule and with terminal lobe of *lower l.* obovate. *fr.* with a deciduous, 2-edged, less compressed, conical or awl-shaped beak, seeds 8 to 13, dark reddish-brown or blackish, about 1/20 in. wide. Europe, &c. (E.B. 1748.) A persistent annual weed, especially of farm-land.

SINARUNDINA'RIA. Included in **Arundinaria.**

Sinclair'ii, in honour of Dr. Sinclair, R.N., Colonial Secretary for New Zealand.

sindjaren'sis -is -e, of Djebel Sindjar, Mesopotamia.

sinen'sis -is -e, Chinese.

singalen'sis -is -e, of Singalang, Sumatra.

singaporen'sis -is -e, of Singapore.

single, of flowers having no more than the normal number of petals, as opposed to double or semi-double.

singula'ris -is -e, unusual.

singuliflo'rus -a -um, with solitary flowers.

sin'icus -a -um (***sino-,*** in compound words), signifying Chinese.

sinistror'sus -a -um, twisted to the left.

SINNING'IA (in honour of Wilhelm Sinning, 1794–1874, head gardener at the University of Bonn). FAM. *Gesneriaceae.* A genus of about 20 species of usually low-growing, hairy herbs, natives of Brazil, often called Gloxinias. Rhizome tuberous. Stem simple or only slightly branched, sometimes almost wanting. Leaves opposite, often large, long-stalked, upper small. Flowers showy, rarely rather small, solitary or clustered in the axils, on long or short pedicels; calyx tube short or broadly turbinate, limb leafy, deeply 5-cleft or 5-parted; corolla tube sometimes gibbous at back, long, broadly cylindrical or bell-shaped, limb of 5 broad, spreading lobes; stamens included. Fruit a capsule. Treatment as for Gloxinia. Hybrids have been raised between *S. barbata* and other species and species of Gloxinia.

S. barba'ta. Stem decumbent or ascending. *l.* oblong to oblong-lanceolate, up to nearly 12 in. long, narrowed at both ends, acute, crenate-serrate, velvety above, crimson beneath; stalks ½ to 1 in. long. *fl.* white with red marks within, much swollen at base, contracted at throat, hairy, 1½ in. long, cal. nearly 1 in. long; peduncles solitary or twin, ½ to 1½ in. long. Summer. 1867. (B.M. 5623; F.d.S. 1847.) SYN. *Tapeionites Carolinae.* var. **ma'jor,** larger in all parts.

S. Carolin'ae. A synonym of *S. barbata.*

S. concin'na.* Stem very short and, like l.-stalk, veins, and peduncles, red. *l.* roundish-ovate, rather small, deeply crenate. *fl.* lurid-purple above, yellowish beneath, spotted within, about 1 in. long, tube dilated towards throat; cal. rather small, segs. longer than tube; peduncles longer than l. Summer. 1860. (B.M. 5253 as *Stenogaster concinna*; F.d.S. 1533 as *Stenogastra concinna.*) var. **multiflo'ra,** *fl.* lilac-blue, *l.* larger. (I.H. 1894, 390 as *Stenogastra multiflora.*)

S. conspic'ua.* Hairy, about 1 ft. h. *l.* ovate-oblong, with a short point, somewhat heart-shaped at base, toothed. *fl.* yellow, paler without, lower part of tube with purple lines and dots within, obliquely funnel-bell-shaped; cal. segs. lanceolate, spreading. Summer. 1868. (G.F. 712 as *Rosanowia conspicua.*)

S. Hel'leri.* Stem 3 or 4 in. h., thick, somewhat woody. *l.* ovate-oblong, 4 to 7 in. long, acute, wedge-shaped at base, crenately toothed, velvety. *fl.* white, throat greenish with red spots, up to 3 in. long, tumid at base, limb broad and round; cal. red, up to 2 in. long; peduncles erect, scarcely 1 in. long. June. 1820. (B.M. 4212 as *S. velutina.*) **S. gutta'ta** (B.R. 1112) greatly resembles this.

S. hirsu'ta. Stem short, prostrate, covered with coarse white hairs. *l.* few, broadly ovate, obtuse, 3 to 5 in. long, heart-shaped at base, deeply crenate, purplish beneath; stalks 1 to 1½ in. long. *fl.* lilac, about 1 in. long and as wide, limb dotted violet, lobes somewhat emarginate, palely hairy without, purple-spotted within; cal. red, ½ in. long, very hairy, sub-erect; peduncles clustered, shorter than l. June, July. 1824. (B.M. 2690, B.R. 1004 as *Gloxinia hirsuta.*)

S. Regi'na. Related to *S. speciosa.* Stem erect, about 6 in. long. *l.* in 4 to 6 pairs, ovate or elliptic-ovate, 4 to 8 in. long, finely crenate, velvety above, with pale-green veins, downy and purple beneath. *fl.* pale violet with a pale-yellowish band spotted with purple within, nodding, tube curved-trumpet-shaped, lobes spreading, about ½ in. long; peduncles axillary, 3 to 4 in. long, 4 to 6 in each axil. Brazil. 1903. (B.M. 8182.) Hybrids have been raised with *S. speciosa.* Very free-flowering.

Sinningia speciosa

S. specio'sa.* Stem short. *l.* oblong, obtuse or nearly so, convex, usually narrowed at base, crenate, velvety and somewhat hairy. *fl.* usually violet in the wild plant, large, bell-shaped; cal. segs. ovate-lanceolate, shortly hairy. September. 1815. (B.M. 1937 and B.R. 213 as *Gloxinia speciosa.*) From this species the greenhouse plants popularly called Gloxinia (q.v.) have been raised. The variations from the wild type, especially in colour and size, are very numerous and striking; many of them have been figured in various works. var. **albiflo'ra,** *fl.* white; **caules'cens,** *l.* larger than in type, stem long, thick. 1826. (B.R. 1127.); **macrophyl'la,** *l.* very large, with white veins. 1844. (B.M. 3934 as *Gloxinia speciosa macrophylla variegata.*); **ru'bra,** *fl.* red. (P.M.B. 7, 271 as *Gloxinia rubra.*)

S. veluti'na. Stem erect, up to 18 in. h., slender, leafy. *l.* ovate, acute, rounded or somewhat heart-shaped at base, 2 to 4½ in. long, green on both sides, veins and stalks at length purplish. *fl.* pale greenish. 1½ to 2 in. long, gibbous at base, throat constricted, limb spreading; cal. funnel-bell-shaped, 1 in. long, segs. 3-angled. 1827. (L.B.C. 1398.)

S. × Youngia'na (*S. speciosa* × *S. velutina*). *rhiz.* very thick. Stem erect, 12 to 18 in. h., purplish. *l.* oblong or ovate, crenate, whitish-green beneath. *fl.* axillary or terminal, solitary, deep violet or purple, tube bell-shaped, yellowish-white at base and in spotted throat, lobes almost equal, round; cal. lobes ovate, acuminate. Summer. (B.M. 4954.)

SINOFRANCHET'IA (*sino,* Chinese; in honour of Adrien René Franchet, 1835–1900, French botanist, who described many Chinese plants). FAM. *Lardizabalaceae.* A single species native of Cent. and W. China constitutes this genus. A deciduous twining shrub related to Holboellia, with long-stalked 3-foliolate leaves, leaflets with a midrib and pinnate veins (in Sargentodoxa there are 2 or 3 veins from the base of the leaflet and they fork). Flowers 1-sexual, inconspicuous, parts in sixes, carpels 3, fruit a many-seeded berry. A vigorous, hardy climber with leaves much like the Scarlet-runner in size and shape but glaucous beneath, succeeding in any good ordinary soil.

S. chinen'sis. Glabrous, climbing to about 30 ft. or more; young shoots and l.-stalks with purplish bloom. *l.* entire, shortly pointed, glabrous, glaucous beneath, terminal lflet. stalked, obovate, lateral oblique, ovate, 3 to 5 in. long, stalks short. *fl.* in drooping racemes about 4 in. long, on short leafy shoots, small, white, inconspicuous. May. *fr.* roundish, about ¾ in. long, on short leafy shoots, small, white, inconspicuous. May. *fr.* roundish, about ¾ in. long, lavender-purple. 1908. (B.M. 8720.)

sino-gran'dis -is -e, Chinese form of the species *grandis*.

SINOJACK'IA (in honour of J. G. Jack, of the Arnold Arboretum, U.S.A., a student of Chinese plants). FAM. *Styracaceae.* Three deciduous trees, natives of China. Leaves alternate, shortly stalked. Flowers few, in loose, lateral, leafy racemes; calyx top-shaped, shortly 5- to 7-lobed; petals 5 to 7; stamens 10 to 14; flower-stalks very slender. Fruit 1-seeded. They like an open, rich, loamy soil. *S. Rehderiana* is hardy, the other probably so.

S. Rehderia'na.* Tree to 16 ft. *l.* obovate or elliptic, 1 to 3 in. long, shortly pointed, base cuneate to subcordate, sparsely minutely toothed; glabrous or nearly so. *fl.* in loose leafy racemes of 5 to 6; pet. usually 6 or 7, oblong, ½ in. long, stalk slender, up to 1 in. long. June. *fr.* cylindric oblong, 1 in. long, beaked. E. China. 1930.

S. xylocarp'a. Tree up to 20 ft., shoots, l.-stalks, and cal. stellately hairy. *l.* elliptic or inclined to obovate, 1½ to 3 in. long, cordate and smaller on the fl.-shoots, short-pointed, base rounded, toothed, soon glabrous. *fl.* 1 in. across, white, in leafy racemes of 3 to 5; pet. elliptic-oblong, ½ in. long. May. E. China. 1934.

W. J. B.

sino-lis'teri, Chinese form of the species *Listeri*.

SINOMEN'IUM (*sino*, Chinese, *men*, moon; Chinese moonseed). FAM. *Menispermaceae.* A genus of 1 species allied to Cocculus but with flowers in long, drooping panicles (not clusters or spikes) and stamens 9 to 12 (not 6 to 9). Fruit a drupe. A hardy and vigorous deciduous twining shrub with entire or lobed deep-green shining leaves and inconspicuous, dioecious flowers. Ordinary soil will suit it.

S. acu'tum. Deciduous, glabrous, twining shrub up to 20 ft. h. *l.* very variable, ovate-cordate and entire, or lobed, lobes often 3 to 5, shallow or deep, with 3 to 5 veins from base, deep bright-green. *fl.* 1-sexual, in pyramidal panicles 6 in. long or more, small, yellow, stalks downy. June. *fr.* about ¼ in. across, globose, black. With blue bloom. Cent. and W. China, Japan. 1901. SYN. *S. diversifolium, Cocculus diversifolius, C. heterophyllus, Menispermum acutum.*

S. diversifo'lium. A synonym of *S. acutum.*

sino-nuttal'lii, Chinese form of the species *Nuttallii.*

sino-orna'tus, Chinese form of the species *ornatus.*

SINOWILSON'IA (*sino*, Chinese; in honour of Dr. E. H. Wilson, 1876–1930, who between 1900 and 1910 introduced many Chinese plants). FAM. *Hamamelidaceae.* A genus of 1 Chinese species allied to Hamamelis but flowers monoecious, without petals, in long, slender, drooping racemes, stamens (or staminodes) 5. Fruit a capsule. Hardy, but flowers of little beauty.

S. Hen'ryi. Deciduous shrub or small tree, about 20 ft. h. *l.* Tilia-like, 3 to 7 in. long, short-stalked, covered like shoots with starry down, teeth bristle-like. *fl.* green, inconspicuous; male spikes 1 to 2 in. long, cylindrical, catkin-like; female spikes shorter in fl. but lengthening in fr. to 6 or 7 in. *fr.* an ovoid capsule ⅔ in. long. *Seeds* jet-black. May. Hupeh, China, 1908.

Sintenis'ii, in honour of the plant collector Paul Ernst Emil Sintenis, b. 1847, who travelled in many parts of the world including W. Asia and Puerto Rico.

sinua'tus -a -um, sinuate, having a strongly waved or recessed margin.

sinuo'sus -a -um, wavy, undulated.

SINUS. The recess between 2 lobes, or formed by a fold.

siph'o, tubular, or with a marked tube.

SIPHOCAMP'YLUS (*siphon*, tube, *kampylos*, curved; from the form of the corolla). FAM. *Campanulaceae.* A genus of about 100 species of herbs, sub-shrubs, or shrubs, sometimes climbing, natives of S. America, with 1 also in Cent. America and the W. Indies, closely allied to Centropogon but ovary almost always cone-shaped above, not flat as in Centropogon. Fruit a capsule, opening at apex by 2 lobes. The 2 smallest anthers are hairy at the tip, the other 3 naked. Leaves alternate or rarely in whorls, usually entire or toothed, rarely pinnately lobed or deeply cut. Flowers red, orange, or purplish, rarely greenish, usually large; corolla straight or incurved, lobes equal or not, sometimes 2-lipped, the side lobes sometimes connate with the upper ones; staminal tube adnate to base of corolla; peduncles 1-flowered, axillary, or forming clustered corymbs or loose racemes at tips of branches. These beautiful stove greenhouse plants succeed in light turfy loam and peat and are propagated by cuttings. Except where otherwise indicated the following are herbaceous perennials.

S. betulifo'lius. Stems branched, terete, glabrous, 3 ft. h. *l.* ovate, slender-pointed, cordate-triangular, 2 in. long, somewhat doubly toothed, smooth above, downy beneath on nerves; stalks nearly 1 in. long. *fl.* 2¼ to 3 in. long, slightly curved, tube bright red, lobes 5, nearly equal, yellow; stamens and style slightly exserted; pedicels axillary, solitary, longer than l. July. Organ Mts. 1842. (B.M. 3973.) Warm greenhouse. One of the supposed parents of *Centropogon × Lucyanus.*

S. coccin'eus. A synonym of *Centropogon coccineus.*

S. crenatifo'lius. About 3 ft. *l.* oblong-elliptic, 5 to 6 in. long, irregularly crenate. *fl.* scarlet, tipped yellow, axillary, solitary. Summer. Brazil. Before 1870. (Ref. B. 227.) Showy warm greenhouse shrub.

S. gigan'teus. Stem 14 ft. or more, branches hairy. *l.* lanceolate, cuspidate, 6 to 9 in. long, narrowed at base, wrinkled, crenately toothed, smooth above, hairy beneath; almost sessile. *fl.* reddish-yellow; cor. falcate, velvety, tube as long as cal. teeth, lobes lanceolate-ovate; pedicels often longer than l. July. Colombia. Stove.

S. glandulo'sus. Softly hairy, 3 ft. h. *l.* heart-shaped, wrinkled, doubly toothed; stalk rather long. *fl.* rose, nodding; cal. lobes spreading, margins reflexed, glandular-toothed; cor. tube curved, compressed, club-shaped; segs. nearly equal, erecto-patent; peduncles axillary, solitary, 1-fld., shorter than l. July. Colombia. 1845. (B.M. 4331; F.d.S. 401.) Stove.

S. harma'tus. Hairy, about 6 ft. h. *l.* oblong-ovate or somewhat heart-shaped, slender-pointed, narrowed to the base, irregularly toothed, nerves prominent beneath; stalked. *fl.* violet; cal. lobes hooked, spreading; cor. tube curved, laterally angular-compressed, segs. nearly equal, long. June. Brazil. 1849. Greenhouse.

S. Humboldtia'nus. About 3 ft., branches angular, densely hairy. *l.* ovate to lanceolate, acute at both ends, sharply toothed, almost smooth above; stalked. *fl.* scarlet; cal. lobes ovate-triangular, shorter than tube; cor. tube straight, segs. ovate-lanceolate, upper longer; pedicels axillary, compressed, as long as l. Summer. Peru. 1866. (B.M. 5631.) SYN. *S. fulgens.* Warm greenhouse.

S. lantanifo'lius. About 3 ft., branches straight, somewhat woody, terete. *l.* ovate, 1½ in. long, acute, base obtuse, somewhat heart-shaped, wrinkled and smooth above, brown-hairy beneath, toothed; stalk short. *fl.* purplish, 8 to 10 together; cal. velvety; cor. narrow, incurved, lobes slender-pointed; pedicels corymbose. Venezuela. 1841. Stove. var. **glabrius'culus,** scarcely hairy. (B.M. 4105 as *S. lantanifolius.*)

S. longepeduncula'tus. Stem 3 ft., terete. *l.* alternate, ovate, slender-pointed, 3 to 4 in. long, membranous, sharply toothed, base heart-shaped; stalked. *fl.* purplish; cal. segs. acute, much shorter than cor.; cor. nearly 2 in. long, narrow, somewhat curved; pedicels axillary, longer than l. Brazil. 1822. (B.M. 4015; G.F. 600 as *S. fimbriatus.*) Stove.

S. macropo'dus. 2 to 3 ft. h., branched, hairy. *l.* ovate, 3 in. long, acute, crenate, slightly hairy above, hairy beneath; stalk short. *fl.* bluish-red; cal. hairy; cor. 4 times as long as cal., tube ventricose above, lower lobes reflexed; pedicel about as long as l., downy. June. Brazil. Stove.

S. manettiiflo'rus. Erect, 12 in. h. *l.* oblong-ovate, slightly toothed, shining above, netted; short-stalked. *fl.* solitary, red and yellow, as long as l.; cal. segs. awl-shaped, toothed; cor. laterally compressed, segs. nearly equal, nearly erect; peduncles 3 or 4 times as long as l. April. Colombia. 1848. (B.M. 4403.) SYN. *S. nitidus* of gardens. Stove.

S. microsto'ma. Erect sub-shrub, 2 to 3 ft. h. Stem glabrous, branches terete. *l.* alternate, ovate, 2 in. long, acute, glandular toothed, glabrous; stalk short. *fl.* scarlet; cal. segs. obtuse, spreading; cor. hairy, swollen above, laterally compressed, segs. small, linear, obtuse, connivent; umbels terminal, peduncle short. Colombia. 1844. (B.M. 4286; F.d.S. 444.) Stove.

S. Orbignia'nus. 2 ft. h. or more, branches terete, erect. *l.* ternate, ovate, 3 to 4 in. long, slender-pointed, downy beneath, unequally sharply toothed; stalk short. *fl.* yellow and red, many in upper axils; cal. lobes 3 times as long as tube; cor. much longer than cal., lobes linear; pedicels half as long as l. July. Bolivia. 1849. (B.M. 4713; F.d.S. 544.) Stove.

S. penduliflo'rus. Glabrous, climbing shrub, 2 ft. h. *l.* opposite, ovate-oblong, distantly toothed, rather acute, thick; stalk long. *fl.* scarlet, nodding; cal. segs. 3 times as long as tube; cor. segs. linear; pedicels 1 in. long; racemes long, terminal, loose. Venezuela. 1847. (F.d.S. 763.) Stove.

Siphocampylus revolutus

S. revolu'tus. Erect, somewhat branched, hairy. *l.* ovate-lanceolate, 3 in. long, slender-pointed, toothed, tips revolute. *fl.* $2\frac{1}{2}$ in. long, purplish-red, tube contracted at throat and base; segs. linear-lanceolate, acute, almost equal, paler within, lowest revolute, nearly white within; stamens bearded. Habitat? 1841.

S. scan'dens. Climbing. *l.* oblong, 1 to $1\frac{3}{4}$ in. long, rather acute at base, slightly fleshy, entire, margins revolute; stalked, reflexed. *fl.* scarlet; cor. tube about 1 in. long, falcate, nearly equal, reflexed; pedicels about $\frac{1}{4}$ in. long, axillary. Peru. 1847. Stove.

S. villos'ulus. Branched, about 3 ft. h. *l.* alternate, oblong-lanceolate, slender-pointed, narrowed to stalk, silky and green above, downy beneath. *fl.* reddish-orange, small, cor. segs narrow, acute; racemes terminal, many-fld.; pedicels longer than cal. Brazil. 1832. (F.d.S. 619.) SYN. *S. amoenus, Lobelia villosula.*

F. G. P.

SIR'EX. *See* **Woodwasps.**

Siris'sa, the native name in Bengal.

SISAL HEMP. *See* **Agave sisalana** in article under **Agave.**

sisala'nus -a -um, of Sisal, Yucatan.

sissoi'des, like Sissoo.

SIS'SOO. *See* **Dalbergia Sissoo.** A native name.

sisymbriifo'lius -a -um, with leaves like Sisymbrium a genus of Cruciferae, mostly considered as weeds in this country.

SISYRINCH'IUM (ancient Greek name used by Theophrastus). FAM. *Iridaceae.* Satin Flower. A genus of about 60 species of annual or perennial herbs of dwarf or middle size, natives of N. and S. America. Differing from Libertia and its allies where they are free by the filaments being joined into a tube at the base. Rootstock usually creeping. Leaves linear to almost cylindrical. Flowers clustered at end of stem with 2 spathe valves, the outer herbaceous, inner membranous; perianth yellow, blue, or red, regular, more or less funnel-shaped; segments joined at base, oblong to lanceolate. Fruit an oblong to globose capsule. They are mostly hardy and grow well in sandy loam and leaf-mould or peat. Several are the better for moist soil conditions, provided drainage is thorough. Some species, like *S. striatum,* grow very readily, and may become naturalized as has *S. angustifolium*; others are less easy and need care in suiting the compost to their liking, as the beautiful *S. filifolium* and *S. Douglasii.* Propagated by seeds or division. Some species are known as Pigroot. **A**

S. angustifo'lium. Blue-eyed Grass. Much like *S. Bermudiana* but *basal l.* much narrower, about $\frac{1}{8}$ in. wide, stem winged to base, longer than l. *fl.* 1 to 4 in cluster, smaller, segs. oblong-obovate, bright blue. *fr.* about half as large. N. America, naturalized in many places, including British Is. in grassy places. (B.M. 464 as *S. gramineum.*) SYN. *S. gramineum.* Hardy.

S. bel'lum. Closely related to *S. angustifolium.* Tufted. Stem branched with narrow wings, leafless below branches. *Spathe* valves shorter than in *S. angustifolium* with a broader white margin. *fl.* well clear of bracts, blue-violet with yellow throat. N. America. Hardy.

S. Bermudia'na. Perennial up to about 1 ft. h., winged, about $\frac{1}{8}$ in. wide. *Basal l.* linear, about $\frac{1}{4}$ in. wide, as long as stem. *fl.* in 2 or 3 stalked clusters of 6 to 8; perianth segs. obovate, mucronate, violet-blue, yellow at base, about $\frac{1}{8}$ in. long. May, June. *fr.* about $\frac{1}{8}$ in. long. Bermuda. (B.M. 94 as *S. iridioides.*) Hardy.

S. californ'icum. Stem over 2 ft. h., unbranched, curved. *l.* 1 to 2 ft. long, linear-ensiform, about $\frac{1}{2}$ in. wide. *fl.* yellow, expanded, opening in succession in a many-fld. cluster; perianth segs. obovate-oblong, obtuse; anthers orange. Autumn. California. 1796. (B.M. 983 as *Marica californica.*) Half-hardy.

S. chilen'se. Stem 6 to 12 in. h., flexuous. *Radical l.* linear-ensiform, striated, 3 to 12 in. long, $\frac{1}{12}$ to $\frac{1}{8}$ in. wide. *fl.* purple, yellow at base; spathe linear, about 3-fld. July. Brazil, &c. 1826. (B.M. 2786.) Half-hardy.

S. convolu'tum. Stem 12 in. h., broadly winged, usually forked. *l.* linear. *fl.* 3 or 4, yellow, veined brown, segs. $\frac{1}{2}$ in. long. Trop. America. Greenhouse.

Sisyrinchium filifolium (p. 1962)

S. Douglas'ii.* Spring Bell. Stem 8 to 10 in. long, unbranched. Root creeping. *l.* erect, broadly linear, spreading, striated, 6 to 8 in. long, base sheathing. *fl.* dark-purple, striated;

segs. obcordate, ⅜ to ⅝ in. long, clawed; spathe 2-fld., erect, leafy N. America. 1826. (B.M. 3509; B.R. 1364.) Hardy. Syn. *S. grandiflorum, Olsynium Douglasii.* var. **al'bum,** *fl.* white.

S. filifo'lium.* Habit rush-like. Stem 6 to 8 in. h. *fl.* bell-shaped, erect; white, the segs. delicately lined pale purplish-red. May. Falkland Is. 1885. (B.M. 6829; G.C. 23 (1885), 696.) Hardy.

S. gramin'eum. A synonym of *S. angustifolium.*

S. graminifo'lium. Stem erect, 7 to 9 in. h., branched. *Radical l.* 8 in. long, scabrid on margins, slender-pointed, sheathing at base; *stem-l.* 3 to 6 in. long. *fl.* yellow, segs. obovate, mucronate; spathes few- or many-fld., outer 1½ in. long, inner 1 in. April. Chile. 1825. (B.R. 1067.) Half-hardy. var. **ascend'ens,** stem 5 to 9 in. long, *radical l.* 4 to 6 in. long, *stem-l.* 2 to 3 in. long, *spathes* very hairy, equal. (B.R. 1914 as var. *pumilum.*); **maculat'um,** *fl.* spotted blood-red. (B.M. 3197 as *S. maculatum.*)

S. grandiflo'rum. A synonym of *S. Douglasii.*

S. idahoen'se. Stem 6 to 16 in. h., narrowly winged, usually unbranched. *l.* 3 to 12 in. long, up to ⅛ in. wide. *fl.* 1 to 6, deep blue; segs. ½ to ¾ in. long. Western N. America. Hardy.

S. iridifo'lium. Stem 4 to 12 in. h., branched. *l.* linear-ensiform, tip incurved, roughly ciliate at margin; radical l. 4 to 8 in., stem-l. 2 to 4 in. long. *fl.* yellowish-white, downy; segs. about ½ in. long, wedge-shaped, slightly mucronate; spathes keeled, outer 1½ in., inner 1 in. long; peduncles flexuous; pedicels slender. June. Brazil to Chile. 1822. (L.B.C. 1979; B.M. 2312 as *S. laxum*; B.R. 646 as *Marica iridifolia.*) Half-hardy.

S. iridioi'des. A synonym of *S. Bermudiana.*

S. lax'um. A synonym of *S. iridifolium.*

S. longifo'lium. A synonym of *Solenomelus chilensis.*

S. lutes'cens. A synonym of *S. striatum.*

S. micran'thum. Stem 1-lvd., 2 to 9 in. h., unbranched, flexuous, glabrous. *l.* linear-ensiform, glabrous; radical l. 1 to 4 in., stem-l. 1 in. long, all glabrous. *fl.* 3 to 10, small, pedicellate, yellow, ⅙ in. long; spathe, outer about 1 in. long, inner ½ in. June. Mexico to Brazil. 1815. (B.M. 2116.) Half-hardy.

S. palmifo'lium. A synonym of *Eleutherine plicata.*

S. peduncula'tum. A synonym of *Solenomelus chilensis.*

S. stria'tum. Stem 1 to 2 ft. h. *Radical l.* about 1 ft. long, distichous, sheathing; stem-l. rather distant, stem-clasping. *fl.* 9 to 12, in a spike, longer than the ovate, cuspidate spathe, perianth yellowish, its tube ⅙ in., segs. over ½ in. long; pedicels as long as spathe. June. Chile. 1788. (L.B.C. 1870 as *S. lutescens*; B.M. 701 as *Marica striata.*) Hardy.

S. tenuifo'lium. Stem ascending, simple or branched, up to 12 in. h. *l.* linear-ensiform, scabrid on margins, striated; radical l. 2½ to 9 in., stem-l. 2 to 4 in. long. *fl.* yellow; segs. oblong, acute; pedicels somewhat hairy, longer than spathe; spathe 1- to many-fld. Mexico. 1816. (B.M. 2117, 2313.) Hardy.

sitchen'sis -is -e, of the Isle of Sitka, NW. America.

SITKA CYPRESS. *See* **Chamaecyparis nootkatensis.**

SITKA SPRUCE. *See* **Picea sitchensis.**

SITOLO'BIUM. Included under **Dicksonia.**

SITO'NES. *See* **Pea and Bean Weevils.**

SIUM (*Sion*, the old Greek name used by Dioscorides). Fam. *Umbelliferae.* A genus of about 5 species of glabrous herbs, natives of the north temperate regions, S. Africa, and St. Helena. Leaves pinnate; pinnae toothed. Flowers white, in compound umbels; involucral bracts numerous. The only species of horticultural interest is *S. Sisarum*, the Skirret, which see for treatment.

S. Sisar'um. Perennial. Root of clustered cylindrical or ellipsoid tubers. Stem smooth below, striate above. *Lflets.* sharply toothed; lateral ovate-lanceolate, terminal ovate with cordate base; upper l. 3-nate, lflets. narrow. Altai, Siberia.

SKIM'MIA (adapted from the Japanese *skimmi*). Fam. *Rutaceae.* A genus of 9 species of evergreen bushy shrubs, semi- or 2-sexual. Leaves dotted with glands, and odorous (not always pleasantly) when crushed, alternate, entire, shortly stalked. Flowers white, in close terminal panicles; petals and stamens 4 or 5. Fruit a drupe, carrying 2 to 4 1-seeded stones.

They succeed in both well-drained open loam or peaty soil, in a sunny place, and are easily propagated by cuttings for the hybrid or named varieties or by seeds for the species. Their beauty is chiefly in the fruits, and crops are better and more certain when plants are grown in groups. With *S. japonica,* which is 1-sexual, it is essential for the production of fruits that a male plant should be in close association with one or more females. Artificial fertilization of the blossoms is often practised.

KEY

1. *Lvs. mostly oblong-ovate, blunt; fl. usually 4-merous* S. japonica
1. *Lvs. mostly oblong-lanceolate, slender-pointed* 2
2. *Lvs. 3 to 6 in. long, clustered at ends of branches* S. Laureola
2. *Lvs. 2 to 4 in. long; fl. 5-merous* S. Reevesiana

S. × Fore'manii* (*S. japonica* × *S. Reevesiana*). *fr.* scarlet, roundish or obovoid on the same panicle, long persisting. *See also* **S. × Rogersii.**

S. Fortu'nei. A synonym of *S. Reevesiana.*

S. frag'rans, S. fragrantis'sima. *See* **S. japonica.**

Skimmia japonica

S. japon'ica. Evergreen 1-sexual bush 3 to 5 ft. h., more in width, mostly glabrous. *l.* clustered at end of twig, 3 to 4½ in. long, 1 to 1½ in. wide, narrowly obovate or oval, glandular beneath, leathery, pale green. *fl.* dull white, ⅓ in. wide, in erect terminal panicles 2 to 3 in. long. Spring. *fr.* orange-shaped or sub-globose, bright red, ⅓ in. wide. Japan. 1838. (B.M. 8038.) Syn. *S. oblata.* vars. **frag'rans** and **fragrantis'sima** are especially sweet-scented male forms. Male fl. are always more fragrant than the female; **macrophyl'la,** a male form with larger *l.* and panicles.

S. Laureo'la. Evergreen glabrous shrub up to 4 or 5 ft. *l.* 3 to 6 in. long, 1 to 2 in. wide, lanceolate, obovate or oblong, in a terminal cluster, heavily scented when crushed. *fl.* white, in terminal oval panicles 1 to 1½ in. long. *fr.* red, roundish-oval, ¼ to ⅓ in. long. Himalaya. 1850. Rather tender and rarely seen.

S. oblat'a. A synonym of *S. japonica.*

S. Reevesian'a.* Evergreen glabrous shrub about 2 ft., more in width. *l.* narrowly oval to lanceolate, 2 to 4 in. long, ¾ to 1¼ in. wide, slender-pointed, cuneate. *fl.* 2-sexual, ½ in. wide, crowded in terminal panicles 2 to 3 in. long. *fr.* crimson, oval or obovoid, ⅓ in. long. China. 1849. (B.M. 4719 as *S. japonica.*) Syn. *S. Fortunei.*

Hardy but most beautiful in the southern counties where it retains its fruit until spring. Dislikes chalk. var. **argent'ea,** *l.* with white margins; **rubel'la,** peduncles, petioles, and buds reddish; a staminate form.

S. × **Rogers'ii.** Probably a hybrid between *S. japonica* and *S. Reevesiana*. *fl.* 2-sexual. *fr.* crimson and flattened at top as in the former. *See also* **S.** × **Foremanii.**

S. rubel'la. A variety of *S. Reevesiana*.

W. J. B.

SKIN IRRITANTS. Many plants are rightly accused of causing irritation of the skin or the mucous membranes, producing redness of the affected parts, itching, blisters, and sometimes acute pain. The symptoms vary in kind and degree and are the result of varying causes. The reaction of individuals varies also so that it is rare to find that all persons exposed to the conditions which bring about irritation in some are affected; many indeed are immune to some though susceptible in a marked degree to others, which again may pass over other persons without causing them any inconvenience.

Perhaps the most widely recognized of these troubles is 'hay-fever'. Here there is no need for contact between the plant and the susceptible person, for the symptoms are produced by pollen floating in the air. Not the pollen of grasses, including cereals, alone is capable of causing running at the eyes and nose and general discomfort and even debility, but the pollen of other plants, such as hazel, sweet chestnut, and other wind-borne pollen may affect some people. Various measures of alleviation have been proposed but avoidance is only certain in pollen-free atmosphere such as high in the mountains or on the ocean. Susceptibility may be outgrown as time passes. Similar symptoms may be produced by other minute air-borne particles such as are produced by the break-up of the fruit-balls of the plane-tree.

With most other forms of skin-irritation direct contact with the plant capable of producing it is necessary, though the contact is not necessarily long. The two main exciting causes appear to be acids, especially formic acid, produced in thin-walled, usually acutely pointed hairs, and essential oils, produced usually on glands at the tips of hairs, or sometimes in glands sunken in the leaf tissue, or even substances in the sap distributed through the plant, the last, perhaps, more often affecting persons working with tropical woods.

The stinging nettles, Urtica sp., are a familiar example of the first group where the broken off tip of the stinging hairs makes a small wound into which the acid enters and produces painful blisters, redness of the skin, and prolonged irritation. The common species, *U. dioica*, is virulent but some species are much worse, and the annual weed, *U. urens*, often makes the hand collection of vegetables from rich market-garden land a painful process. Species of Blumenbackia, Caiophora, and Loasa, often grown in the flower garden, possess similar properties, and some species of the family Malpighiaceae and of Laportea carelessly handled cause very painful symptoms not restricted to the part of the body actually in contact with the plant.

The most familiar example of the second group is *Primula obconica* which in some persons produces effects resembling eczema. Many people are able to handle these most useful decorative plants with impunity, others are so sensitive that the merest contact, so slight as to be unknown to the person concerned, is sufficient to produce marked irritation. The mere presence of the plant in the same room is not a sufficient exciting cause, for the trouble is not due to any emanation from the plant. Where susceptible persons are concerned immediate and thorough washing with soapy water of the part touched, or with a dilute solution of lead acetate, will usually check the troubles. The exciting cause may be carried on the hands to other parts, and it is important not to touch other parts of the body or the skin of other persons with hands which have handled the plant. This applies only to susceptible persons. Other species of Primula do not usually cause any inconvenience, but even handling the seeds of some species may produce irritation in a very few.

Probably a much larger number of persons are affected, and much more seriously, by handling or momentarily touching *Rhus Toxicodendron*. The temptation to plant this shrub or climber for its brilliant autumn foliage is great but should be resisted, unless it can be placed where there is no risk of contact with the skin. It has on some occasions caused very considerable illness as well as irritation, and it has unfortunately been at times offered as *Ampelopis Hoggii*. Other species of *Rhus*, including *R. venenata* and *R. verniciflua*, also have poisonous properties, but mostly confined to the sap. *Umbellularia californica* also causes irritation to the mucous membrane of some people handling it, though apparently to a much more restricted number.

It is not always easy to say whether the skin irritation suffered is due to mechanical effects alone or to a combination of this and some substance produced by the plant. Among the plants causing irritation to the skin of some, and especially to those handling them freely, are Ivy, Sunflower, Helenium, Chrysanthemum, Strawberry, Parsnip, Mucuna, and Stizolobium.

Those employed in gathering Narcissi may suffer from the entry of the minute needle-shaped crystals (*see* **Raphides**) of calcium oxide in the sap, if the latter is allowed to find its way into any small cracks in the hand or on the wrists. Much can be done to prevent this by greasing the hands with tallow before the work is begun and washing them thoroughly when it is finished. The handling of bulbs of these and similar plants, may have similar effects.

No useful purpose would be fulfilled by attempting an exhaustive list of plants which may cause symptoms of this kind, for the great majority of the cases which occur are due to personal idiosyncrasies. Only a proportion of the persons handling a plant capable of producing untoward symptoms are likely to be affected, and it cannot be predicted beforehand who will be susceptible and who immune. Where any mysterious skin irritation may occur, the handling of some plant may be one of the causes to be investigated.

Skin'neri, in honour of Mr. G. Ure Skinner, 1804–67, of Newcastle, who collected orchids in Guatemala, &c., for Mr. James Bateman.

SKIPJACKS. *See* **Wireworms.**

SKIRRET (*Sium Sisarum*). A perennial sometimes grown for its rather large roots which are composed of fleshy, tuberous prongs. The roots are white and are cooked and served in the same way as Salsify. Skirret may be propagated by taking off the side roots just before growth begins in spring and dibbling them in, but the usual method is by seeds sown in drills a foot apart in early April. The seedlings should be thinned to 6 or 8 in. apart when large enough. A rather light soil, manured for a previous crop, deeply cultivated, best suits this plant. The roots may be used from the end of September onwards, being lifted as required through the winter. For use later they should be lifted just before growth begins, and stored in moderately dry sand.

Skorpil'ii, in honour of M. Skorpil, friend of Velenovsky.

SKULL CAP. *See* **Scutellaria.**

SKUNK CABBAGE. *See* **Symplocarpus foetidus.**

slashed, *see* ***laciniatus.***

SLATERS. *See* **Woodlice.**

SLEEP. A condition, generally found at night, characterized by flowers closing and often drooping, and by leaves folding. The movements which result in this sleep seem to be concerned with the need for protecting developing anthers and pistils from loss of heat during the colder hours of the night and the young leaves likewise. Drooping, at least on cold nights, is readily seen in the umbels of the Carrot, in some species of Scabiosa, and in the young flowers of the Pansy. The cotyledons of seedlings, expanded flat in the warm rays of the sun, often close together and so present a much smaller surface to the cold air on cold evenings, opening again in the morning, a phenomenon easily seen, for instance, in Clover, Mimosa, Wood Sorrel, Cucumber, Mimulus, Chickweed, and in many others. Many compound leaves exhibit similar phenomena, their opposite leaflets becoming pressed together so as to present as little surface as possible to the air. There is little doubt that these or similar movements also protect in no small measure from undue loss of moisture for they are frequently seen to occur when the sun is bright and the air unusually dry, and on the other hand the closing of flowers in dull weather will protect the pollen, &c., from damage by rain. *See* **Mimosa.**

SLEEPY DISEASE. A well-known Tomato disease caused by the fungus Verticillium and sometimes called Verticillium Wilt. *See* **Tomato diseases.**

SLIME FUNGUS. *See* **Myxomycetes.**

SLIPPER FLOWER. *See* **Calceolaria.**

SLIPPER, LADY'S. *See* **Cypripedium.**

SLIPPER SPURGE. *See* **Pedilanthus.**

SLIPS. Pieces of a plant taken up and divided, each with a few roots attached, which will, when placed under proper conditions, form plants themselves. The common Box, *Buxus sempervirens*, is thus readily increased, so too may be Pinks and many other plants. The term is also sometimes applied to other forms of stem-cuttings taken without roots.

SLOAN'EA (in honour of Sir Hans Sloane, born in Ireland, 1660, President of the Royal Society, Founder of the British Museum and Chelsea Physic Garden, d. 1753). FAM. *Elaeocarpaceae.* A genus of about 50 species of Trop. American trees with alternate leaves (sometimes nearly opposite), entire or toothed, pinnately nerved. Flowers in racemes, panicles, or clusters, axillary or terminal, rarely solitary; sepals 4 or 5, valvate, rarely joined; petals usually absent, when present 1 to 4, sepaloid; stamens numerous. The Sloaneas need stove conditions and form fine trees with large leaves. A compost of loam and peat suits them and they can be propagated by cuttings of ripe wood in sand under glass with heat.

S. denta'ta. Tree to 50 ft. *l.* ovate, acute, bluntly toothed; stipules cordate-triangular, toothed. *fl.* large, white. August to November. 1752. SYN. *S. grandiflora.*

S. sinemarien'sis. Tree to 50 ft. *l.* roundish-ovate, entire, 1 ft. long; stipules long, slender-pointed, deciduous. *fl.* small, white, in axillary racemes. July, August. 1820. SYN. *S. Aubletii.*

F. G. P.

SLOE. *See* **Prunus spinosa.**

SLOPES. Any piece of land on an inclined plane, but usually applied to lawns naturally or artificially undulated. Such grassy slopes have to be laid out in conformity with the space they occupy and the disposition of the land above and below them. In forming a slope the soil should be made equally firm throughout to prevent subsidence in one part more than another after the work is finished, and an experienced eye is a better guide to the form of a slope than instrumental aid when once its limits are fixed. The formation of a slope or pleasantly undulating ground often effects a great saving in labour when alterations are in progress, for spare soil can be used on the spot instead of carting it away. Gardens sloping to the south or south-west have a better exposure to the sun than those on the level, and sloping ground, no matter what the direction of the slope, is more easily drained than flat.

SLOW-MATCH TREE. *See* **Careya arborea.**

SLOW-WORM, *Anguis fragilis*, is a limbless, non-poisonous Lizard though its appearance suggests that it is a Snake. It feeds on earthworms, slugs, and insects, attains a length of 9 to 12 in., and prefers dry grassy places and ditch-sides shaded by herbage. The eggs hatch immediately after they are laid, and some 6 to 12 young are produced in August. It is a shy creature, which will break off its tail by a jerking movement when captured—a common feature among Lizards. The term 'Blindworm' is a misnomer.

G. F. W.

SLUGS. These widespread and pernicious pests are the most familiar of all creatures which attack plants, and the toll they take every year of agricultural and horticultural crops is very great. They feed chiefly after dark, both above and below ground, on all kinds of living plants, and hide away during the day-time beneath dense herbage, stones, leaves, pots, boards, and in other dark, cool, and moist situations. Damage to plants may occur throughout the year if the weather is favourable, and severe injury is often done to Lettuces and other plants protected beneath cloches even in the depth of winter. During intensely cold weather and in hot, dry periods, they creep into rubbish heaps, shelter among the basal leaves of plants, or burrow into the soil. Slugs, like Snails, are hermaphrodite, and each individual is capable of laying a considerable number of eggs. The oval or round, white, transparent, jelly like eggs are deposited in clusters in the soil, beneath dead and decaying vegetation and in other moist situations. The young Slugs feed for a time on dead and decaying organic matter, but soon turn their attention to seedlings, leaves, roots, and tubers according to the habits of the particular species. The tongue, which is provided with cross rows of small horny teeth, is used for rasping off their food. Some species ascend plants to feed on the leaves, often high above ground-level, others feed at or just below soil level, while the subterranean species attack roots and tubers often far below the surface of the ground. An important feature of these Molluscs is their ability to excrete slime which, while assisting them in crawling, enables them to rid themselves of irritant dressings which may fall upon them. Certain conditions are favourable to Slugs, especially moist soil and an abundance of decaying organic matter. Heavy, wet, and sour soils are invariably heavily infested with Slugs, and even alkaline, water-retaining soils rich in humus often harbour large numbers. Slugs have a number of natural enemies, including birds (especially Rooks, Starlings, Blackbirds, and Ducks), Toads, Shrews, and Moles, and insects (especially certain Ground or Carabid beetles), but none is effective in keeping their numbers in check. There are a number of species of Land Slugs, many of which are common, which are distinguishable by their colour, size, the development of the rudimentary shell enclosed in the mantle, and the number and forms of the teeth on the file-like tongue. The most destructive species are the Grey Slug, *Agriolimax reticulatus*; the Large Black Slug, *Arion ater*; and the Keeled or Subterranean Slugs, *Milax sowerbii* and *M. gagates,* which are so destructive to Potato tubers.

Complete eradication of Slugs in heavily infested areas is not possible, but the persistent use of one or other of the following measures will reduce injury to cultivated plants. Large numbers of Slugs may be caught in traps consisting of Orange or Grapefruit peel, Cucumber rind, Lettuce and Cabbage leaves, and small heaps of Bran laid on the ground among attacked plants. The traps should be examined every day, the captured creatures destroyed, and the traps reset. Slates, tiles, boards, and pieces of sacking may be used in a similar manner to attract the pests, which collect beneath the traps during the day. The old method of stabbing Slugs with a hat-pin after dark has been superseded by the use of Meta-Bran bait. Metaldehyde is purchased in the form of tablets or as a fine powder, and should be thoroughly mixed with bran, dried tea-leaves, crumbled stale brown bread, or bone meal at the rate of 1 oz. of Metaldehyde to 3 lb. of the attractant. The dressing is broadcast over the ground between the plants on mild, damp, but not wet evenings at the rate of 3 oz. of the mixture to each square rod; or the bait may be placed in small heaps about 1 ft. apart, and covered with a tile, stone, or board to protect the dressing from birds and from heavy rain. Metaldehyde is too expensive for the treatment of large areas, and an effective substitute is a mixture of 6 lb. finely ground copper sulphate and 1 cwt. kainit, which is distributed over the ground towards evening at the rate of 3 cwt. to the acre. In gardens where the soil is undrained and has received annual heavy dressings of manure, garden refuse, or spent hops, an effort should be made to devise a simple method of drainage to reduce the soil humidity, and to withhold dressings of organic matter for a year or so and to substitute with inorganic, chemical fertilizers. Proprietary irritant dressings for killing Slugs are available, but their success depends largely upon hitting the creatures during their nocturnal period of activity. It is necessary to make several dressings on successive nights owing to the faculty of these Molluscs of casting off the irritant with the slime that they excrete. Clean cultivation in the matter of weed destruction and the proper disposal of garden refuse is necessary, for clumps of weeds provide shelter for the pests, and compost heaps harbour them.

G. F. W.

SLUGS, CARNIVOROUS. These slugs, sometimes called Snail-Slugs, prey on earthworms, slugs, and other small soil animals, so should be preserved. There are 3 British species, of which *Testacella haliotidea* is the commonest. They can be distinguished from herbivorous Slugs by the presence of an ear-shaped flat shell towards the tail end. They are often seen on lawns and paths at night seeking their prey.

G. F. W.

SLUGWORMS. The larvae of Sawflies belonging to the tribe Caliroini, which includes the genera Caliroa and Endelomyia. They are slug-like and the body of Caliroa is obscured by a dark slime or exudation. The leaves upon which they feed are skeletonized as the surface layer only is eaten. (*See* **Pear and Cherry Slugworm, Rose Sawflies.**)

G. F. W.

SMALL BULB FLIES, *Eumerus tuberculatus* and *E. strigatus*, are much smaller than the Narcissus Fly (q.v.), being about ¼ in. long and resembling Hover Flies. The former species is commonly associated with injury to Narcissus bulbs, the latter with Irises, Hyacinths, and Potatoes. The flies have a metallic green thorax, and a black body with a series of white, crescent-shaped marks along the abdomen. The larva is legless, yellowish-white, though usually stained dark brown by the decaying tissues in which it lives. It is ⅓ in. long, and there is a conspicuous brownish-red projection at the hind end of the body with 2 smaller but easily visible tubercles on either side. As many as 30 to 40 larvae may be found in a single bulb, sometimes associated with a solitary Merodon larva. The puparium is hard, horny, whitish, and nearly ¼ in. long. The flies appear in early May, and successive generations are found until the autumn. The female lays her eggs in batches in the same positions as Merodon, and the resulting maggots enter the bulb through the neck and feed on the bulb scales causing a speedier decay of the bulb than do those of the larger fly. The larvae soon become mature, and pupate in and around the necks of the bulbs. Flies of the second generation appear about early July, when more eggs are laid. The majority of this second brood remain as larvae in the bulbs and emerge as flies the following year.

The measures of control are similar to those advocated against the Narcissus Fly (q.v.). In addition, it is inadvisable to expose drying bulbs to bright sunshine, but to dry them off under cover of a shed as the exposed bulbs are open to attack by the flies. The number of Eumerus in a heavily infested area may be reduced considerably by providing decoy heaps of worthless bulbs, which should be left on the ground during the summer to attract the flies. Egg-laying will take place in the heaps, which should be burned after an exposure period of not longer than a month.

G. F. W.

SMALL ERMINE MOTHS. *See* **Ermine Moths.**

SMALL FLAX LILY. *See* **Phormium Colensoi.**

SMALL REED. *See* **Calamovilfa.**

smarag'dinus -a -um, emerald green.

SMEATHMANN'IA (in honour of Henry Smeathmann who collected plants in Africa). FAM. *Passifloraceae.* A genus of 4 species of evergreen shrubs, natives of W. Trop. Africa. Branches terete, robust. Leaves oblong, leathery, toothed, the stalks with 1 to 4 glands at apex. Flowers white, rather large, scentless, axillary; calyx with a very short tube, lobes 5, oblong; petals 5, rather longer than calyx; corona leathery, ciliate, urceolate, crenate or lobed; stamens about 20. Beautiful stove shrubs, erect in habit, needing a compost of loam, peat, and sand, and propagated by half-ripe cuttings in sand under glass in heat.

S. laeviga'ta. About 6 ft. h. with spreading branches. *l.* alternate, somewhat distichous, 4 in. long, coarsely toothed, narrowed to a short stalk. *fl.* white, 1½ in. across, solitary, axillary, on a short, silky stalk, curved downwards; pet. oblong, like sep. spreading; stamens and pistil long, on a short, thick anthophore. July. 1823. (B.M. 4194.)

S. pubes'cens. About 6 ft. h., branches terete, reddish-hairy, as are also l.-stalks and veins beneath, peduncles and cal. *l.* alternate, oblong, glossy, acute, toothed, rounded at base; stalk short. *fl.* white, solitary; sep. and pet. acute and spreading, outer green and 3-ribbed, inner white; ovary and stigma downy. February. 1845. (B.M. 4364.)

Smeea'nus -a -um, in honour of Alfred Hutchinson Smee, 1841–1901, of Carshalton, Surrey.

SMERINTH'US. *See* **Hawk Moths.**

smilacifo'lius -a -um, with foliage like a Smilax.

SMILACI'NA (diminutive of Smilax). FAM. *Liliaceae.* False Solomon's Seal. A genus of about 25 species of mostly hardy perennials, natives of N. and Cent. America and temperate and mountainous Asia, related to Polygonatum and Maianthemum, differing from the former by its racemose or paniculate terminal inflorescence and almost or quite distinct spreading perianth segments, and from the latter by having floral parts in threes, not twos. Leaves alternate, ovate, lanceolate, or rarely narrow; stalk very short. Flowers small, on short pedicels; perianth at length deciduous; stamens 6; inflorescence terminal; peduncle short; bracts small or absent. They succeed best in a good moist, but not wet, loam in a shady place, most of them being hardy.

S. bifo'lia. A synonym of *Maianthemum bifolium.*

S. borea'lis. A synonym of *Clintonia borealis.*

S. canaden'sis. A synonym of *Maianthemum bifolium.*

S. olera'cea. Stem sub-erect, simple, about 4 ft. h. *l.* oblong-acuminate, 6 to 7 in. long, minutely downy beneath. *fl.* in a deltoid, terminal panicle, minutely bracteate; perianth white, tinged rose without, globose, about ¼ in. long and broad; pedicels ¼ in. long, deflexed or ascending. May. *Berry* rose-purple with dark spots. Sikkim. 1877. (B.M. 6313 as *Tovaria oleracea.*)

Smilacina paniculata

S. panicula'ta. Glabrous. *l.* ovate-lanceolate, 5 in. long, long-pointed, main veins 5 to 7. *fl.* in a terminal panicle, 2¼ in. long as the same width, snowy-white in all parts; pedicels about ⅓ in. long; perianth about ⅓ in. across, segs. elliptic, rounded at tip. March. Guatemala, S. Mexico. 1913. (B.M. 8539.) Needs greenhouse conditions.

S. racemo'sa.* False Spikenard. 2 to 3 ft. h. *l.* 10 to 15, ascending, oblong or lanceolate, slender-pointed, 3 to 9 in. long, paler and downy beneath. *fl.* on solitary pedicels; perianth whitish, $\frac{1}{12}$ in. long; panicle oblong or deltoid, 2 to 6 in. long, branches ascending, dense-fld.; peduncles short. May. N. America. 1640. (B.M. 899 as *Convallaria racemosa*; R.L. 230.)

S. stella'ta. Star-flowered Lily of the Valley. 1 to 2 ft. h. *l.* 6 to 15, ascending, oblong or lanceolate, 2 to 6 in. long, acute or acuminate, sessile and stem-clasping, glaucous and mealy beneath. *fl.* white, ⅛ to ¼ in. long; racemes somewhat dense, 10- to 20-fld., 1 to 1½ in. long; peduncle very short. May. NW. America. 1633. (R.L. 185; B.M. 1043 and L.B.C. 1080 as *Convallaria stellata.*)

S. uniflo'ra. A synonym of *Clintonia uniflora.*

SMI'LAX (ancient Greek name). FAM. *Liliaceae.* A genus of some 200 species of woody or herbaceous climbers (rarely erect in habit), 1-sexual, widely spread over the temperate and tropical regions of both hemispheres, often with a tuberous rootstock. Stems round or angled, often spiny, prickly, or bristly. Leaves alternate, prominently 3- to 9-veined; stalks often very short; stipules usually terminated by a curling tendril. Flowers greenish, whitish, or yellowish, of little beauty, borne in small axillary umbels; perianth segments and stamens 6. Fruit a globose or ovoid berry, black, blue-black, or red, ¼ to ⅓ in. wide.

Not many species are in general cultivation; the most attractive is *S. aspera*, but it can only be grown in the open air in our mildest counties. The tropical species are very rarely seen, even in botanic gardens. *S. excelsa*, *S. hispida*, and *S. rotundifolia* may be planted to clamber over large trees. The Smilaxes generally are not particular as to soil and can be propagated by division.

The genus is well known as the source of the drug sarsaparilla, which is, or has been, obtained from the rootstocks of at least 8 species. Once very popular, it is now regarded in modern medicine as valueless.

S. argyrae'a. Climber with very prickly stems. *l.* lanceolate, 5 to 6 in. long, slender-pointed, bright green with white spots, short-stalked. Bolivia. 1892. (J.H. 1892, 152.) Stove.

S. asp'era.* Evergreen climber; shoots zigzag, angled, spiny. *l.* 1½ to 4 in. long, mostly narrowly ovate-lanceolate, abruptly narrowed above the usually cordate base, but sometimes triangular, sometimes nearly as broad as long, 5- to 9-nerved, margin prickly. *fl.* pale-green, fragrant, in axillary and terminal racemes up to 4 in. long. August, September. *fr.* ¼ in. wide, red. S. Europe and eastwards. 1648. (G.C. 22 (1884), 785.) var. **macula'ta,** *l.* blotched with white. SYN. var. *variegata*; **mauritan'ica,** not so spiny, *l.* larger. Cool greenhouse; hardy in the mildest counties only.

S. Bo'na-nox. Deciduous or semi-evergreen climber; shoots 4-angled, prickly; rootstock tuberous. *l.* roundish, cordate, triangular-ovate, or spear-shaped, 1½ to 4½ in. long, prickly on margins and on veins beneath, 5- to 9-veined, shining on both surfaces. *fl.* greenish-white; stalk of umbels ⅗ to 1¼ in. long. June. *fr.* black, ⅕ in. wide. N. America. 1739.

S. Chi'na. Deciduous climber up to 15 ft., stems sparsely prickly or unarmed. *l.* broadly oval to roundish-ovate, 2 to 3 in. long, sometimes wider than long, abruptly pointed, sometimes slightly cordate, 5- to 7-veined; stalk ⅓ to 1 in. long. *fl.* yellowish-green, stalk of umbel about 1 in. long. May. *fr.* red, ⅜ in. wide, globose. China, Japan. 1759. 'China root', a drug once valued as a cure for gout, is obtained from the root.

S. disco'tis. Deciduous climber up to 16 ft., shoots angled, armed with hooked spines ⅛ in. long. *l.* ovate or narrowly oval, pointed, mostly cordate, 1½ to 3½ in. long, half as wide, glaucous beneath, 3- to 5-veined; stalk $\frac{1}{12}$ to ⅛ in. long. *fl.* greenish-yellow, stalk of umbel slender, up to 1½ in. long. June. *fr.* blue-black. China. 1908. Fairly hardy.

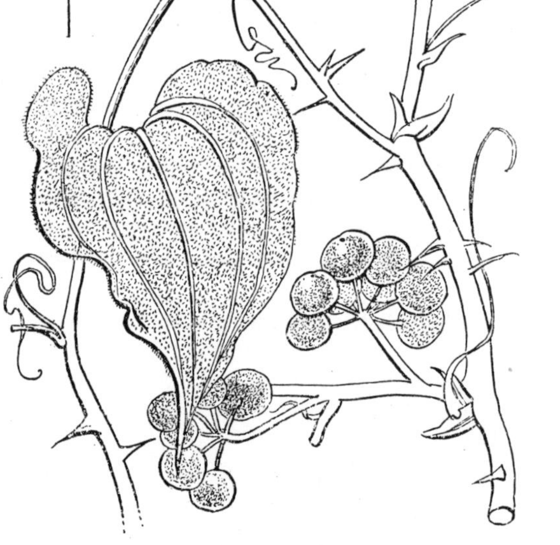

Smilax excelsa

S. excel'sa.* Deciduous climber reaching the top of lofty trees; stems thorny. *l.* broadly ovate, cordate or rounded at the base, sharply pointed, mostly 2 to 3½ (sometimes up to 5) in. long, scarcely as wide, 5- to 7-nerved, stalks ⅓ to ½ in. long. *Umbels* 5- to 10-fld., mainstalk ½ to ¾ in. long. June. *fr.* ⅗ in. wide, red; seeds 3. Orient. 1739. (B.M. 9067.)

S. glau'ca. Deciduous or semi-evergreen climber; branches angled, prickly. *l.* ovate, 1½ to 3½ in. long, broadly tapered or cordate at base, glaucous beneath (sometimes above also), 5-veined. *fl.* greenish-white, 5 to 11 in axillary umbels. June. *fr.* globose, ¼ in. wide, black covered with glaucous bloom. Eastern N. America. 1664. (B.M. 1846.)

S. herba'cea. Herbaceous unarmed climber; stem annual, glabrous. *l.* leathery, triangular-ovate to lanceolate, 7- to 9-veined, entire or nearly so; stalk up to 3 in. long. *fl.* greenish, carrion-scented, numerous in rounded umbels which have a stalk 4 to 9 in. long. *fr.* blue-black, sub-globose, ¼ in. wide. Eastern N. America. 1699. (B.M. 1920.) Two vars. **acumina'ta** and **oblong'a,** are natives of China.

S. hisp'ida.* Deciduous climber, 40 to 50 ft., stems round, the lower part densely furnished with slender prickles and bristles; branches angled. *l.* ovate to broadly ovate, cordate, 2 to 5 in. long, ½ to 3½ in. wide, abruptly pointed, 5- to 9-veined; margins roughened; stalk ¼ to ¾ in. long. *fl.* in axillary umbels of up to 25; main-stalks 1 to 2 in. long. June. *fr.* bluish-black, ¼ in. wide. Eastern N. America.

S. lanceola'ta. Evergreen climber up to 35 ft., tuberous rooted; stem round, usually with recurved prickles towards the base; branches slightly angled, mostly unarmed. *l.* 2 to 3½ in. long, ½ to 1½ in. wide, thinnish, lanceolate, slender-pointed, cuneate, shining green above, dull or slightly glaucous beneath, 5- to 7-veined. *fl.* numerous in axillary, short-stalked umbels. June. *fr.* globose, ¼ in. wide, dark-red. SE. United States. 1785. Rather tender.

S. laurifo'lia. Tall evergreen climber; rootstock tuberous; stems round, prickly; branches angled, mostly unarmed. *l.* leathery, narrowly oval to oblong-lanceolate, cuneate, 2 to 4½ in. long, ⅝ to 2 in. wide, 3-veined, rather glaucous beneath. Stalk of umbel ⅛ to ⅘ in. long. *fl.* greenish. July, August. *fr.* ovoid, ¼ in. wide, black, 1-seeded, ripening the 2nd year. United States. 1739. Not very hardy.

S. long'ipes. Deciduous climber, 10 to 16 ft., branches armed with short recurved prickles. *l.* oval to ovate-oblong, 2 to 5 in. long, 1½ to 3 in. wide, short-pointed, base rounded to broadly cuneate, rather glaucous beneath, 5- to 7-veined. *fl.* yellowish; stalk of umbel 1 to 3 in. long. May. *fr.* blue-black, ¼ in. wide. China. 1907.

S. megalan'tha.* Evergreen climber up to 20 ft., shoots grey, angled, armed with stout spines up to ½ in. long. *l.* broadly ovate, rounded at base, largest up to 9 by 6 in., smaller more lanceolate, leathery, dark glossy green, rather glaucous beneath, 3-nerved; stalk ½ to 1 in. long. *fl.* greenish, in corymbose umbels. *fr.* globose, coral-red, ½ in. wide. China. 1907. Finest in foliage of the hardier species.

S. microphyl'la. Climber 6 to 15 ft., branches angular, armed with short stiff prickles. *l.* oblong to oblong-lanceolate, 1 to 2½ in. long, ¼ to 1 in. wide, shortly pointed, glaucous beneath, 3- to 5-veined, leathery; stalk ¼ in. long. *fl.* greenish-yellow; stalk of umbel ⅛ in. long. *fr.* blue-black, ¼ in. wide. China. 1908.

S. Old'hamii. Herbaceous erect, unarmed plant; stems angled. *l.* broadly oval, ovate or oblong, cordate, 3 to 6 in. long, 1½ to 3½ in. wide, mucronate or slender-pointed, veins 7 or 9, thin in texture; stalk ⅜ in. long. *Umbel* with a stalk 1½ to 3½ in. long, 20- to 40-fld. *fr.* black, ⅜ in. wide. Japan, Korea.

S. pseudo-chi'na. Deciduous climber; rootstock tuberous, sending up stout tendrilled stems 5 or 6 ft. h., weakly or not at all armed. *l.* ovate-cordate, pointed, 3 to 4 in. long, 2 to 3 in. wide, 5-ribbed. *fl.* greenish-yellow, in axillary umbels of 10 to 12. *fr.* ⅓ in. wide, black. N. America. 1739.

S. rotundifo'lia. Horse Brier. Very vigorous deciduous climber up to 30 or 40 ft., stems round, 4-angled, spiny. *l.* ovate to broadly cordate or roundish, lustrous, 2 to 6 in. long, margins entire or roughened; 5-veined; stalk ¼ to ½ in. long. *fl.* greenish-yellow. June. *fr.* ¼ in. wide, black with glaucous bloom. N. America. 1760. Very free-growing and hardy.

S. scobinicau'lis. Deciduous climber up to 15 ft., branches slender, grooved, varying from densely bristly to unarmed. *l.* ovate to ovate-oblong, pointed, 5- or 7-veined, 3 to 5 in. long, 1 to 3 in. wide; stalk ¼ to ⅜ in. long. *fl.* yellowish-white, in axillary umbels ¾ in. wide; mainstalk ⅛ to ⅓ in. long. June. *fr.* black, ¼ in. wide. China. 1907.

S. Siebold'ii. Deciduous or semi-evergreen climber; stems prickly; branches angled. *l.* ovate-cordate with a short slender point, 5- to 7-veined, margins minutely jagged, 1½ to 3½ in. long, both sides green. *fl.* green, in umbels of 4 to 7, mainstalk ½ to ⅝ in. long. June. *fr.* black, ¼ in. wide. Japan. 1905.

S. tamnifo'lia. Stems herbaceous, glabrous unarmed. *l.* leathery, ovate-hastate, broadened at base, 1½ to 3 in. long, ½ to 2 in. wide, pointed, 5- to 7-veined. *Umbels* 1 to 3 in l.-axils, each with up to 30 fl. on a stalk 3 to 4 in. long. *fr.* ⅕ in. wide, black. E. United States. Near *S. herbacea* which has thinner, more ovate l. and longer stalked umbels.

S. trachypo'da. Deciduous, erect or sub-scandent shrub 4 to 12 ft., stems unarmed, round. *l.* ovate, cordate, slender-pointed, 3 to 4 in. long, 1½ to 2¼ in. wide, margin slightly roughened, veins 5 or 7, downy towards base; stalk ½ to 1¼ in. long. *Umbels* with a stalk 1½ to 2 in. long. *fr.* blue-black, ¼ in. wide. China. 1901.

S. Walt'eri. Deciduous climber; stems slightly angled, spiny towards base, branches squarish, unarmed. *l.* ovate to ovate-lanceolate, broadly cuneate to cordate at base, 2 to 4½ in. long, ¾ to 2½ in. wide, 5- to 7-veined. *fl.* greenish, 6 to 15 in short-stalked umbels. June. *fr.* ⅓ in. wide, coral-red. E. United States. 1820.

W. J. B.

Smil'liae, in honour of Mrs. E. J. Smillie, of Australia, *c.* 1867.

Smirnow'ii, in honour of Michael Smirnow, 1849–89, of Odessa, student of the flora of Caucasus.

SMITH'IA (in honour of Sir James Edward Smith, 1759–1828, founder of the Linnean Society, joint author with Sibthorp of *Flora Graeca*). FAM. *Leguminosae.* A genus of about 20 species of herbs, sub-shrubs or shrubs, natives of Trop. Asia and Africa. Leaves pinnate; leaflets small, often falcate, without stipels; stipules persistent. Flowers mostly yellow, rarely purple or violet streaked yellow, often in 1-sided axillary racemes; calyx deeply cut, lobes connate in 2 lips; stand suborbicular, shortly clawed; keel incurved, obtuse or slightly beaked; bracts persistent. For treatment *see* **Mimosa.**

S. purpu'rea. Annual. Stem erect, 6 to 12 in. h., branched, glabrous. *lflets.* oblong, ciliate, long, apiculate; stipules adnate, ovate, bristle-tipped. *fl.* purple, standard round, white spotted like wings; bracts ovate, ciliate; peduncles bristly, as long as wings. E. India. 1848. (B.M. 4283.)

Smith'ii, Smithia'nus -a -um, see above and also in honour of (2) Prof. Christen Smith, 1785–1816, Norwegian botanist who introduced *Aeonium Smithii,* 1815?; (3) John Smith, 1798–1888, of Aberdour, gardener at Kew; (4) Joannes Jacobus Smith, 1867–1947, Dutch botanist, specialist on Indonesian orchids.

SMOKE. Plants in industrial towns and in the neighbourhood of brickworks, lime kilns, smelting furnaces, and coke-ovens suffer greatly from the smoke and acid-fumes arising from coal fires and at times from oil-burning furnaces. Smoke contains particles of unburnt carbon and small quantities of various compounds, some of them oily, arising mainly from incomplete combustion of the fuel. The soot forms a deposit on the foliage of plants which interferes with photosynthesis, since it impedes the access of light, and with transpiration and respiration, since it obstructs the passage of gases through the stomata and lenticels. These are all vital processes and through interference with them the whole plant suffers. Evergreens naturally suffer most and it is rare to find either broad-leaved evergreens, even the common laurel and box, or conifers thriving in smoke-polluted districts. The deposit is not infrequently so thick that it is easily discernible, but care should be exercised in ascribing a black deposit on leaves to this cause, since the sooty fungi, Fumago sp. (q.v.), also produce a black covering in certain circumstances equally detrimental.

Damage from smoke-polluted atmosphere is, however, not confined to the obstructions just referred to, due to the soot-deposit, but is also due to gases escaping from chimneys, the chief of which is sulphurous acid. Plants are very sensitive to the presence of sulphurous acid gas in the air, some showing damage when only 1 part to 1,000,000 is present, if the exposure to the mixture be continued for an appreciable time. Leaves poisoned by sulphurous acid first show translucent spots between the veins which become dull green and then brown, dry, and shrivelled. The amount of sulphurous acid in the air of ordinary large towns appears sufficient to inhibit the growth of certain fungi, including rust fungi which rarely attack plants seriously in towns, and lichens which are rarely seen on trees or roofs within the boundaries of towns. Only acid-resisting grasses will grow in towns where the air is polluted by chimney-fumes; thus *Poa annua* is often the only grass to survive on town lawns. In certain instances hydrochloric acid and arsenic are carried in the fumes to act upon plants to an injurious degree. The fumes from the stoke-hole chimney are of course likely to be injurious to plants especially if they find their way into the houses while the plants have any moisture upon them in which the fumes may dissolve, and this is not infrequently a cause of damage to greenhouse plants.

SMOKE TREE. *See* **Rhus Cotinus.**

SMOKE-WOOD. *See* **Clematis Vitalba.**

A→

SMOOTH FLOWER. *See* **Leianthus.**

SMOOTH SUMACH. *See* **Rhus glabra.**

SMOOTH-FRUITED HORSE-CHESTNUT. Horse-chestnuts without prickles on the husk were at one time excluded from the genus Aesculus and formed the genus Pavia, now combined.

SMUTS or **SMUT FUNGI.** The common name of the Ustilaginales, a large group of fungi in the class Basidiomycetes. The name is derived from the characteristic production of spores which are released in sooty black masses. They are all obligate parasites living on many kinds of wild and cultivated plants and are very destructive to certain crops, especially cereals in which the infection of the inflorescence or grains causes great loss. These diseases being seed-carried necessitate treatment of the seed either by hot water when the smut fungus lives inside the seed tissues or by chemical treatments where it lives on and contaminates the outside of the seed coats (*see* **Seed disinfection**). The typical spore produced by smut fungi is the brand spore which is dark-coloured and on germination produces a promycelium on which basidiospores (sometimes called sporidia) are formed. Many species of smuts contain biologic forms (*see* **Biological Races**). Although the main interest of smut fungi lies in their attacks on cereals there are several which can be very dangerous to garden crops. Examples are *Urocystis cepulae*, causing Onion Smut; *Urocystis violae*, Violet Smut; *Entyloma dahliae*, Dahlia Smut; *Urocystis anemones*, Anemone Smut. Another term used for certain smut diseases is 'Bunt', another name for Stinking Smut of wheat (*Tilletia caries*) which has been known since very ancient times and was probably one of the troubles referred to as 'blightings and blastings' in early historic and religious writings, the cause being ascribed to 'distempers of the air' or displeasure of some god, and similar superstitious theories.

D. E. G.

SMYRN'IUM (ancient Greek name used by Dioscorides, derived from *smyrra*, myrrh, in allusion to the odour of the plants). FAM. *Umbelliferae*. A genus of 6 or 7 species of erect, glabrous, biennial herbs, natives of Europe, W. Asia, and N. Africa. Radical and lower leaves ternato-pinnately cut, upper entire or with fewer segments. Flowers yellow, polygamous, in compound, many-rayed umbels. The plants are now of no horticultural interest but before Celery was introduced, *S. Olusatrum* was cultivated as a salad plant; it is of strong flavour less agreeable than Celery.

S. Olusa'trum. Alexanders, Alisanders, Black Pot-herb, Horse Parsley. 3 to 4 ft. h., stout, branched, leafy, furrowed. *l.* very large, 3- or 4-ternate, with membranous sheaths, shining, serrate. *fl.* greenish-yellow in dense, rounded umbels. May, June. *fr.* nearly black, aromatic.

SNAIL FLOWER, CLIMBING. *See* **Phaseolus Caracalla.**

SNAIL FLOWERS, flowers pollinated by snails, as Alocasia, Aspidistra, and Rohdea.

SNAILS. The general habits of these Molluscs are similar to those of Slugs (q.v.), from which they differ chiefly by the possession of a large and conspicuous spiral shell into which they withdraw at the approach of cold weather and during dry periods. Snails feed in a manner similar to Slugs, and tend to hibernate in clusters among rubbish, in heaps of stones, rubble, and plant pots, and in other dry and sheltered positions. They are less destructive to plants than Slugs, and are never as abundant. Their natural enemies include Birds, especially Thrushes, and certain Ground Beetles and the Glow-worm which devour the Molluscs within their shells. A number of species occur in Britain, including the Large Garden Snail, *Helix aspersa*; the Strawberry Snail, *H. rufescens*, and the Banded Snails, *H. nemoralis* and *H. hortensis*. The first-mentioned is widely distributed in gardens, and is readily identified by its large greyish-brown shell with paler markings. The so-called Strawberry Snail, which is much smaller and with a flatter shell, occurs in sheltered and walled gardens where it does much damage to the leaves and fruits of Strawberry, and to foliage of Violets and other flowering plants, especially in frames. The Banded Snails are chiefly agricultural pests and attack Clover and upland pastures. In some districts there occurs a very large species, namely, the Roman or 'Apple' Snail, *H. pomatia*, which is not reported as being harmful to cultivated crops in this country, and is cultivated on the Continent in 'farms' for the enjoyment of the gourmet. Snails are more difficult to kill than Slugs owing to the protection afforded them by their shells, into which they withdraw at will. It is desirable to examine heaps of bricks and rubble, stacks of plant pots, and similar sites during the winter for the presence of Snails, which may at this season be collected and destroyed without great exertion. Handpicking after dark is a useful measure on rock-gardens, where ample shelter during the daytime is afforded by the stones. For other measures *see* **Slugs.**

G. F. W.

SNAKE GOURD. *See* **Trichosanthes Anguina.**

SNAKE MILLEPEDES. *See* **Millepedes.**

SNAKE-PLANT. *See* **Dracunculus vulgaris.**

SNAKE-ROOT. A name given popularly to many plants reputed to possess curative properties for snake-bites, among them, *Actaea alba*, *Aristolochia Serpentaria*, *Casearia ulmifolia*, *Cimicifuga racemosa*, *Liatris scariosa*, *L. squarrosa*, and *Polygala Senega*.

SNAKE'S BEARD. *See* **Ophiopogon.**

SNAKE'S HEAD. *See* **Fritillaria Meleagris, Hermodactylus tuberosus.**

SNAKE'S MOUTH ORCHID. *See* **Pogonia ophioglossoides.**

SNAKE'S TONGUE. *See* **Ophioglossum.**

SNAKEWEED. *See* **Polygonum Bistorta.**

SNAKEWOOD. *See* **Cecropia.**

SNAPDRAGON. *See* **Antirrhinum majus.**

SNAPWEED. Name used for several species of Impatiens.

SNEEZEWORT. *See* **Achillea Ptarmica.**

SNOW. For the most part snow may be regarded as beneficial in the garden. Plants covered with a few inches of loose snow suffer little damage from frosts that would prove much more harmful to hardier species without such a covering. Snow may, however, act harmfully if a slight thaw is followed by frost so as to cause the formation of a surface-crust of ice, which continuing for some days may cut air supply. Many plants of alpine-regions pass a long winter under snow, well protected from changes of temperature, whereas the same plants subject to the changes of atmospheric and soil conditions at low levels without the protective covering of snow succumb. Little can be done to protect seedlings caught by the ice-crust mentioned above, but the breaking of it as far as possible may save some. Evergreen trees are more liable to damage than most plants, for the heavy weight resting upon their foliage may break off or distort the branches. Deciduous trees are much less liable to suffer in this way as rarely can snow adhere in sufficient quantities to cause injury. The danger is greatest during snowfalls in calm weather with the temperature about freezing-point as the snow then clings to the branches and leaves and collects in heavy masses. In windy weather and in temperatures too low for the snow to ball together, the risk is comparatively slight. The trees that suffer most are the Spruces and Firs with horizontal branches where the leaves are so arranged as to afford a considerable surface for the snow to lie upon, but even trees with upright branches may suffer as the branches are apt to be forced asunder and may crack off or be distorted. The snow should be shaken off the trees with the aid of long poles while it is loose. If a branch is beginning to yield before the snow is shaken off, as soon as it is cleared it should be supported by stays of any convenient kind. If a branch is entirely broken off or so far as to hang down, the surface of the wound on the tree should be made smooth and covered with Stockholm tar or lead paint to prevent the entrance of moisture and parasites.

SNOW FLOWER. *See* **Chionanthus.**

SNOW GLORY. *See* **Chionodoxa Luciliae.**

SNOW IN SUMMER. *See* **Cerastium tomentosum.**

SNOW PEAR. *See* **Pyrus ussuriensis.**

SNOW TREE. *See* **Pyrus nivalis.**

SNOWBALL TREE. *See* **Viburnum Opulus sterile.**

SNOWBERRY. *See* **Chiococca, Chiogenes, Symphoricarpos.**

SNOWDEN'II, in honour of J. D. Snowden of the Dept. of Agriculture, Uganda, *c.* 1906.

SNOWDROP. *See* **Galanthus.**

SNOWDROP TREE. *See* **Halesia carolina.**

SNOWDROP TREE, AFRICAN. *See* **Royena lucida.**

SNOWDROP WINDFLOWER. *See* **Anemone sylvestris.**

SNOWFLAKE. *See* **Leucojum.**

SNOWY FLIES. *See* **Aleyrodidae.**

SOAP. At one time soap-suds were much used as a preventive or cure for depredations of insects, either for watering or for spraying. Their use has been entirely superseded by the various insecticides (q.v.) now available. Soap is still used to mix with some of the insecticides to cause them to wet the surface sprayed more easily or to increase their power of penetrating into crevices, and for this purpose a good brand of soft-soap is best. It is used especially with Nicotine to produce the very effective Nicotine-soap-spray (4 oz. nicotine, 4 lb. soft-soap, 40 gallons water) and with sulphur to make a dip for use against red-spider-mites. The mixtures must be thoroughly effected. Care should be exercised where foliage naturally covered with wax, like that of Carnations and some of the glaucous conifers, has to be sprayed, that the soap-solution is not sufficiently strong to dissolve the wax. Soapy water is useful for sponging the leaves of plants growing in rooms, conservatories, &c.

SOAP BARK TREE. *See* **Quillaja Saponaria.**

SOAP BERRY TREE. *See* **Sapindus.** *S. Muckerossii* is largely grown in warm countries for the soapy sap of its fruits. It does not appear to be in cultivation in Britain.

SOAP BULB. *See* **Chlorogalum pomeridianum.**

SOAP PLANT. *See* **Chlorogalum, Feronia, Sapindus.**

SOAP PODS. Popular name for pods of some species of Caesalpinia and *Acacia concinna.*

SOAP TREE. *See* **Gymnocladus chinensis, Quillaja.**

SOAPERS' ASHES. This refuse has sometimes been offered as a manure. It consists mainly of carbonate of lime with some sulphides and sulphites, a small quantity of sand, and other rubbish. When fresh the sulphur compounds are liable to injure plants, but on standing they become oxidized to sulphates and are not then injurious. The value of the material is small, and may be taken as that of an impure carbonate of lime.

SOAPWORT. *See* **Saponaria officinalis.**

SOBOLE. A shoot, particularly one arising from the ground.

SOBOLEWSK'IA (in honour of Professor Gregor Sobolewski, author of *Flora Petropolitana*). FAM. *Cruciferae.* A genus of 4 species of perennial herbs flowering in their first year, natives of Caucasia and Armenia. Plants leafy and branching at base, leaves stalked, fan-shaped, flowers small, in racemes, white. Fruit short, oblong, roundish, not beaked, indehiscent, usually 1-seeded. Propagated by seed sown in spring. The species closely resemble one another.

S. clava'ta. Much like *S. lithophila* but usually dwarfer, and fruit and pedicels both decurved. Asia Minor, Armenia.

S. lithophil'a. *Rhiz.* much-branched; stems erect, 8 to 18 in. h., hairy and violet in lower parts. *l.* greyish, thin; lower long-stalked, roundish-cordate, toothed; upper with shorter stalks. *fl.* 20 to 50 in a raceme, elongated after flowering; pet. $\frac{1}{8}$ in. long. June. Crimea.

sobolif'erus -a -um, bearing soboles, vigorous shoots, especially those from the ground.

SOBRA'LIA (in honour of Don F. M. Sobral, *c.* 1790, a Spanish botanist). FAM. *Orchidaceae.* A genus of about 60 species of leafy, non-tuberous, free-growing, usually terrestrial orchids, natives of the Andes of S. America from Peru to Mexico. Flowers of most species large and showy, few in a terminal raceme or produced in succession from a cone-like terminal head as in *S. macrantha.* A few species are said to have the inflorescence lateral. In many the flowers, usually produced in summer, are very large, some more or less fleshy, others of very thin texture; they vary in duration but none are long lived. In the *S. macrantha* group a week is considered a long time, but as one flower fades another is produced, to 6 or more on strong plants, thus prolonging the flowering season. The sepals are more or less connate near their bases; the petals are free; the general outline of the lip may be likened to the lip of *Cattleya labiata* as the side lobes are convolute over the column and there is no decided division between them and the expanded front lobe which is often broadly orbicular, often crimped, undulate, undivided or 2-lobed, sometimes slightly fimbriate. Beginning near the stigma are often 2 fleshy, curved, horn-like processes very apparent in some species. Pseudobulbs are absent, stems reed-like, usually closely set, the heights varying in the species, in some thinly clothed with short black hairs. Leaves scattered, rather leathery, plicate, broadly lanceolate, their bases clasping or forming sheaths round the stems, persistent, remaining on the old stems for a considerable time, giving a slight decorative value to the plants, particularly if, after flowering, the dead remainder of each inflorescence is carefully removed. Until devoid of foliage and dead, or nearly so, old stems should not be entirely cut away. Sobralias usually have rather fleshy roots, hence the pots used should be of ample size. They should be well drained. Compost should consist chiefly of rough fibrous loam, not of heavy consistency, a proportion of Osmunda fibre or peat added, varied in quantity according to the nature of the loam used. Very coarse sand or finely broken pot-sherds may also be incorporated. In the growing season water should be liberally given, and though applied less frequently in winter, the compost should never be allowed to become really dry as the stems are often in different stages of growth. Repotting should be done in early spring if necessary. Propagation by dividing the plants which should be of considerable size, weak reeds often result from dividing small plants. The intermediate house meets their requirements as regards temperature, &c. If grown cooler or warmer in the summer, the plants should be rested in a night temperature of about 55° F. in winter. Thrips and scale insects will attack the plants, but the syringe may be freely used in summer and they seldom damage the plants seriously.

S. Brandt'iae. *fl.* from a cone-like head; sep. and pet. rosy-purple, linear-oblong; lip convolute, disk yellow with 5 slightly raised lines, margins undulate. Stems 2 to 5 ft. h. l.-sheaths marked with black spots. S. America. 1896. Habit of *S. macrantha*, *fl.* smaller.

S. Catt'leya. *fl.* rather fleshy, resembling a Cattleya; sep. and pet. purplish-brown; lip purplish with 3 yellow, crested keels, making a sharp angle by its side lobes overlapping the column; infl. several, lateral. *l.* oblong, slender-pointed, plaited, shining. Stem stout, 4 to 12 ft. or more h., its base sometimes thickening and becoming bulb-like. Colombia. 1877.

S. Charlesworth'ii.* *fl.* rich rose-purple with a broad purple band round the lip; sep. 3½ in. long, 1 in. wide; pet. broader, crest bright yellow. Colombia. 1910. Allied to *S. Ruckeri*, but with larger fls.

S. chloran'tha. A synonym of *S. macrophylla.*

S. Clifton'iae. *fl.* white with a purple tinge in throat, rather fleshy. Resembles a dwarf *S. macrantha* in habit. Ecuador. 1910.

S. deco'ra. Allied to *S. sessilis* but without black hairs, smaller, with whitish *fl.* lip rose, wedge-shaped; pet. overlaying sep. Stem about 2 ft. h. Guatemala. 1836. (B.M. 4570 as *S. sessilis.*)

S. dichoto'ma. *fl.* fragrant, white without, violet within, or whitish-rose with rose and purple lip, or wholly deep red, fleshy; lip cucullate, 3-lobed, side lobes entire, mid-lobe emarginate, crisped, crested-lacerate at tip; racemes lateral, drooping, dichotomous, flexuous, many-fld. March. Stems 6 to 20 ft. h., resembling bamboos. *l.* hard, plicate, slender-pointed, 7 to 12 in. or more long, up to 3½ in. wide. Peru.

S. Elizabeth'ae. A synonym of *S. Liliastrum.*

S. frag'rans. *fl.* very fugacious, 1½ in. across, sweetly scented, sep. dirty purplish-green or creamy-white, keeled; pet. pale yellow, thin, flat, lanceolate, lip bright yellow, mid-lobe deeply fringed, having 9 jagged crests. July. Stem 2-edged, up to 12 in. h. *l.* smooth, rather fleshy, with a short keeled sheath. Colombia. 1854. (B.M. 4882.)

S. Hol'fordi. A variety of *S. macrantha.*

S. Klotzschea'na. *fl.* white with a deep yellow disk to lip. Resembles *S. leucoxantha* but fl. have shorter, broader sep. and pet. Peru. 1916.

S. Lanthoin'ei. A synonym of *S. Ruckeri.*

S. leucoxan'tha.* *fl.* large; sep. white, recurved, oblong-ligulate; pet. white, rather shorter and broader; lip deep golden-yellow, flushed orange in throat and disk, white at edge, oblong fan-shaped, convolute at base, front 2-lobed and crenulate; bracts dry, spotted brown. August. Stem up to 5 ft. *l.* plicate, cuneate-oblong, slender-pointed, sheaths warted. Costa Rica. (B.M. 7058; W.O.A. 271.)

S. Liliast'rum.* *fl.* white, large, pendulous; disk of lip yellow. *fl.* in succession from axils of spathe-like bracts, on 2 sides of a zigzag rachis. July, August. *l.* lanceolate, very acute, striate, sheathing at base. Stem 8 to 10 ft. h. British Guiana, Brazil. 1840. SYN. *S. Elizabethae, Epidendrum Liliastrum.* var. **ro'sea,** pet. and lip rich rose, lip veined white.

S. Lin'denii.* *fl.* 10 in. across; sep. and pet. white, tinged rose; lip crimson-purple in front, white in folded part with a few chocolate lines in throat; scape flexuous. Ecuador. 1895. (L. 585.)

S. Louis Sander.* Sep. 3¾ in. long, 1½ n. wide; pet. 2 in. wide, mauve-purple with deeper basal, central, and marginal shades; lip almost orbicular, 4 in. broad, deep mauve-crimson, throat whitish with an ochre-yellow flush beneath the column. Stems 3 to 6 ft. h. Trop. America. 1925 to 1930. Allied to *S. macrantha.*

S. Low'ii. *fl.* deep purple, freely produced, short-lived; sep. and pet. about 2 in. long; lip rather shorter. *l.* narrow-lanceolate, slender-pointed. Stem 1 to 3 ft. h. Colombia. 1890. Allied to *S. sessilis.*

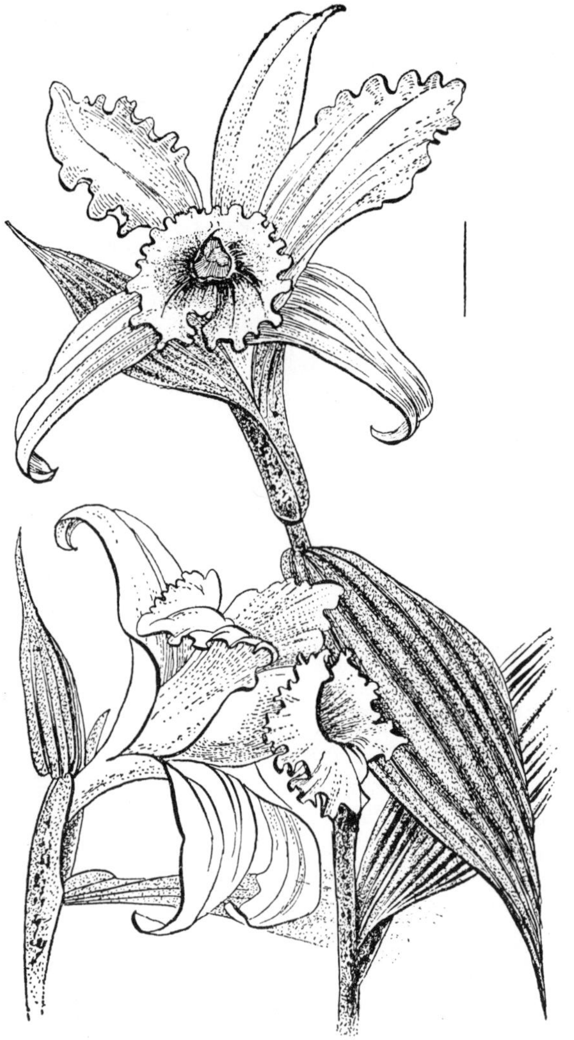

Sobralia leucoxantha

S. Lucasia'na.* *fl.* large, like that of *S. xantholeuca* but sep. and pet. white, faintly tinged rose; lip rosy purple with yellow throat. Trop. America. 1892. (B.M. n.s. 144.)

S. luteo'la. *fl.* light yellow, 3 in. across, with darker veins on lip and a few traces of brown between keels. *l.* oblong-lanceolate, plicate, 6 in. long. Stem 3 ft. h. Trop. America. 1898. Allied to *S. suaveolens.*

S. macran'tha.* *fl.* large, 6 in. across, rich purple and crimson, fragrant; sep. oblong; pet. broader, crisped in upper part; lip folded round column at base, very broad, 2-lobed at apex, margin wavy, throat whitish-yellow; racemes short. Summer. *l.* ovate, slender-pointed, plicate. Stems 6 to 8 ft. h. Mexico, Guatemala. 1842. (B.M. 4446.) var. **al'ba,** a synonym of var. *Kienastiana*; **al'ba na'na,** *fl.* pure white, stem 1 ft. h. 1897; **al'bida,** sep. and pet. creamy-white, lip pale rose; **al'bida na'na,** *fl.* smaller than type, lip dark violet with yellow base, stem 1 to 3 ft. h.; **delica'ta,** *fl.* almost wholly white, sep. and pet. slightly tinged lavender, lip edged soft lilac. 1891; **Hodgkinson'ii,** *fl.* large, sep. light rose-lilac, pet. rosy-lilac, lip brilliant rose-purple, throat orange. 1894; **Holfordii,** *fl.* large rich rose-carmine deepest on front lobe of lip, throat whitish. 1894; **Kienastian'a,** *fl.* pure white except for a small yellow blotch at base of lip. 1888; **lilaci'na,** identical with home-raised forms of *S.* × *Veitchii*; **Princess May,** *see* **S. Princess May**; **purpu'rea,** *fl.* rich purple; **ro'sea,** sep. light-rose, pet. and lip deep rose, 1890; **ru'bra,** *fl.* rich crimson, throat shaded yellow; **Schroder's var.,** *fl.* large, deep crimson-purple; throat orange-yellow below column; **splen'dens,** *fl.* darker and smaller than type. 1846; **Woolley's var.** is a very dwarf form of var. *splendens.*

S. macrophyl'la. *fl.* pale yellow; sep. and pet. about 2½ in. long, narrow, forming a partial tube; lip clawed, front lobe recurved, margin crisped. Stems 3 to 4 ft. h. Brazil. 1852? (B.M. 4682 as *S. chlorantha.*)

S. Princess May. Probably a distinct species, but has been regarded as a variety of both *S. macrantha* and of *S. xantholeuca. fl.* of medium size; sep. and pet. flushed white, front lobe of lip rosy-mauve, throat lemon-yellow; sep. connate to nearly one-third of their length. Colombia. About 1893.

S. Ruck'eri.* *fl.* over 4 in. across; sep. and pet. spreading, rose-purple; lip rich purple-crimson, undulate, disk yellow, whitish edged; rachis elongated, flexuose with sometimes 4 fl. open together. Stems 3 to 6 ft. Colombia. 1878. (X.O. 1 42; W.S.O. 3, 19.) This species has been confused with *S. rosea* of Poeppig and Endl., a Peruvian species which has apparently never been in cultivation.

S. Sand'erae.* *fl.* larger than in *S. leucoxantha* to which it is allied, sulphur-white, with orange throat markings. Cent. America. 1890.

S. Sanderia'na.* *fl.* large; sep. and pet. white tinged with rose, blade of lip bright crimson-purple, throat orange. Allied to *S. macrantha* but stronger with larger fl. and stouter stems. Habitat? 1897.

S. ses'silis. *fl.* deep rose, solitary, sessile; lip tinged yellow in lower half, rhomboid-oblong, with 2 lamellae at base. *l.* beneath and stem covered with dark hairs. British Guiana. 1840. (B.R. 27, 17; B.M. 7376.) SYN. *S. Galeottiana. S. sessilis* of Hooker is *S. decora.*

S. suaveo'lens. *fl.* yellowish-white, strongly scented; lip white, disk brown, keels yellow. Cent. America. 1878. Habit of *S. decora.*

S. val'ida. *fl.* whitish-yellow; lip with a deeper yellow band shading to orange in front. Veins in lip crested. Stems 8 to 12 in. h. Panama. 1907.

S. × Veitch'ii (*S. macrantha* × *S. xantholeuca*) has been raised artificially and also occurs naturally.

S. viola'cea. *fl.* fragrant, pale violet, larger than in *S. decora*; lip convolute as in a Cattleya; bracts imbricate, somewhat leafy. July. *l.* hard, lanceolate, deeply plicate; sheaths slightly warted. Colombia. Plant larger than in *S. decora.* (L. 320.) Variable. var. **al'ba,** *fl.* white, throat and disk of lip orange, lip 1¼ in. across. 1904.

S. virgina'lis. *fl.* white lightly flushed rose, deepest on front of frilled lip, throat yellow. Habit as in *S. violacea* of which it has been considered a variety.

S. Warscewicz'ii. *fl.* very bright purple, larger than in *S. Liliastrum*; pet. cuneate, acute; lip fan-shape, emarginate. *l.* broad-oblong, firm. Stems firm, compact. Costa Rica. 1890.

S. × Wigan'iae.* Possibly a natural hybrid between *S. xantholeuca* and *S. macrantha* or an allied species. *fl.* large, soft yellow tinged rose. Habitat? 1898.

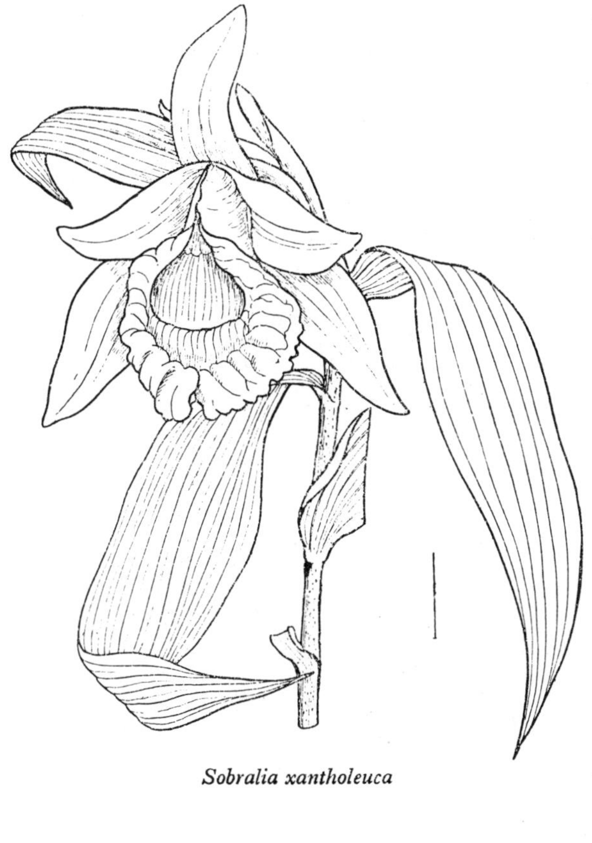

Sobralia xantholeuca

S. Wils'oni. *fl.* white, faintly suffused rose; sep. slender-pointed, over 4 in. long; lip emarginate, crisp-undulate, light rosy-mauve, throat sulphur shading to white with a few darker, slightly raised lines beneath column. *l.* lanceolate, very slender-pointed, 7 in. long. Cent. America. 1890.

S. xantholeu'ca.* *fl.* large, deflexed; sep. and pet. pale yellow; sep. oblong-lanceolate; pet. broader and wavy at edges; lip longer, deeper yellow, much-frilled, emarginate. *l.* lanceolate, slender-pointed, plicate, sheaths dotted brown. Stems rather stout, 3 to 8 ft. h. Cent. America. (W.O.A. 250; B.M. 7332; L. 678; R. 1, 44.) var. **albes'cens,** *fl.* pale primrose, throat golden-yellow, 1889; **na'na,** only 2 ft. h.; **superb'a,** *fl.* deep cream-yellow, throat of lip marked orange-brown; **Wigan's var.,** sep. and pet. creamy-white slightly suffused with pale primrose; lip creamy-white, throat creamy-yellow. When young the fl. are faintly flushed pink. 1894.

E. C.

SOCIAL PEAR SAWFLY, *Neurotoma flaviventris,* is occasionally found attacking Pears, and sometimes Cherry and Plum, on the shoots and leaves of which the larvae construct 'nests' or 'tents'. The black Sawflies with yellow legs and feelers appear in May and June when the oblong, yellow eggs are laid on the underside of the leaves. The caterpillars, which are orange-yellow with a pale stripe down each side of the body, make webs in which they live. When fully fed, they descend to the soil and pupate. This pest is seldom so abundant as to warrant spraying, but the nests should be looked for in July, cut out, and burnt.

G. F. W.

socia'lis -is -e, sociable, forming colonies.

socotra'nus -a -um, of Socotra.

SOCRA'TEA (after the Greek philosopher Socrates). FAM. *Palmaceae.* A genus of 3 or 4 species of unarmed Palms, natives of N. Brazil and Colombia. Leaves few, terminal, equally pinnatisect; segments oblique, wedge-shaped, flabellate, deeply laciniate, laciniae narrow, sinuately toothed. Spathes 5 to 8, deciduous, upper complete; spadices horn-like, recurved after flowering, solitary. Fruit ellipsoid or oblong-obovoid, 1- or rarely 2-seeded. *S. exorhiza* has aerial roots studded with small spines which are used by the Indians as Cassava graters. For treatment *see* **Iriartea.**

S. exorhi'za. Zanona Palm. 60 to 100 ft. h. with 8 to 20 or more aerial roots arising about 6 ft. above ground. *l.* 12 to 20 ft. long; pinnae oblique, subtrapezoid, sinuately toothed, flat; stalks cylindrical, convolute at base. *Spathes* 5 or 6, deciduous; spadix 1½ ft. long, spreading in flower, pendulous in fruit. *fr.* yellowish or yellowish-green, scarcely fleshy, ovate-elliptic, ⅝ to 1 in. long. Guiana. 1849. SYN. *Iriartea exorhiza.* Stove.

SODA. A compound of sodium and oxygen, Na_2O, with a certain amount of water. Sodium is one of the most widely diffused of elements and exists in every soil in combination with various acids. Most of its compounds are readily soluble in water and it is therefore present in all soil solutions and in the ash of all plants. It does not, however, appear to be one of the main nutrients of the plant and the part it plays in plant growth, if any, is obscure. It seems, however, that it may replace potassium to some extent, especially in beet and mangel, and it may well be that all plants benefit by a trace of it.

SODIUM CHLORIDE. *See* **Salt.**

SOFT GRASS. *See* **Holcus.**

SOFT ROT. Plant tissues attacked by various fungi and bacteria either parasitic on living plants or saprophytic on dead material may show different kinds of rots. Generally speaking, woody tissues suffer a dry kind of rot while fleshy structures show soft, slimy or watery disintegration of the tissues, but this is not invariably so. Examples of Soft Rots are seen in carrots and many other root vegetables attacked by *Bacterium carotovorum* especially when stored, Celery Heart Rot due to the same organism, Iris Rhizome Rot due to *B. aroideae.* Many other stems and fruits may be destroyed by soft rot after being damaged by frost, &c., owing to the entrance of various saprophytic organisms.

D. E. G.

SOFT SCALE, *Lecanium hesperidum*, is unlike other species of Lecanium inasmuch as it remains soft throughout its life and never possesses a hard covering. The scale is long-oval, yellowish to brown, and very flat, and gives rise to living young so that there is no need for the provision of a protective covering for the eggs. It is primarily a pest of glasshouse plants, being partial to Figs, Orange-trees, and Vines among fruits, and Aralia and Hibiscus among ornamental plants. It occurs occasionally on Ivy and Holly growing outside in sheltered positions. A constant watch should be kept for this pest in houses of mixed plants where routine fumigation may be attended with some risk of injury to tender plants. The scales may be sponged or removed from tender leaves with the aid of a soft brush dipped in a solution of Soft Soap or with a pointed wooden skewer. The application of a dilute Nicotine-soap wash, Derris extract, or Eucalyptus Oil emulsion is effective provided such washes are applied to both surfaces of the foliage.
G. F. W.

A→

SOIL-LESS CULTIVATION. The first recorded experiment in growing land plants without soil was made in 1699 by Woodward, who grew spearmint in several different kinds of water. Little notice was taken of this work, but early in the nineteenth century Boussingault carried out experiments with plants grown in sand, quartz, and charcoal. The real history of the method as a means of scientific study of plant nutrition begins, however, with the publication in 1840 of Liebig's work on *Chemistry in its Application to Agriculture and Physiology*. Sachs in 1860 dispensed with the use of solid media and was the first to grow plants with their roots directly immersed in a nutrient solution of inorganic salts. From that date the various methods became of increasing importance for studies on mineral nutrition.

It was not, however, until 1936 that the application of these methods to practical crop production was proposed. In that year Dr. F. Gericke of California published results of experiments on the large-scale growing of tomatoes by the 'water-culture' system in tanks of solution. For this system he proposed the name 'hydroponics', a term meaning 'water-growing' in contradistinction to 'geoponics' or 'earth-growing'. His results led to a great deal of interest in the idea on the part of growers, amateurs, and research workers, and practical systems of crop production have been evolved.

The methods proposed fall into two main classes, cultivation in tanks of liquid nutrient solution (Gericke's 'hydroponic' system) and cultivation in an inert medium to which the nutrient solution is applied either periodically or in a continuous slow drip.

Hydroponic System. In this method the solution is contained in shallow waterproof tanks or troughs constructed of metal, wood, concrete, or brick. The tanks, which are set level, may be of any length, but should not exceed about 4 ft. in width and should be between 6 and 12 in. deep. Whatever the material used for construction it must be suitably protected and waterproofed on the inside either by applying a coat of hot bitumen or by painting with a suitable bituminous paint. This material must be free from any tarry or oily substance. The trough is provided with a grid cover made of wire-netting or wire mesh on a suitable framework. If galvanized wire is used it must be protected by bituminous paint as zinc is highly toxic to plant growth except in very minute amounts. This grid is covered with a 2-in. layer of peat, wood-shavings, or other relatively inert absorbent medium which serves partly to exclude light from the solution and partly for the growth of roots in the early stages of establishment. In Gericke's earlier work this covering was kept dry, but later he modified his recommendations, advising the saturation of the medium with solution to encourage root growth in it.

In the case of large seeds or rooted cuttings these may be set directly in the medium on the grid, but with fine seeds Gericke recommends sowing them in either soil or sand and transferring them as soon as they can be handled to the tanks.

A space of 2 to 3 in. should be left between the grid and the surface of the solution, and in his latest accounts Gericke recommends that this space should be increased as the plants grow in order to allow the growth of what he considers to be aerating roots in the saturated atmosphere of the air space. The main mass of the root system will grow down into the solution and absorb the water and nutrients required for the growth of the plant.

The solution may either be tested regularly for concentration of the essential elements and the necessary additions made or the whole solution may be changed at regular intervals of 7 to 14 days, the time depending upon the volume of solution supplied per plant.

Consideration of the solutions recommended for use will be deferred until after discussion of the other methods.

This system has been tested by a number of workers in the United Kingdom and has so far not given very satisfactory results, due, apparently, to the inadequate aeration of the solution. Forced aeration of the solution greatly improves matters but the chief advantage of the system over the other methods, namely, economy in cost of installation, is largely lost. The experience of workers in the eastern United States has been similar and the method is not now widely advocated outside California.

Sand Culture. In the sand-culture system, which is in many ways the simplest to control and operate, the plants are grown in washed sand, the nutrient solution being applied to the surface of the sand by hand or by a system of perforated spray-lines. On a small scale the plants may be grown in pots or boxes, but in large-scale production beds of any convenient width up to 4 ft. are constructed of cement-faced brick, concrete, or wood. The floor of the bed is made of concrete, slightly 'dished' to the middle, down which is placed a row of 2-in. tile drain-pipes running to a drain at the lower end. Where very long beds are necessary, or where it is impossible to provide a fall from end to end of the bed, an alternative method is to make the floor slightly convex upwards and to provide drainage holes in the sides of the beds at intervals of about 1 ft. so that excess water or solution can drain out on to the paths. It is advisable to paint the inside of the beds with a coat of bituminous paint to protect the cement. The beds should be about 12 in. deep, i.e. 3 courses of bricks laid on edge. The sand should be clean, non-calcareous, of medium coarseness, and preferably containing a fair proportion of fine gravel.

The beds should be filled to within about 1 in. of the top and the sand well leached with plain water before use. If the sand contains any appreciable lime it will be necessary to use water acidified with about 1 oz. of sulphuric acid per gallon, washing until the drainage water is no longer alkaline.

The nutrient solution may be applied to the sand in a variety of ways. For beds up to 30 ft. long, $\frac{1}{2}$ in. copper pipes perforated at 6-in. intervals down each side with $\frac{1}{64}$-in. holes diametrically opposite are satisfactory. One pipe is necessary for beds up to 2 ft. wide and 2 for wider beds. The pipes may be connected through a header pipe with stopcocks to a supply tank of solution at the upper end of the beds, the tank being raised on piers to give a minimum head of 1 ft. The solution is then applied when required by opening the stopcock for the necessary length of time.

For beds longer than 30 ft., difficulties in obtaining an even distribution of solution arise, and it may be necessary either to sectionalize the spray-lines or to have recourse to hand-watering by means of a pump and hose fitted with a rose. A machine is available, operating on the pressure of the water-main, which provides a constant dilution of a concentrated nutrient solution independent of the rate of flow. This method, though somewhat expensive in initial outlay, has the advantage that large supply tanks of diluted nutrient solution are unnecessary and reduces greatly the labour of preparing solutions, since a solution 100 times the required final concentration is prepared.

The plants are raised from seed or cuttings in pots or boxes of sand watered with nutrient solution diluted 1 : 5, the strength of the solution being raised to the full amount before final planting. In planting it is unnecessary and indeed undesirable to wash the sand from the roots; a hole is scooped in the sand and the 'ball' dropped in, firming not being needed.

In the early stages of growth, especially with a crop planted in the early months of the year, application of the solution once or twice a week will usually be found sufficient, but the frequency of dosage will need to be increased gradually to once daily with fast-growing plants such as tomatoes. Whatever the method or frequency of application of the solution, sufficient should be applied at each dose thoroughly to saturate the sand, without, however, much excess, since this is wasteful of chemicals. Occasional waterings with plain water between applications of solution may be necessary in very hot weather.

At intervals of 3 to 4 weeks the sand should be thoroughly leached through with plain water to wash out unassimilated residues of the nutrient salts.

Apart from the application of solution, normal cultural practice with regard to staking, stopping, disbudding, pest and disease control, &c., should be followed. While planting may sometimes be a little closer than in soil, free development of the aerial growth must not be hindered. Special care must be taken when spraying plants with insecticides or fungicides that excessive amounts of the spray do not drip on to the sand. It is a good practice, in any event, after spraying to give the sand a good leaching with plain water before the next application of solution.

It will be seen that this method most closely resembles normal soil cultivation and its chief advantages over cultivation in soil lie in the more accurate control of the nutrition of the plant, the more efficient aeration of the rooting medium, and the greater cleanliness and freedom from soil-borne diseases. If such disease should infect a crop, sterilization of the sand is easily and effectively achieved by saturating it with a 1 : 50 dilution of formaldehyde (40 per cent. commercial) after the crop is cleared and subsequently leaching very thoroughly with water before the next crop is planted.

SUB-IRRIGATION SYSTEM. In this method the plants are grown in a waterproof tank or trough as in the hydroponic system, but filled with a coarse aggregate composed of gravel, cinders, crushed clinker, rock chippings, or similar medium, which is periodically flooded from below with the nutrient solution.

The growing tank, which must be completely waterproof, may be constructed in the same way as described for the hydroponic system, but is preferably made with a slight slope in the floor towards the middle. The tank should be set level or with a very slight fall to the end to which the inlet pipe is connected, and if a shallow channel down the middle can be provided, this will aid complete drainage of the solution. The channel is covered with lengths of inverted black iron guttering, painted with 2 coats of bituminous paint. The tank is filled completely with the aggregate, which should be thoroughly washed and graded between ⅛ and ⅝ in. For tomatoes, crushed clinker has given excellent results, although clean silica gravel is satisfactory. Carnations and many other flower crops appear to do better in gravel. Furnace ash should be used with caution as it may contain toxic substances and it tends to disintegrate rapidly. Limestone chippings are only suitable for lime-loving plants, but granite chippings appear to be satisfactory. Entirely non-porous materials such as silica, gravel and granite require more frequent flooding than porous aggregates like clinker.

The nutrient solution is contained in a separate supply reservoir placed at a lower level. This supply tank, which should have a capacity not less than half that of the growing tank, may be constructed in any convenient way. For large installations an underground tank of brick, faced with cement and coated with bituminous paint, provides the best reservoir, but wooden, metal, or concrete tanks may be used, provided the inner surface is protected in the same way. This tank is connected through a centrifugal pump to the growing tank by black iron piping. An electrically driven, direct-coupled pump is satisfactory, but in this case the pump should be mounted in a separate chamber at the side of the supply tank and below the level of liquid in the latter to avoid priming difficulties. A centrifugal pump of the sump type with the motor mounted vertically over the supply tank is more satisfactory, but this type of pump is more expensive.

The outlet from the pump is connected to the bottom of the growing tank either in the middle of the latter or at the lower end. In operation, the pump floods the growing tank from below and when the solution reaches within ½ in. of the surface of the medium an overflow device switches the pump off, allowing the solution to flow back into the reservoir by gravity, ready for use again. The overflow device most easily constructed consists of a glass or metal tube projecting from the tank and bent at right angles. This directs the overflow into a small bucket or glass bottle, hung on a Burgess micro-switch provided with an extension arm. The weight of liquid in the bucket trips the switch, stopping the pump. A small hole bored on the upper side of the bend in the tube ensures immediate flow when the solution reaches the tube and prevents siphoning. The complete cycle of the operation should not take longer than 1½ hrs., but on the other hand too rapid pumping is to be avoided. Switching on of the pump may be either by hand or by means of a time-switch provided with a number of contacts. In the latter case, the 'off' contacts should be set to switch off the supply to the pump soon after the pump is stopped by the overflow device. The latter may then be reset by emptying out the water in the bucket.

Frequency of pumping will depend upon the crop, stage of growth, and weather conditions. Generally, once daily will be sufficient in the seedling stage, increasing to 3 times daily for a large, rapidly growing crop such as tomatoes.

With this system, since the solution is used repeatedly, regular testing at weekly intervals to determine the amount of each of the main nutrients absorbed by the plants is necessary in order that additions may be made to restore the concentration. A simple system of colour tests for this purpose has been devised, which requires the minimum of laboratory facilities and skilled knowledge. (See *The Chemical Testing of Plant Nutrient Solutions*, by G. S. Fawcett and R. H. Stoughton, 1944.)

At approximately 6-week intervals the whole solution should be pumped away, the bed washed through with clean water, and fresh solution made up in the supply tank. With slow-growing crops the intervals between changes of the solution may be longer, but the same solution should never be used for more than about 3 months.

On a small scale the supply tank and pump may be replaced by a bucket or drum of sufficient capacity to flood the tank. This container is provided with an outlet pipe near the bottom which is connected by rubber tubing to the growing trough. Flooding is effected by raising the container above the top of the trough, subsequently lowering it again to allow the solution to flow back by gravity.

The sub-irrigation system possesses certain definite advantages over the sand-culture method. The greater degree of automatic control achieves more economy of labour, while the nutritional and aeration factors are even more nearly optimal. Greater economy in consumption of chemicals and water also results. Against these advantages must be set the fact that the cost of installation is somewhat higher, while the necessity for frequent testing of the solution entails the provision of skilled assistance and simple laboratory facilities or, alternatively, the services of a technical laboratory able to carry out the analyses by contract.

SOLUTIONS. A very great variety of formulae for the preparation of a nutrient solution have been proposed. Basically, the essential feature of a solution is that it shall supply all the chemical elements known to be required for normal growth in a form in which they are readily available to the plant. These elements are nitrogen (in the form of a nitrate), phosphorus (as a phosphate), potassium, calcium, magnesium, iron, sulphur, boron, manganese, copper, and zinc and possibly certain other of the so-called trace elements, to which the last 4 belong. Using commercial grade fertilizers it is normally only necessary to supply the first 9 of these, since the others will usually be present in sufficient amount as impurities for normal growth.

From the nutritional point of view it is relatively immaterial what chemical is used to supply each of these elements, provided that the other part (or 'ion') of the salt is not harmful. Thus, nitrogen could equally well be provided as the nitrate of sodium, potassium, or calcium. Certain other considerations make it desirable to use some salts in preference to others, but on a large scale these refinements are offset by the necessity to use chemicals which are obtainable readily and reasonably cheaply.

It has been found most convenient to calculate the quantities of each element required in terms of parts per million (p.p.m.) of the final solution. The following factors for the commoner fertilizer or commercial-grade chemicals give the fraction of an ounce of each required to be dissolved in 100 gal. of water to give a concentration of 1 part per million of the element required. This factor multiplied by the number of p.p.m. actually needed, and the result multiplied again by the number of hundreds of gallons of solution required, will give the number of ounces and fractions of an ounce to be dissolved in the stated amount of water. Thus, if 50 gal. of a solution containing 200 p.p.m. of nitrogen is required, using nitrate of soda, it is necessary to dissolve $0{\cdot}103 \times 200 \times 0{\cdot}5 = 10{\cdot}3$ oz., or 10¼ oz., in 50 gal. of water.

TABLE

Chemical	*Fraction of 1 oz. required to give 1 p.p.m. of element specified*
Sodium nitrate	0·103 (N)
Calcium nitrate	0·135 (N) Supplies also 1·4 p.p.m. Ca
Ammonium sulphate . .	0·076 (N)
Potassium nitrate . . .	0·122 (N) Supplies also 2·8 p.p.m. K
Potassium sulphate . . .	0·040 (K)
Potassium chloride (Muriate of potash) . . .	0·033 (K)
Superphosphate of lime (16% sol. P_2O_5) . . .	0·268 (P) Supplies also 3·8 p.p.m. Ca
Monocalcium phosphate . .	0·118 (P) Supplies also 0·6 p.p.m. Ca
Magnesium sulphate (Epsom salt)	0·172 (Mg)
Ferrous sulphate (Sulphate of iron)	0·089 (Fe)
Calcium sulphate (Gypsum) .	0·076 (Ca)
Manganese sulphate . . .	0·065 (Mn)
Boric acid	0·090 (B)

The concentrations of each element required will vary with the kind of plant, stage of growth, season of the year, and weather conditions, but as a rough guide the following concentrations are suggested for crops such as tomatoes during the spring months.

Nitrogen (N) .	150 p.p.m.	(=650 p.p.m. nitrate)
Phosphorus (P)	70 ,,	(=210 ,, phosphate)
Potassium (K) .	200 ,,	
Magnesium (Mg)	50 ,,	
Calcium (Ca) .	400 ,,	
Iron (Fe) .	5 ,,	
Boron (B) .	1 ,,	
Manganese (Mn)	1 ,,	

With increasing sunshine and growth of the plants the nitrogen may be increased slowly to about double this figure and the potassium and phosphorus halved.

Iron presents a difficulty through the very insoluble nature of iron phosphate which forms when iron sulphate is added to a solution of a phosphate. In the sand culture system this may be overcome by applying the required amount of iron separately in solution once per week. With the sub-irrigation system satisfactory results are usually obtained if iron sulphate equivalent to 5 p.p.m. is added weekly to the solution immediately before a flooding of the bed.

A formula on these lines, which has been much used with satisfactory results for a wide variety of crops, is that known as the WP solution devised by the Ohio State University, and has the following composition:

Potassium nitrate . .	11¼ oz.
Ammonium sulphate .	1¾ ,,
Magnesium sulphate .	8½ ,,
Monocalcium phosphate .	4½ ,,
Calcium sulphate . .	20 oz.
Water	100 gal.

(It should be noted that in any American formula the U.S. gallon (= 0·83 Imperial gallon) is used. The above formula has been recalculated in terms of the Imperial gallon.)

It will be noticed that this solution contains a small amount of ammonium sulphate. This chemical cannot be used alone as a source of nitrogen but in small quantities is useful as a stimulant in the early stages of growth. It may well be omitted later.

With the above formula manganese and boron should be added monthly by dissolving 1 oz. each of manganese sulphate and boric acid in 1 gal. of water acidified with 4 drops of sulphuric acid and adding 1 pint to the above. Iron may be added weekly at the rate of ½ oz. of ferrous sulphate per 100 gal. of solution.

With many crops the above solution may be doubled in concentration when the plants are growing strongly.

Whatever formula is used the pH (acidity or alkalinity) must be adjusted by any of the recognized methods before use. In the case of the sub-irrigation system the solution should be tested weekly and adjusted accordingly. In general, a pH of 6·0 to 6·5 will be satisfactory for most crops. To increase the acidity (i.e. lower the pH value) a stock solution of 2 oz. of commercial sulphuric acid in 1 gal. of water may be used (on a large scale the concentrated acid may be added directly to the solution, if care is used) and to decrease the acidity (i.e. raise the pH) a stock solution of 2 oz. of sodium hydroxide (caustic soda) in 1 gal. of water. R. H. S.

SOIL FUNGICIDES AND INSECTICIDES. *See* **Fungicides, Insecticides.**

A→

SOILING-UP. A term sometimes used for earthing-up (q.v.).

A→

Soj'a, from the Chinese name *shōyū*. *See* **Glycine Soja,** the Soya bean. **A**

SOLANA'CEAE. Dicotyledons. A family of about 1,800 species of herbs, erect or climbing shrubs, and, rarely, trees, comprised in over 70 genera, widely distributed over temperate and tropical regions. Leaves alternate, upper often twin, occasionally whorled, entire, toothed, lobed or dissected. Flowers hermaphrodite, regular or slightly irregular; calyx 5- (rarely 4-, 6-, or 7-) parted, toothed or lobed, gamosepalous, inferior; corolla gamopetalous, tubular, funnel-, bell-, or salver-shaped, or rotate; limb 5- (rarely 4-, 6-, or 7-) parted or lobed, lobes equal or slightly 2-lipped; stamens alternating with corolla lobes, affixed to tube; ovary 2- to 5-celled, superior, oblique. Fruit a many-seeded capsule or berry. Inflorescence usually cymose, often leaf-opposed owing to adnations. Many plants of the family are of economic importance, the potato (*Solanum tuberosum*) being the chief. Tobacco, manufactured from the leaves of *Nicotiana Tabacum* and a few other species, Chillies, the berries of *Capsicum annuum*, Cayenne Pepper, the ground fruits of a somewhat woody species of Capsicum, Tomato, the fruit of *Lycopersicon esculentum*, Aubergine, the fruit of *Solanum Melongena*, and the medicinal herbs *Atropa Belladonna*, Henbane (*Hyoscyamus niger*) and Stramonium (*Datura Stramonium*) are others of importance. Several species are poisonous. The genera treated here are: Anthocercis, Atropa, Browallia, Brunfelsia, Capsicum, Cestrum, Datura, Duboisia, Fabiana, Grabowskia, Hyoscyamus, Iochroma, Jaborosa, Juanulloa, Latua, Lycium, Lycopersicon, Mandragora, Metternichia, Nicandra, Nicotiana, Nierembergia, Petunia, Physalis, Physochlaina, Retzia, Salpichroa, Salpiglossis, Saracha, Schizanthus, Schwenkia, Scopolia, Solandra, Solanum, Streptosolen, Vestia.

solana'ceus -a -um, Solanum-like.

SOLAND'RA (in honour of Daniel Carlsson Solander, F.R.S., 1736–82, Swedish disciple of Linnaeus and fellow traveller with Sir Joseph Banks and Captain Cook.) FAM. *Solanaceae.* A genus of about 4 species of tall-climbing shrubs with showy flowers, natives of Trop. America. Leaves entire, leathery, shiny. Flowers large, solitary; calyx long-tubular, 2- to 5-cleft at apex; corolla funnel-shaped with a wide, bell-shaped throat and 4 broad lobes; stamens 5, declinate above middle; peduncle thick. Berries globose, pulpy. The Solandras need a warm greenhouse with plenty of light and exposure to sunshine. If given much space and abundance of water they grow rapidly and this should be the treatment at first, but if persisted in they fail to flower. When growth has progressed sufficiently, therefore, water should be withheld entirely until the leaves begin to drop off from drought, and thereafter an abundant crop of flowers will result. Propagation is by seed or by cuttings. If small plants are required the cuttings should be taken from flowering shoots.

S. grandiflo'ra. Peach-coloured Trumpet Flower. Climber to 15 ft. *l.* elliptic or elliptic-oblong, 2½ to 5 in. long. *fl.* greenish-white at first, becoming slowly rich brownish-yellow, fragrant; cal. 2 to 3½ in. long, 3- or 4-cleft, cor. 7 to 10 in. long, lobes undulate-crenate. March, April. *fr.* greenish, ovoid-globose, sweetly sub-acid. Jamaica. 1781. (B.M. 1874.)

S. gutta'ta. Climber to 10 ft. *l.* broadly elliptic-oblong, 3 to 6 in. long, acute, downy beneath. *fl.* erect, terminal fragrant; cor. pale yellow with purple spots or ridges in throat, funnel-shaped, lobes crispate, spreading, cal. tubular, downy, 3 in. long. Mexico. 1830. (B.R. 1551.)

S. Hartweg'ii. Branching shrub of 12 to 15 ft. *l.* elliptic, acute or obtuse, glabrous. *fl.* yellow, 6 to 8 in. across; cal. unequally 3- to 4-lobed; cor. glabrous, tube 5-ribbed, ribs green outside, brownish-purple within, lobes 5, more or less crisped and reflexed. Mexico.

S. laev'is. A variety of *S. longiflora.*

S. longiflo'ra. Shrub to 6 ft. *l.* elliptic-, lanceolate-, or obovate-oblong, 2½ to 4 in. long. *fl.* white with a purplish tinge, 1 ft. long, lobes undulately toothed; cal. about 3 in. long. November. *fr.* 1½ in. across. Jamaica. 1846. Var. **laev'is,** *l.* rather small; *fl.* fragrant, greenish-cream, limb white, cal. 3 in. long. (B.M. 4345 as *S. laevis.*)

F. G. P.

solanifo'lius -a -um, having leaves resembling Solanum.

Solandra guttata

SOLA'NUM (ancient Latin name of a plant). FAM. *Solanaceae.* A genus of over 900 species of mainly herbs distributed over tropical and temperate regions. Leaves simple or compound. Flowers solitary or in terminal cymose corymbs, small; stamens 5, all fertile forming a cone of anthers opening at the tip; ovary 2-celled, many-seeded. Fruit a berry. The most important member of the genus is the Potato (q.v.). *S. nigrum* and *S. Dulcamara* are British but most of the species are only half-hardy or tender. Many of them are showy in flower and a few like *S. crispum*, *S. jasminoides*, and *S. Wendlandii* as well as the British *S. Dulcamara*, ornamental woody climbers. They all grow well in ordinary garden soil.

The diseases of the Potato are dealt with under Potato diseases. Other species of interest to horticulturists are the Winter Cherry, *S. Capsicastrum*, which may be affected by the Spotted Wilt disease (q.v.) which is so severe on Tomatoes, and Winter Cherries so affected are therefore a source of danger as they carry over the disease from season to season. The symptoms appear on the leaves as light-coloured concentric circles and are easily identified. The Potato Blight fungus *Phytophthora infestans* may also on occasion attack Winter Cherry foliage. There is also a Foot Rot due to *P. parasitica* on young plants, and the Grey Mould fungus, *Botrytis cinerea*, may be a nuisance in moist conditions. Stem Canker (due to *Didymella Lycopersici*) may occur and require destruction of affected plants and spraying with Bordeaux mixture. The non-parasitic trouble called Dropsy or Oedema can be severe on Winter Cherries, taking the form of light warty pustules on leaves and stems and requiring reduction in watering and improved ventilation to rid the atmosphere of excessive moisture. Other species of Solanum are likely to be affected by the foregoing troubles, one being *S. Melongena esculentum*, the Egg-plant, which in addition can be attacked by the virus known as Tobacco Ringspot (Nicotiana virus), affected plants showing ringspot-like yellow discolorations on their leaves. Even the weed, Black Nightshade, *S. nigrum*, is dangerous because it is affected by various Potato virus diseases and thus may act as a source of infection.

(D. E. G.)

Solanum aculeatissimum

S. aculeatis'simum.* Annual, 1 to 1½ ft. or more h., erect, branched, very prickly. *l.* ovate-oblong, sinuately lobed, stalked; lobes 5 (sometimes 3 or 7), ovate, entire or repand, prickly. *fl.* white, about ⅝ in. across, nodding; cal. deeply 5-cleft; racemes short, few-fld., peduncles solitary or twin. Summer. *fr.* scarlet, as large as a Tangerine orange (in var. **macrocarp'um,** 1½ in. wide), globose. Tropics. 1871. (F.d.S. 1988 as *S. ciliatum.*) SYN. *S. myriacanthum.* Greenhouse.

S. acutilo'bum. Shrub or small tree with downy, sparingly thorny shoots. *l.* cordate, long-stalked; lobes acute, downy on both sides, not prickly. *fl.* whitish, in hairy corymbs. Brazil. Warm house.

S. aethiop'icum. Annual, 1 to 2 ft. h. *l.* ovate-lanceolate, 5 in. long, repandly angled, unequal at base; paler beneath, stalked. *fl.* white; cal. leafy, 5- to 7-cleft; cor. deeply 5- to 7-cleft, lobes triangular-oblong; racemes drooping, few-fld. *fr.* red, large, globose, edible. Asia, Trop. Africa. 1597. Hardy.

S. ala'tum. A synonym of *S. robustum.*

S. al'bidum. Perennial. Branches white-hairy. *l.* large, 2 ft. long, pinnatifid, bright green above, white-hairy beneath. *fl.* white, small, numerous in cymes. August. Andes of Peru. 1886. (R.H. 1886, p. 232, f. 67.)

S. anthropophago'rum. A synonym of *S. Uporo.*

S. arbo'reum. Large tree to 40 ft. with zigzag branches. *l.* oblong, slender-pointed, wedge-shaped at base, entire, in unequal pairs, one l. very small, subsessile, glabrous. *fl.* white, about ⅓ in. across, lobes oblong, acute. Venezuela. Stove.

S. atropurpur'eum. Erect sub-shrub, branches dark blood-red with unequal prickles, dark purple at base. *l.* 6 to 7 in. long, unequally sub-cordate, 5- to 7-lobed, with strong prickles nearly 1 in. long; long-stalked. *fl.* in lateral racemes 6- to 8-fld., nearly 1 in. long; cal. tinged purple, deeply 5-cleft; cor. purple on yellow base, somewhat 5-parted, segs. acute, about ⅓ in. long. *fr.* at first white, then yellow. Brazil. 1870. Ref. B. 207.) Greenhouse.

S. auricula'tum. Annual. *l.* 6 to 7 in. long, soft, ovate-oblong, with long slender point, smooth green above, greyish and hairy beneath, often with 2 stipule-like growths. *fl.* violet, with white stripe up middle of segs., ⅝ in. across, in sub-terminal, many-fld. corymbs. *fr.* reddish, globose, as large as a Sloe. Madagascar, &c. Half-hardy.

S. avicula're.* Kangaroo Apple. Shrub to 6 ft., erect. *l.* lanceolate, acute, or rarely blunt, pinnatifid or almost entire on old plants, 6 to 10 in. long. *fl.* few, in short loose racemes in axils of upper l., violet, ¾ to 1 in. across; cal. lobes short; cor. lobes short and broad. *fr.* green or yellow, rather large. Australia, New Zealand. 1772. (B.M. 9154 and 349 as *S. laciniatum.*) Greenhouse, or against a warm wall when it behaves as an herbaceous perennial and needs the root-stock to be covered in winter. The Australian form is sometimes distinguished as *S. laciniatum* with flatter, often deeply emarginate cor. lobes.

S. Balbis'ii. A synonym of *S. sisymbrifolium.*

S. beta'ceum. A synonym of *Cyphomandra betaceum.*

S. Capsicas'trum.* Sub-shrub, of 1 to 2 ft., branched, shoots more or less stellately downy. *l.* twin, one much smaller than other, entire or slightly wavy at margin, slightly downy above; larger l. oblong-lanceolate, 1½ to 2 in. long, smaller, lanceolate or obovate. *fl.* small, white, similar to those of *S. Pseudocapsicum* in short racemes nearly opposite l. *fr.* orange-red or scarlet, about as large as a hazel-nut. Brazil. (F.d.S. 1242.) Very ornamental in fruit. var. **Melvin'ii,** compact, about 1 ft. h., berries ovoid; **variega'tum,** *l.* variegated.

S. citrullifo'lium. Hairy annual, 1½ to 2 ft. h., stem branched, prickles straight. *l.* deeply pinnatifid, lobes 5 to 7, obtuse, deeply toothed. *fl.* violet, 1½ in. across; cor. lobes acute; anthers orange; cymes few-fld., near tips of branches. July. *fr.* enclosed in the prickly cal. Texas. 1820. SYN. *S. heterodoxum.* Hardy.

S. cornu'tum. Annual, about 4 ft., branched, prickly. *l.* pinnatipartite, 5 to 7 in. long, 3 to 4 in. wide; lobes pinnatifid, prickly, prickles straight, awl-shaped, yellow. *fl.* yellow, 1 to 1¼ in. across, plicate, star-shaped; anthers unequal, one long, horn-shaped; cymes terminal, simple, few-fld. *fr.* small, spiny. Mexico. Greenhouse. (G.C. 22 (1897) p. 311, f. 94.)

S. crisp'um.* Sub-shrubby, 12 to 14 ft. h., spreading widely, the branches herbaceous. *l.* undivided, ovate, ovate-lanceolate, or sub-cordate, 3 to 4 in. long, often cuspidate, loosely crisped at margins; stalked. *fl.* in corymbs 3 or 4 in. long at ends of shoots, becoming lateral; cal. 5-toothed; cor. bluish-purple, 5-cleft, about ⅔ in. across. *fr.* yellowish-white, as large as peas. Chile. 1824. (B.M. 3795; B.R. 1516; L.B.C. 1959.) Hardy against a wall. var. **ligustri'num,** branches green, glabrous, *l.* sub-cordate, 1½ in. long, glabrous, *fl.* in few-fld. corymbs. Chile. 1831. (L.B.C. 1963 as *S. ligustrinum.*)

S. cyanan'thum. About 6 ft. h., branches stellately hairy, whitish, prickly. *l.* cordate, ovate-elliptic, 14 in. long, almost without prickles, sinuately repand or lobed; stalks about 3 in. long, hairy. *fl.* blue, 2 to 2½ in. across; cal. spreading, 5-parted; peduncles 2 in. long, prickly, whitish, hairy; racemes about 5-fld., 4 in. long. Brazil. 1880. Greenhouse.

S. Dulcama'ra. Bittersweet, Felonwood, Woody Nightshade. Trailing perennial, stems 4 to 6 ft. long, shrubby. *l.* ovate or cordate, sometimes 3- to 5-parted, 1 to 3 in. long, slender-pointed. *fl.* many, drooping, in l.-opposed cymes; cal. lobes obtuse; cor. purple or white, ½ in. across, lobes revolute. Summer. *fr.* red, rarely yellow-green, ½ in. across, poisonous. Europe, including Britain, Asia, N. Africa. (E.B. 930.) var. **mari'num** on English and Irish sea coasts has fleshy *l.* and prostrate habit; **variega'tum,** *l.* variegated, creamy-white. Hardy.

S. elaeagnifo'lium. Erect, branched perennial of about 4 ft. with a few remote prickles. *l.* linear-oblong, entire, stalked. *fl.* bluish-violet or white in forked cymes, 2 or 3 in. long and as broad; cal. deeply 5-cleft; cor. thrice as long as cal., about ⅝ in. across. *fr.* orange, globose. Peru. 1825. (B.M. 2697.) Greenhouse. SYN. *S. saponaceum.* The unripe fruits, called Killo-Killo by the natives, were at one time used as soap for washing clothes.

S. Engleria'num. Shrub to 4½ ft. h., branches stellately hairy. *l.* lanceolate, rusty beneath, slightly sinuate, to 3½ in. long. *fl.* in few-fld. racemes; cal. lobes short; cor. pale blue, 1$\frac{1}{10}$ in. across. Trop. E. Africa.

S. frag'rans. A synonym of *Cyphomandra betaceum.*

S. gigante'um. Biennial. Tree-like of 10 to 25 ft., stem thick, soft, prickly, white-woolly. *l.* oblong, wedge-shaped at ends, 8 in. long, undulate. *fl.* blue, ⅝ in. across; cor. cut half-way; cymes terminal, densely many-fld., with starry white wool. *fr.* red, about as large as a pea. E. Indies. (B.M. 1921.) Greenhouse. Useful in sub-tropical gardening.

S. glau'cum. Perennial to 6 ft. h., stem erect, simple, smooth, glaucous. *l.* oblong-lanceolate, 5 to 6 in. long, slender-pointed, glaucous, margined white; stalk whitish, winged. *fl.* blue, about 1 in. across; cal. 5-cleft; cor. star-shaped; corymbs terminal, then lateral, 3 in. long. *fr.* oblong-ovoid, purple-violet, ¾ in. long. S. Brazil, Uruguay. (B.M. 7945.) Stove. SYN. *S. glaucophyllum.*

S. Henderson'ii. Much like *S. Pseudocapsicum.* *fl.* white, abundant. *fr.* orange-red, ovoid. Of garden origin. 1878. Greenhouse.

S. heterodox'um. A synonym of *S. citrullifolium.*

S. integrifo'lium. Chinese Scarlet Egg-plant. Annual bushy herb, about 3 ft. h., hairy, with strongly hooked prickles. *l.* with lobes sharper than in *S. Melongena*, prickly on veins and l.-stalk. *fl.* small, white, in clusters of 2 to 6. *fr.* bright scarlet or yellow, 1 to 2 in. across, nearly globular. Africa?

S. James'ii. Perennial about 9 in. h., with minute tubers; stem short, slender. *lflets.* 9 to 11, oblong-lanceolate, slender-pointed. *fl.* white, cor. lobes lanceolate-deltoid, as long as tube; cymes few-fld. *fr.* globose. SW. United States, Mexico. 1884. (B.M. 6766.) Hardy. A curiosity only.

Solanum jasminoides

S. jasminoi'des.* Potato Vine. Deciduous twiner with many stems, 3 to 4 ft. long or more, twiggy. *l.* ovate-acuminate, mostly subcordate, $1\frac{3}{4}$ in. long, entire or almost so, sometimes 2- to 5-parted and $2\frac{1}{2}$ in. long; stalked. *fl.* bluish-white, about $\frac{3}{4}$ in. across; cal. short, 5-toothed; cor. deeply 5-cleft, segs. spreading. Racemes 1 to $1\frac{1}{4}$ in. long, about 10-fld. S. America. 1838. (B.R. 33, 33.) Cool greenhouse but hardy against a wall in many parts of the country. var. **al'bum,** *fl.* white; **floribund'um,*** more floriferous than type, *l.* less pinnatifid. 1886; **grandiflo'rum,** more robust, racemes larger; **variega'tum,** *l.* blotched creamy-white.

S. lacinia'tum. *See* **S. aviculare.**

S. lanceola'tum. Perennial of 6 ft. or more, with a few straight prickles at base. *l.* lanceolate or oblong-lanceolate, 6 to 9 in. long, acute, unequal at base, greenish-hairy above; stalks $\frac{1}{2}$ to $\frac{3}{4}$ in. long. *fl.* blue, 1 in. across; cal. 5-cleft; cor. lobes ovate-triangular; cymes 1 to 4 in. long. Many. *fr.* orange, globose. Mexico. 1800. (B.M. 2173.) Greenhouse.

S. macran'thum. 6 to 14 ft. h., stem branched near top, prickly. *l.* ovate, lanceolate, or lanceolate-elliptic, 10 to 15 in. long, 9- or 10-lobed or -angled, lobes entire or nearly so, prickly on veins; l.-stalk short, winged. *fl.* bluish-violet, $1\frac{1}{2}$ to $2\frac{1}{2}$ in. across; cal. $\frac{1}{2}$ to $\frac{3}{4}$ in. across, sometimes prickly; cor. 5- or 6-cleft, segs. acute; racemes 1 to 5 in. long, 7- to 12-fld. Brazil. (B.M. 4138.) Greenhouse. Useful also for subtropical gardening. SYN. *S. maroniense.*

S. margina'tum. Biennial, 3 to 4 ft. h., erect, white-hairy, prickly. *l.* subcordate, sinuately lobed, prickly on both sides, white-hairy beneath, whitish-margined above. *fl.* white, purple-centred; cal. 5- or 6-cleft, sometimes prickly; cor. 5- or 6-cleft, downy-hairy without as are peduncles and pedicels; cymes sub-umbellate. *fr.* yellow, drooping, 1 in. across, globose. Abyssinia. 1775. (B.M. 1928.) Greenhouse, and useful for subtropical gardening.

S. maronien'se. A synonym of *S. macranthum.*

S. Melonge'na. Annual, 2 to 8 ft. h. *l.* ovate, sinuate or lobed, 3 to 6 in. long, with starry wool beneath, prickly. *fl.* blue, 1 to $1\frac{1}{2}$ in. across; cal. $\frac{1}{4}$ to $\frac{1}{2}$ in. long; cor. shortly lobed, hairy without; cymes lateral, few-fld. *fr.* variable in colour, form, and size, edible. Africa, S. Asia. 1597. Greenhouse. var. **esculen'tum,** Aubergine, Brinjal, Egg-plant, Jew's Apple, Mad Apple. Differs from type in having few prickles and solitary fl. *See* **Aubergine; ovig'erum,** *fr.* white, as large as a hen's egg; **specio'sa atropurpu'rea,** *fr.* reddish-scarlet; **serpenti'num,** Snake Egg-plant, *fr.* up to 12 in. long, curled at ends.

S. murica'tum. Melon Pear, Melon Shrub. Erect, spineless bushy herb or sub-shrub. *l.* oblong-lanceolate or ovate, margin undulate; stalk more or less winged. *fl.* blue, small, cor. deeply 5-lobed; clusters long-stalked. *fr.* ovoid, drooping, yellow with splashes of purple, 4 to 6 in. long, flesh yellow, juicy, aromatic. Peru, Chile. Greenhouse. (G.C. 33 (1903), 309.) SYN. *S. guatemalense.*

S. ni'grum. Black Nightshade. Annual, erect, 6 to 12 in. h., usually warted. *l.* rhomboid-ovate, 1 to 3 in. long, sinuate or toothed, narrowed to a stalk. *fl.* few, drooping, white, $\frac{1}{3}$ to $\frac{3}{8}$ in. across; cal. lobes obtuse; cor.-lobes ciliate, recurved; cymes lateral, umbellate. *fr.* black, yellow, or red, $\frac{1}{3}$ in. across. Europe, &c., including Britain. (E.B. 931.) var. **guineen'se,** Garden Huckleberry, stem smooth, *l.* broadly ovate, smooth above, sometimes hairy beneath, cal. deeply cut, *fr.* larger. Used in pies and preserves; **minia'tum,** *fr.* scarlet, *l.* toothed. (E.B. 932.) There seem to be differences in the edibility of different varieties, some of which appear to be more or less poisonous.

S. pen'sile.* Tall, branching climber. *l.* ovate or cordate-ovate, 2 to 4 in. long, paler beneath. *fl.* bright violet-blue with white, star-shaped centre, $1\frac{1}{2}$ in. across; cor. segs. incurved at tip; panicles large, pendulous, hairy. May. *fr.* pale violet, as large as a small cherry, globose. British Guiana, Surinam. 1887. (B.M. 7062.) SYN. *S. amethystinum.* Stove. Very attractive.

S. Pseudocap'sicum.* Jerusalem Cherry. Shrub to 4 ft., glabrous. *l.* oblanceolate or oblong, often repand, bright green, narrowed to short stalk. *fl.* white, small; cor. 5-parted; solitary or few in lateral clusters. *fr.* scarlet, rarely yellow, globose, about $\frac{1}{2}$ in. across. Madeira. 1596. Greenhouse. Usually grown as an annual in small pots for its showy fr. in winter. Variable. var. **na'num,** dwarf, much-branched; **rig'idum,** *fr.* bright orange, globose. 1868; **Weatheril'lii,** *fr.* bright orange, oval, pointed, *l.* strongly veined. 1868. These may be hybrids, perhaps with *S. Capsicastrum.* Compare *S. Hendersonii.*

S. pyracan'thum. Biennial or subshrub, prickly, 3 to 6 ft. h., stem terete, leafy. *l.* oblong, 5 to 6 in. long, acute, unequal at base, pinnatifid, lobes ovate-lanceolate; stalked. *fl.* bluish-violet, 1 in. across; cal. 5-cleft; cor. segs. cuspidate; racemes simple, many-fld., up to 6 in. long, peduncle 2 in. long. *fr.* globose, about $\frac{1}{2}$ in. across. Madagascar. Trop. Africa. 1789. Greenhouse. Best raised annually from seed. Useful for sub-tropical garden.

S. Rantonnet'ii. Shrub to $4\frac{1}{2}$ ft. *l.* lanceolate, slender-pointed, entire, glabrous or nearly so above, hairy beneath. *fl.* violet-blue with yellow centre, about 1 in. across, clustered in axils. *fr.* reddish, as large as hazel-nut, heart-shaped, drooping. Paraguay. 1870. (G.F. 1894, t. 1401 as *S. muticum.*) Greenhouse.

S. robus'tum. Vigorous sub-shrub, 2 to 4 ft. h., with robust, densely woolly prickly branches. *l.* ovate-elliptic, slender-pointed, 5 to 8 in. or more long, sinuately lobed, green and velvety, hairy above, reddish-woolly beneath, prickly on both sides. *fl.* white, 1 in. across; cal. cyathiform, deeply 5-cut; racemes $1\frac{1}{2}$ to 2 in. long with clustered fl. Brazil. 1868. (Ref. B. 37.) Valuable for the sub-tropical garden. SYN. *S. alatum.*

S. rostra'tum. Annual. Stems prickly, hairy. *l.* pinnatifid prickly. *fl.* yellow, in 5- to 8-fld. racemes; cor. lobes broadly ovate acute. *fr.* globose, included in the prickly cal. Mexico. Half-hardy.

S. Seaforthia'num. Trailing. *l.* ovate, $1\frac{1}{2}$ to 3 in. long, acute; lower or all pinnate, terminal seg. $1\frac{1}{2}$ to 3 in. long; stalked. *fl.* pale red or lilac, about $\frac{1}{2}$ in. long; cal. small with 5 minute teeth; cor. deeply 5-cleft; cymes lateral, spreading. *fr.* yellowish-red, globose. S. America. 1804. (B.M. 1982; B.R. 969; L.B.C. 971; B.M. 5823 as *S. venustum.*) var. **al'bum,** *fl.* white. Warm greenhouse.

S. sisymbrifo'lium. Annual or perennial, very prickly, about 4 ft. h. *l.* deeply pinnatifid; lobes oblong, sinuate, or sometimes again pinnatifid. *fl.* light blue or white, 1 in. or more across; cal. and cor. 5-parted; infl. racemose. Brazil, &c. (B.M. 2568; B.R. 148 as *S. decurrens.*) var. **bipinna'tum,** *fl.* white or purple, *l.* bipinnatifid. (B.M. 3954 as *S. Balbisii bipinnatum.*); **purpu'reum,** *fl.* purple, *l.* pinnatifid. (B.M. 2828 as *S. Balbisii purpureum.*)

S. Upor'o. Cannibal's Tomato. About 6 ft. h. *l.* ovate, acute, entire or lower l. angularly lobed, glabrous; stalked. *fl.* white, small, downy; pedicels few, drooping; cal. 5-lobed. *fr.* red, obscurely 2-lobed, with projection at tip. Fiji. (B.M. 5424 as *S. anthropophagorum.*) Stove. Fruit said to have been eaten by natives as accompaniment to human flesh.

S. valdivien'se. Deciduous shrub. *l.* of fascicles obovate to obovate-oblong, up to $\frac{3}{4}$ in. long, smallest roundish, narrowed to a short stalk; of young shoots lanceolate to elliptic, mostly blunt, wedge-shaped at base, with scattered stiff hairs on both surfaces. *fl.* mauve to white, about $\frac{1}{2}$ in. across, sweet-scented, drooping, in umbel-like, 8- to 10-fld. corymbs. Summer. *fr.* dull olive-green, as large as a small pea. Chile. 1927. (B.M. 9552.) SYN. *S. euonymoides.* Needs a sheltered position.

S. Warszewicz'ii. Sub-shrub, prickly. *l.* large, up to 1 ft. long, soft, oval, sub-cordate, deeply 9-lobed; stalk and midrib covered with red, starry prickles. *fl.* white, $1\frac{1}{2}$ in. across, numerous. S. America? (R.H. 1865, p. 430.) Half-hardy. Useful for sub-tropical garden.

S. Wendland'ii.* Climber to 20 ft. or more h., glabrous, with a few scattered, short, hooked prickles. *l.* bright green, variable, upper simple, oblong, cordate, or 3-lobed, sometimes with side lobes, or otherwise cut; lower on branches 6 to 10 in. long, pinnate below, pinnatifid above with 4 to 6 pairs of lflets. or lobes which are ovate or oblong, entire. *fl.* lilac-blue, $2\frac{1}{2}$ in. across in large cymes 6 in. or more across at ends of pendulous branches. August. *fr.* globose. Costa Rica. 1882. (B.M. 6914.) Stove.

S. Wright'ii. Shrub or small tree. *l.* large, 12 in. long, 6 to 8 in. wide, pinnatifid with irregular, ovate or lanceolate lobes, with bristly hairs above, coarse starry hairs beneath. *fl.* white or pale lilac, $2\frac{1}{2}$ in. across; cal. hispid; cor. 5-lobed, midrib of lobes hairy without; cymes 2-fid, lateral; pedicels $\frac{1}{2}$ in. long, hispid. Bolivia.

SOLA'RIA (in honour of Francisco de Borja Solar, an eminent Chilean mathematician). FAM. *Liliaceae*. A genus of 1 or 2 Chilean species with a fleshy corm. *S. miersioides* grows well in a compost of sandy loam and leaf-mould. It should be kept nearly dry during the rest period, gradually lessening the water-supply until the leaves begin to die down. Propagation by seeds or by offsets.

S. miersioi'des. About 4 in. h. *l.* radical, solitary, broadly linear. *fl.* green, small, and inconspicuous, stalked, erect, 3 or 4 in a terminal umbel; tube campanulate, spreading above; fertile stamens 3; involucral bracts 2, scarious; scape simple, leafless. Spring. Chile. 1871. (Ref. B. 260 as *Symea gillesioides*.)

SOLDANEL'LA (from Italian *soldo*, a coin; alluding to the form of the leaf). FAM. *Primulaceae*. A genus of 8 species of dwarf, alpine herbs with perennial rhizomes, 1- to 6-flowered scapes, and radical, stalked, circular or kidney-shaped leaves. Flowers 5-partite; corolla longer than calyx, more or less campanulate, with or without 5 notched scales at throat, lobes fringed; stamens 5, alternate with scales; ovary superior. Capsule oblong-conical, many-seeded. Very charming dwarf alpine plants for moist, cool soil in an open, i.e. free from overhead shrubs or trees, position with moist and cool air around them. There they form spreading mats of green, often glossy foliage, and in early spring produce their beautiful flowers, at times in numbers. It is sometimes found better to protect the buds, which are formed early, from winter wet by a pane of glass over the clump. Propagation is by division or by seed sown as soon as ripe. In nature the Soldanellas at times throw up their flowers through the alpine snow, melted around the scape by the heat generated by the active respiration of the growing stems.

Hybrids occur between the species where they meet in nature. These hybrids are often very difficult to recognize, especially when the parents are closely related, but are characterized by having partially (25–80 per cent.) sterile pollen. The known hybrids are listed below, but cannot be adequately described in a few words; they may be exactly intermediate or vary towards either parent. No hybrids of the geographically isolated plants *S. pindicola* and *S. villosa* are known.

KEY

1. *Cor. broadly funnel-shaped, divided to about half-way, with distinct scales near the base. Anthers prolonged at the tip. Scape usually* 2- *to* 6-*fld. Lvs. about* 1 *in. across* (*Sect.* Crateriflores) 2
1. *Cor. narrowly funnel-shaped or tubular, divided only for* $\frac{1}{5}$ *to* $\frac{1}{3}$ *of its length, with scales very small or lacking. Scape usually* 1-*fld., rarely* 2-*fld. Lvs. usually under* $\frac{1}{2}$ *in. across* (*Sect.* Tubiflores) 5
2. *L.-stalks and pedicels at first with distinctly stalked glands. Lvs. usually crenate and deeply cordate with narrow sinus* 7
2. *L.-stalks and pedicels at first with sessile glands or very shortly stalked glands* 3
3. *Glands sessile* S. alpina
3. *Glands short-stalked* 4
4. *Lvs. green or violet beneath* S. hungarica
4. *Lvs. bluish-grey beneath* S. pindicola
5. *L.-stalks and pedicels at first with sessile glands, later glabrous. Nerves standing out on upper side of lvs. Anthers with pointed basal lobes* S. pusilla
5. *L.-stalks and pedicels with stalked glands. Nerves not evident on upper side of lvs. Anthers with rounded basal lobes* 6
6. *Lvs. orbicular or longer than broad, not cordate; stomata only on lower side* S. minima
6. *Lvs. orbicular or a little broader than long, shallowly cordate, stomata on both sides* S. austriaca
7. *Mature lvs. more or less glabrous above and below, but the petiole sparsely hairy. Cal.-lobes* 1-*nerved* S. montana
7. *Mature lvs. with many persistent hairs, especially below, the petiole villous. Cal.-lobes* 3-*nerved* S. villosa

S. alpi'na. *l.* roundish-kidney-shaped, cordate at base, glands of petiole sessile, margin entire. Scape 1- to 3-fld., about 4 in. h. at flowering time. *fl.* widely bell-shaped, bluish with crimson marks inside, about $\frac{2}{5}$ to $\frac{3}{5}$ in. long, lobes cut to middle or beyond; anthers purple-tipped. April. Pyrenees and Alps to the Tirol. 1656. (B.M. 49; F.d.S. 994.)

S. × Aschersonia'na (*S. austriaca* × *S. montana*).

S. austri'aca. *l.* orbicular, subcordate, $\frac{1}{5}$ to $\frac{2}{5}$ in. across entire; glands almost sessile. Scape 1-fld., $1\frac{1}{2}$ to $3\frac{1}{2}$ in. h. Cor. tubular bell-shaped, $\frac{2}{5}$ to $\frac{3}{5}$ in. long, cut to about quarter-way, bluish-lilac lined with violet streaks. April. North-east (Austrian) Alps. SYN. *S. minima* subsp. *austriaca*.

S. Clus'ii. *See* **S. montana.**

S. Dimon'iei. *See* **S. pindicola.**

S. × Gand'eri. (*S. alpina* × *S. minima*).

S. × Handel-Mazzet'tii (*S. austriaca* × *S. montana*).

S. hunga'rica. *l.* roundish kidney-shaped, cordate at base, up to 1 in. wide, thick, entire, purplish beneath. Scape 1- to 3-fld., about 4 in. h. at flowering time. *fl.* widely bell-shaped, $\frac{2}{5}$ to $\frac{3}{5}$ in. long, lobes cut to middle or beyond, bluish. April. Carpathians to Balkans.

S. × hyb'rida (*S. alpina* × *S. pusilla*).

S. × Janchen'ii (*S. minima* × *S. pusilla*).

S. × lungovien'sis (*S. montana* × *S. pusilla*).

Soldanella minima

S. min'ima. *l.* orbicular, not cordate, thick, $\frac{1}{5}$ to $\frac{2}{5}$ in. across, entire, glands of petiole sessile. Scape 1-fld., $1\frac{1}{2}$ to 3 in. h. Cor. tubular bell-shaped, $\frac{2}{5}$ to $\frac{1}{2}$ in. long, cut to about quarter-way, pale blue or snow-white, lined with violet streaks. April. Southern Alps. 1823.

S. × mix'ta (*S. austriaca* × *S. pusilla*).

S. monta'na. *l.* more or less orbicular, deeply cordate at base, margin remotely scalloped, $\frac{4}{5}$ to $2\frac{1}{4}$ in. wide, l.-stalk glandular-hairy, up to 4 in. long. Scape 3- to 10-fld., about 6 in. h. at flowering time. Cor. widely bell-shaped, $\frac{1}{3}$ to $\frac{2}{3}$ in. long, cut to $\frac{1}{2}$ or beyond, blue or bluish-lilac. April. Northern Alps, Carpathians, Balkan Peninsula. 1816. (B.M. 2163 as *S. Clusii*.)

S. × neglec'ta (*S. minima* × *S. pusilla*).

S. pindico'la. *l.* roundish, cordate at base (about $\frac{1}{2}$ to $1\frac{1}{2}$ in. wide), dull green above, ashy blue beneath. Scape 1- to 3-fld., to $3\frac{1}{2}$ in. h. Cor. broadly funnel-shaped, about $\frac{2}{5}$ in. long, deeply divided, rose-lilac, about 1 in. Northern Greece (Mt. Pindus), Albania. 1928. var. **Dimon'iei,** *l.* smaller (about $\frac{7}{10}$ in. wide). Albania. SYN. *S. Dimoniei*.

S. pusil'la. *l.* cordate kidney-shaped or roundish, about $\frac{1}{2}$ in. wide, entire, leathery, glossy dark green; l.-stalk glabrous. Scape 1- (rarely 2-fld.), 2 to 4 in. h. Cor. narrowly bell-shaped, $\frac{1}{3}$ to $\frac{1}{2}$ in. long, cut to about $\frac{1}{4}$, blue or pale violet, lobes obtuse. Alps of Europe.

S. × Rich'teri. *See* **S. × transsilvanica.**

S. × transsilvan'ica (*S. hungarica* × *S. pusilla*). SYN. *S.* × *Richteri*.

S. villo'sa. *l.* more or less orbicular; l.-stalk persistently villous. Pyrenean counterpart of *S. montana*. Pyrenees. SYN. *S. montana* subsp. *villosa*

S. × Wettstein'ii (*S. alpina* × *S. montana*).

S. × Wiemannia'na (*S. alpina* × *S. austriaca*).

soleiform'is -is -e, sandal-shaped.

Soleirol'ii, in honour of Lieut. Henri Augustine Soleirol, b. 1792, who collected in Corsica, &c.

SOLENAN'THUS (*solen*, tube, *anthos*, flower; from the form of the corolla). FAM. *Boraginaceae*. A genus of about a dozen species of biennial or perennial herbs, natives of the Mediterranean region and Cent. Asia. Stems usually hollow, basal leaves long-stalked, upper alternate. Flowers in racemes, cylindrical or funnel-shaped with short lobes, throat with scales, stamens exserted. Cultivation as for Cynoglossum.

S. apenni'nus. Stem thick, hollow, hairy, 2 to 4 ft. h. *Basal l.* ovate or elliptic, 10 to 16 in. long, hairy above; long-stalked; *upper l.* linear, sessile. *fl.* in a large terminal thyrse, purplish-blue, cylindrical, about ½ in. long, lobes oval, short. May to July. Italy.

S. circina'tus. Habit of *S. apenninus*. *Basal l.* large, elliptic or oblong-lanceolate, up to 2 ft. long with a wide stalk, densely hairy above. *fl.* in short dense heads, then racemose in a terminal thyrse; ashy-blue, about ½ in. long. April, May. Syria to Himalaya.

SOLENID'IUM (*solen*, tube, *eidion*, like; from the form of the lip). FAM. *Orchidaceae*. A genus of 2 species of epiphytic orchids allied to Oncidium and sometimes included in it. Habit of Oncidium but differing by the long keel-like claw of the lip which has 2 parallel hairy lamellae. Compost and treatment as for Oncidiums with a winter minimum temperature of about 60° F.

S. luna'tum. *fl.* several, about ¾ in. across; sep. and pet. narrowed to base, yellow with yellow-brown or brownish spots; sep. rather larger than pet., the lower free or connate at base; lip shorter than sep., deflexed, claw rather long and narrow, blade crescent- or kidney-shaped more or less concave, about ½ in. wide, white with brown-red spots, crest lined red; scape 6 to 10 in. long. Summer. *Pseudobulbs* under 2 in. long, clustered. *l.* 1 or 2, leathery, 3 to 4½ in. long, scarcely ¾ in. wide. Guiana. 1837. (B.R. 1929 as *Oncidium lunatum.*)

S. racemo'sum. *fl.* 10 to 15, about ¾ in. across, yellow, spotted red, in a loose raceme; sep. and pet. free, spreading; sep. rather the larger; lip as long as sep. with a broad claw and 2 long, white, hairy, calli, blade about ½ in. wide; scape about 12 in. long. *Pseudobulbs* 2 to 3 in. long, clustered. *l.* 2, about 8 in. long, ½ in. wide, thin-leathery, narrowed to base. Andes of Colombia.

E. C.

SOLENOME'LUS (*solen*, tube, *melos*, limb; the perianth is tubular). FAM. *Iridaceae*. A genus of 4 species of rhizomatous herbs, natives of Chile. Leaves radical or clustered at base of stem, linear; a few also on stem. Flowers many, shortly pedicellate, in a spathe; perianth yellow with a slender tube and spreading lobes; stamens attached in throat. For treatment *see* **Sisyrinchium.**

S. chilen'sis. Stems 12 to 18 in. h., zigzag, leafy. *Radical l.* 6 to 8 in. long; *stem-l.* distant, shorter towards top of stem, linear-ensiform with a sheathing base. *fl.* deep yellow, segs. obovate, spreading, somewhat concave in lower half, there narrow with a small, dark purple spot at base; spathe 4- or 5-fld.; peduncles solitary or 2 or 4. June. Chile. 1868. (B.M. 2965 as *Sisyrinchium pedunculatum*; F.d.S. 255 as *S. longistylum.*) Half-hardy.

SOLENOPH'ORA (*solen*, tube, *phorein*, to bear; the corolla is tubular). FAM. *Gesneriaceae*. A genus of 4 species of evergreen, branching, roughly hairy shrubs, natives of Mexico. Leaves opposite, large, membranous, often dissimilar, long-stalked. Flowers scarlet or yellow, large, solitary or few, on short axillary peduncles; calyx 5-lobed; corolla tube long with a broad throat, lobes short, broad, suberect. Treatment as for Gloxinia.

S. Endlicheria'num.* Sub-shrub. Stem 1 to 2 ft. h., erect, purplish, with aerial roots. *l.* spreading, broadly elliptic, up to 12 to 18 in. long, long-pointed, hairy; stalk 3 to 4 in. long. *fl.* orange, marked with purple, 1 to 5 in axils; cor. funnel bell-shaped, hairy without, somewhat curved, 2½ to 3 in. long. April. 1849. (F.d.S. 546 as *Arctocalyx Endlicherianus.*)

SOLENOSTE'MON (*solen*, tube, *stemon*, stamen; the filaments being connate in their lower part). FAM. *Labiatae*. A genus of 7 species of perennial herbs, natives of the warmer parts of Africa, closely related to Plectranthus and Coleus but distinct by the near-equal 2-lipped calyx, with the upper lip entire, the lower notched at the tip. Conditions suiting the more tender Begonias suit *S. Godefroyae*.

S. Godefroy'ae. Branched herb to 2 ft., branches 4-angled; finely downy. *l.* wide, ovate or deltoid, ¾ to 1¼ in. long, slightly crenate; stalk about ½ in. long. *fl.* in terminal, spike-like racemes 6 to 8 in. long; whorls separated somewhat; cal. 2-lipped with 2 minute lateral teeth; cor. blue, ⅓ in. long, tube much curved, upper lip very short, 4-toothed, lower ½ in. long, flattened sideways. Autumn. Angola, Congo. 1903. (B.M. 8511.)

SOLIDA'GO (*solido*, to join or make whole; from reputed healing qualities). FAM. *Compositae*. Golden Rod. A genus of about 130 species of perennial herbs, rarely shrubby at base. Most species are natives of N. America, a few are found in S. America, in temperate Europe and Asia, 1 in the Azores. Leaves alternate, entire or frequently toothed. Flower-heads usually yellow, small, in racemes or clusters; involucre oblong or narrowly bell-shaped, bracts mostly appressed, in many series; ray-florets ligulate, spreading, or rarely small and erect. Achenes almost cylindrical or angled. Most species are hardy and grow well in ordinary soil. They are, for the most part, rather coarse and apt to impoverish the soil, but their bright-yellow flowers contrast well with the Michaelmas Daisies which flower at the same time and qualify them for a place in the large border. They are also useful for planting in rough places and on the borders of shrub gardens. They are easily propagated by division in autumn or spring.

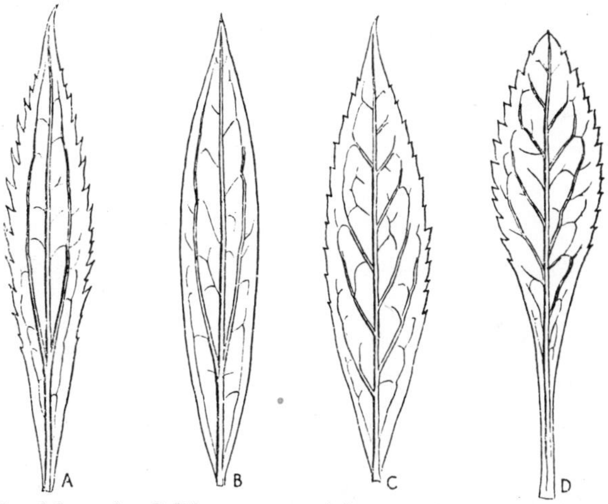

Leaf-form in *Solidago*: A, B, triple-nerved; C, D, pinnately veined; A, C, D, serrate; B, entire; A, B, C, sessile; D, narrowed into petiole.

Botanically the genus Solidago is a difficult one to classify, as the species are numerous, vary much according to conditions of growth, and hybridize both in the wild and under cultivation; a number of the golden-rods found in botanic gardens cannot be identified with certainty and many names are misapplied. The commonest is *S. canadensis* which has become naturalized in Britain. As generally accepted it includes Euthamia and Oligoneuron which are treated as separate genera in some American floras. H. D. House, *Wild Flowers of New York* (1918), illustrates several species in colour.

KEY

1. *Plant very dwarf, mat-forming, scarcely* 1 *in. high* — S. minutissima
1. *Plant taller* (4 *in. to* 9 *ft. high*) — 2
2(1). *Involucral bracts with outward spreading tips* — 3
2. *Involucral bracts erect with appressed* (*not spreading*) *tips* — 4
3(2). *Lvs. not more than* 4 *in. long; lower lvs. not conspicuously larger than middle and upper lvs.* — S. petiolaris
3. *Lvs. up to* 10 *in. long; lower lvs. much larger than middle and upper lvs.* — S. squarrosa
4(2). *Fl.-heads mostly sessile, in compact clusters* (*glomerules*) *of* 2 *to* 5, *the whole infl. a corymb. Lvs. linear* (10 *to* 15 *times as long as broad*), *narrow* (⅓ *in. or less broad*), *entire* — 5

4. *Fl.-heads short-stalked. Lvs. otherwise* 6
5(4). *Stem and lvs. glabrous* S. graminifolia
5. *Stem and lvs. pubescent* S. graminifolia Nuttallii
6(4). *Fl.-heads on mostly spreading or recurving one-sided branches, forming a terminal often large and wide panicle* 7
6. *Fl.-heads on erect or ascending not markedly one-sided branches, which may be axillary or form a terminal usually narrow truss or a corymb* 20
7(6). *Lvs. pinnately veined (lateral veins few and inconspicuous in* S. sempervirens *and* S. uliginosa) 8
7. *Lvs. triple-nerved (i.e. with two lateral veins more prominent than other veins and more or less parallel to margin)* 15
8(7). *All lvs. entire* 9
8. *Many or all lvs. toothed* 10
9(8). *Lvs. fleshy, firm-textured, the lowermost oblanceolate, to 18 in. long, much larger than lanceolate upper lvs. Ray-florets 8–14* S. sempervirens
9. *Lvs. thinner, the lowermost to 6 in. long, not much larger than upper lvs., all lanceolate or linear-lanceolate. Ray-florets 3 to 4.* S. odora
10(8). *Stem densely pubescent* 14
10. *Stem more or less glabrous below infl.* 11
11(10). *Infl. branches few. Ray-florets usually 4* S. ulmifolia
11. *Infl. branches numerous (often 15 or more). Ray-florets usually 5 to 12 (1 to 4 in* S. uliginosa linoides) 12
12(11). *Fl.-heads 5–12 fld.* S. uliginosa
12. *Fl.-heads 15–20fld.* 13
13(12). *Lvs. firm; upper lvs. entire or sparsely toothed. Infl. branches glabrous. Ray-florets 8 to 12* S. juncea
13. *Lvs. thin; upper lvs. closely toothed. Infl. branches pubescent. Ray-florets 5 to 8* S. arguta
14(10). *Stem with long spreading hairs. Lvs. prominently many-veined, rather rugose* S. rugosa
14. *Stem with minute close hairs. Lvs. obscurely few-veined* S. nemoralis
15(7). *Stem glabrous up to infl.* 16
15. *Stem more or less hairy or rough* 18
16(15). *Lvs. thin, mostly sharply serrate; upper lvs. not markedly different from lower lvs.* S. gigantea
16. *Lvs. firmer, shallowly toothed or entire; upper lvs. usually much smaller than lower lvs.* 17
17(16). *Plant markedly stoloniferous* S. missouriensis
17. *Plant with compact rootstock* S. Gattingeri
18(15). *Basal and lower lvs. mostly oblanceolate, much larger than upper lvs.* S. nemoralis
18. *All lvs. very narrowly elliptic, and not differing greatly in size and form* 19
19(18). *Involucre about* $\frac{1}{10}$ *in. long* S. canadensis and some forms of S. × hybrida
19. *Involucre about* $\frac{1}{5}$ *in. long* S. altissima
20(6). *Ray-florets white* S. bicolor
20. *Ray-florets yellow* 21
21(20). *Infl. rounded or flat-topped, corymbose, the fl.-heads in one terminal cluster or in many compact clusters at tips of almost ascending branches* 22
21. *Infl. usually narrow and rather spike-like or fastigiate or with the fl.-heads in short axillary clusters* 23
22(21). *Infl. large (5 to 8 in. across). Plant tall (2 to 5 ft. high), densely hairy* S. rigida
22. *Infl. small (to 2 in. across). Plant dwarfer (6 to 18 in. high), glabrous or sparsely hairy.* S. multiradiata
23(21). *Fl.-heads mostly in short axillary clusters. Lvs. sharply toothed, acuminate* 24
23. *Fl.-heads mostly forming a narrow terminal truss* 25
24(23). *Stem terete, often glaucous. Lvs. mostly lanceolate, narrowed to a sessile base* S. caesia
24. *Stem angled. Lvs. ovate, distinctly stalked* S. flexicaulis
25(23). *Fl.-heads very small (about* $\frac{3}{16}$ *in. across the ray-florets); involucre narrow (about* $\frac{1}{10}$ *in. or less broad)* 26
25. *Fl.-heads larger (about* $\frac{3}{16}$ *to* $\frac{3}{8}$ *in. across the ray-florets); involucre broader (about* $\frac{1}{5}$ *in. broad)* 29
26(25). *Stem pubescent* 27
26. *Stem glabrous below infl.* 28
27(26). *Plant tall (5 to 9 ft. high), with many lateral branches in upper third. Lower lvs. narrowly oblong. Ray-florets numerous (about 15)* S. californica
27. *Plant dwarf (1 to* $1\frac{1}{2}$ *ft. high), not or only sparsely branched. Lower lvs. oblanceolate* S. mollis
28(26). *Lvs. triple-nerved* S. Gattingeri
28. *Lvs. obscurely pinnately veined* S. uliginosa
29(25). *Plant robust (4 ft. or so high). Lvs. to 14 in. long, 3 in. broad* S. glomerata
29. *Plant more slender and smaller (4 in. to 2 ft. high). Lvs. less than 4 in. long, 1 in. broad* S. Virgaurea and allied species.

S. alpes'tris. *See under* **S. Virgaurea.**

S. altis'sima. 4 to 6 ft. h. Stem closely pubescent. *l.* narrowly lanceolate, 3 to 7 in. long, acuminate, remotely serrate or almost entire, closely pubescent beneath, rough above, 3-nerved. *fl.-heads* small, in 1-sided spreading or recurved branches, forming a broad pyramidal panicle. August, September. 1728. Eastern N. America (Add. 2. 75.) Very like *S. canadensis* but fl.-heads bigger, with involucres to $\frac{1}{5}$ in. h.

S. × **Arend'sii.** *See* **S.** × **hybrida.**

S. argu'ta. 3 to 4 ft. h. Stem glabrous or only sparsely pubescent above. *l.* thin, sharply serrate, pinnately veined; *lower l.* narrowly ovate, to 1 ft. long, narrowed into petiole; *upper l.* lanceolate, sessile. *fl.-heads* small, on 1-sided spreading branches, forming an open panicle. August, September. Eastern N. America. 1758.

S. as'pera. A synonym of *S. rugosa aspera.*

S. bi'color. 2 to 3 ft. h. Stem pubescent. *l.* thickish, pubescent; *basal* and *lower l.* narrowly obovate, narrowed into petiole, crenate or serrate; *upper l.* lanceolate, sessile, often entire. *fl.-heads* small, clustered in upper l.-axils and sometimes forming a narrow terminal thyrse; *ray-fl.* white or creamy; *disk-fl.* yellow. August, September. Eastern N. America. (House, W. F. 237.) Distinguished by its 2-coloured fl.-heads, but of no garden value.

S. brachy'stachys. *See under* **S. Virgaurea.**

S. Buck'leyi of gardens. *See* **S. mollis.**

S. cae'sia. 2 to 3 ft. h. Stem glabrous, often glaucous, terete. *l.* lanceolate or oblong-lanceolate, to 5 in. long, acuminate, sharply serrate, glabrous, pinnately veined. *fl.-heads* small, mostly in axillary clusters, a few forming a short terminal thyrsus. August to October. Eastern N. America. (House, W. F. 235.) 1732.

S. califor'nica. 5 to 9 ft. h. Stem pubescent, branched in upper third, with numerous, long, ascending branches to 2 ft. long. *Lower l.* very narrowly oblong (cultrate), to 5 in. long, 1 in. broad, acute, sessile, sparingly serrate, pubescent, 3-nerved; *upper l.* smaller. *fl.-heads* small, about $\frac{1}{5}$ in. across, on ascending branches, forming a long loose thyrse. September, October. California. A tall late-flowering kind.

S. camb'rica. *See under* **S. Virgaurea.**

S. canaden'sis. 3 to 6 ft. h. Stem rough-hairy. *l.* very narrowly elliptic, 3 to 6 in. long, sharply serrate or almost entire, closely pubescent beneath, rough above, 3-nerved. *fl.-heads* small, scarcely $\frac{1}{12}$ in. across, on 1-sided spreading branches, forming a broad pyramidal panicle; involucres about $\frac{1}{10}$ in. h. August to October. Eastern N. America; naturalized in Britain. 1648. (House, W. F. 238.) The commonest species in gardens and a parent of many hybrids, e.g. 'Golden Wings', up to 7 ft. h., much branched above, with very numerous fl.-heads, a very ornamental plant.

S. Cut'leri. N. American alpine counterpart of dwarf European forms of *S. Virgaurea.* 8 to 12 in. h. *Basal l.* oblanceolate, 2 to 4 in. long, serrate above middle with low teeth; *stem-l.* few, oblanceolate. *fl.-heads* large, mostly forming a short thyrse. Maine, New Hampshire, New York State.

S. flexicau'lis. 1 to 3 ft. Stem almost or quite glabrous, somewhat zigzag and angled. *l.* thin, ovate, 1 to 3 in. broad, acuminate, narrowed into petiole, sharply serrate, pinnately veined. *fl.-heads* small, mostly in axillary clusters, a few forming a short terminal thyrsus. July to October. Eastern N. America. (House, W. F. 236.). 1725. SYN. *S. latifolia.* Notable for the flexuose stem and broad leaves.

S. Gatting'eri. 2 to 3 ft. h. Stem glabrous. *l.* glabrous, firm, almost or quite entire; *basal* and *lower l.* narrowly oblanceolate, to 8 in. long, bluntish or acute but not acuminate, narrowed into petiole, 3-nerved; *upper l.* very short. *fl.-heads* small, $\frac{1}{4}$ in. across, on ascending slender branches, forming a narrow somewhat corymb-like panicle. September, October. Tennessee, Missouri. Late-flowering graceful plant of neat habit.

S. gigante'a. 3 to 6 ft. h. Stem glabrous below the inflorescence, often glaucous. *l.* lanceolate or oblong-lanceolate, to $5\frac{1}{2}$ in. long, sharply serrate, glabrous above, pilose on the veins beneath, triple-nerved. *fl.-heads* small, on 1-sided spreading or recurving branches forming a pyramidal panicle. August, September. N. America. 1758. SYN. *S. serotina gigantea.* var. **leiophyl'la,** *l.* glabrous above and below. SYN. *S. serotina* of Aiton not Retzius.

S. glomera'ta. 3 to 4 ft. h. Stem glabrous, angled. *Basal l.* very large, oblanceolate, to 14 in. long, 3 in. broad, narrowed into petiole, sharply serrate, ciliate at margin, otherwise glabrous. *Stem-l.* much smaller, sessile. *fl.-heads* large, $\frac{3}{8}$ in. across, clustered on ascending axillary branches, to 4 in. long, the upper forming a narrow terminal thyrse. August, September. N. Carolina, Tennessee.

S. × **Golden Wings.** *See under* **S. canadensis.**

S. graminifol'ia. 2 to 4 ft. h. Stem glabrous, much branched above. *l.* linear, or linear-lanceolate, to $\frac{3}{8}$ in. broad, entire glabrous. *fl.-heads* small, $\frac{1}{8}$ in. across, sessile, closely set in small clusters on long ascending branches forming a large corymb. September. Eastern N. America. (B.M. 2546 as *S. lanceolata.*) 1758. SYN. *S. lanceolata, Euthamia graminifolia.* var. **Nuttal'lii,** stems and *l.* pubescent. SYN. *Euthamia Nuttallii.*

S. × **hy'brida.** A name of vague application covering many 4 to 7 ft. h. garden forms, derived mostly from *S. canadensis* crossed with other species, with *l.* 3-nerved, *infl.* branches recurving, *fl.-heads* small but very numerous. SYN. *S.* × *Arendsii.*

S. jun'cea. 3 to 4 ft. h. Stem glabrous below the inflorescence. *Lower l.* oblanceolate to narrowly elliptic, to 12 in. long, 2-in. broad, acuminate, narrowed into petiole, sharply serrate, glabrous, pinnately veined; *upper l.* smaller, sessile, entire. *fl.-heads* small, on 1-sided spreading or recurving branches, forming a large panicle. July to September. Eastern N. America. (Add. 2. 51.)

S. latifo'lia. A synonym of *S. flexicaulis.*

S. linoi'des. A synonym of *S. uliginosa linoides.*

S. Milleria'na. A synonym of *S. petiolaris.*

S. minu'ta. *See under* **S. Virgaurea.**

S. minutis'sima. 1 in. h. *l.* ovate to broadly elliptic, less than 1 in. long, acute, slightly toothed. *fl.-heads* small. August. Japan (Yakushima). SYN. *S. Virgaurea minutissima.* A very dwarf, close-growing, mat-forming plant for trough gardens.

S. missourien'sis. 2 to 4 ft. h. Stem glabrous. *Lower l.* oblanceolate, narrowed into petiole, entire or sparingly serrate, glabrous except for the rough (scabrous-ciliolate) margin; 3-nerved; *upper l.* much smaller, sessile, entire. *fl.-heads* small, on ascending or slightly recurving glabrous 1-sided branches, forming a short small panicle. July to September. N. America. The name *S. missouriensis* has been misapplied in gardens to ×*Solidaster luteus.* **S. Short'tii** is a related species, native to Kentucky, with the branches of the inflorescence minutely hairy.

S. mollis. 15 to 24 in. Stem closely pubescent. *l.* mostly oblanceolate, firm, 2 to 4 in. long, blunt, sparsely toothed towards tip, almost entire, narrowed into petiole, closely pubescent above and below, 3-nerved. *fl.-heads* small, on short ascending or erect branches, forming a narrow thyrse. August, early September. Middle N. America. (G.C. iii. 72 (1922), 192 as *S. Buckleyi.*)

S. multiradia'ta. 9 to 18 in. h. Stem glabrous except in lower part, hairy above. *Basal l.* oblanceolate, firm, to 5 in. long, narrowed into petiole, sparingly serrate, net-veined; *upper l.* much smaller, sessile, entire. *fl.-heads* large, few, clustered on short villous branches into a rather dense corymb-like head. July to September. Northern N. America, extending into Arctic (var. *arctica,* SYN. *S. arctica*).

S. nemora'lis. 2 to 3 ft. h. Stem closely pubescent, greyish. *Basal* and *lower l.* mostly oblanceolate, to 6 in. long, narrowed into petiole, crenate, pubescent, obscurely 3-nerved; *upper l.* much smaller, sessile, entire. *fl.-heads* small, on spreading or recurving 1-sided branches, forming a rather 1-sided small panicle. August to October. Eastern N. America. 1769.

S. odo'ra. 2 to 4 ft. h. Stem glabrous or slightly pubescent. *l.* linear-lanceolate, to 4 in. long, acute or acuminate, entire, rather thick, glabrous, with pellucid dots, anise-scented when crushed. *fl.-heads* small, on spreading or recurving 1-sided branches, forming a rather 1-sided small panicle. July to August. Eastern N. America. 1699.

S. petiola'ris. 3 to 5 ft. h. Stem pubescent in upper part. *l.* mostly narrowly elliptic, to 4 in. long, narrowed into a very short petiole, acute, entire or toothed, pubescent, pinnately veined. *fl.-heads* large, $\frac{7}{12}$ in. across, forming an erect narrow thyrse. September to October. Eastern N. America. Noteworthy, like *S. squarrosa,* for the outward-spreading or recurving tips of the outer involucral bracts, giving the involucre a ragged appearance. A decorative late-flowering species.

S. rig'ida. 3 to 4 ft. h. Stem pubescent, stout. *l.* narrowly elliptic-oblong, thick, rigid, to 4 in. long, almost entire, harshly pubescent, pinnately veined; *lower l.* long-petioled, *upper l.* sessile. *fl.-heads* medium, $\frac{3}{8}$ in. across, on ascending branches, forming a long rounded corymb. September. Eastern N. America. 1710. SYN. *Oligoneuron rigidum.*

S. rugo'sa. 4 to 6 ft. Stem conspicuously pubescent. *l.* lanceolate or narrowly elliptic, to 4 in. long, sharply serrate, wrinkled, pubescent, pinnately veined. *fl.-heads* small, $\frac{1}{5}$ in. across, on spreading or recurved branches, forming a large panicle. August, September. Eastern N. America. (Add. 5. 182.) 1732. var. **as'pera,** stem less pubescent; *l.* broader, more wrinkled (rugose), rougher but less villous. 1758. SYN. *S. aspera.*

S. sempervi'rens. 4 to 7 ft. Stem glabrous below the inflorescence. *l.* fleshy, smooth, entire, obscurely 3-veined; *lower l.* narrowly oblanceolate, to 1 ft. long, narrowed into a broad clasping petiole; *upper l.* much smaller. *fl.-heads* medium, $\frac{3}{8}$ in. across, crowded on short 1-sided recurved branches, forming a dense rather 1-sided raceme. September, October. Eastern N. America. (House, W. F. 2. 235.) 1699. A very distinct and ornamental late-flowering maritime species, inhabiting salt-marshes in nature but thriving in any good garden soil.

S. Shor'tii. *See under* **S. missouriensis.**

S. squarro'sa. 3 to 5 ft. h. Stem glabrous or pubescent. *Basal* and *lower l.* large, elliptic, to 14 in. long, narrowed into a winged petiole, coarsely serrate, almost glabrous, pinnately veined; *upper l.* much smaller, shallowly serrate or entire. *fl.-heads* medium, $\frac{3}{8}$ in. across, in short clusters, forming a narrow thyrse; tips of involucral bracts recurved. August to October. Eastern N. America. (Add. 3. 102.)

S. uligino'sa. 2 to 4 ft. Stem glabrous. *Lower l.* firm, ovate-lanceolate to oblong, to 3 in. broad, acute, narrowed into petiole, shallowly toothed, glabrous, pinnately veined: *upper l.* much shorter, entire, sessile. *fl.-heads* small, $\frac{1}{4}$ in. across, on ascending rather 1-sided branches, forming a narrow panicle. August to October. Eastern N. America. var. **linoi'des** more slender, with *lower l.* narrowly oblanceolate, to 1 in. broad and panicle narrower, minutely hairy. SYN. *S. linoides, S. uniligulata.* Graceful and late flowering.

S. ulmifo'lia. 2 to 4 ft. h. Stem glabrous below the inflorescence. *Basal* and *lower l.* elliptic-ovate, to 9 in. long narrowed into petiole, sharply serrate, hairy beneath, pinnately veined; *uppermost l.* entire. *fl.-heads* small, on recurving 1-sided branches, forming a small sparsely branched panicle. August, September. Eastern N. America.

S. uniligul'ata. A synonym of *S. uliginosa linoides.*

S. Virgau'rea. 4 in. to 2 ft. h. Stem usually glabrous below the inflorescence. *l.* mostly lanceolate, 1 to 4 in. long, obscurely toothed, pinnately veined. *fl.-heads* large, to $\frac{3}{8}$ in. across, on ascending leafy branches, forming a narrowly obconical thyrse. July to October. Europe, including Britain. (E.B. 778.) A very variable species; the common lowland form is 1 to 2 ft. h.; dwarfer mostly mountain forms under 1 ft. h., which have been named var. **minuta** (SYN. *S. minuta*), var. **cambrica** (SYN. *S. cambrica*; E.B. 779) and **alpestris,** are good rock plants. *S. Cutleri* (see above) is a related American representative of this group. Here belongs the 6 to 9 in. h. garden plant with pubescent stem called *S. brachystachys.*

W. T. S.

×**SOLIDAS'TER** (combining the names of the parent genera *Aster* and *Solidago*; *aster* is here a generic name and not the usual derogatory suffix *-aster* or *-astrum* indicating incomplete resemblance and hence inferiority). FAM. *Compositae.* Intergeneric hybrid group. One member common in gardens. Easily cultivated in any good soil and sunny position. Propagated by division. SYN. *Asterago.*

×**S. lu'teus.** Stem 2 to $2\frac{1}{2}$ ft. h., smooth below pubescent above. *Basal l.* narrowly oblanceolate, acute, narrowed into long petiole; *stem-l.* linear-elliptic, entire, 3-nerved. *infl.* much-branched, corymb-like, about 4 in. wide. *fl.-heads* numerous, $\frac{1}{2}$ in. wide; ray-fl. bright yellow, becoming creamy-yellow; disk yellow. (G.C. 101. 6.) SYN. *Aster hybridus luteus, Solidaster hybridus, Asterago lutea.* A good plant for front of border. Derived from *Aster ptarmicoides* (which it resembles in habit) crossed with a Solidago at Lyons, France, about 1909.

W. T. S.

soli'dus -a -um, not hollow.

SOLIS'IA (in honour of Octavio Solis of Mexico City). FAM. *Cactaceae.* Plants very small, solitary; tubercles milky; areoles long and narrow, spines from the 2 sides, closely pressed against the plant and interlacing. Flowers yellow, borne in the axils of old tubercles; fruit small, naked. **A**

S. pectina'ta. The only species. Mexico. This species used to be considered as related to, or a form of, *Pelecyphora aselliformis,* but it differs markedly in the position of the *fl.* and in having milky juice. (B.R.C. 4, f. 63.)

V. H.

solitary, growing singly.

SOLITARY BEES are non-social bees whose females work singly to provide a nest and food for the grubs. Though they are solitary, some species live in colonies fairly close together on heaths, and in fields, hedgebanks, lawns, and garden paths. Several families of Bees are included in this category, for instance, the Mining Bees (*Andrena* and *Halictus*), which are important agents in the pollination of fruit blossom; the Leaf-cutter Bees (*Megachile*); and the Mason Bees (*Osmia*), which construct cells of soil, sand, or clay particles in wood, mortar, key-holes, overflow pipes from cisterns, empty snail shells, and similar convenient hollow spaces. (*See* **Pollination, Leaf-cutter Bees, Tawny Mining Bee.**)

G. F. W.

SOL'LYA (in honour of Richard Horsman Solly, 1778–1858, vegetable physiologist and anatomist). FAM. *Pittosporaceae.* A genus of 2 species of evergreen twiners, natives of Australia. Leaves narrow. Flowers blue, nodding, on slender pedicels, in terminal, loose, few-flowered cymes, or rarely solitary; sepals small, distinct; petals spreading from base, obovate; anthers connivent forming a cone round pistil. Well-drained peaty soil is best for these ornamental greenhouse climbers. Propagated by cuttings in sand under glass.

S. Drummond'ii. A synonym of *S. parviflora.*

Sollya fusiformis

S. fusifor'mis.* Australian Blue-bell Creeper. Twining to 6 ft. *l.* ovate-lanceolate to ovate-oblong, $1\frac{1}{2}$ to 2 in. or more long, or lanceolate or oblong-linear, 1 to $1\frac{1}{2}$ in. long, obtuse or somewhat slender-pointed, entire, usually narrowed to the short stalks. *fl.* in cymes, terminal or opposite l., drooping, usually 4- to 8-, sometimes 12- or more-fld.; pet. about $\frac{1}{3}$ in. long. July. 1830. (B.M. 3523; B.R. 1466.) SYN. *S. heterophylla.* var. **angustifo'lia,** less twining than type, *l.* narrow-lanceolate. (B.R. 1840, 3 as *S. linearis.*)

S. linea'ris. A synonym of *S. fusiformis angustifolia.*

S. parviflo'ra. *l.* lanceolate or oblong-linear, larger, often over 1 in. long, but sometimes not over $\frac{1}{2}$ in., stalk short, texture thinner than in *S. fusiformis. fl.* small, 1, 2, or 3 in cyme, pedicels very slender; pet. about $\frac{1}{4}$ in. long. July. *fr.* $\frac{1}{2}$ to $\frac{3}{4}$ in. long, tapered to both ends. 1838. (G.F. 261, f. 1 as *S. Drummondii.*)

solomonen'sis -is -e, of the Solomon Is., Pacific Ocean.

SOLOMON'S SEAL. *See* **Polygonatum multiflorum.**

SOLOMON'S SEAL, FALSE. *See* **Smilacina.**

SOLOMON'S SEAL SAWFLY, *Phymatocera aterrima,* is a common pest in the southern counties, and very frequent in London gardens. The adult 4-winged sawflies are black with smoky wings and longish antennae (feelers), and appear in May, during which month the female, with the aid of her saw-like ovipositor, inserts the eggs in slits in the leaves of Solomon's Seal. The larvae, which are bluish-grey with the body covered with minute black warts, feed on the leaves which are completely devoured with the exception of the main veins which usually remain intact. They are fully fed in July when they descend to the soil and pupate within cocoons.

This pest is readily controlled owing to the open manner of feeding on the foliage, so that a light application of Arsenate of Lead or D.D.T. emulsion will destroy them, or the foliage may be dusted with Nicotine or Derris dusts at the first appearance of the larvae.

G. F. W.

solstitia'lis -is -e, pertaining to the summer solstice (i.e. about 21 June), hence mid-summer flowering or growing and fading rapidly in summer.

solu'tus -a -um, loose, unrestrained.

soma'lius -a -um, of Somaliland, NE. Africa.

somni'ferus -a -um, sleep-bringing.

somnolen'tus -a -um, sleepy; applied to some plants which show sleep-movements.

sonchifo'lius -a -um, with Sonchus-like leaves.

SONCH'US (*Sonchos,* ancient Greek name used by Theophrastus). FAM. *Compositae.* A genus of about 24 species of annual or perennial herbs or shrubs, with milky sap, natives of Europe and N. and W. Africa. Leaves radical or alternate, the stem-leaves often clasping and auricled, margin entire or variously toothed or cut. Flower-heads yellow, small or of moderate size, in irregular corymbs or sub-umbels, rarely solitary; involucre conical after flowering, its bracts in several series; receptacle flat, naked; florets all ligulate; pappus bristles many. Few of the species are of any garden merit. The shrubby species mentioned below have been grown in conservatories because of their elegant foliage. They need only ordinary soil and may be increased by seeds or by cuttings in sand under a glass. Three species are tall-growing common weeds, known as Sow-thistles, *S. oleraceus* which was at one time cultivated as a pot herb, and the prickly-leaved *S. asper,* both annuals growing rapidly and seeding freely, not difficult to keep in check with the hoe, and *S. arvensis,* a troublesome perennial with thick underground structures giving rise very freely to buds and very persistent. The flowers of the last are handsome but not to be encouraged.

S. arbo'reus. Stem woody, terete, unarmed. *l.* pinnatifid; lobes linear, $\frac{1}{12}$ to $\frac{1}{8}$ in. wide, entire. *fl.-heads* larger than in *S. pinnatus,* numerous in terminal corymbs; florets 15 to 20. Canary Is. Tender.

S. conges'tus.* Sachuza de Pastor. Stout, erect, slightly branched, woody near base, with a few patches of white woolly hairs; 1 to 2 ft. h. *l.* crowded, 1 to 2 ft. long, 2 to 3 in. wide, spreading and recurved, base cordate, half-amplexicaul; blade oblanceolate, pinnatifid to, or beyond, middle, toothed, ciliate; lobes triangular, acute. *fl.-heads* deep golden-yellow, 2 to 3 in. across; involucral bracts slightly woolly, obtuse. March. Canary Is. 1882. (B.M. 6142 as *S. Jacquinii.*) Tender.

S. gum'mifer.* 2 to 3 ft. h. *l.* glabrous, pale beneath; lower pinnatifid, lobes 3-angled, slightly toothed, acuminate, terminal lobe oblong-lanceolate; upper l. auricled, rounded, amplexicaul. *fl.-heads* few in an irregular glabrous corymb; involucral scales blackish, slightly appressed, acuminate. Summer. Canary Is. 1861. (B.M. 5219.) Tender.

S. leptoceph'alus. Shrubby, unarmed. *l.* pinnatipartite, lobes linear-filiform, entire, scarcely $\frac{1}{24}$ in. wide. *fl.-heads* many in a terminal corymbose panicle. Canary Is. Tender.

S. pinna'tus. About 3 ft. h. *l.* glabrous, pinnatipartite; lobes linear-lanceolate, slightly toothed or entire, terminal long. *fl.-heads* in a corymbose, branched panicle; involucral scales appressed, glabrous, acuminate, linear or scarcely lanceolate. Summer. Madeira. 1777. Tender.

S. radica'tus. 1 ft. h. *Radical l.* somewhat lyrate, pinnatipartite, glaucous beneath, lobes ovate, obtuse, slightly toothed, terminal, obtusely 3-angled; *cauline l.* auricled, rounded, stem-clasping. *fl.-heads* in a glabrous, irregular corymb; involucral scales blackish, outer broadly ovate, inner linear-lanceolate. Summer. Canary Is. 1780. (B.M. 5211.)

sonda'icus -a -um, *see* **Sundaicus.**

SONERIL'A (from the native Malabar name of one species, *Soothi- Soneri-ila*). FAM. *Melastomataceae.* A genus of about 70 species of herbs and small shrubs of varying habit, natives of the E. Indies and S. China, related to Gravesia, Salpinga, and Bertolonia, but with parts of flower in threes. Leaves sometimes unequal, often thin, entire or toothed, 3- or 5-nerved. Flowers in spikes or scorpioid racemes, often rose; calyx with an oblong, turbinate, or bell-shaped tube, 3-lobed; petals 3, ovate, obovate, or oblong; stamens usually 3, then equal, sometimes 6 with alternate stamens smaller. The Sonerilas require a warm humid atmosphere like the Bertolonias, and partial shade. The compost should consist of fibrous peat broken small, a little chopped Sphagnum, some sand, with small pieces of charcoal or crocks intermixed. Pans or baskets may be used. All the species are summer-flowering. Seed is usually freely borne and can be used for increasing the plants, or they may be raised from cuttings (which must be used for the named varieties or hybrids) taken in spring, inserted in small pots, and put into a close case in the propagating house.

A number of cross-bred forms, mostly with *S. margaritacea* as one parent, have been offered from time to time with very attractive foliage. Hybrids have also been raised with Bertolonia, *see* **Bertonerila.**

S. argen'tea. A variety of *S. margaritacea.*

S. Benson'ii. Close to *S. speciosa* but with 6 instead of 3 stamens. 1873. (B.M. 6049.)

S. el'egans. A synonym of *S. speciosa.*

S. grandiflo'ra. Woody below, branching, about 12 in. h. *l.* crowded, oblong or elliptic, 1 to 2 in. long, glabrous, teeth bristly. *fl.* mauve, in terminal, dense-fld., short-stalked racemes. 1856. (B.M. 5354.)

S. guttula'ta. A variety of *S. orientalis.*

S. lae'ta. Erect herb, 6 in. h. Stem cylindrical, glandular-downy. *l.* ovate or elliptic-ovate, often with one half larger than other, up to 4 in. long, 2 in. wide, green, spotted white above, purple, spotted green beneath, margin not ciliate (in the nearly related *S. maculata* it is ciliate); stalked. *fl.* purplish; cal. oblong-cylindrical; pet. oblong, pointed. China.

S. macula'ta. *See* **S. laeta.**

S. margarita'cea. Stem rather weak, procumbent, 8 to 10 in. long, scarlet. *l.* opposite, oblong or ovate-lanceolate, more or less slender-pointed, dark glossy green with oval pearly-white spots in single lines between veins above; pale with red-purple veins beneath. *fl.* rose in an 8- to 10-fld. corymb. Java. (B.M. 5104.) var. **argen'tea,** *l.* silvery, veins dark green; **Henderson'ii,** plant compact, 6 to 8 in. h., *l.* ovate, dark olive-green, covered with pearly-white spots. (I.H. 23, 230; G.F. 897.); **marmora'ta,** *l.* banded silver-grey. The various silvery varieties, at times figured, appear to originate in var. *argentea*, and those with irregular blotches in var. *Hendersonii.*

S. orbicula'ta. A synonym of *S. speciosa.*

S. orienta'lis. *l.* broad-ovate, acute, cordate at base, crimson-maroon, sometimes with a whitish feathered band down middle, or dotted white on a light or dark green band. *fl.* numerous, bright rose or purple. Burma. 1890. var. **guttula'ta,** *l.* slightly striped, **pic'ta,** *l.* with irregular feathered white stripe down middle; **puncta'ta,** *l.* dotted with white.

Sonerila speciosa

S. specio'sa. Stem nearly glabrous below; peduncle terminal, hairy, 9 to 12 in. h. *l.* ovate-elliptic, 2 to 3 in. long, glabrous or nearly so, slightly toothed; stalked. *fl.* mauve, showy; pet. about ⅝ in. long, round-elliptic, acute. 1856. (B.M. 5026; 4978 as *S. elegans.*) SYN. *S. orbiculata.*

S. stric'ta. Erect, often branched, 3 to 7 in. h., downy and with spreading hairs. *l.* lanceolate or elliptic, ½ to 1 in. long, hairy. *fl.* rose-purple, small; pet. obovate. 1848. (B.M. 4394.)

F. G. P.

songar'icus -a -um, of Dzungaria, central Asia.

SONNERA'TIA (in honour of Pierre Sonnerat, 1749–1841, who travelled into New Guinea, the E. Indies, and China and sent many new plants to European botanists). FAM. *Sonneratiaceae.* A genus of 5 or 6 species of glabrous shrubs and small trees, natives of tropical sea-shores in the E. Hemisphere. Leaves opposite, leathery, oblong, entire, stalked. Flowers large, without bracteoles, in threes at tips of branchlets, or axillary and solitary; calyx thick, leathery, tube bell-shaped, limb 4- to 8-lobed; petals 4 to 8, small or wanting; stamens numerous. Berry subglobose, 10- to 15-celled, many-seeded. The 3 species mentioned below need stove conditions and treatment like Lagerstroemia. **A**

S. ac'ida. Small tree. Shoots 4-angled. *l.* oval-oblong. *fl.* 6-cleft; pet. red. June. *fr.* with acrid pulp. E. Indies. 1822. The fruit is eaten by the natives as a condiment.

S. al'ba. Small tree. Shoots terete. *l.* roundish-oval, 2 to 4½ in. long, rounded or retuse at apex. *fl.* white, 6- to 8-cleft, apetalous. May. *fr.* obconic at base, depressed above. E. Indies. 1824.

S. apet'ala. Kambala-tree. Tree to 40 ft. Shoots terete, pendulous. *l.* ovate-lanceolate. *fl.* white, 4-cleft, apetalous. June. E. Indies. Grows in Mangrove swamps.

SONNERATIA'CEAE. Dicotyledons. A family of 3 genera with 12 species of African and Asiatic trees with opposite entire leaves without stipules. They are related to Lythraceae but have the ovary united to the receptacle and parietal placentation. Stamens many. The many-seeded fruits are half capsule, half berry. The only genus dealt with is Sonneratia.

SOOT. The unburned carbon, mostly from coal fires, which collects in chimneys has long been valued by gardeners. The carbon thus deposited is in a very fine state of subdivision and therefore absorbs various gases, and it is no doubt to this property that it owes its fertilizing value, and especially to the amount of nitrogen it contains in the form of salts of ammonia. The amount varies mainly according to the mineral matter which it may also contain, and lies between 0·5 and 6 per cent., the average being about 4 per cent. Light soot is best, for heavy weight indicates contamination with mineral matter: the weight of a bushel should be about 28 lb. Applied as a top dressing its effect upon the growth of young plants is usually rapid but it should not be used in contact with lime as this would result in the liberation of ammonia in quantity likely to damage foliage, causing burning. Soot is also used at times as 'soot-water' for watering plants, thus applying a small amount of fertilizer. Soot has also a physical effect, for the darkening of the soil ensures the more ready absorption of heat and the soil is warmed up more rapidly. It also has a beneficial effect on the texture of clay soils. The odour of soot no doubt disguises the scent of plants and is perhaps also obnoxious to insects as a dusting of soot is a useful means of checking egg-laying and preventing to a considerable extent the eating of foliage upon which it rests. It should not, of course, be dusted on plants which are ready for use as food.

SOOTY BLOTCH. A minor disease of Apples and Pears caused by the fungus *Gloeodes pomigena* which forms its mycelium on the skin of the fruit in irregular black blotches. The trouble is most prevalent after heavy rains and where the trees are dense in foliage, but as the growth is quite superficial little harm is done.

D. E. G.

SOOTY MOULDS. Certain fungi, e.g. species of Capnodium and Meliola, which grow on the 'honey dew' deposited by insects on leaves and fruits. The mycelium of these fungi is dark or black and although it covers the surfaces of tissues it is entirely superficial, but interferes with access of light and is unsightly. The only remedy is to take steps for the destruction of the insects.

D. E. G.

Sophe'ra, from the Arabian name *çufair*.

SOPH'ORA (from *Sophera*, Arabian name for a tree with pea-shaped flowers). FAM. *Leguminosae*. Deciduous and evergreen trees or shrubs, rarely herbs. Leaves alternate, unequally pinnate; leaflets opposite, sometimes very numerous. Flowers in racemes or panicles, white, yellow, or violet-blue. Pods always, sometimes very markedly, constricted between the few to many seeds. The genus is in 2 sections once kept apart as separate genera: (1) Sophora proper in which the corolla is papilionaceous and (2) Edwardsia, in which the flowers are much larger and have the petals all pointing forward. The species of the Edwardsia section are rather tender and in most places need wall protection. All are sun-lovers. Propagation is best effected by seeds.

KEY

1. *Evergreen* — 2
1. *Deciduous. Fl. papilionaceous* — 4
2. *Lflets. 7 to 9 on old plants. Fl. papilionaceous, violet and white, in terminal racemes* — S. secundiflora
2. *Lflets. 13 to 25 or more on old plants. Fl. with all pet. pointing forwards, yellow* — 3
3. *Pods not winged. Lflets. 13 to 25* — S. macrocarpa
3. *Pods 4-winged. Lflets. 7 to 9 on young, many more on old plants* — S. tetraptera
4. *Lvs. up to 2½ in. long. Spiny shrub. Fl. bluish-white* — S. Davidii
4. *Lvs. 4 to 10 in. long* — 5
5. *Sub-shrub with long annual shoots. Infl. long, terminal. Fl. yellowish-white* — S. flavescens
5. *Tree or shrub* — 6
6. *Shrub. Lvs. yellow-downy at first. Lflets. 17. Racemes axillary* — S. chrysophylla
6. *Tree* — 7
7. *Racemes terminal. Fl. creamy or rosy-white. Lflets. 9 to 17* — S. japonica
7. *Racemes axillary. Fl. rosy-white. Lflets. 13 to 19* — S. affinis

S. affin'is. Round-headed, deciduous tree up to 20 ft. *l.* 6 to 9 in. long; *lflets.* 13 to 19, oval, 1 to 1½ in. long. *Racemes* 3 to 6 in. long, slender, downy, axillary on new growths. *fl.* papilionaceous, ½ in. long, rose-tinted white; cal. downy. June. *Pod* 1½ to 3 in. long, black, downy. SW. United States. 1890. (S.S. 3. 122.)

S. chatham'ica. A synonym of *S. tetraptera microphylla.*

S. chrysophyl'la. Deciduous shrub of 6 to 10 ft. h. *lflets.* 17, obovate, at first yellow, downy. *fl.* papilionaceous, yellow, in axillary racemose spikes; keel pet. elliptic with dorsal margin straight. May, June. Sandwich Is. (B.R. 738 as *Edwardsia chrysophylla.*) Greenhouse.

S. David'ii.* Deciduous, spreading shrub, 6 to 10 ft., shoots slender, grey-downy, afterwards spiny. *l.* 1½ to 2½ in. long; *lflets.* 13 to 21, oval to obovate, ¼ to ⅜ in. long, silky-hairy beneath. *fl.* papilionaceus, ¾ in. long, in terminal racemes of 6 to 12; pet. bluish-white; cal. blue, downy, toothed. June. *Pods* 2 to 2½ in. long. China. 1897. (B.M. 7883.) SYN. *S. viciifolia* Hance non Salisb.

S. flaves'cens. Sub-shrub sending up annual shoots 3 ft. or more long, or, in mild climates, a shrub up to 6 ft. *l.* 6 to 9 in. long; *lflets.* up to 19, narrowly ovate, 1½ to 2½ in. long. *fl.* papilionaceous, yellowish-white, ½ in. long, in cylindrical racemes or panicles up to 1 ft. long, terminal on current season's shoots. July, August. China.

S. japon'ica.* Deciduous tree, 60 to 80 ft., with a rounded head and corrugated bark. *l.* 6 to 10 in. long; *lflets.* 9 to 17, oval to ovate, 1 to 2 in. long, appressed-downy beneath. *Panicles* terminal, 6 to 10 in. long and wide. *fl.* papilionaceous, creamy-white, ½ in. long. September. *Pod* 2 to 3½ in. long. China, Korea. (B.T.S. 2. 520.) var. **pen'dula,** picturesque weeping tree with stiff branches, should be grafted high; **pubes'cens,** *l.* up to 3 in. long, narrow in proportion, young wood and l. more downy. SYN. *S. Korolkowi*; **variega'ta,** *l.* with creamy-white margins; **viola'cea,** wing pet. and keel, rose-violet, later flowering. 1858. A

S. macrocarp'a.* Evergreen tree 20 to 40 ft., shoots downy. *l.* 3 to 5 in. long; *lflets.* 13 to 25, ¾ to 1½ in. long, ¼ to ⅜ in. wide, downy, especially beneath. *fl.* in short axillary racemes of up to 12, yellow, 1 to 1¼ in. long, pet. pointing forward; cal. ¼ in. long, bell-shaped, toothed, downy. May. *Pod* 4 in. or more long, not winged. Chile. 1822. (B.M. 8647.) SYN. *Edwardsia chilensis.*

Sophora macrocarpa

S. secundiflo'ra. Evergreen tree 25 to 35 ft. *l.* 4 to 6 in. long; *lflets.* 7 or 9, 1 to 2 in. long, oblong to obovate, notched at apex. *Racemes* 2 or 3 in. long, terminating leafy young shoots of the current year. *fl.* papilionaceous, 1 in. long, violet-blue and violet-scented. Texas to Mexico. (R.H. 1854, 201.) It requires a south wall in a mild, sunny climate. Attractive in colour and fragrance.

S. tetrap'tera. Kowhai. New Zealand Laburnum. Evergreen or semi-deciduous shrub or small tree, 15 to 40 ft.; shoots, l.-stalks, fl.-stalks, and cal. all tawny-downy. Branchlets zigzag, slender. *l.* 1½ to 4½ in. long, with 7 or 9 lflets. on young plants but many more (sometimes up to 80) on older plants. *fl.* somewhat tubular in outline, golden-yellow, 1 to 2 in. long, pendulous, in racemes of 4 to 8. May. *Pod* 2 to 8 in. long, 4-winged, constricted between each seed. Chile, New Zealand. 1772. SYN. *Edwardsia Macnabiana.* var. **grandiflo'ra,** *fl.* larger (full 2 in. long), lflets. larger, fewer; **microphyll'a,** *lflets.* smaller, more numerous, *fl.* 1 to 1½ in. long. (B.M. 3735.) SYN. *Edwardsia microphylla.*

S. viciifo'lia. A synonym of *S. Davidii.*

W. J. B.

***SOPHROCATT'LEYA.** FAM. *Orchidaceae.* Hybrids between species of Cattleya and Sophronitis. The cultivation calls for individual consideration, some plants thriving better when grown cool, others needing temperatures suitable for Cattleyas.

***SOPHROLAE'LIA.** FAM. *Orchidaceae.* Hybrids between species of Laelia and Sophronitis. *See note under* **Sophrocattleya.**

***SOPHROLAELIOCATT'LEYA.** FAM. *Orchidaceae.* Hybrids including Cattleya, Laelia, and Sophronitis in their parentage. The cultural treatment is that recommended for Cattleyas and Laelias.

SOPHRO'NIA. *See* **Sophronitis.**

SOPHRONI'TIS (*sophron*, modest; in reference to the pretty little flowers of the original species). FAM. *Orchidaceae.* A small genus of about 8 dwarf, tufted, epiphytic orchids, inhabiting the Organ Mts. of Brazil. Flowers very showy, scarlet or violet, borne in short, few-flowered racemes, or solitary, from the top of the pseudobulb; sepals free, equal, flat, spreading; petals similar or broader; lip erect, the lateral lobes broad and connivent, wholly concealing the short and rather thick column, the middle lobe sub-recurved, entire; pollen masses 8. Leaves leathery or fleshy, complicated, at length unfolding, spreading. Pseudobulbs clustered on a rhizome, 1- or 2-leaved. The species are well worthy the attention of cultivators, and have the advantage of occupying but little space. They require to be grown in small pans, which can be suspended in the cool or Odontoglossum house. Compost should be similar to that given to Cattleyas cut rather more finely, to which may be added a little crushed charcoal. Perfect drainage is necessary. All the Sophronites require abundance of moisture when growing. After growth is finished water should be given less frequently but the compost should not be allowed to become really dry. Propagation may be effected by divisions, made just as growth begins.

S. cern'ua. *fl.* 2 to 4 small, rose- or cinnabar-red; lip yellowish in the centre; column white with dark purple wings; racemes short, effuse. Winter. *Pseudobulbs* clustered, ⅓ to ⅔ in. h. (B.M. 3677; B.R. 1129 as *Sophronia cernua.*) SYN. *S. isopetala, S. modesta, S. nutans.*

S. coccin'ea.* Better known as *S. grandiflora. fl.* 1 or 2, brilliant scarlet or cinnabar-red, 1½ to 3 in. across; sep. elliptic-oblong, tapered; pet. very much broader, often over 1 in. wide, broadly oval; lip with erect side lobes which partially conceal the whitish or purplish column; mid-lobe rather narrow, oblong, acute, concave or somewhat conduplicate, orange-yellow, streaked scarlet at base and on side lobes; peduncles 1 to 2 in. h. *Pseudobulbs* fusiform, ovoid or sometimes nearly globose, about 1 in. h., 1-leaved. *l.* oblong, lanceolate, 2 to 3 in. h., ½ to 1 in. wide, fleshy, rigid, channelled above, keeled beneath. Winter. Brazil. 1841. (F.d.S. 1716; B.M. 3709; W.S.O. 3, 3; W.O.A. 504 as *S. grandiflora.*) A beautiful species but very variable in habit, size of fl., &c. The type specimen had rose-scarlet fl. This species has been of great value to the hybridist, beautiful hybrids having been derived from its use with Cattleya, Laelia, and allies. The following varieties have all been known as varieties of *S. grandiflora.* var. **auranti'aca,** *fl.* dark orange-red. 1886. (R.H. 1886, 492.); **gigant'ea,** *fl.* 3¾ in. across. 1892; **militar'is,** *fl.* 3 in. across, bright cinnabar or scarlet-red. 1837. SYN. *S. militaris;* **purpu'rea,** *fl.* carmine-purple, 3½ in. across, pseudobulbs short and thick. 1878. SYN. *S. purpurea;* **ro'sea,** *fl.* rather smaller but rounder, purplish-rose, *pseudobulbs* shorter and *l.* rounder than in type. 1884. (Gn. 25 (1884), 474.)

S. grandiflo'ra. A synonym of *S. coccinea.* var. **Rossiteria'na,** a synonym of *S. Rossiteriana.*

S. Low'ii.* Differs from *S. coccinea,* of which it may be a variety, in its rather smaller *fl.* which are deep yellow. 1908.

S. militar'is. A variety of *S. coccinea.*

S. modes'ta. A synonym of *S. cernua.*

S. pterocarp'a. *fl.* small, rosy-purple; lip ovate, crested; ovary 6-winged, long-beaked; raceme short, corymbose, 3- to 7-fld. March. *Pseudobulbs* seldom over 1 in. h., usually less. *l.* leathery, roundish-oblong, ¾ to 1½ in. long, often 1 in. wide. Very similar to *S. cernua* but with stouter pseudobulbs, wider l., and rather larger fl. Brazil.

S. purpu'rea. A variety of *S. coccinea.*

S. Rossiteria'na.* *fl.* 2 to 2½ in. across, pale yellow with orange striations, pet. twice as broad as sep. and slightly longer, the small scale-like callus at base of lip 2-lobed instead of entire. Brazil. 1877. Very near to *S. coccinea* and perhaps a variety.

S. viola'cea. *fl.* 1 or 2, violet; lip obovate, acute, gibbous at base; column with large, fleshy, obtuse, falcate wings; scape with many bracts at base. Winter. *Pseudobulbs* oval, small, ½ to 1¼ in. h. *l.* solitary, linear, dark green, 1½ to 3 in. long. 1838. (B.M. 6880; W.O.A. 291.)

E. C.

soporif'erus -a -um, sleep-bringing.

SOPU'BIA (from the native Indian name). FAM. *Scrophulariaceae.* A genus of 8 or 9 species of erect, usually annual herbs, natives of Trop. and S. Africa, Madagascar, SE. Asia, and Australia. Leaves opposite or upper alternate, narrow, often laciniate. Flowers bracteate, in spikes or racemes, calyx bell-shaped, 5-toothed or lobed; corolla tube short, lobes 5, spreading; stamens 4; pedicels 2-bracteolate. *S. delphinifolia* needs stove conditions and peaty soil. It is a handsome perennial easily increased by cuttings under glass or by seeds.

S. delphinifo'lia. Stem 3 to 4 ft. h., 4-grooved, spotted purple. *l.* 1 in. long, pinnatisect; segs. almost as long; filiform, flexuous. *fl.* rose, nearly sessile; cor. 1 to 1½ in. long, 1 in. across, nearly bell-shaped. July. India. 1800. SYN. *Gerardia delphinifolia.*

SORBA'RIA (resembling Sorbus). FAM. *Rosaceae.* Deciduous shrubs with pithy young shoots and long pinnate leaves. Leaflets toothed, either simply or doubly. Flowers white, ⅓ in. or less wide, profusely borne in large panicles; petals 5, rounded; stamens numerous. Akin to Spiraea but well distinguished by the pinnate leaves. All the species are hardy and succeed in any soil of good quality in full sunshine. To keep plants at a moderate size and more compact, the shoots that have flowered may be cut back in February almost to the old wood. Propagated by seed, or in some species by suckers.

KEY

1. *Lflets. simply serrate, about ½ in. wide, glabrous*	S. Aitchisonii
1. *Lflets. doubly serrate, over ½ in. wide*	2
2. *Stamens much exceeding pet.*	3
2. *Stamens not or scarcely exceeding pet.*	4
3. *Shrub up to 6 ft.; lvs. glabrous beneath*	S. sorbifolia
3. *Shrub up to 18 ft.; lvs. more or less hairy beneath*	S. arborea
4. *Fl. in narrow panicles*	S. assurgens
4. *Fl. in spreading downy panicles*	S. tomentosa

S. Aitchison'ii.* Shrub up to 10 ft., glabrous, shoots reddish. *l.* 9 to 15 in. long with 11 to 23 lflets. which are narrowly lanceolate, slender-pointed, simply toothed, 2 to 4 in. long, ¼ to ⅝ in. wide. *fl.* ⅓ in. wide in pyramidal panicles 1 to 1½ ft. long, 9 to 15 in. wide. July, August. *fr.* red. Afghanistan, Kashmir. 1895. (G.C. 28 (1900), 255; B.T.S. 1, 526 as *Spiraea Aitchisonii.*) Differs from *S. Lindleyana* in its narrower, glabrous, simply toothed l. SYN. *S. angustifolia.*

S. arbo'rea.* Shrub up to 20 ft. or more, shoots and l. stellately downy. *l.* 8 to 15 in. long, with 13 to 19 lflets. which are ovate-lanceolate, 2 to 4 in. long, doubly toothed; veins parallel, numerous, deeply impressed. *fl.* ¼ in. wide in pyramidal panicles over 1 ft. long and wide; stamens longer than pet. July, August. China. 1908. (K.B. 1914, 53.) SYN. *Spiraea arborea. S. tomentosa* differs by its less prominent venation of the l. and its simple (not stellate) hairs. var. **glabra'ta** has narrower, finally glabrous lflets. and stamens twice or thrice as long as pet.

S. assur'gens. Shrub up to 10 ft., erect in growth, shoots glabrous. *l.* up to 1 ft. long with 11 to 17 lflets. which are lanceolate, with a long, slender, curved apex, 2 to 3½ in. long, ½ to 1 in. wide, doubly toothed, slightly downy beneath; veins in 25 or more pairs. *fl.* ⅜ in. wide in narrow, erect, pyramidal panicles 6 to 12 in. long; stamens about 20. July, August. China. 1903.

S. grandiflo'ra. A synonym of *S. sorbifolia alpina.*

S. Lindleya'na. A synonym of *S. tomentosa.*

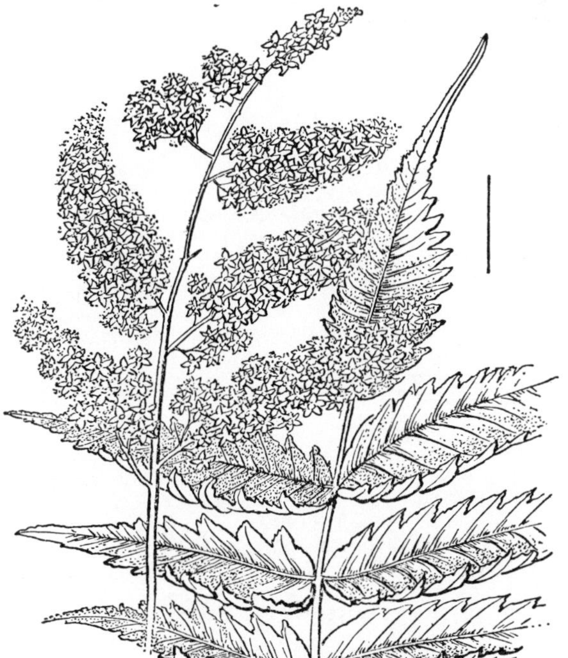

Sorbaria tomentosa (p. 1986)

S. sorbifo'lia. Shrub 3 to 6 ft., suckering freely. *l.* 8 to 12 in. long, with 13 to 25 lflets. which are lanceolate, 2 to $3\frac{1}{2}$ in. long, $\frac{1}{2}$ to 1 in. wide, conspicuously double-toothed, veins in about 20 pairs, usually quite glabrous. *fl.* $\frac{1}{3}$ in. wide, in stiff, erect panicles 6 to 10 in. h., stalks downy; ovaries glabrous; stamens 40 to 50. July. Ural Mts. to Japan. 1759. var. **alpi'na,** habit dwarfer, 2 to 3 ft. h., fewer and shorter *lflets.*, larger *fl.* in broader infl. Siberia. 1852. SYN. *S. grandiflora*; **stellipi'la,** *l.* stellately downy beneath, ovaries downy. Japan. SYN. *S. stellipila.*

S. stellipi'la. A synonym of *S. sorbifolia stellipila.*

S. tomento'sa. Shrub up to 18 ft., graceful and spreading, shoots glabrous. *l.* 10 to 18 in. long, with 11 to 23 lflets. which are lanceolate, slender-pointed, doubly toothed, 2 to 4 in. long, slightly hairy beneath. *fl.* white, $\frac{1}{4}$ in. wide, in terminal pyramidal panicles 1 to $1\frac{1}{2}$ ft. long; stalks downy. July, August. Himalaya. 1840. (B.R. 31, 33 as *Spiraea Lindleyana.*)

W. J. B.

×SORBARO'NIA. FAM. *Rosaceae.* Hybrids between Sorbus and Aronia with characters intermediate between the two. Hardy.

×S. alpi'na (*Sorbus Aria × Aronia arbutifolia*). Shrub. *l.* similar to those of whitebeam, but smaller and with fewer veins. May. *fr.* red, $\frac{1}{3}$ in. wide. 1809.

×S. Dip'pelii (*Sorbus Aria × Aronia melanocarpa*). Bushy shrub with grey-felted young shoots. *l.* elliptic to oblanceolate, $1\frac{1}{2}$ to $3\frac{1}{2}$ in. long. *fl.* $\frac{1}{2}$ in. wide, with rosy anthers. May. *fr.* $\frac{1}{3}$ in. long, blackish-purple. 1870.

×S. hyb'rida. Shrub or small tree, shoots downy. *l.* 2 to $3\frac{1}{2}$ in. long, very variable, usually pinnate or pinnatifid, but the smaller ones are ovate and may be entire and there are intermediate shapes. *fl.* white, $\frac{3}{8}$ in. wide in small corymbs. May. *fr.* sub-globose or pear-shaped, $\frac{3}{8}$ in. long, black-purple. Parents given as the Rowan and *Aronia arbutifolia* which seems doubtful considering both are red-fruited. SYN. *Sorbus spuria.* (B.R. 1196 as *Pyrus spuria.*) Known in 1785.

W. J. B.

sorbifo'lius -a -um, with Sorbus-like foliage.

×SORBOPY'RUS. FAM. *Rosaceae.* Hybrids between Sorbus and Pyrus.

×S. auricula'ris. Bollwyller Pear. (*Sorbus Aria × Pyrus communis.*) Deciduous tree, 30 to 50 ft. *l.* ovate to oval, 3 to 4 in. long, coarsely toothed, grey, felted beneath. *fl.* white, $\frac{3}{4}$ to 1 in. wide, in clusters 3 in. wide; cal. white-woolly; anthers rosy-red. May. *fr.* pear-shaped, 1 to $1\frac{1}{4}$ in. long, red or yellowish-red. Originated at Bollwyller in Alsace before 1619. (B.T.S. 2, 279; B.R. 1437 as *Pyrus bollwylleriana.*)

×S. malifo'lia. Much resembles ×*S. auricularis* but *l.* shorter, more rounded, nearly always cordate, not so coarsely toothed, nor so much felted beneath. *fl.* larger, 1 to $1\frac{1}{2}$ in. wide. *fr.* pear-shaped, 2 in. long, deep yellow. Originated before 1834. May be a seedling from *auricularis.*

W. J. B.

SORB'US (from the Latin *sorbum*, the fruit of *S. domestica*; name used by Cato, Pliny, &c.). FAM. *Rosaceae.*

A genus of European, N. American, and N. Asiatic deciduous trees and shrubs, allied to and often included in Pyrus. Leaves alternate; simple in one group (Aria), pinnate in a second group (Aucuparia). Flowers white or rarely pink, borne in corymbose or racemose clusters; sepals and petals 5; stamens 15 to 20; styles 2 to 5, free or united at the base. Fruit a pome, nearly always globose or ovoid-globose, red, pink, or white, and $\frac{1}{4}$ to $\frac{1}{2}$ in. wide. The Aucuparia or Rowan group comprises many species much admired for their autumnal colouring, and both groups are handsome in fruit. With the exception of *S. Harrowiana*, all the species are hardy and succeed in well-drained open loam; they flower and fruit most freely in sunny situations. The abundant seed they produce renders their propagation easy, but new, rare, or hybrid kinds are mostly grafted on seedling stocks of common Rowan. The members of the 2 groups are distinguished by the figure in parentheses following the specific name, (1) Aria, (2) Aucuparia.

KEY

1. *Lvs. simple or with up to 3 pairs of free lflets. at the base* 2
1. *Lvs. pinnate, lflets all similar* 20
2. *Lvs. mostly with 1 or more pairs of free lflets* 3
2. *Lvs. simple* 4
3. *Lvs. whitish-grey beneath; veins in 8 to 10 pairs* S. hybrida
3. *Lvs. greenish-grey beneath; veins in 10 to 12 pairs* S. × pinnatifida
4. *Lvs. distinctly lobed* 5
4. *Lvs. not distinctly lobed* 9
5. *Lvs. green and nearly glabrous below at maturity* S. torminalis
5. *Lvs. grey or white and downy below at maturity* 6
6. *Veins of lvs. in 7 to 9 pairs; lvs. greenish or yellowish-grey below* 7
6. *Veins of lvs. in 9 to 12 pairs; lvs. whitish-grey or white below* 8
7. *Lvs. oblong, lobes not triangular. Fr. scarlet* S. intermedia
7. *Lvs. broadly ovate, lobes triangular. Fr. orange-brown* S. latifolia
8. *Cal. persistent on the ripe fr.* S. Mougeotii
8. *Cal. absent on the ripe fr.* S. japonica
9. *Lvs. mostly over $4\frac{1}{2}$ in. long* 10
9. *Lvs. mostly less than $4\frac{1}{2}$ in. long* 13
10. *Shoots glabrous or soon nearly so* 11
10. *Shoots woolly or densely hairy* 12
11. *Shoots purplish. Lvs. 5 to 10 in. long, soon glabrous* S. megalocarpa
11. *Shoots purplish-brown. Lvs. 4 to 7 in. long; veins in 18 to 24 pairs* S. meliosmifolia
12. *Shoots white woolly* S. cuspidata
12. *Shoots rusty hairy* S. epidendron
13. *Lvs. not usually over 3 in. long* 14
13. *Lvs. up to 4 in. or more long* 18
14. *Veins of lvs. usually in 6 to 9 pairs* 15
14. *Veins of lvs. usually in 8 pairs or more* 16
15. *Shrub 3 to 6 ft. Fl. pink, pet. erect. Fr. ovoid* S. Chamaemespilus
15. *Tree. Fl. white. Fr. flat-round* S. umbellata
16. *Shrub to 12 ft. Fl. pinkish, pet. erect. Fr. oval, red* S. × Hostii
16. *Tree, or large shrub. Fl. white* 17
17. *Veins of lvs. in 7 to 12 pairs. Fr. bright red* S. alnifolia
17. *Veins of lvs. in 10 to 16 pairs. Fr. brown, spotted* S. caloneura
18. *Lvs. up to 5 in. long, shining green above, grey beneath* S. Zahlbruckneri
18. *Lvs. up to $4\frac{1}{2}$ in. or more long, white-hairy beneath* 19
19. *Veins of lvs. in 8 to 13 pairs. Shoots downy* S. Aria
19. *Veins of lvs. in 8 to 10 pairs. Shoots white-felted at first. Lvs. white-felted beneath* S. Folgneri
20. *Lflets. rarely exceeding 11* 21
20. *Lflets. usually over 11* 23
21. *Lflets. 7 to 11* 22
21. *Lflets. 3 to 9, $2\frac{1}{2}$ to 8 in. long* S. Harrowiana
22. *Lflets. 9 to 11, 1 to $2\frac{1}{2}$ in. long* S. decora
22. *Lflets. 7 to 11, 3 to $5\frac{1}{2}$ in. long* S. Sargentiana
23. *Lflets. 11 to 21* 24
23. *Lflets. often over 21* 37
24. *Dwarf shrub less than $2\frac{1}{2}$ ft. high.* 25
24. *Large shrub or tree* 26
25. *3 to 12 in. h. Lflets. up to $\frac{1}{2}$ in. long. Fl. rose. Fr. white* S. pygmaea
25. *6 to 28 in. h. Lflets. up to 1 in. long. Fl. white. Fr. crimson* S. reducta
26. *Lflets. up to 4 in. long* 27
26. *Lflets. rarely exceeding 3 to $3\frac{1}{2}$ in. long* 28
27. *Lflets. 11 to 17. Lvs. sharply toothed, soon glabrous* S. americana
27. *Lflets. 11 or 13. Lvs. coarsely sharply toothed, whitish downy beneath* S. Esserteauiana
28. *Shoots reddish* S. Matsumurana
28. *Shoots not markedly reddish* 29
29. *Winter buds neither downy nor sticky* S. hupehensis
29. *Winter buds downy or sticky* 30
30. *Winter buds downy* 31
30. *Winter buds sticky* 35
31. *Lvs. glabrous at least in age* 32
31. *Lvs. grey, downy beneath* 33
32. *Tree. Lflets. acute, at first downy acuminate* S. Aucuparia
32. *Usually shrubby. Lflets. glabrous from first* S. tianshanica
33. *Lflets. scarcely toothed* S. Wilsoniana
33. *Lflets. toothed* 34
34. *Infl. glabrous or almost so. Fr. white or pinkish* S. discolor
34. *Infl. downy. Fr. red* S. pohuashanensis
35. *Growth erect* 36
35. *Growth somewhat spreading. Winter buds shining* S. domestica
36. *Midrib, veins and pedicels rusty-hairy* S. rufo-ferruginea
36. *Midrib, &c., not rusty-hairy* S. commixta
37. *Shoots chocolate-red. Winter buds downy* S. Koehneana
37. *Shoots not markedly red* 38
38. *Lvs. more or less hairy* 39
38. *Lvs. glabrous. Shoots downy* S. Vilmorinii
39. *Lflets. 21 to 29, ovate-oblong, up to $\frac{7}{8}$ in. long, cobwebby* S. Prattii
39. *Lflets. 21 to 37, narrow oblong, $\frac{1}{2}$ to $1\frac{1}{2}$ in. long, grey-felted beneath* S. scalaris

S. alnifo'lia (1). Tree 40 to 60 ft. of erect growth when young. *l.* $1\frac{1}{2}$ to 3 in. long, half as wide, veins parallel in 7 to 12 pairs. *fl.* white, $\frac{1}{2}$ in. wide, in corymbs 2 to 3 in. across. May. *fr.* oval, bright red,

⅛ to ½ in. long, the cal. fallen away. Autumnal colour orange and red. Japan, Korea. 1892. (B.M. 7773.)

Sorbus alnifolia (p. 1986)

S. america'na (2). American Mt. Ash. Tree up to 30 ft., winter buds glutinous. *l.* 6 to 10 in. long with 11 to 17 lflets., each 2 to 4 in. long, oblong-lanceolate, sharply toothed, soon glabrous. *fl.* creamy-white, ⅓ in. wide, in clusters 3 to 5 in. across. May, June. *fr.* globose, bright red, ¼ in. wide. E. United States. 1782. (S.S. 171, 172.) Differs from *S. Aucuparia* by its smaller, more compact shape and gummy winter buds.

S. Ar'ia (1). Whitebeam. Tree 30 to 50 ft., shoots downy. *l.* oval to obovate, 2 to 4½ in. long, white with down beneath; veins in 10 to 14 pairs, conspicuous, parallel. *fl.* in clusters 3 to 4 in. across, white, ½ in. wide. May. *fr.* scarlet-red, ovoid or sub-globose, ⅓ to ⅝ in. wide. Europe (Britain). (E.B. 482; E.H. 51.) var. **angustifo'lia,** *l.* twice as long as wide; **chrysophyll'a,** the best of several yellow-leafed forms; **majest'ica,*** finest var., *l.* up to 6 or 7 in. long. *fr.* larger. (B.M. 8184.) Syn. var. *Decaisneana.*

S. Aucupar'ia (2). Ranty, Rowan, Mountain Ash. Tree 40 to 60 ft., winter buds downy. *l.* 5 to 9 in. long with 11 to 15 lflets., each lanceolate-oblong, sharply toothed, 1 to 2½ in. long, glabrous by autumn. *fl.* white, ⅓ in. wide, in clusters 4 to 5 in. wide. May. *fr.* globose, ⅓ in. across, bright red, pendulous. Europe (Britain), W. Asia. (E.B. 486.) var. **asplenifo'lia,** *lflets.* more deeply toothed; **integer'rima,** *lflets.* almost wholly entire; **lanu'ginosa,** *l.*, shoots and infl. very downy; **morav'ica (edulis),** *fr.* larger, used for preserves (**lacinia'ta** is a very attractive form of this with deeply lobed lflets.); **pen'dula,** a gaunt weeping tree; **xanthocarp'a** (*Fifeana*), *fr.* yellow.

S. caloneur'a (1). Small tree or shrub, 15 to 20 ft., shoots and winter buds glabrous. *l.* oval to oblong, 2 to 3½ in. long, soon nearly or quite glabrous, veins in 10 to 16 pairs. *fl.* white, ½ in. wide, crowded in clusters 2 to 3 in. across; anthers violet-purple. May. *fr.* pear-shaped, brown, spotted, the cal. fallen away. China. 1904. (B.M. 8335 as *Micromeles caloneura.*)

S. Chamaemes'pilus (1). Shrub 3 to 6 ft., compact, stiff, slow-growing. *l.* oval to oblong, 1½ to 3 in. long, half as wide, veins in 6 to 9 pairs, green and glabrous on both surfaces. *fl.* pink, with erect pet., densely packed in small clusters. May. *fr.* ⅓ to ½ in. long, ovoid, red. Cent. Europe. June. 1683.

S. commix'ta (2). Tree 30 ft. and upwards, of columnar shape when young, winter buds glutinous. *l.* 5 to 7 in. long, with 11 to 15 lflets., each ovate-lanceolate, slender-pointed, sharply toothed, 1 to 3½ in. long. *fl.* ⅓ in. wide, in clusters 3 to 5 in. across. May. *fr.* globose, ⅓ in. wide, bright red. Japan. 1906. Distinct in its Lombardy poplar-like growth, at least when young, useful for streets.

S. Conradi'nae. A synonym of *S. Esserteauiana.*

S. cuspida'ta* (1). Tree of medium size, shoots stout, white-woolly. *l.* 5 to 7 (occasionally 9) in. long, 2½ to 5 in. wide, veins in 10 to 17 pairs, soon glabrous above, densely white-felted beneath. *fl.* white, ⅝ in. wide, numerous, in clusters 4 in. across., pet. woolly within, anthers purple. May. *fr.* globose, ⅝ in. wide, reddish-brown, spotted. Himalaya. June. 1820. (B.M. 8259.) Syn. *Pyrus vestita.* Handsomest of the Aria group in foliage.

S. deco'ra* (2). Very near *S. americana* but with fewer (9 or 11) *lflets.* that are broader, more rounded at the apex. May, June. *fr.* larger, ⅜ in. wide, globose-ovoid. E. United States. (S.S. 173, 174 s *Pyrus sambucifolia.*)

S. dis'color* (2). Tree up to 35 ft., winter buds downy. *l.* up to 10 in. long with 11 to 17 lflets., each 1½ to 3 in. long, narrow-oblong, pointed, the terminal two-thirds sharply toothed, grey beneath. *fl.* ⅓ in. wide, white, in thin clusters 4 to 6 in. across. May. *fr.* ⅓ in. wide, globose-ovoid, white or pinkish. China. 1903. Much valued and grown for its fine red autumn tints.

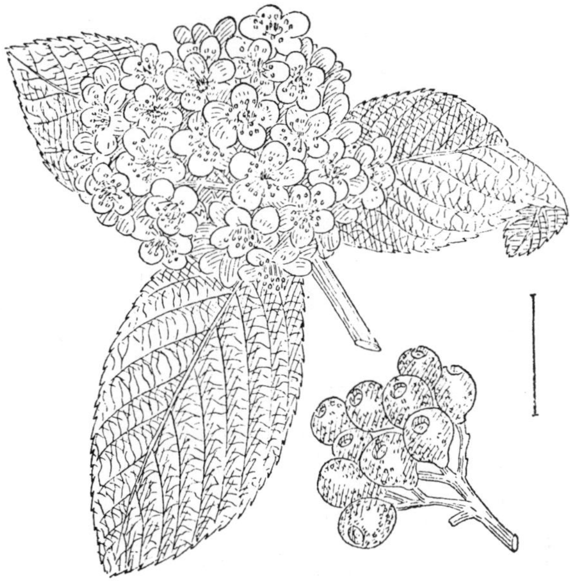

Sorbus caloneura

S. domes'tica (2). Service Tree. Tree 40 to 80 ft., winter buds glutinous and shining. *l.* up to 9 in. long, with 13 to 21 lflets., each narrow-oblong, 1¼ to 2½ in. long. *fl.* white, ½ in. wide, in panicles 4 in. long. *fr.* pear-shaped (**pyriform'is**) or apple-shaped (**maliform'is**), 1 to 1¼ in. long, green or brown, reddish on the sunny side, sometimes eaten but only when bletted. Europe. (E.B. ed. 3, 487.) Syn. *Pyrus Sorbus.* Very distinct by its large, dull-coloured fr.

S. epiden'dron (1). Tree up to 30 ft., shoots, fl.-stalks, and under-surface of l. densely clad with rust-coloured down. *l.* up to 6 in. long, half as wide, slender-pointed, finely toothed. *fl.* creamy-white, packed in clusters 4 in. wide. *fr.* globose, ⅓ in. wide, bluish. China. 1925. Very distinct by its rusty pubescence.

S. Esserteauia'na* (2). Tree up to 50 ft. *l.* 7 to 12 in. long, with 11 or 13 lflets. each 1½ to 4 in. long, oblong-lanceolate, coarsely and sharply toothed, permanently white or greenish-white with down beneath, rich red in autumn. *fl.* crowded in panicles up to 6 in. across, white, ⅓ in. wide. May. *fr.* globose, ¼ in. wide, rich scarlet. China. 1907. (B.M. 9403.)

S. fen'nica. A synonym of *S. hybrida.*

S. Folg'neri (1). Graceful tree up to 30 ft., shoots slender, at first white-felted. *l.* lanceolate to narrowly ovate, 2 to 4 in. long, finely pointed, vividly white-felted beneath; veins parallel in 8 to 10 pairs. *fl.* ⅓ to ½ in. wide, white, numerous in clusters 3 to 4 in. across. May. *fr.* ½ in. long, red, ovoid. China. 1901. (J.R.H.S. 40, 216.) var. **pen'dula.** More pendulous than usual.

S. Harrowia'na (2). Tree 25 to 40 ft. *l.* up to 10 in. long with 3 to 9 lflets., of stout texture, oblong or narrowly obovate, minutely toothed, 2½ to 8 in. long, 1 to 2 in. wide, glaucous beneath. *fl.* small, dull white. May. *fr.* ¼ in. long, pink. China. 1912. Distinct from all others of the Aucuparia group by the striking dimensions of the lflets. Only suitable for mild districts.

S. × Host'ii (1) (*S. Chamaemespilus × S. Mougeotii*). A shrub up to 12 ft. h. In *l.* and habit it is nearer the latter, whilst the pinkish, rather erect pet. suggest the former. *fr.* red, oval, ⅓ in. long. Austrian Alps. (Gn. 20 (1881), 376.)

S. hupehen'sis (2). Tree up to 40 ft., shoots loosely hairy at first; winter buds neither hairy nor gummy. *l.* 8 to 10 in. long, with 11 to 17 lflets., each narrowly oblong, 1½ to 3 in. long, abruptly tapered at the apex. *fl.* small, white, thinly disposed in long-stalked clusters. June. *fr.* globose, ¼ in. wide, white tinged with pink. China. 1910. (B.M. n.s. 96.) Syn. *S. oligodonta.* Confused in gardens with *S. discolor* which has downy winter buds. Autumnal colour good. *See also* **S. Wilsoniana.**

S. hyb'rida (1). Tree 20 to 40 ft. *l.* 3 to 5 in. long, mostly with 2 pairs of free lflets. at the base, lobed in the upper part, with whitish-grey down beneath; veins in 8 to 10 pairs. *fl.* white, ⅝ in. wide. May. *fr.* globose, ½ in. across, red. N. Europe. Syn. *S. fennica.*

S. interme'dia (1). Swedish Whitebeam. Tree up to 40 ft. *l.* 3 to 5 in. long, elliptic with broad acute lobes, with yellowish-grey down beneath; veins in 7 to 9 pairs. *fl.* white ⅝ in. wide, in clusters up to 4 in. across. May. *fr.* oblong, $\frac{1}{2}$ in. long, scarlet. Europe. (B.T.S. 2, 285; E.B. suppl. 484*a*.) SYN. *S. scandica.* Valuable for exposed, windy sites.

S. japon'ica (1). Tree 40 to 60 ft., shoots downy. *l.* ovate to elliptical, $2\frac{1}{2}$ to 4 in. long, lobed and doubly toothed, closely grey- or white-felted beneath, veins in 9 to 12 pairs. *fl.* white on white-woolly stalks. May. *fr.* ovoid, $\frac{1}{2}$ in. long, scarlet. Japan, Korea. 1915. (G.F. 50, 409.) var. **calocarp'a** has purer white pubescence and larger, bright orange *fr.* Handsome Japanese whitebeam. *l.* turns yellow in autumn. SYN. *Pyrus Aria kumaonensis.*

S. Koehnea'na (2). Mostly a shrub up to 14 ft., winter buds downy; shoots chocolate-red. *l.* 6 in. long on virgin shoots, with 17 to 31 lflets. each oblong to ovate, toothed, $\frac{1}{4}$ to $1\frac{1}{4}$ in. long, less than half as wide. *fl.* $\frac{1}{3}$ in. wide, white, in corymbose panicles 2 to 3 in. across. May. *fr.* globose, white, $\frac{1}{4}$ in. wide. China. 1907.

S. latifo'lia (1). Tree 40 to 70 ft. *l.* roundish ovate, 2 to 4 in. long, nearly as much wide at the base, jaggedly toothed and triangularly lobed, grey-felted beneath. *fl.* white, $\frac{5}{8}$ in. wide, in clusters 3 in. across. *fr.* globose, $\frac{1}{2}$ in. wide, brownish-red. Europe (Britain). May. Sometimes considered a hybrid between *S. Aria* and *S. torminalis.* Resembles *S. intermedia* in l. but these are usually wider at the base with the lobing more open and triangular. (G.C. 18 (1882), 749 as *Pyrus latifolia.*)

S. Matsumura'na (2). Japanese Mt. Ash. Tree of small or medium size, shoots reddish. *l.* 4 to 9 in. long with 9 to 13 lflets., each $1\frac{1}{2}$ to 3 in. long, oblong, toothed above the middle only, colour well in autumn. *fl.* white, $\frac{3}{8}$ in. across in clusters 2 to 3 in. wide. May, June. *fr.* ovoid, $\frac{3}{8}$ to $\frac{1}{2}$ in. long, orange-red. Japan. 1912. (G.F. 50, 409.)

S. megalocar'pa (1). Tree up to 25 ft. or a large shrub; shoots stout, purplish; winter buds $\frac{3}{4}$ in. long. *l.* 5 to 10 in. long, half as wide, ovate, obovate or oval, finely toothed, soon glabrous. *fl.* dull white, $\frac{3}{4}$ in. wide, numerous in clusters 4 to 6 in. across. May. *fr.* ovoid, $\frac{3}{4}$ to $1\frac{1}{4}$ in. long, up to $\frac{7}{8}$ in. wide, russet-brown. China. 1903. Remarkable for its large winter buds and fr. Foliage occasionally a good red in autumn. (B.M. n.s. 259.)

S. meliosmifo'lia (1). Tree 20 to 30 ft., shoots glabrous, purplish-brown. *l.* ovate-elliptic, slender-pointed, 4 to 7 in. long, half as wide, green on both sides; veins parallel in 18 to 24 pairs. *fl.* white, in clusters 2 to 4 in. wide. April. *fr.* sub-globose, $\frac{1}{2}$ in. long, dull red, the cal. fallen away. China. 1910. Distinct by the numerous veins of the l. and the short petioles ($\frac{1}{4}$ in. or less long).

S. Mougeot'ii (1). Shrub or small tree. *l.* resembling *S. intermedia* but broader and with whitish-grey down beneath; veins in 9 to 12 pairs. *fr.* $\frac{1}{3}$ in. long, red. Mts. of Cent. Europe.

S. mun'da arachnoi'dea. A synonym of *S. Prattii.*

S. oligodon'ta. A synonym of *S. hupehensis.*

S. × **pinnatif'ida** (1 × 2) (*S. Aria* × *Aucuparia*). Tree of erect habit, up to 50 ft. *l.* 3 to 5 in. long, oblong, mostly with 1 to 3 pairs of free lflets. at the base, lobed in the upper part, or some l. without free lflets., greenish-grey with down beneath; veins in 10 to 12 pairs. *fl.* white, $\frac{1}{2}$ in. wide. May. *fr.* sub-globose, $\frac{1}{3}$ in. across, scarlet. Europe (Britain). G.C. 20 (1883), 493 (E.B. Suppl. 485b). SYN. *S. semipinnata.*

S. pohuashanen'sis (2). Small tree, winter buds downy. *l.* with 11 to 15 lflets. each conspicuously doubly toothed, 1 to $2\frac{1}{4}$ in. long, grey-downy beneath; stipules large and persistent. *fl.* in clusters 4 in. wide. May. *fr.* sub-globose, $\frac{1}{4}$ in. wide, orange-red. N. China. 1909. (B.M. n.s. 133.)

S. Pratt'ii (2). Tree 20 to 30 ft. or a large shrub. *l.* up to $5\frac{1}{2}$ in. long with 21 to 29 lflets., each ovate-oblong, $\frac{1}{2}$ to $\frac{7}{8}$ in. long, toothed, sometimes cobweb-like downy all over beneath, sometimes only on the midrib. *fl.* white, $\frac{1}{3}$ in. wide, in clusters 2 to 3 in. across. May. *fr.* white, $\frac{1}{3}$ in. across, globose. China. 1904. (B.M. 9460.) SYN. *S. munda arachnoidea, S. munda tatsienensis.*

S. pyg'maea. Shrub 3 to 12 in. h.; shoots thinly hairy. *l.* pinnate, up to 3 in. long; lflets. 9 to 15, up to $\frac{1}{2}$ in. long, $\frac{1}{4}$ in. wide, oval, pointed, sharply toothed. *fl.* pale rose to crimson, in terminal clusters of 2 or 3; pet. $\frac{1}{10}$ in. wide, round; pedicels up to 1 in. long, hairy. July. *fr.* white, globose, $\frac{1}{3}$ in. wide. Burma, Tibet, Yunnan. Closely related to *S. reducta* but differing by colour of fl. and fr.

S. reduct'a. Shrub of 6 to 28 in. h. forming dense thickets; shoots thinly bristly; winter buds glabrous. *l.* pinnate, 3 to 4 in. long; lflets. 9 to 15, ovate or oval, coarsely toothed, pointed, $\frac{1}{3}$ to 1 in. long, downy above, smooth beneath. *fl.* in terminal clusters, few, white, $\frac{1}{2}$ in. across; cal. glabrous without, downy within. *fr.* crimson, globose, $\frac{1}{4}$ in. wide. 1943. W. China, Burma.

S. rufo-ferrugin'ea (2). Sometimes considered a var. of *S. commixta,* this differs from it chiefly by having rust-coloured down on the fl.-stalks and on the midrib and veins beneath the lflets. Japan. May. 1913.

S. sambucifo'lia. This confusing name belongs properly to a tree native of NE. Asia, probably not in cultivation. But passing under the name also have been *S. decora, S. Matsumurana,* and (not in cult.) *S. scopulina* and *S. sitchensis.*

S. Sargentia'na (2). Tree 20 to 30 ft., winter buds slightly downy. *l.* 8 to 12 in. long with 7 to 11 lflets. which are oblong-lanceolate, 3 to $5\frac{1}{2}$ in. long, 1 to $1\frac{1}{2}$ in wide, green and downy beneath. *fl.* white, $\frac{1}{4}$ in. wide, in clusters 5 or 6 in. across. May. *fr.* scarlet, globose, $\frac{1}{6}$ in. wide. China. 1908. Next to *S. Harrowiana* in size of lflet., but handsomer in fr. and hardier.

S. scala'ris (2). Tree up to 20 ft. or a shrub, shoots downy. *l.* 4 to 8 in. long, with 21 to 37 lflets., each narrow-oblong, $\frac{1}{2}$ to $1\frac{1}{2}$ in. long, grey-felted beneath, rich red in autumn. *fl.* in clusters 4 or 5 in. wide, dullish-white, $\frac{1}{4}$ in. wide. May, June. *fr.* globose, $\frac{1}{6}$ in. wide, bright red. China. 1904. (B.M. n.s. 69.)

S. semipinna'ta. A synonym of *S.* × *pinnatifida.*

S. tianshan'ica* (2). Shrub or small tree up to 14 ft., winter buds downy. *l.* 5 or 6 in. long, with 9 to 15 lflets. each $1\frac{1}{2}$ to 2 in. long, lanceolate, glabrous, sharply toothed. *fl.* white, $\frac{5}{8}$ in. wide, numerous in clusters 4 to 5 in. across. May. *fr.* globose, $\frac{1}{3}$ in. wide, bright red. Cent. Asia. 1895. Usually shrubby and very charming in fl. (B.M. 7755 as *Pyrus tianschanica.*)

S. tormina'lis (1). Wild Service. Tree 60 to 80 ft. *l.* 3 to 5 in. long and wide, broadly ovate, boldly and deeply cut into 3 to 5 pairs of pointed lobes, dark glossy-green, soon glabrous. *fl.* white, $\frac{1}{2}$ in. wide, in clusters 3 to 4 in. across. June. *fr.* (known as 'chequers') oval, $\frac{1}{2}$ in. long, speckled brown. Europe (Britain). (E.B. 481.) Very handsome tree, the l. changing to red or golden-yellow in autumn.

S. umbella'ta (1). Tree about 20 ft. often regarded as a var. of *S. Aria* under the name *flabellata* but really very distinct. *l.* $1\frac{1}{2}$ to $2\frac{1}{4}$ in. long, tapered to a wedge shape at base; broad rounded and jagged at apex; veins in rarely more than 6 pairs. May. *fr.* depressed globose, late to ripen. SE. Europe, Asia Minor. 1830.

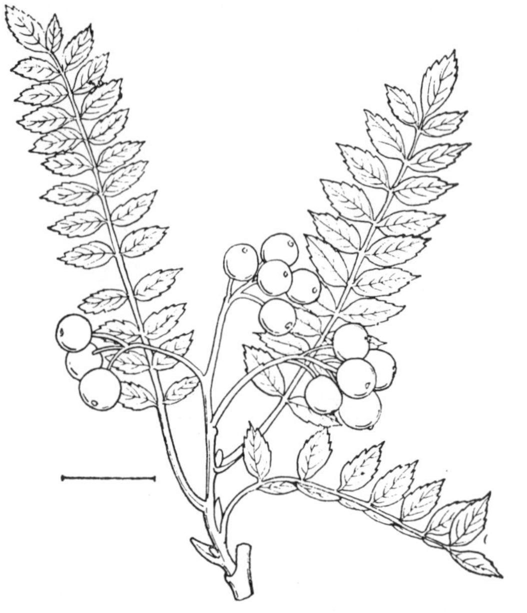

Sorbus Vilmorinii

S. Vilmorin'ii* (2). Tree up to 20 ft., more often a shrub as wide as h., shoots downy. *l.* 3 to 5 in. long with 11 to 31 lflets., each $\frac{1}{3}$ to $\frac{3}{4}$ in. long, elliptic, toothed in upper part, glabrous. *fl.* in loose clusters 3 in. across, $\frac{1}{4}$ in. wide, white. June. *fr.* globose, rosy-pink, $\frac{1}{4}$ to $\frac{1}{3}$ in. wide. China. 1905. (B.M. 8241.) A dainty shrub.

S. Wilsonia'na (2). Tree 30 to 40 ft., winter buds downy. *l.* up to 10 in. long, with 13 to 17 lflets., each oblong-lanceolate, shallowly or scarcely toothed, 2 to $3\frac{1}{2}$ in. long, greyish beneath. *fl.* small, white, in clusters 4 to 6 in. across. May. *fr.* globose, $\frac{1}{6}$ in. wide, crimson. China. Stipules large, strongly toothed persistent. Confused in gardens with *S. hupehensis,* and possibly not in cultivation.

S. Zahlbruck'neri (1). Small tree, up to 20 ft., shoots purplish-brown, almost glabrous. *l.* $2\frac{1}{2}$ to 5 in. long, ovate-elliptic, glossy-green above, grey beneath, turning yellow in autumn. *fl.* white, in clusters 2 to 3 in. wide. May. *fr.* egg-shaped, $\frac{1}{3}$ to $\frac{1}{2}$ in. long, shining red. China. 1901.

W. J. B.

sor'didus -a -um, appearing dirty or neglected.

SORE SHIN. The thin and shrunken appearance of bases of the stems of seedlings, e.g. cabbage, when attacked by the fungus *Corticium solani* is sometimes called sore-shin. The attack does not always kill the seedlings and they may recover when planted out.

D. E. G.

SORGHAS'TRUM (*Sorghum*; *-aster*, like). FAM. *Gramineae.* Similar in structure of inflorescence to Sorghum but having no stalked spikelet, the stalk alone being present. A genus of about 16 species, in tropical and sub-tropical regions, 10 being American, among them *S. nutans* a handsome perennial grass for dry soils but apparently not hardy in England.

S. nut'ans. Indian Grass. Perennial, forming large clumps. Stem 3 to 5 ft. h., unbranched. *l.* pale green. *Panicle* 6 to 13 in. long, narrow; hairs numerous, golden, anthers yellow, thus giving a very bright effect in flower, becoming bronzy-brown later. United States. SYN. *Andropogon avenaceus.*

sorghoi'des, Sorghum-like.

SORG'HUM (Sorgho, the Italian name). FAM. *Gramineae.* A genus of grasses with about 30 wild species and 30 main cultivated races, annual or perennial, mostly natives of the warmer parts of the earth. Spikelets numerous, paired, one sessile, the other stalked; panicle terminal, large, dense, or spreading. Leaves flat, often long and broad. Here belongs Millet (*S. vulgare*) widely cultivated in warmer countries under various names and for different uses, as, for example, Broomcorn with long, branched panicles which are used as brooms; Sugar Sorghums with drooping panicles and red-brown spikelets, grown for their sugary sap and for forage; Kaffir Corn, African Millet, Durra or Egyptian rice corn, Guinea Corn, &c., grown for their seed and Sudan Grass, Tunis Grass for forage. These are all annuals. The perennial *S. halepense* is grown for ornament in borders, and is best in a warm spot, needing only ordinary garden soil.

S. halepen'se. Johnson Grass, Millet Grass. Perennial, spreading; rhizome stout. Stems 2 to 10 ft. h., erect. *l.* up to $\frac{3}{4}$ in. wide, surface smooth, margins rough, sheath smooth, ligule short. *Panicle* up to 10 in. long, spreading. *Spikelets* yellowish-brown, small. Warm temperate regions.

Soria'nus -a -um, in honour of F. Soriano, *c.* 1845.

so'ridens, having sori on the leaf-teeth.

sori'ferus -a -um, bearing sori.

SORINDEI'A (native Madagascar name). FAM. *Anacardiaceae.* A genus of 6 small, glabrous trees, natives of Trop. Africa, Madagascar, and Java. Leaves alternate, unequally pinnate; leaflets entire. Flowers purple or yellow, small; calyx cup-shaped, 5-toothed; petals 5, rarely more; stamens in hermaphrodite flowers 5, in male flowers 10 to 20; panicles terminal, branched, bracteate. Fruit a compressed drupe, 1-seeded. The fruit is said to have a pleasant, sour-sweet mango flavour, somewhat acrid. The inflorescence is produced not only from the branches but from the trunk and the fruits sometimes hang in bunches of 200 or more, 2 ft. long. For treatment of these stove plants, *see* **Anacardium.**

S. madagascarien'sis. About 10 ft. h. *l.* on woody stalks. *fl.* purple, small in axillary racemes. May. Madagascar.

SOROCEPH'ALUS (*soros*, heap, *kephale*, head; the flowers are clustered in heads). FAM. *Proteaceae.* A genus of about 10 species of erect or rarely spreading heath-like, densely leafy shrubs, natives of S. Africa. Leaves scattered, clustered, or almost overlapping, lanceolate or narrow, sometimes awl-shaped, entire or lower deeply cut. Flowers in small heads, clustered in corymbose or capitate spikes; perianth slender, limb globose or oblong. Greenhouse plants needing the same treatment as Protea.

S. diversifo'lius. Stem 2 to 6 ft. h., slender, scarcely branched, hairy above. *l.* spatulate-lanceolate, smooth, glabrous, lowest 2 in. long, 3-fid, 2-pinnatifid, channelled, upper $\frac{1}{2}$ in. long, entire, overlapping, blunt, somewhat concave. *fl.* purple, heads about 1 in. across, solitary sessile, ovate, blunt. June. 1803.

S. imbrica'tus.* About 3 ft. h., branches slightly hairy at first, then glabrous. *l.* overlapping, oblong-lanceolate, acute, with a small inflexed point, at length somewhat spreading, $\frac{1}{3}$ in. long, rough-dotted on back. *fl.* lilac $\frac{1}{3}$ in. long, lamina bearded; heads nearly ovate, about 1 in. across, often 2 or 3 in a close cluster; peduncle scarcely $\frac{1}{2}$ in. long. June. 1791. (A.B.R. 517 as *Protea imbricata.*)

S. lana'tus. About 2 ft. h., branches slightly hairy. *l.* overlapping, linear-awl-shaped, $\frac{1}{3}$ to $\frac{3}{8}$ in. long, channelled above, obtusely keeled at back, or rounded, slightly rough-dotted, ciliate. *fl.* purple, plumosely bearded, in heads as large as a hazel nut; involucre 5- to 7-leaved, coloured; peduncle short, ebracteate or nearly so. August. 1790.

S. seta'ceus. 2 ft. h., branches straight, slightly hairy. *l.* bristly, slender, smooth, 1 to $1\frac{1}{2}$ in. long, mucronate, hairy. *fl.* purple, claw loosely hairy, lamina bearded; head rather larger than a cherry; spike sessile, ovate. July. 1823.

soro'rius -a -um, sisterly, applied to a species nearly resembling another.

SORO'SERIS (*soros*, heap, *seris*, a kind of chichoriaceous plant; in allusion to the dwarf humped habit of the plant). FAM. *Compositae.* A genus of 8 species of dwarf alpine perennial herbs with milky juice, native to the Himalaya, Tibet, and W. China. Leaves entire or toothed, orbicular to lyrate-pinnatifid, stalked, clustered into rosettes. Flower-heads crowded in centre of rosette, white or yellow; involucre with bracts in 2 or 3 series, the outer narrowly linear; florets ligulate. Achenes oblong, many-striate. This genus is related to Crepis, and may interest some rock-garden enthusiasts. The species are *S. bellidifolia, S. Deasyi, S. Gillii, S. glomerata, S. Hookeriana, S. pumila, S. rosularis,* and *S. umbrella.* None is known to have been in cultivation up to 1950.

W. T. S.

SOROSIS. A fleshy mass formed by the conjunction of numerous flowers, seed-vessels and their receptacles, as in Breadfruit, Mulberry, Pineapple.

SORREL (*Rumex Acetosa*). The British wild Sorrel and the more acid French Sorrel, *R. scutatus*, sometimes naturalized in Britain, are sometimes grown as substitutes for Spinach, for use in salads and in cooking. Several forms have been named but all need the same treatment, growing best in a deep moist soil, and all are perennial. They may be raised from seeds sown in drills 15 in. apart in autumn or spring, or by division in March or April. When the seedlings are about 3 in. high they should be thinned out to 12 in. apart, the ground between them being occasionally hoed. Some leaves may be gathered for use about 2 months after seed is sown in spring.

SORREL-TREE. *See* **Oxydendrum arboreum.**

SORROWFUL-TREE. *See* **Nyctanthes Arbor-tristis.**

SORUS (*pl.* sori). A group of sporangia on the frond of a fern. The sporangia of ferns are usually produced in groups in connexion with the veins of the frond and are usually isolated, but occasionally, as in Pteris, a continuous marginal sorus is formed. The sori are sometimes bare, as in Polypodium, but are commonly covered by a membrane called the indusium. The indusia vary considerably in form, attachment, and consistence, and these characters, together with the position of the sori on the frond, are of value in distinguishing the genera of ferns from one another.

SOUARI-NUT TREE. *See* **Caryocar.**

SOULANG'IA. Included under **Phylica.**

Soulangia'nus -a -um, in honour of the chevalier Étienne Soulange-Bodin, 1774–1846, of Fromont, French horticulturist.

Sou'liei, in honour of Father Jean André Soulie, 1858–1905, of the French Foreign Missions in Tibet, who collected many plants there and was murdered at Paan.

SOUR. Soils are said to be sour when they contain an excess of organic acids due to the decomposition of vegetable matter in the absence of sufficient basic material to combine with them, the most frequent base being calcium which can be supplied as chalk or some other form of lime. The formation of these acids is most rapid in wet soils, and borders under glass and soil in pots rapidly become sour if the drainage is not good, and wet land in the open is also frequently sour. The majority of vegetables and all our commonly grown fruits need soils free from excess of organic acids and, therefore, require periodic dressings of some form of lime unless the soil already contains sufficient (*see* **Lime**). Certain weeds, especially Sorrel and Sheep Sorrel, Spurrey, and the yellow *Chrysanthemum segetum*, grow well on acid soils and their presence is an indication of the need for liming to ensure soil fertility for most crops. Peat soils and many alluvial and woodland soils are rich in organic acids, so also is leaf-mould from wet woods.

SOUR GOURD. *See* **Adansonia digitata.**

SOUR SOP. *See* **Annona muricata.**

SOUTH AFRICAN YELLOW-WOOD. *See* **Podocarpus elongata.**

SOUTHERNWOOD (*Artemisia Abrotanum*), also called Old Man and Lad's Love, is a well-known plant in old gardens, grown mostly for the pleasant scent of its leaves, though sometimes also for its medicinal properties which are somewhat similar to those of Wormwood. In S. Europe, where it occurs wild, it is a culinary herb, the young shoots being used for flavouring cakes, &c. It will grow well in any soil, making a bush to 2 ft. high, and is readily propagated by cuttings taken in early summer or by its minute seeds.

SOW-BREAD. *See* **Cyclamen.**

SOW-BUGS. *See* **Woodlice.**

SOWERBAE'A (in honour of James Edward Sowerby, 1759–1824, botanical artist). FAM. *Liliaceae*. A genus of 3 species of tufted perennial herbs with fibrous roots, natives of Australia. Leaves radical, linear-loriform. Flowers pink, in a globular terminal umbel, perianth persistent, not twisting, segments 6, free, or inner connate at base, oblong or ovate; stamens 3; scapes leafless, simple or rarely branched at base. They need greenhouse protection and a compost of sandy loam and peat. Propagation easy by division.

S. junc'ea. Stem unbranched, slender, 1 to 2 ft. h. *l.* somewhat 2-ranked, linear-filiform, terete, all short or some equalling stem, margins scarious at and near base. *fl.* segs. oval-oblong; umbel many-fld. May. 1792. (B.M. 1104.)

S. laxiflo'ra. Stem sometimes slightly branched at base, 1 to 2 ft. h. *l.* crowded at base, sometimes extending some way up stem, not at all scarious on basal margins. *fl.* segs. about ½ in. long, much narrower than in *S. juncea*. 1839. (B.R. 27, 10.)

SOW-THISTLE. *See* **Sonchus.** Troublesome yellow-flowered weeds which should on no account be permitted to seed. *Sonchus oleraceus* and *S. asper* with spiny leaves are annual, *S. arvensis* a widely running handsome perennial with very brittle rhizomes difficult to eradicate. Constant hoeing is the best way of dealing with them.

SPADES. Spades are probably the most indispensable tools for any garden. More can be done with the spade than with any other implement and although the digging fork can be used with advantage on some soils where straightforward thorough turning of the soil, whether light or heavy, is to be done, the best tool for the purpose is the spade. Spades are made in several sizes, that known as No. 3 being generally regarded as suitable for most soils, though No. 2 is also a generally useful one, especially where the soil is heavy. No. 1 spade is the smallest size and No. 4 the largest. For special work such as digging drains a spade with a blade narrow in proportion to its length is made. Local custom governs to a considerable extent the exact form preferred and both the shape of the blade and the form of the handle vary. In very stony or rocky ground an implement with a triangular blade with rounded apex and a long, somewhat curved handle is sometimes used. The blade may have treads affixed or may be quite plain along the top edge; this is called a 'Norfolk' spade. Whatever the form the handle should be straight-grained, made of wood that will not splinter readily, and of a diameter easily grasped. The blade should be firmly fixed to the handle by metal straps carried well up and strongly riveted. The blade should be slightly dished and so constructed that one surface wears more quickly than the other so that friction through the soil keeps the lower edge sharp and bright, so that it will not bend or be liable to break. As with other implements spades should immediately after use be cleaned and wiped with an oily rag before being hung up in the tool shed, for a rusty blade will not do its work properly and will make labour harder. Spades are made of rustless steel at times but these need to be cleaned after use. When the blade of a spade becomes shortened through use it should be set aside for it cannot then dig as deeply as is desirable.

spadic'eus -a -um, furnished with, or like, a spadix.

SPADIX. A fleshy inflorescence with the flowers imbedded in pits, or less frequently sessile on its surface. Such an inflorescence is almost always enclosed, before the flowers open, in one or more spathes growing from the peduncle as in Arum. In some Palms, e.g. Calamus and related genera, there are numerous small spathes (spathellae) each enclosing a group of flowers only. Rarely the spadix is enclosed in neither spathes nor spathellae, as in Acorus. The spadix is usually unbranched as in Anthurium, Zantedeschia, and some Palms but it is usually branched in the family Palmaceae. The spadix usually bears 1-sexual flowers as in Araceae and most Palms, but both sexes may occur on the same spadix, or may be restricted to different spadices or even to different plants. In some Palms hermaphrodite flowers occur, sometimes along with male or female flowers. A spadix is thus a more or less fleshy spike, usually enclosed before flowering in one or more spathes, and bearing 1-sexual flowers. But there are many exceptions and variations.

SPADOSTYL'ES Sieb'eri. A synonym of *Pultenaea euchila*.

SPAN. A length of about 9 in.

SPANIARD. *See* **Aciphylla Colensoi.**

SPANISH BLUEBELL. *See* **Scilla hispanica.**

SPANISH BROOM. *See* **Spartium junceum.**

SPANISH CHESTNUT. *See* **Castanea sativa.**

SPANISH GARLIC. *See* **Rocambole.**

SPANISH IRIS. *See* **Iris Xiphium.**

SPANISH LIME. *See* **Melicocca bijuga.**

SPANISH LIQUORICE. *See* **Glycyrrhiza glabra.**

SPANISH MOSS. *See* **Tillandsia usneoides.**

SPANISH OYSTER PLANT. *See* **Scolymus hispanicus.**

SPANISH VIPER'S GRASS. *See* Scorzonera.

SPARAX'IS (*sparasso*, to tear; the spathes are lacerated). FAM. *Iridaceae*. A genus of about 6 species of S. African herbs. Rootstock a corm. Leaves few, flat, ensiform or broadly linear, erect or falcate. Flowers rather large, showy, 1 to a spathe; perianth yellow with a short straight tube, somewhat funnel-shaped, and 6 obtuse, erecto-patent lobes; stamens short, affixed near base of throat; bracts 2-toothed, much narrower than spathes; spathes few, scattered, sometimes solitary, broad, scarious, striate, often marked with brown lines, fringed at apex. Treatment as for Ixia.

S. bulbif'era. *l.* lanceolate-ensiform, 2-ranked, acute, $\frac{1}{3}$ to $\frac{1}{2}$ in. wide. *fl.* 3 to 5, distant; perianth yellow, funnel-shaped, segs. ovate-oblong, 1 in. long; spathe striped purple at apex; scape sometimes branched, leafy, 1 to 2 ft. h. May. 1758. (B.M. 545 as *Ixia bulbifera.*)

Sparaxis grandiflora

S. grandiflo'ra.* *l.* lanceolate-ensiform, 2-ranked, acute, $\frac{1}{3}$ to $\frac{1}{2}$ in. wide. *fl.* 3 to 5; perianth purple, white or variegated, 2 in. long; segs. equal, spreading star-wise, oblong-wedge-shaped, rounded at apex; scape simple or forked, terete, leafy, 1 to 2 ft. h. April. 1758. (B.M. 541 as *Ixia grandiflora*; 779.) Variable in colouring and form of flower. Many seedlings have been raised differing in some degree from the type and several were at one time named and propagated vegetatively. var. **Lilia'go,** *l.* shorter than stem, finely striated, *fl.* white, spathe white, almost transparent, about as long as tube. (B.R. 258.); **linea'ta,** *l.* 5 to 8 in. long, *fl.* throat yellow, segs. with a longitudinal red line, more or less tinged pink, yellow at base, with a brown mark in middle, upper part white; scapes 2- to 4-fld. (S.B.F.G. s. 2, 131 as *S. lineata.*); **stella'ris,** *l.* erect, acute, *fl.* rich-purple within, rather paler without, tube short, filiform, exserted, mouth deep purple within surrounded by an irregular, starry, white band. (S.B.F.G. s. 2, 383 as *S. stellaris.*); var. **purpu'rea** much resembles var. *stellaris.*

S. pend'ula. A synonym of *Dierama pendulum.*

S. pulcher'rima. A synonym of *Dierama pulcherrimum.*

S. tric'olor.* *l.* as *S. grandiflora*, $\frac{1}{3}$ in. wide, erect. *fl.* 3 to 6, distant, forming a 2-ranked spike; perianth orange, yellow in throat, segs. oblong, 1 in. long, with a 3-angled black spot in middle; spathe valves equal, spotted blackish-brown, sharply cut at apex; scape 1 to 2 ft. h., erect, simple, leafy. May. 1789. (B.M. 381 as *Ixia tricolor.*) Variable and with much variation in colouring of seedlings as in *S. grandiflora*, many having been named. var. **bland'a,** *fl.* segs. flushed rose on a whitish ground, throat yellowish. (B.M. 1482 as var. *subroseo-alba.*); **Griffin'ii,** *fl.* throat yellow with a dark blotch between throat and violet-purple upper part of segs. (B.M. 1428 as var. *violaceo-purpurea.*); **versicol'or,** *fl.* bright purple with lighter margins, more or less clouded or diluted, with a dark mark near base and below it bright yellow; spathe striped brown and purple. (S.B.F.G. 160 as *S. versicolor.*)

SPARGANIA'CEAE. Monocotyledons. A family of 1 genus, Sparganium, with about 20 species in temperate and cold regions of the earth. Herbs with 2-ranked leaves and flowers in globular heads, the lower heads all female, the upper male. Perianth of 3 to 6 segments; stamens 3 to 6; carpels 1 or 2, united, ovule 1. Fruit a drupe. Plants of shallow water.

sparganiifo'lius -a -um, with leaves resembling Sparganium.

SPARGAN'IUM (old Greek name used by Dioscorides for a waterside plant, probably Butomus). FAM. *Sparganiaceae*. Characters as described under family. Two species sometimes offered are of no horticultural merit, but they are useful for fish ponds and wild fowl shelter as are other species, and all are hardy.

S. min'imum. *l.* floating on surface, flat, without a keel, sheaths not inflated. Stems slender, unbranched, 1 to 3 ft. long, upper part floating. *Male fl.-heads* 1 or 2. *Drupe* obovoid. Widely distributed, including Britain.

S. ramo'sum. Bur-reed. Erect, branched, 1 to 4 ft. h. *l.* erect, 2 to 5 ft. long, 3-cornered at base, keeled. *fl.-heads* $\frac{1}{2}$ to $\frac{3}{4}$ in. across. *Drupe* sessile, $\frac{1}{4}$ in. wide. Widely distributed in N. Hemisphere, including Britain.

F. P.

SPARMANNIA (in honour of the Swedish traveller, Dr. Anders Sparrman, 1748–1820, who accompanied Capt. Cook on his second voyage). FAM. *Tiliaceae*. A genus of about 4 species of shrubs or trees covered with soft, starry hairs, natives of Trop. and S. Africa. Leaves cordate, toothed or lobed. Flowers white; stamens numerous; sepals and petals 4. Inflorescence a cymose umbel, with short bracts forming an involucre. Fruit a 4- or 5-celled capsule. Quick growing, especially *S. africana*, needing greenhouse conditions, and a compost of loam and peat. Freely increased by cuttings in sandy peat under a glass in heat. The sensitive stamens are interesting, moving outwards when touched.

S. africa'na.* African Hemp. Shrub of 10 to 20 ft. with patently hairy branches. *l.* cordate, slender-pointed, 5 to 6 in. long, 3 to 4 in. wide, 7- to 9-veined, unequally toothed, hairy on both sides; stalks long. *fl.* on many-fld. peduncles, conspicuous; pet. white, large; barren filaments yellow with purple tips. May. *Capsule* 5-celled. S. Africa. 1790. (B.M. 516.) var. **flore ple'no,** *fl.* double.

S. palma'ta. Smaller in all parts than *S. africana* and more slender, branches half-woody. *l.* 5- to 7-lobed, lobes long-acuminate, unequally toothed, prominently 5- to 7-veined beneath. *fl.* white or purplish, in dense cymose umbels. *Capsules* 4-celled. S. Africa.

SPARROW-GRASS. A corruption of Asparagus.

spars'us -a -um (***sparsi-*** in compound words), scattered.

SPARTI'NA (from Greek *spartine*, a variant of *sparte*, rope or cord; the leaves are fibrous). FAM. *Gramineae*. A genus of about 16 species of perennial tufted or rhizomatous grasses of salt- or fresh-water marshes, occurring on the coasts of Europe, N. and S. Africa, Atlantic Islands, S., Cent., and N. America and across N. America. Stems erect, rigid, often tall. Panicle erect, few to many straight spikes. Spikelets strongly flattened, closely over-lapping on one side only of the spike-axis, stalkless, falling entire at maturity; glumes 3, narrow, keeled. Economically important and easily cultivated but of no garden merit. Propagation by division or seed.

S. pectina'ta. Prairie Cord Grass. Stems 3 to 6 ft. h., forming compact clumps. *l.* up to 2 ft. or more long and $\frac{2}{3}$ in. wide, flat. *Panicle* of 10 to 30 erect spikes. *Spikelets* about $\frac{2}{5}$ in. long; glumes awned. Fresh-water and brackish marshes of N. America. Recommended for cultivation along the margins of lakes and ponds. A form with the leaves longitudinallv striped and margined with yellow has been cultivated in gardens as *S. cynosuroides* var. *aureo-marginata.*

S. Townsend'ii. Rice Grass. Townsend's Cord Grass. Stems 2 to 4 ft. h., forming large clumps, spreading by long rhizomes. *l.* up to 1½ ft. long and ½ in. wide, flat, becoming inrolled. *Panicle* of 3 to 10 erect spikes. *Spikelets* about ⅝ in. long; glumes awnless. England. (B.M. 9125.) This valuable mud-binding grass originated on the foreshore of Southampton Water before 1870 when it was first noticed at Hythe. It is considered to have originated by hybridization between the indigenous *S. maritima* (*S. stricta*) and the introduced N. American *S. alterniflora.* It has spread rapidly on both sides of the English Channel, covering thousands of acres of bare tidal mud-flat with a luxuriant green growth. By means of its deeply penetrating roots and abundant branching rhizomes it consolidates the mud, whilst its stems and leaves collect silt and debris, thus raising the level of the foreshore. On account of its importance in prevention of erosion and in the fixing of coastal muds, it has now been introduced and naturalized in many temperate countries.

C. E. Hb.

spartioi'des, Spartium-like.

SPAR'TIUM (*sparton*, a kind of grass used for making cordage and weaving). FAM. *Leguminosae.* A genus of a single species closely allied to Cytisus and Genista but differing by its 1-lipped, spathe-like calyx which terminates in 5 teeth. Easily grown in porous soil, particularly if lime-free. Should be planted out of pots. Sows itself freely and would probably soon naturalize itself in parts of the country if given an opportunity, but greedily eaten by rabbits when young.

Spartium junceum

S. jun'ceum.* Rather gaunt shrub when allowed to grow naturally, up to 10 ft. h. with almost erect branches and reed-like shoots. *l.* very sparse, fall early, narrow-elliptical or oblong-linear, appressed-pubescent beneath, ½ to ¾ in. long. *fl.* fragrant in loose, terminal racemes; cor. large, shining yellow, standard 1 in. wide; cal. smooth, membranous, with awl-shaped teeth. June to September. *Pods* up to 3 in. long, hairy. Mediterranean region, Canary Is. 1548. (B.M. 85 as *Genista juncea.*) SYN. *G. odorata.* Probably introduced as a medicinal plant. var. **ochroleuc'um,** *fl.* very pale, almost white; **ple'num,** *fl.* double but only worth growing as a curiosity. May be badly cut in severe winters but this, and pruning back, results in the production of a thicket of basal shoots which give the shrub a bush-like compactness. Deciduous but, by reason of the younger and green branches, appearing evergreen.

F. S.

SPARTOCYT'ISUS. Included in **Cytisus.**

SPARTOTHAM'NUS (*sparton*, cordage; *thamnos*, branch; from the use of the plant). FAM. *Verbenaceae.* The only species is an Australian evergreen shrub or sub-shrub. It needs a cool, airy greenhouse and a compost of sand, peat, and loam. Propagation by cuttings in sand under glass.

S. jun'ceus. Broom-like, 2 ft. h., appearing almost leafless, branches spreading, 4-angled. *l.* small, distant, opposite, often scale-like, up to ¼ to ½ in. long, lanceolate or ovate-lanceolate. *fl.* white, very small, solitary in axils, with small bracteoles; cal. and cor. 5-lobed. August. Australia. 1819.

SPATAL'LA (*spatalos*, delicate; alluding to the flowers). FAM. *Proteaceae.* A genus of about 18 species of heath-like shrubs, natives of S. Africa. Leaves scattered, filiform or awl-shaped, entire. Flowers rather small, solitary, in heads, sessile or shortly pedicellate, forming a loose spike or terminal raceme; perianth slender, scarcely dilated towards base, limb straight or incurved, ovoid or oblong; hypogynous scales 4, awl-shaped. Nuts often hairy. The flowers of all mentioned are purple. Treatment as for Protea.

S. curvifo'lia. 2 ft. h. *l.* about 1 in. long, 3-angled, filiform, rather blunt, narrowed to base, incurved-falcate above, straight and silky-hairy at first. *fl.* claw hairy; involucre sub-campanulate, 2-lipped, shaggy at length nearly glabrous; spike solitary, 1 to 2 in. long, finally rather loose; peduncle 1 to 1½ in. long, bracts few, appressed. 1822. SYN. *S. pedunculata.*

S. mol'lis. 2 ft. h. *l.* erecto-patent, about ½ in. long, straight, silky-hairy. *fl.* involucre, hairy, 2-leaved; spike solitary, sessile, erect, dense, oblong-cylindrical, branched, scarcely 1 in. long. June. 1826.

S. niv'ea. 2 ft. h. *l.* overlapping, 2⅓ to ⅓ in. long, slender, acute, straight or slightly curved, slightly silky-hairy. *fl.* involucre bell-shaped, one-third as long as perianth, spike subsessile, erect, dense, overlapping, 1 to 1½ in. long. June. 1806.

S. pa'rilis. 3 ft. h., branchlets umbellate. *l.* crowded, erecto-patent, ½ to ⅝ in. long, slender, acute, straight then slightly recurved, slightly hairy. *fl.* yellowish-downy; involucre shortly stalked, hairy, 4-leaved; spike 1 to 1½ in. long, solitary, sessile, erect, oblong-pyramidal, dense, sometimes branched at base. June. 1821. SYN. *S. pyramidalis.*

S. pro'cera. 2 ft. h. *l.* rather loosely spreading, ½ to 1 in. long, incurved, slender, bristly mucronate, scarcely narrow at base, glabrous; slightly hairy at first. *fl.* involucre hairy, 4-lvd., with 3 or 4 fl.; racemes solitary or often clustered, 1 to 2 in. long. May. 1789. SYN. *S. incurva.*

S. prolif'era. 2 ft. h., branches reddish, nearly glabrous. *l.* erect, or finally spreading, clustered, overlapping, up to ⅗ in. long, slender, straight or nearly so, mucronulate, silky at first. *fl.* involucre nearly sessile, 4-lvd.; spikes sessile, conical-capitate, bracts leafy. July. 1800.

spatha'ceus -a -um, bearing, or having the nature of, a spathe.

SPATHAN'THEUM (*spathe*, *anthos*, flower; the spadix being adnate to the spathe for its whole length). FAM. *Araceae.* A genus of 2 species of tuberous-rooted perennials, natives of the Andes of Bolivia. Tubers large, flattish. Leaves with a long stalk, blade 2-lobed, lobes pinnatifid with numerous lanceolate segments. Peduncle slender, longer than leaves. Spathe oblong-elliptic, slender-pointed, at first convolute, white within, green without. Spadix linear, shorter than the spathe, *S. heterandrum* needs stove conditions and a well-drained soil of rich loam and peat, with plenty of water during growth. The tubers may be divided, and offsets are formed.

S. heterand'rum. Tuber producing a solitary l. after fl. *l.-stalk* about 2 ft. long; blade cordate-ovate, deeply pinnatifid, over 12 in. long, bright green, fleshy, segs. lanceolate, about 4 in. long. *Peduncle* erect, shorter than l.-stalk, almost round. *Spathe* green, fleshy, boat-shaped, acute, 4 to 5 in. long; spadix half as long as spathe to which it is adnate for whole length. 1876.

SPATHE. A bract enclosing 1 or a number of flowers. The spathe may be membranous as in Narcissus, leafy as in Arum, or fleshy or woody as in many of the larger Palms such as Cocos.

SPATHEL'IA (*spathe*, see below). FAM. *Rutaceae*. A genus of 3 species of evergreen unbranched trees, natives of W. Indies. Leaves alternate, unequally pinnate with many leaflets; leaflets alternate, linear-oblong or sickle-shaped, margins glandular. Flowers large, short stalked, panicles long, large, terminal; calyx 5-parted; petals 5, scarcely longer than calyx, overlapping; stamens 5. *S. simplex* grows well under stove conditions in a compost of loam and peat. Patrick Brown gave this the name of *Spathe* (which in Greek referred to a palm spathe or frond as well as many other broad-bladed objects), in allusion to its palm-like growth; Linnaeus amended the name to *Spathelia*, obviously to avoid confusion with the technical term *spatha*.

S. sim'plex. May Pole, Mountain Green, Mountain Pride of the W. Indies. Stem slender, unbranched, 20 to 50 ft. h. *l.* in 20 to 40 pairs, oblong- or linear-lanceolate, slender-pointed or falcate, sometimes crenately toothed. *fl.* red; panicle spreading, several ft. long, powdery. 1778. (B.R. 670.)

SPATHICARP'A (*spathe*, spathe, *karpos*, fruit; the fruits are on the adnate spadix). FAM. *Araceae*. A genus of 6 species of evergreen Brazilian herbs with oblong tuberous rhizomes. Leaves membranous, lanceolate or hastate- or sagittate-cordate, or hastately 3-partite; stalks long, slender, terete, with a long sheath. Peduncles longer than leaves, slender. Spathe oblong-lanceolate with a long slender point, at first convolute, then opening except at base and apex, persistent; spadix adnate to spathe; ovary with 1 ovule. Stove plants needing rich sandy loam; increased by division or seed.

S. hastifo'lia. *l.-stalk* about 8 to 10 in. long; blade more or less distinctly 3-partite, front lobe 2½ in. long, up to 2 in. wide, oblong or ovate-lanceolate, obtuse. *Peduncle* longer than l., 12 to 16 in. long. *Spathe* oblong-lanceolate, greenish, spadix occupying about ⅔ of its length. S. Brazil.

S. sagittifo'lia. *rhiz.* oblique, stout. *l.-stalk* 6 to 12 in. long, about twice as long as blade; blade sagittate, mid-lobe ovate-lanceolate, side lobe sometimes bent back, obtuse, much shorter than mid-lobe. *Peduncles* longer than l. *Spathe* oblong-lanceolate, green, decurrent at base, with a longer or shorter cusp; spadix slender, rather shorter than spathe. S. Brazil. 1860. var. **longicusp'is,** *l.* and *spathe* long-pointed; **platyspath'a,** *spathe* dilated below apex, shortly cuspidate.

SPATHIPHYL'LUM (*spathe*, *phyllon*, leaf; in allusion to the leaf-like spathe). FAM. *Araceae*. A genus of about 27 species of almost stemless, evergreen, perennial herbs, natives of Trop. America, one in Malaya. Leaves oblong, narrowed to a point, midrib prominent; stalk equitant, sheathing at base, sharply bent near summit. Peduncle as long as petiole or longer. Spathe cuspidate, convolute at first, then expanded. Spadix erect, shorter than spathe, densely many-flowered. Flowers hermaphrodite, usually 3- (rarely 2- or 4-) merous, stamens as many as sepals, ovary usually 3-celled. Equal parts of leaf-mould and peat with a little loam and small pieces of charcoal make a suitable compost, and they require a moist stove atmosphere and abundance of moisture. Propagation by seed or by division of rootstock. The small species, *S. cannifolium*, *S. floribundum*, and *S. Patinii* are excellent as contrasts to *Anthurium Andreanum* and *A. Scherzerianum*.

S. bland'um. *l-stalk* about 10 in. long, sharply bent; blade elliptic-oblong or oblong, acute about as long, 4 in. wide. *Peduncle* about 4 in. long. *Spathe* pale green, elliptic-oblong, narrowed to base, cuspidate, 6 to 8 in. long. Surinam.

S. can'didum. A synonym of *S. Patinii*.

S. cannaeform'e. A synonym of *S. cannifolium*.

S. cannifo'lium. *l.-stalk* 12 to 16 in. long, sharply bent, blade ovate-oblong or elliptic-oblong, shortly slender-pointed, 12 to 20 in. long, rather thin, dark shining green above, dull and pale beneath. *Peduncle* about 6 in. long. *Spathe* rigid, green without, white within lanceolate or elliptic-oblong, 5 to 8 in. long; spadix white. Venezuela, Colombo, British Guiana. (G.F. 1870, 640; B.M. 603 and L.B.C. 471 as *Pothos cannaefolia*; I.H. 1877, 269 as *Anthurium Dechardii*.) *See* **S. × hybridum.**

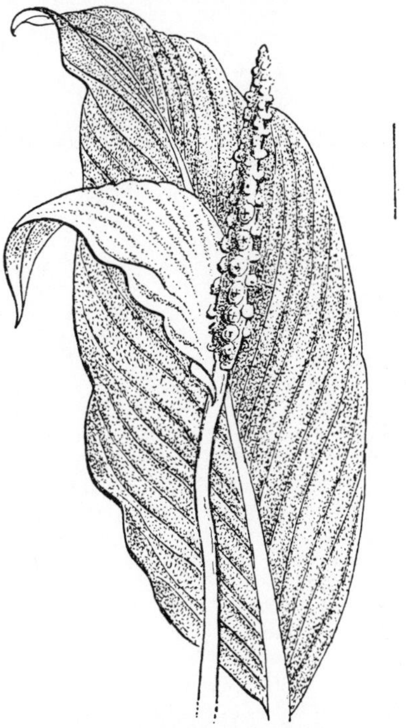

Spathiphyllum cannifolium

S. cochlearispath'um. *l.-stalk* 18 to 30 in. long, sharply bent, blade rather thin, broadly oblong, margin undulate, 20 to 30 in. long, 8 to 10 in. wide. *Peduncle* 4 ft. long. *Spathe* oblong, 6 to 10 in. long, cuspidate, green; spadix whitish. Mexico. 1875. (I.H. 189 as *S. heliconiifolium*.)

S. commuta'tum. *l.-stalk* about 16 in. long, sharply bent, blade widely ovate, 12 to 14 in. long, about 8 in. wide, midrib whitish. *Peduncle* over 20 in. long. *Spathe* white, oblong-lanceolate, 10 to 18 in. long, with a long cusp; spadix white. E. Indies, Philippines. 1870. (G.F. 637 as *Spathiphyllum Menahassae*.)

S. floribund'um. *l.-stalk* 4 to 6 in. long, sharply bent, oblong-elliptic or oblong-lanceolate, about 6 in. long, with an acute slender point. *Peduncle* 8 to 10 in. long. *Spathe* white, oblong-lanceolate, 2½ in. long; spadix yellowish-green or white. Colombia. 1874. (I.H. 159 as *Anthurium floribundum*.)

S. heliconiifo'lium. A synonym of *S. cochlearispathum*.

S. × hyb'ridum (*S. cannifolium* × *S. Patinii*). Intermediate between parents but with spathe whiter on both sides and as large in *S. cannifolium*. (I.H. 1882, 450.)

S. Ortgies'ii. *l.-stalk* 5 to 7 in. long, blade widely elliptic or elliptic-oblong, about 12 in. long, margin undulate, apex somewhat slender-pointed. *Peduncle* 16 to 20 in. long. *Spathe* bright green, oblong-elliptic, about 10 in. long; spadix white. Mexico. 1873. (G.F. 1872, 738.)

S. Patin'ii. *l.-stalk* slender, 10 to 12 in. long, sharply bent, blade oblong-lanceolate with a long narrow point, 8 to 10 in. long. *Peduncle* slender, 14 to 20 in. long. *Spathe* whitish or with a green midrib, spreading or recurved, oblong-lanceolate, about 3 in. long; spadix whitish. Colombia. 1874. (I.H. 397.) SYN. *S. candidum*, *Anthurium candidum*, *A. Patinii*.

S. pict'um. A synonym of *Rhodospatha picta*.

S. Wallis'ii. *l.-stalk* 5 to 8 in. long, sharply bent, blade bright green, oblong-lanceolate, rounded at base, cuspidate, 6 to 10 in. long. *Peduncle* 10 to 12 in. long. *Spathe* bright green, oblong-elliptic. Colombia. (G.F. 920.)

SPATHO'DEA (*spathe-like*, referring to the calyx). FAM. *Bignoniaceae*. A genus of 2 or 3 species of evergreen trees, natives of Trop. Africa, with large flowers in terminal racemes or panicles; calyx split on one side, recurved, corolla large, bell-shaped, tube swollen on one side. Leaves large, odd-pinnate, opposite or in threes; leaflets entire. The Spathodeas need stove treatment and a rich, well-drained soil with plenty of water during the growing season. Only a large house will suit them for they rarely flower until of large size. Propagated by seeds or cuttings. **A**

S. campanula'ta. Tree of 50 ft. *l.* large, pinnate; lflets. lanceolate, stalked. *fl.* orange-scarlet, in a short, slightly branched raceme; cal. long, spathe-like, densely hairy; cor. bell-shaped, 3 in. long, 2½ in. across, limb somewhat 2-lipped, lobes 5. June. Trop. Africa. 1858. (B.M. 5091; F.d.S. 830.)

F. G. P.

SPATHOGLOT'TIS (*spathe*, spathe, *glottis*, tongue; in allusion to the form of the lip). FAM. *Orchidaceae.* A genus of about 40 species of terrestrial orchids, natives of the E. Indies, S. China, Malaya, the Pacific Is., and Australia. Sepals free, sub-equal, spreading; petals similar, sometimes broader or longer; lip sessile at base of column, concave or saccate at base, deeply 3-lobed, the middle lobe spreading more or less in the apical portion, contracted behind into an often long and strap-shaped claw and bearing prominent tubercles or calli; pollen masses 8, of which 4 are usually smaller; bracts erect, or deflexed; racemes on erect scapes, leafless, except for sheathing scales, umbel-like in some, but the rachis elongates and produces flowers for a considerable time. Leaves on the caudex usually 2 or more, plicate, somewhat grass-like, elongated; petioles at length more or less thickened into corm-like pseudobulbs. In some species the pseudobulbs are above the ground, in others a position just below the surface seems more suitable. The foliage is retained on a number of species, but some are deciduous or practically so. The wide distribution of the genus necessitates slightly different temperatures, but those under cultivation thrive in a stove temperature during the summer or growing season with a winter night temperature of approximately 60° F., the deciduous species 55°. Compost should consist of 1 part of Osmunda fibre, 1 part of Sphagnum moss, and 2 parts of fibrous loam. A little leaf-mould and coarse sand may be added. Drainage must be free as abundance of water should be given when growth is active. In winter infrequent watering must be the rule, particularly with the deciduous species which may not require any. Annual repotting carried out in early spring, though not essential, is preferable. Propagation may then be effected by dividing the rhizome leaving 3 or 4 bulbs behind the leading one. The graceful character, and the long duration of the inflorescence gives the genus on the whole considerable merit, and in Ceylon and other suitable climates *S. plicata*, in particular, has been utilized in the outdoor garden.

S. Augusto'rum. A synonym of *S. Vieillardii.*

S. au'rea.* *fl.* 2 or 3 in. across, golden-yellow, with a few dark blood-coloured spots on lip; infl. about 6-fld. at end of scape. July. *l.* narrow, similar to those of a Phaius. 2 to 3 ft. h. Malacca. 1849. *See* **S. Kimballia'na.**

S. elobula'ta. Differs from *S. plicata* in the narrow *l.*, smaller *fl.* with narrower sep. and pet., side lobes of lip less dilated at apex, mid-lobe without basal lobules, column thinner and less arched, infl. often branched. New Guinea.

S. For'tuni.* *fl.* 1 to 1½ in. across, yellow; sep. ovate, obtuse; pet. broader, oblong, subsessile; side lobes of lip blotched red, oblong, erect, mid-lobe cuneate, emarginate; column markedly long and narrow; raceme 5- to 9-fld. secund, pubescent; bracts slender-pointed. January. *l.* twin, linear-lanceolate, longer than scape, deciduous or nearly so. Hong Kong. (B.R. 31, 19.) Greenhouse. Differs but little from *S. pubescens*, of which it is sometimes considered a synonym. The column is broader and the side lobes of lip hairy in the lower corner.

S. grac'ilis. *fl.* bright yellow, 2 in. across, with a few streaks of red on incurved side lobes of lip. Borneo. Has been grown in gardens as *S. aurea*, which it resembles in every character except the broader-lobed and differently formed lip. (B.M. 7366.)

S. ixioi'des. *fl.* 1 to 3, bright golden-yellow, ¾ to 1¼ in. across, nodding; lip having some reddish specks on disk; scapes slender, erect. Summer. *l.* 2 or 3 from each pseudobulb, 8 to 18 in. long, grass-like, often deciduous, sheath purplish, pubescent. E. Himalaya. 1881. (B.M. 7060.)

S. Kimballia'na.* *fl.* about 3 in. across, golden-yellow within, sep. and pet. copiously spotted with reddish-brown or copper-red without, with some faint red marks on lip, the side lobes of which are large. *l.* 2 ft. or more long, 1 to 1½ in. wide, long-acuminate. Borneo. (B.M. 7443; R. 2, 88.) Allied to *S. aurea* of which it is sometimes considered a variety.

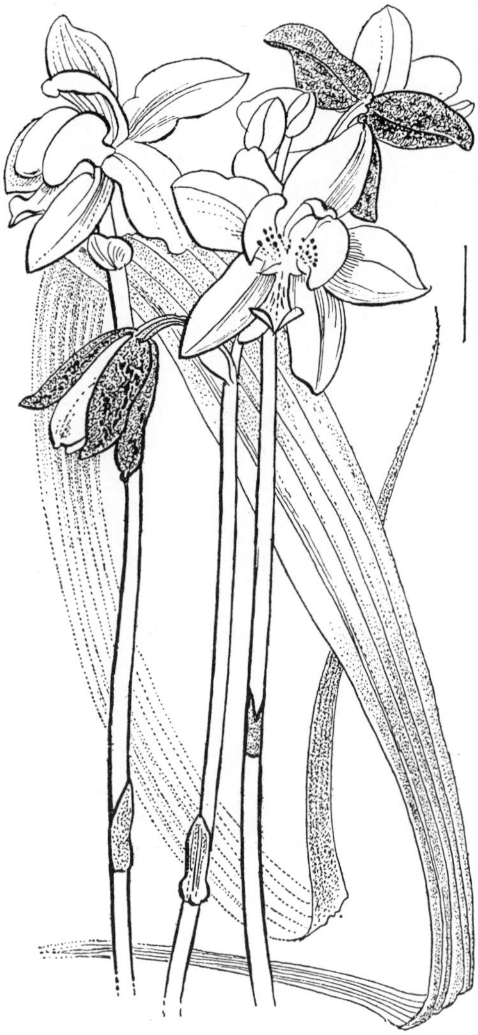

Spathoglottis Kimballiana

S. lilaci'na. A synonym of *S. plicata.*

S. Lobb'ii. *fl.* 4 to 7, sulphur, about 1 in. across, long-stalked; side lobes and base of lip streaked with 3 or 4 brown lines; pet. broader than sep.; raceme loose, scape slender, firm, loosely hairy. Burma. 1876. (Gn. 22 (1882), 188.)

S. Micholitz'ii. A variety of *S. plicata.*

S. pacif'ica. Sep. and pet. whitish-lilac with darker markings; lip lilac, edged yellow, side lobes blunt, curved, mid-lobe stalked, reniform, undulate, disk orange, stalk with 2 white tubercles at base. *l.* oblong-lanceolate. *Pseudobulbs* conical. Pacific Is. 1883.

S. Paul'inae. *fl.* many, about 1 in. across, light rose-purple. *l.* 15 to 24 in. h. *Scapes* taller. Australia. (F.A.O. 1, 62.)

S. Pet'ri.* *fl.* 9 to 12, 1½ in. across; sep. ligulate, acute, like the much broader pet. lilac; lip 3-fid, side lobes purplish, disk white, a rhomboid callosity with 3 furrows and 2 lines of long hairs between side lobes, ochre-yellow; bracts large, conspicuous; scape 2 ft. long, green, becoming purplish at top. *l.* 12 to 18 in. long. South Sea Is. 1877. (B.M. 6354.)

S. plica'ta.* *fl.* many, 1 to 2 in. across, purple; sep. spreading; pet. obtuse, connivent; side lobes of lip truncate, cuneate-oblong, mid-lobe clawed, with 2 whitish tubercles at base; bracts petaloid, lanceolate, coloured; scape 2 ft. or more h. June. *l.* many, ensiform, plicate. Java, Burma. 1844. A variable species. var. **al'ba,** *fl.* white; **Micholitz'ii,** *fl.* larger than in type, rose-purple, plant slightly smaller. New Guinea. 1894.

S. pubes'cens. *fl.* dirty-yellow, slightly violet at base of lip; sep. acute; pet. obtuse; side lobes of lip erect, mid-lobe 3-keeled, with 2 tubercles at base; raceme 2- to 8-fld., secund; scape ascending, pubescent, 1½ ft. long. June. *l.* twin, linear-lanceolate, acuminate at both ends, shorter than scape. Tubers as large as hazel nuts. Sylhet. Allied to *S. Fortuni.*

S. Reg'nieri. Closely allied to *S. Lobbii*, but *fl.* smaller, with no stripes on lateral sep.; stalked ovaries shorter; side lobes of lip shorter and broader; callus standing further back; peduncle with shorter hairs. *l.* much broader. Cochin China. 1887.

S. ro'sea.* *fl.* rose, pretty, about 1½ in. across; sep. and pet. oblong, acute; bracts spreading, as long as pedicels; scape erect, slender, distantly sheathed, taller than leaves. July. *l.* lanceolate, plicate, narrowed at base, nearly 2 ft. long. *Pseudobulbs* densely aggregated, 3-leaved. Philippines. 1837. (B.R. 24, 60 as *Paxtonia rosea.*) Sometimes regarded as a synonym of *S. plicata.*

S. tomento'sa. *fl.* crimson; sep. and pet. very obtuse; side lobes of lip erect, truncate; mid-lobe reniform at apex, claw long; raceme 20-fld.; bracts and space coated with a close fur. June. *l.* twin, broadly lanceolate, longer than scape. Manila.

S. Vieillard'ii.* *fl.* many, 2 in. across, pale lilac or whitish in an elongating raceme; lip usually darker than sep. and pet., side lobes rectangular, retuse, mid-lobe long-clawed, oblong, 2-lobed at apex. *l.* broadly cuneate-oblong, acute, 2½ to 3 ft. long. *Pseudobulbs* ovoid, tinted brown, 2½ in. h. Sunda Is. 1886. A fine but variable species. (B.M. 7013; L. 25 as *S. Augustorum.*) var. **ru'bra**, *fl.* darker and larger than in type, bright purple; lip deeper. 1892.

E. C.

spathula'tus -a -um, spatulate; oblong with the lower end narrowed; having the shape of spatula. **A**

spatio'sus -a -um, occupying much space, large.

spatula'tus -a -um. *See* ***spathulatus.***

SPAWN. The mass of hyphae which is technically known as the mycelium of a fungus. It is the vegetative part of the fungus of which certain threads will later begin to grow together and form special bodies or fructifications on or within which the spores will be produced for reproductive purposes. In some fungi the mycelium is very conspicuous and this is especially so in the common mushroom, *Psalliota campestris*, so that the name 'spawn' is applied to pieces of mycelium of this and some other fungi. Formerly mushroom growers thought highly of what was called 'Virgin spawn' which was dug from fields and old pastures where mushrooms were abundant. This was then inoculated into bricks made from a wet mixture of horse and cow manure and loam, the bricks being piled one on the other and pieces of the virgin spawn placed between each pair of bricks. They became permeated with the spawn and were allowed to dry when it was said to keep for years but in fact probably became unfit for use in less than 1 year. This spawn when moist has a pleasant odour of fresh mushrooms which is lost on drying. Present-day growers use pure culture spawn grown on sterilized manure under sterile conditions. The mycelium is obtained from selected young mushrooms out of which a piece of the inner tissues is cut to inoculate the manure in the containers and so start the spawn. With this method of spawn-making selection can be practised to obtain the best strains of mushrooms and the spawn is said to be more vigorous and give better and bigger crops. Spawn does not correspond with seed but is a means of propagating mushrooms vegetatively.

D. E. G.

SPEARGRASS. *See* **Aciphylla squarrosa.**

SPEARMINT. *See* **Mint, Mentha.**

SPEARWORT. *See* **Ranunculus Lingua.**

SPECIES. A group of individuals which have the same constant and distinctive characters. These individuals may vary in colour of flower, size of leaf, degree of hairiness, &c., but only in such characters as experience teaches us are liable to vary in the seedlings raised from one individual.

SPECIFIC EPITHET. The part of a botanical name which is peculiar to the species: it follows the name of the genus and applies to all individuals which can be regarded as belonging to the particular species. The valid specific epithet is the earliest that has been applied to the species in conformity with the Rules of Nomenclature. *See* **Trivial Name.**

specio'sus -a -um, good-looking, showy.

specta'bilis -is -e, worth seeing, admirable.

SPECULA'RIA (*Speculum Veneris*, Venus's Looking-glass, was an early name of the common European species). FAM. *Campanulaceae.* A genus of about 10 species of erect or decumbent, hispid or glabrous annual herbs, natives of the N. Hemisphere, one extending into S. America. Leaves alternate, entire or toothed. Flowers blue, violet or white, subrotate or bell-shaped, 5-lobed, with a long calyx tube, stamens free of corolla, filaments flat. Differing from Campanula by the long slender tube of the calyx, the inferior 3-celled ovary and the oblong or linear capsules. Easily grown annuals for ordinary good garden soil. Hardy.

S. pentago'nia. Stem about 1 ft. h., branched. *Lower l.* obovate, entire; *upper* ovate-oblong or lanceolate, nearly entire. *fl.* blue; cal. shorter or as long as cor. with spreading lobes; peduncles 1-fld. E. Mediterranean. 1686. (B.R. 56 as *Campanula pentagonia.*)

S. Spec'ulum. Venus's looking-glass. About 1 ft. h., stem branched. *l.* as in *S. pentagonia. fl.* purple, about ¾ in. across; cal. glabrous or hairy, as long as cor., lobes finally reflexed; peduncles 3-fld. Europe. 1596. (B.M. 102 and F.G. 216 as *Campanula Speculum.*) A variable plant. var. **al'ba**, *fl.* white; **grandiflo'ra**, *fl.* about 1 in. across; **procum'bens**, stems spreading; a double-fld. form is also known.

Spec'ulum, looking-glass.

SPEEDWELL. *See* **Veronica.**

Spegazzin'ii, in honour of an Italian botanist, Professor Carlo Spegazzini, 1858–1926, who emigrated in 1879 to the Argentine and became the country's leading botanist as well as Director of Agriculture.

SPEIRAN'THA (*speira*, wreath, *anthos*, flower; in allusion to the inflorescence). FAM. *Liliaceae.* A genus of a single species of Chinese perennial herb with a thick, oblique, stoloniferous rhizome. Related to Convallaria and Theropogon. Hardy in southern England and thriving in a cool, half-shady, position and leafy soil.

S. Garden'ii. *l.* 6 to 8 in a basal rosette, sub-erect, oblanceolate, 5 to 6 in. long, 1 to 1½ in. wide, acute, sessile, evergreen. *fl.* white, starry, about ⅛ in. long, stamens 6; racemes 20- to 30-fld., 1 to 2 in. long, on a slender scape 3 to 4 in. long. June. China. 1854. (B.M. 4842 as *Albuca Gardeni.*) SYN. *S. convallarioides.*

spelun'cae, of a cave.

Spen'ceri, in honour of Sir Walter Baldwin Spencer, 1860–1929, Professor of Biology, Melbourne.

SPENCER'IA (in honour of Spencer le Marchant Moore, 1851–1931, British botanist). FAM. *Rosaceae.* A genus of 2 species of perennial herbs related to Agrimonia. Hardy and useful for a nook in the rock-garden. Not particular as to soil or aspect.

S. ramala'na. *l.* in a basal rosette, flat on ground. *fl.* bright yellow, large, in a spike. Western China. 1919. (B.M. 9007.)

sperab'ilis -is -e, hoped for.

SPERAGE. An old name for Asparagus.

SPER'GULA pilif'era. A synonym of *Sagina pilifera.*

SPERMAPHY'TA. Seed-producing plants. One of the great divisions of the Vegetable Kingdom now often called Embryophyta Siphonogama and including all the plants sometimes known as Phanerogams comprising the divisions Gymnospermae and Angiospermae (q.v.).

SPERMATOZOID. A small cell consisting of a naked filament of protoplasm usually thickened at one end and often spirally coiled, bearing usually 2 or more cilia which enable it to propel itself through the water. The spermatozoids constitute the male cells in most plants below the rank of flowering plants, and even here they are exceptionally found as when the pollen of Ginkgo and a few near relatives germinates.

SPERMOGONIA. Small flask-shaped bodies resembling pycnidia which are formed by some Rust fungi. They contain small spore-like bodies known as spermatia which at one time were thought to be functionless, but recent research has shown that they play an important part in the formation of the aecidium. Some Ascomycetous fungi may produce similar structures but much more work is required to find out their true function in this group. They are often called pycnia and the spermatia pycniospores.

D. E. G.

-spermus -a -um, in compound words, signifying seed, as *polyspermus*, many-seeded.

sphacela'tus -a -um, gangrened.

SPHACE'LE (*Sphakos*, Greek name for Sage which these plants resemble in foliage). FAM. *Labiatae*. A genus of about 20 species of shrubs and sub-shrubs, one of which is a native of the Sandwich Is., the remainder of America from Brazil and Chile to California. Leaves opposite, often bullate-wrinkled and hoary beneath, upper small. Flowers red, violet, blue, or whitish; calyx 5-toothed; corolla tube large, limb short, scarcely 2-lipped, 4-cleft with broad more or less erect lobes; stamens 4; racemes or spikes of loosely 2- to 6-fld., or densely 6- to many-fld. whorls. All the species need greenhouse treatment and cultivation as for the tender species of Salvia.

S. caeru'lea. Soft-wooded sub-shrub. *l.* ovate, toothed. *fl.* in numerous spikes, pale lavender-blue. Winter. 1866.

S. campanula'ta. A synonym of *S. chamaedryoides*.

S. chamaedryoi'des. Shrub of 2 to 3 ft. *l.* oblong-lanceolate, ½ to 1 in. long, narrowed to a short stalk; uppermost much wrinkled. *fl.* pale bluish, ⅝ in. long with broad, crenate lobes; cal. ⅓ in. long; racemes loose with fl. in secund pairs. July. Chile. 1795. (B.R. 1382.)

S. Lind'leyi. Shrub of 3 to 4 ft. *l.* ovate, 1½ to 3½ in. long, cordate at base, much wrinkled, white-woolly beneath. *fl.* purplish-violet; cor. twice as long as cal., hairy without, slightly incurved; racemes dense with many-fld. whorls. July. Chile. 1825. (B.M. 2993; B.R. 1226 as *Stachys Salviae.*)

sphaer-, in compound words, signifying globular.

SPHAERA'LCEA (*sphaira*, globe, *Alcea*, Marsh Mallow; Globe Mallow; the carpels form a round head). FAM. *Malvaceae*. A genus of about 70 species of herbs, sub-shrubs, or shrubs with the habit of Malva or Malvastrum, 5 S. African, the remainder natives of the warmer parts of America. Leaves usually angled or lobed. Flowers violet, rarely red, or flesh-coloured, solitary or clustered in the leaf-axils or in terminal spikes or racemes; calyx 5-cleft with 3 free or coherent bracteoles at base (none in the allied genus Abutilon); staminal column divided into numerous branches near top. Fruit subglobose, of many 2-valved, 2- or 3-seeded carpels, united in a ring around the central receptacle. The best compost is a rich, well-drained loamy soil. The temperature requirements vary, a few being hardy, others needing greenhouse or even stove treatment. Some species are difficult to propagate vegetatively and some rarely set seed if grown in isolation. Cuttings of young shoots in sand under a shaded bell-glass offer the best means of propagation.

S. abutiloi'des. Shrub of about 4 ft. *l.* roundish, toothed, lobes angular. *fl.* rose; pet. twice as long as cal.; peduncles axillary, 1- to 5-fld. August. Bahamas. 1725. (B.M. 2544 as *Malva abutiloides.*) Greenhouse.

S. acerifo'lia. Starry-haired perennial of about 4 ft. *l.* 3 to 4 in. long, 5-lobed, more or less cordate; lobes acute, unequally toothed. *fl.* in terminal more or less spicate clusters, pink to white, 2 in. across. July. NW. America. 1861. (B.M. 5404.) Half-hardy.

S. ambig'ua. Sub-shrub, up to 3 ft. with numerous erect or spreading shoots. *l.* broadly ovate to nearly orbicular, usually shallowly 3-lobed, *fl.* large, grenadine pink, in an open, few to many-fld. panicle. S. United States, N. Mexico.

S. angustifo'lia. Shrub of 3 to 4 ft. *l.* lanceolate, toothed, powdery. *fl.* pink in 1- to few-fld. clusters on solitary or twin axillary peduncles; bracts bristly, deciduous. August, September. Mexico. 1780. (B.M. 2839 as *Malva angustifolia.*) Greenhouse.

S. cisplati'na. Sub-shrub of 2 to 4 ft., erect. *l.* ovate, 1 to 2 in. long, 3-lobed, coarsely roundish-toothed, hairy. *fl.* vermilion, 1 to 1¼ in. across, in 1- to few-fld. axillary racemes. May to July or later. S. America. 1798. (B.M. 5938 and S.B.F.G. s. 2, 120 as *S. miniata.*) Greenhouse.

S. el'egans. Procumbent perennial sub-shrub, stems numerous, 2 ft. or more long. *l.* rather distant, deeply 3-lobed, stalked; lobes wedge-shaped, deeply cut, wavy, starry-haired, teeth blunt. *fl.* pale with dark purple veins, usually solitary in axils of upper l.; peduncles short. July. S. Africa. 1791. Greenhouse.

S. Em'oryi. Hardy perennial of 1 to 2 ft. *l.* broadly ovate, pinnatifidly lobed and toothed. *fl.* orange-red, small, clustered on slender pedicels from l.-axils. California. 1888. (G.F. 1266.)

S. Fend'leri. Sub-shrub up to 2½ ft. with erect or spreading shoots. *l.* ovate, shallowly to deeply 3-lobed, minutely stellate-hairy on both sides. *fl.* pale reddish-orange (Saturn Red), about 1 in. across, in mostly 2-fld. clusters forming a narrow interrupted inflorescence. Summer and autumn. S. United States, N. Mexico. (B.M. n.s. 140) Tender, should be grown in a warm sunny sheltered position.

S. grossulariifol'ia. Perennial, densely whitish tomentose. *l.* broadly ovate, pedately deeply divided with cuneate-obovate divisions themselves usually deeply cleft, more or less cordate. *fl.* small, grenadine, in a many-fld. crowded inflorescence. W. United States. var. **peda'ta** with pubescence less canescent.

S. minia'ta. A synonym of *S. cisplatina*.

Sphaeralcea Munroana

S. Munroa'na. Hardy perennial of 1 to 2 ft. *l.* slightly 3-lobed, sometimes cut, with roundish teeth, base broad. *fl.* scarlet or rose, 1 in. across, numerous in axillary and terminal panicles. Summer. British Columbia southwards. (B.M. 3537 and B.R. 1306 as *Malva Munroana.*)

S. nu'tans. Shrub with branching stem of about 2 ft. *l.* cordate, 5-lobed, lobes acute, unequally toothed, starry-haired; stipules filiform. *fl.* reddish-purple, nodding, on axillary, usually 3-fld. peduncles longer than l.; bracts awl-shaped. July. Guatemala? 1852. (F.d.S. 726.) Stove.

S. obtusilo'ba. Starry-haired shrub of 3 to 4 ft. *l.* heart-shaped, somewhat 5-lobed, crenate; lobes blunt. *fl.* purple with obcordate pet. with darker claws; crowded on many-fld. axillary and terminal corymbose racemes. Chile. 1827. (B.M. 2787 as *Malva obtusiloba.*) Greenhouse.

S. peda'ta. A variety of *S. grossulariifolia*.

S. umbella'ta. Erect, branched shrub up to 10 ft. h. *l.* sub-peltate, 5- to 7-lobed, blunt; long-stalked. *fl.* fiery-violet or scarlet, large, on usually 3- (rarely 2- or 5-) fld. axillary peduncles; bracts obovate, shortly stalked, deciduous. January to April. Mexico. 1814. (B.R. 1608 as *Malva umbellata.*) Stove.

SPHAEREL'LA fragar'iae. The fungus causing Strawberry Leaf-spot. *See* **Strawberry diseases.**

SPHAERIALES. A group of fungi in the class Ascomycetes distinguished by their forming typical hard dark perithecia having a definite and distinct wall and opening by a pore or ostiole. Parasitic species of the groups include the Apple Scab fungus *Venturia inaequalis* and its near relative the Pear Scab fungus, *Venturia pirina, Mycosphaerella Fragariae* causing Strawberry Leaf-spot, *Physalospora Miyabeana* causing Black Canker in Willows and many others equally destructive, dealt with under their appropriate headings.

D. E. G.

SPHAEROCION'IUM. Included in **Hymenophyllum.**

SPHAEROCO'DON (*sphaira*, a sphere, *codon*, a bell; probably referring to the shape of the corolla). FAM. *Asclepiadacea.* A genus of 5 species of perennial herbs, native of Trop. and S. Africa. Greenhouse.

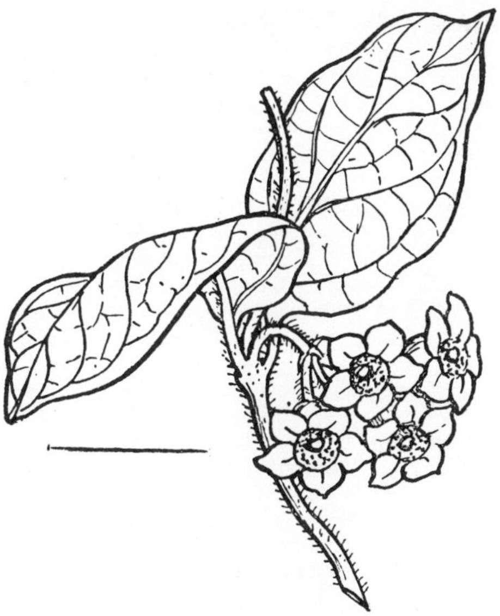

Sphaerocodon obtusifolium

S. obtusifo'lium. Herb, perennia lwith a woody rootstock. Stems erect or twining 1 to 3 ft., pubescent. *l.* oblong-ovate. *fl.* purple-red, pendulous in cymes or false umbels of 5 to 15; cor. campanulate. Nyassaland. (B.M. 7925.)

SPHAEROGY'NE. Included in **Tococa.**

SPHAEROLO'BIUM (*sphaira*, a sphere, *lobos*, a pod; in allusion to the often globular pods. FAM. *Leguminosae.* A genus of 13 species of low, glabrous shrubs, natives of Australia and Tasmania, with rush-like usually leafless stems and papilionaceous yellow or red flowers. Leaves, when present, very slender, small, and entire, sometimes alternate, sometimes opposite or in threes. Pods small, globular or compressed. Greenhouse shrubs thriving in a compost of loam, sand, leaf-soil or peat. Propagated by cuttings; seed sometimes ripens.

S. acumina'tum. A synonym of *S. medium.*

S. grandiflo'rum.* Shrub 1 to 3 ft., stems terete, rush-like, pendulous, leafless in adult plants. *l.* of young plants ⅛ to ½ in. long, linear. *fl.* in lateral pairs forming elegant racemes up to 5 in. long; standard ⅝ in. wide, notched, yellow with a red semicircle at the base; wings ¼ in. long, red; keel rather shorter, yellow. April. W. Australia. (B.M. 7308.)

S. me'dium. Shrub 1 to 2 ft., stems erect, very slender, rush-like, mostly leafless. *l.* on barren shoots only, small, thread-like, in pairs or threes. *fl.* ¼ in. long, red or orange, densely clustered in terminal spikes 3 to 6 in. long; standard orbicular. Summer. W. Australia. 1803. SYN. *S. acuminatum.*

S. vimin'eum. Shrub 1 to 2½ ft., shoots slender, wiry, mostly leafless. *l.* when present (usually on barren twigs) linear, ¼ in. long. *fl.* with standard ¼ in. wide, yellow except for a semicircle of red spots; wings and keel yellow. May to August. Australia, Tasmania. 1753. (B.M. 969.) Differs from *S. medium* in its broad, obtuse keel and shorter cal.

W. J. B.

SPHAEROPHY'SA (*sphaira*, a sphere, *physa*, a bladder; alluding to the inflated pods). FAM. *Leguminosae.* A genus of 3 species of hardy perennial herbs or sub-shrubs, natives of Russia, the Orient, and N. China. They often grow in saline soil. The following species is the only one in cultivation and should be grown in light, sandy loam in full sunshine. It occasionally bears seeds but is often short-lived. Probably a little sea-salt mixed with the soil would help.

S. salsul'a. Sub-shrub about 1½ ft., with a woody rootstock; stems erect, pale, slender, appressed, downy at first. *l.* alternate, pinnate, 1½ to 3½ in. long; lflets. in 6½ to 10½ pairs, oval to obcordate, ¼ to ⅝ in. long, downy beneath. *Racemes* axillary, 2 to 3 in. long, with 4 to 8 fl. towards the top. *fl.* papilionaceous, ⅝ in. long, purplish-red; standard ½ in. wide, rounded, notched. July, August. *Pod* oval, membranous, 1 to 1½ in. long, inflated. Russia to N. China. 1818. SYN. *Colutea caspica.*

SPHAEROP'SIDALES. A group of fungi in the class Fungi Imperfecti in which the typical fructification is the pycnidium, but no ascus-bearing fruit-body has yet been found. The group includes many well-known parasitic species, see, for example, *Septoria Apii* causing Celery Leaf-spot, *Phoma lingam* causing Swede and Turnip Dry Rot and *Ascochyta Pisi* causing Pea Pod Spot.

D. E. G.

SPHAEROP'SIS. A genus of fungi in the class Fungi Imperfecti, the chief parasitic species being *S. malorum* which causes black rot in apple fruits, serious in N. America but of little importance in Great Britain.

D. E. G.

SPHAEROP'TERIS barba'ta. A synonym of *Peranema cyatheoides.*

SPHAEROSTEPH'ANOS (*sphaeros*, globular, *stephanos*, crown; from the shape of the indusium). FAM. *Polypodiaceae.* A genus of 5 species resembling Dryopteris but with elliptical indusia emarginate at the base, attached to the linear receptacle and free all round the edge. For treatment *see* **Dryopteris.**

S. polycarp'a. *cau.* erect; rachis and lower surface villose. *Fronds* tufted, short, 2 to 3 ft. long, 1 to 1½ ft. broad, simply pinnate; pinnae close, very numerous, spreading, dwindling below to mere auricles. *Sori* small, close, ultimately confluent. Malaya. SYN. *Didymochlaena polycarpa, Mesochlaena polycarpa, Nephrodium javanicum.* var. **asplenioi'des** is a hairy form, with narrower pinnae and short oblong-deltoid lobes.

SPHAEROTHE'CA. A genus of fungi in the Erysiphaceae. In includes many well-known parasitic species, e.g. *S. mors-uvae* causing American Gooseberry Mildew, *S. pannosa* (*see* **Peach** and **Rose diseases**), and *S. humuli* on Hop.

sphagnic'ola, growing in Sphagnum.

SPHAG'NUM (*sphagnos*, moss). A genus of mosses found in all countries of the cold temperate zones. The number of species is large, the number stated being dependent upon the limits conceived to be sufficient to distinguish them adopted by different botanists. They are all alike in growing in swamps or actually in water and are therefore often called Bog Mosses. They can scarcely be confused with any other mosses. The stems are erect and often several inches long, closely packed as a rule and destitute of root-hairs; branches in clusters of 2 to 6 occur at close intervals along the stems, in some species spreading, in others reflexed. The spores are produced in short-stalked capsules and are usually conspicuous and globular, liberating the spores by a lid which often bursts off explosively. The leaves are of peculiar structure. They are numerous and have no midrib but consist of a single layer of cells of 2 different kinds, the one long and narrow containing protoplasm and chlorophyll grains, the other large, devoid of protoplasm and lying in the meshes made by the network of chlorophyllose cells. This second form of cell is kept distended by spirally arranged thickenings in the walls, the latter being pierced by holes. The outer layers of cells of the stem are similar in structure to this second type. It is to this peculiar form of cell that Sphagnum owes much of its value in horticulture. The presence of the minute holes in the cell walls make the moss almost as absorbent of water as a sponge. The species all grow in compact tufts and often cover considerable areas. The plants tend to grow upwards, the lower parts of the stems with their leaves dying at a proportionate rate below, the dead portions still retaining their power of absorbing water. Because of their environment they fail to decay and gradually add to the depth of the moss bed, finally becoming packed compactly and forming peat, which may often become feet thick in beds of great age.

When dry, being very light but firm and elastic, it makes admirable packing material. As it absorbs water so readily and retains it to a considerable extent it is very useful for packing around cuttings and young plants which are to be sent for some distance, as it keeps them moist, yielding up water as they need it. Its faculty of absorbing water also makes it an excellent medium in which to grow epiphytic orchids and plants of similar habit, which need plenty of moisture. Used in potting orchids it may often be a guide as to the condition of the rooting medium for these plants by its appearance of healthy growth or the contrary. The plants which benefit by its use have the fact noted in recommendations for potting-composts under their several genera.

SPHEDAMNOCARP'US (*sphedamnos*, maple, *karpos*, fruit; from the form of the fruit). FAM. *Malpighiaceae*. A genus of about 10 species of mostly tall climbing shrubs closely related to Acridocarpus and often included with it. They are useful for greenhouse decoration and succeed in good fibrous loam with a little peat and sand. Cuttings of half-ripe shoots will root in sand under a bell-glass with a little bottom heat.

S. prur'iens. Climber of 6 to 12 ft. *l.* opposite, 1 to 4 in. long, ovate-oblong, mucronate, silky-hairy beneath, base rounded or cordate. *fl.* golden-yellow, 1½ in. across, in sub-corymbose clusters at ends of branches; pet. shortly clawed, roundish, crisped at margins. Autumn. S. Africa. 1899. (B.M. 7894.) SYN. *Acridocarpus pruriens.*

F. G. P.

SPHENAN'DRA (*sphen*, wedge, *andros*, male or anther; from the shape of the anthers). FAM. *Scrophulariaceae*. A genus of a single species of annual or perennial herb, native of S. Africa, needing greenhouse conditions and loamy soil. Propagated by seed.

S. visco'sa. Clammy, hairy, about 1 ft. h. *l.* mostly opposite, oblong-lanceolate with a few teeth; upper l. much smaller, ovate, entire, very acute. *fl.* violet, in a loose raceme, broadly rotate with 5 broad, spreading lobes; stamens 4. June. 1773. (B.M. 217 as *Buchnera viscosa.*)

spheno-, in compound words signifying wedge-shaped.

SPHENODES'MA (*sphen*, wedge, *desme*, cluster; from the form of the inflorescence). FAM. *Verbenaceae*. A genus of about 8 species of climbing shrubs, natives of E. Indies and Malaya. Leaves opposite, entire. Flowers in rather small cymes; calyx 5-toothed; corolla tube short, limb spreading, lobes 5, ovate or oblong; stamens 5. *S. pentandra* needs stove conditions and grows well in sandy loam. It may be increased by cuttings in sand under a glass in heat.

S. pentan'dra. Climber to about 6 ft. *l.* shortly stalked, oblong, obtuse at base, attenuate-acuminate at apex, glabrous and shining above, hairy beneath. *fl.* 6 in a cluster, purple, tube as long as cal., throat white, very hairy; panicle large, leafy below; peduncles filiform. June. E. Indies. 1823. SYN. *S. Jackiana.*

SPHENOGYN'E. Included under **Ursinia.**

SPHENOT'OMA. Included under **Dracophyllum.**

SPHING'IDAE. Sphinx Moths. *See* **Hawk Moths.**

Spi'cant, from the ancient German name.

spica'tus -a -um, spike-like.

SPICE BUSH. *See* **Lindera Benzoin.**

Spiceria'nus -a -um, in honour of Mr. Spicer, tea-planter, who introduced and first cultivated many species of Orchids in this country.

spicif'erus -a -um, spicig'erus -a -um, bearing a spike or point.

spicula'tus -a -um, having a short point or spike.

SPIDER FLOWER. *See* **Cleome spinosa.**

SPIDER ORCHID. *See* **Bartholina pectinata, Ophrys sphegodes.**

SPIDERS. The true Spiders (Order *Araneae*) belong to the Class *Arachnida*, which includes Scorpions, Mites, and Gall-mites. They are characterized by having 2 body regions, the cephalothorax (a fusion of the head and thorax) and the abdomen. They have neither wings nor antennae (feelers), but possess 4 pairs of legs, several simple eyes, and spinnerets towards the tip of the abdomen, through which silk is extruded. The so-called Red Spider is a Mite, being 6-legged when young and 8-legged when adult, and with no clearly defined body-segments (*see* **Mites**). All Spiders are predatory and live on the juices of insects, especially Midges, Flies, and Aphides and are, therefore, beneficial creatures from the gardener's point of view. Some do not spin webs, but either hunt their prey (Zebra-spider) or lie in wait for their victims (Crab-spiders). The greater number, however, rely on webs and snares for capturing their prey. The silk is used not only for webs and snares, but also for spinning a cocoon for the eggs and for letting the spider down from a height. The young of many web-spinning species pay out threads of silk (Gossamer) from their spinnerets to enable them to take an aerial voyage helped by a breeze and in this way are transported from place to place.

Crab-spiders are often seen lurking in flowers where their body colour tones with that of the flower in which they are resting awaiting the visit of some pollinating insect. The Garden Spider, *Aranea diadema*, constructs a beautifully patterned web which is a conspicuous object on shrubs and palings, especially when the silken threads are outlined with droplets of water in late summer. The 'Harvesters' or 'Harvest Men', which belong to a closely related Order (*Opiliones*), are long-legged creatures resembling wingless Crane Flies which feed on insects and small spiders. They are seen stalking through long grass and amongst stubble, and are often caught on grease-bands attached to the stems of fruit-trees.

G. F. W.

SPIDERWORT. *See* **Tradescantia virginiana.**

SPIELMAN'NIA africa'na. A synonym of *Oftia africana*.

SPIGE'LIA (in honour of Adrian van der Spiegel, 1578–1625, Professor of Anatomy at Padua, and botanical writer). FAM. *Loganiaceae*. A genus of about 30 species of glabrous or starry-hairy annual or perennial herbs or rarely sub-shrubs, natives of Trop. and N. America. Leaves opposite, often membranous, usually penninerved, rarely with 3 or 5 veins, connected by stipules or a transverse membrane. Flowers red, yellow, or purplish, long or small, in 1-sided, many- or few-flowered spikes; calyx 5-parted, segments narrow; corolla tubular or salver-shaped, lobes 5, valvate, at length spreading; stamens 5, affixed to tube. A compost of loam and peat is best. *S. anthelmia* may be propagated by seeds, the other two also by cuttings.

S. anthel'mia. Pink Root (of Demerara). Annual, 1½ ft. h. *l.* near base opposite, upper in whorls of 4, ovate-oblong, narrowed to both ends, nearly sessile. *fl.* purplish-white; cor. slender, ½ in. long; spikes 1 to 4 in upper l.-axils. July. Guatemala to Brazil. 1759. (B.M. 2359.) Stove.

S. marilan'dica.* Indian Pink; Maryland Pink Root; Worm Grass. Perennial with unbranched erect stems, 6 to 18 in. h. *l.* ovate-lanceolate, acute, sessile. *fl.* red without, yellow within; cor. 1½ in. long, lobes lanceolate; spikes simple or forked, short. July. N. America. 1694. (B.M. 80; L.B.C. 930.) Hardy.

S. splen'dens.* Perennial, about 18 in. h. *l.* obovate-oblong, acuminate, 4 to 5 in. long, slightly hairy, narrowed to a short stalk. *fl.* bright scarlet, over 1 in. long; cor. cylindric, slightly inflated upwards; spikes several near apex of stem, recurved. July. Mexico, Guatemala. 1860. (B.M. 5268; G.F. 481.) Perennial.

SPIGNEL. *See* **Meum athamanticum.**

SPIKE. An inflorescence with the flowers sessile along an unbranched axis or rachis.

SPIKELET. A secondary spike, especially the small collection of florets in grasses or sedges.

SPIKENARD or **NARD.** *See* **Nardostachys Jatamansii.**

SPIKENARD, PLOUGHMAN'S. *See* **Baccharis.**

SPILOGRAPH'A alterna'ta. *See* **Rose-hip Fly.**

Spin'a Christi, Christ's thorn.

SPINACH (*Spinacia oleracea*). An annual grown for its leaves to be cooked and served as a vegetable. It may be raised in any quantity from seed sown successionally through spring and summer. It does best in a deep rich soil in a rather moist situation through the summer; for the winter crop a drier and rather warm position should be selected. The summer crops are usually grown in spaces between other vegetables as they only need a few weeks from sowing to gathering and so can be grown without interfering with their neighbours. The quicker it is grown the better the production of large succulent leaves, and therefore the soil should be thoroughly manured and cultivated. It is waste of time to sow on dry, poorly worked soil. The first sowing should be made at the latter end of February or early in March as soon as weather and the condition of the soil permit. If sown by itself the drills should be 1 ft. apart and 1 in. deep but space is better utilized by sowing between other crops such as peas and beans. No more should be sown at one time than is needed, for it quickly runs to seed. Sowings should follow at fortnightly intervals through summer until the middle of August or middle of September when crops to stand the winter are sown. If the ground is dry it is a good plan to water it thoroughly a little before the seed is sown or to sow the seed, after soaking it for some hours (4 to 24) in water, on newly turned ground. When the seedlings are up they should be thinned to 6 to 8 in. apart so as to give room for the development of large leaves. Overcrowding gives small plants which run quickly to seed and are useless. Well-developed plants may measure 15 in. across and give a correspondingly large and useful crop. In picking, the largest leaves should be taken, especially in winter and spring when new growth is slow.

For the crop to stand the winter the first sowing should be made in mid-August and this should be followed by 2 others at fortnightly intervals. These sowings are best made on raised beds to prevent any stagnation of moisture and the plants may be allowed to stand more closely, say, in rows 9 in. apart with 4 or 5 in. between the plants after thinning. Arrangements should be made to protect part of the crop when severe weather is forecast so that picking may not be interfered with. Picking from these sowings should be possible from October to May when the first spring-sown crop will be ready.

Weeds must be kept down and in dry weather frequent watering is called for. Heavy dressings of organic matter added during digging are a great aid in preventing premature drying of the soil and rapid running to seed and an application of nitrate of soda at the rate of ¾ lb. to the square rod, twice during the development of the crop, is valuable; 1 oz. of seed will suffice to sow a square rod. The seed has an average life of at least 5 years. There are 2 main forms, round-seeded and prickly seeded. It has long been thought that the prickly seeded varieties are hardier and therefore better for winter crops but experience shows that the round-seeded varieties stand equally well and grow away well in spring, and from the point of view of hardiness can be equally relied upon, while in many instances they are preferred from other points of view. For varieties *see* Supplement.

Among the substitutes for Spinach, Spinach Beet (q.v. and *see* **Beet**) has come to be called Spinach in some districts, but the 2 plants are quite distinct and should not be confused.

DISEASES. The commonest disease of Spinach is Downy Mildew due to the fungus *Peronospora effusa* which may do serious injury to this crop. The leaves show yellowish patches above and the fungus can be detected as a violet-grey mealy growth beneath, which spreads rapidly in moist weather. Spraying is not advisable on Spinach and remedial measures must take the form of picking off affected leaves or dusting with sulphur. It is essential to have well-drained soil for Spinach so as to avoid damp conditions as far as possible. There is also a virus disease of Spinach known as Blight, caused by the virus of Cucumber yellow-mottle mosaic in which the Spinach plant shows yellowing of the leaves starting with the younger ones which become distorted and puckered with the margins inrolled, while the older ones become limp and lie flat. They gradually die until only a few are left in the centre. The disease possibly comes from vegetable marrows but certainly all affected Spinach plants should be destroyed. It is said that this virus is to a large extent averted by sowing in late September, as early sown crops are more likely to be affected. The Leaf Spot due to *Heterosporium variabile* causes circular greyish-brown sunken spots about ¼ in. across but they may increase so much as to destroy the leaves. Weak plants are most affected so that good cultivation and removal of affected leaves are the best methods of control. With many Spinach diseases, especially those of the virus type, it is well to remember that Spinach Beet can also be infected and as this plant overwinters it may carry a disease from one season to another.

D. E. G.

SPINACH BEET (*Beta vulgaris Cicla*). Spinach Beet or Perpetual Spinach is a variety of *Beta vulgaris* grown for its leaves which are used as a substitute for Spinach. It withstands hot weather better than true Spinach and is by some people preferred as a vegetable. It is treated in the same way as the Garden Beet (q.v.), being sown in April for the summer and autumn crop of leaves and about the first week in July for winter and spring supplies, the rows being 15 in. apart and seedlings thinned to 8 in. apart. The soil should be richer than for the growing of beetroots as it is important to encourage the development of large foliage and as soon as the leaves are large enough they should be gathered to encourage the growth of further young leaves. For use in severe winter weather the roots of the July-sown plants may be lifted and grown on in the greenhouse or frame. Half oz. of seed should be enough for 1 sq. rod.

SPINACH, MOUNTAIN. *See* **Atriplex hortensis.**

Spinach, New Zealand. *See* **Tetragonia expansa** and **New Zealand Spinach.**

SPINACH, WILD. Name sometimes used for *Chenopodium Bonus-Henricus*.

SPINA'CIA (*spina*, prickle; from the prickly processes of the fruit in some forms). FAM. *Chenopodiaceae*. A genus of 4 species of annual, erect, glabrous herbs, natives of the E. Mediterranean region. Leaves alternate, stalked, often large, triangular-ovate or hastate, entire or sinuately toothed. Flowers dioecious, rarely hermaphrodite, glomerate; male clusters in terminal interrupted spikes, female often axillary. *S. oleracea* is the valuable Spinach, q.v. for cultivation.

S. olera'cea. Erect, large. Stem hollow, about 2 ft. h. *l.* large, thick, succulent, somewhat triangular, deep green; stalks long. *Male fl.* green, in long, terminal spikes; *female* axillary, sessile, clustered. June. *Fr.* in some varieties round (**glab'ra**), in some prickly (**spino'sa**). 1568.

spinal'ba, having white prickles or spines.

SPINDLE-TREE. *See* **Euonymus europaeus.**

SPINE. A sharp-pointed woody leaf-stalk, stipule, branch, &c.

spines'cens, spiny.

spi'nidens, having prickly teeth.

spinosis'simus -a -um, very spiny.

spino'sus -a -um, spiny.

SPINOVI'TIS. Included in **Vitis.** *See* **V. Davidi.**

spinulif'erus -a -um, bearing small spines.

spinulo'sus -a -um, having small spines.

SPIRAE'A (*speiraia*, an ancient Greek name for a plant used for garlands). FAM. *Rosaceae*. A genus of about 80 species of deciduous shrubs with alternate leaves usually toothed or lobed and shortly stalked. Flowers small, ranging from $\frac{1}{6}$ to $\frac{2}{5}$ in. in width, white, pink, or carmine, borne in fascicles, umbel-like racemes, roundish or flattish corymbs, or panicles; petals 5, rounded; stamens 15 to 60; pistils 5. Fruit dry, erect, with the style adhering at the top and the calyx at the base. The genus is widely spread over the N. Hemisphere. In the Bentham and Hooker conception of the genus, it included the following genera of shrubs, here treated separately: Chamaebatiaria, Holodiscus, Luetkea, Petrophytum, Sibiraea, Sorbaria, as well as several herbaceous plants (Aruncus, Filipendula).

From the cultivator's point of view Spiraea proper may be divided into 2 sections: (1) Flowers white, in simple umbels or umbel-like racemes, or in corymbs produced at the end of short leafy twigs springing from the branches made the previous season, e.g. *S. Thunbergii*, *S. hypericifolia*, *S. canescens*, *S. nipponica*, &c., flowering April to June. (2) Flowers pink to rosy crimson as well as white and produced later on the current season's shoots in compound panicles, either flattish as in *S. japonica* or pyramidal as in *S. Douglasii*; flowering June to September.

Very many hybrids have been raised in gardens, some of the best of which are dealt with in the following notes.

Cultivation is simple. All like a sunny position and a soil of at least moderate quality, enriched if necessary by occasional top-dressings of manure. As regards pruning, the first or early blooming section should be pruned immediately after flowering by thinning out and cutting clean away weak and worn-out shoots; the second section may be pruned at any time during winter by shortening, even nearly back to the old wood, the shoots that have flowered. The flowering period of the japonica group may be lengthened by removing the flower-clusters as soon as they fade.

Nearly all the species can be propagated by late summer cuttings, by layers, or by seeds. The suckering species can be increased by division.

[Catalogues offer plants of several other genera not mentioned above under Spiraea, e.g. Astilbe, Neillia, Physocarpus, Sorbaria often so appear. They should be sought under their correct names.]

KEY:

1.	*Fl. white, in simple umbels or umbel-like racemes*	2
1.	*Infl. compound, i.e. paniculate or with rays of umbel branched*	26
2.	*Umbels, upper at least sessile, sometimes with a very few basal l.*	3
2.	*Umbel-like racemes, lower at least on leafy shoots*	8
3.	*Lvs. entire or toothed near apex only; stamens about as long as pet.*	4
3.	*Lvs. toothed; stamens much shorter than pet.*	6
4.	*Shrub dwarf, shoots angled, lvs. obovate to elliptic*	S. calcicola
4.	*Taller, shoots nearly round*	5
5.	*Lvs. often toothed at apex; umbels sessile*	S. hypericifolia
5.	*Lvs. entire, lower umbels stalked*	S. × cinerea
6.	*Lvs. linear-lanceolate, glabrous*	S. Thunbergii
6.	*Lvs. ovate to oblong-lanceolate*	7
7.	*Umbels all sessile, 3- to 6-fld.*	S. prunifolia
7.	*Lower umbels stalked*	S. × arguta
8.	*Lvs. entire or toothed only near apex*	9
8.	*Lvs. toothed or slightly lobed*	15
9.	*Lvs. 3-nerved*	S. crenata
9.	*Lvs. pinnate-nerved*	10
10.	*Infl. and lvs. pubescent*	11
10.	*Infl. and lvs. glabrous or nearly so*	12
11.	*Buds pointed, longer than l.-stalks*	S mollifolia
11.	*Buds ovoid, obtuse, shorter than l.-stalks*	S. cana
12.	*Buds long-pointed*	13
12.	*Buds ovoid, small*	S. alpina
13.	*Lvs. oblong, entire, buds longer than l.-stalk*	S gemmata
13.	*Lvs. often toothed at apex, buds shorter than l.-stalk*	14
14.	*Lvs. oblanceolate to oblong, $1\frac{1}{2}$ to 2 in. long*	S. trichocarpa
14.	*Lvs. oblong to roundish, $\frac{1}{2}$ to $1\frac{1}{4}$ in. long*	S. nipponica
15.	*Stamens longer than pet., infl. racemose*	16
15.	*Stamens not longer than pet., infl. umbel-like*	18
16.	*Shoots angled*	17
16.	*Shoots round; shoots and lvs. beneath often downy*	S. media
17.	*Shoots and lvs. glabrous*	S. chamaedryfolia
17.	*Shoots downy, lvs. glabrous*	S. virgata
18.	*Lvs. downy*	19
18.	*Lvs. glabrous*	23
19.	*Lvs. obovate with yellowish or tawny tomentum*	20
19.	*Tomentum not yellowish or tawny*	21
20.	*Tomentum yellowish; lvs. $1\frac{1}{2}$ to 2 in. long; fl. $\frac{2}{5}$ in. wide*	S. chinensis
20.	*Tomentum tawny; lvs. $\frac{1}{2}$ to $1\frac{1}{4}$ in. long; fl. $\frac{1}{3}$ in. wide*	S. sinobrahuica
21.	*Lvs. ovate, sharply serrate, downy*	S. Gieseleriana
21.	*Lvs. grey tomentose beneath*	22
22.	*Lvs. rhombic-ovate, downy above*	S. pubescens
22.	*Lvs. ovate to oblong, glabrous above*	S. blanda
23.	*Lvs. acute*	24
23.	*Lvs. obtuse*	25
24.	*Lvs. pinnate-nerved, rhombic-lanceolate*	S. cantoniensis
24.	*Lvs. indistinctly 3-nerved, rhombic-ovate, often 3- to 5-lobed*	S. × Vanhouttei
25.	*Lvs. doubly serrate, dark green above*	S. Schinabeckii
25.	*Lvs. incised, often 3-lobed and palmately veined, pale bluish-green beneath*	S. trilobata
26.	*Infl. corymbose*	27
26.	*Infl. paniculate*	47
27.	*Corymbs on short lateral shoots*	28
27.	*Corymbs terminal on tall shoots of the year*	36
28.	*Fl. pink, dioecious; a spreading shrub*	S. bella
28.	*Fl. white, perfect*	29
29.	*Winter buds about as long as l.-stalks*	30
29.	*Winter buds short, ovoid*	31
30.	*Lvs. and shoots glabrous*	S. longigemmis
30.	*Lvs. downy on veins beneath, shoots downy when young*	S. Rosthornii
31.	*Stamens much longer than pet.*	S. Miyabei
31.	*Stamens about as long as pet.*	32
32.	*Shoots angled, winter buds pointed, with 2 scales*	S. canescens
32.	*Shoots more or less rounded, winter buds blunt, with many scales*	33
33.	*Infl. downy*	34
33.	*Infl. glabrous or nearly so, lvs. downy above*	S. Wilsonii
34.	*Lvs. entire or nearly so, glabrous above, shoots reddish*	S. Veitchii
34.	*Lvs. toothed, at least near apex*	35

35. *Lvs.* 1 *in. or less long* — S. Sargentiana
35. *Lvs.* 1¼ *to* 3 *in. long* — S. Henryi
36. *Stamens about as long as pet.; fl. white; dwarf shrub* — 37
36. *Stamens longer than pet.; in upright shrub* — 38
37. *Glabrous* — S. decumbens
37. *Greyish downy* — S. Hacquetii
38. *Infl. very large, flat, with later single corymbs below* — 39
38. *Infl. a single corymb* — 45
39. *Lvs. under* 1 *in. long, wrinkled; plant of* 9 *in. h.* — S. bullata
39. *Lvs. over* 1½ *in. long, not wrinkled* — 40
40. *Shoots angled, fl. white* — S. albiflora
40. *Shoots striped or nearly round, fl. rose (rarely white)* — 41
41. *Shoots striped, glabrous* — 42
41. *Shoots and lvs. more or less downy, at least, when young; shoots nearly round* — 43
42. *Lvs. ovate-lanceolate* — S. japonica Bumalda
42. *Lvs. elliptic* — S. × Foxii
43. *Lvs. yellow-pubescent on veins beneath* — S. × revirescens
43. *Lvs. not yellow-pubescent* — 44
44. *Fl.* ⅛ *to* ¼ *in. across, ripe follicles spreading* — S. japonica
44. *Fl.* ⅙ *to* ⅓ *in. across, ripe follicles upright* — S. × Margaritae
45. *Fl. rose* — S. densiflora
45. *Fl. white* — 46
46. *Shoots quite round* — S. corymbosa
46. *Shoots striped* — S. betulifolia
47. *Panicle about as broad as long* — 48
47. *Panicle much longer than broad* — 50
48. *Panicle small, pale rose* — S. brachybotrys
48. *Panicle large* — 49
49. *Lvs. pale green, downy beneath* — S. × sanssouciana
49. *Lvs. grey, downy beneath* — S. × Watsoniana
50. *Lvs. downy beneath; fl. pink* — 51
50. *Lvs. glabrous or nearly so* — 53
51. *Shoots and lvs. beneath light brownish, lvs. oblong-ovate, acute* — S. tomentosa
51. *Lvs. grey- or white-downy beneath* — 52
52. *Lvs. acute at both ends, grey-downy beneath* — S. Billiardii
52. *Lvs. obtuse, white-downy beneath* — S. japonica
53. *Lvs. coarsely serrate above middle, obtuse* — S. Menziesii
53. *Lvs. finely serrate, acute* — 54
54. *Fl. light pink, lower branches of infl. not longer than their bracts* — S. salicifolia
54. *Fl. whitish, lower branches of infl. spreading, longer than their bracts* — 55
55. *Infl. downy; lvs. oblong or oblanceolate* — S. alba
55. *Infl. glabrous; lvs. elliptic* — S. latifolia

S. acutifo'lia. A variety of *S. hypericifolia.*

S. Aitchison'ii. A synonym of *Sorbaria Aitchisonii.*

S. al'ba. Erect suckering shrub up to 6 ft., shoots red-brown, angled. *l.* narrowly ovate to oblanceolate, 1½ to 2 in. long, sharply toothed. *fl.* white, in much branched panicles 6 to 8, sometimes 12 in. long. July, August. E. United States. 1759. (G.C. 11 (1879), 753.) Syn. *S. lanceolata, S. salicifolia paniculata.*

S. albiflo'ra. Closely akin to, and often regarded as a var. of, *S. japonica*, but of dwarfer, compact habit, shoots angled, glabrous. *l.* 2 to 3 in. long, lanceolate, coarsely toothed, glabrous and glaucous beneath. *fl.* white, in dense clusters, 1½ to 2 in. wide, from the uppermost l.-axils. June. Japan. 1868. Syn. *S. leucantha.*

S. alpi'na. Shrub up to 5 ft., shoots downy at first, angled, red-brown. *l.* ½ to 1 in. long, ⅛ in. wide, oblanceolate to narrowly oblong, entire, glabrous. *fl.* yellowish-white, ⅙ in. wide, in small umbels terminating short leafy twigs. May, June. 1806. NE. Asia. Distinct by its small, narrow l.

S. Anthony Waterer. *See under* **S. japonica.**

S. ariaefo'lia. A variety of *Holodiscus discolor.*

S. × argu'ta.* Shrub 6 to 8 ft., of rounded, bushy shape; twigs very slender, downy. *l.* oblanceolate, pointed, ¾ to 1½ in. long, entire or toothed towards the apex. *fl.* ⅓ in. wide, pure white, in clusters of 4 to 8, borne thickly along the twigs, each on a slender glabrous stalk ½ in. long. April, May. Hybrid from *S. crenata, S. Thunbergii,* and *S. hypericifolia.* The most beautiful of early Spiraeas. (G.C. 22 (1897), 3; B.T.S. 1. 26.)

S. bel'la. Shrub to 4 ft., shoots angled, slightly hairy. *l.* 1 to 2 in. long, ovate, slenderly pointed, doubly toothed above the middle, glaucous beneath. *fl.* ⅓ in. across, rose, in loose terminal clusters ¾ to 1½ in. wide. June. Himalaya. 1820. (B.M. 2426; L.B.C. 1268.)

S. betulifo'lia. Shrub to 2 or 3 ft., shoots glabrous, red-brown. *l.* broadly oval, rounded at apex, 1 to 1½ in. long, bluntish-toothed, grey-green beneath and almost or quite glabrous. *fl.* white, densely set in corymbose clusters 1½ to 2½ in. across; fl.-stalks glabrous. June. NE. Asia, Japan. Akin to *S. corymbosa* which has downy fl.-stalks.

S. × Billiar'dii.* Shrub up to 6 or 7 ft., shoots downy. *l.* oblong to oblong-lanceolate, pointed, cuneate, sharply toothed, 2 to 3½ in. long, grey-downy beneath. *fl.* ¼ in. wide, bright rose, in several dense, downy, pyramidal panicles 4 to 8 in. long at and near the end of the shoot. Summer. A fine hybrid between *S. Douglasii* and *S. salicifolia* raised in France about 1850. Near *S. Menziesii triumphans.*

S. × blan'da. Shrub up to 6 or 7 ft. with arching branches. *l.* ovate to oblong, 1 to 2½ in. long, cuneate, pointed, sharply toothed, grey-downy beneath. *fl.* pure white, ⅜ in. wide, borne on downy-stalked hemispherical umbels 1½ in. wide. May, June. Hybrid between *S. cantoniensis* and *S. chinensis.* About 1876. Syn. *S. Reevesiana nova.*

S. × brachybot'rys (*S. canescens × S. Douglasii*). Vigorous shrub up to 8 ft. with much of the vigour and grace of *S. canescens. l.* oblong or ovate, ¾ to 1¾ in. long, ⅓ to ⅝ in. wide, sparsely toothed, grey-felted beneath. *fl.* bright pink, in panicles 1½ to 3 in. long and wide. June. Syn. *S. pruinosa.*

S. bractea'ta. A synonym of *S. nipponica.*

S. bulla'ta.* Shrub of compact habit, 10 to 15 in., shoots rusty-downy. *l.* ½ to 1¼ in. long, nearly as wide, roundish-ovate, strongly toothed, puckered. *fl.* small, scarlet-rose, borne very freely in clusters 2 to 3 in. across, terminating the shoots and covering the whole plant. July. Japan. 1879. (G.F. 1886, 1215.) Suitable for the rock-garden.

S. Bumal'da. A synonym of *S. japonica Bumalda* or may be a hybrid between *S. japonica* and *S. albiflora.*

S. caespito'sa. A synonym of *Petrophytum caespitosum.*

S. callo'sa. A synonym of *S. japonica.*

S. calcic'ola. Shrub 3 to 6 ft., shoots long, slender, arching, glabrous, reddish. *l.* ¼ in. long, ⅙ in. wide, obovate to oval, cuneate, rounded at the apex, not toothed, glabrous. *fl.* white, rosy tinted outside, borne in numerous umbels of 6 to 8, forming altogether a slender infl. 4 to 5 in. long. June. China. 1910. Graceful, very distinct shrub with very small l., found wild on limestone.

S. ca'na. Shrub 3 to 4 ft., of dense twiggy habit, shoots grey-downy. *l.* narrowly oval to ovate, tapered at both ends, ⅓ to 1 in. long, half as wide, mostly entire, covered, especially beneath, with grey, silky down. *fl.* white, ¼ in. wide, in dense clusters up to 1 in. across. May. SE. Europe. 1825.

S. canes'cens.* Shrub 6 to 12 ft., branches arching or pendulous; shoots angular, downy. *l.* ½ to 1 in. long, ⅓ to ⅝ in. wide, oval or obovate, toothed at apex, tapered to a very short stalk, greyish-green, downy beneath. *fl.* white in hemispherical corymbs 1 to 2 in. across at ends of short leafy twigs. June, July. Himalaya. 1843. Syn. *S. flagelliformis.* (G.C. 43 (1908), 90). One of the finest species sending out long shoots each year which the following season bear the crowded corymbs from end to end.

S. cantonien'sis. Glabrous shrub of spreading, graceful growth up to 6 ft. *l.* lozenge-shaped, 1 to 2½ in. long, ½ to ¾ in. wide, deeply toothed or 3-lobed, rather glaucous beneath. *fl.* white, ⅓ in. wide, borne in hemispherical clusters 1 to 2 in. across on a leafy stalk. June. China, Japan. 1824. (B.R. 30, 10 as *S. Reevesiana.*) var. **flore ple'no,*** *fl.* many-petalled, ½ in. across, very popular in Italy and S. France, where it succeeds to perfection and is very beautiful in April. Too tender to be a real success in most parts of Britain. (F. d. S. 1097.)

S. carpinifo'lia. A synonym of *S. latifolia.*

S. chamaedryfo'lia. Suckering shrub, 6 to 8 ft., shoots angled, glabrous, zigzag. *l.* ovate to ovate-lanceolate, tapered at the base, 1½ to 3 in. long, half as wide, coarsely toothed, slightly downy beneath. *fl.* ⅓ in. across, white, borne at ends of leafy shoots in corymbose racemes 1½ in. across. May. NE. Asia. 1789. (B.R. 1222.) Syn. *S. flexuosa.* var. **ulmifo'lia,** *l.* ovate, rounded at the base, doubly toothed, *fl.* larger. (L.B.C. 1042 as *S. ulmifolia.*)

S. chinen'sis. Shrub 5 or 6 ft., shoots yellowish-downy. *l.* 1½ to 2 in. long, ¾ to 1¼ in. wide, broadly ovate, sometimes obscurely 3-lobed, clothed beneath with yellowish felt. *fl.* white, ⅜ in. wide, borne on densely downy-stalked clusters 1 to 2 in. across. June. N. China. 1843. Distinguished by its yellowish pubescence. (B.R. 33, 38 as *S. pubescens.*) Not very hardy.

S. × ciner'ea. Shrub up to 5 or 6 ft. *l.* oblong, pointed, 1 to 2 in. long, usually entire but sometimes with 1 or 2 teeth at the apex. *fl.* white, ¼ in. wide, in many-fld. umbels borne on short leafy stalks at the upper part of the shoot, but stalkless near the apex. May. Hybrid between *S. cana* and *S. hypericifolia.* About 1880.

S. confu'sa. A synonym of *S. media.*

S. corymbo'sa. Shrub 1 to 2½ ft., shoots glabrous, round. *l.* 1 to 3 in. long, oval, ovate or roundish, coarsely toothed, glabrous and rather glaucous beneath. *fl.* white, ⅙ in. wide, densely packed in rounded clusters 2 to 4 in. across. June. E. United States. 1819. (L.B.C. 671.)

S. crena'ta. Shrub 3 to 5 ft., shoots downy at first. *l.* oblanceolate to broadly obovate, ¾ to 1¼ in. long, ¼ to 1 in. wide, shallowly toothed at the apex, distinctly 3-veined, greyish-green, downy beneath at first. *fl.* white, ⅜ in. wide, crowded on hemispherical umbels scarcely 1 in. across terminating short leafy twigs. May. SE. Europe to Siberia. 1800. (L.B.C. 1252.)

S. crispifo'lia. A synonym of *S. bullata.*

S. decum'bens. Glabrous shrub, often prostrate, up to 8 or 10 in. h., shoots slender erect. *l.* ½ to 1½ in. long, obovate to oval, tapered at both ends, sharply and coarsely toothed towards the apex. *fl.* white, ⅓ in. wide, in loose clusters about 1½ in. across. June. Mts. of SE. Europe. 1830. (G.C. 11 (1879), 752.) Suitable for the rock-garden. Syn. *S. procumbens.* var. **tomento'sa,** a synonym of *S. Hacquetii.*

S. densiflo'ra.* Shrub up to 2 ft., shoots glabrous, round, brown. *l.* oval or ovate, toothed near the rounded ends, $\frac{2}{3}$ to $1\frac{3}{4}$ in. long, glabrous. *fl.* rose, densely packed in dome-shaped clusters 1 to $1\frac{1}{2}$ in. wide. June. Western N. America. 1854. Attractive free-flowering, dwarf shrub.

S. dis'color. A synonym of *Holodiscus discolor.*

S. Douglas'ii. Shrub 4 to 6 ft., forming a thicket of erect stems, reddish and finely downy when young. *l.* narrow-oblong, $1\frac{1}{2}$ to 4 in. long, coarsely toothed towards apex, grey-felted beneath. *fl.* purlish-rose, densely set in erect panicles 4 to 8 in. long; fl.-stalk and cal. grey-downy. June, July. Western N. America. 1827. (B.M. 5151.)

S. flagellifor'mis. A synonym of *S. canescens.*

S. flexuo'sa. A synonym of *S. chamaedryfolia.*

S. × **Fox'ii** (*S. corymbosa* × *S. japonica*). Compact shrub 2 to 3 ft., shoots nearly glabrous. *l.* oval to lanceolate, toothed except at the base, 1 to $2\frac{1}{2}$ in. long, glabrous. *fl.* white or pinkish in clusters 1 to $1\frac{1}{2}$ in. wide, forming collectively a flattish compound panicle 4 to 8 in. wide. June. About 1860. (R.H. 1900, 117.)

S. gemma'ta. Shrub 6 to 9 ft., shoots slender, angled, reddish, glabrous; buds slender, longer than the l.-stalk. *l.* narrowly oblong, $\frac{1}{2}$ to 1 in. long, $\frac{1}{8}$ to $\frac{1}{3}$ wide, entire and pointed, or with about 3 teeth at the apex, glabrous. *fl.* white, $\frac{1}{4}$ in. wide, in corymbs 1 in. across. May. China. 1886. SYN. *S. mongolica.* Distinct by its long, pointed l.-buds.

S. × **Gieseleria'na** (*S. cana* × *S. chamaedryfolia*). Shrub 4 to 6 ft., shoots downy. *l.* 1 to $1\frac{1}{2}$ in. long, ovate, usually more or less sharply toothed, sometimes entire, downy. *fl.* white, $\frac{1}{3}$ in. wide, borne on leafy-stalked umbels. May, June. Of garden origin. About 1880.

S. Hacquet'ii. Shrub 8 to 12 in., with often prostrate stems. *l.*, fl.-stalk, and cal. all downy. *l.* $\frac{1}{2}$ to 1 in. long, obovate, coarsely and sharply toothed at the end. *fl.* white, $\frac{1}{4}$ in. wide, in loose clusters 1 to $1\frac{1}{2}$ in. across. June. Italy. 1885. Akin to *S. decumbens,* but distinct by its downiness. Useful for the rock-garden. SYN. *S. decumbens tomentosa, S. lancifolia.*

Spiraea Henryi

S. Hen'ryi.* Shrub 6 to 10 ft., spreading more in width. *l.* $2\frac{1}{2}$ to $3\frac{1}{2}$ in. long, oblanceolate to narrowly oblong, coarsely toothed towards apex, downy beneath. *fl.* white, $\frac{1}{4}$ in. wide, in rounded clusters 2 in. across, at end of short, leafy twigs; fl.-stalk and cal. downy. June. China. 1900. (B.M. 8270.) Handsome species akin to *S. Wilsonii* which has infl. and fl.-stalks glabrous.

S. hypericifo'lia. Bushy shrub up to 6 ft., shoots arching, twiggy, downy when young. *l.* narrowly obovate, $\frac{3}{4}$ to $1\frac{1}{4}$ in. long, $\frac{1}{4}$ to $\frac{1}{2}$ in. wide, often with a few teeth at apex, greyish-green, slightly downy beneath. *fl.* pure white, $\frac{1}{4}$ in. across, in stalkless clusters of 5 or more, each fl. on a slender, downy stalk $\frac{3}{5}$ in. long. May. SE. Europe to Siberia and N. Asia. 17th century. var. **acu'ta,** *l.* oblanceolate, *fl.* yellowish-white. SYN. *S. acutifolia.*

S. japon'ica.* Erect shrub, 3 to 5 ft., shoots soon glabrous. *l.* lanceolate to ovate-oblong, 2 to 4 in. long, cuneate, coarsely and sharply toothed, soon glabrous, rather glaucous beneath. *fl.* $\frac{1}{4}$ in. wide, rosy-red, in flat clusters springing from uppermost l.-axils, making altogether a compound infl. 6 to 12 in. wide. June, July Japan. 1870. SYN. *S. callosa.* var. **atrosanguin'ea,** *l.* reddish when young, *fl.* crimson; **Bumal'da,** dwarf, 1 to 2 ft., *fl.* carmine **'Anthony Waterer'*** is a superior form of this, with *fl.* brilliant carmine, *l.* often variegated. 1890. (G.C. 14 (1893) 365.); **Fortun'ei,** tall, *fl.* pink. (B.M. 5164.); **glabra'ta,** *l.* and infl. glabrous, *fl.* pink; **macrophylla,** *l.* up to 6 in. long, puckered, *infl.* poor; **ruber'rima,** more compact, up to 4 ft., *fl.* deep rose.

S. laeviga'ta. A synonym of *Sibiraea laevigata.*

S. lanceola'ta. A synonym of *S. alba.*

S. lancifo'lia. A synonym of *S. Hacquetii.*

S. latifo'lia. Shrub, 5 to 6 ft., shoots glabrous, angled, reddish-brown. *l.* roundish oval or ovate, $1\frac{1}{2}$ to 3 in. long, coarsely toothed, glabrous and rather glaucous beneath *fl.* white or blush-tinted, in glabrous, broadly pyramidal panicles. June to August. N. America. 1789. SYN. *S. carpinifolia, S. salicifolia latifolia.* Differs from *S. salicifolia* by its white fl. and glabrous character.

S. leucan'tha. A synonym of *S. albiflora.*

S. Lindleya'na. A synonym of *Sorbaria tomentosa.*

S. longigem'mis. Shrub, 4 to 5 ft., shoots angular, glabrous; winter buds, $\frac{1}{3}$ in. long. *l.* $1\frac{1}{2}$ to 3 in. long, ovate-lanceolate, sharply toothed, slender-pointed, bright green and glabrous above, at first hairy on the veins beneath. *fl.* white, $\frac{1}{4}$ in. wide, in loose rounded clusters terminating leafy twigs and 2 to $3\frac{1}{2}$ in. across. May. China. 1887. (G. and F. 7, 345.) Distinct by its long slender buds; the similar *S. gemmata* has much smaller l.

S. × **Margari'tae.*** Hybrid shrub up to 4 or 5 ft., parentage shared by *S. albiflora, S. japonica,* and *S. corymbosa*; shoots downy, reddish-brown. *l.* 2 to $3\frac{1}{2}$ in. long, narrowly oval or oblong, cuneate, coarsely and doubly toothed. *fl.* $\frac{1}{3}$ in. wide, bright rosy-pink, in large flat corymbs up to 6 in. across. July to September. Originated before 1890.

Spiraea media

S. media.* Shrub 4 to 6 ft., of upright growth, shoots round. *l.* ovate to oblong, 1 to 2 in. long, $\frac{1}{3}$ to $\frac{3}{4}$ in. wide, toothed towards the apex, usually more or less downy beneath. *fl.* white, $\frac{1}{3}$ in. wide, in umbellate racemes terminating leafy shoots, sometimes constituting collectively an erect panicle. April, May. E. Europe to NE. Asia. 1789. (J.H. 14 (1887) 464 as *S. confusa.*) Much used for forcing early into fl.

S. Menzies'ii. Suckering shrub, 3 to 5 ft., stems brown. *l.* $1\frac{1}{2}$ to 3 in. long, lanceolate, oblong or broadly oval, coarsely toothed except at the lower part, nearly glabrous. *fl.* purplish-rose, crowded on erect pyramidal panicles 3 to 8 in. h. July, August. Western N. America. 1838. var. **exim'ia,** *l.* grey-felted beneath, panicles up to 8 in. long and 6 in. wide; **triumph'ans,*** *l.* ovate-lanceolate, toothed nearly to the base, *fl.* bright purplish-rose, panicles broadly pyramidal, 8 in. long. (*S. Menziesii* has been confused with the tomentose *S. Douglasii* and it may be these 2 varieties are hybrids between that species and *S. salicifolia.*)

S. Miya'bei. Shrub 3 to 4 ft., young shoots downy. *l.* ovate to ovate-lanceolate, coarsely, doubly and sharply toothed, $1\frac{1}{2}$ to 2 in. long, green and glabrous on both sides. *fl.* white, $\frac{1}{3}$ in. wide, in downy, flattish corymbose clusters up to 3 in. across; stamens unusually long. June. Japan. 1915. Akin to *S. japonica.* var. **glabra'ta,** *infl.* glabrous. China. 1907. **pilos'ula,** *l.* up to $3\frac{1}{2}$ in. long, downy on the veins beneath. The best form. China. 1907.

S. mollifo'lia. Shrub to 6 ft., shoots very downy, purplish; buds elongated. *l.* ½ to ¾ in. long, half as wide, oval, oblong or obovate, entire or 3-toothed at the apex, silky all over. *fl.* white, ⅓ in. wide, borne in corymbs about 1 in. across and terminating short leafy twigs on the upper side of arching branches. June, July. China. 1909. Akin to *S. gemmata* and with similar l.-buds, but very distinct by its silky character.

S. mongol'ica. A synonym of *S. gemmata*.

S. nippon'ica.* Shrub 6 to 8 ft., of shapely bushy form, shoots, l. and fl.-stalks glabrous. *l.* broadly obovate to oval, ½ to 1¼ in. long, usually with a few teeth at the apex. *fl.* ⅓ in. wide, pure white, thickly packed in rounded or conical clusters 1 to 1½ in. across and terminating leafy twigs 1½ to 3 in. long. The lower fl. have a small leaf-like bract at the base of the stalk. June. Japan. 1830. (B.T.S. 2, 529.) Syn. *S. bracteata*. var. **rotundifo'lia,*** *l.* and *fl.* larger. (B.M. 7429.) Both charming shrubs; fl.-clusters borne on the upper side of stiff shoots.

S. × Noblea'na. A synonym of *S. sanssouciana*.

S. procum'bens. A synonym of *S. decumbens*.

S. pruino'sa. A synonym of *S. brachybotrys*.

S. prunifo'lia ple'na.* The typical, single-fld. form of this species is not worthy of cultivation. The double-fld. one is a shrub, 6 ft. or more h.; shoots downy. *l.* lustrous green, ovate, 1 to 1¾ in. long, half as wide, finely toothed, downy beneath. *fl.* in stalkless clusters of 3 to 6, ½ in. wide, pure white, built up of very numerous pet., each fl. on a slender stalk up to ¾ in. long. May. Japan. 1845. (F.S. 2, 153.) Beautiful shrub bearing its fl., wreath-like on twigs, 1 to 2 ft. long. Autumn foliage red.

S. pubes'cens. Shrub 4 to 6 ft. with arching branches and downy shoots. *l.* ovate to oval, broadly cuneate, 1 to 1¾ in. long, sharply toothed or slightly 3-lobed, downy above, grey-felted beneath. *fl.* white, ¼ in. wide, densely packed in umbels 1 in. across. May. China. 1883. *S. pubescens* of Lindley is *S. chinensis*.

S. Reevesia'na. A synonym of *S. cantoniensis*.

S. Reevesiana nova. A synonym of *S.* × *blanda*.

S. × revires'cens (*S. amoena* × *S. japonica*). Shrub 2½ to 4 ft., shoots angled, downy when young. *l.* oblong-ovate, slender-pointed, cuneate, 2 to 4 in. long, sharply and coarsely toothed, rather glaucous and with downy veins beneath. *fl.* ¼ in. wide, rose, in downy corymbs 4 to 5 in. wide. June, July, with a second crop in September if the decayed infl. are removed. About 1885. There are several sub-varieties or forms.

S. Rosthor'nii. Shrub up to 6 ft., of spreading habit, shoots slightly downy at first, buds elongated. *l.* 1½ to 3 in. long, half as wide, ovate to lanceolate, slender-pointed, jaggedly toothed, downy especially beneath. *fl.* white, ¼ in. wide, at end of leafy shoots in flattish corymbs 2 to 3½ in. across; fl.-stalks downy. June. China. 1909. Resembles *S. longigemmis* in the curious elongated buds, but that species is glabrous.

S. salicifo'lia. Shrub 3 to 6 ft., spreading vigorously by suckers and forming dense thickets of erect stems. *l.* lanceolate, 2 to 3 in. long, pointed, sharply and often doubly toothed, green and glabrous above and beneath. *fl.* pale rose or rosy-white, crowded in erect pyramidal panicles 4 in. h. June. SE. Europe to NE. Asia. Naturalized in England. (E.B. 414.) Apt to get thin and poor unless divided up and replanted in good soil occasionally. var. **latifo'lia** is *S. latifolia*; **panicula'ta** is *S. alba*.

S. × sanssoucia'na (*S. Douglasii* × *S. japonica*). Shrub to 5 ft., shoots downy. *l.* lanceolate to oblong, 2 to 4 in. long, strongly toothed except near base, grey-downy beneath. *fl.* bright rose, densely packed in a crowd of rounded corymbs, each 1 in. across, the whole forming a panicle 6 to 10 in. wide. July. (B.M. 5169 as *Spiraea Nobleana*.)

S. Sargentia'na. Graceful shrub 6 to 8 ft., shoots slender, arching, round, downy at first only. *l.* ½ to 1 in. long, ⅛ to ½ in. wide, narrowly oval to narrowly obovate, cuneate, toothed near apex, downy beneath. *fl.* creamy-white, ¼ in. wide, borne at end of short, leafy twigs in dense rounded clusters 1 to 1½ in. across; fl.-stalks downy. June. China. 1909. Akin to *S. canescens*, which has angled shoots and is more robust.

S. × Schinabeck'ii (*S. chamaedryfolia* × *S. trilobata*). Shrub 4 to 6 ft. *l.* ovate to roundish, doubly toothed, up to 2 in. long. *fl.* white; stamens shorter than the pet. June. Handsome.

S. sinobrahu'ica. Shrub 4 to 7 ft., shoots thickly tawny downy, buds woolly. *l.* broadly ovate to obovate, lobed and toothed towards the apex, cuneate, ½ to 1⅛ in. long, velvety beneath. *fl.* creamy-white, ⅓ in. wide, borne at the top of short leafy twigs in rounded clusters 1 in. across; fl.-stalks and cal. downy. June. China. 1910. Akin to *S. chinensis*; distinguished by its tawny-downiness.

S. × subvillo'sa. A synonym of *S.* × *Watsoniana*.

S. × syringiflo'ra (*S. albiflora* × *S. salicifolia*). Shrub about 3 ft. *l.* lanceolate, slender-pointed, toothed above middle, nearly smooth. *fl.* pink in downy panicles with small panicles below; stamens twice as long as pet. 1885.

S. Thunberg'ii. Twiggy, bushy shrub up to 5 ft., shoots wiry, angled, downy. *l.* narrowly lanceolate, 1 to 1½ in. long, ⅛ to ¼ in. wide, pointed, toothed, pale green, glabrous. *fl.* ¼ in. wide, pure white, in stalkless clusters of 3 to 5; pet. obovate. Clusters thickly set, wreath-like, on the arching twigs. April. China, Japan. 1863. Autumn colour orange and scarlet. (Add. 112.)

S. tomento'sa. Shrub 3 to 5 ft., shoots brown-felted. *l.* ovate, 1½ to 3 in. long, half as wide, coarsely toothed almost to the base, yellowish- or grey-felted beneath. *fl.* rose or purplish-rose, densely borne in erect, pyramidal panicles 4 to 8 in. h., 1½ to 2½ in. wide. August, September. Eastern N. America. 1736. (B.B. ed. 2, 2, 245.) Differs from *S. Douglasii* by the thicker, browner pubescence, by the l. being toothed much nearer the base, and by the woolly ovaries. var. **alba,** *fl.* white.

S. trichocar'pa.* Spreading shrub up to 6 ft., shoots angled, glabrous. *l.* oblanceolate to oblong, 1 to 2½ in. long, entire or toothed near apex, glabrous, rather glaucous beneath. *fl.* white, ⅓ in. wide, borne in rounded corymbs 1 to 2 in. wide, at ends of short, leafy twigs, the whole forming a graceful spray over 1 ft. long; pet. rounded, notched. June. Korea. 1917. (B.T.S. 3. 464.)

S. triloba'ta. Glabrous shrub up to 4 ft. *l.* roundish, ½ to 1¼ in. long and about as wide, coarsely toothed or obscurely 3- or 5-lobed, broadly tapered or rounded at base, bluish-green beneath. *fl.* white, packed numerously in umbels ¾ to 1½ in. across, each umbel at the end of a short leafy twig. June. N. China to Turkistan. 1801. (L.B.C. 1272.) Pretty shrubs of neat habit.

S. × Vanhout'tei* (*S. cantoniensis* × *S. trilobata*). Shrub up to 6 ft., with graceful, arching, glabrous stems. *l.* rhomboidal or obovate, ¾ to 1½ in. long, coarsely toothed or even 3- to 5-lobed, rather glaucous beneath. *fl.* pure white, ⅓ in. wide, numerous in clusters 1 to 2 in. across. Raised near Paris about 1862. Much used for forcing early into bloom.

S. Veitch'ii.* Shrub up to 10 ft., with long, arching branches, shoots downy, reddish. *l.* ¾ to 2 in. long, ⅓ to ¾ in. wide, oblong or obovate, entire, downy and rather glaucous beneath. *fl.* white, ⅕ in. wide, densely packed in corymbs up to 2½ in. across. June, July. China. 1900. (B.M. 8383.) A fine species of the *S. canescens* group, with similar long shoots crowded on the upper side with bloom. Distinct by its entire l.

S. virga'ta. Shrub 4 to 6 ft., shoots angled, downy. *l.* ¼ to ⅝ in. long, oval, entire, or obscurely toothed at the rounded apex, glabrous, glaucous beneath. *fl.* white, ¼ in. wide, in rounded clusters ½ to 1 in. wide, borne at the end of short leafy shoots. June. China. 1910.

S. × Watsonia'na. Shrub up to 5 or 6 ft., shoots downy. *l.* 2 to 3 in. long, oval to oblong, rounded at the base, terminal half toothed, grey-downy beneath. *fl.* rose, in dense, downy-stalked panicles. June, July. Natural hybrid between *S. Douglasii* and *S. splendens*, found wild in Oregon. Syn. *S.* × *subvillosa*.

S. Wilson'ii. Shrub 6 to 9 ft., with arching branches, shoots downy at first, purplish. *l.* 1 to 2 in. long, oval to obovate, entire or toothed near the apex, downy above and still more so beneath. *fl.* white, ¼ in. wide, in dense clusters up to 2 in. across, terminating short leafy shoots; fl.-stalks and cal. glabrous. June. China. 1900. (B.M. 8399.) Closely akin to *S. Henryi* and *S. Veitchii*.

W. J. B.

SPIRAEA SAWFLY, *Pteronidea spiraeae*, is a frequent pest on *Aruncus silvester* (*Spiraea Aruncus*), the leaves of which are eaten by the larvae. The oval, greenish-white eggs are deposited on the underside of the leaves in May, and the pale greenish larvae with brown heads congregate on the lower surface and eat out roundish holes between the veins. In severe attacks, the entire leaf is eaten with the exception of the main veins. Pupation takes place in a cocoon in the soil beneath attacked plants. There are usually 2 broods a year, the larvae being found from May to early September.

This pest is readily controlled with DDT, which should be applied at the first signs of attack.

G. F. W.

spira'lis -a -um, twisted, as though wound like a spring.

SPIRAN'THERA (*speira*, spiral, *anthera*, anther; from the form of the anthers). Fam. *Rutaceae*. A genus of a single species of fragrant, glabrous, evergreen shrub, a native of Brazil. It needs stove conditions and a compost of peat and sandy loam. Propagation by cuttings of half-ripe wood in sand under a glass. The glass must be removed and wiped frequently as a safeguard against damping-off, to which the cuttings are prone.

S. odoratis'sima.* Shrub of 6 ft. *l.* alternate, 3-foliolate; stalked; lflets. gland-dotted, acuminate, entire, glaucous beneath. *fl.* white; showy, fragrant, in axillary and terminal corymbs; cal. 5-toothed, cup-shaped; pet. 5, long-linear, hairy, overlapping; disk thick, erect, forming a column; stamens 5, hypogynous. July. 1823.

SPIRAN'THERA of Hooker, *see* **Pronaya.**

SPIRAN'THES (*speiros*, spiral, *anthos*, flower; alluding to the spiral inflorescence). Lady's Tresses. FAM. *Orchidaceae*. A large genus of probably over 200 species of terrestrial orchids, widely dispersed over temperate and tropical regions, represented in the British flora and in Australia. Flowers small or rather large, in unilateral or dense, sessile spikes, in some distinctly spiralled around the rachis; dorsal sepals and petals erect, usually connivent or slightly coherent in a helmet or hood, or the ends alone spreading; lateral sepals free and more spreading, all nearly equal, lip sessile or distinctly clawed, often embracing the terete column by its broad base, spreading at apex, undivided or 3-lobed. Column more or less terete. Pollen powdery-granulate. Leaves variable. Stem leafy, or leafless when flowering. Root-fibres often fascicled on a short rhizome, sometimes thickened into a tuber. Though many are of interest, few species are of horticultural value. Except where otherwise indicated, stove treatment is necessary. The hardy species thrive in turfy loam, amongst which pieces of chalk or limestone should be mixed; the stove and greenhouse species succeed in well-drained pots filled with a mixture of turfy loam and fibrous peat, and during the season of rest the latter should be kept rather dry. Propagation is effected by carefully dividing the root-stocks of old plants, just before growth commences.

The group now forming the genus Stenorrhynchus has been separated from Spiranthes. Species not found here should be sought under Stenorrhynchus. In Spiranthes a few natural hybrids are recognized.

S. acau'lis. A synonym of *S. picta*.

S. aestiva'lis. *fl.* and bracts as in *S. autumnalis*, but rather larger; spike slightly pubescent, slender, many-fld. July, August. *l.* 2 to 6 in. long, narrowed below; lower ones on fl.-stem linear, resembling the radical l. Stem 6 to 18 in. h., glabrous. W. Europe (Britain). (E.B. 1473.) Hardy. Damp situations.

S. albes'cens. *fl.* greenish, hairy; pet. linear, forming a helmet with the upper sep.; lip brown-tipped, dilated in front. *l.* oblong, acute, spotted white; stalked. Colombia. SYN. *S. leucosticta*.

S. austra'lis. A synonym of *S. sinensis*.

S. autumna'lis. A synonym of *S. spiralis*.

S. bi'color. *fl.* greenish, with a white lip; sep. gibbous below lip; lip keeled on back, cucullate at dilated base; spike loose, secund, 2 to 4 in. long, densely glandular-pubescent. January. *l.* lowest rosulate, oblong lanceolate, acuminate, disappearing before fl. Stem distantly sheathed with minute l. 1 ft. h. W. Indies, Brazil. 1823. (B.R. 794 as *Neottia bicolor*.) Greenhouse.

S. bracteo'sa. *fl.* white and yellow, many, small; lateral sep. connate at base; mid-lobe of lip 3-lobed; bracts linear-lanceolate, leafy, longer than fl.; spike rarely straight. May. *l.* rosulate, oblong, acute. 1 ft. h. Brazil. 1835. (B.R. 1934.)

S. cern'ua. *fl.* pure white, sweet-scented, pubescent or nearly smooth; lip oblong and very obtuse when outspread (or conduplicate, or margins much incurved), callosities at base prominent; spike cylindrical, rather dense, 2 to 5 in. long. September, October. *l.* linear-lanceolate, lowest elongated, 4 to 12 in. long. Stem leafy below, 6 to 20 in. h. N. America. 1796. (B.M. 5277; B.R. 823; B.M. 1568 as *Neottia cernua*.) Hardy.

S. cinnabari'na. A synonym of *Stenorrhynchus cinnabarinus*.

S. colora'ta. A synonym of *Stenorrhynchus speciosus*.

S. ela'ta. *fl.* small, greenish-white or whitish, ½ in. long; lip linear, blunt, entire; spike long, spiral, pubescent, 3 to 8 in. long; scape glabrous, sheathed with clasping, tubular, slender-pointed scales. July. *l.* rosulate, elliptic or elliptic-oblong, acute, stalked, 2 to 6 in. long. 1½ to 2 ft. h. W. Indies, Brazil. 1790. (B.M. 2026, L.B.C. 343 as *Neottia elata*.) SYN. *Neottia minor*. A variable species.

S. gemmip'ara. A synonym of *S. Romanzoffiana*.

S. grac'ilis. *fl.* small, numerous, spiralled, white tinged green in middle. *l.* ovate or elliptical in a radical tuft. Resembles *S. autumnalis*. About 12 in. h. Roots fascicled. N. America. Hardy or cool house.

S. grandiflo'ra. A variety of *S. picta*.

S. Lindleya'na. *fl.* in pairs, secund, greenish-white; lip dilated. *l.* variegated, shorter than in *S. bicolor*. Caracas.

S. margaritif'era. A synonym of *Stenorrhynchus Esmeralda*.

S. metal'lica. Allied to *S. acaulis*, but with *fl.* only about half the size. Sep. and pet. light green, lip whitish. *l.* 4 to 6 in. long, 1½ to 3 in. wide, of a peculiar olive-brown metallic shade, often with a number of small spots. 1 to 2 ft. h. Brazil. 1882.

S. pic'ta. *fl.* greenish-white or variegated, about ¾ in. long; sep. and pet. linear-oblong, lateral sep. decurrent; lip included, oblong, channelled below the veined summit, dilated at base; spike 4 to 6 in. long, hairy; scape glabrous below, sheathed with slender-pointed scales. February. *l.* with fl., lanceolate or elliptic-oblong, 4 to 6 in. long, narrowed to petioles, green or spotted. 1 to 2 ft. h. W. Indies, Brazil, &c. 1843. (B.M. 1562 and L.B.C. 214 as *Neottia picta*.) var. **grandiflo'ra,** *fl.* greenish within, *l.* almost unspotted. Brazil, Guiana. (B.R. 1043 as *S. grandiflora*; B.M. 2730 as *Neottia grandiflora*.); **variega'ta,** sep., pet., and lip white within, *l.* variegated.

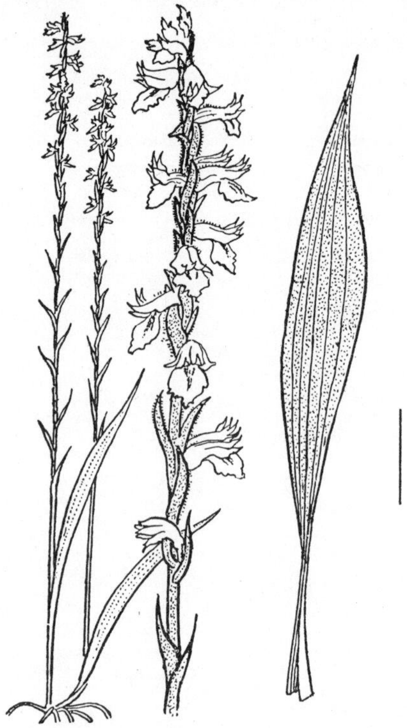

Spiranthes cernua

S. Romanzoffia'na. *fl.* white, much larger and broader than in *S. aestivalis*; lip tongue-shaped, contracted below the recurved tip, tubercles at the base smooth and shining; spike 2 to 3 in. long, stout, glandular-pubescent. August, September. *l.* radical ones on fl.-stem narrow obovate-lanceolate, 3 to 6 in. long. Stem from 6 to 10 in. long, leafy throughout. N. America, Ireland. (E.B. 1474 as *S. gemmipara*.) Hardy.

S. Saurogloss'um. *fl.* sep. green, broader towards apex; upper pet. agglutinate, lateral arcuate; lip white, parallel with column, linear, channelled, sessile; bracts subulate; raceme 1 ft. or more long, dense, cylindrical; scape nearly 2 ft. long, sheathed with distant, leafy scales. April. *l.* radical, oblong-lanceolate, sub-erect, fleshy, not plicate, one-third length of scape. Brazil. 1832. (B.R. 1618 as *Sauroglossum elatum*.) Greenhouse.

S. sinensis. *fl.* generally pink, with white lip, sessile; lateral sep. obscurely dilated at base, but not saccate; the broad base of lip sessile, or appearing raised on a very short claw, with a tubercle each side; spike spiral, very dense or rather loose. June. *l.*, lower ones linear or narrow-lanceolate, 1½ to 4 in. long; upper reduced to scales. Stem 6 to 12 in. or more h. Australia, New Zealand, tropical and temperate Asia. 1823. (A.B.G.C. 8, 369; F.A.O. 1, 63.) SYN. *Neottia australis*. Greenhouse. A variable species.

S. Smith'ii. *fl.* in one variety, yellow, lip marked with a few green veins; in another, brownish, lip yellowish striped green; peduncle many-fld. Costa Rica, 1868. Allied to *S. picta*.

S. spira'lis. *fl.* white, spirally arranged, small, numerous, fragrant, sheathed by the cucullate, cuspidate bracts; lip channelled at base, tip exserted, crenate; spike slender. August, September. *l.* 1 in. long, in lateral rosettes, ovate, acute, after fl. Stem 4 to 8 in. h.; upper part and infl. pubescent. Root tuberous. Europe (Britain), &c. (E.B. 1472.) Hardy.

S. uligino'sa. *fl.* usually 2, greenish-yellow; sep. nearly 1 in. long; pet. shorter; lip at first erect, then reflexed, end lobe broad, somewhat rounded. Winter. Brazil. 1877?

E. C.

SPIRE LILY. *See* **Galtonia candicans.**

SPIRONE'MA (*speira*, spiral, *nema*, thread). FAM. *Commelinaceae*. A genus of a single species of robust, creeping, or stoloniferous herb, more curious than beautiful. It needs stove conditions and a light, rich soil. Increased by division.

S. frag'rans. About 2 ft. h. Stem leafy, short, thick. *l.* large, oblong-lanceolate, sessile, sheaths slightly overlapping. *fl.* small, white, fragrant, in dense head-like cymes, forming a tall, rigid, few-branched panicle; sep. and pet. almost equal, distinct; stamens 6, all perfect. May. Mexico. 1839. (B.R. 26, 47.)

spitham'aeus -a -um, a span, i.e. about 9 in., long.

splashed, having broken stripes of various sizes, as frequently in apples.

SPLEENWORT. *See* **Asplenium.**

splen'dens, gleaming.

splen'didus, strikingly fine.

SPLICE-GRAFTING. Another name for whip or whip-and-tongue grafting, the commonest method of grafting shoots of approximately equal size.

SPLITZERB'ERA. A synonym of Boehmeria.

spodo-, in compound words, signifying ash-grey.

spolia'tus -a -um, plundered.

spondia'um, growing on trees of Spondias.

SPON'DIAS (ancient Greek name used by Theophrastus for the plum, which the fruit in this genus much resembles). FAM. *Anacardiaceae*. A genus of about 10 species of tropical trees. Leaves often clustered near tips of branches, alternate, unequally pinnate; leaflets opposite, often with a long point. Flowers small, on short pedicels; calyx 4- or 5-cleft, deciduous; petals 4 or 5, spreading, sub-valvate. Fruit a fleshy drupe. A compost of loam and sand suits these trees, which need stove conditions. Large cuttings will root in heat, in either sand or potting compost.

S. borbon'ica. Tree of 40 ft. *lflets.* many, entire, slender-pointed. *fl.* dark purple, in axillary and terminal compound racemes. Réunion, Mauritius. 1825.

S. dul'cis. (Sweet) Otaheite Apple. Tree of 50 ft. *lflets.* elliptic-oblong, acuminate, repandly crenulate, smooth; veins parallel. *fl.* yellowish-green in a spreading panicle. June. *fr.* golden-yellow; flavour somewhat resembling pine-apple. Society Is. 1793.

S. lu'tea. Golden Apple; Jamaica or Hog Plum. Tree of 30 ft. *lflets.* 3, in 3 to 8 pairs, stalked, ovate-lanceolate or lanceolate, slender-pointed, toothed or almost entire. *fl.* yellowish-white, in panicles often longer than l. Summer. *fr.* yellow, ovoid, 2 in. long, with an agreeable acid, aromatic flavour. W. Indies. 1739.

S. purpu'rea. Tree of 30 ft. *lflets.* in 8 to 10 pairs, shortly stalked, elliptic-oblong, somewhat blunt, usually toothed. *fl.* purplish, in lateral, few-fld. racemes much shorter than l. Summer. *fr.* yellow or tinged purple. W. Indies. 1817.

spondylophyl'lus -a -um, round-leaved.

SPONGE-TREE. *See* **Acacia Farnesiana.**

spongio'sus -a -um, sponge-like.

SPONGOS'PORA. A genus of Fungi included among the Myxomycetes or Slime Fungi (q.v.). Only *S. subterranea* is known to be parasitic upon cultivated plants, causing powdery or corky scab of potatoes. *See* **Potato Diseases.**

D. E. G.

spontaneous, occurring without the purposeful intervention of man.

SPONGY TISSUE. Tissue consisting of cells with thin unlignified walls with large intercellular spaces as seen, e.g. in the tissues of the lower part of the leaf and in pith.

SPOONFLOWER. *See* **Labisia pothoina.**

SPOONWORT. *See* **Cochlearia.**

sporadic, widely dispersed or scattered; occurring here and there.

SPORANGIUM (*pl.* **sporangia**). The organ in which the asexual production of spores takes place. In the simplest of plants the whole body may become a sporangium, as in Yeast and some 1-celled Algae, or every cell may eventually act as a sporangium, as in some Algae like Ulva, but in higher plants special parts are set aside for this function. The sporangium varies in structure and position, and for details a text-book of Botany should be consulted. Instances in which the Sporangia are of special interest in horticulture are provided by Fungi (see below); Mosses, where the elaborate structure of the fruit derived from a cluster of sporangia appears as a single sporangium; Ferns, where the numerous sporangia are usually borne on leaves; and flowering plants, where there are 2 forms of sporangium, the pollen sacs (or microsporangia) and the ovules (or macrosporangia), the pollen sacs being nearly always borne on leaves, the ovules either on the stem as in, e.g. Tamus, and where there is a single ovule in the ovary as in Compositae and Gramineae, or where the placentation is truly free-central as in Primulaceae, or more usually on the margins of the carpellary leaves. *See* **Pollen, Ovary.** In the class Phycomycetes (q.v.) among the Fungi the sporangia are generally borne on aerial hyphae, at the ends of which a special cell is separated from the rest of the hypha by a cross-wall. The contents of this cell divide and form a number of spores which are released by rupture of the sporangial wall. In aquatic fungi the sporangium produces motile spores (zoospores or swarm spores) and the sporangium is there called a zoosporangium. Some fungi, though now terrestrial, are so closely related to aquatic ancestors that they produce swarm spores, e.g. *Pythium de Baryanum,* which causes damping-off of seedlings (q.v.).

SPORE. The common reproductive bodies of fungi are microscopic bodies called spores, which are either cut off as separate cells from the fungal threads or are produced in specialized bodies known as spore fruits. A spore is generally made up of 1 to several specialized cells which, disseminated, germinate to reproduce the fungus, and are thus equivalent in function to the seeds of higher plants. Spores vary greatly in colour: they may be clear-coloured or dark, and in form may be globular, ellipsoidal, ovate, cylindrical, filamentous, club-shaped, star-shaped, &c. In many fungi we distinguish 2 types of spore, (*a*) asexual spores, which are cut off directly from the hyphae, and (*b*) sexual spores, which are produced as a result of fusion between 2 cells, male and female—an example being the oospores formed by fungi of the class Phycomycetes (q.v.). In general, the sexual spores are formed by the fungus over-wintering and are often called resting spores. These, in many plant-disease fungi, bring about soil contamination. The asexual spores or conidia in general cause immediate infection of other plants, and these are often called summer spores, as with the uredospores of the rust fungi (q.v.), but in some instances spores produced directly on or in the hyphae are thick-walled and can resist unfavourable conditions for long periods, e.g. chlamydospores. In some of the Phycomycetes swarm spores and zoospores are produced in sporangia, and when released these are motile and have the power to swim about in water owing to their possession of fine thread-like attachments or cilia. The kind of spore and sporangium produced is used in classifying fungi. Thus Phycomycetes are classified by their oospores, Ascomycetes by various types of fruit bodies producing ascospores, and Basidiomycetes by different types of sporophores that give rise to basidiospores. The Rust fungi have special types of spores produced at different stages in their life-history (*see* **Rusts**).

Spores are also formed by all the higher plants, both asexually and sexually. *See* **Mosses, Ferns, Spermaphyta, Ovary, Pollen.**

D. E. G.

SPORIDIUM (*pl.* **Sporidia**). The secondary spores formed by the teleutospores of Rust fungi when they germinate. The teleutospore puts forth a specialized germ tube called a promycelium, and this divides into 4 cells, each of which forms a sporidium. The Rust fungi are looked upon as primitive forms of Basidiomycetes, the promycelium as a primitive basidium, and the sporidia as basidiospores (*see* **Rusts**).

D. E. G.

sporiferous, bearing spores.

SPOROCARP. The leaf-branch produced in the Marsileaceae enclosing a number of sori, each of which contains both microspores and macrospores; in Marsilea it is pod-shaped and usually on a long stalk (petiole), in Pilularia it is globular. The term is also sometimes applied to the sori of Salvinia, which are borne on the basal branches of a submerged leaf, containing either microspores or macrospores, not both, enclosed by an inferior indusia. The sporocarps in the 2 families thus have a different origin.

SPOROPHORE. The fruit body of Basidiomycetous fungi which produces the basidia and basidiospores (q.v.). Its form differs widely in the different sections of the Basidiomycetes, which are classified according to its structure. For details see notes on Bracket Fungi, Mushrooms, &c., and books dealing with fungus classification. **A**

SPOROPHYLL. A leaf bearing sporangia, as in most Ferns, Stamens, and Carpels of flowering plants.

SPOROPHYTE. The generation in the life-history of a plant which produces asexual reproductive organs, represented in Ferns and Flowering Plants by the leafy plant, in Mosses by the 'fruit'. *Cf.* **Gametophyte.**

SPORT. A shoot different in character (usually in a single character) from the typical growth of the plant that produced it. Thus a pink-flowered rose, Dorothy Perkins, produced shoots bearing only white flowers, afterwards propagated and called White Dorothy; the well-known Potato, Up-to-Date, produced a plant with tubers having a rough skin, afterwards propagated and called Field Marshal. Such sports or bud variations are by no means uncommon, and give rise to new horticultural varieties which must usually be propagated vegetatively. What may be called incipient sports are often seen where one section of a flower or fruit is of a different colour from the rest, or where part of a plant is hairy and part of the same organ glabrous, as is sometimes seen in the Peach, where part of the skin may be smooth like the Nectarine. The extent of such difference depends largely upon the point at which the change (usually the loss of a character) arose. The existence of such difference may be of long duration before it becomes apparent because its position may be such that the organ in which it could be manifested is not within its range. Such sporting cells may, for instance, be deep in the interior and cannot affect the colouring of flowers until, as sometimes happens on root-cuttings, a growth bud is produced from these internal cells. Such sports are not uncommon, e.g. in *Phlox paniculata* and Bouvardia, when raised from root-cuttings.

SPOTTED WILT. Spotted Wilt is one of the Virus diseases and is caused by Lycopersicum Virus 3. It attacks a great number of different plants, but is best known on the Tomato and is often called Tomato Spotted Wilt disease. From the symptoms on the tomato plant it gets its name of Spotted or Bronzy Wilt. In infected Tomato plants veins are thickened and the young leaves tend to curl downwards, there is a characteristic bronzing or varnishing of the leaves, showing as a rather shiny brownish discoloration on the topmost ones, and on the older ones there may be bronze circular markings or rings or even yellowish mottling. If young, such plants may be killed outright, but in any case they stop growing and remain stunted. The fruit may show no symptoms, but often develops pale yellow or even whitish areas in the normal red skins, showing blotchiness or as concentric circles. On other plants the symptoms of Spotted Wilt disease may be very different. On Arum Lilies they show as white or pale yellow streaks or spots on leaves and stems, with sometimes great distortion. On Gloxinia they show as broad brown circular bands on the leaves, while in *Solanum Capsicastrum* the signs are of definite ringspot type in which the leaves show pale concentric rings, sometimes in great numbers.

Spotted Wilt is spread by Thrips, so that these must be kept down in glasshouses and care must be taken that the trouble is not spread by using the trimming knife on healthy plants after diseased ones. The knife and hands, after dealing with affected plants, ought to be well washed in some disinfectant such as Lysol or Carbolic. Plants affected by Spotted Wilt cannot recover, and as they will act as sources of infection on which the insects feed they must be destroyed as soon as identified. This ruthless weeding-out is the only way to keep the disease in check. Potential danger lies in long-lived plants such as Winter Cherry, Arum Lily, and Gloxinia, which may be infected and carry the virus through the winter in glasshouses. These plants should be watched very carefully and, if possible, young Tomatoes, Lettuces, &c., should not be grown in the greenhouse with them. Some other plants likely to be infected by the Spotted Wilt virus are Amaryllis, Arum, Begonia, Browallia, Calceolaria, Callistephus, Capsicum spp., Chrysanthemum, Dahlia, Delphinium, Gloxinia, Hippeastrum, Limonium, Tomato, Paeony, Penstemon, Primula, Schizanthus, Solanum, Stock, Trachelium, Tropaeolum, Zinnia, and there are many others. Even weeds such as the Deadly Nightshade, *Atropa Belladonna*, and Plantain, *Plantago major*, can be affected, and may in some instances be sources of infection if near to a horticultural crop.

D. E. G.

SPRAGUEA (in honour of Isaac Sprague, American botanical draughtsman). FAM. *Portulacaceae*. A genus of a single species of half-hardy, dwarf, perennial herb, which may be treated as a half-hardy annual, and is suitable for the rock-garden and useful for its late-flowering habit, or for edging. Ordinary well-drained soil suits it. Propagation by seed sown in cold frame in spring, or by cuttings.

S. umbella'ta. *Lower l.* forming a radical rosette, spatulate, somewhat fleshy; *stem-l.* smaller, alternate. *fl.* densely overlapping one another; sep. 2, whitish, large, persistent, scarious; pet. 4, rosy-lake, just protruding; anthers purple; umbel terminal, compound, many-rayed. July. California. 1858. (B.M. 5143.)

SPRAY. I. An arrangement of flowers, longer than broad, composed of a single branch or of several flowers, facing one way, to be worn lying upon a garment, or on the side of the head. II. A shoot bearing several long-stalked flowers, as a spray of Chrysanthemums or Roses. III. Water broken up in very fine particles as from a syringe or from a spraying machine; or solutions similarly treated.

SPRAY DAMAGE. The application of materials designed to check the spread of parasitic diseases and insect attacks upon plants sometimes results in injury to the plant. The reason is often obscure, for there are many factors which may aggravate such damage. In some instances the spray fluid may be too strong, for it is often difficult to be sure of a safe strength; in other instances the strength of a spray must be varied to suit different varieties of the same plant. A good example is found in the spraying of Apple-trees against Scab disease (*Venturia inaequalis*) where lime sulphur at the concentration used on most varieties must be made weaker for use on some varieties, such as Cox's Orange Pippin, while Stirling Castle must not be sprayed with lime sulphur at all. Similarly, against American Gooseberry Mildew (*Sphaerotheca mors-uvae*) sulphur sprays are most effective, but the tender varieties, so-called sulphur-shy varieties, are very sensitive to sulphur sprays and may show scorching on their foliage. On Pears, Scab disease (*Venturia pyrina*) is controlled with Bordeaux mixture rather than with Burgundy as the latter is more likely to injure the young foliage, but some Apples, especially Cox's Orange Pippin, if sprayed with Bordeaux mixture, may suffer injury in the form of a russeting of the fruit. Potatoes are sprayed with Burgundy or Bordeaux mixture against Blight disease (*Phytophthora infestans*) but if they are growing near smoky towns or if the leaves have suffered from injury by aphis the result of such spraying may be that severe damage is done. It is possible that climatic factors, e.g. very hot sunshine, may aggravate spray injury. In lime sulphur spraying, perhaps the most common injury is the scorching of the foliage, seen as a dull brown spotting or tip and marginal browning of the leaves, but in Apples there may also be a considerable dropping of the young fruits. With Bordeaux and Burgundy mixtures the damage may range from mild russeting or cracking of the fruit skin to intense blighting and blackening of the young leaves and blossoms. On some herbaceous plants the damage may be severe. In some fruits even a slight injury may be regarded as serious, e.g. a spray which causes staining of the skin of Peaches. Where shoots are injured there is the danger that they may be invaded by fungi which otherwise would be unable to attack them. Bad mixing of spray materials is also a fruitful cause of damage, and other methods of treatment for disease other than spraying, such as seed disinfection, fumigation, and so on, are all liable to cause damage if done inadvisedly.

SPRAY-FLUIDS. *See* **Fungicides, Insecticides.**

SPRAYING. Spraying is the operation carried out on plants to protect them from fungus and insect parasites. There are many indirect methods of controlling disease, such as clean cultivation and hygiene involving careful pruning and cutting out of dead wood, thinning plants and painting wounds in trees, which can be called indirect methods of plant protection, while spraying and dusting or even seed disinfection may be called direct methods. The chemicals used must destroy the parasite or in fungus attacks prevent germination of its spores and at the same time not injure the host plant. Many chemicals are found to be of use, but the chief are copper and sulphur and certain compounds of these (*see* **Insecticides, Fungicides**). There are many appliances used for spraying and dusting (*see* **Spraying apparatus**) and the grower will choose the one to suit his convenience and special requirements. The aim in spraying against fungal and bacterial parasites is to obtain a fine misty spray and to cover the foliage (upper and lower surfaces) with a thin film of the fungicide so as to get as complete protection as possible from parasitic attack. The spraying may need to be repeated as new growth develops and needs protecting, and this is especially so in a wet season. A substance called a spreader is often mixed in the spray to make it spread more easily and adhere more closely to the surface of the plant. The modern tendency in large plantations (e.g. Apple, &c.) is to use powerful high-pressure spraying machines which produce a driving effect, and this is claimed to eliminate the need of spreaders. In general it can be said that sprays can be applied most effectively when the weather is fine and there is little or no wind. Apart from Powdery Mildews there are few fungus parasites which can be directly killed by spray treatment, and in most diseases the operation is intended not to cure affected plants but to protect the remaining healthy ones from infection. For this reason spraying is best done early, in some cases, e.g. Potato Blight, before the disease appears or at least as soon as the first signs of it are noticed.

Spraying against insect pests on the other hand may be directed towards the destruction of the actual pest or its eggs and here the importance of covering the insect is emphasized. This is the aim with all contact sprays. Stomach poisons are distributed on the foliage likely to be affected and should be such as will adhere and be effective for some time like the sprays used against fungus parasites. *See* **Insecticides.**

SPRAYING APPARATUS. The successful control of plant pests and diseases by spraying and dusting is possible only when the standard insecticide and fungicide is applied in the correct manner at the right time and with the aid of reliable spraying equipment. There are many kinds of spraying and dusting machines and, while the small grower must be guided in his choice of apparatus by the amount of work to be done, the capital cost of the apparatus, and the size of the plants to be sprayed, the commercial grower must consider the availability and permanence of a water-supply, the cost of upkeep, the labour requirements, and the field performance of a central spraying plant with its accompanying underground system of mains and pipe-lines over a mobile spraying unit. It is essential to practise economy by estimating in advance of any spraying performance the cost of labour and concentrated wash, the amount of water required to be conveyed to the orchard or plantation, the time available for the successful completion of the operation, and the availability of spare parts to avoid delay in application. Time is of paramount importance in large-scale spraying, which often entails the speedy application of washes to fruit-trees especially during the pre- and post-blossom periods of top fruits. Unfavourable weather may delay the operation and derange the entire spraying calendar. The quantity of wash required will vary enormously in different conditions, for instance, with the size and density of the trees, the effect of pressure and the type of spray cone in the nozzle, and the kind of spray required for the operation in hand —a cover wash in the case of arsenicals (Lead arsenate) and fungicides (Bordeaux mixture and Lime Sulphur) or a drench when contact washes (e.g. Nicotine, Derris, Pyrethrum, and Oil emulsions) are being applied against sucking insects (e.g. Capsid Bugs, Aphides, and Leaf-hoppers).

The types of (A) *Spraying Apparatus* used are: (1) *Hand Syringe*, which may be adequate for the work required in small gardens and greenhouses, but is wasteful of spray, low in pressure, and takes time for its continuous recharging. (2) *Double-action* or *Continuous Spray Syringe* is preferable to a hand syringe as it is fitted with a length of suction hose to give a continuous jet of spray with slow pumping. (3) *Bucket Sprayer*, which may be obtained with either a detachable or fixed pump, is a convenient machine for medium-sized gardens. (4) *Hand-worked Knapsack Sprayer*, also known originally as a Vermorel Sprayer, has a limited use owing to the fatigue of continuous pumping which soon tires the arm of the operator resulting in a steady decrease in pressure and therefore poor application. (5) *Pneumatic* or *Compressed-air Hand* and *Knapsack Sprayers* vary in capacity from 2 to 5 pints for the former type and 1 to 3 gallons for the latter. The advantages of these types are that the machines are charged with air prior to spraying to a working pressure of 75 to 90 lb. per sq. in., and that both hands of the operator are free to manipulate a tall lance for reaching high branches. (6) *Barrel* and *Tank Sprayers* with capacities of 10 to 20 gal. are mounted on 1- or 2-wheeled carriages the wheels of which should have wide rims and a large circumference to allow for easy traction, and the container should be sufficiently clear of the ground to avoid injury to low-growing plants as the machine is pushed over crops. Such machines when fitted with pneumatic tyres have the advantage of not marking lawns and grass paths over which they are drawn. Barrel sprayers are occasionally mounted in a farm-cart and provided with a movable boom supplied with a number of jets to allow several rows of low crops to be sprayed at one time. (7) *Headland Sprayers* are portable manual pumps which are suitable for small orchards, and are capable of maintaining 2 delivery hoses at pressures of 120 to 180 lb. per sq. in. (8) *Power Sprayers* comprise both *Mobile Units* in which the supply tank and the spray pump unit are mounted on a 4-wheeled carriage drawn by a horse or tractor, and *Stationary Plants* where the pump, mixing and supply tanks are centralized and the wash is conveyed to the operators through a system of underground mains and portable pipes. Power is supplied by means of a petrol or petrol-paraffin engine, while a Diesel engine or electric motor is more suitable for central plants. The capacities of portable outfits are 100 gal. if horse-drawn and up to 250 gal. if tractor-drawn.

The types of (B) *Dusting Apparatus* are: (1) *Hand-dusters* and *Shaker-bellows*, which hold ¼ to 1 lb. of powder, are suitable for the application of Derris, Nicotine, and Sulphur dusts by the amateur gardener. (2) *Knapsack Dusters* work with a single or double bellows action —the latter being preferable in supplying a continuous cloud of dust, thereby giving a more even distribution of powder over the plants. Their capacity is 10 to 15 lb. of dust, the flow of which is regulated by a screw-control. (3) *Rotary Blowers* are highly efficient fan-driven machines. Various sizes are procurable, the smaller with capacities of 10 to 15 lb. being carried in front of the operator and suspended by shoulder-straps, the larger with capacities of 28 to 56 lb. being mounted on a 1- or 2-wheeled carriage. Both types are hand-driven, the latter requiring 2 operators. (4) *Power Dusters* are designed for use in orchards and plantations, in Hop-fields, and in large Potato-growing areas, the motive power being a petrol or a petrol-paraffin engine which drives powerful fans capable of supplying 2 or more nozzles. (*See Commercial Fruit Tree Spraying*, by J. Turnbull, Ministry of Agriculture's Bulletin No. 5, 1939.)

G. F. W.

SPREAD EAGLE. *See* **Oncidium carthaginense.**

SPREADERS. In applying fungicidal sprays to plants to protect them from parasitic fungi and bacteria it is often advisable to include in the spray fluid a substance known as a spreader, sticker, or wetter. This has the effect of making the spray spread better and giving a better covering film on the leaves so that the fungicide adheres more closely and evenly on them. Soft soap, for instance, is used with some sprays, but it has a curdling effect with sprays containing lime, e.g. Bordeaux mixture and Lime Sulphur, and nowadays to avoid this there are many spreading agents available, e.g. saponin, calcium caseinate, sulphite lye, and materials under proprietary names. The use of modern spraying apparatus giving a high-pressure driving spray rather than a low-pressure fine misty spray is said to do away with the necessity for adding a spreader.

G. F. W.

SPREKEL'IA (in honour of J. H. von Sprekelsen of Hamburg who wrote on Yucca Draconis foliis, died 1764; from him Linnaeus received *Sprekelia formosissima*). FAM. *Amaryllidaceae*. A genus of a single species of bulbous plant differing from Hippeastrum by its solitary, distinctly 2-lipped flower and by its spathe, tubular at the base; native of Mexico and Guatemala. Cultivation as for Hippeastrum.

S. Cybis'ter. A synonym of Hippeastrum Cybister.

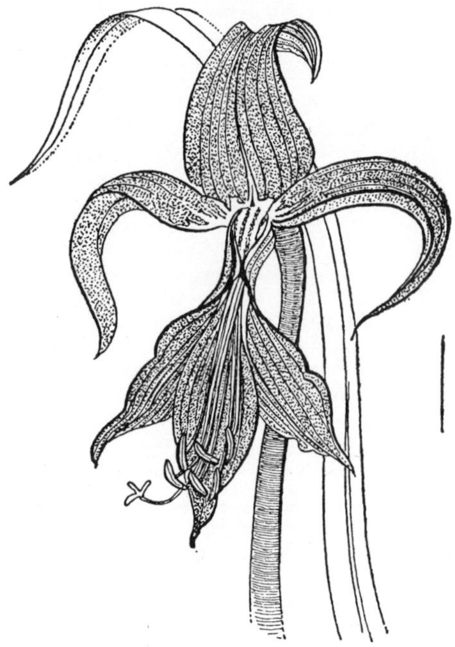

Sprekelia formosissima

S. formosis'sima. Jacobaea Lily. Bulb tunicated. *l.* after fl., loriform-linear. *fl.* crimson or white, large, showy, pedicellate, bract spathe-like, perianth declinate, 2-lipped, without a tube, segs. almost equal; stamens fixed at base of segs; scape hollow, 12 to 18 in. h. Mexico. 1658. (S.B.F.G. s. 2, 144; B.R. 1841, 16, as *S. glauca*; B.M. 47 as *Amaryllis formosissima*.) var. **glauc'a,** *fl.* smaller and paler than type, *l.* glaucous; **Karwinsk'ii,** *fl.* brilliant red, segs. keeled and bordered white; **ring'ens,** *l.* grey-green; *fl.* pendent, upper seg. with middle yellow band.

SPRENGEL'IA (in honour of Christian Conrad Sprengel of Brandenburg, 1750–1816; published a celebrated work in 1793 on the fertilization of flowers). FAM. *Epacridaceae*. An Australian genus of 5 or 6 species of evergreen shrubs. Leaves alternate stem-clasping and concealing the stems, pungent, rigid, hard in texture. Flowers solitary, terminal, surrounded by leaf-like bracts; calyx of 5 sepals; corolla deeply 5-lobed, alternating with the sepals. Fruit a capsule. These 2 attractive species require the same cultural treatment as Epacris.

S. incarnat'a.* Shrub 3 to 10 ft. *l.* ¼ to ½ in. long, ovate, stiff, hard, broad and stem-clasping at the base, tapered to a recurved, pungent point. *fl.* about ½ in. wide, terminal and solitary on short crowded twigs near end of shoot; cal. and cor. pink, both with deep, narrowly triangular segs.; anthers mostly hairy. May. Australia, Tasmania. 1793. (L.B.C. 262.)

S. Poncelet'ia.* Shrub only a few ft. h. *l.* ⅛ to ¼ in. long, ovate, the base sheathing round the stem, apex slender and pungent. *fl.* ½ in. across, white; sep. resembling but narrower than l. blunt; cor. lobes lanceolate, almost cordate at the base, overlapping; anthers glabrous. May. Queensland and New S. Wales. 1824.

W. J. B.

Sprengel'ii, in honour of Kurt Polykarp Joachim Sprengel, 1766–1833, Professor at Halle.

Sprenger'i, in honour of Carl L. Sprenger, 1846–1917, German nurseryman at Vomero, near Naples.

SPRING BEDDING. *See* **Bedding.**

SPRING BELL. *See* **Sisyrinchium Douglasii.**

SPRING SNOWFLAKE. *See* **Leucojum vernum.**

SPRING STARFLOWER. *See* **Brodiaea uniflora** (and note under **Triteleia**).

SPRINGTAILS. These primitive, wingless insects (Order *Collembola*) derive their name from their habit of taking sudden leaps into the air with the aid of a jumping organ (furcula) in the form of a forked tail attached to the underside of the abdomen of the greater number of species. Under certain conditions, these small, delicate, active, jumping insects are extremely destructive to plants, being especially abundant in Mushroom houses, into which they are introduced with the manure. Many species are harmless to plants for they are free-living and feed upon dead and decaying organic matter and only invade the tissues of plants when they have been attacked by other soil organisms (eelworms, insects, fungi, or bacteria). The presence of large numbers of Collembolids on and in roots, bulbs, corms, and tubers is, therefore, no certain indication that these insects are concerned primarily with the injury, for they may be only secondary agents and their presence may mask the effect of the pest or disease primarily concerned with the damage. The colour varies, some being white, others greyish, greenish, dark brown, or black, and their bodies are covered with scales or bristles. The eggs are laid in moist situations, and the young resemble their parents but are smaller and paler. Springtails often abound in glasshouses, where they feed on seedlings, the aerial roots and pseudobulbs of Orchids, and the foliage of a great variety of plants. They flourish in waterlogged soils, especially those containing humus, and they readily succumb when subjected to dry conditions. The stems, caps, and gills of Mushrooms are attacked to such an extent that the crop is greatly injured.

As these insects abound in moist places, all measures for removing superfluous soil moisture by effective drainage and deep cultivation should be employed. Glasshouse cleanliness is specially necessary to avoid outbreaks of these pests, which browse on the slimy Algal covering of inside walls and on plant refuse thrown carelessly beneath the staging. The walls should be lime-washed every year, while all weeds and plant refuse should be periodically cleared from the house and its environs, and dead and dying leaves removed from the base of plants.

Seedlings may be dusted with finely ground Lime and sprayed lightly with a dilute Nicotine-Soap wash, or dusted with Nicotine or Pyrethrum dust.

Heavily infested manure and composts should be subjected to steam sterilization prior to their use.

Routine fumigation of glasshouses with Nicotine vapour will keep these pests in check. **A**

G. F. W.

SPROUT. I. Any quickly grown shoot of a plant, usually a side shoot. II. Brussels Sprouts (q.v.) are commonly called 'Sprouts'.

SPROUTING. Beginning to grow.

SPRUCE CHERMES. *See* **Pine-apple Galls** and **Larix Pests.**

SPRUCE FIR. *See* species of Picea, especially **P. Abies.**

SPRUCE GALLS. *See* **Pine-apple Galls** and **Larix Pests.**

SPRUCE, HEMLOCK. *See* **Tsuga canadensis.**

SPRUCE, NORWAY. *See* **Picea Abies.**

Sprucea'nus -a -um, in honour of Richard Spruce, 1817–93, Yorkshireman who travelled in Trop. S. America.

SPRUE. Market name for the smallest shoots of Asparagus.

Spruner'i, in honour of Wilhelm von Spruner, 1810–95, who collected plants in Greece.

spumarius -a -um, froth-like.

SPUR. I. A hollow, narrow extension of some part of a flower, usually nectariferous, e.g. of the calyx of Delphinium, and the corolla of Viola. II. Rarely, a solid, spur-like projection. III. A short lateral branch with the nodes close together.

SPURGE. *See* **Euphorbia.**

SPURGE, CAPER. *See* **Euphorbia Lathyris.**

SPURGE FLAX. *See* **Daphne Mezereum.**

SPURGE LAUREL. *See* **Daphne Laureola.**

SPURGE NETTLE. *See* **Jatropha urens.**

SPURGE OLIVE. *See* **Cneorum tricoccum, Daphne Mezereum.**

SPURGE, SLIPPER. *See* **Pedilanthus.**

spu'rius -a -um, of illegitimate birth, false.

SPURLESS VIOLET. *See* **Viola hederacea.**

SPURRING. The cutting back of lateral shoots of fruit-trees to a few buds produces spurs and the operation of pruning thus is called Spurring-in. Black Currants, Morello Cherries, Peaches, and Nectarines which produce flowers on the long shoots of the previous year are not spurred-in. The spurs are apt to become congested on old trees spurred-in every year and when this happens the spurs should be reduced in size, and, if it seems desirable, in number, at the time of winter pruning since congested spurs are rarely fruitful.

SPYRID'IUM (from *spyris*, a basket, *eidos*, resemblance; in allusion to the shape of the calyx). FAM. *Rhamnaceae*. A genus of about 30 species of Australian and Tasmanian shrubs. Leaves alternate, usually small, and, like the shoots, more or less downy or hairy. Flowers small, sessile in heads surrounded by small, brown, persisting bracts; parts in fives. Cool greenhouse; thriving in the usual compost of loam, peat, or leaf-soil and sand. Propagated by cuttings.

S. globulo'sum. Evergreen shrub 6 to 8 ft. shoots, underside of l., fl.-stalks, and cal. closely downy. *l.* ovate, obovate or oval, 1 to 1¾ in. long, ½ to ¾ in. wide, pale beneath, glabrous above; stalk ⅛ to ¼ in. long. *fl.* white, small, sessile, crowded in axillary rounded heads ½ to 1 in. across, forming corymbose cymes. W. Australia. 1874. (G.F. 23, 795.)

S. parvifo'lium. Evergreen, much branched shrub about 4 ft., of neat habit; shoots, l. and l.-stalk downy or softly hairy. *l.* roundish-oval to obovate, ¼ to ½ in. long, apex rounded, white when young becoming green and glabrous above; veins deeply sunken. *fl.* white, tiny, closely sessile in small heads forming terminal leafy cymes. Australia, Tasmania.

S. spathula'tum. Evergreen shrub, 3 to 6 ft., much branched, shoots slender, downy. *l.* ¼ to ½ in. long, obovate, cuneate, apex rounded but emarginate; yellowish or white silky-downy beneath, green and nearly glabrous above. *fl.* white, minute, dense in small heads forming cymes or racemes. S. and W. Australia.

W. J. B.

squa'lens, rough, stiff, untidy.

squal'idus -a -um, untidy, dingy.

SQUAMA, a scale, usually a modified leaf.

squama'tus -a -um, scaly.

squamif'erus -a -um, bearing scales.

squamo'sus -a -um, squami- in compound words, scaly or with small, scale-like leaves.

squamula'tus -a -um, covered with small scales.

squamulo'sus -a -um, covered with minute scales.

squarro'sus -a -um, squarrose; having overlapping leaves with pointed tips which are very spreading or recurved.

squarrulo'sus -a -um, minutely squarrose.

SQUASH. *See* **Cucurbita Pepo.**

SQUIL. *See* **Scilla, Urginea maritima.**

SQUILL, ROMAN. *See* **Hyacinthus.**

SQUILL, STRIPED. *See* **Puschkinia scilloides.**

SQUIRREL. *See* **Grey Squirrel.**

SQUIRREL-TAIL GRASS. *See* **Hordeum jubatum.**

SQUIRTING CUCUMBER. *See* **Ecballium Elaterium.**

STAAV'IA (named by Dahl in memory of Martin Staaf, a correspondent of Linnaeus). FAM. *Bruniaceae.* An exclusively S. African genus of 10 species of low, evergreen shrubs. Leaves small, linear or needle-like, hard-pointed. Flowers small, in heads with one exception (*S. Zeyheri*) which has them in spikes; calyx 5-lobed, attached to the base of the ovary; petals free. Greenhouse plants needing the same conditions as Cape heaths; propagated by cuttings.

S. glutino'sa. Shrub 3 ft. and upwards, shoots erect, loosely hairy. *l.* 1/8 to 3/8 in. long, linear, erect or spreading, so densely set as almost to hide the stem; obtuse, 3-sided, heath-like. *fl.-heads* usually solitary, resembling composites, 3/8 in. across; bracts pinkish-white, the true fl. forming a central glutinous disk. April. 1793. (L.B.C. 852.)

S. radia'ta. Shrub 1½ to 3 ft., shoots hairy at first, finally glabrous. *l.* 1/8 to 1/3 in. long, narrowly linear, pointed, crowded, keeled, heath-like. *fl.-heads* 1/4 to 3/8 in. wide, solitary, terminal; bracts white or pale-pink; fl. not glutinous. Widely spread in S. Africa.

W. J. B.

stab'ilis -is -e, firm, lasting.

STACHELI'NA (in honour of Benedict Stachelinus, 1695–1750, Swiss botanist). FAM. *Compositae.* A genus of about 6 species of sub-shrubs, natives of the Mediterranean region. Leaves alternate, entire or wavy-toothed, white-hairy beneath. Flower-heads purplish, narrow, solitary or in dense corymbs; involucral bracts in many series, acute or obtuse; receptacle flat. Achenes glabrous or silky hairy. Nearly hardy.

stachy- or ***-stachys,*** in compound words, signifying spike-like, as *brachystachys*, having a short spike.

STACHYPHRYN'IUM (*stachys*, spike; the inflorescence is a spike). FAM. *Marantaceae.* A genus of 8 species of perennial herbs with foliage from the base, natives of SE. Asia, related Phrynium but with the flowers arranged in solitary pairs on a spike and fruit nut-like. Leaves moderately oblique. For cultivation *see* **Calathea.**

S. Griffith'ii. Densely tufted perennial up to 5 ft. h. *l.-stalk* 3 or 4 ft. long, its apical swelling glabrous, blade oblong, about 2 ft. long, deep green above, glaucous beneath. *fl.-stem* about 6 in. long, the fragrant fl. in 3 or 4 pairs on the spike, white. Malaya.

S. Jagoria'num. Densely tufted, scarcely 1 ft. h. *l.-stalk* about 5 in. long, its apical swelling minutely downy, blade rather obliquely linear-oblong or oblong-lanceolate, about 6 in. long, dark green above with black spots, paler beneath. *fl.* in an almost sessile spike, white. Malaya.

STACHYS (ancient Greek name used by Dioscorides for a plant with a spicate inflorescence). FAM. *Labiatae.* A genus of species of tall perennial or spreading annual herbs, or rarely sub-shrubs or small shrubs, widely dispersed, especially in the north temperate and oriental regions. Leaves entire or toothed, opposite, decussate. Flowers purplish, scarlet, pale yellow or white, sometimes showy but often small, sessile or shortly stalked; calyx tubular bell-shaped, 5-toothed; corolla cylindric, usually having a ring of hairs within, often incurved above, not or scarcely dilated at throat; upper lip erect or spreading, lower longer, spreading, 3-lobed, mid-lobe largest; stamens 4; whorls 2- to many-fld., axillary or clustered in terminal spikes. Fruit, ovoid or oblong nutlets. Several species are natives of Britain, but these are of little horticultural interest, though at one time *S. Betonica* was much used in medicine and *S. palustris* shared with some other plants the name All-heal. All the U.S. native species are known as Hedge Nettle.

Some of the species are of rather weedy habit, and most will thrive in any ordinary garden soil. They may be increased by seed or by division. Some species are listed in catalogues under Betonica, a number of botanists regarding Betonica as a genus distinct from Stachys. All the following are hardy herbaceous perennials unless otherwise indicated.

S. affi'nis. Chinese Artichoke, Crosnes. 12 to 18 in. h. *l.* ovate, acute, net-veined, rough to touch. *fl.* pink, in spike, rarely formed. China, Japan. 1885. (G.C. 3 (1888), 13, 16.) SYN. *S. tuberifera, S. Sieboldii.* The swollen ends of the underground shoots are edible. For cultivation *see* Crosnes. The name *S. affinis*, published by Bunge for this plant in March 1833, must be retained, being earlier than *S. Sieboldii* and *S. tuberifera*, and not invalidated by *S. affinis* of Fresenius published in October 1833, which is a synonym of a Sinai species, *S. pauciflora* (SYN. *S. Boveana, S. aegyptiaca?*).

S. alpi'na. Tall, erect herb. *l.* green, ovate, obtuse or slightly acute, crenate-serrate, cordate at base, roughly hairy, wrinkled. *fl.* purplish or brownish-red, woolly without, in remote, many-fld. whorls; cor. scarcely twice as long as the spiny-toothed cal. Summer. S. Europe. var. **interme'dia,** a large form with more wrinkled *l.* sometimes woolly beneath. (S.B.F.G. 100 as *S. sibirica.*)

S. as'pera. 2 to 4 ft. h., sparsely hairy or somewhat hispid. *l.* oblong-ovate, 1½ to 4½ in. long, acute or acuminate, bluntly toothed, usually distinctly stalked, base truncate or subcordate. *fl.* purple or rose-red, glabrous, sessile, in much interrupted spikes. Summer. Eastern U.S.A., Japan. (L.B.C. 1412.) Wet places.

S. Beton'ica. A synonym of *S. officinalis.*

S. citri'na. Grey-hairy sub-shrub. *l.* radical, elliptical, 1 to 1½ in. long, obtuse, narrowed to base, entire, minutely crenulate, long-stalked; bracts narrower. *fl.* sulphur-yellow, hairy without, included in cal., in small terminal heads, dense, the lower whorls often interrupted. Greece.

S. coccin'ea.* 1 to 2 ft. h., softly hairy. *l.* ovate-lanceolate with cordate base, or oblong-deltoid, obtuse, crenate, 1 to 2 in. long, distinctly stalked; *stem-l.* slender, uppermost sessile. *fl.* scarlet, cor. tube 2 or 3 times as long as cal., narrow, cylindrical; spike interrupted. Summer. Texas to Mexico. 1798. (B.M. 666.) Greenhouse.

S. cors'ica.* Procumbent, mat-forming, shoots slender. *l.* ovate, blunt, about ½ in. long, bright shining green, base rounded or cordate, stalked. *fl.* pinkish-white, in 2- to 4-fld. rather distant whorls, freely produced; cor. twice as long as cal., tube exserted; cal. bell-shaped, hispid, teeth somewhat spiny. Summer. Mediterranean region. Rock-garden in well-drained loam.

S. cre'tica. A synonym of *S. germanica Boissieri.*

S. densiflo'ra. Hairy, erect, 18 in. h., stem nearly simple. *l.* ovate-oblong, obtuse, 2 to 3 in. long, crenate, wrinkled, glossy, cordate at base, stalked; lower bracts ovate, almost sessile. *fl.* flesh-coloured; cal. teeth spiny; cor. twice as long as cal., roughly hairy outside, tube incurved; spike dense, thick, 1½ to 2 in. long. June. S. Europe. 1759. (B.M. 2125 as *Betonica incana.*) SYN. *Betonica hirsuta.*

S. dis'color.* About 1 ft. h., woody at base, densely roughly hairy. *l.* oblong-lanceolate, 1 to 1½ in. long, obtuse, deeply roundish-toothed, wrinkled above, white woolly beneath; stalked, upper narrower. *fl.* large, rose, or rarely yellowish-white, hairy, in many-fld. whorls. June, July. Caucasus. 1820. SYN. *S. nivea, Betonica nivea.*

S. Ehrenberg'ii. 18 in. to 3 ft. h., hairy. *l.* ovate-cordate, 3/4 to 1¼ in. long, strongly wrinkled, grey-woolly on both sides, with roundish teeth; upper oblong. *fl.* small pink, hairy, upper lip retuse; cal. woolly; whorls distant. June to September. Lebanon.

S. german'ica. Downy Woundwort. Shaggy biennial, white-hairy, 1 to 3 ft. h., stout, branched. *l.* coarsely crenate-serrate, often cordate; radical l. 2 to 5 in. long, stalk long; stem-l. ovate-oblong or lanceolate, stalk short. *fl.* pale pink with white variegation, ½ in. long; cal. teeth longer than tube; whorls 4- to 6-fld. April to November. Europe, included in Britain. (B.R. 1289; E.B. 1068.) var. **Boissie'ri,** *l.* oblong or linear-lanceolate, upper shorter, *fl.* rose, upper lip woolly. E. Mediterranean. SYN. *S. cretica.*

S. grandiflo'ra. A synonym of *S. macrantha.*

S. lanat'a.* Lamb's Tongue. Whole plant densely and persistently white-woolly, 12 to 18 in. h. *l.* thick, soft, oblong-elliptic, narrowed to both ends, scarcely toothed, wrinkled. *fl.* small, purplish or striped, in many-fld. whorls in an interrupted spike. July. Caucasus to Persia. 1782. Often used for summer-bedding.

S. lavandulifo'lia.* Dwarf, procumbent undershrub about 18 in. h., running underground. *l.* grey-velvety, oblong-lanceolate, entire, blunt, narrowed to both ends; upper ovate-lanceolate, sessile. *fl.* rose-purple, hairy without, in 2- to 6-fld. whorls. Summer. Armenia. Needs a sunny, well-drained spot.

S. libanot'ica. 2 to 3½ ft. h. Stem often reddish, bristly. *l.* oblong, 1 to 4 in. long, wrinkled, silky hairy, hairs appressed, rounded at base; upper l. lanceolate. *fl.* pink, ½ in. long; cor. somewhat longer than cal.; cal. funnel-shaped, teeth spine-tipped; whorls 6- to 15-fld., remote. Summer. Lebanon, Antilebanon.

S. macran'tha. 1 to 2 ft. h. *l.* broadly ovate, obtuse, crenate, broadly cordate, wrinkled, roughly hairy; upper sessile. *fl.* violet, over 1 in. long, glabrous; cal. about ½ in. long, purplish at tip, roughly hairy; whorls many-fld., distinct, lower remote. May. Caucasus. 1800. (B.M. 700 as *Betonica grandiflora.*) SYN. *Betonica macrantha, S. grandiflora.* Variable. var. **ro'sea,** *fl.* rose; **super'ba,** *fl.* of deeper and richer purple-violet; **viola'cea,** *fl.* violet.

S. niv'ea. Of gardens. A synonym of *S. discolor.*

S. officina'lis. Bishop's-wort; Wood Betony. 6 to 12 in. h., erect or ascending. *l.* oblong-cordate, obtuse, 1 to 4 in. long, deeply crenate; stem-l. few, much narrower than radical l. *fl.* red-purple, hairy, ¾ in. long, tube longer than the spine-tipped cal.; whorls in an oblong spike 1 to 3 in. long; peduncle long. June to August. Europe. (E.B. 1067.) SYN. *S. Betonica, Betonica officinalis.* var. **al'ba,** *fl.* white; **grandiflo'ra,** *fl.* soft rose, larger than type.

S. olympi'ca. Possibly a synonym of *S. lanata.*

S. Siebold'ii. A synonym of *S. affinis.*

S. tuberife'ra. A synonym of *S. affinis.*

STACHYTARPHE'TA (*stachys*, spike, *tarphys*, thick; from the form of the inflorescence). Bastard Vervain. FAM. *Verbenaceae.* A genus of about 50 species of herbs, sub-shrubs, or shrubs, natives of Trop. and Sub-trop. America, one species being widely distributed over Trop. Asia and Africa. Leaves opposite or alternate, toothed, often wrinkled. Flowers white, blue, purple, or scarlet, solitary in the axils of bracts, sessile or half-immersed in the axis of the spike; calyx 5-toothed; corolla tube straight or incurved, limb of 5 broad, spreading, obtuse or retuse lobes, sometimes equal; perfect stamens 2; bracts various; spike terminal. Warm-house treatment is needed. A compost of sandy loam and leaf-soil or peat suits them. The shrubby species may be increased by cuttings in sand under a bell-glass with bottom heat; the herbaceous perennials may be divided. The annuals need to be raised from seed. The leaves of *S. mutabilis* have sometimes been imported from S. America and used for adulterating tea.

S. arista'ta. A synonym of *S. orubica.*

S. bi'color. Shrub of about 3 ft. *l.* ovate to ovate-lanceolate, acute, toothed except near base. *fl.* at first purple, becoming pale greenish-blue, throat persistently white, tube long, funnel-shaped; spike terminal, slender, longer than l.; bracts erect, awl-shaped. June. Brazil. 1865. (B.M. 5538.)

S. cajanen'sis. Shrub of about 3 ft. *l.* ovate, blunt, narrowed to stalk. *fl.* blue, sunk in grooves of spike; spike slender; bracts linear, bristly above. May. Cayenne. 1882.

S. crassifo'lia. Shrub, 2 ft. h. *l.* elliptic or oblong-obovate, 2 to 3 in. long, entire at base, obtuse, margins revolute, lower surface hairy. *fl.* azure-blue; bracts hard, ovate; spikes long, slender, terete, straight, glabrous. June. Brazil. 1826.

S. dichot'oma. Sub-shrub about 2 ft. h. with forked branches; shoots 4-angled. *l.* ovate or ovate-oblong, 2 to 4 in. long, decurrent, deeply toothed. *fl.* blue; bracts very narrow; spikes slender, 6 to 18 in. long. June. S. America. (B.M. 1848 as *S. urticifolia.*)

S. in'dica. Brazilian Tea-tree. Annual, woody at base, 2 ft. h. *l.* oval or oblong, coarsely toothed, narrowed to stalk. *fl.* blue, sunk in deep depressions in axil; bracts appressed; spikes slender, 6 to 10 in. long. July. W. Indies. 1714. (B.M. 1860 as *S. jamaicensis.*)

S. muta'bilis.* Sub-shrub about 3 ft. h. *l.* ovate, narrowed to stalk, scabrid above, hairy beneath. *fl.* crimson then rose, large, sunk in furrows of spike; bracts awl-shaped, spreading above middle; spikes long, erect. All year. S. America. 1801. (B.M. 976.) SYN. *Verbena mutabilis.*

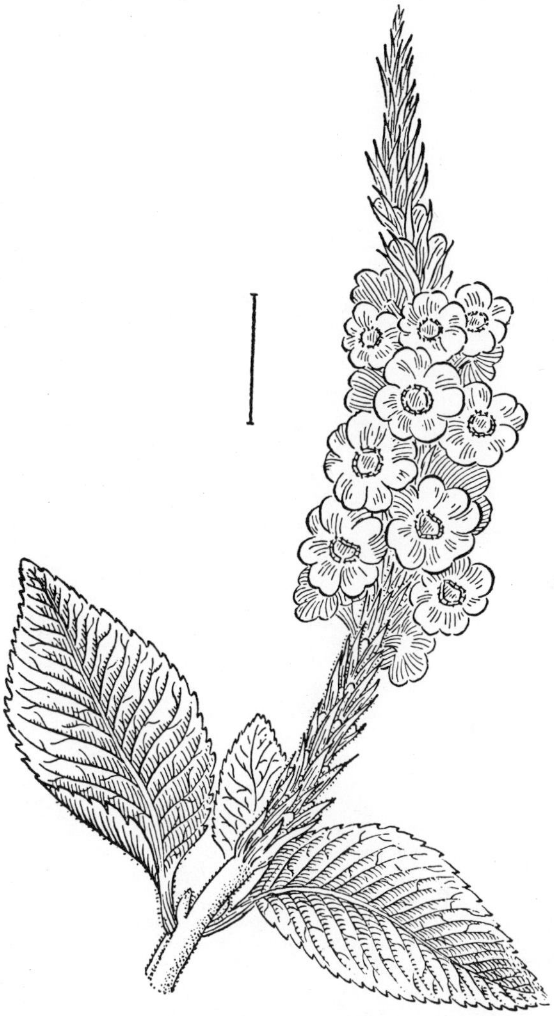

Stachytarpheta mutabilis

S. oru'bica. Sub-shrub about 2 ft. h. *l.* opposite, ovate or rhomboid-ovate, acute, coarsely toothed except at base, tapering to a short stalk, wrinkled. *fl.* rich, deep, blackish-purple; cor. tube curved; spike very long, with numerous leafy bracts suddenly contracted to a long point. October. S. America. 1845. (B.M. 4211, F.d.S. 55 as *S. aristata.*)

STACHYURA'CEAE. Dicotyledons. A family of a single genus, Stachyurus (q.v.), related to Flacourtiaceae but sepals and petals 4 and stamens 8.

STACHYU'RUS (*stachys*, a spike, *oura*, a tail; referring to the shape of the racemes). FAM. *Stachyuraceae.* A genus of 5 or 6 shrubs native of Japan, China, and the Himalaya. Leaves alternate, toothed. Flowers small, scarcely stalked, in pendent racemes; sepals and petals 4; stamens 8, free. Fruit globose, berry-like. The 2 species here described are quite hardy and grow well in an open sandy loam or peaty soil. They should be in full sunshine. Propagated by cuttings or seed. Both are valued for blooming so early in the year.

S. chinen'sis.* Deciduous shrub up to 10 ft. h. and as much wide, shoots green or brown, rarely reddish. *l.* ovate to oblong-ovate, 3 to 5 in. long, abruptly contracted to a shortish, slender point. *fl.* in pendent racemes 2 to 4 in. long, pale yellow, ¼ in. long, opening a fortnight later than those of *S. praecox*; pet. more spreading. March. *fr.* globose, smaller than in *S. praecox*. China. 1908. (G.C. 79 (1926) 229.)

S. prae'cox. Deciduous shrub, 5 to 10 ft. h., shoots reddish-brown, glabrous. *l.* 3 to 6 in. long, ovate-lanceolate, long- and slenderly-pointed, toothed. *fl.* pale yellow, borne 12 to 20 on stiffly drooping racemes 2 to 4 in. long; pet. erect, ¼ in. long. February, March. *fr.* globose, ⅓ in. wide, greenish-yellow. Japan. 1864. (B.M. 6631.)

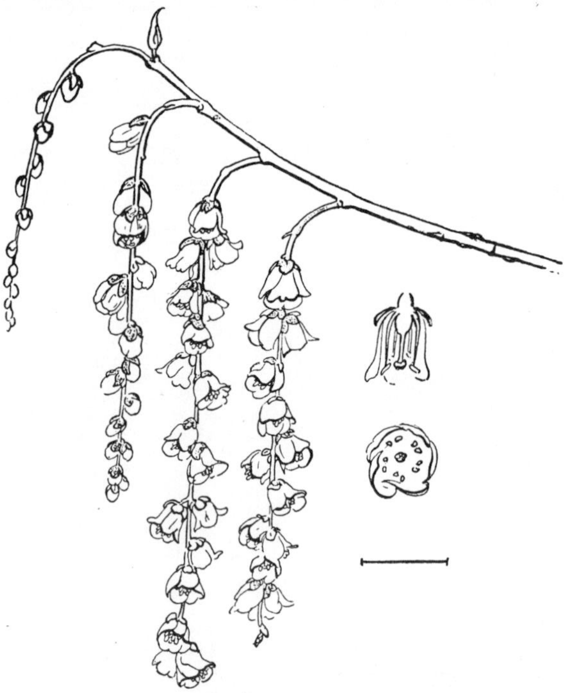

Stachyurus praecox

STACKHOUSIA (in honour of John Stackhouse, 1740–1819, British botanist, who wrote on Algae). Fam. *Stackhousiaceae*. A genus of about 20 species with the characters given under the Family. *S. monogyna* grows well in ordinary soil and may be increased by cuttings of young shoots in sandy soil in a cold frame.

S. monogyna. Perennial with slender, simple or slightly branched stems; 12 to 18 in. h. *l.* linear or lanceolate, sometimes crowded or few and distant, ½ to 1 in. long, rarely up to 2 in. *fl.* white; cor. tube about ½ in. long; racemes at first dense, often lengthening to 4 or 5 in. April. Australia. Syn. *S. linariifolia*.

STACKHOUSIA'CEAE. Dicotyledons. A family of a single genus, Stackhousia, with about 20 species of plants with erect, slightly branched, twiggy stems, often yellowish, from a usually perennial stock. Leaves alternate, narrow, entire, often rather fleshy; stipules none or very small. Flowers white or yellow, in terminal spikes, rarely solitary, with 3 bracts at base; calyx small, 5-lobed or -cleft; petals 5, perigynous, with long claws, usually free at base, united upwards in a tubular corolla with spreading lobes; stamens 5, included in corolla tube, of very unequal lengths. The species are Australian with one species extending to New Zealand, another to the Philippines.

STAFF-TREE. *See* **Celastrus.**

STAG BEETLE (*Lucanus cervus*). The largest British beetle, the male distinguished by the enormously developed jaws or mandibles which resemble the antlers of a stag. The largest individuals are as much as 3 in. long, including the jaws; but there is considerable variation in the size of the body and of the jaws, the smaller males not exceeding half the above size. The female is somewhat smaller than the male, but resembles the latter with the exception of the jaws which are proportionate to the size of the body. They are found flying at dusk on summer evenings and rest during the day on palings, tree trunks, and elsewhere. The female lays her eggs in dead and decaying posts, palings, tree trunks, and in the larger branches of forest trees, especially Oak and Willow. The large, white, Cockchafer-like grubs feed for 3 to 4 years on the decayed wood and may even extend their feeding into neighbouring living wood. The cocoons, in which the grubs pupate, are formed of wood chippings. These beetles are frequently plentiful, especially in the southern counties, but do not occur in the north. This beetle is not a pest of healthy trees since the grubs prefer decaying wood.

G. F. W.

STAGES. Stages are erected in greenhouses, &c., on which to stand plants to be grown in pots. They are generally constructed of wood but are more substantial when the uprights are made of iron. The shelves themselves may be of wooden battens, kept painted to preserve them, or of slate or tiles resting on angle-iron cross bars, or even of concrete or corrugated iron, the last being the least satisfactory material. If the slate or concrete dries too quickly, a layer of fine ashes or small pebbles or shells beneath the pots will ensure the retention of moisture.

Step-stages are frequently used in the middle of span-roofed houses or at the back of a lean-to, the stages being arranged like the steps of a staircase. These are sometimes made to be portable.

Where battens are used, and they are almost universal in step-stages, they should be fixed so as to permit medium-sized and small pots to stand safely upon them.

STAG-HEADED. Trees with dead branches at the top are said to be stag-headed. Sudden changes of environment, such as the removal of neighbouring trees in a plantation, prolonged drought, or interference with drainage may bring about this condition.

stagna'lis -is -e, growing in pools.

STAGONOSPORA. A genus of fungi in the class Fungi Imperfecti, some species of which are parasitic on plants, e.g. *Stagonospora Curtisii*, causing brown spots on flower-stems of Narcissus and brown spots and browning of the tips of the leaves.

D. E. G.

STAG'S HORN FERN. *See* **Platycerium.**

STAG'S HORN MOSS. *See* **Lycopodium.**

STAG'S HORN SUMACH. *See* **Rhus typhina.**

Stahl'ii, in honour of Christian Ernst Stahl, 1848–1919, professor at Strasbourg, then Jena.

STAKES, STAKING. Stakes are indispensable in the garden for supporting plants both in pots and in the open ground, and they should be chosen to fit the purpose they have to fulfil. Wire stakes either simple or with a movable ring are often used for carnations and a few plants of similar habit, the simple ones often having a loop or a spiral form to give better fixing. On the whole, for other plants in pots bamboo or slender deal stakes answer best. Bamboo stakes last well if taken care of and where bamboos can be grown the shoots are often sufficiently strong for this use; many are imported and can be bought in various sizes. Deal stakes can be cut out of ordinary laths of double thickness. Small annual growths from the base of hazel stocks, where they are usually produced in abundance, serve well for young plants being grown on, and the prunings of fruit-trees and bushes may also be used where appearances are immaterial. Strong stakes for fruit and ornamental trees, raspberries, and other plants that need supporting by horizontal wires may be obtained from plantations where the common ash grows well, as this wood generally grows fairly straight and lasts a long time. Sweet Chestnut and hazel are also useful for this and many other purposes.

Hazel is also useful in a green or partially green state for packing since it can then be readily bent as needed. Deal stakes of 2 to 3 in. quartering are also useful as permanent stakes if the lower part is treated with a wood preservative after being cut more or less to a point, as all stakes must be to enable them to be driven into the ground. Deal cut 1 in. square also makes excellent stakes for herbaceous plants.

The importance of staking newly planted trees cannot be over-estimated, for it not only maintains them, if properly done, in an upright position but prevents them from rocking about when the wind blows. When a single stake is likely to be wanted for permanent support it should be put in place at the time of planting; if this is left until planting is finished the stake may be driven in where the best roots are and cause considerable injury to them. Where the site is exposed to wind it is often a good plan to drive the stake in obliquely so that after tying it will support the tree against the pressure of the prevailing wind. Another method is to drive 3 stakes in just clear of the roots and tie the tree to each of them near the top. Whatever method of placing the stakes is adopted the tree should be firmly tied to them with strong cord which will stand the weather, placing a piece of sheet rubber (old tubes from pneumatic tyres are useful for providing these), carpet, or some other soft and durable material round the stem where the ties are made to protect the bark from chafing. These ties will need annual attention to see that they do not restrict the expansion of the stem and to renew them if necessary, and the knots made should be such that they will not draw. Special tree ties are made of somewhat elastic webbing or rubber which gives a little in use and can be attached without fear of injury to the bark.

In the kitchen garden, long, clean, straight rods of moderate diameter, 8 to 10 ft. long are needed as bean poles, and there is nothing better than hazel, ash, or sweet chestnut for these. Carefully stacked for the winter they will last for some years. For peas thinner branches with the twigs left on are needed and hazel is probably the best for this purpose as the twigs formed in a hazel copse are more or less in one plane or can be made so by bundling while still fresh, but other wood can be made use of at need.

For staking herbaceous plants twiggy shoots are often best as the growth of the plant makes them less conspicuous than stouter stakes, they need less tying, and if fairly rigid give sufficient support without unduly interfering with the natural habit of the plant. A not uncommon fault in staking of all types is the failure to drive the stake in sufficiently deep to give it a firm hold in the soil.

STALK. Any kind of lengthened support on which an organ of the plant is elevated. The term is often qualified according to the organ supported, as leaf-stalk (petiole), flower-stalk (pedicel or peduncle), fruit-stalk (pedicel).

STAMEN. In the flowering plants (Spermaphyta) the plant itself is the sporophyte generation (q.v.) and the reproductive organs it bears are of 2 kinds borne on modified shoots constituting the flowers. The flower usually consists of other floral leaves besides those bearing the reproductive organs, protective or attractive structures forming the perianth, but these may be absent and the bare essentials of the flower are the special leaves bearing the pollen sacs, the stamens, and the ovules, usually produced in an ovary. The stamen in its fully developed form consists of a stalk of varying length, called the filament, and a terminal structure called the anther. The anther bears the pollen sacs or microsporangia (*see* **Sporangium**) either singly or in a sorus of 2 or more, sometimes many as in Cycas. In Angiosperms there are usually 4 pollen sacs to the anther, 2 to each lobe. In the sacs the pollen (q.v.) is developed and the sacs eventually dehisce, setting the pollen free. The dehiscence is usually by a longitudinal slit, but sometimes by a transverse slit or by a pore as in Berberis and Erica. The 2 lobes of the anther are joined by tissue called the connective in which the fibro-vascular bundle carrying food through the filament to the developing pollen from the parent plant is to be seen. The connective is sometimes modified as an aid to pollination, e.g. in Salvia where it is often lengthened, so placing the 2 lobes of the anther some distance apart, or it may be continued beyond the apex of the lobes to form a flattish scale as in Viola, or modified in various other ways. In many plants the filaments are long, carrying the anthers beyond the mouth of the corolla as in Fuchsia, but they are often shorter than the corolla and may be absent, as in Orchids, where the anther and style are adherent to one another, or they may be carried up with the tissues of the corolla so that the anthers are seated directly on the corolla tube; the anthers are then said to be sessile. The filaments when present are usually free of one another, but they may be more or less joined in one or more groups, when they are said to be monadelphous, diadelphous, polyadelphous, &c., as the case may be. The amount of coherence varies and may be such that a tube (staminal tube) is formed as in Malva and many Leguminosae. A peculiar arrangement is seen in many Leguminosae, where 9 filaments form a sheath around the ovary, the tenth being free. The filament, usually thread-like, may be flattened in part or throughout its length and may be toothed as in Deutzia. The anthers may bear but one lobe and occasionally some filaments may be devoid of anthers and are then known as staminodes. The anthers are usually free of one another, but may be joined into a tube (syngenesious) as in Compositae.

The stamens in a flower collectively form the androecium, and their number is very variable, though constant or varying within narrow limits in each particular kind of flower, so constant that the number and arrangement of the stamens form one of the chief characters upon which the classification of plants is founded. The androecium may consist of but 1 stamen as in Hippuris, and of any number up to the indefinite condition seen in Ranunculus and Rosa, but 3, 4, 5, 6, 8, and 10 are the numbers most frequently found, arranged in 1 or 2 circles. *See also* **Flower.**

stamin'eus -a -um, having conspicuous stamens.

staminiferous, bearing stamens.

STAMINODE. A rudimentary stamen producing no pollen.

STAMINODY. Production of stamens in place of some other organ.

STANDARD. I. Plants with an upright stem clear of branches for some considerable distance supporting a head. The term is applied to many fruit trees so trained, e.g. Apple, Pear, Plum, Cherry, Damson, Peach, but also to trees grown for ornament, to fruit bushes on a single stem as Gooseberries, Red Currants, to Roses, Hollies, &c., and to such plants as Fuchsias, Heliotropes, Pelargoniums, Chrysanthemums, Mignonette, and so on. Special root-stocks have been selected as most suitable for growing Standard Apple-trees and these should be used in preference to 'free stocks', i.e. mixed seedling apples which were at one time commonly used. The clear stems of Standard Apples and Pears are usually 6 to 7 ft. long and such trees of vigorous varieties in good soil need planting about 40 ft. apart; in poorer soil and with varieties of but moderate vigour, 30 ft. apart may serve, but it is better to err on the liberal side if in doubt. Half-standards are trees with a clear stem of 3 to 4 ft. and are planted from 15 to 24 ft. apart. They are handier to deal with, less exposed to damage by gales, and frequently come earlier into bearing than full Standards (*see* **Apples,** &c.). Standard Roses have a clear stem of about 4 ft., and Weeping Standards of 6 to 8 ft. The stems of other plants trained as Standards vary very much.

STANDARD. II. The back petal of a papilionaceous flower.

Standish'ii, in honour of a member of the firm of Standish and Noble, nurserymen of Sunningdale, Berks. (John Standish, b. 1809, Yorkshire, d. 1875.)

STANGER'IA (in honour of William Stanger, Surveyor-General of Natal, d. 1854). FAM. *Cycadaceae.* A genus of a single species related to Zamia, differing by the pinnate venation of its pinnate leaves. For treatment *see* **Zamia,** requiring a warm greenhouse.

S. eriop'us. Hottentot's Head. Stem about 1 ft. long, nearly subterranean, more or less cylindrical or turnip-shaped, narrowed at base; full height 2 ft. *l.* few, pinnate, smooth; pinnae opposite and alternate, linear-lanceolate, spiny-toothed, rarely pinnately-lobed, lower stalked and sometimes bifid at base, upper sessile; stalk long. *Cones* stalks, hairy, covered with over-lapping scales, male cylindrical, female shorter, oblong-cylindrical. Natal. 1851. (B.M. 5121.) var. **Kratzeri,** smaller, pinnae in about 11 pairs, roundish and mucronate at tip. (G.F. 798 as *S. Kratzeri.*); **schizo'don,** pinnae irregularly cut, more robust. 1872.

F. G. P.

STANHOP'EA (in honour of Earl Stanhope, 1781–1855, President of Medico-botanical Society). FAM. *Orchidaceae.* A genus of about 50 species of beautiful epiphytic orchids, natives of Trop. America from Mexico to Brazil. Flowers large, showy, often strongly scented, but of short (a few days) duration. Considerable variation exists, but the greater number are characterized by stout bract-sheathed peduncles which bear 2 to 7 pedicellate flowers. The sepals and petals are free, spreading, usually wide at the base, then broadly oblong, shortly and bluntly tapered. The petals are similar, generally slightly smaller, often undulate and of thinner texture, in some species strongly reflexing, often more sharply tapered than the sepals. The lip is always very thick and fleshy; its structure, though variation exists, is remarkable. In the greater number of species it is well marked in 3 divisions, the basal portion (hypochil) is saccate, globose, oblong or somewhat shoe-shaped, sometimes with 2 short horns. The mesochil, or central portion, in many species bears 2 fleshy horns of considerable size, clearly distinct, running nearly parallel with the variously shaped epichil (front lobe of the lip), or curved at angles varying in the species. Between the epichil and mesochil there is often a marked constriction and the junction of the mesochil and hypochil is often distinguishable. A groove, narrow or comparatively wide, is often apparent, running from the mesochil to the hypochil. The column is erect or arched over the labellum and is more or less winged. Pollen masses 2. In a few species the horns are absent. The peduncles are generally pendent directly beneath the plant, but in some are shorter and assume a lateral position. In habit there is a strong resemblance between the species, so much so that pseudobulb and leaf characters are not definitely diagnostic. The pseudobulbs are clustered, usually more or less ovoid, often furrowed, 2 or 3 in. high, and bear a single large, rather leathery, plicately veined, persistent leaf, broadly oblong-lanceolate, contracted into a short stalk. Orchid baskets should be used as receptacles, with a few fairly large crocks placed on the bottom, so arranged as to allow the scapes to pass through. Even for the species with lateral spikes baskets are preferable as the inflorescences are often deflexed and may be injured by coming into contact with a pot-rim. Compost should consist of Osmunda fibre and Sphagnum moss, the fibre in slightly greater proportion. When growing, the plants may be suspended in the warm house as they enjoy a warm, moist atmosphere, but usually the intermediate or Cattleya house provides the right temperatures throughout the year. As soon as the young leaves are fully developed the syringe may be freely used, especially on those plants which develop aerial roots, often in such numbers as to conceal the pseudobulbs. In autumn the plants should be exposed to more light. Except when the new leaves are young and tender, shading should be light. In winter the night temperature should be about 55° F. and the plants should then have a rather decided rest, water being given infrequently. The firm feeling of the foliage should never be lost and at the first indication of loss of substance, water should be given. The fact that the plants should be hung near the glass offers facilities for Thrips and Red Spider to attack the leaves, which should be occasionally sponged as a preventive. Propagation is effected by dividing plants. Each division should have 3 to 5 bulbs behind the leading bulb. Though the flowers are rather transient, their size, colour, fragrance, and curious shape render the greater number of the genus worth growing.

S. Amesia'na. A variety of *S. Lowii.*

S. amoe'na. A variety of *S. Wardii.*

S. anfract'a. *fl.* rather small, deep buff-yellow with a few brown spots on each side of the hypochil channel; lip zigzag in profile, as the upper half of the hypochil is bent nearly to the base, mesochil bent at right angles, horns also bent at approximately the same angle as the upper half of the mesochil, strongly constricted beneath in front of sac; column greenish, with narrow, slightly purple spotted wings. Ecuador, Peru. (L. 315 as *S. Wardii venusta.*)

S. au'rea. A variety of *S. Wardii.*

S. Buceph'alus.* *fl.* strongly fragrant; sep., pet., and hypochil pale rich yellow, with purple dots and small blotches everywhere except on hypochil; hypochil, long, narrowed towards blade much as in *S. oculata*; mesochil 2-horned; epichil roundish-ovate, cuspidate; raceme deflexed, several fld. August. *l.* stalked, oblong, acuminate, plicate. S. Mexico. 1843. (B.M. 5278; B.R. 31, 24.) var. **gutta'ta,** sep., pet., and hypochil deep apricot, each pet., and the hypochil, marked with 4 brown blotches; **Roez'lii,** sep., pet., and base of lip deep saffron-yellow, spotted brown, horns and column white, the latter dotted with purple. Nicaragua. 1874. (G.F. 785.) A

S. Calceo'lus. Allied to *S. ecornuta.* *fl.* fragrant, comparatively small, $2\frac{1}{4}$ in. across; sep. concave; pet. sharply reflexed about the middle, deep buff-yellow; lip pandurate, somewhat boot-shaped, flattened at toe, practically entire, saccate behind. Cent. America. 1894.

S. cirrha'ta. *fl.* solitary; sep. white, obtuse, much longer than the ovate, yellow pet.; the short, fleshy lateral horns of the yellow and violet lip produced from the hypochil, which is 3-ribbed within, and rounded outside; mesochil wanting; epichil ovate, undivided; bracts spathe-like, imbricate, longer than ovaries; column wingless, extended into a pair of short tendrils. 1 ft. h. Nicaragua. 1840.

S. conna'ta. *fl.* deep yellow; lower halves of pet. blotched and spotted maroon; hypochil broad, short, globose, banded brown inside, blotched maroon outside, united as far as middle to column base, strongly constricted at junction with mesochil; mesochil and epichil not articulated; epichil very fleshy as are the horns which are nearly parallel with column. Peru. 1854. (X.O. 3, 277.)

S. convolu'ta. Allied to *S. tricornis* but with larger *fl.* Sep. and pet. white tipped buff; lip buff with an orange hypochil. Antioquia. 1909. (B.M. 8507.)

S. costaricen'sis.* Allied to *S. graveolens, fl.* larger, creamy-yellow to yellow or creamy-white with numerous ring-like spots on the sep. and pet.; hypochil stained with purplish-brown at base. The sac beneath the hypochil appears bigibbous. Costa Rica. 1915. (B.M. 8830.)

S. cymbiform'is. Sep. and pet. dirty straw-colour, connivent, latter undulate, with a few small, blood-red spots; hypochil yellow; mesochil and epichil white, spotted purple; raceme often many-fld., lax. Cent. America. (X.O. 124.) Allied to *S. Ruckeri.*

S. deltoi'dea. *fl.* palish yellow, dotted with crimson specks, large; lip orange, blackish-brown at base, and marked each side with a reddish-brown spot. Peru. 1862.

S. devonien'sis.* *fl.* fragrant, pale creamy-yellow, thickly and irregularly spotted with deep crimson-purple; dorsal sep. and pet. barred near base; lip whitish, purple-spotted; hypochil subglobose, with a deep purple stain over lower half; mesochil short, 2-horned; epichil obtusely angled, rhomboid, obsoletely 3-toothed at end; peduncle bearing 2 or more fl. July, August. *Pseudobulbs* ovate, ribbed. $1\frac{1}{2}$ ft. h. *l.* shortly petiolate, lanceolate, plicate, pale green. Guatemala, Mexico. 1853. (F.d.S. 974.) SYN. *S. maculosa.*

S. eburn'ea. A synonym of *S. grandiflora* Lindl.

S. ecornu'ta. *fl.* in pairs 3 to 4½ in. across; hypochil somewhat slipper-shaped, extremely fleshy, bright orange, passing into pure white towards point, purple-blotched on its sides, hornless, but having 4 little tumours; rest of flower pure white, except a few purple spots near base of the firm, concave pet.; whole lip somewhat shoe-shaped; bracts shorter than ovary; scape short, usually lateral. Costa Rica, Guatemala. 1854. (B.M. 4885; F.d.S. 181; X.O. 43, as *Stanhopeastrum ecornutum.*)

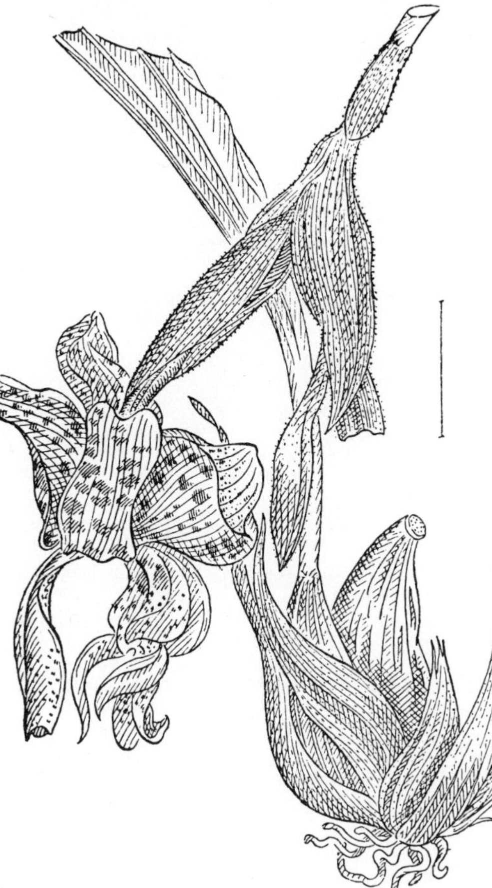

Stanhopea devoniensis (p. 2014)

S. elegant'ula. Allied to *S. saccata. fl.* primrose-yellow; base of pet. and hypochil orange, sparsely dotted brown. Habitat? 1907.

S. flo'rida. *fl.* white, large; sep. and pet. marked on inside with small, purple spots; lip covered with small, purple dots, and having a large blotch on each side between the 2 keels. S. America. 1879.

S. Fregea'na.* *fl.* intense egg-yolk-colour, irregularly spotted dark purple, 2 to a peduncle; sep. oblong-triangular; pet. shorter, acute, usually twisted; lip white, with small, dark purple spots. *l.* and *pseudobulbs* as in *S. Hernandezii.* Mexico. 1855. (X.O. 82.)

S. Fuerstenberg'iae. *fl.* white, blotched crimson at base of lip. Resembles *S. oculata* but fl. smaller and more numerous. Habitat? 1899.

S. gibbo'sa. *fl.* about 6 in. across, dull yellow, blotched and barred dull crimson; colour darker on sep.; hypochil incurved, keel each side; mesochil with ligulate-falcate horns, epichil oblong, acute. June, July. Cent. America. 1870. Somewhat like *S. Wardii.*

S. grandiflo'ra *Lindl. fl.* usually 2, fragrant, ivory white, with a few purple marks on mesochil and hypochil; sep. 2½ in. long; pet. as long, narrower; lip narrow, hypochil long, boat-shaped with 2 horn-like processes at base, mesochil hornless; epichil small, sub-acute; column slender, arched, with 2 rounded wings on upper part; scape short, pendulous or laterally arched. June. Venezuela, Guiana, Brazil, Trinidad. (B.M. 3359; B.R. 1529; L. 336; L.B.C. 1414 as *Ceratochilus grandiflorus.*) var. **spectab'ilis,** *fl.* pale straw-colour, strongly scented, sep. broad; pet. narrow, lip white except a pair of crimson lines and a few crimson spots at base, varnished. Venezuela. 1868. (I.H. 531.)

S. grandiflo'ra *Robb. f.* A synonym of *S. Bucephalus.*

S. graveo'lens.* *fl.* 2 to 6 or more, unpleasantly scented; sep. and pet. delicate straw-colour; lip at base, and centre of fl. generally rich deep apricot-yellow, horns and upper end of lip like ivory, turning yellow, hypochil oblong; column very broad, winged near base, so as almost to form a parallelogram; bracts narrow, scarcely as long as ovary; spike pendent. Guatemala? Brazil. 1843. (B.R. 31, 65 and X.O. 2, 165 as *S. inodora.*) var. **auri'ta,** *fl.* wholly deep apricot; **Leitz'eri,** sep. and pet. more decided yellow than type, orange mark on hypochil replaced by a faint red band, front lobe white, dotted purple. Brazil. 1891. (R.G.F. 1345.) Possibly a distinct species.

S. guttula'ta.* *fl.* fragrant; lower sep. broadly triangular, 2½ in. long, 1½ in. wide, upper narrower, more deeply concave, and like the smaller undulate pet. light yellow with many small red spots, confluent in places; lip 2¼ in. long with narrow strongly curved hypochil groove, sac open, light yellow spotted red, with a broad triangular recess beneath, mesochil very short with a reflexed tooth at base, horns creamy-yellow, red spotted, epichil heart-shaped with a decided apiculus. Sometimes regarded as a variety of *S. oculata.* Peru? 1843.

S. Haselowia'na. *fl.* very large, 5 to 7 in raceme; sep. and pet. creamy-white with numerous ring-like red-purple spots; lip and column spotted purple, channel of hypochil wide, nearly ¼ in. at greatest width; column winged and lobuled at top. *l.* petiolate, oblong-lanceolate. Peru. 1896. (B.M. 7452; X.O. 72.) Allied to *S. Wardii* but mesochil much longer.

S. Hernandez'ii.* Better known as *S. tigrina. fl.* very large, up to 8 in. across, usually 2, deep orange-yellow, richly blotched purplish-brown, strongly scented; hypochil roundish, yellow, with radiating, toothed lamellae within cavity; mesochil 2-horned; epichil oval, equally 3-fid, equalling the flat, falcate horns; column very broad. July to September. *l.* large, broadly lanceolate, deep green, plicate. Mexico. 1836. (B.M. 4197; B.R. 25, 1 as *S. tigrina*; F.d.S. 713–15, as *S. tigrina superba.*) The finest species of the genus. var. **lutes'cens,** *fl.* brilliant yellow, inclining to orange, barred deep chocolate, very large and handsome. Guatemala; **nigro-viola'cea,** *fl.* deep brown-purple, except edges of sep., pet., and upper half of lip.

S. impres'sa. *fl.* About 4 in. across; sep. and pet. bright buff-yellow, sparsely spotted purple; lip buff-yellow, hypochil orange-yellow; bracts large, ovate; scape 6 in. long, 4-fld. *l.* elliptic-oblong, 1 ft. long. *Pseudobulbs* 3 in. long. W. Andes. 1898. Allied to *S. inodora.*

S. inodo'ra. *fl.* several, scentless or nearly so, pale straw, with short, saccate hypochil yellow with a purple-brown blotch on each side, mesochil two-horned, 2-toothed, deeply sulcate between teeth, epichil somewhat rounded-ovate, entire, longer than the incurved horns; wings of column gradually narrowing downwards until they disappear; bracts broadly oblong, equalling ovary. May. Mexico. 1844. (B.R. 31, 65; R.X.O. 165.) var. **amoe'na,** hypochil deep yellow, with brownish-red eyes, epichil rose, dotted, horns dotted inside, very slender pointed.

S. insig'nis.* *fl.* pale dull yellow, richly spotted and stained purple, large, showy, fragrant; hypochil globose, split in front; mesochil with falcate, incurved horns; epichil roundish-ovate, entire, shorter than horns; column remarkable for its broadly-winged margin, giving it almost the shape of a battledore; spike drooping, fl. 3 or more. August, September. *l.* broadly lanceolate, dark green, plicate. *Pseudobulbs* clustered, ovate, furrowed. Brazil. 1826. Variable. Very handsome. (B.M. 2948–9; B.R. 1837; L. 352; L.B.C. 1985.) var. **fla'va,** *fl.* wholly yellow, very sweet scented.

S. Langlassia'na. Sep. and smaller pet. yellowish-white, tinged rose, with small purplish-brown spots near base; lip waxy-white, with pet. pressed against the whitish orange-yellow-tinged column; sep. spreading; hypochil short, broad, shallowly globular, epichil almost square, top inrolled with a blunt projection at base, mesochil fleshy, horns somewhat ligulate. Colombia. 1901.

S. Lowii.* *fl.* scented; sep. and pet. whitish-buff with numerous minute brown spots; lip ivory-white, upper half of globose hypochil with bands of maroon-suffused spots, mesochil solid, horns absent, epichil fleshy, tapered tongue-like; column pale green with ivory-white wings. Colombia. 1892. var. **Amesia'na.** *fl.* very fragrant, porcelain-white, inside of the hypochil suffused rose.

S. macrochi'la. *fl.* white or cream with lines of crimson spots. Mexico. 1859.

S. maculo'sa. A synonym of *S. Devoniensis.*

S. Madouxia'na.* *fl.* 5 to 7, 6 in. across, creamy-white, spotted pink, fragrant; hypochil deeply tinged violet-black, long boat-shaped, incurved, horns fleshy, epichil oval, blunt-pointed, slightly convex; column with 2 large wings in upper part. *l.* 20 to 30 in. long, 5 to 9 in. wide. *Pseudobulbs* ovoid. Colombia. 1898.

S. Martia'na.* Sep. pale straw-coloured with a few purplish spots; pet. white with larger spots and a broad crimson blotch at base; lip white, hypochil short, sessile, pouch-shaped, mesochil short with nearly straight, broad, cirrhose horns, epichil oblong-linear slightly 3-toothed; column pubescent, margins scarcely dilated; peduncles 2-fld. Autumn. *l.* lanceolate, plicate. *Pseudobulbs* ovate, furrowed. Mexico. 1843. (F.d.S. 2112–3; B.R. 29, 44 as *S. Martiana bicolor.*) SYN. *S. velata.*

S. mi'nor. Allied to *S. oculata. fl.* considerably smaller; sep. and pet. creamy-white, thickly spotted purple; pet. with 2 dark purple spots at base; hypochil with an eye-like purple blotch on each side, mesochil and epichil white, spotted light red. S. Brazil. 1907.

S. Molia'na.* Sep. yellowish-white; pet. white; both with rose, ring-like spots; lip white, dotted purple. Peru. 1891. (L. 331.) Allied to *S. Ruckeri* and *S. Wardii*.

S. nig'ripes. Resembles *S. Ruckeri* except in lip. Sep. and pet. yellow with many small, purple blotches and 2 black eye-spots on hypochil, the cavity black. Habitat? 1893.

S. ocula'ta.* *fl.* 4 to 10, usually lemon, or deeper yellow, with many eye-spots on sep., fewer on pet., a deep yellow eye, and 2, or occasionally 4, large, dark brown spots on side of hypochil, which is very much lengthened out, horns half-cylindrical, ascending, acute; raceme drooping. July to November. *l.* large, broad-lanceolate, nerved. *Pseudobulbs* small. Mexico. 1829. A free-flowering and very showy species. (B.M. 5300; B.R. 1800; L.B.C. 1764 as *Ceratochilus oculatus*.) Numerous varieties occur in gardens, varying in colour and in spotting of lip. Most are sweet scented. var. **Barkeria'na,** probably same as var. *Lindleyi*; **cro'cea,** a synonym of *S. ornatissima*; **Lind'leyi,** *fl.* dull wine-red, little spotted.

S. ornatiss'ima. *fl.* deep orange-spotted red, and marked towards base with large blotches of reddish-brown; spikes drooping, 6- to 7-fld. *l.* plicate. Mexico. 1862. (I.H. 325; G.F. 189, as *S. oculata crocea*.) Possibly a variety of *S. oculata*.

S. peruvia'na. *fl.* large, golden-yellow with a few purple spots; hypochil suffused dark purple; column spotted dark purple near top. Peru. 1910. (B.M. 8417.)

S. platyce'ras. *fl.* 3 to 7, nankeen-yellow, marked with purplish-brown dots and circles of small points, large; hypochil broad boat-shaped with 1 large, brownish-purple spot each side, mesochil and epichil whitish, spotted red-purple, horns broadly sickle-shaped; column narrowly winged in upper half. Granada. 1867. (Ref. B. 108; Gn. 33 (1888), 534.)

S. pul'la. *fl.* apricot-yellow, small; lateral sep. oblong, acute, reflexed, dorsal narrower; pet. very bright yellow, shorter, narrower, ligulate, acute, lip very bright, shining, like a plump shoe with a roundish knob at its top and with sharp, semi-oblong side borders; inside stands a nearly square body with four keels, converging like the letter V; between this and the apical knob is an inconspicuous, transverse slit; knob white; side borders and V-like keels brownish-purple; peduncle short, strong, 2-fld. *Pseudobulbs* short, conical, ribbed, dark. Costa Rica. 1877. (X.O. 205.)

S. quadricorn'is. *fl.* usually 3, buff-yellow, sparingly spotted crimson; hypochil oblong, having two short but prominent horns standing erect on lower edge of cavity; mesochil 2-horned, fleshy, hollowed; epichil ovate, entire, broad, shorter than the terete, in-curved horns; bracts very short, narrow. Cent. America. (B.R. 24, 5.)

S. radio'sa. A synonym of *S. saccata*.

S. Rand'ii. Allied to *S. eburnea*. *fl.* 2 to 4, smaller, fragrant, ivory-white, orifice of oval-oblong hypochil slit-like, with an erect short horn on each side and crowded with small papillae inside; column with rounded wings. *Pseudobulbs* about 1 in. h. *l.* about 9 in. or more long, about 3 in. wide. Brazil. 1894.

S. Reichenbachia'na.* *fl.* delicate shining white; sep. and pet. becoming ochre; hypochil becoming rosy, semi-globose, prolonged on upper border into an angle, mesochil solid, with a deep channel, abrupt in front, epichil triangular, rather convex. Colombia. 1879. Resembling *S. eburnea*, but larger and more conspicuous.

S. Rodigasia'na. *fl.* 6 in. across, solitary on pendulous scapes; sep. creamy-white, spotted rose and purple; column green, spotted purple; lip dark purple, with an ivory-white blotch and numerous red spots on mesochil, horns somewhat hatchet-shaped. June. Colombia. 1895. (B.M. 7702.)

S. Ruck'eri. Habit and general colour of *S. Wardii* but paler, epichil stained pink, its eyes very faint. Distinct by form of hypochil which is not oblong but narrowed to base, lateral teeth absent, a strong inflexed tooth in the wide, open fissure at end of mesochil. Nicaragua. 1845. SYN. *S. Ruckeri speciosa*.

S. sacca'ta. *fl.* greenish-yellow, regularly speckled, not blotched, with brown, deep yellow at base, small; sep. and pet. turned completely back on ovary; hypochil very deep and incurved, ochre-yellow marked red; mesochil reduced to space sufficient for development of 2 broad, flat horns, terminating in a short sinus with a central tooth; epichil oval, yellowish-white, flecked red within; bracts shortened. Guatemala. 1836. SYN. *S. radiosa*. (I.H. viii. 270.)

S. Shuttleworth'ii.* *fl.* 3 to 7; sep., pet., and basal part of lip apricot, with dark purple blotches, hypochil orange-yellow with maroon blotches, mesochil and horns whitish, epichil whitish with yellow shading and purple dots; column whitish, spotted purple on wings. Colombia. 1876. (R. 1, 35.) Allied to *S. insignis*.

S. stenochi'la. Allied to *S. tricornis* but fl. smaller. Hypochil globose, inset with thick fleshy warts, with a sharp constriction between it and the fleshy callused mesochil; callus with a compressed knife-shaped process on both sides, epichil narrow, tongue-like with a triangular reflexed point; column appressed to lip; sep. white, pet. apricot, purple-spotted near base; hypochil ivory white, purple blotched, mesochil and epichil yellow. Colombia. 1900.

S. tigri'na. A synonym of *S. Hernandezii*.

S. tricorn'is. *fl.* whitish-ochre, darker tips, spotted crimson on disk, base of pet. and sep.; dorsal sep. reflexed over ovary, lateral spreading; pet. entirely covering lip; hypochil marked outside with white, longitudinal lines, rough within and purple dotted, half-globular; mesochil orange-ochre, a third horn at the base in addition to 2 at the side; horns ligulate, acute; peduncle pendent, 2-fld. *Pseudobulbs* small. Peru. 1879. (X.O. 275, 280.)

S. vela'ta. A synonym of *S. Martiana*.

S. venus'ta. A form of *S. Wardii*.

S. Ward'ii.* *fl.* showy, deliciously scented; sep. and pet. golden-yellow, much dotted purple; lip pale yellow, with 2 large, dark velvety-purple spots on the deep yellow, oblong, boat-shaped, depressed hypochil; mesochil with 2 fleshy horns dotted with purple; epichil roundish-ovate, acute, often thickly spotted purple; column yellow, winged in upper half, spotted red; racemes drooping, 6- to 10-fld. *l.* broad, acuminate, plicate. Guatemala, Venezuela. 1828. (B.M. 5289.) Very variable. var. **amoen'a,*** sep. and pet. lemon-yellow, dotted with purple inside, hypochil orange with large eye-like maroon spots on each side and a maroon stain on each side of median line, mesochil lemon-yellow with small purple dots, column with greenish sides and a green rib down middle. Panama? 1923 or earlier; **au'rea,*** *fl.* deep orange-yellow, large, fragrant; hypochil with 2 large spots. Summer, autumn. 1835. SYN. *S. aurea*; **venust'a,** *fl.* deep uniform orange-yellow hypochil, epichil, and column may be dotted purple. 1896. (L. 315.)

S. Warscewiczia'na. *fl.* fragrant; sep. and pet. yellowish; pet. very acuminate; hypochil yellowish-white, globose, highly glabrous within, with a purplish blotch each side, mesochil and epichil nearly white, mesochil 2 horned, deeply sulcate, with a reflexed tooth; epichil finely dotted, red; horns very acute, incurved; column broadly winged, clawed; bracts much shorter than ovary. Chiriqui Mountains. Costa Rica. 1852. (X.O. 125.)

S. xytrioph'ora. *fl.* pale straw-yellow, with purple markings on base of lip and purplish dots on the rhomboid epichil; hypochil remarkably short. Peru. 1868.

E. C.

STANHOPEAS'TRUM ecornutum. A synonym of *Stanhopea ecornuta*.

STAN'LEYA (in honour of Edward Stanley, Earl of Derby, 1775–1851, student of ornithology, &c.). FAM. *Cruciferae*. A genus of 3 species of stout, hardy, glaucous, perennial herbs, natives of California. Leaves sometimes pinnatifid. Flowers yellow, in long, straight racemes; sepals short, spreading; petals narrow, long-clawed. *S. pinnatifida* grows well in vegetable soil in the open border. It may be increased by seeds or by division.

S. pinnatifi'da. About 3 ft. h. *l.* interruptedly pinnatifid, thick, much resembling a Brassica. *fl.* yellow, closely resembling those of a species of Cleome. 1812.

stans, erect.

STAPE'LIA (named by Linnaeus after Johannes Bodaeus van Stapel, a physician of Amsterdam and commentator on Theophrastus, who died in 1631). Carrion Flower. FAM. *Asclepiadaceae*. A genus of some 90 species closely related to Caralluma, Hoodia, Huernia, Piaranthus, and Trichocaulon and all of which have at various times been included under Stapelia. The plants are leafless succulents with 4- (rarely 6-) angled stems, the angles often compressed and usually toothed, rudimentary leaves being borne on the teeth in the young state; the stems may be decumbent at the base but the numerous branches stand erect and close together. The flowers appear singly or in clusters from the base or higher up the stems; they are usually reddish-brown or purple, often marked with yellow, and in many (but not all) species there is a pronounced smell of bad meat or fish. The 5 petals are joined at the base, which is cup- or bell-shaped, and the free lobes vary in shape but are usually widespread or reflexed; the inner surface is often wrinkled, sometimes papillose, and with or without hairs; the edges of the lobes often have simple or vibratile hairs; the corolla is thick and fleshy, especially towards the centre, where a definite fleshy ring is formed in some species. The inner structure of the flower is remarkable; as in all members of the family Asclepiadaceae, the pollen is not dry and dusty but aggregated into sticky masses (as in orchids);

the anthers are embedded below a central disk which is the style and bears stigmatic surfaces on the under side; surrounding the disk are 2 (sometimes 1) series of outgrowths forming the inner and outer corona; in a typical case the inner corona segments resemble erect horns and the outer ones are narrow strips lying more or less at right angles to the horns, their tips toothed. The shape and colouring of the 2 coronas is used as a generic and specific character in classifying the Stapeliads. Fertilization is effected by flies which may remove the pollen masses if foot or proboscis is inserted into narrow cracks above the anthers and transferred to the stigmatic surfaces by similar means; the lurid coloration and unpleasant smell of the flowers serve to attract flies. The fruit consists of 2 slender pods which, when ripe, split to release the flattened seeds, to each of which is attached a silky pappus. The development of the fruit is often delayed for a year, so that the ripe pods of one year may appear at the same time as the flowers of the succeeding year. The seeds germinate freely and often very rapidly (24 hours).

The Stapelias occur only in Trop. and S. Africa; they have no economic uses, but some species are eaten by the natives.

To grow Stapelias successfully a nice balance must be maintained between the amount of water required by the plant and the amount given to it. The commoner species such as *S. variegata* will grow luxuriantly if overwatered but will become too lush and lose their character; other species treated in the same way speedily rot off; and the allied genera such as Hoodia and Trichocaulon need even more care. The soil, therefore, must be very porous, a suitable mixture being good loam, coarse sand, broken brick, and leaf-mould or, better still, peat, and there should be plenty of crocks at the bottom of the pot. Cow manure is sometimes recommended, but it is unsafe for the rarer varieties. During the winter little or no water is needed and the plants are best stood on a sunny shelf in a greenhouse where the minimum temperature is about 45 to 50° F.; during the growing period the soil should be kept moist but never allowed to become saturated. Stapelias grow naturally in the shade of bushes, not in full sun, and a light shading of the glass during the hottest part of the summer is beneficial; they can be grown in a greenhouse with other plants more easily than the desert cacti, as they do not need so dry an atmosphere. Stapelias should be repotted about every 2 years and the older stems cut back or removed; when the operation is undertaken all traces of root mealy bug should be removed; this pest often multiplies in the dry soil during the winter.

As they hybridize readily, seed produced in a greenhouse where several species have been in flower at the same time is unlikely to be of pure strain. Propagation is easy by cuttings, which should be laid aside for a day or two to dry before being placed in sand where they will quickly root at any time of the year if the temperature can be kept at about 60° F.

The chief pests are mealy bug and root mealy bug, which should be removed as soon as seen; they do little harm unless allowed to accumulate. During the dormant period Stapelias are apt to develop black patches which may cause them to rot away at the base; the sound tips should be removed; they can often be broken off with a clean scar and re-rooted.

S. Aste'rias. Stems up to 10 in., 4-angled, not much toothed. *fl.* 3 to 4 in. across, lobes long and slender, inner surface with dark-purple stripes on a pale ground, transversely wrinkled, thinly covered with erect purple hairs, edges ciliate. Karroo. (W. & S. 568–75; B.M. 536; L.B.C. 453.)

S. deflex'a. Stems erect, slender, angles compressed, green and puberulous. *fl.* 2 to 3½ in. across, lobes fairly slender, slightly wrinkled on the dark-purple inner surface, with long white or purple hairs on the edge. S. Africa. (W. & S. 421–3; B.M. 1890; L.B.C. 135.)

S. Desmetia'na. Stems stout, up to 1 ft. h., angles much compressed, green and velvety; teeth not prominent. *fl.* large, pale to dark purple, with transverse yellow lines and wrinkles; entire inner surface covered with long pale-purple hairs. SE. Cape Province. (W. & S. 356, 504–10.)

S. Engleria'na. Stems prostrate with ascending tips, sides flat, with short teeth on the angles. *fl.* small, lobes rolled back like a Turk's Cap, dark purple-brown with lighter lines. Cape Province. (W. & S. 609, 610.)

S. flaviros'tris. Stems very stout, erect, sides concave, green and velvety. *fl.* 5 to 6 in. across, transversely wrinkled, dark purple with paler lines towards base of lobes; edges with long white or pale-purple hairs. Orange Free State, Griqualand West, Basutoland, Little Namaqualand. (W. & S. 513–20.)

S. gemmiflo'ra. Stem 3 to 4 in. h., glabrous, slightly glaucous. *fl.* 2½ to 3½ in. across; inner surface minutely wrinkled, violet-purple mottled with pale purple or yellow; lobes broad and recurving, edges ciliate; evil smelling. Cape Province. (W. & S. 352, 413–17; B.M. 1839.)

S. Gettlef'fii. Stems decumbent at the base, green and velvety, rudimentary l. unusually long. *fl.* 6 in. lobes long and slender, pale yellow with fine transverse purple lines and purple tip; long hairs on edges. Transvaal. (W. & S. 496–503; B.M. 8681.)

S. gigan'tea. Stems up to 8 in., pale green and velvety, angles compressed. *fl.* the largest in the genus, up to 16 in. across, pale ochre-yellow with fine transverse crimson lines. Natal, Zululand. (W. & S. 478–86; B.M. 7068.)

S. grandiflo'ra. Stems up to 12 in., angles compressed and notched green and velvety. *fl.* 6 in. across, wrinkled and a uniform dark brown and very hairy especially along the edges of the short lobes. Cape Province. (W. & S. 488–90; B.M. 585.)

S. hirsu'ta. Stems about 8 in. h., angles compressed. *fl.* 2½ to 5 in. across, wrinkled, cream-coloured, with purple lines; edges of the lobes hairy and the centre of the fl. shaggy with long white and purple hairs. Cape Province. (W. & S. 547–62.) Very variable.

S. irrora'ta. Branches numerous, decumbent then erect. *fl.* sulphur-yellow spotted blood-red, and base blood-red, tips purple; segs. lanceolate, long-pointed; pedicels usually solitary. July to September. 1795. (L.B.C. 127.) SYN. *Podanthes irrorata.* Possibly a form of *S. verrucosa.*

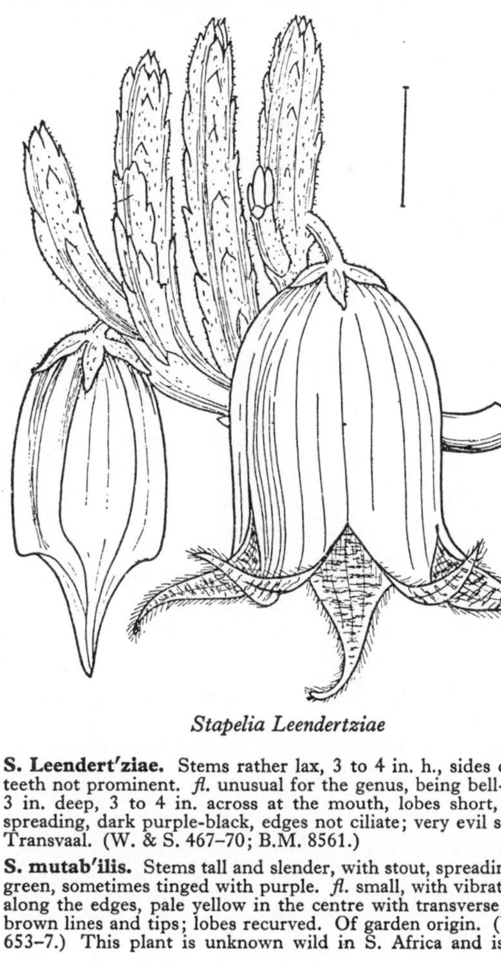

Stapelia Leendertziae

S. Leendert'ziae. Stems rather lax, 3 to 4 in. h., sides concave, teeth not prominent. *fl.* unusual for the genus, being bell-shaped, 3 in. deep, 3 to 4 in. across at the mouth, lobes short, slightly spreading, dark purple-black, edges not ciliate; very evil smelling. Transvaal. (W. & S. 467–70; B.M. 8561.)

S. mutab'ilis. Stems tall and slender, with stout, spreading teeth, green, sometimes tinged with purple. *fl.* small, with vibratile hairs along the edges, pale yellow in the centre with transverse purple-brown lines and tips; lobes recurved. Of garden origin. (W. & S. 653–7.) This plant is unknown wild in S. Africa and is almost certainly a hybrid, which has in turn given rise to a series of hybrids some of which have been given varietal names.

S. nob′ilis. Stems erect, up to 8 in., angles much compressed, green and velvety. *fl.* large, 10 in. across, lobes long and slender, centre bell-shaped; pale buff with fine purple lines, wrinkled, thinly covered with long purple hairs, stouter on the edges. Transvaal. (W. & S. 473–7; B.M. 7771.)

S. oliva′cea. Stems slender, very obtusely angled, not toothed, greyish-green, darker in the grooves. *fl.* less than 2 in., very wrinkled, olive-green with the wrinkled lines brown; evil smelling. Cape Province. (W. & S. 354, 461–5; B.M. 6212.)

S. parvipuncta′ta. Stems erect, obtusely angled, with transverse grooves across the angles. *fl.* about 1 in. across, on long stalks; lobes broad and rounded at the tip, smooth, pale green thickly dotted with purple-brown; vibratile hairs along the edges. Cape Province. (W. & S. 382–5 and Pl. 9.)

S. Peg′lerae. Stems erect, teeth not prominent, quite glabrous. *fl.* 2½ in. across, dark purple-brown, wrinkled, edges of the slender lobes ciliate. Cape Province. (W. & S. 595–600.)

S. Pillans′ii. Stems square with concave sides, blunt angles and conspicuous teeth. *fl.* 5 in. across, remarkable for the lobes which are extended into long tails; purple-brown, without markings, edges ciliate; evil smelling. Cape Province. (W. & S. 523–31.)

S. Plant′ii. Stems about 8 in. h., angles compressed, toothed, green and velvety. *fl.* 5 in. across, purple-brown with yellow lines along the wrinkles, lobes smooth with ciliate edges. Cape Province. (W. & S. 577–9; B.M. 5692.)

S. pulchel′la. Stems like those of *S. variegata*. *fl.* 2 in. across, sulphur-yellow with purple-brown dots. Cape Province. (W. & S. 667 and 668.)

S. pulvina′ta. Stems 4 in. h., angles compressed, teeth prominent, dull green and velvety. *fl.* 4 in. across, lobes slender, pointed, purple-brown with yellow lines, edges with long hairs and a cushion of soft pale-purple hairs in the centre. Cape Province. (W. & S. 536–9 and Pl. 7; B.M. 1240; L.B.C. 206.)

S. revolu′ta. Stems up to 15 in., sides concave, teeth short and spreading, glaucous green. *fl.* with the lobes curved back so far that it appears circular; purple, paler towards the centre, normally without yellow bands hairless except for the ciliate edges. Cape Province. (W. & S. 627–32; B.M. 724.)

S. variega′ta. Stems glabrous, branching freely, up to 6 in. h., angles obtuse with spreading teeth, green mottled with purple. *fl.* very variable, 2 to 3 in. across; inner surface wrinkled, hairless and without cilia on the edges, pale yellow with dark-purple spots and lines. Widely distributed in Cape Province. (W. & S. 672–708 and Pl. 17; B.M. 26; 1169 as *S. picta*.) SYN. *S. normalis*. More than 80 forms have been given names, but they are so variable and inconstant that they can hardly be propagated true to type.

S. verruco′sa. Stems short, angles obtuse, teeth spreading, green and glabrous. *fl.* saucer-shaped with widespreading lobes whose inner surface is covered with short wrinkled lines or tubercles; pale yellow with blood-red spots. Cape Province. (W. & S. 371–80; B.M. 786.) SYN. *Podanthes pulchra verrucosa*.

V. H.

Stapfia′nus -a -um, in honour of Dr. Otto Stapf, 1857–1933, keeper of the herbarium, Royal Botanic Gardens, Kew.

Staphisag′ria (i.e. *staphis*, raisin, *agria*, wild), Greek name for a medicinal plant, with somewhat vine-like leaves, used by Dioscorides.

STAPHYLE′A (from the Greek *staphyle*, cluster; referring to the arrangement of the flowers). FAM. *Staphyleaceae*. A genus of about 10 species of hardy, deciduous shrubs or small trees scattered all round the north temperate zone. Leaves opposite, toothed mostly 3-foliate, but some species have leaves with 5 or 7 leaflets. arranged pinnately. Flowers in terminal panicles (except in *S. holocarpa*, which has them axillary), white or tinted rose; sepals and petals usually of about the same length; stamens 5; fruit a membranous inflated capsule 2- or 3-celled. Seeds few, hard and shining.

All the species love a rich loamy soil and a sunny position. *S. colchica* and *S. Coulombieri* are much valued for forcing into flower in late winter and early spring and they, along with *S. pinnata* and *S. holocarpa*, are the best for ordinary cultivation.

Seeds are sometimes available and propagation can also be effected by cuttings.

KEY

1. *Lflets. 5 to 7, occasionally 3, especially on flowering shoots*	2
1. *Lflets.* 3	4
2. *Panicles pendulous, 2 to 4½ in. long; sep. erect*	S. pinnata
2. *Panicles upright, broad, 5; sep. spreading*	3
3. *Panicles 5 in. long and wide; pet. linear-spatulate*	S. colchica
3. *Panicles more compact; sep. and pet. shorter and wider*	S. Coulombieri
4. *Lvs. downy at least when young*	5
4. *Lvs. glabrous or nearly so (hairy on midrib in* S. holocarpa rosea)	6
5. *Fl. about ⅓ in. long; panicles 1 to 2 in. long*	S. trifolia
5. *Fl. about ½ in. long; panicles 2 to 4 in. long*	S. emodi
6. *Panicles sessile; middle lflet. short-stalked*	S. bumalda
6. *Panicles stalked; middle lflet. long-stalked*	7
7. *Lvs. oblong to oblong-lanceolate, long-pointed*	S. holocarpa
7. *Lvs. broadly ovate to roundish, shortly-pointed*	S. Bolanderi

S. Boland′eri. Glabrous shrub mostly from 6 to 10 ft. but sometimes a slender tree up to 20 ft. *lflets.* 3, broadly ovate to sub-orbicular, 1½ to 3 in. long (often longer on sterile shoots), finely toothed, very shortly-pointed, middle one long-stalked. *fl.* white, ¼ to ⅓ in. long, few in racemes 1½ in. long; sep. and pet. erect. April, May. *fr.* 1 to 2 in. long, obovoid, 3-lobed. California. 1883.

S. Bumald′a. Shrub 3 to 6 ft. *lflets.* 3, ovate to ovate-lanceolate, 1½ to 3 in. long, sharply toothed, downy on midrib and veins beneath. *fl.* dull white, ⅓ in. long in loose terminal clusters 1½ to 3 in. wide. *fr.* an inflated capsule about 1 in. long, 2-lobed. May. Japan. 1812. (S.Z.F.J. i. 95.) Of little garden value.

Staphylea colchica

S. col′chica.* Shrub 8 to 12 ft. *lflets.* 3 or 5, ovate-oblong, 2½ to 3½ in. long, finely toothed, nearly or quite glabrous, shining-green beneath. *fl.* ¾ in. long, in erect panicles up to 5 in. long and wide; sep. narrow-oblong, spreading, whitish; pet. pure white, erect. May. *fr.* 3 to 4 in. long, 2- or 3-lobed, obovoid; an inflated capsule. Caucasus. (B.M. 7383.) var. **laxiflo′ra,** *lflets.* usually 3, panicles more slender, pendulous.

S. Coulombier′i.* Possibly a hybrid between *S. colchica* and *S. pinnata*. *lflets.* 3 or 5, terminal one up to 5 or 6 in. long, dark green, shining beneath. *fl.* white, in panicles more compact than those of *S. colchica*; sep. and pet. shorter and wider. *fr.* 1½ to 3 in. long. var. **grandiflor′a,** panicles longer and laxer, *l.* and *fl.* larger.

S. emo′di. Shrub 6 to 12 ft., occasionally a small tree 20 ft., shoots glabrous. *lflets.* 3, very variable in size, the largest 8 by 4 in. but ordinarily 2½ to 5 in., oval, pointed, toothed, loosely downy beneath when young. *fl.* white, ½ in. long in terminal drooping panicles 2 to 4 in. long; sep. and pet. erect. May. *fr.* 1½ to 2½ in. long. Himalaya.

S. holocarp′a.* Shrub, 8 to 12 ft. but also a tree 20 to 30 ft. *lflets.* 3, oblong to oblong-lanceolate, 2½ to 4 in. long, pointed, finely toothed, glabrous and dark green above, downy on midrib beneath. *fl.* rose in bud, becoming pure white, ½ in. long, in drooping axillary panicles 2 to 4 in. long; sep. erect, oblong; pet. slightly longer. May. *fr.* obovoid, 2 in. long. China. 1908. (B.M. 9074.) var. **ros′ea,** *l.* more downy beneath; *fl.* rose. Probably joined to the type by intermediates.

S. pinna′ta.* Bladder nut. Shrub up to 12 or 15 ft. *l.* pinnate with 5 or 7 lflets. but sometimes only 3; they are ovate or ovate-oblong, 2 to 4 in. long, toothed, dull green, almost or quite glabrous. *fl.* white, ½ in. long, in terminal, pendulous panicles 2 to 4½ in. long; sep. and pet. erect. May, June. Europe, Asia Minor, naturalized in Britain. 1596. (E.B. 322.)

S. trifo'lia. Shrub 10 to 15 ft. *lflets.* 3, broadly ovate, 2 to 4 in. long, sharply and finely toothed, slender-pointed, pale green and downy all over beneath; middle lflet. long-stalked. *fl.* ⅓ in. long, dull white in drooping panicles 1 to 2 in. long. May. *fr.* usually 3-lobed, 1¼ to 1½ in. long; seeds yellowish. Eastern N. America. 1640. Of little garden value.

W. J. B.

STAPHYLEA'CEAE. Dicotyledons. A family of 25 species in 5 genera of trees or shrubs natives of the north temperate zone with odd-pinnate leaves with stipules. Flowers perfect, regular, in panicles; sepals and petals 5, imbricate; stamens 5, at the edge of the disk; ovary usually 3- (rarely 1-) celled; ovules usually many. Fruit a capsule with leathery or fleshy walls, seeds 1 or a few in each cell. Genera dealt with are Euscaphis, Staphylea, Tapiscia, Turpinia.

staphyli'nus -a -um, like a bunch of grapes.

A→

STAR-ANISE. *See* **Illicium anisatum.**

STAR APPLE. *See* **Chrysophyllum Cainito.**

STAR GRASS. *See* **Aletris.**

STAR HEAD. *See* **Centaurea.**

STAR HYACINTH. *See* **Scilla amoena.**

STAR IPOMOEA. *See* **Quamoclit coccinea.**

STAR OF BETHLEHEM. *See* **Ornithogalum umbellatum.**

STAR OF JERUSALEM. *See* **Tragopogon pratensis.**

STAR OF NIGHT. *See* **Clusia rosea.**

STAR THISTLE. *See* **Centaurea.**

STARCH is the most abundant of the non-nitrogenous food reserves in plants. It is found not only in the stems of perennials but in abundance in seeds and tubers and in general in all parts of green plants by which they are carried over the winter. It occurs in the form of small solid granules of various shapes, but often oval. The grains always show layers round a centre, the result of successive depositions of material one on the other. These starch grains are produced by means of plastids (tiny masses of protoplasm), by chloroplastids in parts exposed to light, and by leucoplastids elsewhere. The primary place of production is in the chloroplastids where by the process of photosynthesis (q.v.) starch is produced from carbon dioxide and water. It is insoluble in water, and in order to convey it from the place of formation to the place of storage it has to be changed into a soluble form. This is effected by an enzyme called diastase which converts the solid starch $(C_6H_{10}O_5)_n$ into the soluble sugar, maltose $(C_{12}H_{22}O_{11})$, and in that form it can be carried in the sap stream wherever it is needed for growth and any surplus for storage, where the leucoplasts reconvert it into starch. This process is most noticeable at night when most of the starch formed during the hours of light is removed from the leaves, and if the darkness be prolonged they become completely depleted of starch. The starch-grains vary a good deal in form and size in different plants, and their shape is often characteristic of the plant by which they were formed. The starch of commerce is obtained by crushing the organs of plants containing it and washing it out of the crushed mass.

STARFISH FLOWER. *See* **Stapelia.**

starry, arranged with rays like the points of a star.

STARWORT. *See* **Stellaria.** The name has also been applied to Aster.

STARWORT, ITALIAN. *See* **Amellus Lychnitis.**

STARWORT, WATER. *See* **Callitriche.**

STATI'CE. *See* **Limonium.** The genus Statice as defined by Linnaeus included both the sea-pinks (now called Armeria) and the sea-lavenders (now called Limonium). Although horticulturists have long used the name Statice for the sea-lavenders alone, its use by many botanists for the sea-pinks has made it ambiguous and it is no longer used for any genus.

STATIONS for fruit trees were, in the past, often carefully prepared by forming a bed of concrete, stones, brickbats, or slabs of stone at the bottom of the hole prepared for the planting of a tree, with the object of preventing the penetration of the tap-root into the subsoil. Apart from the fact that a true tap-root is very rarely present on a fruit tree since it or its stock is raised vegetatively, the process was not only costly but often resulted in preventing the adequate development of anchoring roots and increasing thereby the probability of the tree being blown over by a violent wind. It is, therefore, now seldom or never practised.

In preparing stations for planting at the present time the method is first to make sure the drainage is thoroughly good so that the hole does not act as a sump into which excess water from the neighbourhood drains but is rather such that excess water passes from it quickly. The hole is taken out rather wider than is necessary for the roots to go in without bending any back, and the sides and bottom of the hole are well broken up. The tree is then planted, using a planting board (q.v.), the upper roots being only an inch or two beneath the surface, the soil being made firm by treading as the work proceeds after being well placed between the roots, and the tree is firmly attached to the stake which has already been placed in position (*see* **Stakes**). A mulch of strawy manure is an addition well worth while.

STATUARY. Statuary, like most garden furniture, if used in the garden, must be associated with features in harmony with it, otherwise it will detract from instead of enhancing the beauty of the garden. It can rarely be introduced except in connexion with architectural features or geometrical lines. Such positions may be found on terraces, along the sides of long straight walks, sometimes where backed by a carefully kept yew or holly hedge, or as a terminal object to such walks or at places where walks intersect, and sometimes at the end of a vista or avenue. Not only the position but the relative size of the statuary must be considered, and before it is placed it is desirable to ascertain its probable effect by erecting a model of approximately equal size where it is proposed the statue should be.

Whatever the nature of the statue it should be of material known to stand the test of exposure to the climate and atmospheric impurities common to the district. Statuary exposed to the outside air may be rendered more durable by the application of one of the patent colourless solutions sold for such purposes, but paint should not be used.

STAUNTON'IA (in honour of Sir Geo. C. Staunton, 1737–1801, Irish traveller in China). FAM. *Lardizabalaceae.* A genus of evergreen twining shrubs, natives of NE. Asia. The number of species is doubtful owing to the genus being mixed up with Holboellia, but there are at least 4 or 5. That genus differs in having free stamens (united in Stauntonia). The following species is only hardy on a wall except in places like Devon and Cornwall. It needs no special treatment, but as a wall plant it requires an annual winter shortening back of long shoots. Propagated by cuttings.

S. coria'cea. A synonym of *Holboellia coriacea.*

S. hexaphyl'la. Glabrous, twining shrub up to 30 ft. *l.* long-stalked, with mostly 3 or 5, sometimes 6 or 7 lflets. which are ovate to oval, shortly pointed, 2 to 4 in. long, leathery; stalk 1 to 2 in. long. *fl.* 1-sexual, in axillary slender-stalked clusters of 3 to 7, white, tinged violet, fragrant; sep. 6, ¾ in. long, stamens 6 in the males, ovaries 3 in the females. April. *fr.* roundish-ovoid, 1 to 2 in. long, containing a sweet, watery, edible juice. Japan, Korea. 1874.

S. latifo'lia. A synonym of *Holboellia latifolia*.

W. J. B.

STAURAN'THERA (*stauros*, cross, *anthera*, anther; from the coherent anthers forming a cross). FAM. *Gesneriaceae*. A genus of 2 or 3 species of herbs, natives of the E. Indies and Malay Archipelago. Leaves large, membranous, solitary at nodes or opposite and stipule-like. Flowers blue, of medium size, in loose cymes or 1-sided racemes; calyx broadly bell-shaped, 5-cleft; corolla somewhat rotate-bell-shaped, 2-lipped, the posterior lip 2-fid; perfect stamens 4. *S. grandifolia* needs stove conditions and treatment like Klugia.

S. grandifo'lia. About 12 in. h. Stems and branches succulent. *l.* often 10 in. long by 4 in. wide, oblong, unequal-sided; stalk stout, 2 to 4 in. long. *fl.* 1 in. long; cor. tube white, tinged purple and pale yellow, limb pale purple, throat white with a deep-yellow spot on lower side; cal. hairy. *infl.* paniculate. August. Moulmein. 1862. (B.M. 5409.)

STAUROCHIL'US (*stauros*, cross, *cheilos*, lip). FAM. *Orchidaceae*. An epiphytic genus, separated by some from Trichoglottis, Stauropsis, and Cleisostoma, to include a few plants which hardly agree with those genera. They are distinguished by the 5-lobed lip, with the edges of the column adherent to the lip. Column short with horn-like processes.

S. Dawsonia'nus. *fl.* many, fleshy, starry, about 1 in. across; sep. and pet. greenish-yellow, spotted or barred brown or purple-brown; lip shorter than sep., 5-lobed, orange-yellow, blotched and streaked brown, disk golden-haired; column small with 2 penicillate ears; panicle stiff, about 18 in. long. Stem 1 to 2 ft. h. *l.* 3 to 6 in. long, ¾ to 1½ in. wide, 2-lobed. Burma. 1868. (A.B.G.C. 5, 54.) SYN. *Cleisostoma Dawsonianum, Trichoglottis Dawsoniana.*

S. fascia'tus. *fl.* 4 to 9, about 2 in. across; sep. and pet. yellowish, more or less barred with chestnut-brown, whitish without; lip 5-lobed, front lobe longest, tongue-like, pointed, often spotted red-brown, keels hairy. 1 to 3 ft. h. *l.* 2-lobed, 3 to 4 in. long. E. Trop. Asia. SYN. *Stauropsis fasciata.*

S. ionos'ma. Habit of *S. Dawsonianus*. *fl.* violet-scented, over 1 in. across; sep. and pet. somewhat elliptical, yellow, marked brown; lip broadly triangular, whitish, marked red. *l.* 7 to 10 in. long, 1 to 2 in. wide. Philippines. 1843. (B.R. 33, 41 as *Cleisostoma ionosmum.*)

E. C.

STAUROGLOT'TIS. Included in **Phalaenopsis.**

STAUROP'SIS (*stauros*, cross, *opsis*, appearance; in allusion to the shape of the flower). FAM. *Orchidaceae*. A genus of about 8 species of epiphytic Orchids, natives of Malaya. Sepals and petals free, much spreading; lip continuous with the column, spreading, concave, not spurred, narrow, the lateral lobes short, the middle one rather long; pollen masses 2; raceme few or many-flowered; peduncles lateral. Leaves distichous, spreading, coriaceous, flat. Stem leafy, not pseudobulbous. By some the genus has been reduced to 1 species. Reference should be made to Vandopsis, under which several of the species are included; by some *S. fasciata* has been referred back to Trichoglottis but is now under Staurochilus. *S. philippinensis* would probably be correctly placed in Trichoglottis. For treatment *see* **Vanda.**

S. Batemann'ii. A synonym of *S. lissochiloides*.

S. fascia'ta. A synonym of *Staurochilus fasciatus*.

S. gigan'tea. *fl.* 6 to 12, 3 in. across; sep., pet., and lip deep yellow, blotched cinnamon-brown, oblong, obovate; lip with white raised lines, fleshy, small, incurved, channelled, hatchet-shaped with short, rounded basal auricles; racemes axillary, about half as long as l. Spring. *l.* bold, distichous, dark green, broadly lorate, recurved, tough, 1½ ft. or more long, obtuse, emarginate. Burma. 1858. (L. 474; B.M. 5189 and R.X.O. 112 as *Vanda gigantea.*) *See* **Vandopsis.**

S. Imthurn'ii. *fl.* white with a few purple markings on the lip, and yellowish tips to sep. and pet., in a large panicle about 4 ft. long, the side branches produced for a considerable time (1 or 2 years). *l.* long. Solomon Is. about 1915. (B.M. 8714.)

S. lissochiloi'des.* *fl.* 12 to 20, about 3 in. across, fleshy; sep. and pet. yellow, spotted crimson within, rosy-purple without, fading to violet at edge, falcate; lip purple-crimson, saccate at base, front part furrowed and incurved, boat-shaped, side lobes erect, buff-yellow or purple-crimson, disk having an elevated tooth, its base a short, transverse crest; scapes long, erect or inclined. July to September. *l.* lorate, obtuse, obliquely lobed at apex, light green, 18 to 24 in. long, leathery. Stem stout. Philippine Is. (B.R. 32, 59 as *Vanda Batemannii.*) SYN. *S. Batemannii, Fieldia lissochiloides.*

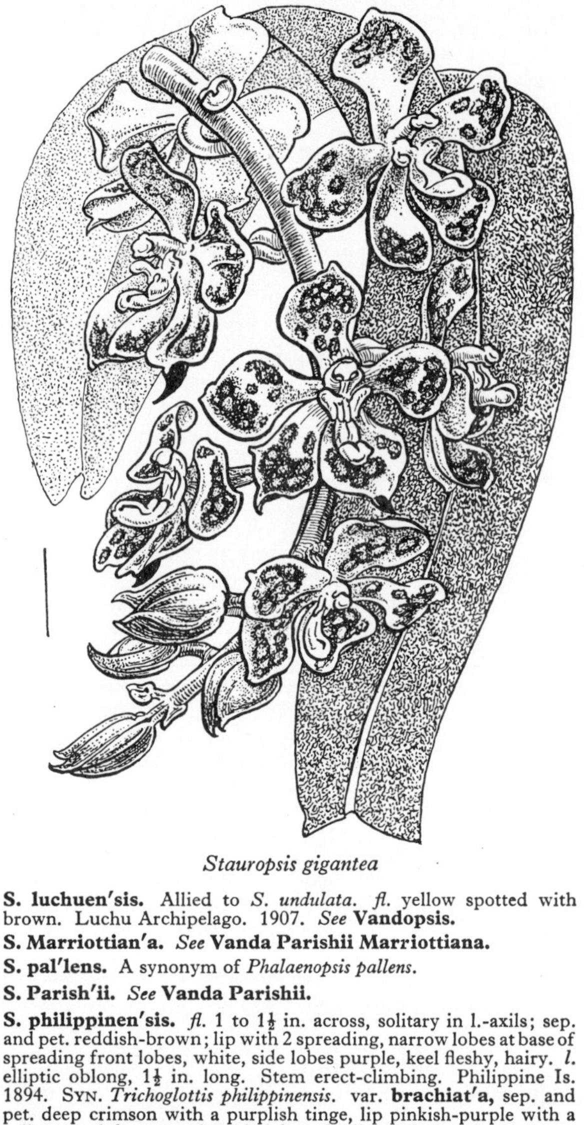

Stauropsis gigantea

S. luchuen'sis. Allied to *S. undulata*. *fl.* yellow spotted with brown. Luchu Archipelago. 1907. *See* **Vandopsis.**

S. Marriottian'a. *See* **Vanda Parishii Marriottiana.**

S. pal'lens. A synonym of *Phalaenopsis pallens*.

S. Parish'ii. *See* **Vanda Parishii.**

S. philippinen'sis. *fl.* 1 to 1½ in. across, solitary in l.-axils; sep. and pet. reddish-brown; lip with 2 spreading, narrow lobes at base of spreading front lobes, white, side lobes purple, keel fleshy, hairy. *l.* elliptic oblong, 1½ in. long. Stem erect-climbing. Philippine Is. 1894. SYN. *Trichoglottis philippinensis*. var. **brachiat'a,** sep. and pet. deep crimson with a purplish tinge, lip pinkish-purple with a yellow patch between the side lobes; fl. slightly larger than in type. *l.* 2 to 3 in. long, grooved in middle. Philippine Is. SYN. *Trichoglottis brachiata, Stauropsis purpurea.*

S. purpu'rea. A synonym of *S. philippinensis brachiata*.

S. undula'ta. *infl.* long-stalked, rachis thickened, densely set with fl., with long, nearly similar sep. and pet.; lip rather long, somewhat boat-shaped, tapering in front to a high keel; column short and thick; pollinia 2 with slender stipes and broad viscid disks. *fl.* 8 to 15, about 1¼ in. across, whitish, lip yellowish-green with red edges. Stem ascending with fleshy, fairly long leaves. Himalaya. 1878. Probably identical with *Vanda undulata*. (A.B.G.C. 5, 55; 8, 275.)

S. Warocquea'na.* *fl.* about 1¾ in. across, many in panicles; sep. and pet. yellow, dotted pale reddish-brown; lip white, spotted rose, keels whitish, stem stout, 1 to 4 ft. h. *l.* 6 to 12 in. long, 1½ to 2 in. wide. New Guinea. 1892. (L. 319.)

STAUROSTIG'MA. A synonym of Asterostigma.

STAVESACRE. *See* **Delphinium Staphisagria.**

stawkia'nus -a -um, of Stawki, near Lemberg.

STEAM HEATING. *See* **Heating.**

Steenis'ii, in honour of C .G. G. J. van Steenis, b. 1901, Dutch botanist and writer on Malayan flora.

STEEPING. Seeds with a very hard testa, like those of some Acacias and Canna, germinate more quickly if soaked in water for 24 hrs. before sowing. Some other seeds may be induced to germinate more regularly by soaking for a few hours in water. Where birds are troublesome seeds are sometimes steeped in paraffin, but it is usually sufficient to damp them only by, for example, shaking them up in a vessel containing a little paraffin.

Steerei, in honour of Joseph Beal Steere, b. 1842, Professor of Zoology, Michigan.

Steffens'ii, in honour of H. F. Steffens, German consul at Mendas, *c.* 1910.

Stein'ii, in honour of G. Stein, Zoologist, New Guinea, *c.* 1931.

steirole'pis, with sterile scales.

STEIRONE'MA. Included in **Lysimachia.**

STE'LIS (ancient Greek name used by Theophrastus for some parasitic plant). FAM. *Orchidaceae.* A genus of over 250 species of epiphytic orchids, natives of Trop. America, from Brazil and Peru to W. Indies and Mexico. Leaves leathery narrowed to stalk. Stems tufted or creeping with simple branches, 1-leaved at apex often with 1 to 3 sheaths below the leaves, without pseudobulbs. Flowers small, or minute, on short pedicels, usually in long, terminal racemes, rarely sub-distichous; sepals spreading, more or less connate; petals much shorter, broad with thickened margins, often including the column and lip; lip sessile at base of column, similar to petals or occasionally narrowed, or 3-lobed; pollinia 2; bracts alternate, often distichous. Few of the species are attractive for their beauty but many are interesting in structure. Flowers are often produced in profusion and several species form flower-spikes from an axis that has previously flowered. A curious character shown by some is that the flowers open and close at irregular periods, numbers on a spike being open, others shut at the same time. Most species are well suited in the cool or the Odontoglossum house. They need treatment like Pleurothallis.

S. atropurpu'rea. A synonym of *S. ciliaris.*

S. barba'ta. *fl.* ochreous-green; pet. and lip marked red-purple; sep. bearing purple hairs. Costa Rica. 1912. Related to *S. Endresii.*

S. Bino'ti. *fl.* small, distichous, green, in many-fld. spikes, 2½ to 4 in. long. *l.* including stalk 4 to 6 in. long. Brazil. 1901.

S. Brueckmuel'leri. *fl.* 10 to 20, yellowish-purple without, pale purple within, at intervals of ⅛ in. along rachis; sep. broadly ovate, acute, united at base, with spreading hairs within; pet. and lip very minute, latter entire; racemes 2 or 3 times as long as l. December. Mexican Andes? (B.M. 6521.)

S. canalicula'ta. *fl.* yellowish-green, very small, secund in a dense raceme; bracts and rachis whitish. *l.* wedge-shaped-oblong, blunt, thick, channelled. About 8 in. h. Bogota. 1872.

S. cilia'ris. *fl.* deep purple; sep. ovate, long ciliate; pet. oblate-rhomboid, fleshy; lip ovate, fleshy, channelled at base; spike naked for half length, then dense-fld. February. *l.* broadly oblong, narrowed at base, 6 in. h. Mexico. 1842. (B.M. 3975 as *S. atropurpurea.*)

S. Endres'ii. *fl.* greenish-white; sep. joined towards base; lip fleshy, transversely sub-rhomboid, hollowed; raceme distichous. December, July. *l.* wedge-shaped, oblong-ligulate, blunt, emarginate, apiculate, thick. Costa Rica. 1870.

S. gi'gas. Sep. deltoid, fleshy, greenish-white, purplish at base; pet. small, dark brown, spikes about 6 in. long. *l.* 4 to 5 in. long, fleshy. About 4 in. h. Brazil. 1832?

S. glos'sula. *fl.* brownish, in 2 transverse rows; dorsal sep. longer than all the rest of fl.; lip fleshy. *l.* wedge-shaped, oblong-ligulate, very slightly 2-lobed, apiculate. Stems densely tufted. Costa Rica. 1870.

S. grandiflo'ra. *fl.* chocolate, among largest of genus; sep. equal, blunt; pet. ovate; lip ovate, concave, emarginate; spike dense; spathe large, acuminate. July. *l.* oblong, emarginate, stalked, 4½ in. long, 1½ in. wide. Stem 3 in. h. Brazil. 1836.

S. grossila'bris. *fl.* light greenish, small; lip thick, fleshy; racemes shorter than l. Growth tufted. *l.* wedge-shaped, spatulate. Habitat? 1881.

S. micran'tha. *fl.* many, whitish, red within, nodding; sep. deltoid; pet. and lip truncate; raceme slender, spike-like. April. *l.* lanceolate-oblong, rather blunt, narrowed at base, 1 to 2½ in. long, 3 to 6 in. h. Jamaica. 1805. (L.B.C. 1011.)

S. Miers'ii. *fl.* very small, pale, yellowish or greenish-white; spikes 2 to 4 in. long, numerous, many-fld. *l.* 1 to 2½ in. long, narrow. Stems ½ to 1 in. h. Brazil. 1843.

S. ophioglossoi'des. *fl.* many, small, greenish-yellow tinged purple; raceme slender, 1-sided, 4 to 8 in. long. September. *l.* 2½ to 6 in. long, oblong-linear, rather blunt, long-tapered to base. Stem shorter than l. W. Indies, Brazil, &c., widely distributed. 1791. (B.R. 935; L.B.C. 442.)

S. sesquipeda'lis. *fl.* pale yellow, secund, large; sep. roundish-ovate, blunt; pet. oblate; lip cucullate; spike 7 to 10 in. long. August. *l.* broadly oval, 1½ to 4 in. long; stalk short. About 6 in. h. Sierra Nevada. 1848.

S. smaragdi'na. *fl.* bright green; spikes 4 in. long. Stems 1½ to 2 in. h. *l.* leathery, 3 to 4 in. long, 1 in. or more wide. Brazil. 1882.

S. tristy'la. Sep. broadly triangular, concave, flushed purple; dorsal sep. with yellowish-green margin; pet. fleshy, yellow; lip purplish; spikes about 8 in. long. Stem 1 to 2 in. long. *l.* 4 to 5 in. long, somewhat oblong. Brazil. 1838.

S. tuba'ta. A synonym of *Physosiphon Loddigesii.*

S. zona'ta. *fl.* light ochre; sep. brown at base; pet. with mauve mid-zone; raceme 1-sided. *l.* very thick, wedge-shaped oblong, blunt. Stem short. Demerara. 1883.

STELLA'RIA (*stella*, star; from the star-like flowers). FAM. *Caryophyllaceae.* A genus of about 100 species of usually diffuse herbs, distributed over temperate regions, in the tropics only on high mountains. Stems usually swollen at nodes. Leaves opposite, narrow or broad. Flowers white, small, in dichotomous cymes; sepals and petals 5, rarely 4; stamens 10, rarely 8, 5, or 3. *S. media* is the common chickweed, ubiquitous annual in gardens and very vigorous in fertile soils. *S. Holostea* is an early hedge-flower, very bright but scarcely to be admitted to the garden. Most of the species grow readily in garden soil but are of little value as garden plants.

S. cerastoi'des. A synonym of *Cerastium trigynum.*

S. gramin'ea au'rea. Perennial. Stems 1 to 3 ft. long, sub-erect, 4-angled. *l.* very narrow, sessile, ciliate, pale golden-yellow. *fl.* numerous, white, ½ in. across; pet. as long as the 3-nerved sep. May to August. The green-leaved parental type is common in Europe, including Britain, Siberia, and W. Asia to N. India. The variety is sometimes used in carpet-bedding.

S. Holos'tea. Adder's Meat, Greater Stitchwort, Moon Flower, Latin Flower, &c. Perennial. Stems 1 to 2 ft. long, decumbent at base, brittle at nodes. *l.* sessile, connate at base, lanceolate, 1 to 4 in. long, acuminate, rigid, ciliate. *fl.* white, up to ¾ in. across, on slender pedicels; pet. twice as long as the almost nerveless sep. April to June. Europe, including Britain. (E.B. 230.)

S. monan'tha atlan'tica. Low carpeting perennial. Stems decumbent; fl. shoots 3 to 6 in. h., 1- or 2-fld. *l.* narrow, sessile, narrowly lanceolate, $\frac{3}{10}$ to ½ in. long, acute, rigid, glabrous, glaucous. *fl.* white, small, on long pedicel arising from axil of an ordinary foliage leaf low on stem; pet. $\frac{3}{10}$ in. long. June, July. Greenland; other vars. of *S. monantha* in Canada, Alaska, Siberia. (Bot. Not. 1943, 266.) Dwarf enough for rock-garden but not of much merit.

S. radi'cans. A synonym of *Cerastium trigynum.*

stella'ris -is -e, star-like.

STELLATE HAIRS. Hair having several branches arranged in a star-like manner.

stella'tus -a -um, star-like.

STEL'LERA (in honour of Georg Wilhelm Steller, 1709–46, German botanist who travelled and collected widely in Russia). FAM. *Thymeleaceae.* A genus of perhaps 8 species of perennial herbs, sub-shrubs, or shrubs, natives of temperate Asia from Persia to China. Leaves alternate, flat. Flowers in heads or dense spikes, at tips of branches, hermaphrodite; perianth tube cylindrical, lobes 4, rarely 5, spreading; stamens 8, rarely 10, attached in middle and at mouth of perianth tube. Cultivation as for *Daphne Cneorum*. Rock-garden or alpine-house.

S. alta'ica. Stems slender, erect or ascending, about 1 ft. h., many from rhizome. *l.* lanceolate or oblong, rather acute, about 1 in. long. *fl.* white, perianth lobes 4; stamens 8; head ovoid, 10- to 15-fld., eventually becoming a leafless spike about 1 in. long. July. Altai. 1824.

Stellera Chamaejasme

S. Chamaejas'me. Stems often many, from a thick rhizome, slender, up to 1 ft. h. *l.* lanceolate or oblong, acute, ½ to ¾ in. long. *fl.* white, about ⅓ in. across, tube reddish, perianth lobes 5; stamens 10; heads dense, globose, many-fld. 1 to 1½ in. across, the uppermost l. forming an involucre. June. Cent. Asia. 1817. (B.M. 9028.)

stellipi'lus -a -um, having starry hairs.

stellula'tus -a -um, starry.

STEM. The part of the plant supporting the leaves and, in flowering plants, the flowers. It is always present in Vascular Plants though sometimes so short that the plants are called stemless or acaulescent. In these the top of the so-called root is, in fact, a stem in which the internodes are extremely short. In the Spermaphytes the stem is developed from the plumule of the embryo in the seed; in the vascular Cryptogams it develops from one of the 4 primary divisions of the fertilized egg-cell. In most plants the stem grows upwards towards the light, contains chlorophyll in some of the cells exposed to light and therefore can take part in photosynthesis, is covered by a true epidermis, and bears leaves and buds at the nodes—characters that are in marked contrast to those of roots. Exceptions to all these may occur, but they are exceptional. The stem, like the root, is increased in length by the division of cells at its tip, known as the growing point, and the elongation of these cells a little behind it, where also are laid down the initials of leaves and buds, nearly always in successional order, the youngest nearest to the actual growing point. Unlike the root branches these outgrowths arise from the outer tissues, not from the inner. If roots are produced they arise from cells farther in as they do when formed from an older root. The original growing point may persist, apart from accident, through the life of the plant, as it does in a pine or ash, but not infrequently it has a comparatively short life of a year or less, its place being taken by the topmost bud (for every bud has a growing point of its own), as it does, for example, in the elm.

The main function of the stem is to place the leaves of the plant in such a position that they shall receive the light necessary for photosynthesis, and the flowers where seed production can be best ensured, and to convey water and food materials collected by the roots, through the vessels of the wood (xylem) to the leaves, and manufactured food from them, through the sieve-tubes of the bast or phloem, to where it may be required for growth or for storage.

Wide differences are found in stems. They may be extremely short, as in the acaulescent plants already referred to and in some minute annuals, or hundreds of feet long as in some species of Eucalyptus (q.v.). They may be simple and unbranched as in most palms or much branched as in most shrubs and round-headed trees and conifers. They vary in thickness from those not thicker than cotton thread to stems of vast bulk like those of Sequoia, Thuja, or Castanea, measuring many feet through. There may be a main stem or many stems of almost equal size and strength. They may grow stiffly erect as in fastigiate trees, or spread more or less horizontally, or droop as in 'weeping trees', and all these forms may be found within the range of 1 species.

In internal structure there are also great differences. There are 2 well-marked types, easily seen in woody stems, perhaps less easily recognized at a casual glance in herbaceous ones. In one if it becut across, a distinct ring of woody tissue will be seen, a condition characteristic of Dicotyledons and Conifers. As these stems age so a fresh ring of wood is laid down each year in succession outside those made before, and as the part of the ring formed in autumn is harder and denser than that formed in spring, the annual rings are usually easily discerned. These rings are formed by the activity of a single ring of cells called the cambium, situated on the outside of the youngest ring of wood, which also forms successive rings of phloem on its outer side, which, however, are not evident since they are of soft, easily compressed tissue (phloem) forming part of the bark which easily separates from the wood at the ring of cambium. These stems are also characterized by the possession of a definite pith and lines of cellular tissue radiating from it towards the circumference dividing the wood into wedge-shaped masses. These are called medullary rays and form the silver-grain of the cabinet-maker; they are for the most part living cells and often contain a store of food, whereas in old stems both the pith and the inner part of the wood is dead, only the part near the cambium still retaining life. In the other type of stem, belonging to Monocotyledons, a transverse section shows no rings, but the woody vessels and fibres, and with them the phloem, form scattered bundles embedded in cellular tissue—there is no definite pith, no separate bark, no medullary rays, no cambium, and their age cannot be told, as can that of Dicotyledons, by the number of rings of wood. Only in exceptional instances, as in Dracaenas, does increase of thickness take place through the activity of a sort of cambium, and though some increase of girth occurs in some other monocotyledonous stems there is no evidence of growth in annual rings.

Certain forms of stem have received special names. The columnar, erect stem of palms and tree-ferns marked by the leaf-bases of former foliage or their scars is called a **caudex.** The cylindrical, jointed stem of grasses, often hollow in the internodes, is known as a **culm.** A **scape** is a leafless, erect stem, ending in an inflorescence of one or more flowers. The term **haulm**, often applied to the stems of potatoes, peas, &c., has no special meaning. Decumbent stems may be **runners** when slender, lying on the surface of the ground and rooting at the nodes, **stolons,** if similar to a runner but often slightly underground and forming erect stems from the terminal buds which tend to produce new plants; **offsets,** if very short stolons; **suckers,** if underground and otherwise like a stem; **rhizomes,** if like a stolon but thick and often forming lateral as well as terminal shoots; **tubers,** if much swollen and produced at the ends of stolons, less often along their length; **corms,** if swollen bases of stems.

While most perennial stems act as storehouses of food, placed in the cells of cortex and medullary rays, &c., the rhizome, tuber, and corm afford examples of special modification for the purpose of storing food. Various other modifications serve particular purposes, among the most remarkable being **thorns** and **tendrils.** Thorns are branches or the terminal part of a main stem which have remained short, in which the woody tissue is strongly developed so that they are very rigid and which end in sharp points. These form an efficient protection against browsing animals and are well seen in hawthorns and blackthorns. In a few plants, e.g. vines and passion-flowers, tendrils, very slender stems with the power of twining round firm supports in a spiral fashion, aid the plants to reach the light. These special stems are not to be confused with twining stems, and, as pointed out elsewhere, not all tendrils are modified stems.

STEM CANKER. Canker-like lesions on stems caused by various fungi which attack and destroy the tissues of woody and half-woody stems. *See*, e.g., **Gardenia diseases, Canker.**

STEM EELWORM, *Ditylenchus dipsaci.* This microscopic nematode is the most common and widely distributed eelworm pest in this country, attacking a wide range of agricultural and horticultural crops, including Cereals, Clover, Potatoes, Onions, Narcissi, and Phlox, and numerous other plants both cultivated and wild. The adult eelworm is $\frac{1}{25}$ to $\frac{1}{20}$ in. in length, eel-shaped, and with the body tapering slightly towards the head (which is provided with a spear-shaped point or stylet), and sharply towards the tail. Eggs are laid within the tissues of the host plant, and hatch into larvae which resemble the adults except in size. Breeding continues within the plant tissues, which eventually decay, when the worms either remain in the dead cells and become dried up or enter the soil and at some time invade other plants. The pre-adult larval forms are capable of remaining in a desiccated state for long periods—3 to 7 or more years—again becoming active when placed in moist conditions. The signs of attack vary with the host plant and to the degree of infection, and such terms as 'Tulip Root' in Oats, Clover 'Sickness', 'False Blight' in Potato tubers, 'Bloated' Onion bulbs, 'Spickles' in Narcissus foliage, Phlox 'Disease', denote attack by this nematode in such crops and plants as those mentioned. The eelworms may attack bulbs (Narcissus and Onion), tubers (Potato), underground stems (Phlox), and stems, shoots, leaves (Oenothera), and may even invade the flowers, capsules, and seeds (certain Composites). There exist biologic races or strains which are restricted to a few or to several host plants. For instance, the Narcissus strain is capable of infecting Onions though not Potatoes or bulbous Irises; the Phlox race may infect annual Phloxes, Oenothera, and Gilia, but not Narcissi or Onions, and so on. A knowledge of the behaviour of such races is desirable so that such rotation practices may be followed as to avoid infection of a subsequent crop grown in infected land. Many weeds, e.g. Plantains, and 'volunteer' plants (e.g. Potatoes 'ground-keepers' due to incomplete lifting of the crop), may act as 'reservoir' hosts and their presence will ensure the continuance of a particular race in that area, so that clean cultivation by the destruction of weeds, the complete lifting of root-crops, the burning of infected stubble, and the proper disposal of all infected plant remains will reduce the chance of survival of the nematodes in the soil.

There is no effective chemical method of eradicating the eelworms from infected ground, and steam sterilization is practically restricted to glasshouse borders. A rotation of crops is the most effective method by starving out the pest, and infected land should be kept clear of susceptible crops for at least 3 years. All weeds should be destroyed by regular hoeing, and focal areas of infection eliminated by lifting and destroying diseased plants. Narcissus bulbs may be subjected to the Hot-Water treatment—their immersion in water at a constant temperature of 110° F. for 3 hours, while Phlox stools may receive similar treatment for a period of 1 hour, but cleaned-up stocks must be planted in fresh, eelworm-free ground otherwise reinfection will follow. The raising of clean Phlox plants from diseased plants is practicable provided that the cuttings are taken from well-washed roots and inserted in clean soil. Potato 'seed' should never be saved from an infected crop.

A dressing of nitrogenous manures or sulphate of potash on slightly affected crops will mask the attack by encouraging growth so that the plants may grow away vigorously even though infected. Reasonable precautions should be taken to avoid the transport of infected soil on tools or on the wheels of barrows, &c., or on the boots of persons working on or walking over the ground.

G. F. W.

STEMMA'TIUM (diminutive of Greek *stemma*, wreath, garland). FAM. *Liliaceae.* A genus of 1 species, a Chilean plant with sub-globose tunicated bulb. Leaves basal, few, linear. Flowers few in a terminal umbel, stalked; perianth salver-shaped with a cylindric tube and 6 almost equal spreading lobes; corona of 6 small scales. Scape simple, leafless; spathe 2-valved. This genus has been confused with Tristagma which has no corona. *S. narcissoides* somewhat resembles a Narcissus. It needs greenhouse treatment, a rich sandy loam and not much water, and can be propagated by seeds or offsets.

S. narcissoi'des. Bulb about 1 in. thick; tunics brown, membranous. *l.* about 4, erect, 6 in. or more long, linear, glabrous. *fl.* 5 or 6 in an umbel; scape terete, purplish, 1 ft. or more long; perianth tube greenish-white, less than ½ in. long; segs. white, oblong, with a slender 2-nerved greenish keel; corona bright orange. September. Chile. 1875. SYN. *Stephanolirion narcissoides, Tristagma narcissoides.*

STEM ROT. Term applied to diseases characterized by the rotting of the tissues of the stems of, usually, herbaceous plants, due to the attacks of fungi, e.g. *Didymella lycopersici. See* **Tomato diseases,** &c.

STEMO'NA (*stemon*, stamen; the stamens are foliaceous). FAM. *Stemonaceae.* A genus of 4 or 5 species of climbing plants, natives of the E. Indies, Malaya, and Trop. Australia, with tuberous rootstocks. Closely related to Liliaceae. Leaves opposite, alternate or whorled, lanceolate, ovate or cordate, rather shining, with thick, transverse veinlets; leaf-stalks not jointed. Flowers rather large, handsome, but evil-smelling; perianth segments 4, distinct, in 2 series, erect, slender pointed; stamens nearly hypogynous. Light turfy loam suits these stove plants which are readily increased by suckers.

S. Curtis'ii. Habit and l.-form as in *S. tuberosa*, but *l.* alternate, stalks long and slender, *fl.* red and green, sometimes unisexual, axillary, 1- to 3-fld. April. India. 1890. (B.M. 7254.)

S. gloriosoi'des. A synonym of *S. tuberosa.*

S. tubero'sa. Climber to 6 ft. *l.* sometimes nearly opposite, ovate-lanceolate, loosely cordate, slender-pointed, slightly mucronate, 4 to 6 in. long. *fl.* green, bell-shaped, glabrous; segs. narrow, slender-pointed, nerves purplish; peduncles solitary, 1- to 3-fld. July. E. Indies. 1803. (B.M. 1500 as *Roxburghia gloriosa.*) SYN. *S. gloriosoides, Roxburghia viridiflora.*

F. G. P.

STEMONA'CEAE. Monocotyledons. A family of about 8 species in 3 genera. Herbaceous plants with a short or creeping rhizome, erect or twining, often climbing to considerable heights. Leaves lanceolate or cordate. Inflorescence in the axils of the stem-leaves with a few large or many small flowers. Perianth of 4 segments. Stamens 4. Carpels 2, superior or half-inferior; stigma sessile, small. Fruit a 2-valved capsule. The family was once known as Roxburghiaceae. The only genus dealt with is Stemona.

sten-, steno-, in compound words, signifying narrow.

STENAC'TIS. Included in **Erigeron.**

STENAND'RIUM (*stenos*, narrow, *aner*, man; the stamens being narrow). FAM. *Acanthaceae.* A genus of about 20 species of usually stemless herbs, natives of the warmer parts of America. Leaves usually at the base of the plant, entire. Flowers small in spikes; calyx 5-parted; corolla oblique 5-lobed; stamens 4, didynamous, included. *S. Lindenii* is a dwarf foliage plant. For cultivation *see* **Eranthemum.**

S. igne'um. A synonym of *Chamaeranthemum igneum.*

S. Linden'ii. Dwarf. *l.* elliptic-obovate, dark green, paler towards midrib and with yellow veins. *fl.* yellow in erect spikes. Peru. 1891. (I.H. 1891, 136.)

STENAN'THERA. *See* **Astroloma.** *S. ciliata = A. longiflorum.*

STENAN'THIUM (*stenos*, narrow, *anthos*, flower; both perianth segments and panicles are narrow). FAM. *Liliaceae.* A genus of 5 species of bulbous plants with long grass-like radical leaves, 3 natives of W. America, 1 of Mexico, 1 of Sakhalin Is. Stem erect, with few leaves. Radical leaves long, linear. Inflorescence racemose or paniculate, often nodding with many narrowly campanulate whitish or greenish or dark-purple flowers, the 6 segments connate in a short tube, their free parts spreading above. Fruit an ovoid capsule. At their best these plants are very beautiful but they rarely prove satisfactory in our gardens even in the light, moist, rich soil and warm, sheltered situations they demand. They may be increased by division or by seeds.

S. angustifo'lium. Stem 2 to 3 ft. h. *l.* 1 to 2 ft. long, channelled. *fl.* greenish-white, lower often sterile, about ⅓ in. wide; panicle of simple spike-like racemes, 1 to 2 ft. long, ⅓ to ½ in. wide. June, July. Habitat? Hardy. var. **graminifo'lium,** *l.* narrower and *fl.* few than in type. (B.M. 1599 as *Helonias graminea.*)

S. occidenta'le. Stem 10 to 20 in. h. *l.* 2 to 4, linear-lanceolate, slender-pointed, 6 to 10 in. long. *fl.* brownish-purple, about ½ in. long, bell-shaped, nodding; racemes simple or branched at base. W. America. 1846. (G.F. 1035, 1132.)

S. robust'um. Stems stout, 3 to 5 ft. h., usually very leafy. *l.* about 1 ft. long, upper small. *fl.* greenish or white, about ½ in. across; panicles dense, usually compound, branches spreading or ascending. July. U.S. America. (Gn. 74 (1910), 513.)

stenau'lum, with narrow grooves.

STEN'IA (*stenos*, narrow; from the form of the pollinia). FAM. *Orchidaceae.* A genus of 2 or 3 species of epiphytic orchids, natives of Guiana, Colombia, and Peru. Flowers rather large; sepals equal in length, spreading, the lateral rather the broader, adnate at base to the short foot of the comparatively thick erect column; petals similar to dorsal sepal; lip continuous with the foot of the column, fleshy, broad, nearly saccate, side lobes small, mid-lobe undivided, or all broad and fimbriate, disk transverse, crested; pollen masses 4, oblong-linear; scapes short, recurved, 1-flowered. Leaves oblong or narrow, leathery. Pseudobulbs clustered, 1- or 2-leaved. Cultivation as for Huntleya.

S. fimbria'ta. A synonym of *Chondrorhyncha fimbriata.*

S. gutta'ta. Closely related to *S. pallida*, but with blunter sep. and pet., spotted purple on a straw-coloured ground, the lip blotched and with only 7 callous teeth. Peru. 1880.

Stenia pallida

S. pal'lida.* *fl.* pale citron, 1½ in. or more across, sep. and pet. linear, about 1 in. long, acute; lip faintly spotted red, saccate, 3-lobed, fleshy, ovate, shorter than pet.; scapes radical, prostrate. August to October. *l.* oblong, 3½ to 5 in. long, 1 to 1½ in. wide, acute, slightly narrowed and keeled at base, sheathed with brownish scales. *Pseudobulbs* inconspicuous, 2-, rarely 3-, leaved. Demerara. 1837. (B.R. 24, 20.)

E. C.

A→

STENOCARP'US (*stenos*, narrow, *karpos*, fruit; alluding to the usually narrow, nearly flat follicles). FAM. *Proteaceae.* A genus of about 18 species of evergreen trees and shrubs, natives of Australia and New Caledonia. Leaves alternate, entire or deeply pinnatifid. Flowers in umbels, hermaphrodite, red, yellow, or white; perianth tubular, opening along the lower side, limb globose. Fruit a usually narrow, leathery follicle. Of the following species, *S. sinuatus* is the most beautiful, and, although capable of becoming a large tree, it flowers whilst still shrubby. It and *S. salignus* are hardy in Scilly.

S. Cunningham'ii (of Robt. Brown). Tall bushy shrub or small tree, nearly or quite glabrous. *l.* oblong-lanceolate, pointed or blunt, 2 to 4 in. long, short-stalked. *fl.* exactly similar to those of *S. salignus* except that the ovary, silky-downy in that species, is quite glabrous in this. N. Australia. *S. Cunninghamii* of Hooker is *S. sinuatus.*

S. Forst'eri. Shrub 6 ft. *l.* 1½ to 2½ in. long, ½ to 1¼ in. wide, obovate, cuncate, blunt or notched at the apex. *Umbels* axillary and terminal, 1 to 1½ in. across, on a stalk about ¾ in. long, 6- to 8-fld., pet. ⅜ in. long, reflexed, white. June. New Caledonia. 1850.

S. salig'nus. Tree 20 to 50 ft., nearly or quite glabrous. *l.* ovate-lanceolate, 2 to 4 in. long, ¼ to 1 in. wide, cuneate, pointed. *fl.* axillary or terminal on slender stalked umbels of 10 to 30; perianth ¼ to ½ in. long on a stalk scarcely as long, yellowish, fragrant. June. Queensland, New S. Wales. 1819. (B.R. 441.)

S. sinua'tus.* Tree 30 to 100 ft., glabrous or nearly so. *l.* either deeply pinnately lobed and 1 to 1½ ft. long, the lobes oblong and in 1 to 4 pairs; or oblong-lanceolate, unlobed, and 6 to 10 in. long. *fl.* in umbels, each of 12 to 20 fl., either solitary or up to 5 forming a compound umbel; perianth bright red, 1 in. long, 3 of its segs. hanging down, 1 erect, the globose limb yellow; pistils brilliant red, erect, forming a crown to the umbel, which altogether is 3 in. long and 2 in. wide. August to November. Queensland, New S. Wales. 1830. (B.M. 4263 as *S. Cunninghamii*).

W. J. B.

STENOCHIL'US. Included in **Eremophila.**

STENOCHLAE'NA (*stenos*, narrow, *chlaina*, cloak; indusium absent). FAM. *Polypodiaceae*. About 50 species of tropical usually epiphytic climbing ferns with once-pinnate fronds, like Blechnum in shape, leathery and with fine close veins. Sori as in Elaphoglossum. *S. palustris*, though often recommended as a stove fern, grows well in the intermediate house where the winter temperature may occasionally fall below 50° F. The compost for it should be an open one of fibrous loam, fibrous peat, partly decayed leaf-mould, and silver-sand in equal parts, with abundant water at the roots all the year round. For treatment *see* **Acrostichum.**

S. laurifol'ia. *cau.* firm, erect, naked. *Fronds* pinnate, 3 ft. long, 1½ ft. broad, leathery; barren pinnae 6 to 9 in. long, 1½ in. broad, gradually narrowed from the cordate base, sharply but finely toothed; fertile a little longer, about ¼ in. broad, lower 1 to 2 in. apart. Philippines, Celebes, Solomon Is. (L.F. 7, 59 as *Acrostichum laurifolium.*)

S. palus'tris.* *rhiz.* woody, wide climbing. *sti.* 3 to 4 in. long, firm, erect, naked. *Fronds* 1 to 3 ft. long, 1 ft. or more broad, simply pinnate; barren pinnae, 4 to 8 in. long, ¾ to 1½ in. broad, acuminate, edge thickened, serrulate, base cuneate, sessile, or slightly stalked, articulated; fertile pinnae, 6 to 12 in. long, ⅛ to ⅙ in. broad, lower distant. Asia, Polynesia, Australia. 1841. Stove or greenhouse. (B.C.F. 1, 222, 224; F.B.I. 422.) SYN. *Acrostichum scandens.*

S. scan'dens. A synonym of *S. palustris.*

S. sorbifo'lia.* *rhiz.* thick, woody, often 30 to 40 ft. long, clasping trees like a cable, sometimes prickly. *Fronds* 12 to 18 in. long, 6 to 12 in. broad, simply pinnate; barren pinnae 4 to 6 in. long, about ½ in. broad, 3 to 20 pairs, articulated at the base, entire or toothed; fertile pinnae 1 to 2 in. apart, 2 to 4 in. long, about ¼ in. broad. Tropics. 1793. There are several varieties of this species, chiefly differing in the number of pinnae. Stove. (F.B.I. 423.) SYN. *Acrostichum sorbifolium.* var. **cuspida'ta** has long-stalked, ligulate-cuspidate pinnae; **buxifo'lia** has sessile, leathery, dark-green, oblong, obtuse pinnae, under 1 in. long, ⅜ in. wide; **Smith'ii** has sessile, 3-pinnatifid fronds with numerous pinnules, small and dichotomously forked; **varia'bile** has the lower pinnae deeply pinnatifid with round dented lobes.

S. tenuifo'lia.* *rhiz.* wide scandent, woody, slightly scaly. *Barren fronds* simply pinnate, stipes 4 to 6 in. long, naked, firm, erect, fronds 3 to 5 ft. long, 12 to 18 in. broad; pinnae 6 to 9 in. long, ¾ to 1½ in. broad, acuminate, edge thickened, serrulate, short-stalked. *Fertile fronds* 2-pinnate, with longer stipes; pinnae long-stalked, with numerous distant pinnules. S. Africa. Stove or greenhouse. (F.S.A. (2) 85, 86; L.F. 4, 47–8 as *S. Meyeriana.*) SYN. *Acrostichum, Meyerianum.*

STENOCORYNE. A synonym of Bifrenaria.

STENOGLOT'TIS (*stenos*, narrow, *glotta*, tongue; the lip is narrow). FAM. *Orchidaceae*. A terrestrial genus of 3 species, allied to Habenaria, of which 2, natives of Africa, are in cultivation. The roots are fleshy, tuberous, and produce a rosette-like tuft of deciduous leaves from the centre of which in autumn rises an erect, many-flowered bracteate spike. The flowers are not large, but pretty and attractive. The sepals and lip are prominent, the petals smaller and partially enclose the column. The lip is spurless, longer than the other segments, divided and toothed at apex. The spikes continue to lengthen and give flowers for a considerable time. The plants should be potted in fibrous loam, with a little leaf-mould and coarse sand. Drainage must be free as the plants should be liberally watered when in full growth. After flowering the leaves fall and during winter few if any applications of water are required until the new growth is seen. Propagation is by separating the crowns in early spring. The cool and Odontoglossum houses give the required temperatures, or when in growth the plants may be removed to a cool position in the intermediate house.

S. fimbria'ta.* *fl.* up to 25 or more, rosy-pink or purplish, rather small; sep. free, almost equal, finally spreading; pet. similar but smaller; lip spreading from column, narrow, as long as sep., 3-fid at apex, often spotted purple; column very short; spike 12 in. or more long. *l.* about 6 in. long, rather narrow, usually with dark spots, margins crenate-undulate. S. Africa. 1891. (B.M. 5872.)

S. longifo'lia.* More robust than *S. fimbriata*. *fl.* 20 to 100; lip ½ in. long with 5 to 7 divisions at apex; sep. ¼ in. long; spike 12 to 30 in. h. *l.* 9 to 12 in. long, usually green, sometimes spotted but more sparsely than in *S. fimbriata.* Natal. 1889. (B.M. 7186.) Fl. colour variable. var. **al'ba,** pure white; **splen'dens,** deeper mauve-purple than in type, and stronger in growth.

E. C.

STENOLO'BIUM. Included in **Tecoma.**

STENOLO'MA (*stenos*, narrow, *lomas*, plate; indusia narrow). FAM. *Polypodiaceae*. A genus of 18 species of tropical ferns related to Loxoscaphe but with indusium terminal instead of at the side of the segments as in Odontosoria. Pinnules wider at apex than at base. For treatment *see* **Davallia.**

S. chusa'num.* *rhiz.* stout, creeping, densely fibrillose. *sti.* strong, erect, 6 to 12 in. long. *Fronds* 1 to 1¼ ft. long, 6 to 9 in. broad, ovate, 4-pinnatifid; lower pinnae ovate-lanceolate, 4 to 6 in. long, 2 to 3 in. broad; pinnules lanceolate, their segs. cut to rachis below with toothed cuneate lobes. *Sori* terminal, usually solitary. Trop. Asia, Polynesia, Japan, Madagascar. SYN. *Davallia tenuifolia.* (L.F. 8, 14.) var. **Burk'ei** a finely cut form with pendent fronds about 2 ft. long; **Veitchia'na** has fronds spreading, broadly ovate, 4-pinnate, ultimate lobes cuneate, simple or 2-fid.

S. Mel'leri. *sti.* wide-creeping, climbing, not prickly. *Fronds* 4-pinnatifid; pinnules of lower pinnae 2 to 3 in. long, 1 in. broad, ovate; segs. 1 in. long, ⅜ in. broad, cut to rachis below, lobes ¼ to ⅜ in. broad, cuneate at base, both deeply toothed and shallowy crenate. *Sori* small, marginal, shallow. Madagascar. 1887. SYN. *S. ferruginea, Davallia ferruginea.*

S. retu'sum.* *rhiz.* close-growing, underground. *sti.* smooth, erect, crimson, 1 ft. long. *Fronds* elongate-triangular, 2 to 3 ft. long, 1½ ft. broad, 3-pinnate; pinnules rhomboid. *Sori* on dilated ends of margins of pinnules. Sumatra. (H.S. 1, 52.) SYN. *Davallia retusa, Lindsaya retusa.*

STENOMES'SON (*stenos*, narrow, *messon*, middle; from the shape of the perianth). FAM. *Amaryllidaceae*. A genus of about 12 species of bulbous plants, natives of Trop. America. Leaves appearing with the flowers, linear or rather broad, loriform. Flowers many in an umbel, very rarely reduced to 1, often on pendulous, recurved pedicels; perianth red, orange or fulvous, showy segments tipped green; tube long, funnel-shaped, often slightly contracted above base or towards middle; lobes nearly equal, erect or more or less spreading; stamens 6, inserted at throat of perianth tube; filaments united towards base into a distinct cup which is often toothed between them. Except where otherwise indicated the species need greenhouse treatment. For cultivation *see* **Hippeastrum.**

S. angustifo'lium. A variety of *S. viridiflorum.*

S. auranti'acum. About 1 ft. h. *l.* ligulate, margins revolute. *fl.* nodding, yellow; segs. ovate, erect; stamens included; bracts shorter than pedicels; umbels 2-fld. Quito. 1843. (B.R. 1844, 42; R.H. 1883, p. 396 as *S. Hartwegii.*)

S. coccin'eum.* *l.* 4 or 5, 1 ft. or more long, rather fleshy. *fl.* 4 to 8 in umbels, drooping, bright crimson; segs. 1½ in. long, oblong-lanceolate, half as long as tube; scape 1 ft. or more h., firm, terete. May. Andes of Peru. 1850. (Ref. B. 309; B.M. 3865 as *Coburgia coccinea.*)

S. cro'ceum. *l.* linear-lanceolate or oval-lanceolate, solitary, green above, whitish beneath. *fl.* 4 in umbel, nearly erect, golden, 1½ in. long, segs. connivent; tube curved; bracts 1 in. long, marcescent; scape 1 ft. long, terete, glaucous. May. Peru. 1820.

S. curvidenta'tum. A variety of *S. flavum.*

S. fla'vum. Bulb 1 in. across. *l.* oblanceolate, 1 ft. long, 1 in. wide, obscurely stalked. *fl.* 4 to 6 in umbel, bright yellow; 1½ to 2 in. long; tube dilated at middle; segs. ½ in. long; scape slender, 1 ft. long.

May. Peru. 1824. (B.M. 2641; B.R. 978 as *Chrysiphiala flava.*) var. **curvidenta'tum,** edge of staminal cup having a 2-fid tooth between each of the filaments. SYN. *S. pauciflorum, Chrysiphiala pauciflora*; **latifo'lium,** edge of staminal cup having an entire tooth between each filament. SYN. *S. vitellinum.*

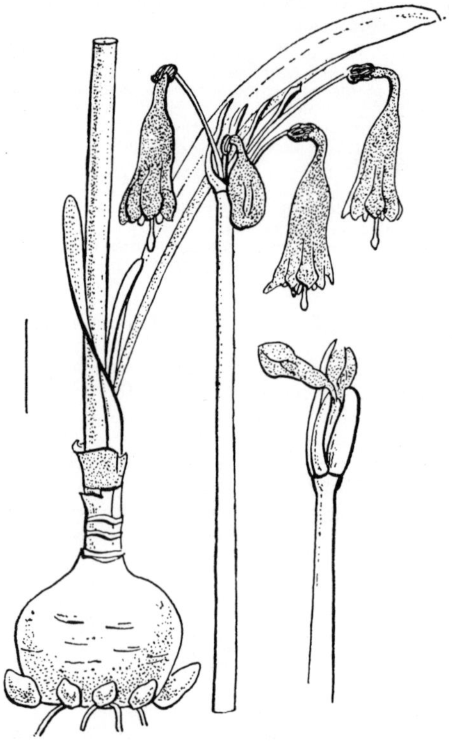

Stenomesson coccineum (p. 2025)

S. ful'vum. A variety of *S. incarnatum.*

S. Hartwe'gii. A synonym of *S. aurantiacum.*

S. hu'mile. *l.* green, glabrous, shining, sub-acute, slightly channelled, nearly 12 in. long, ¼ in. wide. *fl.* scarlet, nearly 3 in. long, tube cylindrical, enlarged above, limb somewhat spreading; scape 1-fld. March. Cordilleras. 1841. (B.R. 1842, 46 as *Coburgia humilis.*)

S. incarna'tum.* *l.* linear, narrowed above, blunt, entire, succulent, net-veined, glabrous, erect, 18 in. long, 1 in. wide. *fl.* 4 or 5 in umbel, variable in colour, usually red, nearly 5 in. long, glabrous; segs. ovate-elliptic, somewhat blunt, spotted, nearly 1 in. long; scape erect, about 2 ft. long; pedicels short. August. (G.F. 1147; S.B.F.G. s. 2, 17 as *Coburgia incarnata.*) var. **ful'vum,** *l.* about 6, linear-ligulate, 18 in. or more long. *fl.* tawny, 4½ in. long, bracts persistent; scape over 2 ft. long. (B.M. 3221; B.R. 1497 as *Coburgia fulva.*); **trichro'mum,** *l.* glaucous, blunt, sub-erect, *fl.* scarlet, green above middle, paler within, 4¾ in. long, slightly curved. (B.M. 3867, 5686 as *Coburgia trichroma.*); **versicol'or,** *l.* 2½ ft. long, 2 in. wide, *fl.* scarlet to whitish-fulvous, lower part curved, 1 in. long, upper ventricose, 1½ in. long, limb 1 in. long, segs. acute, spotted green without, whitish within. (B.R. 28, 66 as *Coburgia versicolor.*)

S. latifo'lium. A variety of *S. flavum.*

S. luteo-vi'ride. *l.* about 4, linear-lorate, glabrous, 12 in. long, 1 in. wide, narrowed gradually to the point. *fl.* 5 or 6 in umbel, tube greenish-yellow, cylindrical, 2 to 3 in. long, segs. yellow with a distinct green keel, 1 in. long; corona green, ⅛ in. long; scape 18 in. long, pedicels very short. Spring. Andes. 1878. (B.M. 6508.)

S. pauciflo'rum. A synonym of *S. flavum curvidentatum.*

S. Pearc'ei. *l.* lorate-lanceolate, 18 in. long, narrowed to an acute apex, and to a flattish stalk 2 to 3 in. long, margins somewhat revolute. *fl.* 6 to 8 in umbel, greenish-yellow, nodding, funnel-shaped, segs. primrose-yellow tinged green without, oblong, erecto-patent; scape 2½ to 3 ft. long, firm, slightly compressed; pedicels 2 to 4 in. long. May. Andes of Bolivia. 1872. (Ref. B. 308.)

S. recurva'tum. Bulb 1 to 1½ in. wide. *l.* 3 to 6, linear, 1 ft. long, ⅓ in. wide. *fl.* 6 to 12 in umbel, tube reddish-yellow, 2 to 2½ in. long, segs. ½ in. long; peduncle 12 to 18 in. long. S. America. SYN. *Carpodetes recurvata, Chrysiphiala recurvata, Coburgia recurvata.*

S. Strickland'ia. A synonym of *Stricklandia eucrosioides.*

S. suspen'sum. *l.* 2, linear, acute, 1 ft. long, ½ in. wide, fleshy. *fl.* 4 to 6 in umbel, drooping, bright scarlet, 1½ in. long, tube half its length, segs. ½ in. deep; scape firm, erect, 12 in. long; pedicels about 1 in. long; spathe 2-leaved, 1½ in. long. May. Peru. 1865. (Ref. B. 22.)

S. trichro'mum. A variety of *S. incarnatum.*

S. viridiflo'rum.* *l.* long, flat, ensiform, about ¾ in. wide, erecto-patent, diverging. *fl.* green; pedicel short; bracts marcescent, deciduous; scape 6 ft. h., erect, terete, smooth. May. Peru. 1839. (B.M. 3866 as *Callithauma viridiflorum.*) var. **angustifo'lium,** *l.* narrower than type, *fl.* with stamens shorter than perianth (B.M. 2866 b as *Callithauma angustifolium.*); **Elwe'sii,** staminal cup deeply 6-cleft, lobes quadrate, emarginate. 1876.

S. vitelli'num. A synonym of *S. flavum latifolium.*

STENORRHYNCH'US (*stenos*, narrow, *rhynchos*, beak; from the form of 'chin'). FAM. *Orchidaceae.* This genus differs from Spiranthes with which it is often combined, chiefly by the bases of the lateral sepals forming a distinct chin or sac. The flowers are rarely very small, often shortly stalked, racemose. The bracts near the flowers are often coloured. Cultivation is the same as recommended for Spiranthes but more heat is needed.

S. aphyl'lus. *fl.* 12 to 15, reddish or brownish-red; upper sep. ½ to ¾ in. long, lower nearly 1 in., all narrow, sac comparatively large, long-adnate to ovary; pet. rather shorter than upper sep.; lip as long as sep., downy at base, its tip reflexed. Bracts about 1 in. long, slender-pointed. Stem leafless, but with large sheaths, 20 to 30 in. h., reddish, smooth in lower, hairy in upper part. Brazil, W. Indies. 1827. (B.M. 2797 as *Neottia aphylla.*)

S. bonarien'sis. *fl.* small, apple-green edged or lined white on sep., pet., and epichil, with white lines on ovary, bright-green median lines on pet. and epichil (which are crenately edged), mesochil thick, orange-yellow; gland to pollinia blue, 1 to 2 ft. h. *l.* 3 to 6 in. long. Buenos Aires. 1924.

S. cinnabari'nus.* *fl.* many, light orange-red or yellowish, urceolate, slightly tomentose; segs. yellowish within, approximating, reflexed at apex; bracts coloured, acute; spike conical, thyrsoid, spirally twisted. June. *l.* lanceolate, sheathing, acute. Stem cylindrical, pale reddish, 2 to 3 ft. h. Mexico. 1846. (B.R. 33, 65.) SYN. *Spiranthes cinnabarina.*

S. colora'ta. A synonym of *S. speciosus.*

S. Esmerald'a. *fl.* small, greenish-white, finally yellowish; dorsal; sep. ligulate, acute, lateral nearly equal, glandular without; pet. lanceolate, acute, unequal-sided; lip oblong, pandurate or ovate, acute, with 2 conical, retrorse calli at base; spike spiral, elongate, many-fld., glandular-hairy; scape above 1½ ft. h., with many sheaths. *l.* rosulate, cuneate-oblong, acute, dark green, with a few small white blotches. Brazil. 1862. (Ref. B. 121 as *Spiranthes Esmeralda.*) SYN. *S. margaritifera.*

S. euphleb'ius. *fl.* not numerous, crowded, horizontal, shortly stalked, white, with red and brown veins on free portions of sep. and pet. pubescent without; sep. united in a tube ½ in. long; pet. semi-lanceolate, erect; scape light greenish-brown. November. *l.* all radical, 5 to 6 in. long, 1½ to 2 in. broad, linear or obovate-oblong, pale green, sparsely spotted white. 1 to 1½ ft. h. Brazil. 1882. (B.M. 6690 as *Spiranthes euphlebia.*)

S. orchioi'des.* Sep. red or rosy cinnabar; pet. rosy, about ½ in. long, puberulous; sac a bluntly conical, free spur, half as long as ovary; lip oblong, pointed, rosy; spike 3 to 5 in. long. November. *l.* late in appearing, long, broadly lanceolate, pointed. 2 to 3 ft. h. W. Indies, Mexico to Brazil. 1826. (B.M. 1036; B.R. 701 as *Neottia orchioides.*) SYN. *Spiranthes orchioides.*

S. specio'sus.* *fl.* and bracts scarlet or bright purplish-red, glabrous, ⅝ in. long, approximate; lip oblong-linear, shortly acuminate; bracts oblong-lanceolate, acuminate, as long as fls.; spike 2 to 3 in. long. April. *l.* elliptic or elliptic-oblong, acute, 4 to 6 in. long. 2 ft. h. W. Indies, Mexico to Venezuela. 1790. (Gn. 25 (1884) 494; B.M. 1374 and L.B.C. 838 as *Neottia speciosa.*) SYN. *Spiranthes colorata.* var. **macula'ta,** *l.* variegated with bright-green spots on darker ground. 1883; **Ortgies'ii,** *fl.* rose. *l.* with large white blotches. 1873.

S. Weir'ii. *fl.* reddish, rather small, sep. and pet. about ½ in. long; lip ¾ in. long, narrow, concave, whitish and yellowish; raceme about 15 in. long, with white, cuspidate bracts, ½ in. or more long. *l.* in a rosette, petiolate, oblong, 4 to 6 in. long, 2 to 3 in. wide, acute, dark purple, freely spotted cream above, purplish below. New Grenada. 1870. SYN. *Spiranthes Weirii.*

E. C.

STENOSE'MIA (*stenos*, narrow, *sema*, standard; the fertile frond bears some resemblance to a flag). FAM. *Polypodiaceae.* Three species of tropical ferns related to Elaphoglossum but with fronds pinnatifid and veins forming 1 or 2 rows of meshes near the midrib, the rest free. For treatment *see* **Acrostichum.**

S. auri'ta.* *cau.* erect, woody. *Barren fronds* with stipe 6 to 9 in. long, deltoid, 8 to 12 in. each way, ternate, central segs. deeply pinnatifid, with lanceolate entire lobes; lateral unequal-sided, with lanceolate, oblong-lobed, lower pinnules. *Fertile fronds* with stem 12 to 18 in. long, deltoid, with distant linear pinnae $\frac{1}{12}$ in. broad; upper simple, lower pinnatifid. Melanesia, Solomon Is. (L.F. 7, 52–3.) Stove. SYN. *Acrostichum auritum.*

STENOSPERMA'TION (*stenos*, narrow, *sperma*, seed). FAM. *Araceae*. A genus of about 20 species of sub-shrubby plants, natives of Trop. America. Stems erect, densely covered with distichous leaves, rooting at nodes. Leaves oblong-elliptic, or lanceolate, oblique, somewhat leathery, bent at junction with petiole which is sometimes sheathing for its whole length. Peduncles long, at first nodding at apex, later erect. Spathe boat-shaped, white. Spadix white. Flowers hermaphrodite, naked; stamens 4; ovary 2-celled. Fruit a small berry; seeds slender. These stove plants require treatment similar to that of Spathiphyllum.

S. multiovula'tum. Stem robust, about 6 ft. long. *l.-stalk* 8 to 10 in. long, blade rigid, leathery, oblong or narrowly elliptic-oblong, narrowed to a short point, about 12 in. long. *Peduncle* 12 to 18 in. long. *Spathe* white, broadly elliptic, 5 to 6 in. long. *Ovules* many. Colombia, Guatemala. 1894. SYN. *S. Spruceanum multiovulatum.*

S. pompayanen'se. Stem about 3 ft. long. *l.-stalk* bent at apex, 6 to 7 in. long, blade leathery, opaque green, elliptic-oblong or oblong-lanceolate, 9 to 12 in. long. *Peduncle* 10 to 12 in. long, somewhat compressed. *Spathe* white, leathery, about 4 in. long with a point about ½ in. long. *Seeds* 8. May. Colombia, Ecuador. 1875. A variable plant. var. **Walli'sii,** *spathe* 3 to 3½ in. long. Colombia. (B.M. 6334 as *S. Wallisii.*)

S. Sprucea'num multiovula'tum. A synonym of *S. multiovulatum.*

S. Wallis'ii. A synonym of *S. pompayanense Wallisii.*

STENOSTO'MUM. Included in **Antirrhoea.**

STENOTAPH'RUM (*stenos*, narrow, *taphros*, trench; from the cavities in the rachis in which the spikelets are seated). FAM. *Gramineae*. A genus of 3 species of creeping tropical grasses. Stems flattened, leaf-blades spreading, spikes narrow, flat. Spikelets like those of Panicum, but embedded in the broad rachis forming a terminal spike. *S. secundatum* grows well in light loamy soil in the warm house, the variegated form making a good basket plant. These grasses make good lawn grasses in warm countries, especially in sandy soils, which they bind with their creeping rhizomes.

S. america'num. A synonym of *S. secundatum.*

S. secunda'tum. St. Augustine Grass. About 6 in. h., erect. *l.* flat, blunt, ciliate at mouth of sheath. Tropics. Sometimes called *Stephanophorum glabrum.* var. **variega'tum,** *l.* striped creamy-white, 2 to 4 in. long. 1874.

STEPHANAND'RA (*stephanos*, crown, *andros*, male; referring to the disposition of the stamens). FAM. *Rosaceae*. A genus of 4 species of deciduous shrubs akin to Spiraea, of graceful bushy growth. Leaves alternate, more or less lobed and toothed. Flowers small, white, disposed in panicles; sepals and petals 5, stamens 10 to 20. Fruit a dry capsule. Natives of E. Asia. The 2 species in cultivation are quite hardy and easily grown in any well-drained loamy soil. Propagated by division or by cuttings.

S. flexuo'sa. A synonym of *S. incisa.*

S. inci'sa. Deciduous shrub 4 to 8 ft., shoots glabrous, zigzag, wiry. *l.* broadly ovate to triangular, 1 to 3 in. long, often cordate, slender-pointed, deeply lobed and toothed; stalk ⅛ to ⅜ in. long. *fl.* greenish-white, ⅙ in. wide, crowded in panicles 1 to 3 in. long; terminate, lateral shoots; stamens 10. June. Japan, Korea. 1872. SYN. *S. flexuosa.* Grown for its graceful habit, elegant foliage, and bright brown stems in winter.

S. Tan'akae. Shrub of twiggy habit up to 6 ft., shoots slender, glabrous. *l.* broadly ovate or triangular, 2 to 5 in. long, slender-pointed, sharply doubly toothed, rounded or cordate at base, hairy on veins beneath; stipules cordate, toothed, stalk up to ½ in. long. *fl.* dull white, ⅙ in. wide, in lax terminal panicles, 2 to 4 in. long. June, July. Japan. 1893. (B.M. 7593.) Autumn colour orange.

W. J. B.

STEPHAN'IA (in honour of Prof. Frederick Stephan of Moscow, d. 1817). FAM. *Menispermaceae*. A genus of 3 species of climbing plants, natives of Trop. Africa, Asia, and Australia. Leaves usually peltate. Flowers dioecious, in simple or compound umbels; sepals in male flowers 6 to 10, in female 3 to 5. They should be treated like Morisonia.

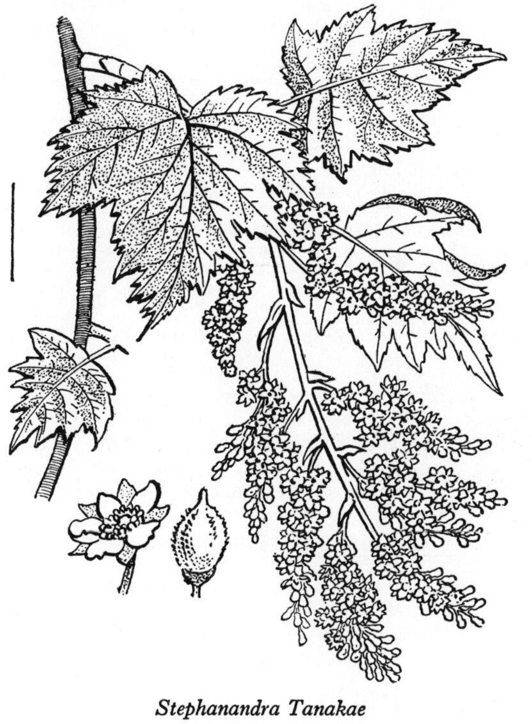

Stephanandra Tanakae

S. hernandifo'lia. *l.* ovate or somewhat deltoid, 3 to 6 in. across, glabrous or thinly downy beneath or on both sides; stalks 1½ to 4 in. long. *fl.* in capitate umbels of 8 to 12 rays; bracts awl-shaped; pet. 3 or 4; peduncles axillary, long or short. June. India. Warm house.

S. rotun'da. *l.* broad-ovate to nearly round, irregularly sinuate-lobed or repand, glabrous; stalks long. *fl.* orange, in loose cymes. June. Himalaya. 1866. Greenhouse.

STEPHANI'TIS RHODODEND'RI. *See* **Rhododendron bug.**

STEPHANOCO'MA (*stephanos*, crown, *kome*, hair; the pappus is crown-like). FAM. *Compositae*. A genus of a single thistle-like herb, native of S. Africa. *S. carduoides* needs greenhouse treatment and otherwise similar to Berkheya.

S. carduoi'des. Herb of 2½ ft., erect, striate, nearly smooth. *l.* sometimes roughly hairy, spiny-toothed or -lobed, usually smooth on both sides, long decurrent. *fl.-heads* yellow, without rays, small, in terminal corymbs; scales of involucre shorter than disk, in many rows, awl-shaped, with solitary, slender spines. Autumn. 1864. (B.M. 5715 as *Stobaea sphaerocephala.*)

STEPHANO'TIS (*stephanos*, crown, *otos*, ear; in reference to the auricles of the staminal crown). FAM. *Asclepiadaceae*. A genus of about 15 species of smooth, twining, often tall shrubs, natives of Madagascar, Peru, Cuba, Malaya, and S. China. Leaves opposite, leathery. Flowers white, large, in umbel-like axillary cymes; calyx 5-parted, segments somewhat leafy; corolla salver- or nearly funnel-shaped, tube cylindrical, broadest at base, throat dilated, limb of 5 twisted lobes; scales of corona 5, erect, often free at tip. Fruit a fleshy follicle. The 2 species introduced grow well in turfy loam with a temperature of 65° F. (55° in winter when the plants should be kept on the dry side). Established plants do best planted in a bed of prepared soil about 3 ft. square, the growths being trained to a trellis beneath the roof. They can, however, be well grown in pots with care, and if fed can be left in the same pot for many years. Propagation by cuttings of previous year's wood taken in spring, inserted singly in pots and rooted in a close frame with a temperature of 60° F. Weak wood should be cut out in spring. Mealy bug and scale insects are the worst pests of Stephanotis, but fumigation in winter and syringing during the growing season will do much to keep these pests in check. The pure white, very fragrant flowers, freely produced, make Stephanotis one of the first favourites among stove plants.

S. floribun'da.* Clustered Wax Flower; Madagascar Chaplet Flower, Madagascar Jasmine. Twiner to about 10 ft. *l.* large, oval or ovate-elliptic, thick, sometimes with a hooked mucro. *fl.* pure white, very fragrant, produced in large bunches; sep. ovate, obtuse, quarter as long as cor. tube; cor. segs. ovate-oblong; coronal scales ovate, shorter than anthers; peduncles short, hardly as long as l.-stalks. May. Madagascar. 1839. (B.M. 4058.) **Elvaston var.,** compact, very free-flowering.

S. Thouar'sii. Habit of *S. floribunda. l.* obovate or obovate-oblong, with a short slender point. *fl.* white, in threes; sep. ovate-lanceolate, one-third as long as cor. tube; coronal scales lanceolate, longer than anthers; peduncles as long as l.-stalks. May. Madagascar. 1842.

Stephens'ii, in honour of Arthur Bligh Stephens, 1855–1909, conservator of forests in Perak.

STEPS in gardens are best constructed in stone or brick which will withstand frost and exposure to all weathers. Steps are necessary to afford means of entering glass-houses when these are above or below ground-level, for passing from one terrace walk to another when the ground is too steep or inconveniently situated for a slope instead, and in any case are safer for use in frosty weather.

Folding steps made of wood or metal hinged at the top are very valuable for standing upon where a ladder cannot be used. Two pairs of steps with a plank resting on their tops or on corresponding steps make a good movable stage for use during hedge clipping, training on walls, &c. Steps convertible with ease into ladders are also made, which are extremely useful.

stercora'rius -a -um, smelling of dung, or growing in dung.

STERCUL'IA (*Sterculius*, a god; derived from *stercus*, dung; the flowers and leaves of some of the species are fetid). FAM. *Sterculiaceae.* A genus of deciduous or evergreen trees most abundant in Trop. Asia but also inhabiting S. America and Africa. Over 250 species have been named, but the generic limits are uncertain and variously defined. Leaves alternate, often very large, sometimes entire, sometimes more or less lobed or digitate. Flowers 1-sexual, sometimes large and few in axillary clusters; sometimes small and borne numerously in panicles. There is no corolla; calyx 5-lobed, sometimes very beautiful; stamens 10 to 15, coalesced into a column. Fruit carpels ultimately splitting apart, spreading and becoming woody or leathery, but sometimes coloured at the early stage.

The Sterculias are easily grown in a good, well-drained loamy soil. Some require stove conditions, others greenhouse, but none is genuinely hardy although a few species have been grown in the Scilly Isles. The genus comprises some very noble foliaged trees, but on account of their size they are ill suited for under-glass cultivation although some flower at comparatively small sizes.

S. acerifo'lia.* Flame Tree. Glabrous, semi-deciduous tree up to 100 ft. *l.* deeply 5- or 7-lobed, 5 to 12 in. across, lobes sinuate; stalk 3 to 9 in. long. *fl.* in panicles up to 1 ft. long, crowded in the terminal l.-axils; cal. rich red, broadly bell-shaped, ¾ in. long, shallowly lobed. New S. Wales, Queensland. Hardy in Scilly. (B.M. 8437 as *Brachychiton acerifolia.*)

S. austro-caledon'ica.* Tree with a slender, erect trunk, 10 ft. or more h., bearing a crowd of l. at the top. *l.* glabrous, 6 in. to 2 ft. across, deeply palmately 5-lobed, strongly veined. *fl.* in dense panicles 4 or 5 in. long springing horizontally from the trunk; cal. ½ in. wide, red, 5-lobed, the lobes with yellow divided tips. April. New Caledonia. (B.M. 7382.) Stove. Probably a distinct genus.

S. Balangh'as. A synonym of *S. nobilis.*

S. Bidwil'lii.* Compact shrub or tree up to 20 ft., softly downy in all its parts. *l.* 3 to 6 in. long and wide, 3-lobed, cordate, central lobe pointed; stalk of equal length. *fl.* almost stalkless, clustered in l.-axils; cal. 1¼ in. wide, pale red, base bell-shaped, with a limb of 5 recurved, broadly ovate, pointed lobes. Autumn. Queensland. 1851. (B.M. 5133 as *Brachychiton Bidwillii.*) Greenhouse.

S. colora'ta. Tree; young shoots downy. Palmately 3- to 5-lobed to 12 in. wide. *fl.* in short dense panicles; cal. tubular, coral-red, covered with fine pubescence. *fr.* conspicuous, with 2 to 5 pendulous leafy valves, pink or greenish outside, yellowish inside; seeds yellow, bean-like. India, Burma, Ceylon, Indo-China, Siam. A showy tree, flowering before the leaves, needing greenhouse treatment in Britain, but becoming too big. It is now placed in a genus distinct from Sterculia as *Erythropsis colorata.*

S. dis'color.* Tree up to 40 ft. or more; shoots and l. thinly downy. *l.* 5- or 7-lobed, 4 to 6 in. wide, cordate, pale beneath; lobes pointed. *fl.* 1 to 3 together, axillary, forming a terminal spike; cal. 1½ in. long, broadly funnel-shaped, rose-red, deeply 6-lobed; lobes erect, pointed, rusty-downy outside. August. Australia. 1858. (B.M. 6608.) Cool greenhouse.

S. diversifo'lia. Tree 20 to 60 ft., shoots and l. glabrous. *l.* variable; entire and ovate, or narrowly lanceolate, or 3- (rarely 5-) lobed with a long middle lobe and 2 lateral ones, all slenderly pointed; they vary from 1½ to 5 in. long and from ½ to 2½ in. wide; stalk long and slender. *fl.* in irregular, axillary panicles 3 or 4 in. long; cal. broadly bell-shaped, about ⅝ in. wide, yellowish white or greenish. Australia. 1824. SYN. *Brachychiton diversifolia, B. populnea.* Greenhouse.

S. foet'ida. Tall tree. *l.* and panicles crowded at the end of the shoots. *l.* palmate, 5- or 7-lobed; lobes oval-lanceolate, 4 to 9 in. long, 1 to 3 in. wide, slender-pointed; stalk 4 to 12 in. long. *Panicles* up to 12 in. long; cal. ½ to 1 in. wide, orange, deeply cut into 5 linear lobes, woolly inside. *Seeds* edible when roasted. Widely spread in the Old World. Tropics. Stove.

S. Gregor'ii. Tree 40 to 50 or more ft., l. and shoots glabrous. *l.* glossy, mostly 3-, sometimes 5-lobed; lobes 2 to 5 in. long, ¼ to ⅝ in. wide, slenderly tapered. *fl.* in axillary, downy panicles 1½ in. long; cal. pale-yellow or salmon, bell-shaped, ⅝ in. long, deeply lobed, downy outside. S. Australia. Much admired in California. SYN. *S. diversifolia occidentalis, Brachychiton Gregorii.* Greenhouse.

S. lanceola'ta. Small tree, 10 to 20 ft. *l.* simple, entire, oval or obovate, shortly pointed, 3 to 6 in. long, 1 to 2½ in. wide, conspicuously veined, glabrous. *Panicles* axillary, clustered along shoots, 1 to 2 in. long, downy; cal. ½ in. across, with 5 spreading, deep lobes, red. China. 1822. (B.R. 1256.) Greenhouse.

S. lu'rida. Tree 20 to 80 ft. *l.* 5 to 8 in. wide, palmately 5- or 7-lobed, lobes often toothed or wavy, sparsely hairy beneath especially on the prominent veins. *fl.* few, scarcely stalked, clustered in l.-axils; cal. 1½ to 2 in. long, bell-shaped, deeply lobed, described as 'livid variegated'. New S. Wales. Greenhouse.

S. macrophyl'la. Tree 100 to 150 ft. *l.* simple, entire, 6 to 16 in. long, 5 to 12 in. wide, blue-grey, downy, strongly ribbed beneath; stalk hairy, 2 to 6 in. long. *Panicles* up to 1 ft. long, deflexed; cal. cup-shaped, very small, yellow 5-lobed, stellately hairy. E. Indies. 1822. Stove.

S. nobi'lis. Large tree; trunk 2 to 3 ft. diam. *l.* simple, entire, oval to broadly oblong, 6 to 12 in. long, 2 to 6 in. wide, membranous, abruptly short-pointed, glabrous or nearly so. *Panicles* clustered near end of shoot, 4 to 12 in. long; *fl.* fragrant, thickly disposed, females scarce; cal. ½ in. long, white or rose, base bell-shaped, lobes 5, much incurved, hairy. Summer. China. 1787. (B.R. 185.) SYN. *S. Balanghas.*

S. platanifo'lia. A synonym of *Firmiana simplex.*

S. rupes'tris. Queensland Bottle Tree. Semi-deciduous tree, 20 to 50 ft., with a huge bottle-shaped trunk girthing up to 35 ft. *l.* glabrous, either simple, linear-oblong, and 3 to 6 in. long by ⅓ to ¾ in. wide, or palmately divided into 5 to 9 linear-lanceolate lflets. 2 to 7 in. long by ⅛ to ⅝ in. wide; both shapes occur on the same tree. *fl.* in axillary downy panicles, 1 to 2 in. long; cal. ½ in. long, bell-shaped, deeply lobed. Queensland. (G.C. 6 (1876), 818–19.) Greenhouse.

S. Tragacan'tha. Deciduous tree up to 40 or 50 ft., shoots, underside of l., fl.-stalks and cal. rusty-downy. *l.* simple, oval, 3 to 9 in. long, 2 to 5 in. wide; stalk 1 to 2 in. long. *Panicles* axillary, clustered terminally, 2 to 4 in. long; *fl.* small, numerous, brownish-purple; cal. lobes cohering at tips. *May. fr.* red when ripe. Trop. W. Africa. (B.R. 1353.) Exudes a gum like tragacanth when wounded. Stove.

S. u'rens. Soft-wooded, wide-spreading tree; bark pale, papery, peeling. *l.* terminal, palmately but often shallowly 5-lobed, 4 to 12 in. long and wide, closely velvety beneath. *Panicles* clustered, up to 8 in. long, glandular-hairy; *fl.* very closely packed and numerous, small, yellow. *fr.* of 4 or 5 carpels 3 in. long, red, covered with stinging hairs. India. 1793. Greenhouse.

S. villo'sa. Deciduous tree, 20 to 50 ft., shoots, l. and fl.-stalks downy. *l.* 8 to 18 in. wide, terminally clustered, palmately 5- or 7-lobed, often deeply so, and toothed, downy; stalk as long as blade. *Panicles* in terminal clusters, 4 to 12 in. long, crooked; cal. yellow, ½ in. wide, base campanulate, limb 5-lobed, stellately downy India, Burma, &c. 1805. Greenhouse.

W. J. B.

STERCULIA'CEAE. Dicotyledons. A family of about 50 genera with 750 species of mostly tropical trees, shrubs and herbs, sometimes climbing, with alternate, stipulate leaves, often simple sometimes digitate. Flowers regular, sometimes 1-sexual, sepals 3 to 5, more or less joined, valvate, petals convolute, sometimes absent; anthers united into a tube; ovary superior; styles 4 or 5. Fruit usually dry. The genera dealt with are: Abroma, Astiria, Cheirostemon, Cola, Dombeya, Firmiana, Fremontia, Guazuma, Guichenotia, Helicteres, Heritiera, Hermannia, Herrania, Kleinhovia, Lasiopetalum, Mahernia, Melhania, Pentapetes, Pterospermum, Reevesia, Ruizia, Rulingia, Seringia, Sterculia, Theobroma, Thomasia, Trochetia.

sterculiifo'lius -a -um, with Sterculia-like leaves.

stereophyl'lus -a -um, having hard leaves.

STEREOSPERM'UM *stereos*, rigid, hence solid, *sperma*, seed). FAM. *Bignoniaceae.* A genus of about 12 species of evergreen trees, natives of Asia and Africa. Leaves once or twice pinnate. Flowers large, Bignonia-like, pale yellow or rose to purple in large, loose, terminal panicles; corolla funnel-bell-shaped with crisped or toothed lobes. Stove conditions are needed. Propagated by seed or cuttings.

S. si'nicum. A synonym of *Radermachia sinica.*

S. suaveo'lens. Tree, 30 to 60 ft. h. *l.* pinnate, 12 to 18 in. long; lflets. 7 to 9, elliptic, 5 in. long, slender-pointed or acute, entire or toothed, hairy when young. *fl.* pale or dark purple, 1½ in. long; cor. downy without, lobes crisped; cal. bell-shaped; panicles many-fld., clammy-hairy. India. SYN. *Heterophragma suaveolens, Tecoma suaveolens.*

STE'REUM. A genus of fungi in the class Basidiomycetes, some species being well-known parasites of cultivated plants, especially trees and shrubs. The fruit bodies (sporophores) of the genus are usually leathery to woody, being expanded into thin wavy plates growing in layers, the upper surfaces velvety or hairy and the lower smooth or even. The chief parasitic species is *S. purpureum*, attacking many kinds of ornamental and fruit-trees and shrubs, especially plums, and causing the well-known disease called Silver Leaf (q.v.). *S. hirsutum* grows on oak branches, stumps, and posts and may occasionally attack the living branches by entering through wounds. The affected wood shows yellow or white stripes and is then described as 'yellow piped' or 'white piped'. The fungus fruit body is 4 or 5 in. across, leathery, hairy, the upper surface yellow or grey with a yellowish margin and the under surface smooth and yellow or tan. Another species causing rot of oak logs is *S. frustulosum* which produces in the wood a dark brown coloration broken at intervals by white spots or hollow cavities, and this is often described as Partridge Wood. The fruit body is much cracked, hard and crust-like, cinnamon, later turning grey. It differs from *S. hirsutum* in that no part of it is separated from the surface on which it grows.

D. E. G.

sterile, barren; a staminate (i.e. male) flower is said to be sterile. *See also* **Self-sterile.**

ste'rilis -is -e, sterile, bearing useless fruit.

STERIPHO'MA (*steriphoma*, foundation; in allusion to the large fruit-stalk). FAM. *Capparidaceae.* A genus of 4 species of unarmed shrubs, natives of Trop. S. America. Leaves of 1 leaflet, lanceolate, entire, the long stalk thickened at apex. Flowers orange, showy; calyx 2- to 4-lobed, irregularly split, torus very short; petals 4, sessile; stamens 6; racemes terminal, peduncles thick, the 1-flowered pedicels thickened at apex, recurved. *S. paradoxum,* worthy of cultivation for the beauty of its flowers, needs stove conditions, and a compost of equal parts of loam, peat, and sand. Cuttings of young wood may be struck in sand, under a glass, with bottom heat.

S. paradox'um. Shrub of 6 ft. *l.* oblong-lanceolate, with long slender points, stalks nearly as long as blades. *fl.* with reddish-brown cal., and yellow pet. and stamens. April to July. Venezuela. 1823. (B.M. 5788 and F.d.S. 564–5 as *S. cleomoides.*) SYN. *Capparis paradoxa.*

F. G. P.

STERNBERG'IA (in honour of Count Kaspar Moritz von Sternberg of Prague, 1761–1838, botanist, author of *Revisio Saxifragarum*, 1810, &c.). FAM. *Amaryllidaceae.* A genus of about 4 species of bulbous plants, natives of S. Europe and the Orient to Caucasus and Persia. Flower often solitary; perianth yellow, funnel-shaped, straight, with a short or rather long tube, and linear or lanceolate, equal lobes; stamens fixed at the throat or the bases of the lobes; bract membranous, hyaline, tubular at base; scape short, sometimes very short, solid. Leaves late or contemporary with the flowers. Bulb tunicated. *S. lutea* is a valuable plant for its yellow flowers in autumn. The genus is divided into Sternbergia proper with autumnal flowers, with a cylindrical tube, and leaves produced in spring; and Oporanthus, with short-tubed, funnel-shaped flowers, produced with the leaves. To the first section belong *S. colchiciflora* and *S. macrantha*; to the second *S. lutea* and *S. Fischeriana*. They succeed best in soil of a good depth in a sheltered sunny place planted from 4 to 6 in. below the surface. They should be left undisturbed after planting. Propagated by bulb increase.

KEY

1.	*Autumn-fld.*	2
1.	*Spring-fld.*	S. Fischeriana
2.	*Lvs. vernal*	3
2.	*Lvs. autumnal*	S. lutea
3.	*Scape subterranean*	S. colchiciflora
3.	*Scape 4 to 6 in. long*	S. macrantha

S. colchiciflo'ra. *fl.* sessile, erect, scented; perianth tube yellowish-white, straight, partly subterranean, about 1 in. long; limb yellow,

Sternbergia lutea (p. 2030)

erecto-patent, 1 to 1⅓ in. long, segs. narrow, striate-nerved; scape subterranean, 1-fld. Autumn. *l.* 4 to 6, vernal, rarely autumnal, erect, twisted, keeled, obtusely callous, 4 in. long, ⅛ in. wide. Hungary and Roumelia on limestone. 1816. (B.R. 2008.)

S. Fischeria'na. *fl.* bright yellow; tube funnel-shaped, under ½ in. long; segs. oblong-spatulate, 1½ in. long; peduncles 2 or 3 to a bulb, short, 1-fld.; spathes white, usually 2-fid. March. *l.* 8 or 9 to a bulb, with the fls., linear, obtuse, 6 in. long at flowering time, afterwards lengthening. *Bulb* 1½ to 2 in. across. Caucasus. 1868. (B.M. 7441.)

S. lu'tea.* *fl.* yellow, 1¾ to 2¼ in. long, turbinate-campanulate; tube straight, funnel-shaped, about ⅓ in. long; segs. slightly concave, obtuse or emarginate, 1½ to 1¾ in. long; scape 2 to 4 in. long, 1- or 2-fld. Autumn. *l.* 5, 6, or more, with the fls., arcuate-reflexed, linear-lorate, obtusely keeled, canaliculate, obtuse, dark green, 6 to 12 in. long, ⅕ to ⅝ in. wide. Cent. Europe. 1596. (B.M. 290 as *Amaryllis lutea*; Gn. 31 (1887). 582.) Known to the Turks as 'Lale', i.e. Lily. var. **angustifo'lia,** a narrow-lvd. form. (Gn. 31 (1887), 582.); **graec'a** has a short peduncle, *l.* short at fl.-time, finally 4 to 5 in. long, 1/12 in. wide. Greece; **sic'ula,** *fl.* larger, perianth segs. more acute, and narrower. Sicily.

S. macran'tha. *fl.* bright yellow; tube cylindrical, 2 in. long; segs. oblong, 1 to 1½ in. long; peduncle cylindrical, 4 to 6 in. long; spathe 3 to 4 in. long. Autumn. *l.* lorate, obtuse, glaucescent, ¾ in. wide, fully developed in June. *Bulb* 1 to 1½ in. wide, neck 4 to 6 in. long. Asia Minor. 1896. (B.M. 7459; Gn. 47 (1895), 174.)

S. sic'ula. A variety of *S. lutea.*

STETSON'IA (in honour of F. L. Stetson of New York). FAM. *Cactaceae.* Tree-like cacti, branching from a short trunk; stems stout; ribs 8 or 9, rounded, crenate, spines unequal, the longest 2 in. long. Flowers up to 6 in. long, white, nocturnal. Fruit unknown. **A**

S. cory'ne. The only species. Argentina. (B.R.C. 2, t. 9, f. 95–6.) SYN. *Cereus coryne.*

V. H.

Steudelia'nus -a -um, in honour of Ernst Gottlieb Steudel, 1783–1856, German botanist, author of *Nomenclator Botanicus* (1821–4, 1840–4), which was the predecessor of *Index Kewensis.*

STEUD'NERA (in honour of Dr. Steudner of Gorlitz, who botanized in Abyssinia, 1832–63). FAM. *Araceae.* A genus of 8 species of perennial plants with thick ascending stems covered with the remains of scale leaves, and peltate, concave, ovate or oblong-ovate leaves, natives of Assam, Burma, and W. China. Related to Remusatia but with staminodes in the female flowers. They need stove conditions and a compost of rich sandy loam, leaf-mould, and bits of broken charcoal, well mixed and drained. A moist atmosphere suits them best and they should have a rest period. They may be propagated by suckers, cuttings, and division of the rootstock.

S. colocasiifo'lia. Stem short, 1½ in. thick. *l.* ovate, acute, 10 to 12 in. long, rigid, leathery, green, paler beneath without spots; stalk 12 to 20 in. long, green, rarely violet. *Spathe* yellow outside, purplish at base, dark purple within, ovate-lanceolate, about 6 in. long. Burma. 1869. (B.M. 6762.)

S. colocasioi'des. Robust large plant, stem long, about 1½ in. thick. *l.* widely ovate, acute, 10 to 24 in. long, thin leathery, pale green above, glaucous beneath; stalk 12 to 18 in. long, green. *Peduncles* many, slender, 5 to 7 in. long. *Spathe* erect, tube green, about 1 in. long, blade yellow, narrow-lanceolate, 5 to 8 in. long; spadix whitish. Trop. Himalaya, Assam.

S. dis'color. Similar to *S. colocasiifolia* but *l.* brownish-spotted, *spathe* yellow outside, and for the most part yellow, with violet in lower third. Burma. (B.M. 6076 as *S. colocasiifolia.*)

Steven'i, in honour of Christian von Steven, 1781–1863, of Finland, director Botanic Garden, Nikita, Crimea.

STEVENSO'NIA (in honour of Sir William Stevenson, a governor of Mauritius 1857–63). FAM. *Palmaceae.* A genus of a single species of tall palm, at first spiny throughout, finally smooth with a ringed caudex, native of the Seychelles, needing a hot, moisture-laden atmosphere, and suffering if the temperature falls too low or the air becomes too dry. It needs well-drained fibrous peat with pieces of charcoal, turfy loam, and sand. Propagation by seeds.

S. Borsignia'na. Tree to 40 ft. h. Stem very spiny when young, less so later. *l.* wedge-shaped-obovate, 2-fid, oblique at base, deeply laciniate with incised segs.; stalk 9 to 18 in. long, glabrous, pale green, convex below; sheaths 2 to 3 ft. long, hoary, scaly, spiny. *Lower spathes* 15 in. long, *upper* club-shaped, smooth, 2 to 3½ ft. long; spadix 3 to 6 ft. long; peduncle 1½ to 3 ft. long, compressed at base. *fr.* orange-red, ⅓ to ⅜ in. long. 1865. (I.H. 433 as *Phoenicophorum sechellarum.*) SYN. *S. grandiflora, Areca sechellarum, Astrocaryum Borsignyanum.*

STE'VIA (in honour of Dr. Peter James Esteve, Professor of Botany at Valencia, d. 1566). FAM. *Compositae.* A genus of about 100 species of herbs or sub-shrubs, usually erect, natives of the warmer parts of America. Leaves opposite or upper alternate, often 3-nerved, toothed, entire or sometimes 3-sect. Flower-heads white or purplish in panicles or corymbs; involucre cylindrical; bracts 5 or 6; receptacle flat, naked; florets 5, regular, 5-cleft, tubular. Achenes narrow; pappus, paleae or bristles, 2 or many. The species mentioned below are perennial herbs unless otherwise stated, succeeding in the open border in summer but needing the protection of a frame in winter. Propagation by seeds, cuttings, or division. The name Stevia has been applied in error to species of Piqueria (q.v.). They are best planted rather deeply in sandy soil and in some districts will come through the winter outdoors if the crowns are protected. Several species besides those mentioned have been introduced from time to time but few are in cultivation now.

S. ivifo'lia. About 2 ft. h., erect. Stem shaggy-hairy, corymbosely branched at top. *l.* rhomboid-lanceolate, deeply sharply toothed, upper sessile. *fl.-heads* white, in fastigiate corymbs; involucre and florets glandular and downy. August. Mexico. 1816. Greenhouse.

S. ova'ta. About 2 ft. h. Stem erect. *l.* ovate, toothed, wedge-shaped at base; upper oblong, sub-entire. *fl.-heads* white, in rather compact fastigiate corymbs. August. Mexico. 1816.

S. purpu'rea. About 18 in. h., erect. Stem velvety-hairy, much branched. *l.* lanceolate, alternate, lower obovate, channelled, narrowed to stalk, toothed at apex. *fl.-heads* purple, in somewhat fastigiate corymbs; involucre pale greenish. August. Pappus paleaceous, 3-awned. Mexico. 1812. (B.R. 93 as *S. Eupatoria.*)

S. Rebaudia'na. Annual herb, 1 to 1½ ft. h. Stem puberulous. *l.* opposite, oblanceolate, crenulate. *fl.-heads* very small, whitish, in a corymb. Paraguay. (Hook. I. 2816.) Known as Caa-ehe or azucacaa. Lvs. have a sugary flavour. SYN. *Eupatorium Rebaudianum.*

S. salicifo'lia. Glabrous shrub, 18 in. h. *l.* opposite, narrow-lanceolate, nearly or quite entire, very shortly stalked, almost connate. *fl.-heads* white, in spreading corymbs. June to September. Mexico. 1803. (B.M. n.s. 80.) Greenhouse.

S. serra'ta. About 18 in. h. Stem erect, branched, hairy. *l.* alternate, somewhat clustered, linear-lanceolate, almost glabrous, toothed, entire at base, contracted to stalk. *fl.-heads* white or pink, in fastigiate corymbs. August. Pappus bristly, 2- or 3-awned. Mexico. 1827. This name has been misapplied to species of Piqueria (q.v.).

STEWART'IA (after John Stuart, Earl of Bute, 1713–92). FAM. *Theaceae.* A genus of about 8 species of deciduous trees and shrubs, inhabiting Eastern N. America and E. Asia. Leaves alternate, toothed, short-stalked. Flowers solitary in the leaf-axils, opening in summer on the current season's shoots. Sepals and petals 5, sometimes 6, silky outside; stamens numerous; styles 5, separate in *S. ovata,* united in all the others. Fruit a woody capsule splitting into 5 valves.

Stewartias dislike a limy soil and prefer one, at least partly, of a peaty nature. With the possible exception of *S. monadelpha,* little known in gardens, they are all fairly hardy in the south of England. They resent disturbance at the root and should be put in their permanent places early. They prefer a site over which a shadow is cast in the hot hours of the day rather than full sunshine. The foliage of most of them acquires fine autumn colours before falling. They are propagated by seed which is best soaked for a few days before sowing, or by cuttings of short side branches about 3 in. long, with a heel, in heat. They should be kept growing through the following winter if possible.

The generic name was published as Stewartia by Linnaeus in 1741 and 1753, but, as it commemorates John Stuart, was amended to Stuartia by L'Héritier in 1781, the original spelling being regarded by him and many later authorities as a manifest orthographic error. The family name Stuart or Stewart is a variant of Steward and derived from the historic office of the family in Scotland. There is thus some justification for the Linnaean spelling.

KEY

1. *Styles united; pet. usually* 5	2
1. *Styles not united; pet. sometimes* 6; *lvs. rounded at base*	S. ovata
2. *Shoots glabrous*	3
2. *Shoots downy, at least at first*	4
3. *Cor. cup-shaped; lvs. ovate or obovate*	S. pseudocamellia
3. *Cor. spreading; lvs. widely elliptic*	S. pseudocamellia koreana
4. *Stamens purple, anthers bluish; lvs. ovate to obovate, ciliate*	S. Malacodendron
4. *Stamens white, anthers violet or yellow*	5
5. *Stamens united at base*	6
5. *Stamens free; bark peeling*	S. sinensis
6. *Lvs. ovate or obovate, sharply toothed*	S. serrata
6. *Lvs. ovate-lanceolate, remotely toothed*	S. monadelpha

S. korean'a.* A synonym of *S. pseudocamellia koreana.*

Stewartia Malacodendron

S. Malacodend'ron.* Small tree or shrub, 15 ft. or more, shoots downy. *l.* 2 to 4 in. long, ovate, oval, or obovate, cuneate, ciliate, downy beneath. *fl.* 2½ to 3½ in. wide; pet. obovate; stamens purple, anthers bluish; styles united. June, July. SE. United States. 1741. (B.M. 8145.) SYN. *S. virginica.* Now quite rare. Succeeds in peaty soil and partial shade.

S. monadelph'a. Tree to 80 ft., trunk 2 to 3 ft. in diameter, shoots downy. *l.* ovate-lanceolate, 2 to 3 in. long, toothed, downy beneath. *fl.* 1 to 1½ in. wide, white; pet. spreading; stamens united at base; anthers violet; ovary appressed downy. *fr.* ⅜ in. long, the smallest in the genus. Japan. (S.Z.F.J. i. 96.)

S. ova'ta. Shrub up to 15 ft., shoots glabrous. *l.* 2½ to 5 in. long, ovate to oval, rounded at base, pointed, sparingly toothed to almost entire, downy beneath. *fl.* creamy-white, 2½ to 3 in. across, stalk downy, ¼ in. long; pet. 5 or 6; stamens yellow, anthers orange; styles 3 to 5, not united. July, August. S. United States. 1785. (B.M. 3918.) var. **grandiflo'ra,*** *fl.* up to 4 in. across, anthers purple. SYN. *Malacodendron pentagynum.*

S. pentagy'na. A synonym of *S. ovata.*

S. pseudocamel'lia. Tree up to 50 ft., shoots glabrous. *l.* 2 to 3½ in. long, ovate or obovate, cuneate, sparsely toothed; stalk ⅛ to ⅜ in. long. *fl.* white, cupped, 2 to 2½ in. across; pet. incurved, margins jagged; sep. densely silky; stamens white, anthers orange-yellow. July, August. Japan. 1874. (B.M. 7045.) Autumn colour red and yellow. var. **korea'na,** *l.* mostly broad-elliptic; *fl.* pet. wide-spreading. Korea. 1917. (B.M. n.s. 20.) SYN. *S. koreana.*

S. serra'ta. Tree probably 30 ft. or more. *l.* oval or obovate, 1½ to 3 in. long, cuneate, pointed, sharply toothed, dull green, downy in vein-axils and on midrib beneath; stalk ⅛ to ¼ in. long. *fl.* cup-shaped, 2 to 2¾ in. across; pet. creamy-white, stained red outside; sep. ½ to ⅝ in. long, glabrous; stamens white, free; anthers yellow; ovary glabrous. June, July. Japan. 1908. (B.M. 8771.)

S. sinen'sis.* Tree up to 30 ft., bark peeling, leaving stem smooth and grey; shoots downy at first. *l.* oval or ovate-oblong, 2 to 4 in. long, cuneate, toothed, downy and ciliate at first, bright green on both sides; stalk ⅛ to ¼ in. long. *fl.* white, fragrant, 2 in. wide; stamens downy, anthers yellow; ovary downy. China. 1901. (B.M. 8778.)

S. virgin'ica. A synonym of *S. Malacodendron.*

W. J. B.

Stewartia'nus -a -um, in honour of Laurence Baxter Stewart, 1876–1934, Curator, Botanic Garden, Edinburgh.

STIBAS'IA. Included in *Marattia.*

-stichus, in compound words, signifying a rank or row, e.g. distichus, 2-ranked.

sticto-, in compound words, signifying spotted or punctured, as *stictanthus,* with spotted flowers.

STIFF'TIA (in honour of A. J. Stifft, 1760–1836, physician to the Imperial Court, Austria). FAM. *Compositae.* A genus of 4 or 5 glabrous trees and shrubs, natives of Brazil and Guiana. Leaves alternate, leathery, entire. Flower-heads yellow or orange, large and solitary or few together, or smaller and panicled; involucral bracts in many series, overlapping, obtuse, appressed, outer progressively shorter; receptacle naked, pitted; florets tubular, the 5 narrow lobes revolute; achenes long; pappus bristles in many series. *S. chrysantha* is a showy shrub, requiring a stove temperature and a light, airy situation with a compost of well-drained turfy loam. Cuttings of young wood in sandy soil under glass with bottom heat afford means of propagation.

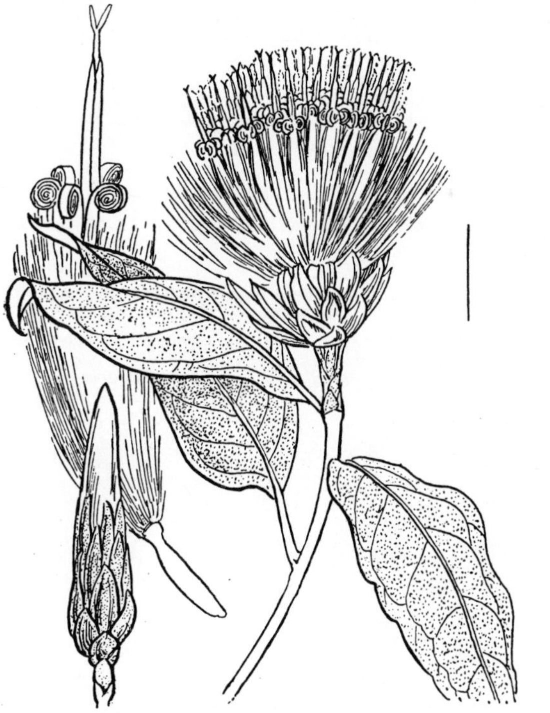

Stifftia chrysantha

S. chrysan'tha. Evergreen shrub of about 6 ft. *l.* lanceolate, slender-pointed. *fl.-heads* orange, 2 in. across, solitary; pappus saffron. February to April. Brazil. 1840. (B.M. 4458.)

STIGMA. That part of the pistil of a flower which is fitted to receive the pollen when mature, and to permit the passage of the pollen tubes for the fertilization of the ovules. The stigma is peculiar in having no epidermis, its surface being covered with long cells which secrete a sticky fluid which serves to retain the pollen grains when they touch it and probably also helps in their germination and growth through the style or ovary wall. The stigmatic surface is usually at the tip of the style (or in its absence at the top of the ovary) but may be on the side of it or occasionally (as in Berberis) beneath the cap which terminates the style. In insect-pollinated flowers the stigma is usually small as it is in cleistogamous flowers, while in wind-pollinated flowers it is usually large and feathery from the presence of long hairs.

STIGMAPHYL'LON (*stigma*, *phyllon*, leaf, the stigma is somewhat leaf-like). FAM. *Malpighiaceae*. A genus of about 60 species of handsome, Trop. American, climbing shrubs. Leaves usually opposite, of 2 forms, entire or toothed, rarely lobed, petioles with 2 glands, stipules minute. Flowers yellow, in umbel-like corymbs, terminal and axillary; calyx 5-parted with 8 glands; petals stalked, unequal, glabrous; stamens 10, unequal, 6 only perfect. Fruit of 1 to 3 samaras. These fine climbers need a stove temperature, and grow in a mixture of loam, leaf soil, and peat, with some sharp sand to ensure good drainage, keeping them moderately dry in the resting season. Cuttings of new ripened wood, not necessarily with a heel or at a joint, root freely in sandy compost with bottom heat. The young plants should be grown on in small pots during the winter.

S. arista'tum. Climber to 15 ft. *l.* on stem, glabrous, sagittate-hastate, angled, acute; on younger branches often oblong, entire; glands at apex of stalk. *fl.* in few-fld., pedunculate umbels; pet. fringed. June to August. Brazil. 1832. (B.R. 1659.)

S. cilia'tum. Golden Vine. Tall climber. *l.* opposite, cordate, oblique at base, smooth, ciliate, glaucous. *fl.* large, 3 to 6 in umbel; pet. fringed, clawed. October. Brazil. 1796.

S. diversifo'lium. Lofty climber. *l.* ovate or oblong-linear, rounded or almost cordate at base, shining above, hairy beneath; glands on petiole close to blade. *fl.-stalks* jointed at base. June. W. Indies. 1826.

S. ful'gens. Tall climber. *l.* cordate-rounded, mucronulate, entire, the basal sinus open, smooth above, silky-silvery beneath; glands of petioles not quite at apex. *fl.* on forked peduncles. Summer. W. Indies. 1759.

S. heterophyl'lum. Tall climber. *l.* opposite, mostly ovate, entire, waved, obtuse, mucronate, sometimes broader, almost cordate, 3-lobed, lobes oblong. *fl.* in several-fld. axillary umbels; sep. erect; pet. orbicular. December. Tucuman. 1842. (B.M. 4014.)

S. Humboldtia'num. Climber. *l.* roundish-ovate, more or less cordate, mucronate, smooth above, softly hoary, like the young branches, beneath. *fl.* yellow in sessile terminal and axillary umbels. S. America. 1824. SYN. *Banisteria Humboldtianum.*

S. jatrophaefo'lium. 6 ft. h. *l.* palmately 5- to 7-cleft, acute, serrate-ciliate, clear light green; glands of petioles at apex. *fl.* in many-fld. umbels; pet. shell-shaped, fringed. Summer. Uruguay. 1841. (B.R. 30, 7.)

S. littora'le. Tall, leafy climber. *l.* opposite and alternate, variable in shape, 2 to 5 in. long, long-stalked. *fl.* in many-fld. axillary corymbs, 1 in. across; claw of pet. longer than cal.; pedicels $\frac{1}{2}$ to $1\frac{1}{2}$ in. long. Autumn. S. Brazil. 1882. (B.M. 6623.) SYN. *Banisteria bonariensis.*

F. G. P.

stigmatic, belonging to the stigma.

stigmat'icus -a -um, dotted.

stigmatiferous, stigma-bearing.

stigmo'sus -a -um, spotted.

Stillmann'ii, in honour of Dr. Jacob Davis Babcock Stillman, d. 1888, friend of Torrey and collector of Californian plants.

stim'ulans, goading, prickly.

STING. A hair capable of penetrating the skin of an animal and introducing an acid such as formic acid.

STINGING BUSH. *See* **Jatropha urens.**

STINGING NETTLE. *See* **Urtica.**

STINKHORN FUNGUS. The common name of the Basidiomycetous fungus *Phallus impudicus*, which grows on rotting debris in woods, thickets, gardens, &c., and has a very disagreeable smell which can be detected some feet away. The fungus appears underground first as a white, egg-like body. This is soon ruptured at the top to allow the rapid growth from the interior of a thick spongy stem which develops at its top a perforated, spongy, evil-smelling, hood-like cap, intended to attract flies to spread its spores.

D. E. G.

STINKING CEDAR. *See* **Torreya taxifolia.**

STINKING GLADWIN. *See* **Iris foetidissima.**

STINKING YEW. *See* **Torreya.**

STINKWOOD, TASMANIA. *See* **Zieria Smithii.**

STIPA (*stupa*, tow, or oakum; the inflorescence is sometimes feathery). FAM. *Gramineae*. A genus of about 100 species of usually tall, perennial or annual, more or less tufted grasses, widely distributed over warm temperate regions. Panicle terminal, often slender. Spikeless 1-flowered, narrow, jointed above the outer glumes; glumes 3, narrow, the 2 outer usually persistent, the inner hard, with a long, sometimes very long, twisted awn. Leaves usually rolled and then almost thread-like. The species mentioned below, especially *S. pennata*, are ornamental and useful in making dry bouquets (*see* **Briza**); they are all hardy except *S. elegantissima*, and grow well in ordinary soil if well drained, being propagated by seed or by division. The twisted, hygroscopic awn of some species is apt to cause the sharp-pointed fruit to work its way through the skin of an animal in whose coat it is caught, and may, by getting into a vital part, cause death. In Nature it is a device for burying the fruit. *S. tenacissima*, Esparto Grass of Spain, Alfa or Halfa of Africa, contains in its foliage very strong fibre valuable in making paper (including cigarette paper), mats, ropes, &c.

KEY

1.	*Panicle-branches feathery-hairy*	S. elegantissima
1.	*Panicle-branches rough or smooth, not hairy*	2
2.	*Awns conspicuously feathery-hairy*	3
2.	*Awns rough, or only shortly and obscurely hairy*	4
3.	*Awns* 6 *in. or more long, hairy in the upper part*	S. pennata
3.	*Awns* 1 *to* 3 *in. long, hairy in the lower part*	S. tenacissima
4.	*Spikelets* $\frac{1}{8}$ *to* $\frac{3}{8}$ *in. long*	5
4.	*Spikelets* $\frac{3}{4}$ *to* $1\frac{1}{2}$ *in. long*	7
5.	*Panicle loose and spreading; spikelets about* $\frac{1}{8}$ *in. long*	S. arundinacea
5.	*Panicle contracted, rather dense; spikelets* $\frac{1}{8}$ *to* $\frac{3}{8}$ *in. long*	6
6.	*Flowering glume long-haired; awn becoming bent when dry*	S. Calamagrostis
6.	*Flowering glume short-haired; awn straight or curved*	S. splendens
7.	*Spikelets* $\frac{3}{4}$ *to* 1 *in. long*	8
7.	*Spikelets* $1\frac{1}{4}$ *to* $1\frac{1}{2}$ *in. long; awn up to* 8 *in. long*	S. spartea
8.	*Awn rough only in the lower part, becoming curled in the upper part*	S. capillata
8.	*Awn downy or nearly smooth in the lower part, becoming bent and not curled*	9
9.	*Awn softly and very shortly hairy in the lower part*	S. juncea
9.	*Awn nearly smooth in the lower part*	S. gigantea

S. arundina'cea. Stems 2 to 5 ft. long. *Panicles* drooping, up to 3 ft. long, spreading; spikelets about $\frac{1}{8}$ in. long, purplish-brown, awn $\frac{1}{3}$ in. long. New Zealand. 1882. SYN. *Apera arundinacea.*

S. Calamagros'tis. Densely tufted. Stem about 3 ft. h., erect. *l.* finely bristly, sheath smooth, ligule almost absent. *Panicle* up to about 1 ft. long, spreading; spikelets about $\frac{3}{8}$ in. long, often violet, awns about as long. S. Europe. SYN. *S. Lasiagrostis, Lasiagrostis Calamagrostis.*

S. capilla'ta. Densely tufted. Stem about 2 ft. h. *l.* grey-green, rolled, rigid, slender, ligule long. *Panicle* scarcely spreading, branches slender; spikelets numerous, about 1 in. long, white, awn 3–6 in. long, rough in lower part. S. Europe, Asia Minor. 1815

S. elegantis'sima. Tufted. Stems 2 to 3 ft. h., erect. *l.* narrow, rolled, erect. *Panicle* 6 to 8 in. long, very loose and spreading, branches very slender, feathery with fine, spreading hairs; spikelets about $\frac{1}{3}$ in. long, awns $1\frac{1}{4}$ in. long. Australia.

S. gigantea. Densely tufted, with erect stems 1⅓ to 2½ ft. h. *l.* rolled, very slender; panicles loose; spikelets purplish, about 1 in. long; awn 4 to 6 in. long, hairless. Spain. Distinguished from *S. juncea* by the hairless awns.

S. jun'cea. Allied to *S. capillata* but more slender and delicate in all parts. Stem about 3 ft. h. Awns 4 to 6 in. long, shortly bristly hairy. SW. Europe. 1772.

S. Lasiagrost'is. A synonym of *S. Calamagrostis.*

S. penna'ta. Feather Grass. Densely tufted. Stems about 2½ ft. h. *l.* green, rarely flat, narrow. *Spikelets* ½ in. or more long, both outer and inner glumes awned, awns of the outer about an inch long, of the inner about a foot long, the lower part smooth, the upper feathery. Europe, Siberia.

S. spar'tea. Allied to *S. capillata* but with fewer, larger spikelets, 2 to 3 ft. h. *Panicles* close; spikelets about 1½ in. long, awn about 6 in. long, rough. W. United States.

S. splen'dens. Stems 3 to 6 ft. h. *Panicles* about 1 ft. long, rather dense, nodding; spikelets about ⅛ in., shining, awns ¼ to ½ in. long, W. Asia.

S. tenacis'sima. Esparto Grass. Densely tufted. Stems 2 to 3 ft. h. *l.* narrow, cylindrical, smooth, long. *Panicles* close; spikelets with awns 1 to 3 in. long, feathery in lower part. Spain, N. Africa.

C. E. Hb.

stipa'tus -a -um, compressed, crowded.

STIPE. (1) The leaf-stalk in ferns. (2) The stalk supporting the cap (pileus) in Mushroom-like fungi. (3) The erect, cylindrical stem of a palm or tree-fern; for which 'caudex' is better, when a special term is needed. (4) More rarely, a prolongation of the floral axis between any 2 whorls of a flower, e.g. between the calyx and corolla as in Silene, when it is better called 'anthophore', or between stamens and pistil, as in *Geum rivale,* better called 'gynophore' or, when the fruit is ripe, 'carpophore'.

STIPEL. A small stipule-like growth at the base of the leaflets of a compound leaf, not infrequent in Leguminous plants, e.g. Phaseolus; in Erythrina they take the form of glands.

stipella'tus -a -um, having stipels.

stipifor'mis -is -e, Stipa-like.

stipita'tus -a -um, having a stalk.

stipularis -is -e, having prominent stipules.

STIPULARY BUD. Accessory buds in the axils of stipules, as seen in Apple, Pear, &c., additional to and at the sides of the axillary bud.

stipula'tus -a -um, having stipules.

STIPULE. Outgrowths from the base of the leaf-stalk, seen in the leaves of many flowering plants, when they are said to be stipulate (cf. **exstipulate**). The stipules are usually 2, 1 on each side of the leaf-base, and usually alike. Their chief function is to protect the as yet unfolded leaves from loss of water and heat and from excess of light. When this is the only function they act as bud scales, as in the Fig, the Oak, the Beech, and in many other trees and are shed as the buds expand, but they may enlarge and protect the young leaf for some time longer as they do in the Tulip-tree, or persist when the leaf is expanded, becoming green and taking on similar functions to the leaf-blade as in the rose, become exactly similar to the leaves in form and size and colouring as in Rubia and Asperula, become even larger than the leaf-blade as in the Pansy, or replace it altogether as in the Yellow Vetch, *Lathyrus Aphaca,* where the blade is completely transformed into tendrils, leaving all the normal functions of the leaf to the stipules. In Polygonaceae the stipules form a peculiar and characteristic sheath (ochrea) clasping the stem above the leaf-base, as is well seen in Rhubarb, and in all but 1 section of the family. In some Acacias (q.v.) and in Robinia they are spines, in Smilax they form tendrils. The presence or absence of stipules is often and, indeed, usually a family characteristic, but sometimes they are so small, or fall so early, that they are easily overlooked, and in the section of Rubiaceae to which Asperula belongs, so like the foliage leaves that they can be distinguished only by the absence of buds from their axils.

stipulo'sus -a -um, having large stipules.

stiria'cus -a -um, native of Styria (Steiermark), Austria.

STIRPS. A race or permanent variety, e.g. the red cabbage.

STITCHWORT. *See* **Stellaria.**

STIZOLO'BIUM (*stizo,* to prick; from the stinging hairs of the fruit). FAM. *Leguminosae.* A genus of about 12 species of annual climbers, natives of the tropics of the Old World. Closely related to Mucuna, the species of which are perennial, but having nearly spherical or flattened oval seeds, not round flat ones as in Mucuna, the hilum occupying only about one-sixth of the circumference instead of nearly three-quarters; the early leaves of Mucuna on germination are scale-like, those of Stizolobium 3-foliolate. Most of the species are of value as fodder and have pods either smooth or covered with velvety down; *S. pruriens,* however, has the pods densely covered with bristly stinging hairs. The species are scarcely worth cultivating except for their interest as economic plants. They require warm-house treatment. *S. Deeringianum* with purple flowers and *S. niveum* with white flowers in racemes about 3 ft. long have smooth downy pods.

S. pru'riens. Cow-itch. *l.* grey-silky beneath; lflets. 6 to 9 in. long. *fl.* in shortly peduncled drooping racemes, 6 to 12 in. long; cor. purplish, 1¼ to 1½ in. long. *Pod* covered with dense persistent bristles, usually brown or pale grey. Tropics. SYN. *Mucuna pruriens, M. utilis.*

STIZOPHYL'LUM (*stizo,* to prick, *phyllon,* leaf; application doubtful). FAM. *Bignoniaceae.* A genus of about 12 species of twining shrubs, more or less hairy when young, natives of Trop. America, closely related to Bignonia. Leaves 2- or 3-foliolate, with translucent dots. Tendrils unbranched. Flowers showy, in a short, sometimes only 2-flowered, terminal raceme; corolla bell-funnel-shaped, lobes overlapping downwards; stamens included; disk distinctly saucer-shaped; calyx membranous, bell-shaped, inflated, irregularly 5-lobed and 5-nerved; ovary linear, compressed. Capsule long and narrow, much flattened. For treatment *see* **Clytostoma.**

S. perfora'tum. Hairy climber. *l.* 3-foliolate; lflets. stalked, ovate. *fl.* 2 in. long, hairy without; cal. margins torn. August. Brazil. 1881. SYN. *Bignonia perforata.*

STOBAEA. Included in **Berkheya.**

STOCK. (1) The rooted portion of a plant to which a graft is applied, usually a stem, occasionally a root. *See* **Rootstock.** (2) The rhizome or crown from which roots proceed. (3) A race of plants or a collection from which plants can be drawn for any purpose.

STOCK, CAPE. *See* **Heliophila.**

STOCK, TEN WEEKS, EAST LOTHIAN, &c. *See* **Stocks.**

STOCK, VIRGINIAN. *See* **Malcomia maritima.**

STOCKS (*Matthiola*). These, the Stock Gilliflowers of the gardeners of the early years of the 19th century, are derived from *M. incana,* using that name in the broad sense to include what was at one time distinguished as *M. annua* and possibly also the Cretan form, *M. fenestralis,* which, if not belonging to *M. incana,* is certainly very closely related. *M. incana* is a native of S. Europe and occurs wild in Britain. There is much variation within the group but in all, the delightful perfume, free-flowering, and generally sturdy habit of these plants have made them general favourites both for the outdoor border and for pots.

The 2 main groups are the Summer Stocks and the Winter Stocks. The Summer Stocks are usually called Ten-week Stocks since they flower in 10 or 12 weeks from the sowing of the seeds. The seeds of this type may be sown outdoors in April but are better sown in pans under glass at the beginning of March. The seedlings should be pricked out into boxes of light, rich soil as soon as large enough and grown on, giving plenty of air, for stock seedlings are very apt to be attacked by damping-off fungi, especially in the seed-pan. These seedlings should be ready to transplant to beds and borders in mild, showery weather after mid-May, protecting from late frosts if necessary, or delaying planting out until fear of frost is past. The Ten-week Stocks are less suitable for pots than other types but are good for cutting from the open. The soil for them can scarcely be too rich or too well prepared and a mulch of leaf-mould is very useful as an aid during dry, hot weather.

Winter Stocks are those which are sown in one year to flower the next. They include the Intermediate, East Lothian, and Brompton Stocks. The Emperor or Perpetual Stocks also belong here but if sown in March they will usually flower in autumn of the same year. The normal time for sowing all these types is June or early July. The Brompton Stocks are robust, vigorous plants, branching and good for flowering in May and June. The Perpetual Stocks treated in the same way usually flower in June. They also are vigorous and branching, growing about 18 in. high. The Intermediate and East Lothian Stocks, also sown in early July, are of dwarfer habit and useful for flowering outdoors in early summer, and especially useful for flowering in pots for the cold greenhouse. All these should be sown in pans in the cold frame, pricked out as soon as possible, and grown on in pots in a cold frame during winter, except in mild districts with dry winter weather and well-drained soil. Stocks are apt to suffer much more from excessive damp than from low temperatures and in many districts it is safer to delay planting until March, rather than to plant in flowering quarters in autumn.

For flowering in pots under glass the seedlings should be planted singly in thumb pots early in autumn and plunged in ashes in a cold frame. In late autumn or early spring, when well established, they should be moved into 5- or 6-in. pots in which to flower. The compost should be of good fibrous loam with enough sand to keep it open and about 1 part in 5 of sifted mortar rubble. They may be grown in their flowering pots in the cool greenhouse from October onwards, but great care must be taken over watering, ventilation be freely given at all suitable times, and no attempt made to force growth by high temperatures. While the East Lothian and Intermediate Stocks sown about the third week in July are probably best for pot cultivation, Ten-week Stocks may also be used and Brompton Stocks sown at the end of June also answer well in pots.

The desire in all methods of using Stocks is that the flowers shall be double, both because they are more lasting and because on the whole the growth is more compact. The structure of the double flower of stocks is that there is repeated formation of calyx and corolla on the floral axis throughout the life of the flower, no stamens and no carpels ever being produced. The production of seeds from a double flower is therefore impossible. Double-flowered plants can only be produced from single flowers belonging to a strain apt to throw double flowers. There is no doubt that strains differ in their proneness to doubling but the best strains produce normally only about 50 per cent. of doubles. A great number of suggestions have been put forward from time to time as to methods of increasing the percentage of plants bearing double flowers, and Miss E. R. Saunders, who investigated the genetics of Stocks with very great thoroughness, found that the 13 methods which had been confidently advocated and were tested by her all failed of their purpose. (See *Journal R.H.S.*, 40, pp. 459–65.) She suggested (*Journal of Genetics*, 5 (1915), pp. 137–43) that the abnormal percentages of doubles sometimes recorded were due to unconscious selection of the most vigorous plants at planting time, a view corroborated at Wisley in 1916–17 (*Journal R.H.S.*, 44, pp. 74–82), where conscious selection of the most vigorous seedlings from good strains was made. An average of over 70 per cent. proved to have double flowers while from the weak plants of the same strains the percentage of doubles was only 53. The selection of seedlings was made at pricking-out time. This result seems in line with the fact that the seeds which would produce single-flowered plants have a shorter life than those which give rise to double-flowered plants so that of the seedlings derived from old seed a higher proportion are double-flowered than of those from fresh seed.

For varieties of merit see Supplement.

DISEASES. Stocks may be attacked by black rot due to *Pseudomonas campestris* and by downy mildew caused by *Peronospora parasitica* as on cabbage. Various damping-off troubles may be caused by *Fusarium*, *Pythium*, and *Phytophthora*. Canker of the stem is caused by *Phoma lingam* and this may be seed-borne. Where the soil is wet root-rots due to *Corticium solani* and *Thielaviopsis basicola*, and attacks of grey mould, *Botrytis cinerea*, may occur. Virus diseases in Stocks show as a mosaic on the foliage accompanied by 'breaking' in the flower causing splashes and streaks of white in the petals. It is also suspected that Stocks can be attacked by the Spotted Wilt virus.

(D. E. G.)

stoechadifo'lius -a -um, with Lavender-like leaves.

STOECH'AS. Included in **Lavandula.**

Stoerckia'nus -a -um, in honour of Anton von Stoerck, 1741–1803, physician of Vienna.

STOKES'IA (in honour of Dr. Jonathan Stokes, 1755–1831, coadjutor of Withering in his arrangement of British plants). FAM. *Compositae.* A genus of a single species of erect, sparingly branched, perennial herb with handsome flower-heads of various colours. It grows well in the open border in summer and may be propagated by seeds or by division.

S. cyan'ea. A synonym of *S. laevis.*

S. lae'vis.* Stem 12 to 18 in. h. *l.* alternate, smooth, lanceolate, entire or somewhat spiny-ciliate at base; lower stalked, upper amplexicaul. *fl.-heads* typically blue, 1 in. or more across, few or solitary at ends of branches, pedunculate; involucre sub-globose, outer scale with a leafy, bristle-fringed terminal appendage, inner lanceolate, entire; florets narrowly 5-cleft. August. *Pappus* of 4 or 5 chaffy scales. N. America. 1766. (B.M. 4966.) SYN. *S. cyanea.* Varieties in colour, size of fl.-head, and early flowering are offered. The colour range is white, yellow, blue, lilac, and purple.

STOKING. *See* **Heating.**

Stollea'nus -a -um, in honour of A. Stollé, b. 1876, geologist, who travelled in New Guinea and Indonesia.

STOLON. A branch arising from near the base of the parent stem, resting on the surface of the soil or growing just below it, rooting at the tip and tending to form a new plant capable of independent growth when the branch is cut or dies away between the parent and the terminal bud of the stolon. *See also* **Offset, Runner.**

stolonif'erus -a -um, bearing or propagating by stolons.

stoloniform, like a stolon, applied to the stems of lilies (Lilium species) which creep horizontally before emerging from the soil and terminating in a leafy shoot.

Stokesia laevis (p. 2034)

STOMA (*pl.* stomata). The stomata are small openings in the epidermis of leaves and young stems through which gases, including water-vapour, can pass from the intercellular spaces of the leaf or cortex to the outer air and from the outer air into the intercellular spaces. The main interchange during the hours of daylight will be water-vapour and oxygen from the plant, the latter the result of photosynthesis, and during the hours of darkness water-vapour and carbon dioxide formed during respiration, while the intake will be during the day mainly carbon dioxide and at night oxygen. The form and structure of the stomata do not vary greatly in different plants though there is considerable difference in the arrangement and in the form of the epidermal cells in their neighbourhood. The opening of the stoma lies between 2 sausage-shaped cells called the guard cells which, unlike the other cells of the epidermis, contain chlorophyll grains. These guard cells are joined at their ends and their walls are so thickened that when they are distended with water ('turgid') the slit between them is opened wide. When the plant loses more water by transpiration than is replaced by intake by the roots, and the guard cells in common with others lose their turgidity, the slit is closed and the loss of water-vapour much diminished. Light has also considerable effect upon their condition and the stomata are usually more or less closed towards the end of the afternoon. Stomata are rarely found on underground parts of plants or those that are submerged in water. They are usually about equally distributed when both surfaces of the leaf, like those of the common Iris, are equally exposed to the light, but in most leaves where there is a distinct upper and lower surface, the upper has far fewer than the lower surface and the upper surface may be devoid of them entirely. In Conifers where, very frequently, the upper surface of the leaf is less exposed than the lower they are usually more numerous on the upper surface, as they are in floating leaves, those of Nymphaea and Hydrocharis, for example. The number on a given area varies greatly in different plants, being much smaller in plants greatly exposed to dry conditions than in those fitted for moister air, where the number may be as high as 300,000 to the square inch, whereas in the dry-country plants it may be only a few hundred. It usually lies between 20,000 and 150,000.

Behind each stoma lies an air space into which the stoma opens, and this communicates with smaller spaces between the cells in the interior of the leaf, &c., and through these intercellular spaces gases may be conveyed all over the plant.

In a few plants there are permanent openings called water-pores or water-stomata usually near the leaf-margin over the ends of veins through which drops of water are exuded when the plant is turgid. They are readily seen in *Zantedeschia aethiopica* at the tip of the leaf and on the teeth of Fuchsia leaves when the plants are in a very moist atmosphere, or on the tips of grass leaves on damp evenings when the drops of water there seen are often mistaken for dew-drops. In some plants, e.g. some of the Saxifrages, as the water so exuded evaporates, lime which was dissolved in it is left behind in the form of a lime encrustation, and such are often called lime-glands.

STOMACH POISONS. *See* **Insecticides.**

stomatiferous, stoma-bearing: in leaves of conifers the area bearing the stomata is frequently marked by a conspicuous band of wax on the leaf-surface.

STOMA'TIUM (*stoma*, mouth; the pairs of toothed leaves looking like an open mouth). FAM. *Aizoaceae* (Mesembryanthemum). Dwarf succulent plants from Cape Province, with very short stems, branching to form clumps; one growth consists of 2 or 3 pairs of leaves which are united at the base, very thick, lanceolate or spatulate, the edges with broad teeth; the surface may be tuberculate, the colour usually dull glaucous green. The flowers are small with narrow petals and produced in summer; they often open in the late afternoon or evening. For cultivation *see* **Mesembryanthemum** (2).

S. agni'num. *See* **Mesembryanthemum agninum.**

S. ermin'inum. Stem very short, branching. *l.* crowded, $\frac{3}{4}$ in. long, face flat, back convex and keeled, tip blunt, 3 or 4 short teeth on the edge, pale grey-green. *fl.* 1 in. across, yellow, scented. SYN. *Mesembryanthemum ermininum.* (M.A.S. 5. 6.)

S. Ful'leri. Similar to *S. ermininum* but a little larger, green with pale-grey dots. *fl.* $\frac{3}{4}$ in. across, yellow, scented.

S. mustelli'num. Similar in habit to *S. ermininum* but *l.* smaller, with 5 to 7 acute teeth, pale grey-green with large, translucent, slightly raised dots. *fl.* $\frac{3}{4}$ in. across, yellow. SYN. *Mesembryanthemum mustellinum.* (M.A.S. 5. 5.)

V. H.

STONE. The hard body within certain fruits, e.g. Cherry, Plum, Peach, formed by lignification of the inner layer of the pericarp (i.e. the endocarp). The stones of each horticultural variety (i.e. clone) vary little in form and sculpturing, and on careful study are often found to possess a combination of minute features which, taken together, distinguish the stones of one variety from those of other varieties. Hence they can be used in the recognition of varieties.

STONE FRUITS. This collective term covers those fruits (technically called drupes) in which a soft fleshy exterior (developed from the pericarp) surrounds a comparatively large stone (i.e. the hard woody endocarp enclosing usually a solitary seed), e.g. Almond, Apricot, Cherry, Cherry-Laurel, Peach, Plum, Sloe, all usually placed in the genus Prunus. It is used to distinguish them as a group from the pome fruits (i.e. Apple, **Pear,**

Quince, in which a fleshy exterior developed from the receptacle surrounds a several-seeded core) and the berried fruits (botanically a heterogenous group, comprising Strawberry, Blackberry, Raspberry, and Mulberry, as well as Currant, Gooseberry, and Grape).

STONE ORPINE. *See* **Sedum reflexum.**

STONE PINE. *See* **Pinus Pinea.**

STONECROP. *See* **Sedum acre.**

Stone'i, in honour of Mr. Stone, gardener to Mr. J. Day, the orchid grower, *c.* 1862.

STONING. A period in the development of fruits at which, in stone-fruits, the endocarp starts lignification or the seeds, as in grapes, begin to acquire their hard testas. There is then, usually, a period of little increase in size in the fruit and special care in water-supply is often necessary. As a rule many of the fruits partially grown by this time are not able to secure all they need for further development and they are soon overpassed by those better favoured and either remain small or fall. See Thinning of Grapes.

STONNORD. An old name for Stonecrop.

STOOL. A stemless mother plant from which layers are annually propagated by bending into the soil, or rooted branches obtained by earthing up.

STOPPING. The operation of stopping or pinching back the growths of trees and plants is a kind of pruning, with the object of inducing the development of lateral buds or directing the flow of sap into lateral growths already formed instead of to the terminal bud as is normal in the untouched shoot. Reference is made to the operation in various articles in the Dictionary and notes given where special methods of carrying it out are advisable. No hard-and-fast rules can be laid down. Where trees are concerned it is in greatest use for training in fancy forms, a type of gardening now much less in vogue than in earlier times, but is also an operation of value for inducing the growth of shoots wherever they may be desired, and for correcting the form of plants apt to be leggy instead of compact. A very important factor is the time at which pinching or stopping is done and another the extent to which it is carried out at any one time. Injudicious application of the operation may well lead to the production of numerous lateral shoots at a season when there is no hope of their reaching maturity and bearing either flowers or fruit.

STORAGE ROTS. Fruits, vegetables, bulbs, &c., when stored may suffer rotting due to attack by fungus and bacterial organisms. This rotting may be encouraged by unsuitable conditions of storage, especially dampness, whether in fruit stores, vegetable clamps, pits, boxes, &c. Root crops such as carrots, beetroot, turnips, &c., may develop a soft rot due to *Bacterium carotovorum* or be destroyed by the fungus *Sclerotinia sclerotiorum*. Often the beginning of the rotting is due to slightly infected specimens being included among the others in the store as with Blackleg (*Bacterium phytophthorum*) and Dry Rot (*Fusarium caeruleum*) among potatoes in clamps or with Brown Rot (*Sclerotinia fructigena*) among apples in store, thus emphasizing the importance of careful selection of fruits, &c., intended for store as well as strict attention to ventilation and general storage conditions. Many of these storage rots are, however, due to common fungi not parasitic on the crop when growing, e.g. Penicillium, the Green Moulds Rhizopus, and *Botrytis cinerea*, any of which may appear on bruised or injured fruits in store or on bulbs of tulips, daffodils, and similar dormant plant structures in the presence of moisture.

D. E. G.

STORAX. *See* **Styrax officinalis.**

STORAX, LIQUID. *See* **Liquidambar.**

Stor'iei, in honour of James G. Storie, *c.* 1880.

STORING. See treatment under individual Fruits and Vegetables.

STORING OF APPLES AND PEARS. A ripening fruit is a living entity which breathes and gives off water-vapour and various gases. To delay its ultimate breakdown and death it must be provided with conditions so cool that they reduce to the minimum its rate of breathing, but not cold enough to damage its tissue by freezing; at the same time they should be humid enough to reduce its loss of water-vapour to a minimum and so prevent shrivelling, but not damp enough to encourage moulds. Temperature and humidity should accordingly remain fairly constant. A temperature of about 32 to 35° F., with humidity of about 85 per cent. is considered to be best for apples; the amateur without special facilities will have to make do with a temperature of about 40 to 50° F., in which event the humidity can be higher. Pears should be stored at 40 to 45° F.

A certain amount of ventilation is also necessary to remove the exhaled gases which accelerate ripening or produce asphyxiation and death if allowed to accumulate. Commercial growers now construct large, ventilated, cool but frost-free well-insulated underground stores, from which rats and mice are excluded. The amateur with less fruit to handle can adopt for the purpose a brick out-house, a cellar, an air-raid shelter, &c. The floor of a fruit store should preferably be of earth, as this ensures a more constant humidity. When it is of concrete or brick, wet sacks can be laid upon it. The entry of rats and mice should be prevented as they will destroy the fruit for the sake of the pips. Dusting the floor with DDT. is a good precaution against woodlice. To prevent frost-damage when the walls are only one brick through, they should be insulated with a thick layer of clean straw. The store should be dark.

Apples and pears to be stored should be sound and unblemished; they should be handled carefully, not tipped or rolled, as bruising will lead to premature rotting. Moreover, they should be taken into the store when cool, i.e. fruit picked one day should be placed in the store early next morning. A decaying fruit liberates thousands of spores liable to infect other fruits, hence stored fruit should be examined once a month at least and any unsound fruit immediately removed.

The older type of fruit store is provided with permanent wooden racks, on which the fruit is stacked, or on which shallow boxes of fruit are placed, or with shelves on which the fruit is stacked, apples preferably several layers deep, but pears should always be in single layers. In many modern stores these are not used as they make the thorough summer cleaning of the store more difficult. Instead, the fruit is stored in portable orchard boxes or trays which can be stacked one above the other.

It is good policy to wash racks, boxes, and trays used the previous season with a copper sulphate solution before using them again in order to remove spores likely to set up decay of the new fruit.

When an outhouse or old stable or similar building with a brick or concrete floor is being used for storing apples, the floor should first be made clean by scrubbing. When dry the floor should then be covered with a layer of clean straw about 6 in. thick with a similar layer against the walls or wooden partitions and the apples then carefully stacked to depth of up to 2 ft. They should then be covered with paper or a thick layer of clean straw in cold weather.

Stored pears need especially careful examination from time to time so that they can be consumed at their best.

The right time for picking varies from variety to

variety. In general, fruits for storing should be harvested before they are completely mature, so as to give a longer period in the store for the purpose of ripening. **A**

Wrapping of the individual fruits in oiled wraps is recommended. Fuller particulars can be found in standard works such as R. Bush, *Harvesting and Storing Garden Fruit* (1947), W. P. Seabrook, *Modern Fruit Growing*, 7th ed. (1945), F. Keeble and A. N. Rawes, *Hardy Fruit Growing*, 2nd ed. (1946).

STORK'S BILL. *See* **Erodium.**

STOVE. A glasshouse devoted to the cultivation of plants needing a high temperature, many of them among the most beautiful in fine foliage or in flowers. In most gardens a single house or a house with a division in the middle fills requirements. Where large specimens are grown the accommodation must be more extensive, and where a large number of different species have to be provided for it will be found that some will need a higher temperature than others. While a divided house can be kept hotter in one section than the other, something can be done in a single house by keeping the plants requiring greater heat at the warmer end and by admitting whatever air is needed at the other end. A further advantage of a divided house is that the atmosphere in one section can be kept drier than that of the other, and by this, not only are the general life conditions of the plants most easily secured, but the period of rest which many need can be arranged for.

The best form of house for a stove is the span-roofed; the hip-roofed type will also answer but the wall on one side is apt to exclude light which a span-roofed house would admit. For the successful cultivation of stove plants, particularly those with brilliant flowers, the admission of all possible light is one of the most important conditions. Where plenty of light is available the foliage takes on more beautiful colouring, and the plants have a shorter-jointed growth than when less light reaches them. For this reason the side walls of the house should be glazed from about 3 ft. above ground-level. Most of the plants will require a little protection from direct sunshine on bright days in spring and summer and this should be provided by roller-blinds of a convenient type so that the shading can be rapidly removed when the weather becomes cloudy.

For maintaining the proper temperature hot-water pipes should be arranged on the walls or above the staging or under the paths with iron gratings above to allow the heated air ready passage into the house. A plunging bed should be provided heated by hot-water pipes with coconut fibre above, and this is best placed in the middle of the house with a path all round, if the house is 15 ft. or more across, the sides being occupied by staging. If the pipes are beneath the staging, the latter should be of slate or so constructed that ashes, pebbles, or shells may be put beneath the pots to retain moisture, otherwise the staging may be of open woodwork.

Ventilation should be so arranged that air entering the house cannot come into direct contact with the plants; it is therefore best to place side ventilators in the walls near the pipes and others near the top of the structure, making most use of the roof ventilators. Cold draughts must, of course, be avoided and the ventilators should be closed as early in the afternoon as is consistent with safety to make the best use of the sun heat which is more beneficial to the plants than indiscriminate use of fire-heat.

In general plenty of water and a moist atmosphere are necessary in the stove; the plants must, therefore, be well and carefully drained, and the soil used be of an open nature, whether of loam or peat, so that water may pass through it readily. It is probably best to use water, both for watering and syringing, at approximately the same temperature as the air of the house. In watering give sufficient to wet the whole ball of soil quite through, but be careful not to apply water unless it is required or the soil will become sodden and sour and the roots soon suffer. Clean rain-water is the best but failing this well-water which has been exposed to the air for some time. Water containing much lime should not be generally used both on account of the harm lime may do in the soil for many plants and because it will mark the foliage syringed with it as the water evaporates.

In arranging the plants overcrowding must be avoided. Growth of many stove plants is rapid and if overcrowded the plants soon become drawn and one-sided. The plants should be encouraged to make their growth in the spring and summer when there is plenty of sunlight. Repotting should be done in spring as they are beginning to grow, and the heat and moisture in the house should be increased. In repotting, as always, clean, dry pots should be used, with clean crocks sufficient to give efficient drainage, and soil in a proper state as regards moisture and sufficiently warmed to avoid chilling the roots.

The materials for potting should be carefully chosen and prepared. The materials required are as follows: good loam from the top spit of a pasture with plenty of fibrous roots in it, taken from a stack made several months before it is required, the turf having been stacked grass-side downwards. Good fibrous peat, if possible of a sandy nature, broken up into lumps with the hands for use; for some plants, especially those often growing as epiphytes in nature, such as Anthuriums, it is well to remove some of the fine particles, which can be done by beating the broken lumps lightly with a stick. Leaf-mould from leaves of Oak, Beech, Elm, or Lime, made into a large heap and occasionally turned is very useful for many plants, but it must be sweet; it should never be collected from a deposit lying under water for long and if at all sour should be replaced by clean granular peat. Coarse silver sand for mixing in the composts to keep them open is of much value in striking cuttings. Well-decayed cow-dung may be used when it is considered a plant needs a little stimulant. Charcoal, in lumps, for mixing in composts to keep them open and to provide something for roots to cling to. Live Sphagnum moss from which all grass, leaves, and refuse have been picked out before use. Coconut refuse is the best material for hot-beds and for plunging plants requiring bottom heat when the heat is derived from hot-water pipes or electric cable.

The need for cleanliness cannot be too greatly stressed. All decaying leaves, &c., should be removed and everything should be neat. Any outbreak of pests should be dealt with immediately, mealy bug and mites being especially liable to occur and to multiply rapidly in the high temperature that must be maintained.

The following is a list of genera among which may be found some of the chief decorative plants for the stove, exclusive of Ferns which are listed under that heading (q.v.) and Palms. The list is by no means complete and is given to draw attention to some of those generally worth cultivation. Many plants suitable only for very large structures are omitted.

FLOWERING PLANTS. Achimenes, Aechmea, Aerides, Aeschynanthus, Agalmyla, Allamanda, Alpinia, Amasonia, Androlepis, Angraecum, Anoectochilus, Anthurium, Aphenandra, Arachnanthe, Ardisia, Aregelia, Argyreia, Begonia, Billbergia, Bollea, Brocchinia, Bromelia, Brunfelsia, Bulbophyllum, Burbidgea, Caesalpinia, Calanthe, Centropogon, Cirrhopetalum, Clerodendron, Clivia, Crinum, Dendrobium, Dendrochilum, Diacrium, Didymocarpus, Echinocactus, Epidendrum, Epiphyllum, Eranthemum, Erythrorhipsalis, Eucharis, Eupatorium, Euphorbia, Gardenia, Gesneria, Gloxinia, Grammatophyllum, Graptophyllum, Gymnocalycium, Hedychium, Heliamphora, Hibiscus, Hippeastrum, Hylocereus, Impatiens, Isoloma, Ixora, Jacobinia, Leuchtenbergia, Luculia, Magnolia, Medinilla, Miltonia, Monochaetum, Muscaenda, Naegelia, Nautilocalyx, Nymphaea, Oncidium, Pancratium, Paphinia, Pentas, Pereskia, Peristeria, Pescatorea, Phalaenopsis, Phauis, Phyllocactus, Pilea,

Pilocereus, Platyclinis, Plumbago, Poinciana, Portlandia, Posoqueria, Promenaea, Pseuderanthemum, Psychotria, Reinwardtia, Renanthera, Rhipsalis, Rhododendron, Rivina, Rondeletia, Russelia, Saccolabium, Saintpaulia, Schaueria, Scutellaria, Strelitzia, Streptocarpus, Tabernaemontana, Tacca, Talauma, Thyrsacanthus, Tillandsia, Torenia, Toxicophaea, Urceolina, Vanda, Vinca, Vriesia, Warscewiczella, Zygocactus.

PLANTS WITH ORNAMENTAL FOLIAGE. Acalypha, Alocasia, Ananassa, Andropogon, Anthurium, Aphelandra, Asparagus, Begonia, Bertolonia, Brexia, Brownea, Caladium, Calathea, Clidemia, Croton, Curculigo, Cymbopogon, Cyperus, Dichorisandra, Dieffenbachia, Dizygotheca, Dracaena, Eriocnema, Erythrina, Ficus, Fittonia, Heliconia, Hoffmannia, Isolepis, Jacaranda, Leea, Maranta, Mimosa, Musa, Nepenthes, Nidularium, Oplismenus, Panax, Pandanus, Panicum, Pavetta, Peperomia, Phrynium, Phyllanthus, Phyllotaenium, Polyscias, Rhopala, Roupala, Sanchezia, Schefflera, Sonerila, Sphaerogyne, Strobilanthes, Tillandsia, Tradescantia, Zebrina, Zingiber.

CLIMBING, WALL, AND PILLAR PLANTS. Allamanda, Anemopaegma, Araujia, Aristolochia, Arrabidaea, Bougainvillea, Cissus, Clerodendron, Combretum, Dipladenia, Ficus, Gloriosa, Hoya, Ipomoea, Jasminum, Manattia, Marcgravia, Oxera, Pandorea, Passiflora, Paullinia, Pellionia, Pothos, Schubertia, Solanum, Stephanotis, Strophanthus, Tecoma, Thunbergia.

strach'eyi, in honour of General Sir Richard Strachey, F.R.S., 1817–1908, who collected plants in the central Himalaya (Kumaon, adjacent Garhwal and Tibet) in 1846–9.

stragula'tus, -a -um, mat-forming.

STRAIN. A stock of a particular variety selected with special attention to some minor though perhaps important character and breeding true to it; sometimes used in the same sense as race.

stramineus -a -um, straw-coloured.

stramoniifo'lius -a -um, with Stramonium-like leaves.

STRAMON'IUM. Included in **Datura.**

strangulatus -a -um, strangling.

STRANVAES'IA (in honour of William Thomas Horner Fox Strangways, Earl of Ilchester, English botanist, 1795–1865). FAM. *Rosaceae.* A genus of 5 species, native of China and N. India. Evergreen trees or shrubs. Leaves simple, alternate. Flowers white, numerous in corymbs or panicles; petals 5; stamens 20; styles 5, united at the lower half. Fruit haw-like. They grow well in either loamy or peaty soil in full sunshine.

Stranvaesia Davidiana

Increased by seed. Their chief attraction is in the handsome fruits; the flowers are fleeting.

KEY

1. *Lvs. entire* 2
1. *Lvs. finely toothed* S. Nussia
2. *Lvs. lanceolate or oblanceolate* 3
2. *Lvs. narrow-oblong, tapered to both ends, downy on midribs only above* S. salicifolia
3. *Growth more or less erect. Lvs. 2 to 4½ in. long. Anthers dark red* S. Davidiana
3. *Growth spreading. Lvs. 1½ to 4 in. long, often wavy at margin. Anthers red* S. undulata

S. Davidian'a. Evergreen shrub or small tree up to 30 ft. *l.* lanceolate or oblanceolate, acuminate, 2 to 4½ in. long, dark green. *fl.* thinly disposed in panicles 2 or 3 in. long, each ⅓ in. wide; pet. white, concave; anthers dark red; fl.-stalk and cal. downy. June. *fr.* globose, brilliant crimson, ⅓ in. wide. China. 1917. (B.M. 9008, as *Photinia Davidiana.*) Hardy, but best in the south and west. Over 20 ft. h. at Exbury, Hants.

S. glauces'cens. A synonym of *S. Nussia.*

S. Nuss'ia. Evergreen tree of 25 ft. or more. *l.* leathery, lanceolate to obovate, 2½ to 4 in. long, 1 to 2 in. wide, dark glossy green above, finely toothed. *fl.* in clusters 3 in. across, white, ½ in. wide; fl.-stalk and cal. woolly. July. *fr.* spherical, orange, ⅓ in. wide, downy. Himalaya. 1828. (B.R. 1956, as *S. glaucescens.*) Tender and only suitable for a wall near London, but 20 ft. h. at Binstead, I. of W.

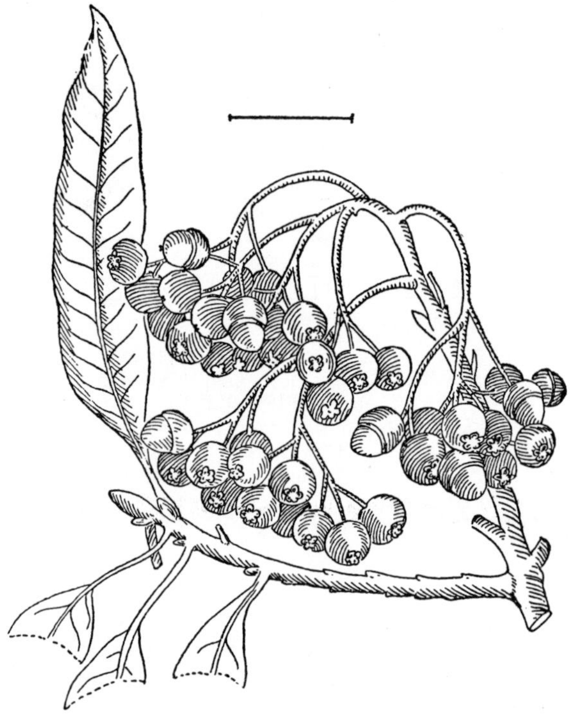

Stranvaesia salicifolia

S. salicifo'lia. Evergreen shrub or small tree of erect habit. *l.* narrow-oblong, pointed, entire, tapered at both ends, 1½ to 4 in. long, ½ to 1 in. wide, downy only on the midrib above. *fl.* in downy panicles 3 in. across, each fl. ¼ in. wide, white; pet. orbicular; anthers red. June. *fr.* orange-shaped, ⅓ in. wide, red. China. 1910. (B.M. 8862.) Very close to *S. Davidiana,* but of more erect growth; l. willow-like and with more numerous veins.

S. undula'ta. Evergreen, widespreading shrub, often twice as wide as high; 8 to 10 ft. *l.* lanceolate or oblanceolate, 1½ to 4 in. long, ½ to 1¼ in. wide, entire; petiole downy, red. *fl.* in downy panicles 3 in. wide, each fl. ⅓ in. wide, white, pet. soon falling; anthers red. June. *fr.* brilliant red, ⅓ in. wide. China. 1901. (B.M. 8418.) Akin to *S. Davidiana* and *salicifolia,* but distinct in its low, spreading habit. var. **fructu-luteo** has yellow fruits.

W. J. B.

STRASBURG TURPENTINE. *See* **Abies.**

strateumaticus -a -um, forming a company or army.

STRATIFICATION. Seeds which quickly lose their power of germination may often be preserved, and others whose testa, if exposed to air, becomes too impervious for the needed water to enter when the time for growth has come, may be kept in a state ready for germination by stratification. The simplest way of stratifying seeds is to take a receptacle with holes to ensure drainage, and of a size suitable for the quantity of seeds to be preserved. On the bottom lay a thin bed of breeze or unburnt coke and cover it with sand. On this the seeds should be laid as closely as possible, and over them another layer of sand, then more seeds, and so on until the pan is filled, when the whole must be covered with more breeze as a deterrent to the entry of worms. The seed should be stratified as soon as it is collected. The receptacle should be stood in the coolest place available. Burial at a depth just sufficient to avoid freezing is a good plan, mounding the earth above into a cone so as to shed off water, for wet conditions in the receptacle are liable to bring about rotting. Stratification has been found useful in preserving many tropical and sub-tropical seeds during their passage to this country, though doubtless the speed of air-travel will largely do away with the necessity for it in future. **A**

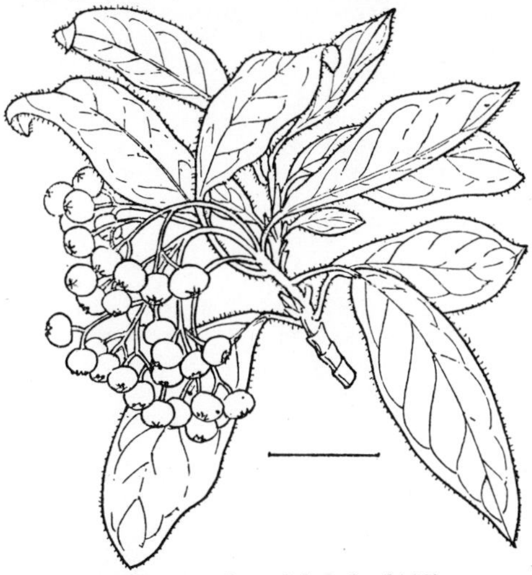

Stranvaesia undulata (p. 2038)

STRATIOTES (*stratiotes*, soldier; from the sword-shaped leaves). FAM. *Hydrocharitaceae.* A genus of a single species of submerged aquatic herbs inhabiting Europe, including Britain. It floats to the surface in summer where it produces its dioecious flowers, afterwards sinking and coming to the surface again in August or later. Meanwhile at the bottom of the ponds it has produced many axillary shoots terminated by big buds, and when it floats in August these grow into young plants which become free and sink to the bottom, there to remain during the winter. While interesting it is a plant, like many aquatic plants, to introduce with discretion since it may increase too rapidly.

S. aloi'des. Soldier's Yarrow, Water Soldier, Water Aloe. *l.* all radical, 6 to 18 in. long, tapering with spiny teeth, rigid, brittle, deep green. *fl.* white, 1½ in. across, on short, stout, axillary peduncles; male with many stamens, 12 bearing anthers; female with many staminodes. June to August. Europe, including Britain, Siberia.

STRATUM (*pl.* Strata). Anything spread out to form a layer. The term is used to denote the layers which constitute many rocks and soils, such as may be seen in many sand-pits, bog-cuttings, slate-quarries, and chalk-pits. They arise from the manner in which the materials of the rock, &c., have been deposited through the ages, for particulars of which a good text-book on Geology should be consulted. The arrangement of these layers in a natural fashion in building rock-gardens is important and should be carefully studied. The strata, it will be found, are usually inclined and often undulated. Not all rocks show them; those, like granite, which have been exposed to such great heat that they have been melted, are not stratified.

STRAVID'IUM. *See* **Barringtonia.**

STRAW. The aerial part of the stems of grasses. The straw of cereals is of value in gardens in many ways. It is used for covering plants and vegetable crops as a protection against frost; for laying under strawberry plants in summer to prevent the fruits being splashed and soiled when rain falls, and as a partial protection against slug damage; for covering potatoes and other root crops in the clamp to keep them from frost damage and to give some ventilation in the clamp. For these and similar purposes the straw should be clean and dry. It is also of value for making straw-mats for covering frames in severe weather. Of recent years it has come into use as a fertilizing agent both in the open and under glass, being laid on the ground in suitable lengths and driven in by the spade so that it stands upright in the spade cut, and not only enriches the soil by its decay but assists in keeping it open.

STRAWBERRY (*Fragaria* × *Ananassa*, &c.). The Strawberry has a unique position among our fruits. The plant itself is herbaceous and consequently requires different cultivation from bush and tree fruits. It is the quickest to crop and the first in season. The delicious flavour of the 'fruit' (technically an enlarged fleshy receptacle covered with numerous very small partly or wholly embedded achenes) ensures its popularity as fresh fruit and for preserving; it is as rich in vitamin C as oranges and lemons. Moreover, its development under cultivation has taken place in comparatively recent times.

Although wild Strawberries grow naturally in many parts of Europe and possess fruits so well-flavoured as to have prompted the remark by the celebrated physician William Butler (1535–1618) that 'Doubtless God could have made a better berry but doubtless God never did', they seem to have received little attention from gardeners until the late Middle Ages. Then *Fragaria vesca*, the commonest species, was transplanted from woods to the garden and cultivated on a large scale in the Royal Gardens at the Louvre, Paris, during the reign (1364–80) of King Charles V. The Alpine Strawberry, *F. vesca semperflorens*, though known to the Swiss naturalist Conrad Gesner (1516–56), did not come to the notice of northern gardeners until the 18th century. By then two other European species, *F. moschata* and *F. viridis*, had also been taken into cultivation. All of these have small flowers and small fruits, about ⅓ to ¾ in. across, and they yielded hybrids of no importance. The chromosome number is $2n = 14$ in *F. vesca* and *F. viridis*, $2n = 42$ in *F. moschata*. Cultivation over a long period neither improved the flavour of the fruits nor greatly increased their size.

The modern large-flowered and large-fruited garden Strawberries owe their origin to the American species *F. virginiana*, with its variety *illoensis* (*F. Grayana*), and *F. chiloensis*. These have the same high chromosome number ($2n = 56$) and produce fertile hybrids in cultivation but occupy different areas in nature, *F. virginiana* inhabiting eastern N. America and *F. chiloensis* the Pacific seaboard of both S. and N. America. *F. virginiana* which possesses a small but aromatic fruit, was introduced into France in 1624 and thence to England. Later introductions probably included its var. *illoensis*, although this was not properly distinguished until 1858 when Mme Élisa Vilmorin named it *F. Grayana*, noting the spreading hairs of the peduncle as a diagnostic feature; typical *F. virginiana* has the hairs of the peduncle appressed. The most important event in the history of the garden Strawberry was the introduction from Chile in 1714 of the large-flowered, large-fruited *F. chiloensis*. Thanks to the enterprise of a French naval officer, Amedée François Frézier (1682–1773), five plants reached France alive after a voyage of six months. All seem to have been females and though they flowered freely they gave no fruit until interplanted among other species, notably *F. virginiana*. Cross-pollination enabled them to set seed, from which fertile plants were raised. Of these the most celebrated was the 'Fraisier-ananas' (i.e. Pineapple Strawberry) which the French botanist Antoine Nicolas Duchesne (1747–1827) named *F. Ananassa* in his *Histoire naturelle des Fraisiers* (1766). This remarkable book, published when the author was but nineteen years, remains a classic of horticultural literature and gives a clear detailed well-documented account of all the Strawberries then known, their history and characteristics. Although some of his contemporaries supposed the 'Fraisier-ananas' to be an introduction from N. America or even Surinam, Duchesne himself correctly regarded it as a hybrid derived from *F. chiloensis* crossed with *F. virginiana*. These two species and the first generation hybrid *F.* × *Ananassa* thus provided the material out of which, in the 19th century, the modern large-fruited Strawberry developed. It may be noted here the name Strawberry (derived from Anglo-Saxon *streawberige* in use as long ago as A.D. 1000) is in no way connected with the practice of laying straw beneath the fruits.

The first important new Strawberry raised in England was Keens's Imperial, figured in *Trans. Hort. Soc.* 2: 101, pl. 7 (1814); from this Michael Keens, a market gardener at Isleworth, Middlesex, later raised Keens's Seedling figured in *Trans. Hort. Soc.* 5: 261, pl. 12 (1823). His contemporary, Thomas Andrew Knight (1759–1838), raised over 400 seedlings, among them Downton and Elton Seedling. The success of these pioneers encouraged others to breed new Strawberries, among the most notable of them being Bradley's Sir Joseph Paxton (1862) and Thomas Laxton's Royal Sovereign (1892). In the United States Charles Mason Hovey (1810–87) began to raise new Strawberries about 1834 and introduced in 1838 his celebrated Hovey variety.

W. T. S.

Whilst Strawberries can be grown successfully on a wide range of soils, rich medium loams and soils with a high organic matter content are best. Very dry soils or soils with a very high lime content are not suitable. The low-growing habit of the strawberry plant makes it especially liable to spring frost damage and, therefore, hollows where the cold air collects should be avoided.

For good results it is essential to plant only healthy stocks, free from pests and diseases, especially virus diseases which pass to all the runners of an infected parent. The best stocks are those raised in isolated conditions by specialist nurserymen for the 'Special Stock Certificate' of the Ministry of Agriculture. This certificate requires the greatest possible freedom from pests and virus and other diseases (see below). The 'A' or Ordinary Certificate is of lower standard, but such plants are suitable for commercial fruiting beds. Raising runners from fruiting beds in the garden is not recommended.

Strawberry varieties differ in their reaction to viruses. Some varieties can carry certain viruses without showing any symptoms of disease. These are called 'virus-tolerant' and an example is Huxley (a coarse variety not recommended for the garden). Other varieties, such as Royal Sovereign, are called 'sensitive' because they exhibit symptoms of disease when infected with virus and give very poor crops. It is therefore important not to grow these 'sensitive' varieties in the neighbourhood of 'tolerant' ones which may be carrying virus infection. The variety Auchincruive Climax is to some extent an exception in that, although semi-tolerant of virus infection, the Special Stock runners have been raised from a virus-free clone, and they can probably, therefore, be grown satisfactorily alongside either 'sensitive' or 'tolerant' varieties.

Planting can be done either in autumn or spring. Autumn planting is better whenever possible. On a small scale excellent results can be got by planting in August, or even July, and watering in dry weather. If this is done a good crop can be taken in the first year. A distance of 15 in. between plants in rows 30 in. apart is suitable for garden culture. On a larger scale where mechanical cultivation is employed 18 in. by 36 in. is more usual. A matted row about 18 in. wide, obtained by allowing runners to root alongside the parent plants, has been shown to crop more heavily than a row of single spaced plants. It is necessary to lay in only the first few runners, and the row width can then be restricted by the use of a sharp hand hoe.

Strawberries respond well to good dressings of dung or other bulky organic manures such as shoddy. Dung at the rate of 20 tons per acre (10 lb. per sq. yd.) can be dug in before planting, or surface mulches at the rate of 10 tons per acre (5 lb. per sq. yd.) applied at intervals during the life of the bed. A useful non-bulky organic manure is meat and bone meal which should be given at the rate of 5 to 10 cwt. per acre with 1 to 2 cwt. of potash. Inorganic forms of nitrogen should be applied in moderation to avoid excess vigour, but where organic manures are not available the following fertilizer mixture should prove satisfactory: Sulphate of ammonia 1 to 2 cwt. per acre (1 oz. per sq. yd.); Superphosphate 3 to 5 cwt. per acre (2 oz. per sq. yd.); Sulphate of potash 1 to 2 cwt. per acre (1 oz. per sq. yd.). Liming is necessary only on strongly acid soils.

Early removal of the flower-stems from plants in their first year will give a second-year crop heavier than the two years total from plants allowed to flower and fruit, but one-year plants produce earlier and larger fruits than older plants. In fruiting beds, runners should be cut off as they form, except where needed to form matted rows.

In dry seasons watering before and during cropping has been found profitable. Not less than ½ in. of water (2 gallons per sq. yd.) should be given at a time. Straw, preferably barley straw, is used to keep the fruit free of grit and soil. It should be spread just before the developing fruit begins to weigh down the truss; if applied too early the risk of frost damage is increased. Some protection from birds is usually necessary in gardens and is best achieved by covering the bed with netting.

Fruit to be marketed is picked straight into chip baskets or punnets, grading being done as it is picked.

After the crop has been harvested the straw and dead leaves can be raked up and removed or burnt off. It is usually necessary to loosen the straw with a fork to enable it to dry out before burning. This practice destroys the old leaves and many insects and fungus diseases with them, and it has no harmful effect on the plants themselves.

For *forcing purposes*, strong early runners of a suitable variety such as Royal Sovereign, in 5 in. or 6 in. pots are brought into the greenhouse during December for March fruiting. Great care is required in control of moisture, heat, diseases, and pests.

Continuous cloches are successful for forwarding Strawberries. Cloches are placed over early planted rows of one year old plants in February and March; the fruit is ripe from 14 to 28 days earlier than from unprotected plants.

Suitable Strawberry varieties, including Alpines and Perpetuals, are listed in the Supplement.

A key for the identification of the varieties of the large-fruited garden Strawberry (*F.* × *Ananassa*), commonly grown commercially in England, has been published by J. Floor and W. S. Rogers in *Journal of Pomology and Horticultural Science*, 21: 34–40 (1945) and reprinted in Ministry of Agriculture and Fisheries, Great Britain, *Bulletin* no. 95, 'Strawberries', 4th ed. (1949). This key is based on characters of the leaflet, notably its length to breadth ratio, wrinkling, serration, outline of base and direction of hairs on the petiole, which are of especial value when inspecting runner beds.

W. S. R. and D. J. W.

DISEASES. Many failures with Strawberries arise from unsuitable soil conditions, especially waterlogging during winter, but the chief root disease of this plant is that known as Red Core or Lanarkshire disease due to the fungus *Phytophthora fragariae*. Attacked plants are small and sickly and the older leaves die. The affected roots are dark brown or black and the outer layers easily strip off leaving the central cylinder which is coloured red. There is no method of curing the plants or any efficient soil treatment, but the variety Auchincruive Climax is resistant. Leaf Spot, due to *Mycosphaerella fragariae*, appears as small reddish spots, later turning greyish-white. It is rarely serious, but where troublesome the plants should be covered with straw as soon as the fruit is picked, burnt over, and sprayed with Bordeaux mixture early in the season. Leaf Scorch, due to *Marssonina fragariae*, is similar to Leaf Spot but the spots are more regular and remain dark purple. The remedy is the same as for Leaf Spot. *Sphaerotheca humuli*, one of the powdery mildews, produces a white powdery coating on leaves and fruit, the margins of affected leaves often curling upwards. It can be checked by dusting with sulphur or spraying from late April with lime sulphur 1 in 100, this being stopped as the fruit develops. Burning over the beds after the fruit is picked as for Leaf Spot is also beneficial against mildew. The most serious diseases in Strawberry plants are due to viruses of which 2 forms are common. Yellow Edge virus causes general dwarfing of the younger leaves with a yellowish coloration principally at the margins, their petioles being thicker and shorter so that the plant is flattish and the leaves become smaller each season so that this disease is often called Little Leaf. The virus is spread by aphides and control must take the form of destroying affected plants on sight and spraying against the aphides with nicotine spray (8 oz. nicotine and 6 lb. soft soap in 100 gal. water) about the end of May. The time to recognize the affected plants is April or better still September; in mid-summer the symptoms are not so distinct. No runners must be taken from even suspected plants and new runners ought to be protected against aphis infection by the warm-water treatment. This is done by submerging the runners in water at a temperature of 110° F. for 20 min. then plunging them into cold water immediately and planting soon after. The variety Royal Sovereign is quickly affected by the virus but some do not suffer so badly and there are varieties which do not show obvious symptoms but are dangerous because they are carriers and the more susceptible varieties will become infected from them. The second virus disease of Strawberries is called Crinkle and this shows as yellowish spots anywhere on the leaf surface and the leaf tends to be crinkled and wrinkled. There is Mild Crinkle and Severe Crinkle; the first is hardly noticeable and is not serious but the latter is very obvious and the plants become dwarfed and unfruitful. The aphis is considered to be responsible for spread to healthy plants in the same way as in Yellow Edge, and where Severe Crinkle occurs the precautions to be taken are the same as for Yellow Edge. Mild Crinkle can usually be ignored.

The fruit of Strawberries may become diseased especially if the weather is wet as the fruit is maturing. As already mentioned, Mildew sometimes occurs on the fruit, but more serious is Grey Mould (*Botrytis cinerea*) which covers the berries with its grey mouldy growth and makes them soft and rotten. It is difficult to control but care should be taken to straw evenly so that the fruit does not touch the ground and also that all infected fruit be collected when picking and carefully burnt. Another fruit disease is Leathery Rot caused by the fungus *Phytophthora cactorum*, in which the fruit does not become soft but is tough and leathery and later brown and shrivelled. Against this disease proper strawing is important and the plants should be dusted with sulphur dust at the beginning of May and twice again at intervals of a fortnight. Apart from the foregoing diseases strawberry flowers are often damaged by frosts causing the condition known as Black Eye in which the central part of the flower becomes quite black although the petals remain uninjured. Such flowers of course yield no berries.

(D. E. G.)

PESTS. Aphides. A number of species of greenfly feed upon the cultivated Strawberry, some of which do injury both directly and indirectly owing to their ability to carry the virus disease known as 'Yellow Edge', one of the chief troubles of the grower. Massee (*The Pests of Fruits and Hops*, 1937, pp. 226–8) names five species found on wild and cultivated Strawberries, namely: the Strawberry Aphis, *Pentatrichopus* (*Capitophorus*) *fragariae* (*fragaefolii*); the Raspberry Aphis, *Amphorophora rubi*; the Rose Aphis, *Macrosiphum rosae*; together with *M. gei* and *M. rogersii*. Of these, the first named is the most common and is the chief culprit concerned in the transmission of the virus. It can be distinguished from other species by its primrose-yellow body and reddish-brown eyes, and the presence here and there on the body of numerous club-headed small hairs, which may be seen with the aid of a good hand-lens. It is found on the Strawberry plant from late August to the following July, when winged forms appear and migrate to other plants, including Silverweed, *Potentilla anserina*. While some of the Strawberry-feeding Aphides cause some leaf-curl, it is found that frequently only slight injury is done to the plants, but all are suspected of carrying the virus until it is proved otherwise. **A**

These pests are not readily destroyed owing to their habit of feeding in the folds of the unopened leaves and on the underside of the older leaves which lie close to the ground, where it is difficult to reach them with a wash or dust. The most effective control is to spray thoroughly the crowns of the plants and the lower leaf surface in April with a Nicotine–Soap wash. Further applications should be given to the runner beds and young plants to keep them virus-free. The fruiting-plants should be burned over immediately after the crop is gathered by covering the beds with straw and setting fire to it on a windy day. This treatment exterminates Red Spider, Leaf-hoppers, and other pests, but not the Tarsonemid Mite. Young runners prior to planting should be given the warm-water treatment as advocated against the Strawberry Mite (q.v.).

Blossom Weevil, *Anthonomus rubi* is common and is also known as the Elephant Beetle and Needle Bug. It is a pest of great importance in certain Strawberry-growing areas in Cambridgeshire, Devonshire, Hampshire, Kent, and Worcestershire. It attacks, also, Blackberry and Raspberry, but to a less extent than Strawberry, of which certain varieties are more prone to attack than others. The adult weevil, which is closely related to the Apple Blossom Weevil (q.v.), is black and appears in the Strawberry plantation in April and May when the eggs are laid in the unopened blossoms through a puncture made by the snout of the female. After the eggs are laid, the female severs the bud-stalk partially or completely so that it wilts. The severed buds are often seen on the ground around the attacked plants. The small, legless grubs feed in the severed stalks, and eventually pupate in them. The weevils emerge about mid-July through a circular hole cut in the dried-up flower-bud. They feed for a time on the foliage, and then seek hibernating quarters beneath the loose bark of trees, among dead leaves, at the base of hedges, in wood-piles and elsewhere. The complete eradication of this pest in Strawberry plantations is difficult, but in gardens it is desirable to rake up and burn all severed buds and stalks in June and early July. Dusting the plants in early May with 5 per cent. DDT. is a measure of control.

STRAWBERRY EELWORM, *Aphelenchoides fragariae*, has been associated for many years with the diseased conditions known as 'Cauliflower' disease and 'Red Plant', though it is possible that the former is due to a bacterium, and the latter to virus infection. It is difficult to diagnose with certainty the symptoms of attack due to eelworm owing to other organisms, including Tarsonemid Mites, being associated with similar signs of attack. The leaf-stalks of eelworm-infected plants become greatly thickened and growth is checked. The eelworms live in the buds, leaf-axils, and leaves, and spread to the growing-points of the runners so that young plants become directly infected from the parent plant.

Runners raised from diseased plants should be immersed in water at a constant temperature of 110° F. for 20 minutes, after which they should be drained, potted into sterilized soil, and planted in clean ground. An infected Strawberry bed should be cleared by burning all the plants, and Strawberries should not be planted on the same site for at least 3 years.

STRAWBERRY MOTH, *Peronea comariana*, is a pest in several districts. This moth is double brooded, the adults of the first generation appearing from late June to mid-July, those of the second in August and September. The eggs are laid on the stipules at the base of the plant and on the leaf-stalks—the winter being spent in the egg stage on the plants. The active, greenish caterpillars feed from late April to mid-June on the foliage, flowers, and fruits, and fasten the leaves together with silken threads. When fully fed, they spin cocoons among their webbing on the lower leaf surface. The second brood larvae feed on the leaves during August and September. The eradication of this pest with the aid of chemical sprays is difficult owing to many of the caterpillars feeding within the unopened leaflets, and more effective control is possible with Nicotine dust blown well into the crowns of the plants before and after the blossoming period. The tops of the plants may be cut with a scythe or mowing-machine in September, or the beds may be burned over by setting light to a loose mulch of dry straw soon after the crop is gathered. The pest is occasionally destroyed completely in a district by a Chalcid parasite, *Copidosoma tortricia*.

SHOOT-CUTTING WEEVILS, *Rhynchites germanicus* and *R. minutus*, occur more often in gardens than in plantations. Both weevils have pronounced snouts, with which they puncture and partially or completely sever the stems of the fruits and leaf-stalks in a manner similar to the Apple Twig-cutter (q.v.). The damage is noticeable from the end of May and in June, and the effect is that the foliage wilts and the fruits shrivel. *R. germanicus* is blue-green and about $\frac{1}{10}$ in. long, *R. minutus* is larger and brassy-green. Eggs are laid in the severed portions, and the legless grubs feed on the decaying stems and stalks. It is advisable to collect and burn all severed and dead stems in June, and to dust the infested plants with 5 per cent. DDT. at the first sign of attack.

(G. F. W.)

STRAWBERRY BEETLES. *See* **Ground Beetles.**

STRAWBERRY BUSH. *See* **Euonymus americanus.**

STRAWBERRY RASPBERRY. *See* **Rubus illecebrosus.**

STRAWBERRY SNAIL. *See* **Snails.**

STRAWBERRY TOMATO. *See* **Physalis peruviana,** Cape Gooseberry.

STRAWBERRY TREE. A common name for *Arbutus Unedo.*

streblo'ceras, having a twisted spur.

STREBLORHIZ'A (*streblos*, twisted, *rhiza*, root; from the shape of the root). FAM. *Leguminosae.* A genus of a single species of glabrous climbing shrub, closely related to Clianthus, native of Norfolk Is. *S. speciosa* is half-hardy and needs loamy soil with a little leaf-mould and charcoal. The compost should not be sifted but broken up by hand and pressed firmly into the pots. After potting the plants should be placed in a pit and kept close for a few weeks, being syringed daily. If the plants are to be grown on in pots they can be trained out on sticks or on a trellis, or on pillars or walls, for which they are very suitable. When grown in pots the plants will need to be shifted in March or April previous to which all the laterals should be pruned hard back and the leaders shortened. Thorough drainage must be ensured when planting out in the border and the same compost will serve as for potting, a depth of 18 in. being sufficient. Propagation is by seeds or cuttings.

S. specio'sa. Climbing shrub to about 3 ft. *l.* unequally pinnate; *lflets.* few, rather large, entire, without stipels; stipules small. *fl.* flesh-coloured, rather large, in axillary racemes; 2 upper cal. teeth very short; standard ovate, erecto-patent, nearly sessile; wings short. May. 1840. (B.R. 1841, 51 as *Clianthus carneus.*)

STRELITZIA (in honour of Charlotte of Mecklenburg-Strelitz, 1744–1818, Queen of George III of England). FAM. *Musaceae.* Bird of Paradise Flower; Bird's Tongue Flower. A genus of 4 species of large perennial herbs with a rhizome or with a woody trunk, natives of S. Africa. Leaves large, long-stalked, in 2 ranks. Scape terminal, or in upper leaf-axils, shortly exserted from the leaf-sheaths; bracts 1 or 2, large, boat-shaped, slender-pointed, more or less coloured. Flowers large, sepals free, long, keeled; petals very dissimilar; stamens 5; ovary 3-celled. Fruit a leathery, many-seeded capsule. Strelitzias are very striking plants and need a warm greenhouse with a night temperature not below 50° F., a strong soil of 2 parts good loam, 1 part peat, and a little sand, a liberal supply of water during summer, and drier conditions in winter. They are usually propagated by suckers or by division, but seeds (set only after hand-pollination) will germinate in light soil plunged in a frame with moist bottom heat.

KEY

1. *Stem not elongated, fls. yellow-blue*	2
1. *Stem tall, fls. white or white-blue*	3
2. *Lvs. ovate or ovate-oblong*	S. Reginae
2. *Lvs. linear-lanceolate*	S. parvifolia
3. *Base of l. cordate, inner fl.-segs. white*	S. augusta
3. *Base of l. obtuse, inner fl.-segs. blue*	S. Nicolai

S. august'a. Stem short. *l.-stalk* about 6 ft. long, blade about 3 ft. long, shining green. *Spathe* purple; outer fl.-segs. white, inner white, unequal, very short. March. 1791. (B.M. 4167–8.)

S. × kewensis. *See* **S. Reginae.**

S. Nicola'i. Stem up to 15 ft. h. *l.* similar to *S. augusta* except that base of blade is obtuse. *Spathe* chestnut-red, outer fl.-segs. white, inner blue. May. 1849. (B.M. 7038.)

S. parvifo'lia. About 4 ft. h. *l.* linear-lanceolate, margin flat. *fl.* purple and yellow. May. var. **jun'cea,** *l.-blade* very small or absent. 1796. (B.R. 516.)

S. Regin'ae. Stemless or nearly so, plant about 5 ft. h. *l.-blade* about 18 in. h. with a l.-stalk of equal length. *Peduncle* about as tall as l. *fl.* large, purple and orange, abundantly produced. April. 1773. (B.M. 119–20.) A variable plant. Among the forms are var. **farino'sa,** *l.* oblong, base truncate, long-petioled; **glau'ca,** *l.* large, glaucous, oblong-lanceolate; **hu'milis,** dwarf, *l.* ovate, long-stalked; **ovat'a,** *l.* ovate, base cordate, l.-stalk shorter; **rut'ilans,** *fl.* very highly coloured, midrib purple. A hybrid (**S. × kewensis**) between this and *S. augusta*, intermediate between the parents with pale watery-yellow fl. with lilac-pink patches at the base of the pet., has been raised at Kew.

strep'ens, creaking, rattling.

STREPOCA'LYX (*streptos*, twisted, *calyx*). FAM. *Bromeliaceae*. A genus of 14 species of showy, usually epiphytic herbs, natives of Guiana, Brazil, and Peru. Related to Androlepis but filaments without auricles and flowers loosely arranged on the branches; sepals contorted. For treatment *see* **Aechmea.**

S. Fuerstenberg'ii. *l.* in a rosette, linear, 2 ft. long, 1½ in. wide, narrowed to a spiny point; margin spiny. *fl.* violet, about 1¼ in. long, in a compact, many-fld. panicle, more or less white-farinose; scape stout, short; bracts bright red. Peru. (B.H. 1879, 42, as *Aechmea Fuerstenbergii.*)

S. Valleran'dii. *l.* about 40 in a dense rosette, ovate, and 3 to 4 in. wide at base, blade linear, 3 to 4 ft. long, 1½ in. wide, spines small and close. *fl.* violet, about 1½ in. long, in a compact, erect, oblong-cylindrical panicle, 1 to 1½ ft. long, white-farinose; bracts as long as branches, bright red, the lower 3 to 4 in. long. (B.H. 1883, 13, 1 and 2; R.H. 1887, 129, as *Lamprococcus Vallerandii.*)

strept-, strepto-, in compound words, signifying twisted.

STREPTANTH'ERA (*streptos*, twisted, *anthera*, anther; in allusion to the shape of the anthers). FAM. *Iridaceae*. A genus of 2 species of S. African dwarf bulbous plants. Leaves ensiform-lanceolate, erect or falcately spreading. Flowers solitary in the spathe, sessile; perianth tube very short, bell-shaped, lobes spreading; stamens attached to the throat of the tube; spathes 1, 2, or 3 in the upper axils. Greenhouse plants growing best in sandy loam, increased by offsets.

S. cu'prea. About 9 in. h. *l.* distichous, acute, mucronate, lower smallest. *Scapes* 2 or 3, smooth, somewhat flexuous, 2- to 4-fld.; perianth tube purple, segs. yellowish-copper, purple at base with a pale yellow spot each side. June. 1825. (P.M.B. 1, 8; S.B.F.G. s. 2, 122.) var. **coccin'ea,** *fl.* glowing orange with almost black centre

Streptanthera elegans

S. ele'gans. About 9 in. h. *l.* distichous, rather blunt, shortly mucronate, narrowing a little above middle. *Scapes* 2 or 3, 1- or 2-fld. *fl.* white tinged faint blush, with a bright-purple centre above which is a velvety-black circle marked with large, bright-yellow spots; tube purple, shorter than spathe which is streaked with irregular, broken lines. 1827. (L.B.C. 1359; S.B.F.G. 209.)

STREPTAN'THUS (*streptos*, twisted, *anthos*, flower; the claws of the petals of some species are twisted). FAM. *Cruciferae*. A genus of about 13 species of annual or perennial herbs mostly natives of western N. America. Leaves entire or lower lyrate-pinnatifid, stem-leaves sessile or amplexicaul. Flowers purple, rarely white or yellow, sometimes pendulous; sepals saccate at base (or only 2 of them), often coloured, sometimes very broad; petals clawed. The 2 species mentioned below are annuals. The seed should be sown late in spring or under glass earlier, like Asters.

S. hyacinthoi'des. Annual, 2 to 3 ft. h. *l.* sessile, narrow below, stem-clasping, oblong-linear, slender-pointed. *fl.* deep bluish-purple; sep. lanceolate, slender-pointed; pet. spatulate-linear, limb reflexed. September. 1834. (B.M. 3516.)

Streptanthus maculatus

S. macula'tus.* Annual, 18 in. or more h. *l.* ovate-oblong, 3 to 6 in. long, glaucous, rather acute; stem-l. clasping, lobes long, obtuse. *fl.* in simple or panicled racemes; cal. purplish; pet. deep velvety-purple in middle, lighter towards the crenulate edge; pedicels 3 to 4 in. long, spreading. August. 1833. (B.M. 3317, as *S. obtusifolium.*)

STREPTOCARPUS (*streptos*, twisted; *karpos*, fruit; the capsule being spirally twisted). FAM. *Gesneriaceae*. A genus of about 80 species of herbs found in Trop. and S. Africa, Madagascar, Burma, and Siam. The S. African species are all stemless and some of this type are also found in E. Africa: others in E. Africa and all those from W. Africa, Madagascar, and Asia are caulescent. Humus-loving herbs with a shallow rooting system. The stemless ones have either a single leaf or a rosette of several leaves, the caulescent ones have leaves in opposite pairs. The single leaf may be from 3 in. to 5 ft. long and develops from one of the cotyledons; growth is basal and long continued and is accompanied by a gradual dying back from the tip; the second cotyledon shrivels early. When there are several leaves these are in the form of an irregular rosette and the first leaf is developed from one cotyledon, the other cotyledon shrivelling; the remaining leaves arise later. Occasionally in both these groups the second cotyledon also enlarges. Some single-leaved species may produce several leaves on occasion (e.g. *S. Comptonii*, *S. gracilis*) and form a bridge between the two groups. In the caulescent species the leaves are small (2 to 3 in. long), stalked, and arranged in opposite pairs, except the first 'leaf' which is developed from one cotyledon and is carried up to a higher level than the other, which soon shrivels.

The inflorescences arise in the stemless species in acropetal succession from the basal inch or two of the midrib, in the caulescent ones from the leaf-axils. They are cymose but characteristically bear 2 flowers at each branching, and these open not at the same time but successively. In a few species, however, the inflorescence may be 1-flowered. Calyx 5-parted, generally (except in *S. Daviesii*) inconspicuous. Corolla varied in form and colour but always with a well-defined tube and a more or less 2-lipped limb. Fertile stamens 2, anthers coherent. Several species may produce cleistogamous flowers in which the corolla fails to develop fully and never opens, self-pollination being obligatory (*see also under* **S. nobilis**). Fruit a cylindrical capsule varying in length from ¾ to 5 in.

All the species grow well under greenhouse conditions in a rich compost. They may be increased by seed (which is extremely small), or by division, or by leaf-cuttings made by nicking the main veins and laying on the surface of sand compost in a propagating frame, or by shoots taken from the base of the cutback cotyledon. Some strains of *S. Rexii* and *S. Johannis* produce adventitious leaves from roots near the surface, and these become centres of new rosette formation. Some of the single-leaved species are monocarpic and die after flowering and seeding, others are perennial. Rosette-leaved species may, under optimum conditions, begin to flower within 4 months from seed, but the single-leaved species are of slower growth.

The species first introduced all had bluish or ivory-white flowers, but when the brick-red *S. Dunnii* flowered at Kew in 1886 it was used for pollinating *S. Rexii* and *S. parviflorus*, and mauve-purple (*S.* × *kewensis*) and bright rosy-crimson (*S.* × *Watsonii*) flowers were secured. These were intercrossed, and the best of the offspring were crossed with *S. cyaneus*, *S. polyanthus*, *S. Saundersii*, *S. Wendlandii*, and *S. Woodii*; considerable back-crossing to *S. Rexii* was carried out and eventually the race of large-flowered garden plants with the habit of *S. Rexii* was produced. (*See below under* **S. × hybridus.**) (See *Journal R.H.S.* 65, p. 17, 1940). The caulescent species (subgenus *Streptocarpella*) are not interfertile with the stemless ones (subgenus *Streptocarpus*).

The species may be classified into 4 main groups as follows:

1. Plants with well-developed stems and stalked leaves about 2 to 3 in. long in opposite pairs (subgenus *Streptocarpella*): *S. caulescens*; *S. Holstii*; *S. Kirkii*; *S. nobilis*; *S. orientalis*; *S. saxorum.*
1. Plants without leafy stems, leaves solitary or few, at least 3 in. long and usually much more (subgenus *Streptocarpus*), 2.
2. Mouth of the corolla-tube laterally compressed: *S. Baudertii*; *S. Comptonii*; *S. Daviesii*; *S. gracilis*; *S. Haygarthii*; *S. Johannis*; *S. polyanthus*; *S. prolixus*; *S. Reynoldsii.*
2. Mouth of the corolla-tube not compressed laterally, 3.
3. Leaves solitary: *S. denticulatus*; *S. Dunnii*; *S. Eylesii*; *S. Fanniniae*; *S. Galpinii*; *S. grandis*; *S. Mahonii*; *S. Michelmorei*; *S. pusillus*; *S. Saundersii*; *S. Vandeleurii*; *S. Wendlandii*; *S. Wilmsii*; *S. Woodii.*
3. Leaves rosulate: *S. Meyeri*; *S. montigena*; *S. parviflorus*; *S. Rexii* and its close allies *S. cyaneus*, *S. Gardenii*, *S. insignis*, and *S. Polackii.*

S. × achimeniflo'rus (*S. × hybridus × S. polyanthus*).

S. × Bank'sii (*S. × hybridus × S. Wendlandii*).

S. Bauder'tii. Stemless. *l.* in a rosette, similar to those of *S. Meyeri*, 2 to 3½ in. long, dark green. *fl.* pale bluish-mauve, yellowish-white, and laterally compressed in the throat with a deep-purple line radiating to each of the lower segs., nearly 2 in. long and 1½ in. across the strongly oblique limb; peduncles 1 to 6-fld. E. Cape Prov. 1939. (B.M. 9650.)

S. × bifloro-polyan'thus. *See* **S. × grandiflorus.**

S. × Blythi'nii (*S. cyaneus × S. Wendlandii*).

S. × Bruan'tii (*S. polyanthus × S. Rexii*).

S. × cantabrigien'sis (*S. cyaneus × S. Dunnii*).

S. caules'cens. Stem gouty, erect and branched, about 1½ to 2 ft. h. *l.* opposite, elliptic, blunt; stalks short. *fl.* violet-purple or pale lilac, ½ in. across, in pedunculate cymes, throat almost closed dorsiventrally. E. Trop. Africa. 1885. (B.M. 6814, pale form.)

S. Compto'nii. Stemless. *l.* usually solitary. *fl.* small, pale lilac, yellow and laterally compressed in throat, limb oblique; infl. about 6 in. h. Transvaal. 1936.

S. cyan'eus. Stemless. *l.* several in a rosette, narrowly oblong or oblong-lanceolate, 2½ to 8½ in. long, obtuse, somewhat rugose. *fl.* on erect 2-fld. scapes 3 to 6 in. long; cor. funnel-shaped; tube ⅝ to 1¼ in., white with a yellow streak; lobes spreading bright mauvish-pink, the lower lined with red. Transvaal, Swaziland. 1907. (B.M. 8521; F.S.P.A. 666 as *S. Rexii.*)

S. Davie'sii. Stemless. *l.* solitary, 6 to 8 in. long and as broad. Infl. about 8 in. h. *fl.* pale violet, greenish and laterally compressed in the throat, 2 in. long and nearly as much across the oblique limb; cal. segs. united for one-third of their length, the lobes large and broadly triangular, standing away from the cor. tube. Natal. 1940. The large leafy cal. is unique in the genus.

S. denticula'tus. Stemless. *l.* solitary, 7 to 8 in. wide, much wrinkled. *fl.* numerous in branching glandular-hairy infl. 8 to 10 in. h.; cor. rose-purple with white tube, the upper lobes purplish at the base, the lower crimson-streaked, ¾ in. long and ½ in. across the limb, lobes rounded, denticulate on the margins. Transvaal. 1912. (B.M. 8632.)

S. Dunn'ii. Stemless. *l.* solitary, up to 3 ft. or more long, decurved, silvery-grey with appressed hairs. *fl.* about 1½ in. long, at length drooping; cor. brick red tubular funnel-shaped, lobes rounded; scapes 6 or more, 1 ft. h., many-fld. *fr.* 1 in. long. Whole plant beset with granules of a solid red pigment. Transvaal. 1886. (B.M. 6903; F.P.S.A. 27.)

S. × Dy'eri (*S. Dunnii × S. Wendlandii*).

S. Eyle'sii. Stemless. *l.* solitary, a foot or so long and about 8 in. broad, with silvery-grey hairs especially towards the base. *fl.* nearly 2 in. long; cor. violet-purple, tube curved, limb oblique; scapes 1 to 3, 1 ft. h., many-fld. *fr.* 3 in. long. S. Rhodesia.

S. Fannin'iae. Stemless. *l.* solitary, 15 in. long, 3 to 4 in. broad, sparsely hairy. *fl.* 1¼ in. long; cor. blue, slightly widened upwards, slightly curved; scape 1 ft. h., many-fld. Natal. The plant at one time grown under this name is *S. Woodii.*

S. Galpin'ii. Stemless. *l.* solitary, ovate-oblong, 8 in. long, 5 in. wide, silky hairy. *fl.* mauve, white in the throat; cor. tube only 1 in. long, broadly funnel-shaped, 1½ in. across the limb whose lobes are almost equal. Transvaal. 1890. (B.M. 7230.)

S. Garden'ii. Stemless. *l.* about 5 in a rosette, narrowly ovate, heart-shaped at base. *fl.* 2¼ in. long, tube pale green outside, somewhat curved downwards; limb pale lilac, green in throat, lower lobes marked with broken purple lines, upper with short continuous lines; scapes 6 in., 1 to 2-fld. Natal. 1854. (B.M. 4862; F.d.S. 1214.)

S. gra'cilis. Stemless. *l.* at first solitary, 3 or 4 subsidiary leaves being produced later, cordate at base, about 3 in. long and broad. *fl.* 1 in. long, pale lilac-yellow in throat; tube sharply curved downward then horizontal, and laterally compressed at the throat; lobes narrowly oblong; scapes several, 6 in. h., several-fld. Natal. 1936.

S. × grandiflo'rus (*S. Gardenii × polyanthus = S. × bifloro-polyanthus*). 1859. The first hybrid to be recorded in the genus.

S. gran'dis. Stemless. *l.* solitary, ovate-cordate, 2 to 3 ft. long, 1 to 2½ ft. wide, rather thin for the genus. *fl.* ½ to ¾ in. long, light purple, darker in the throat and the centres of the lower lobes whitish; tube slightly curved, widening upwards; scapes several to many, 1½ to 3½ ft. h., many-fld. from near the base, the lower bracts sometimes leaf-like. Natal. 1904. (B.M. 8042; F.P.S.A. 803.) A form with pure white flowers is also known.

S. × gra'tus (*S. Dunnii* × *S.* × *hybridus*).

S. × Gree'nii (*S. Rexii* × *S. Saundersii*). 1875. One of the earlier hybrids, but not, apparently, contributing to the development of the modern types.

S. Haygar'thii. Stemless. *l.* solitary, ovate, about 10 in. long and 6 in. broad. *fl.* ¾ in. long, bright cobalt violet; tube slightly curved, laterally compressed at throat, limb oblique. *fr.* slender, 2½ in. long. Scapes about 3, slender, 1 to 1½ ft. h., naked in lower half, loosely branched above, fls. tending to open only 2 or 3 at a time. Natal. 1936.

S. Hols'tii. Erect branching herb about 1½ ft. h., stem more slender than in *S. caulescens* but somewhat swollen at the nodes. *l.* ovate, 1½ to 2 in. long, entire, somewhat hairy, especially on veins beneath; stalk 1½ to 2 in. long. *fl.* purple with white open throat, 1 in. or slightly longer, ⅝ in. across, on slender pedicels in 2 to 6-fld. axillary, long-stalked cymes; upper lip of cor. very short. E. Trop. Africa. (B.M. 8150.)

S. × hyb'ridus. Under this name are grouped the hybrid forms which have been derived from crossing *S. Rexii* with other species and hybrids and back-crossing to *S. Rexii* so that the general appearance is very close to that species. The original species-crosses have usually been given distinctive names (e.g. *S.* × *Bruantii*, *S.* × *kewensis*, *S.* × *Greenii*), as have the further crosses between the *Rexii* type hybrids and the true species (e.g. *S.* × *achimeniflorus*, *S.* × *Banksii*, *S.* × *pulchellus*). Most of the garden plants now grown as *S. Rexii* contain an admixture of other species and are better classed as *S.* × *hybridus*. The *S. Rexii* characters have been enhanced most noticeably in the range of colour, especially as a result of crossing with *S. Dunnii*, and blue, mauve, magenta, rose, pink, salmon, and ivory-white flowers now occur with variations in the depth of colour. In some strains the dark pencilling in the throat is well developed, and in the latest (e.g. Bodnant vars. [1936]) these lines have so broadened as to produce a distinctly coloured lower lip, the upper lip remaining normal; in other strains the pencilling is entirely absent, giving self-coloured flowers with a yellow throat. Variations in size of flower also occur, as in Cuthbert's Giant Flowering (1920) where the plants are also somewhat taller.

S. insig'nis. Stemless. *l.* in a rosette, elliptic or oblong-elliptic, narrowed to the base, 8 to 12 in. long and 4 to 5 in. broad. *fl.* very similar to a large form of *S. Rexii*, but the base of the lobes and throat magenta with darker stripes, tips of the lobes light purple. E. Cape Prov. 1940. (F.P.S.A. 755 as *S. Rexii.*)

S. Johan'nis. Stemless. *l.* in a rosette, oblong, up to a foot long and 2½ in. broad. *fl.* mauve, white in the throat; tube curved, laterally compressed at the mouth, ⅞ in. long; limb oblique, 1¼ in. across; scapes about 6 in. h., 2- to 6-fld. *fr.* 2 in. long. Pondoland. 1939.

S. × kewen'sis (*S. Dunnii* × *S. Rexii*). 1886.

S. Kir'kii. Stem erect. *l.* opposite, elliptic-heart-shaped, blunt, hairy, stalked. *fl.* lilac, ½ in. long in loose axillary stalked cymes. E. Trop. Africa. 1884. (B.M. 6782.)

S. × lichtensteinen'sis (*S.* × *Watsonii* × *S. Wendlandii*).

S. lu'teus. A synonym of *S. parviflorus*.

S. Maho'nii. Stemless. *l.* 1 ft. long and nearly as broad. *fl.* mauve, 1 in. long; tube curved and limb oblique, nearly 1 in. across; scapes many-fld., a foot h. *fr.* 2½ in. long. Nyasaland. 1900. (B.M. 7857.)

S. Mey'eri. Stemless. *l.* in rosette, up to 9 in. long and 3½ in. broad, softly hairy. *fl.* with outside of tube pale blue or purple, ⅞ in. long, limb almost white, lobes nearly equal, throat yellow; scapes 3- to 10-fld. E. Cape Prov. 1899. (B.M. 7036 as *S. parviflorus*; F.P.S.A. 756.)

S. Michelmo'rei. Stemless. *l.* solitary, ovate, a foot or more long and as wide. *fl.* 1¼ in. long, blue-purple, deeper reddish-purple in the mouth of the tube and yellow in the throat; tube slightly curved, widening upwards; lobes only slightly spreading; scapes up to 1 ft. h., *fr.* 4½ in. long. S. Rhodesia. 1935. (B.M. n.s. 54.)

S. monti'gena. Stemless. *l.* in rosette, ovate, 6 in. long and 4 in. wide, yellowish-green with felt of grey hairs. *fl.* nearly 2 in. long, white flushed pale lilac, yellow in throat, tube slightly curved, widening upwards; scapes about 18 in. h., branched in upper third. E. Cape Province. 1940.

S. Mud'dii. A synonym of *S. Wilmsii*.

S. × multiflorus. A garden name applied to a form of *S.* × *hybridus*.

S. no'bilis. Stem erect, branched, up to 2 ft. *l.* ovate-cordate, about 4 in. long, stalk 2 in. *fl.* purple, in axillary cymes with stalks, except uppermost, shorter than leaves; tube nearly 2 in. long, narrow below, broadly funnel-shaped above; lobes small, broader than long, not very unequal. Often cleistogamous both in wild and in cultivation (i.e. the cor. is scarcely developed beyond a short tube and closed lobes; the fl. is thus necessarily self-fertilized; the fr. either retains the cor. as a withered brown cap or grows through it so that it appears as a withered collar; *see* G.C. ser. 3, 113 p. 156: 1943). Trop. W. Africa. 1943.

S. orienta'lis. Stem erect, simple, solitary, 6 to 16 in. h., glandular hairy. *l.* opposite, ovate to elliptic ovate, 1 to 3½ in. long, toothed, glandular hairy above and on veins beneath, with stalks about 2 in. long or shorter on upper leaves. *fl.* pendulous in long-stalked axillary cymes; cor. purple outside, paler within; tube slightly curved and funnel-shaped, over 1 in. long; limb about ¾ in. across, lobes somewhat reflexed, wide oblong. Siam. 1912. (B.M. 8526.)

S. parviflo'rus. Stemless. *l.* in a rosette, 5 to 12 in. long and up to 2 in. wide, oblong or ovate- to lanceolate-oblong, densely velvety. *fl.* white, pencilled with mauve within on the 3 lower lobes and yellow in the throat; tube ⅞ in. long, narrowly funnel-shaped, straight, lobes ¼ in. long. Transvaal. 1882. (B.M. 6636.) Syn. *S. luteus*.

S. Polac'kii. Stemless. *l.* in rosette, oblong or lanceolate, 8 to 10 in. long, 2 in. wide. *fl.* narrowly funnel-shaped, 1 in. or more across, mauve, lower lobes deeper with continuous red lines running into the throat and a broad yellow stripe in the throat itself; scapes up to 6 in. h., mostly 3- to 6-fld. Transvaal. 1940. (B.M. 9668.)

S. polyan'thus. Stemless. *l.* solitary, up to 12 in. long and nearly as broad. *fl.* pale blue, about 1½ in. long, tube curved, laterally compressed and yellow at the throat, limb very oblique, scapes 1 to 3, 12 in. or more h. Natal. 1854. (B.M. 4850; F.d.S. 1168; G.F. 206 R.H. 1862, 250.)

S. proli'xus. Stemless. *l.* solitary, 1 ft. long and 4 to 5 in. wide. *fl.* white; tube curved and laterally compressed at throat; limb oblique. Very close to *S. Haygarthii* but l. relatively narrower and fls. white. Natal. 1940.

S. × pulchel'lus (*S.* × *hybridus* × *S. Woodii*).

S. pusil'lus. Stemless. *l.* solitary, 3 in. long and 3½ in. wide. *fl.* white; tube ½ in. long and almost straight; lobes spreading at right angles, almost equal, short and broad; scapes several, 4 in. h. *fr.* ½ in. long. Natal. 1940.

S. Rex'ii. Stemless. *l.* in rosette, more or less linear-oblong, 4 to 10 in. long and 1 to 2½ in. wide. *fl.* white, bluish, or mauve, with purple stripes on the lower lobes; tube with very slight curve, widening upwards, 1½ in. long; scapes 4 to 6 in. h. and 1- to 2-fld. Cape Prov. from Knysna eastwards. (Populations from different localities show noticeable differences, especially in flower colour.) 1824. (B.R. 1173; G.F. 204; B.M. 3005 as *Didymocarpus Rexii.*) Many of the garden plants grown under this name are of hybrid origin; *see* **S. × hybridus.**

S. Reynol'dsii. Stemless. *l.* solitary, dark green above with short more or less erect hairs, reddish-purple below. *fl.* pale mauve, about 1 in. long; tube curved, laterally compressed at the mouth, throat greenish-yellow outside in bud, very pale when expanded without any yellow band; lobes directed forwards, not forming a flat limb. Natal. 1940. (F.P.S.A. 804.)

S. Saunder'sii. Stemless. *l.* solitary, 12 in. long, 8 to 9 in. wide, heart-shaped, dark green above, rose-purple and very hairy beneath. *fl.* 1½ in. long, pale lilac with 2 purple patches laterally in the throat and a median yellow band; tube broad, slightly curved; scape about 1 ft. h., unbranched almost to top. Natal. 1860. (B.M. 5251; F.d.S. 1802.)

S. saxo'rum. Stems prostrate, bare and somewhat woody on the old parts, somewhat fleshy and bearing rather crowded leaves on the young parts. *l.* 1 in. long including the short stalk. *fl.* with white tube ⅞ in. long, throat open, limb oblique, lobes pale lilac; peduncles axillary 1- to 2-fld., 3 to 6 in. long. E. Trop. Africa.

S. × Taylor'ii (*S.* × *achimeniflorus albus* × *S. denticulatus*).

S. Vandeleur'ii. Stemless. *l.* solitary, more or less heart-shaped, 1 ft. long and broad. *fl.* 2 in. long, tube curved in the middle at its narrowest point, widening upwards, throat open yellow-green, otherwise fl. white, 1½ in. across limb; scapes 1 ft. or more h., many-fld. Transvaal. 1940. (B.M. n.s. 341.)

S. × Watson'ii (*S. Dunnii* × *S. parviflorus*).

S. Wendlan'dii. Stemless. *l.* solitary, up to 2½ ft. long and 2 ft. wide, dark purplish-green above and reddish-purple below. *fl.* blue-purple, 1⅝ in. long, tube sub-cylindrical at top, limb oblique, 1½ in. across; scapes about 1 ft. h. with about 30 fl. from about half-way upwards. Natal. 1890. (B.M. 7447.)

S. Wilm'sii. Stemless. *l.* solitary, up to 1 ft. long and nearly as broad, deep green and shining, rather thin for the genus. *fl.* white, about 1 in. long, foxglove-like, tube slightly curved, mouth open oblique, purple spotted in the throat, lobes only slightly spreading; scapes 10 in. h., unbranched below the middle. *fr.* 3½ in. long. Transvaal. 1939. Syn. *S. Muddii*.

S. Wood'ii. Stemless. *l.* solitary, 12 in. long, 3½ in. wide. *fl.* bluish-mauve with lines of purple spots in the throat, tube ¾ to 1 in. long, slightly curved, mouth open, lobes only slightly spreading; scapes 9 in. h., many-fld. Natal. 1890. (Originally introduced under the name *S. Fanniniae.*) B. L. B.

STREPTOPUS (*streptos*, twisted, *pous*, foot or stalk; the peduncles are abruptly bent or contorted near the middle). Fam. *Liliaceae*. A genus of 4 species of perennial herbs, natives of Europe, temperate Asia, and N. America. Allied to Polygonatum but with the perianth segments distinct, or nearly so, and almost equal. Leaves alternate, ovate or lanceolate, membranous, sessile or amplexicaul. Flowers solitary or twin in the axils, nodding, pink or whitish, bell-shaped or spreading, deciduous; stamens 6; bracts minute or wanting. They thrive in moist, light soil containing peat or organic matter, in shade. They are easily propagated by seed or by division.

S. amplexifo'lius. Stem 2 to 3 ft. h., very smooth except at base. *l.* very smooth, glaucous beneath, strongly stem-clasping. *fl.* on long peduncles which are abruptly bent above middle; perianth greenish-white, segs. ½ in. long; anthers tapering to a point; stigma entire. N. America, Europe, &c. 1752. (B.B. Ed. 2, 520; R.L. 259.) SYN. *S. distortus.* Hardy.

S. distor'tus. A synonym of *S. amplexifolius.*

S. ro'seus.* 18 in. h. Branches with a few short, bristly hairs. *l.* green both sides, finely ciliate. *fl.* rose-purple, longer than half the slightly bent peduncle; anthers 2-horned; stigma 3-cleft. N. America. 1806. (L.B.C. 1603, B.M. 1489, as *Uvularia rosea.*) Hardy.

S. simp'lex. 2 to 3 ft. h. *l.* oblong, 2 to 4 in. long, slender-pointed, deeply heart-shaped at the amplexicaul base, glaucescent beneath. *fl.* whitish, broadly funnel-shaped. ½ in. long, mostly solitary, rarely twin; pedicels 2 to 3 in. long. Nepal. 1822. Greenhouse.

STREPTOSO'LEN (*streptos*, twisted, *solen*, tube; from the form of the corolla tube). FAM. *Solanaceae.* A genus of a single species of evergreen, roughly hairy, climbing shrub with the characters given below, native of Colombia. It needs greenhouse protection and while it will grow in ordinary soil is best suited by a sandy compost. Propagated by cuttings in sand under glass.

Streptosolen Jamesonii

S. Jameson'ii.* Climber to 6 or 8 ft. *l.* ovate, 1 to 2 in. long, acute at both ends, entire, rugose-bullate; stalks long. *fl.* orange, in terminal, corymbose panicles; cal. 5-cleft, segs. short, tubular-bell-shaped; cor. tube long, spirally twisted below, widened above; segs. 5, broad, spreading; stamens 4, perfect. June. Colombia. 1847. (G.C. 21 (1884), 797; R.H. 1883, 36; B.M. 4605 and F.d.S. 436, as *Browallia Jamesonii.*)

Streseman'nii, in honour of Erwin Stresemann, b. 1889, Professor of Zoology, Berlin.

striaefor'mis -is -e, apparently formed of fine parallel layers.

striatel'lus -a -um,
striat'ulus -a -um,
stria'tus -a -um,
} striate; marked with fine parallel lines, streaks, or minute grooves or ridges.

Strib'rnyi, in honour of Vaclav Stribrny, botanist of Lidice, nr. Prague, b. 1853.

STRICKLAND'IA (in honour of Sir C. W. Strickland). FAM. *Amaryllidaceae.* A genus of a single species of bulbous plant, native of Ecuador, closely related to Phaedranassa from which it is distinguished by its monadelphous stamens. Cultivation as for Phaedranassa.

S. eucrosioi'des. *l.* 1 or 2, oblong, acute, stalked; developing after the fl. *fl.* drooping in a 3- or 4-fld. umbel; perianth tube green, about 1 in. long; segs. red; scape terete, 12 to 15 in. long. Ecuador. 1878. SYN. *Phaedranassa eucrosioides, Leperizia eucrosioides, Stenomesson Stricklandii.*

strictus -a -um (***stricti-*** in compound words), strict; very straight and erect.

strid'ulus -a -um, hissing, creaking.

strigillo'sus -a -um, minutely strigose.

strigo'sus -a -um, strigose; beset with sharp, close-pressed, rigid hairs or bristles.

strigulo'sus -a -um, somewhat strigose.

STRIKE. To take root; usually used of cuttings.

STRIKING. The process of propagating by taking cuttings; when the cutting has produced roots it is said to have 'struck'.

STRINGY-BARK TREE. *See* **Eucalyptus.**

striola'tus -a -um, marked with lines or fine ridges.

STRIPED KING OF THE WOODS. *See* **Anoectochilus regius.**

STRIPED SQUILL. *See* **Puschkinia scilloides.**

strobila'ceus -a -um, cone-shaped.

STROBILAN'THES (*strobilos*, a cone, *anthos*, flower; from the form of the young inflorescence). FAM. *Acanthaceae.* A genus of about 300 species of erect herbs or sub-shrubs, many of them monocarpic, native of E. and SE. Asia with outliers in Africa. Leaves opposite, often in unequal pairs. Flowers in heads or cone-like or interrupted spikes or panicles; calyx deeply and nearly equally 5-cut, or sometimes 2-lipped, one lip being shortly 3-toothed; corolla with a swollen tube with 5 ovate or round, nearly equal lobes; stamens 4 or 2. Many species are very beautiful and some, like *S. amabilis* from Sispara, *S. pulcherrimus* from Ceylon, and *S. rubicundus* from Coorg, all perennials with paniculate inflorescences, ought to be introduced for they are sufficiently striking and free-flowering in their native homes. The species described below need the stove, or greenhouse; all sub-shrubs. Any good light soil suits them and they are readily struck by cuttings under a close frame, in heat.

As commonly accepted, Strobilanthes is an extremely variable, large, ill-defined group. In a monographic study by C. E. B. Bremekamp, published in *Verhandl. Nederland. Akad. Wetensch., Naturk*, sect. II, 41. 1–306 (1944), it has been divided into 54 genera, of which 9 are represented by the plants listed below. The genus Strobilanthes as here redefined consists of about 11 shrubby species native to Java and Sumatra, with short ellipsoid spikes of white bracts and white flowers, having 4 stamens, and is distinguished by microscopic characters of the pollen-grains and seed-coat from related genera. *S. cernua* is the type-species. The other genera are: BAPHICACANTHUS (from Greek *baphe*, dying, *acanthus*), comprising only *S. Cusia*; CARVIA (from Indian vernacular name *karvi*), comprising only *S. callosa*; DIFLUGOSSA (an anagram of *Goldfussia*), comprising *S. laevigatus* and 15 other species; GOLDFUSSIA (commemorating Georg August Goldfuss, 1782–1842, German zoologist and mineralogist), comprising *S. anisophyllus*, *S. pentastemonoides*, and about 25 other species; PERILEPTA (in allusion to the stem-clasping leaf-bases), comprising *S. auriculatus*, *S. Dyerianus* and 6 other species; PHLEBOPHYLLUM (referring to the prominently veined leaves), comprising *S. cuspidatus*, *S. Kunthianus*, *S. spicatus*, and 5 other species; PLEOCAULUS (referring to the many stems which arise yearly from the rhizome), comprising *S.*

sessilis; PTERACANTHUS (referring to the winged base of the leaves), comprising *S. attenuatus* and about 19 other species; and SERICOCALYX (referring to the calyx silky on the inside), comprising *S. scaber*.

S. ala'tus. A synonym of *S. attenuatus.*

S. attenua'tus. 2 to 4 ft. h., stem 4-angled. *l.* ovate, acute, slender-pointed, up to 5 in. long, hairy, dark green; stalk 1 to 4 in. long, sometimes winged in upper parts. *fl.* violet-blue with a yellow spot in throat, in loose panicles; cor. tube 1¼ in. long, swollen with a short, narrow base. Temperate Himalaya. 1886. (G.F. 1243.) Greenhouse. SYN. *Pteracanthus attenuatus.*

S. anisophyl'lus. 2 to 3 ft. h. *l.* very unequal, lanceolate, about 3½ in. long, the opposite one of the pair 1¼ in. long, toothed. *fl.*, &c., as in *S. isophyllus.* India. 1823. (B.M. 3404 as *Goldfussia anisophylla*; H.E.F. 191 as *Ruellia anisophylla*; B.R. 955 as *R. persicifolia.*) SYN. *Goldfussia anisophylla.*

S. auricula'tus. *l.* auriculate, sessile. *fl.* pale purple, 1 in. long, in linear, oblong, velvety, cone-like spikes 3 to 4 in. long; cor. tube curved. India. SYN. *Perilepta auriculata.*

S. callo'sus. About 6 ft. h. with stems often warted. *l.* elliptic, 6 to 9 in. long, narrowed to both ends, lined and hairy above. *fl.* pale violet-blue, 1½ in. long, very hairy within; spikes 1 to 4 in. long. India. 1897. (B.M. 7538.) SYN. *Carvia callosa.*

S. colora'tus. 3 to 6 ft. h. *l.* ovate to elliptic, 5 to 7 in. long, often with a long, narrow tip, toothed, dark green above, reddish-purple beneath. *fl.* pale bluish-purple, 1½ in. long, short-stalked, in wide spreading, much-branched panicles 6 to 12 in. h., the bracts falling early; cor. tube swollen, lobes rounded. January. Sikkim. 1886. (B.M. 6922.) SYN. *Diflugossa colorata.*

S. consanguin'eus. *l.* ovate, acute, long-stalked. *fl.* white or pale blue, ¾ in. long, on simple or branched, filiform spikes 3 to 4 in. long; cor. tube swollen from a narrow base; stamens 2. S. India. A variable plant. SYN. *Phlebophyllum spicatum.*

S. Cu'sia. Glabrous. *l.* elliptic-lanceolate, 2 to 4 in. long, acute, toothed, bright green. *fl.* lilac-purple, 2 in. long, in loose, leafy spikes; cor. tube bent; lobes notched. Cult. in India, China, &c.; origin uncertain. (B.M. 6947.) Yield the blue dye called 'Room'. SYN. *S. flaccidifolius, Baphicacanthus Cusia.*

S. cuspida'tus. *l.* ovate, white-silky beneath, long-stalked. *fl.* blue-purple, 1 in. long, nearly smooth, in linear-oblong spikes 3 in. long; stamens 2. S. India. SYN. *Phlebophyllum versicolor.*

S. Dalhousia'nus. A form of *S. pentastemonoides.*

Strobilanthes glomeratus

S. Dyeria'nus. Rather straggling when old. *l.* ovate, slender-pointed, dark green with rich rosy-purple all over middle of l. *fl.* pale blue, 1½ in. long, funnel-shaped in small axillary spikes. Penang. 1893. (B.M. 7574; J.H.S. 26, 66.) A beautiful foliage plant best propagated frequently as young plants show the colour best and are more shapely. SYN. *Perilepta Dyeriana.*

S. flaccidifo'lius. A synonym of *S. Cusia.*

S. glomera'tus. 2 to 6 ft. h. *l.* ovate, 4½ in. long, acute, toothed, hairy especially above, stalked. *fl.* purple, 2 in. long, in heads 1½ in. long, with persistent bracts; cor. tube swollen from a narrow base. Sikkim, Burma. 1838. (B.M. 155, 3881.) SYN. *Goldfussia glomerata.* var. **specio'sus,** deeper purple. (B.M. 4767 as *G. glomerata speciosa.*)

S. isophyl'lus. 1 to 2 ft. h. *l.* linear-lanceolate, glabrous. *fl.* lavender, 1 in. long, numerous in terminal heads, in groups ½ in. across of up to 4 fls.; cor. tube curved, swollen from a short, narrow base, lobes short, round. Khasia Hills, NE. India. 1845. (B.M. 4363.) SYN. *Goldfussia isophylla.*

S. Kunthia'nus. *l.* elliptic, rigid, strongly nerved beneath, toothed. *fl.* bluish, 1 in. long, tube swollen from near base; stamens 2; spikes 3 in. long, hairy. Nilgiri Hills, S. India. SYN. *Phlebophyllum Kunthianum.*

S. Micholitz'ii. About 4 ft. h. with 4-angled stems. *l.* lanceolate, 6 in. long, opposite l. smaller; stalked. *fl.* white, almost covered by the rounded, white, green-tipped bracts of the cone-like, axillary racemes. Sumatra. 1907. A genuine Strobilanthes.

S. pentastemonoi'des. Much branched shrub or sub-shrub; shoots 4-angled. *l.* lanceolate-elliptic, narrowed to both ends, 4½ in. long, opposite pairs unequal, toothed; stalked. *fl.* violet, 1 in. across, in a few-fld. terminal head; cor. tube strongly curved in lower narrow part, 1½ in. long, ⅜ in. wide at throat. India. (B.M. n.s. 86.) Cool greenhouse. SYN. *S. Dalhousianus, Goldfussia pentastemonoides, G. Dalhousiana.*

S. Sabinia'nus. 2 to 5 ft. *l.* broadly elliptic, 6½ in. long, narrowed to both ends, upper ones cordate. *fl.* lavender, about 1¼ in. long, nearly smooth, in linear, downy, cone-like spikes, 4 in. long, mostly solitary; cor. tube curved, swollen from a short base. March. Khasia Hills, NE. India. 1826. (B.R. 1238 as *Ruellia Sabiniana.*)

S. sca'ber. 1 to 3 ft. h., hairy. *l.* elliptic or obovate, slender-pointed, 4½ in. long, sometimes very rough; stalked. *fl.* yellow, 1 in. long, hairy within, swollen upwards; lobes rounded; spikes dense, often clustered, 2 in. long. May. N. India, Burma. 1836. (B.R. 27, 32.) SYN. *Sericocalyx scaber.*

S. ses'silis. Stems numerous, erect, 12 to 18 in. h. *l.* ovate, ¾ to 1½ in. long, acute, hairy, sessile. *fl.* purple, 1¼ in. long, in cylindrical, cone-like spikes, 1 to 2 in. long, axillary and terminal; cor. tube straight, swollen upwards. Nilgiri Hills, S. India. 1833. (B.M. 3902.) SYN. *Pleocaulus sessilis.*

S. Wallich'ii. 6 to 24 in. h. *l.* elliptic, 3 in. long, slender-pointed, nearly smooth; lower stalked, upper sessile. *fl.* blue, 1¼ in. long, solitary or in pairs in loose 1-sided often flexuose spikes 6 in. long; cor. tube nearly straight, swollen upwards. (B.M. 5119 as *Goldfussia Thomsonii.*)

STROBILE. Cone. A fruit formed from a number of flowers close together on a central axis each in the axil of a bract which becomes woody and hard, as in most Conifers, but thin in Cedrus and fleshy and soft in Juniperus (a variety of strobile sometimes called a galbulus); or which remain thin and membranous in Humulus. *Cf.* **Catkin.**

STROBILORACH'IS PRISMAT'ICUS. A synonym of *Aphelandra Hydromestus.*

STROBILUS. A cone or strobile.

STROMANTH'E (*stroma*, bed, *anthos*, flower; from the form of the inflorescence). FAM. *Marantaceae.* A genus of 12 species of rhizomatous herbs, natives of Trop. S. America. Stems often leafy, leaves reversed; flowers in a raceme or panicle; bracts coloured, deciduous; staminode small or none. Related to Ctenanthe from which the coloured bracts distinguish it, and to Maranta where the leaves are not reversed. For cultivation *see* **Calathea.**

KEY

1. *Lvs. green on both sides*	2
1. *Lvs. red beneath*	3
2. *Fl. blue and white; l.-stalk hairy throughout*	S. Tonckat
2. *Fl. orange or yellow*	S. lutea
3. *Lvs. leathery, thick, mid-rib white above*	S. sanguinea
3. *Lvs. less leathery, lateral veins silver-striped*	S. Porteana

S. Lubbersia'na. A synonym of *Ctenanthe Lubbersiana.*

S. lu'tea. Perennial herb over 3 ft. h. with a thickened rhizome, stem leafy. *l.-stalk* about $2\frac{1}{2}$ in. long, its apical swelling smooth or almost so, blade elliptic to linear-lanceolate, margin downy, sheath glabrous. *fl.* yellow, bracts about 1 in. long, orange-yellow. May. Colombia, Venezuela. SYN. *Phrynium luteum.*

S. Portean'a. Perennial herb about 18 in. h. *l.-stalk* very short, thickened, blade ovate-oblong or lanceolate, up to 12 in. long. *fl.* blue or violet; bracts about 1 in. long, red; spikes solitary or twin. Brazil. 1859. var. **Oppenheimian'a,** a synonym of *Ctenanthe Oppenheimiana.*

S. sanguin'ea. Perennial herb about 18 in. h. with a thickened rhizome. *Lower l.-stalks* up to 12 in. long; *upper* short, blade lanceolate, up to 18 in. long, deep green above, purple beneath. *fl.* white; bracts $1\frac{1}{4}$ in. long, red, like rachis, &c. Winter, spring. Brazil. 1845. (B.M. 4646 as *Phrynium sanguineum.*) var. **spectab'ilis,** *l.* green beneath.

S. Tonck'at. Perennial herb with leafy stem up to 6 ft. h., more or less hairy on the swollen nodes. *l.-stalk* very short, hairy, blade ovate-lanceolate to ovate-oblong, about 5 in. long, downy on margin and midrib. *fl.* white; infl. variable. Trop. S. America. (B.M. 2398 as *Maranta angustifolia.*) SYN. *Maranta Tonckat.*

STROMBOCAC'TUS (*strombos*, a top; referring to the shape of the plant). FAM. *Cactaceae.* Low, flat plants, nearly spineless; ribs divided into flat tubercles; flowers small, from the centre, bell-shaped. Fruit smooth. **A**

S. disciform'is. Plants flattened like a disk, greyish-green, with 12 to 18 spiral ribs divided into flat, rhomboidal tubercles; spines 1 to 4 when young but old areoles naked. *fl.* whitish. Mexico. (B.M. 3984 as *Mammillaria turbinata.*) SYN. *Echinocactus turbiniformis.*

S. macrohe'le. Very small, less than 3 in. h., globular; areoles with white wool and 3 or 4 long, curved, papery spines. *fl.* white. Mexico.

S. Schmiedickianus. Very small, flattened on the top, grey-green; ribs 10 to 12, divided into low, 4-angled tubercles; areoles woolly when young, later bare; spines 1 to 4, up to 1 in. long, erect, curved, greyish. *fl.* pale pink. Mexico.

strombuliform, twisted into a screw-form, as the pods of some species of Medicago.

strongylophyl'lus -a -um, round-leaved.

STROPHAN'THUS (Greek *strophos*, twisted cord, *anthos*, flower; from the form of the corolla-lobes). FAM. *Apocynaceae.* A genus of about 30 species of shrubs and small trees, often climbing, natives of Trop. and S. Africa and Trop. Asia. Leaves opposite, pinnately veined. Flowers white, yellowish, orange, red, or purple, usually showy; inflorescences terminal or lateral, sometimes dense and few-flowered, or laxly branched and many-flowered; calyx 5-parted; corolla funnel- or salver-shaped, the mouth furnished with 10 claw-like scales, lobes 5, frequently produced into very long, twisted, thread-like tails. Fruit of 2 divaricate follicles. Seeds with a stalked comose appendage. The species are easily grown in a compost of sandy loam and peat, and readily propagated by cuttings in sand under a glass in a little heat. The seeds provide drugs valuable in cardiac complaints, and of possible use in the treatment of rheumatoid-arthritis.

Strombocactus disciformis

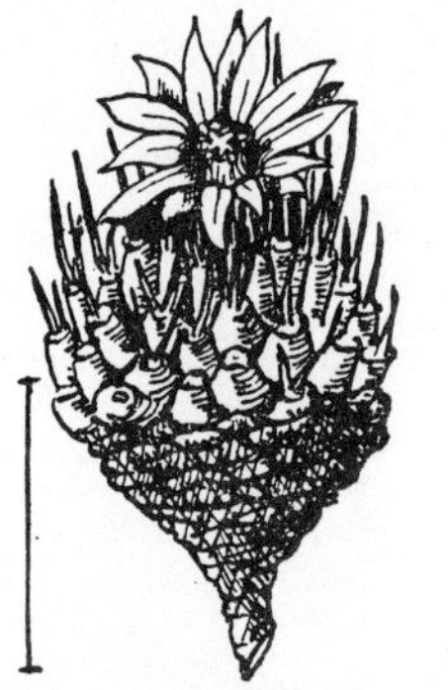

Strombocactus Schmiedickianus

KEY

1.	*Lvs. roughly hairy or pubescent*	2
1.	*Lvs. glabrous*	4
2.	*Stems and lvs. with stiff bristly hairs*	3
2.	*Stems and lvs. softly pubescent*	S. Ledienii
3.	*Cor. tails 6 in. or more in length*	S. hispidus
3.	*Cor. tails less than 1 in. long*	S. Bullenianus
4.	*Cor. lobes not tailed*	5
4.	*Cor. lobes tailed*	7
5.	*Lvs. thick, laurel-like; fl. in dense clusters*	S. gratus
5.	*Lvs. thin; infl. 1- to 2-fld.*	6
6.	*Fl. medium size, produced before lvs.*	S. Welwitschii
6.	*Fl. very large, produced with lvs.*	S. Courmontii
7.	*Fl. large; cor. tube funnel-shaped, 1 in. or more wide at apex*	8
7.	*Fl. small; cor. tube narrow, less than 1 in. wide at apex*	9
8.	*Fl. solitary or almost so; bracts minute, deciduous; cor. tails 3 to 6 in. long*	S. grandiflorus
8.	*Fl. clustered; bracts conspicuous; cor. tails 2 to 3 in. long*	S. sarmentosus
9.	*Cor. tails very long (often 1 ft. or more) thread-like, purple*	S. Preussii
9.	*Cor. tails less than 8 in. long, pale*	10
10.	*Stems densely leafy; lvs. small, narrowly oblong-lanceolate or lanceolate, leathery*	S. speciosus
10.	*Stems not densely leafy; lvs. rather large, oblong or elliptic, not very leathery*	11
11.	*Lvs. rounded above, apex mucronate*	S. Arnoldianus
11.	*Lvs. narrowed at both ends, elliptic-oblong*	12
12.	*Lvs. 1 to 3 in. long; cor. tails $1\frac{1}{2}$ to 3 in. long*	S. divaricatus
12.	*Lvs. 3 to 8 in. long; cor. tails 3 to 8 in. long*	S. caudatus

S. Arnoldia'nus. A glabrous climbing shrub. *l.* 2 to 3 in. long, broadly oblong, rounded above, usually with a mucronate apex, shortly stalked. *fl.* rather small, yellowish, with pallid cor. tails 6 or more in. long. Congo. Stove.

S. capen'sis. A synonym of *S. speciosus.*

S. cauda'tus. A trailing or climbing shrub. *l.* oblong or oblong-obovate, 3 to 8 in. long, abruptly acuminate, narrowed at base, stalk about $\frac{1}{4}$ in. long. *fl.* yellowish or white stained purple; cor. tails 3 to 8 in. long. February, March. Trop. Asia. 1816. Stove. SYN. *S. dichotomus.*

S. Courmont'ii. A rambling shrub. *l.* $1\frac{1}{2}$ to 3 in. long, glabrous, broadly oblong or elliptic; stalks $\frac{1}{2}$ in. long. *fl.* very large, funnel-shaped, cor. white or yellowish stained rose-purple, lobes not tailed. E. Africa. Stove. A most attractive plant. The seeds are employed by Africans in the manufacture of arrow-poison.

S. divarica'tus. Lax shrub of about 4 ft. *l.* elliptic-oblong, 1 to 3 in. long, narrowed to both ends, mucronate glabrous. *fl.* greenish-yellow with red stripes in throat, lobes $1\frac{1}{2}$ to 3 in. long; cymes few-fld. June. China. 1816. Stove. SYN. *S. divergens.*

S. grandiflo'rus. Glabrous woody climber. *l.* ovate, 3 to 5 in. long, somewhat blunt, wavy, pale beneath. *fl.* dull yellow, streaked red, tube over 1 in. wide at mouth, tails reflexed, loosely twisted, 6 in. long or more, yellow stained red. May. S. Trop. Africa. 1884. (B.M. 7390.) Stove. SYN. *S. Petersianus* var. *grandiflorus.*

S. gra'tus. A robust climber. *l.* oblong-elliptic, nearly 12 in. long, shortly acuminate, leathery; stalk short, stained red, scarcely dilated at base. *fl.* pale pink, fragrant, in dense cymes; cor. lobes rounded, not tailed, scales forming a rich-pink corona. May. W. Africa. (B.M. 4466.) SYN. *Roupellia grata.* Stove.

Strophanthus grandiflorus (p. 2048)

S. his'pidus. A stout climbing shrub. Stems and lvs. roughly hairy. *l.* 3 to 10 in. long, oblong, abruptly pointed, sessile or very shortly stalked. *fl.* in lax corymbs; cor. small, yellowish spotted brown or purple internally, lobes with very long, pallid, thread-like tails. W. Africa. Stove. Seeds a source of the drug strophanthin, also used throughout W. Africa in the manufacture of arrow-poison.

S. Ledien'ii. Climbing shrub. *l.* obovate, abruptly pointed, softly pubescent, almost sessile. *fl.* buff-yellow, star-shaped, the cor. tube purple internally with 5 white rays, cor. tails long, twisted, pale yellow. Congo. 1887. Stove.

S. Preus'sii. Climber to 12 ft. or more; branches glabrous, red-brown. *l.* elliptic or oblong, acuminate or abruptly pointed, 2 to 5 in. long. *fl.* cream to orange with purple spots and streaks in throat; cor. lobes ovate, abruptly constricted to purple tails often 1 ft. long. W. Africa. (B.M. 8250.) Stove.

S. sarmento'sus. A stout woody climber. *l.* elliptic, acuminate above and acute below, glabrous, stalk $\frac{1}{2}$ in. or more long. *fl.* large, creamy-yellow with crimson stripes internally, often stained purple; cor. tails 2 to 3 in. long, pale yellow, twisted. Sometimes flowering when leafless. W. Africa. 1824. Stove.

S. specio'sus. Erect or rambling glabrous shrub. *l.* in whorls of 3 or 4, oblong-lanceolate to lanceolate, acute or obtuse above, $1\frac{1}{2}$ to $3\frac{1}{2}$ in. long, narrowed to a short stalk, leathery. *fl.* yellowish, spotted red, lobes $1\frac{1}{2}$ in. long; peduncles as long as, or longer than, l., 2- to 6-fld. June. S. Africa. 1860. (B.M. 5713 as *S. capensis.*) Greenhouse.

S. Welwit'schii. A climbing or trailing shrub. *l.* produced after flowers, $1\frac{1}{2}$ in. long, oblong or elliptic, pale below, with wavy margins; stalks $\frac{1}{8}$ to $\frac{1}{4}$ in. long. *fl.* medium size, cor. funnel-shaped, white stained rose or crimson-purple, lobes not tailed. S. Trop. Africa. Stove. SYN. *S. ecaudatus.*

R. D. M.

STROPHIOLE. A swelling surrounding the hilum of certain seeds.

STROPHOLIR'ION CALIFORN'ICUM. A synonym of *Brodiaea volubilis.*

STRUMA. A cushion-like swelling.

STRUMA'RIA (*struma*, cushion-like swelling; the style is swollen in the middle). FAM. *Amaryllidaceae.* A genus of 6 species of bulbous plants, natives of S. Africa. Leaves lorate. Flowers numerous, in an umbel on a solid scape; pedicels filiform, scarcely spreading; perianth bell-shaped, tube almost absent, segments equal, erecto-patent; filaments more or less connected. Spathes 2, lanceolate, inner smaller. Well-drained sandy loam suits these greenhouse plants, which need a thorough season of rest when the leaves begin to fade. Propagation by seed or division.

S. angustifo'lia. About 6 in. h. *l.* few, linear, flat, entire, rather blunt, shining; sheath radical, erect, 1 to 2 in. h. *fl.* white, flesh-coloured without, segs. widely spreading; scented like *Lilium Martagon*; scape lateral, erect, about 8-fld. April. 1795.

S. rubella. About 1 ft. h. *l.* narrow-linear, oblique, entire, 5 to 9 in. long, rather blunt; sheath absent. *fl.* reddish and flesh-coloured, scentless; segs. widely spreading; scape lateral, 6- to 10-fld.; bracts purplish. May. 1795.

S. trunca'ta. *l.* tongue-like, 6 to 8 in. long, $\frac{1}{2}$ in. wide, blunt, nearly erect; sheath dark blood-red. *fl.* white, reddish at base, scentless, segs. spreading; scape many-fld., pedicels erect; bracts purplish, erect. April. 1795.

strumarius -a -um, strumose.

struma'tus -a -um, strumose.

strumose, strumiferous, bearing a swelling.

STRUTHIO'LA (*struthion*, a little sparrow; in allusion to the resemblance of the seeds to a beak). FAM. *Thymelaeaceae.* A genus of about 50 species of evergreen shrubs and undershrubs, natives of S. and Trop. Africa. Leaves opposite or (rarely) alternate, small, often sheath-like. Flowers stalkless, solitary or rarely in pairs in the upper leaf-axils, forming leafy spikes 1 to several in. long. Flowers small, the calyx constituting the chief feature, being tubular at the base with a limb of 4 lobes; petals 4, 8, or 12, whorled, usually quite minute; stamens 4, included in the calyx tube. Fruit small, dry. The following species require the same treatment as S. African heaths. Propagated by cuttings.

KEY

1. *Pet.* 8	2
1. *Pet.* 4. *Lvs. ovate-oblong*	S. striata
1. *Pet.* 12. *Cal. hairy,* $\frac{1}{2}$ *in. long*	S. tomentosa
2. *Cal. glabrous*	3
2. *Cal. hairy*	5
3. *Lvs. broad, overlapping. Branches glabrous*	S. ovata
3. *Lvs. narrow*	4
4. *Cal. lobes linear*	S. leariloba
4. *Cal. lobes more or less ovate. Lvs. acute*	S. erecta
5. *Cal. tube over* $\frac{1}{2}$ *in. long. Branches twiggy. Lvs. ovate- or linear-lanceolate*	S. longiflora
5. *Cal. tube not over* $\frac{1}{2}$ *in. long*	6
6. *Cal. lobes broadly ovate, acute*	S. lucens
6. *Cal. lobes ovate, obtuse. Lvs. oblong*	S. virgata

S. cilia'ta. A synonym of *S. virgata.*

S. erec'ta. Undershrub, $1\frac{1}{2}$ ft., shoots 4-angled at the apex, glabrous like the l. and cal. *l.* opposite, erect, linear-lanceolate, pointed, $\frac{1}{4}$ in. long, $\frac{1}{24}$ in. wide. *fl.* fragrant, axillary, pink or white; cal. tube $\frac{1}{3}$ in. long, lobes ovate-oblong, pointed, $\frac{1}{8}$ in. long; pet. 8, very tiny, surrounded by hairs. Spring, autumn. S. Africa. 1798. (B.M. 2138.) (B.M. 222 under this name represents *S. leariloba.*)

S. imbrica'ta. A synonym of *S. striata.*

S. inca'na. A synonym of *S. virgata.*

S. juniperi'na. A synonym of *S. leariloba.*

S. learilo'ba. Shrub 5 to 6 ft., shoots 4-angled, quite glabrous, like the l. and cal. *l.* opposite, $\frac{1}{4}$ to $\frac{1}{3}$ in. long, linear, pointed. *fl.* white, axillary at the upper part of the shoots; cal. tube cylindrical, $\frac{1}{3}$ in. long, its lobes linear, $\frac{1}{6}$ in. long, $\frac{1}{20}$ in. wide; pet. 8, oblong, $\frac{1}{24}$ in. long, reddish. June. S. Africa. 1758. (B.M. 222 as *S. erecta*; L.B.C. 75 as *S. juniperina.*)

S. longiflo'ra. Shrub 2 to 3 ft., shoots 4-angled, downy. *l.* densely set, ovate-lanceolate to linear-lanceolate, $\frac{1}{3}$ in. long, $\frac{1}{16}$ to $\frac{1}{8}$ in. wide. *fl.* axillary towards top of shoots; cal. red, tube very slender, cylindrical, $\frac{2}{3}$ in. long, lobes ovate-oblong, blunt, $\frac{1}{6}$ in. long; pet. 8, $\frac{1}{12}$ in. long, yellow. May. S. Africa. 1800. (B.M. 1212 as *S. pubescens.*)

S. lu'cens. Shrub, 2 ft., shoots downy at first. *l.* $\frac{1}{2}$ to $\frac{3}{4}$ in. long, $\frac{1}{12}$ in. wide, lanceolate to narrow-oblong, pointed, ciliate. *fl.* axillary yellow; cal. tube $\frac{1}{2}$ in. long, downy, lobes ovate, pointed, $\frac{1}{12}$ in. long; pet. 8, $\frac{1}{16}$ in. long, surrounded by hairs. June. S. Africa. 1817.

S. ova'ta. Undershrub 2 ft., shoots alternate, glabrous. *l.* opposite, ovate, up to $\frac{1}{2}$ in. long, $\frac{1}{6}$ in. wide, glabrous. *fl.* fragrant, white or pinkish, axillary in the upper parts of the shoot; cal. tube glabrous, $\frac{3}{4}$ in. long, slender, cylindrical, limb $\frac{1}{2}$ in. across of 4 ovate, pointed lobes; pet. 8, oblong, $\frac{1}{16}$ in. long. Spring. S. Africa. 1792. (A.B.R. 119.)

S. pubes'cens. A synonym of *S. longiflora.*

S. stria'ta. Shrub, 2 ft., young shoots downy. *l.* opposite, closely imbricate, ovate-oblong, $\frac{1}{4}$ to $\frac{1}{2}$ in. long, $\frac{1}{12}$ to $\frac{1}{8}$ in. wide, ciliate at first. *fl.* fragrant, axillary, clustered towards end of shoot; cal. tube downy, $\frac{1}{3}$ in. long, cylindrical, lobes $\frac{1}{8}$ in. long, $\frac{1}{24}$ in. wide, white; pet. yellow, $\frac{1}{16}$ in. long. April, July. S. Africa. 1794. (A.B.R. 113 as *S. imbricata.*)

S. tomento'sa. Undershrub, 2 ft., shoots slender, hairy at first. *l.* oval-oblong, up to $\frac{1}{2}$ in. long, $\frac{1}{4}$ in. wide, closely imbricated, grey-downy at first. *fl.* yellow, hairy, axillary for $1\frac{1}{2}$ to 4 in. of upper part of shoot; cal. tube $\frac{1}{4}$ in. long, cylindrical, the lobes oblong, $\frac{1}{20}$ in. long; pet. 12, rather longer than cal. lobes. August. S. Africa. 1799. (A.B.R. 334.)

S. virga'ta. Shrub, 2 ft., shoots at first white with down. *l.* oblong, blunt, $\frac{1}{3}$ to $\frac{5}{8}$ in. long, $\frac{1}{16}$ in. wide, margins white-ciliate at first, grooved at back. *fl.* white, clustered near top of shoots; cal. tube $\frac{1}{2}$ in. long, downy, lobes ovate, obtuse, $\frac{1}{8}$ in. long; pet. 8, oblong, $\frac{1}{24}$ in. long. May. S. Africa. (A.B.R. 149 as *S. ciliata*; L.B.C. 11 as *S. incana.*) var. **ru'bra,** *fl.* red. (A.B.R. 139.)

W. J. B.

STRUTHIOP'TERIS. Included under **Onoclea.**

STRYCHNINE PLANT. *See* **Strychnos Nux-vomica.**

STRYCH'NOS (ancient Greek name used by Theophrastus for a Solanaceous plant). FAM. *Loganiaceae.* A genus of about 70 species of tropical evergreen trees and shrubs, often tall climbers. Leaves opposite, 3- or 5-nerved at or above the base, membranous or leathery. Flowers small or rather long, usually white, 4- or 5-parted, in cymes; corolla lobes valvate. Fruit a berry, mostly globose, indehiscent. The species contain in the bark of the root and in the seed-coats 2 poisonous alkaloids, strychnine and brucine. The flesh of the fruits is harmless. Strychnine is obtained mostly from the seeds of *S. Nux-vomica,* but sometimes from those of *S. Ignatii. S. toxifera* yields Wourali or curare poison used by the S. American Indians to poison their arrows; it is obtained by macerating the scraped bark in water. *S. Ignatii* (Ignatius bean) has been used in India as a remedy for cholera, and *S. potatorum,* also Indian, is said to clarify foul water if the inside of the vessel into which it is poured has been rubbed with it. The climbing species have curious hook-tendrils arising in the axil of a leaf which does not develop like the one opposite to it on the stem, but becomes a scale leaf. If the hook catches a support the tendril twines close round it, much as does the petiole of Clematis, thickens, and becomes lignified. Other species have axillary thorns. The species need stove conditions but have no particular value as garden plants. A few have been in cultivation, among them those mentioned below.

S. Nux-vom'ica. Tree up to 40 ft. h. *l.* ovate, $3\frac{1}{2}$ in. long, 2 in. wide, 5-nerved, glabrous. *fl.* greenish, in terminal, many-fld. cymes 1 to 2 in. across; pedicels very short. *Berry* globose, many-seeded, about $1\frac{1}{2}$ in. across. India, Burma.

S. potato'rum. Clearing Nut. Tree up to 40 ft. h. *l.* elliptic, $2\frac{1}{2}$ in. long, 1 in. wide, 3-nerved, glabrous or nearly so; almost sessile. *fl.* greenish, in axillary cymes about 1 in. across. *Berry* up to $\frac{2}{3}$ in. across. India, Ceylon.

S. spino'sa. Low tree with slender branches and axillary thorns. *l.* obovate or roundish, 5-nerved, rather leathery, glabrous. *fl.* greenish, in short, dense terminal, very compound. *fr.* orange, with leathery shell, 2 in. or more across, pulp abundant, edible; seeds large. Madagascar. Trop. and S. Africa.

STRYPHNODEN'DRON (*stryphnos,* stringent, *dendron,* tree; from the rough taste of the bark). FAM. *Leguminosae.* A genus of about 9 species of small trees, natives of Trop. S. America, closely related to Piptadenia. Leaves 2-pinnate; leaflets small, in many pairs. Flowers small, hermaphrodite or somewhat polygamous, in axillary spikes, 5-merous, sessile; calyx bell-shaped; petals connate to middle, later free; stamens 10, free. Fruit linear, compressed, thick, many-seeded. Stove conditions are needed.

S. guianen'se. Shoots nearly round, rusty-haired. *l.* with 6 to 12 pairs of pinnae; lflets. in 8 to 10 pairs on pinna, oblique, oval-oblong, about $\frac{1}{3}$ in. long, shining above, reddish beneath. *fl.* smooth; cor. about 3 times as long as cal. *Pod* straight or slightly incurved. Guiana.

STUAR'TIA. A synonym of Stewartia.

Stuartia'nus -a -um, in honour of Mr. Henry Stuart Low, orchid grower, *c.* 1880.

Stuhlmann'ii, in honour of F. Stuhlmann, 1863–1928, zoologist of Hamburg, who collected in German E. Africa.

stuppo'sus -a -um, having mats or tufts of long hair.

styla'ris -is -e, having a conspicuous style.

STYLE. The narrow part of most carpels connecting the ovary and stigma, placing the stigma in a position favourable for pollination. The stigma is sometimes sessile upon the ovary and the style absent. The inner tissues of the style consist of loosely arranged cells forming the 'conducting tissue' through which the pollen tube grows from the pollen grains held on the stigma to the ovules inside the ovary.

STYLIDIA'CEAE. Dicotyledons. A family of about 120 species of mostly Australian herbs or sub-shrubs falling into 3 genera; a few species occur in New Zealand, Trop. Asia, and S. America. They are usually somewhat xerophytic. Leaves entire, often narrow and small. Flowers usually 5-partite, often 1-sexual, usually zygomorphic. Stamens 2 with extrorse anthers, united with the style. Carpels 2, joined, inferior. Fruit a capsule. Inflorescence a raceme or thyrse. The genera treated are Candollea, Stylidium.

STYLI'DIUM (*stylos,* column; the styles and stamens are joined). FAM. *Stylidiaceae.* A genus of nearly 100 species of mostly herbaceous perennials, mainly natives of Australia, with 1 or 2 in Trop. Asia and the E. Indies, those mentioned below being Australian. Flowers in racemes, panicles, or corymbs on terminal peduncles or radical scapes; calyx lobes 5, more or less united into 2 lips; corolla lobes irregular, the labellum much smaller and turned down or nearly as long and curved upwards, the other 4 ascending in pairs; column elongated and bent down or folded, elastic. Fruit 2-celled, globose, linear or lanceolate. A compost of sandy loam and peat suits these greenhouse plants which are best propagated by seeds. A few may be divided and the few shrubby species may be increased by cuttings.

S. adna'tum. Stem 2 to 12 in. long. *l.* scattered, upper crowded into a whorl-like tuft, linear; sometimes all very narrow, sometimes rather wide, $\frac{1}{2}$ to $1\frac{1}{2}$ in. long. *fl.* pink in nearly sessile clusters along rachis; the spike-like racemes or panicles dense, usually rather short and nearly sessile, sometimes 6 to 10 in. long. July. 1824. (B.M. 3816 and B.R. 1459 as *S. fasciculatum.*) var. **abbrevia'tum,** *l.* narrow or broad, *infl.* very dense, rarely over 2 in. long. (B.M. 2598 and B.R. 914 as *S. adnatum.*)

S. Arme'ria. *See* **S. graminifolium.**

S. Brunonia'num. *Lower l.* linear to oblanceolate, acute, rarely bluntish, 1 to over 2 in. long, rather flaccid. *fl.* pink; cal. lobes free; cor. with appendages to throat; raceme loose, 2 to 4 in. long, many-fld.; scapes 12 to 18 in. long, with 2 to 5 whorls of narrow l. June. 1841. (B.R. 1841, 1, 5.)

S. bulbif'erum macrocarp'um. About 6 in. h. *l.* very narrow-linear, $\frac{1}{4}$ to $\frac{1}{2}$ in. long, in dense tufts at ends and bases of branches. *fl.* greenish-purple; cal. lobes free, blunt; cor. without appendages; scapes $\frac{1}{2}$ to 2 in. long with a loose corymb of 3 to 7 fl. May. *fr.* almost sessile, about $\frac{3}{4}$ in. long. 1840. (B.M. 3913 as *S. recurvum.*)

S. cilia'tum. *l.* linear, 1 to $1\frac{1}{2}$ in. long, with a hair-like point. *fl.* yellow, occasionally white or pink, of variable size, with or without small appendages; panicle or raceme short and pyramidal or narrow and 3 to 4 in. long; scape 6 to 12 in. long. June. 1842. (B.M. 3883; B.M. 4529 as *S. saxifragoides.*)

S. crassifo'lium. Tall, rigid, erect, nearly glabrous. *l.* linear, 4 to 8 in. long, fleshy. *fl.* pink, 4-lobed, ¾ in. across; on a scape 2 ft. long with numerous small branches. 1899? (B.M. 7679.)

S. dichoto'mum. *l.* crowded at bases and tips of branches, scattered between the tufts, up to 1 in. long, narrow-linear, acute. *fl.* yellow in a thyrse or panicle, scapes 2 to 4 in. h., glandular-pubescent. April. 1850. (B.M. 4538 and F.d.S. 606 as *S. mucronifolium*; F.d.S. 229 as *S. Hookeri.*)

S. graminifo'lium. Trigger Plant. *l.* linear, rather rigid, nearly flat, varying in width, 2 to 9 in. long, sometimes with cartilaginous teeth. *fl.* pink; cor. lobes nearly equal, lip rather long; scapes 6 to 18 in. long, with a narrow raceme or interrupted spike of nearly sessile fl. 1803. (B.M. 1918; B.R. 90.) *S. Armeria* is a form of this with broad l.

S. hirsu'tum. *l.* narrow-linear, acute, 2 to 8 in. long, glabrous or glandular-hairy. *fl.* pink or red in a dense, spike-like raceme, rarely more than 1 in. long, very hairy; lip with crisped margins, and usually short appendages; scapes 6 to over 12 in. long, with spreading hairs. June. (B.M. 3194.)

S. Hoo'keri. A synonym of *S. dichotomum.*

S. laricifo'lium. Sub-shrub of about 1 ft. h. *l.* rather crowded along branches, not in terminal tufts, narrow-linear, mucronate, ½ to 1 in. long. *fl.* pink; cor. with appendages to lip but usually none in throat; infl. a loose raceme or panicle often over 6 in. long, pedunculate. 1818. (B.R. 550; H.E.F. 32; B.M. 2249 as *S. ternifolium.*)

S. mucronifo'lium. A synonym of *S. dichotomum.*

S. reduplica'tum. *l.* radical, linear, 3 or 4 to nearly 12 in. long, slender-pointed, narrowed to a long stalk, nearly flat or with revolute margins, glabrous or minutely glandular-pubescent. *fl.* yellowish-white or pale pink, lower on long pedicels; 2 larger cor. lobes ½ to ¾ in. long, connate to middle; raceme short, loose; scape leafless 6 to 18 in. long with spreading hairs. (B.R. 1842, 41 as *S. pilosum.*)

S. saxifragoi'des. A synonym of *S. ciliatum.*

S. scan'dens. Climber to 2 ft. *l.* all in dense, whorl-like, distant tufts, linear, 1 to 2 in. or more long. *fl.* pink; cor. with more or less prominent appendages to throat and lip; racemes solitary or 2 or 3 together, terminal, on short peduncles. 1803. (B.M. 3136.)

S. spathula'tum. About 6 in. h. *l.* in a radical rosette, obovate to oblong-spatulate, blunt or acute, more or less hairy or glandular, ½ to 1½ in. long including stalk. *fl.* pale yellow, small; cor. with appendages to throat and lip; raceme unbranched, loose, long; scape sometimes 18 in. long, glabrous or hairy. Summer. 1872. (B.M. 5953.)

stylif'erus -a -um, with a well-marked style.

STYLOME'CON (*stylos*, style, *mekon*, poppy; the pistil has a distinct style). FAM. *Papaveraceae.* A monotypic genus, *S. heterophylla* being a Californian annual. Flowers with 2 sepals coherent only in the bud; petals

Stylomecon heterophylla

usually 4, reddish-orange with a dark-purple base; stamens many; ovary turbinate, glabrous, placentas 4 to 11; style short, slender, stigma capitate. Fruit a turbinate capsule with numerous seeds. Cultivation as for annual species of Meconopsis.

S. heterophyl'la. Annual, 15 to 24 in. h. *l.* few, remote, pinnately divided; segs. of lower ones ovate, deeply toothed, stalked, of upper linear entire. *fl.* coppery-orange, with dark crimson centre, 1½ in. across, fragrance of Lily of the Valley, long-lasting, well above foliage. Summer. California. 1826. (B.M. 7636.) SYN. *Meconopsis heterophylla.* Hardy.

STYLOPH'ORUM (*stylos*, style, *phero*, I bear; the style is columnar). FAM. *Papaveraceae.* A genus of 3 species of perennial herbs with yellow or reddish sap occurring in Atlantic N. America and E. China. Stem downy, erect, striate. Leaves more or less in a rosette at base, long-stalked, pinnately cut, the segments irregularly toothed, glaucous beneath; cauline leaves few, similar to radical leaves but sessile or almost so. Flowers yellow or reddish in a slender corymb or umbel; sepals 2, hairy; petals 4; stamens many. Capsule ovoid or linear-downy with soft hairs. Cultivation as for Hylomecon, a light soil of woodland type being best. Propagation by seed sown in open in April or by division.

Stylophorum diphyllum

S. diphyl'lum. Celandine Poppy. Downy herb, about 1 ft. h., bare of l. in lower part of stem. *l.* 8 to 15 in. long, deeply cut into 5 or 7 oblong, sinuately lobed divisions, basal l. often with a pair of distinct lflets. *fl.* deep yellow, 1 in. or more across, on clustered terminal pedicels 1 to 3 in. long; fl.-stem solitary. May. *Capsule* nodding. In shady woods, Eastern N. America. 1854. (B.M. 4867.)

S. japon'icum. A synonym of *Hylomecon japonicum.*

S. lasiocarp'um. Herb of about 18 *in.* h. with reddish sap. *Basal l.* 8 to 18 in. long, long-stalked. *fl.-stems* 2 or 3, each with 4 or 5 fl. clustered at end; pet. obovate-roundish. Cent. and E. China.

S. sutchuenen'se. Herb of about 12 to 15 in. h. covered with reddish, shaggy hair. Stem leafy in lower part. *fl.* yellow, rather smaller than in *S. diphyllum*; fl.-stem solitary; pedicels about 2 in. long in a terminal cluster. *Capsule* narrowly ovate-oblong. W. China.

STYLOPHYL'LUM. Included in **Echeveria.**

stylo'sus -a -um, having a prominent style.

STYPAN'DRA (*stype*, tow, *andros*, anther; the stamens are downy). FAM. *Liliaceae.* A genus of 3 species of perennial herbs with short rhizomes and fibrous roots, natives of Australia. Related to Dianella but with woolly stamens. Stems leafy at base only or throughout, branched. Leaves distichous. Flowers blue, yellowish, or whitish in a loose, terminal, forked cyme; perianth segments 6, spreading, deciduous; stamens 6; pedicels filiform. Capsule oblong. Stypandras are only half-hardy and are best grown in a cool greenhouse; if in a warm border outside they need protection in severe weather. Sandy loam and peat is the best compost and propagation is by division.

S. caespito'sa. Erect, 1 to 2 ft. h. *l.* mostly radical, erect, rigid, 6 to 12 in. h., about $\frac{1}{6}$ in. wide; sheaths short. *fl.* blue or yellowish inside, rarely white, erect; segs. about $\frac{1}{2}$ in. long; pedicels 1 to 2 in. long, usually 3 or 4 in an umbel. June. 1824.

S. glau'ca. Low or ascending, 1 to 3 ft. h. *l.* erect or spreading, linear or lanceolate, 3 to 4 in. long or more, about $\frac{1}{4}$ in. wide; sheaths concealing stem. *fl.* blue, drooping; segs. acute, about $\frac{1}{2}$ in. long; cyme leafy at base; pedicels $\frac{1}{2}$ to 1 in. long, usually solitary. 1823. (B.M. 3417 as *S. propinqua.*)

S. umbella'ta. Nearly allied to *S. caespitosa.* Stem 8 to 10 in. h. *l.* at base many, 5 to 8 in. long, about $\frac{1}{8}$ in. wide. *fl.* white or yellowish, about $\frac{1}{2}$ in. long, often in a single umbel of 2 to 4 fls. June. 1826.

STYPHEL'IA (*styphelos*, hard; in allusion to the stiff, hard-textured leaves). FAM. *Epacridaceae.* Scores of species formerly placed in this genus are now referred to Leucopogon, Astrolome, and other allied genera. Bentham's conception of the genus comprised 11 species, natives of Australia and Tasmania and his nomenclature is here adopted. In later years its geographical limits have been extended to include New Guinea. Leaves alternate, closely set, sessile or nearly so. Flowers axillary, solitary, rarely in twos or threes; corolla tube with a limb of 5 revolute lobes; calyx 5-lobed; stamens 5, exserted. Fruit a dry drupe, bony in the middle. Cool greenhouse plants needing the same conditions and treatment as Epacris, the same peaty, sandy soil, and the same careful watering. They can be propagated, but not very readily, by cuttings.

S. longifo'lia. Shrub 3 to 4 ft., shoots softly downy. *l.* linear-lanceolate, 1 to $2\frac{1}{4}$ in. long, $\frac{1}{6}$ in. wide, tapering from a stalkless base to a slender point. *fl.* green, axillary, solitary, scarcely stalked; cor. tube cylindrical, $\frac{3}{4}$ in. long, $\frac{1}{8}$ in. wide; lobes rolled back, hairy. Spring. New S. Wales. 1807. (B.R. 24.)

S. triflo'ra. Shrub 3 to 4 ft. nearly or quite glabrous. *l.* obovate-oblong to oblong-lanceolate, closely set and overlapping, $\frac{3}{4}$ to $1\frac{1}{4}$ in. long, $\frac{3}{8}$ in. wide, stiffly sharply pointed. *fl.* pale pink and yellow, axillary, usually solitary but sometimes in pairs or threes; cor. tube $\frac{3}{4}$ to 1 in. long, $\frac{1}{6}$ in. wide, lobes much recurved, hairy. June to August. New S. Wales. 1796. (B.M. 1297.)

Styphelia tubiflora

S. tubiflo'ra. Shrub 4 to 5 ft. *l.* about $\frac{1}{2}$ in. long, $\frac{1}{8}$ in. wide, oblong-linear, often narrowed towards the base, abruptly mucronate. *fl.* solitary, axillary; cor. tube red, about 1 in. long, $\frac{1}{8}$ in. wide, narrowing downwards, hairy inside; lobes short, rolled backwards, bearded. Summer. New S. Wales. 1802. (L.B.C. 1938.)

S. vir'idis. Shrub, 4 ft., *l.* oblong-lanceolate or obovate-oblong, sessile, shortly and stiffly pointed, about $\frac{3}{4}$ in. long, $\frac{1}{4}$ in. wide. *fl.* green, solitary, axillary, scarcely stalked; cor. tube $\frac{5}{8}$ to $\frac{3}{4}$ in. long, $\frac{1}{4}$ in. wide, hairy at the base inside; lobes much recurved, hairy; stamens and pistil much exserted. April to June. New S. Wales. 1791. (A.B.R. 312.)

W. J. B.

STYRACA'CEAE. Dicotyledons. A family of about 80 species of shrubs and trees, without latex, in 6 genera, distributed in Brazil to Peru and Mexico, Virginia to Texas, and Japan to Java, with 1 species, *Styrax officinalis*, in the Mediterranean region. Leaves alternate, usually entire, often leathery, with star-shaped hairs. Flowers 5- to many-parted, hermaphrodite (unlike Ebenaceae), regular; stamens twice as many as petals, united at base or into a tube. Carpels 3 to 5, joined, superior. Fruit a drupe, with dry or fleshy pericarp; seeds 1 or few. The genera treated are Halesia, Pterostyrax, Sinojackia, Styrax.

styraciflu'us -a -um, producing storax.

styracoi'des, Styrax-like.

STYR'AX (ancient Greek name for *S. officinalis*). FAM. *Styracaceae.* A genus of about 100 species of deciduous or evergreen trees and shrubs, all those described below being deciduous. Natives of tropical and temperate parts of Asia and America, also of SW. Europe. Leaves alternate, short-stalked, pubescence mostly stellate. Flowers white, in racemes, clusters or solitary; frequently on short, lateral, leafy twigs; calyx bell-shaped, shallowly 5-lobed or entire; corolla 5-, sometimes 8-lobed; fruit a globose or ovoid drupe.

Several of the cultivated species are not very hardy and need wall protection except in the south and south-west, where they are admirable in the open ground. Those quite hardy are indicated below. All of them are beautiful. They like a lightish, loamy soil or a semi-peaty one, and are best raised from seed, but layers and cuttings can be rooted. July cuttings in a warm sand-frame are usually found best.

KEY

1.	*Fls. in few-fld. clusters or racemes*	2
1.	*Fls. in many-fld. racemes*	7
2.	*Lvs. distinctly toothed, though sometimes minutely*	3
2.	*Lvs. entire or almost so*	6
3.	*Lvs. glabrous or nearly so*	4
3.	*Lvs. downy*	5
4.	*Fl.-stalks short, downy, lvs. minutely toothed, narrow-oval*	S. americana
4.	*Fl.-stalks $\frac{3}{5}$ to 1 in. long, glabrous; lvs. sparsely toothed, oval*	S. japonica
5.	*Lvs. white and soft downy beneath*	S. langkongensis
5.	*Lvs. velvety on both surfaces, greyish beneath*	S. schweliensis
6.	*Lvs. $\frac{1}{2}$ to 1 in. long, sometimes with a few teeth, glaucous and downy beneath*	S. Wilsonii
6.	*Lvs. $1\frac{1}{2}$ to 2 in. long, entire, hairy when young*	S. officinalis
7.	*Lvs. usually under 4 in. long*	8
7.	*Lvs. often over 4 in. long*	10
8.	*Shoots smooth or minutely downy*	9
8.	*Shoots and l. beneath white tomentose*	S. Benzoin
9.	*Lvs. minutely toothed, downy beneath at first*	S. dasyantha
9.	*Lvs. coarsely toothed towards apex, downy at first*	S. Shiraiana
10.	*Lvs. obovate to nearly round*	11
10.	*Lvs. lanceolate, nearly glabrous, faintly toothed*	S. Veitchiorum
11.	*Shoots and l. beneath grey-downy*	S. grandifolia
11.	*Shoots finally glabrous*	12
12.	*Lvs. thinly downy beneath, obovate to obliquely ovate*	S. Hemsleyana
12.	*Lvs. densely downy beneath, nearly round*	S. Obassia

S. america'na. Shrub 6 to 10 ft., shoots and l. nearly glabrous. *l.* $1\frac{1}{2}$ to $3\frac{1}{2}$ in. long, narrowly oval or oblong, pointed, cuneate, minutely toothed; stalk $\frac{1}{6}$ in. or less long. *fl.* white, pendulous, 1 to 4 in clusters terminating short, leafy twigs; cor. $\frac{3}{4}$ to $1\frac{1}{4}$ in. wide, with

5 narrow lobes; cal. triangularly lobed. June, July. *fr.* roundish-oval, ¼ in. wide. SE. United States. 1765. (B.M. 921 as *S. laevigata.*) Not very hardy.

S. Benzo'in. A moderate-sized tree, wild in Sumatra, of no horticultural value. It is only of interest as yielding by incision the resinous drug Benzoin, one of the ingredients of 'Friar's Balsam'. Stove.

S. dasyan'tha. Shrub or small tree up to 25 ft. *l.* obovate to broadly oval, 2 to 4 in. long, 1½ to 3 in. wide, pointed, minutely toothed, sparsely downy at first. *Racemes* slender, terminal, 2 to 4 in. long, often with a few fl. in the top l.-axils. *fl.* white, ½ to ¾ in. long; cor. lobes lanceolate, downy outside; cal. ¼ in. long, felted outside. July. China. 1900. Rather tender. Wall.

S. grandifo'lia. Shrub 5 to 12 ft., shoots and racemes grey-downy. *l.* obovate or oval, 2½ to 6 in. long, usually cuneate, slightly toothed to entire, grey-downy beneath. *fl.* in racemes 3 to 6 in. long, fragrant; cor. white, ⅓ to ⅔ in. long; pet. oblong, spreading, downy. May. *fr.* obovoid, downy, ⅓ in. long. SE. United States. 1765. (L.B.C. 1016.) Not really hardy.

S. Hemsleya'na.* Tree 20 to 30 ft., shoots downy at first. *l.* obovate to obliquely ovate, 3 to 5½ in. long, toothed, prominently veined, thinly starry-downy beneath. *fl.* pure white, in semi-erect or pendulous, downy racemes 4 to 6 in. long; cor. ¾ in. long, 1 in. across the spreading ovate lobes; cal. rusty-downy. June. China. 1900. (B.M. 8339.) Hardy.

Styrax japonica

S. japon'ica.* Tree 10 to 25 ft., branches spreading or semi-pendulous. *l.* oval, 1 to 3½ in. long, sparsely toothed, glabrous except for tufts of down in the vein-axils beneath. *fl.* quite pendulous, on slender stalks 1 to 1½ in. long, hanging in rows beneath the shoots; cor. pure white, ¾ in. wide, with 5 deep oval lobes; cal. obscurely lobed. June. *fr.* ovoid, ½ in. long. Japan. 1862. (B.M. 5950 as *S. serrulata.*) Hardy. var. **Farges'ii,** *fl.* larger, nearly 1 in. across, cal. tinged brown. 1925.

S. laeviga'ta. A synonym of *S. americana.*

S. langkongen'sis. Bushy shrub up to 6 ft., shoots brownish with minute down. *l.* 1 to 2½ in. long, ovate to obovate, faintly toothed, dull green above, white and soft with down beneath. *fl.* white or creamy-white, 1 in. across, borne singly or in pairs in the l.-axils of shoots 1 to 2 in. long. China. 1910. Rare and probably tender.

S. Obas'sia. Tree 20 to 30 ft., shoots soon glabrous. *l.* broadly oval to almost orbicular, 4 to 8 in. long, nearly as much wide, distantly and shallowly toothed, densely downy beneath. *fl.* fragrant, in terminal racemes 6 to 8 in. long; cor. pure white, 1 in. wide, deeply 5-lobed; cal. downy, ¼ in. long, with 5 to 10 shallow lobes. June. *fr.* ovoid, ¾ in. long, velvety. Japan. 1879. (B.M. 7039.) Likes slight shade and shelter but is hardy.

S. officina'lis. Shrub or small tree, 12 to 20 ft., shoots, l. and fl.-stalks downy. *l.* broadly oval to ovate, 1 to 2½ in. long, entire, starry-hairy when young. *fl.* pendulous, in terminal clusters of 3 to 6, fragrant; cor. pure white, 1¼ in. wide, very downy, 6- to 8-lobed, the lobes narrow-oblong. June. SE. Europe, Asia Minor. 1597. (B.M. 9653.) Not very hardy, but admirable in the south and south-west. Storax, a fragrant resin, is obtained by incision. **A**

S. schwelien'sis. Shrub or small tree up to 25 ft., shoots reddish-brown, downy. *l.* oval, 2 to 4 in. long, ¾ to 2 in. wide, cuneate, pointed, shallowly toothed, dull green above, greyish beneath, velvety on both surfaces; stalk ⅛ in. or less long. *fl.* white, 1 in. across, single or in pairs on short shoots; cor. lobes downy, cal. bell-shaped, very downy, scarcely toothed. June, July. China. 1913. Good in the south-west.

S. serrulat'a, of Bot. Mag. *See* **S. japonica.**

S. Shiraia'na. Small tree, shoots minutely downy. *l.* obovate to roundish, cuneate, coarsely toothed towards the apex, 1½ to 4 in. long, downy beneath. *fl.* white, shortly stalked, borne in terminal racemes about 2½ in. long on short side-shoots; cor. ¾ in. long, funnel-shaped, lobes ovate, downy, half as long as the tube. Japan.

S. Veitchio'rum. Tree 20 to 30 ft., shoots, l.-stalks, and cal. grey with down. *l.* oval-lanceolate to lanceolate, 3 to 5 in. long, cuneate, long- and taper-pointed, faintly toothed; stalk ¼ to ⅓ in. long. *fl.* white, 1 in. wide, borne on a cluster of terminal and axillary racemes 4 to 8 in. long. China. 1900. Hardy.

S. Wilso'nii. Shrub 8 to 12 ft., of twiggy habit, shoots very slender, downy. *l.* ovate, ½ to 1 in. long, varying from nearly entire to 3- or 5-toothed, glaucous and appressed-downy beneath. *fl.* nodding, terminal on short twigs, often solitary, sometimes in twos or threes; cor. pure glistening white, the 5 lobes ovate-oblong, downy outside; stamens 10 in a columnar cluster. June. *fr.* roundish-ovoid, ¼ in. long. China. 1908. (B.M. 8444.) Blooms when only a few in. high. Rather tender. Wall.

W. J. B.

SUAE'DA (from the Arabian name). FAM. *Chenopodiaceae.* A genus of about 40 species of herbs or shrubs, widely distributed, especially in salt soils. Leaves 3-nate, fleshy, entire. Flowers small or very small, axillary or clustered. None of the species is of horticultural value, but *S. maritima*, Sea Blite, is used in S. Europe in the manufacture of Barilla (*see* **Salicornia**) and the shrubby, grey *S. fruticosa* occurs on British coasts.

suaveo'lens, sweet scented.

sua'vis -e, sweet, agreeable.

suavis'simus -a -um, very sweet scented.

sub-, in compound words, signifies nearly, or slightly, as sub-rotund, roundish; sub-cordate, somewhat heart-shaped.

subbiflo'rus -a -um, nearly like *biflorus.*

SUB-CLASS. A group of Families next in importance to a Class.

Suber, cork.

subero'sus -a -um, corky.

sub-e'rosus -a -um, slightly bitten.

SUB-KINGDOM, the highest subdivision of the Vegetable Kingdom.

submerged, submersed, growing under water.

sub-petiolar, beneath the petiole.

SUB-SHRUB. *See* **Under-shrub.**

SUBSOIL. The layer of earth or rock existing at such a depth below the surface that the ordinary operations of gardening do not reach it, i.e. usually about 1 ft. below the surface downwards. In nature it may be much nearer the surface than this. The subsoil is sometimes of almost the same composition as the soil but there is usually considerable difference between them. The soil is the part usually occupied by the roots of plants from which they draw water and earth salts. Unless the earth salts are renewed there is therefore a tendency for the soil to become depleted of necessary minerals and furthermore, as the soil is usually more permeable, soluble materials are apt to be washed out of the soil into the subsoil, as is often seen with calcium carbonate, so that the subsoil may become relatively richer in mineral salts than the soil. Air, however, usually finds its way to the subsoil in very small quantities and the salts, or some of them, may not be fully oxidized and be poisonous to plants. The subsoil, too, is almost always very deficient in organic matter and in bacteria. While, therefore, it is most desirable to work the subsoil so as to admit air to it and to furnish it with organic matter and the conditions under which nitrifying organisms can work, it is usually unwise to bring the subsoil to the surface until it has assumed to a great extent the characters of soil.

Where the subsoil is sandy or gravelly or chalky, water can usually percolate freely through it, whereas if it be clayey water will be held up unless the subsoil is broken or adequately drained. Sandy soils also are at times in such a condition that they neither permit the passage of moisture down through them in wet weather nor its rise to the surface in dry, owing to the formation of a 'pan' or layer of soil particles cemented together into a solid mass, often by oxides of iron, just below the depth to which air freely penetrates. This is sometimes called a plough pan, but it often develops in soils the plough or other implement of cultivation has never touched. Such land lies wet in winter, depriving roots of air in that season, and is so dry in summer that vegetation has little chance to obtain enough water from it. If the pan be broken up such soils often become quite fertile—another reason for deep digging.

Many of the reported instances of excellent results following the bringing of the subsoil to the surface on investigation show that the results have followed a second trenching when the subsoil enriched and aerated has for the most part been returned to its original position and the soil thereby deepened.

Soil has its origin, of course, in the action of the weather, air, rain, wind, and frost upon the subsoil together with the gradual accumulation of the remains of plants and animals acted upon by bacteria and fungi, the agents of decay. The result of wise cultivation is to hasten these actions and so increase the volume of the earth's crust of which plants can make use.

SUB-SPECIES. A rank higher than that of a variety but lower than that of a species; a well-marked geographical race which might be considered a species by some botanists.

subtended by, having a structure immediately below an organ, usually said of a bract below a flower.

SUBTERRANEAN FRUITS. Fruits buried beneath the surface of the soil during their development and ripening there, as those of the ground-nut, *Arachis hypogaea*, and *Trifolium subterraneum*, which has two forms of inflorescence one of which becomes subterranean. Other examples of geocarpy, as this mode of fruit development is called, occur in the genera Factorovskya, Voandzeia (*V. subterranea*), Morisia, Geococcus, Amphicarpaea, Begonia (*B. hypogaea*), &c. An account of such plants by N. Hylander has been published in *Botaniska Notiser*, 1946, 432–70.

subterra'neus -a -um, growing underground.

SUB-TROPICAL GARDEN. A flower-garden or pleasure-ground devoted during the summer to plants with stately foliage, arranged with a view to represent tropical vegetation. Many of the plants used are natives of tropical countries and are, in consequence, available for placing outside only during the hottest part of the year; but there are others of stately aspect which are quite hardy and invaluable for associating with them. Tropical plants of slow growth which have to be kept under glass all the winter are not only expensive to obtain in the first place but need a great deal of space and considerable attention for their well-being in the colder parts of the year, and this can be given in but few gardens. A most important condition for the sub-tropical garden is shelter; the leaves of the plants used are, in most instances, easily torn by wind and the plants soon disfigured. Shade and moisture are also necessary for some, e.g. Tree and other Ferns and Cycads. There are several sub-tropical plants readily raised from seed each spring, quick-growing, and capable of making large plants before autumn if planted out in rich soil about the middle of June. Of these *Albizzia lophantha*, Castor-oil plants (*Ricinus* sp.), Nicotianas, Solanums, Wigandias, and varieties of *Zea Mays* are especially valuable. Cannas may be easily raised from seeds in spring and the plants are nearly hardy and may be increased by division of the rootstock each spring. The most serviceable of tropical plants are the Palms, *Chamaerops humilis*, *Livistona australis*, *L. chinensis*, *Phoenix dactylifera*, *Ptychosperma elegans*, and *Trachycarpus Fortunei*; the Musas, *M. Basjoo* (hardy or nearly so), *M. Ensete*, and *M. superba*; and the Tree Ferns *Alsophila australis*, *A. excelsa*, *Cyathea dealbata*, and *Dicksonia antarctica*. *Cycas circinalis* and *C. revoluta* may be plunged in sheltered positions among these plants and there are also the Bamboos in the genera Arundinaria, Bambusa, and Phyllostachys, Centaureas, Cordylines, Erythrinas, Fatsias, some species of Ficus, Hostas, New Zealand Flax (Phormium), Pampas Grass, *Arundo Donax*, and, if water is available in the area, some of the fine water-side plants which also make rapid growth in rich soil. For treatment of the plants referred to see under their respective headings.

subula'tus -a -um (***subuli-*** in compound words), awl-shaped.

subulo'sus -a -um, somewhat awl-shaped.

succedan'eus -a -um, following, supplying place of.

succiru'ber -ra -rum, with red sap.

SUCCI'SA. Included in **Scabiosa.**

SUCCISEL'LA. Included in **Scabiosa.**

succi'sus -a -um, abruptly ended as though cut or broken off at the lower end.

SUCCORY. *See* **Chicory.**

succotrin'us -a -um, of Socotra.

SUCCULENT PLANTS. The chief characteristic of succulent plants is their possession of very fleshy foliage or stems or both. They are, for the most part, plants of dry, open situations in nature capable of retaining sufficient moisture to maintain life through long spells of dry, hot weather. They show great diversity of form, and many of them differ so much from the general appearance of plants that they excite interest on that ground alone, but besides this many are very ornamental and bear handsome flowers. They include, therefore, both objects of curiosity and interest from their peculiar mode of existence and sometimes strange and even grotesque form, and objects of outstanding beauty.

Very few succulents are quite hardy, many must have in winter some artificial heat, and some, especially among the Cacti, at times require a high temperature to grow at their best, but, on the whole, few plants are more easily cultivated than succulents or require so little attention, provided a few essentials are satisfied.

While there are many that can be grown with a certain amount of success along with others requiring totally different conditions, the results obtained are far below those given when the plants are grown in a house by themselves. The house they should occupy should be very light, airy, and well drained. The drainage is very important. For a great part of the year the house will need to be kept dry and at no time should water be allowed to remain on the floors, though with a few plants of the type an exception may be made. It is therefore advisable to have the floor of the house above the level of the surrounding ground and to have a damp-course in the walls, an unusual feature in most plant-houses. It is also better for a partition to be made so that one part of the structure may be warm, with a temperature of from 55 to 65° F., the other cool, from 45 to 55° F., but with as much sun-heat in both divisions as the plants can get in summer. If this division cannot be made most succulents will grow in a temperature ranging from 50 to 60° F. in summer with a drop as low as 45° F. at times in winter.

The following notes apply generally, but there are many exceptions, and in particular instances the notes on the various genera in the body of the Dictionary should be consulted, especially under the article **Cactus.**

Most succulent plants inhabit tropical or sub-tropical regions and grow in arid areas where they are baked up for the great part of the year, and during the other portion are subject to torrential rains interspersed with bright sunshine and considerable heat: this is perhaps especially the case with Cacti. It is during this period that they make their growth and flower. During the remainder of the year they are more or less at rest so far as actual increase in size goes. To secure these conditions as nearly as possible under artificial treatment, the plants should be started into growth in spring. They then need copious supplies of water and syringing overhead during April, May, and June. Towards the end of June the water-supply should be gradually reduced and little will be needed for the rest of the season, the plants being allowed to become almost dry. In winter, unless the plants show signs of shrivelling, no water will be required. This treatment ensures the ripening of the growth made and enables the plants to pass safely through the dull winter weather. No shade will be needed but plenty of ventilation in hot weather, and, except during the growing period, a thoroughly dry atmosphere.

Usually large pots will not be needed (but *see* **Cactus**) and the soil should generally consist of good fibrous loam mixed with plenty of sharp silver sand, broken bricks, and mortar rubble. Plenty of drainage must be given. The texture of the roots should be studied in making up the composts for particular plants. Frequent repotting is not often necessary. In fact, if the drainage is good many succulents will do for several years in the same pot, but when it is required the best time for the operation is during April and May.

Propagation is usually simple and few plants root so easily from cuttings. Many are readily raised from seed and many also form suckers or may be propagated from leaf-cuttings. When propagating from suckers it is usually best to let the cut portion dry well before inserting it in the soil, which should have plenty of sand mixed with it and be nearly dry.

For the various genera of Cacti and the Mesembryanthemum group see under those headings. Other genera in which succulents occur include Adromischus, Aeonium, Agave, Aichryson, Aloe, Anacampseros, Apicra, Bryophyllum, Bulbine, Caralluma, Ceropegia, Chiastophyllum, Cotyledon, Crassula, Echeveria, Echidnopsis, Euphorbia, Fouquiera, Furcraea, Gasteria, Graptopetalum, Greenovia, Haworthia, Hoodia, Huernia, Huerniopsis, Kalanchoe, Kleinia, Manfreda, Monanthes, Othonna, Pachyphytum, ×Pachyveria, Pedilanthus, Pelargonium, Penthorum, Piaranthus, Portulacaria, Rochea, Sedum, Sempervivum, Sesuvium, Stapelia, Synadenium, Tillaea, Umbilicus, and Vauanthes.

succulen'tus -a -um, soft, juicy.

SUCKER (1). Shoot of underground origin. (2) The short branch sent into its host by a parasite by which it obtains food, haustorium.

SUCKERING-IRON. Tool used for removing suckers from fruit-trees, &c. It consists of a narrow steel blade about 6 in. long and 3 in. wide at the cutting edge, with a long shank and socket in which is fitted a handle like that of a spade, the whole being about as long as a spade.

suco'sus -a -um, sappy.

sudet'icus -a -um, of the Sudeten region on the borders of Bohemia and Silesia.

sue'cicus -a -um, Swedish (*see also* **suionum** *below*).

Suenderman'nii, in honour of F. Sündermann, b. 1864, nurseryman of Lindau, student of alpine plants.

suffrutes'cens, slightly shrubby, becoming shrubby.

suffrutico'sus -a -um, low and shrubby at base, somewhat shrubby.

suffult'us -a -um, supported from beneath.

SUGAR APPLE. *See* **Annona squamosa.**

SUGAR BEET. *See* **Beta vulgaris crassa.**

SUGARBERRY. *See* **Celtis occidentalis.**

SUGAR BUSH. *See* **Protea mellifera.**

SUGAR CANE. *See* **Saccharum officinarum.**

SUGAR, MAPLE. *See* **Acer saccharum.**

SUGAR PALM. *See* **Arenga pinnata, Caryota urens, Cocos nucifera.**

SUGAR PEA. Edible-podded Pea, *see* **Pea.**

SUGAR PINE. *See* **Pinus Lambertiana.**

A→

SUION'UM, of the Suiones, Sviones, Sveones, or Swear, the Scandinavian people inhabiting in ancient times the Mälar region of Cent. Sweden, from which the medieval and modern names of the whole country (e.g. Suecia, Sverige, Sweden) have been derived.

sulca'tus -a -um (***sulci-*** in compound words), furrowed, grooved.

sulfu'reus -a -um, sulphur-coloured, pale yellow.

sulia'nus -a -um, of Soela Is., Celebes.

suling'ii, of Mt. Soeling, Java.

A→

SULPHUR is one of the chemical elements essential for the growth of plants, for it is a constituent of protoplasm and is found also in other compounds in plants such as mustard oil. The sulphur is derived from sulphates in the soil where they are usually sufficiently abundant in the form of calcium, potassium, or sodium sulphates. The addition of pure sulphur to the soil is usually detrimental to plants, but as a means of controlling certain vegetable and animal parasites it is exceedingly useful. For this purpose it is applied as Flowers of Sulphur or Green Sulphur which is less conspicuous, in the form of a very fine powder, dusted on so as to cover the whole of the plants. The powdery mildews (q.v.) on roses, vines, hops, &c., are controlled by it and so are red-spider-mites. It is also used in plant-houses, being vaporized by heat, special lamps being used for the purpose lest it become ignited, when the vapour will do great harm to the plants. In both instances the destruction of the parasite is brought about by the sulphur-dioxide which is gradually produced from the sulphur particles in contact with air. Sulphur compounds are also very effective for use as sprays. *See* **Fungicides, Insecticides.**

A→

SULPHURATOR. An apparatus for distributing Flowers of Sulphur over plants attacked by mildew or red-spider-mites, consisting of a small bellows with a tin box above the tube, having holes in the bottom, or of a piston arrangement to drive air laden with the sulphur dust over the plants. Usually now called Powder Bellows or Dusting Machines since other dusts may be similarly distributed.

sulphu'reus -a -um, sulphur-coloured, pale yellow.

SULPHURIC ACID. Dilute sulphuric acid is sometimes used as a weed-killer, either in the form of a spray, or injected into the root of such weeds as dandelions by means of a suitable implement. It is also used for spraying the haulms of diseased or late potatoes before lifting to kill the fungus as a preventive of infection of the tubers or to render the lifting of the crop easier. *See* **Fungicides, Weed-killers.**

SULPHUR VAPORIZER. A lamp specially constructed to enable sulphur to be vaporized without igniting, for the distribution of sulphur in plant-houses.

Sultani, in honour of Seyyid Bargash, ibn Seyyid Said, Sultan of Zanzibar, d. 1888.

SUMACH. *Rhus Coriaria*, the leaves of which are used in dyeing and tanning; also applied to *R. typhina* (q.v.).

SUMACH, MYRTLE-LEAVED. *See* **Coriaria myrtifolia.**

SUMATRA CAMPHOR. *See* **Dryobalanops aromatica.**

sumatra'nus -a -um, of Sumatra, Indonesia.

SUMMER BEDDING. The planting out of ornamental plants in beds for summer display usually carried out between May 24 and June 15 or later in cold districts. *See* **Bedding.**

SUMMER CHAFER. *See* **Chafers.**

SUMMER SNOWFLAKE. *See* **Leucojum aestivum.**

sunda'icus, sunden'sis, of Soenda Is., Java.

SÜNDERMANNII. *See* **Suendermannii.**

SUNDEW. *See* **Drosera.**

SUNDROPS. *See* **Oenothera fruticosa.**

SUNFLOWER. *See* **Helianthus.**

SUNFRUIT. *See* **Heliocarpus americanus.**

SUNIP'IA. A synonym of Ione.

SUNN HEMP. *See* **Crotalaria juncea.**

SUN PLANT. *See* **Portulaca grandiflora.**

SUN ROSE. *See* **Helianthemum.**

super (***supra-*** in compound words), implying above.

su'perans, outstanding.

superb'iens, very fine.

superb'us -a -um, magnificent.

superficia'lis -is -e, on the surface.

superior, growing above anything. The upper or posterior lip of a corolla is said to be the superior lip. A calyx is superior when it appears to grow from the top of the ovary, and half-superior when it appears to grow from above the base of an ovary. An ovary is superior when it grows from above the origin of the calyx or perianth.

SUPERPHOSPHATES. *See* **Phosphates.**

superposed, placed vertically above some other part.

superstitio'sus -a -um, connected with religious ceremony.

Supfia'nus -a -um, in honour of Karl Supf, 1855–1915, of Berlin, amateur of Cacti.

supin'us -a -um, lying flat, face upwards.

SUPPRESSION, complete abortion of an organ.

supra-, *see* ***super.***

supranu'bius -a -um, above the clouds.

suratten'sis -is -e, of Surat, West coast of India.

surculo'sus -a -um, producing shoots from below ground (suckers).

sureil, of Sureil in N. Bengal.

SURFACE CATERPILLARS or **CUTWORMS,** are the larvae of a number of species of Noctuid Moths, including the Turnip Moth, *Agrotis segetum*; the Heart and Dart, *A. exclamationis*; and the Yellow Underwing, *Triphaena pronuba*. The caterpillars of these species spend the day beneath stones, turf, and leaves and buried in the soil, and become active after dark when they feed on the lower leaves and partially or completely sever the base of the stem of many plants just above and below ground-level. The effect of their feeding is that the attacked plants wilt and frequently snap off at the portion attacked. The adult Turnip and Heart and Dart Moths somewhat resemble each other, while the Yellow Underwing is larger and possesses yellow hind-wings which are conspicuous only when the moth is on the wing. The larvae of the first two moths are closely similar, being

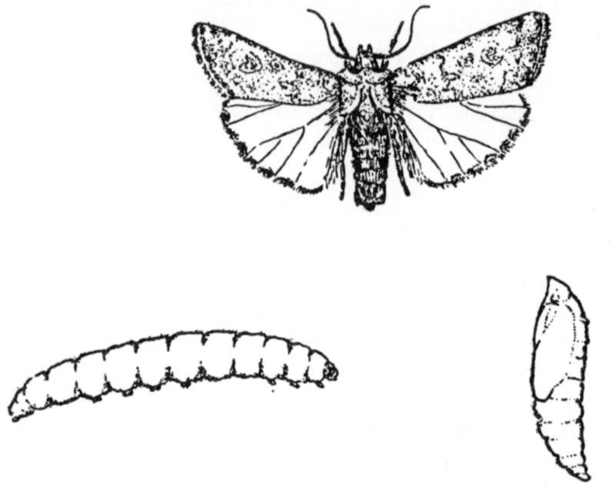

Surface caterpillar
Heart and Dart Moth and its Larva and Pupa

dirty grey, sometimes tinged with brown, and having rows of blackish dots along their sides; those of the Yellow Underwing are larger and yellowish or greenish-grey, with a series of oblique dark green or black stripes along the sides of the body. All 3 species of moth appear from early June to late July, and the eggs are laid on the leaves or stems of many common weeds and cultivated plants. The larvae hatch in about a fortnight and feed on the stems and underground portions of a great variety of plants, including Brassicas (e.g. Cabbage), Root Crops (e.g. Turnip), Chrysanthemums, Dahlias, China Asters, Marigolds, and Zinnias. A number of the caterpillars may, under favourable conditions, pupate in August and produce a second brood of moths in late August and September. Most of them, however, continue to feed throughout the autumn and winter, and are reinforced by young larvae which have developed from the moths of the second brood. They become fully fed in February, March, and April, and then pupate in earthen cells. In small gardens handpicking the caterpillars is a simple method of dealing with the pests which are found in the soil near wilted plants, or they may be collected after dark when they are crawling on the surface of the soil. The ground round susceptible plants should be hoed frequently during the months in which the larvae are active. This operation is effective not only in destroying weeds, which serve as food plants, but in injuring the larvae mechanically with the hoe-blade as they are resting beneath the ground. The most effective method of control is to lay a poison bait between the attacked plants towards evening. The bait consists of Paris Green (½ lb.) and Bran (14 lb.), thoroughly mixed and moistened with about ½ gall. of water to form a moist, but not wet, mash which should be distributed evenly and thinly over the ground. Care must be taken to exclude domestic animals, poultry, and wild birds from the treated area as far as possible. **A**

G. F. W.

surinamen'sis -is -e, of Surinam, S. America.

Suringaria'nus -a -um, in honour of Willem Frederik Renier Suringar, 1832–98, Professor of Botany, Leiden.

Susan'nae, in honour of Mrs. Susanna Muir, wife of Dr. John Muir (q.v.) who also collected in the Riversdale district, S. Africa.

SUSCEPTIBILITY. Plants differ very much in their reaction to attack by disease organisms, and even in the same variety some individuals are more easily attacked than others. The plants which are easily attacked are referred to as susceptible. It is considered that susceptibility to disease and its opposite, resistance to disease, are inherent qualities possessed by different plants, but the degree of susceptibility or resistance is likely to be modified by variations in the conditions under which the plants are grown. For instance, tomato plants which are soft and sappy are far more likely to be affected by *Botrytis cinerea*, the Grey Mould fungus, and by Streak disease (*see* **Tomato diseases**) than are those of a harder, sturdier type, irrespective of the variety grown.

susia'nus -a -um, of Susa, Persia.

suspen'sus -a -um, pendent.

susquehan'nae, of Susquehanna, near Philadelphia.

sutchuenen'sis -is -e, of Szechwan, W. China.

Sutera grandiflora

SU'TERA (in honour of Johann Rudolf Suter, 1766–1827, Swiss botanist, professor at Berne and author of *Flora Helvetica*, 1802). FAM. *Scrophulariaceae.* A genus of about 50 species of annual or perennial herbs, natives of S. Africa, related to Chaenostoma. Leaves mostly opposite, sometimes with short shoots in axils. Flowers axillary or in terminal racemes, rarely in panicles; calyx 5-toothed; corolla tubular, not spurred, deciduous, tube long or short, nearly straight or somewhat curved at apex; stamens 4, didynamous. Fruit a capsule. Greenhouse plants calling for no special soil and propagated by seed or by division.

S. caeru'lea. Clammy hairy annual or perennial 6 to 18 in. h. Stem nearly round, branches many, wiry, leafy. *l.* sometimes clustered, upper alternate, linear, oblanceolate or oblong, spreading, ⅓ to 1½ in. long, more or less toothed; sessile or nearly so. *fl.* blue, bright purplish-blue, or pale rose, ⅓ to ½ in. across, tube funnel-shaped, whitish below, yellow above; stamens exserted. S. Africa. (B.M. 217 as *Buchnera viscosa.*)

S. Dielsia'na. Clammy annual, 6 to 12 in. h., branches moderately leafy. *Upper l.* alternate, all ovate-lanceolate or narrowly elliptic, ½ to 1¾ in. long, toothed, stalked. *fl.* mauve or white with purplish-maroon markings about ¾ in. across, tube cylindrical below, a little dilated and curved above, ⅝ in. long. Namaqualand. SYN. *Chaenostoma racemosum.*

S. grandiflo'ra. Much-branched, glandular-hairy perennial from a woody base up to 3 ft. h. *l.* opposite, about 1 in. long, coarsely toothed. *fl.* freely produced, lavender, in a terminal raceme up to 12 in. long, sometimes branched at the base, pedicels 1 in. long, slender; sep. awl-shaped; cor. tube slender, 1 in. long, somewhat dilated and curved near apex, greenish; limb oblique, 1 in. across, segs. 5, spreading, obovate, mouth white. June to October. S. Africa. (B.M. 9452.)

SUTHERLAND'IA (in honour of James Sutherland, an early Superintendent of the Edinburgh Botanic Garden, author of *Hortus Medicus Edinburgensis* (1683); d. 1719). FAM. *Leguminosae.* A genus of S. African shrubs usually regarded as monotypic but by some authorities as of 3 or 4 closely related species, varying chiefly in foliage. The following species is hardy in Scilly but needs cool greenhouse conditions in most places. Easily grown in ordinary compost and propagated by cuttings or seeds.

S. frutes'cens.* Shrub 5 to 15 ft. h., young shoots downy. *l.* 2½ to 3½ in. long, pinnate; lflets. in 6½ to 10½ pairs, ⅓ to ¾ in. long, lanceolate to oblong, thinly downy. *infl.* an axillary raceme, 1 to 2 in. long, 6- to 10-fld.; stalks stiffly hairy; cor. 1½ in. long, the standard, wings, and keel all rich scarlet, and pointing forwards; cal. bell-shaped, with 5 triangular lobes. June. Pod inflated like a Colutea, up to 2 in. long by 1½ in. wide. 1683. (B.M. 181 as *Colutea frutescens.*) var. **microphyl'la,** *lflets.* smaller, glabrous above; *fl.* fewer. SYN. *S. microphylla*; **tomento'sa,** *lflets.* ½ in. long, obovate to roundish, silvery-white with down on both surfaces. SYN. *S. tomentosa.*

W. J. B.

Sutherlandii, in honour of Dr. Sutherland, Surveyor-General of Natal.

SUTTON'IA (in honour of the Rev. Dr. Sutton, English botanist, 1756–1846). FAM. *Myrsinaceae.* This genus is sometimes merged in Myrsine or Rapanea. If kept separate it includes 8 species in New Zealand and a few in New Hebrides. Flowers usually very small, often 1-sexual, parts in fours or fives, petals free to base; stigma subsessile. Fruit a 1-seeded drupe, sometimes dry. The following species usually require a cool greenhouse, but are hardy in Scilly, and *S. nummularia* in many less-favoured places. Easily cultivated.

S. austral'is. Mapou. Evergreen tree 10 to 20 ft., or a tall shrub; shoots red, dotted with pellucid glands. *l.* alternate, reddish-brown when young, oblong to ovate-oblong, 1 to 2 in. long, margins wavy, glabrous. *fl.* 1-sexual, white, about $\frac{1}{12}$ in. long, crowded in close clusters on the lower, leafless parts of the shoot, forming a cylindrical mass ½ in. across. *fr.* a rounded, black drupe ⅛ in. wide. New Zealand. SYN. *Myrsine Urvillei, Rapanea Urvillei.*

S. chatham'ica. Evergreen tree to 20 ft., young shoots covered with stiff hairs. *l.* alternate, obovate, entire, notched at apex, leathery, 1 to 2½ in. long, ¾ to 1½ in. wide, downy, only on midrib beneath, pale green, gland-dotted beneath; stalk about ⅛ in. long, *fl.* 1-sexual, about $\frac{1}{10}$ in. wide; pet. 4, ciliate, thickly dotted with reddish glands; clusters dense in l.-axils and on lower leafless part of shoot. *fr.* purplish, globose, about ⅓ in. wide. Chatham Is. 1910. SYN. *Rapanea Chathamica.*

S. nummular'ia. Prostrate evergreen shrub; shoots very slender, wiry, reddish-brown, slightly hairy. *l.* alternate, close, broadly ovate or roundish, 1/6 to 1/3 in. long, entire, sometimes notched at apex, dark green, glabrous, slightly wrinkled, dotted beneath with many translucent glands; stalk very short. *fl.* 1-sexual, 1/6 in. wide, yellowish-white, inconspicuous, singly or in twos or threes in l.-axils. *fr.* globose, blue-purple, about 1/5 in. wide. New Zealand. Rock-garden. Fairly hardy.

S. salici'na. Toro. Small tree; *l.* long, narrow, smooth, pale green. New Zealand. The least hardy of the species mentioned; a tree of tropical aspect, growing in more or less shade. SYN. *Myrsine salicina.*

S. Urvil'lei. A synonym of *S. australis.*

SUTURE. Line of junction of carpels, often well seen in the fruit, e.g. Pea, Plum.

SUWARROW NUT. *See* **Caryocar nuciferum.**

Suworowi, in honour of Herr J. P. von Suworow, Medical Inspector in Turkistan, *c.* 1886.

SWAINSO'NA (in honour of Isaac Swainson, 1746–1812, famous grower of plants at Twickenham at the end of the 18th century). FAM. *Leguminosae.* A genus of about 52 species of herbs or sub-shrubs, natives of Australia, one in New Zealand. Leaves unequally pinnate with numerous entire leaflets without stipels; stipules usually herbaceous, rarely bristly. Flowers papilionaceous, bluish-violet, purple, red, rarely white or yellow, in axillary, often stalked racemes; calyx teeth nearly equal or upper shorter; standard round or kidney-shaped, spreading or reflexed; wings oblong, falcate or slightly twisted, often shorter than the broad, incurved keel; bracts membranous, narrow or small. Pods ovoid or oblong, more or less inflated. Very ornamental greenhouse plants needing a compost of sandy loam and peat. Propagation by young cuttings in sand under a bell-glass or by seeds. A revision of the genus Swainsona by Alma T. Lee has been published in *Contrib. New South Wales Herb.* 1: 131–271 (1948).

KEY

1. *Standard with marked plate-like callosities above the claw*	2
1. *Standard without marked callosities above claw, though sometimes slightly ridged there*	4
2. *Keel straight. Style tip not hooked*	3
2. *Keel with a sideways twist at tip. Style tip hooked. Standard ridged rather than callose*	S. occidentalis
3. *Fl. about 1/2 in. long to tip of keel; cal. usually glabrous outside*	S. galegifolia
3. *Fl. about 7/10 in. long; cal. usually woolly outside*	S. Greyana
4. *Fl. about 1 1/4 in. long*	S. Macculochiana
4. *Fl. 3/5 to 4/5 in. long*	5
5. *Fl. about 4/5 in. long*	S. ecallosa
5. *Fl. about 3/5 in. long*	6
6. *Style curved but straight at tip, not hooked*	S. lessertifolia
6. *Style curved with hooked tip*	7
7. *Keel with a sideways twist at tip but pet. not thickened there*	S. occidentalis
7. *Keel not twisted but pet. with thickened tips*	S. canescens

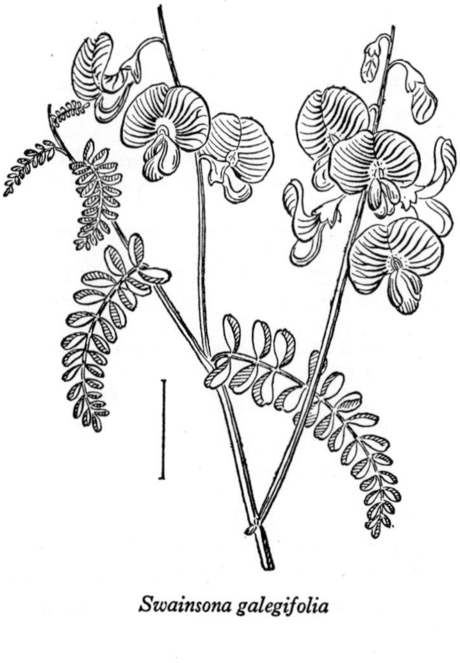

Swainsona galegifolia

S. canes'cens. 1 to 2 ft. h. with herbaceous branches from a woody stock. *lflets.* 9 to 15, obovate or oblong-elliptic, 1/2 to 1 in. long, obtuse or retuse, softly hairy on both sides but more glabrous above. *fl.* blue or violet-blue, variegated pink, with a green blotch at base of standard, nearly sessile; cal. silky-hairy; keel much curved; racemes many-fld., peduncles long, silky-hairy. 1839. W. Australia, S. Australia, Northern Territory. (Paxt. M.B. 7. 199.) SYN. *Cyclogyne canescens.*

S. coronillifo'lia. A form of *S. galegifolia* with light purplish-pink fl.

S. ecallo'sa. Perennial herb, 2 1/2 ft. h., somewhat hairy. *lflets.* 13 to 21, elliptic-oblong, 1/2 to 3/4 in. long, obtuse or emarginate. *fl.* purplish; standard with no callosities above claw. 1903. W. Australia.

S. galegifo'lia.* Glabrous perennial or sub-shrub with erect, flexuous branches about 1 ft. h., sometimes climbing to several feet. *lflets.* 11 to 21 or rarely more, oblong, 1/3 to 2/3 in. long, obtuse or emarginate. *fl.* rather large, orange-red in the type, but varying from 'blue or pink, through all shades of mauve to deep cyclamen-red, red, maroon, brownish-red and yellowish' on wild plants (according to A. T. Lee); standard with prominent callosities above claw; racemes pedunculate, longer than l. July. Queensland, New S. Wales. 1800. (B.M. 792 as *Colutea galegifolia*; B.M. 1725 as *S. coronillifolia.*) SYN. *S. Osbornii, Vicia galegifolia.* A variable plant. var. **albiflo'ra,** *fl.* white. (B.R. 994; L.B.C. 642.)

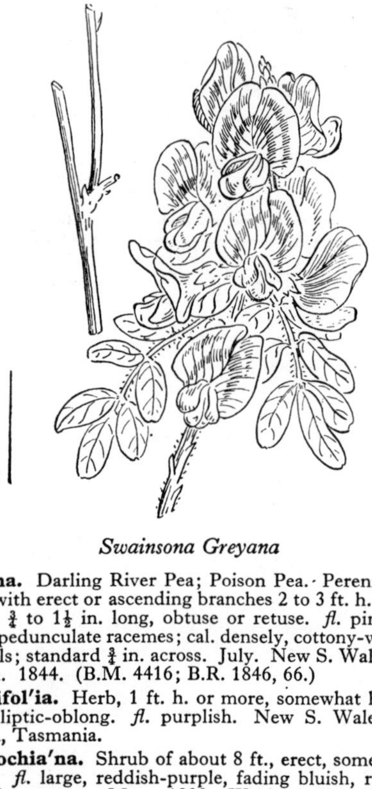

Swainsona Greyana

S. Greya'na. Darling River Pea; Poison Pea. Perennial herb or sub-shrub with erect or ascending branches 2 to 3 ft. h. *lflets.* 11 to 23, oblong, 3/4 to 1 1/2 in. long, obtuse or retuse. *fl.* pink, large, in long, erect, pedunculate racemes; cal. densely, cottony-white, longer than pedicels; standard 3/4 in. across. July. New S. Wales, Victoria, S. Australia. 1844. (B.M. 4416; B.R. 1846, 66.)

S. lessertiifol'ia. Herb, 1 ft. h. or more, somewhat hairy. *lflets.* 5 to 20, elliptic-oblong. *fl.* purplish. New S. Wales, Victoria, S. Australia, Tasmania.

S. Macculochia'na. Shrub of about 8 ft., erect, somewhat hairy. *lflets.* 27–9. *fl.* large, reddish-purple, fading bluish, rarely white, in many-fld. racemes. May. 1900. W. Australia. (B.M. 7995.) The showiest species introduced.

S. occidenta'lis. Perennial spreading sub-shrub 2 to 3 ft. h. *lflets.* 11 to 17, elliptic or oblong, narrowly ovate, 3/4 to 1 in. long. *fl.* violet, in long pedunculate racemes; cal. sparsely pubescent outside, hirsute inside; standard 1/2 in. across. 1863. W. Australia. (B.M. 5490.)

S. purpu'rea. A form of *S. galegifolia.*

S. splen'dens. A form of *S. galegifolia.*

W. T. S.

SWALLOW-WORT. *See* **Asclepias** and **Chelidonium majus.**

SWAMP CYPRESS. *See* **Taxodium distichum.**

SWAMP DOGWOOD. *See* **Ptelea trifoliata.**

SWAMP HICKORY. *See* **Carya aquatica.**

SWAMP LAUREL. *See* **Magnolia virginiana.**

SWAMP LILY, PERUVIAN. *See* **Zephyranthes candida.**

SWAMP LOCUST TREE. *See* **Gleditschia aquatica.**

SWAMP POST OAK. *See* **Quercus lyrata.**

SWAMP ROSE-MALLOW. *See* **Hibiscus Moscheutos.**

SWAMP SAXIFRAGE. *See* **Saxifraga pensylvanica.**

SWAMP WHITE OAK. *See* **Quercus bicolor.**

SWAN FLOWER. *See* **Aristolochia grandiflora.**

Swania'nus -a -um, in honour of J. M. Swan, A.R.A., 1847–1910, of Worcester and London.

SWAN NECK or **SWANWORT.** *See* **Cycnoches.**

SWAN RIVER DAISY. *See* **Brachycome iberidifolia.**

SWARM SPORES. Certain fungi of the Class Phycomycetes, e.g. Chytridiales and Peronosporales, produce spores in their sporangia in the form of microscopic pieces of protoplasm provided with threadlike projections called cilia. These are called swarm spores and by the movement of the cilia they are able to swim about in water. The result is that in damp conditions the fungus is able to spread rapidly. A good example of this may be seen in damping off caused by the fungus *Pythium de Baryanum* (*see* **Damping Off**).

D. E. G.

Swartzia'nus -a -um, in honour of Olof Peter Swartz, 1760–1818, Swedish botanist, Professor at Stockholm.

SWEDE. *See* Supplement.

SWEDE MIDGE, *Contarinia nasturtii*, is a Gall-midge which gives rise to a variety of symptoms on various Cruciferous crops, causing 'blindness' of the terminal bud often followed by the 'many-necked' condition in Swedes and Turnips, the absence of any inflorescence in Cauliflowers, 'curly' or 'crumpled leaf' disease, swollen flowers, distorted and swollen shoots and leaf-stalks, and decay of the underground portions of root crops. Serious outbreaks occur from time to time in the British Isles and in many European countries. The small midges appear in early June, when the eggs are laid in strings or clusters of 15 to 20 on the youngest portions of the food plants, on the flower-buds, and leaf-blades, but chiefly near the base of the leaf-stalks. The larvae emerge in 3 or 4 days, and feed on various parts of the plants which quickly react to the injury sustained. When fully fed, the pale yellow larvae 'jump' from the plant to the ground where pupation takes place in silken cocoons covered with particles of soil. Three or 4 generations occur in 1 year, the second and third in July and August being the peak period of attack. The larvae of the last generation overwinter in the soil, and pupation takes place in spring. Clean cultivation and judicious crop rotation aid considerably in reducing infestations of this Gall-midge by destroying weed hosts, removing crop remnants (e.g. Swede remains), and by forcing the midges to seek elsewhere for their host plants. It is advisable to lift and burn early in the season all young Brassicas, especially Cauliflowers, which are seen to have become 'blind'. Regular hoeing between crops will tend to dry out the surface layers of soil, thereby destroying the larvae, which are very susceptible to drought, as they are preparing to pupate. Early-sown crops are more susceptible to attack than later sowings. Weekly spraying with Nicotine-Soap wash or dusting with Nicotine dust are effective in checking attacks, but are restricted to small areas owing to the cost of material and labour. The wash or dust must be directed into the hearts of the plants to destroy the larvae.

G. F. W.

SWEDISH JUNIPER. *See* **Juniperus communis suecica.**

SWEDISH WHITEBEAM. *See* **Sorbus intermedia.**

SWEEPING. In the hands of a good workman the besom or birch broom is the best appliance for cleaning up fallen leaves on lawns or walks. The worker should always sweep in the same direction as the wind is blowing. The springbok lawn rake is useful for clearing leaves from lawns.

SWEET ACORN OAK. *See* **Quercus Ilex Ballota.**

SWEET ALMOND. *See* **Prunus communis dulcis.**

SWEET ALYSSUM. *See* **Lobularia maritima.**

SWEET AMBER. *See* **Hypericum Androsaemum.**

SWEET BALM. *See* **Melissa officinalis.**

SWEET BASIL. *See* **Basil, Sweet.**

SWEET BAY TREE. *See* **Laurus nobilis.**

SWEET BUCKEYE. *See* **Aesculus octandra.**

SWEET CALABASH. *See* **Passiflora maliformis.**

SWEET CASSAVA. *See* **Manihot dulcis Aipi.**

SWEET CHESTNUT. *See* **Castanea sativa.**

SWEET CICELY (*Myrrhis odorata*). A hardy perennial, native of S. Europe and found wild also in mountain pastures in the north of Great Britain. Its thick root was at one time boiled and eaten with vinegar and oil in salad, and its sweet-scented foliage was added to salads, while its seed has been used to scent oak floors and furniture in the north of England. The leaves have a strong flavour of anise and the plant is sometimes called Anise Chervil; Spanish Chervil, Giant Sweet Chervil, and Myrrh are other names by which it has been known. It is easily grown from seed sown in ordinary soil in autumn and may be propagated by division.

A→

SWEET FENNEL. *See* **Fennel, Foeniculum vulgare dulce.**

SWEET FLAG. *See* **Acorus Calamus.**

SWEET GALE. *See* **Myrica Gale.**

SWEET GUM. *See* **Liquidambar styraciflua.**

SWEET HERBS. Plants possessing an aromatic principle which renders them of value in flavouring soups, stews, dressings, salads, sauces, &c., and some part of which is used for this purpose. A special part of the kitchen garden is usually set aside for the cultivation of sweet herbs where the soil, while good, is not very rich, and where all the sunlight possible is available. The number of kinds of plants grown at present in gardens for this purpose is usually much smaller than of old, but notes on the following will be found in their alphabetical order. *Raised annually from seed*: Angelica, Anise, Basil, Borage, Caraway, Cayenne Pepper, Chervil, Clary, Coriander, Cumin, Dill, Marigold, Parsley, Peppers, Summer Savory.

Perennials increased by division or by cuttings: Balm, Bay, Burnet, Catmint, Chives, Fennel, Horehound, Hyssop, Lovage, Marjoram, Mint, Rosemary, Rue, Sage, Southernwood, Sweet Cicely, Tansy, Tarragon, Thyme, Winter Savory.

SWEET LIME. *See* **Citrus medica.**

SWEET MARJORAM. *See* **Origanum Majorana.**

SWEET MAUDLIN. *See* **Achillea Ageratum.**

SWEET NANCY. *See* **Achillea Ageratum.**

SWEET ORANGE. *See* **Citrus sinensis.**

SWEET PEA (*Lathyrus odoratus*) was introduced to England in 1699 when Father Cupani sent seeds from Italy to Dr. Uvedale at Enfield. The plant is a native of S. Italy and Sicily and was known to botanists before 1700, but there is no evidence that it was grown in gardens in this country till then. The flowers of these early plants were purple, pale purple and red, or white and red with hooded standards and close wings and keel, attractive by a certain grace of poise and by their perfume. Comparatively little change in type or range of colour occurred for a long time, but self-coloured forms were raised and in 1865 one was given an award by the Royal Horticultural Society under the name Scarlet Invincible, and between that date and 1870 only one other received an award. In 1870 Henry Eckford began to cross Sweet Peas, and others also were at work, but most of the 31 awards made between 1870 and 1900 went to varieties of his raising. There arrived forms with a much greater range of colour, with large flowers, and with erect standards, still with their old fragrance. These were known generally as Giant or Grandiflora varieties and they became generally and widely grown for both garden decoration and cutting. It was during this period that bunches of flowers in distinct colours—white, pink, carmine, mauve, and purple—first appeared in Covent Garden Market; before 1880 bunches of mixed colours were the vogue, and sweet peas were generally grown as mixtures. The year 1900 saw a new form of Sweet Pea introduced with standards so ample that, instead of being flat as in the Grandiflora types, they were waved and frilled at the edges. This was the shell-pink variety Countess Spencer raised and shown by Silas Cole, and in the same year the rather smaller and paler Gladys Unwin from W. J. Unwin. Both varieties traced back to the pale pink variety Prima Donna, Cole's after crossing, Unwin's without. There is also evidence that the waved type occurred in other gardens out of Prima Donna. Countess Spencer did not prove to be fixed but Gladys Unwin bred true, and out of those two as a basis a whole range of colour-varieties with waved standards was raised, and a great impetus to the cultivation and raising of new varieties in Britain and America resulted. The years 1901–20 saw 92 new varieties receive awards and numbers of new varieties continue to appear—indeed the names given to varieties run into thousands. Variations in colouring, though neither true blue nor yellow have yet been achieved, but nearly everything else, size, degree of waviness and frilling, doubling of the standard, length of stalk, looseness or closeness of flowers as well as number in the raceme have all occurred, and certainly a clarity of colouring has been secured not seen in the early varieties. Fragrance is still an attribute of the modern Sweet Pea though it is perhaps less heavy than in the old hooded types, but there are complaints of a greater tenderness, a greater risk of mortality when the seedlings are exposed to frost. Whether this is due to a change in the constitution of the plants or to new methods of cultivation is not clear. In any case the waved forms have almost entirely ousted the hooded and grandiflora types from gardens of present time.

Sweet Peas will grow in most types of soil and in most districts, but give their best results in districts of mild sunshine, not objecting to partial shade, a moist atmosphere, and moist but well-drained soil. Deep cultivation and rich soil with plenty of decayed organic matter in it suit them well, but the practice of making deep but narrow trenches of well-dug soil and manure sandwiches does not conduce to the best results: the one often results in the rooting area becoming a sump for surplus water, the other in a poor distribution of roots.

Sweet Peas may be grown for garden decoration either in clumps or in rows, and either sown in the open or raised in pots and planted out. The old style of growing was to sow in drills 2 or 3 in. deep in spring or in autumn in the same manner as culinary peas are sown, and this method is still sometimes adopted, 6 ft. or so being allowed between the rows and little regard being paid to the distance between the plants. Better plants, lasting much longer in flower and giving many more flowers, are to be had by sowing the seeds singly in 3-in. pots in late February or early March in frames and planted out as soon as large enough. Whether in rows or clumps ample room should be given, 10 to 12 in. at least between the plants and if the soil is in really good order, still more—some growers would say a yard was not too much. If growing in clumps is decided upon the clumps will naturally be proportioned in size to the borders, and the temptation to crowd the plant should be avoided here as well. A circular clump on a planting area of 5 ft. across will not need more than 25 plants and may well contain fewer. The plants should have small twiggy sticks put to them as soon as planted out and their main supports should be in place early and sufficiently tall to serve them through their life. Weeds should of course be rigorously suppressed and in dry spells a mulch of some kind will be found a great help. If watering is attempted it should be thorough, not mere driblets that damp the surface soil an inch or so down; they do more harm than good. The only other attention demanded is the prompt removal of spent flowers to prevent the formation of seeds. If this is attended to a good display of flowers may be expected for from 3 to 5 months, usually longer in the moister parts of England than in the drier south-east. The season of flowering may be prolonged if after good growth has been made and the plants begin to show signs of exhaustion they be cut back with the shears and topped to promote the production of fresh growths.

Sweet Peas may be grown in window-boxes, being sown thickly in the front and not staked. They droop over and flower freely if kept watered, but large flowers with long stalks are not to be expected by this method.

Sweet Peas may also be grown under glass for early flowering in April and May. The seed should be sown in September and the plants kept growing slowly, i.e. under quite cool conditions, until January, when they should be potted on and given a little heat. They may be planted out or grown on in 8 to 10-in. pots. At no time should they be forced, and except for sun-heat the temperature should not be above 50° F. There is a specially selected group of varieties for flowering in winter, but speaking generally the plants are not so vigorous nor are the flowers so large as in the normal types; they seem, however, to be more suited to warmer countries.

Still another system of growing has come into common use in recent years, suggested, it is said, by observation of the results following storm damage to plants which were left with only 1 or 2 stems. The seed is sown usually in autumn (a method adopted by some growers for preparing the plants grown in the normal way) in small pots or boxes in frames and given all the air possible. They are planted out as early in March as weather and soil will permit, a good tilth being obtained first, and if desired a fertilizer mixture incorporating at least 1 in 5 of sulphate of potash is raked or hoed in. The plants are put out in double rows 12 to 18 in. apart with 6 to 8 in. between the plants in the rows, the supports, in this instance 7 or 8 ft. bamboos or bean poles, being put in at the same time. The young plants are immediately tied to their support and after about 3 weeks the side growths made are removed leaving the strongest stem (or perhaps 2) to carry on. With the onset of warmer weather growth will be rapid and all side shoots must be removed as soon as large enough to handle and tendrils also should be cut off. The stem must be regularly tied and every care taken to preserve the foliage from harm. Spraying in dry weather when the sun is not on the foliage will be a help. Stronger and longer stems with larger flowers may be expected from this restricted growth than from branching plants if ground preparation has been done thoroughly and in good time. If growth goes on beyond the capacity of the support the plants may be loosed and the lower part carefully coiled so as not to break it and to bring the productive upper end into a position to be tied. It may be noted that a tendril-less Sweet Pea has recently been raised.

The colour classes of Sweet Peas may be arranged as follows:

BLUE-PURPLE SHADES: Lavender, pale blue, rosy-lavender, pale bluish bicolors, mauve, dark bicolors, dark blue, purple, blue-flaked, marbled blue. (True blue is not yet available.)

PINK SHADES: Pink on white ground, pink on cream ground, rose or cerise-shaded salmon on white ground, salmon-cerise or rose-salmon on cream, carmine-rose on white ground, pink or cerise-shaded salmon on cream ground, pink picotees on white ground, pink picotees on cream ground, flaked pink on white ground, marbled carmine on cream ground, deep pink on white ground, deep pink on cream ground, pink bicolors.

ORANGE AND RED: Orange-pink, salmon, orange, orange-scarlet, cerise, deep cherry-cerise, cerise-toned orange-scarlet, cerise-scarlet, scarlet.

WHITE: ivory, pure white.

A dwarf race which does not climb, called Cupid Sweet Peas, has been raised and several colour forms have been produced. These are good in pots and suitable for edging beds.

Sweet Peas are pollinated before the flowers open and are therefore little likely to be crossed by insect agency. If therefore crossing is attempted it must be done just before the flower opens. By breeding from a selected individual, collecting and keeping and sowing the seed from each plant raised from that individual a pure-breeding strain can usually be secured, and once secured it is little likely to vary. Seed is usually set freely in dry summer weather, but in wet weather little is to be expected. Mr. E. R. Janes, who has an excellent paper on modern Sweet Peas in *Journal R.H.S.* 73, p. 95, reports that in some modern varieties individual plants fail entirely to set seed.

For varieties *see* Supplement.

DISEASES. Sweet Peas are subject to many root diseases, e.g. Foot Rot (due to Fusarium), Black Root Rot (*Thielaviopsis basicola*), Wilt (*Verticillium* sp.), Root Rot (*Aphanomyces euteiches*), and various Damping-off troubles due to Pythium and Phytophthora, all of these being encouraged by wet heavy soil conditions either in the compost used in pots or in the soil of the open ground. When planting from pots any plant showing browning of roots and having a scanty root system with few nodules should be discarded. Plants may sometimes be attacked by *Bacterium fascians*, causing Leafy Gall. On the foliage there may occur Downy Mildew, *Peronospora viciae*, or Powdery Mildew, *Erysiphe polygoni*, which may require spraying with Bordeaux mixture or dusting with sulphur (*see* **Powdery and Downy Mildews**). On the leaves of indoor plants White Mould, *Cladosporium album*, may appear, and this requires treatment similar to that for mildews. A virus disease of the mosaic type may appear on the leaves as white to yellow spots and blotches with some distortion of the shoots, and these plants must be destroyed. Another virus is the one called Streak which causes brown to black stripes and streaks on the stems and spots on the leaves, and in these the most severely affected plants should be pulled out and the others watered with a solution of potash fertilizer in water, 1 oz. to 2 gall. Potash should always be included in the soil of the Sweet Pea trench because it is plants which are soft owing to excessive feeding with nitrogen which are particularly liable to Streak disease.

SWEET PISHAMIN. *See* **Carpodinus.**

SWEET POTATO. *See* **Ipomoea Batatas.**

SWEET SCABIOUS. *See* **Scabiosa atropurpurea.**

SWEET-SCENTED CRAB. *See* **Malus coronaria.**

SWEET-SCENTED VERBENA. *See* **Lippia citriodora.**

SWEET SOP. *See* **Annona squamosa.**

SWEET SULTAN. *See* **Centaurea moschata.**

SWEET WILLIAM (*Dianthus barbatus*) has long been grown in British gardens and valued there because of the heartiness of its behaviour, the diversity of colouring in its flowers, the long season over which they are produced, and the sweetness of their perfume, a combination of qualities sufficient to recommend any plant to gardeners who do not value novelty above everything. So well known has it been for centuries that in many books on flower-growing it has been passed over as too well known to need comment, and it never became a florist's flower as did its relatives the Carnation and the Pink, but it has, nevertheless, been a favourite in the gardens of those who delight in simple beauty all along. It is a native of S. Europe and was certainly introduced into English gardens by 1575 and probably earlier. The wild plant has light- or dark-red flowers often striped and with white spots, but in cultivation much variation of colouring has arisen. There are white, light and dark violet, the former sometimes referred to as blue, light and dark red, from pink to blackish-red, the flowers may be striped (var. **striatus**) and there may be red, pink and white, and parti-coloured flowers in the same inflorescence (var. **mutabilis**); a special race is that known as Auricula-eyed (var. **auriculiflorus**), where the flowers have a white or pale centre and a wide rim of colour stretching out to the toothed margin of the petals. Where colour schemes are wanted the true-breeding strains of red (Scarlet Beauty), pink (Pink Beauty) and white can be relied upon, but the plants of mixed colouring are excellent in early summer if well grown. It is perhaps in the fixing of the Scarlet and Pink Strains that the greatest advance has been made in relatively modern times. Double strains are also offered, but they cannot be relied upon to come true, though a proportion of the seedlings will be double, and they are best propagated by cuttings or layers in the same way as Border Carnations. Raising from seed is the common practice where singles are concerned. The double strains are on the whole less pleasing than the single.

Though a perennial, the Sweet William is best treated as a biennial. It produces seed very freely and if permitted will reproduce itself freely in the open, being quite hardy. The best results, however, are obtained by sowing the seed in cold frames or boxes in May, pricking the seedlings out into nursery beds as soon as large enough, giving at least 5 or 6 in. between the plants, and planting in their flowering quarters in autumn. They grow in almost any soil but live longest in good health in rich, well-drained, loamy soil in a sunny place. In partial shade they are apt to become straggly. The best cuttings are those of half-ripe shoots in July, or divisions may be made in September, but except for very special plants seedlings give the best results. A strain has been developed and is offered under the name of Annual Sweet Williams which flower in the year of sowing the seed.

Dianthus barbatus has hybridized in gardens and in nature with several other species of Dianthus. The first recorded hybrid (in 1718) was Fairchild's Sweet William, probably *D. barbatus* × Carnation or Pink, and this was followed by several other hybrids between the Sweet William and Border Carnations made on the Continent and in England, the best known at the present day being probably Napoleon III. These hybrids and others raised from time to time are sterile and must be propagated vegetatively. There are records of hybrids between the Sweet William and *D. arenarius*, *D. Armeria*, *D. Carthusianorum*, *D. Caryophyllus*, *D. chinensis*, *D. collinus*, *D. deltoides*, *D. diutinus*, *D. japonicus*, *D. monspessulanus*, *D. prolifer*, *D. pulchellus*, and *D. superbus*.

In 1920 Messrs. Allwood of Wivelsfield raised and in 1929 introduced a race of hybrids between *D. barbatus* and their hybrid pinks, *Dianthus* × *Allwoodii*, under the name Sweet Wivelsfield. These proved fertile and moreover easy to grow and with a long flowering season. They have the foliage and habit of the Sweet William but a looser inflorescence with larger flowers; they vary in colour and markings as does the Sweet William. Sown in gentle heat in mid-March and grown on in the greenhouse with plenty of air and a temperature not over 50° F. they can be planted out in their flowering quarters in a sunny place in well-drained soil where they will flower until hard frost occurs. They may also be sown outdoors in April. Sown in September singly in 3-in. pots under glass and moved on into 6-in. pots they make good pot-plants for spring and early summer flowering under glass. Double varieties, also fertile, have been raised. The plants are more or less perennial but are best raised annually from seed.

Sweet Williams may suffer from Leafy Gall, q.v. The foliage may suffer in wet seasons from *Botrytis cinerea*, the Grey Mould fungus (q.v.), and from the more serious Rust caused by *Puccinia lychnidearum* which causes brown pustules on the leaves. Badly affected leaves should be removed and the plants sprayed with Bordeaux mixture in spring, while every effort is made to encourage them to grow by good cultivation. There are several leaf spots due to fungi, such as Phomopsis, *Gloeosporium dianthi*, &c., but the most serious is Ring Spot, due to *Heterosporium echinulatum*, which forms pale spots and sometimes causes shot-holing. The control is as for Rust mentioned above.

(D. E. G.)

SWEETBRIER. *See* **Rosa Eglanteria.**

SWEET WILLOW. *See* **Myrica Gale.**

Sweginzow'ii, in honour of Nicolas A. Zvegintzov (or Sweginzow), 1848–1920, from 1905 to 1914 Russian governor of Latvia (Livland), who encouraged a local Riga landowner, Maximilian von Sievers, to found the Römersdorf nursery for trees and shrubs.

SWERT'IA (in honour of Iman. Swert, of Haarlem, author of *Florilegium*, 1620). FAM. *Gentianaceae*. A genus of over 200 species of annual or perennial herbs chiefly natives of India, China, Japan, and America, with outliers in Europe, N. and S. Africa, and Trop. America. Leaves opposite and stalked, the topmost often alternate and sessile. Flowers blue, purplish, or greenish-yellow to white, in cymes or panicles, often forming dense spike-like inflorescences; parts in fours or fives; corolla rotate with a very short tube, the stamens attached to its base. The following species are perennial unless otherwise noted and are hardy or need a cool greenhouse. Very few species are of garden value, the following being the best. The hardier species may be raised from seed in a cold frame or house, the seedlings being transplanted to their permanent quarters as soon as large enough and with as little root disturbance as possible. Several of the perennial species may be increased by division.

S. ala'ta. Annual, branched, stem 1 to 2 ft. h., winged or angled. *l.* ovate, 1½ to 2 in. long. *fl.* in panicles, lurid green-yellow dotted and veined purple; cal. lobes 4, ¼ in. long; cor. lobes 4, often shorter than cal. lobes, one gland to each lobe, fringed. September. Himalaya. (B.M. 5687 as *Ophelia alata.*)

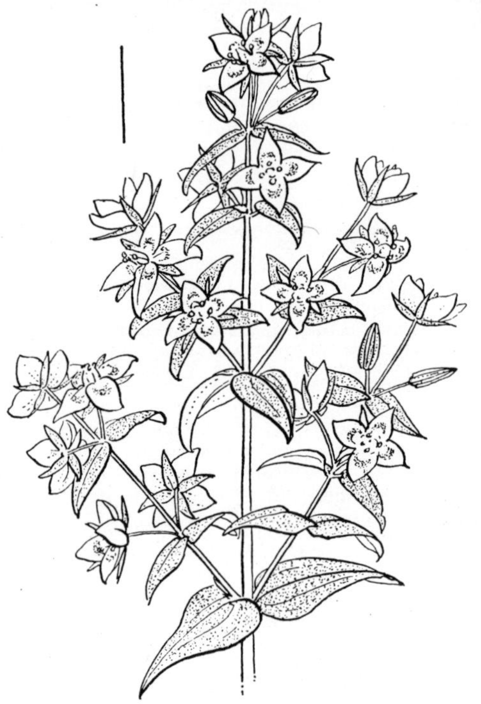

Swertia alata

S. alpes'tris. Erect, 4 to 9 in. h., unbranched. *Basal l.* broad-ovate to round, 2 to 4 in. long, long-stalked. *fl.* in raceme-like spikes, greenish-yellow; cal. lobes 4 or 5, lanceolate, ¼ in. long; cor. lobes 4 or 5, greenish-yellow, narrow-ovate, ½ in. long, 2 glands to each lobe. August, September. Europe. Asia.

S. atroviola'cea. Erect, 6 to 12 in. h. *Basal l.* broad-ovate to spatulate, 2 to 4 in. long, long-stalked; *stem-l.* ovate, sessile. *fl.* in panicles, deep purple-maroon, green within; cal. lobes 5, ovate-lanceolate, ½ to ⅓ in. long; cor. lobes 5, narrow-ovate, ½ to ¾ in. long, 2 glands to each lobe, long-fringed. August. China.

S. bel'la. Annual, stem erect, branched, slender, 4 to 12 in. h. *l.* ovate to broad-ovate, ½ to 1 in. long, thick, sessile or subsessile. *fl.* in panicles, purplish-blue; cal. lobes 5, narrow-ovate, blunt, ¼ in. long; cor. lobes 5, oblong to obovate, ¾ to 1 in. long, one gland to each lobe, fringed. August. China.

S. bimacula'ta. Annual, much branched, 2 to 6 ft. h. *l.* ovate, narrowed at base, 3 to 6 in. long. *fl.* whitish or yellowish, spotted black on upper half, numerous, in corymbs; cor. lobes 4 or 5, ⅓ to ½ in. long, broadly elliptic, pits not depressed; cal. lobes 4 or 5, ¼ in. long, elliptic. September. Himalaya. (M.F.J. 246.) SYN. *Ophelia bimaculata.*

S. caeru'lea. Erect, 6 to 8 in. h., the fl. in a dense terminal panicle. *Basal l.* spatulate, up to 3 in. long; *stem-l.* oblong, 1 to 1½ in. long, sessile. *fl.* bluish, veined green; cor. lobes 5, ⅓ to ¾ in. long, ovate, acute, glands with fimbriate scales; cal. lobes 5, ⅓ to ½ in. long, narrow-lanceolate. September. Himalaya.

S. calici'na. Erect, 5 to 18 in. h., little branched. *Basal l.* narrow-oblong to spatulate; *stem-l.* ovate-oblong, sessile or nearly so. *fl.* panicled, whitish to pale yellow, veined purple; cal. lobes 5, narrow-ovate to oblong, ¾ to 1 in. long; cor. lobes 5, about as long as cal. lobes, 2 glands to each lobe, long-fringed. September. China.

S. chinen'sis. Annual, erect. *l.* lanceolate, 1 to 4 in. long. *fl.* in dense spreading panicles, yellow with a purplish base; cal. lobes 5, narrow-ovate to lanceolate, ½ to ¾ in. long; cor. lobes 5, as long as cal. lobes, ovate, glands long-fringed. September. China.

S. Chira'ta. Annual, branched, 2 to 5 ft. h., stem stout. *l.* narrow-ovate to ovate, 1½ to 6 in. long, lowest stalked. *fl.* in panicles, greenish-yellow, tinged purple; cal. lobes 4, lanceolate, ⅓ in. long; cor. lobes 4, ovate, ¾ in. long, 2 glands to each lobe, fringed with long hair. September, October. Himalaya.

S. corda'ta. Annual, much branched, 9 to 30 in. long. *l.* broad-ovate, 1 to 1½ in. long, often rounded at base, sessile. *fl.* whitish to cream, veined purplish, in panicles; cor. lobes 4 or 5, ¼ to ⅓ in. long, elliptic to oblong; cal. lobes 4 or 5, ⅓ in. long, ovate-lanceolate, acute. September. Himalaya. SYN. *Ophelia cordata, O. nuda.*

S. corymbo'sa. Erect, 6 to 18 in. h., stem 4-winged, topped by a flat corymb. *Basal l.* obovate to spatulate, ¾ to 1¼ in. long, blunt; *stem-l.* ovate to oblong, sessile. *fl.* white or pale blue, veined blue; cor. lobes 4, ⅓ in. long, broad-oblong with short point, glands hairy at margin; cal. lobes 4, ¼ in. long, narrow-lanceolate. September. Himalaya. 1836. (B.M. 4489 as *Ophelia corymbosa.*)

S. de'cora. Annual, erect, 4 to 16 in. h., branched from base. *Basal l.* oblong to obovate, 1 to 2 in. long; *stem-l.* shorter and narrower. *fl.* in panicles, violet-blue; cal. lobes 5, linear, ½ to ¾ in. long; cor. lobes 5, rather longer than cal., lanceolate to ovate-lanceolate, 2 glands to each lobe, fringed. September. China.

S. Delavay'i. Annual, erect, 6 to 15 in. h., branched. *l.* narrow-ovate to lanceolate, 1 to 2 in. long. *fl.* in spreading panicles, pale purplish-blue; cal. lobes 5, broad-ovate, ½ to ¾ in. long; cor. lobes 5, rather shorter, narrow-ovate, 2 glands to each lobe, shortly fringed. September, October. China.

S. dilata'ta. Annual, much branched. *l.* lanceolate. *fl.* greenish-yellow, banded purplish near base; cor. lobes 4 or 5, under ½ in. long, gland horseshoe-shaped; cal. lobes 4 or 5, ½ in. long, narrow-elliptic to elliptic with slender point. September. Himalaya.

S. ela'ta. Erect, 2 to 2½ ft. h. *Basal l.* narrow-ovate to spatulate, 6 to 9 in. long, long-stalked; *stem-l.* short-ovate. *fl.* in close panicles, pale blue, much-spotted green; cal. lobes 5, lanceolate, ¼ in. long; cor. lobes 5, broad-ovate, ½ in. long, 2 glands to each lobe, heavily fringed. September. China.

S. Handelia'na. Tufted, 1 to 2 in. h. *Basal l.* round to kidney-shaped, ½ to 1 in. long, stalked. *fl.* solitary, terminal; pale purple-blue; cal. lobes 5, ovate, under ¾ in. long; cor. lobes 5, ovate to round, ¼ to ⅓ in. long. September. China. SE. Tibet.

S. Hook'eri. Stout, 2 to 4 ft. h. *Basal l.* spatulate, 4 to 9 in. long; *stem-l.* elliptic, narrowed to both ends, 3 in. long, nearly sessile. *fl.* purplish, veined blue, cor. lobes 4, ¾ in. long, broadly ovate to roundish, blunt, glands deep, not fringed; cal. lobes 4, ¼ in. long, ovate, rather acute. September. Himalaya.

S. King'ii. Stout, 2 ft. h. including the dense fl.-spike. *Basal l.* elliptic, 3 to 12 in. long, narrowed to a broad stalk; *stem-l.* oblong to oblong-ovate, up to 5 in. long. *fl.* greenish-white; cor. lobes 5, 1 in. long, oblong, blunt, 2 glands to each lobe with fringe of long hairs; cal. lobes 5, ⅔ in. long, broadly lanceolate. August, September. Himalaya. (H.I.P. 1442.)

S. margina'ta. Erect, 12 to 15 in. h., branched. *Basal l.* ovate to oblong, 4 to 6 in. long, long-stalked. *fl.* in panicles, green, margined yellow; cal. lobes 5, lanceolate, ¼ to ⅓ in. long; cor. lobes elliptic, ½ to ¾ in. long. July, August. N. Asia.

S. multicau'lis.* Much branched from base, 2 to 6 in. h. *Basal l.* narrow-spatulate to oblong, 1 to 4 in. long; *stem-l.* narrow and shorter. *fl.* deep blue in compound cymes; cor. lobes 5, ½ in. long, oblong, glands fringed; cal. lobes 5, ¼ to ⅓ in. long, narrow-oblong. August, September. Himalaya.

S. obtu'sa. A synonym of *S. perennis.*

S. palus'tris. Erect, stem 6 to 18 in. h., slender. *Basal l.* oblong to oblanceolate, 4 to 6 in. long, long-stalked; *stem-l.* much shorter, sessile. *fl.* in panicles, deep to purple-blue; cal. lobes 5, narrow-ovate, ⅓ in. long; cor. lobes 5, oblong, ½ to ¾ in. long, 2 glands to each lobe, fringed. August. N. America.

S. panicula'ta. Annual, erect, 1 to 3 ft. h., much branched. *l.* oblong to lanceolate, 1½ to 2 in. long. *fl.* in panicles, white, spotted purple at base; cal. lobes 5, oblong, ⅙ to ⅓ in. long; cor. lobes ovate, ¾ in. long, one gland to each lobe. September. Himalaya. (B.M. 5687 as *Ophelia paniculata.*)

S. peren'nis. Erect, 6 to 12 in. h. *Lower l.* broadly ovate to round, 2 to 6 in. long with long stalks; *stem-l.* broadly ovate to ovate, narrowing in upper part of stem. *fl.* pale slate-blue; cor. lobes 5, ½ to ¾ in. long, ovate; cal. lobes 5, ⅓ to ½ in. long, narrow-ovate to lanceolate. August, September. North temperate regions. SYN. *S. obtusa.*

S. petiola'ta. Stem stout, hollow, erect, 1 to 3 ft. h. *Basal l.* oblong, up to 3½ in. long; *stem-l.* narrower; all sessile. *fl.* whitish, veined blue-green, 3 to 5 together in panicles; cor. lobes 5, ⅜ in. long, narrow-ovate, acute, sometimes toothed; glands 2 to each lobe, yellow, tipped green, fringed; cal. lobes 5, ⅓ to ½ in. long, lanceolate, acute. September. Himalaya.

S. pubes'cens. Annual, erect, 1 to 2 ft. h., branched. *l.* narrow-lanceolate to linear, 1 to 2 in. long. *fl.* in panicles, whitish, purple at base; cal. lobes 5, unequal, ovate to ovate-lanceolate, ¼ to ¾ in. long; cor. lobes 5, ovate, shorter than cal. lobes, one gland to each at base. September. China.

S. puncta'ta. Stems erect, 6 to 12 in. h., branched. *Basal l.* broad-ovate to round, 4 to 6 in. long, long-stalked; *stem-l.* narrower and shorter. *fl.* in panicles, greenish-yellow; cal. lobes 5, lanceolate, ⅓ in. long; cor. lobes 5, narrow-ovate, ½ to ¾ in. long, 2 glands to each lobe. September. Europe and Caucasus.

S. purpuras'cens. Annual, much branched, 6 in. to 3 ft. h. *l.* oblong to lanceolate, 1½ to 2½ in. long, narrowed to base, lower blunt, upper acute. *fl.* purple to reddish-purple, numerous, in panicles; cor. lobes 4 or 5, reflexed, ¼ in. long, ovate, acute, pits horseshoe-shaped, not fringed; cal. lobes 4 or 5, ⅓ in. long, oblong. September. Himalaya. SYN. *Ophelia purpurascens.*

S. specio'sa. Stem erect, hollow, 1½ to 4 ft. h., little branches, fl. in a close panicle. *Basal l.* broad-ovate, 2 to 5 in. long, long-stalked; *stem-l.* elliptic, slender-pointed. *fl.* yellowish-green; cor. lobes 5, ¾ in. long, oblong to spatulate with a short point, 2 glands to each lobe, fringed; cal. lobes 5, ⅓ to ½ in. long, ovate, acute, toothed, overlapping. Himalaya.

S. tetrago'na. Annual, erect, 6 to 24 in. h., branched. *l.* lanceolate to linear, ¾ to 1 in. long. *fl.* in panicles, nearly white; cal. lobes 5, lanceolate, about ½ in. long; cor. lobes 5, ¾ in. long; 2 glands to each lobe. September. Himalaya.

S. Thomson'ii. Annual, erect, stem hollow, not spreading. *Lower l.* stalked; *upper* oblong to elliptic. *fl.* in panicles, blue-grey; cal. lobes 5, lanceolate, ¼ in. long; cor. lobes 5, oblong to ovate, ⅓ in. long, 2 glands to each lobe. Himalaya.

S. tibet'ica. 2 to 3 ft. h., stem erect, stout. *Basal l.* 6 to 8 in. long, long-stalked; *stem-l.* broader. *fl.* solitary, yellowish-white with pale-blue base, peduncle long; cal. lobes 5, ovate, ¾ in. long; cor. lobes 5, broad-ovate, 2 glands to each lobe. August, September. E. Tibet, China.

S. Ward'ii. 12 to 16 in. h., stem stout, erect. *Basal l.* oblong, 2 to 5 in. long; *stem-l.* narrow-oblong. *fl.* solitary or in pairs, slaty-grey, peduncle long; cal. lobes 5, ovate to lanceolate, about ⅓ in. long; cor. lobes 5, oblong, ¾ to 1 in. long, gland fringed. SE. Tibet, China.

D. W.

SWIETE'NIA (in honour of Gerard von Swieten, 1700–72, Dutch botanist and author). FAM. *Meliaceae.* A genus of a single species of tall tree, native of Cent. America and the W. Indies. It has brownish-red wood, well known as Mahogany. *S. Mahagoni* grows well in a compost of sand and loam. It may be propagated by ripe cuttings with leaves intact in a close frame in heat. Stove conditions are necessary. **A**

S. Maha'goni. Mahogany Tree. Tree of about 70 ft. with glabrous, equally pinnate l. *lflets.* opposite, oblique, ovate, long-pointed, stalked. *fl.* reddish-yellow, small, in axillary panicles; cal. 5-cleft; pet. 5, overlapping. May. 1734.

SWIFT MOTH, *Hepialus* species. The caterpillars of 2 species, the Garden Swift (*H. lupulinus*) and the Ghost Swift (*H. humuli*), are destructive to a great variety of plants. The white, active, shiny caterpillars live in the soil and feed indiscriminately upon roots of grasses, weeds (Dandelion and Docks), vegetables, Strawberry and herbaceous plants, and tunnel into bulbs (Narcissus), corms (Gladiolus), tubers (Dahlia, Paeony, and Potato), and rhizomes (Bearded Iris). The Garden Swift Moth is more common and destructive in gardens than the Ghost Swift. The moths, which fly at dusk during June and July, are smaller than those of the Ghost Swift and have a wing expanse of 1 in. The fore-wings are yellowish-brown with white markings, and the hind-wings are greyish. The white caterpillars have a reddish-brown head, and tend to wriggle backwards when handled or disturbed. They may live for 2 years in the ground before they pupate, the pupae being somewhat active, brown, and armed with small spines which aid them to move upwards through the soil prior to the emergence of the moths.

The female Ghost Swift Moth has a wing expanse of 2½ in., the wings being yellowish with brick-red markings, the male is smaller and has silvery or greyish-white wings, which give the insect a ghost-like appearance when flying. These moths appear about the same time as the Garden Swift, and their eggs are dropped singly over grass and other herbage during flight. The caterpillars closely resemble those of the last species, and the life-cycle is similar. Mummified caterpillars of both moths are commonly found in the soil, the blackened and stiffened larvae having been destroyed by parasitic fungi. Cultural methods will tend to reduce their numbers, and regular hoeing and light forking of infested soil result both in the exposure of the caterpillars to the attacks of insectivorous birds and to mechanical injury inflicted by the hoe-blade. Newly broken grass- and waste-land should not be planted with susceptible crops, e.g. Strawberry, until a season has been devoted to thorough cleansing of the ground by cultivation, which

will destroy coarse-rooted weeds, e.g. Docks. Where the caterpillars abound in gardens, it is advisable to lift and replant bulbous, tuberous, and herbaceous plants annually, and to collect the grubs from the roots and rootstocks. The larvae of these moths are rather susceptible to Naphthalene, which should be applied in the form of Flake or Whizzed Naphthalene at the rate of 2 to 3 oz. to the square yard, and forked, hoed, or watered in. **A**
G. F. W.

Swinhoe'i, in honour of Robert Swinhoe, 1836–77, Consul in China, ornithologist and plant-collector.
A→

SWISS STONE PINE. *See* **Pinus Cembra.**

SWORD FERN. *See* **Polypodium duale.**

SWORD LILY. *See* **Gladiolus.**

SYAG'RUS (Greek *syagros*, wild boar; name of a kind of date-palm mentioned by Pliny, transferred to this American genus by Martius). FAM. *Palmaceae.* A genus of about 12 species of Palms closely related to Cocos and sometimes included in it. Unarmed Palms, natives of S. America, with a terminal crown of pinnatisect leaves. Flower-spike enclosed in a double spathe. Shell of fruit hard and bony with a fibrous rind, with a broad smooth band or channel running from each of the 3 pores and meeting at the top. Seed oily, sometimes hollow. For treatment of these stove Palms *see* **Cocos.** **A**

S. ama'ra. A synonym of *Rhyticocos amara.*

S. botryopho'ra. A synonym of *Arecastrum Romanzoffianum botryophorum.*

S. campes'tris.* Trunk swollen at base. *l.* spreading, 2 to 6 ft. long or more; pinnae 1½ to 2 ft. long, not over ½ in. wide; stalks broadly sheathing, very thick, edges clothed with woody, brown fibres, a few stout, dark reddish-brown spines on naked part. *Spadix* 1½ ft. long, spreading when in flower, nodding in fruit; spadix as long as spathe. Brazil.

S. coccoi'des. Trunk 8 to 10 ft. long, 2 to 3 in. thick. *l.* 4 to 6 ft. long, rather loose, arching; pinnae linear, narrow, slightly curled, 9 to 12 in. long, glabrous. *fl.* yellowish-white, rather larger. *Spadix* slightly branched, 1½ ft. long, drooping, 2 ft. long when in fruit; outer spathes 1 ft. long, obtuse, boat-shaped, reddish-brown hairy outside; inner spathe with peduncle about 18 in. long. Brazil. 1823.

S. como'sa. Trunk 10 ft. h., or somewhat more, ringed below. *l.* 3 to 4 ft. long, spreading; pinnae erect, close, lanceolate. *Spadix* 1 ft. or more long, with 5 to many flexuous branches; spathe fusiform, sulcate. Brazil.

S. macrocar'pa. About 15 ft. h. *l.* 15 to 20 in a crowded head; segs. usually in threes or fours, crisped, spreading, lower 2 ft. long, about ⅝ in. wide, upper shorter. *Spadix* 16 in. long; spathe thick, woody, narrow fusiform. Brazil. SYN. *Cocos Procopiana.*

S. petrae'a. Usually almost stemless. *l.* few, slender, 1½ to 3 ft. long, or more with a short stalk; segs. grouped in twos or threes, solitary towards tip, linear, slender-pointed. *Spadix* usually about 1 ft. long rachis sometimes with 2 or 3 branches; lower spathe shortly 2-winged, upper woody, fusiform-rostrate. Brazil, Bolivia. 1889.

S. Weddelia'na.* Stem slender, clothed with netted black fibres. l. 1 to 4 ft. long, gracefully arched; pinnae long, narrow, arching, dark green above, glaucous beneath. S. America. Perhaps the most elegant small stove-palm. var. **Pynaert'ii,** pinnae rather broader and more closely spaced.

SYCAMINE TREE of the Bible. *See* **Mulberry,** *Morus alba* or *M. nigra.*

SYCAMORE. *See* **Acer Pseudoplatanus.**

SYCOMORE FIG-TREE of the Bible. *See* **Ficus Sycomorus.**

SYCOMOR'US ANTIQUOR'UM. *See* **Ficus Sycomorus.**
A→
A→

SYLVA or **SILVA.** The trees of a particular region.

sylvat'icus -a -um,* *sylves'tris -is -e, of a wood or forest; growing wild in contrast to a cultivated related species (often named *sativus*). The classical spelling (*silvaticus* and *silvestris*) is preferable to the medieval spelling (*sylvaticus* and *sylvestris*).

SYMBEGO'NIA (*sym*, united, *Begonia*, from the united perianth segments of the female flower). FAM. *Begoniaceae.* A genus of 4 species of herbs similar to Begonia, natives of New Guinea, but with the segments of the perianth of the female flowers united, of the male free. Treatment as for Begonia of the more tender species.

Symbegonia fulvo-villosa

S. ful'vo-villos'a. 5 to 8 in. h., branching. Stems crisply hairy, tinged red. *l.* lanceolate-oblong, oblique, about 2½ in. long, deeply, doubly toothed, shining green and finely spotted above, more or less tinged red, finely hairy on veins beneath, white spotted, stalk short. *fl.* 1-sexual, male, perianth segs. 2, free, stamens 12 to 20; female, pale yellow, bell-shaped, hairy, lobes 5, ovate, toothed, spreading, ovary inferior, winged, styles 3. New Guinea. 1908. (B.M. 8409.)

SYMBIOSIS, literally a living together, applied to the numerous instances where one organism lives in close company with another, each contributing something to the well-being, and often the survival, of the other. Examples of this are seen where fungi living in or on the root of a flowering plant collect some of the materials the latter wants and receive from it some it makes, *see* **Mycorrhiza, Leguminosae, nodules** (where bacteria are concerned). In Lichens the plant body is composed of both a fungus and green algae which, living in partnership, ensure the survival of both and the propagation of the combination. Symbiosis may also occur between insects and plants, as in the Myrmecophilous Plants (q.v.), in the Yucca where a particular moth alone pollinates the flower which then produces seeds, which in turn provide food for the caterpillars of the pollinating moth; even the relation between bees and other insects and flowers which results in pollination of the flowers and in providing food for the insects may be looked upon as a form of symbiosis, though in this instance the two participants live in different homes and do not actually feed at the same table.

symmetrical, regular in the number and form of its parts, as a flower having 5 sepals, 5 petals, 5, 10, or 15 stamens.

Sy'monsii, in honour of Rev. Jelinger Symons, 1778–1851, of Leyton and Radnage.

sympatric, inhabiting the same area.

sympetalous, gamopetalous, having the petals joined to one another.

SYMPHORICARP'OS (*symphoreo*, to bear together, *karpos*, fruit; the berries being clustered). St. Peter's wort, Snowberry. FAM. *Caprifoliaceae.* A genus of about 18 species of hardy shrubs, natives of N. America and W. China, allied to Lonicera, but fruit berry-like with 2 fertile cells each containing 1 ovule. The shrubs are small, deciduous, with opposite, short-stalked, usually entire but occasionally lobed, exstipulate leaves. Flowers small, white or pink, in terminal or axillary clusters; corolla 5- or 4-lobed, stamens 5 or 4, equal or nearly so growing on the corolla; ovary inferior. The plants thrive in ordinary soil and may be propagated by the suckers which are produced in great abundance. The flowers of some species, including the commonest, *S. rivularis*, are much visited by bees, and the fruits are eaten by game. The latest monograph is by G. N. Jones in the *Journal of the Arnold Arboretum*, 21, p. 201, from which the key and nomenclature following have been adapted.

KEY

1.	*Fr. blue-black; lvs. and shoots glabrous; fl.-spike terminal*	S. sinensis
1.	*Fr. red or white; fl. clusters mostly axillary*	2
2.	*Fl. shortly campanulate, cor. lobes as long as tube*	3
2.	*Fl. long campanulate or tubular funnel-shaped; cor. lobes shorter than tube*	8
3.	*Fr. white*	4
3.	*Fr. red; shrub erect, twigs hairy*	S. orbiculatus
4.	*Style and stamens not exserted*	5
4.	*Style and stamens shortly exserted*	S. occidentalis
5.	*Erect shrubs*	6
5.	*Low spreading or trailing shrubs*	7
6.	*Young twigs glabrous; bush of 3 to 8 ft.*	S. rivularis
6.	*Young twigs hairy; bush of 1 to 2½ ft.*	S. albus
7.	*Young twigs glabrous or with curved hairs*	S. mollis
7.	*Young twigs with spreading hairs*	S. acutus
8.	*Anthers at least as long as the cor. lobes*	S. microphyllus
8.	*Anthers shorter than the cor. lobes*	9
9.	*Young twigs glabrous*	S. oreophilus
9.	*Young twigs hairy*	S. rotundifolius

S. acu'tus. Low or trailing, young shoots and l. hairy. *l.* oval, $\frac{2}{5}$ to $1\frac{1}{5}$ in. long, usually sinuate, toothed or lobed. *fl.* pink, lobes about as long as tube. June, July. *fr.* $\frac{1}{6}$ to $\frac{1}{4}$ in. wide, in pairs or solitary. California, Oregon. 1888. SYN. *S. mollis acutus.*

S. al'bus. Erect, 1 to 2½ ft. h., young shoots with short curved hairs. *l.* ovate to nearly round, $\frac{2}{5}$ to $1\frac{1}{5}$ in. long, not mucronate, ciliate, usually entire, hairy at least on veins beneath. *fl.* pink, 1 to 5 in axillary clusters, lobes shorter than tube. July to September. *fr.* $\frac{1}{4}$ to $\frac{1}{3}$ in. wide, in pairs or solitary. Eastern N. America. Often confused with *S. rivularis.* (B.B. ed. 2, 3, 276 as *S. racemosus.*) SYN. *S. racemosus pauciflorus, S. albus pauciflorus.* var. **laeviga'tus,** a synonym of *S. rivularis.*

S. × Chenaul'tii (*S. microphyllus × S. orbiculatus*). Habit and l. characters of *S. microphyllus* but usually more hairy on lower surface of l., *fl.* clustered or in spikes, *fr.* bright purplish-red with light spots on exposed, and pinkish-white with purplish dots on shady, side. SYN. *S. parviflorus conglomeratus.*

S. glomera'tus. A synonym of *S. orbiculatus.*

S. Hey'eri. A synonym of *S. occidentalis.*

S. microphyl'lus. Erect, 5 to 8 ft. h., young shoots with curved hairs. *l.* ovate, acute, entire, ½ to 1 in. long, hairy at least on veins beneath. *fl.* pinkish, in pairs or solitary; axillary or in short terminal spikes, narrowly campanulate, lobes short. August. *fr.* translucent, about $\frac{1}{3}$ in. wide. Mexico. 1829. (B.M. 4975.) SYN. *S. montanus.*

S. mol'lis. Low, trailing, young shoots with short curved hairs, 1 to 3 ft. h. *l.* oval to round, $\frac{2}{5}$ to 1½ in. long, obtuse, more or less hairy, ciliate. *fl.* pink, in small axillary clusters, lobes as long as tube. April, May. *fr.* about $\frac{1}{5}$ in. wide. California. var. **mol'lis,** a synonym of *S. acutus.*

S. monta'nus. A synonym of *S. microphyllus.*

S. occidenta'lis. Erect, young shoots usually hairy. *l.* oval, 1 to 4 in. long, entire or on young shoots lobed, obtuse, apiculate, leathery, generally more or less hairy. *fl.* pale pink, campanulate, deeply lobed, many, in short, dense axillary and terminal spikes. June, July. *fr.* greenish-white, quickly discolouring, about ¼ in. wide. 1 to 3 ft. h. Western N. America. (B.B. ed. 2, 3, 277.) SYN. *S. Heyeri.*

S. orbicula'tus. Erect, young shoots hairy. *l.* ovate to nearly round, ½ to 2 in. long, thick, hairy at least beneath. *fl.* pinkish, broadly campanulate, lobes as long as tube, many in crowded axillary spikes. July to September. *fr.* coral red to pink or purplish, elliptical, $\frac{1}{6}$ in. wide. 2 to 6 ft. h. United States. 1730. (Add. 111; B.B. ed. 2, 277 as *S. Symphoricarpos.*) SYN. *S. vulgaris, S. rubra vulgaris.* var. **variega'tus,** *l.* green and yellow.

S. oreoph'ilus. Erect, shoots smooth. *l.* oval, glabrous, $\frac{2}{5}$ to 1 in. long, acute, sometimes toothed or lobed, petioles very short, enclosing the buds. *fl.* rose, in axillary pairs or in few-fld. terminal spikes, tubular-funnel-shaped, lobes short. *fr.* white, about $\frac{2}{5}$ in. long. 3 to 5 ft. h. W. United States.

S. parviflo'rus conglomera'tus. A synonym of *S.* × *Chenaultii.*

S. pauciflo'rus. A synonym of *S. albus.*

S. racemo'sus. A synonym of *S. albus, S. rivularis.* var. **laeviga'tus,** a synonym of *S. rivularis*; **pauciflo'rus,** a synonym of *S. albus.*

Symphoricarpos rivularis

S. rivula'ris.* Erect, young shoots glabrous. *l.* oval, about 1 in. long, glabrous or almost so, generally entire except on strong shoots. *fl.* pink to white, lobes equal to tube, in short terminal racemes. July to September. *fr.* white, ½ in. wide, usually abundant. 3 to 10 ft. h. N. America. 1817. (B.M. 2211; L.B.C. 230 as *Symphoria racemosa.*) SYN. *S. racemosus, S. racemosus vulgaris.* Naturalized in Britain. A variegated form (**variega'tus**) is known.

S. rotundifo'lius. Erect-straggling, young shoots with spreading hairs. *l.* nearly round, $\frac{2}{5}$ to 1¼ in. long, usually entire. *fl.* pale pink, tubular-funnel-shaped, lobes about one-fifth length of cor., sessile, axillary. August. *fr.* ¼ in. wide, white. 2 ft. h. SW. United States.

S. ru'bra vulgaris. A synonym of *S. orbiculatus.*

S. sinen'sis. Erect, young shoot smooth. *l.* oval, ¾ to 1 in. long, smooth, glaucous below. *fl.* white, campanulate, glabrous within and without, solitary, axillary. July. *fr.* bluish-black, about ¼ in. long, shortly beaked, seeds hairy, white. 3 to 5 ft. h. China. 1907.

S. vulga'ris. A synonym of *S. orbiculatus.*

SYMPHYAN'DRA (*symphio*, to grow together, *andros*, anther; the anthers being connate). FAM. *Campanulaceae.* A genus of about 7 species of perennial herbs, natives of the East, differing from Campanula by the connate anthers. Leaves broad, often heart-shaped, toothed; radical leaves long-stalked; stem-leaves few, alternate. Flowers white, yellow, or blue, often nodding, rather large, in racemes or loose panicles. Rich sandy loam with good drainage suits these plants, which can be increased by seed, by division of roots, or by young cuttings in spring. Hardy plants for the rock-garden or border.

S. arme'na. About 2 ft. h. *l.* ovate, acute, deeply toothed, velvety-hoary. *fl.* blue, terminal, solitary, erect; cal. hoary, lobes triangular; cor. tubular, velvety. June. Caucasus. 1836.

S. asiati'ca. Up to 2½ ft. h. *l.* ovate or ovate-lanceolate, up to 3 in. long, base variable, coarsely toothed, with a few white hairs above, glabrous beneath, stalk 1 in. or more long. *fl.* violet, nodding, in a loose infl., about 5-fld.; cor. bell-shaped, about $1\frac{3}{5}$ in. long, glabrous, lobes slightly spreading, about 1½ in. across. Summer. Korea. 1918. (B.M. 8837.) SYN. *Hanabusaya asiatica.*

S. Hofman'nii. 1 to 2 ft. h., softly hairy, more robust than *S. pendula.* *l.* lanceolate, acute, toothed. *fl.* white, nodding, 1 to 1½ in. long; cal. lobes ovate-lanceolate, acute, entire. Summer. Bosnia. 1884. (B.M. 7298.)

S. pen'dula. Pendulous, somewhat woody below, hairy, about 2 ft. h. *l.* ovate, acute, with roundish teeth, velvety. *fl.* cream, in a panicle; cal. lobes lanceolate; cor. funnel-shaped, velvety. Caucasus. 1823. (S.B.F.G. s. 2, 66.)

S. Wan'neri. Erect, to 6 in. h., stems terete, hairy, striped. *l.* lanceolate, unequally toothed, roughly hairy, lower stalked. *fl.* blue, on 1-fld. axillary or terminal peduncles; cor. tubular-bell-shaped. Alps of Europe. SYN. *Campanula Wanneri.*

SYMPHYOSTE′MON (*symphyo*, to unite, *stemon*, stamen; the filaments are connate at base into a cylindrical tube). FAM. *Iridaceae*. A genus of 2 or 3 species of herbs with fibrous roots, natives of extra-tropical S. America and the Andes. Leaves radical, linear, clustered. Flowers sometimes several in a spathe, pedicellate; perianth yellow, whitish or striped with purple, tube rather long, funnel-shaped, lobes nearly equal, erecto-patent; stamens affixed to throat. A compost of sandy loam and leaf-mould or peat suits these plants, which may be propagated by seeds or by offsets in spring.

Symphyandra asiatica (p. 2065)

S. narcissoi′des. 1 to 1½ ft. h. *l.* very narrow, awl-shaped at apex, glaucous, *fl.* dirty white, veined with brown-purple, very fragrant, nodding, funnel-shaped; pedicels short; spathe valves membranous at margin, lowermost more acute than others. South coast of S. America. 1828. (B.R. 1283 as *Sisyrinchium odoratissimum.*) Greenhouse.

S. Sege′this. Stem creeping. *l.* rush-like, 3 to 4 in. long. *fl.* blue, solitary, bases of segs. orange; spathe valves 2. Chile. (G.F. 1117 as *Susarium Segethi.*) Hardy. Curious and interesting.

SYMPHYSIS. Growing together.

SYMPHY′TUM (ancient Greek name used by Dioscorides; the plant was supposed to have the power to heal wounds). FAM. *Boraginaceae*. A genus of about 25 species of erect, sometimes tuberous-rooted herbs, natives of Europe and Western Asia. Leaves alternate, mostly radical; stem leaves at times decurrent; uppermost sometimes crowded and opposite. Flowers white, yellowish, blue or purple, stalked, in cymes or racemes; calyx 5-cleft or 5-parted; corolla broadly tubular, enlarged above, with 5 scales in the throat; lobes 5, very short and tooth-like or scarcely spreading; stamens 5, affixed at about middle of tube. Nutlets 4, smooth or granulated. Mostly showy plants, though at times rather coarse, growing well in almost any soil or situation, even under the shade of trees. They flower through the greater part of the summer. Propagated by seed or by division.

The only British species are *S. officinale*, which exists in both white- and purplish-flowered forms, and *S. tuberosum*, which has yellowish flowers. During the nineteenth century, blue-flowered Caucasian plants, identified as *S. asperum* and *S. peregrinum*, were introduced into cultivation and became naturalized, hybridizing with both forms of *S. officinale* and producing intermediate plants with blue or blue-tinged or purple flowers which have been named *S.* × *caeruleum*, *S.* × *densiflorum*, *S.* × *discolor*, and *S.* × *lilacinum*. There is some doubt as to whether the naturalized blue comfrey, known in Britain as *S. peregrinum*, is a species from the eastern Caucasus or a hybrid between *S. asperum* and *S. officinale*; in Sweden a plant believed to be of this parentage is known as *S.* × *uplandicum*. Although their origin and nomenclature may thus be controversial, the plants themselves are handsome and robust enough for a wild part of the garden.

They are sometimes infected by a fungus *Melampsorella Symphyti* which perennates in the rootstock and produces rusty patches on the leaves. A revision of the genus by Cedric Bucknall has been published in *Jour. Linn. Soc. Bot.* 41: 491–556 (1913).

KEY

1.	*Cor. scales protruding from cor. tube*	2
1.	*Cor. scales enclosed within cor. tube, not protruding*	3
2.	(1) *Stem much branched, many-fld.*	S. ottomanum
2.	*Stem not branched or only slightly branched, few-fld.*	S. bulbosum
3.	(1) *Cal. divided to or below the middle*	4
3.	*Cal. not divided to the middle*	13
4.	(3) *Fl. white or yellowish*	5
4.	*Fl. purplish, red, or blue*	10
5.	(4) *L.-base prolonged downwards on stem from node to node as flange. Stem much branched, 1½ to 4 ft. h.*	S. officinale
5.	*L.-base not markedly prolonged downwards on stem*	6
6.	(5) *Basal or lowermost lvs. cordate or rounded at base*	7
6.	*Basal or lowermost lvs. gradually narrowed at base*	9
7.	(6) *Stem much branched, many-fld.*	S. tauricum
7.	*Stem unbranched, few-fld.*	8
8.	(7) *Lvs. rough with short stiff hairs. Barren shoots decumbent*	S. grandiflorum
8.	*Lvs. almost glabrous. Barren shoots erect*	S. cordatum
9.	(6) *Stem* 8 *to* 20 *in. h.; stem-lvs.* 6 *to* 12, *oblong-lanceolate*	S. tuberosum
9.	*Stem* 6 *to* 12 *in. h., stem-lvs.* 3 *to* 6, *elliptic or ovate*	S. Leonhardtianum
10.	(4) *Fl. purplish or crimson*	11
10.	*Fl. rose in bud, then clear blue*	12
11.	(10) *Lvs. pilose with long hairs; l.-base markedly prolonged downwards on stem as flange*	S. officinale
11.	*Lvs. becoming almost glabrous but rough with tubercles; l.-base often not prolonged downwards on stem*	S. tanaicense
12.	(10) *Cal. very short* ($\frac{1}{10}$ *to* $\frac{1}{6}$ *in. long*), *teeth blunt*	S. asperum
12.	*Cal. longer* ($\frac{1}{8}$ *to* $\frac{3}{8}$ *in. long*); *teeth acute*	S. peregrinum
13.	*Fl. blue*	S. caucasicum
13.	*Fl. white*	S. orientale

S. asper′rimum. A synonym of *S. asperum.*

S. as′perum. Prickly Comfrey. About 4 to 6 ft. h., stem branched, bristly. *l.* ovate-lanceolate, acute at both ends, scabrid; lower stalked; uppermost almost sessile; none decurrent. *fl.* at first rose, then blue; cor. 4 times as long as cal.; cal. lobes blunt. Caucasus. 1799. (B.M. 929.) SYN. *S. asperrimum.* var. **au′reo-variegatum,** *l.* margined yellow.

S. bohem′icum. A variety of *S. officinale.*

S. bulbo′sum. Root creeping, tubers roundish. Stem simple, 8 to 15 in. h. *l.* ovate, 3 to 7 in. long, often rounded at base, mostly stalked, base dilated, stem-clasping. *fl.* yellowish-white, subcylindrical, about ½ in. long, in a few-fld. raceme; cor. about twice as long as cal.; cal. segs. lanceolate. Summer. Europe.

S. cauca′sicum. 1 to 2 ft. h., softly hairy. *l.* ovate-oblong to ovate-lanceolate, 8 in. long, narrowed to a stalk, upper l. up to 6 in.

long, narrower and shortly decurrent. *fl.* blue; cor. 2 or 3 times as long as cal.; cal. segs. triangular, blunt. Summer. Caucasus. 1820. (B.M. 3188; S.B.F.G. s. 2, 294.) SYN. *S. Donii.* A beautiful species worth a place in the large rock-garden for its clear blue fl.

S. corda'tum. Up to 18 in. h., unbranched. *l.* roundish-ovate, 5 to 6 in. long, deeply cordate, slightly setulose, lower long-stalked, upper ovate-lanceolate. *fl.* yellowish-white, about twice as long as cal., in a short, few-fld. raceme; cal. hairy, segs. lanceolate, ciliate. Hungary to Russia. (R.I.F.G. 1303.)

S. grandiflo'rum. Tufted perennial about 8 in. h., with many branches from the rhizome. Stem rarely branched, roughly hairy. *l.* ovate, more or less rounded at base, on fl.-shoots about 1½ in. long, on sterile shoots up to 7 in. long; stalked. *fl.* pale yellow, buds tipped red. March to June. Caucasus. 1900? (B.M. 8944.) Hardy. Tolerant of shade. Distinct by the decumbent barren shoots.

S. Leonhardtia'num. Root tuberous. Stems 6 to 12 in. h., simple or slightly branched, retrorsely setose. *l.* elliptic or ovate, rarely lanceolate, acute, more or less hispid with short bristly hairs; lower narrowed into a winged stalk; uppermost sessile. *fl.* pale yellow, ½ to ¾ in. long; cor. twice as long as cal.; cal. segs. lanceolate or linear-lanceolate. Europe. 1927. (Hegi, I. F. 5. 3. 219.) Dwarfer than typical *S. tuberosum* and of less compact and robust growth but with brighter fl.; possibly not specifically distinct.

S. officina'le. 1½ to 4 ft. h. Stem branched, winged by the decurrent l., covered with deflexed white hairs. *l.* ovate-lanceolate, 6 to 10 in. long, contracted into stalk, upper oblong-lanceolate, 6 to 8 in. long, decurrent. *fl.* white, creamy-white, purple, or rose, ¾ in. long; cor. twice as long as cal.; cal. segs. lanceolate; rachis softly hairy. Britain and Spain eastwards to Siberia and Turkey. (E.B. 1115.) var. **ochroleu'cum,** *fl.* white or yellowish-white. SYN. *S. bohemicum*; **purpu'reum,** *fl.* purple; **coccin'eum,** *fl.* crimson; habit less robust than in other varieties; a good garden plant. (S.B.F.G. s. 2. 304 as *S. officinale bohemicum* but not *S. bohemicum* Schmidt.) SYN. *S. coccineum* of gardens. There is also a form with white-variegated l. and purplish fl. (var. **argen'teum**).

S. orienta'le. Root fusiform. Stem tufted, about 2 ft. h., branched, hairy. *l.* ovate or oblong, rounded or cordate at base, lower about 5½ in. long, stalked, upper 4½ in. long, sessile. *fl.* white, about ¾ in. long, 2 or 3 times as long as cal.; cal. tubular, segs. oblong or ovate, blunt. Near Istanbul; widely naturalized. 1752. (B.M. 1912 as *S. tauricum.*) A pleasing plant for an unconsidered place.

S. ottoma'num. Root fusiform. Stem 12 to 20 in. h., hairy, slender, sub-erect, much branched; branches long and slender. *l.* ovate or oblong, 2 to 3 in. long, acute, roughly hairy; lower cordate and narrowed to a winged stalk; upper sessile with a wedge-shaped base. *fl.* yellowish-white, about ¼ in. long, scarcely twice as long as cal.; cal. segs. ovate-lanceolate. Racemes many-fld. Hungary to Greece. (R.I.F.G. 1305.) Weedy-looking and of no garden value.

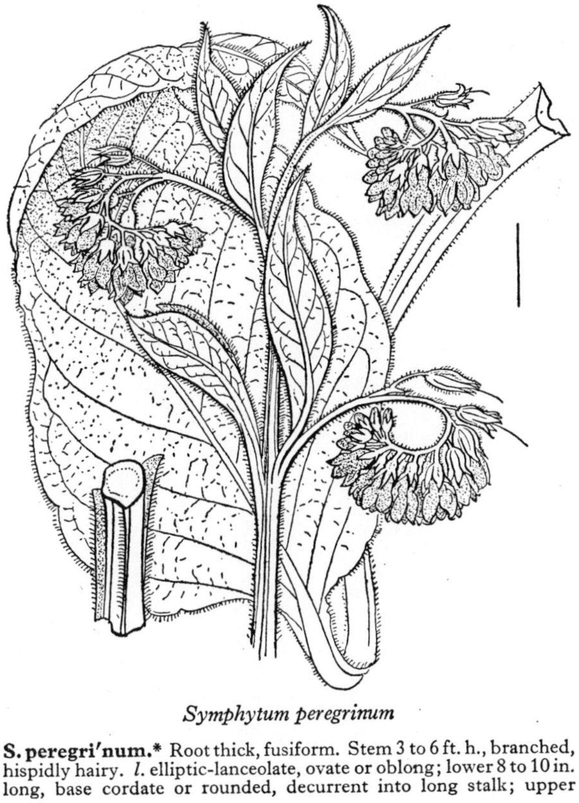

Symphytum peregrinum

S. peregri'num.* Root thick, fusiform. Stem 3 to 6 ft. h., branched, hispidly hairy. *l.* elliptic-lanceolate, ovate or oblong; lower 8 to 10 in. long, base cordate or rounded, decurrent into long stalk; upper ovate, 2 to 3 in. long, sessile; all softly hispid. *fl.* rose, then blue, about ⅝ in. long, cor. 3 or 4 times as long as cal.; cal. segs. hispid, triangular-lanceolate. E. Caucasus, N. Persia?; naturalized widely in Britain and elsewhere. (B.M. 6466; E.B. 1516 as *S. officinale patens.*) Much confused with *S. asperum* but is less strongly setulose and has sessile upper l. and a larger cal. with acute lobes. The status of the very decorative plant cultivated as *S. peregrinum* is uncertain (*see above*). Its correct name may be *S.* × *uplandicum* if it is proved to be a hybrid between *S. asperum* and *S. officinale,* and the original *S. peregrinum* of Ledebour is proved to be not such a hybrid but a true species of the E. Caucasus.

S. pic'tum of gardens is *S. officinale.*

S. tanaicen'se. Root fusiform. Stem about 2 ft. h., branched, not or only partly winged, sparsely setose. *l.* lanceolate; lower long-stalked, upper short-stalked. *fl.* purplish, about ⅜ in. long; cor. twice as long as cal.; cal. segs. lanceolate. E. S. and Cent. Europe. SYN. *S. uliginosum.*

S. tau'ricum. Root fusiform. Stem 12 to 16 in. h., branched, hairy, and somewhat setose. *l.* ovate or ovate-oblong, acute, bullate, somewhat wavy on margin, hairy; lower cordate or rounded at base, 2 to 3 in. long; upper sessile, ovate. *fl.* yellowish-white, about ½ in. long; cor. 2 or 3 times as long as cal.; cal. segs. long, lanceolate. S. Russia. 1806. (B.M. 1787.)

S. tubero'sum. Root tuberous, nodose. Stem 8 to 20 in. h., simple or sparsely branched, retrorsely setose. *l.* oblong-lanceolate, acute, more or less densely hispid; lower, narrowed to a winged stalk, uppermost sessile. *fl.* yellowish-white, ¾ in. long, 1½ to 2 times as long as cal.; cal. segs. lanceolate, acute. Europe, including Britain. (E.B. 1517.)

S. uligino'sum. A synonym of *S. tanaicense.*

S. × **uplan'dicum.** *See under* **S. peregrinum.**

W. T. S.

SYMPIE'ZA (*sympiezo,* to press; the stamens are adherent to the corolla tube). FAM. *Ericaceae.* A genus of 8 species of heath-like shrubs confined to S. Africa. Leaves in whorls of 3, small or minute, linear or elliptic, sulcate at back. Flowers small, clustered in terminal heads; calyx rather thick, complanate and 2-lipped, or tubular-bell-shaped and 4-toothed; corolla oblique or curved with a shortly 2-fid limb, lobes broad and connivent; stamens 4, exserted. Greenhouse plants requiring the same treatment as Cape heaths. *See* **Erica.**

S. capitella'ta. Shrub of 1 to 2 ft. h. *l.* linear-trigonal, erecto-incurved, those near fl. scarcely longer than cal. *fl.* pink, in subglobose, drooping heads, ½ in. wide; cor. $\frac{1}{16}$ to $\frac{1}{24}$ in. long; cal. one-third as long, glabrous. 1812.

SYMPLOCA'CEAE. Dicotyledons. A family of about 150 species all in 1 genus, Symplocas. At one time included in Styraceae but distinct by its inferior ovary completely divided into 2 to 5 cells instead of divided only at the base; the stamens, too, are often more numerous, and the anthers round or ovate instead of narrow or linear.

SYMPLOCARP'US (*symploke,* connexion, *karpos,* fruit; the ovaries coalesce into a compound fruit). FAM. *Araceae.* A genus of a single species found in Atlantic N. America, NE. Asia, and Japan. Characters as described under *S. foetidus,* which is a large, robust, marsh perennial herb preferring peaty soil, and a striking plant for the bog garden. The fetid odour as of a skunk is not so marked as to exclude it from gardens. Increased by division.

S. foe'tidus. Skunk Cabbage. About 12 in. h. from a descending rootstock. *l.* 1 to 2 ft. long, ovate-cordate, acute, thick, and rather leathery, veins thick; stalks short, sheathing. *Spathe* spotted and striped purple and yellowish-green, swollen or shell-shaped, curved at tip, of similar texture to l., persistent; spadix violet, included, globular, short-stalked, entirely covered with thickly crowded fls., all fertile; peduncle very short. Feb., March. (B.M. 3224; B.M. 836 as *Pothos foetidus.*)

SYMPLO'COS (*symploke,* connexion; the stamens are united at base). FAM. *Symplocaceae.* A genus of about 150 species of trees and shrubs, usually glabrous, but sometimes hairy, widely distributed over the warmer parts of Asia, Australia, and America. Leaves alternate, leathery or membranous. Flowers in dense or loose axillary racemes or spikes, sometimes in few-flowered clusters or even solitary; calyx 5-lobed, lobes overlapping; corolla lobes 5 and in 1 series, or 6 to 10 in 2 series, free or more or less connate; stamens often many, in many series. A compost of loam, peat, and sand suits them. Propagation by seed or cuttings in sand under a glass; those of *S. coccinea* need heat.

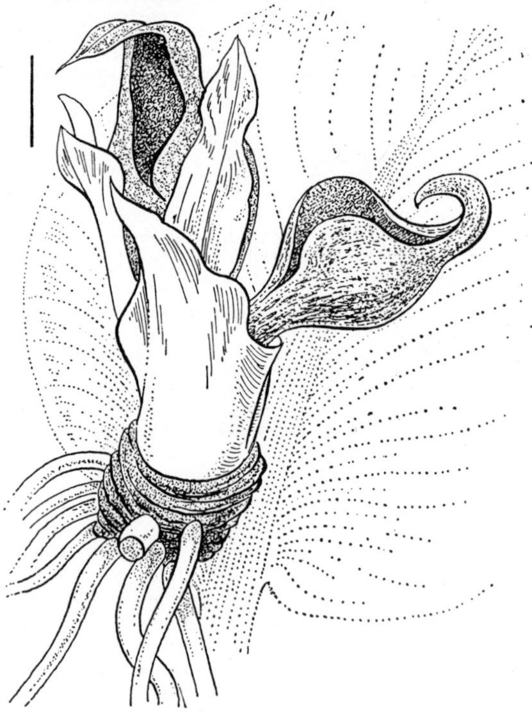

Symplocarpus foetidus (p. 2067)

S. coccin'ea. Up to 10 ft. h. *l.* elliptic-oblong, 3 to 4 in. long, acuminate, obtuse at base, crenulate, glabrous above, hairy beneath; stalk ½ in. long. *fl.* red, solitary in l.-axils, 1 in. across, sessile; cor. 10-lobed; pet. nearly connate at base. May. Mexico. 1825. Stove.

S. crataegoi'des.* Shrub or small tree; young shoots hairy. *l.* oval, ovate to obovate, 1½ to 3½ in. long, up to 1¾ in. wide, narrowed to both ends, finely toothed, slightly hairy above, hairy, especially on veins, beneath, stalk ⅛ to ¼ in. long. *fl.* white, fragrant, ⅓ in. across, in hairy terminal panicles up to 2½ in. long, and in l.-axils on small side-shoots; pet. 5, united at base; stamens about 30 in 5 clusters, 1 at base of each pet. May, June. *fr.* roundish-oval, mostly 1-seeded, becoming bright blue in autumn. China, Himalaya, Japan. 1824? Hardy, but fr. rarely produced in Britain.

S. japon'ica. Shrub up to 10 ft. h. *l.* oblong to ovate-elliptic, 2 in. long, acute at both ends, toothed, glabrous; stalk ¼ in. long. *fl.* pale yellow, nearly sessile in axillary racemes much shorter than l., 3- to 5-fld. June. Japan. 1850. (S.Z.F.J. 24 as *S. lucida.*) Greenhouse.

S. sin'ica. Shrub about 3 ft. h., shoots hairy. *l.* elliptic, 1½ to 2 in. long, acute at both ends, toothed, hairy. *fl.* white, fragrant, in terminal and axillary panicles as long as l. May. China. 1822. (B.R. 710.) Greenhouse.

S. tincto'ria. Horse Sugar; Sweet Leaf. *l.* long-oblong, 3 to 5 in. long, acute, obscurely toothed, thickish, almost evergreen, minutely downy and pale beneath. *fl.* yellow, fragrant, in clusters of 6 to 14 in l.-axils. April. SE. United States. 1780. Greenhouse. The leaves are sweet and greedily eaten by cattle. After drying they are used for the production of a yellow dye.

SYMPODIUM. A stem made up of a succession of shoots from lateral buds which replace the terminal buds, the result appearing like a single axis as seen, for example, in Ulmus.

SYN-. A suffix signifying union, or adhesion, e.g. syncarpus, having joined carpels.

SYNADE'NIUM (*syn*, united, *aden*, gland). FAM. *Euphorbiaceae.* A genus of 2 or 3 species allied to Euphorbia but with the glands of the involucre united, natives of S. and Trop. Africa. *S. Grantii* needs a well-drained sandy loam with a little well-rotted cow-dung. It may be increased by cuttings, which, after becoming thoroughly dry at base, should be inserted in sand, and occasionally very slightly moistened.

S. Grant'ii. Spineless, succulent shrub up to 10 ft. h. Stems round, fleshy at first, becoming woody. *l.* obovate, shortly petioled, green with darker veins, paler beneath, often tinged with red. *fl.* in branched cymes, dark red, small. Zambesi Valley. 1867. (B.M. 5633.)

SYNCARP. A multiple fruit composed of the fruits of several flowers combined, or an aggregate fruit where several carpels of a single flower combine as in Magnolia or Blackberry.

SYNCHYTRIUM. A genus of fungi in the class Phycomycetes in which the members are peculiar in possessing no mycelium. The fungus-body consists only of thin-walled sporangia which release either zoospores or gametes, the first again forming thin-walled sporangia and the latter fusing in pairs to form, later, thick-walled resting sporangia, these again releasing zoospores. In the genus there is one notable parasitic species, *Synchytrium endobioticum* causing wart disease in potatoes, q.v.

D. E. G.

SYNECHAN'THUS (*syneches*, continuous, *anthos*, flower; in allusion to the arrangement of the inflorescence). FAM. *Palmaceae.* A genus of 2 Cent. American and 1 Colombian species of unarmed Palms. Trunk slender, ringed, often with stolons. Leaves in a terminal crown, equally pinnatisect; segs. broad or narrow, membranous, slender-pointed, plicate, often interrupted, margins recurved at base; rachis convex at back, deeply keeled above; stalks channelled above; sheaths short, opening. Flowers greenish, or males purplish, minute; spathes many, tubular, membranous, persistent; spadices many, peduncles long and slender, erect in flowering, branches straight, flattish or 2-edged. Fruit reddish-yellow, shining, ellipsoid, 1-seeded. *S. fibrosus* is a very graceful species needing the same treatment as Chamaedorea.

A

S. fibro'sus. Trunk about 4 ft. h., green. *l.* 4 ft. long, erect and spreading; pinnae many, 1 to 1½ ft. long, spreading and rather drooping, linear-lanceolate. *fl.* in short, linear, 2-ranked clusters; spathes several; spadices ⅓ as long as l., branches many, very slender, forked. *fr.* orange-red, sessile, 1 to 1¼ in. long. Cent. America. (B.M. 6572.)

syngenesious, having the anthers united by their edges so as to form a tube, as seen in Compositae.

SYNGO'NIUM (*syn*, joined, *gone*, womb; the ovaries being united). FAM. *Araceae.* A genus of about 14 species of climbing shrubs, natives of Trop. S. and Cent. America. Leaves sagittate or 3-cut or pedately cut. Sap milky. Flowers monoecious, males and females remote; spathe boat-shaped. They are easily grown in a house with a high temperature and a moist atmosphere. They need an open compost of loam and peat or leaf-mould with some coarse sand, but they are not fastidious as to soil.

S. affin'e. A synonym of *S. Vellozianum oblongisectum.*

S. aurit'um. Five Fingers. Climbing, rarely tree-like, branches about ¾ in. thick, green. *l.* triangular or ovate in outline, about 8 in. long, 3- or somewhat 5-sect, bright shining green, segs. widely ovate-oblong, acute, the side ones unequal, obtuse, with auricles 1 to 2 in. long; stalk 6 to 8 in. long. *Peduncle* about 2 in. long. *Spathe* tube 1½ in. long, cylindrical, purple, blade ovate-oblong, 3 in. long, purplish in throat, yellow or pale purple elsewhere. Jamaica.

S. grac'ile. A synonym of *S. Vellozianum oblongisectum.*

S. podophyl'lum. *l.* of young plants sagittate, 5 to 6 in. long, of adults 5- to 7-pedatisect, segs. oblong-lanceolate, obtuse, longest about 8 in. long; stalk 18 to 20 in. long. *Peduncle* with many whitish scales, 8 in. long. *Spathe* white or rose within, green without, blade about 2½ in. long, ovate, cuspidate. Autumn. Cent. America. var. **albo-lineat'um,** *l.-segs.* 7 to 9, midrib and veins whitish; **multisect'um,** *l.-segs.* 9 to 13, acute, distant at base.

S. Reidelia'num. A synonym of *S. Vellozianum latilobum.*

S. Vellozia'num. Climbing, branches of young plants slender, old with shorter brownish-green internodes. *l.* broadly sagittate, adult. 5-sect, segs. ovate or oblong-ovate, acute, side lobes oblong, obtuse, unequal; stalk about as long as blade. *Peduncle* long, slender, numerous. *Spathe* ovate, pale yellow without, greenish-white within. Brazil var. **latilob'um,** mid-lobe of *l.* about 8 in. long, 6 in. wide, peduncles short. SYN. *S. Reidelianum*; **oblongisect'um,** mid-lobe, 3-cut, lateral, oblong-obtuse. SYN. *S. affine, S. gracile.*

S. Wendlan'dii. Stems ascending, internodes green, lower $1\frac{1}{2}$ in. long, upper $\frac{1}{2}$ in. long. *l.* of young plants sagittate, adult 3-sect, segs. oblong-lanceolate, 4 to 6 in. long; stalk about 6 in. long. *Peduncle* about 2 in. long, solitary or in pairs. *Spathe* oblong-lanceolate, green without, purple within, about 3 in. long. Costa Rica.

SYNNOT'IA (in honour of W. Synnot who collected many plants in S. Africa). FAM. *Iridaceae.* A genus of about 3 species of S. African bulbous plants. Stem simple or slightly branched. Leaves few, flat, linear-ensiform, flaccid. Flowers rather large, sessile; perianth funnel-shaped, lobes erect-spreading, unequal; stamens affixed at base of throat; spathes 1-flowered, scattered, rather broad, cut or fringed at tip. Synnotias need greenhouse treatment and cultivation like Freesias. Propagation is by seed sown in September, seedlings flowering in third or fourth year, or by offsets.

S. bic'olor. *l.* distichous, striate, $\frac{2}{3}$ in. broad, acute. *fl.* alternate, distant; violet or yellow, or lower segs. yellowish, upper white tinged red, tube curved, segs. ovoid; scape erect, simple or branched, 6 to 10 in. long, leafy. March. 1786. (B.M. 548 as *Ixia bicolor.*) SYN. *S. galeata.*

S. galea'ta. A synonym of *S. bicolor.*

S. Meterlerkamp'iae. Stem slender, terete, glabrous, 6 to 10 in. long. *l.* 6 or 7, broadly linear, 2 to 4 in. long, aequitant. *fl.* large, deep violet; tube filiform, obliquely funnel-shaped above, $1\frac{1}{2}$ in. long; outer segs. oblong-ovate, $\frac{1}{2}$ in. long, inner rather larger, undulate on margins, upper seg. broadly ovate; anthers purple; style very long. Temperate house.

Synnotia variegata

S. variegat'a. *l.* ovate-lanceolate, ensiform, lower distichous, upper alternate. *fl.* distant, alternate, yellow and violet, tube $1\frac{1}{2}$ in. long, uppermost seg. erect, 2 side segs. recurved; scape simple, 18 in. long, May. 1825. (S.B.F.G. 150.)

SYNONYM. A superseded name. The accepted name of a plant consists of the name of the genus to which it belongs in combination with the first properly constituted specific epithet given to it, provided that epithet has not been applied previously to another plant of the same genus; all other names for the plant are synonyms. This term may also be applied to sub-species or varieties.

synsepalous, gamosepalous, having the sepals joined to one another.

SYNTHY'RIS (from Greek *syn*, together, *thyris*, a little door; referring to the closed valves of the capsule). FAM. *Scrophulariaceae.* A genus related to Veronica and Wulfenia comprising about 14 species of tufted rhizomatous low-growing perennial herbs, natives of NW. America. Leaves mostly basal, long-stalked, heart-shaped or kidney-shaped or deeply cleft; stem-leaves few, small, bract-like, alternate. Peduncle scape-like, unbranched; pedicels short. Flowers small, blue or violet-blue, in a narrow raceme; calyx 4-parted, segments narrow; corolla tube short, lobes 4, erect or spreading; stamens 2, protruding. Capsule flattened, 2-lobed; seeds minute, disk-like. Growing naturally in mountain woods or moist crevices of rocks, these neat and attractive rock-garden plants like a cool rich soil in sun or shade and are intolerant of places becoming dry in summer. They can be grown in pans for the alpine-house. Increase by seed or careful division in August or September or in May after flowering.

A closely related genus BESSEYA (commemorating Prof. Charles Edwin Bessey, 1845–1915, American botanist, author of the Bessey classification of flowering plants) has often been included in Synthyris or Wulfenia. It comprises about 8 species, native to temperate N. America, with the leaves rather oblong and minutely toothed, the corolla violet-purple, yellow, or white or else lacking (sect. Lunellia), in which event the filaments are conspicuously coloured red, violet, or purple. The best-known species is *B. Bullii* (syn. *S. Houghtoniana*) with yellow or whitish flowers; the more attractive *B. alpina* (syn. *S. alpina*) has violet-purple flowers. A revision of both genera by F. W. Pennell has been published in *Proc. Acad. Nat. Sci. Philadelphia,* 85: 77–106 (1934).

KEY

1. *Cor. blue or violet-blue, always much longer than cal.; posterior lobe a little longer than anterior lobe. Lvs. distinctly toothed or deeply cleft*
1. *Cor. purplish, yellow, or white, sometimes shorter than cal. or lacking, the filaments then red, violet, or purple and conspicuous; posterior lobe much longer than anterior lobe. Lvs. minutely crenate, not deeply toothed or divided* — species of Besseya (see above)
2. *Lvs. heart-shaped or kidney-shaped, lobed to less than ½, palmately veined* — 3
2. *Lvs. deeply and pinnately cleft, with numerous narrow segments* — S. cymopteroides and allied species
3. *Cor. lobes rounded, minutely erose only* — 4
3. *Cor. lobes deeply cut, sharp-toothed. Lvs. pilose. Sepals glabrous.* — S. schizantha
4. *Lvs. glabrous. Sepals only minutely ciliate. Cor. lobes longer than the tube* — 5
4. *Lvs. pilose above. Sepals long-ciliate. Cor. lobes a little shorter than the tube* — S. reniformis
5. *L.-teeth sharply pointed* — S. stellata
5. *L.-teeth blunt.* — S. missurica

S. alpi'na. A synonym of *Besseya alpina* (see above).

S. Bul'lii. A synonym of *Besseya Bullii* (see above).

S. cymopteroi'des. $3\frac{1}{2}$ to $5\frac{1}{2}$ in. h. *l.* 2-pinnatifid, ultimate lobes almost linear, pointed, whitish tomentose when young. *fl.* violet-blue, $\frac{1}{5}$ in. long, in a dense raceme. May. Montana, Idaho. Other species with deep-cut l. are *S. Canbyi, S. dissecta, S. Hendersonii, S. lanuginosa, S. Paysonii,* and *S. pinnatifida.*

S. Houghtonia'na. A synonym of *Besseya Bullii* (see above).

S. missu'rica. About 6 in. h. *l.* heart-shaped to almost orbicular, 1 to $2\frac{1}{2}$ in. wide, leathery, dark green, shallowly lobed with short blunt teeth, glabrous. *fl.* clear violet-blue, about $\frac{1}{4}$ in. long, in an erect many-fld. raceme. April. N. California, Oregon, Washington, Idaho. 1881. (B.M. 6860 as *S. reniformis.*) The specific epithet perpetuates an unfortunate geographical error by Pursh and Rafinesque; the species does not grow on the banks of the Missouri River.

S. renifor'mis. About 3 or 4 in. h. *l.* kidney-shaped to almost orbicular, $\frac{3}{4}$ to 2 in. wide, bluntly toothed, pilose above. *fl.* blue, in a short raceme. March, April, Washington, Oregon, California. SYN. *S. rotundifolia.* var. **corda'ta,** *l.* heart-shaped (i.e. always broader than long), *fl.* darker blue in cultivated form. SYN. *S. rotundifolia Sweetseri.*

S. rotundifol'ia. A synonym of *S. reniformis.*

S. schizan'tha. 6 to 10 in. h. *l.* heart-shaped or kidney-shaped $1\frac{1}{2}$ to 4 in. wide, shallowly lobed, double-toothed, pilose especially on petiole. *fl.* violet-blue, $\frac{1}{5}$ in. long; cor. lobes deeply and sharply cut. Washington, N. Oregon.

S. stella'ta. 4 to 9 in. usually 6 in. h. *l.* heart-shaped to almost orbicular, 1 to 3 in. wide, shallowly lobed with sharp teeth (giving the l.-blade a somewhat starry outline), glabrous. *fl.* violet-blue, about ¼ in. long, in an erect, dense, many-fld. raceme, the sharply toothed bracts rather conspicuous. Oregon, Washington. 1932. (B.M. 9427.) The commonest species in gardens; a neat and elegant plant.

W. T. S.

syphiliti'cus -a -um, once used in treating venereal diseases.

syri'acus -a -um, Syrian.

SYRIAN MAPLE. *See* **Acer syriacum.**

SYRING'A (from the Greek *syrinx*, pipe or tube, originally applied to Philadelphus, some species of which are still frequently called 'syringa'). Lilac. FAM. *Oleaceae.* A genus of some 25 to 30 species of deciduous shrubs or small trees native of NE. Asia and E. Europe. Leaves opposite, nearly always simple and entire, but pinnate in *S. pinnatifolia* and lobed in *S. persica laciniata.* Flowers in terminal or axillary panicles, mostly fragrant; calyx bell-shaped, with 4 teeth; corolla with a usually cylindrical tube and a limb, ¼ to ½ in. across, of 4 more or less spreading lobes; stamens 2; fruit a capsule of oblong or spindle shape.

The genus has 2 distinct sections:

1. LIGUSTRINA or privet-like. Corolla white, its tube short, stamens protruded (3 species, *S. amurensis, S. japonica, S. pekinensis*).

2. TRUE LILACS. Corolla tube slender; stamens enclosed. They are subdivided into 2 groups, one of which (VILLOSAE) produces its panicles at the end of leafy shoots of the current year, usually in June; the other (VULGARES) produces its panicles usually in pairs in May at the end of leafless shoots of the previous year, as in common lilac.

Lilacs are easily grown. They like a sunny position and a rich, moist, loamy soil, and are benefited by an occasional top-dressing of farmyard manure. Where lime is absent an application of bone meal is useful. They require no systematic pruning but should have the panicles cut off as soon as they fade to prevent wastage of vigour involved in needless seed development. Those who desire trusses of extra size, more especially of the garden varieties, not only do this but remove weak, useless, or over-crowded shoots at the same time. Common lilac is much addicted to the production of suckers at the base; these should be rigorously cut out.

Propagation can be effected by means of seeds, cuttings, and layers, the surest method being the last, especially for garden varieties. Most of the species can be raised from cuttings made of half-ripened shoots, but some of the named garden varieties of *S. vulgaris* are reluctant rooters. New varieties of high quality are almost necessarily increased by grafting at first in order to get a preliminary stock, but there is now a general disposition to avoid grafted plants as much as possible owing to the often persistent suckering of stocks of common lilac. The practice of grafting on privet is universally condemned and is probably no longer in use. Own-rooted plants are comparatively slow to reach saleable size and are consequently more expensive.

For forcing, the best varieties are usually grafted on stocks of the common lilac. They are grown on for 2 years, the growth being restricted to a number of strong shoots, generally from 6 to 12 shoots, at the end of the second year, the number varying according to the variety and strength of the plant. Plants required for winter forcing are root-pruned about the beginning of August. This is done by cutting round the plants with a sharp spade, in such manner that the resulting balls will go into 7- or 8-in. pots, or where required in quantity for cut flowers, they may be packed closely in beds in the forcing house. Cutting round the roots helps to ripen the wood and flower-buds. During September they are lifted and potted and plunged outdoors until required for forcing. When required for Christmas, they are put into a darkened house with a temperature of 70° to 80° F. and kept syringed with tepid water. The heat and darkness blanch the coloured varieties; if colour is required they are exposed to the light for several days.

After flowering, they are cut hard back to 2 or 3 buds, and stood in a cool house to start into fresh growth. When all danger of frost is past, they are planted out in the nursery, to be grown on for 1 or 2 years, according to how hard they were forced.

While growing in the nursery all weak wood and suckers must be cut out, retaining only a few strong shoots.

From the foregoing it will be seen how important it is to maintain a regular succession of young stock. By growing them on, if so desired, large specimens may in time be acquired.

By etherization or by the warm-bath method the flowering time may be hastened considerably, and by cold storage it may be retarded so that the flowering season of lilacs may be very considerably extended. **A**

DISEASES. Lilacs may be attacked at the roots by *Armillaria mellea*, the Honey fungus. The foliage may suffer from attack by the Grey Mould fungus and from leaf-spotting and blotching caused by Ascochyta, Phyllosticta, or *Heterosporium syringae,* but none of these should do much harm to a vigorous tree and, if severe, may generally be taken as an indication of weakness due probably to poor root development. The most serious disease of outdoor lilacs is Blight disease caused by *Bacterium syringae,* which causes blackening of young shoots and flower trusses and is very often confused with frost damage. Later effects show as brown spotting on the leaves, but the first blackening effect is the more serious and kills shoots and flowers. The remedy is to cut out all affected shoots as thoroughly as possible back to healthy wood. In forced Lilacs under glass there is a disease of the shoots and buds due to infection by *Phytophthora syringae,* which also sometimes attacks Apples and Pears. In Lilacs this trouble should be remedied by removing all affected shoots and spraying with Bordeaux mixture. Very often Lilacs show pale leaves with yellowish blotches, a condition known as Chlorosis, generally due to unsuitable soil. This can usually be remedied by proper attention to drainage, liming, and the usual feeding by means of artificial fertilizers and humus or even mulching on light soils inclined to dryness.

(D. E. G.)

PESTS. The foliage is often attacked by the Lilac Leafminer, *Gracilaria syringella,* a small Tineid Moth, whose caterpillars live within conically rolled leaves of Lilac (Syringa) and Privet (Ligustrum). The presence of the blistered and rolled leaves on Lilacs is disfiguring and growth is checked. There are 2 generations a year, the moths of the first brood appearing in May, those of the second during July. The eggs are laid on the leaves, and the young caterpillars eat into the leaves and feed on the soft tissue. They later leave their mines and feed on the leaf, causing it to roll up laterally or conically from the apex. Pupation takes place in the leaf-axils, and the winter is passed in the pupal stage. Control measures include handpicking and burning the mined leaves in June and August, thorough and forcible application of Nicotine-soap wash to both leaf surfaces, and 2 or 3 sprayings of Paraffin emulsion or Gammexane in May to deter the females from egg-laying.

G. F. W.

KEY

1. *Cor. tube scarcely longer than cal. Anthers exserted* 2
1. *Cor. tube much longer than cal. Anthers included or almost so* 4

2. *Lvs. generally rounded at base, ovate to broadly ovate* 3
2. *Lvs. narrowed to base, ovate to ovate-lanceolate* S. pekinensis
3. *Shrub. Lvs. abruptly tapered at apex, glabrous* S. amurensis
3. *Tree or shrub. Lvs. gradually tapered, downy beneath at first* S. japonica
4. *Panicles produced from terminal buds, leafy at base* 5
4. *Panicles from lateral buds* 13
5. *Panicles upright* 6
5. *Panicles drooping or arching* 12
6. *Lvs. glabrous and glaucous beneath* 7
6. *Lvs. green or only slightly glaucous and more or less hairy beneath* 8
7. *Lvs.* $1\frac{1}{2}$ *to 4 in. long. Cor. lobes at length reflexed* S. emodi
7. *Lvs. 3 to 8 in. long. Cor. lobes more or less spreading* S. yunnanensis
8. *Cor. lobes more or less upright* 9
8. *Cor. lobes spreading* 10
9. *Lvs. oval, 2 to 5 in. long, whitish beneath* S. Josikaea
9. *Lvs. oval-lanceolate, 3 to 7 in. long, downy on veins beneath* S. Wolfii
10. *Lvs. glabrous or downy on veins only beneath* 11
10. *Lvs. hairy beneath* S. tomentella
11. *Anthers reaching cor. mouth* S. villosa
11. *Anthers not reaching cor. mouth* 22
12. *Fl. whitish within in long pendulous panicles* S. reflexa
12. *Fl. purplish-pink or lilac in dense drooping panicles* S. Komarowii
13. *Lvs. hairy at least on midrib beneath* 14
13. *Lvs. usually glabrous or broad at base* 19
14. *Shoots downy. Lvs. downy above* 15
14. *Shoots finally glabrous* 16
15. *Shoots slender. Lvs. 1 to 2 in. long. Cal. glabrous* S. Julianae
15. *Shoots slender. Lvs.* $1\frac{1}{2}$ *to 3 in. long. Cal. downy* S. Potaninii
15. *Shoots purplish, glandular. Lvs. 2 to* $3\frac{1}{2}$ *in. long* S. velutina
16. *Cor. tube not over* $\frac{2}{5}$ *in. long* 17
16. *Cor. tube over* $\frac{2}{5}$ *in. long, very slender* 18
17. *Lvs. slightly downy, ciliate,* $\frac{1}{2}$ *to 2 in. long* S. microphylla
17. *Lvs. densely downy on veins beneath, 1 to 3 in. long* S. Palibiniana
18. *Shoots glabrous. Lvs. downy on veins beneath, roundish* S. pubescens
18. *Shoots rather downy. Lvs. with 2 pairs of veins from base to apex* S. Meyeri
19. *Lvs. entire or lobed* 20
19. *Lvs. pinnate* S. pinnatifolia
20. *Lvs. broadly ovate, more or less heart-shaped* S. oblata
20. *Lvs. ovate, heart-shaped to ovate, 2 to 6 in. long* S. vulgaris
21. *Lvs. entire,* $1\frac{1}{2}$ *to* $2\frac{1}{2}$ *in. long, ovate* S. × chinensis
21. *Lvs. often lobed, 1 to* $2\frac{1}{2}$ *in. long, lanceolate* S. persica
22. *Buds somewhat pointed* S. Sweginzowii
22. *Buds rounded at apex* S. Tigerstedtii

S. Adamia'na. A synonym of *S. tomentella.*

S. albo-ro'sea. A synonym of *S. tomentella.*

S. amuren'sis. Shrub up to 12 ft. *l.* broadly ovate, 2 to 5 in. long, $1\frac{1}{2}$ to $2\frac{1}{2}$ in. wide, abruptly tapered at apex, glabrous. *Panicle* loose, pyramidal, erect or drooping, up to 6 in. long. *fl.* creamy-white, not fragrant; cor. $\frac{1}{4}$ in. wide, its tube very short. June. Manchuria, N. China. 1876. SYN. *S. Ligustrina amurensis.* Very subject to injury by spring frost.

S. Bretschnei'deri. A synonym of *S. villosa.*

S. × chinen'sis* (*S. persica* × *S. vulgaris*). Rouen Lilac. Shrub of bushy, dense growth, 10 ft. or more h. and wide. *l.* ovate, $1\frac{1}{2}$ to $2\frac{1}{2}$ in. long, taper-pointed, glabrous. *fl.* of common lilac colour, very fragrant and, like the entire panicle, intermediate between parents in size. May. SYN. *S. dubia, S. rothomagensis.* Very free-flowering. var. **al'ba,** *fl.* white; **du'plex,** *fl.* purplish-lilac, double; **meten'sis,** *fl.* rosy-lilac; **Saugean'a,** *fl.* lilac-red (*rubra*).

S. Dielsia'na. A synonym of *S. microphylla.*

S. du'bia. A synonym of *S. × chinensis.*

S. emod'i. Shrub or small tree up to 15 ft., shoots warty. *l.* 3 to 8 in. long, oval, ovate or obovate, dark dull green above, whitish beneath, glabrous. *Panicles* terminal on young leafy shoots, compound, up to 6 in. long, densely fl.; cor. $\frac{3}{8}$ in. long, white or tinged purple. June. *fr.* $\frac{3}{4}$ in. long, tapered at both ends. Himalaya. 1840. (B.R. 31, 6.) var. **ro'sea,** a synonym of *S. villosa*; **variega'ta,** *l.* blotched with yellow.

S. formosis'sima. A synonym of *S. Wolfii.*

S. × Hen'ryi (*S. Josikaea* × *S. villosa*). Habit of *S. villosa*, intermediate in other respects. *infl.* 8 to 10 in. long, cor. $\frac{3}{4}$ in. long, pale violet-purple. Raised at Paris. var. **Lutece,** *fl.* violet, belongs to it; also **eximia,** reddish-rose, paling with age; and **Zabeli,** reddish-lilac.

S. × hyacinthiflor'a (*S. oblata* × *S. vulgaris*). The following varieties are of this origin and from *S. oblata* they inherit an early flowering, being usually in fl. by the end of April; **Descartes,** mauve; **Lamartine,*** mauve-pink, large panicles; **Mirabeau,** mauve, the earliest; **Necker,** rose-pink; **Vauban,** mauve-pink, double.

S. japon'ica. Tree 30 to 35 ft. or a shrub, shoots glabrous. *l.* ovate, taper-pointed, 3 to 8 in. long, half as wide, downy beneath when young. *Panicles* in terminal pairs, each 8 to 12 in. long, 6 to 8 in. wide. *fl.* white; not fragrant, cor. short-tubed, $\frac{1}{4}$ in. wide, lobes spreading; stamens and style protruded. June, July. Japan. 1876. (G. & F. 2, 293.) SYN. *Ligustrina amurensis japonica.*

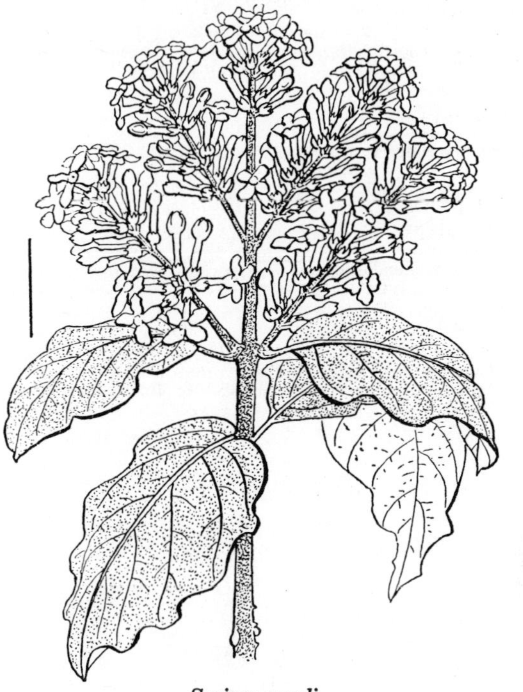

Syringa emodi

S. Josik'aea. Shrub up to 12 ft., shoots stout, downy at first. *l.* 2 to 5 in. long, oval, whitish beneath. *Panicles* terminating young leafy growths, slender, 4 to 8 in. long, half as wide; cor. deep lilac, $\frac{1}{2}$ in. long, $\frac{1}{4}$ in. wide; cal. downy. June. Hungary. 1830. (B.M. 3278.) var. **pal'lida,** *fl.* pale violet; **rubra,** *fl.* reddish-violet.

S. Julian'ae. Shrub up to 6 ft. or more, bushy, shoots slender, very downy. *l.* 1 to 2 in. long, half as wide, oval, cuneate, finely pointed, dull dark green, appressed-hairy above, very hairy beneath. *fl.* very fragrant, in panicles 2 to 4 in. long; cor. $\frac{1}{4}$ to $\frac{1}{3}$ in. long, half as wide, deep lilac; cal. violet. May, June. China. 1900. (B.M. 8423.) Notable for its downiness and fragrance.

S. Koehnea'na. A synonym of *S. velutina.*

S. Komarow'ii. Shrub up to 15 ft., shoots pale brown, warted, downy. *l.* 3 to 7 in. long, obovate or ovate-lanceolate, tapered at both ends, downy beneath. *fl.* not fragrant, densely packed in whorls on drooping, cylindrical panicles, 4 to 6 in. long, terminal on leafy shoots; cor. $\frac{1}{2}$ in. long, deep rose-pink or lilac, lobes erect. China. 1908. var. **Sargentia'na,** panicles longer and, like the l. and cal., more downy.

S. Mey'eri. Shrub 3 to 6 ft., of dense, compact growth, shoots squarish, rather downy. *l.* oval, sometimes obovate, $\frac{3}{4}$ to 2 in. long, with 2 pairs of veins extending from base to apex parallel with margin. *fl.* purple-violet, densely packed in panicles up to 4 in. long; cor. $\frac{1}{2}$ in. long, $\frac{1}{4}$ in. wide. May, June. China (gardens only). 1923. Blooms when only 10 or 12 in. h.

S. microphyl'la. Shrub 5 ft. or more, of spreading habit, shoots slender, downy. *l.* roundish-ovate, $\frac{1}{2}$ to 2 in. long, $\frac{1}{3}$ to $1\frac{1}{4}$ wide, slightly downy, ciliate. *fl.* lilac, very fragrant, borne in panicles 2 to 4 in. long, half as wide. cor. slender-tubed, $\frac{3}{8}$ in. long, $\frac{1}{4}$ in. wide; cal. helmet-shaped, downy, with short triangular lobes. June. China. 1910. SYN. *S. Dielsiana, S. Schneideri.*

S. obla'ta. Shrub up to 10 or 12 ft., occasionally a small tree, shoots glabrous. *l.* broadly cordate to kidney-shaped, often wider than long, $1\frac{1}{2}$ to 3 or 4 in. wide, glabrous, often red in autumn. *fl.* in short broad panicles, pale to purplish-lilac; cor. $\frac{1}{2}$ in. long, $\frac{2}{3}$ in. across, cal. slightly glandular. April, May. N. China. 1856. Akin to *S. vulgaris* but fl. earlier and l. very different. (B.M. 7806.)

S. Palibinian'a. Shrub up to 10 ft., shoots purplish and slightly downy at first. *l.* broadly oval to ovate, 1 to 3 in. long, densely downy on midrib and veins beneath. *fl.* in downy panicles up to 6 in. long, pale lilac-mauve to nearly white; cor. $\frac{1}{3}$ in. long with short, blunt, recurved lobes; cal. purple, glabrous. May, June. Korea. 1917. Akin to *S. velutina* but less downy.

S. pekinen'sis. Small glabrous tree or shrub, 10 to 20 ft. of spreading graceful shape, shoots slender, minutely warty. *l.* ovate to ovate-lanceolate, 2 to $4\frac{1}{2}$ in. long, half as wide, tapered to both ends. *Panicles*

4 to 6 in. long, the creamy-white fl. densely clustered and smelling like privet; cor. $\frac{1}{4}$ in. long, stamens conspicuously exserted. June. China. 1881. (G. & F. 3, 165.) SYN. *Ligustrina pekinensis*. var. **pend'ula,** branches elegantly pendulous.

S. pers'ica.* Persian Lilac. Shrub up to 6 or 7 ft., bushy, rounded, shoots glabrous. *l.* 1 to $2\frac{1}{2}$ in. long, lanceolate to narrowly ovate, long-pointed, sometimes 3-lobed, glabrous. *fl.* lilac, very fragrant, in broad panicles 2 to 3 in. wide and long; cor. $\frac{1}{3}$ in. long, $\frac{1}{4}$ in. wide; cal. funnel-shaped with short lobes. May. Persia to China. 1640. (B.M. 486.) var. **al'ba,** *fl.* white; **lacinia'ta,** *l.* deeply 5-, 7-, or 9-lobed, panicles smaller.

S. pinnatifo'lia. Glabrous shrub up to 8 or 10 ft., shoots slender. *l.* pinnate, $1\frac{1}{2}$ to $3\frac{1}{2}$ in. long, with 7, 9, or 11 lflets. which are ovate-lanceolate, $\frac{3}{4}$ to $1\frac{1}{4}$ in. long, rounded at base. *fl.* white or lilac-tinted, in several axillary panicles $1\frac{1}{2}$ to 3 in. long, produced on previous year's shoots; cor. $\frac{1}{2}$ in. long, $\frac{1}{4}$ in. wide. May. China. 1904. Very distinct in its pinnate (not merely lobed) l. (G.C. (3) lv. 269.)

S. Potanin'ii. Shrub of graceful shape, 9 to 12 ft., shoots minutely downy. *l.* $1\frac{1}{2}$ to 3 in. long, oval, slender-pointed, cuneate, densely downy on both surfaces, especially beneath. *fl.* fragrant, in erect, loosely pyramidal, panicles 3 to 6 in. long, downy; cor. white to rosy-purple, $\frac{1}{3}$ to $\frac{1}{2}$ in. long, lobes $\frac{1}{8}$ in. long. June. China. 1914. (B.M. 9060.)

S. × Preston'iae* (*S. reflexa* × *S. villosa*). The foliage takes after *S. villosa*, but drooping panicles show the influence of *S. reflexa*. *fl.* $\frac{7}{8}$ in. long, $\frac{1}{4}$ in. wide, purple to pinkish-lilac. Raised in Canada where several forms of varying colour are grown.

Syringa pubescens

S. pubes'cens.* Shrub or small tree up to 15 ft., shoots slender, angled, glabrous. *l.* 1 to $2\frac{1}{2}$ in. long, broadly ovate to almost orbicular, short-pointed, downy beneath chiefly on the veins. *Panicles* 3 to 5 in. long, usually in pairs. *fl.* fragrant, pale lilac; cor. $\frac{1}{2}$ in. long, $\frac{1}{4}$ in. wide. April, May. N. China. 1881. (B.M. 7064 as *S. villosa.*) Beautiful shrub but subject to injury by late spring frosts. **A**

S. Rehderia'na. A variety of *S. tomentella.*

S. reflex'a.* Shrub up to 12 ft., shoots angular, stout, warty. *l.* oval, oblong, oval-lanceolate or obovate, pointed, 3 to 8 in. long, nearly half as wide, downy on the midrib and chief veins beneath. *Panicles* terminal on leafy shoots, pendulous or arching, narrowly pyramidal or arching, 4 to 8 in. long. *fl.* densely packed, not fragrant; cor. funnel-shaped, $\frac{1}{3}$ in. long, $\frac{3}{8}$ in. wide, rich pink, whitish inside, lobes incurved. June. China. 1910. (B.M. 8869.) Very distinct by its cylindrical, pendulous racemes.

S. rothomagen'sis. A synonym of *S.* × *chinensis.*

S. Sargentia'na. A variety of *S. Komarowii.*

S. Schnei'deri. A synonym of *S. microphylla.*

S. Sweginzow'ii. Shrub up to 12 ft., shoots slender, glabrous, purplish-brown. *l.* ovate to ovate-lanceolate, 2 to 4 in. long, hairy on the chief veins beneath. *Panicles* 6 to 8 in. long, terminal on leafy shoots. *fl.* fragrant; cor. $\frac{1}{3}$ in. long, pale rosy-lilac, white inside the lobes; cal. glabrous, purplish. June. China. 1914. SYN. *S. tetanoloba.* var. **al'bida,** a paler form.

S. tetanolo'ba. A synonym of *S. Sweginzowii.*

S. Tigersted'tii. Shrub to 10 ft. or more, shoots slender. *l.* ovate, acuminate, rounded at base, to 3 in. long, glabrous above, somewhat greenish-white below and densely pilose along the midrib. *Panicles* terminal on leafy shoots, erect, about 8 in. long, 4 in. wide; pedicels glabrous. *fl.* fragrant; cor. whitish lilac, tube $\frac{1}{4}$ in. long. June. W. China. 1934.

Syringa reflexa

S. tomentel'la.* Shrub 10 to 15 ft., shoots brownish, warty. *l.* 2 to 6 in. long, oval to ovate, cuneate, pointed, pale and softly downy beneath, ciliate. *Panicles* up to 8 in. long and 5 in. wide, terminal on leafy shoots. *fl.* fragrant; cor. $\frac{1}{2}$ in. long, $\frac{1}{3}$ in. wide, pale pink-lilac, white inside; anthers slightly protruded. June. China. 1904. (B.M. 8739 as *S. Wilsonii.*) SYN. *S. albo-rosea*, *S. Adamiana.* var. **Rehderia'na,** shoots and *l.* densely downy; anthers enclosed.

S. veluti'na. Shrub 10 to 12 ft., shoots purplish, often glandular. *l.* oval, ovate, or lanceolate, cuneate, 2 to $3\frac{1}{2}$ in. long, $\frac{1}{2}$ to 2 in. wide, downy beneath. *fl.* fragrant, in panicles 4 to 6 in. long; cor. very slender, $\frac{1}{3}$ in. long, in various shades of purple outside, white inside; lobes recurved; anthers purple. May, June. Korea, N. China. 1910. SYN. *S. Koehneana.*

S. villo'sa.* Bushy robust shrub up to 10 ft., shoots stout, glabrous. *l.* broadly oval, pointed, 2 to 6 in. long, dark green above, rather glaucous and slightly hairy beneath. *Panicles* at and near end of leafy shoots, 6 to 10 in. long, half as wide; cor. lilac-rose, $\frac{1}{2}$ in. long, $\frac{1}{4}$ in. across. May, June. N. China. 1885. (B.M. 8292 as *S. Bretschneideri.*) SYN. *S. emodi rosea.*

S. vulgar'is.* Common Lilac. Shrub or small tree up to 20 ft., shoots and l. glabrous. *l.* cordate to ovate, pointed, 2 to 6 in. long. *Panicles* pyramidal, 6 to 8 in. long, usually in terminal pairs. *fl.* very fragrant, 'lilac' colour in the type, but more or less deeply tinged with blue, violet, purple, or rose in garden varieties; cor. $\frac{1}{3}$ to $\frac{5}{8}$ in. long. May. E. Europe. 16th century. (B.M. 183.) For varieties *see* Supplement.

S. Wilson'ii. A synonym of *S. tomentella.*

S. Wolf'ii. Shrub to 20 ft., shoots glabrous. *l.* 3 to 7 in. long, oval-lanceolate, slender-pointed, veins downy beneath. *Panicles* 8 to 12 in. long, terminal on leafy shoots, downy. *fl.* fragrant; cor. $\frac{1}{2}$ in. long, lilac, lobes erect; anthers primrose-yellow, inserted half-way down the tube. June. Korea, Manchuria. 1909. SYN. *S. formosissima.*

S. yunnanen'sis. Shrub 9 to 12 ft., shoots slender, reddish, warted. *l.* oval, oblong-lanceolate, obovate, tapered at both ends, $1\frac{1}{2}$ to 4 in. long, glaucous beneath, margined with minute hairs. *Panicles* terminal on leafy shoots, up to 8 in. by 6 in. long. *fl.* fragrant; cor. pink or almost white, $\frac{1}{4}$ to $\frac{3}{8}$ in. long, $\frac{1}{4}$ in. across; cal. glabrous, reddish. June. China. 1907.

syringan'thus -a -um, with flowers like Lilac.

SYRINGE. The syringe is an indispensable part of the garden equipment where plants are grown in houses and frames. It is of use for spraying both the plants and the walls and floors. The best syringes are provided with

2 or 3 nozzles of different sizes so that a fine or coarse spray or a jet may be used at will, although a skilful man can vary the type of spray delivered by the use of the finger applied to the nozzle while driving the water out of the syringe with the other hand. Roses of different sizes are also sometimes attached and, where used for insecticide spraying, a detachable bend, so that the underside of foliage may be more easily reached. Ball-valves are now the usual type of fitting and refinements are the non-slip grip on the barrel, of particular value when spraying with soapy materials or when rubber gloves have to be worn, and the outer corrugated case with which some types are provided, a valuable guard against denting the barrel. Syringes are made of different sizes from 14 to 20 in. long and with diameter varying from 1 to $1\frac{3}{4}$ in. The barrel of the syringe should be of a non-corrodible alloy, especially important when it is to be used for spraying sulphur compounds. Attention should be paid to see that nozzles are always clear and washers fitting properly and that the syringe is thoroughly cleansed after using anything but pure water and before it is put aside.

SYRINGO'DEA (*syriggodes*, fistula; in reference to the slender perianth tube). FAM. *Iridaceae*. A genus of about 7 species of small S. African herbs. Leaves filiform. Flowers solitary in the spathe, pedicel short or absent; perianth salver- or funnel-shaped, tube long and slender, lobes spreading, nearly equal; stamens attached to throat; spathes narrow, hyaline. *S. pulchella* needs greenhouse protection and treatment as for Ixia.

S. pulchel'la. Bulb globose, thick. *l.* 4 to 6, setaceous, curved, 3 to 4 in. long, glabrous. *fl.* pale purple, tube $1\frac{1}{2}$ to 2 in. long, thickened above, segs. obovate-wedge-shaped, deeply emarginate, valves of spathe lanceolate, $\frac{1}{2}$ to $\frac{3}{4}$ in. long. Autumn. S. Africa. 1873. (B.M. 6072; F.d.S. 2096.)

syringoi'des, Syringa-like.

syrmat'icus -a -um, sleep-inducing.

SYRPHUS. *See* **Hover Flies.**

systy'lus -a -um, having joined styles.

SYZYG'IUM. Included in **Eugenia.**

szechua'nicus -a -um, of Szechwan, China.

Szovitsia'nus -a -um, in honour of Johann Nepomuk Szovits, d. 1830. Hungarian apothecary and plant-collector, who travelled in the Caucasus and Armenia, 1828–30.

T

tabaci'comus -a -um, having a tobacco-coloured head.

tabaci'nus -a -um, tobacco-like.

Tabacum, from the Spanish name, *tabaco*.

TABASCHIR. Curious stony formations (of silica) found in some bamboos and used medicinally in the East.

Tabbersia'nus -a -um, in honour of Lambertus Johannes Josephus Maria Tabbers, b. 1878, of the Dutch Army, who collected in New Guinea.

TABEBU'IA (native name in Brazil). FAM. *Bignoniaceae*. A genus of about 60 species of trees and shrubs natives of Trop. America. Leaves opposite simple, 3-triolate or digitately 5- to 7-foliolate; leaflets stalked, sometimes toothed. Flowers often large, in racemes or cymes; calyx tubular variously cut at apex; corolla tube long, straight or scarcely curved; limb spreading, somewhat 2-lipped, lobes 5, roundish, nearly equal; stamens 4, didynamous. Capsules oblong or long cylindrical. For treatment *see* **Tecoma** to which they are related.

T. aesculifo'lia. About 20 ft. h. with downy shoots. *l.* digitate; lflets. 7, obovate-oblong, with a short point, narrowed to base, membranous, downy above, hairy beneath. *fl.* orange, somewhat bell-shaped, 3 lower lobes with yellow spots; in a terminal, sub-corymbose panicle. Mexico, Cent. America, Northern S. America. Now more often placed in the genus **Godman'ia** (named after Frederick DuCane Godman, 1834–1919, English naturalist) on account of its pilose anthers and ribbed fruit.

T. aralia'cea. A synonym of *T. serratifolia*.

T. chrysan'tha. Tree of 12 to 15 ft. *l.* digitate; lflets. 5, ovate, slender-pointed, hairy, stalks to 5 in. long. *fl.* yellow, 2 in. long, crowded, terminal. May. Cent. America, S. America. 1823. SYN. *Bignonia chrysantha*.

T. Donnell-Smith'ii. Primavera. Tree *l.* digitate; lflets. 7, oblong to ovate, truncate or rounded. *fl.* golden-yellow, freely borne, usually before the young l. Mexico, Cent. America. A beautiful tree with valuable timber. Now more often placed in the genus **Cybistax** (apparently from *kubistao*, to tumble) on account of its membranous calyx and ribbed fruit.

T. heterophyl'la. *l.* digitate; lflets. 3 to 7, oblong-lanceolate, entire, 1 to $1\frac{1}{2}$ in. long, glabrous. *fl.* rose-pink or nearly white suffused pink, 2 in. long; panicles loose, few-fld. W. Indies. SYN. *T. triphylla*.

T. pal'lida. Tree, shoots terete. *l.* with 1 to 3 lflets., oblong obtuse, somewhat cordate at base. *fl.* tube yellow, limb lilac; cor. funnel-shaped 2 in. long, lobes crenate ciliate; usually few in l.-axils. July. W. Indies (B.R. 965.) SYN. *Bignonia pallida*.

T. Palm'eri. *Lflets.* 5, oblong, somewhat slender-pointed, base obtuse. *fl.* somewhat Paulownia-like, white and purplish with yellow spots, 1 to 2 in. long, in close clusters at ends of naked branches.

T. ro'sea. Small to medium tree. *l.* digitate; lflets. 5, acuminate. *l.* simple in young plants. *fl.* pale mauve, in large clusters. Mexico, Cent. America, north-west S. America. Needs to be kept fairly dry during resting season. SYN. *T. pentaphylla* of many authors but not *Bignonia pentaphylla* of Linnaeus.

T. serratifo'lia. Tree to 20 ft. *l.* papery, not scaly; lflets. 5, oblong-lanceolate, 3 to 5 in. long, shortly pointed, nearly entire. *fl.* yellow, narrowly funnel-shaped, 2 to $2\frac{1}{2}$ in. long, corymbs close. Trinidad, Tobago, S. America. 1822. SYN. *Tecoma serratifolia, Tabeuia araliacea*.

T. specta'bilis. *l.* digitate; lflets. ovate-oblong, obtusely pointed, toothed. *fl.* orange-yellow, funnel-shaped, 3 in. long; in short terminal panicles, the lowest 2 pedicels 3-fld., others 1-fld. Colombia. 1820. (F.d.S. 948 as *Tecoma spectabilis*.) SYN. *Bignonia spectabilis*.

TABERNAEMONTA'NA (in honour of Jacob Theodore of Bergzabern who latinized Bergzabern into Tabernaemontanus, physician and herbalist at Heidelberg, d. 1590). FAM. *Apocynaceae*. A genus of about 160 species of evergreen, often glabrous trees or shrubs, with milky sap, distributed in tropical regions. Leaves opposite, pinnate-nerved, thin or leathery. Flowers white or yellowish in terminal scarcely branched, or in forked cymes, calyx usually small, 5-parted; corolla salver-shaped, throat not scaly, lobes contorted, anthers sagitate, acute; follicles 2, globose, oblong, ovoid or recurved-kidney-shaped, smooth or 3-ribbed. Some species yield rubber. A mixture of loam, sand, and peat is the most suitable for Tabernaemontana. They need stove conditions. Propagated by cuttings in sand under glass in moist heat. Unless stated to the contrary the following species are shrubs with white flowers.

T. amygdalifo'lia. About 6 ft. h. *l.* oval-lanceolate or obovate-oblong, 2 to 5 in. long, acute at both ends, shining; stalks up to ½ in. long. *fl.* very fragrant; segs. obovate, undulate, nearly as long as tube; cymes dichotomous, one-third to half as long as l. Cent. and S. America. 1780. (B.R. 338.)

T. Bar'teri. About 6 ft. h., branches pale. *l.* oblong, upper 2 to 3 in. long, in unequal whorls, narrowed to both ends, stalks dilated, slightly connate at base. *fl.* 1 in. long; cal. tube slightly dilated at base and apex, segs. oblong-obovate, obtuse, rather shorter than tube; cymes few-fld., dichotomously branched, shorter than l. W. Trop. Africa. 1870. (B.M. 5859.)

T. citrifo'lia. About 6 ft. h. *l.* oblong to oblong-ovate, 3 to 5 in. long. *fl.* about ⅝ in. wide; cor. lobes as long as tube; cymes terminal, compound. W. Indies.

Tabernaemontana coronaria

T. corona'ria. Adam's Apple; Crape Jasmine; E. Indian or Broad-leaved Rosebay; Nero's Crown. About 4 ft. h., dichotomously branched. *l.* unequal elliptic-oblong, narrowed to base, 3 to 4 in. long, membranous. *fl.* fragrant at night; cor. tube ⅝ in. long, segs. oblong, obtuse, rather longer than tube, crimped at margins; peduncles in pairs from the forks of branches, 4- to 6-fld. July. India. 1770. (B.R. 1064; L.B.C. 406; B.M. 1865 as *Nerium coronarium.*) SYN. *Ervatamia coronaria.* A

T. dicho'toma. Forbidden Fruit; Eve's Apple. About 6 ft. h., branches terete. *l.* oblong, 2½ to 5 in. long, narrowed to base, blunt at apex; stalks ½ to ⅔ in. long, stipules sheath-like. *fl.* slightly scented, 1 in. long, cor. segs. slightly longer than tube; cymes terminal, dichotomously branched, many-fld., nearly as long as l.; peduncles 3 to 6 in. long, naked. September. *fr.* pendulous orange-yellow, half-round, with a clear cut depression along one side which, supposed to resemble a partly eaten apple, suggested the popular name. India. 1840. (B.R. 1841, 53; L.B.C. 1516 as *Cerbera dichotoma.*)

T. grandiflo'ra. About 6 ft. h., dichotomously branched. *l.* oval or elliptic-obovate, 2 to 4 in. long, acute at base, acutely cuspidate at apex; one of each pair smaller, glabrous. *fl.* yellow, without scent; cal. lobes ⅜ in. long, leafy, with glands towards base; cor. tube 1¼ in. long, lobes obovate, obtuse, shorter than tube; peduncles twice-forked, few-fld. Summer. British Guiana, Venezuela. 1823. (B.M. 5226.)

T. Hol'stii. Tall tree, wood hard. *l.* oblong to elliptic-oblong, up to 10 in. long, 4 in. wide, acute at both ends or tips apiculate, rather leathery. *fl.* white with yellow centre, fragrant, cor. tube fleshy, 1 in. long, densely hairy within; stamens inserted in middle or cor. tube; sep. suborbicular, ciliate; corymb loose. *fr.* a globose, blackish-brown berry. Trop. E. Africa.

T. laurifo'lia. About 10 ft. h. *l.* oval to oval-oblong, 4 to 8 in. long, blunt at both ends. *fl.* creamy-yellow; cor. lobes linear-oblong, shorter than tube; cymes contracted, peduncles about as long as l.-stalks. May. W. Indies. 1768. (B.R. 716.)

T. longiflo'ra. Tree. *l.* oblong-elliptic, abruptly slender-pointed, narrowed to the stalk which is dilated at base. *fl.* clover-scented, large; cor. tube very long, slightly swollen in middle; peduncles lax, about 3-fld. Summer. Sierra Leone. 1849. (B.M. 4484; F.d.S. 534.)

T. longifo'lia. About 6 ft. h. *l.* oblong, 6 to 10 in. long, 1½ to 2½ in. wide, membranous, narrowed to both ends. *fl.* ⅝ in. long; cor. lobes obovate-oblong, reflexed, as long as tube; cymes axillary, dichotomously branched, many-fld., much shorter than l.; peduncles thick. July. British Guiana. 1849.

T. recur'va. About 6 ft. h., branches terete. *l.* broad-lanceolate, 4 in. long, acute at base, blunt, apiculate; stalks ⅓ to ½ in. long. *fl.* fragrant; cor. tube glabrous, throat fleshy, segs. about ⅝ in. long, obtuse; cymes in forks of branches, much shorter than l., many-fld. June to September. India. 1824. (B.R. 1084 as *T. gratissima.*)

T. usambaren'sis. Shrub or small tree, 12 to 20 ft. h., with terete branches. *l.* oblong to linear-oblong, 5 to 8 in. long, 1½ to 2½ in. wide. *fl.* cream to yellow, fragrant; cor. tube about ½ in. long, narrowed below mouth, velvety between filament ridges, otherwise glabrous, lobes oblong, wavy; stamens inserted just below middle of tube; corymbs dense on rather short peduncles. Berries orange-like, 2½ in. wide. Trop. E. Africa.

T. Wallichia'na. 2 to 3 ft. h. *l.* broad-lanceolate, 3 to 4 in. long, obtuse, apiculate, shortly narrowed to the very short, channelled stalks. Cor. tube about ⅓ in. long, lobes narrow, falcate, blunt; cymes twin in forks of branches, 3- to 5-fld., spreading; pedicels twice as long as cal. Summer. Sumatra. 1873.

tabes'cens, wasting away.

TABLE MOUNTAIN PINE. *See* **Pinus pungens.**

tabula'ris -is -e, almost flat like a board; growing on Table Mountain (this meaning is rare).

tabuliform'is -is -e, almost flat and circular in outline like a plate.

TACAMAHAC. A resin yielded by species of Calophyllum and Populus.

tacazzea'nus -a -um, of the Taccaze River, NE. Africa.

TAC'CA (Malayan name). Fam. *Taccaceae.* A genus of about 30 species of perennial herbs with creeping

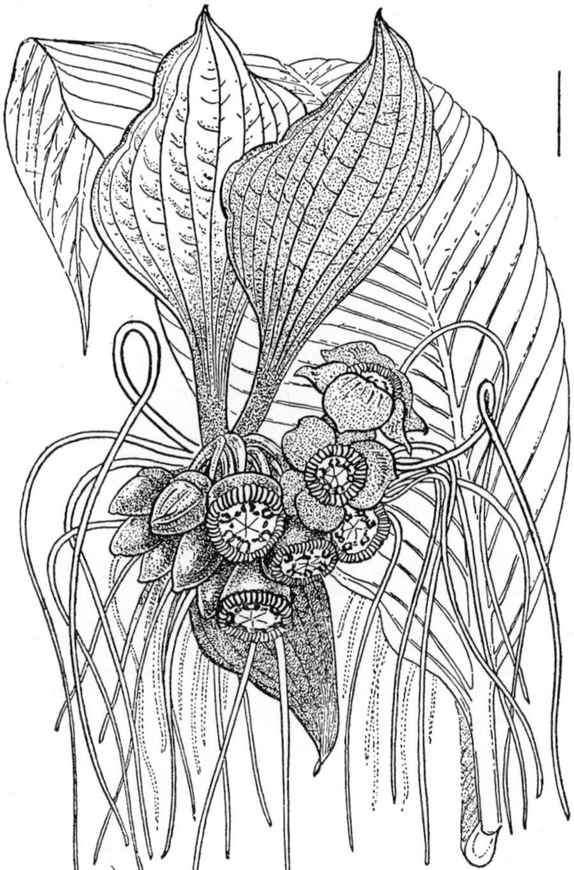

Tacca aspera (p. 2075)

swollen rhizomes and large entire or pinnately or pedately divided leaves, natives of the tropics. For characters *see* **Taccaceae.** A compost of loam, peat, and sand suits them and they require stove conditions, with a resting period during which they must be very sparingly watered. Propagation by division of the rhizomes. The rhizomes of *T. Leontopetaloides* contain much starch which, extracted, is known as E. Indian or South Sea Arrowroot and is largely used for food throughout the tropics. They are mostly grown as foliage plants or curiosities, but the sombre flowers arising out of an involucre of leafy bracts and long thread-like bracteoles give them a weird and sinister appearance.

T. artocarpifo'lia. *rhiz.* tuberous. *l.* usually 3, 2 to 3 ft. across, trisected, segs. stalked, pinnatifid; petioles 2 ft. long, stout, erect. *fl.* green, brown at base, glabrous; segs. broadly ovate; involucre of 6 or 7 l.; scape 5 to 6 ft. h., bearing very numerous fl. on pedicels 1 to 3 in. long, the sterile ones, filiform. May. Madagascar, &c. 1872. (B.M. 6124.)

T. as'pera. 1½ to 2 ft. h. *l.* lanceolate-oblong; stalks long, channelled cylindrical. *fl.* dull purplish-brown, nodding, in a many-fld. lateral umbel; involucre of 4 l., the lower smaller, sessile the upper 2 large, flat, erect, purple. Summer. NE. India, Burma, Malaya. 1812. (B.M. 4589; F.d.S. 860–1 as *Ataccia cristata.*) SYN. *T. cristata.*

T. Chantri'eri. *l.* oblong-elliptic, slender-pointed; stalks reddish brown. *fl.* dark brownish purple, in a loose umbel; involucral l. 4, ovate-cordate to lanceolate. Probably Burma and Siam. 1900. (R.H. 1901. 241.) var. **macran'tha,** *l.-stalks* green. SYN. *T. macrantha.*

T. crista'ta. A synonym of *T. aspera.*

T. integrifo'lia. *l.* oblong, 8 to 16 in. long, slender-pointed, shining green, recurved. *fl.* 4 to 11, green variegated with purple and yellow; at first nearly erect, finally nodding, on long pedicels; involucral l. ovate, twisted; scape axillary, solitary. June. NE. India. 1810. (B.M. 1488.)

T. lae'vis. *l.* oblong, about 1 ft. long, slender-pointed, glabrous. *fl.* 6 to 12 in. in an umbel; greenish-violet tube cup-like; involucre of 4 l.; scape axillary, solitary, shorter than l.-stalks. July. India, Burma. 1820. Doubtfully distinct from *T. integrifolia.*

T. Leontopetaloi'des. *rhiz.* tuberous. *l.* 3-parted, the forked segs. pinnatifid, cut down to a narrow wing into irregular ovate, acute lobes. *fl.* purplish, funnel-shaped, in a dense umbel; involucre of several l. June. E. Tropics. 1793 (L.B.C. 692). (B.M. 7299.)

T. macran'tha. A synonym of *T. Chantrieri macrantha.*

T. pinnatifi'da. A synonym of *T. Leontopetaloides.*

TACCA'CEAE. Monocotyledons. A family of about 32 species in 2 genera. Perennial herbs, natives of SE. Asia, &c., with swollen rhizomes and large entire or variously divided leaves on long stalks. Flowers on leafless stems in umbels with conspicuous leafy bracts; perianth fused at base with ovary, cup-shaped, regular, segments large 6, persistent; stamens 6, filaments broad; ovary inferior, 1-celled. Fruit a many-seeded berry (in (Tacca) or capsule (in Schizocapsa). The family was monographed in *Das Pflanzenreich*, iv. 42 (Heft 92) in 1928 by W. Limpricht.

Tacca'da. Sinhalese name.

TACCA'RUM (from generic names Tacca and Arum). FAM. *Araceae.* A genus of 3 or 4 species of tall, tuberous, Brazilian herbs. Leaves long-stalked, broadly hastate-ovate, 2-pinnatifid; pinnae undulate. Flowers monoecious; spathe erect, tube short, convolute, blade gaping or expanded, oblong, acute; spadix not appendiculate, shorter than spathe, short-stalked, loosely flowered, male inflorescence ovoid or longer than leaf-stalks. Closely related to Staurostigma and needing the same treatment.

T. cylin'dricum. Tuber sub-hemispherical. *l.* solitary, appearing with fl., large, 3-partite, pinnatifid; stalks long, terete, spotted, 3 ft. h. *Spathe* olive-green, ovate, acuminate, slightly longer than spadix; spadix sub-cylindrical, narrowed from base to tip, clothed with fl., male and female infl. of equal length. 1873. (G.F. 732 as *Endera conophalloidea.*) SYN. *T. peregrinum, Lysistigma peregrinum.*

T. Warmingia'num. *l.* solitary, bright green, 2 to 2½ ft. across, with 3 main 2-pinnatifid divisions; stalk 3 ft. h., stout, light green, marked with many white lines. *Spathe* brown, tinted with light copper, 15 in. long, convolute below, open above; spadix shorter than spathe; ovaries green, surrounded by 4 or 6 fleshy, dirty-brown staminodes; stamens of male fl. united into a thick, fleshy, round-topped, pinkish column; scape 8 in. long. October to January. 1882. (G.C. 16 (1881), 661; G.F. 1124.)

taccifo'lius -a -um, with Tacca-like leaves.

TACHIADE'NUS (*Tachia*, a related genus, *aden* gland; the ovary is surrounded by a ring of glands as in Tachia). FAM. *Gentianaceae.* A genus of 5 species of herbs or sub-shrubs, natives of Madagascar. Leaves sessile or stalked, often 3-nerved. Flowers pink or white, sometimes violet with a white tube, large, few in a terminal cyme or solitary; calyx tubular, with many internal glands, 5-cleft at apex, 5-keeled or 5-winged; corolla salver-shaped or funnel-like, with a long tube and 5 spreading, twisted lobes; stamens 5. *T. carinatus* grows well in a mixture of sand, loam, and peat. It needs to be kept rather dry in winter. Propagated by cuttings, inserted in sand under a hand-glass, in heat.

T. carina'tus. Sub-shrubby, 4-angled. *l.* oval, sessile, 3-nerved. Cal. ⅜ in. long, obverse wings half-lanceolate, lobes linear; cor. tube white, 2 in. long, swollen at tip, lobes violet, rounded, blunt, under 1 in. long; cyme terminal, twice dichotomous. October. 1858. (B.M. 5094.)

TACHINID FLIES. These thick-set, bristly flies which are nearly related to the House Fly though belonging to a different family (**Tachinidae**), are parasitic on other insects, especially upon the caterpillars of Moths. The eggs are usually deposited on the host, and the larva feeds within its host insect and breathes either by means of a perforation in the body-wall or by tapping the breathing-tubes of its victim. These flies exert a powerful check on insects in general, and those species which parasitize destructive insects are of considerable economic importance.

G. F. W.

TACHYPODOJU'LUS nig'er. *See* **Millepedes.**

TACSON'IA. Included in **Passiflora.**

Taed'a. Latin name for a pitch pine, hence resinous pine-wood.

taege'tus -a -um, of Mt. Taygetos, Greece.

taenia'tus -a -um (***taenio-*** in compound words), ribbon-like.

TAENIOP'SIS. Included in **Vittaria.**

TAE'NIOTHRIPS. A genus of Thrips some of which are pests in gardens. *See* **Pear Thrips** (*T. inconsequens*), **Rose Thrips** (*T. fuscipennis*).

TAENI'TIS (*tainia*, fillet or ribbon; from the linear sori). FAM. *Polypodiaceae.* A genus of 4 species of tropical ferns with narrow linear pinnae, the veins forming a network. Sori linear, but the line sometimes interrupted, central or sub-marginal. Soil should be 2 parts peat to 1 of loam and the plants should have a moist atmosphere and heavy shade. Propagation is usually by division.

T. blechnoi'des. Fillet or Ribbon Fern. *rhiz.* creeping. *sti.* 8 to 12 in. long, firm, naked, glossy. *Fronds* 1 to 2 ft. long, 8 to 12 in. wide, simply pinnate; pinnae of barren fronds 2 or 3 on each side, 6 to 9 in. long, 1 to 2 in. wide, oblong-lanceolate, slender-pointed, wedge-shaped at base, margin thickened and wavy, lower stalked; fertile pinnae narrower and more numerous. *Sori* in a continuous line about midway between margin and midrib. Malaccas and Philippines. (F.B. i, 54.) var. **interrup'ta,** similar to type but pinnae smaller, *sori* interrupted and much nearer margin. Malaya.

TAGE'TES (from *Tages*, one of the Etruscan deities). FAM. *Compositae.* A genus of about 30 species of erect, branched or diffuse, annual or perennial herbs, natives of the warmer parts of America. Leaves opposite, pinnately dissected or rarely undivided or toothed. Flower-heads yellow or orange, long-pedunculated or densely corymbose; ray florets in 1 series, solitary or rarely absent; receptacle flat, often small. Achenes linear, glabrous or pilose. For treatment *see* **Marigold.**

They may suffer from Foot-rot through the attack of a species of Phytophthora, particularly if in ill-drained soil, and the foliage may be attacked by the Grey-Mould Fungus, *Botrytis cinerea*, in wet seasons. Stem-rot also occurs at times, caused by *Sclerotinia sclerotiorum* (q.v.), and if this is present the attacked plants should be removed and burnt.

KEY

1. *Lvs. pinnately divided*	2
1. *Lvs. simple*	T. lucida
2. *Rays very short (under* $\frac{1}{10}$ *in. long)*	3
2. *Rays longer (over* $\frac{3}{10}$ *in. long)*	4
3. *Lflets. narrowly linear-lanceolate, serrate*	T. minuta
3. *Lflets. linear or thread-like, entire*	T. pusilla
4. *Rays numerous; heads* $1\frac{1}{2}$ *to 4 in. across*	5
4. *Rays few (about 5 to 8); heads 1 in. across*	6
5. *Rays marked with red; heads* $1\frac{1}{2}$ *in. across*	T. patula
5. *Fl. not red-marked; heads 2 to 4 in. across*	T. erecta
6. *Plant perennial. Involucre smooth*	T. lacera
6. *Plant annual. Involucre ribbed*	T. tenuifolia

T. corymbo'sa. A synonym of *T. patula.*

T. erec'ta.* African Marigold. Annual. About 2 ft. h. Stems and branches erect. *l.* pinnatisect; segs. lanceolate, toothed, the teeth, especially in upper l., aristate. *fl.-heads* citron-yellow, much larger than in *T. patula*; involucre somewhat angled; peduncles 1-headed, thickened upwards. July. Mexico.

T. flo'rida. A synonym of *T. lucida.*

T. glanduli'fera. A synonym of *T. minuta.*

T. la'cera. Sub-shrubby perennial of compact habit. *fl.* clear orange-chrome or yellow in small heads freely produced in loose, terminal panicles. February to May. 1898. California. (G.C. 23 (1898), 355.) Half-hardy.

T. lu'cida. Sweet-scented Mexican Marigold. Annual. About 1 ft. h., scarcely branched, erect. *l.* lanceolate, sharply toothed, basal teeth aristate. *fl.-heads* yellow; involucre cylindrical. August. Mexico, S. America. 1798. (B.M. 740; S.B.F.G. s. 2, 35 as *T. florida.*) Half-hardy.

T. minu'ta. Annual, up to 4 ft. h., erect, branches short. *l.* pinnatisect; segs. 13 to 17, linear to lanceolate, narrowed to each end, $1\frac{1}{2}$ in. or more long. *fl.-heads* pale yellow, in corymbose clusters; involucre cylindric. October. S. America. 1826.

T. pa'tula.* French Marigold. Annual, 18 in. h., stem erect, branches spreading. *l.* pinnatisect; segs. linear-lanceolate, toothed, teeth, especially upper ones, aristate. *fl.-heads* brownish-yellow or brownish; involucre smooth; peduncles long, 1-headed, nearly cylindrical. August. Mexico. 1573. (B.M. 150, 3830 and S.B.F.G. 151 as *T. corymbosa.*)

T. signa'ta. A synonym of *T. tenuifolia.*

T. tenuifo'lia. Striped Mexican Marigold. Annual, 18 in. h., erect, branched. *l.* pinnatisect; segs. in 6 pairs, oblong-lanceolate, deeply toothed, lower teeth aristate. *fl.-heads* yellow, involucre, oblong-ovate, 5-angled; peduncles 1-headed, scarcely thickened upwards. 1795. Summer. Mexico. (B.M. 2045.) SYN. *T. signata.* var. **pu'mila,** dwarfer and more compact. (R.H. 1863, 11.)

Taggia'nus -a -um, in honour of Harry Frank Tagg, 1874–1933, botanist, Royal Botanic Garden, Edinburgh.

taheiten'sis -is -e, of Tahiti, Society Is., Pacific.

TAIL. A term applied to any long flexible appendage.

TAIL FLOWER. A common name for Anthurium.

TAI'NIA (*tainia*, a band or fillet; in allusion to the shape of the lip). FAM. *Orchidaceae.* Distributed in Burma, E. Indies, S. China, and Malaya. Flowers pedicellate, scattered, rather large or mediocre; sepals and petals narrow, slightly acute or long-acuminate; lip erect; column rather long; pollen masses 8; scape tall, leafless, few-sheathed at base; raceme terminal, several-flowered, simple. Leaves solitary, plicate, at length thickened into somewhat flask-shaped pseudobulbs. Ania has again been separated by some and has also been called Ascotainia and placed systematically near Bletia and Plocoglottis, while Tainia is placed near Mischobulbon and Nephelaphyllum; some species have indeed been transferred to Mischobulbon. In Ania the lip is produced into a short spur or chin, free from the sepals, in Tainia it has no spur. The species which should properly be placed in Ania are marked with a (1) after the name. In the combined genera about 20 species are known, but under further revision it is probable that some of these will be reclassified. Horticulturally the species have little value. Compost should consist of light fibrous loam 3 parts, Sphagnum moss 1 part, and 1 part or more of Osmunda fibre. After growth a decided rest is required, but not as drastic as that given deciduous Calanthes. Pots are preferable to pans. The flowering season is usually spring. The winter night temperature should be near 60° F. When in growth they enjoy a tropical or nearly tropical atmosphere.

T. angustifo'lia (1). Allied to *T. latifolia. fl.* slightly larger, greenish-brown; pet. broader than sep.; lip 3-ridged, narrowly oblong; spur somewhat globose, incurved. Burma.

T. bicor'nis. Sep. and pet. green, tinged reddish; lip yellow, blotched red, mid-lobe emarginate, apiculate, not spurred, with 2 lamellae at base; anthers 2-horned. March. *l.* oblong-lanceolate, fleshy, shorter than scape. Ceylon. About 1842. (B.R. 30, 8 as *Ania bicornis.*)

T. Fuerstenbergia'na. A synonym of *T. viridifusca.*

T. Hennisia'na (1). Sep. and pet. olive-green, nearly 1 in. long; lip whitish, with short side lobes and 3 low keels; spur short, somewhat square. *l.-blade* about 8 in. long, narrow. *Pseudobulbs* small. Burma. 1911.

T. hongkongen'sis (1). Allied to *T. Hennisiana*, but stronger, lip entire and shorter, spur thicker, about as long. *Fl.*-colour much the same. Hong Kong. 1896.

T. Hookeria'na (1). *fl.* $1\frac{1}{2}$ in. across; sep. and narrower pet. yellowish-green, lined and suffused brown; lip keeled, side-lobes inclined over column, mid-lobe heart-shaped, whitish, with faint red dots. Burma. 1895. (A.B.G.C. 8, 143.)

T. latifo'lia. *fl.* small, green and brown; pet. slightly spreading; lip, lobes small, mid-lobe somewhat orbicular, disk with a narrow central and 2 broader lamellae, sac or chin short, rounded, side lobes obtuse, mid-lobe acute; scape 2 ft. long. *l.* oblong, plicate, shorter than scape. India. 1852. (A.B.G.C. 5, 35; 8, 142.)

T. penangia'na (1). *fl.* yellow and brown, 2 in. across; sep. acuminate; pet. narrower; lip whitish with 3 lamellae; column broadly winged; spur short, broad; scape 12 to 18 in. h., few-fld. *l.* 8 to 12 in. long or more, $1\frac{1}{2}$ to 2 in. wide, elliptic-lanceolate, plicate. *Pseudobulbs* clustered, flagon-shaped. Penang. 1897. (B.M. 7563.)

T. specios'a. *fl.* white; sep. and pet. with long, filiform, rather yellowish tails; lip many-nerved; scape 1 to 2 ft. long. *l.* 4 to 6 in. long, $\frac{3}{4}$ in. wide; stalk 6 to 10 in. long. Perak.

T. viridifus'ca (1). Allied to *T. penangiana. fl.* olive-green, lip yellowish-white with 5 keels. *l.-blade* 20 in. by 3 in. wide, stalk as long. *Pseudobulbs* comparatively large. *Scape* 3 to 5 ft. long. Assam, Burma. (B.M. 4669 as *Calanthe viridi-fusca.*) SYN. *T. Fuerstenbergiana.*

E. C.

TAINIOP'SIS BARBATA. A synonym of *Eriodes barbata.*

taipei'cus -a -um, of the Taipei Shan range, Shensi, N. China.

TAIWA'NIA (from Taiwan, the Chinese name for Formosa). FAM. *Pinaceae.* A monotypic genus closely allied to Cunninghamia but bearing a closer resemblance to Cryptomeria.

T. cryptomerioi'des. Evergreen tree, 150 to 200 ft. h., with long clean trunk, girth up to 20 ft., and spreading head of branches. Young shoots covered by spreading leaf bases. *Winter buds* hidden by leaves. *l.* spirally arranged, on young trees, $\frac{1}{3}$ to $\frac{2}{3}$ in. long, triangular, base clasping shoot, strongly keeled above and below, sides flattened, green with faint stomatic lines on each surface, apex a very sharp point, as the trees age l. become much smaller, $\frac{1}{8}$ to $\frac{1}{6}$ in. long. *Cones* terminal, widely cylindric, $\frac{1}{2}$ in. long, rather less wide, composed of numerous small, overlapping scales. *Seeds* 2 on each fertile scale. Formosa. 1920. Less hardy than Cryptomeria although, sheltered from cold winds, 2 small plants withstood the severe winter of 1939–40 in the National Pinetum at Bedgebury. Cultivation similar to that required by *Cryptomeria japonica.* Freely grown young trees are of graceful outline with drooping branchlets. (B.T.S. 3, 475.)

W. D.

TALAU'MA (perhaps a vernacular name of the W. Indian species). FAM. *Magnoliaceae.* A genus of about 40 evergreen trees, natives of Trop. America and Asia, related to Magnolia but the fruits have a different mode of dehiscence. Leaves and inflorescence as in Magnolia. Sepals 3, petals 6 to many, overlapping; stamens and carpels numerous, carpels in heads or spikes, 2-ovuled. Like the Magnolias these have beautiful and fragrant flowers, but they need warm greenhouse conditions. A compost of loam, peat, and sand suits them. Propagation may be by layers or by inarching on strong-growing Magnolia seedlings. Imported seed seems of no value as the albumen rapidly decays.

Talauma Candollii

T. Candol'lii. About 6 ft. h. *l.* oblong, narrowed to both ends. *fl.* cream, large; pet. 9 to 12, outer ones short; peduncles 1–fld., rather drooping, and, like the young l.-stalks clothed with reddish-brown hairs. June, July. Java. 1828. (B.M. 4251, 6614; B.R. 1709.)

T. dodecapeta'la. About 12 ft. h. *l.* oval-oblong, 6 in. long, 3 to 5 in. wide, leathery, glabrous. *fl.* white, large, terminal, solitary; pet. 10 to 12. Continuous. W. Indies. 1829. SYN. *T. Plumieri.*

T. Hodg'sonii. Tree of 50 to 60 ft. *l.* obovate-oblong, 8 to 20 in. long, leathery, glabrous, slightly sinuate. *fl.* creamy-white, 6 in. across, terminal, solitary; sep. tinged red outside, thick; pet. 6, inner smaller. Winter, spring. Trop. Himalaya. About 1850. (B.M. 7392.)

T. Plumi'eri. A synonym of *T. dodecapetala.*

T. pu'mila. A synonym of *Magnolia Coco.*

J. E. D.

TALI'NUM (perhaps a native African name). FAM. *Portulacaceae.* A genus of about 15 species of herbs, sometimes sub-shrubs, widely distributed over warm regions of the world, especially America. Glabrous, fleshy plants with flat, alternate or nearly opposite leaves without stipules. Flowers in terminal panicles, cymes, or racemes, rarely solitary, axillary or lateral; sepals 2, usually deciduous; petals 5, short-lived; stamens 5 or many; ovules numerous. Fruit a globose capsule, papery, 3-valved. The Talinums are pretty succulent plants growing best in sandy peat, the temperature requirements depend upon their native home, but none can be regarded as hardy. The sub-shrubby species may be increased by cutting, *T. reflexum* by seeds. *T. patens* and some others make good house-plants but, like other succulents, must not be overwatered.

T. Arnott'ii. Sub-shrub with woody stock 5 to 8 in. long, branches succulent, about 1 ft. long. *l.* orbicular-oblong, about 1½ in. long and nearly as wide, rounded at both ends, apiculate, fleshy, entire, almost sessile. *fl.* pale golden-yellow, 1 in. across, solitary in l.-axils; pet. obovate, acute; peduncles longer than l., spreading. Summer. S. Africa. (B.M. 6220.) Greenhouse.

T. caf'frum. Succulent, leafy, biennial or perennial herb, branches spreading or almost erect from a stoutish rootstock. *l.* lanceolate, elliptic-lanceolate to oval or nearly linear, 1 to 1½ in. long, ¼ to ½ in. wide. *fl.* yellow or sulphur on 1- to 3-fld. axillary peduncles. S. and Tropical Africa. Stove.

T. cuneifo'lium. A synonym of *T. portulacifolium.*

T. pa'tens. Puchero. Sub-shrub, stem erect, almost simple, 1 to 2 ft. h. Young shoots pink, succulent, becoming woody. *l.* mostly opposite, oval, tapering to the base. *fl.* carmine in long, terminal leafless panicles; pet. obovate, ¼ in. long; stamens 15 to 20. Autumn. W. Indies and Eastern S. America. 1776. (A.B.R. 253.) var. **variega'tum,** *l.* variegated with white and pink. Greenhouse.

T. portulacifo'lium. Sub-shrub, stem erect, 18 in. h. *l.* flat, wedge-shaped, obtuse, mucronate. *fl.* reddish-violet in a terminal panicle; lower peduncles 3-fld. July, August. India, Arabia, Africa. 1820. Greenhouse. *T. roseum* from Abyssinia is probably identical with this. SYN. *T. cuneifolium.*

T. reflex'um. Erect biennial, 12 in. h. *l.* flat, lanceolate or oval, obtuse, usually opposite. *fl.* yellow, usually on opposite dichotomous peduncles in a terminal panicle. S. America. 1800. Stove.

T. teretifo'lium. Fame Flower. Low tuberous perennial. *l.* linear, cylindrical. *fl.* pink, ⅝ in. across, on naked peduncles 3 to 6 in. long, in an open cyme; stamens 15 to 20. N. America. 1823. (B.R. 29, 1; L.B.C. 819.) Greenhouse.

T. triangula're. Sub-shrub, stem simple, about 2 ft. h. *l.* alternate, obovate-lanceolate, tapering to base. *fl.* red or white in terminal corymbs on 3-cornered pedicels; pet. rounded, ½ in. long; stamens about 30. Autumn. W. Indies to Peru. 1739. Stove.

TALIPOT PALM. *See* **Corypha umbraculifera.**

TALIS'IA (native name in Guiana). FAM. *Sapindaceae.* A genus of about 20 species of evergreen trees or shrubs, natives of Brazil, Colombia, and Guiana. Leaves alternate, equally pinnate, without stipules; leaflets leathery, oblong, entire. Flowers rather small, in branched panicles; sepals erect, in 2 series; petals 5 (rarely more), clawed; margins hairy; stamens 8 (rarely 5 or 7). A compost of turfy loam and peat suits these stove plants, which can be increased by large cuttings with leaves intact, in sand under a glass, in moist heat.

T. guianen'sis. About 4 ft. h. *lflets.* in many pairs, ovate-lanceolate, slender-pointed, glabrous on both surfaces. *fl.* rose in much-branched panicles; cal. shorter than pet. June. Guiana. 1824.

T. prin'ceps. Unbranched. *l.* forming a fine plume, spreading, broad, up to 6 ft. long. *fl.* whitish, small, very numerous; panicles large. Venezuela. 1888.

F. G. P.

TALLIES. *See* **Labels.**

TALLOW SHRUB. *See* **Myrica cerifera.**

TALLOW-TREE, CHINESE. *See* **Sapium sebiferum.**

TALLOW-TREE, SIERRA LEONE. *See* **Pentadesma butyracea.**

TAL'PA EUROPAE'A. *See* **Mole.**

TAMARACK. *See* **Larix laricina.**

TAMARICA'CEAE. Dicotyledons. A family of about 100 species of shrubs or small trees, often heath-like, or rarely herbs, comprised in 4 genera, natives of temperate and sub-tropical regions from Europe and the Mediterranean region to E. Asia and India. Leaves alternate, sessile, without stipules and often scale-like or needle-shaped. Flowers regular, solitary or in spikes; sepals and petals 4 or 5; stamens 4 to many; ovary superior, 1-celled with 3 to 5 parietal placentae. Fruit a capsule with 2 to many bearded seeds. Often seaside, desert, or mountain plants. Fouquiera, at one time placed in this family, has petals joined, not free. The genera included here are Myricaria, Reaumaria, and Tamarix.

TAMARIND. *See* **Tamarindus indica.**

TAMARIN'DUS (Arabic, *tamr*, ripe date, *Hind*, India). FAM. *Leguminosae.* A genus of but 1 species of tropical unarmed tree. A compost of fibrous loam and sand suits *T. indica* which needs stove conditions. Imported seeds should be sown on a hotbed and the young plants when 3 in. high should be potted singly. Cuttings also root readily in sand under a glass in heat. *T. indica* yields the Tamarind of commerce, which is used medicinally in both European and native medicines, and the pulp around the seeds of which is eaten. Bark, wood, leaves, flowers, and seeds are also economically useful.

Tamarindus indica

T. in'dica. Tamarind-tree. Tree of 40 to 60 ft. *l.* equally pinnate, lflets. 20 to 40, opposite, close, oblong, blunt, smooth, or becoming so. *fl.* yellow, striped red, under $\frac{1}{2}$ in. long, only the upper 3 on the racemes developed; racemes few-fld., loose, at ends of branchlets; pedicels jointed at base of cal. June, July. *Pods* 3 to 6 in. long, about 1 in. wide, 3- to 10-seeded, strap-shaped. Tropics. 1633. Probably native of Asia and Africa. (B.M. 4563 as *T. officinalis.*)

F. G. P.

tamaris'ci-, in compound words, signifying Tamarisk-like.

TAM'ARIX (ancient Latin name). FAM. *Tamaricaceae.* Tamarisk. Estimates of the number of species in this genus are very variable, but there are probably not fewer than 60, spread widely over the northern parts of the Old World. Shrubs or trees with plumose branches, bearing tiny scale-like leaves resembling some of the junipers. Flowers pink or white, very small, thickly packed in slender cylindrical racemes, often in bulk making large panicles. In the following species the spring-flowering *T. parviflora* and *T. tetrandra* have 4 stamens; the other have 5 stamens and flower later on the shoots of the current season. Fruit a 3- to 5-celled capsule; seeds tufted at the top.

Tamarisks are essentially maritime shrubs, but often occur also in inland places with a soil of a saline nature. Although they are often found in hot, dry regions, they enjoy a good loamy soil under cultivation. They should be grown in full sunshine. Easily increased by late autumn cuttings out of doors. The following species are all hardy unless otherwise stated.

KEY

1. *Lvs. with a tubular sheath encircling the twig, the blade reduced to a minute triangular projection*	10
1. *Lvs. base not sheathing*	2
2 (1). *Racemes forming large terminal panicles, rarely lateral, on branches of current year, appearing after lvs.*	5
2. *Racemes lateral on branches of previous year, appearing before or with lvs.*	3
3 (2). *Sep., pet., stamens 4; anthers mucronate*	4
3. *Sep., pet., stamens 5; anthers blunt*	T. juniperina
4. *Pet. persistent on fruit*	T. parviflora
4. *Pet. deciduous*	T. tetrandra
5 (2). *Branchlets and lvs. glabrous*	6
5. *Branchlets and lvs. downy*	T. hispida
6 (5). *Pet. persistent on fruit*	7
6. *Pet. deciduous*	8
7 (6). *Fl. buds ovoid*	T. anglica
7. *Fl. buds almost globose*	T. gallica
8 (6). *Disk 10-lobed*	9
8. *Disc 5-lobed. Bracts subulate*	T. odessana
9 (8). *Bracts subulate*	T. chinensis
9. *Bracts ovate-lanceolate*	T. pentandra
10 (2). *Fl. unisexual. Lvs. sheath minutely ridged longitudinally*	T. dioica
10. *Fl. bisexual. Lvs. sheath minutely pitted*	T. aphylla

T. ang'lica. English Tamarisk. Shrub 3 to 10 ft., shoots reddish-brown. *l.* minute, ovate-lanceolate, glabrous. *fl.* $\frac{1}{8}$ in. wide, ovoid in bud, in slender racemes 1 to 2 in. long, white, tinged pink; stamens 5. July to September, later in the south-west coasts of England and France. (E.B. 261.)

T. aphyl'la. Bush or small tree, 10 to 25 ft. h. Branches fastigiate, long, slender, cylindrical, jointed, with *l.* reduced to a very short sheath with a minute point. *fl.* pink, $\frac{1}{8}$ in. across, nearly sessile, in a slender, more or less interrupted spike. July. India. SYN. *T. orientalis, T. articulata.* Greenhouse.

T. articula'ta. A synonym of *T. aphylla.*

T. chinen'sis. Chinese Tamarisk. Shrub or small tree up to 15 ft., branches very slender, often pendulous. *l.* very minute to $\frac{1}{12}$ in. long, rather glaucous. *fl.* pink, in cylindrical racemes $1\frac{1}{2}$ to 2 in. long, forming in the mass large pendulous panicles on current season's growths. July to September. China. 1907.

T. dioi'ca. Small tree, about 6 ft. h., branches long, spreading-fastigiate, drooping at ends. *l.* sheathing, glabrous, green, obliquely truncate, acuminate. *fl.* pink, $\frac{1}{8}$ in. across, dioecious; spikes dense, in panicles 1 to 2 in. long. June. India. 1823. Greenhouse.

T. gal'lica. French Tamarisk. Shrub or small tree usually up to 10 or 12 ft., but sometimes 30 ft. in warm localities; shoot glabrous, purplish. *l.* lanceolate, rather glaucous. *fl.* globose in bud, pink, densely set in cylindrical racemes 1 to 2 in. long, lobes of the disk rounded. June to August. Coasts of France and W. Europe.

T. german'ica. A synonym of *Myricaria germanica.*

T. his'pida.* Shrub 3 or 4 ft., erect, compact, downy on shoot and l. *l.* very glaucous, $\frac{1}{8}$ in. or less long, ovate-lanceolate, sharply pointed. *fl.* bright pink in erect racemes 2 or 3 in. long, forming terminal panicles. August, September. Caspian Sea region. 1893. SYN. *T. kashgarica.* Very handsome in its glaucous foliage and abundant blossom. var. **aestivalis,** a synonym of *T. pentandra.*

T. juniperi'na. Feathery branched shrub or small tree, 12 to 18 ft., branchlets very slender, closely set, making the habit very dense. *l.* pale fresh green, $\frac{3}{16}$ in. long at their largest, down to scale-like and minute. *fl.* bright pink, opening on previous season's growths in racemes $1\frac{1}{2}$ in. long. May. China. 1875.

T. kashga'rica. A synonym of *T. hispida.*

T. Pallas'ii. A synonym of *T. pentandra.*

T. parviflo'ra. Shrub, sometimes tree-like, 12 to 18 ft., branches slender, dark purple. *l.* ovate, scale-like, with hard points. *fl.* pale pink, in slender racemes about 1 in. long; stamens 4. April, May. SE. Europe. 1853. (F.d.S. 9, 898.)

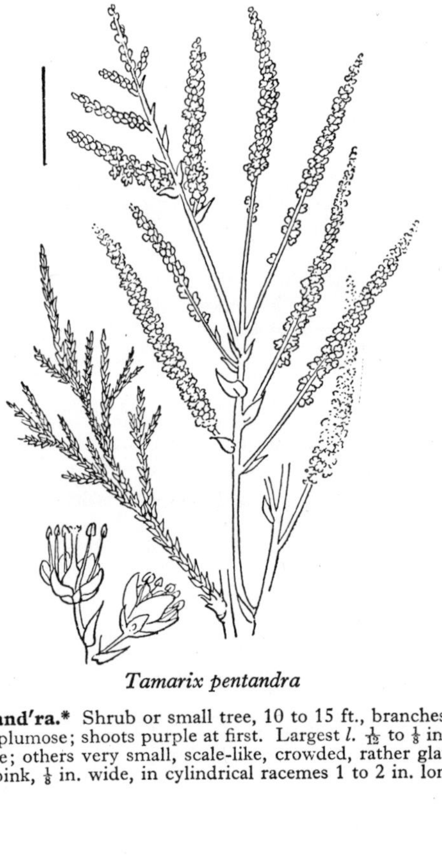

Tamarix pentandra

T. pentand'ra.* Shrub or small tree, 10 to 15 ft., branches long, slender, plumose; shoots purple at first. Largest *l.* $\frac{1}{12}$ to $\frac{1}{8}$ in. long, lanceolate; others very small, scale-like, crowded, rather glaucous. *fl.* rosy-pink, $\frac{1}{8}$ in. wide, in cylindrical racemes 1 to 2 in. long, the current season's shoots transformed into slender panicles; stamens 5. August to September. SE. Europe. 1880. (B.M. 8138.) SYN. *T. Pallasii.* Valued for its late fl. May be pruned hard back in winter.

T. tetrand'ra.* Shrub 10 to 15 ft., stems very dark, glabrous; twigs very slender, densely clothed with minute, scale-like, closely overlapping, pointed l. *fl.* bright pink, very small, packed on cylindrical spikes 1 to 2 in. long from the previous year's shoots; stamens 4. May. SE. Europe, W. Asia. 1821.

tamnifo'lius -a -um, having leaves like Black Bryony (*Tamus communis*).

TA'MUS (variant of Latin *tamnus*, old name for a climbing plant, probably *Tamus communis*). FAM. *Dioscoreaceae.* A genus of 4 species of herbaceous perennial twining plants with alternate shining heart-shaped or 3-lobed long-pointed leaves. Roots tuberous. Flowers dioecious, small, yellowish-green, in axillary racemes; perianth with 6 divisions, male flowers having 6 stamens with slender filaments, female flowers an inferior ovary. Fruit a red berry; seeds globose, not winged.

T. commu'nis. Black Bryony (E.B. 1508), fairly common in hedges, &c., over most of England, is widely distributed in W. Europe and the Mediterranean region. The whole plant contains raphides. The rootstock is rich in starch but too acid and purgative for consumption. The attractive but poisonous berries have caused the death of children and cattle. A detailed account of its life history is given by I. H. Burkill in *Journal of Botany*, 75 (1937). Male plants are about twice as numerous as females. It should not be confused with White Bryony, *Bryonia dioica*, a member of the Cucurbitaceae. Other species, none of special garden merit, are *T. cretica, T. edulis,* and *T. parviflora,* possibly not specifically distinct from one another.

T. elephan'tipes. A synonym of *Dioscorea elephantipes.*

TAN or **TANNER'S WASTE** consists of the bark of various trees, especially Oak, Larch, and Willow from which tannin has been extracted for the purpose of tanning leather. The refuse may be used for the making of hotbeds as it gives a steady heat for a considerable time, the heat being more easily regulated and maintained for a longer period than that obtained from pure stable-manure. In general, however, a mixture of manure and dead leaves is preferred as when it has lost its heat it still forms a valuable manure for adding to the soil, whereas tanner's waste decays slowly and has little manurial value. The greater part of the nitrogenous materials contained in the fresh bark is lost in extracting the tannin, while some of the tannin remains and hinders decay of the refuse. The ash of the waste consists very largely of carbonate of lime and silica, only a very small amount of potash and phosphates being present. If the tan is used as a manure it should be mixed with earth, lime, and farmyard manure and thoroughly saturated occasionally with liquid manure and allowed to ferment for a considerable time before use.

tanacetifo'lius -a -um, with leaves resembling Tanacetum.

TANACE'TUM (altered from medieval Latin *tanazeta*, used in E. Europe). FAM. *Compositae.* A genus of about 35 species of usually erect, often scented, annual or perennial herbs, often woody at base, natives of Europe, N. Africa, W., Cent., and N. Asia, and N. America. Leaves alternate, variously dissected or rarely entire and toothed. Flower-heads yellow, small or of medium-size, in corymbs or rarely solitary, with long peduncles, disk-like; involucre hemispherical or bell-shaped, rarely ovoid, bracts in many series; receptacle flat or slightly convex, naked. Achenes and florets often glandular. Some of the species are showy in a mass but have little individual beauty. Most are hardy and thrive in ordinary soil. Propagation by division.

T. adenan'thum. Densely tufted perennial, 6 to 12 in. h. *l.* covered with silky-white hairs, much cut. *fl.-heads* golden-yellow, about ½ in. across. W. China. Rock-garden.

T. alpi'num. A synonym of *Chrysanthemum alpinum.*

T. argent'eum. A synonym of *Chrysanthemum argenteum.*

T. Aucheria'num. A synonym of *Chrysanthemum Aucherianum.*

T. Balsami'ta. A synonym of *Chrysanthemum Balsamita.*

T. camphora'tum. Silvery-velvety, erect perennial, about 18 in. h., branching, camphor-scented. *l.* 2-pinnate; lobes short, rounded, entire or 3-lobulate, margins revolute. *fl.-heads* golden-yellow, twin or somewhat corymbose; involucre bell-shaped; florets thickened at base and summit. Summer. N. America. (F.d.S. 1191 as *T. elegans.*)

T. fruticulo'sum bractea'tum. Hoary perennial. Stems very numerous, 10 to 14 in. long; root woody. *l.* ¼ to ½ in. long, 1- or 2-pinnatisect. *fl.-heads* yellowish, one to a bracteate peduncle with several coloured bracts crowded beneath the head, appearing like a double involucre; infl. a loose corymb. Tibet. 1878.

T. Herd'eri.* Dwarf, stems rather thick, branched. *l.* in compact silvery rosettes, freely produced. *fl.-heads* bright yellow. Turkistan. Rock-garden.

T. huronen'se. 1 to 2 ft. h., villous or woolly when young. *l.* oblong, pinnatifid, pinnae oblong or oblanceolate. *fl.-heads* long-peduncled, ¾ in. across, in a loose corymb. Eastern N. America.

T. leucophyl'lum. Silky-silvery, about 9 in. h. Stems ascending. *l.* sessile or shortly stalked, roundish-ovate, lower 2-pinnatisect, upper pinnatisect. *fl.-heads* golden-yellow, corymbose; involucre hemispherical, bracts overlapping; florets slightly longer than involucre; peduncles solitary in upper leaf axils. June to August. Turkistan. Rock-garden.

T. vulga're. Buttons; Tansy. 2 to 3 ft. h., stem grooved and angled, leafy. *l.* oblong, 1- or 2-pinnatifid, gland-dotted, 2 to 5 in. long; upper l. half-amplexicaul, lower stalked. *fl.-heads* many, ⅓ in. across, in corymbs; peduncle stout. August, September. Europe including Britain. (E.B. 716.) A variety of this with curled l. (var. **crisp'um**) is grown as an ornamental garnish for dishes. *See* **Tansy.**

TANAKAE'A (in honour of Yoshio Tanaka, Japanese botanist). FAM. *Saxifragaceae.* A genus of a single species of perennial herb with an oblique rhizome. Closely related to Leptarrhena but having 10 stamens and no petals. It grows well in sandy peat in half-shade. Propagation by division in spring.

T. radi'cans.* *rhiz.* oblique, densely fibrillose, giving rise to numerous runners. *l.* evergreen, in a basal rosette, ovate-lanceolate, rounded or heart-shaped at base, acute, 1 to 2½ in. long, rather fleshy, unequally toothed, bristly; stalk long. *fl.* dioecious or monoecious, white, in paniculate cymes, very small; lower peduncles 3-fld., upper 1-fld.; scape slender. April to June. Japan. (B.M. 7943.)

tanasty'lus -a -um, having a long style.

TANEKAHA. *See* **Phyllocladus trichomanoides.**

TANGHINIA. Included in *Cerbera.*

TANGIER PEA. *See* **Lathyrus tingitanus.**

Tang'shen, Chinese name for Bastard Ginseng, *Codonopsis Tangshen.*

tangu'ticus -a -um, belonging to the Tangut region, also called Amdo, of north-eastern Tibet and western Kansu, the territory, once a kingdom of the Tangutans, a northern Tibetan people.

TANIA. *See* **Colocasia antiquorum.**

TANK. A cistern or reservoir for holding rain or spring water until required for use. Although rain-water collected from roofs is apt to be contaminated by bacteria or spores of fungi causing certain plant diseases, or by the spores of mosses or algae, yet it is in most ways and for most plants the best source of water-supply, and like spring water it should usually be kept in tanks until near the temperature of the soil which is to be watered with it. The use of water at a low temperature is not usually detrimental to any but very sensitive plants, but where the temperature of the soil and air are near the minimum the use of water at a lower temperature may well be detrimental to growing plants. Movable tanks may be made of galvanized iron or slate but permanent tanks should be of stone or brick coated inside with cement. These tanks can be below or above ground, either in or adjoining the plant-houses and should be connected to another source of supply in case rain-water fails. Iron tanks should always be galvanized to prevent the formation of iron-rust affecting the water. Where hard water is the source of supply exposure to air in large tanks goes a considerable way towards softening it, but it is, on the whole best to exclude light to prevent the growth of algae in the water. The tanks should be provided with an overflow pipe and with an outlet at the bottom so that they may be periodically emptied for cleaning. It is possible at times to utilize a tank either inside or outside a house for growing water-plants, but care should be taken that the tank in form and proportions is not out of keeping with its surroundings if the use of the house is for ornament.

A supply tank is necessary in connexion with the heating apparatus. It should always be placed a few feet above the highest point of the pipes it has to supply. Its size is immaterial so long as it is kept filled with water. Exposed pipes leading to and from it and the cistern itself should be lagged to prevent freezing in severe weather.

TANKERVIL'LIA. *See* **Phaius Tankervilliae.**

Tankervilliae, in honour of Emma, Lady Tankerville, *c.* 1750–1836, wife of Charley Grey, 4th Earl of Tankerville, who encouraged the introduction of new plants into British gardens.

TANNER'S TREE. *See* **Coriaria myrtifolia** and other species.

TANNIN is an astringent, colourless, soluble material ($C_{14}H_{10}O_9$) found in plants, often in considerable quantity, especially in gall-nuts and in all kinds of bark, but also in other parts, as in seedlings, developing roots and shoots, and probably wherever nitrogenous organic substances are being formed. It is a waste product of metabolism and parts of plants cast off often contain considerable quantities of it. It is of value commercially for it is used in making inks, as a mordant as it makes insoluble compounds with many dyes, and in tanning, for on combining with animal skin it converts it into a much tougher material. Among plants of value for the tannin they contain are Acacia, Betula (used in tanning Russian leather), Butea, Brysonima, Caesalpinia, Castanea, *Geum urbanum* roots, Gordonia, Pterocarpus, Quercus, Rhus, *Rumex hymenosepalus* (Canaigré).

TANSY (*Tanacetum vulgare*) was at one time grown for use in flavouring puddings, cakes, omelettes, salads, and stews, but now its use is confined to the garnishing of dishes with the leaves of the curled form. Tansy is a common roadside plant of vigorous habit, conspicuous in late summer by its flat yellow flower-heads, and easily recognizable at any time by its much-cut leaves with their characteristic scent somewhat resembling camphor. It will grow in almost any soil and is easily propagated in spring by division of its rootstocks. They should be planted at least a foot apart, should be kept free of weeds, and will need restraint lest they spread unduly.

TAPA CLOTH. *See* **Broussonetia.**

TAPE, MEASURING-. A stout tape marked in feet and inches, 33 ft. or 66 ft. (1 chain) long, made to wind into a stout leather case for protection; useful in land measuring, but more subject to change through atmospheric conditions than the measuring-chain (Gunter's chain).

TAPEGRASS. *See* **Vallisneria spiralis.**

TAPEINAN'THUS (*tapeinos*, low, *anthos*, flower; from the low stature of the plant). FAM. *Amaryllidaceae.* A genus of a single species of herb with a tunicated bulb, difficult of cultivation in Britain.

T. hu'milis. *l.* 1, appearing late, filiform, with a small stipitate sheath at base. *fl.* 1 or 2, ⅜ in. across, yellow, funnel-shaped, tube very short, segs. narrow-oblong, erecto-patent, subequal, with a small scale at base; scape very slender, 3 to 4 in. h. Spain, Tangiers. 1887. (G.C. (1887), 53.)

TAPEINID'IUM (*tapeinos*, low, comparatively dwarf). FAM. *Polypodiaceae.* A genus of a dozen species of tropical ferns related to Davallia with once-pinnate fronds and long narrow pinnae but having the stipes continuous with, not jointed to, the caudex, and membranous indusia forming a shallow half-cup attached by both sides and base. For treatment *see* **Davallia.**

T. pinna'tum. *rhiz.* creeping, fibrillose. *sti.* strong, erect, 6 to 12 in. long. *fronds* 9 to 15 in. long, 4 to 8 in. broad, with distant linear, slightly toothed pinnae, 6 in. long, ¼ to ⅜ in. broad. *sori* 1 to each tooth, small. Malaya. (H.S. 1, 60.) SYN. *Davallia pinnata.*

TAPEINOCHI'LUS (Greek *tapeinos*, low, *cheilos*, lip; referring to the small labellum). FAM. *Zingiberaceae.* A genus of about 15 tropical species of perennial herbs, related to Costus, natives of Malayasia and NE. Australia (Queensland). The yellow or brownish flowers are in dense cone-like spikes with conspicuous red bracts. They require stove conditions with shade and considerable warmth and humidity.

T. Ananas'sae. To 6 ft. h. *l.* scattered, narrowly obovate, to 6 in. long, acuminate. *Spike* ovoid, 6 to 8 in. long, 3½ to 4 in. broad, on a leafless erect peduncle, covered with brown bracts and arising direct from the rootstock, 18 to 48 in. h., sometimes with leafy shoots arising immediately below the spike; bracts deep scarlet to crimson, recurving, acuminate, hard, glabrous. *fl.* yellow, shorter than bracts. July, August. Moluccas (Ceram). 1933. (Ann. Mus. Lugduno-Batav. 4. 4.). SYN. *T. pungens.* A remarkable stove plant, the inflorescence suggesting a red pine-apple but having no leafy crown.

W. T. S.

TAPEINOPHAL'LUS. Included in **Amorphophallus.** *See* **A. Rivieri.**

TAPHRI'NA. A genus of Ascomycetous fungi many species of which are plant parasites, including *T. deformans* causing Peach Leaf-curl, *T. Pruni*, the cause of Bladder or Pocket Plums, and *T. Cerasi*, which produces witch's brooms in cherries. The genus was formerly called Exoascus. The asci are formed naked on the surface of the attacked plant tissues, not, as is usual, in some form of fruit.

D. E. G.

TAPIOCA. *See* **Manihot utilissima.**

tapir'iceps, resembling a tapir's head.

tapiro'rum, of the tapirs.

tapi'rus -a -um, tapir-like.

TAPIS'CIA (anagram of *Pistacia*, which it resembles). FAM. *Staphyleaceae.* Monotypic genus akin to Staphylea but differing by its alternate leaves. Some plants have only male flowers, others have only 2-sexual ones. Not very hardy and very rare.

T. sinen'sis. Deciduous tree usually about 30 ft. but has been found 80 ft. with a trunk girthing 12 ft. *l.* pinnate, 12 to 18 in. long, lflets. 5 to 9, ovate, cordate, 3 to 5 in. long, toothed, greyish beneath; stalk ¼ to ½ in. long. *fl.* very small, yellow, honey-scented. *Male panicles* 4 to 6 in. long, with very slender branches; *females* up to 4 in. long. *fr.* ovoid, ⅓ in. long, black, 1-seeded. China. 1908. The foliage turns a good yellow in autumn.

TAP-ROOT, a long, usually central root descending vertically far into the sub-soil; the primary root of a plant formed by the elongation of the radicle.

A→

TAR derived from the distillation of coal or the wood of *Pinus sylvestris* (Stockholm tar) was at one time largely employed as a means of capturing the wingless females of various moths where tacky grease has now taken its place; for making 'tar water' to spray on plants to prevent egg-laying; and for capturing such insects as the flea and raspberry beetles (q.v.). Its use for these purposes has now been entirely superseded and it is now used in the garden only for its preservative value and for painting large wounds on trees made in the course of pruning. It is considered that Stockholm tar is to be preferred for this purpose, but probably a good lead paint is better still, giving a waterproof cover of lasting quality, excluding the spores of fungi, and containing nothing detrimental to the tree. A comparatively recent use of a derivative of tar has, however, gone far towards keeping orchards free from spring attacks by caterpillars, for it has been found that 'tar-oil washes' applied during the dormant season not only kill exposed insects and tend to cleanse the stems of trees of algae, lichens, and loose bark, but also kill the eggs of most pests, including the aphides and Psylla. Unfortunately they are not discriminating between friends and foes of the fruit-grower and leave unharmed the eggs of the red-spider mite while killing the friends that prey upon that pest; continued use of these tar-oil winter-washes, the first of which, introduced from Holland, was known as Carbolineum, may result in a great and detrimental increase of red-spider mite, and other washes have had to be derived for use against it, and against other pests which winter-washes cannot deal with. Many modifications of winter-washes have since been made and they are often offered under proprietary names. Care is necessary in their use, for they are likely to kill any green vegetation under the trees and to damage buds if applied out of the dormant season. *See* **Insecticides.**

TARATA. *See* **Pittosporum eugenioides.**

taraxacifo'lius -a -um, with Dandelion-like leaves.

TARAX'ACUM (derived through medieval Latin *tarasacon* and Arabic *tarakhshagog* from Persian *talkh chakok*, bitter herb). FAM. *Compositae.* A genus of perhaps 60, but according to some botanists, very many, species of herbaceous, nearly stemless herbs, widely dispersed in temperate regions. Leaves radical, entire, or various toothed and jagged. Flower-heads yellow or whitish, homogamous; involucre bell-shaped or oblong, inner bracts in 1 series, outer shorter and in many series; receptacle flat; scapes leafless, usually 1-headed but sometimes branched at top and 2- or 3-headed. The species are hardy and grow in any ordinary soil. The British species, *T. officinale*, the Dandelion, is a troublesome weed, especially in grass, forming buds on its roots if any portion is left in the ground, and producing seeds parthenogenetically, even after the stigmas are cut off. Poisoning is the best means of destroying it (*see* **Weed-killers**). It has considerable medicinal value, especially in the roots of wild plants, and is sometimes grown as a salad (*see* **Dandelion**). The bright colour of the flower-heads of *T. officinale* when open in sunshine and the freedom with which they are produced would doubtless, if it were an exotic plant, commend it as an ornament to the garden, but its invasive qualities condemn it. Other species are sometimes offered but though hardy have, on the whole, less to recommend them. Over 1,200 specific names have been given by Scandinavian and other botanists to apomictic forms of Taraxacum.

T. bico'rne. *l.* not so deeply lobed as in some forms of *T. officinale*, sometimes almost entire. *fl.-heads* bright yellow; involucral bracts with horn-like appendages, not recurved. Turkistan. 1943. (Rev. Bot. Appl. **25** (1945), 4.) SYN. *T. Kok-Saghyz.* A Russian rubber-producing plant of some importance.

T. officina'le. Dandelion. Root long, stout. *l.* radical, oblong-ovate to spatulate, much and very variously cut, and of greatly varying size. *fl.-heads* ½ to 2 in. or more across, bright-yellow; outer rays often brown at back; inner involucral bracts erect, outer recurved. March to October. Europe, &c. (E.B. 802.)

TARCHONAN'THUS (*Tarchon*, the Arabic name for *Artemisia Dracunculus*; *anthos*, a flower; in allusion to the resemblance of its flower-heads to those of that plant). FAM. *Compositae.* A small genus of 3 species from Africa. Leaves stalked, alternate, leathery, finally glabrous above, hairy beneath. Flower-heads small in terminal and axillary panicles, rarely almost solitary. Growing well in sandy fibrous loam with a little peat. Propagated by cuttings under a close frame in early summer.

T. camphora'tus. Shrub with a strong balsamic odour, sometimes a small tree 15 ft. or more, dioecious. *l.* grey and rather sage-like, 3 to 5 in. long, 1 to 1½ in. wide, lanceolate, oblong or ovate, cuneate, mostly entire, very downy at first, pale and net-veined beneath. *fl.-heads* purple, about ½ in. wide, globose, in axillary and terminal panicles forming large compound panicles up to 10 in. by 8 in.; male fl. with the anthers exerted. June to October. S. and Trop. Africa. 1690. (L.B.C. 382.) Greenhouse.

tard'us -a -um (***tardi-*** in compound words), late or slow.

TARE. *See* **Vicia.**

TARNISHED PLANT BUG, *Lygus pratensis*, often known as the Bishop Bug or Fly, is destructive to many kinds of plants, especially Chrysanthemums both under glass and in the open. Considerable malformation of the flowers occurs on such plants as Arctotis, Dahlias, Venidiums, and Zinnias to which it migrates from weeds, e.g. Groundsel, Docks, and Sorrel. The adult bug is pale yellowish-green, often mottled with reddish-brown giving the insects a dark appearance, and is about ¼ in. long. The creamy-white, flask-shaped eggs are inserted in the shoots and stems and among the florets of Composite blooms. The young greenish larvae are wingless and very active, running about over the leaves and shoots and feeding by inserting their sucking rostrum into the tissues and abstracting the sap. At least 2 generations occur in the year, the adults of the second brood overwintering in the cut stems of herbaceous plants, among coarse herbage, in hedge bottoms, and elsewhere. They again become active in spring, laying their eggs on weeds, especially in Groundsel flowers. The most serious damage to Chrysanthemums is done during August and September, when the feeding of the bugs causes spotting and distortion of the leaves, blindness of the buds, stunting and malformation of the shoots, and deformity and discoloration of the blooms.

Clean cultivation, including the destruction of weeds by regular hoeing and scything of ditch-sides near flower-borders will tend to reduce the number of bugs and lessen the chance of massed migration from wild hosts to cultivated plants. A number of immature and mature bugs may be shaken off herbaceous and other plants on dull days into an open inverted umbrella. Attacked plants should be thoroughly sprayed with a D.D.T. emulsion, taking special care to wet both sides of the leaves. Dusting with Nicotine dust is also effective, and the deposit of dust remaining on the foliage tends to repel further attack. Two or three applications are necessary both to cover the fresh growth with dust and to destroy fresh arrivals from their wild hosts. The overwintering quarters of the adults may be reduced by cutting down herbaceous stems to ground-level, by raking out dead leaves from hedge bottoms, by cutting down coarse herbage on ditch-sides, and by clearing away all accumulations of plant refuse in the vicinity of flower borders.

G. F. W.

TARO. Native name of *Colocasia antiquorum.*

taronen'sis -is -e, from the Taron Valley, Yunnan.

TARRAGON (*Artemisia Dracunculus*). Perennial native of S. Europe, grown for the use of its leaves in seasoning salads, and fish sauces, and in the making of tarragon vinegar. It grows best in warm, rather dry positions and may need a little protection in severe winters. In damp soils it is particularly liable to winter injury. It has numerous branching stems about 2 ft. high and long, narrow leaves, the basal ones 3-pointed at apex, upper at the most minutely toothed. It flowers in August but rarely produces ripe seeds. Propagation is by pulling (not chopping) apart the underground runners in March or April, and by cuttings in a little warmth in spring or in summer under a hand-light, outside. The leaves are fit for picking from mid-June to the end of September and are usually used fresh, but may be dried in autumn for use later. If fresh leaves are desired from October onwards they may be had by lifting a few plants and replanting in frames. They are not much used in England except in the making of tarragon vinegar, for which purpose the leaves are picked on a dry day just before the plant flowers, removing them from the stems, and drying slightly before a fire. They are then placed in a jar and covered with the best white vinegar, allowed to stand some hours, and then strained through a flannel jelly-bag, the resulting vinegar being bottled and corked. Two varieties are available, French tarragon with very smooth dark green leaves and Russian tarragon (from Siberia) with less smooth leaves of a fresher green and with less of the tartness of the French variety. The French variety is usually preferred.

TARSONEMID MITES. A group of very minute, often microscopic, Mites which are of great economic importance owing to the injury caused by them to cultivated plants. They are widely distributed throughout the warmer regions of the world, and a great variety of plants are attacked by them (*see* **Tarsonemus**). *Acarapis woodi* belongs to the sub-family *Tarsopolipinae*, members of which are parasites of insects.

G. F. W.

TARSON'EMUS. A genus of destructive mites. *See* **Bulb Scale Mite** (*T. laticeps*), **Fern Mite** (*T. tepidariorum*), **Strawberry Mite** (*T. pallidus*), under **Strawberry,** PESTS, in Supplement.

G. F. W.

tartar'eus -a -um, of the underworld, from the colour.

TARTARIAN LAMB. The rhizome of *Cibotium Barometz* (q.v.).

tasman'icus -a -um, of Tasmania.

tatar'icus -a -um, of Tartary, Central Asia.

Tatarinow'ii, in honour of Alexander Tatarinow, author of a catalogue of Chinese drugs (1856).

Tatu'la, from Datura.

Tauhinu. *See* **Cassinia leptophylla.**

TAUHINU-KOROKIO. *See* **Cassinia retorta.**

tauri, of the Taurus range in Southern Asia Minor.

tau'ricus -a -um, of the Crimea, in ancient geography called *Taurica Chersonese.*

tauri'nus -a -um, of Turin, N. Italy, from the Roman colony *Augusta Taurinorum.*

tauruli'nus -a -um, like a little bull.

Tausch'eri, in honour of Gyula Tauscher, 1832–82, physician of Ercsi, Hungary.

TAVARE'SIA (in honour of José Tavares de Macedo, official of the Portuguese Ministry of Colonies, amateur botanist who assisted Welwitsch in Angola, where *T. angolensis* was found). FAM. *Asclepiadaceae.* Leafless, succulent plants which differ from the other Stapeliads in that the tubercles into which the many angles of the stem are divided are each tipped with 3 bristles. The flowers are tubular funnel-shaped, the internal structure resembling Stapelia (q.v.). For treatment *see* **Stapelia.**

T. Bark'lyi. Stems 10- to 12-angled, glaucous, tubercles white, the 3 bristles purple. *fl.* from base of stem, tubular with a spreading, 5-pointed limb, pale yellow, spotted with red. Cape Province. (W. & S. 1177–80; B.M. 6203 as *Decabelone Barklyi.*)

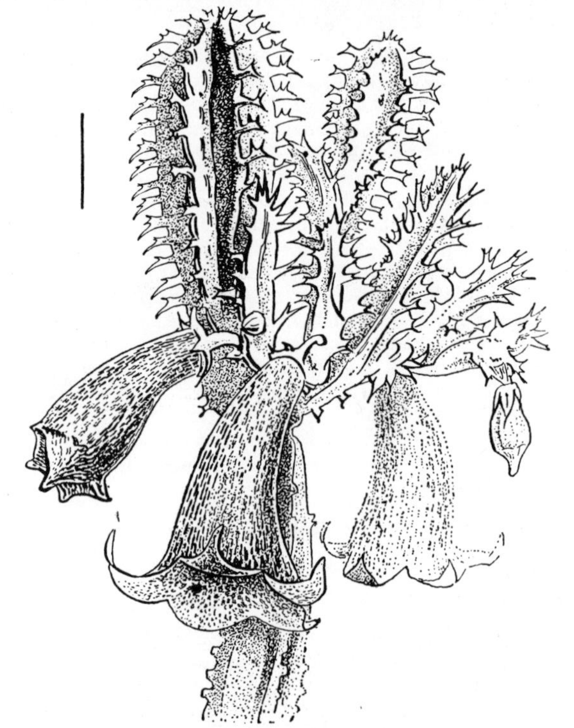

Tavaresia elegans

T. e'legans. Stems tufted, 7- to 9-angled, with 3-branched spines at angles, 6 in. h. *fl.* similar to those of *T. Barklyi*; cor. yellowish-white, spotted blood-red, funnel-shaped, 2 in. long, $1\frac{1}{2}$ in. wide at mouth. Angola. 1873. (B.M. 6115.)

T. grandiflo'ra. Stems about 14-angled, deep green, bristles white. *fl.* similar to *T. Barklyi* but much larger, up to 4 in. long. SW. Africa. (W. & S. 1181–3 and Pl. 23.)

V. H.

TAVERNIE'RA (in honour of J. B. Tavernier, 1605–89, who travelled in the Levant). FAM. *Leguminosae.* A genus of about 7 species of grey-hairy or glabrous undershrubs, natives of the E. Indies and the Orient. Leaves few, 1-foliolate or pinnately 3-foliolate; leaflets often obovate or orbicular; stipules scarious. Flowers papilionaceous, pink or white, few in axillary, stalked racemes; calyx teeth sub-equal or 2 upper more remote; standard broadly orbicular, narrowed at base, scarcely clawed; bracts minute or caducous. Pods flat, indehiscent. Greenhouse plants needing treatment like Mimosa.

T. lappa'cea. Stems procumbent, branched, spreading, terete. *l.* 3-foliolate; lflets. fleshy, obcordate, villous. *fl.* yellow, solitary or twin in l.-axils, pedicels short. August. Arabia Felix. 1820.

T. nummula'ria. E. Indian Moneywort. Much branched, 1 to 2 ft. h. *l.* usually 3-foliolate; lflets. $\frac{1}{4}$ to 1 in. long, obovate-oblong or nearly round, thick, thinly grey-hairy beneath; stipules free. *fl.* red, glabrous, about $\frac{1}{2}$ in. long; racemes few- or many-fld., usually longer than l. June, July. India, eastwards. 1826.

TAWHEWHEO. *See* **Quintinia serrata.**

tawny, reddish-brown, fulvous.

TAWNY MINING BEE, *Andrena fulva* and some other solitary bees make nests in lawns and garden paths, the females digging burrows and throwing up small mounds of fine soil in early spring. The small bees appear in April, emerging then from the burrows made by their parents in the previous year. The shaft is dug 6 to 12 in. deep and a series of short side galleries are made into which pollen and honey are placed as food for the larvae which hatch from eggs laid one in each cell. The mounds may be dispersed by brushing and daily rolling the turf during the period of emergence. A dressing of 3 to 4 oz. of Naphthalene to the sq. yard will discourage the bees from making nests in the treated area.

A G. F. W.

TAXA'CEAE. Coniferae. A family of evergreen resinous trees with 11 genera and about 100 species distributed over the whole world except in the Arctic and Antarctic regions. Leaves alternate (rarely opposite), often in 2 ranks, needle- or scale-like, rarely broad, entire. Flowers usually dioecious, stamens in a cone-like inflorescence; ovules usually solitary. Fruit a seed with a hard shell partly or completely surrounded by a fleshy aril. Embryo with 2 cotyledons. The genera dealt with here are Acmopyle, Cephalotaxus, Dacrydium, Microcachrys, Phyllocladus, Podocarpus, Saxe-Gothaea, Taxus, and Torreya.

taxifo'lius -a -um, yew-leaved.

taxiform'is -a -um, yew-like.

A→

taxodioi'des, resembling Taxodium.

TAXO'DIUM (*Taxus*, the Yew, *eidos*, resemblance; referring to a similarity in the shape of the leaves). Deciduous Cypress. FAM. *Pinaceae.* A small genus of ornamental, hardy or half-hardy trees natives of south-eastern N. America and Mexico, closely allied to the Chinese genus Glyptostrobus. They are semi-aquatic trees, occupying extensive areas of swampy land about the Gulf of Mexico, where the trees are often surrounded by water several feet deep, but they also succeed on drained land. In wet land the lower part is much enlarged but not so in dry-land trees. From the roots of trees growing in very wet ground or those covered by water, hollow, conical protuberances or 'knees' are produced which rise above the water and conduct air to the roots. When young the trees are pyramidal or fastigiate, but old trees have spreading branches. The secondary branchlets are deciduous. Male and female flowers are on the same tree, the male in numerous tassel-like catkins from the ends of branches, the female solitary or a few together, also from near the ends of shoots. Cones rounded, with woody scales. They are very beautiful trees in spring when the leaves are pale green, and again in autumn when the leaves are bright brown. Although the wood is weak and soft, it has long-lasting properties when exposed to weather or excessive damp, and is in demand for many purposes, including vats and water-pipes. It contains a fragrant oil which is repellent to white ants, and can therefore be used for house-building in countries where this pest is prevalent. They succeed in ordinary good garden soil and may also be planted in wet boggy places. Seeds form the best means of increase, but cuttings can be rooted.

T. ascend'ens. Differs from its close relation *T. distichum* by its smaller size, denser habit, much shorter l. pressed close to shoot except at tip. Usually found on dry land, inland from Gulf of Mexico. SYN. *T. distichum imbricarium.* var. **nu'tans,** branches pendulous.

T. dis'tichum. Deciduous Cypress. Large tree, 100 to 120 ft. h., pyramidal when young, but with widespreading head at maturity, bark reddish-brown, fibrous. In wet places the base of the trunk may be much enlarged, and from the roots, long protuberances or 'knees' may rise well above the surrounding land or water level. Young shoots green or glaucous-green at first, brown later, many secondary branches deciduous, and falling in autumn with l. Winter buds rounded and covered with closely pressed, pointed scales. *l.* spirally arranged, but owing to a basal twist appearing 2 ranked on many branchlets, particularly on the deciduous ones, 1/2 to 3/4 in. long on secondary branchlets, shorter on others, pale green in spring, rich brown in autumn, stomata beneath, short-pointed. *Male fl.* purplish, in tassel-like, terminal clusters, usually 3 to 6 in., or more, long. *Cones* solitary or several together, rounded, resinous, 1/2 to 1 1/4 in. wide, scales few, woody, quadrangular, with 2 ovules on each scale. *Seeds* triangular, surface rough. SE. United States to Mexico. 1640. (D.J.C. 498.) Perfectly hardy in many parts of the British Is. and there are numerous trees 80 to 100 ft. h. With young trees it is sometimes difficult to get a single leading shoot and pruning may be necessary. var. **imbricar'ium,** a synonym of *T. ascendens*; **mucrona'tum,** Montezuma Cypress, the Mexican form, chiefly differing by being less hardy with rather larger sub-evergreen l. SYN. *T. mucronatum*; **pend'ulum,** branches drooping; **heterophyl'lum,** synonym of *Glyptostrobus pensilis.*

taxoi'des, Taxus-like.

TAXON (plural **TAXA**). A taxonomic group of any rank; a unit of classification; a species is a taxon. Other commonly used taxa are form, subspecies, series, section, genus, and family.

TAX'US (old Latin name for the Yew, used by Virgil and Pliny, akin to Greek *Taxos* of Dioscorides). Yew. FAM. *Taxaceae.* A genus of a few species of hardy, evergreen trees or large shrubs with a dense branch system, widely distributed over north temperate regions. Leaves sub-spirally arranged but appearing more or less in 2 ranks, short-stalked, narrow, flat, often sickle-shaped. Male and female flowers in leaf-axils on different trees, the male in small rounded heads, the female as tiny solitary green bodies. Fruit a hard nut-like seed surrounded by a fleshy aril which is bright-coloured when ripe. They thrive in almost any soil, succeeding in limy as well as in acid soils, but the ground must be well drained; the sudden waterlogging of ground often results in the death of trees. Propagation of the species is readily effected by seeds. These should be collected when ripe and be mixed with sand and left in a shed for winter, then be sown out of doors in spring. Varieties can be increased by short cuttings inserted in sandy soil in a close, cold frame or under a handlight in August, and shaded from bright sun, or they may be grafted on stocks of the common Yew. The lower branches may also be layered. The wood is hard, strong, and elastic. It can be used for furniture, and was at one time in great esteem for the manufacture of bows. An account of the most venerable British Yew and Irish Yew trees is given in the book *The Churchyard Yew* (1946) by Vaughan Cornish.

DISEASES. Occasionally Bracket fungi may occur on old Yew trees, but they cannot be considered dangerous or common. Two diseases of Yew foliage may cause damage, one being Yew Leaf-scorch due to the fungus *Sphaerulina taxi* which is not common but may cause browning of the leaves, on the upper surfaces of which appear minute rather thickly crowded pustules. For this disease spraying with Bordeaux mixture may be required as the trouble may spread rapidly. Very similar to the above is Yew Leaf-blight due to *Macrophoma taxi* which causes similar symptoms but that small black perithecia are scattered over the *under* surface of the affected leaves. Removal of first-affected branches should be sufficient, although spraying would be a wise additional precaution especially for young trees.

(D. E. G.)

PESTS. YEW GALL MIDGE, *Oligotrophus taxi*, produces an artichoke-shaped gall on the terminal shoots of Yew, especially in the southern counties. The gall consists of numerous short soft leaves within which may be seen the reddish larva. Pupation takes place towards the end of May, and the Gall Midges are on the wing in June.

It is seldom necessary to take special measures against this pest, but an attack on young specimen trees may be controlled by handpicking and burning the cone-shaped galls in spring, and by dusting the growths with Nicotine dust as soon as the shoot deformation is observed.

YEW GALL MITE, *Phytoptus psilaspis*, causes 'Big Bud' on Yew. The infested buds become enlarged, minutely granulated, yellowish or reddish-brown, and contain large numbers of the microscopic mites within the inner fleshy portions. Migration from attacked to healthy buds occurs in spring.

Spraying against this Gall Mite is seldom necessary, but severely galled branches should be removed and burned in spring.

YEW SCALE, *Lecanium corni crudum*, has in recent years become a serious pest of Yew, both specimen trees and hedge plants being attacked. The mature scales resemble the European Brown or Peach Scale, but are paler and somewhat flatter. They attack both shoots and branches. The dust-like, white eggs are found beneath the female scales in July, and the winter is passed in the younger larval stages on the leaves, shoots, and branches. The scales excrete a considerable amount of honeydew, which drops down on to the leaves, shoots, and lower branches and there forms a medium favourable to the growth of Sooty Moulds, the presence of which is often the first indication of an attack. This pest is readily controlled by thoroughly drenching both leaf surfaces, shoots, and branches in early September and in March with a White Oil and Nicotine emulsion (*see* **Scale Insects**).

(G. F. W.)

T. adpres'sa. A variety of *T. baccata*.

T. bacca'ta. Heavily branched tree 40 to 60 ft. h., developing in woods with a long, rather slender trunk, but, if isolated, with a short trunk of considerable girth, and living to a very great age, sometimes upwards of 1,000 years. Branches alternately arranged and widespreading, young shoots green by reason of attached l.-bases. *l.* spirally arranged and appearing so on erect shoots, on side shoots appearing more or less 2-ranked by a basal twist, ½ to 1¼ in. long, narrow, dark glossy-green above, pale green beneath with stomata not easily seen, short-pointed. *Male fl.* yellow, in small rounded heads. February. *Seeds* dark green with a hard shell enclosed in a red, fleshy, edible aril, seed poisonous. Europe (including British Is.), Asia from Himalaya northwards. (D.J.C. 63.) A large number of varieties have developed which vary in habit, size, and colour of foliage. All thrive throughout the British Is. where the ground is not waterlogged, even on thin soil overlying chalk. They withstand regular clipping and at one period were very popular for topiary work. Next to the Holly Yew is the best plant for a permanent evergreen hedge. A Yew hedge should be planted in carefully prepared ground in May or September, and the early trimming should be carried out with a view to making a regular dense bottom. After the hedge is well established, one annual clipping in September will suffice. Varieties are usually grown as decorative specimens, and should not be clipped but allowed to grow freely and kept in shape by light pruning. Yews are often credited with very great age, but it is usually impossible to verify the age. Undoubtedly they may live for many hundreds of years, and after they have reached a particular state may show little variation over a period of 50 or more years. The branches and leaves of Yews are exceedingly poisonous and have caused the death of many cattle and horses. The toxic principle appears to be particularly virulent when the leaves are partly withered; therefore, hedge trimmings should never be left within the reach of animals. var. **adpres'sa,** bush 6 to 8 ft. high differing from type by shorter, relatively broader, dull green l., and dense habit. At Chester about 1838. Female form with red seed arils; a very good garden shrub. Of this the form **au'rea** is golden-yellow, less vigorous than type, and **stric'ta** has stiff, erect branches; **al'ba variega'ta,** points of young shoots and l. silvery; **argen'tea,** *l.* striped silvery-white, changing to straw-colour; **au'rea,** compact bush, *l.* golden, turning green in second year; **Barron'i,** *l.* and young shoots orange, turning copper with age, best growing in a little shade; **canaden'sis,** a synonym of *T. canadensis*; **Cavendish'ii,** branches prostrate, widespreading; **cheshunten'sis,** habit intermediate between type and var. *fastigiata*, with leaf arrangement of latter; **columna'ris,** very narrowly fastigiate, very slow growing, *l.* edged gold, smaller than in var. *fastigiata aurea*; **compact'a,** compact, slow-growing dwarf bush; **contort'a,** branchlets twisted; **Dovaston'ii,** Westfelton Yew, branches long and horizontal, branchlets pendent, a very handsome Yew, about 1777. Male and female fl. have been found on the same plant. Of this the form **aureo-variega'ta** has habit of type with golden variegated l.; **elegantiss'ima,** vigorous, graceful bush. *l.* golden variegated, can be used for hedges. SYN. var. *horizontalis elegantissima*; **elvastonen'sis,** *l.* at first bright orange colour, becoming dull; **epacridioides,** dwarf, erect bush, *l.* short, turning bronze in autumn, green in spring; **erect'a,** bush of dense, erect habit. Of this the form **au'rea,** has golden *l.*; **ericoi'des,** slender, slow-growing, *l.* very small, dark green; **expan'sa,** erect, of pleasing habit, *l.* 1 to 1½ in. long, very dark green above, pale beneath; **fastigia'ta,** Irish Yew, Florence Court Yew, dense, fastigiate, the erect branches with tufted branchlets, *l.* surrounding shoot, female, found wild by a farmer near Florence Court, Ireland about 1780. The form **argent'ea** has silvery l. with the green, **au'rea,** *l.* golden, **Standish'ii,** *l.* golden, of rather slow growth, very attractive; **Fish'eri** has no leading shoot, branches spread horizontally, *l.* green; **Fox'ii,** a dwarf, about 2 ft. h., *l.* small, very dark green; **fructu-lu'teo,** *see* var. **lutea**; **glau'ca,** young *l.* glaucous beneath; **grac'ilis pend'ula,** very decorative tree with erect leader, horizontal branches, long pendent branchlets, and glaucous-green l.; **horizontal'is,** low-growing bush with no distinct leader and long, horizontal branches; **horizontalis elegantis'sima,** a synonym of var. *elegantissima*; **Jack'sonii,** vigorous tree with definite leader, horizontal branches, long pendent branchlets, *l.* rather light green; **lu'tea,** like type but aril yellow. SYN. var. *fructu-luteo*; **na'na,** dwarf, compact, conical bush with dark, glossy green l. longer than in type; **nidpathensis,** very free-growing tree, *l.* green; **nu'tans,** dwarf dense, *l.* very small; **pend'ula,** less vigorous, but otherwise like var. *gracilis pendula*; **procum'bens,** more spreading than var. *nana*; **pyg'maea,** very small rounded bush, the smallest of the dwarf varieties; **pyramid'alis,** branches erect, crowded, rather wide at base. The form **variegat'a** has golden variegated *l.*; **recurva'ta,** branches wide-spreading, horizontal, leaf-margins recurved; **repan'dens,** low-growing, widespreading bush; **semperaur'ea,** very attractive golden-leaved variety; **stric'ta,** dense, erect bush, *l.* pale green; **Washington'ii,** synonym of *T. canadensis Washingtonii*. Several additional dwarf varieties are described in *Dwarf and Slow-growing Conifers*, Hornibrook, ed. 2, 1938.

T. brevifo'lia. Californian or Oregon Yew. Tree, 20 to 30 ft. h., with thin, reddish bark and slender branches; winter buds covered with loose, yellowish scales. *l.* ½ to ⅝ in. long, $\frac{1}{16}$ in. wide, yellowish-green above, paler beneath, pointed. *fr.* as in *T. baccata*. Western N. America. 1854. Very rare in the British Is. and often confused with a variety of *T. baccata*.

T. canaden'sis, bush, 4 to 6 ft. h., with loose straggling branches resembling a low-growing form of *T. baccata*. Eastern N. America. 1800. var. **au'rea,** *l.* golden, but not very bright; **mi'nima,** very dwarf; **Washington'ii,** pendent-branched form, *l.* golden. SYN. *T. baccata Washingtonii*.

T. chinen'sis. Tree 18 to 50 ft. h. with light brown, open branchlets and pale brown winter buds. *l.* more widely disposed than in *T. baccata*, ½ to 1½ in. long, $\frac{1}{12}$ to ⅛ in. wide, sickle-shaped, dark green, spreading horizontally, short-pointed. *Seeds* smaller than in *T. baccata*, aril red. Cent. and W. China. 1908. SYN. *T. baccata chinensis*, *T. cuspidata chinensis*.

T. cuspida'ta. Japanese Yew. Tree up to 50 ft. h., erect or spreading, with red or greyish-brown bark. *Winter-buds* oblong, brown. *l.* more or less upright on the branches, ½ to 1 in. long, $\frac{1}{12}$ to ⅛ in. wide, straight or slightly curved, dark green above, yellowish-green beneath, apex a short, stiff point. *Seeds* longer in proportion than in *T. baccata*, aril red. Japan. 1855. var. **aures'cens,** slow, low-growing bush, *l.* yellow; **chinen'sis,** a synonym of *T. chinensis*, **contor'ta,** branchlets much twisted; **na'na,** dwarf compact, *l.* short.

T. × hyb'rida (*T. baccata* × *T. cuspidata*). Intermediate in habit, *l.* very similar to those of *T. cuspidata*. var. **Sargen'tii,** erect conical, with l. surrounding the shoot as in the Irish Yew. Female.

T. × me'dia (*T. baccata* × *T. cuspidata*). *l.* very like those of *T. cuspidata* but 2-ranked as in *T. baccata*. Raised in N. America. Introduced 1931. var. **Hatfield'ii,** branches stiff, erect like those of the Irish Yew with a similar leaf arrangement, becoming conical with age; **Hicks'ii,** rather similar to last but more columnar.

W. D.

Tazet'ta, a little cup, from the form of the corona in *Narcissus Tazetta*.

T-BUDDING. *See* **Budding.**

Tchihatchew'ia (in honour of Count Pierre A. de Tchihatchef, 1808–90, famous Russian traveller and writer). FAM. *Cruciferae*. A genus of a single species of perennial herb related to Isatis. Hardy. Suited by well-drained loamy soil in sun.

T. isati'dea. Perennial with stout stem 6 to 10 in. h. *l.* linear, spreading and recurved, 1½ to 2½ in. long, gradually larger towards top of stem, hispidly hairy; sessile. *fl.* bright rose-red, vanilla-scented, in a hemispheric much-branched corymb, 4 in. across; limb of pet. oblong, half as long as claw. May. Armenia. 1893. (B.M. 7608.)

Tchonos'kii, in honour of the Japanese plant collector Tchonoski, *c.* 1873.

TEA. The dried leaves of several different plants are used in different parts of the world in the same way as those of *Camellia sinensis* which provides the different types of tea used in European countries; among them are *Catha edulis* (the Arabian Khat), *Ledum palustre* (Labrador tea), *Neea theifera* (the S. American Caparrosa), *Priva echinata* (America), and *Stachytarpheta dichotoma* (W. Indies). The following are said to have medicinal properties:

TEA BERRY or **CANADA TEA.** *See* **Gaultheria procumbens.**

TEA, MEXICAN. *See* **Chenopodium ambrosioides.**

TEA, OSWEGO. *See* **Monarda didyma.**

TEA, PARAGUAY. *See* **Ilex paraguariensis.**

TEA-TREE. *See* **Lycium.**

TEAK, INDIAN. *See* **Tectona grandis.**

TEASEL. *See* **Dipsacus.**

TEC'LEA. *See* **Toddalia.**

TECO'MA (from the Mexican name *Tecomaxochitl*). FAM. *Bignoniaceae.* A genus, as now understood, of about 5 species of erect shrubs, natives of the warmer parts of America. Leaves opposite, unequally pinnate, lflets. toothed, rather thin. Flowers in terminal racemes or panicles; calyx tubular-bell-shaped; corolla funnel-bell-shaped; stamens included, anther cells spreading with the connective leaf-like; disk cup-shaped with crenate edge. Fruit a linear capsule with leathery valves and many narrow-elliptic 2-winged seeds. The Tecomas succeed in good fibrous loam, well-drained, require plenty of water in summer and little in winter, and full light and air so that the growths ripen well, otherwise flowering is sparse. Propagation is by cuttings of partly ripened shoots, or by layers. The supposed hybrid, *T.* × *Smithii*, comes true from seed. The plants commonly called Tecomas should be sought under Campsis.

T. amboinen'sis. Probably a species of Pandorea.

T. austral'is. A synonym of *Pandorea australis.*

T. austro-caledon'ica. A synonym of *Pandorea austro-caledonica.*

T. capen'sis. A synonym of *Tecomaria capensis.*

T. filicifo'lia. A synonym of *Pandorea pandorana*, juvenile state.

T. ful'va. Erect shrub to 15 ft., branches round, smooth. *lflets.* in many pairs, wedge-shaped-ovate, subsessile, toothed at tip, hairy when young, finally smooth; stalks jointed. *fl.* brownish without, yellow within, 1½ in. long; racemes 7- to 9-fld. Peru. 1855. (B.M. 4896.) Stove.

T. Garroch'a. Much like *T. stans*, but more graceful. *Lflets.* oblong-ovate, slender-pointed, toothed, stalked. *fl.* scarlet and yellow, tube slender, narrowing towards base, nearly 1 in. across; in slender racemes forming panicles 5 to 6 in. long. Summer. Argentina. Greenhouse.

T. grandiflo'ra. A synonym of *Campsis chinensis.*

T. jasminoi'des. A synonym of *Pandorea jasminoides.*

T. mol'lis. Softly hairy, erect shrub to 6 ft. Branches rather flattened. *l.* unequally pinnate; lflets. usually in 4 pairs, oblong, slender-pointed, nearly entire, slightly toothed at tip, velvety on both sides. *fl.* yellow or reddish in a terminal panicle. Mexico to Chile. 1824. Greenhouse.

T. radi'cans. A synonym of *Campsis radicans.*

T. Ricasolia'na. A synonym of *Podranea Ricasoliana.*

T. sambucifo'lia. Glabrous, erect shrub to 6 ft., with slightly flattened branches. *l.* unequally pinnate; lflets. in 2 or 3 pairs, oblong, slender-pointed, toothed. *fl.* yellow, funnel-shaped; panicle terminal. July. Peru. 1824. Stove.

T. × **Smith'ii** (? *T. mollis* × *Tecomaria capensis*). *l.* pinnate; lflets. oblong, 1½ to 2 in. long, acute. *fl.* bright yellow, tinged orange; cor. tubular-funnel-shaped, 1½ to 2 in. long; lobes reflexed; panicles up to 8 in. long and as wide. Introduced from Australia. Parentage somewhat doubtful. A useful winter-flowering plant for growing in pots. (G.C. 3 ser. 14 (1893) 649.)

T. stans. Yellow Elder. Erect, glabrous shrub to 12 ft., branches terete. *l.* unequally pinnate; lflets. 5 to 11, lanceolate, slender-pointed, deeply toothed. *fl.* yellow, 1½ in. long, in racemes or panicles. Summer. W. Indies, Mexico to Peru. 1730. (B.M. 3191.) Greenhouse. SYN. *Bignonia stans.* var. **apifolia,** *lflets.* nearly pinnatifid. SYN. *Bignonia incisa* of gardens *Stenolobium stans*; **veluti'na,** lflets. hairy beneath. SYN. *T. velutina.*

T. undula'ta. A synonym of *Tecomella undulata.*

T. valdivia'na. A synonym of *Campsidium chilense.*

T. Whyt'ei. A synonym of *Tecomaria shirensis.*

TECOMAR'IA (from *Tecoma* to which it is very closely related). FAM. *Bignoniaceae.* A genus of 5 species of half-climbing or nearly erect evergreen shrubs with slender or low-spreading branches, natives of Cent. and S. America and S. Africa. Leaves odd-pinnate, opposite; leaflets toothed. Flowers in terminal racemes or panicles; calyx bell-shaped, regularly 5-toothed; corolla funnel-shaped, slightly curved; stamens mostly exserted, with pendulous spreading cells; disk cup-shaped. Capsules linear, compressed. For treatment *see* **Tecoma.** *T. capensis* will succeed in large pots, the others are best planted out.

Tecomaria capensis

T. capen'sis. Glabrous climber to 15 ft. *lflets.* in 4 pairs, ovate, toothed. *fl.* orange-scarlet, 2 in. long, incurved; stamens exserted; racemes stalked. S. Africa. 1823. (B.R. 1117; L.B.C. 1672.) SYN. *Tecoma capensis.* Cool greenhouse.

T. shiren'sis. Erect shrub. *l.* 5 to 9 in. long, sometimes in whorls of 3; lflets. in 4 to 6 pairs, ovate, toothed, acute, glabrous above, with tufts of hair in vein-axils beneath. *fl.* orange, striped red, funnel-shaped, curved, upper lip erect, lower deflexed; stamens exserted. May to September. Trop. Africa. 1902. (B.M. 7970 as *Tecoma Whytei.*) Stove.

TECOMEL'LA (diminutive of Tecoma). FAM. *Bignoniaceae.* A genus of erect shrubs with entire leaves and flowers much resembling those of Tecoma, needing stove conditions.

T. undula'ta. Tall, erect, glabrous shrub. *l.* linear-lanceolate, obtuse, 6 to 7 in. long, wavy, entire; stalk nearly 1 in. long. *fl.* orange, large, bell-shaped; racemes few-fld. at ends of side branches. Summer. Arabia, India. SYN. *Bignonia undulata, Tecoma undulata.*

TECOPHILAE'A (in honour of Tecofila Billiotti, daughter of Professor Colla of Turin, *c.* 1830). FAM. *Amaryllidaceae.* A genus of 2 species of Chilean herbs. Rootstock a fibrous-coated corm. Leaves radical, few or solitary, spreading, linear or lanceolate, sheath scarious. Flowers with a short perianth-tube above the half-inferior ovary, lobes much longer, obovate-oblong, flat, nearly equal; scape leafless but partly enclosed in leaf-sheaths, 1- or loosely few-flowered. *T. cyanocrocus* needs a compost of rich, sandy loam but does not prove an easy plant in many places possibly because it starts early into growth. Retarding by cold-storage has been suggested as a means of treatment. Propagation by cormlets (as in Gladiolus) or by seed.

T. cyanocro'cus. Chilean Crocus. Corm flattish, about ½ in. across, fibrous-coated. *l.* usually 3, radical, linear to linear-lanceolate, 3 to 5 in. long, often with wavy margins. *fl.* blue with a whitish throat, 1¼ to 1½ in. long, segs. obovate, many-nerved; peduncles 1 to 3, 1-fld., 1 to 2 in. long, slender. Chile. 1872. (B.M. 8987.) var. **el'egans,** perianth segs. and *l.* somewhat narrower than in type (G.F. 718 as *T. cyaneo-crocea*). SYN. var. *Regelii*; **Leichtlin'ii,** *fl.* with somewhat more white in throat. 1886; **Regel'ii,** *see* var. **elegans.**

TECTA'RIA (*tectum,* roof; from the indusia). FAM. *Polypodiaceae.* A genus of over 200 species, generally large with reniform or cordate indusia fixed by the sinus as in Dryopteris but with the veins making a network with free veinlets in the meshes. Very few if any species are difficult to suit and whether stove or greenhouse treatment is required a mixture of 3 parts of sandy peat and 1 of fibrous loam will serve. Most species thrive also where the light is not abundant. They should not be potted hard and if planted out the soil around them should be kept moderately loose. They need abundant water at their roots and frequent syringing while growing, but watering should be done sparingly during winter. Propagation by spores is best, the spores being sown as soon as ripe.

Most of the following are sometimes classed under Aspidium.

T. Bar'beri. *sti.* tufted, 6 to 12 in. long, slightly scaly at base. *Fronds* palmately 5-lobed or more usually pinnate, of a terminal seg. and 1 to 4 pairs of pinnae 4 to 6 in. long, 1 in. broad, nearly entire, leathery, naked. *Sori* abundant, principally in 2 rows near main veins. Malaya. (F.B.I. 322.) SYN. *Dictyopteris Barberi, Polyponium Barberi.*

T. cicuta'ria.* *sti.* 1 ft. or more long. *Fronds* 1 to 2 ft. long, sub-deltoid, apex deeply pinnated, with sinuate-lanceolate lobes; below this, 3 to 6 pinnae each side, lowest sub-deltoid, deeply pinnatifid or pinnate below. *Sori* rather large, in 2 rows near main veins, on connected or free veinlets. W. Indies. (F.S.A. (2) 25.) SYN. *Sagenia cicutaria, Nephrodium cicutarium.*

T. crena'ta. *sti.* 1 to 2 ft. long, naked. *Fronds* 2 ft. or more long, 12 to 18 in. broad, apex deeply pinnatifid, with linear-oblong, slightly sinuate lobes; lower pinnae 4 to 8 each side, 6 to 8 in. long, 1¼ to 1½ in. broad, acuminate, bluntly sinuate, lowest stalked and forked. *Sori* in 2 distinct rows near main veins. Philippines. Stove (L.F. 7, 2.) SYN. *Aspidium repandum.*

T. decur'rens. *rhiz.* creeping. *sti.* narrowly winged, often nearly or quite to base. *Fronds* 2 to 4 ft. long, 1 ft. or more broad, cut to winged rachis into 4 to 8 pairs of sinuate linear-oblong pinnae, 6 to 12 in. long, 1 to 2 in. broad, lowest sometimes forked. *Sori* large, in 2 regular rows between principal veins. Trop. Polynesia, Asia. SYN. *Sagenia decurrens, Nephrodium decurrens.* var. **mamillo'sa** has entire pinnae and sori deeply immersed. Moluccas. 1886. SYN. *Sagenia mamillosa.* (I.H. 1886, 598.)

T. irregula'ris. *sti.* tufted, erect, 1 ft. or more long, scaly below. *Fronds* 3 to 4 ft. long; upper pinnae lanceolate, entire, or with broad, blunt, or falcate lobes reaching half-way or more down to rachis; lower pinnae often deltoid, with lobes of the lower side prolonged and pinnatifid. *Sori* scattered, abundant. *Areolae* also copious. Malaya. (F.B.I. 77.) SYN. *Dictyopteris irregularis, Polypodium diffore, P. irregulare.* var. **macrophyl'lum** has bright green fronds, 5 ft. long; pinna 9 in. long, 2 in. broad, toothed. 1898.

T. latifo'lia. *sti.* blackish, 1 ft. or more long. *Fronds* 2 to 3 ft. long, 1 to 1½ in. broad, deeply pinnatifid at apex; pinnae 3 to 5 each side, lowest (much the largest) 8 to 12 in. long, 6 to 8 in. broad, soft, greyish. *Sori* disposed in rows, principally close to main veins. Polynesia. SYN. *Nephrodium latifolium.*

T. Lawrencea'na. *cau.* 3 to 4 in. high. *sti.* (rachis and costa beneath) blackish. *Fronds* 2 ft. or more long, gracefully arching, ovate, pinnate below, pinnatifid above; pinnae falcate, pinnatifid, lower about 1½ ft. long. Madagascar. 1881. SYN. *Sagenia Lawrenceana.*

T. Leuzea'na.* *cau.* sub-arborescent, densely scaly at crown. *sti.* 2 to 3 ft. long, stout, striate. *Fronds* 4 to 6 ft. long, sub-deltoid; pinnae 1 to 1½ ft. long, 6 to 8 in. broad, simple, or lowest with 2 or 3 large pinnate pinnules from lower side; segs. 3 to 4 in. long, ¾ to 1¼ in. broad, with oblong, sub-falcate, entire, or sinuate lobes reaching to a broadly winged rachis. *Sori* copious, usually in close single rows in lobes. N. India to Fiji. 1874. (B.C.F. 2, 539.) SYN. *Pleocnemia Leuzeana, N. Leuzeana.*

T. macro'don. *rhiz.* decumbent. *sti.* 1 ft. or more long, scaly below. *Fronds* 2 to 3 ft. long, 1 to 1½ ft. broad, apex deeply pinnatifid; pinnae below apex numerous, lanceolate, lowest sometimes 1 ft. long and 6 to 8 in. broad, cut to a narrow wing on rachis into close, lanceolate, pinnatifid pinnules. *Sori* small, in rows near main veins. *Areolae* copious. Philippines, &c. 1840. SYN. *Dictyopteris macrodonta, Polypodium macrodon.*

T. martinicen'sis.* *sti.* tufted, dull brownish, 1 to 2 ft. long, scaly below. *Fronds* composed of a large terminal (often forked at base) and from 4 to 8 lanceolate pinnae each side, entire or slightly lobed, lowest pair distinctly forked at base. *Sori* reniform in 2 rows between each primary vein, usually situated on middle of a veinlet. Trop. America. (L.F. 6, 46.) SYN. *Aspidium macrophyllum, Sagenia macrophylla.* There is a garden var. *calvatum.*

T. Moor'ei. *Fronds* 1 to 1½ ft. long, 6 to 9 in. broad, cordate-deltoid in general outline, pinnate below; lower pinnae 6 to 9 in. long, 4 to 6 in. broad, cut to rachis into deeply pinnatifid lobes. *Sori* copious, extra marginal, or stipitate. New Caledonia. (F.d.S. 7, 207.) SYN. *Cionidium Moorei, Deparia Moorei, Trichocarpa Moorei.*

T. Muel'leri. *Fronds* deltoid, 1 to 1½ ft. each way, 3-pinnatifid; lowest pinnae largest, deltoid, unequal-sided; pinnules large, lanceolate, lowest deeply lobed; ribs densely hairy. *Sori* large, disposed in 1 row near main veins; indusium small, fugacious. Queensland. Greenhouse. SYN. *Aspidium confluens, Sagenia confluens, Nephrodium confluens.*

T. polymor'pha. *rhiz.* creeping. *sti.* brownish, naked, 1 ft. or more long. *Fronds* 2 to 4 ft. long, 1 to 1½ ft. broad, impari-pinnate; pinnae 5 to 13, oblong, variously forked, especially lower ones, leathery. *Sori* small, abundant, scattered on connected veinlets. S. China, Malaya. SYN. *Sagenia polymorpha, Nephrodium polymorphum.*

T. Ridley'ana.* *sti.* 4 to 6 in. long, slender, upper part and rachis, transparently winged. *Fronds* 1 to 1½ ft. long, 3 to 4 in. broad, with 12 to 20 horizontal sessile pinnae each side, 1 to 1½ in. long, and about ½ in. broad, bluntish; edge uniformly inciso-crenate, base nearly equal on both sides. *Sori* distant, not reaching either midrib or margin. W. Indies, &c. Stove. SYN. *Aspidium alatum.*

T. subtriphyl'la. *rhiz.* creeping. *sti.* brownish, 1 ft. or more long. *Fronds* 1 to 1½ ft. long, 8 to 12 in. broad, sub-deltoid, having a large, deeply cleft terminal pinna, with lanceolate lobes, and 1 or 2 each side. *Sori* large, scattered on connected veinlets. India, Formosa. (F.B.I. 48.) SYN. *Aspidium subtriphyllum, Sagenia subtriphylla.*

T. trifolia'ta. *sti.* tufted, 1 ft. or more long, base only scaly. *Fronds* 12 to 18 in. long, 6 to 12 in. broad, with a large ovate-acuminate terminal pinna, narrowed or forked at base, and 1 or 2 lateral each side, lowest mostly forked. *Sori* in rows near main veins. Trop. America. Stove. (L.R. 6, 29.) SYN. *Aspidium trifoliatum.* var. **heracleifo'lia** has pinnae pinnatifid on both sides at base; **Plumie'ri** is large and has more numerous and scattered sori with less distinctly peltate indusia.

T. va'rians. *sti.* 4 ft. long, glossy. *Fronds* 3 to 4 ft. long, 2 ft. broad, upper part pinnatifid, with deep, lanceolate lobes; lower pinnae deltoid, over 1 ft. long, 6 to 8 in. broad, cut below nearly to rachis into lanceolate, pinnatifid lobes. *Sori* in rows near main veins. *Areolae* copious. W. Trop. Africa. SYN. *Dictyopteris cameroonianis, Polypodium cameroonianum.*

TECTO'NA (*teka, teku* or *thekku,* S. Indian names of *T. grandis*). FAM. *Verbenaceae.* A genus of 3 species of tall timber trees with large opposite or ternate entire leaves and small white or bluish flowers in terminal panicles. Calyx bell-shaped, with 5 or 6 teeth. *T. grandis,* the teak tree, is grown to a great extent in Java, India, &c., for its durable, heavy wood, used for many purposes. It has been introduced but can be grown only while young, needing stove treatment, being too large for accommodation under glass.

T. gran'dis. Teak Tree. Tree 80 to 150 ft. h., young shoots 4-angled. *l.* ovate, 8 to 12 in. long (larger in seedlings), hairy beneath. *fl.* small, in panicles 18 in. across. India, Burma, E. Indies, &c.

tecto'rum, of roofs.

tec'tus -a -um, roofed or covered.

TEED'IA (in honour of J. G. Teede, a German traveller and botanist who died in Surinam). FAM. *Scrophulariaceae.* Two S. African species of semi-woody plants, biennial or perennial, disagreeably scented. Leaves opposite, toothed; stems 4-angled; calyx 5-lobed, finally subtending the fruit; corolla with a short tube and 5 spreading lobes; stamens 4; fruit a 2-celled, globose berry. Greenhouse, rather attractive plants, propagated by seeds.

T. lu'cida. Glabrous, slightly woody shrub, 2 to 4 ft. *l.* variable, shining, mostly 1½ to 3, but sometimes 5, in. long, ovate or oval; stalks winged, stem-clasping. *fl.* in stalked, axillary, and terminal clusters of 3 to 7; cor. ½ in. wide, lilac or rosy with a purple spot at the base of each lobe. April, May. S. Africa. 1774. (B.R. 209.) Grown as an outdoor annual in California.

T. pubes'cens. Biennial, downy plant, 2 ft. *l.* ovate to oval, pointed 1 to 3½ in. long, half as wide, base partly clasping the stem. *fl.* ⅜ in. across, in axillary, stalked clusters of 3 to 5, pink with a purple spot at the base of each lobe. April. *Berry* black-purple, ¼ to ½ in. across. S. Africa. 1816. (B.R. 214.)

W. J. B.

TEETH. Any small marginal division of leaf, petal, &c.

tege'tum, mat-like, covering.

TEGULE. Bract of involucre in Compositae, also called a phyllary.

TEGUMEN. Inner layer of seed-coat.

TELAN'THERA. Included in **Alternanthera.**

TELEGRAPH PLANT. *See* **Desmodium gyrans.**

TELEK'IA. Included in **Buphthalmum.**

telephioi'des, like *Sedum Telephium.*

Telephium, from the ancient Greek name of a herb *telephion* (*tele*, at a distance, *philos*, lover), used to ascertain whether love was reciprocated.

TELFAIR'IA (in honour of Dr. Charles Telfair, 1778–1838, an Irish botanist who died in Mauritius). FAM. *Cucurbitaceae.* A genus of 2 species of climbing shrubs, natives of Trop. Africa. Leaflets 3 or 5, oblong, auricled at base, repand-toothed or cut. Flowers dioecious. Male moderate to rather large, in racemes on braceate pedicels; calyx tube short, lobes lanceolate, toothed; corolla white or pale purple, rotate, 5-parted, segments fringed with long threads; stamens 3 or 5. Female solitary; ovary oblong, swollen and lobed at base, 3- to 5-celled. Fruit large, globular-compressed. Seeds edible. Telfairias produce their fine flowers very freely but require a large space in the stove and to be pruned frequently before flowering. Sandy loam with a little peat suits them. Cuttings of the flowering shoots will root readily in soil or sand under a glass in heat. The oil expressed from the seed of *T. pedata* is said to be, when fresh, as palatable as almonds.

T. occidenta'lis. Tendrils 2-fid. *l.* alternate, pedately 5-foliolate, stalked; lflets. 3 to 6 in. long, elliptic-ovate, obtuse acuminate, sinuate-toothed, 3-nerved from near base, short-stalked. *fl.* white with purple eye, 1½ to 2 in. across; stamens 5; male racemes 6- to 10-fld., 1 ft. long. September. W. Africa. 1870. (B.M. 6272.) Seeds boiled and eaten by negroes.

T. peda'ta. *l.* long-stalked; lflets. 3 to 5 in. long, slender-pointed, repand-toothed, nerves at angle of 45° from midrib; scent unpleasant when bruised. *fl.* purplish; male 2 in. across in 6- to 8-fld. racemes; peduncles 6 to 8 in. long; female solitary, 4 in. across. *fr.* fleshy, always green, 18 to 36 in. long, often 8 in. across with 10 to 12 deep furrows; seeds as large as a very large kidney bean. Zanzibar. 1825. (B.M. 2751–2; 2681 as *Feuillaea pedata.*)

F. G. P.

Telfair'iae, in honour of Annabella Telfair (*née* Chamberlain), d. 1832, wife of Charles Telfair.

TELIPO'GON (*telos*, summit, *pogon*, beard; the column is bearded to the summit). FAM. *Orchidaceae.* A genus of about 50 species of epiphytic orchids, natives of Colombia, Peru, and Costa Rica. Leaves distichous, short, leathery or fleshy, distant or crowded, growth stem-like. Flower few at apex of the peduncle, in a loose raceme, showy; sepals nearly equal, free, spreading, narrow, often almost hidden by the much broader petals; lip sessile, spreading, entire, rarely smaller than the petals; column very short and thick, bristly or hairy; pollen masses 4; peduncles pseudo-terminal, rather long, erect, simple, usually ancipitous. The flowers are generally yellow with purple netting on the lip. Unfortunately the species are almost unknown in cultivation. *T. Croesus* does best in small baskets full of finely cut Osmunda fibre, potsherds, and Sphagnum suspended in the intermediate house.

T. Croe'sus. Stem narrow, thin. *fl.* yellow, netted, 1½ in. across; sep. triangular, acuminate, awned, 3-nerved, middle nerve keeled beneath; pet. wedge-shaped, rhomboid, 5-nerved, angles obtuse; lip very broad, fan-shaped, rounded, many-nerved, base velvety. Colombia. 1877.

E. C.

TEL'LIMA (anagram of *Mitella* to which this genus is related). FAM. *Saxifragaceae.* A genus of about a dozen species of hardy herbaceous perennials, natives of Western N. America. Leaves roundish-heart-shaped, lobed, toothed; stipules absent or adnate to base of stalk. Flowers greenish or white, pedicellate, nodding, in long, many-flowered, terminal racemes, calyx tube large, limb 5-toothed or 5-cleft; petals 5, rarely reddish, inserted at mouth of calyx, entire, 3-fid or pinnatifid; stamens 10. Fruit a capsule, 1-celled, many-seeded, with 2 beaks (in Mitella there is no beak to the capsule). Plants for the wild garden and wood. For cultivation *see* **Mitella.**

T. affin'is. Stem stout, about 2 ft. h. *Basal l.* roundish, crenately lobed; *stem-l.* usually 3-lobed, lobes cut or toothed. *fl.* with turbinate cal., and pet. 3-lobed at tip. Oregon, California.

T. grandiflo'ra. Hairy perennial. Stem stout, about 2 ft. h. *Basal l.* heart-shaped or roundish, toothed; *stem-l.* similar, 2 to 4; stalks somewhat stipulate at base. *fl.* greenish, not scented, about ½ in. long and broad, becoming reddish; cal. bell-shaped; pet. pinnate, segs. filiform. Alaska to California. (B.R. 1178.) var. **purpur'ea,** about 1 ft. h., *l.* red, *fl.* yellow; foliage good in autumn. SYN. var. *rub'ra.*

T. odora'ta. Much like *T. grandiflora* but *fl.* red, scented. Oregon, &c. A plant for damp spots.

T. parviflo'ra. Greyish hairy, perennial, about 12 in. h. *Basal l.* 3- to 5-parted nearly to base, segs. narrowly wedge-shaped, 3-cleft. *fl.* pink or white, rather large, pet. on a slender claw, palmately 3- to 7-cut; raceme short, lengthened in fruit. British Columbia to Colorado. SYN. *Lithophragma parviflora.*

telma'teius -a -um, of the marshes.

TELOP'EA (*telopas*, seen at a distance; alluding to the great distance from which the crimson flowers are discernible). FAM. *Proteaceae.* A genus of 3 species of evergreen trees and shrubs of great beauty and distinction, 2 native of Australia, 1 of Tasmania. Leaves alternate; flowers crowded in a terminal head subtended by bracts; perianth tubular at first soon splitting on the underside, the style protruding through the opening. Fruit a recurved pod 2 to 4 in. long. For notes on cultivation see below. Propagation may be by layering in pots in winter, allowing the layers to remain undisturbed until rooted.

T. orea'des. Tree up to 30 or 40 ft. or a shrub, shoots at first downy. *l.* linear-oblong to oblanceolate, entire, 6 to 8 in. long, 1 to 2 in. wide, deep green above, inclined to glaucous beneath; stalk up to 1 in. long, downy. *fl.* crimson, numerous in a terminal head 3 or 4 in. across; perianth about 1 in. long, the tube splitting to the base on one side, the protruding style over 1 in. long becoming much curled. Australia. 1910. (B.M. 8684.) Hardy in S. Cornwall under conditions that suit Australian plants generally.

T. speciosis'sima.* Waratah. Evergreen glabrous shrub, 6 to 8 ft. *l.* 5 to 9 in. long, 1½ to 2½ in. wide, obovate, bluntly and coarsely toothed except towards the base, rarely entire. *fl.* deep coral red, packed in a globose head 3 to 4 in. across, subtended by numerous crimson, narrow, pointed bracts 1½ to 3 in. long; perianth 1 in. long. New S. Wales. 1789. (G.C. 17 (1882), 677; B.M. 1128 as *Embothrium speciosissimum.*) Difficult shrub, very rarely seen in fl. Greenhouse. Requires warmth and copious waterings when growing, but to be kept on the dry side in winter.

T. trunca'ta.* Evergreen shrub or a small tree; shoots downy. *l.* 2 to 5 in. long, ⅛ to ¾ in. wide, oblanceolate, apex tapered or rounded, sometimes with 2 or 3 teeth, sometimes 2-lobed. *fl.* rich crimson, crowded in a terminal head 2 to 3 in. across; perianth slender, curved, about 1 in. long; style 1¼ in. long, protruding through the

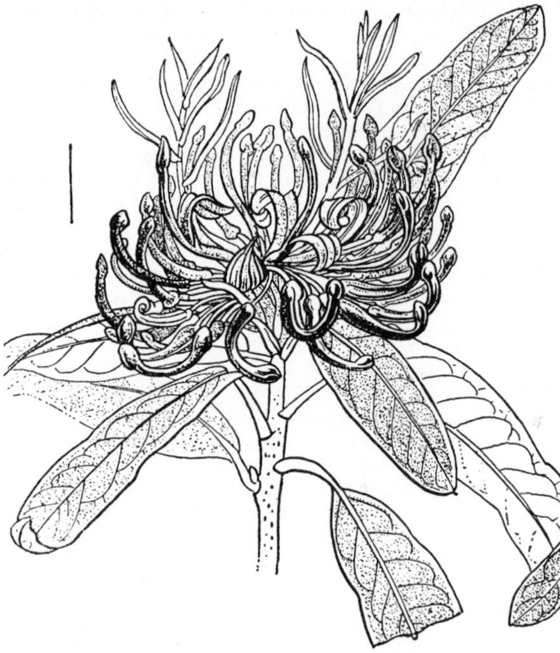

Telopea oreades (p. 2087)

slit perianth. June. Tasmania. 1930. (B.M. 9660.) Hardy, but succeeds better in the warmer counties under conditions suitable for rhododendrons. It is producing fr. freely there; these are spindle-shaped, about 3 in. long.

W. J. B.

TEMPERATE HOUSE. A glass-house constructed for the cultivation of plants of temperate climates which cannot be grown well outdoors in the British climate, especially those which will not, without injury, put up with temperatures below about 40° F. and do not need temperatures above 55 to 60° F. except with sun-heat. The largest house of this kind, the Temperate House at Kew, is about 628 ft. long and 144 ft. wide in its widest part and is large enough to accommodate tall trees.

TEMPERATURE. Seeing that all the functions of a plant are carried out between certain limits of temperature and that between those limits there is a temperature, the optimum, at which they reach their greatest activity, and that, moreover, the minimum, optimum, and maximum for one plant may differ markedly from that required by another, the study of temperatures on the part of the gardener who has in charge anything beyond plants of the hardiest type is an important duty. Temperatures fluctuate so suddenly, and as they depend in nature upon forces beyond control it becomes necessary for the gardener to take such steps as are possible to prevent such changes in the environment of his plants from affecting them injuriously by giving constant attention and anticipating the changes likely to occur. Thermometers (q.v.) enable him to ascertain temperatures; it is not enough to depend upon one's own feelings. A knowledge of the extreme temperatures his plants will withstand with impunity and of the proper degree of heat needful for bringing them to perfection is one of the first essentials for success. Temperature in forcing operations and in the cultivation of fruits under glass is of great importance. Forcing is intimately connected with the regulation of temperature in the forcing house by means of the heating apparatus, and use of the ventilators whenever necessary. To know the country to which a given plant is indigenous, or to ascertain from a reliable source the degree of hardiness of the plants concerned, is often a good guide to its proper treatment so far as heat is concerned, but it is not enough. If that be relied upon alone where the various occupants of a well-stocked garden are concerned and where forcing operations are being carried out while outside temperatures often fluctuate rapidly will lead to very indifferent and perhaps disastrous results. Practical experience and unremitting attention are both essential as well and these combined with properly installed heating and ventilating apparatus maintained as they should be will, if intelligently exercised, go far to overcome the difficulties attending the cultivation of plants under glass, among which temperature fluctuations are not the least formidable.

TEMPLES. Architectural buildings, often based on the designs of ancient temples, were at one time frequently erected in large gardens to form distinct, attractive features in themselves, and sometimes to afford resting-places or places of shelter. They were expensive to erect, for they had to be massive, durable structures. They do not fit well into gardens of the modern taste.

TEMPLETO'NIA (in honour of John Templeton, an Irish botanist). FAM. *Leguminosae.* A genus of about 7 species of evergreen shrubs limited to Australia. Leaves alternate, simple. Flowers 1 to 3 in the leaf-axils. Cool greenhouse, with the same treatment as Acacias. Propagated by cuttings.

T. retu'sa. Glabrous shrub up to 6 ft., shoots angular. *l.* ½ to 1½ in. long, ⅛ to ½ in. wide, obovate, blunt or notched at the apex, often mucronate, scarcely stalked. *fl.* usually solitary, red; standard pet. erect, 1 in. long, sides often doubled inwards; lip ovate, ⅝ in. wide, often bent downwards; keel narrow. March to June. S. and W. Australia. 1817. (B.M. 2334; B.R. 383; L.B.C. 526; and as *T. glauca*, B.M. 2088; B.R. 859; L.B.C. 644.)

W. J. B.

tem'ulus -a -um, intoxicated, bewildered.

TENA'RIS (native name in S. Africa). FAM. *Apocynaceae.* A genus of 2 species of slender, erect, perennial S. African herbs. Leaves opposite, narrow-linear. Flower pink or whitish, in cymes; calyx deeply 5-cleft, lobes acute; corolla tube shortly bell-shaped, lobes 5, long, linear-spatulate; scales of corona 10, attached to staminal tube; stamens attached to base of corolla, filaments connate in a short tube. The species need greenhouse protection. For cultivation *see* **Ceropegia.**

T. rostra'ta. About 18 in. h., slender. *l.* in about 4 pairs, distant, linear, 2 to 3 in. long, acute, arched. *fl.* whitish, densely dotted purple near base, ¾ in. across, rotate; outer corona of 5 small, yellowish lobes; inner pinkish; peduncles 1- or 2-fld., about ¼ in. long. E. Trop. Africa. 1885.

te'nax, holding fast, tough, firm, matted.

TENDRIL. A twisting thread-like growth by which some plants lay hold of a support, enabling them to climb. The tendrils may be metamorphosed terminal shoots and its branches as in the vine, leaves or parts of leaves as in peas, leaf-stalks as in Clematis and Tropaeolum. Tendrils are very sensitive to contact and react so as to twine round supports. They afford one means of bringing leaves and flowers into the light.

tenel'lulus -a -um / ***tenel'lus -a -um*** } somewhat tender or delicate.

tenens, holding fast, enduring.

tene'rus -a -um (***teneri-,*** in compound words), delicate, soft.

Tengwall'ii, in honour of Dr. Tor Ake Tengwall, b. 1892, of Uppsala, Inspector of rubber plantations in Java.

Tenorea'nus -a -um, in honour of Michele Tenore, 1780–1861, Professor of Botany, Naples.

TENT CATERPILLARS, the name given to larvae of Moths and Sawflies which live in colonies in webs or 'nests' formed of silken threads. The caterpillars as they grow make new tents either on some other part of the tree or bush or on an adjoining tree to which they migrate. The most familiar tent-forming species in this country are the Lackey Moth (q.v.), the Apple and Euonymus Ermine Moths (*see* **Ermine Moths**), and the Social Pear Sawfly (q.v.). Apart from the spraying of the foliage of plants attacked by these caterpillars, it is well to cut out and destroy the 'nests' or to burn them with the aid of a painter's blow-lamp as soon as they are seen.
G. F. W.

TENTACLES. Sensitive hairs or filaments, such as those on leaves of Drosera.

tentacula'tus -a -um, having tentacles.

TENTHREDIN'IDAE. *See* **Sawflies.**

tenui'culus -a -um, somewhat slender.

tenu'ior, thinner or more slender than *tenuis.*

ten'uis -is -e (***tenui-*** in compound words), thin, slender.

Teocote, native name for *Pinus Teocote* (q.v.).

TEPALS. H. G. Reichenbach's name for the inner perianth segments (petals) of Orchids; afterwards used for the inner whorl of segments in other petaloid monocotyledons; now used for all the segments of the perianth (perigone), especially when those of the outer and inner whorls are not markedly different in form and texture; it has thus become synonymous with perianth segments or perigone segments. The word *tepal* is an anagram of *petal.* When the lower part of the perianth is tubular this may be called the *tepaltube* and the upper free segments above the tube the *tepalsegs,* the outer or sepaline being then distinguished as the *setepalsegs* from the inner or petaline *petepalsegs* (cf. Traub in *Herbertia,* 13 (1946), 98–100; 1948). This terminology has been used in describing the flowers of Amaryllidaceae.

tephro-, in compound words, signifying ash-grey.

TEPHRO'SIA (*tephros,* ash-coloured; from the appearance of the leaves). FAM. *Leguminosae.* A genus of about 100 species of herbs, sub-shrubs or rarely shrubs widely dispersed over the warmer parts of the world. Leaves usually unevenly pinnate; leaflets opposite, often silky beneath. Flowers red, purple, or white, in leaf-opposed racemes or solitary or twin in the leaf-axils, papilionaceous; calyx tube bell-shaped, teeth distinct, nearly equal; petals clawed, standard nearly round, keel incurved, not beaked; stamens diadelphous. Pods 2-valved, flattish. Several species are economically valuable but few are very ornamental. They all grow well in a compost of sandy peat and leaf-mould. Propagation is by seeds or by cuttings inserted in sand, under a close frame, those of the stove species in heat.

T. can'dida. Small shrub. *l.* 6 to 12 in. long, shortly stalked; lflets. 19 to 25, ligulate, acute, 1½ to 2 in. long. *fl.* reddish or white, ¾ to 1 in. long; standard densely silky; racemes terminal and lateral, 6 to 9 in. long. India. 1816. Stove.

T. capen'sis. Sub-shrub, stems procumbent or trailing, 2 to 3 ft. long. *l.* long-stalked; lflets. in 3 to 6 pairs, elliptic, wedge-shaped-oblong, or lanceolate, obtuse or acute. *fl.* purple, ¼ in. long, standard hairy; racemes interrupted, distantly many-fld.; peduncles long, slender. S. Africa. 1825. Greenhouse.

T. grandiflo'ra. Erect shrub, 1 to 2 ft. h. *l.* short-stalked; lflets. in 5 to 7 pairs, wedge-shaped or linear-oblong, obtuse or acute, retuse or mucronulate. *fl.* red, brownish-red without, ⅜ to ⅘ in. long, in terminal and l.-opposed racemes forming a corymbose cluster at summit. June. S. Africa. 1774. (B.R. 769 as *Galega grandiflora.*) Greenhouse.

T. pal'lens. Erect or ascending sub-shrub. *l.* spreading or recurved, short-stalked; lflets. in 5 to 9 pairs, narrow, wedge-shaped-oblong, ¾ in. long, point recurved. *fl.* pink, about ⅓ in. long, standard hairy, other pet. glabrous; racemes dense, many-fld.; peduncles curved, 4 to 6 in. long. July. S. Africa. 1787. Greenhouse.

T. purpu'rea. Perennial, 1 to 2 ft. h. *l.* 3 to 6 in. long, short-stalked; lflets. 13 to 21, narrow-oblanceolate, obtuse, almost glabrous above, silky beneath. *fl.* pale red, ¼ to ⅜ in. long, silky; racemes 3 to 6 in. long, leaf-opposed, loose, lower fl. clustered. Tropics. 1768. Stove.

T. suber'osa. A synonym of *Mundulea suberosa.*

T. virginia'na. Perennial with simple, erect stem, 1 to 2 ft. h.; leafy at top. *lflets.* 17 to 29, linear-oblong. *fl.* yellowish-white, with purple marks, large, numerous, clustered in a terminal, oblong, dense raceme or panicle. N. America. 1765. Half-hardy.

teph'rus -a -um, ashy-grey.

A→

terato- in compound words implying of strange form.

TERATOLOGY. The study of aberrant growth in plants.

TEREBINTH-TREE. *See* **Pistacia Terebinthus.**

TEREBINTH'US. A synonym of Pistacia.

teres (***tereti-*** in compound words), free from angles; terete; cylindrical or nearly so.

tergemi'nus -a -um, applied to a leaf having each of 2 secondary petioles bearing a pair of leaflets near its summit, a third pair being at the origin of the secondary petioles.

tergesti'nus, of Tergeste, ancient name of Trieste.

terminal, at the end of a shoot or other structure, not lateral or axillary.

TERMINA'LIA (*terminus,* end; in allusion to the frequent terminal clustering of the leaves on the shoots). FAM. *Combretaceae.* A genus of about 100 species of evergreen trees and shrubs widely spread in tropical and sub-tropical regions. Leaves alternate or sub-opposite, often short-stalked. Flowers quite small, of little beauty, green or white, usually arranged in slender spikes but sometimes in heads; calyx 5-toothed; petals absent; stamens 10, anthers exserted. Fruit a drupe, mostly ovoid, flattened or winged; the kernels of some species are edible, others are imported for dyeing and tanning. Several species are valuable timber trees, and some are planted for ornament in tropical countries. They grow easily in open loam and require stove conditions, but have little garden value in this country.

T. Arju'na. Evergreen tree, 60 to 80 ft. *l.* subopposite, not clustered, oblong to narrowly oval, usually 3 to 6 in. long, shallowly toothed, base tapered to subcordate, nearly glabrous; stalk ½ in. or less long. *fl.* small in cylindrical spikes 1½ to 2 in. long, ⅜ in. wide, terminal and axillary, forming leafy panicles. April, May. India.

T. Benzo'in. Tree 30 to 40 ft. *l.* clustered at the curious thickened ends of the shoots, oblanceolate, 3 to 5 in. long, ¾ to 2 in. wide, shallowly toothed, glabrous, slenderly tapered to a glandular stalk up to 2 in. long. Spikes axillary, very slender, about as long as the l. *fl.* very small. Mauritius. 1824. SYN. *T. mauritania.* A milky juice from this tree is said, when dried, to be used as incense.

T. Catap'pa. Olive-bark Tree; Tropical Almond; Indian Almond. Tree 60 to 80 ft. *l.* in terminal clusters, 5 to 13 in. long, 2½ to 7 in. wide, obovate, cuneate, apex broad and rounded or tapered, reddish-downy when young, becoming nearly glabrous; stalk ¼ to ⅝ in. long. Spikes axillary, cylindrical, up to 9 in. long by ½ in. wide. *fl.* closely packed, whitish, the chief feature being the yellow anthers. April. Trop. Asia. 1778. (B.M. 3004.) Ornamental tree much planted throughout the tropics, kernels of nuts palatable.

T. Che'bula. Tree up to 100 ft., shoots and l. varying from nearly glabrous to coppery pubescent (in var. **tomentel'la**). *l.* not clustered, 2½ to 6 in. long, 1½ to 3½ in. wide, ovate or oval, apex blunt or pointed, base rounded; stalks with two glands near the blade. *fl.* white, small, in terminal spikes 2 to 5 in. long, cylindrical, often forming sparse panicles. India, Ceylon, Burma. 1796.

T. latifo'lia. Tree up to 100 ft. *l.* obovate or oblanceolate, clustered, 4 to 8 or 10 in. long, about half as wide, apex notched to short-pointed, soon glabrous; stalk ⅓ to 1¼ in. long. *fl.* small, in very slender spikes 3 to 6 in. long. *Drupe* ovoid flattened on one side, up to 2 in. long; kernel edible, with a sweet almond taste. W. Indies. 1800.

T. maurita'nia. A synonym of *T. Benzoin.*

T. seri'cea. Evergreen, silvery-grey tree from 20 to 70 ft., shoots downy. *l.* mostly crowded at the end of the shoot, narrow-oblong, obovate or oblanceolate, 2 to 4 in. long, ½ to ⅓ in. wide, short-stalked. *fl.* small, in axillary, silky-cylindrical spikes up to 2 in. long, ⅛ in. wide. *fr.* flattened, reddish, broadly winged to make it 1 to 1¼ in. wide. S. Africa. 1816.

W. J. B.

TERMINA'LIS. A synonym of Dracaena.

terminal, -e, at end of shoot, not axillary.

term'inans, ending.

A→

Terna'tea, an old generic name from Ternate Is., Moluccas.

terna'tus -a -um (***terni-,*** in compound words), whorls of 3; having 3 parts arranged around a common axis.

TERNSTROE'MIA (in honour of Christopher Ternstroem, Swedish naturalist and traveller in China, d. 1745). FAM. *Theaceae.* A genus of about 45 species of evergreen trees and shrubs, natives of warmer parts of Asia and of Trop. America and Trop. Africa. Leaves leathery, entire or crenate-serrate. Flowers solitary or clustered on 1-flowered recurved axillary or lateral peduncles; sepals 5, closely overlapping; petals 5, overlapping, joined at base; stamens many, attached to base of corolla. Compost of well-drained fibrous loam suits them and they may be propagated by cuttings of half-ripe shoots under a bell-glass with bottom heat.

T. japo'nica. Tree or shrub to 10 to 12 ft. *l.* alternate, stalked obovate-oblong or oblong, glabrous, pinnately veined. *fl.* white, *Berries* as large as peas. Japan. Warm greenhouse. SYN. *Cleyera japonica* of Thunberg, not Sieb. and Zucc.

TERNSTROEMIA'CEAE. A synonym of Theaceae.

TERRACE. A raised space of ground sometimes formed round a mansion, or on the side of a hill, usually in order to make a level walk. Care must be taken in constructing a terrace that views from the mansion are not obstructed and that it will not prevent the building from being seen to advantage when approaching it. A strongly built wall to retain the terrace in position often has places for large vases or tubs arranged in its length and these may cause obstruction to the view. There is less fear of this happening when the retaining wall is little higher than the terrace and its face can be used as a home or support for plants. There are difficulties in keeping a grass slope neatly mown but if they can be overcome the slope is often to be preferred to an obtrusive wall.

terres'tris -is -e, terrestrial, growing on ground, not on trees or in water.

ter'sus -a -um, clean, neat.

tessella'tus -a -um, chequered with square spots, sometimes spelt *tessalatus*, or *tesselatus.*

Tessendorffia'nus -a -um, in honour of F. Tessendorff, 1879–1924, of Berlin, collected in Russia, N. Germany, and E. Prussia.

TESTA. The skin of a seed enclosing the embryo and, when present, endosperm and perisperm.

TESTACEL'LA. *See* **Slugs, Carnivorous.**

testa'ceus -a -um, brownish-yellow, like unglazed earthenware in colour.

testicula'ris -is -e, testicle-like.

TESTUDINA'RIA. Included in **Dioscorea.**

testudina'rum, like tortoise shells.

TETEAWAKA. *See* **Olearia angustifolia.**

tetra-, in compound words, signifying 4; as tetragonous, with 4 angles.

TETRACENTRA'CEAE. A family with only one species in China and Burma. Trees with alternate, palmate-veined, long-stalked leaves. Flowers with 4 sepals, in a slender spike; stamens 4; carpels 4, ovules several. Fruit a 4-celled capsule. Sometimes placed in Magnoliaceae, sometimes in Trochodendraceae, but according to A. C. Smith, I. W. Bailey, and C. Nast in *Journal of Arnold Arboretum*, 26, 123–54 (1945), best maintained as an independent family.

TETRACEN'TRON (*tetra-*, four, *kentron*, spur; from the 4 spur-like appendages of the fruit). FAM. *Tetracentraceae.* A single species of a tall deciduous Chinese tree constitutes this genus. The leaves resemble those of Cercidophyllum but are alternate. Flowers in slender pendulous spikes, small, sessile, perfect; sepals 4, overlapping, ovate; stamens 4, exserted; carpels 4. Fruit a 4-celled deeply lobed capsule with linear-oblong seeds. Hardy in sheltered situations but liable to damage by spring frosts, but otherwise useful for its pleasant foliage. The flowers, however, are not ornamental.

T. sinen'se. Deciduous tree to 90 ft. h. in the wild; shoots dark, smooth, marked with numerous pale lenticels. *l.* ovate or cordate, 3 to 5 in. long, evenly bluntly toothed, slender-pointed, veins 5 to 7, palmate; solitary also on short spurs on the year-old wood where the fl.-spikes, 4 to 6 in. long, are borne. *fl.* very small, yellowish. June, July. South-Central China, N. Burma. 1901.

TETRACE'RA (*tetra-*, four, *keras*, horn; the 4 capsules are horn-shaped.) FAM. *Dilleniaceae.* A genus of about 40 species of climbing shrubs or trees, natives of the tropics. Leaves parallel-veined. Flowers in panicles; sepals 4 to 6, spreading; petals usually 4 to 6; carpels usually 3 to 5, rarely fewer. *T. sarmentosa* needs stove conditions, thorough drainage, and a compost of peat and turfy loam with a little silver sand and small pieces of charcoal added. Cuttings of young shoots will root in April, in sand with bottom heat.

T. sarmento'sa. Evergreen climber. *l.* obovate to broadly lanceolate, rigid, very roughly hairy. *fl.* white, in terminal panicles. Trop. Asia. 1820. (B.M. 3058 as *Delima sarmentosa.*) SYN. *Trachyptella aspera.*

TETRACHLORETHANE ($C_2H_2Cl_4$) was used against White Fly before the introduction of the White Fly parasite, Encarsia (q.v.), and the discovery of Cyanogas. It could be used where Tomatoes were grown in the early part of the season, but is very harmful to Chrysanthemums and several other plants. *See* **Fumigation.**

TETRACLI'NIS (*tetra-*, four, *cline*, bed; from the 4-ranked leaves). FAM. *Pinaceae.* A monotypic genus allied to Callitris and Widdringtonia, differing from Callitris by its 4-scaled (not 6- or 8-scaled) cone.

T. articula'ta. Tender evergreen tree, 40 to 50 ft. h., with erect branches and flattened, articulated branchlets divided into fine spray. *l.* scale-like, in fours, the lateral pair larger than the facial pair, bases attached to the shoot, tips free and pointed. *Cones* solitary at ends of shoots, rounded, ⅓ to ½ in. wide; scales 4, 2 blunt, 2 pointed, woody, glaucous. *Seeds* oval with 2 wide wings. N. Africa, Malta. SYN. *Callitris quadrivalvis, Thuja articulata.* Wood reddish or yellowish, hard, fragrant, often prettily marked, and esteemed for cabinet work. A hard resin called Sandarac exudes from trunk and branches. It is used in the manufacture of varnishes. Hot, dry conditions appear to be necessary for its successful cultivation. Warm greenhouse.

W. D.

TETRA'DIUM. Included in **Evodia.**

tetradynamous, having 6 stamens of which 2 are shorter than the others and stand on opposite sides of the ovary. Characteristic of Cruciferae.

TETRAGAST'RIS (*tetra-*, four, *gaster*, belly; from the form of the fruit). FAM. *Burseraceae.* A genus of 4 or 5 species of glabrous trees, natives of Brazil, Guiana, and the W. Indies. *T. balsamifera* is a tall evergreen tree needing stove conditions and a compost of sandy loam with a little peat. It can be propagated by ripe cuttings in sand with rather strong heat. It yields a balsamic exudant.

T. balsami'fera. Tree to 60 ft. *l.* alternate, unequally pinnate; lflets. opposite, ovate to oblong, entire, leathery, stalked. *fl.* small. whitish, in axillary panicles. W. Indies. 1820. SYN. *Hedwigia balsamifera.*

F. G. P.

TETRAGO'NIA (*tetra*, 4, *gonia*, angle; from the form of the fruit). FAM. *Aizoaceae.* A genus of about 20 species of prostrate or somewhat climbing herbs or sub-shrubs, mostly S. African, others natives of the shores of E. Asia, Australia, and temperate S. America. Leaves alternate, oblong, linear, ovate or deltoid, entire, rather thick; without stipules. Flowers green, yellowish, or reddish, axillary, solitary or few, sessile or on long pedicels, sometimes in spikes; calyx lobes 3 to 5, petals none. One species only is of horticultural interest, *T. expansa*, for the treatment of which *see* **New Zealand Spinach.**

Tetragonia expansa

T. expan'sa. New Zealand Ice Plant; New Zealand Spinach. Prostrate or decumbent, stems 2 ft. or more long. *l.* ovate, triangular or broadly hastate, 2 to 4 in. long, entire, obtuse or acute, smaller l. narrower, all stalked. *fl.* yellow, small, pedicels very short, axillary, solitary or twin. Australia, New Zealand. (B.M. 2362.) A

TETRAGONOLO'BUS (*tetragonos*, 4-angled, *lobos*, pod; from the 4-winged pod). FAM. *Leguminosae.* A genus of about 10 species of annual or perennial trailing herbs closely related to Lotus but with a 4-winged pod, natives of the Mediterranean region. Easily grown in ordinary soil from seed sown where the plants are to flower. The young pods of *T. purpureus* are sometimes eaten, the ripe seeds used as a substitute for coffee.

T. mari'timus. Perennial trailer, hairy, with ascending stems. *l.* oblong or obovate; stipules shortly adnate. *fl.* pale yellow, solitary, peduncles much longer than fl. June. *Pods* with straight wings much narrower than body. Mediterranean region. SYN. *Lotus siliquosus, T. siliquosus.*

T. purpu'reus. Asparagus Pea; Winged Pea. Annual, 6 to 12 in. h. *lflets.* obovate, entire; stipules ovate. *fl.* dark purple, solitary or twin, in l.-axils. June to August. *Pods* winged, edible. S. Europe. (B.M. 151.) SYN. *Lotus Tetragonolobus. See* **Asparagus Pea.**

Tetragonolobus purpureus

T. siliquo'sus. A synonym of *T. maritimus.*

tetragonus -a -um, having 4 angles.

TETRAMIC'RA bi'color. A synonym of *Leptotes bicolor*, **T. serrati'folia.** A synonym of *Octadesmia montana*, **T. serrula'ta.** A synonym of *Leptotes serrulata.*

TETRANE'MA (*tetra*, 4, *nema*, filament; from the 4 stamens). FAM. *Scrophulariaceae.* A genus of 2 Mexican and Guatemalan species of perennial herbs, with short or ascending stems, and almost radical, opposite, glabrous, obovate or oblong leaves with slightly crenate margins. Flowers 2-lipped, upper lip 2-lobed, lower 3-lobed; stamens 4. Fruit a rather compressed capsule. *T. mexicanum* needs warm greenhouse conditions. It should be potted in spring in a compost of leaf-mould and sandy loam. It flowers freely throughout the summer and may be propagated by seeds or by division. It may be used as a window-plant.

T. mexica'num. Mexican Foxglove. Stems very short, or somewhat ascending. *l.* as described above. *fl.* purplish-violet with paler variegation; on short pedicels at the summit of slender purple axillary scapes 6 to 8 in. long. Summer or continuously. Mexico. 1843. (B.M. 4070; B.R. 29, 52.)

TETRAN'YCHUS tela'rius. *See* **Red Spider Mite.**

TETRAPAN'AX. Included in **Fatsia** in this Dictionary but kept distinct by many botanists, the calyx-lobes, petals, and the stamens being 4- and the ovary 2-celled with 2 styles in Tetrapanax (*T. papyriferus*), whereas they are 5 in *Fatsia* (*F. japonica*).

TETRAP'TERYS (*tetra*, 4, *pteron*, wing; the samaras have 4 wings). FAM. *Malpighiaceae.* A genus of about 100 species of usually climbing shrubs, mostly Brazilian but extending into other parts of Trop. America. Leaves opposite, entire, often transparent, not glandular; stipules 2, variable. Flowers yellow or reddish; calyx 5-parted, with 8 glands, rarely 10 or none; petals clawed; stamens 10, all perfect, the alternate ones longer; umbels or racemes or often panicles, terminal, rarely sub-sessile. These stove plants are difficult to bring to flower in this country. A compost of peat and sand forms the most desirable soil for them. Cuttings of ripe shoots will root in sand under a glass in heat.

T. dis'color. *l.* elliptic to elliptic-oblong, bluntish or slightly acute, leathery, glabrous; stipules interpetiolar, deciduous. *fl.* yellow, in 4-fld. umbels in panicles; pedicels, hoary, jointed in middle. May. Guiana, Trinidad. 1827. SYN. *T. trinitensis.*

T. inaequa'lis. *l.* ovate or elliptic, acute, leathery; stipules interpetiolar, deciduous. *fl.* yellow, in 4-fld. umbels in panicles; pet. jointed at or below middle. May. Brazil, Jamaica. 1818. SYN. *T. citrifolia.* A high-trailing climber.

F. G. P.

tetraque'trus -a -um, with 4 very sharp, almost winged, corners or angles.

tetras'tichus -a -um, having 4-cornered spikes.

TETRASTIG'MA (*tetra*, four, *stigma*; in allusion to the 4-lobed stigma). FAM. *Vitaceae.* A genus of about 40 species of deciduous or evergreen tendril-climbing shrubs closely related to Cissus but with axillary (not leaf-opposed) inflorescences, digitate or pedate leaves, and distinct from Columella by the exceedingly short style, 4-lobed stigma, and leaflets little over $2\frac{1}{2}$ in. long. Natives of Trop. and Sub-trop. Asia and needing greenhouse protection; their graceful, delicate growth makes them very suitable for large greenhouses. For cultivation *see* **Cissus.**

T. Harmand'ii. Tall climber with twining tendrils. *l.* large; lflets. 3 to 5, short-stalked, narrowly lanceolate, toothed, glabrous. *fl.* in axillary short-stalked cymes. *fr.* globose, edible. Philippines. Stove.

T. obtec'tum. Evergreen or half-evergreen climber, stems hairy, tendrils with adhesive disks. *l.* long-stalked; lflets. 5, digitate, sessile, obovate to elliptic, acute, glabrous, with remote, rounded, mucronate teeth. *fl.* greenish, in slender, stalked umbels, pedicels slender, pubescent. Himalaya, W. and Cent. China. 1904. SYN. *Cissus obtectum.*

T. serrula'tum. Climber with twining tendrils. *l.* pedate, petioles $1\frac{1}{2}$ to $2\frac{1}{2}$ in.; lflets. 5 (or 3), $1\frac{1}{2}$ to $2\frac{1}{2}$ in. long, lanceolate, to narrow-ovate, acute, bristly toothed. *fl.* in stalked cymes; axillary or terminal on short branches. *fr.* black, globose, as large as a currant. Himalaya, W. China. 1880. SYN. *Cissus serrulata, Vitis capreolata.*

TETRATHEC'A (*tetra*, four, *theke*, cell; the anthers are often 4-celled). FAM. *Tremandraceae.* A genus of about 20 species of low, evergreen shrubs, native of Australia and Tasmania. Leaves varying from alternate to opposite and verticillate. Flowers 4- or 5-parted, solitary in the leaf-axils; fruit a 2-celled, flattened capsule. Peat-loving shrubs requiring the same treatment as Cape heaths.

KEY

1. *Lvs.* $\frac{1}{2}$ *in. long or less*	2
1. *Lvs. usually over* $\frac{1}{2}$ *in. long, usually alternate*	T. hirsuta
2. *Lvs. strongly revolute*	T. pilosa
2. *Lvs. not strongly revolute*	3
3. *Lvs. whorled*	4
3. *Lvs. not whorled*	5
4. *Lvs. in whorls of* 4 *to* 6, *narrow-linear*	T. ericifolia
4. *Lvs. in whorls of* 3 *or* 4, *oval-lanceolate*	T. thymifolia
4. *Lvs. in whorls of* 3, *broadly ovate*	T. ciliata
5. *Plant glandular and hairy*	T. glandulosa
5. *Plant glabrous. Shoots rush-like*	T. juncea

T. cilia'ta. Shrub with tufted branches, 6 to 18 in. h. Stem slender, densely hairy below. *l.* in whorls of 3, broadly ovate, $\frac{3}{8}$ in. long, ciliate; upper smaller. *fl.* rose-pink, 1 to 3 in axils on slender pedicels $\frac{1}{8}$ in. long; sep. 4, ovate, ciliate; pet. oblong, $\frac{1}{2}$ in. long. S. Australia, Victoria. 1846. (B.M. n.s. 62.)

T. ericifo'lia. Heath-like shrub, 1 to $2\frac{1}{2}$ ft., more or less downy and bristly. *l.* 4 to 6 in a whorl, stalkless, narrowly linear, $\frac{3}{8}$ to $\frac{1}{2}$ in. long. *fl.* solitary, $\frac{1}{2}$ to $\frac{5}{8}$ in. wide, drooping on a slender stalk, $\frac{1}{4}$ in. long; pet. obovate, round-ended, rosy pink; anthers purplish-brown. July. New S. Wales. 1803.

T. ericoi'des. A synonym of *T. pilosa.*

T. glandulo'sa.* Shrub 2 to 3 ft., shoots downy and glandular-hairy. *l.* alternate or sometimes opposite, not in whorls; linear-lanceolate, $\frac{1}{4}$ to $\frac{1}{2}$ in. long; margin glandular-ciliate or toothed. *fl.* solitary, drooping, on glandular-downy stalks about as long as the l. forming racemes 2 or 3 in. long, pet. dark rose, obovate, $\frac{3}{8}$ in. long, round ended; ovary glandular. Victoria, Tasmania. 1822. var. **al'ba,** *fl.* white.

T. hirsut'a.* Shrub 1 to 2 ft., shoots and l. downy and often hairy as well. *l.* mostly alternate, occasionally in whorls, $\frac{1}{2}$ to 1 in. long, $\frac{1}{12}$ to $\frac{1}{4}$ in. wide, elliptic-oblong. *fl.* $\frac{3}{4}$ in. wide, solitary on a slender, glabrous or thinly bristly stalk $\frac{3}{4}$ to $1\frac{1}{4}$ in. long; pet. 5, bright rose, ovate; ovary glabrous or slightly glandular. March. W. Australia. 1843. (B.R. 1844, 67.)

Tetratheca hirsuta

T. jun'cea. Glabrous shrub 2 to 3 ft., shoots long, rush-like, slender, acutely angled or winged, often partly leafless. *l.* always very sparse and distant, linear, $\frac{1}{4}$ to $\frac{1}{2}$ in. long. *fl.* in the axils of the upper very small l. forming an open raceme 2 or 3 in. long; pet. 4, rose, obovate, round-ended, $\frac{1}{3}$ in. long; ovary glabrous. July. New S. Wales. 1803.

T. pilo'sa. Heath-like shrub, 1 to $2\frac{1}{2}$ ft., much branched; varying from glabrous to bristly. *l.* usually linear, strongly revolute, broadly lanceolate. *fl.* on stalks about as long as l. often assembled near end of shoot; pet. rose; oboval-oblong, $\frac{1}{3}$ to $\frac{2}{5}$ in. long; ovary sparsely downy. Australia, Tasmania. 1823. (F.d.S. 1065 as *T. ericoides.*) A white form is sometimes found.

T. thymifo'lia. Shrub 1 to 3 ft., shoots and l. downy or bristly. *l.* in whorls of 3 or 4, oval-lanceolate, $\frac{1}{4}$ to $\frac{1}{2}$ in. long, $\frac{1}{8}$ to $\frac{3}{16}$ in. wide, margins recurved, bristly ciliate. *fl.* drooping, $\frac{1}{2}$ in. across, stalk about as long as the l.; pet. deep rose, obovate to oval, anthers purple; ovary downy. July. Australia. 1824. (B.M. 8028.)

W. J. B.

TETRAZYG'IA (*tetra*, four, *zugos*, yoke; parts of flower in fours). FAM. *Melastomataceae.* A genus of about 13 species of usually furry shrubs or trees, natives of the W. Indies. Leaves stalked, oblong, ovate or ovate-lanceolate, sometimes toothed, 3- to 5-nerved. Calyx tube urn-shaped, or globose, constricted above the ovary, limb 4- or 5-lobed; petals 4 or 5, obovate, obtuse; stamens 8 or 10, equal, filaments awl-shaped; panicles or corymbs terminal, many-fld. For treatment *see* **Melastoma.**

T. angustiflo'ra. Tree of about 20 ft. Branchlets and infl. powdery-downy. *l.* elliptic or elliptic-lanceolate, 3 to 5 in. long, abruptly narrowed to a slender point, entire, whitish-downy beneath. *fl.* white, large; cal. narrow; pet. 5 (rarely 4), about $\frac{1}{2}$ in. long; panicles oblong, the main branches ending in corymbose cymes. May. *Berry* small, black. (B.M. 4383 as *T. elaeagnoides.*)

T. dis'color. Low shrub to 3 ft. *l.* ovate or ovate-lanceolate, entire, 3 to 5 in. long, sharp-pointed, white with scaly down beneath. *fl.* white, small, densely crowded in a corymbose panicle; pet. oval. May. *Berry* small, blue. 1793.

T. elaeagnoi'des. Shrub of about 2 ft. *l.* elliptic-lanceolate or lanceolate, sharply pointed, narrower than in *T. angustiflora,* hairy-white-downy beneath. *fl.* pink or white in a corymbose or raceme-like panicle; pet. 4, about $\frac{1}{4}$ in. long. 1848.

teucrioi'des, Teucrium-like.

TEUCRIUM (ancient Greek name used by Dioscorides, probably from Teucer, King of Troy, who is said to have first used the plant medicinally). FAM. *Labiatae.* A genus of about 100 species of herbs, sub-shrubs or shrubs of varying habit, natives of the temperate and warmer parts of the world. Leaves entire, toothed or cut, sometimes multifid, the bracts sometimes similar, sometimes much reduced. Flowers with calyx tubular or bell-shaped, rarely inflated, 5-toothed; corolla somewhat 2-lipped, obliquely 5-lobed, 2 upper lobes very small, 2 lateral larger, lowest largest; stamens 4. Inflorescence in whorls of 2, rarely many, flowers, axillary or in spikes, racemes or heads. Nutlets obovoid, netted and wrinkled. Few of the species are of horticultural merit, but several are of medicinal value. All thrive in any moderately good soil. The shrubby species may be propagated by cuttings in sandy soil under a glass in spring or summer; the herbs, by division. SYN. Scordium, Scorodonia.

T. au'reum. A synonym of *T. Polium.*

T. beto'nicum. Evergreen shrub, 18 in. h., branches shaggy. *l.* ovate-oblong, 3 to 3½ in. long, crenate, woolly beneath, sometimes above; stalks long. *fl.* purplish, cor. tube exserted, hairy without, throat inflated, incurved; racemes 3 to 6 in. long, secured, whorls 2-fld. May to August. Madeira. 1775. (B.M. 3334.) Greenhouse.

T. bi'color. Glabrous perennial; branches 1 to 2 ft. long, sharply 4-angled. *l.* ovate, oblong or lanceolate, nearly 1 in. long, entire or cut, sometimes 3-fid; upper l. often linear, entire or 3-fid. *fl.* blue, solitary in l.-axils, upper somewhat racemose; bracts longer than fl. July. Chile. 1826. (B.R. 1255 as *T. orchideum.*) Greenhouse.

T. canaden'se. Perennial up to 3 ft. h., softly hairy. *l.* ovate-lanceolate to oblong-ovate, 2 to 3 in. long, toothed, base rounded, somewhat hairy beneath; stalk short; upper l. lanceolate. *fl.* purple to cream, in a rather loose, unbranched spike; cal. hoary, bell-shaped. Summer. Canada, United States. Hardy. Moist soil.

T. Chamaed'rys.* Wall Germander. Hispidly hairy perennial, 6 to 18 in. h., stems ascending, much branched, from a creeping rootstock. *l.* ovate, deeply crenate, ½ to 1½ in. long, gradually narrowed to stalk. *fl.* rose, ¾ in. long, lower lip spotted white and red; whorls about 6-fld. in axils of leafy bracts or sub-secund in leafy terminal spikes. July to September. Europe, naturalized in Britain. (E.B. 1094.)

T. fla'vum. Much-branched sub-shrub, 8 to 15 in. h. crisply grey-hairy. *l.* obovate, crenate above middle, narrowed to a wedge-shaped base and short stalk. *fl.* yellow in a loose raceme 2 to 8 in. long; cal. hairy, half as long as cor. Summer. Syria. Hardy.

T. fru'ticans.* Tree Germander. 2 to 5 ft. h., branches forked. *l.* evergreen, ovate, obtuse, entire, flat, glabrous above, white or reddish-brown-hairy beneath; stalk very short. *fl.* blue in terminal, few-fld. racemes, often on short branches; peduncles shorter than hairy cal. Summer. S. Europe. 1869. (Ref. B. 204; S.B.F.G. 527; B.M. 245 as *T. latifolium.*) Greenhouse or half-hardy. Wall in most places. var. **azu'reum** is a deeper blue in colour but rather more tender.

T. hyrca'nicum. Perennial, 1 to 2 ft. h., hairy, little branched. *l.* ovate-cordate, 1 to 3 in. long, deeply crenate, obtuse, scarcely hairy above, softly hairy beneath; stalked. *fl.* purple in simple dense spikes 3 to 8 in. long; cor. hairy without; pedicels short, erect, hairy. September. Persia. 1763. (B.M. 2013.) Hardy.

T. latifo'lium. A synonym of *T. fruticans.*

T. Ma'rum. Cat Thyme. Shrubby, erect, up to 1 ft. h. *l.* oval or lanceolate, ¼ to ½ in. long, green and hairy above, white-woolly beneath; stalk short. *fl.* reddish-purple in pairs in axils of upper l. forming a more or less one-sided rather crowded infl. 1 to 2 in. long; cal. teeth lanceolate, nearly equal; mid-lobe of cor. roundish. Summer. W. Mediterranean. Hardy. Rock-garden in dry places. A pretty but dangerous plant to admit for cats are inordinately fond of it, tear it to pieces, and trample on its neighbours to their hurt.

T. monta'num. Sub-shrub, prostrate and hoary, much branched at base, branches ascending 2 to 4 in. h. *l.* oblong-linear, entire, narrowed to a short stalk, hoary beneath, sometimes above. *fl.* white, becoming yellow, in a dense terminal head, cal. tubular-bell-shaped, teeth lanceolate. Summer. S. Europe, W. Asia.

T. multiflo'rum. Sub-shrub about 1 ft. h. *l.* ovate, ⅓ to ½ in. long, acute, sometimes hoary beneath. *fl.* light-red; whorls 2- to 6-fld., distant in a raceme. August. Spain. 1738. Half-hardy.

T. orchi'deum. A synonym of *T. bicolor.*

T. orienta'le. Erect perennial about 1 ft. h. *l.* 1- or 2-pinnatisect, 1½ to 2 in. long, broadly ovate; segs. linear, entire or cut; upper l. minute. *fl.* blue, in a loose, sometimes roughly hairy panicle; peduncles 1-fld., nearly twice as long as the acutely toothed cal. Summer. Lebanon, &c. 1725. (B.M. 1279; L.B.C. 1871.) Rock-garden.

T. Po'lium.* Hoary evergreen shrub with procumbent or sub-erect branches, 5 to 6 in. long; branches many from base. *l.* wedge-shaped, oblong or linear, ⅓ to 1 in. long, crenate, softly rugose, obtuse, sessile. *fl.* white, yellowish or purple, small; whorls few, in globose or oblong, terminal heads. Summer. Europe. W. Asia. 1562. Rock-garden in well-drained sandy soil. Variable in form of l. and colour of fl.

T. pyrena'icum.* Stem trailing, silvery-downy, branched. *l.* round, ½ to ⅔ in. wide, crenate, stalked; upper l. oblong-linear, acute, entire. *fl.* purplish and white in few-fld. whorls, in solitary, dense, terminal heads 1 in. across. June to August. S. Europe.

T. sandra'sicum. Sub-shrub, much branched, to 10 in. h. *l.* linear-lanceolate, whitish tomentose beneath, evergreen, ½ to 1¼ in. long, entire, sessile, acute or acuminate. *fl.* lavender-blue, small, in few-fld. axillary cymes. Summer. S. Turkey.

Teusch'eri, in honour of Herr R. Teuscher, 1827–84, planter in Java.

TEXAN UMBRELLA TREE. *See* **Melia Azedarach umbraculifera.**

texa'nus -a -um, of Texas, United States of America.

texen'sis -is -e, of Texas, United States of America.

tex'tilis -is -e, used in weaving.

TEYSMAN'NIA (in honour of J. E. Teysmann, 1808–82, Dutch gardener, author of *Catalogus Plantarum*). FAM. *Palmaceae.* A genus of a single species of low, unarmed Palm, closely related to Corypha, from which it differs mainly in habit. Its large leaves are used by the natives of Sumatra for thatching. For treatment *see* **Corypha.** Warm house.

T. altif'rons. Stem underground. *l.* erect, long-rhomboidal, obtuse, 6 to 7 ft. long, 1½ ft. wide, acute at base, plicate, laciniate, segs. obtusely 2-fid; stalks keeled at back, somewhat concave above, angles rounded with hooked prickles. *Spathes* papery-leathery, sheathing the reddish-hairy peduncle and the deflexed branches of the short spadix. *fr.* as large as an apple, globose or flattish, 1-celled, 1-seeded. Sumatra.

thalamiflorous, having petals and stamens arising directly from the receptacle below the ovary.

THALAMUS. The receptacle of a flower on which the carpels arise.

thalas'sicus -a -um, growing in the sea.

THALE'SIA. *See* **Orobanche.**

THA'LIA (in honour of Johann Thal, 1542–83, German physician and botanist). FAM. *Marantaceae.* A genus of 7 American perennial aquatic herbs 1 of which also occurs in Africa. Usually tall, often covered with waxy bloom. Leaves rather few, leathery, long-stalked; differing from Maranta by the solitary (not 2) hooked staminode, and from Monotagma and Pleiostachya by the bracts falling after flowering instead of persisting until the fruit ripens, as well as in some small differences in the flowers. *T. dealbata* is a good aquarium plant sufficiently hardy to survive most winters in the open if planted about 2 ft. beneath the surface of the water, and excellent in shallow water in a frost free house. It is the hardiest member of a family most of which require the conditions of a stove.

T. dealba'ta.* Perennial aquatic herb about 5 ft. h., covered with whitish bloom. *l.-stalks* about 1 ft. long, its apical swelling smooth, blade ovate-oblong, up to 18 in. long, leathery. *fl.* in a leafless panicle about 8 in. long, violet. June to September. Carolina, Texas. 1791. (B.M. 1690.)

T. genicula'ta. Perennial aquatic herb about 6 ft. h. *l.-stalk* 15 in. or more long, its apical swelling downy, blade ovate-oblong or ovate-lanceolate up to 2 ft. long but usually smaller. *fl.* violet in a large spreading panicle. Florida south to Argentine, Cent. Africa.

thalictrifo'lius -a -um, with Thalictrum-like leaves.

thalictroi'des, Thalictrum-like.

THALIC'TRUM (Greek *thaliktron*, a name used by Dioscorides for a plant with Coriander-like leaves, possibly a member of this genus). FAM. *Ranunculaceae.* A genus of about 130 species of perennial herbs, mostly natives of north temperate regions, with outlying species of no horticultural value on mountains of S. America, Trop. and S. Africa, the Philippines, Java, Sumatra, and

New Guinea. Roots usually fibrous but tuberous in a few species. Leaves often many times ternately or pinnately divided into numerous leaflets (i.e. decompound), but with only one leaflet (i.e. unifoliolate) in one species (*T. rotundifolium*) and only 3 leaflets (i.e. trifoliolate) in a few others (e.g. *T. virgatum*); leaflets usually lobed or toothed. Flowers small, green, yellow, mauve, purple, or white, in most species bisexual (i.e. perfect or hermaphrodite) but in many American species unisexual (i.e. male or female), the plants being then dioecious (i.e. with the male and female flowers on different individuals) or polygamo-dioecious (i.e. with most flowers on an individual plant male or female but some hermaphrodite) or polygamous (i.e. with male, female, and hermaphrodite flowers on the same individual), paniculate or rarely racemose; involucre lacking; perianth with 4 or 5 segments (sepals), usually small and falling quickly but in some species larger, petal-like, and more persistent; stamens numerous, usually with long filaments. Achenes often compressed or ribbed. Botanically the genus is a very difficult one, to which over 700 specific names have been applied, and the number of species is accordingly doubtful. The achenes vary considerably from species to species and are very useful for identification, but their minute characteristics cannot be described concisely here.

Several of the species are well worth a place in the flower garden, as much for the elegance of their intricately divided leaves as for their flowers, which individually are often insignificant. Any fairly good garden soil suits most of them. *T. Delavayi*, *T. dipterocarpum*, *T. diffusiflorum*, *T. reniforme*, and *T. Chelidonii*, the most beautiful members of the genus, need a light, rich, moist but well-drained soil in half-shade; as they start late into growth care must be taken that the crowns are not injured by early hoeing. These species are best propagated by seed, although the double form must be increased by careful division in spring. The others can be readily propagated by seed or division. *T. aquilegiifolium*, *T. flavum*, and *T. speciosissimum* are good border plants. Dwarfer species such as *T. tuberosum* are best on the rock-garden. Very dwarf species like *T. kiusianum* may be grown in pans for the alpine house.

As regards their flowers, the Meadow-rues may be divided for garden purposes into three groups: (1) flowers ornamental on account of their petal-like sepals which are usually longer and more conspicuous than the slender stamens, and which are normally mauve or purplish in *T. Chelidonii*, *T. diffusiflorum*, *T. dipterocarpum*, and *T. reniforme*, white or rose-tinged in *T. foeniculaceum*, *T. orientale*, and *T. tuberosum*; (2) flowers ornamental on account of their conspicuous stamens with broadened and rather club-shaped filaments in *T. aquilegiifolium*, *T. calabricum*, *T. kiusianum*, *T. petaloideum*, and *T. polygamum*, but slender filaments in *T. flavum* and *T. speciosissimum*, the sepals usually small and quickly falling; (3) flowers rather inconspicuous, the sepals small and quickly falling, the filaments slender, e.g. *T. alpinum*, *T. lucidum*, *T. minus*, *T. simplex*, &c. The plants of the last group have only their elegant foliage to recommend them for garden purposes.

Excellent descriptions of the 69 species known in 1885 are given in the monograph by J. C. Lecoyer in *Bull. Soc. Bot. Belgique*, 24 (1885–6). A revision of the American species by B. Boivin has been published in *Rhodora*, 46 (1944).

KEY

1. *Lflets. peltate* — 2
1. *Lflets. not peltate* — 3
2 (1). *Stamen filaments thickened above, club-shaped* — T. ichangense
2. *Stamen filaments slender, thread-like* — T. peltatum
3 (2). *Most or all lflets. thread-like or linear, less than $\frac{1}{8}$ in. wide, and at least 4 times as long as wide, excluding lobes if lobed* — 4
3. *Lflets. not thread-like, more than $\frac{1}{8}$ in. wide* — 5
4 (3). *Infl. many-fld. Fl. very small, scarcely $\frac{1}{5}$ in. across; sep. about $\frac{1}{10}$ in. long, inconspicuous. Some lflets. at least $\frac{1}{12}$ in. wide* — 23
4. *Infl. few-fld., loose. Fl. large, about* 1 *in. across; sep. about $\frac{1}{2}$ in. long, conspicuous, petal-like. Lflets. thread-like, under $\frac{1}{20}$ in. wide* — T. foeniculaceum
5 (3). *Plant very dwarf,* 3 *to* 7 *in. h.* — 6
5. *Plant taller,* 9 *in. to* 10 *ft. h.* — 9
6 (5). *Sep. conspicuous, petal-like, $\frac{3}{10}$ to $\frac{5}{10}$ in. long, longer than stamens. Lflets. usually more than $\frac{1}{2}$ in. wide* — 7
6. *Sep. inconspicuous, falling quickly, less than $\frac{1}{8}$ in. long, shorter than stamens. Lflets. less than $\frac{1}{2}$ in. wide* — 8
7 (6). *Stem bearing several alternate l. with numerous lflets.* — T. orientale
7. *Stem leafless except for* 2 *or* 3 *sessile whorled* 3*-foliolate lvs. forming an involucre for the umbellate fl.* — Anemonella thalictroides (p. 116
8 (6). *Infl. a simple raceme. Stamen filaments thread-like, narrower than anthers. Ovaries and achenes sessile* — T. alpinum
8. *Infl. corymbose. Stamens filaments club-shaped, broader in upper part than anthers. Ovaries and achenes stalked* — T. kiusianum
9 (5). *Some or all stem-l. distinctly stalked, with numerous* (9 *to* 130) *lflets.* — 10
9. *All stem-l. sessile, with* 3 *lflets.* — T. virgatum
10 (9). *Infl. few-fld.* (*fl. usually* 1 *to* 10, *rarely up to* 20). *Sep. white, conspicuous, $\frac{3}{10}$ to $\frac{5}{10}$ in. long, longer than stamens. Achenes sessile, ribbed. Plant usually less than* $1\frac{1}{2}$ *ft. h.* — 11 (also dwarfed specimens of *T. petaloideum* in fruit)
10. *Infl. usually many-fld. Plant not showing above combination of characters (thus if sep. are conspicuous, then achenes are stalked)* — 12
11 (10). *Stem erect, straight,* 7 *to* 20 *in. h. Lvs. mostly crowded at base of stem,* 2*-pinnate; lflets. small, mostly less than $\frac{2}{5}$ in. wide, with lobes entire* — T. tuberosum
11. *Stem often flexuous,* 5 *to* 10 *in. h. Lvs. alternate up stem,* 2*-ternate; lflets. larger, to* $1\frac{1}{5}$ *in. wide, with lobes often crenate-toothed* — T. orientale
12 (10). *Flowering specimens available* — 13
12. *Fruiting specimens available* — 34
13 (12). *Sep. inconspicuous or quickly falling, often green or yellowish, less than $\frac{3}{10}$ in. long* — 14
13. *Sep. conspicuous, fairly persistent, petal-like, usually mauve or purplish, sometimes $\frac{3}{10}$ to $\frac{6}{10}$ in. long; filaments pendulous, thread-like. Achenes stalked* — 30
14 (13). *Stamens and pistils both present in some fl. or on same infl., i.e. plants hermaphrodite or monoecious* — 15
14. *Stamens and pistils not both present on same infl., i.e. plants dioecious* — 25
15 (14). *Stamen filaments club-shaped, as broad as or broader than anthers* — 16
15. *Stamen filaments thread-like, narrower than anthers* — 18
16 (15). *Stamens less than $\frac{3}{10}$ in. long; filaments white; ovaries and achenes more or less sessile* — 17
16. *Stamens about $\frac{4}{10}$ in. long; filaments usually purplish, sometimes white; ovaries and achenes distinctly stalked* — 29
17 (16). *Plant* 9 *to* 20 *in. h. Lflets. small ($\frac{1}{10}$ to $\frac{7}{10}$ in. wide). Filaments often much wider than anthers* — T. petaloideum
17. *Plant* 3 *to* 10 *ft. h. Lflets. larger ($\frac{2}{10}$ to* $1\frac{1}{4}$ *in. or more wide). Filaments little wider than anthers* — T. polygamum
18 (15). *Stigma short (less than $\frac{1}{20}$ in. long). Lflets. usually glabrous, sometimes glandular* — 19
18. *Stigma long ($\frac{1}{10}$ to $\frac{2}{10}$ in. long), about equalling ovary. Lflets. usually hairy beneath but not glandular. Plant* 2 *to* 6 *ft. h.* — T. dasycarpum
19 (18). *Infl. loose, often broad; branches widespreading; stamens pendulous. L. outline about as long as wide; lflets. about as long as wide or shorter than wide* — 22
19. *Infl. rather crowded or else narrow; branches erect or ascending. L. outline longer than wide; lflets. much longer than wide or else rather large* ($\frac{1}{2}$ to $1\frac{1}{2}$ *in. long*) — 22
20 (19). *Anthers $\frac{1}{10}$ in. long. Achenes sessile, ribbed. Lflets. small or minute (less than* 1 *in. wide) mostly* 3*- to* 5*-toothed* — 21
20. *Anthers nearly $\frac{2}{10}$ in. long. Achenes stalked, flattened.* — 45
21 (20). *Plant usually glabrous. Stem markedly grooved. Lflets. very variable in size, mostly over $\frac{2}{5}$ in. wide* — T. minus
21. *Plant usually glandular, odorous. Stem round in section, not or scarcely grooved. Lflets. always very small (mostly under $\frac{2}{5}$ in. long and wide)* — T. foetidum
22 (19). *L. divisions to* $1\frac{1}{2}$ *in. wide, only* 2 *to* 4 *times as long as wide* — 24
22. *L. divisions very narrow, usually many times longer than wide* — 23
23 (22 or 4). *Fl. closely crowded; filaments erect; anthers rounded at tip* — T. lucidum
23. *Fl. not closely crowded; filaments pendulous; anthers often with a minute projection at tip* — T. simplex
24 (22). *Stem green* — T. flavum
24. *Stem glaucous* — T. speciosissimum
25 (14). *Lflets. entire or* 3*-lobed, the lobes entire. Plant* 3 *to* 10 *ft. h.* — 26
25. *Lflets.* 3*-lobed but the lobes toothed, hence* 5*- to* 9*-toothed or -lobed. Plant* 1 *to* 4 *ft. h.* — 27

26 (25) *Infl. rounded or flattened on top. Sep. blunt. Stamen filaments thickened in upper part, club-shaped, white. Style shorter than ovary* T. polygamum
26. *Infl. pointed at top. Sep. distinctly pointed. Stamen filaments slender, thread-like, pendulous, often becoming entangled. Style about as long as ovary* T. dasycarpum
27 (25). *Upper stem-l. short-stalked, almost sessile. Achenes compressed* 28
27. *Upper stem-l. long-stalked. Stamen filaments yellow. Achenes not compressed* T. dioicum
28 (27). *Stamen filaments purplish. Achenes somewhat compressed, about $\frac{3}{10}$ in. long* T. occidentale
28. *Stamen filaments yellow. Achenes much compressed, about $\frac{3}{10}$ in. long* T. Fendleri
29 (16). *Plant robust. Lvs. with stipels (small membranous appendages on l.-stalk) when young. Achenes long-stalked, pendulous, 3-winged* T. aquilegiifolium
29. *Plant slender. Lvs. always without stipels. Achenes short-stalked, not pendulous, ribbed but not winged* T. calabricum
30 (13) *Lflets. 3-lobed or entire, the lobcs usually entire, rarely toothed, usually small* 31
30. *Lflets. crenately 5- to 11-lobed or -toothed, the lobes or teeth blunt, $\frac{2}{10}$ to 1 in. across* 32
31 (30) *Lflets. mostly longer than broad, glabrous. Panicle glabrous* T. Chelidonii
31. *Lflets. mostly broader than long, minutely glandular Panicle glandular* T. reniforme
32 (30). *Lflets. variable in size, mostly $\frac{1}{10}$ to $\frac{5}{10}$ in. wide, glabrous* 33
32. *Lflets. always very small, less than $\frac{2}{5}$ in. wide, minutely glandular. Sep. $\frac{5}{10}$ to $\frac{9}{10}$ in. long, much longer than stamens* T. diffusiflorum
33 (32). *Achenes not or scarcely winged, $\frac{4}{10}$ in. long Sep. $\frac{4}{10}$ to $\frac{6}{10}$ in. long* T. Delavayi
33. *Achenes distinctly winged (the wing about $\frac{1}{50}$ to $\frac{1}{20}$ in. wide), $\frac{2}{5}$ in. long. Sep. about $\frac{3}{10}$ in. long* T. dipterocarpum
34 (12). *Achenes sessile or almost so, not narrowed at base into a distinct stalk* 43
34. *Achenes narrowed at base into a stalk* 35
35 (34). *Achenes short-stalked; stalk $\frac{1}{10}$ in. or less long* 36
35. *Achenes long-stalked, pendulous; stalk $\frac{2}{10}$ in. long, thread-like* T. aquilegiifolium
36 (35). *Achenes broadest at or below the middle* 37
36. *Achenes broadest above the middle, flattened. Asiatic species* 38
37 (36). *Achenes with curved or branched nerves. American species* 25
37. *Achenes with straight longitudinal ribs.* T. calabricum
38 (36). *Achenes not or scarcely winged* 39
38. *Achenes with two membranous wings about $\frac{1}{50}$ in. wide* T. dipterocarpum
39 (38). *Lflets. 3-lobed or entire, the lobes usually entire, rarely toothed, usually small* 40
39. *Lflets. crenately 5- to 18-lobed or toothed* 41
40 (39). *Lflets. always very small, less than $\frac{2}{5}$ in. wide, glandular* T. diffusiflorum
40. *Lflets. variable, mostly $\frac{1}{10}$ to $\frac{5}{10}$ in. wide, glabrous* 44
41 (39). *Lflets. mostly broader than long, glandular* 42
41. *Lflets. mostly longer than broad, glabrous* T. Chelidonii
42 (41). *Veins of achene few, curved, but not sinuous and much branched. Lvs. 1 to 3 in. across* T. neurocarpum
42. *Veins of achene numerous, sinuous and branched forming a network. Lvs. 1 to $1\frac{1}{2}$ in. across* T. reniforme
43 (34). *Achenes not compressed but prominently and evenly ribbed, mostly less than $\frac{2}{10}$ in. long* 20
43. *Achenes slightly or distinctly compressed, about $\frac{2}{10}$ to $\frac{3}{10}$ in. long. American species* 25
44 (40). *Lflets. glabrous. Chinese species* T. Delavayi
44. *Lflets. glandular. West Himalayan species* T. cultratum
45 (20). *Lflets. often large (to 3 in. wide), many-toothed, often with base cordate* T. neurocarpum
45. *Lflets. small (to $\frac{3}{10}$ in. wide), entire or few-toothed, with base rounded or wedge-shaped* T. cultratum

T. adiantifo'lium. *See under* **T. minus.**

T. Albin'ii. *See under* **T. speciosissimum.**

T. alpi'num.* Alpine Meadow Rue. 3 to 6 in. h., rarely more, usually stoloniferous. *l.* basal, ternate, with 3 pinnate divisions; lflets. 3- or 5-lobed or -toothed, $\frac{1}{8}$ to $\frac{1}{4}$ in. long, glaucous beneath; lobes blunt. *fl.* bisexual, erect, then drooping, in a simple few-fld. raceme; sep. $\frac{1}{10}$ in. long; stamens nearly $\frac{2}{10}$ in. long; filaments thread-like, purplish; anthers yellow. *Achenes* sessile, ribbed. July, August. Europe, including Britain, N. Asia, N. America. (B.M. 2237; E.B. 2.) A neat-foliaged little rock-garden plant.

T. anemonoi'des. A synonym of *Anemonella thalictroides.*

T. angustifo'lium. This ambiguous name has been discarded as a source of confusion. For *T. angustifolium* of Linnaeus according to Fritsch *see* **T. simplex galioides.** For *T. angustifolium* according to Jacquin *see* **T. lucidum.**

T. aquilegiifo'lium.* 2 to 3 ft. h.; stem hollow, glaucous. *l.* 2- or 3-pinnate; lflets. 3- to 6-lobed, up to $1\frac{1}{2}$ in. wide; stipels present on l.-stalks. *fl.* bisexual or occasionally unisexual, large, in a corymbose many-fld. panicle; sep. obovate, greenish or white, quickly falling, to $\frac{2}{10}$ in. long; stamens erect or ascending, about $\frac{4}{10}$ in. long; filaments broadened in upper part, as broad as anthers, usually purple. *Achenes* long-stalked, drooping, 3-winged, somewhat inflated. May to July. Europe, N. Asia. Before 1731. (B.M. 1818, 2025.) A very graceful and ornamental border plant, variable in colouring. var. **al'bum,** stamens white. Syn. *T. Cornuti*; **atropurpu'reum,** stems and stamens dark purple. Syn. *T. formosum*; **ro'seum,** stamens lilac-rose.

T. Arsen'ii. *See under* **T. peltatum.**

T. Babington'ii. *See under* **T. minus.**

T. Bauhin'ii. *See under* **T. simplex.**

T. calab'ricum. 14 to 36 in. h. *l.* ternately or pinnately decompound; lflets. 3-lobed or entire, the lobes entire or few-toothed, small, $\frac{2}{10}$ to $\frac{7}{10}$ in. wide; no stipels on l.-stalks. *fl.* bisexual, large, in a few-fld. corymb; sep. less than $\frac{2}{10}$ in. long; stamens erect or ascending, about $\frac{2}{10}$ to $\frac{4}{10}$ in. long; filaments broadened in upper part, nearly as broad as anthers, purple. *Achenes* short-stalked, not drooping, ribbed. May to July. S. Italy (Calabria), Sicily. Like a small version of *T. aquilegiifolium.*

T. Chelidon'ii. About $1\frac{1}{2}$ to 3 ft. or more (up to 10 ft.) h. *l.* ternately or pinnately decompound; lflets. usually longer than broad, mostly ovate to narrowly obovate, 7- to 13-lobed or -toothed, glabrous, $\frac{2}{10}$ to $1\frac{3}{10}$ in. wide. *fl.* bisexual, large, about $\frac{7}{10}$ in. across in a loose few- or many-fld. glabrous panicle; sep. petal-like, mauve, about $\frac{3}{10}$ in. long; stamens drooping, about $\frac{2}{10}$ in. long; filaments thread-like; anthers yellow, about $\frac{1}{10}$ in long. *Achenes* stalked, flattened, not winged. Cent. and E. Himalaya (Kumaon, Nepal, Sikkim, Assam). Syn. *T. cysticarpum.* A beautiful plant related to *T. Delavayi* and often confused with *T. reniforme.* It sometimes bears bulbils in the axils of the l.

T. Cornut'i. A synonym of *T. aquilegiifolium album.*

T. corynel'lum. A synonym of *T. polygamum.*

T. cultra'tum. *See under* **T. neurocarpum.**

T. cysticar'pum. A synonym of *T. Chelidonii.*

T. dasycar'pum. 3 to 7 ft. h., usually dioecious; stem stout, leafy, purplish. *l.* decompound, upper l. sessile or nearly so; lflets. oblong, 3-lobed, the lobes entire, usually finely pubescent beneath, not glandular or glaucous, to about 1 in. wide. *fl.* mostly unisexual, in a large narrowly pyramidal many-fld. panicle pointed at the top; sep. lanceolate to narrowly ovate, pointed, $\frac{1}{10}$ in. long; stamens drooping, nearly $\frac{3}{10}$ in. long; filaments thread-like, often entangled. *Achenes* almost sessile, often hairy. July, August. Canada and United States, in central region from Saskatchewan south to New Mexico. 1856. Syn. *T. purpurascens* of gardens.

T. Delavay'i. 2 to 4 ft. h., slender. *l.* ternately or pinnately decompound; lflets. longer than broad or as long as broad; lflets. mostly 3-lobed, the lobes entire or sometimes few-toothed, small, glabrous, $\frac{3}{10}$ to $\frac{9}{10}$ in. wide. *fl.* bisexual, large, $\frac{6}{10}$ to 1 in. across, in a loose usually many-fld. glabrous panicle; sep. petal-like, mauve, rarely white, $\frac{4}{10}$ to $\frac{6}{10}$ in. long; stamens drooping, $\frac{3}{10}$ to $\frac{4}{10}$ in. long; filaments thread-like; anthers yellow, less than $\frac{1}{10}$ in. long. *Achenes* long-stalked, flattened, scarcely or not winged, about $\frac{4}{10}$ in. long. July, August. W. China. 1890. (B.M. 7152; G.C. 3 ser. 7 (1890), 124: G.C. 3 ser. 38 (1905), 450.) A very beautiful plant commonly cultivated as *T. dipterocarpum*, which is closely allied. To this probably belongs Hewitt's Double (Syn. *T. dipterocarpum plenum*)

T. diffusiflo'rum. 3 to 10 ft. h., slender. *l.* ternately or pinnately decompound; lflets. very small and numerous, 3- to 5-toothed, minutely hairy beneath, less than $\frac{4}{10}$ in. long and wide. *fl.* bisexual, very large, $\frac{8}{10}$ to $1\frac{1}{2}$ in. across, few or many, in a diffuse infl.; sep. petal-like, delicate mauve to light-violet, $\frac{5}{10}$ to $\frac{8}{10}$ in. long; stamens drooping, $\frac{3}{10}$ to $\frac{4}{10}$ in. long; filaments thread-like; anthers yellow, about $\frac{1}{10}$ in. long. *Achenes* distinctly stalked, flattened. SE. Tibet. 1938. Closely allied to *T. reniforme* and *T. Delavayi*; noteworthy for its very small lflets. and very large fl.; a lovely plant but not easy to grow.

T. dioi'cum. 9 to 26 in. h., dioecious, glabrous. *l.* 3- or 4-ternate, all distinctly stalked, even the uppermost; lflets. 3-lobed, the lobes crenately toothed, to 1 in. wide. *fl.* unisexual, small, numerous, in a small loose panicle; sep. greenish or purple, $\frac{1}{10}$ to $\frac{2}{10}$ in. long; stamens drooping, $\frac{3}{10}$ to $\frac{4}{10}$ in. ong; filaments thread-like, yellow; anthers $\frac{1}{12}$ to $\frac{2}{12}$ in. long; stigma purple. *Achenes* almost sessile, ribbed, less than $\frac{2}{10}$ in. long, ribbed. April. Eastern N. America, from Quebec to Georgia. 1759. (B.B. 2. 120.) Foliage elegant, but fl. insignificant.

T. dipterocar'pum. 2 to 5 ft. h., slender. *l.* ternately decompound; lflets. mostly 3-lobed, the lobes entire or sometimes few-toothed, small, glabrous, $\frac{3}{10}$ to $\frac{8}{10}$ in. wide. *fl.* bisexual, large, about $\frac{1}{2}$ in. across, in a loose usually many-fld. glabrous panicle; sep. petal-like, delicate mauve, about $\frac{3}{10}$ to $\frac{4}{10}$ in. long; stamens drooping, nearly $\frac{3}{10}$ in. long; filaments thread-like; anthers less than $\frac{1}{10}$ in. long. *Achenes* short-stalked, flattened, about $\frac{2}{10}$ in. long, with 2 narrow wings about $\frac{1}{50}$ to $\frac{1}{20}$ in. wide (whence the name *dipterocarpum* with 2-winged fruit). W. China. 1908. (R.H. 1915, 568.) A beautiful plant, with slightly smaller fl. and a broader shorter fr. than *T. Delavayi.* Although the name *T. dipterocarpum* is commonly used in catalogues, it is probable that most of the plants listed should be referred to *T. Delavayi.*

T. Fendler'i. 2 to 5 ft. h., dioecious, often minutely pubescent. *l.* 3-ternate, upper l. with very short stalks or almost sessile; lflets. 3-lobed, the lobes mostly crenate-toothed, to 6/10 in. wide. *fl.* unisexual, small, numerous, in a small panicle; sep. less than 2/10 in. long, those of female fl. much smaller than those of male ff.; stamens about 3/10 in. long; filaments thread-like, yellow; anthers about 1/10 in. long. *Achenes* almost sessile, flattened, about 2/10 to 3/10 in. long. July, August. Western N. America, from Oregon and Wyoming to Lower California and Texas. var. **Wright'ii,** 1 to 3 ft. h., usually glabrous. Arizona, N. Mexico. SYN. *T. Wrightii.*

T. fla'vum. Yellow Meadow-rue, 2 to 3 ft. h., deep green; rootstock stoloniferous, yellow; stems stout, furrowed. *l.* 2- or 3-pinnate, longer than wide; lflets. obovate to narrowly elliptic, 3-lobed or entire, usually less than 1 in. wide. *fl.* bisexual, small, numerous, in an erect, rather compact, corymbose or pyramidal panicle; sep. yellow, about 1/10 in. long; stamens bright yellow, about 2/10 to 3/10 in. long; filaments thread-like; anthers about 1/20 in. long. *Achenes* sessile, ribbed, about 1/10 in. long. July, August. Europe, including Britain. (E.B. 8.). var. **specio'sum,** a synonym of *T. speciosissimum.*

T. foenicula'ceum. 6 to 20 in. h., slender, glabrous. *l.* 3- to 5-ternate, intricately divided; lflets. thread-like, about 1/50 in. wide. *fl.* bisexual, large, to 1½ in. across, usually few, in a loose corymb; sep. petal-like, white, sometimes rose-tinged, 3/10 to 6/10 in. long; stamens erect, nearly 2/10 in. long; filaments thread-like; anthers yellow, with greenish-yellow pollen. *Achenes* sessile, ribbed, slightly curved, 2/10 in. long. May, June. 1939. N. China. (Hook. I. 3428.) SYN. *T. psilotifolium.* A graceful plant for alpine house, distinguished by its very finely divided l. and large erect fl.

T. foe'tidum. 9 to 24 in. h., normally covered with minute odorous glands; stem round, 3- or 4-pinnate, triangular in outline, broader than long; lflets. very small, 3- to 7-lobed, usually less than 4/5 in. wide. *fl.* bisexual, small, numerous, in a loose panicle; sep. greenish, about 1/10 in. long; stamens drooping, about 2/10 long; filaments thread-like; anthers 1/10 in. long. *Achenes* sessile, ribbed. June. Cent. Europe. 1640. For garden purposes like a small form of *T. minus*, from which it cannot always be easily distinguished. Rock-garden.

T. galioi'des. A synonym of *T. simplex galioides.*

T. glau'cum. A synonym of *T. speciosissimum.*

T. ichangen'se. 6 to 14 in. h., glabrous. *Basal l.* 2-ternate, *upper stem-l.* with lflets. peltate, ovate to very broadly ovate, crenate, ¾ to 1¾ in. wide. *fl.* bisexual, small, few or many, in a loose corymb; sep. quickly falling, about 1/10 in. long; stamens erect, 2/10 in. long; filaments thickened in upper part and broader than anthers, white; anthers 1/10 in. long, not appendaged. *Achenes* slender, stalked, ribbed. Cent. China. (Hook. I. 1765.) SYN. *Isopyrum multipeltatum.*

T. jalisca'num. *See under* **T. peltatum.**

T. kiusia'num. 4 to 6 in. rarely more h., glabrous; roots tuberous; *l.* 2-ternate to 3-foliolate; lflets. 5- to 3-lobed, to ½ in. wide. *fl.* bisexual, few, 3/10 in. across, in a small loose corymb; sep. purple, hardly 10 in. long; stamens erect, 2/10 in. long; filaments thickened in upper part, broader than anthers, rose-purple; anthers about 1/20 in. long. *Achenes* long-stalked. var. **al'bum,** *fl.* white. Spring. S. Japan (Kyushu). 1932. (Bull. Alp. Gn. Soc. 1. 79.) Neat and attractive, for pans in alpine house.

T. Koch'ii. *See under* **T. minus.**

T. laserpitifo'lium. A synonym of *T. lucidum laserpitifolium.*

T. lu'cidum. 2 to 4 ft. h. *Stem-l.* sessile, numerous, ternate with pinnate divisions; lflets. mostly entire, sometimes 2- or 3-lobed, narrowly lanceolate to linear, much longer than broad, usually less than 3/10 in. wide. *fl.* bisexual, small, numerous, crowded in an ovoid or narrow panicle; sep. greenish, about 1/10 in. long; stamens ascending, 2/10 to 3/10 in. long; filaments thread-like; anthers yellow, blunt, about 1/20 in. long. *Achenes* sessile, ribbed. Europe. 1739. SYN. *T. angustifolium* of Jacquin and other authors. A very variable species, often called *T. angustifolium.* var. **laserpitifo'lium,** *lflets.* broader, lanceolate. SYN. *T. laserpitifolium.*

T. ma'jus. *See under* **T. minus.**

T. mi'nus. 1 to 4 ft. h., often stoloniferous; stem furrowed. *l.* 3- or 4-pinnate, triangular in outline, broader than long; lflets. small but variable, usually 3-lobed, 1/10 to 1 in. wide. *fl.* bisexual, small, very numerous, in a loose panicle with spreading branches; sep. greenish, about 3/20 in. long; stamens drooping, 2/10 to 3/10 in. long; filaments thread-like; anthers 1/10 in. long. *Achenes* sessile, ribbed. Europe, including Britain; N. Asia. (E.B. 3.) Extremely variable, with many local races, to which over 220 specific names, including *T. adiantifolium*, *T. Babingtonii*, *T. Kochii*, *T. majus*, have been given. Botanic gardens distribute more forms of *T. minus* than of any other species, frequently under names which are incorrect. The l. are elegant, the fl. insignificant.

T. neurocar'pum. About 2 to 4 ft. or more h.; stem flexuose. *l.* ternately or pinnately decompound; lflets. about as broad as long or broader than long, often cordate, 7- to 18-lobed or -toothed, 3/10 to 2½ in. wide, minutely hairy beneath. *fl.* bisexual, small, in a large loose panicle; sep. about 2/10 in. long; stamens about 4/10 in. long; filaments thread-like; anthers nearly 2/10 in. long. *Achenes* stalked, flattened. W. Himalaya (Kashmir to Kumaon). This is said to smell of peppermint. It has been confused with *T. reniforme* and is described as such in Hooker's *Flora of British India* 1: 11 (1872) but has less conspicuous flowers. The allied **T. cultra'tum,** likewise Himalayan, has rather similar fl. and achenes but much smaller sparsely toothed lflets. less than ½ in. wide, with the base rounded or wedge-shaped.

T. occidenta'le. 2 to 4 ft. h., dioecious, glabrous or slightly hairy. *l.* 3-ternate, upper l. with short stalks; lflets. 3-lobed, the lobes crenately toothed; sep. less than 2/10 in. long, those of female fl. much smaller than those of male fl.; stamens about 4/10 in. long; filaments thread-like, purplish; anthers about 1/10 in. long. *Achenes* almost sessile, somewhat flattened, about 3/10 in. long. Western N. America (Washington, Oregon, with vars. in other States).

T. orienta'le. 4 to 10 in. h.; stem flexuose, sometimes sprawling. *l.* alternate and well-spaced on stem, 2-ternate; lflets. 3-lobed, the lobes often crenately toothed, 2/10 to 1 2/10 in. wide. *fl.* bisexual, large, 4/10 to 1 1/10 in. across, few, in loose infl.; sep. petal-like, white, 3/10 to 3/5 in. long; stamens erect, nearly 2 2/10 in. long; filaments thread-like; anthers yellow. *Achenes* sessile, ribbed, 2/10 in. long. Spring, Greece, Asia Minor, N. Syria. 1938.

T. pelta'tum. About 3½ ft. *l.* 2- to 4-ternate; lflets. peltate, with 3 to 10 rounded teeth, 1 to 2½ in. ; sep. less than 2/10 in. long; stamens about 4/10 in. long; filaments thread-like; anthers about 1/10 in. long, with a long thread-like appendage. *Achenes* almost compressed. Mexico. Included here as a representative of an American group with peltate l., e.g. *T. Arsenii*, *T. jaliscanum*, *T. Roseanum*, &c.

T. petaloi'deum. To 20 in. h. *l.* 3-ternate; lflets. entire, 2- or 3-lobed, to 1 3/10 in. wide. *fl.* bisexual, medium-sized, 4/10 to 5/10 in. across, few or many, in a corymb; sep. quickly falling, about 1/10 in. long; filaments club-shaped, broadened in upper part, wider than anthers, uneven in length and width, to 2/10 in. long, white; anthers yellow, 1/20 in. long. *Achenes* sessile, ribbed. June, July. Siberia, Mongolia, N. China, Korea. 1799. (L.B.C. 891.)

T. poly'gamum. 3 to 10 ft., dioecious or polygamous. *l.* 3- to 4-ternate, upper l. sessile or nearly so; lflets. entire or 3-lobed, the lobes entire, sometimes finely pubescent beneath but not glandular, to 2 in. across. *fl.* unisexual or bisexual, 2/10 to 3/10 across, in a large many-fld. panicle rounded or flattened at the top; sep. oblong or obovate, blunt, about 1/10 in. long; stamens ascending, about 2/10 in. long; filaments club-shaped, as broad as anthers, white; anthers yellow; ovaries with long curved style. *Achenes* almost sessile. Summer. Eastern N. America, from Newfoundland and Ontario south to Tennessee and Georgia. 1914. (B.B. 2. 121.) SYN. *T. corynellum*, *T. purpurascens* of Linnaeus ? *T. pubescens* ?

T. psilotifo'lium. A synonym of *T. foeniculaceum.*

T. pubes'cens. *See under* **T. polygamum.**

T. purpuras'cens of gardens. A synonym of *T. dasycarpum*; *see also* **T. polygamum.**

T. renifor'me. 1½ to 3 ft. or more h. *l.* ternately or pinnately decompound; lflets. usually as broad as long or longer than broad, almost orbicular to very broadly ovate, 5- to 11-lobed or -toothed, minutely glandular, 2/10 to 1 in. wide. *fl.* bisexual, large, 8/10 to 1 2/10 in. across, in a loose few- or many-fld. minutely glandular panicle; sep. petal-like, mauve, about 4/10 to 6/10 in. long; stamens drooping, 3/10 to 4/10 in. long; filaments thread-like; anthers yellow, about 1/10 in. long. *Achenes* stalked, flattened, not winged. E. Himalaya (Nepal to SE. Tibet and Bhutan). A very beautiful species often confused with *T. Chelidonii*, which is glabrous, and *T. neurocarpum*, which has smaller fls.; it is also very like *T. Delavayi.*

T. Rosea'num. *See under* **T. peltatum.**

T. rugo'sum. A synonym of *T. speciosissimum.*

T. sim'plex. 12 to 36 in. h. *Basal l.* stalked, stem-l. sessile, numerous, ternate with pinnate divisions; lflets. 3-lobed or entire, often narrowly lanceolate, much longer than broad, usually less than ¼ in. wide. *fl.* bisexual, small, numerous, in a narrow loose panicle; sep. greenish, about 1/10 in. long; stamens drooping, to 3/10 in. long; filaments thread-like; anthers yellow, sometimes with a minute projection at tip. *Achenes* sessile, ribbed. Summer. Europe. 1778. A very variable species, sometimes called *T. Bauhinii.* var. **galioi'des,** *lflets.* very narrow, almost thread-like. SYN. *T. galioides*, *T. angustifolium* of Linnaeus but not most authors. No horticultural value, but found in botanic gardens.

T. speciosis'simum. 2 to 5 ft. h., glaucous; rootstock stoloniferous; stem stout, furrowed. *l.* 2- or 3-pinnate, longer than wide; lflets. 3-lobed or entire, to 1½ in. wide. *fl.* bisexual or unisexual; small, numerous, crowded, in an erect rather compact corymbose or pyramidal panicle; sep. pale yellow, 1/10 in. long; stamens mostly ascending, bright yellow, about ¼ in. long; filaments thread-like; anthers almost 1/10 in. long. *Achenes* sessile, ribbed, about 1/10 in. long. July, August. Spain, Portugal, NW. Africa. 1774. SYN. *T. flavum* var. *speciosum*, *T. rugosum*, *T. glaucum.* An ornamental border plant, notable for its glaucous foliage. **T. Albin'ii,** S. Spain, is closely allied but glandular all over and strong-smelling.

T. tubero'sum. 7 to 20 in. h.; roots tuberous; stem erect. *l.* mostly crowded at base of stem, 2-pinnate; lflets. mostly 3-lobed, the lobes entire, under 4/10 in. wide. *fl.* bisexual, large, 8/10 to 1 2/10 in. across, usually few (1 to 10), sometimes many (up to 20) under cultivation, in an erect corymb; sep. petal-like, white, 4/10 to 6/10 in. long; stamens erect, about 2/10 in. long; filaments thread-like; anthers yellow. *Achenes* sessile, ribbed, 2/10 in. long. June. Spain, SW. France. 1713. Attractive rock-garden plant; under cultivation it becomes taller with more but smaller fl. than in the wild.

T. virga'tum. 7 to 20 in. h. *l.* sessile, with only 3 lflets.; lflets. short-stalked, broader than long, with 3 to 12 rounded teeth, less than 1 in. wide. *fl.* bisexual, few or many; sep. petal-like, $\frac{2}{10}$ in. long, white; stamens about $\frac{3}{10}$ in. long; filaments thread-like; anthers about $\frac{1}{10}$ in. long. *Achenes* stalked. Cent. Himalaya eastward to W. China.

T. Wright'ii. A synonym of *T. Fendleri Wrightii.*

W. T. S.

THALLOPHY'TA. A name used in some classifications to include all the plants below the rank of the mosses, i.e. the Algae in which the green colouring matter Chlorophyll is present though often masked by blue-, brown-, or red-colouring matters, and the Fungi from which it is absent. In this classification the Fungi would include the bacteria and their allies, and the slime fungi (Myxomycetes) as well as the plants usually recognized as Fungi. Notes on these groups will be found under their separate headings.

THALLUS. The body of a plant which is either not divided into separate members or, if divided, has all the divisions of a similar form. Such a plant is a Thallophyte.

THAM'NEA (*thamnos*, shrub; from the habit). FAM. *Bruniaceae.* A genus of a single undershrub. It grows well in the greenhouse in a compost of peat and sand and can be propagated by cuttings in sand under a glass.

T. uniflo'ra. Undershrub about 1 ft. h. with filiform, fastigiate branches. *l.* alternate, very small, somewhat rhomboidal, short, bluntly keeled, closely pressed, upper rather longer forming an involucre. *fl.* white, small, terminal, solitary; cal. adnate to the ovary, 5-lobed; pet. 5, with 2-keeled claws and an ovate, spreading limb; stamens 5, included. April. S. Africa. 1810.

THAMNOCAL'AMUS. Included in **Arundinaria.**

THAMNOP'TERIS. Included in **Asplenium.**

THAP'SIA (ancient Greek name used by Theophrastus). FAM. *Umbelliferae.* A genus of 4 species of tall perennial herbs, sometimes with a shrubby stem, natives of the Mediterranean region and Madeira. Leaflets pinnately decompound, segments pinnatifid. Flowers yellowish, dirty white, or purplish in compound, many-rayed umbels; calyx teeth small; petals inflexed at apex, shortly slender-pointed; involucre often absent. *T. garganica* has long had a reputation among the Moors for its healing qualities. Greenhouse or half-hardy treatment is necessary and propagation by seeds or by breaks from the carrot-like root.

T. deci'piens. Black Parsley. Stem terete, unbranched, 6 ft. h., naked and shrubby below. *l.* 3-pinnate; lflets. ovate, acuminate, toothed, terminal ones often connate; stalk sheathing. *fl.* white, obovate, emarginate, involucre of many cut l. June, July. Madeira. 1867. (B.M. 5670.)

T. edu'lis. About 4 ft. h. *l.* large, decompound, fern-like, in tufts, 1 to 3 ft. long including stalk. *fl.* white, involucres, both involucre and involucels of entire lflets. May. Madeira. 1857. (B.M. 5724 as *Monizia edulis.*) Roots with long, curved, horn-like divisions are black outwards and white within. They are eaten in Madeira.

T. garga'nica. Drias-plant. 2 to 4 ft. h., stem terete, glabrous. *l.* twice 3-pinnatisect, shining; segs. linear, acute, long, entire, decurrent or confluent. *fl.* yellow; involucre few-lvd. July, August. Mediterranean region. 1683. (B.M. 6293; S.B.F.G. 287.)

T. villo'sa. 3 to 4 ft. h., stem terete, glabrous. *l.* 3-pinnate, villous; lflets. oblong, sinuately pinnatifid, lower deflexed. *fl.* yellow; involucre and involucels almost wanting. June, July. S. Europe. 1710.

thapsifor'mis -is -e, like Thapsus, a kind of Verbascum.

THATCH PALMS. *See* **Euterpe, Sabal, Teysmannia, Thrinax.**

Thayeria'nus -a -um, in honour of the Massachusetts family of Thayer, interested in the botanical exploration of China.

THE'A (from the Dutch rendering of the Chinese dialect word *t'e*, hence English *tea*; the Mandarin word is *ch'a*). Included in **Camellia.**

THEA'CEAE. Dicotyledons. A family of about 200 tropical and sub-tropical shrubs and trees in about 16 genera. Leaves simple, usually alternate and evergreen, without stipules. Flowers often showy, perfect, regular; usually solitary or paired; sepals 5 to 7; petals 5, rarely 4, 9, or many, joined at base, often to stamens; stamens usually many (rarely 5, 10, or 15), free, in bundles, or united into a tube; ovary superior, 2- to 10-celled. Fruit a 1- to many-seeded capsule or drupe. The family contains many ornamental plants but only one of major economic importance, *Camellia sinensis.* The genera treated of here are Camellia, Cleyera, Eurya, Gordonia, Hartia, Schima, Stewartia, Ternstroemia, Tutcheria.

theca'tus -a -um, bearing receptacles.

theifo'lius -a -um, having leaves like *Camellia sinensis* (*C. Thea*).

theioglos'sus -a -um, smoke-tongued.

theionan'thus -a -um, smoke-flowered.

THECOSTE'LE (*theke*, receptacle, *stele*, column; in allusion to the shape of the gynostemium). FAM. *Orchidaceae.* About 5 species of epiphytic orchids found in Burma, Malacca, Java, and Borneo. Flowers small; sepals and petals free; column long, terete, 2-horned at top, the lip connate with column foot forming a tube, then spreading; side lobes of lip small; mid-lobe velvety. Pollen 2. Scape slender, from base of the 1-leaved pseudobulbs. Allied to Acriopsis. The plants should be placed in small pans and suspended in the intermediate or warm house. Compost should consist of Osmunda fibre and Sphagnum moss in equal quantities. The only species which has appeared in cultivation is

T. ala'ta. *fl.* many, $\frac{3}{4}$ in. across, yellowish, spotted red-purple; side-lobes of lip small, rounded, mid-lobe obovate, rounded at end, hairy in centre; column slender, S-shaped. *Pseudobulbs* ovoid, clustered, about 2 in. h. *l.* 5 in. long, 2 in. wide. *Scape* drooping, 15 in. or more long. Burma, Borneo, Java. In cultivation. 1912. (X.O. 147 as *T. Zollingeri.*) SYN. *Cymbidium alatum.*

E. C.

THELESPER'MA (Greek *thele*, nipple, *sperma*, seed; referring to the papillose achenes). FAM. *Compositae.* SYN. *Cosmidium.* A genus of about 10 species of glabrous annual or perennial herbs, sometimes woody at base, between 8 in. and 2 ft. high, one (*T. megapotamicum*, syn. *T. scabiosoides*, *T. gracile*) occurring in temperate S. America, the others in Mexico and SW. United States. Leaves opposite or the upper alternate, once or twice pinnately divided into linear or filiform segments, the upper sometimes undivided and linear. Flower-heads rather small, many-flowered, on long peduncles; involucre double, the outer bracts free and smaller than the inner bracts which are joined for about their length into a cup and have conspicuous whitish or yellowish margins; ray-florets, when present, about 8, usually yellow but partly red-brown in *T. Burridgeanum*; disk-florets purplish or brownish. Achenes glabrous, cylindrical, smooth or with small protuberances, beakless. The two following are treated as hardy annuals; the others probably need cool greenhouse treatment. In general appearance they suggest Coreopsis and Cosmos.

T. Burridgea'num.* Loosely branched annual, 1 to 2 ft. h. *l.* 2-pinnate, segs. filiform. *fl.-heads* $1\frac{1}{4}$ to $1\frac{1}{2}$ in. across; outer involucral bracts small, hairy; ray-florets slightly 3-lobed at tip, about $\frac{1}{2}$ in. long, to $\frac{1}{4}$ in. wide, deep orange with a red-brown basal blotch or almost entirely red-brown with the tip and upper margin orange. June to September. Texas. Before 1857. (F.d.S. 1860, 1321). SYN. *T. hybridum, Cosmidium Burridgeanum, Coreopsis Burridgei.* At one time erroneously considered a bigeneric hybrid (*Coreopsis tinctoria* × *T. trifidum*) raised by F. K. Burridge of Colchester, England, sometime before 1857. This species was not recorded in a wild state until 1928 (cf. Proc. Biol. Soc. Washington, 41. 146).

T. tri'fidum. Loosely branched annual or biennial, 1 to 2 ft. h. *l.* 2-pinnate, segs. filiform. *fl.-heads* $1\frac{1}{4}$ to $1\frac{1}{2}$ in. across; outer involucral bracts, glabrous; ray-florets slightly 3-lobed, about $\frac{1}{2}$ in. long, deep orange with no red-brown blotch. June to September, SW. United States. 1835. (B.M. 3505 as *Coreopsis filifolia.*) SYN. *T. filifolium, Cosmidium filifolium.*

W. T. S.

THELOCAC'TUS (*thele*, a nipple; referring to the tuberculate ribs). FAM. *Cactaceae*. Smallish cacti, often densely spiny; ribs few, broken into large tubercles; flowering tubercles grooved. Flowers large, borne on the young areoles; fruit dry, dehiscing by a basal pore. **A**

T. bi'color. Plants round, solitary, glaucous, very spiny; areoles close; radial spines 9 to 18, highly coloured, sometimes bright red or red and yellow; centrals 4, stouter. *fl.* large, purplish-pink. Texas, Mexico. (B.M. 4486, 4634.) SYN. *Echinocactus rhodophthalmus.*

T. hexaedro'phus. Plants round or flattened, glaucous; strongly tuberculate; radial spines 6 to 9, awl-shaped, annulate; one erect central, stouter. *fl.* large, purplish. Mexico. SYN. *Echinocactus hexaedrophus.*

T. Mandrago'ra. Plants round with a turnip-like root; tubercles close, 4-sided; radial spines about 12, white; centrals 2, thicker with brown tips. *fl.* white with pink stripes. Mexico. SYN. *Echinocactus Mandragora.*

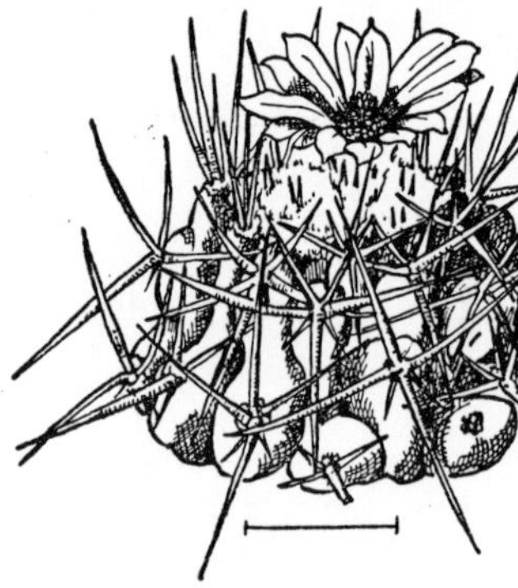

Thelocactus nidulans

T. nid'ulans. Plants round, depressed, solitary, glaucous, grey; spines about 15, all radial, up to 2½ in. long. *fl.* creamy. Mexico. (B.R.C. 4, f. 8.)

T. Potts'ii. Plants round, glaucous; ribs 8 or 9, broad, more or less tubercled; areoles close; radial spines 7 to 10, banded in red and yellow; centrals several, somewhat flattened. *fl.* pale purple. Mexico. SYN. *Echinocactus Pottsii.*

T. subterra'neus. A most unusual little plant; the stem is round or ovoid, very spiny, connected to the turnip-like root by a thin woody stem which may branch. *fl.* unknown. Mexico.

V. H.

THELYG'ONUM (*thelygonos*, begetting girls; Pliny reports that it gives the power of producing female offspring). FAM. *Cynocrambaceae*. One species only, *T. Cynocrambe*, Dog's Cabbage, is a hardy, slightly fleshy, procumbent, annual herb, common in the Mediterranean region, occasionally grown as a pot-herb like Spinach, but it has no horticultural value.

THELYMIT'RA (*thelys*, woman, *mitra*, cap; alluding to the hood-shaped column). Woman's Cap Orchid. FAM. *Orchidaceae*. A genus of about 50 species of terrestrial orchids, with ovoid tubers, needing greenhouse treatment; represented in New Caledonia and Malaya, and 3 or 4 indigenous to New Zealand, but the greater number are Australian. Flowers blue, purple, red, or yellow, occasionally white, usually several in a terminal raceme; sepals, petals, and lip all nearly equal and spreading; column rather short, erect, broadly winged. In one section the column wing forms a hood above the anther and is beautifully fringed or haired, in others it does not form a hood and in still others may be simply lobed; pollen masses granular; bracts shorter than the flowers. Leaves linear, lanceolate, or rarely ovate, sometimes rather thick, but not terete. Stems simple, 1-leaved, the leaf comparatively large, sheathing, near the base of the stem, tapered. The stems bear one or more bracts. The flowers are among the most interesting and beautiful of the minor terrestrial orchids. In Australia they are known as sun orchids as many only expand their flowers in bright sunshine. Compost should be as for Bletias, but temperatures must be governed by that of their native habitat: from New S. Wales a cool greenhouse would probably suit, others would require the intermediate, possibly the warm house. A rest is necessary for the majority when the plants are dormant but some are found in boggy places. All the following are Australian.

T. carn'ea.* *fl.* pink, 1 to 4, fragrant; sep. and pet. oval-elliptic, oblong or obtuse, usually ⅓ in. long; column lobes hairless, yellow. May. *l.* narrow-linear. Stem slender, often flexuous, less than 6 to nearly 12 in. h. 1820. (F.A.O. 1, 64.)

T. Forst'eri. A synonym of *T. longifolia.*

T. gramin'ea. A synonym of *T. longifolia.*

T. grandiflo'ra.* *fl.* greyish-blue to purplish-blue, about 30 in a dense spike; sep. and pet. concave, ½ in. long; hood very flat with two large tufts of white hairs. *l.* lanceolate, 9 in. long, forming a closed sheath for 3 to 4 in. 1½ to 2½ ft. h. Australia. (F.A.O. 2, 49.)

T. ixioi'des. *fl.* 5 to 16, 1 to 2 in. across, blue, pedicellate, usually forming a raceme 4 to 6 in. long; sep., pet., and lip, elliptic-oblong; column with 3 short yellowish lobes and 2 horizontal lobes with a tuft of white hairs. May. *l.* long-linear or linear-lanceolate, flat or channelled, with 1 or 2 shorter ones. Stem usually above 1 ft. h. 1810. (F.A.O. 2, 47.) Variable.

T. longifo'lia.* *fl.* blue, lilac, or pink, rather large, several in raceme; column wings produced behind and over the anther into a broad hood, usually conspicuous from its dark colour with erect white hair tufts. May. *l.* long, narrow. h. variable, usually about 1 ft. 1824. (F.A.O. 1, 64.) SYN. *T. Forsteri, T. graminea, T. pauciflora.*

T. pauciflo'ra. A synonym of *T. longifolia.*

T. variega'ta. *fl.* purple, 2 to 4, large; sep. and pet. lanceolate, shortly acuminate or acute, ¾ to 1 in. long, spotted; column lobes orange, toothed. May, June. *l.* with a villous sheath, blade usually glabrous, linear, much dilated at base and often undulated. Stem not stout, 1 ft. h. or rather more. (F.A.O. 2, 52.) SYN. *Macdonaldia spiralis, M. variegata.*

T. veno'sa.* *fl.* blue, 6 to 10; sep. and pet. ½ to ¾ in. long with deeper blue veins; column broadly winged, its lobes hairless. April. *l.* long, narrow. Stem 1 to 2 ft. h. Variable. 1826. SYN. *Macdonaldia venosa.*

THELYP'TERIS, name used by Theophrastus for a fern. The genus Thelypteris is now included in Dryopteris.

THEMISTOCLE'SIA (in honour of the Greek statesman Themistocles). FAM. *Ericaceae*. A genus of 4 species of glabrous or hairy evergreen shrubs with slender, pendulous branches, natives of Peru, Bolivia, and Venezuela. Leaves alternate, ovate, with a long slender point, rounded or cordate at base, leathery. Flowers in short racemes; cal. bell-shaped or obconical, minutely 5-toothed; corolla tubular, slightly swollen at middle or base, 5-toothed, teeth small, recurved; stamens 10, as long as corolla. A compost of turfy loam, peat, and sand suits these stove plants. Cuttings root readily in sand or soil under glass.

T. corona'ria. Small softly hairy shrub with stout branches. *l.* numerous, ½ in. long, spreading and deflexed, entire, pale beneath. *fl.* dark red, shining; cal. short, pale green, hairy; cor. narrow urn-shaped or tubular, inflated beneath, obscurely 5-angled; pedicels solitary or twin in l.-axils, hairy. January. Venezuela. 1866. (B.M. 5575 as *Thibaudia coronaria.*)

THENARD'IA (in honour of L. J. Thenard, a French biochemist). FAM. *Apocynaceae*. A single species of climbing, glabrous shrub, needing similar treatment to that of Dipladenia.

T. floribun'da. Climber to 10 ft., with terete, slender branches. *l.* opposite, 2½ to 3½ in. long. *fl.* pink, broad, in umbels; cal. somewhat 5-parted; cor. tube very short, more or less rotate, lobes 5, spreading, twisted; pedicels long. June. Mexico. 1823.

THEOBRO'MA (*theos*, god, *broma*, food; referring to the products of the seeds of *T. Cacao*). FAM. *Sterculiaceae*. A genus of about 20 species of trees, natives of the warmer parts of America, the most important species being *T. Cacao*, which produces most of the seed from which cocoa and chocolate are derived. Leaves large, oblong, undivided, pinnately nerved or with 3 or 5 nerves from base. Flowers lateral on branches, small, calyx 5-cleft or 5-parted; petals 5, hooded, narrowed to a claw at base; stamens opposite sepals; peduncles 1-

flowered and clustered or in many-flowered racemes. Fruit often large, drupaceous, with a woody, 5-celled stone; seeds enveloped in pulp. *T. Cacao* will grow with the same treatment as Ticorea.

T. Ca'cao. Cocoa; Chocolate Nut Tree. Tree of 16 to 18 ft. *l.* oblong, slender-pointed, glabrous, quite entire. *fl.* clustered; cal. rose-coloured, segs. lanceolate, slender-pointed, longer than the yellowish cor. May. *fr.* yellow or reddish, ovoid-oblong, 6 to 8 in. long with 50 to 100 bean-like seeds. Trinidad, &c. 1739. (L.B.C. 545.) Productive varieties are propagated by budding.

THEODO'REA. This genus was named Theodorea in 1877 by the Brazilian botanist João Barbosa Rodrigues in honour of a Brazilian statesman Theodoro M. F. P. da Silva. It was renamed **Rodriguezіel'la** (which is now the more usually accepted name of the genus) by O. Kuntze in 1891 as the names Theodorea and Theodora had already been used for other plants. FAM. *Orchidaceae.* A monotypic genus closely allied to Gomeza and included in that genus by some. The sepals and petals are similar, narrowly lanceolate, sub-connivent, erect not undulate as in Gomeza. The lip is at first erect then sharply bent and projecting between the lateral sepals, disk with 2 haired callosities. Column and rostellum short.

T. gomezoi'des. *fl.* 9 to 12; sep. hardly ½ in. long; pet. slightly shorter, greenish-yellow outside, flushed purplish-brown within; lip oblong-ovate, whitish, callosities yellow; scapes arched or sub-erect, 3 to 6 in. long. *Pseudobulbs* clustered, oblong-conical, more or less compressed, ancipitous, 1 to 1¾ in. h., 2-leaved. *l.* 3 to 6 in. long, about ½ in. wide. Brazil. 1903. SYN. *Gomeza Theodorea.*

E. C.

THEOPHRAS'TA (in honour of Theophrastus, Greek botanist, 370–285 B.C.). FAM. *Theophrastaceae.* A genus of perhaps 2 species of glabrous evergreen shrubs, with stout, simple, erect stems. Leaves spreading, linear-oblong, spiny-toothed, net-veined, with short stalks. Flowers white, in many-flowered racemes; calyx 5-parted; corolla cylindrical-bell-shaped, 5-lobed; stamens 5, staminodes 5. Fruit apple-shaped, fleshy, many-seeded. They thrive in a compost of peat and loam under stove conditions. Cuttings of half-ripe shoots will root in sandy loam, under a glass, with bottom heat.

T. america'na. Shrub of 1 to 3 ft. *l.* linear-lanceolate, 16 to 18 in. long, 2 in. wide, gradually narrowed to base, teeth small. *fl.* dull brown, becoming black; sep. rounded at tip; cor. urn-shaped; racemes rusty, tomentose, dense-fld., cylindrical. St. Domingo. SYN. *T. fusca.*

T. Jussieu'i. Shrub of 3 ft. *l.* near top of stem, clustered, spreading, linear-oblong; stalk short. *fl.* white, rather large; cal. segs. ovate-erect; cor. lobes spreading; stamens fixed at base of cor.; racemes short. St. Domingo. 1818. (B.M. 4239.) SYN. *T. densiflora.*

T. smaragdi'na. A synonym of *Deherainia smaragdina.*

THEOPHRASTA'CEAE. Dicotyledons. A family of about 70 species in 4 genera, natives of Trop. America and the Sandwich Is. Shrubs or trees with alternate leaves usually at the tops of the stems or with the branches crowded together, lanceolate and without stipules. Flowers regular, perfect or 1-sexual. Stamens 5 and 5 staminodes. Ovary superior, 1-celled with many ovules on a free central placenta. Fruit a drupe. The only genus treated here is Theophrasta.

therma'lis -is -e, growing under warm conditions.

THERMOMETER. An instrument for measuring the intensity of heat; one of the most useful in gardens, particularly in glasshouses where the plants need to be given heat regulated to meet their requirements. An ordinary thermometer consists of a fine glass tube with a bulb at one end. The bulb and lower part of the tube contain either mercury or alcohol suitably coloured, and as it expands or contracts in the tube, the amount of rise or fall in the temperature is indicated. When a thermometer is made, all the air in the tube above the liquid is expelled and the end is hermetically sealed. The space not occupied by the mercury or spirit is therefore a vacuum and there is nothing in the tube to impede the rise of the liquid as it expands with the rise of temperature. The tube is usually fixed to a frame of some sort on which the scale of degrees is marked, but in some thermometers the scale is marked on the tube itself. Three different scales are in use. Fahrenheit's scale is in general use in Britain and is used as the scale in referring to temperatures in this Dictionary. The others are the Réaumur and the Centigrade, the last being the most generally used on the Continent. In Fahrenheit's scale the freezing-point of water is fixed at 32° and the point at which water boils at sea-level at 212°. In Réaumur's scale the freezing-point is fixed at zero and the boiling-point at 80°, in the Centigrade scale the freezing-point is zero, and the boiling-point 100°. The 3 are therefore quite different to read, because the spaces on the scales between the freezing-point and boiling-point are differently divided.

To convert Centigrade temperature to the Fahrenheit scale divide the number of degrees registered by 5 and multiply by 9, then add 32. Thus 60° on the Centigrade

$$\text{thermometer} = \frac{60\times 9}{5}+32 = 140^\circ\ \text{F}.$$

Ordinary thermometers, *if correctly graduated* to the scale, are well adapted for all horticultural purposes under glass, but cheap thermometers are often some degrees out of truth. There are special forms made for use in mushroom beds and hot beds where there is bottom heat.

There are various kinds of thermometers in use where meteorological observations are taken; many of these are made in special ways for special purposes. There is, for example, a maximum thermometer registering the highest, and a minimum the lowest temperature reached since the indicators in either of the instruments were last set. Solar radiation thermometers are made for indicating the highest temperature in the sun's rays. There is also a minimum thermometer for laying on the grass. Where a minimum thermometer is in use in a garden for ascertaining the lowest degree reached in frosty weather during any period, it should be suspended in a position with a north aspect with a fair exposure. For accurate comparable thermometer readings the thermometers should be placed in a Stevenson screen. A useful application of the thermometer is the hygrometer for ascertaining the humidity of the atmosphere. Two thermometers are mounted side by side, the bulb of one being dry, the other kept moist by means of a wick dipping into water. The difference between the readings of the two thermometers enables the humidity of the air to be calculated, the nearer they are together indicating the greater the relative humidity. A scale is sometimes fitted between the two to be used as a prognosticator of frost.

THERMOP'SIS (*thermos*, lupin, *opsis*, like). FAM. *Leguminosae.* A genus of about 20 species of perennial herbs, natives of N. America, Siberia, and Himalaya. Leaves digitately 3-foliolate, stipulate. Flowers yellow or rarely purple, rather large, in terminal or leaf-opposed racemes; papilionaceous; calyx 2-lipped, upper lip truncate or emarginate, tube campanulate. Pods at most shortly-stalked, not inflated as they are in the nearly related Baptisias. The species are hardy, growing best in light, rich soil. Propagation is best by seed, for divided plants do not establish readily.

T. barba'ta. Hairy, 1 ft. or more h. from a woody rootstock. *l.* often opposite, sessile; lflets. oblanceolate; often hairy; stipules oblanceolate. *fl.* 6 to 12, opposite or 3-nate, stalked; cor. deep purple, 1 in. long. June. Himalaya. 1854. (B.M. 4868.)

T. carolinia'na.* Little branched, 2 to 3 ft. h. *l.* stalked; lflets. obovate, glaucous and finely-hairy beneath, 2 to 3 in. long, 1 in. wide; stipules leafy. *fl.* yellow in a compact erect raceme 6 to 10 in. long. July. E. United States.

T. faba'cea. A synonym of *T. montana.*

T. lanceola'ta. A synonym of *T. lupinoides.*

T. lupinoi'des. About 1 ft. h. *l.* nearly sessile, lowest and highest often simple; lflets. oblong-lanceolate, silky-hairy; stipules half as long as lflets. *fl.* yellow, twin or somewhat whorled; cal. cleft to middle; bracts large; raceme terminal. June, July. Siberia. (B.M. 1389 as *Podalyria lupinoides.*) SYN. *T. lanceolata.*

T. mol'lis. Stem diffusely branched, whole plant softly hairy, 1 to 2 ft. h. *l.* shortly stalked; lflets. elliptic to ovate, tawny-hairy on veins beneath, ¾ to 1½ in. long; stipules ovate to lanceolate, up to ½ in. long. *fl.* yellow, in compact flexuous racemes, 2 to 6 in. long. July. E. United States. (B.B. ed. 2, 343.)

T. monta'na.* 1 to 2 ft. h. *l.* stalk 1 to 3 in. long; lflets. linear to linear-lanceolate, 1¼ to 3 in. long; stipules linear-lanceolate, about 1 in. long. *fl.* yellow in erect, compact racemes 4 to 8 in. long. June, July. Western N. America. 1818. (B.M. 3611; B.R. 1272; L.B.C. 1856.) SYN. *T. fabacea.*

T. rhombifo'lia. Stem slender, somewhat branched, 8 to 15 in. or more long. *l.* shortly stalked; lflets. obovate to oblanceolate, about 1 in. long, ½ in. or more wide, appressed, hairy. *fl.* yellow, loosely arranged in a raceme 4 in. long. June to August. Middle United States. (B.B. ed. 2, 344.)

THEROPO'GON (*theros*, summer, *pogon*, beard; tufted in habit and summer-flowering). FAM. *Liliaceae.* A genus of a single species of herbaceous perennial of tufted habit with grass-like leaves, much like Ophiopogon, common in the Himalaya. Hardy or nearly so, growing in sandy loam and leaf-mould. Propagation by seeds sown in heat in spring or by division.

T. pal'lidus. *l.* 6 to 8, nearly 1 ft. long, persistent, glabrous, ⅙ to ¼ in. wide, distinctly ribbed, green above, glaucous beneath. *fl.* white, sometimes tinged red, ¼ to ⅓ in. long; segs. broad, overlapping; raceme terminal, 2 to 3 in. long, 10- to 20-fld.; scape slender, firm, shorter than l. Spring. 1875. (B.M. 6154.)

THERORHO'DION. *See* **Rhodothamnus.** A

THESPE'SIA (*thespesios*, divine; *T. populnea* frequently planted about temples in the tropics). FAM. *Malvaceae.* A genus of about 10 species of trees or tall herbs, natives of Trop. Asia, Madagascar, and the Pacific Is. Leaves entire or angularly lobed. Flowers showy, often yellow; calyx not conspicuously dotted, truncate, rarely 5-cleft, persistent; ovary 5-celled. Stove conditions are necessary and a compost of loam and peat. Ripened cuttings root freely in sand under a glass in heat. A closely related genus sometimes included in *Thespesia* is **Montezu'ma** (named after the Aztec war-chief Montezuma) which has a deciduous calyx and 3 to 4-celled ovary; it comprises 2 species. **M. speciosis'sima** (SYN. *Thespesia grandiflora*), a native of Puerto Rico, becomes a tree of 30 ft., with long-stalked ovate-cordate acuminate leaves and large glossy red flowers 4 to 6 in. across on pedicels 4 in. long.

T. grandiflo'ra. A synonym of *Montezuma speciosissima.*

T. popul'nea. Mahoe, Portia Oil-nut, Umbrella-tree. Tree of 40 ft. *l.* roundish, heart-shaped, narrowed to apex, 5- to 7-nerved, covered beneath with dot-like scales. *fl.* at first yellow with purple centre, becoming entirely purple by evening; pedicels 1½ to 2 in. long, as long as l.-stalks. June. Tropics of Old World. 1770. var. **guadalupen'sis,** pet. narrower than in type, fringed at base, pedicels 1 in. long. Cultivated in Guadaloupe.

THEVET'IA (in honour of André Thévet, 1502–92, French monk, who travelled in Brazil and Guiana). FAM. *Apocynaceae.* A genus of about 10 species of glabrous shrubs or small trees, natives of Mexico south to Paraguay. Leaves alternate, 1-nerved, or slenderly pinnate-veined. Flowers yellow, large, in terminal cymes; calyx 5-parted with acute, spreading segments; corolla funnel-shaped, tube cylindrical, abruptly expanded to a bell-shaped throat, lobes broad, twisted; stamens at top of tube. Drupe broader than long. Stove conditions are necessary. Propagation by cuttings in sand under a glass in heat.

T. Ahoua'i. Tree of 20 ft. *l.* oblong-obovate, acute, narrowed at base, 4 in. long, glabrous above, sparsely hairy beneath. *fl.* pale yellow on thick pedicels; cor. ribbed, lobes spreading; cymes terminal, many-fld., dense. June. Brazil. 1739. (A.B.R. 231; B.M. 737 as *Cerbera Ahouai.*)

T. nereifo'lia. A synonym of *T. peruviana.*

T. peruvia'na. Yellow Oleander. Tree of 12 ft. *l.* linear, 3 to 6 in. long, glabrous, shining above. *fl.* saffron-yellow, about 3 in. long; cal. segs. about ½ in. long; cymes sub-terminal, much shorter than l., few-fld. June. Trop. America. 1735. (B.M. 2309 as *Cerbera Thevetia.*) SYN. *T. nereifolia.*

T. Yccot'li. Shrub of 8 ft. *l.* narrow-linear, narrowed to both ends, glabrous above, slightly hairy beneath, margins revolute. *fl.* much like those of *T. peruviana*, 3 in. long; cor. lobes 3 times as long as tube; cymes sub-terminal, 1- to 3-fld. June. *fr.* green, warted, as large as a small apple. Mexico. 1800.

thianschan'icus -a -um, of the Tien Shan (Chinese *t'ien*, heavenly, *shan* mountain) range in Cent. Asia.

THIBAU'DIA (in honour of J. M. B. Thibault de Chanvalon, 1725–88, Secretary of the Linnean Society of Paris, botanical writer). FAM. *Ericaceae.* A genus of 2 species of handsome shrubs, natives of the Andes of Colombia and Peru. Leaves alternate, evergreen, leathery, entire, pinnately veined. Flowers scarlet, stalked, numerous, in axillary racemes; calyx tube terete, limb short, obtusely 5-lobed or -toothed; corolla tubular, terete, lobes 5, small, suberect; stamens 10, as long as corolla tube; pedicels bracteate at base, sometimes bracteolate. Stove conditions are required and a compost of turfy loam, peat, and sand. Cuttings will root readily in sand or soil. Several plants at one time put in this genus are now regarded as species of Agapetes, Corallobotrys, Pentapterygium, Proclesia, Psammisia, or Themistoclesia.

T. floribun'da. Branches terete, smooth, greyish. *l.* oblong-lanceolate, acuminate, net-veined. *fl.* glabrous on very long pedicels; racemes solitary, nearly 2 in. long, with overlapping bracts at base. Colombia.

T. pichinchen'sis. 6 to 12 ft. h. *l.* oval-oblong or oblong-lanceolate, obtuse, rounded at base, 3 to 4 in. long; stalk short. *fl.* about ½ in. long; cal. furry, teeth mucronulate; cor. glabrous; racemes shorter than l. Pichincha. 1849.

thibeti'cus -a -um, of Tibet.

THICK-LEAF. *See* **Crassula.**

THIELAV'IA. *See* **Thielaviopsis.**

THIELAVIOP'SIS. A genus of fungi in the class Ascomycetes, some species of which are parasitic on plants, the chief being *Thielaviopsis basicola* which may cause Black Root Rot of many herbaceous ornamental and crop plants. *See*, for example, **Primula.**

D. E. G.

THIMBLEBERRY. *See* **Rubus occidentalis.**

THINNING-OUT, the work of reducing the number of plants on a given area so that they are not too crowded to permit of the proper development of all. Thinning-out should be attended to among seedlings at an early stage, if it is necessary at all, otherwise the whole lot will suffer, by becoming either drawn or stunted. Thinning-out of trees, &c., in a plantation must usually be done gradually, i.e. at intervals, as it becomes necessary to prevent interference with the desired growth of those that are to remain. Thinning-out of branches of trees and shrubs and of spurs of fruit-trees must be attended to periodically to ensure that each of those left has the light and air it requires.

A→

Thiselto'nii, in honour of Sir William Turner Thiselton-Dyer, 1843–1928, Director of Kew from 1885 to 1905.

THISTLE. A name widely applied to herbaceous plants with spiny leaves and usually flowers in heads. *See*, for instance, **Cnicus.**

THISTLE, BLESSED. *See* **Silybum Marianum.**

THISTLE, CARLINE. *See* **Carlina vulgaris.**

THISTLE, COTTON. *See* **Onopordon Acanthium.**

THISTLE, GLOBE. *See* **Echinops.**

THISTLE, GOLDEN. *See* **Protea scolymocephala, Scolymus hispanicus.**

THISTLE, HEDGEHOG. *See* **Echinocactus.**

THISTLE, HOLY. *See* **Silybum Marianum.**

THISTLE, MELON. *See* **Melocactus.**

THISTLE, OUR LADY'S MILK. *See* **Silybum Marianum.**

THISTLE, RUSSIAN. *See* **Salsola.**

THISTLE, SCOTS'. *See* **Onopordon Acanthium;** the name has also been used for **Carduus nutans** and **Cirsium vulgare.**

THISTLE, SOW. *See* **Sonchus.**

THISTLE, WEATHER. *See* **Carlina vulgaris.**

THLADIAN'THA (Greek *thladias*, eunuch, *anthos*, flower; some of the flowers on the type-specimens of *T. dubia* had the anthers suppressed as if castrated). FAM. *Cucurbitaceae.* A genus of about 20 species of climbing herbs, natives of N. China, Java, and the Himalaya. Leaves ovate-heart-shaped, the sinus deep, toothed. Flowers dioecious, golden, large, calyx tube bell-shaped, closed at base by a horizontal scale, segments 5, lanceolate, corolla bell-shaped, 5-parted, segments revolute half-way down; male, solitary or in a raceme, with 5 stamens; female solitary, ovary oblong, style deeply 3-fid, stigmas kidney-shaped. Fruit green, oblong, fleshy, many-ribbed. *T. dubia* is hardy and will grow in almost any soil, but it succeeds best against a sunny wall.

T. du'bia. Tendril climber. *l.* deeply heart-shaped ovate, 4 in. long, $2\frac{1}{2}$ in. wide, acute, toothed, not angular, usually hairy beneath, stalk 1 to $1\frac{1}{2}$ in. long. *Male fl.* rather crowded; racemes 2 to 3 in. long, cal. teeth very narrow; pet. $\frac{3}{4}$ in. long; filaments downy; *female fl.* on a peduncle 2 to 3 in. long and more or less hairy; ovary densely woolly. *fr.* $1\frac{1}{2}$ in. long, $\frac{3}{4}$ in. wide, glabrous, obtuse at both ends. China. (B.M. 5469, male fl. only.)

T. Oliver'i. Vigorous tendril climber. *l.* deeply heart-shaped ovate to 9 in. long, 6 in. wide; stalk to 4 in. long. *Male fl.* paniculate. *Female fl.* solitary. Summer. China. 1894 (R.H. 1903, 473.) Distinguished from *T. dubia* by its glabrous state, its bigger *l.*, more abundant *fl.*, 2-fid tendrils, &c.

THLAS'PI (ancient Greek and Latin name for a Cress). FAM. *Cruciferae.* A genus of about 60 species of low-growing herbs widely distributed over the world, annual or perennial. Basal leaves forming a rosette; stem-leaves often stem-clasping. Flowers white, pink, or pale purple in racemes. Seed-pods compressed, often winged, with usually more than 1 seed in each cell. The following are sometimes grown on rock-gardens where the best need moraine conditions, but a few will grow in well-drained spots. Slugs are very fond of them. Propagated by seed, or the perennials by cuttings taken in April or May. Frequent, even annual, propagation is desirable. The larger annual species like *T. arvense* are weeds. Apart from dwarf alpine species such as *T. bellidifolium, T. cepeifolium, T. limosellifolium,* and *T. rotundifolium,* which are closely allied, the genus has little horticultural interest.

The plant described below as *T. macrophyllum* and known in gardens as *T. latifolium* differs so much from the others in its habit of growth, broad basal leaves, and stalked stem-leaves, as well as in having the partition of the seed-pod thick and ribbed, instead of thin and transparent, that it is now often placed in a genus by itself as **Pachyphrag'ma** (Greek *pachys*, thick, *phragma*, partition) **macrophyl'lum.**

T. alpes'tre. Biennial or short-lived perennial, 4 to 6 in. h. *Basal l.* obovate, entire, to $\frac{3}{10}$ in. wide, narrowed into the stalk; *stem-l.* few, ovate, stem-clasping with usually acute basal lobes. *fl.* white or sometimes lilac; pet. $\frac{1}{8}$ in. long, about twice as long as sep.; anthers often violet; style $\frac{1}{10}$ in. long. *infruct.* elongated, loose. June to August. Europe, including Britain.

T. alpi'num. Perennial, 4 to 6 in. h., forming loose tufts of rosettes; stem unbranched. *Basal l.* obovate or elliptic, to $\frac{2}{5}$ in. wide, narrowed into a long stalk; *stem-l.* few (2 to 5), mostly oblong-lanceolate, stem-clasping. *fl.* white; pet. $\frac{1}{5}$ in. long, nearly 3 times as long as sep.; anthers yellow. *infruct.* elongated, loose. European Alps. *T. Kerneri*, W. Alps, and *T. silvium*, E. Alps, are almost identical with this.

T. bellidifo'lium. Perennial, about 1 to 2 in. h., tufted. *Basal l.* narrowly obovate, sparsely and shallowly toothed, to $\frac{1}{4}$ in. wide, gradually narrowed into the stalk; *stem-l.* few (5 or 6), broadly ovate, stem-clasping, with acute or blunt basal lobes. *fl.* lilac; pet. $\frac{1}{3}$ in. long, 3 times as long as the purplish sep.; anthers yellow. *infruct.* dense, short. Balkan Peninsula.

T. cepeifo'lium. Perennial, 1 to 2 in. h. *Basal l.* elliptic, entire, to $\frac{1}{5}$ in. wide, gradually narrowed into the stalk; *stem-l.* few (about 4), elliptic, sessile. *fl.* lilac; pet. $\frac{1}{4}$ in. long, twice as long as sep.; anthers yellowish; style $\frac{1}{12}$ in. long. *infruct.* dense, short. E. Alps.

T. densiflo'rum. *See under* **T. violas'cens.**

T. goesingen'se. Perennial, 6 to 20 in. h., tufted; rhizome woody; stem sometimes branched. *Basal l.* obovate or oblong, to $\frac{1}{2}$ in. wide, narrowed into the stalk; *stem-l.* numerous (7 to 9), stem-clasping. *fl.* white; pet. $\frac{1}{8}$ in. long, about 3 times as long as sep.; anthers yellow; style $\frac{1}{12}$ in. long. *infruct.* elongated, loose. Austria, Hungary, Balkan Peninsula. SYN. *T. alpinum* var. *goesingense.* Close to *T. alpinum*, but more robust.

T. Kern'eri. *See under* **T. alpinum.**

T. latifo'lium. A synonym of *T. macrophyllum.*

T. limosellifo'lium. Perennial, $1\frac{1}{2}$ to $2\frac{1}{2}$ in. h., tufted. *Basal l.* elliptic, usually entire, to $\frac{1}{4}$ in. wide, gradually narrowed into the stalk; *stem-l.* few (3 to 7), elliptic, sessile. *fl.* lilac; pet. $\frac{1}{4}$ in. long, nearly 3 times as long as sep.; style $\frac{1}{12}$ in. long. W. Alps. SYN. *T. rotundifolium* var. *limosellifolium.*

T. macrophyl'lum. Perennial, 9 to 16 in. h., with creeping root-stocks. *Basal l.* very broadly ovate, acute, slightly toothed or repand, deeply cordate, to 4 in. wide, with an oniony smell when crushed, long-stalked; *stem-l.* few (2 to 6), broadly or very broadly ovate, cordate stalked. *fl.* white; pet. $\frac{1}{4}$ in. long; anthers yellow. *infruct.* elongated, loose. Spring or early summer. Caucasus, E. Asia Minor. 1856. SYN. *T. latifolium, Pachyphragma macrophyllum.* Useful for carpeting beneath deciduous shrubs, but easily grown in full sun, attractive for its profuse racemes of white fl. and bright green l.

T. monta'num. Perennial, 3 to 8 in. h., forming loose tufts of rosettes. *Basal l.* obovate or narrowly obovate, entire or slightly toothed, to $\frac{3}{8}$ in. wide, gradually narrowed into the stalk; *stem-l.* 4 to 8 ovate, stem-clasping with rounded basal lobes. *fl.* white; pet. $\frac{1}{5}$ in. long, about twice as long as sep.; anthers yellow; style $\frac{1}{12}$ in. long. *infruct.* loose. Europe.

T. perfolia'tum. Perfoliate Penny-cress. Annual or biennial, 2 to 9 in. h., sometimes branched. *Basal l.* narrowly obovate, sparsely toothed, to $\frac{3}{4}$ in. wide, gradually narrowed into the stalk; *stem-l.* few (3 or 4), ovate, stem-clasping with rounded basal lobes. *fl.* white; pet. $\frac{1}{10}$ in. long, nearly twice as long as sep.; anthers yellow; style minute. *infruct.* loose, short. Spring. Europe, including Britain. (E.B. 145.)

T. rotundifo'lium. Perennial, glaucous, 2 to 4 in. h., tufted. *Basal l.* broadly ovate or almost circular, entire or sparsely toothed, to $\frac{2}{5}$ in. wide, usually rounded at base, long-stalked; *stem-l.* few (about 4 to 6), ovate, entire, stem-clasping. *fl.* rosy-lilac, rarely white, fragrant; pet. $\frac{2}{10}$ to $\frac{3}{10}$ in. long, 3 times as long as sep.; anthers yellow; style $\frac{1}{16}$ in. long. *infruct.* short, rather dense. European Alps. 1868. (B.M. 5749 as *Iberidella rotundifolia.*)

T. sil'vium. *See under* **T. alpinum.**

T. stylo'sum. Perennial, $\frac{1}{2}$ to 1 in. h., tufted. *Basal l.* elliptic entire to $\frac{1}{8}$ in. wide, narrowed into the stalk; *stem-l.* few (2 to 4) sessile. *fl.* lilac; pet. $\frac{1}{5}$ in. long, about twice as long as sep.; style about $\frac{1}{10}$ in. long. *infruct.* short, dense. Cent. Italy. SYN. *Noccaea stylosa.*

T. violas'cens. Biennial, from 4 in. h. in fl. to 14 in. h. in fruit. *Basal l.* narrowly obovate, to $\frac{3}{4}$ in. wide, narrowed into the long stalk; *stem-l.* 4 to 8, ovate, acute; all *l.* rather glaucous, often violet-tinged or reddish. *fl.* whitish; pet. $\frac{1}{5}$ in. long, slightly longer than sep.; anthers yellow; style very short (about $\frac{1}{30}$ in. long). *infruct.* elongated, loose. Asia Minor, Syria. **T. densiflo'rum** is closely allied.

W. T. S.

tholifor'mis -is -e, dome-shaped (from Greek *tholos*, Latin *tholus*, dome, cupola of temple).

THOMAS'IA (in honour of Peter and Abraham Thomas, collectors of Swiss plants about 1750). FAM. *Sterculiaceae.* A genus of about 28 species of evergreen shrubs (rarely small trees), natives almost wholly of W. Australia, nearly always furnished, often densely, with stellate down. Leaves alternate, mostly lobed, more or less showy; petals none, or minute and scale-like; stamens 5, often alternating with 5 staminodes. Cool greenhouse shrubs, to be grown in a compost of loam, peat, and sand. Thomasia has been much confused in the *Bot. Mag.* and other works with the genus Lasiopetalum which also has no proper petals, but differs in having no stipules and a much more deeply lobed calyx. Cultivation as for Lasiopetalum.

KEY

1.	*Cal. white or brown*	2
1.	*Cal. purple*	3
2.	*Cal. white with rosy stripes*	T. solanacea
2.	*Cal. reddish-brown*	T. foliosa
3.	*Cal.* 1 *to* 1$\frac{1}{4}$ *in. across*	4
3.	*Cal.* $\frac{1}{4}$ *to* $\frac{5}{8}$ *in. across*	5
4.	*Lvs. glabrous or almost so,* $\frac{1}{2}$ *to* 1$\frac{1}{2}$ *in. long*	T. grandiflora
4.	*Lvs. downy, up to* 2$\frac{1}{2}$ *in. long and as wide*	T. macrocarpa
5.	*Lvs. entire, linear-oblong*	T. purpurea
5.	*Lvs. lobed*	6
6.	*Lvs. deeply lobed, leathery*	T. quercifolia
6.	*Lvs. broadly cordate-ovate, much wrinkled*	T. rugosa

T. folio'sa. Much-branched evergreen shrub, 1 to 3 ft., shoots starry-bristly and downy. *l.* $\frac{1}{2}$ to 1$\frac{1}{2}$ in. long, broadly ovate, shallowly cordate, 3- or 5-lobed; starry-hairy, especially beneath. *fl.* in numerous axillary slender racemes up to 1$\frac{1}{2}$ in. long; cal. $\frac{1}{4}$ in. wide, deeply lobed, reddish-brown. June. W. Australia. 1823.

T. grandiflo'ra. Evergreen shrub, 1$\frac{1}{2}$ to 2$\frac{1}{2}$ ft., shoots bristly-hairy and scabrid. *l.* linear-oblong to broadly ovate, entire, slightly cordate, $\frac{1}{2}$ to 1$\frac{1}{2}$ in. long, glabrous or slightly starry-hairy. *fl.* few in terminal slender-stalked clusters; cal. purplish-red, up to 1 in. across, hairy outside; pet. none. June. W. Australia.

T. macrocar'pa.* A bushy shrub 2 to 5 ft., shoots downy and hairy. *l.* triangularly ovate-cordate, up to 2$\frac{1}{2}$ in. long, often nearly as wide, sinuately lobed, downy especially beneath; stipules small, rarely $\frac{1}{2}$ in. long, kidney-shaped. *fl.* few in a loose raceme; cal. 1 to 1$\frac{1}{4}$ in. across, pale purple; anthers darker. June. W. Australia. (B.M. 4111 as *Lasiopetalum stipulaceum.*)

T. purpu'rea. Evergreen shrub 1 to 2 ft., shoots slender, grey-downy. *l.* linear-oblong, $\frac{1}{2}$ to 1$\frac{1}{2}$ in. long, $\frac{1}{4}$ to $\frac{1}{2}$ in. wide, entire, starry above, densely hairy below. *fl.* 3 to 6 in axillary racemes, 1 to 2 in. long; cal. corolla-like, $\frac{1}{4}$ in. wide, pale purple, 5-lobed; pet. minute or absent; anthers 5, black-purple. June. W. Australia. 1803. (B.M. 1755 as *Lasiopetalum purpureum.*)

T. quercifo'lia.* Low, much-branched shrub, shoots stiffly hairy. *l.* broadly ovate, deeply 3- to 7-lobed, $\frac{3}{4}$ to 1 in. long, the lobes rounded, leathery, starry-hairy above and on margins, hairy beneath. *fl.* about 6, clustered towards top of a downy raceme, nodding; cal. $\frac{1}{2}$ in. across, rosy-purple, corolla-like, 5-lobed; pet. none. April to June. W. Australia. 1803. (A.B.R. 459; B.M. 1485, as *Lasiopetalum quercifolium.*)

T. rugo'sa. Shrub 2 to 3 ft., densely clothed with starry down in most parts. *l.* broadly cordate-ovate, 1 to 3 in. long, very much wrinkled with sunken veins and harsh to the touch above; thickly downy beneath. *fl.* few, in slender-stalked racemes 1 to 2$\frac{1}{2}$ in. long; cal. $\frac{1}{2}$ to $\frac{5}{8}$ in. wide, purple, deeply 5-lobed, lobes obtuse. June. W. Australia.

T. solana'cea. Shrub, sometimes a small tree, covered when young with starry down, especially underneath l. *l.* deeply ovate-cordate and coarsely sinuately lobed, 1$\frac{1}{2}$ to 3 in. long, 1 to 2 in. wide; stipules kidney-shaped, $\frac{3}{4}$ to 1 in. long. *fl.* in racemes 2 in. long, sometimes branched and nearly as much wide; cal. $\frac{1}{2}$ in. across, white, each lobe striped with rose down middle; lobes reflexed; pet. none. May to July. W. Australia. Before 1812. (B.M. 1486 as *Lasiopetalum solanaceum.*)

W. J. B.

THOMASINIA'NA OCULIPER'DA. *See* **Red Bud-Borer.**

THOMAS'S PHOSPHATE. *See* **Basic Slag.**

Thompsonia'nus -a -um, in honour of the Rev. George Thompson.

Thomse'ni, in honour of Andreas Christian Thingberg Thomsen, b. 1881, explored Dutch New Guinea.

Thomso'nae, in honour of the wife of the Rev. W. C. Thomson, missionary at Old Calabar, W. Tropical Africa, who found *Clerodendron Thomsonae* in 1860.

THOMSON'IA (in honour of Anthony Todd Thomson, 1778–1849, professor of Materia Medica, University College, London). FAM. *Araceae.* A genus of 1 species of tuberous E. Indian herb with solitary leaves on long spotted stalks. Leaves 3-partite, segments pinnatisect. Peduncle long. Spathe leathery, boat-shaped, deciduous. Spadix sessile, nearly equalling spathe. Flowers 1-sexual, naked, densely covering spadix; stamens 3 to 5; ovary 2-celled, 2-ovuled. Related to Anchomanes but upper staminate flowers sterile. For treatment *see* **Caladium.**

T. napalen'sis. Tuber about 4$\frac{1}{2}$ in. across, flattened-globose. *l.-stalk* 2 to 2$\frac{1}{2}$ ft. long, reddish below, irregularly spotted with brownish-green; blade 3-sect, segs. pinnatipartite, ultimate segs. ovate or oblong-lanceolate, slender-pointed, 4 to 6 in. long, spreading. *Peduncle* 1$\frac{1}{2}$ to 3 ft. long, pale green with brownish spots, *Spathe* 8 to 20 in. long, oblong-boat-shaped, leathery, green without, dirty green within; spadix green, perfect male-fl. purplish-yellow, sterile one yellow. Trop. Himalaya, Nepal, Sikkim, Assam. 1816.

Thomsonia'nus -a -um, Thomson'ii, in honour of (1) Anthony Todd Thomson, 1778–1849, see above; (2) Thomas Thomson, 1817–78, superintendent of Calcutta Botanic Garden, 1854–61, who travelled and worked with Sir Joseph D. Hooker on flora of India; (3) George Thomson, 1819–78, missionary in W. Africa, 1871–8; (4) Joseph Thomson, 1858–95, naturalist and geologist, celebrated as explorer of equatorial Africa.

Tho'ra, medieval plant name of obscure origin.

THORN. *See* **Acacia, Crataegus,** &c.

THORN. Similar to spine, but applied only to sharp-pointed branches.

THORN APPLE. *See* **Datura Stramonium.**

THORN BROOM. *See* **Ulex europaeus.**

THORN, CHRIST'S. *See* **Paliurus Spina-Christi Zizyphus Spina-Christi.**

THORN, GARLAND. *See* **Paliurus Spina-Christi.**

THORN, GOAT'S. *See* **Astragalus Tragacantha.**

THORN, JERUSALEM. *See* **Parkinsonia aculeata.**

THORN, KAFFIR. *See* **Lycium afrum.**

THORN, SALLOW. *See* **Hippophaë rhamnoides.**

Thorncrof'tii, in honour of George Thorncroft, d. 1934 aged 77, who collected plants near Barberton, Transvaal, from 1886 onwards.

Thouar'sii, in honour of Louis M. A. du Petit-Thouars, 1758–1831, of the French navy. Writer on the Orchidaceae of Africa, &c.

Thouin'ii, in honour of André Thouin, 1747–1824, Professor of Agriculture, Paris.

THREE BIRDS ORCHIS. *See* **Pogonia pendula.**

THREE FACES UNDER A HOOD. *See* **Viola tricolor.**

THRIFT. *See* **Armeria maritima.**

THRIFT, PRICKLY. *See* **Acantholimon.**

THRI'NAX (*thrinax*, a fan; from the form of the leaves). FAM. *Palmaceae.* A genus of about 18 species of slow-growing unarmed Palms, natives of the W. Indies and Florida. Stems solitary or tufted, low or medium, ringed below, covered above by the persistent fringed leaf-sheaths. Leaves in a terminal crown, orbicular or truncate at base, fan-like, pleated, multifid; segments 2-fid; stalks slender, 2-convex; sheaths fringed. Spadices long; sheaths papery, split. Flowers perfect on long slender pedicels; stamens 6, filaments united below; ovary 1-celled. Fruit as large as a pea. Some very beautiful plants are included in this genus, and for the most part they are not exacting in their cultural requirements. Young plants grow best in a compost of loam, peat, and sand, turfy loam and sand being best for older plants. Freshly imported seeds sown in well-drained pots or pans of sandy loam, in bottom heat, afford means of propagation. Stove conditions are needed. It is now customary to divide this into two genera, the distinguishing features given by L. H. Bailey in *Gentes Herbarum*, 8: 99 (1949) being as follows:

THRINAX. Stamens 6. Seed with solid albumen divided through the centre by a cavity.

1 *Fl. and fr. distinctly stalked* T. parviflora
1. *Fl. and fr. sessile* 2
2. *Lvs. usually silvery beneath; tree* T. microcarpa
2. *Lvs. green beneath; bushy* T. Morrisii

COCCOTHRINAX. Stamens 8 to 13, commonly 9. Seed with several deep furrows almost dividing it into parts, e.g. *T. argentea* and *T. radiata.*

T. argen'tea.* Broom Palm, Silver Thatch. Stem 12 to 15 ft. h., 2 to 3 in. thick. *l.* shorter than stalk, silvery-grey beneath, segs. united at base; ligule concave, somewhat crescent-shaped. W. Indies. 1830. SYN. *Coccothrinax argentea.*

T. microcar'pa. Stem 10 to 30 ft. h. *l.* 3 to 4 ft. across, orbicular, leathery, pale silvery-green beneath, pale green above, much cut. *Spadix* 1 to 2 ft. long, with slender branches. *fls.* sessile. *fr.* about size of peas. Florida to Puerto Rico. 1896.

T. Morris'ii. Stem club-shaped, 3 to 6 ft. h. *l.* sub-orbicular; greyish beneath; segs. about 30, slender-pointed, about 1 ft. long, free for two-thirds to three-quarters of length; margins yellowish-green. *Spadix* 2 ft. long, branches 9 to 12, recurved. *fls.* sessile. W. Indies. (G.C. 11 (1892), f. 20, 21.)

T. parviflo'ra. Palmetto Thatch; Royal Palmetto Palm. Stem 10 to 30 ft. h. *l.* 10 in. to 2 ft. long, glabrous and green beneath eventually, down above; segs. joined a quarter to one-sixth of length; ligule bluntly deltoid. *Spadix* 2 to 3 ft. long, paniculate. *fl.* pedicellate. *fr.* dry, rather rough. Jamaica, Haiti, Cuba, Bahamas, Florida. 1778.

T. radia'ta. Stem short. *l.* 12 to 24 in. long, green, sometimes minutely downy beneath; segs. united about one third of length; ligule broadly rounded, with a blunt appendage at middle. *Spadix* 2 to 2½ ft. long, paniculate. Trinidad, 1838. SYN. *Coccothrinax radiata.*

THRIPS. These small insects, often termed Thunder Flies or Thunder Bugs, are among the most injurious pests in gardens and glasshouses for they attack the foliage and flowers of a great variety of plants, causing mottled and bleached areas on the leaves, stunted and malformed shoots, and spotting and distortion of the blooms. They pierce and scrape the tissues with the aid of their imperfectly suctorial mouthparts and abstract the sap. One species, *Thrips tabaci*, is concerned with the spread of the Virus disease 'Spotted Wilt', which is transmitted from infected Tomatoes, Arums, Gloxinias, Calceolarias, &c., to healthy plants (*see* Onion Thrips). The adult Thrips are active, slender, elongated insects, seldom exceeding $\frac{1}{10}$ in. in length, and are yellow, brownish, or black. They possess 2 pairs of narrow, deeply fringed wings, and are seen usually on the underside of the leaves, on shoots, and in various flowers. The eggs are inserted within the tissues of shoots, leaves, and blooms, and hatch into small, wingless replicas of their parents, but usually paler. The nymphs excrete minute globules of liquid that dry and darken, thereby rendering the areas between the veins on the lower leaf surfaces unsightly. They undergo a pupal stage, during which period they are quiescent. Numerous broods occur under glasshouse conditions, and all stages —egg, larval, pupal, and adult—may be found on the plants at the same time. A

There are a number of important species which occur both in the open and in glasshouses, and these are considered under their respective headings (*see* **Greenhouse Thrips, Lily Thrips, Onion Thrips, Pea Thrips, Pear Thrips,** *and* **Rose Thrips**).

G. F. W.

THRIXSPERM'UM. Included in **Sarcochilus.**

THROAT. The upper part of the tube of a flower.

THROAT-ROOT. *See* **Geum virginianum.**

THROATWORT. *See* **Trachelium.** A

thrum-eyed, having the anthers at the top of the tube of the flower, as in one form of Primrose (*see* **Heterostylism;** *cf.* **pin-eyed**).

THRUST HOE, the same as Dutch Hoe, *see* **Hoes** *and* **Hoeing.**

THRYAL'LIS (old Greek name used by Theophrastus for Verbascum). FAM. *Malpighiaceae.* A genus of 3 species of starry-haired climbing shrubs, natives of Brazil. Flowers yellow; calyx 5-parted, without glands; petals with short claws, glabrous, limb fringed; stamens 10, perfect; corymbs paniculate, spreading, axillary and terminal; pedicels jointed above base. Stove conditions and a compost of peat and loam suit these plants, which can be propagated by cuttings in sand under a glass in heat.

T. brachysta'chys. Climbing shrub. *l.* opposite, ovate-lanceolate, entire, glaucous-green above, white beneath. *fl.* in short panicles. August. 1823. (B.R. 1162.)

THRYPTOME'NE (*thrypto*, to break or crush; probably meant to allude to the humble appearance of the first species described). FAM. *Myrtaceae.* A genus of about twenty species of evergreen shrubs confined to Australia. Habit of Baeckia. Leaves opposite, small, entire; flowers small, axillary, solitary or rarely in twos or threes; calyx lobes and petals 5; stamens 5 alternate with petals, or 10. Cool greenhouse plants; cultivation as for Baeckia.

T. calyci'na. Shrub 3 to 5, sometimes 10 ft., shoots slender, virgate. *l.* densely set, darkly dotted, oblong or obovate, flat, $\frac{1}{8}$ to $\frac{1}{2}$ in. long. *fl.* pink or white, $\frac{3}{16}$ in. wide, one to three in the upper l.-axils, forming leafy racemes 1 to 2 in. long; sep. and pet. about equal, roundish oval; stamens 5, short. Victoria. SYN. *T. Mitchelliana.*

T. saxi'cola. Erect glabrous shrub, 3 to 4 ft., shoots slender. *l.* densely set, obovate or oblong, $\frac{1}{8}$ to $\frac{1}{4}$ in. long. *fl.* white, 1 to 3 in a l.-axil, borne near end of twigs, about $\frac{1}{8}$ in. wide; pet. pale rose, rounded; stamens 10, anthers purple. April. W. Australia. 1822. (B.M. 3160 as *Baeckia saxicola.*)

T. thymifo'lia. Small, quite glabrous, aromatic shrub. *l.* obovate or oblong, $\frac{1}{12}$ to $\frac{1}{6}$ in. long, $\frac{1}{16}$ to $\frac{1}{8}$ in. wide, scarcely stalked, blunt, dark green, gland-dotted on both surfaces. *fl.* axillary, single or in pairs, $\frac{3}{16}$ in. wide, milk-white, short-stalked, forming leafy racemes 1 to 2 in. long; sep. orbicular; pet. similar but rather smaller; stamens 5. Australia. 1920. (B.M. 8995.)

W. J. B.

THU'JA (from *Thuia*, the old Greek name used by Theophrastus). FAM. *Pinaceae.* A genus of 6 species of evergreen trees from N. America, China, and Japan; of dense, pyramidal habit when young, with a dense branch system and slender flattened branchlets; winter buds hidden by leaves. Leaves scale-like, densely arranged, overlapping. Male and female flowers on different parts of the same tree. Male flowers in small cylindrical or globular bodies from the lower branchlets on the shoots, the female flowers cone-shaped, from near the points of the shoots. Cones solitary but often produced in profusion, conical, composed of 3 to 10 scales. Seeds variable in shape in the several species. They succeed under similar conditions to the species of Chamaecyparis, are quite hardy, and form excellent decorative trees. One species is sometimes grown under forest conditions in this country. Propagation is by seeds sown in beds of fine soil out of doors or in pots or boxes of fine soil indoors. The numerous varieties are increased by cuttings or by grafting. Cuttings are made in early autumn and inserted in sandy soil in a close, cold frame or under a handlight. In grafting, the varieties should be worked upon stocks of their respective species previously established in pots, indoors in spring. The timber of the larger-growing species is light in weight, fragrant, and very long-lasting, even when subjected to very exacting conditions and exposed to such breaking-down fungi as dry rot. *T. sutchuenensis*, a native of NE. Szechwan, is not yet introduced. A

KEY

1. *Branchlets in horizontal planes. Cone scales thin* 2
1. *Branchlets in vertical planes. Lvs. pale green beneath. Cone scales thick* T. orientalis
2. *Lvs. of leading shoots ending in a long point parallel with the shoot, widely spaced* 3
2. *Lvs. of leading shoots ending in a short spreading point, close together. Branchlets with white markings beneath* 4

3. *Leading shoots flattened. Lvs. with a conspicuous gland, yellowish or bluish-green beneath* T. occidentalis
3. *Leading shoots nearly round. Lvs. not conspicuously glandular, usually with whitish markings beneath* T. plicata
4. *Lvs. without glands, not or scarcely concave beneath. Branchlets thickish, at most slightly flattened only* T. Standishii
4. *Lvs. glandular, concave or grooved beneath with conspicuous white markings. Branchlets much flattened* T. koraiensis

T. articula'ta. A synonym of *Tetraclinis articulata.*

T. cauca'sica. A synonym of *T. occidentalis robusta.*

T. dolabra'ta. A synonym of *Thujopsis dolabrata.*

T. gigante'a. A synonym of *T. plicata.*

T. japo'nica. A synonym of *T. Standishii.*

T. kongoen'sis. A synonym of *T. koraiensis.*

T. koraien'sis. Low, broadly pyramidal tree up to 30 ft. h., or widely spreading shrub, branches slender, lower inclined to root and spread the plant in all directions, branchlets flattened. *l.* small, overlapping, light green with a prominent oil or resin gland on the upper surface, glaucous beneath, pointed, the point varying in length on differently placed leaves, with a Tansy-like odour when bruised. *Cones* rather like those of *T. Standishii.* Korea. About 1920.

T. Lobb'ii. A synonym of *T. plicata.*

T. occidenta'lis. American Arbor-vitae, Northern White Cedar. Tree about 60 ft. h. with a strongly buttressed trunk divided near ground into several secondary trunks, or a large bush; branches densely arranged, branchlets divided into many segs. *l.* small, in opposite pairs, those on leading shoots up to ¼ in. long, pointed, with a single well-marked oil gland on back, on secondary branchlets smaller, blunt, with ill-defined glands or glandless, all dark green above, paler beneath, with a strong but pleasant odour when bruised. *Cones* oblong, yellowish and erect when young, brown and pendulous when mature; scales 8 to 10 in opposite pairs, thin, flexible, only middle ones fertile. *Seeds* small, thin, margins winged. Eastern N. America, 1596. (D.J.C. 509.) Gives the best results in ground that is permanently moist. On dry soils it may be attacked by scale insects. There are many varieties, some of which are very decorative. The l. of the type and some of the varieties turn bronze in winter. var. **asplenifo'lia,** branchlets fern-like; **au'rea,** *l.* golden; **aureo-spi'ca,** points of shoots and *l.* golden; **Bod'meri,** distinct with thickened, angular branchlets and densely overlapping *l.*; **Booth'ii,** low compact bush; **Buchan'ani,** main branchlets long and slender with distant secondary branchlets and sparse, grey-green *l.*; **caucas'ica,** a synonym of var. *robusta*; **columna'ris,** narrowly columnar, *l.* dark green; **compac'ta,** erect narrow tree with compact branch system; **crista'ta,** dwarf with ends of branchlets in small, dense tufts resembling a cockscomb; **dens'a,** dwarf, dense, rounded bush; **Dick'sonii,** small slender tree with bright-green *l.*; **dumos'a,** dwarf, rounded bush; **Ellwangerian'a,** narrow, pyramidal bush with both juvenile and adult types of *l.*; the form **au'rea** has golden *l.* and is very attractive; **erec'ta,** tall, stiff, pyramidal tree; a form **vir'idis,** has brighter green *l.*; **ericoi'des,** pyramidal plumose bush with juvenile type of soft, needle-like *l.* which turn bronze in autumn, and back to green in spring; **filifor'mis,** a synonym of var. *flagelliformis*; **flagelliform'is,** main branches long and whip-like, with long, slender branchlets in small dense clusters; **globo'sa,** dwarf, rounded bush 2 to 3 ft. h.; the form of this, **na'na,** is very dwarf, sometimes called **Little Gem**; **grac'ilis,** branches long, slender, drooping, branchlets thinly placed with long, slender bright-green laterals; **Hov'eyi,** dwarf, rounded, compact bush with bright-green *l.*; **lu'tea,** young branchlets and *l.* yellow; **lutes'cens,** branchlets and *l.* golden in 1st year. SYN. var. *Wareana lutescens*; **Ohlendorf'ii,** distinct form with slender whip-like branchlets with juvenile *l.* SYN. var. *Spaethii*; **pen'dula,** branchlets pendulous; **plica'ta,** branches stiff, rigid, *l.* brownish-green; **pu'mila,** very dwarf, compact shrub; **recurv'a,** bush with recurved branchlets; **'Rheingold',** small attractive bush with juvenile type of *l.*, gold in summer, bronze in winter; **robus'ta,** very vigorous of dense habit, *l.* deep green. SYN. var. *caucasica*, var. *Wareana*; **Rogers'ii au'rea,** dense, pyramidal, slow-growing bush, *l.* golden; **Spaeth'ii,** a synonym of var. *Ohlendorfii*; **spiral'is,** stiff, pyramidal, branchlets spirally arranged; **Vervaenea'na,** vigorous, *l.* bronzy-gold, branchlets slender; **Warea'na,** compact, pyramidal tree, with neat, close branchlets, a form with young shoots yellow is **lutes'cens.**

T. orienta'lis. Chinese Arbor-vitae. Tree up to 40 ft. h. or bush producing a number of erect branches from the base. Two types are known, one developing a pyramidal or columnar habit, and the other dwarfer and more or less globular; branchlets flattened, standing at right angles with the branches. *l.* very small, closely arranged, triangular, blunt, green on both sides but bearing minute stomata, very slightly fragrant when bruised. *Cones* egg-shaped, ½ to ¾ in. long, glaucous at first; scales usually 6, occasionally 8, thick, woody, with a strong hook near the tip. *Seeds* oblong, hard, wingless. China. About 1740. (D.J.C. 514.) SYN. *Biota orientalis.* Hardy in many parts of the country and useful decorative plants. The varieties require more attention than many conifers and are at their best in cultivated borders in good loamy soil with some peat or leaf-mould added. The dwarf forms are useful in the rock-garden. var. **argent'ea,** patches of white *l.* amongst the green; **ascoten'sis,** *l.* golden variegated; **athrotaxoi'des,** dwarf, branches contorted, *l.* dark green; **au'rea,** slow-growing, broadly pyramidal bush a few ft. h., *l.* golden-yellow, brightest in spring; a form **variega'ta** has patches of yellow shoots; **compac'ta,** dwarf, densely-branched bush; **decussa'ta,** small, broadly pyramidal bush, branches erect, *l.* of juvenile type, glaucous in summer, purplish in winter; **den'sa,** dwarf, slow-growing bush, *l.* glaucous; **elegantis'sima,** slow-growing bush, erect, pyramidal, tips of shoots golden in 1st summer; **ericoi'des,** small *l.* of juvenile type, similar to *T. occidentalis ericoides* but *l.* not fragrant when bruised; **falca'ta,** vigorous, erect, pyramidal tree, cones large with sickle-like spines at apex of scales; **filiform'is,** a synonym of *T. flagelliformis,* **flagelliform'is,** branchlets slender, erect, whip-like, pendent at tips, *l.* longer than in type. SYN. var. *filiformis,* var. *pendula*; **glau'ca,** branchlets and *l.* glaucous; **globo'sa,** dwarf, dense, globular bush; **grac'ilis,** dense bush wide spreading at base, suddenly narrowed to acute apex, *l.* longer, less closely pressed than in type, some of juvenile type; **Hill'ieri,** slow-growing, compact, ovoid bush, *l.* pale yellow in early summer, green later; **Hov'eyi,** dense and compact; **interme'dia,** branches loosely arranged, pendent, *l.* of both adult and juvenile forms; **melden'sis,** *l.* mixed juvenile and adult, glaucous-green; **min'ima,** very dwarf, *l.* glaucous turning bronze in winter. SYN. var. *minima glauca*; **pend'ula,** a synonym of var. *flagelliformis*; **Rogers'ii au'rea,** compact, *l.* golden; **Rosedalis,** dwarf bush, *l.* of juvenile type; **semperaures'cens,** bush rounded, *l.* golden; **Zuccarinian'a,** bush dwarf, rounded, *l.* bright green.

T. plica'ta. Western Arbor-vitae, Western Red Cedar. Large tree up to 200 ft. h. with a widely buttressed trunk, and red or brownish bark shed in small sections. Branches flexible, horizontal or pendent, branchlets flattened, lying in the same plane as branches, segs. finely divided. *l.* closely pressed, on main shoots about ¼ in. long, dark green, pointed, with oil or resin gland on back, on side shoots about ⅛ in. long, blunt and incurved at apex, with very small glands or glandless, dark green above with patches of glaucous stomata beneath, with Tansy-like odour when bruised. *Cones* ⅓ to ½ in. long, erect and green when young, drooping and brown when mature; scales 10 to 12, thin, flexible, with a small point at apex. *Seeds* 2 to 3 on each fertile scale, ¼ in. long, thin, winged. Western N. America. 1853. (D.J.C. 519.) SYN. *T. gigantea, T. Lobbii.* Thrives in most parts of British Isles where soil conditions are suitable. One of the most effective evergreen trees in moist soil with some shelter from violent winds. Grows rapidly and forms a good screen. Often grown as a hedge and also planted under forest conditions. Should not be used for forest planting where very mild and humid, otherwise very soft wood will be formed. Timber from Western N. America is very long-lasting and is much used in this country for unpainted greenhouses and frames. In America highly valued for shingles. The following varieties are distinct: var. **atrovir'ens,** differs from type by its deeper green *l.*; **au'rea,** with patches of golden *l.* among green; **fastigia'ta,** of stiff fastigiate habit; **grac'ilis,** branchlets divided into very fine spray; **Hill'ieri,** dwarf of slow growth with dense, stunted-looking branchlets which sometimes have slender shoots at tips; **pu'mila,** dwarf dense bush about 2 ft. h.; **pyramid'alis,** narrower and denser than type; **recurva'ta,** branches much distorted; **semperaures'cens,** young shoots and *l.* with golden tinge; **zebrin'a,** *l.* banded green and gold.

T. Standish'ii. Tree of 30 to 40 ft. h., with thin reddish bark shed in thin sections. Branches horizontal with branchlets in same plane. *l.* on main shoots triangular, apex thick, blunt, *l.* on secondary branches smaller, yellowish-green above, glaucous-green beneath, without resin glands, not fragrant when bruised. *Cones* oblong, greenish-yellow when young, brown when mature; scales 8 to 10, thin, flexible, middle ones only fertile. *Seeds* small, thin, with marginal wings. Cent. Japan. 1861. SYN. *T. japonica.* Useful decorative tree distinct by its yellowish-green l.

W. D.

THUJOP'SIS (*Thuja, opsis,* resemblance). FAM. *Pinaceae.* A monotypic genus with many characters similar to those of Thuja, differing by its broader, stronger branchlets, larger, thicker leaves, and rounder cones with woody scales and thin seeds. *Thuja orientalis* also has woody cone scales but the seeds are hard, oblong, and wingless.

T. borea'lis. A synonym of *Chamaecyparis nootkatensis.*

T. dolabra'ta. Hiba. Two types of this evergreen tree are known, one a large tree (*Hondai*) the other a tree of moderate size or a shrub (*australis*). Trunk may divide near ground into 2 or more erect stems, or it may form a shapely pyramid with a single stem. Branches horizontal, branchlets broad, flattened. *l.* in 4 ranks, those on main axis little larger than those on side branches, ⅛ to ¼ in. long, lateral ones keeled, broad, thick, overlapping those of middle ranks, apex rounded and incurved, dark glossy green with white patches of stomata beneath. *Cones* ½ to ¾ in. long, rounded or broadly ovate, scales 8, thick, woody, with a prominent hook near tip. *Seeds* thin with marginal wings. Japan. 1853. (D.J.C. 504.) SYN. *Thuja dolabrata.* Succeeds under similar conditions to the Thujas and forms a very decorative small tree or shrub. Should not be planted where it will be crowded by other trees. Propagation is by seeds. var. **austra'lis,** the smaller type up to 40 or 50 ft. h. usually grown in this country, *cones* broadly ovate; **Honda'i,** the large-growing type up to 100 ft. h., *cones* rounded; **na'na,** slow-growing, spreading plant a few feet h. 1861. SYN. var. *lataevirens.* **variega'ta,** white or pale-yellow patches of *l.* amongst the green, less effective than type. 1861.

W. D.

THUNBER'GIA (in honour of Dr. Karl Pehr Thunberg, 1743–1822, a traveller in Batavia and Japan, afterwards Professor of Botany at Uppsala). FAM. *Acanthaceae.* A genus of about 100 species of usually beautiful twining or dwarf sub-erect annual or perennial plants, natives of S. and Trop. Africa, Madagascar, and the warmer parts of Asia. Leaves opposite, ovate, lanceolate, or elliptic to cordate, the base cuneate, obtuse, or hastate. Flowers solitary in leaf-axils, or in terminal, usually pendent racemes; calyx very minute (within the bracts), ring-like or 10- to 15-toothed or -lobed; corolla conspicuous, tube swollen on one side, curved, lobes 5, rounded, twisted to left in the bud; stamens 4, didynamous, attached near base of corolla tube. Bracts at base of pedicels leaf-like; bracts large and foliaceous, usually 2 beneath each pair, their margins coherent at least at first. Fruit a leathery capsule, with a sword-shaped beak. Thunbergias are easily grown in any moderately good soil, but a compost of fibrous loam and sand with a small quantity of decayed manure suits them best. Most species require stove conditions, and there with brisk, moist atmosphere they grow rapidly in well-drained pots and, so far as the larger, often woody, species are concerned, better still planted out. Several species require much room to develop properly, for severer pruning to keep them in bounds in a comparatively small house is likely to interfere with their flowering, but bare and unsightly shoots should always be pruned back in spring before growth begins. Propagation is by seed and by cuttings of moderately firm wood in a propagating frame with a temperature of 65 to 70° F. *T. alata* and its varieties and *T. Gregorii* will succeed in a warm greenhouse and are readily raised from seed sown in 5-in. pots in March or April. When large enough they are planted singly in pots or baskets in rather rich soil (loam, leaf-mould or peat, and decayed manure) when they soon grow into good flowering plants. They should be grown in the stove at first.

KEY

1. *Annual herbs* — 2
1. *Perennial herbs or woody climbers or shrubs* — 5
2. *Fl. purple (the throat or tube may be yellow)* — T. chrysops
2. *Fl. pale yellow to orange (throat may be purple)* — 3
3. *Petiole winged (especially those of lower l.)* — T. alata
3. *Petiole (when present) not winged* — 4
4. *Lvs. suborbicular, glabrescent above, pilose beneath* — T. capensis
4. *Lvs. rhomboid, villous on both surfaces* — T. primulina
5. *Plants erect and shrub-like* — 6
5. *Plants climbing or prostrate* — 10
6. *Fl. subtended by thick leathery rust-coloured bracts* — T. Vogeliana
6. *Fl. subtended by thin membranous greenish bracts* — 7
7. *Lvs. with 3 primary veins from base, mostly rhomboid in outline* — T. Kirkii
7. *Lvs. pinnate-veined (with a single primary vein), ovate to elliptic in outline* — 8
8. *L.-base cordate to obtuse, sessile* — T. natalensis
8. *L.-base wedge-shaped, all but the upper-most with petioles ⅛ to ½ in. long* — 9
9. *Fl.-bracts more than 1 in. long; lvs. mostly 3 in. long or more* — T. affinis
9. *Fl.-bracts usually ¾ in. long or less; lvs. mostly 1½ to 2½ in. long* — T. erecta
10. *Fl. in shades of yellow, orange, or red (at least the spreading limb so coloured)* — 11
10. *Fl. in shades of blue to purple or white in some vars., at least the limb is so coloured; throat often yellow* — 14
11. *Cal. reduced to a short toothless cup or rim within the leafy bracts; fl. in lax pendent few- to many-fld. racemes* — 12
11. *Cal. comprised of a very short tube and 7 or more usually linear or tooth-like segs. or lobes* — 13
12. *Cor.-tube orange-red, the limb red; stigma capitate.* — T. coccinea
12. *Cor.-tube purple, the limb yellow; stigma lobes funnel-form* — T. mysorensis
13. *Fl. deep orange and waxy; bracts reddish and hispid* — T. Gregorii
13. *Fl. pale yellow to nearly white, not waxy; bracts green* — T. Dregeana
14. *Cal. with many linear segs.* — 15
14. *Cal. cup-like or reduced to a minute sub-entire rim* — 16
15. *Stem retrorsely hairy to glabrate; petiole much shorter than l.-blade; bracts about ¾ in. long* — T. fragrans
15. *Stem glabrous; lvs. petiole nearly twice as long as its blade; bracts about ⅓ in. long* — T. angulata
16. *Fl. in l.-axils; lvs. sessile* — T. Hawtayneana
16. *Fl. in rather dense racemes; lvs. (at least the lower ones) petioled* — 17
17. *Lvs. palmately 3-nerved, elliptic to oblong* — T. laurifolia
17. *Lvs. palmately 5 to 7-nerved, ovate* — T. grandiflora

T. affi'nis. More or less erect shrub, very hairy, stem 4-angled. *l.* elliptic, entire, glabrate, margins finely undulate, base cuneate, short-stalked. *fl.* 2 in. across, violet, tube yellow, curved above base; sometimes more than 1 fl. in axil; cal. with many linear lobes. September. Trop. Africa. (B.M. 6975.) Grown in pots it forms an erect shrub but with more root room it rambles.

T. ala'ta.* Softly hairy annual twiner. *l.* ovate, cordate, l.-stalks winged; *fl.* yellow, purple below, 1½ in. long, tube curved, limb bell-shaped; cal. 12-cleft, very small, surrounded by 2 large, inflated bracts. S. Africa. 1823. (B.M. 2591, F.P.S.A. 148.) The flowers vary greatly in colour. var. **alba,** *fl.* white with blackish middle (B.M. 3512); **auranti'aca.** *fl.* deep yellow with dark middle (L.B.C. 1045); **Ba'keri,** *fl.* pure white; **Dodd'sii,** *l.* irregularly bordered white; *fl.* yellowish-orange, rich purplish-violet in middle; **Fry'eri,** *fl.* pale yellow, white middle; **lutea,** *fl.* entirely yellow; **sulphur'ea** *fl.* sulphur-yellow.

T. angula'ta. Mostly glabrous, perennial climber. *l.* ovate with cordate to sagittate base, about 1½ in. long, long-petioled. *fl.* pale blue, about ¾ in. across, with yellow throat 1 in. long; cal. with many linear lobes; bracts 2, about ⅓ in. long, ciliate, 1-nerved; peduncles long. Madagascar. (T.E.F. 166, 177; L.B.C. 1044.)

T. capen'sis. Annual climber. *l.* suborbicular, weakly toothed, palmately 5-veined, setose beneath on veins, glabrescent above, petiole about ⅛ in. long. *fl.* pale yellow, about 1½ in. long; cal. with 7 to 11 filiform lobes, minute; bracts pilose. S. Africa. 1824. (L.B.C. 1529.)

T. chry'sops. Annual climber, slender, downy, about 3 ft. h. *l.* ovate, base heart-shaped, moderately setaceous above, petiole 1 to 3 in. long. *fl.* purplish with blue limb and yellow funnel-shaped tube. Sierra Leone. (B.M. 4119.)

T. cocci'nea. Large, nearly glabrous climber; branches often 10 to 25 ft. long. *l.* ovate or upper oblong, 5 to 8 in. long, obtuse, toothed, 3–5 palmately veined, glabrate, base cordate or angular; cal. a tiny rim. *fl.* red, 1 in. long in loose, pendent racemes 6 to 18 in. long. Spring. India, Burma. 1823. (B.M. 5124; L.B.C. 1195.)

Thunbergia mysorensis (p. 2106)

T. Dregea'na. Woody climber, but at first herbaceous. *l.* ovate, pubescent, toothed, palmately 5-veined, the base subcordate; petiole ½ to 3 in. long. *fl.* yellow, 1¼ in. across, ¾ in. long; cal. of many linear lobes; bracts pubescent. S. Africa. (Natal Pl. t. 280.)

T. erec'ta. Shrub to 6 ft. h. *l.* ovate to oblong, mostly 1½ to 2½ in. long, glabrate, toothed, the base cuneate; petiole ⅛ to ⅛ in. long. *fl.* dark blue with orange throat and yellow tube; cal. with 7 to 10 linear lobes; bracts ¾ in. long or less. July. Trop. to S. Africa. (B.M. 5013 as *Meyenia erecta*; F.P.S.A. 801.) var. **al'ba,** *fl.* white with yellow tube.

T. frag'rans. Climbing perennial. *Stem.* retrorsely hairy to glabrate. *l.* ovate to oblong, 2 to 3 in. long, the base cordate to hastate, toothed, glabrate; petiole ½ to 1½ in. long, shorter than the blade. *fl.* nearly white, about 1¼ in. long, fragrant; cal. lobed; pedicel usually 2 to 3 in. long. India. 1796. (L.B.C. 1913.) var. **lae'vis,** glabrous, *fl.* scentless, tube often greenish. (B.M. 1881, as *T. fragrans.*)

T. Gibson'ii. *See under* **T. Gregorii.**

T. grandiflo'ra.* Large climber. *l.* ovate or lanceolate, up to 6 in. long, acute, toothed or angularly lobed, palmately 5–7 veined, usually downy; stalks 3 in. long. *fl.* blue, 3 in. long and broad, sometimes clustered; cal. cup-like, sub-entire; racemes usually stout. N. India. 1820. (B.M. 2366; B.R. 495; L.B.C. 324.) var. **al'ba,** *fl.* white. A magnificent plant for large houses.

T. Gregor'ii. Perennial climber. *Stem.* hispidulous. *l.* triangular, 2 to 3 in. long, hirtellous, palmately 5- to 7-veined; petiole 1 to 2½ in. long. *fl.* orange, waxy, 1½ in. across, the lobes truncate and about half as long as tube; cal. with 10 to 13 lobes; bracts hispid and reddish, pedicel 2 to 3 in. long, both with spreading hairs E. to S. Africa. (B.M. 8604, F.P.S.A. 800, both as *T. Gibsonii,* a related species with silky appressed hairs on bracts and pedicels.)

T. Harris'ii. A synonym of *T. laurifolia.*

T. Hawtaynea'na. Slender, nearly glabrous climber. *l.* elliptic to ovate, sessile, glabrate, to 3 in. long, entire, the base cordate. *fl.* violet-purple, tube yellowish, about 1½ in. long; cal. reduced to a toothless rim. S. India. 1839.

T. Hookeria'na. A synonym of *T. Kirkii.*

T. Kirk'ii. Erect shrub to 3 ft. h. *l.* elliptic-lanceolate to rhomboid to 3 in. long, pinnately veined, but with 3 primary veins arising from base, the base cuneate; petiole ⅛ to ¼ in. long. *fl.* violet-blue, 1 in. long, lobes spreading, obovate; cal. cup-like; peduncle 2-fld. September. E. Trop. Africa. 1876. (B.M. 6677.) SYN. *T. Hookeriana.*

Thunbergia natalensis

T. laurifo'lia. Like *T. grandiflora* but *l.* smaller, elliptic or oblong, palmately 3-veined, scarcely angled or lobed. Malaya. 1856. (B.M. 4985; B.M. 4998 as *T. Harrisii.*)

T. mysoren'sis. Climber, to 15 ft. *l.* elliptic, 4 to 6 in. long, acuminate, 3-nerved, glabrate, toothed, the base cuneate to obtuse; petiole ¼ to 1½ in. long. *fl.* yellow, tube purplish, 1½ in. long, 2 in. across, in pendent racemes; stigma-lobes 2, funnel-shaped; cal. a minute cup or rim; bracts purplish-green, about 1 in. long. Spring. Nilgiri Hills, India. 1854. (B.M. 4786 as *Hexacentris mysorensis.*)

T. natalen'sis. Erect sub-shrub, 2 ft. or more h. *l.* ovate, toothed, glabrous above, sessile. *fl.* blue with yellow tube, 2 in. long, curved upwards; pedicels axillary, erect. July. S. Africa. 1857. (B.M. 5082; F.P.S.A. 147.) Nearly hardy.

T. primuli'na. Silky hairy perennial. *l.* rhomboid-ovate with small lobe on each side 3- to 5-nerved, villous, to 2½ in. long. *fl.* primrose-yellow with orange rim to throat, 1½ in. across, axillary, solitary, cal. very short with linear lobes; cor. nearly cylindrical, curved. Uganda. (B.M. 7969.)

T. Vogelia'na. Erect shrub, 8 to 15 ft. h. *l.* ovate to oblong, 3 to 6 in. long, entire to denticulate, glabrate, the base cuneate. *fl.* violet with yellow tube and throat; cal. lobed or divided; bracts thick and leathery, reddish, to ¾ in. long, obtuse to mucronulate. Summer. Trop. Africa. 1863. (B.M. 5389 as *Meyenia Vogeliana.*)

G. H. M. L.

THUNDER-BUGS, THUNDER FLIES. *See* **Thrips.**

THUN'IA (in honour of Franz A. Graf von Thun, 1786–1873, of Bohemia). FAM. *Orchidaceae.* A small genus of epiphytic orchids (in favourable situations some of the species adapt themselves to terrestrial habits) in N. India, Nepal, Assam, Burma, the Andamans. The genus has been included in Phaius, but is quite distinct. The large flowers are borne in terminal, nodding racemes, each flower based by a large bract. Sepals and petals thin, lanceolate, nearly equal. The slightly 3-lobed lip is parallel with the column, bluntly and shortly spurred, the side lobes more or less convolute over the column, often toothed, the mid-lobe rounded, often with more or less heavily fringed keels. The pollinia are 4 but are 2-partite forming 8. Stems take the place of pseudobulbs. As in the deciduous Calanthes the current season's new growth develops flowers, loses its leaves, but remains as a support to the young growth through the next season. The stems taper from the base, which is sheathed by small leaves, becoming normal as they ascend, often amplexicaul, distichously arranged. There is a strong family likeness in habit. Though the flowers remain in beauty only about a fortnight the genus is desirable. Annual repotting is necessary to obtain the best results. Compost should be made of 3 parts of rough fibrous loam, and 1 part of Sphagnum moss and Osmunda fibre, or rough peat with a little sand, the amount varying according to the quality of the loam. A 5- to 7-in. pot is large enough for one stem. When first potted, water should be given infrequently, but more and more freely as growth advances. When well rooted, manure water, at first weak, may be given and continued 2 or 3 times a week through and after the flowering season till signs of leaf decay are seen. While growing the plants may be placed in the warm house as they enjoy a buoyant tropical atmosphere. They may be given rather cooler quarters while in flower, but after flowering should again have warmth and moisture as the stems continue to thicken. When the foliage begins to yellow and drop, remove the plants to an intermediate house and expose to more air and light, though even through the summer only thin shading is required, if any. Decrease waterings, and when all the leaves have fallen remove the pots to a cooler house with a winter night temperature around 50° F. and keep dry. New growth will be seen at the base of the old stem usually towards the end of March and the plants should then be repotted, removing all old compost, dead roots, &c. The syringe should not be used while new growths are short, or their centres may become surcharged with moisture; as the leaves become free its use up to and then after the flowering period is beneficial.

Thunias are readily propagated. Two growths are often produced from one stem and may be separated the following season. The previous year's stems may be cut into lengths of 4 or 6 in. after the new growths have become self-supporting, inserted in pots or laid in a propagating case and potted as soon as growths and roots are seen.

Garden hybrids have been raised and natural hybrids also occur. Probably some of the slightly anomalous colour varieties occasionally seen are not true species. Both species and hybrids naturally flower in summer, but the season may be slightly hastened or retarded by extra heat or a longer rest.

T. al'ba.* *fl.* 5 to 12, large; sep. and pet. oblong-lanceolate, white; lip oval-oblong with 5 fringed often purplish keels on disk and a few purple streaks on each side of them, margin fringed. Stems 2 to 4 ft. h. *l.* oblong-lanceolate, 6 to 9 in. long. Variable. Nepal, Assam, Burma, &c. 1836. var. **Dodg'soni,** a synonym of *T. pulchra*; **flavo-tinct'a,** probably a form of *T. pulchra*, *fl.* similar but with a few streaks on the lip. 1883; **gigant'ea,** *fl.* larger than in type, lip golden-yellow. 1896; **nival'is,** *fl.* white.

T. Benson'iae.* *fl.* 2 to 6; sep. and pet. amethyst-purple, paler near base, almost white; lip large, open, side lobes convolute over column, whitish at base, mid-lobe deep amethyst-purple with numerous yellow fringed keels, margin denticulate. Stems usually shorter and more slender than those of *T. alba*, *fl.* as large. Burma. 1867. (B.M. 5694; W.O.A. 67.) var. **superb'a,** *fl.* more richly coloured, with bronze-orange keels on lip; **Winnian'a,** *see* **T. Winniana.**

T. Brymeria'na.* Allied to *T. Marshalliana*. Sep. and pet. white or purple shaded; lip yellow with radiating crimson-purple lines on mid- and side lobes, the yellow fringed keels tinted red. Possibly a natural hybrid between *T. Bensoniae* and *T. Marshalliana*. Burma. 1892. (R.s.2, 82.)

T. candidis'sima. Allied to *T. Marshalliana*. *fl.* entirely white, side lobes of lip toothed in front; spur inflated, 2-lobed. Burma. 1888.

T. Dodg'soni. A synonym of *T. pulchra*. Possibly distinct.

T. × Majoria'na. Believed to be an imported plant, but indistinguishable from the garden-raised *T.* × *Veitchiana* (*T. Bensoniae* × *T. Marshalliana*). Habitat? 1918.

T. Marshal'liae. A synonym of *T. Marshalliana*.

T. Marshallia'na.* *fl.* 3 to 9, whitish, large; sep. and pet. white; lip with basal portion and front often narrowly margined white, remainder covered with forked veins of rich orange and orange-yellow densely fringed keels. Stems 2 to 3 ft. stout. Burma. 1871. (W.O.A. 130; L. 189.) var. **al'ba,** disk of lip sulphur-yellow. 1906; **ionophle'bia,** side lobes of lip streaked with purple, its central area yellow. 1885; **purpura'ta,** lip white, spotted purple, disk with 5 yellow keels and numerous filiform processes, front part veined purple-brown. 1888; **tric'olor,** sep. and pet. white, lip orange-yellow, marked crimson-purple. 1887; **trilo'ba,** lip 3-lobed, broad, having dark reddish-brown veins and 12 darker rows of toothed crests. 1888. It is possible that the last 3 varieties differ from type by the influence of *T. Bensoniae*.

T. Mastersia'na. A synonym of *T. pulchra*.

T. pulch'ra. *fl.* 4 to 8 of medium size; sep. and pet. white; lip white with brown and yellow crests; spur nearly obsolete. Burma. 1881. Syn. *Phaius Dodgsoni*?

T. veno'sa. Allied to *T. alba*, but with a shorter inflorescence. *fl.* smaller, lip with radiating purplish veins, disk not yellow. (B.R. 24, 33; B.M. 3391 as *Phaius albus*.)

T. Winnia'na. *fl.* large, sep. and pet. magenta-rose; lip with deep crimson-purple front lobe, heavily crested. Possibly a natural hybrid but may be a variety of *T. Bensoniae*. Burma. 1891. (L. 452.)

T. xanthophle'bia. A synonym of *T. pulchra*.

THURAN'THOS (*thus*, incense, *anthos*, flower). Fam. *Liliaceae*. A genus of a single species of S. African bulbous plant. Bulb scaly. Leaves linear, appearing after the flowers. Flowers in a long raceme on a tall scape; perianth segments free, long, recurved; stamens equal with lower part of filaments flattened and incurved, leaving interspaces like the longitudinal openings of a lantern, upper parts cylindrical. Fruit an oblong capsule, pedicels erect. For treatment *see* **Ornithogalum,** S. African species.

T. macran'thum. Bulb scaly, 4½ in. across. *l.* appearing after fl., linear, glabrous, 2 ft. or more long. *Scape* 3½ to 6 ft. h. cylindric, purplish near base. *fl.* drooping on pedicels about 1½ in. long; segs. free, equal, recurved, brownish-yellow with a green band down middle, 1 in. long. S. Africa. 1913. (B.M. 8680.)

THU'YA. A synonym of Thuja.

THUYOP'SIS. A synonym of Thujopsis.

Thwaitesii, in honour of George Henry Kendrick Thwaites, 1811–82, of Bristol, botanist in Ceylon.

thylaciochi'lus -a -um, having a pouch-like lip.

THYME (*Thymus* sp.). Two kinds of Thymus are grown in gardens for their leaves and tops, the common Thyme (*T. vulgaris*) and Lemon Thyme (*T.* × *citriodorus*). Both are much in use for culinary purposes, the aromatic flavour being greatly liked. A light, rather dry soil and warm situation suits Thymes best. Thymes may be used as an edging for part of the kitchen garden and a planting will last in good order for 3 or 4 years, when it should be replaced. The plants are easily propagated by seeds sown in April either in a warm border for subsequent transplanting or in a drill where the plants are intended to form an edging. The seedlings should be thinned to 4 to 6 in. apart. Division is also a ready method of increase; it should be done in March or April, but a better method for Lemon Thyme is to cover the branches, which are freely formed, with a little earth into which they will soon root and produce a stock of plants. For drying, branches should be cut when coming into flower, bunched, and hung in a cool place to dry.

THYME, BASIL. *See* **Calamintha Acinos.**

THYME, CAT. *See* **Teucrium Marum, T. Polium.**

THYME, WATER. *See* **Anacharis.**

THYMELAE'A (*Thymos*, Thyme, *Elaia*, Olive; alluding to the Thyme-like foliage and small Olive-like fruit). Fam. *Thymelaeaceae*. A genus of about 20 species of perennial or rarely annual herbs, sub-shrubs, or small shrubs, mostly natives of the eastern Mediterranean region as far east as Persia, with other species in the Canary Is., Cent. Asia, and Europe. Leaves small or narrow as a rule, scattered. Flowers small, sessile in the leaf-axils, solitary or clustered, hermaphrodite or polygamous; perianth urn-shaped or (especially in male flowers) with a slender, cylindrical tube; lobes 4, spreading; stamens 8, on very short filaments; bracts small. Equal parts of loam and peat suit *T. Tartonraira*, which may be propagated by cuttings of mature shoots or side growths taken in autumn, inserted thinly in well-drained pots of peaty soil and covered with a bell-glass. They will callus if kept in a cool house and root if put into gentle heat in early spring. After potting singly, they should be grown on in close conditions but not high temperature and afterwards hardened and kept quite cool during the following autumn and winter so that the wood becomes thoroughly ripened.

T. hirsu'ta. A synonym of *Passerina hirsuta*.

T. Tartonrai'ra. Small shrub covered with silky whitish or brownish hairs, stem freely forking, rigid. *l.* obovate or obovate-oblong, nerved, overlapping, ½ to ¾ in. long, leathery. *fl.* white, in 2- to 5-fld. axillary clusters, freely produced; bracteoles whitish. June. S. Europe. 1640. (S.B.F.G. 354 as *Passerina Tartonraira*.) Syn. *Daphne Tartonraira*. Fairly hardy.

THYMELEA'CEAE. Dicotyledons. A family of about 450 species of trees or shrubs very rarely slender, annual herbs, in 40 genera widely dispersed in temperate and warmer regions of the world. Leaves opposite or often alternate or scattered, simple, entire; stipules absent. Flowers hermaphrodite, or polygamous or dioecious, regular, usually in terminal spikes, panicles or clusters, sometimes axillary; perianth inferior, petaloid or rarely herbaceous; lobes 4 or 5, imbricate in bud; petals, if present, 4 or 5 near mouth of tube, or wanting; stamens as many or twice as many as lobes; filaments filiform, short; disk hypogynous, annular, cup-shaped; ovary sessile or shortly stalked, 1- (rarely 2-) celled, ovule 1.

Fruit nearly always indehiscent, a nut, berry, or drupe. The genera dealt with are Arthrosolen, Dais, Daphne, Edgeworthia, Gnidea, Lachnaea, Lagetta, Lasiosiphon, Ovidia, Passerina, Phaleria, Pimelea, Stellera, Struthiola, Thymelaea, Wikstroemia.

thymifo'lius -a -um, with Thyme-like leaves.

thymoi'deus -a -um, Thyme-like.

THY'MUS (ancient Greek name used by Theophrastus, probably for a plant of this genus). FAM. *Labiatae*. Including Coridothymus. A genus of numerous species (possibly about 100) of small aromatic bushy or more or less prostrate shrubs or sub-shrubs, a few almost herbaceous, all under 14 in. high, natives of the north temperate Old World from Greenland to Kamchatka but mostly in the Mediterranean region and W. Asia, reaching their greatest diversity in the Balkan and Iberian peninsulas. Leaves small, entire. Bracts or floral leaves usually small and scarcely different from stem leaves in most species but large and conspicuous in *T. bracteosus*, *T. Broussonetii*, *T. Cephalotus*, *T. longiflorus*, and *T. membranaceus*. Whorls few-flowered, mostly crowded into dense terminal many-fld. heads. Flowers small; calyx with a cylindric or ovoid tube, rarely flattened, 10 to 13-veined, bristly within throat, 2-lipped, the upper lip 3-toothed or rarely 3-fid, lower lip 2-fid into narrow almost subulate usually ciliate segments; corolla tube almost straight, naked within, the limb 2-lipped, the upper lip notched, lower lip 3-lobed, the middle lobe largest; stamens 4, usually protruding, the anthers free, not appressed and coherent. Nutlets very small.

For garden purposes the Thymes fall roughly into 3 groups: (1) the common Thyme (*T. vulgaris*) grown for culinary purposes (*see* **Thyme**); (2) the neat bushy species, grown for their habit (e.g. *T. carnosus*) or their flowers (e.g. *T. membranaceus*); (3) the prostrate carpeting species (e.g. *T. Drucei*, *T. Serpyllum*), most of which become sheets of mauve, crimson, or white flowers in June. They are easily grown in light soil in sunny, well-drained positions, the carpeting species being quite hardy and very suitable for covering slopes of the rock garden or growing between paving, the bushy species mostly needing winter protection and better grown in the alpine house in pans. The carpeting species can be divided in August, September, or March, as well as by cuttings in May or June; the bushy species are increased by cuttings in May or June. Seed should be sown in March or April; Thymes hybridize readily and may not come true from seed collected in botanic gardens where several kinds are often grown side by side. To keep them compact and prevent excessive seeding, they can be clipped over lightly in August or September and top-dressed with sandy compost at the same time. The Thymes are notoriously difficult to classify and identify and, as the specific limits are often not well defined and local races and variants are very numerous, accounts by different botanists often disagree widely on whether certain plants should be treated as species or varieties. This uncertainty is reflected in their nomenclature, not only in botanical literature but also in catalogues and in gardens. The following account includes probably all the horticulturally interesting main types; for further information about Balkan species the account by K. Ronniger in Hayek's *Prodromus Florae Peninsulae Balcanicae* (*Fedde, Repert. Beih.* 30), 2. 337–82 (1930) should be consulted; for Caucasian species see *Fedde, Repert.* 31. 135–57 (1932). Hybrids between very unlike species occur but are not easily recognized as such. Many kinds possess characteristic scents when bruised, which have been compared with lemon, camphor, terpentine, caraway, &c. The genus comprises many attractive little plants for both rock-garden and alpine house.

KEY

1. *Plant completely prostrate, forming a close greyish hairy mat; lvs. less than $\frac{3}{10}$ in. long, broadly elliptic, conspicuously hairy on both sides with numerous white hairs mostly more than $\frac{1}{20}$ in. long. Stem with 2 opposite sides hairy, other 2 glabrous. Fl. often axillary, few; cor. about $\frac{1}{5}$ in. long* — T. pseudolanuginosus
1. *Plant not showing the above combination of characters* — 2
2 (1). *Cor. $\frac{2}{5}$ to $\frac{7}{10}$ in. long, distinctly longer than cal. Bracts (floral lvs.) usually conspicuous* — 3
2. *Cor. $\frac{1}{10}$ to $\frac{3}{10}$ in. long, scarcely or not longer than cal.* — 11
3 (2). *Plant mat-forming, with prostrate branches, but fl.-stems erect, $\frac{3}{4}$ to $1\frac{1}{2}$ in. h. Bracts less than $\frac{1}{10}$ in. wide* — T. integer
3. *Plant bushy, with erect or ascending branches, 2 to 12 in. h.* — 4
4 (3). *Most bracts with 1 or 2 prominent teeth on each side, villous, to $\frac{3}{10}$ in. long* — T. villosus
4. *No bracts prominently toothed* — 5
5 (4). *Bracts less than $\frac{3}{10}$ in. long* — 8
5. *Some bracts more than $\frac{3}{10}$ in. long* — 6
6 (5). *Cor. about $\frac{2}{5}$ in. long. Shoots decumbent or spreading. Lvs. linear to very narrowly elliptic, under $\frac{1}{20}$ in. wide* — T. ciliatus
6. *Cor. about $\frac{1}{2}$ to $\frac{3}{5}$ in. long. Shoots erect* — 7
7 (6). *Lvs. all linear or linear-lanceolate, sessile, less than $\frac{1}{10}$ in. wide* — T. Cephalotus
7. *Some lvs. elliptic or even rhomboid, short-stalked, up to $\frac{3}{10}$ in.* — 9
8 (5). *Bracts closely overlapping, covered with numerous golden-brown glands. Cal. tube flattened above and below, hence 2-angled, hidden beneath bracts* — T. capitatus
8. *Bracts not closely overlapping, not conspicuously gland-dotted. Cal. tube not flattened, not hidden beneath bracts* — T. Funkii
9 (7). *Bracts mostly ciliate, reddish. Lvs. mostly elliptic, flat. N. Africa* — T. Broussonetii
9. *Bracts rarely ciliate. L. lanceolate to narrowly lanceolate, or rhomboid-elliptic, margins mostly revolute. Spain* — 10
10 (9). *Cor. white. Bracts membranous, white or pink-flushed* — T. membranaceus
10. *Cor. purple. Bracts firm, reddish* — T. longiflorus
11 (2). *Cal. with 5 conspicuously ciliate subulate segs., the upper lip being divided almost to base into 3 segs. more than $\frac{1}{10}$ in. long, the lower lip with 2 segs. more than $\frac{1}{5}$ in. long. Fl.-heads globose, fluffy-looking* — T. Mastichina
11. *Cal. with the upper lip only 3-toothed, not divided to half-way, the teeth less than $\frac{1}{10}$ in. long, much shorter than the 2 subulate segs. of lower lip* — 12
12 (11). *Bracts (floral lvs.) broader than other lvs., usually markedly differing from them in shape* — 13
12. *Bracts no larger than and not essentially different from other l., often small and inconspicuous* — 19
13 (12). *Lvs. of fl.-stems oblanceolate, not rigid, flat, about $\frac{1}{10}$ in. (up to nearly $\frac{1}{5}$ in.) wide, not prominently veined. Fl.-stems 2 to $3\frac{1}{2}$ in. h.; current year's shoots prostrate, mat-forming* — T. bracteosus
13. *Lvs. of fl.-stems linear, narrowly elliptic, lanceolate or narrowly ovate, margins revolute or under-side prominently veined, about $\frac{1}{20}$ in. wide* — 14
14 (13). *L.-margins revolute* — 17
14. *L.-margins not revolute but veins prominent beneath* — 15
15 (14). *Plant a compact bush to 7 in. h.; all shoots erect or ascending* — T. cilicicus
15. *Plant of loose spreading habit; side shoots arching, with fl.-stems erect, 1 to $2\frac{1}{2}$ in. h.* — 16
16 (15). *Bracts to $\frac{3}{20}$ in. wide. Cal. about $\frac{1}{5}$ in. long. Infl. compact, almost globose* — T. striatus
16. *Bracts less than $\frac{1}{20}$ in. wide. Cal. less than $\frac{3}{20}$ in. long. Infl. often interrupted and oblong* — T. comptus
17 (14). *Plant prostrate, forming dense mats $1\frac{1}{2}$ to $2\frac{1}{2}$ in. h.* — T. hirsutus
17. *Plant bushy with erect or ascending shoots* — 18
18 (17). *L.-margins so strongly revolute as to cover most of under-side; lvs. almost cylindric, deeply pitted. Shoots stiffly erect, more or less parallel* — T. carnosus
18. *L.-margins revolute only at edge, leaving most of under-side exposed; lvs. mostly narrowly ovate, shallowly pitted. Shoots flexuous, diverging* — T. capitellatus
19 (12). *Lvs. linear to narrowly oblanceolate, i.e. 5 or more times as long as wide* — 20
19. *Lvs. narrowly elliptic to broadly elliptic, lanceolate to broadly ovate, i.e. less than 4 times as long as wide* — 25
20 (19). *Plant mat-forming; main shoots prostrate with densely crowded lvs. Fl.-stems less than 2 in. h.* — 21
20. *Plant bushy or shrubby, to 1 ft. h.; all shoots erect or ascending. Fl.-stems more than 2 in. h.* — 22
21 (19). *Lvs. ciliate at margin, otherwise glabrous, narrowly oblanceolate. Cal. glabrous except for ciliated lower segs.* — T. caespititius
21. *Lvs. minutely hairy all over, linear. Cal. conspicuously hairy* — T. hirsutus
22 (20). *Lvs. closely hairy beneath, margins revolute* — 23
22. *Lvs. glabrous beneath, margins not revolute* — 24
23 (22). *Lvs. linear, less than $\frac{1}{20}$ in. wide* — T. Zygis

23. *Lvs. linear-lanceolate to narrowly ovate, more than $\frac{1}{20}$ in. wide* 27

24 (22). *Hairs on upper part of stem spreading, some almost equalling diameter of stem. Teeth of upper cal. lip almost equal, all subulate* T. Marschallianus

24. *Hairs of stem rather appressed, all very short, not equal to half diameter of stem. Teeth of upper cal. lip unequal, middle one lanceolate, longer and broader than 2 subulate lateral teeth* T. Pallasianus

25 (19). *Plants bushy; sterile shoots ascending or erect, not completely prostrate* 26

25. *Plants mat-forming; sterile shoots completely prostrate* 35

26 (25). *L.-margin strongly revolute, under-side tomentose with close minute hairs* 27

26. *L.-margin not strongly revolute, under-side not tomentose* 28

27 (23, 26). *Cor. pale lilac or white. Lvs. $\frac{1}{5}$ to $\frac{3}{5}$ in. long, not ciliate at base. Summer flowering.* T. vulgaris

27. *Cor. purple. Lvs. under $\frac{1}{5}$ in. long, ciliate at base. Winter and spring flowering* T. hyemalis

28 (25). *L.-margin thickened all the way round beneath by an evident uninterrupted marginal vein* T. comosus

28. *L.-margin not thickened by an uninterrupted marginal vein* 29

29 (28). *Lvs. ovate, broadly ovate or almost orbicular, not twice as long as wide* T. nummularius

29. *Lvs. more than twice as long as wide* 30

30 (29). *Second internode below infl. hairy all round or almost glabrous, but not evidently hairy on angles only* 31

30. *Second internode below infl. with 2 opposite sides glabrous, 2 other sides obviously hairy along the angles* T. pulegioides

31 (30). *Cal. about $\frac{2}{10}$ to $\frac{3}{10}$ in. long. Cor. nearly $\frac{1}{2}$ in. long* T. Reichardii

31. *Cal. about $\frac{3}{20}$ to $\frac{2}{10}$ in. long* 32

32 (31). *Lvs. $\frac{3}{5}$ to $\frac{4}{5}$ in. long. margin long-ciliate towards the base* T. Marschallianus

32. *Lvs. less than $\frac{3}{5}$ in. long, margin not long-ciliate* 33

33 (32). *L. upper side not or scarcely gland-dotted, glabrous* T. nitidus

33. *L. upper side gland-dotted* 34

34 (33). *Fl.-stems 4 to 12 in. h., mostly erect. Lemon-scented* T. × citriodorus

34. *Fl.-stems 2 to 5 in. h., mostly spreading. Caraway-scented* T. Herba-barona

35 (25). *Second internode below infl. hairy all round* 35

35. *Second internode below infl. hairy on 2 opposite sides, glabrous on 2 other sides* T. Drucei, T. Trachelsianus

36 (35). *L. upper side with numerous long hairs* T. lanuginosus

36. *L. upper side glabrous, rarely with a few scattered hairs; margin ciliate* 37

37 (36). *Fl.-stem with spreading hairs about equalling or longer than diameter of stem* T. longidens lanicaulis

37. *Fl.-stem with rather appressed hairs much shorter than diameter of stem* T. Serpyllum

T. acicula'ris. A synonym of *T. striatus acicularis.*

T. alpi'nus. A synonym of *Calamintha alpina.*

T. angustifo'lius. A synonym of *T. Serpyllum.*

T. arc'ticus. *See under* **T. Drucei.**

T. × aveyronen'sis (*T. Serpyllum × T. vulgaris*).

T. azo'ricus. A synonym of *T. caespititius.*

T. Billardi'eri. A synonym of *T. integer.*

T. Boissi'eri. *See under* **T. hirsutus.**

T. bracteo'sus. Mat-forming; sterile shoots prostrate, long, creeping; fl.-stems erect, about 4 in. h., hairy all round. *l.* elliptic, $\frac{2}{5}$ to $\frac{4}{5}$ in. long, about $\frac{1}{5}$ in. wide, short-stalked, gland-dotted, glabrous except for marginal cilia. *infl.* hemispherical, about $\frac{3}{5}$ in. across; outer bracts broadly ovate, about $\frac{2}{5}$ in. long, $\frac{1}{5}$ in. wide, reddish, glabrous except for marginal cilia; cal. about $\frac{1}{4}$ in. long, hairy; cor. reddish, about $\frac{3}{10}$ in. long. Balkan Peninsula.

T. britan'nicus. *See under* **T. Drucei.**

T. Broussonet'ii. 5 to 12 in. h. much-branched erect bush; shoots erect or ascending, 4-sided, hairy all round but sometimes with 2 opposite sides almost glabrous and other 2 sides markedly hairy with short hairs. *l.* narrowly ovate or elliptic, to $\frac{7}{10}$ in. long, $\frac{1}{5}$ in. wide, short-stalked, profusely gland-dotted, glabrous, except for a few cilia near base, flat, not revolute. *infl.* hemispherical or ovoid, $\frac{1}{2}$ to $\frac{3}{4}$ in. across, $\frac{1}{2}$ to $1\frac{1}{2}$ in. long; bracts large, showy, broadly ovate, to $\frac{3}{5}$ in. long, $\frac{2}{5}$ in. wide, acute or acuminate, purplish-red, prominently veined, not toothed, sparsely hairy or almost glabrous, gland-dotted, margin ciliated; cal. about $\frac{1}{5}$ in. long, hairy; cor. reddish, about $\frac{7}{10}$ in. long. Morocco.

T. caespiti'tius. Mat-forming sub-shrub with long slender woody prostrate shoots bearing dense tufts of l.; fl.-stems erect, 1 to $2\frac{1}{2}$ in. h., hairy all round with minute hairs. *l.* linear or very narrowly oblanceolate, to $\frac{3}{10}$ in. long, $\frac{1}{20}$ in. wide, gland-dotted above and below, margin ciliate, otherwise glabrous. *infl.* oblong, loose, few-fld., $\frac{1}{4}$ to $\frac{1}{2}$ in. across; bracts like l.; cal. about $\frac{3}{20}$ in. long, gland-dotted, sparsely hairy or almost glabrous; cor. light lilac, about $\frac{1}{5}$ in. long. July, August. Spain, Portugal, Azores, Madeira. (L.B.C. 1530 as *T. azoricus.*) SYN. *T. azoricus, T. micans, T. Serpyllum micans.*

T. capita'tus. 5 to 10 in. h. much-branched bush, sometimes spiny with dead leafless branchlets; shoots ascending, densely hairy all round with short hairs. *l.* clustered at nodes, linear, to $\frac{1}{2}$ in. long, $\frac{1}{20}$ in. wide, sessile, firm, profusely gland-dotted, glabrous or ciliate, margin flat, not revolute but sometimes curled upwards. *infl.* ovoid, dense, cone-like, $\frac{1}{4}$ to $\frac{1}{2}$ in. across, $\frac{1}{2}$ to $\frac{3}{4}$ in. long; bracts closely overlapping, narrowly ovate to lanceolate, to $\frac{1}{5}$ in. long, $\frac{1}{10}$ in. wide, profusely gland-dotted, ciliate; cal. about $\frac{1}{5}$ in. long, flattened above and below; cor. rose, about $\frac{2}{5}$ in. long. July to September. Mediterranean region from Portugal to Palestine. SYN. *Coridothymus capitatus.*

T. capitella'tus. 6 to 12 in. h. much-branched bush of loose growth; shoots ascending, flexuous, diverging, hairy all round with minute hairs. *l.* clustered, lanceolate, to $\frac{3}{10}$ in. long, $\frac{1}{10}$ in. wide, short-stalked, shallowly pitted above, closely hairy below, margin revolute. *infl.* with lateral and terminal subglobose or ovoid fl.-heads about $\frac{3}{10}$ in. across; lower bracts ovate or narrowly ovate, to $\frac{3}{10}$ in. long, $\frac{1}{5}$ in. wide, closely hairy beneath; cal. about $\frac{1}{10}$ in. long, minutely hairy; cor. white, about $\frac{3}{20}$ in. long. Portugal. Camphor-scented.

T. carno'sus. 5 to 9 in. h. fastigiate bush; shoots erect, stiff, almost parallel, hairy all round with minute hairs. *l.* clustered at well-separated nodes, thus having a tiered appearance, narrowly elliptic, thick, almost cylindrical, less than $\frac{1}{5}$ in. long, $\frac{1}{20}$ in. wide, sessile, deeply pitted, slightly hairy, strongly revolute. *infl.* subglobose, about $\frac{3}{10}$ in. across; lower bracts ovate, to $\frac{1}{5}$ in. long, $\frac{1}{10}$ in. wide, closely hairy beneath; cal. $\frac{3}{20}$ in. long, minutely hairy; cor. white or pale lilac, about $\frac{1}{4}$ in. long. June, July. Portugal. Before 1874. Aptly described as 'like a miniature Irish Yew'.

T. × Celakovskya'nus (*T. pulegioides × T. Serpyllum*).

T. Cephalo'tus. 4 to 7 in. h. much-branched bush; shoots ascending, hairy all round with short hairs. *l.* clustered at internodes, linear or linear-oblanceolate, $\frac{1}{10}$ to $\frac{3}{5}$ in. long, $\frac{1}{20}$ to $\frac{1}{10}$ in. wide, sessile, glabrous above, glabrous or minutely hairy beneath, margin revolute, ciliate. *infl.* oblong-ovoid, cone-like, about $\frac{1}{2}$ in. across, $\frac{3}{4}$ to $1\frac{3}{4}$ in. long; bracts large, showy, lanceolate to narrowly ovate, to $\frac{4}{5}$ in. long, $\frac{2}{5}$ in. wide, purple-violet, prominently veined, not toothed, closely hairy below, margin long-ciliate; cal. nearly $\frac{3}{10}$ in. long, hairy; cor. pale violet, about $\frac{3}{5}$ in. long. May. Portugal. 1759. One of the most handsome of all Thymes.

T. Chamaed'rys. *See under* **T. pulegioides.**

T. Chamaed'rys var. **como'sus.** A synonym of *T. comosus.*

T. cilia'tus. Sprawling sub-shrub; sterile shoots often arching; fl.-stems ascending, 3 to 6 in. h., hairy all round with short hairs. *l.* very narrowly elliptic to linear, to $\frac{1}{2}$ in. long, less than $\frac{1}{10}$ in. wide, sessile, margin revolute, ciliated with long hairs or almost glabrous. *infl.* hemispherical to ovoid, about $\frac{1}{2}$ in. across, $\frac{1}{2}$ to $\frac{3}{4}$ in. long; bracts large, showy, narrowly ovate, to $\frac{1}{2}$ in. long, $\frac{1}{5}$ in. wide, acute or acuminate, purple, prominently veined, not toothed, closely hairy below, margin long-ciliate; cal. nearly $\frac{3}{10}$ in. long, hairy; cor. purplish, about $\frac{2}{5}$ to $\frac{3}{5}$ in. long. Algeria, Morocco. The correct name for this species is uncertain, the commonly used name *T. ciliatus* (Desf.) Bentham being antedated by *T. ciliatus* Moench.

T. cili'cicus. 3 to 7 in. h. compact bush; shoots ascending, hairy all round with minute hairs. *l.* linear, to $\frac{1}{2}$ in. long, $\frac{1}{20}$ in. wide, sessile, stiff, prominently veined and closely hairy below, margin ciliate. *infl.* hemispherical, $\frac{1}{2}$ to $\frac{7}{10}$ in. across; lower bracts lanceolate, to $\frac{4}{5}$ in. long, $\frac{1}{5}$ in. wide, prominently veined, closely hairy, margin long-ciliate; cal. about $\frac{1}{5}$ in. long, closely hairy; cor. lilac or mauve, $\frac{3}{10}$ in. long. June. Asia Minor. 1947.

T. × citriodo'rus (*T. pulegioides × T. vulgaris*). 4 to 12 in. h. spreading bush; shoots erect or ascending, hairy all round. *l.* narrowly rhomboid-ovate or lanceolate, to $\frac{2}{5}$ in. long, $\frac{3}{20}$ in. wide, short-stalked, gland-dotted, usually quite glabrous, margin usually revolute. *infl.* oblong, interrupted, about $\frac{3}{10}$ in. across; bracts like l., cal. about $\frac{3}{20}$ in. long; cor. pale lilac, about $\frac{3}{20}$ in. long. Lemon-scented. Exists in numerous forms.

T. como'sus. Shoots ascending or sprawling; fl.-stems 3 to 6 in. h., hairy all round. *l.* broadly ovate or broadly elliptic, up to $\frac{3}{5}$ in. long, $\frac{2}{5}$ in. wide, blunt, base cuneate or rounded, long-stalked, gland-dotted above and below, hairy or glabrous, the margin entirely thickened below by a well-marked uninterrupted marginal vein. *infl.* hemispherical or oblong, sometimes interrupted, $\frac{3}{10}$ to $\frac{4}{5}$ in. across; bracts like l.; cal. nearly $\frac{1}{5}$ in. long, hairy; cor. purplish or white, about $\frac{3}{10}$ in. long. June. E. Europe. Before 1933. SYN. *T. transsilvanicus, T. Chamaedrys comosus.* Sometimes confused with *T. nummularius.* Terpentine-scented.

T. comp'tus. Sprawling sub-shrub; sterile shoots woody, prostrate; fl.-stems ascending, 2 to 6 in. h., hairy all round with minute hairs. *l.* linear, to $\frac{1}{2}$ in. long, less than $\frac{1}{20}$ in. wide, sessile, stiff, gland-dotted, margin ciliate near base, otherwise glabrous. *infl.* usually oblong, elongated, interrupted, sometimes hemispherical, about $\frac{2}{5}$ in. across; lower bracts linear or narrowly lanceolate to narrowly ovate, up to $\frac{1}{2}$ in. long, $\frac{1}{10}$ in. wide, closely hairy, prominently veined; cal. about $\frac{3}{20}$ in. long, hairy; cor. rose, about $\frac{1}{5}$ in. long. Balkan Peninsula. Very close to *T. striatus.*

T. Doerf'leri. A synonym of *T. hirsutus Doerfleri.*

T. Dru'cei. Mother of Thyme. Mat-forming; sterile shoots prostrate, long-creeping; fl.-stems erect, $1\frac{1}{2}$ to 3 in. h., 4-sided with 2

opposite sides hairy, 2 other sides almost or quite glabrous. *l.* broadly elliptic or obovate to narrowly elliptic, about $\frac{3}{10}$ in. long, $\frac{1}{10}$ in. wide, short-stalked, blunt, gland-dotted, glabrous or sparsely hairy above, margin ciliate, 5- to 7-veined below. *infl.* hemispherical, $\frac{3}{5}$ to $\frac{4}{5}$ in. across; bracts like l.; cal. about $\frac{3}{20}$ in. long, hairy, with 3 teeth of upper lip about as long as wide. W. Europe, incl. British Is. Commonly known as *T. Serpyllum* and including most of the white and crimson garden plants cultivated as *T. Serpyllum*, this has been separated from the Scandinavian type chiefly on account of the difference in the hairiness of the fl.-stems and in the chromosome number ($2n = 54$ in *T. Drucei*, $2n = 24$ in *T. Serpyllum* proper). As now defined it includes the common British wild Thymes at one time distinguished as *T. neglectus* and *T. britannicus*. The correct name for the whole group may be *T. Trachelsianus*, the type of which grows in the Alps. **T. arc'ticus** of Iceland and Greenland, with fl.-stems $\frac{1}{2}$ to $1\frac{1}{4}$ in. h., is also closely allied.

T. effu'sus. *See under* **T. pulegioides.**

T. ericifo'lius. A synonym of *Micromeria varia*.

T. Funk'ii. 2 to 4 in. h. much-branched compact bush; shoots erect or ascending, hairy all round with minute hairs. *l.* clustered, linear, to $\frac{3}{10}$ in. long, less than $\frac{1}{20}$ in. wide, sessile, closely hairy, margin revolute, sparsely ciliate near base. *infl.* ovoid, few-fld., about $\frac{1}{4}$ in. across, $\frac{1}{4}$ to $\frac{1}{2}$ in. long; bracts narrowly ovate, to $\frac{1}{5}$ in. long, $\frac{1}{10}$ in. wide, not covering cal., purple; cal. about $\frac{1}{5}$ in. long, purplish; cor. purple about $\frac{1}{2}$ in. long. Spain.

T. gla'ber. *See under* **T. pulegioides.**

T. Her'ba-baro'na. 2 to 5 in. h. ascending or procumbent sub-shrub, from a woody base to $\frac{3}{10}$ in. thick; shoots ascending or spreading, hairy all round with minute hairs, sometimes almost glabrous. *l.* ovate to lanceolate, to $\frac{3}{10}$ in. long, less than $\frac{1}{5}$ in. wide, short-stalked, pointed, glabrous or sometimes minutely hairy below and ciliate at margin, gland-dotted above and below. *infl.* hemispherical or oblong, interrupted, about $\frac{2}{5}$ in. across; bracts like l.; cal. about $\frac{1}{5}$ in. long, gland-dotted, sparsely hairy or almost glabrous; cor. rose, about $\frac{1}{4}$ in. long. June. Corsica, Sardinia; 'herba barona' is a Corsican vernacular name. 1908. Fragrant of caraway.

T. hirsu'tus. Mat-forming sub-shrub, with woody prostrate shoots bearing dense tufts of l.; fl.-stems erect, $\frac{1}{2}$ to $2\frac{1}{2}$ in. h., hairy all round with short spreading hairs. *l.* linear, $\frac{1}{5}$ to $\frac{2}{5}$ in. long, $\frac{1}{20}$ in. wide, sessile, grey, closely hairy, margin revolute, ciliate. *infl.* hemispherical, $\frac{2}{5}$ to $\frac{3}{5}$ in. across; outer bracts lanceolate or narrowly ovate, to $\frac{1}{2}$ in. long, less than $\frac{1}{5}$ in. wide, closely hairy; cal. $\frac{3}{20}$ in. long, gland-dotted, hairy; cor. lilac, about $\frac{1}{5}$ in. long. Crimea (type), Balkan Peninsula (several vars.). var. **Doerf'leri,** 2 to $3\frac{1}{2}$ in. h. Balkan Peninsula. **T. Boissi'eri,** Balkan Peninsula, is a closely allied species with l. glabrous except for ciliate margin.

T. hyema'lis. 6 to 12 in. h. bush, very like *T. vulgaris* but *l.* very short, less than $\frac{1}{5}$ in. long, ciliate at base, and cor. purple. Nov. to April. Spain. SYN. *T. Reuteri* var. *ericoides*.

T. in'teger. Mat-forming sub-shrub, with slender woody prostrate shoots bearing dense tufts of l.; fl.-stems erect, 1 to $1\frac{1}{2}$ in. h., hairy all round with long-spreading white hairs. *l.* linear, $\frac{1}{10}$ to $\frac{2}{5}$ in. long, $\frac{1}{20}$ in. or less wide, sessile, gland-dotted, margin revolute and ciliate with long hairs. *infl.* subglobose, few-fld., about $\frac{1}{2}$ in. across; lower bracts oblanceolate to linear, to $\frac{3}{10}$ in. long, less than $\frac{1}{10}$ in. wide, often purplish, ciliate; cal. about $\frac{3}{10}$ in. long; cor. rose, much longer than cal., about $\frac{1}{2}$ in. long. Cyprus. (Sibth. Sm., Fl. Graeca, 578, as *T. villosus*; A.G.S.B. 15, 257). SYN. *T. Billardieri*.

T. lanicau'lis. A synonym of *T. longidens lanicaulis*.

T. lanugino'sus. This name has been used for a large number of very hairy Thymes. Ronniger restricts it to a plant of N. France closely related to *T. Serpyllum*, having the *fl.-stems* $1\frac{1}{2}$ to 3 in. h., very hairy all round, some hairs equalling the diameter of the stem in length and the *l.* thickly hairy on both sides. For the plant commonly cultivated as *T. lanuginosus* see **T. pseudolanuginosus.**

T. lon'gidens var. **lanicau'lis.** Sterile shoots creeping; fl.-stems ascending $2\frac{1}{2}$ to 5 in. h., densely hairy all round with spreading hairs, the longer hairs equalling the stem-diameter. *l.* very narrowly elliptic to elliptic, to $\frac{1}{2}$ in. long, $\frac{1}{5}$ in. wide, short-stalked, gland-dotted above and below, glabrous above, glabrous or hairy on mid-vein below, margin ciliate towards base. *infl.* hemispherical, about $\frac{2}{5}$ in. across; bracts like l.; cal. about $\frac{3}{20}$ in. long, gland-dotted, villous, the middle tooth of upper lip often up to $\frac{1}{20}$ in. long; cor. rose, about $\frac{1}{5}$ in. long. Balkan Peninsula. Cult. in Germany before 1924. SYN. *T. lanicaulis*. It is uncertain whether this should be treated as a species or as a variety of *T. longidens*.

T. longiflo'rus. 4 to 12 in. h. much branched bush; shoots ascending, hairy all round with minute hairs. *l.* very narrowly elliptic or linear, to $\frac{2}{5}$ in. long, less than $\frac{1}{10}$ in. wide, short-stalked, closely hairy above and below, margin revolute. *infl.* ovoid, about $\frac{1}{2}$ in. across, $\frac{3}{4}$ in. long; bracts large, showy, broadly ovate, to $\frac{1}{2}$ in. long, $\frac{2}{5}$ in. wide, purplish, firm, prominently veined, not toothed, closely hairy below, margin not long-ciliate; cal. about $\frac{3}{10}$ in. long, minutely hairy; cor. rose, about $\frac{3}{5}$ in. long. Spain. 1949. var. **cilia'tus,** bracts ciliate. SYN. *T. Moroderi*.

T. Marschallia'nus. Tufted, rather spreading plant with a woody base; shoots ascending; fl.-stems 4 to 8 in. h., hairy all round with hairs spreading or pressed downwards. *l.* narrowly to broadly lanceolate, $\frac{1}{2}$ to $\frac{3}{4}$ in. long, about $\frac{1}{10}$ in. wide, upper and middle l. sessile, lower l. short-stalked, gland-dotted above and below, margin ciliate towards base, otherwise glabrous. *infl.* oblong, often interrupted, $\frac{1}{2}$ in. across; bracts like l.; cal. about $\frac{3}{20}$ in. long, hairy, teeth of upper lip almost equal; cor. rose, $\frac{1}{4}$ in. long. Caucasus, S. Russia, Balkan Peninsula. SYN. *T. Serpyllum* var. *Marschallianus*. A widespread species with many forms. A hybrid of this with *T. Pallasianus* is grown in botanic gardens.

T. Masti'china. 6 to 12 in. h. erect bush; shoots erect, hairy all round with minute hairs. *l.* broadly to narrowly elliptic, to $\frac{3}{5}$ in. long, $\frac{1}{5}$ in. wide, short-stalked, gland-dotted whitish when young, at length glabrous and green. *infl.* globose, somewhat fluffy-looking, $\frac{3}{10}$ to $\frac{4}{5}$ in. across; bracts like l.; cal. $\frac{2}{5}$ in. long, with 5 narrow ciliate segs., the upper lip being deeply 3-fid; cor. white, nearly $\frac{3}{10}$ in. long. Spain, Portugal, N. Africa. 1596. Easily recognized by the deeply divided upper lip of cal.

T. membrana'ceus. 4 to 8 in. h. rounded bush; shoots ascending or spreading, hairy all round with minute hairs. *l.* linear to rhomboid-lanceolate, to $\frac{3}{5}$ in. long, $\frac{1}{5}$ in. wide, short-stalked, closely hairy above and below, margin revolute. *infl.* ovoid, about $\frac{1}{2}$ in. across, $\frac{3}{4}$ in. long; bracts large, showy, ovate or broadly ovate, to $\frac{3}{5}$ in. long, $\frac{2}{5}$ in. wide, greenish-white or pink-flushed, membranous, prominently veined, not toothed, minutely hairy below, margin not long-ciliate; cal. nearly $\frac{3}{10}$ in. long, minutely hairy; cor. about $\frac{1}{2}$ in. long, white. June to August. Spain. Before 1930. (J.R.H.S. 70 (1935), 19; G.C. 88 (1930), 63; B.M., N.S., 58.) An attractive plant for alpine house. var. **mur'cicus,** most *l.* on fl.-stem rhomboid-ovate, to $\frac{3}{5}$ in. long, $\frac{3}{10}$ in. wide, but with smaller very narrowly elliptic *l.* on short axillary shoots. 1948. SYN. *T. murcicus*.

T. mi'cans. A synonym of *T. caespititius*.

T. monta'nus. *See under* **T. pulegioides.**

T. Morod'eri. A synonym of *T. longiflorus ciliatus*.

T. mur'cicus. A synonym of *T. membranaceus murcicus*.

T. neglec'tus. *See under* **T. Drucei.**

T. ni'tidus. 2 to 3 in. h. rather sprawling sub-shrub; shoots ascending, hairy all round with minute hairs. *l.* mostly ovate, rather rhomboid, to $\frac{2}{5}$ in. long, less than $\frac{1}{5}$ in. wide, blunt, short-stalked, glabrous, sparsely or not gland-dotted above, profusely gland-dotted below. *infl.* oblong, $\frac{1}{2}$ in. across, about $\frac{1}{2}$ to $1\frac{1}{2}$ in. long; bracts like l.; cal. about $\frac{1}{5}$ in. long, sparsely hairy; cor. pale lilac, nearly $\frac{2}{5}$ in. long. Island of Marettimo near Sicily. Before 1938. Alpine house. The plant commonly cultivated as *T. nitidus* is *T. carnosus*. **T. Reichard'ii,** Balearic Islands, is a closely related species, with mostly sprawling branches, *l.* up to $\frac{3}{5}$ in. long, $\frac{1}{4}$ in. wide, cal. $\frac{2}{5}$ to $\frac{3}{10}$ in. long, cor. bright purple, nearly $\frac{1}{2}$ in. long.

T. nummula'rius. Spreading bushy sub-shrub; shoots ascending; fl.-stems $3\frac{1}{2}$ to 6 in. (sometimes up to 12 in.) h., 4-sided with 2 opposite sides hairy, 2 other sides glabrous, often branched. *l.* broadly or very broadly ovate, up to $\frac{7}{10}$ in. long, $\frac{3}{5}$ in. wide, blunt, base rounded or subcordate, short-stalked, gland-dotted above and below, hairy or glabrous, the margin usually ciliate towards the base but not entirely thickened below by a stout uninterrupted marginal vein. *infl.* hemispherical or oblong, $\frac{3}{5}$ to 1 in. across; bracts like l.; cal. about $\frac{1}{5}$ in. long, hairy; cor. mauve-pink, about $\frac{3}{10}$ in. long. Caucasus, Asia Minor. Before 1829. (B.M. 2666.) SYN. *T. Serpyllum* var. *nummularius*. This remarkably broad-leaved Thyme has been confused with *T. comosus*, which has the fl.-stem hairy all round and l. smaller with a raised uninterrupted marginal vein.

T. odoratis'simus. *See under* **T. Pallasianus.**

T. ova'tus. *See under* **T. pulegioides.**

T. Pallasia'nus. Sterile shoots prostrate; fl.-stems erect, 2 to 4 in. h., hairy all round with minute appressed hairs. *l.* linear to oblanceolate, to $\frac{1}{2}$ in. long, $\frac{1}{10}$ in. wide, sessile, gland-dotted above and below, the margin sparsely ciliate towards the base, otherwise glabrous. *infl.* hemispherical, about $\frac{1}{2}$ in. across; bracts like l.; cal. about $\frac{3}{20}$ in. long, gland-dotted, sparsely hairy, teeth of upper lip very small, the middle one longer and broader than 2 lateral teeth; cor. purplish, nearly $\frac{1}{5}$ in. long. S. Russia. SYN. *T. odoratissimus* of Bieberstein (1819) not of Miller (1768) which, according to Ronniger, is the same as *T. glabrescens*, an allied species with l. up to $\frac{2}{10}$ in. wide.

T. pseudolanugino'sus. Mat-forming; shoots prostrate, long-creeping, 4-sided with 2 opposite sides glabrous and 2 sides hairy with short and long hairs, some of which equal the diameter of the stem in length. *l.* elliptic or broadly elliptic, about $\frac{1}{5}$ in. long, $\frac{1}{10}$ in. wide, short-stalked, blunt, covered above and below with long spreading hairs, some nearly $\frac{1}{5}$ in. long. *fl.* few, mostly axillary; cal. $\frac{3}{20}$ in. long, hairy with long spreading hairs; cor. pale pink, near $\frac{1}{5}$ in. long. June. Easily recognized by its grey mats of foliage, sometimes sprinkled with pink axillary fl., not heads, this has been cultivated since before 1880 as *T. lanuginosus* but is distinct from many plants to which botanists have applied that name. Its origin and correct name are uncertain. Ronniger and Jalas have identified it as *T. pseudolanuginosus*.

T. pulchel'lus. *See under* **T. pulegioides.**

T. pulegioi'des. 4 to 12 in. h. spreading bushy sub-shrub; shoots mostly ascending; fl.-stems 4-sided with 2 opposite sides short-hairy and 2 sides glabrous, or hairy only on the angles. *l.* very variable, ovate, elliptic or lanceolate, mostly about $\frac{3}{10}$ in. long,

1/10 in. wide, blunt, base wedge-shaped, stalked, gland-dotted and glabrous above and below, the margin not thickened by an uninterrupted marginal vein. *infl.* mostly oblong and interrupted, about 3/10 in. across; bracts like l.; cal. about 1/10 in. long; cor. mauve, sometimes white or crimson, about 3/20 in. long. Europe, including Britain. A widespread species with numerous variants, which have been distinguished as subspecies **pulegioi'des** (including *T. Chamaedrys*, *T. glaber*, *T. ovatus*), **monta'nus** (SYN. *T. montanus*), **effu'sus** (SYN. *T. effusus*), **pulchel'lus** (SYN. *T. pulchellus*), &c. A form with crimson flowers (which has been named **T. pulegioi'des** var. **Chamaed'rys** f. **kermesi'nus**) from Thuringia, Germany, is sometimes grown as **T. Serpyllum coccin'eus.**

T. Reichard'ii. *See under* **T. nitidus.**

T. Reut'eri var. **ericoi'des.** A synonym of *T. hyemalis.*

T. Serpyl'lum. Mat-forming; sterile shoots prostrate, long-creeping; fl.-stems erect, 1 to 3 in. h., hairy all round with downwards pressed hairs. *l.* narrowly elliptic to narrowly obovate, about 1/5 to 3/10 in. long, to 1/10 in. wide, short-stalked, blunt, gland-dotted and glabrous above and below, sometimes with the margin ciliate near base, 7-veined (i.e. with 3 veins each side of mid-vein) below. *infl.* hemispherical, 3/10 to 3/5 in. across; bracts like l.; cal. about 3/20 in. long, purplish, sparsely hairy, with teeth of upper lip less than 1/20 in. long, about as wide as long; cor. purplish, less than 1/5 in. long. Europe, including Britain. SYN. *T. angustifolius.* The name *T. Serpyllum* is often used to cover a large number of plants, which some botanists distinguish as varieties or subspecies and others as species. The above description is based on the Swedish type, which does not seem to be represented among the plants known in gardens as *T. Serpyllum.* Some of these have been derived from *T. Drucei* (see above) and allies, others from *T. pulegioides* and allies. For plants sometimes treated as varieties of *T. Serpyllum see also* **T. lanuginosus, T. Marschallianus, T. nummularius, T. pseudolanuginosus.**

T. stria'tus. Sprawling sub-shrub; sterile shoots woody, arching; fl.-stems erect, 2 to 4½ in. h., hairy all round with minute hairs, covered at base with numerous crowded l. *l.* linear, to 1/2 in. long, 1/10 in. wide, sessile, stiff, sparsely gland-dotted, margin ciliate, otherwise glabrous. *infl.* hemispherical, 1/3 to 1/2 in. across; lower bracts lanceolate to ovate, to 2/5 in. long, 1/5 in. wide, hairy, prominently veined, often reddish; cal. nearly 1/5 in. long, hairy; cor. purple, about 1/5 in. long. Italy, Balkan Peninsula. SYN. *T. striatus* var. *stabianus.* A variable species with numerous forms, incl. var. **acicula'ris,** *l.* less than 1/20 in. wide. Hungary, Balkan Peninsula. SYN. *T. acicularis.*

T. tenuifo'lius. A synonym of *T. Zygis.*

T. Trachelsia'nus. *See under* **T. Drucei,** which differs from it slightly and possibly inconstantly in the teeth of the upper cal. lip. It is common in the Alps. SYN. *T. Serpyllum* var. *Trachelsianus.*

T. transsilva'nicus. A synonym of *T. comosus.*

T. villo'sus. 4 to 7 in. h. rounded bush; shoots ascending, hairy all round with minute hairs. *l.* clustered at internodes, linear, to 3/10 in. long, less than 1/20 in. wide, sessile, margin revolute and ciliate with very long white hairs. *infl.* subglobose, 1/4 to 1/2 in. across; lower bracts narrowly ovate or lanceolate, to 3/10 in. long, less than 1/5 in. wide, acute, green or purplish, usually with 1 or 2 prominent teeth on each margin, villous with long white hairs; cal. about 1/5 in. long; cor. deep pink, about 2/5 in. long. July, August. Portugal. 1759.

T. vulga'ris. Garden Thyme, Common Thyme. 6 to 8 in. h. spreading bush; shoots ascending, stiff, woody, hairy all round with minute hairs. *l.* oblong-lanceolate to linear, 1/5 to 3/5 in. long, less than 1/10 in. wide, short-stalked, gland-dotted, closely grey-hairy beneath, margin revolute, not ciliate. *infl.* short, interrupted; bracts like l.; cal. about 1/10 in. long, hairy, gland-dotted; cor. lilac, about 1/5 in. long. June to August. S. Europe, from Spain to Italy. Before 1548. For cultivation *see* **Thyme.**

T. Zy'gis. 4 to 12 in. h. bush; shoots ascending, hairy all round with minute hairs. *l.* clustered at nodes, linear, to 3/10 in. long, less than 1/20 in. wide, sessile, gland-dotted, minutely hairy, margin revolute, ciliated towards base. *infl.* long, much interrupted and tiered, the clusters separated by internodes up to 1/2 in. or so long; bracts like l.; cal. less than 3/20 in. long, gland-dotted, minutely hairy or glabrous; cor. white, less than 3/20 in. long. Spain, Portugal. 1771. SYN. *T. tenuifolius.*

W. T. S.

thyoi'des, Thuja-like.

THYRSACAN'THUS. Included in **Odontonema.**

THYRSE. A panicle whose greatest diameter is midway between base and apex.

thyrsiflo'rus -a -um, having flowers in a thyrse.

thy'rsiger -era -erum, bearing a thyrse.

thyrsoi'deus -a -um, resembling a thyrse.

THYRSOP'TERIS (*thyrsos*, bunch or raceme, *pteris*, fern; the sori are in racemose bunches). FAM. *Cyatheaceae. T. elegans*, the only species, is a very distinct fern, requiring only greenhouse temperature, shade, and abundance of water at the roots. Propagation is by the rooting of the lateral shoots which are produced on the trunk.

T. e'legans. Tree-like, 15 ft. h. *fronds* decompound, 5 to 6 ft. long, 1/3 being naked; sterile parts 2-pinnate with lanceolate deeply toothed pinnules; fertile 3-pinnate, each pinna becoming a raceme of stalked sori. *Indusium* cup-shaped. Juan Fernandez. 1854.

thysano-, in compound words, signifying a fringe.

thysanole'pis, having fringed scales.

THYSANOPTERA. *See* **Insects, Thrips.**

THYSANO'TUS (*thysanotos*, fringed; from the 3 fringed inner perianth segments). FAM. *Liliaceae.* Fringe Lily; Fringed Violet. A genus of about 20 species of Australian rhizomatous perennials with 1 species extending to the Philippine Is. and S. China. Leaves radical, grass-like. Flowers usually in umbels, rarely solitary; perianth marcescent, persistent, of 6 segments, outer 3 narrow, inner with broad, coloured margins and marginal fringes; stamens 6 or sometimes 3; bracts short, overlapping; scapes leafless or nearly so, simple or variously branched. These plants need greenhouse protection and grow best in sandy loam. Propagation by offsets.

T. dichot'omus. *rhiz.* thick, fibrous. Stems very variable, erect, branched, 1 to 2 ft. h. or almost twining. *Radical l.* few, short, withering early. *fl.* 1, 2, or rarely 3 in terminal umbels; segs. purple; stamens 6. July. (B.R. 1840, 14 as *T. intricatus.*) B.R. 1838, 50 named *T. tenius* is probably a reduced form of this.

T. ela'tior. *See* **T. tuberosus.**

T. intrica'tus. A synonym of *T. dichotomus.*

T. isan'therus. A synonym of *T. tuberosus.*

T. jun'ceus. *rhiz.* thick, fibrous. Stem slender, loosely branched, erect or flexuous, 1 to 2 ft. h., sometimes with a short l. near base. *Radical l.* few, narrow-linear, short, soon withering. *fl.* 1 to 3 in a terminal umbel with sometimes 1 or 2 sessile along lower branches; segs. purple, about 1/2 in. long; stamens 6. August. 1804. (B.M. 2351; B.R. 656.)

Thysanotus multiflorus var. *prolifer*

T. multiflo'rus. Densely tufted, roots fibrous. *l.* all radical, erect, rigid, much shorter than scape. *fl.* purple, outer segs. very acute, inner rather shorter; stamens 3; scape simple, 6 to 18 in. long, with a single terminal many-fld. umbel or rarely a second one lower down. August. var. **pro'lifer,** luxuriant form with more *fl.* in umbel and frequently a second one below, *l.* sometimes longer than scape. (B.R. 1838, 8 and F.d.S. 1911 as *T. proliferus.*)

T. te'nius. *See* **T. dichotomus.**

T. tubero'sus. Fibrous root swollen into tubers. *l.* radical, few, narrow-linear, very short or equalling scape. *fl.* purple, about ½ in. long; stamens 6; scape erect, rigid, terete, 6 to over 12 in. long, branching into a loose, irregularly forked panicle, each branch bearing a terminal umbel of 1 to 4 fl. and sometimes a lateral sessile one. June. (B.R. 655 as *T. isantherus.*) *T. elatior* is a tall, strong form of this.

THYSANU'RA. *See* **Bristle-tails.**

tianscha'nicus -a -um. *See* ***thianscha'nicus.***

TIAREL'LA (*tiara*, a Persian diadem; from the shape of the capsules). FAM. *Saxifragaceae.* A genus of 7 species of low-growing perennial herbs, 1 native of E. Asia, the others N. American. Leaves mostly radical, long-stalked, simple or 3-foliate; stipules small, adnate to leaf-stalks. Flowers white or rose-tinged, ¼ in. or less across; hypanthium ('calyx-tube') cup-shaped, short; sepals 5; petals 5, entire; stamens 10, filaments long; racemes terminal; capsule valves 2, very unequal. Woodland type of soil suits these plants but they will grow in most garden soils. They are generally well suited to the rock-garden. *T. cordifolia* spreads into wide masses by means of stolons, the others form compact clumps. A revision of the N. American species by O. Lakela has been published in *American Journal of Botany*, 24. 344–51 (1937). Propagation by seed or division. *See also* **Heuchera** and ×**Heucherella.**

KEY.

1. *Stamens always* 10. (Tiarella) 3
1. *Stamens varying from 5 to 10 on same infl. often 7 or 8. Infl. a long narrow panicle.* (× Heucherella) 2
2. *Plant spreading by stolons. Lvs. more or less orbicular in outline though shallowly 7-lobed. Fl.-stem to 16 in. h. Fl. pale carmine; anthers yellow* × Heucherella tiarelloides
2. *Plant forming a compact clump without stolons. L. broadly ovate in outline though shallowly 7–9 lobed. Fl.-stem to 2 ft. Fl. white or rose-tinged; anthers brown* × H. alba
3. *L. always divided into 3 lflets.* 4
3. *L. simple, sometimes deeply lobed* 5
4. *Lflets. deeply lobed; divisions reaching half-way or more to midrib* T. laciniata
4. *Lflets. moderately lobed; divisions not reaching half-way to midrib* T. trifoliata
5. *Stamens of markedly unequal length. Infl. a narrow panicle, the fl.-stalks several-fld.* 6
5. *Stamens more or less equal in length. Infl. a simple raceme, the upper fl. stalks always 1-fld., the lowermost fl. stalks sometimes 2-fld.* 7
6. *Petiole glabrous except near tip* T. unifoliata
6. *Petiole hairy from base to tip* T. californica
7. *Pet. elliptic or lanceolate, longer than sep. Fl.-stem usually leafless* 8
7. *Pet. thread-like, hardly noticeable. Fl.-stems usually with 2 or 3 comparatively large lvs.* T. polyphylla
8. *Plant with long stolons. L. irregularly mottled over upper face* T. cordifolia
8. *Plant without stolons. L. blotched near sinus on upper face* T. Wherryi

T. califor'nica. *fl.-stem* 12 to 20 in. h. Very close to *T. unifoliata* but with petioles hairy throughout. California.

T. cordifo'lia. Foamflower. Rootstock producing slender prostrate stolons after flowering. *l.* ovate, cordate, 1 to 4 in. wide, usually 3- to 5- lobed, becoming reddish-bronze in autumn; petiole hairy. *fl.-stem* 6 to 12 in. h. *fl.* starry, white, ¼ in. across, in a simple raceme; pet. spreading, narrowly elliptic or lanceolate, clawed; stamens equal; anthers brown, slightly broader than long after dehiscence. April to June. Eastern N. America. 1731. (B.M. 1589.) var. **albiflo'ra,** anthers white, *l.* as type **purpu'rea,** *l.* bronzy purple, *fl.* rose. The commonest species, easily recognized by its stolons, which enable it to spread into wide masses.

T. lacinia'ta. *l.* with 3 rhombic lflets., middle one deeply 3-cleft, lateral 2-cleft, deeply cut. *fl.-stem* 6 to 14 in. h., *fl.* minute in a loose narrow panicle; pet. thread-like; stamens markedly unequal. Vancouver Island, Washington. Before 1935. (F.B.A. 77).

T. macrophyl'la. A fictitious species, the original description being made from herbarium specimens comprising *l.* of *Heuchera villosa* and *fl.-stems* of southern form of *Tiarella cordifolia.*

T. Menzies'ii. A synonym of *Tolmiea Menziesii.*

T. polyphyl'la. *l.* broadly ovate, cordate, to 2¾ in. wide, 3-lobed, toothed; petiole hairy. *fl.-stem* 9 to 24 in. h. *fl.* minute, white or reddish, in a simple raceme; pet. thread-like, sometimes absent; stamens equal; anthers as long as broad or slightly longer than broad after dehiscence. E. Himalaya, China, Japan. (Hook. I. 1584.)

T. trifolia'ta. *l.* with 3 rhombic lflets., middle one 3-lobed, lateral 2-lobed, coarsely toothed. *fl.-stem.* 6 to 20 in. h. *fl.* minute in a narrow panicle; pet. thread-like; stamens markedly unequal. British Columbia, Vancouver Island, Washington, Oregon. 1902.

T. unifolia'ta. *l.* ovate, 1 to 5 in. wide, 3- to 5-lobed, rarely 3-cleft, petiole hairy only at tip. *fl.-stem* 6 to 18 in. h. *fl.* white, in a narrow loose panicle; stamens markedly unequal; anthers longer than broad after dehiscence. Western N. America from S. Alaska to N. California. (F.B.A. 81).

T. Wher'ryi. Rootstock compact, without stolons, *l.* ovate, cordate, to 3½ in. wide, sharply 3-lobed, becoming reddish in autumn; petiole hairy. *fl.-stem* 6 to 14 in. h. *fl.* white or rose tinged, starry, ¼ in. across, in a simple often dense raceme; pet. spreading, narrowly elliptic, clawed; stamens equal; anthers orange, slightly broader than long after dehiscence. May, June. Tennessee, N. Carolina, Alabama. 1939. (G.C. 124 (1948), 85). An attractive plant, flowering freely and compact in growth.

W. T. S.

iarelloi'des, Tiarella-like.

tiberia'dis, of Tiberias, Palestine.

tibe'ticus -a -um, of Tibet.

tibici'nus -a -um, flute-like.

TIBOUCHI'NA (native name in Guiana). FAM. *Melastomataceae.* A genus of about 150 species of shrubs or sub-shrubs, rarely perennial herbs, sometimes climbing, often with stiff or bristly hairs, natives of Trop. S. America, mostly in Brazil. Leaves often large, leathery, ovate or oblong, entire, 3- to 9-nerved, stalked. Flowers violet or purple, usually in terminal, 3-forked panicles, large, sometimes with concave involucral bracts, very rarely 4-parted; calyx-tube ovoid, bell-urn-shaped or cylindrical; lobes 5, at least as long as tube; petals 5, obovate, often unequal sided, retuse. Turfy loam suits these plants best but they will grow in peat. Propagation by cuttings of half-ripe shoots in a close frame in heat at almost any time when they are available. *T. elegans* was at one time a favourite plant for exhibition. *T. semidecandra* is excellent in pots, especially the variety *floribunda*, but better on trellises or walls either planted out or grown in large boxes after its first year, and while most of the species need stove conditions this will grow well in the greenhouse or cool stove. A season of rest should be given the Tibouchinas in winter, but plenty of water may be used during summer. The following are all shrubs and need stove treatment unless otherwise stated. They all at one time were placed under Pleroma and at times may appear under that name in catalogues.

KEY

1. *Fl. few (mostly 1 to 5) in racemes* 2
1. *Fl. many (usually 7 or more), in panicles* 4
2. *Lvs. with 7 (rarely 5) nerves, thin* T. laxa
2. *Lvs. with 3 (rarely 5) nerves, leathery and thick* 3
3. *Fl. 1 to 2 in. across; lvs. 1 to 2 in. long, hairless above* T. elegans
3. *Fl. 3 to 5 in. across; lvs. mostly 3 to 6 in. long, silky-hairy above* T. semidecandra
4. *Lvs. (except the uppermost) with 9 veins, nearly hairless above* T. Benthamiana
4. *Lvs. with 5 or 7 veins, densely hairy and often silky above* 5
5. *Branches distinctly 4-winged; shrubs 15 to 30 ft. h.* T. granulosa
5. *Branches angled, terete, or grooved but not winged; shrubs 2 to 7 ft. h.* 6
6. *Lvs. sessile* T. holosericea
6. *Lvs. petioled* 7
7. *Fl. white, less than 1 in. across, bractless* T. Gayana
7. *Fl. blue to purple (or rose), 1 in. or more across, each subtended by a small bract* 8
8. *Pet. ½ to ⅝ in. long, style ¼ in. long* T. heteromalla
8. *Pet. ¾ to 1 in. long, style ¾ in. long or more* 9
9. *Fl.-bract ovate-oblong; shrub 5 to 6 ft. h.* T. viminea
9. *Fl.-bract linear-lanceolate; shrub 2 to 5 ft. h.* T. Gaudichaudiana

T. Benthamia'na.* About 4 ft. h. *sts.* 4-winged. *l.* oblong-lanceolate, 9-nerved, petioled, nearly hairless above, the base obtuse to subcordate. *fl.* dark purple with whitish centre, about 2 in. across, many in terminal panicles. Autumn. S. Brazil. 1841. (B.M. 4007.)

T. e'legans.* About 5 ft. h. *sts.* terete. *l.* ovate-lanceolate, 3-nerved, 1 to 2 in. long, glossy green above. *fl.* 1¾ to 2½ in. across, solitary or few but produced in abundance on the plant. May, June. S. Brazil. 1844. (B.M. 4262.)

T. Gaudichaudia'na. 2 to 6 ft. h. *sts.* obtusely 4-angled or grooved. *l.* ovate-lanceolate, sericeous above, 5-nerved, the uppermost ones sometimes sessile, the lower petioled. *fl.* rose-purple, 1¾ in. across. Summer. Brazil. This species and *T. viminea* (treated below) closely related and possibly not distinct. (B.M. 3766 as *Lasiandra petiolata.*) SYN. *Pleionema Gaudichaudiana, Rhexia petiolata, R. petiolaris.*

T. Gaya'na.* Shrub to 2 ft. h. *sts.* terete. *l.* ovate-oblong, 7-nerved, mostly 1½ in. long, sericeous above, the margin entire. *fl.* white, about ¾ in. across, bractless, in large panicles. Late autumn. Peru. 1874. (B.M. 6345.)

T. heteromal'la. Shrub 3 to 5 ft. h. *sts.* terete to obtusely angled. *l.* broadly ovate, 7-nerved, sericeous above, the base cordate, the upper ones sometimes sessile but others petioled. *fl.* purplish-violet, 1 to 1½ in. across, the style very short. July to September. Brazil. 1819. (B.M. 2337 and B.R. 664 as *Melastoma heteromalla.*)

T. holoseri'cea.* Shrub 2 to 6 ft. h. *sts.* 4-angled. *l.* ovate, acute, 5-nerved, sericeous, sessile. *fl.* purple, about 1½ in. across, many in panicles. July. Brazil. 1816. (B.R. 323 and L.B.C. 236 as *Rhexia holosericea.*) SYN. *Lasiandra argentea.*

T. Knuthia'na. A synonym of *T. semidecandra.*

T. la'xa.* Shrub to 7 ft. h. *sts.* terete, densely hirtellous. *l.* ovate, 7-veined, to 2 in. long, acute to acuminate, the base subcordate. *fl.* deep violet to violet-purple, about 2 in. across, few in trichasia or racemes. Peru. 1867. (B.M. 5629.) SYN. *T. sarmentosa, Rhexia laxa, Pleroma sarmentosa.*

T. macran'tha. A synonym of *T. semidecandra.*

T. sarmento'sa. A synonym of *T. laxa.*

Tibouchina semidecandra

T. semidecan'dra.* Shrub 10 to 25 ft. h. *sts.* 4-angled. *l.* oblong-ovate to ovate, 3- to 5-nerved, 3 to 6 in. long, sericeous above, petioled. *fl.* rich purple, 3 to 5 in. across, solitary or few in trichasia, blossoming more or less continuously under glass, but chiefly in autumn. S. Brazil. 1864. (B.M. 4412 as *Pleroma Knuthianum*; 5721 as *P. macranthum.*) SYN. *Lasiandra macrantha.* var. **floribun'da** flowers while the plant is still very small. Greenhouse. This species, with its large royal purple fl. of velvety sheen and its prominently veined l., is among the finest of greenhouse shrubs. It tends, however, to become straggly and should be pruned in early spring.

T. vimi'nea. About 6 ft. h. *sts.* obtusely 4-angled. *l.* ovate-lanceolate, acute, 5-nerved, 2 to 4 in. long, very hairy on both surfaces, petioled. *fl.* violet-purple or blue, about 1½ in. across, each subtended by an ovate-oblong bract, many in panicles. July, August. S. Brazil. 1821. (B.R. 664 as *Rhexia viminea.*)

G. H. M. L.

TICKLE MY FANCY. *See* **Viola tricolor.**

TICKSEED. *See* **Coreopsis.**

TICO'REA (native name in Guiana). FAM. *Rutaceae.* A genus of about 10 species of trees or shrubs, natives of Guiana. Leaves opposite or alternate, simple or with 1 to 3 entire, pellucid-dotted leaflets. Flowers white, yellowish-white, or scarlet, on bracteate pedicels; calyx short, 4- or 5-lobed; corolla tubular-funnel-shaped, tube long, limb of 5 valvate lobes; disk cup-like or urn-shaped; stamens 5 to 8; inflorescence a panicle or cyme at end of branchlets, rarely axillary, leafless. The species need stove conditions and a compost of loam, peat, and sand. They can be propagated by cuttings in sand, under a glass, in heat.

T. foe'tida. Shrub of 10 ft. *lflets.* 3, equal, almost sessile. *fl.* white, 6 or 7 in a corymb, sessile along the branches; pet. 6 times as long as cal. February. Guiana. 1825. The bruised foliage has a disagreeable odour.

T. jasminiflo'ra. A synonym of *Gulipea multiflora.*

TIGER BEETLES (*Cicindela*) are extremely active and fierce. They hunt and devour other insects. Of the 4 British species, the most familiar is the striking green *C. campestris.* The beetles frequent hot sandy places and often abound on heaths and commons in May and June, running and flying very swiftly. Their hump-backed grubs are equally fierce, and live in vertical burrows in the ground lying in wait for their prey as it passes their lairs.

TIGER FLOWER. *See* **Tigridia.**

TIGER LILY. *See* **Lilium tigrinum.**

Tigersted'tii, in honour of Carl Gustaf Tigerstedt, b. 1886, of Mustila, Finland; prominent Scandinavian dendrologist.

TIG'LIUM. Included in **Croton.** The name is from the apothecary's name *grana tiglia.*

TIGRI'DIA (from *tigris,* tiger; see p. 2114, note on *tigrinus*). FAM. *Iridaceae.* A genus of about 12 species of bulbous plants, natives of Mexico, Cent. America, Peru, and Chile. Radical leaves few and narrow, or broader and plicate-veined; stem-leaves and bracts often 2 or 3, scattered. Flowers few in a spathe, very large in *T. Pavonia*; perianth concave, without a tube; segments free, outer very broad, clawed, inner much smaller, erecto-patent, often obtuse, more or less undulate; filaments connate in a cylindrical tube; spathe 1, terminal or 2 in the axils of the bracts, long, unequally pedunculate. *T. Pavonia* and its varieties are very handsome when in flower. All the species grow best in a light, sandy soil. If they are planted outdoors they should have a warm, sunny place facing south. The bulbs must be lifted in autumn when the leaves die down, stored in a frost-free place, and replanted in April. Propagation by seeds or by offsets.

T. atra'ta. 2 ft. h. *l.* plicate, 12 to 18 in. long. *fl.* dark purple, outer segs. with pale-green spots on claws and dark-brown lamina; spathe 2-valved, 2½ in. long. April. S. Mexico. 1843. Greenhouse.

T. bucci'fera.* Stem branched, 1 ft. long. *l.* linear, plicate, nearly 1 ft. long, ¼ in. wide. *fl.* 2 in. across, base greenish-yellow with purple dots, blade of outer segs. purple, obovate, inner segs. tubular-folded in centre; spathe valves 1½ to 2 in. long. Mts. of Mexico. 1888. (G. and F. 1889, 412.) Half-hardy.

T. coelesti'na. A synonym of *Cypella plumbea.*

T. conchiflo'ra. A variety of *T. Pavonia.*

T. curva'ta. Stem slender, 1 ft. long. *l.* plicate, 8 in. long. *fl.* yellowish, spotted purple; peduncles curved; spathe valve 1. April. Real Del Monte. 1843. Greenhouse.

T. grandiflo'ra. A synonym of *T. lutea.*

T. lilia'cea. A variety of *T. Pavonia.*

T. lu'tea. Stem 8 to 10 in. long, terete, arching, glabrous. *l.* ensiform, stem-clasping, very long acuminate. *fl.* fragrant, yellow with obscure dots, outer segs. obovate, 1 in. long, slightly crenate, inner without appendix; spathe 5- or 6-fld.; pedicellate. Peru. 1843. (B.M. 6295.) Half-hardy. var. **immaculata.** *fl.* not spotted.

T. Meleag'ris. A synonym of *Hydrotaenia Meleagris.*

T. Pavo'nia.* Flower of Tigris, Peacock Tiger Flower. Mexican Tiger Flower. Stem cylindrical, forked, leafy, 1 to 2 ft. long. *l.* lanceolate-ensiform, plicate, acute; basal l. 2-ranked, sheathing, 10 to 18 in. long. *fl.* orange, outer segs. broadly ovate, 3 in. long, mucronate, inner 1½ in. long, channelled below middle; spathe 3-fld., 4 in. long; pedicels long. June. Mexico. 1796. (B.M. 532 as *Ferraria Tigridia*; A.B.R. 178 and L.B.C. 1424 as *F. Pavonia.*) Half-hardy. Variable. var. **al'ba,*** habit of var. *conchiflora*, *fl.* pearly-white with large reddish-brown spots at base of segs. on a yellowish-ground. 1882. A form **alba immacula'ta** is snow-white without spots; **albiflo'ra,*** ground colour of *fl.* white; **conchiflo'ra,*** *fl.* rather dark yellow. (F.d.S. 908 and S.B.F.G. 128 as *T. conchiflora.*) SYN. var. *canariensis*; **fla'va,** spathe yellow. 1896; **lilia'cea,** *fl.* reddish-purple with almost white variegation; **ro'sea,** *fl.* yellow tinged with rose. 1893; **ru'bra,** *fl.* reddish-orange; **specio'sa,** *fl.* with deeper orange ground colour than in type. Other varieties with vernacular names are offered, e.g. **Le Géant, Giant Rose.**

Tigridia Pavonia

T. Prin'glei.* Bulb small, roots fusiform. Stem slender, 1 to 2 ft. long with 2 or 3 winged, plicate l. and 1 fl. *fl.* bell-shaped at base, with crimson blotches within; outer segs. 2¼ in. long, reflexed, limb scarlet; inner broadly heart- or kidney-shaped, limb narrower, triangular-ovate, acute, without spots. July, August. S. Mexico. 1883. (B.M. 7089; G. and F. 1, 389.) Half-hardy.

T. Van-Houttei. A synonym of *Hydrotaenia Van-Houttei.*

T. viola'cea. Stem 7 to 14 in. h., terete, erect, forked at apex. *l.* ensiform, plicate; basal l. 8 to 14 in. long. *fl.* violet, bell-shaped, nodding; blade of outer segs. rose-purple, claw white, dotted with rose-purple, ¾ in. long; inner segs. deflexed, white, dotted in middle; spathe 3- or 4-fld., 2-valved. May. S. Mexico. 1838. SYN. *Beatonia purpurea*. Greenhouse.

tigri'nus -a -um, striped somewhat like a tiger (*Felis tigris*); spotted profusely somewhat like a jaguar (*Felis onca*) which the early Spanish naturalists in America confused with the Asiatic tiger; toothed like a tiger.

TILE-ROOT. *See* **Geissorhiza.**

TI'LIA (ancient Latin name for the lime). FAM. *Tiliaceae*. Lime, Linden. A genus of about 30 species of large or medium-sized trees; winter buds prominent. Leaves alternate but in 2 ranks, mostly roundish-ovate with an oblique, more or less cordate base, always toothed, often with tufts of down in the axils of the veins beneath. Flowers dull white or yellowish, ½ to ¾ in. wide, borne on leafy shoots of the current year from June to August in pendent (rarely upright) cymes, sometimes in threes, sometimes up to 40. They are always produced on a long narrow membranous bract to which the lower half of the stalk of the inflorescence is united. Sepals 5; petals 5; stamens numerous. Fruit dry, nut-like, about the size of a pea, carrying usually 1 (occasionally 2 or 3) seeds.

The limes like a good, loamy soil, moist if possible because they lose their foliage early in dry, hungry soil. They can be transplanted safely to a good size. Seeds when obtainable are best for propagating the species but they are largely infertile. Layering is usually practised for *T.* × *europaea* and other of the commoner limes. Grafting is used for the increase of rare species and garden varieties.

The flowers of Limes secrete an abundance of nectar and in suburban areas are the chief source of honey to bee-keepers. It has accordingly been suggested that municipal authorities should keep this in mind when planting trees for amenity. For street planting *T. mongolica*, *T. euchlora*, and *T. Miqueliana* are recommended as they form moderate-sized trees and together have a long flowering season. *T. Maximowicziana*, *T. insularis*, and *T. tomentosa*, which make larger trees, are suggested for park planting. Unfortunately there seems to be a substance poisonous to bees in the flowers of *T. petiolaris* and it is not recommended for extensive planting. For further details of limes as amenity trees and bee pasturage an article by R. Melville in *Kew Bulletin*, 1949, 147–51 should be consulted.

Lime timber is one of the best obtainable for the manufacture of pianoforte keys. The inner bark of the European species, tough and fibrous, is used to make the bast mats much used for covering glass frames in cold weather. Shoes are made by Russian peasants from the same material, plaited.

Duhamel states that French gardeners, when they want a supply of young Lime-trees, cut over an old one close to the surface of the ground, which soon sends up a great number of shoots: among these they throw a quantity of soil, which they allow to remain 1, 2, or 3 years, after which they find the shoots well rooted, and of a sufficient height and strength to be planted at once where they are finally to remain.

The Limes are the best trees for pleaching, i.e. for making into a narrow screen of interlacing branches. The trees should be planted in line about 8 ft. apart and allowed to grow until they have sufficiently firm stems to allow topping; they should all have their tops cut off at the same height. It is necessary to provide a firm framework on which the branches may be trained. A good procedure is to tie bamboo rods horizontally from tree to tree, the uppermost one near the lopped top, the next about 3 ft. below, and so on. As the bamboos will need to be in place for 3 years or more they should be tied on to the tree with good, thick, lasting string or rope, not wire. The branches on the same plane as the bamboos are bent round and tied securely, not wired, on to these. Those branches to the back and front which cannot conveniently be bent and fastened on to the bamboo framework are cut away. As the trees grow the new shoots are interlaced and tied into place; any which project are pruned back.

Lime-trees may show a leaf-spot due to the fungus *Septoria Tiliae*, the spots being tawny with a pale centre, but usually not much harm is done. The leaves are often blackened by the growth of the fungus *Fumago vagans* which covers the surface of the leaves with its dark-brown threads by growing upon the honey-dew excreted by Aphides (*see* **Sooty Moulds**). *T.* × *europaea*, *T. cordata*, and *T. platyphyllos* suffer more from Aphid attacks than the trees recommended above for amenity planting.

The genus is a very difficult one botanically owing to the readiness with which the species hybridize; a large number of hybrids found in E. and Cent. Europe have been given specific names, mostly by Hungarian botanists. In addition to the species described below, *T. dasystyla* (syn. *T. begonifolia*, *T. caucasica*) of SE. Europe, the Caucasus, and Persia, *T. heterophylla*, *T. monticola*, and *T. neglecta* from N. America have been introduced into cultivation.

KEY

1.	*Lvs. glabrous beneath, except for tufts in vein-axils*	2
1.	*Lvs. hairy beneath*	8
2.	*Lvs. green, or slightly greyish beneath*	3
2.	*Lvs. glaucous beneath*	5
3.	*Lvs. 4 to 8 in. long, coarsely toothed*	T. americana
3.	*Lvs. 2 to 4 in. long*	4
4.	*Lvs. shining green above*	T. euchlora
4.	*Lvs. dull green above*	T. europaea
5.	*Lvs. 3-lobed, coarsely toothed*	T. mongolica
5.	*Lvs. not lobed*	6
6.	*Tufts of hair in vein-axils whitish*	T. insularis
6.	*Tufts of hair in vein-axils brownish*	7
7.	*Lvs. $1\frac{1}{2}$ to 3 in. long and wide, short-pointed*	T. cordata
7.	*Lvs. 2 to $3\frac{1}{2}$ in. long, roundish, abruptly pointed*	T. japonica
8.	*Lvs. densely hairy beneath, hairs simple*	T. platyphyllos
8.	*Hairs tufted or star-shaped*	9
9.	*L.-stalks (and shoots when young) hairy*	10
9.	*L.-stalks and shoots smooth*	17
10.	*Lvs. without vein-axil tufts*	T. Miqueliana
10.	*Lvs. with vein-axil tufts*	11
11.	*Lvs. with bristly teeth*	T. Henryana
11.	*Lvs. denticulate or serrate*	12
12.	*Lvs. grey- or silvery-felted beneath*	13
12.	*Brownish-felt on young branches and veins beneath*	16
13.	*Lvs. minutely toothed in upper part only, obliquely ovate*	T. Tuan
13.	*Lvs. serrate, roundish ovate*	14
14.	*Lvs. silvery beneath, dark green above; l.-stalk up to $1\frac{1}{2}$ in. long; branches erect*	T. tomentosa
14.	*Branches pendulous*	15
15.	*Lvs. silvery beneath; l.-stalk up to $2\frac{1}{2}$ in. long*	T. petiolaris
15.	*Lvs. grey-felted beneath, shining above; l.-stalk shorter*	T. × orbicularis
16.	*Lvs. finely toothed*	T. intonsa
16.	*Lvs. coarsely toothed*	T. Maximowicziana
17.	*Lvs. thinly greyish-hairy beneath*	T. × Moltkei
17.	*Lvs. thickly hairy beneath*	18
18.	*Lvs. silvery beneath with gland-tipped teeth*	T. Oliveri
18.	*Lvs. grey-white beneath, coarsely toothed*	T. Michauxii

T. al'ba. A synonym of *T. tomentosa*.

T. america'na. American lime. Tree up to 130 ft., shoots glabrous. *l.* 4 to 8 in. long, roundish-ovate, usually cordate at base, pointed, coarsely toothed, dark dull green above, pale bright green beneath, glabrous except for tufts of down in vein-axils beneath. *fl.* $\frac{3}{8}$ in. across, yellowish-white, in pendulous cymes of 6 to 15 (rarely seen with us). July. *fr.* not ribbed, roundish oval. N. America. 1752. (S.T.S. 1, 24.) SYN. *T. glabra*. Unsatisfactory tree in Britain. var. **pen'dula,** a synonym of *T. petiolaris*.

T. argen'tea. A synonym of *T. tomentosa*.

T. corda'ta. Small-leaved lime. Tree up to 80 or 100 ft., shoots nearly or quite glabrous. *l.* roundish-cordate, $1\frac{1}{2}$ to 3 in. long and wide; shortly pointed, sharply and finely toothed, dark green and glabrous above, rather glaucous and with red-brown axil-tufts beneath. *fl.* yellowish-white, fragrant, in pendent to erect cymes 2 to 3 in. long; floral bract $1\frac{1}{2}$ to $3\frac{1}{2}$ in. long. June, July. *fr.* globose, $\frac{1}{4}$ in. long, felted. Europe, the only British lime. (E.B. 287.) SYN. *T. microphylla*, *T. parvifolia*, *T. ulmifolia*, *T. europaea* (in part).

T. euchlo'ra.* Tree 40 to 60 ft., branches often rather pendulous, shoots glabrous. *l.* roundish-ovate, cordate, short-pointed, 2 to 4 in. long and wide, finely and regularly toothed, rich glossy green, glabrous except for vein-axil tufts beneath; stalk 1 to 2 in. long. *fl.* in cymes of 3 to 7, yellowish-white, fragrant. July. *fr.* ovoid, pointed, downy, $\frac{1}{4}$ to $\frac{1}{3}$ in. long. Of doubtful origin, probably a hybrid. 1860. A most attractive tree of neat habit, never infested with aphides, the foliage always clean and lustrous.

T. × **europ'aea.** Common Lime. Tree up to 100 ft., shoots glabrous. *l.* broadly ovate, $2\frac{1}{2}$ to 4 in. long, obliquely cordate, short-pointed, glabrous except for vein-axil tufts beneath. *fl.* yellowish-white, fragrant, in pendent cymes of 5 to 10; floral bracts 3 to 4 in. long, oval, faintly ribbed, downy, rarely or never fertile. Supposed to be a hybrid between *T. platyphyllos* and *T. cordata*. (E.B. 286.) SYN. *T. vulgaris*; *T. intermedia*. var. **corallin'a,** red-twigged Lime. Twigs reddish, tree of cleaner growth and free from sucker shoots on trunk.

T. glab'ra. A synonym of *T. americana*.

T. Henry'ana. Tree 30 to 50 ft., shoots downy at first. *l.* obliquely and broadly ovate, cordate, 2 to 5 in. long, $1\frac{1}{2}$ to 3 in. wide, the bristle-like teeth $\frac{1}{10}$ in. long; midrib and veins axil-tufted. *fl.* whitish, up to 20 or more in pendulous cymose clusters, 4 to 6 in. long; floral bracts stellately downy. July. *fr.* oval, 5-ribbed. China. 1901. Distinct by bristle-like teeth of the l.

T. insular'is. Tree 40 to 80 ft., trunk-girth 3 to 10 ft. *l.* roundish-ovate, sometimes approaching kidney-shape, cordate, coarsely toothed, 2 to $3\frac{1}{2}$ in. long, often more wide, with pale tufts of down in vein-axils beneath. *fl.* $\frac{1}{2}$ in. wide, numerous in cymes 3 to 4 in. across; floral bract 2 in. long, glabrous. *fr.* obovoid. Korea. 1919.

T. interme'dia. A synonym of *T. europaea*.

T. inton'sa. Tree up to 65 ft., with a trunk-girth of 9 ft., shoots densely clothed with yellowish-brown hairs. *l.* $1\frac{1}{2}$ to 4 in. long, roundish-cordate, abruptly pointed, evenly toothed, densely clothed beneath with starry down; veins in 7 to 9 pairs with axil-tufts beneath. *fl.* solitary or in threes, yellowish-white, floral bract narrowly oblong, downy. *fr.* $\frac{3}{8}$ in. long, 5-ribbed. China. 1903. SYN. *T. tonsura*. One of the most downy of limes.

T. japon'ica. Japanese Lime. Tree 60 to 70 ft., which appears to be the Japanese counterpart of *T. cordata*; shoots slightly downy. *l.* roundish, 2 to $3\frac{1}{2}$ in. long, cordate, abruptly pointed; axillary tufts on veins beneath. *fl.* sometimes up to 40 in pendulous cymose clusters. July. *fr.* not ribbed, roundish-oval, thin-shelled. Japan. 1886. SYN. *T. cordata japonica*.

T. Maximowiczia'na. Tree 70 to 100 ft., shoots downy. *l.* 3 to 6 in. long, roundish-ovate, cordate, short-pointed, coarsely toothed, stellately grey-down and with vein-axil tufts beneath. *fl.* 10 to 18 in. pendulous downy cymes; floral bracts 3 to 4 in. long. June. *fr.* $\frac{2}{5}$ in. long, ribbed, roundish. Japan. 1890. (G. and F. 6, 113 as *T. Miqueliana*).

T. Michaux'ii. Tree 70 to 80 ft., shoots glabrous. *l.* broadly ovate, 3 to 6 (sometimes 8) in. long, three-fourths as wide, obliquely cordate, coarsely and sharply toothed, stellately grey-downy beneath. *fl.* $\frac{1}{3}$ in. long, yellowish, in pendulous cymes of 9 to 20. July. *fr.* roundish, $\frac{1}{3}$ in. wide. N. America. 1800. SYN. *T. heterophylla Michauxii*. Succeeds better in Britain than *T. americana*.

T. microphyl'la. A synonym of *T. cordata*.

T. Miquelia'na. Tree 40 to 50 ft., shoots grey-felted. *l.* 2 to 5 in. long, $1\frac{1}{2}$ to $3\frac{1}{2}$ in. wide, broadly ovate, cordate, pointed, coarsely toothed, grey-felted beneath, without vein-axil tufts; stalk 1 to $1\frac{3}{4}$ in. long, felted. *fl.* yellowish, in pendulous cymose clusters of 10 to 20. June. *fr.* $\frac{3}{8}$ in. long, roundish oval, felted. Introduced from Japan in 1900 but not known in a wild state.

T. × **Moltk'ei** (*T. americana* × *T. petiolaris*). Vigorous tree with more or less pendulous branches. *l.* roundish ovate, 4 to 8 in. long, greyish downy beneath. *fl.* 5 to 8 in downy-stalked cymes. *fr.* sub-globose, faintly furrowed. Raised near Berlin about 1875. A lime of the same origin has been raised in the Arnold Arboretum, Mass.

T. mongo'lica. Mongolian lime. Tree 30 to 40 ft., of elegant shape, shoots glabrous, reddish. *l.* $1\frac{1}{2}$ to 3 in. long and wide, roundish, often 3-lobed, coarsely triangularly toothed, lobes and apex pointed, lustrous and glabrous above, with conspicuous vein-axil tufts beneath. *fl.* in cymes of 6 to 20 or even 30. July. *fr.* obovoid, downy thick-skinned. China, Mongolia. 1904. Distinct by its maple-like l. with jagged margins.

T. Oliver'i. Tree up to 50 ft., branches rather pendulous, shoots glabrous. *l.* 3 to 4 in. long, nearly as wide, roundish ovate, cordate, finely glandular-toothed, dark green and glabrous above, closely silver-felted and with no vein-axil tufts beneath; stalk 1 to 2 in. long. *fl.* small, in cymes of up to 20; floral bract stalkless. June. *fr.* globose, $\frac{1}{3}$ in. wide, warty, thick-shelled. China. 1900. (R.H. 1924, 189.) Differs from *T. tomentosa* by its glabrous shoots.

T. × **orbicular'is** (*T. euchlora* × *T. petiolaris*). Tree of conical shape with pendulous branches. *l.* very glossy green above, grey-felted beneath. The seed parent is *T. petiolaris* which it most resembles, but its habit is not so pendulous and the l. have shorter stalks and are grey rather than silvery-white beneath. Raised about 1870 near Metz.

T. parvifo'lia. A synonym of *T. cordata*.

T. petiola'ris.* Pendent silver lime. Round-topped, graceful tree 60 to 80 ft., branches pendulous, shoots downy. *l.* 2 to $4\frac{1}{2}$ in. long, not so wide, roundish-ovate, mostly obliquely cordate, slightly downy above, silvery-felted beneath; stalk up to $2\frac{1}{2}$ in. long. *fl.* whitish, fragrant, in cymes of 3 to 10; floral bract 2 to 3 in. long, narrowly obovate. July, August. *fr.* globose to orange-shaped, grooved, warted, $\frac{1}{3}$ in. wide. Of doubtful origin, probably SE. European. 1835 (about). (B.M. 6737.) SYN. *T. americana pendula*. Has been considered a variety of *T. tomentosa*, but the long l.-stalks. and pendulous habit are very distinct.

T. platyphyl'los. Tree 100 to 130 ft., shoots downy. *l.* roundish-ovate, 2 to 5 in. long and wide, obliquely cordate, short-pointed, sharply toothed, densely downy beneath, especially on veins. *fl.* yellow-white, 3 to (rarely) 6 in pendent cymes; floral bract 2 to 5 in. long, downy. June, July. *fr.* roundish to pear-shaped, $\frac{1}{3}$ to $\frac{1}{2}$ in. long, prominently 5-ribbed. Europe. SYN. *T. europaea* (in part), *T. grandifolia*. Differs from *T. cordata* and *T. vulgaris* by its downy shoots and l. var. **asplenifo'lia,** small tree with jaggedly lobed, smaller l. SYN. var. *filicifolia* and *laciniata*; **aurant'ia,** shoots orange-yellow; **obliq'ua,** *l.* more than usually oblique at base; **pyramid'alis,** of tall, more slender shape; **tortuo'sa,** shoots curiously curled and twisted; **vitifo'lia,** *l.* with several slender lobes ½ to 1 in. long.

T. tomento'sa.* White or Silver Lime. Tree 60 to 100 ft., broadly pyramidal, branches erect, stiff, shoots woolly. *l.* 2 to 4½ in. long and wide, roundish-cordate, shortly pointed, toothed, or even with small lobes, dark green above, silvery-white with close felt beneath; stalks ¾ to 1⅓ in. long. *fl.* dull white in pendent cymes of 7 to 10. July, August. *fr.* ⅓ to ½ in. long, ovoid, white, minutely warted, 5-angled. SE. Europe. 1767. SYN. *T. alba, T. argentea.*

T. tonsu'ra. A synonym of *T. intonsa.*

T. Tu'an. Tree 40 to 50 ft., shoots soon glabrous. *l.* 2⅓ to 5½ in. long, broadly and obliquely ovate, slender-pointed, distantly and minutely toothed in terminal half only; grey-felted beneath with tufts of hair in axils of chief veins. *fl.* yellowish-white, 15 to 20 in pendent, slender cymes 3 or 4 in. long. July. *fr.* roundish-oval ⅓ in. long. China. 1901.

T. ulmifo'lia. A synonym of *T. cordata.*

W. J. B.

TILIA'CEAE. Dicotyledons. A family of about 300 species in 35 genera of trees, shrubs, or herbs scattered over the tropical to temperate regions of the world. Leaves usually alternate, simple, stipulate. Flowers perfect, regular; sepals 5 (rarely 3 or 4), free or connate, valvate; petals as many, rarely absent; stamens 10 or more, filaments free or connate only at base, anthers 4-celled, opening by slits or pores; ovary 2- to 10-celled, superior. Fruit usually a capsule or indehiscent and nut-like or drupaceous. Several plants of this family yield articles of economic value, including timber, fibre (jute from Corchorus), bast, &c. Genera dealt with are Antholoma, Apeiba, Entelia, Glyphaea, Grewia, Heliocarpus, Honckenya, Luchea, Muntingia, Sparmannia, Tilia, Tricuspidaria.

tilia'ceus -a -um, like the lime-tree.

TILIACO'RA (Bengalese name). FAM. *Menispermaceae.* A genus of a single species of evergreen climbing shrub needing stove conditions and a compost of sandy loam and peat. Propagated by cuttings under glass in heat.

T. racemo'sa. Climber. *l.* ovate, 3 to 6 in. long, slender-pointed, acute, rounded or heart-shaped at base, glabrous, thin, margin undulate; stalk ½ to 1 in. long. *fl.* yellow in axillary panicles 6 to 12 in. long, hoary at first, at length glabrous; branches 1 in. long, males 3- to 7-fld., females simple, 1-fld. May. *fr.* a drupe, ½ in. long, obovoid, somewhat compressed, red, stalked. E. Indies. 1820.

tiliaefo'lius -a -um, with leaves like Tilia.

Tiling'ii, in honour of H. S. T. Tiling, *c.* 1869, of Nevada.

TILL. A synonym of Lentil. *See* **Lens.**

TILLAND'SIA (in honour of Elias Tillands, a Swedish botanist and Professor of Medicine in the University of Abo). FAM. *Bromeliaceae.* Nearly 400 species of usually stemless herbaceous plants of very various forms occupying a variety of habitats in Trop. and Sub-Trop. America. The genus is characterized in the family by a superior ovary, free petals without ligules, with branches of the inflorescence (when they occur) in 2 ranks, the last character distinguishing it from Catopsis. The scape has usually brightly coloured leaves, the foliage is usually scurfy and unarmed. Fruit a capsule. From Vriesia, Tillandsia is distinguished by the absence of ligules from the petals. Most of the species are epiphytic under natural conditions; but under cultivation it is best to treat the majority of them as pot-plants, the exceptions being such as *T. usneoides* (Old Man's Beard, which could not well be grown in a pot, and, as it makes no roots, does not require soil), *T. bulbosa, T. Gardneri,* and *T. ixioides.* These should be fastened on to blocks of cork or soft wood, and a little sphagnum placed about them to root in. The small, grassy-leaved kinds, of which *T. angustifolia* and *T. virginalis* are examples, may be grown in peat and sphagnum. All the species delight in abundant sunlight, a high temperature during summer, plenty of water (though the soil must not be kept saturated), and syringing overhead twice a day. In winter they should be kept from getting quite dry but need not be syringed. Propagation is effected by seeds and suckers, chiefly by the latter. They should be allowed to grow large before being detached from the parent, and inserted singly in pots just large enough to hold the sucker, using a compost of loam, peat, and leaf-mould. The suckers must not be confined in a close frame for propagating, but kept moderately moist and well shaded. Spring is the best season for detaching them.

Many plants grouped in gardens under Tillandsia belong to Vriesia and should be sought there. A revision of the genus by Carl Mez will be found in Engler's *Das Pflanzenreich,* iv. 32 (Heft 100), 436–598 (1934–5).

A very large number of hybrids have been raised in continental gardens and many of them have been figured in *Gartenflora* and *Revue Horticole* and to a less extent in *Illustration Horticole.*

KEY TO SECTIONS OF THE GENUS

1. *Stamens longer than pet.*	2
1. *Stamens shorter than pet.*	4
2. *Infl. paniculate, or if simple, distichous*	3
2. *Infl. simple, fl. pointing in various directions or reduced to one fl.*	III. PITYROPHYLLUM
3. *Pet. lorate, sub-patent at flowering time, afterwards depended; anthers versatile*	I. PSEUDALCANTAREA
3. *Pet. erect, tubular connivent; stamens erect, anthers erect*	II. PLATYSTACHYS
4. *Sep. free, distinctly asymmetric; fl. all inconspicuous*	IV. PSEUDOCATOPSIS
4. *Sep. generally more or less high and unequally connate, symmetrical, or slightly asymmetric*	5
5. *Style always elongated, longer than, or equalling stamens; infl. if simple, distichous*	6
5. *Style short, not exceeding stamens, or infl. simple and not distichous*	7
6. *Stamens from throat of cor. or emergent*	V. ALLARDTIA
6. *Stamens deeply included, not emergent or exserted*	VI. AEROBIA
7. *Stamens slightly emergent from cor. mouth; infl. if simple, not distichous*	VII. ANOPLOPHYTUM
7. *Stamens deeply included*	8
8. *Lamina of pet. wide, usually obovate or sub-orbicular, conspicuous*	VIII. PHYTARRHIZA
8. *Lamina of pet. narrow, elliptic-lanceolate, or lanceolate, small; fls. minute, not decorative*	IX. DRAPHROANTHEMA

The section to which each species mentioned below belongs is indicated by a roman numeral in parentheses after the name.

T. acau'lis. A synonym of *Cryptanthus acaulis.*

T. aloifo'lia (II). 1½ to 3 ft. h. *l.* in a utricular rosette, linear, acuminate, recurved, pale-lepidote above, transversely zoned beneath; sep. 1 in. long; pet. 2 in. long, white or rose. *infl.* few-fld., simple or with a few spreading branches, axis undulate, bracts rosy, oblong-lanceolate, 2-ranked; scape slender, erect, longer than l. W. Indies, Florida, Guiana, &c. 1790. (H.E.F. 205; B.R. 749 as *T. flexuosa.*)

T. an'cepa (VIII). 1 ft. h. *l.* narrow-linear, acuminate, 6 in. long, ⅓ in. wide, with red stripes at base. *fl.* bluish-mauve, about 1½ in. long; bracts greenish-yellow, boat-shaped, bluntly mucronate; spike 10- to 20-fld., oblong, solitary; scape nearly 1 ft. long. June. Trinidad, Colombia, &c. 1824. (L.B.C. 771; B.H. 1879, 368 as *Phytarrhiza anceps.*)

T. angustifo'lia. A synonym of *T. polystachya.*

T. arequi'tae (VIII). Related to *T. xiphioides* but *fl.* white; scape longer. Uruguay. 1893. (R.H. 1893, 156 as *T. xiphioides arequitae.*)

T. argen'tea. A synonym of *T. Gardneri* and *T. tectorum.*

T. Balbisia'na (II). 1 to 1½ ft. h. *l.* in a utricular rosette, linear-lanceolate, 16 in. long, ⅚ in. wide, convolute, recurved, grey-lepidote; sep. ⅔ in. long; pet. violet, tipped white, erect, convolute, 1¾ in. long; bracts green, red, and yellow, 2-ranked, overlapping, oblong-lanceolate, keeled, acuminate, ¾ in. long; spike compound, compressed; side spikes 3 to 8, 2 to 3 in. long, appressed, alternate. W. Indies, &c. 1874. (B.H. 1879, 98.)

T. bivitta'ta. A synonym of *Cryptanthus bivittatus.*

T. Blok'ii. A synonym of *Vriesia Blokii.*

T. brachycaul'os* (II). 6 in. h. *l.* in a utricular rosette, linear, channelled, about 9 in. long, ⅔ in. wide, recurved, red above, greyish-green beneath, slightly scurfy. *fl.* purple, about 12 in a sessile head. Mexico. 1878. (B.H. 1878, 185.)

T. bryoi'des. A synonym of *T. tricholepis.*

T. bulbo'sa (II). 8 to 12 in. h. *l.* convolute-filiform, greenish, minutely scaly; basal sheath of rosette-l. forming a bulb; flexuous, up to 12 in. long; uppermost longer than spikes; pet. violet, tipped white, 1¼ in. long, apex recurved, convolute spatulate-linear; bracts ⅝ in. long, 2-ranked, overlapping; spikes 5 to 8, about equal, close together, spreading, 2 to 3 in. long; scape erect. November. W. Indies. 1823. (H.E.F. 173; P.F.G. 160 as *T. eminens*; B.M. 4288 as *T. bulbosa picta* (*T. erythraea* of Lindley), bracts scarlet.) Variable. var. **variega'ta,** *l.* variegated.

T. But'zii (II). 1 ft. h. *l.* few in a rosette; base large, dilated, tightly clasping, variegated green and brown; blade setaceous, flexuose, 1 ft. long; pet. lilac, convolute in a tube about 1⅝ in. long; spikes about 3, crowded, dense, 2-ranked, 1½ to 2 in. long; bracts greenish, 1 in. long; scape 3 to 4 in. long. Mexico. 1880. Syn. *T. variegata.*

T. caespito'sa (II). Stemless, about 1 ft. h. *l.* lanceolate from an ovate-base 2 in. wide, blade 1 ft. long, 1 in. wide, tinged purple towards base; sep. 1¼ in. long; pet. violet, 3 in. long; spike dense, simple, 5 to 6 in. long; bracts pink, 1½ to 2 in. long; scape much shorter than l. Mexico. 1883. Syn. *T. Schlechtendahlii, Vriesia caespitosa.*

T. Caput-Medu'sae (II), 8 in. h. *l.* tumid at base, forming a bulb, lanceolate, thick, channelled, spreading, arched, undulate, unequal, shining, silky-grey, up to 8 in. long, ⅝ in. wide. *fl.* erect, 1⅝ in. long; pet. pale blue, erect, tubular; spikes generally 4 in a compound panicle, each 10- to 20-fld., linear-flexuose; scape short, erect, clothed with long bracts. Mexico, &c. 1880.

T. carina'ta. A synonym of *Vriesia carinata* and *V. erythrodactylon.*

T. circina'lis. A synonym of *T. Daratii.*

T. coarcta'ta. *See* **T. tricholepis.**

T. complana'ta. A synonym of *T. tricolor.*

T. compres'sa (II). *l.* in a dense rosette, ensiform, acuminate, ovate at base, 1½ in. wide; blade 1 to 1½ ft. long, convolute in upper half, rigid; pet. white, erect, tubular, shorter than stamens; spike dense, simple, 6 to 8 in. long; bracts reddish-yellow, ovate, keeled, 2 in. long; scape 6 in. long. June. Jamaica, &c. 1863. (B.M. 3275 as *T. setacea.*)

T. corallin'a. A synonym of *Vriesia platynema.*

T. croca'ta (VIII). Stem wavy, branched. *l.* 2-ranked, linear-awl-shaped, 8 in. long, ⅛ in. thick, recurved, silky white-hairy. *fl.* saffron-yellow, about 5; spike short, elliptic, 2-ranked; scape long, slender, hairy, nearly leafless. S. Brazil. 1880. Syn. *Phytarrhiza crocata.*

T. cya'nea (V). 2½ ft. h. *l.* in a rosette, strap-shaped, entire, about 16 in. long, 1 in. wide. *fl.* blue, in a many-fld., branching, pyramidal panicle 15 in. long. Guatemala. 1852. Syn. *Allardtia cyanea, Platystachys cyanea.*

T. cyanes'cens (VII). Differs from *T. pulchella* by its blue pet.; stem long. Brazil. (B.H. 1883, 265 as *Anoplophytum amoenum.*)

T. dianthoi'dea (VII). 9 in. h. Stem 3 to 5 in. long, simple, ascending, nearly terete. *l.* amplexicaul, outer recurved, inner erect or inflexed, leathery, rigid, 3-angled near apex, acute, entire, silky-glaucous; pet. blue, spreading or reflexed; bracts purplish-rose, ovate-lanceolate, acute, persistent; spike 5- to 20-fld., not 2-ranked. Uruguay. 1810. (R.H. 1905, 464; B.R. 1338 as *T. stricta.*)

T. didisticha (VII). 1 ft. h. *l.* in a rosette, thick, robust, lanceolate, channelled, acuminate, grey. *fl.* white in crowded, elliptic spikes, forming a 2-ranked panicle; scape long, arching, clothed with bracts, scaly on back. Argentine, Bolivia. 1881. Syn. *Anoplophytum didistichum.*

T. distach'ya (II). 1 ft. h. *l.* 12 to 15 in a sessile rosette, lanceolate, acuminate, about 1 ft. long, 1 in. wide at base, ½ in. on blade, pale green, concave, glabrous in upper part, scaly in lower above, thinly scaly beneath; sep. ¾ in. long, free to base; pet. white, over 1½ in. long, oblanceolate, long-clawed; bracts green, oblong-lanceolate, about 1 in. long; spikes 2, 2-ranked, 6- to 12-fld.; scape erect, 6 in. long, hidden by linear, falcate l. British Honduras. 1879.

T. Duge'sii (II). *l.* in a dense rosette, up to 2½ ft. long, rigid, ensiform-setaceous from an ovate base, thinly scaly; pet. deep purple, longer than sep.; infl. few-fld., about as long as l.; scape closely sheathed by bracts with glossy crimson bases. Mexico. 1897.

T. Dura'tii (VIII). About 1 ft. h. *l.* 12 to 20, spreading, 6 to 9 in. long, tapering to a thick, awl-shaped, channelled, more or less circinate tip, densely silvery-scaly. *fl.* violet in a compact panicle 3 to 4 in. long, of several dense, few-fld. spikes; scape 6 in. long. Uruguay. (R.H. 1895, 184.)

T. em'inens. A synonym of *T. bulbosa.*

T. erubes'cens (III). Tufted, generally stemless, 3 to 4 in. h. *l.* numerous, closely overlapping, 2 to 2½ in. long, recurved, subulate-lanceolate, very leathery, concave above, ciliate, almost spiny at tip; upper more erect, bright rose, finally green. *fl.* violet, about 2½ in. long; infl. about 5-fld. sessile in l.-rosette; bracts lanceolate, as long as sep. (B.M. 5892 and F.d.S. 1006 as *T. ionantha.*)

T. erythrae'a. *See* **T. bulbosa.**

T. filifo'lia (II).* Dwarf, densely tufted, about 8 in. h. *l.* many, subulate, filiform, spreading green, 8 to 10 in. long, $\frac{1}{12}$ in. or less wide. *fl.* pale blue, small, 2-ranked; pet. reflexed; infl. resembling a species of Limonium, forming a panicle with lax, drooping branches. Mexico. 1871. (B.H. 1871, 177 as *T. staticifolia.*)

T. flexuo'sa. A synonym of *T. aloifolia* and *T. utriculata.*

T. Fuerstenberg'ii. A synonym of *Streptocalyx Fuerstenbergii.*

T. Gard'neri (VII). 5 in. h. *l.* 6 to 8 in. long, flat and ½ in. wide in lower part, narrowed to a reflexed, subulate, convolute point, silver-scaled; inner l. erect; pet. rose, small; spikes 4 to 8, short, 2-ranked, crowded; bracts scaly; scape 2 to 4 in. h., densely sheathed with linear-subulate, scaly l. Trinidad, Brazil. 1879. (B.H. 1881, 209 as *Anoplophytum incanum.*)

T. Geissii (VIII). 6 to 8 in. h. *l.* about 9 in. long, ⅜ in. wide, suberect, linear-subulate, channelled, silvery. *fl.* rose, in a simple spike up to 10-fld.; bracts green at base, carmine above. Chile. 1889. (G.F. 1889, 369.)

T. geminiflo'ra (VII). About 6 in. h. Stemless. *l.* ovate-lanceolate, channelled, acuminate, outer spreading-recurved. *fl.* madder; sep. shorter than pet.; pet. reflexed; bracts red, lanceolate, mucronate, exceeding sep.; spike oblong, sub-compound; scape erect, clothed with red, green-tipped, acuminate sheaths. February. S. Brazil, Argentine. 1840. (B.H. 1880, 191 as *Anoplophytum geminiflorum*; B.R. 28, 63 as *T. rubida.*) var. **inca'na,** *l.* very thick, bracts hoary.

T. gladioliflo'ra. A synonym of *Vriesia gladioliflora.*

T. glaucophyl'la (II). 3 ft. h. *l.* overlapping a slightly tumid base, spreading, recurved, 1 to 1½ ft. long, gradually tapered to a slender point, rigid, somewhat farinose or flocculose; sep. greenish-white; pet. purple, almost white at tip, convolute, erect; filaments banded with purple; lower bracts red, others green, tinged yellow and red; spikes 4 to 9, up to 1 ft. long; scape red, 1 ft. or more long. August. Colombia. 1847. (B.M. 4415; F.d.S. 432 as *Vriesia glaucophylla.*)

T. Glazov'ii. A synonym of *Vriesia procera gracilis.*

T. gra'cilis. A synonym of *Vriesia procera gracilis.*

T. Hamalea'na (VI). About 1 ft. h. Stemless. *l.* many in a rosette, lower arching, upper erect, 1 ft. long, 1½ in. wide, lingulate, concave, uncinate-revolute at tip, unarmed, not scaly. *fl.* sessile, 2-ranked, fragrant; sep. green, ovate-lanceolate; pet. violet, snow-white at base, rhomboid-dilated, spreading-deflexed, obcordate; bracts green and purplish, scaly, conduplicate; spike compound, branches 2-ranked; scape erect, longer than l., with remote, reddish bracts. Ecuador. 1870. (B.A. 1870, 97 as *Wallisia Hamaleana.*) *See* **T. umbellata.**

T. heliconioi'des. A synonym of *Vriesia disticha.*

T. ina'nis. A synonym of *T. bulbosa.*

T. infla'ta. A synonym of *Vriesia incurvata inflata.*

T. ionan'tha. A synonym of *T. erubescens.*

T. ixioi'des (VIII). 6 in. h. *l.* overlapping, linear, 4 in. long, ⅜ in. wide, acuminate, slightly dilated at base, midrib silvery-scaly at back. *fl.* 3 to 7 in a spike, somewhat 2-ranked; sep. hyaline, shorter than pet.; pet. orange; anthers included. Uruguay. var. **occidenta'lis,** 1 ft. h., *l.* longer. Argentine.

T. jun'cea (II). 8 to 18 in. h. *l.* many, clustered, awl-shaped, base brownish-scaly; green above, about 1 ft. long, rigid. *fl.* 1⅜ in. long; pet. bluish-purple, spatulate, twice as long as sep., spreading; bracts scaly, 2-ranked, overlapping, ovate-oblong, pointed, as long as sep.; spike 2 to 3 in. long, compressed, simple or with a few short branches at base, scape shorter than l. Florida, W. Indies to Brazil. 1825. (G.F. 1874, 321.)

T. juncifo'lia. A synonym of *T. juncea.*

T. Karwinskya'na (II). *l.* 20 to 30 in a dense rosette, 1 ft. long, narrowed from a broad base 1 in. wide to a long point, pale green, scaly on back, nearly or quite naked above; pet. lilac, about 1⅝ in. long, twice as long as glossy green sep.; infl. a simple lax, narrow, 2-ranked spike up to 6 in. long; scape 9 to 12 in. long; bracts membranous at margin. Winter. Mexico. 1878.

T. Kra'meri. A synonym of *Vriesia psittacina rubrobracteata.*

T. Leiboldia'na (V). 1 ft. h. *l.* in a dense rosette, ensiform, acuminate, 1 to 1½ ft. long, ¾ to 1 in. wide, not very rigid. *fl.* in a simple, dense spike, 1½ to 2 in. long; pet. lilac, convolute in a tube 1 in. long; bracts bright red, ¾ to 1 in. long; scape erect, much shorter than l. Mexico. 1883. (R.H. 1894, 378.)

T. Lin'deni. A synonym of *T. Lindeniana.*

T. Lindenia'na (VI).* About 2½ ft. h. Stemless. *l.* many in a rosette, arching, about 15 in. long, ½ in. wide, with a dilated more or less purple and lined base and a long narrow point. *fl.* deep blue, throat spotted white; pet. spreading; sep. green, tipped red, half as long as pet.; stamens included; infl. a simple spike about 20-fld.; bracts overlapping, green below, exposed part carmine, keeled; scape erect, about as long as l. Peru. 1867. (G.F. 1869, 193 and R.H. 1872, 230 as *T. Lindeni.*) Many plants have been described as varieties of this variable and showy species, e.g. **luxu'rians,** with several scapes. (B.H. 1871, 289.); **ma'jor,** *fl.* much larger than in type. (F.M. n.s. 529.); **Regelia'na,** bracts green, spike narrow, scape longer. Some others are now referred to *T. Morreniana.*

T. Lorentzia'na (VII). Related to *T. didisticha* but bracts glabrous at back. (G.F. 1891, 313.)

T. microxiph'ion (VII). 1½ ft. h. Stem short, erect, densely leafy. *l.* linear, rigid, pale green, scaly, about 1 in. long, deeply channelled above, rounded at back. *fl.* few, in a dense, terminal spike; bracts pink; pet. violet-purple, lingulate, spreading at tip. February. Paraguay. 1890. (B.M. 7320.)

T. monadel'pha (II). *l.* many, broad and green at base, arching, lanceolate, 8 in. long, ⅜ in. wide, acute, purple on both sides. *fl.* about 20, whitish, tinged rose, rather distant, almost sessile; pet. spreading; filaments united half-way; bracts green, tinged yellow, shining; spike simple, loose, rachis distinctly downy, green; scape erect, longer than l. Trinidad, Guiana. 1882. (B.H. 1882, 168 as *Phytarrhiza monadelpha.*)

T. Morelia'na. A synonym of *Billbergia vittata.*

T. Morrenian'a (VI). Nearly related to *T. Lindeniana* but *fl.* blue without white in throat; scape shorter. (B.H. 1869, 321; F.M. 1872, 44 as *T. Lindeni*; I.H. 1869, 610 as *Vriesia Lindeni.*) Here belongs also *T. Lindeni tricolor* and *T. Lindeni superba rosea.*

T. niti'da. A synonym of *Catopsis nitida.*

T. oligan'tha. A synonym of *Vriesia rubida.*

T. pic'ta. A synonym of *T. splendens.*

T. polystach'ya (II). 1½ to 2 ft. h. *l.* linear-subulate, acuminate, entire, channelled, broad and ventricose at base, 1 ft. long, 1 in. wide, pale green. *fl.* sessile, 1¼ in. long; cal. 2-partite; pet. blue rarely white, linear, channelled, acuminate; bracts scarlet, overlapping above; spikes many, lateral ones about 10, 1 ft. long, alternate. June. W. Indies. 1822. SYN. *T. angustifolia.*

T. polytrichoi'des. A synonym of *T. tricholepis.*

T. pruino'sa (II). 4 to 6 in. h., covered with spreading white scales. *l.* convolute filiform from a dilated base, recurved, as long as stem; pet. violet, tubular, erect; bracts rose, 1 in. long, 2-ranked, approximate, or ovate-oblong, pointed; spike simple, 2 to 3 in. long; scape none. W. Indies, Brazil. (B.H. 1876, 257.)

T. pulchel'la (VII).* Tufted, usually with a stem. *l.* 4 to 6 in. long, awl-shaped, hoary with minute scurfy hair, channelled especially towards base; cal. greenish-white; pet. white; bracts delicate red, overlapping, sheathing, almost hiding fl.; scape and spike about as long as l. Trinidad, Brazil. 1840. (B.M. 5229.) var. **amoe'na,** a synonym of *T. cyanescens*; **pityphyl'la** stem about 1 ft. long, scape shorter than in type, *l.* squarrose. W. Indies, Brazil; **surinamen'sis,** almost stemless, *l.* wider and infl. shorter than in type. Guiana, Brazil.

T. pul'chra. A synonym of *T. pulchella.*

T. pu'mila. A form of *T. bulbosa.*

T. punctula'ta (II). 1 ft. h. *l.* 30 to 40 in a dense rosette, base ovate, blade 6 to 9 in. long, deeply channelled at base. *fl.* lilac; pet. tipped white, convolute in a tube 1 in. longer than cal.; spike dense, simple, or branched, 3 to 4 in. long; lower bracts bright red; scape 6 in. long. Mexico. 1877. (B.H. 1879, 162 as *T. tricolor.*)

T. recurva'ta (IX). About 6 in. h. Stems short, tufted. *l.* 2 to 6 in. long, filiform, recurved, scaly. *fl.* blue; pet. naked within, spreading above the shorter cal.; peduncles axillary or terminal, 1- to 5-fld.; spike included in a sheathing bract, each fl. by a smaller bract, upper somewhat distant. Trop. and Sub-Trop. America. 1793.

T. recurvifo'lia (VII). 6 in. h. Stemless. *l.* 4 in. long, ⅜ in. wide, narrowed to a long point, rigid, grey-scurfy. *fl.* white; pet. spreading; spike 10- to 30-fld., not 2-ranked, about 2 in. long; scape about 3½ in. long; bracts rose-pink. Brazil. 1861. (B.M. 5246; B.R. 1357 as *T. rosea.*)

T. Roez'lii (V). Robust. *l.* linear, 16 in. long, 1½ in. wide, acute, dark green, with large black blotches on upper part, margins incurved. *fl.* rose; spikes 2-ranked, elliptical, in a panicle about 6 in. h. Peru. 1877. (B.H. 1877, 272.)

T. ro'sea. A synonym of *T. recurvifolia.*

T. ru'bida. A synonym of *T. geminiflora.*

T. Schlechtendahl'ii. A synonym of *T. caespitosa.*

T. seri'cea. A synonym of *T. xiphioides.*

T. seta'cea. A synonym of *T. compressa* and *T. juncea.*

T. staticifo'lia. A synonym of *T. filifolia.*

T. streptophyl'la (II). *l.* in a dense basal rosette, base dilated, 3 in. long and wide; blade 6 to 9 in. long, 1 in. wide gradually tapering to a long point, spirally twisted in lower part, densely scaly. *fl.* bright lilac; pet. tubular, 1½ in. long; bracts densely scaly, overlapping; spikes 4 to 8 in a short panicle; scape short, hidden by numerous red-tinted, scaly, overlapping bracts. Jamaica. 1878. (B.M. 6757.)

T. stric'ta (VII). 8 in. h., sometimes caulescent. *l.* about 6 in. long, from a short fleshy rootstock, ⅓ in. wide at base, hoary. *fl.* narrow-cylindrical, about ¾ in. long; cal. pale reddish-brown; cor. deep violet-blue, finally deep red; bracts red-tinged, slightly pellucid; scape short. November. Brazil. 1810. (B.M. 1529; B.H. 1878, 188 and I.H. 1878, 330 as *Anoplophytum strictum.*) *T. stricta* of Lindley is *T. dianthoidea.*

T. tecto'rum (II). Stem long, ascending, leafy. *l.* very many, overlapping, lanceolate-linear, 8 in. long, ⅛ in. wide, spreading, arched, scarious, hairy; sheath very broad, gradually narrowed to blade; sep. free, lanceolate, above, ⅝ long, conduplicate; pet. white, blue in middle, 1 in. long, convolute, tube broadening towards top; bracts light green, tinged rose, lanceolate, conduplicate, rather shorter than sep.; spikes 2-ranked, short, in a short close panicle; scape erect, tall bracts rose at base. Peru. 1865. (B.H. 1877, 328.) SYN. *T. argentea, Pourretia nivosa.*

T. trichole'pis (IX). Moss-like, rarely 5 in. h. *l.* finely awl-shaped, about ½ in. long, densely pruinose. *fl.* greenish-yellow; sep. $\frac{1}{20}$ in. long, pellucid; pet. ⅓ in. long, sub-erect; infl. 2- to 4-fld., simple, 2-ranked, up to ¾ in. long, usually less; scape erect, slender; bracts lanceolate. Brazil, Bolivia, &c. 1880. SYN. *T. bryoides. T. coarctata* is similar in habit but the fl. is solitary.

T. tric'olor (II). *l.* in a rosette, 9 to 12 in. long, from a broad, convex base gradually tapering to a subulate point, entire, dark glaucous-green; lower purplish at base. *fl.* deep rich purple, 3 in. long, opening one at a time; bracts green, becoming tinged bright yellow and bright red towards base, closely placed, sharply boat-shaped; spike flattened, solitary, 3 in. long, ¾ in. wide; scape slender, erect, longer than l. August. Mexico. 1861. (G.F. 1884, 292, and B.M. 5287 as *Vriesia xyphiostachys*; B.H. 1872, 300 as *T. complanata.*) SYN. *T. xiphostachys.*

T. umbella'ta (VI). 1 ft. h. *l.* 9 to 12 in. h., ½ in. wide, linear, light green, shortly sheathing at base, ascending, spreading, acute, glabrous, glossy. *fl.* sapphire, white in centre, 5 or 6 opening simultaneously; cal. green; bracts light green, as large as sep.; infl. a very short flattened spike, scape shorter than l. Ecuador. 1882. (R.H. 1886, 60.) Near *T. Hameleana,* and sometimes regarded as a variety of it.

T. usneoi'des (IX). Long Moss, Old Man's Beard, Spanish Moss. Epiphytic, forming loose, pendulous tufts, sometimes many feet long, covered with spreading, silvery scurf. *l.* alternate, 2-farious, uniform throughout, spreading, 1 to 3 in. long, filiform, grooved above; sheaths ½ to 2 in. long, cylindric. *fl.* yellowish-green, solitary, terminal, about ½ in. long; sep. tinged red. July. Trop. America. 1877. (B.H. 1877, 313; B.M. 6309.)

T. utricula'ta (II). *l.* in a utricular rosette, linear, about 2 ft. long, 2 in. wide, acuminate, gradually tapering from an ovate base, spreading, top recurved; sep. green, margined red, half as long as cor.; pet. greenish-white, spreading at tips; bracts green, margined red, 2-ranked, erect, oblong, blunt; longer than internodes; spike compound, branches long, distant. Florida, W. Indies. 1793.

T. variega'ta. A synonym of *T. Butzii.*

T. vesti'ta (II). 6 in. h. Caulescent. *l.* linear-subulate, 6 in. long, densely scaly. *fl.* yellow; cor. a long, cylindrical tube, exserted about 1 in. from red cal.; spike simple, few-fld.; scape slender, erect, shorter than l. May. Mexico. 1886.

T. vimina'lis. A synonym of *Vriesia viridiflora.*

T. virgina'lis (V). 3 ft. h. *l.* many in a lax rosette, outer filiform, others lorate with a broad sheath, 1 ft. long, 2 in. wide, pale green, pruinose. *fl.* sessile; sep. green, included; cor. club-shaped, 3½ in. long; pet. white, obovate; bracts green, conduplicate large pruinose; spike simple, 2-ranked, elliptical, 8- to 24-fld.; scape erect as long as l. Mexico. 1873.

T. viridiflo'ra (I). *l.* 12 or more in a utricular rosette, 1 ft. long, 1½ in. wide, lorate; pet. green, 3½ in. long, fugacious; spike simple, dense, 12 in. long; bracts 2 to 2½ in. long; scape 1½ to 2 ft. long. Summer. Mexico. 1887. *T. viridiflora* of gardens is a synonym of *Vriesia viminalis.*

T. vitta'ta. A synonym of *Cryptanthus bivittatus.*

T. Warm'ingii. A synonym of *Vriesia ensiformis.*

T. xiphioi'des (VIII).* 8 in. h. covered with silver-grey tomentum, deliciously scented. *l.* crowded in a rosette, 4 to 8 in. long, ⅛ in. wide, broadly subulate, tip involute, margins recurved. *fl.* snow-white, fragrant; sep. linear-lanceolate, acuminate; pet. 3½ in. long, claw slender, linear, blade broadly obovate, acuminate, reflexed, crisped; bracts 2 in. long, closely overlapping; spike about 6-fld., 3 to 4 in. long, reflexed, 2-ranked; scape short. May. (B.M. 5562.) var. **arequi'tae,** a synonym of *T. arequitae.*

T. xiphostach'ys. A synonym of *T. tricolor.*

T. zona'ta. A synonym of *Cryptanthus zonatus.*

TIMO'NIUS (from the Malayan name). FAM. *Rubiaceae.* A genus of about 35 species of dioecious shrubs or small trees, natives of Trop. America. Leaves opposite, leathery, glabrous or silky evergreen; stipules interpetiolar, deciduous. Flowers creamy-white or yellow, in axillary cymes, fragrant; pistillate flowers solitary or in threes on a peduncle, corolla tube usually larger than in staminate flowers, with sterile anthers in lower half; staminate flowers many in a stalked cluster; corolla 4- or 5-lobed; anthers of staminate flowers scarcely exserted. Fruit a round or oblong berry often bluntly 4-angled; seeds many, small, woody, oblong. Stove conditions are needed and a well-drained compost of turfy loam with some dry cow-manure, leaf-soil, and sand. Abundant water is needed throughout the growing season, but drier conditions during rest. Half-ripe shoots can be rooted in sand under a glass with bottom heat.

T. compressicau'lis. Up to 12 ft. h. but flowering at 3 ft. *l.* obovate, blunt or almost so, yellowish-green with midrib pale yellow; stalk short; stipules ¼ to ½ in. long, hairy. *fl.* creamy-white; staminate fl. in a loose cluster, 4 in. across; cor. tube 3 in. long, lobes 4 or 5; pistillate fl. solitary or in pairs on ½ to 1 in. pedicels, smaller, cor. tube 1 to 2 in. long, lobes 6 or 7. *fr.* a round berry. Sumatra, Malaya.

T. flaves'cens. Tree to 40 ft. *l.* with veins purple or blackish. *fl.* yellow; staminate in clusters of 4 to 7; cor. tube 3 to 4 in. long, ¼ in. wide; pistillate solitary, stouter, ⅓ in. wide. *fr.* 4 in. long and wide. W. Malaya. SYN. *T. peduncularis.*

T. Jambosel'la. 6 to 8 ft. h. Very variable, perhaps a form of *T. flavescens.* *l.* elliptic to lanceolate, 3 to 6 in. long, silky on veins beneath. *fl.* white or pale yellow; staminate in 3- to 12-fld. cymes, sessile, peduncle long or short; pistillate solitary on long peduncles. *fr.* globose, ¼ to ½ in. long, rarely oblong, ribbed. Malaya. 1810. SYN. *T. Koenigii, Nelitris Jambosella.*

F. G. P.

timora'nus -a -um, of the island of Timor.

TIMOTHY-GRASS. Phleum pratense. A valuable fodder grass.

TINAN'TIA (in honour of François A. Tinant, 1803–58, of Luxemburg). FAM. *Commelinaceae.* A genus of 3 species of erect herbs, natives of Trop. America, closely related to Tradescantia. Leaves of moderate size or large. Flowers on pedicels from the sides of branches forming a terminal pedunculate cyme. *T. erecta* is a half-hardy perennial and will grow in well-drained loam. Seeds may be sown in a warm, sunny spot in the open ground in spring, or in heat, the seedlings being hardened off before planting out, or may be grown in the greenhouse.

T. erec'ta. Glabrous perennial, 18 in. h. *l.* ovate-lanceolate, hairy above, glabrous beneath, narrowed at base, longitudinally striate; stalk short. *fl.* blue or purplish; pedicels bracteolate at base; peduncle hairy, 1- to 3-parted at apex, branches umbellate. July. 1794. (B.M. 1340 as *Tradescantia erecta*; L.B.C. 1300 as *T. latifolia*; B.R. 1403 as *T. undata.*) SYN. *T. fugax.*

A→

tincto'rius -a -um, of the dyers, applied to plants used at some time in dyeing.

tinc'tus -a -um, coloured.

TINEI'NA. A Superfamily of the *Lepidoptera*, including over 700 British species of small Moths, whose wings are narrow and bordered with long hair fringes. The habits of the caterpillars are diverse, some being leaf-miners (Apple, Azalea and Lilac Leaf-miners), some living in portable cases (*Coleophora* or Case-bearers), some feeding on a variety of stored products (Grain Moths), some forming silken webs (Ermine Moth Tent Caterpillars), some being cosmopolitan and important pests of vegetables (Diamond-back Moth), some domestic pests by attacking carpets, clothing, feathers, furs, wool and hair (Clothes Moths), while the Yucca Moth is closely associated with *Yucca filamentosa* by its habit of pollinating the flowers and ensuring the development of the ovules to provide food for its larvae.

G. F. W.

tin'gens, dyed.

tingita'nus -a -um, of the Roman province Tingitana, now Tangier, N. Africa, taking its name from the ancient city Tingis or Tingi.

tinifo'lius -a -um, with leaves as in *Viburnum Tinus.*

TIN'NEA (in memory of the scientific expedition up the Nile in 1863 by three Dutch ladies, Mme Henriette L. M. Tinne, her daughter, and her sister). FAM. *Labiatae.* A genus of 26 species of tall, hairy, or woolly herbs or undershrubs, natives mostly of Trop. Africa but with 5 species, e.g. *T. Galpinii* (F.P.S.A. 517), in sub-tropical S. Africa. Leaves entire, upper small bracts. Flowers smoky- or violet-purple, fragrant; calyx ovoid, 2-lipped; corolla tube short and broad, limb somewhat 2-lipped, upper lip emarginate or 2-lobed, lower much longer, spreading; stamens 4; whorls often loose, 2-flowered, forming a terminal raceme. *T. aethiopica* needs stove conditions and will grow well in a light, rich compost. It should be grown in a light, airy position and pinched frequently to induce a bushy habit. Cuttings root readily. A monograph of the genus by W. Robyns and J. Lebrun has been published in *Bulletin du Jardin Botanique, Bruxelles,* 8. 161–207 (1931).

T. aethio'pica. Hoary sub-shrub, 4 to 6 ft. h. Stems and branches erect, terete, ribbed, twiggy. *l.* ovate, narrowed to the slender stalks, entire, more or less acute. *fl.* dark maroon-purple, freely produced; tube broad, somewhat longer than cal.; peduncles 2- or 3-fld. Trop. Africa. 1867. (B.M. 5637.) var. **denta'ta.** *l.* elliptic, slightly and irregularly toothed, cal. large, cylindrical, 2-lipped, enclosing cor. tube. 1884. (B.M. 6744.)

TI'NUS. Included in **Viburnum.**

TIP BURN. An injury to plants due to some climatic factor such as excessive heat, although other factors such as excessive humidity in glasshouses, or dry soil, may lead to the condition. The symptoms are that the tips of the leaves or even the margins become brown and dry and inclined to roll up. Any unfavourable condition such as insufficient water or food during hot weather may cause tipburn and, although more common abroad, it is sometimes seen in Great Britain on potatoes or on lettuces under glass.

D. E. G.

TIP'ULA. *See* **Crane-flies.**

TI-RAURIKI. *See* **Cordyline Pumilio.**

tirolen'sis -is -e, of the Tyrol, European Alps.

Tirucal'li, from the Malayan name.

Tisch'leri, in honour of Georg F. Tischler, b. 1878, Director, Botanic Garden, Kiel.

TISSUE. The constituent parts of plants, such as groups of cells, or fibres.

TITANOP'SIS (*titan*, sun, *opsis*, like; from the likeness of the flower to a little sun). FAM. *Aizoaceae* (Mesembryanthemum). Dwarf, stemless succulent plants from Great Namaqualand, S. Africa. Clumps are formed; the growths consist of 4 to 6 or more opposite leaves in rosettes; the leaves are thick and narrow, widening towards the tip which is flattened and closely covered with

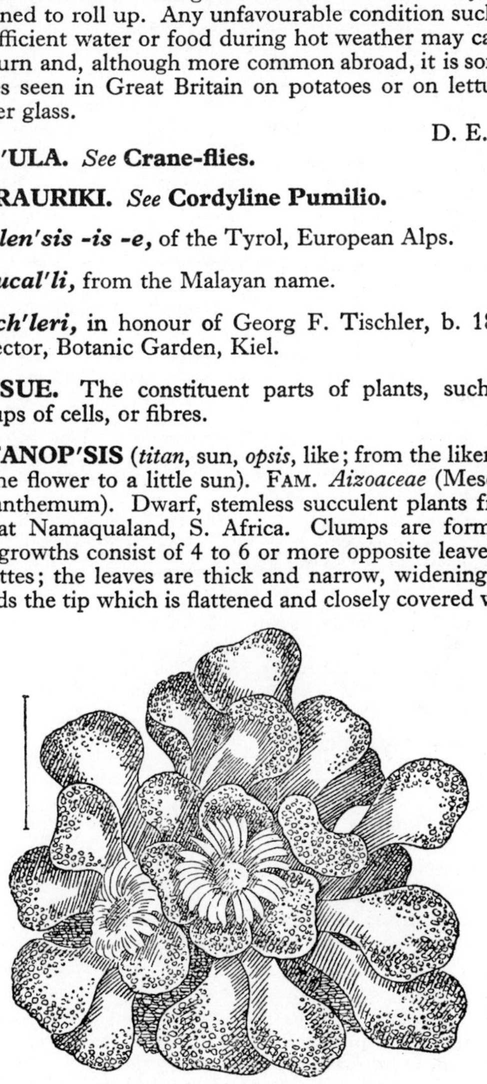

Titanopsis calcarea (p. 2120)

large tubercles; the colouring is grey with a blue or reddish tinge and the plants closely resemble the weathered granite amongst which they grow. The flowers are small with a very short stalk, yellow, and produced in August. For cultivation *see* **Mesembryanthemums (2).**

T. calca'rea. Rosettes up to 3½ in. across. *l.* spreading, spatulate, top truncate, triangular and covered with grey, red-tinged tubercles. *fl.* ¾ in. across, golden-yellow. (NE.Br. 295.) SYN. *Mesembryanthemum calcareum.*

T. Schwante'sii. *l.* erect, widening to the tip, face concave, tips roundish triangular, tips and upper parts of l. covered with blister-like brownish tubercles on a pale blue-green ground. *fl.* ⅝ in. across, pale yellow. (NE.Br. 93.) SYN. *Mesembryanthemum Schwantesii.*

V. H.

TITANO'TRICHUM (Greek *titanos*, lime, chalk, *trix*, hair, on account of the lime-secreting hairs). FAM. *Gesneriaceae.* A genus of a single species of perennial herb, native of Formosa and S. China, related to Rehmannia, but with a deeply divided calyx, corolla with nearly equal lobes and almost cylindrical tube, with stamens affixed in 2 pairs at its base. *T. Oldhamii* is dormant in winter, when it should be kept on a sunny shelf, and can be propagated by leaf cuttings. It grows well in a compost of 2 parts fibrous loam, 1 part peat, 1 part leaf-mould with sand and charcoal.

T. Oldham'ii. Erect perennial herb, 1 to 5 ft. h. with a somewhat woody rootstock and a fleshy cylindrical rhizome. *l.* ovate to oval, 3 to 7 in. long, coarsely hairy, dark green, stalked. *fl.* deep yellow heavily blotched dark crimson, ½ in. long, in a nodding raceme; cor. tube constricted near base. Formosa, S. China. Before 1939. (B.M. n.s. 78.) SYN. *Matsumuria Oldhamii, Rehmannia Oldhamii.* It sometimes produces curious whip-like appendages with rudimentary flowers.

Tita'num, of the mythological Titans, hence gigantic.

TITHO'NIA (*Tithonus*, the mythological favourite of Aurora). FAM. *Compositae.* A genus of about 10 species of robust annual herbs, sometimes shrubby at base, natives of Mexico, Cent. America, and Cuba. Leaves alternate, stalked, entire or lobed. Flower-heads yellow or red, large, heterogamous, on long, thickened peduncles; ray-florets ligulate, spreading, entire or sometimes 2-toothed; involucre hemispherical or broadly bell-shaped, bracts in 2 to 5 series; receptacle convex. Achenes slightly hairy. Any light soil suits these plants which are readily raised from seed. They are half-hardy.

T. diversifo'lia. To 15 ft. h. *l.* ovate, often 3- to 5-lobed. *fl.-heads* 2½ to 6 in. across, yellow; involucral bracts mostly rounded. Mexico, Cent. America.

T. excel'sa. A synonym of *Viguiera excelsa.*

T. ova'ta. A synonym of *Zexmenia ovata.*

T. rotundifo'lia. 4 to 6 ft. h. *l.* heart-shaped, entire or crenately 3-lobed. *fl.-heads* 2 to 3 in. across, with about 12 rich red or orange rays; involucral bracts acute or acuminate. Mexico, Cent. America. Before 1733. (B.M. 3295 as *Helianthus speciosus*; B.R. 591 as *Tithonia tagetiflora*). SYN. *Tithonia speciosa, T. tagetiflora.*

T. tubifor'mis. 3 to 6 ft. h. *l.* simple. *fl.-heads* with oblong rays, peduncles thickened upwards; involucre hairy, somewhat spreading. Achenes usually with 2 awns. Mexico. 1799. (B.R. 1519 as *Helianthus tubiformis.*)

TITOKI. *See* **Alectryon excelsa.**

TI-TREE. *See* **Cordyline.**

TOAD, *Bufo vulgaris*, is one of the most beneficial animals in a garden despite the number of stupid superstitions of which this Amphibian is the subject. It feeds on slugs, woodlice, and insects, and is a useful creature to introduce into a glasshouse for the purpose of ridding the house of certain noxious pests. Toads are nocturnally active, and usually shelter during the day, unless the weather is wet and dull, under stones, in drains, in holes in the ground, or in the shade of broad-leaved plants. Their prey is captured by means of a long tongue which can be shot out to a considerable distance.

G. F. W.

TOAD LILY. *See* **Tricyrtis.**

TOADFLAX. *See* **Linaria.**

TOADFLAX, IVY-LEAVED. *See* **Linaria Cymbalaria.**

TOADSTOOLS. Fungi of the Class Basidiomycetes, producing their spores on radiating gills beneath a stalked cap; applied to those not regarded as Mushrooms, and usually supposed to denote fungi with poisonous properties.

TOATOA. *See* **Phyllocladus glaucus.**

TOBACCO. *See* **Nicotiana Tabacum.**

TOBACCO was at one time largely used as an insecticide in the form of tobacco-paper. It is now superseded by nicotine and other fumigants.

TOBACCO, MOUNTAIN. *See* **Arnica montana.**

TOBACCO, ROCK. *See* **Primulina Tabacum.**

toba'icus -a -um, of the Lake Toba, Sumatra.

Tobi'ra, Japanese name for *Pittosporum Tobira.*

TOCO'CA (*Tococo*, the native name of *T. guianensis*). FAM. *Melastomataceae.* A genus of about 30 species of shrubs, natives of the northern part of S. America. Leaves large, rather thin or sometimes leathery, 3- or 5-nerved, often with a 2-lobed bladder at base of the blade or on the stalk. Flower white or pink, rather large, in panicles, sometimes with large bracts; calyx limb dilated, 5- or 6-lobed; petals 5 or 6, obovate, or oblong, obtuse or retuse; stamens 10 or 12, equal. A compost of 1 part sandy loam and 2 parts rough peat suits these stove shrubs which may be propagated by cuttings of side shoots in February or better by eyes or split shoots in heat.

T. cinnamo'mea. Slender, almost twining tree. *l.* elliptic oblong, 4 to 6 in. long, slender-pointed, entire, leathery, dark brownish and glabrous above, reddish-brown and dotted beneath; stalk ½ to 1 in. long. *fl.* red, ½ in. across, in long-stalked, few-fld. panicles; pedicels thick. Brazil.

T. ferrugi'nea. Stem round, covered with cinnamon scurf. *l.* 3-nerved, elliptic-oblong, with a short point, green above, paler beneath, stained red at first. S. America. 1868. SYN. *Sphaerogyne ferruginea.*

T. guianen'sis. Shrub of 3 or 4 ft. *l.* broadly elliptic or ovate, with a short point, variable, rounded at base, sometimes slightly toothed; stalks ¼ in. long below bladder. *fl.* whitish-pink, in a terminal panicle; pedicels very short or absent; cal. limb entire; pet. obovate-heart-shaped with unequal sides. August, September. Guiana. 1826.

T. imperia'lis.* *l.* large, elliptic, rich dark green with a silky or velvety surface, the main veins reddish at base. Peru. 1869. SYN. *Sphaerogyne imperialis.*

T. latifo'lia. A synonym of *T. platyphylla.*

T. platyphyl'la. Unbranched. *l.* broadly ovate, apiculate, entire or with small teeth below apex, base rounded; long-stalked. *fl.* pink or red in a more or less contracted panicle with slender branches. Trop. America. 1862. SYN. *Sphaerogyne latifolia, T. latifolia.*

TOCOYE'NA (native name in Guiana). FAM. *Rubiaceae.* A genus of about 10 species of erect shrubs, natives of Brazil and Guiana. Leaves opposite or nearly so, ovate or lanceolate with short stalks; stipules small, acute. Flowers white or yellow, showy, subsessile in cymes; corolla funnel-shaped with slender tube and naked throat; limb of 5 spreading twisted lobes; stamens 5, in throat of corolla. Fruit an oblong, many-seeded berry. *T. longiflora* needs stove treatment with a compost of fibrous peat, a little lumpy loam, sand, and charcoal. Cuttings of half-ripe shoots in sand, under a glass, made in May afford means of increase.

T. longiflo'ra. Shrub of about 6 ft. *l.* lanceolate-oblong, narrowed to both ends, 12 in. long, 4 or 5 in. wide, glabrous; stipules triangular. *fl.* clustered, almost sessile; cal. tube turbinate; cor. 8 to 9 in. long, tube yellow, limb white. Guiana. 1826.

TODARO'A. *See* **Campylocentrum.**

TODDA'LIA (*Kaka Toddali*, Malabar name of *T. asiatica*). FAM. *Rutaceae.* A genus of about 8 species of climbing or scrambling shrubs, natives of the tropics of the Old World and S. Africa. Leaves alternate, 3-foliolate; leaflets sessile, lanceolate, leathery, entire or crenate, with pellucid dots. Flowers in axillary or terminal cymes; calyx short, 2- to 5-toothed or lobed; petals 2 to 5, overlapping or valvate; torus small or slightly elongated. The Toddalias are interesting shrubs needing stove treatment with a compost of loam, peat, and sand. Cuttings strike readily in sand under a glass with heat.

T. aculea'ta. A synonym of *T. asiatica.*

T. asia'tica. Lopez root. Climber, often with hooked prickles. *lflets.* oblanceolate-oblong, acute, ½ to 1 in. wide, margins wrinkled, entire or nearly so; stalks 1 in. long, flattened upwards. *fl.* white, in many-fld. hairy panicles shorter than l. May. India, Malaya. 1790.

T. lanceola'ta. Erect, 4 ft. h. or more. *lflets.* oblong-lanceolate, 2 to 3 in. long, acute, margins waved, entire; stalks 1 to 2 in. long, not flattened. *fl.* white on short pedicels, in many-fld., thyrsoid panicles, stamens 8. May. Trop. Africa. 1824. SYN. *Vepris lanceolata.*

T. no'bilis. Shrub. *lflets.* elliptic-oblong or oblanceolate, 5 to 6 in. long, acuminate, margins slightly waved and toothed above or entire; stalks 1 to 2 in. long. *fl.* in terminal and axillary panicles shorter than l.; stamens 4. E. Trop. Africa.

TODDY PALM. *See* **Borassus flabellifer, Caryota urens.**

TO'DEA (in honour of Henry Julius Tode, of Mecklenburg, 1733–97, a mycologist). Crape Fern. FAM. *Osmundaceae.* One species confined to the south temperate zone, having the sporangia of Osmunda but with the sori on the back of the leafy part of the frond. Todeas thrive in the cool house and prove very ornamental if planted in moist, sheltered places in the open fernery. If rapid growth be desired, the plants should be grown in the tropical fernery, in a close case. The soil in which Todeas thrive best is a compost of peat and silver sand, to which a small portion of partly-decomposed sphagnum may be added with advantage.

Todeas are easily propagated from their spores, which are produced in abundance and germinate readily when sown under favourable conditions; but they are of comparatively slow growth, and seedlings require a longer time than most other Ferns to form young plants.

As a decorative Fern, *T. barbara* has few equals, especially where plants are required for very small vases. Good plants of it may be grown in comparatively small pots, and its lasting qualities are unsurpassed by any other known Fern grown for the decoration of the drawing-room, it being but little affected by smoke or gas.

For other species often grown as Todeas *see* **Leptopteris.**

T. bar'bara.* *cau.* sub-arborescent. *sti.* 1 ft. or more long, stout, erect, quadrangular, quite naked. *Fronds* 3 to 4 ft. long, often 1 ft. broad; pinnae close, erecto-patent, 1 to 1½ in. long, ⅛ to ¼ in. broad, more or less distinctly toothed, upper connected at base. *Sori* dense, when mature filling whole undersurface of fertile pinnules. Australia, New Zealand. 1869. (B.M. 5954.) SYNS. *T. africana, T. arborea, T. rivularis.* var. **bipinnatifi'da,** a fine variety, with graceful divisions and incisions in fronds. 1896; **Vrom'ii,*** *fronds* longer than in type, less triangular, pale green, on shorter stipes, furnished nearly to base with longer and less distinctly toothed pinnae. Of quicker growth than type.

TOETOE. *See* **Arundo conspicua.**

TOFIELD'IA (in honour of Thomas Tofield, 1730–79, Yorkshire botanist). FAM. *Liliaceae.* A genus of about 20 species of perennial herbs with a short or creeping rhizome. Leaves radical, in 2 ranks, linear; stem-leaves few or none. Flowers small, sessile or shortly stalked in terminal spikes; perianth of 6 free or slightly joined segments; stamens 6. Fruit a capsule with many seeds. Two species, sometimes placed in a separate genus, Iridogalvia, are natives of the Andes, the others mostly in the north temperate and Arctic zones. The British species, *T. pusilla*, has no garden value. Those mentioned below are hardy and grow best in light, moist soil. They may be increased by division.

T. calycula'ta. 6 to 12 in. h. with 2 or 3 small stem-l. *Radical l.* 2 to 6 in. long, ⅛ to ¼ in. wide. *fl.* greenish yellow, $\frac{1}{12}$ in. long, in a raceme ½ to 3 in. long, 4 to 6 in. wide when expanded. Middle Europe from Latvia to Pyrenees and Balkan Peninsula. Before 1747. (J. Linn. S.B. 53, 197.)

T. pu'bens. A synonym of *T. racemosa.*

T. racemo'sa. Slender, 12 to 24 in. h. *Radical l.* narrow-linear, somewhat rigid, glabrous, 6 to 12 in. long. *fl.* whitish, ⅛ in. long, in a loose raceme 2 to 4 in. long. July. N. America. 1840. (B.M. 3859.)

TOL'MIEA (in honour of Dr. William Fraser Tolmie, d. 1886, surgeon to Hudson's Bay Co., Puget Sound. FAM. *Saxifragaceae.* A genus of a single species of herbaceous perennial with a creeping rhizome, related to Tiarella. Stems more or less leafy. Leaves alternate; radical leaves long stalked, often with a bud at the junction of stalk and blade, heart-shaped, lobed and toothed; stipules thin. Flowers green, nodding, in a slender raceme; calyx tube long, open on one side; petals 5, filiform; stamens 3; ovary 1-celled. A plant for the border or woodland, interesting for the method of multiplication by a bud at the top of the leaf-stalk; quite hardy but sometimes grown as an indoor pot plant, the young plants which arise on the old leaves giving it the names of Pig-a-back plant, Thousand Mothers, and Youth-on-Age.

T. Menzies'ii. Slender, tufted perennial, hairy, 15 to 24 in. h., stems 3- to 5-leaved. *l.* as above. *fl.* greenish, nodding, in a somewhat secund raceme up to 18 in. long; cal. purple-veined. NW. America. 1812. SYN. *Tiarella Menziesii.*

TOL'PIS (derivation ?). FAM. *Compositae.* A genus of about 15 species of annual and perennial herbs, natives of the Mediterranean region and the Canary Is., related to Crepis. Leaves mostly radical, entire, toothed, or pinnatifid, upper ones usually narrow. Flower-heads pale or bright yellow, homogamous; ray florets truncately 5-toothed at apex; involucre bell-shaped; bracts narrow, lower in 1 or 2 series, upper in many series; receptacle naked or honeycombed. Achenes 6- to 8-ribbed; pappus of 6 to 20 bristles. All the following flower in June and seed should be sown on the open border in spring.

T. altis'sima. Branched, erect, to 3 ft. h. *l.* long, linear, lanceolate, toothed; upper linear, entire. *fl.-heads* small; involucre and pedicels mealy. S. Europe. 1823. SYN. *T. virgata.* var. **grandiflor'a,** *l.* lanceolate, densely hairy towards base, *fl.-heads* citron, outer scales of involucre short, awl-shaped. S. Italy, Sicily. 1830.

T. barba'ta. Yellow Hawkweed. Stems erect, branched, leafy. *l.* lanceolate, toothed. *fl.-heads* with slightly mealy involucre, outer scales awl-shaped-falcate. S. Europe, &c. (B.M. 35 as *Crepis barbata.*)

T. macrorhi'za. Stem shrubby, branched, from a thick fleshy root. Whole plant glabrous. *l.* oblong, toothed, slightly fleshy. *fl.-heads* in a large panicle, involucre mealy; pappus of 15 to 20 bristles; pedicels scaly. Madeira. (B.M. 2988 as *Crepis macrorhiza.*)

T. umbella'ta. Erect, branched, about 2 ft. h., stem almost leafless. *l.* oblong-linear, toothed; upper linear, entire. *fl.-heads* pale yellow, small; pedicels hairy at top. S. Europe. 1820.

T. virga'ta. A synonym of *T. altissima.*

TOLU BALSAM-TREE. *See* **Myroxylon toluiferum.**

TOLUIF'ERA. A synonym of Myroxylon.

tolui'ferus -a -um producing Tolu balsam, which is named after the port of Tolu, Colombia.

tolype'phorus -a -um, wound up like a ball of wool.

TOMATO (*Lycopersicon esculentum*). The tomato reaches perfection in this country when grown by modern methods in heated glasshouses. It can also be grown in cold houses, under frames and cloches, and in the open during the summer months.

I. Cultivation in Heated Glasshouses. The main crop in heated glasshouses is planted about the middle of February from seeds sown in December, but in very sunny areas planting can be advanced by 2 to 4 weeks.

Seeds are sown in shallow trays filled with sterilized soil to which some phosphate has been added. If sown thickly they are pricked off into other trays after germination and later potted into 3-in. pots. If sown thinly (1 in. apart) they are allowed to remain until the first pair of rough leaves has begun to open and are then potted into 3-in. pots. The temperature of the propagating house should be 65° F. during germination and for 48 hours after pricking off and potting. During the rest of the propagating period the temperature is normally 60° F., but it should be regulated according to weather conditions. In sunny spells the night temperature can rise up to 65° F., but during dull or foggy weather it may be necessary to reduce the night temperature to 55° F. or even less to prevent the seedlings becoming weak and drawn. Everything possible should be done during propagation to produce a sturdy plant with an abundance of clean roots. Ventilation must be given whenever possible and watering must not be overdone. A

1. *Soil Treatment*. For the first 8 years of a new nursery, soil sterilization should be unnecessary, but later as the crop falls off, the soil must be sterilized either by steam or by some chemical sterilizer such as formaldehyde.

After clearing away the previous crop the soil must be cultivated to a depth of 10 in. every year, but it should be bastard trenched at least 1 year in 3.

(*a*) *Winter flooding*. After digging, the soil should be limed if necessary and flooded with water. This helps to clean the soil and also ensures that the subsoil will not be dry for the next crop.

After forking over and then spreading the lime—hydrated if possible—according to the needs of the soil as determined by analysis, the ground is damped and later flooded heavily with water, applying 80,000 gallons per acre. On heavy soil where drainage is poor, one application is sufficient, but on well-drained soil 2 or even 3 floodings are beneficial.

(*b*) *Base manure applied before planting*. A good supply of organic matter in the soil is necessary for this crop and this should be kept up by annual applications of strawy horse manure for preference. The alternative is composted wheat or oat straw. Cow and other animal manures can be used on very light soil, but not to excess. Horse manure, 30 tons per acre, is the usual dressing. It is dug in so that two-thirds lies 9 to 12 in. deep, the remainder being mixed with the topsoil.

A good base fertilizer mixture is always needed: a mixture of equal parts of hoof and horn, bone-meal, and sulphate of potash is recommended. The rate of application varies from 15 to 30 cwt. per acre and it should be forked into the top 6 in. of soil.

2. *Planting*. Preparations for planting consist of (1) heating the houses for about 14 days to raise the soil temperature to 57 to 60° F. (2) Tying the fillis to the overhead wires in readiness for use. (3) Watering the soil, if dry, to bring it to the correct state for planting. (4) Making the holes to receive the plants.

A cold soil checks growth and sets up root decay, and so soil temperature is important.

Tomatoes are usually planted 14 in. apart in rows which can run either across the house or from end to end. The rows are arranged in pairs, allowing 18 in. from row to row and separating the pairs or double rows by paths 27 in. wide. The plants must be supported to keep them erect. So strings of fillis are fastened to a system of overhead wires, and brought down, one for each plant, and fastened to horizontal wires or strings fixed close to the ground. If an iron stake is driven into the ground at one end of the row and another at the other end, these wires can be stretched tightly between them and will serve to anchor the lower ends of the strings supporting each plant. When planting, a hole is made in the ground to accommodate the ball of soil and roots from the 3-in. pot. This can be made with a solid dibber or with a tool which cuts out the soil. If the soil is too cold, it is wise to stand the plants, pot and all, on the soil and wait until it has warmed up sufficiently. When planting, the 'ball' is knocked carefully out of the pot, placed in the hole and pressed home gently. Do not attempt to level the surface by dragging loose soil over the 'ball'. It only encourages wireworm attack. Next day give a light watering to wet the 'ball' and settle the soil around it.

3. *Training, &c.* As the plants grow, all side-shoots must be removed while they are quite small. The plant is kept in position by pulling down the fillis gently and twisting it around the plant. An occasional raffia tie will keep it in position.

The leaves below the bottom truss should be removed within the first 3 weeks, removing half of them at the end of 10 days, and the remainder about a week later. This forms a clear space below the crop and enables the air to circulate freely over the soil. Tomato plants in good health should not be 'stopped' until they have reached the top wires. The old practice of stopping at 4 or 5 trusses and then again 2 trusses later is not to be recommended as a general practice.

4. *Watering*. Tomatoes should be given only a little water until they have set about 1½ trusses of fruit. This little is just sufficient to keep the ball wet and also that part of the soil entered by the growing roots. Real watering starts about 6 weeks after planting and is repeated every 7 days. About 25,000 gallons per acre is an average application for an established crop, but during the middle of the year this quantity is usually doubled by watering twice each week. The amount, however, must vary with the nature of the soil, the growth, and the weather.

5. *Damping overhead*. Tomato flowers do not set properly in a dry atmosphere, and therefore a programme of overhead damping is essential. In damping, a fine spray of water is cast over the plants, either from a can or by nipping the end of the hose. A house containing 1,000 plants is damped in about 2 minutes. Damping should be done each day between 9 and 10 a.m. G.M.T., unless it is raining. It starts when the first flower opens and continues until the last flower has set. During hot weather it can be done twice or 3 times each day.

6. *Top-dressing Fertilizers*. (*a*) *Potash*. If the plants are very soft during the first 4 weeks, a dressing of 5 cwt. sulphate of potash per acre should be given with the first real watering (about 6 weeks after planting).

(*b*) *Balanced fertilizer*. If the early growth is normal in character apply 5 cwt. of a balanced fertilizer with the first real watering. It should contain about 5 per cent. ammonia, 25 per cent. total phosphates of which 12 per cent. is soluble, and 7 to 10 per cent. potash.

The following is a useful mixture:

	parts by weight
Sulphate of ammonia	3
Dried blood	2
Superphosphate (30 per cent.)	7
Pure dissolved bones	5
Bone flour	½
Sulphate of potash	2½

This mixture should be applied and watered in every 14 days or as the plants require it, except on 2 or 3 occasions when it should be replaced by the dried-blood mixture given below.

(*c*) *Dried-blood mixture*. The tomato plant requires a special stimulant rich in nitrogen occasionally, when it is bearing a heavy strain. The first and most essential application is when the third truss has set in most varieties and when the second truss has set in the case of varieties like Potentate, which bear heavy bottom trusses. The following mixture is recommended:

Sulphate of ammonia	1	parts by weight.
Nitrate of potash	1	
Superphosphate (30 per cent.)	3	
Dried blood	5	

The rate of application is 5 cwt. per acre and it should be given at intervals of 6 weeks, or more frequently if the plants seem to need a stimulant.

7. *Temperature.* The optimum night temperature varies from 60° to 65° F. according to variety. It must be remembered, however, that dull weather tends to make the growth soft while bright sunny weather hardens it. So in dull weather the temperature must be lowered and the rate of growth reduced if the plants are to be kept in a sturdy condition. Advantage can be taken of sunny weather, however, to increase the temperature and so hasten the crop. During the day sun heat will cause the temperature to rise and every attempt must be made to keep it below 80° F. by ventilation and by shading the glass. Damping the paths will also help.

8. *Picking.* Tomatoes are picked when ready for market by turning back the fruit and severing it from the truss by breaking the stalk at the joint just below the calyx, leaving the latter on the fruit. The fruit is then graded for size, shape, and quality and packed preferably in non-returnable boxes holding 12 lb. each.

II. Cold Houses. Tomatoes are grown in cold houses in the same way as for heated houses with a few simple modifications. Usually it is not advisable to plant in cold houses before the middle of April, owing to frosts, except in the warmer parts of the country. Further, it is advisable to plant in single rows 27 in. apart instead of double rows: this improves the circulation of the air. Dressings of fertilizers should be reduced in comparison with those applied in heated houses, especially in the case of nitrogen, because growth must not be allowed to become too strong. Daily overhead damping is unwise because it may encourage attack by **Botrytis.** It should be reduced to hot, sunny days only.

III. Tomatoes Grown Outside in Pots during the summer and taken into the houses in September. A winter crop is possible if tomato plants are planted in 9 or 10-in. pots before 7 July, grown carefully outside until the middle of September and then taken into heated glasshouses and kept at a night temperature of 50° F. to allow the fruit to ripen. The pots should be filled with a mixture of 5 parts good turfy loam (to which lime is added if necessary) and 1 part strawy horse manure, after adding a 3-in. pot each of hoof and horn, bone-meal, and sulphate of potash per barrow load of compost. Every effort must be made to set a full crop and also to combat late blight, *Phytophthora infestans*, by spraying.

IV. Small Glasshouses. Many owners of small glasshouses purchase the plants as they have no facilities for raising them. They should remember that young plants can carry diseases and pests, and therefore must be very careful to get the plants from a good grower. They should make certain they are not infested with White Fly or Red Spider. **A**

The plants can be grown in the ground, but it is much wiser to plant them in large pots, wooden boxes, or on raised benches, for better plants are grown in this way.

The pots, boxes, or benches should be filled with the compost given in Section III and should be top-dressed as recommended in Section I, remembering that 5 cwt. per acre equals approximately 2 oz. per square yard. When benches are used, they should be covered with boards or galvanized sheets to retain the compost which can be placed either in mounds or as a long narrow ridge running parallel to the side of the house. These ridges should be about 9 in. deep and 12 in. wide. Lines of bricks can be used to retain the compost at both the back and the front. The front line can be advanced at regular intervals during the summer and fresh compost filled in behind it to give more soil for the roots.

The plants can be trained up wire or canes fixed parallel to the roof. A roof crop of this kind offers splendid opportunities for a good crop. Tomatoes are usually grown on single stems, but the roof crop can be treated differently. Instead of removing the side shoots they can be allowed to grow and be tied to the wires to keep them in place. Each can be allowed to produce a truss of fruit and should be stopped at the second leaf beyond it. Side shoots will arise from these laterals and can be treated in the same way. By this system of training it is possible to cover the roof with bunches of tomatoes and so produce a truly magnificent crop. The plants will need, of course, to be well fed with fertilizers.

V. In Frames and Cloches. Tomatoes can be grown in frames and continuous cloches by using a little ingenuity to train them in a horizontal position on canes or poles. In frames, the soil at the front is prepared to receive the young plants, and the plants are trained to lie parallel to the surface of the lights. In cloches, the plants are trained to lie horizontally along the line of cloches.

A great number of excellent varieties are available from which to make a selection, and it is often difficult to say which are outstanding. A selection is given in the Supplement.

W. B.

DISEASES. Tomatoes are subject to a large number of diseases, especially when grown under glass. Some are caused by fungus parasites, some by viruses, and some are non-parasitic. Damping-off in the seedlings is due to various soil fungi such as *Pythium de Baryanum*, *Phytophthora parasitica*, and *Corticium solani*, and precautions such as watering with Cheshunt compound, reducing the moisture, and preparing a proper open compost have been described under Damping-off. Treating the seeds with cuprous oxide or watering the soil after sowing with Formalin solution, 1 part Formaldehyde in 600 parts water, have recently been put forward as useful control methods. It must not be forgotten that the water-supply may be contaminated and all tanks, &c., should be properly cleaned each season. *Corticium solani* is not controlled by Cheshunt compound and where this fungus is present watering with mercuric bichloride is advisable. When the young plants have passed the seedling stage and right up to the time of planting out they may suffer from Foot Rot due to attack by the same fungi as mentioned for Damping-off. Low temperatures often aggravate this trouble and care should be taken not to allow the young plants to get cold and wet. It is a wise precaution after potting up to give a first watering with Cheshunt compound. If the disease is continually a nuisance it may be necessary to use sterilized soil for potting, &c., or to practise some form of sterilization of the soil in the beds. Over-watering must always be avoided. Other root rots on older plants show the roots to be infested with fungi such as *Colletotrichum atramentarium*, *Thielaviopsis basicola*, and various species of Fusarium, but most of such troubles are due to damage when potting and planting combined with cold heavy soil and much control is obtained by proper attention to cultivation and drainage. The affected plants wilt during the day and recover at night, and it is recommended that a good top-dressing of peat be applied and kept damp so that new roots are encouraged to grow from the stem bases and then fed by light dressings of fertilizers. Similar to the root rots mentioned is Sleepy disease due to the fungus *Verticillium albo-atrum* which enters the roots and base of the stem, causing wilting. Later the leaves yellow and wither, starting from the base upwards, and when the stem is cut open a reddish discoloration may be seen in the woody tissues. Control is to increase the temperature to 77° F. for about a fortnight, during which time the glass is shaded and the plants syringed overhead but not watered at the roots. A top-dressing of peat is given to encourage new roots in this case also. Severely affected plants may be removed and the holes watered with Cheshunt compound before putting in a new plant. Soil sterilization is advisable after a severe attack of Sleepy disease. A very common leaf trouble is Leaf Mould due to *Cladosporium fulvum* in which yellow blotches on the upper leaf surfaces will be found due to the fungus on the lower surfaces, where it is seen as a velvety brown or purple mouldy growth. The foliage may be severely damaged but the fruit is not usually affected. This disease thrives in warm, moist atmospheres and especially on plants which have been checked from such causes as dryness at the roots. Although it can be prevented from spreading to some extent by sulphur spraying, vaporizing, or dusting, it should be possible to stop it by providing ample ventilation, by encouraging air circulation around the stems and removing some of the leaves, and by special care in watering.

Where Leaf Mould is severe the house when empty should be disinfected with Cresylic acid. Varieties resistant to Leaf Mould are now being investigated.

Tomato plants are sometimes injured by Grey Mould (*Botrytis cinerea*) which, if allowed to flourish on dead leaves or badly trimmed remains of leaf-stalks, may enter the fruit, where it soon shows near the stalk and rapidly rots the fruit. The fungus thrives only where the air is excessively moist and should be easily controlled by reducing this moisture and by thorough removal of infected and dead material. Spraying should not be necessary. Where a stem is slightly infected it may be saved by cutting out the brown infected part and rubbing the cut with liver of sulphur paste or copper-lime dust. Potato Blight disease also attacks tomatoes, usually outdoors, the signs being dark-brown or black patches on the leaves and stems and very soon brown blotches on the fruits, which then rot away. It is not advisable to plant outdoor tomatoes near potatoes, but in any case in a wet season the same precautions ought to be taken as for potatoes and the tomato plants ought to be sprayed *early* with Bordeaux or Burgundy mixture, and this may have to be repeated. Any leaf showing a sign of this disease must be removed.

A less common disease is Stem Rot or Stem Canker caused by the fungus *Didymella Lycopersici* which attacks the stem at the base, causing a shrinking and canker-like effect. In such an attack first-affected plants should be destroyed and the bases of the others sprayed with Cheshunt compound. Where this disease gets severe some form of soil sterilization may be needed.

The tomato suffers from a good number of virus diseases. The chief is perhaps Spotted Wilt, which does serious injury and spreads rapidly. The signs are a browning or varnishing of the young top leaves and sometimes concentric rings appear, whilst the leaves tend to curl downwards and the plant stops growing. Thrips are mainly responsible for the spread, but healthy plants must not be handled or cut with a knife after dealing with diseased ones unless the hands and knife are washed in some disinfectant such as 2 per cent. Lysol. All plants showing Spotted Wilt must be destroyed as soon as seen so as to eliminate the sources of infection. The serious nature of Spotted Wilt virus lies in the fact that it attacks so many other plants (*see* **Spotted Wilt**), and some of these, e.g. Winter Cherry (*Solanum Capsicastrum*), Gloxinia, Arum Lily, Dahlia, &c., being long lived may harbour the disease for years. This is one reason for devoting one glasshouse to tomatoes only and not having different kinds of plants growing near one another. Another virus disease is Bushy Stunt, in which there is enormous production of secondary shoots with a resulting bushy appearance in the plant. Distorting or Enation disease shows very curious leaf malformation, the leaves being reduced to half their width or to thin threads looking like corkscrew tendrils. Also there may be outgrowths from the under surfaces and some proliferation of shoots, so that the plant is very bushy. Ordinary Mosaic shows as mottling with dark- and light-green areas, and this varies in severity from mild mottling to severe mottling with much stunting. This virus does not affect the crop so much as other viruses except in the severe cases, but it may be carried on the seed, so that seed should be taken only from absolutely healthy plants. A dressing of complete fertilizer often helps the plants to outgrow Mosaic to some extent. Aucuba or Yellow Mosaic is more serious and the leaves show bright yellow spots and patches and may become almost all yellow. The fruit is affected by this mottling. Streak disease shows as brown marks on leaves and petioles and long brown stripes on the stems, which when cut open also show brown marks in the pith. The fruits are pock-marked with brown blotches. This trouble is most likely to appear among plants which have been heavily manured with nitrogenous fertilizers and against it the treatment is to give a top-dressing of sulphate of potash, 2 oz. to the square yard and half this amount a fortnight later. It will be seen that with the exception of Mosaic and Streak the virus type of disease must be combated by speedy destruction of affected plants, by fumigation against insects, and by care in handling or trimming the plants.

The fruits of tomatoes may show Water Spot, which occurs as small spots surrounded by a ring. This only occurs with high humidity or outdoors in wet seasons. It is caused by the spores of the Grey Mould fungus *Botrytis cinerea* already mentioned. These spores are able to germinate and injure the skin at one point but then are unable to grow farther and consequently dry out, leaving the small ring-like marks. Buck Eye Rot due to the fungus *Phytophthora parasitica* causes reddish-brown to grey patches in concentric ring-like formation on the fruits. Where common this disease can be checked by careful watering to avoid splashing the ground, removal of affected fruits and the lower leaves to encourage air circulation, and watering the lower part of the plant with Cheshunt compound. Low trusses should be tied up to keep them clear of the ground. There are many non-parasitic disorders in tomato fruits. Greenback in which the stalk end of the fruit remains green and does not ripen is associated with shortage of potash combined with exposure to strong sunlight, which injures the top of the fruit. Shading the house by blinds or white-washing the glass should be effective. Blotchy Ripening shows as irregular patches remaining yellow all over the surface and this also is thought to be caused by some food deficiency, usually potash. The soil should be properly prepared so as to encourage steady uniform growth and a correct balanced fertilizer used for feeding. Scald is caused by fruits growing or being placed too near the glass and shows as a circular white-creamy and wrinkled patch on the fruit. It is not necessary to place tomatoes near glass to ripen off as long as the air temperature is warm enough. A very common disorder is Blossom End Rot or Black Rot in which the blossom ends of tomato fruits show a circular brown or black patch which later becomes sunken. The cause is a shortage of water when the fruits are very young, although the trouble may not show for some weeks afterwards. Plants with large gross foliage or those with diseased roots are more likely to suffer and those grown in pots or boxes are very liable to it. Care must be taken to supply sufficient water and to have proper soil conditions so that the root system is healthy and vigorous. Even if this trouble shows on the bottom trusses there is no reason for it to appear on later ones if care is exercised and the plants properly attended to. The condition known as Dropsy or Oedema shows when greyish furry blisters develop on the stems, leaf-stalks, and under-surfaces of leaves. This is due to roots taking in water that cannot be given off by the leaves, generally because the atmosphere is too moist. It may also be favoured by spraying with oil emulsions against Red Spider. Such spraying should be done on dry foliage and adequate ventilation should be given. Marginal Leaf Scorch is generally due to potash deficiency as in apples (*see* **Apple Leaf Scorch**), but leaves of tomatoes may also be scorched from other reasons, e.g. by woodwork painted with creosote or by fumes from boilers or lamps.

D. E. G.

PESTS. Tomato plants are attacked by a considerable number of insect and allied pests, both in glasshouses and in the open. A list is given of the more widely distributed and destructive pests, all of which are dealt with under their respective headings. A fuller list of the pests of this crop, together with information on glasshouse conditions in relation to the occurrence and control of such pests, appears in *Insect Pests of Glass-house Crops* (1948), by H. W. and M. Miles, which should be consulted by all growers.

The chief pests are: Root-Knot Eelworm, *Heterodera marioni*; Red Spider Mite, *Tetranychus telarius*; Thrips, of which the Onion Thrips, *T. tabaci*, is the most important owing to its ability to transmit the virus disease known as Spotted Wilt; the Glasshouse Leaf-hopper, *Erythroneura pallidifrons*; the Greenhouse White Fly, *Trialeurodes vaporariorum*; the Tomato Moth, *Polia oleracea*; and Wireworms, which tunnel the lower portion of the stems.

TOMATO MOTH, *Polia* (*Hadena*) *oleracea*, is known also as the Bright Line Brown Eye Moth, the caterpillars of which feed on weeds, including Docks, Nettles, and various cruciferous plants. In recent years it has become a serious pest in Tomato houses where the larvae feed on the foliage and tunnel into the fruits and stems. One caterpillar may damage several fruits in a single truss during the night and cause extensive injury to the crop. They are known to attack Cucumbers and Chrysanthemums. The Moth appears in June and July, and has a wing expanse of 1½ to 1¾ in., the fore-wings are purplish-brown with a paler kidney-shaped mark near the centre and a pale wavy line towards the margin, the hind-wings are uniformly grey. The Moths are nocturnally active, and each female is capable of laying several hundred greenish-white eggs, which are deposited in clusters on the underside of the leaves. The caterpillars vary from green to light brown with black and white spots scattered over the body and with a yellow stripe down each side. They are found from July to September and, when fully grown, pupate in the soil, in mulching material, in crevices of walls and woodwork, and even among packing-cases and seed-boxes stacked in the house. A partial second brood may occur in late summer or early autumn in glasshouses. The destruction of weeds in and near Tomato houses is a good measure of preventing a severe attack in glasshouses. All damaged fruits should be removed, for they prove a source of attraction to the moths which enter the houses and proceed to oviposit on the leaves. The fully grown caterpillars may be trapped by providing pupation quarters in the form of loosely folded sacks placed on the staging, borders, and floor of infested houses. The young caterpillars may be killed by lightly spraying the foliage to within a month of gathering the fruit with Arsenate of Lead paste (1½ to 2 lb.), Saponin (½ oz.), and water (25 gall.) or D.D.T. emulsion. This wash is poisonous and must not be used in Tomato houses where Lettuce is grown as an under-crop.

G. F. W.

TOMATO, CANNIBAL'S. *See* **Solanum Uporo.**

TOMATO, GOOSEBERRY. *See* **Physalis peruviana.**

TOMATO-ROOT GALL. *See* **Root-knot Eelworm.**

tombeanen'sis -is -e, of Monte Tombea in Val Vestino, S. Tyrol, between the lakes Garda and Idro.

tomentel'lus -a -um, somewhat hairy.

tomento'sus -a -um, tomentose; thickly hairy, or with matted hair.

TOMENTUM, a covering of dense, often short, rigid hairs, often more or less felted together.

tomiol'ophus -a -um, with a torn helmet.

Tommasinii, Tommasinianus -a -um, in honour of Muzio Spirito de Tommasini, 1794–1879, of Trieste, Italian botanist.

Tonckat, native Malayan name of a related plant, wrongly applied to *Stromanthe Tonckat.*

TONGA PLANT. *See* **Epipremnum mirabile.**

TONGUE. An oblong, often flexible projection.

TONGUE-GRAFTING. *See* **Grafting.**

TONGUE VIOLET. *See* **Schweiggeria fruticosa.**

tonkinen'sis -is -e, of Tonkin, Indochina, SE. Asia.

ton'sus -a -um, shaven, smooth.

TOOLS, IMPLEMENTS, &c. It is necessary to provide a considerable variety of tools for garden work. Some are needed in all establishments whether large or small, the spade, for instance, which is needed at all seasons; some have a less wide use, but the importance of all being of good quality cannot be over-emphasized. On the description and quality of the tools depend to a large extent the amount of work that can be accomplished and the manner in which it is done; workmen generally do more with good and useful tools that are always kept clean than with indifferent or dirty tools, taken in and stored temporarily when wet, becoming rusty or caked with soil. A rule ought to be in force that all who use anything from the tool-shed should return it in a clean, dry condition. Both those who provide and those who use garden tools thus have a share in the quality of the work the tools can be made to do.

The following is a list of tools likely to be necessary in a garden, but the number to be needed must depend upon the extent of the garden and the number of staff employed. Each of the tools is commented upon in its alphabetical position in the Dictionary: Averruncator or long-arm pruner for pruning tall shrubs or trees which cannot be reached by a ladder; axe; bill-hook; brooms, both birch and bass brooms; brushes for pot-cleaning and scrubbing; chisels for pruning and grafting; crow-bars; daisy-grubbers and daisy-rakes; dibbers and bulb-planters; edging-irons or verge-cutters where grass paths and beds in lawns need attention; forks for various purposes; fruit gatherer; grubbing axe; hoes of different types and width and cultivators with spring tines; hooks for trimming banks and hedge-slashers for rough hedges; mattock, hammers and mallet; pick, pickaxe; pruning saws and hand-saws; rakes of different sizes both wooden and iron; rammers for new paths, turf-laying, and erecting posts; reel and line; rollers, light rollers for lawns and seed beds and heavy rollers for gravel or earth paths; scythes or other means of cutting long grass; secateurs; shears; shovels; spades; syringes and spraying apparatus; trowels and hand-forks; turfing-iron and turf-beetle where new turf is to be laid; weeding tools.

TOOL-SHED. A waterproof shed should be provided in every garden in which to store tools. It should be provided with pegs near the roof, or better a rack, on which long-handled tools such as hoes and rakes and scythes can be hung and other pegs for spades, hoes, shovels, &c. Small tools are better kept in a cupboard or fitted into a small rack so that everything should have its place. Means of cleaning and oiling tools after use should also be at hand so that everything may be put away clean at the end of each day, and ready for use without delay on the next occasion when it may be needed. It is well to have all tools branded and where a considerable staff is employed to assign tools and racks to each employee.

TOON'A. Included in **Cedrela.**

TOOTHACHE-TREE. *See* **Zanthoxylum americanum.**

TOOTHBRUSH-TREE. *See* **Salvadora persica.**

toothed, having indentations in the margin.

TOOTHWORT. *See* **Dentaria, Lathraea,** *and* **Plumbago scandens.**

TOP-DRESSING. The addition of fresh soil or some fertilizing material on the surface around plants without disturbance of the roots. Where the top-dressing is applied to oldish trees slightly forking of the surface over the roots should be a preliminary measure. It is an important measure for the maintenance of health in pot plants which have a long period in one pot, and especially of plants that resent root disturbance, for gross-feeding perennials, for trees needing manuring, and for all plants in which new surface roots are desired, e.g. cucumbers and stem-rooting lilies.

TOPIARY. The art of topiary, i.e. of clipping and cutting shrubs and small trees into ornamental or fantastic shapes, takes its name from the Roman *ars topiaria* (ornamental gardening) as practised in the 1st century A.D. and possibly earlier: Pliny the Younger (A.D. 62–113), for example, described the garden of his villa in Tuscany as embellished with Box hedges and shrubs cut into the form of animals, letters, &c. It probably never died out in Italy. When the fashion first became general in Britain is uncertain, but it reached its greatest popularity here in the 16th and 17th centuries. Although sometimes carried to absurdity, topiary work is completely in character with many old buildings and their formal gardens; ingenious, carefully tended examples are often the pride of cottage gardens.

Box (**Buxus sempervirens**) and Yew (**Taxus baccata**), being evergreens with very numerous dark-green leaves, which stand up well to continuous clipping, are generally employed. To train them into the shapes desired calls for much attention over many years; the amount of labour involved and the long time which must pass before large specimens can be grown are, accordingly, serious drawbacks to the employment of topiary work on a large scale for garden ornament. As such plants are intended to last for many years, it is important that the ground should be thoroughly prepared by deep digging before planting, which is best done in October or November. Small plants, e.g. Yews about 3 ft. high, transplant more satisfactorily than large specimens; if they arrive with rather dry roots, these should be soaked in water for about half a day before planting. They should not be clipped until about a year afterwards, i.e. next autumn. Clipping is usually done in August or September. Whatever form is selected, it will be found best to have it broader at the base than at the top, e.g. a dome, pyramid, or cone, although it can be surmounted by a smaller figure to which this does not apply; a peacock or like shape looks best when it stands on a substantial base. When such a base of the proper height exists, the bird can be shaped by taking two leading twigs or bunches of twigs, bending them apart in opposite directions, one being intended to form the head, the other the tail, and then holding them in position by stout wire and tarred string.

During the next season, growth of new shoots and leaves will give body to this and fill in the framework; after 3 years of clipping and tying, the general shape will have been attained; no shoot should be cut away that can be bent into the framework and contribute to its bulk.

For further information the books *Garden Craftsmanship in Yew and Box* (1925) by N. Lloyd, and *The Book of Topiary* (1904) by C. H. Curtis and W. Gibson should be consulted.

W. T. S.

TOPINAMBOUR, native name for *Calathea Allouia* (q.v.).

Topping'ii, in honour of David Le Roy Topping, 1861–1939, of New York and Manila.

top-shaped, inversely conical, contracted towards point.

A→

TORCH LILY. *See* **Kniphofia.**

TORCH THISTLE. *See* **Cereus.**

TORCHES. *See* **Verbascum Thapsus.**

TORE'NIA (in honour of the Rev. Olof Torén, 1718–53, chaplain of Swedish East India Company in India, at Surat, and China, 1750–2). FAM. *Scrophulariaceae.* A genus of about 40 species of herbs, natives of Trop. and Sub-Trop. Africa and Asia. Leaves opposite, usually serrate. Flowers in short, few-flowered racemes, axillary; calyx tubular, plicate, or 3- to 5-winged, obliquely 3- to 5-toothed or 2-lipped at apex; corolla tube cylindrical or broadened above, upper lip broad, notched or 2-fid, lower spreading with 3 nearly equal lobes; stamens 4, in pairs of unequal length. Fruit an oblong capsule. Easily grown plants well fitted for growing in pots or baskets, needing stove or warm greenhouse conditions. They should be raised from seed sown in heat in March or April, the seedlings being pricked off into the pots or baskets in which they are to flower, as soon as large enough to handle. A compost of loam and leaf-mould with a little sand and charcoal suits them. *T. Fournieri*, since it grows erect, is the best for pot cultivation, its branches being supported with small stakes. Aphides are apt to be troublesome to the young plants, necessitating fumigation. Cuttings may be rooted readily under a hand-glass in sand in a warm house. The calyx increases in size after flowering: the measurements below refer to its length before the corolla falls.

The following are all Asiatic species, the most attractive being *T. atropurpurea*, *T. Baillonii*, *T. concolor*, *T. Fournieri*, *T. hirsuta*, and *T. travancorica.*

KEY

1. *Most lvs. narrowly oblong or narrowly oblanceolate, untoothed or scarcely toothed, narrow ($\frac{3}{10}$ in. or less wide)* — T. oblonga
1. *Lvs. ovate to lanceolate, toothed* — 2
2 (1). *Fl. medium-sized or large; cor. tube $\frac{7}{10}$ to 1 $\frac{2}{10}$ in long, often much longer than cal.* — 3
2. *Fl. small; cor. tube $\frac{3}{10}$ to $\frac{6}{10}$ in. long, often little longer than cal.* — 10
3 (2). *Cor. limb bright yellow; upper part of tube purple* — T. Baillonii
3. *Cor. coloured otherwise, the limb usually blue or violet or red-purple, sometimes yellow-blotched, but not completely yellow* — 4
4 (3). *Cal. ellipsoid, with 5 broad prominent wings. Outer stamen filaments unappendaged* — T. Fournieri
4. *Cal. cylindric, ribbed, or keeled but not broadly winged* — 5
5 (4). *Cor. tube narrowly cylindric for lower $\frac{8}{10}$ in., then abruptly swollen, reddish-purple, nearly 3 times as long as cal.* — T. atropurpurea
5. *Cor. tube gradually narrowed from base, rather broad, hardly twice as long as cal.* — 6

6 (5). *Cor. tube blue, violet, or purple* 7
6. *Cor. tube whitish or yellow* T. travancorica
7 (6). *Cal. hairy, not winged; pedicels hairy* T. hirsuta
7. *Cal. glabrous (or sometimes ciliate on wings); pedicels glabrous* 8
8 (7). *Cal. markedly 2-lipped, divided to about half-way, not winged. Lvs. narrowly ovate.* T. concolor
8. *Cal. not divided to more than a third, slightly winged* 9
9 (8). *Lvs. ovate-deltoid* T. asiatica
9. *Lvs. narrowly ovate* T. cyanea
10 (2). *Fl. blue or white* 11
10. *Fl. yellow or yellowish* 13
11 (10). *Cal. not broadly winged; outer stamen filaments with a projection towards base* T. parviflora
11. *Cal. broadly winged; outer stamen filaments unappendaged* 12
12 (11). *Cal. wings continued downwards on to pedicel; cor. limb not uniformly coloured* T. peduncularis
12. *Cal. wings cordate at base, not continued downwards on to pedicel; cor. limb uniformly coloured* T. cordifolia
13 (10). *L.-base mostly wedge-shaped. Cal. ribbed* T. flava
13. *L.-base mostly truncate. Cal. slightly winged* T. Fordii

T. asia'tica. Plant prostrate, rooting at nodes. *l.* ovate-deltoid, small, mostly under 1 in. long, toothed, stalked. *fl.* axillary; pedicels to $1\frac{1}{2}$ in. long; cal. about $\frac{1}{2}$ in. long, glabrous, scarcely winged; cor. violet-purple with white lower lip; tube $\frac{8}{10}$ in. long. S. India. SYN. *T. bicolor*. The Linnaean name *T. asiatica* is used here for a lowland species from the west coast of India agreeing with Linnaeus's specimen collected by Torén, probably near Surat, and with the illustration and description in Rheede's *Hortus Malabaricus*, 9, t. 53 (1689), cited by Linnaeus. It has been applied to a number of other species, e.g. *T. concolor*, *T. cyanea*, *T. hirsuta*, and *T. travancorica*.

T. atropurpu'rea. Plant perennial; branches sometimes decumbent and rooting, up to 2 ft. long. *l.* ovate or narrowly ovate-deltoid, $\frac{3}{5}$ to $1\frac{1}{2}$ in. long, toothed, often rough above, almost glabrous beneath, long-stalked. *fl.* usually solitary; pedicels about $\frac{1}{2}$ to 1 in. long; cal. about $\frac{1}{2}$ in. long, glabrous, not winged; cor. dark red-purple; tube funnel-shaped, 1 to $1\frac{1}{5}$ in. long. Malay Peninsula. 1909. (B.M. 8388.) Noteworthy for the long slender-tubed red-purple fl.

T. auriculifo'lia. A synonym of *Craterostigma pumilum*.

T. Baillon'ii. Branched, erect or sprawling herb. *l.* ovate to narrowly ovate, to $2\frac{1}{4}$ in. long, toothed, stalked. *fl.* terminal and axillary; pedicels about $\frac{3}{4}$ to $1\frac{1}{2}$ in. long; cal. about $\frac{6}{10}$ in. long, glabrous, keeled but not winged; cor. with bright yellow limb; tube $\frac{3}{4}$ to 1 in. long, red-purple in upper part. Indochina. 1876. (I. H. 25. 324; F.M. 1878, 311; B.M. 6700 as *T. flava*.) An attractive plant with sharply contrasting fl.-colours, often confused with *T. flava*, but easily distinguished by its much larger long-pedicelled fl.

T. bi'color. A synonym of *T. asiatica* L. sec. Stearn.

T. con'color. Diffuse herb, 6 to 12 in. h. *l.* narrowly ovate, to $1\frac{1}{2}$ in. long, toothed, stalked. *fl.* usually terminal; pedicels 1 to 2 in. long; cal. $\frac{7}{10}$ in. long, glabrous, keeled but not winged, deeply 2-lipped; cor. purple-blue; tube $\frac{9}{10}$ to $1\frac{1}{10}$ in. long. S. China, including Hong Kong, Formosa. 1844. (B.M. 6797; B.R. 1846. 62; Paxt. M.B. 15. 197.) SYN. *T. asiatica* var. *concolor*.

T. cordifo'lia. More or less erect, much branched, hairy annual, 2 to 8 in. h. *l.* ovate, to 2 in. long, toothed mostly cuneate at base, stalked. *fl.* terminal; pedicels $\frac{1}{5}$ to $\frac{1}{2}$ in. long; cal. about $\frac{2}{5}$ in. long, winged, ciliate on wings; cor. pale blue; tube about $\frac{2}{5}$ in. long. India. 1838. (B.M. 3715.) The name is misleading, but the flattened cal. is cordate.

T. cya'nea. Trailing herb. *l.* narrowly ovate, almost glabrous, to $1\frac{1}{2}$ in. long or more, toothed, long-stalked. *fl.* axillary; pedicels to $\frac{3}{5}$ in. long; cal. about $\frac{1}{2}$ in. long, winged, glabrous except for ciliate wings; cor. lavender-blue with dark-violet blotches; tube about $\frac{7}{10}$ in. long, violet. Ceylon, S. India. (B.M. 4249 as *T. asiatica*.)

T. fla'va. Branched, erect, hairy annual, 3 to 12 in. h. *l.* narrowly ovate, to $1\frac{1}{2}$ in. long, toothed, short-stalked or almost sessile. *fl.* small in a terminal raceme; pedicels $\frac{3}{10}$ to $\frac{3}{5}$ in. long; cal. $\frac{2}{5}$ in. long, ciliate, slightly winged; cor. yellow, inconspicuous; tube $\frac{2}{5}$ in. long. N. India, Malaya, Indochina, China. No horticultural value. *T. flava* of gardens and Bot. Mag. is *T. Baillonii*.

T. Ford'ii. Erect hairy herb, 6 to 12 in. h. *l.* ovate-deltoid, to 3 in. long, toothed, stalked. *fl.* small; pedicels $\frac{1}{5}$ to $\frac{7}{10}$ in. long; cal. about $\frac{2}{5}$ in. long, slightly winged, sparsely hairy; cor. straw-yellow, with lateral lobes violet-blotched; tube about $\frac{2}{5}$ in. long. China. 1884. (B.M. 6797.)

T. Fournier'i. Erect, much branched, glabrous annual, to 1 ft. h. *l.* ovate or narrowly ovate, 1 to 2 in. long, toothed, long-stalked. *fl.* in short terminal racemes or axils of upper l.; pedicels $\frac{1}{5}$ to 1 in. long; cal. ellipsoid, about $\frac{3}{5}$ in. long, broadly winged, ciliate; cor. variously coloured, with upper lip pale lilac, lower lip violet, its mid-lobe yellow-blotched at base; tube $\frac{3}{4}$ to 1 in. long, pale violet, yellow on back. The most popular species, naturalized in warm countries, easily recognized by its prominently winged cal. Indochina. About 1880. (B.M. 6747; G.F. 927; Add. 377.)

T. hirsu'ta. Diffuse annual, sometimes trailing. *l.* narrowly ovate, to 2 in. long, toothed, hairy above and below. *fl.* axillary; pedicels to $1\frac{1}{5}$ in. long, hairy; cal. about $\frac{3}{5}$ in. long, hairy, not winged; cor. with violet-blue limb having lower lip whitish; tube $\frac{4}{5}$ in. long, violet-purple. India. 1859. (B.M. t. 5167.)

T. leucosi'phon. A synonym of *T. travancorica*.

T. oblon'ga. Much branched, sprawling herb, 2 to 10 in. h. *l.* narrowly oblong or narrowly oblanceolate, to $\frac{4}{5}$ in. long, untoothed or scarcely toothed. *fl.* terminal; pedicels $\frac{4}{5}$ to $1\frac{1}{2}$ in. long; cal. nearly $\frac{1}{5}$ in. long; glabrous; cor. pale; tube $\frac{3}{10}$ in. long. China, Indochina.

T. parviflo'ra. Much branched annual, 3 to 8 in. h. *l.* narrowly ovate, to $1\frac{1}{4}$ in. long, toothed, stalked. *fl.* axillary and terminal; pedicels $\frac{1}{5}$ to $\frac{1}{2}$ in. long; cal. about $\frac{1}{5}$ in. long, slightly winged, ciliate on wings; cor. pale blue; tube about $\frac{3}{10}$ in. long. India.

T. peduncula'ris. Decumbent herb about $\frac{1}{2}$ to 1 ft. h. *l.* ovate-deltoid, to $2\frac{1}{2}$ in. long, toothed, stalked, often subcordate. *fl.* in short terminal racemes; pedicels $\frac{1}{5}$ to 1 in. long; cal. about $\frac{2}{5}$ in. long, winged, ciliate on wings; cor. with a pale-blue, purple, and yellow blotched limb; tube about $\frac{1}{2}$ in. long, yellowish. India. 1846. (B.M. 4229 as *T. edentula*.)

T. travanco'rica. Diffuse annual or perennial. *l.* narrowly ovate or lanceolate, to $2\frac{1}{2}$ in. long, toothed, glabrescent, long-stalked. *fl.* terminal or axillary; pedicels to 1 in. long; cal. about $\frac{3}{5}$ in. long, narrowly winged, glabrous or with a few scattered hairs; cor. violet-purple; tube about 1 in. long, pale orange-yellow. S. India, Ceylon. 1938. (B.M. 9615.) SYN. *T. leucosiphon*.

W. T. S.

torfa'ceus -a -um, growing in bogs or mosses.

Toring'o, the Japanese name.

TORINGO CRAB. *See* **Malus Sieboldii.**

toringoi'des, Toringo-like.

TORMENTIL'LA. Included in **Potentilla.**

tormina'lis -is -e, relating to colic.

torna'tus -a -um, round as though turned in a lathe.

TORO. *See* **Suttonia salicina.**

toro'sus -a -um, torose, cylindrical with irregular swellings like a knotted muscle.

torqua'tus -a -um, adorned with a neck-chain or collar.

torqui-, in compound words, signifying twisted.

TOR'REYA (in honour of Dr. John Torrey, 1796–1873, American botanist, one of the authors of the *Flora of North America*). Stinking Yew. FAM. *Taxaceae*. A genus of 4 species of evergreen trees emitting a strong, disagreeable odour when bruised, natives of North America, China, and Japan. Branches opposite or whorled. Leaves spirally arranged but appearing 2-ranked on the branchlets owing to a basal twist, linear, curved in 3 species, straight in *T. californica*, leathery, rigid, acute, resembling those of Cephalotaxus in general appearance but stiffer. Male and female flowers often on different trees but sometimes on different branches of the same tree. Male flowers solitary in leaf-axils on young shoots, female flowers in pairs at base of young shoots. Seeds rather like a large acorn, hard-coated and covered by a fleshy aril as in Cephalotaxus. In one species the seeds are edible and oil is extracted from them. They are not very hardy but succeed in warmer parts of the country in ordinary garden soil, under similar conditions to Cupressus, tolerating some lime in the soil. Propagation should be by seeds whenever possible. They should be sown in sandy soil in a warm greenhouse. Cuttings of short, half-ripe shoots may also be rooted if inserted in sandy soil in a close cold frame or under a handlight towards the end of summer. They should be shaded from bright sun and protected from frost until rooted. Layered branches may also be rooted.

T. califor'nica. California Nutmeg. Tree to 90 ft. h. in its native country, large bush here. Young shoots smooth, green at first, brown later. Winter buds about $\frac{1}{8}$ in. long, brown. *l.* $1\frac{1}{4}$ to 3 in.

long, ⅛ in. wide, straight, stiff, leathery, dark green above with two narrow bands of glaucous stomata beneath, apex a sharp spine. *Seeds* broadly elliptical, 1⅓ to 1¾ in. long, the fleshy covering green with purple marks, thin, containing an oleo-resin. California. 1851. (B.M. 4780 as *T. Myristica*; D.J.C. 74.)

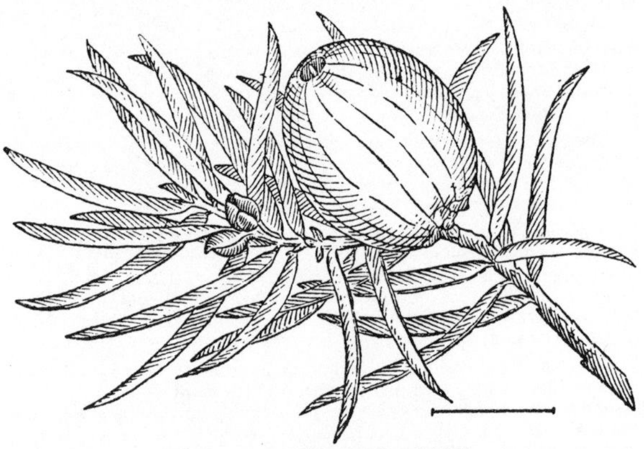

Torreya californica (p. 2127)

T. gran'dis. Varies from a shrub to a tree of 80 ft. h. Young shoots green at first, yellowish-green later. *l.* ¾ to 1¼ in. long, about ⅛ in. wide, rather thin, yellowish-green with 2 sunken, glaucous stomatic bands beneath, inodorous when bruised, apex a sharp point. *Seeds* ¾ to 1 in. long with a reddish-brown covering. China. 1855. (D.J.C. 74.)

T. Myris'tica. A synonym of *T. californica.*

T. nuci'fera. Kaya. Varies in nature from a small to a large tree of 80 ft. h. with many strong, horizontal branches. Young shoots green changing to reddish-brown. Winter buds about ⅛ in. long, glossy. *l.* ¾ to 1¼ in. long, ⅛ in. wide, stiff, curved, dark glossy green above with 2 glaucous stomatic grooves beneath, pointed, emitting a strong, disagreeable odour when bruised. *Seeds* ¾ to 1 in. long, outer covering green, tinged purple. Japan. 1764. (D.J.C. 76.) The seeds contain a good deal of oil and are used for food in Japan.

T. taxifo'lia. Stinking Cedar. Tree up to 40 ft. h. with horizontal or slightly drooping branches. Young shoots bright green with scattered hairs, yellowish-red later. *l.* ¾ to 1½ in. long, dark green above, with 2 glaucous bands of stomata beneath, pointed. *Seeds* 1 to 1½ in. long, rounded, with a disagreeable odour. Florida. 1840.

W. D.

tor'ridus -a -um, parched, tropical.

tort'ilis -is -e (***torti-,*** in compound words), twisted or twined.

TORTOISE-PLANT. *See* **Dioscorea elephantipes.**

TORTOISE-SHELL BUTTERFLY. *See* **Butterflies.**

TORTRIC'IDAE or Tortrix Moths include several hundred species of small moths with wide wings, which are often provided with a dense fringe of hairs, especially on the hind-wings. The moths fly chiefly at dusk, and the oval, usually smooth, eggs are frequently deposited in flattened masses of 'packets' on the leaves and shoots of the host plants. The caterpillars, whose colour range is wide, live either concealed in rolled leaves—'Leaf-rollers'—e.g. Oak Leaf-roller Moth, *Tortrix viridana*; in spun leaves, e.g. Carnation Tortrix, *T. pronubana*; in shoots, e.g. Pine-shoot Moth, *Evetria buoliana*; on the surface of fruits, e.g. the Apple Tortrix, *Cacoecia podana*; in flower-heads, e.g. *Cnephasia chrysanthemana*, on Composites, especially the floral disks of *Chrysanthemum maximum*; in seed-pods, the Pea Moth, *Cydia nigricana*; or in fruits, e.g. Codling Moth, *Cydia pomonella.*

The caterpillars of most species are active and wriggle backwards when disturbed.

The pupa generally protrudes from the cocoon prior to the emergence of the adult and in the situation where the caterpillar has recently been feeding.

The winter is passed in either the egg, larval, or pupal stages according to the species.

Owing to the different habitats taken up by the caterpillars of Tortrix Moths, measures of control must be sought under the name of each pest.

G. F. W.

TORT'RIX. A genus of small moths. *See above and* **Carnation Tortrix Moth** (*T. pronubana*), **Oak Leaf-roller Moth** (*T. viridana*).

tortuo'sus -a -um, tortuous, having an irregular, meandering mode of growth.

tort'us -a -um, twisted, crooked.

TORU. *See* **Persoonia Toru.**

torulo'sus -a -um, thickened at intervals.

TORUS. The floral receptacle from which the parts of flower arise; thalamus.

tor'vus -a -um, fierce, harsh, sharp.

tosarien'sis -is -e, of Tosari, Java.

Tota'ra, native New Zealand name for *Podocarpus Totara.*

Tot'ta, Hottentot.

TOUCH-ME-NOT. *See* **Impatiens Noli-tangere.**

TOURNEFORT'IA (in honour of Joseph Pitton de Tournefort, 1656–1708, author of *Institutiones Rei Herbariae*). FAM. *Boraginaceae.* A genus of about 100 species of trees and shrubs, rarely sub-shrubs, sometimes scrambling or twining, natives of the warmer regions of the world. Leaves alternate, entire. Flowers rather small, in cymes; 5-merous; corolla tube cylindrical, lobes overlapping; stamens attached to and included in tube. The species are of little garden value but a few have been introduced. They grow well in an ordinary compost and can be increased by cuttings.

T. cordifo'lia. Shrub, robust, covered with short hairs. *l.* heart-shaped, about 12 in. long, acute; stalks 3 to 4 in. long. *fl.* white, small, in large terminal corymbs. Trop. America. 1887. (R.H. 1887, 128.) Greenhouse.

T. frutico'sa. Shrub of about 4 ft. *l.* lanceolate or long ovate-lanceolate, slender-pointed, rather obtuse at base, 3 in. long. *fl.* yellow, fragrant, tube longer than cal.; in terminal loose corymbs. June. Canary Is. 1800. (B.R. 464.) Greenhouse.

T. heliotropioi'des. A synonym of *Heliotropium anchusifolium.*

Toveren'ae, in honour of Goyzueta de Toverena, Italian Consul-General in Australia, *c.* 1884.

TOUS-LES-MOIS. *See* **Canna edulis.**

TOWNSENDIA (in honour of David Townsend, botanist of Pennsylvania, *c.* 1840). FAM. *Compositae.* A genus of about 20 species of dwarf perennial herbs, much branched from the base, natives of the western half of N. America. Leaves linear-spatulate, entire. Flower-heads large, much resembling Aster, rays many, violet or rose-purple to white; involucral bracts usually ciliate. Achenes usually bristly. Plants for the well-drained rock-garden or the alpine house, several of which not yet introduced appear to be worthy of a place from their freedom in producing their large flowers and from their habit, but they seem to be somewhat short-lived in cultivation.

T. exsca'pa. Nearly stemless perennial. *l.* linear-spatulate, 1 to 3 in. long, narrowed to the base. *fl.-heads* about ¾ in. across, sessile or almost so among the l., white or purplish-tinged. May, June. Western N. America. SYN. *T. sericea, T. Wilcoxiana* of gardens.

T. grandiflo'ra. Biennial or perennial, 9 to 18 in. h. with several stems from base which may also be branched above. *l.* narrow. *fl.-heads* about 1½ in. across, bright blue or violet; involucral bract narrowed upwards with dry margins. Summer. SW. United States.

Townshend'ii, in honour of Richard B. Townshend of Colorado who sent plants to Kew, *c.* 1878.

A→

toxica'rius -a -um, poisonous.

TOXICODEN'DRON of Miller (from Greek *toxin*, poison, *dendron*, tree). FAM. *Anacardiaceae*. A synonym of Rhus section Toxicodendron to which the Poison Ivy and related species (*Rhus radicans*, *R. Toxicodendron*, *R. orientalis*, &c.) belong. Some American botanists maintain this as an independent genus. *T. vulgare* is a synonym of *Rhus radicans*.

TOXICODEN'DRUM of Thunberg (derivation as above). FAM. *Euphorbiaceae*. A monotypic genus related to Phyllanthus, the cells of the ovary each containing 2 ovules and the sepals of the male flowers being imbricate. Latex is absent. For other characters see below. Greenhouse, in sandy loam. The name Toxicodendrum of Thunberg, published in 1796, has now been discarded owing to the likelihood of confusion with Toxicodendron of Miller, published in 1754; the correct name is accordingly HYAENAN'CHE (from Greek *huania*, Latin *hyaena*, hyena, *agchos*, strangle, the powdered fruit being sprinkled on carcasses to poison hyenas).

H. globo'sa. Shrub or small tree with corky branches. *l.* in whorls of 3 or 4, lanceolate, 2½ to 4 in. long, ½ to 1⅓ in. wide, cuneate; stalk ¼ to ½ in. long. *fl.* dioecious, without pet.; male infl. in axillary clusters about ½ in. long; sep. 5, stamens numerous, white large anthers; female fl. 1 to 3 in the l.-axils; sep. 6 in 2 series. June. S. Africa. 1883. (F.P.S.A. 837.) SYN. *Toxicodendrum capense*, *T. globosum*.

W. J. B.

TOXICOPHLAE'A. *See* **Acokanthera.**

Toxop'ei, in honour of L. J. Toxopeus, b. 1894, biologist of Java.

TOXOSTIG'MA. A synonym of Arnebia.

Toza, native name in S. Africa.

TRACHEAE, TRACHEIDS. *See* **Vessels.**

TRACHELIOP'SIS. Included in **Trachelium.**

TRACHE'LIUM (*trachelos*, neck; the plants were supposed to be efficacious against diseases of the trachea). FAM. *Campanulacae*. Small perennial herbs, usually erect and often woody at the base. Leaves alternate, cauline. Flowers small, almost umbellate or in corymbose panicles; calyx tubular, limb 5-partite; corolla narrow, tubular, with 5 lobes; stamens free; style conspicuously protruding (except in *T. myrtifolium*), with a capitate stigma in *T. caeruleum* and *T. lanceolatum*, shortly 2- or 3-fld. in other species. The limits of the genus which is very close to Campanula are debatable. As defined by Buser in *Bulletin de l'Herbier Boissier*, 2: 501–32 (1894), Trachelium comprises only *T. caeruleum*, *T. lanceolatum*, and *T.* × *halteratum*. The other E. Mediterranean species are placed by Buser in DIOSPHAE'RA (Balkan Peninsula) and TRACHELIOP'SIS (Lebanon, Turkey). In the present account all the species are for convenience retained under Trachelium. The group is Mediterranean in distribution; all except *T. caeruleum* are confined to crevices of limestone rocks. *T. caeruleum* grows well in a compost of sandy loam and leaf-mould. Doubtfully hardy, it can be treated as a half-hardy annual, if sown early, and makes a good pot-plant. It is increased by seed sown in spring on a slight hotbed, or by cuttings in April and August. The other species are neat and attractive species for alpine house cultivation, and may be grown in the rock-garden on limestone soil, when a pane of glass should be provided in winter to keep off excessive rain. They all flower in late summer.

T. asperuloi'des. Tiny cushion plant, 1 to 1½ in. h. *l.* minute, obovate-orbicular, sessile, overlapping, entire. *fl.* lilac, 1 to 5 at tips of shoots; cor. ⅕ in. long, deeply divided into linear lobes. Styx gorge, Greece (Bull. Herb. Boiss. 2. 17). SYN. *Diosphaera asperuloides*.

T. caeru'leum. Erect, about 2 to 4 ft. h. *l.* ovate, acute, not leathery, deeply double-toothed, sometimes hairy beneath, stalked. *fl.* very numerous, in corymbose panicles; cor. violet-blue, about $\frac{3}{10}$ in. long, with a very slender tube and short lobes. W. and Cent. Mediterranean. 1640. (B.R. 72.) var. **al'bum,** *fl.* white. In general appearance this suggests a blue *Kentranthus ruber*. (B.M. n.s. 427).

T. × haltera'tum (*T. caeruleum* × *T. lanceolatum*). Hybrid. Sicily.

T. Jacquin'ii. Resembling *T. rumelianum*, with larger *l.* up to 3 in. long. Crete. 1930. SYN. *Diosphaera Jacquinii*.

T. lanceola'tum. Erect, 6 to 9 in. h. *l.* mainly at the lower part of stem, lanceolate, not leathery, 2½ to 5 in. long, shallowly and simply toothed, glabrous, stalked. *fl.* numerous, in corymbose panicles; cor. violet-blue, about ⅜ in. long, with a very slender tube and short lobes. S. Sicily. 1936. (B.M. 9603.) SYN. *T. caeruleum* var. *lanceolatum*.

T. myrtifo'lium. Tufted with 1 in. h. stems. *l.* minute, elliptic, entire, sessile, hairy. *fl.* 1 to 5 at tips of shoots; cor. lilac or white, hairy, $\frac{3}{10}$ in. long, with short triangular lobes; style not protruding. S. Turkey. 1949. SYN. *Campanula myrtifolia*.

T. Post'ii. Erect, 6 to 12 in. h., thick-stemmed, hairy species with canescent toothed sep., and relatively deeply lobed pale-violet cor. Syria. (Bull. Herb. Boiss. 2. 19.) SYN. *Tracheliopsis Postii*.

T. rumelia'num. Sprawling 6 to 12 in. h. stems. *l.* narrowly ovate or oblong, acute, to 1 in. long, sparsely toothed, sessile. *fl.* numerous, in dense rounded heads; cor. lilac, ⅜ in. long, with linear lobes. Bulgaria, Greece. 1930. (Bull. Herb. Boiss. 2. 16.) SYN. *Diosphaera dubia*, *D. rumeliana*.

T. tubulo'sum. Erect, about 6 in. h. *l.* elliptic, very shallowly toothed, sessile, almost glabrous or shortly hairy. *fl.* corymbose; sep. entire; cor. milk-white, split into short, scarcely spreading triangular lobes. Lebanon, S. Turkey. (Bull. Herb. Boiss. 2. 18.) SYN. *Tracheliopsis tubulosa*.

P. H. D.

TRACHELOSPER'MUM (*trachelos*, neck, *sperma*, seed). FAM. *Apocynaceae*. A genus of about 23 species of climbing shrubs, all from E. Asia except one (*T. difforme*) from S. United States. Stems slender, exuding (like the leaves) a milky juice when cut. Leaves opposite, leathery, markedly veined. Flowers white or pale yellow, in terminal and axillary clusters; corolla with a cylindrical tube and 5 spreading, twisted lobes; stamens very short, the anthers united and attached to the stigma. The 4 species here described are hardy on walls. In cold districts *T. jasminoides* is an attractive greenhouse climber. Propagation is by cuttings.

KEY

1.	*Sep. ovate-lanceolate or lanceolate, acute to acuminate*	2
1.	*Sep. oblong or oblanceolate, blunt or acute*	3
2.	*Sep. about $\frac{1}{10}$ in. long; anther tips barely protruding from cor. tube. W. China*	T. crocostomum
2.	*Sep. about ⅛ in. long; anther tips conspicuously protruding from cor. tube. Japan*	T. asiaticum
3.	*Lvs. ovate to elliptic*	T. majus
3.	*Lvs. ovate-lanceolate*	T. jasminoides

T. asiat'icum. Evergreen climber up to 15 or 20 ft., very leafy, shoots persistently hairy. *l.* ¾ to 2 in. long, ⅜ to ¾ in. wide, dark glossy green. *fl.* yellowish-white, fragrant, in terminal clusters 2 to 2½ in. across; cor. ¾ in. wide, the 5 lobes obovate; cal. lobes erect, pointed. July, August. Korea, Japan.

T. crocos'tomum. Evergreen climber closely allied to *T. asiaticum*. Before 1906. W. China. Probably many plants grown as *T. asiaticum* belong to *T. crocostomum*.

T. jasminoi'des. Evergreen climber up to 20 ft., shoots slender, hairy. *l.* oval-lanceolate, 1½ to 3 in. long, ½ to 1 in. wide, tapered to both ends, dark shining green, at first downy beneath; stalk ⅛ in. long. *fl.* very fragrant, white, about 1 in. wide, in axillary and terminal racemes; cor. lobes narrow, wavy; cal. with 5 reflexed, lanceolate, reflexed lobes. July. China. 1844. (B.M. 4737 as *Rhyncospermum jasminoides*.) Wall or, in cold districts, greenhouse. var. **angustifo'lium,** *l.* ¼ to ½ in. long; **variegat'um,** *l.* shorter, broader, silver-variegated.

T. ma'jus. Vigorous climber up to 40 or 60 ft., shoots persistently downy. *l.* ovate or elliptic, 1 to 3 in. long, ½ to 2 in. wide, dark shining green, paler and at first downy beneath. *fl.* pure white, ½ to ¾ in. wide, cor. lobes, obovate, twisted. *l.* sometimes colour richly before falling. The tallest and largest-leaved of cultivated species; will cover a house like ivy. SYN. *T. japonicum*.

W. J. B.

trachy, in compound words, signifies rough to the touch.

TRACHYCAR'PUS (*trachys*, rough, *karpos*, fruit). FAM. *Palmaceae*. A genus of 5 or 6 species of palms natives of E. Asia, tall, unarmed, and with fan-shaped, plicate leaves. Flower monoecious, small, yellow, in large stout panicles embraced by sheathing spathes; stamens 6; ovary of 3 carpels. Fruit globose or oblong, smooth or tomentose, 1-seeded. Some authorities consider these 3 species, as well as another called *T. Takil*, forms of 1 species. *T. Fortunei* is hardy in many parts of Britain (the other 2 are cool greenhouse); it should be planted in a sheltered spot to avoid or mitigate the shattering of the leaves in high winds. A rich loam with occasional top-dressings of farm-yard manure is recommended.

KEY

1. *Lvs. green beneath; l.-stalk very spiny* 2
1. *Lvs. glaucous beneath; l.-stalk less spiny* T. Martianus
2. *Trunk clothed in upper part with coarse dark fibres* T. Fortunei
2. *Trunk slender, polished, with fibre only near l.* T. khasyanus

T. excel'sus. A synonym of *T. Fortunei.*

T. Fortun'ei. Of varying height according to the climate; thus plants of the same age may vary from 12 ft. in cool places to 40 ft. in warmer ones. Trunk cylindrical, much of upper part clothed with coarse, dark fibres from which ropes and rough fabrics are made. *l.* fan-shaped, up to 2½ ft. long and 3½ ft. wide, divided into numerous narrow lobes; stalk 1½ to 3 ft. long, armed with stout sharp teeth. *fl.* yellow, small, very numerous on a thick-stemmed decurved panicle 2 ft. long, *fr.* a blue-black drupe, ½ in. wide, globose. China. 1844. (B.M. 5221.) SYN. *T. excelsus, Chamaerops excelsa.* Hardy in places in Britain with a moderate climate. var. **surculo'sus,** a very dwarf, suckering form.

T. khasya'nus. Up to 50 ft. or more, stem slender. *l.* fan-shaped, orbicular, very numerously lobed; 2 ft. long, 3 ft. wide; stalk as long as blade. *fl.* yellow, very numerous on a stout panicle 1 to 2 ft. long. *fr.* dull blue. E. Bengal and Burma on mts. 3,500 to 6,000 ft. (B.M. 7128.) Differs from *T. Fortunei* by its more slender, polished trunk only fibred near the l. Cool greenhouse.

T. Martia'nus. Slender stemmed palm up to 40 or 50 ft. *l.* orbicular, 2½ ft. long, 3 ft. wide, with 30 to 40 linear lobes, glaucous beneath; stalk up to 2½ ft. long, semicircular, slightly toothed. *infl.* drooping. *fr.* oblong, yellow at first, finally glossy blue. Himalaya. Differs from *T. khasyanus* by the glaucous under-surface of the l. with the l.-stalk much less spiny, but by some regarded as including that plant.

W. J. B.

TRACHYME'NE. *See* **Didiscus.**

TRACHYPTEL'LA aspera. *See* **Tetracera sarmentosa.**

TRACHYSTE'MON (*trachys*, rough, *stemon*, stamen; the filaments in 1 species are rough.) FAM. *Boraginaceae.* A genus of 2 species of erect, branched, roughly hairy perennial herbs, natives of the Near East. Flowers stalked; calyx 5-cleft; corolla tube cylindrical, 5-scaled within, the 5 lobes linear, spreading, or at length revolute; stamens 5; cymes rather loose. Fruit of 4 erect nutlets. Leaves large, long-stalked, stem-leaves few. *T. orientalis* grows in ordinary soil and is a suitable plant for the wild garden in half-shady places or the edge of woodland. It may be propagated by seeds or division and is quite hardy.

T. orienta'lis. Roughly hairy; stem 1 to 2 ft. h. *Lower l.* about 12 in. long, 8 in. wide, cordate; *upper* ovate-lanceolate, narrowed at base. *fl.* purplish-blue, numerous, about ½ in. across, on long pedicels; cor. lobes revolute, hairy outside at tip; stamens forming a cone. March to May. SE. Balkan Peninsula, Asia Minor, Caucasus. 1752. (B.R. 288 and S.B.F.G. as *Borago orientalis.*) SYN. *Psilostemon orientalis, Nordmannia cordifolia.*

TRADESCANT'IA (in honour of John Tradescant, d. 1638, gardener to Charles I). FAM. *Commelinaceae.* A genus of about 100 species of perennial herbs, natives of N. and Trop. America. Habit and foliage variable. Flowers more or less stalked, many or few in a cyme, rarely solitary, subtended by 1 to 3 bracts similar to the leaves. Sepals 3, distinct, concave, green or coloured; petals 3, free, obovate or orbicular; stamens 6, usually all perfect. Fruit a capsule. *T. virginiana* is the best known of the hardy species. It will thrive in any good, rather moist soil, and although the flowers last but a day they are produced in succession, so the plant has a long flowering period. Its varieties are best propagated by division. The greenhouse and stove species are essentially foliage plants. *T. fluminensis* and *T. albiflora* (plants liable to be confused with *Zebrina pendula* or *Commelina diffusa* which is usually, though incorrectly, known as *C. nudiflora*) are common greenhouse and window plants, and like almost all the species are easy to grow. Variegated forms are most ornamental if grown in good light. These and other tender species are readily increased by cuttings put in light soil in moderate heat. The creeping members of this and related genera are commonly known as 'Wandering Jews', and as they are often confused have been inserted in the key below. They can be grown in hanging baskets in the greenhouse but are frequently used to carpet the soil beneath the staging. It is probable that many of the plants grown as *T. virginiana* are hybrids between that species and others nearly related; in this group individual plants and the clones derived from them are self-sterile; hence one grown in isolation produces no seed, but the species and their varieties intercross readily and then give abundant seed, so that self-sown plants often occur.

A monograph by E. Anderson and R. E. Woodson of the species of Tradescantia indigenous to the United States has been published in *Contributions from the Arnold Arboretum*, no. 9 (1935). **A**

KEY

1. *Plant more or less prostrate, rooting at joints* 2
1. *Plant ascending or erect* 4
2 (1). *L.-sheaths about 1 in. long, tubular, the new growth piercing and emerging from base of sheath; blades narrowly elliptic, bright green above and below, margin undulate, to 4½ in. long. Fl. pale blue* Coleotrype natalensis
2. *L.-sheath not more than ⅜ in. long; new growth not piercing base but emerging from base of sheath* 3
3 (2). *L. upper side with two broad lateral silvery bands separated by green mid-area; lower side purple-red; blade narrowly ovate, elliptic, up to 3 in. long. Pet. 6, joined at base into a tube, purple* Zebrina pendula
3. *Lvs. not as above* 18
4 (1). *Stem absent or very short at least at first* 5
4. *Stem evident, usually branched* 7
5 (4). *Lvs. oblong-ovate, brown hairy* T. fuscata
5. *Lvs. linear-lanceolate* 6
6 (5). *Sep. without glandular hairs. Stem finally lengthening* T. Tharpii
6. *Sep. with glandular hairs. Stem not lengthening* T. longipes
7 (4). *Lvs. in 2 rows on stem, whitish banded above, purple below* T. Reginae
7. *Lvs. in several rows on stem* 8
8 (7). *Fl. umbellate, umbels sessile* 9
8. *Fl. clusters on evident peduncles* 17
9 (8). *Lvs. oblong to ovate* 10
9. *L.-blade linear to lanceolate* 12
10 (9). *Lvs. ovate, keeled, about ¾ in. long, glabrous; stem-ascending* T. navicularis
10. *Lvs. oblong to oblong-lanceolate* 11
11 (10). *Lvs. glabrous, except ciliate margins. Fl. white* T. Crassula
11. *Lvs. softly hairy above, silky beneath. Fl. rose-purple* T. velutina
12 (9). *Upper blades broader than sheaths* 13
12. *L.-blades not broader than sheaths* 14
13 (12). *Peduncles usually white-woolly. Roots tuberous* T. crassifolia
13. *Peduncles more or less glabrous. Roots slender* T. subaspera
14 (13). *Sep. generally hairy all over* 15
14. *Sep. glabrous except at tip* T. canaliculata
15 (14). *Bracts decidedly saccate, blades short* T. gigantea
15. *Bracts not saccate* 16
16 (15). *Sep. not glandular* T. virginiana
16 *Sep. glandular* T. occidentalis
17 (8). *Stamens all equal. Lvs. narrow oblong* Spironema Warscewiczianum
17. *Stamens 3 long, 3 short. Stem procumbent at base ascending above. Lvs. lanceolate* T. elongata
18 (3). *Lvs. purple or reddish on upper side as well as below. Pet. joined at base into a tube* Zebrina Purpusii
18. *Lvs. not purple on upper side, though sometimes purple beneath. Pet. free to base* 19
19 (18). *Sheath surface hairy all round* 20
19. *Sheath surface glabrous except for a single line of hairs; margin often ciliate* 22
20 (19). *L.-blade narrowed into a distinct stalk above sheath, pubescent with very short hairs. Fl. blue, arising out of a boat-like spathe; fertile stamens 3.* Commelina benghalensis

(See p. 532)

20. *L.-blade sessile, i.e. narrowed directly into sheath, villous with longer hairs. Fl. rose or white, not arising out of a boat-like spathe; fertile stamens* 6 — 21
21 (20). *Infl. umbellate, condensed. Fl. rose* — T. Blossfeldiana
21. *Infl. a loose panicle. Fl. white* — T. geniculata
22 (19). *L. surface villous. Infl. a loose much-branched panicle* — T. geniculata
22. *L. surface glabrous* — 23
23 (22). *Lvs. narrow (under ½ in. wide). Internodes short (¼ to 2 in. long). Fl. rose* — T. micrantha
23. *Lvs. broader (to 1 in. wide). Internodes longer. Fl. white or blue* — 24
24 (23). *Plant somewhat ascending; fl. shoots erect,* 4 *to* 8 *in. h.* — 26
24. *Plant prostrate* — 25
25 (24). *Lvs. about twice as long as wide, usually purplish beneath. Anther cells parallel, connective rectangular* — T. fluminensis
25. *Lvs. about* 3 *or* 4 *times as long as wide, usually green beneath. Anther cells diverging, connective triangular* — T. albiflora
26 (24). *L.-blades ovate. Fl. white.* — T. multiflora
26. *L.-blades lanceolate* — Commelina diffusa
(See p. 532 under *C. nudiflora*)

T. albiflo'ra. Wandering Jew. Perennial trailer with shining l. and stems, nodes swollen. *l.* narrowly elliptic or lanceolate, acute, about 1½ in. long, sessile; sheath about 3/10 in. long. *fl.* small, white; stamens 6, all alike; anther cells diverging obliquely, the connective being triangular. S. America. SYN. *T. viridis.* Shy-flowering and often confused with *T. fluminensis.* Greenhouse.

T. Blossfeldia'na. Creeping or trailing perennial, with thick, olive-green, sparsely hairy stems. *l.* narrowly oblong to narrowly elliptic, to 4 in. long, 1¼ in. wide, acute, sessile, leathery, dark green above, purple and pilose with long whitish hairs beneath; sheath about ½ in. long, hairy. *fl.* nearly ½ in. across, in a many-fld. umbel; sep. and pedicels purplish, hairy; pet. rose in upper half, white in lower half. March. Argentine. 1938. Warm greenhouse.

T. brevicau'lis. A name of doubtful application, used by Rafinesque for what would seem to be a dwarfed specimen of *T. virginiana*, but later applied to naturally dwarf species of the S. United States, such as *T. longipes* and *T. Tharpii.*

T. canalicula'ta. Habit of *T. virginiana* but plant glaucous, the l.-blade narrower than the sheath, sep. glabrous or with the tips only with a tuft of glandless hairs. *fl.* purple, blue, to rose, rarely white, with or without blue filaments, occasionally variegated. Summer. Widely distributed in eastern half of United States. (B.M. 3546 as *T. caricifolia.*) SYN. *T. reflexa.* Hardy.

T. caricifo'lia. A synonym of *T. canaliculata.*

T. conges'ta. A synonym of *T. virginiana.*

T. crassifo'lia. Tuberous-rooted perennial. Stems scarcely branched, about 2 ft. h. *l.* elliptic or narrow-lanceolate, woolly beneath. *fl.* in sessile umbels, axillary, upper with 2, lower with 1 bract; similar to those of *T. virginiana* but sep. woolly; pet. purplish-rose or blue. August. Mexico. 1796. (B.M. 1598.) var. **acaul'is** stem short or none. (B.R. 1840, 34 as *T. iridescens.*); **glabrat'a,** *l.* glabrous except the white-woolly margins, sep. white-woolly. Half-hardy.

T. Cras'sula. Somewhat glabrous succulent. Stem ascending, branched, about 18 in. h. *l.* oblong, about 4 in. long, margins ciliate. *fl.* ½ to ½ in. wide, in many-fld. umbels, mostly terminal; sep. hairy; pet. white. July. Brazil. 1825. (B.M. 2935; L.B.C. 1560.) Stove.

T. dis'color. A synonym of *Rhoeo discolor.*

T. elonga'ta. Nearly glabrous perennial with procumbent stems about 18 in. h., rooting at base. *l.* lanceolate or oblong-lanceolate, 3 in. long, slender pointed, sessile, light greyish-green above, striped with silver, reddish-purple beneath. *fl.* rose, sep. green; stamens unequal, 3 long, 3 short, peduncles terminal, 1 to 5. Trop. America. 1892.

T. fluminen'sis. Wandering Jew. Perennial trailer with shining l. and stems, nodes swollen. *l.* narrowly ovate, acute, about 1½ in. long, short-stalked; ciliate at top of the sheath only; sheath about ⅛ in. long. *fl.* small, white; stamens 6, all alike, anther cells parallel, the connective being rectangular; infl. a sessile cluster with 2 unequal foliose bracts. S. America. SYN. *T. viridis vittata, T. tricolor.* In dim light the l. are green, in bright light they are usually purplish-red beneath and forms occur with l. striped yellow and white, the variegation becoming most evident in light. Often confused with *Zebrina pendula, Commelina diffusa,* and *T. albiflora.* Greenhouse.

T. fusca'ta. Stem short, sometimes very short, brown-hairy. *l.* oblong, 6 to 8 in. long, acute, entire, more or less stalked. *fl.* blue or blue-purple, 1 in. or more across, crowded among the l. on very short 1- to 3-fld. peduncles. September. Brazil, &c. 1820. (B.M. 2330; B.R. 482; L.B.C. 374.) SYN. *Pyrrheima Loddigesii.* Stove.

T. genicula'ta. 9 to 12 in. h., the stems procumbent and rooting at base, fl.-shoots ascending. *l.* ovate-lanceolate to lanceolate, acute, rounded or narrowed at base sessile, to 4½ in. long, more or less villous; sheath villous, about 3/10 in. long. *fl.* white, 3/10 in. across, in a loose panicle. Trop. America. Greenhouse.

T. gigante'a. At first l. from cluster near ground, stem finally ascending, straight, little branched, 1 to 2 ft. h. *l.* linear-lanceolate, rather narrower than sheath, glaucous, upper often downy. Bracts conspicuously saccate with blades 1 to 4 in. long, minutely downy. *fl.* in umbels in upper l.-axils, bright magenta to blue, about 1½ in. across; sep. minutely downy without glands. Texas.

T. irides'cens. A synonym of *T. crassifolia acaulis.*

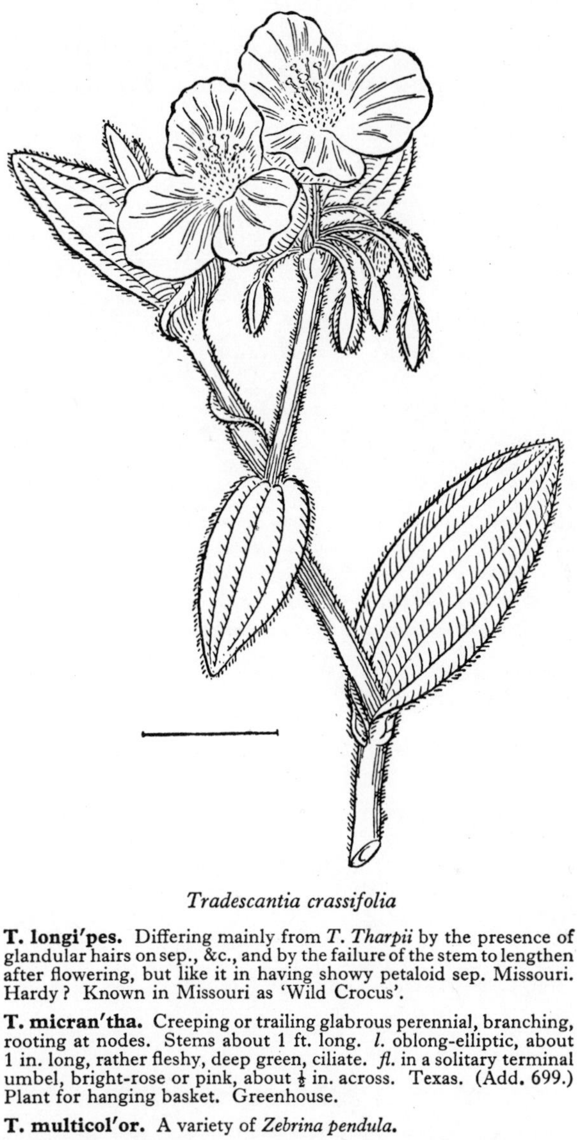

Tradescantia crassifolia

T. longi'pes. Differing mainly from *T. Tharpii* by the presence of glandular hairs on sep., &c., and by the failure of the stem to lengthen after flowering, but like it in having showy petaloid sep. Missouri. Hardy? Known in Missouri as 'Wild Crocus'.

T. micran'tha. Creeping or trailing glabrous perennial, branching, rooting at nodes. Stems about 1 ft. long. *l.* oblong-elliptic, about 1 in. long, rather fleshy, deep green, ciliate. *fl.* in a solitary terminal umbel, bright-rose or pink, about ½ in. across. Texas. (Add. 699.) Plant for hanging basket. Greenhouse.

T. multicol'or. A variety of *Zebrina pendula.*

T. multiflo'ra. Stem ascending. *l.* ovate, somewhat cordate at base, 1 to 2 in. long. *fl.* in terminal and axillary umbels, peduncles hairy, shorter than l., white; sep. ovate, hairy, as long as pet. June. Jamaica. 1824. Stove.

T. navicula'ris. Stoloniferous, glabrous. Stems flexuose, little branched. *l.* ovate, acute, ¾ in. long, rather keeled like sep., ciliate, thickly dotted beneath. *fl.* bright rose, similar to those of *T. virginiana,* pet. twice as long as sep. Summer. Peru. (G.F. 901.) Stove.

T. occidenta'lis. Slender, branched, glabrous, glaucous plant, about 1 ft. h. *l.* narrow-linear, involute. *fl.* blue or rosy, sep. glandular hairy. SE. United States.

T. pilo'sa. A synonym of *T. subaspera.*

T. quad'ricolor. A variety of *Zebrina pendula.*

T. refle'xa. A synonym of *T. canaliculata.*

T. Regi'nae. Erect. *l.* lanceolate, 6 in. long, slender-pointed, whitish-green with middle and margins veined dark green, tinged purple along midrib, purple beneath, glabrous. Peru? 1870. (G.C. 11 (1892), f. 102; I.H. 1892, 147.) The flowering of this species does not appear to have been recorded.

T. subas'pera. Habit of *T. virginiana* but l.-blade broader than sheath and a base narrower than the sheath, stems flexuose, sep. not inflated nor conspicuously leaf-like. Cent. United States. (B.M. 1597.) SYN. *T. pilosa.* Hardy.

T. Tharp'ii. At first often without stem but stem lengthening to 8 in. in fruit, erect, straight, unbranched, shaggy. *l.* linear-lanceolate, 5 to 12 in. long, hairy, green, not glaucous; edged purple or hyaline. *fl.* nearly 2 in. across, in terminal, many-fld. umbels; pedicels and sep. rose or purple; pet. deep rose, purple or blue; filaments hairy. Summer. Cent. United States. SYN. *T. brevicaulis* of some authors. Hardy?

T. veluti'na. Softly white, hairy herb about 18 in. h. Stem branched. *l.* oblong-lanceolate, 5 in. long, dense softly hairy above, shortly silky beneath. *fl.* purplish-rose in terminal and axillary, many-fld. umbels; sep. and pedicels softly downy. May. Guatemala. 1850. Stove.

T. virginia'na. Common Spider-wort. Flower of a Day. Erect, straight, branching, glabrous or somewhat downy above. *l.* linear-lanceolate, 6 to 14 in. long, glabrous or slightly downy on sheath, dull green, not glaucous. Bracts long, foliaceous. *fl.* in few- to many-fld. umbels, usually terminal, blue to purple, rarely rose or white, about 1 in. across; filaments very hairy; sep. rather thin, inflated, hairy all over, but without glands. Summer. E. United States. 1629. (B.R. 1840, 42 as *T. tumida.*) SYN. *T. virginica.* A very variable, hardy species but some of the forms given under this name are probably of hybrid origin or may belong to a nearly related species such as *T. subaspera, T. canaliculata*, or *T. gigantea.* var. **al'ba,** *fl.* white; **al'ba major,** a large-fld. white form; **atrosanguin'ea,** *fl.* dark red; **atroviolac'ea,** *fl.* dark purple; **Azure,** *fl.* rich blue; **Blue Stone,** blue; **caeru'lea,** *fl.* bright blue; **caeru'lea fl. pl.,** *fl.* blue, double; **carn'ea,** *fl.* soft rose-pink; **cocci'nea,** *fl.* bright red; **congesta,** *fl.* purple; **delica'ta,** *fl.* light mauve; **grandiflo'ra alba,** much like *alba major*; **Iris Prichard,** *fl.* mauve with rose shading; **James Crawford Weguelin,** *fl.* lavender blue; **Leonor'a,** *fl.* royal blue with yellow centre; **lilacin'a,** *fl.* lilac purple; **ma'jor,** *fl.* double; **Osprey,** white; **Purple Dome,** purple; **purpu'rea,** *fl.* purple; **ru'bra,** *fl.* dark rose-pink or red; **ru'bra plen'a,** *fl.* double red; **viola'cea,** *fl.* purple-blue or violet. *See also T. brevicaulis.*

T. vir'idis. A synonym of *Zebrina pendula.*

T. vitta'ta. A synonym of *Zebrina pendula.*

T. Warscewiczia'na. A synonym of *Spironema Warscewiczianum.*

T. zebri'na. A synonym of *Zebrina pendula.*

TRAGACANTH, GUM. A product of *Astragalus Tragacantha.*

tragophyl'lus -a -um, with leaves like *Lonicera Caprifolium.*

TRAGOPO'GON (*tragos*, goat, *pogon*, beard; in allusion to the silky pappus). FAM. *Compositae.* A genus of perhaps 40 species of biennial or perennial herbs with alternate, entire, linear, stem-clasping, often grass-like leaves. Flower-heads yellow or purplish, terminal, florets ligulate, truncate, 5-toothed; involucre narrow, bell-shaped or cylindrical, the bracts in a single series, often long; achenes glabrous or somewhat rough; pappus bristles in 1-series. Propagated by seeds sown in spring in ordinary garden soil. This genus has a special interest to geneticists in that it was the subject of hybridization experiments by Linnaeus in 1759, his hybrid *T. porrifolius* × *T. pratensis* being the first deliberately made and scientifically recorded interspecific cross; segregation of characters in the F_1 generation was noted by Koelreuter in 1761. The species readily hybridize but the offspring is usually rather sterile. In America new fertile species *T. mirus* (derived from *T. dubius* × *T. porrifolius*) and *T. miscellus* (derived from *T. dubius* × *T. pratensis*) have arisen through doubling of the chromosomes in hybrids between the species naturalized from Europe.

T. crocifo'lius. Glabrous biennial about 18 in. h. Stem simple or little branched. *l.* narrow-linear, straight. *fl.-heads* purplish-violet; involucral bracts as long as rays. *Achenes* muricate. July. Italy. 1704. (B.M. 479 as *Geropogon glaber.*)

T. dub'ius. Glabrous perennial up to 5 ft. h. *l.* straight, linear-lanceolate, slender-pointed, somewhat glaucous, hairy when young. *fl.-heads* pale lemon-yellow on obconic, hollow peduncles; involucral bracts longer than ray-florets, not purple-margined; pappus whitish. May. Austria. 1788. SYN. *T. major.*

T. gla'ber. A synonym of *T. crocifolius.*

T. ma'jor. A synonym of *T. dubius.*

T. mi'rus. *l.* linear-lanceolate, not undulate, at first slightly hairy, then glabrous and glaucous. *fl.-heads* with ray-florets lilac at tip, yellow below; involucral bracts a little longer than ray-florets, not purple-margined; peduncles swollen; pappus brownish. Originated in America from *T. dubius* × *T. porrifolius.*

T. miscel'lus. *l.* undulate, at first slightly hairy, then glabrous and green. *fl.-heads* yellow; involucral bracts much longer than ray-florets, purple-margined; peduncles swollen; pappus grey. Originated in America from *T. dubius* × *T. pratensis.*

T. porrifo'lius. Salsify. Vegetable Oyster. Glabrous biennial about 3 ft. h. *l.* straight, linear-lanceolate, tapered to a point, sheaths slightly dilated. *fl.-heads* rose- or reddish-purple, up to 2 in. across; involucral bracts longer than ray-florets, not purple-margined; peduncles obconic, hollow at top; pappus brownish. May, June. N. Europe, naturalized in Britain. (E.B. 801.) *See* **Salsify.**

T. praten'sis. Goat's Beard; Jack-go-to-bed-at-Noon; Shepherd's Clock; Noon Flower; Star of Jerusalem. Biennial about 2 ft. h., stem stout, erect. *l.* flexuous, gradually narrowed upwards, lowest channelled above, pale green, slightly hairy when young. *fl.-heads* yellow, up to 2 in. across; involucral bracts about as long as outer ray-florets, purple-margined; peduncles scarcely thickened upwards. Summer. Europe. (E.B. 798–900.)

T. ro'seus. A synonym of *T. ruber.*

T. ru'ber. Cobwebby perennial about 18 in. h. *l.* lanceolate-linear, slightly undulate, glaucous. *fl.-heads* rose or purplish-rose; involucre of about 8 bracts; peduncles terete. Siberia. 1826. SYN. *T. roseus.*

TRAGOPY'RUM. A synonym of Atraphaxis.

Tragus, old generic name in honour of Hieronymus Bock, 1498–1554, German herbalist; 'bock' being German for 'he-goat', Bock adopted the name 'Tragus' (from Greek *tragos*, he-goat).

TRAILER. *See* **Creeper.**

trailing, long and prostrate but not rooting.

Traillia'nus -a -um, in honour of James William Helenus Trail, 1851–1919, Professor of Botany, Aberdeen.

A→

A→

TRANSPLANTING. *See under* **Planting** in Supplement.

TRA'PA (contraction of *calcitrapa*, Caltrop, 4-spiked iron ball, thrown down to maim cavalry horses). FAM. *Onagraceae.* A genus of about 8 species of floating herbs, natives of the warmer parts of Europe, Asia, and Africa. Submerged leaves opposite, root-like, pinnatipartite with thread-like segments; floating leaves in a rosette, rhomboidal, with a spongy swelling near apex of stalk. Flowers axillary, solitary, stalked; calyx tube short, limb 4-parted, 2 or all segments becoming spiny and persisting in fruit; petals 4, white, small; stamens 4. Fruit bony, 1-celled, large, obovoid, 4-angled, indehiscent, with a short cylindrical beak at top. The seeds of *T. bispinosa* and other species are sweet and are eaten in India and China, being known as Singhara or Horn Nuts. The species need a rich loamy soil and to be grown in a cistern or large pot or tub of water. They need a warm house though *T. natans* will grow at fairly low temperature. Raised from seeds which lose their vitality if allowed to dry. This genus is sometimes put in a family, Trapaceae (syn. Hydrocaryaceae) by itself, chiefly on account of its large 1-seeded indehiscent 2- to 4-horned fruit, which is unlike that of any other genus placed in the family Onagraceae (syn. Oenotheraceae).

T. antenni'fera. A synonym of *Trapella antennifera.*

T. bicornu'ta. Ling. *fl.* white, inconspicuous. *fr.* ¾ in. long and wide with 2 strong, opposite, decurved horn-like processes, like horns on a bull's head. China. 1790. Used for food in E. Asia.

T. bispino'sa. Singhara Nut-plant. *floating l.* 2 to 3 in. wide, 2 in. long, very hairy beneath, back margin entire, front lightly crenate; stalks 4 to 6 in. long, woolly. *fr.* ¾ in. across, smooth or hairy; 2 opposite angles with often retrorsely scabrous spines, the other 2 sometimes obsolete. India, Ceylon. 1822. Stove.

T. na'tans. Jesuit's Nut; Water Caltrops; Water Chestnut; Saligot. *Floating l.* 1 in. long, toothed on front margin, rather hairy on veins beneath; stalks 2 to 4 in. long, becoming smooth. *fl.* small, white, hidden beneath l. *fr.* ¾ in. across, all 4 angles spiny, the 2 lateral spines shorter. Persia to Europe and Upper Nile. 1781. Hardy or nearly so.

T. verbanen'sis. Glabrous. *l.* deltoid, 2 upper sides toothed, teeth bimucronulate. *fr.* 3-angled, compressed, with 2 short horns. Lake Maggiore, N. Italy. 1886. Hardy.

TRAPEL'LA (diminutive of Trapa, from a superficial resemblance to that genus in leaf and fruit, though not in flower). FAM. *Pedaliaceae.* A genus of 2 species of annual aquatic herbs, natives of China and Japan. Floating leaves opposite, kidney- or heart-shaped to ovate, toothed, short-stalked. Flowers axillary, solitary, stalked, of 2 kinds, normal and cleistogamous; calyx tube short, with 5 triangular segments; corolla of normal flower funnel-shaped with 5 rounded unequal spreading lobes, of cleistogamous flower very small, cylindric and closed; stamens 4, with long filaments mounted on corolla tube, 2 anthers fertile, 2 sterile. Fruits cylindric, narrow, with 5 long thread-like antennae hooked at tip or 3 antennae and 2 short horns. The inconspicuous cleistogamous flowers much out-number the more showy normal flowers. The fruits should be kept in cold water or continuously damp sand during the winter, then placed in damp earth in a warm glasshouse until germination takes place, and finally transferred to a tank or aquarium 6 to 12 in. deep. The seeds may lie dormant for 2 years or possibly longer, but quickly germinate if a small cut is made in the seed-coat. A detailed account of this interesting genus by Hugo Glück has been published in Engler, *Bot. Jahrbücher*, 71. 267–336 (1940).

T. antenni'fera. Normal *fl.* ¾ to 1 in. long, tube brownish-yellow or light yellow, lobes light rose. *fr.* with 5 antennae. Japan, Manchuria. SYN. *Trapa antennifera.*

T. sinen'sis. Distinguished by its *fr.* with 3 antennae and 2 short horns. China, Japan (rare).

W. T. S.

trapeziformis -is -e, 4-sided but no sides parallel.

Traunstei'neri, in honour of Joseph Traunsteiner, 1798–1850, student of flora of Tyrol.

TRAUTVETTER'IA (in honour of Ernst Rudolf von Trautvetter, 1809–89, Russian botanist). FAM. *Ranunculaceae.* A genus of a single species of perennial herbs, natives of Japan and N. America, related to Thalictrum but with simple palmate leaves. Flowers without petals, sepals white, small, usually 4, overlapping in bud. Fruit a 1-seeded achene. Hardy and growing in any ordinary soil. Easily increased by division in spring or autumn. *T. carolinensis* is widely spread and somewhat variable so that some have divided it into several species, the Japanese form being offered as *T. japonica.*

T. carolinen'sis. False Bugbane. Herbaceous perennial 2 to 3 ft. h. *l.* palmately lobed; *radical* ones large, the lobes toothed and cut; *cauline l.* few, alternate. *fl.* white, small, in a corymbose panicle; sep. 3 to 5, usually 4, concave, very soon falling. July, August. N. America, Japan. (B.M. 1630 as *Cimicifuga palmata.*) SYN. *T. palmata.* var. **occidenta'lis,** much like type but with thin *l.* more deeply cut. Western N. America. SYN. *T. grandis, Actaea grandis.*

T. palma'ta. A synonym of *T. carolinensis.*

travancoren'sis -is -e, of Travancore, S. India.

Traver'sii, in honour of William Thomas Locke Travers, 1819–1903, botanist and ornithologist of Limerick and New Zealand.

TRAVELLERS' JOY. *See* **Clematis Vitalba.**

TRAVELLERS' TREE. *See* **Ravenala madagascariensis.**

Treacheria'nus -a -um, in honour of Mr. W. H. Treacher, Colonial Secretary, Labuan, *c.* 1880.

TREASURE FLOWER. *See* **Gazania.**

TRECU'LIA (in honour of M. Auguste Trécul of Paris, author of a monograph on *Nuphar lutea* in 1843). FAM. *Moraceae.* A genus of 2 or 3 species of glabrous trees or shrubs, natives of Trop. Africa. Leaves alternate, entire, leathery, penniveined; stalk short; stipules lanceolate, rather small, caducous. Flowers dioecious; heads sessile or shortly stalked, at nodes. *T. africana* needs stove treatment, a compost of rich loam and leaf-mould, and a moist atmosphere. Propagation is by cuttings of ripe shoots inserted in sandy loam under a bell-glass with bottom heat.

T. africa'na. African Bread-fruit Tree; Okwa-tree. Evergreen tree to 80 ft. *l.* oblong-ovate or lanceolate, 6 to 14 in. long, half as wide, abruptly and obtusely acuminate, sometimes cordate at base, thickly leathery; stipules 1 in. long. *fl.* green in a globose head, short-stalked. September. *fr.* in a head, 1 ft. or more wide. Trop. Africa. 1872. (B.M. 5986.)

TREE. Woody perennial rising from the ground with a distinct trunk.

TREE CARROT. *See* **Thapsia edulis.**

TREE CELANDINE. *See* **Bocconia frutescens.**

TREE FERN. A fern with a tree-like stem, e.g. species of Cyathea, Dicksonia.

TREE-GUARDS. Guards in some form are needed to protect stems of trees planted in public streets, avenues, and places where cattle graze and also where rabbits are troublesome. Protection is often needed for several years after planting and a lasting form of protection which will also act as a support against injury by strong winds is desirable. Where mere protection against damage to bark by grazing animals or by mischievous persons who may cut the bark is required, ordinary fine-mesh wire-netting tied round the stems or put round a little way from the stem to a height sufficient for the purpose may serve, but more substantial guards are often needed. They should be such as can be fixed with a minimum of damage to the roots, and they are best put in place when the trees are planted.

TREE MALLOW. *See* **Lavatera arborea.**

TREE MIGNONETTE. Mignonette plants grown singly to flower in large pots on tall stems as single specimens. *See* **Mignonette.**

TREE OF CHASTITY. *See* **Vitex Agnus-castus.**

TREE OF HEAVEN. *See* **Ailanthus.**

TREE OF LIFE. *See* **Thuja.**

TREE OF SADNESS. *See* **Nyctanthes Arbor-tristis.**

TREE ONION. *See* **Allium Cepa.**

TREE PANAX. *See* **Dendropanax.**

TREE ROOT-ROT. *See* **Honey fungus.**

TREE TOMATO. *See* **Cyphomandra betacea.**

TREES, DWARFING OF. The oriental practice of dwarfing trees originated in China whence it passed to Japan; here it became popular during the first half of the 19th century. It is only in the hands of the Japanese that it has become a highly skilled art. In Japan these dwarf trees are called *bonsai* (from *bon*, a tray or shallow pot), but actually the term has a wider application and may also be applied to other subjects grown in ornamental containers for indoor decoration. The aim of the cultivator of these dwarf trees is to produce in miniature an imitation of an old specimen that has been picturesquely shaped by exposure to wind and snow. The finest examples, and consequently the most prized by the Japanese, are those which have been naturally stunted in the wild state. These are mostly to be found in mountain regions near the uppermost limit of tree growth where they have been dwarfed not only by the poor rocky nature of the ground, but also by the rigorous climatic conditions. The collector is often obliged to root-prune these *in situ* for several successive years before it is reasonably safe to transplant them. Ancient trees starved through growth on cliffs are sometimes collected by breaking and chiselling away the rock around their roots, but inevitably many such plants die soon after collection. They are planted in moist sand and frequently sprayed. Prior to their final transference to a pot, all wild-collected plants are usually grown for some time in open ground where they have to be very carefully tended until a new system of 'close-in' roots has been formed.

The secret of their subsequent treatment lies in maintaining an equilibrium between the aerial and subterranean parts of the plant, both being reduced to a minimum compatible with their health. Therefore not only root restriction, as some suppose, but a corresponding curtailment of the foliage area is necessary. The latter is best achieved by a constant 'nibbling' process of pruning, which, of course, should always be done with the desired shape of the tree borne in mind. Branches which cannot be so trained may be forced, and temporarily held, in position by stout copper wires wound spirally round the stem, or they may be bent downward by nicely adjusted hanging weights. After 2 or 3 years these unsightly contraptions may be removed, any further shaping will be confined to the nipping back of the young shoots. Miniature trees can also be created from seedlings and cuttings, although much patient and continuous loving care over a long period is needed. Too much nutriment will make them grow excessively, too little will kill them. The number of trees and shrubs which will stand up to this semi-starvation treatment is, however, large. Thus those dwarfed by the Japanese include forms of Acer, Chaenomeles, Chamaecyparis, Citrus, Crataegus, Cryptomeria, Elaeagnus, Ginkgo, Juniperus, Ilex, Ligustrum, Lycium, Malus, Picea, Pinus, Prunus, Rosa, Punica, Salix, Spiraea, Taxus, and Wistaria, as well as Bamboos (Arundinaria, &c.). Seedlings are raised in pans and boxes not more than 4 in. deep, then transplanted to thumb-pots. Training to a preconceived shape should begin as soon as possible by pinching off the tips of the young shoots. As a rule only a few leaves are allowed to remain on each shoot. Rooted cuttings receive the same treatment. Alternatively plants several years old are lifted from the nursery and planted on a slant in small pots. The branches are then bent and held in position by annealed copper wire twisted spirally around them, or are pulled downwards by hanging weights. At first a fine wire is used; thick copper wire is only used when hard limbs and trunks have to be bent. The wire must be taken off and replaced every year. This process of training must be kept up for several years until the tree has assumed the desired height and shape and all the wood is hardened. After that the main branches will be set in position and the wires and weights can be discarded; further shaping is achieved by continually pinching off the shoots. As the roots fill the container and exhaust the nutriment available, the vigour of the plant declines, its annual growth becomes much shorter and its leaves smaller. To prevent its dying, part of the soil must be renewed from time to time. The Japanese usually repot deciduous trees every year, renewing about half of the soil, but Pines may be left for as long as 3 or 4 years. Repotting is best done in spring. If the specimen is too vigorous the longer roots of deciduous trees are cut back; those of Conifers are twisted and tied in a knot. Part of the soil is always removed from the pot-bound ball of roots by means of a stick or blunt skewer. The plant is then usually put back in the same pot, new soil having been added to the bottom of this while other new soil is packed firmly around the ball, thus raising it to or above its original height. A weak fertilizer made from crushed rape-seed cake is used by the Japanese. This is steeped in water until it is putrid and stinks and the trees are watered with the resulting fluid. Alternatively moistened marble-sized balls of it are placed on the soil in the pans and allowed to dissolve slowly in the course of watering. A sprinkling of wood-ash, dried blood, and bone-meal can be used instead.

The choice of a pleasing container is important. The Japanese use unglazed pots for young trees being trained, but later move them into glazed pots varying from 2 to 25 in. in diameter and 5 to 10 in. in depth. Shallow glazed pans or trays without drainage, and no more than 1 in. deep are only used when the tree is raised on a little mound to ensure drainage and then forms part of a miniature landscape of water and carefully chosen rocks and stones among which a few naturally dwarf plants (e.g. *Thalictrum kiusianum*) may also be grown. According to Shinobu Nozaki, evergreen Conifers are usually planted in whitish or brownish pots, deciduous broad-leaved trees and shrubs likewise or in grey or blue pots; white pots are chosen for plants with red flowers, reddish pots for white flowers, and blue pots for yellow flowers.

Japanese gardeners vary the composition of their soil mixtures to meet what they consider the special needs of each plant. Their ingredients are coarse sand, manured and partially sterilized garden soil, a reddish soil formed from volcanic ash, leaf-mould, and clay. These are thoroughly mixed in the right proportions and then passed through sieves of different meshes from $\frac{1}{2}$ in. to $\frac{1}{30}$ in., the last being to eliminate dust which might hinder drainage. The drainage hole is covered with a crock, then comes a layer of coarse silver sand (in small pots) or fine gravel (in deeper pots), followed by coarse particles of soil (from a $\frac{3}{8}$-in. sieve) for an inch or so, then soil from an $\frac{1}{8}$-in. sieve, and finally soil from a $\frac{1}{16}$-in. sieve. According to Nozaki, a compost of 70 per cent. sand and 30 per cent. manured garden soil suits *Pinus Thunbergii*; flowering cherries are given a compost of 70 per cent. red earth, 30 per cent. sand, and so on. Close adherence to these proportions is not, however, essential; an English grower, Collingwood Ingram, has used the same compost for all his dwarf trees over a number of years and obtained satisfactory results. This compost is made up of 2 parts of fibrous turf loam, 1 part of finely sifted leaf-mould, 1 part of silver sand; for some Conifers the amount of sand is increased. An alternative and more desirable compost is 2 parts fibrous loam rubbed between the hands to a granular condition, 1 part flaky leaf-mould, 2 parts coarse silver sand.

Dwarfed trees should be grown out of doors in a partly shaded position rather than full sun. Spraying of the foliage is advisable in hot weather. They can be brought indoors for decoration but must not be kept for long inside the house; it is advisable to put them outdoors at night. They must be watered with care, often 2 or 3 times a day in summer. During winter the pots and soil are covered with straw to prevent freezing of the soil and splitting of the pots.

For further information reference may be made to S. Nozaki, *Dwarf Trees* (Tokyo, 1940), and C. Ingram, *Ornamental Cherries* (London and New York, 1948), and articles by A. Maumerné in *J. Royal Hort. Soc.* 33. 53–70 (1908), D. Wyman in *Arnold Arb. Bull.* (4), 6. 31–9 (1938), and K. Yashiroda in *Brooklyn, Bot. Gdn. Record*, N.S. 6. 68–79 (1950).

The above account is based on these works and information kindly supplied by Mrs. G. Anley, Mr. Shozaburo Aki, and Mr. Collingwood Ingram.

W. T. S.

TREFOIL. *See* **Trifolium.**

TREFOIL, BIRD'S-FOOT. *See* **Lotus corniculatus.**

TREFOIL, MILK. *See* **Cytisus,** of which this is an old name.

TREFOIL, MOON. *See* **Medicago arborea.**

TREFOIL, SCENTED. *See* **Melilot.**

A

TREFOIL, SHRUBBY. *See* **Ptelea trifoliata.**

Treleas'ei, in honour of William Trelease, 1857–1945, first Director of Missouri Botanical Garden, later Professor of Botany, University of Illinois, specialist on Quercus, Piperaceae, and Yucca.

TRELLIS. A framework of crossing wires or narrow wooden slats upon which plants can be trained. Trellis may be used in glass houses or in the open on walls, or of rather stouter construction as an open fence. Under glass it is used as a means of training Peaches, Nectarines and Vines, Cucumbers, and Melons as well as various ornamental plants which could not receive adequate attention without such means. A trellis may also be fixed in a large pot on which to train an individual plant such as Stephanotis or Bougainvillea, and this means of training was often seen in the past for Fuchsia, the scented musk, *Tropaeolum peregrinum*, and other plants grown in rooms. Where wire trellises are used the wire should be galvanized and sufficiently strong and well fastened to take the weight it has to bear without sagging. It may be made in pieces so as to be removable, but for Vines, Peaches, and Nectarines it is usually fixed permanently, for vines the horizontal wires being 9 in. apart, for Peaches and Nectarines, 6 in. The wires should be not less than 1 ft. from the glass. When permanently fixed, horizontal wires are often used alone, but where they cross, making a square or diamond mesh, training is easily possible in any direction. For pots balloon- or pyramidal-trellises were often constructed, or they might take the form of a ladder widening upwards so as to give a flat face.

TREMAC'RON (from Greek *trema*, aperture, *macron*, large, referring to dehiscence of anthers). FAM. *Gesneriaceae.* A genus of 2 species of perennial herbs with a short, thick rhizome, a rosette of coarse-toothed rather stiff-haired leaves and panicles of yellowish-white flowers on slender hairy scapes. Related to Oreocharis but with a ventricose-tubular corolla with small straight lobes and exserted stamens, the anther-cells divergent and opening by slits. For treatment *see* **Ramonda.** Plants of shady rocks and probably best grown in the alpine house.

T. Forrest'ii. Up to 8 in. h. *l.* narrow-oblong or oblong-ovate, 3 in. long, 2¼ in. wide, sometimes larger, blunt, papery, coarsely toothed, hairy on both sides; long-stalked. *fl.* pendulous on slender hairy scapes; pedicels about 1¼ in. long in umbels and cymes; cor. tubular-bell-shaped with an oblique, shortly 5-lobed mouth, pale greenish to yellowish-white, minutely hairy, about ½ in. long, ¼ in. wide; stamens 4 with a filiform staminode; ovary glabrous. NW. Yunnan, Szechwan. 1918? (B.M. 9224.)

T. Mair'ei. Distinct from *T. Forrestii* by its thicker, more leathery lanceolate-ovate or ovate *l.* 3 in. long, 1½ in. wide, with short stalks about ½ in. long, and glandular-hairy ovary. Yunnan. 1913.

TREMAND'RA (*tremo*, to tremble, *andros*, male; the anthers are shaken by the least movement of the air). FAM. *Tremandraceae.* A genus of 2 small Australian shrubs with entire or toothed leaves and solitary axillary flowers with their parts in fives, free. The whole plant is covered with starry down. They need the protection of a cool greenhouse and treatment like Tetratheca. **A**

T. stelli'gera. Densely stellately-hairy shrub of 2 ft. *l.* opposite, ovate, 1 to 1½ in. long, obtuse, usually coarsely and irregularly toothed. *fl.* about ⅓ in. long on pedicels shorter than l.; anthers purple. Summer.

TREMANDRA'CEAE. Dicotyledons. A family of about 23 species in 3 genera of heath-like shrubs with simple, alternate, opposite or whorled leaves without stipules and solitary axillary flowers. Flowers perfect, sepals 4 or 5 (usually free); petals 4 or 5; stamens 8 or 10 (rarely 6); ovary superior, 2-celled with 1 or 2 ovules in each cell. Fruit a capsule. The genera dealt with are Platytheca, Tetratheca, Tremandra.

TREMBLING TREES. *Populus tremula* and *P. tremuloides* have their leaf-stalks flattened and so slender that the leaf-blade is constantly quivering in the slightest breeze.

TREMEL'LA. Gelatinous or waxy fruits of these Basidiomycetous fungi are often found on dead wood. They are saprophytic, not disease-producing.

tremu'lus -a -um, constantly slightly moving.

Treubia'nus -a -um, in honour of Melchior Treub, 1851–1910, Director, Botanic Garden, Buitenzorg, Indonesia.

Treut'leri, in honour of Dr. Treutler who collected near Darjeeling, *c.* 1860.

TREVES'IA (in honour of the family of Treves de Bonfigli of Padua, supporters of botanical research). FAM. *Araliaceae.* A genus of 8 or 9 species of shrubs or small trees, natives of Trop. Asia, Malaya, and the Pacific Is. Leaves large, palmatifid or digitate or pinnate. Flowers polygamous in panicled umbels; petals 8 to 12, often joined and forming a cap in the fertile flowers; stamens as many as petals. Pedicels not jointed. They need stove conditions and a compost of sand, loam, and leaf-mould. A moist atmosphere suits these jungle plants best. Cuttings root readily in sand with heat under glass.

T. palma'ta. Prickly shrub of 5 to 8 ft., shoots covered with reddish hair. *l.* very large, up to 2 ft. long, palmate or digitate, nearly glabrous; segs. lobed or pinnatifid. *fl.* greenish-white, about 1 in. across, the umbels forming panicles 18 in. long, clothed when young with reddish hairs. March. India. 1818. (B.M. 7008; B.R. 894 as *Gastonia palmata.*)

T. Sand'eri. *l.* general outline circular, 2 ft. across, deeply digitately cut, stalk long cylindrical. Annam. A handsome foliage plant. Probably a form of *T. sundaica.*

T. sunda'ica. *l.* digitate, irregularly pinnatifid. *fl.* in panicled umbels, becoming recurved. Malaya.

F. G. P.

TREVO'A (in honour of Señor Trevo, a Spanish botanist.) FAM. *Rhamnaceae.* A genus of 5 species of shrubs or small trees, spiny, natives of S. America. Leaves opposite, the parts of the flower in fours or fives; petals curiously hood-shaped, each enclosing a stamen. Greenhouse shrubs or trees.

T. triner'vis. Tall bush or tree, 8 to 10 ft., branches widespreading, armed with stiff, stout, sharp spines ½ to 1 in. long, in decussate pairs. *l.* obovate to oblong, ½ to 1 in. long, ⅓ to ½ in. wide, minutely toothed to entire, 3-veined, glabrous. *fl.* in axillary clusters of 2 to 4 on short, lateral, slender twigs forming a leafy spike; ⅛ to ⅙ in. wide, cal. yellowish-white, pet. hooded, snow-white. Chile.

W. J. B.

TREVOR'IA (in honour of Sir Trevor Lawrence, 1831–1913, President of The Royal Horticultural Society, 1885–1913). FAM. *Orchidaceae.* Three epiphytic species constitute this genus of which only one seems to have appeared in cultivation. Allied to Sievekingia, Stanhopea, Schlimia, &c., the spikes are drooping, the blooms broadly bell-shaped, with oval sepals, smaller petals and 3-lobed lip. The species are distributed in Ecuador and Colombia. Cultivation, compost, &c., as for Stanhopeas. On account of the drooping nature of the spikes, baskets are preferable to pots, though the inflorescence does not appear to descend as sharply as in many Stanhopeas.

T. Chlo'ris of Rolfe. A synonym of *T. Lehmannii.*

T. Lehman'nii. *fl.* 3 to 5, inverted; sep. broadly elliptic, tapered, over 1 in. long, pale green, dorsal recurved; pet. undulate, ligulate, white, lip and column white, the concave side lobes forming a rounded sac at base, front lobe rather attenuated; surrounding the column base in front is a curious fringed margin. *Pseudobulbs* pyriform, 2 or 3 in. h., monophyllous. *l.* plicately veined, about 8 in. or more long, 1½ to 2 in. wide. Colombia. About 1897. (B.M. 7805 as *T. Chloris*; O.R. 1910, 297.)

E. C.

Trewia'nus -a -um, in honour of Christoph Jacob Trew, 1695–1769, of Nürnberg, Germany, celebrated physician, naturalist, and bibliographer.

tri-, in compound words signifying three, as *triacantha*, with 3 thorns.

triadelphous, having the stamens in 3 bundles.

TRIALEURO'DES vaporarior'um. *See* **Greenhouse White-fly.**

Tria'nae, in honour of José Triana, 1828–90, botanist and traveller in Colombia.

TRIANAE'A bogoten'sis. A synonym of *Limnobium stoloniferum.*

triand'rus -a -um, having 3 stamens.

TRI'AS (*treis*, three; alluding to the arrangement of the floral envelopes). FAM. *Orchidaceae.* A small genus of only 5 or 6 species of dwarf, tufted, or creeping Orchids, allied to Bulbophyllum. Sepals sub-equal, fleshy, spreading, the lateral ones adnate at base with the foot of the column; petals small, oblong or linear; lip slightly spreading at apex, narrow, rather thick, articulated to column base, mobile; scapes lateral, shorter than the fleshy leaves, leafless, freely produced, one-flowered. Pseudobulbs rather small, sub-globose, clustered, 1-leaved at apex. Cultivation, compost, &c., should be as for the smaller Bulbophyllums.

T. Daya'num. A synonym of *Bulbophyllum Dayanum.*

T. disciflo'ra.* *fl.* comparatively large; sep. about 1 in. long, somewhat triangular, upper ½ in. wide at base, lateral slightly larger, connate at base forming a cup-like chin, yellow, spotted red; pet. horn-like, dark red; column yellow; lip tongue-like. *Pseudobulbs* about 1 in. h. *l.* 2 or 3 in. fleshy, tapered, both in this species and in *T. picta* often bluish. Siam. Before 1896.

T. oblon'ga. *fl.* about 1 in. across or less; sep. and pet. brownish- or fuscous-green, with a purplish lip; scapes erect, much shorter than l. April. *l.* small, oblong, acute, leathery, about 1½ in. long, 3 in. h. Moulmein. 1837. (W.P.A.R. 1, 70.)

T. pic'ta.* *fl.* honey-coloured, densely spotted reddish-purple, fleshy, ¾ to 1 in. across; sep. and pet. pointing forward; lip tongue-like, similarly coloured or darker red-purple. *Pseudobulbs* 4-angled, narrow-obovate, acuminate, fleshy, ¾ in. thick. *l.* 2 to 3 in. long. Burma. 1888. SYN. *Bulbophyllum pictum.* (B.M. 9150.)

T. vitri'na. *fl.* shining green, pet. and lip with a few marks of red-brown. *Pseudobulbs* ovoid. *l.* solitary, 3 in. long. *rhiz.* creeping. Tenasserim. 1895.

E. C.

TRICHAN'THA (*thrix, trichos*, hair, *anthos*, flower; the pedicels being slender). FAM. *Gesneriaceae.* A genus of 2 species of climbing or creeping shrubs, natives of Colombia. Leaves opposite, one of each pair ovate or oblong, slender-pointed, the other very small. Flowers solitary or clustered in the leaf-axils, stalked, without bracts; calyx coloured, 5-cleft; corolla violet with 5 longitudinal yellow marks on limb and tube; limb somewhat oblique with 5 short, equal lobes. *T. minor*, a beautiful stove climber, needs well-drained pots of peat, leaf-mould, and sand, and is easily increased by cuttings with bottom heat.

T. mi'nor. Climber, often rooting. *l.* opposite of 2 sizes, larger short-stalked, ovate, slender-pointed, entire, hairy beneath, rather thick. *fl.* dark purple, mouth yellow, about 2 in. long; cor. tubular, constricted above base; hairy; peduncles slender, 1-fld., clustered in l.-axils. Guayaquil. 1864. (B.M. 5428.)

TRICHI'LIA (*tricha*, in three parts; ovary and capsule usually 3-celled). FAM. *Meliaceae.* A genus of about 200 species of trees and shrubs, natives of Trop. Africa and America. Leaves 3-foliolate or unequally pinnate; lflets. opposite or alternate. Flowers rather large, in axillary many-flowered panicles; calyx 4- or 5-toothed or cut; petals 4 or 5, overlapping; staminal tube usually 8- to 10-cleft, rarely entire. The species need stove conditions and as they rarely flower in this country have little to recommend them horticulturally. A compost of loam and peat suits them.

T. Dre'gei. Tree. *l.* large, unequally pinnate; lflets. in 2 to 5 pairs, oblong-lanceolate, 3 to 4½ in. long, smooth or almost so. *fl.* in short axillary panicles, 1 to 2 in. long, pet. hairy, about ½ in. long, finally spreading; stamens forming a deeply 10-cleft tube. Natal.

T. glab'ra. About 20 ft. h., a shrub or small tree. *lflets.* in 3 pairs, sessile, opposite, obovate, firm, somewhat shining. *fl.* white, densely crowded on an umbellate panicle; long-stalked. June. Havana. 1791. SYN. *T. havanensis.*

T. hir'ta. Bastard Ironwood. About 12 ft. h. *lflets.* in about 5 pairs, elliptic or oblong-lanceolate, the lower smaller, glabrous. *fl.* whitish in downy panicles much shorter than l. W. Indies. 1800.

T. odora'ta. Low tree or shrub. *lflets.* in 5 pairs, elliptic or oblong, 5 to 6 in. long, stalks naked. *fl.* yellowish, fragrant, in many-fld. cymes; pedicels much longer than fl. June. W. Indies. 1801. (A.B.R. 637; H.E.F. 128.)

T. spondioi'des. White Butterwood. Tree of 15 to 20 ft. *lflets.* in 10 pairs, ovate-oblong, oblique at base, acute, glabrous. *fl.* greenish-yellow; anthers 10, hairy; panicles downy, about a quarter as long as l. June. Trop. America. (Ref. Bot. 293.)

T. undulatifo'lia. Tree. *l.* pinnate, 6 in. or more long; lflts. in 2 or 3 pairs, rigid-membranous, obovate, 2 in. long, terminal one larger, glabrous, margins undulate. *fl.* pale green, in small, 4- or 5-fld. cymes. Probably of garden origin.

F. G. P.

TRICHI'NIUM (*trichinos*, covered with hairs; the flowers appear shaggy). FAM. *Amaranthaceae.* A genus of about 50 species of herbs, under-shrubs, or rarely small shrubs, natives of Australia. Leaves alternate, narrow or rarely obovate. Flowers in dense globular, ovoid, or cylindrical spikes, rarely long and interrupted; pink or straw-coloured with a short, hard tube and 5 hairy segments; stamens 5, usually 1 to 3 without anthers. Cool greenhouse plants needing a rich compost of loam, rotten manure, and sand, doing best on an airy shelf in full sunlight and needing plenty of water in the growing season, but almost none after flowering. Propagation by pieces of the thick roots about an inch long inserted in sand with bottom heat. The following are all perennials.

T. exalta'tum. Robust, 2 or 3 ft. h. *Lower l.* oblong-lanceolate, 3 to 5 in. long, narrowed into long stalks; *upper* small, sessile. *fl.* about ¾ in. across; segs. yellow with dull red tips; spikes erect on long peduncles, oblong-cylindrical, about 2½ in. thick. 1838. (B.R. 1839, 28 as *T. alopecuroideum.*)

T. Man'glesii.* Stems decumbent or ascending, rarely erect, 6 to 12 in. long. *l.* ovate to linear, obtuse or acute, 1 to 3 in. long, long-stalked; upper few, narrow, acute. *fl.* ¾ to 1 in. long; segs. with pink or whitish tips; spikes globular or ovoid, about 2 in. thick, covered with long white hairs. 1838. (B.M. 5448; G.C. (1864), 555.) SYN. *Ptilotum Manglesii.*

T. Stirling'ii. Stems procumbent or ascending, like l. covered with white hairs. *l.* lanceolate, oblong or almost linear, lower obtuse, short stalked; upper small, acutish. *fl.* scarcely ½ in. long; segs. feathery with pink tips; spikes globular, solitary or in loose panicles, ¾ to 1 in. thick. 1838.

TRICHLO'RIS (*tri*, three, *Chloris*; like Chloris but with 3-awned spikelets.) FAM. *Gramineae.* A genus of 5 or 6 species of perennial grasses native of Mexico and S. America like Chloris but with 3- (instead of 1-) awned spikelets. Requiring ordinary soil only, ornamental for borders and dry bouquets, readily raised from seed.

T. medoci'na. Perennial. *infl.* of several slender, erect spikes close together near top of stem, feathery with the thin awns. Argentine. SYN. *T. Blanchardiana.*

tricho-, in compound words, signifying hair-like, or hairy.

TRICHOCAU'LON (*trichos*, a hair, *caulon*, stem; referring to the bristles on the tubercles in some species). FAM. *Asclepiadaceae.* In the form of the flower this genus resembles Caralluma but the stems are stouter with many vertical rows of tubercles, each tipped with a spine or bristle. The genus may need revision but, as at present constituted, consists of about 25 species. **A**

T. cactifor'me. Stems very stout, up to 4 in. h. and 2 in. in diameter, covered with roundish, spineless tubercles, whitish-green. *fl.* small, pale yellow spotted with red, at top of stem. Cape Province. (W. and S. 1097, 1098; B.M. 4127 as *Stapelia cactiformis.*)

T. Delaetia'num. Stems up to 8 in. h., many-ribbed, the ribs broken into numerous tubercles tipped with purple bristles. *fl.* small, brownish-yellow, near top of stem. SW. Africa. (W. and S. 1084–6.)

T. Eng'leri. The largest of the spineless Trichocaulons, with stems up to 7 in. h., club-shaped, covered with low, irregular, hexagonal tubercles. *fl.* small, pale yellow with red or purple spots, near top of stem. SW. Africa. (W. and S. 1105, 1106.)

T. fla'vum. Stems resemble *T. piliferum* but the spines are darker brown. *fl.* small, dull yellow. Cape Province. (W. and S. 1087–9.)

T. keetmanshoopen'se. Stems with low, irregular, spineless tubercles. *fl.* greenish with reddish spots on upper half of stem. SW. Africa. (W. and S. 1107–9.)

T. Marlot'hii. Stems similar in habit to *T. cactiforme*. *fl.* dark purple-brown. Cape Province. (W. and S. 1111 and 1112.)

T. melofor'me. Stems almost round, or a little elongated with low, spineless tubercles. *fl.* yellow spotted with dark purple, at top of stem. SW. Africa. (W. and S. 1062, 1104.)

T. pili'ferum. Stems cylindric, branching at base with about 25 rows of close-set tubercles, each tipped by a stiff brown bristle. *fl.* dark purple-brown. Cape Province. (W. and S. 1067–70 and Pl. 31; B.M. 6759.) SYN. *Stapelia pilifera.*

V. H.

TRICHOCENT'RUM (*thrix, trichos,* a hair, *kentron,* a spur; alluding to the long, thin spur of the labellum). FAM. *Orchidaceae.* A genus of 30 species of dwarf epiphytic orchids, natives of Trop. America. Flowers medium-sized or rather large; sepals and petals sub-equal, free, spreading; lip at base connate with the column, forming a pitcher, produced into a descending spur, above the pitcher erect, 2-auriculate or naked; lateral lobes scarcely dilated, nearly erect; column short, thick; pollen masses 2, ovoid; scapes short, many-sheathed, 1- or rarely 2-flowered. Leaves leathery, sometimes equitant or erect. Stems very short, 1-, occasionally 2-, leaved, at length usually thickened into a small, fleshy pseudobulb. Though the scapes are short and seldom more than 1-flowered, the bright colouring of the flowers and their size render a number of the species very attractive. A compost similar to that given Bulbophyllums may be used and the plants placed in small pans which can be suspended in the warm house, near the glass. Shading should be carefully attended to as strong sunlight is detrimental to the foliage. Water is required throughout the year, freely given in summer, with discretion in the winter. The winter night temperature should be about 60° F., rather over than under. Propagation is slow. Only occasionally are plants large enough to be divided. Stale or stagnant compost is quickly inimical. The plants often succeed better when pans are slightly tilted. The compost should be slightly mounded so that water cannot remain round the small rhizomes on which the pseudobulbs are often closely set.

T. ala'tum. Allied to *T. fuscum*, but with smaller fl. *fl.* white, base of lip yellow with 7 light red veins; spur yellowish. Colombia. 1898.

T. albiflo'rum.* *fl.* white, tinged purple at base of lip, about 1 in. across; spur short, sac-like, 2-toothed; raceme 1 in. long. *l.* ovate, about 1 in. long. Mexico. 1893.

T. albococci'neum.* *fl.* large, fragrant, freely produced, sep. and pet. bright cinnamon-brown outside, tawny-yellow inside, nearly 1 in. long, lip white, with 2 large, purple spots near base, disk veined rosy-purple, passing to yellow, crest of 4 rosy-purple keels. *l.* sessile, oblong, acute, shining green, 4 to 6 in. long. *Pseudobulbs* very small. Brazil. 1865. (B.M. 5688; L. 748; W.O.A. 204 as *T. albopurpureum.*) SYN. *T. amazonicum.* var. **stria'tum,** *fl.* with large purple blotch each side of base of lip, striped purple near tip.

T. capistra'tum. *fl.* one to a peduncle; sep. and pet. yellow; lip white, dotted and blotched with purple, remarkable for its base extended into 5 short spurs. *l.* oblong-lanceolate, purplish. Costa Rica. 1871.

T. cornuco'piae. Small, with yellowish-white fls.; lip with orange keels. *Pseudobulbs* very small or obsolete. *l.* 3 to 4½ in. long, about 1 in. wide. Rio Negro (?), 1866. (Ref. B. 77.)

T. fus'cum.* *fl.* over 1 in. across on short peduncles; sep. and pet. purplish-green, spreading; lip much longer than pet., cuneate, white with 2 purplish blotches at base, waved, 2-lobed at apex; spur slender, greenish-white, 1 in. long. *l.* oblong, acute, spreading, somewhat twisted, purplish-green, minutely dotted. Mexico. 1841. (B.M. 3969; B.R. 1951.) var. **Kram'eri,** *fl.* larger, spur longer and thinner. Brazil. 1885.

T. Hart'ii. *fl.* about 1 in. across; sep. and pet. light yellow; lip white and reddish-brown. *l.* fleshy, oblong, 2 in. long. Venezuela. 1894. Allied to *T. fuscum.*

T. Hoeg'ei.* *fl.* very large, on a zigzag peduncle; sep. and pet. greenish-yellow, with a purple middle area; lip white, with brilliant purple lines and blotches, and 2 blunt, yellow calli at base, pandurate, undulate, notched at tip; spur with a clavate, notched apex. *l.* robust, horny, cuneate-oblong, acute. Mexico. 1882. (X.O. 234.) A small but distinct plant.

T. ionophthal'mum.* *fl.*, upper sep. and pet. very light yellowish-maroon-brown, with brown dots at top, clawed, blunt; lateral sep. wholly brown; lip whitish, with a large, violet blotch on each basal angle, pandurate. *l.* broader and shorter than those of *T. albococcineum* (which this plant resembles). Amazons. 1876.

T. longicalcara'tum. *fl.* small, white tinged green; disk of lip yellow with 2 orange keels and a small maroon blotch at their apex; column short, broad, with fimbriate wings; anther case purple, pubescent; spur 1½ in. long. Habitat? 1896.

T. macula'tum.* *fl.* 1 or 2, over 1 in. across; sep. and pet. white, spotted rose-purple, oblong, obtuse; lip white, spotted rose, with a yellow crest, obovate, 2-lobed, very obtuse; spur very long. February. *l.* very thick, fleshy, linear-oblong, obtuse, spotted red, 2 to 4 in. long. Sierra Nevada. 1844.

Trichocentrum orthoplectron

T. orthoplect'ron.* *fl.* large; sep. and pet. over 1 in. long; light cinnamon-brown, tipped yellow, cuneate-oblong; lip white, longer than sep., nearly as long as wide with a crimson-lake blotch each side of base, and five bars or semi-abortive keels of same colour between blotches, disk in front of crest yellow; spur whitish, ½ in. long, tapering to an acute point. October. Brazil. (W.O.A. 272.) Curious and beautiful. 1587.

T. panamen'se. Allied to *T. capistratum.* Sep. and pet. light green; lip white with red-purple blotch at base; scape short; spur short, dilated and divided at apex into 4 short lobes. Panama. 1911.

T. Pfav'ii.* *fl.* often 2, about 1½ in. long, sep. and pet. rather broadly spatulate, white with a brown blotch or blotches at base; lip cuneate, 2-lobed, white with a red blotch towards base; spur very short. *Pseudobulbs* small. *l.* 3 to 5 in. long, about 1 in. wide. Costa Rica, Cent. America. 1881. (I.H. (1886), 587.) var **zona'le,** sep. and pet. brown at base, or blotched brown, lip with 1 large, purple blotch or 2 smaller ones before base. 1880. Variable.

T. porphy'rio.* *fl.* solitary, about 2 in. across; sep. and shorter pet. brown, cuneate-oblong, acute, unequally margined and tipped yellow; lip rich magenta-purple, with faint white margin near point with a rectangular, sulphur-yellow blotch on disk in front of the 3 purple lines on crest. *Pseudobulbs* yellow. *l.* cuneate-oblong, 2 to 3½ in. long, ½ to 1 in. wide. S. America. 1884. (I.H. 1884, 508.)

T. pulch'rum.* *fl.* 1½ in. across, white with red marks; sep. and pet. much spreading, oval-elliptic; lip erect, obovate, cuneate at base, emarginate, over 1 in. long; spur slender, about 2 in. long. July. *Pseudobulbs* very small, or obsolete. *l.* 2 or 3, thickened at base, oblong, blunt or acute, sometimes mucronate. Peru.

T. purpu'reum. *fl.* 1 or 2; sep. and pet. dull olive-green; lip purple obovate-oblong, emarginate; spur thick, curved $\frac{3}{4}$ in. long; scapes small. Demerara.

T. tenuiflo'rum. *fl.* dingy brown and white, small; sep. and pet. narrow, sep. acute, pet. blunt; lip linear-obovate, with whole of base occupied by 2 plates. Bahia.

T. tigri'num.* *fl.* 1 or 2; sep. and pet. greenish-yellow with distinct purplish-brown bars or spots; lip pure white, $1\frac{1}{2}$ in. long, nearly 2 in. across the dilated apex, with yellow crest on disk, on each side at base a wedge-shaped blotch of purple; spur short. *l.* oblong, more or less dotted with deep red. Ecuador. 1869. (B.M. 7380; W.O.A. 484.) Flowering while very small. var. **splen'dens,** fine in fl. with base of large, obcordate lip rich purple. (L. 24.)

T. triquet'rum. Sep. and pet. pale straw; lateral sep. prolonged behind, and adnate to spur of lip; lip straw-yellow, irregularly variegated and almost suffused with orange; spur $1\frac{1}{2}$ in. long; ovary 3-angled; peduncles axillary, 1 in. long. *l.* erect, equitant, 6 in. long, $\frac{1}{2}$ in. wide, tapered to point. Peru. (L. 311.)

E. C.

TRICHOCE'REUS (*trichos*, hair, *Cereus*, the flowering areoles being hairy). FAM. *Cactaceae.* Columnar ribbed plants, ribs varying; flowers nocturnal, large, mostly white, scented, with scales and hairs on the tubes; somewhat resembling those of Echinopsis. Fruit with scales but without spines. Most of the species like full sunshine and not too low a temperature. **A**

T. Bridges'ii. Stems tall, slightly glaucous; 4 to 8 ribs, rounded; areoles large, close, spines yellow, very unequal. *fl.* about 7 in. long, white. Bolivia. SYN. *Cereus Bridgesii.*

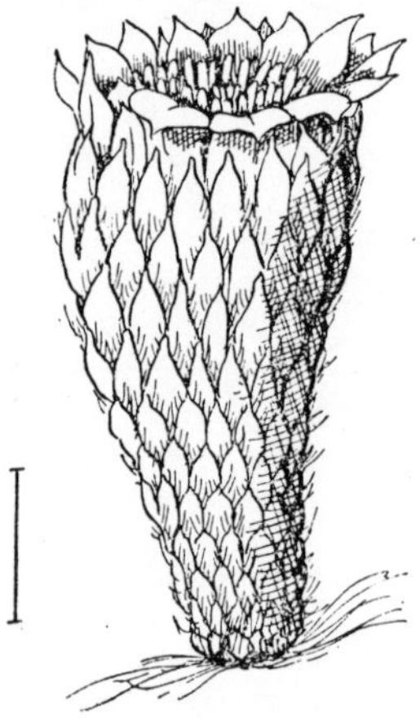

Trichocereus candicans

T. can'dicans. Stems stout, 9 to 11 ribs, rounded; areoles large; spines brownish, radials spreading, centrals several, longest up to 4 in. *fl.* very large, very sweet-scented. Mendoza. (B.R.C. 2, f. 195.) SYN. *Cereus candicans, Echinopsis candicans.* 1063.

T. chiloen'sis. Stems usually branched, ribs 16 or 17, broad, divided into tubercles; radials spreading, stout, one central very stout. *fl.* large, white. Chile. (B.R.C. 2, f. 198–200.) SYN. *Cereus chiloensis.*

T. coquimba'nus. Stems branched, ribs 12 or 13; areoles large, filled with brownish wool and spines very formidable, up to 4 in. long. *fl.* with acute white pet. and black hairs on the tube. Chile. (B.R.C. 2, f. 201–2.) SYN. *Cereus coquimbanus, C. nigrispilis.*

T. lamprochlo'rus. Stems ribbed, ribs tuberculate, spines yellow, not very long. *fl.* about 10 in., from large tufts of brown wool at the top of the stem. Argentina. (B.R.C. 2, f. 192.)

T. macro'gonus. Stems columnar, stout, bluish-green; ribs 7, low; areoles large, spines brown. *fl.* large, white, from the top of the plant. S. America. SYN. *Cereus macrogonus.* A very useful grafting stock.

T. pasaca'na. Stems very stout, with 20 to 38 low ribs; areoles large, close; spines numerous, yellow, stiff, some up to 6 in. long. *fl.* 4 in. long, white, from areoles with long white bristles. *fr.* edible. Argentina, Bolivia. (B.R.C. 2, f. 192–4.) SYN. *Cereus pasacana, Pilocereus pasacana.*

T. Schickendant'zii. Stem stout, not so tall, branching from the base; ribs about 16, low, wavy; spines yellow, short, slender. *fl.* large, lasting several days, scented. Argentina. SYN. *Echinopsis Schickendantzii.*

T. Spachia'nus. Stem branching at the base; ribs 10 to 15, rounded; areoles close, with curly white wool; spines yellow to brown, bristle-like. *fl.* 8 in. long, freely produced on old plants. Argentina. (B.R.C. 2, f. 190.) SYN. *Cereus Spachianus.* Often used as a grafting stock.

T. strigo'sus. Stems very spiny, ribs 15 to 18, low; areoles large, close, with dense white felt; spines numerous, very variable in size and colour. *fl.* large, white, lasting a day or more, scented. Argentina. (B.R.C. 2, f. 211.) SYN. *Cereus strigosus.* Grows quickly and easily in cultivation but does not flower readily.

T. Terscheck'ii. Similar to *T. pasacana* but with fewer ribs and larger fl. Argentina. (B.R.C. 2, f. 203–4.) SYN. *Cereus Terscheckii.*

T. theleg'onus. Stems weak, ribs 12 or 13, divided into prominent 6-sided tubercles; spines slender, brown turning black. *fl.* large, tube woolly. Argentina. (B.R.C. 2, f. 188–9.) SYN. *Cereus thelegonus.*

V. H.

TRICHOCER'OS (*trichos*, hair, *keras*, horn; there are 2 hairy, antenna-like processes from the column). FAM. *Orchidaceae.* A genus of 6 or 7 species of epiphytic Orchids, natives of Peru and Colombia, allied to Telipogon. Flowers loosely racemose at the apices of the peduncles, mediocre or small, rather long-stalked; sepals sub-equal, free, and spreading, larger than the petals; lip sessile at the base of the column, spreading with narrow side lobes; pollen masses 4; bracts shorter than the pedicels. Leaves few, distichous, leathery or fleshy. *T. parviflorus.* Thrives in small pans or baskets of peat and sphagnum and needs a warm house.

T. parviflo'rus. *fl.* green, with purple and brown spots and bars, small; lip 3-parted, minutely ciliolate; peduncle slender, nearly terete, axillary. *Pseudobulbs* small, with a single, fleshy leaf. Colombia. 1870. (R.X.O. 9.)

TRICHOCLA'DUS (*trichos*, hair, *kladon*, branch; referring to the hairy shoots and leaves of some species). FAM. *Hamamelidaceae.* A genus of 5 species of shrubs or small trees, natives of S. Africa. Leaves alternate or opposite, entire. Flowers monoecious or dioecious, in small heads; petals absent from the females, 5 in the males; stamens 5. Fruit a 2-celled capsule. Cool greenhouse; compost, &c., as for Gardenia.

T. crini'tus. Evergreen shrub up to 10 ft., shoots thickly covered with a dark brown, fur-like mass of stellate hairs. *l.* opposite, ovate to pointed, base rounded to cordate, glabrous above, thickly hairy beneath; veins parallel; stalk $\frac{1}{2}$ to $1\frac{1}{4}$ in. long. *fl.* crowded in globose terminal heads, $\frac{1}{2}$ to $\frac{3}{4}$ in. across; pet. yellow, linear. August. S. Africa. 1886.

Trichocladus grandiflorus

T. grandiflo'rus.* Evergreen shrub or small tree, shoots at first minutely downy, spotted red-purple. *l.* alternate, 3 to 4 in. long,

1 to 1½ in. wide, ovate, pointed, base rounded, bronzy brown when young, soon pale and glabrous beneath. *fl.* 1½ in. wide, white in small axillary or terminal racemes; pet. 5, linear, wavy, rosy at base. July. S. Africa. 1890. (B.M. 7418.) 1588.

W. J. B.

TRICHODES'MA (*trichos*, a hair, *desmos*, a bond; the anthers being bound to each other by hair). FAM. *Boraginaceae*. A genus of about 40 species of often rather coarse herbs distributed over the warmer parts of the Old World. Leaves opposite or alternate, entire. Flowers in terminal racemes; calyx deeply 5-cleft, corolla of 5 lobes often with long slender points; stamens exserted; anthers bound together by hairs. The perennial species need a greenhouse, the annuals can be treated as hardy. Ordinary soil suits these often desert plants.

T. Boissier'i. Annual or perennial herb about 18 in. h., silky-grey. *l.* oblong to oblong-lanceolate, about 2 in. long, narrowed to a stalk, upper sessile, heart-shaped, elliptical. *fl.* about 1 in. across, star-shaped, pale blue in slightly drooping racemes on pedicels 2 or 3 times as long as cal. July, August. Syria, Transjordania.

T. physaloi'des. Perennial, 1 to 2 ft. h. with a fleshy rootstock. *l.* glaucous-green, stem-clasping. *fl.* on pedicels up to 2 in. long; cal. purple, 1 to 1½ in. long; cor. white. S. Africa. 1892.

T. zeyla'nicum. Annual, several feet h. *l.* linear to oblong-lanceolate, 3 to 4 in. long, margins usually recurved. *fl.* pale blue, in simple racemes; cal. segs. ¼ to ½ in. long; cor. lobes broader than cal. Trop. E. Africa, S. Asia, Australia. (B.M. 4820.)

TRICHODIADE'MA. *See under* **Mesembryanthemum.**

TRICHOGLOT'TIS (*thrix*, *trichos*, hair, *glottis*, tongue; alluding to the fine hairs on the labellum). FAM. *Orchidaceae*. A genus of about 30 species of tropical Orchids, natives of Malaya, the Philippines, India, New Guinea, differing from Sarcanthus by the thin horizontal lamella in the mouth of spur, at base of column. Flowers small or medium sized, 1, few, or many on lateral peduncles; sepals spreading, the lateral ones very broad, adnate to the foot of the column, the dorsal one and petals oblong; lateral lobes of lip short, erect, the middle one rather broad; column short, wingless. Leaves distichous, scattered at the sides of the stem, narrow. Stem leafy elongated, not pseudobulbous. The species mentioned below thrive in the East India house, and require an abundant supply of moisture when growing, with compost and general treatment as for Vandas. Botanically this genus appears to need further revision as it contains several species which only conform to the genus in its broad outlines. From Staurochilus it is distinguished by the usually short, often single-flowered inflorescence. Few are of horticultural value.

T. brachia'ta. A synonym of *Stauropsis philippinensis brachiata.*

T. cochlea'ris. *fl.* white, with purple bars both sides of sep. and pet. smaller than in *Saccolabium violaceum*; spur conical; lip spoon-shaped, very thick, with few purple blotches; infl. very short, zigzag, 4-fld. *l.* as in *Sarcanthus rostratus* but thicker, obliquely 2-lobed. 8 in. h. Sumatra. 1883.

T. Dawsonia'na. A synonym of *Staurochilus Dawsonianus.*

T. fascia'ta. A synonym of *Staurochilus fasciatus.*

T. flexuo'sa. A synonym of *T. rosea.*

T. Joiceya'na. *fl.* small; sep. and pet. spatulate, white with light purple blotches; lip 3-lobed, white with magenta markings; spur conical, orifice much narrowed by the lamella by 2 callosities on the anterior wall of the lip and by numerous long white hairs; infl. long, branching, many-fld. Stem stout, 12 in. or probably much more, h. *l.* loriform, leathery, often red-tinged, 12 in. long, 1½ in. wide. Celebes (or near). 1929.

T. pal'lida. A synonym of *Phalaenopsis pallens.*

T. philippinen'sis. A synonym of *Stauropsis philippinensis.*

T. ro'sea. *fl.* 1 to 3, small; sep. and pet. about ¼ in. long or less, yellowish-brown; lip white with small side lobes, mid-lobe heart-shaped; spur sac-like. Stem drooping, 12 to 15 in. long. *l.* about 3 in. long, nearly ½ in. wide. Philippines. SYN. *T. flexuosa.*

T. Wenzel'ii. *fl.* fragrant, solitary, axillary; lateral sep. ½ in. long, ¼ in. wide, oblong, bluntly tapered, upper sep. slightly less; pet. smaller all greenish-yellow, barred red; lip white, fleshy, pubescent, with erect side walls each with a purple spot, mid-lobe narrowly hastate, sparsely marked purple, base swollen, 2 narrow purple-faced horns from the sides, fringed with white hairs; spur a short, compressed, blunt sac. Stem 10 in. or more h. *l.* 3½ in. long, ¾ in. wide, almost equally 2-lobed at apex. Philippines. 1914.

E. C.

TRICHOLAEN'A (*thrix*, hair, *chlaena* (Latin *laena*), cloak; in allusion to the hairy coat of the spikelets). FAM. *Gramineae*. A genus of about 10 species of African grasses allied to Panicum, with loose panicles of 2-flowered small spikelets covered with long, silky hairs, awned. Propagated by seed. A light loamy soil suits them. Useful for borders and dry bouquets.

T. ro'sea, sometimes grown as *T. teneriffae*, is **Rhynchelytrum re'pens.** Annual or short-lived perennial, tufted, about 1½ to 2½ ft. h. *l.* linear, scabrid. Panicle rather loose, 3 to 8 in. long; spikelets silky, at first wine-coloured, then purplish. Half-hardy annual. S. Africa. 1895. SYN. *T. repens.*

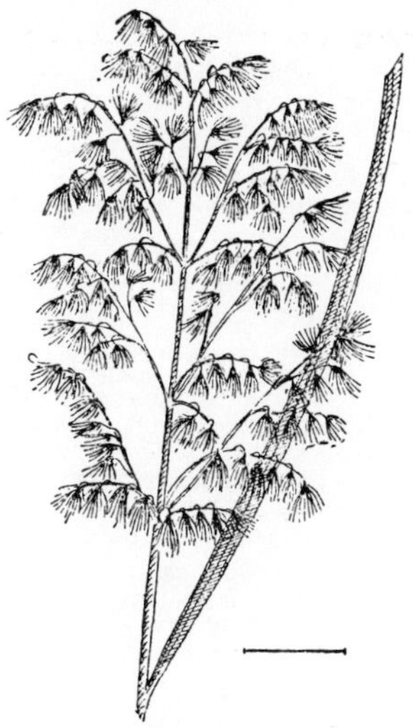

Rhynchelytrum repens (see above)

T. tenerif'fae. Perennial, loosely tufted, 9 to 24 in. h. *l.* linear, becoming rolled, glaucous. Panicle contracted or loose, 1 to 4½ in. long; spikelets long, silky, white-hairy. Mediterranean region. SYN. *Saccharum teneriffae.*

C. E. Hb.

TRICHOLO'MA. A genus of Basidiomycetous fungi with fruit-bodies of mushroom form, many of which are edible, including *T. personatum* (Blewitt or Blue-leg), with grey-brown to lilac cap, at one time an article of commerce.

D. E. G.

TRICHOM'ANES (used by Theophrastus; *thrix*, hair, *manos*, soft; from the texture of the fronds). FAM. *Hymenophyllaceae*. A genus of about 330 species of ferns with delicate fronds, the sori always at the end of a vein, more or less sunk in the frond, indusia tubular, similar to the frond in texture with a truncated or winged mouth, the sessile sporangia on a filiform receptacle (mainly near its base) which generally projects considerably beyond the mouth of the indusium. Widely distributed through temperate and tropical regions, growing mostly on tree-trunks or damp rocks. Except for a few species that require higher temperatures than the greenhouse affords the treatment recommended for Hymenophyllums suits the species of Trichomanes. Stone has not been suggested as a base on which to grow Hymenophyllums and other filmy ferns, but with Trichomanes it is an essential, for in most the rhizomes differ markedly from those of Hymenophyllums for they are able to cling closely to stone. Some species with slender hairy rhizomes like *T. capillaceum*, *T. humile*, *T. pyxidiferum*, and *T. venosum* which grow naturally on tree-trunks, especially the trunks of tree-ferns, do best when rambling through decaying vegetable matter. Others with very slender rhizomes such as *T. Colensoi*, *T. exsectum*, *T. parvulum*, and *T. tenerum* do better when running over or among sandstone or some other soft porous stone. Those with stout, hairy, creeping rhizomes, like *T. javanicum* and *T. radicans*, grow best when near a harder stone to which they cling tenaciously. Whatever stone is used must have a little sandy fibrous peat near its base to establish the plant. Propagation is usually by division of the rhizomes or by means of the buds which some species produce, as for instance *T. pinnatum* which often roots at the tips of its fronds when these touch the ground. There is a variety too of *T. radicans* (*proliferum*) which forms buds on the upper surface of its fronds which may be rooted and produce new plants. Spores may also be used as a means of propagation, though development is slow; plants raised from spores, however, are usually more symmetrical than those raised by division. Where attempts are made to raise these plants from spores, the spores should be sown as soon as they are ripe.

T. ala'tum.* *sti.* tufted, 2 to 4 in. long, winged above. *Fronds* 3 to 12 in. long, 1 to 4 in. broad, lanceolate or ovate-lanceolate, 2- or 3-pinnatifid; main rachis winged throughout; pinnae lanceolate, acute, cut more than half-way to rachis; lobes again often sharply toothed. *Sori* 2 to 12 to a pinna, terminal on segs., mouth spreading. W. Indies. 1824. (H.S.F. i. 39c as *T. attenuatum.*) Greenhouse. Very variable in robustness and hairiness.

T. an'ceps. A synonym of *T. elegans* and *T. maximum.*

T. apiifo'lium.* *sti.* tufted, 4 to 6 in. long, strong, erect, fibrillose, densely at crown. *Fronds* 9 to 18 in. long, 4 to 8 in. broad, ovate, 4-pinnatifid; main rachis only slightly winged towards apex; lower pinnae 4 to 6 in. long, 1 to $1\frac{1}{2}$ in. broad, lanceolate, acuminate; pinnules with numerous segs., again cut into ultimate divisions about $\frac{1}{12}$ in. long. *Sori* 2 to 12 to a pinnule; involucre short, turbinate. Philippines, Malaya, Polynesia. Greenhouse.

T. attenua'tum. A synonym of *T. alatum.*

T. auricula'tum. *rhiz.* strong, wide-creeping, tomentose. *Fronds* nearly sessile, 6 to 12 in. long, $1\frac{1}{2}$ to 2 in. broad, 2-pinnatifid; rachis wiry, very slightly winged throughout or above only; pinnae short-stalked, ovate, rhomboidal, obliquely cuneate at base, irregularly pinnatifid half-way down or more, lowest anterior lobes often considerably prolonged beyond others. *Sori* 2 to 12 to a pinna, the mouth truncate. Japan, &c. 1871. (F.B.I. 182.) SYN. *T. dissectum.*

T. arbus'cula.* *sti.* 1 to 2 in. long, broadly winged to base. *Fronds* 3 to 6 in. long, 1 in. broad, ovate-oblong, pinnatifid down to a broadly-winged rachis; segs. oblong, blunt, crenate, either imbricate or with a small space between them. *Sori* 2 to 6 to a pinna, mouth rather dilated; receptacle long, filiform. Trop. America. (H.G.F. 56.) Greenhouse.

T. bipuncta'tum. *rhiz.* wide-creeping, tomentose, rather slender. *sti.* 1 to 2 in. long, naked, slightly winged above. *Fronds* oblong-lanceolate or oblong-deltoid, 2 to 3 in. long, about 1 in. broad, 3-pinnatifid, rachis winged throughout; pinnae lanceolate, cut away on lower side at base; ultimate segs. strap-shaped, $\frac{1}{8}$ to $\frac{1}{6}$ in. long. *Sori* 1 or more to a pinna; indusium winged. Mauritius. (F.B.I. 283.) SYN. *T. Filicula.*

T. Bo'jeri. A synonym of *T. cuspidatum.*

T. botryoi'des. *cau.* erect, tufted. *Barren fronds* 2 to 3 in. long, 1 in. or rather more broad, on very short stipes, pinnatifid to a slightly-winged rachis, with linear-oblong, deeply-toothed lobes, rooting and proliferous. *Fertile fronds* on stipes 1 to 2 in. long, narrow-linear, tip foliaceous. *Sori*, lower stalked, usually free; upper connected at base. Trop. America. SYN. *Feea nana.*

T. brevise'tum. A synonym of *T. radicans.*

T. capilla'ceum.* *rhiz.* creeping, slender. *sti.* 1 to 2 in. long, very slender, naked. *Fronds* 4 to 8 in. long, 1 to 2 in. broad, pendent, flaccid, lanceolate, 3-pinnatifid, main rachis only slightly winged at apex; pinnae flaccid, 1 to 2 in. long, rachis only winged above; pinnules deeply cut, with distant, linear-filiform segs. $\frac{1}{12}$ to $\frac{1}{8}$ in. long. *Sori* 1 to 4 to a pinna, tube exserted, sometimes stalked. W. Indies. 1862. Greenhouse. SYN. *T. trichoideum.*

T. cellulo'sum. *rhiz.* strong, wiry, tomentose, with numerous long, black fibres. *sti.* 1 to 3 in. long, naked, wiry, winged above. *Fronds* 2 to 6 in. long, 1 to 2 in. broad, erect, rather rigid, ovate-oblong, 2-pinnatifid, main rachis narrowly winged; pinnae erecto-patent, cut to a narrowly-winged rachis; lower pinnules deeply forked; segs. linear-filiform. *Sori* 1 to 8 to a pinna, minute, axillary, tube stalked. S. America. (H.S.C.F. 63.) SYN. *T. gemmatum.*

T. Colen'soi.* *rhiz.* wide-creeping, naked. *sti.* naked, 1 in. long. *Fronds* oblong-lanceolate, 2 to 4 in. long, pinnate; pinnae distant, stalked, cut to stalks into very narrow segs. New Zealand. (H.C.F. 79.)

T. concin'num. *rhiz.* filiform, tomentose. *sti.* $\frac{1}{4}$ to $\frac{1}{3}$ in. long, proliferous, winged upwards. *Fronds* ovate, $\frac{1}{2}$ to $\frac{3}{4}$ in. long, rounded at top, cuneate at base, 2-pinnatifid; lower flabellately pinnatifid, lowest pinnules 2-fid. *Sori* usually lateral, rarely terminal; indusium immersed. Tahiti.

T. crini'tum. *sti.* tufted, $\frac{1}{12}$ to $\frac{1}{4}$ in. long, slender, villous. *Fronds* 2 to 8 in. long, $\frac{1}{2}$ to $\frac{3}{4}$ in. broad, ovate-lanceolate or linear-oblong, 2-pinnatifid; pinnae reaching nearly to rachis, lower ovate-oblong, cut about half-way into broadly linear segs., slightly hairy, ciliate. *Sori* 1 or 2 to a pinna, terminal, mouth dilated. W. Indies to Ecuador.

T. cris'pum. *rhiz.* short or somewhat elongated, strong, tomentose. *sti.* scattered or tufted, 2 to 6 in. long, strong, tomentose. *Fronds* 4 to 12 in. long, $1\frac{1}{2}$ to 2 in. broad, lanceolate, fully pinnate or pinnatifid nearly to rachis; lower pinnae $\frac{3}{4}$ to 1 in. long, oblong, obtuse, spreading, or even deflexed, often incurved and crisped; rachis clothed with reddish-brown hairs. *Sori* 1 to 8 round apex of pinnae, mouth 2-lipped; receptacle long, exserted. Trop. America. 1828. (H.G.F. 27.)

T. curva'tum. A synonym of *T. javanicum.*

T. cuspida'tum. *Fronds* indistinctly but very shortly stalked, about $\frac{1}{2}$ in. broad, outer edge rounded, more or less lobed, base truncate or more or less cuneate. *Indusia* 1 to 6, tube sunk in frond, mouth dilated, scarcely 2-lipped. Mauritius. (G.C. 8 (1890), 100.) SYN. *T. Bojeri.*

T. dissec'tum. A synonym of *T. auriculatum.*

T. e'legans.* *rhiz.* tufted. *sti.* 2 to 8 in. long. *Fronds* dimorphous; barren drooping, pinnatifid, 6 to 18 in. long, 2 to 12 in. broad, broadly lanceolate, with nearly horizontal, crowded, toothed pinnae, often caudate at apex; fertile 6 to 12 in. long, seldom $\frac{1}{2}$ in. broad, erect, undivided, fringed each side with coarse, hair-like, slender spore-receptacles. Trop. America. (H.G.F. 2.) SYN. *T. anceps*, *T. Prieurii*, *Feea elegans.*

T. elonga'tum. Allied to *T. rigidum* but fronds deltoid, segs. broader; pinnae and pinnules imbricate.

T. ero'sum. *rhiz.* thread-like. *sti.* filiform, $\frac{1}{4}$ to $\frac{1}{2}$ in. long. *Fronds* very variable in shape, lanceolate to semicircular, entire or repand-pinnatifid, 1 to 2 in. long, abundantly veined. *Sori* 1 or many along upper margin of frond; indusium immersed, cylindrical, with a large, collar-like limb. SYN. *T. muscoides.* Trop. W. Africa. (F.B.I. 304; L.F. 8, 10.)

T. exsec'tum. *rhiz.* wide-creeping, slender, tomentose. *sti.* slender, naked, 1 to 3 in. long. *Fronds* 6 to 12 in. long, 1 to 2 in. broad, pendent, flaccid, lanceolate, 3-pinnatifid, main rachis narrowly winged in upper half; pinnae distant, flaccid, upper often 3 to 4 in. long, lower ovate or lanceolate, divided to a narrowly-winged rachis, with a few deeply-toothed or pinnatifid pinnules. *Sori* 1 to 4 to a pinna, mouth truncate. Chile.

T. Filic'ula. A synonym of *T. bipunctatum.*

T. fimbria'tum. *rhiz.* strong, wide-creeping. *sti.* 2 to 5 in. long, strong, winged nearly down to base. *Fronds* 4 to 9 in. long, 2 to 4 in. broad, broadly ovate, pinnatifid down to a narrowly-winged rachis; lower pinnae lanceolate, divided more than half way to rachis, with oblong, crenate lobes. *Sori* 2 to 6 to each lobe; receptacle long, filiform. Trinidad. 1863. SYN. *T. superbum.*

T. floribun'dum. A synonym of *T. pinnatum.*

T. foenicula'ceum. A synonym of *T. parvifolium.*

T. Fra'seri. *rhiz.* creeping. *Fronds* small, erect, pale green, naked, somewhat flabellate, lobed. *Sori* confined to top lobes. W. Indies. 1890.

T. fruticulo'sum. A stiff, wiry plant, with deep green fronds. Guiana. 1894.

T. gemma'tum. A synonym of *T. cellulosum.*

T. guineen'se. *cau.* short, slender, sub-erect. *sti.* tufted, 2 to 4 in. long, winged in upper part. *Fronds* deltoid, 3 to 6 in. long, 3-pinnatifid, main rachis distinctly winged; pinnae 8 to 12 pairs, crowded, sessile, all except lowest lanceolate; lowest lanceolate-deltoid; ultimate segs. oblong, obtuse, erecto-patent. *Sori* usually only 1 to each secondary seg., except in deeply pinnatifid, large ones on lower side of lowest pair of pinnae. W. Africa. 1882. SYN. *T. Hartii.*

T. Hart'ii. A synonym of *T. guineense.*

T. hu'mile. *rhiz.* creeping, deeply intermatted. *sti.* $\frac{1}{4}$ to $\frac{1}{2}$ in. long, slender, winged above. *Fronds* 1 to 2 in. long, $\frac{1}{2}$ in. broad, 2-pinnatifid, lanceolate-oblong, cut to a narrowly-winged rachis; segs. pinnatifid, with simple or once-forked, linear lobes. *Sori* solitary on upper side of pinnae, tube more or less exserted, mouth 2-lipped. Java, Formosa, Australia, New Zealand. (B.H. 1864, 239.)

T. inci'sum. A synonym of *T. polypodioides.*

T. javan'icum. *cau.* tufted, with numerous strong, wiry roots. *sti.* 1 to 4 in. long, wiry, erect, naked or villous. *Fronds* 2 to 8 in. long, 1 to 2 in. broad, ovate-lanceolate, acuminate, once fully pinnate; lower pinnae often 1 in. long, $\frac{1}{4}$ in. broad, obtuse or acute, finely toothed. *Sori* 1 to 4 in the axils of linear segs. on upper side of pinnae; receptacle much exserted. India, Java, Trop. Australia. (H.G.F. 37; F.B.I. 180.) SYN. *T. curvatum*, *T. rhomboideum.*

T. Kaulfus'sii. A synonym of *T. trigonum.*

T. Kraus'sii.* *rhiz.* wide-creeping, tomentose. *Fronds* sessile or nearly so, 1 to 3 in. long, $\frac{1}{2}$ in. broad, oblong, attenuate or cuneate at base, once deeply pinnatifid down to a broadly-winged rachis; lobes linear-oblong, nearly entire, or toothed or sinuate-pinnatifid. *Sori* 1 to 6 on the apex of frond, tube more or less exserted, mouth with 2 large lips. Trop. America, Florida. (B.C.F. 3, 370.) Greenhouse.

T. labia'tum. *Fronds* variable in shape, roundish and cordate at one or both ends, or sub-ovate and narrowed at base and apex, pellucid dark green; fertile with a distinct midrib. *Sori* confined to apex, usually 1, rarely 2 to 4; indusia tubular, free or slightly sunk, with tufts of hairs on margined sides; lips large, expanded, rounded. British Guiana. 1885.

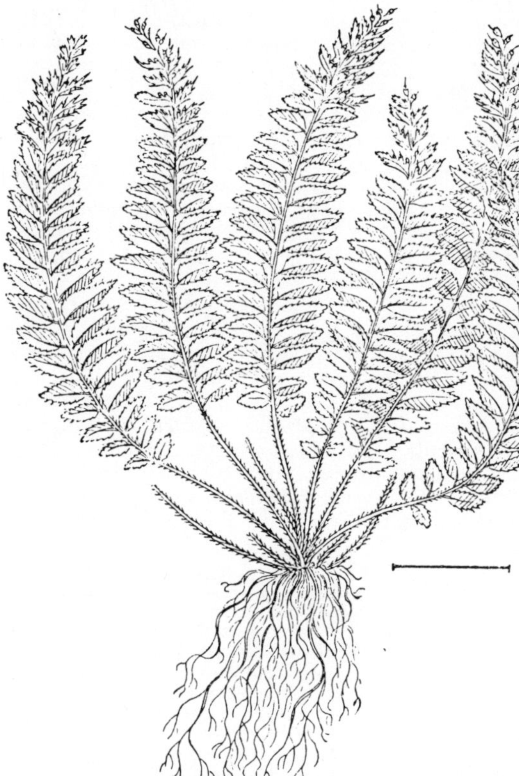

Trichomanes javanicum (p. 2140)

T. Lyall'ii. *sti.* 1 to 2 in. long, slender, filiform. *Fronds* $\frac{3}{4}$ to 2 in. each way, sub-orbicular in general outline, flabellately divided nearly to base into dichotomously-branched, narrow-linear, ciliate, minutely-denticulate segs. *Sori* 3 or 4, terminal on indusia segs., obconical, quite sunk in tube. New Zealand.

T. ma'ximum.* *rhiz.* stout, creeping. *sti.* strong, erect, 3 to 6 in. long. *Fronds* 1 to $1\frac{1}{2}$ ft. long, 6 to 9 in. broad, ovate, 4-pinnatifid; pinnae erecto-patent, ovate-lanceolate, largest 4 to 6 in. long, 2 in. broad; pinnules lanceolate-deltoid, 1 in. or more long, cut to rachis into deeply pinnatifid segs.; ultimate segs. $\frac{1}{8}$ to $\frac{1}{6}$ in. long. *Sori* 2 to 8 to a pinnule; indusium cylindrical, mouth 2-lipped. Malaya, Polynesia, Queensland. 1863. SYN. *T. anceps* (H.S. 40c). Greenhouse.

T. membrana'ceum. *Fronds* sub-sessile, membranous, sub-orbicular, 2 to 3 in. broad, more or less deeply cut from circumference towards centre; lobes broad, rounded, or narrow, margin fringed with a double series of peltate scales. Indusia numerous, round the margin of frond, tube sunk, mouth 2-lipped. Trop. America. (G.C. 8 (1890), 100.)

T. meifo'lium.* *fronds* tufted, 2 ft. high, lanceolate, very finely divided into linear segs., some of which, standing forward as in *Todea fimbriata*, give the whole plant a delightful softness and richness. Reunion, Malaya, Polynesia. 1871.

T. osmundioi'des. *cau.* erect, tufted. *Barren fronds* 4 to 6 in. long, 1 to $1\frac{1}{2}$ in. broad, on stipes 1 to 2 in. long, pinnatifid nearly to rachis, tip not rooting; segs. inciso-crenate, linear-oblong. *Fertile* composed of a rachis and 2 rows of sori, without connecting membrane. Trop. America. (H.G.F. 60.) SYN. *T. spicatum, Feea polypodina.*

T. parvifo'lium. *sti.* erect, wiry, 2 to 4 in. long. *Fronds* 4 to 8 in. long, 2 to 3 in. broad, erect, rigid, broadly ovate; lower pinnae $1\frac{1}{2}$ in. long, cut nearly or quite to stalk; pinnules deeply cleft into thread-like segs. Mauritius, &c. SYN. *T. foeniculaceum.*

T. par'vulum. *rhiz.* wide-creeping, interlaced. *sti.* 1 in. long, wiry, slender, tomentose below. *Fronds* $\frac{1}{4}$ to $\frac{1}{2}$ in. each way, orbicular, flabellately cut about half-way down from outer edge towards base into narrow, irregular segs. *Sori* 4 to 6, terminal on central segs. Japan, Australia, Madagascar, China. (H.S. 39A; F.B.I. 179.) Greenhouse.

T. Peters'ii. *sti.* about $\frac{1}{8}$ in. long. *Fronds* $\frac{1}{4}$ to $\frac{1}{2}$ in. long, linear to obovate-spathulate, crenate or slightly lobed. *Sori* solitary, terminal, tube sunk in frond, mouth much dilated, but entire. United States. 1875. (H.C.F. 86.) Greenhouse.

T. pinnatiner'vium. *rhiz.* dark, tomentose, thread-like. *sti.* up to $\frac{1}{12}$ in. long. *Fronds* scattered, ovate, $\frac{1}{8}$ to $\frac{1}{4}$ in. long, $\frac{1}{12}$ to $\frac{1}{8}$ in. broad, pellucid, clear, bright green. British Guiana. 1886.

T. pinna'tum. *cau.* erect, tufted. *sti.* strong, wiry, erect, naked or slightly hairy, 3 to 12 in. long. *Fronds* simply pinnate in typical state, 4 to 18 in. long, 3 to 12 in. broad, tip often rooting and proliferous; pinnae 2 to 10 opposite or alternate pairs and a terminal one, 2 to 6 in. long, linear, obtuse or acute, sharply and finely toothed, upper edge usually free from stem at base, lower attached and often furnished with a broad, decurrent wing. *Sori* all round pinnae; receptacle long, exserted. Trop. America. 1825. (H.G.F. 8.) SYN. *T. floribundum.*

T. Plu'ma. *rhiz.* short-creeping, clothed with bright brown scales. *sti.* 2 to 4 in. long, terete, wiry. *Fronds* lanceolate, 4 to 6 in. long, 1 to $1\frac{1}{4}$ in. broad, decompound; rachis stiff, terete throughout; pinnae crowded, 20 to 30 pairs, spreading, under $\frac{1}{2}$ in. broad; lower pinnules sparsely pinnatifid, cut into distant, bristle-like, dichotomously-forked lobes, $\frac{1}{8}$ to $\frac{1}{4}$ in. long. *Sori* few, near base of upper pinnae; receptacle very long. Malaya, Samoa. (H.G.F. 97.)

T. polypodioi'des. *rhiz.* wide-creeping, sinuous, rather strong. *sti.* varying from hardly any to 2 in. long. *Fronds* 2 to 9 in. long, 1 to $1\frac{1}{2}$ in. broad, linear-lanceolate, very gradually decurrent below, pinnatifid down to a broadly-winged rachis; lobes oblong, obtuse, crenate-margined. *Sori* 2 to 4 to each lobe; receptacle much exserted. Trop. America. (L.F. 8, 10.) SYN. *T. incisum, T. sinuosum.*

T. Prieur'ii. A synonym of *T. elegans.*

T. puncta'tum. *Fronds* stalked or sub-sessile, $\frac{1}{4}$ to $\frac{1}{2}$ in. broad, sub-orbicular or obovate, undulate or slightly lobed at margin. *Sori* 1 to 4, on outer edge of frond and more or less exserted, mouth distinctly 2-lipped. Trop. America.

T. pusil'lum. *rhiz.* wide-creeping, tomentose. *Fronds* nearly sessile, 2 to 3 in. long, $\frac{1}{2}$ to 1 in. broad, oblong or obovate, cuneate-attenuated below, once deeply pinnatifid down to a broadly-winged rachis; lobes linear or oblong, toothed or deeply pinnatifid. *Sori* 1 to 4 round tip of frond, tube exserted, mouth with 2 large, rounded lobes. Trop. America. (F.B.I. 302; F.S.A. (2) 2.) SYN. *T. quercifolium.*

T. pyxidif'erum.* *rhiz.* wide-creeping, tomentose, rather slender. *sti.* 1 to 2 in. long, naked, winged above. *Fronds* 1 to 6 in. long, 1 to $1\frac{1}{2}$ in. broad, ovate-oblong, 3-pinnatifid, main rachis very narrowly winged; pinnae ovate-rhomboidal, pinnatifid to rachis, lower pinnules again deeply pinnatifid; ultimate segs. often emarginate at apex. *Sori* 1 to 4 to a pinna, axillary, tube more or less winged; receptacle filiform, exserted. Tropics. (F.S.A. (2) 3.) Greenhouse.

T. quercifo'lium. A synonym of *T. polypodioides.*

T. radi'cans.* Cup Goldilocks; Killarney Fern. *rhiz.* wiry, wide-creeping, tomentose. *sti.* strong, wiry, ascending, 2 to 6 in. long naked or nearly so, upper part sometimes winged. *Fronds* 4 to 12 in. long, 2 to 6 in. broad, 3-pinnatifid, main rachis very narrowly winged, often free, except near apex; lower pinnae 1 to 4 in. long, ovate-rhomboidal, cut to a narrowly-winged rachis; pinnules again deeply pinnatifid, ovate-rhomboidal, with deeply-toothed lower segs. *Sori* lateral, 1 to 4 to a pinnule, tube small, more or less exserted; receptacle slender, elongated. N. Hemisphere (Britain). (H.B.F. 42.) SYN. *T. brevisetum.* Hardy. var. **Andrews'ii,** *fronds* deep green, narrow-lanceolate, pinnae more distant than in species, narrower and erect. Ireland; **alabamen'se,** *rhiz.* thin, creeping, 1 ft. long, *sti.* winged to tip of fronds, *fronds* 3 to 7 in. long, 2 in. or less wide, *sori* clustered in a cup at tips of veins. N. America; **dilata'tum,** *fronds* very dark green, much less divided than in type, pinnae and pinnules broadly winged. Hardy; **Luschnatia'num,** *fronds* lanceolate, acuminate, quite sessile. Brazil. Stove; **prolif'erum,** *fronds,* when fully developed, dotted over with small bulbils, from which young plants are easily raised.

T. renifor'me. *sti.* 4 to 8 in. long, naked, wiry. *Fronds* orbicular-reniform, entire, with a deep sinus at the base, 2 to 4 in. broad. *Sori* often encircling whole outer margin; receptacle much exserted, stout, covered with capsules. New Zealand. (L.F. 8, 9.) Greenhouse.

T. rep'tans. *sti.* $\frac{1}{4}$ in. long. *Fronds* $\frac{1}{4}$ to $\frac{1}{2}$ in. each way, obovate-cuneate, often with short, blunt lobes. *Sori* 1 to 4 on outer margin, tube partially or quite exserted, mouth distinctly 2-lipped. Trop. America.

T. rhomboi'deum. A synonym of *T. javanicum.*

T. ri'gidum.* *sti.* tufted, erect, wiry, 2 to 8 in. long, naked or very slightly winged above. *Fronds* 2 to 8 in. long, 2 to 6 in. broad, deltoid or ovate, acuminate, 3- or 4-pinnatifid, main rachis usually only slightly winged towards top; lower pinnae 2 to 3 in. long, erecto-patent, ovate or lanceolate-rhomboid, cut to a rachis which is very narrowly winged throughout or free below; pinnules deeply pinnatifid, with deeply-toothed or pinnatifid, linear lobes. *Sori* 2 to 12 to a pinnule, small, axillary, tube more or less exserted. Tropics. Stove or greenhouse. (F.S.A. (2), 1.) SYN. var. **elongatum.** A synonym of *T. elongatum.*

T. ru'fum. *sti.* and under side of fronds profusely covered with long, rufous woolly hairs. *Fronds* pale green above, about 10 in. long and 1½ in. broad, pinnate; pinnae overlapping, veins exserted at tips. Demerara.

T. saxa'tile. *sti.* terete, hairy. *Fronds* tufted, triangular-ovate, pinnate below; pinnae 2-pinnatifid, upper decurrent; pinnules ovate, margins more or less decurved, giving surface a pretty, undulating character; ultimate segs. broad, short, obtuse-pointed. Indusia cylindrical, supra-axillary, slightly 2-lipped. Borneo. 1862.

T. scan'dens. *rhiz.* wiry, wide-creeping. *sti.* strong, erect, naked, 2 to 4 in. long. *Fronds* 6 to 18 in. long, 3 to 6 in. broad, fully pinnate, or the hairy rachis very slightly winged above, ovate, acuminate; lower pinnae ovate-lanceolate, nearly pinnate, 2 to 4 in. long; pinnules divided to a narrow wing; segs. again pinnatifid about half-way down; margins finely hairy. *Sori* 1 to 4 to a pinnule, mouth with 2 lateral projections. Mexico, W. Indies. 1862.

T. seti'gerum. *sti.* quite terete, 2 to 6 in. long, with hair-like scales. *Fronds* tufted, 9 to 15 in. long, linear or linear-lanceolate, pinnate, smooth, curving; pinnae 2-pinnatifid; pinnules palmate; ultimate segs. elongated, very narrow, almost capillary, lower incurved, sub-erect. Indusia supra-axillary, small, sub-cylindrical, terminal on a narrow seg. Borneo. 1862.

T. sinuo'sum. A synonym of *T. polypodioides.*

T. spica'tum. A synonym of *T. osmundioides.*

T. super'bum. A synonym of *T. fimbriatum.*

T. stric'tum. *Fronds* lanceolate, very pale green, 4 to 6 in. long, 3 or 4 times divided nearly to narrowly-winged stalk; pinnae crowded, lanceolate; lower pinnules deeply cleft into ligulate lobes. New Zealand.

T. tene'rum. *rhiz.* creeping, tomentose, very slender. *sti.* 1 to 2 in. long, slender, naked. *Fronds* 3 to 8 in. long, 1 to 1½ in. broad, pendent, flaccid, lanceolate, 3-pinnatifid, the main rachis only very slightly winged towards apex; pinnae distant, flaccid, cut to a narrowly-winged rachis, with distant, deeply-incised or pinnatifid pinnules; ultimate segs. about ⅛ in. long. *Sori* 1 to 4 to a pinna, tube exserted. Trop. America. (G.C. 8 (1890), 100.) SYN. T. *angustatum.*

T. trichoi'deum. A synonym of *T. capillaceum.*

T. trigo'num. *rhiz.* wide-creeping, strong, tomentose. *sti.* 2 to 4 in. long, strong, compressed, winged above. *Fronds* 4 to 12 in. long, 1½ to 2 in. broad, ovate-lanceolate, acuminate, once-pinnatifid down to a broadly-winged rachis; segs. linear-oblong, rounded or acute, toothed, largest 1 in. long, ¼ in. broad; main rachis densely, fronds surface slightly hairy. *Sori* 2 to 12 to a pinna, tube more or less exserted; receptacle long, filiform. Trop. America. 1862. SYN. *T. Kaulfussii.*

T. trichophyl'lum. *sti.* densely tufted, wiry, terete, 1 to 2 in. long. *Fronds* 2 to 4 in. long, 1 to 1½ in. broad, oblong, decompound; rachis stiff, terete; pinnae 12 to 15 pairs, much imbricated, many deltoid, ½ in. broad; lower pinnules copiously pinnatifid; ultimate divisions bristle-like, ⅛ to ¼ in. long, spreading in all directions. *Sori* copious, free, near base of pinnules on upper side. Borneo, New Caledonia. 1862.

T. veno'sum. *rhiz.* slender, wide-creeping. *sti.* 1 to 2 in. long, very slender, naked. *Fronds* 2 to 5 in. long, 1 to 1½ in. broad, pinnatifid, main veins free in lower half, broadly winged above; lower pinnae about 6 in. long, varying from linear and nearly simple to lanceolate and deeply pinnatifid below. *Sori* only 1 to a pinna, axillary on upper margin, tube slightly 2-lipped. Australia, New Zealand. (L.F. 8, 9.) Greenhouse.

TRICHONE'MA. A synonym of Romulea.

TRICHONIS'CUS. *See* **Woodlice.**

TRICHOPE'TALUM. A synonym of Bottionaea.

tricho'philus -a -um, strongly hairy.

trichophyl'lus -a -um, having hair-like or hairy leaves.

TRICHOPIL'IA (*thrix, trichos*, a hair, *pilion*, a cap; the anther is concealed below a cap). FAM. *Orchidaceae.* A genus embracing about 25 species of beautiful, epiphytic orchids, inhabiting the warmer parts of America, usually at considerable altitudes. Flowers showy, pedicellate; sepals sub-equal, free, narrow, erecto-patent, often twisted; petals similar; lip with the claw adnate to the column, which it closely invests above, the limb spreading, the slightly dilated lateral lobes connivent, the mid-lobe continuous and undulated; the divisions are not clearly defined in some species, the lip then somewhat resembling that of *Cattleya labiata* but more funnel-shaped. Pollen masses 2, obovoid-oblong, not appendiculate; scapes springing from a short rhizome, leafless, few-sheathed, 1-, 2-, or rarely 3- to 5-flowered, bracts small. Leaf rather leathery, erect, conduplicate at base, narrow or rather broad. Pseudobulbs usually flattish and set closely together, 1-leaved. Leucohyle is by some separated from Trichopilia as the lip is somewhat spatulate and concave, its base more free from the column. In the species still often termed Pilumnas, of which *T. fragrans* is an example, the scapes are more or less erect and carry 2 or more flowers, the lip blade is somewhat flat, sub-quadrate or oblong: pots are suitable for these. In the majority the scapes are lateral or arched, and small pans or baskets which can be suspended near the glass are preferable. A compost should be made of 2 parts of Osmunda fibre, 1 part of Sphagnum moss, mixed with a little loam fibre. Good drainage is essential as the plants are impatient of a clogged compost, particularly during winter, when infrequent waterings are required, only often enough to prevent shrivelling. The greater number may be accommodated in the intermediate house throughout the year or may be wintered in that division and grown in the Odontoglossum or cool house during the height of summer. The winter night temperature should be about 55° F. Propagation is better made by the division of large plants, but healthy back bulbs will occasionally yield young growths if placed on sand in a propagating pit or laid on a damp stage in a warm house. Though a few small-flowered species are included in the genus, on the whole the flowers are showy and attractive.

T. al'bida. *fl.* sep. and pet. pale greenish-yellow, nearly straight, margins slightly hyaline; lip longer than pet., 4-lobed, lobes whitish, throat with scattered, brownish-yellow dots; hood 3-lobed; raceme pendulous, about 3-fld. *l.* oblong-lanceolate, flat, sub-cordate at base, acuminate at apex, recurved. Caracas. 1851.

T. Backhousia'na. Plant paler green and more robust and *fl.* more fleshy than in *T. fragrans*, lip much narrower and lobed near end, but twice as broad in middle. *l.* faintly spotted and clouded with darker patches. Colombia. 1876. (O.R. 1944, p. 93.) Often classed as a variety of *T. fragrans.*

T. bre'vis.* *fl.* 2 or 3, 3 in. or more across; sep. and pet. greenish-yellow, blotched and barred chocolate, linear-lanceolate, acute; lip frilled white slightly flushed and veined yellow on front lobe and disk with a few purplish spots at base. *l.* solitary, elliptic-lanceolate, 6 in. long. *Pseudobulbs* conico-cylindrical, 3 to 5 in. long. Peru. About 1891. (G.C. 18 (1895), 641; L. 332.)

T. can'dida. A synonym of *T. fragrans.*

T. coccin'ea.* Sep. and pet. narrow, twisted, 2½ in. long, brownish-green; lip with the basal lobes convolute over column, whitish outside, crimson within, the large front lobe paler, blotched and streaked with rose-carmine, sometimes margined white; scapes deflexed shorter than l., one-fld. Early summer. *Pseudobulbs* oblong, compressed, 2 to 3 in. h., occasionally more. *l.* narrow, 6 to 9 in. long. Cent. America. 1849; var. **crisp'a,** sep. and pet. cherry-crimson, faintly edged white, margins crisped-crenate, lip white outside, deeper than sep. inside, margins irregularly crisped, throat rich deep crimson. April to June. Cent. America. 1857; **le'pida,** *fl.* 4 to 5 in. across, sep. and pet. pale rosy-lilac, irregularly margined white, lip crisped, front lobe deep purple-crimson with irregular white margin; peduncles deflexed. Spring. Costa Rica. 1873. (W.O.A. 197 as *T. lepida.*); **margina'ta,** 1-fld., *fl.* 4 to 5 in. across; sep. and pet. brownish-red or red-crimson, with greenish-yellow or whitish margins, narrow, once-twisted; mid-lobe of lip wavy, reddish-purple, sometimes white margined, throat deep purple, or lip white, throat deep purple; peduncle drooping. May, June, *Pseudobulbs* usually smaller than type. Cent. America. 1880. (B.M. 4857 as *T. coccinea.*); **marginata Champlatreux's form,** sep. and pet. red-crimson, the margins white broken with red spots, lip narrowly white margined, fluted, strawberry-red, darkest beneath the column, whitish without; **marginata crisp'a,** a fine form, *fl.* large, sep. and pet. linear-lanceolate, pale purplish-red with white edges, lip white without, mid-lobe deeply cleft, dull crimson edged white, throat dark crimson. (W.S.O. 5 as *T. crispa marginata*; F.d.S. 1925, 1926.)

T. cris'pa. A variety of *T. coccinea.*

T. frag'rans.* *fl.* 3 to 5, variable in size, fragrant; sep. and pet. nearly uniform, pale yellowish-green, 1 in. or more long, wavy; lip obscurely 4-lobed, pure white, spotted orange near base; scapes erect or nearly so. Winter. *Pseudobulbs* oblong, 4 to 6 in. long, much compressed. *l.* oblong to oblong-lanceolate, 7 to 12 in. long. New Grenada. 1858. (B.M. 5035 as *Pilumna fragrans.*) var. **nob'ilis,** *fl.* larger, segs. white, throat with orange blotch each side which meet. Colombia. (W.O.A. 128 as *Pilumna nobilis*). **nobilis al'ba,** *fl.* white without the yellow eye. 1908?

T. Galeottia'na.* *fl.* 2 in. long, sep. and pet. cuneate-lanceolate, acute, the latter somewhat broader, yellowish; lip closely folded round column, front lobe obreniform, 4-lobed, light yellow, disk dark yellow, sometimes spotted red or red-brown, margin passing to white; peduncles short, procumbent, 1- or 2-fld. August, September. *l.* cuneate-oblong, acute, dark green. *Pseudobulbs* 3 to 5 in. h., ligulate, ancipitous. Mexico. 1860. (I.H. 225 as *T. picta*; B.M. 5550 as *T. Turialvae.*)

T. gra'ta. *fl.* sweetly-scented; sep. and pet. yellowish-green; lip expanded, white, blotched yellow each side of keel; racemes few-fld. *l.* oblong-ligulate. *Pseudobulbs* elongated, ancipitous, 2-leaved. Peru. 1868. Allied to *T. fragrans.*

T. Hennisia'na. Considered a form of *T. fragrans. fl.* larger than in *T. fragrans nobilis*, lip broader with a more undulate margin. Colombia.

T. hymenan'tha. *fl.* 4 to 12, about 1½ in. across, drooping; sep. and pet. whitish or pale straw-yellow, margin fringed, slightly twisted; lip sessile, nearly flat, with erose edges, speckled with deep reddish-purple towards base and sides. Summer. *l.* thick, fleshy, elongated-ensiform, acuminate, narrowed to the base, the lower part representing a stem or pseudobulb. Colombia. 1854. (B.M. 5949; R.X.O. i. 7; W.O.A. 479.) Sometimes separated from Trichopilia under the name *Leucohyle subulata.*

T. Kienastia'na. *fl.* white, with a few yellow lines or spots on disk of lip; sep. and pet. linear-ligulate; lateral lobes of lip median, obtuse-angled; front lobes wavy, emarginate; peduncle usually 2-fld. *l.* and *pseudobulbs* much like those of *T. suavis.* Habitat? 1883.

T. la'xa. *fl.* 5 to 9, fragrant, 2 to 3 in. across, in loose racemes, produced out of broad, obtuse, short, membranous, spotted bracts, arching; sep. and pet. dull rose, with greenish stripe, or green shaded, erect, linear-lanceolate, equal; lip cream. *Pseudobulbs* compressed, 2 to 3 in. h. *l.* lanceolate-oblong, 8 to 12 in. long. S. Colombia. (B.R. 1847, 57 as *Pilumna laxa.*) SYN. *T. Reichenheimii.* var. **flaveo'la**, sep. and pet. yellowish-white. 1884.

T. Lehman'ni. *fl.* white, with a yellow spot in throat of lip; sep. and pet. linear-lanceolate, 1½ in. long; lip with a large, oblong front lobe; scape 2 to 3 in. long, bracteate. *l.* solitary, oblong-lanceolate, obtuse. *Pseudobulbs* ovate-compressed. Colombia. 1888. Perhaps a variety of *T. fragrans*, but with a 1-fld. peduncle. (G.F. 1888, t. 1276, f. 2.) SYN. *Pilumna Lehmanni.*

T. le'pida. A synonym of *T. coccinea lepida.*

T. margina'ta. A variety of *T. coccinea.*

T. modes'ta (Hort). *fl.* small, almost translucent, 2 or 3 or more; sep. and pet. sub-equal, narrowly lanceolate, keeled; pet. inclined upward and forward, ¾ in. long, creamy-white; lower sep. slightly divergent; lip white, side lobes convolute over column, blade with much enlarged corners giving a 2-lobed appearance; crest keeled, ochre-yellow; peduncle 1 in. or more long, bracteate. Habit of *T. sauvis*, but much smaller. *Pseudobulbs* flattish, 1 to 1½ in. h., 1 in. wide. *l.* 5 to 6 in. h., 2 in. wide, keeled, pointed. Costa Rica? 1928.

T. multiflo'ra. A synonym of *Macradenia multiflora.*

T. mu'tica. *fl.* about 1 in. across, dirty white with slight red tinge; sep. and pet. linear, acute; lip broadly ovate, pointed, parallel with column; raceme few-fld., arched. August. *l.* linear-lanceolate, convex at back, 4 to 5 in. long. Trinidad, Surinam, Brazil. 1821. SYN. *Leucohyle mutica, Macradenia mutica.*

T. nob'ilis. A variety of *T. fragrans.*

T. pic'ta. A synonym of *T. Galeottiana.*

T. puncta'ta. Allied to *T. laxa*, but sep. and pet. covered with numerous red-purple spots on a light green ground; lip greenish-white; fl. about 2 in. across; scapes sub-erect. Costa Rica. 1890.

T. Reichenheim'ii. A synonym of *T. laxa.*

T. rostra'ta. *fl.* sep. and pet. pale whitish-green, linear, acute, pet. twice twisted 1½ in. long; lip broad oblong, emarginate, white, with pale orange rays, flabellate, 3-fid towards the apex; peduncle 2- or 3-fld. *Pseudobulbs* linear-lingulate, 4 to 6 in. h., the scales slightly dotted. *l.* broadly ligulate, acute. Colombia. 1872.

T. sanguinolen'ta.* *fl.* rather showy, 2½ in. across; sep. and pet. yellowish-olive, with brownish-crimson transverse bands or ocellate markings; lip emarginate, recurved, white, flabellately veined, veins in basal half marked by broken crimson lines. *Pseudobulbs* ovate, oblong, 1 to 2 in. h. *l.* undulate, shortly petiolate, 4 to 6 in. long. Ecuador. 1843. (As *Helcia sanguinolenta* I.H. ser. iii. 21; L. & P.F.G. 2, 182.) Succeeds in Odontoglossum house.

T. sua'vis.* *fl.* large, variable, white or creamy-white, delicately Hawthorn-scented; sep. and pet. narrowed to base, undulate rather than twisted; lip yellow in the throat, spotted with pale violet-rose on front and sides, closely rolled up at base, funnel-shaped and 3-lobed in front; peduncles 3- or 4-fld. March, April. *Pseudobulbs* oblong-obcordate, rounded, ancipitous, clustered, 2 to 3½ in. h., sometimes nearly 3 in. wide. Considered the finest species. *l.* large, broad-oblong, acute, wavy, nearly sessile, sometimes 12 in. long, 4 in. wide. Costa Rica. 1850. (B.M. 4654; F.d.S. 761; L.J.F. 227; L. & P.F.G. i. 11; W.S.O. iii. 8.) var. **al'ba,** *fl.*, sep. and pet. pure white; lip white, marked in throat with a yellow stain. May, June. (W.O.A. i. 14; R. 31); **grandiflor'a,** *fl.* more highly coloured than in type, and expanding better; sep. and pet. white; lip over 3 in. across, white, with large, rich crimson spots, throat deep orange. *l.* and pseudobulbs very large. A lovely variety.

T. torti'lis.* *fl.* drooping, large and attractive; sep. and pet. yellowish-green, with lurid brownish-purple blotches along middle part, spirally twisted, narrow-lanceolate, 2½ in. long; lip white outside, yellowish-white or white within, thickly spotted rose and blotched yellow about throat, base closely rolled in, front part spreading out and 3-lobed; peduncle procumbent, 1-fld. *l.* oblong, acute, 5 to 7 in. long. *Pseudobulbs* oblong or ligulate, compressed, 2 to 3 in. long. Mexico. 1835. (B.M. 3739; W.O.A. viii. 349; B.R. 1863.) There are several varieties.

Trichopilia tortilis

T. Turial'vae. *fl.* 2 to 3; sep. and pet. oval-lanceolate, about 2 in. long, clear yellow; lip somewhat trumpet-shaped, mid-lobe rounded, clear yellow, throat with brownish dots; scape short. *Pseudobulbs* 2 to 3 in. h. *l.* elliptical, pointed, 4 to 5 in. long, about 2 in. wide. Costa Rica. 1863. (in cultivation?) *T. Turialvae* of Bateman is *T. Galeottiana.*

E. C.

TRICHOSAC'ME (*trichos*, hair, *acme*, point; the corolla has a hairy appendage). FAM. *Asclepiadaceae.* A genus of a single species of climbing shrub, densely woolly all over except on corolla. Cultivation as for Stapelia.

T. lana'ta. *l.* opposite, elliptic or oblong, heart-shaped at base, blunt; stalked. *fl.* purple, rather small, in a 6- to 10-fld. umbellate cymes; cal. segs. 5, lanceolate; cor. tube short, rotate, lobes emarginate, with a long, terminal, filiform appendage to each; peduncles leaf-opposed. July. Mexico. 1850. (F.d.S. 1123.)

TRICHOSAN'THES (*trichos*, hair, *anthos*, flower; the corolla is fringed). FAM. *Cucurbitaceae.* A genus of about 50 species of annual or perennial climbing herbs, sometimes shrubby at base, occasionally tuberous-rooted, natives of Trop. Asia, N. Australia, and Polynesia. Leaves entire or 3- to 9-lobed, toothed; tendrils usually 2- or 3-branched. Flowers usually monoecious; calyx long-tubular, with 5 lanceolate segments; corolla 5-cleft nearly to base, the lobes long-fringed; staminate flowers with 3 stamens, peduncles in axillary pairs, one 1-flowered and caducous, the other racemose; female flowers solitary with an inferior 1-celled ovary, the style 3- or 6-cleft at apex. Fruit lanceolate or globose, smooth, occasionally large, often ornamental and highly coloured. Seeds should be sown on a hotbed in spring, the plants being subsequently treated like Cucumbers. The fruits of *T. Anguina* are eaten as a vegetable in India.

T. Angui'na. Common Snake Gourd, Viper Gourd, Serpent Cucumber. Stem twining, more or less downy. *l.* between cordate and reniform, 3- to 7-lobed, or 5-angled, downy. *Peduncles* 5 to 10 in. long, 8- to 15-fld., the earlier male peduncle sometimes replaced by a female; cal. tube 1 in. long; corolla with oblong pet. about 1 in. long, the fringe occupying ½ in. *fr.* very long, cylindrical, sometimes twisted, striped green and white when young, brilliant orange when ripe, edible. India, &c. 1735. (B.M. 722; B.R. 32, 18 as *T. colubrina.*) SYN. *Anguina sinensis.* Half-hardy.

T. bractea'ta. *l.* broadly ovate, palmately 3- to 7-lobed, acute, toothed, downy, rough above. *Male fl.* in racemes on long stout peduncles, snow-white, fringed; racemes at first capitate then elongated, bracts toothed or lacerate, 1 in. across; *female fl.* solitary, their pedicels short. *fr.* nearly globular, 2 to 3 in. across, red with orange streaks. India, N. Australia. 1825. (B.M. 6873 as *T. palmata.*)

T. colubri'na. A synonym of *T. Anguina.*

T. corda'ta. Robust, tuberous-rooted climber, perennial. *l.* wide ovate-cordate, rarely lobed, acute, slightly toothed. *Male fl.* 4 to 8, on a peduncle 4 to 8 in. long; cal. segs. slender-pointed. *fr.* globose, red, streaked orange. India.

T. cucumeroi'des. Perennial. Root fleshy, tuberous. *l.* more or less palmate, 3- to 5-lobed, margin wavy. *Male fl.* 3 to 15 on a peduncle 1 to 4 in. long; pet. oblong, acute, fringe long. *fr.* oblong, shortly beaked, about 3 in. long, vermilion. Japan.

T. japo'nica. Stem slender. *l.* thin, broadly ovate, glabrous, smooth, 3- to 5-lobed, lobes triangular, acute. *Male* racemes few-fld., bracts large, broadly ovate, deeply toothed, teeth awl-shaped; peduncle robust, grooved. *fr.* ovoid, somewhat acute. Japan. 1872. (G.F. 714.) Greenhouse.

T. Kirilow'ii. Herbaceous perennial, stem branched, root tuberous. *l.* roundish, often deeply 5- to 7-lobed, palmate; lobes oblong or oblong-lanceolate, acute, deeply incised. *fl.* monoecious. *Male* racemes 4 to 18 in. long, 3- to 8-, rarely only 1-fld.; pet. triangular-wedge-shaped, deeply cut, fringe long; bracts sharply toothed. *fr.* ovoid or ovoid-oblong, orange-red. China. 1872. Greenhouse. SYN. *Eopepon vitifolius.*

T. palma'ta. A synonym of *T. bracteata.*

T. tubero'sa. A synonym of *Ceratosanthes tuberosa.*

F. G. P.

TRICHOS'MA. Included in **Eria**. *T. suavis* is *Eria coronaria.*

TRICHOSPO'RUM. *See* **Aeschynanthus.**

TRICHOSTE'MA (*thrix, trichos,* hair, *stemon,* stamen; the filaments are very slender). FAM. *Labiatae.* A genus of about 10 species of N. American herbs or sub-shrubs. Related to Teucrium but of different habit. Leaves entire. Flowers usually blue or violet in dense or loose axillary, many-flowered whorls; stamens 4, lower longest, long exserted. *T. lanatum* is a half-hardy shrub for well-drained sandy loam.

T. lana'tum. Blue Curls. Perennial, sub-shrubby, erect, about 18 in. h. *l.* like those of *Rosmarinus officinalis,* linear, entire, 1 to 2 in. long, margins revolute, rugose above, loosely hairy beneath. *fl.* blue-purple, with very long exserted stamens; spikes about 6 in. long, verticels 10- to 20-fld., wholly clothed with purple, woolly hairs. S. California.

tricho'tomus -a -um, having divisions (usually branches) in threes; cut in a threefold manner.

TRICHOSTIG'MA (*thrix, trichos,* hair, *stigma*; the stigma being hairy). FAM. *Phytolaccaceae.* A genus of 3 Trop. American, erect or climbing shrubs with alternate stalked, entire, oval or elliptic leaves. Flowers in racemes, 4-parted; sepals free, ovate, or elliptic, reflexed in fruit; petals none; stamens 8 to 25; ovary 1-celled; style very short. Fruit globular, berry-like. A stove-house plant, propagated by cuttings in a close frame. *T. peruvianum* is valuable for its ornamental leaves.

T. peruvia'num.* Climbing shrub, 6 ft. h., branches slender. *l.* elliptic slender-pointed, base oblique, thick, shining metallic green above, rosy-violet beneath. *fl.* small, whitish in a long raceme at first erect, but becoming drooping. Andes. (I.H. 16, 591.)

tric'olor, three-coloured.

TRICUSPIDA'RIA (*tricuspis,* 3-pointed, alluding to the 3-toothed petals). FAM. *Elaeocarpaceae.* A genus of 3 species of evergreen trees, natives of S. America. Leaves alternate or opposite, simple, short-stalked, firm-textured. Flowers cup-shaped or urn-shaped, white or red, axillary, on long pedicels; calyx quickly falling; petals 5, somewhat fleshy, 3- (rarely 5-) toothed at tip; stamens 15 to 20, opening by pores. Capsule leathery; seeds ovoid. Although often listed as *Tricuspidaria* (a name published in 1796 by Ruiz and Pavon) the botanically correct name of the genus is CRINODENDRON (from Greek *krinon,* a kind of lily, *dendron,* tree, in allusion to the white, fragrant, somewhat lily-like flowers of *C. Patagua*) published in 1782 by Molina. *C. tucumanum* is not cultivated in Britain and is horticulturally inferior to the 2 Chilean species, *C. Patagua* and *C. Hookerianum.*

Crinodendron Hookerianum (p. 2145)

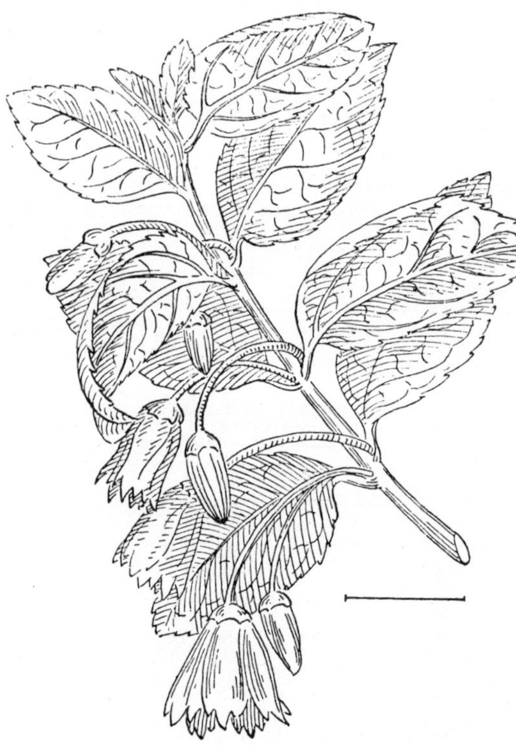

Crinodendron Patagua (p. 2145)

Provided they are given sufficiently mild conditions these grow easily and well in a warm peaty or loamy soil free from lime. They can only be grown in the open in the mildest parts of the British Isles; in cold localities a cool greenhouse will be required; elsewhere they should be given the shelter of a warm wall. Propagation is by seed or by cuttings of partly matured side shoots, about 3 in. long, taken with a heel, in July or August, inserted in a sandy compost around the edges of a pot and kept in a warm, closed propagating frame, where they should root in about a month.

C. Hookeria' num.* Lantern Tree, 10 to 30 ft. h. *l.* very narrowly elliptic, 1½ to 5 in. long, ½ to 1¼ in. wide, coriaceous, toothed, hairy beneath along the main veins. *fl.* urn-shaped, rich crimson; pet. curving inwards, $\frac{7}{10}$ to $\frac{9}{10}$ in. long; anthers nearly ⅖ in. long; ovary densely hairy. May, June. Chile. 1848. (B.M. 7160, as *Tricuspidaria dependens.*) Syn. *Crinodendron lanceolatum, Tricuspidaria Hookeriana, T. lanceolata.* The fl. forms a short-stalked bud in autumn, which remains dormant and the size of a pea until spring. A white-fld. form **al'bum** has been offered. Where it thrives, this is a superb shrub or small tree and can even be clipped to make a wind-screen in light woodland.

C. Pata'gua. Tree, 20 to 30 ft. (sometimes to 70 ft.) h. *l.* elliptic to narrowly obovate, 1 to 3 in. long, ½ to 1¼ in. wide, thus proportionally broader than those of *C. Hookerianum*, coriaceous, toothed, apparently glabrous (microscopically hairy) beneath. *fl.* cup-shaped, white; pet. erect, not curving inwards, ⅗ to $\frac{7}{10}$ in. long; anthers ⅕ in. long; ovary minutely hairy. Late summer. Chile. 1901. (B.M. 8115, as *Tricuspidaria dependens.*) Syn. *Crinodendron dependens, Tricuspidaria dependens, T. Patagua.* The Chilean vernacular name of this species is Patagua. It is not so ornamental as *C. Hookerianum*, the fl. being white and often not freely produced.

C. tucuma'num. Tree, to 90 ft. h. in Argentine. *l.* elliptic to narrowly elliptic, ½ to 3½ in. long, ¼ to 1¼ in. wide, scarcely toothed, glabrous beneath except for tufts of hair in axils of veins. *fl.* cup-shaped, white; pet. ⅖ to ⅗ in. long; anthers ⅒ in. long; ovary glabrous. Argentine, Bolivia. (Lilloa, 2. 352.)

W. T. S.

TRICYR'TIS (*treis*, three, *kyrtos*, convex; the 3 outer petals are bag-like at base). Fam. *Liliaceae*. Toad-lilies. A genus of 9 or 10 perennials with shortly creeping rhizomes, natives of Formosa, Japan, and Himalaya. Stem erect or arching, simple below inflorescence. Leaves alternate, ovate or oblong, cordate-amplexicaul or subsessile. Inflorescence terminal or in upper leaf-axils, loosely dichotomous, erect. Flowers few, rather large, pedicels longish, bell-shaped, often spotted within, segments free, lanceolate, outer saccate at base, inner flat, all spreading in upper part; stamens 6. Sandy loam and peat suits them as it does Trilliums but they are later as a rule in flower and need a warm sheltered spot lest the buds are delayed until autumn frosts. Propagation by seeds or offsets. Descriptions of the Japanese species are given in a survey by G. Masamune in *Journal of Society of Tropical Agriculture* (*Taiwan*), 2. 38–48 (1930).

T. Bak'eri. Habit of *T. macropoda* but *fl.* yellow, spotted red, and veined red near tips, segs. broadly ovate. Japan? (B.M. 6554 as *T. macropoda.*)

T. formosa'na. Stem arching, about 1 ft. h. *l.* few-sessile, oblanceolate, lower 4 to 5 in. long, up to 1 in. wide. *fl.* few, whitish-purple with very few spots, about ¾ in. long, style as long as stigmas. Formosa.

T. hirt'a. Japanese Toad Lily. Stem 1 to 3 ft. h. softly white hairy. *l.* oblong, shortly abruptly pointed, cordate-amplexicaul, 4 to 6 in. long, hairy. *fl.* 6 to 15, about 1 in. long, in racemes; white with large purple dots on outer segs. June, July. Japan. 1863. (B.M. 5355; Gn. 49 (1896), 290.) var. **ni'gra** has darker, earlier fl.

T. latifo'lia. Stem 2 to 3 ft. h., glabrous, flexuous. *l.* broadly oblong, uppermost ovate. *fl.* few, whitish with minute purple spots; style as long as stigmas. June. Japan.

T. macran'tha. About 2 ft. h. *l.* ovate-lanceolate, about 4 in. long, 2 in. wide. *fl.* deep primrose spotted light chocolate within, pendulous, long-stalked. September. Japan. 1935?

T. macropo'da. Stem 2 to 3 ft. h., downy in upper part. *l.* oblong, 4 to 5 in. long, 1½ to 2 in. wide, acute, rounded at base, sessile or with very short stalk, glabrous above, downy beneath. *fl.* whitish-purple with small purple dots, about ¾ in. long; style half as long as stigmas. September. Japan, China. var. **striat'a** ,*l.* striped white.

T. macula'ta. Stem hairy, 2 to 4 ft. h. *l.* oblong, similar to those of *T. hirta.* *fl.* about ¾ in long, whitish with large purple spots; many in a loose terminal corymb. July. Himalaya. 1851. (B.M. 4955.) Syn. *T. elegans, T. pilosa.*

T. pilo'sa. A synonym of *T. maculata.*

T. stoloni'fera. Stem running at base, about 2 ft. h. *l.* lanceolate, slender-pointed, amplexicaul, 4 to 5 in. long, hairy on nerves at first. *fl.* about 1¼ in. long, mauve with deeper spots; many in a loose corymb, pedicels hairy at first. September. Formosa. 1913. (B.M. 8560.) Syn. *T. formosana*, var. *stolonifera.* Doubtfully distinct from *T. formosana.*

TRIDACT'YLE. Included in **Angraecum.**

TRI'DAX (*Thridax*, old Greek name used by Theophrastus for Lettuce, the ligulate ray florets often being 3-toothed). Fam. *Compositae*. A genus of about 15 species of annual or perennial herbs, natives of Trop. America. Leaves opposite, cut or pinnately lobed; segments few, narrow. Flower-heads yellow or disk greenish, rather small, long-stalked, heterogamous; ray florets ligulate or somewhat 2-lipped, outer lip large, sometimes 3-toothed, 3-cleft, or 3-parted, inner small or minute, 2-lobed or parted, sometimes absent; involucral bracts in few series; receptacle flat or convex, achenes turbinate, silky-hairy. Propagated by division or by seeds. These plants grow in ordinary soil but few are worth growing.

T. bi'color ro'sea. Annual of 12 to 15 in. *Basal l.* somewhat triangular, 2 in. long, 1 in. wide, strongly nerved, margin widely toothed; *upper* gradually narrower and smaller, mostly entire. *fl.-heads* 1½ to 2 in. across; rays rose, 15 to 20, rather broad, 3-toothed, disk yellow. Summer. Mexico. 1887. Hardy annual to be sown rather late.

T. coronopifo'lium. About 12 in. h. *l.* variously pinnatifid or 3-fid; lobes linear, acute. *fl.-heads* yellow, rays unequally 5-lobed, outer involucral l. obtuse or mucronate. June. Mexico. Syn. *Ptilostephium coronopifolium.*

T. triloba'ta. About 12 in. h. *l.* 3-lobed, variously cut. *fl.-heads* yellow, rays 5-toothed; pappus bristles very short or longer and plumose; peduncles hairy or glandular-downy near top. June. Mexico. (B.M. 1895 as *Galinsoga trilobata.*)

tri'dens, 3-toothed.

tridentate, with teeth at apex.

tridy'mus -a -um, triple.

TRIENTA'LIS (Latin signifying ⅓ of a foot high). Fam. *Primulaceae*. A genus of but 2 species, natives of the North Temperate zone. Rhizome creeping, perennial, with an erect stem bearing 5 to 7 whorled, obovate-elliptic or lanceolate, entire leaves. Flowers white; calyx 5- to 9-parted, persistent; corolla rotate, 5- to 9-parted, tube very short, segments elliptic-lanceolate; stamens 5 to 9; peduncles 1 to 3, 1-flowered, filiform,

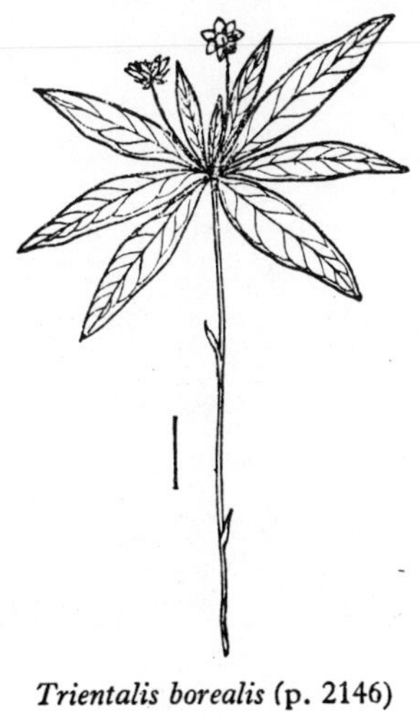

Trientalis borealis (p. 2146)

ebracteate. These plants need a light rich soil with plenty of leaf-mould and a shady situation. Propagated in spring by seeds covered with a handlight, or by division.

T. borea'lis. Star Flower. Stem about 9 in. h. with 5 to 9 *l.* at top. *fl.* with finely acuminate pet. May. NW. America. 1816. SYN. *T. americana.*

T. europae'a. Stem wiry, slender, 4 to 8 in. h., leafy at top. *l.* obovate to obovate-lanceolate, $1\frac{1}{2}$ to $2\frac{1}{2}$ in. long, shining, rigid, narrowed to the short stalks. *fl.* few, erect, $\frac{1}{2}$ to $\frac{3}{4}$ in. across; pet. ovate, acute. June, July. Europe, including Britain. (L.B.C. 105; E.B. 1139.)

trifarious, arranged in 3 rows.

trifascia'tus -a -um, in 3 bundles.

trifid, cut half-way into 3 parts.

trifoliate, bearing 3 leaves.

trifoliolate, having 3 leaflets from the same point.

TRIFO'LIUM (*treis*, three, *folium*, leaf; most species have 3-foliolate leaves). FAM. *Leguminosae.* A genus of perhaps 300 species of annual, biennial, or perennial herbs widely distributed over the temperate and sub-tropical regions of the N. Hemisphere, a few also being found on mountains of Trop. Africa and America and in extra-tropical S. America. Leaves digitately 3- (rarely 5- or 7-) foliolate, sometimes pinnate, 3-, very rarely 5-foliolate; stipules adnate to petioles. Flowers papilionaceous, often purple, red or white, rarely yellow, in spikes, capitula or umbels, or rarely solitary; petals often marcescent, all long-clawed, or the 4 lower ones adnate to the staminal tube; standard oblong or ovate; wings narrow; keel shorter than wings, obtuse; stamens diadelphous. Pod oblong, sub-terete or compressed-obovate, indehiscent. The genus is of greater agricultural than horticultural interest but a few species are useful rock-garden plants and one, *T. incarnatum*, the Crimson Clover, is one of the best plants for green-manuring. *T. repens* is one of the plants commonly recognized as the Shamrock, and the 4-leaved form, by no means uncommon, is regarded as 'lucky'. Some native species are often found in lawns but are not desirable plants either there or on playing fields, though excellent in meadows and pastures, especially *T. hybridum*, *T. medium*, *T. pratense*, and *T. repens*. The following species are perennial unless otherwise stated. All can be grown easily from seed and take kindly to ordinary sweet garden soil, and the perennial species, some of which root as they run, can be increased by division.

T. alpi'num.* 3 to 6 in. h. with a very short, thick underground stem. *lflets.* 3, linear-lanceolate; stalks long; stipules very long and narrow. *fl.* purple, upper pet. pink with purple streaks; in long-stalked umbels. July. European Alps. 1775. Rock-garden. var. **al'bum,** *fl.* white.

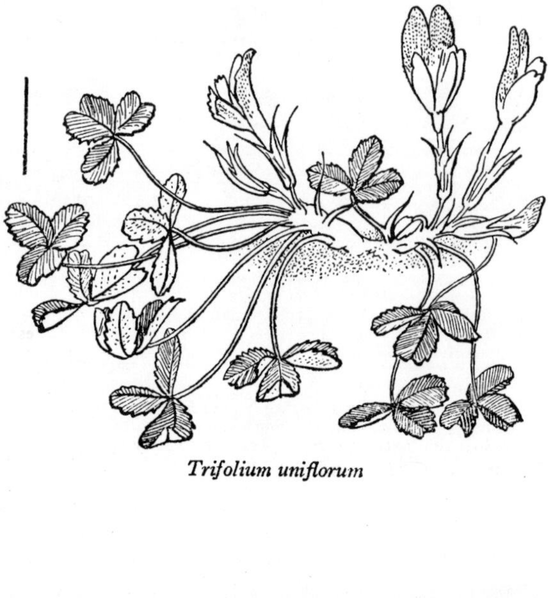

Trifolium uniflorum

T. ba'dium. Usually biennial, 4 to 8 in. h. *lflets.* 3, elliptic to deltoid, $\frac{2}{5}$ to $\frac{4}{5}$ in. long; stalk long; stipules pointed. *fl.* golden yellow, turning chestnut-brown with age. (R.I.F.G. 22, 118.) S. Europe.

T. incarna'tum. Crimson Clover. Annual, about 1 ft. h. Stems slender, hairy, hairs spreading. *lflets.* 3, broadly obovate or obcordate, $\frac{3}{4}$ to $1\frac{1}{2}$ in. long; stalk short; stipules blunt. *fl.* bright scarlet, $\frac{1}{2}$ in. long; cal. hairy; heads terminal, stalked, ovoid or cylindrical, 1 to 2 in. across. June, July. S. Europe. 1640. (B.M. 328.) A good plant for green-manuring, sown in August or early September and dug in in April.

T. re'pens. 3 in. h., creeping and rooting. *lflets.* 3, obovate to obcordate, about $\frac{1}{2}$ in. long; stalk long. *fl.* white in heads. Europe, including Britain. (E.B. 362.) var. **purpuras'cens,*** *l.* bronzy. The form with 4 lflets. is fairly constant, and the best to plant from its interest. The number of teratological forms of this species is very great.

T. uniflo'rum.* Tufted, creeping, about 2 in. h. *lflets.* 3, ovate, toothed, slender pointed; stipules sheathing with a long slender point. *fl.* axillary, solitary, on short peduncles; cor. very long, standard blue-purple, wings and keel purple. May to September. Syria, &c. 1800. (L.B.C. 1882; S.B.F.G. s. 2, 200.) var. **Sternbergia'num,** *fl.* white. Rock-garden or alpine house.

TRIFUR'CIA. A synonym of Herbertia.

TRIGGER-PLANT. *See* **Stylidium graminifolium.**

trigintipe'talus -a -um, having 30 petals.

TRIGLOCH'IN (*treis*, three, *glochin*, point; from the 3 angles of the carpels). FAM. *Juncaginaceae.* A genus of about 13 species of perennial herbs distributed over the temperate and cold regions of the world, growing in fresh or brackish marshes. Leaves long, flat or somewhat terete, sometimes floating. Flowers in erect scapes, small or rather large; segments scale-like, 3, 6, or rarely fewer; stamens 6. *T. maritima* is sometimes offered for planting outdoors in shallow water but has no great value, *T. bulbosa* will grow in pots of loamy soil standing in saucers of water in the greenhouse.

T. bulbo'sa. Rootstock 4 more or less tuberous or shortly rhizomatous. *l.* half-cylindrical, linear, outer often reduced to sheaths. *fl.* purplish, many, very variable, in a long simple raceme on an erect, smooth scape, up to about 12 in. h. Europe, Asia Minor, S. Africa. 1806. (B.M. 1445; L.B.C. 1151.) Greenhouse.

T. mari'tima. Tufted, about 12 in. h. *l.* rather flaccid, somewhat flattened at tip. *fl.* greenish, purple-edged in a rather loose-fld. raceme; scape curved. Coasts of Europe, N. Africa, Asia, N. America. Hardy.

TRIGONEL'LA (*treis*, three, *gonu*, angle; the spreading wings and flat standard give the flowers a triangular appearance). FAM. *Leguminosae.* A genus of about 75 species of annual or perennial herbs, often with a strong smell, natives of Europe, Asia, Africa, and Australia. Leaves 3-foliolate; stipules adnate to stalks. Flowers papilionaceous, yellow, blue or white; calyx tubular or short, its lobes nearly equal; standard obovate or oblong, sessile or with a broad claw; wings oblong; keel obtuse. The species are of small horticultural interest and the undermentioned need only ordinary soil. *T. Foenum-Graecum* was once used in human medicine and in cooking. *T. ornithopodioides* is a British species, but of no horticultural merit.

T. coeru'lea. Annual. Erect, 1 to 2 ft. h. *lflets.* ovate, lower roundish, toothed; stipules lanceolate, toothed at base. *fl.* in dense, stalked heads, white lined blue. July, August. Cent. Europe. 1562. (B.M. 2283 as *Trifolium coeruleum.*)

T. Foe'num-Grae'cum. Fenugreek. Annual. Erect, 1 to 2 ft. h. *lflets.* obovate, faintly toothed; stipules lanceolate-falcate, entire. *fl.* white; cal. hairy, teeth awl-shaped, as long as tube. June to August. S. France. 1597. (F.G. 766.)

TRIGONID'IUM (*trigona*, a triangle, *eidos*, like; alluding to the form of several parts). FAM. *Orchidaceae.* A genus of about 11 species of curious but not striking epiphytic Orchids inhabiting Trop. America. Scapes many-sheathed, 1-flowered, erect. Flowers rather large, pedicels short, bracts spathaceous; sepals sub-equal, connivent or coherent at base in a triquetrous turbinate tube, free above, spreading; petals similar but much smaller; lip rising from base of column, erect, much shorter than sepals, lateral lobes erect, embracing the column, mid-lobe spreading; pollen masses 4. Pseudobulbs with 1 or 2 fleshy leaves. The genus is allied to Maxillaria, though not very closely, and the species require compost and general treatment as for that genus. They will succeed in the cool or Odontoglossum house during summer but need a winter temperature of about 55° F.

T. acumina'tum. *fl.* dull straw-colour without, pencilled rich brown within; sep. acuminate, recurved at apex; pet. oval-lanceolate, mucronate; peduncles 4 to 5 in. long. *Pseudobulbs* ovate, acute, sulcate, 1-leaved. *l.* linear, 6 to 10 in. long. Demarara. 1834.

T. Egertonia'num. *fl.* pale liver-colour, dashed and veined brown; sep. acute, lateral reflexed; pet. slightly acute. *Pseudobulbs* clustered, oval, compressed, 2-leaved. *l.* narrow, often 18 in. long, ensiform. Honduras. 1834. Very distinct.

T. latifo'lium. Sep. and pet. yellow and purple; lip with yellow fleshy front lobe and narrow purplish side lobes; peduncle about 6 in. long. *Pseudobulbs* ovoid, compressed, about 3 in. h., 2-leaved. *l.* 6 to 7 in. h., nearly 2 in. wide, channelled. Brazil. About 1894.

T. monophyl'lum. A synonym of *Neocogniauxia monophylla.*

Trigonidium obtusum

T. obtu'sum. Sep. greenish-yellow, shaded red, obovate; pet. white veined rose, brown at apex, obtuse; lip white, tubercled at back, lateral lobes margined red, mid-lobe yellow in front, recurved; peduncle 3 to 6 in. long. *Pseudobulbs* often shortly distant, oblong-ovoid, hardly 2 in. h., 2-leaved. *l.* linear-lanceolate, 4½ to 9 in. long, nearly 1 in. wide. Demarara. 1834. (B.R. 1923.)

T. rin'gens. A synonym of *Mormolyce ringens.*

T. subre'pens. *fl.* greenish-yellow lined brown. Allied to *T. tenue* but larger in all parts. Habitat? 1906.

T. te'nue. *fl.* brownish-purple; sep. reflexed in upper half, very acuminate; pet. narrow to a slender point; lip obtuse, glabrous, reflexed at apex; peduncle slender, 2½ to 4½ in. h. *Pseudobulbs* oval, compressed, 1-leaved. *l.* ensiform, very acute, 5 to 12 in. long. Demarara. 1836.

TRIGUE'RA. Included in **Hibiscus.**

trigy'nus -a -um, having 3 styles.

TRILI'SA (*trilix,* triple; from the divisions of the pappus). FAM. *Compositae.* A genus of 2 species of erect, perennial herbs, natives of N. America. Leaves alternate, entire, stem-clasping; radical leaves long. Flower-heads purplish or white, rather small, in a panicle; florets regular, tubular, 5-cleft; involucral bracts in 2 or 3 series; receptacle flat, naked. *T. odoratissima* grows well in any moderately good light soil. It is hardy and may be increased by division in spring or by seeds sown early in autumn.

T. odoratis'sima. Vanilla Plant. 2 to 4 ft. h., corymbosely branched at top. *l.* thick; radical l. large, obovate-spatulate, tapering at base, often slightly, bluntly toothed; stem-l. oblong, clasping at base, upper small, scattered. *fl.-heads* bright purple, numerous, pedicellate; involucral scales glandular. September. 1786. (A.B.R. 633 and S.B.F.G. s. 2, 184 as *Liatris odoratissima.*) The leaves are fragrant of vanilla if bruised.

TRILLIA'CEAE. Monocotyledons. A family usually included in Liliaceae but separated by Hutchinson and comprising the genera Medeola, Paris, Scoliopus, and Trillium, natives of the temperate and montane regions of the North Hemisphere. Stem simple. Leaves usually 3 or 4 in a whorl at the top of the stem, sometimes more, sometimes paired and opposite. Flowers solitary or umbellate; perianth segments free; anthers 2-celled; ovary superior.

TRIL'LIUM (*trilix,* triple; the leaves and parts of the flower are in threes). FAM. *Liliaceae.* Wood Lily. A genus of about 30 species of perennial herbs with short, thick, usually erect rhizomes, natives of N. America and extra-tropical Asia from the Himalaya to Japan. Leaves 3, whorled, at apex of stem, broad, sometimes sessile, sometimes with well-developed stalk, 3- to 5-nerved, reticulate-penninerved. Stem simple, erect, with a few short, scarious sheaths at base. Flowers solitary, erect, drooping or reflexed, sessile or pedicellate within the leaves; perianth violet, lurid, white or greenish, persistent; segments distinct, spreading, the 3 outer (sepals) slender, herbaceous, green or rarely coloured, the 3 inner (petals) petaloid, often larger, less spreading or sometimes recurved; stamens 6; style deeply 3-fid or 3-parted from base. Fruit a globose or ovoid berry, indehiscent. A deep, well-drained woodland or peaty soil in a somewhat shady position, moist in summer, is best for these beautiful plants. Open woodland suits them well but they may be grown in the border. They can be forced gently provided the rhizomes are well developed. Transplanting is best done after midsummer or when the foliage dies down. They may be increased rather slowly by dividing the roots. Seedlings flower in 2 or 3 years from sowing. *T. grandiflorum* is the best species and is one of the most beautiful of hardy spring-flowering plants. The species described below are all American. Asiatic species, apparently of less garden value, include: *T. apetalon, T. camschatcense* (syn. *T. Pallasii*), *T. japonicum* (syn. *Trillidium japonicum*), and *T. Morii.*

KEY

1. *Fl. stalked*	2
1. *Fl. sessile*	9
2 (1). *Fl. erect, held above lvs.*	3
2. *Fl. held below lvs. on a recurved stalk*	8
3 (2). *Lvs. sessile or nearly so*	4
3. *Lvs. stalked*	6
4 (3). *Pet. erect in lower part, then spreading outwards*	T. grandiflorum
4. *Pet. spreading from base*	5
5 (4). *Pet. white, becoming rose; anthers yellow*	T. ovatum
5. *Pet. dark purple, brown, yellowish-green, or white. Anthers purple*	T. erectum
6 (3). *Lvs. large, 3 to 8 in. long*	T. undulatum
6. *Lvs. small, 2 in. or less long*	7
7 (6). *Fl.-stalk 1 in. or more long; stamens half as long as pet.*	T. rivale
7. *Fl.-stalk 1 in. or less long; stamens a third as long as pet.*	T. nivale
8 (2). *Style lacking; stamens straight*	T. cernuum
8. *Style evident; stamens curved*	T. nervosum
9 (1). *Lvs. stalked. Sep. reflexed*	T. recurvatum
9. *Lvs. sessile. Sep. ascending*	10
10 (9). *Anthers ⅗ in. or more long; pet. 1½ to 3½ in. long, greenish-yellow or white to maroon*	T. chloropetalum
10. *Anthers mostly less than ⅗ in. long*	11
11 (10). *Pet. ⅘ to 1⅖ in. long, purple or green*	T. sessile
11. *Pet. 1⅖ to 2½ in. long, greenish or bright yellow*	T. luteum

T. cer'nuum. Stem 2 or 3 together, 18 in. h. *l.* broadly rhomboidal, 2 to 6 in. long, abruptly narrowed to tip; stalk short. *fl.* small; pet. white, ⅔ to 1 in. long, oblong-ovate, wavy, recurved, rather longer than the lanceolate sep.; peduncle usually shorter than fl., deflexed. April ,May. Eastern N. America. 1758. (B.M. 954.)

T. chlorope'talum. 1 to 2 ft. h. *l.* round-ovate, 3 to 6 in. long, usually mottled, sessile. *fl.* sessile; pet. greenish-yellow or white to maroon. California, Oregon, Washington.

T. dis'color. Stem stout, solitary, 6 to 12 in. h. *l.* ovate-lanceolate to broadly ovate, 3 to 5 in. long, tapering from near base to apex, green and brown or dark purple above; sessile. Pet. dark purple varying to green, $1\frac{1}{2}$ to 2 in. long, erect, oblong, blunt, narrowed below; sep. shorter, lanceolate, spreading. February, March. N. America. 1831. (B.M. 3097.) SYN. *T. sessile Wrayi.* var. **atra'tum,** *fl.* dark maroon, of medium size, *l.* distinctly marked. 1888.

T. erec'tum. Birth-root, Lamb's Quarters. Stem solitary, 12 in. h. *l.* broadly rhomboidal, abruptly narrowed to apex, acute at base, sessile. *fl.* 1 to $1\frac{1}{2}$ in. long, spreading, odour unpleasant; pet. dark purple, oval or oblong, rather longer than the lanceolate-ovate sep.; peduncles $1\frac{1}{2}$ to 3 in. long, finally declined. May. Eastern N. America. 1759. (B.M. 470; L.B.C. 1838.) SYN. *T. foetidum, T. rhomboideum.* var. **al'bum,** pet. greenish-white or rarely yellowish. (B.M. 1027; L.B.C. 1850.) **ochroleu'cum,** pet. yellowish-white. (B.M. 3250 as *T. erectum viridiflorum.*)

T. foe'tidum. A synonym of *T. erectum.*

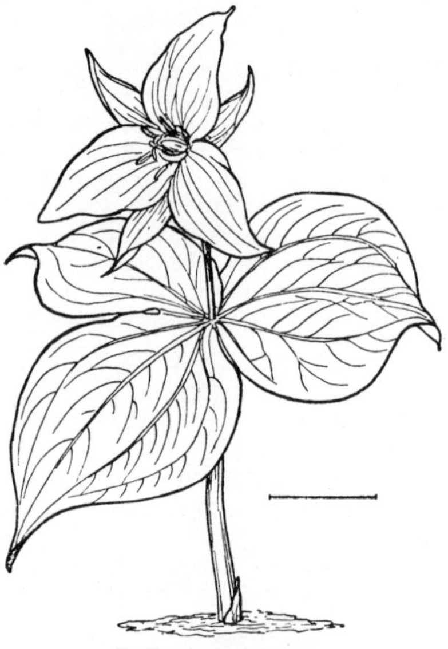

Trillium grandiflorum

T. grandiflo'rum.* Wake Robin. Stem solitary, 12 to 18 in. h. *l.* rhombic-ovate, 3 to 5 in. long, abruptly narrowed to apex, nearly sessile. *fl.* 2 in. long; pet. white, becoming rose, obovate, much longer and wider than sep.; peduncle longer than fl., erect or slightly declined. April to June. Eastern N. America. 1799. (L.B.C. 1349; B.M. 855 as *T. erythrocarpum.*) Rather variable; worth growing from seed in order to select good forms. var. **ro'seum,** *fl.* pink; **ru'brum,** *fl.* becoming deep pink.

T. lu'teum. $\frac{1}{2}$ to 1 ft. h. *l.* round-ovate, 3 to 6 in. long, strongly mottled, sessile. *fl.* sessile; pet. greenish-yellow to bright yellow. E. United States.

T. nervo'sum. Stem slender, solitary, 12 to 18 in. h. *l.* oval or oblong, 4 in. long, acute, shortly stalked. *fl.* $1\frac{1}{2}$ to 2 in. long; pet. tinged rose, oblong, much longer and wider than sep., often undulate; styles united below middle; peduncle $1\frac{1}{2}$ to 2 in. long. April, May. SE. United States. 1823. SYN. *T. stylosum.*

T. niva'le. Stem 6 to 9 in. h. *l.* oval or ovate, 1 to 2 in. long, blunt, rounded at base, spotted purple, distinctly stalked. Pet. white, oblong, 1 in. long, blunt, scarcely wavy, spreading from an erect base; sep. lanceolate, obtuse; peduncle 1 in. long. March, April. SE. United States. (B.M. 6449.)

T. obova'tum. A synonym of *T. erectum.*

T. ova'tum. Stem 8 to 10 in. h. *l.* ovate to round, $2\frac{1}{2}$ to $5\frac{1}{2}$ in. long, abruptly acute. Pet. white, becoming deep rose, 1 to $1\frac{1}{2}$ in. long, oblong-lanceolate to narrow-ovate, spreading, longer and broader than sep.; stalked. March, April. Western N. America. 1810.

T. pic'tum. A synonym of *T. undulatum.*

T. recurva'tum. *rhiz.* horizontal. Stem 12 in. h. *l.* ovate to ovate-oblong, usually acute at both ends, marbled; stalk short. *fl.* sessile; pet. brownish-purple, $\frac{3}{4}$ to $1\frac{1}{2}$ in. long, oblong-lanceolate, narrowed to a claw; sep. reflexed. April. United States. (B.B. ed. 2, 3, 524.)

T. rhomboid'eum. A synonym of *T. erectum.*

T. riva'le. Stem slender, 2 to 10 in. h. *l.* ovate, 1 to 3 in. long, more or less cordate at base; stalk 1 to $1\frac{1}{4}$ in. long; Pet. white with purple dots in centre, about 1 in. long, acute; peduncle 1 to $3\frac{3}{4}$ in. long. April. California, Oregon. 1913. (G.C. 54 (1913), 43.) (B.M. n.s. 444.)

T. ses'sile. Stems slender, 6 to 12 in. h., 2 or more together. *l.* broadly oval, widest in middle, 1 to 3 in. long, abruptly pointed, narrowed to base, variegated with paler and darker green above; sessile; *fl.* $\frac{5}{8}$ to $1\frac{1}{4}$ in. long, sessile; pet. purple, lanceolate, erect, much longer than the lanceolate, spreading sep. March, April. United States. 1759. (B.M. 40; L.B.C. 875.) var. **califor'nicum,** stouter than type, *l.* broadly rhombic-ovate, 3 to 6 in. long, spotted, *fl.* purple, pink or white, 1 to 4 in. long, oblanceolate to rhombic-obovate. California. (G. and F. 1890, f. 44); **Wray'i,** a synonym of *T. discolor.*

T. stylo'sum. A synonym of *T. nervosum.*

T. undula'tum. Stem solitary, 12 in. h. *l.* ovate, 3 to 5 in. long, with a long slender point, base rounded, margin wavy, stalk short. *fl.* $\frac{3}{4}$ to 1 in. long; pet. white, striped purple at base, oblong, wavy, much longer than the lanceolate sep.; peduncle 1 to 2 in. long, erect. April, May. Eastern N. America. 1811. (B M. 3002; L.B.C. 1232; S.B.F.G. 212.)

triloba'tus -a -um, } 3-lobate; 3-lobed.
trilo'bus -a -um, }

trilocular, 3-celled.

Trimenia'nus -a -um, Trimenii, in honour of (1) Henry Trimen, 1843–96, Director of Botanic Garden, Peradeniya, Ceylon, author of *Handbook to Flora of Ceylon,* &c.; (2) Roland Trimen, 1840–1916, entomologist, Curator of S. African Museum 1873–95, brother of H. Trimen.

trimes'tris -is -e, existing for 3 months.

TRIME'ZA (*treis,* three, *megas,* great; the outer flower segments are much larger than the inner). FAM. *Iridaceae.* A genus of 3 or 4 species of bulbous plants, natives of the W. Indies and S. America, with a few basal, long, flat, or rush-like leaves and one or none on the flowering stem. Flowers many in a spathe, segments free to base, shortly clawed, spathe solitary or two or three in the leaf-axils. Stove temperature is needed.

T. martinicen'sis. *l.* about 6, narrow-linear, erect, about 1 ft. long, $\frac{1}{4}$ in. wide, narrowed to the point. *fl.* 4 to 6, bright yellow, very fleeting; outer segs. about $\frac{3}{4}$ in. long, mottled in throat, inner much smaller; scape about 1 ft. long with a single clasping l. April. W. Indies. 1776. (B.M. 416 as *Iris martinicensis.*) SYN. *T. lurida.*

TRIOLE'NA (*treis,* three, *olene,* arm; in allusion to the 3 processes from base of anthers). FAM. *Melastomataceae.* A genus of 3 Trop. America herbs with large leaves, ovate or oblong, stalked. Flowers in scorpioid racemes or spikes; calyx tube short, finally 3-winged, lobes 5; petals 5, obovate; stamens 10, nearly equal; anthers dissimilar. A rich sandy loam with leaf-soil and a moist warm (stove) temperature are required. Propagation is by seed or by cuttings in sandy loam under a bell-glass with bottom heat.

T. hirsu'ta. Perennial About 6 in. h. *l.* ovate, slender-pointed, 3-nerved, bright green with bronzy-red centre, lightly toothed, ciliate. *fl.* white or tinted rose, in racemes; cal., pedicels and *fr.* hairy. Trop. America. SYN. *Bertolonia hirsuta.*

T. scorpioi'des. Perennial. Stem about 1 in. long, somewhat woody. *l.* ovate, rather slender-pointed, lightly toothed. *fl.* rose, in scorpioid axillary cymes; pet. oblong-ovate. Mexico. 1859.

F. G. P.

TRIO'NUM. Included in **Hibiscus.**

TRIOPH'ORA. Included in **Pogonia.**

TRIOP'TERIS (*treis,* three, *pteron,* a wing; the samaras are 3-winged). FAM. *Malpighiaceae.* A genus of about 10 species of climbing shrubs, natives of Mexico and the W. Indies. Leaves opposite, glabrous and shining, veined and stalked, without stipules. Flowers blue or violet; calyx 5-parted with 8 glands; petals clawed; stamens 10, all perfect, alternately long and short. Racemes terminal or axillary; peduncles bracteate. *T. rigida* is difficult to flower in the British Is. It needs stove conditions and a compost of peat and sand.

T. ri'gida. *l.* roundish-obovate, elliptical or oblong-linear, shining with many parallel and netted veins, rigid and leathery. *fl.* blue in a loose panicle. W. Indies. 1822. var. **jamaicen'sis,** *l.* $\frac{1}{2}$ to 1 in. long, half as wide; **lucida,** *l.* retuse or blunt, $4\frac{1}{2}$ in. long, $\frac{3}{4}$ to $1\frac{1}{2}$ in. wide. Cuba.

F. G. P.

TRIOS'TEUM (*treis*, three, *osteon* a bone; from the 3 bony nutlets). FAM. *Caprifoliaceae*. A genus of 8 herbaceous perennials natives of Asia and N. America. Leaves opposite, slightly connate at base, sessile, fiddle-shaped or obovate. Flowers dirty white, yellow or purple, often axillary, solitary or clustered, rarely spicate; calyx 5-lobed; corolla tubular-bell-shaped, swollen at base, limb oblique; stamens 5. Fruit a drupe, 2- to 5- or 6-stoned. Somewhat weedy perennials but hardy, growing well in light sandy soil with some leaf-mould. Propagated by seed or by division in spring.

T. erythrocar'pum. Softly hairy, somewhat glandular. 1½ to 3 ft. h. *l.* ovate-rounded, tip acuminate, base stem-clasping. *fl.* greenish outside, purplish inside. *fr.* red. June. W. China.

T. perfolia'tum. Softly hairy. 2 to 4 ft. h. *l.* oval, abruptly narrowed towards base, downy beneath. *fl.* brownish-purple, clustered, sessile. June. *fr.* orange, ½ in. long. N. America. (S.B.F.G. s. 2, 45.)

T. pinnati'fidum. Softly hairy, somewhat glandular. 1½ to 2 ft. h. *l.* deeply and pinnately lobed, lobes pointed, base wedge-shaped. *fl.* yellowish or greenish. *fr.* white. July, August. NW. China.

tripartite, cut to the base into 3 divisions.

TRIPETALE'IA (*tri*, three, *petalon*, a petal; in allusion to the 3-rayed corolla). FAM. *Ericaceae*. A small genus of deciduous shrubs with entire, alternate leaves, corolla of 3 (rarely 4 or 5) separate, spirally recurved petals, 3 (rarely 4 or 5) sepals and a 3- (usually) valved septicidal capsule. Distinguished by its 3-petalled corolla from Elliottia (4 petals) and Cladothamnus (5 petals). Requires a rather light, well-drained, lime-free soil and enjoys light shade. Propagated by seed and cuttings.

T. bractea'ta. Hardy, deciduous shrub, 3 to 6 ft. h. *l.* obovate, smooth, entire, 1 to 2 in. long, ⅜ to ¾ in. wide. *fl.* in 3 to 6 in. terminal racemes on current year's growths, cor. pink-stained white, made up of 3 (normally) narrow-oblong, pet., transversely and spirally recurved towards tip, about ⅝ in. long; cal. lobes 3 (occasionally 4 or 5), oval, about half length of pet. July, August. Japan. 1892. K.B. 1934, 192 as *Botryostege bracteata*. SYN. *Elliottia bracteata*.

T. panicula'ta. Deciduous, erect shrub 2 to 6 ft. h. *l.* rhomboid, elliptical or obovate, pointed, more or less hairy on midrib and veins, especially beneath, 1 to 2½ in. long, 7/16 to 1⅛ in. wide. *fl.* in terminal, erect panicles up to 6 in. long from current year's growth; cor. 3-radiate, normally of 3 narrow-oblong pet. each 7/16 in. long, recurved as in *T. bracteata*, pink-stained white; cal. cup-shaped, obscurely and shallowly 3- (to 5-) lobed. July to September. Japan. 1877. SYN. *Elliottia paniculata*.

F. S.

TRIPHA'SIA (*triphasios*, triple; parts of flowers in threes). FAM. *Rutaceae*. A genus of a single species related to the orange with characters indicated below. *T. trifolia* needs greenhouse conditions and grows well in a compost of turfy loam and peat, requiring careful watering in winter. The fruit, an ovate berry about as large as a hazel-nut, has an agreeable sweet taste and is sometimes preserved whole in syrup and called Manilla Lime Berries; in some tropical countries it is used for making marmalade.

T. trifo'lia. Lime Berry. Evergreen spiny shrub or small tree up to 15 ft. but usually much smaller. *l.* 3-foliolate, dark green; lflets. ovate, retuse, entire, central one largest; spines in pairs, very sharp, shorter than l. *fl.* white, fragrant, solitary in l.-axils; cal. 3-lobed; pet. 3, free, overlapping, thick; stamens 6, free, shorter than pet.; style thick, longer than stamens. *fr.* ovate, about ½ in. wide, dull red, usually 1-seeded. China? 1798. Widely cultivated in countries nearly frost-free. (L.B.C. 18.) SYN. *T. aurantiola, Limonia trifolia*.

TRIPHYSA'RIA. *See* **Orthocarpus.**

tripinnate, leaflets of a 2-pinnate leaf themselves pinnate.

tripinnatifid, thrice cleft nearly to the base, or midrib.

tripinnatisect, thrice cleft to the base, or midrib.

TRIPLADE'NIA. A synonym of Kreysigia.

TRIPLA'RIS (*triplex*, triple; the floral parts being in threes). FAM. *Polygonaceae*. A genus of about 10 species of Trop. S. American trees. Leaves alternate, short-stalked, often large, ovate, oblong, or lanceolate. Flowers dioecious, sessile or nearly so within bracts; perianth 6-cleft, male funnel-shaped, female narrow, spikes long, softly or silky hairy, often branched. Nut 3-angled, angles acute. Stove conditions are needed.

T. surinamen'sis. Long John. Tree, 40 to 90 ft. h. in British Guiana; branches hollow. *l.* narrowly ovate to narrowly elliptic-oblong, short-acuminate, firm-textured, to 1 ft. long. *fl.* greenish-white, in clustered slender dense-fld. spikes 3 to 5 in. long. *fr.* with enlarged perianth having 3 narrowly oblong lobes to 1 in. long, becoming deep red. British Guiana, Surinam, Brazil. Ornamental when in fruit but suitable only for tropical cultivation. Ferocious stinging ants inhabit the hollow branches of wild trees.

triple-nerved, having 3 prominent veins, the side ones leaving the midrib near its base (*see under* **Solidago**).

***triplo-*,** in compound words indicating three times.

TRIPO'LIUM. Included in **Aster.**

TRIP'TERIS. Included in **Osteospermum.**

TRIPTEROCA'LYX (from *tri*, three, *pteron*, wing, calyx, referring to the 3-winged calyx). FAM. *Nyctaginaceae*. A genus of about 5 species of succulent annual herbs with opposite leaves. Closely related to Abronia but having flower parts usually in fours and the fruit (anthocarp) with thin, broad, transparent wings encircling and extending above and below it. Treatment as for Abronia.

T. Crux-mal'tae. Ascending or procumbent, much branched. Stems to 1 ft. long. *l.* elliptic-oblong, broadly ovate or ovate-rhombic, bright green, 1 to 2 in. long. *fl.* bright purplish-pink, ⅜ to 1 in. long, with throat greenish, in many-fld. heads. W. Nevada adjacent California. The largest fld. species of the genus.

TRIPTERYG'IUM (*tri*, three, *pteryx*, wing). FAM. *Celastraceae*. 2 species of climbing, deciduous shrubs. Leaves alternate, large. Flowers small, with a 5-lobed calyx, 5 petals, 5 stamens. Fruits 1-seeded, with 3 membranous wings (resembling wych elm fruits but with an extra wing). They grow well in any soil of ordinary quality. *T. Regelii* is quite hardy; *T. Wilfordii* is only suitable for the warmer countries.

T. Forrest'ii. A synonym of *T. Wilfordii*.

T. hypoglau'cum. A synonym of *T. Wilfordii*.

Tripterygium Wilfordii (p. 2150)

T. Regel'ii. Deciduous shrub of rambling growth, up to 30 ft., shoots angled, warted. *l.* $2\frac{1}{2}$ to 6 in. long, oval or ovate, cuneate to rounded at the base, long and slender-pointed, toothed; stalk $\frac{1}{4}$ to $\frac{3}{4}$ in. long. *fl.* yellowish-white, $\frac{1}{3}$ in. wide, in terminal panicles up to 9 in. long, 2 to 4 in. wide. *fr.* 3-angled, each angle with a wing, greenish-white, $\frac{5}{8}$ in. long. Japan, Korea. 1905.

T. Wilford'ii.* Deciduous climber 30 to 40 ft., shoots angled. *l.* 2 to 6 in. long, ovate, glabrous, sometimes glaucous beneath. *fl.* greenish-white, $\frac{1}{4}$ in. wide, in compound panicles 1 ft. or more long, terminal and axillary; stalks rusty-downy; cal. whitish-downy; anthers red-purple. Autumn. *fr.* purplish-red, crowded in clusters, each $\frac{3}{4}$ in. long, 3-winged, wings $\frac{1}{6}$ in. wide. S. China, Formosa, Burma. 1913. (B.M. 9488.) SYN. *T. Forrestii, T. hypoglaucum.* Tender, but succeeds in Cornwall and similar climates.

W. J. B.

TRIPTIL'ION (*treis*, three, *ptilon*, wing; from the 3 divisions of the pappus). FAM. *Compositae.* A genus of about 6 species of annual or perennial Chilean herbs. Leaves alternate, scattered, ciliate, spiny-toothed, or pinnatifid. Flower-heads blue or white, rather small, homogamous, in a leafy panicle or corymb at the tips of branches; florets 2-lipped, outer lip entire or 3-toothed, inner entire or 2-fid; involucral bracts few, acute and spiny, outer shorter; receptacle naked or with bristly fibres. Achenes minutely papillose. A light rich soil suits these hardy or nearly hardy plants best. Seeds should be sown in early April on a slight hotbed, the seedlings being pricked out and either planted out in a well-drained sheltered place at the end of May or flowered in pots in a cool, airy greenhouse. *T. spinosum* may be divided.

T. cordifo'lium. Annual of about 6 in., erect, branched at apex. *l.-stem* clasping, nearly round, toothed and remotely spiny. *fl.-heads* white, in clusters of usually 3 at ends of branches. July. Pappus bristles 3, ciliate at apex. Chile. 1824. (B.R. 353.)

Triptilion spinosum

T. spino'sum. Perennial of about 6 in., corymbose at apex. *l.* pinnately lobed, lobes ending in a short spine. *fl.-heads* blue, the inner lips of florets white; involucre glabrous. July. Chile. 1827. (B.R. 27, 22.)

trique'trus -a -um, 3-edged or 3-cornered.

trisected, cut into 3 approximately equal parts.

TRISMERIA (*treis*, three, parts). FAM. *Polypodiaceae.* A genus of 2 species of ferns, nearly related to Pityrogramma. For treatment, *see* **Pityrogramma.**

T. trifolia'ta. *sti.* tufted, 8 to 12 in. long. *Fronds* 2 to 3 ft. long, 6 to 8 in. broad, pinnate; lower pinnae ternate, upper simple, petiolate, 2 to 4 in. long; fertile fronds with white or yellowish powder beneath. Trop. America. 1810. (H.G.F. 4; B.C.F. 2, 276.) SYN. *Gymnogramma trifoliata.* Variable.

TRISTAG'MA (*tri-*, three, *stagma*, something which drips; from the 3 nectarial pores on the ovary). FAM. *Liliaceae.* A genus of 5 species of dwarf Chilean and Patagonian plants with tunicated bulbs. Leaves basal, few, linear. Flowers 2 to 3 in a terminal umbel, small, stalked; perianth with a cylindric tube and 6 linear involute lobes less than $\frac{1}{12}$ in. wide; no corona; stamens mounted on the tube, enclosed. Scape simple, leafless; spathe 2-valved. Of botanical interest only but remarkable for the very narrow, somewhat tubular perianth segments. Cool greenhouse cultivation is suggested.

T. narcissoi'des. A synonym of *Stemmatium narcissoides.*

T. niva'lis. Scape 4 to 8 in. h. *l.* to 10 in. long. $\frac{1}{16}$ in. wide. *fl.* 2 or 3, greenish, erect, tube $\frac{1}{2}$ in. long, lobes $\frac{3}{10}$ in. long. Chile. Other species closely resembling this are *T. Ameghinoi, T. australe, T. inflatum.*

TRISTAN'IA (in honour of Jules M. C. Tristan, 1776–1861, a French botanist). FAM. *Myrtaceae.* A genus of about 20 species of evergreen trees and shrubs. All the cultivated species are Australian but the genus is represented also in New Caledonia and the Indian Archipelago. Leaves alternate or (rarely) opposite. Flowers small, yellow or white, borne in stalked axillary clusters; petals 5. The species here described require greenhouse conditions in most places but 2 are cultivated in the open in Scilly Is. They are easily grown in the usual compost of loam, peat, and sand and propagated by cuttings.

Tristania conferta

T. confer'ta. Tall, densely leafy tree; young shoots hairy. *l.* alternate but usually clustered at the end of the branches, ovate-lanceolate, base cuneate, apex blunt or pointed, 3 to 7 in. long, $1\frac{1}{4}$ to $2\frac{1}{2}$ in. wide, leathery, glabrous; stalk up to 1 in. long. *fl.* in clusters of 3 to 7, usually on the young wood below the cluster of l.; cor. white, $\frac{5}{8}$ to $\frac{3}{4}$ in. wide, stamens on an axis $\frac{1}{2}$ in. long. August. New S. Wales. 1805. (G.F. 1888; B.R. 1839 as *T. macrophylla.*) Hardy in Scilly Is. Flowers when a few ft. h.

T. densiflo'ra. Shrub. *l.* opposite, ovate, leathery, entire. *fl.* crimson in numerous 3-fld. cymes. Australia. 1881.

T. depres'sa. A synonym of *T. suaveolens.*

T. lauri'na. Shrub, small or large tree up to 70 ft. h. *l.* alternate, $1\frac{1}{2}$ to $4\frac{1}{2}$ in. long, $\frac{1}{3}$ to $1\frac{1}{4}$ in. wide, lanceolate to obovate-oblong, glaucous to silky-downy beneath and dotted. *fl.* in short, stoutly stalked, axillary clusters of 3 to 10; cor. orange-yellow, $\frac{1}{3}$ to $\frac{1}{2}$ in. wide; unpleasantly scented. July. E. Australia. (B.M. 7529.)

T. macrophyl'la. A synonym of *T. conferta.*

T. neriifo'lia.* Slender shrub to a small tree. *l.* opposite, lanceolate, pointed, cuneate, 1½ to 3½ in. long, ¼ to ⅝ in. wide. pale and dotted beneath. *fl.* in axillary clusters of about ten, often forming, collectively, leafy terminal corymbs several in. across; cor. bright yellow, ½ in. wide. July to September. New S. Wales. 1804. (L.B.C. 157; B.M. 1058 as *Melaleuca neriifolia*, A.B.R. 485 as *M. salicifolia.*) Hardy in Scilly Is.

T. suaveo'lens. Shrub or small tree; shoots and l. densely covered with soft, hoary down. *l.* alternate, elliptic to ovate and obovate, 1½ to 3 in. long but often twice as much, apex pointed or blunt. *fl.* ½ in. wide, yellow, in axillary clusters with a mainstalk ½ to 1½ in. long. August. Australia. 1820. SYN. *T. depressa.*

W. J. B.

TRISTELLATE'IA (*tri*, three, *stella*, star; in allusion to the 3 star-like fruits). FAM *Malpighiaceae.* A genus of about 22 species of woody climbers, natives of Madagascar, the E. Indies, and 1 in Queensland. Leaves opposite or in whorls, the stalks with 1 or 2 glands at the top; stipules minute. Flowers yellow in terminal or lateral racemes; petals distinctly clawed. Fruit of 3 carpels each with about 7 wings spreading in a star-like manner. Stove plants with showy flowers.

T. australa'siae. Climbing shrub with prominent lenticels and drooping flowering shoots. *l.* ovate or ovate-oblong, 2 to 4 in. long, acute and recurved at tip, dull green, glabrous, entire; stalks up to ⅜ in. long, toothed. *fl.* yellow in terminal racemes of 12 to 16 in opposite pairs; pet. oblong or ovate-oblong, about ½ in. long, clawed with a truncate or somewhat heart-shaped base; filaments 10, yellow at first, finally red. Summer. *fr.* 3-coccous; cocci 8-winged. Malayasia, Australasia. 1902. (B.M. 8334 as *T. australis.*) SYN. *T. australis.*

tris'tis -is -e, sad, of dull colour.

trisulca'tus -a -um, with 3 grooves.

TRITELE'IA (Greek *tri-*, three; the flower-parts being in threes). FAM. *Liliaceae.* Including Calliprora, Hesperoscordum, and Seubertia. A genus of about 14 species, natives of Western N. America. Corm with a straw-coloured fibrous tunic. Leaves usually 2 to corm, linear, keeled beneath, basal. Flowers funnel-shaped, in umbels. Stamens 6, all fertile and essentially alike although they may be inserted at different heights on perianth or be alternately long and short; anthers versatile, not appressed to style. Style slender; stigma-lobes 3, short. The species of this genus have been described in this Dictionary (pp. 313–15) under Brodiaea; *see* **B. Bridgesii, B. crocea, B. Douglasii** (= *T. grandiflora* var. *Howellii*), **B. hyacinthina, B. ixioides, B. lactea,** and **B. peduncularis.** Monographic study has led to the re-definition of the genus Brodiaea which consists of species with a dark-brown corm-tunic, leaves rounded beneath, fertile stamens 3, anthers basifixed and appressed to style, stigma with 3 spreading or recurving lobes; *see* **B. californica** (= *B. elegans*), **B. coronaria, B. minor,** and **B. rosea** (= *B. coronaria* var. *rosea*, with lavender flowers which become pinkish on drying). Other species are now placed in other genera; Dichelostemma comprises *B. Ida-maia, B. congesta* (described as *B. pulchella*), *B. multiflora, B. pulchella* (described as *B. capitata*), and *B. volubile*; Ipheion comprises *B. uniflora*; Triteliopsis comprises *B. Palmeri.* For further information see monographic studies of Brodiaea proper by R. F. Hoover in *American Midland Naturalist*, 22. 551–74 (1939), of Dichelostemma in *A.M.N.* 24. 463–7 (1940), of Triteleia in *A.M.N.* 25. 73–106 (1941) and of Ipheion (syn. Beauverdia) by W. G. Herter in *Boissiera* 7. 503–12 (1943) and W. T. Stearn in *Gard. Chron. III*, 114. 60–1 (1943).

triternate, having the secondary petioles of a 2-ternate leaf again ternately divided, hence with 9 leaflets or divisions.

TRITHRI'NAX (*tri*, three, *thrinax*, fan; from the division and form of the leaves). FAM. *Palmaceae.* A genus of 5 species of rather dwarf Palms, natives of S. America. Leaves in a terminal crown, roundish-ovate, much divided in a fan-like manner, glabrous; sheaths fibrous and spiny, erect or deflexed. Flowers small, hermaphrodite; spathes many, the lower oblong, obliquely cut, the upper obliquely truncate; spadices spreading, on thick peduncles, with flexuous branches. Fruit a berry, 1-seeded. For treatment, *see* **Thrinax.**

T. acanthoco'ma. Stem dwarf, clothed with the persistent netted sheaths, armed with numerous stout, reflexed spines. *l.* large, fan-shaped, cut two-thirds down into many linear, 2-fid segs. *Spadix* branched. Rio Grande. 1879. (G.F. 959; G.C. 9 (1878), p. 661.)

T. brasilien'sis. Stem slender, 6 to 10 ft. h., 2 to 3 in. thick. *l.* fan-shaped, 3 ft. or more long, nearly orbicular; sheaths at base fibrous, fibres at first parallel and longitudinal, then obliquely interlaced and finally plaited at right-angles; at the summit these fibres unite forming a series of very long, stout spines, abruptly curved downwards. *Spadix* within the upper l., much branched. Brazil. 1875. (I.H. 203.)

T. campes'tris. Allied to *T. brasiliensis* but with *lflets.* shortly 2-fid, white hairy above, becoming glabrous beneath; branches of *spadix* stouter. S. Argentine. 1889.

TRITI'CUM (ancient Latin name for Wheat). FAM. *Gramineae.* About 15 species of annual or biennial grasses with erect stems, flat leaves, spike-like inflorescences, spikelets 2- to many-flowered, sessile, placed flat-wise on the rachis, and fruits free of the glumes. The genus contains some of the most important food plants in the wheats; 2 species are cultivated in the British Is., **T. aes'tivum** (syn. *T. sativum, T. vulgare*), the Bread Wheat, being the principal source of flour for bread-making, and **T. tur'gidum,** the Rivet or Cone Wheat, providing flour used in biscuit-making. The spikes of wheat, especially bearded varieties, are often dried and mixed with other grasses for decorative purposes. The perennial species, once placed in Triticum, are now referred to **Agropy'rum** (*agros*, field, *pyros*, wheat). **A. re'pens** (syn. *Triticum repens*: E.B. 1810), Couch Grass, Quitch, Scutch, Twitch, is a very variable and troublesome weed with abundant, widely creeping, tough rhizomes and smooth stems, 1 to 4 ft. high. **A. jun'ceum** var. **boreoatlan'ticum** (E.B. 1813), Sand Couch Grass, is valuable with marram grass for consolidating coastal sand-dunes. C. E. Hb.

TRITOMA. A synonym of Kniphofia.

TRITO'NIA (*triton*, a weathercock, the stamens vary in direction in different species). FAM. *Iridaceae.* A genus of about 16 species of perennial herbs with corms, natives of S. Africa. Stem simply or slightly branched. Leaves few, narrow linear or broader and ensiform, often falcate. Flowers one to a spathe, in a loose spike, sessile; perianth-tube slender, straight, widened upwards, sometimes short, sometimes long, rarely somewhat incurved at apex; limb concave or broadly bell-shaped, usually nearly regular, segments overlapping; stamens 3, affixed to base of limb, filaments free; style exserted, filiform. Fruit a small capsule with usually small, globose, black seeds. All the following grow well in a cool greenhouse; some are hardy in a well-drained, sunny border, liking a fairly dry, rich soil. The less hardy ones may grow at the foot of a south wall but should be housed for the winter. In pots the Tritonias need plenty of water during the growing season and a light, airy position near the glass. When the leaves begin to turn yellow water should be gradually withheld, and then kept dry or nearly so until growth begins again. Propagation by division or by seeds. Like many of the Iridaceae the group to which the Tritonias belong is difficult to classify and here the modern reversion to several genera has been followed so that species often included may have to be sought, as indicated below, in other genera. The most popular plants of the Tritonia group are those known in gardens as Montbretias, crosses between *Crocosmia aurea* and *C. Pottsii* (often known as *T. Pottsii*). For a note on these *see* **Crocosmia.**

T. au'rea. A synonym of *Crocosmia aurea.*

T. capen'sis. A synonym of *Acidanthera capensis.*

T. cris'pa. A synonym of *Acidanthera crispa.*

T. croca'ta.* About 2 ft. h. *l.* 4 to 10, broadly linear-ensiform, curved, striate, acute, shorter than scape. *fl.* 7 to 9, in 2 ranks, saffron, about 1 in. long, bell-shaped, tube about as long as segs., widely expanded, segs. obovate, with an almost transparent spot at base, nearly equal; scape nearly 2 ft. long, terete, flexuous, leafy at base. May, June. S. Africa. 1758. (B.M. 184 as *Ixia crocata.*) Variable in colour: the following forms have been named: **auranti'aca,** *fl.* orange-red; **coccin'ea,** *fl.* scarlet; **purpu'rea,** *fl.* purple; **sangui'nea,** *fl.* bright blood-red. var. **minia'ta** has darker green *l.* and smaller bright red *fl.* 1795. (B.M. 609 as *T. miniata.*) Greenhouse.

T.×crocosmiiflo'ra. A synonym of *Crocosmia×crocosmiiflora.*

T. deus'ta. Habit, &c., of *T. crocata* but scape shorter (up to 12 in.) and *fl.* somewhat smaller, cinnabar-red, the 3 outer segs. with a black spot on the claw. May. S. Africa. (B.M. 622.)

T. fenestra'ta. A synonym of *T. hyalina.*

T. fla'va. A synonym of *Montbretia flava.*

T. fla'vida. 14 to 26 in. h. Stem closely sheathed with l. up to infl. which may have 1 branch. *l.* linear, acute, deep green, striate, up to 14 in. long; stem-l. 4 or 5. *fl.* 8 to 12, pale yellow, up to 1 in. long, tube funnel-shaped, lobes spreading slightly, nearly equal, blunt. May. Natal. 1927. (B.M. 9592.) Hardy.

Tritonia hyalina

T. hyali'na.* About 1 ft. h. *l.* broadly lanceolate-ensiform, acute, striate, dark green. *fl.* 7 to 9 in 2 ranks, pale orange, about 1 in. long, tube short, segs. spreading, rounded, apiculate. S. Africa. 1801. (B.M. 704 as *T. fenestrata.*) Greenhouse.

T. linea'ta. 8 to 18 in. h. *l.* about 6, lanceolate-ensiform, veins and margin whitish. *fl.* 2 to 7, straw-coloured, veined, with orange spots, 1 in. long; tube short, segs. spreading slightly, nearly equal, inner with 3 parallel, yellow lines. May. Cape to Natal and Griqualand. 1774. (B.M. 487 as *Gladiolus lineatus.*)

T. minia'ta. A variety of *T. crocata.*

T. pal'lida. A synonym of *Acidanthera pallida.*

T. Pott'sii. A synonym of *Crocosmia Pottsii.*

T. ro'sea. About 18 in. h., branched. *l.* linear, firm, about 12 in. long. *fl.* 3 or 4, up to 12 in a loose spike, bright red, 1 in. long, tube broadly funnel-shaped; segs. oblong, lower perianth segs. with a yellowish-red spot. June. S. Africa to Natal. (B.M. 7280.) Greenhouse.

T. scilla'ris. A synonym of *Dichone scillaris.*

T. securi'gera. A synonym of *Montbretia securigera.*

T. squa'lida. Stem slender, up to 2 ft. h. *l.* lanceolate-ensiform, thick, ribs and margins yellowish. *fl.* in 2 ranks, whitish-rose, about 1 in. long, veins rose, tube short, funnel-bell-shaped; segs. spreading, rounded-ovate. May. S. Africa. 1774. (B.M. 581.) Greenhouse.

T. undula'ta. A synonym of *Dichone undulata.*

T. vi'ridis. A synonym of *Acidanthera viridis.*

T. Wil'sonii. A synonym of *Gladiolus Wilsonii.*

tri'tus -a -um, in common use.

TRIVIAL NAME. (1) In common speech the vernacular name of a plant; (2) in scientific use (now obsolescent) the specific epithet, e.g. the specific name *Bellis perennis,* consists of the generic name *Bellis* followed by the trivial name or specific epithet *perennis.*

trivia'lis -is -e, belonging to the cross-roads, hence common, commonplace, ordinary.

TRIX'IS (*trixos,* triple; from the 3-angled fruit). FAM. *Compositae.* A genus of about 60 species of herbs or shrubs of various habit, natives of Cent. and S. America and the W. Indies. Leaves alternate, sometimes decurrent. Flower-heads yellow or whitish; florets 2-lipped, outer lip 3-toothed, inner 2-fid; involucral bracts often in 2 series; receptacle small; pappus bristles numerous. Stove or greenhouse protection is needed in winter, with a compost of sandy loam and leaf-mould. The perennial species may be increased by cuttings, planted in sand under a bell-glass in May. Seeds of *T. senecioides* should be sown in the open in April.

T. divarica'ta auricula'ta. Sub-shrubby climber to 18 in. *l.* oval-lanceolate, slender-pointed, toothed, nearly glabrous, obtusely auricled at base; sessile. *fl.-heads* white or yellowish-white; involucral scales long-pointed. August, September. Brazil. 1827. (B.M. 2765 as *T. auriculata.*)

T. senecioi'des. Annual branched, from base, hairy and glandular. *l.* oblong, sinuately lobed, toothed, slightly woolly beneath, stem-clasping. *fl.-heads* white, solitary, involucral scales in 2 or 3 series; peduncles long. August, September. Chile. 1821. (H.E.F. 101.)

TRIZEUX'IS (*tri,* three, *zeuxis,* union; alluding to the cohesion of the 3 sepals). FAM. *Orchidaceae.* Three species of small, epiphytic Orchids of no great beauty, but remarkable in having the lip superior, i.e. with the parts of the flower in their proper position, the ovary not being twisted as in the generality of Orchids. *T. falcata* should be placed in a small pan, which can be suspended. Compost as for Odontoglossums. The cool end of a Cattleya house gives sufficient temperature to plants from Costa Rica and Brazil, but if from Trinidad or warm localities, more heat is required.

T. falca'ta. *fl.* green, minute, densely racemose along the branches of the slender scape, which is 6 to 12 in. h. *Pseudobulbs* very small, about ½ in. h. *l.* distichous-rosulate, oblong-linear, acuminate, slightly falcate, 1½ to 4 in. long, ⅓ in. broad. Trop. America. 1820. (H.E.F. 126; L.B.C. 975; L.C.B. 2.)

E. C.

TROCHE'TIA (in honour of R. I. G. du Trochet, 1771–1847, French physiologist and botanist). FAM. *Sterculiaceae.* A genus of about 6 species of evergreen shrubs and small trees, natives of Mauritius, Madagascar, and St. Helena. Leaves alternate, generally aggregated near the end of the shoot. Flowers axillary, 1 to 3 on a stalk; sep. and pet. 5. The fine species described here are stove-plants and like a compost of peat, leaf-soil, and sand.

T. Blackburnia'na.* Shrub or small tree, shoots downy, ribbed. *l.* oval to obovate-oblong, 3 to 6 in. long, 2 to 3½ in. wide, toothed, 3- or 5-veined; stalk up to 2 in. long, ribbed, downy. *fl.* solitary, axillary, drooping; sep. linear-lanceolate, 1 in. long; cor. bell-shaped, 1¼ in. wide; pet. pinkish, veined with rosy-crimson and suffused with the same at the revolute apex of each; stalk 3 in. long. May. Mauritius. (B.M. 7209.)

T. grandiflo'ra. A synonym of *T. triflora.*

T. triflo'ra.* Shrub up to 10 ft., shoots, l.-stalks, and fl.-stalks thickly overlaid with reddish-brown, stellate down. *l.* ovate to ovate-lanceolate, 3 to 6 in. long, half as wide, margin crenate, closely scurfy beneath; stalk 1 to 1½ in. long. *fl.* borne in threes at end of a drooping axillary stalk 2 or 3 in. long; cor. bell-shaped, 2¼ in. across, white with a yellow blotch at base of each pet., l. and fl. crowded near the end of the branch. December. Mauritius. (B.R. 1844, 21 as *T. grandiflora.*)

W. J. B.

trochlea'tus -a -um, pulley-like.

TROCHOCAR'PA (*trochos,* a wheel, *karpos,* fruit; in allusion to the radiating cells of the fruit). FAM. *Epacridaceae.* A genus of about 6 species of evergreen trees and shrubs, confined to Australia and Tasmania. Leaves mostly alternate, the terminal pair on the shoot often opposite. Flowers small, each in the axil of a small bract or bracteole and forming slender spikes; calyx 5-parted; corolla tube cylindrical or campanulate with 5 rounded lobes. Fruit a globular drupe carrying 10 stones, or less by abortion. Cool greenhouse plants that should be grown in sandy peat. Propagated by cuttings.

T. lauri'na. Tree from 20 to 30 ft., quite glabrous. *l.* rather aggregated at the end of the shoot, 1½ to 2½ in. long, ¾ to 1¼ in. wide, oval, tapered at both ends, conspicuously 5- to 7-veined, shining green, short-stalked. *fl.* $\frac{3}{16}$ in. long, white, sessile in terminal solitary or clustered, slender spikes ¾ to 1½ in. long; tube of cor. $\frac{1}{16}$ in. long. June. *fr.* a flattened globose drupe ⅓ in. wide. Queensland, New S. Wales. 1829. (B.M. 3324.) Hardy in Scilly Is.

TROCHODENDRA'CEAE. Dicotyledons. A family with only 1 species in Japan and Formosa. Trees with alternate, toothed, whorled, pinnate-veined, long-stalked leaves. Flowers without perianth, in a raceme-like cyme, with numerous stamens and 5 to 11 carpels with many ovules. Fruit a follicle. Only genus, Trochodendron. The genus Euptelea is usually placed in the family Trochodendraceae on account of its lacking a perianth, but the investigations of A. C. Smith, C. G. Nast, and I. W. Bailey (summarized in *Journal of the Arnold Arboretum*, 27. 175–91; 1946) have shown that it should be placed in a family **Euptelea'ceae** by itself, differing from Trochodendraceae in many features, the most obvious being its fruit, which is a samara, not a follicle.

W. T. S.

TROCHODEN'DRON (*trochos*, wheel, *dendron*, tree; in allusion to the spreading stamens). FAM. *Trochodendraceae.* Monotypic. Handsome, hardy, spreading, evergreen small tree. Leaves clustered, crenate, long-stalked. Flowers without sepals or petals; stamens many, spreading from the edge of a wide green disk, filaments long; carpels 5 to 11. Fruit of 5 to 11 follicles immersed in the torus, splitting at apex to allow escape of the numerous, long, narrow seeds by which the plant is propagated. Requires similar cultivation to Magnolia. (For a detailed description by A. C. Smith, see *Journal of the Arnold Arboretum*, 26. 130; 1945.)

T. aralioi'des. 12 to 60 ft. h. in Japan, with aromatic bark. *l.* ovate to oblong-ovate, 3 to 5 in. long, long-stalked, leathery, glossy above. *fl.* green, about 1 in. across, in erect, terminal racemes; pedicels 1 to 1½ in. long. June. Japan, Formosa. Before 1894. (B.M. 7375.)

troglodyta'rum, of the Troglodytes or cave-dwellers (from Greek *trogle*, hole); by the name *Musa troglodytarum* Linnaeus probably intended to indicate that the fruits of this Banana were fit only for apes (known scientifically as Troglodytes) to eat, unlike the more appetizing fruits of *M. sapientium* (of the wise) and *M. paradisiaca* (paradisial), once known as 'Apples of Paradise' and reputed to be the forbidden fruit of the Garden of Eden.

troja'nus -a -um, of Troy, Asia Minor.

TROL'LIUS (from the German *Trollblume*, globe flower). FAM. *Ranunculaceae.* Globe Flower. A genus of about 20 species in Europe, Asia, and N. America. Fine herbaceous perennials with erect stems, usually palmately lobed leaves, showy flowers, terminal or axillary, with 5 or more petaloid sepals, yellow or yellow-red, more or less globe-shaped, shorter flat nectaries, free carpels and many-seeded inflated dry fruits. A moist and rather heavy soil suits the Globe-flowers best. They are compact in growth and usually flower abundantly. Propagation is by division of the roots, preferably in September, or by seeds, which, however, often do not germinate until the second year after sowing.

T. acau'lis. 3 to 12 in. h., tufted. *l.* 5- to 7-parted; lflets. much cut, toothed. *fl.* golden-yellow, about 2 in. across, spreading, solitary on very short peduncles; sep. 9, lanceolate, acute, toothed; pet. spatulate, shorter than stamens. June, July. Himalaya. (B.R. 29, 32.)

T. aconitifo'lius. A synonym of *T. europaeus napellifolius.*

T. albiflo'rus. A variety of *T. laxus.*

T. alta'icus. 1 to 2 ft. h. *l.* much as in *T. europaeus. fl.* yellow to pale orange; sep. 15 to 20, broad, obtuse, sometimes only 10; pet. 5 to 15, narrowly linear, obtuse, about as long as stamens. Altai, Siberia.

T. altis'simus. A variety of *T. europaeus.*

T. america'nus. A synonym of *T. laxus.*

T. anemonifo'lius. About 20 in. h. *l.* orbicular in outline, divided almost to base into 3 broad roundish, obovate, shallowly 3-lobed and toothed divisions. *fl.* ½ to 2 in. across, golden-yellow, flat; sep. 5; pet. very narrow. 1909. W. China. Closely related to *T. yunnanensis.*

T. asia'ticus. 1 to 1½ ft. h. *l.* much as *T. europaeus* but smaller, bronzy-green, lobes finely toothed. *fl.* dark yellow; sep. 10, spreading (not globe-shaped); pet. 10, nearly as long as sep., exceeding stamens. May, June. Siberia, Turkistan. Before 1823. (B.M. 325.) var. **aurantia'cus,*** a fine orange var.; **Fortu'nei,** sep. many, appearing double.

T. aurantia'cus. A variety of *T. asiaticus* or of *T. europaeus.*

T. Bud'dhae. About 20 in. h. *l.* divided into 3 deeply 3-lobed and toothed divisions; *basal l.* usually smaller than stem-l. *fl.* 1¼ to 2 in. across, golden-yellow, flat; sep. 5; pet. linear, a little longer than stamens. 1913. NW. China. SYN. *T. stenopetalus.*

T. cauca'sicus. A synonym of *T. ranunculinus*, but the name has also been applied to *T. altaicus.*

T. chinen'sis. Glabrous perennial with stout, grooved stem. *l.* in lower part kidney-shaped, upper more rounded, up to 5 in. long, 7 in. across, 5 partite; segs. widely lanceolate, up to 3 in. long, 2 in. across, lobed, sharply toothed, thin; stalk broad about ⅓ in. long. *fl.* golden-yellow on peduncles up to 12 in. long; sep. 12 or 13, outer wide-ovate, about ¾ in. long, inner rather narrower and longer; pet. 20, linear, over 1 in. long. N. China. 1912. (B.M. 8565.)

T. × culto'rum. A name covering a group of garden hybrid 2 to 3 ft. h., with globular orange *fl.*, derived from *T. europaeus* crossed with *T. asiaticus* and *T. chinensis*; here belong **Earliest of All, Etna, Fire Globe, Goldquelle. Golden Queen, Orange Globe,** and other good forms for the herbaceous border or water garden. May, June.

T. dschunga'ricus. Habit of *T. europaeus*, about 1 to 2 ft. h., but *fl.* open, not globular, golden-yellow within, reddish outside; sep. about 15, rounded, mucronate; style straight; awl-shaped. May, June. Turkistan.

T. europae'us. Glabrous, 1 to 2 ft. h., erect, rarely branched. *l.* ternate, side lobes deeply cut in 2, middle lobe cut in 3, toothed, lower long-stalked, upper sessile. *fl.* lemon yellow, 1½ to 2 in. across, globular, solitary; sep. 10 to 15, ovate; pet. egg-yolk yellow, about as long as stamens. June to August. Europe, including Britain. (E.B. 42.) Very variable. var. **al'bidus,** *fl.* creamy-yellow; **gigan'teus,** up to 2½ ft. h., a robust variety, **na'nus** (or **hu'milis**), 3 to 8 in. h., compact; **napellifo'lius,** a robust var., *l.* deeply divided, stems many-fld.

T. Far'reri. About 3 to 10 in. h. *l.* segs. deeply 3-lobed with a few broad teeth. *fl.* about ¾ to 1¼ in. across, yellow; pet. shorter than stamens, linear-spatulate. NW. China. SYN. *T. pumilus* var. *Farreri.*

T. Gammiea'nus. 1½ to 5 in. h. *l.* deeply divided and dissected into narrow lobes; upper stem-l. long-stalked, usually reaching to fl., base sheathing. *fl.* solitary, about 1¼ in. across, yellow, flat; sep. 5.; pet. shorter than filaments. Nepal. 1928. (G.C. 89 (1931), 490). Probably the true *T. pumilus* of D. Don.

T. gigante'us. A synonym of robust forms of both *T. asiaticus* and *T. europaeus.*

T. hyb'ridus. A name applied to many seedling forms of merit intermediate between species but which cannot confidently be ascribed to any particular species.

T. japo'nicus. 4 to 8 in. h. *l.* radical and forming an involucre. *fl.* yellow, sep. 5 or 6, about 1 in. long. Japan. Nearly allied to *T. laxus.* var. **flore ple'no,** a synonym of *T. asiaticus Fortunei.*

T. la'xus. Stems more or less ascending, slender, 6 to 24 in. long. *Lower l.* stalked; all 5- to 7-parted; lflets. wedge-shaped, much cleft and toothed. *fl.* solitary, greenish-yellow, 1 to 2 in. across; sep. 5 to 7, entire or toothed at tip, spreading; pet. many, much shorter than stamens. May to August. United States. (B.M. 1988 and L.B.C. 56 as *T. americanus.*) var. **albiflo'rus,** lower than type, lflets. 5, *fl.* pale or white, pet. nearly as long as stamens. Alpine form, W. United States.

T. Ledebour'ii. 2 to 3 ft. h. *l.* cleft to base; segs. lobed and toothed. *fl.* deep orange, cup-shaped, 2 to 2½ in. across; sep. 5, spreading, veined, ovate; pet. 10 to 12, narrow linear, longer than the dark orange, erect stamens. May, June. E. Siberia, Amurland.

T. lilaci'nus. 3 to 12 in. h. *l.* cleft to base, much lobed and toothed. Cal. petaloid, tinged lilac, regular; sep. 15 to 20 persistent; cor. of about 10 nectariform, yellowish; pet. with a tubular gibbous base and oblong blade rounded at top. Turkistan, Altai Mts. SYN. *Hegemone lilacina.*

T. napellifo'lius. A variety of *T. europaeus.*

T. pa'tulus. A synonym of *T. ranunculinus.*

T. pu'milus. 1 ft. h. or less. *l.* 1 to 2 in. across, round, 5-parted; segs. broadly ovate, 3-lobed. *fl.* yellow, solitary, 1 to 1½ in. across, flat open; sep. 5 or 6, rounded, emarginate; pet. 10 to 12, as long as stamens, very narrowly wedge-shaped. June, July. N. India, W. China. var. **yunnanen'sis,** a synonym of *T. yunnanensis.*

T. ranunculi'nus. 3 to 12 in. h. *Radical l.* palmately cut, segs. cut and toothed. *fl.* golden-yellow, flat, 1½ to 1¾ in. across; sep. 5 to 10, spreading; pet. linear-spatulate, about as long as stamens. June, July. Caucasus, Armenia. Variable in all parts, especially in size of fl. SYN. *T. patulus, T. caucasicus.*

T. sinen'sis. A synonym of *T. chinensis.*

Trollius yunnanensis

T. yunnanen'sis. Glabrous perennial up to 2 ft. h. *l.* tufted at base, 1½ to 4 in. or more across, more or less 5-angled, deeply 3- or 5-cleft, long-stalked; seg. broadly ovate to obovate, teeth broad, acute, pale beneath; stem-l. 1 or 2, with short sheath. *fl.* 1½ to 2 in. (sometimes more) across, golden-yellow, flat; pedicels ½ to 2 in. long if flowering; sep. usually 5, sometimes greenish near tips; pet. about 12, linear-spatulate, about ⅓ in. long, orange-tipped. May 1913. Yunnan, China. (B.M. 9143.) SYN. *T. pumilus yunnanensis.* Sometimes confused with *T. ranunculinus.*

TROMBID'IUM. *See* **Mites.**

TROMSDORF'FIA specio'sa. A synonym of *Chirita Horsfieldii.*

troodi, of Mt. Troodos, Cyprus.

TROPAEOLAC'EAE. Dicotyledons. A family of about 65 species in 2 genera, Tropaeolum and Magallana, of, frequently, climbing herbs with sensitive leaf-stalks (like Clematis) and peltate, simple but sometimes deeply lobed leaves. Stems occasionally tuberous at the base. Flowers often showy, perfect, zygomorphic, spurred. Sepals and petals 5; stamens 8; ovary superior, the spur being a hollow development of the tip of the pedicel. The genera are TROPAEOLUM (see below), the fruit of which separates into 3 rounded 1-seeded carpels with a fleshy or spongy outer layer (pericarp), and MAGALLANA, a genus of 1 species, *M. porifolia* (Hook. I. 3150), native to Patagonia, with small yellowish-green flowers, deeply 2- to 5-cleft pore-covered leaves and a 3-winged fruit; it is named in honour of the celebrated Portuguese navigator Ferdinand Magellan (Fernando Magallanes), *c.* 1480–1521. The family is sometimes included in Geranianceae.

TROPAEO'LUM (coined by Linnaeus from Greek *tropaion,* Latin *tropaeum,* trophy, i.e. a sign of victory consisting originally of a tree-trunk set up on the battlefield and hung with captured helmets and shields; as gardeners used to grow *T. majus* up pyramids of poles and netting, Linnaeus compared its rounded leaves to shields and its flowers to spear-pierced blood-stained gold helmets ornamenting such a memorial or statue of victory). FAM. *Tropaeolaceae.* A genus of about 64 species. The bright flowers of quaint shapes usually freely produced on long stalks and the rapid growth of many of the climbers render the Tropaeolums very useful and decorative plants for many purposes. The annuals are readily raised from seed sown in the open border in moderately rich soil in spring or they may be sown in pots under glass and planted out at the end of May after hardening off, and this is best for *T. peregrinum.* The climbing species *T. majus, T. peltophorum,* and *T. peregrinum* grow rapidly and can be used for covering a trellis, or fence or even bushes outdoors or for rafters, &c., in the greenhouse either grown in pots or planted out. They do not lend themselves to formal training but support themselves by their twining leaf-stalks. The less vigorous varieties such as Golden Gleam can be used for vases, and baskets and will flower freely until the first autumn frosts, and almost continuously if kept free from frosts as they do in their native homes. The dwarf forms of *T. majus* are among the most valuable summer-flowering annuals and the flowers can be used with excellent effect for table-decorations. The soil should not be too rich, otherwise leafy growth will be made at the expense of flowers. The double varieties do not all produce seed very freely but can be propagated readily from cuttings in sandy moist compost under glass and kept through winter in a frost free, light and airy house. The hardy *T. polyphyllum* needs a warm sunny place in a rather dry or at least well-drained soil and can be well accommodated on the rock-garden. Neither it nor the perennial tuberous rooted species like *T. azureum, T. tuberosum,* and *T. tricolorum,* nor the rhizomatous and beautiful *T. speciosum* like calcareous soils but are best in soils of turfy loam and peat or sandy peat and good leaf-mould. *T. azureum* and *T. tricolorum* should be grown singly in pots in a light house, being provided with a trellis or twiggy sticks over which to climb. During growth they require much water but when the stems die down the pots should be stored away in a dry, cool place and no water should be given until growth begins again. The tubers should then be carefully shaken out and repotted. The tuberous rooted species can also be increased from seeds or by means of cuttings of slender wiry shoots which callus and form small tubers in one season. *T. speciosum* is more at home in the north and west but can be grown anywhere if the right conditions can be given it and will form a beautiful covering for a north wall or growing over evergreen trees or shrubs. It must have a soil constantly moist and free from lime and it must have shade especially for its roots and the lower part of the stem. It is propagated by seeds or by division of the long-creeping fleshy underground rhizomes but it does not like disturbance at the roots; rhizomes should be planted at least 9 in. deep. The tubers of *T. leptophyllum* and *T. tuberosum* may be boiled and eaten.

Tropaeolum species, especially *T. speciosum,* may be attacked by the virus disease Spotted Wilt causing yellowish spots on the leaves which then turn brown and die and the leaves thus grow rather distorted and cupped. All infected plants must be destroyed.

The Cabbage White Butterfly caterpillars often feed on the annual species and aphides also are sometimes troublesome. Where they occur the measures recommended for dealing with these pests should be adopted.

KEY

1. *Lvs. palmately cut almost to stalk into 4 to 7, usually 5 divisions* — 2
1. *Lvs. entire or shallowly or deeply lobed but not cut to more than two-thirds of radius* — 8
2 (1). *Fl. blue or violet, almost regular* — T. azureum
2. *Fl. yellow or red or both, not blue or violet* — 3
3 (2). *Spur very short, conical, $\frac{3}{10}$ in. long; pet. yellow, 3 large, 2 small, red-veined at base* — T. brachyceras
3. *Spur longer, $\frac{3}{5}$ in. or more long* — 4
4 (3). *Pet. small, shorter or little longer than sep., about $\frac{3}{10}$ in. long or less, sometimes lacking* — 5
4. *Pet. large and conspicuous, much longer than sep., to 1 in. or so long* — 6
5 (4). *Sep. pointed, somewhat spreading, thus showing green inside; pet. red; stamens protruding* — T. pentaphyllum
5. *Sep. rounded, blunt, incurved; pet. yellow; stamens enclosed* — T. tricolorum
6 (4). *Pet. deep red, upper 2 narrowed into wedge-shaped base, lower 3 with almost rectangular blade sharply distinct from its linear stalk. Lvs. bright green. Plant high-climbing* — T. speciosum
6. *Pet. yellow, orange, or pinkish-white, all narrowed into wedge-shaped base* — 7
7 (6). *Plant prostrate, very glaucous. Fl. always yellow or orange* — T. polyphyllum
7. *Plant climbing. Fl. yellow, orange, or pinkish-white* — T. leptophyllum
8 (1). *Lvs. entire or shallowly toothed or angled* — 9
8. *Lvs. deeply lobed* — 17
9 (8). *Pet. large, about $\frac{3}{4}$ to 2 in. long, conspicuous, red or yellow, much longer than sep. Lvs. mostly rounded or half-circular in outline, rarely triangular* — 12
9. *Pet. small, $1\frac{1}{2}$ in. or less long, inconspicuous, purple or blue, deeply cut or long-ciliate, not much longer than sep. Lvs. triangular in outline* — 10
10 (9). *Stems and fl. glabrous* — T. Wagenerianum
10. *Stems hairy* — 11
11 (10). *Fl. hairy* — T. Deckerianum
11. *Fl. glabrous* — T. Lindenii
12 (9). *Pet. all toothed and long-ciliate in upper part; sep. red* — T. Moritzianum
12. *Pet. entire or shallowly toothed but not long-ciliate in upper part* — 13
13 (12). *Base of 3 lower pet. ciliate* — 14
13. *Base of pet. not ciliate* — 16
14 (13). *Plant hairy. Lower 3 pet. deeply toothed* — T. peltophorum
14. *Plant glabrous. Lower 3 pet. usually entire* — 10
15 (14). *Nerves of lvs. ending in a projecting point. Pet. mostly pointed* — T. minus
15. *Nerves of lvs. not projecting at ends. Pet. mostly rounded* — T. majus
16 (13). *Lvs. triangular in outline, entire. Lower 3 pet. toothed, upper 2 entire* — T. chrysanthum
16. *Lvs. semicircular in outline, shallowly lobed. Lower 3 pet. with undulate but not toothed edge* — T. crenatiflorum
17 (8). *Fl. umbellate, about 5 together* — T. umbellatum
17. *Fl. solitary* — 18
18 (17). *Pet. entire. Perennial* — T. tuberosum
18. *Pet. deeply toothed. Annual* — 19
19 (18). *Sep. yellowish-green; pet. yellow with a few red spots at base of lower pet.; upper 2 pet. much larger than lower 3* — T. peregrinum
19. *Sep. red; pet. orange-red; upper 2 pet. smaller than lower 3* — T. Smithii

T. adun'cum. A synonym of *T. peregrinum.*

T. albiflo'rum. A synonym of *T. leptophyllum.*

T. azu'reum. Glabrous climber with small tubers. *l.* 5-lobed, about $1\frac{1}{4}$ in. (sometimes 2 in.) across, lobes linear-lanceolate to obovate. *fl.* blue, about $1\frac{1}{4}$ in. across, pet. emarginate, spur conical, about $\frac{1}{8}$ in. long. Autumn. Chile. 1842. (B.R. 28, 65; B.M. 3985; P.M.B. 9, 247; F.d.S. 1160 as *T. violaeflorum.*) Flowers variable in form. Tender.

T. brachy'ceras. Slender, glabrous climber with small tubers. *l.* 5- to 7-lobed, lobes obovate to linear-lanceolate, obtuse. *fl.* about $\frac{1}{2}$ in. long; yellow, upper pet. with purplish lines; pet. more or less emarginate; spur about $\frac{1}{4}$ in. long, obtuse. June. Chile. 1830. (B.M. 3851; B.R. 1926; P.M.B. 4, 55; S.B.F.G. s. 2, 370.) Half-hardy.

T. canarien'se. A synonym of *T. peregrinum.*

T. chrysan'thum. Climber. *l.* triangular, entire. *fl.* about $1\frac{1}{2}$ in. long, yellow; spur conical, nearly $\frac{1}{2}$ in. long; lower pet. toothed. Colombia. (F.d.S. 10 (1854) 1005.)

T. cocci'neum. A synonym of *T. tricolorum.*

T. crenatiflo'rum. Tender annual climber. *l.* 5-lobed, lobes blunt, mucronate. *fl.* pale orange, about $1\frac{1}{2}$ in. long; upper pet. with red lines, curved, lower straight; spur about $\frac{1}{2}$ in. long, nearly cylindrical; peduncle longer than l. June. Peru. 1844. (B.M. 4245.)

T. Deckeria'num. Hairy climber. *l.* triangular, repand. *fl.* with long conical dull-red cylindric spur about $1\frac{1}{2}$ in. long, green at tip; sep. green; pet. shorter than sep., toothed and ciliate, blue; anthers blue. Venezuela, Colombia. (F.d.S. 5 (1849), 490; Belg. H. 2. 245).

T. edu'le. A synonym of *T. leptophyllum.*

T. e'legans. A synonym of *T. tricolorum.*

T. Jarrat'tii. A synonym of *T. tricolorum.*

T. × Leichtli'nii. *See* **T. leptophyllum.**

T. leptophyl'lum. Climber with large tubers. *l.* long-stalked, 6- or 7-lobed. *fl.* about $1\frac{1}{2}$ in. long, much overtopping l., orange, yellow, or pinkish-white, pet. notched; spur straight, about $\frac{3}{4}$ in. long, narrow conical. Summer. Chile, Bolivia. 1841. (P.M.B. as *T. edule*; F.d.S. 2041 as *T. albiflorum.*) Varying much in the sizeof l., notching of pet., and colour of fl., similar to *T. polyphyllum* save for its tubers and climbing habit. Half-hardy. *T. × Leichtlinii* with bright orange-yellow fl. with red spots is a hybrid of this with *T. polyphyllum* (1895).

T. Linden'ii. Hairy climber. *l.* pentagonal-ovate. *fl.* about $1\frac{3}{4}$ in. long with long conical red spur about $1\frac{1}{4}$ in. long; sep. green; pet. about as long as sep., red-violet, fimbriate. Colombia. (I.H. 6. 5 (1894), 17.)

T. Lobbia'num. A synonym of *T. peltophorum.*

T. ma'jus. Indian Cress, Nasturtium. Strong growing glabrous annual climber. *l.* orbicular, its nerves not projecting, rarely lobed. *fl.* large, very variable in colour, orange in wild plant; pet. rounded; spur 1 in. or more long. Summer. Peru. 1686. Half-hardy. (B.M. 23; 3375 as var. *atrosanguineum*). var. **flore ple'no** has double *fl.*; **na'num,** the Tom Thumb Nasturtium, a non-climbing form, smaller in *fl. T. majus* has given rise in cultivation to a great number of forms showing variation in stature, habit and size, in colour of fl. and l., but apparently not in degree of resistance to frost. Variations are still occurring as in **Golden Gleam** which originated in America and has given rise to other semi-double forms quite recently. There is scarcely any doubt that some of the variations have resulted from the crossing of *T. majus* with *T. peltophorum* and *T. minus.* Hybrids of *T. majus* with *T. Moritzianum* and *T. peregrinum,* have also been recorded. The l. of *T. majus* and *T. minus* and the fl. have been used in salads and the young green fr. are pickled and used as a substitute for capers.

T. mi'nus. Non-climbing glabrous annual. *l.* roundish-reniform, nerves projecting in a point. *fl.* smaller than in *T. majus,* deep yellow; pet. ending in a bristle-like point, lower much spotted, its cilia hairy; spur distinctly curved, about $1\frac{1}{4}$ in. long, cylindrical. Summer. Peru. 1585. (B.M. 98.) *T. minus* was first figured by Lobel in 1576 as *Nasturtii indici genuina effigies*, and there is a dried specimen in the herbarium at Genoa collected in the Botanic Garden there in or about 1585, *T. peregrinum* was described by Dodoens in 1574 as *Nasturtium indicum*, and was apparently the first species known.

Tropaeolum polyphyllum (p. 2156)

T. Moritzia'num. Tender climber. *l.* rounded, margins wavy, about as large as in *T. majus*. *fl.* large, orange and red; upper pet. ciliate-toothed, lower ciliate; spur straight, awl-shaped, about 1 in. long. July. Cent. America, Venezuela, Colombia. 1839. (B.M. 3844; P.M.B. 8, 199.)

T. mucrona'tum. A synonym of *T. tuberosum*.

T. pelto'phorum. Tender pubescent annual climber. *l.* roundish, mucronate. *fl.* medium to large, red; upper pet. roundish, lower clawed, toothed, fringed below; spur somewhat curved, 1¼ in. long; peduncles longer than l. Summer. Colombia, Ecuador. 1843. (B.M. 4097 and P.M.B. 11, 271 as *T. Lobbianum*.)

T. pentaphyl'lum. Tall, glabrous, tender, perennial climber, with long, beaded tubers. Stems and l.-stalks purple. *l.* 5-lobed, lobes elliptical, usually obtuse, long-stalked. *fl.* 1 to 1¼ in. long; upper sep. spotted red, pet. about ⅛ in. long, scarlet, entire; spur conical, about 1 in. long, red and green. June, July. *fr.* spotted black. S. America. 1829. (B.M. 3190; L.B.C. 1989 and B.R. 1547 as *T. quinatum*.)

T. peregri'num. Canary Creeper. Half-hardy annual or perennial climber. *l.* 5-lobed, lobes deeply cut. *fl.* long-stalked, rather small; pet. sulphur or lemon yellow, upper erect, red-spotted at base, lobed; spur about ½ in. long, conical. Summer. Peru. 1810. (B.M. 1351; B.R. 718; S.B.F.G. s. 2, 184 all as *T. aduncum*.) SYN. *T. canariense*. *See* **T. Smithii** and **T. minus.**

T. polyphyl'lum. Hardy grey-green herbaceous perennial with long rhizome and prostrate leafy stems. *l.* large, 5- to 7- or more lobed, lobes sometimes cut, variable. *fl.* long-stalked, freely produced; pet. yellow, orange or ochre, nearly equal, obovate, upper notched; spur ¾ in. long, narrowly conical. Summer. Chile, Argentine. 1827. (B.M. 4042; P.M.B. 10, 175.)

T. quina'tum. A synonym of *T. pentaphyllum*.

T. Smith'ii. Climber, half-hardy annual or perennial. *l.* 5-lobed, lobes acute, sometimes cut. *fl.* bright orange-red, all pet. bristle fringed; spur somewhat curved, conical, about ¾ in. long; peduncles longer than l. S. America. 1775. (B.M. 4385 and F.d.S. 384 as *T. peregrinum*.)

T. specio'sum. Flame Nasturtium. Tall hardy climber, perennial with more or less fleshy rhizomes. *l.* 5- or 6-lobed, hairy lobes obovate, notched, shortly stalked. *fl.* of moderate size, scarlet, upper narrow-wedge-shaped, lower squarish, notched, abruptly clawed; spur narrow, 1 to 1¼ in. long, more or less straight. Chile, Chiloé. 1846. (B.M. 4323; P.M.B. 14, 173.)

T. trico'lorum. Variable tall, slender, half-hardy perennial climber with small tubers. *l.* 5- to 7-lobed, lobes usually linear, obovate. *fl.* of various colours; cal. orange-scarlet, tipped black; pet. orange, entire, shorter than spur; spur ¾ to 1 in. long, straight or somewhat curved. The spur varies from red to yellow with blue or greenish tip, the cal. is blue, violet, red, or yellow with greenish margin, and yellow within. Summer. Bolivia, Chile. 1828. (S.B.F.G. 270; B.M. 3169 as *T. elegans*; B.R. 1935 and P.M.B. 3, 123 as *T. coccineum*; P.M.B. 5, 29 as *T. Jarrattii*.)

T. tubero'sum. Glabrous, nearly hardy perennial climber, with large yellow tubers marbled with purple and reddish or bluish stems, l.-stalks, and peduncles. *l.* 5-lobed, truncate at base, long-stalked. *fl.* long-stalked; sep. red; pet. about equal to sep., usually entire, upper rounded lower narrower, all orange or scarlet; spur straight, abruptly narrowed, scarlet, about ¾ in. long. September. Peru, Bolivia. 1827. (B.M. 3714; P.M.B. 5, 49 both as *T. mucronatum*.)

T. umbella'tum. Glabrous tender climber with large tubers. *l.* almost round, 5-lobed, cordate; lobes obtuse. *fl.* 1¼ in. long, scarlet; sep. yellow; spur straight, conical, about ¾ in. long. Distinct by the many-fld. axillary peduncles. June. Bolivia. 1846. (B.M. 4337.)

T. violaeflo'rum. A synonym of *T. azureum*.

T. Wageneria'num. Climber. *l.* triangular, entire, pointed. *fl.* with long cylindric red spur about 1¾ in. long, green-tipped; sep. green; pet. a little longer than sep., violet, deeply cut. Venezuela. 1850. (F.d.S. 6 (1850), 553; Belg. H. 2. 1.)

Tropaeolum speciosum

TROPICAL ALMOND. *See* **Terminalia Catappa.**

TROPICAL DUCKWEED. *See* **Pistia Stratiotes.**

A→

trop'icus -a -um, of the tropics.

tropido-, -tropis, in Greek compound words signifies the keel of a papilionaceous flower, or a part resembling it.

TROS. An old generic name now included in **Narcissus.**

TROUGH AND SINK GARDENING. The growing of dwarf plants in discarded stone pig troughs and kitchen sinks was introduced to the gardening public by an exhibit at The Royal Horticultural Society's Chelsea Flower Show of 1923, and its many advantages have since made it popular.

Room can be found for either or both receptacles in the smallest of gardens; a trough or a couple of sinks will easily accommodate 20 to 40 alpine plants, and many which will tolerate neither open ground nor pan culture can be grown to perfection in trough or sink; raised to a convenient height the plants are brought near the eye for intimate observation, and weeding becomes an easy matter; slugs, snails, and woodlice seldom, if ever, find their way into these little gardens, consequently *Campanula Zoysii*, *Mertensia maritima*, and other plants for which these pests have a special liking can be safely grown.

Both troughs and sinks must be of stone. Those of sandstone are the most usual but slate and limestone examples are sometimes mét with. Old ones can still be found lying about in old cottage gardens and farmyards and also in builders' yards. Excellent hand chiselled modern replicas are frequently seen at horticultural shows; these soon take on the patina of age if lightly brushed over once or twice with rain-water in which cow dung has been steeped. They are generally used for alpine plants, but a charming miniature lily pond can be made in an undrilled trough as several of the pygmy Waterlilies (Nymphaeas) require only from 4 to 9 in. of water. Small aquatics and water snails will add to the interest.

Sinks look well set at intervals along the coping of a low wall, on stone balustrade, or flanking the sides of a broad flight of steps. In such positions they must be raised about an inch above the flat surface on which they stand, otherwise the drainage may be impeded. Troughs look best when raised on four stone blocks or pedestals a foot high and about 9 in. square. Sinks may also be raised on supports of some sort, but in this case the pedestals should be about 18 in. high at least. Rick straddle stones are very suitable for this purpose but are difficult to find. Rough sandstone and cement pedestals are easily made at home. All that is required is a wooden mould (sides only) made to the size and height required, some thin sandstone, walling stones, and cement. The pedestals are built up, layer by layer, starting with a layer of cement on a perfectly level base. The wallers are carefully fitted into the sides and corners of the mould and a layer of cement follows, well worked amongst the stones. Any space in the centre can be filled with rough pieces of stone and cement. In this manner the mould is filled to the top, the last layer being of cement. Before the cement is quite dry one side of the mould is knocked away and the other three will come away easily. Small sandstone chippings can now be pressed into the cement layers if desired. Large sinks may have four such supports, 8 in. square, or one at either end which should extend the whole width of the sink; small sinks need only one central pedestal, 1 ft. square. Brick pedestals are not advocated as they look out of place with the stone.

Drainage is a matter of great importance. Sinks are always provided with outlet holes, but as a rule troughs do not possess them. If alpines are to grow in these, an outlet must be cut with a stonemason's chisel and hammer. To ensure that all superfluous water drains away, the trough or sink should be tilted towards the outlet; it should be tested by pouring in water before filling it with soil. When the water is found to run away satisfactorily, and the sink or trough has been firmly fixed so as to keep it in this state of efficient drainage, two or three large crocks must be placed over the outlet and a few smaller one over these. Gravel about the size of hazel nuts is the best material for drainage as it remains damp and cool in the hottest weather. Sinks, which are seldom more than 5 in. deep, require 1½ to 2 in. of gravel; troughs will need enough to fill them to one-third their depth. A thin layer of roughage, such as waste from sieved peat or partially rotted leaf-mould, must cover the gravel to prevent the soil from clogging the drainage material. At this stage the main rock feature must be arranged in sinks, otherwise it will not give any appearance of stability. In troughs the largest rocks need not be set in place till they are two-thirds full of soil. The compost should be as follows: 1½ parts good old fibrous loam; 2 parts partially rotted leaf-mould (sieved); 1 part coarse sand; 2 parts limestone or sandstone chips (according to the plants to be grown).

Always err on the side of too much grit rather than on the side of too much soil. Avoid using flower-pot grit which is very unsightly in colour. Pack the compost firmly about the rocks and arrange the secondary rocky outcrops before the soil reaches the brim, as the rocks must never appear merely to sit on the surface. Continue packing till the trough or sink is full. The effect of the rocks should be of one bold rock feature with one or two outcrops appearing occasionally. Water-worn limestone, beautiful in colour and grain, is probably the most easy to handle as several pieces can be built up to give the appearance of a single massive rock with crevices in which small plants can be grown. Sandstone is not so pleasing either in colour or shape, but it improves with time when moss softens its colour and veils its angles. Plants are always surprisingly happy in that curious spongy material, tufa, in spite of its lime content. Its form is rugged and picturesque, and a single large block, well bedded down in soil, will provide a most interesting rock-garden. Holes can be bored in it with ease, and Saxifrages, Sempervivums, small Sedums, Phyteumas, Androsaces, and many small cushion plants will thrive in these holes packed with rich soil. In time the roots will work their way into the substance of this soft stone and into the soil below.

The balls of soil on pot-grown plants must be broken and most of the soil shaken out when they are planted in the sink or trough garden. Cushion plants should always occupy the highest positions; miniature trees should be planted on descending slopes with mat plants occupying the lowest levels. After planting, the surface of the soil must be covered with at least ½ in. of chips to match the rocks.

Watering must be carefully attended to, especially that of sinks which stand in full sun. These usually require water every day in hot dry weather. The soil, whether in sink or trough, must always be sufficiently moist to sustain life, but it should not be saturated. This condition cannot, of course, be avoided in wet weather.

A miniature landscape, rock garden, alpine lawn, rose garden, or lake with minute water lilies, all these can be devised and carried out in a space of 2 or 3 ft. with a minimum of expenditure and a maximum of pleasure.

The number of plants suitable for trough and sink gardens is very large. The following lists do not claim to be exhaustive. The letter (G) after the name denotes that a pane of glass is desirable in winter.

BULBS AND CORMS: *Allium crenulatum, A. cyaneum; Crocus ancyrensis, C. Balansae* Zwanenburg, *C. biflorus pusillus, C. chrysanthus fusco-tinctus, C. minimus, C. susianus minor*; *Merendera* various species; *Iris Bakeriana, I. histrioides major*; *Hyacinthus azureus* (syn. *Hyacinthella azurea*); *Narcissus asturiensis* (syn. *N. minimus*), *N. Bulbocodium nivalis, N. juncifolius, N. nanus, N. rupicola, N. scaberulus*; *Oxalis adenophylla, O. enneaphylla rubra, O. lobata.*

CUSHION PLANTS: *Arenaria caespitosa* Bevan's var.; *Draba bryoides imbricata* (G), *D. polytricha* (G), *D. pyrenaica* (G), *D. rigida* (G); *Globularia bellidifolia, G. cordifolia, G. cordifolia alba, G. incanescens, G. nana*; *Gypsophila aretioides* (G), *G. aretioides caucasica* (G); *Petrocallis pyrenaica.*

CUSHION PLANTS, MORE DIFFICULT: *Androsace arachnoidea superba, A. carnea, A. cylindrica, A. glacialis, A. helvetica, A. imbricata, A. pubescens, A. pyrenaica*; *Arenaria tetraquetra*; *Douglasia laevigata, D. Vitaliana praetutiana*; *Draba mollissima*; *Globularia spinosa*; *Trachelium rumelianum* (syn. *Diosphaera dubia*); all the above require glass in the winter.

CHOICE CARPETING PLANTS: *Calceolaria tenella*; *Dianthus Langianus, D. myrtinervis*; *Gypsophila repens*; *Raoulia australis, R. glabra* (G), *R. lutescens* (G); *Saxifraga oppositifolia splendens, S. retusa*; *Sedum album* Coral Carpet; *Talinum okanoganense* (G), *T. spinescens* (G); *Veronica canescens* (G).

DWARF AND SLOW-GROWING CONIFERS: *Abies balsamea hudsonia*; *Chamaecyparis obtusa* vars. *caespitosa, juniperoides, minima, pygmaea*; *C. pisifera* vars. *plumosa compressa, plumosa nana, plumosa Rogersii*; *Cryptomeria japonica Vilmoriniana*; *Juniperus communis compressa*; *Picea Abies humilis, Picea Abies pygmaea, P. albertiana conica, P. mariana nana*; *Pinus sylvestris beauvronensis*; *Taxus baccata pygmaea*; *Thuja orientalis minima glauca.*

DWARF SHRUBS: *Carmichaelia Ensyi*; *Crassula sarcocaulis*; *Escallonia rubra pygmaea*; *Hypericum Coris, H. ericoides*; *Jasminum Parkeri*; *Lithospermum graminifolium*; *Moltkia × intermedia, Moltkia petraea*; *Penstemon cristata, P. Menziesii* (syn. *P. Roezlii*), *P. microphyllus, P. Newberryi, P. rupicola*; *Rosa chinensis minima* forms (including *R. Lawranciana, R. Roulettii*); *Salix herbacea, S. reticulata, S. retusa, S. serpyllifolia, S. Uva-ursi*; *Thymus membranaceus* (G); *Veronica Bidwillii, V. Olsenii.*

DWARF AND SLOW-GROWING TREES: *Ilex nummularifolia*; *Prunus prostrata*, Cretan form; *Rhamnus pumila*; *Salix Boydii.*

General List: *Acantholimon creticum, A. glumaceum*; *Androsace sarmentosa chumbyi, A. sempervivoides*; *Aquilegia akitensis, A. scopulorum*; *Asperula arcadiensis, A. Gussonei*; *Calceolaria biflora*; *Campanula Allionii* in var., *C. arvatica, C. Aucheri, C. cenisia, C. lasiocarpa, C. Morettiana, C. Raineri, C. Saxifraga, C. tridentata, C. Zoysii*; *Cyananthus lobata*; *Dianthus alpinus, D. callizonus, D. Freynii, D. haematocalyx, D. neglectus, D. subacaulis, D. squarrosus*; *Douglasia laevigata*; *Edraianthus carinatus, E. dinaricus, E. graminifolius, E. pumilio, E. serpyllifolius major*; *Erigeron aureus, E. compositus, E. leiomerus, E. trifidus*; *Erodium chamaedryoides roseum, E. corsicum album*; *Gentiana alpina, G. sino-ornata, G. verna angulosa*; *Geranium Farreri, G. subcaulescens splendens*; *Helichrysum bellidioides, H. frigidum, H. marginatum* (G); *Houstonia coerulea*, Millard's form; *Iberis pygmaea*; *Mertensia maritima*; *Morisia monanthos*; *Myosotis explanata* (G), *M. rupicola*; *Papaver alpina*; *Phyteuma comosum*; *Potentilla nitida rubra*; *Polygala calcarea*; *Primula marginata* in var., *P.*×*pubescens* var.; *Pulsatilla vernalis* (syn. *Anemone vernalis*); *Ranunculus alpestris, R. crenatus, Saxifraga Aizoon baldensis, minor, S. Burseriana crenata, sulphurea, S. cochlearis minor, S.*× Cranbourne, *S.*×Hocker Edge, *S.*×*Irvingii, S.*×*Jenkinsae, S. primuloides* Elliott's var., *S. valdensis*; *Sedum acre minus, S. lydium*; *Sempervivum arachnoideum, S. arenarium, S.*×*Hookeri, S. valdense, S. tectorum alpinum*, also a few of the larger good coloured varieties such as *montanum rubrum, Schlehanii bruneifolium*, Hall's hybrids, *ornatum, rubicundum, violaceum*, &c.; *Thalictrum kiusianum*; *Veronica bombycina*.

Trailing Plants (to hang over the sides): *Achillea*× *Lewisii* King Edward; *Androsace lanuginosa*; *Asperula lilaciflora caespitosa, A. pontica*; *Campanula Elatines* (G); *Geranium sanguineum lancastriense*; *Linum salsoloides*; *Petrophytum caespitosum* (syn. *Spiraea caespitosa*); *Phlox Douglasii* in var.; *Phlox subulata* in var.; *Saponaria ocymoides rubra compacta*; *Sedum Praegerianum, S. spurium* Schorbusser Blut; *Veronica rupestris* and vars. Silver Queen, Wedgewood, *V. Teucrium* Trehane.

Water Plants: *Nymphaea pygmaea alba rubra, N. tetragona*.

Invasive Plants: *Acaena*; *Arenaria balearica*; *Campanula carpatica, C. cochleariifolia* (syn. *C. pusilla*), *C. linifolia, C. rotundifolia*; *Cerastium tomentosum*; *Cotula squalida*; *Epilobium nummulariifolium*; *Frankenia*, all; *Mazus pumilio*; *Mentha Requienii*; *Pimelia coarctata*; *Polygonum* probably all; *Potentilla verna nana*; *Pratia angulata Treadwellii, P. repens*; *Thymus Serpyllum*, and similar creeping species; *Veronica filiformis*.

G. A.

TROWEL. The garden Trowel is an indispensable tool most useful for lifting small plants with a minimum of root disturbance and for planting anything out of pots. It is to be preferred to the Dibber at any time for the hole may be made larger with its sides less packed, and the roots of the plant to be inserted may be spread out better. In selecting a Trowel care should be taken to see that the blade is firmly fixed in the handle and that the latter is of sound construction. The Fern Trowel has a narrower and often stouter blade than the Garden Trowel and is used for lifting Ferns, especially by collectors of these plants searching for them in their native habitats and is also useful for lifting plants growing among stones or in crevices.

Troximon. *See* ***Agoseris.***

TRUE LOVE. *See* **Paris quadrifolia.**

TRUFFLES. The popular name of the fruit-bodies of the fungus genus Tuber, in which all species are subterranean and form tuber-like fleshy fruits highly valued as food. They have been so esteemed since classical times and were certainly known in France and Italy in the 14th century. They occur principally in calcareous soils usually under trees at the edges of woods, but are rare in sandy soils. In Great Britain the soil beneath beeches seems to be most favoured and in France that beneath evergreen oaks such as *Quercus Ilex* and *Q. coccifera*, but occasionally under hazel as well. The best British species is *Tuber aestivum* but more delicious ones are said to occur on the Continent, for instance, *T. marginatum*, the Garlic-scented Truffle of Italy and *T. melanospermum* the French Truffle used in Pâté de foie gras and Poulard truffé. The Family of Fungi to which Truffles belong is the Tuberaceae, a member of the Ascomycetes, the most important genus being Tuber. *Tuber aestivum* is 1 to 4 in. across, bluish-black when moist, brown when dry, nearly globose and covered with hard, ribbed, and furrowed warts. The flesh is at first white, then yellow, and finally brown with a network of whitish branched veins. It has a slight, but pleasant odour. As Truffles are hidden in leaf-mould or earth and are sometimes up to a foot deep they are difficult to find, but as they possess a faint smell animals are used to detect them. In France small dogs (poodles) are used and formerly in some English counties similar methods were used. Pigs were also used for truffle hunting, but where these fungi are abundant men are often able to detect them by slight bulging or even cracking of the soil or by observing the habitat of the so-called truffle fly *Anistoma cinnamomea*. Attempts at artificial cultivation of truffles are not very successful although some people go to great trouble to select beech leaf-mould in which are placed truffles or truffle parings. France is probably the only country which includes truffles in its exports.

D. E. G.

trullif'erus -a -um, bearing a structure, usually a leaf, shaped like a pot, pan, or trowel.

TRUMPET CREEPER or CLIMBER. *See* **Campsis.**

TRUMPET FLOWER. Various species of Campsis, Tecoma, &c., are so called.

TRUMPET HONEYSUCKLE. *See* **Lonicera sempervirens.**

TRUMPET LILY. *See* **Zantedeschia aethiopica.**

TRUMPET TREE. *See* **Cecropia peltata.**

TRUMPET WEED. *See* **Eupatorium purpureum.**

TRUMPETS. *See* **Sarracenia flava.**

trunca'tulus -a -um, ***trunca'tus -a -um*** truncate; ending very bluntly and abruptly as though a piece had been broken or cut off.

trunci'cola, a dweller on tree-trunks.

TRUNK. The stem of a tree.

TRUSS. A popular name for a compact, moderate-sized cluster of flowers; an umbel of flowers produced from one centre and growing on one stem, as in Auricula, Pelargonium, Polyanthus, Verbena, &c.

truxillen'sis -is -e, of Truxillo, Mexico.

TRYMA'LIUM (*trymalia*, a perforation; there are small holes at the top of the capsule). Fam. *Rhamnaceae*. A genus of about 5 species of Australian shrubs with the habit and deciduous stipules and bracts of Pomaderris but with smaller flowers and a more slender inflorescence. Petals 5, hood-shaped, entire or 3-lobed, not enclosing the anthers. None of the species is particularly ornamental. *T. Billardieri* is sometimes grown in greenhouses in sandy loam and leaf-mould. It can be increased by cuttings.

T. Billardier'i. Tall shrub. *l.* variable, broadly ovate or obovate and blunt, 1 to 2 in. long, or ovate to ovate-lanceolate, rather slender-pointed, 2 to 3 in. long, entire or crenate, white, hoary or long-haired beneath. *fl.* numerous, in loose, narrow, terminal panicles, 2 to 6 in. long. Syn. *T. expansum, T. floribundum.*

F. G. P.

TRYPHAEN'A. Old name for Graphiphora. *See* **Surface Caterpillars.**

tsangpoen'sis -is -e, from the neighbourhood of the Tsangpo River, S. Tibet.

tsarongen'sis -is -e, from the Tsarong district, SE. Tibet.

Tschonos'kii, in honour of M. Tschonoski, a collector for Maximonwicz, the Russian botanist, in Japan, *c.* 1873.

tsjangpoen'sis -is -e, *see* **tsangpoensis.**

TSU'GA (the Japanese name). Hemlock, Hemlock Spruce. Fam. *Pinaceae.* A genus of about 10 species of evergreen, mostly hardy, trees, natives of N. America, Japan, Formosa, China, and the Himalaya, with horizontal branches and branchlets divided into very fine sprays. Leaves lasting several years, linear, spirally arranged but often appearing on the face of the shoot owing to a basal twist, short-stalked and arranged on a small peg-like base, which is less prominent than in Picea, usually blunt. Male and female flowers on different branches of the same tree a little in advance of the growth in spring. Male flowers from leaf-axils of the previous year's growth, female flowers at the points of last year's shoots. Cones solitary, pendulous, ripening the first year, remaining on the branches for several months after shedding the seed; scales thin, leathery. Seeds 2 to each fertile scale, winged. They succeed under similar conditions to Abies. They are best increased by seeds, sown in beds of light soil out-of-doors, or the rarer and more tender species in sandy soil in a cold frame or greenhouse. The varieties can be propagated by shoot cuttings inserted in sandy soil in a cold frame or under a handlight in July or August, shading from bright sun, or they can be grafted on stocks of their respective types previously established in pots, grafting being carried out in a warm propagating house in spring. The wood is useful for building and other purposes and the bark contains tannin. The nomenclature of the species is difficult to follow for different authors have applied the same name to more than 1 species. The species have also been confused with those of Abies. The resin from *T. canadensis* is sometimes known as Canada Pitch.

KEY

1.	*Lvs. flat, grooved above*	2
1.	*Lvs. rounded or keeled above, with stomata on both sides*	T. Mertensiana
2.	*L.-margin toothed*	3
2.	*L.-margin entire*	5
3.	*Lvs. with 2 white or pale bands with stomata beneath; buds pointed*	4
3.	*Lvs. with stomata near tips above, spreading radially*	T. × Jeffreyi
4.	*Lvs. with 2 clear narrow bands and distinct green margin beneath; buds pointed*	T. canadensis
4.	*Lvs. with 2 broad indistinct bands beneath and indistinct green margin; buds globose*	T. heterophylla
5.	*Shoots glabrous; lvs.* $\frac{1}{3}$ *to 1 in. long*	T. Sieboldii
5.	*Shoots hairy at least in grooves*	6
6.	*Lvs. notched at tip*	7
6.	*Lvs. not or scarcely notched at tip*	8
7.	*Lvs.* $\frac{1}{4}$ *to* $\frac{1}{2}$ *in. long; shoots hairy all over, reddish-brown*	T. diversifolia
7.	*Lvs.* $\frac{1}{3}$ *to 1 in. long; shoots hairy chiefly in grooves, light brown or grey*	T. chinensis
8.	*Lvs.* $\frac{1}{4}$ *to 1 in. long; shoots hairy chiefly in grooves*	T. caroliniana
8.	*Lvs.* $\frac{1}{2}$ *to* $\frac{3}{4}$ *in. long; shoots hairy all over*	T. yunnanensis
8.	*Lvs. 1 to* $1\frac{1}{4}$ *in. long; shoots hairy all over*	T. dumosa

T. Albertia'na. A synonym of *T. heterophylla.*

T. america'na. A synonym of *T. canadensis.*

T. Brunonia'na. A synonym of *T. dumosa.*

T. canaden'sis. Eastern Hemlock; Spruce Hemlock. Large tree up to 100 ft. h. forked near base, sometimes into several strong, erect branches. Young shoots greyish-brown, hairy. *Winter buds* very small, ovate, with hairy scales. *l.* $\frac{1}{4}$ to $\frac{2}{3}$ in. long varying in size on the same shoot, appearing more or less 2 ranked, tapering slightly from base to rounded apex, dark green above with 2 glaucous stomatic bands beneath. *Cones* ovate, $\frac{1}{2}$ to 1 in. long on thin stalks, scales few; rounded. *Seed* small, wing oblong. Eastern N. America. 1736. (D.J.C. 525, 530.) Syn. *Abies canadensis.* var. **albo-spi'ca,** tips of shoots white. Syn. var. *argentea*; **Friend'ii,** stiff, pyramidal tree; **macrophyl'la,** *l.* distinctly larger than in type; **milforden'sis,** dense bush with weeping branches; **na'na,** dwarf compact bush. Syn. var. *minima*; **parvifo'lia,** large bush with heath-like arrangement of very short, dark green *l.*; **pend'ula,** large bush or small tree with dense weeping branches. Syn. var. *Sargentiana.*

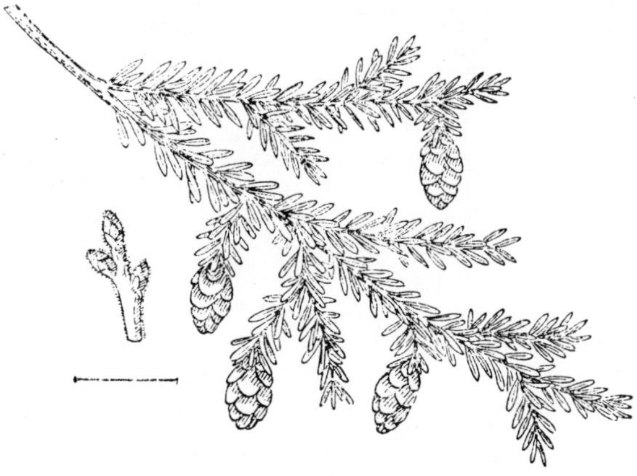

Tsuga canadensis

T. carolinia'na. Graceful pyramidal tree up to 70 ft. h. Young shoots grey, slightly hairy, particularly in furrows. Winter buds ovate, with downy scales. *l.* appearing 2-ranked, $\frac{1}{4}$ to $\frac{3}{4}$ in. long, varying in length on the same shoot, dark green and grooved above, with 2 silvery stomatic bands beneath, blunt. *Cones* oblong, 1 to $1\frac{1}{2}$ in. long, with oblong, rounded, scales. *Seed* small with a long wing. Mts. of SW. Virginia to N. Georgia. 1886. (D.J.C. 532.)

T. chinen'sis. Varies from pyramidal bush to tree up to 100 ft. h. Young shoots pale yellow with scattered hairs. *Winter buds* small, ovate. *l.* variable in size, up to 1 in. long, dark green above with indistinct stomata beneath, blunt, slightly notched. *Cones* ovate, to 1 in. long, scales glossy, rounded and curving inwards at tip. China. 1900. (D.J.C. 533; B.M. 9193.) Syn. *Abies chinensis.* Very liable to injury by late spring frosts.

T. diversifo'lia. Pyramidal tree of 50 to 80 ft. related to *T. Sieboldii.* Young shoots hairy. *Winter buds* pear-shaped, downy. *l.* mostly in 2 opposite ranks, $\frac{1}{4}$ to $\frac{1}{2}$ in. long, dull green, blunt, shallowly notched. *Cones* small with rounded, shining scales. *Seed* small with a very short wing. Japan. 1861. (D.J.C. 535.) Syn. *T. Sieboldii nana, Abies diversifolia.* More liable to frost injury in spring than *T. Sieboldii.*

T. dumo'sa. Himalayan Hemlock. Large, gracefully branched tree up to 120 ft. h. Young shoots light-brown, hairy. *Winter buds* rounded, scales downy. *l.* 1 to $1\frac{1}{4}$ in. long, tapering from base to pointed apex, dark green and grooved above with 2 silvery bands of stomata beneath. *Cones* ovate, stalkless, $\frac{1}{2}$ to 1 in. long, scales rounded, glossy. *Seed* small with well-developed wing. Himalaya. 1838. (D.J.C. 529.) Syn. *T. Brunoniana.* Very beautiful tree but only for the warmest parts of the country.

T. heterophyl'la. Western Hemlock. Large pyramidal tree 200 to 250 ft. h., of graceful outline. Young shoots slender, greyish, hairy. *Winter buds* small, ovate. *l.* more or less 2 ranked $\frac{1}{4}$ to $\frac{3}{4}$ in. long, shorter ones on face of shoot, grooved and dark green above with 2 silvery bands of stomata beneath, margins finely toothed, blunt, not narrowing to apex as in *T. canadensis. Cones* sessile, conical, pointed, scales few, strap-shaped. *Seed* small, wing well developed. Western N. America. 1851. (D.J.C. 525 as *T. Albertiana.*) Syn. *T. Mertensiana* Lindl. and Gord., not (Bong.) Carr; *Abies Albertiana.* Very hardy, decorative tree, which is being planted under forest conditions.

T. Hookeria'na. A synonym of *T. Mertensiana.*

T. × Jeff'reyi. At one time looked upon as a variety of *T. Mertensiana,* now regarded as a natural hybrid between *T. heterophylla* and *T. Mertensiana* with an intermediate character. Habit resembles *T. Mertensiana* but leaf arrangement closer to *T. heterophylla. l.* dull or dark green, spreading at right angles to shoot, $\frac{1}{2}$ in. long, $\frac{1}{16}$ in. wide, flattened and grooved with a few broken lines of stomata above, with several lines of grey stomata beneath. Syn. *T. Mertensiana Jeffreyi.* Raised in 1851 in Edinburgh from seeds collected in British Columbia.

T. Mertensia'na of (Bong.) Carr. Mountain Hemlock. Large pyramidal tree 80 to 100 ft. h., when young with dense branchlets. Young shoots brownish-grey, very hairy. *l.* ¾ to 1 in. long, closely arranged, spreading round shoot, not appearing in ranks, slightly curved, pointing forwards, convex above, rounded beneath, grey-green, stomata on each surface, blunt or short-pointed. *Cones* without stalks, cylindrical, up to 2¼ in. long and 1 in. wide when open, scales thin, broader than long. *Seed* brown with a wing nearly ½ in. long. Western N. America. 1854. SYN. *T. Hookeriana, T. Pattoniana, Abies Pattoniana.* Very handsome, hardy tree, seen at its best when sheltered from rough winds. var. **argent'ea,** *l.* much more glaucous than in type; **Jeff'reyi,** a synonym of *T. Jeffreyi.*

T. Pattonia'na. A synonym of *T. Mertensiana.*

T. Siebold'ii. Japanese Hemlock. Large tree in Japan up to 100 ft. h., usually a large bush in British Is. Branch system dense, young shoots smooth, light brown. *Winter buds* small, reddish, ovate. *l.* ¼ to ½ in. long, variable in arrangement, those on face of shoot shorter than side leaves, dark glossy green and grooved above with 2 bands of silvery stomata beneath, rounded at tip, slightly notched. *Cones* ovate, ½ to ¾ in. long, scales rounded. *Seed*-wing short. Japan. 1853. Excellent evergreen of Yew-like character but less sombre. var. **na'na,** synonym of *T. diversifolia.*

T. yunnanen'sis. Large, strongly branched tree, up to 100 ft. h. Young shoots reddish-grey, hairy, winter buds very small, hidden by l. *l.* ½ to ¾ in. long, green above, with 2 broad glaucous bands of stomata beneath, short-pointed. *Cones* ovate, ½ to ¾ in. long, scales rounded, reflexed at apex. W. China. 1908. (D.J.C. 539.) Very rare in cultivation and very susceptible to injury from late spring frosts.

W. D.

TSUSIOPHYL'LUM (*Tsusia*, modified from the Japanese vernacular name *Tsutsuji*, used by Maximowicz to designate a section of Rhododendron and *phyllon*, a leaf). FAM. *Ericaceae.* A monotypic genus characterized by shrubby growth, an almost general appressed pubescence, alternate entire leaves, flowers in clusters of 2 to 6, tubular corolla with spreading limb, calyx lobes 5, strigose, stamens 5, and a 3-locular, hard, septicidal capsule. Much resembles Rhododendron but differs by the anthers opening by longitudinal slits (not apical pores) and by the 3- (not 5- or 10-) celled capsule. Thrives under the same conditions as Phyllodoce and is propagated by seed, cuttings, and layers.

T. Tanak'ae. Partially evergreen shrub 12 to 18 in. h. with spreading branches and appressed hairy young wood. *l.* oval, ovate-lanceolate to oblanceolate, recurved, appressed hairy especially on upper surface and at edge, ⅜ to ¾ in. long, $\frac{3}{16}$ to $\frac{5}{16}$ in. wide. *fl.* in compact terminal clusters of 2 to 6; cor. white, tubular with 5 spreading, rugose lobes, tube ⅜ in. long, limb ¼ in. across, silky-hairy within, appressed hairy without; cal. lobes 5, of uneven size, oval to lanceolate, acute or blunt, appressed hairy, $\frac{1}{32}$ to $\frac{1}{16}$ in. long. June. Japan. 1915. More interesting than beautiful.

F. S.

tuanen'sis -is -e, of Mt. Tuan, New Guinea.

TUBA-ROOT. *See* **Fish-poison plants.**

tuba'tus -a -um, narrow, cylindrical and hollow with an expanded mouth like a trumpet.

tube, the part of a gamosepalous calyx, or of a gamopetalous corolla, below the lobes; a staminal tube is formed by the union of the staminal filaments in a monadelphous flower.

TUBER. A swollen underground branch, usually roundish, with buds or 'eyes' from which new plants or tubers are produced, e.g. Jerusalem Artichoke, Potato.

TUBER. *See* **Truffles.**

TUBER ROOT. *See* **Asclepias tuberosa.**

TUBERA'RIA. Included in **Helianthemum.**

TUBERCLES. *See* **Nodules.** A

tubercula'tus -a -um, tubercled, covered with little warts or excrescences.

tuberculo'sus -a -um, *see* ***tuberculatus.***

Tubergenia'nus -a -um, Tubergen'ii, in honour of the celebrated bulb firm, Messrs. C. G. van Tubergen, Jr., of Haarlem, Holland, founded in 1868 by Cornelis Gerrit van Tubergen, 1844–1919, and later carried on by his nephews J. M. C. Hoog and T. M. Hoog, and his grand-nephews T. Hoog and C. J. H. Hoog; it has been responsible for the introduction of many new bulbous plants.

tuberif'erus -a- um, bearing tubers.

TUBEROSE. *See* **Polianthes tuberosa.**

tubiflo'rus -a -um, *see* ***tubatus.***

tubiform'is -is -e, *see* ***tubatus.***

TUBILA'BIUM. *See* **Anoectochilus.**

TUBS. Wooden tubs, usually of oak or teak, are sometimes used for large plants, such as Palms, Oranges, Tree Ferns, and Bay Trees, and even Agapanthus and similar plants intended to be put into a frost-free house in winter after standing out in summer. The trees, &c., will often remain in the tubs for several years without renewal of the soil and it is therefore most important that good drainage should be provided and that watering should be carefully attended to. Occasional renewal of the surface soil is necessary.

TUBULAR FLORET. A floret of the disk in flower-heads of Compositae.

tubulo'sus -a -um, tubular, pipe-like.

TULBA'GHIA (in honour of Ryk Tulbagh, Dutch Governor of the Cape of Good Hope, d. 1771). FAM. *Liliaceae.* A genus of about 20 species of rhizomatous perennial herbs with a garlic-like odour, natives of S. and Trop. Africa. Leaves radical, ligulate, the withered sheaths sometimes forming with the rhizome a pseudo-corm. Flowers many in a terminal umbel, pedicellate; perianth urn- or nearly salver-shaped, with 6, nearly equal, spreading lobes; corona rather fleshy at throat, shorter than lobes; stamens 6; involucral bracts 2, scarious, broad; scape simple, leafless. Sandy loam and peat suit these greenhouse plants which can be propagated by offsets or by seeds.

T. acutilo'ba. Corm ampullaeform with brown tunic. *l.* 4 to 6, linear, 4 to 6 in. long, $\frac{1}{12}$ in. wide. *fl.* greenish; ⅓ in. long; tube oblong; segs. lanceolate; corona annular, crenate, purple; *infl.* a 2- to 6-fld. umbel; pedicels ¼ to 1 in. long; scapes 6 to 12 in. long, slender, terete; spathe valves green, lanceolate. S. Africa. Variable.

T. affi'nis. A variety of *T. alliacea.*

T. allia'cea. *l.* 5 or 6, 6 to 9 in. long, ⅛ to ¼ in. wide. *fl.* greenish-purple, about ½ in. long; corona obscurely red, fleshy, entire or crenate; umbels 4- to 12-fld.; scapes 9 to 18 in. long. June. S. Africa. 1820. (Ref. B. 349; F.P.S.A. 653.) var. **affi'nis,** more robust than type, *l.* 1 ft. or more long, ¼ to ½ in. wide, perianth segs. half as long as tube, narrower. SYN. *T. affinis*; **Ludwigia'na,** *l.* lorate, 6 to 8 in. long, ⅜ to ¾ in. wide, scape 18 to 24 in. long. Corona yellow. (B.M. 3547 as *T. Ludwigiana.*) *T. alliacea* of B.M. 806 is *T. capensis.*

T. capen'sis. *l.* 10 to 12, 12 in. or more long, ⅓ to ½ in. wide. *fl.* greenish-purple, segs. half as long as tube; corona obscurely purple, deeply emarginate; umbels 6- to 8-fld.; scapes 18 to 24 in. long. June. S. Africa. 1774. (B.M. 806 as *T. alliacea.*)

T. frag'rans. *See under* **T. pulchella.**

T. Ludwigia'na. A variety of *T. alliacea.*

T. natalen'sis. *l.* 6 to 8, linear, light green, 6 to 12 in. long. *fl.* fragrant, white, ½ in. long; corona greenish-white; umbels 6- to 10-fld.; scape over 12 in. long. May. S. Africa. 1891.

T. pulchel'la. *l.* about 12, to more than 14 in. long, 1 in. wide. *fl.* violet, about ½ in. long; lobes ovate-lanceolate, about equalling cylindrical tube; corona cup-like with 2-fid lobes; 3 stamens inserted half-way up tube, other 3 at mouth of tube; umbels about 20- to 30-fld.; scapes about 1½ ft. long. Transvaal. This species was first described in 1930. *T. fragrans* likewise from the Transvaal (F.P.S.A. 438) is closely allied, if not the same.

T. Simm'leri. Base ovoid. *l.* lorate-lanceolate, obtuse; *fl.* small, rose, ovate-oblong; corona urn-shaped, crenately 3-lobed; scape much longer than l. Transvaal.

T. viola'cea. *l.* 6 to 10, green, 8 to 12 in. long, $\frac{1}{8}$ to $\frac{1}{4}$ in. wide. *fl.* purplish-violet, $\frac{2}{3}$ to $\frac{3}{4}$ in. long; segs. lanceolate, half as long as cylindrical tube; corona segs. ligulate, emarginate; umbels 8- to 20-fld.; scapes 12 to 24 in. long. March. S. Africa. 1838. (B.M. 3555; F.P.S.A. 9.)

TULIP. It is probable that the introduction of the Garden Tulip into Europe is due to Ogier Ghiselin de Busbecq who was Ambassador of the Holy Roman Empire to Suleiman the Magnificent. He first saw it at Adrianople when on his way to Constantinople in 1554 and introduced it to Europe in 1572. Conrad Gesner described some Tulips he saw growing at Augsberg in 1559. From the description it seems probable that these were seedlings of *Tulipa suaveolens*, not *T. Gesneriana* which more nearly approximates to the Tulip of gardens. It is possible that Clusius, who certainly had seeds from Busbecq, first sent Tulips to England from Vienna, for Richard Hakluyt wrote in 1582: 'Within these four years there have been brought into England from Vienna in Austria divers kinds of flowers called Tulipes and these and others procured thither a little before from Constantinople by an excellent man called M. Carolus Clusius.' In 1593 Clusius became Professor of Botany at Leiden and brought Tulips there among other things. He lost them by theft and they were soon distributed widely over Holland, but apparently they were not the first to be grown in Leiden. In 1590 John Hogeland grew Tulips at Leiden from bulbs possibly obtained from George Rye, a merchant of Mechlin, who himself had them from an eastern merchant at Antwerp. Whatever their actual date of introduction there is no doubt that it was from Turkey the garden Tulip first came to Europe, nor that it rapidly became a general favourite. It had been grown in gardens in Turkey for a long time and it had been a 'Royal Flower' for long before the Turkish Tulip Epoch, 1700–30, e.g. in 1574 Selim II sent an order to the Sheriff of Aziz for '50000 bulbs for my royal gardens'. Mr. A. Baker (*Journ. R.H.S.* 56, 238) records the high prices sometimes paid for Tulip bulbs in Turkey, and how the Sultan directed the Mayor of Stamboul to fix prices, those who sold at higher prices than those fixed being sentenced to expulsion from the city. The cult of the Tulip became as extravagant in Turkey during the reign of Ahmed III, 1702–20, as ever it did in Holland during the Tulip mania in 1634–7. In both Holland and Turkey fabulous prices were asked and received for special Tulip bulbs and much speculation went on in Holland for a while, not a little reminiscent of that in England at the time of the South Sea Bubble. Ever since that time Tulips have been an important crop in Holland, not for their food value, although the bulbs have been eaten from time to time, but to supply the enormous demand for bulbs for spring flowering which grew up in many countries. It is still a crop of great importance there, though vast numbers are now raised in parts of England, especially in Lincolnshire and near Wisbech, in W. United States and in British Columbia where climate and soil are eminently suited to the production of bulbs for wide distribution.

Even at the time of Busbecq great numbers of Tulip varieties were known and enumerated. A list of 1,323 varieties is given in a manuscript by Sheik Mohammed Lalizare in the reign of Ahmed III, and there are other very lengthy Turkish lists. The ideal of the Turkish fancier was not quite the same as that of the western growers. His 'six things which make a flower valuable' were: 'The petals should be stiff and smooth and of one colour; the six petals should be of one size and equal in length; they should touch one another; the inner petal should be narrower than the outer; they should conceal the stamens and the pistil should just be visible; the flower should stand erect.' So far there is not much difference from the accepted standards of the present day, but further: 'The flower should resemble an almond. The petals should look like a dagger or needle. If the tulip has not these petal characters it is a cheap flower. The tulip with the needle end is the better of the two; if it has both dagger shape and needle point it is priceless.' The pointed petal was therefore the ideal in Turkey, but it was little valued in Europe. There the rounded broad end to the petal was looked for in the perfect Tulip. The plant known as *Tulipa elegans* shows the pointed petal type well. As time has passed various forms have evolved and have led to the making of classes different from those possible when the Tulip was first introduced. Both English and Dutch raisers have played a part in attaining the present races, but mostly the Dutch. New varieties are obtained by seedling raising and by sporting. Seedlings are not difficult to raise. Seed is produced very freely by most forms of florist's Tulip, germinates well if sown as soon as ripe, and in course of time produces flowering plants, though sometimes as long as 10 years must elapse before the true character of the seedling is evident. The varieties thus raised are increased by offsets. The seedlings are for the most part of self-colours save for the basal blotch, but they are subject to a peculiar form of sporting called 'breaking' in which the flower becomes variously streaked with colour on a white or yellow ground. The 'breaking' takes various forms and was for long looked upon as a mystery. It is now known to be due to infection by a virus carried from plant to plant by aphides, and can be induced by injecting some of the sap from a broken plant into one in which breaking has not yet occurred. The unbroken form is known as a 'breeder' and in the language of the older florists it becomes 'rectified' when it breaks. The rectified form was looked upon as the more perfect form and valued according to whether its markings were clear and clean and regular. It is probably true to say that the popular taste to-day is toward the self-coloured flower, but the broken forms have a striking beauty of their own better seen in the individual than in a mass planting to which the breeder types lend themselves so well.

As late as the end of the 19th century the florist's Tulip in England meant only the May-flowering Tulip with cup-shaped flowers with no other colour than white or yellow in the base of the flower. Others were grown in gardens, derived from the same general source, but they gained little recognition as flowers worthy of the fancier's attention and care. The position is different to-day and though the English florist's Tulip is still grown and justly valued for the perfection of its shape and the clear colours of its best examples, many other forms are recognized and defined and grown very largely. As with many other widely grown plants nomenclature of varieties of these which had not come under the purview of the Tulip fancier was in many instances in a very confused state until in 1913 a Tulip Nomenclature Committee was set up by The Royal Horticultural Society and comparative trials were instituted in its gardens at Wisley. English and Dutch growers co-operated in sorting out the varieties and in preparing a Report which was published in 1917. Meanwhile other groups of Tulips were being evolved in Holland and trials were begun in 1929 at the headquarters of the Algemene Vereniging voor Bloembollencultuur (General Dutch Bulb-Growers' Society) of Haarlem and the Committee was reconstituted to settle questions of classification and synonymity, and to draw up colour descriptions of the numerous additional varieties which were grown there or appeared at exhibitions. In 1929 a Tentative List of Tulip Names was published as a result of co-operation between the two bodies represented on the Committee, with a Supplement in 1930, and in accordance with the resolution adopted at the International Horticultural Conference held at Rome in 1935 this list of garden varieties of Tulips serves as the basis from which the names of garden varieties of Tulips take priority. Other new varieties have been considered since and the two Societies have co-operated in producing the latest *Classified List of Tulip Names*, published in 1948, containing over 4,300 names of which about 500 are synonyms. **A**

The present classification provides 16 divisions as follows:

EARLY-FLOWERING

1. *Duc van Tol Tulips.* Very early Tulips, rarely exceeding 6 in. high. 2. *Single Early Tulips.* 3. *Double Early Tulips.* 4. *Mendel Tulips.** Mid-season, single tall Tulips of medium build. 5. *Triumph Tulips.** Mid-season, single tall Tulips of stouter build than Mendel Tulips and not so tall as Darwin Tulips.

* Double forms of these may appear and would be classed with them.

MAY-FLOWERING

6. *Cottage Tulips.* All Tulips, including lily-flowered, which do not fall within the other classes. 7. *Dutch Breeders.* Flower oval or cupped, brown, purple, or red, but sometimes bronze; base white or yellow, but generally stained blue or green to blue-black. 8. *English Breeders.* Flowers forming one-third to a half of a hollow ball when fully expanded; base always white or yellow, without trace of other colour.

9. *Darwin Tulips.* Lower portion of flower usually rectangular in outline; segments of good substance; stems tall and strong. 10. *Broken Dutch Breeders.* 11. *Broken English Breeders.* 12. *Rembrandt Tulips.* Broken Darwin Tulips. 13. *Broken Cottage Tulips.* 14. *Parrot Tulips.* Varieties with laciniate segments. 15. *Late Double Tulips.* 16. *Species and First Crosses between species.*

In describing the colours of Tulips certain terms have been long used. The breeder Tulips as already stated are self-coloured, but when they 'break' the colour appears in the form of stripes, usually on a white or yellow ground, and each group of broken Tulips (i.e. Divisions 10, 11, 12, and 13 in the above classification) is subdivided according to the colouring and the ground: thus *Roses* have rose or cerise markings on a white ground; *Bybloemen* have violet or purple markings on a white ground; *Bizarres* have brown, red, or purple markings on a yellow ground. The colour may be in streaks in the middle of the segments as well as on the margins, when the flower is said to be *flamed*, or it may be of fine lines, making a border to the segments, when the flower is described as *feathered*.

No wild species as at present known can be pointed to with certainty as the species from which the garden Tulips have been derived. The evidence of the chromosome-behaviour and their invariable interfertility suggest that they are all derived from one species and are not of hybrid origin though they present features, e.g. the white of the flower seen in many of them, which are not known in combination with their other characters in any wild species. As Sir Daniel Hall, in *The Genus Tulipa*, has pointed out, all wild species save the *Clusiana-stellata* group, with which the garden Tulips will not cross, have yellow bases. The garden Tulips therefore probably arose from a yellow-based species which gave white-based mutants under cultivation and the intercrossing of such variants gave rise to the garden Tulips of Turkey from which ours are directly derived. For a discussion on the point the work cited should be consulted. The probability seems to be that the original species was one closely related to *T. Gesneriana.* It has been surmised that the dwarf Duc van Tol Tulips have been derived from a dwarf species of S. Russia sometimes called *T. suaveolens*, but no direct proof is forthcoming. The Dutch and English Breeder Tulips, like the Cottage Tulips, were selected seedlings raised in gardens from the original garden Tulips of Turkey, and their form can be matched among the illustrations of early Turkish and Dutch garden Tulips. The Parrot Tulips are a later garden-raised group, perhaps from the variety of *T. Gesneriana* called *dracontia*. The robust race known as Darwin Tulips with square-based flowers was introduced in 1899, and this group has provided many of the best-known and most widely grown of present-day varieties. Messrs. Krelage of Haarlem were pioneers with this race and in 1915 the same firm first flowered plants derived from the crossing of Darwin and Duc van Tol Tulips, introduced in 1921 and distinguished as Mendel Tulips in 1923. The Tulips of this race are intermediate between their parents, and many varieties of the same breeding have been added since. In 1923, too, Messrs. Zandbergen of Rijnsburg introduced another race raised by Messrs. Zocher and Co. of Haarlem which were probably the result of crossing Single Early varieties with Dutch Breeder, Cottage, and Darwin Tulips. The name Triumph Tulips was given to this race by Messrs. Zandbergen, and many others of the same breeding have since been added. The Cottage Tulips, as might be expected from the definition of the group, vary greatly in form and 4 well-marked types may be distinguished, the true cup type as in Bouton d'Or, the long-pointed type, often with a distinct waist, as in Mrs. Moon, the type with pointed reflexing segments, as in Retroflexa, and the long egg-shaped type as in John Ruskin.

While some Tulips will persist for a long time if left in cultivated ground, and a few will even hold their own in grass, they usually deteriorate when they become crowded and are far better if lifted annually and replanted in late October or early November. If planted earlier they are apt to have their foliage damaged by frosts and laid open to the attacks of the fungus disease called 'Fire'. They grow best in a well-drained sandy soil with some leaf-mould, but no fresh manure should come in contact with the bulbs. Well-rotted cow-dung or soil from an old hotbed may be added with advantage, but this should be done some months before the bulbs are planted. A dressing of fine bone-meal or steamed bone-flour at the time of planting assists in the making of good bulbs for future use. In heavier soils a little sand below and around the bulbs will be of assistance, but every care must be taken to ensure good drainage. The bulbs should be planted 5 or 6 in. apart and should have about 4 in. of soil above them. Except in very sandy soil the bulbs should be planted with a trowel, not a dibber, or, in large plantings in beds from which the soil is taken out to the necessary depth, the bulbs placed on the bottom and covered with soil from the next bed, and so on. Nothing further except hoeing between the rows to keep the surface soil from caking and to repress weeds is necessary until flowering. As the flowers are going over they should be broken off just below the flower so as to prevent the withered petals and stamens from falling into the ground where they are likely to be attacked by the 'fire' fungus and a fruitful source of infection in the succeeding year. The immature seed pod is also removed and the food made in the leaves is then wholly directed to the developing bulb. If seed is needed, this, of course, cannot be done. When the leaves and stems have quite withered the bulbs should be dug up, dried in a shady place or cool airy shed (not in the sun), in a thin layer, cleaned, and graded, and stored in a dry cool place until autumn. They are sometimes attacked by aphides in the store, and this is a frequent cause of the spread of the virus that leads to breaking, and measures should therefore be taken to deal with this attack. If it is necessary to remove the plants to make room for summer-bedding plants, they should be lifted carefully without damage to the leaves and laid in a bed of ashes in a sunny place or planted in a spare border. In mixed borders the bulbs may be left in the ground, but the leaves should not be removed until they have withered. Some varieties are less adversely affected by being left undisturbed than others, among them the early-flowering types especially.

Some Tulips are excellent pot plants, especially the dwarf early-flowering varieties, both single and double. A compost of loam with some sand to lighten it and decayed hotbed manure suits them and 3, 4, or 5 bulbs may be put into a 5-in. pot. The treatment should be the same as for Hyacinths (q.v.). Some varieties are also excellent for forcing, but here the choice of varieties is of great importance. For a list *see* Supplement. Forcing is usually done in boxes as for Narcissi, and the bulbs should be specially prepared for the purpose. The most important thing, given good firm, heavy bulbs of normal size for the variety, is the temperature at which the bulbs are kept after lifting. **A**

Most Tulips, both those of garden origin and the wild species (*see* **Tulipa**), produce offsets freely, and these can be readily removed when the bulbs are cleaned after lifting. As they reproduce the parents they afford a ready and fairly rapid means of propagation. Usually all the offsets of a broken Tulip carry the virus too, but occasionally the virus has not yet spread to all the offsets and the breeder and broken types may both be produced, but that is rare. True sporting occasionally occurs, but apart from this the only way of obtaining new varieties is by seed-raising. The seed is best sown as soon as ripe, but it may be kept until February. It should be sown in boxes of light, sandy soil and put into a cold frame where the seedlings will appear in March or early April. They are best left in the boxes until the following year, being given protection during the winter, but no artificial heat. The following autumn the little bulbs should be planted out in a prepared bed of light soil, giving room to develop, and grown on there until of flowering size, a matter of 4 or 5 years or more. The first flowers, though they show the colour and to some extent the form, rarely give an idea of the true characters of the plant and the most promising at least should be grown on in the ordinary way for another year before it is decided to discard them. Only a very small proportion, as is to be expected, will be an advance upon existing varieties and, as has already been said, all will usually be self-coloured. A further period must elapse before they 'break'. Both offsets and seedlings usually produce only one leaf from a bulb until the flowering stage is reached, such plants are sometimes called widows.

A peculiar type of natural propagation is seen in the 'droppers' which are sometimes formed.

DISEASES. When in store, if conditions are not satisfactory, Tulip bulbs may be rotted by such fungi as Penicillium sp. causing Green Moulds (q.v.) or by Fusarium sp. and similar fungi. When growing, Tulips in forcing houses may suffer from Root Rot due to Pythium sp. especially if the soil is kept very wet. Perhaps the most important disease of this type among forced Tulips is Shanking due to the fungi *Phytophthora cryptogea* and *P. erythroseptica* which cause rotting of the roots and basal part of the bulb with blackening extending up the central parts, the result being that growth of the flower shoot is dwarfed or the bulb does not flower at all. Great care must be taken to destroy affected plants and owing to the oospores of these fungi contaminating the soil it must be carefully discarded and fresh soil obtained for future Tulips. Wet soil must be avoided, but it must be stated that where the disease is serious the soil may require to be sterilized. Probably the most important Tulip disease in outdoor or indoor crops is the one known as Fire due to *Botrytis tulipae*. This shows as specks or streaks on foliage and flowers, the spots are first water-soaked (q.v.), then brown, and the tips of the leaves may become dark brown and scorched in appearance. The flower petals are spotted and the flower-stalk may be attacked in the axil of a leaf so seriously that the plant topples over. The fungus forms sclerotia of very small pin-head size on all affected material and also on the fleshy scales of the bulb which thus carry the disease. The soil of the old bed is also contaminated by sclerotia. It is essential to remove first affected leaves and in severe attacks to remove the flowers before the petals fall. Where the foliage suffers severely this must be removed when it has yellowed and before the fungus is able to grow down to the bulb. Affected beds should not be used for Tulips for some years. Spraying or dusting with sulphur is not effective, and copper-containing sprays are likely to injure Tulip leaves. The disease is rather seasonal and is encouraged by cold moist weather, so that the site for Tulips should be well drained and the bulbs planted deeply and as late as possible, so that the shoots may miss some of the cold wet weather in early spring. Tulips should be lifted every year and bulbs sorted so that diseased ones can be discarded and only healthy flowering-sized ones replanted. In glasshouses it is especially important to give good ventilation, avoid excessive moisture, and remove the first signs of Fire disease on the foliage. Grey Bulb Rot of Tulips is due to the fungus *Sclerotium tuliparum.* This causes a grey soft rot of the bulb, usually at the nose, and affects the young growing stem so that, unlike Fire disease, plants affected by Grey Bulb Rot rarely grow far above ground. The bulb is quickly destroyed and the fungus forms moderately large brownish-black sclerotia on the rotted parts, and these also contaminate the soil. There is no cure for affected bulbs and they should be removed and burnt. Tulips should not be grown for several years in the affected bed. In forcing Tulips it is said that this disease can be avoided to a large extent by planting the bulbs so that the nose is left showing above ground. There is a Rust of Tulips due to *Puccinia Prostii*, causing yellow pustules or spots on the leaves, but this is very rare in Great Britain. Of non-parasitic diseases Topple or Wet Stem is seen when the base of the stem of forced Tulips shrivels and exudes a sugary fluid, while the plant falls over. The cause is somewhat obscure, but the trouble is thought to be encouraged by forcing at too high a temperature when the humidity is excessive. Wide and rapid variations in temperature should be avoided. It is said that Topple can be checked by putting calcium nitrate into the water used for watering at the rate of 2 oz. to the gallon of water, but this may cause injury in some varieties. Chalkiness is a trouble which shows when the outer and perhaps the inner scales assume a hard white appearance resembling chalk. This can be caused either by the attack of such storage fungi as *Penicillium* sp. or Green Moulds, by badly ventilated and humid storage conditions, or even by injury due to drying the bulbs in hot sunshine after lifting. It is not necessary to expose the bulbs to very hot sun for a long period. Hard Base occurs, especially in the variety Couronne D'Or, when there is sometimes a peculiar roundness in the base of the bulbs and no root ridge is present. In such bulbs the roots cannot emerge properly and may grow upwards between the outermost fleshy scale and the one inside it. It is best to treat such bulbs by cutting through the outermost fleshy scale just above the rooting base with the point of a knife. There is a virus disease of Tulips called Breaking due to two viruses (Tulipa Virus 1 and T.V. 2). The symptoms are that self-coloured flowers show white flecks and stripes down the petals. This appearance has been known at least since the year 1576, but has only recently been proved to be due to a virus. Some people like the appearance, but in a pure stock it is necessary to discard the plants showing Breaking or the trouble will increase. Aphides are the chief means of spread. Practically all Tulips are susceptible, but the early-flowering ones are not so likely to be affected, probably because the aphides are not then so prevalent and spread is limited. Nevertheless Tulips showing Breaking should be destroyed.

(D. E. G.)

TULIP, AFRICAN. *See* **Haemanthus coccineus.**

TULIP, CALIFORNIAN. *See* **Calochortus.**

TULIP, DROOPING. *See* **Fritillaria Meleagris.**

TULIP, GOLDEN STAR. *See* **Calochortus pulchellus.**

TULIP TREE. *See* **Liriodendron Tulipifera.**

TULIP TREE, LAUREL-LEAVED. *See* **Magnolia grandiflora.**

TU'LIPA (*tulbend*, the Turkish name for a turban, which the flower much resembles). FAM. *Liliaceae*. A genus of perhaps 100 species of herbs with tunicated bulbs, the tunics sometimes woolly within. Stem simple, few-leaved, 1-, 2-, or 3-flowered. Leaves linear or broadly ovate or lanceolate. Flowers erect or rarely nodding, showy; perianth deciduous, bell- or somewhat funnel-shaped; segments distinct, erect or erecto-patent, sub-equal, often blotched inside near base; base ground colour usually yellow, rarely white; stamens 6, hypogynous, shorter than perianth; filaments more or less flattened, narrowed, or shortly filiform at apex; anthers oblong-linear, erect, dehiscing laterally; ovary 3-celled, many-seeded; stigmas 3-cleft, prominent, sessile or with a style. For general cultivation *see* **Tulip.** The classification followed here is that adopted in Sir A. D. Hall's *The Genus Tulipa* (1940) in the main. Several plants which have been collected wild, mainly in France and Italy, and were regarded and named as species, are now considered to be escapes derived from plants in cultivation and really belonging to the race of Garden Tulips, e.g. *T. aximensis*. The chief of these have been included below, but there are many others; to this group of Tulips the name Neo-tulipae has been applied. A small group, natives of China and Japan, of little horticultural importance, has been separated into a new genus, **Amana** (q.v.). The Tulips proper are natives of Europe, W. and Cent. Asia, and N. Africa, and are hardy. While the great race of Garden Tulips (*see* **Tulip**) takes pride of place in most gardens, many of the species are very beautiful, e.g. *T. Clusiana*, the easily grown *T. Kaufmanniana*, Tulips of the group *T. Eichleri*, *T. Fosteriana*, *T. Greigii*, *T. ingens*, which are better in frames where their large flowers can be protected in inclement weather, *T. sylvestris* and its sweet-scented relatives for naturalizing in stony ground, *T. Celsiana* and *T. tarda* for the rock-garden, to mention only a few. Of some of these, fine seedling variations have been raised.

The main bases of classification are found first in the presence or absence of a tuft of hairs at the base of the filaments, giving the two main groups, Eriostemones and Leiostemones respectively; then in the cottony coating of the inside of the tunic or its absence; and then mainly in habit and floral details.

KEY

1.	*Filaments quite glabrous*	2
1.	*Filaments hairy at base*	43
2.	*Bulb tunic glabrous or nearly so*	3
2.	*Bulb tunic more or less hairy within*	14
3.	*Plant 1-fld.*	4
3.	*Plant with 2 or more fl.*	12
4.	*Fl. nodding in bud*	T. Ostrowskiana
4.	*Fl. erect in bud*	5
5.	*Late-flowering; lvs. shining green, glabrous*	T. Sprengeri
5.	*Lvs. glaucous*	6
6.	*Fl. crimson-scarlet with yellow-edged black blotch*	7
6.	*Fl. yellow*	10
7.	*Perianth segs. broad, not reflexing; fl. campanulate*	T. Gesneriana
7.	*Fl. not campanulate*	8
8.	*Fl. opening flat, segs. narrow*	T. boeotica
8.	*Fl. not opening flat*	9
9.	*Segs. long, incurved*	T. armena
9.	*Segs. reflexing*	T. suaveolens
10.	*Fl. primrose-yellow, segs. reflexing*	T. hungarica
10.	*Fl. suffused green*	11
11.	*Segs. long, incurved, pale yellow suffused green at first*	T. galatica
11.	*Segs. pointed and reflexing, red and green at back*	T. altaica
12.	*Stem with some axillary fls.*	13
12.	*Two or more fls. from ground level*	T. Kolpakowskiana
13.	*Fl. with black blotch, campanulate, segs. incurving*	T. rhodopea
13.	*Fl. without black blotch, segs. narrow, reflexing*	T. iliensis
14.	*Bulb tunic with a little long silky hair*	15
14.	*Bulb tunic lined with much hair or with a tuft at apex*	23
15.	*Anthers long and twisted*	T. Kaufmanniana
15.	*Anthers normal*	16
16.	*Fl. with black blotch half length of segs.*	T. Micheliana
16.	*Fl. without or with a smaller black blotch*	17
17.	*Lvs. marked with purple stripes*	T. Greigii
17.	*Lvs. green*	18
18.	*Lvs. with V-shaped median channel*	19
18.	*Lvs. flat*	20
19.	*Fl. solitary; lvs. numerous*	T. Schmidtii
19.	*Fl. 2 or more; segs. without blotch*	T. praestans
20.	*Black blotch margined*	21
20.	*Black blotch without margin*	T. ingens
21.	*Fl. wide campanulate, buff without*	T. Eichleri
21.	*Fl. opening flat*	22
22.	*Stem glabrous; lvs. up to 4 in. wide*	T. Fosteriana
22.	*Stem pubescent; lvs. up to 3 in. wide*	T. Tubergeniana
23.	*Bulb tunic lined with much straight hair*	T. lanata
23.	*Bulb tunic with tuft of hair at apex or felted within with curled hair*	24
24.	*Bulb tunic lined with curled hair*	25
24.	*Bulb tunic with tuft of hair at apex*	36
25.	*Lvs. with V-shaped median channel*	T. Hoogiana
25.	*Basal lvs. flat*	26
26.	*Fl. wine-red within*	T. cypria
26.	*Fl. scarlet to brown-red*	27
27.	*Lvs. green*	28
27.	*Lvs. glaucous*	29
28.	*Perianth segs. 2¼ to 3¼ in. long*	T. Oculus-solis
28.	*Perianth segs. 1¼ to 2 in. long*	T. Julia
29.	*Stems about 4 in. long; lvs. usually undulate; blotch margined*	T. undulatifolia
29.	*Stem 6 in. or more long; lvs. plane*	30
30.	*Basal lvs. about 3 in. wide*	31
30.	*Basal lvs. usually not over 2 in. wide*	32
31.	*Stem up to 20 in. long, outer segs. with median stripe*	T. praecox
31.	*Stem about 8 in. long, fl. campanulate, broad*	T. Stapfii
32.	*Basal lvs. scarcely over 1 in. wide*	33
32.	*Basal lvs. about 2 in. wide*	35
33.	*Perianth segs. about 1½ in. long, reflexed*	T. sharonensis
33.	*Perianth segs. 2 in. or more long*	34
34.	*Fl. cup-shaped; segs. over 3 in. long, blotch deep olive*	T. Veneris
34.	*Fl. loose, open; segs. 2 to 3 in. long, blotch black-purple*	T. systola
35.	*Perianth segs. equal; fl. cup-shaped; outer segs reflexing*	T. aleppensis
35.	*Fl. opens flat; outer segs. slightly the longer, recurved at margins*	T. kuschkensis
36.	*Plant more than 1-fld.*	T. Aitchisonii
36.	*Plant 1-fld.*	37
37.	*Fl. scarlet*	38
37.	*Fl. yellow or white with or without red markings*	40
38.	*Basal lvs. broad*	T. montana
38.	*All lvs. linear*	39
39.	*Lvs. crowded in basal rosette*	T. linifolia
39.	*Lvs. scattered on stem*	T. Maximowiczii
40.	*Fl. yellow with or without crimson markings*	41
40.	*Fl. white stained crimson at back*	42
41.	*Lvs. about ½ in. wide*	T. stellata chrysantha
41.	*Lvs. about ¼ in. wide; fl. pale buff-yellow*	T. Batalinii
42.	*Stamens and blotch yellow*	T. stellata
42.	*Stamens and blotch deep violet*	T. Clusiana
43.	*Bulb tunic lined with long silky hairs*	44
43.	*Bulb tunic with few short hairs only*	45
44.	*Fl. spreading cup-shaped, segs. nearly 2 in. long, broad, white (except blotch) within*	T. polychroma
44.	*Fl. opening to a pointed star, segs. about 1¼ in. long, ivory (except blotch) within*	T. turkestanica
45.	*Fl. yellow with or without colour on back of segs.*	46
45.	*Fl. white or coloured*	50
46.	*Plant dwarf; lvs. about ¼ in. wide; segs. about 1 in. long*	T. urumiensis
46.	*Plant larger*	47

47. *Fl. without green on back; lvs. narrow; stem slender* — T. Grisebachiana
47. *Fl. greenish or reddish on back* — 48
48. *Stem 6 in. long; fl. reddish at back. May* — T. Celsiana
48. *Segs. 2 in. or more long* — 49
49. *Stems tinged reddish; segs. about 2 in. long* — T. australis
49. *Stems green; segs. over 2 in. long* — T. sylvestris
50. *Fl. white to cream white, at least in upper half* — 51
50. *Fl. coloured* — 53
51. *Stem 6 in. long, 2-fld.* — T. primulina
51. *Stem 3 to 4 in. long, up to 6-fld.* — 52
52. *Fl. ivory with yellow base; segs. ¾ in. long* — T. biflora
52. *Fl. white in upper third, yellow below; segs. 1½ in. long* — T. tarda
52. *Fl. white tinged pink, stained yellow below; segs. 1¼ in. long* — T. cretica
53. *Basal blotch yellow* — 54
53. *Basal blotch dark or undefined* — 57
54. *Fl. light rose to lilac* — 55
54. *Fl. mauve* — 56
55. *Lvs. about ⅜ in. wide, slightly glaucous; fl. opening to wide, flat star, segs. 1¼ in. long* — T. humilis
55. *Lvs. ⅛ in. wide, glabrous; fl. globular; segs. about 1 in long* — T. Lownei
56. *Fl. pale mauve; segs. 2¼ in. long; yellow blotch well defined* — T. saxatilis
56. *Fl. dark mauve, rather smaller; yellow blotch less defined* — T. Bakeri
57. *Stem 2 to 3 in. long* — 58
57. *Stem taller* — 59
58. *Fl. pink with yellow median band outside; segs. 1¼ in. long* — T. Aucheriana
58. *Fl. violet; blotch blue; segs. 2¼ in. long* — T. pulchella
59. *Perianth segs. narrow, pointed; fl. starry* — T. Orphanidea
59. *Perianth segs. wider* — 60
60. *Stem 6 to 8 in. long; segs. copper to scarlet within* — T. Hageri
60. *Stem 12 in. long; segs. orange within* — T. Whittallii

T. acumina'ta. Turkish Tulip. *fl.* of varying colours, 3 to 4 in. long; segs. all alike, narrowed gradually to a long point; peduncle glabrous. April. *l.* and bulb as in *T. Gesneriana.* (B.R. 127 as *T. cornuta.*) A form of the Garden Tulip.

T. Aitchiso'nii. *fl.* 1 or 2, wide starry, white with purple blotch or wholly yellow, marked crimson on back of outer segs.; segs. about 1½ in. long, bluntly pointed. April. *l.* 2 to 4, spreading, 3½ to 4 in. long, about ¼ in. wide, glabrous. Stem 1½ to 2 in. h. *Bulb* round, about ½ in. across. Chitral, Kashmir. 1935. (H.T. 14, 15.) var. **cashmeria'na,** *fl.* yellow, up to 6 in. h., stem 2- or 3-fld. Kashmir. A small tulip best in pots in cool house.

T. aleppen'sis. *fl.* solitary, cup-shaped, crimson-scarlet with rounded yellow-edged black blotch; segs. nearly 3 in. long, inner more rounded, slightly shorter, outer slightly reflexing. April. *l.* 4 or 5, upright, lowest about 12 in. long, 2 in. wide, slightly glaucous and ciliate. Stem about 8 in. h. *Bulb* ovoid, 1½ in. wide. Syria. (H.T. 26, 27.) Stoloniferous. The plant described is that identified by Hall as *T. aleppensis* and differs considerably from the true *T. aleppensis* of Boissier ex Regel.

T. alta'ica. *fl.* solitary, pointed cup-shaped, light primrose yellow, back of outer segs. coloured green and red; segs. 2 in. long, long acuminate. April. *l.* 3, lowest 6 in. long, 2¼ in. wide, slightly glaucous. Stem about 8 in. h. *Bulb* 1½ in. thick. Cent. Asia. (H.T. 37.)

T. arme'na. *fl.* solitary, loosely globular, deep crimson-scarlet with deep blue or olive blotch, sometimes margined yellow or wholly yellow; outer segs. reflexing, 2¼ in. long, 1 in. wide, pointed inner shorter, rounder. *l.* 4, 2 at base 6 in. long, 1 in. wide, slightly glaucous. Stem about 8 in. h. *Bulb* ovoid, about 1 in. thick. Asia Minor, Armenia.

T. Aucheria'na. *fl.* 1 to 3, flat star-shaped when open, pink with yellow-brown-stained blotch, outer segs. with broad greenish-yellow stripe, inner with 2 green or brown veins on backs; segs. 1¼ in. long. April. *l.* 2 to 5, near ground, strap-shaped, about 5 in. long, ⅜ in. wide, slightly wavy at margin. Stem 2 to 3 in. h. *Bulb* about ½ in. thick. Persia, Syria. (H.T. 9.)

T. austra'lis. *fl.* fragrant, in bud urn-shaped, opening to a wide star, clear yellow, outer segs. greenish and often reddish on back; segs. 2 in. long, ⅜ in. wide, pointed, reflexing at tip in age. *l.* 3 to 5, lowest 2 in. long, ⅛ in. wide, strap-shaped, glabrous. Stem 1-, rarely 2-fld., 6 to 10 in. h. *Bulb* ovoid, pointed, 1¼ in. thick. Mediterranean region. (B.M. 717, 9078 as var. *arvorum.*)

T. aximen'sis.† *fl.* deep red with yellow-margined green blotch. Savoy. 1894. (*Neo-tulipae, see* **T. Gesneriana.**)

T. Ba'keri. Closely allied to *T. saxatilis* but much deeper in colour, less shiny *l.*, and aerial stem often unbranched. March. Crete. 1926. (B.M. 9607; H.T. 9.)

T. Baldacci.† *fl.* purplish-red with yellow-grey blotch. N. Italy. 1893. (*Neo-tulipae, see* **T. Gesneriana.**)

T. Batali'nii. *fl.* buff-yellow with pale olive-tinged blotch, otherwise like *T. linifolia.* Bokhara. (B.M. 7991; H.T. 18.)

T. biflo'ra. *fl.* 1 to 5 near top of peduncles, about 3 in. h., opening flat, white with yellow basal blotch, outer segs. stained green and crimson at back, inner with green median line; segs. ¾ in. long. February. *l.* linear, 5 in. long, ⅜ in. wide, slightly glaucous. *Bulb* ovoid, ⅝ in. thick. Caspian and Caucasus regions. (B.M. 6518; H.T. 11.) var. **ma'jor** is somewhat larger, and *T. turkestanica* which differs in the bulb (*see* Key) and in having orange (not yellow) filaments and purple or deep brown (not yellow, purple-tipped) anthers has often been confused with this.

T. Billietia'na. *fl.* yellow. Savoy. 1858. (*Neo-tulipae, see* **T. Gesneriana.**)

T. boeot'ica. *fl.* solitary, opening flat and starry, scarlet-orange, with broadly yellow-margined olive blotch; segs. 2¼ in. long, outer more pointed than inner. April. *l.* 4, lower 2 about 6 in. long, 2¼ wide, glaucous. Stem about 6 in. h., hairy. Greece.

T. Bonarotia'na.† *fl.* yellow and red. Florence, Italy. 1822. (*Neo-tulipae, see* **T. Gesneriana.**)

T. Borszczow'ii. *fl.* crimson to yellow with a large black-purple blotch at base of each seg., bell-shaped; outer segs. ovate, acuminate, inner wedge-shaped, cuspidate. March, April. *l.* long, upright. *Bulb* with long hairs inside tunic. Cent. Asia. Probably not now in cultivation, the plants so named being a form of *T. Oculus-solus.*

T. Celsia'na. *fl.* 1 to 3 on short pedicels, flat star-shaped when open, yellow, much red-tinged without, fragrant, smaller than *T. australis* to which it is nearly allied. May. 6 in. h. *Bulb* round, 1 in. across. Spain, Morocco, Atlas Mts. (B.M. 717 as *T. Breyniana*; B.M. 9078 as *T. australis arvorum.*) SYN. *T. persica.* Stoloniferous.

T. chrysan'tha (of gardens, not Boissier). A synonym of *T. stellata chrysantha.*

T. Clusia'na.* Lady Tulip. *fl.* solitary, flat starry when open, white with small purple blotch, outer segs. red outside; segs. 2 in long, ⅜ in. wide, pointed. April, May. *l.* 4, two lower, 8 to 10 in. long. ⅜ in. wide, folded, slightly glaucous. *Bulb* round, 1 in. across. Persia Iraq, Afghanistan. (B.M. 1390.)

T. conni'vens.† *fl.* scarlet with black blotch narrowly margined yellow. Italy. 1884. (*Neo-tulipae, see* **T. Gesneriana.**)

T. coryneste'mon. *fl.* solitary, opening flat, yellow, unblotched, tinged green and red outside; segs. 1¼ to 2 in. long. April. *l.* glaucous, glabrous. *Bulb* about 1 in. in diam. Cent. Asia. (H.T. 21.) Notable for thickened apex of the filaments.

T. cre'tica. *fl.* whitish tinged pink, stained yellow at base, outer segs. tinged purple and green, inner pink at backs; outer segs. 1¼ in. long, spreading, inner erect. April. *l.* 2 or 3, flattish, dark green, glabrous. Stem 1- to 3-fld., 3 to 4 in. long. *Bulb* ovoid, about 1 in. thick. Crete. (H.T. 9.) Stoloniferous.

T. cuspida'ta. *See* **T. Stapfii.**

T. cyp'ria. *fl.* solitary, cup-shaped, deep wine-red with blue-black blotch; segs. 3¼ in. long, pointed, outer reflexing. April. *l.* 4, lower 8 in. long, 1½ in. wide. Stem 8 in. h. *Bulb* ovoid, 1¼ in. thick. Cyprus. 1930. (B.M. 9363.) Needs cool house.

T. dasyste'mon (of gardens). A synonym of *T. tarda.* The true plant does not appear to be in cultivation.

T. Did'ieri.† *fl.* scarlet with broadly yellow-margined black blotch. N. Italy. 1846. (*Neo-tulipae, see* **T. Gesneriana.**)

T. Eich'leri. *fl.* solitary, wide bell-shaped, bright glossy scarlet with yellow-margined black blotch; segs. 4 in. long, 2 in. wide, light buff outside, outer acuminate, inner obovate. April. *l.* 4 or 5, basal about 8 in. long, 2¼ wide, glaucous. Stem 6 to 8 in. h., hairy. *Bulb* ovoid, about 2 in. wide. Transcaucasus. (B.M. 6191; H.T. 31.)

T. ele'gans. *fl.* bright red, bell-shaped, eye yellow, segs. equal, oblong, narrowed to an acute point; stigma very large; peduncle finely downy. April, May. Belongs to the Garden Tulip group. Probably of garden origin.

T. erythronioi'des. *See* **Amana graminifolia.**

T. etru'sca.† *fl.* crimson with narrow yellow-margined black blotch. Italy. 1884. (*Neo-tulipae, see* **T. Gesneriana.**)

T. Fosteria'na. *fl.* solitary, opening flat, bright glossy scarlet, lighter without, with black blotch margined yellow; segs. over 3 in. long, 1½ in. wide, bluntly pointed, inner rather shorter. March, April. *l.* 3, lowest 8 in. long, 4 in. wide, more or less glaucous. Stem about 8 in. h., glabrous. *Bulb* globose, 2 in. thick. Samarkand. (H.T. 32.) Several varieties have been grown. **Defiance** has a yellow blotch and yellow stamens. **Mme Lefeber** (Red Emperor) is up to 24 in. h.

T. Fransonia'na.† *fl.* rose-red with violet-purple blotch narrowly margined white. Italy. 1854. (*Neo-tulipae, see* **T. Gesneriana.**)

T. galat'ica. *fl.* solitary, globular, pale buff-yellow with smoky stain at base, greenish when young; outer segs. nearly 3 in. long, pointed, inner shorter and less pointed. April. *l.* 4, lower about 5 in. long, ⅜ in. wide, flat, slightly glaucous. *Bulb* about 1 in. thick, ovoid. Asia Minor. (H.T. 21.)

T. Gesneria'na. The name given to the Tulips introduced into W. Europe in the 16th century (1554 onwards) from Turkish gardens. The Turks are said to have grown and admired these plants 'for the variety and beauty of their colours', and the chief characteristic of this cultivated race is its astonishing capacity for variation. To it belongs the whole galaxy of 'garden' Tulips developed in W. Europe (*see* **Tulip**), but to this day the origin of this race of plants remains uncertain. No wild species can confidently be claimed as its progenitor, though certain Tulips from S. Russia and Armenia have been identified with it. In certain places in Italy and SE. France a number of Tulips have been collected and described as distinct species, but it is evident that they are descendants of garden Tulips which have escaped and become naturalized. They are collectively known as *Neo-tulipae* and are nothing more than variants of *T. Gesneriana.* The salient features of this 'species' are bulb tunics glabrous or with very few hairs; *l.* 3 to 4, ovate to lanceolate, long, tapered to the apex, the lowest 1¼ to 3 in. wide, glabrous; stem 1 to 1½ ft. h., glabrous; *fl.* 2 to 4 in. long, extremely variable in shape and coloration. April, May.

T. Greig'ii.* *fl.* solitary, wide cup-shaped, bright scarlet with a dark olive or black blotch on the bright yellow base; outer segs. 3¼ in. long, 2½ in. wide, mucronate, reflexing and with recurved margins, inner slightly larger, erect. April. *l.* 3 or 4, lowest 8 in. long, over 3 in. wide, glaucous, usually with purple-brown stripes. Stem 6 to 8 in. long, downy. *Bulb* ovoid, 1¼ in. thick. Turkistan. (B.M. 6177; H.T. 33.)

T. Grisebachia'na. A tall (up to 12 in. h.) slender, narrow-leaved form closely related to *T. sylvestris,* without green colouring at back of *fl.* Herzegovina, Montenegro.

T. Ha'geri. *fl.* bell-shaped, copper to nearly scarlet within, with an olive blotch sometimes margined yellow, outer segs. buff and green, inner copper with a green median band on backs; segs. 2 in. long, 1 in. wide, rather obtuse. April. *l.* 4 or 5, strap-shaped, lowest 6 to 8 in. long, about ½ in. wide, glabrous, dark green. Stem 1- to 4-fld., about 6 in. h. *Bulb* ovoid, about 1 in. wide. Greece, Asia Minor. (B.M. 6242; H.T. 3 and 4.) var. **ni'tens** has a round bell-shaped *fl.,* orange-scarlet within with a blue-purple blotch, and broader glaucous *l.*

T.×harlemen'sis. A group of hybrids between *T. Greigii* and *T. Kaufmanniana,* including Franz Schubert, Glück, Handel, Robert Schumann, and Rossini.

T. Hoogia'na.* *fl.* solitary, of loose cup form, bright scarlet with a long blotch, black to olive, margined yellow; outer segs. 6 in. long, 2 in. wide, lanceolate, pointed, inner narrower. May. *l.* up to 8, channelled, lowest 8 in. long, 2¼ in. wide, glaucous. Stem 12 in. long, glabrous. *Bulb* ovoid, up to 2 in. thick. Cent. Asia. (H.T. 29.) Needs a warm, sheltered place.

T. hu'milis. *fl.* 1 or 2, long and narrow, pale rose to deep rose-purple with a yellow base, outer segs. dirty white, stained purple and brown, inner with a crimson median line outside, about 2½ in. long, ⅖ in. wide, pointed. February, March. *l.* 2 to 4, linear, lowest 4 in. long, ⅖ in. wide, slightly glaucous, dark green. About 4 in. h. *Bulb* ovoid, ½ in. thick. NW. Persia. (B.M. 9048.)

T. hunga'rica.† *fl.* yellow, with deeper base. Hungary. 1882.

T. ilien'sis. Closely related to *T. Kolpakowskiana,* but stem 1-rarely 2-fl.; only robust cultivated specimens up to 5-fld. *l.* and *fl.* segs. narrower. *fl.* opening to a star with flat yellow segs. stained red and olive at back. March. Turkistan.

T. in'gens.* *fl.* solitary, loosely cup-shaped, bright glossy scarlet with long black blotch; outer segs. buff and downy outside; segs. 4½ in. long, 1½ in. wide, blunt. April. *l.* 3 to 5, lowest 10 in. long, flat, tapering. Stem reddish, up to 10 in. long. *Bulb* long ovoid about 1¼ in. thick. Cent. Asia. (H.T. 30.) Needs shelter and a warm spot.

T. Ju'lia. *fl.* solitary, cup-shaped, deep scarlet with black blotch with narrow yellow margin; segs. 2 in. long, ¾ in. wide, pointed. *l.* 4, narrow, pointed, upright, lowest about 6 in. long. Stem glabrous, about 6 in. long. *Bulb* about 1¼ in. thick. Transcaucasia.

T. Kaufmannia'na.* Water-lily Tulip. *fl.* solitary, opening to a wide flat star, white, primrose, or yellow with yellow base; outer segs. red-streaked, narrow, elliptic, 3½ in. long, pointed, inner rounded. March. *l.* 3 to 5, lowest 10 in. long, 3½ in. wide, slightly glaucous. Stem about 8 in. long, hairy. *Bulb* about 1½ in. thick. Turkistan. (B.M. 6887; H.T. 34.) Seedlings vary considerably and some good forms have been named. **Brilliant** is soft crimson throughout; **coccin'ea,** scarlet; **Josef Kafka,** buttercup yellow, overlaid vermilion on reverse of pet.; **Lady Rose,** *fl.* large, French Rose with deeper blotch at base inside, outside of pet. overlaid with Porcelain Rose. One of the finest varieties; **ryen'sis,** has distinctive scarlet markings. Hybrids have been raised with *T. Greigii.*

T. Kolpakowskia'na. *fl.* 1 or 2, segs. at first opening flat, later fully reflexed, bright yellow without blotch, backs with olive and red flush, 2¼ in. long, lanceolate. April. *l.* 2 to 4, lowest 8 in. long, 1¼ in. wide, flat, glaucous. Stem about 6 in. long. *Bulb* round, 1 in. thick. Turkistan. (B.M. 6635 as *T. Borszczowi*; H.T. 36.) var. **coccin'ea** is *T. Ostrowskiana.*

T. kuschken'sis. *fl.* solitary, cup-shaped, opening flat, blood-red with a yellow-margined black blotch; segs. about 3 in. long, pointed, margin recurved. April. *l.* 4, narrow, upright, lowest 6½ to 8 in. long, glaucous. Stem about 9 in. long, glabrous. *Bulb* ovoid, about 1½ in. thick. Turkistan, &c. (B.M. 9370; H.T. 28.)

T. lana'ta. *fl.* solitary, wide cup-shaped, matt scarlet with deep olive blotch broadly margined yellow; segs. about 5 in. long, 2½ in. wide. April. *l.* 4 or 5, lowest 10 in. long, 2 in. wide, lanceolate, somewhat glaucous. Stem up to 20 in. long, downy. *Bulb* avoid, about 2 in. thick. Stoloniferous. (B.M. 9151; H.T. 29.)

T. linifo'lia. *fl.* solitary, open, segs. about 2 in. long, ¾ in. wide, pointed, glossy scarlet with black-purple blotch. May. *l.* in a rosette, linear, 3 to 5 in. long, ¼ in. wide. Stem up to 6 in. long. *Bulb* round, ¾ in. thick. Bukhara. (B.M. 7998; H.T. 18.)

Tulipa Kaufmanniana

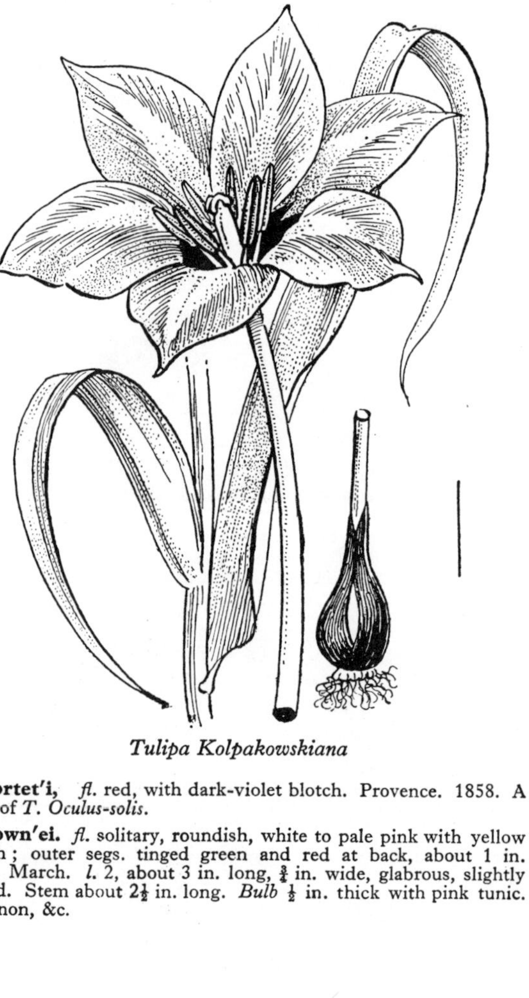

Tulipa Kolpakowskiana

T. Lortet'i, *fl.* red, with dark-violet blotch. Provence. 1858. A form of *T. Oculus-solis.*

T. Lown'ei. *fl.* solitary, roundish, white to pale pink with yellow blotch; outer segs. tinged green and red at back, about 1 in. long. March. *l.* 2, about 3 in. long, ¾ in. wide, glabrous, slightly folded. Stem about 2½ in. long. *Bulb* ½ in. thick with pink tunic. Lebanon, &c.

T. lu'rida. *fl.* crimson-purple, with black blotch. Italy. 1884. (*Neo-tulipae, see* **T. Gesneriana.**)

T. maleo'lens.† *fl.* scarlet with yellow-margined black blotch. Italy. 1823.

T. Marjolet'ti.† *fl.* yellowish, then white, flushed purple outside. Savoy. 1894. (*Neo-tulipae, see* **T. Gesneriana.**)

T. Martellia'na.† *fl.* scarlet with yellow-margined black blotch. Italy. 1884.

T. mauritiana. *fl.* red with yellow base. Savoy. 1858. (*Neo-tulipae, see* **T. Gesneriana.**)

T. Maximowicz'ii. Similar in all respects to *T. linifolia* except that *l.* are scattered, with margins plane instead of undulate. Bokhara.

T. Michelia'na. *fl.* solitary, cup-shaped, pale scarlet with large black blotch broadly margined pale yellow; segs. 2¼ in. long, tapering, pointed. April. *l.* 4, lowest about 6 in. long, glaucous. Stem about 10 in. long with a few purple stripes. *Bulb* ovoid, 1¼ in. thick. Transcaspia and Persia.

T. monta'na. *fl.* solitary, opening nearly flat; deep crimson-scarlet with a small black blotch; segs. 2 in. long. April. *l.* 3 or 4, lowest 4 in. long, ¾ in. wide, lanceolate, flat. Stem about 5 in. long. *Bulb* round, about ¾ in. thick. Persia. (B.R. 1106; H.T. 19; B.M. n.s. 433.) SYN. *T. Wilsoniana.*

T. neglec'ta.† *fl.* lemon-yellow with yellowish base. Italy. 1838. (*Neo-tulipae, see* **T. Gesneriana.**)

T. Oculus-so'lis. *fl.* solitary, opening loosely, dull brownish-scarlet with long black blotch narrowly edged yellow, segs. about 3 in. long, 1 in. wide, pointed, reflexing. April. *l.* 4, lowest 10 in. long, 2 in. wide, upright, pointed, glabrous. Stem about 8 in. long. *Bulb* 1¼ in. thick. Stoloniferous. Italy, France. (H.T. 23.)

T. Orphanid'ea. *fl.* 1 (rarely more), loosely star-shaped when open, dull orange to brown, stained green and purple outside; outer segs. 2 in. long, ⅕ in. wide, inner twice as wide. April. *l.* 3 or 4 towards base of stem, basal *l.* about 8 in. long, folded, narrow. Stem 4 to 8 in. long. *Bulb* ovoid, 1 in. thick. Greece, Turkey. (B.M. 6310; H.T. 5.) var. **Whittal'lii,** *see* **T. Whittallii.**

T. Ostrowskia'na. *fl.* solitary, cup-shaped with bright scarlet, olive blotched segs. reflexing; segs. about 2 in. long, ¾ in. wide. April. *l.* 2 to 4, upright, lowest 8 to 12 in. long, 1¼ in. wide. Stem about 8 in. long. *Bulb* 1½ in. thick. Turkistan. (B.M. 6895; 6710 as *T. Kolpakowskiana*; H.T. 38.) SYN. *T. Korolkovii concolor, T. Kolpakowskiana coccinea.*

T. Passerinia'na.† *fl.* crimson with yellow-margined black blotch. Italy. 1884. (*Neo-tulipae, see* **T. Gesneriana.**)

T. pers'ica. A synonym of *T. Celsiana.*

T. planifo'lia.† *fl.* dark red with black blotch sometimes margined green. Savoy. 1858. (*Neo-tulipae, see* **T. Gesneriana.**)

T. platystig'ma.† *fl.* purplish-rose with blue blotch. France. 1855. (*Neo-tulipae, see* **T. Gesneriana.**)

T. polychro'ma. *fl.* 1 to 5, spreading cup-shaped, white or tinged pink, yellow in lowest third; outer segs. tinged blue-grey at back, up to 1¾ in. long. February. *l.* 2 to 4, upright, up to 6 in. long, glaucous. Stem 4 to 6 in. long, glabrous. *Bulb* ovoid, about ¾ in. thick. Persia, Baluchistan? (H.T. 12.)

T. prae'cox. *fl.* solitary, opening wide, dull scarlet with broad yellow-margined, deep olive blotch; outer segs. dull orange or green without, 2½ in. long, pointed, reflexing, inner shorter and narrower. March. *l.* 3 to 5 upright, lowest 12 in. long, 3¼ in. wide, glaucous. Stem 20 in. long, glabrous, coloured. *Bulb* 1½ in. thick. Stoloniferous. N. Italy. (H.T. 25, 27.)

T. prae'stans. *fl.* 1 to 4, cup-shaped, pale to dark red; segs. 2¼ in. long, 1¼ in. wide, bluntly pointed. April. *l.* 5 or 6 (or more), lowest 10 in. long, 4 in. wide, channelled. Stem up to 18 in. long, more or less downy, coloured below *fl.* *Bulb* ovoid, 1¼ in. thick. Cent. Asia. (B.M. 7920; H.T. 35.) A variable plant.

T. primuli'na. Related to *T. australis.* *fl.* 1 or 2, opening in afternoon, creamy-white, yellowish towards base, marked green and lavender without; segs. about 2 in. long. April. *l.* as in *T. australis.* Stem about 8 in. long. *Bulb* ovoid, about 1 in. thick. Algeria. (B.M. 6786; H.T. 1.) SYN. *T. cuspidata.* Regel.

T. pulchel'la. *fl.* 1 to 3, cup-shaped, opening flat, light crimson to purple with white-margined deep blue blotch; outer segs. green or grey without, about 1¼ in. long, ½ to ¾ in. wide. March. *l.* 2 or 3, strap-shaped, 4 to 6 in. slightly channelled, glabrous. Stem about 4 in. long. *Bulb* ovoid, ¾ in. thick. Asia Minor. 1877. (B.M. 6304; H.T. 6.) Needs protection.

T. retroflex'a. *fl.* bright yellow, about 3 in. long; segs. uniform, oblong, narrowed gradually to acute point; stamens yellow. May. Of Garden Tulip group.

T. rhodo'pea. *fl.* 1 (very rarely 2 or 3 fl. in cultivation), cup-shaped, but star-shaped when open, dull brownish-scarlet, with yellow-margined dark olive or black blotch; segs 2½ in. long, 1 in. wide, outer pointed, inner blunter. April. *l.* 3 to 5, lowest 6 in. long, 2½ in. wide, pointed, glaucous. Stem, about 8 in. long. (up to 12 to 18 in. in wild specimens). *Bulb* ovoid, about 1 in. thick. Bulgaria. (H.T. 22.)

T. saxat'ilis. *fl.* 1 to 3, flat cup-shaped, pale lilac with yellow blotch; segs. 2 in. long, up to 1 in. wide. April. *l.* at base, 6 to 11 in. long, flat, shining green. Stem to 12 in. long. *Bulb* round, over 1 in. thick, tunic yellow-brown, tinged pink. Crete. 1827. (B.M. 6374; H.T. 10.) Needs a well-drained sunny position. Stoloniferous.

T. Schmidt'ii. *fl.* solitary, wide open cup-shape, scarlet with a broadly yellow-margined black blotch; outer segs. 3 to 4 in. long, 1 to 1⅖ in. wide, inner broader. June. *l.* up to 10, upright, lowest 10 to 12 in. long, 1 to 1⅕ in. wide, lanceolate, channelled, slightly glaucous. Stem 16 in. h., glabrous. *Bulb* round, 2 in. thick. Transcaucasia. (B.M. 9535; H.T. 39.)

T. segusia'na. *fl.* deep red with greyish-white blotch with a broad yellow margin. N. Italy. 1894. (*Neo-tulipae, see* **T. Gesneriana.**)

T. seroti'na.† *fl.* crimson with black blotch without margin. Italy. 1838. (*Neo-tulipae, see* **T. Gesneriana.**)

T. sharonen'sis. *fl.* solitary, wide bell-shaped, dark scarlet with dark olive blotch narrowly margined yellow; segs. 1¼ in. long, pointed, reflexing. April. *l.* 3 or 4, upright, narrow, pointed. Stem up to 6 in. long. *Bulb* about 1 to ⅖ in. thick. Palestine.

T. Sommie'ri.† *fl.* rose with yellow base. Italy. 1884. (*Neo-tulipa, see* **T. Gesneriana.**)

T. spathula'ta.† *fl.* scarlet, with narrowly yellow-margined black blotch. Italy. 1839. (*Neo-tulipae, see* **T. Gesneriana.**)

T. Spreng'eri.† *fl.* solitary, opening widely with segs. reflexing, brownish-crimson, much lighter without; outer segs. 2½ in. long, ⅗ in. wide, inner 1 in. wide. May. *l.* 4 to 6, lowest 10 in. long, over 1 in. wide, pointed, glabrous, shining. Stem about 12 in. long. *Bulb* 1 in. or more thick. Asia Minor. 1894. (H.T. 39.) Will put up with shade and naturalize itself.

T. Stapf'ii. *fl.* solitary, cup-shaped, deep crimson-scarlet with small deep-purple blotch with or without a yellow margin; outer segs. 3¼ in. long, 1½ in. wide, inner rather smaller. April. *l.* 4, lower two up to about 10 in. long, 3 in. wide, glaucous. Stem up to about 12 in. long. *Bulb* about 2 in. thick. Persia, Asia Minor. (B.M. 9356; H.T. 24.) SYN. *T. cuspidata* Stapf.

Tulipa stellata

T. stella'ta. *fl.* solitary, star-shaped with recurving segs., white with light-yellow blotch, outer segs. tinged red at back, about 1½ in. long, ⅖ in. wide. April. *l.* 3 to 5, near base, lowest 8 in. long, ⅖ in. wide, somewhat undulate. Stem 6 to 8 in. long, glabrous. *Bulb* nearly round, about ⅘ in. thick. Afghanistan, NW. India. 1827. (B.M. 2762; H.T. 16.) var. **chrysan'tha,** brilliant yellow, with red-tinged back, otherwise like type. (B.M. n.s. 13.)

T. strangula'ta.† *fl.* red, with greyish-black blotch having a broad yellow margin. Italy. 1822. (*Neo-tulipae, see* **T. Gesneriana.**)

T. suaveo'lens. *fl.* solitary, cup-shaped, fragrant, crimson-scarlet with yellow, olive, or black-margined pale yellow blotch; segs. 1⅓ in. long, pointed. March. *l.* 3 to 6, lowest elliptic-lanceolate. Stem about 3 in. long. *Bulb* long ovoid, about ½ in. thick. Hab.? 1608.

T. sylves'tris. *fl.* 1 or 2, long, fragrant clear-yellow with red and green on back of outer segs.; segs. 2 in. long, ⅘ in. wide, reflexing at the reddish tips. April. *l.* 4 or 5, lowest strap-shaped, somewhat channelled, 10 in. long, ⅘ in. wide. Stem rather weak, up to 12 in. long, glabrous, green. *Bulb* ovoid, 1¼ in. thick; tunic yellow, tinged red. Europe (Britain), Persia, N. Africa. (H.T. 3; S.B.F.G. 186 as *T. turcica*; n.s. 4, 97 as *T. repens.*) SYN. *T. florentina.*

T. systo'la. *fl.* of form of *T. Oculus-solis*, scarlet, with deep-purple blotch sometimes margined yellow; segs. 2 to 3 in. long, pointed, inner shorter, rounded. April. *l.* 4, lowest 10 in. long, about 1 in. wide, somewhat glaucous. Stem 6 to 8 in. long, glabrous. *Bulb* ovate, about 1 in. thick. Persia, Iraq, Cyprus, Palestine, &c.

T. tar'da.* *fl.* 1 to 6, flat star-shaped, yellow at base, white in upper fourth, marked green and some red at back of outer and with 2 purple and 1 green line on inner segs.; segs. about 1½ in. long, ⅗ in. wide, lanceolate. May. *l.* 4 to 7, forming a rosette, up to 6½ in. long, ⅘ in. wide, at first folded, glabrous. Stem about 3 in. long. *Bulb* ovoid, up to ⅘ in. thick; tunic yellow. Turkistan. (B.M. 9321; H.T. 13.) SYN. *T. dasystemon* of gardens. Stoloniferous.

T. Tubergenia'na. *fl.* solitary, large and opening to a flat cup, glossy vermilion with a short yellow-margined olive blotch, segs. nearly 4 in. long, 1½ in. wide, pointed or cuspidate. April. *l.* 4 to 5, channelled, lowest to 12 in. long, 2¾ in. wide, glaucous, downy, pointed. Stem about 12 in. long, downy. *Bulb* about 1½ in. thick. Cent. Asia. (H.T. 30.) Near *T. ingens.*

T. turkestan'ica. *fl.* 1 to 7, pointed star-shape, 2 in. across, ivory-white with orange base, outer segs. reddish without; segs. 1⅓ in. long, ⅖ in. wide. February. *l.* 2 or 3 about 8 in. long, ⅘ in. wide. Stem 8 in. long. *Bulb* ovoid, nearly 1 in. thick, tunics bright crimson or purple. Turkistan. (H.T. 11.)

T. undulatifo'lia. Near *T. Stapfii* in form and of variable colour (light red to soft crimson). *l.* shorter, often undulate, stem about 3½ to 6 in. *Bulb* about 1 in. thick. Asia Minor. 1877. (Differs from *T. undulatifolia* of B.M. 6308 in the hairy tunic.)

T. urumien'sis. *fl.* 1 or 2, urn-shaped, yellow, outer segs. olive and red without. April. *l.* 2 to 4, strap-shaped, somewhat channelled, about 5 in. long, ⅖ in. wide, glabrous, dull green. Stem about 2 in. long. *Bulb* nearly round, about ¾ in. thick. NW. Persia. 1928. (B.M. 9288; H.T. 2.)

T. variopic'ta.* *fl.* red, streaked with orange and purple and with grey blotch. Italy. 1838. (*Neo-tulipae, see* **T. Gesneriana**.)

T. Ven'eris. *fl.* solitary, cup-shaped, light scarlet with deep-olive blotch margined yellow; segs. over 3 in. long, 1¼ in. wide, outer long-pointed, inner rounded. May. *l.* 4, lowest about 16 in. long, 1¼ in. wide, somewhat glaucous. Stem 12 in. long. *Bulb* about 1½ in. thick. Cyprus. Stoloniferous.

T. viola'cea. *fl.* solitary, opening to a wide star, crimson-violet or purple with a yellow-margined blue or olive blotch; outer segs. violet without; segs. 1¼ to 2 in. long, about 1 in. wide. March. *l.* 3 to 5, lowest 4 to 6 in. long, about ½ in. wide, glabrous, slightly glaucous. Stem 4 to 5 in. long. *Bulb* about ¾ in. thick. 1894. N. Persia, Kurdistan, &c. (B.M. 7440; H.T. 7.) var. **pal'lida,** white faintly tinged purple. (H.T. 8.) SYN. *T. violacea coeruleo-oculata.*

T. viridiflo'ra. *fl.* pale yellow and green. Belonging to the garden tulip group. (Gn. 32 (1877), 514.)

T. vitelli'na. *fl.* pale yellow; segs. ovate, obtuse. *l.* ovate-lanceolate acute, glabrous. Stem 1 to 2 ft. h. 1889. Of the Garden Tulip group.

T. Whittal'lii. *fl.* solitary, bell-shaped, finally opening widely, bright orange with dark-olive basal blotch; outer segs. 2½ in. long, ⅗ in. wide, pointed, green and buff without; inner wider. April. *l.* 3 or 4, lowest 8 in. long, ⅘ in. wide, slightly folded, glabrous. Stem about 12 in. long. *Bulb* round, 1 in. thick. Smyrna. (B.M. 9649; H.T. 5.)

TUMATAKURU. *See* **Discaria Toumatou.**

TUMBLER SPREKELIA. *See* **Hippeastrum Cybister.**

TUMBO'A. A synonym of Welwitschia.

A→

tumes'cens, inflated.

tu'midus -a -um, tumid, swollen.

TUMOURS. Excrescences which arise on plants, mostly as a result of the attacks of fungus or bacterial parasites.

tumulo'rum, of burial mounds.

Tuna, W. Indian name for a cactus fruit.

tunbridgen'sis -is -e, of Tunbridge Wells, Kent.

TUNIC. A coat or cover of a bulb. Any loose membranous skin not formed from the epidermis.

TU'NICA (*tunica*, under garment referring to bracts at base of calyx). FAM. *Caryophyllaceae.* A genus of about 20 species of annual or perennial herbs with the habit of small-flowered Dianthus or some species of Gypsophila. To the latter genus it is nearly allied, differing especially in the form of the calyx, which is not bell-shaped, is without nerves between the sepals, and is membranous between the nerves; beneath the calyx there are usually 2 glume-like bracts as in Dianthus. Flowers in corymbs or heads. The genus is distributed over middle and Southern Europe, especially in the Mediterranean region with a few in Asia Minor. Rock plants for well-drained sites.

T. grami'nea. Tufted perennial with woody base, 6 to 12 in. h. *l.* narrow, 3-cornered in section, scabrid, those of branches clustered. *fl.* rose; pet. entire, obcordate; cal. more or less hispid without basal scales; in a few-fld. panicle. Summer. Greece.

T. illy'rica. Clammy-haired perennial with many stems 4 to 10 in. h., loosely spreading. *l.* narrow-linear, 3-nerved, rough-edged. *fl.* clustered with bristle-like stems; whitish with purple spots or stripes; cal. rough-hairy with 3-toothed segs. July, August. Dalmatia.

T. olym'pica. Glabrous erect annual about 1 ft. h. with slender more or less spreading branches. *Radical l.* broad linear, others narrow; margins scabrid. *fl.* in a spreading panicle with slender pedicels, white; pet. oblong-linear, entire; cal. glabrous with slender-pointed segs. June, July. Lydia, Cilicia. In woods.

T. proli'fera. Glabrous annual with erect branches. *l.* scabrid on margin; stem-l. short. *fl.* small, rose, in a head with outer involucral l. mucronate, others scale-like. Spring. N. and Middle Europe to Greece. (S.H.Gr. 394.)

T. Saxifra'ga. Tufted perennial with thick woody rootstock. Stems many, spreading or erect, 4 to 8 in. h., mostly smooth. *Lower l.* narrow-linear, about 1/25 in. wide; *upper* small and similar to the green keeled bracts. *fl.* white, tinged rose or lilac, in loose few-fld. corymbs; cal. 5-angled with 5 green nerves, teeth ovate, obtuse, finely ciliate. June to September. S. Europe east to Persia. A variable plant especially in fl. colour and size. A double-fld. var. less hardy than the type has been described. var. **pleniflo'ra,** with white and lilac forms.

tunica'tus -a -um, tunicated; having a coat or coats, especially of bulbs, such as the Tulip.

A→

Tunilla, native name of *Cereus Tunilla.*

tunisen'sis -is -e, of Tunis, N. Africa.

tuolumnen'sis -is -e, of Tuolumne County, California.

TU'PA. Included in **Lobelia.** *See* **L. Tupa.**

TUPE'LO. *See* **Nyssa sylvatica.**

TUPIDAN'THUS (*tupis*, mallet, *anthos*, flower; from the shape of the flower-buds). FAM. *Araliaceae.* A genus of 1 small, glabrous, erect tree at first, then becoming a tall climber. It grows in sandy loam in a warm house. It can be propagated by cuttings in sand under a glass in heat.

T. calyptra'tus. *l.* digitate; lflets. 7 to 9, narrow oblong with a short point, 7 in. long, 2½ in. wide, narrowed to base, their stalks 2 in. long. *fl.* green; buds ⅝ in. through, nearly globose; stamens 50 to 70; main umbel about 3-rayed, its branches 3 in. long, very stout, with large bracts at their bases; partial umbels 5- to 7-cleft. India. 1856. (B.M. 4908.)

TUPIS'TRA (*tupis*, mallet; from the strange form of the stigma). FAM. *Liliaceae.* A genus of about 7 species of perennial herbs, natives of N. India, Burma, and Malaya. Rhizome thick; leaves radical, long, large, narrowed to a stalk. Flowers clustered, almost sessile; perianth yellowish, violet or purple, bell-shaped, with a broad tube, and 6, rarely 8, short, nearly equal lobes; stamens 6 or 8; spike terminal, dense, cylindrical; scape erect or recurved at tip, simple. Rich loam suits them with a stove temperature; they may be increased by suckers or by division in spring.

T. gran'dis. *fl.* shining purple, fleshy in erect spikes; stigma pure white, disk-like, spreading. (B.M. 7829.) SYN. *T. perakensis.* Malaya. 1900.

Tupistra nutans

T. nu'tans. *rhiz.* fleshy. *l.* oblanceolate, 2 to 3 ft. long, 2 to 4 in. wide, erect, long stalked, narrowed to both ends. *fl.* lurid-violet or tube greenish, about ½ in. long, bracts large, dry, deltoid; spike dense, nodding, 3 to 6 in. long; scape 3 to 6 in. long. March. Himalaya. 1820. (B.M. 3054; B.R. 1233.)

T. tupistroi'des. *rhiz.* creeping, much-branched. *l.* lanceolate, over 1 ft. long, acute, papery, bright green, stalks dilated at base, firm, erect, 6 in. or more long. *fl.* dark purple, ½ in. across; spike drooping, loose, 2 to 3 in. long; peduncle dark-purple, erect, as long as spike. December. Khasia. 1872. (B.M. 6280; G.F. 192 as *Macrostigma tupistroides.*) SYN. *T. macrostigma.*

turbina'tus -a -um, turbinate; top-shaped.

Turczaninow'ii, in honour of N. S. Turczaninow (Nikolai Stepanovich Turchaninov), 1796–1864, Russian botanist and author of *Flora Baicalensi-Dahurica.*

TURF. Turf is a peculiar feature of British gardens, for the close-growing grasses of which it is composed need a moist moderate climate such as they enjoy here if they are to be perennial and constant in their growth. The term is applied in horticulture to grass sods which are laid over the surface of ground to form lawns, edging, verges, &c. Turves cut from existing lawns in forming flower-beds may, of course, be utilized but the chief source is the grass field, especially the pasture. Not only is turf cut from pastures of value for lawn-making but it is also stacked grass-side downwards in heaps to decompose and form loam of a fibrous nature of great value in potting and for various other purposes. When used for forming new lawns, &c., that are to be frequently mown, it is most important that the turf should be as free as possible from weeds such as Daisies, Plantains, Dandelions, and the like. Pasture land that has long been laid down and the grass closely eaten off by sheep or deer is generally the best, as, provided the soil is fairly good, the more grazing or cutting is practised, the denser will the turf become at the root, and the better it will be for the quick formation of a new lawn. The turves should be cut of a uniform size and uniformly about 1½ in. thick. Turves 3 ft. long by 1 ft. wide, if tough enough for rolling up, are of a convenient size. They are best cut by a turfing iron or by a turf-plough which is worked in a similar way. After lifting they should be trimmed to a uniform thickness by means of a box in which they are laid grass side down, and at the same time any tap-rooted weeds should be removed. Small turves 9 in. square are sometimes used and are readily fitted together. Before the turf is laid the ground should be thoroughly prepared, by draining, enriching if necessary, treading firmly and raking fine after such levelling as is needed is carried out. Autumn and favourable weather in winter or early spring afford the best seasons for the work of turf-laying. When the turves are laid and fitted as closely as possible all the interstices should be filled with fine soil, swept with a birch broom, and then the whole surface may be rammed or beaten with a turf-beater. It is important to get newly laid turf consolidated and the pieces fitted together while the ground is moist. If for any reason turf is laid late in spring or during summer it is very apt to become dried up and the pieces to separate from one another, and these seasons should be avoided. It is of little use watering from the top in summer to remedy this state of affairs, but new turf stands a much better chance of establishment at these seasons if the ground is watered first and the turves then laid in position. When established subsequent treatment is that of a lawn (q.v.).

TURF ASHES. Ashes from burnt turf are of some value when applied to land, but to burn it is a wasteful mode of dealing with turf. It is of far greater value if dug or ploughed in as turf, as the roots of plants and trees quickly seize upon such material when within their reach. Burning destroys all the fibre and the nitrogen is dissipated, while the ashes soon lose any manurial value they may have if exposed to rain.

TURF ANT, *Lasius flavus*, a small yellow Ant, the nests of which are found in fields and meadows and which often causes considerable inconvenience on lawns, especially in new gardens made on virgin land. This and certain other species of Ants raise mounds, resembling Mole-hills, which are covered with grass, and their eradication on lawns is particularly desirable.

The earth-mounds should be dispersed by vigorous raking as soon as they appear, and the lawn frequently rolled to consolidate the turf. In severe infestations inject Carbon disulphide into the nests. Make a hole 6 to 9 in. deep in the centre of each mound, pour in ⅓ fl. oz. of the liquid, and stamp ground firmly to prevent the loss of the poisonous fumes. (*See* **Carbon disulphide.**)

A G. F. W.

TURF-BEATER, or TURF-BEETLE. This is used for beating the surface of newly laid turf, to consolidate and render it level. A Turf-beater may easily be made from a flat, oblong piece of wood 3 in. thick. A strong handle should be fixed into the centre of the upper side at an angle sufficiently acute to allow the Beater to be brought down flat on the turf when in use.

A→

TURF DISEASES. The most common trouble in turf is the appearance of brown patches due to the death of the grasses, and although this appearance can be caused by various fungi a contributing factor may be that the soil is wet and drainage poor, and these points must be considered when applying a remedy. Brown Patch is due to the fungus *Rhizoctonia solani* and Pink Patch to *R. fusiforme.* Dollar Spot is due to the fungus

Sclerotinia homoeocarpa and Snow Mould or Fusarium patch to the fungus *Fusarium nivale*. The names given to these diseases speak for themselves and all are treated by improvement of the aeration of the soil with a spiking instrument and brushing in sand, as well as watering the affected patches with Bordeaux mixture or one of the proprietary fluids sold for use against these turf troubles. Apart from these there is the occurrence on lawns of Fairy Rings the remedy for which is given under Fairy Rings.

D. E. G.

TURF-RASER. A useful implement where a large quantity of turf has to be cut; it is employed for marking out the proper width for cutting in strips, and is used by a person who works in advance of others lifting the turf. A very simple form, but one which answers most effectually, consists of an ordinary wooden handle with the point of an old scythe fixed into one end of it, at nearly or quite a right angle. This blade cuts into the turf at a uniform depth, and is guided along a line by the workman using it.

TURF-SCRAPER. A scraper, made of wood or iron, similar to those used for roads, answers equally well for scraping lawns when worm-casts or ant-hillocks abound. A Turf-scraper is not, as a rule, otherwise required.

TURFING-IRON, or **TURFING-SPADE.** An implement used for lifting turf that has previously been cut through with an edging-iron or a turf-raser. It has a bent handle, and a heart-shaped, flat blade, and is much handier for the purpose than an ordinary spade, as, if properly used, any quantity of turf may be cut of about a uniform thickness.

TURF-WALKS. Walks formed of turf instead of gravel, stones, or other hard substances. They require in formation exactly the same preparation as lawns, with, of course, the width limited. Occasionally, but not very frequently, Turf-walks are introduced into kitchen gardens.

turfa'ceus -a -um, growing in bogs.

tur'gidus -a -um, turgid, distended, swollen, puffed out.

TURION (from Latin *turio*, a shoot). (1) a scaly sucker or shoot from the ground, later becoming a stem as in Asparagus; (2) a biennial shoot of Rubus in its first year (i.e. a primocane), as distinct from the same shoot in its second year (i.e. a floricane); (3) winter resting shoot of certain water-plants, e.g. Hydrocharis, 'which are stored with food material and protected externally in some way, become detached from the parent and pass the winter either floating or resting at the bottom of the water. In the spring they expand, produce adventitious roots, and rapidly develop into full-fledged individuals' (Arber, *Water Plants*, 219. 1920).

W. T. S.

turkestan'icus -a -um, of Turkistan, Central Asia.

TURKEY CORN. *See* **Dicentra cucullaria.**

TURKEY OAK. *See* **Quercus Cerris.**

TURKEY RED. Yielded by seeds of *Peganum Harmala*.

TURMERIC. *See* **Curcuma longa.**

TURMERIC ROOT. *See* **Hydrastis canadensis.**

TURN'ERA (in honour of William Turner, d. 1568, author of a *New Herbal*, 1551). FAM. *Turneraceae*. A genus of nearly 90 species of herbs or shrubs, natives of S. America, a few found in Madagascar, Mauritius, and S. Africa. Leaves alternate, entire to more or less pinnatifid, often with 2 glands at base. Flowers yellow, usually solitary in leaf-axils, rarely clustered or racemose; calyx 5-parted; petals 5. Peduncles sometimes connate with leaf-stalk. Rather weedy and short-lived plants, but pretty in flower, needing stove conditions and a light sandy soil. Seed is freely produced or the plants may be raised from cuttings or (in the herbaceous perennials) by division.

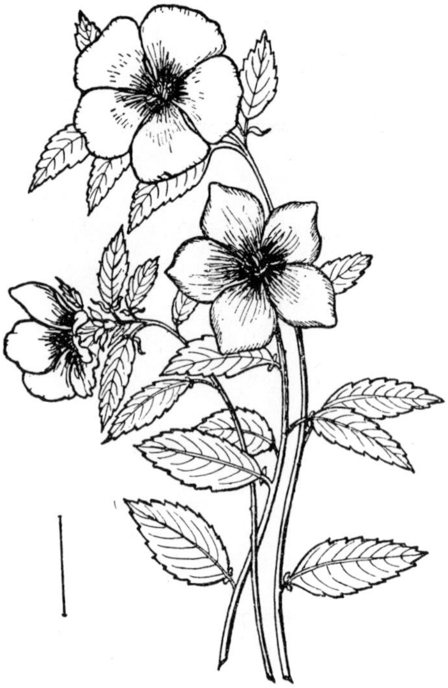

Turnera ulmifolia elegans

T. ulmifo'lia. W. Indian Holly. Sage Rose. Sub-shrub of 2 to 4 ft. *l.* oblong, acute, toothed, downy above, white-hairy beneath, 2-glanded at base. *fl.* yellow, large, almost sessile, peduncles connate with l.-stalks, 2-bracteate. June to September. W. Indies, Mexico, S. America. 1733. (B.M. 4137.) var. **angustifo'lia,** *l.* oblong-lanceolate. 1773. (B.M. 281 as *T. angustifolia*); **cuneiform'is,** 1 to 3 ft. h., *l.* oblong-wedge-shaped, coarsely toothed, claws of pet. brownish. Brazil. 1821; **el'egans,** 1 to 2 ft. h., *l.* oblong-lanceolate, coarsely-toothed, entire, downy. *fl.* pale yellow or sulphur with purple-brown claws, sessile. Brazil. 1812. (B.M. 2106 as *T. trioniflora*.)

TURNERA'CEAE. Dicotyledons. A family of 6 genera with about 100 species for the most part natives of the warmer parts of America. Annual or perennial herbs, shrubs or trees with alternate toothed or lobed leaves, with or without stipules, and axillary flowers solitary or rarely in cymes. Sepals 5-toothed; petals 5, free, regular; stamens 5, free on calyx tube; ovary superior of 3 carpels, 1-celled. Fruit a capsule, with 3 to many arillate seeds. The flowers are nearly always heterostyled as in Primula. The only genus dealt with here is Turnera.

Turn'eri, in honour of Mr. Turner of Manchester, orchid-grower, *c.* 1883.

TURNIP (*Brassica rapa*). A hardy biennial of European origin widely grown for its fleshy roots and for the tender growing tops used in spring as green vegetables or, blanched, as a substitute for Seakale. There seems no doubt that the Turnip was well known to the Ancient Greeks and Romans; there is, however, confusion in the literature between the Turnip and the Rape (*Brassica Napus*). The swollen roundish root is not very nutritious; it consists of about 90 per cent. water, with a little sugar but no starch, its place being taken by pectase, a jelly-like substance which helps jams to set. Turnip roots, have, however, much the same vitamin C (ascorbic acid) content as Potatoes, and an antiscorbutic juice for infant-feeding can be extracted by boiling the grated root in water for about 15 minutes and then squeezing through muslin (see *British Medical Journal*, 1941, no. 4206, p. 226). The iron content of the green leaves is significant, the vitamin C content high. At one time Turnips were regarded as chiefly autumn and winter crops, but with attention to details, especially good cultivation and the proper choice of varieties for different seasons, Turnips may be had practically the year round. They are, or should be, grown rapidly and are useful on this account for catch crops. A light friable sandy loam suits them best, but most soils not very sour and not deficient in phosphates can, with good cultivation, be made to yield good crops. Unless soils are moist Turnips are apt to run to seed, without forming roots of useful size, or to become stringy in dry weather and of an inferior quality. In dry weather especially, the Turnip Flea Beetle is very troublesome, attacking the seedlings as soon as they are above ground. The earliest crops are grown on mild hotbeds, warm manure, leaves, or other fermenting material sufficient to give a gentle warmth only, for Turnips will not stand hard forcing; whether under lights or in trenches, protected from cold by mats laid over the trench or by litter, from the time the seedlings appear until the plants are ready for use they must be given plenty of air and moderate watering daily. This sowing should be made about the end of January to the end of February and the seedlings should be thinned out as soon as large enough. If frames are used standing on the hotbed, they may already have grown a crop of Lettuces and Radishes by the end of February; after the beds have been trodden and covered with 3 in. of fine compost, Turnips may be sown at intervals of 4 to 5 in. in holes about 1 in. deep, the seedlings being then reduced to one at each station. An early variety must be used for this sowing.

By mid-March a sowing may be made in the open on a south border, and successional sowings made thereafter until the end of June or early July. The main crop is sown from mid-July to the end of August. These sowings should be made in drills 1 ft. apart and 1 to 1½ in. deep on moist soil. Where possible watering should be done when needed. The plants should be thinned to 9 in. apart, or for the last sowings at first about 6 in. apart, and finally to 1 ft., to stand the winter, the intermediate roots being pulled for use. Frequent hoeing is desirable to suppress weeds and to aerate the soil. Turnips for use in winter are usually pulled from the open but may be stored in sand or soil against periods of severe weather, for which purpose the tops should be first cut off but not too closely. The young growths made in early spring are very useful as 'greens' at the time when Cabbages are often scarce. Turnip seed has an average life of 5 years and ½ oz. is sufficient to sow a square rod.

Turnips are best grown on land well manured for a previous crop, the most probable extra requirement being, as with most root crops, phosphates which can be conveniently supplied by superphosphate at the rate of 2 lb. to the square rod.

Varieties for various purposes are listed in the Supplement. The main variations are in shape of roots (round, flat, or long), colour of flesh, season of use, and size of foliage.

TURNIP DISEASES. Under this heading may be included the diseases of Swedes. An important trouble is Club Root or Finger and Toe (*Plasmodiophora brassicae*), with its characteristic symptoms showing as swollen and gnarled tumour-like swellings on the roots, causing them to rot away and contaminate the soil with the parasite. The remedy is chiefly concerned with liming the soil, improving the drainage, and practising a long rotation of this crop. Certain varieties of Swedes such as Bangholm, Studsgaad, and Wilhelmsburger are very resistant and among Turnips the yellow-fleshed varieties are more resistant than the white-fleshed ones. Dry Rot caused by the fungus *Phoma lingam* is more severe on Swedes than Turnips, causing brown sunken elongated cankerlike areas on the side of the fleshy root. This disease can be seed-borne, but much infection may come from the soil or from manure containing pieces of rotten roots, and care in avoiding the use of such manure for Swedes is the chief method of avoiding the trouble. Soft Rot (*Bacterium carotovorum*) reduces the inside of Turnips and Swedes to a soft grey putrid mass although the outer rind may remain firm. This rot usually starts at a wound due to cultivation, growth cracks, or even following Dry Rot, but with good cultivation and care that infected refuse is not used for manuring there should be little loss from Soft Rot. Black Rot (*Pseudomonas campestris*) may invade Turnips and Swedes and turn them dark brown inside or show as rings of black dots where the parasite follows the vascular (conducting) system. As with Soft Rot, if affected roots are burnt the disease is not to be feared. Powdery Mildew, *Erysiphe polygoni*, may occur on the leaves as white powdery spots or patches, especially in dry summers, but is not likely to cause much injury in a well-cultivated crop which does not suffer extreme dryness at the roots (*see* **Powdery Mildews**). There are various leaf spots of Turnip and Swede due to fungi such as *Alternaria brassicae*, *Cercosporella brassicae*, &c., and there is White Blister disease due to the fungus *Cystopus candidus* (*see* **Cabbage White Blister**) but none of these is likely to be serious in its effects. An important non-parasitic trouble is Brown Heart or Raan in which the symptoms do not show externally, but when the roots are cut open the flesh contains greyish or brownish areas usually located in the lower half of the fleshy root. The feeding value of such roots is much reduced and they are bitter and stringy when cooked. This trouble is considered to be due to boron deficiency in the soil, but contributory factors may be extreme dryness or overliming. It can be corrected by applying Borax at the rate of 2 oz. to the square rod applied with fine sand or soil to assist even distribution about a week before sowing, but it must not be forgotten that proper preparation of the land and making sure that it contains sufficient humus to prevent extreme dryness, together with good cultivation, will also help to avoid Brown Heart. Properly prepared and cultivated soil will also do much to avoid the splitting of the sides of Turnips known as Growth Cracks which so often allow such diseases as Soft Rot to enter and destroy the root.

D. E. G.

TURNIP CABBAGE. *See* **Kohl-Rabi.**

TURNIP, DEVIL'S. A name for *Bryonia dioica.*

TURNIP FLEA OR FLY. *See* **Flea Beetles.**

TURNIP GALL WEEVIL. *See* **Cabbage Pests, Gall Weevil.**

TURNIP, INDIAN. *See* **Arisaema triphyllum.**

TURNIP, LION'S. *See* **Leontice Leontopetalum**

TURNIP MOTH. *See* **Surface Caterpillars.**

TURNIP RADISH. *See* **Radish.**

TURNIP-ROOTED CELERY. *See* **Celeriac.**

TURNIP, ST. ANTHONY'S. A name for *Ranunculus bulbosus.*

TURNSOLE. *See* **Heliotropium.**

TURPENTINE. *See* **Silphium terebinthinaceum,** and various conifers (Picea and Pinus). A

TURPENTINE, CHIAN-. *See* **Pistacia Terebinthus.**

TURPENTINE, STRASBOURG. *See* **Abies.**

TURPIN'IA (in honour of Pierre Jean François Turpin, celebrated French botanical artist and naturalist, 1775–1840). FAM. *Staphyleaceae.* A genus of about 16 species of trees and shrubs with handsome foliage, natives of the tropics except Africa. Leaves usually unequally pinnate, rarely simple, glabrous; leaflets opposite, toothed, sometimes with stipels, leathery. Flowers white, small, in large terminal or axillary panicles; calyx 5-parted, persistent; petals 5, broadly spatulate to orbicular; stamens 5. Fruit 3-celled, leathery or fleshy with few or many seeds in each cell. All the species need protection and grow in a compost of peat, loam, and sand. They may be propagated by cuttings of ripe wood in sand under a glass in heat.

T. argu'ta. Shrub of 3 to 4 ft. *l.* simple, obovate-oblong, slender-pointed, slightly crenate, 3 to 6 in. long. *fl.* dirty-white or purplish in bud; inner sep. and pet. oblong-ovate, about equal in length, 2 outer sep. rather smaller; panicle dense, terminal. March. S. China. 1826. (B.R. 1819 as *Ochranthe arguta.*) Greenhouse.

T. insig'nis. Tree to 20 ft. *l.* toothed. *fl.* fragrant; cal. segs. unequal; pet. with very short claws; panicle terminal. May. Mexico. 1847. (B.M. 4459 as *Lacepedia insignis.*) Stove.

T. nepalen'sis. Very close to *T. pomifera* but with smaller fl. and fr. Stove.

T. occidenta'lis. Cassava Wood. Tree of 20 to 30 ft. *lflets.* in 2 or 3 pairs, elliptic-oblong, crenate or sharply toothed, with stipels. *fl.* in panicles, the lower branches opposite, bearing small corymbs. W. Indies. 1824.

T. pomi'fera. Shrub or tree up to 25 ft. h. *l.* 5 to 20 in. long; lflets. 3 to 9, elliptic, oblong or ovate, slender-pointed, 2½ to 8 in. long. *fl.* yellowish in large terminal panicles. May. *fr.* red, purplish, yellow, or green, ⅓ to ½ in. across. Himalaya. 1820. Stove.

F. G. P.

TURRA'EA (in honour of Giorgio della Turre or Turra, 1607–88, Professor of Botany at Padua, author of several botanical works). FAM. *Meliaceae.* A genus of about 70 species of trees or shrubs, natives of Trop. and S. Africa, Trop. Asia and Australia. Leaves alternate, stalked, entire or bluntly lobed. Flowers in few-flowered axillary clusters, with bracts, white, long; calyx 4- or 5-parted, petals 4 or 5, free, twisted; staminal tube 8- or 10-toothed; disk annular. A compost of loam and peat suits them and they may be propagated by cuttings of ripe wood, with leaves intact, in sand in heat.

T. floribun'da. *l.* ovate, rounded at base, hairy especially beneath; l.-stalk slender. *fl.* pale yellowish-green, fragrant, in twos or threes on short scaly spurs at ends of branches, pedicels densely downy; cal. cup-shaped, silky; pet. linear, revolute in upper half. April, May. S. Africa. (B.M. 8984.) Greenhouse.

T. heterophyl'la. Shrub. *l.* ovate, 2 to 3½ in. long, often angularly lobed. *fl.* clustered at ends of branches; pet. about 1 in. long, shorter than style; peduncles silky, ¼ to ½ in. long. May. Upper Guinea. 1843. (B.R. 30, 4, as *T. lobata.*) Stove.

T. obtusifo'lia. Shrub of 4 to 6 ft., glabrous. *l.* obovate, 1 to 1¾ in. long, narrowed to a short stalk, entire or bluntly 3-lobed, margins revolute, paler beneath. *fl.* solitary, axillary, peduncles ½ to ¾ in. long; pet. narrow, 1 to 1¾ in. long. May. S. Africa. 1872. (B.M. 6267.) Greenhouse.

T. ri'gida. A synonym of *Quivisia chilosantha.*

F. G. P.

tur'pis -is -e, ugly, unsightly, deformed.

TURRI'TIS. Included under **Arabis.**

TURTLE HEAD. *See* **Chelone.**

TUSSA'CIA (in honour of F. Richard de Tussac, French botanist, 1751–1837, author of a Flora of the Antilles, 1808). FAM. *Gesneriaceae.* A genus of 4 or 5 species of herbs with creeping simple or branched rhizomes, natives of Trop. America. Leaves opposite, often large, the upper floral ones reduced to bracts. Flowers in many-flowered umbels in the upper leaf-axils, forming collectively a terminal corymb, calyx often scarlet, segments free, large, bell-shaped, 5-angled or 5-winged; corolla yellow, lined with purple, tube rather broadly cylindrical, limb oblique somewhat spreading broadly 5-lobed; stamens included. For cultivation *see* **Gesneria.**

Tussacia pulchella

T. pulchel'la. About 1 ft. h. *l.* ovate or ovate-oblong, acute, 3 to 7 in. long, crenate-serrate, stalk short. *fl.* about 1 to 1½ in. long, tube erect, cylindrical; cal. red; lobes deltoid, toothed. July. W. Indies. 1830. (B.M. 1146 and L.B.C. 1028 as *Besleria pulchella.*)

T. semiclau'sa. Branching herb, stems violet or spotted red. *l.* broadly ovate, downy, ciliate-toothed, bright green. *fl.* in short terminal panicles; cor. golden-yellow, striped crimson; cal. cinnabar-red, bell-shaped, truncate. Brazil. 1870. (I.H. 3, 28.)

TUSSILA'GO (*tussis,* cough; name used by Pliny in allusion to the medicinal use of the leaves). FAM. *Compositae.* A genus of 1 species, native of Europe and Asia, naturalized in N. America. Perennial herb with underground rhizomes, flowering before leaves appear. Leaves radical, at first rounded and cordate, cobwebby, becoming large and more or less angular. Flower-heads yellow, solitary on scaly scapes about 4 in. high, elongating in fruit; central florets male (about 40), outer female (about 300); achenes with a pappus of white, toothed, hairs. *T. Farfara* occurs wild in Britain, especially on stiff clay soils where it is one of the earliest flowers to appear. It is not a plant to introduce to the garden indiscriminately for its creeping rhizomes are difficult to keep within bounds or to eradicate. The leaves are used at times for cigar making and are smoked as an alleviator of asthma. Other plants listed under this name belong usually to Petasites.

T. Farfa'ra. Coltsfoot. See above. var. **variegat'a,** *l.* margined or blotched creamy-white. The variety is more commonly planted than the type.

TUSSOCK. Tuft growing from the ground, as in some grasses.

TUTCHER'IA (in honour of William James Tutcher, 1867–1920, of the Botanical and Forestry Dept. of Hong Kong). FAM. *Theaceae.* A genus of 2 species of evergreen trees, natives of SE. China. Leaves alternate, ovate-lanceolate. Flowers white, showy, axillary; sepals imbricate, silky outside, inner series becoming petaloid; petals 5, large; stamens many, connate at base, adnate to petals; ovary 4- to 6-celled; styles united nearly to apex. Fruit a globose, woody capsule deshiscing by 3 to 6 valves with 2 to 5 seeds in each cell. For cultivation *see* **Camellia.**

T. spectab'ilis. Small tree. *l.* ovate-lanceolate, slender-pointed, wedge-shaped at base, 5 to 6 in. long, shining above, stalks short. *fl.* white, about 3 in. across, slightly scented; pet. broadly obovate, emarginate. *Capsules* globose 2 to 3 in. across. (*J.R.H.S.* 74. 255.) SE. China. Tender.

TUTSAN. *See* **Hypericum Androsaemum.**

TUTU. *See* **Coriaria ruscifolia.**

TWEED'IA (in honour of J. Tweedie, 1775–1862, of Glasgow and Argentine). FAM. *Asclepiadaceae.* A genus of about 50 species of erect or twining perennial herbs or sub-shrubs, natives of S. America, mostly in Brazil, 1 in Mexico and the W. Indies. Leaves opposite. Flowers blue, white, yellowish-white or purplish; calyx 5-parted; corolla tube short, campanulate or almost globular and with 5 often narrow lobes; cymes sometimes forming umbels, loosely few-flowered, sometimes capitate, axillary, pedunculate. The following species like a rich, well-drained, loamy soil and do best if planted out in the stove or greenhouse with the shoots trained near the glass. *T. caerulea* is a beautiful climber, remarkable for the changes in colour shown by the flower during its life. At first it is pale blue slightly tinged green; it then becomes purplish and finally lilac. All species can be propagated by cuttings under a bell glass in bottom heat. All have been placed under Oxypetalum, to which genus students of the Asclepiadaceae now return them with the exception of *T. caerulea*, placed in a genus by itself as *Amblyopetalum caeruleum.* The genus Tweedia, as now defined, consists of about 6 Chilean and Argentine species not in cultivation. For further details see Supplement.

T. appendicula'ta. Twiner. *l.* ovate, acuminate, base cordate, downy. *fl.* pale yellow, fragrant; pet. narrow-lanceolate, acute, erect-spreading; peduncles cymose, usually 4-fld. Brazil. Stove.

Tweedia caerulea

T. Banks'ii. Twining sub-shrub. *l.* cordate or ovate-cordate, shortly acuminate, hairy beneath. *fl.* purple; cor. segs. linear or linear-lanceolate; peduncles loosely fld., longer than pedicels. June. Brazil. 1826. Stove.

T. caeru'lea.* Twining sub-shrub. *l.* oblong- or lanceolate-heart-shaped, mucronate, hairy on both surfaces. *fl.* blue; cor. segs. oblong, spreading; peduncles erect, shorter than l. few-fld. July. Buenos Aires. 1832. (S.B.F.G. s. 2, 407; B.M. 3630 as *T. versicolor.*) Greenhouse or Stove. SYN. *Amblyopetalum caeruleum.*

T. solanoi'des. Erect sub-shrub scarcely branched, 6 ft. h. *l.* lanceolate or oblong-heart-shaped, mucronate, acute, hairy; stalked. *fl.* bluish with rose tinge; cor. segs. spreading; in many-fld. corymbose panicles, terminal or extra-axillary. June. Brazil. 1846. (B.M. 4367 as *Oxypetalum solanoides.*) Stove. SYN. *Tweedia floribunda, T. pubescens, T. rosea.*

TWIG. One of the smaller shoots of a tree or shrub.

TWINER, plant climbing by spirally coiling the stem round some support. The spiral is usually for any one species always in one direction.

TWIN FLOWER. *See* **Bravoa geminiflora.**

TWITCH. *See* **Triticum repens.**

TYD'AEA. Included under **Isoloma.**

Tyerman'ii, in honour of Mr. Tyerman of Penlee, Tregoney, Cornwall, *c.* 1871, a Kew Gardens student who became Superintendent of the Botanic Garden, Liverpool.

TYLO'PHORA (*tylos*, swelling, *phoreo*, to bear; application doubtful). FAM. *Asclepiadaceae.* A genus of about 40 species of usually twining, rarely sub-erect sub-shrubs or herbs, natives of Trop. and Sub-Trop. Africa, Asia, Australia, New Caledonia, and Norfolk Is. Leaves opposite. Flowers rather small, sometimes minute; calyx deeply 5-cleft; corolla tube short, subrotate, deeply 5-cleft, lobes rather broad; coronal lobes 5, fleshy; cymes umbel-like or shortly racemose. These stove plants are not very ornamental. Their cultivation is the same as for Hoya. Those mentioned below are all twining sub-shrubs.

T. asthma'tica. E. Indian Ipecacuanha. About 5 ft. h. *l.* ovate to orbicular, slender pointed, often cordate at base, glabrous above; stalks without glands, nearly round. *fl.* green, rather large; cor. segs. acute; peduncles shorter than l. bearing 2 or 3 sessile, few-fld. umbels towards apex, pedicels long. November. India. 1814. (B.M. 1929 as *Cynanchum viridiflorum.*)

T. barba'ta. About 10 ft. h. *l.* ovate or ovate-lanceolate, acute, not cordate, 1 to 2 in. long; stalks slender. *fl.* dingy purple, few in one, rarely 2 umbels; cor. $\frac{3}{8}$ in. across, slightly bearded within. July. Australia. 1822.

T. conspic'ua. Hairy twiner. *l.* oblong or obovate-oblong, more or less cuspidate, base cordate, glabrous except for veins; stalked. *fl.* $\frac{2}{3}$ in. across; cor. lobes ovoid, tuberculate; corona very short. Angola.

T. Flanagan'ii. Tall, glabrous climber with scattered l. *l.* ovate-lanceolate, slender, pointed, 1 to 2 in. long, leathery; stalked. *fl.* purple-red, deeply 5-cleft, lobes $\frac{1}{2}$ in. long; coronal l. fleshy; panicles cymose, axillary or terminal, pedicels much longer than *fl.* S. Africa.

T. grandiflo'ra. About 10 ft. h. *l.* ovate to ovate-lanceolate, with short slender points, more or less cordate, 1 to 2 in. long, hairy; stalks slender. *fl.* purple, 1 to 3 on a short, interpetiolar peduncle; cor. 1 in. across, lobes obtuse. July. Australia. 1822.

T. ocula'ta. *l.* oblong-lanceolate, 3 in. long. *fl.* purple, in short umbellate cymes. Sierra Leone. 1895.

tymphres'teus -a -um, of Mt. Tymphrestus, Aetolia.

TYPE. In common speech, a type is something which exhibits all the characteristic features and qualities of the class to which it belongs. As used in botany and zoology the word has several rather divergent meanings.

In botanical nomenclature, a type is that constituent (normally a dried specimen of one or more individual plants or of part of a plant) of a group of plants to which the name of the group is permanently attached. It is not necessarily the most typical or representative constituent of the group, but simply the one on which the first description associated with the publication of the name was based. To be valid, a botanical name must be published and accompanied by a description or by a reference to a previously published description. When this description has been made from a single specimen, or primarily based on one specimen which is mentioned as the type-specimen, this specimen is called the *holotype.* When the description has been based on two or more specimens without one being indicated as the holotype, these are called *syntypes*; one of them later selected as the type is called the *lectotype.* Often the original description mentions several specimens in addition to the holotype; these other specimens are called *paratypes.* An *isotype* is a duplicate specimen of the holotype. When no material on which the original description was based is available, a specimen selected for working purposes as a standard is called a *neotype.* There exist over 200 other terms for nomenclatural types. The above were approved at the 12th International Botanical Congress, Stockholm, 1950. Different names based on the same type and thus absolute synonyms are called *typonyms.* The place where the type-specimen was collected is called the *type-locality*; a specimen collected in the same locality and closely matching the type is sometimes called a *topotype.*

Modern botanical nomenclature rests on the type-method. Thus the type of the name of a family is a genus, that of a generic name a species, that of a specific or varietal name usually a specimen, less often a description or illustration by an earlier author. This type determines the application of the name. Thus if the reclassification of a genus or species leads to its division, the name must be kept for that part of the group retaining the type, even if this forms only a small part of the group involved, and the rest must be renamed. Many early descriptions of plants are very concise and lack significant detail: by means of the description alone the plant which the original author had in mind cannot be distinguished with certainty from related plants: when this is so, examination of the type-specimen often makes clear the proper application of the name. Such an examination sometimes shows that later authors have misinterpreted the original description and mistakenly applied the name to plants other than the one represented by the type-specimen. Thus the lectotype of the name *Veronica Traversii*, published by J. D. Hooker in 1864, represents a species with a long-tubed corolla. The plant commonly known in gardens as *Veronica Traversii* and figured as such in *Bot. Mag.* 6390 (1878) has a short-tubed corolla and does not agree with the type: hence it has had to receive a new name, *Veronica* (or *Hebe*) *brachysiphon.*

Plant-breeders and geneticists have another set of terms compounded from *-type.* Thus a *biotype* is a true breeding group of organisms agreeing so closely in their minute characters that they are presumed to be identical in their hereditary properties (known collectively as their *genotype*). A biotype is thus usually a small true-breeding group within a larger group. Most species not on the verge of extinction consist of several or many biotypes. The *phenotype* is the form assumed by an individual as the result of interaction between its *genotype* and its conditions of growth. The genotype (i.e. the inherited potentialities) of a seed may be such that this can grow into a tall phenotype; given starved conditions it might produce only a dwarf phenotype. The term *genotype* is sometimes extended to mean a group with similar hereditary properties and breeding potentialities; in systematic botany it is also sometimes used for the type-member of a genus, but this use is confusing and unnecessary. The term *karyotype* refers to the constitution of a nucleus of a cell as shown by the number, form, and size of its chromosomes; it may also be used for a group of species agreeing in the number, form, and size of their chromosomes.

In ecology an *ecotype* is a group of plants distinguishable from other plants of the same species by growing in a particular habitat and possessing distinct characteristics assumed to be connected with adaptation to that habitat. Thus a number of species have sea-side ecotypes tolerant of windy conditions and salt-spray.

W. T. S.

TY'PHA (old Greek name used by Theophrastus). Fam. *Typhaceae.* A genus of 9 to 15 species of marsh herbs natives of tropical and temperate regions. For characters *see* Family. These plants are decorative hardy aquatic perennials for margins of rivers and ponds to be planted in water up to 6 in. deep. They may be used for forming bays on the margins and make excellent cover for waterfowl but need attention lest they become too invasive. Propagated by seed or by division. The genus is easily recognized by its cylindric brown fruiting heads like ramrods which are sometimes dried for indoor decoration and which have given it the English names 'Reed Mace' and 'Cat's-tail' (mentioned by William Turner in 1548 as 'cattes tayle' and now commonly used in America). Unfortunately illustrators of Pharaoh's daughter finding the infant Moses in his 'ark of bulrushes' (Hebrew *gome*, probably Papyrus) usually portray the 'flags by the river's brink' as *Typha latifolia*, and the name 'Bulrush' has now become popularly associated with this species, although it is used in books mostly for the Pool-rush *Scirpus lacustris.*

T. angustifo'lia. Small Reed Mace. About 4 ft. h. Smaller in all parts than *T. latifolia.* *l.* dark green, not glaucous, $\frac{1}{4}$ to $\frac{3}{4}$ in. wide, convex beneath, channelled above towards base. *fl.-spikes* brown, $\frac{1}{2}$ to $\frac{3}{4}$ in. thick, separated by $\frac{1}{2}$ to 1 in., the female often interrupted. July. Britain, &c. (E.B. 1386.)

T. glau'ca. Robust plant with glaucous leaves reputed to be a hybrid *T. angustifolia* × *T. latifolia.*

T. japo'nica. A synonym of *T. orientalis.*

T. latifo'lia. Reed Mace, Cat's-tail. 6 to 8 ft. h. *l.* linear, 3 to 6 ft. long, $\frac{3}{4}$ to $1\frac{1}{2}$ in. wide, obtuse, nearly flat, somewhat glaucous. *fl.-spike,* dark brown, 6 to nearly 12 in. long, 1 in. thick, contiguous or nearly so, silky from the filiform perianth scales. July, August. Britain, &c. (E.B. 1385.) var. **elat'ior,** *l.* narrower, spikes shorter.

T. Laxmann'ii. Slender, $2\frac{1}{2}$ to $4\frac{1}{2}$ ft. h. *l.* very narrow, usually less than $\frac{1}{4}$ in. wide, half-round, grooved above, *convex* beneath. *Spikes* brown, remote, the female ovate-oblong. SE. Europe, Asia Minor to China.

T. mi'nima. Slender, 1 to $2\frac{1}{2}$ ft. h. *l.* of sterile stems very narrow linear, under $\frac{1}{12}$ in. wide, of flowering stem reduced to inflated sheathing bases or almost so. *Female spike* rusty brown ovate or shortly cylindrical, contiguous to male or remote. Europe, Caucasus to E. Asia.

T. orienta'lis. Narrow-leaved Far Eastern counterpart of *T. Shuttleworthii.* *l.* about $\frac{1}{4}$ in. wide. Japan, China.

T. Shuttleworth'ii. Robust, 3 to $4\frac{1}{2}$ ft. h. *l.* linear, $\frac{1}{6}$ to $\frac{1}{2}$ in. wide, longer than the fl.-stems. *Spikes* contiguous, the female thick and longer than male. Europe.

T. stenophyl'la. A synonym of *T. Laxmannii.*

TYPHA'CEAE. Monocotyledons. A family of 9 to 15 species of marsh plants comprised in the only genus, Typha, natives of Europe, temperate and Trop. Asia, Africa, Australia, and temperate N. America. Leaves in 2 ranks, long, sheathing, entire. Stems cylindrical, not knotted, solid, simple, with closely crowded flowers on a terminal spadix, male above, female below. Flowers with perianth; staminate of 2 to 5, rarely 1 stamen, often joined; pistilate of 1 carpel on a hairy axis. Fruit a nut or achene.

ty'phinus -a -um, typhoi'des, Typha-like.

TYPHLOCY'BA ROSAE. *See* **Rose Leaf-hoppers.**

TYPHO'NIUM (ancient Greek name adopted by Schott). Fam. *Araceae.* A family of about 23 species of tuberous, perennial herbs, natives of Trop. Asia, Australasia, and the Pacific Is. Leaves formed with the flowers hastate, sagittate or 3- to 5-lobed, or pedatisect; stalk long. Peduncle usually short; spathe tube persistent, convolute, more or less constricted at the throat; blade ovate-lanceolate or lanceolate, purplish, rarely whitish. Appendix of spadix variable, usually shortly stalked. Related to Arum but with the ovules attached to the base of the ovary; appendix of spadix much exserted, its stalk distinctly truncate above. The species need stove conditions and a light, rich soil with abundant water during the growing season. After the leaves die down water should be withheld until growth beings again, the pots containing the tubers being stored in a warm, dry place. Propagation is by division of the tubers.

T. Brown'ii. *rhiz.* thick, tuberous. *l.-stalk* 8 to 10 in. long; blade hastate, more or less 3-lobed, segs. long lanceolate, 3 to 6 in. long. *Peduncle* about 2 in. long. *Spathe-tube* nearly globose, about 1¼ in. long; blade widely ovate, slender-pointed, about 4 in. long. April. Australia. 1875. (B.M. 6180.)

T. divarica'tum. Tuber about ¾ in. across. *l.-stalk* slender, 4 to 12 in. long; blade cordate- or hastate-sagittate, more or less 3-lobed, 2 to 6 in. long, *Peduncle* about 1¼ in. long. *Spathe-tube* oblong-ovoid, about 1 in. long; blade ovate-lanceolate, dark purple, 5 to 6 in. long. July. India, &c. 1759. (B.M. 2324 as *Arum trilobatum.*)

T. diversifo'lium. Tuber about ¾ in. across. *l.-stalk* 6 to 12 in. long; blade ovate-lanceolate or hastate, mid-lobe ovate-oblong, side-lobes ovate- or oblong-lanceolate about half as long as mid-lobe. *Spathe-tube* oblong, about 1 in. long, pale green; blade oblong-lanceolate, velvety-purple, 3 to 5 in. long. India. var. **Huegelia'num,** adult *l.* 5- to 7-lobed. 1879.

T. flagellifor'me. Tuber flattish-round, small. *l.-stalk* slender, 6 to 12 in. long; blade very variable in shape and size, sagittate or hastate-oblong to 3-lobed, 2 to 4 in. long, the lateral lobes spreading almost horizontally. *Peduncle* slender, 2 to 8 in. long. *Spathe-tube* green, ovoid or oblong, about ½ in. long; blade lanceolate, prolonged into a long flagellum, 3 to 10 in. long, white. India, Malaya, Philippines. 1819. (L.B.C. 396 as *Arum flagelliforme.*)

T. gigante'um. Tuber nearly round, about ¾ in. across. *l.-stalk* about 2 ft. long; blade hastate, 12 in. long or more. *Peduncle* about 6 in. long. *Spathe-tube* oblong-ovoid, 2½ in. long; blade over 6 in. long, convolute below. China. Greenhouse.

T. Girald'ii. Nearly related to *T. giganteum* but smaller; *l.-stalk* variegated, l. usually shorter. *Spathe* ovate oblong, about 5 in. long. China. (B.M. n.s. 156.)

T. trilobat'um. Tuber subglobose, about 1½ in. across. *l.-stalk* 10 to 12 in. long, sheath variegated; blade hastate, deeply 3-cut, segs. all slender-pointed, mid-lobe ovate, 3½ to 7 in. long, side lobes oblique. *Peduncles,* slender, 2 to 3 in. long. *Spathe-tube* oblong, 1 in. long, blade oblong-ovate-lanceolate, 6 in. long or more, pale green without, rose-purple within. India, Malaya. (L.B.C. 442 and B.R. 450 as *Arum orixense.*)

TYPHONODO'RUM (derivation from Greek *tuphov*, typhoon, stormy wind, *doron*, gift, but relevance not clear.) FAM. *Araceae.* A genus of a single species of gigantic, evergreen, glabrous tree-like Aroid. Characters as given below. Spadix female in lower part, neuter in middle, male above. Fruit a large berry. Treatment as for Amorphophallus.

T. Lindleya'num. Evergreen, glabrous, tree-like. Stem 3 to 10 ft. h., up to 1 ft. thick. *l.* in a terminal crown; stalk 2 to 4 ft. long, sheathing at base, blade ovate, 14 to 40 in. long, acute, deeply heart-shaped or arrow-shaped at base, basal lobes roundish, sinus triangular. *Spathe* sub-erect, 16 to 24 in. long, tube oblong, green, blade lanceolate up to 18 in. long, convolute at base, yellow; on a short green peduncle; spadix orange-yellow 10 to 16 in. long. May. Madagascar, Zanzibar. 1905. (B.M. 8307.) It grows wild in water 3 ft. or more deep. The seeds are eaten by the natives.

typ'icus -a -um, agreeing best with the type of a group (*see* **Type**).

tyrian'thinus -a -um, of Tyrian purple dye.

TYRIM'NUS (derivation uncertain, said to be from Greek *turos*, cheese, the plant being reputed to cause milk to curdle, but perhaps connected with the god Tyrimnos). FAM. *Compositae.* A genus of a single species of erect thistle-like, grey-hairy herb, native of S. Europe. Characters as below. Hardy, but of no garden merit.

T. leucograph'is. Biennial 1 to 2 ft. h.; stem unbranched or only slight branched. *l.* alternate, sinuate, dentate or pinnatifid teeth and lobes spiny; stem-l. decurrent. *fl.-heads* purple or white, long-stalked, hemispherical; *fl.* all fertile; involucre receptacle and pappus as in Carduus. Achenes 4-angled. May to July. S. Europe. (R.I.F.G. 881.) SYN. *Carduus leucographus.*

TYTON'IA. A synonym of Hydrocera.

U

uber -is -e, full, fruitful, luxuriant.

ucra'nicus -a -um, of the Ukraine, European Russia.

uden'sis -is -e, pertaining to the Uda River or Udsk district of East Siberia near the Sea of Okhotsk.

uduen'sis -is -e, of Udu, north-east New Guinea.

Uechtrizia'nus -a -um, in honour of Richard von Uechtritz, 1836–86, of Breslau, writer on the flora of Silesia, 1881.

ugan'dae, uganden'sis -is -e, of Uganda, E. Trop. Africa.

Ugni, from the native Chilean name *uñi.*

ugoen'sis -is -e, of Mt. Ugo in Luzon, Philippines.

Uittien'ii, in honour of Hendrik Uittien, 1898–1944, distinguished Dutch systematic botanist, authority on tropical American flora, shot during Nazi occupation of Holland for patriotic activities.

ulcero'sus -a -um, full of excrescences or knots.

U'LEX (old Latin name). FAM. *Leguminosae.* Very spiny shrubs whose genuine leaves are 3-foliolate but only seen on quite young seedlings; in adult plants they are reduced to a spine-tipped petiole. The green colouring of the spines and young shoots give these shrubs an evergreen character. Flowers 1 or 2 in the spine-axils, both calyx and petals yellow; calyx 2-lipped; standard petal ovate. Pod few-seeded. About 6 species are known, all W. European, only 3 of which, all British, are worth cultivation. Of these *U. europaeus* flowers in spring, the other 2 in late summer and autumn. A revision of Ulex and allied genera by W. Rothmaler has been published in Engler, *Bot. Jahrb.* 72. 69–116 (1941). Ulex is here reduced to 6 species and the genera **Ne'pa,** with 1 species, *N. Boivinii*, syn. *U. Webbianus*, and **Stauracan'thus,** with 1 species, *S. genistoides*, syn. *U. spartioides*, are recognized as distinct.

To get the most beauty out of these shrubs they must be grown in full sunshine and in poor, dry soil. In good garden soil they grow too freely and blossom poorly. They are admirable for grouping on dry, hot banks, always remembering that, in *U. europaeus*, the quantity of dead twigs and spines inside the outer living layer makes them very inflammable.

The double-flowered *U. europaeus* is easily struck from late summer cuttings dibbled in very sandy soil in a frame or under a hand-light.

KEY

1. *Main spines* 1 *to* 2 *in. long, cal. densely shaggy* $\frac{5}{10}$ *to* $\frac{7}{10}$ *in. long* U. europaeus
1. *Main spines usually less than* 1 *in. long, cal. pubescent* $\frac{3}{10}$ *to* $\frac{1}{2}$ *in. long* 2
2. *Spines weak. Wings curved, about as long as keel* U. minor
2. *Spines stiff. Wings straight, longer than keel* U. Gallii

U. europae'us. Gorse, Whin, Furze. Densely spiny shrub, 2 to 4 ft. as seen wild, twice as high in gardens; shoots hairy, lateral ones short, spine-tipped; primary spines 1 to 2 in. long, furrowed; lateral spines $\frac{1}{4}$ to $\frac{1}{2}$ in. long. *fl.* golden-yellow, $\frac{7}{8}$ in. long. April, May. *Pod* $\frac{5}{8}$ in. long. W. Europe, including Britain. (E.B. 323.) var. **plenus,*** *fl.* double, most or all the stamens being transformed into pet. of different sizes; **stric'tus,** Irish gorse, of erect, rather columnar growth, shy-flowering. Ireland. SYN. *U. hibernicus, U. strictus.* Commons gorse is occasionally killed back to ground-level in severe winter, but never outright.

U. Gal'lii. Densely spiny shrub, 1½ to 2 ft. in a wild state, taller in gardens; shoots hairy, spines $\frac{1}{4}$ to 1 in. long. *fl.* golden-yellow, $\frac{5}{8}$ in. long; wing pet. curved, differing from that of *U. nanus* in being longer than the keel. August to October. *Pod* $\frac{1}{3}$ to $\frac{1}{2}$ in. long. W. Europe; almost confined to the western side of England. (E.B. 324.) Not so hardy as *U. minor.*

U. hiber'nicus. A synonym of *U. europaeus strictus.*

U. mi'nor.* Dwarf shrub of dense habit, usually 1 to 2 ft. on moors and commons, taller and more lanky in gardens; shoots downy, densely spiny; spines $\frac{1}{4}$ to $\frac{3}{4}$ in. long. *fl.* golden-yellow, $\frac{1}{2}$ in. long; cal. downy; wing pet. about as long as the keel. July to October. Pod $\frac{1}{2}$ in. long, hairy. W. Europe including England. (E.B. 325.) SYN. *U. nanus.*

U. stric'tus. A variety of *U. europaeus.*

ulici'nus -a -um, ulicoi'des, Ulex-like.

uligino'sus -a -um, growing in swamps.

ULLOA. *See* **Juanulloa.**

ULLU'CUS (*Ulluco*, the native name). FAM. *Basellaceae.* A genus of a single species of fleshy, decumbent and twining herbaceous perennial with a creeping rhizome and angular stem producing tuberous roots. Leaves alternate, roundish-heart-shaped, thick-stalked. Flowers in loose, large, axillary racemes, golden, with a 5-parted rotate perianth with a short tube, 5 stamens and a very small ovate. Fruit ovoid, berry-like. *U. tuberosus* is half-hardy, and grows well in any light soil, being reproduced easily by tubers. The small tubers are eaten in Peru and Bolivia, and it has been unsuccessfully tried as a substitute for potatoes in this country.

U. tubero'sus. Description as above. About 1 ft. h. Andes of S. America. 1846. (B.M. 4617.)

ULMA'CEAE. Dicotyledons. About 160 species of trees (rarely shrubs) falling into about 15 genera found in all parts of the world except the polar regions. Leaves alternate, pinnate-veined, usually oblique at base, generally toothed, stipules deciduous. Flowers sometimes unisexual; perianth segments usually connate, 4 to 5, rarely 3 to 8, stamens as many or rarely twice as many; ovary superior, 1-celled, style 2-parted. Fruit a samara, nut, or drupe, 1-seeded. The genera treated here are Aphananthe, Celtis, Hemiptelea, Planera, Pteroceltis, Ulmus, Zelkova.

ULMA'RIA. *See* **Filipendula.**

ulmifo'lius -a -um, elm-leaved.

ulmoi'des, elm-like.

UL'MUS (ancient Latin name). Elm. FAM. *Ulmaceae.* A genus of about 35 species of deciduous trees, mostly of large size, inhabiting the temperate regions of the N. Hemisphere, with numerous hybrids; frequently suckering from the root; shoots often corky winged. Leaves alternate, nearly always more or less obovate and unequal-sided or oblique at base, always toothed, mostly harsh to the touch above, shortly stalked. Flowers bisexual, very small, opening early in spring before the leaves or in autumn in clusters from the leaf-axils. Perianth bell-shaped, mostly with 4 or 5 lobes and the same number of stamens. Fruit (samara) a flat membranous disk notched at top with a flattened seed just below the notch or in the centre.

Elms are mostly hardy trees, easily transplanted and, with the exception of the American species, easily cultivated in any soil of even moderate quality if well drained. Some of them change to a good yellow in autumn, none better than our Common Elm.

As regards propagation not much reliance can be placed on seed produced in this country. *U. glabra*, the Wych Elm, yields fertile seed and, as it does not sucker, provides a useful stock on which to graft or bud other species. Some of the *carpinifolia* group are also quite fertile. The Common Elm is mostly barren, but like some others produces abundant suckers. Layering is quite easy from stool plants or branches low enough to reach the ground.

DISEASES. The most important disease of Elms is that known as Dutch Elm Disease caused by the fungus *Ceratostomella Ulmi* (the name of the imperfect stage of the fungus is *Graphium Ulmi*). The symptoms are to be seen in early summer when the leaves on some branches dry up and shrivel and may remain hanging on the tree in a brown dead state. The dead twigs often twist and curl up at the tips. The disease may persist for several years, killing branches in succession and, if at the top of the tree, the condition known as 'Stag-headed' may be the result. A symptom of the disease is that the sapwood of dead and dying branches shows, when cut across, brownish spots or flecks in the wood near the bark, like broken rings. A long slanting cut with a knife will similarly show irregular brownish streaks. Stripping the bark off an affected branch will also show long dark streaks on the peeled tissues. The spread of the disease is largely carried out by the Elm Bark Beetles (*Scolytus scolytus* and *S. multistriatus*) which ordinarily lay their eggs in weak or dying elm-trees by boring through the bark of the trunk and larger branches. From an infected tree the beetles become contaminated with the spores of the fungus which they carry on their bodies when they fly to healthy trees to feed. The fungal spores gain entrance through the small feeding wounds made by the beetles in the crotches of the twigs of the crown and thus infection is spread. In a year or so, when its vitality has been sapped, the tree is in a fit condition for the beetle to breed in and the vicious circle is complete. Although trees of all ages are attacked, young trees and succulent growths are mostly generally affected. The die-back of branches is due partly to the effect of a toxin produced by the fungus and partly to blockage of the wood-vessels curtailing the water-supply to the leaves. Infected trees may be assisted by a light dressing of dung or a general fertilizer, but too much nitrogen should be avoided. Dead and dying branches should be removed or burnt. Dying trees should be cut down, small branches burnt, and cut timber, if not utilized at once, should be disbarked by the end of February to kill beetle larvae.

There has been much research on the resistance of elms to the Dutch Elm Disease. No species is completely resistant, but the Asiatic *U. parviflora* and *U. pumila* are highly resistant, while the American elm, *U. americana*, is most susceptible. Of British elms, the Wych elm, *U. glabra*, and some of its hybrids are comparatively susceptible, the Jersey or Wheatley elm, *U. stricta* var. *sarniensis*, the most resistant, and the remainder intermediate. British elms often recover from an attack, but drought and other adverse conditions favour the fungus and the beetles. A very resistant elm named 'Christine Buisman' which has been distributed from Holland is not suitable for street planting on account of its spreading habit and pendulous branches, and, moreover, has proved to be susceptible to the coral spot fungus,

Nectria. Breeding and selection of trees resistant to both fungi continues.

D. E. G. and R. M.

U. ala'ta. Wahoo or Winged Elm. Tree of 40 to 50 ft., shoots glabrous, ultimately developing 2 conspicuous corky wings. *l.* 1½ to 2½ in. long, narrowly obovate or ovate-oblong, glabrous above, downy on veins beneath. *fr.* oval ½ in. long, covered with white hairs. S. United States. 1820. (S.S. 7, 313.) Very rare and apparently unsuited for Britain.

U. america'na. White Elm. Tree up to 130 ft. with a broad, open head of branches pendulous at the ends. *l.* 3 to 6 in. long, oval or obovate, slender-pointed, very unequal at the base, doubly toothed, glabrous and rough above, usually downy beneath; veins in about 18 pairs; stalk ½ in. long. *fr.* oval, scarcely ½ in. long, fringed with hairs; seed just below the notch. N. America. 1752. (S.S. 7, 311.) Magnificent tree in its native land but rarely good in Britain.

U. × **bel'gica** (*U.* × *hollandica* noth. *belgica*). Belgian Elm. Tree up to 100 ft. or more; shoots more or less downy. *l.* 3½ to 5 in. long, very unequal at base, abruptly pointed, roughish above, densely downy beneath; veins in 14 to 18 pairs. *fr.* obovate, ¾ in. long; seed near the centre. Popular street tree on the Continent. noth. **Dumont'ii,** habit more pyramidal.

U. campes'tris. A confused name now rejected.

U. carpinifo'lia. Smooth-leaved Elm. Tree, 100 ft. suckering, outer branches pendulous, shoots glabrous or nearly so, slender. *l.* 2 to 4 in. long, ovate or oval, very unequal at base, abruptly slender-pointed, glossy green, smooth and glabrous above, downy in vein-axils beneath; veins in 10 to 12 pairs. *fr.* oval or obovate, ⅜ in. long; seed close to the notch. Europe, including Britain, W. Asia. (E.H. 7, 399–401.) Syn. *U. glabra* (Miller, not Hudson), *U. foliacea.* var. **Berard'ii,** *l.* oval, ½ to 1½ in. long, coarsely toothed, glabrous. Metz. 1863; **pen'dula,** branches slender, pendulous; **subero'sa,** of low, spreading habit, branchlets with 4 corky wings; **variega'ta,** *l.* spotted and stained with white, especially near the margins; **Webbia'na,** columnar tree, *l.* small rounded.

U. corita'na. Coritanian Elm. Tree up to 60 ft. Branches spreading ascending forming an open crown. Branchlets glabrous, chestnut brown. *l.* varying from suborbicular to ovate-acute and ovate-lanceolate in the varieties, bright green, smooth and shining above, paler and with prominent tufts of hairs in the vein axils below, margin bluntly biserrate. Veins 8 to 12 pairs. Midlands and East Anglia. var. **media,** *l.* 1½ to 2½ in. long, ovate-acute, base very unequal; **rotundifo'lia,** *l.* 1 to 2 in. long, broadly ovate-acute, base obliquely subcordate; **angustifo'lia,** *l.* 1½ to 3½ in. long, narrowly ovate to ovate-lanceolate, base very unequal.

U. cornubien'sis. A synonym of *U. stricta.*

U. crassifo'lia. Cedar Elm. Tree up to 80 ft., shoots softly downy, often developing 2 corky wings. *l.* ¾ to 2 in. long, ovate to oval, bluntish at the apex, coarsely toothed, very rough above, softly downy beneath, firm and thick in texture; stalk 1/12 to ⅛ in. long. *fl.* in axillary clusters in early autumn. *fr.* ⅓ in. long, oval, deeply notched, completely downy. S. United States. 1876. (S.S. 7, 315.)

U. diversifo'lia. East Anglian Elm. Erect to spreading tree up to 60 ft., suckering. Branchlets hairy, slender. Short lateral stalk mostly with l. elliptical to obovate-acute, margin rather bluntly 2-serrate, base very unequal or occasionally with all l. elliptical acute with base tapering to rounded and subequal, or with both kinds of l. on the same shoot. *l.* 2 to 3½ in. long, slightly rough above, softly hairy below.

U. exonien'sis. A synonym of *U. glabra fastigiata.*

U. folia'cea. A synonym of *U. carpinifolia.*

U. ful'va. Slippery Elm. Tree 60 to 70 ft., shoots and winter buds very downy. *l.* 3 to 8 in. long, obliquely oblong-ovate, abruptly narrowed to a long, slender point, doubly toothed, rough above, downy beneath. *fr.* orbicular to obovate, up to ¾ in. long, slightly notched; seed central, covered with a patch of red-brown hairs. N. America. 1830. (S.S. 7, 314.) Uncommon.

U. glab'ra.* Wych or Scotch Elm. Tree 100 to 125 ft. with an open, widespreading head of branches; shoots downy. *l.* 3 to 7 in. long, oval or obovate, sometimes 3-lobed near the end, very oblique at the base, rough above, downy beneath; veins in 14 to 20 pairs; stalk ¼ in. or less long. *fr.* oval, ¾ to 1 in. long, downy at the notched apex; seed in the centre. N. Europe, including Britain. (E.H. 7, 394.) Syn. *U. montana.* Much used as a stock for grafting because of its non-suckering habit. var. **Camperdown'ii,** globose-headed tree with pendulous branches; **crisp'a,** *l.* narrowly oblong-oval, up to 3½ in. long, jaggedly and deeply cut into slender teeth; slow-growing; **fastigia'ta,** Exeter Elm, narrow columnar tree with erect branches. Syn. *U. exoniensis*; **fastigiata au'rea,** *l.* yellow; Syn. *U. Wredei*; **lacinia'ta,** *see* **U. laciniata**; **libero-rubro,** inner bark, purplish-red; **lutes'cens,** *l.* yellow; **na'na,** dwarf, rounded bush, 5 or 6 ft.; **pen'dula,*** branches stiffly pendulous. An excellent lawn tree of rounded shape, should be grafted high; **purpu'rea** (*atropurpurea*), *l.* purple when young.

U. × **hollan'dica** var. **ma'jor*** (*U. glabra* × *U. carpinifolia*). Dutch Elm. Tree up to 120 ft., head of branches open, spreading, pendulous at the ends, suckering, shoots soon glabrous. *l.* 2½ to 5 in. long, acute, very unequal at the base, dark shining green and nearly glabrous above, downy in the axils of the 10 to 14 pairs of veins beneath. *fr.* oval-obovate, ¾ to 1 in. long; seed close to the notch. Britain. var. **Smith'ii,** Downton Elm, branches pendulous. Syn. *U. Smithii*; **ve'geta,** Huntingdon Elm, tree up to 100 ft., suckering, *l.* up to 5 or 6 in. long, oval, glabrous or nearly so above, downy beneath in the axils of the 14 to 18 pairs of veins, *fr.* oval, ⅞ in. long; seed below the notch. England. 1750.

U. japo'nica. Japanese Elm. Tree up to 100 ft., shoots very downy, warted, yellowish-brown, sometimes winged. *l.* 3 to 4½ in. long, oval or obovate, abruptly slender-pointed, coarsely double-toothed, rough above, downy beneath especially on the 12 to 16 pairs of veins; stalk ⅛ in. long. *fr.* obovate, ⅝ in. long; seed close to the notch. Japan. 1897. (G. & F. 6, 327.)

U. × **Klem'eri** (*U.* × *hollandica* var. *Klemeri*). Flanders or Klemmer Elm. Tall, narrowly pyramidal tree.

U. lacinia'ta. Tree up to 30 ft., shoots nearly or quite glabrous. *l.* obovate or obovate-oblong, up to 6 or 7 in. long, mostly 3- or sometimes 5-lobed at apex, rough above, densely and softly downy beneath. *fr.* oval, ⅞ in. long, glabrous; seed in the centre. China, Japan. 1900. Akin to *U. glabra* but the lobed l. are very distinct.

U. lae'vis. European White Elm. Tree over 100 ft., shoots grey-downy. *l.* obliquely obovate, 2½ to 5 in. long, doubly toothed, abruptly pointed, glabrous above, densely grey-downy beneath; veins in 16 to 18 pairs; stalk ⅛ to ¼ in. long. *fr.* ovate or oval, ½ in. long, ciliate, with incurved horns at the notch. Cent. and E. Europe. 1800. (E.H. 7, 389, 390.) Old World counterpart of *U. americana,* but succeeds better in Britain. Syn. *U. pedunculata.*

U. macrocar'pa. Tree sometimes 50 ft., but usually smaller and bushy; shoots downy, developing 2 corky wings. *l.* 2 to 4 in. long, broadly obovate to oval, shortly and slender-pointed, rough, bristly, and with axil tufts beneath; veins in 10 to 14 pairs. *fr.* orbicular to obovate, up to 1¼ in. long, ciliate; seed central. China. 1908. Distinct by its large fr.

U. monta'na. A synonym of *U. glabra.*

U. ni'tens. A synonym of *U. carpinifolia.*

U. parvifo'lia. Tree up to 40 ft. with a slender trunk and elegant head of slender branches; shoots grey-downy. *l.* ¾ to 2½ in. long, oval to obovate, bluntly toothed, shining green above, paler bright green beneath; stalk 1/16 to ¼ in. long. *fl.* in axillary clusters opening in early autumn. *fr.* ovate to oval, ⅓ in. long; seed in the centre. China, Korea, Japan. 1794. (R.H. 1909, 399.) Attractive and distinct; retaining its foliage until New Year.

U. peduncula'ta. A synonym of *U. laevis.*

U. pinna'to-ramo'sa. A variety of *U. pumila.*

U. × **Pitteur'sii** (*U.* × *hollandica* var. *Pitteursii*). Belgium.

U. Plot'ii. Plot Elm. Slender, elegant tree up to 80 or 90 ft., suckering, younger branches pendulous. *l.* obovate to oval, 1½ to 2 in. long, dull green, rounded to cordate at the base, downy beneath; veins in 8 to 10 pairs. *fr.* narrowly obovate, notched, seed above the centre. Europe (S. and E. England) (E.H. 7, 403.) Differs from *U. carpinifolia* by its slender habit and small dark green *l.* with fewer veins with nearly equal bases.

U. proce'ra. English Elm. Tree 100 to 150 ft., suckering; shoots downy. *l.* 2 to 3½ in. long, broadly ovate or oval, very unequal at the base, abruptly pointed, rough above, downy and with axil tufts of white down on the 10 to 12 pairs of veins beneath. *fr.* roundish, ½ in. wide, glabrous; seed close to apical notch. England, mostly in hedgerows, possibly also in France. (E.H. 404.) Much planted in the 17th and 18th centuries to form avenues. Syn. *U. campestris.* var. **Van-Houtt'ei,** *l.* yellow; **variega'ta,** *l.* conspicuously blotched and margined with creamy-white. One of the best variegated large trees.

U. pu'mila. Dwarf Elm. Small tree, 12 to 40 ft. h., or a shrub. *l.* ¾ to 2½ in. long, oval to oval-lanceolate, coarsely toothed, dark green, glabrous; stalk 1/12 to ⅛ in. long. *fr.* obovate to round, ½ in. wide, deeply notched; seed near the centre. China, Siberia, Turkistan. 1860. var. **pen'dula,** branches slender and pendulous; **pinnato-ramosa,** branchlets pinnately arranged, *l.* longer-pointed, Syn. *U. pinnato-ramosa.*

U. Rosseel'sii. A synonym of *U. viminalis aurea.*

U. sero'tina. Red Elm. Tree up to 60 ft., shoots often becoming corky. *l.* 2 to 3½ in. long, narrowly obovate, very oblique at base, slender-pointed, doubly toothed, glossy and glabrous above; veins in about 20 pairs; stalk ¼ in. long. *fl.* in racemes opening in September. *fr.* oval, ½ in. long, deeply notched, markedly ciliate. SE. United States. 1898. (S.S. 14, 718.)

U. × **Smith'ii.** A synonym of *U.* × *hollandica Smithii.*

U. stric'ta. Cornish Elm. Suckering tree 80 to 100 ft., of columnar shape due to the shortness of its side branches. *l.* 2 to 2½ in. long, obovate or oval, glabrous and glossy above, tufted in the vein-axils beneath; veins in 10 to 12 pairs. *fr.* ⅜ in. long, resembling that of *U. nitens* but narrower. Cornwall, Devon, Somerset, Brittany. (E.H. 7, 397.) Syn. *U. cornubiensis, U. nitens stricta.* var. **Sarnien'sis,** Jersey Elm, of stiff pyramidal growth, with more erect-branching, *l.* not so downy beneath, proportionately broader. (B.T.S. 1, 86.) Syn. var. *Wheatleyi*; **Wheat'leyi au'rea,** *l.* rich yellow.

U. Thoma'si. Rock Elm. Tree 80 to 100 ft., buds and shoots downy. *l.* 2 to 4½ in. long, oval to obovate, abruptly pointed, doubly toothed glabrous above, downy beneath; veins in 14 to 20 pairs. *fl.* in racemes 1 to 2 in. long. *fr.* oval, ⅜ in. long, completely downy, shallowly notched. N. America. 1875. (S.S. 7, 312.) Of little or no value in Britain. SYN. *U. racemosa.*

U.×ve'geta. A synonym of *U.×hollandica vegeta.*

U. vimina'lis. Tree 30 to 40, rarely 70 ft., of slender graceful habit, branches drooping. *l.* 1 to 2½ in. long, ⅛ to ⅝ in. wide, oblanceolate or narrowly oval, often tapered at base, long- and slender-pointed, very deeply toothed, upper surface very rough, downy beneath on the veins and in the vein-axils. *fr.* like *U. carpinifolia.* Of uncertain origin; probably a seedling sport from a hybrid. SYN. *U. campestris viminalis.* var. **au'rea,** *l.* yellow. SYN. *U. Rosseelsii*; **variega'ta,** *l.* stained with creamy-white.

U. Wilsonia'na. Tree up to 80 ft., shoots downy, often becoming corky. *l.* ovate to oval, unequal at the base, shortly but slenderly pointed, doubly toothed, very rough above, downy beneath on the 16 to 22 pairs of veins; stalk ⅛ to ¼ in. long. *fr.* obovate, glabrous; seed situated just below the notch. China. 1910.

W. J. B. and R. M.

Ulricia'nus -a -um, in honour of Oberlandforstmeister Ulrici, 1824–96.

UMBEL. An inflorescence with stalked flowers arising from a single point; if the umbels arise from similarly arranged peduncles the inflorescence is a compound umbel.

umbella'tus -a -um, umbella'ris -is -e, umbellate, arranged in, or resembling umbels.

UMBELLIF'ERAE. Dicotyledons. A family of about 1,400 species in about 180 genera, chiefly natives of the north temperate regions but also distributed over all other parts of the world. Mostly herbs with hollow internodes and usually much divided leaves with a conspicuous sheath and without stipules. Flowers in umbels, mostly compound, usually with an involucre of bracts at the base of the main umbel and others at the bases of the secondary umbels, the former being called an involucre, the latter involucels. The inflorescence is a simple umbel in several genera and in Eryngium a head, the topmost flowers opening first. Flowers usually perfect and regular; the calyx very small; petals free, 5 (rarely 0), white or yellow; stamens 5; ovary inferior, of 2 carpels each containing one ovule. Fruit a dry schizocarp splitting into 2 mericarps each with 1 seed, held together at first by a thin stalk (carpophore) running between them. The nature of the ripe fruit is in this family a main basis of classification. The plants are usually poisonous but several are useful as food, as condiments, or medicinally. The genera dealt with here are: Aciphylla, Actinotus, Aegopodium, Ammi, Angelica, Anthriscus, Apium, Arracacia, Astrantia, Athamanta, Azorella, Bupleurum, Cachrys, Carum, Chaerophyllum, Coriandrum, Crithmum, Daucus, Didiscus, Dorema, Eryngium, Ferula, Foeniculum, Hacquetia, Heracleum, Hydrocotyle, Laserpitium, Levisticum, Malabaila, Meum, Molospermum, Myrrhis, Opoponax, Petroselinum, Peucedanum, Pleurospermum, Portenschlagia, Seseli, Smyrnium, Sium, Thapsia, Xanthosia. Some botanists now remove the genus Hydrocotyle from the Umbelliferae and place it in an independent family, the Hydrocotylaceae, mainly on account of the woody endocarp of its fruit; it stands between the Umbelliferae and Araliaceae.

UMBELLULA. An umbel on a branch of the main umbel.

UMBELLULA'RIA (*umbella,* umbel; in allusion to the shape of the inflorescence). FAM. *Lauraceae.* Monotypic genus, differing from Sassafras by its umbellate inflorescence and from Laurus by its 4-celled anthers. *U. californica,* although occasionally injured during our severest winters, may be considered hardy in our average climate. It does not like very chalky soils. Propagated by seeds and layers. Handling the foliage is apt to cause skin irritation, running at the eyes, &c., in some persons.

Umbellularia californica

U. califor'nica. Californian Sassafras. A strongly aromatic, evergreen tree, 50 to 80 ft. (sometimes twice as high in its wild state). *l.* alternate, leathery, 2 to 5 in. long, ⅝ to 1½ in. wide, narrowly oval or oblong, tapered to both ends, entire, soon quite glabrous. *fl.* yellowish-green, in stalked umbels ¾ in. wide, in several of the terminal l.-axils; perianth 6-parted; stamens in several whorls. April. *fr.* roundish-obovoid, ⅞ to 1 in. long, green becoming purplish. California to Oregon. 1830. (B.M. 5320 as *Oreodaphne californica.*)

W. J. B.

umbilicate, navel-like; depressed in centre.

UMBILI'CUS (*umbilicus,* navel; from the depression in the leaves). FAM. *Crassulaceae.* There are about 6 nearly related species distributed through S. Europe to W. Asia; they have sometimes been included in Cotyledon (q.v.) and, as now defined, the genus no longer contains the species with leaves in a close rosette (*see* **Rosularia**). The leaves are stalked and peltate, characterized by a depression in the centre; the flowers are small and bell-shaped, very numerous but inconspicuous. The plants are hardy but of more interest than decorative value in the garden. **A**

U. Aizo'on. A synonym of *Rosularia Aizoon.*

U. chrysan'thus. A synonym of *Rosularia pallida.*

U. erec'tus. Rootstock creeping. *l.* toothed. *fl.* yellow, very small, in a dense spike. Balkans, Asia Minor. SYN. *Cotyledon lusitanica.*

U. fimbria'tus. A synonym *Orostachys fimbriatus.*

U. gla'ber. A synonym of *Rosularia glabra.*

U. globulariaefo'lius. A synonym of *Rosularia globulariaefolia.*

U. libanot'icus. A synonym of *Rosularia Sempervivum.*

U. pal'lidus. A synonym of *Rosularia pallida.*

U. penduli'nus. Root tuberous. *l.* in a short-stemmed open rosette, peltate, depressed in the centre, long stalked. *fl.* small, tubular, greenish-white, with red dots, crowded into a simple or branched spike. Chiefly in Europe, including Great Britain. (D.C.Pl.Gr. 162.) SYN. *Cotyledon Umbilicus.*

U. platyphyl'lus. A synonym of *Rosularia platyphyllus.*

U. sedoi'des. A synonym of *Sedum Candollei.*

U. Sempervi'vum. A synonym of *Rosularia Sempervivum.*

U. serra'tus. A synonym of *Rosularia serrata.*

U. spino'sus. A synonym of *Orostachys spinosus.*

U. turkestan'icus. A synonym of *Rosularia turkestanica.*

V. H.

umbona'tus -a -um, raised like the boss of a shield.

umbraculiform, umbrella-shaped.

umbrati'cola, a dweller in shade.

umbra'tilis -is -e, remaining in the shade.

UMBRELLA LEAF. *See* **Diphylleia cymosa.**

UMBRELLA PINE. *See* **Sciadopitys verticillata.**

UMBRELLA PLANT. *See* **Peltiphyllum.**

UMBRELLA TREE. *See* **Magnolia tripetala.**

umbro'sus -a -um, shade-loving or affording shade.

unarmed, without spines, prickles, or thorns.

UNCA'RIA (*uncus,* a hook; the peduncles become hooked spines). FAM. *Rubiaceae.* A genus of about 30 species of tropical climbing shrubs, mostly Asiatic, with opposite, shortly stalked leaves with entire or 2-fid stipules. Flowers yellowish in heads; corolla tube long funnel-shaped, lobes 5, valvate; stamens 5 attached to the throat of the corolla. Related to Nauclea in which the capsules split into two. The oldest name, Ourouparia, is not now recognized. Stove conditions and a compost of loam, sand, and peat suit the plants which can be propagated by cuttings in sand under glass.

U. Gamb'ieri. Gambier Catechu. Climbing to about 10 ft. *l.* ovate to ovate-lanceolate, long pointed, 4 to 5 in. long, leathery, smooth. *fl.* stalked; cal. hairy; cor. ½ in. long; peduncles axillary, about 1 in. long. May. India. 1825. Produces the gambier of commerce.

U. sessilifruc'tus. About 10 ft. h. *l.* elliptic, more or less obtusely pointed, 4 to 4½ in. long, shining above, glabrous and glaucous beneath; stalks ¼ in. long. *fl.* pale red; heads 1 in. across; peduncles 1 to 1½ in. long, axillary and in terminal panicles. India. 1829. SYN. *Nauclea sessilifructa.*

unca'tus -a -um, unciform, bent or curved at tip like a hook.

UNCI'FERA (*uncus,* a hook, *fero,* to bear; the pollen masses are attached to a curved process). FAM. *Orchidaceae.* A genus of 4 epiphytic Orchids, natives of Sikkim and Assam, allied to Saccolabium. Flowers rather small, pale yellow, very shortly stalked, in lateral, dense, spike-like racemes; sepals sub-equal, free; petals similar or rather smaller; lip affixed to the base of the column, the base produced in a rather long, curved spur; lateral lobes small, the middle one entire or slightly 3-lobed; pollen masses 2. Leaves distichous; sheaths persistent, clothing the stem. Of little horticultural interest. Compost and treatment as for Saccolabiums. The species are *U. acuminata, U. heteroglossa, U. lancifolia,* and *U. obtusifolia.*

E. C.

uncina'tus -a -um, uncinate, hooked.

UNCI'NULA. A genus of Ascomycetous fungi, one of which, *U. necator,* is the cause of the Powdery Mildew of the Vine. (*See* **Vine diseases.**)

un'cipes, with hooked stalk.

unda'tus -a -um, wavy.

UNDERGROUND BEAN. *See* **Voandzeia subterranea.**

UNDERGROUND ONION. *See* **Onion, Potato.**

UNDER-SHRUB. A small plant, woody except at tips of branches which perish annually; the term sub-shrub has the same meaning.

undo'sus -a -um, wavy.

undula'tus -a -um (***undulati-*** in compound words), undulate, wavy, usually applied to a leaf-margin alternately concave and convex, not flat.

Une'do, literally, I eat one.

Unequally pinnate, imparipinnate, i.e. pinnate with an odd terminal leaflet.

UNGER'NIA (in honour of Baron Franz von Ungern-Sternberg, 1800–68, of Dorpat). FAM. *Amaryllidaceae.* A genus of 8 species of Asiatic bulbous plants differing from Lycoris by the numerous discoid seeds. Leaves lorate. Flowers many in an umbel; perianth regular, tube funnel-shaped, lobes oblong, keeled with many close green ribs; stamens in 2 rows near the throat of the perianth tube; scape solid; spathe valves 2. For treatment *see* **Amaryllis.** Hardy or nearly so. Except for the doubtful *U. Oldhamii,* said to be Japanese, the species (*U. ferganica, U. flava, U. minor, U. Sewerzowii, U. trisphaera,* and *U. Victoris*) are natives of Cent. Asia and Persia and their bulbs probably require a rest period, during which they are kept dry.

U. trisphaer'a. Bulb 3 in. across, tunics produced 6 in. above its neck. *Scape* 6 to 12 in. long; umbel 6- to 15-fld. *fl.* reddish, 1 to 1¼ in. long, segs. acute. Summer. Turkistan. 1886. (Gr.F. 914 as *Lycoris Sewerzowii.*)

UNGNA'DIA (in honour of Baron David von Ungnad, Austrian envoy at the Court of Constantinople about 1576 to 1582, who sent seeds of the Horse-chestnut and many other Balkan plants to Clusius). FAM. *Sapindaceae.* One species, a shrub or small tree related to Aesculus. *U. speciosa* is not hardy and should be grown outdoors in summer, in a cool conservatory in winter. Almost any soil suits it and it can be increased by layers or by imported seeds.

U. specio'sa. *l.* alternate, unequally pinnate, without stipules; lflets. in 6 or 7 pairs, about 4 in. long, very shortly stalked, ovate-lanceolate, the terminal one long-stalked. *fl.* pink in lateral corymbs or clusters; cal. 4- or 5-partite, segs. nearly equal; pet. 4 or 5, nearly equal, claws crested at apex; stamens 7 to 10. June. Texas. 1850. (F.d.S. 1059.)

unguicula'ris -is -e, unguicula'tus -a -um, having a stalk or claw, usually applied to the petals.

uni-, in compound words, signifying one-, as uniflorus, one-fld.

UNICORN PLANT. *See* **Martynia louisiana.**

UNIFO'LIUM. A synonym of Maianthemum.

unilocular, of an anther, ovary, or fruit, having only one chamber or loculus.

uninterrupted, having parts regularly increasing or diminishing or all of one size and at approximately equal intervals.

UNIO'LA (old Latin name of an unknown plant). FAM. *Gramineae.* Spike Grass. A genus of 8 species of perennial grasses, natives of N. America. Leaves flat or involute. Panicles sometimes long, sometimes large, loose, or dense; spikelets closely 3- to many-flowered, very flat, sharply keeled; glumes lanceolate, compressed-keeled; lemmas lanceolate, awnless. Seeds should be sown in early spring in the open border. Some species resemble superficially *Bromus unioloides* and *Briza maxima* but are distinguished from the one by their awnless lemmas and from the other by their very flattened (not plump) spikelets.

U. latifo'lia. Tufted perennial. Stems 2 to 4 ft. h. *l.* flat, up to 1 in. wide, spreading and drooping. *Panicle* loose; spikelets ⅗ to 1½ in. long, on drooping peduncles. August. E. and Middle United States.

U. panicula'ta. Sea-oats. Stems about 8 ft. h., from creeping rhizomes. *l.* narrow, rolled erect. *Panicle* long, drooping; spikelets up to 1 in. long, narrower than in *U. latifolia,* upright on short pedicels. E. United States and W. Indies; sometimes used there to bind drifting coastal sand-dunes.

untrue, (1) seeds that produce varieties differing from that which they purport to be; (2) trees that do not prove true to name when they flower or fruit; (3) plants that 'sport' in their produce.

UPAS TREE. *See* **Antiaris toxicaria.**

uplan'dicus -a -um, of Upland, the district of Sweden around Uppsala.

URACH'NE. *See* **Oryzopsis.**

uralen'sis -is -e, of the Ural Mts., Russia.

ura'lum, from Urala swa, native name of *Hypericum Uralum.*

uran'thus -a -um, with tailed flowers.

URA'RIA (*oura*, tail; in allusion to the long racemes). FAM. *Leguminosae.* A genus of about 8 species of half-woody perennials, natives of Trop. Asia, Africa, and Australia with compound stipellate leaves and racemes of minute but very numerous papilionaceous flowers; calyx tube very short, 2 upper teeth short, 3 lower longer; standard broad; wings adherent to the obtuse keel; stamens diadelphous. The species grow in a compost of sand, loam, and peat in the stove.

U. crini'ta. 3 to 6 ft. h. *lflets.* 3 to 7, oblong, 4 to 6 in. long, about 1½ in. wide, rather leathery, green and smooth above, paler beneath. *fl.* purplish, ½ in. long, in dense cylindrical racemes over 1 ft. long. July. India.

U. pic'ta. Robust, stem 3 to 6 ft. long, downy. *lflets.* 4 to 6, rarely 9, linear, rigid, rather leathery, smooth above, minutely downy beneath. *fl.* purple; in dense, cylindrical racemes 6 to 12 in. long; cor. slightly exserted. July. Himalaya, Philippines. 1788.

Urbanii, in honour of Ignaz Urban, 1848–1931, of Berlin Botanical Museum, authority on flora of W. Indies.

ur'bicus -a -um, belonging to towns.

URBIN'IA. Included in **Echeveria.**

× URCEOCHA'RIS. Hybrids between species of Eucharis and Urceolina. × *U. Clibranii* was raised by Messrs. Clibran of Altrincham by crossing *Eucharis grandiflora* and *Urceolina urceolata* in 1892. *See* G.C. 12 (1892) 214. For cultivation *see* **Eucharis.**

× U. Clibran'ii. *l.* broadly ovate, acute. *fl.* pure white, intermediate between the parents, 2½ in. long, tube slender, limb cup-shaped, segs. slightly acute; stamens 6, nearly as long as segs.; infl. umbellate. Summer. SYN. *Eucharis Clibranii.*

× U. edenta'ta. Similar to × *U. Clibranii* except that there are no teeth on the corona between the stamens. A natural hybrid. (B.M. 8359.)

URCEOLA'RIA. A synonym of Urceolina.

urceola'tus -a -um, pitcher- or urn-shaped.

URCEOLI'NA (*urceolus*, a small cup or pitcher; from the shape of the perianth). FAM. *Amaryllidaceae.* A genus of 3 species of S. American bulbous plants with flat, ovate, oblong, or narrow leaves contracted into the stalks. Flowers rather long stalked, in a many-flowered umbel; erect at first then recurved or drooping; perianth expanded abruptly from a narrow tube into an oblong tubular or urn-shaped limb, lobes almost equal, connivent or connate, shortly spreading at apex; stamens attached at throat, projecting from the perianth, filaments straight; spathe valves 2, dry; scape solid. For treatment *see* **Amaryllis.**

U. au'rea. A synonym of *U. urceolata.*

U. latifo'lia. *l.* oblong, about 12 in. long, 2 to 3 in. wide, acute, striped above, shining, nerved and smooth beneath; stalked. *fl.* yellowish-red, greenish at tip; segs. ovate, connivent, equal; scape erect, terete, about 12 in. h. April. (B.M. 4952 as *Leperiza latifolia.*)

U. minia'ta. A synonym of *U. peruviana.*

U. pendu'la. A synonym of *U. urceolata.*

U. peruvia'na. Bulb as large as a walnut. *l.* 1 or 2, lanceolate, 6 to 8 in. long, acute, striated, margins reflexed. *fl.* 2 to 6, nodding, cinnabar-red or scarlet, 1½ in. long, segs. broadly ovate, acute; scape 8 to 14 in. long, erect, slightly twisted above. September. Peru, Bolivia. 1836. (B.R. 25, 68 as *Pentlandia latifolia.*) SYN. *U. miniata.* (B.M. n.s. 399.)

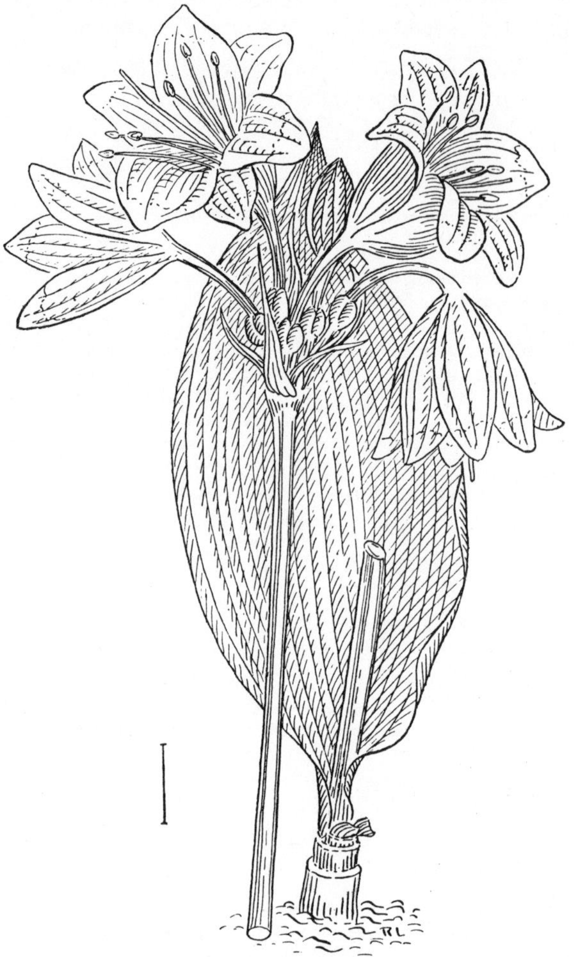

× *Urceocharis edentata*

U. urceola'ta. Bulb about 1½ in. through. *l.* 1 or 2, oblong, about 12 in. long, 3 or 4 in. wide, acute, glabrous; stalk long, compressed above. *fl.* 4 to 6, drooping, 2 in. long, bright yellow in basal half, upper part green margined white; segs. lanceolate, concave, outer 3 longer; scape about 12 in. h. Peru. (B.M. 5464.) SYN. *U. pendula.* Easily recognized by the green 1 in. long narrow stalk-like basal tube of the perianth.

URECHI'TES (*oura*, tail, *Echites*; in allusion to the twisted appendages of the anthers). FAM. *Apocynaceae.* A genus of about 2 species of prostrate or twining sub-shrubs, allied to Mandevilla, natives of the W. Indies and Trop. and Cent. America. Leaves opposite, entire not peltate. Flowers showy; 2 to several in terminal or axillary scopioid cymes; calyx 5-parted with numerous small scale-like appendages at base; corolla funnel-shaped with short cylindrical tube, long-bell-shaped throat, and 5 broad, twisted lobes, stamens 5, attached to top of tube, anthers usually with linear coiled appendages; seeds prolonged into a beak crowded with a tuft of long hair. For treatment *see* **Dipladenia.**

U. suberect'a. Partially erect, woody below. *l.* ovate to oval or elliptical, loosely silky (like shoots) at first. *fl.* large, yellow, in a loose 4- to 6-fld. terminal cyme; peduncle hairy. May. Colombia to Florida. 1845. (B.M. 4702 as *Dipladenia flava*; 1064 as *Echites suberecta.* Add. 131 as *U. pinetorum.*)

UREDINA'LES, Uredi'neae. *See* **Rusts.**

UREDOSPORE. The summer spore produced by many Rust fungi. They are formed on crowded groups of spore-bearing hyphae, so that they produce a pustule. They become free by the rupture of the host epidermis. They are 1-celled, thin-walled, orange or yellow, and germinate without a rest, infecting their host by a germ-tube usually entering through a stoma. Several generations of this summer stage may occur. In a few species growing in acid regions the uredospores may develop thick walls and rest before germination. These spores, intended to tide the fungus over periods of drought, are known as amphispores.

D. E. G.

URE'NA (*Uren*, the Malabar name). FAM. *Malvaceae*. A genus of 3 species of tropical herbs or under-shrubs, with usually angled or lobed leaves and small, usually clustered flowers. Calyx 5-cleft or -toothed with 5 adnate bracteoles; petals 5; staminal tube truncate or minutely toothed; carpels hooked. *U. lobata* is an annual growing well in any rich soil in a stove. Of little beauty.

U. loba'ta. Variable more or less hairy annual herb. *l.* cordate, 5- to 7-lobed to about a third, lobes 1 to 2 in. long, acute or obtuse; stalks shorter than blades. *fl.* pink; bracteoles equally cal. Summer. India. (B.M. 3043.)

u'rens, stinging.

URE'RA (from *uro*, burn, sting, pain acutely). FAM. *Urticaceae*. A genus of about 40 species of tropical trees and shrubs with powerful stinging hairs, natives of Trop. America, Africa, the Mascarene, and Pacific Is. Leaves alternate, feather veined or with 3 to 5 veins, stipulate. Flowers in panicles, unisexual, sometimes monoecious; perianth of male flowers 4- to 5-parted, segments ovate, stamens 4 or 5; female perianth 4-lobed. Achene enclosed in the fleshy perianth forming a pseudoberry. Needs stove conditions. In Latin America members of the genus are often known as 'ortiga' (i.e. nettle); gloves should be worn when handling them.

U. alceifo'lia and **U. caracasa'na,** widespread in Trop. America, have *l.* shallowly crenate-toothed, hairy, but without prickles, *fr.* red or orange.

U. bacci'fera. Cow-itch, Chichicaste. 6 to 21 ft. h. *l.* large, long-stalked; blade narrowly to broadly ovate, to 15½ in. long, 10½ in. wide, base rounded, margin and main veins on lower side prickly. *infl.* axillary, much branched, pink or crimson, 1 to 3 in. long; *pet.* white, very small. *fr.* white, waxy, 1/10 in. long. Trop. S. America, Cent. America, W. Indies. SYN. *Urtica baccifera*. Standley in his *Flora of Costa Rica* (*Field Mus. Publ. Bot.* 18), 1. 397 (1937) describes this shrub as 'one of the most dangerous plants of Central America, well known almost everywhere in the region. When one is struck by the coarse hairs the effect is almost like that of an electric shock and there often follows the most intense pain that may last, in decreasing degree, for several or many hours, with attendant inflammation of the skin. The plant is often used for hedges, which few larger animals care to penetrate.'

W. T. S.

URGIN'EA (*Beni Urgin*, an Arab tribe in Algeria). FAM. *Liliaceae*. A genus of about 30 species of bulbous plants, natives of Europe, the Mediterranean region, E. Indies, Trop. and S. Africa. Leaves radical, often narrow-linear, sometimes broadly loriform or nearly oblong. Scape leafless with small, dry bracts, ending in a usually many-flowered raceme with often rather small flowers; perianth whitish or rather pale yellowish or pink, at length deciduous; segments 6, distinct, more or less bell-shaped or spreading. Fruit a many-seeded globose or oblong capsule, deeply 3-lobed. Seeds brownish-black, more or less winged. *U. maritima* and *U. undulata* may sometimes be grown with success outdoors but are not really hardy and all the other species referred to, being mostly natives of S. Africa, need greenhouse protection. The large bulbs of *U. maritima* are well known in medicine as Squills. The general cultivation required is the same as for Scilla to which Urginea is very nearly allied.

U. altis'sima. Bulb 4 to 6 in. thick. *l.* 5 or 6, lorate-lanceolate, 1 to 1½ ft. long, 1½ to 2 in. wide at base, acute, glabrous. *Scape* 2 to 3 ft. long, raceme 1 to 2 ft. long, dense, cylindrical, 1½ to 2 in. broad. *fl.* nearly bell-shaped, about ⅓ in. long, whitish with a purplish-green keel, segs. ligulate. May. 1789. (B.M. 1074 as *Drimia altissima.*)

U. capita'ta. *l.* linear-lorate, about 12 in. long, ½ in. wide, somewhat fleshy. *fl.* white in a dense, terminal, globose raceme, 1 to 1½ in. wide; scape 6 to 9 in. long. June. Kaffraria. 1862. (B.M. 5388 as *Ornithogalum capitatum.*)

U. exuvia'ta. Bulb 1 to 1¾ in. thick, outer scales long, striped. *l.* 2 to 4, semi-terete, 1 to 1½ in. long, 1/20 in. wide, hard, flexuous, smooth. *fl.* about ½ in. long, whitish with purplish keel in a rather dense raceme, 10- to 20-fld., 2 to 4 in. long. June. 1795. (B.M. 871 as *Albuca exuviata.*)

U. filifo'lia. Bulb about 1 in. thick; reddish-brown. *l.* 3 to 6, 8 to 12 in. long, about 1/30 in. thick, filiform, hard, flexuous, glabrous. *fl.* about ⅓ in. long, whitish, purple-keeled, oblong, on pedicels ¼ to ½ in. long, in rather dense racemes, 6- to 20-fld., on a slender erect scape, 6 to 15 in. long. June. 1820. (B.R. 557 as *Albuca filifolia.*)

U. frag'rans. Bulb 1½ to 2 in. thick. *l.* 12 to 20, semi-terete, 6 to 8 in. long, about 1/24 in. wide, glabrous, persistent. *fl.* about ½ in. long, whitish, purple-keeled, fragrant; segs. oblong; pedicels about ½ in. long; raceme 12- to 20-fld., 4 to 6 in. long, rather loose; scape about 12 in. long, slender, terete, glaucous. July. 1791. (B.R. 311 as *Albuca fugax.*)

U. macrocen'tra. *l.* solitary, cylindrical, erect, 18 in. long. *fl.* ⅛ in. long, white tipped green, in a dense raceme 5 to 6 in. long, 1 in. wide; scape stout, erect up to 3 ft. long; lowest bracts with a dry convolute spur up to 1 in. long. May. 1887.

U. mari'tima. Sea Onion; Squills. Bulb 4 to 6 in. thick, ovoid, much out of ground. *l.* in spring, 10 to 20, lanceolate, 12 to 18 in. long, 2 to 4 in. wide above middle, rather fleshy, glaucous-green, glabrous. *fl.* about ¼ in. long, whitish, with greenish-purple keel, pedicels ½ to ¾ in. long; raceme dense, 12 in. or more long; scape 1 to 3 ft. long, terete, reddish. Mediterranean region. 1829. (B.M. 918 as *Ornithogalum Squilla.*) SYN. *U. Scilla.*

U. physo'des. Bulb purple, 1½ to 1¾ in. thick. *l.* 5 or 6, lanceolate, 6 to 9 in. long, 1 to 1½ in. wide, rather fleshy, glabrous. *fl.* about ¼ in. long, whitish, purple-keeled; pedicels about ¾ in. long; raceme rather dense, 30- to 60-fld., 3 to 5 in. long, cylindrical; scape slender, 6 in. long. June. 1804. (B.M. 1046 as *Albuca physodes.*)

U. undula'ta. Bulb ovate, large. *l.* linear, channelled, distinctly undulate-sinuate. *fl.* pale rose; segs. narrow, linear strap-shaped, obtuse, slightly joined at base; pedicels ascending, about as long as segs.; raceme loose, short; scape slender, erect, much longer than l. June. Is. of Mediterranean, N. Africa.

URINE. The liquid excreta of animals contains, in addition to small quantities of various salts, the nitrogenous waste (mainly urea) collected from all parts of the body of the animal by the blood and extracted from the blood by the kidneys. The presence of this nitrogenous material makes urine a valuable manure, and because of this, litter capable of absorbing it is spread where animals stand. On standing, urea is quickly decomposed by bacterial action into water and ammonium carbonate, the change being as in the following formula:

$$CO(NH_2)_2 = 2H_2O + (NH_4)_2CO_3$$

Urea — Water — Ammonium carbonate

The ammonium carbonate so produced is broken down into ammonia, carbon dioxide, and water, thus:

$$(NH_4)_2CO_3 = 2NH_3 + CO_2 + H_2O$$

Ammonium carbonate — Ammonia — Carbonate — Water

and unless something is present either to combine with or to absorb the ammonia it will pass into the air and be lost. The addition to the Urine of gypsum (calcium sulphate) results in the conversion of the ammonia into the non-volatile sulphate of ammonia, while if the urine be added to the soil the ammonia will be absorbed and retained for a time. It is very useful for such fruits as Black Currants and Raspberries as well as many other plants if diluted with 3 or 4 times its bulk of water. The liquid should not be allowed to drain away from manure heaps but should be collected in a tank to be used as suggested above. The solid matter, including urea, in urine is about 8 per cent. in that of cattle, 11 per cent. of horses, 13 per cent. of sheep, 25 per cent. of pigs; 3 to 6 per cent. in man.

urmien'sis -is -e, of Lake Urmia, NW. Persia.

URN FLOWER, DROOPING. *See* **Urceolina urceolata.**

urni'gerus -a -um, urn-bearing.

uro-, in compound words, signifying a tail.

UROCE'RUS gi'gas. *See* **Woodwasps.**

UROCYS'TIS. A genus of Smut fungi (Ustilaginales), species of which may cause serious plant diseases. *See* **Onion Smut** *and* **Smuts.**

UROMY'CES. A genus of Rust fungi (Uredinales) in which the teleutospores are 1-celled. Important plant diseases are caused by *U. caryophyllinus* (*see* **Carnation Rust**) and *U. fabae* (*see under* **Bean**, p. 243*a*).
D. E. G.

UROPE'DIUM. *See* **Cypripedium caudatum Lindeni.**

UROPE'TALUM. A synonym of Dipcadi.

UROSKIN'NERA (in honour of G. Ure Skinner, merchant, collector of Cent. American plants). FAM. *Scrophulariaceae.* A genus of 2 species of softly hairy herbs, natives of Mexico and Cent. America. Leaves opposite, stalked, soft, crenate. Flowers rosy-violet, rather large, shortly stalked, declinate, in dense, secund, terminal spikes or racemes; bracts bristly; calyx tubular-bell-shaped, with 4 or 5 bristly teeth; corolla tube long, widened above, with 5 spreading nearly equal lobes; stamens 4, included; style long, slightly 2-fid. *U. spectabilis* needs warm house conditions and a sandy loam. It may be increased by seed, or by cuttings in sand under a bell glass in heat.

U. specta'bilis. 12 to 18 in. h., grey with close hairs. *l.* oblong-toothed, 2 to 4 in. long. *fl.* in sessile terminal close spikes about 3 in. long; cal. small, hairy, 4-toothed; cor. smooth, $1\frac{1}{2}$ in. long, funnel-shaped. Mexico. 1856. (B.M. 5009; F.d.S. 1433.)

UROSPA'THA (*oura*, a tail, *spatha*, spathe; the spathe being long-pointed in most species). FAM. *Araceae.* A genus of a dozen species of marsh plants with spongy rhizomes, natives of Brazil and Guiana. Leaves few, arrow or halberd-shaped, usually variegated; stalks long, sheathing at base. Peduncles at least as long as leaves. Spathe erect, coloured without, white within, more or less twisted near narrowed apex, persistent; spadix shortly stalked or sessile, densely flowered. Flowers hermaphrodite; perianth segments 4 to 6, arching; stamens 4 to 6. Berry 2-celled. Stove conditions, light loamy soil, and abundance of water are needed. Propagation may be by division of the rootstock.

U. descis'cens. A synonym of *Dracontioides desciscens.*

U. sagittifo'lia. *l.-stalk* bent at junction with blade, warted; blade sagittate to hastate, broadly lobed, 12 to 20 in. long, lower lobes oblong-lanceolate, narrower than mid-lobe; sinus deep, rounded. *Peduncle* about 2 ft. long. *Spathe* lanceolate, about 10 to 12 in. long, yellowish- or deep-green, mottled or blotched grey or rosy-red, lanceolate, long-pointed; spadix about 2 to $2\frac{1}{2}$ in. long, green, more or less cylindrical. Brazil. 1866.

UROSPER'MUM (*oura*, a tail, *sperma*, seed; the achenes being beaked). FAM. *Compositae.* A genus of 2 species of herbs, natives of the Mediterranean region. Leaves radical or alternate, deeply toothed or lyrate-pinnatifid; those of stem clasping. Flower-heads yellow on long peduncles at tips of branches; involucre bell-shaped; bracts in one series, spiny; receptacle conical, naked; ray-florets ligulate, 5-toothed at apex. Achenes beaked. *U. Dalechampii* is a perennial for any ordinary soil, best propagated by division.

U. Dalechamp'ii. 18 in. h. forming a spreading clump up to a yard across. *l.* variously runcinate, toothed, silvery-grey. *fl.-heads* lemon-yellow, about $1\frac{1}{2}$ in. across, on naked peduncles; involucre velvety-hairy. June to September. S. Europe. 1739. (B.M. 1623 as *Arnopogon Dalechampii.*)

UROSTIG'MA. Included in **Ficus.**

URSIN'IA (in honour of John Ursinus of Regensburg, 1608–66), who wrote *Arboretum Biblicum*). FAM. *Compositae.* A genus of about 60 species of annual or perennial herbs or shrubs, natives of S. Africa, *U. annua* being also in Abyssinia. Strongly scented and gland-dotted plants with deeply pinnately cut leaves. Flower-heads rayed, the ray-florets in 1 row, neuter. Peduncles terminal, usually 1-headed. Ray-florets in 1 row, either wholly yellow or coppery or dark purplish-brown on the reverse; disk yellow. Two types of achene occur within the group. In the genus Ursinia proper, which has about 15 to 20 species, the achene is crowned with 2 series of pappus-scales, outer 5 broad, inner 5 narrow, but is hairless at base. In another group, often separated as an independent genus **Sphenogyne** (from Greek *sphen*, wedge, probably in allusion to the stigmas) which has about 40 or so species, the achene is crowned with a single series of 5 broad pappus-scales and has a tuft of long hairs at base. These differences are just as important as those by which many genera of Compositae are maintained and the recognition of the genus Sphenogyne thus rests on good botanical grounds; as, however, these plants agree so closely in general habit and the achenes of many species are unknown, they are all kept together here. The annual species may be sown outdoors in April where they are to flower; cuttings of the perennial species will root readily in sand under a bell-glass. All the perennial species need greenhouse treatment and both annual and perennial species will grow well in well-drained ordinary garden soil.

KEY

1. *Annuals with pinnatipartite lvs.*	2
1. *Small shrubs or sub-shrubs*	5
2. *Rays dark and purplish on reverse*	U. anthemoides
2. *Rays yellow or orange on reverse*	3
3. *All scales of involucre with a membranous tip, obtuse*	8
3. *Scales of involucre slender or bristle-pointed*	4
4. *Outer scales of involucre ovate-lanceolate slender-pointed, purple-tipped*	U. cakilifolia
4. *Outer scales of involucre ovate, bristle-pointed*	U. pygmaea
5. *Outer scales of involucre with a broad membranous edge*	U. pilifera
5. *Edge of outer involucral scales not or very narrowly membranous edged*	6
6. *Lvs. woolly*	U. abrotanifolia
6. *Lvs. glabrous or nearly so*	7
7. *Rays dark-coloured on reverse*	U. dentata
7. *Rays yellow on reverse*	9
8. *Rays with a purplish blotch near base*	U. versicolor
8. *Rays completely orange, unblotched*	U. speciosa
9. *Lvs. pinnate or 3-fid*	U. crithmifolia
9. *Lvs. pinnate throughout*	U. anethoides

U. abrotanifo'lia. Shrub up to 2 ft. h., the erect branches covered with pale woolly hair, leafy. *l.* 2- or 3-pinnatisect, $1\frac{1}{2}$ to 2 in. long; segs. narrow-linear, hairy. *Ray-florets* wholly yellow; peduncles 6 to 10 in. long. 1789.

U. anethoi'des. Shrubby, 1 to 2 ft. h., glabrous or thinly cobwebby. *l.* 1 to $1\frac{1}{2}$ in. long, pinnately divided into linear filiform segs. *fl.-heads* 1 to 2 in. across; rays orange with a conspicuous purple base; peduncles 6 to 8 in. long. 1928. (G.C. iii. 84 (1928), 3). SYN. *Sphenogyne anethoides.*

U. anthemoi'des.* Annual, up to 12 in. h. *l.* segs. linear-filiform, variable. *fl.-heads* on long drooping peduncles, about $1\frac{1}{2}$ in. across; rays purplish outside. August. 1774. Half-hardy. (B.M. 544 as *Arctotis anthemoides.*)

U. cakilifo'lia. Annual up to 12 in. h. Much like *U. versicolor* but with the somewhat fleshy *l.* less divided, and the involucral scales rather rigid, purple-tipped and long slender-pointed. *fl.-heads* deep yellow or orange, about 2 in. across. 1924. (B.M. 8676.) Hardy.

U. crithmifo'lia. Stout shrub, glabrous or nearly so, up to 2 ft. h. densely leafy. *l.* $1\frac{1}{2}$ to 2 in. long; segs. filiform. *fl.-heads* 1 to $1\frac{1}{2}$ in. across, yellow; rays long, gland-dotted; on peduncles 3 to 10 in. long. July. 1768. (B.M. 3042 as *Sphenogyne crithmifolia.*)

U. denta'ta. Slender shrub up to 2 ft. h., densely leafy. *l.* $\frac{1}{2}$ to $\frac{3}{4}$ in. long; segs. short, bristle-tipped, gland-dotted, almost or quite glabrous. *fl.-heads* rather small; rays coppery beneath; peduncles 6 to 9 in. long. June. 1787.

U. pili'fera. Diffuse sub-shrub about 9 in. h., thinly hairy. *l.* 1 to 1½ in. long; segs. narrow-linear, bristle-tipped. *fl.-heads* about 1 in. across, white within, coppery outside; peduncles 6 to 9 in. long. December. 1821. (B.R. 604 as *Sphenogyne pilifera.*)

U. pul'chra. A synonym of *U. versicolor.*

Ursinia cakilifolia (p. 2182)

U. pygmae'a. Dwarf annual, glabrous, a few in. h., leafy. *l.* about ¾ in. long; segs. filiform. *fl.-heads* small, yellow, 1924.

U. specio'sa. Annual, 1 to 2 ft. h., glabrous. *l.* 1½ to 2½ in. long, pinnatisect; segs. linear or oblong-linear, bristle-tipped. *fl.-heads* about 2¼ in. across; rays orange; disk-florets purplish-black; peduncles to 6 in. long. 1930. (B.M. n.s. 128.) Half-hardy.

Ursinia versicolor

U. versi'color. Annual about 1 ft. h. with pale straw-coloured stems, glabrous. *l.* 1½ to 2 in. long, twice pinnate; segs. linear. *fl.-heads* bright orange, about 2 in. across; peduncles 4 to 6 in. long. 1836. Namaqualand. Hardy. (P.M.B. 6, 77 as *S. speciosa*; B.M. 9317 as *Sphenogyne versicolor.*)

ursi'nus -a -um, smelling or otherwise like a bear.

UR'TICA (old Latin name used by Horace and Pliny from *uro*, to burn). FAM. *Urticaceae.* A genus of about 30 species of annual or perennial herbs, rarely shrubby at base, armed with stinging hairs, widely distributed over temperate and sub-tropical regions. Leaves opposite, toothed or coarsely cut, stalked. Flowers, monoecious or dioecious, in clusters on spikes, racemes, or panicles. None is of any value and 2 of these Stinging nettles are common weeds in Britain, the annual *U. urens,* and the perennial *U. dioica,* while a third, the most virulent as regards its stings, the Roman nettle, *U. pilulifera,* is occasionally found. The sting of *U. urentissima* (Devil's Leaf), a native of Timor, is said to be so virulent that its effects last for months and may even cause death. The perennial stinging nettle is, when quite young, at times used as a substitute for Spinach, and it yields a strong fibre as do others of the genus. These weeds are usually most abundant and vigorous in soils containing much nitrogen. The perennial stinging nettle needs constant cutting over 3 or 4 years to destroy it or spraying when in full growth with sodium chlorate.

URTICA'CEAE. Dicotyledons. A family of about 500 mostly tropical herbs, shrubs, or trees, falling into over 40 genera. Some species having stinging hairs. Leaves usually stipulate. Flowers monoecious or dioecious (rarely perfect), usually in axillary cymes; perianth segments 4 or 5; stamens as many, filaments incurved in bud, uncoiling suddenly when pollen is ripe; ovary 1-celled. Fruit achene or drupe, 1-celled. The genera dealt with here are Boehmeria, Debregeasia, Helxine, Humulus, Laportea, Myriocarpa, Pellionia, Pilea, Pourruma, Urera, and Urtica.

Urvil'lei, in honour of Jules Sébastian César Dumont d'Urville, 1790–1844, French naval officer, author of a flora of the Falkland Islands.

USEFUL INSECTS. Many are unaware of the vast number of insects which are of direct or indirect benefit to mankind, or that many predacious and parasitic insects are utilized for keeping down the numbers of their noxious relations or of the use of certain plant-feeding insects for controlling noxious weeds. Among the more important beneficial insects are the predacious and parasitic species, including among the former group such familiar insects as Ladybirds and Ground or Carabid Beetles and their grubs, and the maggots of Lace-wing flies and Hover Flies; and among the latter a vast host of 4-winged Hymenopterous insects (Ichneumon-flies, Chalcid and Braconid 'wasps') and of the 2-winged Dipterous family of Tachinid flies, all of which play an important part in checking the increase of plant pests. Apart from these groups of insects, there are others which are of direct or indirect benefit to man, as, for example, pollinating agents of fruit and other blossom as Hive and Humble Bees, Drone and Hover Flies, Flower Beetles, and others; insects which produce Silk (*Bombyx mori* and the caterpillars of other moths), Wax (certain oriental Scale insects), Lac (the Indian Lac insect), and Cochineal (Scale insect); those whose wings or bodies are so brilliantly coloured that they are used in the decorative arts (tropical Butterflies, Moths, and Beetles); those that serve as food for man (African and Australian tribes cook and eat wood-boring grubs, Honey-pot Ants, &c.); and those insects whose larvae feed entirely on dead and decaying vegetable matter and reduce it to a state where lower organisms, e.g. Bacteria, can convert it into plant food and humus. A full account of beneficial and useful insects is given in the Ministry of Agriculture's Bulletin No. 20, entitled *Some Beneficial Insects.*

G. F. W.

usitatis'simus -a -um, most useful.

USTE'RIA of Cavanilles. Included under **Maurandia.**

USTILAGINA'LES. *See* **Smuts.**

USTILA'GO. The largest genus of Ustilaginales (Smut Fungi). Most species are of importance in Agriculture since their hosts are cereals and other grasses, but *U. violacea* (formerly known as *U. antherarum*) attacks the flowers of Lychnis and related genera (*see* **Carnation diseases**) and *U. Vaillantii* causes smut in the anthers of Scilla and Chionoscilla.

D. E. G.

ustula'tus -a -um, scorched or having a scorched or singed appearance.

u'tilis -is -e, useful.

utricle, a fruit with a small bladder-like pericarp.

UTRICULA'RIA (*utriculus*, a little bottle; in allusion to the bladders borne on leaves or runners). FAM. *Lentibulariaceae.* Bladderworts. A genus of about 250 species of herbs of tropical and temperate regions, those of the latter being all aquatic, the tropical species include both epiphytes and terrestrial plants usually with peculiar runners in the moss, &c., in which they grow. Leaves of the floating species much divided into capillary segments on which are borne small bladders with trap-door entrances, and often, as in the British *U. vulgaris*, small, entire leaves on short upright shoots which reach the surface of the water. In the land species similar bladders are borne on the runners already referred to. In epiphytic species like *U. alpina* as well as in the land species the leaves are entire, and in the epiphytes tuberous branches are borne which act as water-storage organs. Flowers borne out of the water on a simple or slightly branched scape, solitary or in racemes; calyx deeply 2-lobed; corolla 2-lipped and spurred, upper lip erect, entire or more or less 2-fid, lower often large and spreading, 3- to 6-lobed; spur often incurved. The Utricularias trap insects and other small creatures which are sucked into the bladders, the trap-door, which can only be opened from the outside, then closes and the plant absorbs the results of their decay (*see* **Carnivorous Plants**). The differences in habit necessitate different treatment for the species of these interesting plants. *U. minor*, *U. neglecta*, and *U. vulgaris* are best grown in aquaria and *U. intermedia* in shallow pans of water with Sphagnum growing therein. These are British and hardy, passing the winter as hibernating winter-buds at the bottom of the water. *U. Endresii* and *U. alpina* are best in baskets of fibrous peat and Sphagnum suspended near the glass. *U. Humboldtii*, *U. longifolia*, and *U. reniformis* will grow in large pots of peat and Sphagnum partially plunged in water. *U. bifida* and *U. prehensilis* grow well in ordinary soil in a pot plunged a few inches below the surface of a warm tank.

U. alpi'na.* Epiphytic. Tubers ovoid, stalked, ⅓ to ½ in. long. *l.* elliptic-lanceolate, 4 to 6 in. long, erect, narrowed to slender stalk. *fl.* white, 1½ in. across, with palate and disk of lower lip yellow, edges of upper lip recurved, lower twice as large; cal. pale-green lobes ovate-cordate, obtuse; spur, stout, incurved; scape erect taller than l., 1- to 4-fld. July. W. Indies and S. America. 1871. (B.M. 5923 as *U. montana.*) Stove.

U. bi'fida.* Densely tufted. *l.* erect, filiform or slightly thickened upwards, 1 to 2 in. long, bright green. *fl.* bright yellow with a large and prominent orange-yellow palate, upper lip reflexed, lower very short, 2-lobed; scapes many, 2 to 5 times as long as l. September. Trop. Asia. 1882. (B.M. 6689.) Greenhouse.

U. emargina'ta.* Aquatic. *l.* 1 to 3 in. long, much-divided. *fl.* 1 or 2 on an erect scape 1½ to 3½ in. long, upper lip concave, roundish-ovate, about ⅓ in. across, lower smaller, entire, 2-fid. Brazil.

U. Endres'ii.* Epiphyte with slender creeping rhizomes and ovoid tubercles about ¼ in. long. *l.* solitary, narrow-elliptic-lanceolate, 1 to 3 in. long; stalks stiff, as long as blades. *fl.* drooping on very slender pedicels on an erect scape twice as long as l., about 5-fld.; sep. pale green or reddish, ½ to ¾ in. long; cor. pale lilac with a yellow palate 1¾ to 2 in. across, ciliate. Spring. Costa Rica. 1874. (B.M. 6656.) SYN. *U. montana rosea* of gardens. Stove.

U. Forgetia'na. A variety of *U. longifolia.*

U. Humbold'tii.* Fibrous rooted. *l.* usually solitary, obcordate narrowed to a long stalk. *fl.* in racemes on short pedicels on a long glabrous scape; bluish-purple, large; sep. dark brownish, leafy convex, ovate, acute; upper lip of cor. small, entire, slightly in flexed at apex, lower dilated, truncate, yellow, excavated at base spur awl-shaped, ascending-decurved. Guiana. 1886. (F.d.S.1390. Stove.

U. interme'dia. Stems slender, 4 to 8 in. long. *l.* in 2 ranks, closely set, ¼ to ½ in. wide, orbicular; segs. awl-shaped; pitchers on leafless branches, ⅛ to ¼ in. long. *fl.* pale yellow, in racemes of 3 or 4; upper lip twice as long as palate, lower broad, flat. July to September. N. Europe, including Britain, N. Asia, N. America. (E.B. 1127.)

U. janthi'na. A synonym of *U. reniformis.*

U. longifo'lia. Densely tufted. *l.* strap-shaped, narrowed to the stalk, up to 12 in. long, bright green. *fl.* mauve, with a golden blotch on palate, on a 10-fld. scape up to 2 ft. h. Brazil. 1888. Stove. var. **Forgetian'a,** *fl.* violet-blue, nearly 2 in. across with an orange palate, on tall scapes. Brazil. 1897. (B.M. 8516; Gn. 52 (1897) 142 as *U. latifolia.*)

U. ma'jor. A synonym of *U. neglecta.*

U. mi'nor. Stems very slender, 3 to 10 in. long. *l.* orbicular, ⅛ to ¼ in. wide, much cut; segs. awl-shaped, entire; pitchers in l.-axils 1/12 in. long, on slender stalk. *fl.* pale yellow, ⅓ in. across; spur minute; scape 2 to 6 in. long, 2- to 6-fld. Summer. N. Hemisphere, including Britain. (E.B. 1126.)

U. monta'na. A synonym of *U. alpina.*

U. neglec'ta. Stems very slender, 6 to 8 in. long. *l.* smaller than in *U. vulgaris*, rather remote, nearly orbicular; segs. awl-shaped, entire, somewhat ciliate; pitchers very short-stalked. *fl.* pale-yellow, upper lip longer than palate; spur acute; scape 2- to 8-fld., very slender. W. Europe, including Britain. (E.B. 1125 bis).

Utricularia reniformis (p. 2185)

U. prehen'silis.* Growing in mud or very shallow water; stems twining; annual. *l.* linear-lanceolate to lingulate, obtuse, up to 1 in. long, narrowed to slender stalk, often disappearing before fl. open., bladders numerous on l. and rhizoids, nearly globose, about $\frac{1}{24}$ in. wide. *fl.* yellow, upper lip broadly oblong-spatulate; palate erect, crested; spur straight, descending, about $\frac{1}{4}$ in. long. Trop. Africa. 1909. (G.C. 48 (1910) 447.) Warm house.

U. renifor'mis. Epiphytic. *l.* reniform, 2 to 4 in. across, pale green stalk dull red, slender, 4 to 6 in. long. *fl.* pale violet, in racemes on slender pedicels, scape about 18 in. long; upper lip hemispheric with two vertical golden bands, edged deep violet, lower much larger, $1\frac{1}{2}$ in. across, sides rounded. July. Brazil. 1886. (B.M. 7466 as *U. janthina.*) Stove. SYN. *U. janthina.*

U. vulgar'is. Stems 6 to 18 in. long, leafy. *l.* broadly ovate, $\frac{3}{4}$ to 1 in. long, spreading, pinnately multifid; segs. remotely toothed; pitchers at base of and on segs. $\frac{1}{8}$ to $\frac{1}{4}$ in. long, short-stalked. *fl.* yellow, $\frac{1}{2}$ to $\frac{3}{4}$ in. long; spur conical, appressed to lower lip; scape 4 to 8 in. long, 2- to 8-fld. July, August. Europe, including Britain, N. Africa, Siberia, N. America. (E.B. 1125.)

utricula'tus -a -um, bladdery.

utriculo'sus -a -um, bladder-like.

u'va ur'si, bear's grapes.

UVA'RIA (*uva*, a cluster of grapes; from the fruits of some species). FAM. *Anonaceae.* A genus of about 80 species of mostly climbing or scrambling shrubs with curved hooks, natives of Trop. Africa and Asia. Leaves alternate, entire, without stipules. Flowers yellow, purple or brown, hermaphrodite, terminal or leaf-opposed, rarely axillary; sepals 3, often joined near base, broad, valvate; petals 6, overlapping in 2 rows, sometimes joined at base; stamens indefinite. Sandy loam and peat make a suitable compost for these stove plants which can be rooted from cuttings of ripe wood in sand under glass in heat. *U. purpurea* from Java, with purple-red flowers is cultivated in some tropical countries.

U. Kirk'ii. Small shrub 3 to 4 ft. h., with rusty hairy branches. *l.* oblong, $1\frac{1}{2}$ to 5 in. long, rusty-hairy beneath at first, then glabrous of nearly so; stalks very short. *fl.* pale dirty straw-colour, tinged verdigris green, 3 in. across, solitary in l.-axils. October. Zanzibar. 1868. (B.M. 6006.)

U. zeyla'nica. Large woody climber to 20 ft. *l.* lanceolate to oblong-lanceolate, 2 to 4 in. long, dark shining green above, red or pale beneath. *fl.* dull red, 1 in. across, solitary or twin on hairy peduncles $\frac{1}{2}$ in. long. Ripe carpels ovoid, pubescent, yellowish. Ceylon, S. India. 1794.

uviform'is -is -e, clustered like bees in a swarm.

UVULA'RIA (diminutive of *uva*, a bunch of grapes; from the form of the fruit). FAM. *Liliaceae.* A genus of about 3 species of hardy rhizomatous perennial herbs, natives of N. America, related to Tricyrtis but with loculicidal capsules. Leaves alternate, sessile or perfoliate, ovate or lanceolate. Flowers solitary or twin at tips of branchlets on rather thin pendulous pedices; usually pale yellow, bell-shaped, segments distinct, erect or spreading above, outer foveolate at base within, deciduous; stamens 6. Hardy, spring-flowering, needing a light, sandy soil, and increased by division.

U. fla'va. A variety of *U. perfoliata.*

Uvularia grandiflora

U. grandiflo'ra. Habit of *U. perfoliata* but more robust. *l.* oblong, membranous, perfoliate, glabrous, 2 to 4 in. long. *fl.* 1 to 3, $1\frac{1}{4}$ to $1\frac{1}{2}$ in. long; segs. lanceolate, acute, about $\frac{1}{4}$ in. wide; pedicels $\frac{1}{2}$ to $\frac{3}{4}$ in. long. May. 1802. (B.M. 1112.) var. **pal'lida,** *fl.* sulphur-yellow.

U. lanceola'ta. A variety of *U. perfoliata.*

U. perfolia'ta. Stems forked above, about 1 ft. h. *l.* 6 to 12, oblong perfoliate, subacute, $1\frac{1}{2}$ to 3 in. long, membranous, green above, paler beneath. *fl.* 1 or few, $\frac{3}{4}$ to $1\frac{1}{4}$ in. long; segs. lanceolate, acute, papillose within. 1710. (B.M. 955; R.L. 184.) var. **fla'va,** *fl.* larger and of deeper colour; **lanceola'ta,** *l.* narrower than in type.

U. ro'sea. A synonym of *Streptopus roseus.*

U. sessilifo'lia. A synonym of *Oakesiella sessilifolia.*

V

VACCA'RIA (*vacca*, cow; the plant is said to be good fodder). FAM. *Caryophyllaceae.* A genus of 3 species in Middle and S. Europe extending to Siberia and Persia. Annual herbs with flat leaves, allied to Saponaria with which they are sometimes combined, differing by having no outgrowth at the base of the petals. Branching of stems forked; calyx swollen, sharply 5-angled and winged, 15- to 25-nerved. Fruit a many-seeded capsule. *V. pyramidata* will grow in any soil and may be sown like any other hardy annual in the open border.

V. pyramida'ta. A glabrous annual. Stem single, about 12 to 24 in. h., much branched above. *l.* lanceolate or ovate-lanceolate, sessile, about 2 in. long, blue-green. *fl.* many, red; cal. about $\frac{1}{2}$ in. long, whitish, with 5 green wings, pyramidal. July, August. S. Europe east to Mesopotamia. 1596. (B.M. 2290 as *Saponaria vaccaria.*) SYNS. *V. vulgaris, V. segetalis,* var. **al'ba,** *fl.* white.

VACCINIA'CEAE. Included in **Ericaceae.**

vacciniiflo'rus -a -um, with flowers resembling those of Vaccinium.

vaccinifo'lius -a -um, with leaves resembling those of a Vaccinium.

Vaccaria pyramidata (p. 2185)

VACCI'NIUM (old Latin name of disputed origin, used by Virgil and Pliny, probably a corruption of Hyacinthus). FAM. *Ericaceae.* A genus of over 130 species of deciduous and evergreen shrubs and, rarely, small trees characterized by alternate leaves, flowers solitary or in terminal or axillary racemes, corolla urceolate, campanulate or cylindrical with 4 or 5 lobes or 4-parted, calyx lobes 4 or 5, stamens 8 or 10, ovary entirely inferior, fruit a berry crowned by persistent calyx lobes. For distinction from Chiogenes, Gaultheria, and Pernettya see those genera. The genus inhabits the northern hemisphere, with most species in N. America and E. Asia. As accepted here, it includes the groups sometimes separated as independent genera under the names Batodendron, Cyanococcus, Epigynium, Hugeria, Oxycoccoides, Oxycoccus, Polycodium, and Vitis-idaea.

The Vacciniums grow well under the same conditions as Gaultheria. Propagated by seed, cuttings, layers, and, when available, offshoots.

The genus has considerable economic importance in the United States and Canada, where many thousands of acres of otherwise rather barren land with acid soil are used for the cultivation of Blueberries and Cranberries. These fruits are made into tarts, pies, jams, sauces, and preserves, a great quantity being canned. The genus divides fairly readily into subgenera. Of these the Cranberries, i.e. Oxycoccus (often considered an independent genus Oxycoccus) and Oxycoccoides (Hugeria), are easily recognized by the corolla being split almost to the base into 4 narrow recurving lobes. Oxycoccoides with 2 species, the American *V. erythrocarpum*, and the E. Asiatic *V. japonicum* consists of erect bushes 3 to 6 ft. high with deciduous leaves and mostly insipid or sweetish berries, although some forms are recorded as tart and highly flavoured. The 2 species of Oxycoccus, *V. Oxycoccos* and the larger fruited *V. macrocarpon*, are very dwarf small-leaved evergreen trailing shrubs with acid berries. Of *V. macrocarpon* several forms have been selected and are cultivated on a large scale in the E. United States in Cranberry bogs, the water-level of which can be artificially controlled, so that from December to April the plants are under a foot or so of water, but are above the water-level during their season of growth. These bogs are prepared by flooding for about 2 years to kill the natural vegetation and are then smoothed and covered with about 3 in. of clean sand. Cuttings 5 to 10 in. long are then pushed through the sand into the peat below at 12 to 18 in. apart. Subgenus Vitis-idaea, with evergreen leaves, short racemes, campanulate corolla, and hairy filaments, comprises *V. crassifolium*, *V. Delavayi*, *V. floribundum*, *V.*×*intermedium*, *V. moupinense*, and *V. Myrsinites* as well as *V. Vitis-idaea*, the Cowberry or Red Whortleberry. The red berries of the last are often gathered on a large scale from wild plants, but the members of this group are mostly cultivated for ornament. Subgenus Batodendron has only one species, *V. arboreum*, the Farkleberry or Sparkleberry, which forms a large bush or small tree with campanulate flowers, included anthers, and dry hard berries. Subgenus Polycodium, the Deerberries, consists of *V. stamineum*, *V. caesium* and allies, notable for their campanulate flowers with protruding anthers; the berries are inedible in some forms, edible in others. Subgenus Vaccinium (Euvaccinium) has numerous species, the best known being *V. uliginosum*, the Bog Whortleberry, and *V. Myrtillus*, the Bilberry, Blaeberry, or Whortleberry, with pleasant-tasting blue-black glaucous berries which can be gathered in great quantity on many British moorlands, especially in areas where sheep are excluded or where the heather has been too frequently burned (see *Journal of Ministry of Agriculture*, 45. 546–52; 1938).

Horticulturally, the most important subgenus is Cyanococcus, the true Blueberries, with 'species freely hybridizing, their classification difficult, contradictory and confused' (Fernald). An attempt by W. H. Camp to clarify this perplexing group will be found in *Brittonia*, 5. 203–75 (1945). It includes *V. angustifolium* (Lowbush Blueberry), *V. Ashei* (Rabbit-eye Blueberry), *V. atrococcum*, *V. australe* (South-eastern High-bush Blueberry), *V. corymbosum* (North High-bush Blueberry), *V. myrtilloides* (Sour-top Blueberry, Canadian Blueberry), *V. hirsutum*, *V. Oldhamii*, *V. pallidum* (Dryland Blueberry), &c. Some of the American species are highly variable, apparently as a result of past hybridization, and have yielded good material for selection and breeding work, which was begun in 1906 by Frederick V. Colville of the U.S. Department of Agriculture, and has resulted in the introduction of many improved varieties. In northern regions only the low-bush Blueberries (mostly *V. angustifolium*) which are about 6 to 18 in. high can be grown. Fields of these are often burned over every third year. The high-bush Blueberries (derived mostly from *V. Ashei*, *V. australe*, and *V. corymbosum*) reach a height of 6 to 15 ft. They prefer a very acid (pH 4·3 to 5·5) moist soil, with the water-table about 8 in. below the surface in summer. The named varieties, e.g. Concord, Jersey, Pioneer, Rancocas, and Rubel, are single clones and appear to give the best yields when interplanted with other varieties for cross-pollination. Being shallow-rooted and not drought-resistant they benefit from mulches of leaves, sawdust, &c., but not of farmyard manure. Up to 500 lb. of a complete fertilizer have been applied to an acre. Flower-buds are produced on the new shoots of the previous season's growth; hence to maintain good crops the bushes should be lightly pruned in the dormant season by the thinning out of small branches and of a few of the older stems, especially those 4 years or more old. In small plantations the bushes are set about 5 or 6 ft. by 5 or 6 ft. apart; for ease of mechanical cultivation the rows are better 8 to 10 ft. apart with the bushes 5 ft. apart in the rows. They are propagated by layering or by cuttings. Hardwood cuttings 4 to 6 in. long, the tip with flower-buds being cut off, are inserted during the dormant season in a mixture of half sand, half peat and should be rooted by June. Softwood cuttings of the current year's growth, taken about 4 in. long in July and stripped to 2 upper leaves, root in about 8 weeks in a propagating frame. For further information bulletins issued by the Canadian and U.S.A. Departments of Agriculture and various agricultural experiment stations should be consulted.

W. T. S.

DISEASES. Vacciniums are generally very hardy, but 1 or 2 parasitic diseases are known. The fungus *Sclerotinia Oxycocci* infects the leaves and fruits of the Cranberry, *Vaccinium Oxycoccos*, and similar attacks on the Cowberry, *V. Vitis-idaea*, and the Bilberry, *V. Myrtillis*, are due to *Sclerotinia Vaccinii* and *S. baccarum* respectively. The fungus *S. Ledi* is said to be heteroecious, the conidia from the leaves of *Vaccinium uliginosum* attacking the flowers of *Ledum palustre* and then producing sclerotia which give rise to apothecia, the ascospores from which again infect *V. uliginosum.*

KEY

1. *Pet. united at least half-way* 2
1. *Pet. separated almost to base of cor., recurved, linear-oblong* 50
2. *Cor. campanulate or cylindrical* 3
2. *Cor. more or less urceolate* 17
3. *Pet. united half-way* V. modestum
3. *Pet. united more than half-way length, usually much more* 4
4. *Shrubs normally evergreen* 5
4. *Shrubs deciduous* 10
5. *Shrubs of 6 ft. or more in height* 6
5. *Shrubs under 6 ft. in height* 9
6. *Young wood quite glabrous* V. Dunalianum
6. *Young wood more or less downy* 7
7. *Fl. about ½ in. long, yellowish, striped and tinted red* V. padifolium
7. *Fl. about ¼ in. long, white or pink* 8
8. *Shoots glabrous or slightly pubescent; stamens much shorter than pistil; style protruding; ovary* 10-*celled* V. arboreum
8. *Shoots pubescent; stamens almost as long as pistil; ovary* 4- *or* 5-*celled* V. ovatum
9. *Cor.* 4-*lobed* V. Vitis-idaea
9. *Cor.* 5-*lobed* V. crassifolium
10. *Shrubs of over 6 ft. in height* 11
10. *Shrubs of not more than 6 ft.* 12
11. *Lvs. bristly on both surfaces and ciliate* V. ciliatum
11. *Lvs. feebly puberulent on upper surface only, not ciliate* V. Arctostaphylos
12. *Shrub of low creeping habit, to 6 in. h.; lvs. glabrous, toothed; fl.* 1 *to* 3; *ped. longer than cal. tube; fr. red* V. praestans
12. *Shrubs not with this combination of characters* 13
13. *Stamens prominently protruding from cor.* 14
13. *Stamens not protruding* 34
14. *Fr. dark purple* V. melanocarpum
14. *Fr. pale in colour* 15
15. *Lvs. glabrous* V. neglectum
15. *Lvs. downy on lower surface* 16
16. *Fr. greenish or yellowish; lvs. green beneath* V. stamineum
16. *Fr. blue-green; lvs. glaucous beneath* V. candicans
17. *Evergreen shrubs* 18
17. *Deciduous shrubs* 28
18. *Shrubs tall, up to 6 ft. or more h.* 19
18. *Shrubs dwarfer, mostly 1 to 4 ft.* 20
19. *Anthers without awns. Disk of fl. not lobed. American species (subgenus Cyanococcus)* 47
19. *Anthers with awns on back. Disk of fl. distinctly* 5-*lobed (subgenus Epigynium)* 48
20. *Lvs. notched at apex* 21
20. *Lvs. not notched at apex* 22
21. *Cor. ovoid-urceolate, white striped red* V. retusum
21. *Cor. globose-urceolate, creamy-white tinged rose* V. Delavayi
22. *Young wood glabrous or nearly so* 23
22. *Young wood bristly or pubescent* 24
23. *Anthers not drawn out into awn-like tips. Bracts small* V. Rollisonii
23. *Anthers with 2 elongated tips. Bracts conspicuous* 47
24. *Young shoots bristly* 25
24. *Young shoots pubescent* 26
25. *Lvs. glandular-pubescent on surfaces and margin* V. fragile
25. *Lvs. slightly pubescent at base above and bristly-serrulate* V. Nummularia
26. *Lvs. entire; cor. chocolate-red* V. moupinense
26. *Lvs. more or less serrulate* 27
27. *Lvs. dotted with tiny pits or pitted bristles beneath; cal. lobes ciliate* V. Mortinia
27. *Lvs. not pitted; cal. lobes glabrous* V. Myrsinites
28. *Shrubs over 6 ft. h.* 29
28. *Shrubs under 6 ft. h.* 34
29. *Fl. solitary from axils* 30
29. *Fl. in axillary racemes* 31
30. *Fr. oval, translucent coral-red; lvs. serrulate* V. parvifolium
30. *Fr. rounded, dark blue; lvs. entire* V. ovalifolium
31. *Lvs. quite glabrous* 47
31. *Lvs. more or less pubescent or glandular* 32
32. *Lvs. densely pubescent beneath, entire, 1¼ to 2½ in. long; cor. about ⅕ in. long* V. atrococcum
32. *Lvs. less pubescent beneath, entire or toothed* 33
33. *Lvs. with scattered or numerous glands beneath* V. Ashei
33. *Lvs. without glands beneath* V. corymbosum
34. *Filaments pubescent; anthers awnless; ovary* 10-*celled (subgenus Cyanococcus)* 35
34. *Filaments glabrous; anthers awned on back; ovary* 4- *to* 5-*celled (subgenus Vaccinium)* 43
35. *Ovary and fr. hairy* V. hirsutum
35. *Ovary and fr. glabrous* 36
36. *Lvs. glandular beneath* 37
36. *Lvs. not glandular beneath* 39
37. *Shrub over 3 ft. h.; lvs. 1½ to 2 in. long; cor. $\frac{3}{10}$ to ⅗ in. long* V. amoenum
37. *Shrub 3 ft. or less h.; lvs. ¾ to 1¾ in. long; cor. ⅕ to $\frac{3}{10}$ in. long* 38
38. *Shrub 1½ to 3 ft. h.; cor. about $\frac{3}{10}$ in. long* V. virgatum
38. *Shrub 6 to 16 in. h.; cor. about ⅕ in. long* V. tenellum
39. *Lvs. toothed* 40
39. *Lvs. entire* 42
40. *Lvs. sparsely toothed; cor. usually greenish-white* V. vacillans
40. *Lvs. closely and sharply toothed; cor. usually white* 41
41. *Shrubs 3 to 8 ins. h.; lvs. ⅕ to ⅖ in. wide* V. angustfolium
41. *Shrubs 6 to 16 in. h.; lvs. ⅖ to ⅗ in. wide* V. Lamarckii
42. *Lvs. pubescent on both sides* V. myrtilloides
42. *Lvs. glabrous or pubescent only below* V. vacillans
43. *Shoots round in section* 44
43. *Shoots angled* 46
44. *Lvs. glaucous on both sides* V. uliginosum
44. *Lvs. glaucous on one side only if at all* 45
45. *Lvs. bright green on both sides* V. caespitosum
45. *Lvs. somewhat glaucous below* V. deliciosum
46. *Cor. pink; lvs. $\frac{3}{10}$ to $\frac{7}{10}$ in. long* V. Myrtillus
46. *Cor. greenish-white; lvs. $\frac{7}{10}$ to 2 in. long* V. membranaceum
47. *Fr. bright blue* V. australe
47. *Fr. dull black* V. Ashei
48. *Lvs. entire; cor. pink* V. urceolatum
48. *Lvs. toothed; cor. white* 49
49. *Fr. white* V. leucobotrys
49. *Fr. black* V. Sprengelii
50. *Creeping evergreen shrubs; lvs. ⅕ to $\frac{7}{10}$ in. long (subgenus Oxycoccus)* 51
50. *Upright deciduous shrubs; lvs. ¾ to 2¾ in. long (subgenus Oxycoccoides)* 52
51. *Lvs. blunt, only slightly glaucous beneath; filaments scarcely ⅓ length of anthers* V. macrocarpon
51. *Lvs. acute, very glaucous beneath; filaments half length of anthers* V. Oxycoccos
52. *Shoots and lvs. glabrous* V. japonicum
52. *Shoots pubescent; lvs. slightly pubescent on veins* V. erythrocarpum

V. amoe'num. *See under* **V. virgatum.**

V. angustifo'lium. Low-bush Blueberry. Twiggy deciduous shrub about 3 to 8 in. h. with glabrous or slightly downy shoots. *l.* narrowly elliptic or lanceolate, tapered to both ends, bristly serrulate, glabrous or slightly pubescent on midrib, ⅖ to 1⅕ in. long, ⅕ to ⅖ in. wide. *fl.* $\frac{3}{10}$ to ⅘ in. in short, compact, axillary racemes; cor. white with reddish streaks, cylindrical-campanulate, slightly narrowed at mouth, ⅕ in. long with 5 blunt, recurved lobes; cal. lobes triangular, acute. April, May. *fr.* blue-black, bloomy, sweet, rounded, ⅕ to $\frac{3}{10}$ in. across. E. United States. 1772. Syn. *V. pensylvanicum angustifolium.* Grown commercially in United States since 1850, and now occupying a very large acreage (probably 150,000 acres) in the NE. States and Canada, the fields being burned over every second or third year. Its chromosome number is $2n = 24$, that of the larger and less fire-resistant *V. Lamarckii* $2n = 54$. It is hardier than the high-bush Blueberries.

V. arbo'reum. Farkleberry. Large evergreen (in cold areas deciduous) shrub or small tree up to 30 ft. in nature with glabrous or slightly downy young wood. *l.* ovate, oval, oblong or obovate, acute or blunt, entire or obscurely toothed, glabrous above, usually slightly downy beneath, ¾ to 2⅜ in. long, ⅜ to 1¼ in. wide. *fl.* solitary from axils or in terminal, leafy racemes 1 to 2 in. long; cor. white, campanulate, ¼ in. long with 5 recurved lobes; cal. lobes short, ovate-triangular. July, August. *fr.* inedible, black, globose, ¼ in. across. S. and SE. United States. 1765. (B.M. 1607 as *V. diffusum.*) Syn. *Batodendron arboreum, B. andrachneforme.* var. **glauces'cens.** *l.* glaucescent. United States.

V. Arctosta'phylos. Caucasian Whortleberry. Fine deciduous shrub up to 10 ft. h. with red young shoots. *l.* ovate-oblong, acute to acuminate, serrulate, more or less undulate, sparsely downy on veins, 1 to 4 in. long, $\frac{3}{4}$ to $1\frac{3}{4}$ in. wide, become a lovely red in autumn. *fl.* nodding in downy, bracteate, axillary racemes; cor. greenish-white marked with purplish-pink, campanulate, $\frac{1}{4}$ in. or a little more long with 5 short, more or less recurved lobes; cal. lobes shorter than cor., ovate-triangular, subacute to acuminate. May, June. *fr.* globose, purple, about $\frac{5}{16}$ in. across. Caucasus, Lazistan. 1800. (B.M. 974.) *V. padifolium* was confused with *V. Arctostaphylos* for a long time and is still occasionally supplied in its stead. *V. padifolium* is (usually) evergreen and has smooth stamens, whereas *V. Arctostaphylos* is deciduous and has pubescent stamens.

V. Ash'ei. Rabbit-eye Blueberry. Bush $4\frac{1}{2}$ to 18 ft. h., usually deciduous, but some forms almost or quite evergreen. *l.* broadly elliptic or sometimes broadly obovate, serrate or entire, dark green, pale green, or even glaucous, usually glandular beneath, densely pubescent to glabrous, $1\frac{1}{2}$ to 3 in. long, $\frac{4}{5}$ to $1\frac{3}{5}$ in. wide. *fl.* pale to bright pink, sometimes white or red, usually broadly urceolate, about $\frac{3}{10}$ to almost $\frac{1}{2}$ in. long. *fr.* black or dull, often insipid but some forms well flavoured, $\frac{3}{10}$ to $\frac{7}{10}$ in. across. SE. United States. A very variable species, selected forms of which are grown commercially on a large scale in the southern States.

V. atrococ'cum. Downy Swamp or Black Huckleberry. Deciduous, branching shrub 6 to 10 ft. h. *l.* oval or oblong, entire, acute, smooth above, densely pubescent beneath, $1\frac{1}{2}$ to 3 in. long, $\frac{1}{2}$ to $1\frac{1}{2}$ in. wide. *fl.* in axillary and terminal short, crowded, bracteate racemes; cor. pink or green flushed red, cylindrical-urceolate, about $\frac{1}{4}$ in. long with 5 small, erect or spreading lobes; cal. lobes triangular about $\frac{1}{12}$ in. long. May. *fr.* black, rounded, sweet, $\frac{1}{4}$ in. or more across. Eastern N. America from Canada to Alabama. In cult. 1898. (B.B. 2. 702.) Syn. *V. corymbosum atrococcum*, var. **leucococ'cum** has translucent greenish- or yellowish-white fr. 1925.

V. austra'le. Deciduous bush 6 to 12 ft. h. *l.* broadly elliptic to ovate-lanceolate, entire, glaucous, glabrous, 2 to $3\frac{1}{4}$ in. long, 1 to $1\frac{1}{2}$ in. wide, *fl.* white, sometimes pink-tinged, rather cylindric, $\frac{3}{10}$ to $\frac{2}{5}$ in. long. *fr.* blue, usually well flavoured, $\frac{3}{10}$ to $\frac{1}{2}$ in. across. Eastern N. America. According to W. H. Camp (1945) this species more than any other has contributed to the excellent qualities of the modern high-bush commercial blueberries; in fact, until recently, the better varieties were mostly selections of *V. australe* taken from the wild.

V. bractea'tum. Evergreen shrub 3 to 5 ft. h. with smooth or nearly smooth young wood. *l.* elliptic to elliptic oblong, pointed, thin, smooth or nearly so, 1 to $2\frac{1}{2}$ in. long, about half as wide. *fl.* in axillary, conspicuously bracted, puberulent racemes; cor. white, fragrant, cylindrical-urceolate, downy, $\frac{1}{4}$ in. long with 5 small triangular lobes; cal. lobes downy, triangular. *fr.* red, globose, downy, $\frac{1}{4}$ in. across. July, August. China, Japan. 1829. (L.B.C. 1648 as *Andromeda chinensis*.) Syn. *V. chinense*.

V. caespito'sum. Dwarf Bilberry. Dwarf, deciduous, rapidly spreading shrub 3 to 12 in. h. *l.* obovate to oblong-cuneate, smooth, bluntly toothed, $\frac{1}{2}$ to 1 in. long, about half as wide. *fl.* nodding, solitary from l.-axils; cor. pink or nearly white, oval-urceolate, $\frac{3}{16}$ in. long with 5 (rarely 4) small, erect lobes; cal. undulate rather than toothed. May to July. *fr.* blue-black, globose, sweet, about $\frac{1}{4}$ in. across. Canada, N. and W. United States. 1823. (B.M. 3429.)

V. canaden'se. A synonym of *V. myrtilloides*.

V. can'dicans. Deciduous shrub up to 6 ft. h. with pale, hairy, young wood. *l.* elliptic, ovate or obovate, acute, tapered to or rounded at base, entire, glaucous beneath, more or less pubescent on both sides. *fl.* nodding in axillary, glaucous, bracteate racemes; cor. white, open-campanulate, about $\frac{1}{4}$ in. long with 5 lobes; cal. lobes triangular pubescent and sometimes glandular-pubescent; stamens prominently exserted. May, June. *fr.* greenish or bluish, globose, $\frac{3}{8}$ in. or a little more across. SE. United States. Syn. *Polycodium candicans*. Closely related to *V. neglectum* and *V. melanocarpum*.

V. cilia'tum. Deciduous, spreading shrub usually 3 to $7\frac{1}{2}$ ft. h. in cultivation, over 12 ft. in nature, with glandular-hairy young wood. *l.* ovate, obovate or elliptical, acute, ciliate-serrulate, bristly beneath especially on veins, more sparingly above, 1 to $3\frac{1}{4}$ in. long, half as wide, turning red in autumn. *fl.* nodding on downy stalks in axillary, bracteate racemes; cor. greenish-yellow tinted red, campanulate, $\frac{1}{6}$ in. long with 5 short lobes; cal. lobes broadly ovate. June, July. *fr.* edible, black, globose, $\frac{1}{4}$ to $\frac{3}{8}$ in. across. Japan, Korea. 1892.

V. corymbo'sum. Swamp, High-bush, or Tall Blueberry. Branching deciduous shrub 4 to 12 ft. h. with warty young wood which may be pubescent or nearly glabrous. *l.* ovate, oval to elliptical, pointed, usually entire, sparsely downy on nerves beneath, sometimes ciliate, 1 to 3 in. long, half as wide; becoming a beautiful red in autumn. *fl.* in short lateral or terminal bracteate racemes; cor. white tinted pink or pinkish, ovoid- or cylindrical-urceolate, $\frac{1}{4}$ to $\frac{3}{8}$ in. long with 5 short, more or less spreading teeth; cal. lobes bluish-green, broadly-triangular, subacute. May, June. *fr.* edible, blue-black, bloomy, globose, $\frac{1}{4}$ to $\frac{1}{3}$ in. across. E. United States. 1765. (B.T.S. 2, 625.) var. **albiflo'rum,** *l.* bright green, finely serrulate or serrulate-ciliate (B.M. 3428 as *V. albiflorum*); **glab'rum,** *l.* glaucous, almost or quite glabrous beneath, serrulate-ciliate. A most variable species, probably of hybrid origin.

V. crassifo'lium. Thick-leaved Whortleberry. Procumbent, trailing, evergreen shrub with wiry stems up to 3 ft. long. *l.* ovate, oval, elliptic or sub-orbicular, blunt or sub-acute, serrulate, smooth and shining, dark green above, paler beneath, $\frac{1}{3}$ to $\frac{5}{8}$ in. long, $\frac{1}{8}$ to $\frac{3}{8}$ in. wide. *fl.* half-nodding in axillary and terminal scaly-bracted racemes; cor. rosy red or white with red stripes, campanulate-urceolate, $\frac{1}{8}$ in. long with 5 short, erect lobes; cal. lobes broadly triangular, acute. May, June. *fr.* black, globose, just over $\frac{1}{8}$ in. across. SE. United States. 1794. (B.M. 1152.) Syn. *Herpothamnus crassifolius*. Not absolutely hardy and reluctant to flower except in milder areas.

V. Delavay'i. Compact, evergreen shrub 1 to $2\frac{1}{2}$ ft. h. with bristly young shoots. *l.* crowded cuneate-obovate, or broadly ovate, usually notched at apex, entire, smooth, $\frac{3}{8}$ to $\frac{1}{2}$ in. long, $\frac{3}{16}$ to $\frac{1}{4}$ in. wide. *fl.* in short, crowded, axillary or more usually terminal, bristly racemes; cor. creamy-white, tinged rosy pink, globose-urceolate, $\frac{1}{6}$ in. long with 5 small ovate or triangular lobes; cal. lobes triangular, ciliate. June. *fr.* crimson to purplish, globose, about $\frac{1}{6}$ in. across. Yunnan. 1915. Not reliably hardy or free-flowering in Britain.

V. delicio'sum. Closely resembling *V. caespitosum* except for its sub-globose-urceolate cor. and its thicker, slightly larger, obovate or oval l., glaucescent beneath. Western N. America. 1920. Probably confused with *V. caespitosum* until recently. *fl.* nodding, solitary and axillary. May, June.

V. Donia'num. A synonym of *V. Sprengelii*.

V. Dunalia'num. Erect or nearly erect evergreen shrub or small tree up to 20 ft. h. in nature with angular branches, smooth in every part. *l.* oval to oblong-lanceolate, tapering to base, caudate-acuminate at apex, entire, smooth, leathery, slightly recurved, 3 to 5 in. long, 1 to $1\frac{2}{3}$ in. wide. *fl.* in $1\frac{1}{2}$ to 3 in. axillary racemes; cor. white, campanulate, $\frac{1}{5}$ in. long with 5 small triangular lobes; cal. lobes small triangular. *fr.* black, globose, $\frac{1}{6}$ in. across. NE. India, W. China. (Wight, Ic. 1194.) Syn. *Epigynium Dunalianum, Thibaudia revoluta*. var. **urophyl'lum,** shoots and petioles downy. Very vigorous but only to be attempted in mild areas.

V. erythri'num. Evergreen shrub, about 18 in. h. with red twigs. *l.* alternate, ovate, $1\frac{3}{4}$ to 2 in. long, rather blunt, entire, leathery, glossy, reddish when young. *fl.* many in clustered, terminal, 1-sided racemes, $2\frac{1}{2}$ to 3 in. long, sessile or nearly so; cor. moderately large, deep coral-red, urn-shaped, segs. small, reflexed; pedicels red. October. Java. 1852. (B.M. 4688; F. d. S. 1115.) Warm greenhouse.

V. erythrocar'pum. Southern Mountain Cranberry. Deciduous shrub 3 to 6 ft. h. with spreading branches and pubescent young shoots. *l.* ovate, ovate-oblong or lanceolate, acute, bristly-serrulate, slightly pubescent on veins, 1 to 3 in. long, $\frac{1}{2}$ to 1 in. wide *fl.* nodding solitary from l.-axils; cor. pink, deeply divided into 4 narrow, strongly recurved, pointed lobes $\frac{1}{3}$ in. long; cal. lobes acute, triangular. June. *fr.* red ageing to purple-red, broadly oval (nearly round), $\frac{1}{4}$ in. across, very acid. SE. United States. 1806. (B.M. 7413.) Syn. *Oxycoccus erythrocarpus*.

V. fra'gile. Evergreen shrub 1 to 2 ft. h. with bristly new wood. *l.* ovate or oval, tapered to both ends, acute, shortly mucronate, glandular-pubescent on both sides and at edge, finely serrulate, rather soft, $\frac{1}{2}$ to $1\frac{1}{4}$ in. long, about half as wide. *fl.* in 1 to 2 in. pubescent racemes from terminal l.-axils, bracts red; cor. white to deep pink, urceolate, about $\frac{1}{4}$ in. long with 5 small reflexed lobes; cal. lobes ciliate. July. *fr.* rounded, black, nearly $\frac{1}{4}$ in. across. W. China. 1909. Syn. *V. setosum*. Hardy only in milder districts.

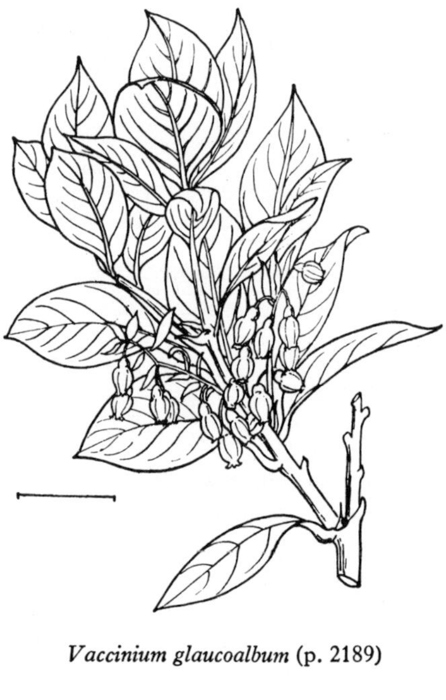

Vaccinium glaucoalbum (p. 2189)

V. glaucoalbum. Dense, evergreen shrub 2 to 4 ft. h. with smooth young wood. *l.* ovate to oblong-obovate, bristly serrulate, pointed, leathery, smooth and green above, very glaucous, and more or less bristly especially on veins beneath, 1½ to 2½ in. long, about half as wide. *fl.* in axillary, 2 to 3 in. racemes, flower bracts glaucous, ciliate; cor. cylindrical-ovoid, white tinted pink, ⅛ to ¼ in. long; cal. lobes small, smooth, triangular. May, June. *fr.* black with glaucous bloom, globose, ⅕ to ⅓ in. across. Sikkim Himalaya. (B.M. 9536.) Not reliably hardy except in south and west. **A**

V. hirsu'tum. Hairy Huckleberry. Deciduous shrub about 2 ft. h. with very downy young shoots. *l.* ovate to elliptic-oblong, acute, entire, pubescent especially beneath, ¾ to 2⅜ in. long, about half as wide. *fl.* in short, crowded, bracteate, axillary racemes; cor. white tinted pink, pubescent, cylindrical-urceolate, ⅜ in. or more long with 5 short lobes; cal. lobes pubescent, acute. May, June. *fr.* purplish-black, edible, glandular-hairy, roundish, ¼ in. across. SE. United States. 1887. (G. & F. 2, 365.)

V. × **interme'dium** (*V. Myrtillus* × *V. Vitis-idaea*). Bushy, evergreen or nearly evergreen shrub 8 to 12 in. h. with slightly angular and minutely downy young shoots. *l.* obovate or elliptic, tapering gradually to base, abruptly towards a small apical gland, slightly recurved, serrate, bright green, glabrous above and reticulate, paler and sparsely dotted with minute glandular-hairs beneath, ⅝ to 1 in. long, 5/16 to ½ in. wide. *fl.* usually in short, terminal racemes but occasionally solitary and axillary; cor. campanulate, slightly narrowed at throat, about 3/16 in. long, pinkish, lobes 5, triangular, slightly spreading; cal. lobes broadly ovate, pointed, smooth. May, June. *Berry* rounded, dark violet, about ¼ in. across. Europe, including England. 1870. Like many other hybrids, this leans more towards one parent than the other in different individuals; the above description applies to an average plant.

V. japo'nicum. Deciduous shrub 2 to 3 ft. h. with smooth young shoots. *l.* ovate to ovate-oblong, rounded or subcordate at or tapered to base, acute, serrulate, glabrous, rather glaucous beneath, ¾ to 2⅜ in. long, 7/16 to 1¼ in. wide. *fl.* solitary on ½ to ¾ in. slender stalks from l.-axils; cor. pink, about ¼ in. long, deeply divided into 4 strongly recurved lobes; cal. lobes small, triangular, acute. June, July. *fr.* scarlet, globose or roughly pear-shaped, ¼ in. across. Japan, Korea. 1892. Syn. *Oxycoccoides japonicus.* var. **sin'icum,** *l.* narrower, pubescent on midrib beneath. Cent. and W. China. 1907.

V. Lamar'ckii. Deciduous bush, 6 to 16 in. h. *l.* broadly elliptic, serrate, deep green, glabrous or sometimes pubescent along the veins beneath, ⅗ to 1⅕ in. long, ⅖ to ⅗ in. wide. *fl.* in short compact axillary racemes; cor. usually white, cylindrical, about ¼ in. long. *fr.* bright blue, well flavoured, 3/10 to ½ in. across. Newfoundland to W. Virginia and N. Carolina. Syn. *V. pensylvanicum* of Lamarck, not Miller. Closely related to *V. angustifolium*, but with a higher chromosome number ($2n = 48$), taller growth, larger l. and fl.

V. leucobot'rys. Evergreen shrub, 4 to 7 ft. h. with whorled branches. *l.* oblong-lanceolate, deeply toothed; stalk very short. *fl.* waxy-white, almost diaphanous, urn-shaped; racemes numerous, axillary drooping, 1-sided, many-fld., longer than l. Summer. *fr.* pure white with 5 dark spots below apex, about as large as peas. Bengal. 1859. (B.M. 5103 as *Epigynium leucobotrys.*) Greenhouse.

V. macrocar'pum. Large or American Cranberry. Creeping evergreen shrub with ascending shoots. *l.* oval to oblong, tapering to or rounded at base, entire, somewhat revolute, glaucescent beneath, ¼ to ¾ in. long, about half as wide. *fl.* (1 to 10 to a single shoot) on slender, pubescent, 2-bracted stalks from l.-axils; cor. white tinted and streaked pink, ⅓ in. long, deeply divided into 4 lobes, each ¼ to ⅜ in. long, so that they are almost separate and so strongly rolled back that the 8 stamens are prominently exserted; cal. cup-shaped with 4 short, ciliate lobes. June to August. *fr.* rounded or broadly oval, scarlet, very acid and astringent, ⅜ to ¾ in. across. Eastern N. American, N. Asia. 1760. (B.M. 2586.) Syn. *Oxycoccus macrocarpus*, *O. palustris* var. *macrocarpus*. Closely related to *V. Oxycoccos*. The commercially grown Cranberry of eastern America having several selected forms; for cultivation see above.

V. maderen'se. A synonym of *V. padifolium*.

V. melanocar'pum. Georgia Blueberry. Deciduous shrub 3 to 4½ ft. h. with richly pubescent young shoots. *l.* ovate, elliptic or oblanceolate, acute to acuminate, pubescent (at least beneath), 1½ to 4¼ in. long, ⅜ to 1½ in. wide. *fl.* in lateral racemes, bracts large; cor. white or greenish, open-campanulate, about ¼ in. long with 5 broad lobes; cal. lobes ovate or triangular, pubescent, ciliate, sometimes sessile-glandular at edge; stamens prominently exserted. May, June. *fr.* dark purple, globose, palatable, ⅜ in. across. SE. United States. Syn. *Polycodium melanocarpum.* Closely related to *V. neglectum.*

V. membrana'ceum. Thin-leaved Bilberry. Erect, deciduous, branching shrub 2 to 5 ft. h. with angular, smooth young shoots. *l.* oval, ovate or oblong, tapered (usually) to, or rounded at base, acute at apex, thin, serrulate, 1 to 2¾ in. long, ⅗ to 1⅛ in. wide. *fl.* usually solitary in l.-axils; cor. depressed globose-urceolate, greenish- or pinkish-white, ¼ in. long and across mouth with 5 small triangular lobes; cal. entire or slightly lobed. June, July. *fr.* dark purple, rounded, ¼ to ⅓ in. across, edible. Michigan, Alaska, Brit. Columbia, Oregon, California. 1828. (B.M. 3447 as *V. myrtilloides.*) Syn. *V. macrophyllum.* Of little garden value.

V. modes'tum. Small shrublet with slender, creeping stems and ascending shoots only a few in. h. *l.* few and collected towards ends of growths, ovate, obovate or elliptical, rounded at, or tapering to, base, rounded, very obtuse, sometimes slightly notched, entire, smooth, reticulate, slightly glaucous beneath, ¾ to 1 3/16 in. long, ⅜ to ⅝ in. wide. *fl.* solitary from upper l.-axils, long-stalked, sparsely distributed, bracteoles conspicuous; cor. rosy-pink, depressed globose, about 3/16 in. long, cleft almost to middle into 5 ovate, rounded, slightly reflexed lobes; cal. lobes reddish, short and triangular. *fr.* glaucous-violet, pleasant to taste. W. Yunnan, Burma-Tibet boundary. Recently introduced.

V. Morti'nia. Evergreen, procumbent shrub 1 to 4 ft. h. with long, spreading, rooting branches and dark-downy young shoots. *l.* close-set, ovate or sub-orbicular, sub-acute, base rounded, glandular-serrulate, firm, leathery, dark green above, downy on midrib, paler and dotted with tiny glandular bristles or dark pits beneath, ⅜ to ½ in. long, 3/16 to ⅜ in. wide. *fl.* in compact, axillary racemes near tips of branchlets; cor. pinkish-white tinted rose, cylindrical-urceolate, 3/16 to ¼ in. long with 5 small lobes; cal. lobes short, triangular. June. *fr.* glaucous-purple, oval, ⅕ in. wide. Ecuador. About 1840. (B.M. 6872.) Syn. *V. coccineum.* Hardy in the south and west of Britain but apt to be cut in very severe winters.

V. moupinen'se. Evergreen, dense shrub, 1 to 2 ft. h. with hairy young shoots. *l.* crowded, oval, oblong or obovate, tapered to base, sub-acute or rounded, slightly recurved, ciliolate towards apex, otherwise glabrous, firm, leathery, entire, ⅗ to ⅝ in. long, 3/16 to ¼ in. wide. *fl.* in axillary, brownish-red, ¾ to 1 in. long, racemes; cor. red or chocolate-red, urceolate, 5-ridged, about 3/16 in. long with 5 small, triangular lobes; cal. dark carmine, smooth, with short triangular lobes. May, June. *fr.* globose, purple-black, ¼ in. across. W. China. 1909.

V. Myrsini'tes. Evergreen Blueberry. Evergreen, more or less decumbent shrub up to 2 ft. h. with slender, often hairy young shoots. *l.* oval, oblong or obovate, tapered to base, acute or sub-acute, irregularly glandular-serrulate, glabrous and dark green above, paler and sparsely pubescent beneath, ⅜ to ¾ in. long, 3/16 to 5/16 in. wide. *fl.* in terminal and axillary umbel-like clusters or red-bracted, short racemes; cor. white or pinkish, ovoid-urceolate, ¼ in. long with 5 blunt or pointed, small and spreading lobes; cal. red, smooth, lobes acute, triangular. April, May. *fr.* blue-black, globose, ¼ in. across. SE. United States. 1813. (B.M. 1550 as *V. nitidum.*) var. **glau'cum,** glabrous throughout, *l.* beneath and *fr.* glaucous.

V. myrtilloi'des. Canadian Blueberry, Sourtop, Velvet-leaf Blueberry. Branching, deciduous shrub up to 18 in. h. with hairy young shoots. *l.* lanceolate or narrow-oblong, entire, acute or acuminate, ciliate, pubescent, especially on nerves, particularly beneath, 1 to 1½ in. long, ⅓ to ⅖ in. wide. *fl.* in axillary racemes; cor. greenish-white or reddish, cylindrical-campanulate, ⅛ to ¼ in. long with 5 erect lobes; cal. lobes green tipped brownish-red, ovate, pointed. May. *fr.* sweet, globose, blue-black, bloomy, about ¼ in. across. Labrador and Manitoba to Virginia and Illinois. 1834. (B.M. 3446 as *V. canadense.*)

V. Myrtil'lus. Bilberry, Whortleberry. Bushy, deciduous shrub 6 to 18 in. h. with 3 or 4 winged stems. *l.* ovate, pointed, serrulate, sparsely glandular-downy on veins beneath, ⅜ to 1 3/16 long, ¼ to ⅝ in. wide. *fl.* solitary, axillary; cor. pink, globose-urceolate, about ¼ in. long with 5 erect-spreading lobes; cal. green, scarcely lobed. May. *fr.* blue-black, bloomy, rounded, ⅓ in. across. Europe, N. Asia. Cult. 1789. (E.B. 456.) var. **leucocar'pum,** berries white.

V. neglec'tum. Bushy, deciduous shrub up to 6 ft. h. with smooth young shoots. *l.* oval to lanceolate or obovate, pointed, rounded at or tapered to base, entire, glabrous, often glaucous beneath at first, 1 to 3½ in. long, ⅓ to 1½ in. wide. *fl.* in lateral, bracteate racemes; cor. pink, pinkish or white, campanulate, about ¼ in. long with 5 fairly large lobes; stamens prominently exserted; sep. smooth. May. *fr.* sub-globose to obovoid, green or yellow, ¼ in. or slightly more across. SE. United States. Syn. *Polycodium neglectum.* Closely related to *V. stamineum.*

V. Nummula'ria. Evergreen, branching, rigid shrub up to 18 in. h. with young shoots thickly clothed with brown bristles. *l.* sub-orbicular, ovate or oval, sub-acute or rounded, rounded at base, rugose and slightly hairy at base above, smooth beneath, bristly-serrulate, recurved, leathery, ½ to 1 in. long, ⅜ to ⅝ in. wide. *fl.* in dense, hairy, ½ to 2 in. axillary racemes from terminal part of branchlets; cor. pink, urceolate, ⅕ in. long with 5 small, erect lobes; cal. lobes small, bluntly triangular, ciliate. April, May. *fr.* black, palatable, broadly ovate, ¼ in. long, 3/16 in. wide. Sikkim, Bhutan. 1850. (A.G.S. Bull. 8, 71.) The most attractive dwarf species in cultivation but hardy only in mildest localities.

V. ovalifo'lium. Tall or Oval-leaved Bilberry. Deciduous, branching, rather straggling shrub up to 12 ft. h. with smooth young shoots. *l.* oval or ovate, sub-acute or rounded at both ends, sometimes mucronulate, entire or nearly so, glaucescent beneath, 1 to 2 in. long, ⅝ to 1¼ in. wide. *fl.* solitary, axillary; cor. pink, ovoid-urceolate, 5/16 to ⅜ in. long with 5 sub-erect or spreading lobes; cal. cup-shaped with very short lobes. June. *fr.* dark blue, bloomy, sub-globose, ⅓ in. or more across, mildly acid. Canada, N. United States. 1880. (B.B. ed. 2, 2,700.)

V. ova'tum. Evergreen, densely-leaved shrub, often spreading when young, up to 12 ft. h. with downy young shoots. *l.* ovate-oblong, pointed or blunt at apex, rounded, subcordate or cuneate at base, bright lustrous green and slightly downy above, paler and sparsely minutely-bristly beneath, serrate, firm, leathery, ½ to 1¼ in. long, about half as wide. *fl.* solitary or in short axillary racemes; cor. white stained pink, campanulate, about ¼ in. long with 5 spreading lobes; cal. lobes broad, shallow, acute. April, May. *fr.* black, round, acid, 5/16 in. across. Western N. America. 1826. (B.M. 4732.)

V. Oxycoc′cus. Small Cranberry. Evergreen, creeping, straggling shrub with wiry, ascending stems. *l.* ovate to ovate-oblong, acute, usually rounded at base, entire or obscurely toothed, revolute, glaucous beneath, 3/16 to ⅜ in. long, a little more than half as wide. *fl.* 1 to 6 in clusters or, rarely, racemes on erect, 2-bracteate, downy, slender stalks from terminal and subterminal buds; cor. pink, about ⅓ in. across, divided almost to base into 4 strongly recurved pet. each ¼ in. long; cal. cup-shaped with 4 (rarely 5) short lobes. May to July. *fr.* red, rounded or broadly oval, ⅓ in. across, edible, very acid. Northern part of N. Hemisphere. In cult. 1789. (E.B. 876.) Syn. *Oxycoccus Oxycoccos, O. palustris, O. quadripetalus.*

V. padifo′lium. Madeiran Whortleberry. Evergreen or partly deciduous large, dense, erect shrub up to 9 ft. in this country but a small tree in nature. *l.* ovate, oval or oblong, pointed, rounded, subcordate or cuneate at base, serrulate, slightly pubescent on midrib and at base, especially beneath, 1 to 2 in. long, about half as wide. *fl.* in 1 to 2 in. long, bracteate, axillary racemes; cor. yellowish, striped red, campanulate, 7/16 in. long with 5 slightly recurved lobes; cal. lobes wide and shallow. June. *fr.* black, rounded, sweet, ⅜ in. across. Madeira. 1777. (B.M. 7305.) Syn. *V. maderense.*

V. parvifo′lium. Red Bilberry. Erect, deciduous shrub with smooth, slender, transversely angular shoots, 6 to 8 ft. h. in cultivation but up to 18 ft. in nature. *l.* thin, ovate, oval or oblong, rounded at base, obtuse at apex, smooth, entire, ½ to 1 in. long, ⅜ to ½ in. wide. *fl* solitary (rarely in 2's), rather sparse, nodding on stalks about ¼ in. long from l.-axils; cor. depressed-globose-urceolate, pale green flushed red, 5/32 in. long, ¼ in. wide with 5 minute, recurved lobes; cal. 1/16 in. long, coloured like cor., lobes broad and rounded. May, June. *Berry* oval, semi-translucent, coral-red, about ⅓ in. long, palatable. California to Alaska. 1881.

V. pensylva′nicum of Lamarck. A synonym of *V. Lamarckii.*

V. pensylva′nicum angustifo′lium. A synonym of *V. angustifolium.*

V. prae′stans. Deciduous shrub about 6 in. h. with creeping stems and ascending, smooth or downy shoots. *l.* broadly elliptic or obovate, obtuse or pointed, mucronulate, tapering to base, obscurely serrulate, smooth above, sparsely pubescent on veins beneath, 1 to 2¼ in. long, ½ to 1½ in. wide. *fl.* on short, pubescent, bracteate stalks with 2 lanceolate bracteoles beneath cal., solitary or in fascicles of 2 or 3 from axils near base of leafy part of stems; cor. white tinged pink, campanulate, about ¼ in. long with 5 erect, ovate, rather large lobes; cal. lobes rounded, ciliate. June. *fr.* bright red, sweet, fragrant, rounded, up to ½ in. across. NE. Asia. 1914. Notable for the size of the fruit.

V. refle′xum. Evergreen, branched from base; branches 1 to 2 ft. long, leafy drooping. *l.* oblong-lanceolate, acute, ½ to ¾ in. long, sharply toothed in upper part; bright pale red at first; stalk very short. *fl.* red, firm, rather 5-angled, in small, short, few-fld. corymbs or in many-fld. almost globose heads. January. Bolivia. 1869. (B.M. 5781.) Greenhouse.

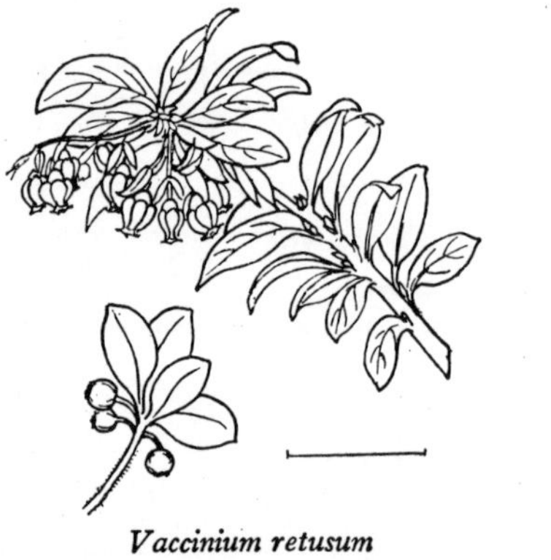

Vaccinium retusum

V. retu′sum. Low, evergreen shrub about 1 ft. h. with downy young shoots. *l.* oblong, obovate or elliptical, obtuse and more or less notched at apex, narrowed to base, leathery, smooth, entire, recurved, ½ to 1 in. long, usually a little more than half as wide. *fl.* solitary or in 1 to 2 in. long clustered racemes; cor. white striped red, ovoid-urceolate, ⅓ in. long with 5 short lobes; cal. lobes very short, triangular, obtuse. May. *fr.* nearly round, ⅓ in. across. E. Himalaya. 1882? (B.M. 9291.) Syn. *Thibaudia retusa.* Rare in cultivation and shy-flowering.

V. Rollison′ii. Evergreen, erect, much branched, branches angled, slightly hairy, leafy, 2 ft. h. or more. *l.* obovate, ¾ in. long, leathery, glossy, entire or sometimes retuse. *fl.* drooping; cor. rich scarlet, lobes 5, acute; raceme terminal, 4- to 6-fld. Java. 1851. (B.M. 4612.)

V. Sprengel′ii. Evergreen, erect, slenderly branched shrub up to 10 ft. h., with smooth or downy young wood. *l.* lanceolate or oblong, acute to acuminate, tapering to both ends, smooth, serrulate, nerves prominent below, 1½ to 3 in. long, ½ to 1⅛ in. wide. *fl.* in 1 to 4 in. long, axillary racemes; cor. white or pinkish, downy within, cylindrical-urceolate, ¼ in. long with 5 lobes; cal. lobes small, glabrous, triangular. May. *fr.* black-purple, globose, ⅛ in. across. NE. India, W. and Cent. China. (Wight, Ic. 1191.) Syn. *V. affine, V. mandarinorum, V. Donianum, Agapetes Sprengelii, Epigynium affine, E. Donianum, E. Sprengelii.* Fairly hardy in milder counties.

V. stami′neum. Deerberry. Bushy, deciduous shrub up to 5 ft. h. with pubescent young shoots. *l.* oval, ovate or obovate, acute base, rounded or abruptly cuneate, entire, pubescent on midrib above, glaucous and pubescent beneath, 1 to 2¾ in. long, about half as wide. *fl.* in downy, axillary racemes up to 2⅜ in. long, bracts leafy; cor. whitish or crimson tinted, campanulate, about ⅛ in. long, deeply cleft into 5 truncate-ovoid, sub-acute lobes; cal. lobes glabrous or slightly downy, triangular; stamens prominently exserted. April to June. *fr.* greenish or yellowish, globose or pear-shaped, ⅓ in. across, inedible. Eastern N. America. 1772. (B.B. ed. 2, 2, 697.) Syn. *Polycodium stamineum.* Closely related to *V. neglectum.*

V. tenel′lum. *See under* **V. virgatum.**

V. uligino′sum. Bog Bilberry. Stiff, deciduous, much-branched shrub 1 to 2 ft. h. with glabrous or puberulent young shoots. *l.* oval, oblong obovate or suborbicular obtuse, tapered, often abruptly, to base, entire, glaucous, slightly pubescent and reticulate beneath, ¼ to 1 in. long, half as wide. *fl.* solitary or from 2 to 4 on separate stalks from axils at terminal part of previous year's shoots; cor. white or pinkish, ovoid-urceolate, about ⅛ in. long with (usually) 4 short, spreading lobes; cal. lobes usually 4, short, acute or subacute. May, June. *fr.* blue-black, bloomy, sweet, rounded, ¼ in. across. Northern part of N. Hemisphere. In cult. 1789. (E.B. 878.)

V. urceola′tum. Evergreen, bushy shrub up to 6 ft. h. in nature with densely pubescent young shoots. *l.* ovate-oblong, acuminate, rounded at base, entire, leathery, pubescent in youth, 2 to 4 in. long, 1 to 2½ in. wide. *fl.* in 1 to 1½ in. long, axillary racemes; cor. pink, urceolate, ¼ in. long with 5, sometimes 4, lobes; cal. lobes triangular; stamens slightly exserted. June. *fr.* rounded, black, ¼ in. across. W. China. 1923. Tender except in mild districts.

V. vacil′lans. Dryland Blueberry. Stiff, branching, deciduous shrub 1 to 3 ft. h. with smooth or minutely hairy, yellow-green young shoots. *l.* oval to obovate, usually rounded at base, blunt or pointed usually mucronulate, entire or sparingly serrulate or ciliate-serrulate except at base, firm, smooth, pale or glaucous beneath, 1 to 1¾ in. long, about half as wide. *fl.* in terminal and lateral bracteate racemes from previous year's wood; cor. white tinged with pink or red, cylindric-urceolate, ¼ in. or a little more long with 5 short lobes; cal. reddish, lobes triangular or rounded, blunt. May. *fr.* globose, black, blue-black, or red, bloomy, sweet, ¼ in. across. E. United States. In cult. 1878. (B.B. ed. 2, 2, 702.) Syn. *Cyanococcus vacillans.* var. **crini′tum,** branchlets and *l.* beneath hairy.

V. virga′tum. Southern Black Blueberry, Rabbit-eye Blueberry. Deciduous upright shrub about 1½ to 3 ft. h. with usually downy young shoots. *l.* oblanceolate or narrowly elliptic, pointed, margin sharply serrulate, shortly mucronate, glandular above, slightly pubescent or glabrous on midrib and veins beneath, 1½ to 2¼ in. long, ½ to ¾ in. wide. *fl.* in short axillary or terminal racemes or clusters; cor. white or pink, cylindrical-urceolate, about ⅓ in. long with 5 short, recurved lobes; cal. lobes triangular. May, June. *fr.* black, rounded, ⅕ to 3/10 in. across. E. and SE. United States. 1770. (B.M. 3522.) Syn. *V. tenellum,* is closely allied with *l.* smaller, racemes shorter and denser, cor. shorter, almost white. (B.B. 2, 703.) Syn. *V. virgatum tenellum.* The l. become splendid red before falling. **V. amoe′num,** Large-cluster Blueberry, is a closely allied species, somewhat larger in growth, *l.* and *fl.* SE. United States. 1765. *V. vacillans* and *V. Lamarckii* are sometimes grown under the name *V. amoenum.*

V. Vit′is-idaea. Cowberry, Mountain Cranberry. Evergreen shrub 6 to 12 in. h. with creeping stems and ascending shoots which are black-pubescent at first. *l.* obovate or oval, obtuse or rounded, often notched, tapered to base, firm, leathery, lustrous, quite smooth or minutely ciliate at base above, paler and black-dotted beneath, ⅓ to 1⅓ in. long, about half as wide. *fl.* in sub-terminal bracteate racemes; cor. white or pinkish, campanulate, ¼ in. long with 4 rather large lobes; cal. 4-lobed. May, June. *fr.* dark red, rounded, about ⅓ in. across, edible. Europe, N. Asia, NE. America. In cult. 1789. (E.B. 877.) Syn. *Vitis-idaea Vitis-idaea.* var. **ma′jus,** *fl.* larger, *l.* up to 1½ in. long; **mi′nus,** dwarfer than type, displays its *fl.* and *fr.* to advantage, more useful garden plant than type. NW. America and NE. Asia.

F. S. and W. T. S.

vaccinio′ides, Vaccinium-like.

vacci′nus -a -um, relating to cows, of the colour of a red cow.

Vachel′lii, in honour of the Rev. George Harvey Vachell, chaplain to the Hon. East India Company at Macao from 1825 to 1836.

vacil′lans, variable.

va'gans, wandering, of wide distribution.

VAGA'RIA (from *vagus*, roaming; the plant being first described from a specimen of uncertain origin grown in Paris, whither it had evidently wandered from the Levant). FAM. *Amaryllidaceae.* A genus of a single species of bulbous plant, native of Syria, allied to, and sometimes included in, Pancratium but with the corona in the form of 12 linear-awl-shaped teeth. Cultivation as for Pancratium in a cool house.

V. parviflo'ra. Bulb ovoid, about 2 in. thick with a long neck; tunic dull brown. *l.* 4 to 6 strap-shaped, about 6 in. long at flowering time, later 2 ft. long, finely grooved on face with a median white band. *Scape* up to 10 in. long, stout, glabrous, umbel 6- to 9-fld., pedicels at first very short. *fl.* funnel-shaped, up to 1½ in. long, tube ⅓ in. long, white with a broad green keel outside; corona of 12 narrow teeth about ¼ in. long. Autumn. Syria. 1837? (B.M. 9406.)

VAGINA. Sheath, e.g. a winged petiole from which a stem apparently issues.

vagina'tus -a -um, having a sheath.

Vah'lii, in honour of M. Vahl, 1749–1804, of Norway. Director of Botanic Garden, Copenhagen.

Vaillan'tii, in honour of S. Vaillant, 1669–1722, French botanist.

VALDIV'IA (in honour of Pedro Valdivia, conqueror of Chile). FAM. *Saxifragaceae.* A monotypic genus of more botanical than horticultural interest.

V. Gaya'na. Evergreen shrub or sub-shrub from a few in. to 1 or 2 ft. h. *l.* crowded in a terminal cluster, 3 to 8 in. long, 1½ to 3 in. wide, oblanceolate, pointed, coarsely often doubly toothed, teeth gland-tipped, tapered at the base to a short hairy stalk. *fl.* few in hairy, erect racemes up to 2 in. long; pet. 5 to 7, red, linear, ⅜ in. long with a patch of down on the inside; cal. bell-shaped with 5 pointed lobes. Chile. 1863. Grows in shady woods, greenhouse.

W. J. B.

valdivia'nus -a -um, of Valdivia, Chile.

Valentinia'nus -a -um, in honour of Pére S. P. Valentin of the Tsedjong Roman Catholic Mission, China, *c.* 1919.

valenti'nus -a -um, of Valencia, Spain.

VALERIAN. *See* **Valeriana.**

VALERIAN, GREEK. *See* **Polemonium coeruleum.**

VALERIAN, RED. *See* **Kentranthus.**

VALERIA'NA (medieval name, perhaps from *valere*, to be healthy; in allusion to its powerful medicinal qualities). FAM. *Valerianaceae.* A genus of about 150 species of perennial herbs, sub-shrubs or shrubs, mostly natives of the north temperate regions and extra-tropical S. America with a few in Brazil and the E. Indies. Leaves at base entire or toothed, or stem leaves (or all) pinnatifid, or 1-, 2-, or 3-pinnatisect. Flowers white or pink; calyx at first inrolled but forming a feathery crown at fruiting time; corolla with a short, rarely a long tube and a 5-cleft, spreading limb; stamens 3, usually saccate near the base. Fruit compressed, one-seeded, with a feathery pappus. Few of the species are of horticultural value, but *V. officinalis* has distinct medicinal qualities. The species mentioned below are hardy perennials growing without trouble in ordinary soil and readily increased by division. The dwarf species are good rock plants, bearing a strong resemblance to one another as a rule. The genus Kentranthus (Red Valerian) differs in having a distinctly spurred corolla with only one stamen.

V. alliariifo'lia. Erect from a thick, branching rhizome, glabrous; stem tall, sulcate. *Lower l.* broadly heart-shaped, coarsely toothed, long-stalked; *stem-l.* smaller, sessile or almost so. *fl.* pink in a terminal compound corymb. Summer. E. Europe, W. Asia. SYN. *V. macrophylla.* Borders.

V. alpes'tris. About 6 in. h., glabrous. *Lower l.* ovate-oblong, toothed; *upper* sometimes unequally 2- or 3-lobed, progressively smaller. *fl.* pinkish in numerous small heads. May to August. Caucasus. Rock-garden.

V. angustifo'lia. A synonym of *Kentranthus angustifolius.*

V. arizo'nica. About 3 in. h., glabrous, from a creeping rhizome. Stem erect. *l.* rather fleshy, radical entire or nearly so, 1 in. long; upper lobed. *fl.* pink, in corymbs; cor. ½ in. long, gradually broadened upwards. April to July. Arizona. (G.C. 29 (1901), 198.) Rock-garden.

V. asarifo'lia. About 12 in. h., compact. *fl.* red, in many umbels. June to August. Crete. Rock-garden.

V. Calcitra'pa. A synonym of *Kentranthus Calcitrapa.*

V. cel'tica. About 3 in. h., very fragrant in all parts. *rhiz.* creeping. *l.* small, ovate, tapered to base; lower entire. *fl.* yellowish in a loose panicle. May to July. European Alps. Rock-garden. Collected in the Alps for its fragrance.

V. Cornuco'piae. A synonym of *Fedia Cornucopiae.*

V. edu'lis. A synonym of *V. obovata.*

V. globulariifo'lia. 3 to 4 in. h. *l.* small, oval, entire; stem-l. pinnatifid. Stem grooved. *fl.* pink, in rather large heads. Pyrenees. Rock-garden. Plant fragrant.

V. monta'na. About 6 in. h., erect, glabrous or slightly hairy. *Lower l.* oblong or obovate, blunt, slightly toothed; *upper* lanceolate, acute; all shining. *fl.* pink in corymbs, lengthening in fruit. July. European Alps, Caucasus. 1748. (L.B.C. 317.) var. **rotundifo'lia,** dwarfer, *lower l.* nearly round. (B.M. 1825.)

V. obova'ta. 2 to 4 ft. h., pubescent or glabrous, from a fleshy tap-root. *l.* thickish, not toothed; lower oblanceolate to spatulate, sometimes laciniate-pinnatifid, stalk margined; upper few or none. *fl.* yellowish white, in a long panicle. N. America including Mexico. Roots edible when cooked. Borders. SYN. V. *edulis.*

V. officina'lis. All-heal, Cat's Valerian, Common Valerian, St. George's Herb. About 3 ft. h., stems sulcate. *l.* all or nearly all pinnatisect; segs. in 7 or 8 pairs, lanceolate, toothed. *fl.* pink in a corymb, lengthening in fruit. June. Europe, including Britain, Asia. (E.B. 666.) Very variable. Borders, wild garden. Cats are very fond of this plant, especially the powdered root.

V. Phu. About 3 ft. h., glabrous, stem erect, round, smooth. *Lower l.* oblong or elliptic, entire; *stem-l.* pinnately lobed, lobes oblong. *fl.* white, in a paniculate corymb. August. Caucasus, Europe. **'Aurea',** young growths bright golden in spring. Borders.

V. pyrena'ica. 2 to 4 ft. h., hairy from a large rhizome, without stolons; stem erect sulcate. *l.* glabrous; radical large, heart-shaped, coarsely unequally toothed; stem-l. toothed, 3-lobed, terminal lobe largest. *fl.* pale rose. Pyrenees. Borders.

V. saliu'nica.* About 4 in. h. *l.* dense, small, entire, dark green. *fl.* pink, sweet, in corymbs. S. Europe. Rock-garden.

V. sambucifolia. About 4 ft. h., erect. Habit of *V. officinalis. l.* pinnatisect. *fl.* small, white, tinged pink, in large loose corymbs. June to August. Europe. SYN. *V. officinalis sambucifolia.* Borders.

V. septentriona'lis. About 2 ft. h., stem slender, erect. *fl.* white, in loose panicles. June, July. Rocky Mts. Borders.

V. supi'na.* About 4 in. h., carpet-forming. *l.* small, oval, ciliate, almost entire, dark shining green. *fl.* white, tinged pink in loose corymbs, almost sessile, fragrant. June to August. Cent. Europe. Rock-garden, moraine.

VALERIANA'CEAE. Dicotyledons. A family of about 350 species of herbaceous plants and a few shrubs scattered over the N. Hemisphere and extending to the Andes, distributed over 8 genera. Leaves opposite, without stipules. Inflorescence a long or short cyme. Flowers often small but numerous and sometimes showy, perfect or unisexual, irregular. Calyx scarcely developed at flowering time but later enlarging to a hairy pappus at the top of the fruit. Corolla 3- to usually 5-lobed, frequently spurred at the base. Stamens 1 to 4, inserted on the corolla tube, anthers introrse. Ovary inferior, 3-celled, but one only fertile with one ovule. Fruit an achene with adnate calyx (i.e. a cypsela). The genera dealt with here are Fedia, Kentranthus, Nardostachys, Patrinia, Valeriana, Valerianella.

VALERIANEL'LA (diminutive of Valeriana). FAM. *Valerianaceae.* A genus of about 50 species of small, annual herbs with forked branching, natives of Europe, N. Africa, W. Asia, and N. America. Radical leaves in a rosette, entire; cauline leaves entire, toothed or rarely pinnately cut. Flowers whitish, pale lilac or pink; calyx limb toothed, lobed, or absent; corolla tube usually short, not spurred or saccate at base, limb spreading, 5-cleft; stamens 3; cymes sometimes fastigiately corymbose, sometimes densely globose at tips of shoots; bracts free.

Fruit without a feathery pappus, the calyx forming nearly a short or obsolescent rim. For cultivation of these hardy salad plants *see* **Corn Salad.**

V. carina'ta. Similar in all characters to *V. Locusta* except in *fr.* which is oblong, boat-shaped with the fertile cell not corky; cal. limb indistinct. Europe, including Britain. (E.B. 670.)

V. Locus'ta.* Corn Salad, Lamb's Lettuce, White Potherb. 6 to 12 in. h. *l.* linear-oblong or oblong-lanceolate, entire or toothed, 1 to 3 in. long; stem-l. half clasping. *fl.* pale lilac, minute, in capitate cymes. April to June. *fr.* minute, glabrous or hairy; fertile cell corky at back; cal. limb absent. Europe, including Britain. (E.B. 669.) SYN. *V. olitoria.*

valesia'cus -a -um, of Wallis (Valais), SW. Switzerland.

Valeton'ii, in honour of Theodore Valeton, 1855–1929. Dutch bacteriologist in Java.

va'lidus -a -um (***validi-*** in compound words), strong, well developed.

VALLA'RIS (*vallus*, stake, palisade; said to be used in Java for fences). FAM. *Apocynaceae.* A genus of 5 or 6 species of twining shrubs, natives of Trop. Asia and Malaya. Leaves opposite, minutely doted. Flowers white, in cymes or clusters; calyx 5-parted, sometimes glandular within; corolla salver-shaped, tube short, throat naked, lobes broad; stamens at top of tube; filaments very short, club-shaped. For treatment of these stove-climbers *see* **Vallesia.**

V. dichot'oma. A synonym of *V. Heynei.*

V. Heyn'ei. Tall climbing shrub, with pale bark. *l.* elliptic or linear-oblong, 2 to 4 in. long, ½ to 1½ in. wide, slender pointed, sometimes hairy. *fl.* white, in forked cymes, fragrant, ⅜ in. across; sep. ovate-oblong, obtuse; disk ciliate. *fr.* straight, 6 in. long, 2 in. wide, tapered from a rounded base to a stiff point. Himalaya to Burma and Ceylon. SYN. *V. dichotoma.*

V. Pergula'na. Climbing shrub, with pale bark. *l.* broadly elliptic or obovate, or abruptly rounded, 4 to 7 in. long, 3 to 4 in. wide, membranous, shortly pointed, sometimes downy beneath. *fl.* white, odour goat-like. India. 1818.

F. G. P.

Vallerand'ii, in honour of Eugene Vallerand.

VALLES'IA (in honour of Francisco Valles, physician to Philip II of Spain; d. 1592). FAM. *Apocynaceae.* A genus of 2 species of much-branched glabrous shrubs or small trees, natives of Trop. America. Leaves alternate, lanceolate or oblong. Flowers small, in cymes; calyx 5-parted, without glands; corolla salver-shaped, throat hairy, lobes 5, ovate or lanceolate, twisted; stamens included. Stove treatment is necessary with a compost of sandy loam and peat. Propagation by cuttings in sand, under glass, in heat.

V. cymbifo'lia. Shrub of 3 ft., dichotomously branched, branches terete. *l.* ovate-oblong, 2 to 2½ in. long, rugosely tubercled and with pellucid dots, acute. *fl.* white, ½ in. long, many, in branched cymes half as long as l. Peru. 1822. SYN. *V. dichotoma.*

F. G. P.

vallesi'acus -a -um, *see* ***valesiacus.***

Vallea stipularis pyrifolia

VAL'LEA (in honour of Felice Valle, d. 1747, who wrote *Florula Corsicae*, published in 1761). FAM. *Elaeocarpaceae.* Nearly hardy but apt to be cut back by winter frosts. Good in a cool greenhouse either in pots or planted out and growing rapidly in a well-drained compost. Propagated by either seed or cuttings.

V. stipula'ris pyrifo'lia. Bush to 15 ft. h., glabrous, branches slender. *l.* very variable, lanceolate to broadly ovate or palmately lobed, 1 to 4½ in. long, herbaceous to somewhat leathery, dark green above, more or less glaucous beneath with tufts of hair in vein axils; stalk slender; stipules sometimes present. *fl.* in small terminal or lateral cymes; sep. 5, pale rose with darker veins; cor. cup-shaped, pet. 5, overlapping, deep rose, obovate, 3-lobed to half-way, ⅓ to ½ in. long; stamens 30 to 40. Andes from Colombia to Bolivia. 1928. (B.M. 9365.)

VALLISNE'RIA (in honour of Antonio Vallisnieri, 1661–1730, Professor at Padua). FAM. *Hydrocharitaceae.* A genus of 2 species of submerged aquatics, found in freshwater lakes, ditches, &c., in warm and temperate regions of the world. *V. spiralis* is frequently planted in aquaria or even in outdoor fish-ponds for oxygenating the water. Propagated by the rooted runners.

V. gigante'a. More vigorous and larger than *V. spiralis. l.* 3 ft. long, broad, deep green. S. America. A plant for large aquaria and deep water outdoors. var. **marmora'ta,** *l.* pale green, spotted and barred purple and eventually yellow; **mi'nor,** smaller, *l.* pale green, almost transparent; **rubrifo'lia,** *l.* broad, bronzy crimson lined purple.

V. spira'lis. Eelgrass, Tapegrass. Stem very short, sometimes stoloniferous. *l.* very long in deep, short in shallow water, translucent green, often minutely toothed at apex. *fl.* dioecious; male in a dense ovoid spike not quite as long as the bifid or trifid spathe, the fl. breaking off when ready to open and floating to the surface of the water; female solitary with green perianth and 3 large stigmas, raised to the surface on a slender peduncle which after pollination twists in a close spiral carrying the young fruit to the bottom to ripen. Europe. 1818. var. **tor'ta,** *l.* twisted like a corkscrew, light green.

VALLO'TA (in honour of Pierre Vallot, 1594–1671, French botanist, who wrote a description of the gardens of Louis XIII in 1623). FAM. *Amaryllidaceae.* A genus of a single species of bulbous plant, native of S. Africa. *V. speciosa* needs a compost of good fibrous loam, leaf-

Vallota speciosa (p. 2193)

soil and sand in equal parts. The best season for planting a fresh stock is June and July when their roots will become active before the flower stems are sent up. The bulbs should be placed 6 to 8 in. below the surface of the soil and surrounded with sand, then covered with compost which should be firmly pressed around them. They should not be disturbed for years and when ultimately established will produce masses of flower. During the growing season and in dry weather an occasional soaking of water or liquid manure will be beneficial. Vallota differs from Amaryllis and Brunsvigia by its almost regular perianth. Crosses with related genera have been attempted without success except that *Cyrtanthus sanguineus* has been crossed with *V. speciosa*, producing an intermediate plant sometimes called *V.* × *hybrida*.

V. purpu'rea. A synonym of *V. speciosa.*

V. specio'sa. Scarborough Lily. Bulb rather large, ovate. Stem 1 to 2 ft. h., compressed. *l.* broad-linear up to over 18 in. long. *infl.* 3- to 10-fld. with oblong-lanceolate spathe valves. *fl.* bright scarlet, 3 to 4 in. long, funnel-shaped, straight, erect, tube short, lobes oblong-ovate; stamens shorter than perianth. S. Africa. 1774. (R.H. 1870, 50). var. **al'ba,** *fl.* white; **delicat'a,** *fl.* delicate salmon-pink. 1893; **elat'a,** *fl.* smaller, cherry red; **exim'ia,*** *fl.* about 4 in. across, throat white with a crimson feathering; **magnif'ica,** a synonym of var. *eximia*; **maj'or,** *fl.* reddish-scarlet, throat with transparent areas; **min'or,** smaller in all parts than type.

VALONIA OAK. *See* **Quercus Aegilops.**

VAL'SA. A genus of fungi of the Class Ascomycetes containing some species which are often found associated with dieback in stone-fruit trees, e.g. *Valsa ambiens* on cherries and plums. It is most probable that the fungus is but a weak parasite and attacks only shoots that are dying back from some other cause. (*See* **Dieback.**)

D. E. G.

valvate, of sepals or petals in the bud in contact with one another by margins only.

VALVE. The door by which a body opens; the pieces into which a capsule splits.

valverden'sis -is -e, of Valverde, chief town of Hierro, Canary Is.

VALVES. *See* **Heating.**

Valvular dehiscence, opening by valves, seen both in anthers and fruits.

VANCOUVE'RIA (in honour of Capt. George Vancouver, 1757–98, of the *Discovery*, who explored the north-west coast of America). FAM. *Berberidaceae.* A genus of 3 species of perennial herbs, native to Western N. America, related to Epimedium but with 6 (instead of 4) inner sepals, petals, and stamens. Leaves normally all basal, usually with 9 cordate, rounded often somewhat 3-lobed leaflets. Flowering stem normally leafless, about 8 to 16 in. h. Flowers small, white or yellow, with reflexed sepals and petals. The Vancouverias are graceful, hardy, creeping woodland plants with slender rhizomes, suited to cool shady places in peaty soil and propagated by division. A monograph of Vancouveria and Epimedium by W. T. Stearn will be found in *J. Linnean Soc. Bot.* 51. 409–535 (1938); the 3 species are illustrated here and in L. R. Abrams, *Fl. Pacific States*, 2. 222 (1944).

V. chrysan'tha. 8 to 16 in. h. *l.* 2-ternate or with 3 or 5 lflets., evergreen; lflets. firm, margins cartilaginously thickened and somewhat undulate, to $1\frac{1}{2}$ in. long and wide. *fl.* yellow, about $\frac{1}{2}$ in. long, in a few-fld. usually simple infl.; pedicels, stamens, and ovary glandular; pet. hooded at tip. May. S. Oregon, N. California. 1935.

V. hexand'ra. 4 to 16 in. h. *l.* 2- or 3-ternate, perishing in autumn; lflets. thin, not thickened at margin, up to 3 in. long and wide, often much less. *fl.* white, about $\frac{1}{2}$ in. long, in a many-fld., usually paniculate infl.; pedicels glabrous; stamens and ovary glandular; pet. hooded at tip. May. Washington to California. In cultivation in 1886. SYN. *Epimedium hexandrum.*

V. planipe'tala. Redwood Ivy. 7 to 12 in. h. *l.* 2- or 3-ternate, occasionally with 5 lflets., evergreen; lflets. firm, margins cartilaginously thickened and slightly or distinctly undulate, to $2\frac{1}{2}$ in. long and wide, often much less. *fl.* white or lavender-tinged, about $\frac{3}{16}$ in. long, in a many-fld. paniculate infl.; pedicels glandular; stamens and ovary glabrous; pet. flat, slightly 3-toothed at tip. May. N. Oregon, California. In cultivation 1909. SYN. *V. parviflora.* Sometimes grown under the unsuitable and incorrect name *V. sibirica.*

W. T. S.

VAN'DA (Indian name of the original species). FAM. *Orchidaceae.* A polymorphic genus embracing probably fifty species of often very beautiful epiphytic orchids, natives of India, Ceylon, the E. Indies, Malaya, Borneo, Philippines, Java, one also in Trop. Australia. Flowers showy or rarely rather small, shortly pedicellate, usually fragrant; sepals and petals free, sub-equal, much spreading, often narrowed or nearly clawed at base; in a number the petals are so twisted as to bring their reverse surface into full or partial view; lip continuous with the column, spreading, saccate or obtusely spurred at base, the lateral lobes erect, rounded or reduced to auricles, the middle one spreading or thickened; column short, thick, wingless; pollen masses 2; bracts short; racemes usually simple; peduncles lateral. Capsules often on rather long pedicels. Considerable variation is seen in the genus, in colour, size, and number of the flowers, and in their habit. The leaves are always distichous, but they may be spreading, leathery, slightly fleshy, often unequally 2-lobed, and ragged or shortly 2-lobed and emarginate at apex, terete or approaching terete. Some species are quite dwarf, others reach considerable size. Stem leafy, not pseudobulbous, in the larger species becoming somewhat woody with age. The Vandas require more light than do most other Orchids; but light shading is required during very bright weather. During growth, say from March or April until about October, a high temperature and abundance of moisture are essential; the temperature should not fall below 70° or 75° F. during the day, and may be allowed to rise to 85° or even higher in sunny weather. The night temperature during the growing season should not fall more than about 10° below that maintained during the day. In the winter months 60° or 65° F. at night will be sufficient, and less water will be required—none being allowed to lodge in the axils of the leaves. Though most species require a warm house, species such as *V. caerulea* and *V. Amesiana* from higher altitudes are better suited in the cool house, rising to sub-tropical conditions during summer. The roots, including those emitted from the stem, are usually thick and fleshy and extend a considerable distance. While the roots are extending and further proof of their activity is seen in their tips which are greenish and smooth, abundance of water should be supplied, the syringe freely used, and the highest temperatures given. When, particularly in the cooler-growing species, the root tips are seen to be calloused over, applications of water must be governed by the winter temperature of the house. In the greater number of the E. Indian species some root activity may be apparent throughout the year and the compost must be allowed only to approach dryness. With *V. Amesiana*, *V. caerulea*, *V. Kimballiana*, and *V. teres* a decided rest is beneficial in a cooler, drier atmosphere, water being given only to compensate for the pipe-heat used, the syringe discarded for the time. With *V. caerulea* especially, though the leaves must not be allowed to become flaccid, water may be withheld and the plants exposed to light until a portion of their chlorophyll is lost—it will be replaced in early summer. A winter atmosphere too humid, or then too much water at the roots, is largely productive of brown-black disfiguring blotches appearing on the leaf-margins of this fine species. Conversely, during growth, hardly too much moisture can be used on a hot day, nor too high a temperature reached during and following midday, though the morning temperature may fall to 50° F. and air should be freely admitted by night. *V. teres* may have tropical temperature and atmosphere when growing, with a sunny position near the glass with little if any shading. In winter 50° to 55° F. is sufficient with full exposure to light and very occasional waterings. *V. Hookeriana*, a most beautiful species, has often adapted itself to a practically terrestrial condition in swampy places and should have full sunlight, a tropical temperature, and abundance of water throughout the year—conditions difficult to obtain in English winters. On the whole the genus is easily cultivated and so many fragrant or beautiful species are included that the very slight cultural differences required are worth studying. *V. Sanderiana*, considered by some to be the finest of all orchids, should have a minimum temperature of 70° F. and be placed in a basket which can be suspended away from direct pipe heat. For all the smaller species baskets suitable to the size of the plant are preferable to pots, which should be used for the taller, stronger-growing kinds like *V. tricolor*. The compost used should be as for Aerides, the nodules of charcoal, pot sherds or broken bricks of size in proportion to that of the plant and well mixed with the compost, clear drainage being essential. As with Aerides, if plants become leggy the stems may be severed in spring, below active roots, and potted, the old base being kept, on the possibility of new growths being formed. *V. teres* is readily propagated as the stems are more inclined to develop lateral growths, and lengths of 12 in., more or less, may be laid in a propagating case until roots are seen, or potted and placed with the main batch.

V. alpi'na. *fl.* 2 or 3, pale green, small; sep. and pet. oblong; lip yellowish with dull purple streaks, gibbous below apex, emarginate, hollow at deep purple base; raceme almost sessile, erect. *l.* channelled recurved, obliquely 2-lobed. Khasya. 1837. Syn *V. Griffithii, Luisia alpina.* Allied to *V. cristata.*

V. Amesia'na.* *fl.* 1 to 12, creamy-white tinted rose especially on lip at first, fading to light yellow, fragrant, 1½ in. across; sep. and pet. oblong-cuneate; side lobes of lip small, nearly square, mid-lobe reniform, 2-lobed; spur conical; scape erect, often tall, branched. *l.* thick, grooved, tapered. Stem short, thick. India. 1887. (B.M. 7139; W.O.A. 296.) var. **al'ba,** *fl.* white.

V. × amoe'na. A natural hybrid (*V. caerulea* × *V. tessellata*). Intermediate as regards habit, &c. *fl.* 2 to 3 in. across; sep. and pet. bluish-grey with violet spots; lip violet-blue with whitish side lobes. 1897. var. **Sand'erae,** sep. and pet. cream-white, reticulated with lilac, lip violet-purple with small divergent apical lobes. 1908.

V. Arbuthnotia'na. *fl.* 2½ in. across, golden-yellow with transverse bars of purple; mid-lobe of lip fiddle-shaped. *l.* thin. Malabar. 1892. Allied to *V. tessellata.*

V. Bateman'ni. *See* **Stauropsis lissochiloides.**

V. Ben'soni.* *fl.* 10 to 15, 2 in. across, white without; sep. and pet. yellowish-green, dotted and reticulated with reddish-brown within, obovate, nearly equal; lip pink or rose-purple, with 2 oblong-falcate divergent lobes at apex, 3 lamellae on disk, basal auricles small, white; spur conical, white; scapes rigid, 18 in. long. *l.* leathery, lorate, channelled, 7 to 10 in. long, ½ to 1 in. wide, toothed at tip. Rangoon. 1866. (B.M. 5611.) var. **trist'is,** *fl.* sulphur-yellow without, dark brown within, lip whitish-yellow with green side lobes. 1896.

V. bi'color. *fl.* 2½ in. h., white without, yellowish-brown within, with obscure livid tessellations; sep. and pet. falcate; lip lilac, with large, white yellow-bordered auricles, giving the base a broad, cordate appearance, dotted with lilac and tinged with yellow; column short, stout, whitish at base; spur short, blunt; raceme erect, rigid, few-fld., longer than l. *l.* lorate, leathery, 6 to 9 in. long, very oblique and somewhat 3-toothed at apex. Bhutan. 1875.

V. Boxal'lii. A variety of *V. lamellata.*

V. brun'nea. *fl.* as large as in *V. concolor*, olive-brown within; sep. and pet. elongated-cuneate, obtuse; lip pale yellowish-white; spur long, conical, acute. July. *l.* long, ligulate, toothed. Burma, Siam. About 1892.

V. caerul'ea.* *fl.* 7 to 20, up to 5 in. across; sep. and pet. pale blue, usually with deeper tessellations, membranous, oblong, obtuse, short-stalked; lip deep blue, small, leathery, oblong-linear, obtuse with two diverging lobes; scapes erect, much longer than l. Autumn. *l.* lorate, channelled, leathery, unequally truncate, 5 to 12 in. long, about 1 in. wide. Stem erect, 2 to 3 ft. or more h. Assam, Burma, Siam. 1849. var. **al'ba,** *fl.* rather small, sep. and pet. white, lip blue. 1912; **albid'ula,** *fl.* white with blue veining on lip. 1912; **albocaerul'ea,** sep. and pet. white, lip blue, 1913; **Bluebeard,** *fl.* nearly circular, sep. and pet. indigo-blue with whitish mottling, lip dark violet. 1911; **Bodnant Rose,** *fl.* medium size, mottled and tinged with rose-pink, lip suffused with rose-pink. 1921; **Charlesworth'ii,** *fl.* pure white, with only a little yellow at base of lip. 1918; **delica'ta,** *fl.* pale pink, lip bright red. 1924; **Dreadnought,** *fl.* large, dark blue with deeper tessellations. 1909; **Fascination,** sep. and pet. reticulated with rose, bluish at apex, lip dark rose. 1927; **King of the Blues,** *fl.* large, dark blue. 1920; **Lady Holford,** *fl.* large, reticulated with bright blue on a lighter ground. 1912; **Luton Hoo var.,** *fl.* 5 in. across, richly tessellated with deep blue on a paler ground. 1912; **Paetersia'na,** *fl.* white, tinted rose, showing no blue, lip deeper rose. Khasya. 1897; **R. Chollet,** *fl.* large, bright blue. 1908; **Rochfordia'na,** *fl.* nearly white, tinted rose on lip; **Sand'erae,** *fl.* clear pink or with sep. and pet. paler at base. 1910; **The Node,** *fl.* flushed with rose-pink, lip rose colour. 1930; **Westonbirt var.,** *fl.* large, rich blue, the sep. and pet. reticulated with deeper blue. 1910; **Wrig'leyi,** *fl.* smaller than in type, sep. and pet. rather narrow, pure white, lip rose-pink, spur slender, distinct, possibly a natural hybrid (*V. caerulea* × *V. Moorei*). 1911. There are many other varieties.

Vanda caerulescens

V. caerules'cens.* *fl.* 10 to 20 or more, about 1 in. across; sep. and pet. pale mauve-blue, cuneate-ovate, twisted at base which is clawed; lip deep blue-violet, obovate, emarginate, auricles lilac-purple, spur tipped green; scape slender, erect, axillary. Spring. *l.* leathery, ligulate, dark green, 5 to 7 in. long, truncately 2-lobed, tip spiny. Burma. 1869. (B.M. 5834; W.O.A. 48.) var. **Blue King,** *fl.* brighter, lip deeper blue. 1930; **Boxall'i,** a synonym of *V.* × *confusa*; **Lowiana,** probably a form of *V.* × *confusa*. *V. caerulescens* of Lindley is *V. caerulea.*

V. Cathcart'ii. *See* **Arachnanthe Cathcartii.**

V. × Charlesworth'ii. A supposed natural hybrid (*V. Bensoni* × *V. caerulea*). *fl.* 2½ in. or more across; sep. and pet. much as in *V. coerulea*, yellowish-white dotted and reticulated with lilac-purple, veined and suffused at margins with light rose-purple; lip fleshy, lobes at apex broadly rounded, light red-purple, mid-lobe purplish with 3 fleshy keels, side lobes whitish; column with 2 orange blotches at base. Burma. 1894.

V. Clark'ei. *See* **Arachnanthe Clarkei.**

V. con'color. *fl.* 7 to 10, 2 in. across; sep. and pet. white without, yellow-brown within, oblong-obovate, wavy; lip 3-lobed, downy at base, side lobes white with rosy dots, mid-lobe constricted in middle, basal half yellow with raised lines, remainder cinnamon-brown, 2-lobed at apex; spur short, conical; raceme long, lateral. *l.* membranous, evergreen, 3-lobed at tip, 7 to 9 in. long, about 1 in. wide. China, Java, Sumatra. 1835. (B.M. 3416 as *V. Roxburghii unicolor.*) Habit of *V. tesselata.*

V. × confu'sa. A supposed natural hybrid (*V. caerulescens* × *V. parviflora*). Sep. and pet. whitish; lip violet bordered white, less dilated at apex than that of *V. caerulescens*, spur short, conical. 1887. (B.M. 6328 as *V. caerulescens Boxallii.*)

V. crista'ta. *fl.* 2 to 6, 2 in. across; sep. and pet. yellow-green, oblong, obtuse, pet. incurved; lip buff, striped rich purple between 5 to 7 raised white lines, with 2 divergent, narrow, acute lobes at tip and a short middle one; racemes erect, shorter than l. March to July. *l.* channelled, recurved, truncate and 3-toothed at tip, 5 to 7 in. long, narrow. Stem short, erect. Nepal. 1818. (B.M. 4304; B.R. 28, 48; W.O.A. 290.)

V. Cuming'ii. A synonym of *V. lamellata.*

V. Dear'ei.* *fl.* 4 or 5, 3½ in. across, soft yellow; sep. and pet. shortly stalked, elliptic, obtuse; lip side lobes small, mid-lobe squarish broad, transverse, pandurate, spur conical with a short, rounded, grooved crest over front of mouth. Stem stout, 2 to 8 ft. h. *l.* fleshy, 12 in. or more long. Sunda Isles. 1886.

V. Denev'ii. A synonym of *Phalaenopsis Denevei.*

V. Denisonia'na.* *fl.* 5 or 6, 2½ in. h., thick, fleshy; sep. and pet. white, slightly tinged green, undulate, dorsal sep. and pet. spatulate; lip white, fiddle-shaped, with 4 or 5 raised lines, apex 2-lobed, base with 2 nearly square auricles; spur short, conical; racemes axillary, peduncle stout. April. *l.* lorate, rigid, recurved, sharply 2-lobed at tip, 7 to 12 in. long, ¾ to 1 in. wide, dark green. Stems erect. Burma. 1869. (B.M. 5811.) var. **al'ba,** *fl.* white; **hebra'ica,** sep. and pet. sulphur, darker within with markings resembling Hebrew letters, spur orange within. July. Burma. 1885. (W.O.A. 248.); **puncta'ta,** *fl.* sulphur, with some brown spots on dorsal sep. and pet., middle and base of lip white.

V. densiflo'ra. A synonym of *Saccolabium giganteum.*

V. fur'va. *fl.* few, about 1½ in. across, with a slightly fishy smell; sep. and pet. dull brown, with a little greenish-yellow at edge; pet. clawed, falcate, broader than sep.; lip greenish-yellow, hairy at base, 5-furrowed, 2-lobed; spur cylindrical; racemes short. Spring. 1 ft. h. Java. 1848. SYN. *V. fuscoviridis.*

V. fuscovi'ridis. A synonym of *V. furva.*

V. gigante'a. A synonym of *Stauropsis gigantea.*

V. Gow'eri. A synonym of *Stauropsis undulata.*

V. Griffith'ii. A synonym of *V. alpina.*

V. hasti'fera. *fl.* about 9, in a loose raceme, larger than in *V. lamellata Boxallii*; sep. and pet. light yellow, blotched red inside; lip white, marked with brown and mauve, side lobes semi-oblong, triangular, mid-lobe halberd-shaped, covered with hairs at base. Tall. *l.* linear-ligulate, erose at apex, 8 in. long, 1 in. wide. Borneo. 1884. SYN. *Renanthera trichoglottis.*

V. helvo'la. *fl.* 3 or more, 2 in. across, yellowish to wine-red, shading to pale purple; lateral sep. connivent under lip; lip side lobes bright purple, short, mid-lobe purple or rose-purple, triangular-hastate, tumid inside and a little furrowed, concave beneath, the little sac having a pair of small callosities on side opposite column; spur short, conical; raceme erect, shorter than l. March, April. *l.* carinate at base, oblique and obtuse at apex. Habit of *V. tricolor* but smaller. Java. 1850.

V. Hookeria'na.* *fl.* 2 to 9, 2½ to 3 in. across, sep. white, tinted rose; pet. larger, white, spotted magenta, undulate, broadly spatulate-oblong; lip cuneate at base, 3-lobed, 1½ in. broad, white, lined with magenta-purple, with a large deep purple auricle on each side of column; peduncle l.-opposed. September. *l.* erect, 2 to 3 in. long, terete, pale green, subulate-pointed. Stems rooting, elongated, terete. Borneo. 1879. (W.O.A. ii. 73; R. ii. 74.) var. **al'ba,** *fl.* pure white, with calli faintly yellow.

V. insig'nis.* *fl.* 5 to 7, 2½ in. across; sep. and pet. tawny yellow, spotted chocolate-brown within, colour more or less confluent on margins and tips, yellowish-white without, obovate-spatulate; lip large, almost fiddle-shaped, side lobes white, short, mid-lobe white, suddenly expanded to a half-moon shaped, concave, purplish-rose limb; spur conic, compressed, recurved; raceme about as long as l. May, June. *l.* channelled, rigid, linear-ligulate, curving, unequally cut or toothed at tip, 9 to 12 in. long, about 1 in. wide, keeled. Stem sub-erect. Moluccas. 1846. (B.M. 5759.) var. **Schroederia'na,** sep. and pet. light yellow, lip pure white with a large, concave mid-lobe and 2 orange lines in front of spur mouth. Autumn, Malaya. 1883. *V. insignis* of Warner is *V. tricolor insignis.*

V. Kimballia'na.* *fl.* 8 to 20 or more, 1½ to 2 in. across; upper sep. and pet. white or faintly flushed purple, purple-nerved; lateral sep. white, falcate; side lobes of lip yellowish, spotted reddish-brown inside, ending in an incurved tendril, mid-lobe amethyst-purple, with three keels; spur pale purple, incurved, nearly 1 in. long. *l.* sub-cylindric, 6 to 9 in. long, bronzy. Stem 6 to 24 in. h. Shan States (at 4,000 to 5,000 ft.). 1889. (B.M. 7112; Gn. 27 (1890), t. 747; W.S.O. 3, 36.) var. **Lack'nerae,** *fl.* snow-white, with light yellow spots at mouth of spur. 1894. (G. F. 1894, t. 1428.)

V. lamella'ta. *fl.* 1 to 2 in. across, pale yellow, streaked dull, pale red, in long, loose, erect racemes; sep. and pet. obovate, undulate, lower larger and slightly incurved; lip with 2 diverging elevated lines, acute, obcuneate, retuse; auricles small, rounded; spur short, cylindrical-conical, hairy within. August. *l.* leathery, obliquely and acutely 2-dentate, 12 to 15 in. long, usually under 1 in. wide, keeled. Philippines. 1837. var. **Boxall'ii,** *fl.* 14 to 20; dorsal sep. creamy-white, inner part of lateral reddish-brown tinged purple; pet. white or dorsal sep. yellowish, lower reddish-brown near base; limb of lip rich magenta-rose towards front, disk with six reddish-purple stripes running back to mouth of tube. November, December. *l.* much recurved, longer than type. (L. 32; W.O.A. 338 as *V. superba.*) Stems erect. 1880.

Vanda insignis

V. limba'ta.* *fl.* about 12, 2 in. across; sep. and pet. cinnamon-brown, blotched and tessellated with darker reddish-brown, evenly bordered with yellow, tinged with lilac without, lip rosy-lilac, margined white, quadrate, slightly fiddle-shaped, disk tumid, with 5 to 7 parallel furrows; racemes loose, erect. June. *l.* 8 to 10 in. long, channelled, leathery, obliquely retuse at apex, ¾ to 1½ in. wide. Stems stout, with long, thick roots. Java. 1875. (B.M. 6173; W.S.O. 3, 9.)

V. Lind'eni. *fl.* sep. and pet. light yellow, with red dots on disk, cuneate-oblong, wavy; lip whitish-yellow, with nearly square side lobes and a triangular, 2-edged mid-lobe produced into a sharp angle with 2 tumours at apex, sulcate beneath, with a linear, velvety, ascending auricle on each side at base, and 3 furrows over disk, tumours and side lobes purple-spotted, disk marked with 4 purple lines, tip under the tumours brownish; spur conical, hairy inside. Sunda Isles. 1886. (L. 56.)

V. Lindleya'na. A synonym of *Stauropsis gigantea.*

V. lomboken'sis.* *fl.* fleshy, 2 to 2½ in. across, segs. sub-equal, spatulate, 1 in. or more long, mauve, faintly mottled white, variable, margins undulate; lower sep. about 1 in. wide; lip 1 in. long, more or less oblong, margins reflexed except at base, forming a constriction behind the strongly recurved blunt apex, side lobes small, erect, white, base whitish with a few purplish lines, column short, stout, white with a raised yellow callosity at its base; anther marked with red; spur short, blunt. *Spikes* ascending, 6- or more-fld. *l.* strap-shaped, 8 to 10 in. long, 1 to 1½ in. wide, thick, leathery. Summer. Lombok, Malay Archipelago. 1942. var. **Virginia Courtauld** has brick-red sep. and pet. faintly mottled white, lip mauve.

V. Low'ii. *See* **Arachnanthe Lowii.**

V. luzo'nica.* *fl.* 10 to 20, about 2 in. across; sep. and pet. white with an occasional violet-purple or crimson-purple spot and a narrow transverse purple line at base, mid-lobe of lip violet-purple or amethyst. Resembling *V. tricolor* in habit, but with longer, recurved, narrower l. and longer, more slender roots. Philippines. About 1914. (B.M. 8709.) var. **dul'cis,** *fl.* white, with marginal bands of rose-violet on all segs. 1922.

V. × Mansell'ii. At first thought to be a natural hybrid (*V. Ameseana* × *V. caerulea*) but the spur length suggests it is probably a form of *V.* × *Moorei.* 1927.

V. Merrill'ii. Allied to *V. luzonica.* Sep. and pet. yellowish, stained on basal halves with carmine-red with further striations; side lobes of lip white dotted purple, mid-lobe yellow, flushed red with 4 raised purple lines. Philippines. In cultivation?

V. × Moor'ei. A natural hybrid (*V. caerulea* × *V. Kimballiana*). *fl.* near to those of *V. Kimballiana* in shape; sep. and pet. lilac; front lobe of lip dull purple, obcordately 2-lobed, broader than that of *V. caerulea*; spur ⅝ in. long cylindrical, curved. *l.* 6 to 9 in. long, about ½ in. wide, fleshy. Upper Burma. 1897.

V. multiflo'ra. A synonym of *Acampe multiflora*.

V. panicula'ta. A synonym of *Sarcanthus paniculatus*.

V. Parish'ii.* *fl.* several, 2 in. across, fleshy, strongly scented; sep. and broader pet. greenish-yellow, dotted reddish-brown, cuneate-oblong, acute; mid-lobe of lip magenta-purple, narrowly margined white, rhomboid, gibbous below apex, with a median keel and a violet, conical callus at base; spur short, gibbous; auricles white, orange-striped; scape erect. Summer. *l.* broadly elliptic-oblong, 6 to 9 in. long, 2 to 3 in. wide, unequally 2-lobed, fleshy, bright green. Burma, Siam. 1870. Dwarf. (W.O.A. 15.) Placed by some under Stauropsis or Vandopsis. var. **Capstone var.**, sep. and pet. purplish-mauve, flushed brownish- or bronzy-red in upper halves; lip whitish, apex bluish-purple, keel raised, compressed, magenta-purple, very prominent, side lobes whitish, tipped and margined purple. Much stronger than var. *Marriottiana*; **Marriottian'a,** *fl.* not scented, sep. and pet. bronzy-brown, suffused with magenta, lip with a rich magenta, rhomboid mid-lobe and white basal auricles; raceme about 6-fld. *l.* slightly emarginate. Stems closely leafy. 1880. (W.O.A. 61.) SYN. *V. purpurea.* By some regarded as a distinct species.

V. parviflo'ra. *fl.* hardly 1 in. across; sep and pet. pale yellow, oval; lip funnel-shaped, the broadly oblong, rounded mid-lobe white, with purple crests on the fleshy disk, dotted with lilac; spur short, conical; racemes short, erect, many-fld. Summer. *l.* lorate, obliquely and obtusely 2-lobed at apex, with an intermediate cusp. India, Burma, Ceylon. 1844. (B.M. 5138; F.d.S. 1452.) SYN. *V. testacea, Aërides testaceum, A. Wightianum.*

V. pulchel'la. A synonym of *Saccolabium calceolare*.

V. pu'mila. Allied to *V. cristata* which it resembles, but smaller and fl. without the horns at apex of the lip. Sep. and pet. creamy-white, lip streaked purple; spur comparatively large, conical. Bhutan, Sikkim, Siam, &c. (B.M. 7968.)

V. purpu'rea. A synonym of *V. tricolor*.

V. Roeblingia'na. *fl.* 2 to 6 or more, 2 in. across; sep. and pet. brown and green; lip narrow, white with purple and yellow streaks, apex dilated in a pair of halberd-shaped lobes, side lobes white, streaked purple. *l.* linear-oblong, recurved, 6 in. long. Stem 1 ft. h. Philippines. 1894. Allied to *V. limbata*.

V. Roxburgh'ii. A synonym of *V. tessellata.* var. **unic'olor,** a synonym of *V. concolor*.

V. Sanderia'na.* *fl.* up to 15, about 4 in. across, flat; dorsal sep. and smaller pet. pink, slightly stained buff-yellow, lateral sep. 2 in. across, pale nankeen outside, greenish- or tawny-yellow within, reticulated with dull crimson; lip small, fleshy, concave, pale purplish-red at base, tip chocolate-purple, strongly recurved, 3 prominent keels extending from base to apex; racemes axillary. September, October. *l.* broadly ligulate, leathery, recurved, 9 to 15 in. long, about 1 in. wide, deeply channelled. Philippines. 1881. (B.M. 6983; W.O.A. 124; R. 62.) SYN. *Euanthe Sanderiana, Esmeralda Sanderiana.* var. **al'ba.** *fl.* white; **alba'ta,** dorsal sep. and pet. white with a few purple spots at base, lateral sep. red-veined; hypochil sulphur, striped brownish-purple, mid-lobe brownish-sulphur (sometimes purple-striped) at base. 1887; **Chillingham var.,** rather dwarf form with exceptionally rich-coloured flowers. 1905; **Holmewood var.,** *fl.* nearly circular, pet. broader and rounder, sep. shorter than type. 1897; **labello-vir'idis,** lip green. Mindanao. 1886; **Lawson's var.,** sep. and pet. rounder than in type, dorsal sep. and pet. soft rose, flushed crimson, spotted at base, lower sep. greenish-veined and marked rich red-brown. 1931; **Olympia,** *fl.* large, upper sep. and pet. deep blush, greenish with red-brown markings at base, lower sep. buff-green, heavily marked and veined with rich chocolate-brown. 1937; **Rann Lea var.,** *fl.* 4 in. across of brilliant colouring. 1914; **rosea,** *fl.* tinged rose. 1898; **roseo-alba,** upper sep. and pet. nearly white, purple spotted on inner halves, lower sep. greenish-purple, veined at base. 1902.

V. spathula'ta. *fl.* $1\frac{1}{4}$ in. across, golden-yellow; sep. and pet. spatulate-oblong; lip clawed, side lobes very small, mid-lobe slightly 3-fid; scape 1 to $1\frac{1}{2}$ ft. long. *l.* 2 to 4 in. long, bluntly 2-lobed. Stem 2 ft. h. India, Ceylon.

V. Stangea'na. *fl.* 4 or 5 or more, $1\frac{1}{2}$ in. across; sep. and pet. at first greenish within, becoming ochre, tessellated with dark purple-brown; column, spur, and base of lip whitish, mid-lobe broad at base, then contracted, front part cordate, with 2 diverging, depressed, rounded lobes at apex, centre of lip with 3 prominent keels. *l.* 4 to 6 in. long, unequally 2-lobed. Assam. 1886. (R.X.O. 102.) Allied to *V. tessellata*.

V. stria'ta. Closely allied to *V. cristata* of which it may be a form, differing by its smaller flowers, disk of the lip less strongly ridged and spur more obtuse. NW. Himalaya. 1874. (R.X.O. 150.)

V. suaveo'lens. A synonym of *V. tricolor*.

V. sua'vis. A variety of *V. tricolor*.

V. sumatra'na. *fl.* 2 to 10, fragrant; sep. and pet. clawed, broadly ovate, undulate, nearly 1 in. long, slightly less wide, yellow, marked, spotted, or suffused red-brown; lip olive-green, lined and spotted red-brown, side lobes small, mid-lobe hastate, constricted in middle, expanded in front, obtusely sub-orbicular with 2 ribs running to the puberulous mouth of the short, compressed spur, in the mouth of which are 2 calli. *l.* closely set, strap-shaped, arched, up to 12 in. long, less than 1 in. wide. Sumatra. 1907? Allied to *V. limbata*.

V. super'ba. A synonym of *V. lamellata Boxallii*.

V. te'res.* *fl.* 2 to 5, 3 to 4 in. or more across; sep. oblong, dorsal white slightly tinged rose, lateral creamy-white, twisted, parallel with lip; pet. rosy-magenta, paler towards margins, larger, sub-orbicular, undulate, spreading horizontally; lip bright rose-magenta, cucullate, large, strongly veined, side lobes convolute over column; throat orange, striped and spotted crimson, apex dilated and emarginate; spur conical; racemes l. opposed. June to August. L. and stems terete, dark green. *l.* 4 to 5 in. long. Burma, Siam. 1828. (B.M. 4114; B.R. 1809.) Straggling or climbing, several feet long; requires a stake or to be attached to a support. var. **al'ba,** synonym of var. *candida*; **Anderson'ii,** *fl.* 5 to 8, larger and more richly coloured than type, mid-lobe of lip purple-rose. (W.S.O. 3, 2.); **auror'ea,** sep. white, pet. white slightly tinted rose, throat light ochre with rosy lobes, having 2 rows of small purple dots, column light rose-purple. 1884. (W.O.A. 409 as *V. teres candida.*); **candi'da,** *fl.* white, throat light yellow. 1875; **candida, Gatton Park var.,** fine form with side lobes of lip yellow, paler without. 1939. SYN. var. *alba*, Gatton Park, Coleman's var.; **gigan'tea,** *fl.* large and richly coloured, stems and *l.* stouter than in type. 1896. There are many other varieties.

V. teretifo'lia. A synonym of *Sarcanthus teretifolius*.

V. tessella'ta.* *fl.* 6 to 12, 2 in. across, often fragrant; sep. and pet. pale green or grey-green with chequered lines of olive-brown, oblong-obovate, white without; lip violet-purple and convex in front, deeper purple near apex, side lobes white, lanceolate; spur pinkish, short; raceme erect. Summer. *l.* ligulate, recurved, channelled, leathery, obliquely 3-toothed at tip, 5 to 9 in. long, narrow. Stems erect, 6 to 12 in. h., stout. Bengal, Ceylon, Burma, &c. 1850. (B.M. 2245; B.R. 506; W.O.A. 59 as *V. Roxburghii.*) A variable plant. In var. **ru'bra** the lip is pink.

V. testa'cea. A synonym of *V. parviflora*.

V. trichorhi'za. A synonym of *Luisia trichorhiza*.

Vanda tricolor

V. tric'olor.* *fl.* 7 to 12, fleshy, $2\frac{1}{2}$ to 3 in. across, white without, fragrant; sep. and pet. pale yellow, spotted brownish-red within, oblong-obovate, obtuse; pet. twisted so as to show their outer surface; lip 3-lobed, mid-lobe rose-magenta, paler at tip, convex, cuneate, deeply emarginate, disk with 5 white lines, basal lobes white, short, thick; racemes dense, axillary. *l.* lorate, channelled, recurved, obliquely 2-lobed, 12 to 18 in. long. Stems tall, erect. Java. 1846. (F.d.S. 641; W.O.A. 77.) A very variable species. One group of varieties with white ground is known in gardens as *V. suavis* and these are placed under var. *suavis* here. The *tricolor* group has a yellow ground.

Varieties of tricolor group: var. **Corning'ii,** sep. and pet. rich yellow, spotted and streaked deep crimson, margin rose-purple, lip dark plum-colour, passing to pale rose towards base, *l.* very broad, dark green; **Dalkeith var.,** sep. and pet. pale yellow densely spotted red-purple in irregular rows, lip red-purple, streaked white at base; **Dodg'sonii,** *fl.* numerous and very fragrant, sep. and pet. light amber streaked and blotched reddish-brown, margin violet, lip rich violet-purple with some white blotches near base; **formo'sa,** sep. and pet. bright yellow with regular rows of oblong, reddish-brown spots; **Hov'eae,** sep. and pet. yellowish, thickly spotted red, lip rose-crimson. (L. 396.); **insig'nis,** sep. and pet. light yellow, spotted crimson, lip pale lilac. (W.O.A. 3 as *V. insignis.*); **Lewis'ii,** *fl.* light coloured, spotted reddish-brown; **Patersonii,** *fl.* 2 in. across, sep. and pet. creamy-white, densely spotted cinnamon-brown, broad, lip bright magenta; **planilab'ris,** *fl.* larger and brighter than in type, sep. and pet. citron, thickly spotted rich brown, very broad, clawed or narrowed at base, lip large, flat, rose, margin purplish-mauve, disk striped chocolate-purple. (W.O.A. 87.); **purpu'rea,** *fl.* about 3 in. across, sep. and pet. cream, densely spotted red-brown, lip with white faintly purple-striped side lobes, mid-lobe, whitish, with light or dark purple blotch at base, column white with yellow dot at base: a variable variety. Alor. 1932. Syn. *V. purpurea*; **Russellia'na,** *fl.* very bright, in long racemes, habit robust, pendulous; **Wallich'ii,** sep. and pet. yellow, spotted brown, lip lilac. 1893; **Warn'eri,** sep. and pet. margined, deep rose, lip deep rosy-purple, *l.* linear, ribbed. (W.S.O. 2, 39.)

Varieties of *suavis* group: **sua'vis,** the racemes have typically larger fl. with longer pedicels than in *V. tricolor*, the sep. and pet. white with brown-purple or purple dots, mid-lobe of lip narrower above than below, lower part deep purple. (B.M. 5174; W.O.A. 180 as *V. suavis.*) It is difficult, however, so numerous are the gradations, to determine with certainty the place of the numerous varieties of both type *V. tricolor* and this major variety, *suavis*; **suavis al'ba,** sep. and pet. creamy-white, lightly flecked with pale buff, side lobes of lip white, mid-lobe pale yellow; **suavis Chatsworth var.** sep. and pet. thickly spotted and streaked blood-purple, lip rose-purple with deeper dots, side lobes purple, margined white. (W.O.A. 324.); **suavis flav'a,** *fl.* yellow with broad, oblong, rich brown spots. (B.M. 4432 as *V. tricolor.*); **suavis Gottschalckei,** sweetly scented, larger and stouter than type, more densely spotted, lip bright rosy-purple, tipped white, pedicels tinged rose. 1869; **suavis Linden'ii,** sep., pet., and base of lip white, rest of lip purple, 1886; **suavis magni'ficens,** *fl.* larger and richer in colour than in type. 1886. (L. 60.); **suavis pal'lida,** *fl.* whitish with greenish-yellow spots. 1905; **suavis ru'bra,** sep. and pet. suffused orange, lip red. Java. (I.H. 32, 579); **suavis Sand'erae,** *fl.* large, pure white with light greenish-yellow in place of the typical purple spots, side lobes of lip rose and brown; **suavis Veitch'ii,** *fl.* strongly scented, cinnamon-yellow, with very dark spots, margins pinkish, mid-lobe of lip bright pink. 1894.

V. tricuspida'ta. Allied to *V. teres*. *fl.* up to 13, opening 2 or 3 at a time; dorsal sep. broadly ovate, lateral roundly rhomboid, narrow at base, closely set; pet. twisted with ovate-orbicular blade, side lobes of lip erect, almost linear, falcate, embracing column, mid-lobe convex, saddle-shaped with longitudinal keel and 3 subulate laciniae; spur conical appressed to back of lip; sep. and pet. rose-purple, obscurely dotted, lateral sep. lighter; mid-lobe of lip velvety, pale purple, keel and laciniae darker, side lobes rose-purple spotted at base. Alor. 1909. In cultivation? (O.R. 1933, 209.)

V. undula'ta. A synonym of *Stauropsis undulata*.

V. Vida'lii. A synonym of *V. lamellata*.

V. viola'cea. A synonym of *Rhynchostylis coelestis*.

V. Vipan'i. *fl.* 5 to 7, 2 in. across; sep. and pet. blunt, clawed, undulate, white without, within pale at base, marked with short brownish-purple lines, rest of sep. brownish-olive, of pet. inclining to ochre, all striped dark brown-purple; mid-lobe of lip olive-green or rose-purple, contracted in middle, side auricles yellow; spur short, conical. *l.* linear, about 12 in. long, unequally 2-dentate. Burma. 1882.

V. vitelli'na. A synonym of *V. parviflora*, or possibly a form of *V.* × *confusa*.

V. Wat'soni.* *fl.* numerous, pure white, lip margin denticulate, crest and interior of short sac-like spur yellow, dotted red-brown. Annam. 1904. A beautiful species. *fl.* shape and habit much that of *V. Kimballiana* but *infl.* more dense, *l.* longer, more tapered, more closely set, stem shorter. Cool or Odontoglossum house. **A**

V. Wightian'a. A synonym of *Acampe Wightiana*.

×**VANDAENOP'SIS.** Fam. *Orchidaceae.* Hybrids combining species of the genera Phalaenopsis and Vanda.

Vandas'ii, in honour of Dr. Karel Vandas, 1861–1923, Czech botanist, for many years Professor at the Technische Hochschule, Brno.

Vandewa'teri, in honour of A. van de Water, b. 1879, botanist in Sumatra, &c.

vandoi'des, Vanda-like.

VANDOP'SIS (*Vanda*, *opsis*, resemblance; Vanda-like). Fam. *Orchidaceae.* A genus into which some authors have placed species from Vanda, Arachnis, Stauropsis, &c., which presented discrepancies with the genera under which they had been included. As defined at present, as will be seen below, plants varied in habit are included, and so though an incomplete list is appended, the species under cultivation have been retained in the genera under which they are better known. Vandopsis is allied to Esmeralda and Arachnis, the main distinction being the lip structure which is fleshy, concave at base, compressed laterally at the extremity, with a high keel, familiar in *Vanda Parishii*, which merges into the front of the lip. Under cultivation treatment should follow that given to warm-growing Vandas.

For **V. breviscap'a** *see* **Arachnanthe**; **V. chinens'is, V. gigant'ea,** and **V. lissochiloi'des** *see* **Stauropsis**; **V. Low'ii** *see* **Arachnanthe**; **V. luchuen'sis** *see* **Stauropsis**; **V. Parish'ii** *see* **Vanda**; **V. Warocquean'na** and **V. Woodford'ii** *see* **Stauropsis.**

E. C.

VANESSA. A genus of Butterflies which are conspicuous by their size (varying from 2 to 3 in. in wing expanse) and their attractively coloured wings, the upper surfaces being conspicuous by their brilliance, pattern, and colour range. The wings in repose are generally erected and appressed, thereby exposing the duller undersides with a view to concealment. Several species are familiar visitors to the flowers of garden plants, more especially the Peacock, Small Tortoiseshell, and Red Admiral, all of which are seen on sunny days in summer and early autumn sucking the nectar from the flowers of Buddleias, Perennial Asters, Phloxes, Scabious, and other plants, both wild and cultivated. These Butterflies are beautiful additions to the garden, and none can be considered in the light of potential pests. Their caterpillars are rather elongated in form and are covered with stiff spines. The pupae (chrysalides) are angular, and hang downwards from shoots and leaves and are not enclosed in any type of cocoon. While many species are single-brooded, some are double-brooded (Comma) or even many-brooded (Small Tortoiseshell). Several hibernate in the adult stage (Comma, Peacock, Small Tortoiseshell) in barns, buildings, tree-trunks, and in rabbit-holes. A few even are immigrants from the Continent (Camberwell Beauty, Painted Lady, and Red Admiral). The several species—a list of which is given—are readily distinguished from one another by the colour pattern of the upper wing surfaces.

Comma, *V. c-album* (Syn. *Polygonia c-album*) is again becoming abundant after several years of scarcity, and the adults are found in June, and again from September to May. The food plant of the caterpillar is the Stinging Nettle (*Urtica*).

Small Tortoiseshell, *V. urticae*, is one of the most familiar of British butterflies, and hibernated specimens are common objects in houses, buildings, barns, and sheds. The larvae are gregarious and feed in colonies on the Stinging Nettle.

Large Tortoiseshell, *V. polychlores*, is a less familiar species, its caterpillars feeding on the foliage of Elm, Willow, and Aspen, and occasionally as a pest on Cherry and Pear.

Camberwell Beauty, *V. antiopa*, is the most striking Butterfly found in this country, being an occasional migrant from the Continent. The food plants are Birch, Willows, and Poplar.

Peacock, *V. io*, is another familiar species, especially in gardens. Its caterpillars are gregarious and feed in a web on the Stinging Nettle.

Red Admiral, *V. atalanta*, is a common visitor to fruits and flowers, and feeds in its caterpillar stage solitarily on Stinging Nettle in a chamber formed by a spun leaf.

Painted Lady, *V. cardui*, like the last, is an immigrant from the Continent. The larval food plants are Thistles (*Carduus*), Stinging Nettle, and Mallow (*Malva*).

G. F. W.

VANGUER'IA (*Voa-Vanguer*, the native name of the fruit in Madagascar). FAM. *Rubiaceae*. A genus of about 30 species of shrubs and small trees, sometimes spiny, natives of tropical and sub-tropical regions, except Australia. Leaves opposite, leathery or membranous; stipules interpetiolar, frequently joined to form a persistent ring. Flowers white or greenish, small, in cymes or clusters; calyx tube short, limb 5; rarely 4-toothed or lobed, or irregular 5- to 10-toothed; corolla tube rather short, limb of 5, rarely 4 or 6, ovate, slender-pointed, appendiculate, finally reflexed lobes; stamens 5. Fruit a dry or fleshy drupe, sometimes edible and rather large. The following species need stove conditions and a compost of loam and peat. They may be propagated by cuttings in similar soil, under glass, in heat.

V. madagascarien'sis. Unarmed, about 12 ft. h. *l.* ovate, membranous, glabrous. *fl.* green; cymes from below l. June. *fr.* apple-like without persistent sep., succulent, edible, containing 5 stones. Madagascar. 1809. SYN. *V. edulis.*

V. veluti'na. Softly hairy shrub to 3 ft. *l.* large, cordate-ovate, entire, much waved, usually downy beneath; stalk short. *fl.* pale yellowish-green in short dense cymes in axils of lower l. May. Madagascar. 1829. (B.M. 3014.)

Vanhassel'tii, in honour of F. J. F. van Hasselt, b. 1870, who botanized in New Guinea.

Vanhout'tei, in honour of L. B. van Houtte, 1810–76, Belgian nurseryman.

VANILL'A (Spanish *Vainilla*, a little sheath; in allusion to the shape of the fruit). FAM. *Orchidaceae*. A genus of about 70 species of tall, climbing, branched Orchids, scattered over tropical regions of both hemispheres. Flowers large, but usually dull and uninteresting in axillary, often short racemes or spikes, sometimes solitary, sepals and petals sub-equal, free, spreading but not always fully; claw of the lip adnate to the elongated column, the limb broad, concave, its base rolled around the column, obscurely, but sometimes distinctly 3-lobed; bracts ovate. Capsule often elongated, fleshy, not (or at length scarcely) dehiscent. Leaves leathery or fleshy, nerved, sessile or shortly petiolate. The genus includes both leafless and leafy species. Terrestrial or epiphytic, many of the species seem to begin growth in the earth, but the stems quickly ascend the supporting trees, often attaining considerable height, and if their connexion with the ground is severed, many at any rate, continue to grow without inconvenience, the roots emitted by the stems being sufficient. In the leafless species the plants assimilate food by means of both stems and roots. Under cultivation the species require a warm moist atmosphere. In summer the temperature should reach the tropical; in winter, a night temperature should be maintained of 65° F.; occasional falls to 60° seem harmless to *V. fragrans*, *V. Pompona*, &c., but even with them growth may be checked. *V. fragrans* may be trained to wires along the roof, but the majority of the species should be placed against a wall or stout piece of wood. Compost should consist of Sphagnum moss and Osmunda fibre in equal parts. Small pots only need be used as once the stem roots are produced much of the required nourishment seems to be derived from the moist air. The plants require water throughout the year and the syringe may be freely used, even in winter if temperature is about 70° F. Propagation by cutting the stems into lengths and placing in a propagating case. The leafy species, in particular, usually break into growth quickly. The leafless species are seldom seen in cultivation and do not appear to respond as readily as the more common kinds to attempts at propagation. In addition to the species described a few others have appeared in cultivation but have little interest other than botanical. Vanilla is remarkable in being the only genus of Orchidaceae which possesses any decided economic value. The fruit of several species is largely employed, under its botanical name, for flavouring chocolate, liqueurs, ices, &c. *V. fragrans* (*planifolia*) produces the best Vanilla and has been largely grown for commercial purposes, but the Vanilla flavouring is now largely produced synthetically. **A**

V. aromat'ica. *fl.* 3 to 5 or solitary, whitish tinted, green, sep. 2 to 3 in. long, narrow; pet. slightly smaller; lip obscurely 3-lobed, cucullate at base. Stem slender, branching. *l.* 4 to 7 in. long, 1½ to 3 in. wide. Brazil, W. Indies. In cultivation? In gardens the name has been applied to both *V. fragrans* (*planifolia*) and *V. Pompona.*

V. bi'color. *fl.* 3 in. long, very fragrant; sep. and pet. dull red, acute, spreading; lip cream, half-free, convolute, apiculate, undulate, column bearded. *l.* ovate-oblong, nearly sessile, acute, striate, margins reddish. Demerara.

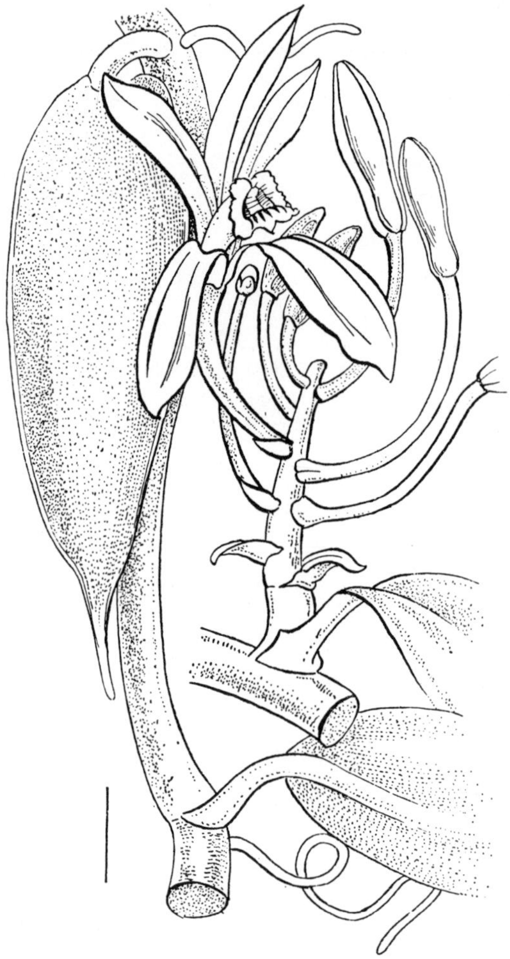

Vanilla fragrans

V. frag'rans.* *fl.* 2 in. across, wholly green, or white within or with a white lip; sep. and pet. lanceolate-oblong; lip with callus below the toothed apex, crested in middle with minute, recurved scales. *fr.* 6 in. long, nearly cylindrical. Stem cylindrical, branching, said to attain a length of 300 ft. *l.* fleshy, 5 to 7 in. long, oblong or ovate-oblong, acute. W. Indies. 1800. (B.M. 272, 7167; L.B.C. 733 as *V. planifolia.*) var. **variega'ta,** *l.* green with cream-white stripes. The dried fruit of this species provided the vanilla of commerce, now produced synthetically. Under cultivation artificial pollination is usually needed.

V. grandiflo'ra. A synonym of *V. Pompona.*

V. Humblot'ii.* *fl.* many, very large, bright yellow; sep. ligulate-acute; pet. rhombic, broad, acuminate; lip rhombic, blunt, angled, undulate in front, with a brown, ribbon-like zone over front part of disk and many strong, twisted hairs scattered from base to disk. Madagascar. 1885. Leafless. **A**

V. imperia'lis.* *fl.* fleshy; sep. and pet. golden-yellow, over 2 in. long; lip dark purple, veined yellow. Stem stout, scandent. *l.* sessile, fleshy, 6 to 9 in. long, 4 to 5 in. wide. *Spikes* axillary with closely imbricating bracts about 1 in. long. Gold Coast, Cameroons, Uganda. 1876. In cultivation 1917.

V. lutes'cens. A synonym of *V. Pompona.*

V. Phalaenop'sis.* *fl.* 6 or 7 in umbel, 3 in. across; sep. faint blush-white, keeled behind, acute, lateral divided to base; pet. same colour but less acute, channelled; lip pale rosy-blush outside, tawny-orange within, over 1 in. long, broadly funnel-shaped. Stems long rooting, leafless. Seychellas. 1869. (F.d.S. 1769.)

V. planifo'lia. A synonym of *V. fragrans.*

V. Pompo'na.* *fl.* 2 or more together in l.-axils, 6 in. across, with general aspect of *Cattleya citrina*; sep. and pet. yellowish-green; lip very bright-yellow. Habit of *V. fragrans* but more robust. *fr.* stouter, triquetrous. Tropical America. 1859. (F.d.S. 2218 as *V. lutescens.*) SYN. *V. grandiflora.*

V. Rosch'eri. *fl.* many, white, large; sep. lanceolate-oblong, 3 to 3½ in. long; pet. as long and rather wider; lip entire, undulate, 2½ to 2¾ in. long; column 1 in. long; pedicels 1½ in. long. Stem stout, leafless. Kenya, Tanganyika, Zanzibar, Pemba.

V. Walk'eriae. *fl.* many, white, 2 in. long; sep. oblanceolate; pet. broader, acute, margins undulate; lip epichil ovate, acute, margins undulate, disk with 2 ridges below middle; racemes 5 to 6 in. long. Stem 1 in. thick, leafless. S. India, Ceylon.

V. Wightia'na. *fl.* 1 to 1¼ in. long, fragrant; sep. and pet. pale yellow or whitish, tipped green, linear-oblong; lip 3-lobed with a hairy, red-dish-purple crest, the hairs pale yellow near tip of lip. Stems leafless. S. India. 1899.

Vanleeuwe'nii, in honour of W. M. Docters van Leeuwen, b. 1880, botanist in the Dutch E. Indies.

VAPORIZER. The name given to the type of apparatus used to heat sulphur in glasshouses. Vaporizers are specially constructed vessels in which the sulphur can be heated so that it vaporizes without catching fire and burning, which would be highly injurious to living plants. The sulphur vapour condenses on the foliage as a very fine film of particles and so protects the plants from fungus diseases such as mildews, &c. The type known as Campbell's Sulphur Vaporizer is a household word to horticulturists.

D. E. G.

VAPOUR. The gaseous state of a substance usually seen as a solid or a liquid. The change of form is brought about by heat and is most familiar as the invisible moisture in the air. This vapour arises in heated houses (whether heated artificially or not), from the soil walls, paths, &c., when watered and from evaporating-troughs filled with water and placed on hot pipes. It also arises from the transpiration of leaves, and the feeling of dampness in the air may be due to any of these causes and is sometimes particularly noticeable after rain outdoors. For most plants a certain amount of water-vapour in the air is beneficial, and this requirement varies considerably with different plants. A knowledge of the special requirements in this direction and a means of measuring the atmospheric humidity by, e.g., the wet and dry bulb thermometer (q.v.) are an advantage to the cultivator. Various insecticides and fungicides depend for their action upon their capacity for vaporization, e.g. sulphur and, to a large extent, nicotine.

VAPOURER MOTH, *Orgyia antiqua*, is a pest of many trees, both forest and fruit, shrubs, Roses and, occasionally, herbaceous plants. It is sometimes troublesome on Hawthorn and other ornamental trees. The male has rich chestnut-brown wings 1 to 1½ in. across, with a white mark in the centre of the fore-wing. It is on the wing during August and September. The female is brownish-grey, wingless, and emerges from its cocoon on the branches and shoots and *not* in the ground, so that grease-banding is a useless operation against this species of wingless female moth. The caterpillar is strikingly coloured, hairy, with four large yellow tufts of hair on the back and longish pencils of hair on the head and thorax. The eggs hatch in May and June, and the caterpillars devour the leaves until they are fully fed in August when cocoons are spun round the brown chrysalides attached to branches, shoots, and spurs.

The egg-masses laid on the cocoons of female moths should be collected and destroyed during pruning operations, as Tar-disillate washes only destroy a small number of these eggs. Spraying the foliage of fruit-trees with Arsenate of Lead after blossoming is effective against the caterpillars; while a thorough application of a Derris wash gives an effective control against the young larvae on plants on which it is considered inadvisable to apply a poisonous spray.

G. F. W.

varia'bilis -is -e, variable.

VARIABILITY. Variation implies that a plant may differ more or less widely from its parent or parents, often showing some altogether new characters. Variability is the capacity for this variation, and it is usually greatest in sexual reproduction, most common in the offspring resulting from the union of different species, i.e. in hybrids and their progeny, frequent when 2 varieties of a species are crossed, less common when the offspring is derived from 2 individuals exhibiting the same characters or from self-fertilized unions. The cause of this type of variability no doubt has its origin in the union of unlike gametes resulting in cells of a different genetical constitution from those of the seed parent, new characters or factors modifying characters being brought in from the pollen parent (*see* **Mendel's Law**). Crossing is not the only cause of the production of new varieties, however. From time to time variations arise which cannot be directly attributed to this cause, and indeed appear to be far removed from it. When these variations occur in seedlings, as, e.g., the waved type of flower in Sweet Peas which suddenly appeared in more than one place, the possible effect of some unsuspected cross within the species cannot be altogether ruled out, but when it occurs in the body of a plant which hitherto has appeared to have constant characters it appears probable that it has its origin in some other cause. Certain variations which do not always affect the constitution of the germ cells, but which can be perpetuated by vegetative propagation, are familiar to all horticulturists, e.g. the presence of a virus injected into a plant by an insect in almost infinitesimal doses may bring about variety in flower colouring as in Gladioli and Tulips (*see* **Tulip, Diseases**), changes in the shape of the foliage, in the habit of the plant, and in the structure of its flowers, as in the Nettle-leaf modification of Black Currants (*see* **Currant, Black, Diseases**); or variegation of certain types as in Abutilon and other Malvaceous plants. Some of these variations are such as to interfere with the nutrition of the plant which would not survive for long in competition with unaffected plants of the same species but which can be maintained in the garden. Though causes bringing about somewhat similar results are known, e.g. exposure to extremes of temperature, treatment by drugs such as colchicine (q.v.) and to a certain extent some of the growth substances or hormones (q.v.), exposure to X-rays, and certain types of mutilation, it is not possible at present to put others, indeed many others, down to anything but accident. It seems impossible to rule out change of environment as a fruitful cause of changes affecting not only the individual plant generally but also its genetical constituent. It is no uncommon thing to find that a newly introduced plant that has appeared to present constant characteristics in its native home begins almost at once to show variations in its progeny. Many instances could be given, but one will suffice, the great range of variety now seen in *Primula malacoides*, a plant of comparatively recent introduction. Few indeed of the species regularly raised from seed in the garden fail to show considerable variation in the course of time without any crossing with other species, even those that appear morphologically invariable or almost so are found on analysis of their behaviour to show differences of, e.g., earliness in maturing, susceptibility to forcing, and the like. Seakale well exemplifies this and would no doubt show greater variability if it were more regularly raised from seed instead of being usually raised from root-cuttings. Among the 'accidents' bringing about variation sometimes occurring in the body of, sometimes during the cell-divisions at the time of the formation of, pollen grains and egg-cells, both affecting the genetic constitution of the cells concerned, are the doubling of the chromosomes in a cell, apparently due to the failure of the dividing cell to form a cross wall cutting the contents into two as normally occurs, and the loss of one or more character-determinants from the chromosomes during the process. If either of them occurs in the plant body then all the cells derived from the one in which the accident occurred, and all the parts built up from this cell and its offspring, will be affected, and the results may or may not be evident in the plant according to the position of that cell and its derivatives. If the parts affected are in the outer layers of the stem then in all probability they will soon make themselves evident and the plant will be said to be sporting or to show bud-variation. The commonest manifestation of this is seen in the production of a streak of colour in a flower or the whole of one section, even to the extent that a longitudinal half of the plant may produce flowers or parts (as in variegation) of a different colour, or abnormally smooth, and so on. Propagated from the abnormal part a new variety may be multiplied, but if parts of both normal and abnormal sections are used in propagation then 'sporting' will continue to be evident, though the tendency may be hidden for a time. The original plant will in fact consist of two varieties and constitute what is called a 'chimaera'. If the accident occurred in a deep-seated cell then the change may not be seen until the course of events leads to the production of buds from the deeper tissues, as, e.g., when root-cuttings are made and found to yield, as is not very unusual, a form differing from the parent. This is now well known in Bouvardia and may occur in almost any plant capable of reproduction by root-cuttings. It is seen in some potatoes, e.g. Golden Wonder with a russet skin, the Variety Langworthy clothed with an abnormal integument—abnormal so far as Langworthy is concerned; similarly Field Marshal has Up-to-Date constituting its inner part; and so on. The outer covering may be 1, 2, 3, or many cells thick and a similar state of affairs has been produced experimentally by grafting, e.g. Solanums, and accidentally by grafting, e.g. *Cytisus purpureus* on Laburnum (*see* × **Laburnocytisus Adami**) and in Craetogomespilus (q.v.). These are called Graft-hybrids and are constitutionally of the same order as the chimaeras already referred to.

Where doubling of chromosomes occurs the plants derived from the abnormal cells will usually be larger in all parts than normal, and this form of 'accident' thus leads to giant forms, some at least of which have resulted in the development of useful food plants from their wild ancestors. Such plants showing double the normal number of chromosomes in their cells are known to the geneticist as tetraploids and may be the start of various other combinations of chromosomes, so that triploids are often produced and various other polyploid forms. The knowledge that colchicine brings about the doubling of chromosomes has put a means of inducing variation into the hands of the plant breeder which may have far-reaching results when combined with the application of Mendel's laws.

It seems unlikely that the behaviour of the chromosomes will give an explanation of all the phenomena of variability which plants exhibit, but their study certainly helps to an understanding of the mechanism of variation and enables more certain results to be obtained more quickly than before, even though they may be no more startling.

va'rians, varying.

VARIEGATED LAUREL. *See* **Aucuba.**

VARIEGATION. The appearance shown by the foliage of some plants in which the leaves display yellow or whitish patches scattered on the normal green colour. Such a condition may be called chlorosis (q.v.) if the reason for this loss of colour or lack of chlorophyll is due to some derangement due to unhealthy condition, and such chlorosis may be only temporary, or the symptoms may be due to infection by a virus (q.v.), when the condition is often called 'infectious chlorosis', or in some plants variegation is not infectious but inherent in the plant, and the appearance is then known as 'variegation'. Such plants are often valued by horticulturists. Although some may come true from seed the majority must be propagated from buds and cuttings and even then may tend to revert to the normal green colour. They are in general not so robust as normal green plants and may be more liable to succumb to drought or severe weather conditions. Examples are variegated periwinkle, nasturtium, Miscanthus, elder, holly, elm, maple, privet. Many well-known variegated plants such as Abutilon, ash, mountain ash, and laburnum show examples of infectious chlorosis.

variega'tus -a -um, variegated, irregularly coloured.

VARIETY. This term is used in classification with a number of meanings; it refers generally to a group within a species or to individuals which diverge in greater or less degree from what is regarded as the type or as the typical state (*see* **Type**) of the species, but is sometimes applied to a member of a hybrid group or even a graft-chimaera. A variety in the horticultural sense is any plant with distinctive characters not worthy of specific rank, these characters being permanent in that they can be maintained by vegetative or seminal propagation. The term may thus apply to a sub-species, a variety in the botanical sense, a cultivar, a form, or a nothomorph (i.e. a member of a hybrid group). A variety in the botanical sense is a population within a species, this population having several distinctive characters which are fairly constant over an area and which enable it to be distinguished from other populations forming part of the species; it is thus a geographical race, intermediate between a form (which occurs here and there within a population, from typical members of which it differs in only one or two minor characters) and a sub-species (which is a fairly well-distinguished major geographical race almost worthy of specific rank and likely to be considered a species by some botanists), the differences between these categories being less than those usually found between species. From the standpoint of botanical nomenclature a species is now regarded as the sum of its varieties, the specific name thus covering them all and the type being designated by using the specific epithet as a varietal epithet; thus the type of *Lilium nepalense* is distinguished as *L. nepalense* var. *nepalense* from *L. nepalense* var. *concolor*. Many garden varieties are not varieties in the botanical sense but are forms, cultivars, or nothomorphs. A cultivar (horticultural variety) is a variety or race subordinate to a species that has originated and persisted under cultivation. The term variety is abbreviated as 'var.', sub-species as 'subsp.' or 'ssp.', form as 'f.', cultivar as 'hv.', nothomorph as 'nm.', and mixomorph (a variety of a graft-chimaera, the two components being differently combined in various chimaeras derived from the same two plants) as 'nmx'. Garden varieties may arise in several ways (*see* **Variation**) and may be such that they can be propagated true only by vegetative means.

W. T. S.

variola'tus -a -um, marked as if by pustules or pittings of smallpox.

va'rius -a -um, vari- in compound words, differing.

VARNISH-TREE. *See* **Aleurites moluccana, Melanorrhoea usitata, Rhus verniciflua.**

Varta'ni, in honour of Dr. Vartan of Jerusalem, *c.* 1885, who sent Irises from Palestine to Sir Michael Foster.

vascular, furnished with or relating to the vessels or ducts formed in all the higher plants from the Ferns to Flowering Plants.

VASCULAR SYSTEM. Those parts of plants in which true Vessels (q.v.) occur. A vascular system is present in roots, stems, and leaves, and their modifications in all Ferns, Horse-tails, Club-mosses and their allies, and in all Spermaphytes; and as parts are lignified, forms a skeleton or framework which is the last part of the plant to decay. The chief uses of the Vascular System are (1) to give strength and mechanical support to all parts of the plant, serving as a framework for the cellular tissues in which photosynthesis and storage of food go on; (2) to act as a channel for conveying water and the substances taken in from the soil to the aerial parts of the plant and the substances made in the leaves, &c., to the various parts where they may be needed or stored.

vasculo'sus -a -um, pot- or pan-shaped.

Vasculum. Botanist's collecting box; a metal box with a large lid and means of slinging so as to be carried over the shoulder. The term is also applied to a pitcher-shaped leaf.

VASES. Various kinds of Vases are made both for growing plants in and also for displaying cut flowers. Vases for terrace walls and other positions in formal gardening and for use in conservatories are made in various sizes and in a great variety of designs. They must be made to withstand all weathers and of a material which will not be deleterious to the plants growing in them. Terra-cotta and stone (natural or artificial) vases are probably the most satisfactory but other materials are sometimes used, even cast iron. For the arrangement of flowers glass vases are best, but silver, China and other materials serve well, while for use at exhibitions metal vases are most serviceable. All vases should have a base sufficiently large to prevent them becoming top-heavy when filled with flowers. The sizes and shapes must be determined by individual tastes and requirements, but Trumpet Vases or Glasses are among the most useful. For table-decoration the vases should be low and the flowers lightly arranged so that they do not obstruct the view from one side of the table to the other.

Va'seyi, in honour of Dr. George Vasey, b. 1822 at Scarborough, England, d. 1893 at Washington, D.C., U.S.A., from 1872 to 1893 Botanist, U.S. Dept. of Agriculture, or his son George Richard Vasey, who discovered *Rhodendron Vaseyi* in 1878 in N. Carolina.

Va'sica, a Bengal plant name.

vas'tus -a -um, very large.

VAUAN'THES (*vau*, V, and *anthos*, a flower; there being a V-shaped marking often found on the petals). FAM. *Crassulaceae*. A genus of 1 species, allied to Crassula, but differing in the bell-shaped flower.

V. dicho'toma. Annual. Stem 4 to 6 in. h. *l.* opposite, fleshy, linear, sessile, glaucous-grey. *fl.* yellow, orange, or cream, often with a dark V-shaped mark; opening in full sun. S. Africa. 1774. (B.M. 4607.) SYN. *Crassula dichotoma, Grammanthes chloraefolia, G. gentianoides.*

Vayre'dae, in honour of Estanislao Vayreda y Vila, 1848–1901, student of Catalonian flora.

VEGETABLE. (1). Of the plant kingdom. (2) Derived from plants. (3) In a horticultural sense, a plant either cooked or raw eaten as part of the savoury rather than the sweet course of a meal. In this sense, a vegetable is often a plant grown for vegetative structures, i.e. roots, tubers, leaves, and stems, but Peas and Beans are always considered vegetables and for exhibition purposes Cucumbers and Tomatoes are also included among vegetables. *See* **Salads.**

Vauanthes dichotoma

VEGETABLE BUTTER. *See* **Madhuca butyracea.**

VEGETABLE FIRE-CRACKER. *See* **Brodiaea Ida-Maia.**

VEGETABLE HAIR. *See* **Tillandsia usneoides.**

VEGETABLE HORSEHAIR. The fibres of *Chamaerops humilis* and *Tillandsia usneoides.*

VEGETABLE IVORY. Nuts of *Phytelephas macrocarpa.*

VEGETABLE MARROW (*Cucurbita Pepo ovifera*). Half-hardy usually trailing annual, easily grown and widely cultivated during the summer for its fruits which are mostly used when half-grown or even younger for cooking in various ways, but some are allowed to ripen for the purpose of making jam from the fleshy part or for storing in a dry place for cooking in winter. While young the flesh is very tender, but as the fruits become old the flesh becomes drier. Seeds should be sown singly or two in a 3 in. pot about the end of April, and placed in gentle heat. When the plants have 2 rough leaves they should be hardened by being placed in an airy place. Early in June they may be planted out where they are to grow either on the flat or on an old manure heap. The plants should be covered with hand-glasses or cloches for a few days until established in their new places, when the covering should be removed. All fruits should be cut when large enough to cook unless they are required for seed or for use as already mentioned. The plants need plenty of water in dry weather, and the growths need some thinning when they become too crowded. While the normal growth is trailing or climbing by tendrils, a variation occurs in the bush-type which makes no trailers. Considerable variation occurs in the form and colour of the fruits and their ultimate size. The Supplement should be consulted for varieties.

The vegetable Marrow is only grown in glasshouses as a catch crop, by training one plant up each purlin or gutter post in houses where tomatoes are grown.

The variety chosen is usually the 'Long Green', although some markets seem to prefer the cream and green hybrids.

The successful combination of Marrows with Tomatoes depends upon having the former ready to plant in the houses, when the fires are started to warm the soil about 14 days before planting the tomato crop.

With this end in view Marrow seeds are sown at the beginning of January to be ready for planting out early in February. Seed trays containing a compost suitable for cucumbers are employed and the seeds are germinated at 70° F. When the first pair of leaves appear, the seedlings are potted into size 48 pots half-filled with Cucumber compost and kept at a temperature of 65° F. Later the pots are filled up by adding more compost and kept at 60° F. until planting time. The young plants have a thin spindly appearance and must be staked with a thin wooden stake to support them.

When planting at the foot of the purlin or gutter post, a spadeful of soil is taken out. Half of it is mixed with an equal quantity of composted strawy horse manure and returned to the hole, shaping the surface like a basin, in the bottom of which the young Marrow plant is planted. This is done so that the Marrow can be watered without allowing too much water to flow towards the adjoining tomato plants. If the soil around the plant is kept moist, the marrow will start into growth about 7 days after planting. If a hot-water pipe is near to the marrow plant, it should be wrapped round with a double thickness of newspaper to prevent scorching.

The fruit should be set only on lateral branches and not in the main stem. This is done by pollinating the female flowers in the same way as for Melons.

As the growth approaches the overhead wires it becomes stronger and should be trained towards the centre of the house. It will produce strong thick stems and large leaves, which must be stopped and thinned to prevent it from casting too much shade over the tomatoes. Pruning can be carried out without harming the plant, for once it has reached the top of the house it is very difficult to injure.

Planted early in February, cutting should begin early in April and continues until the price falls in June or the shade becomes excessive for the Tomatoes.

Occasionally an autumn crop of bush Marrows may be attempted in houses where Tomatoes have failed, but they are rarely profitable.

Marrows are cut when they are about 9 in. long, graded for size, and packed 6 in a Cucumber box or 3 in a handle basket. The marrows are packed firmly in wood-wool or sweet hay after lining the container with blue tissue paper.

W. B.

DISEASES. With diseases of vegetable Marrows may be mentioned those of Pumpkins and Gherkins. Powdery Mildew due to the fungus *Erysiphe cichoracearum* often causes a white coating on vegetable Marrow leaves and can be checked by dusting the plants with green sulphur every fortnight. Much of this trouble, however, is due to dryness at the roots which reduces the resistance of the plants, so that every care should be taken by supplying the soil with plenty of humus to ensure that ample moisture is available. *Botrytis cinerea*, the Grey Mould fungus (q.v.), often destroys flowers and fruits, and any such infected material should always be destroyed and if necessary some foliage removed to admit sunshine and facilitate circulation of air. Minor troubles may be Anthracnose (*Colletotrichum lagenarium*) or Gummosis (*Cladosporium cucumerinum*) which are described on cucumber (*see* **Cucumber**). Marrows also suffer from a virus disease called Mosaic which causes marked yellow mottling and perhaps puckering of the young leaves, and the shoots are stunted. The fruit may also be mottled and covered with wart-like areas and the crop reduced. This virus is thought to be the same as that causing Cucumber Yellow Mottle Mosaic and Spinach Blight. All infected Marrow plants should be rogued out and destroyed and seed taken only from definitely healthy plants. The virus also attacks weeds such as wild Solanum spp. and *Bryonia dioica*, so that solanaceous weeds and bryony in hedgerows should be grubbed out where the disease continually appears.

D. E. G.

VEGETABLE OYSTER. *See* **Tragopogon porrifolius, Salsify.**

VEGETABLE REFUSE. *See* **Compost Heap.**

VEGETABLE SCULPTURE. *See* **Topiary.**

VEGETABLE SHEEP. *See* **Raoulia.**

VEGETABLE TALLOW TREE. *See* **Sapium sebiferum.**

VEGETABLE WAX. A wax-like substance or 'bloom' formed on many leaves and fruits acting as a check to loss of water from the surface thus protected. The wax is formed in the cuticle and sometimes attains considerable thickness as in fruits of *Myrica cerifera* and on the trunks of some Palms.

ve'getus -a -um, of vigorous growth.

VEIN. Any part of the fibro-vascular system in a leaf or other flattened structure of a plant through which sap flows to and from its cells. Veins are sometimes called nerves, and when they are thicker than the rest of the leaf, especially when they project on the under surface, they are often called ribs (compare midrib). In Monocotyledons the veins usually run parallel with the midrib, in Dicotyledons they usually form a network (reticulated veining). The arrangement of the veins is a constant characteristic of a species, and to a large extent determines the form of the leaf (*see also* **Venation**).

VEINLET. One of the smaller branches of a vein.

VEITCH'IA (in honour of James Veitch jun., 1815–69, and his son John Gould Veitch, 1839–70, of Chelsea, the leading nurserymen of their day). FAM. *Palmaceae.* A genus of about 4 species of tall Palms with pinnate leaves, natives of the Fiji Is. and New Hebrides. Leaves forming a crown, equally pinnatisect, not prickly; pinnae linear or tapering to the obliquely truncate apex, margins thickened. Allied to Hedyscepe but the male flowers have papery sepals connate at base and the female flowers are much the larger; spadix branched. Stove conditions are needed for *V. Joannis* and treatment as for Latania.

V. Joan'nis. *l.* pinnate; pinnae minutely toothed, midrib ending in a small curve, apex obliquely truncate. *fl.* very small; spadix much branched, forming a large bunch. *fr.* green at first, finally bright orange, red at base, ovoid-ellipsoid, about 2 in. long. Fiji. 1868.

Veitchia'nus -a -um, Veitchii, Veitchiorum, in honour of the celebrated nursery firm Messrs. Veitch of Exeter and Chelsea who raised and introduced so many good plants into gardens and trained so many good gardeners in the 19th and early 20th centuries. The firm was founded at Killerton near Exeter in 1808 by John Veitch, 1752–1839, moved to Exeter in 1832, extended to Chelsea in 1853, and divided in 1854 into the independent firms of Robert Veitch & Son of Chelsea. The latter firm was brought to an end in 1914 by Sir Harry James Veitch, 1840–1924, on his retirement. **A**

VELAMEN, the external layer of the aerial root of Orchids and Araceae, consisting of a many-layered series of empty tracheids with netted, perforated walls (*see* **Vessels**) by which moisture is obtained from the atmosphere.

Velenovsk'yi, in honour of Josef Velenovsky, 1858–1949, Professor of Botany at the Charles University of Prague.

VEL'LA (*veller,* Celtic name for Cress). FAM. *Cruciferae.* A genus of 3 deciduous or evergreen low shrubs in the western Mediterranean region. Leaves simple, entire, sessile. Flowers in a loose raceme, shortly stalked, small, yellow, sometimes veined violet. Ovary shortly stalked, 2-jointed with 2 ovules in the lower, none in the upper joint, stigma capitate. Seeds not winged. Low shrubs for the rock-garden, in a sunny, rather dry position. Liable to be damaged or killed in severe winters, though *V. spinosa* is apparently the hardier of the two species in cultivation. Propagation by cuttings of half-ripe wood in gentle heat.

V. glabres'cens. Small, dense, unarmed shrub, erect, branched at base. *l.* more or less evergreen, few, clustered in axils, oblong, obtuse, narrowed below, entire, glabrous except of rigid hairs on face and margin. *fl.* pale yellow with deeper veins, in erect, ebracteate racemes; pedicels very short. April to July. Algeria, Morocco.

V. Pseudocy'tisus. Evergreen shrub to 2 ft. (higher in warm districts), branches erect, at first spiny-bristly, later smooth. *l.* obovate, $\frac{1}{2}$ to $\frac{3}{4}$ in. long, covered with stiff bristly hairs. *fl.* in an erect terminal raceme 4 to 8 in. long; pet. about $\frac{1}{8}$ in. long. May to July. Mts. of Central Spain. 1759. (B.R. 293.) Sometimes put in a genus Pseudocytisus.

V. spino'sa. Deciduous shrub to 1 ft., dense and compact, branches rigid, erect, soon smooth, upper spine-tipped. *l.* grey-green, dull, linear, fleshy, smooth or almost so. *fl.* about $\frac{3}{8}$ in. across, in terminal corymbs; pet. with brown veins. June. Spain.

VELLE'IA (in honour of Major Velley, algologist, d. 1806). FAM. *Goodeniaceae.* A genus of about 12 species of perennial herbs all except *V. macrophylla* having a short, thick rootstock and radical leaves. Natives of Australia. Flowers yellow as in Goodenia, but with the calyx free from the ovary; scapes or peduncles erect or ascending, 2- or 3-times forked, many-flowered; bracts opposite, free or connate. Cultivation as for Goodenia, needing greenhouse protection.

V. lyra'ta. *l.* oblong-spatulate, deeply toothed in basal half or lyrate-pinnatifid, 5 or 6 in. long. *fl.* with 3 sep.; cor. about $\frac{1}{2}$ in. long, lobes broadly winged; scapes 6 to 12 in. h., dichotomous, branches spreading. April. 1819. (B.R. 551; H.E.F. 24.)

V. macrophyl'la. Erect, 3 to 4 ft. h., leafy, branching. *l.* usually 2 to 6 in. long, toothed, narrowed to stalk. *fl.* in large, loose, dichotomous panicles; peduncles axillary. July. 1839. (B.R. 1841, 3 as *Euthales macrophylla.*) Closely related to *V. trinervis.*

V. parado'xa. *l.* broadly ovate and under 2 in. long, or narrowly oblong and over 4 in. long, coarsely toothed or entire or almost so. *fl.* with 5 free sep.; cor. hairy without, sometimes spurred; scapes 6 to 18 in. h., 2- or 3-forked. July. 1824. (B.R. 971.)

V. triner'vis. *l.* oblong, entire or remotely toothed; stalks long. *fl.* with bell-shaped cal. with 5 unequal lobes; about $\frac{1}{2}$ in. long, lobes all broadly winged; scapes dichotomous, low or ascending to 12 in. h. July. 1803. (B.M. 1137, as *Goodenia tenella.*)

veller'eus -a -um, densely long-haired.

VELLO'ZIA (in honour of J. M. de la Conception Velloss, 1742–1811, Capuchin monk, of Rio de Janeiro, who edited the works of Vandelli on Brazil). FAM. *Velloziaceae.* A genus of about 40 species of plants with woody, fibrous, erect, sometimes tree-like stems, natives of Trop. and S. Africa, Madagascar, and Brazil. Leaves clustered at tips of branches, sometimes short, narrow and straight, sometimes long, narrow- or broad-linear, rigid, often sharp. Flowers white, sulphur, violet, orange-red or blue, often showy; perianth campanulate or funnel-shaped, with scarcely any tube, segments equal and erecto-patent, ovate, oblong or gradually narrow to a slender base; stamens 6, sometimes indefinite, and clustered; peduncles terminal 1-flowered. They need stove or greenhouse conditions and a compost of well-drained, sandy peat. Care is needed in watering. Propagation by seed or suckers.

V. can'dida.* Tufted with short branches, leafy at apex. *l.* linear, grass-like, narrowed to a filiform tip, rigidly keeled, remotely spine-toothed. *fl.* pure white; stamens 18 in 6 bundles; peduncle long, glandular-scabrid in upper part like the ovary and perianth. Summer. Brazil. 1865. (B.M. 5514.) Stove.

Vellozia elegans

V. el'egans. Stem rigid, flexuous, 6 in. h. *l.* 3-ranked, linear-lanceolate, slender-pointed, 4 to 8 in. long, sharply keeled, toothed near tip. *fl.* pale lilac in bud, then pure white, $1\frac{1}{4}$ in. across, segs. spreading; peduncle terminal, sheathed at base, bearing 3 to 5 slender pedicels 2 to 6 in. long. May. Natal. 1866. (B.M. 5803.) SYN. *Talbotia elegans.* Greenhouse.

V. retiner'vis. Trunk 12 ft. h. with a terminal tuft of l. *l.* long-linear, recurved, rigid, glabrous. *fl.* blue, $1\frac{1}{2}$ in. across; segs. $1\frac{1}{4}$ to $1\frac{1}{2}$ in. long, $\frac{1}{4}$ to $\frac{1}{3}$ in. wide, glabrous without; anthers $\frac{1}{2}$ in long, nearly sessile, peduncles dark above, somewhat bristly beneath ovary; ovary oblong, densely covered with ascending brown bristles. Natal, Transvaal. 1877. (Ctf. 26 (1877) 903; G.C. 6 (1876) 837 as *Xerophyta retinervis.*) Greenhouse.

V. squama'ta. Stem short, forked, covered with scale-like l.-bases. *l.* linear, slender-pointed, 4 to 6 in. long, spreading, glaucous, keeled. *fl.* orange-red, tube slightly widened upwards, segs. somewhat spreading; scape longer than l. Summer. Organ Mts. 1841. (B.M. 4136, as *Barbacenia squamata.*) Stove.

VELLOZIA'CEAE. Monocotyledons. A family of 70 species of xerophytic plants in 2 genera, natives of Brazil, S. Africa, and Madagascar. Perennial herbs or with a woody base, the upper part of the stems covered with the fibrous sheaths of old leaves, the lower with numerous adventitious roots which are capable of absorbing quantities of water like a sponge, thus enabling the plant to make use of dew in the dry season. Leaves linear in a rosette. Flowers solitary at the end of a naked stalk. The flowers are closely similar in structure to those of the Amaryllidaceae in which family this was at one time included, but the stamens may be numerous and arranged in 6 bundles and the numerous ovules are on projecting plates in the 3 cells of the ovary, the plates being shield-shaped or otherwise thickened on their outer side. The genera are Barbacenea, Vellozia.

VELTHEIM'IA (in honour of August Ferdinand Graf von Veltheim, 1741–1801, German patron of botany). FAM. *Liliaceae*. A genus of 3 species of bulbous perennials with tunicated bulbs, natives of S. Africa. Leaves radical, several, oblong or strap-shaped, rather thick. Flowers in a dense spike or raceme on a leafless scape, nodding; perianth tubular cylindrical with very short teeth, persistent; stamens 6, affixed about middle of perianth tube. Fruit a 3-celled, winged capsule, seeds 2 in each cell, nearly round. Light loamy soil and a cool greenhouse suit the Veltheimias, but they cannot be forced with success. They should have 2 months rest after the leaves die down. Propagation is by offsets or by leaves pulled off close to the bulbs which inserted in pots of soil make bulbs at the lower end. *V. glauca* is less easy to grow than *V. viridifolia*.

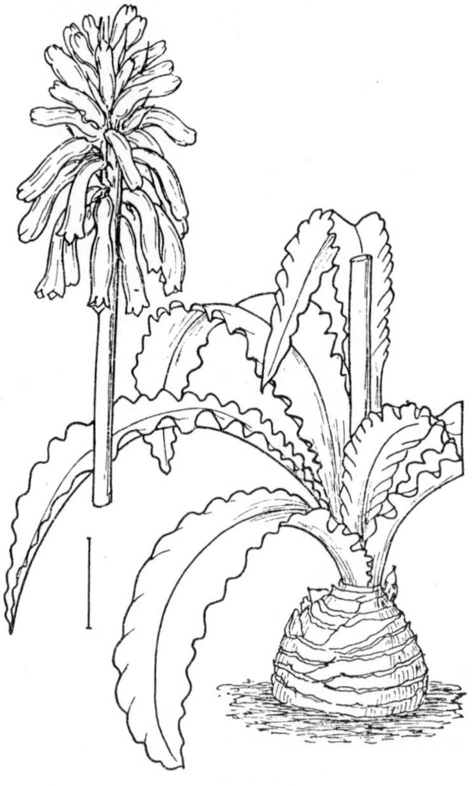

Veltheimia Deasii

V. Deas'ii. *l.* 9 to 12, strap-shaped, 4 to 12 in. long, to about 1 in. wide, glaucous, much undulated. *fl.* pink with green tip, yellow inside, about $1\frac{1}{5}$ in. long; pedicels up to $\frac{1}{5}$ in. long; raceme 2 to 3 in. long, many-fld.; scape up to 10 in. or so long, bracts about $\frac{1}{2}$ in. long. December. 1928. (G.C. 88 (1930), 450; G.F. 82 (1933), 248; B.M. 8931.) Closely related to *V. glauca* but smaller and with more undulate l. and the stamens inserted below the middle of cor. tube, instead of at the middle.

V. glau'ca. *l.* about $1\frac{1}{2}$ in. wide, glaucous, much undulated. *fl.* red-spotted or yellowish, $\frac{1}{2}$ to $\frac{3}{4}$ in. long; pedicels very short; raceme 2 to 6 in. long, bracts about $\frac{1}{3}$ in. long; scape 1 ft. or more h. March. 1781. (B.M. 1091, and a reddish-fld. form, B.M. 3456, as var. *rubescens*.)

V. viridifo'lia. *l.* 8 to 12, strap-shaped, 8 to 12 in. long or more, 2 to 4 in. wide, intense green, often as though varnished, margins undulate. *fl.* reddish or yellowish, spotted, $1\frac{1}{4}$ to $1\frac{1}{2}$ in. long; pedicels up to $\frac{1}{4}$ in. long; raceme 3 to 5 in. long, with up to 60 fl.; scape 1 to $1\frac{1}{2}$ ft. long; bracts about $\frac{1}{3}$ in. long. April onwards. 1768. (L.B.C. 1245; B.M. 501, as *Aletris capensis*.)

veluti'nus -a -um (***veluti-*** in compound words), velvety, covered with soft, fine, silky down.

VELVET FLOWER. *See* **Amaranthus caudatus.**

VELVET LEAF. *See* **Cissampelos Pareira** and **Lavatera arborea.**

VELVET MOULD. *See* **Grey Mould** (q.v.).

VELVET TAMARIND. The fruit of *Dialium guineense*.

VENATION, arrangement of veins. The main veins forming the midrib and its chief branches show the course of the larger fibrovascular bundles and from these numerous branches are spread through the blade of the leaf. The venation follows the main form of the leaf, *pinnate* in a pinnate leaf, *palmate* in a palmate leaf, *pedate* in a pedate leaf, *furcate* in a forked leaf. The minor branches may be free, that is with ends free of one another, or they may form a network as in most Dicotyledons, when the venation is said to be *reticulate*. It is convenient in descriptions to distinguish between the principal and lesser veins. The central vein running from the base towards the tip is called the *midrib*; other veins almost equally prominent and passing from the base or from near the base towards the tip are often called *secondary veins* or *nerves*, though not comparable in function to the nerves of animals; their arrangement is sometimes called nervation. Smaller veins arising from the midrib and these primary lateral veins are called *veinlets*; the areas between the veins are called *intervenia*. In many Monocotyledons the veins start from near the base, curve outwards without branching, and then curve inwards towards the tip and unite. Such veins are described as *parallel-veined*; they may be straight and almost mathematically parallel, as in many grasses, these being described as *straight-veined*, or the lateral veins may be markedly curved, as in Hosta, and hence described as *curve-veined*. Special terms are used to describe certain types. Thus in Thymus the nervation may be *marginal* (with the margin thickened all round by a raised continuous vein) or *camptodrome* (with the lateral veins becoming thinner towards the margin and the margin not thickened) or *pseudomarginal* (with the lateral veins more prominent but not joining a continuous marginal vein). Some other terms describing the course of the secondary veins are: *craspedodrome*, when the secondary veins run from the midrib to the margin without dividing, *acrodrome* when they arch from the base to the tip and there converge, as in the curve-veined leaves of Monocotyledons already mentioned, and *brochidodrome* when they run out towards the margin but curve markedly, forming loops.

W. T. S.

vena'tor, hunter, referring in *Rhododendron venator* to the flowers being red like a fox-hunter's coat.

VENEER GRAFTING. *See* **Grafting.**

venena'tus -a -um, poisonous.

veneno'sus -a -um, very poisonous.

VENICE SUMACH. *See* **Rhus Cotinus.**

VENICE TURPENTINE. A product of *Larix decidua*.

VENI'DIUM (apparently from *vena*, vein, with reference to the ribbed achenes). FAM. *Compositae*. A genus of about 18 perennial or annual herbs, natives of S. Africa, with the characters of Arctotis but without a pappus. Leaves alternate, often cut pinnately and usually woolly. Flower-heads large, showy; ray-florets female, ligulate, disk-florets perfect, 5-toothed. Achenes smooth, winged or ridged. Half-hardy or greenhouse plants propagated by seed. *V. fastuosum* is a somewhat coarse-growing plant but very showy and useful for cutting. Seed should be sown in March in gentle heat, but is often difficult to germinate. It grows well in sun in ordinary soil, as do the other species mentioned, provided it is well drained. All described below can be grown as half-hardy annuals.

V. calendula'ceum. A variety of *V. decurrens.*

V. decur'rens. Diffusely branched, softly hairy, stems 12 to 18 in. long, angled. *l.* more or less lyrate with the terminal lobe largest, cobwebby at first, later smooth above, white-hairy beneath. *fl.-heads* about 1½ in. across, rays bright yellow, disk nearly black or dark brown, peduncles long. July to October. In the type the petioles, about 2 in. long, are decurrent and eared at the base, but in var. **calendulaceum** the ears are usually wanting.

Venidium fastuosum

V. fastuo'sum. Branched from the base, hoary, 2 to 3 ft. h., up to 2 ft. through. Stem hollow. *l.* many, lyrate-pinnatifid becoming less cut in upper part of plant, 5 to 6 in. long, grey-hairy on both sides. *fl.-heads* up to 5 or 6 in. across, ray-florets golden-yellow with purplish blotch at base, disk about 1 in. across, brownish-purple or black; involucral bracts in several series, hoary; closing in dull weather. (B.M. 9127; F.P.S.A. 198, as *V. Wyleyi.*)

V. macroce'phalum. Silvery tomentose annual about 18 in. h. with branching stems. *l.* deeply lobed, cauline eared at base. *fl.-heads* about 3 in. across, rays cream or straw-colour, disk orange. August. (B.M. 8845; F.P.S.A. 117.)

V. Wy'leyi. A synonym of *V. fastuosum.*

veno'sus -a -um, having conspicuous veins.

Ventena'tii, in honour of Étienne Pierre Ventenat, 1757–1808, French botanist and librarian, author of important folio botanical works, illustrated by P. J. Redouté.

VENTILA'GO (*ventilo,* to be exposed to wind; in allusion to the linear wings in the upper part of the fruit). FAM. *Rhamnaceae.* A genus of about 10 species of climbing shrubs, natives of the tropics. Leaves alternate, almost in 2 ranks. Flowers small, usually in leafless panicles at ends of branches, rarely axillary; calyx lobes 5, spreading; petals 5, somewhat hooded; stamens 5. For cultivation of *V. maderaspatana,* which needs stove conditions.

V. maderaspata'na. Shrub, shoots and l. glabrous. *l.* oblong-lanceolate to ovate, acute or nearly so, crenate or entire. *fl.* green in slender spikes, sometimes panicled. India. 1822.

F. G. P.

VENTILATION. Ventilation is one of the most important operations in the management of all kinds of plants under glass, and the provision of ventilators properly placed is a requisite in all types of horticultural structures for the regulation of temperature and humidity and for the interchange of air. The size and position of the ventilators needed depend on the kind of plants to be cultivated. In peach houses and vineries provision should be made for the admission of abundant air whenever it is required and weather permits, while in plant stoves and houses where a high temperature is needed at all times, a smaller number of ventilators will suffice. It is always advisable to provide ventilators near the top of the house so situated that the full amount of air can be admitted without rain getting in and available for use at all times irrespective of the direction of the wind. Where no side or front sashes are provided, as in many lean-to houses, wooden door ventilators fixed in the front wall are best. If air from these can be made to pass over the heating pipes it will be warmed before reaching the plants. Wooden ventilators may be similarly placed in the back wall, but wherever possible lifting sashes are to be preferred. Both side and top ventilators can be easily opened or closed by means of a lever at one end of the house, thus saving much time compared with the old method of dealing with each sash separately.

There are many factors to be considered in the use of the ventilators and only practical experience is likely to result in their use to the full advantage. The most important perhaps are the state of the weather, which is often very changeable, and the difference between the outside and inside temperatures. Almost of equal importance is the fact that at different seasons the same plants will need dissimilar treatment, for they will be at different stages of growth. During spring sudden changes of temperature caused by improper ventilation will soon make their evil effects evident on young and tender foliage. The modern use of large panes of glass makes the rise of temperature by sun-heat much more rapid than in old houses with small panes, and consequently the need for early attention to ventilation is more imperative. When it is known that air will have to be admitted to a house the ventilators should be opened very gradually as soon as the temperature begins to rise in the early part of the day. It is never good practice to allow the temperature to rise high and then to open the ventilators to their full extent in one step or even in two. Such a measure causes a sudden change which leads to tender young foliage losing too much water and wilting. Few plants can stand this and their foliage becomes scorched and insects and mites are encouraged, doing damage which the plants cannot overtake. In spring in the forcing house and other structures the ventilation may need different management nearly every day in order to keep near the requisite temperature for the plants in relation to the light available. In general, ventilating should begin early in the day when it appears likely that it will be necessary and should be increased at intervals until the full amount required is reached; draughts should always be avoided; if the wind is rough or the outside air cold, front and back ventilators should not be open at the same time unless it is certain that the occupants of the house will not suffer—which is rarely the case. In summer when inside and outside temperatures are approximately the same, air may usually be admitted freely without causing much injury.

ventral, belonging to the upper or inner face of an organ; opposed to dorsal.

ventrico'sus -a -um, ventricose; swelling unequally; inflated on one side; e.g. the corolla tube in many Labiatae.

VENTUR'IA. A genus of fungi of the Class Ascomycetes. Several species are important plant parasites. *See*, e.g., **Apple and Pear Scab** under **Apple Diseases.**

venulo'sus -a -um, finely veined.

VENUS'S COMB. The fruit of the Umbelliferous plant *Scandix Pecten-veneris.* Native to Britain.

VENUS'S FLY-TRAP. *See* **Dionaea muscipula.**

VENUS'S HAIR. *See* **Adiantum Capillus-Veneris.**

VENUS'S LOOKING-GLASS. *See* **Specularia Speculum.**

VENUS'S NAVELWORT. *See* **Omphalodes linifolia.**

VENUS'S OR VENICE SUMACH. *See* **Rhus Cotinus.**

venus'tus -a -um, lovely, graceful.

VEP'RIS. Included under **Toddalia.**

VERAT'RUM (ancient Latin name used by Lucretius and Pliny from *vere*, truly, and *ater*, black, from the colour of the root). FAM. *Liliaceae.* A genus of about 20 species of perennial herbs, natives of Europe, Siberia, and N. America. Rhizome thick (very poisonous), root fibres somewhat poisonous, containing veratrin, present also in Schoenocaulon. Stem erect, leafy. Leaves often broad, pleated, narrowed to a large sheath, upper leaves rarely all narrow, uppermost usually narrow. Flowers numerous in a terminal panicle, pedicels short, perianth purplish, greenish or whitish, persistent, broadly bell-shaped or spreading; segments (in hermaphrodite flowers) connate towards the base in a very short tube, in others oblong, spreading, nearly equal, scarcely narrowed at base, many-nerved; stamens 6. Propagation may be effected by division or by seeds. Veratrums are hardy and thrive in any rich soil. The rhizome of *V. album*, powdered and sold as Hellebore Powder, is used to destroy caterpillars, especially those of the Gooseberry Sawfly.

Veratrum viride

V. al'bum. Langwort, White Hellebore. Stem erect, 3 to 4 ft. h., downy, with 10 to 12 l. *l.* green, plicate; radical l. 1 ft. long, oblong, 5 to 6 in. wide, firm. *fl.* whitish within, greenish without at base, crisped-toothed, almost sessile, in dense raceme, rachis downy. July. Europe, N. Africa, Siberia. 1548.

V. califor'nicum. Stout, 3 to 7 ft. h. *l.* ovate-acute, upper lanceolate, rarely slender-pointed. *fl.* drooping, bell-shaped, broader than in *V. viride*, segs. obtuse, whitish with a greener base. W. United States.

V. Maac'kii. Stem slender, 2 ft. h., slightly thickened at base, few-lvd. *Lower l.* lanceolate, 6 in. long, 1 in. wide in middle, stalked; *upper* sessile. *fl.* dark purple, $\frac{1}{5}$ to $\frac{1}{4}$ in. long, segs. oblong, blackish at base; lower pedicels $\frac{1}{4}$ to $\frac{1}{3}$ in. long; lateral racemes ascending; panicle loose, 6 to 12 in. long. E. Siberia. 1883. (G.F. 1070.)

V. nig'rum. 2 to 4 ft. h., somewhat swollen at base, erect, many-lvd. *Lower l.* oblong, 12 in. long, 6 to 8 in. wide, narrowed at base, plicate. *fl.* blackish-purple, $\frac{1}{6}$ to $\frac{1}{4}$ in. long, segs. oblong, obtuse; lower pedicels $\frac{1}{12}$ to $\frac{1}{4}$ in. long; racemes densely fld., lateral short, making a narrow panicle 1 to 3 ft. long. June. S. Europe, Siberia. 1596. (B.M. 963.)

V. vi'ride. Indian Poke. 2 to 7 ft. h. with a rootstock 2 to 3 in. long. *l.* plicate, acute; lower oval, about 12 in. long, upper gradually smaller. *fl.* yellowish-green; segs. lanceolate or oblong, ciliate, toothed; pedicels $\frac{1}{12}$ to $\frac{1}{2}$ in. long; lateral racemes loosely fld., often reflexed. July. N. America. 1742. (B.M. 1096 as *Helonias viride.*)

V. Wilson'ii. Much-branched, up to 3 ft. h., leafy at base. *l.* about 10, overlapping, strap-shaped, acute, up to 2 ft. long, 1 in. wide, glabrous. *fl.* white with a green band in lower half, about 1 in. across, in large pyramidal panicles about 2 ft. long. Summer. *fr.* a 3-celled capsule; seeds about 20 in each cell. S. China. 1908. (B.M. 8925.)

VERATRUM ROOT. The source of Hellebore Powder.

verbanen'sis -is -e, from Lake Maggiore (Lacus Verbanus).

verbascifo'lius -a -um, with leaves resembling Verbascum.

VERBAS'CUM (ancient Latin name used by Pliny). FAM. *Scrophulariaceae.* A genus of nearly 300 species of mostly biennial herbs, rarely perennial or sub-shrubs, more or less hairy or woolly, natives of Europe, N. Africa, and W. and Cent. Asia, some species very widely distributed and naturalized in other parts of the world. Leaves alternate, often soft, entire, or crenately or sinuately toothed or pinnatifid, often in a large basal rosette. Flowers yellow, brownish-red, purple, or red, rarely white, in spikes or racemes on short pedicels; calyx deeply 5-cleft or parted, rarely with short teeth; corolla with a very short tube, lobes 5, broad, nearly equal; stamens 5, attached to base of corolla. Fruit a globose, many-seeded capsule. Some of the species are distinctly ornamental and showy and some have white-woolly foliage in a rosette in their first year, making them worthy of a place in the border or the wild garden on that account. Except *V. nigrum*, *V. phoeniceum*, *V. pinnatifidum*, and *V. simplex*, they are biennials, however, and are mostly difficult to keep true from seed since they cross very readily. *V. nigrum* and *V. phoeniceum* can be propagated by division, and *V. pinnatifidum* by cuttings. Some of the hybrids have received names and some can be propagated by cuttings, but though they do not usually come true from seed most are worth a place for the contrast their frequently tall, erect, densely flowered inflorescences make with perennials of looser habit. As will be seen, there is great difference in the stature of the different species. These hardy plants are not particular as to soil, so long as it is well drained, and they thrive on chalk. A

V. banat'icum. Biennial, 2 to 6 ft. h., greyish-green, much branched with long ascending spikes. *Basal l.* oblong or obovate-oblong, sometimes pinnately lobed, to 1 ft. long; *stem-l.* smaller, sessile, undulate. *fl.* primrose, $\frac{3}{8}$ to nearly 1 in. across, on pedicels $\frac{1}{10}$ to $\frac{3}{8}$ in. long, forming long slender spikes; cal. densely tomentose; filaments with whitish hairs; anthers orange; capsules almost globose. Summer. SE. Europe. 1935. (B.M. 9608.) A very graceful plant, with a long flowering season.

V. Blatta'ria. Moth Mullein. Glabrous, green biennial, 8 in. to 4 ft. h., simple or branched. *Basal l.* oblong-lanceolate, 4 to 10 in. long, obtuse, crenate, lobed, or somewhat pinnatifid; *stem-l.* small, sessile, ovate or oblong, more or less toothed. *fl.* bright yellow, rarely cream, $\frac{3}{4}$ to $1\frac{1}{4}$ in. across, on pedicels $\frac{1}{4}$ to 1 in. long, forming slender, glandular panicles; filaments purple-haired. Summer. Europe, including Britain. (E.B. 942.) var. **grandiflo'rum,** larger in all parts, *fl.* white, about 2 in. across. (B.M. 8863.) **V. virga'tum** is nearly allied but more glandular, with *upper l.* shortly decurrent, racemes more densely fld., pedicels more clustered and shorter than cal.

V. Boerhaav'ii. About 2 ft. h. covered with white floccose hairs at first. *Basal l.* obovate or oblong, stalked; *upper l.* cordate-amplexicaul or shortly decurrent, acute or long-pointed. *fl.* yellow, sessile, clustered or rarely solitary, large, in a simple or slightly branched spike. S. Europe. 1731.

V. × Caledonia. Robust and branched; *fl.* of various colours, buff to bronzy yellow.

V. Chaix'ii.* Nettle-leaved Mullein. About 3 ft. h., whitish tomentose. *l.* green or whitish-hairy, crenate; lower stalked, wedge-shaped at base, truncate or cut; upper sessile, rounded at base. *fl.* yellow, in panicles, the clusters loosely many-fld.; cal. segs. lanceolate, awl-shaped; filaments purple-haired. S. and Cent. Europe. 1821. var. **al'bum,** *fl.* white. **V. orienta'le** is nearly allied to this.

V. crassifo'lium. 3 to 4 ft. h., densely covered with yellow hairs. *l.* obovate-spatulate, 6 to 8 in. long, crenulate, woolly; stem-l. long decurrent. *fl.* yellow, large, clustered in a spike-like raceme; filaments glabrous. Portugal.

V. cu'preum. A synonym of *V. phoeniceum.*

V. densiflo'rum. A synonym of *V. thapsiforme.*

V. gigan'teum. A synonym of *V. Thapsus.*

V. × hyb'ridum. Name mostly applied to hybrids of *V. phoeniceum* or perhaps to forms of that variable species.

V. leian'theum. Up to 14 ft. h., covered with dense white felted hair. *Basal l.* up to 4 by 2 ft.; *stem-l.* oblong, crenate, rugose, with a decurrent base, covered with white hair on both surfaces. *fl.* bright yellow, $\frac{3}{4}$ in. across in a large much-branched panicle up to 7 ft. long and $2\frac{1}{2}$ ft. wide, loosely many-fld.; cal. segs. small, oblong-lanceolate, blunt; cor. and infl. generally glabrous. Summer. Asia Minor. (G.C. 44 (1908), 171.)

V. liba'ni. About 5 ft. h. with white woolly l. and tall spikes of pale yellow fl. July to September. Probably of garden origin.

V. longifo'lium. Yellowish or whitish hairy, 3 to 4 ft. h. *l.* very numerous, densely placed, undulate; lower $1\frac{1}{2}$ to 2 ft. long, narrowly ovate or oblong-lanceolate, short stalked; upper sessile, stem-clasping. *fl.* golden-yellow, about 1 in. across, in a densely branched infl. about 1 ft. long, $3\frac{1}{2}$ in. wide; cal. hairy, segs. lanceolate, filaments with pale violet hairs. June to September. S. Europe. 1898. (B.M. 7707.) var. **panno'sum.**

V. Lychni'tis. 2 to 3 ft. h., stem angled. *l.* oblong-lanceolate, obtuse, 4 to 10 in. long, coarsely crenate, green above, white beneath, stalked; upper ovate, sessile. *fl.* whitish, $\frac{1}{3}$ in. across, in an erect many-fld. narrow panicle; cal. woolly; filaments with white hairs. July, August. Europe, including Britain, W. Asia. (E.B. 939.)

V. nig'rum.* Dark Mullein. 2 to 3 ft. h., rather loosely covered with long hairs; stem angled. *Basal l.* ovate-oblong or oblong-lanceolate, up to 1 ft. h., often heart-shaped, crenate, stalked; *upper l.* ovate-heart-shaped, scarcely white beneath, only uppermost sessile. *fl.* yellow, $\frac{1}{2}$ to $\frac{3}{4}$ in. across, clustered, in an erect, slender raceme, slightly branched, 1 to $1\frac{1}{2}$ ft. long; segs. lanceolate, hairy, filaments with purple hairs. June to October. Europe, including Britain, Asia. (E.B. 940.) var. **al'bum,** *fl.* white. More or less perennial.

V. olym'picum.* 5 to 6 ft. h., branching from near base, forming a candelabra. *Basal l.* lanceolate, broad, 6 in. long, acuminate, woolly. *fl.* bright golden yellow, 1 to $1\frac{1}{4}$ in. across; filaments white-hairy. June to September. Bithynia. 1883. Filaments with whitish or yellowish hairs. (G.C. 101 (1937), 135; Ctf. 31 (1882), 1078.) Worth growing for the large rosette of grey-felted l.; a plant of this raised at Kew in 1927 flourished until 1940.

V. orienta'le. *See* **V. Chaixii.**

V. ovalifo'lium. About $2\frac{1}{2}$ ft. h., grey hairy. *l.* ovate, large; lower doubly or deeply crenate, upper cordate-amplexicaul. *fl.* orange-yellow, solitary, sessile or nearly so, $1\frac{1}{2}$ in. across, in a dense spike; cal. densely white-woolly, segs. lanceolate; filaments with orange or purple hairs. July. Caucasus. 1804. (B.M. 1037; B.R. 558 as *V. formosum.*)

V. panno'sum. A variety of *V. longifolium.*

V. phlomoi'des. Woolly Mullein. About 4 ft. h., white to yellowish hairy. *Basal l.* oblong, doubly or deeply crenate; *upper* short, blunt; all glabrous above, hairy beneath. *fl.* yellow, in clusters on a long raceme; pedicels shorter than the hairy cal.; cal. segs. triangular-lanceolate; filaments white-woolly. June to September. S. Europe. Caucasus. 1739. (S.B.F.G. 221.)

V. phoeni'ceum.* Purple Mullein. Perennial, 2 to 3 ft. h. or in rich soil up to 5 ft. *Radical l.* in a rosette, ovate or oblong, entire or with large crenatures; *upper* few, small; all glabrous or nearly so above, hairy beneath. *fl.* variable in colour, $1\frac{1}{4}$ in. across, solitary in a long slender raceme; pedicels much longer than cal.; raceme glandular, sometimes slightly branched, many from the base; cor. glabrous. May to September. S. Europe, N. Asia. 1796. (B.M. 885.) The colour is typically violet or red but varies to white and shades of pink, lilac, rose, and purple. It appears to be a parent of some of the hybrids offered. It seeds freely and may therefore spread unduly.

V. pinnati'fidum. Sub-shrub, 1 ft. or more h. *l.* green, usually glabrous, lower 2-pinnatifid, upper pinnatifid, segs. oblong, toothed. *fl.* yellow in distant, few-fld. clusters or almost solitary on a rigid, slightly branched raceme. Caucasus. 1813. (S.B.F.G. 228; B.M. 1777 as *V. bipinnatifidum.*)

V. pulverulen'tum. Hoary Mullein. Habit of *V. Lychnitis* but *l.* much wider, sessile, with small crenatures, more matted with white, woolly hairs; upper l. heart-shaped. Stem round. *fl.* bright yellow, $\frac{1}{2}$ to $\frac{3}{4}$ in. across, several to each bract; infl. a pyramidal panicle; cal. segs. small, lanceolate; filaments white-woolly. July. Europe, including Britain.

V. pyramida'tum. 3 ft. h. or more, hairy. *Lower l.* large, gradually narrowed to base; *upper* sessile, heart-shaped, auriculate. *fl.* yellow in a grey-hairy pyramidal panicle 1 to 2 ft. long; branchlets densely fld. or sometimes racemose. Summer. Caucasus. 1804. (S.B.F.G. 31.)

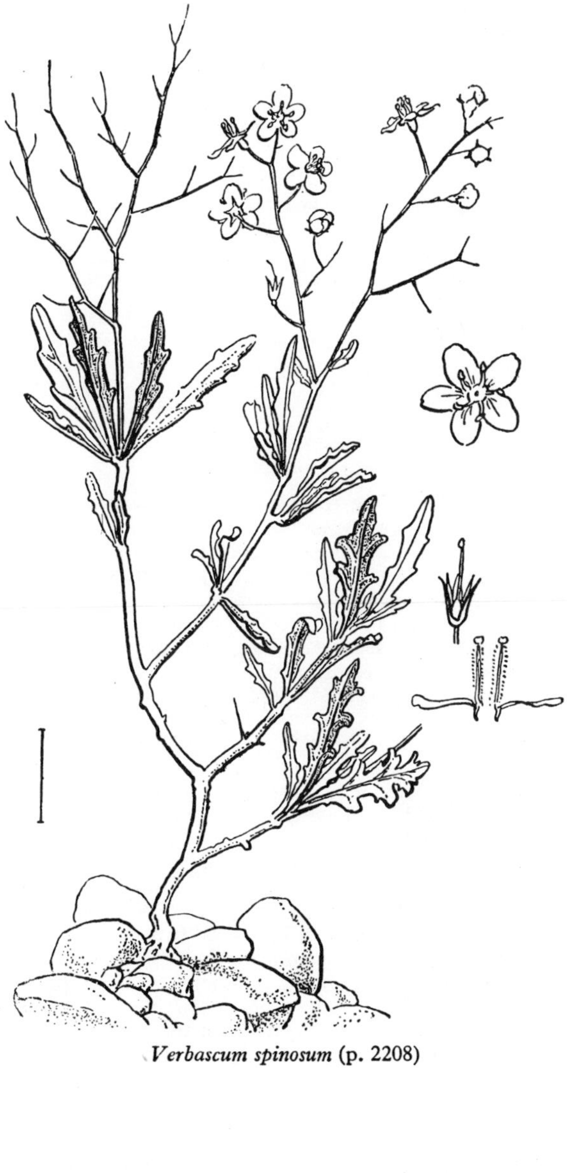

Verbascum spinosum (p. 2208)

V. × rubigino'sum. *V. Chaixii* × *V. phoeniceum*, 2 to 3 ft. h. *l.* crenate, hairy beneath; upper sessile or amplexicaul, lower stalked. *fl.* yellow and red; usually in twos or threes in a loose raceme, rarely solitary; pedicels much longer than cal. June to August. Hungary. 1817. **V. × tau'ricum,** also a *phoeniceum* hybrid, has *fl.* larger, pedicels shorter, raceme simpler. (B.M. 3799.)

V. sim'plex. Perennial, about 2 ft. h. from a shrubby base, many-stemmed, densely white- or yellowish-haired, almost shaggy. Stem leafy below. *l.* ovate or oblong-spatulate, obtuse, 1 to 2 in. long; stalk long, upper l. sessile, in clusters of 2 to 5. *fl.* yellow, in a branched raceme; cal. white-hairy, segs. oblong-mucronate; filaments white-hairy. Summer. Syria. (G.C. 36 (1904), 2.)

V. sinua'tum. 2 to 3 ft. h., yellowish- or grey-hairy. *Basal l.* oblong-spatulate, sinuately pinnatifid, usually undulate, nearly sessile; *stem-l.* oblong, acute, entire, shortly decurrent. *fl.* small, yellow, or rarely white, in distant rounded clusters in a pyramidal panicle with long twiggy branches; cal. downy, segs. shortly lanceolate; filaments purple-hairy. Summer. Mediterranean region, Canary Is.

V. soonga'ricum. 5 or 6 ft. h., covered with white hairs. *Lower l.* lanceolate, acute, narrowed to stalk; *stem-l.* sessile, oblong, cordate-auriculate; uppermost roundish. *fl.* yellow, clustered, in a panicle; cal. segs. lanceolate; filaments white-woolly. Dzungaria.

V. specio'sum. About 6 ft. h. *l.* thick, entire, or lower crenate, long, oblong, gradually narrowed to stalk; upper sessile or amplexicaul. *fl.* yellow in loose often many-fld. clusters on a very long panicle; pedicels longer than cal. Summer. Hungary. 1818.

V. specta'bile. About 2 ft. h. *l.* doubly crenate, sometimes hairy above, somewhat long-haired beneath; lower oblong-ovate with a cordate base, stalked, upper sessile, half-amplexicaul. *fl.* yellow and purple, solitary or a few together on a long nearly simple, clammy raceme. Caucasus. 1820.

V. spino'sum. Dwarf spreading bush to 12 in. h. with intricately branched woody grey shoots ending in short spines. *l.* small, narrowly oblanceolate, to 2 in. long, $\frac{3}{8}$ in. wide, grey-tomentose, entire or shallowly toothed. *fl.* yellow about $\frac{3}{8}$ in. across, in a small twiggy panicle; cal. tomentose; filaments orange. Crete. A very distinct species for the rock-garden or sink-garden, easily recognized by its dwarf shrubby habit.

V. thapsifor'me. 2 to 5 ft. h., densely covered with yellow hair. *Basal l.* oblong-elliptic or oblong-lanceolate, crenulate, narrowed to stalk; *stem-l.* narrowly decurrent. *fl.* large, yellow, in clusters forming a spike; cal. hairy, segs. lanceolate; cor. rather flat. June to August. Europe, Siberia. SYN. *V. densiflorum* of Visiani.

V. Thap'sus. Aaron's Rod, Hag Taper, Torches, Adam's Flannel, Jacob's Staff, Shepherd's Club, Blanket Leaf. Densely woolly, with an unbranched stout, round stem 2 to 3 ft. h., not glandular. *Basal l.* obovate-lanceolate, 6 to 18 in. long, entire or crenate; *stem-l.* oblong, decurrent, acute. *fl.* yellow, $\frac{3}{4}$ to 1 in. across in a simple spike 6 to 10 in. long; cor. woolly without; filaments white-hairy. June to August. Europe, Asia. (E.B. 937.) Wool once used for lamp wicks.

V. verna'le. A synonym of *V. Chaixii* and *V. nigrum.*

V. virga'tum. *See under* **V. Blattaria.**

V. Wiedemannia'num. 3 to 4 ft. h. *l.* evergreen, cobwebby; basal-l. 3 to 5 in. long, oblong or elliptic, crenate or almost entire, narrowed to a stalk; stem-l. small, sessile. *fl.* indigo-blue, becoming purplish-lilac, $1\frac{1}{2}$ in. across, in very long racemes; *cal.* densely glandular-hairy, segs. linear-lanceolate; filaments purple-hairy. June to September. Asia Minor. 1893.

VER'BENA (ancient Latin name for the European Vervain, *V. officinalis*, used by Virgil and Pliny). FAM. *Verbenaceae.* A genus of about 200 species, mostly annual or perennial herbs, but a few slightly woody at the base, almost all American. Leaves opposite or rarely ternately whorled, toothed or deeply cut, rarely entire. Flowers small or of moderate size, solitary in the axils of usually very narrow bractlets; calyx tubular, 5-ribbed, 5-toothed, the teeth often unequal; corolla salverform, its tube straight or incurved, equal in diameter throughout or slightly enlarged upwards, the limb spreading, somewhat 2-lipped, the 5 lobes oblong or broad, obtuse or retuse; stamens 4, didynamous, very rarely 2, affixed at about the middle of the tube, included; the anther-connective often with a glandular appendage which may protrude somewhat from the corolla-mouth; spikes terminal, rarely axillary, sometimes very short and with crowded flowers in fascicles. Fruit separating into 4 narrow nutlets.

All the Verbenas are readily raised from seed sown in early spring in heat, or from cuttings of shoots which have no flowers. The hardy perennial species may also be raised by division of the rootstock. All require a well-drained rich soil and a sunny position and may be planted in the open border during summer from the middle or end of May. Most species are somewhat tender, even *V. rigida* being apt to suffer in hard winters. The Garden Verbena (*V.* × *hybrida*) was at one time commonly propagated by cuttings to keep the various varieties true, but the plants were found to be difficult to keep through winter and seedsmen developed strains which gave good results, and the clonal stocks were dispensed with, excepting two recently introduced varieties of exceptional merit for bedding and garden decoration, namely **Lawrence Johnston,** with large heads of deep crimson flowers and **Firefly** with bright scarlet flowers. The Garden Verbena is of somewhat diffuse habit, free-flowering, and with a considerable range of colour, making it excellent for summer bedding; some forms also are pleasantly scented. The various strains offered in the trade are doubtless of hybrid origin, the result of crossing *V. peruviana*, *V. incisa*, *V. phlogiflora*, and *V. platensis.* Treated like other half-hardy annuals, the seedlings should be planted out about the end of May about 1 ft. apart. By this time they will be beginning to flower and any clashing colours may thus be avoided. The growth is semi-trailing and may be pegged down to give good ground cover, and the plants may thus be used as a carpet for other taller plants. Their flowering will continue until November if the weather is open. They need a sunny position and a well-drained soil. They may also be grown as pot plants with the necessary stopping and supports to counteract the sprawling habit. Verbenas appear to be worthy of wider cultivation for summer bedding, especially where snapdragons suffer from rust and its consequent disfigurement.

The European (and British) *V. officinalis*, in common with some American species, had at one time a great reputation for medicinal purposes; its flowers, too, were in demand as a restorative for defective vision. It has no claim to a place in gardens except on this account. For general garden purposes the best are *V. bonariensis* and *V. corymbosa* as border plants, and *V.* × *hybrida*, *V. peruviana*, and *V. rigida* as bedding plants. The following Key does not include *V. scabrido-glandulosa* and *V. tridens*, which are not herbaceous plants but shrubs with interlacing branches, very small leaves giving them a heath-like appearance, and few-flowered inflorescences; they belong to a group of about 30 species of like habit, native to Argentina, Chile, and Patagonia, which have been placed in a genus distinct from Verbena under the name **Junel'lia** (in honour of the Swedish botanist Sven Junell). They are interesting shrubs for the rock-garden, needing a well-drained soil and full sun and are easily propagated by cuttings. For reasons of space, particulars of the hair-covering have been omitted from the following descriptions.

KEY

1. *Anthers unappendaged. Cor. mostly small, individually not showy. Cal. rarely twice as long as fr., not twisted beyond it (Sect. Verbenaca)* 2
1. *Anthers-connective usually appendaged. Cor. mostly large and showy. Cal. usually more than twice as long as fruit, constricted or twisted beyond it (Sect. Glandularia)* 35
2 (1). *Spikes crowded and short, at least during anthesis, often forming a head, usually neither greatly elongated nor open after anthesis* 3
2. *Spikes slender and open or compact at anthesis, greatly elongating afterwards* 12
3 (2). *Stems densely villose, canescent* V. hirta
3. *Stems neither villose nor canescent* 4
4 (3). *Lvs. much reduced, $\frac{3}{20}$ to $\frac{7}{10}$ long when mature* V. alata
4. *Lvs. larger* 5
5 (4). *Lvs. obviously sessile and cordate or clasping at base* 6
5. *Lvs. short-stalked or almost sessile or, if sessile, neither cordate nor clasping at base* 10
6 (5). *Bractlets conspicuously longer than cal.* 7
6. *Bractlets equalling or but slightly longer than cal.* 9
7 (6). *Cor. usually 3 times as long as cal. Lvs. rigid, mostly oblong or oblong-lanceolate, scabrous and more or less hispidulous on both sides* 8
7. *Cor. twice as long as cal. Lvs. soft, mostly ovate-lanceolate, strigose-hairy, not scabrous* V. hispida

8 (7). *Cor. purple or magenta* — V. rigida
8. *Cor. lilac* — V. rigida lilacina
9 (6). *Lvs. obviously clasping at base. Spikes compact, mostly short, commonly sessile and crowded into dense fasciculate cymes* — V. bonariensis
9. *Lvs. not clasping. Spikes more elongate, stalked, solitary or in open panicles* — V. × Dermenii
10 (5). *Bractlets and cal.* $\frac{3}{20}$ *to* $\frac{1}{4}$ *in. long. Lvs. rigid, veins deeply impressed above* — V. corymbosa
10. *Bractlets and cal.* $\frac{1}{10}$ *to* $\frac{3}{20}$ *in. long. Lvs. not rigid, the veining flat above* — 11
11 (10). *Cal. minutely puberulous, obscurely short-apiculate. Bractlets almost glabrous* — V. recta
11. *Cal. densely white-strigose, long-cuspidate. Bractlets distinctly ciliate* — V. brasiliensis
12 (2). *Spikes conspicuously bracteate with many leafy bracts often to* $\frac{3}{5}$ *in. long.* — V. bracteata
12. *Spikes not conspicuously bracteate. Bractlets not leafy, less than* $\frac{3}{10}$ *in. long* — 13
13 (12). *Bractlets usually about twice as long as cal.* — V. gracilis
13. *Bractlets mostly equalling cal.* — 14
14 (13). *Spikes solitary or in threes at tips of shoots and branches* — 15
14. *Spikes normally panicled at tips of shoots and branches* — 19
15 (14). *Plants prostrate or nearly so. L. dissected* — V. supina
15. *Plants erect. Lvs. not dissected* — 16
16 (15). *Spikes coarse, thick, about* $\frac{3}{10}$ *in. wide in fr., very dense, the fruiting cal. closely overlapping* — 17
16. *Spikes slender, graceful, about* $\frac{3}{20}$ *in. wide in fr., not specially dense, the fruiting cal. usually not at all overlapping or scarcely so* — 18
17 (16). *Lvs. elongate-elliptic to ovate-acuminate, short-stalked. Cor. limb about* $\frac{1}{5}$ *in. wide* — V. Macdougalii
17. *Lvs. ovate-orbicular, sessile. Cor. limb about* $\frac{7}{20}$ *in. wide.* — V. stricta
18 (16). *Lvs. incised-pinnatifid or 3-fid. Stems densely hirsute hispid* — V. xutha
18. *Lvs. merely serrate. Stems glabrous or strigillose* — V. simplex
19 (14). *Lvs. pinnatifid, 2-pinnatifid, 3- to 5-cleft or incised-laciniate* — 20
19. *Lvs. merely dentate, serrate or incised, rarely hastate* — 27
20 (19). *Spikes densely spreading-pubescent* — 21
20. *Spikes merely strigillose or pubescent* — 22
21 (20). *Stems and branches glabrescent; infl. hairs short, glandular* — V. Runyonii
21. *Stems and branches densely hirsute; infl. hairs long, not glandular* — V. lasiostachys
22 (20). *Spikes dense-fld., the fl. almost overlapping. Fr. sparse* — 23
22. *Spikes loosely fld., the fl. distant. Fr. usually abundant* — 24
23 (22). *Spikes greatly elongated, 12 to 16 in. long. Lvs. mostly 3-fid* — V. × Suksdorfii
23. *Spikes shorter, 2 to 4 in. long. Lvs. merely irregularly and deeply incised-laciniate* — V. × Baileyana
24 (23). *Lvs. densely strigillose on both sides; stems and branches sparsely and minutely hispidulous or strigillose* — V. menthifolia
24. *Lvs. glabrous or almost glabrous above, sparsely strigillose beneath only on the larger veins; stems and branches glabrous except for the angles* — 25
25 (24). *Spikes mostly short, 4 to 12 in. long.* — 26
25. *Spikes always much elongated, 16 in. or more long.* — V. officinalis macrostachya
26 (25). *Lower l. lanceolate, elliptic or oblanceolate, often broad.* — V. officinalis
26. *Lower lvs. linear-oblong, narrow.* — V. officinalis Gaudichaudii
27 (19). *Spikes thick, dense, usually with fr. touching* — 28
27. *Spikes very slender, loose-fld., the fr. usually not touching* — 30
28 (27). *Infl. conspicuously densely glandular-pubescent. Lvs. obtuse at the tip* — V. robusta
28. *Infl. obscurely puberulous, not glandular. Lvs. attenuate at the tip* — 29
29 (28). *Lvs. very narrowly lanceolate or oblong-lanceolate, never incised or hastate. Spikes few Fr. sparingly and irregularly produced* — V. × Blanchardii
29. *Lvs. usually more broadly lanceolate or ovate-lanceolate, often incised or hastate. Spikes numerous, dense-fld. Fr. densely and regularly produced* — V. hastata
30 (27). *Spikes sparsely fruited* — 31
30. *Spikes abundantly fruited* — 32
31 (30). *Stems rather densely hirsute with whitish stiff spreading hairs* — V. × matritensis
31. *Stems appressed pilose or puberulent* — V. × Engelmannii
32 (30). *Bractlets usually equalling cal.,* $\frac{1}{10}$ *to* $\frac{3}{20}$ *in long* — V. litoralis
32. *Bractlets shorter than cal., about* $\frac{1}{20}$ *in. long* — 33
33 (32). *Plants to 5 ft. h. Lvs. 3 to 8 in. long, to 3 in. wide, obviously stalked, with rounded-cuneate base* — 34
33. *Plants 1 to 3 ft. h. Lvs. 2 to* $2\frac{3}{4}$ *in. long,* $\frac{1}{2}$ *to* $\frac{3}{4}$ *in. wide, almost sessile on short-stalked with an attenuate base* — V. carolina
34 (33). *Lvs. glabrous beneath or with scattered long stiff hairs on the veins beneath* — V. urticifolia
34. *Lvs. densely and uniformly puberulent beneath* — V. urticifolia leiocarpa
35 (1). *Infl. congested, forming a head, not elongating after anthesis* — 36
35. *Infl. elongating after anthesis* — 39
36 (35). *Lvs. merely serrate. Cor. tube to* $1\frac{1}{10}$ *in. long, its limb to* $\frac{3}{5}$ *in. wide* — V. phlogiflora
36. *Lvs. pinnatifid-dissected. Cor. tube to* $\frac{2}{5}$ *in. long, its limb to* $\frac{3}{10}$ *in. wide* — 37
37 (36). *Lvs. strigose-pubescent on both sides* — 38
37. *Lvs. glabrous on both sides* — V. radicans
38 (37). *Cor. yellow. Anther-appendages protruding from cor. mouth* — V. sulphurea
38. *Cor. violet or white. Anther-appendages not protruding* — V. pulchella
39 (35). *Lvs. merely serrate, dentate or somewhat incised* — 40
39. *Lvs. pinnatifid-dissected or 2-pinnatifid* — 43
40 (39). *Lvs. sessile or nearly so, small, usually* $\frac{4}{5}$ *in. or less long. Cal.* $\frac{1}{20}$ *in. or less long, short-pubescent, not canescent* — V. peruviana
40. *Lvs. stalked, larger, more than* $\frac{4}{5}$ *in. long. Cal. over* $\frac{1}{20}$ *in. long, somewhat hirsute, canescent* — 41
41 (40). *Lvs. thick-textured, mostly revolute at the margin, densely soft-pubescent or spreading-hirsutulous on both sides, the veins conspicuously impressed above and raised beneath* — 42
41. *Lvs. thin-textured, not revolute, appressed-strigose or short-strigose on both sides, the veining flat or almost so. Cor. scarlet* — V. incisa
42 (41). *Cor. white* — V. platensis
42. *Cor. of various colours* — V. × hybrida
43 (39). *Bractlets equalling or longer than cal.* — 44
43. *Bractlets usually much shorter than cal.* — 48
44 (43). *Cor. tube* $\frac{3}{5}$ *to 1 in. long. Bractlets mostly almost equalling cal.* — 45
44. *Cor. tube* $\frac{2}{5}$ *to* $\frac{3}{5}$ *in. long. Bractlets mostly longer than cal.* — 47
45 (44). *Bractlets glabrescent except for long-ciliate margins* — V. canadensis
45. *Bractlets uniformly hirsutulous throughout* — 46
46 (45). *Spikes dense and compact, rather few-fld., mostly not much elongating after anthesis. Plants prostrate or decumbent* — V. elegans
46. *Spikes densely many-fld., elongating after anthesis. Plants ascending, decumbent only at base* — V. elegans asperata
47 (44). *Lvs. 2-pinnatifid, the ultimate segs. linear-oblong* — V. bipinnatifida
47. *Lvs. mostly only 3-cleft, with segs. remotely incised or lobed, the ultimate segs. broad* — V. bipinnatifida latilobata
48 (43). *Cal. hairs very glandular* — V. Wrightii
48. *Cal. hairs less or not glandular* — 49
49 (48). *Cal. hairs appressed strigose, strigillose or almost strigose* — 50
49. *Cal. hairs spreading, not appressed* — 56
50 (49). *Cal. merely strigillose* — V. × monacensis
50. *Cal. densely strigose or almost strigose* — 51
51 (50). *Cor. tube* $\frac{3}{5}$ *to* $\frac{4}{5}$ *in. long. Lvs. irregularly incised or 3-parted* — V. × Teasii
51. *Cor. tube about* $\frac{2}{5}$ *in. long or less. Lvs. pinnatifid-dissected or 2-pinnatifid* — 52
52 (51). *Cal. merely almost strigose, the hairs short and not completely appressed. Lvs. segs. oblong, about* $\frac{1}{20}$ *in. wide* — V. pogostoma
52. *Cal. obviously strigose, the hairs longer, white and closely appressed* — 53
53 (52). *Lvs. segs. all uniformly narrowly linear, mostly less than* $\frac{1}{20}$ *in. wide.* — 54
53. *Lvs. segs. broader, oblong, not uniform, mostly* $\frac{1}{20}$ *in. or more wide* — 55
54 (55). *Cor. blue, purple, violet, rose or lilac* — V. tenuisecta
54. *Cor. white* — V. tenuisecta alba
55 (53). *Cor. tube* $\frac{2}{5}$ *in. long, its limb* $\frac{1}{5}$ *in. wide. Bractlets about* $\frac{1}{10}$ *in. long. Spikes greatly elongated and lax after anthesis* — V. mendocina
55. *Cor. tube less than* $\frac{2}{5}$ *in. long its limb about* $\frac{3}{20}$ *in. wide. Bractlets about* $\frac{3}{20}$ *in. long. Spikes densely congested even after anthesis, not elongating* — V. santiaguensis
56 (49). *Cor. lobes conspicuously white-margined* — V. tenera Maonettii
56. *Cor. lobes uniformly coloured* — 57
57 (56). *Cor. tube* $\frac{1}{2}$ *to* $\frac{3}{4}$ *in. long. Lvs. irregularly incised or 3-parted* — V. × Teasii
57. *Cor. tube* $\frac{2}{5}$ *to* $\frac{1}{2}$ *in. long. Lvs. pinnatifid-dissected* — 58
58 (57). *Cal. hairs more or less glandular* — G. Gooddingii
58. *Cal. hairs not glandular* — 59
59 (58). *Cor. with dense short hairs on the outside. Cal. hairs wide-spreading* — V. Berteri
59. *Cor. glabrous on the outside. Cal. hairs ascending* — 60
60 (59). *Bractlets about* $\frac{1}{5}$ *in. long. Cal. about* $\frac{2}{5}$ *in. long* — V. tenera
60. *Bractlets* $\frac{1}{10}$ *to* $\frac{1}{5}$ *in. long. Cal. about* $\frac{1}{5}$ *in. long* — 61
61 (60). *Bractlets glabrous except for the ciliate margins. Cal. very sparsely short-puberulent, not canescent* — V. laciniata
61. *Bractlets densely white-pubescent throughout. Cal. densely white-pubescent* — V. dissecta

V. ala′ta. Erect perennial to 6 ft. h., with broom-like appearance; stems and branches very sharply 4-angled, with almost winged angles. *l.* sessile, $\frac{1}{2}$ to 1 in. long, ovate or triangular-oblong, acute, entire or serrate, 3-nerved, rugose. *fl.* in terminal panicles, the spikes subcylindric, dense, short; bractlets lanceolate, acuminate, shorter than cal.; cor. blue. Brazil. 1830. (S.B.F.G. 2. 41.)

V. arrai'ana. A synonym of *V. phlogiflora*, although some plants offered in the trade under this name are *V. incisa.*

V. Auble'tia. A synonym of *V. canadensis.*

V.×Baileya'na. Hybrid between *V. officinalis* and *V. hastata.* Erect perennial. Garden origin. 1819.

V.×Beal'ei. Hybrid between *V. hispida* and *V. litoralis*, with intermediate characters. Garden origin. 1936.

V. Bert'eri. Procumbent, branches ascending. *l.* 3-fid-pinnatifid, the middle lobe 3-dentate, attenuate and entire at base, stalked, the lobes oblong-lanceolate, rather acute. *Spikes* very dense, capitate, many-fld., stalked; bractlets linear-lanceolate, a third or half as long as the cal.; cal. $\frac{3}{10}$ in. long; cor. lilac or rose, tube $\frac{2}{5}$ to $\frac{3}{5}$ in. long. Peru and Chile.

V. bipinnati'fida. Diffusely branched perennial; stems ascending, 6 to 18 in. h., occasionally rooting at the lower nodes. *l.* 2-pinnately divided or 3-partite with the divisions again more or less 2-pinnatifid, $\frac{3}{4}$ to $2\frac{1}{2}$ in. long, the lobes linear or oblong, stalked. *Spikes* stalked, capitate or fascicle-like in anthesis, elongating in fr.; bractlets mostly longer than the cal., linear-subulate; cal. about $\frac{7}{20}$ in. long, its lobes very slender, subulate-setaceous from a broader base, unequal; cor. pink, purple, violet, lavender, or violet, tube about $1\frac{1}{2}$ times as long as cal., limb $\frac{3}{10}$ to $\frac{1}{2}$ in. wide, the throat hairy; anther-appendages purplish. Cent. United States, Mexico. Grown as an annual. 1819. var. **latiloba'ta,** *l.* mostly only 3-cleft, the segs. only remotely incised or lobed and all much broader. Texas, Arizona, NW. Mexico. 1946.

V.×Blanchard'ii. Hybrid between *V. simplex* and *V. hastata*, with intermediate characters. From both it differs in producing fr. only very sparingly and irregularly. E. and Cent. United States. 1854.

V. bonarien'sis.* Coarse erect perennial, 3 or more ft. h.; stems conspicuously 4-angled. *l.* oblong-lanceolate, sessile, $1\frac{3}{4}$ to 4 in. long, $\frac{1}{4}$ to $\frac{3}{8}$ in. wide, cordate and clasping at base, acute, sharply serrate from below the middle, entire toward the base, rugose. *Spikes* compact, mostly short, commonly sessile and crowded bractlets lanceolate-acuminate, barely equalling or slightly surpassing cal.; cal. $\frac{3}{20}$ in. long, pubescent, subulate-lobed; cor. bright blue, violet lilac, or purple, tube scarcely twice as long as cal., limb small, about $\frac{1}{10}$ in. across. Brazil, Paraguay, Argentina. 1737. A good border plant if grown in a mass; sometimes seeds itself to death.

V. bractea'ta. Stems usually several, diffusely branched, decumbent or ascending, rarely erect. *l.* $\frac{1}{3}$ to $2\frac{1}{4}$ in. long, pinnately incised or usually 3-lobed, narrowed at base into a short margined petiole, the lateral lobes narrow, spreading far apart, the middle lobe large, cuneate-obovate, incised-dentate or cleft. *Spikes* terminal, sessile, comparatively thick; bracts conspicuous, much longer than cal., spreading-ascending, recurved in age, leafy; cal. about $\frac{3}{20}$ in. long, cor. bluish, pale violet, lavender, lilac, or purplish, tube slightly onger than cal., limb about $\frac{1}{20}$ in. wide. S. Canada to N. Mexico. 1818. (B.M. 2910 as *V. bracteosa.*)

V. bracteo'sa. A synonym of *V. bracteata.*

V. brasilien'sis. Erect perennial, 3 to 5 ft. h., differing chiefly from *V. bonariensis* in having its l. cuneate-attenuate to the sessile or scarcely stalked base. Trop. America. 1904.

V. canaden'sis. Pubescent or glabrate perennial, to 2 ft. h.; stems decumbent or ascending, rooting at the lower nodes, slender, usually branched. *l.* membranous, ovate or ovate-oblong, 1 to $3\frac{1}{2}$ in. long, $\frac{3}{8}$ to $1\frac{1}{2}$ in. wide, truncate or cuneate at base and narrowed into a margined petiole, incised or incised-pinnatifid or 3-cleft. *Spikes* stalked, fascicle-like in anthesis, elongated in fr.; bractlets shorter than or rarely as long as cal., cal. glandular-hirsute, $\frac{2}{5}$ to $\frac{3}{5}$ in. long, the lobes subulate-setaceous, unequal; cor. lavender, blue, rose-pink, purple, or magenta, rarely white, tube twice as long as cal., limb $\frac{2}{5}$ to $\frac{3}{5}$ in. wide. Cent. and S. United States. 1774. (B.M. 9. 308 and B.R. 4. 294 as *V. Aubletia.*) Hardy and variable. var. **atroviola'cea,** *fl.* dark violet; **candidiss'ima,** *fl.* white; **compac'ta,** habit compact; **Drummond'ii,** *l.* 2-pinnatifid, cal. only $\frac{2}{5}$ in. or less long (B.R. 10. 1925 as *V. Aubletia Drummondii.*); **grandiflo'ra,** especially large *fl.*; **Lambert'i,** *l.* pinnatifid lanceolate or ovate-lanceolate, cuneate at the base, cal. more than $\frac{2}{5}$ in. long (B.M. 48. 2200 as *V. Lamberti*, S.B.F.G. 2. 4. 363 as *V. Lamberti rosea* with paler, fragrant, larger fl.). Typical *V. canadensis* has l. pinnatifid broadly ovate to deltoid, cordate or broadly truncate at the base, cal. $\frac{9}{20}$ in. long. Border.

V. caroli'na. Slender perennial, 2 to 3 ft. h., erect or ascending; stems 4-angled. *l.* lanceolate or lanceolate-oblong, 1 to 3 in. long, $\frac{1}{3}$ to $\frac{3}{4}$ in. wide, cuneate-based, short-stalked, acute, coarsely and irregularly serrate. *infl.* paniculate, the spikes very slender; bractlets ovate-subulate, about half as long as cal.; cal. $\frac{3}{5}$ to $\frac{4}{5}$ in. long; cor. pale lavender, blue, mauve, or light purple. W. United States to El Salvador. 1814.

V. chamaedrifo'lia. A synonym of *V. peruviana.*

V. chamaedryoi'des. Applied to a race of *V. peruviana.*

V. cocci'nea. A trade name applying mostly to *V. peruviana.*

V. compac'ta. Trade name for a compact-growing race of *V. canadensis.*

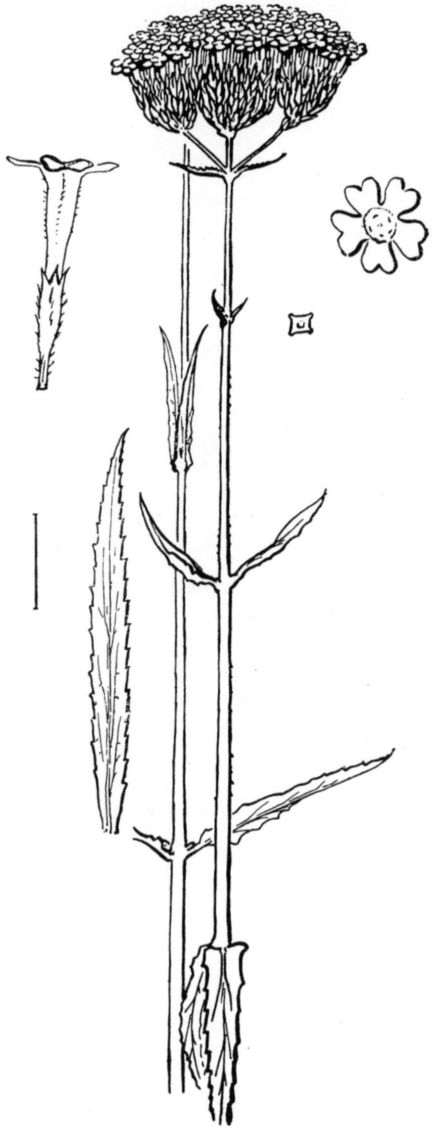

Verbena bonariensis

V. corymbo'sa.* Perennial, about 3 ft. tall, spreading underground; stems 4-angled, corymbosely branched above *l.* oblong or ovate, often almost triangular, 1 to $2\frac{1}{2}$ in. long, to 1 in. wide, short-stalked, truncate at base, acute, rigid, rugose, unequally toothed, often with a small toothed or entire lobe on each side near the base. *infl.* a terminal corymbose panicle, the spikes short, very dense; bractlets from half as long to almost equalling cal.; cal. about $\frac{1}{6}$ in. long, cor. tube twice as long as cal. reddish-purple, limb heliotrope-blue, lobes about $\frac{1}{8}$ in. long. Summer. Southern S. America. 1928. (B.M. 9361.) Hardy; best in moist soil in sun.

V.×Covas'ii. Hybrid between *V. santiaguensis* and *V. laciniata*, with intermediate characters. Garden origin. 1945.

V.×Dermen'ii. Hybrid between *V. hispida* and *V. bonariensis*, with intermediate characters. Bolivia and Paraguay. 1936.

V. dissec'ta. Whitish-hairy annual, with decumbent stems; branches slender, erect. *l.* ovate 3-partite-pinnatifid, $\frac{3}{8}$ to $1\frac{1}{2}$ in. long, cuneate at base, decurrent into the petiole, the segs. linear-oblong, rather blunt. *Spikes* fastigiate, very densely many-fld., hardly elongating in fr.; bractlets oblong, about $\frac{1}{10}$ in. long, much shorter than the densely white-pubescent cal.; cor. violet, tube slightly longer than cal.; anther-appendages blackish. Southern S. America. 1920.

V. e'legans. Spreading annual, with procumbent hairy stems and ascending hispidulous branches, often purplish. *l.* ovate, pinnatifid-laciniate, 1 to $2\frac{1}{2}$ in. long, $\frac{1}{2}$ to $1\frac{1}{3}$ in. wide, cuneate at base and decurrent into the petiole, segs. broadly oblong, rather blunt. *Spikes* terminal, capitate, rather few-fld. but dense, compact, usually not much elongating after anthesis; bractlets lanceolate, about equalling cal.; cal. almost $\frac{2}{5}$ in. long; cor. magenta-purple, tube about twice as long as cal., limb about $\frac{1}{2}$ in. wide. Mexico. 1891. var. **asper'ata** stouter, more erect, with spikes densely many-fld., elongating after anthesis, and the hairs coarser and hardly or not at all glandular. Texas, Mexico. 1883.

V. ×Engelman'nii. Hybrid between *V. hastata* and *V. urticifolia*, with intermediate characters. Cor. pale blue. N. and cent. United States. 1814.

V. erinoi'des. A widely misapplied name, strictly a synonym of *V. laciniata*, but in the trade applied to various species, including *V. Berteri*, *V. dissecta*, and *V. tenuisecta*.

V. Goodding'ii. Stems usually several from a common base, erect or decumbent-ascending. *l.* $1\frac{1}{4}$ to 2 in. long, tapering at base into a short margined petiole, 3-cleft, the divisions coarsely toothed or incised. *Spikes* fascicle-like in anthesis, somewhat elongate in fr.; bractlets lanceolate, acuminate, usually a little shorter than cal.; cal. $\frac{7}{20}$ to $\frac{9}{20}$ in. long; cor. pink, lavender, or blue, tube very little longer than the cal., limb $\frac{3}{10}$ to $\frac{9}{20}$ in. wide. SW. United States, N. Mexico. 1929.

V. gra'cilis. Low diffusely branched annual or perennial; stem mostly erect, 8 to 16 in. h. tall, round-angled, branches decumbent to ascending. *l.* ovate or obovate, $\frac{3}{4}$ to $3\frac{1}{4}$ in. long, cuneate at base and narrowed into a margined petiole, incised-pinnatifid to pinnately cleft or 2-pinnatifid, the segs. oblong or lanceolate, rather acute. *Spikes* terminal, sessile, slender, rather sparsely fld.; bractlets linear, usually much longer than cal.; cal. about $\frac{1}{10}$ in. long; cor. lilac, tube somewhat longer than cal., limb about $\frac{1}{10}$ in. wide. SW. United States, Mexico. 1829.

V. hasta'ta. Slender, mostly unbranched perennial, 3 to 7 ft. h., sometimes short-branched above. *l.* oblong-lanceolate or lanceolate, stalked, acute or acuminate, 3 to 6 in. long, 2 to 3 in. wide, narrowed at base, serrate or incised-dentate, rarely pinnatifid, the lower sometimes 3-lobed at base. *Spikes* stiffly erect, paniculate, usually numerous, densely many-fld., compact; bractlets lanceolate-subulate, usually a little shorter than cal.; cal. about $\frac{3}{20}$ in. long; cor. violet, tube somewhat longer than cal., limb nearly $\frac{1}{5}$ in. wide. Canada, United States. 1827. (B.R. 1102, as *V. paniculata*.) var. **al'ba,** cor. white.

V. hir'ta. Low perennial; stems procumbent; branches ascending. *l.* often ternate, ovate, obovate, or rounded, sessile, cuneate at the base, coarsely serrate or few-toothed and almost 3-lobed. *Spikes* dense-fld.; bractlets lanceolate, acute, equalling or slightly shorter than cal.; cal. $\frac{3}{20}$ in. long; cor. blue or reddish, throat bearded, limb about $\frac{3}{20}$ in. wide. Brazil, N. Argentina. 1825.

V. his'pida. Perennial, 1 to $1\frac{1}{2}$ ft. tall; stems erect or ascending, sharply 4-angled, many-branched. *l.* ovate-lanceolate or lanceolate, acute or acuminate, sessile, cuneate-attenuate to the cordate-clasping base, soft-textured, coarsely and unequally serrate or incised, sometimes 3-fid. *Spikes* terminal, often ternate, very dense, cylindric, to about 3 in. long; bractlets lanceolate, equalling or surpassing the cal.; cal. about $\frac{1}{10}$ in. long; cor. pale lilac, violet, purple, or blue, tube about twice as long as cal., limb very small. Southern S. America. 1835.

V. horten'sis. A synonym of *V.×hybrida*.

V. ×hybrida.* Common Garden Verbena, Florists' Verbena. Perennial (grown as an annual), with spreading or compact growth; stems mostly procumbent or ascending, rooting at the nodes; branches numerous. *l.* lanceolate or ovate, $\frac{1}{2}$ to $2\frac{3}{4}$ in. long, $\frac{1}{3}$ to $1\frac{1}{2}$ in. wide, acute, truncate at base or cuneately narrowed into the petiole, thick-textured, veins conspicuously impressed above and raised beneath, the margins irregularly incised-dentate with often lobe-like teeth. *infl.* terminal, large and showy, stalked. *Spikes* at first depressed and fascicle-like, later elongating, very densely many fld., the fl. close together; bractlets lanceolate, much shorter than cal.; cal. $\frac{3}{10}$ to $\frac{3}{5}$ in. long; cor. of various colours, usually with a white, cream, or yellow 'eye' of varying diameter, often very fragrant, tube $\frac{3}{5}$ to $1\frac{1}{5}$ in. long, limb $\frac{2}{5}$ to $\frac{9}{10}$ in. wide. Garden origin. 1837. There are at least 122 named varieties in the trade, most of which fall into the following: var. **auriculiflo'ra,** with the conspicuous central 'eye'; **stria'ta,** with striped cor.-lobes; **al'ba,** with white cor.; **caeru'lea,** blue; **ro'sea,** pink; **purpu'rea,** purple; **compac'ta,** of compact growth; **na'na,** very dwarf; **cocci'nea,** scarlet; **lu'tea,** yellow; **nigroviola'cea,** dark violet; **grandiflo'ra,** especially large-fld. Two of the best colours are **Lawrence Johnston,** deep crimson; **Firefly,** bright scarlet.

V. inci'sa. Spreading perennial, to 2 ft. h., often slightly woody at the base; stems ascending; branches erect. *l.* thin-textured, oblong-ovate or triangular (or the uppermost ones lanceolate), truncate or subcordate at base and cuneately attenuate into the petiole, coarsely incised-serrate. *Spikes* terminal, often in 3's or in a corymbose panicle, densely many-fld., at first fascicle-like, later elongating; bractlets ovate, one-quarter to one-third as long as the cal.; cal. about $\frac{2}{5}$ in. long, cor. scarlet, tube about $\frac{3}{5}$ in. long, limb $\frac{3}{10}$ in. wide. Southern S. America. 1826. (B.M. 3628.) Greenhouse.

V. ×Kond'ai. Hybrid between *V. racemosa* and *V. tenuisecta*, with intermediate characters. Garden origin. 1936.

V. lacinia'ta. Low annual, with creeping stems, rooting at the nodes, much branched; branches short, ascending. *l.* 3-parted or pinnatifid-laciniate, $\frac{1}{2}$ to $\frac{3}{4}$ in. long, the segs. oblong-lanceolate, acute or obtuse, entire or dentate. *Spikes* terminal, small, fascicle-like or slightly elongating, many-fld., stalked; bractlets about half as long as cal.; cal. about $\frac{1}{5}$ in. long; cor. red-violet, lavender, or blue, tube slightly longer than cal. Summer. Hardy. S. America. 1818. var. **contrac'ta** more compact (B.R. 1766 as *V. multifida contracta*); **Sabin'ii** is dwarfer, denser, more glabrous, with rich-purple cor. (S.B.F.G. 2. 347, as *V. Sabini*.)

V. Lambert'i. A narrow-leaved race of *V. canadensis*.

V. lasio'stachys. Perennial, with prostrate stems or erect and several ft. h., diffuse, much branched from the base. *l.* oval or oblong, $1\frac{1}{2}$ to $2\frac{1}{2}$ in. long, cuneately attenuate into the petiole, obtuse or acute, coarsely and irregularly serrate or incised, sometimes 3-fid at base. *Spikes* terminal, panicled, much elongated, often 18 to 20 in. long, slender, densely many-fld.; bractlets one-third to half as long as cal.; cal. about $\frac{3}{20}$ in. long; cor. bluish, tube somewhat surpassing cal. Western N. America. 1812.

V. ×Lecoc'qi. Hybrid between *V. hispida* and *V. lasiostachys*, with intermediate characters. Garden origin. 1936.

V. litora'lis. Perennial, to 3 ft. h.; stems 4-angular, branched above. *l.* lanceolate or oblong, tapering into a very short petiole or almost sessile, $1\frac{1}{4}$ to 4 in. long, more or less sharply and coarsely serrate. *Spikes* terminal, cymose or paniculate, often elongate, slender, loosely fld.; bractlets usually about as long as cal. about $\frac{1}{10}$ in. long; cor. blue, lavender, or purple, tube somewhat longer than cal., limb about $\frac{1}{10}$ in. wide. S. United States to Argentina and Chile. 1875.

V. Macdougal'ii. Coarse perennial; stems stout, rarely branched, 1 to 3 ft. h. *l.* oblong-elliptic or elongate-ovate, $2\frac{1}{2}$ to 4 in. long, shortly or scarcely petioled, coarsely and irregularly serrate. *Spikes* solitary or several, short-stalked, thick, dense both in anthesis and fr., 2 to 10 in. long; bractlets usually surpassing the cal.; cal. $\frac{1}{5}$ in. long; cor. deep purple, tube scarcely longer than cal., limb about $\frac{1}{4}$ in. wide. SW. United States. 1927.

V. ×matriten'sis. Hybrid between *V. carolina* and *V. hastata*, with intermediate characters. Garden origin.

V. melin'dres. A race of *V. peruviana*.

V. melindroi'des. A variety of *V. peruviana*.

V. melissoi'des. A synonym of *V. peruviana*.

V. mendoci'na. Very similar to *V. tenuisecta*, but with l.-segs. broader, oblong, not uniform in diameter, mostly $\frac{1}{20}$ in. or more wide, cor.-tube $\frac{2}{5}$ in. long, limb $\frac{1}{5}$ in. wide, bractlets about $\frac{1}{5}$ in. long, and whole plant usually more persistently whitish-strigose. Uruguay, Argentina. 1945.

V. menthifo'lia. Very similar to *V. officinalis*. SW. United States, NW. Mexico.

V. ×monacen'sis. Stems prostrate, ascending toward the tips, branched, sharply 4-angled. *l.* deeply 3-fid, narrowed at base into the winged petiole, the segs. incised, the individual lobes elliptic or oblanceolate, mostly blunt. *infl.* solitary, terminal, at first fascicle-like, later elongating, densely many-fld.; bractlets about $\frac{1}{5}$ in. long; cal. $\frac{3}{10}$ in. long; cor. large, showy, tube half again as long as cal., limb about $\frac{3}{10}$ in. wide. Garden origin. 1823.

V. multi'fida. A synonym of *V. laciniata*.

V. ×Noack'ii. Hybrid between *V. hispida* and *V. hastata*, with intermediate characters. Garden origin. 1936.

V. officina'lis. Vervain, Pigeon's Grass. Annual; stems 4-angled, ascending or spreading, 1 to 3 ft. h., diffusely branched. *l.* the lower ones ovate, oblong, or obovate, 1 to 3 in. long, narrowed into margined petioles, deeply incised or 1 to 2-pinnatifid, the upper ones linear or lanceolate, acute, entire, sessile. *Spikes* paniculate, very slender, mostly 4 to 5 in. long; bractlets shorter than the cal.; cor. purplish or lavender, very tiny, limb $\frac{1}{20}$ to $\frac{1}{10}$ in. wide. Europe. 1737. var. **Gaudichaud'ii,** an Australian variety with the body even of the lower l. linear-oblong and narrow; **macrosta'chya,** spikes uniformly elongated, to 18 in. long and very coarsely glandular-puberulent.

V. panicula'ta. A synonym of *V. hastata*.

V. peruvia'na. Low procumbent half-hardy perennial with slender creeping forking stems rooting at the nodes, the tips and branches ascending. *l.* oblong or ovate, broadly cuneate at base and narrowed into an extremely short petiole, crenate or almost incised-dentate. *Spikes* solitary, long-stalked, ascending, densely corymbose-fld.; bractlets less than half as long as the cal.; cor. bright scarlet, very showy, tube somewhat surpassing cal., limb almost $\frac{2}{5}$ in. wide. Southern S. America. 1827. (B.M. 3333 as *V. chamaedrifolia*; S.B.F.G. 2. 9 as *V. melissoides*.) Often recommended for rock-gardens, but tender. Plants offered in the trade as var. **melind'res** have oblong to oblong-lanceolate unequally incised-serrate less hairy l. (B.R. 1184 and L.B.C. 1514, as *V. melindres*.) The strain called *V. chamaedryoides* has somewhat more numerous and more shallow teeth; **melindroi'des** has ovate doubly crenate-serrate more densely hairy l.; **glabriuscula** has almost smooth l.; **rosea,** cor. pink.

V. phlogiflo'ra. Sprawling perennial with ascending stems often several ft. tall and numerous widespreading or erect branches. *l.* oblong or lanceolate, acute, cuneate and narrowed into the petiole at base, otherwise unequally subincised-serrate. *Spikes* terminal, stalked, solitary or ternate, sometimes cymose-paniculate and densely crowded, not elongating after anthesis; bractlets half as long as cal; cal. about $\frac{1}{2}$ in. long; cor. purple, lilac, red, or blue, tube about 1 in. long, limb to $\frac{3}{4}$ in. wide. Summer. Southern S. America. 1834. Greenhouse. (B.M. 3541 and S.B.F.G. 2. 391 as *V. Tweediana.*)

Verbena peruviana (p. 2211)

V. plate'nsis. Tufted perennial; stems and branches ascending-erect or rooting at the nodes near the base. *l.* ovate or oblong-triangular, 1 to 2 in. long, shortly cuneate and entire at the base and narrowed into the short petiole, acute, sinuately serrate with obtuse teeth above the base, thick-textured. *Spikes* terminal, solitary, very dense, mostly considerably elongated even in anthesis with closely imbricate fl.; bractlets about half as long as cal.; cal. about $\frac{3}{4}$ in. long; cor. large, white or rarely pinkish, fragrant at night, the tube $\frac{3}{4}$ to 1 in. long, limb $\frac{3}{5}$ in. wide. Summer, autumn. Southern S. America. 1837. (B.M. 3694, as *V. teucrioides.*) Greenhouse.

V. pogosto'ma. Diffuse greyish perennial to $1\frac{1}{2}$ ft. *l.* 3-fid, the segs. pinnatifid, lobes linear. *Spikes* terminal, cylindric, dense; bractlets almost as long as cal.; cal. $\frac{1}{4}$ in. long; cor. deep blue, limb about $\frac{1}{4}$ in. wide.

V. pulchel'la. Much-branched, creeping perennial with ascending branches. *l.* pinnatifid-dissected, ovate, 1 to $1\frac{1}{2}$ in. long, narrowed into a winged petiole, the segs. broad, oblong, rather acute. *Spikes* terminal, stalked, solitary or ternate, densely congested-capitate, not elongating after anthesis; bractlets less than half as long as cal. cal. $\frac{1}{4}$ to $\frac{7}{20}$ in. long; cor. violet or white, tube scarcely surpassing cal., limb about $\frac{1}{4}$ in. wide. Brazil to Argentina. 1827. (S.B.F.G. 295.)

V. radica'ns. Procumbent perennial, with stems rooting at the base. *l.* 3-fid, the segs. again 3-fid, the lobes oblong-linear, somewhat fleshy. *Spikes* short, almost capitate; bractlets half as long as cal.; cal. about $\frac{3}{10}$ in. long; cor. lilac, fragrant, its tube about twice as long as cal., limb about $\frac{2}{5}$ in. wide. Summer, autumn. Andes of Argentina, Chile. 1832. Almost hardy, but cuttings should be wintered in frames.

V. rec'ta. Low erect perennial; stems 1 to 2 ft. tall, 4-angled. *l.* ovate-lanceolate, thin-textured, 2 to $3\frac{1}{2}$ in. long, $\frac{3}{4}$ to 1 in. wide, acute, sharply and somewhat irregularly serrate, cuneately narrowed into the petiole at base. *Spikes* short, dense-fld., mostly $1\frac{1}{2}$ to 3 in. long, not elongating much after anthesis; bractlets equalling the cal., about $\frac{1}{20}$ in. long; cor. magenta-lavender, tiny, tube barely surpassing cal., limb scarcely $\frac{1}{20}$ in. wide. Mexico. 1819.

V. ri'gida. Stiff perennial with tuberous roots; stems ascending or erect, little-branched,to 2 ft. tall, leafy, 4-angled. *l.* oblong, very rigid, sessile, clasping at base, acute, irregularly dentate with wide-spreading teeth, rough to touch. *Spikes* terminal, in 3's, the lateral ones stalked, densely congested, later elongating to 1 or 2 in. and cylindric; bractlets surpassing cal.; cal. about $\frac{3}{20}$ in. long; cor. purple or magenta, tube 2 or 3 times as long as cal., limb about $\frac{1}{5}$ in. wide. Brazil to Argentina. 1830. (B.M. 3127 and S.B.F.G. 2. 207 as *V. venosa*; S.B.F.G. 2. 318 as *V. rugosa.*) A good bedding plant, the tubers of which may be kept like dahlias over winter. var. **al'ba,** *fl.* white; **lilaci'na,** *fl.* lilac-bluish.

V. robus'ta. Erect perennial $1\frac{1}{2}$ to 2 ft. h., stiffly erect; stems sharply 4-angled, branched from the base; branches ascending or erect. *l.* ovate, $1\frac{1}{2}$ to 3 in. long, rounded at apex, cuneately narrowed at base into the winged petiole, irregularly sharp-serrate, very rough to touch. *Spikes* panicled, thick, densely many-fld. even after anthesis; bractlets equalling or surpassing cal.; cal. about $\frac{1}{10}$ in. long; cor.-tube about $\frac{1}{5}$ in. long, limb to $\frac{1}{10}$ in. wide. Western N. America. 1843.

V. rugo'sa. A name as used by horticulturists synonymous with *V. rigida.*

V. Runyo'nii. Tall annual herb; stems erect, rather stout, sharply 4-angled. *l.* sessile, clasping, $\frac{3}{4}$ to $2\frac{1}{2}$ in. long, more or less 3-parted, each division pinnatifid-incised with broad acute teeth. *Spikes* panicled, $5\frac{1}{2}$ to $9\frac{1}{2}$ in. long, rather closely many-fld.; bractlets equalling cal.; cal. about $\frac{1}{10}$ in. long; cor. blue, tube about $\frac{1}{5}$ in. long, limb about $\frac{1}{10}$ in. wide. Texas. 1901.

V. santiaguen'sis. Very similar to *V. tenuisecta*, but with l.-segs. broader, oblong, not uniform in width, mostly $\frac{1}{20}$ in. or more wide, the cor.-tube less than $\frac{2}{5}$ in. long, its limb only about $\frac{1}{10}$ in. wide, and the spikes densely congested even after anthesis, not elongating. Uruguay, Argentina. 1943.

V. scab'rido-glandulo'sa. Shrub 9 to 18 in. h., up to 3 ft. across, with rigid interlacing branches. *l.* linear, linear-oblong or lanceolate, usually entire, rarely with a short basal lobe on each side, about $\frac{1}{5}$ in. long, $\frac{1}{20}$ in. wide. *infl.* long-stalked, terminal capitate, 5- to 12-fld.; bractlets oblanceolate, $\frac{3}{20}$ in. long; cal. about $\frac{1}{5}$ in. long; cor. light mauve, tube about $\frac{7}{20}$ in. long, limb $\frac{3}{10}$ in. across. Argentina. 1926. (G.C. 88 (1930), 133 as *V. thymifolia*; B.M. n.s. 98.) SYN. *Junellia scabrido-glandulosa.* Delightfully scented rock-garden shrub.

V.×Schnack'ii. A hybrid between *V. peruviana* and *V. megapotamica*, with intermediate characters. Garden origin. 1945.

V. sim'plex. Perennial, 4 to 20 in. h.; stems chiefly erect, simple or sparingly branched above, the branches ascending, *l.* linear, narrowly oblong, lanceolate, or spatulate, $1\frac{1}{4}$ to 4 in. long, tapering to a subsessile base, obtuse or rather acute, rather sparsely serrate. *Spikes* slender, terminal, erect, usually densely many-fld.; bractlets commonly shorter than the cal.; cal. $\frac{1}{5}$ in. long; cor. deep-lavender or purple, tube scarcely longer than cal., limb $\frac{1}{4}$ in. wide. Eastern N. America. 1814.

V. stric'ta. Rather coarse erect perennial, 1 to 3 ft. h.; stems simple or branched above. *l.* oval or suborbicular, $2\frac{1}{2}$ to 4 in. long, sessile or nearly so, thickish, sharply 2-serrate. *Spikes* solitary or several, short-stalked, thick, usually quite dense; bractlets about as long as cal.; cal. about $\frac{1}{5}$ in. long; cor. blue or purple, tube slightly longer than cal., limb $\frac{3}{10}$ in. wide. N. America. 1800.

V.×Suksdor'fii. Hybrid between *V. officinalis* and *V. lasiostachys* var. *septentrionalis*, with intermediate characters; it sets hardly any fr. Garden origin. 1904.

V. sulphu'rea. Perennial, sometimes slightly woody at base, to 2 ft. h.; stems procumbent; branches ascending or erect, 4-angled. *l.* pinnatifid or almost 2-pinnatifid, the segs. all linear, rather uniform, blunt, widespreading. *Spikes* long-stalked, capitate, densely many-fld., not elongating after anthesis; bractlets shorter than or almost equalling cal.; cal. about $\frac{1}{4}$ in. long; cor. pale sulphur-yellow, rather large, tube about $\frac{2}{5}$ in. long, limb to $\frac{3}{10}$ in. wide; anther-appendages violet, exserted. Chile. 1832. (B.R. 1748 and S.B.F.G. 2. 221.) Greenhouse.

V. supi'na. Low annual, usually much branched from the base, the stems and branches procumbent, the tips often ascending or erect. *l.* many-parted or pinnatisect, cuneate at base and decurrent into the petiole, the ultimate segs. oblong, rather blunt, dentate-incised or 3-fid. *Spikes* terminal, solitary, slender, dense and short in anthesis, often elongated to 6 in. in fr.; bractlets about half as long as cal. or sometimes more elongate; cal. about $\frac{1}{10}$ in. long; cor. tiny, tube about $\frac{1}{10}$ in. long, limb $\frac{1}{20}$ in. wide. Mediterranean region and the Near East. 1819.

V.×Teas'ii. Hybrid between *V. tenuisecta* and *V.×hybrida*, with intermediate characters. Stems decumbent or ascending, abundantly branched; branches ascending, slender. *l.* very variable in shape and size, more or less deeply incised-pinnatifid, often more or less 3-parted, the lowest divisions usually again pinnatifid-incised, lobes sharply acute, body of blade and lowest lobes often relatively broad, with recurved secondary lobes. *Spikes* flattened and almost capitate, later elongating to 6 in. or more, very densely many-fld.; bractlets about one-third as long as the cal.; cal. $\frac{3}{10}$ to $\frac{1}{2}$ in. long; cor. showy, blue, purple, pink, or white, tube $\frac{2}{5}$ to $\frac{4}{5}$ in. long, limb $\frac{1}{5}$ to $\frac{7}{20}$ in. wide. Garden origin. 1926. Here belong the races called Albion, Bellaire, Ceres, Madge Roberts, Rowena, and Ruth.

V. tene'ra. A much misunderstood species, the name being often applied to *V. pulchella*, but in *V. tenera* the spikes elongate after anthesis and typically the plant is quite small; also confused with *V. tenuisecta*, from which it may be distinguished by its cal. hairs being ascending-spreading instead of appressed. Cultivated forms have *l.* closely resembling those of *V. dissecta* and *V. laciniata*, from both of which they differ in having bractlets about ⅕ in. long and cal. ⅜ in. long. Brazil to Argentina. 1832. var. **Maonett'ii,** Italian Verbena, cor. reddish-violet, the lobes rayed and margined white. Garden origin. 1855. (F.d.S. 1129; Gartenfl. 4. 142.) Here belongs the *V. alpina* of the trade.

V. tenuisec'ta. Moss Verbena. Perennial, with decumbent stems; branches divergent, ascending. *l.* triangular, ¾ to 1½ in. long, 3-partite-pinnatifid, the segs. all uniformly narrowly linear, mostly less than $\frac{1}{20}$ in. wide, entire or dentate, obtuse or acute. *Spikes* terminal, solitary, stalked, fastigiate, ovate-capitate and dense during anthesis, later elongating to 1½ in. or more; bractlets usually about one-quarter as long as cal.; cal. about $\frac{3}{10}$ in. long; cor. blue, purple, violet, or lilac, showy, tube $\frac{3}{20}$ to ⅕ in. longer than cal., limb about ⅜ in. wide. Southern S. America. 1837. In the trade this species is usually called *V. erinoides.* var. **al'ba,** cor. white. 1915.

V. teucrioi'des. A synonym of *V. platensis.*

V. tri'dens. *l.* crowded sessile, very small, less than $\frac{1}{10}$ in. long, divided into three rigid spiny lanceolate segs., with smaller crowded succulent l. in axil; cal. ⅙ in. long; bractlets much shorter than cal.; cor. tube about ⅜ in. long, limb nearly $\frac{3}{10}$ in. wide, white to lilac. Argentina (Patagonia). SYN. *Junellia tridens.*

V. tri'fida. Shrubby, to 3 ft. h., branches 4-angled, clustered in the l.-axils. *l.* clustered, ½ to 1 in. long, 2-fid or nearly so, cuneate at base, sessile, the segs. lanceolate, acuminate, the central one larger, entire or sometimes laciniate. *Spikes* terminal, conglomerate-capitate, very dense, subsessile, short; bractlets about equalling cal.; cal. about ⅓ in. long, conspicuously 5-parted; cor. purple, tube slightly longer than cal. Mexico, Colombia. 1818. Greenhouse. (P.F.G. 1. 169.) A curious plant.

V. triphyl'la. A synonym of *Lippia citriodora.*

V. Tweedia'na. A synonym of *V. phlogiflora.*

V. urticifo'lia. Erect perennial, 3 to 5 ft. h.; stems solitary, simple or more often branching above, 4-angled, branches upright. *l.* ovate, oblong, or oblong-lanceolate stalked or the uppermost sessile, coarsely serrate-dentate, very thin-textured, acute or acuminate, mostly rounded at base, 1½ to 5 in. long, glabrous or with scattered long hairs on the veins beneath. *Spikes* numerous, usually stiffly ascending and strigose, to 6 in. long, rather sparsely fld., bractlets about $\frac{1}{20}$ in. long; cal. scarcely $\frac{1}{10}$ in. long, stigose; cor. white, tube scarcely exserted, limb scarcely $\frac{1}{10}$ in. wide. Eastern and Cent. N. America. 1810. var. **leiocar'pa,** *l.* densely and uniformly puberulent or velvety beneath, the mature infl. branches usually very slender, loosely ascending or divergent, puberulent. Eastern and Cent. United States.

V. veno'sa. A synonym of *V. rigida.*

V. × **Wing'ei.** Hybrid between *V. tenera* and *V. canadensis*, with intermediate characters. Garden origin. 1938.

V. Wright'ii. Stems usually several from a common base, decumbent-ascending or erect, branched. *l.* almost sessile or contracted into short-margined petiole, ¾ to 1½ in. long, 2-pinnatifid or 3-fid, the divisions rather deeply incised, the ultimate segs. narrowly lanceolate. *Spikes* short-stalked, more or less compact even in fr.; bractlets shorter than cal.; cal. ¼ to $\frac{7}{20}$ in. long; cor. pink, lavender, rose, magenta, or purple, tube about $\frac{3}{20}$ in. long, limb about ¼ in. wide. SW. United States. 1937. (B.M. n.s. 409.)

V. xu'tha. Stems upright, 2 to 3½ ft. h., branched, hirsute-hispid. *l.* oblong or broadly ovate, 2 to 4½ in. long, incised-pinnatifid or more often 3-fid, the segs. coarsely dentate, the laterals much smaller than the middle and close to the sessile base. *Spikes* elongate, compact only at anthesis; bractlets almost equalling or a little shorter than cal.; cal. about $\frac{3}{20}$ in. long; cor. blue, lilac, or purple, tube about as long as cal., limb ⅕ to $\frac{3}{10}$ in. wide. S. United States. 1840.

H. N. M.

VERBENA, LEMON-SCENTED. *See* **Lippia citriodora (Aloysia triphylla).**

VERBENA OIL PLANT. *See* **Lippia citriodora.**

VERBENA, SAND. *See* **Abronia latifolia.**

VERBENA, SWEET-SCENTED. *See* **Lippia citriodora.**

VERBENA'CEAE. Dicotyledons. A family of over 3000 species in about 100 genera scattered over the warm and temperate regions of the Southern Hemisphere with a few in the North Temperate Zone. Herbs, shrubs, or trees with usually opposite or whorled leaves without stipules, simple or divided. Inflorescence spicate, often with a coloured involucre, or cymose. Flowers usually perfect, mostly zygomorphic but sometimes regular. Calyx 4- to 5- rarely 6- to 8-lobed. Corolla 5-lobed, usually with a long, cylindrical tube, and often 2-lipped mouth. Stamens rarely equalling number of petals, usually didynamous, or 2 with 2 or 3 staminodes; anthers introrse. Ovary superior, usually 4-lobed with 1 ovule in each lobe. Carpels 2 each divided into 2-cells; style usually terminal. Fruit drupe-like or a capsule. Several species are of economic importance. *Tectona grandis* is the important timber tree of Malaya, yielding teak. *Lippia citriodora* is the source of Verbena oil. The leaves of *Priva echinata* are used as tea in America. The tubers of *P. laevis* are edible. Citharexylum of S. America yields timber (fiddle-wood), some species of Lantana have edible fruit, and there are many ornamental plants among the genera treated here, viz. Amasonia, Baillonia, Bouchea, Callicarpa, Caryopteris, Citharexylum, Clerodendrum, Cornutia, Duranta, Faradaya, Gmelina, Holmskioldia, Lantana, Lippia, Monochilus, Oxera, Petrea, Premna, Priva, Rhaphithamnus, Spartothamnus, Stachytarpheta, Tectona, Verbena, Vitex.

verben'iflos, Verbena-flowered.

VERBESI'NA (from a supposed resemblance to some species of Verbena). FAM. *Compositae.* A genus of about 50 species of annual or perennial herbs, sub-shrubs, or rarely shrubs, natives of the warmer parts of America, few of which are of horticultural value. Leaves opposite or upper (or all) alternate, sometimes stalked, rarely entire. Flower-heads yellow or ray-florets white; involucral bracts oblong or linear in few series; receptacle convex or conical, paleaceous; ray-florets ligulate, spreading, entire or 2- or 3-toothed. Achenes glabrous or hairy. The genus contains stove, greenhouse, and hardy species all needing rich soil. They may be increased by seed, the perennials also by division. The following are perennial except *V. encelioides.*

V. croca'ta. About 2 ft. h., the branches 4-winged. *l.* opposite, decurrent, irregularly pinnately lobed; lobes oval, erosely toothed, the terminal somewhat deltoid. *fl.-heads* globose, solitary terminal; ray-florets orange-yellow. Summer. Mexico. 1812. (B.M. 1627 as *Spilanthes crocata.*)

V. encelioi'des. Erect, greyish-hairy annual, 2 to 3 ft. h. *l.* ovate or oblong, coarsely toothed; stalk broadly winged, auricled. *fl.-heads* yellow, somewhat corymbose. August. Achenes of rays wingless, 3-toothed, those of disk winged, 2-awned. Mexico. 1785. Greenhouse. SYN. *Ximenesia encelioides.*

V. gigante'a. Stems round, green. *l.* large, winged, glistening, green, alternate; lower ones decurrent; upper sessile, amplexicaul, pinnatipartite. *fl.-heads* white, ovate-oblong, in compound corymbs. Jamaica. Tender; useful in a young state for bedding.

V. pinnati'fida. About 3 ft. h., stem 4-winged, hairy. *l.* opposite, long-decurrent, pinnatifid, long wedge-shaped at base, downy on both sides especially on veins. *fl.-heads* pale yellow; involucral scales blackish, linear-lanceolate, acute; rays about 12, oblong; panicles opposite, branched, corymbose at apex. August. Mexico. 1826. Greenhouse.

V. Pur'pusii. About 1 ft. h. *l.* in a rosette, elliptic, 4 to 5 in. long. *fl.-heads* golden-yellow, 1¾ to 2 in. across, solitary on a scape 8 to 12 in. long. Mexico.

V. virgi'nica. About 2 ft. h. *l.* alternate, ovate-lanceolate, pinnately veined, toothed or lobed, downy below and on the decurrent wings which are sometimes interrupted. *fl.-heads* white in compound corymbs; ray-florets 3 or 4, oval. August. N. America. 1812. Hardy.

verecun'dus -a -um, modest.

VERGE-CUTTER. *See* **Edging-iron.**

ve'ris, of spring (*ver*, spring), hence spring-flowering; the medieval name *Primula veris* (from which the generic name Primula is derived) meant 'firstling of spring'.

vermicula'ris -is -e (***vermi,*** in compound words), worm-like.

VERMICULITE. This substance is formed from a micaceous ore found chiefly in U.S.A. but also in Uruguay, S. Africa, and Uganda. It is heated to about 2,000° F. when the flakes expand so that it forms a sterile highly porous medium. During this process the moisture content is converted to steam and expands the ore about 10 to 15 times its original volume. The resulting product is light in weight and highly absorbent and retentive of both air and water. In this form it is used as a compost for the rooting of cuttings or the raising of seeds. It has also been found successful for the cultivation of Lilies from scales. Before using, the Vermiculite should be soaked in a bucket and the surplus water squeezed out. Care must be taken in subsequent watering since the moisture is retained much longer than in the case of compost made chiefly of sand or pumice. Probably little further water beyond the initial soaking will be required before the cuttings are rooted. Since the Vermiculite contains no nutriment the cuttings should be potted up in other compost as soon as they are rooted. If it is desired to leave the young seedlings in Vermiculite, they should be watered weekly with a solution of a complete fertilizer.

It has been claimed that cuttings root more readily and that seeds, especially Lily seeds, germinate more quickly in this medium than in the more normal composts. In Gt. Britain Horticultural Vermiculite is often marketed under the trade name of 'Exflor', and there are two grades, a fine grade for very small seeds and a coarser grade for larger seeds and cuttings. Dry Vermiculite can be used for the storage of bulbs and tubers. Different kinds of Vermiculite vary in their pH value; some are too alkaline for horticultural use. The pH should be about neutral (pH 7).

Vermiculite is accepted by the U.S. Customs and Bureau of Plant Industry as a sterile substance and need not be washed from the roots of the plants on import as is required in the case of soil.

P. M. S.

Ver'nae, in honour of Verna, daughter of Herr Alwin Berger, one-time curator of the La Mortola garden.

verna'lis -is -e, vernal, appearing in spring.

VERNALIZATION. The word 'vernalization' is the anglicized form of the Russian word 'jarovisation', first coined by the plant physiologist Lysenko and meaning literally 'making spring-like'. Lysenko originally used the word in connexion with his studies on wheat, but it has since come to have a wide connotation. 'Winter' varieties of wheat sown in spring grow and tiller freely but fail more or less completely to form ears, although, when sown in early winter, they produce generally bigger crops than 'spring' varieties. It has been known for nearly a hundred years that if winter varieties are germinated at low temperatures and then stored till sowing in spring they will produce a normal crop. Similar results have been obtained with other cereals and with many other plants. The theory of vernalization embodies the conception that plants require, among other factors, a period at a particular temperature range to enable them to pass from the vegetative to the reproductive condition. In general, plants of temperate regions are enabled to flower, or are accelerated in flowering, by exposure to low temperatures at some time in their vegetative growth, while those of warm climates frequently require the reverse conditions and will only flower successfully if they have received a period at high temperatures. The time at which exposure to the required temperature conditions can occur is relatively independent of the stage of growth reached, and can be as effective on the just-germinated seed as on the growing plant. It is probable that many of the cases of annual and biennial plants 'running-to-seed' abnormally early, e.g. flowering of beet or carrots in the first season, are to be attributed to exposure of the young plants to temperatures low enough to 'vernalize' them. Such conditions may, for example, occur after the early sowing.

Temperature alone, however, is not the only factor concerned in producing the condition of 'ripeness-to-flower', and it is intimately related to the effect of length of day on this condition. The 'photoperiodic effect', as the influence of day-length on flowering is called, may be nullified or reinforced in particular cases by the temperature conditions (*see* **Light** in Supplement).

The concept of vernalization has been extended to other plants than annual and biennial seed-crops, in particular, to bulbs. It has been shown by Dutch and English workers that the temperature conditions during the later stages of growth of bulbs and during storage of the dry bulbs may have profound effects on the subsequent flowering of the new bulb. Thus, in hyacinths, in which the formation of the flower occurs during the storage period, high temperatures during this time accelerate flower formation and result in earlier flowering when the bulbs are later forced. This is the basis of the so-called 'preparation' of hyacinths for early flowering. With daffodils, however, the flower is formed in the bulb before lifting and acceleration of the time of subsequent flowering is obtained by low-temperature storage or 'precooling', a phenomenon analogous to the low temperature vernalization of temperate cereals.

R. H. S.

VERNATION. The disposition of leaves in the bud (cf. **aestivation**).

vernici'ferus -a -um, producing varnish.

vernico'sus -a -um, varnished.

ver'nix, varnish.

VERNON'IA (in honour of William Vernon, botanist and traveller in N. America, d. 1711). Fam. *Compositae*. A genus of about more than 600 species of annual or perennial herbs or shrubs or small trees, chiefly tropical, most widely represented in the warmer parts of America. Leaves alternate, entire or toothed, pinnately veined, sessile or stalked. Flower-heads purple, reddish, bluish, or rarely white, terminal, solitary, cymose or paniculate, homogamous; involucral bracts in many series, inner longest; receptacle naked or pitted, sometimes shortly hairy; florets all equal, tubular, slender, narrowly 5-cleft. Achenes striated, ribbed or angled, rarely terete; pappus of many hairs, often with an outer row of short hairs or flattened bristles. Few of the species are horticulturally valuable, most being of weedy habit. Those mentioned need rich, light-soil, and may be readily increased by seeds, cuttings, or divisions, according to the nature of the plant. A few species are hardy but most need either the greenhouse or the stove.

V. acutifo'lia. A synonym of *V. sericea.*

V. altis'sima. 5 to 10 ft. h. *l.* lanceolate or lanceolate-oblong, toothed, rather thin, veiny, glabrous above, hairy beneath; stalk short. *fl.-heads* purplish-violet, ½ in. h. or less, in a loose cyme, involucral scales blunt or acute, not acuminate. September to November. N. America. 1820. Syn. *V. praealta.* Wild garden. Hardy.

V. arkansa'na. A synonym of *V. crinita.*

V. axilliflo'ra. A synonym of *V. Cotoneaster.*

V. Baldwin'ii. 3 to 7 ft. h., hairy. *l.* oblong to ovate-lanceolate, 4 to 8 in. long. Involucral scales, greenish, acute or slender-pointed, tips spreading or reflexed. *fl.* purplish. July. August. Montana to Texas.

V. Calvoa'na. Stem stout, sulcate, branched, 8 to 12 ft. h., hairy. *l.* oblong-lanceolate, 8 to 14 in. long, slender-pointed, toothed, narrowed to unequally auriculate base; sessile. *fl.-heads* white, 2 in. across, with a purple eye; involucral scales, large, spreading, in many series; corymbs large, branching, spreading, bracts leafy, toothed. January. Cameroons. 1861. (B.M. 5698.) A fine stove shrub.

V. confer'ta. A slender-stemmed small tree, remarkable for its large *l.* up to 20 in. long, crowded at ends of branchlets. *fl.-heads* small, white. Trop. Africa.

V. Cotoneas'ter. Hairy shrub about 18 in. h., branches terete. *l.* oblong-elliptic, 8 to 14 in. long, acute, nearly entire, roughly hairy above, shaggy beneath; sessile. *fl.-heads* violet-purple, sessile, much shorter than bracts, in long, terminal, scorpioid cymes. September. Brazil. (L.B.C. 1690.) Stove.

V. crini'ta. 8 to 10 ft. h. erect, vigorous. *l.* linear-lanceolate, 4 to 12 in. long, glabrous or nearly so, toothed. *fl.-heads* 50- to 70-fld., purple; involucral scales green, tips filiform, often reddish; pappus often purplish. July to September. Montana to Texas. (Add. 166; G.C. 126 (1949), 1134 as *V. arkansana.*) var. **al'ba,** *fl.-heads* white.

V. fascicula'ta. Glabrous, 2 to 5 ft. h. *l.* linear to oblong-lanceolate, 3 to 6 in. long, thickish, veins obscure. *fl.-heads* numerous, crowded on branches of cyme, 20- to 30-fld.; involucral scales mostly blunt, closely appressed. July to September. Ohio to Texas.

V. glau'ca. 2 to 4 ft. h. *l.* ovate-lanceolate. *fl.-heads* purple; involucral scales usually with slender tips; pappus creamy or straw-coloured. E. United States.

V. noveboracen'sis. About 5 ft. h. *l.* lanceolate or oblong, 3 to 9 in. long. *fl.-heads* purple; involucral scales, brownish or purple, tipped with a long bristle; cymes open; pappus purplish or purplish tinged. August. E. United States. 1710. Wild garden. Hardy.

V. odoratis'sima. A synonym of *V. scabra.*

V. pinifo'lia. 1 to 2 ft. h., leafy. *l.* linear, 1 to 4 in. long, $\frac{1}{16}$ to $\frac{1}{8}$ in. wide, crowded, becoming glabrous above, margins revolute; sessile. *fl.-heads* bright purple, in flat-topped, many-fld. corymbs 3 to 8 in. across; involucral scales mucronate, grey-hairy. Summer. S. Africa. 1863. (B.M. 5412 as *Webbia pinifolia.*) Greenhouse perennial.

V. podoco'ma. Tall, branches, stalks and under surface of l. hairy. *l.* large, leathery. *fl.-heads* rose-purple, florets $\frac{1}{2}$ in. long; loosely arranged in a terminal panicle up to 3 ft. long and 3 ft. wide. Eastern Africa, Iran, Abyssinia to the Transvaal, Zululand. 1892. (B.M. 7255.) SYN. *V. Oliveriana.*

V. praeal'ta. A synonym of *V. altissima* and *V. noveboracensis.*

V. scab'ra. Shrub 4 ft. h., with terete branches. *l.* obovate, rigid, wedge-shaped at base, slightly toothed at apex, roughly hairy above, hairy and net-veined beneath. *fl.-heads* purple; involucral bracts slender-pointed; cymes paniculate. October. Venezuela. 1817. Stove.

V. seri'cea. Sub-shrub, 4 ft. h. *l.* lanceolate, slender-pointed, more or less obtuse at base, almost entire, nearly glabrous above, appressed hairy beneath; stalk very short. *fl.-heads* purple or white, sessile, solitary or twin in axils; involucre bell-shaped, outer scales recurved, mucronate, inner blunt. December. Brazil. 1823. (B.R. 522.) Stove.

V. stenoste'gia. Perennial herb about 18 in. h. with branched densely hairy stem. *l.* oblong, up to 5 in. long and 2 in. wide, but variable, sharply toothed, softly downy beneath with glistening glands. *fl.-heads* flattish in clusters of 2 to 4 at ends of branches, about $1\frac{1}{4}$ in. across, 50- to 70-fld., *fl.* rose-purple in bud becoming almost white; involucral bracts linear. Winter. Achenes finely ribbed, blackish. Nigeria. (B.M. 8981 as *Candidea stenostegia.*)

vernonoi'des, Vernonia-like.

ver'nus -a -um, of the spring.

VERO'NICA (possibly in honour of St. Veronica). FAM. *Scrophulariaceae.* Speedwell. A genus of about 250 species of small trees, shrubs, and annual or perennial herbs, the last mostly natives of the cooler parts of the N. Hemisphere, the trees and shrubs of New Zealand, Australia, Tasmania, New Guinea, and S. America. Leaves opposite, rarely alternate or whorled; floral leaves and bracts mostly alternate. Flowers in axillary or terminal racemes, sometimes in spikes or panicles, sometimes solitary; calyx usually 4-lobed, rarely 3- or 5-lobed; corolla with tube usually short and 4 (rarely 3, 5, or 6) lobes usually spreading; stamens 2; ovary and capsule 2-celled; seeds few or many.

The genus Veronica, as defined by Wettstein and accepted here, includes plants showing considerable diversity in size, habit of growth, relative length of corolla tube and lobes, form of the capsule, seed characters and chromosome number. Several botanists have accordingly tried to separate from Veronica proper a number of lesser genera more uniform in character, notably Paederota, Veronicastrum, and Hebe. **Paedero'ta** is a S. European and W. Asiatic group of dwarf herbaceous mountain-loving perennials with opposite leaves, a long corolla tube, and equally long lobes forming a 2-lipped flower; it includes *V. Bonarota* and *V. lutea.* **Veronicas'trum** is an American and E. Asiatic group of tall herbaceous perennials, mostly inhabiting open woodland and prairie, with whorled leaves, a long corolla tube and very short lobes forming an almost cylindric or narrowly funnel-shaped flower; the capsule is swollen and splits open by 4 short slits; this group includes *V. virginica* (*Veronicastrum virginicum*). **He'be** is not so well defined. It includes the shrubby New Zealand, Australian, New Guinea, and S. American species commonly represented in gardens by *V. brachysiphon, V. cupressoides, V. elliptica, V. Hulkeana, V. speciosa,* and hybrids, and is technically distinguished from the typical herbaceous Veronicas of Europe, Asia, and N. America by the capsule being thick-walled and dorsally compressed with the septum across the broadest diameter, and the chromosome numbers ($2n$) being 40, 42, 80, 84, or 120 (i.e. multiples of 20 and 21). Veronica proper has the capsule thin-walled and laterally compressed with the septum across the narrowest diameter; its chromosome numbers ($2n$) are mostly multiples of 7, 8, 9, 10. These characters are not, however, always combined; in some species one or two characters typical of the one group are associated with characters typical of the other group. Thus on the whole Hebe is probably better considered a part of Veronica than treated as generically distinct. It was first published as a genus in 1789, revived by Pennell in 1921, and accepted by many New Zealand botanists in 1926; since then the name Hebe has come into general use among gardeners in New Zealand and the United States. Although not accepted here, the alternative names under Hebe, Paederota, and Veronicastrum are given below.

All the Veronicas are easy to cultivate provided the climate suits them. The herbaceous kinds include excellent border plants, such as *V. longifolia* and *V. Teucrium thracica,* but most of them on account of their low growth are better suited to the rock garden, where such carpeting species as *V. prostrata* provide a good cover for sunny slopes, while others, like *V. bombycina,* are choice enough for the scree or alpine house. A few rank-growing aquatic perennials sometimes appear as weeds in water-gardens and may be grown in aquaria. The annual species are likewise best regarded as weeds since their flowers are mostly small, an exception being *V. persica,* and they seed freely among alpines and tend to overgrow choice plants. The herbaceous kinds are mostly very hardy, but some of the sub-shrubs and many of the truly shrubby species, the typical Hebes, are more or less tender. Practically the whole of the Hebes are perfectly at home in the south-western counties of England and other places with mild climatic conditions, but comparatively few can withstand the hardest winters in eastern England. Some of the New Zealand species, e.g. *V. speciosa,* grow in nature close to the sea and thus are good for sea-side planting. Moreover, like most New Zealand plants, they are usually very wind-resistant; in this connexion *V. Dieffenbachii, V. elliptica,* and *V. salicifolia* and hybrids derived from them, such as Blue Gem, especially deserve mention. The New Zealand Veronicas of this type are handsome both in leaf and flower; indeed, the rather tender *V. Hulkeana* is among the most beautiful of flowering shrubs. Other species such as *V. cupressoides, V. Hectori,* and *V. lycopodioides,* the 'whipcord Veronicas', have very small rather insignificant flowers but are remarkable when mature for their short scale-like leaves in which they mimic plants of such unrelated genera as Cupressus, Lycopodium, and Salicornia; the leaves of young seedling plants are, however, larger and more spreading and shoots with such juvenile leaves sometimes appear on mature bushes. The juvenile forms are said to remain permanent so long as they are kept in a warm moist atmosphere. These shrubby species are propagated by cuttings of young wood about 4 in. long from June to August. The dwarf herbaceous kinds are propagated by division in August or March to April or by cuttings from June to September.

The following key includes most of the species likely to be found in gardens, among them some common and widespread weeds, but not all of those described below.

Hybrids are especially frequent among the shrubby Veronicas, and it is impossible to recognize them by means of a short and simple key. Moreover, some of the species are extremely variable, notably *V. Teucrium* as commonly accepted by botanists. Those who wish for further information on this large and complicated genus are accordingly referred to T. F. Cheeseman's *Manual of the New Zealand Flora*, 2nd ed. (1925), and supplementary papers by L. Cockayne and H. H. Allan in *Transactions of New Zealand Institute* for the New Zealand species and to a systematic list of names and synonyms (but not descriptions) by G. Stroh in *Beihefte zum Botanischen Centralblatt*, 61. B. 384–451 (1942); descriptions in German of most of these will be found in a work by H. Römpp in Fedde, *Repertorium, Beihefte* 50 (1931). A detailed account of *V. Teucrium* and allies by B. Watzl has been published in *Abhandl. zool.-bot. Gesellschaft, Wien* 5, part 5 (1910), of *V. spicata* and allies by A. Härle in *Bibliotheca Botanica*, 104 (1932), and of *V. Chamaedrys* and allies by R. Riek in Fedde, *Repertorium, Beihefte*, 79 (1935). **A**

W. T. S.

KEY

1. *Erect or decumbent shrubs or small trees (Hebe)* 2

1. *Herbs, sometimes woody at base* 49

2 (1). *Lvs. entire, rarely very minutely toothed* 3

2. *Lvs. with roundish or sharp teeth* 45

3 (2). *Shrubs or small trees; lvs.* 1 *to* 6 *in. long. not imbricate; racemes many-fld., longer than lvs.* 4

3. *Shrubs; lvs. usually under* 1 *in. long* 17

4 (3). *Lvs. obovate, oblong-lanceolate, or lanceolate, usually over* $\frac{1}{3}$ *in. wide* 5

4. *Lvs. less than* $\frac{1}{3}$ *in. wide* 14

5 (4). *Erect or spreading shrubs or small trees* 6

5. *Prostrate or trailing; lvs.* $\frac{1}{2}$ *to* $1\frac{1}{2}$ *in. long, oblong to elliptic-oblong, obtuse* V. chathamica

6 (5). *Lvs.* 2 *to* 6 *in. long* 7

6. *Lvs. usually not over* $2\frac{1}{2}$ *in. long* 11

7 (6). *Lvs. obovate, obtuse, dark green; racemes little longer than lvs., broad, dense* V. speciosa

7. *Lvs. linear-oblong to lanceolate* 8

8 (7). *Lvs. linear-oblong, pale green,* 2 *to* 4 *in. long* V. Dieffenbachii

8. *Lvs.* 2 *to* 6 *in. long, lanceolate, acute* 9

9 (8). *Fl.* $\frac{1}{6}$ *in. across; capsule up to* $\frac{1}{6}$ *in. wide, scarcely twice as long as cal.* 10

9. *Fl.* $\frac{1}{4}$ *to* $\frac{1}{3}$ *in. across; capsule* $\frac{1}{4}$ *to* $\frac{1}{3}$ *in. wide,* 3 *times as long as cal.* V. macrocarpa

10 (9). *Shrub; racemes longer than lvs.; cor. tube distinctly longer than cal.* V. salicifolia

10. *Tree; racemes shorter than lvs.; cor. tube scarcely longer than cal.* V. gigantea

11 (6). *Lvs.* 1 *to* 2 *in. long, linear-oblong to oblong-lanceolate, rather blunt, glabrous* V. ligustrifolia

11. *Lvs.* 1 *to* 3 *in. long, obovate-oblong to elliptic-oblong* 12

12 (11). *Lvs. obovate-oblong to linear-oblong; racemes long, curved* V. macroura

12. *Lvs. elliptic-oblong to lanceolate-oblong; racemes straight* 13

13 (12). *Lvs.* 1 *to* 3 *in. long, glabrous; racemes lax; fl. white* V. amabilis

13. *Lvs.* 1 *to* $2\frac{1}{2}$ *in. long, margins softly downy; racemes dense; fl. bluish-white* V. Lewisii

14 (4). *Racemes longer than lvs.* 15

14. *Racemes about equal to lvs; cal.-teeth about half as long as cor. tube* V. parviflora

15 (14). *Lvs. acute* 16

15. *Lvs. obtuse,* $\frac{3}{4}$ *to* $1\frac{1}{4}$ *in. long; cal. teeth as in* V. parviflora V. leiophylla

16 (15). *Lvs. often deflexed, narrow linear; cal. teeth much shorter than cor. tube* V. angustifolia

16. *Lvs. flat, lanceolate; cal. teeth nearly as long as cor. tube* V. gracillima

17 (3). *Shrubs erect or decumbent at base only (but see* V. pimeleoides) 18

17. *Shrubs spreading, decumbent or prostrate; lvs. small* 43

18 (17). *Lvs. fairly large, not scale-like, all of one form* 19

18. *Lvs. small, those of mature plants short, thick, scale-like, those of young plants and reverted shoots longer, spreading* 38

19 (18). *Fl. in racemes* 20

19. *Fl. in usually simple spikes (racemes in* V. decumbens) 30

20 (19). *Racemes branched as a rule* 21

20. *Racemes simple as a rule* 24

21 (20). *Lvs. rarely over* $\frac{1}{2}$ *in. long, obtuse, keeled* V. laevis

21. *Lvs. over* $\frac{1}{2}$ *in. long* 22

22 (23). *Cal.* 4*-toothed, teeth acute; lvs. glaucous* 23

22. *Cal. usually* 3*-toothed, teeth obtuse; fl. white; lvs. dark green* V. diosmifolia

23 (22). *Lvs. oblong-obovate, entire; fl. lavender* V. insularis

23. *Lvs. linear-oblong, often toothed; fl. white or lavender* V. Colensoi

24 (20). *Lvs. usually less than* $\frac{3}{4}$ *in. long* 25

24. *Lvs. usually over* $\frac{3}{4}$ *in. long* 27

25 (24). *Lvs. green or glaucous, minutely ciliate when young* 26

25. *Lvs. bright green with red margins* V. Balfouriana

26 (25). *Lvs. ovate-lanceolate, acute, glaucous* V. Darwiniana

26. *Lvs. obovate-oblong, blunt, often apparently* 2*-ranked* V. vernicosa

27 (24). *Glabrous throughout* 28

27. *Branchlets and l.-margins hairy; fl.* $\frac{1}{2}$ *in. across, fragrant* V. elliptica

28 (27). *Lvs. blunt, flat* 29

28. *Lvs. acute, keeled; fl. white, about* $\frac{1}{4}$ *in. across* 117

29 (28). *Lvs. oblong; fl. often purplish,* $\frac{1}{3}$ *in. across* V. Matthewsii

29. *Lvs. narrow obovate; fl. white* $\frac{1}{3}$ *in. across* V. obovata

30 (19). *Lvs. not over* $\frac{1}{8}$ *in. long* 31

30. *Lvs. usually over* $\frac{1}{8}$ *in. long* 32

31 (30). *Fl. white; lvs. broadly oblong to roundish, concave, nerveless* V. Buchananii

31. *Fl. dark purplish-blue; lvs. glaucous, keeled* V. pimeleoides

32 (30). *Lvs. red-margined* 33

32. *Lvs. not red-margined* 34

33 (32). *Shoots shiny purplish-black; lvs. almost flat* V. decumbens

33. *Shoots with two rows of hair; lvs. concave, glaucous* V. pinguifolia

34 (32). *L.-margins very hairy* V. Gibbsii

34. *L.-margins not hairy* 35

35 (34). *Lvs. keeled* 36

35. *Lvs. nerveless* 37

36 (35). *Lvs. obovate-oblong, closely overlapping, truncate or somewhat heart-shaped at base* V. buxifolia

36. *Lvs. linear-oblong, spreading; cor. often* 3*-lobed* V. anomala

37 (35). *Lvs. obovate to roundish; spikes short, crowded* V. carnosula

37. *Lvs. stem-clasping or cordate at base; spikes* 1 *to* $1\frac{1}{2}$ *in. long* V. amplexicaulis

38 (18). *Lvs. in remote decussate pairs* V. cupressoides

38. *Lvs. densely overlapping with the opposite pairs joined and hiding the branch* 39

39 (38). *Branchlets* 4*-angled* V. lycopodioides

39. *Branchlets more or less terete* 40

40 (39). *Branchlets* $\frac{1}{8}$ *to* $\frac{1}{6}$ *in. in diameter* 41

40. *Branchlets* $\frac{1}{20}$ *to* $\frac{1}{12}$ *in. in diameter* 42

41 (40). *Blackish-brown when dry; ring of lvs.* $\frac{1}{10}$ *in. h.* V. Hectori

41. *Yellowish-green when dry; ring of lvs.* $\frac{1}{12}$ *in. h.* V. salicornioides

42 (41). *Branchlets about* $\frac{1}{15}$ *in. thick; lvs. forming an obconic sheath open at the top* V. Armstrongii

42. *Branchlets* $\frac{1}{20}$ *in. thick; lvs. forming a narrow sheath adnate to stem at base* V. propinqua

43 (17). *Fl.* $\frac{1}{8}$ *to* $\frac{1}{6}$ *in. across, in oblong or ovoid heads* 44

43. *Fl.* $\frac{1}{3}$ *to* $\frac{1}{2}$ *in. across, in loose racemes* V. Bidwillii

44 (43). *Lvs. fleshy, not keeled, erect or spreading* V. Haastii

44. *Lvs. leathery, keeled, spreading or recurved* V. epacridea

45 (2). *Fl. almost or quite sessile, in a many-fld. dense panicle or corymb* 46

45. *Fl. with pedicels* $\frac{1}{4}$ *to* 1 *in. long, in a loose raceme* 47

46 (45). *Lvs.* 1 *to* 2 *in. long; fl. in a large panicle, pale lilac, rarely white* V. Hulkeana

46. *Lvs.* $\frac{1}{3}$ *to* 1 *in. long; fl. in dense corymbs; white, but pink in bud* V. Lavaudiana

47 (44). *Stems prostrate at base, then ascending; lvs.* $\frac{1}{2}$ *to* 4 *in. long, lanceolate to ovate; plants* 6 *to* 24 *in. h.; fl.* $\frac{1}{3}$ *to* $\frac{1}{2}$ *in. across* V. catarractae

47. *Stems mostly prostrate and rooting; lvs.* $\frac{1}{10}$ *to* $\frac{3}{4}$ *in. long, broadly ovate, oblong or obovate, plants usually under* 9 *in. h.; fl.* $\frac{1}{3}$ *in. across* 48

48 (47). *Lvs.* $\frac{1}{4}$ *to* $\frac{3}{4}$ *in. long, broadly ovate or oblong-ovate; plant loosely branched, somewhat erect* V. Lyallii

48. *Lvs.* $\frac{1}{10}$ *to* $\frac{1}{4}$ *in. long, broadly oblong or obovate; plant completely prostrate* V. Bidwillii

49 (1). *Cor. tube very short, much shorter than lobes* 50

49. *Cor. tube well-developed (about* $\frac{1}{5}$ *in. long), about as long as lobes or not much shorter than lobes* 113

50 (49). *L.-blades* $\frac{1}{10}$ *in. or less long, rounded; plant prostrate, minute; fl. axillary on pedicels to* $\frac{1}{5}$ *in. long* V. canescens

50. *L.-blades more than* $\frac{1}{10}$ *in. long* 51

51 (50). *Lvs. pinnately divided or cut almost to midrib* 52

51. *Lvs. entire or toothed* 59

52 (51). *Plant erect, about* 6 *to* 20 *in. h., racemes usually long (often* 6 *in. or more); cor. tube cylindric; capsule glabrous, longer than wide* 53

52. *Plant spreading or much-branched, usually less than* 9 *in. h.* 54

53 (52). *Lvs. always pinnately divided to midrib into well-separated linear segs. less than* $\frac{1}{20}$ *in. wide* V. pinnata

53. *Lvs. deeply toothed or cut but incisions rarely reaching midrib and segs. mostly more than* $\frac{1}{20}$ *in. wide at base* V. incana

54 (52). *Plant greyish-white with close hairs* V. pectinata

54. *Plant not greyish-white* 55

55 (54). *Plant very dwarf, usually under* 4 *in. h.* V. armena

55. *Plant taller, usually between* 4 *and* 12 *in. h.* 56

56 (55). *Cal. segs.* 4, *almost equal in length; fruiting pedicels recurving; fl. usually white* 57
56. *Cal. segs. mostly* 5, *unequal; fl. usually blue* 58
57 (56). *Lvs. pinnately divided into very narrow segs.* V. caucasica
57. *Lvs. deeply cut but not to midrib* V. peduncularis
58 (56). *Capsule rounded at base, slightly longer than wide* V. austriaca
58. *Capsule wedge-shaped at base, wider than long* 112
59 (51). *Infl. terminal, sometimes with lateral branches as well* 60
59. *Infl. axillary or the fl. solitary in l.-axil, the main stem continuing leafy growth and not ending in an infl.* 85
60 (59). *Perennials grown for ornament* 61
60. *Annual, erect or diffuse, occurring as a weed, under* 1 *ft. h.; l. under* 1$\frac{1}{2}$ *in. long; fl. almost sessile; cor. shorter than cal.* 115
61 (60). *Lvs. very small, under* $\frac{7}{10}$ *in. long,* $\frac{3}{5}$ *in. wide; plants dwarf, under* 8 *in. h.; infl. few-fld.* 62
61. *Lvs. larger, some at least over* $\frac{7}{10}$ *in. long; plants often more than* 8 *in. h., infl. many-fld.* 74
62 (61). *Lower lvs. larger than upper lvs., forming a basal rosette and persistent* 63
62. *Lower lvs. no larger than upper lvs., often absent at fl. time* 64
63 (62). *Lvs. almost entire or slightly crenate; infl. compact, umbel-like* V. bellidioides
63. *Lvs. irregularly toothed; infl. a loose raceme with well-spaced fl.* V. senanensis
64 (62). *Lvs. silvery white with closely appressed silky hairs less than* $\frac{3}{10}$ *in. long; plant very dwarf, usually less than* 1 *in. h.; fl. reddish* V. bombycina
64. *Lvs. not silvery white* 65
65 (64). *Lvs. linear with revolute margin* 66
65. *Lvs. elliptic to ovate-orbicular or obovate, margin not revolute* 67
66 (65). *Lvs. grey with long woolly hairs, about* $\frac{1}{5}$ *to* $\frac{1}{2}$ *in. long* V. caespitosa
66. *Lvs. grey with very short hairs, about* $\frac{2}{5}$ *to* $\frac{4}{5}$ *in. long* V. cinerea
67 (65). *Cal. lobes* 5, *one smaller than the others; lvs. elliptic to obovate* V. satureioides
67. *Cal. lobes* 4 68
68 (67). *Infl. mostly elongated, many-fld.* V. serpyllifolia
68. *Infl. usually short, few-fld.* 69
69 (68). *Stems herbaceous* 70
69. *Stems somewhat woody at base* 71
70 (71). *L.-blades up to* $\frac{7}{10}$ *in. long* V. alpina
70. *L.-blades under* $\frac{2}{5}$ *in. long* V. repens
71 (69). *Lvs. elliptic or lanceolate or oblanceolate, more than twice as long as wide, evenly spaced up the stem* 72
71. *Lvs. ovate-orbicular, broadly elliptic or obovate, not twice as long as wide* 73
72 (71). *Pedicels glandular; cor. rose with red veins* V. fruticulosa
72. *Pedicels usually without glands; cor. deep blue* V. fruticans
73 (71). *Lvs. clustered towards tip of stem* V. Nummularia
73. *Lvs. fairly evenly spaced along stem* V. telephiifolia
74 (61). *Pedicels up to* 3 *or* 4 *times as long as cal.* 75
74. *Pedicels no longer than cal.* 76
75 (74). *Lvs. almost entire; stem* 6 *to* 24 *in. h. (often over* 12 *in.)* V. gentianoides
75. *Lvs. irregularly toothed* 4 *to* 12 *in. h. (usually* 5 *to* 7 *in.)* V. senanensis
76 (74). *Plant densely white-tomentose on lvs., stem and cal.* V. incana
76. *Plant green, not white-tomentose throughout* 77
77 (76). *L.-tip blunt or acute, but not acuminate, margin shallowly crenate with blunt teeth* 78
77. *L.-tip markedly acute or acuminate, margin often sharply toothed* 82
78 (77). *Infl. and cal. not glandular or with only a few short scattered glands* 79
78. *Infl. and cal. glandular* 81
79 (78). *Stems and infl. glabrous or nearly so* V. crassifolia
79. *Stems and infl. very hairy* 80
80 (79). *Plant* 3 *to* 12 *in. h.; lvs. ovate, toothed in middle but entire towards base and tip; cal. segs. more than half as long as capsule* V. spicata
80. *Plant* 6 *to* 36 *in. h.; lvs. narrowly ovate, toothed from base to tip; cal. segs. about half as long as capsule* V. hybrida
81 (78). *Lvs. not glandular; ovary and capsule hairy* V. orchidea
81. *Lvs. glandular on both sides; ovary and capsule glabrous* V. euxina
82 (77). *Infl. usually much branched, with lateral racemes diverging at a wide angle* (40° *or more) from the main stem; lvs. usually subcordate at base, deeply toothed, paired* V. Bachofenii
82. *Infl. simple or branched, with lateral racemes more erect (diverging at* 30° *or less from the main stem)* 83
83 (82). *Lvs. subcordate at base, paired, long-stalked* V. grandis
83. *Lvs. usually rounded or wedge-shaped at base, often in* 3*'s, when all paired usually almost sessile* 84
84 (83). *Lvs. rounded at base, sharply toothed; fl. almost sessile* V. longifolia
84. *Lvs. wedge-shaped at base, coarsely toothed; fl. short-stalked* V. spuria
85 (59). *Pedicels long, often* 3 *to* 5 *times as long as cal.* 86
85. *Pedicels very short, shorter or little longer than cal.* 103
86 (85). *Stems and lvs. completely glabrous, or if hairy then lvs. linear-lanceolate and racemes alternate. Marsh and water plants usually occurring in water gardens as weeds* 87
86. *Stems and lvs. slightly or distinctly hairy. Plants of drier places* 91
87 (86). *Lvs. of fl.-stem distinctly stalked* 88
87. *Lvs. of fl.-stem sessile* 89
88 (87). *Chief lvs. of fl.-stem acute* V. americana
88. *Chief lvs. of fl.-stem rounded at tip* V. Beccabunga
89 (87). *Lvs. linear-lanceolate; racemes alternate up the stem, capsule wider than long, much longer than cal.* V. scutellata
89. *Lvs. lanceolate or ovate; racemes opposite, i.e. in pairs up the stem; capsule longer than wide, shorter or scarcely longer than cal.* 90
90 (89). *Fruiting pedicels ascending; cor. pale blue* V. Anagallis-aquatica
90. *Fruiting pedicels horizontal; cor. pinkish or whitish* V. catenata
91 (86). *Annuals, small-fld., occurring as weeds* 92
91. *Perennials grown for ornament* 96
92 (91). *Cal. segs. broadly ovate, somewhat heart-shaped at base; petiole sometimes equalling blade in length* V. hederifolia
92. *Cal. segs. ovate, narrowly elliptic or lanceolate, not heart-shaped at base; petiole much shorter than blade* 93
93 (92). *L.-blade wider than long; pedicels more than twice as long as lvs; style more than* $\frac{1}{10}$ *in. long; plant completely prostrate* V. filiformis
93. *L.-blades usually longer than wide; pedicels not twice as long as lvs.* 94
94 (93). *Cor.* $\frac{1}{4}$ *to* $\frac{1}{2}$ *in. across distinctly longer than cal.* V. persica
94. *Cor. smaller,* $\frac{3}{10}$ *in. or less across, about as long as cal.* 95
95 (94). *Cal. segs. blunt; capsule with long glandular hairs but no short bent glandless hairs* V. agrestis
95. *Cal. segs. acute; capsule with short bent glandless hairs and few long glandular hairs* V. polita
96 (91). *Plant completely prostrate; fl. solitary in l.-axils on pedicels to* 1$\frac{1}{4}$ *in. long; lvs. under* $\frac{1}{2}$ *in. long, wider than long* V. filiformis
96. *Plants with ascending or erect stem* 4 *in. to* 3 *ft. h.; fl. in axillary racemes; lvs. usually longer than wide* 97
97 (96). *Lvs. acuminate, lanceolate, up to* 4 *in. long; plant* 2 *to* 3 *ft., almost glabrous, with long racemes of whitish fl.* V. derwentia
97. *Lvs. usually not acuminate (if acuminate, then not lanceolate)* 98
98 (97). *Lvs. thick, coriaceous; blades elliptic to narrowly oblanceolate* V. Forrestii
98. *Lvs. membranous (except in* V. Hookeriana*); blades lanceolate to broadly ovate* 99
99 (98). *Lvs. deeply toothed or divided* 110
99. *Lvs. shallowly toothed or almost entire* 100
100 (99). *Stem with long hairs in* 2 *narrow opposite longitudinal strips* V. Chamaedrys
100. *Stem more or less evenly hairy all round* 101
101 (100). *Lvs. crowded, thick, coriaceous,* $\frac{1}{4}$ *to* $\frac{1}{2}$ *in. long,* $\frac{3}{10}$ *in. wide; almost sessile; plant creeping with fl.-stems* 3 *to* 10 *in. h.* V. Hookeriana
101. *Lvs. well-spaced, thin, larger* 102
102 (101). *Lvs. long-stalked; plant decumbent,* 6 *to* 10 V. montana
102. *Lvs. sessile; plant erect,* 1 *to* 2$\frac{1}{2}$ *ft. h.* V. urticifolia
103 (102). *Lvs. not acuminate, usually somewhat hairy, less than* 2$\frac{1}{2}$ *in. long* 104
103. *Lvs. acuminate, glabrous; plant* 2 *to* 3 *ft. h.* 116
104 (103). *Cal. segs. usually* 5, *unequal, on occasional fl. with* 4 105
104. *Cal. segs. always* 4 108
105 (104). *Sterile shoots prostrate; fl. shoots ascending or erect* V. prostrata
105. *All shoots more or less ascending* 106
106 (105). *Capsule wedge-shaped at base* V. orientalis
106. *Capsule rounded at base* 107
107 (106). *L.-base rounded or cordate, blade shallowly to deeply toothed but not pinnatisect; terminal sterile shoot very short, with broad deeply toothed lvs.* V. Teucrium
107. *L.-base wedge-shaped, blade often deeply toothed to pinnately lobed; terminal sterile shoot rather elongated with narrow mostly entire lvs.* V. austriaca
108 (104). *Plant very dwarf, under* 2 *in. h.; lvs. on a basal rosette; infl. few* (2 *to* 5)*-fld., solitary and apparently terminal, arising from uppermost l.-axil* V. aphylla
108. *Plant taller, not rosette-forming; infl. few- to many-fld.* 109
109 (108). *Plant almost or quite glabrous; cor. about* 4 *times as long as cal.* V. Allionii
109. *Plant hairy; cor. hardly twice as long as cal.* 110
110 (109). *Stems with hairs in* 2 *narrow opposite longitudinal strips* V. Chamaedrys
110. *Stems more or less evenly hairy all round* 111

111 (110). *Lvs. whitish tomentose, less than ¾ in. long*	V. pectinata
111. *Lvs. not whitish tomentose, ¾ to 2 in. long*	V. officinalis
112 (110). *Lvs. pinnately divided into very narrow segs.*	V. multifida
112. *Lvs. deeply cut but not to midrib*	V. orientalis
113 (49). *Cor. lobes much shorter than tube; plants* 3 *to* 6 *ft. h.; lvs. in whorls of* 3 *to* 6 (*Veronicastrum*)	V. virginica
113. *Cor. lobes about as long as tube; plants less than* 14 *in. h.; lvs. paired* (*Paederota*)	114
114 (113). *Fl. blue*	V. Bonarota
114. *Fl. pale yellow*	V. lutea
115 (60). *Plant hairy; lvs. ovate, coarsely toothed*	V. arvensis
115. *Plant glabrous; lvs. oblanceolate or narrowly oblong*	V. peregrina
116 (103). *Lvs. lanceolate, sharply toothed*	V. derwentia
116. *Lvs. broadly ovate to narrowly ovate, entire or with only* 2 *or* 3 *teeth*	V. perfoliata
117 (28). *Cor. tube* 2 *to* 5 *times as long as cal., slender*	V. Traversii
117. *Cor. tube* 1 *to* 2 *times as long as cal., broad*	V. brachysiphon

V. agrest'is. Procumbent Speedwell. Annual weed, much branched, with procumbent or prostrate stems up to 9 in. long. *l.* ovate, toothed, short-stalked. *fl.* small, blue or pinkish, solitary on long pedicel from l.-axil. Europe, including Britain. (E.B. 972.)

V. Allion'ii. Mat-forming herb, perennial, with habit of *V. officinalis*. Stem creeping, rooting. *l.* obovate-elliptic, about ⅜ in. long, regularly toothed or entire, leathery, opaque dark green; stalks short. *fl.* dark violet in dense spikes about 2 in. h., ⅜ in. wide on short pedicels, from upper l.-axils. Alps. Rock-garden.

V. alpi'na. Rootstock creeping. Stem ascending, branching at base, slender. *l.* opposite or alternate, elliptic or oblong, with or without rounded teeth, upper l. larger than lower; stalk short. *fl.* blue or violet, up to ¼ in. across, in dense spike-like racemes. May. Usually weak but up to 8 in. h. Mts. of Europe, including Britain, Northern Asia. (B.M. 2975; E.B. 980.) Rock-garden.

V. ama'bilis. Evergreen shrub up to about 8 ft. with rather slender, terete branches, slightly downy when young. *l.* oblong- or elliptic-lanceolate 2 to 4 in. long, about ¾ in. wide, firm, flat. *fl.* white ⅓ in. across, in axillary racemes near ends of branches, 4 to 6 in. long, slender and lax-fld.; cal. segs. acute. S. Island, New Zealand. Syn. *Hebe amabilis.*

V. america'na. American Brooklime. Perennial herb, rather fleshy, with creeping base. *l.* lanceolate to narrowly ovate, acute, toothed, stalked, glabrous. *fl.* small, violet or lilac. Summer. N. America. A marsh plant, closely related to *V. Beccabunga* and of no garden value.

V. amplexicau'lis. Evergreen shrub, 1 to 3 ft. *l.* ½ to 1 in. long, ⅓ to ⅜ in. wide, broadly oblong or oval, cordate, apex rounded, the bases partly clasping the stem, glaucous. *fl.* white, ¼ in. wide, in 1 or 2 pairs of spikes near the top, each 1 to 1½ in. long; stalks downy. July, August. New Zealand. 1882. (B.M. 7370.) Syn. *Hebe amplexicaulis.*

V. Anagallis-aquatica. Water Speedwell. Perennial, rather fleshy, glabrous, with creeping base. *l.* usually lanceolate, acute, toothed, sessile, glabrous. *fl.* small, pale blue; fruiting pedicels ascending. Summer. N. America, Europe, incl. Britain. (E.B. 987 as *V. Anagallis.*) Syn. *V. Anagallis.* A marsh plant, found in ditches and by ponds, of no garden value.

V. × Anderson'ii* (*V. salicifolia* × *V. speciosa*). Evergreen shrub, 4 to 6 ft. *l.* 3 to 4½ in. long, 1 to 1½ in. wide, narrow-oblong, fleshy, obtuse. *fl.* densely packed in racemes 3 to 5 in. long, 1½ in. wide, bluish-violet, fading to white, especially towards the base of the raceme. August, September. 1845. (P.F.G. ii. 38.) Syn. *Hebe* × *Andersonii.* var. **variegat'a,** *l.* with white variegation; once very popular in arrangements of summer bedding.

V. angustifo'lia. Evergreen shrub, 3 to 6 ft.; shoots erect, glabrous, shining, afterwards purplish-brown. *l.* stalkless, 1½ to 3½ in. long, ⅛ to ¼ in. wide, entire, pointed, glabrous. *fl.* ⅛ to ¼ in. wide, white tinged lilac, numerous in axillary racemes 2 to 5 in. long near the top of the shoots. July to September. New Zealand. 1868. (B.M. 5965 as *V. parviflora angustifolia.*) Syn. *Hebe angustifolia.*

V. ano'mala.* Erect evergreen shrub, 3 to 5 ft.; shoots nearly glabrous, slender. *l.* ⅓ to ¾ in. long, ⅛ to ⅙ in. wide, oval-lanceolate to narrow-oblong, dark shining green, glabrous. *fl.* white or pale pink, ¼ to ⅓ in. wide, in a cluster of spikes, each of 5 to 10 fl. and 1 to 1½ in. long; anthers blue. June, July. New Zealand. 1883. (B.M. 7360.) One of the hardiest shrubby species. Syn. *Hebe anomala.*

V. aphyl'la. Perennial hairy herb with or without a short creeping stem. *l.* more or less in rosettes, ovate elliptic, ½ to 1 in. long; stalk short. *fl.* lilac-blue or violet, clustered at top of naked peduncles to 3 in. long. S. Europe. Rock-garden. Fl. passing quickly.

V. aqua'tica of Bernhardi, not Gray. A synonym of *V. catenata.*

V. arme'na. Tufted from a rather woody stock. Stems many, to 4 in. h., weak. *l.* small, opposite, pinnately cut into linear segs. *fl.* bright blue in short loose spikes. Armenia. Rock-garden.

V. Armstrong'ii. Evergreen shrub 1 to 3 ft. with often fan-like branching. Shoots slender, clothed in the adult state with appressed, overlapping *l.* which are roundish or blunt-tipped, ⅒ in. long. (In the juvenile state the l. are linear, pointed, spreading, ⅒ to ⅛ in. long.) *fl.* white, ⅕ to ¼ in. wide, in terminal clusters of 4 to 8. July, August. New Zealand. (G.C. 27 (1899), 137.) Akin to *V. cupressoides.* Syn. *Hebe Armstrongii.*

V. arven'sis. Wall Speedwell. Annual weed, hairy, erect or spreading, simple or branched, mostly under 6 in. h. *l.* ovate, toothed, short-stalked to almost sessile. *fl.* small, blue or whitish, almost sessile, in a terminal raceme. Europe, including Britain, (E.B. 976.)

V. austria'ca. Downy herbaceous perennial, 1 to 2 ft. h. *l.* ovate, deeply pinnatifid; segs. often sharply cut. *fl.* blue, rather large, in 2 to 4 axillary, long racemes from near the top of the stem. July. SE. Europe. Hardy border. A very variable species divided by botanists into several sub-species; some forms with much divided l. resemble *V. multifida* and are only to be distinguished by their capsules slightly longer than wide and rounded at base.

V. Bachofen'ii. Perennial herb, 2 ft. h. erect, hairy stems. *l.* opposite, long-stalked subcordate, at base, deeply and sharply toothed from base to tip. *fl.* blue; infl. terminal, much branched with numerous loose, long racemes, spreading at a wide angle from the stem; cal. almost glabrous. July, August. E. Europe. In cult. 1848. Syn. *V. grandis* var. *Bachofenii.* Related to *V. longifolia.*

V. Balfouria'na.* Evergreen shrub, 2 to 4 ft., shoots purplish. *l.* ⅓ to ¾ in. long, ¼ to ⅙ in. wide, oval to slightly obovate, pale shining green, nearly glabrous. *fl.* ⅓ to ½ in. wide, pale purplish-blue, crowded in stalked racemes 2 to 3 in. long. June, July. New Zealand. (B.M. 7556.) Syn. *Hebe Balfouriana.*

V. Barker'i. Large shrub; shoots erect, brownish-purple when young. *l.* about 2 in. long, ⅓ to ⅜ in. wide, lanceolate or oblong-lanceolate, midrib not prominent. *fl.* ⅕ to ¼ in. wide, pale lilac, in dense-fld. racemes about 2 in. long. Chatham Is. Syn. *Hebe Barkeri.* Close to *V. Dieffenbachii.*

V. Baumgarten'ii. Perennial herb, erect, 1 to 4 in. h. *l.* lanceolate to elliptic, sessile or short-stalked, shallowly toothed towards the tip, glabrous, to ¾ in. long, lower l. smaller than upper. *fl.* blue, in 1- to 4-fld. axillary racemes; pedicels 3 to 5 times as long as cal.; capsule glabrous. SE. Europe, from Carpathians to N. Balkan Peninsula. Rock-garden.

V. Beccabun'ga. Brooklime. Perennial marsh herb of no garden value, akin to *V. americana* but l. blunt. Europe, Asia, N. America. (E.B. 990.)

V. bellidioi'des. Akin to *V. alpina* but with basal l. much larger than stem l.; stem 2½ to 8 in. h. *l.* obovate, obtuse, greyish. *fl.* pale blue, in a terminal cluster. May. European mountains from Pyrenees to Carpathians, &c. 1875. Rock-garden.

V. Bidwill'ii. Prostrate, self-rooting shrub, about 6 in., shoots often matted. *l.* ⅒ to ¼ in. long, oblong to obovate, thick and leathery, entire or notched at each side; racemes 3 to 9 in. long, erect, slender, axillary. *fl.* ⅛ in. wide, white lined with pinkish-lilac. June, July. New Zealand. 1850. Syn. *Hebe Bidwillii.* Rock-garden. Akin to *V. Lyallii.*

V. Bieberstein'ii. A synonym of *V. multifida.*

Veronica bombycina

V. bombyci'na. Tufted perennial, white with silky appressed hair, usually under 1 in. h. *l.* ovate or oblong-spatulate, about ⅛ in. long, sessile. *fl.* reddish in a few-fld. terminal raceme, sometimes solitary. July. Lebanon. Rock-garden, moraine. An attractive plant for the alpine house. **A**

V. Bonaro'ta. Downy perennial, 2 to 6 in. h. *Lower l.* almost round; *upper* ovate or lanceolate, more or less deeply toothed, glossy dark green. *fl.* blue, with cor. tube nearly ⅛ in. long, slightly shorter than lobes, in a compact terminal spike about 1½ in. long. July. S. Europe. Rock-garden in stony soil or moraine. SYN. *Paederota Bonarota.* Often placed in a separate genus on account of long cor. tube.

V. brachysi'phon.* Shrub of bushy rounded shape, 6 to 7 ft., much more in width. *l.* narrowly oval, oblong, or slightly obovate, ½ to 1 in. long, ⅛ to ¼ in. wide, short-stalked. *fl.* ¼ to ⅓ in. across, white, in racemes about 2 in. long. July. New Zealand. 1868. (B.M. 6390 as *V. Traversii.*) SYN. *Hebe brachysiphon.* Valuable and popular species, rarely injured by cold, wrongly known as *V. Traversii* in gardens. The true **V. Traversii,** SYN. *V. Traversii* var. *elegans, Hebe Traversii,* has the cor. tube 2 to 5 times as long as the sep. (see *Kew Bulletin,* 1927, 397), whereas in *V. brachysiphon* the sep. are longer and the cor. tube equals the sep. or is only twice as long as them.

V. Buchan'anii. Dwarf evergreen shrub, 6 to 12 in., much-branched, shoots stout, round. *l.* ⅛ to ¼ in. long, oblong to roundish, set closely together, thick and leathery, concave, glabrous. *fl.* white, ⅛ in. wide, in a cluster of 2 or 4 spikes near the top of the shoot, each spike ½ to ¾ in. long, densely fld. June, July. New Zealand. SYN. *Hebe Buchananii.* Rock-garden.

V. Buxbaum'ii. A synonym of *V. persica.*

V. buxifo'lia. Evergreen shrub, 2 to 4 ft., branches erect, young shoots nearly glabrous. *l.* ⅓ to ½ in. long, 3/16 to ¼ in. wide, oblong or slightly obovate, pointed, dark lustrous green, glabrous, minutely dotted beneath. *fl.* white, ¼ to ⅓ in. across, in closely packed spikes ⅓ to 1 in long. June, July. New Zealand. SYN. *Hebe buxifolia.*

V. caespito'sa. Tufted perennial making a greyish cushion 1 to 3 in. h. *l.* linear-spatulate, about ⅓ in. long obtuse, entire, margins revolute. *fl.* pink, in terminal very short racemes, sometimes solitary, scarcely raised above l., about ⅓ in. across. May, June. Asia Minor, Syria. Rock-garden, moraine.

V. canes'cens. Minute creeping perennial with intricately branched stems 1 to 4 in. long, hispidly hairy all over and greyish. *l.* broadly ovate, up to 1/10 in. long. *fl.* pale blue, about ⅓ in. across, axillary, on slender peduncles about ¼ in. long. July onwards. New Zealand. (B.M. 9003 A.) Rock-garden. Seeds itself freely. It is *V. canescens* of Kirk which is described here. **V. canes'cens** of Schrader (1803) is a synonym of *V. incana.* **V. canes'cens** of Bastard (1812) is a synonym of *V. Teucrium vestita.* **A**

V. canterburien'sis. A variety of *V. vernicosa.*

V. carno'sula.* Neat, dwarf, evergreen shrub, decumbent and up to about 1 ft. in cult. *l.* roundish obovate, glaucous green, concave, ⅓ to ¾ in. long, ¼ to ⅜ in. wide. *fl.* white, ¼ in. across, crowded in numerous spikes that form a dense terminal cluster; stalks very downy. July, August. New Zealand. One of the hardiest. (The plant of B.M. 6587 is not this species but *V. pinguifolia.*) SYN. *Hebe carnosula.*

V. catarrac'tae. Sub-shrub, woody at the base; procumbent, with ascending, purplish, slender, herbaceous shoots up to 24 in h. *l.* distant, ordinarily ½ to 1½ in. long, lanceolate to ovate-lanceolate, coarsely toothed. *fl.* white with rosy-purple lines, ⅓ to ½ in. wide, numerous and with stalks ⅓ to 1 in. long in slender racemes 3 to 9 in. long. July to September. New Zealand. SYN. *Hebe catarractae.*

V. catena'ta. Perennial herb, rather fleshy, with creeping base. *l.* lanceolate, toothed or almost entire, sessile, glabrous. *fl.* small, pale blue; fruiting pedicels spreading horizontally. N. America, Europe, including Britain. SYN. *V. aquatica* of Bernhardi not Gray. A marsh plant closely akin to *V. Anagallis-aquatica* and of no garden value.

V. cauca'sica. Perennial herb with erect or ascending stems about 6 in. long. *l.* deeply cut into oblong segs., narrow at base and sometimes toothed. *fl.* white with blue streaks on upper pet. in loose, many-fld. racemes on slender peduncles. June. Caucasus. 1815. (L.B.C. 1369.)

V. Chamaed'rys. God's Eye, Angels' Eyes, Birds' Eyes, Germander Speedwell. Perennial herb with creeping rootstock and slender ascending or erect stem 12 to 18 in. h., hairy on two sides. *l.* broadly ovate, 1½ in. long, roundish toothed, nearly sessile, rather thick. *fl.* bright blue, in many-fld. racemes 3 to 6 in. long in l.-axils. May onwards. Europe, including Britain. (L.B.C. 53; E.B. 986.) Good border plant, common wild.

V. chatha'mica. Small, prostrate or trailing shrub; shoots usually downy. *l.* closely set, ½ to 1 in. long, oval to oblong, glabrous or nearly so. *fl.* ¼ in. wide, purple, densely set in several broad racemes ½ to 1 in. long near the tips of the shoots. July, August. Chatham Is. Rock-garden. SYN. *Hebe chathamica.*

V. cine'rea. Perennial herb with ascending stems up to 6 in. h. *l.* lanceolate to linear, sessile, margin usually inrolled, mostly ash grey with very short hairs. *fl.* rose, in 10- to 20-fld. spikes. Summer. Asia Minor. Rock-garden.

V. circaeoi'des. Trailing, mat-forming herb with stems about 8 in. long. *l.* rhomboidal, crenate towards apex, dark green, often russet or bronzed. *fl.* pearly white, veined pink, rather small, in loose racemes. August. Orient? Rock-garden. The name has no botanical standing. Probably a form of *V. orientalis.*

V. Colens'oi. Evergreen shrub 1 to 2 ft. *l.* crowded, 8 to 12 to the inch, obovate-oblong, ¾ to 1¼ in. long, ⅛ to ½ in. wide, glabrous, spreading, sometimes remotely toothed. *fl.* white, ¼ in. wide, in dense racemes 1 in. long from the terminal l.-axils. July, August. New Zealand. (Cheeseman in his *Manual N.Z. Flora* states that the plant figured under this name in B.M. 7297 is very different from typical *V. Colensoi*). SYN. *V. Hilli, Hebe Colensoi.*

V. crassifo'lia. Perennial herb 8 to 16 in. h. with blue *fl.* in slender spikes, closely akin to *V. spicata* but almost or quite glabrous. July and August. Balkan Peninsula. Border.

V. cuneifo'lia. Tufted perennial with slender ascending or procumbent stems, 2 to 3 in. *l.* of the form of *V. Chamaedrys. fl.* blue, margined white, in solitary, not paired axillary racemes. June, July. Asia Minor. Rock-garden. var. **villo'sa,** a downy form of this. SYN. *V. dichrus.*

V. cupressoi'des. Evergreen shrub 3 to 6 ft., of dense rounded habit resembling a dwarf cypress; shoots 1/80 in. thick, often minutely downy. *l.* scale-like, 1/16 in. long, closely appressed to the stem which is also clasped by their united bases. (On juvenile plants the l. are ¼ in. long and linear.) *fl.* ⅛ in. wide, pale purplish-blue, borne in heads of 3 to 8; anthers red-brown, conspicuous. June, July. New Zealand (B.M. 7348.) SYN. *Hebe cupressoides.* One of the hardiest.

V. Darwinia'na. Evergreen shrub, 3 ft. or more, of compact, rounded shape. *l.* ½ to ¾ in. long, ⅛ to ⅓ in. wide, oval-lanceolate, pointed, stalkless or nearly so, slightly concave, minutely ciliate, glaucous above and beneath. *fl.* white, ¼ in. wide, in 2 or 4 racemes near the top of the shoots, each ¾ to 1½ in. long. July to August. New Zealand. SYN. *Hebe Darwiniana.*

V. decum'bens.* Evergreen shrub with a decumbent base and erect branches 1 to 3 ft., shoots purplish-black. *l.* closely set to rather distant, oval oblong or obovate, ⅓ to ¾ in. long, glabrous. *fl.* ¼ in. wide, white, densely crowded in 2 or 4 racemes each ½ to ¾ in. long near the tips of the shoots. July, August. New Zealand. 1888. The shining, purple-black shoots are distinctive. SYN. *Hebe decumbens.*

V. decussa'ta. A synonym of *V. elliptica.*

V. derwent'ia. Stems herbaceous from a perennial, woody base, 2 to 3 ft., erect. *l.* broadly lanceolate, long and slenderly pointed, glabrous, 3 to 4 in. long, sharply and strongly toothed. *fl.* ⅜ in. wide, pale blue or white, fragrant, in axillary racemes 6 to 8 in. long; anthers purplish. June. Australia, Tasmania. 1802. (B.M. 1660, 3461 as *V. labiata.*) **A**

V. dich'rus. A synonym of *V. cuneifolia villosa.*

V. Dieffenbach'ii. Spreading evergreen shrub, 3 to 5 ft., shoots round, stout and up to ⅛ in. thick. *l.* narrow-oblong, 2 to 4 in. long, ½ to 1 in. wide, leathery, bases clasping stem. *fl.* ¼ in. wide, densely set in racemes 3 or 4 in. long, purplish-lilac; anthers blue. September. Chatham Is. (B.M. 7656.) SYN. *Hebe Dieffenbachii.* Akin to *V. speciosa*; handsome but tender.

V. diosmifo'lia. Evergreen shrub, usually 2 to 5 ft. occasionally a small tree, 15 ft. *l.* closely set, ½ to 1 in. long, 1/10 to ⅛ in. wide, linear to narrowly lanceolate, pointed. *fl.* ¼ in. wide, white to pale lavender-blue, in corymbose racemes ½ to 1¼ in. long; cal. 3- rarely 4-lobed. July. New Zealand. 1835. (B.M. 7539 as var. *trisepala.*) SYN. *Hebe diosmifolia.*

V. × edinen'sis (*V. Hectori* × *V. pimeleoides*). Hebe hybrid.

V. e'legans. A variety of *V. spuria.*

V. ellip'tica.* Evergreen shrub or a tree up to 20 ft., shoots more or less downy. *l.* ½ to 1¼ in. long, ¼ to ½ in. wide, oval or obovate, spreading horizontally, stalked, pale green; margins downy. *fl.* ⅓ to ⅜ in. wide, white with purple lines, fragrant, borne in numerous racemes 1 to 1½ in. long. July, August. Tierra del Fuego, Falkland Is., Chile, New Zealand. 1776. (B.M. 242 as *V. decussata.*) SYN. *Hebe elliptica.* Largest fld. of all the shrubby species. The handsome, hardy, long-flowering **Autumn glory** with violet fl. probably owes its origin to this species.

V. epacri'dea. Low or prostrate, much-branched, evergreen shrub, densely leafy. *l.* overlapping, stiff, V-shaped, ovate, 3/16 in. long, each pair united at the base. *fl.* ⅛ in. wide, white, densely packed in ovoid, terminal clusters ½ to 1¼ in. long, ¾ in. wide. July. New Zealand. 1860. SYN. *Hebe epacridea.*

V. euxi'na. Perennial herb with erect, glandular stems up to 20 in. h. from a decumbent base. *l.* opposite broadly elliptic or ovate-elliptic, shallowly toothed almost from base to tip, densely glandular, to 2½ in. long. *fl.* blue, with 3 lower cor. lobes narrow; infl. terminal, simple or branched, with erect densely fld. spikes; cal. glabrous except for ciliate margin; capsule glabrous. July. 1926. SE. Europe. (Hook. Icon. 3135.) Closely akin to *V. spicata.*

V. × Fairfield'ii. Apparently a hybrid of *V. Hulkeana* and *V. Lavaudiana.* Very like *V. Hulkeana* but smaller in growth, *l.* being mostly less than 1 in. long, red-margined, crenate, and the pale lilac *fl.* in a shorter and broader panicle. New Zealand, but unknown there in a wild state. (B.M. 7323.) SYN. *V. Hulkeana* var. *Fairfieldii, Hebe Fairfieldii.*

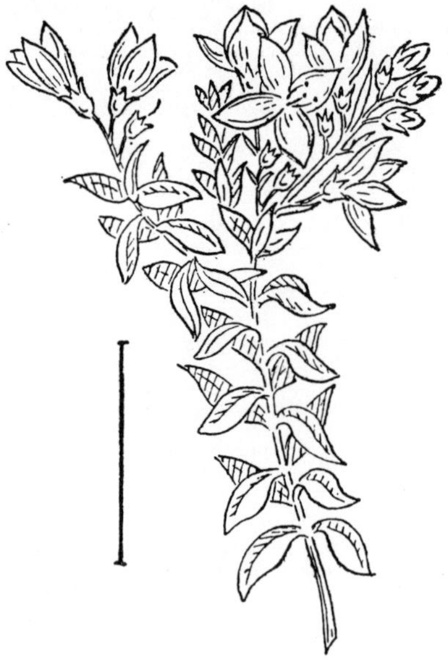

Veronica diosmifolia (p. 2219)

V. filifo'lia. Perennial with several erect or ascending stems 6 to 12 in. h., crisply downy. *l.* sessile, 2-pinnatifid with almost filiform divisions. *fl.* large, white, blue-veined, in loose 4 to 8-fld. racemes in l.-axils. Caucasus. Rock-garden. Not well distinguished from *V. caucasica.*

V. filifor'mis. Annual or perennial, somewhat tufted herb with rather downy filiform prostrate branches, rooting at nodes. *l.* broadly ovate or almost orbicular, subcordate, small, shortly stalked. *fl.* pale blue, on filiform axillary pedicels. May onwards. Asia Minor. A pretty plant but apt to be invasive, colonizing even among grass.

V. folio'sa. Perennial herb closely akin to *V. spuria.* E. Europe.

V. formo'sa.* Evergreen shrub 2 to 4 ft. erect, bushy. *l.* oblong-lanceolate, $\frac{1}{4}$ to $\frac{5}{8}$ in. long, $\frac{1}{8}$ to $\frac{3}{16}$ in. wide, scarcely stalked. *fl.* lilac to purplish-blue, $\frac{1}{2}$ to $\frac{3}{4}$ in. wide, crowded in short axillary racemes about 1 in. across which open successively from July onwards. Tasmania, SE. Australia. 1835. (B.M. 4512.) Tender. SYN. *Hebe formosa.*

V. Forrest'ii. Perennial herb with creeping shoots; stems 6 to 15 in. h., decumbent. *l.* narrow ovate or oblong, up to $\frac{3}{4}$ in. long, glabrous, often purple beneath. *fl.* reddish in terminal or axillary racemes. Yunnan, China. Rock-garden. **V. morrisoni'cola,** Formosa, is closely allied.

V. fru'ticans.* Rock Speedwell. Procumbent sub-shrub, woody at the base, branches erect, 2 to 4 in. h. (6 in. in gardens). *l.* oval to ovate and obovate, $\frac{1}{4}$ to $\frac{1}{2}$ in. long, glabrous or nearly so, entire or slightly blunt-toothed. *fl.* bright blue with a red eye, $\frac{1}{2}$ in. across, 2 to 6 in an erect terminal cluster. July to September. Mts. of Europe, including Scotland. (E.B. 981 as *V. saxatilis.*) SYN. *V. saxatilis.* The best of the dwarf European species for the rock-garden.

V. fruticulo'sa. Sub-shrub a few in. h. with a perennial woody base. *l.* oblong-lanceolate, sometimes rather obovate, 1 to $1\frac{1}{2}$ in. long, $\frac{1}{4}$ to $\frac{1}{2}$ in. wide, entire or shallowly crenate. *fl.* pink (never blue), $\frac{3}{8}$ to $\frac{1}{2}$ in. wide, opposite on racemes at the terminal half of erect annual leafy shoots 6 in. h. July. Mts. of Europe. (E.B. (1st ed.), t. 1028.)

V. gentianoi'des. Tufted perennial with simple erect stems 6 to 12 in. h. *l.* rather thick, lower in a rosette, obovate or oblong, 1 to 3 in. long, almost entire, others distant, oblong or lanceolate. *fl.* pale blue, margined deeper, to $\frac{1}{2}$ in. wide, in a somewhat loose raceme about 10 in. long. June. Caucasus. 1784. (B.M. 1002; S.B.F.G. 5.) var. **pal'lida,** *fl.* white; **variega'ta,** *l.* variegated, *fl.* pale blue. A beautiful plant for border or rock-garden, forming glossy-leaved free-flowering mats.

V. Gibb'sii.* Evergreen shrub, 9 to 18 in., young shoots entirely concealed by the l. which are closely set, overlapping, $\frac{1}{3}$ to $\frac{3}{4}$ in. long, $\frac{1}{3}$ to $\frac{1}{2}$ in. wide, glaucous, often purple-tinged, fringed with white hairs. *fl.* white, $\frac{1}{5}$ in. wide, in 2 or 4 clusters, each about 1 in. long, near the shoot tips. July. New Zealand. The hairy-margined l. are distinctive. SYN. *Hebe Gibbsii.*

V. gigante'a. Evergreen, round-headed tree, 20 to 30 ft. with a distinct trunk. *l.* 2 to 4 in. long, $\frac{1}{3}$ to $\frac{1}{2}$ in. wide, ciliate, lanceolate, pointed. *fl.* white, $\frac{1}{5}$ in. wide, in racemes 2 to 4 in. long. Nearly akin to *V. salicifolia* and sometimes regarded as a variety of it. Chatham Is. where it has been found 40 ft. h. 1909. SYN. *Hebe gigantea.*

Veronica gentianoides

V. Girdwoodia'na. A garden synonym for *V. formosa.*

V. glauco-caeru'lea. A variety of *V. pimeleoides:*

V. gracil'lima. Evergreen shrub 4 to 6 ft. *l.* 1 to $2\frac{1}{2}$ in. long, $\frac{1}{6}$ to $\frac{1}{3}$ in. wide, linear-lanceolate to lanceolate, slender-pointed, leathery. *fl.* $\frac{1}{4}$ in. wide, lilac-rose, densely set on slender racemes 3 to 5 in. long; stalks minutely downy. July, August. New Zealand. SYN. *V. ligustrifolia gracillima.* SYN. *Hebe gracillima.*

V. gran'dis. Herbaceous perennial with erect hairy stems about 1 to 2 ft. h. *l.* opposite, ovate to lanceolate, stalked, subcordate at base, deeply toothed, to 3 in. long, 1 in. broad. infl. terminal, with fl. in long, ascending spikes. *fl.* white. NE. Asia. Closely akin to *V. Bachhofenii.*

V. Griev'ei. A form or perhaps a hybrid of *V. saxatilis* with very bright *fl.*

V. Guthriea'na. Apparently a hybrid of *V. fruticans*, but larger. *fl.* clear blue.

V. Haast'ii. Low, often prostrate, evergreen shrub, shoots erect, up to 12 in. or more, densely leafy. *l.* $\frac{1}{4}$ to $\frac{1}{2}$ in. long, oblong to obovate, blunt, concave, overlapping, each pair united at the base. *fl.* white, small, borne in small spikes forming collectively an ovoid head up to $1\frac{1}{2}$ in. long. July, August. New Zealand. Very hardy.

V. Headfort'ii. A variety of *V. speciosa.*

V. Hec'tori. Evergreen shrub, 6 in. to $2\frac{1}{2}$ ft., shoots round, stout, rigid, covered by closely flattened, scale-like *l.* $\frac{1}{10}$ to $\frac{1}{8}$ in. long, closely overlapping, each pair united up to the middle; ciliate, when young. *fl.* $\frac{1}{4}$ in. wide, white or pinkish, crowded in a small terminal head. July. New Zealand. (B.M. 7415.) SYN. *Hebe Hectori.* Akin to *V. lycopodioides.*

V. hederifo'lia. Ivy-leaved Speedwell. Annual weed akin to *V. agrestis.* Europe, including Britain. (E.B. 970.)

V. Hookeria'na. Stout branched prostrate herb about 8 to 10 in. long. *l.* crowded, broadly ovate, $\frac{1}{4}$ to $\frac{1}{2}$ in. long, spreading, coarsely crenate, leathery, downy. *fl.* white, often streaked pink, $\frac{1}{4}$ to $\frac{1}{3}$ in. across, in a corymbose raceme of 4 to 8 fl. on stout axillary erect peduncles 1 to 2 in. h. N. Island, New Zealand. (Hook. Icon. t. 640 as *V. nivea*). SYN. *Hebe Hookeriana.* Rather tender.

V. Hulkea'na.* Evergreen shrub of lax habit. *l.* in distant pairs, broadly ovate, 1 to 2 in. long, $\frac{1}{2}$ to $1\frac{1}{4}$ in. wide, coarsely toothed, dark glossy green. *fl.* $\frac{1}{4}$ to $\frac{1}{3}$ in. wide, delicate lavender or lilac, in panicles 6 to 18 in. long, half as wide. May, June. New Zealand. 1860. (B.M. 5484.) SYN. *Hebe Hulkeana*. Most beautiful in fl. of all shrubby species. Needs wall protection. var. **Fairfield'ii**, a synonym of *V.* × *Fairfieldii*.

Veronica Hulkeana

V. hyb'rida. Perennial herb with erect hairy but not glandular stems $\frac{1}{2}$ to 2 ft. h. *l.* opposite, narrowly ovate to lanceolate, shallowly toothed almost from base to tip, not glandular. *fl.* blue; infl. terminal in erect densely fld. spikes; cal. hairy; capsule hairy. Europe, including Britain. Closely akin to *V. spicata* and now generally considered a sub-species of it. Not a hybrid.

V. inca'na. Silvery-grey herbaceous perennial 1 to 2 ft. h. *l.* opposite; lower oblong, upper lanceolate, 1 to 3 in. long, white-hairy, often toothed. *fl.* many, blue, on short pedicels, in terminal racemes 3 to 6 in. long. July. Russia. 1759. SYN. *V. canescens* of Schrader. var. **candidis'sima** has larger *l.* and blue *fl.*; **glau'ca** is silvery with deeper blue *fl.*

V. inci'sa. *See under* **V. pinnata.**

V. insula'ris. Evergreen shrub 1 to 3 ft., erect or decumbent. *l.* closely set, $\frac{3}{4}$ to $1\frac{1}{4}$ in. long, $\frac{1}{3}$ to $\frac{1}{2}$ in. wide, oval-oblong or oblong-obovate, very leathery, often glaucous. *fl.* $\frac{1}{4}$ in. wide, pale lavender-blue, numerous in corymbose racemes $\frac{3}{4}$ to $1\frac{1}{2}$ in. long; stalks minutely downy. June, July. New Zealand. SYN. *Hebe insularis*.

V. Kirk'ii. A variety of *V. salicifolia*.

V. labia'ta. A synonym of *V. derwentia*.

V. lae'vis. Evergreen shrub of dense habit, 2 to 4 ft., wholly glabrous. *l.* closely set, overlapping, erect or appressed, $\frac{1}{3}$ to $\frac{2}{3}$ in. long, $\frac{1}{6}$ to $\frac{1}{3}$ in. wide, ovate-oblong to obovate-oblong. *fl.* white, $\frac{1}{4}$ in. wide, crowded in branched corymbose clusters, $\frac{3}{4}$ to $1\frac{1}{2}$ in. long. July, August. New Zealand. SYN. *Hebe laevis*.

V. latifo'lia. The application of this name is controversial. When Linnaeus published the name he referred to descriptions of the species later named *V. urticifolia* by Jacquin, but the specimen in his herbarium belongs to the species which he himself later named *V. Teucrium*. Consequently many authors, notably Kerner and Schinz and Keller, have used the name *V. latifolia* instead of *V. urticifolia*, while others, notably Pennell, have used the name *V. latifolia* instead of *V. Teucrium*. To avoid ambiguity, it has not been adopted in either sense here.

V. Lavaudia'na.* Evergreen shrub under 1 ft. *l.* $\frac{1}{3}$ to 1 in. wide, broadly obovate to roundish, rather coarsely toothed, shortly and stoutly stalked. *fl.* $\frac{1}{4}$ to $\frac{1}{3}$ in. wide, pink, borne in a cluster of spikes forming a corymbose, terminal, slender-stalked panicle 2 in. across. May. New Zealand. 1880. (B.M. 7210.) SYN. *Hebe Lavaudiana*. Akin to *V. Hulkeana*.

Veronica Lavaudiana

V. leiophyl'la. Evergreen shrub, 4 to 12 ft. *l.* $\frac{3}{4}$ to $1\frac{1}{4}$ in. long, $\frac{1}{6}$ to $\frac{1}{3}$ in. wide, glabrous, narrowly oblong. Racemes slender, 4 in. long, closely packed with white fl. $\frac{2}{5}$ in. wide; stalks and margin of calyx minutely downy. July, August. New Zealand. SYN. *Hebe leiophylla*.

V. Lewis'ii.* Erect evergreen shrub, 3 to 6 ft., shoots stout, greyish-white downy. *l.* $1\frac{1}{2}$ to $2\frac{1}{2}$ in. long, $\frac{3}{4}$ to 1 in. wide, oblong to oval, rounded to subcordate at the base, glabrous, pale green above, mid-rib and margins downy. *fl.* pale blue, $\frac{1}{3}$ in. or more wide, densely set on stout racemes 2 in. long and 1 in. wide. July, August. New Zealand.

V. ligustrifo'lia. Evergreen shrub up to 3 ft., shoots glabrous. *l.* $\frac{1}{4}$ to over 1 in. apart, oblong to linear-lanceolate, 1 to $2\frac{1}{4}$ in. long, $\frac{1}{4}$ to $\frac{1}{2}$ in. wide. *fl.* white, scarcely $\frac{1}{4}$ in. wide, in slender cylindrical racemes 2 to 3 in. long; cal. deeply 4-lobed. July, August. New Zealand. SYN. *Hebe ligustrifolia*. var. **gracil'lima,** a synonym of *V. gracillima*.

V. × Lind'sayi (*V. amplexicaulis* × *V. pimeleoides*). Hebe hybrid.

V. linifo'lia. Sub-shrub, with a woody base, shoots slender, herbaceous, lower ones procumbent and rooting, up to 9 in. long. *l.* set 12 to 16 to the in. spreading, linear, $\frac{1}{8}$ to 1 in. long, $\frac{1}{16}$ to $\frac{1}{6}$ in. wide, entire. *fl.* white or pale rose, $\frac{1}{3}$ to $\frac{1}{2}$ in. wide, in slender-stalked racemes of 2 to 5. May, June. New Zealand. Akin to *V. Lyallii*. SYN. *Hebe linifolia*.

V. loganioi'des. Dwarf decumbent, conifer-like evergreen shrub, 6 to 18 in. h., shoots erect, downy. *l.* $\frac{1}{8}$ to $\frac{1}{6}$ in. long, ovate-lanceolate, either entire or with a few teeth, erect or spreading, stalkless, keeled, dull green. *fl.* pure white or sometimes veined with pink, $\frac{1}{4}$ to $\frac{1}{3}$ in. across, in a cluster of racemes forming a corymbose head 1 in. across. June, July. New Zealand. (B.M. 7404.) SYN. *Hebe loganioides*.

V. longifo'lia. Herbaceous perennial about 2 to 4 ft. h., glabrous or nearly so. *l.* opposite or in whorls of 3, oblong-lanceolate, $2\frac{1}{2}$ to 4 in. long, slender-pointed, sharply toothed from base to tip. *fl.* lilac, in dense-fld. long racemes, terminal. July to September. Cent. Europe to N. Asia. 1731. var. **albiflo'ra,** *fl.* white; **glau'ca,** *l.* bluish, *fl.* bright rich purple; **ro'sea,** *fl.* pink, stems branched; **subses'silis,** 2 to 3 ft. h., compact, much branched, *l.* downy beneath, spikes longer than in type, *fl.* purple-blue. Japan. 1878. (B.M. 6407.) SYN. *V. subsessilis*. A fine plant but less hardy than type. Border plants; often confused with *V. spicata* in gardens.

V. lu'tea. Perennial herb of erect habit, 6 to 9 in. h. *l.* opposite lanceolate to broadly ovate, deeply toothed. *fl.* yellow, with cor. tube about $\frac{1}{8}$ in. long, slightly shorter than lobes, in a short compact, few-fld. terminal spike. E. Alps. SYN. *Paederota lutea*, *P. Egeria*. A curious little plant, closely akin to *V. Bonarota*, for rock-garden in rock crevice, stony soil or moraine, but little garden value. Hybridizes in nature with *V. Bonarota*.

V. Lyall'ii.* Sub-shrub, woody at the base, with procumbent rooting stems up to 18 in. long. *l.* ovate to roundish, $\frac{1}{4}$ to $\frac{1}{2}$ in. long, coarsely and bluntly toothed, glabrous, thick and leathery. *fl.* $\frac{1}{2}$ in. across, white veined with rose, in erect slender-stalked racemes 3 to 8 in. h.; anthers blue. July to September. New Zealand. 1876. SYN. *Hebe Lyallii.*

V. lycopodioi'des. Evergreen shrub, $1\frac{1}{2}$ to 3 ft. with stiff, erect, 4-angled branches clothed with scale-like *l.* which are appressed triangular, keeled, pointed, $\frac{1}{16}$ in. long, each pair united at the base. *fl.* $\frac{1}{4}$ in. wide, white, in small terminal heads; anthers blue. June. New Zealand. (B.M. 7338.) SYN. *Hebe lycopodioides.* Occasionally shoots revert to the juvenile conditions and produce awl-shaped or linear, lobed l. $\frac{1}{2}$ in. long, not appressed.

V. macrocar'pa. Erect, evergreen shrub up to 8 ft., shoots glabrous. *l.* 3 to 6 in. long, $\frac{1}{2}$ to 1 in. wide, oblong-lanceolate, glabrous. *fl.* $\frac{1}{2}$ in. or more across, white, numerous in slender racemes 4 to 7 in. long. July, August. *Capsule* up to $\frac{1}{2}$ in. long, large for this genus. New Zealand. Connected by intermediate forms with *V. salicifolia.* SYN. *Hebe macrocarpa.* (B.M. n.s. 358, var. *latisepala.*)

V. macrou'ra. Evergreen shrub, 1 to 5 ft., shoots glabrous. *l.* 1 to 3 in. long, $\frac{1}{2}$ to $1\frac{1}{4}$ in. wide. *fl.* white, $\frac{1}{6}$ to $\frac{1}{4}$ in. wide, in dense racemes 2 to 4 in. long. New Zealand. SYN. *Hebe macroura.*

V. mari'tima. A synonym of *V. longifolia.*

V. Matthews'ii.* Erect evergreen glabrous shrub up to 4 ft., shoots purplish-red when young, glabrous. *l.* closely set, $\frac{3}{4}$ to $1\frac{1}{2}$ in. long, oblong or oval, thick, leathery. *fl.* $\frac{1}{4}$ to $\frac{3}{8}$ in. wide, 2 to 4 in. long, white or purplish, in slender cylindrical racemes 2 to 4 in. long; stalks downy. June, July. New Zealand, where it is a popular garden shrub in the S. Island. SYN. *Hebe Matthewsii.*

V. melissifo'lia. Habit of *V. Chamaedrys.* Perennial herb 1 to 2 ft. *l.* ovate, deeply toothed, sessile. *fl.* blue in loose many-fld. racemes 3 to 9 in. long. Caucasus. Asia Minor.

V. Michaux'ii. Downy herbaceous perennial, 4 to 16 in. *l.* ovate with roundish teeth, those of fl.-stem clasping at base. *fl.* pale blue in a few dense racemes in axils of upper l. Summer. Persia.

V. monta'na. Slender, trailing, hairy herbaceous perennial, 12 to 18 in. long, rooting. *l.* rather few, ovate, coarsely roundish toothed. *fl.* white or pale blue in slender, few-fld. racemes, about 4 in. h. May, June. Europe. Rock-garden.

V. morrisoni'cola. *See under* **V. Forrestii.**

V. multi'fida. Perennial with diffuse, spreading stems about 3 to 12 in. long, somewhat woody at base, hairy. *l.* about $\frac{1}{2}$ in. long, deeply once or twice cut into very narrow segs. *fl.* light blue or pink in short axillary racemes; capsule wedge-shaped at base. June. E. Europe, W. Asia. 1748. (B.M. 1679.) Rock-garden. Easily confused with forms of *V. austriaca* and *V. orientalis.*

V. Nummula'ria. Perennial 1 to 4 in. h. somewhat woody at base, with diffuse much branched creeping, very leafy stems. *l.* ovate-orbicular, about $\frac{1}{8}$ in. long, entire, glabrous. *fl.* blue or pink, large, clustered at the end of the downy raceme. June. Pyrenees. 1820. Rock-garden. A neat ground-covering plant.

V. obova'ta. Erect evergreen shrub, 4 to 5 ft. *l.* $\frac{3}{4}$ to 1 in. long, $\frac{3}{8}$ in. wide, narrowly obovate, blunt-ended, tapered to the short, flat stalk, leathery, the pairs set about $\frac{1}{4}$ in. apart. *fl.* white, $\frac{1}{6}$ in. wide, in slender racemes 1 to 2 in. long. July, August. New Zealand. SYN. *Hebe obovata.*

V. officina'lis. Perennial herb with hairy ascending branches 2 to 18 in. long. *l.* opposite, ovate-oblong or orbicular, $\frac{1}{4}$ to 1 in. long, toothed. *fl.* pale blue or lilac in opposite axillary racemes. May, June. Europe, including Britain. (E.B. 984–5.)

V. Olsen'ii. Prostrate, rooting at the nodes; shoots densely hairy; fl.-stems 3 to 5 in. h. *l.* crowded, $\frac{1}{6}$ to $\frac{1}{4}$ in. long, broadly ovate or almost orbicular, short-stalked, thick and leathery. *fl.* $\frac{1}{4}$ to $\frac{1}{3}$ in. across, white with pink veins. New Zealand. Near *V. Bidwillii,* but more slender with glabrous *l.* and many slender downy, many-fld. racemes. SYN. *Hebe Olsenii.*

V. orchi'dea. Herbaceous perennial with erect glandular stems up to 3 ft. h. from a decumbent base. *l.* opposite, lanceolate or oblong-lanceolate on fl.-stems, shallowly crenate almost from base to tip, rarely almost entire, not glandular, to $2\frac{3}{4}$ in. long. *fl.* dark violet-blue, with 3 lower cor. lobes narrow and pointed, rather twisted and pointing downwards; infl. terminal much branched, with erect densely fld. spikes; cal. glandular; capsule glandular. August. 1819. SE. Europe from N. Italy to Black Sea. (B.M. 2210; Hook. Icon. 3136.) SYN. *V. spicata* var. *orchidea.*

V. orienta'lis. Perennial, woody at the base, with diffuse or decumbent stems about 8 in. long. *l.* linear, lanceolate, or nearly oblong, usually toothed. *fl.* pink or blue in 2 or 4 axillary paired, loose, racemes. July. Asia Minor. 1847. (L.B.C. 419.) Rock-garden in full sun. *V. taurica* is very similar.

V. Orsinia'na. A sub-species of *V. Teucrium.*

V. parviflo'ra. Evergreen shrub usually 4 to 6 ft. in cult. but found in a wild state occasionally 20 to 25 ft., with a trunk girth of 6 ft. *l.* 1 to $2\frac{1}{2}$ in. long, $\frac{1}{8}$ to $\frac{1}{4}$ in. wide, narrowly linear-lanceolate, glabrous. *fl.* white or lilac-tinted, $\frac{1}{8}$ in. wide, on slender racemes 2 to 3 in. long. July, August. New Zealand. 1822. SYN. *Hebe parviflora.* var. **angustifo'lia,** a synonym of *V. angustifolia.*

V. pectina'ta. Low, woody, evergreen prostrate sub-shrub forming a dense mat 3 to 6 in. h., all the parts covered with long white hairs. *l.* oval or obovate $\frac{3}{8}$ to $\frac{3}{4}$ in. long, conspicuously bluntly toothed. *fl.* deep blue with a white centre, numerous in racemes 3 to 5 in. high. May, June. Asia Minor, Syria. 1819.

V. peduncula'ris. Perennial herb with prostrate or ascending stems $\frac{1}{2}$ to 1 ft. h. *l.* ovate to lanceolate, deeply toothed, sometimes pinnately divided, with rounded teeth or lobes, short-stalked or sessile, glabrous or hairy to $1\frac{1}{4}$ in. long. *fl.* white with rose veining, $\frac{3}{8}$ in. across, in long loose many-fld. racemes; pedicels 3 to 5 times as long as cal. May to June. Caucasus, Asia Minor. Nyman's var., *fl.* pale blue. A graceful free-flowering rock-garden plant, with bronzy l.

V. peregri'na. Annual weed akin to *V. arvensis* but glabrous and with oblanceolate *l.* (E.B. 977.) N. America, but now widespread in Europe; first noticed in England about 1680.

V. perfolia'ta. Digger's Speedwell. Sub-shrub or herbaceous perennial; stems erect, 2 to 3 ft. *l.* ovate, pointed, spreading, 1 to $2\frac{1}{2}$ in. long, each pair sometimes united by their broad stalkless bases and clasping the stem. *fl.* bluish-violet with darker lines, $\frac{1}{2}$ in. wide, borne on upper part of erect axillary racemes 6 to 10 in. long. August. Australia. 1834. (B.M. 1936.) Greenhouse. Hardy in favoured districts.

V. per'sica. Annual weed akin to *V. agrestis* but with larger *fl.* Asia, Europe, including Britain. (E.B. 973 as *V. Buxbaumii.*) SYN. *V. Buxbaumii.*

V. petrae'a. Tufted perennial with diffuse or ascending downy stems, 4 to 5 in. h. *l.* oblong, about $\frac{1}{2}$ to $\frac{3}{4}$ in. long, base wedge-shaped, upper l. often entire, lower few-toothed. *fl.* blue, large, in solitary, axillary, rather long-peduncled racemes. Caucasus.

V. pimeleoi'des. Prostrate or partly erect shrub up to $1\frac{1}{2}$ ft., shoots usually downy. *l.* oval, ovate, or obovate, $\frac{1}{2}$ in. long, spreading or rather erect, glaucous, somewhat keeled. *fl.* purplish-blue, $\frac{1}{4}$ to $\frac{1}{3}$ in. across, in cylindrical, solitary, or branched spikes $\frac{3}{4}$ to $1\frac{1}{2}$ in. long. June, August. New Zealand. (B.M. 8967.) SYN. *Hebe pimeleoides.* Rock-garden. var. **glauco-caeru'lea,** larger and more robust, more intensely glaucous. *l.* up to $\frac{1}{2}$ in. long. *fl.* darker purple. SYN. *V. glauco-caerulea, Hebe pimeleoides* var. *glauco-caerulea.*

Veronica pimeleoides

V. pinguifo'lia.* Evergreen shrub 1 to 3 ft., often decumbent, shoots downy when young. *l.* obovate to roundish, stalkless, $\frac{1}{4}$ to $\frac{3}{4}$ in. long, half as wide, blunt, concave, entire, glabrous, glaucous. *fl.* $\frac{1}{4}$ to $\frac{1}{3}$ in. across, white, crowded on spikes $\frac{3}{4}$ to 1 in. long; anthers blue. June to August. New Zealand. (B.M. 6147 and B.M. 6587 as *V. carnosula.*) SYN. *Hebe pinguifolia.*

V. pinna'ta. Herbaceous perennial about 1 ft. with erect stems from a woody rootstock. *l.* very numerous to $2\frac{1}{2}$ in. long, pinnately divided into narrow segs. less than $\frac{1}{20}$ in. wide. *fl.* blue, infl. branched, long racemes; cal. and capsule glabrous. Cent. Asia. In cult. 1815. Akin to *V. spicata* but l. finely divided. **V. inci'sa** is probably a hybrid from *V. pinnata* with l. deeply cut into narrowly triangular or almost linear forward-pointing lobes. In cult. 1789. (L.B.C. 1397.)

V. poli'ta. Annual weed akin to *V. agrestis*, often confused with it. Europe, including Britain. (E.B. 971.)

V. pren'ja. A synonym of *V. austriaca.*

V. propin'qua. Cypress-like, evergreen shrub, 1 to 3 ft. *l.* scale-like, $\frac{1}{10}$ to $\frac{1}{8}$ in. long, closely set on the twigs, each pair united by their margins for much of their length, the free parts rather expanded. *fl.* $\frac{1}{6}$ to $\frac{1}{4}$ in. wide, white in terminal clusters of 4 to 8. July, August. New Zealand. (G.C. 3 (1888), 21 as *V. cupressoides variabilis.*) SYN. *Hebe propinqua.*

V. prostra'ta. Perennial herb with mat-forming prostrate sterile stems and erect or ascending fl.-stems 2 to 8 in. h. *l.* ovate to linear, toothed, wedge-shaped at base, short-stalked, glabrous or hairy, to $1\frac{1}{4}$ in. long. *fl.* deep blue, $\frac{3}{10}$ in. across, in short dense many-fld. racemes; pedicels about as long as cal. May, June. Europe, N. Asia. (B.M. 3683.) SYN. *V. Teucrium* var. *prostrata*, *V. rupestris* of gardens, not Salisbury. A good free-flowering rock-garden plant. var. **al'ba,** *fl.* white, **ro'sea,** *fl.* pink; **Spode Blue,** *fl.* China blue.

V. re'pens. Perennial herb forming wide close mats. Stems prostrate, slender. *l.* ovate, $\frac{1}{4}$ to $\frac{1}{2}$ in. long, vivid green, with few rounded teeth. *fl.* numerous, solitary in l.-axils, whitish or very pale blue, sometimes in short racemes. September. Corsica, Spain. var. **macrocar'pa,** *fl.* pink. Spain. Rock-garden on level site. Good as cover for bulbs.

V. rupes'tris. A synonym of *V. prostrata* as a rule.

V. salicifo'lia. Evergreen shrub up to 10 ft., shoots round, often minutely downy when young. *l.* narrowly lanceolate, slender-pointed, 4 to 6 in. long, $\frac{1}{2}$ to $\frac{3}{4}$ in. wide. *fl.* $\frac{1}{4}$ in. long, lilac-tinged white to bluish-purple, rarely pure white, crowded on slender, cylindrical racemes 4 to 6 in. long; cor. lobes narrow, erect. June to August. New Zealand. SYN. *Hebe salicifolia.* Widely spread and very variable. var. **Kirk'ii,** *l.* smaller, $\frac{3}{4}$ to $1\frac{1}{2}$ in. long, oblong or oblong-lanceolate, *fl.* white, shrub up to 12 ft.

V. salicornioi'des. Evergreen shrub, akin to *V. Hectori* and *V. propinqua.* New Zealand. SYN. *Hebe salicornioides.*

V. satureioi'des. Mat-forming perennial; stems tufted from a woody base, about 3 in. h. *l.* opposite, crowded, oblong or obovate, $\frac{1}{3}$ in. long, slightly toothed at tip. *fl.* dark blue in rather crowded short terminal racemes; cal. 5-partite. April, May. Dalmatia. 1885.

V. saxa'tilis. A synonym of *V. fruticans.*

V. scutella'ta. Marsh Speedwell. Perennial herb, with creeping base. *l.* narrowly linear to linear-lanceolate, entire or slightly toothed, sessile, usually glabrous, sometimes hairy. *fl.* small, pale blue, white, or pink; capsule much longer than cal. Europe, N. America. (E.B. 988.) A marsh plant, of no garden value.

V. senanen'sis. Herbaceous perennial, 4 to 12 in. h. *l.* ovate-oblong, deeply and irregularly toothed, stalked, glabrous or hairy, to 1 in. long. *fl.* pale bluish-purple with deeper veins, $\frac{3}{8}$ in. across, in loose racemes; pedicels much longer than cal. Japan. (Takeda, Alp. Fl. Japan 86.)

V. serpyllifo'lia. Perennial herb, akin to *V. alpina* and *V. repens* Europe, Asia. (E.B. 978.)

V. sibi'rica. A variety of *V. virginica.*

V. specio'sa.* Evergreen shrub up to 5 ft., shoots angled, stout, glabrous. *l.* 2 to $4\frac{1}{2}$ in. long, $\frac{3}{4}$ to $1\frac{3}{4}$ in. wide, obovate to oblong, stout, downy on the midrib above. *fl.* dark reddish-purple or blue-purple, $\frac{1}{3}$ in. across in racemes near tip of the shoots 3 or 4 in. long, 1 to $1\frac{1}{2}$ in. wide. July to September. New Zealand. 1835. (B.M. 4057.) SYN. *Hebe speciosa.* Tender and only suitable for the warmest counties in its typical state. It has produced several beautiful varieties and hybrids: **Cookia'na,** white, *fl.* large; **Evelyn,** rich carmine; **glorio'sa,** bright pink; **Headfort'ii,** purplish-blue; **La Seduisante,** bright crimson; **Purple Queen,** bright purple; **Silver Beauty,** silver-variegated; **Simon Deleaux,** rich crimson; **Veitch'ii,*** deep rich purple.

V. spica'ta. Herbaceous perennial with stems 6 to 18 in. h. from a decumbent base. *l.* opposite, narrow-oblong to oblong-lanceolate, toothed except at base and tip, 1 to $1\frac{1}{2}$ in. long. *fl.* bright blue, in dense racemes, solitary or few at ends of stems, $1\frac{1}{2}$ to 3 in. long; cor. tube shorter than cal., stamens long, purple. Summer. Europe, including Britain. (E.B. 982.) For rock-garden or front of border. Variable in stature and colour. var. **al'ba,** *fl.* white; **ro'sea,** *fl.* purplish-pink. In gardens the name *V. spicata* is often misapplied to the more robust *V. longifolia* and it may also be used for other members of section Pseudolysimachia, e.g. *V. crassifolia*, *V. euxina*, *V. hybrida*, *V. orchidea*, and *V. spuria*, and hybrids.

V. spu'ria. Densely downy herbaceous perennial with erect stems 1 to 3 ft. h. *l.* opposite or whorled, lanceolate, about 1 in. long, crenate-toothed towards apex, smooth or almost so. *fl.* blue, in rather large terminal panicles, rather loose, many-fld. June. SE. Europe. 1797. Border plant. var. **el'egans,** more branched and with downy *l.*

V. subses'silis. A variety of *V. longifolia.*

V. surculo'sa. Dwarf creeping perennial of dense habit. *l.* oblanceolate or lanceolate, very hairy, bluntly toothed, under $\frac{1}{2}$ in. long. *fl.* blue in short racemes; pedicels about as long as cal.; capsule wedge-shaped at base. Asia Minor. Rock-garden.

V. syria'ca. Annual. Stem diffuse or ascending, branched, downy, 6 to 12 in. long. *l.* ovate to ovate-lanceolate, bracts narrower, somewhat toothed. *fl.* blue, large, in slender, terminal racemes 4 to 6 in. long; pedicels about $\frac{1}{2}$ in. long. Syria. 1857. Half hardy. (F.d.S. 1259.) There is a white-fld. form.

V. tau'rica. Closely akin to *V. orientalis.* Crimea. (L.B.C. 901.)

V. telephiifo'lia. Glabrous perennial, creeping or tufted, with short very slender branches. *l.* more or less in rosettes, obovate-spatulate or oblong, scarcely $\frac{1}{4}$ in. long, blue-green, fleshy. *fl.* blue, in short axillary racemes. Summer. Armenia. A choice rock-garden plant.

V. Teu'crium. Perennial 6 to 36 in. h. erect or decumbent stems, more or less hairy. *l.* ovate to linear, more or less toothed or somewhat pinnatifid, more or less round or heart-shaped at base. *fl.* large, blue, in long, opposite, axillary racemes. July. S. Europe, N. Asia. 1596. (L.B.C. 425.) An extraordinarily variable and widespread species, divided by some botanists into 5 sub-species (as well as numerous varieties and forms) to which the names *Teucrium*, *crinita*, *Orsiniana*, *thracica*, and *altaica* have been given; for a detailed account, see *Abh. zool.-bot. Ges. Wien* 5 (1910); var. **thra'cica,** erect, up to 20 in. h., *l.* ovate or roundish, *fl.* azure-blue in dense racemes. Balkans. (B.M. 9215.); **Trehane,** 4 to 8 in. h., *l.* golden-yellow. SYN. *V. Orsiniana chrysophylla*; **vesti'ta,** almost prostrate, *l.* grey-hairy. France, Spain. SYN. *V. canescens* of Bastard not Schrader, *V. Bastardii*, *V. Teucrium* var. *canescens.* They are attractive and showy garden plants. The name *V. latifolia* (see above) is also used for this species.

V. Travers'ii. *See under* **V. brachysiphon.**

V. urticifo'lia. Erect, herbaceous perennial to 2 ft. h., sessile; stem crisply hairy. *l.* ovate, sharply toothed, sessile, usually cordate at base. *fl.* light blue in loosely branched opposite racemes. Europe. Border plant. SYN. *V. latifolia* of many authors.

V. vernicos'a, Evergreen shrub 1 to 3 ft. erect or decumbent, branches spreading, very minutely downy when young. *l.* closely packed on the shoots, $\frac{1}{4}$ to $\frac{1}{2}$ in. long, $\frac{1}{8}$ to $\frac{3}{16}$ in. wide, oval to obovate, pointed, dark lustrous green. *fl.* white, $\frac{1}{4}$ to $\frac{1}{3}$ in. wide in 4 to 8 clustered racemes. $\frac{1}{2}$ to $1\frac{1}{2}$ in. long near the tips of the shoots. June to August. New Zealand. (B.T.S. ii. 640.) SYN. *Hebe vernicosa.* var. **canterburien'sis,** smaller and more prostrate. SYN. *V. canterburiensis.* (B.M. n.s. 136 as *Hebe vernicosa canterburiensis.*)

V. virgi'nica. Herbaceous perennial with erect, downy, unbranched stems, 2 to 6 ft. h. *l.* in whorls of 3 to 6, lanceolate, long slender-pointed, 2 to 4 in. long, closely sharply toothed. *fl.* many, white or pale blue in dense terminal erect racemes 6 to 10 in. long, pedicels short. Autumn. Eastern N. America. 1714. SYN. *Veronicastrum virginica*, *Leptandra virginica.* var. **japo'nica,** *fl.* blue or white with pedicel longer than cal. Japan; **sibi'rica,** *fl.* blue or white with pedicels shorter than cal. or absent. NE. Asia. SYN. *Veronicastrum sibiricum.*

VERONICAS'TRUM. Included in **Veronica.**

verruco'sus -a -um, warted; covered with wart-like excrescences; verrucose.

verruculo'sus -a -um, somewhat verrucose.

VERSAILLES LAUREL. A broad-leaved form of the common Laurel, *Prunus Laurocerasus.*

versatile, turning freely on its support; swinging to and fro.

VERSCHAFFELT'IA (in honour of Ambrose Colletto Alexandre Verschaffelt (1825–86), Belgian author of a work on Camellias, 1848). FAM. *Palmaceae.* A genus of 1 tall palm, at first spiny, native of the Seychelles. A slender tree, ringed, with stilt-roots. Leaves recurved, in a terminal crown, blade oblong, usually laciniate with toothed segments, sheath long, deeply split. Spadix 3 to 6 ft. long, branched, recurved; spathes 2 or 3, long, sheathing, lowest only persistent; flowers very small;

fruit globose, smooth, 1 in. long. Cultivation as for Latania.

V. splen'dida. Tree to 80 ft., 6 to 12 in. thick, very spiny at first, with many aerial roots. *l.* 5 to 8 ft. long, stalk 6 to 12 in., blade obovate, bright green, 3 to 5 ft. wide, 2-fid, deeply toothed at edges. (I.H. 12, 430.)

versi'color, changeable in colour, or variously coloured.

verticil, a whorl.

verticilla'ris -is -e, having whorls.

verticillaster, a false whorl; the verticillaster of Labiatae consists of two opposite cymes.

verticilla'tus -a -um, arranged in a whorl, forming a ring round a common axis.

VERTICIL'LIUM. A genus of Fungi Imperfecti several species of which cause plant diseases, mostly attacking roots and causing wilting. *See* **Tomato Sleepy Disease** (due to *V. alboatrum*), and the wilt of Michaelmas Daisies (*V. Vilmorinii*) described under Aster Diseases.

D. E. G.

VERTICOR'DIA (*verto*, to turn, *cordis*, a heart; a title of Venus to whom the Myrtle was sacred). FAM. *Myrtaceae*. Juniper Myrtle. A genus of about 50 species of shrubs, with, as a rule, the aspect of a Heath or Diosma, all natives of Australia. They are glabrous save for cilia on the leaf edges, having small opposite (or rarely alternate), entire leaves. Flowers whitish, pink, or yellow, in corymbs, spikes, or racemes; calyx lobes 5, often coloured, plumose, radiating; corolla of 5 petals, entire, fringed, or digitate; stamens 10, alternating with staminodes. Easily grown in the greenhouse in a compost of sandy loam and leaf-mould, and propagated readily by cuttings of firm or partially ripened shoots under a glass or close frame. They need abundance of water and syringing

Verticordia niten

throughout the summer and should not be allowed to become dry at the roots at any time.

V. Brown'ii. Shrub 3 to 4 ft. h., very densely branched; young shoots almost thread-like, pale. *l.* 1/12 to 1/8 in. long, oval to obovate, sessile, apex rounded. Keeled and almost 3-sided. *fl.* very small and numerous in terminal corymbs making dense clusters 3 to 5 in. across; cal. cut into numerous hair-like lobes, forming the conspicuous part of the infl.; pet. fringed. April. W. Australia. 1842.

V. densiflo'ra. Bushy shrub, 2 to 3 ft. *l.* linear, almost thread-like, terete or 3-sided, 1/4 to 1/2 in. long, densely crowded in axillary tufts or on short branches. *fl.* white or pink, in dense, terminal clusters, long-stalked, and forming radiating compound clusters 2 to 4 in. across; cal. bristly at base; pet. fringed. June. W. Australia. 1860. Akin to *V. Fontanesii* but with much longer stalk, more open clusters of corymbs.

V. Fontanes'ii. Bushy shrub, 3 to 4 ft. *l.* linear, 1/8 to 1/3 in. long, terete to 3-sided. *fl.* white or pink, 1/4 to 1/3 in. wide, in small terminal corymbs or rounded panicles 1 to 2 in. across; cal. tube bristly hairy, the 5 to 7 lobes fringed and feather-like, silvery white; pet. oblong or ovate, slightly downy, sometimes ciliate. April. W. Australia. 1826.

V. insig'nis. Shrub 1 to 2 ft., much-branched; shoots erect, slender, pale. *l.* obovate to oval, 1/8 to 1/2 in. long, 1/12 to 1/4 in. wide, apex rounded, mucronate, sessile, glabrous. *fl.* pink, 1/2 in. wide, in terminal corymbs making clusters 3 or 4 in. across; cal. deeply fringed; pet. orbicular, fringed; stalk very slender, up to 1 1/4 in. long. April. W. Australia. 1838.

V. ni'tens.* Erect shrub, 3 to 4 ft., stems slender. *l.* opposite or in fours, linear, semi-terete, 1/2 to 1 1/2 in. long, 1/16 to 1/24 in. wide. *fl.* golden-yellow, in terminal corymbs forming a close, flattish mass of blossom 1 1/2 to 4 in. across; cal. deeply divided into 7 to 11 subulate lobes; pet. ovate to obovate, shortly irregularly fringed. August. W. Australia. 1859. (B.M. 5286.)

W. J. B.

ve'rus -a -um, true.

VERVAIN. *See* **Verbena officinalis.**

VERVAIN, BASTARD. *See* **Stachytarpheta.**

VERVAIN SAGE. *See* **Salvia Verbenaca.**

ves'cus -a -um, small, fine, feeble.

VESICA'RIA. (*vesica*, bladder or blister; in allusion to the inflated pod). FAM. *Cruciferae*. A genus of annual or perennial herbs, natives of the Mediterranean Region for the most part, with entire or pinnatifid leaves and yellow flowers. Fruit an inflated pod. At one time many species were included in this genus but are now distributed over several other genera: *V. arctica*, *V. gracilis*, and *V. grandiflora* are to be sought in Lesquerella; *V. cretica*, *V. edentula*, and *V. sinuata* in Alyssum; *V. utriculata* in Alyssoides; *V. didymocarpa* in Physaria. They are easily cultivated in ordinary soil and are in the main hardy and suitable for the rock-garden. The perennial species may be increased by division, the annual species by seeds.

V. grae'ca. Perennial. *l.* of sterile branches thick, oblong-spatulate, slightly pointed, of fertile branches, sessile, erect, acute, margins ciliate, often toothed. *fl.* yellow, elliptic, in racemes; pet. twice as long as sep. Greece.

vesica'rius -a -um, inflated, bladder-like, or composed of little bladders.

vesicato'rius -a -um, blistering.

vesiculo'sus -a -um, inflated, bladder-like, or composed of little bladders.

VESLINGIA SATIVA. A synonym of *Guizotia abyssinica.*

VES'PA. *See* **Hornet.**

vespertil'is, vespertilio'nis, bat-like, as leaves with 2 large lobes.

vesperti'nus -a -um, appearing or expanding in the evening.

VESPUC'CIA. *See* **Hydrocleys.**

A→

VESSELS. Vessels are tubes formed by the union of several cells, the cavities of which have been made continuous by the complete or partial absorption of the walls which originally separated them. These are called tracheae. Elongated cells with pitted lignified walls which conduct water are known as tracheids. They form part of the wood (including the leaf-veins) of most flowering plants and are characterized by their lignified walls which are either pitted or have ring-like (annular), spiral or netted (riticulated) thickening which assists in keeping the cavity open as does the spiral wire in a rubber hose. They early lose their protoplasm, contain air, water, or both, and form an important part of the system by which water is conveyed from one part of the plant to another. In the wood of the Pteridophyta and in the Coniferae long closed cells occur with a similar function and with similar walls and contents. Somewhat similar cells occur in the outer layer (velamen) of the aerial roots of orchids, where their walls are only partially lignified, and in the leaves and cortex of Sphagnum moss, where they are not at all lignified. For their arrangement in the plant *see* Vascular System and Venation and compare Sieve Tubes and Laticiferous Vessels and Cells.

vesta'lis -is -e, white.

VES'TIA (in honour of L. C. de Vest, 1776–1840, Professor at Graz). Fam. *Solanaceae*. Monotypic genus akin to Cestrum. *V. lycioides* is a handsome shrub requiring cool greenhouse conditions and a good loamy soil. Easily propagated by cuttings.

V. lycioi'des. Evergreen, erect, unpleasantly scented shrub; shoots downy. *l.* alternate, oblong-oval to obovate, 1 to 2 in. long, glabrous, entire, base cuneate. *fl.* nodding, axillary; cal. bell-shaped, $\frac{1}{4}$ in. long, green, 5-toothed; cor. tube 1 to $1\frac{1}{4}$ in. long, $\frac{1}{4}$ in. wide, pale-yellow with a limb of 5 spreading lobes $\frac{3}{4}$ in. across. April to June. Chile. 1815.

W. J. B.

vesti'tus -a -um, clothed, covered with.

VETCH. *See* **Vicia.**

VETCH, BASTARD or **BLADDER.** *See* **Astragalus.**

VETCH, BITTER. *See* **Lathyrus.**

VETCH, KIDNEY. *See* **Anthyllis Vulneraria.**

VETCH, MILK. *See* **Astragalus.**

ve'xans, annoying, wounding.

vexilla'ris -is -e, having a standard.

VEXILLUM. The standard or large posterior petal of a papilionaceous flower.

A→

via'lis -is -e }
via'rum } by or of the wayside.

VIBORG'IA (in honour of Eric Viborg, 1759–1822, Professor of Botany at Copenhagen). Sometimes spelt Wiborgia. FAM. *Leguminosae*. A genus of about 10 species of S. African shrubs, sometimes spiny. Leaves 3-foliolate. Flowers papilionaceous, petals long and slenderly clawed, standard ovate. Cool greenhouse, in an ordinary compost of loam, peat, or leaf soil and sand.

V. obcorda'ta. Shrub 3 to 6 ft., shoots long, slender, grooved, appressed-silky. *l.* 3-foliolate; lflets. $\frac{1}{6}$ to $\frac{3}{8}$ in. long, $\frac{1}{12}$ to $\frac{1}{8}$ in. wide, base cuneate, apex rounded or notched, silky. *Racemes* terminal, many-fld., 3 to 8 in. long. *fl.* $\frac{3}{8}$ in. long, yellow. July. Pod oval, $\frac{3}{8}$ in. long, 1-seeded, winged. S. Africa. (L.B.C. 509 as *Crotalaria floribunda.*)

W. J. B.

viburnoi'des, Viburnum-like.

VIBURN'UM (ancient Latin name for *V. Lantana*). FAM. *Caprifoliaceae*. A genus of about 120 species spread over the north temperate zone, including N. Africa, Asia as far south as Java, in the W. Indies, and in S. America. Shrubs, occasionally small trees, evergreen or deciduous. Leaves opposite, simple, entire, toothed or lobed, with or without stipules attached to the stalks; the pubescence is usually stellate. Flowers white or pinkish, borne in flattish, rounded, or pyramidal clusters, sometimes sterile. The fertile flowers are small and have a bell-shaped or tubular corolla with 5 rounded usually spreading lobes, 5 stamens, and a drupaceous 1-seeded fruit, red, black, blue, or yellow. Sterile flowers—large and showy—are borne by several species; they consist of petals only and are situated on the inflorescence margin.

Viburnums are easily cultivated, but they are ill-adapted for dry situations and poor soils. The great majority are quite hardy but a few, like *V. odoratissimum*, *V. rigidum*, and *V. suspensum*, are happiest in the warmer counties. Seeds are available for propagation of most of the species and cuttings taken from half-ripened shoots usually take root readily, most quickly in gentle bottom heat, but also in close unheated hand-lights or cloches.

The garden value of the genus is contributed to by flower, fruit, and often autumn colour. In contrast to the flowers of a good many species, which are exceptionally fragrant, the wood is frequently evil-smelling when bruised. It is to this character that the forbidding specific names *foetidum* and *foetens* refer.

KEY

1.	*Lvs. evergreen*	2
1.	*Lvs. deciduous*	16.
2.	*Fl. in flat umbel-like cymes*	3
2.	*Fl. in paniculate cymes*	14
3.	*Winter-buds without scales*	4
3.	*Winter-buds with one or two pairs of scales*	6
4.	*Outer or all fls. of infl. enlarged and sterile*	V. macrocephalum
4.	*Fl. all alike, perfect*	5
5.	*Lvs. smooth above, 1 to 3 in. long, entire*	V. utile
5.	*Lvs. larger, slightly toothed*	V. × Burkwoodii
5.	*Lvs. wrinkled above, 4 to 8 in. long*	V. rhytidophyllum
6.	*Veins of lvs. curving and branching inside margin*	7
6.	*Veins of lvs. straight, ending in teeth*	13
7.	*Cor. cylindrical*	V. cylindricum
7.	*Cor. rotate*	8
8.	*Lvs. distinctly 3-nerved*	9
8.	*Lvs. not distinctly 3-nerved*	11
9.	*Lvs. entire or nearly so*	V. cinnamomifolium
9.	*Lvs. somewhat toothed*	10
10.	*Lvs. 3 to 5 in. long, 1 to $2\frac{1}{2}$ in. wide*	V. Davidi
10.	*Lvs. 2 to $3\frac{1}{2}$ in. long, $\frac{1}{2}$ to $1\frac{1}{4}$ in. wide*	V. propinquum
11.	*Lvs. $\frac{1}{5}$ to 1 in. long, glabrous*	V. Harryanum
11.	*Lvs. over $1\frac{1}{2}$ in. long*	12
12.	*Lvs. dull green, very hairy*	V. rigidum
12.	*Lvs. glossy green above, less hairy*	V. Tinus
13.	*Lvs. 3 to 6 in. long, with dark dots beneath*	V. japonicum
13.	*Lvs. 1 to $3\frac{1}{2}$ in. long, 3-nerved at base*	V. foetidum
14.	*Young shoots smooth*	V. Henryi
14.	*Young shoots warted*	15
15.	*L.-stalks $\frac{1}{2}$ to $1\frac{1}{4}$ in. long; lvs. hairy in vein-axils beneath*	V. odoratissimum
15.	*L.-stalks $\frac{1}{4}$ to $\frac{1}{2}$ in. long; lvs. glabrous*	V. suspensum
16.	*Fl. after lvs. or with lvs.*	17
16.	*Fl. normally before lvs.; cor. salverform with tube $\frac{3}{10}$ to $\frac{1}{2}$ in. long; lvs. not lobed*	24
17.	*Lvs. lobed, stipulate*	18
17.	*Lvs. not lobed*	22
18.	*Fl. all alike, perfect*	19
18.	*Outer or all fls. of infl. enlarged and sterile*	20
19.	*Lvs. black-dotted beneath*	V. acerifolium
19.	*Lvs. without black dots beneath*	V. orientale
20.	*Anthers yellow*	21
20.	*Anthers purple, l.-stalk $\frac{3}{4}$ to $1\frac{1}{2}$ in. long*	V. Sargentii
21.	*L.-stalk with few large glands*	V. Opulus
21.	*L.-stalk with small, usually stalked glands*	V. trilobum
22.	*Fl. in paniculate cymes*	23
22.	*Fl. in flat umbel-like cymes*	25
23.	*Cor. tubular*	V. erubescens
23.	*Cor. rotate*	V. Sieboldii
24.	*Cor. tube about $\frac{1}{3}$ in. long; l. veins 5 or 6 pairs*	V. fragrans
24.	*Cor. tube about $\frac{1}{2}$ in. long; l veins 7 to 10 pairs*	24 bis
24 bis.	*Infl. hairy, compact*	V. × bodnantense, V. grandiflorum
24 bis.	*Infl. hairy at nodes only, looser*	V. foetens
25.	*Winter-buds without scales*	26
25.	*Winter-buds with 1 or 2 pairs of scales*	34
26.	*Outer or all fls. of infl. enlarged and sterile*	27
26.	*Fls. all alike, perfect*	29
27.	*Veins branching inside margin*	V. macrocephalum
27.	*Veins straight, ending in teeth*	28
28.	*Stamens as long as cor. lobes; bush spreading*	V. alnifolium
28.	*Stamens half as long as cor. lobes, bush erect*	V. furcatum
29.	*Cor. salver-shaped*	30
29.	*Cor. rotate*	31
30.	*Stamens included within about $\frac{2}{5}$ in. long cor. tube*	57

30. *Stamens protruding from about $\frac{1}{2}$ in. long cor. tube* 59
31. *Cor. lobes shorter than tube, cymes 5-rayed* V. cotinifolium
31. *Cor. lobes longer than tube* 32
32. *Teeth of l. close* V. Lantana
32. *Teeth of l. distant* 33
33. *Lvs. ovate* V. Veitchii
33. *Lvs. oblong-lanceolate* V. buddleifolium
34. *Outer or all fls. of infl. enlarged and sterile* V. tomentosum
34. *Fls. all alike, perfect* 35
35. *Veins curving, branching within margin* 36
35. *Veins straight, ending in teeth* 40
36. *Infl. stalked* 37
36. *Infl. sessile or nearly so; l. sharply toothed* 38
37. *L. glossy, entire, finally glabrous; infl. long-stalked* V. nudum
37. *L. obscurely toothed, usually somewhat hairy; infl. short-stalked* V. cassinoides
38. *L.-stalk with broad wavy margin* V. Lentago
38. *L.-stalk with narrow flat margin* 39
39. *Buds, l.-stalks, and shoots rusty-hairy* V. rafidulum
39. *L.-stalks and shoots not rusty-hairy* V. prunifolium
40. *Fruits red* 41
40. *Fruits black or blue-black* 53
41. *Lvs. not stipulate* 42
41. *Lvs. stipulate* 47
42. *Lvs. 3-nerved at base* V. foetidum
42. *Lvs. not 3-nerved at base* 43
43. *Lvs. downy both sides* V. dilatatum
43. *Lvs. glabrous except on veins beneath* 44
44. *Lvs. broadest above middle* V. Wrightii
44. *Lvs. broadest below middle* 45
45. *Stamens very short* V. phlebotrichum
45. *Stamens at least half length of cor.* 46
46. *Lvs. ovate-oblong, acuminate, 3 to 5 in. long* V. setigerum
46. *Lvs. ovate, $2\frac{1}{2}$ to 3 in. long* V. Wrightii Hessei
47. *L.-stalk $\frac{1}{8}$ to $\frac{1}{4}$ in. long* 48
47. *L.-stalk $\frac{1}{3}$ to $1\frac{1}{4}$ in. long* 49
48. *L. hairy beneath* V. ichangense
48. *L. hairy only on veins beneath* V. erosum
49. *L. downy beneath* 50
49. *L. downy on veins beneath at most* 51
50. *L. downy on both surfaces* V. hupehense
50. *Young lvs. bronzy; lvs. downy beneath* V. Wilsonii
51. *Cor. hairy outside* V. dasyanthum
51. *Cor. glabrous outside* 52
52. *Infl. long-stalked* V. lobophyllum
52. *Infl. short-stalked* V. betulifolium
53. *Lvs. stipulate* 54
53. *Lvs. not stipulate* 55
54. *L.-stalk not over $\frac{1}{2}$ in. long, lvs. rounded at base, bark close* V. affine
54. *L.-stalk over $\frac{1}{2}$ in. long, lvs. deeply cordate at base, bark flaky* V. molle
55. *Veins on 7 to 11 pairs; shoots smooth* 56
55. *Veins in 5 to 7 pairs; shoots rough* V. scabrellum
56. *Young shoots glabrous* V. dentatum
56. *Young shoots slightly hairy* V. pubescens
57. *Filaments and anthers about the same length; stamens inserted above middle of cor. tube; lvs. acute, usually rounded at base* V. Carlesii
57. *Filaments much longer than anthers; stamens at or below middle of cor. tube* 58
58. *Infl. $2\frac{1}{4}$ to $3\frac{1}{2}$ in. across; stamens inserted at or slightly below middle of cor. tube with anther tips reaching mouth* V. × Juddii
58. *Infl. $1\frac{1}{4}$ to 2 cm. across; stamens inserted on lower third of cor. tube with anther tips not reaching mouth* V. bitchiuense
59. *Heads nearly 4 in. across; stamens inserted at base of cor. tube* V. × Carlcephalum
59. *Heads about 2 in. across; stamens inserted on tube about $\frac{1}{10}$ in. above base* V. × Burkwoodii

V. acerifo'lium. Deciduous shrub, 3 to 6 ft., shoots at first softly downy. *l.* 2 to 4 in. long, maple-like, 3-lobed, the lobes coarsely toothed and slender-pointed, softly downy and black-dotted beneath. *fl.* yellowish-white, $\frac{1}{5}$ in. wide, in long-stalked clusters 2 to $3\frac{1}{2}$ in. across. June. *fr.* oval, $\frac{1}{4}$ in. long, red then purple-black. N. America. 1736. Crimson in autumn.

V. affi'ne. Deciduous shrub, 5 to 7 ft., shoots glabrous. *l.* broadly oval to ovate, $1\frac{1}{2}$ to $3\frac{1}{2}$ in. long, rounded or subcordate at base, pointed, coarsely triangular-toothed; veins in 4 to 6 pairs; stalk $\frac{1}{12}$ to $\frac{1}{2}$ in. long. *infl.* $1\frac{1}{2}$ to 3 in. wide, densely set with small white fl. May, June. *fr.* oval, $3\frac{1}{2}$ in. long, bluish-black. N. America. 1899. var. **hypoma'lacum,** *l.* densely pubescent beneath. Autumn colour good. (G. & F. 3. 125 as *V. pubescens.*)

V. alnifo'lium. Hobble-bush. Deciduous shrub up to 10 ft., lower branches often self-layered; shoots densely scurfy-downy. *l.* broadly ovate to roundish, cordate, toothed, 4 to 8 in. long, more or less downy on both surfaces. *fl.* white, in flat stalkless clusters 3 to 5 in. across, the marginal ones sterile, 1 in. wide. May, June. *fr.* red then black-purple. N. America. 1820. Loves moisture and some shade. Autumn colour crimson. (B.M. 9373.)

V. Awafu'ki. A synonym of *V. odoratissimum.*

V. betulifo'lium.* Deciduous shrub up to 12 ft., shoots glabrous, purplish-brown. *l.* 2 to 4 in. long, ovate to rhombic, cuneate, coarsely toothed; veins in 4 to 6 pairs, slightly hairy and tufted in their axils. *fl.* white, $\frac{1}{8}$ in. wide, in short-stalked, usually 7-rayed clusters 2 to 4 in. across. June. *fr.* red, sub-globose, $\frac{1}{4}$ in. long. China. 1901. (B.M. 8672.) This species does not fruit freely as a young plant but when mature is one of the finest shrubs for the effect of its berries in autumn.

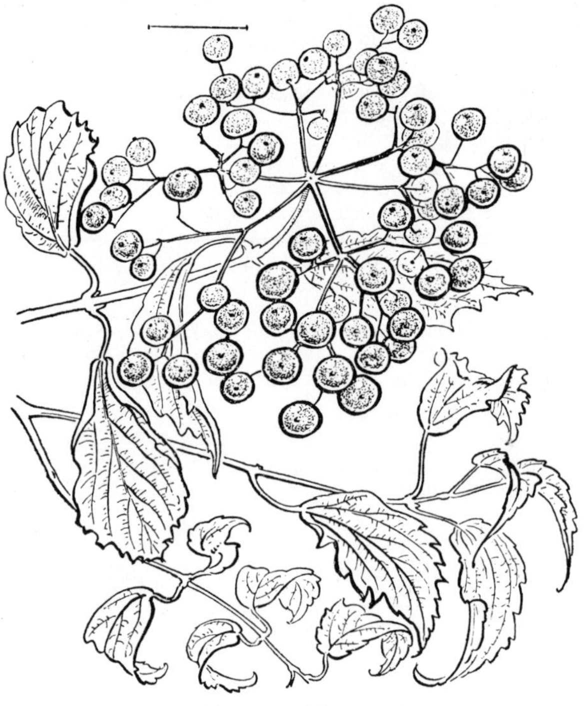

Viburnum betulifolium

V. bitchiuen'se. Deciduous shrub up to 10 ft., of loose open habit, shoots densely downy. *l.* ovate, $1\frac{1}{2}$ to $3\frac{1}{2}$ in. long, slightly toothed, downy above, more so beneath; veins in 5 to 7 pairs. *fl.* pink then white, very fragrant, in rounded clusters up to 3 in. across; cor. $\frac{3}{4}$ in. wide, tube slender, $\frac{1}{3}$ in. long. May. *fr.* $\frac{2}{5}$ in. long, black. Japan. 1911. (B.T.S. 3. 497.) Closely akin to *V. Carlesii*, but of more open habit and looser infl.

V. × bodnanten'se. (Hybrid between *V. fragrans* and *V. grandiflorum.*) Deciduous much-branched shrub up to 11 ft. *l.* lanceolate or ovate to oblanceolate or obovate, $1\frac{1}{2}$ to 4 in. long, $\frac{3}{4}$ to $2\frac{1}{4}$ in. wide, toothed, becoming glabrous beneath except for axil-tufts; veins in 6 to 9 pairs. *fl.* closely packed in clusters to 3 in. wide, deep rose in bud, later almost white; cor. $\frac{2}{5}$ in. wide, the tube about $\frac{3}{10}$ to $\frac{2}{5}$ in. long. October onwards. (J.R.H.S. 73 (1948), 44; B.M. N.S. 113.) There exist several forms of this hybrid, the best being Dawn, which is a very good fragrant winter-flowering shrub.

V. buddleifo'lium. Deciduous shrub up to 8 ft., shoots densely downy. *l.* oblong-lanceolate, 3 to 5 in. long, 1 to 2 in. wide rounded to cordate at base, shallow-toothed, felted beneath. *fl.* white, $\frac{1}{3}$ in. wide, in clusters 3 in. across. June. *fr.* oval, $\frac{1}{3}$ in. long, red then black. China. 1900. Akin to *V. Lantana.*

V. × Burkwood'ii. (Hybrid between *V. Carlesii* and *V. utile.*) Evergreen shrub, 4 to 6 ft. *l.* ovate, pointed, $1\frac{1}{2}$ to 4 in. long, half as wide, cuneate to cordate at base, slightly toothed, dark lustrous green above, thickly downy beneath. *fl.* $\frac{1}{2}$ in. wide, fragrant, pinkish becoming white, in clusters $2\frac{1}{2}$ to $3\frac{1}{2}$ in. wide. March, April, May. 1924.

V. × Carlceph'alum (*V. Carlesii* × *V. macrocephalum*). Deciduous shrub with *l.* and habit similar to *V. Carlesii. fl.-heads* large up to 5 in. in diam., globular, white with very little red colouring on outside of buds; tube shorter than *V. Carlesii* about $\frac{1}{10}$ in. long with anthers protruding. Fragrant. April. Raised about 1932. (J.R.H.S. 1947, fig. 132; G.C. 119 (1946), 217.)

V. Carles'ii.* Deciduous shrub of bushy habit, 4 to 8 ft., shoots densely downy. *l.* 2 to $3\frac{1}{2}$ in. long, broadly ovate to oval, pointed, irregularly toothed, dull green, downy especially beneath; veins in 5 to 7 pairs. *fl.* very fragrant, in close clusters 2 to 3 in. wide, white, $\frac{1}{2}$ in. across, tube slender $\frac{1}{3}$ in. long. April, May. *fr.* $\frac{1}{3}$ in. long, oval, black. Korea. 1902. (B.M. 8114.) Very charming for its fragrance and beauty.

V. cassinoi'des. Deciduous shrub of bushy rounded shape, 6 to 8 ft., shoots scurfy. *l.* $1\frac{1}{2}$ to $4\frac{1}{2}$ in. long, oval, ovate, or oblong, obscurely toothed, dull green, nearly glabrous. *fl.* yellowish-white,

$\frac{1}{3}$ in. wide, in flattish, short-stalked clusters 2 to 4 in. across. June. *fr.* pale green, then bright rose, finally blue-black. N. America. 1761. Described as the best Viburnum in the gardens of New England. (G. & F. 9, 305.) Near *V. nudum* which differs by its glossy l. and much longer-stalked infl.

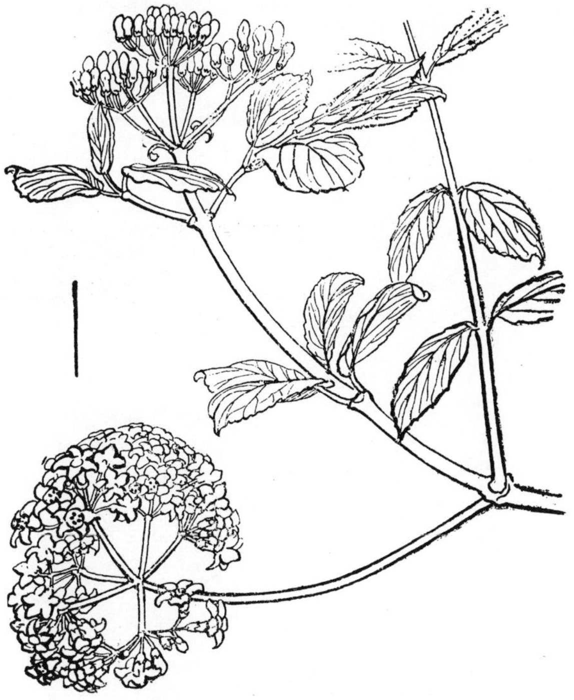

Viburnum × *Burkwoodii* (p. 2226)

V. cinnamomifo'lium. Evergreen shrub up to 18 ft. and as much wide. *l.* 3 to $5\frac{1}{2}$ in. long, 1 to $2\frac{3}{4}$ in. wide, scarcely toothed, glabrous, oval to obovate, conspicuously 3-veined. *fl.* dull white, $\frac{1}{4}$ in. wide, in spreading clusters 4 to 6 in. across. June. *fr.* $\frac{1}{6}$ in. long, ovoid-globose, blue-black, shining. China. 1904. Akin to *V. Davidi*, but larger, infl. wider, fr. smaller. (S.T.S. 2, 119.)

V. coria'ceum. A synonym of *V. cylindricum.*

V. corylifo'lium. Deciduous shrub, up to 10 ft., shoots densely hairy. *l.* $1\frac{1}{2}$ to $3\frac{1}{2}$ in. long, orbicular-ovate to obovate, rounded to subcordate at base, abruptly pointed, toothed; veins in 6 to 9 pairs, downy above, hairy beneath. *fl.* fragrant, white, very small, in compound hairy-stalked clusters $1\frac{1}{2}$ to 3 in. across. June. *fr.* ovoid, $\frac{1}{3}$ in. long, scarlet. India, China.

V. cotinifo'lium. Deciduous shrub, 6 to 12 ft., shoots, l., and fl.-stalks densely downy. *l.* 2 to 5 in. long, ovate to nearly orbicular, wrinkled, finely toothed. *fl.* in rounded corymbs 2 to 3 in. across, white tinged pink, widely funnel-shaped, $\frac{1}{4}$ in. long. June. *fr.* red, finally black, ovoid, $\frac{1}{3}$ in. long. Himalaya (where it represents *V. Lantana*). 1830. (B.R. 1650.) Autumn colour crimson.

V. cylind'ricum. Evergreen shrub or a tree up to 40 ft., shoots glabrous, warty. *l.* oval to oblong, 3 to 8 in. long, half as wide, slightly toothed near apex, dull green above, and covered with a thin layer of wax which cracks or shows grey when l. is bent. *fl.* in clusters 3 to 5 in. across, white, quite tubular, $\frac{1}{4}$ in. long, lobes erect; anthers lilac. July to September. *fr.* ovoid, $\frac{1}{6}$ in. long, black. Himalaya, China. (S.T.S. 2. 143.) Syn. *V. coriaceum.*

V. dasyan'thum. Deciduous shrub up to 8 ft., shoots glabrous. *l.* ovate to oblong, rounded at base, slender-pointed, sparsely and shallowly toothed, $2\frac{1}{2}$ to $4\frac{1}{2}$ in. long, glabrous above; veins in 6 or 7 pairs. *fl.* white, $\frac{1}{3}$ in. across, the corolla hairy outside, borne in open 7-rayed clusters 3 to 4 in. across. June. *fr.* ovoid, $\frac{1}{3}$ in. long, red. China. 1907. (S.T.S. 2. 149.)

V. Davidi. Evergreen shrub, 3 to 5 ft. of dense, compact growth, shoots warty. *l.* oval to obovate, sharply pointed, obscurely toothed, 3 to 5 in. long, conspicuously 3-veined, glabrous except for tufts in vein axils. *fl.* dull white, $\frac{1}{6}$ in. wide, densely set in flat corymbs 2 to 3 in. wide. June. *fr.* ovoid, $\frac{1}{4}$ in. long, shining blue, very handsome. China. 1904. (B.M. 8980.) Good foliage shrub.

V. denta'tum. Arrow-wood. Upright, deciduous bush up to 15 ft., shoots glabrous. *l.* broadly ovate to roundish, $1\frac{1}{2}$ to 3 in. long, pointed, coarsely and sharply toothed, glossy green and glabrous above; veins in 6 to 10 pairs, often tufted in their axils. *fl.* white, $\frac{1}{6}$ in. wide, in clusters 2 to 3 in. across. May, June. *fr.* roundish-ovoid, $\frac{1}{4}$ in. long, blue-black. N. America. 1736. (G. and F. 10, 332.)

V. dilata'tum.* Deciduous shrub up to 10 ft., shoots very downy. *l.* broadly ovate to obovate, 2 to 5 in. long, from tapered to cordate at base, hairy on both sides; veins in 5 to 8 pairs. *fl.* pure white, $\frac{1}{4}$ in. wide, borne in hairy, 5-rayed clusters, 3 to 5 in. across. June. *fr.* roundish-ovoid, $\frac{1}{3}$ in. long, bright red. Japan. 1845. (B.M. 6215.) Handsome in fl., fr., and autumn colour. var. **xanthocar'pum,** *fr.* yellow. (B.M. n.s. 103.)

V. ero'sum. Deciduous shrub, 6 to 7 ft., shoots slender, downy. *l.* $1\frac{1}{2}$ to $3\frac{1}{2}$ in. long, 1 to 2 in. wide, ovate to oblong-obovate, sharply toothed, slender-pointed, downy especially beneath; veins in 7 to 10 pairs; stalk $\frac{1}{4}$ in. or less long. *fl.* $\frac{1}{6}$ in. wide, white, in clusters up to $3\frac{1}{2}$ in. across; ovary glabrous. May. *fr.* red, roundish-ovoid, $\frac{1}{4}$ in. long. Japan. 1844. (G. and F. 9, 85.) Akin to *V. ichangense* which has a woolly ovary. Both have very short l.-stalks.

V. erubes'cens. Deciduous shrub or small tree. *l.* elliptic, 2 to 4 in. long, slender pointed, toothed except near base, with 5 to 7 pairs of veins prominent beneath, slightly hairy beneath, glabrous above; stalk up to 1 in. long, reddish. *fl.* white tinged pink, in sessile pendulous panicles about $2\frac{1}{2}$ in. long, on slender slightly hairy peduncles; cor. tubular, about $\frac{3}{8}$ in. long; lobes 5, spreading, rounded; ovary glabrous. *fr.* at first red, then black, about $\frac{1}{4}$ in. long, broadly elliptic. Nepal, W. China. 1925?

V. foe'tens. Deciduous shrub, up to 10 ft., shoots glabrous. *l.* ovate, pointed, $2\frac{1}{2}$ to 5 in. long, strongly toothed, downy in vein-axils beneath; veins in 7 to 10 pairs. *fl.* white or pinkish, fragrant, in rounded clusters 2 in. or more across; cor. $\frac{3}{8}$ in. wide, the slender tube $\frac{1}{2}$ in. long. January to March. *fr.* $\frac{1}{2}$ in. long, red then black. Himalaya. Akin to, and confused with, *V. grandiflorum*, but much less downy. The name refers to the unpleasant odour of the bruised twigs.

V. foe'tidum. Evergreen, very leafy shrub, 6 to 10 ft., shoots very downy. *l.* 1 to 3 in. long, obovate, oval or ovate, coarsely and shallowly toothed, often 3-lobed at apex, dark green and glabrous above, tufted in vein-axils beneath. *fl.* white, $\frac{1}{6}$ in. wide, crowded in trusses 2 in. wide. July. *fr.* roundish-oval, bright red, $\frac{1}{4}$ in. wide. China, India. 1901. (B.M. 9509.) Very handsome in fr. but rather tender.

Viburnum fragrans

V. fra'grans.* Deciduous shrub 10 to 15 ft. and as much wide, sometimes self-layering. *l.* obovate or oval, $1\frac{1}{2}$ to 4 in. long, 1 to $2\frac{1}{2}$ in. wide, strongly toothed, glabrous except for axil-tufts beneath; veins in 5 or 6 pairs. *fl.* closely packed in clusters $1\frac{1}{2}$ to 2 in. wide, white, tinged with pink or wholly pink; cor. $\frac{1}{3}$ to $\frac{3}{8}$ in. wide, the tube $\frac{1}{3}$ in. long, November onwards. *fr.* scarlet. One of the most attractive of winter-flowering shrubs. N. China. 1909. (B.T.S. 3, 498; B.M. 8887.) There exist several forms of this shrub, not all of them free-flowering; see also *V.* × *bodnantense.*

V. furca'tum. Deciduous shrub up to 12 ft., young shoots downy. *l.* roundish to roundish-ovate, cordate, $3\frac{1}{2}$ to 6 in. long, often nearly as wide; veins in 9 or 10 pairs. *infl.* flat, 4 in. wide, fertile central ones $\frac{1}{6}$ in. wide, marginal sterile ones 1 in. across; all white. May. *fr.* ovoid, $\frac{1}{3}$ in. long, scarlet finally black. Japan. 1892. (S.T.S. 2. 119.) Very near *V. alnifolium* with a similar love of shade and moisture. Autumn colour crimson.

V. grandiflo'rum. Deciduous shrub, sometimes a small tree, shoots at first softly downy. *l.* 3 to 4 in. long, oval-oblong, tapered towards both ends; veins in 6 to 10 pairs, very downy beneath. *fl.* in clusters 2 to 3 in. across, white, flushed rose, $\frac{1}{2}$ to $\frac{3}{4}$ in. wide across lobes, the slender tube $\frac{1}{2}$ in. long. Jan. to March. *fr.* oval, $\frac{1}{2}$ in. long, blackish-purple. Himalaya. 1914. (B.M. 9063.) Syn. *V. nervosum* of some authors. Akin to *V. fragrans* but less hardy.

V. Harrya'num. Evergreen shrub 6 to 10 ft., shoots minutely downy. *l.* ⅓ to 1 in. long, orbicular to obovate or broadly ovate, entire or nearly so, glabrous, dark dull green; stalk 1/12 in. long. *fl.* pure white, ⅛ in. wide, in clusters 1 to 1½ in. across. *fr.* ovoid, ⅛ in. long, shining black. China. 1904. Very distinct in its small l.

V. Hen'ryi.* Evergreen shrub up to 10 ft., of stiff erect habit, shoots glabrous. *l.* 2 to 5 in. long, narrowly oval, ovate or obovate, shallow-toothed, dark shining green, glabrous except on midrib beneath and on stalk. *Panicles* pyramidal, up to 4 in. long and wide. *fl.* ⅓ in. across, white. June. *fr.* oval, ⅓ in. long, red then black. Very handsome in fr. China. 1901. (B.M. 8393.)

V. Hes'sei. A synonym of *V. Wrightii Hessei.*

V. hupehen'se.* Deciduous shrub, 6 to 7 ft., shoots downy, purplish-brown. *l.* rounded ovate, 2 to 3 in. long, slender-pointed, coarsely toothed, downy on both surfaces, but more densely beneath; veins in 7 or 8 pairs. *fl.* white, ¼ in. wide, in usually 5-rayed clusters 2 in. across. May, June. *fr.* ⅓ to ⅜ in. long, ovoid, red. China. 1908. Bears magnificent heavy masses of fr. (B.M. N.S. 41.)

V. ichangen'se. Slender-branched, deciduous shrub, 5 to 10 ft. *l.* ovate to ovate-lanceolate, slender-pointed, wide-toothed, 1½ to 2½ in. long, downy beneath; stalk 1/12 to ¼ in. long. *infl.* 1 to 1½ in. across, downy, 4- or 5-rayed, borne at the end of several lateral as well as terminal shoots. *fl.* ¼ in. wide, white, fragrant; ovary woolly. *fr.* ¼ in. long, downy, bright red. China. 1901. (S.T.S. 2. 150.)

V. japon'icum. Evergreen shrub up to 6 ft., shoots stout, glabrous. *l.* leathery, 3 to 6 in. long, half to nearly as much wide, ovate, oval, roundish, or obovate, glabrous, dark shining green, covered with tiny black dots beneath. *fl.* white, ⅜ in. wide, very fragrant, closely set in rounded trusses 3 to 4½ in. wide. June. *fr.* roundish-oval, ⅓ in. long, red. Japan. 1879. SYN. *V. macrophyllum.* Differs from *V. odoratissimum,* which has a pyramidal infl., by the veins running out to the teeth.

V.×Judd'ii. (Hybrid between *V. bitchiuense* and *V. Carlesii.*) Deciduous spreading shrub of bushy habit, 4 to 8 ft. h.; shoots densely covered with stellate hairs. *l.* ovate to ovate-oblong or elliptic, pointed, shallowly toothed, hairy beneath. *fl.* fragrant, in clusters 2½ to 3½ in. across, pink, becoming almost white; cor. ½ in. across, tube about ⅜ in. long. April, May. Raised in 1920.

V. Ketelee'ri. A synonym of *V. macrocephalum Keteleeri.*

V. Lanta'na. Wayfaring Tree. Vigorous deciduous shrub up to 15 ft., sometimes tree-like; shoots, buds, lower surface of l., and fl.-stalks all coated densely with minute down. *l.* 2 to 5 in. long, broadly ovate to oblong, wrinkled. *fl.* white, ¼ in. wide, borne in usually 7-rayed clusters 2 to 4 in. across. May, June. *fr.* oblong, ⅓ in. long, red, finally black. Europe (S. England). Occasionally turns a good red in autumn.

V. lantanoi'des. A synonym of *V. alnifolium.*

V. Lenta'go. Sheep-berry. Deciduous shrub or small tree, 20 to 30 ft., shoots slightly scurfy. *l.* 2 to 4 in. long, ovate to obovate, taper-pointed, finely toothed, dark and glossy, almost glabrous; stalks often winged. *fl.* creamy-white, ¼ in. wide, in flat stalkless clusters 3 to 4½ in. across. May, June. *fr.* oval, ½ to ⅝ in. long, blue-black. N. America. 1761. (S.S. 223–4.) Autumn colour red or red and orange.

V. lobophyl'lum.* Deciduous shrub 10 to 15 ft. *l.* ovate to roundish or obovate, 2 to 4½ in. long, shallowly toothed, glabrous except on the midrib and veins beneath; veins in 5 to 7 pairs. *fl.* white, ¼ in. wide, in 7-rayed, glandular-downy, long-stalked clusters 2 to 4 in. across. June. *fr.* globose, ⅓ in. long, bright-red. Does not generally fruit well as a young plant but when mature this species is very valuable for the brilliant autumn colour of its fruits. China. 1901. (G.C. 60 (1916), 197; B.M. n.s. 164.)

V. macrocepha'lum.* Chinese Snowball. Deciduous or partially evergreen shrub up to 12 ft., of rounded, bushy form, shoots scurfy. *l.* ovate, oval, or oblong, 2 to 4 in. long, thinly downy above, more so beneath. *fl.* pure white, all sterile, 1¼ in. wide, in heavy, globular trusses up to 6 in. across. May. 1844. (B.R. 33, 34.) Notable as bearing the largest and most showy infl. in the genus. It is really the sterile or garden form of *V. macrocephalum Keteleeri,* a Chinese species which has sterile fl. on the margin only, the infl. being flat, 3 to 5 in. across, the centre filled with small fertile fl. (R.H. 1863, 270). *V. macrocephalum* is best at the foot of a wall in cold localities.

V. macrophyl'lum. A synonym of *V. japonicum.*

V. mol'le. Deciduous bushy shrub with conspicuously peeling bark, shoots glabrous, soon turning grey. *l.* broadly ovate to roundish, cordate, 2 to 5 in. long, coarsely toothed, glabrous above, downy beneath. *fl.* white, ¼ in. wide, in clusters 2 to 4 in. across. June. *fr.* blue, oval, ⅜ in. long. N. America. 1923. Distinct by its flaky bark and blue fr. but rare.

V. nervo'sum of some authors *see* **V. grandiflorum.**

V. nu'dum. Deciduous shrub 10 to 15 ft., shoots slightly scurfy-downy. *l.* 2 to 4½ in. long, oval, ovate or lanceolate, entire or obscurely toothed, dark glossy green above, scurfy downy beneath. *fl.* creamy-white, ¼ in. wide, in flattish clusters, 2 to 4½ in. wide. *fr.* roundish, ⅓ in. long, blue-black. N. America. 1752. (B.M. 2281.)

V. odoratis'simum. Evergreen shrub up to 20 ft., shoots stout, warted, glabrous. *l.* stout, leathery, 4 to 8 in. long, half as wide, dark glittering green and glabrous above; vein-axils tufted beneath. *fl.* pure white, ¼ in. wide, fragrant, borne in pyramidal panicles 3 to 6 in. long and nearly as wide. August. *fr.* red, ultimately black. China, India. 1818. (B.R. 456.) SYN. *V. Awafuki.* Confused in gardens with *V. japonicum.* Not very hardy in cold districts but a magnificent evergreen in the south-west in England.

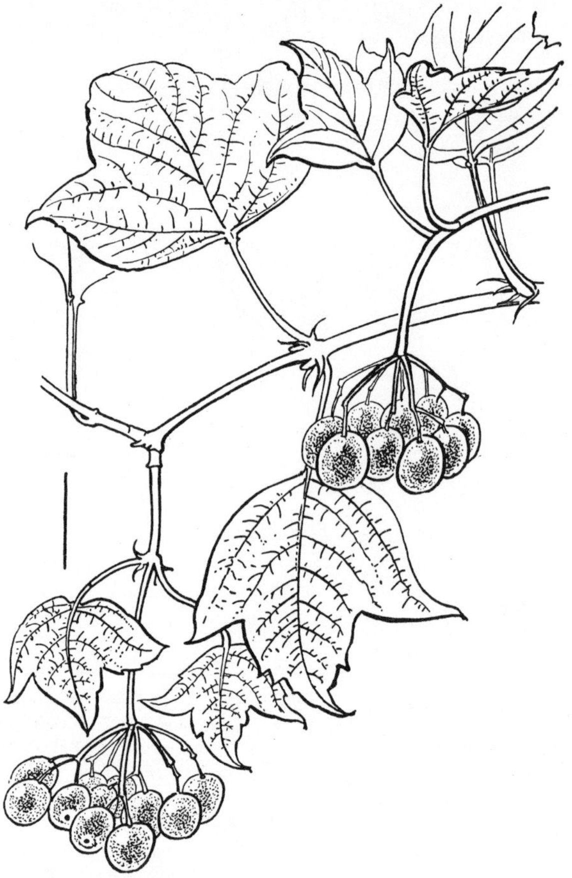

Viburnum Opulus americanum

V. O'pulus. Guelder Rose; Rose Elder. Deciduous shrub, 10 to 12 ft., shoots glabrous. *l.* 2 to 4 in. long and wide, 3-lobed, maple-like, coarsely and irregularly toothed, more or less downy beneath. *infl.* flat, 2 to 3 in. across with a fringe of white sterile fl., each ¾ in. wide; the centre filled with small, yellow-anthered, fertile fl. June. *fr.* bright translucent red, globose, ⅓ in. wide. Europe (Britain), N. Africa. (E.B. 639.) Beautiful in fr. and autumn colour. var. **america'num** (*see* **V. trilobum**); **na'num,** curious dwarf shrub 1 to 3 ft., rarely if ever flowers; **ster'ile,*** Snowball Tree, *fl.* all sterile and closely packed into a globose cluster, 2 to 2½ in. across; there is a rose-tinted form called **ro'seum**; **xanthocarp'um** (*fructu-luteo*), *fr* beautiful translucent yellow. A form with unusually large fr. is known as **Notcutt's var.**

V. orienta'le. Deciduous shrub, 5 to 8 ft. *l.* maple-like, 3 to 5 in. long 3-lobed, cordate, with tufts in vein-axils beneath. *fl.* white, ⅓ in. across, in long-stalked clusters 2 in. wide. June. *fr.* ⅓ in. long, oval, red finally black. Caucasus, Asia Minor. 1827. Very near *V. acerifolium* but never has minute black dots beneath l. like that species.

V. phlebot'richum. Deciduous shrub 6 to 8 ft. *l.* narrowly ovate to oblong, strongly triangular-toothed, 1½ to 3 in. long, tapered at base, glabrous except for silky hairs on midrib and on the 6 to 9 pairs of veins beneath. *infl.* few-fld. slender-stalked, drooping, ¾ to 1¾ in. across. *fl.* ⅓ in. wide, white; cal. purple; stamens very short. May. *fr.* red, oval, ⅓ in. long, pendulous. Japan. 1890. (S.T.S. 2, 120.)

V. propin'quum. Evergreen shrub, 4 to 6 ft., shoots angular, reddish, glabrous, shining. *l.* ovate-lanceolate to oval, 2 to 3½ in. long, ½ to 1¼ in. wide, 3-nerved, glossy green, glabrous. *fl.* greenish-white, ⅛ in. wide, in clusters 1½ to 2½ in. across. June. *fr.* globose-ovoid, ⅛ in. long, blue-black. China. 1901. (S.T.S. 2. 115.) Akin to *V. Davidi* but with much smaller l.

V. prunifo'lium. Black Haw. Shrub or bushy tree, 20 to 30 ft., shoots glabrous, reddish. *l.* ovate, oval, or obovate, 1½ to 3½ in. long, shortly pointed, glabrous. *fl.* pure white, ¼ in. wide, in flattish stalkless clusters, 2 to 4 in. across. June. *fr.* blue-black, oval, ⅓ to ⅝ in. long. N. America. 1731. (S.S. 5. 225.) SYN. *V. pyrifolium.* Confused in gardens with *V. Lentago* which has long- and taper-pointed l.

V. pubes'cens. Deciduous shrub, 6 to 10 ft., shoots downy. *l.* 2 to 4 in. long, ovate to roundish, slender-pointed, rounded at base, coarsely toothed, velvety with down beneath; stalk ⅛ to ⅓ in. long. *fl.* white, ¼ in. wide, in clusters 2 to 4 in. across. June. *fr.* dark purple, oval, ⅓ in. long. N. America. 1736. SYN. *V. venosum.* Often confused with *V. dentatum*; distinct by the short l.-stalk. *V. pubescens* of many authors is *V. affine hypomalacum.*

V. pyrifo'lium. A synonym of *V. prunifolium.*

V. reticula'tum. A synonym of *V. Sieboldii.*

V. × rhydophylloi'des (*V. Lantana* × *V. rhytidophyllum*).

V. rhytidophyl'lum. Evergreen shrub or small tree up to 20 ft. h. by 30 ft. wide, shoots stout, densely downy. *l.* 4 to 8 in. long, 1½ to 3 in. wide, deeply wrinkled and dark green above, grey with thick felt beneath. *fl.* dull yellowish-white, ¼ in. wide, opening during May in clusters 4 to 8 in. across, having remained in the naked bud state through winter. *fr.* oval, ⅓ in. long, red then shining black. China. 1900. (B.M. 8382). Remarkable for its wrinkled l.

V. ri'gidum. Evergreen shrub, 6 to 10 ft., shoots hairy. *l.* ovate to oval, toothless, 2 to 6 in. long, half as wide, dark dull green and scabrid above, softly downy beneath. *fl.* ⅓ in. wide, white, numerous in flattish clusters 3 to 4½ in. across; stigma pink. February to April. *fr.* ovoid, ⅓ in. long, blue finally black. Canary Is. 1778. (B.M. 2082.) SYN. *V. rugosum, Tinus rugosus.* Tender and only suitable for the south-west in England.

V. rufi'dulum. Large shrub or tree sometimes over 30 ft., branches stout, rigid; shoots rusty with down. *l.* 2 to 4 in. long, oval to obovate, usually bluntish, shining and glabrous above, rusty-downy beneath. *fl.* white, ⅓ in. wide, in flattish clusters, 3 to 5 in. across. June. *fr.* oval, dark blue, ½ to ⅝ in. long. N. America. 1902. Distinct from *V. Lentago* and *V. prunifolium* by its rust-coloured downiness. Autumn colour, rich red.

V. rugo'sum. A synonym of *V. rigidum.*

V. Sandank'wa. A synonym of *V. suspensum.*

V. Sargent'ii. The Chinese representative of *V. Opulus*, from which it is distinguished by its purple anthers (yellow in *V. Opulus*). *l.* larger, longer stalked and with a more elongated middle lobe. Bark corky. (S.T.S. 1, 42.) var. **fla'vum,** anthers yellow, *l.* downy on veins beneath. 1904. Autumn colour, yellow and crimson.

V. scabrel'lum. Deciduous shrub, 6 or 7 ft., shoots rough with starry down. *l.* ovate to oblong-ovate, 1½ to 4 in. long, remotely toothed, downy on veins beneath. *fl.* white, ¼ in. wide, in downy-stalked clusters 2 to 3½ in. across. June. *fr.* blue-black, roundish, ¼ in. long. N. America. 1830. Much confused in gardens with *V. molle* which has distinctly peeling bark.

V. Schneideria'num. Evergreen shrub up to 10 ft. *l.* leathery, narrowly ovate to rhombic-oval, 1¾ to 3½ in. long, entire or remotely toothed, lustrous green. *fl.* small, white in long-stalked clusters up to 3½ in. wide and 6- or 7-rayed. June, July. *fr.* ovoid, ⅕ in. long. China.

V. seti'gerum.* Deciduous erect-growing shrub up to 12 ft., shoots glabrous. *l.* 3 to 5 in. long, ovate-lanceolate, rounded at the base, slender-pointed, dark green, glabrous on both surfaces except on the 6 to 9 pairs of veins beneath. *fl.* white, ¼ in. wide, in clusters 1½ to 2 in. across; cal. purple. May, June. *fr.* ⅓ in. long, ovoid, red. China. 1901. (S.T.S. 2, 121.) SYN. *V. theiferum.*

V. Siebold'ii. Deciduous shrub 6 to 10 ft., shoots downy. *l.* 2 to 5 in. long, obovate to oblong, strongly veined, coarsely toothed, dark lustrous green; veins in 7 to 10 pairs. *fl.* creamy-white, ⅓ in. across, in panicles 3 to 4 in. wide. May, June. *fr.* oval, ½ in. long, pink, finally blue-black. Japan. 1880. (G. and F. 2, 559.) SYN. *V. reticulatum.*

V. suspen'sum. Evergreen shrub 6 to 12 ft., shoots warted. *l.* stout and leathery, ovate to oval, pointed, entire or toothed, 2 to 5 in. long, glossy green, glabrous; veins in 4 or 5 pairs. *fl.* fragrant, rose-tinted white, ⅓ in. across, borne in panicles 2½ to 4 in. long and nearly as wide. March. *fr.* globose, red. Japan. 1850. (B.M. 6172.) SYN. *V. Sandankwa.* Suitable for the south-west in England.

V. the'iferum. A synonym of *V. setigerum.*

V. Ti'nus.* Laurustinus. Evergreen, luxuriantly leafy shrub of rounded shape, 10 to 15 ft. *l.* entire, narrowly ovate, 1½ to 4 in. long, ¾ to 1¾ in. wide, dark lustrous green above, with axil tufts beneath. *fl.* white, pinkish in bud, ¼ in. wide, in terminal clusters 2 to 4 in. across. December to April. *fr.* ovoid, ¼ in. long, deep blue, finally black. SE. Europe. 1560. var. **hir'tum,** shoots, l.-stalks, &c., furnished with bristly hairs; **lu'cidum,*** *l.* 4 in. by 2½ in. very lustrous green; *fl.* ½ in. wide, the finest form; **purpur'eum,** *l.* tinged dull purple; **stric'tum,** habit more erect; **variega'tum,** *l.* more or less yellow. One of the most valuable of evergreens; vars. *hirtum* and *lucidum* not so hardy as the type.

V. tomento'sum.* Deciduous shrub 6 to 10 ft. with horizontal branches and minutely downy shoots. *l.* ovate or oval, pointed, 2 to 4 in. long, sharply toothed, more or less downy especially beneath; veins parallel in 8 to 12 pairs. *infl.* a flat cluster 3 to 4 in. wide. *fl.* white, outer sterile ones 1 to 1½ in. across, fertile inner ones ¼ in. wide. June. *fr.* red, then black. China, Japan. 1865. var. **Maries'ii,*** infl. and sterile fl. larger, 1½ to 2 in. wide, the growth more spreading and horizontal; **plica'tum*** (Japanese Snowball); *fl.* pure white, wholly of the large sterile type, borne in globose clusters 2 to 3 in. wide. In the very first rank of white-fld. hardy shrubs. 1844. A

V. trilo'bum. The American type of *V. Opulus*, of which it has generally been regarded as a geographical form. It differs by the usually glabrous l. whose stalks have small glands. In *V. Opulus* these are large and disk-like.

Viburnum utile

V. u'tile. Evergreen shrub of open habit, 6 ft. or more, shoots slender, downy. *l.* narrowly ovate to oblong, 1 to 3 in. long, entire, glossy dark green above, prominently veined and covered beneath with white stellate down; veins in 5 or 6 pairs. *fl.* white, ⅓ in. wide, closely packed in rounded clusters 3 in. across. May. *fr.* oval, ¼ in. long, blue-black. China. 1901. (B.M. 8174.)

V. Veitch'ii. Deciduous shrub, 5 to 7 ft., shoots, l.-stalks, undersurface of l. and fl.-stalks, all densely downy. *l.* 3 to 5 in. long, ovate, cordate, sparsely toothed, wrinkled. *fl.* ¼ in. wide, in flattish clusters 3 to 5 in. across, white. May, June. *fr.* oval, ⅓ in. long, red finally black. China (where it represents *V. Lantana.*) 1901.

V. veno'sum. A synonym of *V. pubescens.*

V. Wilson'ii. Deciduous shrub, 6 to 10 ft., shoots very downy. *l.* ovate to roundish oval, slender pointed, 1½ to 3½ in. long, bronzy when young, downy beneath. *fl.* white, ¼ in. wide, borne in 5- or 6-rayed clusters 2 to 3 in. across; stalks velvety. June. *fr.* ⅓ in. long, ovoid, bright red, downy. China. 1908. Akin to *V. hupehense.*

V. Wright'ii.* Deciduous shrub, 6 to 10 ft. *l.* 3 to 5 in. long, broadly ovate or obovate, short-pointed, downy on veins beneath and in their axils; veins in 6 to 10 pairs. *infl.* 2 to 4 in. across. *fl.* white, ¼ in. wide. May. *fr.* roundish-ovoid, red, ⅓ in. long. Japan. 1892. (S.T.S. 1, 19.) Valued for its handsome fr. and brilliant autumn colour. var. **Hes'sei,** dwarfer, with smaller infl., *l.* ovate with fewer shallower teeth. SYN. *V. Hessei.*

W. J. B.

VI'CIA (ancient Latin name used by Virgil). FAM. *Leguminosae.* Tare. A genus of about 120 species of annual or perennial herbs of various habit, natives of the north temperate regions and S. America. Leaves equally pinnate; leaflets usually numerous, entire or toothed at apex; leaf often ending in a tendril; stipulate. Flowers papilionaceous, often blue, violet, yellowish-white, or white, axillary, racemose; calyx teeth nearly equal, or the lower longer; standard obovate or oblong, emarginate; wings adnate to keel; bracts very caducous. Pods flattened, 2-valved. Few of the species are of horticultural value, the most important being **V. Faba,** the Broad Bean (q.v.). This is one of the oldest of cultivated plants, a form with seeds about ⅖ in. long being widely grown in Europe during prehistoric times and represented in the remains of the lake dwellers at Glastonbury, Somerset, as well as in Switzerland. It has an enormous number of forms grouped into 3 major varieties, var. **mi'nor,** with seeds averaging ⅗ in. long, var. **equi'na,** seeds averaging ½ in. long, var. **ma'jor,** seeds averaging 1 in. long, to which the Broad Beans grown for culinary purposes belong. It evidently originated in the Mediterranean region and is closely related to a species **V. Plini'ana** (SYN. *Faba vulgaris* var. *Pliniana*) which grows wild in the highlands of Algeria. The common Vetch, *V. sativa*, is a valuable fodder plant. The following grow easily in ordinary garden soil and are quite hardy. They may be propagated by seed, and the perennial species by division. Some of the following have not established themselves in British horticulture so far, and some may not have been introduced, but they have features that recommend a trial and are likely to succeed in warm, open, stony, loamy soils.

V. alpes'tris. Many-stemmed, branches prostrate or ascending, 4 to 6 in. long. *l.* without tendrils. *fl.* violet, large, in 8- or 9-fl. secund racemes. Summer. Levant on hills.

V. argen'tea. Tufted about 1 ft. h., perennial. Stem 4-angled. *l.* grey-silvery, without tendrils; lflets. oblong-linear, mucronate. *fl.* with whitish standard veined violet, keels darker with deep purple tips; infl. many-fld., secund. June. Pyrenees. 1827. (B.M. 2946.)

V. canes'cens. Perennial, 15 to 18 in. h.; stems many, erect, densely woolly. *lflets.* in 8 to 12 pairs, crowded linear-elliptical; upper l. sometimes with a short tendril. *fl.* blue in a dense raceme about as long as l. June, July. Top of Lebanon. Larger in l. and fl. and stouter than *V. argentea.* **V. Greya'na** resembles this but has acute lflets. Cilician Taurus. (B.M. n.s. 233.)

V. Crac'ca. Cow Vetch; Tufted Vetch. Perennial. Scrambling or climbing; stem 2 to 6 ft. long. *lflets.* linear-oblong, 1 to 4 in. long, acute or mucronate; l. with branched tendrils. *fl.* bright blue, ½ in. long, drooping in dense 10- to 30-fld. secund racemes on peduncles longer than l. June to August. Europe, including Britain. (E.B. 385.) Wild garden.

V. Fa'ba. Broad Bean, Horse Bean. Erect annual, 2 to 4 ft. h., glabrous or nearly so, leafy. *lflets.* 2 to 6, oval to elliptic, obtuse or mucronate. *fl.* white with a large blue-black spot. May to August. *Pods.* large and thick, 2 to 8 in. long; seeds large, often flat. Habitat? Widely cultivated. SYN. *Faba vulgaris. See* **Bean, Broad Beans.**

V. Greya'na. *See* **V. canescens.**

V. oroboi'des. Perennial, 1 to 2 ft. h. *lflets.* ovate, mucronate. *fl.* blue, on many-fld. racemes in l.-axils, often 3 or 4 together. June. S. Europe, N. Africa. 1758. var. **al'ba,** *fl.* white.

V. Or'obus. Bitter Vetch. Erect, slightly hairy perennial, 1 to 2 ft. h.; stem almost leafless. *l.* 2 to 3 in. long, sessile; lflets. linear-oblong, ¾ to 1½ in. long. *fl.* white, tinged purple, ½ in. long, in loose 6- to 20-fld., secund racemes. June to September. Europe, including Britain. (E.B. 386.)

V. pyrena'ica. Perennial about 1 ft. h. *l.* slightly tendrilled; lflets. obcordate, mucronate. *fl.* purple, solitary in l.-axils; cal. somewhat bell-shaped; segs. shorter than tube. May. Pyrenees. 1818.

V. sylvat'ica. Wood Vetch. Glabrous perennial, stems 2 to 4 ft. long, usually trailing. *lflets.* many, elliptic-oblong, mucronulate; tendrils branched; stipules bristly-toothed. *fl.* white with blue veins in 6- to 18-fld. secund racemes; peduncles longer than l. June, July. Europe, including Britain, N. Asia. (E.B. 387). Wild garden.

V. uniju'ga.* Erect, tufted; stems wiry, 12 to 15 in. h. *lflets.* 2. *fl.* rich violet-purple or blue in dense racemes. June to August. NE. Asia. 1758. (B.M. 2098 as *Orobus Lathyroides.*) Border or rock-garden. SYN. *Ervum gracile.*

viciifo'lius -a -um, Vetch-leaved.

vici'nus -a -um, neighbouring.

VICTO'RIA (in honour of Her Majesty Queen Victoria, 1819–1901). FAM. *Nymphaeaceae.* A genus of 1 or 2 species of aquatic herb, native of Tropical America. A gigantic, prickly perennial (in nature) with a thick rhizome, growing in 4 to 6 ft. of water, with the characters given below. The structure of the leaves with their strong veins projecting on the lower surface gives them great buoyancy, sufficient to sustain the weight of a small child provided it stands on a flat board so that the pressure is distributed evenly over the whole leaf. In Britain the plant is best treated as an annual since it is difficult to keep it alive through the dull days of winter. The seeds, which should be kept in water until ready for sowing, should be put into loamy soil in a pot; the pot is then submerged to the depth of 2 in. in a tank of water at a temperature not allowed to fall below 85° F. The tank should be in full light and as near the glass as possible. The seed should be sown in January and as soon as the seedlings appear they should be pricked out singly into small pots, gradually shifting them into larger pots as they grow stronger. About the beginning of May, the best plant will probably be ready to be placed in the large tank. Two or three cartloads of good strong loam with a fair amount of rotted cow dung will be necessary to enable the plant to attain full size. When well established the temperature of the water may be allowed to fall to 80° F. but not lower. All the sunlight possible is needed to keep the plant in robust health and the house in which it is grown should not be shaded in any way. Where the water can be maintained at 80° F., the tank in which the Victoria is grown may be in the open air in a place sheltered from the wind. In windy places the upturned margins of the leaves will cause them to be damaged and the plant to be spoilt.

V. amazo'nica (V. re'gia). *rhiz.* thick. *l.* usually floating, 4 to 6½ ft. across, at first oval with a deep narrow sinus at one end; later l. almost exactly orbicular, peltate, flat except for the upturned margin 2 to 5 in. broad; full green and netted above; deep purple or sometimes green beneath, with spongy tissue, much veined, and more or less beset with sharp, horny, awl-shaped prickles; stalk terete, very prickly. *fl.* 1 ft. or more across; cal. deeply 4-fid, tube tawny, turbinate, very prickly, adnate to ovary; segs. purple-brown, concave, deciduous, shorter than pet.; torus annular; pet. very numerous, outer white, spreading, oblong, concave, obtuse, inner gradually passing into filaments and becoming deep purple or rose; perfect stamens in about 2 ranks, large, fleshy, awl-shaped, incurved below, the rest erect; peduncles radical, longer than l.-stalk, rising above water level in fl., terete, prickly, sometimes 1 in. thick, 1-fld. Summer. *Berry* large, cyathiform, truncate, fleshy, green, prickly; seeds many, oval, dark brown. Trop. S. America. 1838. (B.M. 4275–4278 as *V. regia.*) The correct name for this plant under the International Rules of Botanical Nomenclature is *V. amazonica* being based on the earliest specific epithet, but the name *V. regia* has been more widely used.

Victo'riae, in honour of Queen Victoria.

Victo'riae-Ma'riae, in honour of Victoria Mary Augusta Louise Olga Pauline Claudine Agnes of Teck, Queen Mary, b. 1867.

victoria'lis -is -e, victorious. Bulbs of *Allium Victorialis* were worn by Bohemian miners as a protection against evil spirits.

VICTORIAN DOGWOOD. *See* **Prostanthera lasianthos.**

VICTORIAN HAZEL. *See* **Pomaderris apetala.**

Vidalia'nus -a -um, Vidal'ii, in honour of (1) Capt. Vidal, R.N., who collected in Azores in 1842; (2) Sebastian Vidal y Soler, 1842–89, Spanish botanist and forester in Philippines.

Vieillard'ii, in honour of Eugène Vieillard, d. 1872, who collected in New Caledonia, 1861–7.

VIG'NA (in honour of Dominico Vigna, d. 1647, Professor of Botany at Pisa, who wrote a Commentary on Theophrastus in 1625). FAM. *Leguminosae.* A genus of about 60 species of twining or prostrate herbs, natives of the warmer parts of the globe. Leaves pinnately 3-foliolate, leaflets stipellate, lateral ones oblique, petioles long. Flowers papilionaceous, in a short racemose cluster terminal on a long axillary peduncle; standard roundish, keel bent inwards but not coiled as it is in Phaseolus. From Dolichos, Vigna is distinct by the lateral stigma just above the line of hair on the inner side of the style:

in Dolichos it is terminal or only slightly oblique. Pods linear, straight or slightly curved, a few inches to over a yard long. Seeds small, kidney-shaped to almost round, of various colours and usually with a distinct colour round the hilum. *V. cylindrica* (Catjang), *V. sesquipedalis*, (Asparagus Pea, Yard-long Bean) and *V. sinensis* are widely grown for cattle food and for green-manuring, but the seeds of all can be used for human consumption like peas, as they are in some parts of the world, and the brittle pods of *V. sesquipedalis* are used like those of the Scarlet Runner Bean. A few species are ornamental. All can be readily raised from seed.

V. cylind'rica. Annual, 18 to 24 in. h., spreading or sub-erect, glabrous. *lflets.* 3 to 5 in. long, ovate-lanceolate. *fl.* white or yellowish, pink at base of petals, in twos or threes. *Pod* about 3 to 5 in. long, erect or ascending when green and often remaining so. Seeds slightly kidney-shaped, about ¼ in. long. Tropics. SYN. *V. Catjang.*

V. sesquipeda'lis. Climbing annual, 6 to 8 ft. h., glabrous. *lflets.* ovate, 5 to 6 in. long, dark green. *fl.* whitish or tinged purple, 1 to 3 on peduncle. *Pod* nearly round, up to 3½ ft. long, pendent. Seed variously coloured, small, ends truncate. S. Asia. SYN. *Dolichos sesquipedalis, V. sinensis* var. *sesquipedalis.*

V. sinen'sis. Habit of *V. cylindrica*, but *pod* 8 to 12 in. long, pendent early, seeds somewhat kidney-shaped to nearly round, ⅜ to ½ in. long. Cent. Asia? (B.M. 2232.)

V. strobilo'phora. Woody twiner, many ft. h. *lflets.* ovate, 2½ in. long. *fl.* Wisteria-like in cone-like racemes, standard pinkish-white, wings and keel purple; standard roundish with two small appendages at base; bracts large, overlapping. Mexico. 1894. (G. & F. 1894, f. 30.)

VIGUIE'RA (in honour of Alexandre Viguier, librarian of Montpellier, author of a book on Poppies, 1814). FAM. *Compositae.* A genus of about 60 species of erect, branched, annual or perennial herbs, rarely shrubs, natives of the warmer parts of America. Lower (rarely all) leaves opposite, upper usually alternate. Flower-heads of moderate size, rarely large, pedunculate, at tips of branches, heterogamous; involucre broadly bell-shaped or hemispherical, the bracts in 3 or more series; receptacle convex, conical, or finally oblong, paleaceous. Achenes often more or less hairy. Half-hardy or greenhouse plants, growing well in ordinary soil, but not distinguished.

V. excel'sa. Stem rough, 6 to 8 ft. h. *l.* elliptic, acute, toothed at apex, 3-nerved, rough on both sides. *fl.-heads* yellow; involucral bracts in many series, ciliate, appressed; peduncles terete. August. Mexico. 1820. SYN. *Helianthus giganteus* of Cavanilles, *Tithonia excelsa.*

V. linea'ris. Half-hardy perennial. Stem erect, branched, rough, 2 ft. h. *l.* rarely opposite, linear, entire, 1-nerved, bristly-hairy on nerves, margin revolute. *fl.-heads* yellow; involucral bracts oblong, with leafy appendix at tip. September. Mexico. 1823. (B.R. 523 as *Helianthus linearis.*)

vi'lis -is -e, common, of little value.

VILLAN'OVA (in honour of Thomas M. Villanova, 1757–1802, Professor of Botany at Valencia). FAM. *Compositae.* A genus of 6 or 7 species of diffuse, glandular-hairy herbs, natives of Peru, Colombia, and Mexico. Lower (or all) leaves opposite, upper often alternate, 3-nately or pinnately cut, often few-lobed. Flower-heads yellow, heterogamous, pedunculate, irregularly paniculate or corymbose; involucre bell-shaped, bracts few, nearly equal; receptacle small, naked; ray-florets ligulate, 3-toothed; disk florets 5-cleft. Achenes glabrous. *V. chrysanthemoides* is a hardy annual and should be sown in the open border in April.

V. chrysanthemoi'des. Stem erect, grooved, 1 to 2 ft. h., leafy. *l.* alternate, 2 in. long and wide, twice 3-nately cut into linear or obovate, laciniate, recurved lobes; stalked. *fl.-heads* yellow, 1 in. across; ray-florets 15 to 20; peduncles stout, glandular, naked or with 1 or 2 rudimentary l. Rocky Mts. 1878. (B.M. 6422.)

VILLARES'IA (in honour of Matthias Villarez, *c.* 1794, Superintendent of Gardens at Santa Espina). FAM. *Icacinaceae.* A genus of about 12 species of evergreen climbing shrubs or small trees, natives of the tropics. Leaves alternate, oblong, entire or spiny-toothed, thick leathery. Flowers white; calyx 5-parted; petals 5, ribbed within; stamens 5; cymes small in panicles. For cultivation *see* **Olax.**

V. mucrona'ta. Tree erect, stem round. *l.* ovate or oblong, mucronate, smooth, shining above, paler beneath, spiny-toothed in young, entire in older trees. *fl.* sessile, fragrant; racemes terminal and in axils of upper l., usually solitary, sometimes in twos or threes, 2 in. long. Autumn. Chile. 1840. (B.M. 8376.) Cool greenhouse. Worth trying in favoured places in south-west of England.

Villa'rii, in honour of Celestine Fernandez-Villar, 1838–1907, Spanish monk, of Manila.

VILLARS'IA (in honour of Dominique Villars, 1745–1814, Professor at Grenoble and writer on plants of Dauphiné). FAM. *Gentianaceae.* A genus of about 10 species of marsh herbs, one S. African, the others Australian. Stem simple and leafless, or slightly branched with a few leaves. Leaves entire or somewhat toothed, long-stalked. Flowers yellow or white in cymes; calyx 5-cleft; corolla broadly bell-shaped, somewhat rotate; filaments filiform. The following need greenhouse treatment with a compost of peat and sand, the pots being stood in water. Propagation is easy by division or by seeds.

V. capita'ta. Stems slightly branched, leafy, 6 in. h. *l.* broadly-ovate, orbicular or reniform, coarsely sinuately-toothed or entire, less than 1 in. long; stalks long. *fl.* yellow, sessile in flattish heads about ½ in. across, peduncles long. Summer. Australia. 1879. (B.M. 6420.)

V. exalta'ta. Habit of *V. parnassifolia*, 6 in. to 3 ft. h. *l.* tufted, ovate to orbicular or reniform, more or less cordate at base, entire or sinuately toothed, 1 to 2 in. long; stalks long. *fl.* yellow, ¾ to 1 in. across, lobes bearded or fringed at base within. July. Australia. 1820. (B.M. 1029 as *Menyanthes exaltata*; 1328 as *M. sarmentosa*, a stoloniferous form.) SYN. *V. reniformis.*

V. nymphaeoi'des. A synonym of *Nymphoides peltata* (p. 1178).

V. ova'ta. Stem ascending, nearly naked, about 6 in. h. *l.* clustered, oval, entire, leathery. *fl.* citron-yellow in terminal, raceme-like cymes; cor. segs. crenate-fimbriate at margins, hairy at base within. June. S. Africa. 1786. (B.M. 1909 as *Menyanthes ovata.*)

V. parnassifo'lia. Loosely branched, 1 to 2 ft. h., stems almost lfless. *Radical l.* ovate or almost orbicular, entire or sinuate-crenate, slightly cordate or rounded at base, mostly under 1 in. long; stalks long. *fl.* yellow, cor. lobes slightly longer than cal. August. Australia. 1825. (B.R. 1533 as *V. reniformis.*)

V. renifor'mis. A synonym of *V. exaltata.*

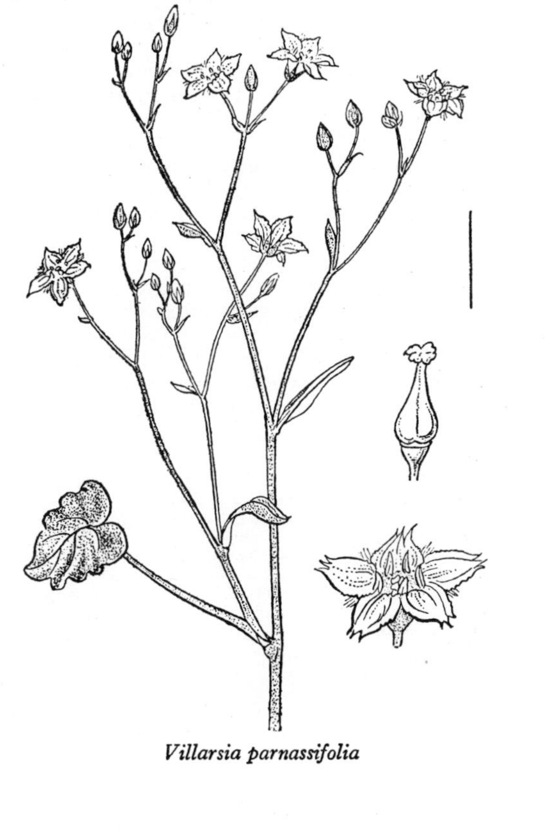

Villarsia parnassifolia

Villeneuv'ei, in honour of Count De Villeneuve, *c.* 1887.

villicau'lis -is -e, having a shaggy stem.

vil'lipes, with a long-haired stalk.

villo'sipes, with a very hairy stalk.

villos'ulus -a -um, slightly hairy

villo'sus -a -um, shaggy, covered with long, soft hairs.

VILMORIN'IA (in honour of Pierre Philippe André Levêque de Vilmorin, 1776–1862, French nurseryman and seedsman). FAM. *Leguminosae.* A genus of a single species, a shrub native of San Domingo, needing similar treatment to Clitoria.

V. multiflor'a. Shrub of 6 ft. *l.* unequally pinnate with 5 or 6 pairs of lflets.; lflets. oval, hairy beneath; stipules rather broad at base, long-pointed. *fl.* purple, papilionaceous, in axillary racemes; calyx cylindrical, obtusely 4-toothed, somewhat 2-lipped; pet. narrow-oblong, wings shorter than keel. May. 1826. SYN. *Clitoria multiflora.*

vimina'lis -is -e, with long slender shoots.

VIMINA'RIA (*vimen*, a twig; in allusion to the twiggy, apparently leafless branches.) FAM. *Leguminosae.* Monotypic genus, native of Australia and Tasmania. Cool greenhouse, in light-loamy soil. Hardy in Scilly.

V. denuda'ta. Rush Broom. Glabrous shrub. 10 to 20 ft., sometimes low and spreading, shoots long, wiry, rush-like. *l.* usually reduced to a slender, filiform, terete stalk 3 to 9 in. long, but occasionally bearing at the top 1 to 3 lflets. each ½ to 1½ in. long. *Racemes* terminal, 3 to 6 in. long. *fl.* nearly ½ in. long; standard yellow with a red semicircular stain at the base, notched, ⅜ in. wide; wings and keel yellow, smaller. August. 1780. (B.M. 1190.)

W. J. B.

vimi'neus -a -um, having long flexible twigs or shoots.

vina'ceus -a -um, wine-coloured.

VIN'CA (*Vinca* or *Pervinca*, the ancient Latin name used by Pliny). FAM. *Apocynaceae.* A genus of about 10 species of erect or procumbent herbs or sub-shrubs, widely distributed, several of them in Europe, *V. rosea* in the Tropics. Leaves opposite. Flowers rather large, solitary in leaf-axils; calyx 5-parted without glands, segments narrow; corolla salver-shaped, tube cylindrical; lobes 5, large; stamens attached above middle of tube, included. The hardy Periwinkles are excellent trailing plants for banks and shady places under trees, for the wild garden and the wood. They will grow in almost any soil and when once established, spread rapidly. They may be propagated by division, any single shoot with roots being dibbled in in autumn to early spring. *V. rosea* needs stove or greenhouse treatment and a compost of fibrous loam with a little decayed manure or peat. It is readily propagated from cuttings of young shoots taken off as soon as new growth begins in spring and inserted in sandy loam in a close frame. The points should be taken out as soon as the young plants are established to make them bushy. The flowers are produced on the young shoots as they lengthen. The old plants can be carried over through the winter and, unless it is desired to increase stock, it is unnecessary to propagate *V. rosea* every winter.

V. acutiflo'ra. A synonym of *V. difformis.*

V. difform'is.* Evergreen, dwarf sub-shrub with prostrate barren and ascending fl. shoots. *l.* ovate, 1¼ to 2¾ in. long, glabrous; stalks about ¼ in. long. *fl.* solitary on pedicels up to 1½ in. long in upper l.-axils; pale blue, 1½ in. across; sep. linear, up to about ⅔ in. long; cor. tube below insertion of stamens cylindric, above funnel-shaped; segs. obliquely obovate, about ½ in. across. Autumn. W. Mediterranean region. (B.M. 8506.) SYN. *V. acutiflora, V. media.* var. **bi'color,** cor. with white centre; **du'bia,** deeper blue. Not quite so hardy as *V. major.*

V. herba'cea. All stems fertile, herbaceous, glabrous, declinate, simple. *l.* elliptic or lanceolate, rather blunt, 1 in. long, margins revolute, ciliate. *fl.* bluish-purple, corolla ⅔ to 1 in. long, bearded in middle and at throat. May, June. E. Europe. 1816. (B.M. 2002; B.R. 301.) Hardy perennial. A tendency to doubling is sometimes found.

V. libanot'ica. Very near *V. herbacea* but l.-margins smooth. Lebanon.

Vinca difformis

V. major.* Band-plant, Cut-finger. Larger in all parts than *V. minor.* Flowerless stems rooting at tip only; flowering stems erect, lengthening after flowering. *l.* ovate or heart-shaped at base, ciliate. *fl.* blue-purple; cal. lobes ciliate, as long as cor. tube. April, May. Europe, including Britain. (E.B. 905.) Hardy perennial. var. **al'ba,** *fl.* white; **pubes'cens,** *l.* narrower, more hairy, *fl.* red-purple, lobes narrower, pointed. SYN. *V. pubescens, V. major* var. *oxyloba.* Caucasus; **reticula'ta,** *l.* netted with golden-yellow; **variega'ta,** *fl.* blue, *l.* blotched creamy-white.

V. me'dia. A synonym of *V. difformis.*

V. mi'nor.* Stems tough. Flowerless stems 1 to 2 ft. long, prostrate, rooting; flowering stems erect, short. *l.* elliptic-ovate, 1 to 1½ in. long, margins smooth; stalk very short. *fl.* blue-purple, 1 in. across; cal. segs. glabrous, one-third as long as cor. tube. April, May. Europe, including Britain. (E.B. 906.) Hardy perennial. var. **al'ba,** *fl.* white; **albople'na,** *fl.* double, white; **argen'teo-variega'ta,** *l.* silver-variegated; **atropur'purea,** *fl.* deep purple; **azu'rea,** *fl.* sky-blue; **caeuru'leo-ple'na,** *fl.* double, blue; **cup'rea,** *fl.* reddish-copper; **La Grave,** *fl.* lavender, very large; **multip'lex,** *fl.* double, purple; **puni'cea,** *fl.* red-purple; **roseople'na,** *fl.* double, reddish; **variega'ta,** *l.* yellow-variegated.

V. pubes'cens. A synonym of *V. major pubescens.*

V. ro'sea. 1 to 2 ft. h., downy, erect. *l.* long; stalks short. *fl.* almost sessile, lobes rose, showy, obovate; cor. tube 1 in. long; throat with a hairy ring over tips of stamens and a slighter one at the narrow opening. March to October. Tropics. 1758. (B.M. 248.) Greenhouse or stove. This is often put in a separate genus as *Catharanthus roseus.*

VINCETO'XICUM (*vincere*, to conquer, *toxicum*, poison; from supposed powers as antidotes). FAM. *Apocynaceae.* A genus of about 80 species of erect or twining perennial herbs or sub-shrubs, mostly natives of temperate and warm regions, with a few in the tropics. Leaves opposite, rarely alternate or in whorls of 4. Flowers usually greenish-yellow or purplish, sometimes nearly black, in cymes; calyx 5-parted; corolla roundish bell-shaped, deeply 5-cleft; corona attached to staminal tube, nearly entire, toothed, shortly 5- to 10-lobed, or nearly 5-partite. The following except *V. pilosum* are hardy perennials needing the same treatment as Cynanchum, in which genus they were at one time included.

V. acu'tum. Twiner. *l.* oblong, ovate-cordate, acute. *fl.* white; pet. oblong, obtuse. July. S. Europe. 1596.

V. fusca'tum. 2 to 3 ft. h., stem twining at top. *l.* ovate. *fl.* yellow; cor. bearded; umbel simple. July. SE. Europe. 1817. SYN. *Cynanchum minus.*

V. japo'nicum. Stem somewhat twining above. *l.* rounded, shortly slender-pointed or retuse, with a very short mucro, paler beneath, downy on veins and somewhat velvety. *fl.* whitish, on slender pedicels; cor. glabrous; cymes loosely fld., shorter than l. Japan. (P.F.G. 3, 150.)

V. me'dium. 2 to 3 ft. h., stem twining at top. *l.* broadly ovate, obtuse or ovate-lanceolate, acute. *fl.* white, beardless; pedicels hardly longer than peduncle; umbels often divided. May. E. Europe.

V. nig'rum. 2 to 3 ft. h., stem twining at top. *l.* ovate-lanceolate, slender-pointed, finely ciliate, narrower than in *V. officinale*. *fl.* brown; cor. bearded; pedicels scarcely longer than peduncle; umbel simple. July. S. Europe. 1596. (B.M. 2390 as *Cynanchum nigrum*.)

V. officina'le. 1 to 3 ft. h., erect, with a downy line each side. *l.* ovate, slender-pointed, finely ciliate at first. *fl.* white, without a beard, pedicels 3 times as long as peduncle; umbel simple. May. Europe. 1596. SYN. *Cynanchum Vincetoxicum*.

V. pilo'sum. Twining sub-shrub. *l.* ovate, rounded, mucronulate at apex, base rounded or somewhat cordate. *fl.* white, on short, erect pedicels; peduncles about as long as l., many-fld. July. S. Africa. 1726. (B.R. 111 as *Cynanchum pilosum*.) Greenhouse.

V. purpuras'cens. Slightly downy; finally somewhat twining. *l.* narrow-oblong, mucronate, upper smaller. *fl.* dull purple, on slender pedicels; cymes long stalked, axillary, many-fld. Japan. 1850. Somewhat tender.

vinciflo'rus -a -um, with Vinca-like flowers.

vincoi'des, Vinca-like.

vin'culans, binding.

VINE. Term sometimes used for any climbing plant, especially in U.S.A., but usually restricted in Britain to the Grape-vine.

VINE (*Vitis vinifera*). The Grape-vine is found growing wild in the temperate regions of W. Asia, S. Europe, and parts of N. Africa. It is supposed to have originated in Asia Minor to the south of the Caucasus and the Caspian Sea, but early became widely distributed. Records of its cultivation and of the making of wine in Egypt go back 5,000 or 6,000 years.

The introduction of the vine into England has been accredited to the Romans in the reign of the Emperor Augustus, about A.D. 10, and vineyards existed in England very early in our history. They are mentioned by the Venerable Bede who wrote in A.D. 731 and in the Domesday Book. Wine was received as tithes by the Bishop of Ely, shortly after the Conquest, from vines grown in his diocese, and the Isle of Ely was called the Isle of Vines by the Normans. Vineyards were probably common in all monastic establishments, but on the suppression of the latter probably led to their neglect, but they were still planted here and there until modern times. They were certainly cultivated in the time of Henry III and were, somewhat later, written of as plentiful in Gloucestershire. The first Earl of Salisbury planted a vineyard at Hatfield, which is noted as existing when Charles I was taken there as prisoner. There are records of vineyards existing in several parts of Surrey and of a notable one at Bury St. Edmunds. The occurrence of such names as Vineyard St. in many old towns testifies to the widespread cultivation in the open in times past. More modern examples of which there are authentic records are the great vine at Northallerton in Yorkshire, which in 1789, growing in the open air, had covered 132 sq. yards and was then reputed to be 150 years old; and the vineyard at Cardiff which existed until recently. No doubt the increasing ease with which cheap foreign wines could be imported, together with the uncertainties of the British climate which sometimes caused the destruction of the crop or failed to ripen it, accounts for the recent neglect, but it is unquestioned that excellent wine can sometimes be made from grapes grown in the open in many parts of England, provided varieties suitable for the purpose and which find the soil and climate congenial are planted and well looked after. Recently some success has been obtained by growing vines under cloches in the south of England.

VINE GROWING OUTDOORS IN ENGLAND. As Phylloxera is not prevalent in England, vines can be grown outdoors without wall protection on their roots, if site and variety are suitable. The site should be in the southern half of England and Wales, preferably on a southerly slope, to avoid spring frosts, which are the most serious trouble.

The best varieties at present are Gamay Hatif des Vosges and Madeleine Royale for wine, and Pirovano I4 and Muscat de Saumur or Pearl de Czaba for eating.

Rows can run north and south, with 4 ft. between vines and 2 ft. 6 in. between rows. The safest pruning method is the Guyot, in which 2 shoots are grown upwards each year from a short stump. In the winter, one is cut off to 4 ft. and is bent down horizontally, and the other is cut back to 2 buds. This latter grows the 2 shoots for the following season and should not bear fruit, while the long bearer bears fruit on all the shoots from its buds. These shoots are pruned back occasionally during the summer to about 6 in. above the bunches of fruit, and in the winter this long bearer with all its shoots is cut right out at the base, and the 2 upright shoots used as in the previous year.

There is sure to be some trouble with fungus diseases, and precautionary treatment should be given. Powder with sulphur powder when the shoots are 4 in. long, and again at 3-weekly intervals until the end of blooming. Then spray with Bordeaux mixture made from 5 lb. copper sulphate, 7½ lb. slaked lime, and 100 gallons water, and repeat the spray at 3-weekly intervals if the weather continues wet.

The fruit will ripen after the beginning of September in a normal year, but for wine may be left to get very ripe, hanging on the vines till well after the first frosts, which do not hurt the ripe grapes.

For greatest success with table grapes, cloches may be employed. These need to give at least 22 in. head room, and must have slots at the top which can be opened to let out the fruiting shoots, while the fruit hangs inside the cloche.

The pruning method can well be exactly the same as for the outdoor grapes, but the cloches advance the ripening by about 30 or 40 days in a good year. This makes it possible to grow much bigger grapes, and the following are recommended: Muscat Hamburgh, Golden Chasselas, Chasselas Rose, White Frontignan, Chasselas 1921.

The Chasselas have the exceptional property of hanging ripe on the vines under cloches for very long periods, and extend the season up to Christmas in a good year.

For further information *see* R. B. Brock, *Outdoor Grapes in cold Climates* (Rep. Viticult. Res. Station, Oxted, no. 1; 1949), *More outdoor Grapes* (Rep. Viticult. Res. Station, Oxted, no. 2; 1950), and E. Hyams, *The Grape Vine in England* (1949).

R. B. B.

The cultivation of the grape-vine became general under glass in the 18th century, and as they were apparently often grown on the extension system some very large vines developed. A notable example was the Black Hamburgh vine at Valentines, Ilford, Essex, which was planted in 1758 and was still flourishing into the 20th century. It was the parent of the even more celebrated vine at Hampton Court which was planted in 1769 and is still in vigorous health and bearing. Many other examples remarkable for their size and for the crops they bore are on record, but they do not exceed the records of vines growing in the open in S. Europe, e.g. a vine in Portico di Romagna is said to have extended 2,000 ft., a Muscat at Balançon is recorded in 1737, which at 20 years of age produced 4,206 bunches of grapes, and vines with trunks over 2 ft. in diameter are mentioned several times, while the wood from vine trunks was used in various temples for pillars, steps, and statues. In the British Is. very large bunches have been produced from time to time, e.g. Speechley at Welbeck about the end of the 18th century produced a bunch of white Syrian grapes weighing about 20 lb., and in the latter part of the 19th century a bunch of Black Hamburgh was exhibited at Edinburgh weighing 21 lb. 12 oz., and bunches of White Syrian and White Nice of over 26 lb. each.

CULTIVATION UNDER GLASS. The vinery range was a prominent feature of all large gardens, most of which had a grape-room. Late grapes are cut with the stem in December. The end of each stem is placed in a bottle of water and placed in the grape-room, which is kept at a cool and even temperature. In this way grapes may be kept for a considerable time. Lady Downes is especially useful for this purpose.

In private gardens it is usually necessary to make special borders for the vines, and the method which has been in use for very many years cannot be improved on. Both indoor and outdoor borders are recommended, the bases of which should be concreted and allowance made for ample drainage. When completed the actual soil depth for the vines should be about 2 ft. 6 in. in front to 3 ft. at the back. The vines should be planted inside the house and allowed to penetrate to the outside borders through arches built in the wall beneath the surface of the soil. The arches should at first be built up and no roots allowed outside till they have first filled the inner border.

For the first year a wall of turf is built about 3 ft. from the front of the house and filled with soil in which the vines are planted. Subsequent additions are made to the border in a similar way, and according to the growth of the vines, till the whole is filled in. The time taken to complete a border is from 4 to 6 years. No elaborate mixture of soil is necessary for the borders. The following has proved satisfactory: 4 parts loam, 1 part well-rotted manure, with a good sprinkling of wood ash and bone-meal.

The gardener is often advised to plant 'fruiting canes' which may be several years old, but it is also possible to raise one's own. This is easily done by inserting eyes—one to a 3-in. pot—in January, and placing in a warm house. Vines raised in this way are ready for planting during the latter end of April, and in almost every case 2 bunches of grapes can be taken from each vine the next year. Allow the vines to make as much growth as possible the first year.

In the autumn prune the vines back according to the growth they have made. If this has been satisfactory the rods should be cut back to approximately one-third of their length. Pruning should be done when the leaves have turned colour, but before they fall. Early pruning will at all times prevent bleeding.

In the following spring, when growth commences, select shoots on each side of the vine about 18 in. apart and alternate them if possible. From these shoots will be formed the spurs from which the grapes will be produced for many years. The shoots should be stopped at the second leaf beyond the bunch. All sub-laterals should be removed from the base of the shoot to the bunch and thereafter stopped at the first leaf. Stopping at the first leaf should continue till the grapes are ripe. At the end of the second year the main rod is cut back to about two-thirds its length, so that it takes 3 or 4 years to reach maximum length. When all fruit is cut, allow the vine to make as much growth as possible.

Vineries should be kept as cold as possible during the resting period. In most gardens it is necessary to use the houses for chrysanthemums and other plants when the fruit is cut. This will do no harm, but assuming the vines are to be started into growth in February, all ventilators and doors should be thrown wide open from Christmas on and as much frost as possible admitted. The vines can be hosed over during hard weather so that they become covered with ice. This is beneficial and will ensure a good 'break' later.

The skilful gardener will know immediately he enters a vinery if the ventilation is correct. But for the training of the journeyman careful attention to the thermometer is essential. When the vines are being started little ventilation is necessary till the buds are about to break. Thereafter air should be admitted when the temperature reaches 68 to 70° F., and added gradually till the maximum is reached. When the temperature begins to fall, ventilation should be gradually reduced, finally closing the house to enclose some sun heat. A more buoyant atmosphere is necessary when the vines are in flower, necessitating a freer circulation of air, returning to the former method when the berries are set. After thinning gradually, admit more air according to weather conditions. Front ventilation should be commenced when the grapes are nearing the end of the stoning period or a fortnight or so before they begin to colour. From this time a little air should be admitted during the night.

A humid atmosphere must be maintained in the vineries during the growing season by frequent damping of floors and walls. Exception must, however, be made during the flowering period, when drier conditions are essential. Damping should then be reduced to once a day—in the afternoons. A little front ventilation may be given at this time on favourable occasions.

Black Hamburgh is an easy grape to set—occasional tapping of the rod is sufficient. Muscat of Alexandra and Canon Hall Muscat are the most difficult. The method for setting these varieties is perhaps unusual. When the vines are in full flower hose them over with a fine spray. Select a sunny day and hose with full pressure. The hosing is done just before midday. The next day the vines are kept dry and the flowers lightly brushed with a rabbit's tail. The following day the vines may be hosed again, and so on. The other varieties are not so difficult to set, but it is wise to use the rabbit's tail on them.

Thinning grapes calls for a deal of intelligence, and the grower must know the varieties he is thinning. He must visualize the size of the berries when fully grown and thin accordingly. Obviously the larger-berried varieties will need harder thinning than the smaller kinds. For instance, Mrs. Pince needs but moderate thinning. Madresfield Court must have far more berries removed. Aim always at cutting out the under-berries and remove all from the centre of the bunch. Few will need taking from the top, for they have more room there, and the bunch needs to be well furnished at the top when ripe.

There are many varieties of grapes to choose from, the best known and commonly grown being: *Black*—Madresfield Court, Black Hamburgh, Muscat Hamburgh, and Lady Downes; *White*—Buckland Sweetwater, Fosters Seedling, Muscat of Alexandra, Canon Hall Muscat, and Mrs. Pearson.

The private gardener should aim to grow only those of the best quality, which give little if any more trouble than those of lesser value. The best of those mentioned are: *Black*—Madresfield Court, Black Hamburgh, and Muscat Hamburgh, for early work. The choice for late use is more limited, the best being Mrs. Pince. Alicante is largely grown, and Lady Downes for late keeping. Gros Colmar is largely grown for market and is favoured for invalids. *White*—The best are Muscat of Alexandra and Canon Hall Muscat. These are of more delicate constitution than the black varieties and are best grown in a house by themselves. It has, however, been proved for many years that Muscats can be grown successfully in a mixed vinery. Success is attributed in some measure to inarching the Muscat on to Black Hamburgh stock before planting. Eyes of Black Hamburgh were inserted in January, and the Muscats were inarched in April close to ground level, being planted early in May. Mrs. Pearson is an excellent white variety for the late house. It is of first-class quality, with a pleasant Muscat flavour, and will keep well.

F. J. R.

DISEASES. In the cultivation of grapes under glass the leaves sometimes show intumescences on the under surfaces which later dry and look yellow or brownish. This condition is not a disease but is the non-parasitic trouble known as Dropsy or Oedema (q.v.). The roots can be attacked by the Honey Fungus (q.v.) or occasionally by Crown Gall (q.v.). There is a Downy Mildew (*Plasmopara viticola*) causing a downy or mealy growth on the undersurfaces of the leaves. Although considered a serious disease on the Continent it is very rare in Britain. The Powdery Mildew, *Uncinula necatrix*, is common in this country with its white powdery coating which occurs on leaves and flowers and young fruits with the effect that the fruit is often cracked and mouldy. It may occur outside or under glass, and to prevent it the foliage should not be allowed to become over-crowded, ventilation should be adequate, and dusting with green sulphur should be done. In dull, cold weather sufficient heat is necessary to keep the atmosphere buoyant. Painting the hot water-pipes with sulphur may result in scorching the leaves, especially the lower ones, but it is a good plan to paint the dormant vines after removing the loose bark with a mixture of sulphur and soft soap. Soft soap and flowers of sulphur are mixed together in equal parts and made up into balls about the size of a golf ball. This is placed in a jam jar with a little water and stirred with the brush used for painting the vines. The Grape berries may suffer from various troubles. From fungi they can contract Ripe Rot caused by the fungus *Glomerella cingulata* which causes Apple Bitter Rot (q.v.). Ripe Rot in grapes shows as spots on the berries with fungus pustules, roughly in rings on the berries which also shrink. All diseased berries should be removed and the air kept free from moisture by the provision of sufficient ventilation. Anthracnose (*Gloeosporium ampelophagum*) is not common, but this shows as spots or holes on the leaves and on the berries. The spots are at first light brown but later turn red and have a darker margin. On the spot appear pustules. The treatment now recommended is to cut out diseased twigs and to spray in winter with strong Lime Sulphur solution, i.e. 1 part to 9 parts of water. The Grey Mould fungus, *Botrytis cinerea*, can be a nuisance in the vinery and cause serious damage to the foliage and destruction of the fruit. This fungus is encouraged by a very moist atmosphere and will live on dead and dying tissues in the greenhouse. It should be prevented by providing sufficient heat and ventilation to avoid excessive humidity and by strict removal of any dead or dying leaves, shoots, fruits, &c. All such infected leaves and other debris should be burnt.

There are two well-known functional disorders which commonly occur in grapes. Scald or Sunscald appears when one side of the berry, generally near the top, becomes scalded looking and sunken. The cause is due to excessive moisture being on the berries during hot sunshine, and Muscat varieties are particularly sensitive to the trouble. Ventilation must be carefully watched and must be adequate to prevent excess moisture on the berries. Early ventilation must not be neglected nor should the night temperature be too low, or the moisture is deposited on the berries. Shanking shows first as a spot on the stalk of the berry, but the stalk quickly withers and turns black and the berry gradually shrinks and becomes sour. The trouble may affect only a few berries, but sometimes all on a bunch show the trouble. The reason is malnutrition owing to unsatisfactory root growth, which must be improved. Overcropping and incorrect pruning may also contribute to the trouble. The condition of the soil must be examined and if waterlogging occurs the drainage must be improved and possibly the whole border remade. The provision of the necessary soil foods must not be neglected. Where the roots of a glasshouse vine are growing in a border outside the house extreme care is necessary in cultivation, especially when cold conditions prevail outside. **A**

D. E. G.

PESTS. Phylloxera vitifoliae (*vastatrix*) is a scheduled pest and its presence in Vineries must be reported immediately to the Ministry of Agriculture. This gall-forming Aphis has an extremely complicated life cycle, one form occurring on the roots, the other on the leaves. The root-infesting form predominates on European Vines—the last record of its occurrence in Britain being in 1934. It is apparently an insect of American origin, and its first appearance in France was between the years 1863 and 1867. The presence of this pest in French vineyards proved a major catastrophe and thousands of Vines were killed. The use of American rootstocks, which are less susceptible to attack from the root form than continental varieties, resulted in a marked diminution of the pest. It then became the practice to graft European varieties—the foliage of which is not usually seriously affected by the leaf-form—on to American rootstocks. Legislative measures to exclude this pest have been made by countries throughout the world.

Details of the measures for controlling this pest are omitted owing to the importance of refraining from taking any active measures against it until official instructions have been received. The presence of any root galls on Vines should be viewed with suspicion, and specimens of the diseased roots should be submitted to the Ministry of Agriculture.

G. F. W.

VINE BOWER. *See* **Clematis Viticella.**

VINE, CONDOR. *See* **Marsdenia Cundurango.**

VINE, GLORY. *See* **Clianthus.**

VINE, GRANADILLA. *See* **Passiflora quadrangularis.**

VINE, GRAPE-FLOWER. *See* **Wisteria.**

VINE, ICE. *See* **Cissampelos Pareira.**

VINE LOUSE. *See* **Vine,** *Pests* (Phylloxera).

VINE MAPLE. *See* **Acer circinatum.**

VINE, PIPE. *See* **Aristolochia macrophylla.**

VINE, POISON. *See* **Rhus radicans, R. Toxicodendron.**

VINE, POTATO. *See* **Ipomoea pandurata.**

VINE, SILK. *See* **Periploca graeca.**

VINE, SILVER. *See* **Scindapsus pictus.**

VINE WEEVIL, *Otiorrhynchus sulcatus*. This weevil is in both its larval and adult stages destructive to a great variety of plants in the open and under glass. The grubs feed on the roots, bulbs, corms, and tubers of such plants as Saxifrages and Sedums, Ferns (e.g. Adiantum), Fruits (especially Strawberry), Begonias, Cyclamens, and Primulas, thereby causing the foliage to turn yellow and the plants to wilt. The adult weevils feed at night on the foliage of fruit-trees (especially Vines and Peaches), indoor and outdoor Ferns, and ornamental trees and shrubs (especially Rhododendrons). The adult weevil is about $\frac{1}{3}$ inch long, dull black minutely speckled with yellow, with roughened wing-cases beneath which there are no wings. The weevils appear under glass in early spring and occur in the open throughout the summer. They feed at night, eating out small portions from the leaves, especially the marginal areas, and hide during the day beneath rubbish and stones, and among the basal leaves of low-growing plants. The eggs are laid in the soil and at the base of plants. The grubs are wrinkled, legless, white with brown heads, and lie in a curled position. They feed from June to the following February. Pupation takes place in late winter or early spring in small earthen cells near the host plants.

The complete eradication of this pest is difficult once it has become established, but its numbers may be considerably reduced by persisting in the methods advocated. The weevils may be trapped on rock-gardens, in shrub borders, and glasshouses from March to May by placing on the ground and staging rolled pieces of sacking, crumpled dusters, strips of corrugated paper or old seed-boxes to provide hiding-places and shelter during the day-time—the traps are examined daily, the weevils removed and destroyed, and the traps reset. Another method is to place greased or tarred boards on the ground beneath attacked plants, e.g. Vines, jarring the rods after dark to dislodge the weevils. Pot plants may be shaken over sheets of paper or linen after dark. When pot plants are attacked by the grubs, they should be removed from their pots, the soil shaken from the roots, the larvae collected and destroyed, and the plants repotted into clean soil. The addition of dry lead arsenate or 5 per cent. D.D.T. to the potting soil into which susceptible plants such as Begonias, Cyclamens, and Primulas are to be potted is desirable, using 6 to 8 oz. to each bushel of compost. A bait similar to that advocated against the Clay-Coloured Weevil (q.v.) has proved effective against the adult weevils in the United States.

G. F. W.

VINE, WONGA WONGA. *See* **Pandorea pandorana.**

vinea'lis -is -e, growing in vineyards.

VINEYARD CANE. *See* **Arundo Donax.**

vini'color, wine-coloured.

vino'sus -a -um, wine-red, wine-like.

VI'OLA (an old Latin name used by Virgil, Pliny, and others, being a variant of the Greek *ion* and applied like that name to 3 groups of plants, *Viola purpurea* or *ion melan* referring to the true Violets, *Viola alba* or *leukoion* to the Stock, Matthiola, and *Viola lutea* or *ion melinon* to the Wallflower, Cheiranthus). FAM. *Violaceae*. A genus of about 400 main species, many having several subspecies and varieties, of mostly perennial herbs widely distributed over the north and south temperate zones, with a few shrubby species in S. Europe, the Andes, and the Sandwich Is. and a few annuals and biennials in Europe belonging to the *Viola tricolor* group. Habit diverse, the stemless species producing leaves and peduncles direct from the tip of the root-stock, the leafy-stemmed species having longer internodes and evident stems with the peduncles arising from the axils of stem-leaves. Leaves very variable in form, often more or less heart- or kidney-shaped, but lanceolate in some species and shallowly or deeply cut in others; stipules persistent, often very large, sometimes as long as the leaf-blade, but very small or lacking in some Andean species; petiole often long. Flowers of two kinds, showy (chasmogamous) with well-developed petals, or permanently closed (cleistogamous) and inconspicuous, without petals. Sepals 5, unequal; petals 5, irregular, the lower one with a slight pouch or a short or long spur; stamens 5, the lower 2 with nectar-producing appendages which fit into the petal spur; ovary superior, hairy or glabrous; style usually club-shaped and slightly or distinctly curved, manifesting great diversity at the tip where the stigmatic opening is situated (*see* Figure, p. 2237). Fruit a many-seeded capsule, lying on the ground, opening at the tip and spilling out the seeds in a few ant-dispersed (myrmecochore) species, but usually held erect and splitting forcibly when ripe into 3 boat-shaped valves, the drying sides of which contract and fling out the seeds; those of the myrmechochore species, e.g. *V. odorata*, are provided with an appendage (oil-body, elaiosome) attractive to ants.

For botanical purposes the genus Viola has been divided into a number of sections and subsections based largely on the form of the style, as detailed below. The inquiring gardener who cares to examine the flowers of a few species with a good lens will find these technical differences worthy of study, as other differences of more horticultural interest are associated with them. For garden purposes the most important groups are Nomimium, which comprises the true Violets (e.g. *V. odorata*, *V. hirta*, *V. canina*, &c.), and Melanium, which comprises the true Pansies (*V. tricolor*, *V. lutea*, &c.). The Violets, i.e. the species of the first group, are often plants of open woodland and scrub, usually on slopes, and do well in the garden among bushes or on the shadier side of the rock-garden; a number grow in pastures and a few, e.g. *V. lanceolata*, *V. palustris*, *V. primulifolia*, and *V. stagnina*, in boggy places. The Pansies inhabit more open places, such as rocky mountain slopes, dunes, rock ledges, &c.; a few (e.g. *V. tricolor*, *V. arvensis*) are weeds of cultivated ground. Most of them are attractive little plants when they bloom freely but some produce seed abundantly from closed self-pollinated flowers (cleistogenes) and tend to dispense with their more showy insect-pollinated flowers.

Viola odorata, the Sweet Violet, is one of our most fragrant wild plants, and is common in woods, in hedges, amongst bushes, and on warm banks. At the beginning of the 19th century several double forms of this, blue, rose, and white, were in cultivation, but the varieties with very large single flowers seem to have appeared first between 1860 and 1865, notably Czar, to which The Royal Horticultural Society gave an Award of Merit in 1865 and which became the parent of many others. To what extent the 60 or so varieties of Sweet Violets now in cultivation are derived from *V. odorata* is uncertain. The large-flowered double Violets, known as Parma or Neapolitan Violets, are evidently of Oriental origin and derived not from *V. odorata* but another species, probably *V. alba*. *V. cyanea* and *V. pontica* (both sometimes regarded as Eastern sub-species of *V. sepincola*) seem also to have contributed to the diversity of the cultivated Sweet Violet. It should be remembered that this has long been grown in Persia, Syria, and Turkey; thus an old Aramaic work, translated into Arabic in A.D. 904 (see *Ber. Deutschen Bot. Ges.* 50. 321–36; 1932) gives detailed instructions for Violet cultivation.

For many years the cultivation of the Sweet Violet has been a market-garden industry, and great quantities are grown in southern England, notably Devon, Sussex, and Kent, for marketing in London and other big cities. The flowers begin in the early autumn and continue throughout the winter and until spring is well advanced. When grown out of doors they thrive best in moderately heavy, rich soil. Where the soil is light and gravelly, some soil of heavy texture must be incorporated with the former, and a liberal application of well-rotted cow dung if possible. The Sweet Violet, however, is not at all fastidious as to soil, and almost any good garden soil will suit, provided it be enriched with a good dressing of manure of a thoroughly decomposed character. Material from the compost heap will serve equally well. The borders should be deeply dug and manured in February if the soil is free from frost, and planting may be done from March up to the end of April. Plant in rows 12 in. apart and allow 12 in. between each plant. As there is always the risk of the flowers being spoiled by autumn rains and frosts, the finer varieties are grown in cold frames during autumn and winter. The frames should be prepared for the reception of the plants in August, and planting done in September. The best position for the frame is a sheltered one with a southern aspect. The proper method is to make a bed of leaves on which the frame should be set. The bed of leaves should be made up 3 ft. above ground level, and must be firmly trodden. When the frame is placed on the bed of leaves, the prepared soil is filled in, and the compost should be from 8 to 10 in. in depth, and consist of 3 parts of light loam and 1 of leaf-mould. The materials should be well mixed and firmly trodden. Allow a space of 1 ft. between each plant. Equally good results are obtained by growing in a frame used earlier for melons, the spent manure being covered by about 8 in. of compost.

Violets can also be grown in pots. For this purpose well-rooted runners should be selected in October and put into pots of any size to suit the particular plants. The compost is made up of loam and leaf-mould in equal parts, and a little sharp silver-sand should be added. After potting place in a cool glass structure where the temperature can be maintained at around 40 to 45 degrees. It should be emphasized that Violets abhor heat, and if subjected to it they become weak and will not flower. During the winter months there must be abundance of air, water, and, of course, the more sunshine the better. Red spider is often a trouble, and in mild weather the plants should get an occasional syringing with water.

Violets are propagated by division, by cuttings, and from seed. Division of the old plants is done as soon as flowering is over, and it is advisable to divide the plants into pieces each with 3 crowns. Weak pieces should be discarded. If runners are used for propagation, they should be removed from the parent plants in April and planted 1 ft. apart. Planting must be done firmly, and just deep enough to embed the base of the crowns. Cuttings can be taken from the parent plants and generally have a few tiny rootlets on them. Prick them off into a cold frame in early March, and plant them in their summer quarters at the end of April. Violet seed should be sown in early autumn; sow in shallow boxes, and make sure that the seed is lightly covered. Place the boxes in a cold frame, and in early spring the seedlings can be transplanted either into other boxes or direct into 3-in. pots. Keep the plants in the frame until the end of April and then plant out.

For further details reference may be made to G. L. Zambra, *Violets for Garden and Market*, 2nd ed. (1951). A history of the development of the Violet by E. A. Bunyard has been published in *New Flora and Silva*, 4. 188–94 (1932). A few garden Violets are scentless and have evidently been derived from species other than *V. odorata*, *V. cyanea*, *V. pontica*, and *V. alba* which are scented.

The Garden Pansy (*V.* × *Wittrockiana*) is a group of mixed origin derived largely from the Heartsease (*V. tricolor*), which varies greatly in habit and flower colour, but having characters derived from *V. lutea* and possibly from *V. altaica*. For centuries *V. tricolor* was esteemed in gardens for its quaintly marked flowers, but it had little horticultural importance and no change in size or colour seems to have taken place until deliberate selection was made by English gardeners from about 1810 onwards. The chief worker was T. Thomson, gardener to Lord Gambier, who grew Pansies on a large scale at Iver, Buckinghamshire. By 1835 about 400 named varieties were on sale. Selection in Britain led to the creation of a special group called Show Pansies conforming to rules laid down by florists and Pansy Societies. The aim was to produce a flower as circular and flat as possible, not less than 2 in. in diameter, with a well-defined circular central blotch, &c. Meanwhile, selection in Belgium and France of Pansies obtained from Britain resulted in another group, the Fancy Pansies, with a greater range of colour and a less formal shape. The modern Exhibition Pansies are largely derived from these. For details of cultivation *see under* **Pansy**; fuller information will be found in H. H. Crane, *Pansies and Violas* (1951).

Botanically every member of this genus is a Viola. In gardens the name Viola is often used as a vernacular term with a restricted meaning for a group of plants (*V.* × *Williamsii*) obtained originally by crossing the Garden Pansy and *V. cornuta* and sometimes called Tufted Pansies; these were first raised about 1863 by James Grieve. In 1887 another prominent Scottish raiser, Dr. Charles Stuart, found among his seedlings one of very compact habit with small white flowers lacking the usually conspicuous rays or guide-lines. Later seedlings of this type have become known as Violettas. A distinction is thus made by gardeners between Violets, Pansies, Violas, and Violettas; all, however, are members of the genus Viola as defined at the head of this article. The last 3 groups are easily distinguished from the true

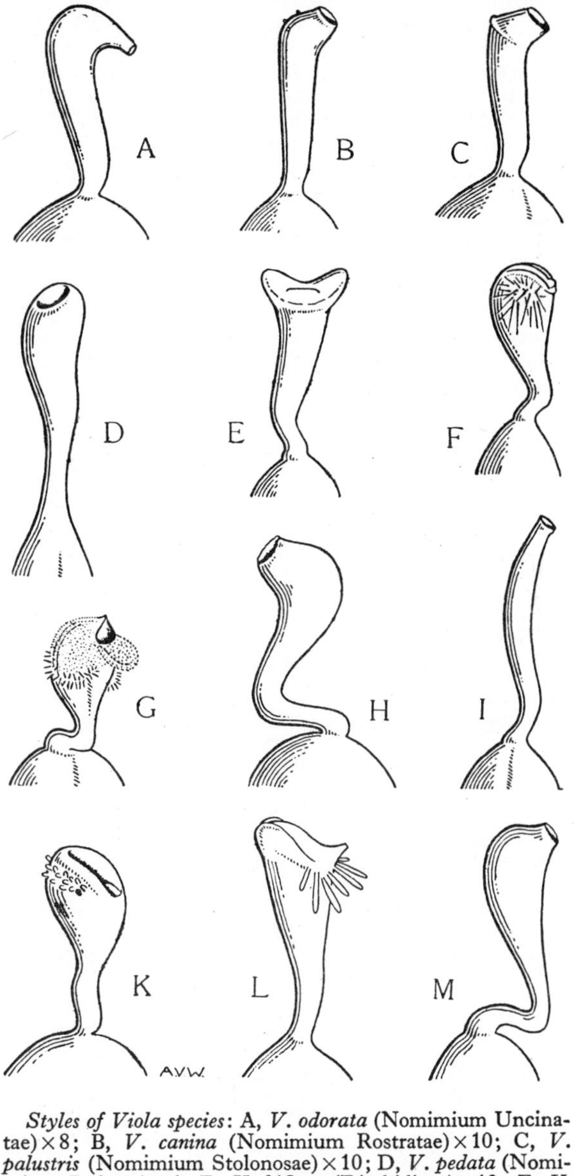

Styles of Viola species: A, *V. odorata* (Nomimium Uncinatae) × 8; B, *V. canina* (Nomimium Rostratae) × 10; C, *V. palustris* (Nomimium Stolonosae) × 10; D, *V. pedata* (Nomimium Pedatae) × 6; E, *V. biflora* (Dischidium) × 12; F, *V. pedunculata* (Chamaemelanium Nuttallianae) × 8; G, *V. lutea* (Melanium) × 8; H, *V. delphinantha* (Delphiniopsis) × 16; I, *V. hederacea* (Erpetion) × 12; K, *V. sempervirens* (Nomimium Orbiculares) × 12; L, *V. Jooi* (Nomimium Adnatae) × 10; M, *V. arborescens* (Xylinosium) × 16; all drawn from herbarium specimens of wild origin.

Violets by their habit of growth and larger rather flat blooms; a good technical distinction is provided by the different form of the style in sections Melanium (Fig. G) and Nomimium (Figs. A, B, C, L).

There are no clear-cut distinctions between the last 3, but most Pansies are annuals or biennials, often of loose growth, with a very short blunt spur to the flower and much divided stipules as in *V. tricolor*, whereas Violas and Violettas are perennial and of more compact growth, sometimes with a longer spur and less divided stipules derived from *V. cornuta*. They are better plants for garden decoration. All of them do well in a sunny position on well-drained deeply worked loam enriched with leaf-mould or manure. They can be planted in spring (i.e. late March or early April) or autumn (not later, however, than mid-October). They are admirable for beds or edgings but mostly out of character for the rock-garden.

Most species are better fitted for the rock-garden than elsewhere. Among the easiest and most free-flowering is *V. cornuta*; hybrids of this and *V. gracilis* have been given the group-name *V.* × *Visseriana*. These thrive in any good well-drained soil. Some of the high alpine species such as *V. cenisia* and *V. delphinantha* grow in nature either in screes or shady rock crevices and hence need specially well-drained positions and careful treatment in the alpine-house or scree; a compost of loam, leaf-mould, coarse sand, and finely broken crock has been found suitable. Some other species, among them the difficult *V. pedata*, also do well in scree. A remarkable group of species, belonging to the section Andinium, inhabits the Andes; these mostly form close rosettes of leaves and are known as the 'penwiper' or rosulate Violas. Attempts to cultivate them have been unsuccessful, possibly because they are short-day plants from high altitudes, but they would need scree or alpine-house treatment; they include *V. Cotyledon*, *V. coronifera*, *V. petraea*, and *V. volcanica*.

Propagation of named forms of the Garden Pansy and its allies is usually by cuttings, about 2 to 2½ in. long for preference, of basal shoots with short internodes. Cuttings should be prepared by making the cut immediately below a joint and all but the upper 2 leaves should be removed. Insert them in pots or boxes in a well-drained sandy soil, place in a cold propagating frame, and keep well syringed each day. Shade if need be from the hot midday sun until they have rooted. Those cuttings inserted in June and July will produce plants which can be planted out in the autumn and will flower early the following spring. Autumn-rooted cuttings are best grown on in a cold frame as the young plants are often not strong enough to stand the winter without protection except in very favoured localities.

Seed sowing produces a large vigorous stock, but the plants will probably vary considerably. Sow the seeds in a light, well-drained soil either in boxes or pots, and germinate in a cold frame, or slightly heated house, during the spring (March, April). Prick out into boxes or pans as soon as large enough to handle, and continue to grow them on under cool conditions in a frame. Plant out into their positions when large enough. Most Violets of a clump-forming or carpeting habit, e.g. *V. hirta*, *V. odorata*, *V. eizanensis*, *V. hederacea*, as well as some of the Pansies, e.g. *V. cornuta*, are easily increased by careful division of clumps in September.

W. T. S. and G. M. T.

PESTS. MIDGE, *Dasyneura affinis*, a gall-midge widely distributed throughout Europe, frequently causes considerable loss in plants grown in frames in the British Is. Attacked plants are distorted and dwarfed, the leaves becoming thickened and the leaf-margins curled upwards which hinders the normal functions of the leaves. There are several generations a year on cultivated plants in frames and glasshouses. The female midge inserts her eggs within the rolled leaf margins of the youngest leaves, and the galled portions are easily seen within 10 days after oviposition. The pale orange, legless maggots are found within the rolled leaf portions and, when fully grown, spin cocoons within the galls. In severe attacks the flowers are likewise galled.

It is advisable to remove and burn the galled leaves as soon as they appear, and to dust the plants with Nicotine dust at temperatures above 65° F. to ensure penetration of the Nicotine vapour within the rolled leaf margins. The site of the crop should be changed, and all galled portions removed from the plants prior to replanting elsewhere. Soil treatment is unnecessary as the larvae pupate on the plants within the galls and not in the ground.

G. F. W.

DISEASES. Several leaf-spotting fungi are apt to attack Violas and Violets, among them *Ascochyta Violae*, *Phyllosticta Violae*, *Ramularia lactea*, and *Septoria Violae*, all at times found on Violets, and in addition *Ramularia agrestis* and species of Cercospora on Pansies and Violas, but these are all more likely to prove troublesome where the plants are crowded than where free movement of air and moderate humidity occurs. Violets in frames can be preserved from such attacks by increasing ventilation, cleanliness, and occasional spraying with Bordeaux mixture. Black Root Rot, caused by *Thielaviopsis basicola*, may be troublesome if soil conditions are not good and there is insufficient drainage and aeration, and the same conditions predispose Violas to attack by Damping Off, Root Rot due to *Aphanomyces euteiches*, Foot Rot to *Myrothecium roridum*, and Collar Rots to *Phytophthora* and *Rhizoctonia*. All these troubles are dealt with under their appropriate headings. A more serious disease of Violets is due to the Smut fungus *Urocystis Violae*, which produces dark bladder-like swellings on leaves and stems which finally burst and release myriads of black spores which contaminate the soil. Affected plants should be destroyed before the swellings burst and the remainder sprayed with Bordeaux mixture. The frames and soil where Smut-affected plants have grown should be treated with Formalin before a new planting is made. The Rust fungus, *Puccinia Violae*, also attacks Violets at times but is not usually serious. A virus infection causing mottling of the leaves and spotting of the petals occurs in Violets, and in Violas one producing white streaks and splashes on the flowers typical of 'breaking' and attributed to infection by the Cucumber Mosaic Virus. Plants showing these symptoms should be immediately destroyed and precautions taken against attacks of Aphis by spraying or fumigating.

D. E. G.

The genus is a difficult one from the botanical standpoint, as many species, notably those of the Melanium section, vary considerably, particularly in colour, while related species hybridize freely. The number of specific names applied to them exceeds a thousand. There is no monograph of the genus as a whole, but for over 30 years an industrious German botanist, Wilhelm Becker (1874–1928), studied it intensively and published a long series of learned and detailed papers, notably 'Violenstudien' in *Beihefte zum Botanischen Centralblatt*, 26. ii (1909–10) and 'Violae Asiaticae et Australenses' in *B.B.C.* 34. ii (1916–17), 36. ii (1918), 40. ii (1923). He dealt mostly with the European, Asiatic, Australasian, and S. American species, while an American botanist, Ezra Brainerd (1844–1924), revised the N. American species; Brainerd's work has been continued by his daughter Viola Brainerd Baird, the authoress of the beautifully illustrated *Wild Violets of North America* (1942). Becker's long study of the genus as a whole resulted in a reclassification of the sections, published in Engler's *Die natürlichen Pflanzenfamilien*, 2nd ed. 21.

363–76 (1925). A number of Becker's sections have never had any members in cultivation. The following synopsis accordingly omits these, but retains his numbering and lettering for the others; the same numbers and letters placed after a name in the list of species indicate the section to which it belongs. The measurements given have mostly been taken from herbarium specimens and should be regarded as approximate rather than precise indications of size. Good coloured illustrations of Eastern N. American species are given in H. D. House, *Wild Flowers of New York*, vol. i (1918), as well as in Baird, *Wild Violets*.

W. T. S.

CLASSIFICATION

1. *Plants herbaceous* 2
1. *Plants shrubby (rarely cultivated)* 15
2. *Style almost cylindric, thickest about* $\frac{1}{2}$ *way up, with a simple erect (not hooked or beaked) stigmatic tip* (Fig. I); *pet. spur almost lacking* Sect. 14
2. *Style thickest above middle, the tip swollen, beaked or hooked; pet. spur usually evident* 3
3. *Plants stemless, the lvs. and fl. arising direct from rootstock* 4
3. *Plants with evident stems bearing lvs. and fl.* 10
4. *Style tip hooked* (Fig. A) Sect. 1A
4. *Style tip not hooked* 5
5. *Style with a swollen rounded head and abruptly bent base* (Fig. G); *fl. Pansy-like, lower pet. flat* Sect. 4A
5. *Style otherwise; fl. Violet-like, lower pet. more concave* 6
6. *Style club-shaped with a wide oblique hollow on one side of tip, beakless* (Fig. D) Sect. 1O
6. *Style beaked at tip* (Figs. K. L, C) 7
7. *Fl. yellow* Sect. 1P
7. *Fl. violet, blue, mauve, or white, not yellow* 8
8. *Stipules joined to petiole for* $\frac{1}{2}$ *their length* Sect. 1G
8. *Stipules free* 9
9. *Rhiz. short, stout, without stolons* Sect. 1N
9. *Rhiz. long and slender* Sect. 1F
10. *Style tip with 2 flanges, hence Y-shaped in front view* (Fig. E) Sect. 2
10. *Style tip without flanges* 11
11. *Style tip beaked* (Fig. B) Sect. 1B
11. *Style tip markedly swollen* (Figs. F, G) 12
12. *European and Asiatic species with pet. spur usually well-developed; stipules usually large and divided; stigmatic opening wide* Sect. 4B
12. *North American and east Asiatic species with pet. spur hardly longer than cal. appendage; stipules usually small and entire; stigmatic opening narrow* 13
13. *Lvs. deeply divided* Sect. 3C
13. *Lvs. not deeply divided* 14
14. *Stem with lvs. on lower part* Sect. 3B
14. *Stem with lower part bare of lvs.* Sect. 3D
15. *South American species with lvs. crowded in regular rosettes; style appendages diverse* Sect. 7
15. *European species with lvs. not crowded in rosettes; style without appendages, curved like a swan's neck* (Figs. H, M) 16
16. *Spur of pet.* $\frac{1}{10}$ *in. or less long* Sect. 5
16. *Spur of pet.* $\frac{2}{5}$ *to* $1\frac{1}{5}$ *in. long* Sect. 6

1. Section Nomimium. Herbaceous, mostly perennial plants; leaf-blade rounded to lanceolate. Flowers mostly violet or blue-violet, occasionally white, rarely yellow; lateral petals spreading sideways; spur varying in length; style straight or curved forward throughout its length, thickened upwards and more or less club-shaped, the tip usually hooked or bent forwards with the stigmatic opening in front at the end of a short beak (Figs. A, B, C, D). This section includes the true Violets; these are very numerous and it has accordingly been divided into a number of subsections:

1A. Subsection *Uncinatae*. Style distinctly hooked at the tip, the hook (measured on the underside) about as long as the greatest diameter of the style; stigmatic opening narrow (Fig. A). Plants stemless, the flowers and leaves arising direct from the rootstock. Capsules on prostrate stems, the seeds falling out or being removed by ants. This section includes the British *V. odorata* (Sweet Violet) and its allies, among them *V. × permixta*.

1. *Well-developed plant without stolons; petioles usually shaggy with long spreading hairs; fl. scentless* V. hirta
1. *Well-developed plant with stolons; petioles almost glabrous or hairy with short downward-pointing hairs; fl. scented* 2
2. *Stipules broadly to narrowly ovate* V. odorata
2. *Stipules lanceolate or linear-lanceolate* 3
3. *Some lvs., especially on stolons, rather triangular-cordate, the margins of the upper half almost straight-sided; bracts on peduncle usually above middle, small* V. alba
3. *All lvs. with margins of the upper half distinctly curved; bracts on peduncle a little below middle* 4
4. *Basal sinus of lvs. narrow; stipules glandular; spur stout, as broad or broader than long* V. pontica
4. *Basal sinus of lvs. rather open; stipules almost glabrous; spur longer than broad* V. cyanea

1B. Subsection *Rostratae*. Style hooked at the tip (but almost straight in *V. rostrata*), the hook or beak shorter than the greatest diameter of the style; stigmatic opening rather wide (Fig. B). Plants caulescent, the flowers and leaves being borne on short stems arising from the rootstock (except in young plants on first flowering which may be stemless). Capsules on erect stems. This subsection, the leafy-stemmed Dog Violets, is widespread in distribution; it includes the European Dog Violet, *V. canina*, representative of the group Arosulantes without a basal rosette of leaves, the peduncle being terminal, and the Wood Violet, *V. Riviniana*, representative of the Rosulantes with a basal rosette of leaves. *V. yakusimana*, remarkable for its leaves less than $\frac{1}{4}$ in. wide and petals about $\frac{1}{5}$ in. long, possibly belongs here.

1. *Stipules serrate* 2
1. *Stipules entire, not serrate* 12
2. *Spur* $\frac{2}{5}$ *to* $\frac{7}{10}$ *in. long; lateral pet. beardless* V. rostrata
2. *Spur* $\frac{3}{10}$ *in. or less long; lateral pet. bearded near the base* 3
3. *Ovary and capsule finely hairy; petiole also usually hairy* V. rupestris
3. *Ovary and capsule glabrous* 4
4. *Lvs. cuneate or rounded at base, broadest at one-third above base* V. lactea
4. *Lvs. truncate or cordate at base* 5
5. *Main axis with a basal rosette of lvs., the fl.-stems lateral* 6
5. *Main axis continued up into fl.-stem without a basal rosette of lvs.* 10
6. *Fl. usually small, about* $\frac{1}{2}$ *in. across, spur* $\frac{1}{8}$ *in. long; plant small, purplish, almost glabrous, except for upper side of lvs. Northern N. America* V. labradorica
6. *Fl. larger* 7
7. *Species of Europe, including Britain; stipules with numerous* (6 *to* 10 *or so each side*) *fine serrations* 8
7. *Species of N. America; stipules with fewer* (3 *to* 6 *each side*) *often coarser serrations* 9
8. *Spur usually violet, slender* V. Reichenbachiana
8. *Spur whitish, stout* V. Riviniana
9. *Plant usually pubescent; fl. deep violet or violet-blue; spur* $\frac{3}{10}$ *to* $\frac{2}{5}$ *in. long* V. adunca
9. *Plant almost glabrous; fl. pale violet or white; spur about* $\frac{1}{6}$ *in. long* 14
10. *Spur about twice as long as cal. appendages* V. canina
10. *Spur scarcely longer than cal. appendages* 11
11. *Plant* 4 *to* 8 *in. h.; stipules shorter than petiole* V. stagnina
11. *Plant* 8 *to* 16 *in. h.; stipules equalling or longer than petiole* V. elatior
12. *Plant robust, with mature lvs. up to* $3\frac{1}{2}$ *in. wide; sep. more than* $\frac{3}{10}$ *in. long; capsule-valves* $\frac{2}{5}$ *to* $\frac{1}{2}$ *in. long* V. mirabilis
12. *Plant not robust, with mature lvs. at most* $1\frac{1}{2}$ *in. wide; sep. less than* $\frac{3}{10}$ *in. long. Capsule-valves* $\frac{3}{20}$ *to* $\frac{1}{4}$ *in. long* 13
13. *Fl. very small, spur* $\frac{1}{8}$ *in. or less long* V. labradorica, V. yakusimana
13. *Fl. longer, spur about* $\frac{1}{5}$ *in. long* V. adunca
14. *Fl. pale violet* V. conspersa
14. *Fl. white with violet veining on lower pet.* V. striata

1F. Subsection *Stolonosae*. Style club-shaped, almost straight with a short almost conical beak at one side of the rather flattened tip (Fig. C). Plants stemless, the flowers and leaves arising direct from the very long slender rhizome. Capsules on erect stems. This subsection includes the British Marsh Violet, *V. palustris*.

1. *Lvs. kidney-shaped to ovate-orbicular, the base deeply cordate with a narrow sinus* 2
1. *Lvs. lanceolate, oblanceolate, oblong or ovate, the base cuneate, slightly cordate or truncate* 4
2. *Pedicel with bracts well above the middle; lvs. sparsely hairy below; fl.* $\frac{1}{2}$ *to* $\frac{7}{10}$ *in. across; spur* 2 *or* 3 *times as long as cal. appendage* V. epipsila
2. *Pedicel with bracts at or below the middle; lvs. glabrous below; fl. smaller, with upper pet. bent back or twisted; spur no longer than cal. appendages* 3
3. *Lvs. glabrous above; fl. lilac, rarely white* V. palustris
3. *Lvs. sparsely hairy above; fl. white with purple veining* V. blanda
4. *Lvs. oblong or ovate, the base rounded, subcordate or truncate* V. primulifolia
4. *Lvs. lanceolate or oblanceolate, the base cuneate, gradually narrowed into petiole* V. lanceolata

1G. Subsection *Adnatae*. Style mostly somewhat flattened and hollowed out at the tip, with a short stigmatic beak (Fig. L). Stipules united for about half their length to the petiole. Stemless perennials. This subsection has numerous mostly Asiatic species.

1. *Lvs. ovate, broadly ovate or oblong, not deeply divided* 2
1. *Lvs. deeply divided into narrow segs.* 4
2. *Lvs. oblong, twice as long as wide, the sides almost parallel for much of their length* V. Patrinii
2. *Lvs. ovate or broadly ovate, less than twice as long as wide, the sides markedly curved, not parallel* 3
3. *Fl. mauve; sep. more than* $\frac{1}{5}$ *in. long; seeds reddish-brown* V. Jooi

3\. *Fl. white; sep. less than $\frac{1}{5}$ in. long; seeds whitish* — V. Cunninghamii
4\. *Lvs. divided to base into 3 main divisions narrowed at base into a distinct stalk; lvs. becoming very large after flowering* — V. chaerophylloides, V. eizanensis
4\. *Lvs. palmately or pinnately cut but divisions not stalked* — V. pinnata

1N. Subsection *Boreali-Americanae*. Style almost straight, flattened and margined on the tip, with a short almost conical beak. Stipules free, lanceolate, membranous. Stemless perennials without stolons, the rhizome short and stout. Flowers violet or blue, rarely white, the lateral petals bearded. The species are all N. American. Those described below may be distinguished as follows:

1\. *Lvs. deeply cut into 5 to 17 lobes* — 2
1\. *Lvs. undivided or with only 1 large lobe at base* — 3
2\. *Petioles pubescent; spurred pet. glabrous* — V. palmata
2\. *Petioles glabrous; spurred pet. bearded at base* — V. pedatifida
3\. *Principal lvs. narrowly ovate or lanceolate (2 or 3 times as long as wide), often with coarse teeth or lobes at base* — V. sagittata
3\. *Lvs. broadly ovate to kidney-shaped (sometimes wider than long)* — 4
4\. *Fl.-stems and most of plant glabrous; sep. mostly glabrous* — 5
4\. *Fl.-stems glabrous, most of plant hairy; sep. always ciliated* — 6
5\. *Spurred pet. shorter than lateral pet.; beard of pet. with club-shaped hairs* — V. cucullata
5\. *Spurred pet. about as long as lateral pet.; beard of pet. with fine hairs* — V. papilionacea
6\. *Spurred pet. densely bearded at base; mature lvs. light green with about 17 (10 to 26) teeth each side* — V. septentrionalis
6\. *Spurred pet. glabrous or only slightly hairy at base; mature lvs. dark green, with about 32 (21 to 52) teeth each side* — V. sororia

1O. Subsection *Pedatae*. Style large, markedly club-shaped, beakless, with a sloping concave tip having the stigmatic opening near the centre of the cavity (Fig. D). Stipules fused in lower part. Stemless perennials without stolons, the rhizome erect. This subsection includes only the N. American *V. pedata* and its varieties and is noteworthy for its pedately divided leaves and large flowers with the lateral petals beardless and the orange tips of the anthers conspicuous.

1P. Subsection *Orbiculares*. Style club-shaped, curved in upper part and papillose on the back with a fairly wide 2-lipped stigmatic opening (Fig. K). Stemless perennials with rounded leaves and short-spurred, rather small yellow flowers. This includes the Western N. American *V. sempervirens* and *V. orbiculata*; the Eastern N. American *V. rotundifolia* diverges from them in style character but is best placed here.

1\. *Plant with stolons; lvs. evergreen* — V. sempervirens
1\. *Plant without stolons* — 2
2\. *Cleistogamous fl. on stems with very small bracts. Eastern N. America* — V. rotundifolia
2\. *Cleistogamous fl. on stems with small lvs. Western N. America* — V. orbiculata

2\. Section Dischidium. Herbaceous perennial caulescent plants, with a few basal more or less rounded leaves; stipules small, free, pointed. Flowers yellow, small, sometimes violet-tinged; lateral petals not bearded, often pointing upwards; style not beaked but deeply cleft at the tip into 2 lips or wings, between which is the stigmatic opening (Fig. E). This includes the widely distributed *V. biflora* and 7 other species, all Asiatic.

3\. Section Chamaemelanium. Herbaceous plants mostly with well-developed stems; stipules small, free; flowers mostly yellow, less often white, the upper petals sometimes brownish or violet; spur very short, hardly or not longer than the calyx appendage; style not beaked, club-shaped, swollen and rounded and hairy at or near the tip, not winged, the stigmatic opening in a hollow or a tiny projection at the front side of the head (Fig. F). This section, the Mock Pansies, is N. American and has many species; it has accordingly been divided into a number of subsections.

3B. Subsection *Nuttallianae*. Leaves undivided, very broadly ovate to lanceolate; lower part of stem bearing leaves.

1\. *L.-blades about as wide as or wider than long; large, to $1\frac{1}{2}$ in. across* — V. pedunculata
1\. *L.-blades longer than wide; fl. smaller, about $\frac{1}{2}$ to $\frac{3}{4}$ in. across* — 2
2\. *Peduncles much shorter than lvs.* — V. Nuttallii
2\. *Peduncles as long or longer than lvs.* — V. praemorsa

3C. Subsection *Chrysanthae*. Leaves deeply divided (but almost entire in *V. lobata* var. *integrifolia*).

1\. *Upper 2 pet. dark violet or purple* — 2
1\. *Upper 2 yellow, sometimes brownish or purplish on back* — 4
2\. *Lower 3 pet. pale yellow or cream except for violet veins, the lowermost pointed* — V. Hallii
2\. *Lower 3 pet. pale lilac with yellow base and violet veining, the lowermost truncate-rounded and notched* — 3
3\. *Lvs. deeply and pinnately dissected, the ultimate segs. 10 to 35 rather oblong, not prominently veined beneath* — V. Beckwithii
3\. *Lvs. divided into 3 to 7 narrowly ovate or lanceolate prominently 3- to 7-veined beneath* — V. trinervata
4\. *Lvs. pinnately divided into very narrow segs., the middle division with a long slender stalk; pet. deep orange-yellow, about $\frac{3}{5}$ in. long* — V. Douglasii
4\. *Lvs. palmately cleft, the middle division not stalked* — 5
5\. *Plant 3 to 6 in. h.; stem very short and l. almost basal; stipules very small* — V. Sheltonii
5\. *Plant coarser, 4 to 15 in. h; stem well-developed and bare of lvs. in lower part; stipules ovate, conspicuous* — V. lobata

3D. Subsection *Erectae*. Leaves undivided, halbert-shaped to broadly ovate or heart-shaped; lower part of stem often bare of leaves for $\frac{1}{2}$ to 3 in.

1\. *Fl. white, violet, or pinkish with a yellow eye* — 2
1\. *Fl. yellow* — 5
2\. *Lvs. broadly kidney-shaped to broadly ovate; fl. reddish-violet on both sides* — V. Flettii
2\. *Lvs. broadly ovate to ovate; fl. white or pinkish, sometimes violet on back* — 3
3\. *Stipules with thread-like teeth* — V. ocellata
3\. *Stipules entire* — 4
4\. *Lvs. almost glabrous beneath; rhizome short, compact, rather thick with many roots* — V. canadensis
4\. *Lvs. pubescent beneath; rhizome slender, long, with few roots* — V. rugulosa
5\. *Lvs. narrowly ovate or lanceolate, rather hastate, often twice as long as wide* — V. hastata
5\. *Lvs. broadly or very broadly ovate or kidney-shaped, not hastate, not twice as long as wide but sometimes wider than long* — 6
6\. *Stipules small, thin, under $\frac{3}{10}$ in. long* — V. glabella
6\. *Stipules larger, about $\frac{3}{10}$ to $\frac{3}{5}$ in. long* — 7
7\. *Stipules ovate, often toothed. Western N. America* — V. lobata integrifolia
7\. *Stipules lanceolate, entire. Eastern N. America* — 8
8\. *Stem sparsely hairy in upper part; 1 to 3 basal lvs. usually present at fl. time* — V. pensylvanica
8\. *Stem densely hairy in upper part; basal lvs. usually lacking at fl. time* — V. pubescens

4\. Section Melanium. Herbaceous, stemless to long-stemmed, mostly perennial plants, a few species annual; stipules mostly free and deeply cut. Flowers mostly yellow or blue, less often white or reddish, often of mixed colours; 3 lower petals bearded; spur mostly longer than the calyx appendage, often very long; style with an abrupt bend at the very base, club-shaped, swollen at the tip into a rounded hairy head, the stigmatic opening wide and in a hollow at one side with a distinct lip (Fig. G). This section includes the true Pansies.

4A. Subsection *Scaposae*. Plant stemless; stipules small, membranous, joined to the petiole. The only species is *V. alpina* of the European Alps.

4B. Subsection *Elongatae*. Plant with stems usually long and well-developed, though sometimes very short in high alpine species; stipules free, green and leafy, mostly large and deeply divided.

4B*a*. Series *Integrifoliae*. Leaves entire or margin only slightly wavy.

1\. *Lvs. very narrowly lanceolate to almost linear, to 2 in. long. $\frac{1}{5}$ in. wide, covered with minute hairs* — V. allchariensis
1\. *Lvs. otherwise* — 2
2\. *Stipules 3- to 7-lobed at base* — V. valderia
2\. *Stipules entire or with a small tooth at base* — 3
3\. *Spur about $\frac{1}{10}$ in. long* — 4
3\. *Spur about $\frac{1}{5}$ to $\frac{3}{10}$ in. long* — 5
4\. *Lvs. almost orbicular or broadly ovate, base rounded or subcordate* — V. Comollia
4\. *Lvs. oblanceolate or elliptic, base narrowly cuneate* — V. Stojanowii
5\. *Longest sep. (exclusive of appendage) about $\frac{1}{5}$ in. long. Balkan Peninsula* — V. Grisebachiana
5\. *Longest sep. (exclusive of appendage) nearly $\frac{3}{10}$ in. long. Alps* — V. cenisia

4B*b*. Series *Crenatifoliae*. Leaves distinctly crenate-toothed.

1\. *Spur long and slender, equalling longest sep. (exclusive of appendage), about $\frac{2}{5}$ to $\frac{1}{2}$ in. long, at least 3 times as long as cal. appendage* — 2
1\. *Spur shorter than longest sep. (exclusive of appendage), $\frac{1}{20}$ to $\frac{2}{5}$ in. long, at most 3 times as long as cal. appendage* — 6
2\. *Dwarf high alpine plants, $1\frac{1}{2}$ to 4 in. h. in fl.; internodes of above-ground stems very short, under $\frac{1}{2}$ in. long, hence lvs. crowded and basal* — 3
2\. *Taller plants 4 to 12 in. h. in fl.; internodes mostly long and lvs. well spaced on the evident ascending stems* — 4
3\. *Stipules entire, stalked, rounded, usually rather like lvs. in form but smaller* — V. Grisebachiana (some forms)
3\. *Stipules toothed, often acute, differing from lvs. in form* — 9
4\. *Stipules broad, palmately lobed or toothed, but not pinnately dissected; upper lvs. ovate, broad, truncate at base* — V. cornuta

4. *Stipules pinnately divided with narrow segs.; upper lvs. cuneate at base and narrowed into petiole* 5
5. *Upper lvs. ovate to almost orbicular. N. Africa* V. Munbyana
5. *Upper lvs. linear or lanceolate, 1/20 to 3/10 in. wide* 22
6. *Fl. very large, mostly 1½ to 3 in. wide, rather circular in general outline, with the lateral pet. very broad and distinctly overlapped by the lower pet.; colours very diverse; plants of garden origin* 26
6. *Fl. smaller, ⅖ to 1½ in. wide, usually much longer than wide, with the lateral pet. scarcely or not overlapped by the lower pet.* 7
7. *Spur slender, about ⅕ to 3/10 in. long, distinctly longer than cal. appendage* 8
7. *Spur short and rather stout, under ⅕ in. long, not much longer than cal. appendage* 14
8. *Dwarf high alpine plants, 1½ to 4 in. h. in fl.; internodes of above-ground stems very short, under ½ in. long, hence lvs. crowded and basal* 9
8. *Taller plants, 4 to 12 in. in fl.; internodes usually long and above-ground stems well developed, with l. usually well spaced* 10
9. *Fl. usually dark violet, rarely pale yellow or white; l.-blade mostly longer than wide and stipules deeply toothed* V. calcarata
9. *Fl. usually bright yellow; l.-blade mostly broadly ovate to almost circular and stipules shallowly toothed* V. Zoysii
10. *Stipules entire or sparsely toothed; upper lvs. broadly ovate to almost orbicular, truncate or subcordate at base; plant glabrous* V. arsenica
10. *Stipules deeply toothed or lobed or dissected; upper lvs. elliptic, ovate or lanceolate, cuneate at base* 11
11. *Stipules deeply toothed, with incisions reaching about half-way but not to base or midrib* V. elegantula
11. *Stipules divided almost to base* 12
12. *Fl. about 1½ in. wide* V. pseudo-Munbyana
12. *Fl. not more than 1 in. wide* 13
13. *Plant more or less glabrous, sparsely branched with few stems* V. declinata
13. *Plant hairy with minute profuse hairs, many-stemmed* V. gracilis
(*See also* V. saxatilis)
14. *Fl. very small, ¼ to ½ in. long, the pet. usually shorter than sep.; plant annual* V. arvensis
14. *Fl. larger, mostly over ⅗ in. long, the pet. usually much longer than sep.* 15
15. *Stipules ovate, leafy, toothed to not more than half-way; plant densely hairy* V. Orphanidis
15. *Stipules deeply divided, segs. narrow* 16
16. *Plant conspicuously hairy on stems and l.; stipules pinnately divided; fl. light violet* V. hispida
16. *Plant glabrous or sparsely hairy* (V. lutea *sometimes distinctly hairy but stipules palmately divided*) 17
17. *Fl. small, usually less than 9/10 in. long and wide* 18
17. *Fl. larger, usually more than 1 in. long and wide* 19
18. *Spur 1 to 1½ times as long as cal. appendages; pet. usually little longer than sep.* V. tricolor
18. *Spur usually twice as long as cal. appendages; pet. much longer than sep.* V. saxatilis
19. *Lower pet. scarcely or not at all overlapping lateral pet.; fl. yellow or violet* 20
19. *Lower pet. overlapping lateral pet.; fl. with great colour range; plants of garden origin, rarely naturalized* 21
20. *Internodes short, less than 3/10 in. long, hence lvs. rather crowded and basal* V. altaica
20. *Internodes longer, to 1 in. long; lvs. often well spaced* V. lutea
21. *Plants annual or biennial; stipules deeply divided with end lobe very large, stalked; spur about as long as cal. appendage* V. × Wittrockiana
21. *Plants perennial; some stipules less divided, the incisions reaching scarcely more than half-way and the end lobe not stalked; spur sometimes twice as long as cal. appendage* V. × Williamsii
22. *Blade of lower pet. truncate and notched. Italy, Balkan Peninsula, widespread and very variable* V. Bertolonii
22. *Blade of lower pet. rounded. Corsica, Sardinia* V. corsica

5. Section Xylinosium. Sub-shrubs to 1 ft. high, with the roots and lower part of the stem woody; leaves and stipules rather narrow. Flowers small, lilac or yellow, with short stout spurs about 1/10 in. or less long; style curved from the base, club-shaped, gradually thickened to the tip, without a stigmatic beak or with only a very short beak (Fig. M). This includes *V. arborescens* and 3 other species.

6. Section Delphiniopsis. Small bushy plants 2 to 5 in. high with a thick woody rootstock and stems woody at base; leaves and stipules narrowly oblanceolate, not more than 1/10 in. long. Flowers reddish-violet with very long slender spurs up to 1 in. long; style curved from the base somewhat like a swan's neck, gradually thickened to the tip, with a fairly wide stigmatic opening but no appendages (Fig. H). A very distinct group of charming little cliff-dwelling plants with remarkably long slender spurs, but not easy to grow.

1. *Spur about ⅗ in. long, little longer than blades of pet.* V. Kosaninii
1. *Spur ⅗ to 1⅕ in. long, much longer than blades of pet.* 2
2. *Blade of lower (spurred) pet. entire or slightly emarginate, about as long as other pet. Balkan Peninsula* V. delphinantha
2. *Blade of lower (spurred) pet. deeply notched, distinctly shorter than upper pet. Spain* V. cazorlensis

7. Section Andinium. Plants with the leaves usually crowded into a regular rosette on a sometimes elongated woody stem; rootstock going deep into the earth; young leaves not rolled; stipules mostly membranous and small or lacking. Flowers often very numerous, not or scarcely overtopping the leaves; style club-shaped, mostly with a well-developed stigmatic beak and very diverse appendages. A curious group, in general appearance very unlike the Violets and Pansies, with numerous species in the mountains of S. America, almost impossible to grow.

14. Section Erpetion. Plant low-growing, herbaceous, small-leaved and stemless, forming rosettes and producing slender stolons which in turn form rosettes; leaf-blade ovate, rounded or kidney-shaped; stipules small, lanceolate. Flowers small; spur very short; style almost cylindric, with a simple stigmatic opening (Fig. I). This section, sometimes given generic rank under the name Erpetion, includes only the Australian *V. hederacea*, an easily grown but somewhat tender species.

V. adun'ca (1B). Hooked-spur Violet. *rhiz.* compact, somewhat woody, branched. Plant in fl. 2½ to 4 in. h., leafy-stemmed, the stems procumbent, usually short and under 3 in. long. *l.* broadly ovate or ovate, ½ to 1 in. wide, pubescent or glabrous, long-stalked; stipules small, usually slightly toothed, sometimes entire. *fl.* deep to light violet or lavender, with a white eye, lower pet. veined with dark violet, to ¾ in. long; pet. ½ in. or more long, spur 3/10 to ⅗ in. long; peduncles usually longer than l. Spring. N. America, widespread. (Baird, Viol. 187.) Syn. *V. canina* var. *adunca*. var. **gla'bra,** *l.* always glabrous; **mi'nor,** a synonym of *V. labradorica*.

V. aeto'lica. A variety of *V. saxatilis*.

V. al'ba (1A). *rhiz.* creeping, usually putting out long stolons. Plant in fl. about 2 to 4 in. h., stemless. *l.* narrowly ovate to very broadly ovate, to about 1½ in. wide, cordate at base, blunt, crenate, more or less hairy on both sides, sometimes almost glabrous; petioles hairy with downward pointing hairs; stipules linear-lanceolate, long, fimbriate, ciliate. *fl.* white or violet, fragrant, about ⅗ in. long; spur nearly ⅕ in. long; peduncles usually a little longer than l. Spring. Cent. and E. Europe. (R.I.F.G. 4498B.) Syn. *V. scotophylla*. A variable species, near *V. odorata*, but with narrower stipules. var. **pic'ta,** *fl.* white suffused with lilac or violet towards pet. tips (Moggridge, Fl. Mentone, 54 as *V. hirta* var. *picta*); **ro'sea,** *fl.* rose; **rub'ra,** *fl.* reddish; **viola'cea,** violet. **V. Dehnhardt'ii,** S. Europe, is very similar.

Viola allchariensis var. *Herzogii*

V. allcharien'sis (4B). *rhiz.* perennial, branched at or near ground-level. Plant in fl. about 4 in. h., leafy-stemmed, the shoots and l. densely covered with short grey hairs. *l.* linear to linear-spatulate, to ⅕ in. wide, acute, entire or with 1 or 2 blunt teeth each side, grey with short hairs; stipules free, divided into several long linear segs. *fl.* large, blue-violet, about 1¼ in. long; pet. broad, to ⅗ in. long, spur blunt, cylindric, about ⅕ in. long. Yugoslavia (Macedonia). var. **Herzog'ii,** *l.* narrower, *fl.* smaller, yellow. (B.M. 9537.)

V. alpest'ris. A synonym of *V. saxatilis*.

V. alpi'na (4A). *rhiz.* short, simple or branched, perennial, not putting out stolons. Plant in fl. 1½ to 4 in. h., stemless. *l.* all basal, broadly ovate to oblong-ovate, truncate or slightly cordate at base, blunt, shallowly crenate, glabrous or almost so; petiole long; stipules oblong, small, joined to petiole for most of their length. *fl.* medium-sized or large, usually rich purple or violet with white eye, ½ to 1 in. long; pet. broad, to ½ in. long; spur blunt, about ⅒ in. long; peduncles longer than l. May to June. Austrian Alps, Carpathians, Transylvania. (R.I.F.G. 4509.) A delightful little alpine Pansy.

V. alta'ica (4B). *rhiz.* creeping, slender, perennial. Plant in fl. 2 to 5 in. h., leafy-stemmed. *l.* elliptic to broadly ovate, to ¾ in. wide, usually much less, wedge-shaped at base, blunt or slightly acute, shallowly crenate, glabrous, long-stalked; stipules free, usually large and deeply cut or toothed. *fl.* large, yellow or sometimes violet, ¾ to 1½ in. long; pet. broad, to ¾ in. long, spur to ⅕ in. long, slightly longer than cal. appendages. March to June. Crimea, Turkistan, Altai Mts. 1805. (B.M. 1776; B.R. 54.) A true Pansy and possibly among the ancestors of the Garden Pansy. *See* **V. × Wittrockiana.**

V. arbores'cens (5). Dwarf shrubby loose-growing plant, up to 1 ft. h., with a woody rootstock and spreading woody branches. *l.* narrowly oblanceolate, up to 2 in. long, ⅖ in. wide, stalked; stipules free, narrowly oblanceolate or linear, much shorter than l.-blade. *fl.* bluish, long-stalked; pet. to ⅖ in. long, entire; spur short, rounded, stout, less than ⅒ in. long. E. Mediterranean region. 1784. (Moggridge, Fl. Mentone, 76.)

V. arena'ria. A synonym of *V. rupestris.*

V. arse'nica (4B). *rhiz.* perennial, branched. Plant in fl. about 6 in. h., leafy-stemmed, more or less glabrous. *l.* broadly ovate to almost orbicular, to 1¼ in. wide, blunt, rounded, shallowly crenate, bright green, glabrous, long-stalked; stipules lanceolate, leafy, toothed. *fl.* large, deep yellow, with darker lines, about 1¼ in. long; pet. broad, to ⅗ in. long, spur blunt, cylindric. Yugoslavia (Macedonia).

V. arven'sis (4B). Field Pansy. Annual weed closely akin to *V. tricolor* with very small creamy-white *fl.* 3/10 to ⅗ in. long, the lower pet. orange or yellow-blotched at base; sep. longer than pet.; spur very short, blunt. Europe, including British Is.; Asia. (E.B. 179.) SYN. *V. tricolor* var. *arvensis.*

V. Beckwith'ii. Akin to *V. trinervata,* but with more divided *l.* not prominently veined beneath. Western N. America, Great Basin area. (Baird, Viol. 67.)

V. Bertolon'ii of Pio (1815), not Salis (1834) (4B). Closely akin to *V. gracilis* but glabrous or with only a few hairs on *l.* and stipules. *fl.* violet, yellow, or white; lower pet. truncate, notched, long-spurred. Italy, Balkan Peninsula. A very variable and beautiful species, easily grown in a sunny place, divided into many local races, e.g. var. **Cavillier'i,** W. Italy, **grae'ca,** Balkan Peninsula, **messanen'sis,** S. Italy, &c. SYN. *V. heterophylla* of Bertoloni, not Poiret. **V. cor'sica** is the Corsican and Sardinian representative of this, with the lower pet. rounded, not notched; *fl.* blue. SYN. *V. Bertolonii* of Salis, not Pio.

V. biflo'ra (2). *rhiz.* creeping, slender, perennial. Plant in fl. 2½ to 6 in. h.; stems glabrous, erect, usually with 2 or 3 l., 1- to 3-fld., usually 2-fld. *l.* kidney-shaped, to 1¾ in. wide, shallowly crenate, sparsely hairy or almost glabrous, lower l. long-stalked, upper l. short-stalked; stipules very small, narrowly ovate, entire. *fl.* bright yellow, veined brownish purple-black, ⅖ in. or less long; pet. narrow, to ⅖ in. long, spur short, blunt, hardly 1/20 in. long; tip of style with 2 short flanges. April, May. Northern Hemisphere, from Europe across N. Asia to N. America. 1752. (B.M. 2089; R.I.F.G. 4489; Baird, Viol. 73.) A charming little plant for a cool half-shady place on rock-garden, ranging in the Alps from subalpine zone up to 13,000 ft.

V. blan'da (1F). *rhiz.* short. Plant in fl. 2 to 4 in. h., stemless then, but producing later long leaf-bearing runners with cleistogamous fl. *l.* ovate, to 2¼ in. wide, usually much less, deeply cordate at base, acute, faintly crenate, almost entire, glabrous except for a few short hairs on upper side, long-stalked; stipules lanceolate, slightly toothed. *fl.* small, white with purple veins, sweet-scented, about ½ in. long; pet. narrow, to ⅖ in. long, spur short, blunt, about ⅒ in. long. Early spring. N. America. 1802. (Baird, Viol. 161.) A pleasing neat little Violet. **V. Pringl'ei,** Mexico, is closely akin but has hairy petioles. (Baird, Viol. 163.)

V. bosni'aca. A synonym of *V. elegantula.*

V. calcara'ta (4B). *rhiz.* very slender, often almost thread-like, long, much-branched, creeping below ground. Plant in fl. 3 to 4 in. h., almost stemless, the internodes very short. *l.* elliptic or lanceolate, ⅖ in. or less wide, wedge-shaped at base, acute, shallowly crenate, long-stalked, glabrous or ciliate; stipules narrow, toothed or lobed, often as long as petiole. *fl.* large, violet or yellow, rarely white, to 1¼ in. long; pet. broad, to ¾ in. long, spur slender, ⅕ to ⅖ in. long. March to July. Alps of Cent. Europe. 1752. (R.I.F.G. 4510.) A very variable and attractive alpine Pansy, not always free-flowering in gardens. var. **Zoys'ii,** a synonym of *V. Zoysii.*

V. calca'rea. A variety of *V. hirta.*

V. canaden'sis (3D). *rhiz.* short, without stolons. Plant in fl. 12 to 18 in. h., erect, leafy-stemmed, the internodes up to 6 in. long. *l.* ovate to very broadly ovate, to 2½ in. wide, cordate at base, acuminate, toothed, sparsely hairy to almost glabrous, long-stalked; stipules lanceolate, entire. *fl.* medium-sized, white tinged with pale violet, yellowish at base, the lower pet. prominently purple-veined, about ¾ in. long; pet. to ½ in. long, spur very short, rounded, about 1/20 in. long. May to July. N. America, widespread in mountain woods. 1783. (S.B.F.G. 2, 5, 62; Baird, Viol. 51.) A lanky species of unusual habit with large pale fl.

V. cani'na (1B). Dog Violet. *rhiz.* short, creeping. Plant in fl. about 3 in. h., leafy-stemmed, with no central non-flowering rosette. *l.* mostly ovate, usually under ¾ in. wide, truncate or subcordate at base, blunt or acute, shallowly crenate, glabrous or slightly hairy, long-stalked; stipules oblong-lanceolate, toothed, much shorter than petiole. *fl.* medium-sized, blue with whitish base, about ¾ in. long; pet. to ⅖ in. long, spur yellowish, stout, about ⅒ in. long. April to June. N. temperate region (Europe, Asia), including Britain. (E.B. 125 as *V. flavicornis.*) SYN. *V. flavicornis.*

V. cazorlen'sis (6). Dwarf compact shrubby plant, 4 to 6 in. h., with a woody rootstock and erect twiggy shoots. *l.* very narrowly elliptic or narrowly oblanceolate, to ⅖ in. long, ⅒ in. wide; stipules free, undivided or divided to base into 2 segs., so that the l. seems to consist of 3 to 5 narrow lflets. *fl.* deep rosy-lilac or reddish-violet, long-stalked; upper pet. about ⅖ in. long; blade of lower pet. deeply notched, spur slightly curved, slender, to 1⅕ in. long. June. S. Spain, on mountains of Jaen. 1935. (J.R.H.S. 73 (1948), 261.) Allied to *V. delphinantha* and requiring similar treatment.

V. ceni'sia (4B). Taproot slender, branching from the crown into numerous long slender shoots up to 9 in. long, each ending above ground in a short stem with a tuft of l. Plant in fl. 1½ to 6 in. h., short-stemmed. *l.* small, broadly to narrowly ovate, to 3/10 in. wide, cuneate or truncate at base, blunt, entire, usually glabrous, sometimes hairy, short-stalked; stipules spatulate, entire or with 2 short lanceolate segs. at base. *fl.* medium-sized or large, light violet, about ¾ to 1 in. long; pet. broad, to ½ in. long, spur slender, pointed, ⅕ to 3/10 in. long. July. European Alps, on limestone. (R.I.F.G. 4512.) Best grown in scree or alpine house.

V. chaerophylloi'des (1G). *rhiz.* short, without stolons. Plant in fl. 2½ to 5 in. h., stemless. *l.* mostly divided into 3 short-stalked segs., these deeply 2- or 3-lobed and toothed, but some later l. ovate-lanceolate, undivided, glabrous or slightly hairy, long-stalked; stipules joined to petiole for half length, upper part lanceolate. *fl.* large, violet or whitish, scented, about 7/10 in. long; pet. about ½ in. long, spur stout, ⅕ in. long. SE. Asia. SYN. *V. pinnata* var. *chaerophylloides.*

V. chrysan'tha of Hooker. A synonym of *V. Douglasii.*

V. Clementia'na (4B). Akin to *V. altaica.* Asia Minor.

V. Comol'lia (4B). Closely akin to *V. cenisia. fl.* light purple or whitish with a central yellow spot; spur slender. Alps of N. Italy.

V. consper'sa (1B). American Dog Violet. *rhiz.* branched. Plant in fl. 2 to 8 in. h., leafy-stemmed, with no central non-flowering rosette. *l.* broadly ovate to almost orbicular, to 1¾ in. wide, cordate at base, acute or rounded, crenate, almost glabrous, long-stalked; stipules lanceolate, toothed, much shorter than petiole. *fl.* medium-sized, pale violet with dark-violet veins, to ¾ in. long; pet. to ⅖ in. long, spur often purplish, about ⅕ in. long. Eastern N. America. (Baird, Viol. 193.) var. **Mason'ii,** *fl.* white. Close to *V. canina.*

V. cornu'ta (4B). Rootstock short, tufted. Plant in fl. 4 to 12 in. h., leafy-stemmed, the stems prostrate at base, then ascending; internodes long. *l.* ovate or broadly ovate, less than 1 in. wide, truncate or slightly cordate at base, blunt or acute, shallowly crenate, glabrous above, somewhat hairy beneath, stalked; stipules leafy, as long as petiole or longer, deeply cut, the end seg. longest. *fl.* large, violet, about 1¼ in. long; pet. to ¾ in. long, spur slender, rather acute, about ½ in. long. Summer. Pyrenees, naturalized elsewhere. 1776. (B.M. 791.) var. **al'ba,** *fl.* white. A good reliable plant which, hybridized with the Garden Pansy (*V. × Wittrockiana*), has given rise to the Tufted Pansies, Violas, and Violettas (*V. × Williamsii*), and hybridized with *V. gracilis* has given rise to *V. × Visseriana,* all plants of high garden merit.

V. cor'sica. *See under* **V. Bertolonii.**

V. cuculla'ta. *rhiz.* short, fairly thick, without stolons. Plant in fl. 3 to 6 in. h., stemless; peduncles overtopping l. *l.* broadly ovate to kidney-shaped, to 3½ in. wide, cordate at base, acute or acuminate, shallowly crenate, usually glabrous (but hairy on upper side in var. *prionosepala*), long-stalked; stipules lanceolate, entire. *fl.* medium-sized, violet with deep violet veins on lower pet., lateral pet. bearded with club-shaped white hairs, about ¾ in. long; pet. to ½ in. long, spur very short, rounded, about ⅒ in. long. *Capsules* green, narrowly ovoid, on erect stalks. April to June. Eastern N. America. About 1760. (Baird, Viol. 121.) Varies to forms with *fl.* white (**albiflo'ra**) or mottled blue and white (**Thurstonii**).

V. cunea'ta. *See under* **V. ocellata.**

V. Cunningham'ii (1G). *rhiz.* creeping. Plant in fl. 3 to 6 in. stemless. *l.* ovate or broadly ovate, almost triangular, to 1 in. wide, truncate or slightly cordate at base, blunt, shallowly crenate or almost entire, glabrous, long-stalked; stipules narrowly oblong, joined to petiole except for lanceolate tip. *fl.* small, white or pale violet, ½ to ⅗ in. long; pet. to ⅖ in. long, spur very short, blunt, less than ⅒ in. long. May. New Zealand. 1915.

V. cya'nea (1A). *rhiz.* short, putting out short stolons. *l.* broadly ovate, deeply cordate, blunt, crenate, almost glabrous, usually rather shining and light green, long-stalked; stipules lanceolate, long-pointed, almost glabrous. *fl.* medium-sized, blue or violet, with lower part white; pet. about ½ in. long, spur less than ⅕ in. long. Spring. E. Europe. SYN. *V. sepincola* subsp. *cyanea.* A fragrant easy-growing little Violet, sometimes grown as a pot-plant under the name Russian Violet (Russischen Veilchen).

V. declina'ta (4B). Plant in fl. 4 to 9 in. h., leafy-stemmed with stems prostrate at base, then ascending; internodes long. *Lower l.* very small, ovate, $\frac{1}{4}$ in. or less wide, truncate or subcordate at base; *upper l.* much longer, narrowly elliptic, to $\frac{1}{4}$ in. wide, cuneate at base, all l. blunt, crenate, glabrous or ciliated; stipules conspicuous, shorter or longer than petiole, palmately divided into about 7 narrow segs. *fl.* medium-sized or large, violet with yellow throat, about 1 in. long; pet. fairly broad, to $\frac{5}{8}$ in. long, spur slender, about $\frac{1}{10}$ in. long. E. Europe. An attractive little short-lived Pansy, closely akin to *V. tricolor.*

Viola cornuta var. *alba* (p. 2242)

V. delphinan'tha (6). Dwarf compact shrubby plant, $1\frac{1}{2}$ to 4 in. h., with a woody rootstock and erect or ascending twiggy shoots. *l.* linear or narrowly oblanceolate, to $\frac{1}{2}$ in. long, less than $\frac{1}{10}$ in. wide; stipules free, undivided or divided to base into 2 segs. so that the l. seems to consist of 3 to 5 narrow lflets. *fl.* deep rosy-lilac or reddish-violet, long-stalked; pet. about $\frac{3}{10}$ to $\frac{5}{8}$ in. long, almost equal; blade of lower pet. entire or scarcely notched, spur curved, slender, $\frac{7}{10}$ to 1 in. long. June, July. Greece, Bulgaria, in clefts of calcareous rock. 1933. (Hook. Ic. 3117.) A delightful choice little plant, remarkable for its bushy habit and long-spurred fl., best grown in sink garden on the side of a tufa rock. *V. cazorlensis* and *V. Kosaninii* are closely allied.

V. delphinifo'lia. A synonym of *V. pedatifida.*

V. dissec'ta var. **eizanen'sis.** A synonym of *V. eizanensis.*

V. domes'tica. A synonym of *V. papilionacea.*

V. Douglas'ii (3C). *rhiz.* short. Plant in fl. 2 to 6 in. h., leafy-stemmed. *l.* pinnately twice-cleft into long narrow linear segs. scarcely $\frac{1}{10}$ in. wide, minutely hairy or almost glabrous, long-stalked; stipules lanceolate, entire or toothed. *fl.* fairly large, bright yellow with brown veining, $\frac{1}{2}$ to $\frac{3}{4}$ in. long; pet. to $\frac{5}{8}$ in. long, spur very short, about $\frac{1}{20}$ in. long. Oregon, California. (Baird, Viol. 65.) Syn. *V. chrysantha* of Hooker, not Schrader.

V. eizanen'sis (1G). *rhiz.* short, stout. Plant in fl. about 4 in. h., stemless. *l.* divided into 3 main segs., in turn deeply divided into lanceolate or linear-lanceolate lobes, at fl. time $1\frac{1}{2}$ in. wide, later to $2\frac{1}{2}$ in. wide, glabrous or slightly hairy, long-stalked; stipules joined to petiole for much of length, upper part lanceolate. *fl.* large, pale rose, about 1 in. long, fragrant; pet. to $\frac{7}{10}$ in. long, spur $\frac{1}{5}$ in. long. March, April. Japan. About 1930. Syn. *V. dissecta* var. *eizanensis.* Doubtfully distinct from *V. chaerophylloides*; a delightful plant for pans in alpine house.

V. ela'tior (1B). *rhiz.* compact. Plant in fl. about 8 to 16 in. h., erect, leafy-stemmed. *l.* lanceolate or narrowly ovate, to $\frac{3}{4}$ in. wide, acute, lower l. somewhat cuneate, upper l. truncate or subcordate at base, shallowly crenate, shortly hairy especially on upper side, stalked, stipules large, lanceolate, equalling or longer than petiole. *fl.* large, pale blue, about 1 in. long; pet. to $\frac{5}{8}$ in. long, spur blunt, scarcely $\frac{1}{10}$ in. long. May, June, Europe, W. Asia, in marshy places. (R.I.F.G. 4508 as *V. persicifolia.*)

V. elegan'tula (4B). Plant in fl. 4 to 12 in. h., leafy-stemmed; stems prostrate at base, then ascending; internodes long. *Lower l.* small, broadly ovate often subcordate, blunt, $\frac{1}{2}$ in. or less wide; *upper l.* much larger, ovate or lanceolate, cuneate at base, acute, all l. crenate, more or less glabrous, stalked; stipules conspicuous, palmately divided into up to 10 narrow segs. *fl.* medium-sized, very variable in colour, $\frac{3}{4}$ to 1 in. long; pet. to about $\frac{1}{2}$ in. or more long, spur slender, about $\frac{3}{10}$ in. long. May to June. Yugoslavia. (B.M. 9021.) Syn. *V. bosniaca, V. latisepala.* var. **ro'sea,** *fl.* rose, the commonest form in gardens; **bi'color,** upper pet. violet, lower yellow; **lu'tea,** *fl.* yellow; **al'ba,** *fl.* white. Short-lived, like many Pansies related to *V. tricolor*, but seeding freely.

V. epipsi'la (1F). *rhiz.* elongated, slender. Plant in fl. about 4 in. h., stemless. *l.* usually 2, sometimes 3, broadly ovate to kidney-shaped, to $2\frac{3}{4}$ in. wide, deeply cordate at base, crenate, glabrous apart from a few hairs on veins beneath, long-stalked; stipules free, ovate-lanceolate. *fl.* medium-sized, lilac or whitish, to $\frac{3}{4}$ in. long; pet. to $\frac{1}{2}$ in. long, spur fairly thick, $\frac{1}{10}$ in. long; peduncle with bracts above middle. Europe, Asia, but not Britain. (Fl. Danica 2405.) '*V. epipsila*' of British authors is a form of *V. palustris.*

V. eriocar'pa. A synonym of *V. pensylvanica.*

V. flavicor'nis. A synonym of *V. canina.*

V. Flett'ii (3D). *rhiz.* creeping. Plant in fl. 4 to 6 in. h., leafy-stemmed. *l.* kidney-shaped to broadly ovate, to $1\frac{3}{4}$ in. wide, cordate at base, blunt and rounded or acute, shallowly crenate, glabrous or slightly hairy, purple-veined above, purplish beneath, long-stalked; stipules lanceolate, entire. *fl.* medium-sized, violet with yellow base and dark violet veins, about $\frac{3}{4}$ in. long; pet. to $\frac{1}{2}$ in. long, spur short, blunt, yellow. Washington, Western N. America. (Baird, Viol. 61.)

V. × **florarien'sis** (4B). Hybrid which appeared in Correvon's garden, Floraire, near Geneva, between *V. cornuta* and a *V. tricolor* form, notable for long fl. season. *fl.* purple and yellow.

V. glabel'la (3D). *rhiz.* creeping, brown. Plant in fl. $2\frac{1}{2}$ to 12 in. h., leafy-stemmed, the stem bearing 2 or 3 l. close together at the top. *l.* kidney-shaped to very broadly ovate, to 2 in. wide, shallowly cordate at base, acute, crenate, glabrous or slightly hairy, short-stalked unless basal; stipules narrowly ovate, entire. *fl.* small or medium-sized, bright yellow, the lower pet. purple-veined, about $\frac{1}{2}$ to $\frac{3}{4}$ in. long; pet. to $\frac{1}{2}$ in. long, spur $\frac{1}{20}$ in. long. April, May. Western N. America. (Baird, Viol. 19.)

V. gra'cilis (4B). Plant in fl. 4 to 6 in. h., leafy-stemmed, stems prostrate at base, then ascending. *Lower l.* broadly ovate, less than $\frac{1}{2}$ in. wide, rounded or subcordate at base; *upper l.* elliptic, cuneate at base, all l. blunt, shallowly crenate to almost entire, hairy with numerous short hairs; stipules conspicuous, pinnately divided into about 5 to 8 segs., the end one much longer and wider than side segs. *fl.* large, deep violet, about 1 to $1\frac{1}{4}$ in. long; pet. to about $\frac{1}{2}$ in. long, spur slender, $\frac{1}{5}$ to $\frac{3}{10}$ in. long. Asia Minor, Balkan Peninsula. (B.M. 8541, not typical.) Syn. *V. olympica.* This description refers to the true *V. gracilis* of the Bithynian Olympus near Bursa, Asia Minor; a dainty species, it unfortunately tends to be superseded in gardens by coarser hybrid forms.

V. Grisebachia'na (4B). *rhiz.* slender, branching below ground. Plant in fl. $1\frac{1}{2}$ to 3 in. h., leafy-stemmed, but internodes short. *l.* crowded, ovate, or spatulate, to $\frac{3}{10}$ in. wide, rounded or cuneate at base, sparsely crenate or entire, glabrous or nearly so, long-stalked; stipules oblanceolate, entire, stalked. *fl.* large, about 1 in. long, violet or blue; pet. to $\frac{5}{8}$ in. long, spur about $\frac{3}{10}$ in. long. Balkan Peninsula. A beautiful little Pansy akin to *V. cenisia* and needing careful cultivation.

V. Hall'ii (3C). Akin to *V. Beckwithii. fl.* with upper 2 pet. violet, lower 3 yellow. Oregon, California. (Baird, Viol. 71.)

V. hasta'ta (3D). *rhiz.* creeping, white, brittle. Plant in fl. 3 to 10 in. h., leafy-stemmed, the stem bearing 3 or 4 l. close together at the top. *l.* narrowly ovate or lanceolate, almost triangular, often hastate (halberd-shaped), to $1\frac{1}{2}$ in. wide, shallowly cordate at base, often with laterally projecting rounded basal lobes, acute or acuminate, crenate, finely hairy, short-stalked unless basal; stipules small, ovate, toothed. *fl.* small, bright yellow, the lower pet. purple-veined, about $\frac{1}{2}$ in. long; pet. to $\frac{3}{10}$ in. long, spur $\frac{1}{20}$ in. long. April, May. Eastern N. America. (Baird, Viol. 21.) Distinguished from other small-flowered yellow Violets by its often hastate l.

V. hedera'cea (14). Australian Violet. *rhiz.* short, vertical, putting out long thread-like stolons with well-separated tufts of l. Plant in fl. $1\frac{1}{2}$ to 3 in. h., stemless. *l.* ovate to kidney-shaped, to $1\frac{1}{2}$ in. wide, usually wedge-shaped and shallowly cordate at base, blunt, rounded, entire or toothed. *fl.* small, violet with white tips to pet., to $\frac{1}{2}$ in. long; pet. to $\frac{3}{10}$ in. long, spur almost absent, the base of lower pet. slightly gibbous. Summer. Australia. 1823. (H.E.F. 225; L.B.C. 1133; S.B.F.G. 170 as *Erpetion reniforme.*) Syn. *Erpetion hederaceum, E. reniforme.* A tender species usually needing glasshouse or frame protection in winter, but growing and flowering freely in a cool position on the rock-garden in summer.

V. heterophyl'la of Bertoloni (1810), not Poiret (1808). A synonym of *V. Bertolonii* of Pio, not Salis.

V. hir'ta (1A). *rhiz.* creeping, rather woody, branched but without stolons. Plant in fl. $2\frac{1}{2}$ to 4 in. h., stemless. *l.* narrowly ovate-oblong to broadly ovate, to 2 in. or more wide, deeply cordate at base, blunt, crenate, very hairy when young, sometimes almost glabrous later, long-stalked; petiole with long spreading hairs; stipules lanceolate, ciliate along margin. *fl.* medium-sized, blue-violet, sometimes white, scentless, to $\frac{3}{4}$ in. long; pet. to $\frac{1}{2}$ in. long, spur $\frac{1}{10}$ in. long, usually violet. N. and Cent. Europe, including British Is.; N. Asia. (E.B. 172.) Closely akin to *V. odorata* but stolons lacking, l. narrower, more triangular, hairs on petiole more spreading, fl. at most faintly scented. Some of the plants known in gardens as 'scentless forms of *V. odorata*' are probably derived from this species. var. **calca'rea,** smaller, with upper 2 pet. almost parallel, the 2 lateral horizontal, narrow, spur very short. May to June. British Is., France. SYN. *V. calcarea*.

V. his'pida (4B). Rouen Pansy. Rootstock perennial, branched at top. Plant in fl. 3 to 8 in. h., much branched, with long internodes, the whole plant (except peduncles) rather shaggy with spreading hairs. *Lower l.* broadly ovate, to $\frac{3}{8}$ in. wide, subcordate at base; *upper l.* lanceolate, longer, cuneate at base, all l. blunt, crenate, hairy, long-stalked; stipules pinnately divided, the end seg. the longest. *fl.* fairly large, light violet, with darker veining, about $\frac{3}{4}$ in. or more long; pet. about $\frac{1}{2}$ in. long, spur blunt, $\frac{1}{10}$ to $\frac{1}{5}$ in. long. May to August. NE. France. 1812. (B.M. 1498 as *V. rothomagensis*.) SYN. *V. rothomagensis*. A hairy little Pansy, akin to *V. tricolor* and *V. lutea*.

V. horten'sis of Schur. A form of *V. odorata*.

V.× horten'sis of Wettstein. A synonym of *V.× Wittrockiana*.

V. Joo'i (1G). *rhiz.* creeping, without stolons. Plant in fl. 2 to 3 in. h., stemless, the peduncles overtopping l. *l.* ovate, to 1 in. wide, cordate at base, blunt or acute, crenate, glabrous, long-stalked; stipules joined to petiole for much of their length, tips free, lanceolate, acuminate. *fl.* small or medium-sized, mauve with purplish streaks, scented, to $\frac{3}{4}$ in. long; pet. to $\frac{1}{2}$ in. long, spur stout, slightly curved, $\frac{1}{5}$ in. long. May, but occasional fl. all summer. Transylvania, SE. Europe. (Gentes Herb. 4, 314.) SYN. *V. transsilvanica*. An attractive easy-growing little Violet; according to Becker not specifically distinct from the Asiatic *V. macroceras*.

V. Juress'ii. A synonym of *V. palustris Juressii*.

V. Kosanin'ii (6). Dwarf compact shrubby plant, to 5 in. h., with a woody rootstock and erect or ascending twiggy shoots. *l.* linear or narrowly oblanceolate, to $\frac{7}{10}$ in. long, less than $\frac{1}{10}$ in. wide; stipules free, undivided or divided to base into 2 segs., so that the l. seems to consist of 3 to 5 narrow lflets. *fl.* rosy-lilac, long-stalked; upper pet. nearly $\frac{3}{10}$ in. long; blade of lower pet. deeply notched, spur straight, about $\frac{3}{8}$ in. long. Albania. Closely allied to *V. delphinantha* and *V. cazorlensis* but less ornamental, the spur being shorter.

V. labrado'rica (1B). *rhiz.* creeping, slender. Plant in fl. $1\frac{1}{2}$ to 3 in. h., leafy-stemmed but stem very short. *l.* very broadly ovate, almost orbicular, usually less than 1 in. wide, shallowly cordate, blunt or acute, shallowly crenate, more or less glabrous, long-stalked; stipules lanceolate, sparsely toothed. *fl.* small, violet with white violet-veined base, about $\frac{3}{8}$ in. long; pet. to $\frac{3}{8}$ in. long, spur short, blunt, less than $\frac{1}{8}$ in. long. (Baird, Viol. 191.) N. United States, Canada, Greenland. Probably only a northern variety (*minor*) of *V. adunca*.

V. lac'tea (1B). *rhiz.* erect. Plant in fl. 2 to 8 in. h., leafy-stemmed. *l.* narrowly ovate or lanceolate, to $\frac{3}{8}$ in. wide, cuneate or rounded at base, acute, shallowly toothed, rather thick, minutely hairy, long-stalked; stipules lanceolate, long-toothed. *fl.* fairly large, pale bluish-white, to $\frac{3}{4}$ in. long; pet. to about $\frac{1}{2}$ in. long, spur about $\frac{1}{10}$ in. long, pale yellowish-green. May, June. W. Europe, including British Is. (E.B. 176.) Akin to *V. canina* and *V. stagnina*.

V. lanceola'ta (1F). *rhiz.* slender, creeping, with stolons. Plant in fl. $2\frac{1}{2}$ to 9 in. h., stemless. *l.* narrowly lanceolate to almost linear, to 12 in. or more long, $\frac{1}{2}$ in. wide, gradually narrowed into the petiole, acute, almost entire, glabrous; stipules lanceolate. *fl.* small, white with purple veining on lower pet., about $\frac{3}{8}$ in. long; pet. about $\frac{3}{8}$ in. long, spur about $\frac{1}{20}$ in. long. Eastern N. America, in damp places. 1785. (Baird, Viol. 147.)

V. loba'ta (3). *rhiz.* short, creeping. Plant in fl. 4 to 15 in. h., leafy-stemmed, the lower part bare. *l.* palmately lobed or divided into 5 to 9 oblong segs., hairy, long-stalked; stipules broad, ovate, toothed. *fl.* medium-sized, yellow with brown veins on lower 3 pet., about $\frac{3}{4}$ in. long; pet. to $\frac{1}{2}$ in. long, spur less than $\frac{1}{10}$ in. long. March to July. California, Oregon. (Baird, Viol. 23.) var. **integrifo'lia,** *l.* entire or toothed, but not divided.

V. lu'tea. *rhiz.* slender, creeping below ground, branched. Plant in fl. 3 to 6 in. h., leafy-stemmed, with fairly long internodes. *Lower l.* ovate, rounded at base; *upper l.* lanceolate, cuneate at base, all l. crenate, sparsely hairy or almost glabrous, long-stalked; stipules palmately divided, middle seg. largest. *fl.* large, bright yellow or shades of violet, to $1\frac{1}{4}$ in. long; pet. to $\frac{3}{8}$ in. long, spur to $\frac{1}{5}$ in. long. Europe, including British Is. (E.B. 181.) The most attractive of British wild Pansies and an ancestor of the Garden Pansy (cf. **V.× Wittrockiana**).

V. macedo'nica. A synonym of *V. saxatilis macedonica*.

V. macro'ceras. *See under* **V. Jooi.**

V. mira'bilis (1B). *rhiz.* stout, creeping, branched. Plant in fl. about 4 in. h., stemless then, but producing later elongated stems 5 to 18 in. h. with cleistogamous fl. *l.* broadly ovate, to $2\frac{1}{2}$ in. wide, shallowly cordate, blunt or acute, crenate, sparsely hairy, long-stalked; stipules narrowly lanceolate, entire. *fl.* fairly large, lilac, scented, about $\frac{3}{4}$ in. long; pet. to about $\frac{1}{2}$ in. long, spur about $\frac{3}{10}$ in. long. Europe, N. Asia. 1732. (R.I.F.G. 4504.)

V. missourien'sis. *See under* **V. papilionacea.**

V. Munbya'na (4B). Plant in fl. 4 to 18 in. h.; stems ascending from a prostrate base; internodes long. *l.* well-spaced, broadly ovate, to 1 in. wide, subcordate, rarely cuneate at base, blunt or acute, crenate, glabrous or sparsely hairy, long-stalked; stipules divided to base. *fl.* large, yellow or violet, about $1\frac{1}{4}$ in. long; pet. to $\frac{7}{10}$ in. long, spur slender, about $\frac{1}{2}$ in. long. N. Africa. An attractive long-spurred Pansy.

V. Nuttall'ii (3B). *rhiz.* erect. Plant in fl. 2 to 5 in. h., leafy-stemmed, but the stem very short and the peduncles usually overtopped by the mostly basal l. *l.* lanceolate or oblong-elliptic to narrowly ovate, to $\frac{1}{2}$ in. wide, cuneate at base, blunt, entire or faintly toothed, minutely hairy, long-stalked; stipules narrowly lanceolate. *fl.* small or medium-sized, deep yellow with brown veins on lower 3 pet., about $\frac{3}{8}$ in. long; pet. to $\frac{3}{10}$ in. long, spur very short. Western N. America. (Baird, Viol. 33.) A yellow Violet closely akin to *V. praemorsa* but with smaller fl. rather hidden beneath the l.

V. obli'qua. Possibly the earliest name for *V. cucullata*, but the description is much too brief and the illustration too crude for certainty.

V. ocella'ta. *rhiz.* slender. Plant in fl. 5 to 12 in. h., leafy-stemmed. *l.* broadly ovate, almost triangular, to 2 in. wide, lower l. cordate at base, upper l. subcordate or truncate, acute, crenate, hairy, long-stalked; stipules small, lanceolate, entire. *fl.* medium-sized, white, the upper 2 pet. violet outside, the lower 3 purple-veined, the lowermost with a yellow eye at base, to $\frac{3}{4}$ in. long; pet. about $\frac{1}{2}$ in. long, spur very short. California, S. Oregon. (Baird, Viol. 57.) A pretty little Violet but of slight garden merit; **V. cunea'ta,** likewise of California and Oregon, is closely akin but has lower l. cuneate at base. (Baird, Viol. 59.)

V. odora'ta (1A). Sweet Violet. *rhiz.* short, stout, putting out long prostrate rooting stolons. *l.* broadly ovate to almost orbicular, to $2\frac{1}{2}$ in. wide, deeply cordate, blunt or acute, crenate, almost glabrous, long-stalked; petioles almost glabrous or with short downward pointing hairs; stipules narrowly ovate with glandular teeth. *fl.* medium-sized, deep violet, lilac, or white, rarely yellowish, about $\frac{3}{4}$ in. long; pet. about $\frac{1}{2}$ in. long, spur less than $\frac{1}{5}$ in. long. February to April. Europe, including British Is., N. Africa, Asia. (E.B. 171.) The above description refers to the wild Sweet Violet. Many forms with bigger fl., some double, and a greater range of colour are grown in gardens; see G. L. Zambra, *Violets* (1951), for garden forms and E. S. Gregory, *British Violets* (1912) for British wild forms, including var. **prae'cox,** small, early flowering (October to March).

V. olym'pica. A synonym of *V. gracilis*.

V. orbicula'ta (1P). *See under* **V. sempervirens.**

V. Orphani'dis (4B). *rhiz.* compact. Plant in fl. 8 to 20 in., leafy-stemmed, the stems softly hairy, numerous, erect or sprawling, internodes long. *l.* ovate or broadly ovate, to 1 in. wide, mostly subcordate or rounded at base, blunt, crenate, hairy, stalked; stipules large, ovate, deeply cut but not divided into segs. *fl.* large, violet or bluish, about 1 in. long; pet. to $\frac{3}{8}$ in. long, spur slender, about $\frac{1}{5}$ in. long. Balkan Peninsula. Habit too lank for garden purposes.

Viola palmata

V. palma'ta (1N). *rhiz.* short, stout. Plant in fl. 3 to 5 in. long, stemless. *l.* palmately lobed or divided into 5 to 11 segs., hairy; stipules narrowly lanceolate. *fl.* fairly large, violet, the lower pet. white at base and veined with darker violet, nearly 1 in. long; **pet.**

about ¾ in. long, spur hardly 1/10 in. long. April, May. Eastern N. America. 1739. (B.M. 535; Baird, Viol. 81.) Variable in degree of l. cutting and width of segs.

V. palus'tris (1F). *rhiz.* slender, creeping, elongated. Plant in fl. about 4 to 5 in. h., stemless. *l.* usually 3 to 5 together, almost orbicular, to 2¼ in. wide, deeply cordate at base, blunt, rounded, shallowly crenate, glabrous, long-stalked; stipules free, ovate. *fl.* small, pale or dark lilac with deeper veins, sometimes white, ⅜ to ⅝ in. long; pet. to ⅜ in. long, spur fairly stout, scarcely 1/10 in. long; peduncle with bracts at or below middle. Europe, including British Is., Asia, N. America. (E.B. 170.) var. **Juress'ii,** later *l.* somewhat acute or acuminate. Syn. *V. Juressii.*

V. papiliona'cea (1N). *rhiz.* stout, branching. Plant in fl. 2 to 5 in. h., stemless. *l.* broadly ovate to kidney-shaped, to 5 in. across, deeply cordate at base, blunt or acute, crenate, almost glabrous, long-stalked; stipules narrowly lanceolate. *fl.* large, rich violet with white centre, about 1 in. long; pet. to ¾ in. long, spur scarcely 1/10 in. long. April, May. Eastern N. America. (Baird, Viol. 93.) Syn. *V. domestica.* Many forms, including var. **albiflo'ra,** *fl.* white, **Pricea'na,** Confederate Violet, pale greyish-blue with blue veins. Syn. *V. Priceana.* Sometimes confused in gardens with *V. cucullata* but having the lowest (spurred) pet. as long as lateral pet. (instead of shorter than lateral pet. as in *V. cucullata*).

V. Patrin'ii (1G). *rhiz.* short. Plant in fl. 3 to 6 in. h., stemless. *l.* at fl. time oblong, to 1 in. wide, truncate or subcordate at base, rounded, almost entire, glabrous or with very minute hairs, long-stalked; petiole narrowly winged in upper part; stipules joined to petiole for most of their length, tips ovate-triangular, small. *fl.* small, about ½ in. long, whitish; pet. to ⅜ in. long, spur scarcely 1/10 in. long. Siberia, &c. A small Violet of no garden value.

Viola pedata var. *concolor*

V. peda'ta (10). Bird's-foot Violet. *rhiz.* short, erect. Plant in fl. 2 to 6 in. h., stemless. *l.* palmately divided into numerous narrow segs., glabrous except for the sometimes ciliate margin, long-stalked; stipules joined to petiole in lower part, linear-lanceolate above, toothed with fimbriae. *fl.* large, upper 2 pet. dark violet, lower 3 pet. light violet with darker veins, about 1 in. long; pet. all bearded, to ⅝ in. long, spur about 1/20 in. long. April to June. Eastern N. America. 1759. (Baird, Viol. 181.) A very beautiful and variable species with several vars. and forms, the most distinct being the southern var. **con'color,** all pet. same colour, usually light violet, *fl.* very large, up to 1¾ in. long. 1789. (B.M. 89 as *V. pedata*; Baird, Viol. 183.) A tricky plant, which has been found to do best in England in a low-lying pocket of the rock-garden planted in almost pure sand with coarse unsifted leaf-soil about 6 in. below.

V. pedati'fida (1N). *rhiz.* short, erect. Plant in fl. about 3 in. h., stemless. *l.* palmately divided into several or many narrow segs., glabrous or minutely hairy, long-stalked; stipules linear-lanceolate, fimbriate. *fl.* fairly large, violet, about ¾ in. long; pet. to ¾ in. long, lower 3 bearded with white hairs at base, spur 1/10 in. long. April to June. N. America. (Baird, Viol. 140.) Syn. *V. delphinifolia.* In habit rather like *V. pedata* but fl. smaller, with lower pet. bearded.

V. peduncula'ta (3B). California Golden Violet, Grass Pansy, Johnny-jump-up, Gallito. *rhiz.* stout, deep in soil. Plant in fl. 4 to 12 in. h., leafy-stemmed. *l.* mostly very broadly ovate, almost triangular, to 2 in. wide, truncate or subcordate at base, blunt, crenate, minutely hairy or almost glabrous, long-stalked; stipules narrowly elliptic-oblong, entire or slightly toothed. *fl.* large, yellow with dark brown veins on lower 3 pet., about 1 in. long; pet. ½ to ¾ in. long, spur very short, 1/20 in. long. May. California, Lower California. About 1856. (B.M. 5004; Baird, Viol. 39.) The most conspicuous of the W. American Mock Pansies, but rather tender; in California it grows and flowers during the winter and spring and dies down completely during the rainless period of summer and autumn.

V. pensylva'nica (3D). Akin to *V. pubescens,* but dwarfer and almost glabrous. *fl.* yellow with purple veins on lower lip. *Capsule* hairy. Eastern N. America. (Baird, Viol. 17 as *V. eriocarpa.*) Syn. *V. eriocarpa, V. scabriuscula.* var. **leiocar'pa,** capsule glabrous.

V. × permix'ta (1A). Natural hybrid of *V. hirta* and *V. odorata,* often very floriferous, some forms with stolons, others without them.

V. persicifo'lia. A name of disputed application generally used for *V. stagnina* but sometimes considered the earliest name for *V. elatior.*

V. pinna'ta (1G). *rhiz.* short. Plant in fl. 2 to 4 in. h., stemless. *l.* divided into numerous narrow segs., minutely hairy, long-stalked; stipules joined to petiole for most of their length except for lanceolate tip. *fl.* small, blue-violet, about ½ in. long, scented; pet. to nearly ½ in. long; spur stout, about ⅛ in. long. European Alps, N. Asia. Remarkable among European Violets for its much divided l.

V. pon'tica. *See under* **V. suavis.**

V. praemor'sa (3B). *rhiz.* erect, short, blunt-tipped (hence the epithet *praemorsa*). Plant in fl. 3 to 10 in. h., leafy-stemmed, the stem at first very short, later more elongated, the peduncles overtopping the mostly basal l. *l.* ovate, broadly oblong-elliptic or almost orbicular, to 1½ in. wide, cuneate at base, blunt, toothed or undulate, hairy with long hairs to almost glabrous, long-stalked; stipules lanceolate. *fl.* fairly large, bright yellow, the lower 3 pet. with brownish-purple veins, about ¾ in. long; pet. to ½ in. long, spur very short. Pacific Coast of N. America from California to Vancouver Is. (Baird, Viol. 37.) Syn. *V. Nuttallii* var. *praemorsa.*

V. praten'sis. A synonym of *V. pumila.*

V. Pricea'na. A variety of *V. papilionacea.*

V. primulifo'lia (1F). *rhiz.* stout, erect. Plant in fl. 2 to 10 in. h., stemless. *l.* oblong-ovate or ovate, to 1½ in. wide, subcordate, truncate or cuneate at base, blunt or acute, shallowly crenate, glabrous or sparsely hairy, usually long-stalked; petiole somewhat winged in upper part; stipules narrowly lanceolate. *fl.* small, white with purple veins on lower pet., to ½ in. long; pet. about 3/10 in. long, spur very short, about 1/20 in. long. Eastern N. America, inhabiting boggy places. 1783. (Baird, Viol. 145.)

V. Pring'lei. *See under* **V. blanda.**

V. pseudo-Munbya'na (4B). Plant in fl. to 8 in. h., the stems ascending from a prostrate base; internodes numerous, short, hence l. crowded. *l.* ovate, to ¾ in. wide, cuneate at base, acute, incised crenate, hairy on mid-vein and margin, long-stalked; stipules conspicuous, deeply divided. *fl.* large, violet with purple streaks, about 1½ in. long; pet. to 1 in. long, spur about ⅜ in. long. Before 1897. Known only in cultivation, probably from NW. Africa. (Acta Horti Berg. 2, 11 f. 173–7 as *V. Munbyana.*) Near *V. Munbyana* but distinguished by its incised-crenate l. and shorter thicker spur.

V. pubes'cens (3D). *rhiz.* short. Plant in fl. 4 to 10 in. h., leafy-stemmed, the stems hairy, with 2 to 4 l. close together at the top. *l.* very broadly ovate, almost triangular, or kidney-shaped, to 4 in. wide, shallowly cordate, acute or acuminate, shallowly crenate, hairy, usually long-stalked; stipules narrowly lanceolate, entire. *fl.* small, bright yellow with brown veins on lower pet., about ⅜ in. long; pet. to ½ in. long, spur very short, about 1/20 in. long. May to July. Eastern N. America, in dry woods. (Baird, Viol. 15.)

V. pu'mila. Akin to *V. elatior* but dwarfer and almost or quite glabrous, with all l. cuneate at base. Plant in fl. 2 to 8 in. h. *fl.* dark or pale violet. Europe, W. Asia. (R.I.F.G. 4507 B.) Syn. *V. pratensis.*

V. Reichenbachia'na (1B). Closely akin to *V. Riviniana* but somewhat dwarfer, with pale violet *fl.* having the spur dark purple and more slender. March to May. Europe, including Britain, N. Africa, Asia. (E.B. 174; R.I.F.G. 4503 as *V. silvestris.*) Syn. *V. sylvestris* of Lamarck as understood by Reichenbach.

V. Rivinia'na (1B). Dog-violet, Wood-violet. *rhiz.* short, erect. Plant in fl. 2 to 8 in. h., leafy-stemmed, with a central non-flowering rosette and ascending axillary stems. *l.* very broadly ovate, almost orbicular, to 3 in. wide, deeply cordate, blunt or acute, crenate, shortly hairy, long-stalked; petiole glabrous; stipules lanceolate, with long spreading teeth (fimbriae). *fl.* large, blue-violet, about 1 in. long; pet. to about ½ in. long, spur paler, whitish-yellowish or pale violet, about ⅛ in. long. April to June. Europe, including British Is.; N. Africa. (E.B. 173; R.I.F.G. 4502.) Commonest of British Dog-violets.

V. rostra'ta. *rhiz.* slender. Plant in fl. 4 to 8 in. h., leafy-stemmed. *l.* broadly ovate, to 1¼ in. wide, cordate at base, acute or acuminate, crenate, glabrous, except for a few hairs on upper side, long-stalked; stipules lanceolate, with long teeth. *fl.* medium-sized, lavender with violet veining on lower pet., about ⅝ in. long excluding spur; pet. to ⅝ in. long, spur slender, usually straight, ⅜ to 7/10 in. long; lateral pet. beardless. Eastern N. America. (Baird, Viol. 195.)

V. rothomagen'sis. A synonym of *V. hispida.*

V. rotundifo'lia (1P). *rhiz.* stout. Plant in fl. about 2 or 3 in. h., stemless then but producing later sprawling purplish stems to 6 in. long with cleistogamous fl. *l.* broadly ovate to almost orbicular, to 2 in. wide, cordate at base, blunt, crenate, hairy, firm, long-stalked; stipules narrowly ovate, entire. *fl.* small, yellow with brown veins on lower pet., about $\frac{3}{8}$ in. long; pet. to $\frac{1}{2}$ in. long, spur $\frac{1}{10}$ in. long. May. Eastern N. America. (Baird, Viol. 167.)

V. rugulo'sa (3D). Akin to *V. canadensis*, but even taller, up to 2 ft. h., with long underground stolons. *l.* distinctly hairy beneath. *fl.* white with yellow base, the lower 3 pet. violet-veined. N. America. (Baird, Viol. 53.)

V. rupes'tris (1B). Teesdale Violet. Akin to *V. Riviniana* but dwarfer, the plant in fl. 1 to 2 in. h., hairy on petiole and capsule. *fl.* pale blue-violet. Europe, including England; Asia, N. America. SYN. *V. arenaria.*

V. sagitta'ta (1N). *rhiz.* short. Plant in fl. about 4 in. h., stemless. *l.* mostly narrowly ovate, to 4 in. long, $1\frac{1}{4}$ in. wide, cordate or truncate at base, unevenly toothed, the basal lobes often hastate, acute, the first and later l. ovate, blunt, glabrous or minutely hairy, long-stalked. *fl.* medium-sized, violet, the lower 3 pet. white at base and violet-veined, densely bearded, to $\frac{3}{4}$ in. long; pet. to about $\frac{1}{2}$ in. long, spur about $\frac{1}{10}$ in. long; sep. glabrous. April, May. Eastern N. America, in damp places. 1775. (L.B.C. 1471; Baird, Viol. 131.)

V. sarmento'sa of Bieberstein. A synonym of *V. alba.*

V. sarmento'sa of Douglas. A synonym of *V. sempervirens.*

V. saxati'lis (4B). Perennial, closely akin to *V. tricolor.* Plant in fl. 4 to 8 in. h., leafy-stemmed, the stems often prostrate at base, then ascending, branched, elongated. *Lower l.* ovate; *upper l.* narrowly ovate or elliptic, to $\frac{1}{2}$ in. wide, all l. cuneate or rounded at base, blunt, crenate, hairy; stipules pinnately divided, the end seg. large, lateral seg. few, small. *fl.* medium-sized, usually yellow, $\frac{1}{2}$ to $\frac{3}{4}$ in. long; pet. much longer than sep., spur to $\frac{1}{5}$ in. long, twice as long as cal. appendages; sep. ciliated. Summer. E. Europe, Asia Minor. SYN. *V. alpestris*, *V. tricolor* var. *alpestris.* var. **aeto'lica,** *fl.* mostly yellow, SYN. *V. aetolica*; **macedo'nica,** *fl.* mostly violet, SYN. *V. macedonica.* The plant figured in B.M. 9599 as *V. Stojanowii* var. *latifolia* is very like *V. saxatilis. V. saxatilis aetolica* is a good rock-garden plant.

V. scabrius'cula. A synonym of *V. pensylvanica.*

V. scotophyl'la. A synonym of *V. alba.*

V. sempervi'rens (1P). *rhiz.* creeping, sending out very long stolons. Plant in fl. 2 to 3 in. h. *l.* very broadly ovate, to $1\frac{1}{4}$ in. wide, shallowly cordate, blunt or acute, shallowly crenate, sparsely hairy above, glabrous and often rusty beneath with minute brown flecks, evergreen, long-stalked; stipules lanceolate, entire. *fl.* small, yellow with brown veins on lower pet., about $\frac{3}{8}$ in. long; pet. to $\frac{1}{2}$ in. long, spur very short, less than $\frac{1}{20}$ in. long. Western N. America. 1937. (Baird, Viol. 29.) SYN. *V. sarmentosa* of Douglas not Bieberstein. **V. orbicula'ta,** also of Western N. America, is very similar but not evergreen; it lacks stolons, as does *V. rotundifolia* (q.v.).

V. sepin'cola (1A). A name of varied application, originally based on a French plant, considered by some authorities to be a hybrid of *V. hirta* and *V. odorata*, but now regarded as an independent species differing from *V. odorata* in its lanceolate stipules, &c.; *V. cyanea* and *V. pontica* (*see under* **V. suavis**) are closely akin and can well be classified as sub-species of *V. sepincola.*

V. septentriona'lis (1N). Akin to *V. sororia*, but lower side of young *l.* with short scattered hairs (not woolly) and the lowest (spurred) *pet.* densely bearded (not glabrous or nearly so as *V. sororia* and *V. cucullata*). *fl.* violet, sometimes white. *Capsule* usually purplish, almost globose, on stalks prostrate before maturity. N. America (Baird, Viol. 111.)

V. Shelton'ii (3C). *rhiz.* short. Plant in fl. 3 to 6 in. h., leafy-stemmed, but stem short. *l.* palmately divided into many short lobes, glabrous. *fl.* small, pale yellow, the upper 2 pet. brownish on the back, the lower 3 purple-veined, about $\frac{1}{2}$ in. long; pet. to $\frac{1}{2}$ in. long, spur very short. Western N. America. (Baird, Viol. 63.)

V. silva'tica. A synonym of *V. Riviniana.*

V. soro'ria (1N). *rhiz.* stout. Plant in fl. about 3 in. h., stemless. *l.* broadly ovate or kidney-shaped, to $4\frac{1}{2}$ in. wide, cordate at base, acute, crenate, densely hairy beneath when young, sparsely hairy above, long-stalked; stipules linear-lanceolate. *fl.* fairly large, blue, violet, or lavender, whitish at base, with deeper violet veins, sometimes white, about $\frac{3}{4}$ in. long; pet. to $\frac{1}{2}$ in. long, spur about $\frac{1}{10}$ in. long. March to June. Eastern N. America. (Baird, Viol. 103.)

V. stagni'na (1B). *rhiz.* slender, creeping. Plant in fl. 2 to 12 in. h., leafy-stemmed. *l.* narrowly ovate, or lanceolate, to $\frac{3}{4}$ in. wide, truncate or subcordate at base, acute, shallowly crenate, glabrous or nearly so, pale green, stalked; stipules linear-lanceolate, lower and middle much shorter than petiole, upper sometimes as long. *fl.* small, very pale blue or almost white, about $\frac{3}{5}$ in. long; pet. to $\frac{2}{5}$ in. long, spur less than $\frac{1}{10}$ in. long, greenish. May to June. Europe, including British Is., N. Asia. (E.B. 177.) Often and perhaps correctly known as *V. persicifolia.* A marsh-loving species, closely akin to *V. elatior.*

V. Stojanow'ii (4B). *rhiz.* slender, erect. Plant in fl. 3 to 4 in. h., leafy-stemmed, the internodes short, hairy. *l.* narrowly oblanceolate, to $\frac{1}{5}$ in. wide, narrowed into petiole, blunt, entire, very hairy; stipules undivided or with a basal tooth. *fl.* small, yellow, about $\frac{1}{2}$ in. long; pet. under $\frac{3}{10}$ in. long, spur scarcely $\frac{1}{5}$ in. long. Balkan Peninsula. var. **latifo'lia,** *see* **V. saxatilis aetolica.**

V. stria'ta (1B). *rhiz.* long. Plant in fl. 6 to 12 in. h., leafy-stemmed, the stems later elongating to as much as 2 ft. *l.* ovate or almost orbicular, to 2 in. wide, deeply or shallowly cordate at base, blunt or acute, crenate, slightly hairy above, glabrous beneath, long-stalked; stipules conspicuous, lanceolate-linear, deeply toothed. *fl.* medium-sized, white or creamy-white with purple veins on lower pet., to $\frac{3}{4}$ in. long; pet. to $\frac{1}{2}$ in. long, spur blunt, nearly $\frac{1}{5}$ in. long. April, May. Eastern N. America. (Baird, Viol. 197.)

V. sua'vis. Some doubt exists as to the correct application of the name *V. suavis* of Bieberstein, which, according to a leading authority, Kupffer, is a synonym of *V. odorata* although others have adopted it for a plant of SE. Europe and W. Asia identified by Kupffer with the W. European *V. sepincola* but distinguished as *V. pontica* by W. Becker and as *V. sepincola* subsp. *pontica* by Hayek. It is closely akin to *V. odorata* and *V. alba. rhiz.* fairly thick, with short often subterranean stolons. *l.* broadly ovate, deeply cordate at base, blunt or acute, crenate, almost glabrous or shortly hairy, long-stalked; stipules lanceolate, elongated, with long glandular teeth (fimbriae). *fl.* fairly large, pale blue with a whitish base, scented; pet. about $\frac{1}{2}$ in. long; spur short, about $\frac{1}{10}$ in. long. Spring. S. European Russia, Caucasus, Asia Minor, Turkistan, Kashmir. About 1830. (? S.B.F.G. s. 2. 126 as *V. suavis.*)

V. sylves'tris of some authors. A synonym of *V. Reichenbachiana.*

V. transsilva'nica. A synonym of *V. Jooi.*

V. tri'color (4B). Heartsease, Wild Pansy, Love-in-idleness, Pink of my John. Annual or short-lived perennial, varying greatly in habit, size and fl. colour. Plant in fl. $1\frac{1}{2}$ to 12 in. h., often branched. *Lower l.* ovate, blunt; *upper l.* lanceolate, acute, all l. cuneate at base, crenate; stipules deeply divided, the end seg. largest. *fl.* medium-sized, in the type form with upper 2 pet. mauve or violet, the lateral 2 pet. whitish with black lines, the lowest pet. whitish with a deep yellow basal blotch and black lines, but some forms almost entirely white, yellow, violet, or pink, about $\frac{3}{4}$ in. long; pet. about $\frac{1}{2}$ in. long, spur short, about $\frac{1}{10}$ in. long. Europe, including British Is., Asia. (E.B. 178; Acta Horti Berg. 2. 1–4.) A parent of the Garden Pansy (*V.* × *Wittrockiana*). var. **arven'sis,** a synonym of *V. arvensis*; **ma'xima,** a synonym of *V.* × *Wittrockiana.*

V. trinerva'ta (3C). *rhiz.* short, erect. Plant in fl. 2 to 3 in. h., leafy-stemmed. *l.* palmately divided into 3 to 7 narrowly ovate or lanceolate acute segs., the terminal ones prominently 3-veined beneath, firm, glabrous, stalked; stipules of lower l. joined to petiole except at tip, of upper l. free, lanceolate. *fl.* small, 2 upper pet. violet, lower 3 paler, lilac, with violet and orange base, $\frac{1}{2}$ in. long, scented; pet. about $\frac{3}{10}$ in. long, spur yellowish, $\frac{1}{20}$ in. long. April. Washington, Oregon. (Baird, Viol. 69.)

V. valde'ria (4B). Closely akin to *V. cenisia* and similar in habit but usually more hairy, with stipules divided into 2 to 7 narrow segs. Plant in fl. 2 to 3 in. h. *fl.* medium-sized to large, pale lilac-purple; spur $\frac{1}{5}$ to $\frac{3}{10}$ in. long. Maritime Alps of Italy and France, on granite. Difficult in cultivation.

V. × **Visseria'na** (4B). A group-name for the hybrids between *V. cornuta* and *V. gracilis*, such as G. Wermig, Lord Nelson, Jersey Gem, &c. SYN. *V. cornuta hybrida*, *V. gracilis hybrida.*

V. × **William'sii** (4B). A group-name for the plants known in gardens as Violas, Tufted Pansies, and Violettas, derived from crossing the Garden Pansy (*V.* × *Wittrockiana*) with *V. cornuta*; it includes Ardwell Gem, Blue Duchess, Maggie Mott, &c. SYN. *V.* × *Stuartii.*

V. × **Wittrockia'na** (4B). Garden Pansy. Annual or short-lived perennial. Plant in fl. about 4 to 9 in. h., leafy-stemmed, the stems elongated, much branched. *Lower l.* ovate, subcordate, crenate; *upper l.* lanceolate-elliptic, cuneate at base, sometimes entire; stipules large, pinnately divided. *fl.* very large, rather rounded in outline, very diverse in colour, to 2 in. across, the pet. almost orbicular, the lateral pair much overlapped by the lowest pet.; spur less than $\frac{1}{5}$ in. long. SYN. *V. tricolor maxima*, *V. tricolor hortensis* of some authors, not of De Candolle (which is small-fld. and belongs to *V. tricolor* proper), *V. hortensis* of Wettstein not of Schur (which is a form of *V. odorata*). A variable group derived by hybridization and intensive selection of *V. tricolor* crossed with other species, apparently *V. lutea* and probably *V. altaica* (see head of article).

V. yakusima'na (1B ?). *rhiz.* compact. Plant in fl. 1 in. or less h., leafy-stemmed. *l.* kidney-shaped, about $\frac{1}{5}$ in. wide, cordate at base, blunt, shallowly toothed, glabrous, short-stalked; stipules minute, lanceolate, entire. *fl.* small, about $\frac{3}{10}$ in. long, the upper 4 pet. white, the lowest violet-veined; pet. about $\frac{1}{5}$ in. long, spur minute, blunt, scarcely $\frac{1}{20}$ in. long. May, June. Yakushima, S. Japan. About 1938. A tiny Violet for the alpine house or a cool part of the rock-garden, forming carpets of deep green l.

V. Zoys'ii (4B). Closely akin to *V. calcarata*, but usually smaller, with stipules not deeply divided, fl. usually yellow, rarely lilac. Plant in fl. $1\frac{1}{2}$ to 3 in. h. *fl.* medium-sized or large, $\frac{3}{4}$ to $1\frac{1}{4}$ in. long; spur $\frac{1}{5}$ to $\frac{3}{10}$ in. long. Eastern Alps, Balkan Peninsula, on limestone. SYN. *V. calcarata* var. *Zoysii.*

W. T. S.

VIOLA'CEAE. Dicotyledons. A family of about 800 species in 17 genera of annual or perennial herbs or shrubs widely distributed in all but arctic regions. Leaves alternate, usually simple, stipulate. Flowers perfect, regular or usually zygomorphic. Sepals 5, persistent. Petals 5, the front petal often spurred forming a nectary. Stamens 5 alternate with petals, filaments short; anthers introrse, connective often prolonged beyond the anthers into a membranous wing. Ovary superior, of 3 carpels, 1-celled with many ovules on 3 parietal placentae. Fruit a capsule or a berry. The genera dealt with here are Alsodeia, (now more generally known as Rinorea), Corynostylis, Hymenanthera, Ionidium, Melicytus, Noisettia, Schweiggeria, Viola.

viola'ceus -a -um, violet-coloured.

VIOLET. *See* **Viola.** The name Violet was applied to many unrelated plants in olden times, a few of which are noted below.

VIOLET, BOG. *See* **Pinguicula vulgaris.**

VIOLET, CALATHIAN. *See* **Gentiana Pneumonanthe.**

VIOLET, CAPE. *See* **Ionidium capense.**

VIOLET, DAME'S. *See* **Hesperis matronalis.**

VIOLET, DOG. *See* **Viola canina, V. Riviniana.**

VIOLET, DOG'S TOOTH. *See* **Erythronium Dens-canis.**

VIOLET, FALSE. *See* **Dalibarda repens.**

VIOLET, FRINGED. *See* **Thysanotus.**

VIOLET, SPURLESS. *See* **Viola hederacea.**

VIOLET, TONGUE. *See* **Schweiggeria.**

VIOLET, WATER. *See* **Hottonia palustris.**

violoi'des, Viola-like.

Viorna, from the French name of *Clematis Vitalba.*

VIPER GOURD. *See* **Trichosanthes Anguina.**

vipera'tus -a -um, viper-like.

VIPER'S BUGLOSS. *See* **Echium vulgare.**

VIPER'S GRASS. *See* **Scorzonera hispanica.**

vi'rens, green.

vires'cens, light green.

VIREYA. Included in **Rhododendron.**

vir'ga-au'rea, golden rod.

virga'tus -a -um, twiggy.

VIRGI'LIA (in honour of the Latin poet, Virgil 70–19 B.C.). FAM. *Leguminosae.* A genus generally regarded as monotypic although an additional species, *V. divaricata,* was described in the *Journal of Botany,* 1934, p. 43, but is probably not sufficiently distinct to warrant specific rank. *V. capensis* is a cool greenhouse plant, easily cultivated in light loamy soil. Hardy in Scilly Is.

V. capen'sis.* Shrub or tree up to 30 ft., younger parts reddish downy. *l.* pinnate, 4 to 8 in. long; lflets. 13 to 41, linear-oblong, $\frac{1}{2}$ to $1\frac{1}{4}$ in. long, $\frac{1}{8}$ to $\frac{1}{4}$ in. wide, apex mostly rounded, mucronate. *fl.* 7 to 12 clustered at the end of axillary racemes 3 to 5 in. long, papilionaceous; cor. uniformly white, pink, purplish, or crimson; standard $\frac{5}{8}$ in. long, wings smaller. July. *Pod* $1\frac{1}{2}$ to 2 in. long, $\frac{3}{8}$ in. wide, flat, softly downy. S. Africa. 1767. (B.M. 1590.)

V. lu'tea. A synonym of *Cladrastis tinctoria.*

W. J. B.

virgina'lis -is -e, virginal, hence white.

virgi'neus -a -um, virginal, hence white.

VIRGINIA CREEPER. This name used by James Petiver in 1704 is a variant of the earlier but now obsolete name Virginia Vine and belongs properly to an American species *Parthenocissus quinquefolia* introduced from Virginia about 1629, with the shoots red in the spring, all the leaves divided into 5 or sometimes 3 leaflets and the tendrils ending in adhesive disks by which it clings to walls and trees. The name is now commonly misapplied to 2 species of later introduction, *P. vitacea* (*P. inserta* of some authors), an American plant introduced before 1824, with the shoots green in the spring, all the leaves divided into leaflets, but the tendrils usually without adhesive disks, and *P. tricuspidata* (*Ampelopsis Veitchii*), a Japanese and Chinese plant introduced about 1862, the leaves varying greatly in shape according to their position on the plant, some being ovate and scarcely lobed, others deeply 3-lobed, others divided into distinct leaflets, while the tendrils have adhesive disks enabling it to cling to walls.

VIRGINIAN COWSLIP. *See* **Mertensia virginica.**

VIRGINIAN DATE PLUM. *See* **Diospyros virginiana.**

VIRGINIAN SILK. *See* **Periploca graeca.**

VIRGINIAN STOCK. *See* **Malcolmia maritima.**

virginia'nus -a -um, of Virginia, United States.

virgin'ieus -a -um, of Virginia, United States.

VIRGIN'S BOWER. *See* **Clematis Viticella.**

virgula'tus -a -um, twiggy.

virgulto'rum, of a coppice.

virides'cens, becoming green, viridescent.

viri'dulus -a -um, greenish.

vi'ridus -a -um, viridi- in compound words, green, as *viridiflorus,* green-flowered.

viro'sus -a -um, poisonous.

VIRUS DISEASES. In addition to diseases directly attributable to wrong cultural conditions or to attacks of fungi or insects, many plants suffer from diseases brought on by inoculation by a virus. The exact nature of a virus is unknown though many of its properties are now familiar.

The first scientific record of virus disease was made by Iwanowski in 1892 when he demonstrated that the sap of tobacco plants suffering from Mosaic (q.v.) disease was infectious to healthy plants even after it had been passed through a bacteria-proof filter. In 1897 Beijerinck repeated these experiments and referred to the infective principle by the name *contagium vivum fluidum,* now called a 'virus'. Viruses cannot be distinguished even with the most powerful microscopes and they can pass through the smallest filter that can retain the most minute of known bacteria. There are now very large numbers of plant disorders attributed to infection by one or other of these viruses. At the present time much research on them and on the symptoms shown by virus-infected plants is being carried out. In such studies methods of control and the development of plants resistant to specified virus diseases are being carefully considered and tested. The effects of virus diseases on different plants vary very much and so do the symptoms, but all have the one common feature that they are transmitted from diseased to healthy plants by an extremely small but infectious principle which is called a virus. The virus has the peculiar power of spreading throughout all the vegetative parts of the plant but they rarely infect the seeds and very few virus diseases are seed-borne. In a virus-infected plant, therefore, the virus is soon present in tubers, corms, bulbs, &c., and affected plants must not be used for propagation or the result will be further virus-infected plants. This is an important point in such economic crops as potatoes. At one time potatoes and similar stocks of plants were described as 'running out' or suffering from 'degeneration diseases' but it is now known that the real reason for failures in cropping, &c., was the increasing virus infection in the stock. In nature the method by which viruses are carried from diseased to healthy plants is by biting and sucking insects, chiefly aphides; the insect acquiring the virus by feeding on the diseased plant and later feeding on a healthy one. There must therefore be a source of the virus (i.e. an infected plant) as well as insects moving about among the plants and remedial measures must be based in general on these two points. To a less extent viruses are spread by handling and cutting diseased plants among healthy ones and it is essential in cases of attack to deal with the diseased ones first and to wash the hands and trimming knife in some disinfectant before dealing with healthy ones. It is also important to realize that infected plants cannot recover and being sources of infection should be destroyed as soon as noticed. If, however, there is much infection in a stock it is often better to destroy it and start again with healthy young plants, e.g. *see* **Strawberry Yellow Edge.** In certain parts of Great Britain weather conditions are much against insects so that by careful selection, regular inspection, and rogueing out of suspected plants it is possible to maintain stocks free from virus infection. An example is the large trade done in potatoes referred to as Scotch or Irish seed which are grown in districts adverse to aphis and are thus not very likely to become virus infected. Although viruses in general do not kill plants quickly they cause a slow but steady degeneration so that perennial plants come up looking more weak and sickly each year and continually act as sources of infection, and with stocks of dahlias, tulips, lilies, strawberries, arums, &c., constant rogueing and destruction of virus-infected individuals is necessary to preserve clean stocks. In glasshouses fumigation against insects is obviously necessary as a precaution against spread of virus disease. The symptoms shown by plants affected with virus disease are seen as mottling or chlorosis in the leaves which may be accompanied by distortion and this type of symptom is usually called the Mosaic type; in others there appear brownish to black streaks or stripes on leaves and stems as in the Tomato Stripe or Streak disease; and there is a large number of miscellaneous troubles where the plant exhibits discoloration and distortion or very great stimulation of some parts of the plant in which group may be placed Leaf Roll or Curl of Potatoes (q.v.). In Mosaic there are many types of chlorosis varying from yellowish mottling due to lighter green areas of tissue appearing over the surface of the leaves, to spots, flecks, &c., or circular ring-like yellow bands, or clearing of the veins, or yellowing of the whole leaf. There are sometimes (e.g. Potato mosaic) both primary and secondary symptoms so that a plant infected late in summer will show slight primary symptoms, but the progeny grown from its tubers will show more severe secondary symptoms the following season. The symptoms are mainly seen on the foliage although occasionally they may affect flowers (*see* **Tulip Diseases**) and sometimes fruits (*see* **Cucumber Diseases**).

An important point about virus diseases is that some plants are less affected than others, and some cases are known in which plants are so little affected that there are no external symptoms to show the presence of virus infection, but other individuals (or clones) of the same plant can be infected from it and may suffer quick and complete degeneration. Such plants are known as 'carriers', a good example being seen in some strawberry varieties which may be infected with Yellow Edge Virus but show no symptoms of the trouble, yet if planted near a variety such as Royal Sovereign the latter is infected and suffers severely. With Tomato Spotted Wilt virus (*see* **Spotted Wilt** and **Tomato diseases**) the tomato is quickly and severely affected by infection from such plants as Winter Cherries and Arum Lilies which show quite distinct symptoms of this virus but are not rapidly killed and so carry it on for some years in the greenhouse. For a fuller discussion see Masters Memorial Lectures 1949 by Dr. Kenneth M. Smith in *J.R.H.S.* lxxiv. 482 and 521, and *The Fruit Year Book*, 1950, 84, for 'Virus Diseases of Fruit Trees' by Dr. L. C. Luckwill.

D. E. G.

VISCA'RIA (*viscum*, bird-lime; referring to the sticky bands on the stem of *V. viscosa*). FAM. *Caryophyllaceae*. A genus of 4 small perennial herbs, natives of Europe and temperate Asia. Allied to Lychnis with which it is often combined but distinct by the capsule being 5-celled at the base instead of completely without division. Plants usually densely tufted, glabrous, or sticky beneath the nodes. Flowers in racemes, whorled, usually red; calyx 10-ribbed, 5-toothed, without bracts at its base; petals with scales at the top of the claw; stamens 10; styles usually 5. Capsule opening by teeth equal in number to the styles. Deep cool soil suits them best and in it they will flourish on the rock-garden, seeding freely, and, if desired, also to be propagated by division.

V. alpi'na. Rootstock short, thick, with a rather dense tuft of l.-rosettes. Stems lateral, 2 to 4 in. h., without sticky bands. *l.* of rosette oblong to lanceolate, narrowed to a petiole, upper linear, all rather thick, deep green. *fl.* many, on short pedicels, almost in a head, chalky pink or white; cal. short, almost bell-shaped, teeth rounded; pet. 2-cleft, with 2 short scales at base of blade. Spring and summer. Europe (including Britain), Siberia, Labrador. (B.M. 394.) SYN. *Lychnis alpina*. var. **al'ba,** *fl.* white. Save that it is taller, *V. lapponica* is similar to this species.

Viscaria atropurpurea (p. 2249)

V. atropurpu'rea. Almost glabrous perennial herb with a tufted rootstock. Stem 18 in. or more high, clammy below nodes, often tinged purple. *Basal l.* linear to linear-oblanceolate, acute, 1 to 4 in. long; *stem-l.* mostly in lower part of stem and shorter, often reddish-purple near base, and densely ciliate there. *fl.* in a panicle, up to 10 in. long, pedicels slender; cal. purplish, about $\frac{3}{8}$ in. long; pet. red-purple, $\frac{1}{2}$ in. long, claw as long as cal., 2 coronal lobes to each pet. May. Balkans. (B.M. 9489.) SYN. *Lychnis atropurpurea.*

V. vulga'ris. Catchfly. Habit of *V. alpina* but larger, stem clammy in upper part, about 12 to 18 in. h., often reddish below the nodes. *Rosette l.* oblanceolate, upper lanceolate, $1\frac{1}{2}$ to 3 in. long. *fl.* in whorl in a raceme, with reddish bracts at the base, bracts ciliate, tips often recurved; cal. tubular, smooth; pet. rose, rarely white, 2-fid, with 2 scales at base of blade. May to July. Europe (including Britain), Siberia, Japan. (E.B. 213 as *Lychnis Viscaria.*) SYN. *V. viscosa, Lychnis Viscaria.* var. **albiflor'a,** *fl.* white; **ple'na,** *fl.* more or less double; **splen'dens flor'e plen'o,** *fl.* larger and of brighter colour.

visca'tus -a -um, clammy.

vis'cidus -a -um, viscous, clammy, sticky.

visco'sus -a -um, clammy, sticky.

VIS'CUM (old Latin name used by Virgil and Pliny.) FAM. *Loranthaceae.* A genus of perhaps 70 species of shrubs parasitic on trees, distributed over temperate and warmer parts of the globe. Leaves sometimes flat and rather thick, often reduced to minute teeth or scales. Flowers dioecious or monoecious, in usually sessile clusters at the nodes or terminal, rarely solitary; perianth-tube of male flower short and thick, of female adnate to the ovary. Fruit a one-seeded berry, sometimes crowned with the perianth. The common Mistletoe, *V. album,* is associated with many legends and superstitions and was at one time regarded as of medicinal value. It is frequently parasitic on Apple trees which are probably its commonest host, but it occurs also on a large number of trees of different families, including Poplars, Hawthorns, Limes, Maples, Mountain Ash, rarely on Oaks, and perhaps less commonly still on Pears; it has been found on the Cedar of Lebanon and is common on the Scots Pine in Switzerland. The investigations of K. Tubeuf, *Monographie der Mistel* (1922), have shown that these Mistletoes belong to 3 physiologically distinct races, alike in appearance and characters but needing different hosts: (1) a race confined to Pinus and other conifers; (2) a race confined to Abies; (3) a race growing on a variety of broad-leaved trees but divided into sub-races with definite preferences. Large quantities are imported to augment native supplies for the Christmas trade. The ripe fruits (they usually ripen about May) may be crushed on young branches of Apple or Hawthorn preferably on the lower side of a branch in order to propagate this parasite. The viscid pulp soon hardens and fixes the seed to the branch and the radicle is able to penetrate the bark on germination.

V. al'bum. Mistletoe. Evergreen unisexual shrub of a tawny or yellowish colour, usually attached to its host in the form of a pendulous, dichotomously branched, rounded bush 2 or 3 ft. wide. *l.* opposite, narrowly obovate or oblong, roundish at the apex, $1\frac{1}{2}$ to $3\frac{1}{2}$ in. long, $\frac{1}{4}$ to 1 in. wide, sessile. *fl.* inconspicuous, sessile, in the forks of the branches, often in threes. *fr.* translucent white, globose, $\frac{1}{3}$ in. wide, with one seed embedded in viscous pulp. Europe (including Britain), N. Asia. (E.B. 635.) **A**

VIS'MIA (in honour of M. de Visme, merchant of Lisbon). FAM. *Guttiferae.* A genus of about 25 species of trees or shrubs, natives of Trop. America and Trop. W. Africa. Leaves entire, usually large, hairy or shaggy beneath, gland-dotted, rarely glabrous. Flowers yellow or whitish; sepals 5; petals 5, often hairy above; stamens in 5 groups; cymes terminal, sometimes with few, sometimes with many flowers in panicles. The under-mentioned species are all shrubs needing stove conditions and a compost of loam and peat. Propagation by cuttings in sand, under a glass, in heat.

V. glab'ra. 6 ft. h. with flattish branchlets. *l.* elliptic-lanceolate, glabrous, on short, flattish stalks. *fl.* in loose panicles; cal. ovate-oblong, obtuse, glabrous. July. Peru. 1824.

V. guianen'sis. American Gamboge, Gutta-Gum Tree. 8 ft. h., branchlets 4-angled. *l.* ovate-lanceolate, slender-pointed, dilated at base, glabrous above, reddish beneath; stalks short. *fl.* in corymbs; cal. hairy. August. Guiana. 1824.

V. guineen'sis. 6 ft. h., branchlets round, forked. *l.* ovate-lanceolate, acute; stalks slender. *fl.* in a spreading panicle; cal. ovate-lanceolate; cor. glabrous. Guinea. 1823.

Visnaga, Spanish name of Ammi.

VIS'NEA (in honour of Senhor Visne, an 18th-century Portuguese botanist). FAM. *Theaceae.* A genus of a single species of evergreen tree with the habit and inflorescence of Eurya and needing the same cultural treatment.

V. Mocane'ra. *l.* smooth, alternate, elliptic or lanceolate. *fl.* rather small, subsessile; sep. overlapping; pet. connate at base; stamens numerous. March. *fr.* berry-like, indehiscent. Canary Is., Madeira. 1815. (R.H. 1882, p. 212.) By some supposed to be the Mocan of old, made into a kind of syrup in the Canary Is.

vistulen'sis -is -e, of the neighbourhood of the R. Vistula.

VITA'CEAE. Dicotyledons. A family of 11 genera with about 450 species of shrubs, mostly climbing, widely distributed especially in tropical and subtropical regions. Closely related to Rhamnaceae, differing mainly by the fruit which in Vitaceae is a berry, in Rhamnaceae a capsule, drupe, or nut. Leaves alternate, often large, stipulate. Inflorescence generally a much-branched cyme. Flowers regular, sometimes unisexual. Calyx with 4 or 5 slight lobes. Corolla of 4 or 5 petals often slightly united at the tip and falling off as a whole. Stamens 4 or 5, opposite petals; anthers introrse. Ovary superior, of usually 2 carpels, sometimes 3 to 6, with a few ovules. Fruit a berry. The important genus Vitis belongs here. Others are Ampelocissus, Ampelopsis, Cayratia (described on p. 528 as Columella), Cissus, Leea, Parthenocissus, Pterisanthes, Rhoicissus, Tetrastigma.

Vital'ba, white vine.

Vitalia'nus -a -um, in honour of Vitaliano Donati, 1717–62, professor at Turin.

A→

vitelli'nus -a -um, of the colour of egg-yolk.

VI'TEX (Latin name used by Pliny for *V. Agnus-castus* or a similar shrub). FAM. *Verbenaceae.* A genus of some 100 species of deciduous shrubs or trees often aromatic. Leaves opposite, digitately 3- to 7-foliolate (rarely simple). Inflorescence terminal or axillary with blue, white, or yellowish flowers. Corolla tubular at base with a 2-lipped, 5-lobed limb; stamens 4, in 2 unequal pairs. Fruit a small, globose or ovoid drupe. Easily cultivated in light loamy soil, provided they are suited in regard to climate, a compost of loam and peat is best for greenhouse cultivation. Propagated in gentle heat by half-ripened cuttings.

KEY

1. *Leaflets 1 to 3*	V. trifolia
1. *Leaflets 3 to 7*	2
2. *Leaflets linear-lanceolate; fl. in terminal racemes*	V. Agnus-castus
2. *Leaflets ovate-lanceolate to obovate*	3
3. *Fls. large, few at end of peduncle*	V. Lindenii
3. *Fls. small in whorls on terminal racemes or panicles*	V. Negundo

V. Ag'nus-cast'us.* Chaste Tree. Deciduous shrub of spreading habit up to 10 ft., shoots grey-downy, aromatic. *l.* of 5 or 7 short-stalked, radiating lflets. of linear-lanceolate shape, 2 to 6 in. long, $\frac{1}{4}$ to $\frac{3}{4}$ in. wide, mostly entire, grey-felted beneath. *fl.* pale violet, fragrant, in terminal racemes 3 to 7 in. long of stalkless clusters; cor. tubular, $\frac{1}{3}$ in. long, 5-lobed. September, October. S. Europe. 1570. (S.F.G. 609.) Requires a wall except in the mildest districts. (B.M. n.s. 400.) var. **al'ba,** *fl.* white.

V. inci'sa. A synonym of *V. Negundo incisa.*

V. Linden'ii. Shrub or small tree; shoots grey-downy. *l.* of 3 or 5 radiating lflets. which are stalkless, oval to obovate, 2 to $3\frac{1}{2}$ in. long, glabrous, entire. *fl.* $\frac{3}{8}$ in. wide, stalkless, borne 3 to 6 at the end of a common stalk 1 to 3 in. long, pale violet outside, streaked purple within. May. Colombia. 1872. (B.M. 6230.) Stove.

V. Negun'do. Deciduous shrub up to 10 or 12 ft. *lflets.* usually 5, but also 3 or 7, up to 4 in. long, 1 to 1½ in. wide, ovate-lanceolate, entire or toothed; stalk 1 in. or more long. *fl.* lilac, ¼ in. long, in distant whorls forming terminal racemes or panicles 6 to 9 in. long. September. China. 1697. South or west wall. var. **heterophyl'la,** *lflets.* always sharply, often deeply toothed, which, with their longer stalks distinguish this from the more attractive *V. Agnus-castus.* N. China. (B.M. 364 as *V. Negundo*). SYN. *V. incisa.*

Vitex Negundo var. *heterophylla*

V. trifo'lia. Shrub (sometimes decumbent) to a small tree. *l.* simple or 3-foliolate; lflets. 1 to 3 in. long, obovate-oblong, entire, closely matted beneath with whitish hairs; stalk 1 in. long. *fl.* blue or lavender, often quite pale, ½ in. wide, cor. downy, in panicles 1 to 4 in. h., the largest rather resembling lilac trusses. July. SE. Asia to Japan, the Philippines, Australia. 1739. (B.M. 2187.) Stove.

W. J. B.

Viticel'la. An old name for *Clematis Viticella,* meaning a small vine.

vitice'nus -a -um, viticoi'des, Vitex-like.

vitien'sis -is -e, Fijian.

vitifo'lius -a -um, vine-leaved.

vitigi'neus -a -um, with vine-like habit.

VITIS (ancient Latin name). FAM. *Vitaceae.* In the *Genera Plantarum* of Bentham and Hooker, this genus is made to comprise Ampelopsis, Cissus, Columella, Parthenocissus, Tetrastigma, and Vitis itself. Later botanists have re-established these genera and they are consequently treated separately in this work. Some species have been placed in 4 of these genera, nearly all in 2 or 3, thereby creating an unwieldy number of synonyms. It may be assumed that practically the whole of Ampelopsis, Cissus, and Parthenocissus have, at one time or another, been included in Vitis. Names not under Vitis here should be sought under the genera indicated above.

Vitis, in its narrower conception, is a genus of some 60 or 70 species of deciduous and evergreen shrubs, almost invariably climbing and supporting themselves by tendrils. Leaves alternate, simple (rarely compound), lobed and toothed. Flowers small, in panicles or racemes opposite a leaf, petals green, adhering together by their tips and falling away unseparated. Fruit (grape) a pulpy berry containing 2 to 4 usually pear-shaped seeds.

The hardy vines here mentioned succeed best in rich loam. The chief difficulty is the provision of suitable support for them, but they are excellent for large pergolas, or for training up poles either solitary or linked together by chains. Under these conditions they must be pruned pretty much as vines are in vineries, that is, the shoots should be shortened back once or twice in summer and hard back in winter. If a failing or unwanted tree, especially an oak, can be given up to them to clamber over unrestrained, that would be copying nature. Some gorgeous effects are produced by the autumn colouring species planted in this way, such, for instance, as *V. amurensis, V. californica, V. Coignetiae, V. Davidi, V. Thunbergii,* and *V. Wilsonae.* These vines can also be grown on walls and trellis work.

Propagation is effected by eyes or by layering.

The tender species may be planted out or grown in large pots and trained to rafters or trellis. They need a rich loamy soil with some manure intermixed.

V. aconitifo'lia. A synonym of *Ampelopsis aconitifolia.*

V. acumina'ta. *fr.* black, large, in long, narrow bunches. *l.* rounded or slightly cordate at base, gradually narrowed to a sharp point, scarcely toothed on the margin, glabrous above, with very short, glaucous-white pubescence beneath. Fiji. 1890.

V. aegirophyl'la. *fl.* small; peduncles opposite the leaves, often twin, longer than l., dichotomously cymose. *fr.* ⅓ in. long. *l.* pale, glabrous, broadly ovate, abruptly acuminate, unequally and deeply acuminate-toothed; lower ones 3 in. long. Branches without tendrils, terete, striated. Turkistan. 1892.

V. aestiva'lis. Summer Grape. Climber, 60 to 80 ft., shoots loosely downy. *l.* roundish ovate, 4 to 8 (sometimes 12) in. wide, dull green, loosely rusty-downy beneath. *Panicles* 4 to 10 in. long, slender. *fr.* black, bloomy, globose, ⅓ in. wide. United States. 1656. Hardy. A few varieties of American grapes are partly derived from this vine like 'Le Noir' and 'Herbemont.'

V. amuren'sis. Vigorous climber, shoots reddish and flossy when young. *l.* broadly ovate, 4 to 10 in. wide, 3- or 5-lobed, green and glabrous or slightly downy beneath. *fr.* ⅓ in. wide, black. Amurland, Manchuria. 1854. Hardy. Its fine foliage turns crimson and purple in autumn.

V. arbo'rea. A synonym of *Ampelopsis arborea.*

V. arma'ta. A synonym of *V. Davidi.*

V. austri'na. A synonym of *V. cinerea floridana.*

V. bi'color. Blue Grape. Vigorous climber; shoots glabrous and blue-white. *l.* broadly ovate, 4 to 12 in. wide, 3- or 5-lobed glabrous or nearly so on both surfaces, vividly blue-white beneath. *fr.* about ⅓ in. wide, purple-black. E. and Cent. United States. Hardy. Readily distinguished by the very glaucous lower surface of its large l. SYN. *V. Lecontiana.*

V. californ'ica. Climber 30 ft. or more h., shoots at first grey-woolly. *l.* roundish cordate to kidney-shaped, 3 to 5 in. wide, sometimes indistinctly 3-lobed, widely toothed, at first woolly like the shoots, finally only downy or glaucous beneath. *fr.* ⅓ in. wide, black covered with whitish bloom. California. 1890. Hardy. Distinct by its smallish, rounded, shallowly and evenly toothed l. which change to crimson in autumn.

V. can'dicans. Mustang Grape. Vigorous high climber; shoots white-woolly. *l.* 2 to 5 in. wide, cordate to broadly ovate, wavy margined, sometimes obscurely 3-lobed, entirely covered at first with white wool which falls away above but persists and remains dense beneath. *fr.* globose, ⅗ in. wide, purplish; flavour disagreeable. Cent. United States. 1860. Hardy.

V. capreola'ta. A synonym of *Tetrastigma serrulatum.*

V. cine'rea. Branches 4- or 5-angled. *l.* about 12 in. wide, glossy above. *fr.* black, very small; peduncles very long, twisting with the tendrils. N. America. var. **canes'cens,** *l.* much smaller and more ornamental than type; **florida'na,** young shoots and veins beneath rusty tomentose. SYN. *V. austrina.*

V. cirrho'sa. Straggling shrub with long, weak, brittle, fleshy stems, tendrils long, 2-fid. *l.* digitate; lflets. 3 to 7, succulent, sub-sessile, obovate, distantly dentate-serrate, glabrous. *fl.* minute in dense cymes. S. Africa. 1866. Greenhouse.

V. Coignet'iae.* Climber 60 to 90 ft., shoots at first loosely flossy. *l.* 4 to 8 in. wide (sometimes 12 in.) roundish ovate, deeply cordate, obscurely 3- or 5-lobed, unequally lobed, soon glabrous above, rusty-downy beneath. *fr.* ½ in. wide, black with purple bloom. Japan. 1875. The largest-leaved of hardy vines and one of the most beautiful in its crimson and scarlet autumnal hues. SYN. *V. Kaempferi.* Hardy.

V. cordifo'lia. Frost Grape. Very vigorous climber with main stem sometimes 1½ to 2 ft. in diameter. *l.* broadly cordate-ovate, 3 to 5 in. wide, not or indistinctly 3-lobed, coarsely and unequally toothed, bright green, glabrous except on veins beneath. *Panicles* up to 12 in. long. *fr.* globose, ⅜ in. wide, black. E. United States. 1806. Grapes said to be moderately well flavoured after frost. Hardy.

Vitis Davidi

V. David'i. Luxuriant climber; shoots with gland-tipped, hooked bristles. *l.* cordate, slender-pointed, toothed, 4 to 10 in. long, 3 to 8 in. wide, shining and glabrous above, rather glaucous, more or less glandular-bristly beneath and on stalk. *fr.* ⅝ in. wide, black, edible. China. 1885. Autumn colour brilliant red. (R.H. 1890, 465.) Syn. *V. armata, Spinovitis Davidi.* Hardy.

V. Endres'ii. Strong growing climber. *l.* cordate, deep velvety green, veins deep purplish-brown. Costa Rica. 1875. Stove.

V. flexuo'sa.* Slender-stemmed climber; shoots reddish-downy when young. *l.* roundish ovate-cordate to triangular and truncate, 2 to 3½ in. long, glabrous and shining above, downy on veins beneath. Infl. slender, 2 to 6 in. long. *fr.* black, ⅓ in. wide. Japan, Korea, China. 1880. Elegant vine, distinct by its small l. Hardy. var. **ma'jor,** a synonym of *V. pulchra*; **parvifo'lia,*** *l.* smaller, rarely up to 3 in. long, deep lustrous bronzy green above, purple beneath; charming for a wall; **Wilson'ii,** a synonym of *Ampelopsis micans.*

V. Henrya'na. A synonym of *Parthenocissus Henryana.*

V. himalaya'na. A synonym of *Parthenocissus himalayana.*

V. incon'stans. A synonym of *Parthenocissus trifoliata.*

V. indivi'sa. A synonym of *Ampelopsis cordata.*

V. Jut'tae. A synonym of *Cissus Juttae.*

V. Kaemp'feri. A synonym of *V. Coignetiae.*

V. Labrus'ca. Fox Grape. Vigorous climber; shoots very woolly at first, with a tendril or infl. at every joint. *l.* roundish cordate-ovate, not or 3-lobed, 3 to 7 in. wide, shallowly toothed, dark green and soon glabrous above, at first whitish—then rusty downy beneath; stalk more than half as long as the blade. *fr.* globose, ⅝ in. wide, black purple, musky flavoured. N. America. 1656. The parent of several varieties of grape vine with berries reddish-brown or amber. Hardy.

V. lana'ta. Young branches tomentose. *l.* cordate-ovate, shortly pointed, 3 to 6 in. long, 1¾ to 3 in. wide, softly hairy, but sometimes felted beneath or glabrous. *fl.* small, in a panicled cyme. *fr.* purple, ⅓ in. wide, 4-seeded, round. China. Himalaya. 1824. Hardy. l. scarlet in autumn.

V. Lecontia'na. A synonym of *V. bicolor.*

V. montic'ola. Mountain Grape. Slender climber, 30 ft., shoots slightly downy. *l.* 2 to 4 in. wide, roundish cordate, often slightly 3-lobed, coarsely triangular toothed, dark shining green above, greyish beneath. *fr.* globose, ½ in. wide, black, sweet. Texas. 1898. Interesting for its small l. Hardy.

V. odora'tissima. A synonym of *V. vulpina.*

V. orienta'lis. A synonym of *Ampelopsis orientalis.*

V. palma'ta. A synonym of *V. rubra.*

V. pentag'ona. Vigorous climber; shoots, tendrils, and undersurface of l. densely clothed with whitish felt. *l.* 3 to 6 in. long, scarcely as wide, ovate, the base cordate or truncate, apex pointed, usually 3- but also 5-angled. *fr.* globose, ⅓ in. wide, blue-black, in slender panicles 4 to 6 in. long. China. 1907. Perhaps the most densely felted of cultivated vines. Hardy. var. **bel'lula,** *l.* only 1½ to 2½ in. long.

V. Piasez'kii. Slender climber; shoots and l.-stalks reddish-downy and glandular-bristly. *l.* variable, from 3-foliate and 5-foliate to simple, ovate and lobed, 2 to 5 in. long, coarsely toothed, glabrous above, downy especially on the veins beneath. *fr.* black, ⅜ in. wide. China. 1903. (B.M. 9565.) Syn. *Parthenocissus sinensis.* Hardy. var. **Pagnuc'cii,** shoots glabrous, *l.* nearly so. China. 1887. Both colour finely in autumn. Syn. *V. Pagnuccii.*

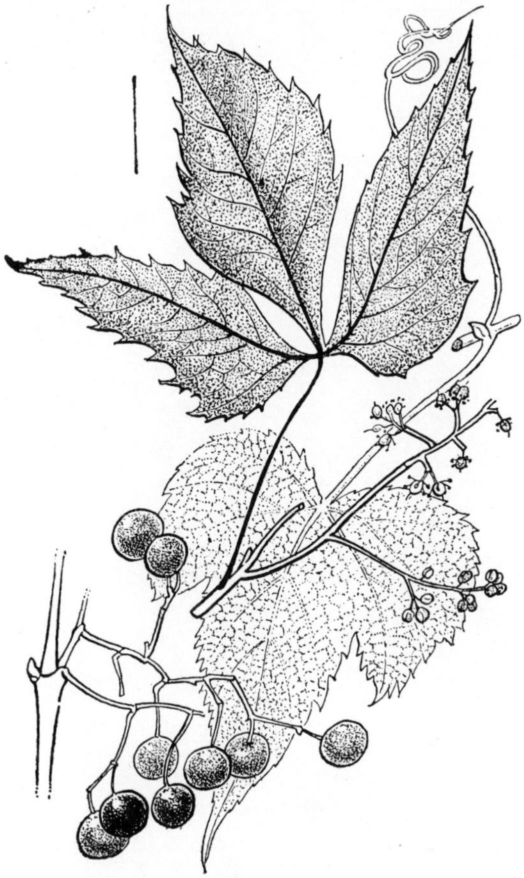

Vitis Piasezkii

V. planicau'lis. Very large glabrous climber, tendrils simple, stems flattened, branches terete. *l.* digitate, long-stalked; lflets. 5, oblong-lanceolate, toothed, short-stalked, base obtuse. *fr.* large, globose, red. India. (B.M. 5685.)

V. poli'ta. A synonym of *Pterisanthes polita.*

V. pteroph'ora. A synonym of *Cissus gongylodes.*

V. pulch'ra. Vigorous climber; shoots reddish, soon glabrous. *l* roundish-ovate, shallowly cordate, 3 to 6 in. wide, often slightly 3-lobed, coarsely toothed, apex shortly and slenderly pointed; glabrous or nearly so and shining above, grey-downy beneath. When young, the l. is reddish, dying into purple and blood red in autumn. *Panicle,* slender 3 or 4 in. long. Origin unknown. Hardy. Syn. *V. flexuosa major* (of gardens).

V. quinquefo'lia. A synonym of *Parthenocissus quinquefolia.*

V. reticula'ta. A synonym of *V. Wilsonae.*

V. ripa'ria. A synonym of *V. vulpina.*

V. Romanet'ii. Vigorous climber; shoots downy and glandular-bristly, purplish. *l.* roundish-ovate, 6 to 10 in. long, 3-lobed, shallowly toothed, each tooth with a bristle-like tip, grey-felted beneath; stalk glandular-bristly and downy. *fr.* black, ⅜ in. wide. China. 1881. (R.H. 1890, 444.) Hardy. Syn. *V. rutilans.* Akin to *V. Davidi* in its glandular bristliness, but the l. of that species are glabrous beneath.

V. rotundifo'lia. Muscadine. Strong climber up to 100 ft., close barked, shoots warted, pith continuous through the joints (nodes), tendrils unbranched. *l.* rounded to broadly ovate, 2 to 4½ in. wide, rarely lobed but coarsely triangular-toothed, shining and glabrous above. *fr.* roundish up to 1 in. wide, dull purple without bloom, skin tough, flavour musky. S. and Cent. United States. 1806. Hardy.

V. ru'bra. High climbing shrub with glabrous, bright red, angled shoots. *l.* deeply 3- or 5-lobed, the lobes long and slender-pointed, coarsely toothed, dark shining green above, bright green and glabrous or with downy veins beneath; stalk red. *Berries* roundish, black, without bloom, often with 1 seed only. Cent. United States. 1882. (G.F. 2, 341 as *V. palmata.*) Hardy.

V. rubrifo'lia. A synonym of *Parthenocissus Thomsonii.*

V. rupes'tris. Bush grape. Scarcely climbing, bushy shrub, 6 or 7 ft., usually without tendrils. *l.* kidney-shaped to broadly cordate, 2½ to 4½ in. wide, scarcely lobed but coarsely and sharply toothed, shortly pointed, bright green, downy only on the veins beneath. *fr.* purple-black, roundish, ½ in. wide, pleasantly flavoured. SE. and Cent. United States. 1860. Remarkable for its dwarf habit. Hardy.

V. rutilans. A synonym of *V. Romanetii.*

V. serjanifo'lia. A synonym of *Ampelopsis serjanifolia.*

V. Thomson'ii. A synonym of *Parthenocissus Thomsonii.*

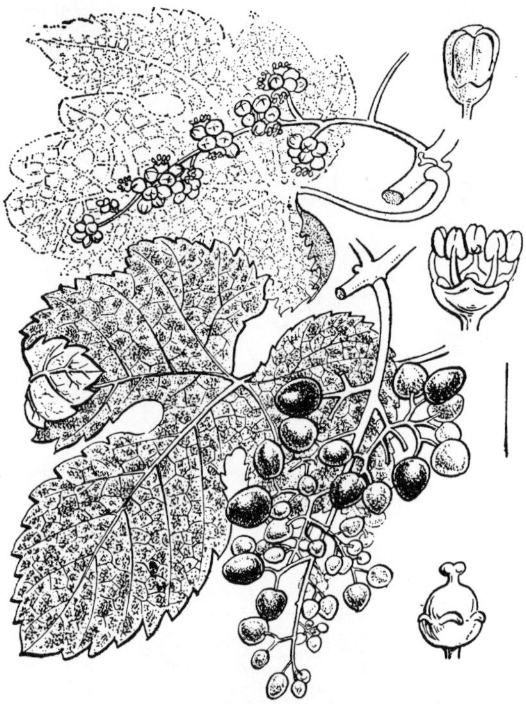

Vitis Thunbergii

V. Thunberg'ii. Slender-stemmed climber of moderate vigour only; shoots angled, downy; a tendril is missing from every third joint. *l.* 3- or 5-lobed, cordate, 3 to 6 in. wide, lobes ovate and separated by broad, rounded sinuses; sharply shallowly toothed, rusty brown-felted beneath, turning rich red in autumn. *fr.* black with a purple bloom. Japan. (B.M. 8558.) Hardy.

V. vini'fera. Common Grape Vine. Climber 50 or 60 ft., shoots glabrous or loosely woolly. *l.* 3- or 5-lobed, 3 to 6 in. long and wide, coarsely toothed, varying from downy to glabrous above, usually downy beneath; stalk half as long as the blade. *fr.* oval or globose, black with a blue bloom, or amber-coloured. Native probably of the Caucasus region. Hardy. var. **apiifo'lia,** Parsley Vine. *l.* in 3 or 5 divisions again cut up into numerous deep lobes; **corinthia'ca,** *fr.* small, black and often seedless, the currant of the grocers' shops when dried; **inca'na,** Miller Grape. *l.* covered with whitish-cobweb-like down; **purpu'rea,** *l.* at first claret-red, finally purple.

V. vita'cea. A synonym of *Parthenocissus vitacea.*

V. Voinieria'na. Stem thick, fleshy, climbing. *l.* 3-foliolate; lflets. stalked, oblong-obovate, 4 in. long, 5 in. wide, serrate, prominently nerved, glossy-green above, hairy beneath. Tonkin. 1897. Stove or greenhouse.

V. vulpi'na. Riverbank Grape. High climber, shoots glabrous. *l.* thin, 3 to 8 in. wide, broadly ovate-cordate, more or less 3-lobed, coarsely triangularly toothed, glossy green on both surfaces. *fl.* in panicles 3 to 8 in. long, sweetly scented. *fr.* globose, ⅓ in. wide, black-purple, covered with bloom. N. America. 1656. (B.M. 2429.) SYN. *V. odoratissima, V. riparia.* Hardy. Charming in May and June for its fragrant fl.

V. Wilson'ae. Very vigorous climber; shoots woolly at first. *l.* roundish ovate-cordate, shortly pointed, wavy margined, 3 to 6 in. wide, at first woolly all over, cobwebby beneath, chiefly on the veins. Panicle 3 to 5 in. long, often unbranched. *fr.* ½ in. long, black with purple bloom. China. 1904. (G.C. 46 (1909), 236.) SYN. *V. reticulata.* Hardy. Rich autumn colour.

W. J. B.

vitis-idae'a, from *vitis* and *idaeus,* of Mt. Ida, Crete.

vit'reus -a -um, glassy.

VITTADI'NIA (in honour of Dr. C. Vittadini, 1800–65, Italian writer on fungi). FAM *Compositae.* A genus of about 14 species of herbs with a thick stem or branching sub-shrubs, natives of Australia, New Zealand, S. America, and Hawaii, closely related to Erigeron from which it differs in habit, and by the long awl-shaped appendages of the style branches which in Erigeron are short. Leaves alternate, flower-heads rather small with a yellow disk and white or blue rays; involucre in several series; ray-florets pistillate, crowded, in more than 1 row. Achenes narrow, flattish; pappus of many fine bristles. Rather tender, needing no special soil. Propagation by seeds.

V. austra'lis. Herb, about 12 in. h., hairy. *l.* obovate or spatulate to linear-wedge-shaped, entire or coarsely 3-toothed or -lobed. *fl.-heads* solitary; ray-florets narrow. Australia, Tasmania. SYN. *V. tricolor, V. triloba.*

V. tri'color. A synonym of *V. australis.*

V. trilo'ba of Gardens. A synonym of *Erigeron mucronatus.*

VITTA'RIA (*vitta,* ribbon; from the shape of the fronds). FAM. *Polypodiaceae.* A genus of over 80 species of tropical ferns with rather hard grass-like fronds having sori in a continuous marginal or almost marginal line without indusia. Veins free. Sandy peat and a moist stove house suit them. Propagation is by division of the crowns.

V. angustifo'lia. *Fronds* 1 to 1½ ft. long, ¼ to ½ in. broad, narrowed very gradually to an acute point and below to base or short stem, flaccid; midrib distinct; veins immersed, forming 2 or 3 rows of vertical, hexagonal areolae. *Sori* sunk in a groove, within margin. Trop. America, Malaya. 1816. SYN. *Pteropsis angustifolia, Taenitis angustifolia.*

V. elonga'ta. *Fronds* 6 to 18 in. long, ⅛ to ¼ in. broad, acute or rather blunt, lower part very gradually narrowed to base; midrib faint or distinct; veins simple, immersed. *Sori* sunk in a marginal groove, with 2 nearly equal lips opening outwards. Himalayas, Australia, &c. (F.S. 1, 21.)

V. linea'ta. Florida Ribbon Fern. *fronds* 6 to 18 in. long, ⅛ to ⅜ in. broad, gradually narrowed downwards to a stout, compressed stem, edges often reflexed; midrib distinct, raised; veins immersed, parallel. *Sori* in a broad, slightly intra-marginal line in a slight furrow, edge of frond at first wrapped over it. Florida, Trop. America. 1793. (L.F. 2, 65; F.S.A. (2) 149.) SYN. *Taeniopsis lineata.*

V. scolopendri'na. *Fronds* 1 to 1½ ft. long, ½ to ⅞ in. broad, acute, entire, lower part very gradually narrowed to base; midrib blackish, thick, grooved in front below; veins oblique, fine, parallel. *Sori* in broad, continuous, sub-marginal lines, the firm, unaltered edge of frond at first wrapped over it. S. Africa, Malaya. (F.S.A. (2) 186.) SYN. *Taeniopsis scolopendrina.*

V. stipita'ta. *Fronds* 1½ to 2 ft. long, ¼ to ½ in. broad, firm, gradually tapering below into a long, slender stem; midrib indistinct except towards base; veins distant, oblique. *Sori* sunk in a groove within margin, the flattened, thickened edge of frond produced beyond it. Colombia to Peru. SYN. *Taeniopsis stipitata.*

vittarioi'des, Vittaria-like.

vitta'tus -a -um, striped longitudinally.

vittifor'mis, -is -e, band-like.

viv'ax, having long-lasting flowers; long-lived.

vivipa'rus -a -um, viviparous, forming young plants or bulbils in the inflorescence instead of flowers, or from flowers, or having seeds which germinate while still attached to the plant.

VOANDZE'IA (from Madagascan native name *voandzou*). FAM. *Leguminosae.* A genus of a single species of shortly creeping hairy herbaceous plant. Leaves 3-foliolate; leaflets oblong or lanceolate, stipellate. Flowers small, yellow, papilionaceous; solitary or up to 3 on a flexuous peduncle; stamens diadelphous. Pod, tuber-like, roundish. The ovary is buried after flowering by the lengthening decurved peduncles as in *Arachis hypogaea,* and the pods ripen in the earth. Widely cultivated in Cent. Africa for its seeds. Cultivation as for Arachis.

V. subterra'nea. Bambarra Ground Nut; Underground Bean. About 3 in. h. *l.* pinnately 3-foliolate; lflets. up to 3 in. long; stipels minute. *fl.* ¼ to ⅓ in. long, yellow, wings as long as the obovate standards. *Pods* sub-globose, 2-valved; seed 1 or 2, mottled with yellow, about ½ in. long. Nigeria. 1823. Stove.

VOCHISIA. *See* **Vochysia.**

VOCHYA. *See* **Vochysia.**

VOCHY'SIA (Vochy, the native name of *V. guianensis*). FAM. *Vochysiaceae.* A genus of about 100 species of shrubs or tall trees, rarely herbaceous, natives of Trop. S. America. Leaves scattered, opposite or whorled, leathery, sometimes prettily veined; stipules small, awl-shaped. Flowers mostly yellow, scented, rather large, in long racemes or panicles; sepals 5, joined at base, unequal, posterior one large and spurred; petals 1 to 3, sometimes lacking, linear or spatulate, 2 smaller than third; fertile stamen 1; staminodes 2. Fruit a leathery or woody 3-celled, 3-winged capsule each cell with 1 winged seed. Both the species described are trees needing stove conditions and a compost of loam and peat. Ripe cuttings will strike in sand, under a bell-glass, in heat. A revision of the genus by F. A. Stafleu has been published in *Recueil Trav. Bot. Néerland.* 41. 397–540 (1948).

V. ferrugi'nea. Tree of about 25 ft. *l.* elliptic or ovate to lanceolate, slender-pointed, narrowed to base, glabrous above, rusty hairy beneath. *fl.* in loose, slightly nodding terminal racemes. Trop. America from Nicaragua and Costa Rica to Peru and Brazil. 1826.

V. guianen'sis. Copai-yé-wood. Tree of 12 ft. or more. *l.* elliptic, oblong or ovate, with a short point, smooth on both sides. *fl.* with a spreading spur, in erect, dense-fld., terminal racemes. Guiana, Brazil. 1822.

VOCHYSIA'CEAE. Dicotyledons. A family of 4 genera including about 180 species of trees, rarely herbs, natives of Trop. America, with opposite or whorled, simple leaves, stipulate or not. Flowers perfect, zygomorphic. Sepals usually joined at the base, the posterior one often spurred. Petals rarely 5, usually 3 to 1, perigynous or epigynous. Fertile stamen 1, the rest staminodes. Carpels 3, with 2 to many ovules. Fruit indehiscent or a capsule. The genera referred to here are Qualea and Vochysia.

Vogel'ii, in honour of J. R. T. Vogel, 1812–41, who accompanied Capt. H. D. Trotter on the Niger expedition, 1841.

VOLES, including the Bank Vole, *Evotomys glareolus*, and the Water Vole or Water Rat, *Arvicola amphibius*, are generally vegetable feeders. The normal food of the former consists of coarse herbage, grasses, roots and shoots, aquatic plants, and small fish. Both species, however, invade gardens on occasion and do damage by devouring bulbs and corms and the foliage of many plants. The natural enemies of these rodents and the measures for preventing extensive damage to crops are similar to those mentioned under Field Mice.

G. F. W.

Volkamer'i, in honour of Johann Georg Volkamer, 1662–1744, writer on the flora of Nuremberg.

Vol'kensii, in honour of Dr. Georg Ludwig August Volkens, 1855–1917, who collected in SE. Africa.

volu'bilis -is -e, twining.

vomer'culus, a little ploughshare.

vomeren'sis -is -e, of Vomero, Naples.

vomito'rius -a -um, causing sickness.

VONIT'RA (a Madagascar vernacular name). FAM. *Palmaceae.* A genus of 1 species of Palm related to Dictyosperma and sometimes included with it. Much dwarfer than *D. album* and with different fruit. Cultivation as for Areca.

V. fibro'sa. Piassava Palm. Stem slender, 3 ft. h. *l.* pinnate 5 ft. long; lflets. 18 in. long, 1 in. wide; stalks 2 ft. long. *fr.* nearly round, ½ in. wide. Madagascar. 1894. SYN. *Dictyrosperma fibrosum.* Yields the Piassava fibre of commerce, used in brush making; this fibre is softer than that obtained from Attalea and Leopodina in Brazil used for the making of Bass brooms.

Vorderman'nii, in honour of Dr. A. G. Vordermann, 1844–1902, of the Dutch navy, in the Dutch Indies.

VOUA'PA *See* **Macrolobium.**

VRIES'IA (in honour of W. H. de Vriese, 1806–62, Dutch botanist). FAM. *Bromeliaceae.* A genus of over 100 species of mostly perennial herbaceous plants, a few dying after flowering, natives of S. and Cent. America, with dense rosettes of unarmed leaves, the flower-stem bearing 1 or more spikes of usually distichously arranged, shortly stalked, showy yellow, red or rarely white flowers. It is closely related to Tillandsia (with which it was at one time combined) and differs by the presence of ligules on the petals.

Vriesia amethystina

V. amethy'stina. *fl.* yellow, 2½ in. long, distichous, distant, subsessile, tubular; pet. twice length of sep.; anthers exserted; bracts greenish-yellow, small; spike simple, distichous, the rachis pulvinate; scape slender, erect, exceeding the l., bracteate. *l.* 12 to 16 in. long, 1 in. wide, lingulate, acuminate, shining green above, amethyst beneath. 18 in. h. Brazil. 1884. (B.H. 1884, 330, t. 15, 16; B.M. 7121 as *Tillandsia amethystina.*)

V. Barille'ti. *fl.* yellow; pet. 2 in. long, shorter than stamens; bracts yellowish-olive, much-spotted dark red, distichous, clustered, keeled; spike simple, about 1 ft. long; scape about as long as l. *l.* green, 16 to 20 in. long, shortly acuminate, with margins rolled in at the middle. 18 in. h. Ecuador. 1883. (B.H. 1883, 33, t. 3.)

V. brachy'stachys. A synonym of *V. carinata.*

V. carina'ta. *fl.* yellow, 2¼ in. long; pet. shorter than stamens; infl. few-fld. distichous, in a spike about 2½ in. long, 2 in. wide, apex, emarginate; bracts keeled, incurved, base red or purple, apex yellow, longer than sep.; scape taller than leaves, sub-erect. November. *l.* ensiform, about 8 in. long, ⅝ in. wide. 10 in. h. Brazil. 1866. (B.M. 6014; R.H. 1875, 331 as *V. brachystachys*; B.H. 1882, 287, t. 10–12 as *V. psittacina carinata.*) SYN. *Tillandsia carinata.*

V. chryso'stachys. *fl.* golden-yellow, about 1 in. long; pet. longer than stamens; bracts yellow, obtusely keeled; spike many-fld. simple, distichous, elliptic, 8 in. long, ¾ in. wide; scape elongated, erect. *l.* numerous, rosulate, lax, arched, coriaceous, 8 in. long, 2 in. wide, loriform, lingulate at base, green, but rosy and glaucescent beneath towards base. Stem short. 16 in. h. Trinidad. 1881. (B.M. 6906.)

V. di'sticha. *fl.* white, about 2½ in. long; pet. longer than stamens; spike simple, few-fld., distichous, about 8 in. long; bracts 1½ in. long, spreading, reddish beyond middle, green above; scape erect. *l.* linear, 8 in. long, ⅗ in. wide, subucate at apex, tinged purple below. 1 ft. h. Guatemala, &c. (I.H. 1883, 490 as *V. heliconioides.*)

V. Duvalia'na. *fl.* yellow, tipped green, about 2 in. long; bracts scarlet, margined greenish-yellow, keeled, incurved; spike about 18-fld., simple, elongated-elliptic, 8 in. long, 2½ in. wide; scape erect, about 1 ft. h. *l.* membranous, 9 in. long, 1½ in. wide, lanceolate, green above, tinged red beneath, the sheath broad. 1 ft. h. Brazil. 1884. (B.H. 1884, 105, t. 7, 8.)

V. ensifor'mis. *fl.* yellow, 2 in. long; pet. shorter than stamens; infl. many-fld., simple, distichous, 15 in. long; bracts citron, about 2 in. long; scape erect, 3 ft. long. *l.* subensiform, 2 ft. long, 1½ in. wide, acute; veins reddish. Brazil. 1884. (B.H. 1884, 260, t. 12, 13, as *V. Warmingii.*)

V. erythrodac'tylon. *fl.* yellow, about 2 in. long; pet. shorter than stamens; infl. distichous in a spike about 6 in. long, 2⅗ in. wide, apex rounded; bracts keeled, incurved, base, bright red, green above, longer than sep.; scape shorter than l., erect. November. *l.* deep purple at base, linear, 10 in. long, 1 in. wide. 1 ft. h. Brazil. 1866. SYN. *Tillandsia carinata.*

V. fenestra'lis. *fl.* greenish-yellow, about 1¾ in. long, longer than stamens; spike simple, distichous, about 18 in. long; bracts green, spotted brown, roundish; scape erect, long, robust. *l.* coriaceous, about 18 in. long, broad, arched, concave, pale, beautifully marked with pellucid reticulations in the upper half, rounded-mucronate at apex, slightly spotted with red at base. 3 ft. h. Brazil. 1875. Plant tufted. (I.H. n.s. 215; B.H. 1884, 65, t. 11, 5; B.M. 6898 as *Tillandsia fenestralis.*)

V. gladioliflo'ra. *fl.* greenish-violet, about 2 in. long, secund, longer than stamens; spike simple, many-fld., cylindrical, about 10 in. long; bracts obtuse, erect; scape stout. *l.* broad-linear, 2 ft. long, 3½ in. wide. 3 ft. h. Costarica. 1863.

V. gra'cilis. A synonym of *V. procera gracilis.*

V. gutta'ta. *fl.* about 2 in. long, sepals citron, with reddish marks, elliptic; pet. yellow, shorter than stamens; bracts light rose-coloured, broad, conduplicate, nearly equalling the cal., farinose; spike, many-fld., simple, 6 in. long, pendulous; scape arched. *l.* 9 in. long, 1 in. wide, slightly acute, mucronate, olivaceous, spotted and blotched dark purple. 1 ft. h. Brazil. 1875. (B.H. 1880, 13, 1–3; I.H. n.s. 200.)

V. hierogly'phica. *fl.* dull yellow; petals longer than stamens; infl. many-fld. paniculate, up to 3 ft. h., branches sub-erect; bracts bluntly keeled, inflated, about 1 in. long; scape stout. *l.* broad-linear, 18 in. long, 4 in. wide, marked above with dark green, blackish-purple below. 5 ft. h. Brazil. 1878. (I.H. 1884, 514; B.H. 1885, 57, t. 10–12.) SYN. *Massangea hieroglyphica.*

V. incurva'ta. *fl.* yellow, spotted green at apex, about 2 in. long; pet. shorter than stamens, bracts red, edged orange, keeled, oval-lanceolate, 2 in. long; spike dense, stout, distichous, about 8 in. long. l. green, lorate, shortly acuminate, widened at base, 10 in. long, 1¼ in. wide. 1 ft. h. Brazil. 1882. var. **infla'ta,** differs by the much inflated bracts. (B.M. 6882 as *Tillandsia inflata*; B.H. 1882, 52, t. 2, as *V. incurvata.*)

V. Jongh'ei. *fl.* tawny-yellow, up to 2 in. long, rather remote, horizontal; sep. greenish, with fuscous margins; bracts fuscous green, plicate, gibbous at base, shorter than sep.; spike simple, 8 in. long, 5 in. wide; scape erect, simple, longer than l., with lanceolate, leafy bracts. *l.* lorate, 18 in. long, 1⅗ in. wide, recurved, fuscous purplish beneath. 2½ ft. h. Brazil. 1874. (B.M. 6945; and B.R. 1874, 291, t. 12, 13 as *Tillandsia Jonghei.*)

V. longebractea'ta. *fl.* yellow; pet. shorter than stamens; spike simple, many-fld., distichous, 1 ft. long, 3 in. broad; bracts keeled, pale red or green, 2 to 2½ in. long; peduncle stiffly erect. *l.* thin, flexible, lorate, almost glabrous, 1½ to 2 ft. long, 1½ to 2 in. broad, narrowed to apex, or rounded and cuspidate. 3 ft. h. Venezuela, Trinidad. 1897.

V. Lubber'sii. *fl.* pet. 1 in. long, white, shorter than stamens, infl. paniculate, lax, branches 4- to 6-fld., simple, distichous spike 2 to 3 in. long; bracts long. *l.* 12 to 20, densely rosulate-utriculate, ensiform from an ovate base, 8 in. long, ½ in. broad, pale glaucous green. 18 in. h. Brazil. 1882.

V. Malzinei. *fl.* white, about 3 in. long; infl. 10- to 24-fld., simple, cylindrical, 6 in. long; scape about as long as l., erect; bracts yellow or red, ovate-navicular, above 1 in. long. April. *l.* 15 to 20 in a dense rosette, about 1 ft. long, 3 in. broad at the dilated base, falcate, chartaceous, deltoid-cuspidate at apex, bright green above, red-brown with fine vertical lines at back. Mexico. 1874. Acaulescent. (B.H. 1874, 313, t. 14; B.M. 6495 as *Tillandsia Malzinei.*)

V. Morre'nii.* *fl.* yellowish-green, 2 in. long, longer than stamens, secund. infl. many-fld., paniculate branches sub-erect, 10- to 20-fld. bracts straw-coloured; scape stout. *l.* erect, 1½ ft. long, 4 in. wide, sub-coriaceous, with broken, zigzag, transverse brownish markings; tip rounded. 3 ft. h. Brazil.

V. parai'bica. *fl.* yellow, about 2¾ in. long, in a densely imbricated, distichous spike; bracts large, purple-red, as long as the golden-yellow cal.; scape erect, short. Summer. *l.* green, shining, lingulate, 6 to 9 in. long, about 1 in. wide, about as long as the scape. 6 to 9 in. h. Brazil. 1885.

V. Pastuchoffia'na. Closely related to *V. Morrenii* but with obtuse instead of acute sep. 3 ft. h. Brazil.

V. Philip'po-Coburg'i. *fl.* yellowish-green, about as long as stamens, secund. Infl. many-fld., paniculate, about 2 ft. long, branches sub-erect, red; lower bracts large, dark red; bracteoles bright red, scarious, very acute. *l.* 2 ft. long, 2½ in. broad, rigidly membranous, light green, shining, the apex reddish-brown; sheath slightly dilated, variegated with pale purplish blotches. 3 ft. h. Brazil.

V. platyne'ma. *fl.* greenish, about 1½ in. long; sep. thick, shining, exuding a colourless gum; infl. about 40-fld., distichous, simple, about 18 in. long; bracts purple-violet, foliaceous, half-amplexicaul, rigid, about 1¾ in. long. *l.* canaliculate, obtuse, mucronate. 1½ ft. long, 2½ in. wide, glaucous violet below, and with a greenish-blue tint above transversely marked with dark, wavy lines. 3 ft. h. Brazil, W. Indies. 1871. (G.F. 1870, 354, t. 671; I.H. 1871, t. 70 and F.M. n.s. 116 as *Encholirion corallinum.*) SYN. *T. corallina.* var. **Libo'nii,** *l.* rounder, *fl.* much smaller (about 1 in. long); **rosea,** *l.* long acute, reddish-violet beneath. Brazil.

V. Platzmann'ii. *fl.* yellow, distichous, rather remote, shortly pedunculate, tubular; bracts purplish, concave; spike simple, secund, about 10-fld.; scape 3 to 4 ft. h., slender, erect, bracteate. *l.* lingulate, broad at base, green, margined with red, spotted beneath. 18 in. h. Brazil. 1875.

V. poenula'ta. *fl.* yellow, 1½ in. long; pet. shorter than stamens; spike 7- to 12-fld., moderately dense, non-distichous, 3 to 4 in. long; bracts 1¼ in. long; peduncle 6 to 8 in. long, erect. *l.* about 20 in a dense rosette, with an ovate base 1 to 1¼ in. broad, reflexing, linear-convolute, rigid, coriaceous 5 in. long, ⅛ in. wide, thinly lepidote. Brazil. SYN. *Tillandsia Glaziovii.*

V. pro'cera gra'cilis. *fl.* yellow, more or less erect, over 1 in. long, shorter than pet.; infl. many-fld., paniculate, about 18 in. long; bracts reddish at base, greenish towards the apex; scape 2 to 2½ ft. h. *l.* entire, of a pleasing green, 12 in. long, 2½ in. broad, semi-amplexicaul at base, narrowed to acute apex. 3 ft. h. Guiana, Brazil. 1886. SYN. *V. gracilis, Tillandsia gracilis.*

Vriesia psittacina (p. 2255)

V. psittaci'na. *fl.* yellow, spotted green at tip, about 2½ in. long; pet. shorter than stamens; infl. simple, lax, distichous, few-fld., about 8 in. long; rachis red; scape 1 ft., erect. July. *l.* radical, 12 in. long, 1 in. wide, linear-ligulate, recurved, acute, entire, yellow-green, thin, more or less waved. 18 in. h. Brazil. 1828. (B.R. 1843, t. 10; B.H. 1882, 287, t. 10–12; B.M. 2841 as *Tillandsia psittacina.*) Several varieties of this striking plant have been named, among them the following: var. **deco'ra,** bracts and rachis green; *fl.* and *l.* smaller. Brazil; **Morrenia'na,** *fl.* more numerous and more closely set. (B.H. 1882, 287, t. 10–12, f. 2 (not 3); **rubro-bractea'ta,** bracts shining red. A garden variety. (B.M. 5108 as *Tillandsia Krameri.*)

V. regi'na.* *fl.* white at first, becoming dull yellow with a strong, Jasmine-like perfume, 2½ in. long; bracts rose; spikes 2-ranked, curved, in a branched panicle; scape stout, developing rapidly, eventually reaching about 7 ft. *l.* about 4 ft. long, 7 in. wide, recurved at apex, broadly sheathing at base. Brazil. 1867. A magnificent plant. (I.H. 1867, t. 516 as *V. gigantea.*)

V. reticula'ta. *fl.* sep. yellow-green; pet. white, about as long as stamens; infl. paniculate, about 18 in. long, branches generally 10- to 15-fld., distichous; bracts about 1 in. long; scape stout. Spring. *l.* lorate-lanceolate, 1½ to 2 ft. long, in a dense rosette, 2½ in. wide, moderately firm, much reticulated with fine transverse lines of dark green on pale green. 3 ft. h. Brazil. 1870. SYN. *Guzmania reticulata.*

V. Rodigasia'na. *fl.* citron-yellow, 1½ in. long; pet. shorter than stamens; bracts yellow tinged red, ovate, short; panicle loose, about 1 ft. long, with branches spreading, few-fld., scarlet spathe; scape nearly erect, slender, with narrow bracts. *l.* sheathing and fuscous at base, linear, slightly channelled, rounded-cuspidate, green, with a few dark blood-red spots. Brazil. (I.H. 1882, t. 467.)

Vriesia splendens

V. ru'bida. *fl.* sep. bright red; pet. white, convolute in a tube more than ½ in. longer than cal.; spike few-fld., lax, simple, 3 to 4 in. long, bracts bright red, ⅜ in. long; peduncle 1 ft. long, erect upper bract-leaves bright red. *l.* densely rosulate, ensiform, acuminate, ovate at base, 9 in. long, ½ in. broad, rigid, coriaceous. 18 in. h. Brazil. 1885. SYN. *Tillandsia oligantha.*

V. sanguinolen'ta. *fl.* 1⅜ in. long; pet. white longer than stamens; infl. paniculate, about 1 ft. long; branches 9 in. long, fl. secund; bracts keeled; scape stout. *l.* broad-linear, 20 in. long, nearly 4 in. wide, with brownish-red blotches on both surfaces. 6 ft. h. Colombia. (I.H. 1875, t. 200.) SYN. *Encholirion sanguinolentum.*

V. Saunder'sii.* *fl.* 2 in. long, sulphur-yellow; sep. keeled; panicle loose, branches 5- to 7-fld.; bracts distichous, concave; scape erect, shining, angled, yellowish-white. *l.* rosulate, broad-linear, about 10 in. long, 1¾ in. wide, obtuse, glaucous green dotted with white, spotted purple-brown below. 1½ ft. h. Brazil. 1872. (I.H. 1873, t. 132 as *Encholirion Saundersii.*

V. scala'ris. *fl.* about 1⅝ in. long; pet. yellow, shorter than stamens; infl. simple, few-fld., distichous about 5 in.; bracts deep rose; scape 1½ to 2 ft. long, pendulous. *l.* 6 in. long, ⅜ in. wide, acuminate, wine coloured on back. 8 in. h. Brazil. 1879. var. **vi'ridis,** bracts green. Brazil.

V. specio'sa. A synonym of *V. splendens.*

V. splen'dens. *fl.* erect, nearly 3 in. h.; pet. yellow, shorter, than stamens; infl. many-fld., simple, distichous, about 15 in. long, 2 in. wide; bracts bright red, keeled, about 3 in. long; scape erect, longer than leaves. *l.* linear, 15 in. long, 2½ in. wide, green above, lighter beneath with dark-brownish transverse bands. 3 ft. Guiana. (B.M. 4382 as *V. speciosa.*) SYN. *Tillandsia vittata, T. zebrina.*

V. tessella'ta. *fl.* sep. green, glutinous; pet. yellow, 2 in. long, about as long as stamens; bracts green; panicle about 3 ft. long, erect, loose, branches 9- to 12-fld., erect, arcuate, fls. secund; scape stout, equalling l. *l.* broad-linear, 15 in. long, nearly 3 in. wide, coriaceous rigid, channelled, tessellated green and yellow, sub-glaucescent, acuminate, sheath broad, dark fuscous. 6 ft. h. Brazil. 1882. (B.H. 1882, 381, t. 14–16; I.H. 1874, t. 179 as *Tillandsia tessellata.*) var. **roseo-pic'ta,** *l.* marked with large rosy spots. 1884; **San'derae,*** *l.* variegated with white and yellow bands on a tessellated green ground. Brazil. 1893; **Sanderia'na,** *l.* more distinctly zoned and marbled than in type. 1892.

V. viridiflo'ra. *fl.* greenish, 1½ in. long, ¾ in. wide; bracts green; spike simple, few-fld. distichous, dense, fusiform; scape twiggy, 2 ft. h., covered with scarious bracts. *l.* in a large open rosette, membranous, shining, ligulate, acute, recurved, entire, 1 ft. long, 1½ in. broad. Costa Rica. 1878. SYN. *Vriesia viminalis* (B.H. 1878, 257, 14–15).

V. Wawran'ea. *fl.* pet. waxy-yellow, longer than stamens; infl. few-fld., simple, about 8 in. long, 4 in. wide; bracts fleshy, green, round; scape stout. Summer. *l.* about 20 in a rosette, 18 in. long, 2½ to 3 in. wide, glaucous, bluish-green, with fine, transverse, wavy lines, a dark brown blotch just under the mucro, and dark chestnut-brown at the base. 1½ ft. h. Brazil.

VRYDAGZYNEA. Included in **Anoectochilus.**

Vua'pa, native name of *Macrolobium bifolium* in Guiana.

vulca'nicus -a -um, fiery, thence growing on an extinct volcano.

vulga'ris -is -e, vulga'tus -a -um, common.

vulnera'rius -a -um, relating to wounds.

vulpa'ria, from vulpes, fox, indicating that the plant could be used to poison foxes.

vulpi'nus, foxy.

×**VUYLSTEKEA'RA** (in honour of Charles Vuylsteke, 1844–1927, of Loochristy, Belgium, nurseryman who specialized in hybridization of Orchids). Hybrids combining species of Cochlioda, Miltonia, and Odontoglossum.

W

WACHENDORF'IA (in honour of E. J. Wachendorf, 1702–58, Dutch botanist, professor at Utrecht). FAM. *Haemodoraceae.* A genus of about 7 species of tuberous-rooted, perennial, S. African herbs. Stem erect, often thickened at base. Leaves few, ensiform or rarely linear, sometimes large, more or less plicate-veined. Flowers in terminal panicles, often hairy, perianth without a tube, yellow; segments narrow or obovate-oblong, outer, especially the back one, different from inner, decurrent to the pedicels; stamens 3. Seeds 1 in each cell of the 3-celled capsule. Greenhouse or frame protection is needed and a mixture of very sandy loam with a little peat suits them. They are better planted out, flowering more freely than in pots but they must be kept free from frost. Little or no water should be given during the resting season. Propagation is by seed or by offsets. They are worth trying in sheltered places in favoured districts. The root yields a red colouring matter.

W. brevifo'lia. A variety of *W. hirsuta.*

W. hirsu'ta. Stem $1\frac{1}{2}$ ft. h., hairy. *l.* linear-ensiform, 3-nerved, hairy. *fl.* drooping, red in bud, golden-yellow when expanded; peduncles 4- or 5-fld., secund; panicle spreading, bracts hairy. April. 1687. (B.M. 614; A.B.R. 398 as *W. villosa.*) var. **brevifo'lia,** *l.* 5-nerved, *fl.* crimson mixed with tawny-yellow. 1795. (B.M. 1666.)

Wachendorfia paniculata

W. panicula'ta. Stem $1\frac{1}{2}$ ft. h., greenish, corymbose-paniculate. *l.* ensiform, 3-nerved, in 2 rows, one-third as long as *W. thyrsiflora. fl.* golden-yellow; segs. hairy without, reddish, obovate; in secund racemes, pedicels 3- to 5- fld. April. 1700. (B.M. 616.) var. **pal'lida,** *fl.* pale yellow. (B.M. 2610; F.P.S.A. 114.)

W. thyrsiflo'ra. Stem nearly simple, about 2 ft. h. *l.* ensiform, 5-nerved, glabrous. *fl.* in a terminal spike, rachis angular; yellow, lobes wedge-shaped-lanceolate; lower branchlets of spike 3- or 4-fld. May. 1759. (B.M. 1060.)

W. villo'sa. A synonym of *W. hirsuta.*

Wagneria'nus -a -um, in honour of M. Wagner, 1813–60, of Munich, who collected in Trop. America.

WAHLENBERG'IA (in honour of Georg Wahlenberg, 1780–1851, of Uppsala, author of *Flora Lapponica,* &c.). FAM. *Campanulaceae.* A genus of about 150 species of annual or perennial herbs or sub-shrubs very closely related to Campanula, mostly natives of S. Africa, India, China, Japan, Australia, and of New Zealand, with a few species in the tropics, also one a native of Britain. From Campanula the genus is distinguished by the capsule opening by valves at the top inside the calyx, not as in Campanula at the sides beneath the calyx. Edraianthus, which is sometimes included in Wahlenbergia, differs from it in capsule and inflorescence. The capsule opens irregularly in Edraianthus but by regular valves in Wahlenbergia. The 2 genera are more easily distinguished by the arrangement of the flowers. In Wahlenbergia the flower is borne on a fairly long pedicel and has no bracts immediately beneath it. In Edraianthus the stem ends in a dense cluster of flowers or in a solitary flower with bracts immediately beneath it. The species of Edraianthus are all dwarf compact perennials native to the Balkan Peninsula; the account on pp. 735–6 includes only those with closely clustered flowers. The 3 species with solitary flowers, often regarded as typical Wahlenbergias by rock-gardeners, are accordingly described below. There are no grounds for separating them generically from Edraianthus. *E. Wettsteinii* has 1 to 3 flowers on a stem, while *E.* × *Murbeckii* is a hybrid between *E. Kitaibelii* with clustered flowers and *E. serpyllifolius* with solitary flowers. All species of Edraianthus are suitable for the choice rock-garden or alpine house and are probably best in limestone scree or on a sunny ledge. Propagation is by seed or by cuttings of non-flowering shoots taken from June to August and inserted in sand in a frame. *W. hederacea* is a bog plant best established by sowing seed on living sphagnum. The annual species from S. Africa, &c., can be treated as half-hardy annuals and planted out in late spring; the perennials for the most part need greenhouse conditions though the New Zealand species can be grown in the alpine house. All the species can be propagated by seed but *W. albomarginata* and some Australian species can also be increased by cuttings taken with an inch or so of the white underground stem in April or May, inserted in sand, and prevented from flowering. The plants often catalogued as Wahlenbergias with flowers in a close cluster at the top of the stem should be sought under Edraianthus. An account of the African species by W. von Brehmer will be found in Engler, *Bot. Jahrb.* 53. 9–143 (1910); the Australian species are described by N. Lothian in *Proc. Linnean Soc. New South Wales,* 71. 201–35 (1947).

KEY

1. *Fls. closely clustered in heads* — Edraianthus sect. Capitati (p. 735)
1. *Fl. solitary or in loose infl.* — 2
2 (1). *Plant with long thread-like creeping stems and small almost orbicular angled lvs.; l.-blades wider than long; cor. bell-shaped, about $\frac{3}{10}$ to $\frac{2}{5}$ in. long* — W. hederacea
2. *Plant otherwise; lvs. longer than wide* — 3
3 (2). *Bracts or small lvs. present immediately beneath fl. and reaching to tip of cal.; dwarf, tufted perennials $\frac{1}{2}$ to $3\frac{1}{2}$ in. h. when in fl.; European (Edraianthus)* — 4
3. *No bracts or small lvs. near the fl.; African, Asiatic, or Australasian (Wahlenbergia proper)* — 7
4 (3). *Lvs. narrowly oblanceolate, to $\frac{4}{5}$ in., $\frac{1}{10}$ in. wide, hairy only on margin* — E. serpyllifolius
4. *Lvs. linear, often less than $\frac{1}{20}$ in. wide, hairy on face* — 5
5 (4). *Fl. sessile on tuft of lvs., the stem extremely short; lvs. rarely more than $\frac{1}{2}$ in. long* — E. pumilio
5. *Fl. borne on an evident stem to 3 in. long; lvs. up to $1\frac{1}{2}$ in. long* — 6
6 (5). *Bracts narrowed into a long point; cal. segs. twice as long as ovary; ovary glabrous* — E. dinaricus
6. *Bracts not narrowed into a long point; cal. segs. about as long as ovary; ovary hairy* — E. Wettsteinii

7 (3). *Lvs. crowded at the base of stem, mostly forming rosettes or basal tufts* 8
7. *Lvs. scattered up the stem* 13
8 (7). *Lvs. with strongly thickened margin, entire, spoon-shaped; cor. divided almost to base into 5 lobes* W. cartilaginea
8. *Lvs. not thickened at margin* 9
9 (8). *Cor. rather saucer-shaped* W. annularis
9. *Cor. bell-shaped* 10
10 (9). *Lvs. linear, rigid, 1 to 1$\frac{1}{2}$ in. long, $\frac{1}{10}$ to $\frac{1}{8}$ in. wide* W. Matthewsii
10. *Lvs. almost orbicular or narrowly oblanceolate* 11
11 (10). *Lvs. almost orbicular, abruptly narrowed into petiole as long as the blade; stems creeping and forming dense mats; capsule globose* W. congesta
11. *Lvs. oblanceolate or narrowly oblanceolate, gradually narrowed at base* 12
12 (11). *Plant 2 to 12 in. h.; lvs. often with reddish-brown underside; cor. $\frac{2}{5}$ to $\frac{7}{10}$ in. long, $\frac{7}{10}$ to 1$\frac{1}{4}$ in. across; New Zealand* W. albomarginata
12. *Plant 1 to 4 in. h.; lvs. green on both sides; cor. small. to $\frac{2}{5}$ in. long, $\frac{1}{2}$ in. across; Tasmania* W. saxicola
13 (7). *Cal. tube (ovary) and capsule hairy* 14
13. *Cal. tube (ovary) and capsule glabrous* 15
14 (13). *Cal. tube (ovary) with long recurved hairs about $\frac{1}{20}$ in. long; cal. segs. narrowly triangular, less than 5 times as long as wide at base; cor. $\frac{2}{5}$ to $\frac{1}{2}$ in. long* W. capensis
14. *Cal. tube (ovary) with short hairs about $\frac{1}{50}$ in. long; cal. segs. narrowly lanceolate or linear, more than 5 times as long as wide at base; cor. $\frac{7}{10}$ to $\frac{4}{5}$ in. long* W. trichogyna
15 (13). *Lvs. thread-like, about $\frac{1}{50}$ in. wide, $\frac{1}{4}$ to $\frac{1}{2}$ in. long, very numerous, in alternate clusters up the stem* W. capillacea
15. *Lvs. otherwise, not thread-like, larger, solitary or in pairs but not clusters* 16
16 (15). *Fl. small; cor. $\frac{1}{5}$ in. or less long* 17
16. *Fl. medium-sized or large; cor. about $\frac{1}{2}$ in. or more long* 18
17 (16). *Plant hairy in lower part* W. gracilis
17. *Plant glabrous* W. multicaulis
18 (17). *Cal. segs. triangular, hardly twice as long as wide at base* W. undulata
18. *Cal. segs. narrowly lanceolate to linear, about 5 times as long as wide at base* 19
19 (18). *Cor. white with red stripes; cor. lobes much shorter than tube; rootstock formed of globose tubers; Juan Fernandez* W. tuberosa
19. *Cor. blue or purple, rarely white, not red-striped; cor. lobes about as long as tube or longer; rootstock without globose tubers* 20
20 (19). *Lower part of stem glabrous* W. denudata
20. *Lower part of stem hairy* 21
21 (20). *Cor. up to $\frac{3}{4}$ in. across; stems usually one from the crown* W. Billardieri
21. *Cor. up to 1$\frac{1}{4}$ in. or more across; stems usually several from the crown* 22
22 (21). *Lvs. hairy on both sides; cal. segs. at anthesis $\frac{3}{8}$ to $\frac{3}{5}$ in. long* W. consimilis
22. *Lvs. glabrous on upper side; cal. segs. at anthesis $\frac{1}{10}$ to $\frac{1}{8}$ in. long* W. gloriosa

W. albomargina'ta. Perennial, of tufted habit; stems up to 5 from a rosette, 2 to 8 in. h., leafless, 1-fld. *l.* basal, spatulate, $\frac{3}{4}$ to 1 in. long, to $\frac{1}{5}$ in. wide, reddish-brown at the margin, often reddish-brown beneath, ciliate on the petiole, otherwise glabrous. *fl.* erect; ovary glabrous, marked with dark lines; cal. segs. almost linear, about $\frac{1}{5}$ in. long; cor. bell-shaped, about $\frac{3}{4}$ in. long, to 1$\frac{1}{4}$ in. across, white or blue. June. New Zealand. 1881. (B.M. 6613 as *W. saxicola.*) var. **pygmae'a,** a dwarf alpine form about 1 in. h.; *fl.* drooping. SYN. *W. pygmaea.* This species is best treated as an annual or wintered under glass.

W. annula'ris. Annual or perennial herb; fl.-stems branched, 6 to 24 in. h. *l.* basal, narrowly oblanceolate or almost linear, to 2$\frac{1}{4}$ in. long, $\frac{3}{8}$ in. wide, hairy, toothed. *fl.* erect; ovary glabrous; cal. segs. narrowly triangular, about $\frac{1}{10}$ in. long; cor. broadly campanulate, almost rotate, white becoming light violet, $\frac{3}{8}$ in. long, nearly 1 in. across. S. Africa. An attractive free-flowering plant.

W. Billardier'i. Erect perennial 9 to 15 in. h.; rootstock thick; stems few or solitary, usually unbranched, hairy in lower part. *l.* well-spaced on lower part of stem in pairs, sometimes alternate, ovate to lanceolate, to 1 in. long, $\frac{1}{8}$ in. wide, entire or sometimes toothed, hairy beneath. *fl.* medium-sized; ovary glabrous; cal. segs. narrowly triangular, to $\frac{1}{5}$ in. long; cor. funnel-shaped, about $\frac{1}{2}$ in. long, $\frac{1}{2}$ to $\frac{3}{4}$ in. across, blue, pale mauve or white. Australia (Victoria). SYN. *Campanula littoralis* of Labillardière.

W. capen'sis. Erect hairy simple or branched half-hardy annual 12 to 18 in. h. *l.* mostly in pairs on lower part of stem, mostly oblong-lanceolate, to 2 in. long, $\frac{3}{4}$ in. wide, irregularly toothed, hairy. *fl.* at first drooping, later erect; ovary densely covered with long white hairs; cal. segs. narrowly triangular, about $\frac{1}{4}$ in. long; cor. rather saucer-shaped, about $\frac{1}{2}$ in. long, to $\frac{3}{4}$ in. across, bluish-green outside, blue inside, with lobes violet, spotted black near sinuses. July. S. Africa, naturalized in Australia. (B.M. 782 as *Campanula capensis*; A.B.R. 238 as *Roella decurrens.*)

W. capilla'cea. Erect annual or perennial, 10 to 18 in. h. *l.* numerous, scattered up the stem in alternate clusters, thread-like, $\frac{1}{4}$ to $\frac{1}{2}$ in. long, about $\frac{1}{50}$ in. wide, glabrous. *fl.* in a terminal panicle; ovary glabrous; cal. segs. linear, about $\frac{1}{10}$ in. long; cor. funnel-shaped, to $\frac{7}{10}$ in. long, dark blue. May. S. Africa. 1822. Greenhouse.

Wahlenbergia capensis

W. cartila'ginea. Dwarf perennial; fl.-stems 1 to 3 in. h., 1-fld. *l.* basal, in rosettes, spatulate, to 1$\frac{1}{4}$ in. long, $\frac{3}{10}$ in. wide, entire, with a strongly thickened cartilaginous margin, glabrous or hairy. *fl.* erect; ovary glabrous or hairy; cal. segs. linear-oblong, to $\frac{1}{2}$ in. long, with thickened margins; cor. to $\frac{1}{2}$ in. long, cut almost to the base into 5 lobes, white. New Zealand.

W. conges'ta. Dwarf, densely tufted perennial, with creeping stems, to 2 in. h. in fl. *l.* almost orbicular or oblong-spatulate, to 1 in. long. *fl.* small; cor. $\frac{1}{4}$ to $\frac{1}{3}$ in. across, pale blue. New Zealand.

W. consi'milis. Erect perennial 8 to 30 in. h.; rootstock thick; stems usually many, branched or unbranched, hairy in lower part. *l.* rather crowded on lower part of stem, paired or alternate, lower l. ovate or spatulate, to 2 in. long, $\frac{1}{2}$ in. wide, entire or sometimes toothed, hairy on both sides, upper l. lanceolate or linear-lanceolate. *fl.* large; ovary glabrous; cal. segs. narrowly triangular, to $\frac{3}{5}$ in. long; cor. broadly funnel-shaped, about 1 in. long, to 1$\frac{1}{2}$ in. across, dark blue. Australia. 1911. (G.C. 52 (1912), 216 as *W. vincaeflora.*) **W. glorio'sa,** Victoria, is closely akin, with deep blue to purple *fl.*

Edraianthus dina'ricus. Dwarf, tufted perennial. *l.* linear, to 1$\frac{1}{2}$ in. long, $\frac{1}{20}$ in. wide, hairy on upper side. *fl.* large, solitary, clasped by an involucre, on a leafy stem to 3 in. h.; ovary glabrous; cal. segs. ciliated, about $\frac{3}{10}$ in. long; cor. funnel-shaped, about $\frac{7}{10}$ in. long, violet. Balkan Peninsula (Dalmatia). SYN. *Wahlenbergia dinarica.*

W. glorio'sa. *See under* **W. consimilis.**

W. gra'cilis. Slender plant, 5 to 14 in. h., apparently annual but said to be perennial; stem usually branched, hairy in lower part. *l.* closely placed on lower part of stem, lower l. oblanceolate, toothed, hairy. *fl.* small; ovary glabrous; cal. segs. subulate, less than $\frac{1}{10}$ in. long; cor. funnel-shaped, about $\frac{1}{5}$ in. long. New Caledonia and elsewhere in Polynesia and SE. Asia. This plant, described from New Caledonian specimens, has no garden value but is mentioned here because the name has often been applied in error to other species. It is doubtfully distinct from *W. marginata* of Japan and China, while *W. quadrifida* of Australia is closely akin. For *W. gracilis* of B.M. 691 *see* **W. trichogyna.**

W. hedera'cea. Dwarf annual or perennial, with thread-like creeping stems. *l.* all stalked, almost orbicular, usually angular, $\frac{1}{3}$ to $\frac{1}{2}$ in. wide. *fl.* small; ovary glabrous; cal. segs. less than $\frac{1}{10}$ in. long; cor. narrowly campanulate, $\frac{3}{10}$ to $\frac{2}{5}$ in. long, pale blue. July, August. W. Europe, including British Is. (E.B. 875.) SYN. *Campanula hederacea.* An exquisite little plant of moist peaty places.

W. Matthew'sii. Perennial of tufted habit; rootstock woody; stems simple or branched, 3 to 6 in. h. *l.* basal, linear, 1 to $1\frac{1}{2}$ in. long, $\frac{1}{10}$ to $\frac{1}{8}$ in. wide, rigid, numerous. *fl.* medium-sized, erect; ovary glabrous; cal. segs. about $\frac{1}{5}$ in. long; cor. bell-shaped, about $\frac{3}{5}$ in. long, pale lilac. July to September. New Zealand. 1916.

W. multicau'lis. Erect perennial, about 1 ft. or more h.; stems numerous, simple or branched, glabrous. *l.* numerous, scattered up the stem, linear. *fl.* small; ovary glabrous; cal. segs. about $\frac{1}{10}$ in. long; cor. about $\frac{3}{10}$ in. long. W. Australia. (? L.B.C. 1406 as *Campanula capillaris.*)

Edraianthus pumi'lio. Very dwarf cushion-forming perennial. *l.* linear, rarely more than $\frac{1}{2}$ in. long, $\frac{1}{20}$ in. wide, hairy on upper side. *fl.* large, sessile on tuft of l.; ovary glabrous; cal. segs. hairy, about $\frac{1}{5}$ in. long; cor. funnel-shaped, about $\frac{3}{5}$ in. long, violet. May, June. Balkan Peninsula (Dalmatia). SYN. *Wahlenbergia pumilio.* A choice rock-garden plant for scree.

W. saxi'cola. Dwarf perennial; stems 1 to 4 in. h., 1-fld. *l.* basal, oblanceolate, spatulate or lanceolate, to 1 in. long, $\frac{1}{4}$ in. wide, green on both sides, usually glabrous, slightly toothed or entire. *fl.* long-pedicelled; ovary glabrous; cal. segs. almost linear, about $\frac{1}{10}$ in. long; cor. bell-shaped, about $\frac{2}{5}$ in. long, up to $\frac{1}{2}$ in. diameter, light blue. Tasmania. SYN. *Campanula saxicola.* The plant commonly grown and figured in B.M. 6613 as *W. saxicola* is *W. albomarginata.*

Edraianthus serpyllifolius (*Wahlenbergia serpyllifolia*)

Edraianthus serpyllifo'lius. Dwarf mat-forming perennial. *l.* basal, in rosettes, oblanceolate, to $\frac{4}{5}$ in. long, $\frac{1}{10}$ in. wide, ciliated on margin, otherwise glabrous. *fl.* solitary on a leafy stem 1 to 6 in. long; ovary glabrous; cal. segs. ciliated, about $\frac{1}{5}$ in. long; cor. bell-shaped, about $\frac{3}{5}$ to $\frac{4}{5}$ in. long, buds deep red, opening to rich-purple-violet. June. Balkan Peninsula (Dalmatia, Bosnia, Albania). (J.R.H.S. 58 (1933), p. 1, as *Wahlenbergia serpyllifolia.*) SYN. *Campanula serpyllifolia, Wahlenbergia serpyllifolia.* var. **ma'jor** has larger *fl.* A good rock-garden plant.

W. trichogy'na. Erect perennial 9 to 24 in. h.; rootstock thick; stems often many, usually unbranched, hairy. *l.* on lower part of stem, paired or alternate, lanceolate or linear-lanceolate, to 2 in. long, $\frac{1}{4}$ in. wide, toothed, hairy. *fl.* large; ovary with short hairs; cal. segs. linear, to $\frac{1}{2}$ in. long; cor. funnel-shaped, about $\frac{7}{10}$ in. long, to $1\frac{1}{4}$ in. diameter, tube whitish with yellow base, lobes spreading, blue. Summer. Australia. Before 1799. (B.M. 691 as *Campanula gracilis*; R.H. 1849, 41 as *W. vincaeflora*; P.F.G. 2 (1851), f. 142 as *W. vincaeflora.*) Often known as *W. gracilis* or *W. vincaeflora.* Best treated as an annual.

W. tubero'sa. Glabrous perennial; rootstock formed of almost globose woody tubers to $1\frac{1}{2}$ in. across; stems erect, 6 to 12 in. h., many-fld. *l.* narrowly oblong, to 1 in. long, toothed, glabrous. *fl.* erect, medium-sized; ovary glabrous; cal. segs. linear; cor. bell-shaped, about $\frac{1}{2}$ in. long, white with 5 longitudinal pink stripes. 1874. Juan Fernandez. (B.M. 6155.) An extraordinary but pretty species for greenhouse cultivation.

W. vinciflo'ra. A synonym of *W. gracilis*, but applied to *W. consimilis* and *W. trichogyna.*

Edraianthus Wettstein'ii. Dwarf tufted perennial. *l.* linear, hairy on upper side, *fl.* solitary or several in a head; cor. funnel-shaped, violet-blue, Balkan Peninsula (Albania, Montenegro).

W. T. S

WAHOO. *See* **Ulmus alata.**

WAILES'IA. A synonym of Dipodium.

Wailes'ii, in honour of G. Wailes, amateur naturalist of Newcastle, *c.* 1842.

WAITZ'IA (in honour of F. A. C. Waitz, b. 1768 at Schaumberg, Germany, State physician to the Dutch at Samarang, Java, who wrote on Javanese plants). FAM. *Compositae.* A genus of 6 species of annual Australian herbs, with alternate linear leaves. The 'everlasting' flower-heads are usually in terminal corymbs, rarely in oblong, leafy racemes; involucral bracts all coloured and petal-like in many overlapping rows; receptacles without scales; florets numerous, all fertile, tubular, 5-toothed; achenes ending in a slender beak. For treatment *see* **Celosia.** Greenhouse plants.

W. acumina'ta. A synonym of *W. corymbosa.*

W. au'rea. About 1 to 2 ft. h. *l.* like those of *W. corymbosa. fl.-heads* rather larger, fewer and in looser corymbs than in *W. corymbosa*; involucre golden-yellow or tinged brown, bracts longer than fl. Summer. 1835. (B.R. 1941 as *Morna nitida.*)

W. corymbo'sa. Roughly hairy or hoary, 1 to 2 ft. h. *l.* linear, lower 2 to 3 in. long, stem-clasping, margins revolute. *fl.-heads* numerous in a dense, terminal corymb; involucre dark or pale yellow, white or light pink, outer bracts passing into small scales. Summer. 1864. (B.M. 5443; G.F. 401 as *W. acuminata.*)

W. grandiflo'ra. 1 to 2 ft. h. *l.* like those of *W. corymbosa* but less hairy. *fl.-heads* bright yellow, much larger than those of *W. aurea.* Summer. 1863. Rather easier to grow than *W. aurea.*

W. ni'vea. A synonym of *W. odontolepis.*

W. odontole'pis. About 18 in. h. *l.* linear, roughly downy, or nearly smooth. *fl.-heads* rather large, usually few, in a dense corymb; involucral bracts pure white or pink or very rarely pale yellowish, not longer than the florets. Summer. 1863. (B.R. 1838, 9 as *Morna nivea.*)

W. Steetzia'na. Under 1 ft. h. *l.* linear. *fl.-heads* solitary or in loose corymbs, smaller than in *W. nivea*; involucre varying from pure white to pale or bright yellow, hemispherical, about $\frac{1}{2}$ in. across. Summer. 1861. (B.M. 5342 as *W. tenella.*)

W. tenel'la. A synonym of *W. Steetziana.*

WAIUATUA. *See* **Rhabdothamnus Solandri.**

WAKE ROBIN. *See* **Arum maculatum, Trillium grandiflorum.**

Wakefield'ii, in honour of the Rev. Thomas Wakefield, 1836–1901, who sent plants to Kew from E. Trop. Africa.

WALAFRI'DA (in honour of the Benedictine monk Wahlafrid Strabo, A.D. 809–49, abbot of Reichenau in Germany in 842, author of a celebrated Latin poem *Hortulus*, 'The Little Garden'). FAM. *Scrophulariaceae.* A genus of about 30 species of shrubs, sub-shrubs, sometimes annual herbs, closely akin to Selago and united with it by Bentham and Hooker but restored in the *Flora Capensis.* Walafrida is distinguished from Selago (which has a 5-lobed calyx) by having a 3-lobed sometimes 2-lobed calyx. In other respects the botanical characters agree with those of Selago. For cultivation *see* **Selago.**

W. myrtifo'lia.* Sub-shrub, 1 to 2 ft., loosely branched; shoots slender, terete, downy. *l.* scattered, narrow-oblong to lanceolate, up to $\frac{3}{4}$ in. long. *fl.* in terminal, corymbose clusters 1 to $1\frac{1}{4}$ in. across; cor. purple, $\frac{1}{4}$ in. wide, tube slender, $\frac{1}{4}$ in. long; lobes $\frac{1}{8}$ in. long. March. S. Africa. 1829. (B.M. 3028 and B.R. 1504 as *Selago Gillii.*)

W. rotundifo'lia. Sub-shrub, 1 to 2 ft. or more; shoots erect, downy. *l.* densely set, orbicular to oval-oblong, $\frac{1}{8}$ to $\frac{3}{8}$ in. long, glaucous. *fl.* purple, closely set in terminal, corymbose clusters or panicles up to 2 in. across; tube of cor. $\frac{1}{4}$ in. long, lobes $\frac{1}{12}$ in. long. S. Africa. 1814. SYN. *Selago rotundifolia.*

WALDSTEIN'IA (in honour of Count Franz Adam Waldstein-Wartenburg, 1759–1823, Austrian botanist and author). FAM. *Rosaceae.* A genus of 5 species of creeping perennial herbs with the general habit of Fragaria, natives of the north temperate zone. Leaves mostly basal, 3- to 5-cleft or 3- to 5-foliolate, toothed, long-stalked; stipules rather large, membranous. Flowers yellow, about $\frac{1}{2}$ in. across, in corymbs; calyx 5-partite, usually with an outer calyx of 5 small segments, persistent; petals 5, obovate; stamens numerous; carpels 2 to 6. Achenes pubescent, borne on a short, dry axis.

Easily grown in ordinary soil, for the rock-garden, front of border or edge of wood, best planted to form large mats; unfortunately the flowers are freely produced at the edge of the mat and not over its whole surface. Propagated by division or by seed.

KEY

1. *Lvs. divided into 3 lflets.*	2
1. *Lvs. deeply lobed*	3
2. *Outer cal. (with very short segs.) present*	W. ternata
2. *Outer cal. lacking*	W. fragarioides
3. *Infl. with glandular hairs*	W. idahoensis
3. *Infl. without glandular hairs*	4
4. *Infl. with bracts only*	W. lobata
4. *Infl. with lvs.*	W. geoides

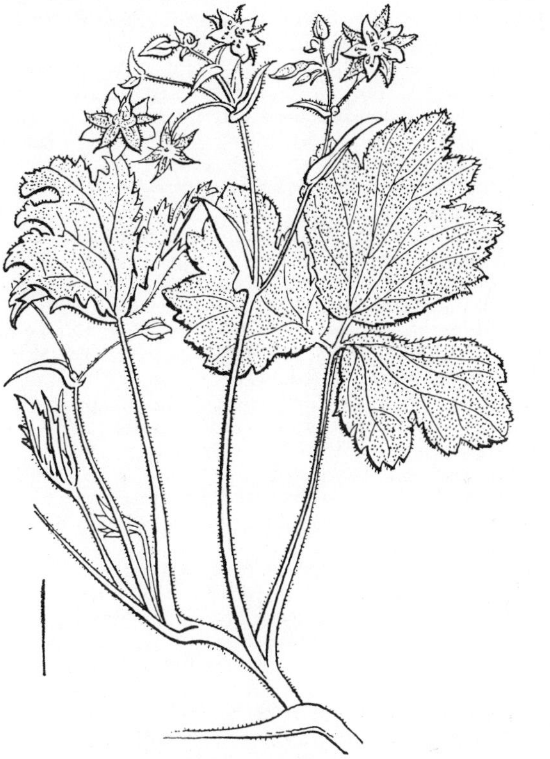

Waldsteinia fragarioides

W. fragarioi'des. Downy or nearly glabrous mat-forming perennial. *l.* 3-foliolate; lflets. broadly wedge-shaped, 1 to 2 in. long, toothed except at base. *fl.* in 3- to 8-fld. corymbs; carpels 4 to 6. May, June. E. United States. (B.M. 1567 and L.B.C. 408 as *Dalibarda fragarioides.*)

W. geoi'des. 2 to 10 in. h. with a shortly creeping rhizome. *l.* palmately deeply 3- to usually 5-lobed, lobes somewhat coarsely toothed; basal l. long-stalked. *fl.* about ¾ in. across, little raised above l.; pet. obovate. April, May. E. Europe. 1804. (B.M. 2595.)

W. idahoen'sis. 4 to 10 in. h. *l.* shallowly 5- to 7-lobed and toothed, cordate, almost orbicular. *fl.* with almost orbicular pet., in loose 2- to 7-fld. racemes; carpels 2. Idaho.

W. loba'ta. Slightly hairy. *l.* cordate, 3-lobed, teeth mucronulate; stalks slender, longer than blades. *fl.* with narrow-oblong or elliptic pet.; carpels 2. Georgia to N. Carolina.

W. terna'ta. Plant rather small, about 4 in. h. *l.* in rosettes at the tips of the shoots, 3-foliolate, hairy, long-stalked; lflets. shortly stalked, middle one broad-obovate, lateral narrower. *fl.* about ½ in. across, long-stalked, erect in 3- to 7-fl. racemes; pet. not auricled at base, longer than sep. April, May. E. Europe, Siberia, Japan. SYN. *W. sibirica*, *W. trifolia.*

W. trifo'lia. A synonym of *W. ternata.*

Walker'ae, in honour of the wife of General Walker who collected ferns, &c., in Ceylon, &c.

Walker'i, in honour of General George Warren Walker, d. 1844, who collected and introduced plants from India, &c.

WALKING LEAF. *See* **Camptosorus rhizophyllus.**

WALL CRESS. *See* **Arabis.**

WALL FERN. *See* **Polypodium vulgare.**

WALL PENNYWORT. *See* **Umbilicus pendulinus. A**

WALL PEPPER. *See* **Sedum acre.**

WALL PLANTS. The term Wall Plants may include plants grown against walls for support and also many others which from their quick growing habit may be used for covering a large surface rapidly, or, being more or less tender, are grown with greater certainty and brought to greater perfection by the shelter which a wall affords.

Another type of wall plant is the dwarf hardy plant of tufted or mat-forming habit that can root into the crevices of a dry wall, that is a wall built of blocks of stone bedded in earth, but not in mortar or cement. Usually backed by a bank of earth, such walls, properly built and preferably planted as the building progresses, often make a very pleasant and enduring feature in a garden, requiring comparatively little attention after their first building.

Walls surrounding the kitchen garden are usually utilized for the cultivation of fruit-trees that will not succeed in the open, and in some places give a suitable position for tomatoes since greater heat can be secured there than in the open ground.

Many ornamental plants are best grown against a wall in most parts of the country and many will be found in the body of the Dictionary with this recommendation, among them the following hardy or nearly hardy plants: *Aristolochia durior*, *Campsis grandiflora*, *C. radicans*, Ceanothus sp., Celastrus sp., Chaenomeles sp., *Chimonanthus praecox*, many species of Clematis and the many beautiful hybrids, Cotoneasters, Eccremocarpus, Eriobotrya, Escallonias, Euonymus sp., *Forsythia suspensa*, &c., *Garrya elliptica*, Ivies, *Jasminum nudiflorum*, *J. primulinum*, *J. officinale*, *J. revolutum*, Loniceras, Magnolias, Pyracanthas, Roses, hardy Vines, Virginia Creepers (Ampelopsis and Parthenocissus), and Wisterias. In choosing plants regard should be given to the colour of the wall. Some species are able to cling to walls by means of aerial roots, e.g. the common Ivy (Hedera), or of adhesive disks on their tendrils, e.g. the Virginia Creepers, but many need support. This can be provided by passing a strip of strong cloth over the stem and nailing the ends either side to the brickwork by long stout nails driven into the mortar. Another method is to fasten horizontal lengths of wire about 8 to 12 in. apart across the wall, the ends of the wire being secured to metal pins with hooks or eyelet holes; the plant is then tied to the wires. For twining plants the supports should be vertical not horizontal.

The walls of cool greenhouses afford space for strong-growing Tea Roses and Bougainvilleas; Fuchsias, Heliotropes, Jasmines, Passionflowers, Streptosolen are other useful plants for this position, while *Ficus pumila* will cover a wall in a cool house with a dense green curtain as will Ivy outside.

Of plants for the dry wall species and varieties of Antirrhinum, Campanula, Cheiranthus, Dianthus, Erinus, Ferns, Iberis, Onosma, Scabiosa, Sedum and Sempervivum all furnish good examples, and many other tufted and mat-forming species may be used if the moisture-supply is suitable.

WALL RUE. *See* **Asplenium Ruta-muraria.**

Wallacea'nus -a -um, in honour of Alfred Russel Wallace, 1823–1913, British naturalist and traveller.

WALLFLOWER. *See* **Cheiranthus Cheiri.**

WALLFLOWER, ALPINE. *See* **Erysimum dubium.**

WALLFLOWER, SIBERIAN. *See* **Cheiranthus Allionii.**

WALLICH'IA (in honour of Nathaniel Wallich, *née* Nathan Wolff, 1786–1854, Danish botanist, author of important works on Indian plants). FAM. *Palmaceae*. A genus of 3 species of Himalayan palms. Low, tufted plants with short branching or tall stems. Leaves in a dense terminal cluster, in 2 ranks, unequally pinnately cut, scurfy; segments sometimes clustered, oblong, obovate or oblanceolate, coarsely toothed; stalks slender, laterally compressed; sheaths short, cut and long-ciliate at margins. Flowers usually monoecious or dioecious, yellowish; spathes many, rather leathery, lower ones narrow, tubular, upper boat-shaped; stamens 6. Allied to Arenga, which has 3 distinct sepals, Didymosperma, where the calyx is cup-shaped and 3-lobed, and Caryota by the uniform albumen of the seed. Fruit reddish or purple, oblong-ovoid, usually 1-seeded. Wallichias need a strong rich soil and stove conditions. They are propagated by gradually separating the suckers so that they become rooted before being completely detached, or by seeds.

W. caryotoi'des. Stem very short or none, often covered with persistent l.-bases. *l.* few, alternate, 3 to 8 ft. long; lflets. 12 to 15 in. long, lower in opposite clusters, upper mostly solitary and alternate, deep shining green above, whitish beneath. *Spadix* about 18 in. long. *Male fl.* numerous, yellowish-white; *female* purplish, few. July. *fr.* ovate-oblong, as large as a nutmeg. India. 1825.

W. densiflo'ra. Habit of *W. caryotoides*. *l.* up to 12 ft. long. *Male spadices* enclosed in large, overlapping, dark purple spathes streaked yellow; *female spadices* clustered, nearly white, *fl.* violet. Assam. 1840. (B.M. 4584.)

W. dis'ticha. 10 to 15 ft. h., stem 5 or 6 in. thick. *l.* 6 to 10 ft. long, alternate in a ⅓ spiral, erect, graceful; lflets. 1 to 2 ft. long, 2 to 2½ in. wide, clustered, linear, toothed at tip with a large tooth each side of middle, glaucous beneath; stalk and sheath short, scurfy. *Spadix* 3 to 8 ft. long. *fl.* green. Himalaya.

Wallichia'nus -a -um, Wallich'ii, in honour of N. Wallich; *see* **Wallichia.**

Wallis'ii, in honour of Gustav Wallis, 1830–78, who collected in the Andes, &c., for William Bull, nurseryman of Chelsea.

Wallroth'ii, in honour of Karl Friedrich Wilhelm Wallroth, 1792–1857, of Nordhausen, writer on the German flora.

WALNUT (*Juglans regia*). The common Walnut is a tree with fine foliage, making a notable ornament for planting in parks, paddocks, &c., useful for its fruits both in the young and in the ripened condition, and for its timber, employed in cabinet-work, &c., and for the making of gun-stocks.

Walnut-trees succeed in any fairly good soil; if it is of good depth overlying gravel so much the better. The trees are winter-hardy but both the young shoots and the fruits are liable to much injury by late spring frosts, and sites where spring frosts are likely to be severe should therefore be avoided. Propagation is effected by seeds, by grafting, budding, and by inarching. For timber and park trees, and for stocks, seed is the usual method of propagation, and where possible for the first two purposes the seed is best sown where the trees are to grow. For stocks and for nursery purposes generally the seed may be stratified through the winter and sown in nursery rows about 2 ft. apart in the following February or March. The seedling trees may be transplanted in the following autumn or allowed to remain a year longer. They form a long tap-root which grows straight down, and if transplanting has to be done it should not be long deferred. Stocks for budding or grafting may be seedlings 1 year old of either *J. regia* or *J. nigra*, the latter being suitable for trees in cultivated land, which does not so well suit *J. regia* stocks, or they may be layered plants of the same species. Where *J. nigra* stocks are used the very long, almost fibreless roots are best shortened by about one-third so that the ends shall not be turned up in planting, for this is apt to delay growth. Ring-budding may be used on trees up to 25 years of age with some success in May, delaying the cutting-back until the following year when the union is thoroughly lignified. Budding is done on 1-year old wood. The greatest success, however, has been attained by grafting under glass in March, provided sound scion wood is used. Another method is to graft with leafy shoots in July, taking great care that the scions are kept turgid. A warm close frame is needed for this.

Pruning should be kept at a minimum as much bleeding usually follows the cutting of branches.

Walnuts rarely come into bearing until they have been established for some years. It is uncommon to see fruit on any trees less than 15 to 20 years of age, but dwarf trees may be induced to fruit at a much younger period by planting a young grafted tree in good but not rich soil and pinching out the tips of the shoots with finger and thumb (not cutting with a knife) just behind the terminal bud when the shoot has attained 5 or 6 leaves. This must be done throughout the year on all moderately strong growths and continued annually. The thin shoots on which the male flowers are produced should not be pinched.

The fruits of the black walnut, *J. nigra*, are of little value in Britain, and those of *J. regia* vary greatly from tree to tree, some bearing excellent nuts of good flavour well filling the shells, others being of poor quality. Care should be taken therefore in selecting scions, using only those from named varieties of good repute, or from trees which are known to bear good crops of fine quality regularly. Walnuts for pickling should be gathered while the shell is quite soft so that a needle can be passed through them readily. The ripe fruits drop and the shells split and disclose the nuts. Squirrels collect and store the nuts in considerable numbers and rooks often cause considerable loss just as the shells begin to harden about the second week in September, usually feeding in the trees during the first hour of daylight.

Walnuts may be preserved for use during winter. Several methods are in use. The nuts may be dried and packed in clean jars or casks with alternate layers of sand, or placed in jars with close-fitting lids and buried in the ground. Another way is to put them in jars and sprinkle them with salt or bury them in sawdust.

For recommended varieties see Supplement.

DISEASES. Walnut-trees may be attacked in their roots by the Honey Fungus (q.v.), so that when planting walnuts old stumps and other debris should be carefully removed from the selected site. Other diseases which may enter through wounds and cause much trouble are Silver Leaf and Coral Spot (qq.v.). In grafting many failures can be caused by the fungus *Chalaropsis thielavioides* which enters the junction and kills the scion. Clean methods are necessary, the stock being painted with 2 per cent. Formalin solution before being cut and the knife also being sterilized. There is a Leaf Blotch due to the fungus *Gnomonia leptostyla* (*Marsonina juglandis*) which is fairly common and appears as large discoloured patches, first yellowish-brown and later dark brown. These dark blotches also appear on the green shells containing the young nuts, so that if required for pickling they are spoilt. The fungus overwinters on the fallen leaves and the best remedy is to rake up these fallen leaves and burn them. Perhaps the most serious disease, however, is Bacterial Blight (*Pseudomonas juglandis*), which causes very small angular blackish spots on the leaves often aggregated towards the leaf-tips. Similar spots may attack the green shells of the young fruits and the shoots may show elongated black patches. The disease is most severe on young trees in nurseries and should be treated by cutting away affected shoots while frequently wiping the knife with a cloth moistened with formalin or lysol, and, in addition, the trees should be sprayed once or twice in the season with Bordeaux mixture. In walnut fruits the shells of the nuts sometimes do not mature or harden properly but show thin places or even holes, so that the kernels are not covered. This seems to be more common in some varieties than in others, but shortage of potash combined with lack of sunshine is considered to be the chief reason. Before storing walnuts they should be thoroughly cleaned and dried, otherwise they may be attacked by *Botrytis cinerea*, the Grey Mould fungus (q.v.) which generally gains entrance at the suture or crack between the two halves of the shell.

D. E. G.

WALNUT-TREE, INDIAN. *See* **Aleurites moluccana.**

Walsh'ae, in honour of Maria Ernestine Walsh, *née* Held, b. 1881, who collected in Australia and E. Indies.

WALUEW'A. Included under **Oncidium.** *W. pulchella* = *O. Waluewa.*

WAMPEE-TREE. *See* **Clausena Lansium.**

WANDERING JEW. A common name for plants with prostrate rooting stems grown in pots or beneath glasshouse staging, e.g. *Saxifraga stolonifera*, *Tradescantia albiflora*, *T. fluminensis*, and *Zebrina pendula*, and sometimes applied also to *Linaria Cymbalaria*.

WANDERING SAILOR. *See* **Linaria Cymbalaria.**

WANGHEE or **WHANGEE CANE.** *See* **Phyllostachys nigra.**

Wan'neri, in honour of Herr Wanner, Conservator of Imperial Forests, Banat, Hungary, *c.* 1814.

WARATAH-TREE. *See* **Telopea speciosissima.**

WARDEN. Old English name for a long-keeping cooking pear used in making 'Warden Pies', named after Warden Abbey, Bedfordshire.

WARDIAN CASE. Wardian Cases are invaluable for packing pot-plants that have to travel long sea voyages. By their aid many new and rare plants of foreign climates have been imported into this country, and others are exported in a similar way. The importation and exportation of plants in Wardian Cases is mostly conducted by some of the principal nurserymen and those in charge of botanic gardens, who usually make special arrangements, so that what they send away or have sent to them shall be of sufficient value and importance to warrant the outlay incurred, which is often somewhat considerable. Certain seasons are also selected for sending plants to particular countries abroad, such as are best calculated to favour a safe voyage in respect of the effect of climatic conditions on the plants during transit. Wardian Cases are made in different sizes to hold small or somewhat large plants, as the case may be. The pots are usually packed in soil or cocoa fibre, and held in position by narrow strips of wood, which are firmly secured by nailing them close down on the top of each inside the Case. The roof, if it may be so called, is made of 2 frames which fit on the ends and meet together at the top, where they form a ridge. They are glazed and the glass protected by thin pieces of wood, which are fixed a short distance apart, so as to allow as much light as possible to pass to the plants inside. One or both of these sash-frames is movable, and may be unscrewed and taken off for the purpose of packing or unpacking. When travelling, Wardian Cases are nearly air-tight, so that but little evaporation or change of air can take place, only a small circular hole, covered with perforated zinc, being allowed at each of the ends near the top. The frames in which the glass is embedded are made air-tight by being fitted up with putty before being screwed. Instructions are invariably given as to the part of a ship where Wardian Cases should be placed during the voyage.

Other kinds of Wardian Cases are those used for plant-growing in drawing-rooms, &c., and in ferneries, for the special accommodation of Filmy Ferns, and such as require a very moist atmosphere. The former, with the stands on which they are placed, are usually rendered ornamental for associating with the surroundings, and have a fine appearance when filled with green Ferns, small foliage plants, and Lycopods. In Ferneries, such cases may be quite plain externally; they, of course, answer their purpose equally well for preserving moisture inside.

Wardii, in honour of (1) Dr. Nathaniel Bagshaw Ward, 1791–1868, inventor of the Wardian case, (2) Frank Kingdon-Ward, b. 1885, botanical collector and explorer, especially in W. China and N. Burma.

warleyen'sis -is -e, of Warley Place, Essex, the home of Miss Ellen A. Willmott.

Warmingia'nus -a -um, in honour of Professor Johannes Eugenius Bülow Warming, 1841–1924, of Copenhagen, celebrated Danish botanist and pioneer ecologist.

Warocques'nus -a -um, in honour of Herr Warocque of Charlroi, Belgium, *c.* 1890.

WARPUR'IA (in honour of G. Warpur who collected *W. clandestina*). FAM. *Acanthaceae.* A monotypic genus. Low herb with opposite leaves, entire or nearly so. Flowers white, minute, in dense many-flowered cymes, collected in heads; calyx hyaline, 5-parted, segments narrow; corolla rather tube-like with 5 minute lobes; stamens 4; disk ring-like. Fruit a capsule with a beak. Warm greenhouse conditions suit it, with cultural conditions as for Fittonia.

W. clandesti'na. Small low herb. *l.* lanceolate, slightly scalloped, veins hairy beneath, of a beautiful crystalline pale green above, with a broad zigzag intensely black band down each side of midrib. *fl.* very minute, in a small globular head on a longish strigose pedicel. Madagascar. 1908. A striking foliage plant. The insignificant fls. are best removed.

WAR'REA (named by Lindley in honour of its discoverer, Frederick Warre, who sent *W. tricolor* to the Loddiges by whom it was figured as *Maxillaria Warreana*). FAM. *Orchidaceae.* A small genus of about 3 species of terrestrial orchids, natives of Brazil, Colombia, Peru, Costa Rica. Flowers showy, open, globose, shortly stalked; sepals and petals very similar; the sepals broad, concave, oblique at base, adnate to the foot of the long clavate column; lip affixed to foot of column, sessile, shortly contracted at base and incumbent, at length erect, broad, concave, lateral lobes not prominent, mid-lobe expanded, entire or 2-fid, disk with elevated fleshy lines. Pollinia 4. Racemes elongated, loose. Scapes leafless, many-sheathed, tall, simple. Bracts short. Leaves few, distichous, often tapered, plicate. Pseudobulbs ovoid or elongated. Several species formerly included in this genus are now placed in Zygopetalum, Paradisanthus, or Aganisia. The plants have a superficial resemblance to Phaius of the *P. grandifolius* section and should be given a similar compost but with a smaller proportion of loam. Winter night temperature should be not less than 60° F. Propagation is by division, but of late years few large plants have been seen. **A**

W. bidenta'ta. Allied to *W. tricolor* and sometimes regarded as a variety of that species. Lip longer and narrower, and not so transverse, with a deep frontal sinus, keel at base very sharp, disk covered with small callosities. Colombia. Before 1844. SYN. *W. Lindeniana.*

W. grandiflo'ra. *fl.* 8 to 10, large; sep. whitish; pet. marbled white and rose; lip flushed crimson with blackish-brown marbling in middle. Peru.

W. Hookeria'na. Allied to *W. tricolor* but with larger fls. Rather more robust. *fl.* reddish-purple, segs. palest in centre; lip darker. Peru. 1910. SYN. *Phaius Hookerianus.*

W. Lindenia'na. A synonym of *W. bidentata.*

W. tri'color.* *fl.* 8 to 10, large, sub-globose, drooping; sep. and pet. yellowish-white often brownish, yellow externally, lateral sep. ending in a short obtuse spur; lip yellow and purple, white on the waved margin, concave at base with 3 ridges; scapes about 2 ft. long, purple at joints. *Pseudobulbs* sub-cylindric, tapered, 3 to 5 in. h. *l.* 4 or 5, 12 to 20 in. long, 2 to 4 in. wide, long stalked, lanceolate. Summer. Brazil. 1829. (X.O. 24; B.M. 4235; L.B.C. 1884 as *Maxillaria Warreana.*) var. **bidenta'ta** *see* **W. bidentata, stapelioi'des,** sep. and pet. yellowish-white with 5 purplish-brown bars and purplish spots, lip brownish-purple at base, margin reddish-yellow. Colombia. 1872; **unijugat'a,** sep. and pet. white, lip purplish, obscurely veined, the front emarginate.

W. unijugat'a. A variety of *W. tricolor.*

E. C.

WARREEL'LA (allied to Warrea). FAM. *Orchidaceae.* A monotypic genus of epiphytic orchids now separated from Zygopetalum and Aganisia. Pseudobulbs are absent or nearly so but the plants differ from Bollea, Huntleya, &c., in that the scapes are several-flowered. The sessile lip bears a somewhat fan-shaped callus from base to middle. Treatment, compost, &c., should be as for Huntleya.

W. cya'nea. *fl.* 4 to 8, about 1 in. across; sep. and pet. oval-oblong, white or faintly tinted blue; lip rhomboidly fan-shape, bluish on margins, whitish at base, apiculate, crest with about 5 lamellae; scapes about 12 in. h. *l.* lanceolate, pointed, plicate, 7 to 12 in. long, 1 in. or more wide. Colombia. 1843. (B.R. 1845, 28 as *Warrea cyanea.*) SYN. *Aganisia cyanea.*

E. C.

WARSCEWICZEL'LA (in honour of Józef Warszewicz, 1812–66; see below). FAM. *Orchidaceae.* A genus of perhaps 18 epiphytic species distributed in Brazil, Costa Rica, Peru. At one time placed under Zygopetalum, the genus has been restored by some as decided differences from true Zygopetalums are apparent. The species more nearly resemble Bollea as pseudobulbs are absent, the habit is tufted, the scapes are single-flowered, usually shorter than the numerous rather thin leaves with raised veins which are distichously arranged. Flowers large, often fragrant, upper sepal free, the lateral affixed to the short foot of the column; petals similar; lip slightly 3-lobed, sessile or shortly clawed to column foot; often somewhat square or rounded; disk transverse, curved, crested; column with or without 2 small wings; pollinia 4. Compost and treatment should be as for Huntleyas, but the plants must be studied. A winter night temperature of 60° F. suits those from Costa Rica and the hills of Brazil. All are impatient of direct sunlight and shading should be carefully attended to in bright weather. Propagation is by division of large plants, but care is required as the rather fleshy roots are often entangled.

W. amazon'ica.* *fl.* white, dorsal sep. about 1¼ in. long, lateral longer; pet. as long as dorsal, sep. slightly wider, all reflexed; lip obscurely lobed emarginate, 2 in. long, 1½ in. wide, with forked purplish or reddish veins on lower half. *l.* 6 to 10 in. long, about 1 in. wide. Brazil. 1854. (R.X.O. 1, 222, 93; J. H. 1892, f. 79 as *W. Lindeni*; L. 337 and G.C. 14 (1893) 493 as *Zygopetalum Lindeni.*)

W. aromat'ica.* *fl.* 3 to 4 in. across; sep. and pet. lanceolate, acute; lip azure blue, purplish at base, obreniform, many lobuled, slightly crisped, disk with a many furrowed callus at the contracted base. *l.* cuneate-oblong, acute. Chiriqui. 1868? (R.X.O. 173 as *Zygopetalum aromaticum.*) SYN. *Huntleya aromatica.*

W. cand'ida.* *fl.* 2½ in. across; sep. white, lanceolate, acute; pet. white, broader, reflexed, lip quadrate-hastate, rosy-purple in centre, margin broad, bluish, disk with large obtriangular callus with a retuse 5-toothed apex and 5 bluish-purple bars. *l.* oblong-lanceolate, 6 to 12 in. long, about 1 in. wide. Bahia. 1852. SYN. *Warrea candida, Huntleya candida, H. radicans, Zygopetalum candidum.*

W. cochlear'is. A synonym of *W. flabelliformis.*

W. cochlea'ta. A synonym of *W. flabelliformis.*

W. dis'color.* *fl.* 2 to 3 in. across; sep. white or straw-yellow, upper erect or inclined forward, lower deflexed; pet. purple-tinted, more or less convolute over column; lip concave, deep velvety purple, whitish at base with a yellow oblong appendage divided at edge into strong diverging teeth, 5 of which terminate in as many ribs, side lobes large, mid-lobe rounded, broader than long, margin almost entire; column short, whitish, with purplish flush in front. *l.* 6 to 12 in. long. Cent. America, Costa Rica. 1848. (X.O. 1, 93 and B.M. 4830 as *Warrea discolor.*) SYN. *Zygopetalum discolor.* var. **atrocoeru'leum,** *fl.* larger than type, sep. cream-white, pet. tinged lilac-blue, lip violet-blue, crest marked with white. Costa Rica. 1905.

W. flabelliform'is.* Sep. and narrow pet. white; dorsal sep. 1¼ in. long, half as wide, lateral longer; lip over 1 in. long, wider than long, concave, rather broadly rounded, sessile, margin undulate, white or stained purple, usually with branching purplish veins, disk broadly sub-orbicular with many furrows, margin minutely crenulate. *l.* up to 12 in. long, 2 in. wide. Variable. West Indies, Brazil. Before 1836. (B.M. 3585 as *Zygopetalum cochleare*; L. 189 as *Z. Gibeziae.*) SYN. *Warscewiczella cochlearis, W. cochleata Gibeziae, Warrea cochleata, W. Gibeziae, Zygopetalum flabelliformis.*

W. Linden'ii. A synonym of *W. amazonica.*

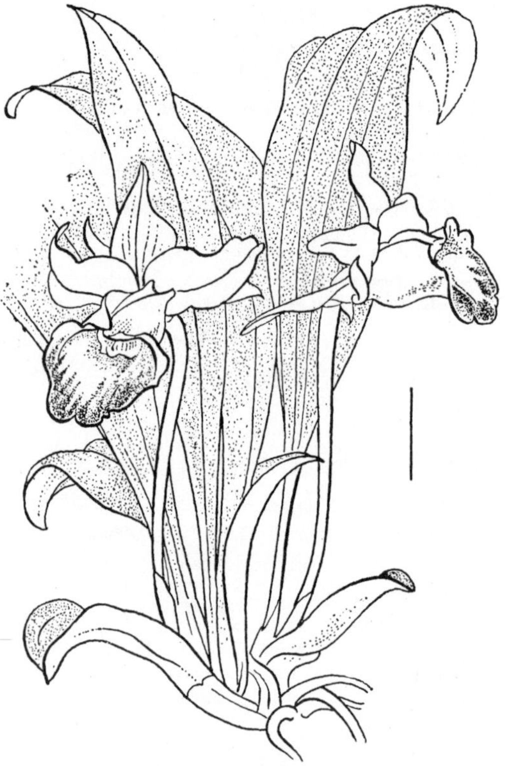

Warscewiczella marginata

W. margina'ta.* Allied to *W. discolor.* Sep. and pet. elliptic, 1¼ in. long; lateral sep. and pet. reflexed, dorsal erect, whitish or pale straw-yellow; lip rounded, retuse, with reflexed edges, more or less flushed and veined purple, claw yellow with a slight tubercle, crest nearly square, marked purple; column white. *l.* oblong-acute, 6 in. or more long. Colombia. Before 1852. (R.X.O. 23, 2; B.M. 4766 as *Warrea quadrata*; B.M. 5582; R.X.O. 23, 1 as *Warscewiczella velata.*) SYN. *W. marginata, Zygopetalum velatum, Z. marginatum, Huntleya marginata.*

W. pic'ta. Much like *W. discolor*, but lip rhomboidal and crisped, yellowish-white, with numerous broad purple marginal lines, brownish basal borders, and a greenish tablet-like basal callus with 2 teeth in front and a few on the sides; sep. pale greenish or yellowish-white. 1883. SYN. *Zygopetalum pictum.*

W. vela'ta. A synonym of *W. marginata.*

W. Wailesia'na. *fl.* of moderate size, scented like sweet peas; sep. and pet. white or cream; lip roundish, concave, white stained and striated in centre with violet, crest of 5 radiating finger-like bars, free except at their origin. *l.* 6 to 9 in. long, about 1 in. wide. Brazil. 1849. (B.H. 1878, 10; P.F.G. 1, 73 as *Zygopetalum Wailesianum*; I.H. iv, 152 as *Warrea digitata.*) SYN. *Warrea Wailesiana.*

W. Wendland'ii.* *fl.* about 4 in. across; sep. and pet. white, lanceolate, somewhat twisted; lip with a cordate or cordate-reniform limb, white, with a large blotch and lines of violet-purple, margin undulate, many-lobuled, crest semi-lunate with 7 or more short violet-purple ridges. *l.* narrow, oblong-ligulate, 7 to 10 in. long. Allied to *W. aromatica.* Costa Rica. 1858. (R. 53 as *Zygopetalum Wendlandii.*) var. **dis'color,** sep. and pet. yellowish-green, lip 1½ in. across, white with a large bright violet blotch in centre, margin much crisped and minutely lobed. (W.O.A. 126.)

E. C.

***Warszewiczia'nus* (*Warscewiczia'nus*) *-a -um*, *Warszewicz'ii* (*Warscewicz'ii*),** in honour of the Polish Lithuanian plant collector Józef Warszewicz (pronounced Var-chev-ich), 1812–66, who left Poland foı his part in the 1830 rebellion and travelled extensively in S. America, collecting orchids, &c., for Messrs. van Houtte; from 1853 he was Inspector of the Krakow botanic garden.

WART-DISEASE. *See* **Potato Wart-disease.**

WARTED GOURD. *See* **Cucurbita Pepo verrucosa.**

WARTS. Hard or firm rounded excrescences on any part of a plant.

WASHINGTON THORN. *See* **Crataegus cordata. A**

WASHINGTON'IA (in honour of George Washington, 1732–99, the great American). FAM. *Palmaceae.* A genus of 2 species of tall palms, natives of the S. United States and California. Trunks covered above with remains of leaves. Leaves terminal, large, spreading, roundish, flabellately plicate, cut nearly to middle; segments filiferous on edges; stalks long, robust, flat-convex, margins very spiny. Spadices long, much branched, branches slender, flexuous. Flowers white, perfect. For treatment *see* **Chamaerops.** **A**

W. fili'fera. Tree of 20 to 40 ft., stem cylindrical. *l.* orbicular, fan-like; stalks with stout, hooked, marginal spines; blade deeply cleft along upper folds, very filiferous. California. var. **robust'a,** taller, l.-stalks grooved above, *l.* more deeply cleft. S. California.

Wason'ii, in honour of Lieut.-Com. Cathcart Wason, R.N., of H.M.S. *Woodlark* at Chungking, 1903–4.

WASP BEETLE. *See* **Longicorn Beetles.**

WASPS. The common Wasp and its relatives are too well known to require any description, but 'Wasps' is a general name to include a number of species, both Solitary and Social. There are 7 species of Social Wasps, including the Hornet (q.v.), and more than twice that number of Solitary Wasps, in which only males and females occur with no workers or neuters. These Solitary insects form cells in dry banks, among heather, and elsewhere and provision them with insects upon which their grubs feed, and are never destructive to fruit. At least 2 species of Social Wasps—the Common, *Vespula vulgaris*, and the German Wasp, *V. germanica*—cause considerable annoyance to gardeners and fruit-growers in August and September by their attacks on ripening Apples, Pears, and Plums and, in glasshouses, to Grapes, Peaches, and Nectarines. They puncture the skin of the fruit, devour the fleshy portion, and leave a shrivelled husk; and often ruin a far greater quantity by biting out portions of odd fruits here and there. Wasps are important pests of these fruits in autumn, but they also do a vast amount of good in spring and summer by hunting insects of all kinds and carrying them back to their nests. Despite the good they do, it is essential to take active measures against them to avoid serious loss of hardy and glasshouse fruits.

The female or queen is the only individual to survive the winter, the torpid insect often being found sheltering in cracks and crevices in sheds, outhouses, barns, glasshouses, and similar places. In spring the queen becomes active and seeks a place suitable for the construction of the nest—some species being ground- others tree-builders and suspend their nests from the branches of trees and shrubs. The nest is formed of wasp-paper, a grey, fragile substance formed of finely triturated wood obtained either from sound or weathered wood according to the habits of the particular species. A small group of cells is attached to the apex of the newly formed nest, and the grubs are tended and fed by the female. The Wasps from these original cells form the first batch of workers and take a share in the work of the nest. Soon the queen remains altogether in the nest and concentrates on egg-laying. Only workers are produced during late spring and summer, but later both males or drones and females or future queens appear. The females after pairing with the males seek out some crevice in which to pass the winter. The remainder—old queen, workers, and males—die during the late autumn on the approach of cold weather.

The hibernating queen Wasps may be destroyed when found, and also captured in spring, especially on the flowers of Cotoneasters and on Paeony and Cistus buds—their destruction disposing for all time of a potential colony later in the year. The usual method of destroying a nest is either to pour a solution of Potassium or Sodium cyanide or to place some granular Calcium cyanide (ALL VERY POISONOUS) into the entrance to the nest, which should be left open. Less poisonous preparations may be used with equal effect, namely, Derris dust, a tablespoonful of the powder being placed at the entrance of the hole, or Tetrachlorethane poured in the entrance. Derris powder does not destroy the grubs and pupae within their cells, so that it is advisable to dig the nest out the following day. It is not always possible to discover every nest, so that numbers of Wasps may still continue to invade vineries and orchards, from the fruit of which they may be diverted by placing narrow-mouthed bottles and jars, baited with syrup or jam mixed with beer, suspended from the wires of glasshouses or branches. The Wasps entering the traps cannot easily escape and are drowned in the mixture. Bunches of Grapes and high-grade Apple and Pear fruits may be protected by enclosing them in wasp-proof netting.

G. F. W.

WATER. Water is indispensable to the existence of plants of all kinds and upon the attention given to its supply depends to a great extent the difference between success and failure in cultivation. It is well, therefore, for cultivators to understand something of its composition and properties as well as the sources from which it is derived and the methods of regulating its supply. Chemically, water is a compound of Hydrogen and Oxygen in the proportion of 2 parts by volume of the one and 1 of the other, i.e. H_2O. But though that is the normal composition of water, it is now known that various modifications occur in the proportions in which these 2 elements are combined, and that these modifications are found in different amounts, often very minute, in samples of water from different sources. In discussing these variations in his Masters Lectures, 1937 (see *Journal Royal Hort. Soc.* 62, pp. 425 and 473), Sir Edward Salisbury suggests that owing to their presence some water, as that from melted snow, may have a different effect from, say, rain-water (which is nearly pure H_2O), or well water. It cannot be said at present that this is proved, but some observations are certainly significant—the great difficulty of proof lies in the great differences in the amount and kind of the substances which waters from different sources carry in solution. It is known, and has been demonstrated, that exceedingly minute quantities of chemical compounds dissolved in water have an apparently grotesquely disproportionate effect upon plants. It has already been pointed out (*see* **Photosynthesis**) that green plants can decompose water and so obtain their necessary supplies, or some of them, of both Hydrogen and Oxygen for the making of food. This, however, is not the only property of water that makes it of importance to the plant and to the cultivator. In its pure state at ordinary temperatures it is a colourless, tasteless, inodorous liquid, leaving no residue when it evaporates (as it does slowly or rapidly at any temperature). Further, at a low temperature (32° F. or 0° C.) it is converted into solid ice, or into snow. Unlike most other liquids as it approaches the solidifying point it expands, so that at just below 40° F. it is so much lighter than at normal temperature that it rises to the top and freezing occurs there instead of at the bottom of the mass as in most liquids when they solidify. At the same time as the change to the solid state occurs the mass expands, so that 10 lb. of ice occupies and must have the same space as 11 lb. of water occupied. This leads to the bursting of vessels in which water is confined and to the splitting of moist clods and the lifting of plants in the soil in winter and to various other phenomena with which frost has made us familiar, for water is practically incompressible. Water also brings about a further change in its surroundings as it evaporates, for it absorbs a great deal of heat, robbing its surroundings, and so 'cooling the air', one of the ultimate effects of the well-known operations of damping-down and syringing. The combined effect of these peculiarities is that the temperature near great bodies of water is more equable and changes more slowly than in great land masses.

Water has remarkable solvent powers and a great number of substances are more or less soluble in it, and on this account it is the means by which earth-salts are brought to the roots of the plant and absorbed by the root-hairs (*see* **Absorption**). By the same vehicle they are carried, along with other substances made in the plant, from place to place in it where they may be needed. The fact also that gases, as well as solids, are soluble in water leads to the increase in its power of dissolving solids, for few natural water-supplies are wholly deficient in dissolved Carbonic acid gas (CO_2), and because of this they are able to dissolve small, but valuable, quantities of carbonate of lime and otherwise insoluble phosphates, &c., and bring them to the roots of the plants in a state suitable for absorption. There seems no doubt, also, that leaves may similarly absorb small quantities of materials from solutions in water, and upon this fact is based the operation of spraying with solutions of salts of such elements as iron, zinc, magnesium, and so on that may, in these days of shortage of animal manures, be deficient in the soil.

The natural sources from which water is derived are (1) rain, (2) ponds and streams, (3) springs. No hard-and-fast rules or facts can be laid down distinguishing these completely from one another, but certain broad facts may be stated.

Rain-water as it falls may dissolve a small quantity of nitrates and ammonia from the air and will also carry with it into the soil a certain amount of dissolved oxygen which will benefit the roots of plants (*see* **Respiration** in Supplement). Rain-water is usually collected from roofs and therefore brings with it the impurities which accumulate on such surfaces, and may also bring into the glasshouses the spores of disease-organisms, as it has been shown, e.g. those of the soft-rot bacteria which attack so many different plants, blown on to the roofs from neighbouring fields. The amount and nature of the soluble matter in it, however, make it safe as a rule to use for spraying and watering without fear of disfiguring foliage. If the rain passes through air impregnated with fumes from chimneys and chemical works it may dissolve enough to be actually detrimental. **A**

Water in streams and ponds usually contains more mineral matter in solution than is likely to be present in rain-water, and may, except in very shallow streams and pools, be considerably colder than the air.

Spring water also usually contains a considerable amount of dissolved mineral matter, the exact nature of which depends upon the strata from which the water is drawn, It may be actually injurious, containing too much iron, or too much lime for Ericaceous plants, or be brackish and unfit for mixing with spraying materials. It is also usually much colder than the air, especially if derived from deep wells.

The amount of water available to plants in the soil is an important factor in fertility. It depends not only on the absolute quantity there but also on the nature of the soil, for plants can withdraw a greater quantity in soils of coarse texture before they reach the point when they cannot overcome the tension with which it is held than they can in those of very fine texture such as clays. It therefore follows, for it is water which holds the plant in its proper position for work, that wilting (q.v.) may occur in clay soils earlier than in sandy or silt soils. The speed with which the wilting-point is reached also depends upon the condition of the plant and upon its nature, for both influence the development of the root system and the structure of the plant governs largely the rate at which water is lost. An over-supply of water in the soil, frequently called water-logging, since it interferes with the air supply, impedes the development of roots and may cause wilting early in hot weather and generally check growth of all aerial parts at all times. The remedy is drainage (q.v.). Another impediment to the full development of roots is shortage of soluble phosphates and probably also shortage of potash, both of which can be remedied by appropriate dressings of manure. Furthermore, water-logged soils are cold soils and crops on them will be late. The ideal to aim at is to ensure a sufficient amount of both air and water in the soil, both free to move readily wherever wanted. This can be largely secured by thorough cultivation and where necessary by some form of irrigation. While it is improbable that large quantities of water can be raised by capillary attraction from very low levels it is certain that water can be obtained from low levels, partly by the roots going after it, and partly by the movement of water-vapour in the air spaces and its condensation on the soil particles, so that even when the surface is dry the soil beneath will for long be moist if it be 'in good heart'. *See also* **Sap, Vascular system, Vessels.** The effects of atmospheric humidity on the opening and closing of flowers and fruits are often profound and its effect on Transpiration has already been dealt with.

WATER ALOE. *See* **Stratiotes aloides.**

WATER ARCHER. *See* **Sagittaria sagittifolia.**

WATER ASH, CAROLINA. *See* **Fraxinus caroliniana.**

WATER AVENS. *See* **Geum rivale.**

WATER BALSAM. *See* **Hydrocera angustifolia.**

WATER BEAN. *See* **Nelumbo.**

WATER CALTROPS. *See* **Trapa natans.**

WATER CHINKAPIN. *See* **Nelumbo lutea.**

WATER CORE. *See* **Apple Diseases,** p. 151*a*.

WATERCRESS is a favourite and valuable salad plant for which there is a steady demand except when the plants are flowering and producing seed in summer. It is a hardy perennial, native of Britain, growing wild in ditches and small streams. It is best grown in shallow streams of running water with a clean bottom free from mud. Where natural water-courses of a suitable type do not exist but a constant supply of clean water, uncontaminated by sewage or cattle watering places and so on, is available, shallow ponds or beds over which the water is kept constantly flowing, and which can be emptied at will for replanting in spring, &c., are best. The water-cress is readily propagated by dibbling in young pieces of old plants, with roots, planting them about 6 in. apart, or by seed. Failing this method of growing, beds may be made in the garden a few inches below the general surface and planted at the end of March with tops from old plants,

6 in. apart each way, or sown with seeds in drills, the seedlings being thinned to 6 in. apart as soon as large enough. The plants must be well supplied with water and all flower heads must be removed as soon as they appear. When established the more the tops are gathered the better, as the removal of the tops induces prolific branching. Such a bed should furnish supplies until autumn. On the approach of autumn some plants should be placed in pans and transferred to a warm house to provide winter supplies, or a bed similar to the first may be made outdoors and planted in August. It may need a frame for protection during winter but air must be given on all possible occasions. The large brown-leaved form is the one generally preferred but the green-leaved has the reputation of being more easily grown. Care must be taken to keep the plants and beds free from pests, an end which periodical re-planting much assists, as does care in keeping the surroundings of the beds free from weeds and rubbish. A dressing of 1 to 2 cwt. of superphosphate per acre, applied after a crop has been taken, has been found beneficial. For details of commercial cultivation reference should be made to *Ministry of Agriculture and Fisheries, Bulletin* no. 136, 'Cultivation of Watercress' by C. H. Sansom. Three main kinds of Watercress occur in the British Isles. Their names depend on their classification. Some botanists regard these white-flowered plants as forming a genus Nasturtium (from *nasus*, nose, *tortusa*, twisted, this old Latin name being borrowed from another kind of Cress; not to be confused with Tropaeolum) distinct from the yellow-flowered land or amphibious Cresses of the genus Rorippa. Others, including the monographer O. E. Schulz, regard Nasturtium as a section (Cardamium) of Rorippa. The cultivated green or summer Watercresses belong to *Rorippa Nasturtium-aquaticum* (SYN. *Nasturtium officinale*); their chromosome number is $2n = 32$ and the seeds are arranged in 2 rows in the pod. A related species, *R. microphylla* (SYN. *N. uniseriatum, N. microphylla*), has a chromosome number of $2n = 64$ and the seeds are arranged in a single row in the pod. Both species produce long pods with abundant seed. The brown or winter Watercresses belong to the hybrid group (*R.* × *sterilis*) derived from *R. Nasturtium-aquaticum* and *N. microphylla*; the pod is small and rarely contains good seed; the chromosome number is $2n = 48$. The 3 kinds are illustrated in *Agriculture*, 53. 435–56 (1947).

WATER CROWFOOT. *See* **Ranunculus aquatilis.**

WATER ELM. *See* **Planera.**

WATER FLAG. *See* **Iris Pseudacorus.**

WATER HAWTHORN. *See* **Aponogeton distachyus.**

WATER LEMON. *See* **Passiflora laurifolia.**

WATER LETTUCE. *See* **Pistia Stratiotes.**

WATER LILIES. *See* **Nuphar, Nymphaea, Water Plants.**

WATER LOCUST-TREE. *See* **Gleditschia aquatica.**

watermalien'sis -is -e, of Watermall, Belgium.

WATER MELON. *See* **Citrullus vulgaris.**

Watermey'eri, in honour of E. B. Watermeyer who discovered the Gladiolus so named.

WATER MILFOIL. *See* **Myriophyllum.**

WATER OAK. *See* **Quercus nigra.**

WATER PLANTAIN, GREAT. *See* **Alisma Plantago-aquatica.**

WATER PLANTS. Plants which grow in water, whether rooted in the mud, floating on the surface, or wholly submerged, hardy or tender. Water plants will be found in the following genera: [(*t*) genus includes tender species.] Acorus, Alisma, Apium, Aponogeton (*t*), Arundo, Azolla, Bacopa (*t*), Brasenia, Butomus, Cabomba (*t*), Calla, Caltha, Cardamine (*t*), Carex, Ceratophyllum, Ceratopteris (*t*), Chara, Cladium, Colocasia (*t*), Cotula, Cryptocoryne (*t*), Cyperus (*t*), Dipidax (*t*), Eichhornia (*t*), Elatine, Eleocharis, Elodea, Eriophorum, Glyceria, Gratiola, Heteranthera (*t*), Hippuris, Hottonia, Houttuynia, Hydrilla, Hydrocharis, Hydrocotyle, Hydrocleis, Hydrolea (*t*), Hypericum, Iris, Isoetes, Juncus (*t*), Jussueua (*t*), Lachnanthes, Lemna, Limnanthemum (*t*), Limnobium (*t*), Limnocharis (*t*), Limnophila (*t*), Limosella (*t*), Lobelia, Ludwigia (*t*), Lysimachia, Marsilea (*t*), Mayaca (*t*), Mentha, Menyanthes, Micranthemum (*t*), Mimulus, Miscanthus, Myosotis, Myriophyllum (*t*), Naias, Nelumbo (*t*), Nesaea, Nuphar, Nymphaea (*t*), Oenanthe, Orontium, Oryza (*t*), Oxalis (*t*), Peltandra, Penthorum, Phragmites, Phyllanthus (*t*), Pilularia, Pistia (*t*), Polygonum, Pontederia (*t*), Potamogeton, Preslia, Proserpinacea, Ranunculus, Rorippa, Rumex, Saccharum (*t*), Sagittaria (*t*), Salvinia (*t*), Saururus, Scirpus, Scutellaria, Spartina, Stachys, Stenotaphrum, Stratiotes, Thalia (*t*), Tilbaea, Trapa, Trapella, Triglochin, Typha, Utricularia, Vallisneria (*t*), Veronica, Villarsia (*t*), Xanthosma (*t*), Zannichellia, Zantedeschia (*t*), Zizania.

In addition to the plants growing actually in the water, those associated with them on its banks or in marshy or boggy spots need careful consideration in the planting of a garden. Many plants of this nature are referred to in the Dictionary, some worthy of inclusion for their fine foliage, some for their flowers, some for other intrinsic interest. Generally, before selecting a site for them consideration must be paid to the seasonal level of the water, for drying out during summer when the demand for moisture in soil and air is greatest must not be risked and for many submergence during winter (or at any period for any considerable time) is a risk to their well-being and perhaps to their existence. The articles on the following may be consulted:

HARDY FERNS. *Adiantum pedatum*, Athyrium, *Blechnum Spicant*, Cystopteris, *Dicksonia punctilobula*, Dryopteris, Lastrea, *Onoclea sensibilis*, Osmunda, Polystichum, Struthiopteris, Woodwardia (not very hardy).

HARDY ORCHIDS. *Calopogon pulchellus*, *Calypso bulbosa*, *Cypripedium reginae* and its relations, Epipactis, Goodyera, Habenaria, *Liparis liliiflora*, Listera, Orchis, *Pogonia ophioglossoides*, *Spiranthes cernua*.

INSECTIVOROUS PLANTS. Darlingtonia, Dionaea, Drosera, Pinguicula, Sarracenia, *Utricularia vulgaris*.

SHRUBS AND TREES. *Alnus glutinosa laciniata*, *Andromeda polifolia*, *Arctostaphylos Uva-ursi*, Arundinaria, Azalea, Bambusa, Betula, *Clethra alnifolia*, *Cornus alba*, *C. Baileyi*, and *C. stolonifera*, *Erica Tetralix*, Gaultheria, *Hippophae*, Kalmia, *Ledum latifolium*. *Liquidambar styraciflua*, *Myrica*, Phyllostachys, Populus, *Rubus arcticus*, *Salix babylonica*, *S. caerulea*, *S. daphnoides*, *S. gracilistyla*, *S. rosmarinifolia*, *S. vitellina*, *Spiraea Aitchisonii*, *S. salicifolia*, Vaccinium, Wisteria.

HERBACEOUS PERENNIALS. Aconitum (some shade), Actaea, Amsonia, *Anagallis tenella*, *Anemone rivularis*, Anthericum, Arnica, Aruncus, *Arundo Donax* (rather tender), *Asclepias incarnata*, *Aster nemoralis*, *A. puniceus*, Astilbe, Astrantia, *Baptisia australis*, *B. tinctoria*, *Buphthalmum speciosum*, *Cardamine pratensis plena*, Chelone, Chrysosplenium, Cimicifuga, Clintonia, Coptis, *Coreopsis rosea*, *Cornus canadensis*, Crocosmia, Epilobium (invasive), Eupatorium

Filipendula, Gentiana, Gunnera, Hemerocallis, *Hibiscus Moscheutos, Inula Helenium*, Iris, *Kirengeshoma palmata*, Lilium, Lobelia, *Lychnis chalcedonica*, Lysichitum, Lysimachia, Lythrum, Mimulus, Miscanthus, Parnassia, Peltiphyllum, *Petasites japonica*, Phormium, Polygonum, Primula, Ranunculus, *Rheum palmatum*, Rodgersia, *Schizostylis coccinea*, Senecio, Tradescantia, Trollius.

Many of the plants that grow best actually in water are particularly beautiful and some of them can be grown in very commonplace homes, such as old barrels cut in halves and sunk in the ground to within a few inches of their tops or even in large earthenware pans so long as they are protected from frost. The majority, however, need large tanks, outdoors or indoors, ponds, or lakes, to give them room to develop. Where tanks and pools for the storage of water exist they may often be utilized for the growing of hardy Nymphaeas, but unless the tanks are very large, only those of neat habit should be chosen, leaving the larger kinds for more commodious places, bearing in mind that the beauty of all, large and small, is enhanced when the gleaming water shines between the plants. Fine effects can be achieved by the aid of aquatic plants when their cultivation is in skilful hands, but when everything has been carefully done they may not be free from casual mishaps. The outstanding adversity comes when, in a long-continued drought, the level of the water sinks abnormally low and so leaves the crowns of the Nymphaeas exposed above its surface. Where natural expanses of water exist, provided there is ample water supply and an efficient outlet to prevent stagnation, it is possible to achieve a beautiful and interesting feature of the garden therein, while the banks may be planted with moisture-loving plants of many kinds and of diverse habits.

Weeds must be removed from both the water and from the banks as soon as they appear. If allowed to establish themselves they will spread rapidly, be very difficult to eradicate, and may do much harm and even swamp the desirable plants before they can be got out. The troublesome 'flannel weed' is dealt with under Nymphaea, where also some account of fungus diseases and insect attacks will be found. Fish do much to keep down both flannel weed and insects. Water-voles may sometimes be troublesome, and waterfowl are apt to do much damage to small plants if unguarded, and it is most desirable that young plants should be grown in reserved quarters until large enough to plant out. For the removal of dead leaves, weeds, or any accumulation of floating refuse, as well as to give the necessary attention to plants requiring it in small areas of water, a strong, light plank or ladder long enough to give secure bearing at both ends might be used; for larger areas wading boots have to be resorted to.

Where artificial pieces of water have to be made the siting must be carefully considered, bearing in mind that water seeks its bed in low-lying ground; where conditions are favourable a low-lying site should therefore be chosen, otherwise an unnatural effect will be produced. The outline should be carefully considered and unnatural shapes avoided. Artificial work should generally be carefully concealed below the intended water-level or by vegetation planted for the purpose. If the soil in which the pool is to be made is clayey and retentive of water the work will be simplified; but if it be porous the whole of the bottom will need to be of puddled clay or be lined with concrete. When the soil has been excavated as deeply as is desired—say to a minimum depth of about 3½ ft. in the middle or deepest part, gradually diminishing to about 1½ ft. at the margins with the sides sloping outwards—the surface of the excavation should be made as firm as possible and finished off regularly ready for the puddling operation. To effect this, clay only should be beaten and worked into a thoroughly tenacious mass in some convenient place, and when this is done the bottom and sides of the pool should be evenly covered throughout with it to a thickness of 9 to 12 in. The clay will need to be well rammed and beaten as the work proceeds so as to leave no chance of water percolating through it, and for the same reason the work should be done expeditiously so that none becomes dry before the puddling is finished. As soon as it is completed water should be gradually admitted. If concrete is to be used for lining the pool, where the subsoil is clayey, it should be covered with a layer of ashes or broken ballast before concreting begins to ensure that cracks which may occur in the clay during drought do not affect the concrete and no loose pockets of earth should be left anywhere. For the concrete use the best Portland cement, sharp sand, and for the aggregate clean gravel, crushed stones, or slag of a size from $\frac{3}{16}$ to $\frac{3}{4}$ in. quite free from organic matter or mineral salts. The mixture should be 1 part of cement to 2 parts by weight of sand and aggregate mixed thoroughly while dry and gradually wetted until the heap is firm enough to keep its shape when thrust into with a spade, not so wet as to be a sloppy mess. The concrete is spread evenly to the depth of 6 in. over the bottom of the pond. The work should not be done in frosty weather nor allowed to dry very quickly in hot, dry weather. If the area is large the concrete should be reinforced by a layer of wire (chicken wire of not less than 1½ in. mesh will serve) mid-way—that is, 3 in. concrete, wire, 3 in. concrete. If the pool is of formal shape wooden shuttering should be used to mould and support the sides during construction. Means of emptying the pool should be arranged when it is constructed and also means of maintaining a constant level, so that when water enters in excess, an equivalent amount may be drained or flow away, but the flow should be slow, and, if possible, water from a cold spring should not be allowed to enter the pool directly. If concrete lining is employed it will be necessary to change the water two or three times before either plants or animals are introduced into it.

A sunny position should always be selected for a water-lily pond and over-hanging trees are a disadvantage since their falling leaves render more frequent cleansing necessary. If the bottom of the pool is of natural earth the plants may be put directly into it, but it may be necessary to put mounds of good earth as planting sites. In any case, planting should be firm and carried out in March or the beginning of April. More tender varieties will be better planted later. Where the bottom is of concrete the planting must be done in mounds or the plants may be planted in wicker baskets and sunk in their positions, means having been taken to avoid the washing of the plant out as it is let down. As the baskets decay the plants root out into the surrounding soil. As already said the planting should not be so thick as to hide the water, indeed, it is best to restrict plant-growth to about one-third of the surface area of the pool.

Where a tank is to be constructed in a house it is best made on a solid brick floor covered with 6 in. of concrete, the walls being of brick, concrete, or stone, the whole being covered inside and out with a 1 in. coating of cement rendering, finished off smoothly to make it watertight. The house should not be very lofty and there should be ample ventilation both at top and sides, for the plants need plenty of air on hot days and shading is undesirable. The house should have sufficient 4-in. piping to enable a minimum temperature of 65° to 70° F. to be kept and the water in the tank should be heated by a 4-in. pipe passing round the tank about 6 in. from sides and bottom. As in the outside pool arrangements should be made for maintaining the water at a constant level, and this should be able to be varied to suit different conditions, and there should also be means of emptying the tank by a pipe at its lowest point. The planting of the indoor tank may be done in brick-enclosed beds but better in tubs made of 1 in. elm boards sunk into the water where needed.

Notes on the treatment of particular plants will be found in the body of the Dictionary.

WATER PORES, or Water Stomata, are large stomata with 2 guard cells which do not close, situated over the end of fine vascular bundles in the leaves or at the leaf-tip. They occur in many plants and extrude drops of water when the root-pressure is high (see, e.g., leaves of *Tropaeolum majus*, Cucumber, Fuchsia, Alchemilla, Crassula, Papaver, Zantedeschia, Colocasia, Ficus). In many Saxifrages they occur in connexion with chalk-glands near the margin of the leaf and the water extruded being highly charged with calcium carbonate leaves behind a white deposit of that substance. The drops of water (often confused with dew) extruded from grass-leaves come not from water-stomata but from gaps in the epidermis. Plants possessing water-stomata are more liable to damage from fumigation than are those without them.

WATER REED. *See* **Arundo.**

WATER-SOAKED. Symptoms shown by leaves or other green tissues of plants when in the normal green colour they develop spots or patches which are darker green and more translucent than the healthy cells. This kind of spot or patch is generally due to the attack of a fungus or bacterial parasite on the tissues and the affected spot or patch is usually described as 'water soaked'. D. E. G.

WATER SOLDIER. *See* **Stratiotes aloides.**

WATER THYME. *See* **Anacharis, Elodea.**

WATER VIOLET. *See* **Hottonia palustris.**

WATER-WEED, AMERICAN. *See* **Anacharis canadensis.**

WATER WHITE OAK. *See* **Quercus lyrata.**

WATERING. The operation of supplying water to plants, especially to those growing in pots or tubs or planted out in glasshouses, is one of the most important connected with horticulture. It is not too much to say that its improper performance is productive of more damage and causes more deaths, directly or indirectly, among a varied collection of plants than any one other factor. Indiscriminate watering at fixed periods is a common fault and no more frequent question is asked by the ignorant than, 'How often does it [this or that plant] need watering?' This question can scarcely ever be answered truthfully for the conditions causing need for water vary continuously and depend not only upon the state of growth of the individual plant but upon the humidity of its surroundings of soil and air. Only very general directions can be given, though with some common and easily cultivated plants they may be more definite when their general behaviour and local conditions have been ascertained. It can be said that, as a rule, soft-wooded plants and all those that grow quickly need more water than the slow-growing, hard-wooded plants, but even here exceptions may be found. The seasons of growth and rest have also to be taken into consideration and the water-supply regulated accordingly.

Soft rain-water is always best for plants, especially those outside the range of the easily grown groups, and it is best stored to attain approximately the temperature of the air, though here again, for the more hardy plants, there is a considerable degree of tolerance. Plants in pots, when they need watering, should be soaked, not slightly damped; it may not be necessary to apply water daily, but surface sprinkling is always to be avoided; on the other hand it may be necessary to water thoroughly 2 or 3 times a day. These remarks do not apply to the operation of 'damping down' which is aimed, not at supplying the plants with water, but to the maintenance of a moist atmosphere, helping to check the loss of water from the foliage. The amount of water and the frequency of its application are matters which can only be judged from personal experience in dealing with the different plants grown: in a general collection every individual plant has its particular requirements which are not to be learned by rule of thumb, nor supplied haphazard, nor judged by mere surface inspection. The time when water is likely to be needed will be anticipated somewhat by the competent cultivator so as to avoid as much as possible having to supply it during the sunniest part of a hot day. In summer, watering should be done in early morning if it is known that the plants will need a supply before the afternoon, the general watering following when it is nearly time to close the house for the day. When a plant has been overlooked and begins to flag the pot should be stood in a pail of water until well soaked and kept shaded for the rest of the day. In winter, on the other hand, when it is desirable to have the foliage dry at night, all watering is best done in the morning. Not that watering necessarily wets the foliage, indeed, as will be found from the directions given concerning various plants, wetting the foliage of some must be carefully avoided, but in winter no water should be standing on the stages during the night. The question of the method of watering, whether by means of hose, or water-pots, with or without a rose is bound to arise, and can only safely be answered by reference to the plants concerned: Which method will supply their individual requirements? not, Which method will get over the job with least effort or most quickly?

For plants in the open various methods of applying water are practised, and on a large scale there is little doubt that over-head oscillating sprinklers, diffusing water approximating to falling rain, are likely to give a well-distributed supply. This type is also excellent for the watering of lawns. The delivery pipes may be fixed or movable according to requirements of use and cultivation of the land, but whatever method is adopted it should be such that all parts needing it receive their equal supply of water at such a rate that the water will enter the soil, not run off or pack the surface, and give the thorough soaking which alone yields the best results. The rock-garden and the dry-wall garden should not be overlooked. The latter is best watered by perforated underground pipes at the back of the wall, and similar pipes laid deep enough to be out of the way of implements of cultivation may well be used in special circumstances in the market-garden or the vegetable-garden. Watering by open channels is less practised in England than in countries with a very light summer rainfall, but the system is worth consideration in some districts. A minor application of this method is used in dry weather where the seed drills are well watered a little before seed-sowing is carried out.

The need for watering trees and shrubs outside depends on the seasons and other circumstances, such as recent transplanting. Whenever it is necessary it is best to water thoroughly and then to mulch the surface with dry, light material such as bracken which will tend to check undue evaporation. This method is, of course, applicable to all kinds of plants set in the open ground, though the nature of the mulch must vary, at times, as for rock-plants, being even stone chips; indeed, small pebbles have been used with advantage in mulching fruit-trees and bushes.

WATERING-ENGINES. Movable tanks with a pump delivering water through a nozzle as a spray; very useful for applying water to trees and one means of watering lawns and borders. Where sufficient pressure is available the place of the hand-worked pump has been taken by sprinklers for many purposes, as referred to above.

WATERING-CANS. A strong can holding 12 to 16 quarts is large enough for carrying and managing when full, the latter capacity being the extreme limit. The ordinary kind, usually galvanized with a braced spout, is generally fitted with a coarse detachable rose and is well adapted for all work outside. Smaller sizes are necessary for use in most glasshouses and are better with longer spouts. The usual sizes are 2, 3, 4, 5, and 6 quarts of water. The spout may be bent downwards or the rose fitted at a right angle so that water emerges without lifting the can so high. For watering seed-pans, boxes, &c., a very fine rose is needed which will fit without permitting drip, and for this the best is a brass rose with a screw fitting. If several roses with a uniform screw are provided, the same can may be utilized for various purposes. Cans are made without a cross-handle for watering closely set pots near the glass as on high shelves. The cans may be galvanized or painted inside and out and should have the spout well supported and be provided with a rim keeping the bottom of the can from contact with the soil or bench when stood down.

Watier'i, in honour of M. Watier, Inspector of Woods and Forests, Morocco, *c.* 1920.

WATSON'IA (in honour of Sir William Watson, 1715–87, apothecary, physician, and naturalist, celebrated for his electrical researches). FAM. *Iridaceae*. A genus of about 60 species of ornamental herbaceous plants with corms, natives of S. Africa. Stem frequently tall. Leaves usually long, sword-like, rather rigid, veined, midrib usually prominent; basal leaves several. Flowers in spikes, sessile, each one wrapped at base by a bract and two fused bracteoles (prophylls); perianth tube slightly or distinctly curved or bent, the lowest part narrowly cylindric, the upper part gradually or abruptly swollen, the lobes nearly equal or the inner 3 wider than the outer 3, ovate, oblong, or lanceolate; stamens attached within tube at junction of lower and upper part; filaments free, filiform, rather long; style slender, stigmatic branches 6 or sometimes 12.

Watsonias are mostly handsome plants when in flower, some being very showy. In Britain they are on the borderline of hardiness. At places with a mild climate, e.g. in some gardens of south-western England and western Scotland, they can be grown as outdoor perennials, but in southern England generally they seem to do best in a sunny well-drained border outside a glasshouse; elsewhere they are better grown in frames or pits. They like a sandy loam enriched with a little peat or leaf-mould, and should always be given a sunny well-drained position. According to experience at Kew, they can be divided for cultural purposes into 2 groups. Those that flower in spring and early summer, e.g. *W. aletroides*, *W. coccinea*, *W. fulgens*, *W. marginata*, *W. Meriana*, *W. pyramidata*, and *W. Versfeldii*, rest during the late summer; consequently the corms of these can be lifted if desired and stored. Those that flower from mid-summer onwards, e.g. *W. Ardernei*, *W. Beatricis*, *W. densiflora*, *W. Galpinii*, *W. longiflora*, and *W. Wordsworthiana*, are more or less evergreen, and drying of the corms is not advisable. Some Watsonias grow wild in moist places; all seem to like abundant water while actively growing. Propagation is by seeds and offsets. In recent years a number of attractive hybrids have been raised. The species are sometimes difficult to distinguish and it is thus advisable to refer to the coloured plates in *Botanical Magazine* and *Flowering Plants of South Africa* when trying to check their identity; probably botanists have tried to distinguish more species than exist in nature.

A group of 7 dwarf species, often included in Watsonia, has now been separated as a genus **Thereian'thus** (from Greek *thereios* summer, *anthos* flower); they have only one basal leaf and the stamens are attached near the mouth of the almost straight perianth tube. The only species sometimes cultivated is *T. spicatus*, SYN. *Watsonia punctata*, about 6 to 12 in. high with purple flowers.

KEY

1. *Perianth lobes under ½ in. long, erect*	2
1. *Perianth lobes more than ½ in. long, usually spreading*	3
2 (1). *Perianth red, 1½ to 2 in. long*	W. aletroides
2. *Perianth yellowish, about 1 in. long*	W. flavida
3 (1). *Perianth tube short, under 1 in. long*	4
3. *Perianth tube long, more than 1 in. long*	7
4 (3). *Lvs. not thickened at margin, 6 to 9 in. long; plant less than 2 ft. h.; infl. usually unbranched*	W. brevifolia
4. *Lvs. with somewhat or distinctly thickened margin, mostly over 1 ft. long; plant more than 2 ft. h.; infl. usually branched*	5
5 (4). *Bracts to ⅖ in. long, much shorter than the internodes, not clasping stem at base but diverging from it; fl. well-spaced, the bracts of one fl. not reaching those of fl. above*	W. alpina
5. *Bracts to ⅘ in. long, as long as or longer than the internodes*	6
6 (5). *Fl. rose-red; l.-margin not yellow*	W. Galpinii
6. *Fl. mauve or purplish; l.-margin yellow*	8
7 (6). *Perianth about 1½ in. long; anthers about ½ in. long*	W. marginata
7. *Perianth about 2 in. long; anthers about ⅗ in. long*	W. vittata
8 (3). *Upper part of perianth tube broadly funnel-shaped, little more than twice as long as width of mouth*	9
8. *Upper part of perianth tube cylindric or narrowly funnel-shaped, 3 or more times as long as width of mouth*	12
9 (8). *Perianth tube abruptly bent at transition from narrow basal part to swollen upper part*	10
9. *Perianth tube gently curved, not abruptly bent*	11
10 (9). *Perianth tube about 1¼ in. long, broadly funnel-shaped in upper part*	W. pyramidata
10. *Perianth tube about 1⅗ in. long, more narrowly funnel-shaped in upper part*	W. Cooperi
11 (9). *Perianth lilac-purple*	W. Wordsworthiana.
11. *Perianth white*	W. Ardernei
12 (8). *Perianth lobes about 1¼ to 1½ in. long*	13
12. *Perianth lobes 1 in. or less long*	15
13 (12). *Inner perianth segs. to 1 in. wide; back of outer segs. coral-red, of inner segs. much paler (except in var.* concolor)	W. tabularis
13. *Inner perianth segs. to ⅗ in. wide; perianth uniformly coloured*	14
14 (13). *Perianth lilac, almost regular*	W. Versfeldii
14. *Perianth red, markedly irregular*	W. spectabilis
15 (12). *Perianth tube abruptly bent at transition from narrow basal part to swollen upper part*	16
15. *Cor. tube gently curved or almost straight*	21
16 (15). *Cormlets produced in quantity in axils of upper stem-lvs. and bracts; fl. reddish-orange*	W. bulbillifera
16. *Cormlets absent from upper stem-lvs. and bracts*	17
17 (16). *Perianth segs. obovate or narrowly obovate, ⅖ to ½ in. wide*	W. knysnana
17. *Perianth segs. narrowly oblong or oblanceolate, ⅕ to ⅖ in. wide*	18
18 (17). *Fl. white, rose-tinged*	W. roseoalba
18. *Fl. otherwise*	19
19 (18). *Fl. purplish; anthers overtopping style and branches*	W. Wilmaniae
19. *Fl. scarlet to pink; style branches overtopping anthers*	20
20 (19). *Fl. rose-red to pink*	W. Meriana
20. *Fl. scarlet*	W. fulgens
21 (15). *Infl. with few (about 3 to 10) fl.; plants low, about 1 to 2 ft. h.*	22
21. *Infl. with many (about 15 to 50) fl.; plant usually tall, 3 ft. and more h.*	25
22 (21). *Perianth tube very slender, scarcely* $\frac{1}{10}$ *in. in diameter near top, almost straight; segs. with prominent purplish mark at base*	W. strictiflora
22. *Perianth tube wide, ⅕ to ⅖ in. in diameter near top, rather curved*	23
23 (22). *Fl. crimson; perianth tube 1½ to 2 in. long*	W. coccinea
23. *Fl. pink; perianth tube mostly 1¼ to 1½ in. long*	24
24 (23). *Perianth segs. unblotched at base; style overtopping anthers*	W. humilis
24. *Perianth segs. with dark spots at base; anthers overtopping style branches*	W. maculata
25 (21). *Infl. very dense, with 40 to 50 fl. crowded on to 1 ft. or so of stem*	W. densiflora
25. *Infl. looser*	26
26 (25). *Bracts small, to ⅖ in. long, diverging from the stem; fl. well-spaced*	W. Fourcadei
26. *Bracts larger, ⅖ to 1½ in. long; fl. usually fairly close together*	27
27 (26). *Bracts not clasping stem but diverging away from it*	W. longifolia

27. *Bracts clasping stem, rather erect* 28
28 (27). *Fl. purplish; bracts about as long as internodes* W. vittata
28. *Fl. orange-red; bracts longer than internodes* 29
29 (28). *L.-margins thickened; perianth segs. spreading widely or recurving* W. Beatricis
29. *L.-margins not thickened; perianth segs. ascending-spreading* W. Pillansii

W. al'ba. A synonym of *W. Ardernei.*

W. aletroi'des. 1 to 2 ft. h. *Basal l.* 6 to 12 in. long, $\frac{1}{4}$ to $\frac{1}{2}$ in. wide. *infl.* usually simple, sometimes branched; spike 6- to 12-fld. *fl.* scarlet; tube sharply bent, about $1\frac{1}{2}$ in. long, $\frac{1}{4}$ in. diameter at throat; lobes very short, almost erect, about $\frac{1}{4}$ in. long, the outer scarlet, the inner whitish. June. Cape Province. 1774. (B.M. 441 as *Antholyza Merianella*, 533; A.B.R. 174 as *Antholyza tubulosa*; G.C. 95 (1934), 131; F.P.S.A. 983.) Easily recognized by its narrow cylindric fl. with very short perianth lobes.

W. alpi'na. About $2\frac{1}{2}$ ft. h. *Basal l.* 10 to 15 in. long, to $1\frac{1}{2}$ in. wide, with a distinctly thickened yellow margin. *infl.* branched; spikes many-fld., loose, the fl. well-separated, the bracts shorter than internodes. *fl.* pink with a deeper stripe down each lobe, small; tube very short, curved, about $\frac{4}{5}$ in. long; lobes ascending, about $\frac{4}{5}$ in. long. Transvaal. (F.P.S.A. 689.)

W. angus'ta. A synonym of *W. fulgens.*

W. Ardern'ei.* 3 to $4\frac{1}{2}$ ft. h. *Basal l.* up to 2 ft. long, 1 in. wide. *infl.* profusely branched; spikes many-fld., loose, the fl. well-separated, the bracts shorter than internodes. *fl.* white, large; tube curved, broadly funnel-shaped in upper part, about 2 in. long; lobes about 1 in. long. September. Cape Province. 1889. (F.P.S.A. 750.) SYN. *W. Meriana Ardernei, W. rosea Ardernei, W. alba, W. iridifolia O'Brieni.* A very beautiful plant of which a single clump was discovered about 1886 in the Tulbagh district of Cape Province; it has not been found again.

Watsonia Beatricis

W. Beat'ricis.* About 3 ft. h. *Basal l.* to $2\frac{1}{2}$ ft. long, $1\frac{1}{8}$ in. wide, with a distinctly thickened yellow margin. *infl.* simple, rarely branched; spikes many-fld., dense, the bracts as long as or longer than internodes. *fl.* deep orange-red, large; tube curved, narrowly funnel-shaped, about 2 in. long; lobes spreading or recurving, about 1 in. long. July to September. Cape Province. 1925. (B.M. 9139; F.P.S.A. 744.) A showy species with many fl. open at the same time.

W. brevifo'lia. 1 to $1\frac{1}{2}$ ft. h. *Basal l.* 6 to 9 in. long, $\frac{1}{8}$ to $\frac{1}{2}$ in. wide. *infl.* simple; spike few-fld., loose, the fl. well-separated, the bracts shorter than internodes. *fl.* orange-red, small; tube curved, short, about $\frac{3}{4}$ to 1 in. long, lobes spreading, $\frac{1}{2}$ to $\frac{3}{5}$ in. long; May. Cape Province. 1794. (B.M. 601.)

W. bulbilli'fera. About 5 to 6 ft. h. with cormlets in axils of upper stem-l. and lower bracts. *Basal l.* to 2 ft. long, $2\frac{1}{4}$ in. wide. *infl.* branched; spike few-fld., loose, the fl. well-separated, the bracts shorter than internodes. *fl.* brick-red, pale outside, large; tube bent, the upper part cylindric, about $1\frac{3}{5}$ in. long; lobes ascending-spreading, about 1 in. long. Cape Province. (F.P.S.A. 726.) Notable for the production of small corms in axils of bracts and stem-l. but not so showy as many species.

W. cocci'nea. About 1 ft. h. *Basal l.* 6 to 9 in. long, about $\frac{1}{2}$ in. wide. *infl.* simple; spike few-fld., loose, the bracts shorter or longer than internodes. *fl.* bright crimson, large; tube curved, cylindric in upper part, about 2 to $2\frac{1}{2}$ in. long; lobes spreading, about 1 in. long; style overtopping anthers. June, July. Cape Province. About 1805. (B.M. 1194 as *W. Meriana* var.)

W. Cooper'i. About $4\frac{1}{2}$ ft. h. *Basal l.* to 3 ft. long, $1\frac{1}{2}$ in. wide. *infl.* branched; spike many-fld., loose, the fl. well-separated, the bracts shorter than internodes. *fl.* purplish-pink, large; tube sharply bent, funnel-shaped in upper part, about $1\frac{1}{2}$ in. long; lobes spreading, about $1\frac{1}{5}$ in. long. Cape Province. 1925. (B.M. 9261 as *W. Wordsworthiana.*) Very close to *W. pyramidata* and probably not specifically distinct.

W. densiflo'ra. 2 to 3 ft. h. *Basal l.* 2 to 3 ft. long, $\frac{1}{2}$ to $\frac{3}{4}$ in. wide. *infl.* simple; spike many-fld., very dense, the membranous bracts overlapping for over half their length. *fl.* rose-red, or sometimes white; tube curved, about $1\frac{1}{4}$ in. long, lobes about $\frac{7}{10}$ in. long, spreading; anthers overtopping style branches. June. Transvaal, Natal, Orange Free State. 1879. (B.M. 6400.)

W. fla'vida. About 2 ft. h. *Basal l.* to 2 ft. long, $\frac{3}{10}$ in. wide, *infl.* simple; spike many-fld., rather dense. *fl.* yellowish, small; tube curved, $\frac{3}{5}$ in. long; lobes erect, $\frac{2}{5}$ in. long. Transvaal. (F.P.S.A. 296).

W. Fourcad'ei. To $4\frac{1}{2}$ ft. h. *Basal l.* to 2 ft. long, $1\frac{1}{2}$ in. wide, margins yellowish. *infl.* branched; spike many-fld., loose, the fl. well-separated, the bracts much shorter than internodes. *fl.* coral-red, large; tube curved, about 2 in. long; lobes ascending-spreading, nearly 1 in. long. June. Cape Province. 1930. (F.P.S.A. 235.)

W. ful'gens. About 3 ft. h. *Basal l.* 1 to 2 ft. long, $\frac{3}{4}$ to 1 in. wide. *infl.* branched; spike many-fld., loose, the fl. well-separated, the bracts mostly shorter but sometimes longer than internodes. *fl.* scarlet, fairly large; tube sharply bent, about $1\frac{1}{2}$ to 2 in. long; lobes spreading, about $\frac{3}{4}$ in. long. June, July. Cape Province. (B.M. 600, F.d.S. 1077 as *W. iridifolia fulgens*; A.B.R. as *Antholyza fulgens.*) SYN. *W. angusta.*

W. Galpin'ii. About $2\frac{1}{2}$ ft. h. *Basal l.* to 14 in. long. *infl.* simple or sometimes branched; spike few-fld., fairly dense, the bracts mostly longer than the internodes. *fl.* orange-red, small; tube curved, about $\frac{3}{4}$ in. long; lobes spreading, to $\frac{3}{4}$ in. long. August. Cape Province. 1925. (F.P.S.A. 45.)

W. hu'milis. 8 to 18 in. h. *Basal l.* 6 to 9 in. long, $\frac{1}{10}$ to $\frac{1}{5}$ in. wide. *infl.* simple; spike few-fld., loose, the bracts mostly shorter than internodes. *fl.* pink, deepest on tube, large; tube curved, $1\frac{1}{2}$ to nearly 2 in. long; lobes about $\frac{3}{4}$ in. long, not spotted at base; stigma branches overtopping anthers. June. Cape Province. 1754. (B.M. 631.) **W. macula'ta** has somewhat larger fl., with a purple blotch between the lobes at base, the anthers overtopping stigma branches. Before 1809. (B.M. 1195 as *W. humilis* var. B.)

W. iridifo'lia ful'gens. A synonym of *W. fulgens.*

W. iridifo'lia O'Brienii. A synonym of *W. Ardernei.*

W. knysna'na. About 40 in. h. *Basal l.* about 18 in. long, $\frac{3}{4}$ in. wide. *infl.* branched; spike many-fld., dense, the bracts longer than internodes. *fl.* rose-pink; tube strongly curved, nearly 2 in. long; lobes spreading nearly 1 in. long. Cape Province. (F.P.S.A. 746.)

W. longifo'lia. About 4 to 5 ft. h. *Basal l.* to 3 ft. long, $\frac{1}{2}$ in. wide. *infl.* usually simple; spike many-fld., fairly dense, the bracts longer or shorter than internodes. *fl.* varying from almost white to pink, coral and terra-cotta; tube curved, to $2\frac{1}{4}$ in. long; lobes spreading, about $\frac{3}{4}$ in. long. Cape Province. 1925. (F.P.S.A. 741.)

W. macula'ta. *See under* **W. humilis.**

W. margina'ta. About 5 ft. h. *Basal l.* to $2\frac{1}{2}$ ft. long, $1\frac{1}{2}$ in. wide, with a distinctly thickened brownish margin. *infl.* branched; spike many-fld., dense, the bracts longer than internodes. *fl.* rose-pink, small; tube curved, about $\frac{3}{4}$ in. long; lobes spreading, nearly 1 in. long. July. Cape Province. 1774. (B.M. 608; F.P.S.A. 748.)

W. Meria'na. About 2 to 3 ft. h. *Basal l.* 1 to 2 ft. long, $\frac{1}{5}$ to $\frac{1}{2}$ in. wide. *infl.* usually simple; few-fld., loose, the bracts longer or shorter than internodes. *fl.* rose-red, salmon-pink or pinkish, large; tube about 2 in. long; lobes spreading, 1 in. long. May, June. Cape Province. 1750. (B.M. 418; Trew, Pl. Selectae, 40 as *Meriana flore rubello.*) var. **Ardern'ei,** a synonym of *W. Ardernei*; **cocci'nea,** a synonym of *W. coccinea*; **ro'seo-al'ba,** a synonym of *W. roseoalba.*

W. Pillan'sii. 4 to 6 ft. h. *Basal l.* to nearly 4 ft. long, 1 in. wide. *infl.* simple; spike many-fld., dense, the bracts longer than internodes. *fl.* orange-red, large; tube curved, 2 in. long; lobes ascending-spreading, nearly 1 in. long. Cape Province. (F.P.S.A. 745.) Near *W. Beatricis* but horticulturally inferior in that fewer fl. are open at the time and the fl. do not open so widely.

Watsonia coccinea (p. 2269)

W. puncta'ta. A synonym of *Thereianthus spicatus* (see above).

W. pyramida'ta. 4 to 5 ft. h. *Basal l.* to 2½ ft. long, 1 in. wide. *infl.* branched; spike many-fld., loose, the bracts mostly much shorter than internodes. *fl.* rose-red, large; tube strongly curved or bent, broadly funnel-shaped in upper part, about 1¼ in. long; lobes spreading, 1¾ to 1½ in. long. June. Cape Province. 1800. (F.P.S.A. 974; B.M. 1072 as *W. rosea*; A.B.R. 335 as *Gladiolus pyramidatus*.) Syn. *W. rosea*. The plants distinguished as *W. Ardernei*, *W. Cooperi* and *W. Wordsworthiana* are closely akin to this.

W. ro'sea. A synonym of *W. pyramidata*.

W. ro'sea Ardern'ei. A synonym of *W. Ardernei*.

W. roseoal'ba. 12 to 18 in. h. *Basal l.* 12 to 18 in. long, ½ in. wide. *infl.* simple; spike many-fld., fairly loose but the bracts longer than internodes. *fl.* white, flushed pink, large; tube abruptly bent, about 2 in. long; lobes spreading, pointed, nearly ¾ in. long. July. Cape Province. About 1800. (B.M. 537.)

W. specta'bilis. About 1½ ft. h. *Basal l.* about 1 ft. long, ⅝ in. wide. *infl.* branched; spike few-fld., rather dense, the bracts longer than internodes. *fl.* bright red, large; tube curved, very swollen in upper part, about 2¼ in. long; lobes about 1¼ in. long, the upper 5 ascending-spreading, the lowest one recurved. Cape Province. (F.P.S.A. 977.) Rather like a Homoglossum in appearance owing to the zygomorphic flower.

W. strictiflo'ra. 12 to 18 in. h. *Basal l.* 6 to 12 in. long, ½ in. wide. *infl.* simple; spike few-fld., loose, the bracts shorter than internodes. *fl.* rose-red, with a dark purple mark at base of lobes; tube almost straight, very slender, about 1¾ in. long; lobes spreading, about ¾ in. long. May. Cape Province. 1810. (B.M. 1406.)

W. tabula'ris. 5 to 6 ft. h. *Basal l.* to 3½ ft. long, 2 in. wide. *infl.* branched; spike many-fld., loose, the bracts shorter than internodes. *fl.* deep coral-red on tube and outside of outer lobes, but paler salmon- or rose-pink on outside of inner lobes, as well as inner side of both, large; tube curved, 1¾ in. long; lobes spreading, 1¼ in. long. Cape Province. (F.P.S.A. 238.) var. **con'color,** *fl.* scarlet or orange-red, the inner perianth lobes same colour as outer.

W. Versfeld'ii. To 5 ft. h. *Basal l.* nearly 3 ft. long, 2 in. wide. *infl.* branched; spike many-fld., loose, the bracts mostly a little longer than internodes. *fl.* rose, large; tube curved, about 2 in. long; lobes spreading, nearly 1¾ in. long. Cape Province. (F.P.S.A. 747.)

W. vitta'ta. 2½ to 3 ft. h. *Basal l.* to 16 in. long, $\frac{7}{10}$ in. wide, with a thickened yellowish margin. *infl.* branched; spike many-fld., loose, the bracts mostly shorter than internodes. *fl.* rose-purple with a purple stripe, fairly large; tube curved, about 1¼ in. long; lobes spreading, 1 in. long. Probably Cape Province. (F.P.S.A. 749.)

W. Wilman'iae. To 4½ ft. h. *Basal l.* to 2 ft. long, 1½ in. wide, with pale yellow margin. *infl.* branched; spike many-fld., fairly dense, the bracts slightly longer than internodes. *fl.* purplish-rose, large; tube abruptly bent, about 1½ in. long; lobes spreading, about ¾ in. long. Cape Province. (F.P.S.A. 743.)

W. Wordsworthia'na. To 5½ ft. h. *Basal l.* about 2 ft. long, 1 to 1½ in. wide. *infl.* branched; spike many-fld., loose, the bracts shorter than internodes. *fl.* purplish-lilac, large; tube curved, broadly funnel-shaped in upper part, about 2 in. long; lobes ascending-spreading, 1¼ in. long. Cape Province. (F.P.S.A. 742; the plant figured in B.M. 9261 as *W. Wordsworthiana* is identified by G. J. Lewis as *W. Cooperi*, which see.)

W. T. S.

Watson'ii, in honour of William Watson, 1858–1925, Curator, Royal Botanic Gardens, Kew.

Watsonia'nus -a -um, Watso'nium, in honour of Sir W. Watson (*see* **Watsonia**).

WATTAKA'KA (native Malabar name for another species). Fam. *Asclepiadaceae*. Three species of S. Asiatic climbing shrubs akin to Marsdenia, differing in the shape and posture of the corolla-lobes. *W. sinensis* is hardy against a wall. Propagated by seed. The other species need a warm house and treatment like Hoya.

W. corruga'ta. Nearly related to *W. sinensis* and perhaps conspecific with it but with yellow *fl.* and transversely lamellate *fr.* China.

W. sinen'sis. Climbing or pendulous shrub, 10 ft., shoots slender, softly downy; bark warty. *l.* broadly ovate, cordate, pointed, 2 to 4 in. long, 1¾ to 3 in. wide, velvety downy beneath; stalk ½ to 1½ in. long. *fl.* 10 to 25 in axillary, long-stalked, downy umbels 2 to 3 in. across; cor. ½ in. wide, 5-lobed, lobes white, red-dotted, rounded, spreading, ciliate; cal. deeply 5-lobed, $\frac{1}{10}$ in. long; stamens 5. Summer. *fr.* of 2 incurved, spreading downy follicles about 2 in. long, ¼ to ⅜ in. wide at base, tapering upwards. China. 1907. (B.M. 8976.) Syn. *Dregea sinensis*.

W. volu'bilis. Twining shrub. *l.* ovate to nearly round, with a slender point, 3 to 6 in. long; stalk 1 to 3 in. long. *fl.* green, about ½ in. across, cup-shaped, cor. lobes triangular; umbels very many-fld., dropping; peduncles 1 to 3 in. long. India. Syn. *Dregea volubilis, Hoya viridiflora, Asclepias volubilis*.

Wat'tii, in honour of Sir George Watt, 1851–1930, author of many books on Indian plants.

WATTLE. *See* **Acacia.**

Wawrea'nus -a -um, in honour of Heinrich Wawra von Fernsee, 1831–1887, Austrian botanist.

WAX. Particles of wax are found in the cuticle of many plants, often in the form of microscopic granules, rods, or flakes. These form the 'bloom' on many fruits, and on such leaves as those of Cabbage, Aloe, some Crassulas and Sedums and other plants of dry situations, and sometimes form a thick layer, as on the stems of the Palm, *Ceroxylon andicola*, the fruits of *Myrica cerifera*, the leaves of the Wax-palm, *Copernicia cerifera*, making this product of the plant of economic importance. The function of the wax appears to be to prevent the surface from being wetted.

WAX DAMMAR. *See* **Podocarpus neriifolius.**

WAX FLOWER. *See* **Hoya carnosa.**

WAX FLOWER, CLUSTERED. *See* **Stephanotis floribunda.**

WAX, GRAFTING. *See* **Grafting Wax.**

WAX MYRTLE. *See* **Myrica cerifera.**

WAX PALM. *See* **Copernicia cerifera.**

WAX TREE. *See* **Rhus succedanea, Vismia guianensis.**

WAY-BREAD. *See* **Plantago.**

WAYFARING TREE. *See* **Viburnum Lantana.**

WEATHER. Weather may be defined as the condition of the atmospheric surroundings in regard to temperature and humidity, air movement, precipitation of water, snow, or ice. It is a matter of continual interest in horticulture both indoors and out the year round, for all work has to be adapted to its changes, and while climate gives a general indication of what may be expected in England the changes in the weather are so irregular and need watching for and, as far as possible anticipating, that, on the whole, weather more preoccupies the mind of the cultivator than does climate. Opportunity must always be seized and provision always be made against change, not only from day to day but from hour to hour. The nature of the provision must depend upon the locality, the soil, and the plants grown. Among the operations greatly dependent upon the weather is transplanting, and for this the weather and the proper season for the work are the controlling factors. Very dry weather is always unfavourable for any transplanting, for even if watering is attended to, evaporation is so constant and rapid that the effects of watering are soon lost. Mild, moist weather should, therefore, be made use of for the operation and this may mean, in some seasons, waiting a long time before the transplanting can be done and the plants re-established. Advantage should be taken of frosty weather to wheel manure, and so on, into places that cannot be well reached when walks and the ground are loose. In snowy weather when work outside may be suspended, everything that can be done under cover should receive full attention. Digging should not be done when the surface is frozen, but a covering of litter may prevent this and enable the work to proceed in spite of frost; snow should not be buried. Pruning may proceed even in frosty weather so far as the plants are concerned, but not to the great discomfort of the operator. Attention to weather changes is even more important where the treatment of glasshouse plants is concerned. Rapid changes outdoors soon make their effect seen in the houses, and means to counteract them must be immediately taken, for the plants in the glasshouse are more tender and suffer more quickly and more severely than those normally grown outside. Successful cultivation thus entails constant vigilance and the taking of every opportunity to forward work as far as may be practicable.

WEATHER PLANT. *See* **Abrus precatorius.**

WEATHER THISTLE. *See* **Carlina acaulis.**

WEB-MAKING CATERPILLARS. *See* **Tent Caterpillars.**

Webbia'nus -a -um, Webb'ii, in honour of (1) Philip Barker Webb, 1793–1854, botanical explorer of the Canary Is., author of *Histoire naturelle des Iles Canaries*; (2) Capt. W. S. Webb, *c.* 1810, who collected in the Cent. Himalaya and was associated with Wallich.

Weber'i, in honour of Georg Heinrich Weber, 1752–1828, professor at Kiel.

Weddellia'nus -a -um, Weddell'ii, in honour of Dr. Hugh Algernon Weddell, 1819–77, of Painswick, botanist and traveller in Peru; most of his work was done in France.

WEDE'LIA (in honour of George Wolfgang Wedel, 1645–1721, German botanist, Professor at Jena). FAM. *Compositae.* A genus of about 60 species of roughly hairy or shaggy annual or perennial herbs and subshrubs, natives of the warmer parts of the world. Leaves opposite, often toothed, rarely 3-fid or entire. Flower-heads yellow, pedunculate, terminal or in upper leaf-axils, heterogamous; bracts of involucre more or less in 2 or 3 series, outer 3 to 5 herbaceous, inner dry; ray-florets ligulate, entire or 2- or 3-cleft at tip; disk-florets 5-toothed or cleft. Achenes smooth or warted. The following species grow in ordinary soil. Most species, however, are of no special horticultural value.

W. au'rea. A synonym of *Zexmenia aurea.*

W. his'pida. Perennial about 18 in. h. with erect hispid branches. *l.* lanceolate to obovate-lanceolate, wedge-shaped at base, slender-pointed, toothed. *fl.-heads* solitary on peduncle, outer involucral bracts hairy, inner glabrous or nearly so. June. Mexico, &c. (B.R. 543.) SYN. *Zexmenia texana.* Half-hardy.

W. radio'sa. Sub-shrub to 2 ft. *l.* ovate to oblong-lanceolate, acute, toothed, downy. *fl.-heads* 1 to 3 on peduncles longer than l.; involucral scales in 3 series, outer leafy, inner membranous. June. Brazil. 1820. (B.R. 610.) Greenhouse.

WEDGE-GRAFTING. *See* **Grafting.**

WEED. A useless or troublesome plant growing without cultivation; a plant out of place.

A→

WEED-KILLERS. Certain chemicals, e.g. salt and ashes, have been used for centuries for the destruction of weeds, but the scientific investigation and practical use of chemicals for controlling weeds did not reach any importance until the beginning of the present century. Since the accidental discovery in 1896 of the effectiveness of copper sulphate as a weed-killer, the herbicidal possibilities of other chemicals have been investigated with the result that many more substances with similar properties have been discovered.

There are at present many chemical weed-killers of proved value, the most recent being those of the hormone or 'growth-promoting' type. While chemical weed-killers have a wider application in agriculture than in horticulture, there are, nevertheless, some which are very useful for the control of weeds in gardens.

Some of these chemicals kill all plant growth and are described as non-selective: their use is limited to gravel paths and drives, and similar uncultivated areas. Others kill various weeds, but owing mainly to differences in habit of growth have no toxic effect on certain cultivated plants: these are styled selective herbicides and can be used for weeds of arable land and of lawns. A few chemicals are toxic to weeds but have a fertilizing effect on the surrounding cultivated plants: these are known as herbicidal fertilizers.

The more important herbicides for the horticulturist are: sodium chloride, sodium arsenite (and other arsenical compounds), fuel oils, coal-tar derivatives, sodium chlorate, copper sulphate, copper chloride, iron sulphate, sulphuric acid (Brown Oil of Vitrol, B.O.V.), ammonium sulphate, calcium cyanamide, the methylchlor and dichlor derivatives of phenoxyacetic acid known by the abbreviations M.C.P. or M.C.P.A. and D.C.P., D.C.P.A., or 2:4-D respectively. M.C.P.A. is the active constituent of Methoxone, Agroxone, Verdone, and other trade preparations: D.C.P.A. is the active principle of Phenoxyl. Other herbicides, e.g. dinitro-ortho-cresyl (D.N.O.C.) and its derivatives, which are widely used in agricultural practice, are of little importance to the horticulturist, since they are toxic to most vegetable crops.

Of the chemicals listed above, the first four are non-selective and their use is limited to paths and uncultivated land.

Sodium arsenite is most effective as it kills all weeds and acts as a soil sterilant, thus preventing plant growth for a considerable period. A 10 per cent. solution (1 lb. to 1 gall. of water) sprayed at the rate of 1 gall. to 8 to 10 sq. yards gives good control. The solution can be applied with a normal spraying appliance or with a water-can with fine 'rose' nozzle.

As it is very poisonous to human beings and livestock, great care must be exercised in using it. Because of its poisonous properties its use has declined in favour of sodium chlorate, which is non-poisonous to animals and is equally destructive of weeds: it has not, however, such a lasting effect as a soil sterilant.

Sodium chlorate. A 10 per cent. solution (1 lb. in 1 gall. of water) will kill deep-rooted perennial weeds; a 5 per cent. solution kills large weeds and grasses; and a 2½ per cent. solution is sufficient for the destruction of annuals. The solution should be applied in the same manner as sodium arsenite, at the rate of 1 gallon to 10 sq. yards. This herbicide is also effective for the eradication of weeds on cultivated land from which the crop has been removed. If applied in the autumn, crops may be safely planted in the following spring or summer, but if used in the spring, subsequent planting must be delayed for from 4 to 6 weeks. Since this chemical is explosive if allowed to come into contact with dust or organic materials, the container should be kept tightly closed. Also, to prevent risk of fire, clothes and boots that have become soaked with the solution should be washed.

Very few chemicals are suitable for the control of weeds among vegetables since they are toxic to most of the latter. The most useful, as determined by experiments up to date is: *Sulphuric Acid* or *Brown Oil of Vitriol* (B.O.V.). This is used for weed control in onions, leeks, parsnips, carrots, beetroot, and any other crop in which germination is slow and weed seedlings become established before seedlings of the crop emerge. Pre-emergence spraying, i.e. *before* the crop plants appear, is effective, and is also safe, because the acid leaves no toxic residues in the soil.

B.O.V., which contains 77 per cent. of the acid, and is much cheaper than the latter, is used at a concentration of 8 to 13 galls. B.O.V. to 100 galls. of water, plus 1 pint of a wetting agent such as a sulphonated oil. The latter increases the penetration of the spray and causes it to spread more evenly over the weed foliage.

In the case of onions and leeks but *not* of other crops, a second spraying is possible after the crop seedlings have appeared and have reached the 2-leaf stage, while in a weedy crop a third application when the plants are in the 4- to 6-leaf stage is quite safe. The acid does not damage onion and leek plants because the growing-points of their stems are protected by the leaf-sheaths, and the waxy surface and almost vertical position of the leaves causes the spray to run off them without having any harmful effect. The rate of application of the spray depends on the size of weeds and type of sprayer and varies from 120 to 150 galls. per acre if a knapsack sprayer is used, and from 80 to 100 galls. if a large power sprayer is employed.

Great care is necessary in using B.O.V. A wooden or non-metal container should be used; the acid must be poured gradually into the water, *never* the reverse process; protective clothing must be worn and an acid-resistant sprayer should be used.

No method of using D.C.P.A. and M.C.P.A. for the control of weeds among vegetables has yet been perfected, since these substances are toxic to all vegetables, particularly to those of the cabbage family. Recent experiments indicate, however, that 2 lb. of D.C.P.A. or M.C.P.A. per acre used as a spray is effective for the control of perennial weeds in asparagus beds if applied when the asparagus is in the advanced 'fern' stage.

For the control of weeds in turf, the most widely used chemical has been *Ammonium sulphate* which is the basis of all 'lawn sands'. These mixtures have a corrosive action on most lawn weeds but at the same time encourage the growth of the grass. The most successful results are obtained by the use of a mixture of 3 parts sulphate of ammonia, 1 part calcined sulphate of iron, and 20 parts lime-free sand, applied at the rate of 4 oz. per sq. yard 3 or 4 times in a season, commencing towards the end of February.

For a small private lawn, a solution of 3 lb. sulphate of ammonia and 2 lb. sulphate of iron in 100 galls. of water, applied at the rate of 100 galls. to 100 sq. yards and followed by ordinary watering gives effective control.

For the eradication of deep tap-rooted weeds, 'spot' treatment with a mixture of 35 parts of weight of sulphate of ammonia, 15 parts by weight of calcined sulphate of iron, and 50 parts by weight of sand is effective. By 'spot' treatment is meant the injection of a herbicide into the crown of the weed by a sharp steel skewer or by a special injecting tool, of which there are many types on the market. Most herbicides are suitable for the 'spot' treatment of weeds in small areas of turf and in inaccessible parts of the herbaceous border or parts of the garden where other methods of control are impracticable.

M.C.P.A., and *D.C.P.A.* or 2 : 4-*D.* The use of these plant hormones or 'growth-promoting' substances for weed control in turf is still in the experimental stage, but the results of experiments carried out since 1945 at the St. Ives Greenkeeping Research Station, Bingley, Yorkshire, are promising.

Synthetic plant hormones have a stimulating effect on the growth of plants. If the concentration is increased and the stimulus thereby exaggerated, some species are killed but others unaffected. In those plants that are susceptible to the growth stimulus, violent physiological disturbance occurs, resulting in abnormal development, contortion, and ultimate death. The difference in susceptibility of plants is not yet fully explained. Grasses are not injured, but the worst lawn weeds, particularly those with a rosette habit of growth, are severely damaged.

The rates of application per acre recommended for established lawns are:

D.C.P.A. (2:4-D)	2 to 4 lb. as spray. 4 lb. as dust.
M.C.P.A.	5 to 6 lb. as spray. 6 to 8 lb. (or more) as dust.

The composition of proprietary 'hormone' weed-killers should be ascertained in order to use correct quantities. Good results are obtained from April to October inclusive. Best results are given when growth is vigorous, and suitable pre-treatment with nitrogenous fertilizer is of value in encouraging speedy and complete eradication.

For 'spot' treatment, only a very small quantity of these chemicals is required, less than 1 oz. of a 5 per cent. M.C.P.A. being sufficient for the treatment of 1 sq. yard. These weed-killers should not be used for weeds in seedling grass as they may have very harmful effects.

Sprayers and other equipment used for these 'hormone' derivatives should be thoroughly cleaned with hot water or a weak solution of ammonia.

The eradication of runner-bearing weeds growing in the herbaceous border or among shrubs and roses is difficult, but can be effected by immersing the cut ends of the creeping stems (stolons or rhizomes) in jars of a suitable weed-killer, e.g. a 40 per cent. solution of sodium chlorate or a 10 per cent. solution of copper sulphate.

Chemical control of water-weeds in pools, lakes, and streams is hazardous to plant and animal life and should only be used when no other method is possible.

Green algae, known as silkweed or blanket-weed, can be destroyed by overhead watering with potassium permanganate at a concentration of 1 teaspoonful per gall. of water. This causes no serious damage to other plants or to animals.

Copper sulphate at the very low concentration of 1 oz. to 1,200 galls. of water may be also used for destroying green algae on garden ponds. The sulphate is placed in a muslin bag tied to the end of a pole and is drawn through the water slowly to ensure even dispersal.

A. G. E.

WEED-WIND or **WITH-WIND.** Old name for *Convolvulus arvensis* (Bind-weed).

weeping, having pendulous branches or branchlets; weeping forms occur in many trees.

WEEVIL PLANT. *See* **Curculigo.**

WEEVILS, a name popularly applied to members of the Coleopterous family *Curculionidae*, distinguishable from beetles by the head being produced in front to form a rostrum or snout upon which are borne the elbowed antennae. The grubs differ from those of beetles by being legless, with the body more or less curved, and with a prominent, usually brownish head attached to

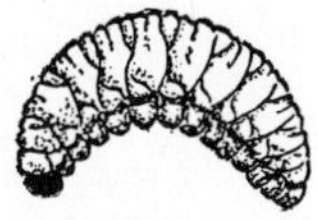

Weevil larva

a greyish or whitish stout body. The term 'Weevil' is also frequently, but incorrectly, applied to members of the family Bruchidae or Seed Beetles. The length of the rostrum varies considerably with the species, some possessing a very long snout (Nut Weevil), others a short one (Pea and Bean Weevils). The function of this organ in the female is often that of a boring instrument, a hole being drilled by it in seeds, buds, shoots, and stems for placing the eggs within the plant tissues. The food habits of weevils vary considerably but the greater number are internal feeders during the larval stage and the legless grubs may be found within buds (Apple Bud Weevil, *Anthonomus cinctus*), flowers (Apple Blossom Weevil, *A. pomorum*), fruits (Nut Weevil, *Balaninus nucum*), shoots (Apple Twig-cutter, *Rhynchites coeruleus*), corms and tubers (Vine Weevil, *Otiorrhynchus sulcatus*), stems (Pine Weevil, *Hylobius abietis*), and roots (Turnip Gall Weevil, *Ceuthorrhynchus pleurostigma*). There are marked differences, also, in the habits of the adults, some of the leaf-feeding weevils being diurnally active (*Phyllobius*), others are nocturnal (*Otiorrhynchus*). Among the most destructive species are the Grain Weevils (*Calandra sp.*), which cause extensive losses to maize and wheat in the world's granaries; the Mexican Cotton Boll Weevil (*Anthonomus grandis*), which is the most serious enemy of the American cotton crop; and the Palm Weevil (*Rhynchophorus ferrugineus*), which infests coco-nut palms.

Control measures against the more important plant-infesting species in this country are described under their respective headings, e.g. Apple Blossom Weevil, Bean and Pea Weevils, Nut Weevil, &c.

G. F. W.

WEIGEL'A (in honour of Christian Ehrenfried von Weigel, 1748–1831, professor at Greifswald, north Germany). Fam. *Caprifoliaceae.* A group of about 12 species of deciduous shrubs, native to E. Asia, with fairly large, nearly regular white, pink, or red (rarely yellow) flowers, and on this account often treated as a genus distinct from Diervilla, which thus restricted comprises 3 species, all N. American, with small 2-lipped yellow flowers; in this Dictionary the species of Weigela are dealt with under **Diervilla.** Thus *D. coraeensis* may also be known as *W. coraeensis*; *D. floribunda* as *W. florida*; *D. hortensis* as *W. hortensis*; *D. japonica* as *W. japonica*; *D. Middendorffiana* as *W. Middendorffiana*; *D. praecox* as *W. praecox*; *D. venusta* as *W. venusta* (or *W. florida* var. *venusta*).

W. T. S.

WEIGHTS AND MEASURES. Garden produce is now almost always sold by weight, avoirdupois weight being used. The containers used vary both in kind and capacity and to some extent according to the market to be supplied, but with improved facilities for conveyance to distant markets, the latter is of less moment than in the past.

The tendency is to make containers of standard sizes holding approximately a given weight.

Several vegetables are bunched or bundled for the market, are usually washed, and frequently several bunches are made into larger ones, the whole being packed in a suitable container. Cellophane wrapping is coming into favour for several articles.

Bunch or Bundle. *Asparagus*, usually 100 or 120 heads, the latter made up of 6 bundles of 20, but sometimes 25, 50, or 150; wrapped in paper or leaves or cellophane. Marketed in baskets. *Early Carrots*, 12 to 50; sent in flats. *Celery*, 8 to 12 sticks. *Herbs*, of varying size. *Horseradish*, 20 roots. *Leeks*, 6 to 8 in a fan in boxes or baskets. *Mint*, in winter 20 to 30 shoots, summer, handful; sent in flats or hampers. *Spring Onions*, 144 in 12 bundles of 12. *Spring sown Onions*, 6 to 20. *Parsley*, in winter small, in summer a handful; sent in flats, pads, or hampers. *Radish*, 12 to 14; sent in baskets. *Rhubarb*, forced early, 2 or 3 to 8 or 10 sticks, later 3 to 6 lb. *Salsify* and *Scorzonera*, 12 roots; sent in flats. *Early Turnips*, 20; sent in pads, hampers, or bushel baskets.

The containers mainly used are:

Bag, used chiefly for Potatoes and contains ½, 1, or 1½ cwt., but the following are also often marketed in bags: Borecole, Sprouting Broccoli, Brussels Sprouts (late) and tops, Carrots, Coleworts, Onions, Peas, Turnips. Waterproof paper bags (standard measure 31 × 19 in.) are suitable for all these crops and offer certain advantages.

Boxes of standard sizes. Market produce was, and no doubt will be again, frequently sold in non-returnable wooden boxes, the chief sizes of which were, for Tomatoes, 14″ × 9″ × 5½″ holding 12 lb.; Cucumbers, 20½″ × 14½″ × 4½″, to hold 2 layers; Apples, bushel, 18″ × 11½″ × 10″ to hold about 40 lb., half-bushel, 14½″ × 9″ × 9″ to hold about 20 lb., quarter-bushel or peck, 12½″ × 7″ × 7″ to hold about 10 lb.

Bushel Sieve made of wicker work to hold 8 gallons. Size varying somewhat; diameter 17½″, depth 10¾″ at sides, 10″ at middle, or diameter 16″, depth 10½″. Holds 40 to 44 lb. Apples, 56 lb. Potatoes. The half-sieve is also used, diameter 12½″, depth 6″. Holds 24 lb. Currants or Cherries, 28 lb. Plums.

Bushel Basket, diameter at top 14½″, bottom 10″, depth 17″. Holds 40 lb. Apples or Pears, 56 lb. Potatoes, Greens cut and packed about 30 lb. ½-bushel and ¼-bushel baskets used to contain choice vegetables.

Grape baskets hold 4 to 6 lb. or may be marketed in 'shallows' holding 10 to 12 lb.

Bushel Flat, a basket with a lid, 21″ long, 16″ wide, 10″ deep. Holds 4 layers of Cucumbers, 40 lb. Apples.

Chip Baskets with handles, holding from 2 to 12 lb., also made of wood pulp, holding up to 4 lb., used for Strawberries, Raspberries, Loganberries, Blackberries, with or without a cover. The best sizes for these fruits are 3 or 6 lb.

Crates, wooden containers with slat sides. Standard size for Broccoli and Cauliflowers, 22¾″ × 13¾″ × 13¾″, holding 18 to 30 heads; for Celery, 17⅛″ × 15″ × 5½″; for Lettuces, 18¼″ × 11½″ × 5⅞″; for Rhubarb, 28″ × 11¾″ × 7⅛″. Crates are also made of wood pulp and measure 20⅞″ × 19″ × 6½″.

Hand, a bunch of 12 to 30 Radishes, according to season.

Punnets, made of chip wood or wood pulp in the form of trays, sometimes circular, sometimes square. They vary much in size. Seakale punnets 8″ diameter at top, 7″ at bottom, 2″ deep; Radish punnets 8″ diameter, 1 in. deep; Mushroom punnets 7″ diameter, 1″ deep; forced Strawberry punnets contain ½ lb. or 1 lb. For dispatch to market the punnets are packed in shallow boxes or flats.

STRIKE, a basket about 12″ in diameter, 7″ deep, holding 12 lb. Tomatoes.

Weilbach'ii, in honour of August Weilbach, 1813–63, gardener in Botanic Garden, Copenhagen.

Weinland'ii, in honour of Dr. C. A. F. Weinland, 1864–91, who collected in New Guinea.

WEINMAN'NIA (in honour of Johann Wilhelm Weinmann, apothecary of Ratisbon, author of *Phytanthoza Iconographica*, 1737–45). FAM. *Cunoniaceae.* A genus of about 50 species of trees or shrubs, natives of Malaya, Madagascar, and the Pacific Is., Australia and New Zealand, and tropical and temperate S. America. Branches opposite, often terete. Leaves opposite, evergreen, stalked, simple, 3-foliolate or odd pinnate; leaflets usually with glandular teeth; rachis often winged; stipules variable, deciduous. Flowers white, small, clustered or scattered, in simple, terminal, and axillary, erect racemes; calyx tube short, limb 4- or 5-partite; petals 4 or 5, spatulate or ovate, sessile; stamens 8 or 10, inserted with the petals. All the species need stove or greenhouse treatment and a light, rich soil. They may be propagated by cuttings in sandy soil in a close frame in heat. The following all need stove conditions.

W. glab'ra. Shrub of 6 ft. *l.* odd pinnate, short-stalked, glabrous; lflets. in 3 to 5 pairs, oblong-elliptic, serrate or crenate-serrate or entire. *fl.* twin; pet. rather longer than cal. segs.; pedicels slightly hairy. January. Jamaica. 1815.

W. hir'ta. Shrub or tree of 6 ft. or more. Branches roughly hairy. *lflets.* in 3 or 4 pairs, $\frac{1}{2}$ to $\frac{3}{4}$ in. long, elliptic, bluish, toothed above base, hairy beneath. *fl.* in clusters in a raceme; stamens 8, exserted. May. Jamaica. 1820.

W. ova'ta. Glabrous tree of 6 ft. upwards. *l.* elliptic-oblong, rather blunt, acute at base, 2 to 3 in. long, 1 to $1\frac{1}{2}$ in. wide, crenate; stalk about $\frac{1}{4}$ in. long. *fl.* in few-fld. clusters in a very loose raceme. May. Peru. 1824.

W. pinna'ta. Near *W. glabra.* Tree of 6 ft. upwards. Branchlets shortly downy. *lflets.* in 3 to 7 pairs, elliptic-oblong, $\frac{1}{3}$ to $\frac{2}{3}$ in. long, bluish, toothed above base, rough-haired on midrib beneath or nearly smooth. *fl.* clustered in a raceme; stamens 8, exserted. May. Jamaica. 1815.

W. trichosper'ma. Shrub of 4 ft. *l.* pinnate; lflets. many, oblong, acute, toothed, oblique at base, glabrous and shining above, slightly hairy beneath. *fl.* in a loose raceme. May. Chile.

W. trifolia'ta. A synonym of *Platylophus trifoliata.*

Weinmann'ii, in honour of J. A. Weinmann, 1782–1858, director, Botanic Garden, St. Petersburg.

Welborn'ii, in honour of G. Welborn, who, *c.* 1908, collected in the Philippines.

WELD. *See* **Reseda luteola.**

WELDEN'IA (in honour of L. von Welden, 1780–1853, of the Austrian army, naturalist). FAM. *Commelinaceae.* A genus of a single species, *W. candida* is a tuberous herb for the alpine house, from the mountains of Mexico and Guatemala where it was first found in the crater of a volcano. It is propagated by root-cuttings, the fleshy root which protrudes through the drainage hole of a pot stood in sand or ash being cut in September into pieces about 1 in. long and inserted in a pot of sandy soil.

W. can'dida. Stem short, unbranched. *l.* 6 to 8, strap-shaped, 2 to 6 in. long, bases folding. *fl.* snow-white, 1 in. across, solitary on an erect scape, several of which arise from the leaf-rosette; cor. lobes broad, spreading. April. Before 1894. (B.M. 7405.)

WEL'FIA (in honour of the Royal Family of Hanover (Guelph)). FAM. *Palmaceae.* A genus of 2 tall unarmed palms, natives of Cent. America and Colombia. Leaves in a terminal crown, deeply pinnately cut, leathery, segments much narrowed to base, many-nerved, plicate. Flowers pale yellowish-white, rather large. Spathes 2, deciduous; spadices thick, pendulous. *W. regia* grows well in a compost of rich loam and leaf-mould mixed with a little old cow-dung, under stove conditions. Propagation by seeds.

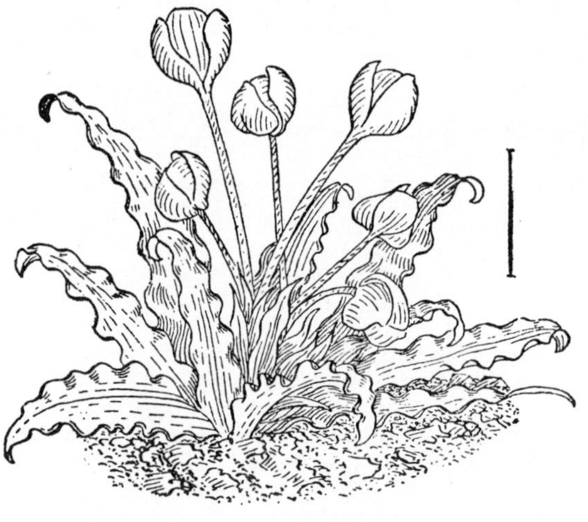

Weldenia candida

W. re'gia. Eventually 60 ft. h. *l.* of young plants divided into 2 oblong, slender-pointed lobes, bronzy; adult up to 20 ft. long, deeply pinnately divided; segs. unequal, whitish beneath. Colombia. 1869. (G.C. 1870, 764.)

Well'byi, in honour of Capt. Wellby, who travelled in Tibet and Abyssinia, 1898, d. of wounds S. Africa, 1899.

WELLINGTON'IA. *See* **Sequoia.** Named in honour of Sir Arthur Wellesley, 1769–1852. Duke of Wellington.

WELSH ONION. A name originally given to *Allium fistulosum*, the epithet 'Welsh' here referring not to Wales but being a transcription of the German 'Welsch' (foreign); it is, however, often though incorrectly transferred to the Ever-ready or Everlasting Onion (*A. Cepa* var. *perutile*), which has narrow leaves usually less than $\frac{1}{2}$ in. wide and semicircular in section, being rather flattened on the inner side and rounded on the outer side; this plant rarely flowers. *A. fistulosum* has wider leaves circular in section (see G.C. 114 (1943), 86–88) and flowers normally every year.

W. T. S.

WELSH POPPY. *See* **Meconopsis cambrica.**

WELWITSCH'IA (in honour of Dr. Friedrich Welwitsch, 1806–72, botanical traveller). FAM. *Welwitschiaceae.* A genus of a single species, native of SW. Africa where rain rarely falls. A remarkable plant, of no beauty, but of unique character. It has been introduced to Kew and other botanic gardens but is unlikely to prove anywhere easy to cultivate. A full account of it will be found in *Transactions of the Linnean Society*, 24. 1–14 (1863) and in *Botanical Magazine*, 5368–9. Said to live more than a century. An article by H. Herre in *J. South African Bot.* 14. 105 (1948) records the first flowering in December 1947 of a plant raised at the University Botanic Garden, Stellenbosch, S. Africa, from seed sown in December 1927. The plants have been grown there in drain-pipes in a mixture of decomposed granite and leaf-mould. They strongly dislike any mica in the soil.

W. Baines'ii. Trunk obconical, to 3 ft. in diameter, rising $\frac{1}{4}$ to 1 ft. above the soil, finally dark brown; the lower part forms a deep stout tap-root, branching downwards at end. *l.* 2 rarely 3 from deep grooves in circumference of trunk, lorate, very leathery, split at end into innumerable curling thongs, dying away gradually at the tip but growing continuously from the base. *fl.* solitary in scales of young cones; cones scarlet, small, erect, at length oblong, in stout forked cymes from near the insertion of the l. 1862 and 1878. SYN. *W. mirabilis, Tumboa Bainesii.*

WELWITSCHIA'CEAE. A family of only 1 species, akin to no other member of the plant kingdom, the remarkable *Welwitschia Bainesii*; see *Flora Capensis* 5, sect. 2, Suppl. 1–3 (1933). It is sometimes included in Gnetaceae but has little in common with Ephedra and Gnetum. A

WENDLAND'IA (in honour of Johann Christoph Wendland, 1755–1828, or of his son, Heinrich Ludolph Wendland, 1792–1869, Curator of Royal Gardens, Herrenhausen). FAM. *Rubiaceae.* A genus of about 56 species of shrubs or small trees, natives of Trop. and Sub-trop. Asia. Leaves opposite or 3-nately whorled; stipules entire or 2-fid. Flowers, white, pink, or yellow, small, 2- or 3-bracteolate, in terminal, thyrsoid or paniculate, many-flowered panicles; calyx lobes 4 or 5, small; corolla tubular, salver- or funnel-shaped, lobes 4 or 5, overlapping in bud; stamens 4 or 5, alternate with corolla lobes. Need warm-house conditions and treatment as for Vangueria. A revision of the genus by J. M. Cowan has been published in *Notes Royal Bot. Garden, Edinburgh*, 16. 233–314 (1932) with a supplement in *Bull. Jardin Bot. Buitenzorg*, 14. 8–46 (1936).

W. specio'sa.* Tree or bushy shrub up to 20 or 30 ft. h.; young branchlets puberulous. *l.* opposite, coriaceous, broadly ovate, entire, 3 to 5 in. long, 2 to 3 in. wide, more or less abruptly acute, narrowed at the base, glabrous or very sparsely pubescent above, glabrous beneath except along the sparsely pubescent nerves; interpetiolar stipules with leafy orbicular expansion at apex. *infl.* terminal; panicle pubescent with linear bracteoles. *fl.* cream coloured, fragrant, very shortly pedunculate, ¾ in. long; cal. with few greyish hairs, lobes lanceolate acute, equalling the receptacle; cor. 5-fid, with tube pilose within and ovate rounded lobes one-third as long; anthers exserted, lanceolate or linear-lanceolate, base 2-fid; style sparsely covered with hairs, stigma prominently 2-lobed. Nov.–Jan. Upper Burma, Yunnan. 1912.

W. tincto'ria. About 6 ft. h. *l.* opposite, elliptic, ovate or obovate, 4 to 8 in. long, narrowed to a point, glabrous and often shining above, paler and usually hairy beneath; stipules erect, large, tip awl-shaped or with a laterally flattened, rigid appendage. *fl.* white, sessile, clustered in large spreading hairy panicles. July. India. 1825.
J. M. C.

Wendlandia'nus -a -um, in honour of Hermann Wendland, 1825–1903, Director, Royal Gardens, Herrenhausen, Hanover, a post which his father and grandfather had likewise held with distinction (*see* **Wendlandia**).

Wentia'nus -a -um, in honour of F. A. F. C. Went, 1863–1935, Professor of Botany, Utrecht.

WERCKLEOCE'REUS (in honour of Carlo Werckle, a Costa Rican collector, *c.* 1898). FAM. *Cactaceae.* Epiphytic cacti, branched, 3-angled, climbing by aerial roots; areoles small, felted, with few spines. Flowers about 5 in. long, with spines and black wool on the tube. They prefer hot-house treatment. A

W. Tonduz'ii. Stems 3- or 4-angled, not glaucous; margins of ribs straight; areoles small, felted, without spines. *fl.* whitish. Costa Rica. (B.R.C. 2, t. 39, f. 296.) SYN. *Cereus Tonduzii.*

WERNER'IA (in honour of Abraham Gottlob Werner, 1750–1817, Professor of Mineralogy, Freiberg, founder of scientific geology). FAM. *Compositae.* A genus of about 37 species of dwarf, tufted, perennial herbs, natives of the Andes of S. America. Leaves radical or clustered on stem, entire or rarely toothed or pinnatisect. Flower-heads large or medium, heterogamous and rayed, rarely homogamous with only disk-florets; involucre broadly bell-shaped or hemispherical, bracts in 1 series; receptacle flat or convex, naked; ray-florets pink, yellow, or white, in 1 series, ligulate; disk yellow. Achenes oblong or turbinate. *W. rigida* grows well in a light soil and may be increased by division. It needs greenhouse conditions. The genus is closely allied to Senecio; a revision by M. Rockhausen has been published in Engler, *Bot. Jahrb.* 70. 248–342 (1939).

W. ri'gida. Loose cushions up to 9 in. h. *l.* linear, obtuse, overlapping, to 1½ in. long. *fl.-heads* yellow, solitary, on a short peduncle; involucral bracts violet, about 13. Ecuador.

WEST INDIAN ARROWROOT. *See* **Maranta arundinacea.**

WEST INDIAN CEDAR. *See* **Cedrela odorata.**

WEST INDIAN LOCUST TREE. *See* **Hymenaea Courbaril.**

WEST WIND, FLOWER OF THE. *See* **Zephyranthes.**

WESTERN YEW. *See* **Taxus brevifolia.**

Westland'ii, in honour of Mr. A. B. Westland, who, *c.* 1884, discovered *Aristolochia Westlandii* at Tai-mo-Shan, China.

WESTRING'IA (in honour of Johan Peter Westring, 1753–1833, physician to the King of Sweden). FAM. *Labiatae.* A genus of about 26 species of shrubs, widely dispersed over extra-tropical Australia. Leaves in whorls of 2 or 6. Flowers all axillary, or rarely in terminal leafy heads, usually having 2 very small bracts beneath the calyx; calyx bell-shaped, 5-toothed; corolla with a short tube usually hairy within, a dilated throat, upper lip erect, flat, broadly 2-lobed, lower 3-lobed, spreading; 2 upper stamens perfect, 2 lower sterile. Greenhouse plants growing in any light, rich compost, and readily propagated by cuttings of young shoots. A synopsis of the genus by B. Boivin has been published in *Proc. Royal Soc. Queensland*, 60. 99–110 (1949).

W. ama'bilis. *l.* in whorls of 3, ovate-lanceolate or narrowly elliptic, acute, flat, ½ to ⅘ in. long. *fl.* rose, crowded along the tips of the branches. Queensland, New S. Wales. Stated to be a very decorative shrub with rather large and abundant fl.

W. cine'rea. A form of *W. rigida.*

W. Dampier'i. Several ft. h. *l.* in whorls of 4, very rarely of 3, linear, about ½ to 1¼ in. long, smooth or scabrous above, often hoary beneath. *fl.* white, with small yellow and purple dots, nearly sessile, about as large as those of *W. rosmariniformis* but cor. more hairy; cal. teeth less than half as long as segs. September. S. Australia, W. Australia. 1803. (B.M. 3308.)

W. eremi'cola. 3 ft. h., branches erect, often twiggy, more or less hoary or silky-hairy. *l.* usually in whorls of 3, narrow-linear, acute or mucronate, rarely over ½ in. long. *fl.* pale blue, rather small, usually distant; cal. hoary; cor. hairy. June. Queensland, New S. Wales, Victoria. 1823. (B.M. 3438; B.R. 1418 as *W. longifolia.*)

W. longifo'lia. Several ft. h. *l.* in whorls of 3, narrow linear, usually over 1 in. long, margins sometimes somewhat revolute. *fl.* lilac, rather small, axillary; cor. hairy without, tube longer than cal. teeth. Summer. 1878. New S. Wales.

Westringia rigida (p. 2276)

W. ri'gida. About 3 ft. h. *l.* mostly in whorls of 3, sometimes of 4, linear, blunt or mucronate, rigid, margins very revolute, usually glabrous above in age, smooth and shining, or rough with minute tubercles, hoary beneath. *fl.* as in *W. Dampieri*; cal. teeth less than half as long as tube. 1823. (B.M. 3307 as *W. cinerea.*) Widespread in Australia. *W. cinerea* is a more hairy form.

W. rosmarinifor'mis. Several ft. h. *l.* in whorls of 4, oblong-lanceolate to linear, acute or blunt, ½ to 1 in. long, leathery, glabrous and shining above, hoary and silvery-white beneath, margins recurved or revolute. *fl.* pale blue, almost sessile, all axillary; cor. hairy outside; cal. teeth about half as long as tube. July. Queensland, New S. Wales. 1791. (A.B.R. 214 as *W. rosmarinacea.*)

WET-ROCK KOROMIKO. *See* **Veronica linifolia.**

WETTING-AGENTS. Materials added to spray-fluids to ensure that they wet the foliage or bodies of insects sprayed, mitigating the presence of wax or minute down which often protects both foliage and the bodies of insects from wetting, and enabling the spray to penetrate minute orifices like the spiracles of insects.

Wettstein'ii, in honour of Dr. Richard von Wettstein, 1862–1931, Professor of Botany, Vienna.

WEYMOUTH PINE. *See* **Pinus Strobus.**

WEYMOUTH PINE RUST. *See* **Pinus, Diseases.**

Weyrich'ii, in honour of Dr. Weyrich, 1826–63, Russian naval surgeon.

WHANGEE or **WANGU CANE.** *See* **Phyllostachys nigra.**

WHARANGI. *See* **Melicope ternata.**

WHARARIKI. *See* **Phormium Colensoi.**

WHAUWHAUPAKU. *See* **Nothopanax arboreum.**

WHEAT. *See* **Triticum.**

WHEAT, GUINEA OR TURKEY. *See* **Zea Mays.**

WHEELBARROW. *See* **Barrow.**

Wherr'yi, in honour of Edgar Theodore Wherry, b. 1885, professor at Philadelphia, authority on Polemoniaceae, &c.

WHIN. *See* **Ulex europaeus.**

WHIN, PETTY. *See* **Genista anglica.**

WHINBERRY. *See* **Vaccinium Myrtillus** and **V. Vitis-Idaea.**

WHIP GRAFTING. *See* **Grafting.**

Whippl'ei, in honour of Lieut. Amiel Weeks Whipple, 1818–63, explorer for the railway route across America in 1853.

WHITE ALDER. *See* **Platylophus trifoliata.**

WHITE ARUM LILY. *See* **Zantedeschia aethiopica.**

WHITE ASH. *See* **Fraxinus americana.**

WHITE BEAM. *See* **Sorbus Aria.**

WHITE BLADDER FLOWER. *See* **Araujia sericofera.**

WHITE BOTHEN, WHITE GOLDES. *See* **Chrysanthemum Leucanthemum.**

WHITE BRYONY. *See* **Bryonia dioica.**

WHITE BUTTERWOOD. *See* **Trichilia spondioides.**

WHITE CAMASSIA. *See* **Camassia Leichtlinii.**

WHITE CEDAR. Variously applied to *Chamaecyparis thyoides, Libocedrus decurrens,* and *Thuja occidentalis.*

WHITE CLIMBING RATA. *See* **Metrosideros albiflora** and **M. scandens** (q.v.).

WHITE CYPRESS. *See* **Taxodium distichum.**

WHITE ELM. *See* **Ulmus americana.**

WHITE FLY. *See* **Aleyrodidae.**

WHITE FLY PARASITE (*Encarsia formosa*). This minute Chalcid 'wasp' is employed for the control of the Greenhouse White Fly (q.v.). The Parasites are just visible to the naked eye, and are introduced into glasshouses infested with White Fly in the form of larvae which are contained within the black parasitized 'scales' of White Fly attached to leaves. The female Chalcid, which is about $\frac{1}{40}$ in. long, thrusts 1 egg into each mature White Fly 'scale'. The parasite larva feeds within the body of its host, destroying it, and eventually emerging as a 4-winged 'wasp' through a circular hole in the upper side of the 'scale'. Success with this method of control will depend upon the presence of White Fly 'scales' prior to the introduction of the parasite and to favourable conditions of temperature, humidity, and illumination. Special consideration has to be given to the maintenance of the Parasites over winter, and this is not possible in many instances owing to low temperatures, to the absence of its host and to the fact that many glasshouses are cleared of crops at the end of the growing season.

The Parasites require about 3 to 4 weeks to complete their development, and will multiply rapidly under temperatures above 70° F., somewhat moist atmospheric conditions, and in bright sunlight. The rate of breeding of the Parasites must necessarily be higher than that of their host—the White Fly—to enable them to overcome even a normal infestation of the pest in a glasshouse, and cool and very dry conditions and partial shade will considerably check the rate of breeding and may result in disappointment following the introduction of the Parasites into an infested house.

G. F. W.

WHITE GUM. *See* **Eucalyptus leucoxylon, E. viminalis.**

WHITE HEART HICKORY. *See* **Carya tomentosa.**

WHITE HELLEBORE. *See* **Veratrum album.**

WHITE HOREHOUND. *See* **Marrubium vulgare** and **Horehound.**

WHITE LIME. *See* **Tilia tomentosa.**

WHITE MUSTARD. *See* **Mustard, Sinapis alba.**

WHITE PINE. *See* **Pinus Strobus.**

WHITE POTHERB. *See* **Valerianella Locusta.**

WHITE ROOT. *See* **Polygonatum multiflorum.**

WHITE SAPOTA. *See* **Casimiroa edulis.**

WHITE TRUFFLE. *See* **Truffles.**

WHITE VINE. *See* **Clematis Vitalba.**

WHITE WATER-LILY. *See* **Nymphaea alba.**

WHITE WOOD. *See* **Liriodendron Tulipifera.**

Whitea'nus -a -um, in honour of W. H. White, gardener to Sir Trevor Lawrence, *c.* 1895.

WHITEHEAD'IA (in honour of the Rev. Henry Whitehead of S. Africa). FAM. *Liliaceae.* A genus of a single species of S. African bulbous plant. It needs greenhouse protection and a rich light soil and may be propagated by offsets.

W. bifo'lia. Bulb brownish; $1\frac{1}{2}$ to 2 in. wide. *l.* 2, opposite, roundish-oblong, glabrous, rather fleshy, 6 to 8 in. long, 4 to 6 in. wide, somewhat acute or emarginate. *fl.* light green, almost sessile, $\frac{1}{3}$ to $\frac{1}{2}$ in. long, segs. nearly equal, spreading above base in a dense raceme 3 to 6 in. long, on a club-shaped scape, $1\frac{1}{2}$ ft. long; stamens 6, exserted; bracts 1 to $1\frac{1}{2}$ in. long. April. S. Africa. 1792. (B.M. 480 as *Eucomis bifolia.*) SYN. *W. latifolia, Melanthium massoniaefolium.*

Whit'ei, in honour of (1) A. S. White of Fandiaweni, Natal; (2) Cyril Tenison White, 1890–1950, Queensland botanist.

WHITETHORN. *See* **Crataegus.**

WHITE-TREE. *See* **Melaleuca Leucadendron.**

WHITFIELD'IA (in honour of T. Whitfield, botanical collector of African plants.) FAM. *Acanthaceae.* A genus of about 10 species of shrubs, natives of Trop. Africa. Leaves opposite, entire. Flowers white or brick-red on short pedicels in a terminal, bracteate raceme; calyx 5-parted; corolla with 5 twisted lobes; stamens 4, didynamous; bracteoles and sometimes the bracts coloured. For treatment *see* **Barleria.**

Whitfieldia lateritia

W. lateri'tia. Evergreen shrub of about 3 ft. with round, spreading, tortuous branches. *l.* ovate or oblong-ovate, leathery. *fl.* brick-red, somewhat bell-shaped; cal. large, brick-red, half as long as cor. October to March. Sierra Leone. 1841. (B.M. 4155.)

W. longifo'lia. Shrub to 8 ft. *Upper l.* 6 to 8 in. long, 2 to 3 in. wide, closely dotted above; stalk short. *Racemes* 1 to 3, simple, downy. *fl.* white, narrow part of cor. tube 1 to $1\frac{1}{4}$ in. long, lobes soft, with white hairs, not glandular; cal. $\frac{3}{4}$ to 1 in. long. *Capsule* 4-seeded, glabrous. Trop. Africa.

Whitford'ii, in honour of Harry Nichols Whitford, b. 1872, of Kansas, forest officer in Manila.

WHITLA'VIA. Included in **Phacelia.**

WHITLOW GRASS. *See* **Draba.**

A

Whit'neyi, in honour of J. Dwight Whitney, 1819–1916, N. American geologist.

Whittal'lii, in honour of Edward Whittall, Smyrna merchant, who collected in Asia Minor.

WHORL. A ring of organs all on one plane.

WHORTLEBERRY. *See* **Vaccinium Myrtillus.**

Whyt'ei, in honour of (1) Mark Whyte, who introduced plants from Chile, *c.* 1867; (2) Alexander Whyte, 1834–1908, who collected in Trop. Africa.

Wichuraia'nus -a -um, in honour of Max Ernst Wichura, 1817–66, German botanist.

WIDDRINGTON'IA (in honour of Captain Widdrington [formerly Cook] who travelled in Spain), Cypress Pine. FAM. *Pinaceae.* A genus of evergreen trees and shrubs natives of S. Africa and the mountains of Cent. Africa, too tender for outdoor cultivation in this country except in a few favoured localities. They are closely related to Callitris but differ in the number of cone scales, which are 4 instead of 6 or 8. Leaves on young plants spirally arranged, linear, soft, flat, pointed, on older specimens scale-like, or there may be a mixture of both kinds. Male and female flowers on different trees, the former solitary and terminating short shoots, the latter axillary and made up of 2 pairs of scales. Cones ovate or globular, scales 4, woody. Seeds up to 5 on each fertile scale, each with 2 wings. The fragrant wood of the larger growing species can be used for a variety of purposes. In this country they must usually be grown in a cool greenhouse.

W. cupressoi'des. Saprae Wood. Bush 6 to 12 ft. h. with dense, erect branches. *l.* of young plants up to $\frac{1}{2}$ in. long, thin and soft, of mature plants scale-like, triangular, closely pressed. *Cones* $\frac{1}{2}$ to $\frac{3}{4}$ in. long and wide, scales smooth, 2 wider than the other 2. S. Africa. 1799. SYN. *Callitris cupressoides.*

W. dracomonta'na. A shrub differing only from *W. cupressoides* by its roughened cone scales. Some regard it as a synonym of *W. cupressoides.* Natal.

W. juniperoi'des. Clanwilliam Cedar. Tree 20 to 60 ft. h., with widely spread branches. *l.* of juvenile plants $\frac{1}{2}$ to $\frac{3}{4}$ in. long, glaucous green, those of mature type scale-like in opposite pairs, closely pressed, both kinds on same tree. *Cones* globular, $\frac{1}{3}$ to $\frac{3}{4}$ in. long and wide; scales woody, warted, spurred near the apex. *Seeds* with narrow wings. Cedarberg Mountains, S. Africa. 1758. The wood is used for cabinet work and furniture. A useful resin is also produced by the tree.

W. Mahon'i. A synonym of *W. Whytei.*

W. Schwarz'ii. Tree of moderate size closely allied to *W. juniperoides* from which it chiefly differs by its smaller, thicker, blunter l. and smaller cones. Cape Province, S. Africa.

W. Whyte'i. Milanji Cedar. Large tree. Commercially the most important species. Branches of young trees pyramidal, in old trees wide spreading. *l.* juvenile, glaucous green, up to 1 in. long. $\frac{1}{16}$ to $\frac{1}{12}$ in. wide, on old trees scale-like in opposite pairs, pressed close to shoot. *Cones* ovate, $\frac{1}{3}$ to $\frac{3}{4}$ in. across the base, $\frac{1}{2}$ to 1 in. long, scales woody, one pair a little larger than other. *Seeds* brown with 2 wide-spreading wings. To 140 ft. h. Mount Milanji, Nyasaland. 1891. SYN. *W. Mahoni.* Wood yellowish or brownish, fragrant and of very good quality. One of the most important coniferous woods of Africa. Has been grown out-of-doors in a few gardens in the British Is. but is not hardy.

A→

WIDOW, MOURNFUL. *See* **Scabiosa atropurpurea.**

Wieman'nii, Wiemannia'nus -a -um, in honour of August Wiemann, grower of alpine plants at Graz, who first grew *Saponaria Wiemannii.*

Wierzbick'ii, in honour of Peter Wierzbicki, 1794–1847, Hungarian botanist.

WIG TREE. *See* **Rhus Cotinus.**

WIGAND'IA (in honour of Johannes Wigand, 1523–87, Bishop of Pomerania, writer on plants). FAM. *Hydrophyllaceae.* A genus of 5 or 6 species of large herbs or shrubs covered with stinging hairs, all natives of mountainous parts of Trop. America. Leaves very large, more or less entire. Inflorescence circinate. Calyx divided to base with linear segments; corolla large, funnel- to salver-shaped, segments 5; stamens 5, usually exserted, attached to lower part of corolla tube; styles 2, long. Fruit a capsule, seeds small, numerous, more or less winged. Their fine foliage makes these plants valuable for sub-tropical bedding. They can be treated as half-hardy annuals, the seed being sown in heat in early spring, the seeds grown on in light, loamy soil, hardened off and planted out in June. They may be grown under glass as perennials and propagated by cuttings.

Wigandia caracasana

W. caracasa'na. Robust, erect, up to 10 ft., softly golden or silky hairy. *l.* ovate, about 18 in. long and 15 in. wide, obtuse, somewhat cordate at base, coarsely crenate, whitish-hairy beneath. *fl.* lilac with white tube, about ¾ in. long, in terminal secund spikes; style about as long as cal. or a little longer. Summer. Mexico to Colombia. 1836. (B.M. 4575; B.R. 1966.) SYN. *W. macrophylla.*

W. Kunth'ii. Bristly hairy, 6 to 15 ft. h. *l.* doubly sharply toothed, hairy above. *infl.* bristly hairy. *fl.* violet-blue in panicles. Autumn. Mexico. SYN. *W. urens* of gardens.

W. Vigier'i. About 6 ft. h. *l.* oval-elliptic, cordate at base, sparsely toothed, channelled; stalks 9 in. long. *fl.* lilac-blue, becoming wine-red to fawn, widely funnel-shaped, woolly without, in large spreading panicles; sep. longer than cor. tube. Origin unknown, 1868. Perhaps a form of *W. caracasana.*

Wight'ii, in honour of Robert Wight, M.D., 1796–1872, Supt. of Madras Botanic Gardens.

Wigramia'nus -a -um, in honour of Clive Wigram, 1st Baron Wigram of Clewer, b. 1873.

WIKSTROEM'IA (in honour of Johannes Emanuel Wikström, 1789–1856, Swedish botanist). FAM. *Thymeleaceae.* A genus of 20 species of shrubs or trees, natives of Trop. and E. Asia, Australia, and the Pacific Is. Leaves opposite or rarely alternate. Flowers with a long perianth tube and 4 spreading lobes; stamens 8; inflorescence a short raceme or spike at tips of branches. *W. viridiflora,* the bark of which yields a valuable paper material, is sometimes grown in the warm house, but has no claim to horticultural merit, nor has any other species.

WILCOX'IA (in honour of General Timothy E. Wilcox, U.S.A., a keen student of plants). FAM. *Cactaceae.* Plants with tuberous, dahlia-like roots and slender, branched stems, weak and with few ribs; all spines similar. Flowers diurnal, large for the size of the plant, with a short tube; fruit spiny. **A**

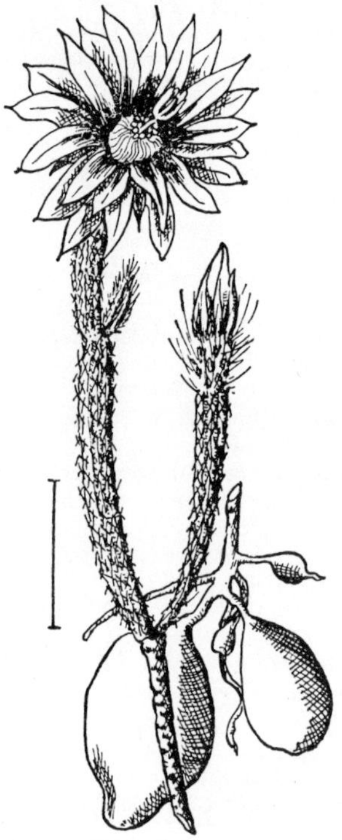

Wilcoxia Poselgeri

W. Poselge'ri. Roots black, tuberous; stems very slender, with 8 to 10 low ribs; spines very small, almost hiding the ribs, dark. *fl.* purple. Texas. (B.R.C. 2, f. 164–5.) SYN. *Cereus tuberosus, Echinocereus Poselgeri.*

W. Schmoll'ii. Similar to *W. Poselgeri,* but with shorter, thicker branches which are hidden by the mass of long grey silky hairs. Mexico. Sometimes listed as *W. senilis.*

W. se'nilis. *See* **W. Schmollii.**

W. viperi'na. Stems very long, trailing, very slender, covered with velvety down; spines dark, very small. *fl.* red. Mexico. SYN. *Cereus viperina.*

V. H.

Wild, native; growing without the intervention of man.

WILD BERGAMOT. *See* **Monarda fistulosa.**

WILD CLOVE. *See* **Pimenta acris.**

WILD DATE. *See* **Phoenix sylvestris.**

WILD HYACINTH. *See* **Scilla non-scripta.**

WILD IRISHMAN. *See* **Discaria Toumatou.**

WILD OLIVE. *See* **Elaeagnus, Olea europaea. A**

WILD POTATO VINE. *See* **Ipomoea pandurata.**

WILD SNOWBALL. *See* **Ceanothus americana.**

WILD WATER LEMON. *See* **Passiflora foetida.**

WILD WILLIAM. *See* **Lychnis Flos-cuculi.**

WILDING. Any uncultivated plant, sometimes used specifically for the crab-apple.

Wildpret'ii, in honour of Mr. Wildpret, Curator, Botanic Garden, Orotava, Teneriffe, *c.* 1897.

Wilkesia'nus -a -um, in honour of Admiral Charles Wilkes, 1798–1877, leader of the U.S. exploring expedition, 1838–42.

WILLDENOW'IA (in honour of Carl Ludwig Willdenow, 1765–1812, Professor of Botany, Berlin). FAM. *Restionaceae.* A genus of about 8 species of S. African herbs with rush-like, leafless stems. Sheaths loose, persistent. Flowers dioecious; male spikelets in an interrupted spike, loosely many-flowered; female 1-flowered sessile. A compost of loam and peat suits *W. teres*, which needs greenhouse treatment and can be propagated by division. *W. teres* is sometimes confused with a species of Restio.

W. te'res. Erect, about 3 ft. h., terete, branched from about middle; branches ascending, covered with white scales and purple spots. *Sheaths* 1½ in. long, convolute, reddish-brown, glabrous, slender-pointed. *Male infl.* 2 to 2½ in. long, erect, sometimes branched; female spikelets 1 to 3 at tip of branch. 1790.

WILLEMET'IA. *See* **Noltea africana.**

Williamsi'anus -a -um, in honour of John Charles Williams, 1861–1939, of Caerhays Castle, Cornwall, a noted amateur gardener.

Williams'ii, in honour of (1) Mr. Williams of Bahia; (2) Robert Statham Williams of New York, 1859–1945, American plant collector in Bolivia and Philippines; (3) Benjamin Samuel Williams, 1824–90, nurseryman at Upper Holloway, London, author of *The Orchid-grower's Manual*; (4) Percival Dacres Williams, 1865–1935, of Lanarth, Cornwall; (5) John Charles Williams, 1861–1939, of Caerhays Castle, Cornwall; (6) Louis Otho Williams, b. 1908, American botanist.

Willink'ii, in honour of Jan Abraham Willink, 1812–87, Dutch botanist.

Willkom'mii, in honour of Heinrich Moritz Willkomm, 1821–95, successively professor of botany at Tharandt, Dorpat, and Prague, student of Spanish flora.

Willmorea'nus -a -um, in honour of Mr. Willmore amateur gardener of Oxford, who raised *Anagallis Monellii Willmoreana* from seed sent from Madeira, *c.* 1834.

Willmot'tiae, Willmottia'nus -a -um, in honour of Miss Ellen Ann Willmott, 1860–1934, of Warley, Essex, a noted amateur gardener who introduced many plants.

WILLOW. *See* **Salix.**

WILLOW, AMERICAN WATER. *See* **Dianthera americana.**

WILLOW GRASS. *See* **Polygonum amphibium.**

WILLOW HERB. *See* **Epilobium.**

WILLOW HERB, FRENCH OR PERSIAN. *See* **Epilobium angustifolium.**

WILLOW, KILMARNOCK WEEPING. *See* **Salix Caprea pendula.**

WILLOW WEEVIL. *See* **Salix, Pests.**

WILLUGHBE'IA (in honour of Francis Willughby, 1635–72, English naturalist, friend of Ray). FAM. *Apocynaceae.* A genus of about 10 species of sarmentose or tall-climbing, Malayan and E. Asiatic shrubs, yielding caoutchouc. Leaves opposite, shortly stalked. Flowers in axillary cymes; calyx short, 5-lobed; corolla salver-shaped, tube nearly glabrous within, mouth naked or with fleshy glands alternate with lobes; stamens included. Berry large, globose or ovoid, many-seeded. *W. edulis* needs treatment of Allamanda.

W. edu'lis. An immense climber. *l.* oblong or obovate-oblong, caudate or with an obtuse point, thinly leathery, base acute; stalk ⅛ to ⅜ in. long. *fl.* pale pink; cymes on short, stout peduncles. *fr.* edible, sub-ovoid, as large as a lemon. July. India. 1818.

Wilman'ae, in honour of Miss M. Wilman of the McGregor Museum, Kimberley.

Wil'sonae, in honour of Helen Wilson, d. 1931, wife of Dr. E. H. Wilson.

×**WILSONA'RA** (in honour of Mr. Gurney Wilson, Chairman, Orchid Committee, Royal Hort. Society). FAM. *Orchidaceae.* Hybrids combining the genera Cochlioda, Odontoglossum, and Oncidium.

Wilsonia'nus -a -um. *See* ***Wilson'ii.***

Wilson'ii, in honour of (1) Dr. Ernest Henry Wilson, 1876–1931, who collected in China for Messrs. Veitch of Chelsea, and in China, Japan, and Korea for the Arnold Arboretum, Massachusetts, of which he became Director; (2) George Ferguson Wilson, 1822–1902, founder of the Wisley Wild Garden.

WILT. Apart from the physiological wilting, with subsequent recovery, which occurs in plants short of water, the term is frequently used to describe diseases, generally caused by fungus parasites attacking the roots, which cause permanent wilting of all or part of the leaves on a plant. Damping Off (q.v.) in seedlings may be preceded by wilting, but in adult plants there are many 'Wilt' diseases of herbaceous plants, shrubs, and trees. Instances are Verticillium wilt of Tomatoes due to the fungus *Verticillium alboatrum* (see **Tomato Sleepy disease**), Wilt disease of Michaelmas Daisies due to *Verticillium Vilmorinii*, and Wilt in Morello cherries due to attack by *Verticillium Dahliae* in the roots. These are cases in which signs of ill health appear at some distance from the seat of attack, i.e. the leaves are affected by poisonous substances in the sap stream although the fungus parasite is situated in the roots.

D. E. G.

A→

Wilton'ii, in honour of Sir E. Colville Wilton, b. 1870, Chinese Consular Service, Ichang.

Wimbushii, in honour of the Rev. John Wimbush who first collected *Crinum Wimbushii* by Lake Nyassa, Cent. Africa.

Wim'meri, in honour of Christian Friedrich Heinrich Wimmer, 1803–68, who studied the flora of Silesia.

Wimset'tii, in honour of Mr. Wimsett who introduced the variety *Wimsetti* of *Pteris cretica.*

Winckel'ii, in honour of W. F. Winckel, 1880–1938, of Java.

WIND. The direction, rate, and regularity of movement, and temperature of the air are matters of daily and sometimes hourly consideration in the proper management of glass-houses and frames, for largely upon these factors the amount of ventilation that can be given and the best methods of securing it depend. But preparation against injurious changes in the wind affect far more than this. Prevailing winds determine the best positions for shelter belts not only for personal comfort but for protection of plants of all kinds. The possible strength of the winds at certain seasons and whether they bring deleterious matter such as salt, sulphurous, or arsenical fumes, dust as from cement works, &c., must be taken into consideration in choosing the trees for planting such belts. The nature of the stakes, and especially the direction of the stakes in relation to the plants, and the prevailing wind must be determined according to local conditions, and this applies particularly to newly planted trees. Plants stood out on standing-grounds for the summer need securing against rough weather and so do plants in the herbaceous border. Growths made by plants trained on walls or on wire fences need timely tying, for strong winds may do much damage. Large trees often have branches torn off by gales, especially perhaps in summer, and if neglected the wounds give entry to germs of disease and moisture which rapidly cause permanent and often irreparable damage to the mutilated tree. So far as possible, therefore, means of avoiding such damage should be taken beforehand and everything made secure against injury.

Gentle movements of the air may be beneficial in promoting transpiration and avoiding the evils of stagnation of moisture and deleterious gases in the air. With some plants, too, the wind is the agent for the carrying of pollen and necessary therefore for the production of fruit, while it plays its part in the ripening of fruits, especially of the 'dry' type, such as capsules, legumes, and the like, while in nature it is an active agent in the distribution of seeds. Strong winds also affect the movements of insects, not infrequently restricting them severely, so that the virus-carrying aphides are rarely present and active in windy places and the hive-bee may not work well there either. The latter fact may impose a severe restriction on the production of seeds of such plants as Cabbages in very windy places.

WIND FLOWER. *See* **Anemone, Gentiana Pneumonanthe.**

WINDBREAKS. Windbreaks are plantings made for the purpose of affording protection from the effects of snow and cutting winds. Their influence in preventing drying out of soil and damage to branches, and in promoting the successful pollination of fruit-trees, is often considerable. Windbreaks divert air currents upward, and although such currents eventually work down to ground level again the area immediately behind the screen is comparatively calm. As regards depth the effect of the screen depends upon the height and density of the trees. A dense screen may cut the force of the wind by 75 per cent. in the area immediately behind it, this effect gradually lessening until protection is completely lost. With a 40-ft. screen protection will probably cease at a distance of 200 yards away. The prevention of ground draughts is most important, so the lower portion of any screen must be as thick as possible. For this reason pines planted pure cannot make a good screen, as they lose their lower branches. Combined with shrubs or hedges they are perhaps the best trees to use, where protection over a fairly large area is required. For ordinary gardens a well-grown hedge, or better still a double hedge with a path between, is usually satisfactory, and has the advantage of taking up a minimum amount of ground. Windbreaks should be curved to cover as many points of the compass as possible. If this cannot be arranged a return screen at each end is desirable, as with a straight hedge the wind forces its way in round the corners, and tends to convert the protected area into a triangle. If a return screen is not possible a group of trees at the ends will help to break up the currents and reduce wind force. To obtain the best results a windbreak should be at least 8 rows thick, but if a strong hedge can be maintained on the windward side the planting of 4 rows only should give good results.

Species to use

Hedges. Whitethorn, Beech, or Privet, preferably in double lines. Lawson's Cypress is a good evergreen, also Thuya. Near the sea-coast Tamarisk makes an excellent rough hedge of considerable height. *Cupressus macrocarpa* grows fast and well, but frequently dies off. All these can be run up to 10 ft.

Trees. Where a tall screen is required occupying little space a double row of Lombardy Poplars, 8 ft. between trees and 6 ft. between rows, will be found very useful. A thorn or similar hedge should be planted behind it to reduce ground draught. A single row of Lombardy poplars, with trees 5 ft. apart kept topped down, will make a thick screen up to 10 ft. in height. For general planting, in places where over 2 rows can be put in, Austrian Pine may be used. Its branching is thick, and the lower branches are more or less permanent. If considered too sombre it can be lightened with cherry or birch. Scots or Corsican Pine is useful, preferably combined with an outer row or two of Sycamore or Beech, and if possible a thorn hedge on the windward side. *Cupressus macrocarpa*, a better tree than hedge plant, can be used in mild climates, especially near the sea. If a mixed plantation is needed, Sycamore, Norway Maple, and Ash, with a backbone of Conifers, will make a good screen, especially on chalk soils. The outer section should be planted with hardy shrubs such as Snowberry (*Symphoricarpos rivularis*), Aucuba, and Elder. White Poplar planted at 10-ft. intervals, and kept topped to 8 ft. or so, is an excellent 'front-line tree', carrying thick twigs and branches. It will grow anywhere, and in the most exposed situations.

Planting. Trees for a windbreak should be planted at 4-ft. intervals, except for the 2 outside rows, which should be planted 6 ft. apart, in order to ensure good rooting. Plants should be small and well-rooted. Until well established they are liable to be rocked by wind so that constant examination and 'treading down' is essential during early life.

A. D. Le S.

WINDFALL. Term frequently used for fruits found lying in an immature condition below trees, e.g. Apples. No doubt the wind knocks or shakes off some healthy fruits but the fall of immature fruits may be due to physiological conditions (*see* **June drop**) or to the presence of grubs feeding on the seeds, e.g. Codling Moth or Sawfly larvae. These larvae usually leave the fruits soon after they fall and enter the ground to pupate. It is therefore desirable that they should be collected without delay and disposed of either by feeding to pigs or removing as far from the orchard as possible.

WINDOW-BEARING ORCHID. *See* **Cryptophoranthus.**

WINDOW-BOXES. Plants can be grown on window ledges in boxes filled with compost or in pots standing in boxes. These should be not less than 6 in. wide and 7 in. deep on the inside. They are usually of wood, but are sometimes manufactured of reinforced concrete, zinc, aluminium, &c. For wooden boxes teak or oak is best owing to its durability; deal will rot within 2 or 3 seasons unless treated with a preservative (*see* **Wood Preservation**), but creosote should not be used for this the inside can be coated with tar or charred by means of a blow-lamp and the outside painted with 2 coats of paint on a lead paint undercoating. The wood should be about 1 in. thick and the joints secured by dovetails or screws; old flooring planks provide suitable timber for boxes. It is usual to bore a number of holes in the bottom for drainage. The inconvenience which drip may cause should not be overlooked; this can be avoided by raising the bottom of the box on wooden wedges high enough for a tray to be slipped underneath the drainage holes. A wise precaution against the box being dislodged is to have a stout wire running horizontally across the front of it, and securely fastened to the brickwork on either side, or to secure it by brackets and screws to the woodwork of the window-frame, allowing a slight space, e.g. ¼ to ½ in., between the box and the frame. The box is best planted when in position. The bottom should be covered with a layer about 1 in. thick of stones or crock, and this then covered with a layer of turf, fibrous peat, or dead leaves; the box is then filled to within 1 in. of the top with compost; the sterilized John Innes Compost is recommended, but good ordinary garden soil enriched with peat or leaf-mould and lightened with sand will serve, especially if given a little superphosphate and bone-meal (about a teacupful of each to a bushel of soil). Wait a week before planting in order to give the soil time to settle. Soil is best changed every other year. Window boxes are usually very exposed and liable to dry out easily; hence they are not favourable for seedlings, and it is better to set young plants rather than try to raise seedlings from a direct sowing in the box; annuals, like Eschscholtzia, which do not readily transplant, must, however, be sown where they are to grow. No plant can be expected to ornament a window-box satisfactorily all the year round. During the winter the box can be planted with broad-leaved evergreens such as small bushes of Aucuba or Skimmia; these are more satisfactory than evergreens with small leaves because they can be more easily washed clean of soot from time to time. In late winter bulbs of Narcissus can take their place. When risk of frost is past, i.e. during the last week of May in southern England, Pelargoniums (Geraniums) and other half-hardy plants for summer decoration should be planted in the boxes. The choice of plants depends on the amount of sun they will receive. In sunny positions, plants such as Calendula, *Lobelia Erinus*, Sweet Alyssum (*Lobularia maritima*), Marguerite (*Chrysanthemum frutescens*), Mesembryanthum (robust kinds), Pelargonium, Petunia (especially the drooping 'Balcony' kinds), Snapdragon (Antirrhinums), *Tropaeolum minus*, Verbena, and Zinnia can be grown; in shady positions, Begonias, Calceolarias, and Pansies are more likely to be successful. The soil should never be allowed to dry out; during the summer a thorough soaking is desirable whenever the soil begins to dry out. To maintain as long a flowering season as possible, blooms should be removed when they fade and seeding be thus prevented.

W. T. S.

WINDOW GARDEN. The term refers to the growing of plants just within a room opposite and close to the window, or on the sill outside. In the latter position the placing of window-boxes (which prevent the falling of pots, perhaps on the heads of passers-by) to fit the window gives the best results, the plants being planted out or sown in them and renewed from time to time. An alternative is the construction of a glass case which can be attended to for watering, &c., through the window from the room, and may make a pleasant feature for those in the house (*see* **Plant Boxes and Cases**), while the window-boxes give pleasure to those without as well. Many plants will also succeed in the room either on an internal window-ledge or on a table in the window. With these it is usually necessary to stand the pots in saucers, but it is important that these saucers should be used only to catch superfluous water from the drainage of the pots and be emptied when the water has run through, not used as a reservoir for supply, which they can do effectively only for aquatic plants, not for plants that need a good supply of air to their roots. When water is required, and this can only be judged by examination, not laid down as a necessity to be supplied at stated times and regular intervals, a good soaking should be given, and in summer a gentle damping over the foliage with a fine rose or syringe will be useful, and help to keep the foliage clean. Potting is best done in spring, and then drainage can be thoroughly attended to. During severe frosts, unless there is a fire in the room, the plants will be safer placed temporarily on the floor. Among the plants which can be readily grown in the Window Garden are Zonal and Ivy-leaved Pelargoniums, and those with scented foliage, Fuchsias, Calceolarias, some dwarf Campanulas, Chinese Primulas and *Primula malacoides* and *P. obconica*, some Cacti, *Sedum lineare*, Echeverias, greenhouse Ferns, spring-flowering bulbs such as Hyacinths, Narcissi, and Tulips, Heliotropes, Myrtles, the Arum Lily, *Zantedeschia aethiopica*, *Vallota speciosa*, Tussilago, and even some Lilies. These plants are liable to suffer from the dryness of atmosphere usual in dwelling-houses; consequently they do better if the pots stand on a waterproof tray of gravel, or pebbles, and water. *See* **Room Plants.**

WINDOW PLANTS. Curious succulent plants, the foliage of which is buried in the desert sand except for an area at the tip of the leaf which is transparent enough to admit light to the chlorophyll-tissue of the leaf within. *See* **Conophytum** and **Mesembryanthemum.**

WINEBERRY. *See* **Rubus phoenicolasius.**

WINE PALM. *See* **Borassus flabellifer.**

WINE PALM, EAST INDIAN. *See* **Phoenix sylvestris.**

Winit'ii, in honour of Phya Winit Wanadorn, Siamese Forest Officer, collector of plants in NW. Siam, *c.* 1924.

Wink'leri, in honour of (1) Moritz Winkler, German botanist who collected in Spain in 1873 and 1876; (2) Constantinus Winkler, chief botanist, Petrograd Bot. Garden, 1893–1900; (3) K. Johannes M. Winkler, b. 1874, German surgeon who collected in Sumatra; (4) Hubert Winkler, b. 1875, professor at Breslau; (5) Hans Winkler, b. 1877, professor at Hamburg.

WINTER BLOOM. *See* **Hamamelis virginiana.**

WINTER CHERRY. *See* **Physalis Alkekengii.**

WINTER CRESS. *See* **Land Cress, Barbarea praecox.**

WINTER DAFFODIL. *See* **Sternbergia lutea.**

WINTER-FLOWERING PLANTS should be given a place in the garden where they are protected as far as possible from strong winds and can be seen from the house or close to a path. Several, such as *Daphne Mezereum*, *Chimonanthus praecox*, and *Viburnum fragrans*, are notable for their strong and sweet scent. Since they are not as conspicuous or showy as many of the summer-flowering plants, careful attention should be given to their placing and if possible they should be given a background of evergreens or walls. The 2 winter-flowering plants that should be in every garden are the yellow Winter Jasmine, *J. nudiflorum*, and the 'Stylosa' Iris, *I. unguicularis*. These can provide a succession of flowers from October till March during all mild spells. These are both best grown against a wall and, though tolerant of all soils, do best in well-drained light sandy soil. In January the Witch-Hazel *Hamamelis mollis* will unfold its twisted yellow petals, and these are extremely frost resistant. An effective January combination is the yellow *H. mollis* and the purple *Rhododendron mucronulatum*. Both of these are suitable for lime-free soils. The Winter cherry *Prunus subhirtella autumnalis* will open flowers during mild spells throughout the winter. Other good January flowering shrubs are *Chimonanthus praecox* and the fine yellow variety *C. praecox luteus*, *Daphne Mezereum*, *Mahonia japonica*, and *M. Bealii*. *Viburnum fragrans* will often begin flowering in November and continue through mild spells, but it is generally at its best during January. A particularly attractive combination is a bed of *V. fragrans* underplanted with *Cyclamen neapolitanum*. *V.×bodnantense* is a very good recent addition to our winter-flowering shrubs. The Korean *Abeliophyllum distichum* with palest blush-pink flowers on the bare branches is well worth a space against a wall.

The dwarf heathers, forms of *Erica carnea* and the hybrid *E.×darleyensis*, provide colour during the winter months, if carefully chosen for a succession, and are good plants for under-planting among some of the shrubs previously mentioned.

In the warmer counties of the south and west of England and Scotland the varieties of *Camellia×Williamsii* will flower freely throughout the winter and will be followed in February and March by varieties of *C. japonica*, and in late February and March by the wonderful rose-crimson goblet flowers of *Magnolia Campbellii*, if the winter has been free of hard frosts. These large Magnolias of the Yulan section are some of the most magnificent winter and early spring-flowering plants that are available for our gardens, but they are best suited to cultivation in the west and south-west since their buds are tender to hard frosts.

Among herbaceous plants the Hellebores are for the most part winter-flowerers and the Christmas Rose *H. niger*, and its fine form *altifolius*, should be planted in a warm sunny position and left undisturbed. Although very hardy they will repay a cloche to keep the flowers clean of mud. The many forms of *H. orientalis* flower freely in February when well established.

There are also several good Primulas for this season, notably forms and hybrids of *P. Juliae* and the pale mauve *P. Edgeworthii*.

Among smaller plants with bulbs, corms, or tubers the genera Galanthus, Crocus, Cyclamen, Iris, and Narcissus provide a number of very attractive winter-flowering species and are most attractive planted in a raised bed or even a raised frame filled with a well-drained compost. They are also attractive planted among the flowering shrubs or on the rock-garden. The Snowdrop season is opened in October or November with *Galanthus nivalis* sub-sp. *Olgae*, while December and January will bring out *G. byzantinus*, *G. graecus* and *G. rhizehensis*. Later the common Snowdrop, *G. nivalis*, with its numerous forms and hybrids will follow with *G. plicatus* and *G. Elwesii*. All these Snowdrops are best moved and divided when in growth soon after their flowering. Among the Crocus species *C. laevigatus* can be relied on for flowers from November till January, while in January and February *C. chrysanthus* and its many forms, *C. Imperati*, and the golden *C. aureus* will bring a touch of spring to winter, opening their flowers in any sunny period. They are all very hardy. Among the Cyclamen, *C. coum*, *C. vernum*, *C. vernum hiemale*, and *C.×Atkinsii* are good winter-flowering plants, the corms increasing in size from year to year. Among the Iris, *I. histrioides*, *I. reticulata*, and *I. histrio* var. *aintabensis* flower during January and February and should be given a sunny position where the soil is well drained. The earliest forms of Narcissus to flower are the varieties of *N. Bulbocodium* var. *Romieuxii* and var. *monophyllus*. Flowering in December and January, these are rather tender and for safety should be given a cloche or grown in a cold frame or alpine house. For the rock-garden the dwarf *N. minimus*, *N. cyclamineus*, and *N. 'February Gold'* will generally be in flower during February.

For further details of these winter-flowering plants the articles under the various genera should be consulted.

P. M. S.

WINTER GARDEN. This term usually denotes a very large, cool, glass-house, from which the frost is merely excluded the plants in it being occupied by subjects not sufficiently hardy to withstand our climate outside during the winter. The Winter Garden is usually of sufficient size to allow the central part of the interior being laid out in walks and large beds. The latter are planted with the stronger-growing occupants which cannot be properly accommodated in pots. Rhododendrons may be specially mentioned, for their foliage is attractive at all seasons while their flowers are very beautiful; Camellias, Australian Acacias and other hard-wooded plants, Araucaria, many Tree Ferns, Palms, and many other plants requiring a little winter protection. If treated like a Conservatory (q.v.) any greenhouse plant in season could be introduced on the shelves around. Tea Roses may be trained on the Pillars and climbers of many kinds are suitable if kept tied.

WINTER HELIOTROPE. *See* **Petasites fragrans.**

WINTER KILLING or **WINTER INJURY.** The kind of injury which plants may suffer owing to very low temperatures can be conveniently considered under the two headings Frost injury and Winter killing. The first refers to damage done by frost after the plants have begun to grow in spring, while the second refers to injury that may occur while the plants are dormant during winter. Frost injury is mainly concerned with sensitive annuals or the foliage and flowers of perennial plants and trees, while winter injury may occur on underground tubers, corms, &c., or even woody structures which are dormant. In general, frost will cause puckering and blistering and curling of young leaves, sometimes chlorotic patches in the normal green leaf, or may cause complete blackening and death of leaves or even young fruits (e.g. Plums and Apples). Sometimes the injury is only slight as in the case of certain Apples which through slight frost injury, although not killed, show a brown russet discoloration of the skin near the eye. Strawberry flowers may become blackened in the centre and show the 'black eye' appearance (*see* **Strawberry diseases**).

In winter injury Potatoes in store turn sweet or are entirely destroyed. The degree of injury to plants varies from root killing, bud injury, cracking of the bark, or even blackening of the internal tissues. In Great Britain perhaps the best-known symptom of severe cold is cracking in the bark of woody plants such as Apples or even large trees such as Oak. Such plants as Ericas may show split stems to such an extent that most or all of the plant is killed. *E. lusitanica* is especially susceptible and even *E. arborea* and *E. mediterranea* are affected. Some Rhododendrons suffer splitting of shoots which later develop into large cankers (e.g. *R. Thomsonii*) which sometimes remain superficial, but rotting organisms may enter the wound and kill the branch. Apple-trees may show longitudinal cracking and splitting so deep as to expose the wood. The degree of injury is also influenced by the condition of the plant, and it will be found that where plants are suffering weakness from such factors as poor soil conditions and malnutrition they will be more susceptible to winter injury. This applies especially in the case of herbaceous plants with soft tissues such as Cabbage, Lettuce, &c. An interesting case of winter injury is seen in fruit-trees which have been loosened in the ground by wind, with the result that water remains in a socket around the collar and during winter causes rotting of the bark at the base of the stem. This kind of injury to fruit-trees is known as 'The Death'.

D. E. G.

WINTER MOTH, *Cheimatobia* (*Operophtera*) *brumata*, is, together with the Mottled Umber and March Moths (q.v.), grouped under the heading 'Winter Moths'. There are other species of Moths, namely, the November, *Asthena dilutata*, and December, *Eriogaster populi*, which emerge from their chrysalids during the winter months, but the caterpillars of the Winter, Mottled Umber, and March are as important pests of fruits and of ornamental species of *Pyrus* and *Prunus* as any with which the fruit-grower and gardener has to contend.

The male has greyish-brown wings, the forewings with an expanse of 1 to 1½ in., while the female is spider-like and practically wingless—the wings being very abbreviated making flight impossible. They appear from early October to late January, during which period the females ascend the stem from the soil and deposit their light-greenish eggs, which later become reddish, singly or in small groups on the branches, spurs, and shoots. The caterpillars, which are at first grey with dark heads and later green with white stripes and greenish heads, feed on the developing buds in early spring, and then openly on the foliage and fruitlets often causing complete defoliation and rendering the fruits worthless by biting pieces out of their sides. When fully fed in mid-June, they descend to the soil and pupate.

Control measures against the 3 species of Winter Moths include grease-banding (q.v.), the application of an arsenical wash in spring (*see* Stomach Poisons), and the use of a delayed dormant Winter Petroleum wash in late March (*see* **Winter Washes**). **A**

G. F. W.

WINTER SPORE. Among fungi there are many species which produce different kinds of spores (*see* **Pleomorphism**). In general the spores are of 2 kinds, some thin-walled (conidia) which germinate quickly and enable the fungus to spread rapidly, while others are thick-walled and require a period of rest before they will germinate. Some of these latter in fact will not germinate before they have been subjected to the low temperatures of winter when they begin to grow with favourable conditions in spring. They are therefore often referred to as winter or resting spores (*see* **Resting spores**). In the different groups we thus find the thick-walled oospores of certain Phycomycetes, especially in the 'damping off' type of fungus, and in the Rust fungi we find the teleutospore or resting spore. In the Ascomycetes the ascospores are often called winter spores because although thin-walled they are protected by being enclosed inside the relatively thick wall of the ascocarp. (*See* **Ascomycetes, Perithecium, &c.**)

D. E. G.

WINTER WASHES. Spray fluids applied during the winter months on trees, &c., especially fruit-trees when they are in a dormant condition and for this reason these sprays are also called Dormant sprays. *See* **Fungicides, Insecticides.**

WINTERA'CEAE. Dicotyledons. A family of trees or shrubs with small flowers often included in Magnoliaceae, but lacking stipules and with the carpels more or less in a single whorl on a short axis instead of spirally arranged on an elongated axis. It includes Drimys and Illicium and is treated in this Dictionary under **Magnoliaceae.**

WINTERA'NA. *See* **Canella.**

WINTERANA'CEAE (Syn. *Canellaceae*). Dicotyledons. A family of tropical plants with 4 species in America, 1 in Africa, 1 in Madagascar, allied to Bixaceae and Violaceae, with entire leaves without stipules, flowers in umbels, perfect, regular. Sepals 4 or 5, petals 4 or 5 or none, stamens 20 or fewer in 1 bundle, carpels superior, 2 to 5, with 2 to many ovules on a parietal placenta. Fruit a berry. The genera dealt with are Canella, Cinnamodendron, Cinnamosma, and Winterana. Some botanists now consider that the more correct name for this family is Canellaceae.

WINTERBERRY. *See* **Ilex laevigata.**

WINTERGREEN. *See* **Gaultheria procumbens, Pyrola.**

WINTERGREEN, CHICKWEED. *See* **Trientalis europaea.**

Win'teri, in honour of (1) Ferdinand Winter, 1835–88, apothecary of Eifel; (2) E. L. Winter, commissioner of Kumaon, N. India, in 1908.

WINTER'S BARK. *See* **Drimys Winteri.**

WINTERSWEET. *See* **Chimonanthus praecox, Toxicophlaea spectabilis.**

WIRE. Galvanized iron wire and copper wire finds many uses in the garden, while soft iron and silvered binding wire is indispensable for florists' work. The foundations of wreaths and other designs are made of wire while stalks of leaves and flowers are strengthened, supplemented, or supplied by stiff wire of various thicknesses sold in 6- or 8-in. lengths. The short lengths are known as 'stubbs'. Binding wire is wound on reels. It is very fine but strong. Galvanized wire is used for both permanent and movable trellises in the glass-houses and for fences on which to train espaliers and roses, blackberries, loganberries, &c., in the open, as well as for strengthening hedges. Barbed wire is an additional protection to tree guards in the orchard and park. Single and stranded galvanized wire is useful for guying trees liable to rock in the wind. Galvanized wire netting of different meshes has various uses, especially in protecting crops from rabbits and birds. Painted or galvanized wire is also used for stakes and for holding glass in cloches. Copper wire should be used for tying labels to trees.

WIREWORMS. The long, thin, 6-legged, pale brown, tough-skinned grubs called wireworms are the most widely distributed and injurious of all soil pests and are the immature stages of Click Beetles or Skipjacks. They are normal inhabitants of turf and grassland where 300,000 to 1,500,000 may occur to the acre. While primarily grass-root feeders, they also attack a wide range of cultivated plants by boring into underground stems, roots, tubers, bulbs, and corms, and by devouring the roots of many Cereals, vegetable and fruit crops, ornamental plants, and glass-house crops owing to their introduction in loam. The term 'Black Wireworm' is often applied to the sluggish, many-legged Millepede (q.v.) and that of 'White Wireworm' to the white, spear-shaped, active, harmless maggot of 2-winged Flies (*Thereva* species), while many beneficial grubs of Carabid or Ground Beetles are too frequently destroyed in mistake for Wireworms. Many species occur in gardens, among the most common being *Agriotes lineatus*, *A. obscurus*, and *Athous haemorrhoidalis*. Wireworms hatch from eggs laid by the female Click Beetle from May to July usually beneath the soil surface among grass tufts and other plants. Young larvae do little harm for they feed at first on decaying vegetable matter and disintegrating turf. As they grow their colour deepens, and they begin to attack the underground portions of plants. They continue to feed for 4 or 5 years according to the species and to the availability of food. When fully grown, the mature Wireworms descend to a depth of 8 to 12 in. in the soil, and pupate in earthen cells. The pupal stage is comparatively brief, and the adult either emerges in autumn and hibernates among refuse, or remains underground in its pupal cell until the following spring.

Wireworms are most troublesome in weedy, neglected gardens, and in gardens and allotments on sites recently converted from broken grassland and waste-ground. There is no speedy and effective method of eradicating these pests in heavily infested ground, and it is necessary to persist with certain cultural methods to reduce their numbers and to render conditions unfavourable to them. Turf should be skimmed from grassland, and placed—grass downwards—at the bottom of the first spit during digging and trenching operations to allow the Wireworms to feed on the disintegrating turf while subsequent crops are establishing themselves. The ground should be consolidated prior to seed-sowing by treading or rolling. Hoeing should be a regular routine operation throughout the growing season, for this ensures weed control while the grubs are exposed to insectivorous birds as well as

Wireworm beetle (p. 2283)

to injury by the mechanical action of the hoe. Some crops are less attractive than others, and Broad, French, and Runner Beans, Peas, Kale, Parsnip, and Spinach should be grown the first year after grass. Potatoes are a favoured food plant, but damage to the tubers may be avoided to some considerable extent by cutting off the haulm in mid-August to hasten the ripening of the tubers, which should be lifted by early September to escape the autumn-feeding period of the Wireworms. Trapping is effective on a small scale, and effective baits consist of Potato tubers, and Carrots spitted on wooden skewers and buried in the ground. Such baits are lifted periodically, the Wireworms removed and destroyed, and the traps reset. Naphthalene dressings have a temporary repellent action on Wireworms, and may be broadcast along seed-rows and round freshly planted seedlings to allow them to become established before any damage occurs. Loam intended for glass-house borders and potting composts should be partially sterilized with steam or fumigated with Carbon disulphide prior to use. Green Manuring, using a Mustard crop, is partially effective when dug in during July owing to its repellent action on the grubs. **A**

G. F. W.

WISTER'IA (in honour of Caspar Wistar, 1761–1818, Professor of Anatomy in the University of Pennsylvania). FAM. *Leguminosae*. A genus of 7 species of beautiful deciduous twining climbers, 2 from N. America, the others from China or Japan. Leaves alternate, unequally pinnate. Flowers blue, violet, purple, rose, or white, in pendulous racemes. Pods velvety in the Asiatic species (except *W. japonica*), glabrous in the American ones.

All the species are hardy in the south of England and like a good loamy soil. *W. sinensis* is often planted (in Italy especially) to clamber over large trees. All of them can be trained on walls and pergolas. *W. floribunda macrobotrys* (*W. multijuga*) is best placed where its long racemes can be allowed to fall their full length freely. A kind of large cage is sometimes constructed for it. Plants restricted in space, as on walls, have to be pruned hard back annually in late winter to keep them within bounds. A second pruning—a mere shortening back of the leafy shoots—is useful in August. By means of these 2 prunings, plants of *W. sinensis*, and *W. venusta* may be grown as standards. Propagation is by layering.

KEY

1. *Fl. about ½ in. long, base of standard without swellings; infl. axillary* — W. japonica
1. *Fl. ½ to 1 in. long, base of standard with swellings; infl. terminal on short branches* — 2
2. *Pedicels not over ⅜ in. long; wings of fl. long-auricled, pods glabrous* — 3
2. *Pedicels ⅜ to 1¼ in. long; wings of fl. not long-auricled, pods velvety* — 4
3. *Racemes* 8 *to* 12 *in. long, glandular; cal. lobes nearly as long as narrow tube* — W. macrostachya
3. *Racemes* 2 *to* 4 *in. long, scarcely glandular; cal. lobes much shorter than broad tube* — W. frutescens
4. *Lvs. downy, especially beneath* — W. venusta
4. *Lvs. almost smooth when mature* — 5
5. *Fl. open successively on slender raceme; lflets.* 11 *to* 19 — W. floribunda
5. *Fl. open almost simultaneously on broader raceme; lflets.* 7 *to* 15 — 6
6. *Lflets.* 9 *to* 15*; fl.* ⅘ *in. long, pale violet* — W. × formosa
6. *Lflets.* 11 (7 *to* 13)*; fl.* 1 *in. long, mauve to white* — W. sinensis

W. brachybot'rys. A synonym of *W. floribunda.*

W. floribun'da. Climber 30 ft. or more. *l.* 10 to 15 in. long; lflets. 11 to 19, soon nearly glabrous and dark glossy green, ovate, 1½ to 3 in. long. *Racemes* slender, 5 to 10 in. long on short leafy shoots. *fl.* opening successively from the base ½ to ¾ in. long, violet or purplish-blue, fragrant; standard pet. ¾ in. wide; cal. ⅓ in. long with triangular teeth. June. *Pod* 3 to 6 in. long, velvety. Japan. 1830. SYN. *W. brachybotrys.* var. **al'ba,** *fl.* white, racemes up to 2 ft. long, (B.T.S. 2, 262–3 as *W. multijuga alba.*); **macrobotr'ys,*** racemes 3 or 4 ft. long (sometimes 6 ft. in Japan), long known as *W. multijuga*; **ro'sea,** *fl.* pale rose tipped purple. SYN. *W. multijuga rosea*; **Russellia'na,** *fl.* darker than the type; **variega'ta,** *l.* poorly variegated; **viola'cea ple'na,** *fl.* violet, double.

W. × formo'sa* (*W. floribunda alba* × *W. sinensis*). Shoots silky downy. *lflets.* 9 to 15. *fl.* ⅘ in. long, pale violet, opening almost simultaneously on racemes 10 in. long. Raised in Massachusetts. 1905.

W. frutes'cens. Climber 30 to 40 ft. *l.* 7 to 12 in. long; lflets. 9 to 15, ovate to oblong-lanceolate, 1½ to 2½ in. long, glabrous at maturity. *Racemes* terminal, 4 to 6 in. long, very downy. *fl.* crowded, lilac-purple, with a yellow spot, ¾ in. long; cal. slenderly bell-shaped with short teeth. June–August. *Pod,* 2 to 4 in. long. E. United States. 1724. (B.M. 2103.)

W. japo'nica. Climber with slender, climbing, glabrous stems. *l.* 6 to 9 in. long; lflets. 9 to 13, ovate, rounded to cordate at the base, 1½ to 2½ in. long, glabrous and glossy. *Panicles* up to 12 in. long,

Wisteria venusta (p. 2285)

many-fld., 6 to 12 in. long; *fl.* pale yellow or white, ½ in. long, cal. glabrous except for the ciliate margins, toothed. *Pod* 3 to 4 in. long, glabrous 6- to 7-seeded. Japan. 1878. SYN. *Millettia japonica.*

W. macrosta'chya. Climber 20 to 30 ft. *lflets.* usually 9, ovate to oval-lanceolate, 1½ to 3 in. long. *Racemes* 8 to 12 in. long, glandular-downy, with up to 90 fl. which are lilac-purple; fl.-stalk and cal. glandular-hairy. May, June. *Pod* 3 to 5 in. long. Cent. United States. Near *W. frutescens* but handsomer and with racemes twice as long.

W. multiju'ga. A synonym of *W. floribunda macrobotrys.*

W. sinen'sis.* Chinese Kidney Bean. Climber up to 100 ft., trunk girthing up to 5 ft. *l.* 10 to 12 in. long; lflets. usually 11, oval to ovate-oblong, 1½ to 3½ in. long, ciliate, downy at first beneath. *fl.* mauve or deep lilac, 1 in. long, in racemes 8 to 12 in. long, opening simultaneously. May. *Pod* 5 to 6 in. long, velvety. China. 1816. (B.M. 2083.) The noblest hardy climber ever introduced. By an annual hard pruning back in late winter and a shortening back of young shoots in August, plants can be grown and kept as standards 6 or 8 ft. h.

W. venus'ta. Climber 30 ft. and upwards, shoots softly downy. *l.* 8 to 14 in. long; lflets. usually 11, oval to ovate, base rounded, apex shortly pointed, 1½ to 4 in. long, downy especially beneath. *Racemes* 4 to 6 in. long, 3 to 4 in. wide. *fl.* white, slightly fragrant, 1 to 1¼ in. long; standard pet. yellow at base. May, June. *Pod* 6 to 8 in. long, velvety. Gardens of Japan. 1912. (B.M. 8811.) Well distinguished by its entirely downy character. var. **ple'na,** *fl.* double; **viola'cea** with violet *fl.* is the wild Japanese form.

WITCH ELM. *See* **Wych Elm.**

WITCH HAZEL. *See* **Hamamelis.**

WITCHES' BROOMS. This is the name used for abnormal appearance of shoots produced on the tree branches which is in most cases due to invasion by parasitic fungi. In a typical Witches' Broom on the affected branch there grows from one point a dense formation of crowded shoots. Usually this crowded mass of small branches is erect and can easily be seen among the larger branches but in cultivated and wild cherries the Witches' Brooms, caused by the fungus *Taphrina Cerasi*, may consist of relatively few shoots in a bunch, but these are very thick and swollen and are obviously much larger and longer than the normal shoot growth. Other Witches' Brooms are those typical ones seen in Birch-trees looking like enormous birds' nests and caused by the fungus *Taphrina turgidus.* Most Witches' Brooms are due to species of the fungus Taphrina (q.v.), but a few are caused by certain Rust fungi, e.g. *Melampsorella Caryophyllacearum* on Silver Fir (*see* **Abies**). It must also be remembered that some are considered to be caused by mites as in willows.

D. E. G.

WITCHES' KNOTS. *See* **Witches' Brooms.**

WITCHES' THIMBLE. *See* **Silene maritima.**

WITHE ROD, SMOOTH. *See* **Viburnum nudum.**

WITHY. *See* **Salix fragilis, S. viminalis.**

WITLOOF. A variety of Chicory (q.v.).

WITSEN'IA (in honour of Nicholas Witsen, Dutch patron of botany). FAM *Iridaceae.* A monotypic genus of an ornamental S. African shrub needing sandy peat and greenhouse conditions. Propagation by seed or by cuttings.

W. corymbo'sa. A synonym of *Nivenia corymbosa.*

W. mau'ra. Stem woody, erect, 2 to 4 in. long, branches leafy at top. *l.* distichous, rigid, ensiform, 6 to 8 in. long. *fl.* tube about 2 in. long, ½ in. wide at throat, brownish near base, bluish-black towards top, segs. yellow, erect, ½ in. long; infl. crowded in oblong heads. S. Africa. 1790. (B.R. 5; P.M.B. 8, 221.)

Wittea'nus -a -um, Witt'ei, in honour of Heinrich Witte, 1829–1917, Dutch horticulturist and writer.

WITTMACK'IA (named in honour of Max Carl Ludwig Wittmack, 1839–1929, for many years editor of *Gartenflora*). FAM. *Bromeliaceae.* A genus of 5 epiphytic herbs, related to Hohenbergia but with a loosely branched inflorescence. Cultivation as for Aechmea.

W. odo'ra. *fl.* sessile, spreading; pet. pale yellow; panicle loose, 2-pinnate, 1 to 1½ ft. long; peduncle 1½ ft. long; bract-l. appressed. *l.* 10 to 12, 2 to 3 ft. long, lorate, lepidote on both sides, but especially at the back. W. Indies. 1879. A distinct but not showy plant. SYN. *Aechmea odora.*

Witsenia maura

Wittmannia'nus -a -um, Wittmann'ii, in honour of Herr Wittmann who travelled and collected in the Caucasian Taurus, *c.* 1840, and was later gardener in Odessa.

Wittrockia'nus -a -um, in honour of Veit Brecher Wittrock, 1839–1914, professor at Stockholm and director of Hortus Bergianus, author of a history of the cultivated Pansy in *Acta Horti Bergiani,* 2 (1896–7).

WITTSTEIN'IA (in honour of Georg Christian Wittstein, 1810–1887, author of books on plant-names and chemistry). FAM. *Ericaceae.* A genus of a single species of prostrate or creeping shrub, native of Australia. Closely related to Themistoclesia. For treatment of this greenhouse plant, *see Erica.*

W. vaccinia'cea. Branches ascending, 6 to 12 in. long, usually slightly hairy. *l.* scattered or in clusters of 2 or 3, obovate-oblong, blunt, thick, about 1 in. long, pale or glaucous beneath; stalk short. *fl.* yellowish-green or reddish, about ⅓ in. long, drooping, solitary in l.-axils. Victoria. 1892.

WOAD, DYER'S. *See* **Isatis tinctoria.**

WOAD, WAXEN. *See* **Genista tinctoria.**

WOAD, WILD. *See* **Reseda Luteola.**

Wockea'nus -a -um, Wock'ei, in honour of Erich Wocke, b. 1863, at one time head gardener at the Botanic Garden, Zürich, later the founder of the Alpenpflanzengarten at Oliva near Danzig, author of *Die Kulturpraxis der Alpenpflanzen* (3rd ed., 1940).

WOLF BERRY. *See* **Symphoricarpos occidentalis.**

Wolff'ii, in honour of Herman Wolff, 1866–1929, German veterinary surgeon and botanist, monographer of genera of Umbelliferae.

Wolfia'nus -a -um, Wolf'ii, in honour of (1) Ferdinand Otto Wolf, 1838–1906, professor of botany at Sitten, many years president of the Société Murithienne du Valais; (2) Franz Theodor Wolf, b. 1841, German geologist and botanist, monographer of the genus Potentilla.

WOLF'S BANE. *See* **Aconitum Lycoctonum.**

WOLF'S CLAW. *See* **Lycopodium clavatum.**

WOLF'S MILK. *See* **Euphorbia.**

wolga'ricus -a -um, volgen'sis -is -e, of the region of the River Volga.

Wollaston'ii, in honour of (1) William Hyde Wollaston, 1766–1820, physician-naturalist and chemist of East Dereham; (2) Alexander Frederick Richmond Wollaston, 1875–1930, naturalist and explorer.

Wolteria'nus, in honour of Paul Wolter, b. 1861, orchid-grower of Magdeburg.

WOMAN'S-CAP ORCHID. *See* **Thelymitra.**

WONGA-WONGA VINE. *See* **Pandorea pandorana.**

WOOD. The hard part of the stem and root. *See* **xylem.**

WOOD ANEMONE. *See* **Anemone nemorosa.**

WOOD ASHES. *See* **Ashes.**

WOOD AVENS. *See under* **Geum** in Supplement.

WOOD BETONY. *See* **Pedicularis canadensis, Stachys officinalis.**

WOOD BRONEY. An old name for the Ash (*Fraxinus excelsior*).

WOOD FERN. *See* **Polypodium vulgare.**

WOOD LAUREL. *See* **Daphne Laureola.**

WOOD LEOPARD MOTH. *See* **Leopard Moth.**

WOOD LILY. *See* **Trillium.**

WOOD NUT. *See* **Corylus Avellana.**

WOOD OIL. *See* **Dipterocarpus.** A

WOOD OIL-TREE. *See* **Aleurites.**

WOOD PRESERVATION. When used for many purposes wood will last almost indefinitely, but under certain conditions, however, it can be seriously damaged or even destroyed by the attack of certain organisms, e.g. fungi and insects. Some timbers such as greenheart, teak and western red cedar have a high natural resistance to these forms of attack and for a long time have been used wherever durability is of special importance. Durable woods such as these have become scarce and expensive in recent years, so that it is now necessary to use less durable woods which must be specially treated if they are to give long service.

The most serious loss of timber in use is from decay caused by wood-destroying fungi, which can attack timber exposed to the air only when its moisture content exceeds about 20 per cent. of its dry weight. Dry timber or timber water-logged or immersed in water out of contact with the air is not subject to decay. Good building construction should aim at providing effective damp-proof courses, good ventilation, and protection of the timber by painting and, if seasoned timber is used, these will generally ensure that the timber will not become sufficiently damp to decay. Under some conditions of use, e.g. in contact with the ground, it is not possible to prevent timber from becoming damp, and in such cases it is essential to treat it with a wood preservative if a long life is to be obtained.

Wood preservatives are liquids containing substances toxic to fungi and insects, and three types are in common use, namely, oil, water-soluble, and solvent types, each of which has some special advantage. The best known of the oil type is coal-tar creosote which has been the standard preservative for over 100 years for timber used out-of-doors or under the most exposed conditions, such as poles, sleepers, and marine timbers, where the dark colour and characteristic odour are not objectionable. Creosote and other tar oils should not be used to preserve horticultural timbers in confined spaces such as in glass-houses, as the vapour can be harmful to plant life. *See under* **Fungicides** (organic) in Supplement.

Water-soluble preservatives, as their name implies, consist of toxic chemicals dissolved in water and 1 to 5 per cent. solutions of zinc chloride, copper sulphate, sodium fluoride, mercuric chloride (corrosive sublimate), and arsenical compounds have all been employed for preserving wood. Being water-soluble they are not so permanent as the oil types when used out-of-doors, as the salts are leached out from the treated wood. Modern preservative mixtures, however, are more resistant to leaching than the single salts, and are being used in increasing amounts for the pressure treatment of building and horticultural timbers. The fact that the treated wood is odourless and can be painted when dry makes these preservatives especially suitable for these purposes. The solvent type consists essentially of toxic chemicals dissolved in volatile liquids such as white spirits or solvent naphtha. Those based on copper naphthenate and pentachlorophenol are efficient preservatives and have become increasingly popular in recent years. These chemicals are practically insoluble in water and are relatively permanent, and wood treated with them can be painted after the solvent has evaporated. They are, however, somewhat costly and this usually restricts their use to a brush or other surface application.

The most effective method of applying wood preservatives is by pressure, though some permeable species, such as alder, beech, hornbeam, lime, sycamore, Scots and Corsican pine, can be readily impregnated by the open-tank hot and cold process. An impregnation treatment which ensures that all sapwood is completely penetrated should always be employed for timber used in contact with the ground or under other severe conditions. There are a number of firms with plants in various parts of the country who specialize in the pressure treatment of timber with creosote or water-soluble preservatives, but the open-tank method can be carried out with very simple equipment.

Surface treatments include brushing, spraying, dipping, and steeping, in increasing order of effectiveness. These are not generally suitable for long-term preservation unless they are repeated periodically. When applying a preservative by brush or spray the preservative should be applied liberally and the timber allowed to absorb the liquid freely along end grain and at joints, where decay usually starts. Timber should be thoroughly dry at the time of treatment.

The following are a few examples of appropriate preservative treatments:

Fencing, poles, stakes, and other timbers used externally or in contact with the ground. Pressure creosoting will give the best results; with permeable timbers the open-tank method will also give good results. Stakes removed each year can be given a brush or dip treatment with a creosote or solvent-type preservative.

Building timbers, timber for glass-houses, frames, bulb and seed boxes, &c., *wheelbarrows and timbers to be subsequently painted.* Pressure treatment with water-soluble preservatives is the most suitable; open-tank treatment also suitable in many cases. Dipping machined components in a solvent-type preservative is also effective but sufficient time must be allowed for the solvent to evaporate before painting or putting plants near to the treated wood.

Tool handles. Dipping in a solvent-type preservative followed by painting, varnishing, or oiling with raw linseed oil will preserve them and make them more comfortable to handle.

Further information will be found in *Forest Products Research Leaflets*, no. 6, 'Dry Rot in Wood. Recognition, Prevention and Cure' (1947); no. 39, 'Timber Decay and its Control' (1946); no. 11, 'The Hot and Cold Open Tank Process of Impregnating Timber' (1945); *Forest Products Research Bulletin*, no. 1, 'Dry Rot in Wood' (4th edn. 1945), by K. St. G. Cartwright and W. P. K. Findlay; *Forest Products Research Records*—no. 9, 'Methods of Applying Wood Preservatives. Part 1. Non-pressure Methods' (1950), by J. Bryan; no. 17, 'Wood Preservatives' (1950), by N. A. Richardson; and the books *Wood Preservation*, by G. M. Hunt and G. A. Garratt (1938); *Decay of Timber and its Prevention*, by K. St. G. Cartwright and W. P. K. Findlay (1946).

N. A. R.

WOOD ROTS. There are many kinds of wood rots due to the attack of wood-destroying fungi which may occur either on the living trees or on the timber from the time it is felled, prepared, and stored, or even when it is in position in buildings and sheds. The chief factor which encourages these wood-destroying fungi is moisture, and it is generally the presence of dampness which is responsible for their attack on building timber. Most of them belong to the Basidiomycetes and a large number are of the type known as Bracket fungi. They have been described under their various hosts in the various tree diseases. (*See also* **Bracket Fungi, Dry Rot**, &c.)

D. E. G.

WOOD RUSH. *See* **Luzula.**

WOOD SORREL (*Oxalis Acetosella*). Hardy native perennial sometimes grown for the use of the young leaves in salads. A cool, shady place is best for it and soil containing plenty of decayed leaves. It should be cut over frequently so that it does not produce seeds, for the seedlings are apt to be too numerous. It is easily raised from seed or can be obtained from wild sources.

WOOD SOWER. An old name for Wood Sorrel.

WOOD TONGUE FERN. *See* **Drymoglossum.**

WOOD VIOLET. *See* **Viola Riviniana.**

WOODBINE. *See* **Lonicera Periclymenum.**

WOODBINE, AMERICAN. *See* **Parthenocissus quinquefolia.**

WOODEN PEARS. *See* **Xylomelum.**

WOODFORD'IA (in honour of James Woodforde, d. 1837, who published a catalogue of the plants round Edinburgh in 1824). Fam. *Lythraceae*. A genus of a single species of shrub with long spreading branches, native of India, &c. For treatment of this stove plant *see* **Leianthus.**

W. floribun'da. Shrub of 1 to 4 ft. *l.* opposite or nearly so, entire, lanceolate, 2 to 4 in. long, usually rounded or heart-shaped at base, often grey-hairy beneath. *fl.* scarlet, in short panicles in l.-axils, rarely solitary; cal. $\frac{1}{3}$ to $\frac{1}{2}$ in. long, 6-toothed; pet. 6, about as long as cal. or wanting. May, June. (B.M. 1906 as *Grislea tomentosa.*) Syn. *W. tomentosa.*

Wood'ii, in honour of John Medley Wood, 1827–1915, Curator, Botanic Garden, Durban.

Woodfordia floribunda

WOODLICE. These very common Crustaceans, also known as Pillbugs, Sowbugs, and Slaters, are a source of considerable trouble in nurseries and gardens. They are characterized by possessing 2 pairs of antennae, 7 pairs of legs, a segmented flattened body, and an abbreviated abdomen. There are a number of marine and fresh-water forms, while the terrestrial species which, with the possible exception on the Common Pill Woodlouse (*Armadillidium*), are dependent on moisture and favour damp and shaded situations. They are destructive pests in glass-houses and Mushroom sheds, and the presence of decomposing rubbish (garden refuse heaps), decayed woodwork (glass-house staging, path edgings and tree stumps) and 'Fern Rockeries' in conservatories provide conditions favourable to their rapid increase. Woodlice are nocturnal, and hide away during the day-time in crevices beneath stones, in posts and brickwork, and in leaf-mould, compost, and rubbish heaps. Their food consists chiefly of dead and decaying organic matter, but several species attack plants by gnawing the stems, eating out irregular holes in the foliage of a variety of plants both in the open and in glass-houses, devouring the finer roots of pot plants, and nibbling the aerial roots of Orchids. The white eggs are carried by the female beneath the body in a manner similar to Prawns and Shrimps. The young Woodlouse resembles its parents, but is paler and delicate in appearance. There are a number of species associated with damage to garden plants, including *Oniscus asellus* (brownish) and *Porcellio scaber* (slate-grey). These, together with *Armadillidium speyeri, Porcellio laevis* and *Trichoniscus roseus*, frequently occur in glass-houses and cause considerable havoc to plants. **A**

Control. Their numbers may be effectively reduced by trapping and baiting. Suitable traps consisting of scooped-out Potato tubers and Mangold roots, Orange and Grapefruit peel, and inverted plant-pots stuffed loosely with straw should be set down on the ground, among pots on glass-house staging and resting on the moss of Orchid pots. The traps should be examined daily, the Woodlice collected and destroyed, and the traps reset. Effective baits consist of ½ lb. of Paris Green (an arsenical preparation) mixed thoroughly with either 14 lb. Bran or 28 lb. of Dried Blood. The bait is broadcast evenly and thinly over the soil, staging or border, towards evening at the rate of ½ to 1 oz. to the sq. yd. Spring and summer applications are more effective than autumn dressings since their natural food in the form of decaying vegetation increases as the season advances. Five per cent. D.D.T. dust may be applied over the ground. Clean cultivation, including the proper disposal of garden refuse, fallen leaves, weeds, and the removal of dead and decaying foliage at the base of plants, should be practised. Rotting tree stumps, old seed-boxes, and decayed wooden edgings to garden paths should be removed, while brickwork in glass-houses may require pointing to reduce all available shelter for these pests. G. F. W.

WOODRUFF or **WOODROWELL.** *See* **Asperula.**

WOODS'IA (named after Joseph Woods, 1776–1864, author of *The Tourists' Flora*). FAM. *Polypodiaceae.* A genus of nearly 40 species of tufted ferns, mostly inhabiting cold or temperate climates, especially N. America. Stipes often jointed and separating at the joint. Sori globose; indusium inferior, soft-membranous, from the first calyciform or more or less globose, and sometimes enclosing the sorus, at length opening at the top, the margin or mouth irregular, lobed or fringed. With the exception of *W. mollis*, all the exotic species thrive in a cool house. *W. alpina* and *W. ilvensis* are British. As a rule, Woodsias flourish where but little soil is allowed around their roots, in crevices of damp rocks or upon the rocks themselves, generally in fairly exposed situations. They are adapted for growing in small intermediate and hardy Ferneries where they form suitable companions to *Asplenium Ruta-muraria, A. Trichomanes, Ceterach officinarum*, &c., and they may also be successfully cultivated in pots. They require a very open soil, of turfy peat and light loam in equal parts, with a free mixture of finely broken charcoal, sandstone, or silver-sand. Thorough drainage is essential, and the crowns of the plants should be kept above the soil and surrounded by a few small stones: the effect of this arrangement is to keep the roots in a permanently moist state without using much water, for they are particularly averse to stagnant moisture.

Woodsias are usually increased by the division of their crowns, best done when they are at rest from November to March. They may also be propagated by means of spores, which are produced in abundance and germinate freely, especially when sown in a temperature of 65 to 70° F.

W. alpi'na. *Rootstock* stout, somewhat elongated. *sti.* shining, clothed with ferruginous scales. *Fronds* 3 to 6 in. long, linear-lanceolate, densely tufted; pinnae distant, ovate-cordate, ¼ to ½ in. long, pubescent and ciliate, with a few broad lobes. *Sori* 3 to 5 on each lobe. Arctic Europe (Britain), &c. (H.B.F. 7; L.F. 7, 27.) SYN. *W. hyperborea.*

W. cauca'sica. A synonym of *W. fragilis.*

W. fra'gilis. *Fronds* lanceolate, 9 in. long, glandular-hirsute on rachis and midrib, firm-membranous, 2-pinnate; primary pinnae sessile, nearly opposite, lanceolate, broadest at base, acuminate-pinnatifid or again pinnate; lobes or ultimate pinnules oblong, acute, serrated. *Sori* large, 2 on each lobe, 1 each side near margin; indusium globose. Caucasus. SYN. *W. caucasica, Hymenocystis caucasica.*

W. glabel'la. *sti.* short. *fr.* linear, slightly tapering below, pinnate; pinnae very remote towards the short stipes, all deltoid, very obtuse, cut into from 3 to 7 shortly rounded or sub-cuneate entire lobes. Arctic and the temperate zones. (B.B. ed. 2, 1, 13.)

W. hyperbor'ea. A synonym of *W. alpina.*

W. ilven'sis. *Fronds* broadly lanceolate; pinnae oblong, obtuse, broader at base, sessile, deeply pinnatifid, with many oblong, sub-crenate lobes. Alpine regions of N. Hemisphere. (H.B.F. 8; L.F. 9, 28.)

W. mol'lis.* *Fronds* lanceolate, pinnate, generally densely clothed, especially beneath, with short, jointed hairs, scarcely attenuated below; pinnae sessile from a broader base, oblong, obtuse, pinnatifid; lobes approximate, oval or nearly round, entire or crenate. *Sori* marginal; involucre opening with a jagged, circular mouth. Mexico, Peru. (L.F. 7, 26.) Greenhouse. SYN. *Physematium mollis.*

W. obtu'sa.* *sti.* tufted, not articulated, 3 to 6 in. long, chestnut towards base. *Fronds* oblong-lanceolate, narrowed to both ends, 6 to 9 in. long, 2-pinnate or 3-pinnatifid; central pinnae sessile, lanceolate-deltoid, 1 to 1½ in. long, lower reduced; pinnules oblong, blunt, crenulate, or lowest sub-pinnatifid, glandular-pilose. *Sori* sub-marginal, 6 to 12 on largest pinnules; indusium a small, membranous, lacerated, white cup. United States to Peru. (H.G.F. 43; L.F. 7, 29.) SYN. *W. Perriniana.*

W. orega'na. *sti.* densely tufted, not articulated, chestnut, 2 to 4 in. long. *Fronds* oblong-lanceolate, narrowed to both ends, 3 to 4 in. long, 2-pinnate, glabrous; pinnae lanceolate, sessile, central ones ⅜ to ½ in. long, cut to rachis or a narrow wing into blunt, oblong, crenate lobes, lower distant, gradually reduced; rachis straw colour. *Sori* sub-marginal; indusium hidden by sorus. N. America. Closely allied to *W. obtusa.* (B.B. ed. 2, 1, 13.)

W. Perrinia'na. A synonym of *W. obtusa.*

W. polystichoi'des.* *Fronds* 9 in. long, opaque, lanceolate, pinnate, sparsely subulate-squamulose; pinnae spreading, approximate, sessile, 6 to 8 in. long, lanceolate, acute, cuneate-truncate at base, acutely auricled at superior base, entire or obsoletely crenate at apex, indistinctly costate. *Sori* marginal in a distinct line or series; involucre globose of 4 or 5 ciliated incurved scales. Japan. 1863. (H.G.F. 32.) var. **Veitch'ii.** *Fronds* very villose (H.G.F. 32, ff. 1, 2, 4–6.)

W. scopuli'na. *sti.* densely tufted, 2 to 3 in. long, chestnut below. *Fronds* 4 to 6 in. long, oblong-lanceolate, 2-pinnate, narrowed to both ends; central pinnae lanceolate, sessile, ⅜ to ½ in. long, cut to rachis or a narrow wing into close, ligulate-oblong, crenate-pinnatifid lobes; slightly glandular-pilose above, densely beneath, with a few minute scales on ribs. Rocky Mts. 1884. (B.B. ed. 2, 1, 13.)

W. sinua'ta. Similar to *W. polystichoides* with pinnae broader, more obtuse, lobed-pinnatifid. Korea, N. China. (H.G.F. 32, 3.) SYN. *W. polystichoides sinuata.*

WOODWARD'IA (named after Thomas Jenkinson Woodward, 1745–1820). Chain Fern. FAM. *Polypodiaceae.* A genus of 10 species of ferns distributed round the world in the N. temperate zone. Fronds usually large, 2-pinnatifid. Sori linear or linear-oblong, sunk in cavities of the frond, in single rows parallel with, and contiguous to, the midribs of the pinnae and pinnules; indusium sub-coriaceous, the same shape as the sorus, closing over the cavity like a lid. Woodwardias possess a decorative character for either the cool greenhouse, the conservatory, or the hardy Fernery, according to their requirements. Few Ferns are as effective as *W. radicans* or *W. orientalis*, grown either on the indoor rockery or in a hanging-basket in the conservatory; while *W. areolata* and *W. virginica* are very ornamental when planted in a marshy part of the hardy Fernery. The compost in which Woodwardias grow most luxuriantly is a mixture of equal parts fibrous loam, peat or leaf-mould, chopped Sphagnum, and silver-sand, with abundance of water at the roots all the year round. It is of most importance that these plants should be kept under cool treatment, as in heat they soon become a prey to Thrips and scale, whereas when grown in a cool atmosphere they are usually very clean.

Although Woodwardias may be, and sometimes are, propagated from spores, they are usually increased by means of the young bulbils produced either towards the end of their fronds, as in *W. radicans* and its varieties, or over the whole of their surface, as in *W. orientalis.* The hardy kinds are easily multiplied by the division of their rhizomes. This is more successfully performed from November to March than at any other time of the year.

W. angustifo'lia. A synonym of *W. areolata.*

W. areola'ta.* *Barren fronds* 9 to 12 in. long, 6 to 8 in. broad, on slender stipes, deltoid-ovate, with numerous oblong-lanceolate, sinuate pinnae each side, lower 3 to 4 in. long, ½ to ¾ in. broad, reaching to rachis, which above has a broad wing, naked. *Fertile fronds* on an elongated, strong, erect, chestnut-brown, naked stem; pinnae 3 to 4 in. long, narrow-linear, ½ to 1 in. apart. United States. 1812. (H.G.F. 61; L.F. 4, 46; B.C.F. 3, 400.) SYN. *W. angustifolia.*

W. Harland'ii. *sti.* 6 to 18 in. long, erect, nearly naked. *Barren fronds* varying from linear-lanceolate, undivided, to broadly ovate, with 1 or 2 spreading, linear-lanceolate lobes, 3 to 4 in. long, $\frac{1}{2}$ to $\frac{3}{4}$ in. broad, reaching to a broadly winged rachis, naked. *Fertile fronds* with more numerous and narrower lobes, lowest often quite free of others. *Sori* in broad lines close to midrib of lobes, with short lines branching from these in an erecto-patent direction. Hong Kong.

W. japo'nica. *sti.* 6 to 12 in. long, erect, scaly below. *Fronds* broadly ovate, 1 to $1\frac{1}{2}$ ft. long, 9 to 12 in. broad; pinnae lanceolate, often 6 in. long, 1 to $1\frac{1}{4}$ in. broad, reaching half or two-thirds of way to rachis, the lines of sori which margin the midrib of the pinnae confined to upper part of upper ones. China and Japan.

W. orienta'lis. *sti.* erect, densely scaly at base. *Fronds* 4 to 8 ft. long, 1 to $1\frac{1}{2}$ ft. broad; pinnae lanceolate, sometimes more than 1 ft. long, cut below nearly to rachis into sinuate or pinnatifid pinnules, sometimes 4 in. long, those of under side shorter, none at base of pinnae; veins copiously anastomosing outside the sori; upper surface often with many buds. Japan to Formosa. Closely allied to *W. radicans*. (Gn. 20 (1881) 530.)

W. radi'cans.* *sti.* strong, erect, naked, scaly at base. *Fronds* 3 to 6 ft. long, 1 to $1\frac{1}{2}$ ft. broad; pinnae lanceolate, lower often 1 ft. long, cut below within a short distance of rachis into finely toothed, lanceolate pinnules 1 to $1\frac{1}{2}$ in. long, those of under side shortest; veins anastomosing once outside line of fruit; gemmae few and large, at base of upper pinnae. Canaries, S. Europe, China, N. India, Java. 1779. var. **Brown'ii** has regularly and symmetrically crested pinnae. 1878. (G.C. 23 (1885) 279.) SYN. *W. cristata*; var. **Burgesia'na,*** *fronds* light and elegant, sometimes $2\frac{1}{2}$ ft. long, of a harsh, leathery texture; pinnae and pinnules uniformly depauperate, serrate throughout. Azores.

W. virgi'nica. *sti.* strong, erect, 1 to $1\frac{1}{2}$ ft. long. *Fronds* oblong-lanceolate, 1 to $1\frac{1}{2}$ ft. long, 6 to 9 in. broad; pinnae linear-lanceolate, 4 to 6 in. long, $\frac{3}{4}$ to 1 in. broad, cut within $\frac{1}{12}$ in. of rachis into linear-oblong lobes, which are $\frac{1}{6}$ to $\frac{1}{4}$ in. broad at base; the lines of sori which margin the midrib of the pinnae often reaching low down in the lower ones. Eastern N. America. 1774. (L.F. 4, 45.)

WOODWASPS or Horn-tails are large 4-winged insects belonging to the Hymenopterous family *Siricidae*. The most familiar species in Britain is the Large Woodwasp, *Urocerus* (*Sirex*) *gigas*, whose black- and yellow-banded body and the female's long stout ovipositor causes many people to confuse it with a Hornet. Its larva bores in the wood of Coniferous trees, including Scot's Pine, Larch, Spruce, and Silver Fir. The smaller Steel Blue Woodwasp, *Sirex noctilio*, metallic blue in colour, is common in Larch and Silver Fir woods. These insects are not garden pests, for they only attack either forest trees whose vigour is reduced as a result of unfavourable soil conditions, inclement weather, or fungal attack, or felled timber. The injury to timber by the burrowing larvae is often considerable. Mention is made of these striking insects by reason of the frequency of the females in gardens bordering woods, and they are often seen alighting on garden plants and flying in bright sunshine during the summer.

G. F. W.

WOODY NIGHTSHADE. *See* **Solanum Dulcamara.**

WOOLLEN. *See* **Verbascum,** for which this is an old name.

WOOLLY APHIS (*Eriosoma lanigerum*). American Blight is the name given to this pest by many gardeners, to whom it is the most familiar of all fruit pests. While the Apple is the chief host, it occurs occasionally on Pear, ornamental species of Pyrus and Pyracantha, and on *Cotoneaster horizontalis*. The presence of masses of cotton-wool-like patches on the stem, branches, and shoots indicates that the pest is active, while tumour- or gall-like growths on the infested portions show that this pest has been present at some former date. This insect not only reduces the vigour of its host, but gives rise to unsightly tumours and permits the entry of Canker and other fungus spores into the lesions made during its feeding. A careful watch should be kept on newly acquired plants for this pest, which is often disseminated on nursery stock. The life cycle of the Woolly Aphis in Europe is somewhat complicated, but it is rendered more so in the United States, Canada, Australia, New Zealand, and elsewhere owing to the occurrence of a root form which, if not unknown, is of little importance in this country. The Aphis hibernates beneath rough bark, in wounds and cankers, and in other sheltered positions on its host plant, but is frequently overlooked during the winter owing to the small amount of 'wool' excreted during this season. It becomes active in April, and the attack reaches its zenith in May and June when severely infested trees are found to be garlanded by masses of 'wool'. The attack dies away in July and little of it is seen during August, but it may recur in September when the sexual forms are produced.

WINTER TREATMENT. Forcible and thorough application of a Tar Oil wash at 8 per cent. will aid in reducing the pest. The strength of this wash should be increased to 10 per cent. for old, neglected, heavily infested trees. Young trees found to be infested should before being transplanted be dipped in the weaker concentration of Tar Oil.

SPRING AND SUMMER TREATMENTS. The colonies of Aphides are readily destroyed by forcibly spraying the infested portions of the tree in May and June with Nicotine-Soap wash; by dusting Cordons and young trees with Nicotine dust at temperatures above 65° F.; by painting the colonies with a stiff brush dipped in Nicotine-Soap wash or Methylated Spirit; or by rapidly moving the flame of a painter's blow-lamp over the colonies.

The idea that this pest is eradicated from attacked trees by growing Nasturtiums round the stems is fallacious. Success has followed the introduction into infested orchards of a N. American Chalcid parasite (*Aphelinus mali*), especially in Australia and New Zealand, and recent promising results have been obtained with this 'wasp' in some districts in the British Is.

G. F. W.

WOOLLY BEAR, the velvety black and grey long-haired caterpillar of the Garden Tiger Moth, *Arctia caia*, which is a conspicuous object in gardens throughout the country. It feeds on a wide variety of plants, including Docks, Plantains and various Grasses and, occasionally, on cultivated plants though never in sufficiently large numbers to warrant any action being taken against it.

G. F. W.

WOOLLY BEECH APHIS. *See* **Fagus, Pests.**

Wordsworthia'nus -a -um, in honour of Mrs. R. Wordsworth (*née* Glover) of Bulawayo, botanist in S. Africa, *c.* 1920.

WORKING. Worked trees are those grafted or budded on root-stocks. *See* **Budding, Grafting.**

WORM. A term often loosely applied to any elongate, slender, soft-bodied, crawling animal. The Group *Vermes* comprises the true worms, which are limbless and includes the Ringed worms (*see* **Earthworms, Enchytraeid Worms**) and a large number of marine creatures (e.g. Bristle-worms, Ribbon-worms, and Arrow-worms). Other groups include Tapeworms (Cestodes), Roundworms (*see* **Eelworms** and **Horse-hair Worms**). In the United States and Canada the larvae of insects, especially Moths, are often called worms, e.g. Cabbage Worm, Corn Ear Worm, Cutworm, and Beet and Parsnip Webworms. The name 'Blood-worm' in this country refers to the larva of certain Midges (*Chironomus*). By 'worm-eaten' wood is meant timber attacked by the grubs of Furniture, Death-watch, and Powder Post Beetles (*Anobium*, *Xestobium*, and *Lyctus*).

G. F. W.

WORM GRASS. *See* **Spigelia marilandica.**

WORMWOOD (*Artemisia Absinthium*) is grown for its leaves and tops which have medicinal value and is one of the materials used in the manufacture of absinthe. The dried tops and leaves are sometimes used to place among clothes to repel moths. It is easily grown, treated as an herbaceous perennial in rather dry soil, and can be propagated by division in spring or by cuttings, and may be readily raised from seed.

WORSLE'YA (in honour of Arthington Worsley, 1861–1943, mining engineer who travelled much in Cent. and S. America and on settling at Isleworth, Middlesex, specialized in growing Amaryllidaceae). FAM. *Amaryllidaceae*. Included here in Hippeastrum but distinguished as a genus by certain botanists on account of the spathe-valves being 4 instead of 2, the seeds D-shaped, the bulb prolonged at the top into a long aerial neck, the leaves sickle-shaped. The only species is *W. Rayneri*, the Blue Amaryllis of Brazil, described on p. 1001 as *Hippeastrum procerum*.

WOUND PARASITE. A parasitic fungus which is able to obtain access to the tissues of its host only through naked wounds.

WOUNDS. Wounds may be divided into 2 classes: (*a*) those caused by pruning or lopping, and (*b*) those caused by breakage, or blows from vehicles or mowing machines. Small wounds, especially those made with a sharp tool, usually heal quickly, but larger wounds may never heal completely, and need protection to prevent the entrance of fungal spores and wood-boring insects. Normally the wound is healed by a covering of 'callus', or wound wood, formed by the cut edges of the cambium, or growing layer found between wood and bark. The rate of occlusion depends on the age and type of tree. In young or quick-growing trees growth of 'callus' is rapid, but with old trees or shrubs growth may be very slow and quite inefficient to protect from disease or decay. To leave such wounds untreated may lead to extensive damage and at times to the loss of the tree.

When pruning, the branch should always be cut back flush with the trunk or to a larger branch. Small wounds can be dressed with white lead paint or grafting wax. Larger wounds can be painted with a 50/50 mixture of creosote and tar. The edges of bark wounds should be cut clean with a sharp knife or chisel, and the wound itself should be trimmed to an elliptical shape to encourage quick healing. If the wood is broken or splintered it must be smoothed off to prevent the lodging of moisture. Small bark wounds can be protected in the same way as pruning cuts.

If the wounds are large the wood tends to dry out and crack. In such cases a tar dressing is often useless, as being inelastic it tends to open with the wood. A brush-applied dressing of plastic bitumen, over a preliminary coating of creosote, is preferable. If tar dressings must be used they should be applied thickly and inspected frequently. Bordeaux paste is sometimes used for such wounds. This consists of copper sulphate worked to a thick paste with linseed oil. It is, however, liable to crack, and the colour is ugly and conspicuous.

Cavities may be cleaned out, disinfected with creosote, and filled with concrete, but if shallow they should simply be cut away at the base to allow moisture to escape, treated in the same way as an ordinary wound, and left open.

A. D. C. Le S.

WOUNDWORT. *See* **Anthyllis Vulneraria, Stachys sp.**

WOURALI-POISON (CURARE). *See* **Strychnos.**

Wray'i, in honour of Leonard Wray, 1853–1942, director of Museums in Federated Malay States, collected in Malaya, 1881–1905.

WREATH. A floral or foliar head-dress which goes all round the head, made of choice flowers of rather small or medium size, or of laurel or bay leaves. Another kind of Wreath is made for funerals and memorials, usually of flowers, but sometimes of evergreens. It is circular in outline and arranged on a framework of wire, thin board or even cardboard, covered with moss or lichen held in place by wire or string, often with a further base of laurel leaves or spruce sprigs wired on before the flowers are placed in position.

WREATH, PURPLE. *See* **Petrea.**

WRIGHT'IA (in honour of William Wright, 1740–1827, Scottish physician and botanist). FAM. *Apocynaceae*. A genus of about 12 species of shrubs or small trees with often cord-like branches, natives of Trop. Africa, Asia, and Australia. Leaves opposite, penni-nerved. Flowers red, white, or yellow, in terminal or sub-axillary, sessile cymes; calyx short, 5-partite with scales or glands within; corolla salver-shaped, tube cylindric, usually short, throat with 1 or 2 series of over-lapping scales; stamens at top of tube; filaments short, dilated. These stove plants need a mixture of peat, loam, and sand. Cuttings root readily in sand in heat. The E. Indian species are known as Palay or Ivory Trees.

W. cocci'nea. 12 ft. h. or more, sometimes glabrous. *l.* elliptic or elliptic-lanceolate, 3 to 5 in. long, membranous, obtusely caudate, acute at base; stalks very short. *fl.* dark-red, 1 in. across; cor. almost fleshy; scales crimson; cymes 3- or 4-fld. July. India. 1822. (B.M. 2696; L.B.C. 894 as *Nerium coccineum*.)

W. du'bia. Shrub. *l.* ovate-lanceolate, 3 to 4 in. long, glabrous, slightly undulate, rather obtusely acuminate. *fl.* lobes yellow outside, orange-red within, ⅝ in. long, spreading, acuminate; pedicels rather shorter than fl.; cymes 3-fld., glabrous. June. Malaya. 1813. (B.M. 1646 as *Cameraria dubia*; H.I. 1521 as *Strophanthus Jackianus*). SYN. *Scleranthera dubia*.

W. pubes'cens. Hairy tall shrub or small tree. *l.* ovate to elliptic-oblong, 2 to 4 in. long, slender-pointed; stalk short. *fl.* white, sessile or almost so; cor. tube about as long as cal., segs. twice as long; cymes terminal, 3-forked, corymbose, not longer than l. March. N. Australia. 1829.

W. tincto'ria. Pala Indigo Plant. Small, glabrous tree. *l.* elliptic-ovate, elliptic-lanceolate, or obovate-oblong, 3 to 5 in. long, obtusely caudate; stalk very short. *fl.* white, ½ to ¾ in. across; cymes sometimes 5 in. across with slender, spreading, forked branches. Summer. India. 1812. (B.R. 933.)

Wrightia'nus -a -um, in honour of Charles Henry Wright, 1864–1941, assistant in the Herbarium, Kew.

Wright'ii, in honour of Charles Wright, 1811–85, of Connecticut, plant-collector in Cuba, &c.

WULFE'NIA (in honour of Franz Xavier Freiherr von Wulfen, 1728–1805, Austrian botanical author). FAM. *Scrophulariaceae*. A genus of 5 species of almost glabrous, tufted, perennial herbs, with thick rhizomes, natives of SE. Europe, W. Asia, and the Himalaya. Leaves radical or almost so, crenate, stalked. Flowers blue or purple, small, in axils of bracts, racemose or spicate at tops of scapes; calyx 5-partite; corolla tube exserted, cylindrical; limb of 4 erecto-patent lobes; stamens 2, inserted at mouth of corolla; peduncles scape-like, simple, with a few alternate bracts. They are pleasing rock-garden plants for a moist, well-drained site. Any rich, light soil suits them, but winter wet is liable to damage them and they are the better for the protection of a glass or frame during winter. Propagation by division or seed. Botanically the genus is of great interest owing to the geographical isolation of the species, which are rare plants in the wild.

W. Amherstia'na. *l.* narrowly obovate to oblanceolate, narrowed into long petiole, 2 to 6 in. long, shallowly or deeply crenate, sparsely hairy on both sides, or glabrous above. *fl.-stems* 5 to 12 in. h.; infl. many-fld., loose, 1½ to 8 in. long; cal. glabrous; cor. purple, about $\frac{3}{10}$ in. long, lobes narrow, acuminate. July. Himalaya. 1846. The least showy of the genus.

W. Baldacc'ii. *l.* narrowly obovate to broadly elliptic, narrowed into long petiole, 1½ to 4 in. long, deeply crenate or toothed or almost lobed, sparsely hairy on both sides, almost glabrous beneath. *fl.-stems* 3 to 6 in. h.; infl. few-fld., loose, 1 to 2½ in. long; cal. glandular; cor. lilac-blue, about ⅜ in. long, lobes broad, rounded. Albania. 1929. (Bull. Alp. Gn. Soc. 1. 45.)

W. Bull'ii. A synonym of *Besseya Bullii*; *see under* **Synthyris.**

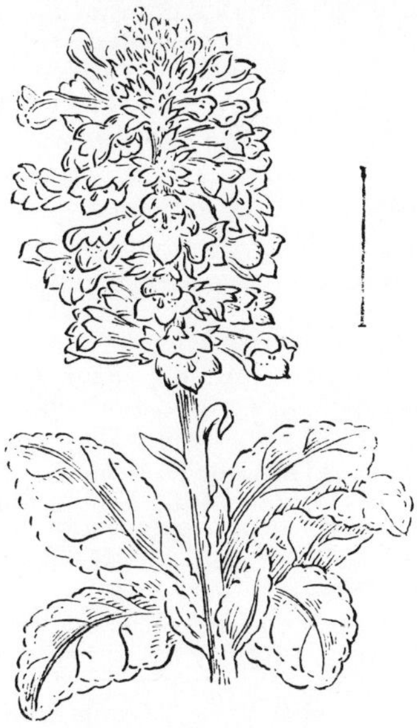

Wulfenia carinthiaca

W. carinthia'ca. *l.* oblong to oblanceolate, narrowed into a winged petiole, 3 to 10 in. long, shallowly or deeply crenate, glabrous above, sparsely hairy beneath. *fl.-stems* 10 to 24 in. h.; infl. many-fld., dense, 1½ to 4 in. long; cal. glabrous except for ciliate margin; cor. dull blue-violet, about ½ in. long, lobes rounded. June to August. E. Alps, Balkan Peninsula. (B.M. 2500; S.B.F.G. 66.)

W. orienta'lis. *l.* oblong to oblanceolate, narrowed into long petiole, 4 to 12 in. long, deeply or shallowly crenate or toothed, coriaceous, glossy, glabrous. *fl.-stems* 7 to 16 in. h.; infl. many-fld., loose, 5 to 8 in. long; cal. glabrous; cor. nearly 1 in. long, heliotrope, lobes rounded. May. Taurus Mtns., Asia Minor. 1949.

W. T. S.

WULF'FIA (in honour of John C. Wulff, d. 1817, author of *Flora Borussica*). FAM. *Compositae.* A genus of about 8 ill-defined species of roughly hairy, perennial herbs, natives of Trop. America. Leaves opposite, stalked, crenately toothed. Flower-heads yellow, at first depressed, finally globose, pedunculate, solitary or 3 to 7 in a corymb; involucre hemispherical, with 2 or 3 series of bracts; receptacle slightly convex, paleae enveloping the florets; ray-florets, when present, entire or minutely toothed. Achenes glabrous or slightly hairy. Stove plants easily growing in light soil, propagated by seed or division.

W. stenoglos'sa. About 3 ft. h. Stem erect, 4-angled, spotted. *l.* oblong-lanceolate, wedge-shaped at base, slender-pointed, toothed, scabrous above, nearly glabrous beneath. *fl.-heads* orange-yellow; ray-florets about 8, twice as long as involucre; peduncles 3-nate, terminal. June. Brazil. 1822. (B.R. 662 as *Gymnolomia maculata.*) SYN. *W. maculata.*

WURMB'EA (in honour of F. van Wurmb, Secretary, Academy of Sciences, Batavia). FAM. *Liliaceae.* A genus of about 7 species of bulbous plants, 4 natives of W. Australia, 2 of S. Africa, 1 of Fernando Po, related to Dipidax. Bulb tunicated. Leaves few, lanceolate at base of stem. Flowers in a short pedunculate spike, without bracts; perianth persistent, tube short, segments long, spreading; filaments filiform, anthers ovate. Fruit a 3-valved capsule. *W. capensis* needs greenhouse protection and a compost of sandy peat with a little loam. It is easily increased by seeds or offsets.

W. campanulat'a. A synonym of *W. capensis.*

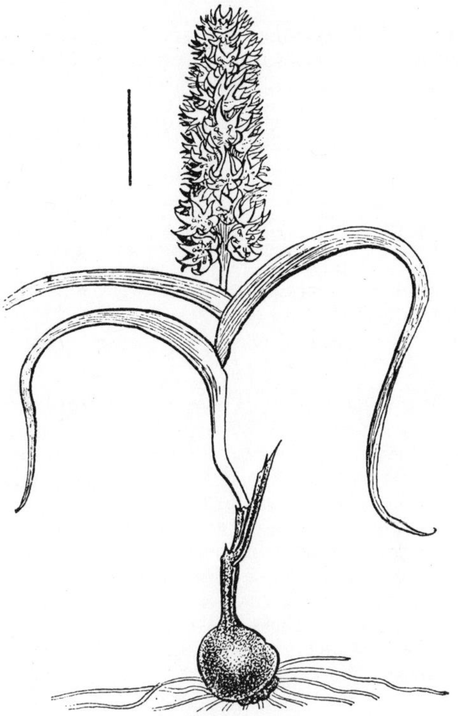

Wurmbea capensis

W. capen'sis. Bulb ovoid, tunic brown. *l.* 3 or 4, firm; lower linear, 3 to 9 in. long, upper lanceolate, base dilated, sheathing stem. Stem 6 to 12 in. long. *fl.* pale, about ½ in. long; tube bell-shaped, segs. lanceolate, acute, with black glands above base; spikes 1 to 3 in. long. S. Africa. 1819. (B.M. 1291 as *Melanthium monopetalum.*) var. **longiflo'ra,** robust, *fl.* pale, ½ to ¾ in. long, segs. about as long as the cylindrical tube. 1788; **pu'mila,** dwarf, *l.* linear, *fl.* 3 or 4 only; **purpu'rea,** *fl.* lurid purple, tube bell-shaped, segs. often longer than tube. (B.M. 694 and A.B.R. 221 as *W. purpurea.*)

Wyattia'nus -a -um, in honour of G. Neville Wyatt of Cheltenham, amateur gardener, *c.* 1883.

WYCH ELM. *See* **Ulmus glabra.**

WYETH'IA (in honour of N. B. Wyeth who discovered the genus). FAM. *Compositae.* A genus of about 7 species of perennial N. American herbs with thick rootstocks. Stems usually not branched with a solitary flower-head. Leaves entire. Flower-heads yellow, large, heterogamous, radiate; involucre hemispherical, bracts in 2 or 3 rows, almost equal; receptacle flat or slightly convex; ray-florets ligulate, spreading, entire or almost so; disk-florets shortly 5-cleft. Achenes glabrous or nearly so. Hardy plants for the border or wild garden.

W. angustifo'lia. 6 to 24 in. h. *Radical l.* long-lanceolate, narrowed to both ends, sometimes toothed, often undulate; stalked; *stem-l.* sessile, broader. *fl.-heads* with ray-florets 1½ in. long, numerous; involucre 1 in. h., bracts foliaceous. Autumn. United States.

W. mol'lis. Woolly when young, becoming almost smooth, 1 to 3 ft. h. with solitary or few heads. *l.* oblong or ovate, rounded to wedge-shaped at base. *Ray-florets* 10 to 15, over 1 in. long. *Achenes* minutely downy at apex. Nevada, California. (B.M. 7772.)

WYMOT. *See* **Althaea officinalis.**

X

xalapensis -is -e, of Xalapa, Mexico.

XANTHIS'MA (yellowness; alluding to the flower colour). FAM. *Compositae.* A genus of 2 species of annual or biennial herbs, natives of the prairies of Texas. Leaves alternate, narrow, usually entire. Flowers all ligulate, fertile, Achenes 4 or 5, ribbed, pappus persistent, the middle bristles longer than the outer. Easily grown in ordinary soil from seed sown outdoors in April.

X. texa'num. Annual, nearly smooth, branched, 1½ to 4 ft. h. *l.* linear-lanceolate entire, about 1 in. long, upper l. sometimes toothed near tip. *fl.-heads* yellow, about 2 in. across, solitary, terminal, disk small. Summer. 1877. (B.M. 6275.) SYN. *Centauridium Drummondii.*

xantho-, in compound words, signifying yellow.

XANTHOCE'PHALUM (*xanthos*, yellow, *kephale*, head). FAM. *Compositae.* A genus of 8 species of herbs or sub-shrubs, one native of Ecuador, the others Mexican. Leaves alternate, narrow. Flower-heads solitary or corymbose at ends of branches, yellow; ray-florets ligulate, spreading, nearly entire; disk-florets 5-cleft at tip; involucre more or less broadly bell-shaped, bracts overlapping in several series. Achenes smooth. The species need only ordinary soil. *X. centauroides* can be increased by cuttings, *X. gymnospermoides* by seed.

X. centauroi'des. Sub-shrub about 18 in. h. *l.* linear, rather thick, wrinkled, glabrous, deeply toothed, sessile. *fl.-heads* yellow, about 1 in. across, involucre clammy, outer scales spreading. Mexico. 1826. SYN. *Grindelia coronopifolia.* Greenhouse.

X. gymnospermoi'des. Annual, 2 to 4 ft. h. *l.* lanceolate-linear, 3 to 6 in. long, lower somewhat spatulate, toothed towards tip, others entire. *fl.-heads* orange-yellow, 1 in. across, in loose corymbs. September. New Mexico. 1859. (B.M. 5155 as *Gutierrezia gymnospermoides.*) Hardy.

XANTHO'CERAS (*xanthos*, yellow, *keras* a horn; in allusion to the horn-like growths between the petals). FAM. *Sapindaceae.* A monotypic genus. Except for its liability to occasional injury by late spring frost this tree is quite hardy. It likes a good loamy soil and is best propagated by seed, but also can be raised from root cuttings.

X. sorbifo'lium. Deciduous tree 20 to 25 ft., of erect habit; shoots very pithy, glabrous. *l.* alternate, pinnate, 5 to 10 in. long; lflets. 9 to 19, stalkless, lanceolate, 1½ to 2½ in. long, coarsely and sharply toothed. *Racemes* axillary, 6 to 10 in. long; cor. about 1 in. across, the 5 pet. white with a carmine spot at base. May. *fr.* globose or pear-shaped, 3-valved, about 2 in. wide; seeds globose, ½ in. wide, purple-brown, several in each valve. China. 1870. (B.M. 6923.)

W. J. B.

XANTHOCHY'MUS. Included in **Garcinia.**

XANTHOPHYLL. A yellow colouring matter which occurs in plants in the form of minute granules called plastids, insoluble in water. To it the yellow colour of flowers is usually, though not always, due, and to it is also due the yellow of autumn leaves of such plants as Elm, Tulip Tree, Maidenhair Tree, and Birch. The xanthophyll is associated with chlorophyll in the green plastids in the leaves and when, with the onset of autumn, the green colouring matter is decomposed the yellow xanthophyll is left unchanged, and is one of the complex chemicals composed of carbon, hydrogen, and oxygen formed by the plant which give rise to autumn tints.

XANTHORHI'ZA (*xanthos*, yellow, *rhiza*, root; the long roots and rootstock arc yellow). FAM. *Ranunculaceae.* A genus of a single species, a native of Eastern N. America. A dwarf, running shrub with yellow inner bark, pinnate leaves, and terminal panicles of small flowers with 5 sepals, 5 nectaries, and 5 or 10 stamens and carpels, related to Actaea. *X. simplicissima* is hardy and will grow in ordinary moist soil. Propagation is easy by division in early spring. The yellow rootstocks are very bitter and have been used medicinally in N. America.

X. simplicis'sima. Yellow Root. Deciduous shrub, 2 to 3 ft. h., little branched, with long creeping rootstock. *l.* with 3 or 5 sessile oblong-ovate, lobed and toothed lflets.; stalks long. *infl.* a loose panicle, appearing before the l. *fl.* small, dark purple, often 1-sexual. March, April. 1766. (B.M. 1736 as *X. apiifolia.*) SYN. *Xanthorhiza apiifolia.* Attractive for its early flowering and its foliage.

XANTHORRHI'ZA. *See* **Xanthorhiza,** the original spelling.

XANTHORRHOE'A (*xanthos*, yellow, *rheo*, to flow; in allusion to the resinous juice extracted from the plants). FAM. *Liliaceae.* A genus of 11 species of long-lived perennial plants called Grasstrees, with a thick, woody stem, 2 wild in West, 2 in South, 6 in East, and 1 in East and South Australia. Stem usually well-developed, but in *X. minor* scarcely rising out of the earth and in *X. pumilio* hardly over an inch long. Leaves in a dense terminal tuft, long-linear, brittle, spreading or recurved, their broad bases overlapping and long persisting. Flowers white on a long terminal peduncle bearing a dense cylindrical spike of nearly sessile flowers; perianth persistent, segments 6, free; stamens 6. Fruit a capsule. These plants need greenhouse conditions, either planted out in a well-drained bed or border or grown in tubs in a compost of peat and loam; they may be increased by offsets. The stems of several species yield a copious, dark or yellow resinous gum, the former called Black Boy Gum, the latter Botany Bay Resin.

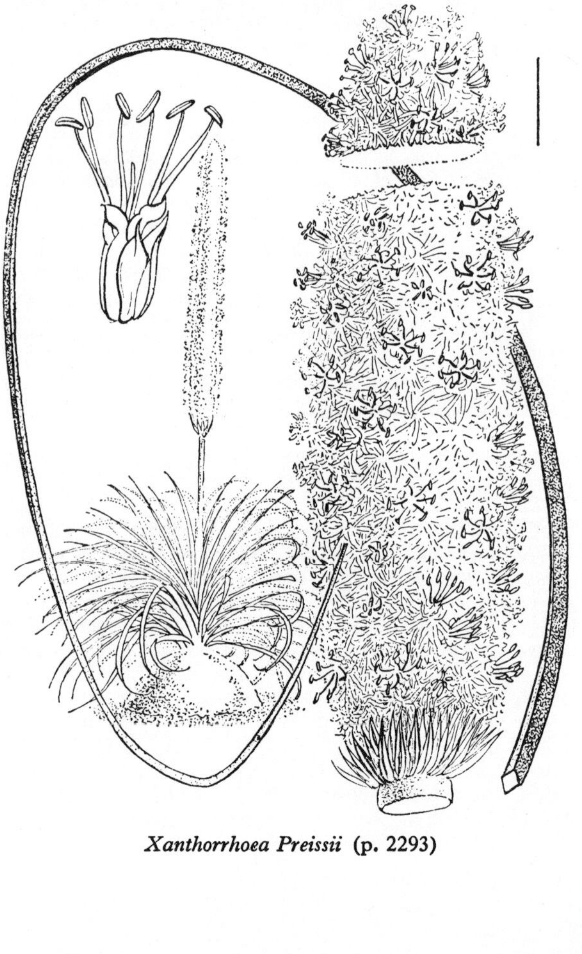

Xanthorrhoea Preissii (p. 2293)

X. arbo'rea. Botany Bay Gum. Stem several ft. h., 6 to 9 in. thick. *l.* flat or 3-cornered, 3 to 4 ft. long, $\frac{1}{8}$ to $\frac{1}{4}$ in. wide. *fl.* about $\frac{1}{2}$ in. across, 3-nerved; spike 3 to 4 ft. long, 1 to 1$\frac{1}{2}$ in. wide; scape 5 to 6 ft. long. April. Queensland.

X. austra'lis. Stem up to 2 ft. long. *l.* about 2 ft. long, about $\frac{1}{10}$ in. wide. *fl.-spike* about 2 ft. long, 1$\frac{1}{2}$ in. thick; scape about 2 ft. long. Summer. Tasmania, Victoria. 1824.

X. bractea'ta. Stem very short. *l.* about 2 ft. long, about $\frac{1}{10}$ in. wide, concave above, tapering to a narrow 3-cornered point. *fl.-spike* 4 to 6 in. long, $\frac{1}{2}$ to $\frac{3}{4}$ in. thick; scape 2 to 3 ft. long. Summer. 1810.

X. has'tilis. Stem very short. *l.* 3 to 4 ft. long, $\frac{1}{8}$ to $\frac{1}{4}$ in. wide, flat in front, back angle more or less prominent. *fl.-spike* 1$\frac{1}{2}$ to 2 ft. long, the ends of the bracts with dense, rusty wool; scape 6 to 8 ft. long. 1803. (B.M. 4722.)

X. mi'nor. Stem scarcely visible. *l.* 1 to 2 ft. long, $\frac{1}{12}$ to $\frac{1}{8}$ in. wide, flat, thick or more or less 3-cornered. *fl.-spike* 3 to 6 in. rarely 8 in. long, up to $\frac{3}{8}$ in. thick; scape often longer than l. New S. Wales to Tasmania. 1804. (B.M. 6297.)

X. Preiss'ii. Blackboy. Stem sometimes short, but up to 15 ft. long. *l.* 2 to 4 ft. long, $\frac{1}{12}$ to $\frac{1}{8}$ in. wide, rigid very brittle when young. *fl.* about $\frac{1}{2}$ in. across, spike 1 to 3 ft. long, 1 in. thick; scape 1 to 3 ft. long. April. W. Australia. (B.M. 6933.)

X. quadrangula'ta. Stem several feet long. *l.* 1$\frac{1}{2}$ ft. long, slender but rigid, 4-cornered, rarely over $\frac{1}{12}$ in. wide. *fl.-spike* 3 to 4 ft. long, 1$\frac{1}{2}$ in. thick; scape 3 to 4 ft. or more long. S. Australia. 1874. (B.M. 6075.)

XANTHORRHOEA'CEAE. Monocotyledons. A family separated by the Liliaceae by some botanists to include various genera with a thick woody stem or rhizome and a dry membranous perianth of 6 free or almost free segments. As defined by J. Hutchinson it comprises Xanthorrhoea, Xeronema, and 6 other genera.

XANTHO'SIA (*xanthos*, yellow; some species are covered with yellow down). FAM. *Umbelliferae.* A genus of 17 species of herbs or small shrubs, spreading or decumbent at base or erect, often covered with long, soft hairs mixed with star-shaped hairs, natives of Australia. Leaves toothed, lobed or ternately divided. Flowers in usually compound umbels; partial umbels with 2 or 3 bracts and several sessile flowers, the general umbel with 3 or 4 rays and as many bracts, but sometimes the whole reduced to very few or but 1 flower; calyx lobes peltate, cordate; petal point incurved, margins recurved. Treatment as for Didiscus.

X. pilo'sa. Erect or decumbent shrub, 1 to 2 ft. h. *l.* coarsely sinuate-toothed, 3- or 5-lobed or rarely 3-parted, middle lobe longer than others, rarely over 1 in. long. *fl.* white; peduncles usually 2 in the nodes, each 2- or 3-fld. or with only 1 fl. June. 1826.

X. rotundifo'lia. Erect, 1 to 2 ft. h., woody at base. *l.* nearly orbicular, irregularly toothed, $\frac{3}{4}$ in. across, glabrous or woolly beneath. *fl.* white, rather numerous, pedicels very short; peduncles long, umbels large, compound. 1836. (B.M. 3582.)

xanthospi'lus -a -um, spotted yellow.

XANTHOSO'MA (*xanthos*, yellow, *soma*, body; referring to the yellow inner tissue of some species). FAM. *Araceae.* A genus of 40 species of milky, perennial herbs, natives of Trop. America. Leaves arrow-shaped, spear-shaped or pedatisect on long and thick stalks. Flowers monoecious, the imperfect male flowers between the perfect ones and the female ones; spathe tube oblong or ovoid, convolute, persistent, at length bursting irregularly, throat constricted, blade boat-shaped; spadix without appendices, shorter than spathe and adnate with it at the base; male inflorescence cylindrical or clavate, long, imperfect portion constricted; female shorter, dense-flowered, narrowed above; peduncles 1 or several, rather long. The species grow well in rich, light, well-drained soil, under stove conditions. Propagation is by the cutting up of the stem or rootstock into small pieces, planting these in light soil or fibre in bottom heat. After a stem has been cut off a large number of shoots are developed which will strike readily under the same conditions. Some species may be used in sub-tropical gardening. They should have a sheltered place in a well-drained bed, principally made up of leaf-mould, and should be given abundance of water. The tubers of *X. sagittifolium* are used as food in the W. Indies, its acrid properties being dissipated by cooking.

X. atrovi'rens. *rhiz.* cylindric. *l.* ovate-arrow-shaped, dark green above, greyish-green beneath, midrib and main veins light green, mid-lobe somewhat oblong, short-pointed, basal lobes about half as long, semi-ovate; stalks deep green shorter than blade. *Spathe* tube oblong-ovoid, 3$\frac{1}{4}$ in. long, green, blade dull green with a somewhat violet tip and reddish veins, 8 in. long; spadix about 1$\frac{3}{4}$ to 4 in. long, yellow or rose; peduncles 4 to 6 in. long. Venezuela; much cultivated in W. Indies. Differs from *X. violaceum* and *X. Lindenii* in the green (not white or purple) veins of the l.

X. belophyl'lum. Stem short, thick. *l.* large, cordate-hastate, 1$\frac{1}{2}$ to 2 ft. long, mid-lobe shortly apiculate, basal lobes semi-ovate, rather acute, opaque, slightly pruinose above, ashy or pale green beneath. *Spathe* 8 in. long, tube greenish-white within, blade yellow; spadix whitish, much shorter than spathe. Venezuela, Guiana.

X. helleborifo'lium. A synonym of *Andromycia cubensis.*

X. Linden'ii. Tuberous. *l.* oblong-hastate, 12 in. long, glabrous except midrib, deep green, midrib and main veins ivory white, mid-lobe oblong, acute, basal lobes obtuse, unequal sided; stalks longer than blades sheathing for one-third of its length. Colombia. 1871. (J.H. 1872, 88 as *Phyllotaenium Lindenii.*) A showy variegated plant which may be used in the dwelling house. var. **magnif'icum,** larger than type.

X. sagittifo'lium. Stem thick, erect, 3 ft. or more high. *l.* broadly ovate-arrow-shaped, pruinose, 16 to 36 in. long, mid-lobe semi-ovate, slender-pointed, twice as long as the acute basal lobes. *Spathe* 7 in. long, tube greenish, blade whitish-green; spadix much shorter, peduncles longer, than spathe. W. Indies. 1710. (B.M. 4989.)

X. viola'ceum. *rhiz.* short. *l.* oblong-ovate-arrow-shaped, midrib and main veins purplish or violet, mid-lobe shortly slender-pointed, basal lobes a quarter to a third as long, sub-triangular; stalks brownish-violet, nearly twice as long as blades. *Spathe* tube oblong, 4 in. long, glaucous and pale green without, yellowish-white within, blade sulphur-white, 6 in. long; spadix 7$\frac{1}{2}$ in. long, violet and white; peduncles 6 to 8 in. long. W. Indies. 1864.

xanthostepha'nus -a -um, with a golden crown.

XANTHOXY'LUM. *See* **Zanthoxylum.**

Xant'ii, in honour of Mr. J. L. Xantus, who collected in South California, *c.* 1875.

XENIA. A term used for an effect alleged to be produced by the pollen parent upon the seed parent or upon part of it: thus it has been claimed that in certain apples the appearance and even form of the fruit depends upon the origin of the pollen which has led to its formation, and that as a result 2 or more distinct forms of fruit may be borne on a single tree if 2 or more distinct varieties furnish the pollen, the forms of the fruits approximating to those produced by the pollen parents respectively. These effects are often claimed but lack substantiation. The changes brought about as a result of pollination or fertilization of the ovules in the normal increase in size of the ovary as it becomes a fruit with the changes that accompany it, often profound, and involving far more than the ovary alone are not included in the term. In some instances, however, the characters of the pollen parent affect the colour of the seed and even its shape, but in all such instances it seems to be only the contents of the seed that are affected, that is not the parent itself but the succeeding generation, either the endosperm as may often be seen when the pollen fertilizing a normally pale-seeded variety of maize comes from a dark-seeded variety, or the embryo itself, as when a variety of pea with yellow seeds furnishes the pollen fertilizing the ovule of one with green seeds—these are instances where perhaps the use of the term 'xenia' is justifiable. Reports of such occurrences as the appearance of rough-coated gooseberries on a smooth-coated variety on the side neighbouring a rough-coated variety are, if true, to be explained by some other cause than pollination from the rough-coated variety.

XERAN'THEMUM (*xeros*, dry, *anthos*, flower; the flower-heads are dry and retain their form and colour for years). FAM. *Compositae.* A genus of 4 or 5 species of annual herbs, natives of the Mediterranean region and extending to Persia. They are valuable for the lasting quality of their flower-heads which retain their colour and form for many years and thus warrant the name of Everlasting Flowers or Immortelles. The erect, branching stems bear alternate, narrow, entire, hoary leaves. Flower-heads solitary on long peduncles without rays, the outer flowers few and sterile, the inner fertile; involucral bracts in many series and of different lengths, glabrous, petal-like, persistent and of various colours, white, purple, and pink. Easily grown but best in light, rich soil, the seed being sown where the plants are to grow in spring, like those of other hardy annuals, or the seedlings may be transplanted.

X. an'nuum. About 2 ft. h. *l.* linear or oblong, margins revolute. *fl.-heads* purple; involucre hemispherical inner bracts longer than outer; florets over 100. July. S. Europe. 1570. A variable species with colour forms, **al'bum** (white), **ro'seum** (pink) and **purpu'reum** (purple) in each of the 3 following varieties: var. **ligulos'um,** heads semi-double; **multiflo'rum,** heads smaller than in type and plant more compact and bushy; **perligulo'sum,** heads double. Syn. *X. superbissimum.*

X. cylindra'ceum. Annual of 12 to 20 in. Stems striate, whitish, branches long. *l.* linear, entire, white-hairy; sessile. *fl.-heads* purple or violet, solitary, oblong-cylindric, 10- to 15-fld.; involucral bracts muticous, outer hairy on back, oval, very obtuse. Summer. Achenes about 1/4 in. long, with 10 unequal apical teeth, longest about 1/8 in. S. Europe.

X. inaper'tum. Habit of *X. annuum* but fl.-heads white; involucre ovoid-oblong, inner bracts scarcely longer than outer, not or scarcely radiating; florets 30 to 40. S. Europe, Persia. 1836.

X. superbis'simum. *See* **X. annuum perligulosum.**

xero- in compound words signifying dry.

XERONE'MA (*xeros*, dry, *nema*, thread; the filaments being dry and persistent). Fam. *Liliaceae.* A genus of 1 species allied to Asphodelus. Rhizome very short, root fibres clustered. Leaves erect, folded. Flowers red, short-stalked in a 1-sided terminal raceme. *X. Moorii* needs stove conditions and a rich sandy loam with leaf-soil. Propagation by seeds or division.

X. Moor'ii. Stem erect, simple, about 20 in. long. *l.* mainly basal, erect, 12 to 16 in. long, those of stem small, and few. *fl.* bright crimson. 1/2 to 3/4 in. long, persistent, in a simple 1-sided terminal raceme; segs. distinct, linear, erect. New Caledonia. 1878. (G.C. 10 (1878) 17; B.M. 8342.)

xeroph'ilus -a -um, loving dry places.

XEROPHYL'LUM (*xeros*, dry, *phyllos*, leaf; the leaves are dry and grass-like). Fam. *Liliaceae.* A genus of 3 N. America plants, 2 in West and 1, *X. asphodeloides*, in East N. America, related to Helonias, growing in moist places. Rhizome short, woody. Stem erect with long, linear, rough-edged leaves, mainly clustered at the base, and usually white, long-stalked flowers in a pyramidal or cylindrical raceme. Perianth pieces 6, withering and persistent; segments linear, erect, 1-nerved; stamens 6. Fruit a short-stalked capsule. A peaty soil suits them best, and they are fairly hardy. Propagation by seed or division.

X. asphodeloi'des. Herb of 3 to 4 ft. *l.* densely clustered at base, long-linear, rather stiff, 12 to 18 in. long, margins rough, 1/12 in. wide; stem-l. short and very narrow. *fl.* yellowish-white, fragrant; segs. longer than stamens, about 1/4 in. long; racemes 3 to 6 in. long. Summer. Eastern N. America. (B.M. 748 as *Helonias asphodelioides.*)

X. setifo'lium. A synonym of *X. asphodelioides*; *see also* **X. tenax.**

X. te'nax. Habit of *X. asphodelioides*, *l.* rather wider, *fl.* white, stamens violet. Western N. America. (B.M. 8964; B.R. 1613 as *X. setifolium.*)

XEROPHYTES. Plants able to live their lives in places where water is difficult to obtain, either because there is little of it for a longer or shorter period of the plant's life or because for some reason, such as prolonged low temperature, the water present cannot readily be absorbed. Xerophytic plants are characterized by one or more of the following features: reduced leaves, rolled leaves spines branches reduced to thorns, much hard tissue, thick cuticle, sunken stomata, thick waxy bloom, or extreme hairiness.

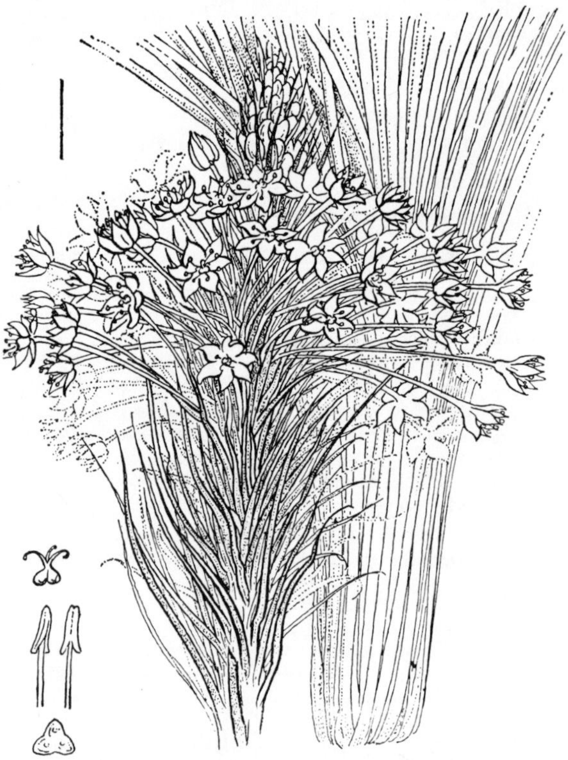

Xerophyllum tenax

xestophyl'lus -a -um, with polished leaves.

XIME'NIA (in honour of Francisco Ximenez, Spanish monk, who wrote on Mexican plants in 1615). Fam. *Olacaceae.* A genus of 4 species of trees or shrubs, 1 Mexican, 1 S. African, 1 native of the S. Pacific Is., the fourth dispersed over the tropics. Leaves alternate, entire, often clustered, rather leathery. Flowers whitish, in short, axillary cymes, or rarely solitary; calyx small, 4- or 5-toothed or lobed; petals 4 or 5, hypogynous; stamens 8 or 10. Fruits an ovoid or globose drupe with fleshy flesh, that of *X. americana* having a sweet, aromatic flavour, but a little rough to the palate. *X. americana* needs stove conditions and a compost of peat and loam. Cuttings root readily in sand under a glass, in heat.

X. america'na. False Sandal Wood; Hog, Mountain, or Seaside Plum. Tree of about 20 ft., branches covered with astringent bark, often ending in a spine. *l.* ovate-oblong or roundish. 1 1/4 in. long, 1 in. wide, or more, emarginate, rounded at base, glabrous. *fl.* fragrant, rather large for the family, in racemes or corymbs; pet. 4, oblong, hairy within, many times longer than cal. April. *fr.* oval or oblong, edible. Tropics. 1759.

X. caff'ra. Kaffer Plum. Much branched, gaunt-looking shrub to 7 ft. h., branches often spiny. *l.* oblong to oblong-ovate, about 1 1/4 in. long. *fl.* green. *fr.* oblong to oblong-orbicular, about 1 1/4 in. long, orange-red or scarlet. Transvaal. (F.P.S.A. 1681.)

XIPHI'DIUM (*xiphos*, sword, *eidos*, like; in reference to the leaves). Fam. *Haemodoraceae.* A genus of 2 species of perennial herbs, natives of Trop. America from the W. Indies to Brazil. From a short rhizome with broad-linear or long lanceolate, distichous, membranous, equitant leaves. Inflorescence panicle with numerous, small, short-stalked flowers on simple branches; perianth without tube, segments equal, oblong, spreading, not decurrent at base; stamens 3 affixed at base of inner segments. *X. caeruleum* grows in equal parts of loam, peat, and sand and needs stove conditions. Increased by division.

X. caeru'leum. 1 to 2 ft. *l.* oblong-lanceolate or oblong, 1 to 2 in. wide, slender-pointed, often rough at edges, glabrous. *fl.* white or blue, 8 to 10 on each branch of the panicle, about ¾ in. across; segs. oblong-lanceolate; panicle downy. May, June. W. Indies. 1856. (B.M. 5055 as *X. floribundum.*) Variable. *X. giganteum* is a broad-leaved form, margins entire.

xiphioi'des, Xiphium-like.

XI'PHION, xi'phium. Old generic name, referring to the sword-like leaves. Included in **Iris.**

xiphochi'lus -a -um, with sword-shaped lip.

xiphophyl'lus -a -um, sword-leaved.

XOLIS'MA. A synonym of Lyonia.

XYLA'RIA. A genus of fungi in the class Ascomycetes (q.v.) some species of which are important from a horticultural standpoint although not true parasites. One is *X. vaporaria* which grows in cucumber and mushroom beds. In the former it is not important, but in the latter its mycelium runs through the compost and thus competes with and crowds out the mushroom spawn, so that failure of the mushrooms may result (*see* **Mushroom Diseases**). Fungi such as *X. vaporaria* are sometimes called 'weed fungi' on mushroom beds.

D. E. G.

XYLEB'ORUS. *See* **Shot-borer Beetles.**

A→

XY'LIA (*xylon*, wood). FAM. *Leguminosae.* A genus of 3 species of Trop. Asiatic and African trees, notable for their good timber. Pyingado is the timber of *X. xylocarpa*, SYN. *X. dolabriformis*; it is extremely hard, heavy, strong, and durable.

xylo-, in compound words, signifying woody.

XYLO'BIUM (*xylon*, wood, *bios*, life; growing on trees). FAM. *Orchidaceae.* A genus of about 25 species of epiphytic orchids found in Trop. America, Mexico, and W. Indies. Flowers in racemes, very shortly stalked; sepals erect, at length somewhat spreading, lateral broader than dorsal, adnate at base to foot of column, forming a chin; petals similar to dorsal sepal, but smaller; lip more or less jointed to foot of column, sessile or contracted and incumbent at base, at length erect, side lobes erect, covering the column, mid-lobe short, broad, spreading; column erect, semi-terete; scapes from bases of pseudobulbs, erect, simple, often many-fld. Pollinia 4. Leaves large or long, plicate-veined, contracted into stalks. Stems short, many-sheathed, mostly thickened into a 1- or 2-leaved pseudobulb.

The genus has been confused with Maxillaria, but is more nearly akin to Bifrenaria and Batemannia. Though of moderate size and often numerous, the flowers are not brightly coloured and as a whole the genus has little to attract horticulturally. A similar compost to that given Maxillarias should be used, with an addition of one-fourth of fibrous loam. Pots are preferable to pans, but thorough drainage is essential. A rest is necessary in winter, particularly with the species which have hard pseudobulbs. The coolest end of the intermediate house suits them, or they may be grown in the cool house during summer and wintered in a night temperature of 55° F.; occasional falls below that temperature do no harm. Propagation is made by division of the plants when large enough. The pseudobulbs are usually walnut shaped or ovoid, small for the size of the leaves, and set closely together in the species seen in cultivation.

X. bractes'cens. *fl.* 15 to 25; sep. and pet. about 1 in. long, greenish-yellow; lip obscurely 3-lobed with 7 to 9 fleshy, undulate, red-brown keels; bracts 1½ to 2 in. long; scape about 30 in. h. *Pseudobulbs* ovoid-conical, 2½ in. h., 2-leaved. *l.*, with stalk, 10 to 20 in. long. Peru. 1842. SYN. *Maxillaria bractescens.*

X. Col'leyi. *fl.* reddish-brown, spotted purple, scented of cucumber; sep. nearly 1 in. long, about ⅓ in. wide; pet. smaller; lip purplish; scape short. *l.* similar to that of Stanhopea, blade 12 to 15 in. long or even much more, stalk stout, 3 to 4 in. long. *Pseudobulbs* round. Trinidad, Guiana. 1890. SYN. *Maxillaria Colleyi.*

X. conca'vum. *fl.* pale yellow; lateral sep. falcate, slender-pointed; pet. half as large as sep.; lip almost truncate, concave, bluntly 3-lobed, mid-lobe somewhat fleshy; tuberculate at edge, with a long, narrow ridge in middle, 3-lobed at point, veins rose. *Pseudobulbs* oblong, deeply furrowed. *l.* 2, 3-ribbed, shining. 9 in. h. Guatemala, Costa Rica. 1844. SYN. *Maxillaria concava.*

X. de'color. A synonym of *X. palmifolium.*

X. ecuadoren'se. Allied to *X. foveatum*, but *fl.* light yellow. Ecuador. 1911.

X. ela'tum.* *fl.* numerous, yellowish-green, marked dull red without; lip with dark red-brown tubercles; scapes 3 ft. h. *l.* nearly as long. Peru. 1913.

X. elonga'tum. Allied to *X. palmifolium. fl.* 10 to 20; sep. and pet. pale yellowish-white, about ¾ in. long; lip 3-lobed, purplish-brown, mid-lobe verrucose. Spring. W. Indies, Cent. America. SYN. *Maxillaria elongata.*

X. fovea'tum. *fl.* uniform pale straw-colour, faintly scented; sep and pet. linear-oblong; lip 3-lobed at tip, mid-lobe rounded, fleshy concave. *l.* lanceolate, undulate, including stalk 15 to 20 in. long, about 2 in. wide, three times as long as raceme. Demerara, Venezuela, Cent. America. Allied to *X. squalens.* SYN. *Maxillaria foveata.*

X. hyacin'thinum. *fl.* 15 to 25, hyacinth-scented, set closely; sep. and pet. yellowish; lip veined red with a 3-toothed callus. Venezuela.

Xylobium leontoglossum

X. leontoglos'sum. *fl.* yellow with red dots; sep. oblong-lanceolate; lip oblong, side lobes narrow, mid-lobe rounded, fleshy, with rough red dots, 5-keeled; raceme dense, oblong or cylindrical; scape robust. March. *Pseudobulbs* clustered, fusiform, about 2 in. long, 1-leaved. *l.* elliptic-lanceolate, acute, plicate, about 12 in. long, including stalk. Colombia. 1889? (B.M. 7085.) SYN. *Maxillaria leontoglossa.*

X. pallidiflo'rum. *fl.* stalked; sep. and pet. pale sulphur; lateral sep. broadly falcate; lip whitish at back, reflexed above, somewhat truncate-emarginate, 5-keeled; racemes erect, 3- to 7-fld. *Pseudobulbs* in dense clusters, cylindrical, 4 to 7 in. long, 1-leaved. *l.* oblong, slender-pointed, glabrous, 8 to 10 in. long, 3-ribbed, arched. 1 ft. h. W. Indies, Venezuela. 1826. (B.M. 2806 as *Maxillaria pallidiflora.*)

X. palmifo'lium. Sep. and pet. sulphur; sep. ovate-oblong, obtuse spreading; pet. half as large connivent; lip whitish, slightly 3-lobed obtuse, hooded, with 5 raised calli; scapes radical, many-fld. *Pseudobulbs* oblong, compressed, 1 to 2½ in. h. *l.* solitary, oblong-lanceolate, narrowed at both ends, 12 to 15 in. long. W. Indies. 1830. (B.M. 3981 and B.R. 1549 as *Maxillaria decolor.*) SYN. *X. decolor.*

X. squa'lens. *fl.* dingy, pale, yellowish flesh-colour, numerous, in a dense thyrse-like raceme; pet. and lip streaked purple, side-lobes of lip deep purple; scape 4 to 6 in. h., brown-scaly. *Pseudobulbs* ovoid, 1 to 2½ in. h., 5 or 6 ribbed, 2-leaved. *l.* including stalk 12 to 24 in. long. Brazil. 1828. (B.M. 2955 as *Maxillaria squalens*; B.R. 732 as *Dendrobium squalens.*)

E. C.

XYLOM'ELUM (*xylon*, wood, *melon*, an apple; referring to the woody fruits). FAM. *Proteaceae.* A genus of 4 species of evergreen trees or shrubs confined to Australia; leaves opposite. Flowers small, borne in pairs in the axils of small, soon deciduous bracts, and closely crowded in opposite spikes. Fruits woody, tapering from near the base towards the apex and splitting lengthwise. Seeds flat, winged. The following species are hardy in Scilly but require cool greenhouse treatment in most places.

X. occidenta'le. Tree or shrub, 12 to 25 ft., shoots and infl. densely reddish- or grey-downy. *l.* broadly ovate to oval or oblong, 3 to 5 in. long, irregularly, coarsely prickly toothed, glabrous at maturity. *Spikes* 3 to 5 in. long, forming collectively a large, leafy terminal panicle; perianth ⅜ to ½ in. long. *fr.* 3 in. long, 1 in. wide near the base. W. Australia. Differs from *X. pyriforme* by its prickly-leaved flowering shoots.

X. pyrifor'me. Tree of medium size; shoots reddish-woolly. *l.* leathery, glossy, those of the flowering branches usually entire, 4 to 6 in. long, lanceolate or ovate-lanceolate, those of the barren branches up to 8 in. long, prickly toothed and shorter stalked. *fl.* creamy-brown, densely crowded in cylindrical, axillary spikes 2 to 3 in. long, 1 in. wide; perianth scarcely ½ in. long. *fr.* woody, 2½ to 3 in. long, 1½ in. wide, inversely pear-shaped; seeds yellow, winged. New S. Wales. 1869.

W. J. B.

XYLOPHA'COS. Included in **Astragalus.**

XYLOPHYL'LA. Included in **Phyllanthus** but kept distinct by some botanists on account of its different habit, the branches being flattened and leafy with flowers along the margin and true leaves obsolete. There are about 10 species.

X. angustifo'lia. A synonym of *Phyllanthus angustifolius.*

X. specio'sa. A synonym of *Phyllanthus speciosus.*

XYLO'PIA (from *xylopicron*, *xylon*, wood, *pikron*, bitter). FAM. *Anonaceae.* A genus of about 30 species of leafy trees or shrubs, 5 Indian, 6 or 7 African, the rest American. Leaves leathery, often distichous. Flowers solitary or clustered in leaf-axils, sessile or shortly pedicellate; sepals 3, more or less connate, valvate; petals 6, in 2 series, the inner ones included; stamens numerous. The undermentioned stove tree needs a compost of sandy loam and fibrous peat, charcoal and dried cow dung. It may be propagated by hard cuttings in heat.

X. glab'ra. Bitter Wood. Tree of 20 ft. *l.* lanceolate, 2 to 3 in. long with a tapered point, downy beneath, clothed with appressed hairs in youth. *Cor.* silky, outer pet. ⅓ to ½ in. long. W. Indies, S. America. 1820.

XYLOS'MA (*xylon*, wood, *osme*, fragrance; in allusion to the fragrant wood). FAM. *Flacourtiaceae.* A genus of over 100 species, widely spread in the warmer parts of both hemispheres. Flower inconspicuous without petals; fruit a small 2- to 8-seeded berry.

X. racemo'sa. Evergreen tree 40 to 80 ft., shoots spiny on young trees. *l.* ovate to roundish, pointed, toothed, 1 to 3 in. long. *fl.* very small, yellow, fragrant, in axillary racemes ⅓ to 1 in. long. August. *fr.* black-purple, ⅛ in. wide, globose, style adhering at top. Japan, Korea, E. China. SYN. *Hisingera japonica.* var. **pubes'cens,** young shoots downy. W. China. 1907. Hardy.

XYLOS'TEUM. Included in **Lonicera.**

XYRIDA'CEAE. Monocotyledons. A family of about 200 species in 2 genera, mostly in the warmer parts of the world, none in Europe, often growing in wet places. Herbs usually with fibrous roots and basal rosettes or clusters of long, linear, or linear-lanceolate leaves, sheathing at the base. Flowers in a terminal spike or head on an erect scape, single in the axils of overlapping, stiff, dry bracts. Outer 3 perianth pieces sepal-like, inner 3 petal-like; stamens 3 fertile, 3 sterile (i.e. represented by staminodes), or absent; anthers opening by lengthwise slits; ovary superior, 1- or imperfectly 3-celled. Fruit a capsule, many-seeded, opening by 3 valves. The leaves and roots are used in the cure of itch in India and S. America. The only genus treated here is Xyris.

XY'RIS (name used by Dioscorides for *Iris foetidissima*). FAM. *Xyridaceae.* A genus of about 190 perennial or rarely annual herbs of rush-like habit distributed over the warmer parts of the earth. Spike globose, ovoid, or shortly cylindrical, with closely overlapping bracts. Petals (inner perianth pieces) yellow, rarely white. Few of the species are of horticultural value. Most need stove or greenhouse conditions, though some are hardy or nearly so, like the Yellow-eyed Grass (a name applied to several closely allied species) of N. America. *X. operculata* needs stove treatment and grows readily in a light, rich soil. It may be increased by division.

X. opercula'ta. Perennial. *l.* almost subulate, about 5 in. long, rigid, tufted; sheaths shining brown. *fl.-heads* ovoid to globular, ⅓ to ½ in. wide; bracts black. *fl.* about ½ in. wide, pet. yellow; scape slender, 12 to 18 in. h., in centre of l.-rosette, sheathed at base. Australia. 1804. (B.M. 1158; L.B.C. 205.)

XYSMALO'BIUM (*xysma*, a fragment, *lobos*, a division; in allusion to the minute divisions of the crown). FAM. *Asclepiadaceae.* A genus of about 40 species of perennial herbs, all African, very closely related to Asclepias. None of the species is hardy and several would need stove conditions. For cultivation *see* **Asclepias.**

X. orbicula're. Stems 1 to 3 ft., usually downy on 2 lines. *l.* opposite, 1½ to 3 in. long, ½ to 2¼ in. wide, sessile, glabrous, oblong and broadly ovate to lanceolate; margins rough. *fl.* in lateral umbels on downy stalks up to 1¼ in. long; cor. chocolate-coloured with a green blotch, with 5 reflexed, glabrous lobes ¼ in. long; staminal column greenish-yellow, ⅛ in. long. S. Africa. 1867. (R.B. 254 as *Gomphocarpus padifolius.*) SYN. *Asclepias orbicularis.* Greenhouse.

Y

YAM. *See* **Dioscorea.**

YAM-BEAN. *See* **Pachyrhizus tuberosus.**

YANG-MAE TREE. *See* **Myrica rubra.**

yargongen'sis -is -e, of Yargong gorge, Tibet.

YARROW. *See* **Achillea Millefolium.**

YARROW, SOLDIER'S. *See* **Stratiotes aloides.**

Yasha, native name of the Japanese *Alnus firma Yasha.*

YATE or **YEIT TREE.** *See* **Eucalyptus cornuta.**

yedoen'sis -is -e, of Yedo (literally 'estuary gate'), the name of which was changed in 1868 to Tokyo (literally 'eastern capital') on its becoming the residence of the Emperor of Japan.

YELLOW ARCHANGEL. *See* **Lamium Galeobdolon.**

YELLOW BARK. *See* **Cinchona Calisaya.**

YELLOW BIRD'S-NEST. *See* **Monotropa Hypopitys.**

YELLOW CRESS. *See* **Barbarea praecox.**

YELLOW CYPRESS. *See* **Chamaecyparis nootkatensis.**

YELLOW DEAL. *See* **Pinus sylvestris.**

YELLOW-EDGE DISEASE. *See* **Strawberry diseases.**

YELLOW ELDER. *See* **Tecoma stans.**

YELLOW EVERLASTING. *See* **Helichrysum arenarium.**

YELLOW-EYED GRASS. *See* **Xyris.**

YELLOW FLAG or **IRIS.** *See* **Iris Pseudacorus.**

YELLOW HORNED POPPY. *See* **Glaucium flavum.**

YELLOW LOOSESTRIFE. *See* **Lysimachia vulgaris.**

YELLOW PIMPERNEL. *See* **Lysimachia nemorum.**

YELLOW PINE WESTERN. *See* **Pinus ponderosa.**

YELLOW ROCKET. *See* **Barbarea praecox.**

YELLOW ROOT. *See* **Hydrastis canadensis.**

YELLOW TOAD-FLAX. *See* **Linaria vulgaris.**

YELLOW STAR FLOWER. *See* **Sternbergia lutea.**

YELLOW STAR OF BETHLEHEM. *See* **Gagea sylvatica** (a synonym of *G. lutea*).

YELLOW SULTAN. *See* **Centaurea moschata flava.**

YELLOW UNDERWING MOTH. *See* **Surface caterpillars.**

YELLOW WATER-LILY. *See* **Nuphar luteum.**

YELLOW-WEED, DYER'S. *See* **Reseda Luteola.**

YELLOW WOOD. *See* **Cladrastis lutea, Ochrosia borbonica, Podocarpus, &c.**

YELLOW-BOY. *See* **Chrysanthemum segetum.**

yemen'sis -is -e, of Yemen, Arabia.

YERBA BUENA. *See* **Micromeria Chamissonis.**

YEW. *See* **Taxus.**

YEW, CHINESE. *See* **Podocarpus macrophyllus Maki, Taxus chinensis.**

YEW, CLUSTER-FLOWERED. *See* **Cephalotaxus.**

YEW, JAPANESE. *See* **Cephalotaxus drupacea fastigiata.**

YEW, JOINTED. *See* **Athrotaxis.**

YEW, LORD HARRINGTON'S. *See* **Cephalotaxus drupacea pedunculata.**

YEW, PRINCE ALBERT'S. *See* **Saxegothaea conspicua.**

YEW, STINKING. *See* **Torreya.**

YOKE ELM. *See* **Carpinus Betulus.**

yosemiten'sis -is -e, of the Yosemite valley, California.

Youngia'nus -a -um, in honour of Messrs. Charles, James, and Peter Young, nurserymen at Epsom, Surrey, during the first half of the 19th century, and Milford; the firm, which came to an end in 1862 with the death of William Young, was famed for its uncommon plants and grew many species from Spain and the Canary Is., introduced by P. B. Webb on whose estate the Milford nursery was situated.

YOUTH AND AGE. *See* **Zinnia elegans.**

A→

YPONOMEU'TA or **HYPONOMEU'TA.** *See* **Ermine Moths.**

YUC'CA (from *yuca*, the Carib name for the manihot, erroneously used). FAM. *Liliaceae.* Including Hesperoyucca. Evergreen trees and shrubs confined to the S. United States, Mexico, and Cent. America. The number of species is variously estimated by different authorities, but there are probably about 30, besides numerous hybrids of garden origin. The differentiation of the species is not easy and few genera of its size are more cumbered with synonyms than this. Some botanists place it with Agave, Cordyline, Dracaena, Phormium, and other genera of similar habit in a family Agavaceae distinct from Liliaceae and Amaryllidaceae.

They vary in stature from trees 50 ft. high down to acaulescent shrubs. Leaves crowded in dense terminal clusters, in shape long and narrow, mostly spine-tipped and often with horny, more or less shredded margins. Flowers of some shade of white, rarely pure, sometimes tinged with purple, from 1½ to 2½ in. long, the 6 rather fleshy segments of the perianth often more erect than spreading; stamens 6, shorter than the perianth; style short; stigmas 3. They are borne very numerously, often very densely, on erect or pendent panicles varying from 1½ to 6 ft. in length. The 6-celled fruit is oblong or ovoid, 1½ to 8 in. long according to the species, and is either dry and dehiscent or fleshy and indehiscent; the latter type is sometimes edible and dried by the Indians for winter food.

Not many of the species are genuinely hardy in the average climate of Britain, but a few like *Y. gloriosa*, *Y. recurvifolia*, *Y. filamentosa*, and *Y. flaccida* are amongst them. Pretty nearly the whole genus is suited by climatic conditions ranging between those, say, of the Isle of Wight to those of the French Riviera. For most cultivators the majority are definitely greenhouse plants. They all like an open loamy soil and all possible sunshine. If grown in pots they can be placed in the open air during the summer months, plunging the pots in ashes. They are propagated by cutting up the thick, fleshy roots into pieces 2 or 3 in. long and placing these in sandy soil in gentle heat. A few species with the suckering habit of *Y. flaccida* may be increased by division. In a wild state the Yuccas (with one or two occasional exceptions) depend for pollination on species of the Pronuba or Yucca Moth (*Tegeticula yuccasella* in the eastern, southern, and western United States, 4 other species in California), which collects pollen from the anthers of one flower, flies with this to another flower, usually on another plant, lays its eggs within the ovary of this, runs up to the stigma and thrusts the pollen into the stigmatic opening. Thus cross-pollination is effected. The larvae feed on the swelling seeds, but do not damage more than a few in each capsule. If seed is required in non-American gardens, the flowers should be hand-pollinated. How successfully this can be done is shown by the many hybrids raised first by J. B. Deleuil at Marseilles from 1874 onwards and later by Carl Sprenger at Naples. Thus between 1897 and 1907 Sprenger (d. 1918) raised and named over 100 hybrid forms of Yucca in his nursery at Vomero, a suburb of Naples, most of which were put in commerce by him or later by Willy Muller at Nocera. Some were introduced into British gardens, including *Y. × vomerensis*, probably the hardiest and most handsome, and it is likely that a number still survive in Italian and French gardens. They are not described below, but an account by Sprenger, listing 112 named forms, will be found in *Mitteilungen der Deutschen Dendrologischen Gesellschaft*, 1920, 96–138; a less complete and less accurate enumeration is given in G. Molon, *Le Yucche* (1914).

The Key below distinguishes only the more commonly cultivated species. For further information 'The Yucceae' by William Trelease in *Annual Rep. Missouri Botanical Garden*, 13 (1902) and *Yuccas of the South-western United States*, Part I (1938), 2 (1947), by Susan D. McKelvey should be consulted.

W. J. B. and W. T. S.

DISEASES. Yuccas occasionally suffer damage from *Botrytis cinerea* (*see* **Grey Mould Fungus**). More common is the Yucca Leaf Spot due to the fungus *Coniothyrium concentricum* which makes leaves very unsightly by producing brown patches on which concentric rings of black dots (pycnidia) appear. Although this fungus does not kill the leaves it is very persistent and should be combated by removal of first affected leaves or parts of leaves and by spraying with Bordeaux mixture.

D. E. G.

KEY

1. *L.-margin without numerous spreading fibres, though often toothed when young or with a few fibres when old* — 2

1. *L.-margin with numerous long spreading, recurved or curled fibres* — 7

2 (1). *Plant stemless, the rosette basal* — 3

2. *Plant with evident stem except when young* — 4

3 (2). *Lvs. broadest at base and tapering gradually from there to tip* — Y. Whipplei

3. *Lvs. broadest above the base* — Y. rupicola

4 (2). *Lvs. flexible, recurving, nearly flat* — Y. recurvifolia

4. *Lvs. stiff, straight, generally concave* — 5

5 (4). *L.-margin horny with numerous minute short teeth; lvs. at middle under $1\frac{1}{2}$ in. wide; ovary short-stalked* — Y. aloifolia

5. *L.-margin entire or sparingly toothed, ultimately with a few fibres; lvs. at middle 2 to $3\frac{1}{2}$ in. wide; ovary sessile* — 6

6 (5). *Lvs. smooth on upper side* — Y. gloriosa

6. *Lvs. roughened on upper side* — Y. Treculeana

7 (1). *Lvs. wide, to 2 in. wide; infl. branched* — 8

7 (1). *Lvs. narrower, $\frac{1}{4}$ to $\frac{1}{2}$ in. wide; infl. unbranched* — 11

8 (7). *Lvs. concave, blue-green; per. 2 to 4 in. long* — Y. baccata

8. *Lvs. almost flat; per. 1 to 2 in. long* — 9

9 (8). *Lvs. flexible, recurving, thin* — Y. flaccida

9. *Lvs. stiff, straight* — 10

10 (9). *Lvs. oblong-lanceolate to oblanceolate, $1\frac{1}{4}$ to 4 in. wide; fl. 2 to $2\frac{3}{4}$ in. long* — Y. filamentosa

10. *Lvs. linear-lanceolate, $\frac{3}{4}$ to $1\frac{1}{2}$ in. wide; fl. $1\frac{1}{4}$ to 2 in. long* — Y. Smalliana

11 (7). *Style bright green, darker than ovary* — Y. glauca

11. *Style white or pale green, lighter than ovary* — Y. angustissima

Y. aloifo'lia.* Stem slender, erect, 10 to 20 ft. *l.* 18 to 21 in. long, 1 to $1\frac{1}{4}$ in. wide, minutely toothed, spine-tipped, glaucous green. *fl.* creamy-white, tinged with purple near the base, 2 in. long, borne on panicles 2 to 3 ft. h. May, June. SE. United States, W. Indies. (B.M. 1700.) Greenhouse. var. **draco'nis,** stem branched, *l.* brighter green, broader and longer. 1605. (G.C. 1870, 828.) SYN. *Y. draconis*; **tri'color,** *l.* with a yellow or whitish band down the middle; **variegat'a,** *l.* with whitish stripes.

Y. angustifo'lia. A synonym of *Y. glauca.*

Y. angustis'sima. Stemless, but with a thick prostrate rootstock. *l.* 8 to 16 in. long, $\frac{1}{12}$ to $\frac{1}{5}$ in. wide, spiny pointed, margins white and curly threaded. *fl.* on a glabrous raceme, or panicle branched near base, 3 to 5 ft. h., segs. dull white, acutely lanceolate; style white or greenish. SW. United States. (McKelvey, Yucca, 2, 36.) Near *Y. glauca* which has a green style.

Y. austra'lis. A synonym of *Y. filifera.*

Y. bacca'ta. Nearly acaulescent or with a short, prostrate stem. *l.* 2 to 3 ft. long, 2 in. wide, concave, stiff, spine-tipped, rough, margins set with coarse thread. *fl.* white, 3 in. long, in an erect dense panicle up to 3 ft. h. August. *fr.* edible, dried for winter eating by Indians. Nevada, Utah, Colorado, New Mexico, Texas, Arizona, S. California. (McKelvey, Yucca, 1. 8–12.) SYN. *Y. circinata.* Hardy only in such places as the Isle of Wight.

Y. Boerhaav'ii. A variety of *Y. flexilis.*

Y. canalicula'ta. A variety of *Y. Treculeàna.*

Y. circina'ta. A synonym of *Y. baccata.*

Y. constric'ta. Stem 3 to 5 ft. or acaulescent. *l.* $1\frac{1}{2}$ to 2 ft. long, about $\frac{1}{2}$ in. wide, linear, rigid, channelled above, margins bearing numerous fine threads. *Panicle* 3 to 5 ft. long, slender-stalked, occasionally branched towards top. *fl.* white, globose-campanulate. 1 to 2 in. long. Summer. SW. United States. 1862. (Fl. d. S. 110; McKelvey, Yucca, 2. 50). Akin to *Y. glauca.* Half-hardy.

Y. Desmetia'na. Stem 10 to 15 ft. *l.* $1\frac{1}{2}$ to 2 ft. long, $\frac{1}{2}$ to 1 in. wide, flat, stiffly recurved, not spine-tipped or toothed, purple when young become glaucous and green, persisting in a dead state and hanging close to the stem for many years. Evidently very shy-flowering. An old plant flowered for the first time at Montserrate, Cintra, Portugal, in 1928. *Panicle* drooping, pyramidal, 3 ft. long, 1 to $1\frac{1}{2}$ ft. wide. Mexico. 1868. (G.C. 86 (1929) 93.) Greenhouse.

Y. draco'nis. A variety of *Y. aloifolia.*

Y. ela'ta. Tree, single-stemmed or few-branched, up to 24 ft. *l.* linear, $1\frac{1}{2}$ to 2 ft. long, $\frac{1}{8}$ to $\frac{1}{2}$ in. wide with a dilated base, spine-tipped, margins white, furnished with numerous threads 2 to 3 in. long. *Panicles* 7 to 10 ft. long, erect, slender-stalked, formed of crowded racemes 6 to 9 in. long occupying the terminal half; *fl.* white, about 2 in. long. Summer. SW. United States. 1886. (B.M. 7650; McKelvey, Yucca, 2. 25–31.) SYN. *Y. radiosa.* Greenhouse.

Y. elephan'tipes. A synonym of *Y. guatemalensis.*

Y. Ellacomb'ei. A synonym of *Y. gloriosa nobilis.*

Yucca filamentosa

Y. filamento'sa.* Adam's Needle. Stemless, spreading by short side growths. *l* stiffly erect to spreading, 1 to $2\frac{1}{2}$ ft. long, $1\frac{1}{2}$ to 4 in. wide, oblong-lanceolate or oblanceolate, pointed, slightly glaucous, with numerous marginal, curly, white threads 2 to 3 in. long. *fl.* pendulous, yellowish-white, 2 to 3 in. long, borne in erect, conical glabrous panicles 3 to 6 ft. h. July, August. SE. United States. 1675. (B.M. 900.) Hardy. var. **variega'ta,** *l.* margined and striped with yellow (Lowe and Howard, Beaut. Lvd. Pl. 51). *Y. Smalliana* is often confused with this species.

Y. fili'fera. Tree 20 to 50 ft., eventually much-branched, trunk 2 to 5 ft. in diam. *l.* 1 to $1\frac{1}{2}$ ft. long, 1 to $1\frac{1}{2}$ in. wide, spine-tipped, green, margins coarsely threaded. *fl.* creamy-white, 2 in. long, crowded in pendent panicles 4 to 5 ft. long, 15 to 18 in. wide. June. Mexico. (G.C. 3 (1888), 743, 751; B.M. 7197.) SYN. *Y. australis.* Greenhouse. Very fine on the French and Italian Riviera.

Y. flac'cida. Acaulescent and spreading by side shoots from the base. *l.* 1 to 2 ft. long, 1 to $1\frac{1}{2}$ in. wide, pointed, green or glaucous, terminal part bent downwards, margin furnished with curly threads 2 in. long as in *Y. filamentosa.* *fl.* yellowish-white, 2 to $2\frac{1}{2}$ in. long, in erect downy panicles. July, August. SE. United States. 1816. (Ref. B. 5, 323.) Hardy. var. **integ'ra,** without marginal fibres. (B.M. 2662 as *Y. glauca*); **ma'jor,** *l.* glaucous, broader; panicle downy. (B.M. 6316 as *Y. orchioides major.*) SYN. var. **glauces'cens; orchioi'des,** *infl.* racemose, *l.* almost without threads.

Y. fle'xilis. Stem short. *l.* 2 to 2½ ft. long, 1 to 1½ in. wide, spine-tipped, entire or obscurely toothed, glaucous at first, becoming green, gracefully reflexed. *fl.* white, 3½ in. long, pendent, loosely disposed on a long-stalked panicle up to 4 ft. long. Origin uncertain. 1859. (R.H. 1859, 400.) Closely akin to *Y. recurva*, from which it differs by its long-stalked panicles and narrower l. Greenhouse. var. **Boerhaav'ii,** *l.* flat, scarcely pungent. SYN. *Y. Boerhaavii*; **Peacock'ii,** *l.* stiffer, not recurved. SYN. *Y. Peacockii.*

Y. × floribun'da. (*Y. filamentosa* × *Y. gloriosa.*)

Y. funi'fera. Stemless, often tufted shrub. *l.* 3 to 4 (sometimes up to 6) ft. long, 1½ in. wide, forming a dense rosette, sword-shaped, concave, the marginal fibres coarse and often 6 to 10 in. long.

On account of its narrow flowers, this is generally placed in a genus distinct from Yucca and it is accordingly treated earlier in this Dictionary (p. 990) as *Hesperaloe funifera.*

Y. gigante'a. Possibly a hybrid between *Y. guatemalensis* and *Y. gloriosa* or more probably a form of *Y. guatemalensis*; does not appear to have been found wild. At its best it is a branching tree 30 ft. and upwards, its trunk 3 ft. in diameter. *l.* 3 to 4 ft. or more long, 4 in. wide. *fl.* resembling those of *Y. gloriosa*, white, 3 to 3½ in. long, in a compact pyramidal panicle 2 to 3 ft. long, half as wide. Magnificent in the Azores. Greenhouse.

Y. glau'ca.* Acaulescent, or with a short prostrate stem. *l.* narrowly linear, 1 to 2½ ft. long, ¼ to ¾ in. wide, tapering to a long slender point, glaucous, the whole forming a horizontal rosette 4 ft. across; margin of l. white, with a few threads. *fl.* pendulous, greenish-white, 2 to 3 in. long in an erect raceme 3 to 5 ft. h. July, August. Cent. United States. 1811. (B.M. 2236 as *Y. angustifolia*; McKelvey, Yucca, 2. 57–59.) Hardy. var. **stric'ta** differs by its distinct erect form and branched infl. (B.M. 2222 as *Y. stricta.*)

Y. glorio'sa.* Stem short, thick, sometimes branched. *l.* 1½ to 2 ft. long, 2 to 3 in. wide, stiff, flat, straight, spine-tipped, glaucous green. *fl.* creamy-white, often tinged with red or purple outside, pendulous, closely packed in a narrowly conical, erect panicle, 3 to 6 ft. h., but known to have been as much as 15 ft. July to September. SE. United States. 1550. (B.M. 1260.) Hardy. var. **medio-striat'a,** *l.* with a whitish stripe down the middle; **nob'ilis,** *l.* quite glaucous, recurved. SYN. *Y. Ellacombei.* Other strong-growing forms difficult to distinguish are vars. *robusta* and *superba.*

Y. guatemalen'sis.* Round-headed tree with usually several trunks springing from a swollen base and ultimately 25 to 45 ft. h., much-branched. *l.* 2 to 4 ft. long, 2 to 4 in. wide, glossy green, obscurely toothed, apex soft. *fl.* ivory-white or cream-coloured, 2½ to 3 in. long, very densely packed in erect panicles 2 to 3½ ft. h. Summer. Cent. America. 1873. (G.C. 18 (1895), 519, 523; B.M. 7997.) SYN. *Y. elephantipes, Y. Lenneana.* Greenhouse.

Y. Harriman'iae. Stemless, often tufted. *l.* linear to lanceolate-spatulate, 8 to 16 in. long, ¼ to ¾ in. (or even more) wide, rigid, glaucous becoming green, spine-tipped, margins brown and set with coarse, curling fibres. *fl.* greenish, about 2 in. long, borne in racemes 10 to 20 in. h., the segs. broad, blunt; style white slender. Utah, Colorado. (McKelvey, Yucca, 2, 54–56.) Closely akin to *Y. glauca* which has a green swollen style. Probably fairly hardy.

Y. Lennea'na. A synonym of *Y. guatemalensis.*

Y. macrocar'pa of Engelmann. A synonym of *Y. Schottii.*

Y. orchioi'des maj'or. A synonym of *Y. flaccida major.*

Y. parviflo'ra. A synonym of *Hesperaloe parviflora.*

Y. radio'sa. A synonym of *Y. elata.*

Y. recurvifo'lia.* Stems up to 6 ft., sometimes branched. *l.* 2 to 3 ft. long, 1½ to 2½ in. wide, at first glaucous, tapered to a spiny point, all except the upper much recurved. *fl.* creamy-white, 2 to 3 in. wide, in an erect panicle 3 to 5 ft. h., much looser and more branched than in *Y. gloriosa* to which it is closely akin. SE. United States. 1794. (B.T.S. i. 58.) The easiest, hardiest, and most generally useful species. var. **marginat'a,** *l.* bordered with yellow; **variegat'a,** *l.* with a median yellow line.

Y. rupi'cola. Nearly or quite stemless, consisting of a rosette of numerous *l.* 2 to 3 ft. long, 1½ in. wide, gradually narrowed to a spiny apex; margins minutely toothed. *fl.* white or yellowish, drooping, 2 to 2½ in. long in a panicle 5 or 6 ft. h., with slender branches. September. SW. United States. 1850. (B.M. 7172; McKelvey, Yucca, 2. 16–187.) Hardy.

Y. schidi'gera. *See under* **Y. Schottii.**

Y. Schott'ii. Stem 10 to 16 ft. rarely branched. *l.* 1½ to 3 ft. long, 1½ to 2½ in. wide, tapering to a fine point, concave; margins without coarse threads. *Panicle* 2 to 3 ft. h., conical. *fl.* white, rather globose, about 1¼ in. long. Arizona. (McKelvey, Yucca, 1. 40–43.) SYN. *Y. macrocarpa* of Engelmann, not Merriam. Near the usually acaulescent *Y. baccata* but with a tall stem and smaller fr. which is edible and made into a fermented beverage by Indians. Greenhouse. The name *Y. macrocarpa* has also been applied to 2 allied species both with the margin breaking into fibres; **Y. schidi'gera** with *l.* about 1½ ft. long, **Y. Torrey'i,** with l. about 3 ft. long.

Y. Smallia'na. Almost stemless. *l.* firm, 1 to 3 ft. long, ¾ to 1½ in. wide, linear-lanceolate, pointed, with numerous marginal white threads. *fl.* pendulous, almost white, 1½ to 2 in. long, in erect finely hairy panicle. SE. United States. Closely akin to *Y. filamentosa.*

Y. strict'a. A variety of *Y. glauca.*

Y. Torrey'i. *See under* **Y. Schottii.**

Y. Treculea'na.* Tree with single or branched stem, usually under 15 ft. *l.* blue-green, thick, stiff, roughened, spine-tipped, 2 to 4 ft. long, 2 to 3 in. wide, sometimes with thready margins. *fl.* white, sometimes purple-tinged, 1½ to 2½ in. long, densely packed in a narrowly pyramidal panicle, 2 to 4 ft. long. June. Texas and Mexico. 1858. (R.H. 1869, 406; McKelvey, Yucca, 1. 31–36) Greenhouse. var. **canalicula'ta,** *l.* broader, channelled, *fl.* smaller, yellowish-white. (B.M. 5201 as *Y. canaliculata.*)

Y. × vomeren'sis (*Y. aloifolia* × *Y. gloriosa.*) Possibly the best of Sprenger's hybrids (*see* heading).

Yucca Whipplei

Y. Whipp'lei.* Stemless, producing from the rootstock a hemispherical mass of l. up to 6 ft. across. *l.* 1 to 3 ft. long, ½ to 1¼ in. wide, glaucous, tapered to a sharp, slender spine; margins finely toothed. *fl.* 2½ to 3 in. across, pendent, greenish-white, tipped and margined with purple, closely set on the upper half of an erect panicle 8 to 15 ft. h. May, June. California to Arizona. 1854. (B.M. 7662 as *Hesperoyucca Whipplei*; McKelvey, Yucca, 2. 1–12.) SYN. *Hesperoyucca Whipplei.* var. **viola'cea,** the whole of the perianth more or less deeply tinged violet. (R.H. 1884, 324.)

W. J. B. and W. T. S.

yuccifo'lius -a -um, with leaves like a Yucca.

Yu'lan, Chinese plant name, originally applied to the white *Magnolia denudata.*

yunnanen'sis -is -e, of Yunnan, W. China.

Z

Zabel'i, in honour of Hermann Zabel, 1832–1912, German dendrologist.

ZACIN'THA (first discovered on Zante, the Greek island *Zacinthos*). FAM. *Compositae.* A monotypic genus, native of the Mediterranean region. A hardy annual calling for no special soil.

Z. verruco'sa. Annual 6 to 12 in. h. *l.* radical lyrate; stem-l. few, alternate, stem-clasping, less cut. *fl.-heads* yellow, rather small; involucre narrow, inner bracts folded, outer spreading, receptacle flat, naked, florets all ligulate, 5-toothed. *Achenes* glabrous. Summer. Mediterranean region. (S.B.F.G. 820.)

ZAHLBRUCKN'ERIA (in honour of Johann Zahlbruckner, 1782–1850, Austrian botanist). FAM. *Saxifragaceae.* A monotypic genus, related to Saxifraga and often included in it, of botanical but not horticultural interest, the petals of the minute greenish flowers being shorter and narrower than the sepals.

Z. parado'xa. Stems creeping or procumbent, 2 to 12 in. h. *l.* kidney-shaped, with 5 to 7 rounded lobes, cordate at base, long-stalked. *fl.* about $\frac{1}{10}$ in. across; pet. linear, greenish-white. European Alps, in damp shady places. SYN. *Saxifraga paradoxa.*

Zahn'ii, in honour of (1) Gottlieb Zahn, drowned 1870 while collecting for Messrs. Veitch in Cent. America; (2) Karl Hermann Zahn, b. 1865, monographer of Hieracium; (3) Heinrich Zahn, b. 1880, missionary in New Guinea.

zaidamen'sis -is -e, of Zaidam, SW. Outer Mongolia.

ZALAC'CA (native name in Moluccas). FAM. *Palmaceae.* A genus of about 14 species of stemless Palms, with creeping roots, natives of Assam and Malaya. Leaves long, equally pinnatisect, segments alternate, clustered or equidistant, lanceolate or oblanceolate, slender-pointed, stalk often armed with spirally placed prickles, sheaths also armed with flattened prickles. Spathes persistent; spadices sometimes branched, drooping, the flowering branches catkin-like. Fruit globose or ovoid, usually beaked, 1- to 3-seeded. Warm house species which may be treated like Cycas. **A**

Z. edu'lis. *l.* many, clustered, erect, clothed with long, often toothed prickles; segs. linear-lanceolate, very long slender-pointed, $1\frac{1}{2}$ to $2\frac{1}{2}$ ft. long, $1\frac{1}{2}$ to 2 in. wide, whitish beneath; stalk with strong prickles. *fl.* spadices drooping, long-branched, the male axillary, longer and more branched than female; female catkins 2 to 3 in. long, thicker than males. *fr.* brownish, pear-shaped, $2\frac{1}{2}$ in. long. Malaya. 1847. SYN. *Z. Blumeana.* var. **Wallichia'na,** *l.* 18 to 20 ft. long, segs. clustered in 2's, 3's, or 4's, about 18 in. long, 3 or 4 in. wide; stalk 4 to 6 ft. long, with strong brown prickles.

zaleu'cus -a -um, very white.

Zaz'il, native Persian name of a Delphinium.

ZALUZA'NIA. *See* **Podachaenium.**

ZALUZIANSK'YA (in honour of Adam Zaluziansky von Zaluzian, 1558–1613, physician of Prague, author of *Methodus Herbariae*, 1592). FAM. *Scrophulariaceae.* A genus of about 40 more or less clammy annual or perennial herbs, natives of S. Africa. Lowest leaves opposite, upper alternate, usually with few teeth. Flowers sessile, usually in dense or interrupted terminal spikes; calyx ovate-tubular, shortly 5-toothed, 2-lipped or 2-parted; corolla persistent, tube long, finally cleft to base, limb 5-lobed, entire of 2-cleft (lobes of those mentioned are 2-cleft); stamens usually 4. Fruit a capsule. All species grow well in sandy loam and peat. Seeds of *S. capensis* and *S. villosa* should be sown in summer in the open; *S. lychnidea* may be increased by cuttings or by division.

Z. capen'sis. Half-hardy annual. Stem erect, 6 to 12 in. h., appressed hairy. *l.* linear, with few or no teeth, margin and nerves usually ciliate. *fl.* whitish; cor. slender, about $1\frac{1}{4}$ in. long, shortly hairy outside; spike usually short and few-fld. SYN. *Nycterinia capensis.* Spring.

Z. lychni'dea. Sub-shrub of 6 to 12 in., appressed hairy. *l.* oblong-linear, with few or no teeth, 1-nerved, nearly glabrous, upper broadly lanceolate or oblong obtuse, margin and nerve ciliate. *fl.* yellowish-white; cor. tube $1\frac{1}{2}$ in. or more long; spikes long. May to July. (B.M. 2504 and B.R. 748 as *Erinus lychnidea*; S.B.F.G. s. 2, 239 as *Nycterinia lychnidea.*)

Zaluzianskya maritima

Z. mari'tima. Perennial herb, but annual in cultivation, sometimes decumbent and branched, densely leafy, hairy, about 3 ft. h. *l.* narrowly elliptic to oblong-lanceolate, 1 to 3 in. long, lower short-stalked, upper sessile. *fl.* deep red or purple-brown outside, shining white within; tube $1\frac{1}{2}$ to 2 in. long, limb 5-cleft, about $\frac{3}{4}$ in. across; spikes long, rather densely fld. S. Africa. 1906. (B.M. 8215.)

Z. selaginoi'des. A synonym of *Z. villosa.*

Z. villo'sa. Half-hardy annual, 3 to 12 in. h. *l.* spatulate, the lower obovate, stalk rather long, the upper oblong- or linear-spatulate; floral l. adnate to cal., dilated at base. *fl.* white, centre orange, fragrant at night, about $\frac{3}{4}$ in. long, nearly glabrous outside; stamens 2; spikes interrupted at base. May. 1854. SYN. *Z. selaginoides.*

ZAMAN. *See* **Pithecolobium Saman.** This tree is sometimes placed in a genus by itself as *Samanea Saman.*

Zam'bac, Arabic and Persian name for *Jasminum Sambac*, sometimes applied for comparison to other white scented flowers.

ZA'MIA (*zamia*, loss; from the sterile appearance of the male cones). FAM. *Cycadaceae.* A genus of about 36 species of handsome perennial plants, resembling Palms and in some ways Ferns, natives for the most part of Trop. America and the W. Indies, one extending to the S. United States. Stem simple, lobed or branched, smooth or scarred sometimes below ground. Leaves few, pinnate; pinnae broad or narrow, entire or toothed, parallel-veined; stalk smooth or spiny. Flowers dioecious in glabrous or rarely furry cones. Cones small, solitary or 2 or more together; males oblong-cylindrical with many series of peltate scales on thick stalks, anthers single; females larger and thicker, the flowers being naked ovules beneath the scales. Equal parts of good loam and peat with a little silver-sand suits them They need to be shaded from bright sun in summer and a temperature of not less than 60° F. in winter, except *Z. pumila* which will survive in a warm greenhouse. In summer they should be watered freely both at the root and overhead. If they are not thriving it is a good plan to shake all the soil away from the roots, wash them carefully, cut away all decayed parts and repot them in fresh soil, then plunge them in bottom heat and water carefully until new growth appears. They can be propagated by division where the stems are clustered, and by seeds and offsets. The underground parts are sometimes ground into flour which, rich in starch, after the removal of a poisonous principle found in most Cycads, makes palatable cakes and puddings when properly prepared.

KEY

1.	*Veins of lflets. usually prominent beneath*	2
1.	*Veins of lflets. scarcely prominent beneath*	12
2.	*Veins striate*	3
2.	*Veins not striate*	9
3.	*Peduncle of male cone longer than cone*	4
3.	*Peduncle of male cone shorter than cone*	5
4.	*Lflets. ovate*	Z. obliqua
4.	*Lflets. linear-lanceolate*	Z. Lindenii
5.	*Lflets. linear-lanceolate, cuspidate*	Z. pseudoparasitica
5.	*Lflets. acuminate*	6
6.	*Lflets. lanceolate to ovate*	7
6.	*Lflets. long lanceolate, with a long point*	Z. Chigua
7.	*Lflets. oblong-lanceolate, slender-pointed*	Z. montana
7.	*Lflets. lanceolate or ovate*	8
8.	*Lflets. broad lanceolate; veins distinct*	Z. Wallisii
8.	*Lflets. lanceolate or ovate, long pointed*	Z. Skinneri
9.	*Lflets. obovate, thickly leathery, margin revolute, nerves prominent*	Z. furfuracea
9.	*Lflets. lanceolate, nerves slender*	10
10.	*Lflets. linear-lanceolate or obovate-oblong, veins immersed, margin revolute*	Z. Loddigesii
10.	*Lflets. wider*	11
11.	*Lflets. obliquely lanceolate, narrowed to a spiny toothed tip*	Z. muricata
11.	*Lflets. narrow lanceolate with a long sharply toothed tip*	Z. Fischeri
12.	*Stem underground*	13
12.	*Stem partly underground. Margin of lflets. more or less revolute*	14
13.	*Lflets. linear, obtuse, margin thick, revolute*	Z. floridana
13.	*Lflets. obovate-wedge-shaped or spatulate*	Z. pygmaea
14.	*Lflets. linear-lanceolate or oblong-wedge-shaped*	Z. media
14.	*Lflets. narrow-linear, blunt*	Z. angustifolia

Z. angustifo'lia. Stem ovoid-conical. *Adult l.* glabrous; lflets. 4 to 20 each side, mostly alternate, narrow-linear, 6 to 8 in. long, rather blunt, scarcely narrowed at base; stalks rounded beneath, unarmed. *Cones* 2 to 2½ in. long; males reddish-hairy, females bluntly cuspidate; peduncles erect, reddish-hairy. W. Indies.

Z. calo'coma. A synonym of *Microcycas calocoma.*

Z. Chig'ua. Stem cylindrical, a few in. to 3 ft. h. *l.* about 4 ft. long, spiny on rachis and stalk; lflets. 14 to 140, alternate, spreading, dense, long lanceolate, 4 to 8 in. long with a slender, fragile point, smooth, rarely toothed, deep green, veins about 16, more or less prominent beneath. *Cones* of male 5 to 7 in. long, of female, much larger. Colombia. 1847.

Z. Fisch'eri. Stem dwarf, thick, ringed with l.-scars. *l.* about 16 in. long, densely hairy at first, not prickly; lflets. 18 to 36, narrow lanceolate, 1½ to 4 in. long, long-pointed, acute, narrowed to base, toothed, glabrous, deep green above, paper beneath. *Male cone* 1½ to 3 in. long, female shorter. Mexico. 1849. (G.C. 19 (1883), f. 29.)

Z. florida'na. Stem underground, beet-shaped, about 10 in. long. *l.* ovate to ovate-lanceolate; stalk angled, reddish-brown-hairy at base; lflets. 28 to 44, usually opposite, linear, straight, 3 to 3½ in. long, blunt, margin thickened and revolute, deep shining green above, paler beneath. *Male cones* numerous 1½ to 2½ in. long; *female* 2 to 8 in. long. Florida. var. **Purshia'na,** *l.* 12 to 30 in. long, lflets. 12 to 40, dark green above, paler beneath, broad-linear to oblong-linear, narrowed to base, more or less obtuse, rarely toothed, 2 to 5 in. long. (B.M. 1838, 2006 as *Z. media.*)

Z. furfura'cea. Stem more or less tuberous, about 6 in. long, sometimes branched. *l.* 3 to 4 ft. long; stalk prickly, at first hairy; lflets. 4 to 26, lanceolate to obovate-oblong, 2 to 8 in. long, abruptly narrowed at base, more or less toothed, thick leathery, veins numerous, hairy above, densely hairy beneath. *Male cones* about 4 in. long, *female* rather shorter. Mexico, Colombia. (B.M. 1969.)

Z. integrifo'lia. A synonym of *Z. media Commeliniana.*

Z. Kickx'ii. A synonym of *Z. pygmaea Kickxii.*

Z. latifo'lia. A synonym of *Z. Loddigesii latifolia.*

Z. Leibold'ii. A synonym of *Z. Loddigesii Leiboldii.*

Z. Linden'ii. Stem cylindrical, 3 to 8 ft. h., stout. *l.* 10 to 15, 6 to 8 ft. long, with an ovate, sheathing base; stalk 6 ft. or more long, prickly, softly hairy at first; lflets. 40 to 80, long linear-lanceolate, 8 to 14 in. long, sometimes curved, sharply toothed from middle upwards, veins 22 to 30, shiny glaucous. *Female cones* 14 in. long. Ecuador. 1875. (I.H. 1875, 195.) Syn. *Z. Noeffiana.*

Z. Loddiges'ii. Stem more or less tuberous, about 8 in. h., thick. *l.-stalk* usually prickly, hairy at first, soon smooth; lflets. 6 to 44, variable, linear-lanceolate to obovate-oblong, up to 7½ in. long, spiny toothed from middle upwards, usually with brownish down beneath. *Male cone* 1½ to 2½ in. long; *female* thick, about 2 in. long. Mexico. 1844. (G.F. 186.) var. **latifo'lia,** *lflets.* obovate-oblong to narrow-oblong, more or less blunt, 4 to 9½ in. long, veins 35 to 43, sometimes spiny toothed. Syn. *Z. latifolia, Z. prasina*; **Leibold'ii,** *lflets.* 5 to 10 in. long, linear-lanceolate, distinctly narrowed to a blunt tip which is usually 2-fid, spiny toothed from middle upwards, bright green above, paler beneath, veins 32 to 36. Syn. *Z. Leiboldii.*

Z. me'dia. Stem short, cylindrical. *l.* about 3 ft. long, not prickly; lflets. 12 to 54, 2 to 8 in. long, jointed to rachis, linear-lanceolate to oblong-wedge-shaped, narrowed to base, and to the long, blunt, emarginate tip, entire or irregularly toothed, leathery, clear deep green or yellowish-green above, paler beneath. *Male cones* 2 to 4 in. long; *female* thicker, 2½ to 5 in. long. Cuba. var. **Commelinia'na,** *lflets.* 12 to 36, linear-lanceolate to oblong, 3½ to 7½ in. long. W. Indies. 1758. (B.M. 1851 as *Z. integrifolia.*) Greenhouse.

Z. monta'na. Stem 4 to 6 ft. h., swollen. *l.* 4 or 5, 4½ to 5½ ft. long, more or less erect; stalk somewhat spiny, rusty hairy at base; lflets. 16 to 20, wide oblong-lanceolate, 7 to 14 in. long, spreading, widest in upper third, narrowed to a wedge-shaped base, obliquely cuspidate, usually 3-toothed, shining. Colombia. 1875.

Z. murica'ta. Stem rarely 6 in. long, more or less bulbous, often branched. *l.-stalks* round, prickly at first; lflets. 6 to 24, finally spreading, 4 to 9 in. long, oblong- or narrow-lanceolate, spiny toothed from middle upwards, rather thin, shining above, yellowish-green or glaucous beneath, jointed to rachis, veins numerous. *Male cones* 2 to 5, 1¼ to 2½ in. long; *female* 2 to 4 in. long, rusty or greyish hairy. Colombia, Venezuela, Mexico. 1849. var. **pic'ta,** more robust than type, *l.* 6 ft. or more long, lflets. 10 to 50, 5 to 14 in. long, irregularly toothed, yellowish or greyish-green, spotted white. Guatemala, Mexico. Syn. *Z. picta.*

Z. Noeffia'na. A synonym of *Z. Lindenii.*

Z. obli'qua. Stem slender, cylindrical, erect, 8 ft. h. *l.* 2 to 3 ft. long, forming an erect terminal crown, at length spreading; stalk slender, smooth; lflets. 4 to 12, 4 to 8 in. long, ovate, oblong or lanceolate, slender-pointed, abruptly narrowed to stalk, jointed in rachis, papery, shining green above, paler beneath, spiny toothed, veins 20 to 50, slender, striate. *Female cone* 6 in. long. Colombia. 1875. (B.M. 7542.)

Z. Otton'is. A variety of *Z. pygmaea.*

Z. pic'ta. A variety of *Z. muricata.*

Z. prasi'na. A synonym of *Z. Loddigesii latifolia.*

Z. pseudoparasi'tica. Stem 3 to 10 ft. h., ringed, naked. *l.* 25 or more, up to 6 ft. long, stalks somewhat prickly; lflets. many, long-linear-lanceolate or wide oblong-lanceolate, curved, 7 to 21 in. long, with a cuspidate point, jointed to rachis, entire, glabrous. *Female cone* up to 16 in. long, 5 in. across. Panama. 1873. (I.H. 1873, 133, 134 as *Z. Roezlii.*)

Z. pu'mila. A synonym of *Z. floridana Purshiana.*

Z. pygmae'a. Stem very short. *l.* 2½ to 20 in. long, glabrous; stalk slender, smooth, about 3 in. long; lflets. 3 to 25, spreading, the middle ones longest, 1 to 3½ in. long, oval-oblong, spatulate, or obovate-wedge-shaped, obtuse or truncate, slightly brownish-hairy, toothed from middle upwards, shining or pale green, jointed to rachis. *Male cones* 1 in. long; *female* up to 2 in. long. Cuba. 1815. (B.M. 1741.) var. **Kickx'ii,** *l.* 2 in. long, short lanceolate, widened from the base upwards. Syn. *Z. Kickxii*; **Otto'nis,** *l.* 12 to 20 in. long, lflets. oblong-lanceolate or lanceolate-elliptic, 2 to 4 in. long, slight brownish-downy beneath. Syn. *Z. Ottonis.*

Z. Roez'lii. A synonym of *Z. pseudoparasitica.*

Z. Skin'neri. Stem cylindrical, 3 ft. or more h. *l.-stalk* prickly, smooth, olive-green, hairy at first; lflets. 2 to 11, oblong-lanceolate or broadly ovate, slender-pointed, spiny toothed above middle, veins 15 to 33, rigid, deep green. *Male cones* 3 or 4, 1½ to 6 in., chestnut-red; *female* 3 to 6 in. long. Cent. America. 1851. (B.M. 5242; F.d.S. 2212.)

Z. tonkinen'sis. A synonym of *Cycas circinnalis undulata.*

Z. Wallis'ii. Stem 12 to 18 in. h., thick, glabrous. *l.* few, finally drooping; stalk prickly, brownish, hairy at base; lflets. 2 to 16,

Zamia obliqua (p. 2301)

widely elliptic-lanceolate or oblanceolate, 12 to 20 in. long, distinctly narrowed to a long point, obliquely acute, yellowish-green. *Male cones* 2 to 3 in. long, oblong-cylindrical. Colombia. 1875. (B.M. 7103 as *Aulacophyllum Wallisii.*) SYN. *Z. amplifolia.*

F. G. P.

zamiifo'lius -a -um, Zamia-leaved.

ZAMIOCUL'CAS (combined of *Zamia* and *Culcas*, the Arabic name for *Colocasia antiquorum*). FAM. *Araceae.* A genus of a single species of herb with a thick horizontal rhizome, native of E. Trop. Africa, allied to Gonatopus, differing botanically by the upper flowers on the spadix having no ovary, the lower having aborted staminodes, and by the short peduncle. Leaves large, unequally pinnate with 6 or 8 pairs of alternate pinnae. Spathe tube convolute, blade lanceolate or boat-shaped; spadix shorter than the spathe, cylindrical. *Z. zamiifolia* needs stove conditions and a compost of sandy loam, leaf-mould, and pieces of charcoal. It must have a moist atmosphere. Propagation may be by division or young plants may be raised from the leaflets after they have been removed from the rachis. If these are laid upon damp soil tubers will soon form at their basal ends and these, with the leaf attached, should be potted singly in small pots with the tuber just buried.

Z. Boivin'ii. A synonym of *Gonatopus Boivinii.*

Z. Loddiges'ii. A synonym of *Z. zamiifolia.*

Z. zamiifo'lia. *rhiz.* short, horizontal, producing large, white, sessile tubers. *l.* unequally pinnate, pinnae in 6 to 8 pairs alternate, elliptic- or obovate-lanceolate, 3 to 6 in. long; stalk 12 to 18 in. long, stout, green, spotted with dark green. *Peduncle* about 1½ in. long, green. *Spathe* tube subglobose, under 1 in. long, blade boat-shaped, spreading, about 2 in. long, nearly as wide; spadix greenish-yellow. Zanzibar, &c. (B.M. 5985 as *Z. Loddigesii*; L.B.C. 1408 as *Caladium zamiaefolium.*)

ZANONA PALM. *See* **Socratea exorhiza.**

ZANTE WOOD. The wood of *Chloroxylon Swietenia* and *Rhus Cotinus.*

ZANTEDESCH'IA (in honour of Giovanni Zantedeschi, 1773–1846, Italian botanist and physician). FAM. *Araceae.* A genus of 8 species of S. African marsh-loving perennial herbs with thick rhizomes. Leaves sagittate, sometimes with white transparent dots; stalks long, thick, sheathing at base. Flowers monoecious, all perfect on a dense-flowered spadix shorter than the spathe, shortly stalked, erect, cylindrical; spathe white or yellow, erect, tube short, convolute, funnel-shaped, persistent, throat opening, blade obliquely expanded, its apex cuspidate, recurved. Fruit a 1- to 3-celled berry. The genus is better known as Richardia; its species are distinct and attractive by their handsome foliage and tall elegant flower spathes. They are easily grown and the spathes, especially those of *Z. aethiopica*, are much grown for cutting. Propagation is easily effected by suckers which are produced in quantity; they may be taken at any time when the old plants are being repotted, but spring is probably the best time as the young suckers will then have time to establish themselves and so flower early in the following season. The plants need a very rich soil composed of good loam and cow manure in about equal parts. The suckers when removed should be placed singly in pots and started in a little heat. *Z. aethiopica*, if grown under glass in summer, should be placed where it is fully exposed to light and about the end of July they may be moved to the open air to ripen thoroughly; alternatively the plants when making new growth may be kept in the beds or borders or they may be potted up and left outside until they have recovered the slight check received and become established. Instead of drying off they may thus be kept growing continuously, being kept fairly cool in the dull months and in spring, and from time to time being given manure, water, or other fertilizer. *Z. Elliotiana* and *Z. angustiloba* should be grown in the warm pit during winter and in the cool one during summer. Where the plants of *Z. aethiopica* are stood out at the end of July they must be housed again before frost comes for exposure to frost is very destructive to the foliage. Another method of treating *Z. aethiopica* when established plants are available is to plant them out each year in the open garden on a piece of ground which has been heavily manured, turning the plants out of their pots, dividing them or not according to their size, and putting them about 15 in. apart. Little attention will be needed during summer except watering, which they need in abundance. About mid-September they must be lifted and potted carefully so as to damage the roots as little as possible, using 5- or 6-in. pots, placing 2 or 3 together in a larger pot.

In all but cold districts *Z. aethiopica* may be grown as an aquatic plant planted in shallow water at least 30 in. deep so that the rhizomes may be out of reach of frost in winter. In gardens these plants are often known as Callas or Richardias. Calla is a different genus, typified by *Calla palustris*, in which *Z. aethiopica* was erroneously placed by Linnaeus. Accordingly in 1818 Kunth proposed a new genus Richardia to accommodate it. The name Richardia had, however, already been used for a genus of Rubiaceae and the present genus was therefore re-named Zantedeschia, which is its correct botanical name. An account of the genus by H. P. Traub has been published in *Plant Life*, 4 (1948), 8–32 (1949).

DISEASES. Arum Lilies may suffer from attacks by leaf-spotting fungi, e.g. *Phyllosticta Richardiae*, causing brown spots on the leaves, but these can usually be checked by careful destruction of badly infected leaves. The corms may be destroyed by Soft Rot due to *Bacterium ariodeae* which causes wet soft rot and increases rapidly if the soil be very wet and heavy. Where this is noticed the corms in the dormant season should be washed and examined, the diseased parts can be cut out cleanly and the corms immersed in 2 per cent. formalin solution for half an hour. Root Rot due to the fungus *Phytophthora Richardiae* does not affect the corms but will destroy the roots and make them hollow and rotten. The leaves will then begin to brown at the tips and margins and the flowers will also brown at the tips; the affected plant can often be lifted out of the soil without any pulling. If young, the plants ought to be taken out of the soil and the corms alone steeped in the 2 per cent. formalin solution for 10 minutes before planting in clean or sterilized soil. If older, give waterings with Cheshunt Compound (*see* **Fungicides**) and in the dormant season soak the corms in 2 per cent. formalin as for Soft Rot. A serious disease of Arum Lilies is Spotted Wilt (*see* **Tomato Spotted Wilt**) which causes white spots or streaks on the leaves and whitish blotches on the stems, sometimes with twisting and puckering of the leaves. This is a Virus disease which may be taken by insects to other plants, such as young tomatoes, lettuces, &c., and all affected Arums should be destroyed.

D. E. G.

KEY

1.	*Lvs. arrow-shaped, heart-shaped, or oblong*	2
1.	*Lvs. lanceolate*	Z. Rehmannii
2.	*Lvs. spotted*	3
2.	*Lvs. not spotted*	5
3.	*Spathe, not purple-blotched*	7
3.	*Spathe with purple blotch at base*	4
4.	*Spathe trumpet-shaped, white*	Z. albomaculata
4.	*Spathe open from base, light yellow*	Z. melanoleuca
5.	*L.-base heart-shaped*	6
5.	*L.-base spear-shaped, with hastate basal lobes*	Z. oculata
6.	*Spathe white*	Z. aethiopica
6.	*Spathe golden yellow, with purple blotch at base*	Z. angustiloba
7.	*L.-base heart-shaped*	Z. Elliottiana
7.	*L.-base truncate*	Z. Sprengeri

Z. aethio'pica. Lily of the Nile; Arum Lily; Calla; Trumpet Lily. About 2 ft. to 2 ft. 6 in. h. *l.* arrow-shaped, twice as long as broad, cuspidate, varying greatly in size, dark green, unspotted; stalk long, stout. *Spathe* dead white, creamy at base within, 3 to 10 in. long, convolute below, expanded above with recurved margins, narrowed to a cuspidate point. S. Africa. 1731. (B.M. 832 as *Calla aethiopica.*) SYN. *Richardia africana.* Variable in stature and size of l. and spathe. Spathes sometimes double or treble. var. **Little Gem,** 12 to 16 in. h., *spathes* 3 to 4 in. long. SYN. var. *compacta*, var. *minor*; **gigante'a,** plant very large; **Childsia'na,** dwarfer and more floriferous than type. Occasionally the l. are partly spathe-like with a large white basal area. There are several other garden forms.

Z. albomacula'ta. About 2 ft. h. *l.* long-arrow-shaped, 12 to 18 in. long, cuspidate, 3 to 4 times as long as broad, with oblong, white, translucent spots all over; stalks short. *Spathe* greenish-white, trumpet-shaped, about 2 in. across, blotched crimson at base. S. Africa. 1859. (B.M. 5140 as *Richardia albomaculata.*) Nearly hardy. var. **sulphu'rea,** *spathe* soft yellow.

Z. angustilo'ba. About 2 ft. h. *l.* long-deltoid or -oblong, acute or acuminate, arrow-shaped with spreading basal lobes and very open sinus, 7 to 17 in. long, 4 to 11 in. wide. *Spathe* deep gamboge-yellow with black-purple blotch at base, paler outside, nearly horizontal. Transvaal, Angola. 1892. (B.M. 7397 as *Richardia Pentlandii.*) SYN. *Z. macrocarpa, Richardia Pentlandii.*

Z. × aura'ta (*Z. albomaculata × Z. oculata*). *l.* spotted. *Spathe* large, spotted.

Z. × cantabrigien'sis (*Z. melanoleuca × Z. Rehmanii*).

Z. Elliottia'na. 2½ to 3 ft. h. *l.-blades* roundish ovate, deeply cordate at base, 12 in. long, about 7 in. wide, apiculate, with transparent blotches; stalks about 2 ft. long. *Spathe* bright golden-yellow, 6 in. long, its tube funnel-bell-shaped, limb 3 in. long and broad, tip caudate; peduncle about 3 ft. long. Transvaal. 1896. (B.M. 7577 as *Richardia Elliottiana*). Warmhouse.

Z. × Elliottiopica (*Z. aethiopica × Z. Elliottiana*).

Z. hasta'ta. A synonym of *Z. oculata.*

Z. Lathamia'na (*Z. albomaculata × Z. Elliottiana*).

Z. Lutwych'ei. A synonym of *Z. oculata.*

Z. melanoleu'ca. About 18 in. h. *l.* oblong- or ovate-arrow-shaped, 6 to 12 in. long, marked with oblong, translucent, white spots. *Spathe* pale yellow with a black-purple spot at base, oblong, widely spreading from base, peduncle slender, with dark bristles in lower part. Natal. 1869. (B.M. 5765 as *Richardia melanoleuca.*) var. **suffus'a,** more robust than type; **tropical'is,** larger and without bristles at base of peduncle.

Z. ocula'ta. About 2 ft. h. *l.* arrow-shaped-ovate, about twice as long as wide, cuspidate, unspotted. *Spathe* greenish-yellow, tube bell-shaped, black-purple at base within, blade long-cuspidate, tip erect. Summer. Cent. and S. Africa. 1859. (B.M. 5176 as *Richardia hastata.*)

Z. Ragioni'eri (*Z. Elliottiana × Z. Rehmannii*).

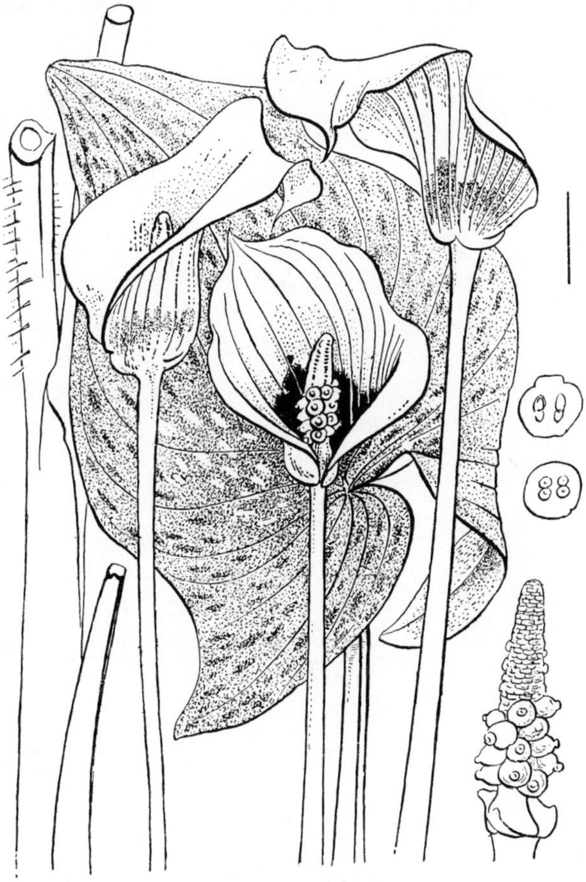

Zantedeschia melanoleuca

Z. Rehmann'ii. Dwarf. *l.* lanceolate, 7½ to 15 in. long, 1 to 2 in. wide, awl-shaped at tip, green- or white-spotted. *Spathe* bright rose, darker rose or sometimes white or greenish-white at base within, margins rosy tinted, erect. Natal. (B.M. 7436 as *Richardia Rehmannii.*) There are several garden forms differing in depth of colour, and ranging from light pink to violet-red.

Z. Spreng'eri. About 18 in. h. *l.* oblong, about 8 in. long, 3 in. wide, acute, white-spotted. *Spathe* bright yellow, sulphur yellow or almost white. Transvaal.

Z. × Tayl'ori (*Z. × aurata × Z. Elliottiana*).

ZANTHOXY'LUM (*xanthos*, yellow, *xylon*, wood). FAM. *Rutaceae.* A genus of about 200 species of deciduous or evergreen shrubs or trees, rarely scandent, usually more or less spiny, the spines in pairs or solitary. Leaves alternate, pinnate; mainstalk often prickly. Flowers small, usually in small panicles and with little beauty; sepals and petals 4 or 5, the latter sometimes absent; stamens 8 or 10. Fruit a 2-valved capsule. Tropical, sub-tropical, and temperate regions of both hemispheres. Most of the parts are aromatic or pungently scented when crushed, and of some species the seeds are ground up and used as a pepper-like condiment. Easily grown in loamy soil and in ordinary positions.

KEY

1.	*Lflets. downy beneath,* 5 *to* 11. *Fl. in axillary clusters before lvs.*	Z. americanum
1.	*Lflets. glabrous or nearly so beneath. Fl. terminal or rarely axillary*	2
2.	*Rachis of lvs. broadly winged*	Z. planispinum
2.	*Rachis of lvs. not or scarcely winged*	3
3.	*Lvs.* 10 *to* 18 *in. or more long. Shoots densely prickly*	Z. ailanthoides
3.	*Lvs. under* 10 *in. long*	4
4.	*Spines hooked*	Z. stenophyllum
4.	*Spines straight*	5

5. *Spines flattened and broad at base*	Z. simulans
5. *Spines slender*	6
6. *Spines solitary*	7
6. *Spines in pairs*	Z. piperitum
7. *Lflets.* 7 *to* 15	Z. capense
7. *Lflets.* 11 *to* 21	Z. schinifolium

Z. ailanthoi'des. Deciduous tree 50 to 60 ft., shoots stout, densely prickly. *l.* pinnate, 10 to 18 in. long (larger on young plants); lflets. 11 to 23, ovate to ovate-lanceolate, 2 to 5 in. long, toothed, glabrous. *fl.* in flattish clusters 5 in. or more across whitish; stamens yellow. Japan, Formosa. Very handsome in foliage but only suitable for the south-west.

Z. ala'tum. *See under* **Z. planispinum.**

Z. alat'um planispi'num. A synonym of *Z. planispinum.*

Z. america'num. Prickly Ash. Deciduous shrub, usually 6 to 10 ft. but also a small tree up to 25 ft., shoots downy, prickly. *l.* pinnate, 6 to 8 in. long; lflets. 5 to 11, ovate or oval, $1\frac{1}{2}$ to $2\frac{1}{2}$ in. long, very downy beneath, finely toothed or entire. *fl.* very small, yellowish-green opening in spring in axillary clusters on previous year's shoots. Eastern N. America. 1740. SYN. *Z. fraxineum.*

Z. Bung'ei. A synonym of *Z. simulans.*

Z. capen'se. Bushy shrub to 10 ft., or a small tree; shoots armed with strong, sharp, solitary prickles. *l.* 3 to 5 in. long; lflets. 7 to 15, obovate or oval, $\frac{1}{2}$ to $1\frac{1}{2}$ in. long, up to $\frac{1}{2}$ in. wide, bluntly toothed, with a gland at base of each tooth; mainstalk prickly. *fl.* very small, fragrant, in axillary and terminal, downy panicles $\frac{3}{4}$ to 3 in. long, mainstalk prickly. *fr.* globose, $\frac{1}{8}$ to $\frac{1}{6}$ in. wide blackish. S. Africa. Greenhouse. SYN. *Fagara capensis.*

Z. fraxi'neum. A synonym of *Z. americanum.*

Z. ni'tidum. A synonym of *Z. Bungei.*

Z. piperi'tum.* Japan pepper. Shrub of compact habit, or a small tree; shoots downy, spines in pairs, flattish, $\frac{1}{2}$ in. long. *l.* 3 to 6 in. long, mainstalk downy, prickly; lflets. 11 to 23, ovate, $\frac{1}{2}$ to $1\frac{1}{4}$ in. long, glabrous, toothed, terminal one notched. *fl.* small, green, in panicles 1 to 2 in. long and terminal on short axillary twigs. *fr.* reddish. N. China, Korea, Japan. 1877. The black seeds, when ground, are used as a condiment in Japan.

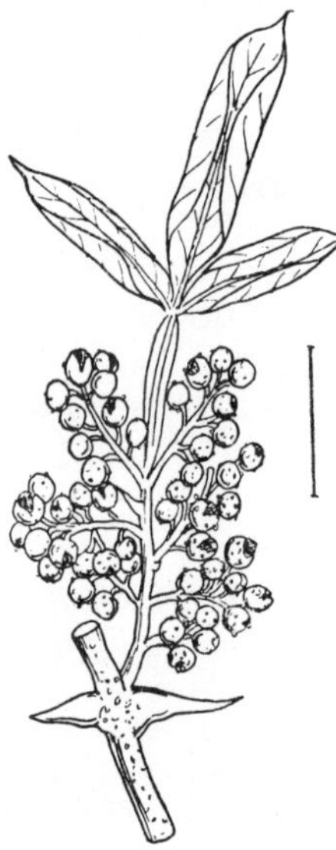

Zanthoxylum planispinum

Z. planispi'num.* Deciduous shrub, 6 to 12 ft., shoots glabrous; spines in pairs, broad and flat, $\frac{1}{4}$ to $\frac{3}{4}$ in. long. *l.* 5 to 10 in. long; mainstalk winged; lflets. 3 or 5, $1\frac{1}{2}$ to 5 in. long, ovate to lanceolate, toothed. *fl.* in panicles $1\frac{1}{2}$ to 2 in. long, yellowish. Spring. *fr.*, red, warted, globose, $\frac{1}{8}$ to $\frac{1}{6}$ in. wide. Japan, China, Korea. 1865. (B.M. 8754.) SYN. *Z. alatum planispinum, Z. alatum subtrifoliolatum.* The closely allied **Z. ala'tum,** Himalaya, has 5 to 13 lflets.

Z. schinifo'lium. Deciduous shrub or small tree; shoots glabrous; spines solitary, $\frac{1}{2}$ in. long. *l.* 3 to 7 in. long; lflets. 11 to 21, lanceolate, $\frac{3}{4}$ to $1\frac{1}{2}$ in. long, bluntly toothed, notched at end, glabrous, mainstalk prickly. *fl.* $\frac{1}{8}$ in. wide, greenish, in terminal flattish clusters 2 to 4 in. across. August. *fr.* green or brown; seeds blue-black. China, Japan, Korea. 1872.

Z. si'mulans. Shrub of spreading habit, 10 ft., or more; spines flat, $\frac{1}{4}$ to $\frac{3}{4}$ in. long. *l.* 3 to 5 in. or more long; lflets. 7 to 11, broadly ovate, $\frac{1}{2}$ to 2 in. long, bluntly toothed, glabrous, shining; mainstalk and midrib prickly. *fl.* in a panicle about 2 in. wide. *fr.* reddish, with dark dots. China. 1869. SYN. *Z. Bungei* of Hance (1875).

Z. stenophyl'lum. Sub-scandent, deciduous shrub up to 10 ft., shoots and l. glabrous; spines short, stout, hooked. *lflets.* 7 to 13, ovate-oblong to lanceolate, $1\frac{1}{2}$ to 4 in. long, abruptly slender-pointed, cuneate, very finely toothed; mainstalk prickly. *fl.* in terminal flattish panicles 2 to $3\frac{1}{2}$ in. across. *fr.* reddish shining beaked globose, $\frac{1}{8}$ in. wide. W. China. 1908. Rather tender.

W. J. B.

zanzibaren'sis -is -e, zanziba'ricus -a -um, of Zanzibar, E. Africa.

Zapo'ta, from the Mexican plant name, *cochil-zapotl.*

ZAUSCHNE'RIA (in honour of Johann Baptist Joseph Zauschner, 1737–99, professor at Prague). FAM. *Onagraceae.* A genus of about 4 species of dwarf perennials, mostly sub-shrubby, natives of Western N. America. Lowest leaves opposite, upper alternate. Flowers large, in racemes, scarlet, Fuchsia-like; calyx tube (hypanthium) globose, inflated just above ovary, then funnel-shaped; lobes 4; petals 4; stamens 8, exserted. Seeds obovoid, with a pappus of long silky hairs. Somewhat tender but in sheltered, warm positions sufficiently hardy to live outside through winter. For safety, however, they should be propagated annually from cuttings of side shoots in September in pots in sandy soil and wintered in a cool house or frame and planted out in spring. Old plants may be divided in spring and seeds sown about March on a gentle hotbed afford other means of increase. Any light soil suits them, but they are not happy in heavy soil. A sunny well-drained ledge of the rock-garden is probably the best place, but *Z. cana* has been effectively used at Kew to fill a bed on the flat. The number of species recognized depends on the opinion of individual botanists. The following Key is adapted from one given in a detailed study of the genus Zauschneria by J. Clausen, D. D. Keck, and W. M. Hiesey, *Experimental Studies on the Nature of Species*, 1. 213–59 (1940) in Carnegie Institution, *Publication* no. 520. According to this, the plants classified as *Z. californica* are tetraploid (with 60 somatic chromosomes), while the other 3 species are diploid (with 30 somatic chromosomes). They are, nevertheless, often difficult to identify owing to the great variation of each and the absence of easily observed clear-cut distinguishing features. In floral characters they are almost identical.

KEY.

1. *Plants herbaceous throughout; lvs. broadly lanceolate to oval, the chief lvs. more than $\frac{1}{4}$ in. wide*	2
1. *Plants shrubby at base; lvs. linear to lanceolate, usually less than $\frac{1}{4}$ in. wide*	4
2. *Broadest lvs. $\frac{1}{5}$ to $\frac{3}{10}$ in. wide, rarely more, almost entire, lowest usually whitish-grey, rarely green; stems less than 8 in. h.*	Z. septentrionalis
2. *Broadest lvs. $\frac{3}{10}$ to $\frac{3}{5}$ in. wide, not whitish-grey*	3
3. *Lvs. rather coriaceous, the lateral veins evident, more or less sharply toothed, only slightly if at all glandular, broadly ovate*	Z. Garrettii
3. *Lvs. not coriaceous, the lateral veins obscure, often glandular, broadly lanceolate to ovate*	Z. californica latifolia
4. *Stems slightly woody; lvs. linear-lanceolate to broadly lanceolate, usually $\frac{1}{10}$ to $\frac{1}{5}$ in. wide, green or greyish but not whitish-grey*	Z. californica
4. *Stems obviously woody at base; lvs. thread-like to narrowly linear, up to $\frac{1}{10}$ in. wide, densely whitish-tomentose*	5
5. *Lvs. linear, nearly $\frac{1}{10}$ in. wide, moderately clustered; fl. $1\frac{1}{4}$ to $1\frac{1}{2}$ in. long*	Z. californica angustifolia
5. *Lvs. thread-like or nearly so, about $\frac{1}{20}$ in. wide, densely clustered; fl. 1 to $1\frac{2}{5}$ in. long*	Z. cana

Z. califor'nica.* Californian Fuchsia; Humming Bird's Trumpet. About 1 ft. h., somewhat woody below. *l.* crowded, linear-lanceolate, $\frac{1}{10}$ to $\frac{2}{5}$ in. wide, entire or somewhat toothed, sessile, hairy, lower opposite, those of branches alternate. *fl.* scarlet, in loose spikes at end of branches, large, erect, spreading; cal. base globosely inflated, lobes spreading; pet. obcordate or rather deeply 2-cleft, rather longer than cal. lobes. Summer, autumn. California, Mexico. 1847. (F.d.S. 414; P.M.B. 15, 195; B.M. N.S. 19.) var. **angustifo'lia,** *l.* narrow, less than $\frac{1}{5}$ in. wide, densely grey-hairy, California; **latifo'lia,** *l.* rather broad, to $\frac{3}{5}$ in. wide. SYN. *Z. latifolia,* &c. Oregon, California, Arizona, Nevada, New Mexico. Before 1850. (B.M. 4493.)

Z. ca'na.* Notable for its narrow crowded grey *l.* less than $\frac{1}{16}$ in. wide. California. Before 1930. SYN. *Z. californica microphylla.*

Z. Garrett'ii. Notable for its rather broad, leathery, prominently veined, broadly ovate l. to $\frac{3}{8}$ in. wide. Utah, Wyoming. SYN. *Z. latifolia Garrettii.*

Zauschneria californica (p. 2304)

Z. latifo'lia. A synonym of *Z. californica latifolia.*

Z. mexica'na. A synonym of *Z. californica.*

Z. microphyl'la. A synonym of *Z. cana.*

Z. septentriona'lis. Notable for its dwarf tufted habit, 3 to 8 in. h. California.

W. T. S.

Zawadsk'ii, in honour of Alexander Zawadzki, 1798–1868, of Brno, Czechoslovakia.

ZE'A (old Greek name for a food grass, probably spelt). FAM. *Gramineae.* A genus of 1 species, the origin of which is unknown. Its only close relative is the Mexican and Guatemalan Teosinte (*Zea mexicana = Euchlaena mexicana*) known only as a weed or from areas where fields have reverted to brush and savannah. Once considered a possible ancestor of Maize, this is now more generally interpreted as a weed which developed from Maize, probably by hybridization with Tripsacum. Maize is the only crop widely cultivated in both tropical and temperate regions, and in the tropics from sea-level to above 12,000 ft. In Mexico and the United States it is the virtual staff of life, the most important crop of the country, in the former being consumed directly, though in the United States about nine-tenths of the crop is fed to animals and reaches the market as meat, milk, and eggs. In the United States and Canada Maize is extensively milled (both wet and dry milling), producing salad oil, corn flour, corn sugar, corn syrup, corn flakes, and a variety of other products. Other parts of the world where it is a crop of first-rate importance are S. Africa, Bessarabia, the Argentine, and SE. Asia. Specialized varieties have been developed for eating as a vegetable ('sweet corn'), for popping, and for making wrappers for cheroots (e.g. Burma). In the United States, Maize, normally one of the world's most variable crop plants, has been standardized by inbreeding, the inbreds ('lines') being crossed to restore vigour, producing 'hybrid corn' with that combination of high yield and uniformity so necessary for the mass production methods of modern mechanized agriculture. Little has been done in breeding ornamental varieties, though the Japanese have long appreciated the interest and beauty of the striped and coloured leaf sorts mentioned below *Zea Mays* is a very vigorous annual grass with tall often branching stems, broad, arching leaves, terminal panicles of staminate flowers (tassels), and axillary spikes of pistillate flowers usually enclosed in a sheath of leaves from the top of which protude the long silky stigmas (silks) at flowering times. For the early history of Maize in Europe, *see* J. J. Finan, *Maize in the great Herbals* (1950), reprinted from *Ann. Missouri Bot. Garden*, 35. 149–91 (1948). It would appear to have been first introduced into Spain by Columbus, probably before 1500. For cultivation of Sweet Corn see article on that vegetable. The following ornamental varieties may be treated like other half-hardy annuals, raised under glass in small pots and planted out, or sown outdoors in May, where they are to grow.

Z. Ma'ys. Maize, Indian Corn, Guinea Wheat, Turkey Wheat, Mealies. Stems 3 to 8 ft. or more h. *l.* 2 to $4\frac{1}{2}$ in. wide, flat, smooth beneath, hairy above, margin ciliate, sheath smooth, ligule about $\frac{1}{8}$ in. long. *fl.* as above. *fr.* (on 'cobs') bright yellow, sometimes red, brown, white, or green. var. **Cura'gua,** very robust, *l.* green, **gracil'lima,** dwarf, slender, with a form **gracil'lima variega'ta** with *l.* striped white; **japo'nica,** dwarfish, *l.* striped white, cobs small, and a form **quadri'color,** larger, *l.* striped green; white, yellow, and rose.

E. A.

ZEBRA PLANT. *See* **Calathea zebrina.**

ZEBRA SPIDER. *See* **Spiders.**

ZEBRA WOOD. *See* **Myrtus fragrans, Guettarda speciosa.**

ZEBRI'NA (latinized from the Portuguese *zebra* and referring to the zebra-like striping on the upper side of the leaves of *Z. pendula*). FAM. *Commelinaceae.* A genus of 4 species of decumbent or pendulous branching herbs, natives of Mexico and S. United States, closely akin to Tradescantia but distinguished by the well-developed corolla tube (about $\frac{1}{3}$ in. long). Leaves mostly narrowly ovate, with a sheathing base. Flowers small, about $\frac{3}{5}$ in. across, almost sessile, in clusters enclosed by 2 bracts, the lower and outer one much larger than the upper and inner one; cal. tubular; corolla with a slender basal tube and 3 spreading lobes; stamens 6, equal; anthers with a wide connective, dumb-bell-like in shape. Warm greenhouse plants growing well in light rich soil, and readily increased by cuttings, good for hanging baskets and as ground-cover beneath staging or on surface of very large tubs or pots. Like the creeping species of Tradescantia, they are sometimes called Wandering Jews.

Z. flocculo'sa. Stems decumbent, hairy. *l.* narrowly ovate, $1\frac{1}{2}$ to 3 in. long, $\frac{3}{4}$ to $1\frac{1}{4}$ in. wide, acuminate, green with whitish hairs on both sides, sessile; sheath about $\frac{3}{8}$ in. long, hairy. *fl.* clustered; cor. lobes blue on upper side, white beneath. March. Origin uncertain, probably Mexico. SYN. *Tradescantia commelinifolia.*

Z. pen'dula. Stems decumbent, almost glabrous except for a line of very short hairs. *l.* narrowly ovate, to 3 in. long, $1\frac{1}{2}$ in. wide, acute or acuminate, short-stalked, the upper side with a central green stripe and broad silvery longitudinal lateral stripes, the lower side purplish-red; sheath about $\frac{1}{2}$ in. long, glabrous except for cilia and a line of hairs. *fl.* clustered; cor. lobes purplish-rose on upper side, white beneath. Summer, &c. Mexico. Before 1850. (R.H. 1855, 141.) SYN. *Cyanotis vittata, Tradescantia tricolor, T. zebrina.* var. **quadri'color,** *l.* striped with green, red, and grey.

Z. Purpus'ii. Stems decumbent, mostly glabrous except for a line of hairs. *l.* narrowly ovate, to $2\frac{3}{4}$ in. long, $1\frac{1}{2}$ in. wide, acuminate, the upper side dull greenish-purple, the lower side bright reddish-purple, almost sessile; sheath about $\frac{3}{8}$ in. long, ciliated. *fl.* clustered; cor. lobes purplish-rose on upper side, white beneath. October. Mexico. (Bonstedt, Parey's Blumeng. 211.) SYN. *Tradescantia purpurea.* Best grown in a temperate house.

W. T. S.

zebri'nus -a -um, striped with different colours.

Zedoa'ria, from the Arabic name, *Zedwar.*

ZEDOARY, ROUND. *See* **Curcuma Zedoaria.**

ZEHNE'RIA. Included in **Melothria. Z. scab'ra** = *M. punctata.*

ZEHNTNEREL'LA (in honour of Dr. Leo Zehntner, formerly of the Horto Florestal, Joazeiro, Brazil). FAM. *Cactaceae.* Stems tall, slender, branched at the base; ribs numerous, very spiny; flowers very small from the upper part of the stem, white with white hairs in the throat. **A**

Z. squamulo'sa. There is only one species which should not be confused with *Rhipsalis squamulosa.* (B.R.C. 2, f. 249–50.) SYN. *Cereus squamulosus.*

V. H.

ZELKO'VA (*Zelkoua* or *Tselkwa*, the Caucasian name for *Z. carpinifolia*). FAM. *Ulmaceae.* A genus of 5 species found in Japan, China, Caucasus, and the Island of Crete. Deciduous trees or shrubs with smooth grey trunks; leaves alternate, always strongly toothed, rough on the upper surface and very shortly stalked. Flowers small, green, unisexual and of no beauty; both sexes on the same twig. Fruit a short-stalked, obliquely roundish drupe, $\frac{1}{6}$ to $\frac{1}{4}$ in. wide.

All the species are hardy and succeed in any good soil, preferably a deep, well-drained loam. They should be propagated by seeds, especially *Z. carpinifolia* and *Z. serrata*, but they are sometimes grafted on elm.

KEY

1. *Shrub or small tree*	2
1. *Tree*	3
2. *Lvs.* $\frac{1}{2}$ *to* 1 *in. long, bristly at first, then nearly glabrous*	Z. cretica
2. *Lvs.* 1$\frac{1}{2}$ *to* 2$\frac{1}{2}$ *in. long, downy beneath*	Z. Verschaffeltii
3. *Shoots nearly glabrous, l.-veins* 8 *to* 14 *pairs*	Z. serrata
3. *Shoots hairy, l.-veins* 6 *to* 12 *pairs*	4
4. *Shoots very downy, l.-veins* 6 *to* 8 *pairs, l.* 1$\frac{1}{2}$ *to* 3$\frac{1}{2}$ *in. long*	Z. carpinifolia
4. *Shoots grey woolly at first, l.-veins* 8 *to* 12 *pairs, l.* 1$\frac{1}{2}$ *to* 2$\frac{1}{2}$ *in. long*	Z. sinica

Z. Abeli'cea. A synonym of *Z. cretica.*

Z. carpinifo'lia.* Tree up to 100 ft., trunk smooth, grey, beech-like, with scaling bark, usually shortish and breaking into a great number of erect crowded branches; shoots very downy. *l.* 1$\frac{1}{2}$ to 3$\frac{1}{2}$ in. long, ovate rounded or cordate at base, with 7 to 10 coarse teeth each side, rough above, downy beneath; stalk $\frac{1}{12}$ to $\frac{1}{8}$ in. long. *fr.* $\frac{1}{5}$ in. wide. Caucasus. 1760. (E.H. 4, 248.) SYN. *Z. crenata, Z. ulmoides.* One of the most distinct, handsome, and interesting of hardy trees.

Z. cre'tica. Shrub 10 to 15 ft. bushy and twiggy; shoots very slender, at first furnished with pale short bristles. *l.* $\frac{1}{2}$ to 1 in. long ovate to oblong, with 7 or 9 large triangular teeth, both surfaces at first bristly like the shoots, soon nearly or quite glabrous; almost stalkless. Mts. of Crete. About 1924. SYN. *Z. Abelicea.*

Z. Da'vidi. A synonym of *Hemiptelea Davidi.*

Z. serra'ta. Tree 100 to 120 ft., trunk smooth, grey. *l.* 2 to 4$\frac{1}{2}$ in. long, ovate to ovate-lanceolate, slender-pointed, rounded to cordate at base, with 6 to 14 coarse slender-tipped teeth, each side, rough with short scattered hairs above, glabrous beneath; stalk $\frac{1}{10}$ to $\frac{1}{4}$ in. long. *fr.* roundish, about $\frac{1}{8}$ in. wide. Japan. 1861. Under cultivation a widely spreading tree, distinct and elegant. SYN. *Z. acuminata, Z. Keaki.*

Z. si'nica. Deciduous tree, 50 to 60 ft., shoots grey-woolly at first, becoming glabrous, brown. *l.* 1 to 2$\frac{1}{2}$ in. long, ovate to ovate-lanceolate, rounded at base taper-pointed, ciliate, with 7 to 12 teeth on each side, dark, dull green and rough above, downy beneath; stalk very short, downy. *fr.* obovoid, $\frac{1}{4}$ in. wide, shortly stalked. China. 1920.

Z. Verschaffel'tii. Small tree or a bush; shoots slender, spreading, slightly hairy at first. *l.* 1$\frac{1}{2}$ to 2$\frac{1}{2}$ in. long, oval or ovate, with 6 to 9 triangular teeth $\frac{1}{4}$ in. deep along each side, rough above, softly downy beneath. Origin unknown, probably Caucasian. 1892. Distinct by its bushy habit and the coarse dentation of the l. SYN. *Ulmus Verschaffeltii.*

W. J. B.

ZENO'BIA (after Zenobia, Queen of Palmyra, *c.* A.D. 266). FAM. *Ericaceae.* A small genus of 2, or possibly only 1, species with alternate, slightly blunt-dentate. Leaves 5-merous. Flowers in axillary clusters on the previous year's shoots appearing like a raceme; stamens 10; sub-globose, 5-valved, capsular, loculicidal fruit. Distinguished from Pieris and Lyonia by its deciduous or almost deciduous foliage and from Leucothoe by its awned anthers. Thrives in well-drained lime-free loam. Old wood should be cut out from time to time. Propagated by seed, cuttings, layers, and offshoots if available.

Z. pulverulen'ta. Rather to be looked upon as a variety of *Z. speciosa.* So different, however, is the superficial appearance of the 2 plants that, from at least the horticultural point of view, *Z. pulverulenta* is often given specific rank. Its principal difference from the type species lies in the intense glaucous bloom which covers leaves and young branches. Found in nature in association with the type and introduced at about the same time. (B.M. 667 as *Andromeda pulverulenta.*) SYN. *Andromeda dealbata, A. glauca.*

Zenobia speciosa

Z. specio'sa. Deciduous or, at the most, half-evergreen shrub 4 to 6 ft. h. with smooth young wood. *l.* oval or oblong, tapering to or slightly rounded at base, apex acute or rounded, slightly and bluntly toothed, 1 to 2$\frac{1}{4}$ in. long, half as wide. *fl.* pendent in axillary clusters on upper usually leafless part of previous year's shoots; cor. glistening white, campanulate, $\frac{1}{2}$ in. long and $\frac{7}{16}$ in. across mouth with 5 shallow, slightly recurved lobes; cal. lobes ovate, pale green, rugose. June, July. SE. United States. 1801. SYN. *Z. pulverulenta nuda, Z. cassinifolia, Andromeda cassinifolia, A. speciosa nitida.* (B.M. 970.) var. **quercifo'lia,** *l.* with a wavy, shallowly lobed edge. A most beautiful plant and quite hardy, at least in S. and W. Britain.

F. S.

ZEPHYRAN'THES (*zephyros*, the west wind, *anthos*, flower; a fanciful name, the species being natives of America and hence introduced into Europe from the west). FAM. *Amaryllidaceae.* A genus of about 35 species of bulbous plants nearly related to Habranthus, Pyrolirion, and Hippeastrum, natives of the warmer parts of America. Leaves filiform, or linear, or narrowly strap-shaped, few, dying off each season or persistent (evergreen). Flowers solitary on a hollow scape; spathe tubular and sheathing below, free, unilateral and often 2-fid above (as in Habranthus; not cut into 2 opposite segments as in Pyrolirion; nor of 2 equal, opposite, and quite free valves as in Hippeastrum); flower usually borne on a pedicel which may be from very short to long, rarely sessile, erect or nearly so; perianth funnel-shaped in lower part, the 6 segments usually united at the base to form a tube (but sometimes almost free), and more or less spreading to recurved upwards; stamens 6, 3 longer alternating with 3 shorter; style from shorter than to much exceeding the stamens, stigma 3-fid with linear segments or capitate and 3-lobulate. Zephyranthes are mostly spring- or summer-flowering plants resting in winter, but the hardy *Z. candida* flowers in September and October and has leaves throughout the year; hence it makes a good edging plant in southern England. A few of the others can be left outside if planted in a dry sunny border. Most of them like to be protected by a glass roof from heavy rains, both winter and summer, but the only heat they need is to keep out the frosts. They should get all the sun available. Thus most of them can be grown in a sunny frame or on a shelf in a cool greenhouse. A compost of turfy loam with a quarter in bulk of coarse sand, another quarter of peat or leaf-mould, well mixed, suits them. Drainage must be perfect, and it is important to exclude worms; a partially sterilized compost, e.g. the John Innes (*see* **Composts**), is the best. When well potted and in good health, the bulbs may be left undisturbed for several years before repotting, as they usually flower better when they are a little pot-bound. Propagation is by separating the offset bulbs or by seeds which most species produce freely.

KEY

1. *Perianth yellow* — 2
1. *Perianth creamy-white, or greenish-white, or white, or white flushed pink to rose* — 5
2 (1). *Stigma 3-fid, segs. linear* — Z. longifolia
2. *Stigma capitate, 3-lobulate* — 3
3 (2). *Perianth ¾ to 1 in. long* — Z. pulchella
3. *Perianth 1⅜ to 2¼ in. long* — 4
4 (3). *Perianth golden-yellow, 1⅜ to 1¾ in. long; lvs. deciduous* — Z. citrina
4. *Perianth soft primrose-yellow, 2 to 2¼ inches long; lvs. evergreen* — Z. Ajax
5 (1). *Stigma capitate, 3-lobulate* — 6
5. *Stigma 3-fid, segs. linear* — 8
6 (5). *Perianth 2¼ to 2¾ in. long, slender trumpet-shaped, tube very narrow greenish as long as the bright rose segs.* — Z. macrosiphon
6. *Perianth 1¼ to 2 in. long, funnel-shaped or crocus-like, tube very short, white to pink* — 7
7 (6). *Fl. sessile; spathe split to apex; lvs. deciduous* — Z. verecunda
7. *Fl. on pedicel ¼ to ⅜ in. long; spathe with narrowly saccate apex; lvs. evergreen* — Z. candida
8 (5). *Style shorter than or subequal to (but not exceeding) the stamens* — 9
8. *Style overtopping the stamens* — 11
9 (8). *Perianth mostly 2¼ to 2¾ in. long* — Z. Simpsonii
9. *Perianth 1¼ to 2 in. long* — 10
10 (9). *Fl. sessile* — Z. verecunda
10. *Fl. on pedicel ⅓ to 1 in. long* — Z. Lindleyana
11 (8). *Perianth creamy-white or greenish-white; scape very stout; lvs. ⅜ to ½ in. wide* — Z. concolor
11. *Perianth white, or white flushed pink, or pink, or rose; scape slender; lvs. not more than ⅓ in. wide* — 12
12 (11). *Perianth white, or white more or less flushed pink outside* — 13
12. *Perianth pale to deep pink or rose* — 18
13 (12). *Perianth 2¾ to 4¼ in. long* — 14
13. *Perianth 1 3/16 to 2¼ in. long* — 15
14 (13). *Lvs. bright shining green, margins thin, ⅛ to 3/16 in. wide* — Z. Atamasco
14. *Lvs. dull grey-green, margins rounded, 1/24 to 1/12 in. wide* — Z. Treatiae
15 (13). *Pedicel shorter than spathe* — Z. mesochloa
15. *Pedicel longer than spathe* — 16
16 (15). *Inner perianth-segs. markedly narrower than the outer* — Z. insularum
16. *Inner perianth-segs. about as wide as the outer* — 17
17 (16). *Perianth 1 3/16 to 1⅜ in. long* — Z. albiella
17. *Perianth 1½ to 2¼ in. long* — Z. tubispatha
18 (12). *Perianth 2¾ to 4 in. long* — Z. grandiflora
18. *Perianth 1 3/16 to 2⅜ in. long* — 19
19 (18). *Perianth 2 to 2⅜ in. long, tube slender, ⅜ to ⅝ in. long; lvs. 1/16 in. wide* — Z. Plumieri
19. *Perianth 1 3/16 to 1¾ in. long, tube short and broad; lvs. ⅛ to ¼ in. wide* — 20
20 (19). *Perianth 1⅜ to 1¾ in. long, pink; spathe ⅝ to ¾ in. long* — Z. Wrightii
20. *Perianth 1 3/16 to 1⅜ in. long, rose; spathe ¾ to 1 in. long* — Z. rosea

Z. A'jax. Garden hybrid between *Z. candida* and *Z. citrina*. *l.* with fl., like those of *Z. candida*, evergreen. *Scape* 6 to 8 in. long; spathe about 1 in.; pedicels ½ to ¾ in.; perianth 2 to 2¼ in., pale primrose-yellow, green at base; style subequal to stamens, stigma capitate and 3-lobulate. June. 1899. (G.F. 1469.) Hardy.

Z. albiel'la. *l.* with fl. ascending, linear, about 4 in. long, 1/12 to ⅛ in. wide. *Scape* 2¾ to 3¼ in. long; spathe ⅝ to ⅞ in. long; pedicels about 1 in.; perianth 1 3/16 to 1⅜ in. white, green at base, segs. ¼ to 5/16 in. wide; style just overtopping stamens, stigma 3-fid. Spring to autumn. Colombia. 1945. Greenhouse.

Z. Anderson'ii. A synonym of *Habranthus Andersonii.*

Z. Atamas'co. Atamasco Lily. *l.* with fl., spreading, narrowly strap-shaped, 6 to 16 in. long, ⅛ to 3/16 in. wide, bright shining green, channelled, margins thin. *Scape* 4 to 10 in. long; spathe 1 to 1⅜ in. long, mostly 1 3/16 in.; pedicel 3/16 to ⅜ in. long; perianth 2¾ to 4¼ in. long, white or white flushed pink, segs. ½ to ¾ in. wide; style exceeding the stamens, stigma, 3-fid. February to May. United States, from Missouri and Virginia to Florida. Before 1629. (L.B.C. 1899; B.M. 239 as *Amaryllis Atamasco*.) Hardy.

Z. can'dida. *l.* with fl., persistent (evergreen), erect, linear, mostly 8 to 12 in. long, ⅛ to ⅙ in. wide, somewhat fleshy. *Scape* 4 to 8 in. long; spathe 1 to 1 3/16 in. long, narrowly saccate at apex; pedicel ¼ to ⅜ in. long; perianth crocus-like, 1 3/16 to 2 in. long, white, sometimes faintly flushed rose, green towards base, segs. ⅜ to ⅝ in. wide; style subequal to or just exceeding the stamens, stigma capitate and 3-lobulate. September, October. Argentina and Uruguay along the La Plata River. 1822. (B.M. 2607; L.C.B. 1419; B.R. 724 as *Amaryllis candida*.) Hardy. var. **ma'jor,** larger in all respects, *l.* to 18 in. long, spathe about 1½ in., pedicel 1 3/16 in., and perianth 2 to 2¼ in. The hardiest species, its easy cultivation, evergreen rush-like l. and freely produced white crocus-like fl. in autumn making it a good edging plant.

Z. cardina'lis. A synonym of *Habranthus cardinalis.*

Z. carina'ta. A synonym of *Z. grandiflora.*

Z. citri'na. *l.* with fl., ascending-spreading, narrowly strap-shaped, blunt, 8 to 14 in. long, ¼ to ⅙ in. wide, channelled. *Scape* 5 to 10 in. long; spathe ¾ to 1⅛ in. long; pedicel 1 to 1½ in. long, exceeding the spathe; perianth mostly 1⅜ to 1¾ in. long, golden-yellow except the green tube, segs. ⅓ to ½ in. wide; style shorter than stamens, stigma capitate and 3-lobulate. June to September. British Guiana and Trinidad (?). 1880. (B.M. 6605.) SYN. *Z. Eggersoniana.* Greenhouse.

Z. con'color. *l.* appearing after the fl., strap-shaped, about 12 in. long, ⅜ to ½ in. wide. *Scape* 6 to 12 in. long, very stout; spathe 1½ to 2 in. long; pedicel 1⅜ to 2⅜ in. long; perianth 1¾ to 2½ in. long, pale greenish-white, or creamy-white, greenish at base; segs. erect, ½ to 1 in. wide; style exceeding the stamens, stigma deeply 3-fid. April to July. Mexico. 1837. (B.R. 31, 54 as *Habranthus concolor*.) Greenhouse.

Z. Eggersonia'na. A synonym of *Z. citrina.*

Z. fla'va. A synonym of *Pyrolirion aureum.*

Z. gracilifo'lius. A synonym of *Habranthus gracilifolius.*

Z. Grahamia'na. A synonym of *Z. verecunda.*

Zephyranthes grandiflora

Z. grandiflo'ra. *l.* with fl., erect-spreading, narrowly strap-shaped, 10½ to 16 in. long, ¼ to ⅓ in. wide. *Scape* 5 to 8 (rarely to 10½) in. long; spathe 1 3/16 to 1½ in. long, pedicel ¾ to 1 3/16 in. long; perianth

$2\frac{3}{4}$ to 4 in. long, rose-pink, segs. $\frac{1}{2}$ to 1 in. wide; style exceeding the stamens, stigma 3-fid. June to July. Guatemala, W. Indies; naturalized in many warm countries. 1824. (B.R. 902; B.M. 2594 and S.B.F.G. ser. 2, 4, as *Z. carinata*.) SYN. *Z. Tsouii*, *Z. carinata*. Half-hardy.

Z. insula'rum. *l.* with fl., sub-erect to spreading, $4\frac{1}{2}$ to $8\frac{1}{4}$ in. long, $\frac{1}{8}$ to $\frac{1}{4}$ in. wide. *Scape* about $5\frac{1}{2}$ in. long; spathe about $\frac{3}{4}$ in. long; pedicels about 1 in. long, perianth $1\frac{3}{8}$ in. long, white flushed pink outside, green at base; segs. markedly unequal, outer longer, about $\frac{5}{8}$ in. wide, inner about $\frac{1}{2}$ in. wide; style much exceeding the stamens, stigma 3-fid. May. W. Indies? (known only in gardens). Before 1935. Greenhouse.

Z. Lindleya'na. *l.* with or after the fl., spreading, linear, 8 to 12 in. long or (in cultivation) to 20 in., about $\frac{1}{8}$ in. wide. *Scape* 2 to 6 in. long; spathe $\frac{3}{4}$ to $1\frac{3}{16}$ in. long; pedicels $\frac{1}{8}$ to $\frac{7}{8}$ in. long, generally included in the spathe; perianth $1\frac{3}{8}$ to $1\frac{3}{4}$ in. long, pale pink; segs. $\frac{1}{8}$ to $\frac{1}{2}$ in. wide; style usually shorter than the stamens, stigma shortly 3-fid. April to July. Mexico. Before 1825. Greenhouse.

Z. longifo'lia. *l.* usually with fl., erect, filiform, 6 to 10 in. long, $\frac{1}{24}$ in. wide. *Scape* $2\frac{1}{2}$ to $4\frac{1}{4}$ in. long; spathe about 1 in. long; pedicels $\frac{1}{4}$ to $\frac{3}{8}$ in. long, rarely $\frac{3}{4}$ in.; perianth $\frac{3}{4}$ to 1 in. long, yellow; segs. free to base, $\frac{3}{16}$ to $\frac{3}{8}$ in. wide; style sub-equal to but not exceeding the stamens, stigma 3-fid. June to August. Arizona, New Mexico, Mexico. Greenhouse.

Z. lon'gipes. A synonym of *Habranthus longipes*.

Z. macrosi'phon. *l.* with fl., narrowly strap-shaped, to about 12 in. long and $\frac{1}{6}$ in. wide. *Scape* $5\frac{1}{2}$ to 8 in. long; spathe $1\frac{3}{16}$ to $1\frac{3}{8}$ in. long; pedicel 1 to $1\frac{1}{2}$ in. long, perianth slender trumpet-shaped with narrow tube as long as the erect segs., $2\frac{3}{8}$ to $2\frac{3}{4}$ in. long, bright rose with greenish tube; segs. about $\frac{1}{2}$ in. wide; style distinctly shorter than the stamens, stigma capitate and 3-lobulate. May to July. Mexico. 1865. Greenhouse.

Z. mesoch'loa. *l.* after or with fl., spreading-decumbent, linear-strap-shaped, 8 to 12 in. long, $\frac{1}{8}$ to $\frac{3}{16}$ in. wide. *Scape* 3 to 6 in. long; spathe $\frac{3}{4}$ to $1\frac{3}{16}$ in. long; pedicel $\frac{3}{8}$ to $1\frac{1}{8}$ in. long, always shorter than spathe; perianth mostly $1\frac{3}{8}$ to $1\frac{3}{4}$ in. but sometimes to $2\frac{1}{2}$ in. long, white, sometimes very lightly flushed pink, green at base (whence the name *mesochloa*, half green), segs. $\frac{1}{4}$ to $\frac{1}{2}$ in. wide; style exceeding the stamens, stigma deeply 3-fid. April to June. Paraguay, Uruguay, Argentina. 1829. (B.R. 1361.) Half-hardy.

Z. Plumier'i. *l.* after fl., filiform, to 9 in. long, $\frac{1}{16}$ in. wide. *Scape* 4 to 8 in. long, slender; spathe $1\frac{3}{16}$ to $1\frac{1}{2}$ in. long; pedicel $\frac{1}{2}$ to 1 in.; perianth 2 to $2\frac{3}{8}$ in. long, funnel-shaped with a slender tube $\frac{3}{8}$ to over $\frac{1}{2}$ in. long, pink; segs. $\frac{3}{8}$ to over $\frac{1}{2}$ in. wide; style much exceeding the stamens, stigma deeply 3-fid. February, March. W. Indies. Greenhouse.

Z. pulchel'la. *l.* with fl., erect, linear, 8 to 12 in. long, $\frac{1}{16}$ to $\frac{1}{12}$ in. wide. *Scape* $7\frac{1}{2}$ to 9 in. long; spathe $\frac{3}{4}$ to 1 in. long; pedicel about $\frac{3}{4}$ to 1 in. long; perianth $\frac{3}{4}$ to 1 in. long, yellow; segs. $\frac{3}{16}$ to $\frac{1}{4}$ in. wide; style shorter than the stamens, stigma capitate and 3-lobulate. September. Texas. Before 1937. Half-hardy.

Z. pu'mila. A synonym of *Hippeastrum roseum*.

Z. robus'ta. A synonym of *Habranthus robustus*.

Z. ro'sea. *l.* with fl., more or less decumbent, narrowly strap-shaped, about 8 in. long and $\frac{3}{16}$ to $\frac{1}{4}$ in. wide. *Scape* $3\frac{1}{2}$ to $6\frac{1}{2}$ in. long; spathe $\frac{3}{4}$ to 1 in. long; pedicel 1 to $1\frac{3}{4}$ in. long, clearly exceeding the spathe; perianth $1\frac{3}{16}$ to $1\frac{3}{8}$ in. long, rose, segs. $\frac{1}{3}$ to $\frac{1}{2}$ in. wide; style clearly overtopping the stamens, stigma deeply 3-fid. July to December. Guatemala, W. Indies. 1823. (B.M. 2537; B.R. 821.) Half-hardy.

Z. ses'silis. A synonym of *Z. verecunda*.

Z. stria'ta. A synonym of *Z. verecunda*.

Z. Simpson'ii. *l.* with fl., erect, linear-filiform, mostly 7 to 11 in. long and $\frac{1}{24}$ to $\frac{1}{16}$ in. wide, dull grey-green, margins rounded. *Scape* 3 to 6 in., sometimes to 8 in. long; spathe 1 to $1\frac{3}{16}$ in. long; pedicel lacking or up to $\frac{1}{2}$ in. long; perianth mostly $2\frac{1}{2}$ to 3 in. long, pink, deeper in middle of outer seg.; segs. $\frac{3}{8}$ to $\frac{5}{8}$ in. wide; style sub-equal to but not exceeding the stamens, stigma 3-fid. February to May. Florida. About 1892. Greenhouse.

Z. texa'na. A synonym of *Habranthus texanus*.

Z. Treat'iae. *l.* with fl., erect, linear-filiform, 8 to 12 in. long, $\frac{1}{24}$ to $\frac{1}{12}$ in. wide, dull grey-green, margins rounded. *Scape* $3\frac{1}{4}$ to 8, rarely 10 in. long; spathe 1 to $1\frac{3}{8}$ in. long; pedicel lacking or up to $\frac{3}{8}$ in. long; perianth $2\frac{3}{4}$ to 4 in. long, white becoming pink with age; segs. $\frac{3}{8}$ to $\frac{3}{4}$ in. wide; style exceeding the stamens, stigma 3-fid. February to May. Florida. 1880. Half-hardy.

Z. Tsou'ii. A synonym of *Z. grandiflora*.

Z. tubispa'tha. *l.* with fl., spreading-decumbent, narrowly strap-shaped, $9\frac{1}{2}$ to 13 in. long, about $\frac{1}{4}$ in. wide. *Scape* 4 to 8 in. long; spathe about 1 in. long; pedicel $1\frac{3}{16}$ to 2 in. long, exceeding the spathe; perianth $1\frac{1}{2}$ to $2\frac{1}{4}$ in. long, white, green at base; segs. $\frac{3}{8}$ to $\frac{2}{3}$ in. wide; style overtopping the stamens, stigma 3-fid. April to June. W. Indies. 1813. (B.M. 1586 as *Amaryllis tubispatha*.) Greenhouse.

Z. verecun'da. *l.* after or with the fl., ascending-spreading, linear, 8 to 12 in. long, $\frac{1}{12}$ to $\frac{1}{8}$ in. wide. *Scape* 2 to $5\frac{1}{2}$ in. long; spathe $\frac{3}{4}$ to $1\frac{3}{16}$ in. long; pedicel lacking; perianth $1\frac{3}{16}$ to 2 (rarely $2\frac{3}{8}$) in. long, white, green towards the base, or more or less flushed red outside, or deep pink; segs. $\frac{1}{4}$ to $\frac{3}{8}$ in. wide; style not exceeding the stamens, stigma capitate and 3-lobulate or very shortly 3-fid. May to July. Mexico. 1824. (B.M. 2583; R.B. 356; B.M. 2593 as *Z. striata*; R.B. 212 as *Z. sessilis*.) SYN. *Z. Grahamiana*, *Z. striata*, *Z. sessilis*. Greenhouse.

Z. versi'color. A synonym of *Habranthus versicolor*.

Z. Wright'ii. *l.* after fl. linear, 8 to 12 in. long, $\frac{1}{6}$ in. wide. *Scape* 3 to 10 in. long; spathe about $\frac{3}{4}$ in. long; pedicel $\frac{5}{8}$ to $1\frac{3}{16}$ in. long; perianth $1\frac{3}{8}$ to $1\frac{3}{4}$ in. long, pink; segs. $\frac{3}{8}$ to $\frac{1}{2}$ in. wide; style much exceeding the stamens, stigma deeply 3-fid. April. W. Indies. Greenhouse.

J. R. S.

zephy'rius -a -um, pertaining to the west wind, hence western, or flowering or fruiting in Indonesia during the western monsoon.

Zerum'bet, Indian plant name.

ZEUXI'NE. Included under **Anoectochilus.**

ZEUZ'ERA PYRI'NA. *See* **Leopard Moth.**

ZEXME'NIA (name based on an anagram of surname of Francisco Ximenez, also commemorated by Ximenia). FAM. *Compositae*. A genus of about 25 species of annual or perennial herbs or sub-shrubs, sometimes tall climbers, natives of the warmer parts of America. Leaves opposite, entire or toothed. Flower-heads yellow, solitary, corymbose or sub-umbellate, heterogamous, radiate; involucre variable, bracts in 2, 3, or several series; receptacle convex, paleae sheathing the flowers; ray-florets ligulate, spreading, entire or 2- or 3-toothed; disk-florets tubular, apex shortly 5-cleft. Achenes usually slightly hairy. A fairly rich soil suits them. Hardiness varies according to habitat. *Z. aurea* can be increased by cuttings in sandy soil under a glass in heat; *Z. ovata* is readily propagated by seed sown in the open.

Z. au'rea. Sub-shrub with terete branches, coarsely hairy, about 18 in. h. *l.* opposite, ovate-lanceolate, obtuse at base, toothed, roughly hairy on both surfaces; sessile. *fl.-heads* golden-yellow, solitary and terminal in upper axils; ray-florets 7 to 9, twice as long as involucre. September. Mexico. 1829. (B.M. 3304 as *Wedelia aurea*.) SYN. *Verbesina aurea*. Half hardy.

Z. ova'ta. Annual, 2 ft. h., with terete, hairy branches. *l.* ovate, acute, toothed, 3-nerved, paler beneath, base stem-clasping. *fl.-heads* deep orange-yellow; ray-florets elliptical; peduncles short, terminal, solitary or corymbose. Autumn. Mexico. 1828. (B.M. 3901 as *Tithonia ovata*.) Hardy.

Z. texa'na. A synonym of *Wedelia hispida*.

Zey'heri, in honour of Karl Ludwig Philipp Zeyher, 1799–1858, of Dillenburg, collector in S. Africa where he died; or of his uncle, Johann Michell Zeyher, 1780–1843, horticulturist.

zeyla'nicus -a -um, of Ceylon.

zibethi'nus -a -um, pertaining to the zibet or Asiatic civet-cat (*Viverra zibetha*), from the use of the decomposing fruit of *Durio zibethinus* as a bait for the civet-cat.

ZIER'IA (named in honour of John Zier, d. 1796, a Polish botanist long resident in London). FAM. *Rutaceae*. A genus of about a dozen evergreen shrubs or rarely small trees, natives of Australia and Tasmania. Leaves 3-foliolate, rarely simple, mostly opposite, rarely alternate. Flowers in axillary cymes, rarely solitary; calyx 4-lobed; petals and stamens 4. Cool Greenhouse. Propagated by cuttings.

Z. arbores'cens. A synonym of *Z. Smithii macrophylla*.

Z. laevigat'a. Glabrous, erect shrub, up to 5 ft. *lflets*. 3, linear, pointed, $\frac{1}{2}$ to 1 in. long, $\frac{1}{24}$ to $\frac{1}{12}$ in. wide, on a common stalk $\frac{1}{12}$ to $\frac{1}{4}$ in. long, margins very revolute. *fl.* $\frac{1}{2}$ in. wide, 5 to 10 in. axillary, slender-stalked clusters; pet. pale pink, spreading. May. New S. Wales, Queensland. 1822. (B. iv. 185.)

Z. lanceola'ta. A synonym of *Z. Smithii*.

Z. macrophyl'la. A synonym of *Z. Smithii macrophylla*.

Z. obcorda'ta. Shrub up to about 2 ft., shoots shaggy with pale hairs. *l.* 3-foliolate, very shortly stalked; lflets. $\frac{1}{8}$ to $\frac{1}{2}$ in. long, obovate or obcordate, shaggy like the shoots beneath, less so above. *fl.* 1 to 3 in l.-axils, white, tiny; pet. $\frac{1}{12}$ in. long. June. New S. Wales, Queensland. 1824.

Z. pilo'sa. Shrub up to 4 ft., shoots densely downy or hairy. *lflets.* 3, with a very short mainstalk, linear to narrowly oblong, pointed, $\frac{1}{2}$ to $\frac{7}{8}$ in. long, $\frac{1}{12}$ to $\frac{1}{8}$ in. wide, hairy beneath, mid-rib deeply sunken, margins much recurved. *fl.* very small, white, 1 to 3 in. l.-axils, shortly stalked. June. New S. Wales. 1822.

Zieria Smithii

Z. Smith'ii. Tasmanian Stinkwood; Sandfly Bush. Shrub or sometimes a small tree; shoots often glandular-warted. *lflets.* 3, on a common stalk $\frac{1}{2}$ to 1 in. long, also warted, 1 to 3 in. long, lanceolate, $\frac{1}{4}$ to $\frac{7}{8}$ in. wide. *fl.* white, $\frac{3}{8}$ in. wide in axillary, trichotomous clusters, 2 to 3 in. long, 1 to $1\frac{1}{2}$ in. across. April. Australia, Tasmania. (R.M. 1395.) SYN. *Z. lanceolata.* var. **macrophyl'la,** the tree-like form, up to 16 ft. *l.* up to 4 in. long and 1 in. wide. *fl.* larger, in cymes up to 5 in. long. (B.M. 4451 as *Z. macrophylla.*) SYN. *Z. arborescens.*

W. J. B.

ZIGADE'NUS (*zygos*, yoke, *aden*, gland; the glands usually in pairs at the base of the perianth segments). FAM. *Liliaceae.* A genus of about 18 species of bulbous or rhizomatous plants, natives of N. America and Asia, some of which are poisonous to stock. Stem erect, scape-like, with or without a few small leaves. Leaves radical or clustered at base of stem, long-linear. Flowers in a terminal, simple or paniculately branched raceme; perianth persistent, segments sometimes connate at base in a very short, turbinate tube, or distinct, sub-equal and flat; stamens 6, nearly equalling perianth segments. A moist, peaty soil suits the following N. American species best. They can be propagated by division or by seeds. *Z. Muscaetoxicum*, having usually no glands, is sometimes separated as a genus Amianthium.

Z. den'sus. Stem slender, 12 to 18 in. long, with many reduced l. *l.* nearly 12 in. long, $\frac{1}{6}$ to $\frac{1}{4}$ in. wide, firmer and more distinctly ribbed than those of *Z. Muscaetoxicum.* *fl.* white, becoming purple, $\frac{1}{8}$ to $\frac{1}{6}$ in. long; segs. usually with a small gland at base; lower pedicels about $\frac{1}{2}$ in. long; raceme 1 to 3 in. long, $\frac{1}{2}$ to $\frac{3}{4}$ in. wide. May, June. 1823. SYN. *Z. angustifolius, Amianthium angustifolium, Helonias angustifolia.*

Z. e'legans.* 6 to 12 in. h. with a few reduced l. *l.* 4 to 6, firm, linear glaucous green, many-nerved, 12 to 18 in. long, $\frac{1}{4}$ to $\frac{1}{2}$ in. wide. *fl.* greenish without, whitish within, about $\frac{1}{2}$ in. long segs., oblong, thickly nerved, with a conspicuous gland on lower half at base of each seg.; pedicels ascending, $\frac{1}{2}$ to 1 in. long; racemes 2 to 4 in. long, 1 to 2 in. wide, simple or loosely paniculate. Summer. 1828. SYN. *Z. glaucus, Anticlea elegans.*

Z. glaber'rimus. 24 to 36 in. h. from a creeping rhizome. *l.* linear, grass-like, acuminate, 12 to 18 in. long, about $\frac{1}{3}$ in. wide. *fl.* white, about $\frac{1}{2}$ in. long, segs. acute, oblong, clawed, with 2 distinct glands near base of each seg.; pedicels ascending, $\frac{1}{4}$ to $\frac{1}{2}$ in. long; racemes 5- to 10-fld., loosely paniculate. June. 1811. (B.M. 1703 as *Helonias bracteata.*)

Z. glau'cus. Closely akin to *Z. elegans* but with middle and upper bracts of infl. herbaceous (not scarious-margined), the creamy-white segs. green, bronze, or purple (not pale) on the back and the capsule hardly longer than (instead of twice as long as) the perianth.

Z. grami'neus. A synonym of *Stenanthium gramineum.*

Z. Muscaeto'xicum. Stem 12 to 24 in. long, slender, with a few very small l., slightly thickened at base. *l.* many, linear-lorate, membranous, nearly 12 in. long, $\frac{1}{4}$ to $\frac{3}{4}$ in. wide, obtuse. *fl.* greenish-white, $\frac{1}{8}$ to $\frac{1}{6}$ in. long; lower pedicels $\frac{1}{2}$ to $\frac{3}{4}$ in. long; raceme dense, oblong, 2 to 4 in. long, 1 to $1\frac{1}{2}$ in. wide. Summer. 1758. (G.F. 1121; B.M. 803 as *Helonias laeta.*) SYN. *Amianthium Muscaetoxicum.* A fly-poison has been made from this plant.

Z. Nuttall'ii. Stem 6 to 18 in. h. with a few small l. *l.* 4 to 6, firm, 12 to 18 in. long, $\frac{1}{4}$ to $\frac{1}{2}$ in. wide. *fl.* white, $\frac{1}{8}$ to $\frac{1}{4}$ in. long; segs. with an obovate small gland at base of each seg.; racemes often simple, dense above, 2 to 3, rarely 4 to 6 in. long; lower pedicels $\frac{1}{2}$ to $\frac{3}{4}$ in. long. June. 1883. (G.F. 1121.)

ZIL'LA (Arabic name for *Z. spinosa*). FAM. *Cruciferae.* A genus of 3 species natives to desert regions from Morocco to Syria and Arabia. *Z. spinosa* needs cool greenhouse treatment and is of more botanical than horticultural interest. Propagation is by seed.

Z. spino'sa. Short-lived much-branched bush 2 to 4 ft. h., herbaceous in texture during its first year, with glaucous fleshy l., then becoming woody, spiny, and leafless; shoots glabrous, grey, with sharp spines. *l.* narrowly oblanceolate, to $1\frac{3}{4}$ in. long, $\frac{3}{10}$ in. wide, entire, glaucous, fleshy. *fl.* small, usually solitary near tips of shoots; sep. erect, about $\frac{3}{10}$ in. long, pale green; pet. pale lilac with deeper veining, $\frac{3}{10}$ in. long, entire. *fr.* beaked. Late winter, spring. N. Africa, W. Asia, in desert region. (F.P.S.A. 1075.)

W. T. S.

zimapan'i, of Zimapan, Mexico.

Zimmerman'nii, in honour of Albrecht W. P. Zimmermann, 1860–1931, German botanist at Amani.

A→

ZIN'GIBER (*Zingiberi*, ginger, name used by Dioscorides, derived from an Indian word; said to be cognate with Malayalam *inchiver*, from *inchi*, root). FAM. *Zingiberaceae.* A genus of over 50 species of perennial herbs with branching, thick aromatic rhizomes, natives of E. Indies, Malaya, and New Guinea. Flowering stem usually distinct from the leafy one. Leaves usually lanceolate 2-ranked. Flowers with minute lateral staminodes or none which distinguishes this from the Hedychium and Globba groups of the family, and with a large, 3-lobed lip. The plants require stove temperature, and grow well in a compost of loam, sand, and peat. Like other rhizomatous members of the family they are readily increased by division just as new growth begins in spring. Most species die down in winter and while at rest should have little water. *Z. officinale* is the source of ginger, the 'coated ginger' being the rhizome with the rind still on, 'scraped ginger' the rhizome with the rind removed.

KEY

1.	*Lvs. striped creamy-white*	Z. Darceyi
1.	*Lvs. green*	2
2.	*Fl.-spike usually terminal on leafy stem*	Z. brevifolium
2.	*Fl. and lvs. on separate stems*	3
3.	*Spike sessile or nearly so*	Z. Mioga
3.	*Spike on erect peduncles, usually many-fld.*	4
4.	*Bracts green or yellow, rounded*	5
4.	*Bracts red or reddish-green, acute*	7
5.	*Bracts green with paler margin*	6
5.	*Bracts yellow*	Z. Parishii
6.	*Lvs. linear, scarcely $\frac{3}{4}$ in. wide; lip purple, spotted yellow*	Z. officinale
6.	*Lvs. lanceolate or oblong-lanceolate; 2 to 3 in. wide, lip yellow*	Z. Zerumbet
7.	*Spike 8 in. long or more, obtuse*	Z. spectabile
7.	*Spike usually not over 4 in. long, if longer, apex acute*	8
8.	*Spike slender; lvs. silky beneath*	Z. coloratum
8.	*Spike thick*	9
9.	*Spike 2 to 3 in. long*	Z. cylindricum
9.	*Spike large, bracts, glabrous, lvs. linear-oblong*	Z. Cassumunar

Z. brevifo'lium. Flower and foliage stems not always distinct, 8 to 12 in. h. *l.* lanceolate or elliptic, about $4\frac{1}{2}$ in. long, slender-pointed. *fl.* in a narrow, cylindrical, acute spike about 3 in. long, small, yellow; bracts orange-yellow, striped red. New Guinea. 1886.

Z. Cassum'unar. Bengal Root. 5 to 6 ft. h. *rhiz.* greenish-yellow with a hot, camphor flavour, not bitter. *l.* oblong-lanceolate, slender-pointed, 8 to 16 in. long, downy beneath. *fl.* in a dense more or less elliptic spike about 4 in. long, peduncle 7 to 10 in. long, bracts red, white edged, greenish-brown, red-edged, or green then red; cor. pale sulphur; lip about $\frac{3}{4}$ in. wide, pale yellow. July, August. India, Malaya. 1807. (B.M. 1426.) SYN. *Z. Cliffordiae.*

Z. Clifford'iae. A synonym of *Z. Cassumunar.*

Z. colora'tum. About 2½ ft. h. *l.* linear-lanceolate, slender pointed, up to 10 in. long, paler and silky hairy beneath. *fl.* in a spike about 1½ in. long, peduncle 3 to 4 in. long, bracts purple, with silky white hairs on margin; cal. white with 3 purple lines; cor. creamy-white. NW. Borneo. 1879.

Z. cylind'ricum. 6 ft. or more h. *l.* oblong-lanceolate or lanceolate slender-pointed, rather thin, about 8 in. long, downy beneath. *fl.* in a dense spike about 3 in. long, acute, peduncle cylindrical, about 3½ in. long; bracts pale, or reddish; cor. lobes greenish; lip obovate, yellowish-white. Ceylon.

Z. Dar'ceyi. 2 to 6 ft. h., robust. *l.* lanceolate 6 to 8 in. long, 2 to 2½ in. wide, bright shining green, with broad margin and oblique stripes of creamy-white. Origin? Introduced from Sydney Bot. Gard., 1890.

Zingiber Mioga

Z. Mio'ga. Moderately robust, about 3 ft. h., stem with 5 or 6 striate sheaths. *l.* linear-lanceolate, narrowed to a long point, about 12 in. long thin. *fl.* in an elliptic spike 2½ to 3 in. long on a short peduncle, bracts white; cor. white; lip yellow. Japan. (B.M. 8570.)

Z. officina'le. Ginger. 3 ft. h. *l.* lanceolate or linear-lanceolate narrowed to a slender point, up to 8 in. long. *fl.* in a dense elliptic spike, peduncle about 10 in. long, bracts pale green sometimes yellow on margin; cor. yellowish-green; lip oblong-ovate, deep purple with yellow spots and stripes. July. E. Indies. 1605.

Z. Parish'ii. About 3 ft. h. *rhiz.* tuberous, creeping. *l.* oblong-lanceolate, shortly auricled at base, about 5 in. long, shining green above, paler and downy beneath. *fl.* in a loose cylindrical spike about 3½ in. long; peduncle about 3½ in. long; bracts yellow or pale green with red margin at tip; cor. white, tube about 1¼ in. long; lip obovate sulphur with brownish veining. July. Burma. 1861. (B.M. 6019.)

Z. specta'bile. Robust. Stem over 6 ft. h., somewhat flattened. *l.* oblong-lanceolate, slender-pointed, 8 to 12 in. long, deep green above, paler and downy beneath. *fl.* in a loose cylindrical spike 8 to 12 in. long; peduncle about 12 in. long; bracts yellow passing to scarlet; cor. yellowish-white; lip obovate, 2-lobed, lemon with a black tip. Malaya. (B.M. 7967.)

Z. Zerumb'et. *rhiz.* white outside, yellow within, at first taste aromatic, becoming bitter. 12 to 20 in. h. *l.* closely set, oblong-lanceolate, slender-pointed, 4 to 6 in. long, smooth above, hairy beneath. *fl.* in a dense, nearly round spike about 3 in. long; peduncle up to 12 in. long, bracts pale green; cor. white; lip nearly round, pale yellow with orange bands. Summer. E. India. 1699. (B.M. 2000.)

ZINGIBERA'CEAE. Monocotyledons. A family of about 800 species in about 40 genera of perennial herbs with often swollen rhizomes, natives of Trop. Asia and Africa. Leaves in 2 ranks or spirally arranged with sheaths, petioles, and entire blades, having a ligule at the top of the sheath as in grasses. Inflorescence a raceme, head, or cyme. Flowers often showy; perianth of 6 segments, outer 3 (sepals) united into a tube at base and usually different in texture and colour from the more conspicuous inner 3 (petals) which are united at base into a long tube. Only 1 stamen is fertile, the other 2 of the inner whorl being sterile, and represented by staminodes, sometimes very small if not absent; the lip or labellum has been variously interpreted but in most genera seems to represent the combination of 3 outer stamens, but in Costus may represent the combination of the 3 outer stamens with 2 of the inner stamens present in other genera as staminodes. Ovary inferior, 3-celled with numerous ovules. Fruit a capsule. Several genera contain plants of economic importance; see under the genera here treated, which are Aframomum, Alpinia, Amomum, Brachychilus, Burbidgea, Cautlea, Costus, Curcuma, Elettaria, Gastrochilus, Globba, Hedychium, Hemiorchis, Kaempferia, Mantisia, Phaeomeria, Pommereschea, Renealmia, Rhynchanthus, Roscoea, Tapeinochilus, Zingiber.

This family was at one time united with Cannaceae, Marantaceae, and Musaceae to form the family Scitamineae, but these groups are now kept distinct as families of the order Scitaminales. **A**

ZIN'NIA (in honour of Johann Gottfried Zinn, 1727–59, Professor of Botany at Göttingen). FAM. *Compositae.* A genus of about 15 species of annual or perennial herbs, or sub-shrubs, mostly natives of Mexico. Leaves opposite, entire. Flower-heads of various colours, heterogamous, radiate, of medium size to large, pedunculate in the forks or at tips of branches; involucre bell-shaped or sub-cylindrical, bracts in 3 or several series, outer gradually shorter; receptacle conical or finally cylindrical; ray florets ligulate, spreading, in 1 series; disk-florets tubular, shortly 5-cleft at apex. Achenes narrow, striated, glabrous or ciliate at angles. The following are all half-hardy annuals flowering in summer and best in an open, sunny situation. The varieties of *Z. elegans* last long in flower if the weather is hot and dry. They do best in a rich, deep, loamy soil, and are particularly useful for hot summer flowering. Seeds should be sown at the end of March or in April and the seedlings pricked off into frames when large enough, then planted in their flowering quarters in early June. If sown too early and starved they never grow very well afterwards. A considerable amount of attention has been given, especially in California, to the selection and perpetuation of races of *Z. elegans*, a naturally variable species, with the result that many colour forms of large size have been placed on the market, see Supplement.

DISEASES. Zinnias may suffer when young from Damping Off and Foot Rot diseases caused by fungi such as Pythium sp. and Phytophthora sp. (*see* **Damping Off** and **Foot Rot**) and there is a Stem Rot of older plants caused by *Corticium solani*. On the foliage there is a seedling leaf blight due to a species of Alternaria, and older plants suffer from *Botrytis cinerea* (*see* **Grey Mould**), especially in wet seasons and in glass-houses where excessive moist atmospheres occur. Grey Mould may be serious on Zinnias and every effort should be made to remove affected plants and give the others plenty of room and air. Zinnias may also take the virus disease known as Spotted Wilt in which the leaves become mottled with flecks of dark green or chlorotic yellowish rings on a darker background, and the growing points may be distorted. Destruction of such plants is essential (*see* **Spotted Wilt**).

D. E. G.

Z. angustifo'lia. Annual, 1 to $1\frac{1}{2}$ ft. *l.* sessile or nearly so, oblong to ovate-oblong, hairy like stems. *fl.-heads* 1 to $1\frac{1}{2}$ in. across, bright golden-yellow or orange; scales of receptacle entire. Summer. Mexico. 1862. (G.F. 1863, 390 as *Z. Haageana.*) SYN. *Z. Haageana.*

Z. e'legans.* Youth and Age. Erect hairy annual, 1 to 3 ft. h. *l.* sessile, stem-clasping, ovate-heart-shaped. *fl.-heads* scarlet, crimson, violet, rose, buff, or white, 2 to $4\frac{1}{2}$ in. across; involucral bracts ovate, obtuse, upper margined black; scales of receptacle with a toothed crest; peduncles round, solitary, longer than l. Summer, autumn. Mexico. 1796. (B.M. 527, var. *violacea*; B.R. 1294, var. *coccinea.*) Very variable.

Z. linea'ris. Neat, dense, erect bush, about 1 ft. h. *l.* linear or linear-lanceolate, dark green. *fl.* bright golden-yellow with light orange margin, $1\frac{1}{2}$ to 2 in. across; scales of receptacle entire. Summer. (G.C. 2 (1887), 597.) Very free-flowering.

Z. pauciflo'ra. Annual about 2 ft. h., erect, hairy. *l.* lanceolate-heart-shaped, somewhat stem-clasping. *fl.-heads* yellow; involucral scales, appressed; paleae entire; ray-florets obovate, obtuse or 1- or 2-toothed at apex; terminal peduncles striated, obconical, lateral more slender. Summer. 1753.

Zinnia tenuiflora

Z. tenuiflo'ra. Annual, about 2 ft. h., erect, almost glabrous. *l.* lanceolate-heart-shaped; stalk very short. *fl.-heads* on very long, cylindrical peduncles; involucre oblong, scales appressed, scarcely margined; ray-florets scarlet, $\frac{1}{2}$ to $\frac{2}{3}$ in. long, entire or 2-toothed, apex revolute. Summer. 1799. (B.M. 555.)

A→

ZIZA'NIA (an old Greek name for some wild grass or other weed). FAM. *Gramineae.* A genus of 2 N. American and 1 Asiatic water-side grasses with tall stems up to 9 ft. high, and broad flat leaves. *Z. aquatica* is a handsome annual species, with robust stems up to 12 ft. h. and long bright-green leaves 1 to $2\frac{1}{2}$ in. wide. The rather large grains, about $\frac{2}{5}$ to $\frac{4}{5}$ in. long, are greedily eaten by fish and water-fowl and were used by the N. American aboriginees for food, and are still gathered for this purpose by some of the northern tribes. They have a high nutritive value (see *Jour. Agr. Res.* 77. 65–79 (1948); *Jour. Washington Acad. Sci.* 30. 185–205 (1940)). It has been introduced into the British Is. on several occasions as an ornamental plant or as food for water-fowl, but has never become permanently established. After flowering the seed should be collected and kept moist throughout the winter, and then sown in pots standing in water, or on the soft muddy bottom in shallow water; for further details, see *Kew Bull.* 1909, 381–3.

Z. aqua'tica. Water Oats, Water Rice, Canada Rice, Indian Rice, Annual Wild Rice. Annual. *See above.* N. America.

Z. aqua'tica var. **angustifo'lia.** Stems more slender, usually not more than 4 ft. h. *l.* up to $\frac{3}{8}$ in. wide. N. America.

Z. caducifo'lia. Manchurian Wild Rice. E. Asia. Manchuria to Indo-china and Assam. Perennial. For long cultivated in China as a vegetable. When cultivated in Britain it forms dense tufts of l. 4 to 5 ft. long and up to $2\frac{1}{2}$ in. wide, but never flowers.

Z. latifo'lia. A synonym of *Z. caducifolia.*

Z. palus'tris. A synonym of *Z. aquatica angustifolia.*

ZIZI'PHORA (name denoting a resemblance to Zizyphus). FAM. *Labiatae.* A genus of about 12 species of dwarf, annual herbs or spreading sub-shrubs, natives of Cent. and W. Asia and the Mediterranean region. Leaves small, entire or with few teeth. Flowers small, subsessile, or on short pedicels; calyx tubular, long, 2-lipped; corolla tube scarcely exserted, upper lip erect, entire, lower spreading, 3-cleft; perfect stamens 2-whorls few-flowered, axillary, clustered on upper part of stem. The following are half-hardy sub-shrubs, suited by any good light, well-drained soil. Propagation by cuttings. Like Thymus in appearance but distinguished by the narrow cylindrical calyx with minute teeth and the 2 (not 4) perfect stamens.

Z. clinopodioi'des. Diffuse sub-shrub, 6 to 12 in. h., often purplish. *l.* nearly all ovate, upper narrow, oblong or ovate, $\frac{1}{2}$ in. long, narrowed to a short stalk. *fl.* blue-purple; cor. nearly twice as long as cal., in few-, 6- to 10-fld. whorls, forming an almost globose, loose head. July. W. Asia. 1821. *Z. Puschkinii* (B.M. 1093) and *Z. serpyllacea* (B.M. 906) are closely allied.

ZI'ZYPHUS (from *Zizouf*, the Arabic name of *Z. Lotus*). FAM. *Rhamnaceae.* A genus of about 40 species of evergreen or deciduous trees and shrubs inhabiting the tropical and warm temperate regions of both hemispheres. Leaves alternate, shortly stalked, 3- or 5-veined, either toothed or entire. Flowers small, yellow or greenish in axillary cymes, inconspicuous; the parts in fives. Fruit a globose, ovoid, or oblong drupe, fleshy or dry. *Z. Jujuba*, the jujube tree, the most important species, is cultivated in many countries for its pleasant, palatable fruits. None of the species is genuinely hardy in the ordinary climate of Britain, but *Z. incurva* and *Z. Jujuba* would be hardy in the mildest parts. The other species here described require greenhouse treatment. They like an open loamy soil. Paliurus, a genus with which this has sometimes been confused, is well distinguished by its winged fruits. Both have a species called 'spina-Christi' which legend credits as being the Tree from which the Crown of Thorns was made.

Z. incur'va. Evergreen tree or large shrub, sometimes 50 ft., shoots glabrous, prickles broad-based but slender. *l.* 2 to 4 in. long, ovate, slender-pointed, obliquely rounded at the base, prominently 3-veined. *fl.* yellow, $\frac{1}{8}$ in. across, numerous in axillary cymes $\frac{1}{2}$ to $\frac{3}{4}$ in. wide. *fr.* globose or obovoid, $\frac{1}{3}$ in. wide. India. 1823.

Z. Juju'ba. Jujube. Deciduous shrub or small tree to 30 ft. h.; shoots glabrous, zigzag, armed with spines in pairs, one longer and straight, the other short and hooked. *l.* oval ovate-lanceolate or oval, 1 to $2\frac{1}{2}$ in. long, mostly blunt or rounded, obscurely toothed, 3-veined glabrous beneath. *fl.* yellowish, $\frac{1}{5}$ in. wide, in axillary twos or threes, short-stalked. *fr.* $\frac{1}{2}$ to $1\frac{1}{4}$ in. long, ovoid, dark red then black, edible. Mediterranean region. 1640. (I.B.F.G. 241 as *Z. sativa.*) SYN. *Z. vulgaris.* Tender. Cult. in many warm temperate countries for its fruit. *Z. mauritiana*, India, &c., differs in the shoots and the lower side of the lvs., being densely hairy and is evergreen.

Z. Lo'tus. Jujube Lotus. Deciduous small tree or shrub; shoots very pale, species in pairs, one straight and up to $\frac{1}{2}$ in. long, the other quite small and hooked. *l.* ovate to elliptic-oblong, $\frac{1}{3}$ to $\frac{3}{4}$ in. long, 3-veined. *fl.* tiny, axillary. *fr.* yellow, roundish-ovoid, $\frac{1}{4}$ in. wide, farinaceous. S. Europe, N. Africa. 1931.

Z. mauritia'na. *See under* **Z. Juju'ba.**

Z. Mis'tol. Spreading, much branched tree up to 40 ft., trunk sturdy; shoots pale, sturdy, zigzagged at first, like the l. covered with close white down; spines twin, about equal, $\frac{1}{2}$ in. long. *l.* 1 to $1\frac{3}{4}$ in. long, ovate, both base and apex often rounded, 3-veined, glaucous beneath. *fl.* green, small, inconspicuous. *fr.* ovoid, $\frac{1}{3}$ in. long edible. Argentine.

Z. mucrona'ta. Tree 20 to 30 ft. or a shrub; shoots, l.-stalks, and infl., thinly downy; species twin one up to 1 in. long, broad based, the other short and hooked. *l.* ovate to cordate-ovate, pointed, often minutely mucronate. *Cymes* axillary, crowded with 10 to 20 small, cream-white, fragrant fl. *fr.* globose, $\frac{1}{3}$ in. wide, red. Trop. and S. Africa. 1810.

Z. Paliu'rus. A synonym of *Paliurus spina-Christi.*

Z. sativ'a. A synonym of *Z. Jujuba.*

Z. spi'na-Chri'sti. Evergreen shrub, or tree 20 to 30 ft., shoots pale, glabrous, spines unequal, twin. *l.* ovate to oval, $\frac{3}{4}$ to $2\frac{1}{2}$ in. long, 3-veined, glabrous, apex blunt or rounded. *fl.* minute, woolly, numerous in short close clusters. *fr.* globose, $\frac{1}{3}$ to $\frac{1}{2}$ in. wide, black when ripe, edible. N. Africa, W. Asia.

Z. vulga'ris. A synonym of *Z. Jujuba.*

W. J. B.

ZOI'SIA [ZOY'SIA] (in honour of Karl von Zois or Zoys, 1756–*c.*1800, Austrian botanist). FAM. *Gramineae.* A genus of about 8 species of low perennial maritime grasses, natives of E. Asia, Polynesia, Australia, New Zealand. Rhizomes and stolons creeping, producing a loose to dense turf; stems short, wiry; leaves short, narrow. Inflorescence a slender spike-like raceme; spikelets small, compressed, awnless or very short-awned from the tip, very short-pedicelled, 1-flowered; lower glume absent; upper glume equalling the spikelet and enclosing the flower glume. Useful for lawns in warm climates.

Z. japo'nica. Korean or Japanese Lawn Grass. *rhiz.* and stolons relatively stout, forming a compact turf. *l.* $\frac{1}{2}$ to 4 in. long, flat, rather stiff, $\frac{1}{10}$ to $\frac{1}{6}$ in. wide; spikelets ovate, $\frac{1}{12}$ to $\frac{1}{8}$ in. long. China, Korea, Japan. Cultivated as a lawn grass in the United States. Tried experimentally in the British Is., but not very hardy.

Z. Matrel'la. Manila Grass. *rhiz.* and stolons relatively stout forming a loose to compact turf. *l.* stiff to rigid, $\frac{1}{2}$ to 2 in. long, inrolled or opening out and up to $\frac{1}{10}$ in. wide; spikelets lanceolate to oblong, up to $\frac{1}{8}$ in. long. SE. Asia. SYN. *Z. pungens.*

Z. tenuifo'lia. Mascarene Grass. *rhiz.* and stolons very slender, producing a dense turf. *l.* thread-like, bristly, $\frac{1}{2}$ to 4 in. long, tightly rolled or opening out and up to $\frac{1}{16}$ in. wide; spikelets narrowly oblong-lanceolate, $\frac{1}{12}$ to $\frac{1}{8}$ in. long. Cultivated as a lawn grass in the United States. Native of the Mascarene Is., Solomon Is., Japan, Formosa, &c.

Zolling'eri, in honour of Heinrich Zollinger, 1818–59, traveller and collector in Java.

ZOMICAR'PA (*zoma*, dress, *karpos*, fruit; the fruit being covered by the tube of the spathe). FAM. *Araceae.* A genus of 3 species of tuberous Brazilian herbs producing leaves and flowers at the same time. Rhizome tuberous, horizontal. Leaves kidney-shaped, 3-partite or pedatisect, segments oblong-elliptic or oblong-lanceolate, the outer smallest; stalk longer than blade. Peduncle slender about as long as leaves. Spathe persistently convolute, base hooded, constricted at throat, blade twice as long as tube, ovate-lanceolate or lanceolate, slender-pointed; spadix adnate to spathe at base; ovary containing 6 to 9 ovules. For treatment *see* **Alocasia.**

Z. Pytho'nium. *l.-stalk* slender, round, 3 to 8 in. long or more, green spotted brownish-purple; blade reniform; segs. 5, lateral half lanceolate and ovate-oblong, middle one broadly elliptic. *Peduncle* as long as or longer than l. *Spathe* 2 to 3 in. long, blade ovate-oblong, slender-pointed, tube white within, lower part livid brown or olive, upper reddish or brownish streaked. 1860. The plant is said to be an antidote to snake bites.

Z. Riedelia'na. *l.-stalk* 2 to 8 in. long, greenish, purple-brown spotted; blade reniform, pedatisect, segs. 5 to 7, middle one 3 to $3\frac{1}{2}$ in. long, distant from lateral ones. *Peduncle* green with dots and stripes of brownish-purple. *Spathe* 3 to $3\frac{1}{2}$ in. long, tube inflated, glaucous without, yellowish-green within, throat constricted, blade twice or thrice as long as tube, arching, oblong, glaucous green. *Spadix* much longer than spathe tube, naked part club-shaped, longer than infl. 1860.

Z. Steigeria'na. *l.-stalk* streaked and spotted brown, 4 to 10 in. long; blade deep green, paler beneath, 3-cut; segs. oblong-lanceolate or ovate-lanceolate, wedge-shaped at base, 2 to 6 in. long. *Peduncle* slightly longer than l.-stalk, spotted and streaked. *Spathe* somewhat curved at top, brownish-purple without. *Spadix* whitish and dark brownish-purple, not reaching beyond middle of spathe; appendage club-shaped. 1860.

ZOMICARPEL'LA (diminutive of Zomicarpa). FAM. *Araceae.* A single species of rather small, slender, tuberous rooted herbs, native of Colombia, differing from Zomicarpa by its 1-ovuled ovaries, and requiring the same cultural treatment.

Z. macula'ta. *l.-stalk,* 3 to 4 in. long, channelled above, olive with brownish variegation; blade bright green with a series of pale blotches arranged around, near the margin. *Spathe* dull green, 1 in. long, lanceolate, becoming nearly flat with revolute margins; spadix blackish, $1\frac{1}{2}$ in. long, very slender. Colombia. 1881.

zona'tus -a -um, having a zone or girdle, usually of a distinct colour.

ZOOSPORE. A type of spore produced in certain fungi belonging to the class Phycomycetes (q.v.), another name for them being swarm spores. They are formed at the ends of special conidiophores in special structures known as sporangia or zoosporangia, which burst to release the zoospores. The zoospores are simply minute pieces of protoplasm which possess delicate processes or projections called cilia by means of which they are able to swim and move about in water; at length they come to rest and grow a germ tube which in parasitic fungi can cause infection and disease. An example is the fungus *Pythium de-Baryanum* causing Damping Off disease (*see* **Damping Off**).

D. E. G.

ZOSTEROSTY'LIS. *See* **Cryptostylis.**

Zuccarini'anus -a -um, in honour of Joseph Gerhard Zuccarini, 1797–1848, professor at Munich, author of a *Flora Japonica* in collaboration with Siebold.

ZYGADE'NUS. *See* **Zigadenus.**

×**ZYGOBATEMANN'IA.** FAM. *Orchidaceae.* Hybrids between species of Batemannia and Zygopetalum.

ZYGOCAC'TUS (*zygon*, a yoke; probably referring to the curiously jointed stems). FAM. *Cactaceae.* Epiphytic plants with stems flattened, jointed, branching dichotomously; margins serrate, with 2 sharp teeth at the end of the ultimate joint with a terminal areole between filled with brown wool and bristles. Flowers terminal, scarlet or white, irregular, the tube curving upwards, perianth leaves reflexed. Fruit purple, smooth. **A**

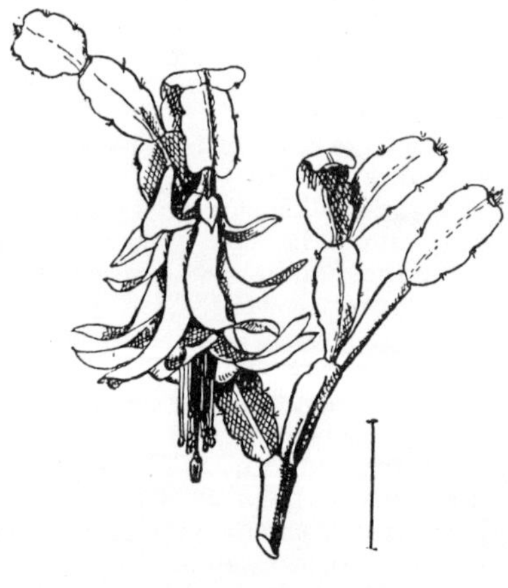

Zygocactus truncatus

Z. trunca'tus. Crab Cactus. The only species. The fl. appear from October to January and last for some days. It can be grown on its own roots but is often grafted on Pereskia or Hylocereus to raise the drooping branches from the ground. Brazil. (B.M. 2562; B.R. 696; L.B.C. 1207.) SYN. *Epiphyllum truncatum.*

V. H.

×**ZYGOCO'LAX.** FAM. *Orchidaceae.* Hybrids between species of Colax and Zygopetalum.

Z.-c. × Veitch'ii Krom'eri. An imported variety slightly stronger than the hybrid *Colax jugosus* × *Zygopetalum crinitum* raised by Messrs. Veitch and flowered in 1877. Sep. and pet. yellowish-green, blotched brown-purple; lip nearly round, whitish, with lines of violet-purple. Brazil. About 1900. (B.M. 7980.)

zygo'meris, having twin parts.

ZYGOMORPHIC, term for an irregular flower, capable of division into 2 similar halves along 1 vertical line only.

ZYGOMYCE'TES. Fungi of the class Phycomycetes characterized by the method of formation of their sexual spores. Besides ordinary conidia they form sexual resting spores from equal and similar sexual cells (gametes) which fuse in pairs. The resulting cell surrounds itself with a thick brown wall and goes into a resting condition and is known as a zygospore.

D. E. G.

× ZYGONIS'IA. FAM. *Orchidaceae.* Hybrids between species of Aganisia and Zygopetalum.

ZYGOPET'ALUM (*zygos*, yoke, *petalon*, petal). FAM. *Orchidaceae.* The genus was originally founded about 1826 on *Z. Mackaii*, the species typical of the plants now given under this heading. Later a number of other plants were included, allied, but presenting many horticultural differences, particularly in their vegetation and with botanical discrepancies also, so, as in the original issue of this work, forming a polymorphic group, sections of which not only required differences in cultivation but superficially had little resemblance to the typical Zygopetalums. The desirability of separating them from Zygopetalum seems evident and here they are distributed over Bollea, Galeottia, Huntleya, Kefersteinia, Pescatorea, Promenaea, Warreella, and Warscewiczella. Zygosepalum is put under Menadenium; Colax, included under Zygopetalum by some, is kept separate. Zygopetalum so treated includes about 20 species distinguished by having nearly equal sepals, free or shortly connected at base, lateral placed on the column foot; petals similar to sepals; the 3-lobed lip affixed to the column foot, is slightly incumbent forming a short chin, its side lobes, usually small and erect embracing the column, may be spreading, the disk has a transverse crest, often fleshy, large, entire, or divided into rib-like lobes. The column produced into a foot is semi-terete, incurved, wingless or with 2 small wings near tip. Pollinia 4. The flowers are often comparatively large and showy. Several species have considerable horticultural value, particularly as the flowers are often produced in winter. The greater number have decided pseudobulbs bearing 2 or 3 leaves at their apex and sheathed in basal leaves. The scapes, usually rather tall and several-flowered, are produced from the base of the pseudobulbs often contemporary with the young growth. The leaves are distichously arranged, moderately stiff, sub-plicate or with raised veins. The genus occurs chiefly in Brazil, Guiana, and Venezuela, but extends to Peru. Some species are strictly epiphytic, others appear to have adapted themselves to a terrestrial or semi-epiphytic habit. Under cultivation the stronger growing *Z. crinitum*, *Z. intermedium*, *Z. Mackaii*, &c., should have a compost of 2 parts of fibrous loam, 2 parts of Osmunda fibre, and 1 part of Sphagnum moss with an addition of finely broken crocks. For large plants use a greater proportion of loam fibre. They may be grown in the cool or Odontoglossum house in summer, but should be wintered in a cool part of the intermediate house at about 55° F. Water is required throughout the year but not too frequently in winter.

Z. maxillare should be placed on a section of tree-fern stem or on a shallow raft, omitting loam from the compost. The Odontoglossum house suits it for the greater part of the year but a winter temperature of 50 to 55° F. should be given it. The leaves of the young growths are enfolded and while in this state, moisture must not lodge in them; when expanded the syringe may be freely used. Thrips are speedily attracted by the flowers and flower-buds, the bracts at the base of each pedicel forming a hiding-place. Gentle fumigation or dipping should be employed if their presence is suspected. Scale and Red-spider Mite will attack the foliage but may be checked by syringing and sponging. Propagation is by the division of large plants, by the manipulation of old healthy pseudobulbs as advised for Cymbidiums. Very rarely small growths are emitted from the apex of old bulbs and when rooted they may be potted and grown on. Several plants are included below under Zygopetalum which are incongruous as the genus is here defined, but until further revision can be made it is difficult to assign them to their correct position. They have not appeared recently in cultivation, but may do so, and as they certainly belong to the Zygopetalum group they are retained here under their old names, their possible synonyms probably indicating their correct genera.

Z. africa'num. A synonym of *Odontoglossum bictoniense.*

Z. aromat'icum. A synonym of *Warscewiczella aromatica.*

Z. Backhousia'num. A synonym of *Pescatorea Backhousiana.*

Z. Ball'ii. A synonym of *Menadenium Ballii.*

Z. Beaumont'ii. A synonym of *Batemannia Beaumontii.*

Z. bel'lum. A synonym of × *Pescatobollea bella.*

Z. Binot'ii. *fl.* 5 to 6; sep. and pet. green; lip 3-lobed, mid-lobe, lanceolate-oblong, white tinged with green with 8 purple ridges at base; scapes shorter than l.; pseudobulbs ovate-oblong, compressed, diphyllous. *l.* linear-lanceolate, 12 in. or more long. Possibly a natural hybrid between Colax and Zygopetalum. Brazil. 1905.

Z. brachypet'alum. Sep. 1 in. long, about ⅓ in. wide; pet. slightly smaller; both brown marbled green, stiff, convex, oblong, obtuse; lip white, veined deep bluish-violet, over 1 in. long, about 1 in. wide, emarginate, crest or frill white, closely striped with blue; scape tall, 5- to 12-fld. *Pseudobulbs* clustered, ovoid-oblong, compressed, 1½ to 2½ in. h., 2- or 3-leaved. *l.* lanceolate ensiform, shorter than scapes. Brazil. 1848. var. **stenope'talum,** sep. and pet. narrow, acute, lip violaceous with white margin, basal crest with about 5 crenatures, *l.* narrower, Brazil. 1888. (G.F. 37 (1888), 1277.)

Z. Burk'ei.* *fl.* 4 or 5 about 3 in. across; sep. and pet. green with thick bands of brown broken here and there into spots; lip 1 in. long, nearly as wide, white, with a ruff of about 13 crimson plaits or folds; scape erect. *Pseudobulbs* clustered, narrow-oblong, furrowed, about 2 in. long, 2- or 3-leaved. *l.* 8 to 12 in. long, about 1 in. wide. Guiana. 1883. (W.O.A. 142.)

Z. Burt'ii. A synonym of *Huntleya Burtii.*

Z. can'didum. A synonym of *Warscewiczella candida.*

Z. caules'cens. A synonym of *Z. Mosenianum.*

Z. ceri'num. A synonym of *Pescatorea cerina.*

Z. chloran'thum. A synonym of *Batemannia armillata.*

Z. citri'num. A synonym of *Promenaea xanthina.*

Z. Claesia'num. A synonym of *Z. crinitum.*

Z. cochlea're. A synonym of *Warscewiczella flabelliformis.*

Z. coeles'te. A synonym of *Bollea coelestis.*

Z. Crepaux'i. A synonym of *Z. crinitum.*

Z. crini'tum.* *fl.* large very fragrant; sep. about 1½ in. long, lateral about ½ in. wide, dorsal sep. and pet. narrower; green, barred with brown; lip broad-obovate, white or cream, veins densely hairy, purplish, callus yellow, small, incurved; spikes sometimes 2 from a pseudobulb, 12 to 18 in. h., 5- to 7- or more-fld. *Pseudobulbs* ovate, 12 to 18 in. h., 3- to 5-leaved. Brazil. 1829. (L.B.C. 1687; B.M. 3402 as *Z. Mackaii crinitum*; L.B.C. 1687 as *Z. stenochilum*; L. 216 as *Z. intermedium.*)

Z. Daya'num. A synonym of *Pescatorea Dayana.*

Z. dis'color. A synonym of *Warscewiczella discolor.*

Z. Dormania'num. A synonym of *Pescatorea Dormaniana.*

Z. euglos'sum. A synonym of *Z. intermedium* or *Pescatorea euglossa.*

Z. expan'sum. Sep. green, acute; pet. brown in upper part, blotched brown in lower, broader than sep.; lip green with 5 interrupted brown stripes in basal half and brown blotches at base of the fringed mid-lobe. *l.* grass-like, cuneate-oblong-ligulate, acute. Ecuador. 1878. Apparently allied to *Kefersteinia graminea.*

Z. fimbria'tum. A synonym of *Pescatorea Klabochorum.*

Z. flabellifor'me. A synonym of *Warscewiczella flabelliformis.*

Z. forcipa'tum. *fl.* whitish-ochre; lip very broad, fringed in front, with two brick-red areas each side of callus and a few purple spots on front part. Trop. America. 1883. Allied to *Kefersteinia graminea.* *Z. forcipatum* of gardens is *Z. laminatum.*

Z. frag'rans. A synonym of *Warscewiczella marginata.*

Z. Gairia'num. A synonym of *Pescatobollea* × *Gairiana.*

Z. Gautier'i. A variety of *Z. maxillare.*

Z. gem'ma. *fl.* very pale, scarcely larger than in *Z. sanguinolentum*; lip marked with many dark blotches, toothed and crisped. Colombia. 1874. SYN. *Kefersteinia gemma.*

Z. Gibez'iae. A synonym of *Warscewiczella flabelliformis.*

Z. grami'neum. A synonym of *Kefersteinia graminea.*

Z. graminifo'lium. *fl.* 2 in. or more across; sep. and pet. bronzy blackish-brown with some green spots and markings, acute; lip violet-blue, streaked white, broadly obovate or obcordate, emarginate, convex; scapes 5- to 7-fld. *Pseudobulbs* size of a filbert, 3- to 5-leaved. *l.* 3 to 5, grass-like, 8 to 12 in. long. S. Brazil. (L. 339.) Should be placed on a raft or section of tree-fern stem.

Z. grandiflo'rum. A synonym of *Galeottia grandiflorum.*

Z. hemixan'thum. A synonym of *Bollea hemixantha.*

Zygopetalum intermedium

Z. interme'dium (Lodd).* *fl.* several, fragrant; sep. $1\frac{1}{4}$ to $1\frac{1}{2}$ in. long, about $\frac{5}{8}$ in. wide; pet. as long, slightly narrower, greenish or greenish-yellow, tinged marked or blotched with brownish-red or purplish-brown; lip $1\frac{1}{4}$ to $1\frac{1}{2}$ in. long, nearly as wide, broadly, shortly clawed, the blade shortly villose, broadly cordate reniform, margin undulate, emarginate, white or whitish with numerous radiating purple-violet lines and suffused spots of same colour, crest horseshoe-shape, ridged; front of column velvety; scape stout, 12 to 30 in. h. Autumn and winter. *Pseudobulbs* clustered, ovoid-conical, $1\frac{1}{2}$ to 3 in. h. 3- to 5-leaved. *l.* 10 to 18 in. long, 1 to $2\frac{1}{2}$ in. wide. Brazil. 1842. (R. 1, 16; L. 71, 72; B.R. 1433 as *Eulophia Mackaiana*; P.M.B. 3, 97 as *Zygopetalum Mackaii.*) SYN. *Z. Mackaii intermedium, Z. Mackaii crinitum, Z. velutinum* (Hoff.), *Z. Rivieri, Z. euglossum* (Rchb). var. **peruvia'num** has smaller fls. Peru. (L. 418.)

Z. Jorisia'num.* *fl.* about $2\frac{1}{2}$ in. across; sep. and pet. green, blotched brown; lip mid-lobe white, side lobes yellow, fimbriated, crest purplish-brown, large. Venezuela. 1890. Habit much as in *Z. crinitum.* (L. 238.)

Z. Klaboch'ii. Sep. and pet. white-ochre; lip white, fringe-toothed. *l.* 5 in. long, $\frac{1}{2}$ in wide. Habitat? 1885. This may be a Kefersteinia.

Z. Klabocho'rum. A synonym of *Pescatorea Klabochorum.*

Z. lac'teum. *fl.* 1, small, white with a few brownish dots and streaks at base; sep. and pet. oblong, acute; lip very broad, cuneate-oblong, retuse, callus depressed, 2-fid at lip; column dilated in middle, sometimes angled. *l.* very stout, cuneate-oblong, acute. Chiriqui. 1872. SYN. *Kefersteinia lactea.*

Z. Lalin'dei. A synonym of *Bollea Lalindei.*

Z. lamello'sum. A synonym of *Pescatorea lamellosa.*

Z. lamina'tum. *fl.* small; sep. and pet. light yellow; lip white, spotted purple, with nearly free laminae at base. *l.* narrow. Habitat? 1885. Possibly a Kefersteinia.

Z. Lawrencea'num. A synonym of *Bollea Lawrenceana.*

Z. Lehman'ni. A synonym of *Pescatorea Lehmannii.*

Z. Linden'iae. A synonym of *Menadenium Lindeniae.*

Z. Linden'ii. A synonym of *Warscewiczella amazonica.*

Z. lu'cidum. A synonym of *Huntleya lucida.*

Z. Macka'ii.* *fl.* 5 to 7 or more, fragrant; sep. up to $1\frac{3}{4}$ in. long, about $\frac{1}{2}$ in. wide; pet. slightly smaller, greenish-yellow, blotched with purplish or chestnut brown; lip with short broad claw, its blade broadly fan-shaped or roundly sub-quadrate, margin undulate, emarginate, $1\frac{1}{4}$ to $1\frac{3}{4}$ in. long, often as broad, white with numerous, radiating, interrupted lines of violet-purple; front of column smooth; callus horseshoe-shaped, ridged, toothed in front; scapes 15 in. to 30 in. h. Autumn, winter. *Pseudobulbs* clustered, ovoid, compressed, $1\frac{1}{2}$ to $2\frac{1}{2}$ in. h. 2- or 3-leaved. *l.* 12 to 20 in. long, $\frac{3}{4}$ to $1\frac{1}{2}$ in. wide. Has been confused with *Z. intermedium* to which it is closely related. Brazil. 1826. (B.M. 2748; H.B. 1, 8; L. 72; W.O.A. 427.) **Charlesworth's var.,** sep. and pet. pale green, lip pure white. 1912; **crini'tum,** a synonym of *Z. crinitum*; **interme'dium,** a synonym of *Z. intermedium.*

Z. margina'tum. A synonym of *Warscewiczella marginata.*

Z. maxilla're.* *fl.* 5 or more, $2\frac{1}{2}$ in. h., showy; sep. and pet. green, transversely blotched and barred chocolate-brown, ovate-oblong, acute; lip rich bluish-purple, with large roundish mid-lobe, spur blunt, ruff large, deeper purple, horse-hoof shaped, joined to the small, erect side lobes; scapes radical, spikes drooping. *Pseudobulbs* oblong, furrowed, $1\frac{1}{2}$ to 3 in. h., at short intervals on creeping branching rhizomes, 2- or 3-leaved. *l.* lanceolate, 8 to 15 in. long, about 1 in. wide. Brazil. 1829. (B.M. 3686; L.B.C. 1776.) The plant should be placed on a raft or on a section of tree-fern stem. var. **Gautier'i,** stronger in habit than type, *fl.* 2 to 3 in. across, sep. and pet. green, heavily blotched and barred brown, lip purplish-blue, paler on margins, crest deep velvety purple. Brazil, Paraguay. 1867. (W.O.A. 28; L. 284 as *Z. Gautieri.*); **Sanderia'num,** more robust than type, sep. $1\frac{1}{4}$ in. long over $\frac{1}{2}$ in. wide, pet. narrower, light green, dotted or suffused at base with purplish-brown, lip broad, blue, paler on margins, crest purplish-blue. Brazil. About 1888. (G.F. 1888, 1287.) SYN. *Z. mandibulare, Z. Sanderianum.*

Z. Meleag'ris. A synonym of *Huntleya Meleagris.* var. **al'bido-ful'vum.** A synonym of *Huntleya albidofulvum.*

Z. microp'terum. A synonym of *Promenaea microptera.*

Z. Mosenia'num. Stems up to 2 ft. clothed with sheathing bases of old l. *fl.* 2 to 4, on axillary peduncles 6 to 12 in. long; sep. and pet. lanceolate-acute, narrow, nearly 1 in. long, pale green, blotched purple-brown; lip cuneate-obovate, 1 in. long, about $\frac{3}{4}$ in. wide, slightly emarginate, hairy, white with radiating violet lines having stronger hairs, disk semicircular, fleshy, with radiating lines and rows of violet hairs. *Pseudobulbs* absent. *l.* many, closely set, distichous, equitant, linear-lanceolate, 3 to 7 in. long. Brazil. 1890. SYN. *Z. caulescens.* The absence of pseudobulbs seems to place this at variance with true Zygopetalums.

Z. Murraya'num. *fl.* 5 to 9; sep. and pet. greenish, ovate-lanceolate, acute; sep. about 1 in. long, $\frac{1}{3}$ in. wide, pet. slightly smaller; lip shorter than sep., furfuraceous, white, side lobes erect, mid-lobe reflexed, 4 times as large, purple-spotted at base, the prominent semicircular callus yellow with 5 straight violet-brown lines. *Pseudobulbs* ovate, deeply furrowed, $1\frac{1}{2}$ to 3 in. h., 3- or 4-leaved. *l.* narrow-lanceolate, 8 to 15 in. long, about 1 in. wide. Organ Mts. of Brazil. 1837. (B.M. 3674.)

Z. mystaci'num. *fl.* yellowish-green, callus, stalk of lip and column white with purple dots, blade of lip broken into numerous fringes, otherwise much like *Kefersteinia graminea.* Colombia. 1881. SYN. *Kefersteinia mystacina.*

Z. obtusa'tum. *fl.* in a long raceme; sep. and pet. green with narrow, transverse, brown bars, narrow, long, obtuse; lip very pale violet, lower callus retuse, purplish; bracts obtuse. Habitat? 1878. Very close to *Z. maxillare.*

Z. pal'lens. A synonym of *Pescatorea pallens.*

Z. pal'lidum. Probably a form of *Z. Mackaii* with smaller, paler fl.

Z. Patin'ii. A synonym of *Bollea Patinii.*

Z. peruvia'num. A synonym of *Batemannia peruviana.*

Z. pic'tum. A synonym of *Warscewiczella picta.*

Z. platan'thera. A synonym of *Colax placantherus.*

Z. Prainia'num. Very similar to *Z. Burkei.* Sep. and pet. dusky brown with obscure green markings near tip; lip white with purple lines on crest ridges; scapes 2- to 5-fld. *Pseudobulbs* 2 to 4 in. h., 2- or 3-leaved. *l.* 8 to 15 in. long, $\frac{1}{2}$ to $1\frac{1}{4}$ in. wide, rather fleshy. Peru. 1914. (B.M. 8610.)

Z. Protheroea'num. A synonym of *Z. triste.*

Z. pulvina're. A synonym of *Bollea coelestis.*

Z. quadra'tum. A synonym of *Warscewiczella marginata.*

Z. Rivie'ri. A synonym of *Z. intermedium.*

Z. Roez'lii. A synonym of *Pescatorea Roezlii* and *Z. intermedium*.

Z. Rollison'ii. A synonym of *Promenaea Rollisonii*.

Z. rostra'tum. A synonym of *Menadenium labrosum*.

Z. Ruckeria'num. A synonym of *Pescatorea Ruckeriana*.

Z. Russellia'num. A synonym of *Pescatorea Russelliana*.

Z. Sanderia'num. A variety of *Z. maxillare*.

Z. sanguinolen'tum. *fl.* pale straw-coloured or greenish with dark blood-red spots; sep. broadly lanceolate; pet. oblong-ovate, both acute; lip cuneate-flabellate, lobed at tip, undulate, toothed, basal callus dark purple, 2-toothed at tip. *l.* 2-ranked, cuneate-lanceolate, acute, glaucous. Venezuela. (R.X.O. 1, 25 as *Kefersteinia sanguinolenta.*)

Z. Schroederia'num. A synonym of *Pescatorea Schroederiana*.

Z. stapelioi'des. A synonym of *Promenaea stapelioides*.

Z. stenochi'lum. A synonym of *Z. crinitum*.

Z. tri'color. A synonym of *Koellensteinia tricolor*.

Z. tris'te.* Allied to *Z. Mackaii*, *fl.* similar in shape, but smaller; sep. and pet. dusky purple-brown, nearly uniform, lip violet-blue with paler marbling, crest white, lined violet. *Pseudobulbs* clustered, ovoid, 2 to 3 in. h. 2- to 3-leaved. *l.* 15 to 18 in. long, about 1 in. wide. Brazil. Before 1899. SYN. *Z. Protheroeanum*.

Z. triumph'ans. A synonym of *Pescatorea triumphans*.

Z. vela'tum. A synonym of *Warscewiczella velata*.

Z. veluti'num. A synonym of *Z. intermedium*.

Z. venus'tum. A synonym of *Warreella venusta*.

Z. Vervae'tii. A variety of *Pescatorea Klabochorum*.

Z. viola'ceum. A synonym of *Bollea violacea*.

Z. vi'ride. A synonym of *Colax viridis*.

Z. Wailesia'num. A synonym of *Warscewiczella Wailesiana*.

Z. Wallis'ii. A synonym of *Pescatorea Wallisii*.

Z. Wendland'ii. A synonym of *Warscewiczella Wendlandii*.

Z. Whit'ei. A synonym of *Bollea Whitei*.

Z. xanthi'num. A synonym of *Promenaea xanthina*.

E. C.

ZYGOPHYLLA'CEAE. Dicotyledons. A family of about 250 species in about 26 genera in warm regions. Usually shrubs or sub-shrubs, occasionally herbs, rarely annuals. Leaves opposite, rarely spirally arranged, usually equally pinnate, stipulate. Flowers solitary or rarely 2 together, regular, perfect. Sepals and petals 4 or 5, stamens twice as many. Carpels superior, 4 or 5, with 1 to many ovules, style 1 or long-forked. Fruit generally a capsule, rarely a berry or drupe. The genera dealt with here are Guaiacum, Larrea, Porlieria, and Zygophyllum.

ZYGOPHYL'LUM (*zygon*, yoke, *phyllon*, leaf; the leaves are usually in pairs). FAM. *Zygophyllaceae*. Caper Bean. A genus of about 80 species of small frequently prostrate shrubs, under-shrubs, or perennial herbs, natives mostly of Australia and N. Africa. Leaves opposite; leaflets 2, very rarely only 1, often fleshy; stipules 2, often spiny. Flowers white or red, usually with a purple or red basal spot; calyx 4- or 5-parted, overlapping; petals 4 or 5, clawed, overlapping and twisted; stamens 8 or 10, exceeding petals; peduncles 1-flowered, axillary, solitary or rarely twin. Fruit 4- or 5-angled or -winged, capsular. Except where otherwise stated the following species all need greenhouse treatment and should be grown in a compost of loam, peat, and sand. Propagation by seeds or by cuttings in sand, under a glass. *Z. Fabago* grows freely in a sunny spot in dry, well-drained soil.

Z. al'bum. Procumbent. *lflets.* cylindrical, club-shaped, fleshy, cobwebby. *fl.* white, pet. crenate, blunt; pedicels erect. October, November. N. Africa. 1779. (S.B.F.G. 371.)

Z. cocci'neum. 12 in. h. *lflets.* cylindrical, fleshy, smooth. *fl.* scarlet; pet. acuminate; pedicels erect. August. N. Africa, W. Asia. 1823.

Z. cordifo'lium. 12 in. or more h., ash-coloured. *l.* simple, usually somewhat cordate at base, or oblique or ½-cordate; sessile. *fl.* yellowish, 4- or 5-cleft; pet. broad, 3 times as long as cal.; peduncles as long as l. October. S. Africa. 1774.

Z. Faba'go. Syrian Bean-Caper. 1 to 4 ft. h. from a thick, fleshy, deep root. *lflets.* flat, smooth, obovate. *fl.* yellow, coppery-brick-red at base; pet. not cut; pedicels erect. July to September. Syria east to Afghanistan. (S.B.F.G. s. 2, 226 as *Fabago major.*) Hardy perennial.

Z. foe'tidum. Sub-shrub, 2 to 4 ft. h., with herbaceous branches. *lflets.* obovate, obtuse, oblique at base ,larger 1 to 1½ in. long; stalk ½ in. long. *fl.* orange-yellow with purple basal spot; pet. 4 times as long as hairy cal.; peduncles nodding, ½ in. long. June. S. Africa. 1790. *Z. insuave* is a form of this with narrow pet.

Z. fruticulo'sum. Diffuse, shrub, branches forked, dwarf. *lflets.* obliquely oblong or lanceolate, rarely ovate. *fl.* 4-cleft, yellow; filaments awl-shaped, without wings. July. Australia. 1820. SYN. *Raepera fabagifolia*. var. **bilo'bum**, *lflets.* narrow. SYN. *Raepera aurantiaca*.

Zygophyllum fulvum

Z. ful'vum. 3 ft. h. *l.* sessile; lflets. lanceolate-ovate, acute, somewhat narrowed at base, up to 1 in. long very fleshy. *fl.* brownish red or yellow with a red basal blotch; pet. twice as long as cal.; peduncles ½ to 1 in. long, finally reflexing. July. S. Africa. 1713. (B.M. 2184 as *Z. sessilifolium.*)

Z. insua've. *See* **Z. foeti'dum.**

Z. Morgsa'na. 4 ft. h., stem terete. *l.* up to 1½ in. long, short stalked; lflets. obovate, obtuse, somewhat oblique at base. *fl.* nodding, 4- or 5-cleft; pet. yellow, obovate, 3 times as long as the glabrous cal.; peduncles ½ to ¾ in. long. August. S. Africa. 1732.

Z. spino'sum. 1 to 2 ft. h. with grey branches. *l.* sessile; lflets. linear, flat, or margins slightly revolute, ⅛ to ⅝ in. long, fleshy, acute. *fl.* 5-cleft, nodding, yellowish or cream with red streaks or a purple spot towards base, 2 or 3 times as long as cal.; peduncles equal to or exceeding l. July. S. Africa. 1830.

ZYGOSE'PALUM. A synonym of Menadenium.

zygospore. A sexually produced spore characteristic of the fungus Class Zygomycetes (q.v.).

ZYGOSTA'TES (*zygos*, yoke, *statos*, standing; alluding to 2 processes which stand out more or less horizontally from the base of column and together somewhat resemble a yoke). FAM. *Orchidaceae*. A genus of about 4 dwarf epiphytes, natives of Brazil. Flowers small, racemose, on axillary peduncles; sepals sub-equal, free, spreading or reflexed; petals similar or broader; lip continuous with the column-base, spreading, concave, undivided, with a fleshy often incurved appendage at base. Column arched semi-terete, the 2 processes at the base, linear, fleshy, dilated at apex. Rostellum long, horizontal at first, then recurved. Pollinia 4. Leaves fleshy or leathery, imbricate, the limb articulate, the sheaths thickening but hardly into pronounced pseudobulbs. One or 2 species have occasionally been introduced. Cultivation should be as for Ornithocephalus to which the genus is allied.

Z. Allenia'na. *fl.* 3 to 5, pellucid, very small; sep. reflexed, shortly clawed; pet. broader, clawed, spatulate, margins serrulate; lip boat-shaped, acute, margin entire; processes pointing forward. *Pseudobulbs* very small. *l.* about 1 in. long. Paraguay, Brazil. 1898.

Z. cornu'ta. *fl.* many, closely set, very small; pet. broader than sep., rhomboid, acute, serrated on margins, lip concave, oblong, acute, purplish, the appendage oblong, the processes more or less 2-lobate, margin fimbriate-serrulate. *l.* oblong-ligulate, 1¼ to 2½ in. long, ⅓ to ½ in. wide. Brazil.

Z. Greenia'na. *fl.* 2; sep. oblong, obtuse; pet. white, ovate, tooth-letted; lip white, streaked green, foveate, rounded, peduncles short. *Pseudobulbs* minute, somewhat pear-shaped. *l.* cuneate-ligulate, 3-angled, fleshy; superposed. Brazil. 1869.

Z. luna'ta. *fl.* many, closely set, very small; sep. free or thel ateral briefly connate, ovate, acute, greenish-white; pet. broader, rounded, serrate, greenish-yellow; lip white, concave, ovate, fimbriate-serrulate, the appendage sub-quadrate, yellow, the processes globose at apex. *l.* somewhat spatulate 1½ to 3 in. long. Brazil. SYN. *Ornithocephalus navicularis.*

E. C.

ZYGOTRITO'NIA (from *zygos*, yoke, *Tritonia*; in allusion to the markedly zygomorphic flowers and its affinity with Tritonia). FAM. *Iridaceae.* A genus of about 7 species of slender perennial herbs up to 18 in. high, natives of Trop. Africa, related to Gladiolus and Tritonia. Corms with fibrous coats. Leaves sword-like. Flowers small, $\frac{3}{10}$ to $\frac{7}{10}$ in. long, yellow, white, or purplish, sessile, in loose spikes; perianth tube narrowly funnel-shaped, upper lobe erect, curved and rather hooded, narrow, much longer than the other 5 more or less equal lobes which are directed downwards; stigma undivided or weakly lobed. The species are *Z. bongensis*, *Z. crocea* (Hook. I. 3120), *Z. Giorgii*, *Z. gracillima*, *Z. nyassana*, and *Z. praecox*, needing cultivation in a warm greenhouse, of interest for their curiously shaped flowers but of no decorative value.

W. T. S.